HANDBOOK OF MOLECULAR CYTOLOGY

Edited by

A. LIMA-DE-FARIA

Institute of Molecular Cytogenetics,
University of Lund, Sweden

1969

NORTH-HOLLAND PUBLISHING COMPANY
AMSTERDAM · LONDON

Library of Congress Catalog Card Number: 69-18387

Standard Book Number: 7204 7115 X

PUBLISHERS:

NORTH-HOLLAND PUBLISHING COMPANY – AMSTERDAM
NORTH-HOLLAND PUBLISHING COMPANY, LTD. – LONDON

SOLE DISTRIBUTORS FOR THE WESTERN HEMISPHERE:

WILEY INTERSCIENCE DIVISION
JOHN WILEY & SONS, INC. – NEW YORK

PRINTED IN THE NETHERLANDS

Previous volumes in the series **FRONTIERS OF BIOLOGY**

Volume 1: **Microbial models of cancer cells**
G. F. GAUSE, Academy of Medical Sciences, Moscow

Volume 2: **Interferons**
Edited by N. B. FINTER, Imperial Chemical Industries, Macclesfield, Cheshire

Volume 3: **The biochemical genetics of vertebrates except man**
I. E. LUSH, Rowett Research Institute, Aberdeen

Volume 4: **Delayed hypersensitivity**
J. L. TURK, University of London

Volume 5: **Human population cytogenetics**
W. M. COURT BROWN, Western General Hospital, Edinburgh

Volume 6: **Thymidine metabolism and cell kinetics**
J. E. CLEAVER, University of California

Volume 7: **The cell periphery, metastasis and other contact phenomena**
L. WEISS, Roswell Park Memorial Institute, Buffalo, N.Y.

Volume 8: **The electrostatics of biological cell membranes**
R. M. FRIEDENBERG, University of Maryland

Volume 9: **The pyrrolizidine alkaloids. Their chemistry, pathogenicity and other biological properties**
L. B. BULL, C. C. J. CULVENOR and A. T. DICK, Commonwealth Scientific & Industrial Research Organization, Australia

Volume 10: **Antagonists and nucleic acids**
M. EARL BALIS, Sloan Kettering Institute for Cancer Research, Rye, N.Y.

Volume 11: **Macrophages and immunity**
D. S. NELSON, Department of Bacteriology, The University of Sydney, Australia

Volume 12: **The biological code**
M. YČAS, Department of Microbiology, College of Medicine, State University of New York, Syracuse, N.Y.

Volume 13: **The biochemistry of folic acid and related pteridines**
R. L. BLAKLEY, Department of Biochemistry, Australian National University

Volume 14: **Lysosomes in biology and pathology** (complete in 2 volumes)
Edited by J. T. DINGLE and HONOR B. FELL, Strangeways Research Laboratories, Cambridge

Acknowledgement

The publisher wishes to acknowledge the permission to use illustrations previously published by various molecular cytologists. Full reference to this material is to be found in the bibliography at the end of each chapter.

General preface

The aim of the publication of this series of monographs, known under the collective title of '*Frontiers of Biology*', is to present coherent and up-to-date views of the fundamental concepts which dominate modern biology.

Biology in its widest sense has made very great advances during the past decade, and the rate of progress has been steadily accelerating. Undoubtedly important factors in this acceleration have been the effective use by biologists of new techniques, including electron microscopy, isotopic labels, and a great variety of physical and chemical techniques, especially those with varying degrees of automation. In addition, scientists with partly physical or chemical backgrounds have become interested in the great variety of problems presented by living organisms. Most significant, however, increasing interest in and understanding of the biology of the cell, expecially in regard to the molecular events involved in genetic phenomena and in metabolism and its control, have led to the recognition of patterns common to all forms of life from bacteria to man. These factors and unifying concepts have led to a situation in which the sharp boundaries between the various classical biological disciplines are rapidly disappearing.

Thus, while scientists are becoming increasingly specialized in their techniques, to an increasing extent they need an intellectual and conceptual approach on a wide and non-specialized basis. It is with these considerations and needs in mind that this series of monographs, '*Frontiers of Biology*' has been conceived.

The advances in various areas of biology, including microbiology, biochemistry, genetics, cytology, and cell structure and function in general will be presented by authors who have themselves contributed significantly to these developments. They will have, in this series, the opportunity of bringing together, from diverse sources, theories and experimental data, and of integrating these into a more general conceptual framework. It is unavoidable, and probably even desirable, that the special bias of the individual authors will become evident in their contributions. Scope will also be given for presentation of new and challenging ideas and hypotheses for which complete evidence is at present lacking. However, the main emphasis will be on fairly complete and objective presentation of the more important and more rapidly advancing aspects of biology. The level will be advanced, directed primarily to the needs of the graduate student and research worker.

Most monographs in this series will be in the range of 200–300 pages, but on occasion a collective work of major importance may be included exceeding this figure. The intent of the publishers is to bring out these books promptly and in fairly quick succession.

It is on the basis of all these various considerations that we welcome the opportunity of supporting the publication of the series '*Frontiers of Biology*' by North-Holland Publishing Company.

E. L. TATUM
A. NEUBERGER, *General Editors*

Preface

Cytology has made great advances during the past decade. At the turn of the century, the rediscovery of Mendel's laws aroused particular interest in the nucleus, more especially in the chromosomes which were sought as the carriers of hereditary factors. Rapid expansion of chromosome studies led to a great development in cytology, which for several decades consisted mainly of the study of the nucleus. The application of the techniques of electron microscopy to the cytoplasmic organelles after World War II changed this trend, making the cytoplasm an equally important field of research in cytology. Investigation in this last area expanded so rapidly that workers concerned with the nucleus and those concerned with the cytoplasm had only limited points of scientific contact. However, with the development of molecular biology there has been a rapid increase in our knowledge of the molecular organization of both cytoplasmic and nuclear components, and of molecular interactions between cellular structures. Molecular cytology became common ground for the two groups of cytologists.

The gathering of contributions from the diversified fields of molecular cytology into a handbook is the result of the pressing need for a deeper understanding of the molecular interactions within the cell.

In planning the Handbook it was found appropriate to have about half of the chapters written by European authors and the other half by American colleagues. The same principle was applied in choosing the Advisory Editorial Board which consisted of: W. Beermann, W. Bernhard, H. Fernández-Morán, K. Porter, and H. Swift. An attempt was also made to have the nuclear structures represented by about the same number of chapters as the cytoplasmic organelles, to permit a better understanding of the macromolecular interactions between the two cellular compartments.

It is apparent that in a number of cytological fields our knowledge has not yet reached the molecular level. Cytology is, however, coming closer to this stage every day. We are near the threshold of a synthesis that embraces the information from the light microscopic studies, ultrastructural analysis and the biochemical data. The purpose in preparing the Handbook has been to bring together this knowledge at a moment when it has not yet crystallized into a coherent body of molecular organization and interaction. By having in one book most of the information available on the evolution of DNA, the ultrastructure and biochemistry of chromosomes, and the ultrastructure and biochemistry of cytoplasmic organelles, the reader may be in a better position to get a general picture of the molecular interactions within the cell, to see the areas which are least developed, and to find out where new and significant trends in research lie.

DNA is present not only in the nucleus, but also in the mitochondria and the chloroplasts. This is confirmation that there are three genetic systems in the cell. A pressing problem is to find out how the three genetic systems interact and their degree of independence. Extra DNA copies are released from the chromosomes and find their way to the cytoplasm in the oocytes of several species of invertebrates and vertebrates. This phenomenon brings the nuclear and the mitochondrial DNA's closer and one wonders in what way mitochondrial DNA activity may be affected by the presence of nuclear DNA in the cytoplasm.

The study of the evolution of DNA is the basis of the understanding of the evolution of the chromosome from viruses to higher organisms.

In the Handbook the treatment of the evolution of DNA starts with the study of the evolution of base sequences in this macromolecule (McCarthy). It is followed by the occurrence of repetition of nucleotide sequences in chromosomes of lower and higher organisms (Britten and Kohne). Special attention is paid to the highly repetitive DNA of rodents (Walker, Flamm and McLaren) and to the doublet pattern of the nucleic acids of viruses since this study has a direct bearing on their origin (Subak-Sharpe).

The pattern of DNA in viruses leads to the study of the viral chromosome (Kleinschmidt) and to the organization of the chromosome in bacteria (Caro). At this point it seemed appropriate to insert three chapters on the fine structure of the bacterial cell (Van Iterson).

The next step in the evolution of the chromosome leads us to the molecular organization of chromosomes in higher organisms. This subject is first treated by Ris, and is followed by two chapters on the organization of heterochromatin at the molecular level: one on the biochemistry and molecular biophysics of hetero- and euchromatin, which describes the interactions between histones and DNA (Frenster), and the other on the DNA replication and gene amplification in heterochromatin, which deals mainly with the occurrence of ribosomal cistrons in this chromosome material (Lima-de-Faria). The problem of crossing-over has not yet completely reached the molecular level but Henderson discusses the information available at this level. The relation between this phenomenon and DNA replication has become clearer by the finding that DNA synthesis not only occurs at the interphase of meiosis but also at the early stages of the meiotic prophase (see the chapters by Stern and Hotta, Callan, and Lima-de-Faria).

Only by combining our knowledge of the ultrastructure with the study of the biochemical activity can we expect to reach an understanding of the function of the nucleus and of the chromosomes. The information on the ultrastructure of the interphase nucleus, spermatids, mitotic and meiotic chromosomes has been assembled by Kaye, Lafontaine and Lord, and Sotelo, respectively. The treatment of the biochemistry of the interphase nucleus and of mitotic and meiotic chromosomes starts with the nuclear protein fractions (Fambrough), is followed by the DNA, RNA and protein synthesis during the mitotic cell cycle (Monesi), and the biochemistry of meiosis (Stern and Hotta). Due to their importance, the biochemical activity of polytene and lampbrush chromosomes is treated separately (Berendes and Beermann, and Callan, respectively). Chromosome movements have long been a subject of speculation but at present ultrastructural and biochemical data are yielding information on the molecular mechanisms involved in this process (Forer).

Special attention is paid to the nucleolus due to its central role in the production of ribosomes. The ultrastructure and function (Miller and Beatty) and its synthetic activity (Perry) are discussed in detail.

Differentiation, which for many years has been one of the least developed areas of cytogenetics, seems to have entered a new period of expansion. New data are emerging on the regulation of DNA and RNA synthesis in cells, and the work of Gurdon, Tarkowski and Beatrice Mintz receives special attention in the chapter by McLaren. Cell hybrids induced by viruses and other aspects of nuclear function are described in the chapter by Ringertz.

Cancer is a central problem in cell differentiation, but its study has only partly reached the molecular level. However, the interaction between viruses and chromosomes (Nichols) is one of the fields of research which has brought this problem to the level of macromolecular interactions between these two types of structures. The relation between chromosome abnormalities and carcinogenesis as well as the ultrastructure of the cancer cell are an integral part of this problem (Levan, and Bernhard, respectively). Within the general context of chromosome abnormalities are those which involve the sex chromosomes and the autosomes in man and mammals. It was felt that these should not be left out due to their importance in differentiation and their medical interest (Hamerton, and Taylor, respectively).

The study of the structure and function of the nuclear envelope closes the section of the Handbook dealing with the nucleus (Stevens and André).

Mitochondria and chloroplasts fulfil basic functions in the cell, but the discovery of nucleic acids, and in particular DNA, in these organelles has further increased their functional significance. Five chapters written by Munn, Borst, Kroon, Swift and Wohlstenholme, and Lefort-Tran are concerned with the ultrastructure, biogenesis, biochemistry and function of these organelles.

Polysaccharides are synthesized and coupled in the Golgi apparatus (Favard) with proteins coming from the cavities of the endoplasmic reticulum (Goldblatt). This last cell structure is the main site of protein synthesis where ribosomes play a basic role (De Man and Noorduyn). However, information is largely lacking about the molecular arrangement of the membranes of the endoplasmic reticulum, associated enzymes, and even the structural arrangement of the ribosomes on the endoplasmic reticulum.

Lysosomes are known for their nutritive role in the cell, their active part in the defence against various pathogenic bodies and their role in lytic phenomena leading to the disappearance of intracellular organelles or structures during differentiation (Wattiaux). On the other hand peroxisomes are a special type of respiratory particle with the ability of reducing oxygen to water by a two-step mechanism involving hydrogen peroxide as an intermediate (Baudhuin).

Specialized cell structures involved in chromosome and cell movements are the centrioles (Pitelka), the cilia and the flagella (Afzelius, and Sleigh). These organelles are intimately interrelated since centrioles can produce cilia. Their ultrastructure, biochemistry and physiology are treated in three chapters.

The Handbook closes with seven chapters on the cell surface, pynocytosis, cell membranes and walls. Although this is the last part of the book it is not the least significant. Our knowledge of these structures and their function is in many ways rudimentary, but this is also an area that is expanding rapidly as the methods of molecular biology are being applied more extensively to these structures. This problem is treated by Bennett (two chapters), Schoffeniels (two chapters), Stockem and Wohlfart-Bottermann, Robertson, and Kreger.

A Handbook of this kind can make no claim to be complete or exhaustive. It is only intended as an introductory work to Molecular Cytology.

It is a great pleasure to acknowledge the collaboration of the Advisory Editorial Board and of other colleagues who have made valuable suggestions in the preparation of the Handbook. These are: W. Beermann, E. L. Benedetti, W. Bernhard, M. Birnstiel, J. Bonner, P. Borst, H. Burström, J. E. Cummins, H. Fernández-Morán, H. Holter, T. Laurent, D. Mazia, M. J. Moses, A. Neuberger, D. S. Parsons, K. Porter, R. D. Preston, J. Prichard, H. Swift, and E. L. Tatum.

I would like to thank Dr. E. van Tongeren, director of the North-Holland Publishing Co., for his active and personal interest in this work and his two collaborators Mr. H. L. Woudhuysen and Mrs. K. Koning for their kind assistance.

Lund, May 30, 1969

A. LIMA-DE-FARIA

Contents

For a detailed list of contents the reader is referred to the first page of each chapter.

GENERAL PREFACE VII
PREFACE IX

Part I – Evolution of DNA

1 B.J.MCCARTHY: The evolution of base sequences in nucleic acids 3
2 R.J.BRITTEN and D.E.KOHNE: Repetition of nucleotide sequences in chromosomal DNA 21
3 R.J.BRITTEN and D.E.KOHNE: Implications of repeated nucleotide sequences 37
4 P.M.B.WALKER, W.G.FLAMM and A.MCLAREN: Highly repetitive DNA in rodents 52
5 J.H.SUBAK-SHARPE: The doublet pattern of the nucleic acid in relation to the origin of viruses 67

Part II – Chromosome organization in viruses and bacteria

6 A.K.KLEINSCHMIDT: Chromosomes of viruses 91
7 L.G.CARO: Chromosomes of bacteria 126

Part III – Bacterial fine structure

8 W.VAN ITERSON: The bacterial surface 149
9 W.VAN ITERSON: Bacterial membranes, flagella and pili 174
10 W.VAN ITERSON: The internal organization of bacteria 197

Part IV – Chromosome organization in higher organisms

11 H.RIS: The molecular organization of chromosomes 221
12 J.H.FRENSTER: Biochemistry and molecular biophysics of heterochromatin and euchromatin 251
13 A.LIMA-DE-FARIA: DNA replication and gene amplification in heterochromatin 277
14 S.A.HENDERSON: Chromosome pairing, chiasmata and crossing-over . . . 326

Part V – Ultrastructure of the interphase nucleus and chromosomes

15 J.S.KAYE: The ultrastructure of chromatin in nuclei of interphase cells and in spermatids 361

16 J.G.LAFONTAINE and A.LORD: Organization of nuclear structures in mitotic cells 381
17 J.R. SOTELO: Ultrastructure of the chromosomes at meiosis 412

Part VI – Biochemistry of the interphase nucleus, chromosomes and spindle

18 D.M.FAMBROUGH, JR.: Nuclear protein fractions 437
19 V.MONESI: DNA, RNA, and protein synthesis during the mitotic cell cycle 472
20 H.D.BERENDES and W.BEERMANN: Biochemical activity of interphase chromosomes (polytene chromosomes). 500
21 H.STERN and Y.HOTTA: Biochemistry of meiosis 520
22 H.G.CALLAN: Biochemical activities of chromosomes during the prophase of meiosis 540
23 A.FORER: Chromosome movements during cell-division 553

Part VII – Ultrastructure and biochemistry of the nucleolus

24 O.L.MILLER, JR. and B.R.BEATTY: Nucleolar structure and function 605
25 R.P.PERRY: Nucleoli: the cellular sites of ribosome production 620

Part VIII – Control mechanisms of cellular differentiation

26 A.MCLAREN: Recent studies on developmental regulation in vertebrates. . 639
27 N.R.RINGERTZ: Cytochemical properties of nuclear proteins and deoxyribonucleoprotein complexes in relation to nuclear function 656

Part IX – Chromosome abnormalities and other pathological conditions

28 W.BERNHARD: Ultrastructure of the cancer cell 687
29 A.LEVAN: Chromosome abnormalities and carcinogenesis 716
30 W.W.NICHOLS: Interactions between viruses and chromosomes 732
31 J.L.HAMERTON: Sex chromosomes and their abnormalities in man and mammals 751
32 A.I.TAYLOR: Autosomal abnormalities 804

Part X – The nuclear envelope

33 B.J.STEVENS and J.ANDRÉ: The nuclear envelope 837

Part XI – Ultrastructure and biochemistry of mitochondria and chloroplasts

34 E. A. MUNN: Ultrastructure of mitochondria 875
35 P. BORST: Biochemistry and function of mitochondria 914
36 A. M. KROON: DNA and RNA from mitochondria and chloroplasts (biochemistry) 943
37 H. SWIFT and D. R. WOLSTENHOLME: Mitochondria and chloroplasts: nucleic acids and the problem of biogenesis (genetics and biology) 972
38 M. LEFORT-TRAN: Cytochemistry and ultrastructure of chloroplasts 1047

Part XII – Ultrastructure and biochemistry of ribosomes, endoplasmic reticulum and Golgi apparatus

39 J. C. H. DE MAN and N. J. A. NOORDUYN: Ribosomes: properties and function. 1079
40 P. J. GOLDBLATT: The endoplasmic reticulum 1101
41 P. FAVARD: The Golgi apparatus 1130

Part XIII – Ultrastructure and biochemistry of lysosomes and peroxisomes

42 R. WATTIAUX: Biochemistry and function of lysosomes 1159
43 P. BAUDHUIN: Peroxisomes (microbodies, glyoxysomes). 1179

Part XIV – Ultrastructure and biochemistry of centrioles, flagella and cilia

44 D. R. PITELKA: Centriole replication 1199
45 B. A. AFZELIUS: Ultrastructure of cilia and flagella 1219
46 M. A. SLEIGH: The physiology and biochemistry of cilia and flagella. . . . 1243

Part XV – Cell surface and function

47 H. S. BENNETT: The cell surface: components and configurations 1261
48 H. S. BENNETT: The cell surface: movements and recombinations 1294
49 E. SCHOFFENIELS: Uptake mechanism of the cell, active transport 1320
50 E. SCHOFFENIELS: Cellular aspects of membrane permeability 1346
51 W. STOCKEM and K. E. WOHLFARTH-BOTTERMANN: Pinocytosis (endocytosis). 1373

Part XVI – Cell membranes and walls

52 J. D. ROBERTSON: Molecular structure of biological membranes. 1403
53 D. R. KREGER: Cell walls 1444

SUBJECT INDEX 1481

PART I

Evolution of DNA

CHAPTER 1

The evolution of base sequences in nucleic acids

BRIAN J. MCCARTHY

Departments of Microbiology and Genetics, University of Washington, Seattle, Washington 98105

Contents

1. Introduction and methods of approach
2. The DNA content of various genomes
3. Base composition and nearest-neighbor relationships in DNA
4. Satellite DNAS
5. Inter- and intra-genome base sequence homology
6. Conservative and non-conservative genes
7. Ribosomal RNA genes
8. Extranuclear DNA
   (a) Mitochondrial DNA
   (b) DNA of chloroplasts and other organelles
9. Conclusions

1. Introduction and methods of approach

Although there is an almost complete lack of detailed sequence information for DNA or RNA, a considerable body of data exists relating to the overall base composition and to differences and similarities among the base sequences of DNAs of related organisms. A large number of determinations of base composition have been made on a variety of organisms. This has proved useful for taxonomic purposes especially in micro-organisms where the base composition is highly variable. In higher plants and animals only small differences in base composition exist so that such measurements are not useful for comparative purposes.

Chemical analyses of DNA samples show the equivalence of A to T and G to C. Thus, the overall base composition of DNA may be described in terms of the % G + C. Chemical analyses of the relative amounts of the four bases present are essential where the possibility exists of the presence of unusual bases. Otherwise, this analysis has been largely replaced by less tedious methods. The two most popular of these indirect methods involve measurements of the buoyant density in cesium chloride (Schildkraut et al. 1962a) or the mean thermal denaturation temperature, T_m (Marmur and Doty). The great advantages of the former method derive from the fact that only 1 μg is required and adequate determinations may be made on a crude homogenate without purification of the DNA.

More detailed sequence data have been obtained only with the smallest DNA molecule known, that of the coliphage ΦX174 (Hall and Sinsheimer; Sedat and Sinsheimer). Since there are no known deoxyribonucleases of sufficient specificity for sequence work, the most useful degradative methods are chemical procedures selectively destroying the purines or the pyrimidines. Such procedures allow the estimation of purine and pyrimidine sequences of various lengths (Burton; Hall and Sinsheimer; Sedat and Sinsheimer). Using these methods, Burton and co-workers have shown that sequences of polydeoxythymidylic acid exist in higher than statistically expected proportions in all DNAs, whereas corresponding polydeoxycytidylic acid sequences were very rare.

Measurements of nearest neighbor or dinucleotide frequences in DNA may be made by means of *in vitro* copying of DNA by DNA polymerase (Josse et al.). Using a given DNA primer and the four 5′-deoxyribotriphosphates, one of which is labeled with P^{32}, a faithful copy of the primer is made. Degradation of the synthesized DNA leading to 3′-nucleotides leads to the 'nearest neighbor' pattern of that particular base residue. By repeating the analysis with the other three labeled nucleotides, the frequencies of all sixteen dinucleotide sequences may be established. This kind of analysis may be extended to larger nucleotide sequences by allowing the incorporation of a mixture of ribonucleotides and deoxyribonucleotides in the presence of Mn^{2+} (Berg et al.). Degradation with alkali leads to oligonucleotide fragments. This is a promising, but yet largely unexplored approach to detailed sequence data.

Thus, the problem of complete sequence determination of DNA is far from solution and indirect means must be used to obtain comparative sequence data. At the present time a very productive indirect approach is offered by the use of annealing reactions between nucleic acids. Following the discovery that the two strands of DNA may be physically separated and reassociated (Doty et al.), the possible value of this reaction for comparisons of related nucleic acids became apparent. The formation of heteroduplex DNA molecules by the separated DNA strands originating from two related organisms is a function of their base sequence divergence. These reactions may be studied by the CsCl density gradient method if one of the DNAs is labeled with a heavy isotope such as N^{15}, C^{13} or H^2. Other procedures, such as the DNA agar method, (McCarthy and Bolton; Hoyer and Roberts) or Denhardt's adaptation of the membrane filter method of Gillespie and Spiegelman demand only radio-labeled DNA and are consequently much more convenient. Recent developments of this methodology allow the quantitative estimation of the extent of nucleotide sequence divergence (McCarthy 1967).

2. *The DNA content of various genomes*

The evolution of the more complex from the simpler forms of life has been accompanied by a large increase in the total amount of DNA per cell nucleus. This is consistent with increase in the total information content necessary for more developmental, structural and behavioral complexity. A selection of some of the available data for a variety of organisms is given in Table 1. The total complement of DNA increases by a factor of about 10^3 from bacteria to mammals. Viruses contain even smaller amounts of DNA. In general, the amount of DNA per haploid cell nucleus increases systematically with the complexity of the organism although several exceptions exist. The *Urodela* contain much larger amounts of DNA per cell nucleus than do the other amphibia, the subclass *Anura*. The values for all amphibians are higher than those for mammals. Other exceptions to this general rule exist in the plant kingdom, some of which may be explained by polyploidization (Stebbins). Within a closely related group of organisms, such as placental mammals, reptiles or birds, the amounts of DNA per cell nucleus differ by no more than 10% (Atkin et al.).

Several possible mechanisms may be proposed to account for this steady increase in the amount of DNA per genome (McCarthy 1965). The simplest is 'end addition' of nucleotides to an intact DNA molecule (Kornberg). It is possible for a DNA molecule to increase in length during replication through this end addition. This process would create random sequences upon which selection might act. Another possibility involves the acquisition of genetic material from another organism. This process occurs in bacteria through the transfer of episomes and by viral transduction. It is conceivable that viruses may play a part in genetic transfer in eucaryotic organisms. However, gene duplication appears to be the most important process at the present time. Many examples of the operation of this process have been suggested from work on amino

TABLE 1

DNA content per nucleus of various organisms[a]

Organism	Daltons	Nucleotide pairs	Reference[b]
Viruses			
bacterial			
ΦX174	1.6×10^6	5500	Thomas and McHattie
λ	30×10^6	45×10^3	Thomas and McHattie
T5	85×10^6	130×10^3	Thomas and McHattie
T2	130×10^6	200×10^3	Thomas and McHattie
animal			
Shope papilloma	5×10^6	7.5×10^3	Thomas and McHattie
Adenovirus 12	14×10^6	20×10^3	Thomas and McHattie
Fowlpox	230×10^6	350×10^3	Thomas and McHattie
Bacteria[c]			
Mycoplasma gallisepticum	0.2×10^9	0.3×10^6	McCarthy (1967)
Hemophilus influenzae	0.7×10^9	1×10^6	McCarthy (1967)
Escherichia coli	2.6×10^9	4×10^6	McCarthy (1967)
Pseudomonas sp.	2.4×10^9	4×10^6	McCarthy (1967)
Bacillus subtilis	1.3×10^9	2×10^6	McCarthy (1967)
Fungi			
Saccharomyces cerevisiae	13×10^9	20×10^6	McCarthy (1967)
Invertebrates			
Tube sponge	0.06×10^{12}	0.1×10^9	McCarthy (1965)
Jelly fish[c]	0.2×10^{12}	0.3×10^9	McCarthy (1965)
Sea urchin[c]	0.5×10^{12}	0.8×10^9	McCarthy (1965)
Nereid worm[c]	1×10^{12}	1.4×10^9	McCarthy (1965)
Snail, *Tectorius muricatus*[c]	4×10^{12}	6.3×10^9	McCarthy (1965)
Cliff crab	1×10^{12}	1.4×10^9	McCarthy (1965)
Drosophila melanogaster	0.12×10^{12}	0.2×10^9	McCarthy (1967)
Vertebrates			
Lung fish	60×10^{12}	94×10^9	McCarthy (1965)
Frog	28×10^{12}	45×10^9	McCarthy (1965)
Amphiuma	120×10^{12}	180×10^9	McCarthy (1965)
Shark, *Carcharias obscurus*	3.4×10^{12}	5.2×10^9	McCarthy (1965)
Carp	2×10^{12}	3.3×10^9	McCarthy (1965)
Chicken	1.2×10^{12}	2.1×10^9	McCarthy (1965)
Mouse	3.0×10^{12}	4.7×10^9	McCarthy (1965)
Human	3.6×10^{12}	5.6×10^9	McCarthy (1965)
Plants			
Arabidopsis thaliana	2.6×10^{12}	4×10^9	Stebbins
Zea mays	20×10^{12}	30×10^9	Stebbins
Tradescantia paludosa	40×10^{12}	60×10^9	Stebbins

[a] More extensive data are given in: Handbook of Biochemistry, ed. H.A. Sober (1968) Chemical Rubber Co, Cleveland, Ohio. [b] These sources are reviews. Original references are contained within them. [c] Haploid cells. Other numbers are for diploid cells.

acid sequences in proteins as well as from studies of DNA itself (see chapters by Britten and Kohne).

3. Base composition and nearest-neighbor relationships in DNA

The base composition of bacterial DNA is extremely variable. The range covered is from approximately 24–75% GC (Table 2). Similar, although not quite as extensive, variation exists in the composition of DNA of other groups of microorganisms and in viruses. In metazoans, much more limited variation exists, although the more primitive invertebrate phyla such as Sponges include members differing by 25% GC. The more advanced invertebrate phyla such as the Echinoderms and the Chordates and higher plants have very restricted DNA base compositions mostly in the range of 35–45% GC. Thus, the most highly developed forms of both animals and plants have selected a DNA base composition of approximately 40% GC. This means, of course, that measurements of base composition alone are not sufficiently sensitive to distinguish and compare the DNA of higher organisms.

A higher level of resolution is provided by measurements of nearest-neighbor relationships in DNA. Some examples selected from the literature are given in Table 3. Perhaps the most striking feature of these measurements is given by the relative occurrence of the dinucleotides CpG and GpC. These are nearly equal in bacteria, but the

TABLE 2

Range of base compositions[a] in the DNA of various groups of organisms

Organism	Base composition[a] (% GC)	Reference
Bacteria	24–75	Hill
Blue-green algae	35–71	Edelman et al. (1967)
Fungi	38–63	Storck (1966)
Protozoa	22–66	Sueoka
Algae	36–66	Sueoka
Sponges	35–60	Antonov
Molluscs	31–47	Antonov
Arthropods[b]	32–45	Antonov
Echinoderms	35–45	Antonov
Chordates[c]	38–47	Antonov
Higher plants	37–50	Vanyushin et al.
Viruses	28–74	Thomas and McHattie; Bellett (1967)
Mitochondria	25–52	Borst et al.
Chloroplasts	26–47	Edelman et al. (1967)

[a] An extensive compilation of base composition data is given in: Handbook of Biochemistry, ed. H. A. Sober (1968) Chemical Rubber Co, Cleveland, Ohio. [b] An exception to this restricted range is the dAT satellite DNA of the genus cancer. [c] Some minor components (satellites) fall outside this range (see Table 3).

TABLE 3

Nearest-neighbor frequencies (expressed as parts per thousand) of various DNAS

Dinucleotides	*E. coli*[a] 50% GC	*Chlamydomonas*[b] 64% GC	Wheat[b] 38% GC	Sea urchin[b] *Paracentrotus lividus* 40% GC	Human[b] 41% GC	Hamster[c] 42% GC	SV_{40} virus[b] 41% GC	Vaccinia virus 35% GC	*Physarum polycephalum* Nuclear 41% GC	*Physarum polycephalum* Mitochondrial 26% GC
ApA, TpT	72, 74	60· 59	72, 89	110, 102	97, 97	98, 108	105, 116	106, 112		
CpA, TpG	72, 70	77, 73	68, 70	67, 67	74, 74	68, 79	68, 79	52, 57	55	45
GpA, TpC	56, 55	44, 46	62, 71	57, 59	61, 67	62, 57	62, 57	65, 61		
CpT, ApG	54, 56	57, 60	67, 60	59, 53	71, 70	68, 69	62, 73	53, 55	68	46
GpT, ApC	54, 55	55, 60	56, 53	53, 58	49, 54	60, 52	60, 52	53, 49		
GpG, CpC	56, 56	71, 74	51, 59	33, 38	50, 47	44, 40	49, 44	28, 26	69	26
TpA	51	53	58	90	67	73	68	111		
ApT	67	54	75	104	81	82	74	124		
CpG	68	63	39	20	10	8	6	28	20	13
GpC	84	92	50	31	43	35	44	22		

[a] Josse et al.; [b] Swartz et al.; [c] Morrison et al.

frequency of CpG is always much lower in higher organisms. This feature has been used by Cummins et al. as an argument for the procaryotic nature of mitochondrial DNA where again the frequency of CpG is near to that expected for a random arrangement of nucleotides (Table 3).

A similar argument has been advanced by Morrison et al. who have suggested that the small DNA tumor viruses (e.g. SV_{40}) are related in an evolutionary sense to the host mammalian DNA, whereas the larger DNA viruses (e.g. vaccinia) which have different base compositions and nearest-neighbor relationships originate from some other group of organisms. Bellett (1967a, b) has made use of base composition and nearest-neighbor data in constructing a classification of viruses.

4. Satellite DNAs

Certain DNA samples which have been analyzed contain a satellite of different base composition from the main band. These satellites are to be distinguished from extranuclear DNA present in cytoplasmic organelles. Bacterial DNAs are of unimodal distribution except for the case of various species of halophilic bacteria (Table 4). In these cases a second band of lower % GC represents some 10 or 20% of the total. Other, presumably related, strains of halophilic bacteria contain only the main high GC band (Joshi et al.). Satellite bands of DNA in bacteria may be added to some bacteria through the introduction of an episome of different base composition (Falkow and

TABLE 4

Base composition of satellite DNAS

Organism	Main component (% GC)	Satellite % GC	% of total	Reference
Bacteria				
Halobacterium salinarium	67	58	20	Joshi et al.
H. cutirubrum	68	59	10	Joshi et al.
Invertebrates				
Cancer antennarius	40	3	30	Smith
Cancer magister	41	3	12	Smith
Cancer productus	41	3	31	Smith
Gecarcinus lateralis	38	5	17	Skinner
		57	5	
Balanus nubilis (barnacle)	47	55	—	Smith
Vertebrates				
Mouse	41	32	11	Waring and Britten
Bovine	44	52		Cheng and Sueoka; Polli et al.
Guinea pig	37	43		Kit

Citarella). It is not yet known whether the satellite band in halobacteria is episomal.

The best-known satellite DNA is probably the poly dAT component of various species of crabs. This is unusual in that it contains only 3–4% GC being similar to the alternating dAT polymer synthesized *in vitro*. The relative amount of satellite DNAs varies in different species of the genus (Smith). A species of land-crab *Gecarcinus lateralis* contains a small high GC satellite in addition to the dAT component (Skinner) (Table 4). A high GC satellite occurs also in a species of barnacle (Smith). The intracellular location of these satellites in invertebrates is not known, although they do seem to be present in all tissues.

Satellite components have also been detected in some mammals (Table 4). The mouse satellite, undoubtedly chromosomal, is a particularly well-studied example. It appears to consist of many closely similar base sequences (Waring and Britten). For more detailed information regarding the properties of the mouse satellite DNA, see the chapters by Britten and Kohne, and by Walker, Flamm and MacLaren. The satellite in calf-thymus DNA seems also to contain partially related sequences as judged from its rate of renaturation (Polli et al.).

5. *Inter- and intra-genome base sequence homology*

The relative extent of homology among the base sequences of related DNAs may be measured by DNA–DNA duplex formation. Several variants of the techniques are used.

(a) An estimate may be obtained from the relative binding of one radio-labeled DNA to several unlabeled DNA preparations. The results are then expressed as percent reaction relative to that with homologous DNA since reactions are never quantitative (McCarthy and Bolton 1964). This method is limited in its precision since it is difficult to obtain several DNA-agar or DNA-filter preparations of equal quality.

(b) A more precise estimate may be made from the results of competition experiments. Several unlabeled DNA preparations are used as competitors in the reaction of one labeled DNA with homologous unlabeled DNA. Greater precision derives from the use of a single batch of DNA-filters. An example of this type of assay is shown in Fig. 1 illustrating the relationships of three DNAs isolated from various species of *Drosophila*. A plateau value in the competition curve is taken to indicate the fraction of the total DNA too dissimilar in base sequence to react. With complex DNA these measurements are relative estimates of base sequence divergence, and are highly dependent on the reaction conditions (McCarthy 1967; Laird and McCarthy).

(c) An estimate of the extent of base sequence divergence may be obtained from studies of the thermal stability of heteroduplexes. The decrease in stability is proportional to the extent of mismatching of bases, and thus, to the amount of base substitution. Fig. 2 illustrates the decreased stability of heterospecific DNA duplexes of *Drosophila* compared to homologous duplexes. These thermal stability measurements may be calibrated to yield quantitative measurements of base sequence divergence

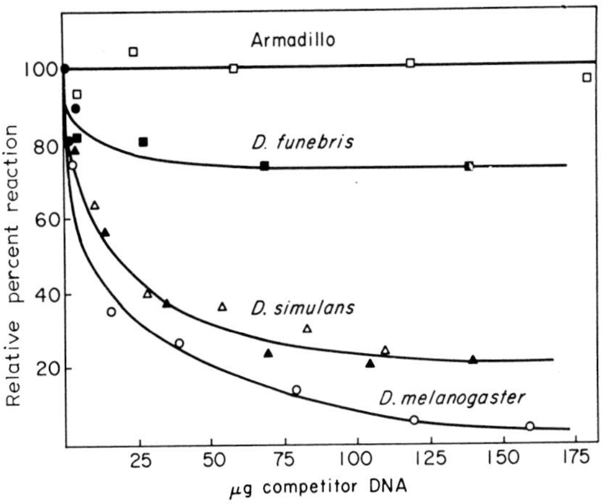

Fig. 1. Competition by DNA isolated from different *Drosophila* species in the reaction of H^3-labeled *D. melanogaster* DNA to filter-bound *D. melanogaster* DNA. Increasing amounts of unlabeled DNA from *D. funebris*, *D. simulans*, Amherst (△), *D. simulans*, Hawaii (▲), *D. melanogaster* or Armadillo were incubated with 1 μg H^3-labeled *D. melanogaster* DNA and 15 μg filter-bound *D. melanogaster* DNA.

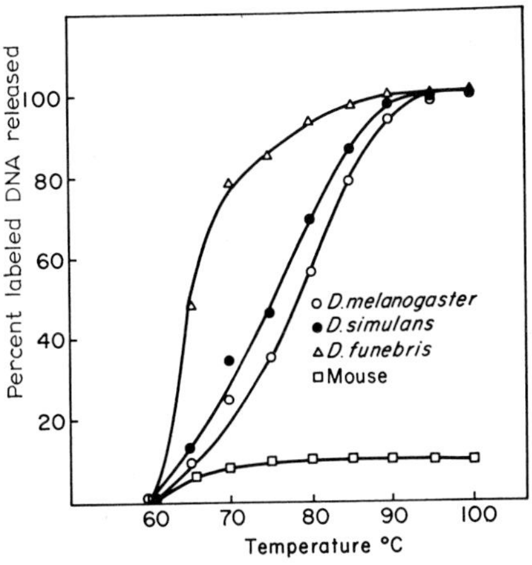

Fig. 2. Thermal stability of profiles of homologous and heterologous *Drosophila* DNA–DNA duplexes. 2 μg H^3-labeled *D. melanogaster* DNA (4200 cpm) was incubated at 60 °C for 30 hr in 0.4 ml 1 × SSC with filters containing *D. melanogaster* DNA (60 μg), *D. simulans* DNA (44 μg), *D. funebris* DNA (56 μg) or mouse DNA (60 μg). The filter-bound hybrids were incubated for 5 min in 5 ml 1 × SSC at each of the indicated temperatures. The eluted H^3 DNA was precipitated with 200 μg serum albumin in 10% TCA at 0 °C, collected on filters, and the radioactivity determined by liquid scintillation spectrometry. Of the input H^3 DNA, 8%, 5.6%, 2.8% and 0.8% reacted and was recovered by thermal denaturation from the *D. melanogaster*, *D. simulans*, *D. funebris* and mouse DNA filters, respectively. H^3 *Drosophila* DNA released from the mouse DNA filters is plotted relative to percent homologous DNA released. (SSC = 0.15 M NaCl + 0.015 M Na citrate.)

through similar studies of DNA chemically modified to give known extents of base changes. The study of interactions of oligodeoxyribonucleotides of known chain length with DNA provides another means for the quantitative estimation of base sequence divergence (McCarthy 1967).

Similar methods may be used for studies of intra-genome base sequence homologies deriving from gene duplications. This topic is covered in the chapters by Britten and Kohne.

6. *Conservative and non-conservative genes*

The most detailed information regarding the evolution of base sequences in a very restricted part of the genome comes from studies of amino acid sequence in proteins, such as hemoglobin and cytochrome C (Zuckerkandl and Pauling; Fitch and Margoliash). The amino acid sequences of hemoglobin and cytochrome C have been completely determined for a variety of organisms. In the latter case, it is clear that cytochrome C amino acid sequences are so extremely conservative that similarities may be seen among proteins of extremely distant organisms such as yeast and man (Fitch and Margoliash). No such detailed information exists for nucleic acid base sequences although it is equally evident that different sections of the genome evolve at different rates. In mammals, a particular fraction of the genome is relatively conserved in all the species examined (Hoyer et al.; McCarthy 1965). Any two mammalian DNAS of organisms placed in different orders cross-react to form DNA–DNA heteroduplexes to approximately the same extent. Furthermore, a small fraction of the DNA of mammals will react with that of birds or fish (Hoyer et al.). All of these experiments demonstrate variability of the rate of fixation of nucleotide substitutions in various parts of the genome. A special example of relatively conservative gene loci is afforded by the genes for ribosomal RNA.

7. *Ribosomal RNA genes*

The fraction of the genome which specifies ribosomal RNA synthesis is, by virtue of its accessibility, the most widely studied in terms of its variation among related organisms. In all cases, there are multiple genes for both the 16–18S and the 23–28S ribosomal RNA. These cistrons, which are usually contiguous, vary in number from 2–5 in bacteria to several hundred in higher organisms and normally comprise some 0.1 to 0.3% of the total DNA.

The base composition of ribosomal RNA is almost identical in all bacteria (Table 5), and not correlated with the base composition of the bacterial DNA (Midgley). Significant differences exist between the composition of the two ribosomal RNA size classes. In higher plants and animals the base composition is likewise very similar for all species. In all of these cases the overall base composition of ribosomal RNA is about

TABLE 5

Base composition of various ribosomal RNAS

Source	% GC in DNA	A	U	G	C	% GC	Reference
Bacteria							
Proteus vulgaris	38	26.2	20.7	31.4	21.7	53	Midgley
Bacillus subtilis	42	25.9	20.8	31.0	22.3	53	Midgley
Escherichia coli	50	25.1	20.4	32.6	21.9	54	Midgley
Pseudomonas aeruginosa	64	25.7	21.0	31.6	21.7	53	Midgley
Rhodopseudomonas spheroides	52	25.7	17.7	31.0	25.5	56	Gray et al.
Fungi							
Neurospora crassa							
cytoplasm	54	24.7	24.2	27.4	23.7	57	Storck (1966)
mitochondria	41	33.9	31.9	19.2	15.0	34	Rifkin et al.
Saccharomyces cerevisiae	41	26.6	26.5	25.7	20.1	47	Storck (1966)
Mucor racemosus	38	27.9	27.5	25.4	19.2	45	Storck (1966)
Protozoa							
Tetrahymena pyriformis	25	31.4	25.1	26.3	16.7	43	Lyttleton
Euglena gracilis							
cytoplasm	53	22.7	19.6	29.5	27.1	56	Brawerman
chloroplasts	24	29.3	23.9	27.4	19.4	47	Brawerman
Insect							
Drosophila melanogaster	40	29.9	27.4	23.0	19.7	43	Hastings and Kirby
Plants							
Pea	42	24.3	22.0	31.4	22.3	54	Wallace and Ts'o
Animals							
Rabbit	42	18.6	18.6	34.1	28.7	63	Wallace and Ts'o
Sheep	42	17.8	19.3	32.7	30.2	63	Wallace and Ts'o

53–63% GC. Some fungi and protozoa and *Drosophila melanogaster* are anomalous in having ribosomal RNA of the AT type. It seems likely that both chloroplast and mitochondrial DNA have genes for specifying ribosomal RNA since these organelles contain ribosomal RNA which differs both in size and base composition (Table 5).

Studies of various groups of bacteria have demonstrated that the base sequence of ribosomal RNA cistrons is more resistant to change than sequences elsewhere in the genome (Dubnau et al.; Moore and McCarthy 1967). This may be inferred from the high interspecies cross-reaction of ribosomal RNA and DNA or from the relatively high thermal stability of the ribosomal RNA hybrids formed. Fig. 3 illustrates the fact that

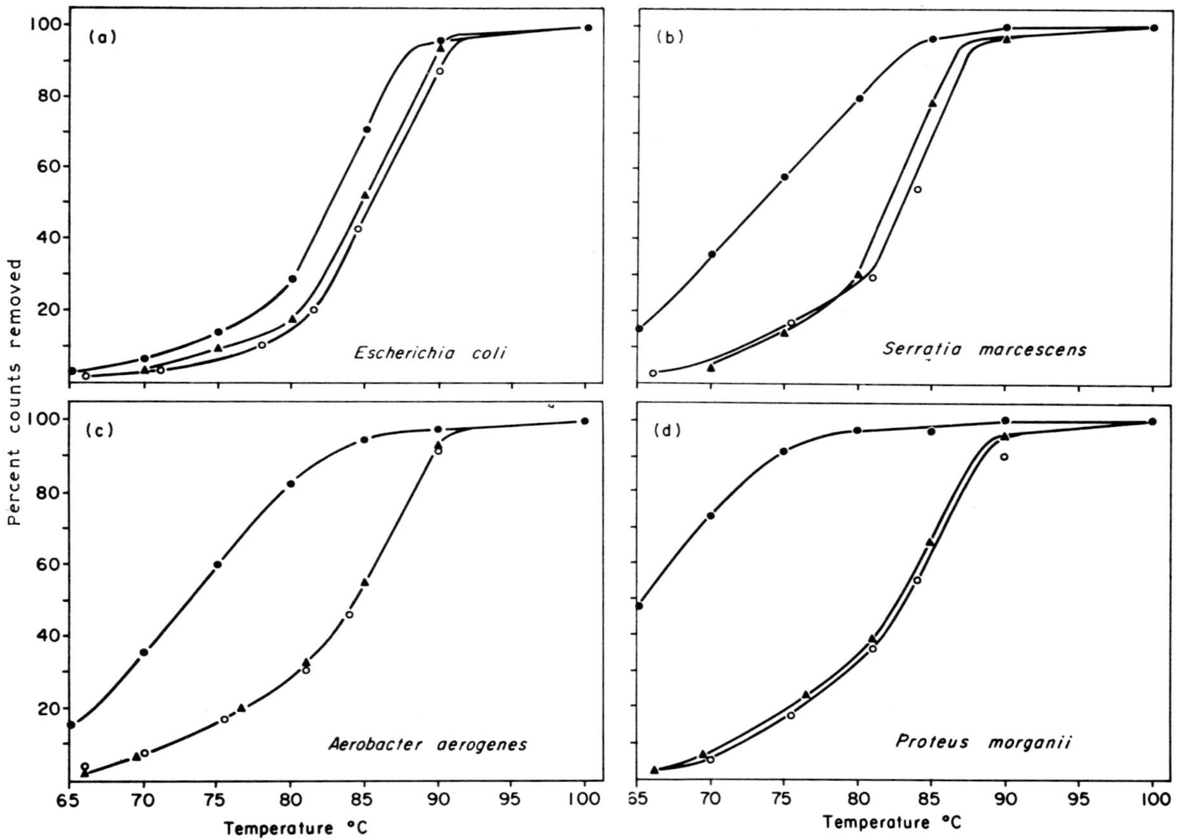

Fig. 3. Comparison of the thermal denaturation profiles of hybrids formed with either *Escherichia coli* ribosomal RNA or *E. coli* pulse-labeled RNA. The profiles for C^{14} pulse-labeled RNA (179 cpm/μg) were obtained by incubating 33.3 μg of RNA with filters containing 50 μg of DNA from various sources: pulse-labeled RNA, ●; 23S RNA, ▲; and 16S RNA, ○ (from Moore and McCarthy 1967).

interspecies hybrids of bacterial ribosomal RNA are of higher stability relative to homologous hybrids than is the case for hybrids of pulse-labeled or messenger RNA. Thus, the limited fraction of the genome represented by ribosomal RNA is conservative in base sequence relative to the remainder of the genome which specifies genetic messages. Similar results were obtained with *Drosophila* ribosomal RNA (Laird and McCarthy). Other published data dealing with ribosomal RNA of plants and mammals suggest that this relative conservation of base sequence in ribosomal RNA is universal in all groups of organisms. In spite of this overall conservatism, it seems likely that the base sequence differs among individual ribosomal RNA cistrons within an organism. This conclusion is based on the imperfect nature of the base-pairing in ribosomal RNA hybrids of mammals (Moore and McCarthy 1968).

8. Extranuclear DNA

(a) *Mitochondrial DNA*

In recent years it has become clear that mitochondria possess many independent biochemical capabilities. In addition to the presence of a unique DNA component, these organelles contain RNA polymerase and ribosomes distinguishable from those in the cytoplasm. In particular, mitochondrial DNA from vertebrate tissues was identified as a circular molecule of about 11×10^6 molecular weight (Borst et al.). All available evidence suggests that mitochondrial DNA is a unique and indispensable component distinct from the nuclear DNA.

The buoyant density and base composition of mitochondrial DNA isolated from various organisms is summarized in Table 6. Considerable variation exists so that the base composition may be higher, lower or nearly equal to that of nuclear DNA. In fungi where the base composition of the nuclear DNA is quite variable, Storck (1967) has observed some correlation between nuclear and mitochondrial base compositions such that fungi having high GC DNA tend to harbor mitochondrial DNA of high GC. In most cases, the mitochondrial DNA of related organisms is similar in base composition, although the large difference between mitochondrial DNAs of *Tetrahymena pyriformis* and *Paramecium aurelia* is an obvious exception (Table 6).

Nearest-neighbor frequencies of the mitochondrial DNA of *Physarum polycephalum* have been determined by Cummins et al. (see Table 3). These authors point out that these frequencies, particularly that of CpG, are closer to those occurring in bacterial DNAs than those of eucaryotic organisms, in accordance with the procaryotic nature of these organelles.

(b) *DNA of chloroplasts and other organelles*

The most convincing evidence for the presence of DNA in chloroplasts is offered by analytical centrifugation of DNA from complete plant or algal lysates or preparations enriched in chloroplasts. In many cases, satellite DNA components are observed.

TABLE 6

Density and base composition of mitochondrial DNA

Organism	Nuclear DNA ρ	Nuclear DNA % GC[a]	Mitochondrial DNA ρ	Mitochondrial DNA % GC[a]	Reference
Protista					
Saccharomyces cerevisiae	1.700	41	1.685	25	Corneo et al.
Neurospora crassa	1.712	53	1.701	42	Luck and Reich
Paramecium aurelia	1.689	30	1.702	43	Suyama and Preer
Tetrahymena pyriformis	1.688	29	1.682	23	Suyama and Preer
Euglena gracilis	1.707	48	1.691	32	Ray and Hanawalt
Plants					
Allium cepa	1.688	29	1.706	47	Suyama and Bonner
Animals					
Mouse	1.701	42	1.701	42	Corneo et al.
	1.690	31			
Guinea pig	1.700	41	1.702	43	Corneo et al.
Chicken	1.701	42	1.708	49	Corneo et al.
Duck	1.700	41	1.711	52	Borst et al.

[a] % GC estimated from the relationship established by Schildkraut et al. (1962b) assuming no unusual bases.

TABLE 7

Density and base composition of chloroplast DNA

Organism	Nuclear DNA ρ	Nuclear DNA % GC[a]	Chloroplast DNA ρ	Chloroplast DNA % GC[a]	Reference
Algae					
Euglena gracilis	1.707	48	1.686	26	Ray and Hanawalt; Edelman et al. (1965)
Chlamydomonas reinhardii	1.723	64	1.695	36	Chun et al.
Chlorella ellipsoida	1.716	57	1.695	36	Chun et al.
Higher plants					
Beta vulgaris	1.695	36	1.705	46	Chun et al.
Spinacia oleracia	1.689	30	1.700	42	Kislev et al.
Nicotiana tabacum	1.696	37	1.706	47	Green and Gordon
Dianthus caryophilus	1.695	36	1.706	47	Green and Gordon
Brassica rapa	1.692	33	1.695	36	Suyama and Bonner

[a] Base composition estimated for the relationship established by Schildkraut et al. (1962b), assuming no unusual bases.

These may be attributed to chloroplasts in the algae since aplastidic non-photosynthetic variants lack the satellite DNA (Table 7). In the case of microorganisms, the base composition of chloroplast DNA is higher in GC than that of the nuclear component, while in higher plants the base composition of chloroplast DNA is lower in % GC.

Estimates of the amount of DNA per chloroplast are in the range of 1×10^{-16} – 4×10^{-15} g/chloroplast, which would suggest a content of $10^8 - 4 \times 10^9$ daltons per chloroplast (Gibor and Granick). Studies of the rate of renaturation suggest a non-redundant DNA of about 80×10^6 molecular weight (Wells and Birnstiel).

The question of the origin of chloroplasts and their possible relationship to blue-green algae has been recently discussed by Edelman et al. (1967). Since both chloroplast and blue-green algal DNA are heterogeneous in base composition, the origin of chloroplasts by invasion of eucaryotic cells is likely to have occurred more than once. The putative relationship of blue-green algal and chloroplast DNA will be further explored by physical studies of the DNAs and through molecular hybridization.

Some studies of the DNA associated with the kinetoplasts of protozoa have been published. Kinetoplast DNA can be detected as a satellite in DNA extracted from whole cells of *Crithidia fasciculata* and *Leishmania enriettii* (Schildkraut et al. 1962b; Dubuy et al.). Since these organisms contain only one kinetoplast per cell, the amount of kinetoplast DNA would seem to be larger than that present either in chloroplasts or mitochondria. In both cases, the kinetoplast DNA is about 40% GC while the nuclear components are about 60% GC.

9. *Conclusions*

Although very little actual sequence data exist, a considerable body of information is available regarding similarities and differences in DNA base sequences of related organisms. Recent advances in the methods for fractionating DNA both at the level of organization of the chromosome and at the level of pure nucleic acid make it possible to examine different base sequences in terms of their distribution and relative lability to evolutionary divergence. Refinements in the methodology are likely to facilitate the quantitative measurement of the average base sequence divergence between two genomes as well as that at a given locus. These advances will surely increase our understanding of evolutionary mechanisms at the molecular level.

References

ANTONOV, A.C.: The relationship of the base composition of DNA to systematics and evolution of animals. Progr. Modern Biol. (USSR) 60 (1965) 161.

ATKIN, N.B., G.MATTINSON, W.BECAK and S.OHNO: The comparative DNA content of 19 species of placental mammals, reptiles and birds. Chromosoma 17 (1965) 1.

BELLETT, A. J. D.: Numerical classification of some viruses, bacteria and animals according to nearest neighbor base sequence frequency. Proc. Natl. Acad. Sci. U.S. 54 (1965) 491.

BELLETT, A. J. D.: Preliminary classification of viruses based on quantitative comparisons of viral nucleic acids. J. Virol. 1 (1967) 245.

BERG, P., H. FANCHER and M. CHAMBERLIN: The synthesis of mixed polynucleotides by purified preparations of DNA polymerase from *E. coli*. In: V. Bryson and H. J. Vogel, eds.: Informational macromolecules, Rutgers symposium. New York, Academic Press (1963).

BORST, P., A. M. KROON and G. J. C. M. RUTTENBERG: Mitochondrial DNA and other forms of cytoplasmic DNA. In: D. Shugar, ed.: Genetic elements, properties and function. New York, Academic Press (1967).

BRAWERMAN, G.: The isolation of a specific species of ribosomes associated with chloroplast development in *Euglena gracilis*. Biochim. Biophys. Acta 72 (1963) 317.

BURTON, K.: Sequence determination in nucleic acids. In: P. N. Campbell and G. D. Greville eds.: Essays in biochemistry, Vol. 1, p. 57, New York, Academic Press (1966).

CHENG, T. Y. and N. SUEOKA: Heterogeneity of DNA in density and base composition. Science 141 (1963) 1194.

CORNEO, G., C. MOORE, D. R. SANADI, L. I. GROSSMAN and J. MARMUR: Mitochondrial DNA in yeast and some mammalian species. Science 151 (1966) 687.

CUMMINS, J. E., H. P. RUSCH and T. E. EVANS: Nearest neighbor frequencies and the phylogenetic origin of mitochondrial DNA in *Physarum polycephalum*. J. Mol. Biol. 23 (1967) 281.

DENHARDT, D. T.: A membrane-filter technique for the detection of complementary DNA. Biochem. Biophys. Res. Commun. 23 (1966) 641.

DOTY, P., J. MARMUR, J. EIGNER and C. L. SCHILDKRAUT: Strand separation and specific recombination in DNAs. II. Physical chemical studies. Proc. Natl. Acad. Sci., U.S. 46 (1960) 461.

DUBNAU, D., I. SMITH, P. MORELL and J. MARMUR: Gene conservation in *Bacillus* species. I. Conserved genetic and nucleic acid base sequence homologies. Proc. Natl. Acad. Sci., U.S. 54 (1965) 491.

DUBUY, H. G., C. F. T. MATTERN and F. L. RILEY: Isolation and characterization of DNA from kinetoplasts of *Leishmania enriettii*. Science 147 (1965) 754.

EDELMAN, M., J. A. SCHIFF and H. T. EPSTEIN: Studies of chloroplast development in Euglena. XII. Two types of satellite DNA. J. Mol. Biol. 11 (1965) 769.

EDELMAN, M., D. SWINTON, J. A. SCHIFF, H. T. EPSTEIN and B. ZELDIN: DNA of the blue-green algae (Cyanophyta). Bacteriol. Rev. 31 (1967) 315.

FALKOW, S. and R. V. CITARELLA: Molecular homology of *F. menogenote* DNA. J. Mol. Biol. 12 (1965) 138.

FITCH, W. M. and E. MARGOLIASH: Construction of phylogenetic trees. Science 155 (1967) 279.

GIBOR, A. and S. GRANICK: Plastids and mitochondria: Inheritable systems. Science 145 (1964) 890.

GILLESPIE, D. and S. SPIEGELMAN: A quantitative assay for DNA–RNA hybrids with DNA immobilized on a membrane. J. Mol. Biol. 12 (1965) 829.

GRAY, E. D., A. M. HAYWOOD and E. CHARGAFF: Rapidly labeled RNA of *Rhodopseudomonas spheroides* under varying conditions of catalase synthesis. Biochim. Biophys. Acta 87 (1964) 397.

GREEN, B. A. and M. T. GORDON: The satellite DNAs of some higher plants. Biochim. Biophys. Acta 145 (1967) 378.

HALL, J. B. and R. L. SINSHEIMER: The structure of the DNA of bacteriophage ΦX174. IV. Pyrimidine sequences. J. Mol. Biol. 6 (1963) 115.

HASTINGS, J. R. B. and K. S. KIRBY: The nucleic acids of *Drosophila melanogaster*. Biochem. J. 100 (1966) 532.

HILL, L. R.: An index to DNA base compositions of bacterial species. J. Gen. Microbiol. 44 (1966) 419.

HOYER, B. H., B. J. MCCARTHY and E. T. BOLTON: A molecular approach in the systematics of higher organisms. Science 144 (1964) 959.

HOYER, B.H. and R.B.ROBERTS: Studies of DNA homology by the DNA-agar technique. In: H.J. Taylor, ed.: Molecular genetics. New York, Academic Press (1967).

JOSHI, J., W.GUILD and P.HANDLER: The presence of two species of DNA in some halobacteria. J. Mol. Biol. 6 (1963) 34.

JOSSE, J., A.D.KAISER and A.KORNBERG: Enzymatic synthesis of DNA. VIII. Frequencies of nearest neighbor base sequences in DNA. J. Biol. Chem. 236 (1961) 864.

KISLEV, N., H.SWIFT and L.BOGORAD: Nucleic acids of chloroplasts and mitochondria in Swiss chard. J. Cellular Biol. 25 (1965) 327.

KIT, S.: Equilibrium sedimentation in density gradients of DNA preparations from animal tissues. J. Mol. Biol. 3 (1961) 711.

KORNBERG, A.: Synthesis of DNA-like polymers *de novo* or by reiterative replications. In: V.Bryson and H.J.Vogel, eds.: Evolving genes and proteins. Rutgers symposium. New York, Academic Press (1965).

LAIRD, C.D. and B.J.MCCARTHY: Magnitude of interspecific nucleotide sequence variability in *Drosophila*. Geneticis, in press.

LUCK, D.J.L. and E.REICH: DNA in mitochondria of *Neurospora crassa*. Proc. Natl. Acad. Sci., U.S. 52 (1964) 931.

LYTTLETON, J.W.: A simple method of isolating ribosomes from *Tetrahymena pyriformis*. Exptl. Cell Res. 31 (1963) 385.

MCCARTHY, B.J.: The arrangement of base sequences in DNA. Bacteriol. Rev. 31 (1967) 215.

MCCARTHY, B.J.: The evolution of base sequences in polynucleotides. Progr. Nucleic Acid Res. Mol. Biol. 4 (1965) 129.

MCCARTHY, B.J. and E.T.BOLTON: An approach to the measurement of genetic relatedness among organisms. Proc. Natl. Acad. Sci., U.S. 50 (1963) 156.

MARMUR, J. and P.DOTY: Determination of the base composition of DNA from its thermal denaturation temperature. J. Mol. Biol. 5 (1962) 109.

MIDGLEY, J.E.M.: The nucleotide composition of RNA from several microbial species. Biochim. Biophys. Acta 61 (1962) 513.

MOORE, R.L. and B.J.MCCARTHY: Comparative study of ribosomal RNA in Enterobacteria and Myxobacteria. J. Bacteriol. 94 (1967) 1066.

MOORE, R.L. and B.J.MCCARTHY: Variability in the base sequence of the reduplicated genes for ribosomal RNA in the rabbit. Biochem. Genetics 2 (1968) 75.

MORRISON, J.M., H.M.KEIR, H.SUBAK-SHARPE and L.V.CRAWFORD: Nearest neighbor base sequence analysis of the DNAs of a further three mammalian viruses: SV_{40} human papilloma virus and adenovirus type 2. J. Gen. Virol. 1 (1967) 101.

POLLI, E., G.CORNEO, E.GINELLI and P.BIANCHI: Fractionation of calf thymus DNA by density gradient centrifugation. Biochim. Biophys. Acta 103 (1965) 672.

RAY, D.S. and P.C.HANAWALT: Properties of the satellite DNA associated with the chloroplasts of *Euglena gracilis*. J. Mol. Biol. 11 (1965) 760.

RIFKIN, M., D.WOOD and D.LUCK: Ribosomal RNA and ribosomes from mitochondria of *Neurospora crassa*. Proc. Natl. Acad. Sci., U.S. 58 (1967) 1025.

SCHILDKRAUT, C.L., M.MANDEL, S.LEVISOHN, J.E.SONNEBORN and J.MARMUR: DNA base composition and taxonomy of some protozoa. Nature 196 (1962a) 795.

SCHILDKRAUT, C.L., J.MARMUR and P.DOTY: Determination of the base composition of DNA from its buoyant density in CsCl. J. Mol. Biol. 4 (1962b) 430.

SEDAT, J. and R.L.SINSHEIMER: Structure of the DNA of bacteriophage ΦX174. V. Purine sequences. J. Mol. Biol. 9 (1964) 489.

SKINNER, D.M.: Satellite DNAs in the crabs *Gecarcinus lateralis* and *Cancer pagurus*. Proc. Natl. Acad. Sci., U.S. 58 (1967) 103.

SMITH, M.: Deoxyribonucleic acid of Crustacea. J. Mol. Biol. 9 (1964) 17.

STEBBINS, C.L.: Chromosomal variation and evolution. Science 152 (1966) 1463.

STORCK, R.: Nucleotide composition of nucleic acids of fungi. II. Deoxyribonucleic acids. J. Bacteriol. 91 (1966) 227.

SUEOKA, N.: Variation and heterogeneity of the base composition of DNA: A compilation of old and new data. J. Mol. Biol. 3 (1961) 31.

SUYAMA, J. and W.D.BONNER: DNA from plant mitochondria. Plant Physiol. 41 (1966) 393.

SUYAMA, J. and J.R.PREER: Mitochondrial DNA from protozoa. Genetics 52 (1965) 1057.

SWARTZ, M.M., T.A.TRAUTNER and A.KORNBERG: Enzymatic synthesis of DNA. XI. Further studies on nearest neighbor base sequences in DNAs. J. Biol. Chem. 237 (1962) 1961.

THOMAS, C.A., JR and L.A.MACHATTIE: The anatomy of viral DNA molecules. Ann. Rev. Biochem. 36 (1967) 485.

VANYUSHIN, B.F., A.N.BELOZERSKY and N.A.KOKURINA: Nucleic acids and plant evolution. Trans. Moscow Soc. Naturalists 24 (1966) 7.

WALLACE, J.M. and P.O.P.TS'O: Nucleotide composition of various ribosomes. Biochem. Biophys. Res. Commun. 5 (1961) 125.

WARING, M.J. and R.J.BRITTEN: Nucleotide sequence repetition: A rapidly reassociating fraction of mouse DNA. Science 154 (1966) 791.

WELLS, R.D. and M.L.BIRNSTIEL: A rapidly renaturing DNA component associated with chloroplast preparations. Biochem. J. 105 (1967) 53.

ZUCKERKANDL, E. and L.PAULING: Evolutionary divergence and convergence in proteins. In: V. Bryson and H.J.Vogel, eds.: Evolving genes and proteins. New York, Academic Press (1965).

CHAPTER 2

Repetition of nucleotide sequences in chromosomal DNA

R. J. BRITTEN and D. E. KOHNE

Department of Terrestrial Magnetism, Carnegie Institution of Washington, Washington, D.C. 20015

Contents

1. Introduction
2. DNA, strand separation and reassociation
3. The rate of reassociation of DNA without sequence repetition
4. Repetitious DNA in higher organisms
5. The occurrence of repetitious DNA
6. The precision of repetition
7. Length of repeated sequences

1. Introduction

The DNA of all organisms contains some nucleotide sequences that occur more than once. Some repetition of short sequences is expected by chance alone. In reality very much more repetition is present than would be expected by chance. In higher organisms between $\frac{1}{3}$ to $\frac{2}{3}$ of the total DNA is made up of sequences hundreds of nucleotides long which recur a thousand to a million times. This chapter discusses much of the experimental evidence concerning repeated nucleotide sequences reported by Britten and Waring, Waring and Britten, and Britten and Kohne (1967a, b, 1968). The following chapter discusses principally the implications of these findings.

In order to deal with this essentially novel subject some concepts must be introduced and our usage of certain words clarified. Therefore, as a brief introduction we have taken some definitions from 'An instructive glossary' recently prepared by Bolton et al., and arranged them in logical rather than alphabetical order, with minor changes in phraseology.

nucleotide sequence. A specifically ordered row of nucleotides in the DNA (or RNA) of an organism. In the DNA, the complementary sequence is always present (except for single-stranded viruses) and the two strands are often considered together as in: The rate of reassociation is a measure of the degree of repetition of a nucleotide sequence.

repeated sequence. A segment of nucleotide sequence which occurs many times in the DNA of one cell of a higher organism. A coined word would be preferable since precise repetition appears to be the exception within the large, greatly divergent families of repeated sequences.

family of repeated sequences. The set of related sequences in the genome of a given higher organism which will reassociate with each other. The concept of family is useful. At the moment, however, different families with equal numbers of members and equal degree of divergence are not resolvable.

unique. Designates that a particular sequence occurs only once in a genome, as in: The concentration of a unique sequence is known from the genome size and the total DNA concentration. The situation for almost all of viral and bacterial DNA.

divergence. (1) The increasing degree of mismatch among a set of nucleic acid sequences that occurs on an evolutionary time scale, as in: The divergence between the DNA of *Salmonella* and *E. coli* has lowered the average melting temperature of interspecies pairs compared to that of intraspecies pairs. (2) The act of speciation which leads to two distinct species lines, as in: The paleontological record indicates that about 300 million years have elapsed since divergence of the lines leading to the amphibians and the reptiles.

cation concentration (κ). The concentration of cations determines the dimensions of the charge cloud around the negatively charged nucleic acid molecules and thus controls the repulsive Coulomb forces. Symbolized by κ, representing the molarity of monovalent cations. Divalent ions are immensely more effective and must be considered separately. The rate of reassociation is very sensitive to the cation concentration. A standard buffer used in this work is sodium phosphate, *p*H 6.8, abbreviated PB. For 0.12 M PB the value of κ is 0.18.

criterion. The standard of precision of pairing set by the cation concentration in combination with the temperature during incubation. Now expressed in terms of these two parameters because the fraction of unpaired nucleotides implied is unknown.

dissociate. To separate completely the two strands of a pair so that one may diffuse away from the other.

reassociate. To incubate nucleic acids under conditions such that dissociated complementary strands may collide with each other and form base-paired double strands. Also the act of forming such a double strand. Reassociation does not imply that the particular strands were paired *in vivo*. The optimum temperature is 20 to 30° below the melting temperature and the rate of the reaction increases with the cation concentration. See C_0t.

C_0t. (k_0t) The product of the concentration of DNA or RNA and the time of incubation (Mols nucleotides × seconds per liter). The effectiveness of the C_0t in inducing reassociation depends on the genome size, the presence of repeated sequences, the fragment size, the cation concentration and the temperature of incubation.

pair. To form a base-paired structure between two nucleic acid strands due to complementary or partially complementary nucleotide sequences. To reassociate. Also the product of this process.

related. Signifies that nucleic acid fragments contain complementary nucleotide sequences and thus will pair. It is presumed that complementary sequences of any significant length, greater than say 20 or 25 nucleotides, cannot arise independently. Thus relatedness in this sense implies common origin. The boundary between relationship and chance similarity is not yet clearly defined experimentally.

genome size. (1) The haploid DNA content of a cell or virus particle. In rapidly growing cells partially completed new chromosome sets are not to be counted. (2) The amount of DNA per typical unique sequence in the genome. (1) is measured by chemical assay and (2) by rate of reassociation. The comparison of these results indicates that chromosome pairs of a diploid cell are nearly identical in sequence. There are difficulties with these definitions, for example: sex chromosomes; polyploid plant hybrids; significantly different genes in a diploid heterozygote, etc.

higher organism. Here used in a somewhat vague sense to include all organisms with highly repetitive DNA sequences. To date only viruses, bacteria and a blue-green alga have been found not to contain gross quantities of repeated sequences. It thus appears possible that the line between organisms that contain many or few repeated sequences will lie between eukaryotic and prokaryotic creatures.

saltatory replication. The hypothetical event by which a family of hundreds of thousands of similar nucleotide sequences is produced in the DNA of an organism. Large, closely similar (presumed evolutionarily young), as well as greatly divergent (presumed evolutionarily old), families are observed. Thus, families are produced in a time short compared to the time required for their loss by divergence (a few hundred million years).

2. DNA, strand separation and reassociation

The capacity of the complementary strands of DNA to reassociate specifically supplies an immensely powerful tool for studies of relationship. Conditions can be chosen such that reassociation occurs only between nucleotide sequences having common ancestry.

DNA carefully isolated from tissues is in the form of long double-stranded molecules. These molecules are termed 'native' as long as the two strands have not been separated although they may have been broken into relatively short but still double-stranded pieces. The two strands of the native molecule may be completely dissociated from each other in solution by boiling. Under the proper conditions the separated complementary strands may reform stable double-stranded molecules with a helical structure like native DNA. A basic paper in this area is that by Marmur et al. Other useful papers are those by Bolton and McCarthy and McCarthy and Bolton (1964). We have chosen to call these processes dissociation and reassociation. They have been termed denaturation and renaturation by many authors. However, the term renaturation is not properly applicable to pairs formed between DNA strands from different animals as well as between different segments of the DNA from one animal.

The process of reassociation can be measured in a variety of ways, each of which depends upon some easily detected physical difference between single-stranded dissociated DNA and doublestranded reassociated DNA. In the DNA-agar method of McCarthy and Bolton (1963) reassociation is monitored by measuring the binding of labeled single-stranded DNA to DNA which is physically immobilized in a supporting substance. Unbound DNA can then be very effectively washed away. It has been demonstrated by this method that the reassociation reaction is species dependent. DNA from a given species binds most effectively with immobilized DNA from the same species. DNA from closely related species will bind nearly as well, while DNA from a distantly related organism will bind hardly at all to the immobilized DNA.

It is also possible to measure the amount of reassociation which has occurred between single strands of DNA that are in free solution. The fraction of reassociated DNA may be estimated from the change in the physical properties of the molecules. For example, dissociated DNA absorbs more ultraviolet light than does reassociated DNA and it is therefore possible to follow the reassociation of DNA by monitoring the quantitative change in the absorbance of ultraviolet light during the course of the reaction. Double-stranded DNA has a greater degree of optical activity than single-stranded DNA and it is possible to follow the reassociation reaction by recording the changes in optical rotation as helical structure is formed.

Another very useful technique for measuring reassociation depends on the ability of a calcium phosphate (hydroxyapatite) column to separate reassociated, double-stranded DNA from single-stranded DNA. Reassociation reactions can be followed by passing the reaction mixtures through hydroxyapatite columns and determining the amount of double-stranded DNA adhering to the column. The technique for separating single strand and double strand DNA was described by Bernardi and by Miyazawa and Thomas and utilized by Britten and Kohne (1967a) to measure reassociation.

The stability of the reassociated double-stranded molecules can be compared with that of native DNA. In this way the precision of sequence matching between the two strands of the reassociated molecule may be estimated. Reassociated DNA molecules which are imperfectly matched have a lower temperature of dissociation than those reassociated with a higher precision of sequence matching or, of course, native DNA molecules.

3. The rate of reassociation of DNA without sequence repetition

The presence of many repeated nucleotide sequences in the DNA of higher organisms brings a totally new significance to studies of the rate of reassociation of DNA. Previously, the *fact* of reassociation was emphasized while the *rate* of the process was principally of technical interest. The rate of reassociation is a direct measure of the concentration of complementary sequences and thus the degree of sequence repetition.

The reassociation of a pair of complementary strands results from their collision. While most collisions between single-stranded fragments are ineffective, an occasional collision leads to the formation of a structure with the two sequences properly opposed, 'in register' so that a stable helical double-stranded molecule results. The time measured for the reassociation of one-half of the DNA is just proportional to the number of different fragments originally present, for a given DNA concentration. The DNA of a small virus (SV_{40}) cut to one-tenth of its original length yields 10 different fragments, each 1200 nucleotides long. The phage T4 has 35 times as much DNA and yields 350 different fragments of the same size. If the fragmented preparations of DNA are adjusted to the same *total* concentration under conditions suitable for reassociation, it is observed that the T4 viral DNA takes 35 times as long as the SV_{40} DNA for one-half of the pieces to become reassociated. From reassociation rate measurements it is thus possible to determine the number of different nucleotide sequences present in the genome of a particular species by comparing its DNA reassociation rate to that of an appropriate standard DNA.

In order to achieve reproducible rates of reassociation and be able to interpret the relative rates for different DNA preparations, the temperature, salt concentration and fragment size must be controlled. The DNA used in this work has been sheared to fragments about 500 nucleotides long by two passages through a needle valve with a pressure drop of 3.4 kilobar.

Fig. 1 illustrates a useful graphical method for the presentation of measurements of the time course of reassociation. The progress of an ideal second-order reaction is plotted as a function of the logarithm of the time after initiation of the reaction multiplied by the DNA concentration. The logarithmic scale is convenient for comparing reactions which differ in rate by large factors. Further, since the horizontal axis is the logarithm of the product of initial concentration (C_0) and the time (t), reactions carried out at different concentrations may be intercompared and the data combined to give a more complete view of the time course of the reaction.

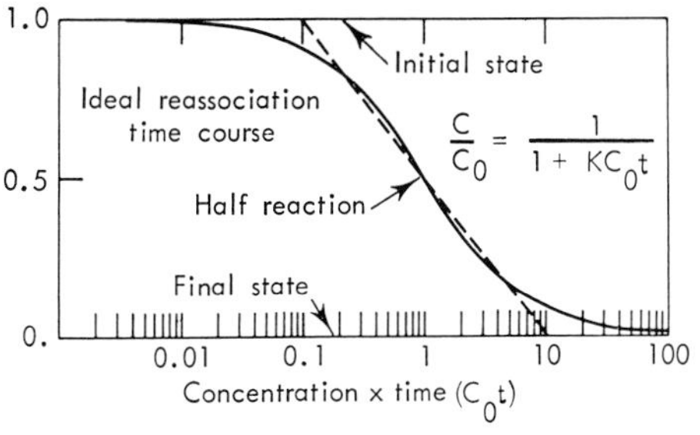

Fig. 1. Ideal second-order reaction time course as an illustration of the features of the log C_0t plot. (From Britten and Kohne 1967a.)

The symmetrical shape of an ideal second-order curve plotted in this way is pleasing and convenient. The central two-thirds of the curve follows closely a straight line, shown dashed. The ratio of the values of the C_0t at which the line passes through zero and 100 percent reaction is a useful diagnostic. This ratio is about 100 for an ideal reaction when estimated as shown in Fig. 1. If the ratio is much greater than 100 the reaction is surely heterogeneous; i.e., species with widely different rates of reassociation are present.

Fig. 2 shows the time course of reassociation of a number of double-stranded nucleic acids. Within the precision of the measurements the reassociation of these various preparations follows the time course of a single second-order reaction. The value of the C_0t at which each of these curves reaches 50 percent reassociation is marked with an arrow on the upper nomographic scale. Cairn's measurement of the size of the *E. coli* genome (4.5×10^5 nucleotide pairs) has been used to locate the nomographic scale shown above the figure. The T4 bacteriophage chromosome length has also been carefully measured by Burgi and Hershey to be 2×10^5 nucleotide pairs. The molecular weight of MS-2 viral RNA is 2.4×10^6 or 4,000 nucleotide pairs in the double-stranded replicative form as estimated by Billeter et al. The rate of

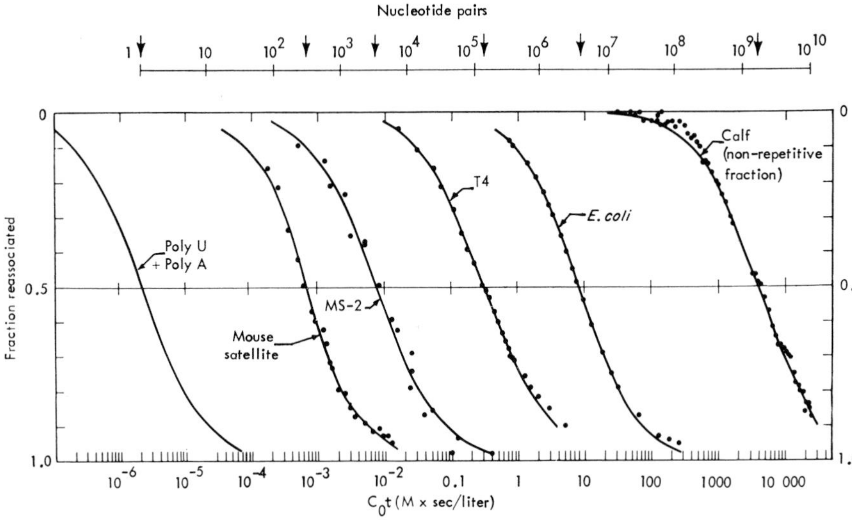

Fig. 2. Reassociation of double-stranded nucleic acids from various sources. The C_0t required for half reaction is indicated by the arrows near the upper nomographic scale. Over a factor of 10^9 this value is proportional to the number of different nucleotide sequences in the nucleic acid preparation. The curves shown are those that would be observed with $\kappa = 0.18$ at the optimum temperature for the particular nucleic acid. Poly U + Poly A from Ross and Sturtevant (optical hypochromicity as measure). MS-2 RNA from Billeter et al. (increase in RNAase resistance as measure). The remainder are from Britten and Kohne (1967a) with optical hypochromicity as the measure for T-4, *E. coli* and mouse satellite. The calf non-repetitive fraction was measured by the increase in optical rotation at 370 mμ.

reassociation of the homopolymer pair (poly U + poly A) is consistent with the fact that these molecules are complementary in all possible registrations.

The curve on the far right of Fig. 2 shows the reassociation measured by optical rotation of a slowly reassociating fraction of calf thymus DNA prepared on hydroxyapatite. The rate of reassociation of this fraction is just that expected if it were made up of unique sequences. The genome size of the calf is 3.2×10^9 nucleotide pairs and the slowly reassociating fraction amounts to about 60 percent of the calf DNA.

It appears that the C_0t required for half reassociation of DNA is proportional to the genome size. This is only true, however, in the absence of repeated DNA sequences. The curve on Fig. 2 labeled mouse satellite refers to a 10 percent fraction of mouse DNA which was estimated by Waring and Britten to be repeated about a million times.

4. *Repetitious DNA in higher organisms*

When the time course of reassociation is measured for the DNA of higher organisms, a fraction of the DNA reassociates slowly as would be expected for DNA derived from a large genome where each sequence is present in low concentration. In addition, however, there are fractions which reassociate with much greater rapidity, indicating that multiple copies of these sequences exist in the genome. The resulting curve is highly complex and spreads over a wide range of C_0t.

Fig. 3 shows the time course of reassociation of calf thymus DNA, assayed

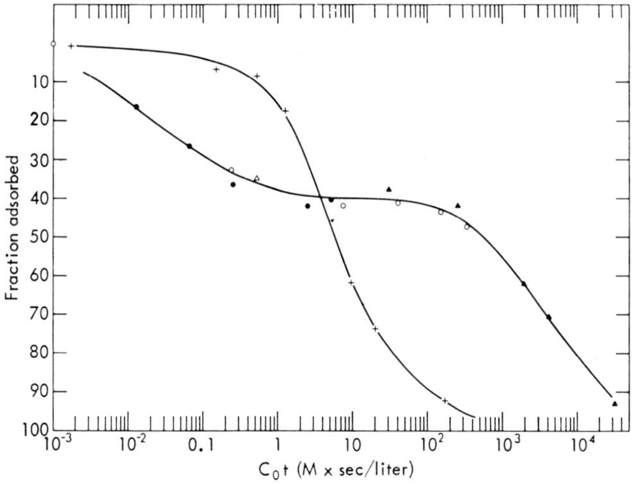

Fig. 3. The kinetics of reassociation of calf thymus DNA measured with hydroxyapatite. The DNA was sheared at 3.4 kilobar and incubated at 60 °C in 0.12 M PB. At various times samples were diluted, if necessary (in 0.12 M PB at 60 °C), and passed over a hydroxyapatite column at 60 °C. The DNA concentrations during the reaction were: △, 2; ●, 10; ○, 600; ▲, 8600 μg/ml; +, radioactively labeled *E. coli* DNA at 43 μg/ml present in the reaction containing calf thymus DNA at 8600 μg/ml. (From Britten and Kohne 1967b.)

with hydroxyapatite. Evidence that this technique indeed measures reassociation has been reported by Britten and Kohne (1967a, b). In the case of the calf DNA (as for the DNA of many but not all higher organisms) a clear separation exists between DNA which reassociates very rapidly and very slowly. The rapid fraction in calf DNA requires a C_0t of 0.03 for half reassociation while the slow fraction requires a C_0t of 3,000. Thus the concentration of DNA strands which reassociate rapidly is 100,000 times the concentration of those which reassociate slowly. If the slow fraction is made up of unique sequences each of which occurs only once in the calf genome then the sequences of the rapid fraction must be repeated 100,000 times on the average.

The measurements shown on Fig. 3 were done in several series at widely different DNA concentrations. Nevertheless the results are concordant. The points fall on a single curve with good accuracy. This establishes that the measured reassociation process results from a bimolecular collision. In turn the rapidity of the early part of the reassociation reaction can result only from a high concentration of reacting species.

In one of the series of measurements on Fig. 3 in addition to the 8600 μg per ml of sheared calf DNA there was present 43 μg per ml of P^{32}-labeled sheared *E. coli* DNA which serves as an 'internal standard'. The simultaneous assay of the reassociation of the two DNAs present together controls a variety of possible experimental errors. Thus they give a more precise measure of the relative concentration of complementary sequences in the *E. coli* DNA compared to those in the calf DNA.

The DNA content of bull sperm is 3.2×10^9 nucleotide pairs per cell and Cairn's

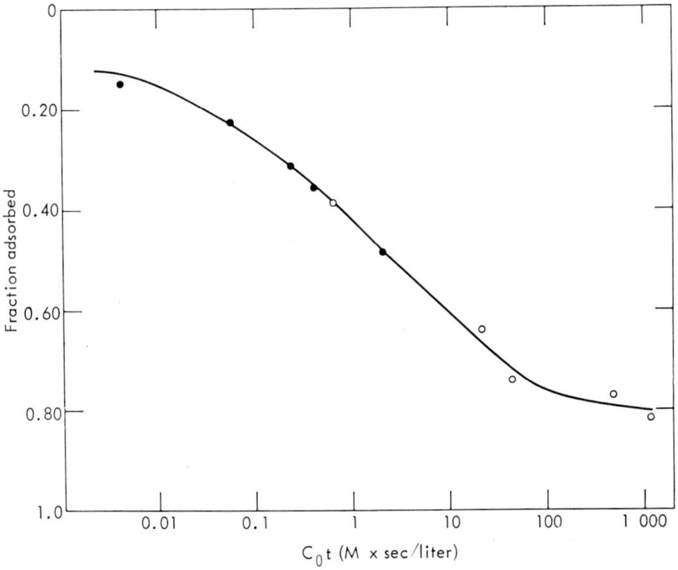

Fig. 4. The kinetics of reassociation of salmon sperm DNA measured with hydroxyapatite. The DNA was sheared at 3.4 kilobar and incubated at 50 °C in 0.14 M PB. The samples were diluted into 0.14 M PB at 50 °C, if necessary, and passed over hydroxyapatite at 50 °C. The DNA concentrations during the incubation were: ●, 8; ○, 1600 μg/ml. (From Britten and Kohne 1967b.)

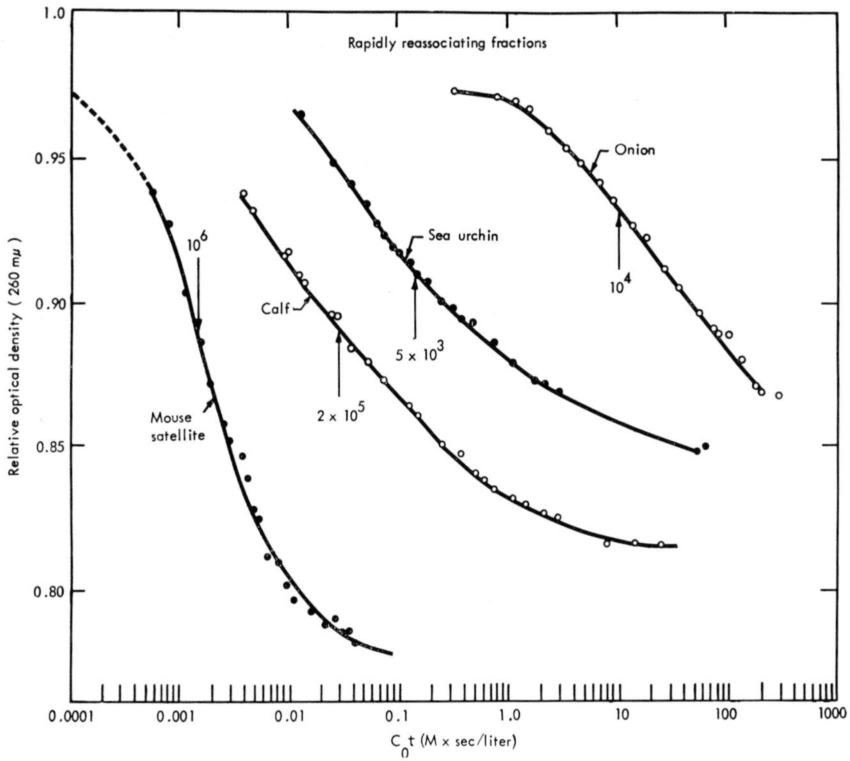

Fig. 5. Optical reassociation curves of repetitious DNA fractions from various organisms. All of the fractions were purified on hydroxyapatite with only minor modifications in the procedure for each different DNA. All of the fractions, except onion, were reassociated in 0.08 M PB at 60 °C. The onion fraction was reassociated at 0.24 M PB at 60 °C and the data from this run adjusted to 0.08 M PB incubation conditions. The average degree of repetition per genome for these fractions is indicated. (From Britten and Kohne 1967a.)

measurement gives 4.5×10^6 nucleotide pairs for the size of the *E. coli* genome. The ratio of these numbers is 710 and the ratio of the C_0t for half reaction of the slow part of the calf curve to that for *E. coli* is 690. This establishes with greater accuracy the conclusion drawn from Fig. 2 that a large fraction (about 60%) of the calf DNA does not exhibit repeated sequences.

Fig. 4 shows the reassociation of salmon sperm DNA measured with hydroxyapatite. By far the majority of the salmon DNA appears to be made up of repeated sequences. The average degree of repetition is not so great as it is for the repeated fraction of calf DNA. A great deal of heterogeneity is evident in the population of repeated sequences.

Fig. 5 shows measurements of reassociation assayed by ultraviolet hypochromicity of fractions of the DNA from four organisms. In each of these cases sheared DNA was incubated under conditions such that partial reassociation occurred and the reassociated fraction was collected on hydroxyapatite. These fractions were then denatured and the time course of reassociation measured in the spectrophotometer. It is clear that all of these organisms contain repetitive DNA. However, the pattern observed is quite different in these four cases. The sea urchin and calf curves are probably representative of the bulk of the repeated DNA in these organisms. However, the mouse satellite curve represents only the most repetitive fraction of mouse DNA. In the case of the onion DNA an intermediate fraction has been observed which reassociates with a repetition frequency between 10 and 1,000.

5. *The occurrence of repetitious DNA*

The DNAS of a variety of organisms have been investigated to determine the distribution of repetitious DNA among life forms. This limited survey was accomplished by utilizing the techniques of hydroxyapatite fractionation and optical reassociation rate determination. The species of bacteria and blue-green algae (*E. coli, Clostridium perfringens, Plectonema boryanum*) that have been examined do not contain repetitious DNA detectable by these methods. While the sensitivity of the test for repeated sequences is high the existence of a small amount of repetition cannot be ruled out. A summary of the characteristics of DNA reassociation is presented in Table 1.

TABLE 1

Characteristics of DNA reassociation

Type of DNA	Nonrepetitive*	Repetitive
Source:	Bacteria Viruses Blue-green algae	Vertebrates Invertebrates Higher plants *Euglena* Dinoflagellate
Rate of reassociation (uniform fragment size)	One single rate, inversely proportional to DNA content per cell or particle	Many different rates. Slowest inversely proportional to DNA content per haploid cell. Fastest up to 1,000,000 times faster
Extent of reassociation	Excellent, up to 90% reformed helices (no strong effect of fragment size)	Good if DNA cut into very small fragments. Poor if DNA is of high molecular weight
Stability of reassociated DNA	Temperature at which strands separate (T_m) almost equal to that of native DNA	Some with T_m near that native DNA and many lower degrees of stability
Molecular weight of product	Several times the fragment size due to pairing of free single-stranded ends. (Concatenation)	Enormous if DNA fragments are large due to multiple interconnections. (Network formation)

* Meaning no gross repetition, although a minor quantity may well be present.

The list of higher organisms with repetitious DNA is further expanded by considering the results obtained from DNA-agar measurements. The reassociation conditions, standard for the DNA-agar technique, utilize a C_0t of from 1 to 100. In higher organism DNA only repetitious fractions will reassociate appreciably at these C_0ts. Therefore, the reassociation detected in the DNAs of higher organisms by the DNA-agar technique is due primarily to reassociation of repetitious DNA. A list of organisms in which repeated nucleotide sequences have been detected is shown in Table 2. Since such a broad range of types of organisms are represented it seems virtually certain that repetitious DNA is universally present in higher organisms. In assembling this table we have made use of measurements published by Hoyer et al., Bolton et al. (1963, 1964) and Denis.

No fungi or higher algae have been examined. These intermediate forms are now of great interest. Thus far the line between organisms which do and do not contain repetitious DNA follows that between eukaryotic and prokaryotic forms. Eukaryotes contain repetitious DNA while prokaryotes do not. A number of measurements will be required to be certain of the boundary between those life forms which do and those which do not possess repetitious DNA.

6. *The precision of repetition*

Repeated nucleotide sequences comprise a large fraction of the DNA of all higher organisms thus far examined. The repetitious fraction of the DNA is made up of many families of repeated nucleotide sequences. A family of repeated nucleotide sequences can only arise from the manifold duplication of an existing nucleotide sequence. Evidence discussed in the following chapter suggests that the production of a family occurs relatively rapidly. Therefore at some time the members of a family were probably nearly identical. With the passage of time and the occurrence of mutations and other chromosomal events the members of a family diverge from one another in nucleotide sequence to produce a family of similar but not identical sequences.

Thus a wide range of precision of matching occurs among reassociated pairs formed among the repeated sequences of DNA from a given species. The degree of divergence can be taken to be a measure of the age of the family and is of interest in relation to the history of the evolution of the species, and evolutionary processes in general.

When DNA strands which are similar but not identical reassociate with each other the resulting pair has reduced stability. At a given cation concentration it will dissociate at a lower temperature than a perfectly complementary or native double-stranded molecule. A rough estimate of the effect has been made by Britten and Waring indicating that, for poly U–poly A double-stranded 'helices', 1% mismatched bases reduce the melting temperature 1 °C.

Hydroxyapatite is a convenient method for the examination of the thermal stability of DNA. When the temperature of a hydroxyapatite column is raised, adsorbed double-

TABLE 2

Occurrence of repetitious DNA

Protozoans
- Dinoflagellate (*Gyrodinium cohnii*)[a]
- *Euglena gracilis*[a]

Porifera
- Sponge (*Microciona*)[a]

Coelenterates
- Sea anemone (*Metridium*) (tentacles)[a]

Echinoderms
- Sea urchin (*Strongylocentrotus*) (sperm)[a-c]
- Sea urchin (*Arbacia*) (sperm)[a-c]
- Starfish (*Asterias*) (gonads)[a]
- Sand dollar (*Echinarachnis*)[a]

Arthropods
- Crab (*Cancer borealis*) (gonads)[a]
- Horseshoe crab (*Limulus*) (hepatopancreas)[a]

Molluscs
- Squid (*Loligo pealii*) (sperm)[a]

Elasmobranchs
- Dogfish shark (liver)[a]

Osteichthyes
- Salmon (sperm)[a-c]
- Lungfish[a, c]

Amphibia
- Amphiuma (liver, red blood cells, muscle)[a]
- Frog (*Rana pipiens*)[b]
- Frog (*Rana sylvatica*)[c]
- Toad (*Xenopus laevis*) (heart, liver, red blood cell)
- Axolotl (*Ambystoma tigrinum*)[c]
- Salamander (*Triturus viridescens*)[c]

Aves
- Chicken (liver, blood)[a-c]

Mammals
- Tree shrew[c]
- Armadillo[c]
- Hedge hog[c]
- Guinea pig[c]
- Rabbit[c]
- Rat (liver)[a-c]
- Mouse (liver, brain, thymus, spleen, kidney)[a-c]
- Hamster[c]
- Calf (thymus, liver, kidney)[a-c]

Primates
- Tarsier[c]
- Slow Loris[c]
- Potto[c]
- Capuchin[c]
- Galago[c]
- Vervet[c]
- Owl monkey[c]
- Green monkey[c]
- Gibbon[c]
- Rhesus[b, c]
- Baboon[c]
- Chimp[a, c]
- Human[a-c]

Plants
- Rye (*Secale cereale*)[c]
- Tobacco (*Nicotiana glauca*)[c]
- Bean (*Phaseolus vulgaris*)[c]
- Vetch (*Vicia villosa*)[c]
- Barley (*Hordeum vulgare*)[a, b]
- Pea (*Pisum sativum* var. Alaska)[a, b]
- Wheat (*Triticum aestivum*)[a, c]
- Onion (*Allium sp.*)[a]

[a] Rate of reassociation measured directly by hydroxyapatite fractionation and/or measurement of optical hypochromicity as a function of time.

[b] Labeled, sheared fragments bind to DNA from the same species imbedded in agar at a C_0t so low that repetition must be present.

[c] Sheared non-radioactive fragments of DNA from the listed organism compete with the DNA-agar reaction (b) of a related species, reducing the amount of labeled DNA which binds to the imbedded DNA.

stranded DNA dissociates and is eluted in the single-stranded form. Miyazawa and Thomas, and Britten and Kohne (1967a) have shown that for precisely matched sequences the temperature of dissociation measured in this way is quite close to that measured by optical hyperchromicity. Fig. 6 shows the results of fractionation of reassociated salmon sperm DNA. Sheared DNA was dissociated and incubated at 50 °C in 0.14 M phosphate buffer (PB) for a C_0t of 270, and the reassociated DNA adsorbed on hydroxyapatite at 50 °C, 0.14 M PB. The resulting thermal chromatogram (Fig. 6, dashed line) shows the expected broad range of thermal stability. In order to establish the specificity of the fractionation samples eluted at 65 and 85 °C were reincubated at 50 °C. They were then readsorbed and reanalyzed in the same way.

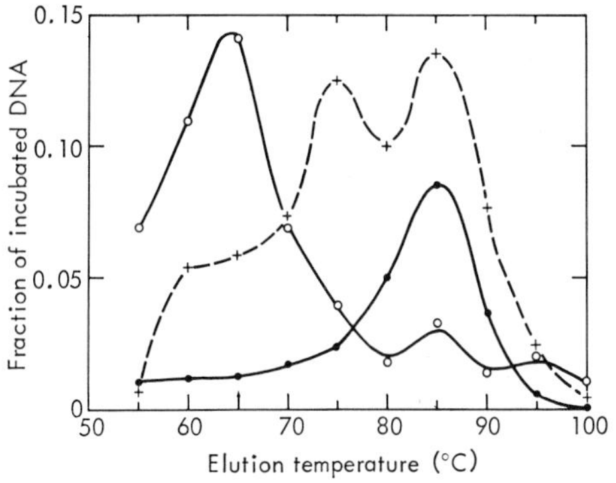

Fig. 6. Hydroxyapatite thermal fractionation of reassociated salmon sperm DNA. DNA sheared at 3.4 kilobar was incubated at 50 °C in 0.14 M PB (C_0t = 370) and passed over hydroxyapatite at 50 °C in 0.14 M PB. The adsorbed DNA was eluted by exhaustive washing (0.14 M PB) at 5 °C temperature intervals (+). Four fractions (65, 70, 85, and 90 °C) were separately denatured (100 °C, 5 min) and reincubated (50 °C, 0.14 M PB, C_0t about 10) and readsorbed on hydroxyapatite at 50 °C. Two of these were again thermally eluted from a column: ○, 65 °C fraction; ●, 85 °C fraction. The other two were eluted with 0.4 M PB and melted in the spectrophotometer as shown in Fig. 7. The fraction bound and the details of the shape of the elution curves depend on the degree of incubation. (From Britten and Kohne 1967b.)

The strand pairs formed during the second incubation are not necessarily the ones that were originally eluted. Instead they are new duplexes formed by randomly assorted pairings among this selected set of strands. In each case, however, the same average degree of precision of relationship results. The 65° peaks cut again at 65° and the 85° cut at 85°. The degrees of divergence are thus characteristic of these populations. The members of the families presumably have been randomly mutated, and all differ from each other to about the same extent. Similar studies have been done with calf thymus DNA with entirely comparable results. In addition, experiments with labeled calf DNA fractions indicate that little sequence homology exists between precisely and imprecisely reassociating sets of repetitive DNA. Thus these are apparently distinct young and old sets of families. It appears legitimate to think of families being formed and then diverging. A diagram appearing in the following chapter schematizes this view.

7. Length of repeated sequences

Are reassociated pairs complementary only in short regions or are they complementary over most of their length? The thermal stability of a pair does not by itself answer this question since it appears that complementary sequences 100 nucleotide pairs long will have a thermal stability approaching that of very long complementary sequences. However, ultraviolet hyperchromicity is a measure of the extent of sequence matching. Therefore, the hyperchromicity of a preparation of strand pairs gives a measure of the average length of the complementary regions present. Results for two such preparations are shown in Fig. 7. Native, completely complementary salmon DNA has a hyperchromicity of about 0.25 (calculated as 1.00–0.75 on the scale of the figure). Single-stranded DNA has a hyperchromicity of 0.06 and melts mostly at lower temperatures as shown by the upper curve.

The 70 and 90° fractions each have a little more than half the hyperchromicity of native DNA. From this we may conclude in each case that the potentially complementary regions are certainly as long as half and perhaps as long as the whole fragments.

Several complicating factors interfere with drawing a more firm conclusion. Reassociated sheared fragments will in general have single-stranded regions since two

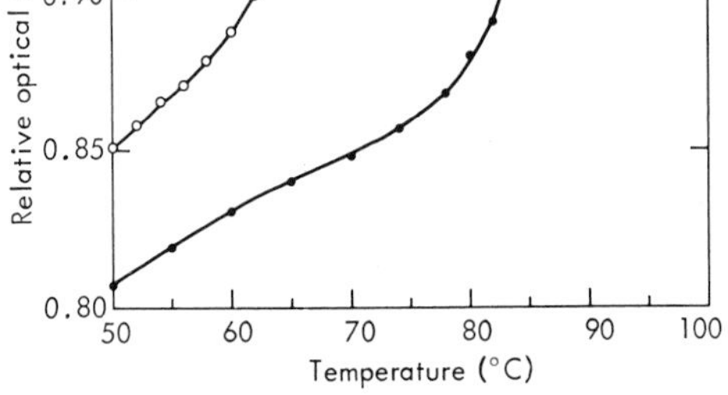

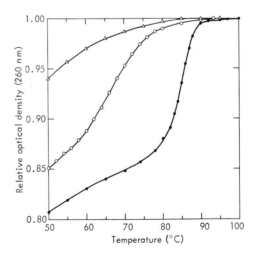

Fig. 7. Optical melting curves in 0.14 M PB of fractions of salmon sperm DNA. Fractions prepared as described in Fig. 6: ●, fraction eluted at 90 °C; ○, fraction eluted at 70 °C. The upper curve (△) is for the DNA which did not bind to hydroxyapatite (50 °C, 0.14 M PB) in the first incubation and is therefore purely single-stranded. (From Britten and Kohne 1967b.)

complementary fragments rarely terminate at the same points in the sequence. All degrees of overlap will occur. For first pairing the expected hyperchromicity for perfectly complementary pairs is perhaps only two-thirds that for native DNA. We do not know the extent of pair formation involving the single-stranded ends in later collisions. Finally, of course, the sequences in these families have diverged from each other and the unmatched nucleotides occurring within the paired sequences reduce the hyperchromicity.

These measurements are corroborated by the hyperchromicity of reassociated repetitive DNA fractions from many organisms. It usually falls between 0.16 and 0.20. The few CsCl density measurements we have made show a marked decrease in density upon reassociation which also implies a good extent of complementary pairing of repetitive DNA.

It appears that, on the average, repeated sequences are *not* extremely short (not less than 300 nucleotides) and may be much longer than our fragments, which average perhaps 500 nucleotides. One imagines that a wide distribution of lengths will be present after a family diverges since translocations as well as nucleotide substitutions probably occur.

References

BERNARDI, G.: Chromatography of nucleic acids on hydroxyapatite. Nature 206 (1965) 779.

BILLETER, M. A., C. WEISSMANN and R. C. WARNER: Replication of viral RNA. IX. Properties of double-stranded RNA from *E. coli* infected with bacteriophage MS2. J. Mol. Biol. 17 (1966) 145.

BOLTON, E. T.: Plant nucleic acids. In: Carnegie Institution of Washington Year Book 64, Washington, D.C. (1965) 314.

BOLTON, E. T., D. J. BRENNER, R. J. BRITTEN, D. B. COWIE, S. FALKOW, D. E. KOHNE, A. RAKE and R. B. ROBERTS: An instructive glossary. In: Carnegie Institution of Washington Year Book 66, Washington, D.C. (1967) 68.

BOLTON, E. T., R. J. BRITTEN, T. J. BYERS, D. B. COWIE, B. HOYER, Y. KATO, B. J. MCCARTHY, M. MIRANDA and R. B. ROBERTS: Carnegie Institution of Washington Year Book 63, Washington, D.C. (1964) 366.

BOLTON. E. T. and B. J. MCCARTHY: Fractionation of complementary RNA. J. Mol. Biol. 8 (1964) 201.

BRITTEN, R. J. and D. E. KOHNE: Nucleotide sequence repetition in DNA. In: Carnegie Institution of Washington Year Book 65, Washington, D.C. (1967a) 78.

BRITTEN, R. J. and D. E. KOHNE: Repeated nucleotide sequences. In: Carnegie Institution of Washington Year Book 66, Washington, D.C. (1967b) 73.

BRITTEN, R. J. and D. E. KOHNE: Repeated Sequences in DNA. Science 161 (1968) 529.

BRITTEN, R. J. and M. WARING: 'Renaturation' of the DNA of higher organisms. In: Carnegie Institution of Washington Year Book 64, Washington, D.C. (1965) 316.

BURGI, E. and A. D. HERSHEY: A relative molecular weight series derived from the nucleic acid of bacteriophage T2. J. Mol. Biol. 3 (1961) 458.

CAIRNS, J.: The chromosome of *E. coli.* Cold Spring Harbor Symp. Quant. Biol. 28 (1963) 43.

DENIS, H.: Species specificity of DNA–RNA and DNA–DNA hybridizations. In: Carnegie Institution of Washington Year Book 64, Washington, D.C. (1965) 455.

HOYER, B. H., B. J. MCCARTHY and E. T. BOLTON: A molecular approach in the systematics of higher organisms. Science 144 (1964) 959.

MARMUR, J., R. ROWND and C. L. SCHILDKRAUT: Denaturation and renaturation of DNA. In: Progress in Nucleic Acid Research 1. New York, Academic Press (1963) 232.

MCCARTHY, B. J. and E. T. BOLTON: An approach to the measure of genetic relatedness among organisms. Proc. Natl. Acad. Sci., U.S. 50 (1963) 156.

MCCARTHY, B. J. and E. T. BOLTON: Interaction of complementary RNA and DNA. J. Mol. Biol. 8 (1964) 184.

MIYAZAWA, Y. and C. A. THOMAS JR: The nucleotide composition of short segments of DNA molecules. J. Mol. Biol. 11 (1965) 223.

ROSS, P. D. and J. M. STURTEVANT: On the kinetics and mechanism of helix formation: The two stranded poly (A + U) complex from polyriboadenylic acid and polyribouridylic acid. J. Am. Chem. Soc. 84 (1962) 4503.

WARING, M. and R. J. BRITTEN: Nucleotide sequence repetition: A rapidly reassociating fraction of mouse DNA. Science 154 (1966) 791.

CHAPTER 3

Implications of repeated nucleotide sequences

R. J. BRITTEN and D. E. KOHNE

Department of Terrestrial Magnetism, Carnegie Institution of Washington, Washington, D.C. 20015

Contents

1. Introduction
2. The expression of repeated nucleotide sequences
3. Ribosomal and S-RNA genes
4. Redundancy of extranuclear DNA
5. Patterns of repetition
6. Saltatory events of replication
7. The flow of DNA replication
8. Relation between age and divergence
9. Why repeated sequences?
10. A role in evolution?

1. Introduction

In the previous chapter the evidence concerning the occurrence of repeated nucleotide sequences in chromosomal DNA was examined. In this chapter the following questions are explored. (1) To what extent are the repeated sequences expressed? (2) How do families of repeated sequences arise? (3) What role do repeated nucleotide sequences play during evolution? None of these questions have complete answers as yet. There is, however, sufficient evidence to provide tentative answers to the first two questions and to stimulate provocative speculation concerning the third.

2. The expression of repeated nucleotide sequences

At this time there is no direct proof of the phenotypic expression of the bulk of the repeated nucleotide sequences occurring in higher-organism DNA. Genetics certainly does not suggest that genes in general occur in numbers of tens or hundreds of thousands.

The only known exceptions are the immunoglobulin genes where there is limited genetic evidence for gene multiplicity in the sense suggested here. Recent evidence of Gray et al. for example, suggests that there may be genetic multiplicities of a high order in the immunoglobulin. One might suppose that the function of the repeated DNA sequences is related to the existence of the immune response system. However, repetitive DNA is present in the invertebrates and plants which do not have an immunoglobulin system. Nevertheless the immune system may have developed out of the potentiality supplied by repeated DNA sequences.

However this may be, some repeated sequences are commonly expressed at least up to the stage of rapidly labelled RNA (presumably 'messenger' RNA). The existing measurements of the reassociation of RNA with DNA in higher organisms have all been carried out with a small effective C_0t (see previous chapter). Under these conditions only reassociation of RNA molecules with families of repeated DNA sequences can be observed. Furthermore, RNA which reassociates with repeated DNA sequences makes up a large fraction of the rapidly labelled RNA. For example, Church and McCarthy (1967a) showed that in regenerating mouse liver, 25% of the pulse-labelled RNA hybridizes with DNA after a C_0t (calculated on the basis of the DNA concentration) equivalent to about 100 under the conditions of Fig. 2 of the previous chapter.

In earlier experiments McCarthy and Hoyer using the DNA-agar system hybridized mouse L-cell steady state labelled RNA with mouse DNA. About 1.5% of this RNA was hybridized after an effective C_0t of about 50. On reincubation with DNA ($C_0t = 4$) this selected RNA reacted to the extent of 30%.

In this same work measurements done with high ratios of RNA to DNA suggest that at least 5% of the DNA can hybridize with the RNA. The large fraction of the pulse-labelled or selected RNA which can react with the DNA at small C_0t indicates that much 'messenger' RNA is homologous to repeated DNA sequences. Thus it appears likely that members of families of repeated nucleotide sequences have genetic functions. It is not possible to say how many members of a family of repeated sequences are expressed as RNA. Suppose part or all of the nucleotide sequence of a gene were a member of a family of repeated sequences. If this gene were expressed, RNA would be produced which could hybridize with all of the members of that family of repeated DNA sequences.

McCarthy and Hoyer showed that hybridizable RNA of the mouse differs in different tissues. Church and McCarthy (1967a, b) showed that marked changes occur in the hybridizable RNA during liver regeneration as well as during mouse embryonic development. Denis has also reported changes in the hybridizable RNA during the development of *Xenopus laevis*.

These results suggest that certain families or members of these families have to do only with a particular genetic function which is called into play at certain times in development or in certain tissues. The role of the repeated sequences in such a function could be regulatory or involve coded structural information.

The interpretation given here differs somewhat from those in the original papers since those papers antedate the knowledge that the measured hybrids were formed only with families of repeated DNA sequences.

3. Ribosomal and S-RNA genes

Multiple ribosomal genes are present in the DNA of all species examined thus far. Yankofsky and Spiegelman, and Attardi et al. (1965a, b) have reported that for several bacteria about 0.2–0.3% of the DNA reassociates with the ribosomal RNA. This is enough DNA to specify 4 to 6 copies of each ribosomal RNA subunit, or 4 to 6 different pairs of ribosomal subunits. The multiplicity of ribosomal genes in higher organisms is much greater than in bacteria. Rittossa et al. have reported ribosomal RNA saturation values of 0.03% for chicken and 0.27% for *Drosophila melanogaster*. Wallace and Birnstiel have reported a value of about 0.11% for *Xenopus laevis*, while Attardi has reported a value of about 0.01% for HeLa cells. The estimates of the multiplicity of the ribosomal genes range from 130 in the *Drosophila*, to 600 in the chicken to about 2000 in *Xenopus*.

The 23S and 16S ribosomal RNAs of bacteria have different nucleotide sequences. It is possible in bacteria that each of the multiple ribosomal genes has a completely different nucleotide sequence. In this event the multiple ribosomal genes would not resemble the families of repeated nucleotide sequences described in the previous chapter.

Fragmentary evidence indicates that the multiple ribosomal genes of higher organisms probably constitute at least one family of similar nucleotide sequences. However it is possible that several families of both 28S and 18S ribosomal RNA genes are present. The heterogeneity of ribosomal genes is an open question of evident importance.

Multiple S-RNA genes are very probably present in higher organisms. Rittossa et al. have demonstrated that 0.018% of *Drosophila* DNA is complementary to S-RNA. This amount of DNA corresponds to about 15 copies of each of 60 S-RNAs if each type of S-RNA were represented equally.

Giacomoni and Spiegelman, and Oishi et al. have reported that from 35–80 S-RNA genes are present in bacteria. No conclusion can be drawn concerning the multiplicity of each S-RNA in these bacteria until more evidence is obtained. Again, however, it is clear that the multiplicity of the bacterial genes is much lower than that of higher organisms.

4. Redundancy of extranuclear DNA

Mitochondrial DNA is also present in multiple copies in most higher organisms' cells. Kroon et al. have reported that mitochondrial DNA comprises about 1% of the total DNA from several animals. Mitochondrial DNA appears to be much less complex than nuclear DNA. Borst et al. have shown that chicken liver mitochondrial DNA reassociates very rapidly and completely with no evidence of the nucleotide sequence mismatches which are characteristic of reassociated repetitive nuclear DNA. Borst et al. further have interpreted their reassociation rate studies to mean that the information content of mitochondrial DNA was equivalent to that in a DNA molecule of 10 million molecular weight. This is the amount of DNA in one circular molecule of which several are present in each mitochondrial particle. This suggests that the DNA molecules in different chicken liver mitochondria are identical.

This interpretation is probably correct. A certain conclusion, however, cannot be drawn until comparison of the rate of reassociation of mitochondrial DNA with other DNA of known genome size is available with the cation concentration, temperature and fragment size carefully matched. The present data however rule out large scale heterogeneity of the DNA in chicken liver mitochondria. It will be of great interest to determine the degree of similarity between mitochondrial DNAs from different tissues.

It is not known whether mitochondrial DNA holds sequences in common with nuclear DNA. Dawid has reported that there are no detectable sequences in common between mitochondrial and nuclear DNA of *Xenopus*. The experimental technique, however, was relatively insensitive. The question of nuclear representation of mitochondrial DNA is therefore still open.

Many plant cells have a number of chloroplasts which contain DNA. While it may be presumed that this DNA exists in multiple copies, there is no evidence concerning its heterogeneity. Richard's measurements suggest some homology between chloroplast DNA and nuclear DNA of *Euglena*: However, the question of the existence of a nuclear representation for chloroplast DNA remains unanswered.

5. *Patterns of repetition*

The rate of reassociation of the DNA of one organism can be evaluated over the whole course of the reaction (C_0t from 10^{-4} to 10^4). Individual measurements of reassociation at several concentrations are required and fractionation of the DNA may be useful. From these measurements the amount of DNA with various degrees of repetition may be calculated. The result is a repetition frequency spectrogram for the DNA of the particular organism, such as the tentative one for mouse DNA shown in Fig. 1. This curve is correct in its broad aspects but has some indefiniteness in detail. The width of the peaks results in part from the difficulty of resolving reassociation rates that differ by less than a factor of 10. Repetition frequency spectra could also be derived for calf DNA and salmon DNA from Figs. 3 and 4 of the previous chapter. They would differ from that of Fig. 1. Neither would show the large isolated peak of 10^6 copies although both would have some DNA in that region. The calf DNA would show a large broad peak in the region of 10^4 to 10^5 copies (40% of the DNA), little if any DNA with a small degree of repetition, and of course, a large peak of unique DNA.

Very much more calf DNA occurs in families with a high degree of repetition than in those families with just a few members. No DNA with a repetition frequency between 2 and 10 has been detected in mouse or calf. This paucity of DNA with a low frequency of repetition has a definite implication for understanding the origin of families which will be discussed in the following section.

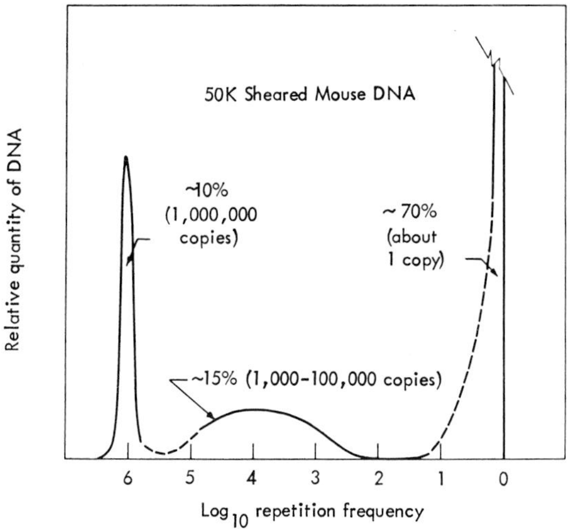

Fig. 1. Spectrogram of the frequency of repetition of nucleotide sequences in the DNA of the mouse. Relative quantity of DNA plotted against the logarithm of the repetition frequency. These data are derived from measurements of the quantity and rate of reassociation of fractions separated on hydroxyapatite. The dashed segments of the curve represent regions of considerable uncertainty. (From Britten and Kohne 1967a.)

What quantity of DNA has been replicated to form families of repeated sequences? Forty percent of the calf DNA behaves as repetitious DNA. The average repetition frequency is about 100,000. A single length of DNA 15,000 nucleotide pairs long, copied 100,000 times would have the same average repetition frequency and total quantity as the repetitious DNA of the calf. Such a homogeneous set of fragments would have the smallest possible information content that could be present in the repeated DNA of the calf. The situation is known to be more complex, however and the potential information content of the repetitious DNA fraction is very much greater. Four factors may contribute: (1) Many different families of repeated sequences are present. (2) Small quantities of very long DNA sequences may be repeated with much lower than average frequency. (3) Family members have diverged from each other as a result of many changes in their nucleotide sequences. (4) The repeated sequences (or perhaps, fragments of them) have been translocated into positions adjoining unrelated sequences.

In this regard an observation of Britten and Waring is significant. When a preparation of higher-organism DNA of moderate fragment size (5 to 10 million molecular weight) is denatured and incubated (for example $C_0t = 100$, $\kappa = 0.18$, 60 °C), large particles form that create a visible haze in the solution, and most of the DNA may be sedimented in a desk-top centrifuge. Reassociation of repeated sequences links the fragments into a network. Apparently regions of each fragment are members of families of repeated sequences. The repeated sequences must be scattered throughout the genome with few large gaps between them. This extensive interspersion throughout the DNA of the members of the families of repeated sequences may be related to their function. They could for example have regulatory or structural roles which would lead to such a distribution. Alternatively this dispersion may simply represent the degree of translocation of sequence fragments which occurs in higher organisms.

6. *Saltatory events of replication*

Families of repeated nucleotide sequences probably originated in rather sudden events of excessive replication of particular sequences. An event of this type is here designated a *saltatory replication* since the members of a family must undergo sudden jumps in number when viewed on an evolutionary time scale. It is impossible to say how rapid such jumps are but they must occur in a time much shorter than 100 million years.

The random duplication (production of one extra copy) of lengths of nucleotide sequence would not produce the pattern of repetition frequencies shown in Fig. 1. In this case only rarely would families with a great many members result. The expected curve would peak at the right and slope rapidly and steadily down to the left. The curve shown in Fig. 1 could not result from the production of a small number of extra copies of randomly selected sequences. It could, however, result from the manifold copying of particular 'marked' sequences, or from events in which very many copies of a randomly selected sequence are made in a short time. The replication process must then continue until tens or hundreds of thousands of copies of the nucleotide sequence are present. The mechanisms which initiate and halt these events are not known.

The mouse satellite, the peak at the extreme left in Fig. 1, is an outstanding example of the result of a saltatory event since a million copies of a sequence about 300 nucleotide pairs long are present in each cell.

Suppose that family formation were a continuous process in which members were added in small numbers. Since divergence occurs it is presumed that the ancient members of any family have diverged from each other. Newer members must be copied from pre-existing members and therefore must reflect their divergence. In a continuously produced family then, recent members are each closely related to only a small fraction of the whole. Thus sequences selected for relatively precise relationship would show a lower frequency of repetition than those selected for imprecise relationship.

Quite the opposite seems to be true. For those cases which have been examined, young families of repeated sequences which have not diverged very much have as many or more members than do the older, more divergent families. The reassociation kinetics of the two fractions of salmon DNA shown in Fig. 7 of the previous chapter were measured. Both fractions showed heterogeneity, but the 90 °C fraction started to reassociate at one-fourth of the C_0t required for the 70 °C fraction. Thus some young families had even more members than any of the older families. This observation is substantiated for both calf and mouse DNA. Future and more precise observations of the correlation between number of members and the age of families will be very informative regarding the historical pattern of saltatory events.

What is a saltatory replication? The appearance in the genome of a family of repeated sequences involves a number of events: (1) many copies must be made of a segment of DNA; (2) a number of these copies must be integrated into the genome in such a way that they are duplicated and transmitted to progeny; (3) the resulting family must either determine a favorably selected phenotype or be associated with a favorable genetic element; (4) sufficient time must pass for its dissemination throughout the population; (5) if the set of events can be described as a saltatory replication the growth of the family must be terminated within a reasonably short time.

No known processes combine all five of these events. Virus infection, however, does involve some of them. In virulent infection very many copies are made of the virus genome. In a lysogenic state a chromosomally integrated segment is transmitted to progeny. Further it is known that segments of DNA which are capable of genetic activity in the host may, in some living systems, be carried in the virus' life cycle. Cases are not known where large numbers of viral DNA copies are integrated into the host genome nor are any cases clearly established in higher organisms where new host-type genes are carried in a virus life cycle.

We are not proposing here that saltatory replications are the result of virus infection but the relationships may suggest new experimental approaches. There are cases in which a quantity of DNA results from the production of many copies of particular segments of DNA; for example, the tremendous quantity of DNA (mainly mitochondrial) in certain eggs and the mitochondrial or chloroplast DNA in more typical cells. In none of these cases is it known that the copies may become integrated in such a way that *their* descendants are transmitted to the progeny. Such an event is necessary in order that the members of a repeated family may diverge from each other. Only the small fraction of the repetitive DNA which does not show divergence (and thus has high thermal stability after reassociation) can be DNA which has been recently replicated from a master copy.

7. *The flow of DNA replication*

Fig. 2 shows in the form of a block diagram the processes that have been deduced from the observations of repeated and non-repeated nucleotide sequences in higher organisms. It is not ruled out that occasional random duplications also occur. DNA may be lost as well but since this work has not produced evidence on this point DNA loss is not shown on the diagram.

An 'original' sequence of DNA starting in box 1 would occasionally be replicated many times and become a family of identical sequences in box 2. The members of the family in box 2 would undergo mutations and deletions and perhaps be translocated to other segments of the chromosome or other chromosomes, thereby reaching box 3. After a longer period of time, these nucleotide sequences would diverge from each other to such an extent that sequence homology could no longer be recognized. Some sequences ending up in box 4 might not be distinguishable from those in box 1 by experimental test. Sequences might pass from box 2 to 4 at different rates depending on selection pressure, statistical fluctuations, or unknown mechanisms.

Much saltatory replication of DNA sequences has occurred over evolutionary history and these repeated sequences have diverged from each other fairly rapidly on an evolutionary time scale. The rate of production of new repeated families or family

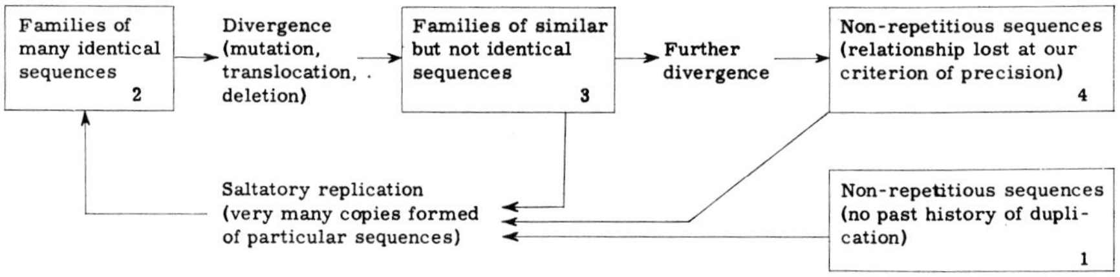

Fig. 2. A schematic diagram representing events occurring during evolutionary history which would give rise to the observed pattern of repeated and unrepeated DNA sequences. (From Britten and Kohne 1967a.)

members must, broadly speaking, be as great as the loss of family members by divergence. The universal occurrence in large quantity of repetitious sequences in higher organisms indicates that loss of repeated DNA by divergence is compensated by further production of repeated DNA. Saltatory replications therefore add a considerable quantity of DNA to the genome. It is not an unreasonable proposal that the many ancient events of replication have been the source of the majority of the DNA in the chromosomes of higher organisms. In fact for salmon, onion and amphiuma the majority of the DNA is in the form of repeated sequences.

A quantitative estimate of the rate of production of repeated sequences in the vertebrates can be obtained from the data of Hoyer et al. They have measured the fraction of the repeated sequences held in common among a series of vertebrates. The results correlate nicely with the known times (from the paleontological record) since divergence of the species lines leading to the modern forms. At the criterion used in their measurements half of the repeated sequences differ sufficiently not to reassociate when the period since divergence of two species is one hundred million years. Thus since 40% of the calf genome is made up of repeated DNA we may estimate that the average flux of saltatory replication would supply, for example, 20% of the calf genome in one hundred million years.

Such a rate of saltatory replication, maintained throughout the course of evolution, would be an important source of genome growth. The data of Hoyer et al. does indicate a fairly steady rate of saltatory replication during the evolution of the vertebrates but there is little useful data outside this phylum and very likely some surprises await us within it.

With the knowledge that saltatory replications could be a source of genome growth the following questions arise. Has the genome actually grown over the course of evolutionary time? Is DNA loss quantitatively important? How important are other potential sources of genome growth such as ploidy changes compared to saltatory replications? None of these questions yet have definite answers but there is evidence bearing on each of them.

Hinegardner's measurements of the DNA content of many species suggest that both increase and decrease of genome size occur. A wide range of the genome size of species can be present within an order or even a genus. It appears that the loss of DNA must on occasion be important and that the evolutionary history of genome sizes is probably quite varied.

Amphiuma contains about 30 times as much DNA per haploid cell as does man. These two forms have had a common ancestor at some time in the past. Since the genome sizes now differ by a factor of 30, one or the other organism has gained or lost DNA while evolving to its present state. It is very probable that amphiuma has gained in genome size since many vertebrates have about the same DNA content per cell as does man.

According to Britten and Kohne (1967b) the majority (80–90%) of amphiuma DNA is made up of families of repeated sequences while a smaller portion is made up of unique sequences. Saltatory replication has supplied the major portion of the DNA of the amphiuma genome. The genomes of onion and salmon are also mainly composed of repeated DNA while a large fraction of all other higher organism genomes which have been examined consists of repeated DNA. Still we cannot say that ploidy changes are unimportant since they might well increase both the repeated and the unique sequences in the same ratio.

The continued divergence of family members from each other implies, as indicated in Fig. 2, that the non-repeated fraction of the DNA should retain many short sequences, 'fossil repetitions', which may be just recognizably related to each other. In fact, as the criterion of precision of relationship is lowered more repeated DNA is observed. This observation raises the intriguing question, 'Do all of the DNA sequences of higher organisms have a history of repetition?' No answer can as yet be given.

8. *Relation between age and divergence*

Since families of many degrees of divergence are observed, we must assume that a long series of saltatory events has occurred in each of the species lines leading to present higher organisms. Fig. 3 shows a three-dimensional schematic diagram suggestive of the history of families produced by saltatory replications. The scale on the left represents the period of time since each of the families of repeated sequences was produced. The lower scale is a measure of the divergence within each family. The cutouts represent a prediction of the differential melting curves to be observed for the families if the DNA were reassociated under conditions such that only repeated sequences pair. Thus all the members of a young family are closely related and all pairs melt at a temperature near that of native DNA. In ancient families a great deal of divergence has occurred and the average melting temperature is far below that of native DNA. Some members will have suffered more changes than others and the melting curve thus broadens with time. Melting curves are also broadened due to initial spread in GC content. The range of quantities of DNA in the various families reflects the wide range of repetition frequences observed.

In order to bring this diagram to concrete form, a number of arbitrary decisions were made which are not central to the underlying ideas. For example, the average rate of divergence is not well known. The degree of spreading is hardly known at all but has been estimated from the width of the 65 °C fraction on Fig. 6 of the previous chapter. It is not known how often the saltatory events occur. There is some suspicion that they are quite rare. The diagram suggests 10^7-year intervals but as far as definite evidence goes, they could occur 10 or 100 times more often. If about 10 families are observable each would contain (e.g. in calf) about 5% of the DNA and would contain, on the average, 10^5 copies of a sequence several thousand nucleotide pairs long.

It is possible to visualize, on this diagram, the divergence of the sequences shared

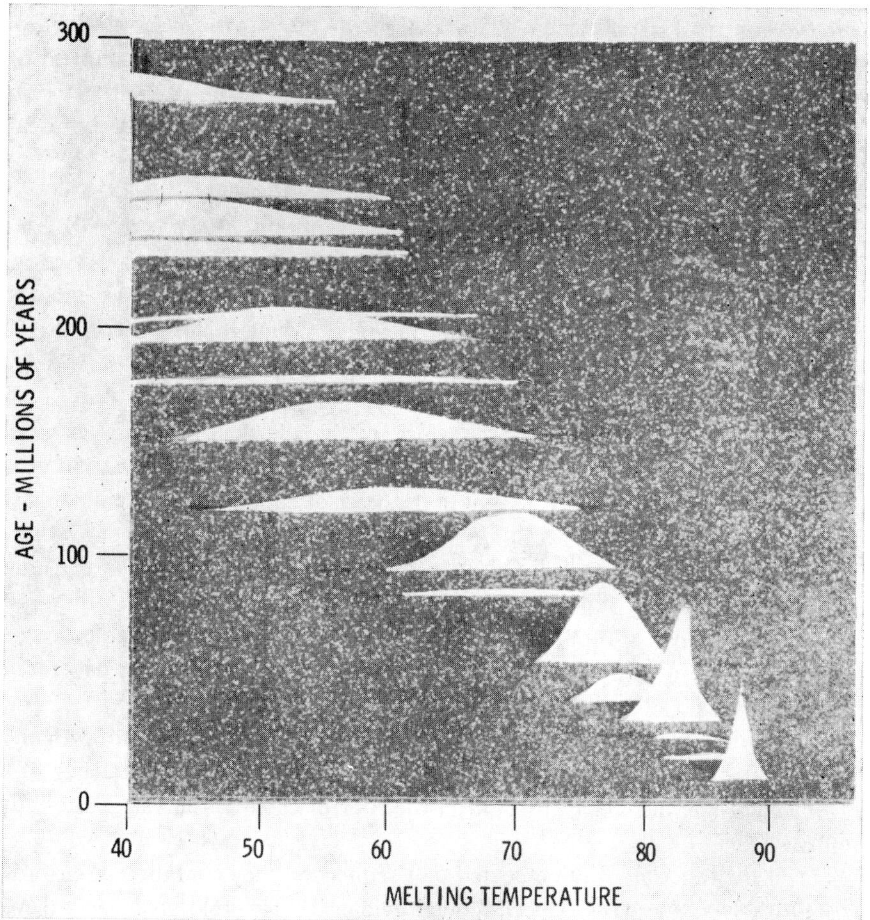

Fig. 3. A schematic diagram proposed by R. B. Roberts to suggest the relationship between age and thermal stability of families of repeated sequences. The height of a cutout represents the quantity of reassociated DNA with a particular thermal stability belonging to a family of repeated sequences. Each family is supposed to have originated in a sudden event of saltatory replication at a time in the past shown by the scale of age. (From Britten and Kohne 1967b.)

between species. Suppose, for example, that the species lines to modern horse and cattle diverged about 70 million years ago. If this diagram represents the DNA of cattle, horse DNA would contain all the families older than 70 million years. In place of the younger families, it would have a quite distinct set of its own.

9. *Why repeated sequences?*

Any discussion of the function or long-term evolutionary significance of repeated sequences in DNA, at this stage of knowledge, is bound to be speculative. Nevertheless it is just this potential significance which makes their study worthwhile and speculation unavoidable. It seems certain that repeated nucleotide sequences of DNA have played an important role in evolution. Few would hold that a majority of the DNA of many higher forms could be maintained as repetitive sequences in the face of all the selective forces unless it was involved in the survival or change of species.

However, it is not known at what level their importance lies. Are the repeated sequences actually repeated genes in sets of hundreds of thousands? Is their role more subtle but still directly genetic? Perhaps they are only important to the structure of the chromosome or as markers for chromosomal pairing. It is even conceivable that they exist as punctuation marks in the genetic message although there seems to be an exorbitant quantity for such a purpose. The degree of divergence of the sequences among vertebrates also makes this appear unlikely.

Another unlikely possibility is that they are involved in the differential expression of genetic information in various tissues. There is no evidence for variation of DNA content from cell type to cell type except in the cases of haploid or polytenic cells. The DNA-agar studies of McCarthy and Hoyer may now be interpreted to show that the quantity of repeated sequences varies little if any from tissue to tissue in the mouse. Further, the majority of repeated sequences have diverged from each other. Only nearly identical copies of DNA sequences would be useful in increasing the degree of expression of certain genes in particular tissues or would be likely to be produced within an individual's lifetime.

The fascinating question remains. What possible usefulness is there for as many as 100,000 members of a family of repeated sequences? A repetition frequency of this order of magnitude has been observed in the DNA of each of the vertebrates so far examined.

Whatever the function of the repeated DNA sequences, they contain in their present pattern (intra-species and inter-species) much evidence bearing closely on actual events in the history of the evolution of the species.

10. A role in evolution?

We postulate that repeated sequences have a direct genetic role, as suggested by the RNA homology measurements. We also propose that saltatory replications underlie major events in evolution. As yet there is no way of knowing whether the repeated element is a set of genes, a gene, or a gene fragment. It seems probable that only a fraction of repeated sequences would be expressed in any tissue at any stage of the life of an organism. Repeated genes, however, could meet a requirement for an extreme rate of production, for example, of a given protein. The individual members of such a set would not be under selection pressure and they would diverge from each other in the course of time. If a gene fragment were multiply replicated, the expression of the whole set of copies would probably be suppressed in the selected population and again divergence would be free to occur.

Translocation into new assemblages would yield combinatorial possibilities for novelty. In an individual line of organisms a fortunate (from the point of view of their descendants) set of saltatory replications might occur and gene fragments carrying the information specifying useful structural or metabolic potentialities would be present in many copies. The development of a gene specifying a new function from a set of elements of older genes appears to be far more probable than its development *de novo* from a random nucleotide sequence. A structural gene for a new enzyme might be assembled by accident through the translocation of multiple copies of fragments of existing genes. These fragments are presumed to carry information for parts of the primary structure useful in broad classes of enzymes and some would be modified by nucleotide sequence changes. Once the new enzyme had made its appearance it would be subject to mutation and selection, and risk the chance of improvement or loss in the same way as the pre-existing enzymes in the population. Novel cellular functions hardly recognizably related to their precursors might result from rare combinations of repeated elements (genes or gene fragments). The very large numbers of copies of the repeated DNA sequences might play their role by increasing the probability of such rare events.

An extraordinary variety of forms has appeared in the course of evolution, reflecting a restless source of originality. The nature of the forces behind the acts of speciation and divergence remain central problems in the study of evolution. We may look forward to surprises before a full understanding of these forces and processes is achieved. Momentous genetic events must occur that are capable of inducing grand deviations in the course of evolution. Consider the issues raised in the following quotation from G.G.Simpson:

> 'The history of life is decidedly nonrandom. This is evident in many features of the record, including such points already discussed as the phenomena of relays and of major replacements at defined times. It is, however, still more striking in two other phenomena copiously documented by fossils. Both have to do with evolutionary trends: first, that the direction of morphological (hence also functional and behavioral) change in a given lineage often continues without significant deviation for long periods of time and, second, that similar or parallel trends often appear either simultaneously or successively in numerous different, usually related, lineages. These phenomena are far from universal; they are not "laws" of evolution; but they are so common and so thoroughly established by concrete evidence that they demand a definite, effective directional force among the evolutionary processes. They rule out any theory of purely random evolution such as the rather naive mutationism that had considerable support earlier in the twentieth century. What directional forces the data do demand, or permit, is one of the most important questions to be asked of the fossil record.'

Suppose that an event occurs in which a large number of unexpressed genes or better, a class of genetic potentiality is produced in the genome but only a small part appears phenotypically. The small expressed part, 'the top of the iceberg', if favorably selected, will introduce the as yet unexpressed class into the population. In effect a hidden package of potential genetic effects would have been selected which, after spreading through the population could lead to radically new features that could not result from a detailed balance of mutation and selection.

A saltatory replication producing a hundred thousand copies of the 'right' sort of gene is a candidate for a genetic event with immense potentiality. Not all of the copies would be initially expressed. Perhaps not many ever would be. But mutation, translocation and recombination with other genes would yield a whole range of potential genetic activity which would perhaps come into view at times long after the appearance of the first effects that resulted from the saltation. If the early effects were selectively advantageous, the whole set of products of the saltatory replication would be introduced into the population. The dynamics of selection would be fundamentally altered. The species might then appear to take a surprising and even an apparently purposeful course of evolutionary change. Owing to the great multiplicity of copies their selective elimination might be impossible short of eradicating the species. Potentialities important in the longer term would then have an opportunity to survive and reach fruitful expression.

Events of this general type would be capable of causing a striking divergence of two genetically isolated populations even though the environments in which the two populations existed were identical.

One must ask whether an excess of currently useless DNA would not be lost under selection pressure in a population. Some characters are indeed severely selected and their frequency in a population undergoes relatively rapid change. Other characteristics have significance over a longer period of time; for example, the potential for genetic adaption to changing environment. In those lines of species which have persisted through many changes, surely the loss of such long term potentials has been guarded against. The potential for really striking innovation is perhaps tested and selected for over immense periods of geologic time. The thread of life itself might have been lost if small minorities did not continually appear which in some way could protect themselves against major environmental changes, or adapt to new modes of existence. Such a potential seems now to be a central characteristic of life. It nevertheless must be selected for, and mechanisms must be present which integrate the effects of selection over periods of billions of years.

References

ATTARDI, G., P.C.HUANG and S.KABAT: Recognition of ribosomal RNA sites in DNA. I. Analysis of the *E. coli* system. Proc. Natl. Acad. Sci., U.S. 53 (1965a) 1490.

ATTARDI, G., P.C.HUANG and S.KABAT: Recognition of ribosomal RNA sites in DNA. II. The HeLa cell system. Proc. Natl. Acad. Sci., U.S. 54 (1965b) 185.

BORST, P., G.RUTTENBERG and A.M.KROON: Mitochondrial DNA I: Preparation and properties of mitochondrial DNA from chick liver. Biochim. Biophys. Acta 149 (1967) 140, 156.

BRITTEN, R.J. and D.E.KOHNE: Carnegie Institution of Washington Year Book 65, Washington, D.C. (1967a) 78.

BRITTEN, R.J. and D.E.KOHNE: Carnegie Institution of Washington Year Book 66, Washington, D.C. (1967b) 68.

BRITTEN, R.J. and M.WARING: Carnegie Institution of Washington Year Book 64, Washington, D.C. (1965) 324.

CHURCH, R.B. and B.J.MCCARTHY: RNA synthesis in regenerating and embryonic liver. I. The synthesis of new species of RNA during regeneration of mouse liver after partial hepatectomy. J. Mol. Biol. 23 (1967a) 459.

CHURCH, R.B. and B.J.MCCARTHY: RNA synthesis in regenerating and embryonic liver. II. The synthesis of RNA during embryonic liver development and its relationship to regenerating liver. J. Mol. Biol. 23 (1967b) 477.

DAWID, I.B. and D.R.WOLSTENHOLME: Renaturation and hybridization studies of mitochondrial DNA. Biophys. J. 8 (1968) 65.

DENIS, H.: Gene expression in amphibian development. II. Release of the genetic information in growing embryos. J. Mol. Biol. 22 (1966) 285.

GIACOMONI, D. and S.SPIEGELMAN: Origin and biologic individuality of the genetic dictionary. Science 138 (1962) 1328.

GRAY, W., W.J.DREYER and L.HOOD: Mechanism of antibody synthesis: Size differences between mouse kappa chains. Science 155 (1967) 465.

HINEGARDNER, R.: Personal communication.

HOYER, B.H., E.T.BOLTON, B.J.MCCARTHY and R.B.ROBERTS: The evolution of polynucleotides. In: V.Bryson and H.J.Vogel, eds.: Evolving genes and proteins. New York, Academic Press (1965) 581.

KROON, A., P.BORST, E.VAN BRUGGEN and G.RUTTENBERG: Mitochondrial DNA from sheep heart. Proc. Natl. Acad. Sci., U.S. 56 (1966) 1836.

MCCARTHY, B.J. and B.H.HOYER: Identity of DNA and diversity of messenger RNA molecules in normal mouse tissues. Proc. Natl. Acad. Sci., U.S. 52 (1964) 915.

OISHI, M., A.OISHI and N.SUEOKA: Location of genetic loci of soluble RNA on *Bacillus subtilis* chromosome. Proc. Natl. Acad. Sci., U.S. 55 (1966) 1095.

RICHARDS, O.C.: Hybridization of *Euglena gracilis* chloroplast and nuclear DNA. Proc. Natl. Acad. Sci., U.S. 57 (1967) 156.

RITTOSSA, F., K.ATWOOD, D.LINDSLEY and S.SPIEGELMAN: On the chromosomal distribution of DNA complementary to ribosomal and soluble RNA. Natl. Cancer Inst. Monograph #23. International Symposium on the nucleolus: its structure and function (1966) p. 449.

SIMPSON, G.G.: This view of life. New York, Harcourt Brace & World, Inc. (1964) 164.

WALLACE, H. and M.BIRNSTIEL: Ribosomal cistrons and the nucleolar organizer. Biochim. Biophys. Acta 114 (1966) 296.

YANKOFSKY, S.A. and S.SPIEGELMAN: The identification of the ribosomal RNA cistron by sequence complementarity. II. Proc. Natl. Acad. Sci. U.S. 48 (1962) 1466.

CHAPTER 4

Highly repetitive DNA in rodents

P. M. B. WALKER, W. G. FLAMM and ANNE MCLAREN

Department of Zoology, The University of Edinburgh

and

Agricultural Research Council Unit of Animal Genetics, The University of Edinburgh

Contents

1. Introduction
2. Properties of satellite DNA of the mouse (*Mus musculus*)
3. Are sequences similar to those in mouse satellite present in other DNA?
4. The single-strand interaction
5. Are the mouse satellite sequences expressed?
6. How far are these properties peculiar to the mouse?
7. Discussion

1. *Introduction*

In previous chapters in this handbook Britten and Kohne have provided excellent evidence that the DNA of many higher organisms can be placed in families, in which the number of related members may range from 10^2 to 10^6 per genome. They deduce from this that we are seeing in each organism a snapshot of an evolutionary process, which they believe to consist of a 'saltatory' replication of a random sequence followed by the divergence of this sequence and the consequent recruitment of the families not so highly repeated.

In this chapter we will discuss only the properties of the highly replicated DNAS occurring 10^5–10^6 times, which can sometimes but not always be isolated as satellite bands from nuclear DNA. In particular we want to raise the question whether their properties are consistent with their being a product of a recent 'saltatory event' or whether they have a functional importance which has ensured their integrity and preserved their sequences.

We will first consider mouse satellite DNA, about which we know most. We will then discuss some of the relevant properties of comparable DNA from other organisms, before discussing the implications of our results.

2. *Properties of satellite DNA of the mouse (Mus musculus)*

A large proportion of the most highly replicated fraction of native mouse DNA can be isolated by caesium chloride gradient centrifugation from the remainder of the DNA as a light satellite component (Flamm et al. 1966). It is very homogeneous and of high molecular weight (10^7 daltons), as shown by the sharpness both of its band pattern in the centrifuge and of its thermal transition on melting in the spectrophotometer, and by suitable viscosity measurements (Bond et al.). It is 34% CG compared to 42% for the main band, and if it consists of a number of members of a related family then 90% of them must have a CG content with ± 1.5% of the observed mean.

Despite this homogeneity in banding properties, the sequences may still differ slightly among themselves while preserving an overall similarity. The main evidence that they are not identical stems from the observation that the renatured duplex of mouse satellite DNA melts some 5.5° lower than the native duplex. Curiously the T_m of the renatured duplex is as near the expected value for a DNA of this base composition as the native duplex; in the native state it is abnormally stable to heat denaturation. The 5.5° discrepancy loses some of its force since we have shown (Walker and McLaren 1965) that DNA, cross-linked with nitrous acid (Geiduschek) under conditions which cause little deamination (Vielmetter and Schuster), also melts 5° lower than the native molecules after heating at 100° and then cooling, despite the presence of cross-linking which maintains the complementary strands in register.

From the molecular weight data, from Britten's evidence for the length of the repeated sequence and from its size relative to the whole genome, we can calculate that satallite DNA must consist of blocks containing at least 100 tandem reduplications of a sequence 300–400 base pairs long. If these blocks are spread evenly throughout the genome, there would be on average about 300 of such blocks per chromosome. If, on the other hand, the sequences are gathered in blocks of the maximum size, there would, in the mouse, need to be at least four chromosomes entirely composed of satellite DNA.

Such is the measure of the genetic and evolutionary problem. When we look more deeply into the properties of this DNA it appears even more unusual. The two strands are so different in base composition that they can be easily isolated on an alkaline caesium chloride gradient to give a heavy (H) and a light (L) strand. Mouse satellite thus became the first non-viral DNA in which this separation was achieved (Flamm et al. 1967). Since centrifugation in alkaline caesium chloride separates DNA single strands on the basis of their content of guanosine and thymidine (Vinograd et al. 1963), this separation implies that the individual strands are homogeneous in the proportion of these bases also.

Information on the mouse DNA is summarized in Table 1.

TABLE 1

Properties of mouse DNA

DNA fraction	% of genome	ρ 7.0 (g/cm^3)*	ρ 12.5 (g/cm^3)**	σ (cm)†	T_m (°C)††	Melting range (°C)	Base ratios (%) A	T	G	C	%GC	%GT
Main peak		1.702		0.035	74.5	12.0						
Denatured	90		1.758				29	29	21	21	42	50
main peak		1.717		—	45	50						
Native satellite		1.691		0.008	74.2	3.5						
Renatured	10						33	33	17	17	34	50
satellite		1.696		—	70.0	11.0						
H strand	5	1.723	1.752	—	40	60	21	45	13	22	35	58
L strand	5	1.699	1.725	0.020	40	60	44	22	20	14	34	42

* Buoyant density in neutral CsCl based on a buoyant density of 1.710 g/cm^3 for *E. coli* DNA at atmospheric pressure.

** Buoyant density in alkaline CsCl (*p*H 12.5) determined from the root mean square position and expressed in terms of the initial density of the solution at atmospheric pressure (see Vinograd and Hearst).

† Standard deviation calculated from the band width at $^6/_{10}$ peak height (Vinograd and Hearst).

†† T_m, the temperature corresponding to a 50% increase in relative absorbance during heat denaturation. Melting was conducted in a medium of 0.06 M sodium phosphate, *p*H 6.8.

3. *Are sequences similar to those in mouse satellite present in other DNA?*

Isolated single strand DNA facilitates very sensitive tests of homologies, if the hydroxyapatite technique for detecting the reassociation of an isotopically labelled component is used (Walker and McCallum; Flamm et al. 1967). Our method has been to measure only those reassociations which are stable at 70 °C in 0.12 M PO_4, and to ignore for the present, those less perfect fits between polynucleotides stable only at lower temperatures. Such a high temperature of fractionation ensures that we only take account of those duplexes most like the native molecule (Walker and McLaren 1965).

Under these conditions 15 to 20% of the DNA from either the heavy or the light strand alone of mouse satellite, labelled with P^{32}, will reassociate; this unexpected property is discussed more fully below. In the presence of its unlabelled complement, however, either strand reassociates to between 80 and 90%, and this is little affected by the presence of denatured heterologous DNA. We can therefore investigate whether main-band DNA from the mouse contains sequences complementary to the isolated satellite strands. We find that a further 2–3% of satellite-like sequences are contained in the main-band DNA. The size of this fraction and of the satellite itself depends on the molecular weight of the preparation. In very high molecular weight preparations a smaller proportion of DNA is found in the satellite position. This indicates that some blocks of sequences are shorter than others and band at higher densities because they are covalently bonded to main-band DNA.

In these experiments DNA from one strand of mouse satellite was incubated at 2×10^{-5} mg/ml and was half renatured in 20 min if the same amount of the complementary strand was present. It was only necessary to add 2×10^{-3} mg/ml of main-band DNA to detect the 2–3% of satellite sequences. This sensitivity can be considerably improved; at least 1 mg/ml of a low-molecular weight sample of a denatured heterologous DNA can be added to the incubation mixture and if this DNA contains 2×10^{-5} mg/ml of sequences complementary to the single-stranded DNA, we can expect complete renaturation of the latter. Since there are about 6×10^9 base pairs in the mammalian genome it is possible to detect at least 1.2×10^5 of these (400 sequences 300 base pairs long) which might be complementary to a mouse satellite strand.

In Fig. 1 we show experiments designed to test whether the technique could detect sequences at very low relative concentrations, then to measure the effect of heterologous DNA on the rate of reassociation of the satellite strands and finally to show whether rat DNA alone can react with a single strand. The first tests (Fig. 1a) involved deliberately adding duplex satellite DNA to a 18,250 fold excess of low molecular weight rat DNA, at concentrations at which the complementary strand was $\times \frac{1}{4}$, $\frac{1}{2}$ and 1 that of the P^{32}-labelled strand. It will be seen that this added duplex material is easily detected and that the rate of reassociation is little different from that of the control experiments without rat DNA (Fig. 1b). With rat DNA alone no significant reassociation

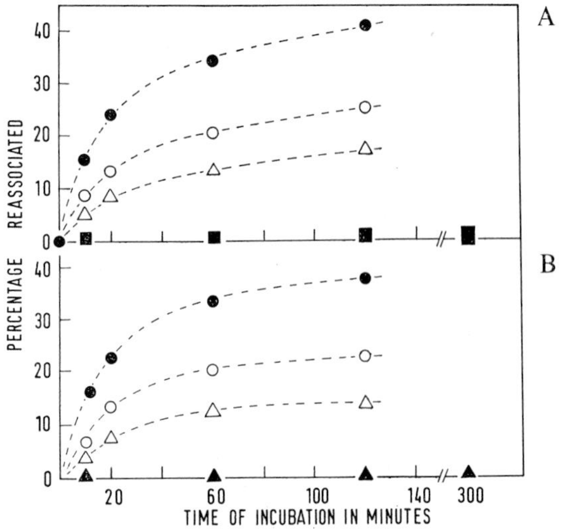

Fig. 1. The absence of satellite sequences in rat DNA. P^{32}-labelled heavy strands from mouse satellite DNA at 10^{-3} mg/ml were incubated for 100 min at 60° and fractionated on hydroxyapatite at 70°, to remove the single-strand reacting material. 68% of this DNA eluted at 0.12 M PO_4. This fraction was diluted with 0.12 M PO_4 to 2×10^{-5} mg/ml in the final incubation mixture, which also contained low molecular weight unlabelled DNA as indicated. Each mixture was heat-denatured before incubation. (A) With added rat DNA at 3.6×10^{-1} mg/ml and duplex satellite mouse DNA at the following concentrations, (■) 0.0 mg/ml (pairs of readings from two separate experiments at each time); (△) 10^{-5} mg/ml; (○) 2×10^{-5} mg/ml; (●) 4×10^{-5} mg/ml.
(B) Without added rat DNA but with duplex mouse satellite DNA at the following concentrations, (▲) 0.0 mg/ml; (△) 10^{-5} mg/ml; (○) 2×10^{-5} mg/ml; (●) 4×10^{-5} mg/ml.

is found and the very low backgrounds in these experiments show that it would have been easy to detect complementary sequences at a concentration of 5% of the P^{32}-labelled strand. This would have allowed us to see one part in 365,000 of the rat DNA.

In a second series of experiments with DNA from the rat, guinea pig, *Apodemus sylvaticus*, *Peromyscus polionotus* and *P. maniculatus*, we were able to use DNA at higher concentrations ranging from 0.5 to 1.0 mg. In all these experiments the results were negative and we therefore conclude that there are less than 1:1,000,000 sequences like mouse satellite in these rodents, that is less than 20 sequences 300 base pairs long. One such sequence may exist, but there seems little evidence in these rodents of the few or many sequences from which we must presume mouse satellite to have arisen.

4. *The single-strand interaction*

The last experiments show that the test for reassociation on hydroxyapatite fails to give positive results with 10^5 excess of heterologous DNA. It is therefore the more remarkable that between 10–15% of either of the mouse satellite single strands will, after incubation, associate to give an apparently duplex molecule (Fig. 2a), consisting of light and light or heavy and heavy strands, which dissociates on heating in a typical co-operative manner. These duplexes can be separated from the unassociated single strands on hydroxyapatite, and, after heat-denaturing the separated materials can be reincubated and rechromatogrammed. Formerly associated duplexes reassociate a second time to 30%, while the unassociated materials from the first incubation now associate hardly at all (Fig. 2b).

This interaction is not due to contamination by complementary strands during isolation since: (1) The overall base composition is like the parent strand and easily distinguishable from a true light-heavy duplex (see Table 1); (2) Addition of a $\times 10$ excess of a cold identical strand prepared in the same way will not increase the fraction associated above 15%, but will only increase the rate of reassociation.

It can also be shown that these light–light or heavy–heavy associated duplexes still have binding sites for whole complementary strands unlike the normal light–heavy duplex. We conclude that there may be some short self-complementary sequences in each strand; for example, 20–30 alternating CG bases might be sufficient. These, if

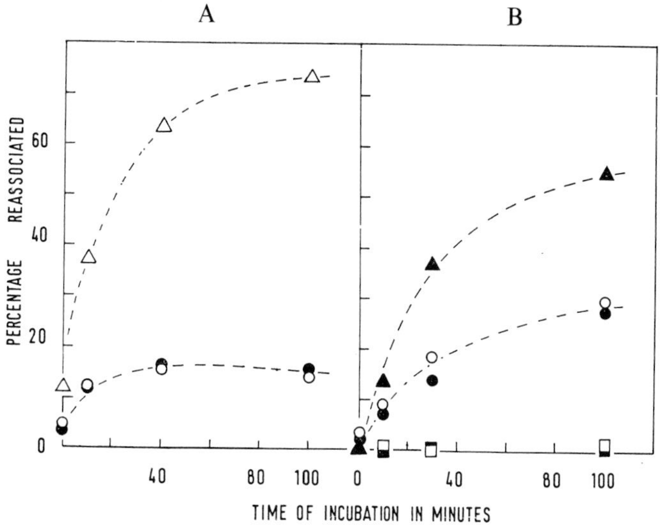

Fig. 2. Renaturation of homologous strands of DNA. All samples were incubated in 0.12 M PO_4'' at 60° for the times stated at a total concentration of 4×10^{-5} mg/ml. Percentage reassociation refers to the fraction of the radioactivity eluting at 0.3 M PO_4'' from hydroxyapatite.

(A) Whole heavy (● ?) and light (○) strands incubated alone. Heavy and light strands incubated together (△).

(B) Heavy or light strands were first fractionated on hydroxyapatite after incubation at 5×10^{-4} mg/ml, when 12.2% of the heavy and 18.8% of the light strands eluted at 0.3 M PO_4. The DNA from both 0.3 M and 0.12 M fractions were then diluted to 4×10^{-5} mg/ml and heat-denatured before incubation and refractionation. 0.12 M light (□) and heavy (■) strand fractions incubated alone. 0.3 M light (○) and heavy (●) strand fractions incubated alone. 0.12 M light and heavy strand fractions incubated together (▲).

scattered among the repeated satellite sequences and in the absence of a complementary strand, would allow the homologous strands to reassociate over part of their length and so stabilise the molecule on hydroxyapatite. Provided there was little chance of two such sequences appearing in one molecule of the denatured and fractionated material, we would expect the concentration dependence of the association which we in fact observe. Such a small fraction would not significantly alter the base composition of the 15% of the molecules in which it occurred, and would explain the low reassociation maximum (30%) after the second incubation, since heat denaturation can be shown to reduce molecular weight.

5. *Are the mouse satellite sequences expressed?*

Just as it is possible to devise with a single strand very sensitive tests for DNA–DNA homology, so too can we test whether there are RNA sequences homologous to one or the other strand in a mixed population of RNA molecules. Homologous RNA sequences can be expected to increase the rate of reassociation of one isolated strand or, as in our earlier experiments, of one strand of a denatured duplex. Provided that the RNA is rigorously purified of contaminating DNA by caesium chloride centrifugation, we have so far found no sequences in RNA preparations from the mouse able to associate with mouse satellite DNA even if the RNA is added in ×1,000 or ×5,000 excess. RNA from various tissues has been tested including that from the murine myeloma 5563 (Williamson and Askonas). Parallel experiments with main band DNA do, on the other hand, show a marked reassociation with the RNA tested. It should be noted that *in vitro* experiments with RNA polymerase (Weissman) show that an RNA product can be made from mouse satellite.

In summary the mouse genome has from 10–15% of its DNA organised in a class with special properties; they appear to have sequences repeated many times, one strand of all the sequences has a very different composition from the other, they are apparently untranscribed, but not untranscribable. The sequences are isolated in blocks of about 100 reiterations, and within some of these blocks there is evidence for a short sequence which allows the homologous strands to reassociate. Further the sequences are not found in other related DNAs.

6. *How far are these properties peculiar to the mouse?*

So far we have also investigated DNA from the guinea pig (*Cavia porcellus*), the European wood mouse (*Apodemus sylvaticus*), the brown rat (*Rattus norvegicus*) and two species of North American deer mouse (*Peromyscus maniculatus* and *P. polionotus*). All these show patterns strikingly different both from each other and from *Mus musculus*.

Fig. 3 shows a series of tracings from analytical centrifuge photographs of whole DNA in a neutral caesium chloride gradient. In those instances where a definite satellite band could be identified, we isolated and then reran it in alkaline caesium chloride (Fig. 4). We then found even greater diversity. *Apodemus sylvaticus* has a light satellite comparable to *Mus musculus* but it does not separate into discrete light and heavy strands. The guinea pig satellite, on the other hand, shows an even more extreme and complex band pattern than *Mus*. Reassociation experiments show that

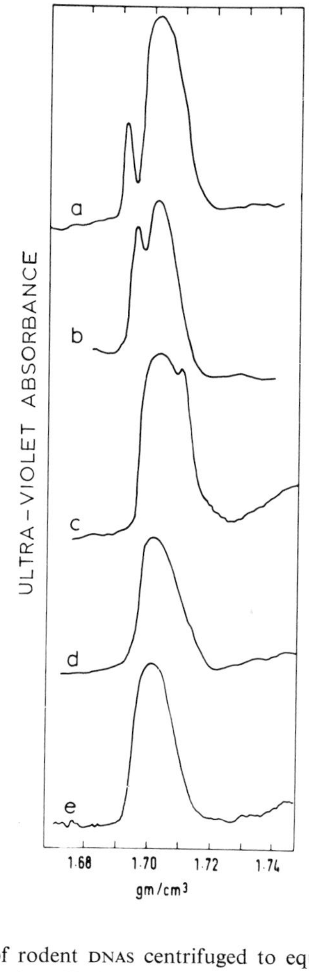

Fig. 3. Densitometer tracings of rodent DNAs centrifuged to equilibrium in neutral gradients of CsCl. All samples were centrifuged at 45,000 rev./min for 24 hr in an M.S.E. analytical centrifuge containing approximately 2 μg of either mouse (a), *Apodemus sylvaticus* (b), guinea pig (c), *Rattus norvegicus* (d), or *Peromyscus maniculatus* (or *Peromyscus polionotus*) (e) DNA. Buoyant densities were determined relative to *E. coli* DNA taken as 1.710 g/cm³ at atmospheric pressure (see Schildkraut et al.).

the satellite has split into two pairs of strands, a pair with extreme compositional bias (αL and αH) and a pair not so widely separated (βL and βH).

Since we have identified similar satellites both lighter and heavier than the main band DNA, there seems to be no reason to doubt that analogous sequences might be concealed within the main band DNA of other organisms like the rat and *Peromyscus*. A rapidly reassociating component has indeed been isolated from both rat and *Peromyscus* DNA by hydroxyapatite salt fractionation; agar binding studies indicate that in *Peromyscus* at least this component is analogous to mouse satellite (Walker and McLaren 1968). Such cryptic sequences might also be identified by their capacity to separate into single strands of different GT–CA ratio. Alkaline caesium chloride runs have been made on whole DNA extracted from a number of these rodents (Fig. 5) and there is evidence that both rats and *Peromyscus* have strand-biased sequences which show as shoulders on either side of the main peak of the DNA.

Rates of reassociation can also be measured for these fractions, which in the case

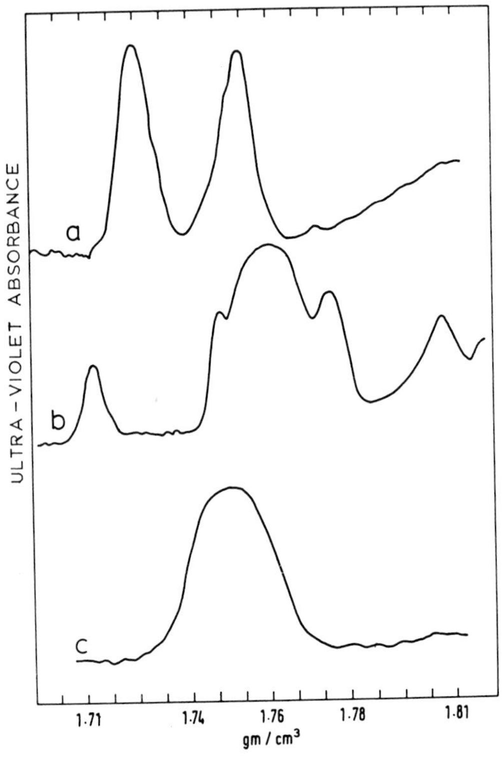

Fig. 4. Densitometer tracings of satellite DNAs from mouse (a), guinea pig (b) and *Apodemus sylvaticus* (c) centrifuged to equilibrium in alkaline gradients of CsCl as specified in Fig. 3. Buoyant densities were determined from root mean square positions and are expressed in terms of the initial density of solution at atmospheric pressure.

of *Mus*, guinea pig and *Apodemus sylvaticus* have been identified with the satellite fraction. Guinea pig and *Mus* data both indicate a repeated sequence of 300–400 base pairs, although in the former it must be shared between two distinct sequence sets. Satellite DNA from *Apodemus* reassociates some ten times more slowly than that from mouse, indicating either a longer repeating sequence or a greater number of different sequences of the same length. Rat and *Peromyscus* spp. also have fractions which reassociate at rates comparable to that of the mouse, although the size of the fraction may be less. In *Peromyscus* this fast renaturing fraction has not yet been shown to be identical with the shoulders on the curve in Fig. 5.

7. Discussion

There are grave difficulties in explaining either the formation or the continued preservation of these highly repetitive DNA fractions, whose properties distinguish them

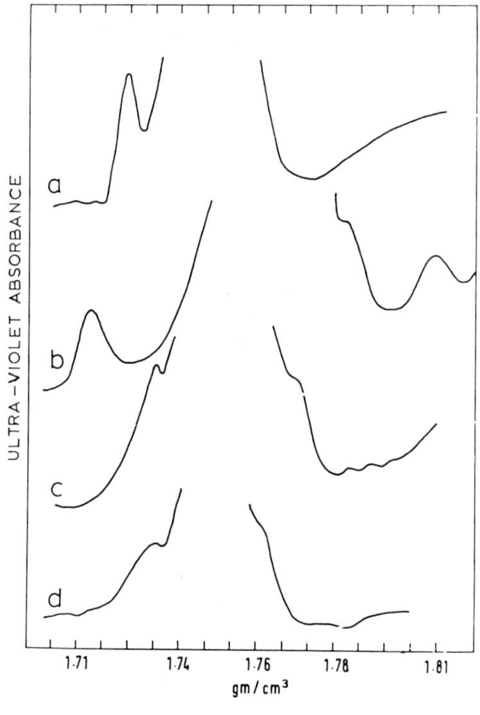

Fig. 5. Densitometer tracings of unfractionated mouse (a), guinea pig (b), *Rattus norvegicus* (c), and *Peromyscus* (either *maniculatus* or *polionotus*) (d) DNA at equilibrium in an alkaline CsCl density gradient. Conditions of centrifugation were as specified in Fig. 3. In order to emphasise the presence of minor components (which we believe represent single strands), the samples were overloaded with approximately 50 μg of DNA per centrifuge cell and tracing of the major band is left open. Buoyant density positions were determined as described in Fig. 4.

sharply from the families of sequences repeated 10^3–10^4 times, with which Britten and Kohne are mainly concerned. If the formation of highly repetitive DNA is a rare event, it is unlikely that we shall observe it or discover whether it occurred suddenly or gradually over the course of many generations. The preservation of such a fraction would seem to be a more tractable problem. At present, however, our techniques are unable to detect whether all the sequences in mouse satellite DNA, for example, are nearly identical and therefore consistent with a high selective pressure, arising from their functional significance, or whether they are rapidly diverging after a 'saltation', when selection pressure may be minimal and any base substitution retained. The problem is aggravated because we know neither when the sequences arose nor the rate of base substitution in such an unselected system.

It may be possible to answer some of these questions soon. The study of sub-species and races may help in discovering the rate of divergence of the highly replicated DNAS. So far as we know, all laboratory mouse strains have indistinguishable satellite DNA, but a more promising system is perhaps the island races of *Apodemus sylvaticus* where it is possible to make an intelligent guess about the date of their isolation (Berry, Evans and Sennitt). We are also studying the distribution of the oligomers formed by random and selective degradation of the complementary strands, preparatory to an attempt at sequencing mouse satellite DNA. Clearly the number of oligomers of a given composition will give direct evidence on the degree of heterogeneity.

The bias in base sequence of some satellites is relevant to this discussion in another way; of the first three satellites studied two have sufficient bias to allow strand isolation. Guinea pig strands are crucial here, since mutation would quickly be expected to eliminate the extreme bias in which either G or C is very deficient in one strand. Only if the strands had arisen recently or if they were subject to selection pressure would we expect such a divergence between the strands in the face of random base substitution.

We must also consider whether strand divergence is compatible with any possible function for these sequences. They appear not to be transcribed in the mouse, and reference to coding assignments would indicate that guinea pig α-strands would give a very aberrant protein lacking about a third of all the amino acids. Their high degree of redundancy also argues against a role in determining polypeptide sequence.

Before considering functions which do not involve transcription, some discussion of the origin of this DNA is necessary, if only because the presence of two different and unrelated satellite sequences in two species of mice, *Mus musculus* and *Apodemus sylvaticus*, indicates the presence of a puzzling process, which cannot but have some evolutionary significance. With the analogy of virus replication in mind, 10^6 replications of a random sequence would seem possible if one accepts the formation of a new DNA polymerase of unique specificity and subject to an abnormal control. It is the next stage which is difficult to envisage; as the result of this replication one chromosome has a supernumerary part four times its original size. Throughout many subsequent mitotic and meiotic divisions these sequences must be preserved until they are safely translocated into other chromosomes.

The only virtue of postulating this single magnificent event would be to explain why all the sequences were originally identical. Suppose however that there already existed in the genome a number of blocks containing certain sequences which were stringently preserved for some specific functional requirement. Our mutant polymerase could now multiply a larger number of one of these sequences to a much more limited extent than in the first hypothesis. This reduces the structural difficulties, and provided the multiplication occurs simultaneously, need not alter the functioning of such sets of sequences, as we shall show later.

The origin and distribution throughout the genome of the original blocks might result from duplication and subsequent translocation. That these are in fact rather frequent events in the mammalian genome is suggested by genetic evidence. Harris, for example, has identified three unlinked loci in man, each determining a set of phosphoglucomutase isozymes which resemble one another so closely in physical and biochemical properties that it seems only reasonable to argue that the loci must originally have arisen by duplication, followed by translocation (Harris).

Although no direct evidence exists for the occasional multiplication of scattered sequences, it seems that if two closely related species differ in their DNA content, the additional DNA tends to be spread throughout all members of the chromosome complement. Conceivably this extra DNA could have originated as the replication of one particular scattered sequence. In the case of *Allium cepa* and *A. fistulosa*, the pachytene configuration of at least one chromosome of the species hybrid suggests that the interpolated region is indeed made up of segmental duplications (Rees and Jones).

Are there chromosomal properties which might require a large number of similar sequences scattered over the genome? We should now like to consider the case for what we will call 'housekeeping' sequences. They could be concerned with some or all of the following functions:

(1) Initiation regions. There may be recognition sequences for the replication or transcription of the DNA, although there seems no reason to expect that the blocks should contain so many reiterated sequences or why different species should need different sequences. Taylor has however suggested the need for an AT-rich sequence of at least 100 base pairs, with a strong strand bias, to explain his bromodeoxyuridine results in the Chinese hamster and *Vicia*.

(2) Recombinator regions. To explain observations on genetic recombination in fungi, Holliday has proposed that a particular sequence of bases recurs at irregular intervals along the length of the chromosomes; this sequence would act as a specific substrate for an enzyme which would initiate a recombinational event by causing single strand breaks at corresponding points on homologous chromatids. Such a function would demand repetition of one sequence many times over; however, the repeats would be expected to occur singly, rather than in large blocks.

(3) Pairing sites in meiosis. Holliday has also postulated the existence of specific short base sequences, probably distinct from those in the recombinator regions, which would form the attachment sites for a fibrillar, contractile protein linking homologous

chromosomes during the prophase of meiosis. The specificity of pairing would be brought about by the pattern of distribution of the sites: non-homologous chromosomes might also show a tendency to pair, but any such arrangement would be unstable as the binding sites would not be opposite each other. Again, the repeated sequences would presumably occur singly, and need only be long enough to provide specificity for the pairing enzyme.

(4) Centromere recognition. There is genetic evidence in mice, and also in fungi, that in crosses between distantly related stocks, centromeres of the same origin may show affinity for one another and assort together at meiosis, thus giving rise to disturbed segregation ratios (see Michie 1953, 1955; Wallace 1953, 1959). The centromeric region of the chromosome is clearly large enough to accommodate substantial amounts of DNA.

(5) Chromosome folding.

The last four functions all involve recognition between parts of chromosomes. It seems that higher organisms have their genetic material organised so that the chromosomes can respond to changes in their cellular environment by folding, unfolding or pairing in specific ways. Patterns change as between interphase and mitosis, in the 'lampbrush' chromosomes of oocytes, in the highly organised packing of the sperm head, in the patterns of chromomeres in different tissues (Lima-de-Faria et al.) and in the bands of dipteran salivary chromosomes. In some instances, e.g. salivary chromosomes, the pattern is clearly genetically determined; in others, its genetic basis can be inferred from, for example, the distinctiveness of different karyotypes. It therefore seems highly likely that base sequences must be in some way involved in chromosomal 'housekeeping'. For example, the base sequence and pattern of the lengths of the genome concerned with folding (folding sites) could allow certain parts of the chromosome to interact directly, giving a folded structure. Alternatively or additionally, these folding sites might be concerned with the attachment of, say, proteins which would therefore mediate and possibly control the particular folding pattern required.

The preservation of similar patterns of sequences in the folding sites throughout the genome can be understood if each site has to interact sequentially with a number of others both in the same and different chromosomes. For example, mitotic folding is likely to involve pairs of folding sites different from those in the lampbrush chromosome, which would in turn be different from a possible association between chromosomes in interphase. If we extend the hypothesis further to include a mechanism for the pairing of homologous chromosomes in meiosis, such as Holliday's pairing sites or the 'effective pairing segments' suggested by Pritchard, there are additional strong reasons for the preservation of similar sequences.

The stronger the reasons for preserving a large number of sequences in the genome, the more difficult is it to explain the difference in the satellite sequences in *Mus* and *Apodemus*. But let us suppose that in a species without a 10^6 replicated sequence there are 10^4 folding sites spread throughout the genome and that each consists of 10 sequences similar to each other but not identical. The permutations of these ten, together with the decision about which of the 10 are to be operative, are presumed to determine the specificity of folding in each chromosomal situation. The specific new polymerase, postulated earlier, which is responsible for the sudden increase from 10^5 to 10^6 reiterated sequences per genome, multiplies a hundred-fold one only of the ten sequences in each folding site throughout the genome of an individual. Such a replication would simply intercalate a number of redundant sequences and would not materially alter the pattern by which folding site recognition is mediated in different situations. The redundant information would not be easily lost from any individual folding site however, since this would immediately alter the pattern recognised by a number of other sites. But if our preliminary results, showing that other rodents lack mouse satellite sequences, are more widely confirmed, we must postulate that it is advantageous for other organisms to amplify different sequences and to lose those represented in highly reiterated DNAS elsewhere.

To return now to our original antithesis between the purely evolutionary role ascribed by Britten and Kohne to the 10^6 reiterations and our view that they may have a functional significance: we are impressed by their interstrand compositional bias, by their apparent similarity within an organism, and by the possibility of associations between single strands both *in vitro* and in nature, and by the difficulty of envisaging a 10^6 replication of one cistron selected by chance. They may be the stuff of evolution but there is something to be said for the view that families of sequences have been preserved because they are needed and not observed because they are young.

Acknowledgments

We would like to thank Dr. K. Atwood of the University of Illinois, who first suggested to one of us (P. M. B. Walker) that satellite DNA might be concerned with chromosome folding and Dr. N. A. Mitchison of the National Institute of Medical Research for supplying the mice carrying the 5563 plasmacytoma.

We gratefully acknowledge the support of this work by the Medical Research Council and the Nuffield Foundation. W. G. Flamm is on foreign assignment from the National Cancer Institute, Bethesda, Maryland.

References

BERRY, R. J., I. M. EVANS and B. F. C. SENNITT: The relationships and ecology of *Apodemus sylvaticus* from the Small Isles of the Inner Hebrides, Scotland. J. Zool. 152 (1967) 333.

BOND, H. E., W. G. FLAMM, H. E. BURR and S. B. BOND: Mouse satellite DNA; further studies on its biological and physical characteristics and its intracellular localisation. J. Mol. Biol. 27 (1967) 289.

FLAMM, W. G., H. E. BOND and H. E. BURR: Density gradient centrifugation in a fixed-angle rotor; a higher order of resolution. Biochim. Biophys. Acta 129 (1966) 310.

FLAMM, W. G., M. MCCALLUM and P. M. B. WALKER: The isolation of complementary strands from a mouse DNA fraction. Proc. Natl. Acad. Sci. U.S. 57 (1967) 1729.

GEIDUSCHEK, E. P.: 'Reversible' DNA. Proc. Natl. Acad. Sci. U.S. 47 (1961) 950.

HARRIS, H.: Personal communication, Galton Laboratories, University College, London.

HOLLIDAY, R.: Genetic recombination in fungi. In: Replication and recombination of genetic material. Canberra, Aust. Acad. Sci., in (1968) press.

LIMA-DE-FARIA, A., P. SARVELLA and R. MORRIS: Different chromomere numbers at meiosis and mitosis in *Ornithogalum*. Hereditas 45 (1959) 407.

MICHIE, D.: Affinity: a new genetic phenomenon in the house mouse. Evidence from distant crosses. Nature 171 (1953) 26.

MICHIE, D.: 'Affinity'. Proc. Roy. Soc. (London) Ser. B 144 (1955) 241.

PRITCHARD, R. H.: The bearing of recombination analysis at high resolution on genetic fine structure in *Aspergillus nidulans* and the mechanism of recombination in higher organisms. Microbial Genetics, Xth Symp. Soc. Gen. Microbiol. Camb. Univ. Press (1960) 155.

REES, H. and R. N. JONES: Structural basis of quantitative variation in nuclear DNA. Nature 216 (1967) 825.

SCHILDKRAUT, C. L., J. MARMUR and P. DOTY: J. Mol. Biol. 4 (1967) 430.

TAYLOR, J. H.: The regulation of DNA replication in chromosomes in higher cells. 2nd Inter. Symp. Cell Chem. 1967.

VIELMETTER, V. W. and H. SCHUSTER: Die Basenspezifität bei der Induktion von Mutationen durch Salpetrige Säure im Phagen T2. Z. Naturforsch. 15b (1960) 304.

VINOGRAD, J. and J. E. HEARST: Equilibrium sedimentation of macromolecules and viruses in a density gradient. Fortschr. Chem. Org. Naturstoffe 10 (1962) 395.

VINOGRAD, J., J. MORRIS, N. DAVIDSON and W. DOVE: The buoyant behaviour of bacterial and viral DNA in alkaline cesium chloride solution. Proc. Natl. Acad. Sci. U.S. 49 (1963) 12.

WALKER, P. M. B. and A. MCLAREN: Fractionation of mouse deoxyribonucleic acid on hydroxyapatite. Nature 208 (1965) 1175.

WALKER, P. M. B. and A. MCLAREN: Studies on the heterogeneity of rodent DNA. In preparation.

WALKER, P. M. B. and M. MCCALLUM: Renaturation of T_4 bacteriophage deoxyribonucleic acid in the presence of excess heterologous DNA. J. Mol. Biol. 18 (1966) 215.

WALLACE, M. E.: Affinity: a new genetic phenomenon in the house mouse. Evidence from within laboratory stocks. Nature 171 (1953) 27.

WALLACE, M. E.: Experimental evidence for a new genetic phenomenon. Phil. Trans. Roy. Soc., London, Ser. B 241 (1958) 211.

WEISSMAN, S. M.: Personal communication. Yale University School of Medicine.

WILLIAMSON, A. R. and B. A. ASKONAS: Biosynthesis of immunoglobulins: The separate classes of polyribosomes synthesizing heavy and light chains. J. Mol. Biol. 23 (1967) 201.

CHAPTER 5

The doublet pattern of the nucleic acid in relation to the origin of viruses

J. H. SUBAK-SHARPE

Institute of Virology, University of Glasgow

Contents

1. DNA, base composition and base sequence
2. What is doublet analysis?
3. What is the random expectation for doublet frequencies?
4. How can doublet frequencies be related to amino acid frequencies?
5. Doublet pattern and overall use of the genetic code
6. The experimental evidence – direct comparison of the doublet patterns of virus and host
7. The stability of the doublet pattern
8. Which selective forces could overcome the stability of the doublet pattern?
9. Is there an unbiased way of comparing the doublet patterns of nucleic acids which have different base compositions?
10. The experimental evidence – comparison of the general designs of the nucleic acid of viruses and host
11. Do the general designs provide information relative to the phylogenetic problem of the origin and evolution of mammalian viruses?

1. DNA, base composition and base sequence

Today it is generally accepted that the genetic information of all organisms is encoded in the sequential arrangement of bases in their nucleic acid. In the great majority of cases this nucleic acid is double stranded deoxyribonucleic acid (DNA), although in the case of viruses some are known which contain only single stranded DNA, others have only single stranded ribonucleic acid (RNA) and still others have only double stranded RNA (Fenner). For our purposes discussion of double stranded DNA will suffice.

Pre-eminently only the four bases guanine (G), cytosine (C), adenine (A), and thymine (T) are present in DNA where these bases exhibit a very unusual structural arrangement: They are ordered into two antiparallel complementary polynucleotide strands (Fig. 1) which are wound round one another to form a double stranded helical molecule. The complementary nature of the base pairing *between* the two strands is such that A in one strand always pairs with T in the other and similarly G always pairs with C. It follows that a characteristic property of double stranded DNA is that the amount of A always equals that of T, and likewise the amount of G always equals that of C. However within a single polynucleotide strand of DNA there exists no such simple relationship and A, T, G and C may be present in any proportions.

The amount of (G+C) found in the DNA of any individual species is constant and highly characteristic for that species and is also known as the base composition. DNAS from many taxonomically different organisms have been investigated and found to be distributed over the whole range of base compositions from about 20% (G+C) to about 80% (G+C). Several investigators have concluded from the clustering of the base compositions of apparently related groups of organisms that phylogenetic relationships seem to be reflected by the DNA base composition (Lee et al.; Sueoka 1961). Comparisons of (G+C) content have been frequently used for the elucidation and definition of taxonomic relationships, and it has been suggested that such data should in future be included in species description (Hill).

Sueoka (1961, 1962) has also investigated both from experimental data and by theoretical considerations whether there exists in bacteria any correlation between the DNA base composition and the amino acid composition of the bulk protein. But the information which is inherent in the base composition is very limited (Subak-Sharpe 1967) for, though it defines the relative proportions of the four bases in DNA, it contains no information concerning the sequential arrangement of these bases in the DNA.

Final characterisation of a DNA in terms of the complete sequence of bases along the polynucleotide chain is not yet feasible, but some characterisation of DNA in terms of the distribution of its two-base (doublet) sequences has become possible since 1961 when Josse et al. introduced the elegant technique of 'nearest neighbour base sequence analysis'. It is, therefore, now possible to ask, whether the highly characteristic patterns of doublet distributions, which result from 'nearest neighbour analysis' of the nucleic acid of viruses and their host cells, provide information relevant to the problem of the origin of these viruses and the problem of their evolutionary relationships.

2. *What is doublet analysis?*

The technique of doublet analysis estimates the overall frequency with which a given base is adjacent to each of the four bases in the polynucleotide chains of the DNA under investigation. The four bases which generally occur in DNA allow the formation of only $4 \times 4 = 16$ possible doublets and the frequencies of these sixteen doublets characterize the DNA.

Experimentally the relative frequencies of the sixteen doublets are determined *in vitro* in four separate reactions, which are primed with a sample of the same DNA. On this template-DNA the enzyme 'DNA polymerase' synthesizes product-DNA from the deoxyribonucleoside 5′-triphosphates of the four bases, of which only one is supplied labelled in the a position with P^{32} (a different one in each of the four reactions). The product-DNA is later degraded enzymatically to deoxyribonucleoside 3′-monophosphates, which are separated, and their P^{32} contents measured.

The essential point is, that the radioactive label is transferred from the 5′ position of the supplied labelled nucleotide to the 3′ position of the nearest neighbour nucleotide in the synthesized product-DNA. (For example when [aP^{32}] deoxyguanosine 5′-triphosphate is supplied the P^{32} in the four 3′-monophosphates, obtained from the enzymic degradation of the product-DNA, describes the relative frequency distribution of the four doublets GpG, CpG, ApG and TpG). The analysis is completed by combining the data from the four separate reactions and this gives the frequencies of occurrence of all sixteen doublets in the DNA under study. It is of course essential that the supplied template-DNA be highly pure in the sense that it must be uncontaminated by any other DNA.

To be of value in characterizing DNA the method clearly depends on the synthesis of a faithful (though not necessarily a perfect) copy of the nucleotide sequence of the supplied template-DNA or a representative part of it, and the evidence suggests that this is so. It has been shown that the enzyme forms the product-DNA by copying both strands of the template-DNA, that the two strands of the product (as of the template) have opposite polarities, that the product itself can be used as template, and that the doublet frequencies are reproducible and characteristic of any DNA supplied as template (Josse et al.; Swartz et al.; Josse and Swartz). The technique as used here has limitations which are of little relevance to our present considerations but which have been discussed (Josse and Swartz; Smellie; and Inman et al.). Moreover, most of these limitations have recently been overcome by the use of a further enzyme – a ligase (Mitra et al.; Goulian and Kornberg; Goulian et al.). Variations have been described which employ single-stranded DNA as template (Swartz et al.), or use DNA-dependent RNA polymerase as enzyme with ribonucleoside 5′-triphosphate as substrate (Weiss and Nakamoto; Furth et al.; Chamberlin and Berg; review by Smellie), but their details do not need to be considered here.

There exists conclusive evidence today that the information for the synthesis of any one polypeptide resides in only the one strand of DNA which is transcribed into mRNA (Marmur et al.; Kahan; Hall et al.; Bautz; Tocchini-Valentini et al.). However the DNA polymerase used for doublet analysis copies both strands. It is, therefore, important to understand the precise relationship which theory demands must exist between the doublet frequency pattern in DNA and the thus delimited pattern of the corresponding messenger RNA. The complete pattern in both cases is formed by 16 doublets. Of course it should be remembered that thymine (T) in DNA is equivalent to uracil (U) in RNA.

The sixteen doublets of DNA can be placed into two 'natural' groups. The four doublets ApT, TpA, GpC and CpG are their own anti-parallel complement – they are *independent* (Fig. 1). They occur in identical amounts in both DNA strands and therefore the frequency of these independent doublets found by doublet analysis is in fact their frequency of occurrence in the genetic message. The remaining twelve doublets form six anti-parallel complementary pairs, i.e. ApA-TpT; ApG-CpT; ApC-GpT; TpG-CpA; TpC-GpA and GpG-CpC (Fig. 1). The sum of the frequencies of the two

messenger-like strand

5' → 3'... pGpAp<u>Ap</u>Tp<u>Tp</u>ApGpTpCpApCpTpGp<u>Gp</u>Cp<u>Cp</u>Gp...

double-
stranded
DNA

3' ← 5'... pCpTp<u>Tp</u>Ap<u>Ap</u>TpCpApGpTpGpApCp<u>Cp</u>Gp<u>Gp</u>Cp...

complementary strand

messenger
RNA

5' → 3'... pGpAp<u>Ap</u>Up<u>Up</u>ApGpUpCpApCpUpGp<u>Gp</u>Cp<u>Cp</u>Gp...

(The independent doublets are underlined; the direction of reading is from 5' to 3').

The 16 doublets in DNA are

independent: ApT; TpA; GpC; CpG

dependent: ApA-TpT; GpT-ApC; TpG-CpA; GpA-TpC; ApG-CpT;
GpG-CpC

Fig. 1. Base relationships in deoxyribonucleic acid (DNA) and ribonucleic acid (RNA).

complementary doublets of such a pair in double stranded DNA delimits the maximum frequency with which either doublet could be present in the coding strand of DNA, in which case the other doublet would be totally absent from this strand. The average frequency of a complementary pair in double stranded DNA gives the expectation for each doublet in the coding strand if both doublets occur there equally often. Because the precise frequency in the genetic message of either doublet of a complementary pair cannot be deduced, such doublets are 'dependent'. Therefore the frequency estimates for *independent* doublets have a much greater information content than those for *dependent* doublets.

3. *What is the random expectation for doublet frequencies?*

Assuming the distribution of bases in a double stranded DNA is random, with what frequency are the various doublets expected? If x is the frequency of the base G or C and $(\frac{1}{2}-x)$ that of A or T, then the expected frequencies of the 16 doublets are:

$$\mathrm{GpG} = \mathrm{CpC} = \mathrm{CpG} = \mathrm{GpC} = x^2$$
$$\mathrm{ApA} = \mathrm{TpT} = \mathrm{TpA} = \mathrm{ApT} = (\tfrac{1}{2}-x)^2$$
$$\text{and } \mathrm{ApG} = \mathrm{CpT} = \mathrm{TpC} = \mathrm{GpA} = \mathrm{TpG} = \mathrm{CpA} = \mathrm{ApC} = \mathrm{GpT} = x(\tfrac{1}{2}-x)$$

Note that the sixteen doublets all fall into one of three frequency groups, except only in the special case when G=C=A=T, that is at 50% (G+C) content in which case all expected frequencies are identical. At any other (G+C)% value the expected frequencies are different for the three groups. In a doublet frequency diagram the random expectation is therefore illustrated by three straight lines drawn at x^2, $(\frac{1}{2}-x)^2$ and $x(\frac{1}{2}-x)$.

The DNA of many organisms has been subjected to nearest neighbour analysis and it has been found almost always that the frequencies of the 16 doublets are not in accord with their random expectation. As these deviations are highly reproducible, both in direction and in magnitude, this shows that in nature the sequence of bases in DNA is not random.

4. *How can doublet frequencies be related to amino acid frequencies?*

Now that the genetic code is known, one can attempt to relate doublet frequency data to the expected frequencies of the appropriate amino acids in average (but not bulk) protein. To do this one has to assume first, that only a negligible amount of the DNA does not *at least potentially* specify proteins and second, that synonym codons are used at random. The first assumption is probably reasonable, although it is already known that DNA which codes for ribosomal RNA, transfer RNA and 5S RNA is most probably not translatable into protein. But in most organisms this only accounts for a fraction of 1% of the DNA. The second assumption is almost certainly wrong, but it may be some time yet before the real situation is understood and a more justifiable working hypothesis becomes available.

In this article evidence for colinearity of gene (DNA) and protein (Yanofsky et al.; Sarabhai et al.), the evidence that the genetic message is read in triplets from a fixed starting point (Crick et al.; Steisinger et al.), and the codon assignments for individual amino acids (Crick) will not be discussed but are assumed to be known to the reader.

Within a genetic message of three-base sequences any doublet can be present in three positions only (Fig. 2). Doublets in positions 1 or 2 are confined within the codon and therefore their frequencies are directly relatable to the frequencies of

Given that the message is read from left to right, and that X may stand for A, U, G or C, consider the sequence CpG:

1. In position 1, the sequence CpG occurs as first and second bases in a codon.
   messenger RNA → . XpXpXp. CpGpXp. XpXpXp.
   possible codons: CGU, CGC, CGA, CGG,
   amino acid coded by these: arginine

2. In position 2, the sequence CpG occurs as second and third bases in a codon.
   messenger RNA → . XpXpXp. XpCpGp. XpXpXp.
   possible codons: UCG, CCG, ACG, GCG,
   amino acids coded by these: serine, proline, threonine, alanine.

3. In position 3, the sequence CpG occurs as third base in one codon and first base in the next codon.
   messenger RNA → . XpXpXp. XpXpCp. GpXpXp.
   possible codons: there are 256 two-codon combinations and the general case is XXC and GXX

   75 different dipeptides are coded by these codons, and individual amino acids are affected to differing extents owing to the degeneracy of the code.

Fig. 2. The three positions which a doublet sequence can occupy in messenger RNA.

certain amino acids. All position 1 doublets relate to either one or two amino acids, while all position 2 doublets relate to either three or four amino acids (chain termination here is taken as equivalent to an amino acid); e.g. CpG in position 1 codes only for arginine CGU, CGC, CGA, CGG and in position 2 codes for serine UCG, proline CCG, threonine ACG and alanine GCG. A doublet in position 3 bridges two codons and may, therefore, be present in 256 two-codon combinations coding 65, 70, 75, 91, 98 or 105 different dipeptides (depending on the nature of the doublet), which diminishes the predictive value of the analysis.

In addition there are three major sources of intrinsic 'noise' which vitiate the usefulness of correlating doublet frequency to amino acid frequency. First, in double-stranded DNA the information obtainable from the dependent doublets is severely restricted. This does not apply to single-stranded DNA. Second, the observed frequency of a doublet is the sum of its frequency of occurrence in the three positions along the reading frame. Therefore the abundance or scarceness of occurrence of a doublet, caused by its restricted or favoured use at one or more of the three positions, can be obscured through the composite nature of the doublet frequency. It is self-evident that the different positions may be affected in opposite ways, so that the effects could cancel out and be undetectable by doublet analysis. Third, the degeneracy of the code constitutes a severe restriction on predictions of average amino acid composition based on doublet analysis.

One illustration will suffice. Although the independent doublet CpG is extraordinarily rare in all vertebrate DNA (Swartz et al.), this still does not enable one to make accurate predictions: double strandedness is here irrelevant, and its rarity demands some restriction on use in every one of the three positions. Even if CpG were totally absent from both positions 1 and 2 its use would still be under restraint in position 3. Unfortunately every one of the five amino acids which has CpG-containing codons also has alternative unaffected codons (e.g. arginine: *AGA*, *AGG*, CGU, CGC, CGA, CGG; serine *AGU*, *AGC*, *UCU*, *UCC*, *UCA*, UCG; proline *CCU*, *CCC*, *CCA*, CCG; threonine *ACU*, *ACC*, *ACA*, ACG; and alanine *GCU*, *GCC*, *GCA* and GCG.)

5. *Doublet pattern and overall use of the genetic code*

Accurate predictions based on doublet analysis are clearly ruled out although useful 'working' predictions of relative amino acid frequencies can often be made (Subak-Sharpe et al. 1966b). But the doublet patterns provide other important clues, for they contain information concerning the overall use which the organism makes of the genetic code. The cells of every organism are endowed with a population of transfer RNA molecules (separable into different classes by virtue of their codon recognition) which translate messenger RNA transcribed from the DNA in the cell nucleus into polypeptides. As a consequence of natural selection the population of transfer RNA molecules should be optimally adapted to the translation of messenger RNA transcribed from cell DNA *with that particular doublet pattern.* Unless there is extensive redundancy in the translation apparatus, such a population of transfer RNA molecules cannot simultaneously be even tolerably well adjusted to the translation requirements of messenger RNA transcribed from DNA with a widely different doublet pattern (Subak-Sharpe and Hay; Subak-Sharpe et al. 1966b).

This line of reasoning leads to two different sets of problems:

First, it is clear that the doublet pattern in the DNA is a direct measure of the organism's overall use of the genetic code. As overall use of the code is likely to be one of the most stable characteristics of an organism, the doublet patterns are in all probability the best remaining clues to the most ancient evolutionary relationships between living organisms. In this context it is of interest that the echinoderm pattern shows many relationships to the vertebrate pattern (Subak-Sharpe 1969) and also that the six bacterial DNAS analysed by Josse et al. (1961) fall into only two pattern types (Subak-Sharpe 1967).

Second, it allows one to take a new look at the problems of host–virus interactions. Unless the above arguments contain a fallacy, viruses which are unable to modify the translation apparatus of the uninfected host would be expected to have a doublet pattern in their nucleic acid which conforms with that of host DNA. The normal host would satisfy all the translation requirements of such viruses. *A priori* one expects this to apply to the very small viruses, which contain only enough nucleic acid to code for a very few proteins.

On the other hand some viruses may be able to alter the host's translation apparatus, either qualitatively by adding one or more virus coded species of transfer RNA to the pre-existing population, or quantitatively by regulating the relative amounts of the molecular species produced by the host or by modifying their structure. If a virus can modify the translation apparatus its doublet pattern would not have to resemble that of the host but could differ markedly from it. *A priori* this may, but need not, apply to some of the larger viruses.

6. *The experimental evidence – direct comparison of the doublet patterns of virus and host*

Four typical representative comparisons of the doublet frequencies in viral nucleic acid and in human DNA (which is representative of all mammalian DNAS), are given in diagram form in Fig. 3. Herpes simplex is a virus containing a large molecule of double-stranded DNA (mol. wt. $\sim 70 \times 10^6$), SV_{40} contains a small molecule of double-stranded DNA (mol. wt. $\sim 3 \times 10^6$), MVM and EMC respectively contain a small molecule of single-stranded DNA or RNA (mol. wt. 1.7 and 3×10^6). For ease of presentation the individual doublet frequencies which are obtained in units per thousand have been superimposed. Where a doublet's frequency in the viral nucleic acid exceeds that in human DNA, the excess is shown by shading, and where the converse is the case the excess of the host's doublet is shown by hatching. The open parts of the columns indicate the amount of overlap. In all the fourteen cases which our group in Glasgow has examined so far, one of two general situations has been observed.

Fig. 3. Superimposed doublet patterns of the DNA of human spleen and the DNAS of four mammalian viruses. Doublet frequencies of the DNA of human spleen and superimposed (1) herpes virus (2) minute virus of mouse (MVM) (3) encephalomyocarditis virus (EMC) (4) simian virus 40 (SV_{40}). The raw data are presented in histogram form which emphasizes similarities (open part of columns) and differences: excess of viral doublet over host doublet is indicated by solid top of column; excess of host doublet over viral doublet by hatched top of column. Values on the ordinates are in doublet per thousand. For source of the data, see the legend to Figs. 5–7.

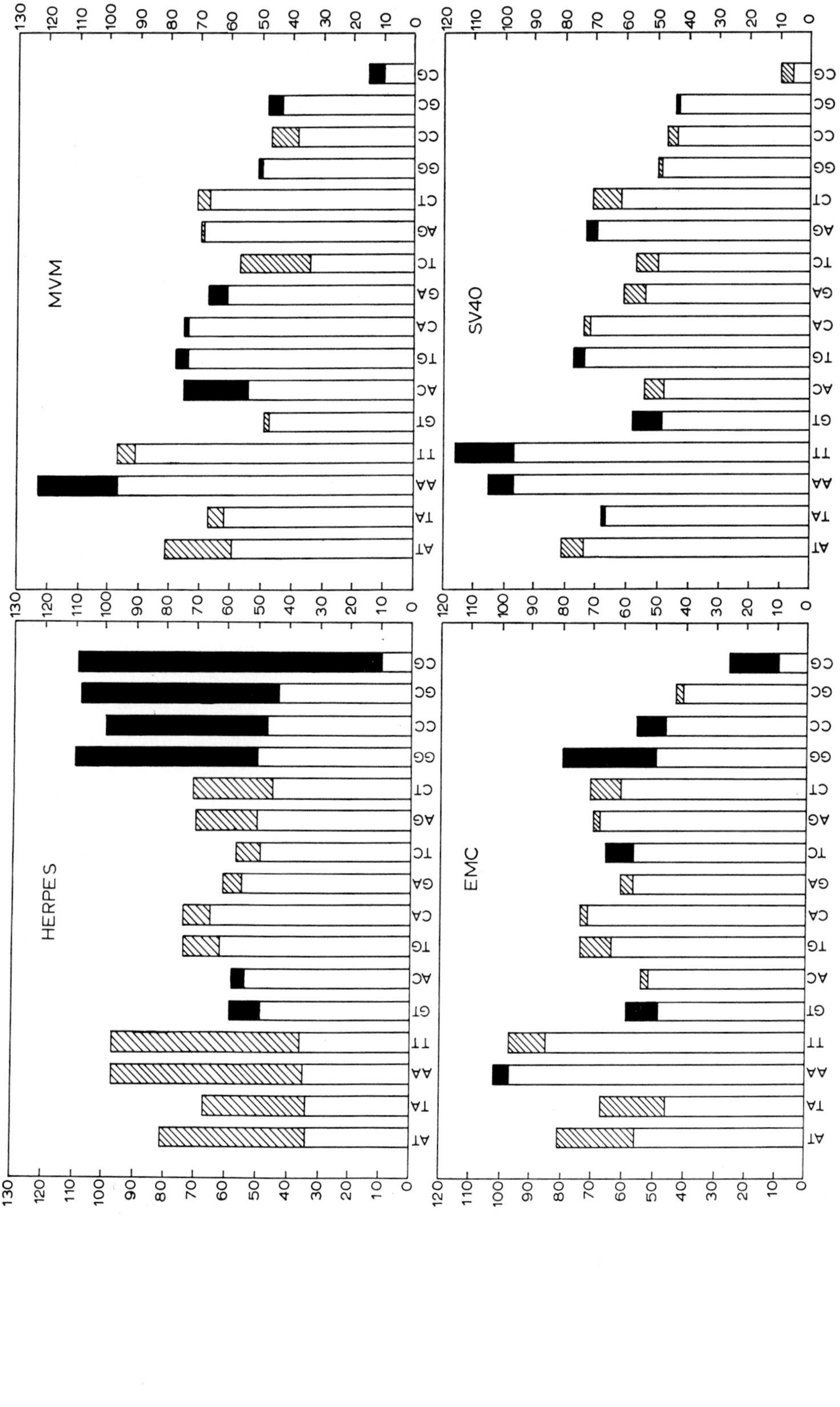
MVM
SV40
HERPES
EMC
CG
GC
CC
GG
CT
AG
TC
GA
CA
TG
AC
GT
TT
AA
TA
AT
0
10
20
30
40
50
60
70
80
90
100
110
120
130

The first is illustrated by SV_{40}, MVM and EMC – in every instance the superimposed doublet patterns of virus and host overlap to a remarkable degree. This very extensive overlap suggests that there are only small differences between virus and host doublet patterns, particularly if allowance is made for single strandedness in EMC and MVM. The concordance between the doublet patterns of all the small viruses examined (mol. wt. of N.A. $< 5 \times 10^6$) with that of mammalian DNA only makes sense in terms of some causal evolutionary relationship.

The second situation is illustrated by herpes virus, and superimposition shows large differences with much less overlap and hardly any similarities in doublet pattern between virus and host (Fig. 3). Four other large viruses gave analogous results, but the viral patterns themselves differ quite considerably.

Of the fourteen virus nucleic acids whose analysis has been completed to date (Subak-Sharpe et al. 1966a; Morrison et al.; Hay and Subak-Sharpe; McGeoch and Crawford), four are like SV_{40} (i.e. SV_{40}, polyoma, Shope papilloma and human papilloma) three are like MVM (i.e. MVM, Hl and Kilham RV), two are like EMC (i.e. EMC and polio) and five resemble the herpes type of situation (i.e. pseudorabies, herpes, equine rhinopneumonitis, adenovirus type 2 and vaccinia).

7. *The stability of the doublet pattern*

At this point it is worth considering the evolutionary stability of the doublet pattern. There is experimental evidence indicating enormous enduring quality. Swartz et al. have obtained almost identical results in doublet analyses done on the DNAs from man, cattle, mice, rabbits, chickens and even salmon. The pre-existing doublet pattern in the DNA must therefore have remained virtually unchanged, despite subsequent divergent evolution of these vertebrates from a common ancestor.

On purely theoretical grounds doublet patterns are also expected to have great stability even in evolutionary time. The major reasons for such stability are as follows: first, as the pattern is due to the statistical frequency of the 16 doublets in the DNA, the resistance to change of the pattern must be directly proportional to the size of the genome. Thus just to change the frequency of the independent doublet CpG by 10 doublets per 1000 in a DNA of 10,000 nucleotides (the size of the SV_{40} genome) would take 50 selected mutational steps that are directionally consistent (because of its independent nature 50 such changes result in 100 changed CpG doublets.) For DNAs like herpes, *E. coli* and bovis, which respectively consist of 2.3×10^5, 1.3×10^7 and 6×10^9 nucleotides, the comparable numbers of mutational changes are 1150, 65,000 and 30,000,000. The equivalent number of mutational steps for most dependent doublets is double this. In other words even 10,000 selected and directionally consistent mutational steps would not detectably alter the vertebrate doublet pattern or even that of bacteria.

Second, by no means all base changes alter the doublet frequencies to the same extent. The actual effect which base change has on the doublet frequency depends on the adjacent bases on both sides. A single base change maximally alters by one each the frequencies of 8 doublets (e.g. mutation in the triplet AGA → ACA results in loss of ApG, CpT, GpA and TpC and gain in ApC, GpT, CpA and TpG), but in other cases it results in only four doublet changes (e.g. mutation CCA → CAA results in loss of CpC and GpG and gain in ApA and TpT), and in still others the net result is no change (e.g. mutation GGC → GCC) (Fig. 4). Thus not every mutation affects the doublet pattern. Net changes in the frequency of any doublet must of course lead to correlated but complex changes in the frequencies of others.

C	A	C
...Ap~~G~~pAp...	...Cp~~C~~pAp...	...G~~G~~C...
⟶	⟶	⟶
⟵	⟵	⟵
...Tp~~C~~pTp...	...Gp~~G~~pTp...	...C~~C~~G...
G	T	G

(All sequences written in direction 5' → 3'.)

Net loss:	ApG, GpA, TpC, CpT.	CpC, GpG	none
Net gain:	ApC, CpA, TpG, GpT.	ApA, TpT	none

(Direction of reading is as indicated. The selected single-base change is shown above or below the base it replaces.)

Fig. 4. The consequences of selected single-base changes on doublet sequences.

Third, some base changes must result in changed amino acids in the polypeptides coded by the nucleic acid. The likelihood of such amino acid replacement depends both on the position in the codon of the altered base and on the particular base sequence. All changes of the first base of a codon (except some U ↔ C changes for leucine and some C↔A changes for arginine) and all changes of the second base, but only about $\frac{1}{3}$ of all changes of the third base, result in a changed amino acid sequence. This inevitable alteration in protein which results from most base substitutions must exert a powerful brake on selective forces which are tending to move the doublet pattern consistently towards a new equilibrium.

8. Which selective forces could overcome the stability of the doublet pattern?

First, there are the selective forces which operate at the level of translation. In some lines of descent the presence of a particular doublet in a codon or set of codons may *inherently* engender difficulties at translation – codon–anticodon recognition may be faulty, or too stable or unstable. As the lineage evolves, such codons would become systematically replaced by synonym or related unaffected codons which must alter the doublet pattern. This proposition could explain the extraordinary rarity of the doublet CpG in all vertebrate DNAS.

At this fundamental level continuously operating selective forces are probably irresistible unless the translation apparatus itself is more readily modified, which does not seem very probable.

Second, there are the forces which bring about the adaptation of a line of descent to a particular environmental niche. If extensive incorporation of a particular amino acid into the great majority of the different proteins coded is favoured, the doublet pattern will in consequence become altered. If extensive exclusion were favoured, this would also happen. As all 4 alanine codons contain the doublet GpC and all 3 isoleucine codons the doublet ApU, such forces could bring about excess or shortage respectively of these doublets.

The third category of special forces of selection apply to viruses and operate at the level of host–virus interaction. These forces are a product of the constantly recurring (although dynamically changing) environment provided by the host and must *a priori* exert their influence on every virus generation; their perpetual action could eventually have its effect on the viral doublet pattern, even though the viral genome may be able to modify the pre-existing translation apparatus of the host at each generation.

A group of fourth selective forces are those, which result in particular shortish stretches of DNA becoming many times duplicated within the haploid genome, so that these stretches finally constitute a substantial proportion of the total DNA of the organism. Such stretches could even be wholly composed of or include DNA which does *not* specify polypeptides. Whenever satellite DNA is observed in the density profile of the whole DNA these forces are likely to have operated.

9. *Is there an unbiased way of comparing the doublet patterns of nucleic acids which have different base compositions?*

To compare the doublet patterns of two DNAS with very similar (G+C) content poses little problem, because their direct comparison by histograms as in Fig. 2 is informative. But such direct comparison becomes less meaningful as the difference in base composition increases. By definition there must exist differences in the raw doublet patterns of DNAS with say 40 and 70% G+C content. And yet it would be of particular interest to compare, without bias, DNAS with widely different (G+C) content and investigate whether their doublet patterns show any relationship in their underlying general design.

The 'general design' of the doublet pattern of a DNA is the consequence of the DNAS summed history of responses to selection pressures, and *is defined by the pattern of deviations from random expectation of the 16 doublets.* Only consistent selection exerted differentially on a base or the bases of particular doublets can mould the general design; randomly occurring base substitutions do not affect it. Change in (G+C) content *per se* need not alter the general design, though such change must result in altered doublet frequencies.

When the doublet patterns of the DNAs of different organisms are compared it is of interest whether one can find traces of any evolutionary relationships. Comparison of the DNAs' general designs investigates whether the DNAs resulted from adaptive response to similar or different selective situations during their evolution. The doublet frequencies of related DNAs should show departures from random expectation which are similar in direction and magnitude. Unrelated DNAs would be expected to show only chance similarities. Thus very different general designs suggest only remote evolutionary relatedness.

The general design of a DNA is obtained by normalizing the doublet frequencies individually to the value they would have in a DNA of 50% (G+C) content (Subak-Sharpe et al. 1966a). In such DNA A=T=G=C and the random expectation is that the 16 doublets will be present in equal amounts, that is 62.5 each per 1000. By measuring for every normalized doublet the departure from this expectation, the direction and size of the deviation for all the 16 individual doublets can be determined. The general design can then be plotted and compared with that of any other DNA.

In practice, the experimentally found value 'z' of a doublet is divided by its expected frequency assuming randomness, and then multiplied by 0.0625. Thus the observed frequency of say ApG when normalized is 0.0625 z/ag (where the frequencies of A=a; T=t; G=g; and C=c; and a, t, g and c are obtained from the experimental data by the procedure of Josse et al.). The only sources of error stem from the experimental determinations of the doublet frequencies and of the base composition.

Doublet patterns obtained for single stranded DNA or RNA can be similarly normalized to A=T=G=C or A=U=G=C and the corresponding general designs may then be plotted. It only has to be remembered that the doublet pattern obtained is that of only one of the two strands, thus none of the doublets here are dependent.

10. The experimental evidence – comparison of the general designs of the nucleic acid of viruses and host

Is there any evidence of relatedness from comparison of the general design of nucleic acid of mammalian viruses and mammalian cells?

Figs. 5, 6 and 7 show the general designs of human DNA and the nucleic acid of thirteen mammalian viruses. The general design of all the small viruses, that is the four double stranded oncogenic DNA viruses, SV_{40}, polyoma, Shope papilloma and human papilloma (Fig. 5), the three single-stranded DNA viruses, MVM, Hl and Kilham rat virus and the two single-stranded RNA viruses EMC (Fig. 6) and polio (not shown) closely resemble the characteristic general design of the vertebrate host

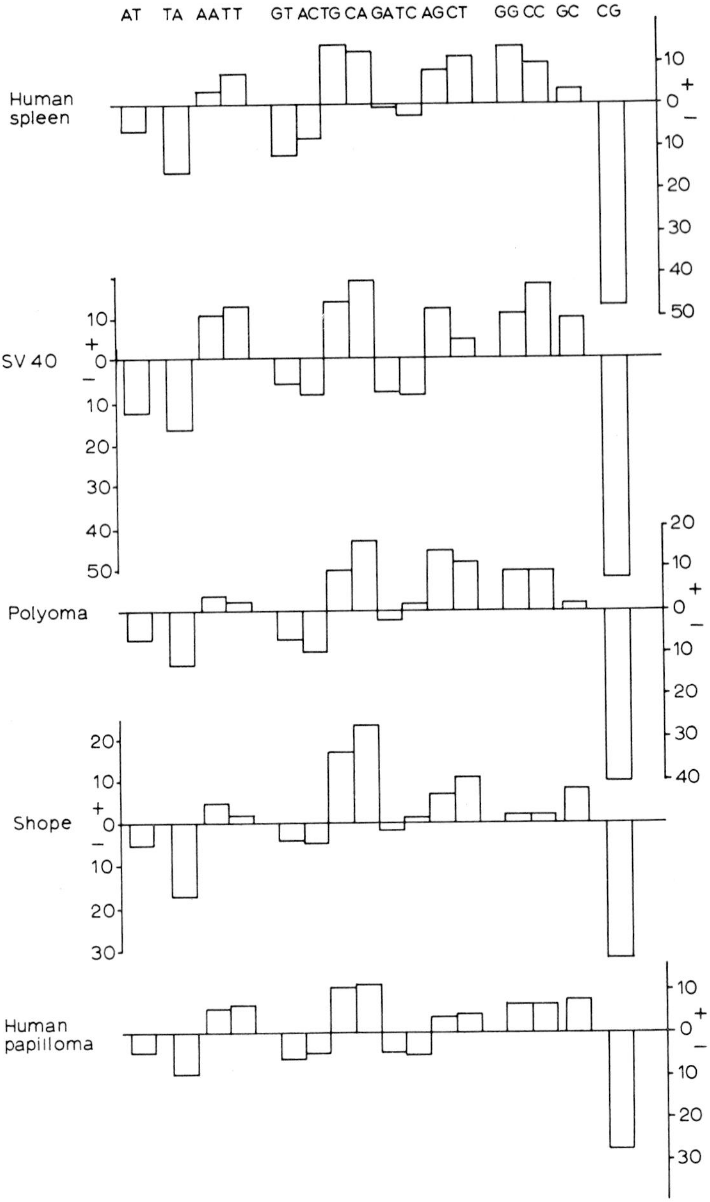

Fig. 5 (*legend see p. 82.*)

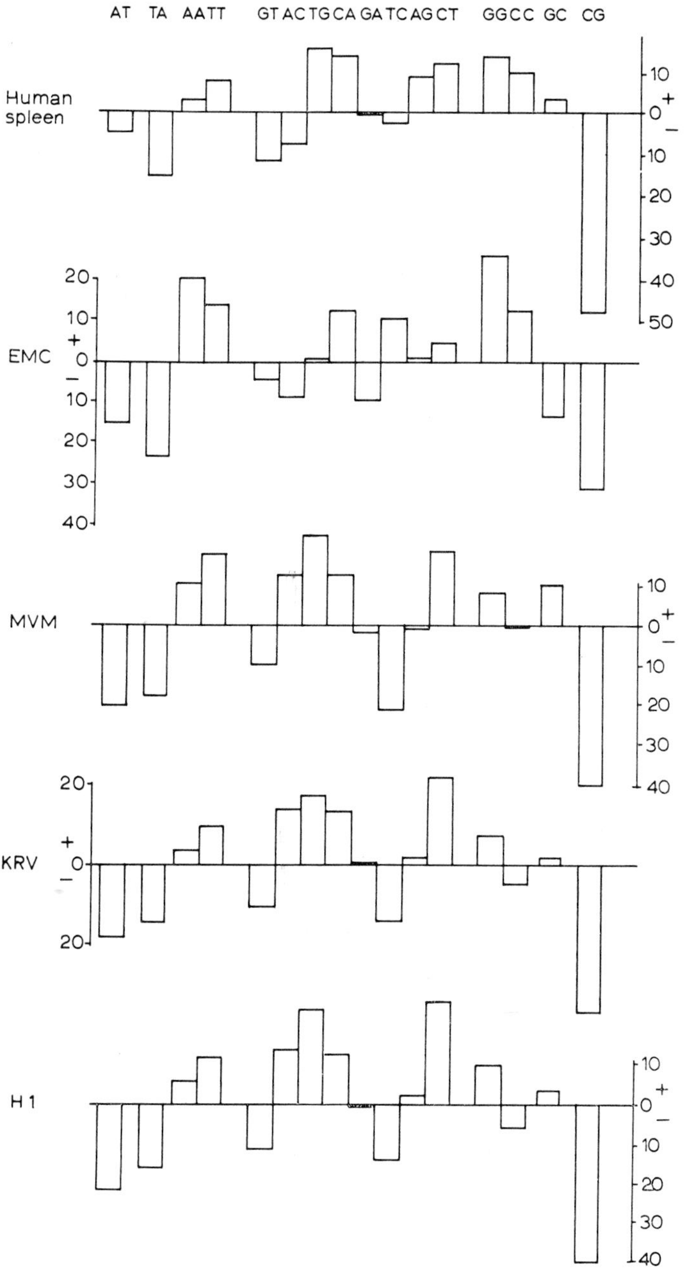

Fig. 6 (*legend see p. 82.*)

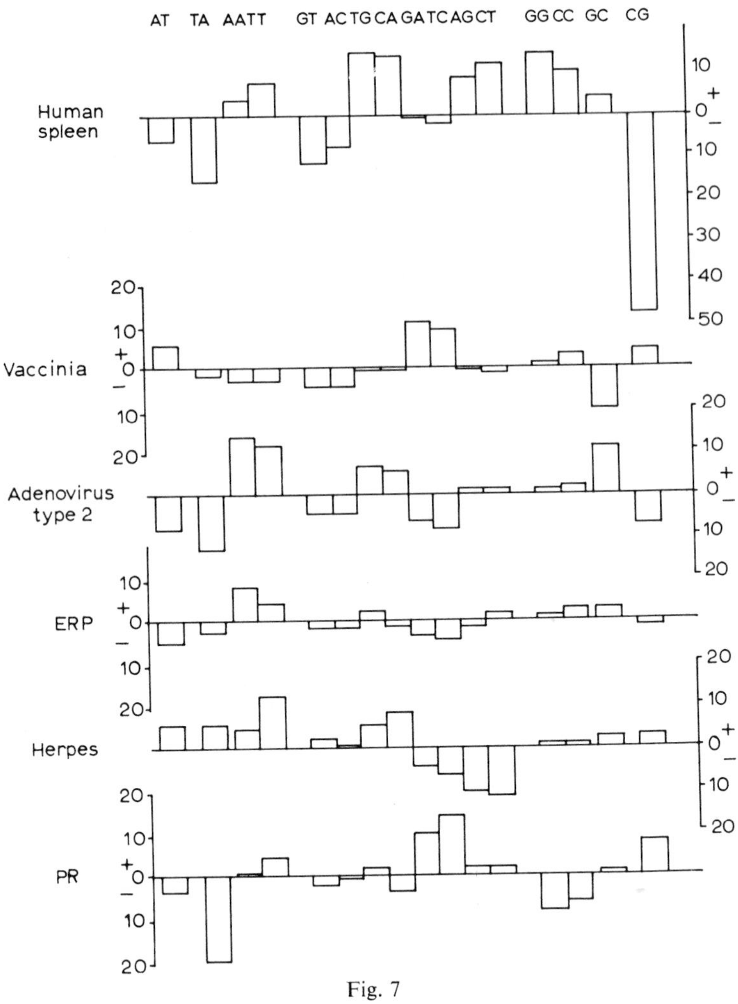

Fig. 7

Figs. 5–7. The general design of the DNA of human spleen cells and of the nucleic acid of thirteen mammalian viruses. Doublet frequency patterns of DNA or RNA (EMC) were normalized to G=C=A=T (U) = 25% and expressed as deviations from random expectation (i.e. 62.5) in doublets/10^3. The sources of the data are human spleen from Swartz et al.; polyoma, Shope papilloma, pseudorabies, herpes from Subak-Sharpe et al. (1966a); SV_{40}, human papilloma, vaccinia, equine rhinopneumonitis, adenovirus type 2 from Morrison et al.; encephalomyocarditis (EMC) from Hay and Subak-Sharpe; minute virus of mice (MVM), Hl virus and Kilham rat virus from McGeoch et al.

DNA. These viruses all are small (their nucleic acid has a molecular weight of $< 5 \times 10^6$ daltons), all have icosahedral symmetry of particles, and all have a (G+C) content of 41–48% (Table 1). The general designs of the four large double-stranded DNA viruses, pseudorabies, herpes, vaccinia and equine rhinopneumonitis (Fig. 7), neither resemble one another, nor vertebrate DNA. All four viruses are large (their DNA has a

TABLE 1

Comparison of the base composition and nucleic acid content of the examined mammalian viruses

Virus	(G+C)%	Molecular weight of genome $\times 10^6$
Single-stranded RNA		
EMC	47	3
Polio	46	2
Single-stranded DNA		
MVM	41	1.7
H1	45	1.7
Kilham RV	43	1.7
Double-stranded DNA		
Polyoma	48	3
SV_{40}	41	3
Shope papilloma	47	5
Human papilloma	41	5
Adenovirus type 2	57	23
Vaccinia	35	160
Equine rhinopneumonitis	55	70
Herpes	68	70
Pseudorabies	74	70
Host cells		
Human spleen	41	1.8×10^{12}

molecular weight of 70–160 $\times 10^6$ daltons), their (G+C) content spans the range from 35% for vaccinia to 74% for pseudorabies, and all have a wide host range. The remaining analysed virus is adenovirus type 2 (Fig. 7) which is intermediate in size having a DNA content of 23 $\times 10^6$ daltons. Its general design shows slight resemblance to that of vertebrate DNA but this is limited and does not extend to the characteristic CpG doublet. Recent evidence indicates that this adenovirus is 'mildly' oncogenic (Freeman et al.).

11. Do the general designs provide information relative to the phylogenetic problem of the origin and evolution of mammalian viruses?

The nucleic acid of all nine small mammalian viruses examined conforms closely in general design to that of their host's DNA, while the DNA of at least four large viruses lacks such resemblance. As has already been discussed, the near identity of all the vertebrate doublet patterns, and also theoretical considerations, indicate the great stability of this character. Needless to stress, this applies equally to the general design. Two alternative evolutionary explanations could account for the remarkable resemblance between the general design in the nucleic acid of a virus and the highly characteristic general design of the DNA of its mammalian host. The virus genome could have originated directly from the polypeptide specifying stretches of host DNA recently or at any time during the host's evolutionary history. Thus when it arose the nascent genome would already have been fully adapted for translation by the host and subsequent minimum response to the forces of selection would have kept the evolving genome so adapted. Alternatively the virus genome could have originated from some foreign DNA in a distal line of descent with a different general design and, as a consequence of continually occurring steps of mutational change followed by selective survival, have subsequently changed its general design to that of the host. This alternative appears the less probable one, because an enormous number of selected mutational changes have to be postulated even for the smallest viruses which must involve very large numbers of amino acid changes in every one of the virus-specified proteins. Subak-Sharpe (1967) calculated that the change from an initially random general design to that characteristic of vertebrates would require at least a change in one in every three amino acids in every polypeptide specified by the nucleic acid. It seems very unlikely that many polypeptides could undergo such extensive changes and yet retain their original function. We, therefore, favour the view that all viruses whose nucleic acid closely reflects in general design the host doublet pattern probably originated from within polypeptide specifying stretches of the DNA of ancestors of their host or related organisms at any time during the host's evolutionary history up to the present. This, of course, is a general conclusion and is not confined only to mammalian viruses.

The DNAs of the large mammalian viruses have general designs which are quite different to that of their hosts, nor do they greatly resemble one another. The above considerations force one to the view that these large viruses are likely to have originated in distal lines of descent and that they probably carry genetic information which enables them to modify their host's translation apparatus where necessary. This has so far only been confirmed in the case of herpes virus (Subak-Sharpe and Hay; Subak-Sharpe et al. 1966b). The general design of the DNA of large mammalian viruses may still afford a clue to their ancestry. It is difficult to rationalize that such large viruses could have originated in vertebrate polypeptide-specifying DNA long ago and, responding to natural selection, have since evolved in a divergent manner to arrive at their present day general designs.

Considerations of the general design of the nucleic acid of mammalian viruses and of their host cells have forced us to conclude that these viruses are of at least diarch origin. But the surprising conclusion really is that, irrespective of their strandedness or type of nucleic acid, all small viruses appear to have their origin from essentially the same information *source* – namely the polypeptide-specifying stretches of DNA of 'ancestral' host cells. This of course does not mean that all originated from one *particular* stretch, nor that single- and double-stranded RNA and DNA viruses arose by essentially the same *processes*. The information source from which the large viruses originated lies probably in distal lines of descent. They may have evolved from stretches of the DNA of organisms from different phila which were frequently in close environmental contact with the present day host or its ancestors (e.g. symbionts or parasites); an alternative possibility is, that a pre-existing virus of such an organism might have succeeded to survive in and then adapt to the new mammalian host.

Postscript

The only virus which may not quite fit the above considerations is adenovirus type 2 and there is circumstantial evidence which encourages us to speculate that its DNA may be compound in origin, formed by fusion of a smaller piece ($\sim 3 \times 10^6$) of DNA with the general design of the host, and a larger piece which has a quite different general design. This model would fit some of the known facts and is now under experimental investigation.

Since this manuscript was submitted, doublet analysis of adenovirus 7 and adenovirus 11 have been completed (McGeoch et al. to be published). Both the doublet patterns and the general designs of these adenoviruses are closely similar to that of adenovirus type 2.

Acknowledgements

I wish to express my gratitude to my colleagues Dr. J. M. Morrison, Dr. J. Hay, Prof. H. M. Keir and Mr. D. McGeoch in the Department of Biochemistry and Miss W. M. Shepherd and Dr. R. R. Bürk in the Department of Virology in Glasgow. Without their continuing collaboration in experiments and discussions, the ideas described above could not have developed very far.

I also thank The British Medical Bulletin for permission to use material from my article published in Vol. 23, pages 161–168 in 1967.

References

BAUTZ, E. K. F.: The structure of T4 messenger RNA in relation to messenger function. Cold Spring Harbor Symp. Quant. Biol. 28 (1963) 205.

CHAMBERLIN, M. and P. BERG: Deoxyribonucleic acid directed synthesis of ribonucleic acid by an enzyme from *Escherichia coli*. Proc. Natl. Acad. Sci. U.S. 48 (1962) 81.

CRICK, F. H. C.: The genetic code – yesterday, today and tomorrow. Cold Spring Harbor Symp. Quant. Biol. 31 (1966) 1.

CRICK, F. H. C., L. BARNETT, S. BRENNER and R. J. WATTS-TOBIN: General nature of the genetic code for proteins. Nature (Lond.) 192 (1961) 1227.

FENNER, F.: The biology of animal viruses, Vol. 1. New York and London, Academic Press (1968).

FREEMAN, A. E., P. H. BLACK, E. A. VANDERPOOL, P. H. HENRY, J. B. AUSTIN and R. J. HUEBNER: Transformation of primary rat embryo cells by adenovirus type 2. Proc. Natl. Acad. Sci. U.S. 58 (1967) 1205.

FURTH, J. J., J. HURWITZ and M. GOLDMAN: The directing role of DNA in RNA synthesis specificity of the deoxyadenylate deoxythymidylate copolymer as a primer. Biochem. Biophys. Res. Commun. 4 (1961) 431.

GOULIAN, M. and A. KORNBERG: Enzymatic synthesis of DNA, XXIII Synthesis of circular replicative form of phage ΦX 174 DNA. Proc. Natl. Acad. Sci. U.S. 58 (1967) 1723.

GOULIAN, M., A. KORNBERG and R. L. SINSHEIMER: Enzymatic synthesis of DNA, XXIV Synthesis of infectious phage ΦX 174 DNA. Proc. Natl. Acad. Sci. U.S. 58 (1967) 2321.

HALL, B. D., M. GREEN, A. P. NYGAARD and J. BOEZI: The copying of DNA in T2-infected *E. coli.* Cold Spring Harbor Symp. Quant. Biol. 28 (1963) 201.

HAY, J. and J. H. SUBAK-SHARPE: Analysis of nearest neighbour base frequencies in the RNA of a mammalian virus: encephalomyocarditis virus. J. Gen. Virol. 2 (1968) 469.

HILL, L. R.: An index to deoxyribonucleic acid base compositions of bacterial species. J. Gen. Microbiol. 44 (1966) 419.

INMAN, R. B., C. L. SCHILDKRAUT and A. KORNBERG: Enzymic synthesis of deoxyribonucleic acid. XX Electron microscopy of products primed by native templates. J. Mol. Biol. 11 (1965) 285.

JOSSE, J., A. D. KAISER and A. KORNBERG: Enzymatic synthesis of deoxyribonucleic acid. VIII Frequencies of nearest neighbour base sequences in deoxyribonucleic acid. J. Biol. Chem. 236 (1961) 864.

JOSSE, J. and M. SWARTZ: Determination of frequencies of nearest neighbour base sequences in deoxyribonucleic acid. Methods in Enzymology 6 (1963) 739.

LEE, K. Y., R. WAHL and E. BARBU: Contenu en bases puriques et pyrimidiques des acides desoxyribonucléiques des bactéries. Ann. Inst. Pasteur 91 (1956) 212.

MCGEOGH, D. J., L. V. CRAWFORD and E. A. C. FOLLET: The DNAs of three parvoviruses. J. Gen. Virol. (1969) in press.

MARMUR, J., C. M. GREENSPAN, E. PALACEK, F. M. KAHAN, J. LEVINE and M. MANDEL: Specificity of the complementary RNA formed by *Bacillus subtilis* infected with bacteriophage SP8. Cold Spring Harbor Symp. Quant. Biol. 28 (1963) 191.

MITRA, S., P. REICHARD, R. B. INMAN, L. L. BERTSCH and A. KORNBERG: Enzymic synthesis of deoxyribonucleic acid. XXII Replication of a circular single-stranded DNA template by DNA polymerase of *Escherichia coli.* J. Mol. Biol. 24 (1967) 429.

MORRISON, J. M., H. M. KEIR, J. H. SUBAK-SHARPE and L. V. CRAWFORD: Nearest neighbour base sequence analysis of the deoxyribonucleic acids of a further three mammalian viruses: simian virus 40, human papilloma virus and adenovirus type 2. J. Gen. Virol. 1 (1967) 101.

SARABHAI, A. S., A. O. W. STRETTON, S. BRENNER and A. BOLLE: Co-linearity of the gene with the polypeptide chain. Nature (Lond.) 201 (1964) 13.

SMELLIE, R. M. S.: Biochemistry of deoxyribonucleic acid and ribonucleic acid replication. Brit. Med. Bull. 21 (1965) 195.

STREISINGER, G., Y. OKADA, J. EMRICH, J. NEWTON, A. TSUGITA, E. TERZAGHI and M. INOUE: Frameshift mutations and the genetic code. Cold Spring Harbor Symp. Quant. Biol. 31 (1966) 77.

SUBAK-SHARPE, J. H.: Base doublet frequency patterns in the nucleic acid and evolution of viruses. Brit. Med. Bull. 23 (1967) 161.

SUBAK-SHARPE, J. H.: The doublet pattern of the nucleic acid of oncogenic and nononcogenic viruses and its relationship to that of mammalian DNA. 8th Canadian Cancer Conference (1969), in press.

SUBAK-SHARPE, J. H., R. R. BÜRK, L. V. CRAWFORD, J. M. MORRISON, J. HAY and H. M. KEIR: An approach to evolutionary relationships of mammalian DNA viruses through analysis of the pattern of nearest neighbour base sequences. Cold Spring Harbor Symp. Quant. Biol. 31 (1966a) 737.

SUBAK-SHARPE, J. H. and J. HAY: An animal virus with DNA of high guanine + cytosine content which codes for S-RNA. J. Mol. Biol. 12 (1965) 924.

SUBAK-SHARPE, J. H., W. M. SHEPHERD and J. HAY: Studies on sRNA coded by herpes virus. Cold Spring Harbor Symp. Quant. Biol. 31 (1966b) 583.

SUEOKA, N.: Variation and heterogeneity of base composition of deoxyribonucleic acids: A compilation of old and new data. J. Mol. Biol. 3 (1961) 31.

SUEOKA, N.: On the genetic basis of variation and heterogeneity of DNA base composition. Proc. Natl. Acad. Sci. U.S. 48 (1962) 582.

SWARTZ, M. N., T. A. TRAUTNER and A. KORNBERG: Enzymatic synthesis of deoxyribonucleic acid. XI Further studies on nearest neighbour base sequences in deoxyribonucleic acids. J. Biol. Chem. 237 (1962) 1961.

TOCCHINI-VALENTINI, G. P., M. STODOLSKY, A. AURISICCHIO, M. SARNAT, F. GRAZIOSI, S. B. WEISS and E. P. GEIDUSCHEK: On the asymmetry of RNA synthesis *in vivo*. Proc. Natl. Acad. Sci. U.S. 50 (1963) 935.

WEISS, S. B. and T. NAKAMOTO: The enzymic synthesis of RNA: nearest neighbour base frequencies. Proc. Natl. Acad. Sci. U.S. 47 (1961) 1400.

YANOFSKY, Č. B., B. C. CARLTON, J. R. GUEST, D. R. HELINSKI and U. HENNING: On the colinearity of gene structure and protein structure. Proc. Natl. Acad. Sci. U.S. 51 (1964) 266.

PART II

Chromosome organization in viruses and bacteria

CHAPTER 6

Chromosomes of viruses

ALBRECHT K. KLEINSCHMIDT

Department of Biochemistry, New York University School of Medicine, New York, N.Y.

Contents

1. Introduction – structural aspects of nucleic acids
2. Viral DNA – size and shape
3. Viral RNA – size and shape
4. The replication of viral chromosomes
5. Structural phenomena in transcription and translation
6. Toward structural mapping of chromosomes

1. Introduction – structural aspects of nucleic acids

Viral chromosomes are nucleic acids. They consist of either of the two fundamental types: deoxyribonucleic acid (DNA) or ribonucleic acid (RNA). These linear polymers in turn are condensation products of a monomer unit, the nucleotide, which contains a phosphopentose and a heterocyclic base. The pentose moieties, ribose in RNA or deoxyribose in DNA, are joined by 3′-5′ phosphodiester bonds to form a continuous chain or strand from which the bases protrude. Within this pattern sufficient variation can be accomodated to provide the uniqueness of structure that permits the nucleic acid to function as the viral chromosome, i.e., to code for the proteins required to carry out the replication of the viral nucleic acid and to provide the protein complement of the mature virus particle. The uniqueness resides in the nucleotide sequence – the primary structure of a given polynucleotide. In general, four different bases, two purines (adenine and guanine) and two pyrimidines (cytosine and either uracil (RNA) or thymine (DNA)) are present in a nucleic acid. In a specific sequence of three nucleotides, the information is coded for the insertion of an amino acid into a polypeptide chain. Sequential permutation of these triplets so that a series of specific proteins can be determined, implies a specific and essentially unique sequence of nucleotides and thus provides a unique nucleic acid molecule as the chromosome of a given virus.

The primary structure of a single strand of nucleic acid is thus the chemical basis of its informational function in determining the primary structure of the proteins that will be synthesized. In contrast, the secondary structure is the chemical basis for the perpetuation of the primary structure through the process of the replication of the virus. The aspect of the secondary structure that permits the specification of the nucleotide sequence in the replicative process is the complementary relationship of the bases that is exhibited in the Watson and Crick double-stranded helix. In this structure two strands of nucleic acid, arranged in a double helix, are held in a fixed position with respect to each other by hydrogen bonds between pairs of bases, along the entire length of the structure, one member of the pair being located in each strand. The specificity of the pairing is dictated by requirement that guanine can form hydrogen bonds with cytosine and adenine with thymine (or with uracil in RNA). Thus each strand is the complement of the other in the sense that the sequence of one implies a related specific sequence of the other. This relationship allows one strand to serve as a template for the biosynthesis of its complement. The details of the biosynthetic mechanism vary and are not entirely understood in most cases, but it is probable that complementary pairing by the formation of specific hydrogen bonds between adenine and thymine or guanine and cytosine determines the insertion of a specific nucleotide at a specific position in the chain.

The DNA or RNA of the virus may be either single-stranded or double-stranded. Either variety may be tightly packed within the virus particles, but assumes a different and characteristic configuration when released into solution and separated from viral protein. Single-stranded nucleic acids have a limited rotation about the covalent bonds between the phosphate and sugar residues of the backbone. Because they have no regular pattern of weak, intrachain bonds they tend to collapse to form coils of a random configuration. In contrast, double-stranded forms are stabilized in the Watson–Crick structure with the ordered, multiple weak bonds between neighboring and opposite bases. This results in a partially rigid configuration in solution forming an extended chain or worm-like shape. The differences are reflected in the hydrodynamic properties of the two kinds of molecules. A nucleic acid of a given molecular weight will have a much higher viscosity in the double- than in the single-stranded configuration; and while sedimenting in an ultracentrifuge, the sedimentation coefficient will be lower for double strands than for single strands.

The stability of the secondary structure of double-stranded nucleic acids (Watson and Crick) depends in part on the hydrogen bonds between the N atoms or N and O atoms of the heterocyclic bases. This leads to the complementary pairing of purines and pyrimidines in which two hydrogen bonds are formed between adenine and thymine (or uracil) and three between guanine and cytosine. In addition, strong stabilizing forces exist between each pair of bases and the pair stacked above and below it. These arise primarily from dipole interactions, both permanent and fluctuating, between the atoms of the layers of base pairs extending over the entire length of the double-stranded molecule. Additional stabilization results from hydrophobic bonds, i.e., differences in the interaction of the double helix and the single-stranded coil with the solvent.

The double-stranded helix can be denatured in solution, for example, by heating, leading to collapse of the ordered structure and separation of strands. Because the stabilizing forces are the result of a series of weak interactions along the molecule, they are cooperative and reinforce each other. As a result, denaturation consists of a helix–coil transition or melting out of the entire structure over a temperature range of only a few degrees. This transition is most easily observed by recording the ultraviolet absorption of the solution as a function of temperature. Since the double-stranded form is hypochromic with respect to the single strands, a large increase in absorbance coincides with denaturation. The temperature at which the absorbance change is one-half completed is referred to as the mid-point temperature (T_m) and serves to characterize the process. In neutral solution the T_m will be greater for nucleic acids having a higher content of guanine and cytosine. For a nucleic acid of a given composition, the T_m will increase as the ionic strength is decreased or as substances such as alcohols are added to the solvent. DNA can also be denatured by raising the *p*H to about 12 to 13. Under these conditions the protons that are involved in the hydrogen bonds are titrated and the helix–coil transition is initiated.

Renaturation or the reversal of denaturation can be accomplished if the single strands are allowed to anneal at a temperature a few degrees below the T_m. The annealing process allows the complementary strands to rejoin so that their bases are in register and the hydrogen-bonded, stacked structure is reconstituted.

The viral chromosome can exist as the nucleic acid moiety of a stable, mature virus particle or virion, or may reside, devoid of its protein coat or capsid, inside infected cells. The viral chromosome may enter a competent or permissive cell through injection, as it occurs with large DNA bacteriophages. Also, naked DNA is transferred to a cell, either penetrating a recipient bacterial protoplast, or a naked cell of higher organization. This process, called transformation, utilizes also fractured DNA to produce virions if a complete viral genome is transferred. In virulent bacteriophages the term transfection is used when their naked DNA transforms without altering the bacterial cell walls. Mainly with animal or plant viruses infection occurs through engulfing processes of the whole or part of the virus particle (pinocytosis or viropexis). In the latter case, decoating with liberation of the nucleic acid from its capsid, occurs within the cell. Entry of viral DNA may lead to multiplication of the virus inside the cell, and release of the virus progeny, or the viral genome may be integrated into the cellular chromosome by insertion and replicate in rhythm with the host chromosome (transduction). The resulting provirus (prophage) is carried through subsequent cellular generations.

Viral nucleic acids and viral proteins are produced during the vegetative stage. Viral DNA is replicated semi-conservatively by DNA polymerase (Kornberg) using precursors synthesized by the host. If the infected DNA is single-stranded, it is first converted to a double-stranded replicative form. With viral DNA as template, DNA-dependent RNA polymerase synthesizes messenger RNA which, in turn, uses cellular enzymatic systems, transfer RNA, ribosomes, etc., for the synthesis of viral proteins. The nucleic acid of RNA viruses can be considered to be a messenger RNA. In replication, a complementary strand is synthesized first, which acts as a template for synthesis of new strands. The mechanism of viral RNA replication has been reviewed (Weissmann and Ochoa).

The nucleic acid of small viruses can code for only a few proteins; the genomes of more complex, larger viruses contain information for a large number of proteins including those for biosynthesis and assembly of the nucleic acid and of structural proteins of the virus and for amino acyl-transfer RNAS.

In structural or microscopic terms, the stages of replication, recombination and transcription occur on the filamentous nucleic acid molecule. These processes are transient and dynamic.

The complexes engaged in synthesis at a given time are portions of segments of nucleic acid molecules with the appropriate enzymes attached and represent a very small part of the total amount of nucleic acid present. In cytological studies, we may see static aspects of these dynamic processes. More frequently, we see the products of such transient reactions, such as newly synthesized nucleic acid filaments, assemblies of proteins, or packed virions. The future holds the prospect of visualizing microscopically in detail the transient complexes involved in replication, regulation and morphogenesis.

After synthesis of viral constituents, small viruses mature by spontaneous assembly of nucleic acid and viral protein to produce virions (Pirie). A similar process, more complex as to the number of components, but basically consisting of self-assembly in sequential steps, is assumed to occur with large, more differentiated viral particles. Morphopoiesis, i.e., the intracellular organization in sequential steps, is genetically directed, as shown in studies of T2 bacteriophages (Kellenberger 1966).

Viral nucleic acids range in molecular weight from about one million to 200 million. Some satellite virus nucleic acids are reported to be a fraction of 10^3 molecular weight. One of the aims of microscopy is to correlate the molecular weight of polynucleotides accurately with length. When their configuration is known, length measurements of microscopic images of viral nucleic acids can be used for measuring molecular weights. Viral genomes are tightly packed within their capsids. The capsid determines the conformational arrangement of the nucleic acid within the core. However, a double-stranded viral chromosome in solution assumes an extended filamentous form that may be from 500 to 1000 times longer than the diameter of the virion. When a linear nucleic acid is released from the virus particles by chemical or other means, it shows filamentous properties as judged by a variety of physical methods (viscosity, ultracentrifugation, light scattering, etc.) and by electron microscopy.

The microscopic appearance of these filaments is the result of many interactions. Size and shape in solution are transformed into forms of dry, two-dimensionally fixed individual molecules of DNA or RNA. Denaturation of double-helical forms by physical or chemical means, or through enzymatic attack leading to local strand separation, produces also local changes of shape, with appearance of loops. Single-stranded nucleic acids appear in solution as tightly coiled filaments, although these have a tendency to base-pair between sections of the chain with single-stranded regions looping out, thus lending stability to the structure. When stretched chemically or physically, the changes in structure may be greater than for double-stranded material. Size and shape depend therefore on the methods used for preparation and fixation of the samples.

The light microscope is used to observe appropriately labeled single nucleic acid molecules, e.g., with tritium or P^{32} label, by autoradiographic techniques (see for example Cairns for T2 phage DNA). P^{32}-labeling has been used mostly in star counting of compact bacteriophage DNA (Rubenstein et al.). In addition, cytochemical and cytological methods have been widely used for the study of cells containing large numbers of virions. The virions may be seen scattered or forming a paracrystalline array within the cell.

The electron microscope is presently the most suitable instrument to visualize viral chromosomes. Limitations are the high vacuum (it requires completely dry preparations), the temperature of the electron beam and the poor contrast of biological material.

Several preparative methods are used to visualize individual filamentous macromolecules. In the droplet technique one obtains, by streaking nucleic acid from a dilute solution (or blotting of a droplet in one direction), adsorbed macromolecules

Fig. 1. Electron micrograph of DNA of bacteriophage SP50 (Biswal et al.) prepared by the 'diffusion method'. The contrast arises after rotary-shadowing with uranium. The bar indicates 1 μ.

which appear mostly parallel and oriented (Beer). Using a basic protein monolayer as an adsorptive film (Kleinschmidt), one obtains a less disturbed, less stretched configuration. Under these conditions, the nucleic acid molecules are 'fixed' onto a two-dimensional protein layer on an aqueous surface, giving a better image of the structure of unbroken, large nucleic acids both *in vitro* and *in vivo*; fixation artifacts are thereby minimized. Nucleic acids can also be observed in the process of being released from viral particles by so-called 'one-step release' techniques. For these purposes, one may also use viral chromosomes within infected cells at any stage of virus replication. All these preparations use a procedure for contrasting of nucleic acids, such as a heavy metal deposition (shadow-casting) or staining with heavy metal salts.

Nucleoproteins, as they occur stoichiometrically complexed as helical subunit structure of some RNA viruses, can be studied with negative staining techniques. Phosphotungstate and uranyl acetate have been shown to be most successful.

Electron microscopy of viruses or virus-infected tissues shows mainly the packed viral chromosomes. Thin sections are widely used to study relations between intracellular structures and virions. Freeze-etching of such cells gives preparations similar to thin sections. Nuclease-treated embedded and sectioned virus particles can be analyzed for DNA or RNA-containing cores. Configurational details of viral chromosomes in packed form have been described only for some large viruses. The viral chromosome assumes the rod-like or the isometric shape of the viral capsid (Caspar and Klug). However, during and after replication and recombination of nucleic acids, details of molecular reaction sites are veiled by the loosely structured nucleic acid pools of primer or completed products.

Useful books and review articles not referred above are cited.

2. *Viral DNA size and shape*

DNA of virions can be linear or circular. All known examples of linear DNA are double-stranded (Fig. 1). However, covalently closed circular DNA is known to occur both in the single- and double-stranded forms.

There are two types of linear DNA molecules: (1) those with a circular genetic map (e.g., phages T2, T4, P22) in which the genes are circularly permuted (Fig. 2a) and (2) those (e.g., phages T3, T5, T7, λ, SP50) with linear genetic maps and, therefore, no circular permutation (Fig. 2b); these are referred to as 'unique' (Thomas 1966). Some viral DNAs may have one or more breaks (nicks) on different parts of each strand (e.g., T5), or single-stranded breaks may occur randomly distributed (e.g., SP50).

The ends of all viral DNA molecules thus far examined are terminally redundant or repetitious, i.e., the nucleotide sequence at both ends of each strand are the same (cf. Fig. 2a, b). The shortest terminal repetition (20 nucleotides) is found in phage λ DNA (Kaiser and Wu), the longest (about 6000 nucleotide pairs) in T2 DNA (MacHattie et al.; Thomas 1967).

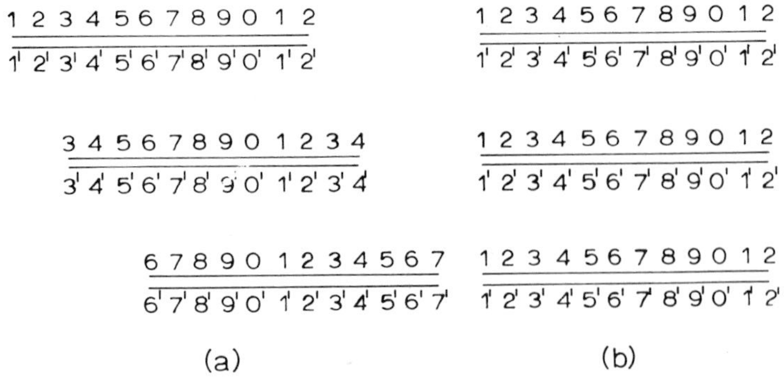

Fig. 2. (a) Permuted and (b) non-permuted collection of DNA molecules (according to Thomas 1967).

In phage λ and other related transducing phages (Kaiser and Wu), the redundant DNA sections at the 3′-ends are exposed, i.e., are single-stranded. Since both these ends are complementary in the anti-parallel sense, annealing of these DNAs leads to the formation of non-covalently closed rings with one break in each strand (Fig. 3). The length of the double-stranded section between the two breaks is the same as that of the terminal redundancy. Both breaks can be closed by formation of phosphodiester bonds between the adjoining 3′- and 5′-ends of each strand through a reaction catalyzed by the enzyme polynucleotide ligase (Gellert et al.; Olivera et al.; Richardson et al.; Sadowski et al.). Ring formation and covalent closure of λ DNA normally occurs intracellularly following infection of the host bacterium (*E. coli*) by λ phage (Bode and MacHattie).

In another form of terminal redundancy, DNA can be repetitious in its double-stranded ends. These linear forms of phage DNA may be converted to non-covalent circles (Thomas 1967) by annealing, following brief exposure to exonuclease III. The enzyme removes nucleotides, one at a time, from the 3′-end sequences with the formation of a molecule similar to λ DNA, with single-stranded ends which can undergo ring formation upon annealing (cf. Fig. 3). In the case of unique but not circularly

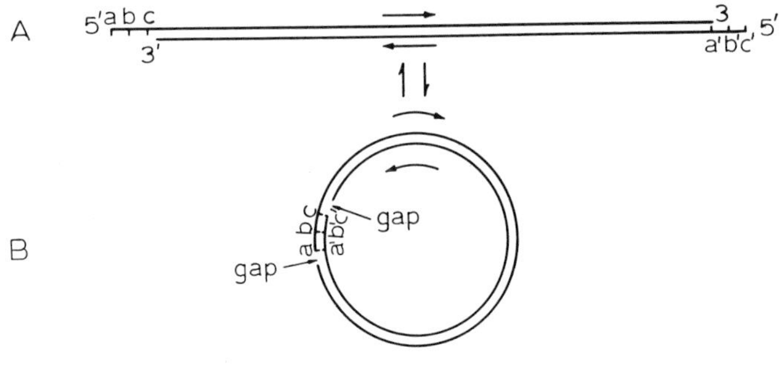

Fig. 3. Schematic representation of the conversion of linear λ DNA (A) to a non-covalently closed ring (B). The undirectional arrows indicate the polarity (5′→3′) of each strand.

permuted DNAs, the ends of different molecules are complementary and, after treatment with exonuclease III, may anneal with each other. This can result in the formation of rings and of concatenate molecules having two, three, or more times the length of the original DNA. Some of these concatemers may be circular.

Transducing phages (λ, Φ80, 186, P2 and others of *E. coli*; N1 of *Micrococcus lysodeikticus*) insert their chromosome into the genome of the host cell (prophage stage). There it replicates in synchrony with the chromosome of the host unless induction, through UV irradiation or other agents, occurs, leading to proliferation of the phage. All these phage DNAs have short, cohesive ends, which may have identical sequences in related phages (Kaiser and Wu; Mandel and Berg).

Covalently closed, double-stranded circular DNA of some viruses has a supertwisted configuration (Fig. 4, form I). Mild treatment with endonuclease produces one or more single strand breaks and the molecule untwists to an open ring form (Fig. 4, form II). Stronger endonuclease treatment produces further breaks and it eventually becomes linear (Fig. 4, form III). Each of the two strands of form III has a number of breaks, but the fragments are held together by base-pairing (Vinograd et al. 1965). Form I can also be converted to an open, although unnicked ring (Fig. 4, form I′) that remains covalently closed. This may happen by exposure to alkali, as shown by centrifugation studies on polyoma DNA (Vinograd et al. 1968). As further illustrated in fig. 4, form I may also be denatured (e.g., by alkali) to a covalently closed supercoil

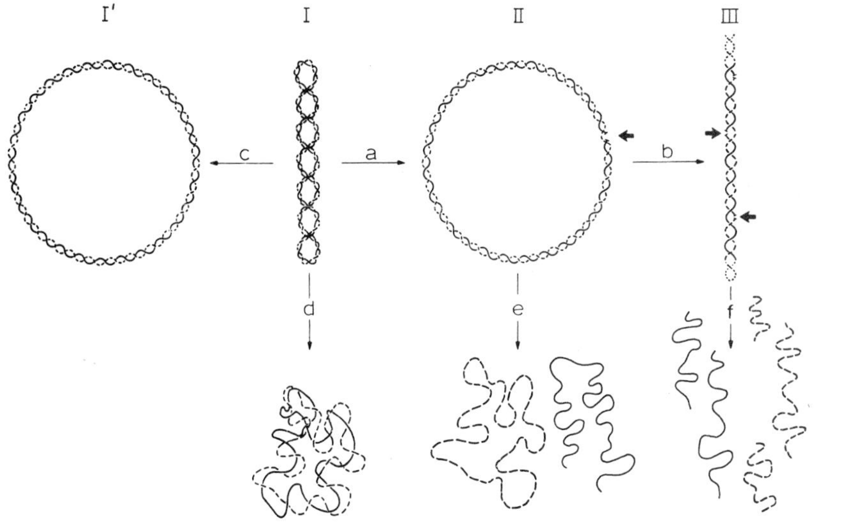

Fig. 4. Diagram showing various configurations of circular, double-stranded DNA and their denaturation products (from Vinograd et al. 1965). The small heavy arrows indicate single-stranded nicks. $\xrightarrow{a}$, transition produced by mild endonuclease treatment, $\xrightarrow{b}$, by stronger endonuclease treatment, $\xrightarrow{c}$, transition produced by alkali or during spreading on protein monolayers in preparation for electron microscopy. ↓ d,e,f, alkali denaturation of forms I, II and III, respectively.

TABLE 1*

DNA viruses

Name[a]	Host[b]	Diameter (Å)[c]	Particle weight[d] (M.W.×10⁻⁶)	Number of capsomers[e]	Nucleic acid[f] (M.W.×10⁻⁶)	Nucleic acid[g] length (μ)	Ratio[h] G+C (%)	Remarks[i]
			Double-stranded DNA viruses, cubical naked					
Tipula iridescent	Insects	1300[1]	1200[2]	812[3]	126[4]	60[4]	34[4]	
Adeno-viruses	Man	700[5]	87–145[6]	252[5]	23[7]	12[7]	58[8]	Fiberlike protein (type 5)[9]
					22[7]	11[7]	49[8]	Type 12, 18, 31 highly oncogenic
Papilloma	Mammals	550[10]	47[11]	72[12]	5[13]	2.5[14]	46[15]	DNA rings,[13] twisted[16]
Polyoma	Mammals	450[17]	22[18]	72[19]	3.0[20]	1.5[21]	48[22]	DNA rings,[23] twisted[24]
SV40	Monkey	450[25]	44[26]	72[25]	3.3[27]	1.7[27]	41[28]	DNA rings,[27] twisted[28]
			17.3[29]		2.4[30]	1.5[30]		
			Double-stranded DNA bacteriophages, tailed					
T even T2, 4, 6	*E. coli*	Head: 700×1000[31] Tail: 120×1100	220[32]		110[33] (—130)	55[34]	35[35] (Hydroxy-methyl-cytosine)	Head: bipyramidal + hexagonal prism[32]
T1	*E. coli*	Head: 650[36] Tail: 100×1500			31[37]	16[37]	48[35]	
T3	*E. coli*	Head: 500[36] Tail: 100×1800	49[38]		23[38]	12[14]	50[35]	
T5	*E. coli*	Head: 800[36] Tail: 100×1800			85[33]	39[33]	39[35]	DNA strands 3+1 nicks[39]
T7	*E. coli*	Head: 500[36] Tail: short	38[40]		24[41]	12[41]	48[35]	
λ	*E. coli*	Head: 500[42] Tail: 100×1500	66[42]		33[43]	17[43,44]	49[45]	DNA: cohesive ends[46,47]

* a-i: *see p. 102*; 1-47: *see p. 103*

TABLE 1*, *continued*

Name[a]	Host[b]	Diameter (Å)[c]	Particle weight[d] (M.W.×10^{-6})	Number of capsomers[e]	Nucleic acid[f] (M.W.×10^{-6})	Nucleic acid[g] length (μ)	Ratio[h] G+C (%)	Remarks[i]
b_2 b_5	*E. coli*	Head: 600[48] Tail: 140×1400			26[49]	13[43]		DNA: cohesive ends[46,47]
80	*E. coli*	Head: 710[50] Tail: 1800×			29[51]	14[50]	53[50]	DNA: cohesive ends[46,47]
	E. coli	Head: 680[52] Tail: 180×1400			20[53]	10[53]		DNA: cohesive ends[54]
2	*Salmonella*	Head: 600[52] Tail: 40×70			26[55]	14[55]	48[55]	
29	*B. subtilis*	Head: 315×415[56] Tail: 60×415			11[56]	5.8[56]		
50	*B. subtilis*	Head: 750[57] Tail:2300	200[58]	252[59]	100[58]	50[58]	44[58]	Nicked DNA[58]
84	*B. stearothermophilus*	Head: 530[60] Tail: 1300	50[60]		28[61]	15[62]	42[60]	
		Single-stranded DNA bacteriophages, cubical naked						
X174	*E. coli*	250[63]	6.2[64]	12[63]	1.7[65]	1.8[66]	A:25[65] T:33 G:24 C:18	Rings[67]
3	*E. coli*	250[68]	6.2[69]	12[69]	1.7[69]		A:25 T:33 G:24 C:18	Rings genetically related to ΦX174[69]
	E. coli	7600×50[70] rods	11[70]		1.7[70]		A:24[70] T:34 G:20 C:22	Rings[70]
		Single-stranded DNA bacteriophages, helical naked						
3	*E. coli*	8000×60[71] rods	11[71]				A:23[71] T:36 G:21 C:20	Rings

3-88: *see p. 103*

TABLE 1, *continued*

Name[a]	Host[b]	Diameter (Å)[c]	Particle weight[d] (M.W. × 10^{-6})	Number of capsomers[e]	Nucleic acid[f] (M.W. × 10^{-6})	Nucleic acid[g] length (μ)	Ratio[h] G+C (%)	Remarks[i]
f1	*E. coli*	8500 × 50[72] rods	11[72]		2.3[72]			Rings
			Double-stranded DNA viruses, cubical enveloped					
Herpes virus	Man	1050[73]		162[73]	100[74]	53[74]	68[75]	Ether-sensitive
Pseudo-rabies	Mammals				68[71]		74[72]	
			Double-stranded complex DNA viruses					
Pox-viruses	Man Mammals	2000–2500 ×[76] 2000–2500 × 2500–3200	3200[77]	Helical capsomers[78, 79]	160[80]	89[81, 82]	37[80]	Brick-shape virion,[83] en-veloped, an multilayere nucleoid: triplet[84]
Fowlpox	Birds	2500 ×[76] 2500 × 3200–3400		Helical capsomers[78, 79]	200–240[85]	91[86]	35[87]	~25% larg (linear dim. than vaccin poxvirus[88]

[a] Ordered after Lwoff and Tournier, and Davis et al.

[b] Main host studied extensively.

[c] Mostly from maximum diameters of negatively stained virions. First value: diameter (mean); secon value: length (rod).

[d] Calculated (chemical data), or from counting particle concentration, or other data.

[e] Number of capsomers (morphological units) from Caspar and Klug (1962). For triangulation point symmetric structure see also Caspar; Klug et al.

[f] The value chosen mostly reliable to length measurements.

[g] The best mean value chosen, rounded off.

[h] From buoyant density, melting (T_m) and/or chromatography; G+C = guanine + cytosine, A = adenin C = cytosine.

[i] All are two-ended filaments, exception: rings (indicated).

TABLE 1, *continued*

References

[1] Williams, R.C. and Smith
[2] Thomas, R.S.
[3] Smith
[4] Bellett and Inman
[5] Horne et al.
[6] Ginsberg and Dingle
[7] Green, M.H. et al.
[8] Piña and Green
[9] Wilcox et al.
[10] Williams, M.G. et al.
[11] Neurath et al.
[12] Finch and Klug (1965)
[13] Kleinschmidt et al. (1965)
[14] Lang et al.
[15] Crawford and Crawford
[16] Follett and Crawford
[17] Wildy et al. (1960a)
[18] Calculated from: Winocour
[19] Klug
[20] Crawford (1963)
[21] Stoeckenius
[22] Crawford (1964)
[23] Dulbecco and Vogt
[24] Vinograd et al. (1965)
[25] Bernhard et al. (1962)
[26] Mayor et al.
[27] Crawford et al.
[28] Crawford and Black
[29] Koch et al.
[30] Anderer et al.
[31] Horne and Wildy
[32] Cohen
[33] Thomas, Jr. and MacHattie (1967)
[34] Thomas, Jr. and MacHattie (1964)
[35] Sinsheimer (1960)
[36] Williams, R.C. and Fraser
[37] Bresler et al.
[38] Bendet et al.
[39] Abelson and Thomas
[40] Davison and Freifelder
[41] Freifelder and Kleinschmidt
[42] Kaiser
[43] MacHattie and Thomas, Jr.
[44] Caro
[45] Ledinko
[46] Hershey et al.
[47] Ris and Chandler
[48] Arber and Kellenberger
[49] Kellenberger, G. et al.
[50] Shinagawa et al.
[51] Yamagishi et al.
[52] Anderson, T.F.
[53] Kleinschmidt (unpublished)
[54] Mandel and Berg
[55] Rhoades et al.
[56] Anderson, D.L. et al.
[57] Földes and Trautner
[58] Biswal et al.
[59] Pohjanpelto and Nyholm
[60] Saunders and Campbell (1965a)
[61] Saunders and Campbell (1965b)
[62] Kleinschmidt and Saunders
[63] Hall et al.
[64] Sinsheimer (1959a)
[65] Sinsheimer (1959b)
[66] Freifelder et al.
[67] Fiers and Sinsheimer
[68] MacLean and Hall
[69] Tessman
[70] Marvin and Hoffmann-Berling
[71] Salivar et al.
[72] Zinder et al.
[73] Wildy et al. (1960b)
[74] Becker et al.
[75] Russell and Crawford
[76] Joklik (1966)
[77] Smadel et al. (1939)
[78] Herzberg et al.
[79] Nagington and Horne
[80] Joklik (1962)
[81] McCrea and Lipman
[82] Easterbrook
[83] Green, R.H. et al.
[84] Peters and Muller
[85] Gafford and Randall
[86] Hyde et al.
[87] Randall et al.
[88] Ruska and Kausche

in which the two strands are separated but remain physically linked, whereas denaturation of form II gives rise to both single-stranded filaments and rings. Denaturation of form III yields fragmented, single-stranded filaments. In electron microscopy of DNA rings, a similar kind of conversion from the supertwisted form to an open, or a denatured supercoil can be achieved utilizing the denaturating effects of urea and the surface tension of a DNA-containing protein film (Vasquez et al. 1968). The hydrogen-bonded duplex is thereby lost in all or in part of the molecule.

Some data pertaining to shape, size and nature of individual DNA viruses, as well as features of their genomes, are summarized in Table 1.

The DNA is packed inside the virion as one molecule filling a core of variable size and shape. Models of packing must (a) explain packaging as it occurs as an intracellular sequential assembly process from a pool of nucleic acid filaments; (b) provide enough space in the capsid for one semi-rigid, double-stranded DNA filament; and (c) allow an explanation of how infection occurs by injection of DNA through the tail, when this is present. Generally speaking, the space, provided for the viral DNA by the virion, depends on the capsid design. Rod-like or helical capsid structure gives a helical symmetry also to its DNA, and cubical symmetry of isometric or icosahedral viruses gives a spherical tertiary structure or a condensed coil of the DNA (Caspar). In large DNA viruses, examples have been described in more detail: a model of DNA packed in the head of T even phages has been proposed which gives a packed DNA thread in form of a beehive (Kilkson and Maestre). When examined as a negatively stained extracted complex (Klimenko et al.), it appeared as flattened twists with a polar tail. In these T2 DNA preparations and in packed λ DNA (Kaiser), a central space, free of DNA, was observed. The phage tail may contain DNA because it was found that *in vitro* ejection of DNA through the tail can be initiated enzymatically (T5; Frank et al.) or chemically (SP50; Biswal et al.). In the case of the complex poxviruses, the viral chromosome structure is best described as a sequential morphological assembly occurring by the apposition of the outer layers (Dales). The 'nucleoid' first appears spherical. The viral chromosome residing inside the mature virion is finally described as in a 'triplet' or horseshoe-like form (Peters).

3. *Viral RNA – size and shape*

The RNA of plant viruses, animal viruses and RNA bacteriophages shows variations in size similar to those of viral DNA (Table 2). Viral RNA is linear; single-stranded filaments are much more common than double-stranded filaments. No single- or double-stranded RNA rings have yet been described.

Some RNA viruses yield a regular series of RNA strands of different length when they are opened by various extraction procedures (double-stranded RNA of reovirus: Gomatos and Stoeckenius; Vasquez and Kleinschmidt). In some cases single-stranded viral RNA consists of a few pieces packed in a single virus particle (influenza virus:

TABLE 2*

RNA viruses

Name[a]	Host[b]	Diameter (Å)[c]	Particle weight[d] (M.W. × 10^{-6})	Number of capsomers[e]	Nucleic acid[f] (M.W. × 10^{-6})	Ratio[h]	Remarks[i]
Small, single-stranded RNA viruses, cubical naked							
Turnip yellow mosaic	Cruciferae	280[1]	5.7[2]	32[3]	1.9[4]	A:23[5] U:22 G:17 C:38	
Foot and mouth disease	Cattle	230[6]	6[7]	32[8]	3.1[9]	A:26[7] U:22 G:24 C:28	
Polio-myelitis	Man	300[10]	5.5[11]	60[12]	2[11]	A:28[13] U:25 G:25 C:22	Type 1 (similar type 2, 3)
Coxsackie A	Man	280[14]	7[15]	60[16]	2[15]	A:27[15] U:25 G:28 C:20	Type A 9 (different from type B)
ECHO	Man	270[17]		32[18]		A:27[19] U:25 G:25 C:23	
Encephalo-myocarditis	Mice	270[20]	10[20]	32[18]	3.1[21]		
Single-stranded RNA bacteriophages, cubical naked							
MS2	*E. coli*	260[22]	3.6[22]		1.1[22]	A:22[22] U:26 G:27 C:25	
f_r	*E. coli*	210[23]	4.1[23,24]		1.2[23,24]	A:24[23,24] U:24 G:27 C:25	
R17	*E. coli*	230[25]	3.6[26]	32[25]	1.1[27]	A:25[28] U:23 G:27 C:25	Length 1.1 μ[29]
f2	*E. coli*	200[30]	3[31]		1.8[32]	A:22[32] U:25 G:27 C:26	

* [a-i]: see p. 102; [1-68]: see p. 108.

TABLE 2*, *continued*

Name[a]	Host[b]	Diameter (Å)[c]	Particle weight[d] (M.W. × 10^{-6})	Number of capsomers[e]	Nucleic acid[f] (M.W. × 10^{-6})	Ratio[h]	Remarks[i]
Q_β	*E. coli*	200[33]	4.2[34]		1.5[35]	A:22[36] U:29 G:24 C:25	Length 1.4 μ[33]
			Double-stranded RNA viruses, cubical naked				
Reovirus	Mammals	600[37]	>70[38]	180[39] (trimers)	17[40]	A:38[41] U:28 G:17 C:17	Total length 8.3 μ[40] Trimodal: 1.1; 0.7; 0.3 μ[42,43]
Wound tumor	Clover	700[44]		92[44]	>10[45]	A:31[44] U:32 G:19 C:19	Fragmented[42]
Rice dwarf	Rice	700[46]	107[47]		10[48]	A:28[48] U:28 G:22 C:22	Fragmented[49]
Cytoplasmic polyhedrosis	Silkworm	400[50]	29[50]		4.7[50]	A: } U: } 57[50] G: } C: } 43	Bimodal: 1.3 and 0.4 μ[50]
			Single-stranded RNA viruses, cubical enveloped				
Arbovirus A	Mammals	650[51]	50[52]		2[53]	A:29[54] U:20 G:26 C:25	Sindbis
Arbovirus B	Mammals	500[55]	47[55]		3.3[55]	A:31[55] U:22 G:26 C:21	Dengue
			Single-stranded RNA viruses, helical naked				
Tobacco mosaic	Tobacco	170 × 3000[56]	50[57]	2130[58] (structural units)	2.1[59]	A:30[60] U:26 G:25 C:19	
Potato X	Potato	130 × 5150[56]			2.0[61]	A:34[60] U:21 G:22 C:22	

* [a-i]: see p. 102.

TABLE 2*, *continued*

Name[a]	Host[b]	Diameter (Å)[c]	Particle weight[d] (M.W. $\times 10^{-6}$)	Number of capsomers[e]	Nucleic acid[f] (M.W. $\times 10^{-6}$)	Ratio[h]	Remarks[i]
		Single-stranded RNA viruses, helical enveloped					
Influenza	Man	90[62] long filaments	300[63]		2.9[64]	A:23[64] U:33 G:20 C:24	5 pieces[65]
Myxo para-influenza	Man	170[62] long			6.8[66]	A:26[67] U:22 G:25 C:27	
Vesicular stomatitis	Cattle	150[68] long			7[69]		Pieces: $>6\mu$[70] 3 components
Newcastle disease	Fowl	170[62] helical filaments	800[71]		7.5[72]	A:26[67] U:22 G:25 C:27	One piece[65]
Mumps	Man	170[62] helical filaments					
Measles	Man	160[73] helical filaments			3.3[74]		
		Single-stranded RNA viruses, complex enveloped					
Avian myeloblastosis	Fowl	400[75]			15[76]	A:25[77] U:23 G:29 C:23	Pieces: $8.7\,\mu$[78] 4 pieces[76]
Rous sarcoma	Fowl	600[79]			9.5[80]	A:25[81] U:23 G:28 C:24	Several pieces[82]
Murine leukemia	Mice	700[83]	220[84]		13[85]	A:25[84] U:23 G:25 C:27	Rauscher's virus Several pieces[86]

* [a-i]: *see p. 102.*

TABLE 2, *continued*

References

[1] Markham
[2] De Rosier and Haselkorn
[3] Huxley and Zubay
[4] Mitra and Kaesberg
[5] Matthews and Ralph
[6] Bachrach and Breese
[7] Bachrach et al.
[8] Breese et al.
[9] Strohmaier and Mussgay
[10] Horne and Nagington
[11] Anderer and Restle
[12] Finch and Klug (1959)
[13] Schaffer et al.
[14] Breese and Briefs
[15] Mattern
[16] Klug and Caspar
[17] Benyesh et al.
[18] Mayor
[19] Fukada et al.
[20] Faulkner
[21] Burness et al.
[22] Strauss and Sinsheimer
[23] Hoffmann-Berling and Marvin
[24] Hoffmann-Berling et al.
[25] Vasquez et al. (1966)
[26] Gesteland and Boektker
[27] Mitra et al. (1963)
[28] Paranchych and Graham
[29] Granboulan and Franklin (1966)
[30] Schwartz and Zinder
[31] Zinder
[32] Loeb and Zinder
[33] Vasquez and Kleinschmidt (unpublished)
[34] Overby et al.
[35] Bishop et al.
[36] Mills et al.
[37] Vasquez and Tournier (1962)
[38] Gomatos and Tamm (1963a)
[39] Vasquez and Tournier (1964)
[40] Vasquez and Kleinschmidt (1968a)
[41] Bellamy and Joklik
[42] Kleinschmidt et al. (1964)
[43] Dunnebacke and Kleinschmidt
[44] Bils and Hall
[45] Gomatos and Tamm (1963b)
[46] Fukishi et al.
[47] Kawade et al.
[48] Miura et al. (1966)
[49] Sato
[50] Miura et al. (1967)
[51] Simpson and Hauser
[52] cited from: Luria and Darnell
[53] Wecker
[54] Pfefferkorn and Hunter
[55] Stollar et al.
[56] Brandes and Bercks
[57] Markham et al.
[58] Fraenkel-Conrat
[59] Gierer
[60] Dorner and Knight
[61] Schuster
[62] Waterson and Cruikshank
[63] Frisch-Niggemeyer
[64] Ada
[65] Duesberg (1968a)
[66] Compans and Choppin
[67] Scholtisseck and Rott
[68] McCombs et al.
[69] Simpson and Harper
[70] Huppert et al.
[71] Rott
[72] Duesberg and Robinson (1965)
[73] Norrby and Magnusson
[74] Waterson
[75] Bernhard et al. (1958)
[76] Bonar et al.
[77] Robinson
[78] Granboulan et. al.
[79] Bernhard
[80] Crawford and Crawford
[81] Robinson et al.
[82] Duesberg (1968b)
[83] De The and O'Connor
[84] Boiron et al.
[85] Duesberg and Robinson (1966)
[86] Blair and Duesberg

Duesberg 1968a). However, most of the viruses of Table 2 show only one filament of short, single-stranded RNA.

The contribution of the electron microscope towards the study of viral RNA size is still small. Single-stranded RNA collapses easily because there is very little ordered stabilization and stacking. Single-stranded RNA is highly sensitive to cellular and extracellular RNases, which act during the extraction of virions or cells, and may be but incompletely protected by the use of protein-denaturing agents (formaldehyde, urea) in preparation for electron microscopy. Hence, size heterogeneity may be more apparent than real. For example, the single-stranded RNA of avian myeloblastosis virus when extracted and studied by microscopy (Granboulan et al.) gives a trimodal size distribution with a wide spread in each peak presumably indicating an intrinsic variation in size and some preparative degradation. At present, molecular weight calculations based on these measurements are not very accurate.

Some viral RNAs have been used successfully for *in vitro* reconstitution of virus particles. Using TMV protein (17,570 minimal M.W.: Fraenkel-Conrat) and RNA (2×10^6 M.W.; Knight) rods of TMV are formed which have the structure and infectivity of native TMV (Fraenkel-Conrat and Williams). The length of the rods, built up from a stoichiometric association, depends primarily on the size of the RNA. Other RNAs (e.g., from MS2 phage; Sugiyama) can be reconstituted with TMV proteins to rods. Small RNA viruses of cubical symmetry which have more than one protein (MS2, f2, etc.) are more difficult to reconstitute (e.g., fr bacteriophage: Hohn). In recent experiments (Roberts and Steitz), phage R17, consisting of one molecule of A-protein, 180 coat protein subunits (14,000 M.W.) and one molecule of RNA (1.1×10^6 M.W.), was reconstituted to yield a high percentage of infectious particles.

4. *The replication of viral chromosomes*

The replication of viral DNA has been studied at different levels: (a) *in vitro* experiments utilizing nucleic acid as a primer, nucleoside triphosphates as building blocks and polymerizing enzymes; (b) intracellular replication followed by isolation and studies of replicated material; and (c) *in situ* microscopic studies of replicated viral DNA and of virions.

Double-stranded DNA replicates semi-conservatively (Meselson and Stahl). The enzymatic process is in part understood; details, however, are still a matter of conjecture. Recombination also occurs presumably as a separated process. It is believed to be due to breakage and reunion of the DNA strands. Little is known of the enzymatic mechanism, although several enzymes have been identified that may be involved: a DNA polymerase (Englund et al.) and endonuclease activity producing single-stranded breaks (Lehman 1967) and a DNA ligase which repairs nicked DNA (Lehman 1968). The details of the replication of viral chromosomes that can be observed by microscopy are summarized in Table 3.

TABLE 3

Virus	Nucleic acid form	Product	Contour length (μ)	Remarks	References
		(a) *DNA replication in vitro*			
T7	Double-stranded, partly degraded by exonuclease III	Double-stranded complete	11	Extensive replication: branches, DNA polymerase required	Richardson et al. Inman et al.
M13	Single-stranded circular	Double-stranded circular, + trailing single strands	2	Extensive replication: branches, DNA polymerase required	Mitra et al. 1967
ΦX174	Single-stranded circular	Double-stranded circular	2	DNA polymerase and polynucleotide joining enzyme (ligase) required; no branches	Goulian and Kornberg Goulian
		(b) *DNA replication in vivo*			
ΦX174 + *E. coli*	Infective ΦX174 phage DNA (rings, single-stranded)	Replicative form (RF), ring	1.6–1.8 1.6	Multiple size rings (<3%) found	Kleinschmidt et al. 1963 Rush et al.
λ phage + *E. coli*	Infective linear double-stranded DNA	Circular form	17–18	Early stage	Bode and Kaiser
				Supertwists	Bode and MacHattie
		Circles with double-branched loops	17 + 2–10		Tomizawa and Ogawa
		Circular forms and concatenate linear forms		Late stage	Weissbach et al.
T4 + *E. coli*	Linear permuted double-stranded DNA	Replicative form	1–2 times phage DNA size	No rings found	Frankel
				Branches	Kozinski et al.
		Pools of entangled replicative forms	Up to 6 times of *E. coli* chromosomes	Branches	Huberman
		(c) *RNA replication in vitro*			
Q_β	Single-stranded	Complementary strand	1.0	Specific RNA-polymerase required	Haruna and Spiegelman August et al.

TABLE 3, *continued*

Virus	Nucleic acid form	Product	Contour length (μ)	Remarks	References
		(d) *RNA replication in vivo*			
R17 + *E. coli*	Single-stranded	RF and replicative intermediates (RI) (branched)	1.1	RI double-stranded, single-stranded combined	Granboulan and Franklin 1968
MS2 + *E. coli*	Single-stranded	RF	1.1–0.2	Degraded by preparative RNAase treatment	Weissmann and Ochoa
M12 + *E. coli*	Single-stranded	RF	1.1	T_m (RF) = 90 °C 100% infectivity after renaturation	Ammann et al.
Polio + HeLa cells	Single-stranded	Replication complex	0.1–2.2	Complexed with RNA polymerase	Girard et al.
TYMV + cabbage	Single-stranded	RF	0.24	Rare branches	Wolstenholme and Bockstahler
TMV + tobacco	Single-stranded	RF	0.42	Rare branches	Wolstenholme and Bockstahler

For single-stranded DNA such as that of ΦX174 phage, a double-stranded ring structure called a replicative form (RF) (Fig. 5) is first made which, in further steps, serves as the template for the production of single-stranded viral DNA rings. The initial production *in vivo* of the replicative form is accompanied by its attachment to a membrane fraction of the host. In a model for the replication of this DNA (Gilbert) one strand is presumed to remain attached to the cytoplasmic membrane, while the RF rotates as it is replicated. This rolling circle model would result in the formation of molecules of more than one genome in length which could be made circular by the use of their redundant parts. It was suggested that the model is also applicable to the replication of λ and T4 DNA.

5. *Structural phenomena in transcription and translation*

Transcription and translation of viral genes is a process of high complexity. During intracellular viral growth, microscopic studies have disclosed phenomena which are related to the biosynthesis machinery of the viral components. A part of the general

Fig. 5. ΦX174 replicative forms, isolated from injected *E. coli* cells. Uranium rotary-shadowed. About 2% are of multiple-size contour length of rings (Rush et al.). The bar indicates 1 μ.

process, centered around the ribosome, can be outlined as follows: messenger RNA binds amino acyl-transfer RNA active ribosomes (30S and 50S units) in closely connected but sequential steps to form a complex for protein synthesis. Activating enzymes and a series of other factors are necessary. The polymerization of amino acids proceeds after initiation at the ribosomal complex and finally a complete protein is released. Several ribosomes are simultaneously engaged in translation of a given messenger RNA forming structures known as polysomes. Some examples of polysomes involved in viral replication that have been observed by electron microscopy are listed in Table 4.

TABLE 4

Polysomes in viral infection

Virus	Host	Number of ribosomes per polysome	References
T4 phage	*E. coli* spheroplast	First 10–11	Rolfe and Rich
Polio virus	HeLa cells	27	Rich et al.
		35	Summers et al.
TMV	Tobacco leaves	60-80	Kiho
MS2	*E. coli* protoplast	11–14	Hotham-Iglewski and Franklin
MS2	Cell-free *E. coli* system	28–30	Vasquez (unpublished)

Actual molecular events can rarely be observed by electron microscopy of thin sections of virus-infected cells. Other important features of the viral replication cycle may however be disclosed. The electron microscopic studies of Kellenberger (1961) and others of the assembly of particles of phage T2 from their individual components are a good case in point.

6. *Toward structural mapping of chromosomes*

One of the main problems of the primary structure of viral chromosomes is the sequence of nucleotides in the functional units (genes) of a specific chromosome. Nucleotide sequence analysis of nucleic acids of high molecular weight seems to be an

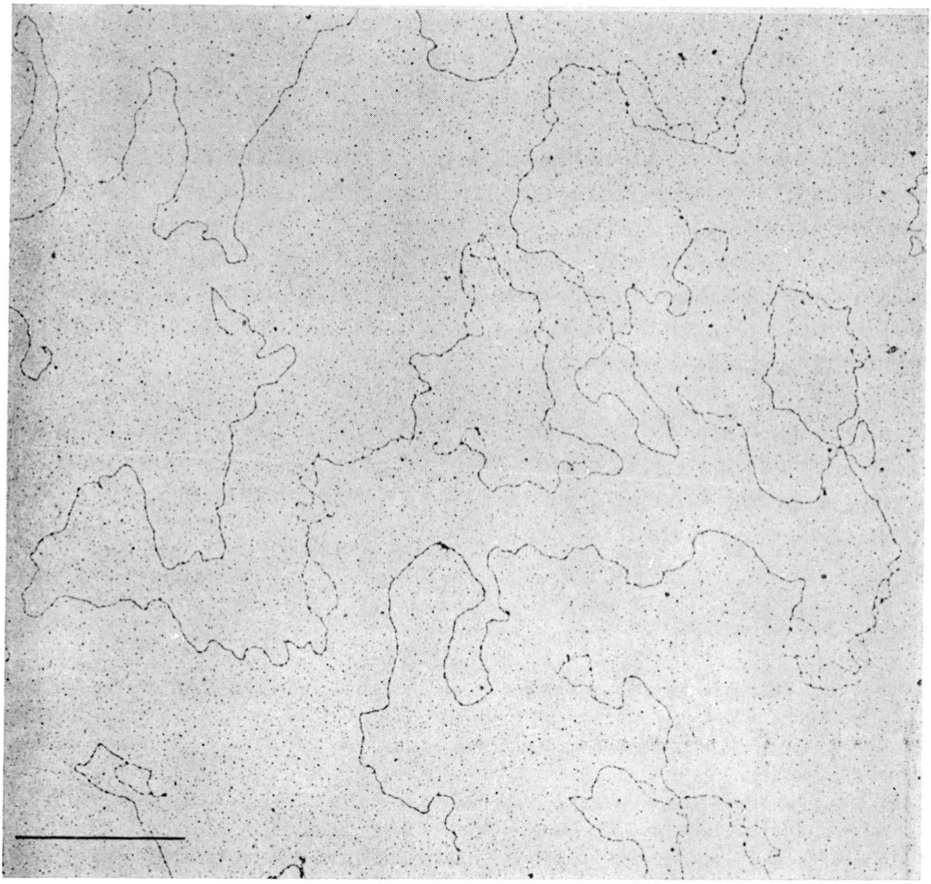

Fig. 6. Lambda phage DNA, after partial melting (46 °C, 10 min) in formaldehyde (12%). The loop (about 12 along the 'right arm' of each molecule) are visible in *all* molecules spread. Contrast by uranyl acetate staining (Gordon and Kleinschmidt). The bar indicates 1 μ.

insurmountable task if one uses conventional biochemical methods (RajBhandary and Stuart). For example, the short single-stranded DNA of ΦX174 phage is more than 50 times the length of various transfer RNAs whose sequence is presently known (Miura). However, electron microscopic studies have shown, in general, that localized marking of non-randomly distributed regions of the DNA molecule is indeed possible. Several methods are promising: one possibility may be the staining of certain adenine (Beer and Moudrianakis), guanine (Moudrianakis and Beer), thymine (Beer et al.), or cytosine residues of nucleic acids (Zobel and Beer). This resolution of specific staining is not yet clearly achieved. Another possibility presently shown is local denaturation at presumably A-T rich sites along a double-stranded nucleic acid molecule (Inman 1966). A third possibility is the mapping of unmatched regions of renatured double-stranded viral DNA. In the latter case one of the two strands is a wild type strand, the other a mutant strand which has deletions of known size. The resulting formation of single-stranded regions looping out from the filaments of a double strand indicates accurate hybridization of the two strands except at the deletion site. Lambda phage was used to show a series of deletion regions of non-homology in the form of bushes (Davis and Davidson) or open loops (Westmoreland et al.).

Also for lambda DNA, A-T rich regions could be identified after the molecules were melted in 10% formaldehyde at temperatures higher than 45 °C (Inman 1966, 1967). Similar denaturation profiles were found in DNA rings (form II) of papilloma virus and polyoma virus (Follett and Crawford). An example of denaturation of λ DNA molecules is shown in Fig. 6. It demonstrates a kind of molecular structural analysis that may permit correlation of regions mapped by a morphological method with those identifiable by genetic methods.

I am much indebted to Dr. C. Vasquez for help with the preparation of the tables and to Dr. S. Ochoa and Dr. R. C. Warner for improving the manuscript. The work in this laboratory was supported by a grant from the J. A. Hartford Foundation, Inc., New York.

Selected bibliography

CANTONI, G. L. and D. R. DAVIES, eds.: Procedures in nucleic acid research. New York, Harper and Row Publishing Co. (1966).

CHARGAFF, E. and J. N. DAVIDSON, eds.: The nucleic acids, vols. 1–3. New York, Academic Press (1955 and 1960).

Cold Spring Harbor symposia on quantitative biology, vols. 28, 31, 33, Cold Spring Harbor, Cold Spring Harbor Laboratory on Quantitative Biology, 1963, 1966, 1968.

DAVIDSON, J. N. and W. E. COHN, eds.: Progress in nucleic acid research and molecular biology, vols. 1–17. New York, Academic Press (1963 ff.).

DAVIS, B. D., R. DULBECCO, H. N. EISEN, H. S. GINSBERG and W. B. WOOD: Microbiology. New York, Harper and Row Publishing Co. (1967).

FENNER, F.: The biology of animal viruses, vol. 1. New York, Academic Press (1968).

FINEAN, J.B.: Engström-Finean, biological ultrastructure, 2nd ed. New York, Academic Press (1967).

FLORKIN, M. and E.H.STOTZ, eds.: Comprehensive biochemistry, vol. 8 part B: Nucleic acids. New York, Elsevier (1963).

GROSSMAN, L. and K.MOLDAVE, eds.: Methods in enzymology XII. Nucleic acids, part A and B. New York, Academic Press (1967 and 1968).

HALL, C.E.: Introduction to electron microscopy, 2nd ed. New York, McGraw-Hill (1967).

HARBER, E.: Die Nucleinsäuren. Stuttgart, Georg Thieme Verlag (1964).

HAYES, W.: The genetics of bacteria and their viruses. New York, Wiley and Sons (1964).

HORSFALL, F.L. and I.TAMM, eds.: Viral and rickettsial infections of man, 4th ed. Philadelphia, J.B. Lippincott and Co. (1965).

KAY, D., ed.: Techniques for electron microscopy, 2nd ed. Philadelphia, F.A.Davis Co. (1965).

LURIA, S.E. and J.E.DARNELL, JR.: General virology, 2nd ed. New York, John Wiley and Sons (1967).

MAHLER, H.R. and E.H.CORDES, eds.: Biological chemistry. New York, Harper and Row Publishing Co. (1967).

MICHELSON, A.M.: The chemistry of nucleosides and nucleotides. New York, Academic Press (1963).

PEASE, D.P.: Histological techniques for electron microscopy, 2nd ed. New York, Academic Press (1964).

REIMER, L.: Elektronenmikroskopische Untersuchungs- und Präparationsmethoden, 2nd ed. Berlin, Springer-Verlag (1967).

SIEGEL, M., ed.: Modern developments in electron microscopy. New York, Academic Press (1964).

SPIRIN, A.S.: Macromolecular structure of ribonucleic acids. London, Reinhold Publishing Corp. (1964).

STENT, G.S.: Molecular biology of bacterial viruses. San Francisco, W.H.Freeman and Co. (1964).

References

ABELSON, J. and C.A.THOMAS, JR.: The anatomy of the T5 bacteriophage DNA molecule. J. Mol. Biol. 18 (1966) 262.

ADA, G.L.: Ribonucleic acid in influenza virus. In: G.E.W.Wolstenholme, ed.: The nature of viruses. London, Ciba Foundation Symposium (1957) p. 104.

AMMANN, J., H.DELIUS and P.H.HOFSCHNEIDER: Isolation and properties of an intact phage specific replicative form of RNA phage M12. J. Mol. Biol. 10 (1964) 557.

ANDERER, F.A. and H.RESTLE: Untersuchungen über ein attenviertes Poliomyelitis-virus Type 11, Reindarstellung und physikalisch-chemische Eigenschaften des Virus. Z. Naturforsch. 19b (1964) 1026.

ANDERER, F.A., H.D.SCHLUMBERGER, M.A.KOCH, H.FRANK and H.J.EGGERS: Structure of simian virus 40 II. Virology 32 (1967) 511.

ANDERSON, D.L., D.D.HICKMAN and B.E.REILLY: Structure of *Bacillus subtilis* bacteriophage Φ29 and the length of Φ29 DNA. J. Bacteriol. 91 (1966) 2081.

ANDERSON, T.F.: One the fine structures of the temperate bacteriophages P1, P2 and P22. Europ. Regional Conference on Electron Microscopy, Delft (1950) p. 1008.

ARBER, W. and G.KELLENBERGER: Study of the properties of seven defective-lysogenic strains derived from *E. coli* K 12 (λ). Virology 5 (1958) 458.

ARNOTT, S., M.H.F.WILKINS, W.FULLER and R.LANGRIDGE: Molecular and crystal structures of double-helical RNA II. J. Mol. Biol. 27 (1967) 525.

AUGUST, J.T., A.K.BANERJEE, L.EOYANG, M.T.FRANZE DE FERNANDEZ, K.HORI, C.H.KUO, U.RENSING and L.SHAPIRO: Synthesis of bacteriophage Qβ RNA. Cold Spring Harbor Symp. Quant. Biol. 33 (1968) 73.

BACHRACH, H.L. and S.S.BREESE, JR.: Purification and electron microscopy of foot and mouth disease virus. Proc. Soc. Exptl. Biol. Med. 97 (1958) 659.

BACHRACH, H.L., R.TRAUTMAN and S.S.BREESE, JR.: Chemical physical properties of virtually pure foot and mouth disease virus. Am. J. Vet. Res. 25 (1964) 333.

BECKER, Y., H.DYM and I.SARKOV: Herpes simplex virus DNA. Virology 36 (1968) 184.

BEER, M.: Electron microscopic determination of the length of single polynucleotide chains. In: L.Grossman and K.Moldave, eds.: Methods in enzymology, vol. XII B. Academic Press, New York (1968) p. 377.

BEER, M. and E.N.MOUDRIANAKIS: Determination of base sequence analysis in nucleic acids with the electron microscope: visibility of a marker. Proc. Natl. Acad. Sci. 48 (1962) 409.

BEER, M., S.STERN, D.CARMALT and K.H.MOHLHENRICH: Determination of base sequences in nucleic acids with the electron microscope V. Biochemistry 5 (1966) 2283.

BELLAMY, A.R. and W.K.JOKLIK: Studies on reovirus RNA II. J. Mol. Biol. 29 (1967) 19.

BELLETT, A.J.D. and R.B.INMAN: Some properties of DNA preparations from Chilo, Sericesthis and Tipula iridescent viruses. J. Mol. Biol. 25 (1967) 425.

BENDET, I.J., E.SCHACHTER and M.A.LAUFFER: The size of T3 DNA. J. Mol. Biol. 5 (1962) 76.

BENYESH, M., E.C.POLLARD, E.M.OPTON, F.L.BLACK, W.D.BELLAMY and J.L.MELNICK: Size and structure of ECHO, poliomyelitis and measle virus determined by ionizing radiation and ultrafiltration. Virology 5 (1958) 256.

BERNHARD, W.: Electron microscopy of tumor cells and tumor viruses. Cancer Res. 18 (1958) 491.

BERNHARD, W., R.A.BONAR, D.BEARD and J.W.BEARD: Ultrastructure of virus of myeloblastosis and erythroblastosis isolated from plasma of leukemic chickens. Proc. Soc. Exptl. Biol. Med. 97 (1958) 48.

BERNHARD, W., C.VASQUEZ and P.TOURNIER: La structure du virus SV40 étudiée par coloration négative au microscope électronique. J. Microscopie 1 (1962) 343.

BILS, R.F. and C.E.HALL: Electron microscopy of wound tumor virus. Virology 17 (1962) 123.

BISHOP, D.H.L., N.R.PACE and S.SPIEGELMAN: The mechanisms of replication: a novel polarity reversal in the *in vitro* synthesis of Q_β-RNA and its components. Proc. Natl. Acad. Sci. 58 (1967) 1790.

BISWAL, N., A.K.KLEINSCHMIDT, H.C.SPATZ and T.A.TRAUTNER: Physical properties of the DNA of bacteriophage SP50. Molec. Gen. Genetics 100 (1967) 39.

BLAIR, C.D. and P.H.DUESBERG: Structure of Rauscher mouse leukemia virus RNA. Nature 220 (1968) 396.

BODE, V.C. and A.D.KAISER: Changes in the structure and activity of λ DNA in a superinfected immune bacterium. J. Mol. Biol. 14 (1965) 399.

BODE, V.C. and L.A.MACHATTIE: Electron microscopy of superhelical circular λ DNA. J. Mol. Biol. 32 (1968) 673.

BOIRON, M., J.P.LEVY and J.PERIES: *In vitro* investigations on murine leukemia viruses. Progr. Med. Virol. 9 (1967) 341.

BONAR, R.A., L.SVERAK, D.P.BOLOGNESI, A.J.LANGLOIS, D.BEARD and J.W.BEARD: Ribonucleic acid components of BA1 strain A (myeloblastosis) avian tumor virus. Cancer Res. 27 (1967) 1138.

BRANDES, J. and R.BERCKS: Gross morphology and serology as a basis for classification of elongated plant viruses. Advan. Virus Res. 11 (1965) 1.

BREESE, JR., S.S. and A.BRIEFS: Certain physical properties of a herpangina strain and a pleurodynia strain of Coxsackie virus. Proc. Soc. Exptl. Biol. Med. 83 (1953) 119.

BREESE, JR., S.S., R.TRAUTMAN and H.L.BACHRACH: Rotational symmetry in foot and mouth disease virus and models. Science 50 (1965) 1303.

BRESLER, S.E., N.A.KISELEV, V.F.MANJAKOV, M.I.MOSEVITSKY and A.K.TIMKOVSKY: Isolation and physiochemical investigation of T1 bacteriophage DNA. Virology 33 (1967) 1.

BURNESS, A.T.H., A.D.VIZOSO and F.W.CLOTHIER: Encephalomyocarditis virus and its ribonucleic acid: sedimentation characteristics. Nature 197 (1963) 1177.

CAIRNS, J.: An estimate of the length of the DNA molecule of T2 bacteriophage by autoradiography. J. Mol. Biol. 3 (1961) 756.

CARO, L.G.: The molecular weight of lambda DNA. Virology 25 (1965) 226.

CASPAR, D.L.D.: Design principles in virus particle construction. In: F.L.Horsfall and I.Tamm, eds.: Viral and rickettsial infections of man, 4th ed. Philadelphia, Lippincott Co. (1965) p. 51.

CASPAR, D.L.D. and A.KLUG: Physical principles in the construction of regular viruses. Cold Spring Harbor Symp. Quant. Biol. 27 (1962) 1.

COHEN, S.S.: The biochemistry of bacteria infected by viruses. In: F.L.Horsfall and I.Tamm, eds.: Viral and rickettsial infections of man, 4th ed. Philadelphia, Lippincott Co. (1965) p. 175.

COMPANS, R.W. and P.W.CHOPPIN: Isolation and properties of the helical nucleocapsid of the parainfluenza virus SV5. Proc. Natl. Acad. Sci. 57 (1967) 949.

CRAWFORD, L.V.: The physical characteristics of polyoma virus II. Virology 19 (1963) 279.

CRAWFORD, L.V.: The physical characteristics of polyoma virus IV. Virology 22 (1964) 149.

CRAWFORD, L.V. and P.H.BLACK: The nucleic acid of simian virus 40. Virology 24 (1964) 388.

CRAWFORD, L.V. and E.M.CRAWFORD: The properties of Rous sarcoma virus purified by density gradient centrifugation. Virology 13 (1961) 277.

CRAWFORD, L.V., E.A.C.FOLLETT and E.M.CRAWFORD: An electron microscopic study of DNA from three tumor viruses. J. Microscopie 5 (1966) 597.

DALES, S.: Penetration of animal virus into cells. Progr. Med. Virol. 7 (1963) 1.

DAVIS, B.D., R.DULBECCO, H.N.EISEN, H.S.GINSBERG and W.B.WOOD: Microbiology. New York, Harper and Row Publishing Co. (1967) p. 1016.

DAVIS, R.W. and N.DAVIDSON: Electron microscopic visualization of deletion mutations. Proc. Natl. Acad. Sci. 60 (1968) 243.

DAVISON, P.F. and D.FREIFELDER: The physical properties of T7 bacteriophage. J. Mol. Biol. 5 (1962) 635.

DE ROSIER, D.J. and R.HASELKORN: Particle weight of turnip yellow mosaic virus. J. Mol. Biol. 19 (1966) 52.

DE THÉ, F. and T.E.O'CONNOR: Structures of a murine leukemia virus after disruption with tween-ether and comparison with two myxoviruses. Virology 28 (1966) 713.

DORNER, R.W. and C.A.KNIGHT: The preparation and some properties of some plant virus nucleic acids. J. Biol. Chem. 205 (1953) 959.

DUESBERG, P.H.: The RNA's of influenza virus. Proc. Natl. Acad. Sci. 59 (1968a) 931.

DUESBERG, P.H.: Physical properties of Rous sarcoma virus RNA. Proc. Natl. Acad. Sci. 60 (1968b) 1151.

DUESBERG, P.H. and W.S.ROBINSON: Isolation of the nucleic acid of Newcastle disease. Proc. Natl. Acad. Sci. 54 (1965) 794.

DUESBERG, P.H. and W.S.ROBINSON: Nucleic acid and protein isolated from the Rouscher mouse leukemia virus (MLV). Proc. Natl. Acad. Sci. 55 (1966) 219.

DULBECCO, R. and M.VOGT: Evidence for a ring structure of polyoma virus DNA. Proc. Natl. Acad. Sci. 50 (1963) 737.

DUNNEBACKE, T.H. and A.K.KLEINSCHMIDT: RNA from reovirus as seen in protein monolayers by electron microscopy. Z. Naturforsch. 22b (1967) 159.

EASTERBROOK, K.B.: Morphology of deoxyribonucleic acid extracted from cores of vaccinia virus. J. Virol. 1 (1967) 643.

ENGLUND, P.T., M.P.DEUTSCHER, T.M.JOVIN, R.B.KELLEY, N.R.COZZARELLI and A.KORNBERG: Structural and functional properties of *Escherichia coli*. Cold Spring Harbor Symp. Quant. Biol. 33 (1968) 1.

FAULKNER, P., E.M.MARTIN, S.SVED, R.C.VALENTINE and T.S.WORK: Studies on protein and nucleic acid metabolism in virus-infected mammalian cells II. Biochem. J. 80 (1961) 597.

FIERS, W. and R.L.SINSHEIMER: The structure of the DNA of bacteriophage ΦX714 I, II. J. Mol. Biol. 5 (1962) 408, 424.

FITCH, J.T. and A.KLUG: Structure of poliomyelitis virus. Nature 183 (1959) 1709.

FITCH, J.T. and A.KLUG: The structure of viruses of the papilloma-polyoma type III. J. Mol. Biol. 13 (1965) 1.

FÖLDES, J. and T.A.TRAUTNER: Infectious DNA from a newly isolated B. subtilis phage. Z. Vererbungslehre 95 (1964) 57.

FOLLETT, E.A.C. and L.V.CRAWFORD: Electron microscopy study of the denaturation of human papilloma virus DNA I. J. Mol. Biol. 28 (1967) 455.

FRAENKEL-CONRAT, H.: Structure and function of virus proteins and of viral nucleic acid. In: H. Neurath, ed.: The proteins, 2nd ed., vol. 3. New York, Academic Press (1965) p. 99.

FRAENKEL-CONRAT, H. and R.C.WILLIAMS: Reconstitution of the TMV from its inactive protein and nucleic acid. Proc. Natl. Acad. Sci. 41 (1955) 690.

FRANKEL, F.K.: Evidence for long DNA strands in the replicating pool after T4 infection. Proc. Natl. Acad. Sci. 59 (1968) 131.

FRANK, H., M.L.ZARNITZ and W.WEIDEL: Über die Rezeptor-substanz für den Phagen T5. Z. Naturforsch. 18b (1963) 281.

FREIFELDER, D. and A.K.KLEINSCHMIDT: Single-stranded breaks in duplex DNA of coliphage T7 as demonstrated by electron microscopy. J. Mol. Biol. 14 (1965) 271.

FREIFELDER, D., A.K.KLEINSCHMIDT and R.L.SINSHEIMER: Electron microscopy of single-stranded DNA: circularity of DNA of bacteriophage ΦX174. Science 146 (1964) 254.

FRISCH-NIGGEMEYER, W.: The internal structure of influenza virus. Z. Naturforsch. 14b (1959) 168.

FUKADA, M., T.FUKADA, H.NAKAI and Y.KAWADE: Purification and characterization of ECHO7 virus. Ann. Rep. Inst. Virus Res. Kyoto Univ. 9 (1966) 79.

FUKUSHI, T., E.SHIKATA and I.KIMURA: Some morphological characteristics of rice dwarf virus. Virology 18 (1962) 192.

GAFFORD, L.G. and C.C.RANDALL: The high molecular weight of fowlpox genome. J. Mol. Biol. 26 (1967) 303.

GELLERT, M., J.W.LITTLE, C.K.OSHINSKY and S.B.ZIMMERMAN: Joining of DNA strands by DNA ligase of *E. coli*. Cold Spring Harbor Symp. Quant. Biol. 33 (1968) 21.

GESTELAND, R.F. and H.BOEDTKER: Some physical properties of bacteriophage R17 and its ribonucleic acid. J. Mol. Biol. 8 (1964) 496.

GIERER, A.: Structure and biological function of ribonucleic acid from tobacco mosaic virus. Nature 179 (1957) 1297.

GILBERT, W. and D.DRESSLER: DNA replication: the rolling circle model. Cold Spring Harbor Symp. Quant. Biol. 33 (1968) 473.

GINSBERG, H.S. and J.H.DINGLE: The adenovirus group. In: F.L.Horsfall and I.Tamm, eds.: Viral and rickettsial infections of man, 4th ed. Philadelphia, Lippincott, Co. (1965) p. 860.

GIRARD, M., D.BALTIMORE and J.E.DARNELL, JR.: The poliovirus replication complex, site for synthesis of poliovirus RNA. J. Mol. Biol. 24 (1967) 59.

GOMATOS, P.J. and W.STOECKENIUS: Electron microscope studies on reovirus RNA. Proc. Natl. Acad. Sci. 52 (1964) 1449.

GOMATOS, P.J. and I.TAMM: The secondary structure of reovirus RNA. Proc. Natl. Acad. Sci. 49 (1963a) 707.

GOMATOS, P.J. and I.TAMM: Animal and plant viruses with double-helical RNA. Proc. Natl. Acad. Sci. 50 (1963b) 878.

GORDON, C.N. and A.K.KLEINSCHMIDT: High contrast staining of individual nucleic acid molecules. Biochim. Biophys. Acta 155 (1968) 305.

GOULIAN, M.: Initiation of the replication of single-stranded DNA by *Escherichia coli* DNA polymerase. Cold Spring Harbor Symp. Quant. Biol. 33 (1968) 11.

GOULIAN, M. and A. KORNBERG: Enzymatic synthesis of DNA XXIII. Proc. Natl. Acad. Sci. 58 (1967) 1723.

GRANBOULAN, N. and R. M. FRANKLIN: Electron microscopy of viral RNA replicative form and replicative intermediate of the bacteriophage R17. J. Mol. Biol. 22 (1966) 173.

GRANBOULAN, N. and R. M. FRANKLIN: Replication of bacteriophage RNA: analysis of the ultrastructure of the replicative form and the replicative intermediate of bacteriophage R17. J. Virol. 2 (1968) 129.

GRANBOULAN, N., J. HUPPERT and F. LACOUR: Examen au microscope électronique du RNA du virus de la myéloblastose aviaire. J. Mol. Biol. 16 (1966) 571.

GREEN, M. H., P. PIÑA, R. KIMES, P. C. WENSINK, L. A. MACHATTIE and C. A. THOMAS, JR.: Adenovirus DNA I. Proc. Natl. Acad. Sci. 57 (1967) 1302.

GREEN, R. H., T. F. ANDERSON and J. E. SMADEL: Morphological structure of the virus of vaccinia. J. Exptl. Med. 75 (1942) 651.

HALL, C. E., E. C. MACLEAN and I. TESSMAN: Structure and dimensions of bacteriophage ΦX174 from electron microscopy. J. Mol. Biol. 1 (1959) 192.

HARUNA, I. and S. SPIEGELMAN: Specific template requirements for RNA polymerase. Proc. Natl. Acad. Sci. 54 (1965) 579.

HERSHEY, A. D., E. BURGI and L. INGRAHAM: Cohesion of DNA molecules isolated from phage lambda. Proc. Natl. Acad. Sci. 49 (1963) 675.

HERZBERG, K., A. K. KLEINSCHMIDT, D. LANG, K. REUSS: Vaccinevirus und Kanarienpockevirus electronenmikroskopisch bei Negativkontrastierung. Naturwissenschaften 48 (1961) 725.

HOFFMANN-BERLING, H. and D. A. MARVIN: Physical and chemical properties of two small bacteriophages. Nature 197 (1963) 517.

HOFFMANN-BERLING, H., D. A. MARVIN and H. DÜRWALD: Ein fädiger DNS-phage (fd) und ein sphärischer RNS-phage (fr) wirtspezifisch für männliche Stämme von *E. coli*. Z. Naturforsch. 18b (1963) 198.

HOFSCHNEIDER, P. H.: Untersuchungen über 'kleine' *E. coli* K12 Bacteriophagen I. Z. Naturforsch. 18b (1963) 136.

HOHN, T.: Self assembly of defective particles of the bacteriophage fr. European J. Biochem. 2 (1968) 152.

HORNE, R. W., S. BRENNER, A. P. WATERSON and P. WILDY: The icosahedral form of an adenovirus. J. Mol. Biol. 1 (1959) 84.

HORNE, R. W. and J. NAGINGTON: Electron microscope studies on the development and structure of poliomyelitis virus. J. Mol. Biol. 1 (1959) 333.

HORNE, R.W. and P.WILDY: Virus structure revealed by negative staining. Advan. Virus Res. 10 (1963) 102.

HOTHAM-IGLEWSKI, B. and R. M. FRANKLIN: Replication of bacteriophage RNA: alternations in polysome patterns and association of double-stranded RNA with polysomes in *E. coli* infected with phage R17. Proc. Natl. Acad. Sci. 58 (1967) 743.

HUBERMAN, J. A.: Visualization of replicating mammalian and T4 bacteriophage DNA. Cold Spring Harbor Symp. Quant. Biol. 33 (1968) 509.

HUPPERT, J., M. ROSENBERGOVA, L. GRESLAND and L. HAREL: Properties of RNA from vesicular stomatitis virus. In: J. Colter and W. Paranchych, eds.: The molecular biology of viruses. New York, Academic Press (1967) p. 463.

HUXLEY, H. E. and G. ZUBAY: The structure of the protein shell of turnip yellow mosaic virus. J. Mol. Biol. 2 (1960) 189.

HYDE, J. M., L. G. GAFFORD and C. C. RANDALL: Molecular weight determination of fowlpox DNA by electron microscopy. Virology 22 (1967) 112.

INMAN, R. B.: A denaturation map of the λ phage DNA molecule determined by electron microscopy. J. Mol. Biol. 18 (1966) 464.

INMAN, R.B.: Denaturation maps of the left and right sides of the lambda DNA molecule determined by electron microscopy. J. Mol. Biol. 28 (1967) 103.

INMAN, R.B., C.C.RICHARDSON and A.KORNBERG: Enzymatic synthesis of DNA XVII. J. Mol. Biol. 9 (1964) 46.

JOKLIK, W.K.: The purification of four strains of poxviruses. Virology 18 (1962) 9.

JOKLIK, W.K.: The poxviruses. Bacteriol. Rev. 30 (1966) 33.

KAISER, A.D.: On the internal structure of bacteriophage lambda. J. Gen. Physiol. 49 (1966) no. 6, part 2, 171.

KAISER, A.D. and R.WU: Structure and function of DNA cohesive ends. Cold Spring Harbor Symp. Quant. Biol. 33 (1968) 729.

KAWADE, Y., I.KIMURA, T.KODAMA and N.SUZUKI: On the size of RNA from dwarf rice virus. Ann. Rep. Inst. Virus Res. Kyoto Univ. 9 (1966) 145.

KELLENBERGER, E.: Vegetative bacteriophage and maturation of the virus particle. Advan. Virus Res. 8 (1961) 1.

KELLENBERGER, E.: Control mechanisms in bacteriophage morphopoiesis. In: G.E.W.Wolstenholme and N.O'Connor, eds.: Principles of biomolecular organization. Ciba Foundation Symposium. Boston, Little, Brown and Co. (1966) p. 192.

KELLENBERGER, G., L.ZICHICHI and J.J.WEIGLE: Exchange of DNA in the recombination of bacteriophage lambda. Proc. Natl. Acad. Sci. 47 (1961) 869.

KIHO, Y.: Isolation of polyribosomes from tobacco plants infected with TMV. Japan. J. Microbiol. 12 (1968) 211.

KILKSON, R. and M.F.MAESTRE: Structure of T2 bacteriophage. Nature 145 (1962) 494.

KLEINSCHMIDT, A.K.: Monolayer techniques in electron microscopy of nucleic acid molecules. In: L.Grossman and K.Moldave, eds.: Methods in enzymology, XIIB. New York, Academic Press (1968) 361.

KLEINSCHMIDT, A.K., D.LANG, D.JACHERTS and R.K.ZAHN: Darstellung und Längenmessungen des gesamten DNA-Inhaltes von T2-Bacteriophagen. Biochim. Biophys. Acta 61 (1962) 857.

KLEINSCHMIDT, A.K., A.BURTON and R.L.SINSHEIMER: Electron microscopy of the replicative form of the DNA of the bacteriophage ΦX174. Science 142 (1963) 961.

KLEINSCHMIDT, A.K., T.H.DUNNEBACKE, R.S.SPENDLOVE and F.K.SCHAFFER: Electron microscopy of RNA from reovirus and wound tumor virus. J. Mol. Biol. 10 (1964) 282.

KLEINSCHMIDT, A.K., S.J.KASS, R.C.WILLIAMS and C.A.KNIGHT: Cyclic DNA of shope papilloma virus. J. Mol. Biol. 13 (1965) 749.

KLEINSCHMIDT, A.K. and D.G.SAUNDERS: Physical properties of TP84 phage DNA (in preparation).

KLIMENKO, S.M., T.I.TIKCHONENKO and V.M.ANDREEV: Packing of DNA in the head of bacteriophage T2. J. Mol. Biol. 23 (1967) 523.

KLUG, A.: Structure of viruses of the papilloma-polyoma type. J. Mol. Biol. 11 (1965) 424.

KLUG, A. and D.L.D.CASPAR: The structure of small viruses. Advan. Virus Res. 7 (1960) 225.

KLUG, A., J.T.FINCH, R.LEBERMAN and W.LONGLEY: Design and structure of regular virus particles. In: G.E.W.Wolstenholme and N.O'Connor, eds.: Principles of biomolecular organization. Ciba Foundation Symposium. Boston, Little, Brown and Co. (1966) 158.

KNIGHT, C.A.: Chemistry of viruses. Protoplasmatologia IV, 2. Wien Springer-Verlag (1963).

KOCH, M.A., H.J.EGGERS, F.A.ANDERER, H.D.SCHLUMBERGER and H.FRANK: Structure of simian virus 40 I. Virology 32 (1967) 503.

KORNBERG, A.: Enzymatic synthesis of DNA. New York, John Wiley and Sons (1961).

KOZINSKI, A.W., P.B.KOZINSKI and R.JAMES: Molecular recombination in T4 bacteriophage deoxyribonucleic acid I. J. Virol. 1 (1967) 758.

LANG, D., H.BUJARD, B.WOLFF and D.RUSSELL: Electron microscope of size and shape of viral DNA in solutions of different ionic strength. J. Mol. Biol. 23 (1967) 163.

LEDINKO, N.: Occurrence of s-methyldeoxycytidylate in the DNA of phage lambda. J. Mol. Biol. 9 (1964) 834.

LEHMAN, I.R.: Deoxyribonucleases: their relationship to DNA synthesis. Ann. Rev. Biochem. 36 (1967) 645.

LOEB, T. and N.D.ZINDER: A bacteriophage containing RNA. Proc. Natl. Acad. Sci. 47 (1961) 282.

LWOFF, A. and P.TOURNIER: The classification of viruses. Ann. Rev. Microbiol. 20 (1966) 45.

MCCOMBS, R.M., M.BENYESH-MELNICK and J.P.BRUNSCHWIG: Biophysical studies of vesicular stomatitis virus. J. Bacteriol. 91 (1966) 803.

MCCREA, J.F. and M.B.LIPMAN: Strand length measurements of normal and 5-iodo-2′-deoxyuridine-treated vaccinia deoxyribonucleic acid released by the Kleinschmidt method. J. Virol. 1 (1967) 1037.

MACHATTIE, L.A. and C.A.THOMAS, JR.: DNA from bacteriophage lambda: molecular length and conformation. Science 144 (1964) 1142.

MACHATTIE, L.A., D.A.RITCHIE, C.A.THOMAS, JR. and C.C.RICHARDSON: Terminal repetition in permuted T2 bacteriophage DNA molecules. J. Mol. Biol. 23 (1967) 355.

MACLEAN, E.C. and C.E.HALL: Studies on bacteriophage ΦX174 and its DNA by electron microscopy. J. Mol. Biol. 4 (1962) 173.

MANDEL, M. and A.BERG: Cohesive sites and helper phage function of P2, lambda and 186 DNA's. Proc. Natl. Acad. Sci. 60 (1968) 265.

MARKHAM, R.: The biochemistry of plant viruses. In: F.M.Burnet and W.M.Stanley, eds.: The viruses, vol. 2. New York, Academic Press (1959) p. 33.

MARKHAM, R., J.H.HITCHBORN, G.J.HILLS and S.FREY: The anatomy of tobacco mosaic virus. Virology 22 (1964) 342.

MARVIN, D.A. and H.HOFFMANN-BERLING: A fibrous DNA phage (fd) and a spherical RNA phage (fr) specific for male strains of *E. coli*. Z. Naturforsch. 18b (1963) 884.

MATTERN, C.F.T.: Some physical and chemical properties of Coxsackie virus A9 and A10. Virology 17 (1962) 520.

MATTHEWS, R.E.F. and R.K.RALPH: Turnip yellow mosaic virus. Advan. Virus Res. 12 (1966) 273.

MAYOR, H.D.: Picornavirus symmetry. Virology 22 (1964) 22.

MAYOR, H.D., R.M.JAMISON and L.E.JORDAN: Biophysical studies of the simian papova virus particle (vacuolating SV40 virus). Virology 19 (1963) 359.

MESELSON, M. and F.W.STAHL: The replication of DNA in *Escherichia coli*. Proc. Natl. Acad. Sci. 44 (1958) 671.

MILLS, D.R., N.R.PACE and S.SPIEGELMAN: The *in vitro* synthesis of a non-infectious complex containing biologically active viral RNA. Proc. Natl. Acad. Sci. 56 (1966) 1778.

MITRA, S., M.D.ENGER and P.KAESBERG: Physical and chemical properties of RNA from the bacterial virus R17. Proc. Natl. Acad. Sci. 50 (1963) 68.

MITRA, S. and P.KAESBERG: Biophysical properties of RNA from turnip yellow mosaic virus. J. Mol. Biol. 14 (1965) 558.

MITRA, S., P.REICHARDS, R.B.INMAN, L.L.BERTSCH and A.KORNBERG: Enzymatic synthesis of deoxyribonucleic acid XXII. J. Mol. Biol. 24 (1967) 429.

MIURA, K.I.: Specificity in the structure of transfer RNA. Progr. Nucl. Acid Res. Mol. Biol. 6 (1967) 39.

MIURA, K.I., I.FUJII, T.SAKAKI, M.FUKE and S.KAWASE: Double-stranded RNA from cytoplasmic polyhedrosis virus of the silkworm. J. Virology 2 (1968) 1211.

MIURA, K.I., I.KIMURA and N.SUZUKI: Double-stranded ribonucleic acid from rice dwarf virus. Virology 28 (1966) 571.

MOUDRIANAKIS, E.N. and M.BEER: Base sequence determination in nucleic acids with the electron microscope III. Proc. Natl. Acad. Sci. 53 (1965) 564.

NAGINGTON, J. and R.W. HORNE: Morphological studies of Orf and vaccinia virus. Virology 16 (1962) 248.

NEURATH, H., G.R.COOPER, D.G.SHARP, A.R.TAYLOR, D.BEARD and J.W.BEARD: Molecular size, shape and homogeneity of the rabbit papilloma virus protein. J. Biol. Chem. 140 (1941) 293.

NORRBY, E.C.J. and P.MAGNUSSON: Some morphological characteristics of the internal component of measles virus. Arch. Ges. Virusforsch. 17 (1965) 443.

OLIVERA, B.M., Z.W.HALL, Y.ANRAKU, J.R.CHEN and I.R.LEHMAN: On the mechanism of the polynucleotide joining reaction. Cold Spring Harbor Symp. Quant. Biol. 33 (1968) 27.

OVERBY, L.R., G.H.BARLOW and R.H.DOI: Comparison of two serologically distinct ribonucleic acid bacteriophages II. J. Bacteriol. 91 (1966) 442.

PARANCHYCH, W. and A.F.GRAHAM: Isolation and properties of an RNA-contained bacteriophage. J. Cellular Comp. Physiol. 60 (1962) 199.

PAULING, L.: The nature of the chemical bond and the structure of molecules and crystals, 3rd ed. Ithaca, Cornell University Press (1960).

PETERS, D.: Electron microscopic studies on the localization of deoxyribonucleic acid inside of DNA viruses. VI. Internatl. Congr. for Electron Microscopy, Kyoto, 2 (1966) 195.

PETERS, D. and G.MÜLLER: The fine structure of the DNA-containing core of vaccinia virus. Virology 21 (1963) 266.

PFEFFERKORN, E.R. and H.S.HUNTER: The source of ribonucleic acid and phospholipid of Sindbis virus. Virology 20 (1963) 446.

PIÑA, M. and M.H.GREEN: Biochemical studies on adenovirus multiplication III. Proc. Natl. Acad. Sci. 54 (1965) 547.

PIRIE, N.W.: Biological organization of viruses. In: G.E.W.Wolstenholme and N.O'Connor, eds.: Principles of biomolecular organization. Ciba Foundation Symposium. Boston, Little, Brown and Co. (1966) p. 136.

POHJANPELTO, P. and M.NYHOLM: Fine structure of subtilis phage SP50. Arch. Ges. Virusforsch. 17 (1965) 481.

RANDALL, C.C., L.G.GAFFORD, R.L.SOEHNER and J.M.HYDE: Physicochemical properties of fowlpox virus DNA and its anomalous infectious behavior. J. Bacteriol. 91 (1966) 95.

RAJBHANDARY, U.L. and A.STUART: Nucleic acids – sequence analysis. Ann. Rev. Biochem. 35 (1966) 759.

RHOADES, M., L.A.MACHATTIE and C.A.THOMAS, JR.: The P22 bacteriophage DNA molecule. J. Mol. Biol. 37 (1968) 21.

RICH, A., S.PENMAN, Y.BECKER, J.DARNELL and C.E.HALL: Polyribosomes: size in normal and polio-infected HeLa cells. Science 142 (1963) 1658.

RICHARDSON, C.C., R.B.INMAN and A.KORNBERG: Enzymatic synthesis of DNA XVIII. J. Mol. Biol. 9 (1964) 46.

RICHARDSON, C.C., Y.M.MASAMUNE, T.R.LIVE, A.JACQUEMIN-SABLON, B.WEISS and G.C.FAREED: Studies on the joining of DNA by polynucleotide ligase of phage T4. Cold Spring Harbor Symp. Quant. Biol. 33 (1968) 151.

RIS, H. and B.L.CHANDLER: The ultrastructure of genetic systems in prokaryotes and eukaryotes. Cold Spring Harbor Symp. Quant. Biol. 28 (1963) 1.

ROBERTS, J.W. and J.E.A.STEITZ: The reconstitution of infective bacteriophage R17. Proc. Natl. Acad. Sci. 58 (1967) 1416.

ROBINSON, W.S.: In: J.J.Colter and W.Paranchych, eds.: The molecular biology of viruses. New York, Academic Press (1967).

ROBINSON, W.S., A.PITKANEN and H.RUBIN: The nucleic acid of the Bryan strain of Rous sarcoma virus: purification of the virus and isolation of the nucleic acid. Proc. Natl. Acad. Sci. 54 (1965) 137.

ROLFE, R. and A.RICH: Polyribosomes from bacteriophage T4 infected protoplasts. Biophys. J. 5 (1965) 153.

ROTT, R.: Antigenicity of Newcastle disease virus. In: R.P.Hanson, ed.: Newcastle disease virus: an evolving pathogen. Madison, Wisconsin University Press (1964) p. 133.

RUBENSTEIN, I., C.A.THOMAS, JR. and A.D.HERSHEY: Molecular weights of T2 bacteriophage DNA and its first and second breakage products. Proc. Natl. Acad. Sci. 47 (1961) 1113.

RUSH, M.G., A.K.KLEINSCHMIDT, W.HELLMANN and R.C.WARNER: Multiple length rings in preparation of ΦX174 replicative form. Proc. Natl. Acad. Sci. 58 (1967) 1676.

RUSKA, H. and G.A.KAUSCHE: Über Form, Grössenverteilung und Struktur einiger Virus-Elementarkörper. Zentr. Bakteriol. Parasitenk., Abt. I. Orig. 150 (1943) 311.

RUSSELL, W.C. and L.V.CRAWFORD: Properties of the nucleic acid from some herpes group viruses. Virology 22 (1964) 288.

SADOWSKI, P., B.GINSBERG, A.YUDELEVICH, L.FEINER and J.HURWITZ: Enzymatic mechanism of the repair and breakage of DNA. Cold Spring Harbor Symp. Quant. Biol. 33 (1968) 165.

SALIVAR, W.O., H.TZAGOLOFF and D.PRATT: Some physical-chemical biological properties of the rod-shaped coliphage M13. Virology 24 (1964) 359.

SATO, T.: A preliminary investigation on the molecular structure of dwarf virus ribonucleic acid. J. Mol. Biol. 16 (1966) 180.

SAUNDERS, G.F. and L.L.CAMPBELL: Characterization of the thermophilic bacteriophage for *Bacillus stearothermophilus*. J. Bacteriol. 91 (1965a) 340.

SAUNDERS, G.F. and L.L.CAMPBELL: Properties of the DNA of the thermophilic bacteriophage TP84. Biochemistry 4 (1965b) 2836.

SCHAFFER, F.L., H.F.MOORE and C.E.SCHWERDT: Base composition of the ribonucleic acid of three types of poliovirus. Virology 10 (1960) 530.

SCHOLTISSECK, C. and R.ROTT: Behavior of virus-specific activities in tissue cultures infected with myxoviruses after chemical changes of the viral nucleic acid. Virology 22 (1964) 169.

SCHUSTER, A.: The ribonucleic acids of viruses. In: E.Chargaff and J.N.Davidson, eds.: The nucleic acids, vol. 3. New York, Academic Press (1960) p. 245.

SCHWARTZ, F.M. and N.D.ZINDER: Crystalline aggregates in bacterial cells infected with RNA bacteriophage f2. Virology 21 (1963) 276.

SHINAGAWA, H., Y.HOSAKA, H.YAMAGISHI and Y.NISHI: Electron microscopic studies on Φ80 and Φ80pt phage virions and their DNA. Biken's J. 9 (1966) 135.

SIMPSON, R.W. and R.E.HARPER: Structural components of vesicular stomatitis virus. Virology 29 (1966) 654.

SIMPSON, R.W. and R.E.HAUSER: Basic structure of group A arbovirus strains Muddelburg, Sindbis and Semliki forest examined by negative staining. Virology 34 (1968) 358.

SINSHEIMER, R.L.: Purification and properties of bacteriophage ΦX174. J. Mol. Biol. 1 (1959a) 37.

SINSHEIMER, R.L.: A single-stranded DNA from bacteriophage ΦX174. J. Mol. Biol. 1 (1959b) 43.

SINSHEIMER, R.L.: The nucleic acids of the bacterial viruses. In: E.Chargaff and J.N.Davidson, eds.: The nucleic acids, vol. 3. New York, Academic Press (1960) p. 187.

SMADEL, J.E., T.M.RIVERS and E.G.PICKELS: Estimation of the purity of preparations of elementary bodies of vaccinia. J. Exptl. Med. 70 (1939) 379.

SMITH, K.M.: The arthropod viruses. Advan. Virus Res. 9 (1962) 195.

STOECKENIUS, W.: Appendix. In: R.Weil and J.Vinograd, eds.: The cyclic helix and cyclic coil forms of polyoma viral DNA. Proc. Natl. Acad. Sci. 50 (1963) 737.

STOLLAR, V., T.M.STEVENS and R.W.SCHLESINGER: Studies on the nature of Dengue virus. Virology 30 (1966) 303.

STRAUSS, J.H. and R.L.SINSHEIMER: Purification and properties of bacteriophage MS2 of its ribonucleic acid. J. Mol. Biol. 7 (1963) 43.

STROHMAIER, K. and M.MUSSGAY: Density gradient centrifugation with infectious ribonucleic acid of foot and mouth disease virus. Science 130 (1959) 217.

SUGIYAMA, T.: TMV-like rods formed by 'mixed reconstitution' between MS2 RNA and TMV protein. Virology 28 (1966) 488.

SUMMERS, D.F., J.V.MAIZEL, JR. and J.E.DARNELL, JR.: The decrease in size and synthetic activity of poliovirus polysomes late in the infectious cycle. Virology 31 (1967) 427.

TESSMAN, E.S.: Complementation groups in phage S13. Virology 25 (1965) 303.

THOMAS, JR., C.A.: The arrangement of information in DNA molecules. J. Gen. Physiol. 49 (1966) no. 6, part 2, 143.

THOMAS, JR., C.A.: The rule of the ring. J. Cellular Comp. Physiol. 70 (1967) suppl. 1, 13.

THOMAS, JR., C.A. and L.A.MACHATTIE: Circular T2 DNA molecules. Proc. Natl. Acad. Sci. 52 (1964) 1297.

THOMAS, JR., C.A. and L.A.MACHATTIE: The anatomy of viral DNA molecules. Ann. Rev. Biochem. 36 (1967) 485.

THOMAS, R.S.: The chemical composition and particle weight of Tipula iridescent virus. Virology 14 (1961) 240.

TOMIZAWA, J.I. and T.OGAWA: Replication of phage lambda DNA. Cold Spring Harbor Symp. Quant. Biol. 33 (1968, in press).

VASQUEZ, C., N.GRANBOULAN and R.M.FRANKLIN: Structure of the RNA bacteriophage R17. J. Bacteriol. 92 (1966) 1779.

VASQUEZ, C. and A.K.KLEINSCHMIDT: Electron microscopy of RNA strands from individual reovirus particles. J. Mol. Biol. 34 (1968) 137.

VASQUEZ, C., A.K.KLEINSCHMIDT and C.BASILICO: Electron microscopic studies of polyoma DNA released in protein monolayers. (Submitted).

VASQUEZ, C. and P.TOURNIER: The morphology of reovirus. Virology 17 (1962) 503.

VASQUEZ, C. and P.TOURNIER: New interpretation of the reovirus structure. Virology 24 (1964) 128.

VINOGRAD, J., J.LEBOWITZ, R.RADLOFF, R.WATSON and P.LAIPIS: The twisted circular form of polyoma viral DNA. Proc. Natl. Acad. Sci. 53 (1965) 1104.

VINOGRAD, J., J.LEBOWITZ and R.WATSON: Early and late helix-coil transitions in closed circular DNA. The number of superhelical turns in polyoma DNA. J. Mol. Biol. 33 (1968) 173.

WATERSON, A.P.: The morphology and composition of Newcastle disease virus. In: R.P.Hanson, ed.: Newcastle disease virus: an evolving pathogen. Madison, Wisconsin University Press (1963) p. 119.

WATERSON, A.P. and J.G.CRUIKSHANK: Form of the nucleoprotein component as a taxonomic criterion for the myxoviruses. Nature 201 (1964) 640.

WATSON, J.D. and F.H.C.CRICK: A study of deoxyribose nucleic acid. Nature 171 (1953) 737.

WECKER, E.: Eigenschaften einer infektiösen Nucleinsäure-fraktion aus Hühnerembryonen, die Encephalitis-virus infiziert wurden. Z. Naturforsch. 14b (1959) 370.

WEISSBACH, A., P.BARTL and L.A.SALZMAN: The structure of replicative DNA – electron microscopic studies. Cold Spring Harbor Symp. Quant. Biol. 33 (1968) 525.

WEISSMANN, C. and S.OCHOA: Replication of bacteriophage RNA. Progr. Nucl. Acid Res. Mol. Biol. 6 (1967) 353.

WESTMORELAND, B.C., W.SZYBALSKI and H.RIS: Mapping of the deletions and substitutions in heteroduplex DNA molecules of coliphage λ by electron microscopy. Science (submitted).

WINOCOUR, E.: Purification of polyoma virus. Virology 19 (1963) 158.

WILCOX, W.C., H.S.GINSBERG and T.F.ANDERSON: Structure of type 5 adenovirus II. J. Exptl. Med. 118 (1963) 307.

WILDY, P., M.G.P.STOKER, I.A.MACPHERSON and R.W.HORNE: The fine structure of polyoma virus. Virology 11 (1960a) 444.

WILDY, P., W.C.RUSSELL and R.W.HORNE: The morphology of herpes virus. Virology 12 (1960b) 204.

WILLIAMS, M.G., A.K.HOWATSON and J.D.ALMEIDA: Morphological characterization of the virus of the human common wart (*Veruga vulgaris*). Nature 189 (1961) 895.

WILLIAMS, R.C. and D.FRASER: Morphology of the seven T bacteriophages . J. Bacteriol. 66 (1956) 458.

WILLIAMS, R.C. and K.M.SMITH: The polyhedral form of the Tipula iridescent virus. Biochim. Biophys. Acta 28 (1958) 464.

WOLSTENHOLME, D.R. and L.E.BOCKSTAHLER: Electron microscopy of double-stranded RNA induced by TYMV and TMV. Molec. Gen. Genetics 100 (1967) 349.

YAMAGISHI, H., F. HOSHIZAKO and K. SATO: Characteristics of DNA molecules extracted from bacteriophages Φ80 and Φ80pt. Virology 30 (1966) 29.

ZINDER, N. D.: Properties of a bacteriophage containing RNA. In: M. Pollard, ed.: Perspectives in virology, vol. 3. New York, Harper Row (1963) p. 58.

ZINDER, N. D., R. C. VALENTINE, M. ROGER and W. STOECKENIUS: f1, a rod-shaped male-genetic bacteriophage that contains DNA. Virology 20 (1963) 638.

ZOBEL, C. R. and M. BEER: The use of heavy metal salts as electron stains. Intern. Rev. Cytol. 18 (1965) 363.

CHAPTER 7

Chromosomes of bacteria

LUCIEN G. CARO

Biology Division, Oak Ridge National Laboratory,
*Oak Ridge, Tennessee**

Contents

1. Introduction

2. The bacterial nucleus
   (a) Light-microscope studies
   (b) Electron-microscope studies

3. The bacterial chromosome
   (a) Nature and morphology of the bacterial chromosome
   (b) Genetic composition of the nuclear material
   (c) Interactions between genetic elements
   (d) Transfer of genetic information

4. Replication of the bacterial chromosome
   (a) General properties of chromosome replication in bacteria
   (b) Control of replication
   (c) Origin of replication
   (d) Segregation of genetic material

5. Conclusions

* Operated by Union Carbide Corporation for the United States Atomic Energy Commission under contract No. W-7405-eng-26.

1. *Introduction*

The bacterial chromosome has been studied more extensively than any other and is the source of much of our information on the structure and mode of replication of the genetic material, on the control and the mechanism of gene expression, and on the exchange of genetic material occurring in recombination.

In this chapter we shall examine some of the properties of the bacterial chromosome. We shall first consider briefly the cytology of the bacterial nucleus. We shall then discuss the structure of the bacterial chromosome, its genetic composition, its interaction with other genetic elements, and the various ways in which genetic information can be transferred from one cell to another. We shall, finally, examine the self-replication property of the chromosome, the control and the mechanism of this replication, and the segregation of the replication products at cell division. We shall ignore the study of gene expression which will be treated in subsequent chapters.

2. *The bacterial nucleus*

(a) *Light-microscope studies*

The nature and, indeed, the existence of the bacterial nucleus were for a long time controversial subjects. The controversy was finally settled when it was recognized that the large amount of RNA contained in bacterial cells complicates the interpretation of staining procedures specific for nucleic acids. In the 1940's, suitable staining procedures were developed: after hydrolysis of the RNA with HCl, basic dyes (e.g. Giemsa stain) reveal deeply staining bodies of a variety of shapes and dimensions located along a central axis in rod-shaped cells (Fig. 1) (Robinow; Murray). Each cell contains two to four or more such 'chromatin bodies'. Their shape and disposition are strongly influenced by physiological conditions, the stage in the life cycle of the cell, and the methods of fixation and staining used. By placing living cells in a medium of high refractive index (gelatin solution), light bodies that are similar in appearance and in location to the chromatin bodies can be seen with the phase-contrast microscope (Mason and Powelson). They increase in size in parallel with cell growth, divide, and are segregated between the daughter cells. It is well-established that these clear structures correspond to the chromatin bodies. The evidence for this came mostly from electron microscopy.

(b) *Electron-microscope studies*

Early electron micrographs of thin sections of bacteria revealed, in the center of the cell, clear, irregularly shaped regions containing either clumps of dense material or a network of fibrillar substance more or less aggregated. It was soon recognized that

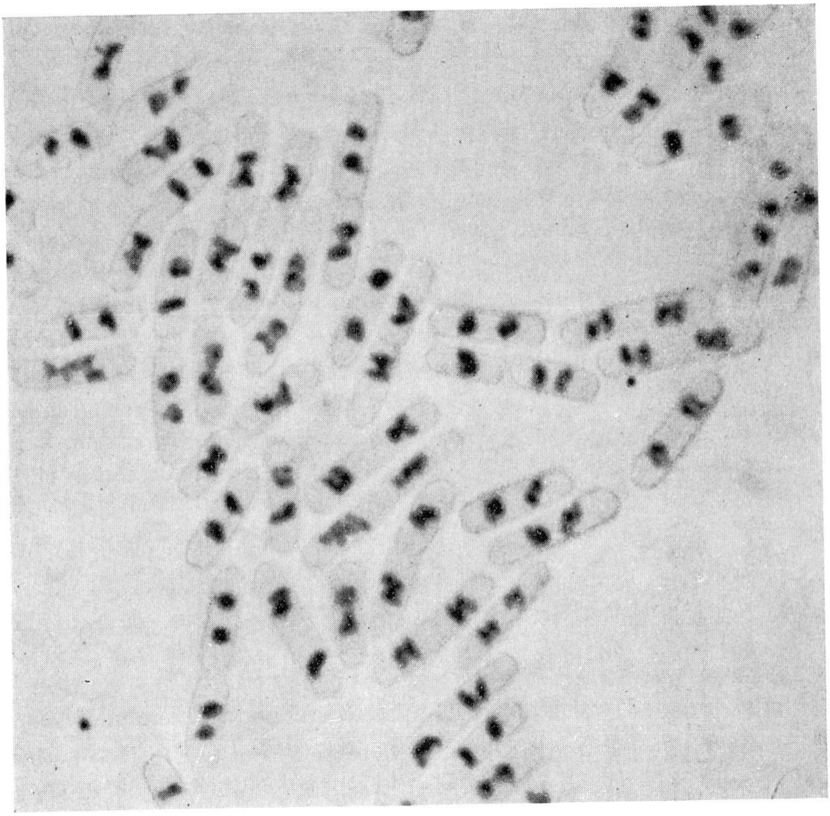

Fig. 1. Light micrograph of *Bacillus cereus*. Fixed in osmium tetroxide vapors. Ten minutes before fixation the cells were placed in medium containing 3 % NaCl, thus causing a more compact geometry of the nuclear material. Feulgen strain; × 4500. (Courtesy Dr. C. Robinow.)

these morphological variations were due to fixation and embedding differences. The fixation procedure now commonly accepted as giving the most accurate picture of the cell is that developed by Ryter and Kellenberger. Schreil demonstrated that this fixation gels a solution of DNA and preserves its fine fibrillar structure, whereas other fixations do not. It seems likely, therefore, that this fixation is the best one for nuclear material.

In *Escherichia coli*, the nuclear material appears as a network of very fine fibrils, as thin as 20 Å with no sign of organization (Fig. 2). In *Bacillus subtilis* or in *B. megaterium*, the fibers are packed more closely (Fig. 3) and may show some evidence of a periodic arrangement (Giesbrecht). The significance of this type of organization is not clear. It does not seem to be a feature essential for chromosomal segregation or expression since many bacteria do not show it. No other obvious structural element is present in the nuclear region: the fibrils seem simply imbedded in a very light-density matrix.

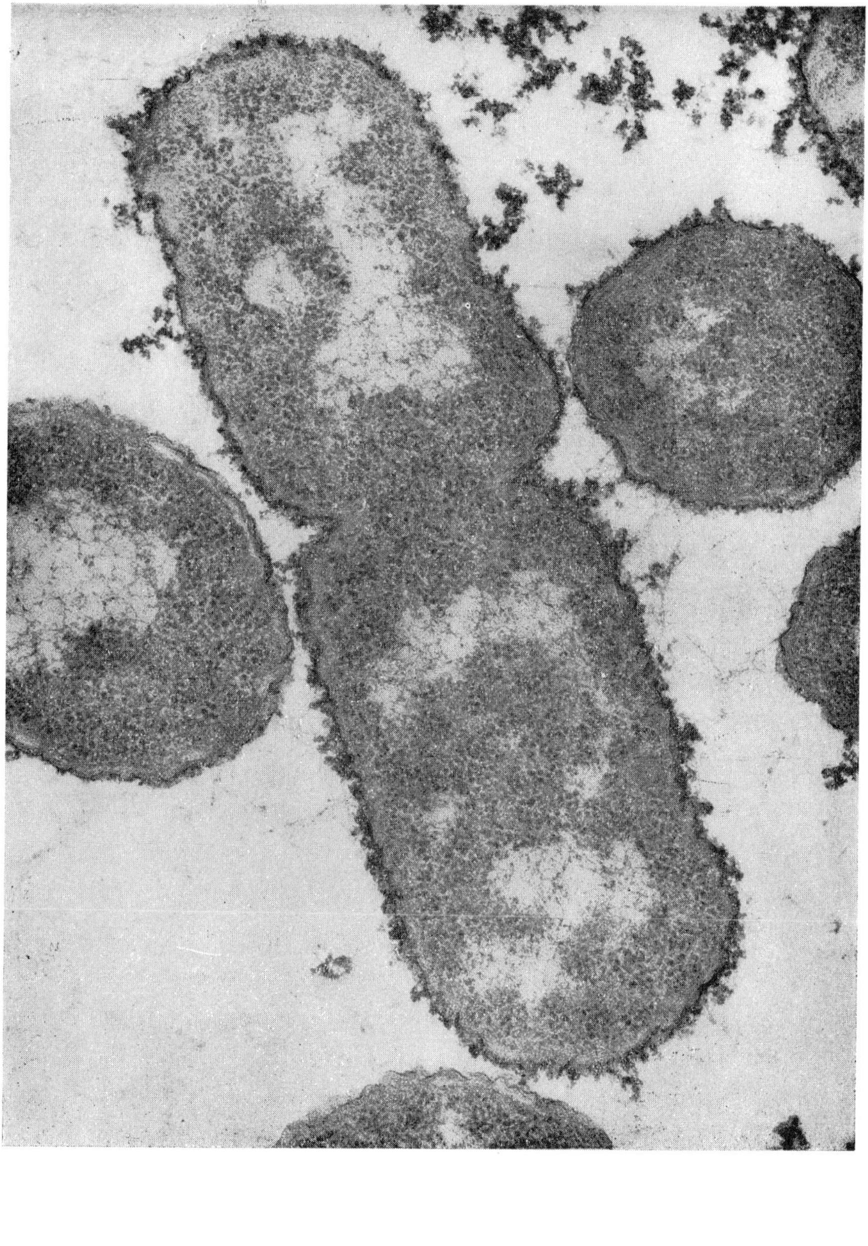

Fig. 2. *Escherichia coli* K12. Electron micrograph of a thin section. Fixed according to Ryter–Kellenberger procedure; embedded in Epon; stained with uranyl acetate followed by lead citrate. The dense material outside the cell is precipitated during fixation. Note the finely stranded nuclear material in direct contact with the ribosomes which comprise most of the cytoplasm; × 53,000.

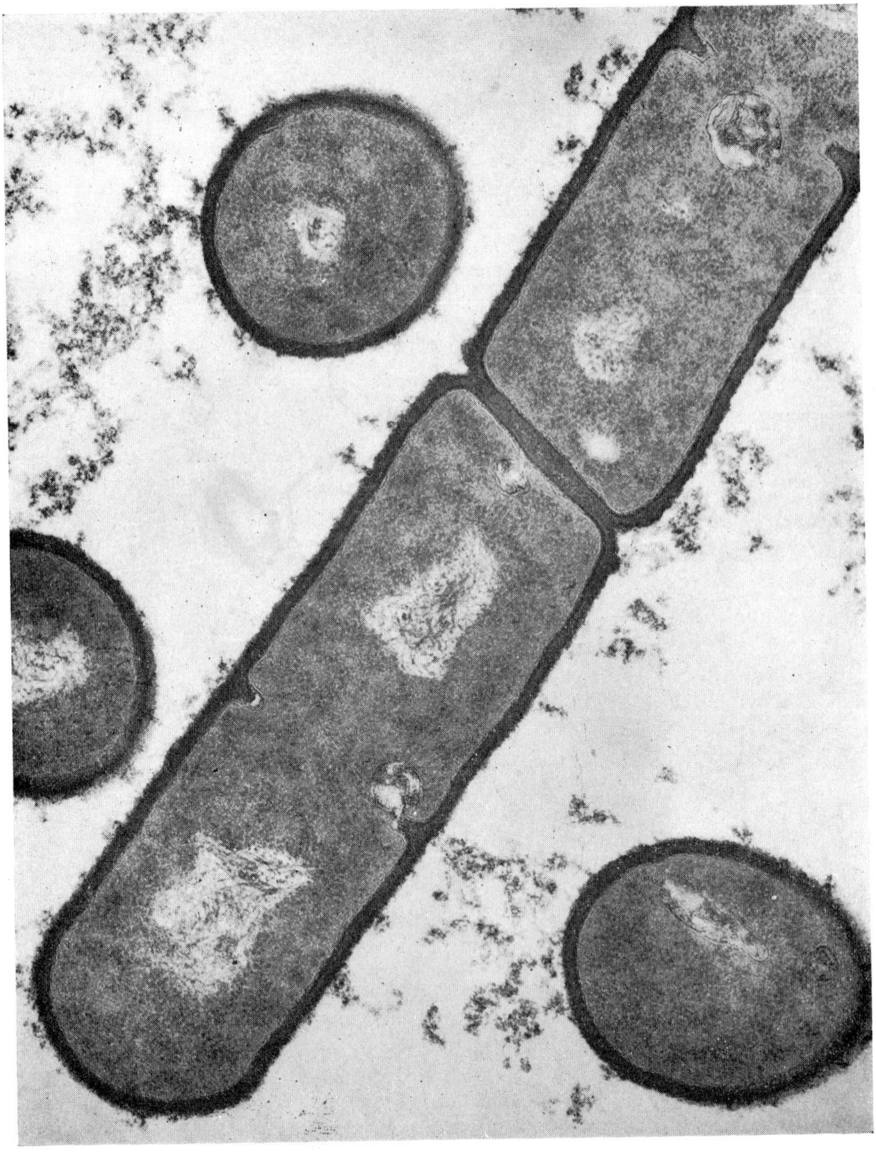

Fig. 3. *Bacillus subtilis* W168. Fixation and embedding as in Fig. 2. Note compactness of nuclear region with some evidence of organization of the DNA. Invaginations of the cell membrane (mesosomes) can be seen at various points with a particular prominent one associated with the formation of a septum; × 48,000.

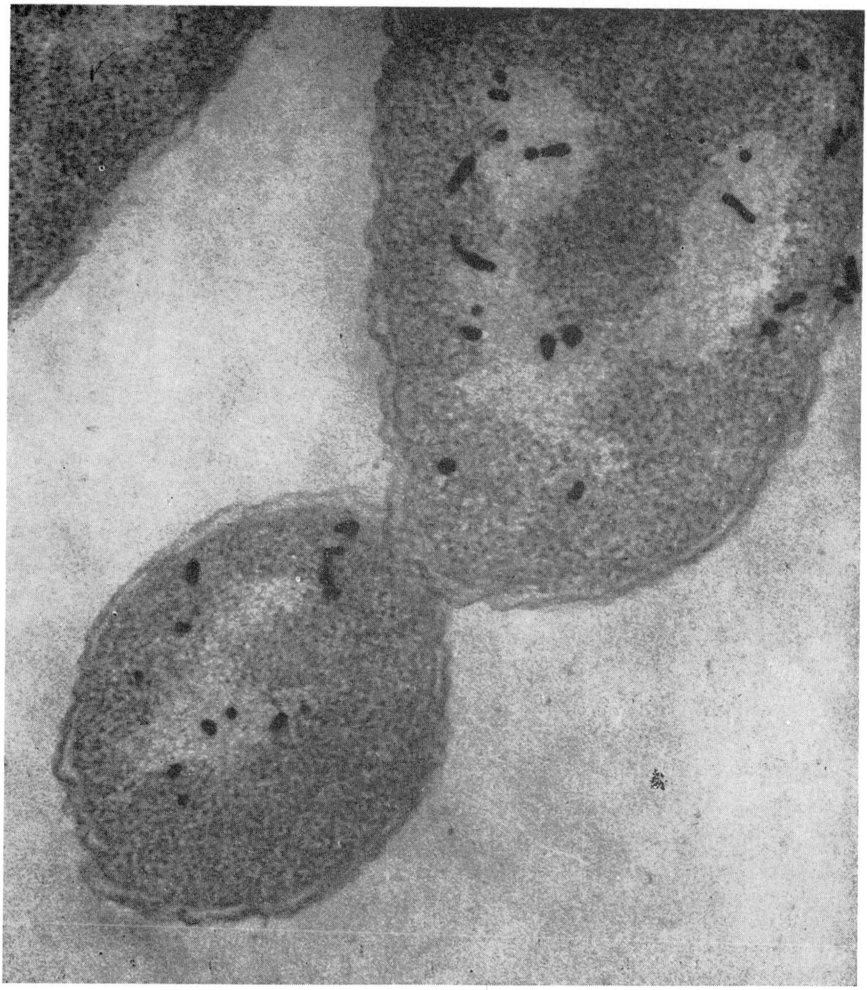

Fig. 4. Electron-microscopic autoradiograph of mating bacteria. The Hfr cell (large cell at top of picture) was labeled, previous to mating, with H^3-thymine. The F^- cell (small cell at bottom) was unlabeled, and mating took place in cold medium. The autoradiographic grains indicate the presence of labeled DNA in the nucleus of the Hfr and its transfer to the nucleus of the F^-; × 72,000.

The central clear regions of the bacterial cell were commonly identified, mostly on circumstantial evidence, as containing the chromatin (Chapman and Hillier; Maaløe and Birch-Andersen; Ryter and Kellenberger; Murray). We used autoradiographs of thin sections of bacteria labeled with H^3-thymidine to show that these regions contain most or all of the cell's DNA (Caro et al.; Caro 1961). Later on we developed techniques for the direct examination of autoradiographs in the electron microscope which gave an even clearer demonstration of this (Fig. 4) (Caro 1962; Caro and Van Tubergen). It is thus clear that the central clear regions contain the bacterial DNA.

The nuclear region is not bounded by any membrane, the nuclear material coming into direct contact with the cytoplasm. The outline is very irregular especially in *E. coli*. The shape and disposition in the cell of the nuclear region depend upon the physiological state of the cell. In cells growing in the presence of 2% NaCl, for example, the nuclear region becomes more compact, with regular outlines (Kellenberger et al.). In presence of the antibiotic aureomycin, the nuclear region becomes spherical with a dense core of cytoplasmic material at the center (Kellenberger 1960). A very similar picture is obtained with treatment with chloramphenicol (Kellenberger et al.). Phage infection with the virulent bacteriophage T2, which causes a general breakdown of the cell's DNA, results in a fragmentation of the nuclear region with small pools of nuclear material dispersed throughout the cytoplasm (Kellenberger 1962). A temperate phage, such as λ, which does not break down the cell's DNA, has no visible effect on the nuclear region.

The nuclear region could be considered as a gel of DNA, with little other material present. The stability of the gel can be impaired by a variety of agents. The forces which hold this mass of DNA in place are completely unknown. They exert their influence on exogenous DNA as well. Thus, after infection with λ phages labeled with H^3-thymidine, the label appears immediately in the nucleus of the cell (unpublished observations). Similarly, in conjugation, the donor cell's DNA entering the recipient cell is found immediately in the nuclear region of that cell (Fig. 4). It would seem therefore that DNA is kept condensed in the nuclear region by nonspecific forces which can be applied to exogenous as well as endogenous DNA.

The physiological activities of the nuclear region are not known in detail. Newly replicated DNA appears in the entire nucleus (Caro 1961; unpublished observations), but the actual replication point could well be located on the membrane or some extension of the membrane as suggested by some recent observations (Ganesan and Lederberg). Autoradiography has shown (Caro and Forro; Franklin and Granboulan) that RNA is synthesized in a region in or near the nucleus and is subsequently transferred to the cytoplasm. It seems likely, therefore, that the RNA polymerase activity takes place either in the nuclear region or on its periphery at the interface with the cytoplasm.

There is no evidence in bacteria for a mitotic apparatus such as is found in higher cells. But this does not rule out the possibility, as we shall discuss later, that bacteria have a primitive form of the mitotic apparatus.

3. *The bacterial chromosome*

(a) *Nature and morphology of the bacterial chromosome*

Most of our knowledge of the structure of the bacterial chromosome came, until recently, from the studies of Cairns (1963a, b). He labeled the DNA of *E. coli* K12 with

H^3-thymidine, lysed the cells gently with lysozyme and drained the lysate on a membrane filter. The filter was autoradiographed. The resulting photographic grain patterns showed that the chromosome is a single linear structure, 1100 μ long, forming a ring with, usually, a replicated portion comprised between two forks: one, presumably, the origin of replication, the other, the growing point (Fig. 5). These observations of Cairns have been confirmed by Bleecken et al.

Stronger evidence on the nature of the bacterial chromosome was provided by Bode and Morowitz who examined by electron microscopy the chromosome of *Mycoplasma hominis* which has the useful property of being unusually short. They found it to be a ring of DNA, approximately 265 μ long with a single replicating point. The isolated chromosome had been treated with pronase, a strong proteolytic enzyme. Since the structure was kept whole, it is likely that there are no protein 'linkers' and that the bacterial chromosome is a single DNA molecule.

(b) *Genetic composition of the nuclear material*

In the simplest case, all the genes of *E. coli* K12 form a single linkage group or chromosome. In conjugation, genetic markers can be transferred and integrated into the chromosome of a recipient cell. Genetic analysis has shown that the chromosome of *E. coli* K12 Hfr cells is circular (Jacob and Wollman). The genetic and the physical studies of the chromosome are therefore in agreement.

Certain classes of genetic markers can exist outside the chromosome. Typical of one of these classes is the sex factor F. It is constituted entirely or primarily of DNA (Driskell-Zamenhof), and it is presumed to have a circular structure. The presence or absence of F determines three main mating types in *E. coli* K12 and closely related bacteria: F^-, F^+, and Hfr. F^- cells lack F entirely and can only act as recipients in matings with donor cells. In F^+ cells the sex factor is established in the cell, replicating at the same rate as the chromosome, but not as part of it. F^+ cells transfer the sex factor F to recipient cells but transfer chromosomal markers with extremely low efficiency. F can become integrated into the chromosome, giving rise to an Hfr cell. An Hfr cell transfers chromosomal markers with high efficiency. It can transfer its entire chromosome, starting from the point at which F had become integrated but with the sex factor itself being transferred after all the chromosomal markers. (See reviews by Gross; Hayes; Jacob and Wollman.)

Other autonomous genetic elements such as the drug resistance transfer factors (Watanabe) or certain colicinogenic factors (Kahn and Helinski; Monk and Clowes) share with F the property of self-transfer and of low-frequency chromosomal transfer but they do not seem to integrate stably into the chromosome and do not produce Hfr cells.

Other genetic elements have very different properties but share with F the ability to replicate either independently of or integrated into the chromosome. Such an element, for example, is the bacteriophage λ. Upon entering a sensitive cell, the DNA of λ

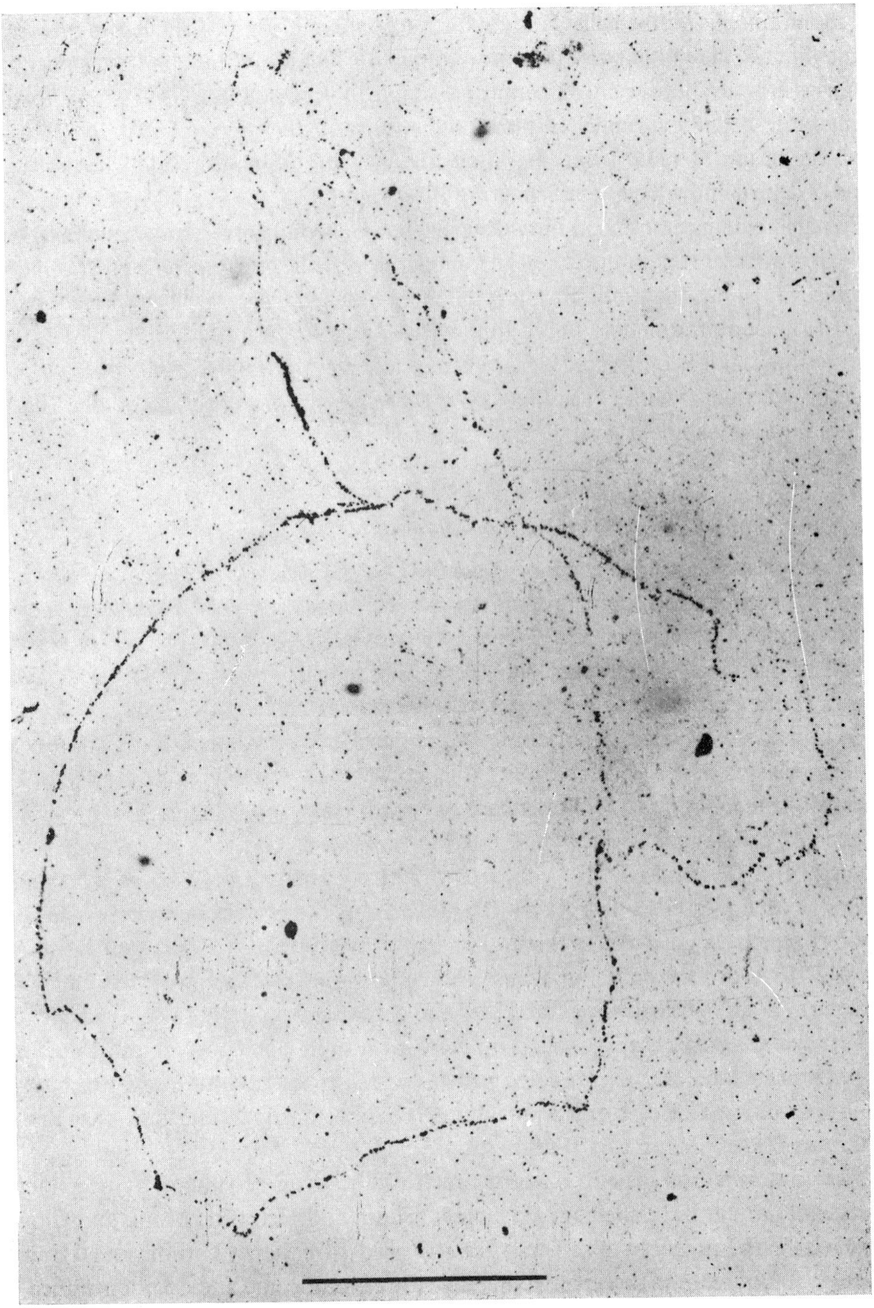

Fig. 5. Autoradiograph of the chromosome of *Escherichia coli* K12 Hfr, labeled with tritiated thymidine for two generations and extracted with lysozyme. Scale = 100 μ (From Cairns 1963b, by courtesy of Dr. J. Cairns).

can either replicate itself, in an uncontrolled manner, resulting in the production of a large number of phages and the death of the cell, or it can become integrated into the continuity of the chromosome and replicate with it. Such genetic elements which can either have an autonomous existence within the cell or as components of the bacterial chromosome have been called episomes by Jacob and Wollman.

(c) *Interactions between genetic elements*

The genetic interactions between chromosome and episomes are best explained by assuming that both are circular (Campbell). An episome, according to Campbell's model, becomes integrated into the bacterial chromosome by a single reciprocal crossover. It can be excised, and become autonomous again, by another such crossover. A good example of this is the formation of F′ factors.

An F′ factor is an episome which carries, in addition to the sex factor F, a fragment of the chromosome. It arises, as illustrated in Fig. 6a, by a single reciprocal exchange within an Hfr chromosome. Presumably because of the presence on the fragment of the sex factor F, it is capable of autonomous replication. Since there is not genetic homology between the F′ factor and the rest of the chromosome, there is no tendency for pairing and exchange, and the two genetic units are perfectly stable (Scaife and Pekhov; Berg and Curtiss). The net result is that the genome, while remaining haploid, is divided into two smaller chromosomes.

Such an F′ factor can be introduced, by conjugation, with high efficiency, into an F^- cell, where it can establish itself and replicate autonomously. Such a situation is usually unstable: there is diploidy for the markers present on the F′, and frequent pairing and crossing-over occur between them and their homologs on the chromosome.

Pairing, resulting in reciprocal crossing-over, between two nonhomologous portions of the chromosome can occur in two ways, depending on the relative orientation of the two segments involved. In an Hfr cell, one way results, as we have seen, in the formation of an F′ factor, leaving a corresponding deletion on the chromosome. The other results in an inversion of the portion of the chromosome between the two pairing segments (Berg and Curtiss) (Fig. 6b).

(d) *Transfer of genetic information*

There are three principal manners in which some of the genetic information in the chromosome can be transferred to a suitable recipient cell. One is conjugation, already described. Another is transduction, in which a fragment of the bacterial genome is packed up into the head of a bacteriophage and transferred to a recipient cell by the same mechanism as the injection of phage DNA. Some temperate phages (i.e., phages capable of intergrating stably into the chromosome thus giving rise to a lysogenic cell) give a specific kind of transduction. The temperate phage λ, for example, integrates very close to the *gal* markers which code for the enzymes used in the utilization of

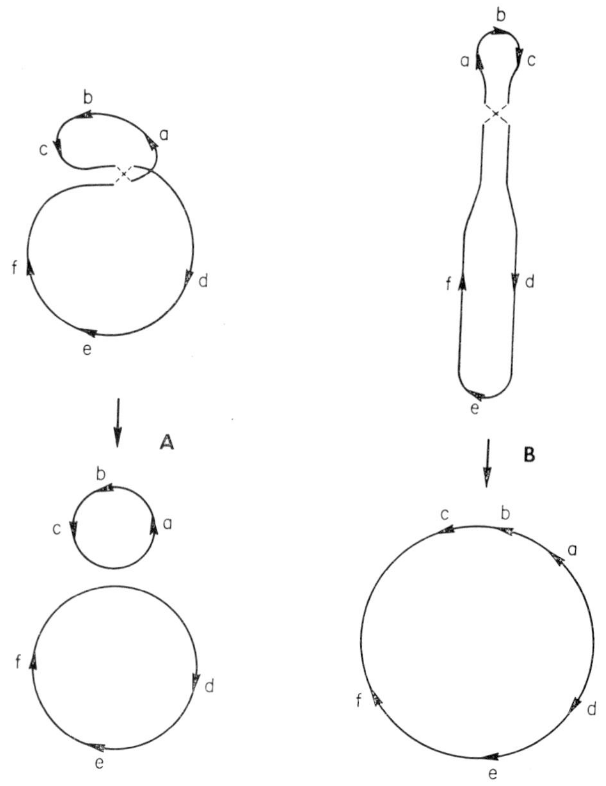

Fig. 6. Reciprocal exchange within a ring chromosome. (A) Formation of two rings by pairing, in one direction, of two segments of the chromosome followed by breakage and exchange. If this occurs in an Hfr cell, and if the two rings produced are capable of autonomous replication, the events described in the diagram will result in the formation of an F′ factor. (B) Formation of an inversion of part of the chromosome by pairing in the opposite direction. (From Berg and Curtiss, by courtesy of Dr. Berg and the editors of Genetics).

galactose. When λ is induced, the single crossing-over which removes it from the chromosome takes place occasionally in such a way that instead of a complete λ genome what comes out is a fragment of the λ genome plus the *gal* genes. Such a defective phage, named λdg, transduces only the *gal* character (see Jacob and Wollman for review). Conversely the phage P1 is capable of generalized transduction, that is to say it can transfer any genetic marker present on the chromosome or on an episome. In transducing particles of P1, the only DNA present is that of the bacterium (Ikeda and Tomizawa).

The third way of transferring genetic information is by transformation. It is the most direct way since genetic markers are introduced into a recipient cell in the form of free DNA molecules (Avery et al.). This has been a great advantage in that it is possible to study directly the biological effect of various physical treatments applied to DNA. The effects of heat, ionizing radiations, ultraviolet light, shear degradation, various chemicals and mutagenic agents, and enzymes have been thus studied (Schaeffer).

Transformation, transduction, and conjugation have been used extensively to study the genetic composition of the bacterial chromosome. Unfortunately, it is not possible to use all three on any one strain. Thus, conjugation and transduction have been found in *E. coli*, but transformation (except for very special cases such as that of λ bacteriophage DNA) has not; whereas in *B. subtilis* transformation and transduction, but not conjugation, have been demonstrated.

4. *Replication of the bacterial chromosome*

(a) *General properties of chromosome replication in bacteria*

The autoradiographs of Cairns (1963a, b) (Fig. 5) and of Bleecken et al. indicate that in *E. coli* growing with glucose as a carbon source replication takes place at only one growing point, without opening of the circular chromosome, and results in the formation of two complete rings held together at one point. Separation produces two circular daughter chromosomes. Other lines of evidence have confirmed the existence of a single growing point for *E. coli* (Bonhoeffer and Gierer), *B. subtilis* (Yoshikawa and Sueoka) and *Mycoplasma hominis* (Bode and Morowitz). In glucose medium, replication of the chromosome goes on during all of the generation time (Schaechter et al.). The rate at which the growing point describes the chromosome is the same for all cells in a culture, as evidenced by the length of DNA labeled by a very short pulse of H^3-thymidine (Cairns 1963a).

There seem to be three ways in which the cell can regulate chromosome replication: number of growing points, length of the interval between two rounds of replication, and rate of displacement of growing point. We have discussed so far the case of cells growing in a simple salts medium with glucose as a carbon source. In *B. subtilis* cultures that are growing rapidly in a very rich medium (Pennassay broth), Oishi and co-workers have found that a new round of replication starts at the origin before the end of the previous round, with the result that during approximately one half of the generation time a chromosome has three growing points (Fig. 7a). Thus, the number of growing points acts as a regulatory mechanism to speed up chromosome replication. Conversely, when cells are grown in poorly utilized carbon sources such as succinate, aspartate, acetate or proline, with very long generation times, the required slowing down of chromosome replication is obtained both by increasing the interval between two rounds of replication and by decreasing the rate of displacement of the growing point (K. G. Lark and C. Lark; C. Lark 1966; Helmstetter).

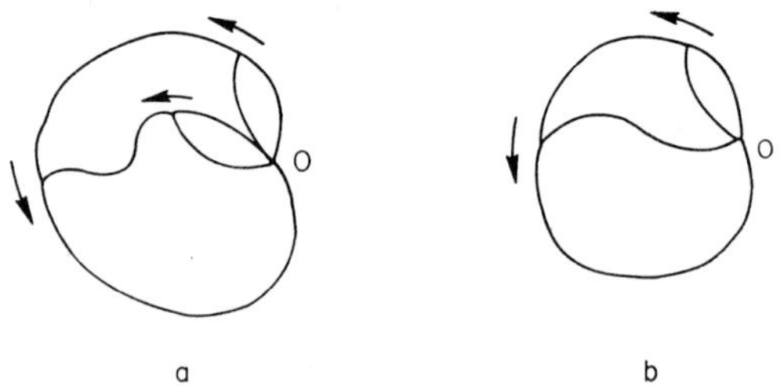

Fig. 7. Postulated chromosome configuration in special cases of replication. (a) Premature initiation from the origin on both branches of a partially replicated chromosome, occuring in fast growing cells of *Bacillus subtilis* (dichotomous replication, after Oishi et al.). (b) Premature initiation on one branch only occurring after a period of thymine starvation (after K.G. Lark and Bird 1965a). 0 is the origin of replication; arrows indicate position and direction of displacement of growing points.

(b) *Control of replication*

Many of the known facts concerning the control of chromosome replication in *E. coli* come from the works of Maaløe and his co-workers (Maaløe and Kjeldgaard) and of Lark and his group (K. Lark 1966). It seems clear, from their results, that chromosome replication can take place to a limited extent in the absence of protein and RNA synthesis. Under these conditions the replication does, however, eventually come to a stop. If the possibility of synthesizing proteins is restored to the cell a new round of DNA replication becomes possible. K.G. Lark's results (1966) show that the region of the chromosome where this reinitiation takes place remains the same for at least six generations.

Jacob and Brenner proposed a model which accounts for most of the known facts about replication (Jacob et al. 1963). They call each unit of DNA (chromosome, episomes, nonintegrated phage, etc.) capable of autonomous replication a 'replicon'. They propose that each replicon contains (1) a structural gene coding for the synthesis of an 'initiator', and (2) a site, the 'replicator', specifically recognized by the initiator. The interaction of the initiator and the replicator triggers a round of DNA replication. Each replicon being a circular structure, the completion of this round of replication brings the growing point back to the replicator. The production of a new molecule of initiator is needed to start replication again.

Thus, the protein essential to the initiation of a new round of DNA replication, and which cannot be synthesized during starvation for an essential amino acid (Hanawalt et al.; Maaløe and Kieldgaard) may be the Jacob and Brenner initiator.

The regulation of initiation of chromosome or episome replication is clearly under genetic control since it has been possible to isolate mutations affecting it. There are, for example, temperate phages unable to multiply in the autonomous state but which can multiply as prophages (Jacob et al. 1957). It is presumed that in the second case the phage genome having become part of the chromosomal replication is replicated with it. There are also temperature-sensitive mutations affecting the F episome

(Cuzin and Jacob 1967a) or the bacterial chromosome (Kohiyama et al.).

In either case the affected replicon replicates normally at low temperature but stops replication at high temperature. In the case of a temperature-sensitive F factor, the inability to replicate is corrected by the introduction in the cell of a wild-type episome. It seems, therefore, that a diffusible gene product of the wild-type episome can initiate replication of the mutant episome (Cuzin and Jacob 1967a).

We have already seen that initiation can occur before the completion of the previous round of replication if the cells are growing in very rich medium. Another type of premature initiation has been described by Pritchard and Lark. They found that if thymine is restored to thymine-requiring cells, after a period of starvation, chromosome replication resumes not only at the position of the growing point, but also in a new location. Further experiments showed that a new round of replication, involving only one of the two partially replicated daughter chromosomes, was started at the point of 'origin' of replication defined by amino acid starvation (Pritchard and Lark; Lark and Bird 1965a; Fig. 7b).

(c) *Origin of replication*

The classical experiment of Meselson and Stahl indicated that for most cells in a culture a new round of replication starts at the point where the previous round had terminated. The work of Lark and his co-workers (K. G. Lark 1966) showed that the point of reinitiation of DNA synthesis following amino acid starvation, remains the same for the progeny of each cell for at least six generations. These experiments did not, however, demonstrate either that the origin of replication is completely stable, or that it is the same for all cells in a culture.

The replicon model of Jacob and Brenner (1963) postulates a fixed genetic site, the replicator, for the origin. On the other hand, Nagata (1963) proposed a model according to which the origin is variable in F^- cells, while it is located at the site of integration of the F factor in Hfr cells. A number of experiments, mostly unpublished, have been performed to differentiate between the two models and to map the genetic site of the origin of chromosome replication.

Using transduction with P1 as the analytical tool, we (Berg and Caro), have measured gene frequencies in isogenic Hfr strains in order to evaluate the influence of the integrated F factor on the origin and direction of chromosome replication. No significant difference in transduced gene frequency was found, and we concluded that the integrated F factor does not normally affect chromosome replication.

Further experiments on the same strains showed (Caro and Berg, in preparation) that during amino acid starvation chromosome replication stops in a region of the chromosome located between the tryptophan and $adenine_3$ markers and starts again in the same region when the essential amino acid is restored. The replication proceeds in a counterclockwise direction. Further evidence indicated that the stopping and reinitiation point is the true origin of replication.

In a different series of strains, however, the origin seems to be located in a diametrically opposite position, and the direction of replication is clockwise.

From this and from work from several other laboratories, it would appear that there is a fixed genetic site for the origin of replication (replicator). This site is stable but is strain-specific.

(d) *Segregation of genetic material*

The autoradiographic studies of Forro and Wertheimer, of Forro, of Van Tubergen and Setlow, and of Lark and Bird (1965b) interpreted in the light of our knowledge of the nature of the bacterial chromosome, show that chromosome segregation in *E. coli* is accomplished by a mechanism fully as precise as that of higher organisms. Under the usual conditions of cells growing in a minimal glucose medium, each cell contains one to two replicating chromosomes. They are segregated at division into each of the two daughter cells and, at the next division, each of the products of the replication is similarly separated.

Recent evidence obtained by Forro, by Clark and Maaløe, and by Helmstetter indicates that the completion of a round of replication and the initiation of a new round take place, not at the end and beginning of the cell's division cycle, but nearer to the middle of that cycle. From all the evidence available, the number and state of the chromosomes at various times in the life cycle of a cell are as shown in Fig. 8.

Cuzin and Jacob (1967b) have studied the segregation of an episome F-lac during cell division. They discovered that a DNA strand of the episome segregates for several generations with the corresponding chromosomal strand (that is to say the chromoso-

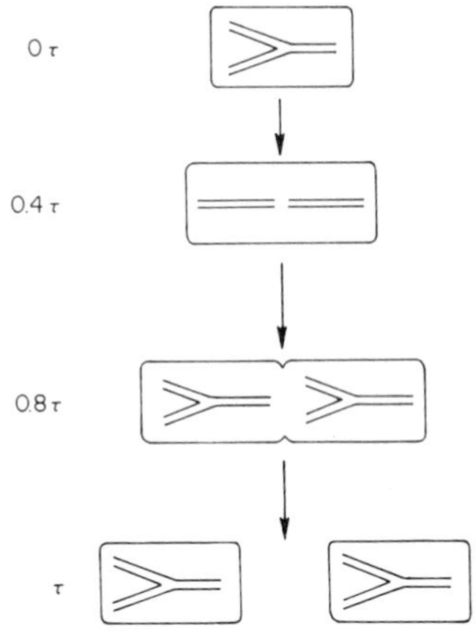

Fig. 8. Diagrammatic representation of chromosome configuration at various times during the cell division cycle, valid for *Escherichia coli* grown in glucose minimal medium. For convenience the chromosomes are represented as linear structures rather than rings. τ is generation time.

mal DNA strand synthesized during the same replication cycle). They conclude that when the genome of a cell is formed of several replicons that all the replicons are part of a single unit of transmission.

Jacob et al. (1963) have proposed that the replicons are attached to the cell membrane. Growth of the cell membrane between two newly replicated units would provide a mechanism for their orderly separation and segregation. Morphological evidence for a link between the cell membrane and the nucleus has been found in *B. subtilis*. This link is provided by the mesosomes (Fig. 9; Ryter and Jacob 1964). In *E. coli*, connections between the nuclei and fine projections of the membranous system have also been demonstrated (Ryter and Jacob 1966). Not enough information is available to determine which part, if any, of the chromosome is attached to the membrane, or to evaluate the nature of this attachment. In view of the results of Ganesan and Lederberg the growing point seems a good candidate. Jacob et al. (1963) and K.G. Lark (1966) chose the replicator as point of attachment, mostly on theoretical grounds. Jacob et al. have postulated further that the replicator of the sex factor F, in either its autonomous or its integrated form, is also attached to the membrane at a site corresponding to that of effective sexual contacts with an F^- cell. Such a contact would, in their view, trigger a cycle of DNA replication different in nature and in

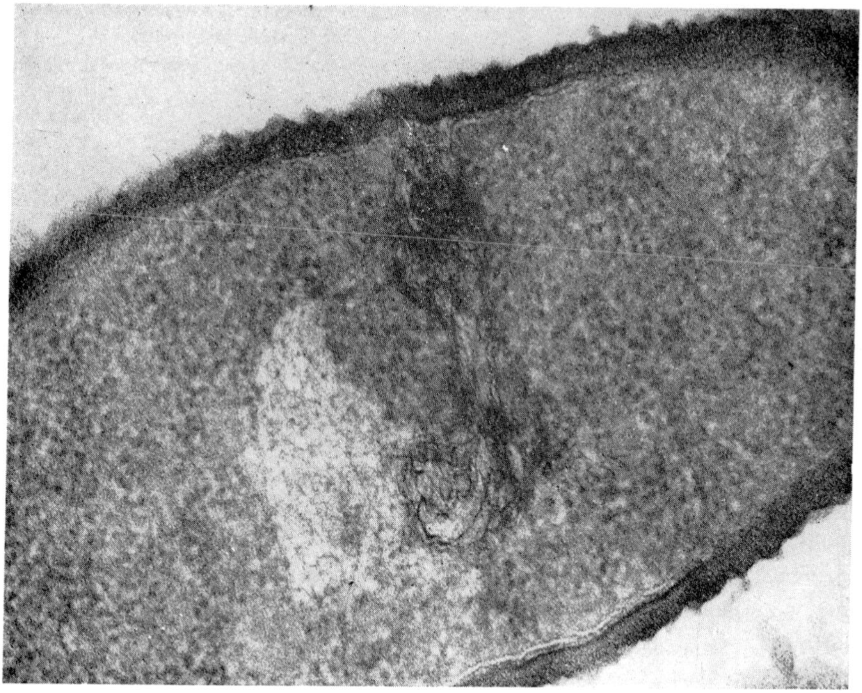

Fig. 9. *Bacillus subtilis* W128. Oblique section showing large mesosome uniting nuclear region to cell membrane; × 120,000.

regulation from the vegetative replication cycle. In the case of an Hfr cell, this replication would provide the driving mechanism for the transfer of one of the two replicas of the chromosome (Fig. 10). Autoradiographic experiments (Gross and Caro 1966) as well as several other lines of evidence, have supported this model (for review, see Gross and Caro 1965). It has not, however, been shown conclusively that the replication was *necessary* for transfer and it has not been proven that the enzyme system (DNA polymerase) involved belongs to the Hfr cell (Bonhoeffer).

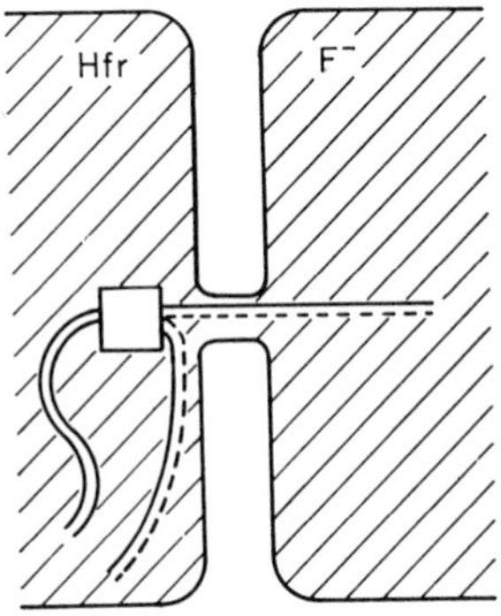

Fig. 10. Diagrammatic representation of the Jacob and Brenner model of DNA transfer in conjugation. The DNA replicates at the point of contact; one copy passes, as it is formed, into the female cell; replication provides the driving force for transfer.
——, DNA synthesized before the cells are mixed. ----, DNA synthesized after the cells are mixed.

5. *Conclusions*

We may summarize some of the information and reasonable speculations discussed in this chapter by outlining the properties of a 'typical' bacterial chromosome: It is a giant DNA molecule more than 1 mm long (200 times longer than the nucleus which contains it), covalently linked to form a ring. Its topological structure is not dependent on any protein. In a growing culture, it is most likely to be partially replicated. The fork at one end of the replicated region is at the origin, or replicator, a fixed genetic site. The fork at the other end is the growing point where a DNA polymerase produces, at a constant rate, two copies of the unreplicated portion of the chromosome. This growing point may be attached to the membrane and thus be a fixed point through which the chromosome passes during replication. The chromosome is attached to the membrane perhaps by its growing point, perhaps by its replicator, and perhaps by both. The completion of a round of replication results in the formation of two rings of DNA which begin replicating themselves almost without interruption. The growth of the membrane between the attachment sites of the rings separates the structures and ensures their orderly segregation into each of the two daughter cell divisions. Separate elements of the genome (episomes and chromosome) are segregated together, so that DNA strands made in the same cycle of replication remain associated with each other at each cell division. Each round of replication is triggered by the interaction with the replicator of a specific initiator protein.

Each replicating chromosome probably constitutes one nuclear region. There is no sign of organization within this nucleus which seems to be constituted by a pool of DNA held together in the central axis of the cell. Fragments of chromosome introduced into a suitable recipient cell by transformation, transduction, or conjugation are able to find their way to this nucleus rapidly to pair and to recombine with its chromosome with very high efficiency.

This picture of the bacterial chromosome is constructed from experiments done with a very small number of strains. Yet, evidence from new strains has not, so far, contradicted what we have learned from *E. coli* or *B. subtilis*. It seems, therefore, to be a general picture, applying with only small variations to most bacteria. Many details, some of which may affect drastically our present concepts, are still unknown, and it is likely that this simplified picture will be changed as our knowledge increases.

Acknowledgements

I am indebted to Mr. David P. Allison for excellent technical assistance and in particular for the preparation of some of the electron micrographs appearing in this chapter. I thank D. C. Robinow, Dr. J. Cairns and Dr. C. M. Berg for authorization to use some of their pictures, and Dr. R. Curtiss and Miss Jane Ann Mays for critical reading of the manuscript.

References

AVERY, O.T., C.M.MACLEOD and M.MCCARTY: Studies on the chemical nature of the substance inducing transformation of pneumococcal types. J. Exptl. Med. 79 (1944) 137.

BERG, C.M. and L.G.CARO: Chromosome replication in *Escherichia coli*. I. Lack of influence of integrated F factor. J. Mol. Biol. 29 (1967) 419.

BERG, C.M. and R.CURTISS III: Transposition derivatives of an Hfr strain of *Escherichia coli* K12. Genetics 56 (1967) 503.

BLEECKEN, S., G.STROHBACH and E.SARFERT: Autoradiography of bacterial chromosomes. Z. Allgem. Mikrobiol. 6 (1966) 121.

BODE, H.R. and H.J.MOROWITZ: Size and structure of the *Mycoplasma hominis* H39 chromosome. J. Mol. Biol. 23 (1967) 191.

BONHOEFFER, F.: DNA transfer and DNA synthesis during bacterial conjugation. Z. Vererbungslehre 98 (1966) 141.

BONHOEFFER, F. and A.GIERER: On the growth mechanism of the bacterial chromosome. J. Mol. Biol. 7 (1963) 534.

CAIRNS, J.: The bacterial chromosome and its manner of replication as seen by autoradiography. *J.* Mol. Biol. 6 (1963a) 208.

CAIRNS, J.: The chromosome of *Escherichia coli*. Cold Spring Harbor Symp. Quant. Biol. 28 (1963b) 43.

CAMPBELL, A.: Episomes. Advan. Genet. 11 (1962) 101.

CARO, L.G.: Localization of macromolecules in *E. coli*. J. Biophys. Biochem. Cytol. 9 (1961) 539.

CARO, L.G.: High-resolution autoradiography, J. Cell Biol. 15 (1962) 189.

CARO, L.G. and F.FORRO, JR.: Localization of macromolecules in *E.coli*. J. Biophys. Biochem. Cytol. 9 (1961) 555.

CARO, L.G. and R.P.VAN TUBERGEN: High-resolution autoradiography. J. Cell Biol. 15 (1962) 173.

CARO, L.G., R.P.VAN TUBERGEN and F.FORRO, JR.: The localization of deoxyribonucleic acid in *E.coli*. J. Biophys. Biochem. Cytol. 4 (1958) 491.

CHAPMAN, G.B. and J.HILLER: Electron microscopy of ultrathin sections of bacteria. J. Bacteriol. 66 (1953) 362.

CLARK, D.J. and O.MAALØE: DNA replication and the division cycle in *Escherichia coli*. J. Mol. Biol. 23 (1967) 99.

CUZIN, F. and F.JACOB: Mutations de l'épisome F d'*Escherichia coli* K12. Ann. Inst. Pasteur Lille 112 (1967a) 397.

CUZIN, F. and F.JACOB: Existence chez *Escherichia coli* K12 d'une unité génétique de transmission formée de différents réplicons. Ann. Inst. Pasteur Lille 112 (1967b) 529.

DRISKELL-ZAMENHOF, P.: Bacterial episomes. In: I.C.Gunsalus and R.Y.Stanier, eds.: The bacteria, Vol. V: Heredity. New York, Academic Press (1964) 155.

FORRO, F. JR.: Autoradiographic studies of bacterial chromosome replication in amino acid deficient *Escherichia coli* 15T⁻. Biophys. J. 5 (1965) 629.

FORRO, F. JR. and S.A.WERTHEIMER: The organization and replication of deoxyribonucleic acid in thymine-deficient strains of *E.coli*. Biochem. Biophys. Acta 40 (1960) 9.

FRANKLIN, R.M. and N.GRANBOULAN: High-resolution autoradiography of bacteria labeled with tritriated uridine. J. Mol. Biol. 14 (1965) 623.

GANESAN, A.T. and J.LEDERBERG: A cell-membrane bound fraction of bacterial DNA. Biochem. Biophys. Res. Commun. 18 (1965) 824.

GIESBRECHT, P.: Vergleichende Untersuchungen an den Chromosomen des Dinoflagellaten *Amphidinium elegans* und denen der Bakterien. Zentr. Bakteriol., Parasitenk., Abt. I. Orig. 187 (1962) 452.

GROSS, J.D.: Conjugation in bacteria. In: I.C.Gunsalus and R.Y.Stanier, eds.: The Bacteria, Vol. V: Heredity. New York, Academic Press (1964) 1.

GROSS, J.D. and L.CARO: Genetic transfer in bacterial mating. Science 150 (1965) 1679.

GROSS, J.D. and L.G.CARO: DNA transfer in bacterial conjugation. J. Mol. Biol. 16 (1966) 269.

HANAWALT, P., O.MAALØE, D.J.CUMMINGS and M.SCHAECHTER: The normal DNA replication cycle. II. J. Mol. Biol. 3 (1961) 156.

HAYES, W.: The genetics of bacteria and their viruses. New York, John Wiley & Sons, Inc. (1964).

HELMSTETTER, C.E.: Rate of DNA synthesis during the division cycle of *Escherichia coli* B/r. J. Mol. Biol. 24 (1967) 417.

IKEDA, H. and JUN-ICHI TOMIZAWA: Transducing fragments in generalized transduction by phage P1. J. Mol. Biol. 14 (1965) 85.

JACOB, F. and S.BRENNER: Sur la régulation de la synthèse du DNA chez les bactéries: l'hypothèse du réplicon. C. R. Acad. Sci. 256 (1963) 298.

JACOB, F., S.BRENNER and F.CUZIN: On the regulation of DNA replication in bacteria. Cold Spring Harbor Symp. Quant. Biol. 28 (1963) 329.

JACOB, F., C.R.FUERST and E.L.WOLLMAN: Recherches sur les bactéries lysogènes défectives. Ann. Inst. Pasteur Lille 93 (1957) 724.

JACOB, F. and E.L.WOLLMAN: Sexuality and the genetics of bacteria. New York, Academic Press (1961).

KAHN, P. and D.R.HELINSKI: Relationship between colicinogenic factors E_1 and V and an F factor in *E. coli* J. Bacteriol. 88 (1964) 1573.

KELLENBERGER, E.: The physical state of the bacterial nucleus. In: W.Hayes and R.C.Clowes, eds.: Microbial genetics, 19th symposium of the Society for General Microbiology (1960) 39.

KELLENBERGER, E.: Vegetative bacteriophage and the maturation of the virus particles. Advan. Virus Res. 8. New York, Academic Press P1962) 1–61.

KELLENBERGER, E., A.RYTER and J.SÉCHAUD: Electron microscope study of DNA containing plasm. J. Biophys. Biochem. Cytol. 4 (1958) 671.

KOHIYAMA, M., D. COUSIN, A. RYTER and F. JACOB: Mutants thermosensibles d'*Escherichia coli* K12. Ann. Inst. Pasteur Lille 110 (1966) 465.

LARK, C.: Regulation of desoxyribonucleic acid synthesis in *Escherichia coli*: Dependence on growth rates. Biochim. Biophys. Acta 119 (1966) 517.

LARK, K.G.: Regulation of chromosome replication and segregation in bacteria. Bacteriol. Rev. 30 (1966) 3.

LARK, K.G. and R. BIRD: Premature chromosome replication induced by thymine starvation: restriction of replication to one of the two partially completed replicas. J. Mol. Biol. 13 (1965a) 607.

LARK, K.G. and R. BIRD: Segregation of the conserved units of DNA in *Escherichia coli*. Proc. Natl. Acad. Sci. U.S. 54 (1965b) 1444.

LARK, K.G. and C. LARK: Regulation of chromosome replication in *Escherichia coli*: Alternate replication of two chromosomes at slow growth rates. J. Mol. Biol. 13 (1965) 105.

MAALØE, O. and A. BIRCH-ANDERSEN: Bacterial anatomy. Sixth symposium of the Society for General Microbiology, Cambridge, Cambridge Univ. Press (1956) 261.

MAALØE, O. and N.O. KJELDGAARD: Control of macromolecular synthesis; a study of DNA, RNA and protein synthesis in bacteria. New York, W.A. Benjamin (1966).

MASON, D.J. and D.M. POWELSON: Nuclear division as observed in live bacteria by a new technique. J. Bacteriol. 71 (1956) 474.

MESELSON, M. and F. STAHL: The replication of DNA in *E. coli*. Proc. Natl. Acad. Sci. U.S. 44 (1958) 671.

MONK, M. and R.C. CLOWES: Transfer of the colicin I factor in *Escherichia coli* K12 and its interaction with the F fertility factor. J. Gen. Microbiol. 36 (1964) 365.

MURRAY, R.G.E.: The internal structure of the cell. In: I.C. Gunsalus and R.Y. Stanier. eds.: The bacteria, vol. I. New York, Academic Press (1960) 35.

NAGATA, T.: The molecular synchrony and sequential replication of DNA in *Escherichia coli*. Proc. Natl. Acad. Sci. U.S. 49 (1963) 551.

OISHI, M., Y. HIROSHI and N. SUEOKA: Synchronus and dichotomous replications of the *B. subtilis* chromosome during spore germination. Nature 204 (1964) 1069.

PRITCHARD, R.H. and K.G. LARK: Induction of replication by thymine starvation at the chromosome origin in *E. coli*. J. Mol. Biol. 9 (1964) 288.

ROBINOW, C.F.: The chromatin bodies of bacteria. Bacteriol. Rev. 20 (1956) 207.

RYTER, A. and F. JACOB: Etude au microscope électronique de la liaison entre noyau et mésosome chez *Bacillus subtilis*. Ann. Inst. Pasteur Lille 107 (1964) 384.

RYTER, A. and F. JACOB: Etude morphologique de la liaison du noyau à la membrane chez *E. coli* et chez les protoplastes de *B. subtilis*. Ann. Inst. Pasteur Lille 110 (1966) 801.

RYTER, A. and E. KELLENBERGER: Etude au microscope électronique de plasmes contenant de l'acide désoxyribonucléique. Z. Naturforsch. 13b (1958) 597.

SCAIFE, J. and A.P. PEKHOV: Deletion of chromosomal markers in association with F-prime factor formation in *Escherichia coli* K12. Genet. Res. 5 (1964) 495.

SCHAECHTER, M., M.W. BENTZON and O. MAALØE: Synthesis of deoxyribonucleic acid during the division cycle of bacteria. Nature 193 (1959) 1207.

SCHAEFFER, P.: Transformation. In: I.C. Gunsalus and R.Y. Stanier, eds.: The bacteria, Vol. V: Heredity. New York, Academic Press (1964) 87.

SCHREIL, W.: Studies on the fixation of artificial and bacterial DNA plasms for the electron microscopy of thin sections. J. Cell Biol. 22 (1964) 1.

VAN TUBERGEN, R.P. and R.B. SETLOW: Quantitative radioautographic studies on exponentially growing cultures of *Escherichia coli*. Biophys. J. 1 (1961) 589.

WATANABE, T.: Infectious heredity of multiple drug resistance in bacteria. Bacteriol. Rev. 27 (1963) 87.

YOSHIKAWA, H. and N. SUEOKA: Sequential replication of the *Bacillus subtilis* chromosome. Proc. Natl. Acad. Sci. U.S. 49 (1963) 806.

PART III

Bacterial fine structure

CHAPTER 8

The bacterial surface

WOUTERA VAN ITERSON

Laboratory of Electron Microscopy, University of Amsterdam, Amsterdam, The Netherlands

Contents

1. Introduction

2. The cell wall
   (a) The outermost layers
   (b) The cell wall proper

3. Forms defective in cell wall materials
   (a) General remarks
   (b) Semi-gymnoplasts (spheroplasts)
   (c) Gymnoplasts (protoplasts)
   (d) L-forms
   (e) Mycoplasma (the pleuropneumonia and pleuropneumonia-like organisms or PPLO

1. Introduction

The bacteria – or Schizomycetes (Von Naegeli) – constitute a large, diversified group of small organisms comprising species with more fundamental variations in their energy-yielding processes than are encountered anywhere else amongst other living organisms. Those in the order *Eubacteriales* are unicellular and may be arranged in chains, sheets or regular packages. Bacteria in the order *Actinomycetales* show branching in the manner of fungal mycelia. Most bacteria multiply by the device called 'binary transverse fission', but some unicellular eubacteria reproduce by 'budding', while the mycelium of actinomycetes is divided by transverse partitions and develops chains of conidia or even sporangia at the end of aerial hyphae. The mode of reproduction of the wall-less *Mycoplasmatales* is at yet insufficiently understood. A number of bacteria are endowed with the property of forming peculiar resting cells which may be either 'endospores' or 'cysts'.

Eubacteria may have the shape of a sphere, or of a straight or curved or helically twisted rod. A few types are, during part of their life cycle, sessile by means of a stalk that forms part of the organism (e.g. *Caulobacter*). Some species are motile by means of flagella; the *Beggiatoales*, on the other hand, glide, rotate on their long axis and oscillate, but lack flagella. The *Myxobacteriales* glide over surfaces and are capable of rapid bending and twisting movements. Bacteria are encased in a more or less flexible cell wall, but 'pleomorphic forms' have also been described, and the typical feature of the *Mycoplasmatales* is that they are devoid of a cell wall, and are separated from the environment only by an easily deformable cytoplasmic membrane.

Many bacteria are free-living; some, however, are parasites of animal or plant cells, and even of other bacteria (Starr and Baigent). Those from 'root nodules' of plants may be regarded as symbiotic. Bacterial life exists in a remarkably wide range of environments, including extremes of temperature, salinity, and acidity. There are 'psychrophilic' bacteria which can live at unusually low temperatures; such as *Bacillus maquariensis* which forms spores at temperatures down to and including 0 °C (Marshall and Ohye). Others are 'thermophilic' and can live at temperatures up to 65–70 °C. Some again can live in distilled water with only traces of nutrients, whereas others belonging to the *Halobacteria* demand high concentration of salts. Gram-positive cocci are described as having internal osmotic pressures of 20–30 atm, whereas in Gram-negative rods it appears to be no higher than 4–8 atm (Razin). Some bacteria are so constructed that they can live at a *p*H of even less than 1, and still maintain their protoplasm in a normally functioning state.

The species preferred for laboratory study are readily cultivated on solid or in liquid media in artificial environments which have supplied data for the construction of so-called 'life cycles'. Descriptions of the morphology and physiology of micro-organisms are generally based exclusively on artificial cultures of this type. The behaviour of the same organisms in their natural habitat has been far less thoroughly explored. Few bacteriologists seem to be aware that colonies of bacteria from strains long maintained in the laboratory may differ from their undomesticated prototypes in nature as much as for instance the tulips of our hothouses from their ancestors in their native Asia Minor.

The dimensions of micro-organisms can vary over an approximately 50-fold range. Among bacteria are found the smallest free-living cells known sofar. There are strong morphological and chemical reasons for conceding bacterial status also to the *Rickettsiae* and the viruses of the psittacosis-lymphogranuloma group. What then does there exist to unify this diversified class of organisms? The cardinal common feature of these organisms is their small volume, as may be seen from Fig. 1. This has fundamental implications for the anatomy of the bacterial cell. In this figure various types of cells have been drawn to the same scale. Electron microscopy has brilliantly confirmed the fact derived from light microscopy: that important analogies exist in the general ultrastructural pattern of the higher animal and plant cells. In both these cell types lipoprotein membranes are employed as envelopes of various organelles (plastids, mitochondria, lysosomes), as part of the endoplasmic reticulum and Golgi complexes, and in separating the cytoplasm from the nucleoplasm. In the cells of higher organisms most, if not all hereditary information is carried by a number of structural sub-units, the chromosomes, which in most instances become visible only at the time of nuclear division. In the process known as mitosis, two complete sets of chromosomes are equitably distributed between two newly formed daughter nuclei.

A bacterium corresponds in size to a single mitochondrion (Fig. 1), and the pattern of its ultrastructure differs in important features from that found in the cells of animal or plant tissue. A major difference is the disposition of membranes inside the cells. Furthermore, a most important feature of the bacteria is that their hereditary material is not distributed over a set of separate chromosomes confined within a common nuclear envelope as in higher organisms. Instead one finds a single, long, circular, much folded 'genophore' (Ris) or 'chromosome' (see chapter by Caro) which is over much of its surface in close contact with the cytoplasm, from which it is not separated by a membranous envelope. Morphologically the replication of this element bears no resemblance to a process of mitosis. Although 'sexuality' has been established for a number of bacteria this does not imply that fertilization necessarily involves a complete fusion of the genetic equipment of the two mating cells. Only part of the chromosome is transferred to the recipient cell; the product of such a conjugation is therefore only a partial zygote (merozygote), and the haploid condition is normally re-established after parts of the genome of the recipient have been exchanged for parts of the introduced fraction of the hereditary material of the donor.

The chromosome material of blue-green algae is organized in the same way as it is in bacteria. These two classes of organisms are therefore designated as 'procaryotes'. Sexuality seems to be lacking in the blue-green algae.

Special conditions of fixation and embedding have to be observed for the faithful preservation of the molecular cytology of micro-organisms. Where this has been successfully accomplished as in specimens fixed by the procedure introduced by Ryter

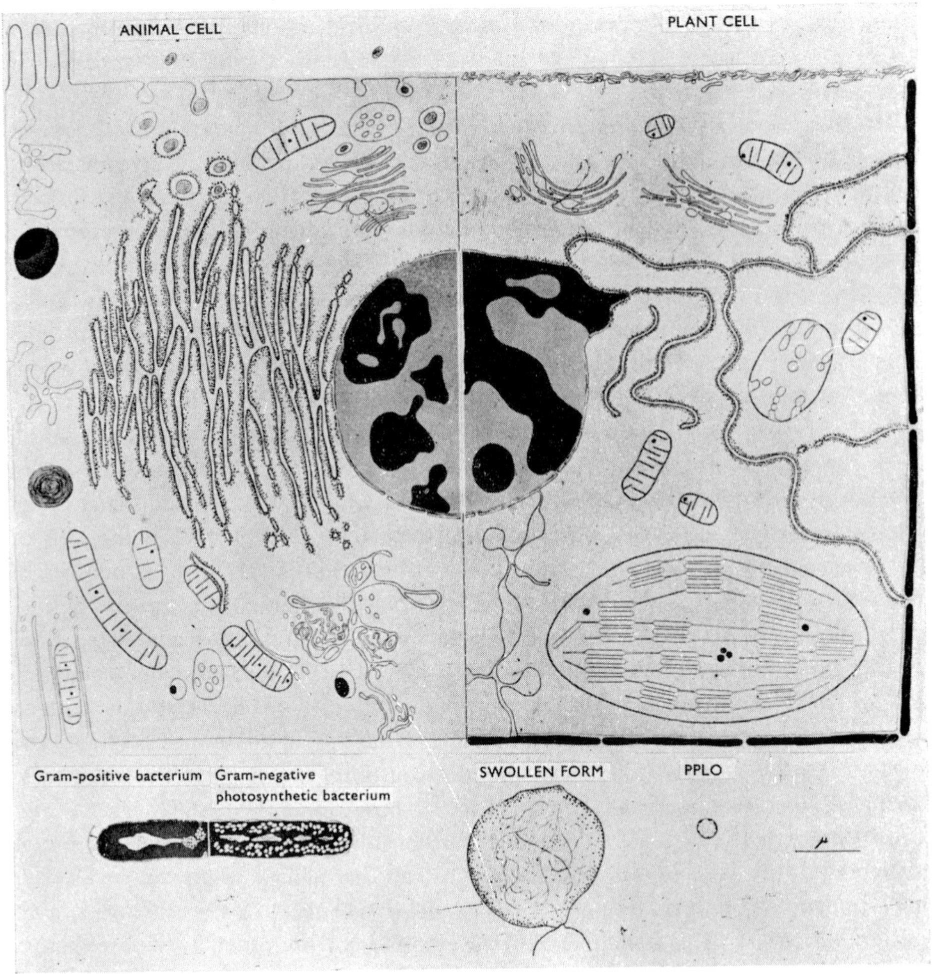

Fig. 1. Schematic drawing of portions of a generalized tissue cell of an animal and a higher plant, a Gram-positive bacterium (*B. subtilis*) and a Gram-negative photosynthetic bacterium (*Rhodospirillum rubrum*); furthermore a *Proteus* cell deprived of its cell wall and therefore swollen, and a *Mycoplasma* element. The drawing has been made at a scale of 10,000 ×, and was then reduced to its present form. In this way the dimensions of the various organelles and elementary structures can, to a certain degree, be compared. It can be seen how small bacteria compare to eucaryotic cells. They are so small that they cannot possess the same morphological pattern as the eucaryots. (From 'Recent Progress in Microbiology', University of Toronto Press.)

and Kellenberger, an architecture can be revealed which corresponds, to a surprisingly high degree, with that in frozen-etched specimens prepared according to Moor and Mühlethaler.

The physiological diversity of microbes stressed in the beginning of this section is not paralleled by an equally great diversity of basic organization. It is therefore possible to arrive at the 'concept of a bacterium' ably developed by Stanier and Van Niel. It should be realized that beneath the morphological peculiarities of bacteria, considerable functional similarity exists with the machinery of eucaryotic cells. Because of their relatively simple fine structure bacteria are potentially useful objects for studies of the relationships of structure and function at the molecular level.

2. *The cell wall*

(a) *The outermost layers*

On their outside, bacteria may carry layers that are not considered to be integral components of their walls. Loose slime, extracellular gums and polysaccharide material belong to this class; they tend to be loosely attached to the surface and are easily removed by washing, without detriment to the viability of the cells. Capsules are superficial layers of rather specific organization, as was suggested in particular by the observations of Tomcsik and his collaborators (see Tomcsik). Their observations were made with the phase contrast microscope on capsulated bacteria suspended in certain antisera. The dimensions of the capsules seen in Fig. 2 have been exaggerated through flattening of the preparation. It is possible to preserve the capsules around

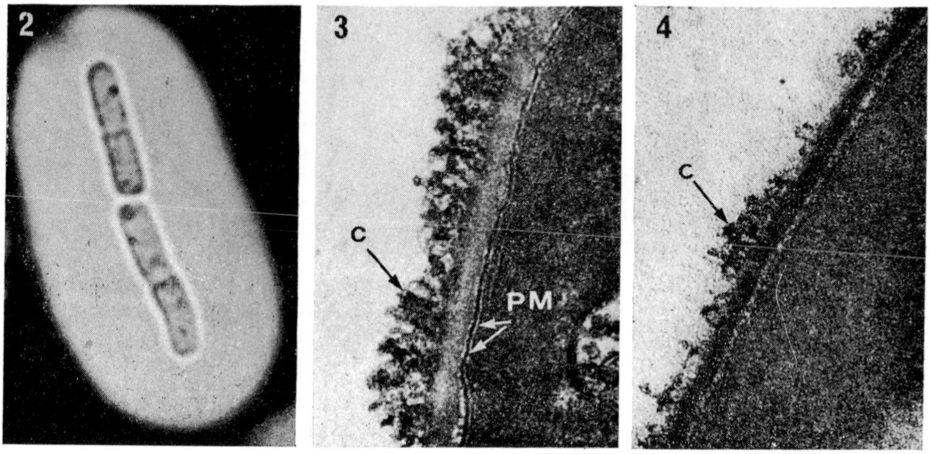

Fig. 2. India-ink preparation of *Bacillus megaterium*, light microscopy. The cells have been squashed under a cover slip, which in part explains the very considerable diameter of the capsular material. (Courtesy of Dr. C. F. Robinow.)

Fig. 3. Capsular material (c) of *B. megaterium* preserved for the e.m. by embedding the cells in agar prior to their fixation. In the segment of cell wall profile shown it is not easy to distinguish the rigid layer from the plastic layer on its outside. Note that the outer dense layer (PM) of the plasma membrane is more opaque to the electron beam than the one adjacent to the cytoplasm.

Fig. 4. Fragment of cell wall of *B. megaterium* covered with less capsular material (c) than in Fig. 3, since the culture was grown in a peptone-yeast extract medium to which no glucose had been added. ×120,000.

the bacteria, in sections for the electron microscope, by first embedding the organisms in agar and then fixing them through the agar. After this treatment (Figs. 3, 4) the diameter of the capsules is, understandably, much smaller than in squashed preparations for the light microscope (Fig. 2). The presence of capsules, and the extent to which they develop on certain bacterial species is, amongst others, dependent on metabolic factors. When the medium in which *Bacillus megaterium* was grown overnight was enriched with 2% glucose (Fig. 3), more capsular material developed than in the same basal medium (Fig. 4) without glucose.

Some bacterial species have the peculiarity that their cells remain cemented together with material which is anatomically and functionally different from capsules (Canale-Parola et al.; Murray 1963; Pangborn and Starr). *Acetobacter xylinum* is unusual in that it develops extensive layers of extracellular cellulose. Other bacteria live within a sheath (*Sphaerotilus natans*). The cells of *Gallionella ferruginea* were found to be attached, either sideways or terminally, to ferriferous bands composed of strands with iron in the ferric and ferrous state, and containing an organic matrix (Fig. 5; Van Iterson).

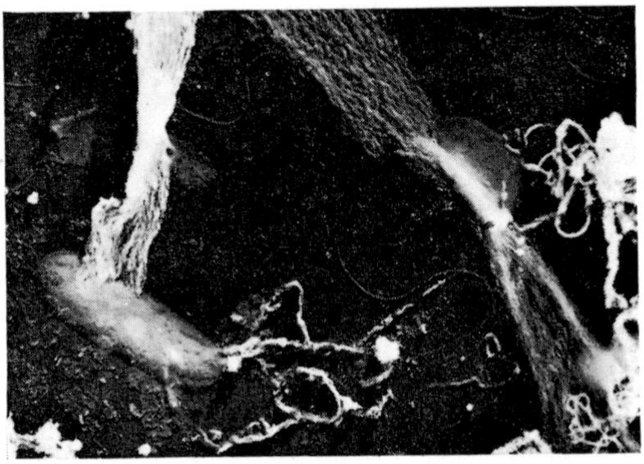

Fig. 5. *Gallionella ferruginea.* On the left a typical, so-called end-cell can be seen attached to a ferruginous band, whereas to the right a side-cell can be seen at the site of the helical twist of such a band. The bands are composed of strands in which an organic matrix has been found. × 40,000.

(b) *The cell wall proper*

Empty cell wall husks obtained by the disruption of cocci, rods or curved cells preserve the original shape of the intact bacterium. From this it has been inferred that the shape of Gram-positive as well as Gram-negative bacteria is maintained by a 'rigid layer', chemically complex, which also serves to protect the underlying plasma membrane from mechanical damage. In the complete cell wall the rigid layer is associated with varying amounts of several other high molecular compounds (see reviews by Rogers 1965, 1966; Martin; Weidel and Pelzer; Salton). External to the rigid layer lies a more plastic fabric. The particular component which confers rigidity on the cell has sofar been called by too many names, as for instance: 'mucopeptide', 'glycopeptide', 'muropeptide', 'peptido-glycan', 'R-layer', 'basal structure', 'Stütz Membran' and 'murein sacculus'. The latter term, which has advantages over the others by its greater specificity, was coined by Weidel (Weidel and Pelzer) who considers the sacculus to be 'one enormous macromolecule kept together by covalent bonds throughout' (Fig. 6). Weidel and Pelzer introduced the term 'murein', which is analogous to 'protein', after the Latin *murus* (wall), to designate the unique type of heteropolymer from which the bacterial sacculi are made. Chemically the murein sacculus is defined by the presence of two amino sugars: N-acetyl-muramic acid (i.e. the 3–0-ether of D-glucosamine and

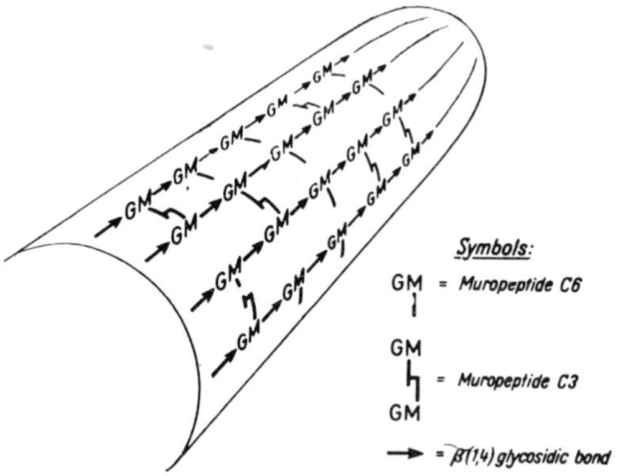

Fig. 6. Stereochemical model of the murein sacculus of *E. coli* as suggested by Weidel and Pelzer. The symbols are further specified in Fig. 7.

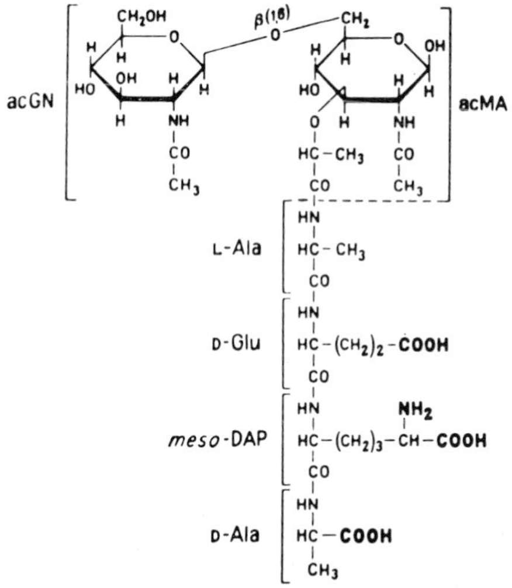

Fig. 7. Structural formula of a simple *E. coli* muropeptide consisting of acetyl-glucosamine glycosidically linked to acetyl-muramic acid. To the free carboxyl group of the acetyl-muramic acid the amino acids are attached through peptide bonding.

D-lactic acid) and N-acetyl-glucosamine. As alternative constituents, may be present 2,6-diaminopimelic acid and lysine, and D-glutamic acid, L- and D-alanine. In addition a number of more common amino acids have been found in close association with these murein compounds (Weidel and Pelzer). So far this small set of amino sugar derivates and amino acids appears to be unique in nature for the walls of bacteria and blue-green algae. Lysozyme can break the sacculi down into small fragments of 'muropeptides' (Fig. 7; Weidel and Pelzer).

Skilful stepwise degradation of the cell wall of *E. coli* by Weidel, Martin and Frank (see Martin and Frank) eventually revealed the naked murein framework (Fig. 8a-c). Such an *E. coli* sacculus would constitute less than 10% of the weight of the original cell wall, though varying with the conditions of cultivation higher values have been found for other bacteria. Martin and Frank inferred that the cell wall of *E. coli* is composed of three superimposed layers of which two are plastic and are peeled off in the process leading to the cell structure seen in Fig. 8c. These two are a superficial

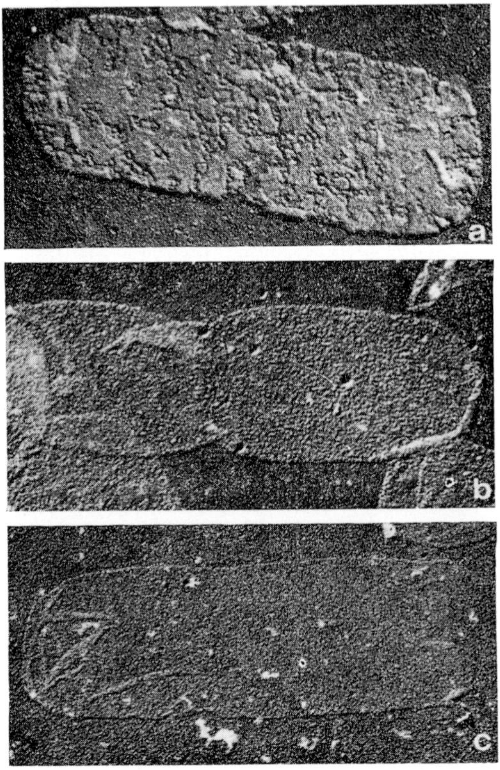

Fig. 8. Stepwise degradation of the *E. coli* cell wall. The cell wall has been gradually stripped of all accessory layers until the naked murein sacculus was left (c). (a) Cell wall prepared in the Mickle disintegrator with Na-dodecylsulphate. (b) After phenol extraction of the non-covalently bound lipoprotein and lipopolysaccharide. (c) The surface pattern of protein, bound covalently to the murein sacculus and still visible in (b), has been removed with pepsin. (From Martin and Frank.) ×27,500.

lipoprotein with perhaps an intermediate liposaccharide layer (see below). The third layer, the cell-shaped murein sacculus, would be the innermost.

The cell walls of Gram-negative bacteria are often considered to have higher structural and chemical complexity than those of some Gram-positive species, though this is not certain. Their walls have been reported to contain, in association with the murein sacculus, protein and lipid as major components with small amounts of lipopolysaccharide and mucopeptide (Rogers 1965; Salton). In transverse sections, in the electron microscope, the Gram-negative wall appears as a number of layers of different electron-scattering capacity, and these have been assigned to the different chemical components. The various authors have not, however, reached agreement on this point as yet. In the case of the cell wall of *E. coli*, which is the most extensively studied, Frank and Dekegel deny the presence of a third dense layer when the cells are in the logarithmic phase of growth, and therefore locate the murein sacculus differently from most authors. On the basis of the work of Martin and Frank; Murray et al.; Nermut; De Petris, and the combined electron microscope and X-ray study by Burge and Draper, the following tentative interpretation of the wall of some Enterobacteriaceae seems likely (see also Fig. 9). The width of the wall of *Proteus vulgaris* is

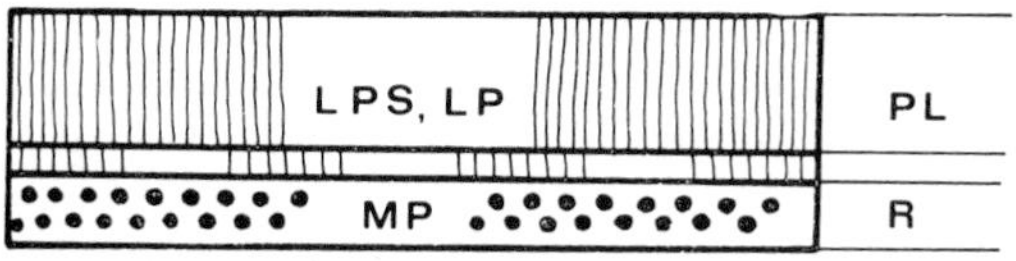

Fig. 9. Schematic drawing of the cell wall of enterobacteria after Nermut. R: rigid layer (murein sacculus), MP, mucopeptide. Pl: plastic layer consisting of lipoproteins and lipopolysaccharides (LP and LPS).

144 Å (Burge and Draper), and that of *E. coli* may be approximately the same (Fig. 10). It consists of two parts: a 52-Å wide rigid component covered on its outside by a 92-Å wide soft component which superficially resembles a unit membrane. The soft component is identical with the spheroplast wall which remains when the rigid layer is destroyed (Fig. 10), for instance by the combined action of lysozyme and EDTA. The innermost dense layer of the rigid component, close to the plasma membrane, is the murein sacculus (mucopeptide, MP) with on its outer circumference rows of globular proteins covalently linked to it. The soft layer (identical with the spheroplast wall (cf. Fig. 10) contains lipoprotein (LP) and lipopolysaccharide (LPS). In view of the fact that in *E. coli* the phage receptor sites are contained in the lipoprotein and lipopolysaccharide moiety and located at the surface of the cell, and that the lipopolysaccharide component acts as the 0-antigen site, it is highly probable that both components are arranged in such a way that they penetrate each other forming a mosaic pattern at the surface of the cell. For an illustration of cell wall fragments of a frozen-etched *E. coli* cell, see Fig. 11.

In several Gram-negative species, such as *Spirillum* species, *Halobacterium halobium*,

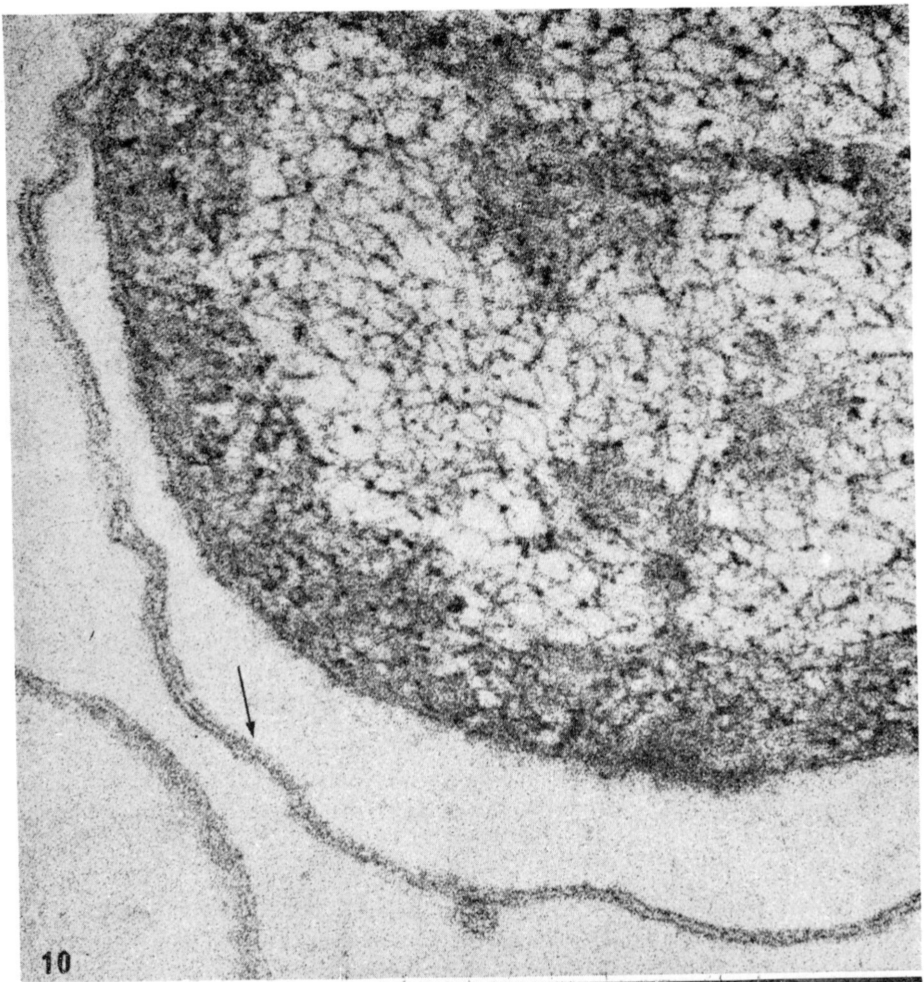
10

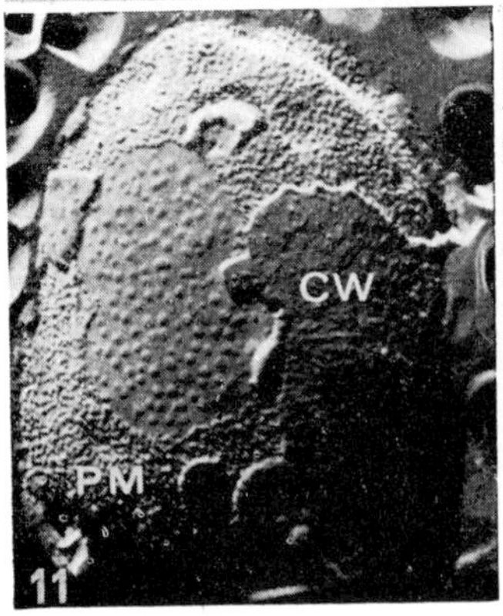
CW
PM
11

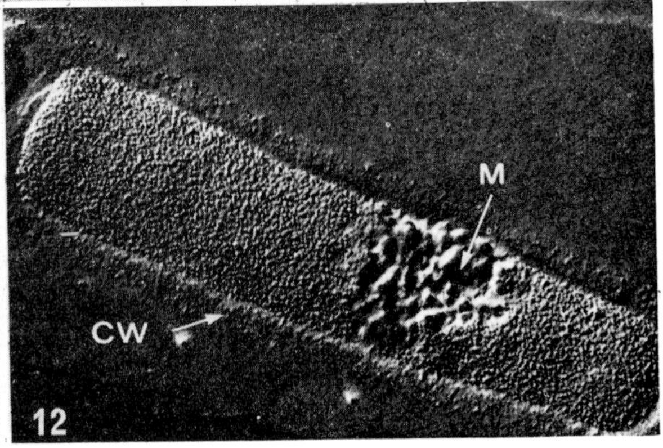
M
CW
12

Vibrio metchnikovii, Selenomonas palpitans, Rhodospirillum rubrum and *Lampropedia* (cf. Salton), beautiful regular patterns have been observed which are arrangements of spherical macromolecules. It has not yet been ascertained whether such regular patterns of spheres are a constant feature of the Gram-negative wall. When, however, the walls of *E. coli* were treated with sodium lauryl sulphate, regular rows of subunits of about 75 Å were revealed (Boy de la Tour et al.). A straightforward demonstration of the macromolecules in sectioned wall profiles of *Spirillum serpens* was obtained by Murray (1967).

The walls of Gram-positive bacteria are generally thicker than those of the Gram-negative species; they are poor in lipids and rich in polysaccharides. The murein network is probably multi-layered. Lysozyme liberates relatively few monomers or dimers of mucopeptide, but rather fragments of higher molecular weight (Salton). In the Gram-positive walls polysaccharides, mucopolysaccharides and teichoic acid are often a major component. Furthermore, teichuronic acid, antigenic M-protein and other substances have been found. Fig. 12 is an illustration of a frozen-etched *B. subtilis* cell showing the cross-fractured cell wall. The wall of *B. megaterium* contains a relatively thick rigid component (approx. 100 Å), covalently bound to a plastic layer made up of teichoic acid (Nermut) (see Fig. 13). In *B.polymyxa* a murein

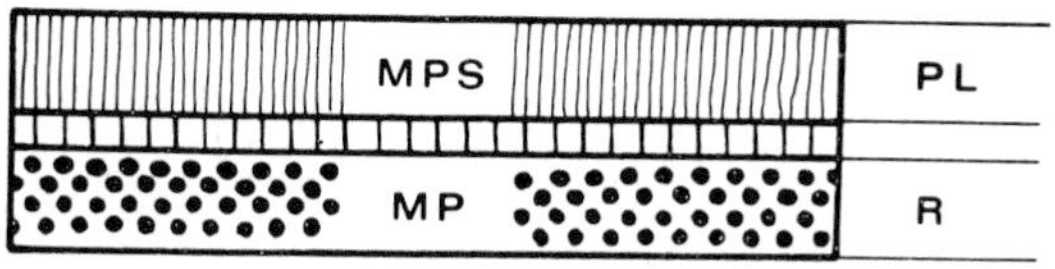

Fig. 13. Schematic drawing by Nermut of the cell wall of *B. megaterium*. In this Gram-positive wall the murein sacculus (R) is thicker than in the Gram-negative wall (cf. Fig. 9). The plastic layer consists here of mucopolysaccharides (MPS).

layer of approx. 60 Å is covalently linked to a plastic layer of polysaccharides of unknown chemical composition, and weakly bound externally to this is an additional layer which has a rectangular pattern of protein-containing globules (Nermut and Murray). The total width of this wall amounts to approx. 240 Å. Rectangular

Fig. 10. Cell wall of *Proteus mirabilis* lightly affected by penicillin. On the left three dense lines can be distinguished, whereas on the right two remain, which may be due to loss of the rigid layer (murein sacculus) so that only the plastic surface is left. The transition between intact and penicillin-affected cell wall is in the neighbourhood of the arrow. The cell wall has lost its rigidity and is no longer molded to the protoplast. × 193,000.

Fig. 11. Replica of *Escherichia coli* cell, frozen-etched according to Moor and Mühlethaler's method. At CW cell wall fragments, at PM plasma membrane covered with granular particles. (Courtesy N. Nanninga.) × 57,000.

Fig. 12. *Bacillus subtilis*, frozen-etched. Unlike the situation shown in Fig. 11, the surface of the cell has here been freed completely from the cell wall, which can now only be seen edge-on (arrow CW). Note the granular appearance of the plasma membrane. M: mesosome. (Courtesy N. Nanninga.) × 40,000.

patterns were also recently found in *B. lineola*, *Clostridium tetani* and *Listeria monocytogenes* (see Nermut). *Micrococcus radiodurans* possesses a layer in a beautiful hexagonal pattern which is considered representative for the lipoprotein (Thornley et al.).

An interpretation for the growth of the murein sacculus has been put forward by Weidel and Pelzer who assume that the three-dimensional macromolecule is extended by incorporation of building blocks after the breaking down of certain links by degradative enzymes. In the case of Gram-negative bacteria the wall appears to grow by diffuse intercalation of new components (Cole), whereas in Gram-positive cells growth of the wall is said to be restricted to special sites (Chung).

Halobacterium and *Mycoplasma* provide two exceptions from the general rule that a murein sacculus is essential for the maintenance of the morphological integrity of the cell envelopes of bacteria. In *Halobacterium halobium* a cell wall has been demonstrated (Cho et al.; Stoeckenius and Rowen), but it is lacking in murein; the envelope of *Mycoplasma* is discussed below.

From the point of view of classification it is of importance that the typhus rickettsiae, which were once included amongst the viruses, are now found to have a cell wall which is structurally and chemically very similar to that of bacteria. Their walls contain the materials characteristic of the walls of the bacteria and blue-green algae, namely diaminopimelic acid, muramic acid, and other compounds, and therefore these organisms resemble in this respect Gram-negative bacteria (Wood and Wissemann). Even members of the psittacosis-lymphogranuloma-trachoma group of organisms have now been shown to contain muramic acid, and to have a penicillin-sensitive, double-layered limiting envelope (cf. Armstrong and Reed).

Although it is generally believed that the function of the cell wall is mainly the protection of the protoplast against its own osmotic pressure, there are now also indications that it may harbour certain enzyme systems; alkaline phosphatase has been found for instance (Kushnarev et al.; Munkres and Wachtel). Moreover, the wall may have barrier functions in addition to those of the plasma membrane.

3. *Forms defective in cell wall materials*

(a) *General remarks*

It has been widely accepted that when the stiffening function of the murein sacculus is weakened by either enzymatic breakdown (e.g. with lysozyme) or by the inhibition of its normal synthesis (e.g. by addition of glycine, penicillin – (cf. Figs. 10, 14) – or another suitable antibiotic, or in the absence of an indispensable precursor), the shape of the bacterium is usually no longer maintained (see below). The operations of removing the cell wall materials are usually performed in a 'stabilizing medium', i.e., a medium in which the osmotic pressure is raised with the aid of a non-penetrating solute such as sucrose or polyethylene-glycol. The hydrodynamic pressure of the medium which counteracts the osmotic pressure of the cell sap will prevent the cell from bursting, and the 'protoplast' or 'spheroplast' will then assume a globular shape. These spherical forms are sensitive to osmotic shock. It is customary to call them 'spheroplasts' when they are not completely stripped of all cell wall material, and 'protoplasts' when they are genuinely free from all those compounds. Frey Wyssling points to the fact that these terms are used incorrectly, prefering the term 'gymnoplast' to 'protoplast' and 'semi-gymnoplast' to 'spheroplast'. When, on the other hand, forms defective in cell wall materials are obtained under cultural conditions that enable them to be indefinitely propagated in their soft, plastic state devoid of any set shape, they are designated as L-forms of the bacterium from which they were derived. All three bacterial forms deficient in cell wall materials are products of the laboratory, but there are reasons to think that stable as well as unstable forms of this kind arise also in natural environments.

From warm-blooded animals and human beings, a group of organisms has been isolated: the pleuropneumonia-like organisms or *Mycoplasmataceae*, which consist of small, deformable elements lacking a cell wall but endowed with plasma membrane more stable and elastic than that of bacteria. A true bacterial ancestor with a cell wall has never been established with any degree of certainty. These organisms can be cultivated on enriched media.

Bacterial forms defective in cell wall materials are of considerable biological interest, since they represent morphologically unusually simple systems that are nonetheless capable of performing life's most essential physiological activities.

(b) *Semi-gymnoplasts (spheroplasts)*

A typical spheroplast is illustrated in Fig. 14. It was obtained by a few hours' treatment with penicillin of *Proteus mirabilis* in its logarithmic phase, in a medium in which the osmotic pressure had been adjusted with 0.25 M sucrose. The treatment with penicillin results in a considerable increase in the surface area of the cell wall which has apparently lost its rigidity. Gram-negative bacteria are on the whole more resistant to lysozyme than several species of Gram-positive bacteria. Semi-gymnoplasts, in many respects similar to the one in Fig. 14, can be obtained from Gram-negative bacteria, when these are exposed at an alkaline *p*H to lysozyme in the presence of ethylene-diamine-tetra-acetate (EDTA) and an osmotically stabilizing solute. After lysozyme degradation of the wall of *E. coli*, the shape of the bacterium remained at first unaltered, but when the external osmotic pressure was lowered below that of the cell, sufficient water was taken up to produce the spherical form (Birdsell and Cota-Robles). Weinbaum et al. arrived at the interesting conclusion that not only the mucopeptide (murein sacculus), but also phospholipids may play an important part in the maintenance of the structural rigidity of the *E. coli* B cell envelope.

When rod-shaped cells are converted into 'spheroplasts' or 'protoplasts' their nucleoids are affected, in the sense that they fuse and can no longer be distinguished as separate entities (Figs. 10, 14). This will be further discussed in the chapter on the internal organization of bacteria.

(c) *Gymnoplasts (protoplasts)*

The use of the term 'protoplasts' or 'isolated protoplast' (Brenner et al.) is at present restricted to spherical bacterial forms from which all cell wall components have been removed. Naked protoplasts retain no residual cell wall demonstrable in the electron microscope, neither by chemical or immunological methods, nor by phage receptor activity. It is included in the definition of an isolated protoplast that it is lysed unless a medium of suitable composition is present to balance its internal osmotic pressure. Only a limited number of Gram-positive organisms seem to fulfil the requirement that the rigid mucopolymer (murein sacculus) can be completely solubilized by one of the lytic procedures in present use. The classical case of 'protoplast', or better of 'gymnoplast' formation, is Weibull's experiment of 1953 (cf. also Tomcsik and Guex-Holzer) in which the walls of *Bacillus megaterium* were removed with lysozyme in a stabilizing medium, and all the rod-shaped cells changed into spherical bodies. Fig. 15 shows naked protoplasts from a recent, rather similar experiment (Op Den Kamp et al.) performed in acetate veronal buffer of which the osmotic value had been raised with 0.3 M sucrose. That such gymnoplasts are indeed sensitive to lysis can be seen in Fig. 16, in which they had been exposed to the same buffer, but without added sucrose. In contradiction to current ideas, it proved possible in parallel experiments, to produce 'protoplasts' that retained the longitudinal shape, although they were free from cell wall materials as checked by electron microscopy and by a chemical test for the presence of diaminopimelic acid. In Fig. 17 such a *B. megaterium* protoplast can be seen enveloped only by its plasma membrane (compare Figs. 15, 16 with Fig. 17), still retaining the shape it had before the cell wall was removed. These protoplasts even tended to preserve their shape and internal structure when they were suspended in sucrose-free buffer (cf. next chapter). The factor which in the two experiments produced this difference in the 'protoplasts' (Figs. 15 and 16, as compared with Fig. 17) is to be sought in the *p*H of the original growth medium of the bacilli before they were converted into 'protoplasts'. The rounded 'protoplasts' sensitive to lysis were

---

Fig. 14. Semi-gymnoplast (spheroplast) obtained from *Proteus mirabilis* by growth in the presence of penicillin. The cell wall remains after such treatment, but it loses rigidity. ×100,000.

Fig. 15. Gymnoplast (naked protoplast) obtained from *Bacillus megaterium* grown overnight in a medium buffered at *p*H 7. The gymnoplast is stabilized by the suspension in a hypertonic milieu in which it rounds up during the cell wall removal with lysozyme. At the empty space L an inclusion of poly-β-hydroxybutyrate has been dissolved during the embedding procedure. ×28,000.

Fig. 16. A gymnoplast obtained from *B. megaterium* grown at *p*H 7 is sensitive to osmotic lysis, and therefore loses its contents in an hypotonic environment. Only the limiting surfaces of the lipid granules and some cytoplasmic fibrils remain. ×70,000.

Fig. 17. A gymnoplast or protoplast obtained from *B. megaterium* grown in a culture in which the *p*H had dropped overnight to about 5. The shape of the cell departs little from the norm, despite its having been suspended in a hypotonic medium during lysozyme treatment. The cell content of this cell appears largely intact, in contrast to that in Fig. 16 which has lost almost all of its constituents. G: area of a storage product, presumably glycogen. In such protoplasts the mesosomes are sometimes not expelled to the medium but remain preserved in the gymnoplast. ×48,000.

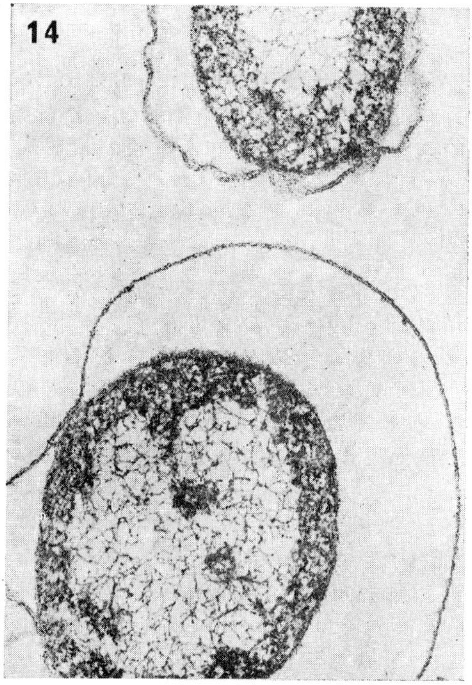
14

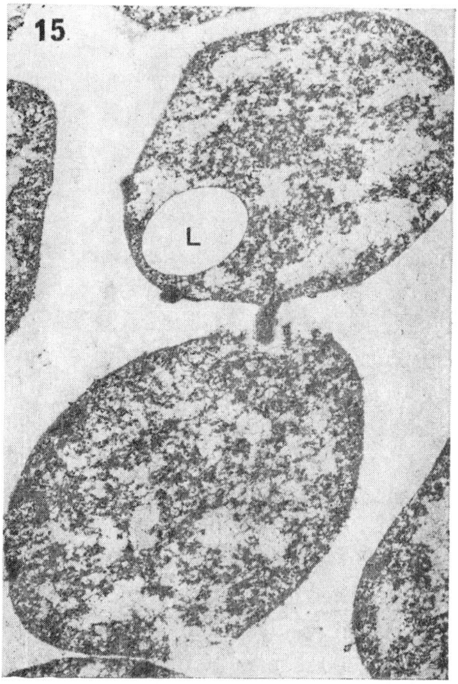
15
L

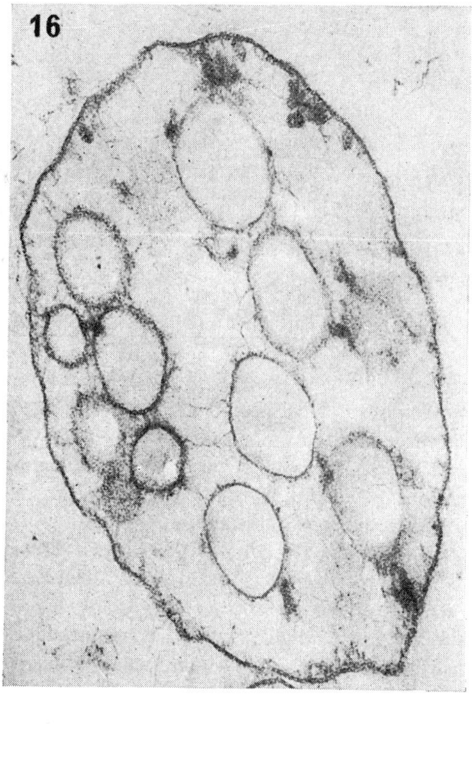
16

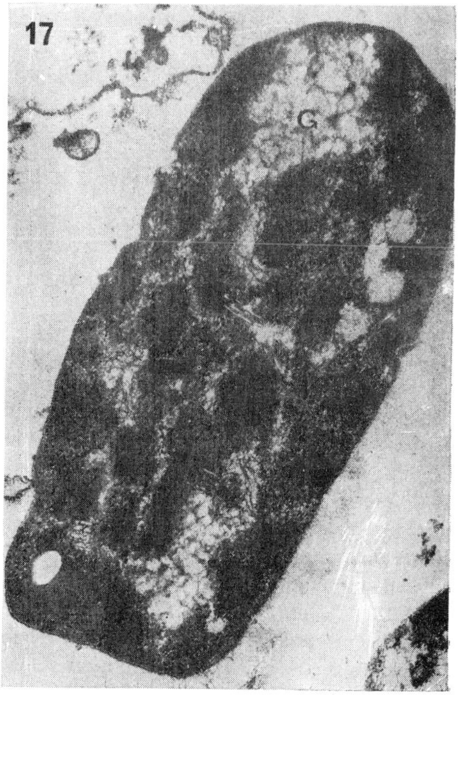
17
G

made from cells harvested at *p*H 7 of the culture medium, whereas the rod-shaped 'protoplasts' which were more resistant to lysis had been made from cells grown in medium in which the *p*H had dropped to 5. Chemical analysis revealed that a lowering of the *p*H of the culture medium markedly changed the composition of the phospholipids of the membrane fractions of the cells. In cells cultured at *p*H 7, the membrane fraction was found to consist of 5% cardiolipin, 40% phosphatidyl ethanolamine, 40% phosphatidyl glycerol, and 15% 0-lysyl phosphatidyl glycerol, whereas in the cells harvested at *p*H 5 the membrane content of phosphatidyl glycerol was reduced to 8%, and a newly identified phospholipid: glycosaminyl phosphatidyl glycerol, appeared to constitute 32% of the total phospholipids, while the other phospholipids remained constant. It may be concluded that in the bacilli harvested at low *p*H, the physical properties of the plasma membrane have changed, as is apparent from the shape of the protoplast, the behaviour of the intracellular membrane systems, and the preservation of the original fine structure of the cytoplasm and nucleoplasm. It is not our intention to imply that the decisive factor here is the change in the phospholipid composition of the membrane. There may, for instance, also be an effect of the growth condition on the structural proteins of the cytoplasmic membrane. These observations, on the production of rod-shaped 'protoplasts', suggest that the definition of protoplasts, as agreed upon by the workers cited above (Brenner et al.), may be too restricted.

(d) *L-forms*

The striking feature of the bacterial L-phase variant of growth, is the great diversity in shape and size its elements assume. In 1935 Klieneberger (working at the Lister Institute) isolated aberrant, soft forms from cultures of *Streptobacillus moniliformis*; she kept these in pure culture and designated them as L-form, in contrast to the bacterial form. Since then, numerous reports have appeared describing highly pleomorphic growth when normal bacteria were subjected to an unfavourable environment, normal sera, antibiotics like penicillin, certain amino acids and enzymes, certain

---

Fig. 18. The L-form *Proteus* L9 in section. A 'large body' is nearly filled with nucleoplasm in the shape of several perhaps interconnected areas, and with some cytoplasm mostly situated alongside the plasma membrane. Small forms are to be seen inside vacuoles, and also outside the cell. × 28,000.

Fig. 19. The L-form *Proteus* L9 in a shadowed preparation. The small forms appear to adhere to each other, and to the collapsed larger elements. (Printed in reverse.) ×11,700.

Fig. 20. *Proteus* L9 in frozen-etched preparation. The cell surface, although uneven, is of a totally different appearance from that of the plasma membrane of *E. coli* or *B. subtilis* when stripped from its cell wall layers by the fracturing during the freeze-etching procedure (cf. Figs. 11 and 12, and next chapter, Figs. 4 and 6). (Printed in reverse.) × 68,000.

Fig. 21. *Proteus* L9, frozen-etched. The L-form has been fractured all through. The intra-cellular compartments may now be seen, as well as some small forms inside them. At I (arrow) is visible the inner surface of the cell envelope of such a small element, and at O the outer surface. (Printed in reverse.) × 53,000.

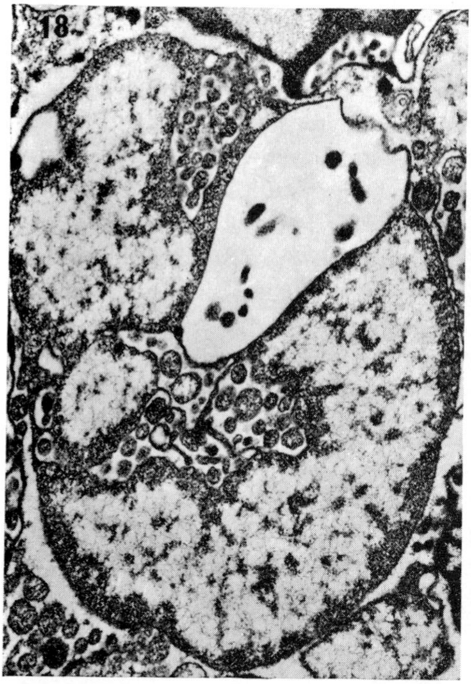
18

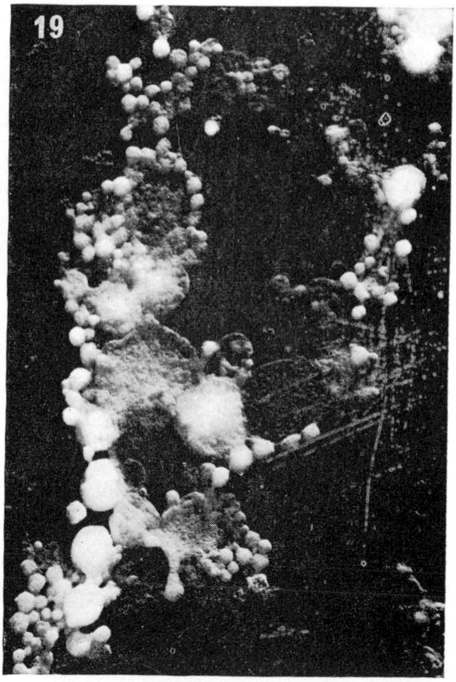
19

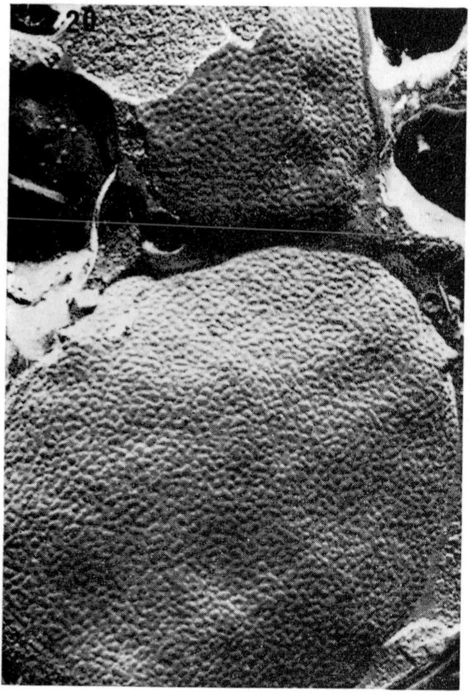
20

21
I
O
O

bacteriophages, etc. The way these factors act in initiation of transformation of bacteria into their L-form has so far been insufficiently analyzed. The physical state of the culture medium appears to influence the morphology of the growth. Similarly to mycoplasma, bacterial L-forms penetrate into soft agar and develop in the interstices of the fibrillar network of the agar gel (Razin and Oliver) from where they grow in all directions. When the growth reaches the agar surface it spreads to form the typical, often strongly vacuolated, lace-like peripheral zone, which lends the colony the well-known 'fried egg' appearance. Based on light-microscopical observations 'large bodies' and small 'granules' have been described in the colonies, as well as elements ranging in size between these two extremes. Freshly produced colonies are usually 'unstable' and revert to the bacterial form, but numerous cases have been described where stable L-forms were obtained for which it proved impossible to regain the parent bacteria.

Colonies of L-forms are generally larger than those of mycoplasmas, and they usually require for their growth higher salt concentrations. This sensitivity to the osmotic tension of the culture media may be due to the internal osmotic pressure (turgor) which in L-forms, as with most bacteria, is apparently higher than that of the culture medium. On the other hand, the much used stable L-form *Proteus* L9, originally isolated from *Proteus mirabilis* by E. Klieneberger-Nobel, grows well in ordinary nutrient broth (Difco brain–heart) in which it is strongly pleomorphic. In Figs. 18–21 elements of this *Proteus* L9 are illustrated. The larger elements are not rounded, but they can, presumably because of a comparatively low turgor, assume all sorts of shapes. In sections, in the electron microscope, they are seen to be bordered by a membrane of the usual appearance, but in frozen-etched specimens we recently observed striking differences of visible detail between the plasma membrane of the normal parent and the limiting membrane of the stable L-form (Fig. 20). In frozen-etched specimens the plasma membrane of *Proteus* closely resembles that of *E. coli* (Fig. 11) or *B. subtilis* (Fig. 12). The observed differences in membrane structure between *Proteus* and its L-form are in need of further investigation.

In electron microscope sections, *Proteus* L9 (Fig. 18) and other L-forms appear to be filled with often very irregular areas of cytoplasm and nucleoplasm, and frequently there are variously shaped vacuoles. Inside these vacuoles there are often small forms which are occasionally also seen on the outside of the large elements. In serial sections it was found that these small forms are attached by means of some sort of stalk to either the vacuolar membrane or the outer membrane of the L-form (Fig. 22a-d). The smallest of such particles measured 80–100 mμ, and can be seen to consist merely of a membrane enveloping a small amount of cytoplasm, and occasionally also some nucleoplasm. Weibull and Beckman wrote that only particles of at least 0.6–0.7 μ are viable, i.e. can form colonies, but that the smaller particles were capable of vigorous respiration, though to a lesser degree than the parent bacterium. The biosynthetic activity of these smallest particles was low. In our opinion only those particles can grow out and reproduce which have, in addition to some cytoplasm, a sufficiently

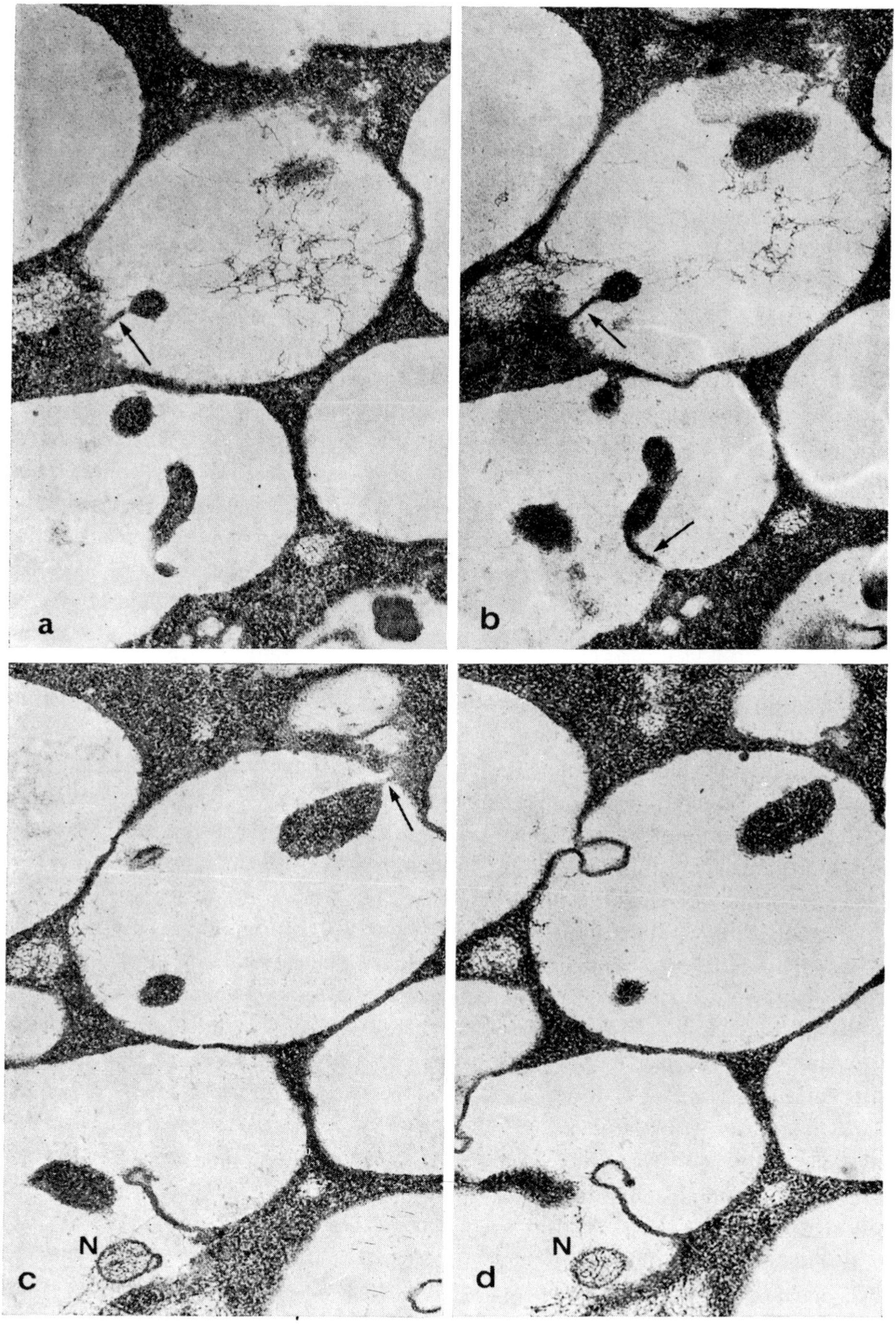

Fig. 22. Serial sections through a small, strongly vacuolated area of *Proteus* L9. The vacuoles include small forms, some of which (arrows) can be seen to be attached to the vacuolar wall by a thin stalk. In (a) and (b) remnants of nuclear fibrils are visible in one of the vacuoles, and in (c) and (d) can be seen a small element that may contain some nucleoplasm (N). $\times 60{,}000$.

long complement of the genophore (DNA molecule). The small L-form particles appear to originate inside the parent L element from an inclusion within a membrane of cytoplasm and nucleoplasm (Fig. 18, Fig. 22a-d). Normal bacterial growth presumably requires the presence of the shape-rendering cell wall, whereas the remarkable feature of L-forms is, of course, the absence of a cell wall. Morrison and Weibull, on the other hand, detected some diaminopimelic acid (DAP) and hexosamine in preparations of *Proteus* L9, but apparently these quantities are too small to suffice for a complete rigid cell wall layer. The surface of *Proteus* L9 and other L-forms requires further investigation, as is shown by the morphology in frozen-etched cells in Figs. 20 and 21.

(e) *Mycoplasma (the pleuropneumonia and pleuropneumonia-like organisms or PPLO)*
The mycoplasmas are the smallest organisms that have been cultivated on cell-free media. These are viable elements which easily pass bacteria-proof filters. On solid media they develop in very small colonies generally about 250–270 μ. They may vary, however, from 10 μ to 1 mm; the smallest are those of the T strains which reach 10–80 μ, dependent on the medium used. This is a smaller size than that of most of the L-phase variants of bacteria. They resemble the latter colonies in the way the elements in their centres embed themselves in the agar, and by the sometimes lace-like pattern of the colony periphery, although the edge is often entire. Two types of mycoplasmas exist. The first, with *Mycoplasma laidlawii* as the type species, is saprophytic. It is found in sewage, compost, earth, etc. The second type is parasitic in the sense that the mycoplasmas are found associated with cells and cell exudates of warm-blooded animals. The culture media of the second group must be enriched with sufficient amounts of ascitic fluid or blood serum. They require cholesterol, and much of it is found in their membranes. In this respect there is a certain resemblance with the cell membrane of the animal cell. For their optimal growth an alkaline *p*H is desirable, but some prefer *p*H 6, especially the T strains. Most parasitic species grow best under anaerobic conditions.

A recent review of the group has been presented by Morton, where it is stated: 'It is current practice to designate as L-forms those pleuropneumonia-like organisms which can revert to a bacterial form, and as PPLO those for which no reversion has as yet been demonstrated.' It is therefore surprising that now a 'Subcommittee on the Taxonomy of Mycoplasmatales' (Edward et al.) has recommended to recognize the order *Mycoplasmatales* as a new class separate from the Schizomycetes. It is even stated that: '... the requirement for sterols and the absence of a cell wall, place the mycoplasmas in some ways much closer to the protozoa than to bacteria ..., although on the other hand mycoplasmas are distinguished from protozoa by their procaryotic cell structure.'

Although many problems remain to be solved, it appears justified to discuss the mycoplasmas in the present context. According to the experience of the author, when colonies of mycoplasma species are fixed through their agar medium with OsO_4 after Ryter and Kellenberger, the sectioned elements are, under the electron microscope, indistinguishable from those of species of bacterial L-forms. In common with any wall-less bacterium that has lost its rigid organization, here too a cytoplasmic membrane of the usual structure envelops cytoplasmic material in direct contact with fibrils of DNA (Fig. 23). Kandler et al. found in PPLO and in bacterial L-phase variants a comparatively higher DNA content in the cells than in complete bacteria, which, apart from the swollenness of these elements, may be explained by the relatively large size of the nuclear areas in many of these cells. Like the rounded bacterial gymnoplasts and the L-forms, mycoplasmas also lack internal membranes (mesosomes), except for those that delimitate vacuoles or the so-called 'elementary reproductive corpuscles'. Furthermore the enzymatic activities so far detected in mycoplasma membranes resemble those of the bacterial 'protoplast' membrane (Razin). Even the (uncorrected) sedimentation coefficient for the ribosomes as estimated by Maniloff et al. seems to correspond to that of the bacterial ribosomes. Like bacteria and their L-forms, mycoplasma species appear to possess the biosynthetic pathway to lysine involving the intermediate meso-α, Σ-diaminopimelic acid (Smith).

Much evidence appears to be in favour of classifying the mycoplasmas together with

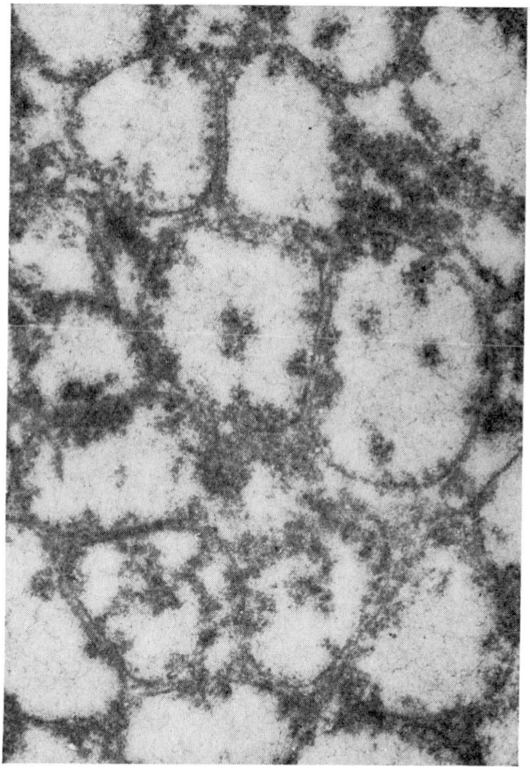

Fig. 23. *Mycoplasma fermentans*. A membrane envelops nucleoplasm and some cytoplasm. $\times$ 66,000.

the bacteria. With their small size and simplicity of organization allied with ordinary metabolic capabilities, the mycoplasmas come close to the theoretical values for 'minimum cell size consistent with the requirements of self replication' (Morowitz), and invite speculations on 'the possibility of the synthetic assembly of very small cells' (Morowitz). However, despite the use of electron microscopy, the literature on the shapes and mode of propagation of the mycoplasma elements has remained contradictory.

In our opinion it may be of importance for a better appreciation of the mycoplasma problem that Spears and Prevost (1967) estimated for *Mycoplasma hominis* an internal pressure of 3 to 4 atm. This is less than the osmolarity value of the growth medium (0.250), whereas the saprophitic *M. laidlawii* possessed 5 to 6 atm which was equal to that of the medium. At low osmolarities of the surrounding fluid, wall-less cells will tend to be swollen, whereas at high osmolarities they may shrink. Swollen cells are, of course, rounded, but in iso-osmotic milieus and in those of lower values there is no reason to assume the globular shape. This may explain the irregular shapes so often encountered in electron microscope preparations of elements of mycoplasma and L-forms (Fig. 18).

Mycoplasmas are far less sensitive to osmotic lysis than ordinary bacterial gymnoplasts. Their membranes must be very elastic, since the cells can swell to an enormous size without bursting (Razin et al.). The lipid composition of the membranes depends markedly on the fatty acid composition of the growth medium, and this may influence the physical properties of the membranes. Changes in these physical properties in turn influence the cell morphology and stability (Razin et al.).

No wonder that workers who have sampled mycoplasmas at different stages of their growth, and have used widely differing media and techniques, have arrived at different and often contradictory conclusions. Spherical elements, rings, rods, long branching filaments, and large bodies have been described. Some investigators, amongst them Klieneberger-Nobel and Dienes, believe that 'elementary particles' can grow out into large bodies and in turn develop inside these, while others consider them involution forms. Razin and Cosenza, using phase contrast optics, confirmed that cells during growth can go through a cycle of morphological changes, starting with an elementary body out of which grow branching filaments which further develop into chains of coccoid elementary bodies. A completely different mode of replication, namely a rather precise symmetrical binary fission, has so far only been claimed for *M. gallisepticum* (Morowitz and Maniloff).

Great care is certainly required when efforts are made to discover generalities in the developmental cycles of these pleomorphic organisms that are so sensitive to physical influences. A critical attitude is desirable, in particular where negative staining is used, since it has been found to produce artefacts (Reuss). Small elements have been described, the smallest hardly more than 0.1 μ, but there can only be viability if the particle contains an adequate share of the genome and of ribonucleoprotein; only then can it be expected to have a chance to develop further, and to reproduce.

References

ARMSTRONG, J.A. and S.E.REED: Fine structure of *Lymphogranuloma venereum* agent and the effects of penicillin and 5-fluorouracil. J. Gen. Microbiol. 46 (1967) 435.

BIRDSELL, D.G. and E.H.COTA-ROBLES: Production and ultrastructure of lysozyme and ethylenediaminetetraacetate-lysozyme spheroplasts of *Escherichia coli*. J. Bacteriol. 93 (1967) 427.

BOY DE LA TOUR, E., A.BOLLE and E.KELLENBERGER: Nouvelles observations concernant l'action du laurylsulfate de sodium sur le paroi et la membrane d'*E. coli*. Pathol. Microbiol. 28 (1965) 229.

BRENNER, S., F.A.DARK, P.GERHARDT, M.H.JEYNES, O.KANDLER, E.KELLENBERGER, E.KLIENEBERGER-NOBEL, K.MCQUILLEN, M.RUBIO-HUERTOS, M.R.J.SALTON, R.E.STRANGE, J.TOMCSIK and C.WEIBULL: Bacterial protoplasts. Nature 181 (1958) 1713.

BURGE, R.E. and J.C.DRAPER: The structure of the cell wall of the Gram-negative bacterium *Proteus vulgaris*. I. An electron microscope and X-ray study. II. Distribution of electron density across the wall. J. Mol. Biol. 28 (1967) (I: 173; II: 189).

CANALE-PAROLA, E., R.BORASKY and R.S.WOLFE: Studies on *Sarcina ventriculi* III. Localization of cellulose. J. Bacteriol. 81 (1961) 311.

CHO, K.Y., C.H.DOY and E.H.MERCER: Ultrastructure of the obligate halophilic bacterium *Halobacterium halobium*. J. Bacteriol. 94 (1967) 196.

CHUNG, K.L.: Autoradiographic studies of bacterial cell wall replication I. Cell wall growth of *Bacillus cereus* in the presence of chloramphenicol. Can. J. Microbiol. 13 (1967) 341.

COLE, R.M.: Cell wall replication in *Salmonella typhosa*. Science 143 (1964) 820-822.

DE PETRIS, S.: Ultrastructure of the cell wall of *Escherichia coli* and chemical nature of its constituent layers. J. Ultrastruct. Res. 19 (1967) 45.

DIENES, L.: Morphology and reproduction processes of the L-forms of bacteria. I. Streptococci and Staphylococci. J. Bacteriol. 93 (1967) 693.

EDWARD, D.G., F.F.EDWARD, E.A.FREUNDT, R.M.CHANOCK, J.FABRICANT, L.HAYFLICK, R.M.LEMCKE, S.RAZIN, N.L.SOMERSON and P.G.WITTLER: Recommendations on nomenclature of the order Mycoplasmatales. Science 155 (1967) 1694.

FRANK, H. and D.DEKEGEL: Electron microscopical studies on the localization of the different components of cell walls of Gram-negative bacteria. Folia Microbiol. (Prague) 12 (1967) 227.

FREY-WYSSLING, A.: Gymnoplasts instead of "Protoplasts". Nature 216 (1967) 516.

KANDLER, O., C.ZEHENDER and J.MULLER: Vergleichende Untersuchungen über den Nucleinsäuren und Atmungsstoffwechsel von *Proteus vulgaris*, dessen stabiler L-phase und den pleuropneumonieähnlichen Organismen. Arch. Mikrobiol. 24 (1956) 219.

KLIENEBERGER, E.: The natural occurrence of pleuropneumonia-like organisms in apparent symbiosis with *Streptobacillus moniliformis* and other bacteria. J. Pathol. Bacteriol. XL (1935) I 93.

KLIENEBERGER-NOBEL, E.: L-forms of bacteria. In: I.C.Gunsalus and R.Y.Stanier, eds.: The Bacteria, Vol. I. New York/London, Academic Press (1960) 361.

KUSHNAREV, V.M., J.DONE, C.D.SHOREY, J.P.LOKE and J.K.POLLAK: The cytochemical localization of alkaline phosphatases in *Escherichia coli* at the electron microscope level. Biochem. J. 96 (1965) 27c.

MANILOFF, J., H.J.MOROWITZ and R.J.BARRNETT: Ultrastructure and ribosomes of *Mycoplasma gallisepticum*. J. Bacteriol. 90 (1965) 193.

MARSHALL, B.J. and D.F.OHYE: *Bacillus macquariensis* n.sp., a psychotrophic bacterium from subantarctic soil. J. Gen. Microbiol. 44 (1966) 41.

MARTIN, H.H.: Bacterial protoplasts. A review. J. Theoret. Biol. 5 (1963) 1.

MARTIN, H.H. and H.FRANK: Quantitative Bausteinanalyse der Stützmembran in der Zellwand von *Escherichia coli*-B. Z. Naturforsch. 17b (1962) 190.

MOOR, H. and K.MÜHLETHALER: Fine structure in frozen-etched yeast cells. J. Cell Biol. 17 (1963) 609.

MOROWITZ, H.J.: The minimum size of cells. In: G.E.W. Wolstenholme and M. O'Connor, eds.: Principles of biomolecular organization. Ciba Foundation Symposium. London, J. and A. Churchill, Ltd. (1966) 446.

MOROWITZ, H.J. and J. MANILOFF: Analysis of the life cycle of *Mycoplasma gallisepticum*. J. Bacteriol. 91 (1966) 1638.

MORRISON, H. and C. WEIBULL: The occurrence of cell wall constituents in stable *Proteus* L-forms. Acta Pathol. Microbiol. Scand. 55 (1962) 475.

MORTON, H.E.: The pleuropneumonia and pleuropneumonia-like organisms. In: Bacterial and mycotic infections of man, 4th ed. London, Pitman Med. Publ. Co. Ltd. (1965) 786.

MUNKRES, M. and A. WACHTEL: Histochemical localization of phosphatases in *Mycoplasma gallisepticum*. J. Bacteriol. 93 (1967) 1096.

MURRAY, R.G.E.: Role of superficial structures in the characteristic morphology of *Lampropedia hyalina*. Can. J. Microbiol. 9 (1963) 593.

MURRAY, R.G.E.: Personal communication (1967).

MURRAY, R.G.E., P. STEED and H.E. ELSON: The location of the mucopeptide in sections of the cell wall of *Escherichia coli* and other Gram-negative bacteria. Can. J. Microbiol. 11 (1965) 547.

NERMUT, M.V.: Structural arrangement of bacterial cell walls. Folia Microbiol. (Prague) 12 (1967) 201.

NERMUT, M.V. and R.G.E. MURRAY: Ultrastructure of the cell wall of *Bacillus polymyxa*. J. Bacteriol. 93 (1967) 1949.

OP DEN KAMP, J.A.F., W. VAN ITERSON and L.L.M. VAN DEENEN: Studies on the phospholipids and morphology of protoplasts of *Bacillus megaterium*. Biochim. Biophys. Acta 135 (1967) 862.

PANGBORN, J. and M.P. STARR: Ultrastructure of *Lampropedia hyalina*. J. Bacteriol. 91 (1966) 2025.

RAZIN, S.: The cell membrane of Mycoplasma. Ann. N.Y. Acad. Sci. 143 (1967) 115.

RAZIN, S. and M. ARGAMAN: Lysis of mycoplasma, bacterial protoplasts, spheroplasts and L-forms by various agents. J. Gen. Microbiol. 30 (1963) 155.

RAZIN, S. and B.J. COSENZA: Growth phases of *Mycoplasma* in liquid media observed with phase-contrast microscope. J. Bacteriol. 91 (1966) 858.

RAZIN, S. and O. OLIVER: Morphogenesis of mycoplasma and bacterial L-form colonies. J. Gen. Microbiol. 24 (1961) 225.

RAZIN, S., M.E. TOURTELOTTE, R.N. MCELHANEY and J.D. POLLACK: Influence of lipid components of *Mycoplasma laidlawii* membranes on osmotic fragility of cells. J. Bacteriol. 91 (1966) 609.

REUSS, K.: Influence of fixation on gross morphology of *Mycoplasma*. J. Bacteriol. 93 (1967) 490.

RIS, H.: Ultrastructure and molecular organization of genetic systems. Can. J. Genet. Cytol. 3 (1961) 95.

ROGERS, H.J.: The outer layers of bacteria: the biosynthesis of structure. In: Function and structure in micro-organisms. XV Symp. Soc. Gen. Microbiol. London (1965), 186.

ROGERS, H.J.: Separable polymers in bacterial cell walls. Brit. Med. Bull. 22 (1966) 185.

RYTER, A., E. KELLENBERGER, A. BIRCH-ANDERSON and O. MAALØE: Étude au microscope électronique de plasma contenant de l'acide désoxyribonucléique I. Les nucléoides des bactéries en croissance active. Z. Naturforsch. 13b (1958) 597.

SALTON, M.R.J.: The bacterial cell wall. Amsterdam, Elsevier Publ. Co. (1964).

SMITH, P.F.: Comparative biosynthesis of ornithine and lysine by *Mycoplasma* and L-forms. J. Bacteriol. 92 (1966) 164.

SPEARS, D.M. and PH.J. PROVOST: A comparison of the osmotic and passive permeability properties of *Mycoplasma laidlawii* and *Mycoplasma hominis*. Can. J. Microbiol. 13 (1967) 213.

STANIER, R.Y. and C.B. VAN NIEL: The concept of bacterium. Arch. Mikrobiol. 42 (1962) 17.

STARR, M.P. and N.L. BAIGENT: Parasitic interaction of *Bdellovibrio bacteriovorus* with other bacteria. J. Bacteriol. 91 (1966) 2006.

STOECKENIUS, W. and R. ROWEN: A morphological study of *Halobacterium halobium* and its lysis in media of low salt concentration. J. Cell Biol. 34 (1967) 365.

THORNLEY, M. J., R. HORNE and A. M. GLAUERT: The fine structure of *Micrococcus radiodurans*. Arch. Mikrobiol. 51 (1965) 267.

TOMCSIK, J. and S. GUEX-HOLZER: Änderung der Struktur der Bakterienzelle im Verlauf der Lysozym-Einwirkung. Schweiz. Z. Allgem. Pathol. Bakteriol. 15 (1952) 517.

TOMCSIK, J.: Antibodies as indicators for bacterial surface structures. Ann. Rev. Microbiol. 10 (1956) 213.

VAN ITERSON, W.: *Gallionella ferruginea* Ehrenberg in a different light. Trans. Neth. Roy. Acad. Sci. II LII 2 (1958) 1.

WEIBULL, C.: The isolation of protoplasts from *Bacillus megaterium* by controlled treatment with lysozyme. J. Bacteriol. 66 (1953) 688.

WEIBULL, C. and H. BECKMAN: Chemical and metabolic properties of various elements found in cultures of a stable *Proteus* L-form. J. Gen. Microbiol. 24 (1961) 379.

WEIDEL, W. and H. PELZER: Bagshaped macromolecules – a new outlook on bacterial cell walls. Advan. Enzymol. 26 (1964) 193.

WEINBAUM, G., R. RICH and D. A. FISCHMAN: Enzyme-induced formation of spheres from cells and envelopes of *Escherichia coli*. J. Bacteriol. 93 (1967) 1693.

WOOD, W. H., JR. and CH. L. WISSEMAN, JR.: The cell wall of *Rickettsia mooseri*. J. Bacteriol. 93 (1967) 1113.

CHAPTER 9

Bacterial membranes, flagella and pili

WOUTERA VAN ITERSON

Laboratory of Electron Microscopy, University of Amsterdam, Amsterdam, The Netherlands

Contents

1. Membranes
   (a) General remarks
   (b) The cell membrane
   (c) Intracellular membranes

2. Flagella and pili (fimbriae)
   (a) Introductory remarks
   (b) Flagella
   (c) Pili (fimbriae)

1. *Membranes*

(a) *General remarks*

The main membrane fraction of bacteria consists of protein (40–70% dry weight) and lipid (15–40%). Sometimes there is carbohydrate (10–20%) (Weibull 1965). Contrary to most membranes, those in bacteria contain enough protein to cover five times the area occupied by the lipid (Korn). The lipid is of a few types; for instance, *Azotobacter agilis* and *E. coli* have only one type of phospholipid, namely phosphatidyl ethanolamine. In *B. cereus* about 50% of the lipids were found to consist of phospholipids, the major component being phosphatidyl ethanolamine (46%) and phosphatidyl glycerol (35%) (Houtsmuller and Van Deenen). Until quite recently it had been insufficiently appreciated that environmental conditions induce remarkable differences in the chemical make-up and physiological properties of these lipoprotein membranes. The effect of a slight change in the *p*H of the culture medium on the composition of the phospholipids in *B. megaterium* has been discussed in chapter 8. When cells were harvested at *p*H 5 instead of *p*H 7, the contents of phosphatidyl glycerol dropped to 8% of the total phospholipids, concomitant with the appearance of a new phospholipid identified as glucosaminyl phosphatidyl glycerol.

Unlike the situation in eucaryotic cells, the lipids in all bacteria except mycoplasmas are described as having no sterols, polyunsaturated fatty acids or sphingolipids (Hagen et al.), whereas phosphatidyl choline (lecithin) would be rare. Phosphatidyl choline is the major phospholipid of the endoplasmic reticulum of higher organisms. It is therefore of interest that a few bacteria are known to possess extensive intracellular membrane systems, but to contain no phosphatidyl choline.

Mycoplasma species alone among the bacteria possess membranes containing variable amounts of free and esterified cholesterol, a feature which they share with the membranes of animal cells. Unsaturated fatty acids in the growth medium reduced the osmotic fragility of mycoplasma and caused a pronounced change in the morphology of the cells (cf. chapter 8). In the mycoplasma membrane adenosine triphosphatase activity could be demonstrated; this activity bore resemblance to similar systems in bacteria but differed from those associated with ion transport in membranes of mammalian cells, and also from mitochondrial adenosine triphosphatase (Rottem and Razin).

(b) *The cell membrane*

The existence of a cytoplasmic membrane underneath the cell wall has been inferred *inter alia* from plasmolysis experiments before it was revealed in the electron microscope in sectioned cells. Robinow and Murray had demonstrated in the light microscope the presence of a boundary separate from the cell wall by staining with Victoria blue 4 R or B. Plasmolysis was studied by several authors by following in principle the lines set out in 1895 by Alfred Fischer. For a good description see Robinow (1960). The protoplasm in Gram-negative bacteria pulls away from the cell wall in hypertonic

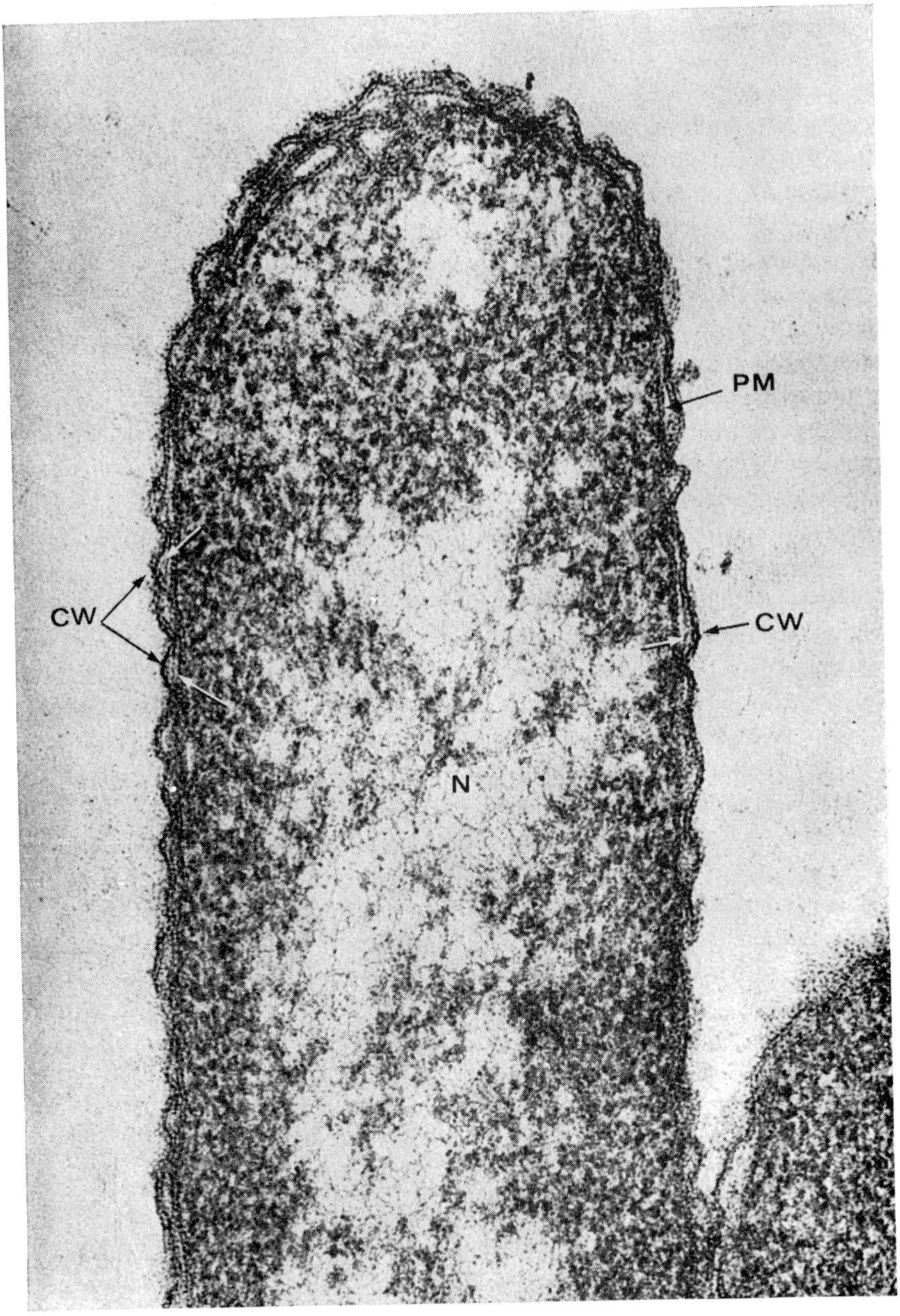

Fig. 1. *Escherichia coli* B. Example of a Gram-negative organism fixed with the Ryter-Kellenberger method. The cell wall in which frequently three layers can be distinguished (arrows CW) is wrinkled and only here and there in contact with the underlying plasma membrane (PM). *E. coli* is poor in intracellular membrane systems. The nucleoplasm is highly dispersed, and part of its fibrils appear to extend into the cytoplasm (cf. chapter 10). ×157,000.

solutions, whereas in Gram-positive species this is more difficult to achieve. The high osmotic pressure of the cell sap of the Gram-positive cells (up to 20–30 atm in some cocci), as compared with the much lower pressure in many Gram-negative rods might be partly responsible for this. But it should also be pointed out that the linkages between the plasma membrane and the straight, smooth Gram-positive wall (indicated by arrows (Br) in Figs. 2 and 3) might be stronger, more numerous or even of a different nature than those connecting the Gram-negative wall to the plasma membrane. This seems to be borne out by the appearance of these walls in sections, in particular after Ryter-Kellenberger fixation, by which perhaps an artefact is introduced in Gram-negative bacteria. The wall appears to be wrinkled and wider than the plasma membrane, to which it remains attached only here and there (Fig. 1), whereas in Gram-positive cells a smooth continuity is maintained.

After glutaraldehyde fixation the walls of Gram-negative cells are less wrinkled. The attachment of the two integuments to each other is not everywhere alike. Cota-Robles observed in electron micrographs of growing plasmolysed *E. coli* cells that the

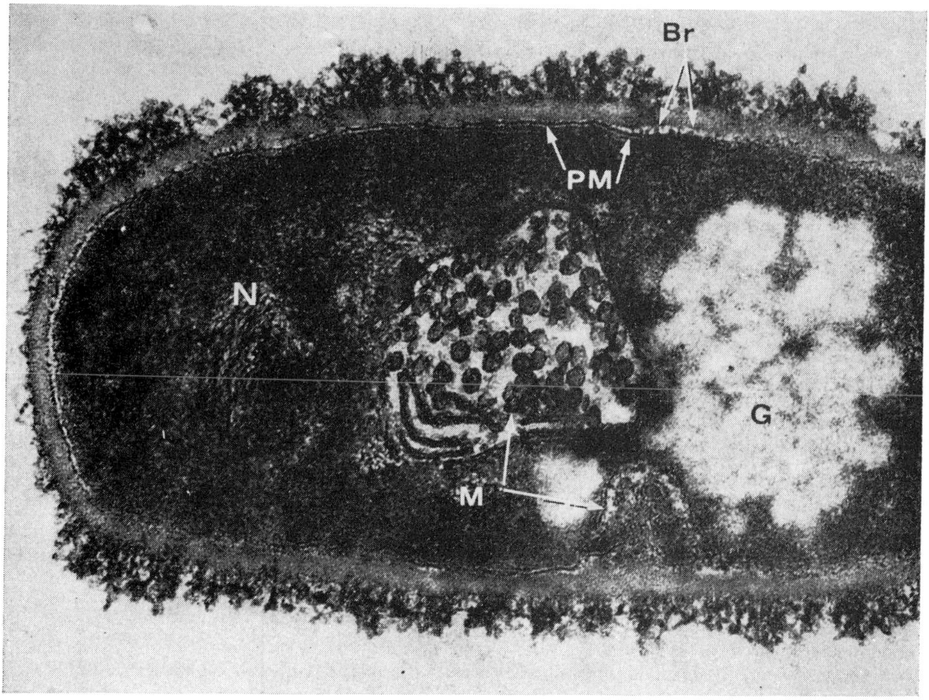

Fig. 2. *Bacillus megaterium*. After 18 hr growth in a glucose-rich medium. This figure and Fig. 3 provide examples of the relationship between the cell wall and the plasma membrane in a Gram-positive bacterium. The two integuments are parallel and cover each other closely and smoothly. Where they are separated by a retraction of the cytoplasm the connection is not easy to break, as is indicated by the 'bridges' Br. M: membranous organelle (mesosome); N: nucleoplasm; G: accumulation of reserve material, probably glycogen; PM: plasma membrane. × 94,000.

protoplast is more tightly attached to the cell wall along the sides of the cell than at its tip, or at the centre of dividing cells.

The cytoplasmic membrane or plasma membrane is considered to function as an osmotic barrier. It can, of course, hardly be conceived of as a semi-permeable membrane (cf. Schögl), but rather as one that is selectively permeable and actively engaged in the uptake of various nutrients and other materials. Bacteria maintain an osmotic balance in relation to their environment.

Inside practically all bacteria, the electron microscope reveals intracellular membranes in continuity with the plasma membrane, which are usually regarded as invaginations of the latter (see below). The fine structure of the membrane has been described as triple-layered and corresponding to the Davson–Danielli model. The inner profile of the plasma membrane is usually but little prominent, and difficult to distinguish from the dense cytoplasm (Figs. 2, 3). It can be studied to better advantage in partly plasmolysed cells, or after treatment with ether (Robinow 1962). Reinvestigation of the fine structure of bacterial membranes seems advisable in view of Sjöstrand's recent contention that in the same micrographs of animal cells on correct focussing some cytoplasmic membranes display a globular pattern, whereas in adjacent membranes a triple-layered structure is seen, in which the opaque layer facing the cytoplasm is thicker than that facing the extracellular space.

In frozen-etched preparations of *B. subtilis* we recently observed that the outside of the plasma membrane is studded with numerous granules and short fibrils (Figs. 4, 6), whereas the profile facing the cytoplasm is very much smoother.

(c) *Intracellular membranes*

Micro-organisms were formerly considered to be so small and primitive that they did

---

Fig. 3. *Bacillus subtilis.* A large mesosome M can be seen to extend, from the cell wall and plasma membrane, all through the cytoplasm to the nuclear area N. The organelle M is a cluster of delicately bordered vesicles which were found to be well preserved in frozen-etched specimens (Figs. 4, 6). The organelle's location on a developing cross wall, and its smooth continuity with it, suggest that it has a function related to the wall formation. Such an organelle therefore is a peripheral body in the sense of Chapman and Hillier. Br: 'bridges', i.e. connections between the cell wall and the somewhat retreated plasma membrane. PM: plasma membrane; M: membranous organelle (mesosome); N: nucleoplasm. ×150,000.

Fig. 4. *Bacillus subtilis.* In this frozen-etched specimen a cluster of vesicles (M) is clearly distinguishable from the plasma membrane PM by its much finer granular appearance. The plasma membrane is one its outside studded with numerous granules and short fibrils, apparently composed of these granules. ×104,000. (From Nanninga.)

Fig. 5. *Bacillus subtilis.* Section through a mesosome with the shape of a membranous whorl. ×147,000.

Fig. 6. *Bacillus subtilis.* Frozen-etched specimen. A mesosome is seen in a position comparable to that in Fig. 3. The fracturing, however, may have occurred alongside the site of septum development. Note the granules and short fibrils on the exterior of the plasma membrane; other pictures have shown that this membrane is on its inside less covered with protrusions (cf. Nanninga). × 62,400.

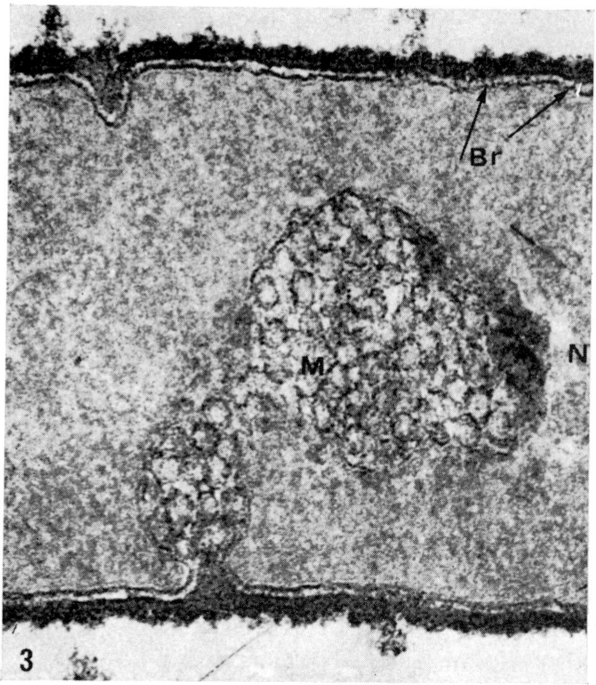
Br
M
N
3

PM
M
4

5

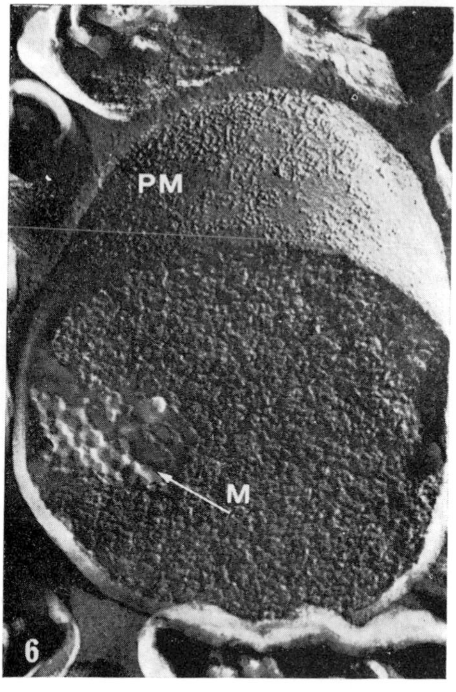
PM
M
6

not require special membranes, although elsewhere biochemical activities concerned with energy transfer are generally associated with membranous structures. Consequently the finding of an extensive system of membranes in the cytoplasm of an actinomycete (Glauert and Hopwood 1959, 1960b) came somewhat as a surprise. Chapman and Hillier had earlier described certain empty 'peripheral bodies' close to ingrowing septa in dividing *B. cereus* cells, but in their preparations the fine structure of these delicate organelles was disturbed. With the advent of more refined methods a number of authors (Van Iterson 1960–61; Glauert and Hopwood 1960a; Fitz-James 1960; Giesbrecht), soon followed by several others, provided ample evidence of the existence of complex membranous organelles inside a number of Gram-positive bacteria. In the Enterobacteriaceae, the Spirillae and in some other Gram-negative species, organelles of similar complexity proved not to be a regular feature, but later on they were in fact revealed in other species, so that in this group they are not lacking altogether.

It has often been suggested that the complex membranous organelles arise from repeated infoldings of the cell membrane, the continuity with which is often readily demonstrable (Fig. 3). It is important to note that these organelles occur not only in the cytoplasm, but also in the nuclear area. They are of somewhat variable organization: appearing as clusters of vesicles (Figs. 3, 4, 6) and tubules, as membranous whorls (Fig. 5), and as combinations of these two types of structures; they are enwrapped in a membrane in which triple-layered structure can often be recognized. Imaeda and Ogura ascribe these different appearances to sectioning a system of tubules under different angles. However, this cannot be so in all cases, as follows from frozen-etched preparations of *B. subtilis* (Figs. 4, 6) in which the separate vesicles can be recognized. In some instances, like the S membranes of Tomasz et al., the intrusions appear as single loops.

An interesting feature of the mesosomes is that through them a means of access to the extracytoplasmic environment is carried into the very interior of the cell. This observation, originally derived from work on sections, is confirmed by negative staining of whole cells: the stain enters the organelles, and by virtue of its opacity reveals the internal contours. Such a construction would facilitate the exchange of solutes between the cell's interior and the environment without materials having to pass through the cytoplasm proper (Van Iterson 1965).

The membranous organelles (plasmalemmosomes of Mercedes Edwards) are now usually called 'mesosomes' (Fitz-James 1960). To avoid confusion it should be borne in mind that not all of the membranes found in bacteria need be uniform in composition or function. After bleaching sections of Ryter-Kellenberger fixed material, Silva, by removing the lower oxides of osmium, found that the mesosomes are denser than the cytoplasmic membrane. Morphological differences between the outer membrane and mesosomes are also very evident in replicas of frozen-etched bacilli (Nanninga, Figs. 4, 6). Both sets of observation suggest the possibility that the two types of membranes differ in composition and function.

An important difference in the biochemical properties between the cell membrane and the internal organelles was revealed in *B. subtilis* with potassium tellurite and tetranitro-blue tetrazolium (see Van Iterson 1965). Under suitable conditions of oxygen limitation, reduction products were in both cases found to cover the membranes of the mesosomes. With reduction of tellurite, however, a few crystal-like precipitates were also found in the neighbourhood of the plasma membrane. Tetranitro-blue tetrazolium (TNBT) was less affected by the embedding procedures than the 2,3,5-triphenyl tetrazolium used previously by Van der Winkel and Murray, but the precipitates delimited the membranes less precisely and were less opaque than the reduced tellurite. Although certain problems remain unsolved, the conclusion seems warranted that mesosomes function as chondrioids (mitochondrial equivalents), and Sedar and Burde suggested that they are the bearers of the succinic dehydrogenase system. This contention is supported by the finding by Ferrandes et al. that the mesosomal fraction of *B. subtilis* is rich in cytochromes, and further by the observation of Cohen-Bazire et al. of the parallelism between an increased haem content in dividing organisms of *Caulobacter crescentus* during oxygen limitation and a larger than usual number of small, less involuted, membranous intrusions. The *Caulobacter* possessed an additional organelle which was superficially similar to the others, but not in open connection with the environment. This structure may have a function in the differentiation of the stalk. Mesosomes are not confined to aerobic bacteria; they also occur in e.g. *Clostridia* (Murray) and in *Lactobacillus plantarum* (Kakefuda et al.), which does not carry out an oxidative energy-yielding reaction.

It has been recognized that the internal structures might play a role in the production of the cell wall material (e.g. Van Iterson 1961; Imaeda and Ogura) and in forming the layers that envelop the endospore in bacilli (Fitz-James 1960; Young and Fitz-James; Robinow 1962). In plant cells, Golgi vesicles contribute material to the plasmalemma and the wall, and are involved in the synthesis of wall precursors. In this respect it would almost seem permissible to relate at least some of the membranous structures in the bacteria to the Golgi apparatus of the larger cells. Multivesicular bodies which superficially resemble mesosomes would move outward in order to fuse with the cell membrane, whilst dumping their content into the wall space. Even in bacteria a situation is known in which constituent vesicles of mesosomes travel separately through the cytoplasm, namely, on their extrusion into the infra-wall space during plasmolysis. Conversion into naked 'protoplasts' (gymnoplasts) is customarily performed in media of higher tonicity than the growth medium, the first cytological change then obtained is the displacement of intracytoplasmic and DNA-associated membrane systems towards the cell periphery (for an exception, see chapter 8). In a later stage small rounded vesicles appear to accumulate in large numbers in the empty space between the cell wall and the retracted protoplast. After removal of the cell wall with lysozyme, the vesicles are extruded into the medium (Fitz-James 1964; Ryter and Landman). According to Ryter, the membrane which enwraps the organelle is perhaps stretched out and incorporated into the cytoplasmic membrane during this process. L-phase variants of *B. subtilis*, which arise when this experiment is performed in a suitable medium, lack mesosomes and the capacity to make walls and transverse partitions (Ryter and Landman).

At present there is no evidence that the component vesicles of mesosomes are capable of acting like the Golgi bodies in the organization and redirection of cell products. The membranous invaginations resemble the endoplasmic reticulum in that they form enclosed systems within the cell, but as yet this analogy cannot be carried very far.

The membranous organelles of *B. subtilis* were recently revealed in frozen-etched cells (Nanninga; Figs. 4, 6) and appear to differ importantly in fine structure from that of the cell membrane. From this, and from what has been said above, it becomes doubtful whether the mesosomes, despite their apparent continuity with the cell membrane, are actually derived from it.

A most intriguing function recently postulated for the mesosomes by Ryter and Jacob (see Jacob et al.) is that they should control the replication of the genetic equipment in co-ordination with cellular division. The replicating units are considered to be connected to the membrane, and their distribution to the two daughter cells at every division would result from the growth of the membrane between the two attachment points. Support for this postulate is found in a number of experimental data. In serial sections of *B. subtilis* each nucleus, dependent on its stage of division, is in contact with one or two mesosomes. Moreover it became evident from the investigation of germinating spores (Ryter) that during replication of the chromosomes there are always two points of attachment of the nucleus to the membranes, either by the two mesosomes or by a mesosome and a smaller 'intermediate structure'. On plasmolysis, when the mesosomes have left the cytoplasm, the nucleus remains attached to the membrane by means of the intermediate structure. That growth of the membrane occurs between the two attachment points was inferred by Ryter from the distribution of tellurium needles along the cell membrane, and from cell elongation that occurred during germination of spores of *B. subtilis*.

The many functions suggested for the membrane systems seem to raise a problem for such Gram-negative micro-organisms as *E.coli* and *Proteus*, in which organelles of the tubular vesicular and the concentric membrane type are seldom revealed. When *Proteus* is incubated at low oxygen concentration with potassium tellurite, for the right period of time, the reduced product is found to be restricted to rounded areas contiguous to the plasma membrane. Nermut favours the explanation that tellurium deposits in *Proteus* correspond to sites of glycine oxidase activity; in our experience, however, there was a close correspondence with the sites where tetranitro-blue tetrazolium is reduced to its diformazan. Moreover, it was found (Fond and Leene, unpublished) that the polarographic reduction potentials of potassium tellurite and tetranitro-blue tetrazolium are approximately equal (i.e., between -0.20 V and -0.25 V), the potentials of both compounds being measured in the medium in which *Proteus* cells were incubated.

Ryter and Jacob (1966) have confirmed that in *E. coli* the structures, which are morphologically identical with the mesosomes in bacilli, are usually absent. However, in cells grown in synthetic media they skilfully demonstrated delicate, simple membrane intrusions near the nucleus, at the poles, or at the site of division. These membranes might be obscured by the cytoplasm in cells from nutrient broth. Although these membrane structures are not extruded during plasmolysis, similarly to what happens in bacilli, they may become part of the cytoplasmic membrane, the nucleoid remaining attached.

Azotobacter, sometimes selected for biochemical work on the electron transport chain, can have a cytoplasm packed with internal membranes (Fig. 7). It needs to be found out whether these membranes play a major role in the process of nitrogen fixation.

In the bacteria the process of ATP synthesis is not confined to electron transport mechanisms which are linked to oxygen. In chemo-autotrophic bacteria, certain chemical substrates are used as terminal acceptors. Evidence is accumulating that elaborate internal membranes are required for these chemosynthetic processes. Murray and Watson (cf. Murray) presented beautiful examples of nitrifying bacteria: *Nitrosomonas europea* and *Nitrosocystis oceanus*, which both oxidize ammonium ions to nitrite, and *Nitrobacter agilis*, which oxidizes nitrite to nitrate, all of them with highly organized membranes in the cytoplasm. On cell division in *Nitrosomonas* the whole lamellar structure divides and passes into the sister cells. These membranes therefore appear to be elements of a stable, self-reproducing cell organelle. For further discussion of interesting organelles like the one found in *Thiovullum*, cf. Murray.

The production of ATP by photophosphorylation is again coupled to internal membranes; i.e., the photosynthetic pigment is incorporated in a possibly continuous system of membranes connected to the plasma membrane. Like the photosynthetic apparatus of higher plants, that of bacteria consists of a system of vesicles which are either large and flattened and stacked as in grana, or smaller and rounded (Fig. 9). Menke coined the term 'thylakoid' for this membranous unit. Systems of the first type of plastid lamellae or thylakoids, resembling the lamellae in the three nitrifying organisms mentioned above, are found in the non-sulphur purple bacteria *Rhodospirillum molischianum* and *Rhodomicrobium vannielli*, and are much the same as the plastids in blue-green algae. On the other hand *Rhodospirillum rubrum* (Figs. 8, 9), the most studied of the non-sulphur purple bacteria, and *Rhodopseudomonas spheroides* will, under conditions of oxygen limitation, develop small vesicles whose formation can be suppressed by growing these facultative aerobic bacteria in air. An excellent review on the organization of the photosynthetic apparatus (chromatophores) in purple and green bacteria has been written by Germaine Cohen-Bazire. The author found that the cytoplasm of two large purple sulphur bacteria: *Chromatium okenii* and *Thiospirillum jenense* was also filled with vesicles 50 mμ in diameter and structurally indistinguishable from those in *Rhodospirillum rubrum*. The photosynthetic

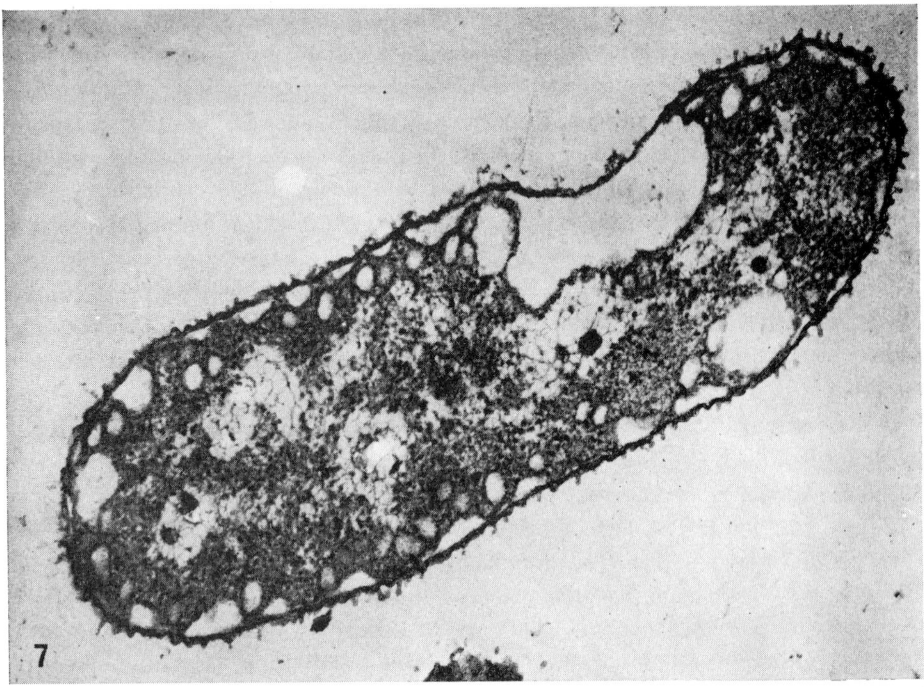
7

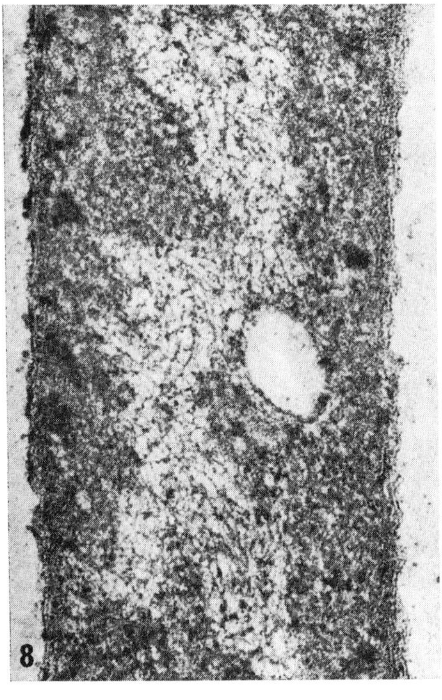
8

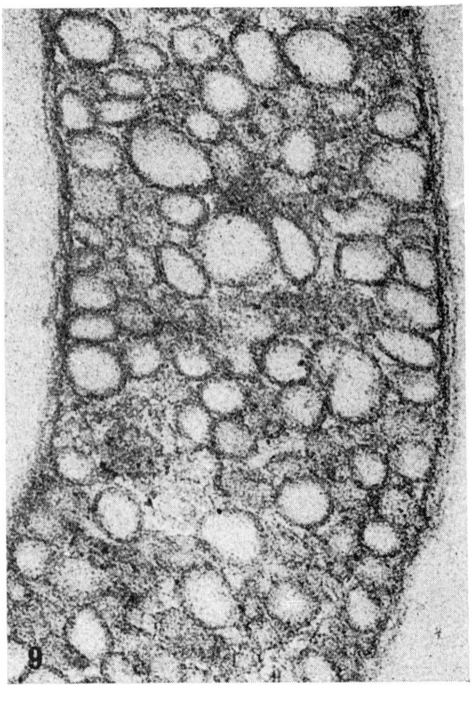
9

apparatus of the green sulphur bacteria: *Chlorobium* and *Chloropseudomonas* is considered to be somewhat different, namely, a system of ellipsoidal structures 100–150 mμ long and 30–50 mμ wide, close to the surface. An exact analysis of the molecular fine structure of the membranes and of the location of the quantasomes remains a difficult matter, even after Giesbrecht and Drews' analysis (by freeze-etching and other methods) of the thylakoids of *Rhodospirillum viridis.* This study revealed a beautiful pattern of 100-Å periodicity besides granula protruding into the vesicle lumen.

The pigments in non-photosynthetic carotenoid-containing bacteria have also been found associated with membranes (Mathews).

Thus, it appears that even in bacteria, membranes play essential parts in primary physiological functions.

2. *Flagella and pili (fimbriae)*

(a) *Introductory remarks*

The filamentous appendages of bacteria, because of their thinness, were the first components to be successfully demonstrated in the electron microscope. Notwithstanding the fact that individual flagella are hardly more than 10 mμ wide, the existence of locomotor organelles has been inferred since the middle of the 19th century. (For early literature, see Houwink and Van Iterson). Pili or fimbriae, on the other hand, were first discovered with the electron microscope.

(b) *Flagella*

It was the motility of bacteria which first drew Van Leeuwenhoek's attention to their very existence. The shape and behaviour of the locomotor organelles has been studied in the dark field and phase contrast microscopes, but much remains to be known. There also exist bacteria, such as the myxobacteria, *Beggiatoa* and *Vitreocilla*, which are capable of translational and rotating movements over solid surfaces, despite the fact that no type of motor organelle has been discovered so far. Recently, however, Gräf, and Pate and Ordall have related the movement of myxobacteria to the presence

---

Fig. 7. *Azotobacter vinelandii.* Unusual features of this organism are: (1) numerous small vesicles some of which may be continuous to large vacuoles; (2) small peg-like extensions of the cell envelope. Both these features may be connected with the uptake and the fixation of nitrogen. The vesicles resemble those of *Rhodospirillum* (see Fig. 9). × 62,500.

Fig. 8. *Rhodospirillum rubrum.* After heterotrophic growth in the dark this organism has been exposed anaerobically to light for 6 hr. Under the conditions of this experiment hardly anything can be observed of the photosynthetic vesicles that developed during longer illumination (see Fig. 9). The dark granules may be polyphosphate. × 130,000.

Fig. 9. *Rhodospirillum rubrum.* Grown anaerobically, exposed to moderately strong illumination for many hours. Numerous vesicles have developed that are interconnected and connected to the plasma membrane, and thus form a reticulum continuous with the plasma membrane. The photosynthetic pigments are integrated in this reticulum. × 115,500.

of 'peripheral fibrils' within the cell envelope, which are parallel to each other along the length of the cell. The speed developed by such organisms (5 μ/sec) remains far below that of flagellated organisms (50 μ/sec).

Bacteria move through water with one or more 'tails' or 'fascicles' which, when they have come to rest, split up into separate flagella; after proper mordanting and staining, these flagella can be seen even in the light microscope. The individual flagella, constituting the flagella bundle, emerge from different areas on the cell, and this phenomenon is used as a characteristic in the identification of bacteria. Flagella originate from one or two sites, usually the poles, i.e. *lophotrichous*, as in *Spirillum*; or they may emerge from all over the surface, i.e. peritrichous implantation, as in bacilli and enterobacteria. A close correlation exists between the presence of flagella and motility. However, some authors, amongst them Pijper, have held the view that motility is due to changes of the cell shape, rather than to the activity of its flagella. Pijper produced excellent motion pictures of swimming bacteria to prove his point that flagella are mere passive appendages, a product of movement instead of a mechanism for propulsion. Various arguments, which will not be repeated here, invalidate this viewpoint. It is of interest that the bacterial body can rotate either more slowly than the flagella bundle (Metzer) or more rapidly (Stocker). Bacterial motility has been discussed by Weibull (1960); Doetsch; Newton and Kerridge; Jahn and Bovee; Burge and Holwill.

When prepared for the light or electron microscopes the flagella tail usually splits up. The originally helical filaments, when flattened on the supporting surface, assume a sinusoidal shape with a wave length that is fairly constant for a given species. Sometimes there is 'biplicity', which means that two different wave lengths occur either amongst the flagella on the same cell, or even on the same flagellum. The shorter wave length is half that of the normal value. Mitani and Iino, using a curly mutant of *Salmonella abortivoequina*, were able to obtain information on the arrangement of individual flagella. The conformation of the bundled flagella of a swimming bacterium could be as follows: 'single flagella are parallel with each other and form a bundle consisting of five or more flagella; the bundles gyrate spirally, with the characteristic flagella wave.'

Are the thin threads as seen in electron micrographs flexible ropes, or are they contractile? Doetsch assumes that 'they are *inert*, rigid or semirigid helical structures, whose precise form reflects their macromolecular configuration and the influence of the physicochemical *milieu* thereon'. In view of the observation that flagella can be reconstituted *in vitro* from flagellin molecules (Abram and Koffler; Asakura et al.; Lowy and McDonough), and are then indistinguishable from intact flagella in thickness and sine-wave shape, Doetsch's suggestion does not sound too unlikely. This process of spontaneous reconstitution has been considered similar to crystallization (Asakura et al.). However, Martinez and Gordee put forward the idea that *in vivo* a biologically controlled mechanism is involved in aggregating the flagellum in an ordered structure.

According to Kerridge (1960) the phenotypic expression of the ability to produce flagella is affected by the environment, e.g. the temperature of incubation. Mechanically deflagellated *Salmonella* will regenerate functionally and morphologically normal flagella in a buffered-salts medium containing a complete amino acid mixture. When the phenylalanine of the mixture was replaced by 0.005 M DL-fluorophenylalanine, the regenerated flagella were not functioning, and in stained preparations had half the wavelength of normal flagella (Kerridge 1959).

Flagella consist almost exclusively of a protein (99%), although in some cases the presence of carbohydrate has been recorded (cf. Newton and Kerridge; Abram and Koffler). This protein of the flagella is of relatively low molecular weight (approximately 20,000–40,000). It has been called 'flagellin' by Astbury, and was classified by him with the keratin-myosin-epidermis-fibrinogen group of fibrous proteins, which he considered 'monomolecular muscles'. Flagella and muscle filaments are indeed of comparable width. A flagellum consists of isodiametric flagellin monomers polymerized into long, multi-stranded threads. Different types of arrangement of flagellin molecules in flagella of one kind of bacterium, have been suggested by Lowy and Hanson after a detailed analysis of negatively stained specimens. The authors point out that helices of globules in bacterial flagella resemble the helices of globules in actin molecules. The question whether the fine structure observed in flagella has anything to do with contraction, or whether flagella are rigid helices, has not been clarified thus far.

The base of the flagellum at the point where it pierces the cell wall is often thickened and bent to form a basal hook. Interesting illustrations of such hooks, differing in fine structure from the rest of the flagellum, have been given by Lowy. With the possible exception of the thick sheath enclosing the stout single flagellum of *Vibrio metschnikovii*, flagella and cell wall have little in common. When the cell wall is dissolved by lysozyme action, the flagella remain inserted in the naked protoplast (Weibull 1953). From shadowed preparations of cells that were old, or had been allowed to autolyze to make them more transparent in the electron microscope, it had been inferred that flagella originate from basal structures. However, later it was considered that such basal bodies could be artefacts caused by cytoplasmic coagulation around the base of the flagella. Recently the presence of basal structures has received renewed attention in the interpretation of negatively stained preparations of *Vibrio* (Glauert et al.), of *Proteus* (Abram et al. 1965; Hoeniger and Van Iterson 1963) of *Bacillus* (Abram et al. 1966), and of *Rhodospirillum* (Cohen-Bazire and London), but the conclusions arrived at by various authors remain controversial. Sometimes the hook at the base of the flagellum has been observed to be connected with a broadened part called 'collar' (c in Figs. 11 and 12) in the terminology of Hoeniger and Van Iterson. Two layers have been distinguished in the collar (see Abram et al. 1965; Cohen-Bazire and London). The collar (c) is connected, by means of a narrowing 'neck' part, to a small disc or cup (d, Figs. 11, 12) which can also have the appearance of a paired disc (Cohen-Bazire and London). But, whereas Cohen-Bazire and London

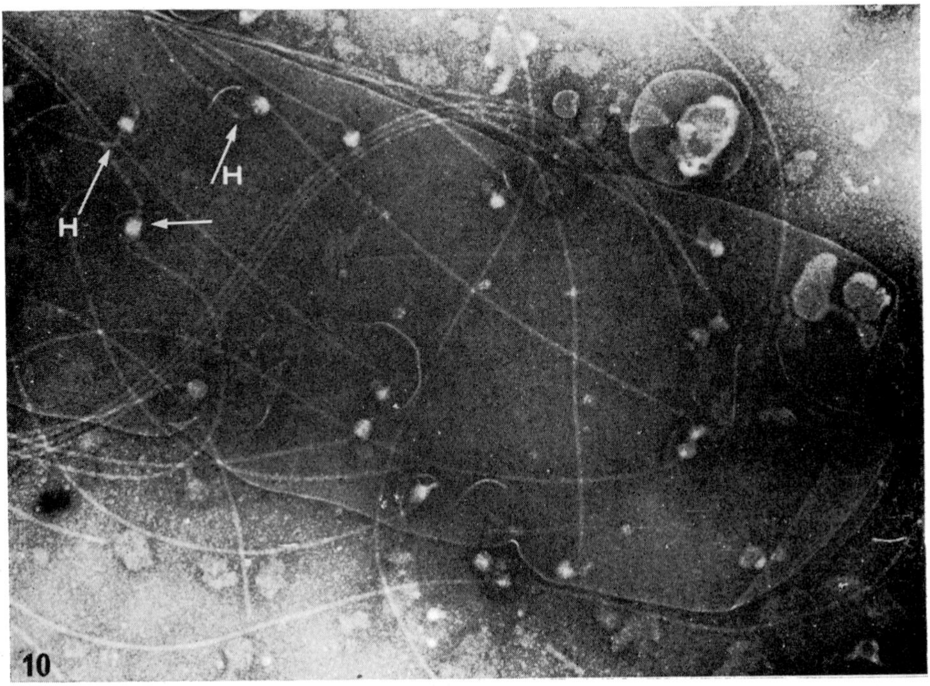
H
H
10

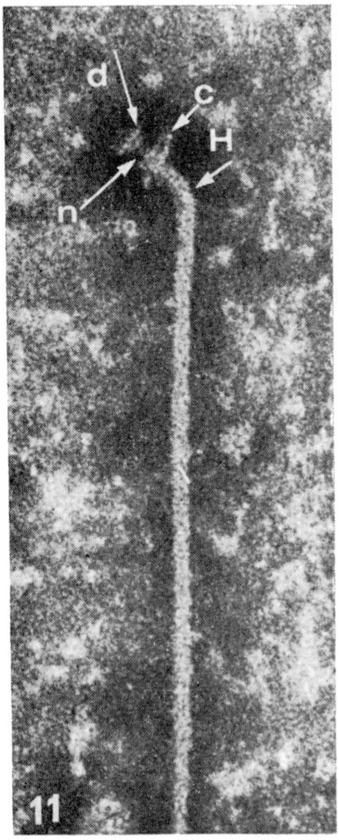
d
c
H
n
11

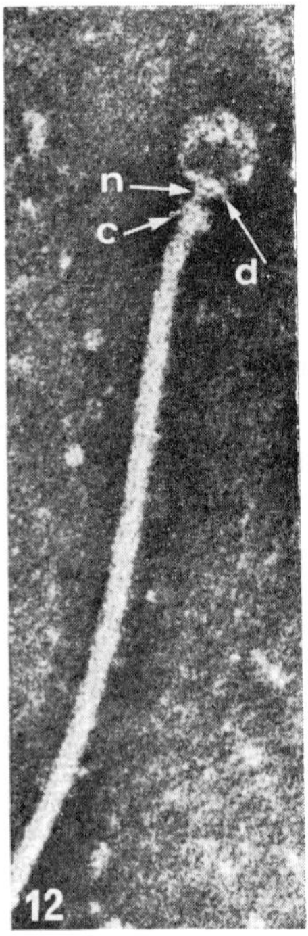
n
c
d
12

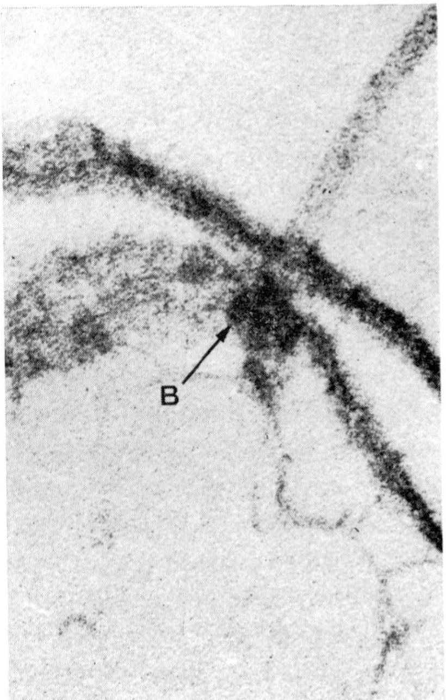
B
13

consider this whole structure, consisting of two paired discs connected by a narrower part, to represent the basal body, in our view the proximal 'paired disc' (d) is merely a specially dense component which apparently becomes easily detached from the rest of the spherical basal body (Fig. 12). The collar (c) is interpreted as a fragment of cell wall material. The basal organelles are apparently fragile, and not easily revealed in thin sections (Van Iterson and Hoeniger), although it has been seen that flagella originate beneath the plasma membrane (Murray and Birch-Andersen). In Fig. 13, in a section of *Proteus* released of most of its cell contents, a flagellum is seen to terminate in the basal body. Ritchee et al. show a very similar basal body on the flagellum of *Vibrio fetus*. Flagella probably have no ATPase activity, and Doetsch points out that the system converting chemical into mechanical energy should reside in the flagellar basal bulb.

The question of contractility may well be posed again for the spirochaetes, with their curious movements. These slender coiled organisms are held in shape by an axial filament or bundle of flagella-like fibrils situated between the cell wall and the cytoplasmic membrane (cf. Ryter and Pillot; Listgarten and Socransky). The cytoplasm is helically coiled around the bundle stretched between its two extremities. When the cell is flattened on a surface the axial rope sometimes unravels, displaying the separate fibrils (Fig. 14).

(c) *Pili (fimbriae)*

In the early stages of electron microscopy it was observed that bacteria may have a coat of straight filamentous appendages differing from flagella in their smaller diameter, their usually shorter length, and their lack of undulation (Houwink and Van Iterson). Now, more than eight morphologically distinct organelles of this type have been recorded (Brinton 1967). A single cell may have two or more kinds of them in addition to flagella and capsular material. The structures have been named 'fimbriae' by Duguid et al., and 'pili' by Brinton (1959). For reviews on this subject, see Brinton (1965, 1967).

Fig. 10. *Proteus mirabilis*. Preparation negatively stained with potassium phosphotungstate. Most of the picture is taken up by a hollow tube of cell wall freed from cytoplasm and plasma membrane. It is clearly seen that the flagella arise from a basal organelle. At the unlettered arrow two flagella seem to originate in a double basal structure. At H flagella are bent into a hook. × 68,300.

Fig. 11. Flagellum of *Proteus mirabilis* from which the basal body has been broken off (compare this figure with Fig. 12). At H hook-like bend. At c broadened part or 'collar', here interpreted as a remnant of the cell wall. At n the narrow 'neck' part, and at d a small disc which, as is evident from Fig. 12, forms the part where the flagellum is connected to the basal body. ×169,000.

Fig. 12. Flagellum of *Proteus mirabilis* on which the basal organelle has been well preserved. For legend, see Fig. 11. ×169,000.

Fig. 13. Flagellum of *Proteus mirabilis*, in a section of a cell relieved of most of its cytoplasmic contents, is seen to pierce both the cell wall and the plasma membrane, and to terminate in a basal body B. The thickness of the cell wall and the plasma membrane on the left of the picture are due to a tangential cutting in a relatively thick section. × 319,000.

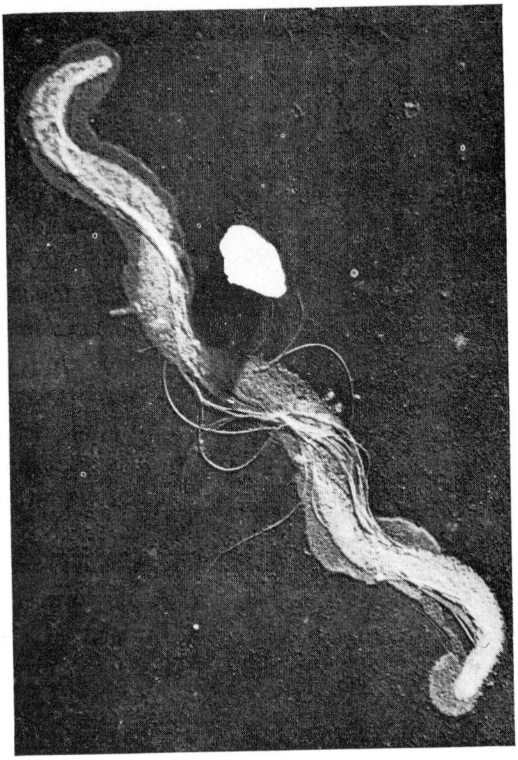

Fig. 14. A spirochete from the cecum of the guinea pig. A cable of fibrils between the cell wall and cytoplasm has partly unwound itself; it is still intact in the upper part of the picture. ×110,000.

The pili are long, thin appendages that grow out from all parts of the surface of many Gram-negative bacteria (Fig. 15). Some pili of polarly flagellated cells are polar (Schmidt 1966). Depiliation does not seem to affect the cell's viability. A characteristic of pili is their adhesiveness, which causes the bacteria to adhere to one another or to particles of e.g. polysterene latex, or to various cells such as red blood corpuscles, thus causing haemagglutination. Pili are antigenic; Gillies and Duguid prepared antisera which agglutinated only piliated strains.

Only 'type I pili' and 'F type pili' have been studied in detail. They consist of pure protein 'pilin' with a molecular weight of 16,600. It is possible to depolymerize pili into pilin subunits, which can repolymerize spontaneously to form pili indistinguishable from native pili in electron micrographs. In the presence of chloramphenicol,

---

Fig. 15. *Escherichia coli* with pili, probably of the type I. (Brinton, see text.) ×15,000.

Fig. 16. *Escherichia coli* with F pili which are here covered with male-specific RNA phages. (Courtesy Dr. C.C. Brinton.) ×20,000.

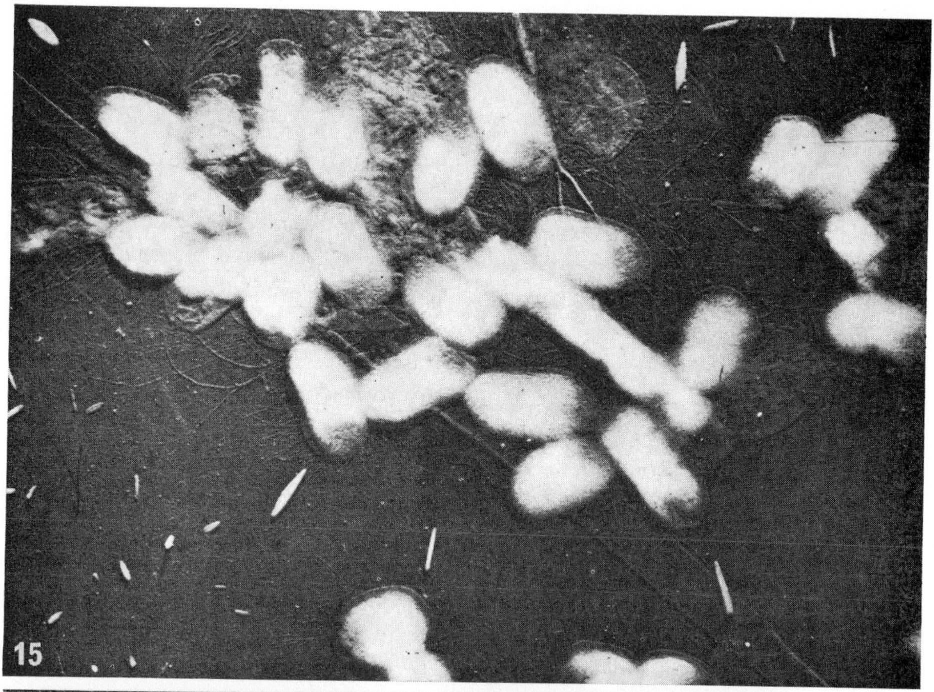
15

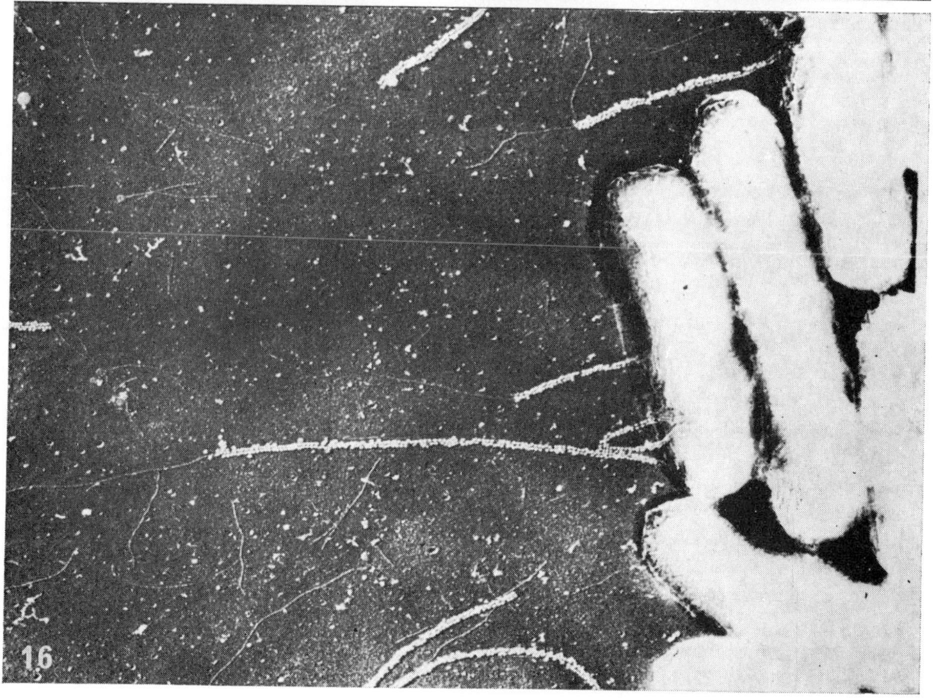
16

cells depiliated from type I or F type pili continue to regenerate these appendages, which may indicate that their growth is an assembly of presynthesized subunits from a pool rather than a *de novo* synthesis, as has been suggested also for flagella.

The type I pilus is a hollow rod, 70 Å wide. Based on X-ray diffraction studies, a model is proposed of the protein subunits assembled in a right-handed helix of pitch distance 24 Å, with $3\frac{1}{8}$ subunits per turn of helix, around an approx. 20–25 Å wide axial core (Brinton 1965). The presence or absence of type I pili is considered to be mutational in nature, cells having either hundreds of pili or none, but environmental conditions are also considered to play a part (Bösenberg). The piliated cells may have certain growth advantages: under limited oxygen and high cell concentration piliated cells, according to Brinton, grow twice as fast as non-piliated cells.

The interesting feature of F pili is that they have been found to be involved in the transport of bacterial and viral nucleic acid. The synthesis of this pilus was shown to be directed by the fertility factor F. Furthermore, the F pilus, as predicted by Brinton et al., has been found to be identical with the f^+ antigen (Ishibashi). The F pili of *E. coli* are rods, 85 Å in diameter, with an axial hale of about 20–25 Å (Fig. 16); they easily form longitudinal aggregates. Depiliated cells restore maximum F piliation within 5–10 min. They appear sometimes to have a 'terminal knob' (Lawn). It has been shown that a group of spherical male-specific RNA phages and a group of rod-shaped male-specific DNA phages attach to F pili (Crawford and Gesteland). In electron micrographs the RNA phages are then situated all along the length of the pilus, while the DNA phages attach to their tips. According to Brinton and Beer the F pilus is active in the transfer of DNA and RNA into the bacterium, a condition that may be analogous to the way nucleic acid is injected through phage tails, the pili serving as their tails for these tail-less phages. Schmidt noticed that in *Caulobacter*, too, bacteriophages contained RNA attached to the pili of their host. The F pilus is considered to serve during conjugation as conductor of the bacterial DNA, which would pass through the axial hole, from the donor to the recipient cell.

References

ABRAM, D. and H. KOFFLER: *In vitro* formation of flagellin-like filaments and other structures from flagellin. J. Mol. Biol. 9 (1964) 168.

ABRAM, D., H. KOFFLER and A. E. VATTER: Basal structure and attachment of flagella in cells of *Proteus vulgaris*. J. Bacteriol. 90 (1965) 1337.

ABRAM, D., A. E. VATTER and H. KOFFLER: Attachment and structural features of flagella of certain bacilli. J. Bacteriol. 91 (1966) 2045.

ASAKURA, S., G. EGUCHI and T. IINO: Reconstitution of bacterial flagella *in vitro*. J. Mol. Biol. 10 (1964) 42.

BÖSENBERG, H.: Beobachtungen über das Auftreten von Fimbrien und Geiszeln bei *Proteus vulgaris* in flüssigen Kulturen. Zentr. Bakteriol. Parasitenk., Abt. I. Orig. 203 (1967) 468.

BRINTON, C. C., JR.: Non-flagellar appendages of bacteria. Nature 183 (1959) 782.

BRINTON, C. C., JR.: The structure, function, synthesis and genetic control of bacterial pili and a molecular model for DNA and RNA transport in Gram-negative bacteria. Trans. N. Y. Acad. Sci. II 27 (1965a) 1003.

BRINTON, C. C., JR.: Contributions of pili to the specificity of the bacterial surface, and a unitary hypothesis of conjugal infectious heredity. In: Davis and Warren, eds.: The Specificity of Cell Surfaces, Englewood Cliffs, N. J., Prentice Hall, Inc. (1967) 37.

BRINTON, C. C., JR. and H. BEER: The interaction of male-specific bacteriophages with F pili. In: Colter and Paranchych, eds.: Molecular Biology of Viruses. New York, Academic Press (1967) 251.

BRINTON, C. C., JR., P. GEMSKI, JR. and J. CARNAHAN: A new type of bacterial pilus genetically controlled by the fertility factor of *E. coli* K12 and its role in chromosome transfer. Proc. Natl. Acad. Sci. U.S. (1964) 776.

BURGE, R. E. and M. E HOLWILL: Hydrodynamic aspects of microbial movement. In: 15th Symp. Soc. Gen. Microbiol. Cambridge University Press (1965) 250.

CHAPMAN, G. B. and J. HILLIER: Electron microscopy of ultrathin sections of bacteria. I. Cellular division in *Bacillus cereus*. J. Bacteriol. 66 (1953) 362.

COHEN-BAZIRE, G.: Some observations on the organisation of the photosynthetic apparatus in purple and green bacteria. In: H. Gent, A. San Pietro and L. P. Vernon, eds.: Bacterial photosynthesis. Yellow Springs, O., The Antioch Press (1963) 89.

COHEN-BAZIRE, G., R. KUNISAWA and J. S. POINDEXTER: The internal membranes of *Caulobacter crescentus*. J. Gen. Microbiol. 42 (1966) 301.

COHEN-BAZIRE, G. and J. LONDON: Basal organelles of bacterial flagella. J. Bacteriol. 94 (1967) 458.

COTA-ROBLES, E. H.: Electron microscopy of plasmolysis in *Escherichia coli*. J. Bacteriol. 85 (1963) 499.

CRAWFORD, E. M. and R. F. GESTELAND: The adsorption of bacteriophage R-17. Virology 22 (1964) 165.

DOETSCH, R. N.: Some speculations accounting for the movement of bacterial flagella. J. Theoret. Biol. 11 (1966) 411.

DUGUID, J. P., I. W. SMITH, G. DEMPSTER and P. N. EDMUNDS: Non-flagellar filamentous appendages ("fimbriae") and hemagglutinating activity of *Bacterium coli*. J. Pathol. Bacteriol. 70 (1955) 335.

EDWARDS, M. R.: Electron microscopic observations on the morphological characteristics of *Listeria monocytogenes*. In: M. L. Gray, ed.: Sec. Symposium on Listeric infection. Bozeman, Montana State College (1963).

FERRANDES, B., P. CHAIX and A. RYTER: Localisation des cytochromes de *Bacillus subtilis* dans les structures mésosomiques. Compt. Rend. 263 (1966) 1632.

FITZ-JAMES, PH. C.: Participation of the cytoplasmic membrane in the growth and spore formation of bacilli. J. Biophys. Biochem. Cytol. 8 (1960) 507.

FITZ-JAMES, PH. C.: Fate of the mesosomes of *Bacillus megaterium* during protoplasting. J. Bact. 87 (1964) 1483.

GIESBRECHT, P.: Über organisierte Mitochondriën und andere Feinstrukturen von *Bacillus megaterium*. Zentr. Bakt. Parasitenk. Abt. I Orig. 179 (1960) 538.

GIESBRECHT, P. and G. DREWS: Über die Organisation und die makromolekulare Architektur der Thylakoide 'lebender' Bakterien. Arch. Mikrobiol. 54 (1966) 297.

GILLIES, R. R. and J. P. DUGUID: The fimbrial antigens of *Shigella flexneri*. J. Hyg. 56 (1958) 303.

GLAUERT, A. M. and D. A. HOPWOOD: A membranous component of the cytoplasm in *Streptomyces coelicolor*. J. Biophys. Biochem. Cytol. 6 (1959) 515.

GLAUERT, A. M. and D. A. HOPWOOD: Membrane systems in the cytoplasm of bacteria. In: Proc. European Regional Conf. Electron Microscopy, Delft. II (1960a) 759.

GLAUERT, A. M. and D. A. HOPWOOD: The fine structure of *Streptomyces coelicolor* I. The cytoplasmic membrane system. J. Biophys. Biochem. Cytol. 7 (1960b) 479.

GLAUERT, A. M., D. KERRIDGE and R. W. HORNE: The fine structure and mode of attachment of the sheathed flagellum of *Vibrio metchnikovii*. J. Cell Biol. 18 (1963) 327.

GRÄF, W.: Bewegungsorganellen bei Myxobakterien. Arch. Hyg. Bakteriol. 149 (1965) 518.

HAGEN, P.O., M.GOLDFINE and P.J.LE B.WILLIAMS: Phospholipids of bacteria with extensive intracytoplasmic membranes. Science 151 (1966) 1543.

HOENIGER, J.F.M., W.VAN ITERSON and E.NIJMAN VAN ZANTEN: Basal bodies of bacterial flagella in *Proteus mirabilis* II. Electron microscopy of negatively stained material. J. Cell Biol. 31 (1966) 603.

HOUTSMULLER, U.M.T. and L.L.M.VAN DEENEN: Studies on the phospholipids and phospholipase from *Bacillus cereus*. Proc. Koninkl. Ned. Akad. Wet., Ser. B 66 (1963) 236.

HOUWINK, A.L. and W.VAN ITERSON: Electron microscopical observations on bacterial cytology II. A study on flagellation. Biochim. Biophys. Acta 5 (1950) 10.

IMAEDA, T. and M.OGURA: Formation of intracytoplasmic membrane system of Mycobacteria related to cell division. J. Bacteriol. 85 (1963) 150.

ISHIBASHI, M.: F.Pilus as f^+ antigen. J. Bacteriol. 93 (1967) 379.

JACOB, F., A.RYTER and F.CUZIN: On the association between DNA and membrane in bacteria. Proc. Roy. Soc. (London), Ser. B. 164 (1966) 267.

JAHN, TH.L. and E.C.BOVEE: Movement and locomotion of micro-organisms. Ann. Rev. Microbiol. (1965) 21.

KAKEFUDA, T., J.T.HOLDEN and N.M.UTECH: Ultrastructure of the membrane system in *Lactobacillus plantarum*. J. Bacteriol. 93 (1967) 472.

KERRIDGE, D.: The effect of amino acid analogues on the synthesis of bacterial flagella. Biochim. Biophys. Acta 31 (1959) 579.

KERRIDGE, D.: The effect of inhibitors on the formation of flagella by *Salmonella typhimurium*. J. Gen. Microbiol. 33 (1960) 519.

KORN, E.D.: Structure of biological membranes. Science 153 (1966) 1491.

LAWN, A.M.: Morphological features of the pili associated with *Escherichia coli* K12 carrying R factors or the F factor. J. Gen. Microbiol. 45 (1966) 377.

LISTGARTEN, M.A. and S.S.SOCRANSKY: Electron microscopy of axial fibrils, outer envelope, and cell division of certain oral spirochetes. J. Bacteriol. 88 (1964) 1087.

LOWY, J.: Structure of the proximal ends of bacterial flagella. J. Mol. Biol. 14 (1965) 297.

LOWY, J. and M.W.MCDONOUGH: Structure of filaments produced by re-aggregation of *Salmonella* flagellin. Nature 204 (1964) 125.

LOWY, J. and J.HANSON: Electron microscope studies of bacterial flagella. J. Mol. Biol. 11 (1965) 293.

MARTINEZ, R.J. and E.Z.GORDEE: Formation of bacterial flagella. I. Demonstration of a functional flagellin pool in *Spirillum serpens* and *Bacillus subtilis*. J. Bacteriol. 91 (1966) 870.

MATHEWS, M.M.: Ultrastructure of nonphotosynthetic carotenoid-containing bacteria. J. Bacteriol. 91 (1966) 1369.

MENKE, W.: Structure and chemistry of plastids. Ann. Rev. Plant Physiol. 13 (1962) 27.

METZNER, P.: Die Bewegung und Reizbeantwortung der bipolar begeisselten Spirillen. Jahrb. Wiss. Botanik 59 (1920) 325.

MITANI, M. and T.IINO: Electron microscopy of bundled flagella of the curly mutant of *Salmonella abortivoequina*. J. Bacteriol. 90 (1965) 1096.

MURRAY, R.G.E.: The organelles of bacteria II. In: A.Tyler and D.Mazia, eds.: The General Physiology of Cell Specialization. New York, McGraw Hill (1963) 28.

MURRAY, R.G.E. and A.BIRCH-ANDERSON: Specialized structure in the region of the flagella tuft in *Spirillum serpens*. Can. J. Microbiol. 9 (1963) 393.

NANNINGA, N.: Structural features of mesosomes (chondrioids) of *Bacillus subtilis* after freeze-etching. J. Cell Biol. 39 (1968) 251.

NERMUT, M.V.: Sites of 'glycine oxidase' activity in *Proteus vulgaris*. Can. J. Microbiol. 13 (1967) 551.

NEWTON, B.A. and D.KERRIDGE: Flagellar and ciliary movement in micro-organisms. In: Function and structure in micro-organisms. 15th Symp. Soc. Gen. Microbiol. Cambridge University Press (1965) 220.

PATE, J. L. and E. J. ORDAL: The fine structure of *Chondrococcus columnaris*. III. The surface layers of *Chondrococcus columnaris*. J. Cell Biol. 35 (1967) 37.

PIJPER, A.: Bacterial flagella and motility. Ergebn. Mikrobiol. Immunitätsforsch. Exptl. Therap. 30 (1957) 37.

RITCHIE, A. E., R. F. KEELER and J. H. BRYNER: Anatomical features of *Vibrio fetus*: Electron microscopic survey. J. Gen. Microbiol. 43 (1966) 427.

ROBINOW, C. F.: Outline of the visible organization of bacteria. In: J. Brachet and A. E. Mirsky, eds.: The Cell, IV. New York, Academic Press (1960) 45.

ROBINOW, C. F.: One the plasma membrane of some bacteria and fungi. Circulation 26 (1962) 1092.

ROBINOW, C. F. and R. G. E. MURRAY: The differentiation of cell wall, cytoplasmic membrane and cytoplasm of Gram-positive bacteria by selective staining. Exptl. Cell Res. 4 (1953) 390.

ROTTEM, S. and S. RAZIN: Adenosine triphosphatase activity of mycoplasma membranes. J. Bacteriol. 92 (1966) 714.

RYTER, A.: Relationship between synthesis of the cytoplasmic membrane and nuclear segregation in *Bacillus subtilis*. Folia Microbiol. (Prague) 12 (1967) 283.

RYTER, A. and F. JACOB: Étude au microscope électronique de la liaison entre noyau et mésosome chez *Bacillus subtilis*. Ann. Inst. Pasteur 107 (1964) 384.

RYTER, A. and F. JACOB: Étude morphologique de la liaison du noyau à la membrane chez *E. coli* et chez les protoplastes de *Bacillus subtilis*. Ann. Inst. Pasteur 110 (1966) 801.

RYTER, A. and O. E. LANDMAN: Electron microscope study of the relationship between mesosome loss and the stable-L state (or protoplast state) in *Bacillus subtilis*. J. Bacteriol. 88 (1964) 457.

RYTER, A. and J. PILLOT: Étude au microscope électronique de la structure externe et interne du Tréponème reiter. Ann. Inst. Pasteur 104 (1963) 496.

SCHMIDT, J. M.: Observations on the adsorption of *Caulobacter bacteriophagus* containing ribonucleic acid. J. Gen. Microbiol. 45 (1966) 347.

SCHÖGL, R.: General aspects of the transport of matter across non-semipermeable membranes. Protoplasma LXIII (1967) 288.

SEDAR, A. W. and R. M BURDE: The demonstration of the succinic dehydrogenase system in *Bacillus subtilis* using tetranitro-blue tetrazolium combined with techniques of electron microscopy. J. Cell Biol. 27 (1965) 53

SILVA, M. T.: Electron microscopic study on the effect of the oxidation of ultra-thin sections of *Bacillus cereus* and *Bacillus megaterium*. J. Ultrastruct. Res. 18 (1967) 345.

SJÖSTRAND, F. S.: The structure of cellular membranes. Protoplasma LXIII (1967) 248.

STOCKER, B. A. D.: Cellular organization in bacteria. In: Bacterial Anatomy, 6th Symp. Soc. Gen. Microbiol. Cambridge University Press (1956) 19.

TOMASZ, A., J. D. JAMIESON and E. OTTOLENGHI: The fine structure of *Diplococcus pneumoniae*. J. Cell Biol. 22 (1964) 453.

TOMCSIK, J. and S. GUEX-HOLZER: Änderung der Struktur der Bakterienzelle im Verlauf der Lysozym-Einwirkung. Schweiz. Z. Allgem. Pathol. Bakteriol. 15 (1952) 517.

VANDERWINKEL, E. and R. G. E. MURRAY: Organelles intracytoplasmiques bactériens et site d'activité oxydoréductrice. J. Ultrastruct. Res. 7 (1962) 185.

VAN ITERSON, W.: Membranes, particular organelles and peripheral bodies in bacteria. Proc. European Regional Conf. Electron Microscopy, Delft. II (1960) 763.

VAN ITERSON, W.: Some features of a remarkable organelle in *Bacillus subtilis*. J. Biophys. Biochem. Cytol. 9 (1961) 183.

VAN ITERSON, W.: Symposium on the fine structure and replication of bacteria and their parts. II. Bacterial cytoplasm. Bacteriol. Rev. 29 (1965) 299.

VAN ITERSON, W., J. F. M. HOENIGER and E. NIJMAN VAN ZANTEN: Basal bodies of bacterial flagella in *Proteus mirabilis*. I. Electron microscopy of sectioned material. J. Cell Biol. 31 (1966) 585.

WEIBULL, C.: The isolation of protoplasts from *Bacillus megaterium* by controlled treatment with lysozyme. J. Bacteriol. 66 (1953) 688.

WEIBULL, C.: Movement. In: I.C.Gunsalus and R.Y.Stanier, eds.: The Bacteria, I. Academic Press (1960) 153.

WEIBULL, C.: Morphology and chemical anatomy of bacteria. In: Bacterial and mycotic infections of man, 4th ed. Pitman Med. Publ. Cy. Ltd., (1965) 37.

YOUNG, E. and PH.C.FITZ-JAMES: Chemical and morphological studies of bacterial spore formation. J. Cell Biol. 12 (1962) 115.

CHAPTER 10

The internal organization of bacteria

WOUTERA VAN ITERSON

Laboratory of Electron Microscopy, University of Amsterdam, Amsterdam, The Netherlands

Contents

1. Nucleoplasm and cytoplasm
   (a) Introductory remarks
   (b) The nucleoplasm
   (c) The cytoplasm
2. Cell inclusions
   (a) General remarks
   (b) Storage compounds
   (c) The spore
   (d) Crystalline inclusions
   (e) Phage-like objects and inclusions of microtubule structure
3. Concluding remarks

1. *Nucleoplasm and cytoplasm*

(a) *Introductory remarks*

In bacteria nucleoplasm and cytoplasm are not properly separated from one another by means of a nuclear envelope, nor by any other distinct boundary. On the contrary: in sections of cells fixed by the Ryter-Kellenberger method, or pre-fixed with a suitable aldehyde-containing solution, an intermingling of these two phases can be observed, in particular in such Gram-negative organisms as *Escherichia coli* or *Proteus mirabilis* (Van Iterson 1965).

(b) *The nucleoplasm*

The picture of a neat ring-shaped bacterial chromosome, derived from experimental data and discussed by Caro in his chapter of this Handbook, has no morphological counterpart in the published works of electron microscopists, concerned with the behaviour of bacterial chromatin *in situ*. How the long molecule of DNA, which is about 1,000 times longer than the cellular compartment which houses it, is folded within it, remains as yet unsolved.

After the universal adoption of the Ryter-Kellenberger technique of fixation the bacterial nuclei appeared in sections as electron transparent vacuoles filled with a nucleoplasm composed of fibres. In numerous cases these fibres are seen crossing at random, seemingly unrelated to the shape of the nuclear area and the state of its division. The beginnings of the division of the 'genophore' (Ris 1961) are nowhere with certainty distinguishable from its terminal phases. Much of this unintelligible organization of the bacterial nucleus is undoubtedly accounted for by the fact that most electron microscopists have studied the chromatin of bacteria growing in relatively rich media. Under these conditions, as Yoshikawa et al. have shown, the bacterial chromosome may initiate fresh rounds of replication in newly replicated portions before the first round has been completed. In the confinement of the small nuclear volume *in situ* this is bound to produce highly complicated patterns.

Furthermore the entire genome must be transcribed, and it has been suggested (Doudney) that "RNA formation on the DNA template is required 'at the molecular or genetic level' for subsequent DNA replication". Does this take place at the sites of intimate contact between the nucleoplasm and cytoplasm? As yet it has not been sufficiently analysed whether all the fibrils in the nuclear area are parts of the single DNA molecule.

The work of Lark's group and that of Maaløe and Kjeldgaard has shown how DNA synthesis in growing bacteria may be regulated through the choice of a suitable culture medium. The continuous synthesis of DNA in cultures of randomly multiplying bacteria is now contrasted with sequences of slow increases in DNA per cell, sometimes followed by intervals of arrested replication. (For a different interpretation of the latter, see Koch and Pachler). The application of these techniques to the morphological study of the bacterial 'chromosome' replication promises to provide more readily interpretable images. The contrast between Figs. 2 and 3 of *B. subtilis* grown in a medium of simple salts with 2% glucose, and Fig. 1 of a cell grown in heart infusion broth, illustrates the degree of improvement that may be expected. This difference in the appearance of the nuclei, however, can be caused by the 'salt effect' described by Whitfield and Murray, and Kellenberger (1960), which changes the state of aggregation of chromatin in living bacteria. The two media used here are of not quite comparable osmotic values (calculated from freezing-point depression, i.e. −0.60 °C (345 milli-osmolar) in the heart infusion broth, and −0.85 °C (485 milli-osmolar) in the synthetic medium).

Curved and twisted patterns of fibre bundles are found in bacilli even in rich broth during the first few generations obtained from germination of spores (Robinow 1962b). In most other cases, as in the minute cocci found by Ruys in human strains of mycoplasma (Van Iterson and Robinow) the coiled rope-like organization within the nuclear areas may be caused by the slow growing of the cells (see also the micrographs of Fuhs).

It is interesting to note that dinoflagellates, as has been shown repeatedly, have

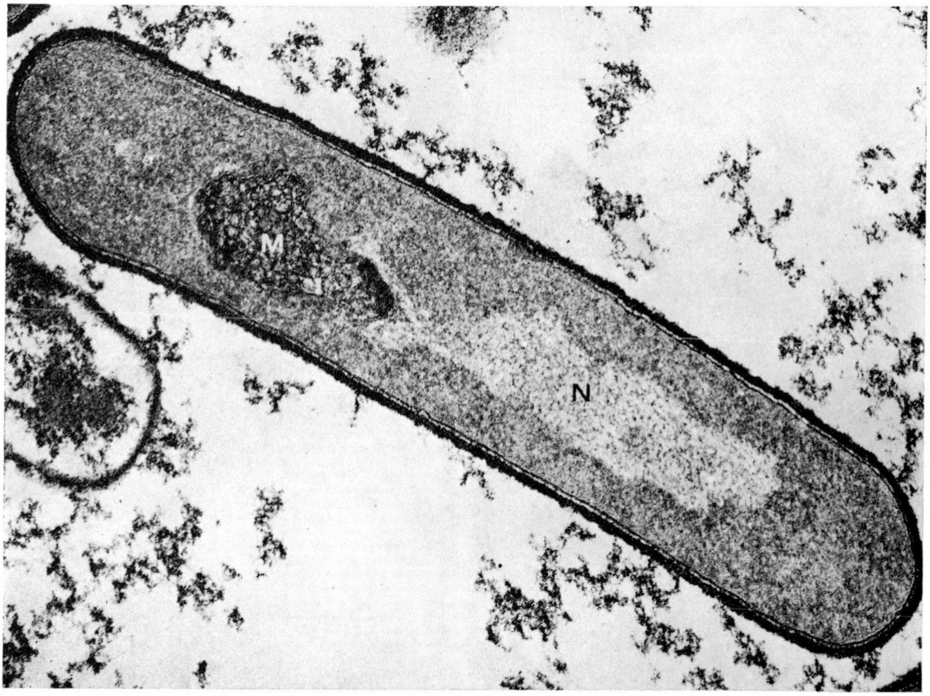

Fig. 1. *Baccillus subtilis* strain Marburg. Grown in heart infusion broth, the nuclear area (N) appears filled with a felt-work of criss-crossing fibrils. In bacilli from heart infusion broth cultures patterns of ordered nuclear fibrils are encountered only very rarely in germination (Fig. 12). Note the well-developed mesosome M. × 85,000.

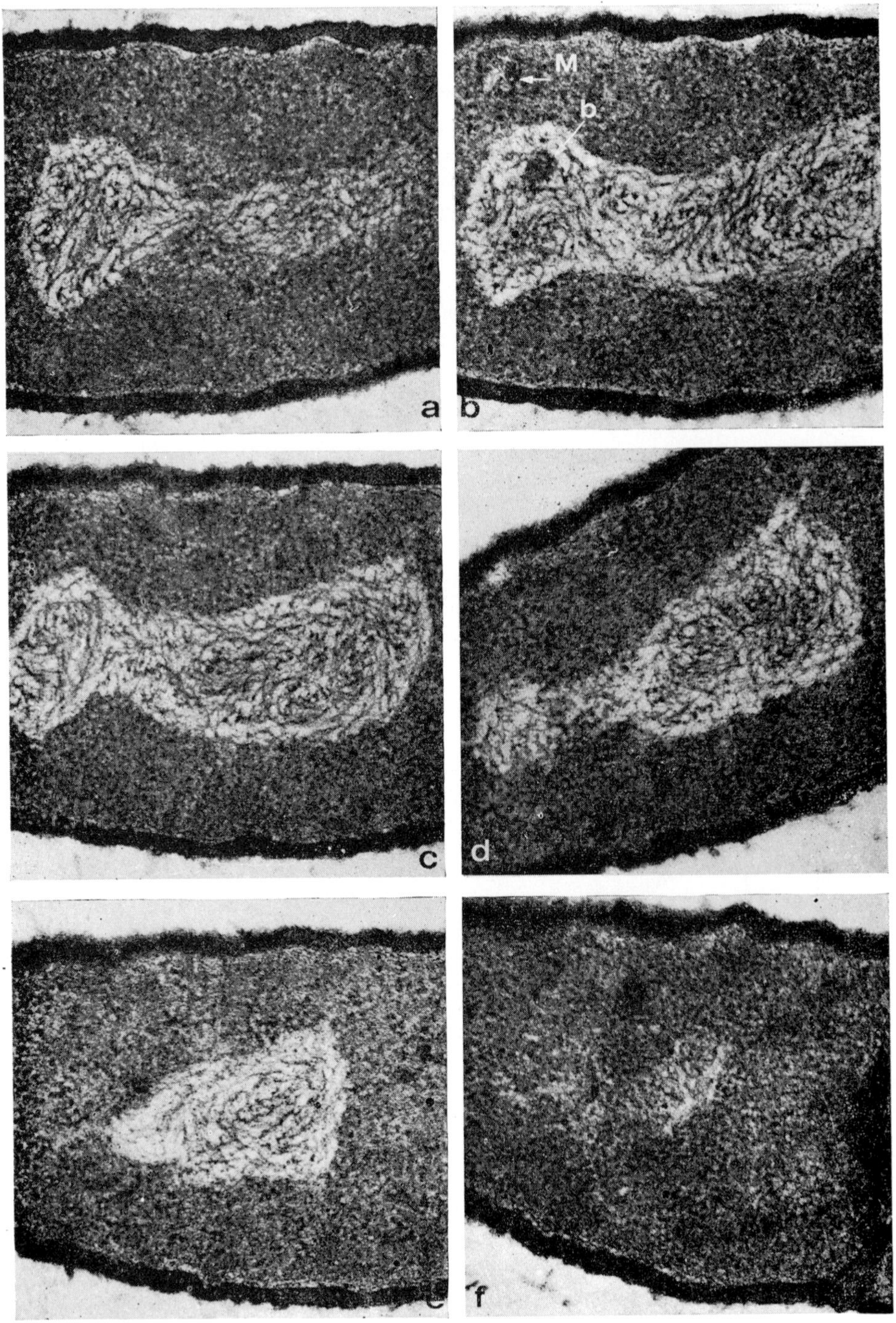

Fig. 2. *Bacillus subtilis* strain W23. Loose, swirling patterns of fibrils in serial sections of the nuclear area of a bacillus from a culture grown in a synthetic salt medium supplemented with 2% glucose. Compare with the dense felt-work of fibrils in the nuclear area of Fig. 1. It is remarkable that under these conditions the mesosomes are far less developed than in the rich broth, and are not easily visible in the dense cytoplasm. × 94,000.

chromosomes which lack histones. Their chromosomes closely resemble bacterial genophores in their fine structure, and separate after division by an unusual form of mitosis (Giesbrecht; Kellenberger 1962; De Haller et al.; Dodge; Leadbetter and Dodge). In ordinary bacteria such as *E. coli*, *B. subtilis* and *B. cereus*, the cycle of growth and division of the nuclei is more or less intelligible at the level of the light microscope, but it must be pointed out that this is not true of the nuclei of many other species, e.g. *Vitreoscilla* and the giant bacteria from the gut of tadpoles described by Delaporte (1964a, b). For further details the reader should consult the reviews of Robinow (1960a, b), and Murray.

The behaviour of nuclear material during spore formation is also not easily interpreted. In the presence of chloramphenicol the nuclear material aggregates in the centre of the cell (Kellenberger and Ryter; Morgan et al.), whereas UV irradiation causes its dispersal in the form of an extended tortuous vacuole (Ryter 1960). In spheroplasts, protoplasts and large L-forms the fibrillar material seems to fuse, and its subdivision in small compartments when the small L-phase variants each receive their part of the genomes is an interesting problem.

Ris (1966) has rightly stressed that "since the term 'chromosome' has been applied to the complex nucleoprotein structure of the eukaryote nucleus, it is unwise to use it also for the DNA molecule of viruses or bacteria", and he suggests "'genophore' as a general term to designate the physical counterpart of a linkage group". The bacterial 'chromosome' or 'genophore' is functionally the equivalent of all the chromosomes in the nucleus of the eucaryotic cell. DeLamater held that one or two centrioles take part in the separation of divided bacterial chromosomes. Robinow (1960b), confirming the presence of these structures, equated the 'centrioles' or 'accessory chromatin granules' as he called them with the systems of membranes in contact with the nuclear material found in electron micrographs of *B. cereus* and *B. subtilis* (Van Iterson 1960). Giesbrecht believed that the nuclei are chromosomes in close contact with 'membrane bodies' capable of dividing, and stated: "Since the 'membrane bodies' themselves could have either a direct or an indirect connection with the cell surface, there seems to exist at least a temporary connection between the chromosomes of the bacteria and the cell surface". These earlier views on the importance of the contact between the nuclear DNA (cf. Van Iterson 1960, 1961) with the membrane systems have received a fresh impetus from the interesting studies of serial sections of *B. subtilis* by Ryter and Jacob (cf. chapter 9).

Much remains to be clarified about the replication, unwinding and segregation of the DNA within the nuclear space, the attachment point(s) to the membrane, and the relationships to other important macromolecules.

(c) *The cytoplasm*

It is a curious fact that so little is known with certainty about the details of the structural organization of the bacterial cytoplasm, in view of the present well-established information on the structure and properties of ribosomes in *in vitro* systems.

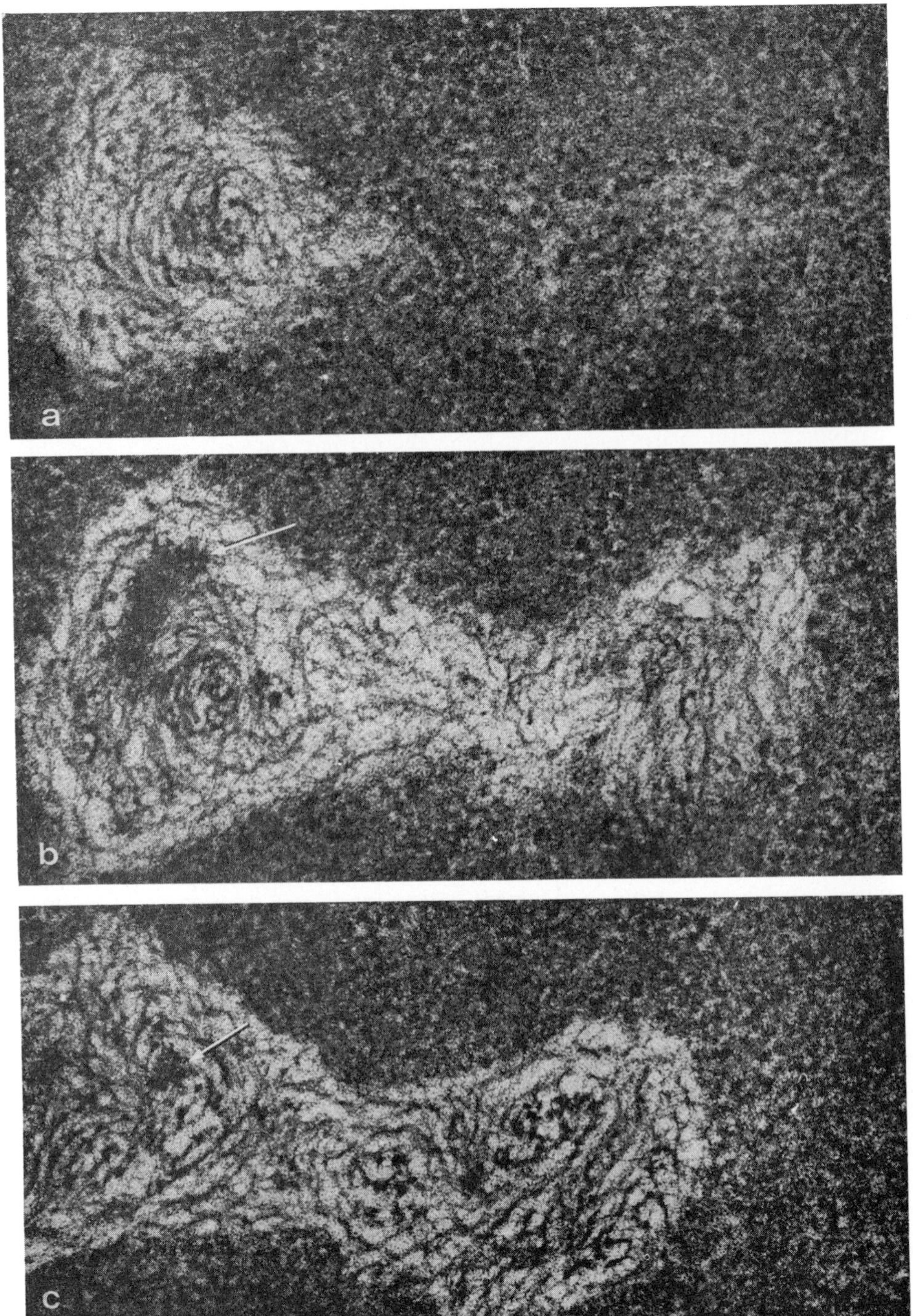

Fig. 3 (*For legend see p. 203.*)

The study of serial sections has revealed nothing in support of the theory that bacteria (*E. coli*) contain free ribosomes. Data are accumulating to confirm that in protein synthesis in micro-organisms 'microbial membranes' are involved (cf. Hendler). There is, however, no evidence that the 'membranes' are the intracellular membrane systems or mesosomes.

In sections, at good resolution, there seems to exist no contact between the comparatively electron-opaque ribonucleoprotein component of the cytoplasm and the mesosomal membranes. Even if such a contact would exist it cannot be essential, in view of the fact that in hypertonic solutions the mesosomal vesicles are displaced and expelled from the cytoplasm without effecting the cell's viability.

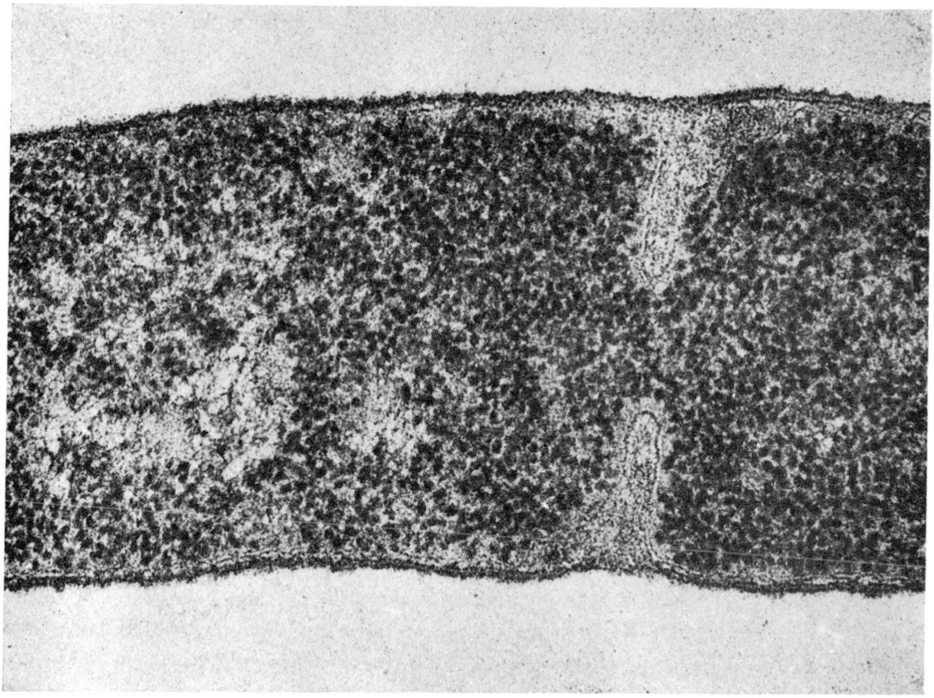

Fig. 4. *Bacillus subtilis*. Prepared according to Silva. The cells have first been fixed in glutaraldehyde followed by osmium tetroxyde, which was later removed with periodic acid. Further treatments include: uranylacetate, and poststaining with lead. A clear distinction can now be made between the ribosomes and diffuse, less densely stained background material. (Courtesy N. Nanninga.) ×100,000.

Fig. 3. *Bacillus subtilis* strain W23. The patterns of the nuclear fibrils in the nucleoids of cells grown in the synthetic, glucose-enriched medium are as yet, even at high magnification, difficult to analyze. The delimitation of the nucleoplasm against the cytoplasm is not sharp, but fibrils are seen to continue in the cytoplasmic region at least in these comparatively thick sections (cf. also Van Iterson 1966). Note the extent to which the dumbbell-shaped nucleoid of Fig. 2 resembles that of Fig. 3, even down to the presence of a dark area; possibly cross-sections of fibrils at the arrows in Figs. 2b, and 3b and c. ×178,000.

Since 1964 the author has advanced the view that the ribonucleoprotein in bacteria appears to be 'part of an all pervading fibrous continuum connected to the plasma membrane' (Van Iterson 1965, 1966). Fibrillar material from the nuclear area, which need not all be DNA, was observed to extend all through the cell, and seemed to provide a fibrillar framework for the cytoplasm. Schlessinger et al. arrived at an almost as extreme conclusion: 'the ribosomes are distributed on a reticular matrix which extends throughout the cytoplasm'.

Fitz-James (1964) has shown festoons of ribosomes to be suspended from the protoplast membrane of *B. megaterium*, and Pfister and Lundgren, after rupturing cells of *B. cereus* by freezing and thawing, also found that clusters of ribosomes remained associated with the cell membranes.

Electron micrographs obtained after freeze-etching of cells which remained perfectly viable after glycerol impregnation and cooling, provide further evidence for the point of view that the cytoplasm consists of three-dimensionally interconnected 'cords' (see e.g. Fig. 5). These cords, which are about 30 mμ wide in the frozen-etched preparations, probably correspond with the much shrunken cords of material found in the fixed, dehydrated and sectioned cell (Van Iterson 1966).

The 'particulate' nature of the ribosomes, on the other hand, is exceptionally clear in Fig. 4 where the cell has been prefixed with glutaraldehyde before osmium fixation, the osmium having been removed later.

Taylor and Storck suggest that the unique sedimentation coefficient of 70 S ribosomes of bacteria and blue-green algae should be used to define this group further in distinction of the eucaryotic organisms.

2. Cell inclusions

(a) *General remarks*

It seems that the cell inclusions to be described hereafter usually, if not always, result from a change in the metabolic processes of the bacteria, a change which can occur either naturally towards the end or after completion of exponential growth, or can be induced by the introduction of foreign DNA or RNA.

(b) *Storage compounds*

The composition of the environment affects the constitution of bacteria. When, for example, growth is restricted in the presence of a suitable carbon and energy source lipids accumulate which are sometimes considered as a storage form of carbon atoms at relatively high-energy levels. In *E. coli* the lipid granules may contain pure phosphatidyl ethanolamine, but in many other organisms they consist of poly-β-hydroxybutyrate (see Fig. 5, and chapter 8, Figs. 15 and 16). According to Lundgren et al. the poly-β-hydroxybutyrate polymer is *in vivo* crystalline with a fiber repeat of 5.9 Å. In sections in the electron microscope the lipids, after being extracted during the

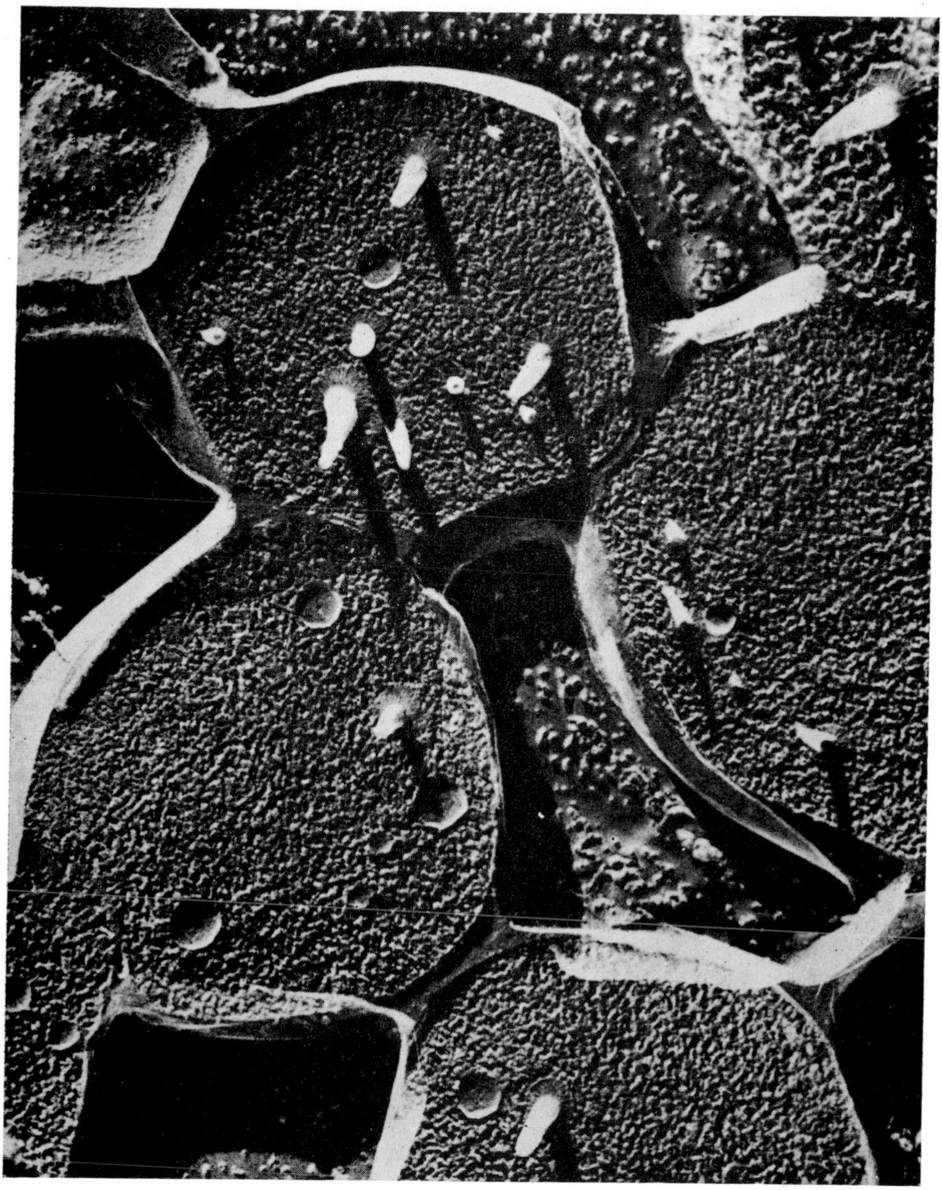

Fig. 5. Frozen-etched naked protoplast (gymnoplast) of *Bacillus megaterium*. Cells from an overnight culture grown at *p*H 7 first freed from their cell walls by lysozyme in a stabilizing medium, and then submitted to Moor and Mühlethaler's freeze-etching procedure. The poly-β-hydroxybutyrate accumulations that appear to be empty rounded areas in sections (chapter 8, Figs. 15, 16) are here seen as elongated structures with long shadows sticking out from the surface replica. Where they were severed from the cytoplasmic surface they have left behind rounded imprints. $\times$ 29,000.

processing, are often seen to have left behind empty rounded areas (chapter 8, Figs. 15 and 16). It is rather surprising that in the frozen-etched *B. megaterium* cells the same 'sudanophilic granules' appear elongated with a fan-shaped basis (Fig. 5). This phenomenon is perhaps an artefact introduced by the cleavage process.

Several bacterial species accumulate intracellular polysaccharides; in *E. coli*, and probably also in *B. megaterium* (Fig. 7 and chapter 9, Fig. 2), this takes the form of glycogen.

Metachromatic or volutin granules develop in some bacteria, when their growth becomes restricted, in medium containing a source of energy, phosphate, and sufficient Mg and Ca ions. The structure, the metabolism and the – largely hypothetical – functions of this inorganic phosphate have recently been discussed by Harold. In electron micrographs these accumulations appear as uniformly opaque structures that are not readily extractable. They can probably be complexes of polyphosphate with protein and RNA. Voelz et al. found, in *Myxococcus xanthus* electron micrographs, the granules to be associated with glycogen inclusions, and dispersed in the cytoplasm or in the nucleoid. A competitive relationship has been postulated between inorganic polyphosphate and nucleic acid metabolism (cf. Harold). In the large polar bodies in coryne- and myxobacteria the physiological pathways of the inorganic polyphosphate may be rather complex.

In certain sulphur bacteria accumulations of sulphur occur. In the light microscope they appear as highly refractile droplets. They serve as an energy reserve; the sulphur, an oxidation product of hydrogen sulphide, can be further oxidized to sulphate.

(c) *The spore*

In the genera *Bacillus* and *Clostridium* and in some other bacteria a small resting cell surrounded by various integuments can develop. It differs from the parental cell in chemical and morphological structure, in content of enzymes and in physiological functions. The dormant spore is resistant to heat, metabolically inactive, and in the light microscope recognizable by its high refractility. This latter property and heat resistance are usually related to the presence, in relatively large quantity, of an uncommon substance: the calcium salt of dipicolinic acid.

Several authors (e.g. Young and Fitz-James; Ryter and Jacob; Ryter 1965; Freer and Levinson) have now analyzed the morphological changes which take place during sporulation, and the following is a summary of their main results. When cells start to form spores they stop growing exponentially in an environment rich in various minerals; they then often contain two nucleoids. Ryter distinguishes six stages of spore formation. The onset of sporulation is the appearance of an axially disposed cord of chromatin. It has been suggested that such a cord could result from fusion of several vegetative chromatin bodies (cf. Robinow 1960c), often two (Young and Fitz-James), but this is interpreted by Ryter as the result of an incomplete separation of the two parts of one replicated nucleoid from the vegetative cell. The axial chromatin rod breaks up into two nucleoids in the process of the formation of the forespore. One

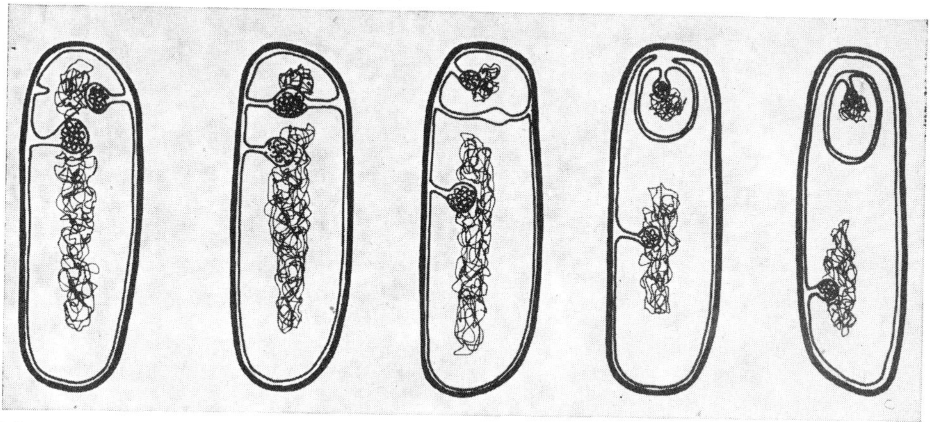

Fig. 6. Schematic drawing of the sequence of events during the formation of the endospore after various authors (see text).

nucleoid moves to the cell pole where it becomes secluded from the remainder of the spore mother cell by an inward growing invagination of the plasma membrane, which eventually closes by fusion, thus giving rise to a double forespore membrane (see Figs. 6 and 7). In this way an interesting continuity is preserved between the plasma membrane of the sporangium, that of the spore, and that of the next vegetative generation. A mesosome accompanies the chromatin in the forespore, and another one remains attached to the nucleoid of the sporangium (Fig. 6). Mesosome activity is also associated with the delineation of the two membranes around the forespore. Apart from the closure where they meet, there is also growth of the membranes towards the cell pole (Figs. 6 and 7). Eventually the forespore becomes enwrapped completely. The space between these two forespore membranes corresponds with the space where normally in the vegetative cell division the cross wall is formed, but here the cortex develops in it. At the same time the spore becomes refractile. The innermost layer of the cortex has been called 'cell wall primordium' (Freer and Levinson) because this layer appears to give rise to the cell wall during spore germination. In sequence (starting from inside) the layers surrounding the spore core are: a plasma membrane, the cell wall primordium, the cortex i.e. a sometimes very thick, intricately organized envelope (Robinow 1953; Mayall and Robinow), the outer cortical layer, a multilayered outer spore coat, and lastly, in some species, the exosporium. It is generally agreed that spore coat synthesis is a function of the spore mother cell rather than of the forespore. It is now understood that the cortex and outer cortical layer probably consist essentially of mucopeptide similar to that found in the walls of vegetative cells (Warth et al. 1963b), and that it has a low mineral content (Thomas). The spore coats would mainly be proteinaceous (Warth et al. 1963a); on micro-incineration Thomas obtained a highly ordered fine structure of minerals in the middle layer of the coats. Even the core cytoplasm turned out to be unusually rich in minerals. The exosporium is sometimes of a complicated structure (not visible in Figs. 9–12). Gerhardt and Ribi

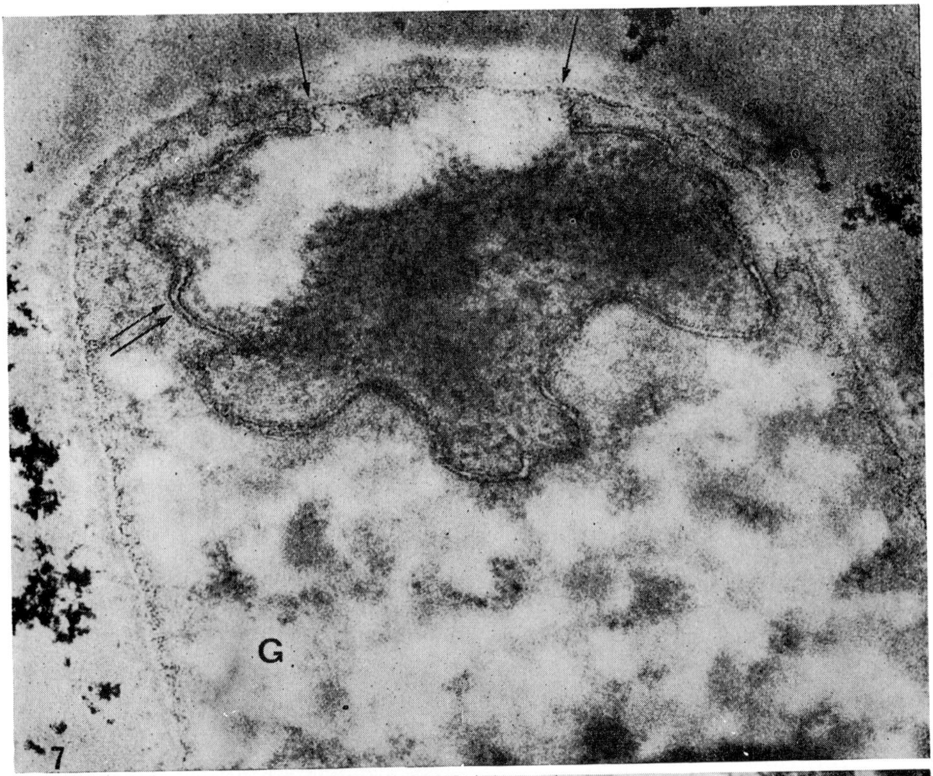
G
7

8

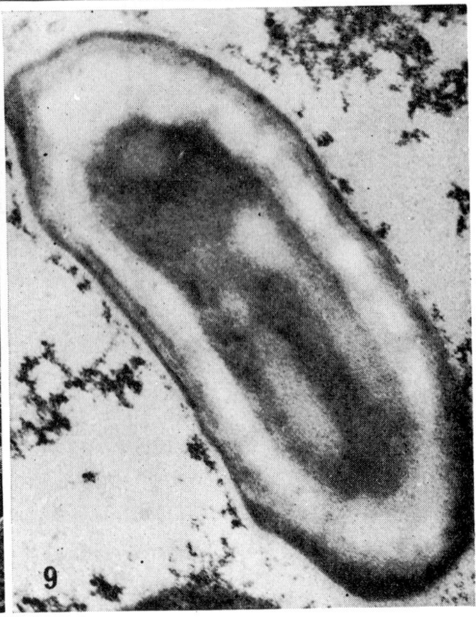
9

found it to consist, for the *B. cereus* spore, of two main layers: an outer one with a nap of hair-like projections, and an inner basal layer with a hexagonally perforate surface pattern of holes. Spores are often provided with a characteristic surface structure which can be valuable as a taxonomic aid. Here we will only mention the curious tubular, approximately 200 Å wide appendages on the surface under the exosporium of *Clostridium* spp., which are either sealed at the distal end and bear a hemispherical cap, or are open (Hodgkiss et al.). Hirsute appendages have been described by Pope et al.

The transformation of the dormant spore into the vegetative cell (Figs. 10–12) involves three steps: activation, for instance by pre-heating in water; germination in a suitable medium which does not involve protein synthesis but leads to enzyme activation; and finally outgrowth. Germination is accompanied by loss of refractility, heat resistance, and excretion of sometimes 30% of the spore's dry weight in the form of dipicolinic acid, calcium, peptide and enzymes. The cortex disintegrates, the cell wall primordium thickens and becomes the cell wall of the germling cell. (Figs. 10, 11).

The fate of the nuclear material in the entire process from spore formation to germination remains at present obscure. From the axial chromatin the DNA equivalent of one 'chromosome' is included in the spore together with a mesosome; in the more mature spore the nuclear material becomes arranged against the plasma membrane and is then rather voluminous (Robinow 1953; Fitz-James 1953; Ryter 1965). Halverson et al. isolated from the spore of *B. subtilis* a form of DNA that proved to be unusually heavy in a caesium chloride gradient; it appeared shortly before the onset of thermal resistance and disappeared during the outgrowth after germination.

Undoubtedly spore formation provides a most intricate example of cell differentiation.

The cysts, such as they develop, in for instance *Azotobacter* ssp., or the microcysts of the Myxobacteria, are formed by a shortening and rounding up of a vegetative cell followed by the formation of a thick envelope consisting of a sort of capsule, the intine, covered on the outside by a laminated structure, the exine or cyst coat. The cysts are resistant to elevated temperatures, etc., but they are not comparable with spores, in particular not in the way they originate.

(d) *Crystalline inclusions*

In the cells of certain bacilli, e.g. *B. thuringensis* or *B. cereus* var. *alesti*, pathogenic for

---

Fig. 7. Spore formation in *Bacillus cereus*. Note that two membranes (double arrows) envelop the spore primordium, and are still in contact with the plasma membrane (at arrows). (From Robinow 1962.) ×86,000.

Fig. 8. Carbon replica of *Bacillus subtilis* spores. The surface ridges are not known to correspond to any structures seen in sections. × 45,000.

Fig. 9. Spore of *B. subtilis* in section. Due to the imperviousness to liquids of spores before they have been 'woken up', they cannot be fixed adequately. This figure should be compared with Fig. 10. × 95,000.

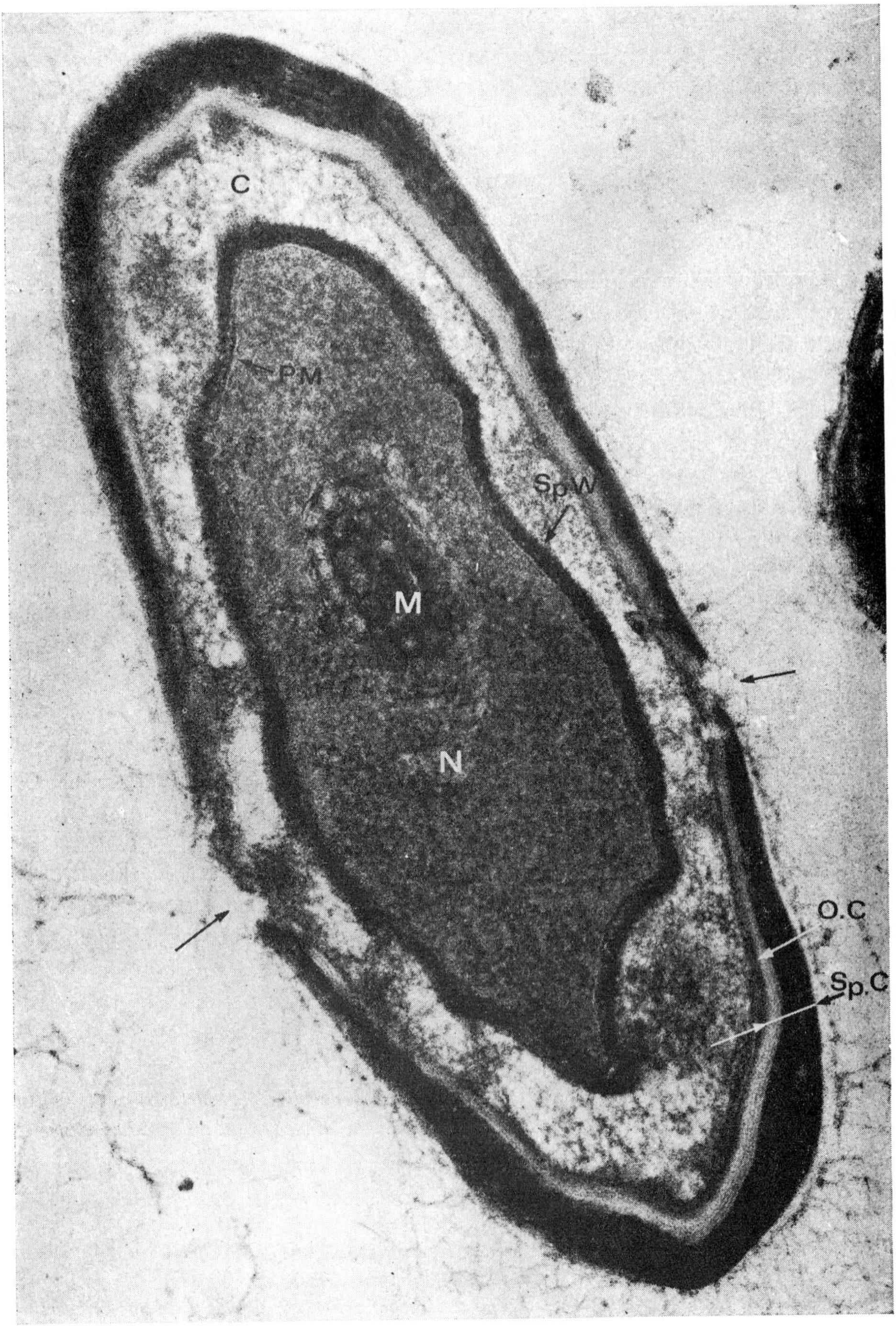

Fig. 10 (*For legend see p. 212.*)

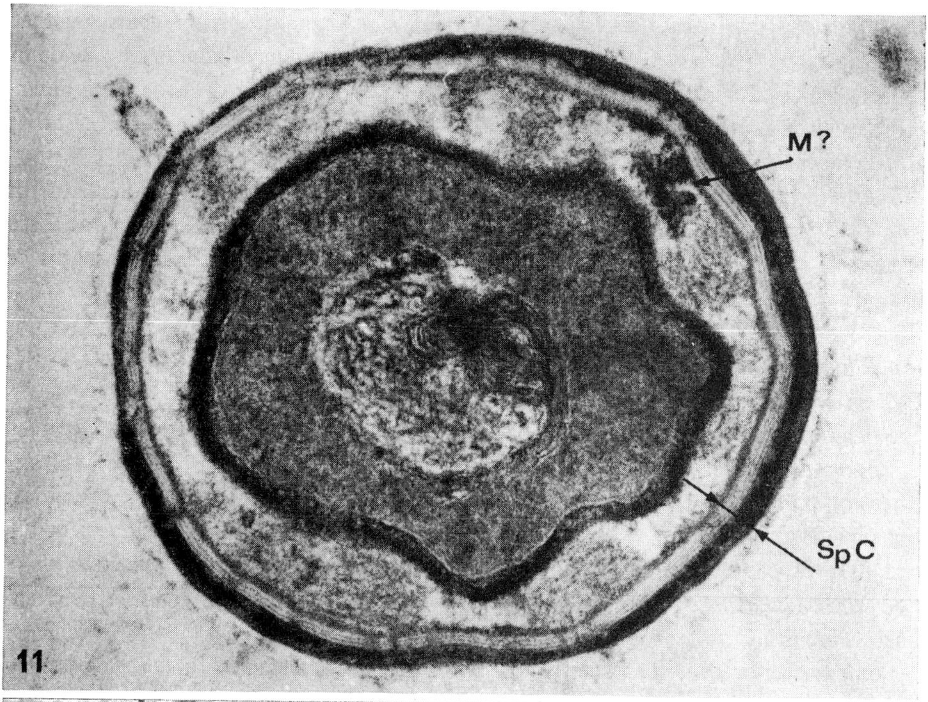

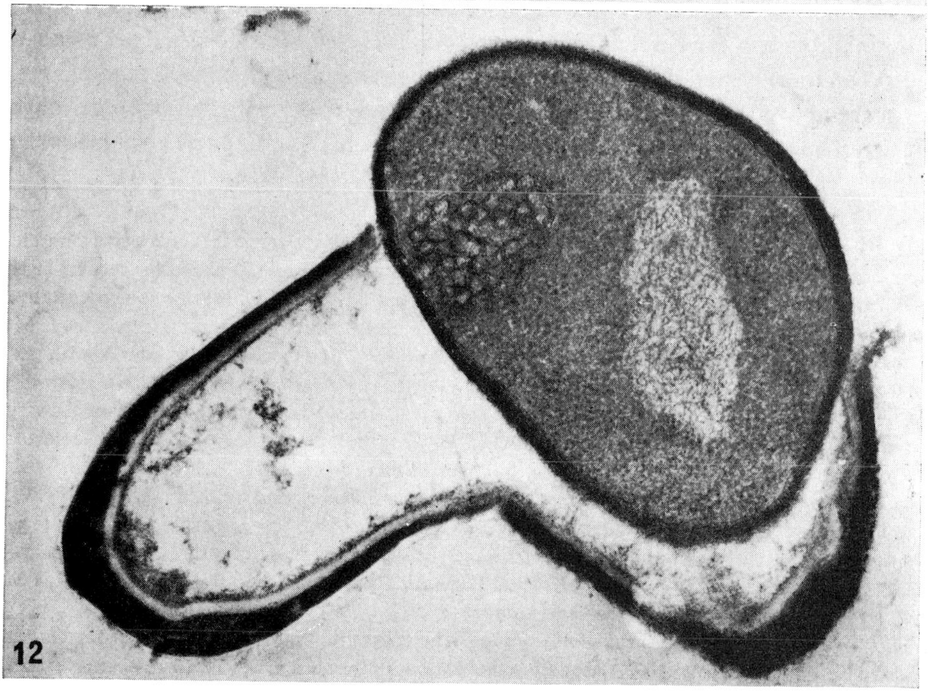

Figs. 11 and 12 (*For legend see p. 212.*)

the larvae of some insects, a bipyramidal crystal of a toxic protein is formed together with the spore (Hannay). The crystals are synthesized *de novo* from amino acids in the culture medium and contain no nucleic acid. Holmes and Monroe have determined with X-ray diffraction the parameters of the tetragonal unit cell of the crystal of *B. thuringensis*.

Furthermore paracrystalline arrays have been demonstrated in *E. coli* infected with RNA of bacteriophage f2 (Schwartz and Zinder; Franklin and Granboulan), but these consist of the RNA-containing virions. Such a crystal formation resembles that of various viruses in plant and animal cells.

(e) *Phage-like objects and inclusions of microtubule structure*

Bacterial inclusions of these types form a controversial subject.

A number of references exist of particles shaped like bacteriophages but deprived of heads. Lewin observed them inside and outside the cells of *Saprospira grandis*. These objects were of two types: hollow rods and solid rods of the same dimensions, but furnished with a tail or wicklike axial filament extending beyond one end of the rod. Lewin coined for both the term 'rhapidosomes' (Gr. *rhapis* = rod; *soma* = body). Similar rhapidosomes have been described for several myxobacteria (Reichenbach; Pate et al.).

Some bacteriocins – i.e. some highly specific antibiotics – appear also to be shaped as head-less bacteriophages (Bradley and Dewar). Vieu et al. elegantly demonstrated how in the case of the bacteriolytic agent of *Yersinia enterolitica* rod-shaped particles adsorbed to cells, and contracted their sheaths in the manner of the T even phages.

In the above cases the evidence supports the view that the particles are defective bacteriophages of the tailed type. On the other hand, Correll and Lewin made the

---

Fig. 10. Spore of *Bacillus subtilis* in a stage of germination. At the arrows there are cracks in the spore core (SpC); note the laminations of this integument. The cortex (C) and outer cortical layer (OC) are breaking up, and dissolving. The spore core is well on its way to become a young vegetative cell. From the cell wall primordium a new cell wall has been formed. The plasma membrane (PM) has been the innermost membrane in the former sporangium. The nucleus (N) is now central, and in it is a mesosome (M). A remarkable feature, little stressed by other authors, is that the cortex must be a very stiff gel that during its swelling compresses the vegetative cell, causing it to assume the very irregular outline. In this figure as well as in Fig. 11 there are thicker accumulations of the cortex material at the sites where the cell appears most compressed. ×127,000.

Fig. 11. Spore of *Bacillus subtilis* in a stage of germination. This picture is similar to that of Fig. 10, but in cross section. The cortex appears to consist of material with the properties of springs; local concentrations of this material have deeply indented the wall of the developing cell. Note the laminations of the spore coat (SpC). The mesosome looks as if it is folded into the nuclear area. At M perhaps mesosomal vesicles. ×107,000.

Fig. 12. Spore germination in *Bacillus subtilis*. The spore has cracked open, perhaps by forces exerted by the cortex. The cell, released from the tensions of the cortex, which is here in an advanced stage of disintegration, has now acquired a smooth outline. Nucleus and mesosome appear to be separate in this section of the cell. ×91,000.

surprising observation that the *Saprospira* rhapidosomes would contain RNA–protein in an even higher ratio than does tobacco mosaic virus.

Not only bacteria that lyse spontaneously, like *Saprospira*, contain the inclusions, but apparently also quite normal cells (Van Iterson et al.; Yamamoto). Several bacteria, like *Proteus*, possess rods of undetermined length (Fig. 13). The rods consist of a wall surrounding a central cavity, which in some instances appears to be obstructed at intervals along its length by materials of unknown composition. On their outside such rods are much smoother than the tails of imperfect phages with their contractile sheaths and structured cores (Fig. 14). The smooth rods resemble in structure the microtubules of the cells of higher organisms (Van Iterson et al.). It would seem far-fetched to relate such tubules to the aberrant formation of phage tails, were it not for their possible identity with the smooth type of polysheaths (Kellenberger and Boy de

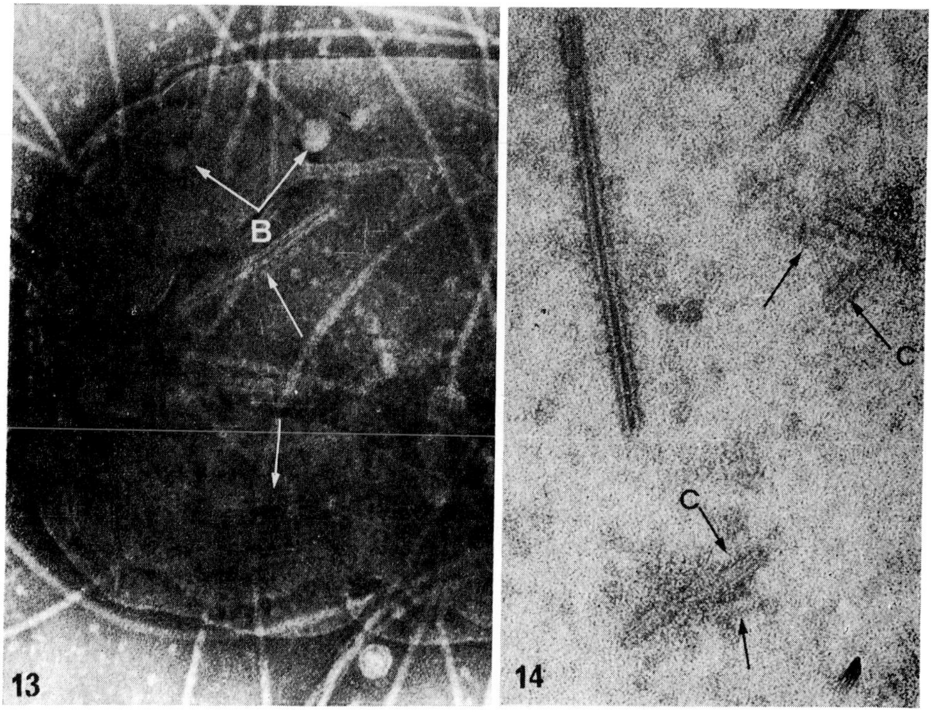

Fig. 13. *Proteus mirabilis* from which most of the cytoplasm and plasma membrane have been released by osmotic shocking in distilled water after mild penicillin treatment. Negative staining. The cell is now sufficiently transparent to permit the recognition of a number of rod-like objects with hollow cores (arrows). At B, basal granules on the flagella. × 88,000.

Fig. 14. Structures resembling microtubules, and phage-like objects without heads (released from *Proteus mirabilis*). When a certain strain of *Proteus mirabilis* was treated with 1 γ mitomycin C per ml medium, particles resembling head-less bacteriophages with contracted sheaths (arrows, c), and also with uncontracted sheaths (arrows), were seen together with hollow rods, resembling those seen in the adjoining figure. × 78,000.

la Tour), which are held to be aberrant phage tail formations. Rods of the microtubule type possess no end plate, nor a core structure. In the morphogenesis of the tail of the T4 phage, however, the earliest structure so far identified is the end plate (Wood and Edgar). The core is then assembled on this end plate. Excellent electron micrographs of cell sections, in which complete bacteriophages of the T4 type including tails can be seen, have recently been published by Margaretten et al., but loose tails are not visible in these pictures.

Pate et al. suggest that in the myxobacterium *Chondrococcus columnaris* the membranes of the mesosomes break down to give rise to tubular, smooth 'rhapidosomes'. If this should be true, the tubules would consist of lipoprotein.

It appears to be of first importance to ascertain the exact chemical nature of the various tubules and loose tails. Preliminary studies of Yamamoto provide a fresh example of smooth tubules, this time from *Pseudomonas*, which contain large quantities of RNA; an observation which, if confirmed, makes their nature the more mysterious.

3. *Concluding remarks*

Heslop-Harrison wrote: 'indeed, in a sense, development is the progression through time of organogenetic acts, each in itself differentiative.' Comparison of the procaryotic cell structure of bacteria with that of the eucaryotic cell has brought to light certain important facts. These are the following. The absence in the procaryotic cells of structures built and behaving like true chromosomes. Absence of a nuclear envelope, and instead intimate contact of fibrils from the nuclear area with cytoplasmic components amongst which are fibrils and membranous elements. Integrated in the cytoplasm are 70 S ribosomes instead of the larger ones common amongst the eucaryotic cells. The organization of respiratory and photosynthetic enzyme systems in comparatively simple membranous elements which – although of a different nature from the cell membrane – are often in close contact with it. Flagella that diverge in structure from the pattern that is the general rule in the eucaryotic cell. A cell wall of a particular structure and with components that are unique for the procaryotes.

Undoubtedly more differences could be mentioned, and still more may be discovered. The bacteria thus show a basic organization that diverges importantly – although probably not fundamentally – from that of the eucaryotic cells, but also amongst the procaryotes themselves by the 'progression through time of organogenetic acts' an impressive amount of cell differentiation has taken place.

References

BRADLEY, D.E. and A. DEWAR: The structure of phage-like objects associated with non-induced bacteriocinogenic bacteria. J. Gen. Microbiol. 45 (1966) 399.

CORRELL, D.L. and R.A. LEWIN: Rod-shaped ribonucleoprotein particles from *Saprospira*. Can. J. Microbiol. 10 (1964) 63.

DE HALLER, G., E. KELLENBERGER and CH. ROUILLER: Etude au microscope électronique des plasmas contenant de l'acide désoxyribonucléique. III. Variations ultrastructurales des chromosomes d'*Amphidinium*. J. Microscopie 3 (1964) 627.

DELAMATER, E. D.: Bacterial chromosomes and their mechanism of division. In: Bacterial Anatomy, VI Symp. Soc. Gen. Microbiol. Cambridge, Cambridge University Press (1956) 215.

DELAPORTE, B.: Etude comparée de grandes spirilles formant des spores etc. Ann. Inst. Pasteur 107 (1964a) 246.

DELAPORTE, B.: Etude descriptive de bactéries de très grandes dimensions. Ann. Inst. Pasteur 107 (1964b) 845.

DODGE, J. D.: Chromosome structure in the Dinophyceae. I. Cytochemical studies. Arch. Mikrobiol. 48 (1964) 66.

DOUDNEY, C. O.: Requirement for ribonucleic acid synthesis for deoxyribonucleic acid replication in bacteria. Nature 211 (1966) 39.

FITZ-JAMES, PH. C.: The structure of spores as revealed by mechanical disruption. J. Bacteriol. 66 (1953) 312.

FITZ-JAMES, PH. C.: Polyribosomes in protoplasts of *Bacillus megaterium*. Can. J. Microbiol. 10 (1964) 92.

FRANKLIN, R. M. and M. GRANBOULAN: Ultrastructure of *E. coli* cells infected with bacteriophage R17. J. Bacteriol. 91 (1966) 834.

FREER, J. H. and H. S. LEVINSON: Fine structure of *Bacillus megaterium* during microcycle sporogenesis. J. Bacteriol. 94 (1967) 441.

FUHS, G. W.: Symposium on the fine structure and replication of bacteria and their parts. I. Fine structure and replication of bacterial nucleoids. Bacteriol. Rev. 29 (1965) 277.

GERHARDT, PH. and E. RIBI: Ultrastructure of the exosporium enveloping spores of *Bacillus cereus*. J. Bacteriol. 88 (1964) 1774.

GIESBRECHT, P.: Vergleichende Untersuchungen an den Chromosomen des Dinoflagellaten *Amphidinium elegans* und denen der Bakterien. Zentr. Bakteriol. Parasitenk., Abt. I Orig. 187 (1962) 452.

HALVERSON, H. O., J. SZULMAJSTER and R. COHEN: Etude de l'acide désoxyribonucléique des spores de *Bacillus subtilis*. J. Mol. Biol. 28 (1967) 71.

HANNAY, C. L.: Inclusions in bacteria. In: Bacterial Anatomy; Symp. Soc. Gen. Microbiol. (1956) 318.

HAROLD, F. M.: Inorganic polyphosphates in biology: structure, metabolism, and function. Bacteriol. Rev. 30 (1966) 772.

HENDLER, R. W.: Protein synthesis as a membrane-oriented cellular activity. In: H. Peeters, ed.: Protides of the Biological Fluids. Amsterdam, Elsevier Publ. Cy. 15 (1967) 37.

HESLOP HARRISON, J.: Differentiation. Ann. Rev. Plant Physiol. 18 (1967) 325.

HODGKISS, W., Z. J. ORDAL and D. C. CANN: The comparative morphology of the spores of *Clostridium botulinum* type E and the spores of the "os mutant". Can. J. Microbiol. 12 (1966) 1283.

HOLMES, K. C. and R. E. MONROE: Studies on the structure of parasporal inclusions from *Bacillus thuringiensis*. J. Mol. Biol. 14 (1965) 572.

KELLENBERGER, E.: The physical state of the bacterial nucleus. In: Microbial Genetics, X Symp. Soc. Gen. Microbiol., Cambridge (1960) 39.

KELLENBERGER, E.: The study of natural and artificial DNA-plasms by thin sections. In: R. J. C. Harris, ed.: The Interpretation of Ultrastructure. New York/London, Academic Press (1962) 233.

KELLENBERGER, E. and A. RYTER: Contribution à l'étude du noyau bactérien. Schweiz. Z. Allgem. Pathol. Bakteriol. 18 1(955) 1122.

KELLENBERGER, E. and E. BOY DE LA TOUR: On the fine structure of normal and "polymerized" tail sheath of phage T 4. J. Ulstrastruct. Res. 11 (1964) 545.

KOCH, A. L. and P. F. PACHLER: Evidence against the alternation of synthesis of identical chromosomes in *Escherichia coli* growing at low rates. J. Mol. Biol. 28 (1967) 531.

LARK, K.G.: Regulation of chromosome replication and segregation in bacteria. Bacteriol. Rev. 30 (1966) 3.

LEADBETTER, B. and J.D.DODGE: An electron microscope study of nuclear and cell division in a Dinoflagellate. Arch. Mikrobiol. 57 (1967) 239.

LEWIN, R.A.: Rod-shaped particles in *Saprospira*. Nature 198 (1963) 103.

LUNDGREN, D.G., R.ALPER, C.SCHNAITMAN and R.H.MARCHESSAULT: Characterization of poly-β-hydroxybutyrate extracted from different bacteria. J. Bacteriol. 89 (1965) 245.

MAALØE, O. and N.O.KJELDGAARD: In: Control of Macromolecular Synthesis. New York/Amsterdam, W.A.Benjamin, Inc. (1966).

MARGARETTEN, W., C.MORGAN, H.S.ROSENKRANZ and H.M.ROSE: Effect of hydroxyurea on virus development. J. Bacteriol. 91 (1966) 823.

MAYALL, B.H. and C.F.ROBINOW: Observations with the electron microscope on the organization of the cortex of resting and germinating spores of *B. megaterium*. J. Appl. Bacteriol. 20 (1957) 333.

MORGAN, C., H.S.ROSENKRANZ, H.S.CARR and H.M.ROSE: Electron microscopy of chloramphenicol-treated *Escherichia coli*. J. Bacteriol. 93 (1967) 1987.

MURRAY, R.G.E.: The internal structure of the cell. In: I.C.Gunsalus and R.Y.Stanier, eds.: The Bacteria, Vol. I. New York/London, Academic Press (1960) 35.

PATE, J.L., J.L.JOHNSON and E.J.ERLING: The fine structure of *Chondrococcus columnalis*. II. Structure and formation of rhapidosomes. J. Cell Biol. 35 (1967) 15.

PFISTER, R.M. and D.G.LUNDGREN: Electron microscopy of polysomes within *Bacillus cereus*. J. Bacteriol. 88 (1964) 1119.

POPE, L., D.P.YOLTON and L.J.RODE: Appendages of *Clostridium bifermentans* spores. J. Bacteriol. 94 (1967) 1206.

REICHENBACH, H.: Die wahre Natur der Myxobakterien-"Rhapidosomen". Arch. Mikrobiol. 56 (1967) 371.

RIS, H.: Ultrastructure and molecular organization of genetic systems. Can. J. Genet. Cytol. 3 (1961) 95.

RIS, H.: Fine structure of chromosomes. B. Chromosomes and genes. Proc. Roy. Soc. (London), Ser. B 164 (1966) 246.

ROBINOW, C.F.: Spore structure as revealed by thin sections. J. Bacteriol. 66 (1953) 300.

ROBINOW, C.F.: The chromatin bodies of bacteria. Bacteriol. Rev. 20 (1960a) 207.

ROBINOW, C.F.: Outline of the visible organization of bacteria. In: J.Brachet and A.E.Mirsky, eds.: The Cell, Vol. IV. New York, Academic Press (1960b) p. 45.

ROBINOW, C.F.: Morphology of bacterial spores, their development and germination. In: I.C.Gunsalus and R.Y.Stanier, eds.: The Bacteria, Vol. I. New York/London, Academic Press (1960c) 207.

ROBINOW, C.F.: On the plasma membrane of some bacteria and fungi. Circulation 26 (1962a) 1092.

ROBINOW, C.F.: Morphology of the bacterial nucleus. Brit. Med. Bull. 18 (1962b) 31.

RYTER, A.: Etude au microscope électronique des transformations nucléaires de *E. coli* K12S et K12S (λ 26) après irradiation aux rayons ultraviolets et aux rayons X. J. Biophys. Biochem. Cytol. 8 (1960) 399.

RYTER, A.: Etude morphologique de la sporulation de *Bacillus subtilis*. Ann. Inst. Pasteur 108 (1965) 40.

RYTER, A. and F.JACOB: Etude au microscope électronique de la liaison entre noyau et mésosome chez *Bacillus subtilis*. Ann. Inst. Pasteur 107 (1964) 384.

RYTER, A. and E.KELLENBERGER: Etude au microscope électronique de plasmas contenant de l'acide désoxyribonucléique I. Les nucléoides des bactéries en croissance active. Z. Naturforsch. 13b (1958) 597.

SCHLESSINGER, D., V.T.MARCHESI and B.C.K.KWAN: Binding of ribosomes to cytoplasmic reticulum of *Bacillus megaterium*. J. Bacteriol. 90 (1965) 456.

SCHWARTZ, F.M. and D.ZINDER: Crystalline aggregates in bacterial cells infected with the RNA bacteriophage f2. Virology 21 (1963) 276.

SILVA, M.T.: Electron microscopic study on the effect of the oxidation of ultrathin sections of *Bacillus cereus* and *Bacillus megaterium*. J. Ultrastruct. Res. 18 (1967) 345.

TAYLOR, M.M. and R.S.STORCK: Uniqueness of bacterial ribosomes. Proc. Natl. Acad. Sci. U.S. 52 (1964) 958.

THOMAS, R.S.: Ultrastructural localization of mineral matter in bacterial spores by microincineration. J. Cell Biol. 23 (1964) 113.

VAN ITERSON, W.: Membranes, particular organelles, and peripheral bodies in bacteria. Proc. Eur. Conf. on EM, Delft. II (1960) 763.

VAN ITERSON, W.: Some features of a remarkable organelle in *Bacillus subtilis*. J. Biophys. Biochem. Cytol. 9 (1961) 183.

VAN ITERSON, W.: Symposium on the fine structure and replication of bacteria and their parts. II. Bacterial cytoplasm. Bacteriol. Rev. 29 (1965) 299.

VAN ITERSON, W.: The fine structure of the ribonucleoprotein in bacterial cytoplasm. J. Cell Biol. 28 (1966) 563.

VAN ITERSON, W., J.F.M.HOENIGER and E.NIJMAN VAN ZANTEN: A microtubule in a bacterium. J. Cell Biol. 32 (1967) 1.

VAN ITERSON, W. and C.F.ROBINOW: Observations with the electron microscope on the fine structure of the nuclei of two spherical bacteria. J. Biophys. Biochem. Cytol. 9 (1961) 171.

VIEU, J.F., O.CROISSANT and Y.HAMON: Ultrastructure d'un agent antibactérien produit par *Yersinia enterocolitica*. Compt. Rend. 264 (1967) 181.

VOELZ, H., U.VOELZ and R.O.ORTIGOZA: The 'polyphosphate overplus' phenomenon in *Myxococcus xanthus* and its influence on the architecture of the cell. Arch. Mikrobiol. 53 (1966) 371.

WARTH, A.D., D.F.OHYE and W.G.MURRELL: The composition and structure of bacterial spores. J. Cell Biol. 16 (1963a) 579.

WARTH, A.D., D.F.OHYE and W.G.MURRELL: Location and composition of spore mucopeptide in *Bacillus* species. J. Cell Biol. 16 (1963b) 593.

WHITFIELD, B.J. and R.G.E. MURRAY: The effects of the ionic environment on the chromatin structures of bacteria. Can. J. Microbiol. 2 (1956) 245.

WOOD, W.B. and R.S.EDGAR: Building a bacterial virus. Sci. Am. 217 (1967) 61.

YAMAMOTO, T.: Presence of rhapidosomes in various species of bacteria and their morphological characteristics. J. Bacteriol. 94 (1967) 1746.

YOSHIKAWA, H., A.O.SULLIVAN and N.SUEOKA: Sequential replication of the *Bacillus subtilis* chromosome. III. Regulation of initiation. Proc. Natl. Acad. Sci. U.S. 52 (1964) 973.

YOUNG, F.E. and PH.C.FITZ-JAMES: Chemical and morphological studies of bacterial spore formation. I. Formation of spores in *Bacillus cereus*. J. Biophys. Biochem. Cytol. 6 (1959) 467.

PART IV

Chromosome organization in higher organisms

CHAPTER 11

The molecular organization of chromosomes

HANS RIS

Department of Zoology, University of Wisconsin, Madison, Wisconsin

Contents

1. Introduction
2. Molecular components in chromosomes
   (a) DNA
   (b) RNA
   (c) Histones
   (d) Non-histone protein
   (e) Metal ions
3. Arrangement of molecular components in chromosomes
   (a) The structure of inactive chromatin
   (b) Molecular complexes in active chromatin
   (c) The nature of structural continuity of chromosomes

Supported by a Public Health Service research career program award (K6-GM-21,948) and a research grant (GM-04738) from the National Institutes of Health.

1. Introduction

The stretches of DNA which code for the various proteins of a cell are always integrated in specific order into larger units which correspond to the linkage groups of genetic analysis. In prokaryotic cells, one generally finds a single linkage group and, therefore, a single genophore (Ris 1961) consisting of one large molecule of DNA. Eukaryotes, on the other hand, have at least two and often more than a hundred genophores. These eukaryote genophores, the chromosomes, differ markedly from the genophore of prokaryotes in morphology and behavior. Their DNA is always associated with an equal mass of basic proteins (histones or protamines) and variable amounts of other proteins to form characteristic fibers which are coiled and folded into thicker threads; these threads in turn compose the chromonema visible in the light microscope. The chromosomes are separated from the rest of the cell by the nuclear envelope, a part of the endoplasmic reticulum. The eukaryote cell, thus, is characterized by a clearly defined nucleus. In connection with the multiplicity of genophores, the eukaryotic cell has evolved complex mechanisms for nuclear division including the condensation of chromosomes through helical coiling and a mitotic apparatus. Chromosomes are clearly defined individually only during division stages. In the interphase nucleus, they are unravelled and hydrated and, therefore, not individually visible. The term 'chromatin' is used to indicate chromosomal material when individual chromosomes cannot be recognized. During interphase, some parts of chromosomes remain coiled (condensed chromatin, heterochromatin) while others are more unraveled (extended chromatin, euchromatin). There is good evidence that DNA-dependent RNA synthesis occurs in the extended regions (active chromatin) but is absent in the condensed parts (inactive chromatin).

Chromosomes have two major functions: They maintain and replicate the genetic information contained in their DNA; and this information is transcribed at the right time in proper sequence into the specific types of RNA which direct protein synthesis. The control of these chromosomal functions is obviously of great interest and still quite mysterious. It seems likely that the chromosomal proteins are involved with this control. A better knowledge of the morphology of the DNA–protein complexes in both active and inactive chromatin is necessary for an understanding of chromosome functions. This chapter will review what has been learned about the structure of chromosomal nucleoproteins through chemical, physical and electron microscopic investigations.

2. Molecular components in chromosomes

The major constituents of chromosomes are deoxyribonucleic acid (DNA), histones, non-histone proteins and ribonucleic acids (RNA). It will be useful to review briefly the major structural features of these molecules insofar as they relate to the organization of chromatin.

(a) *DNA*

The physical properties of DNA molecules have recently been reviewed by Josse and Eigner. DNA isolated from chromosomes has the structure of a typical Watson–Crick double helix. At low humidity, DNA fibers from all organisms give X-ray diffraction patterns indicative of the A-structure. At high humidity, this is changed reversibly into the B-form in which the bases are 3.36 Å apart and at right angle to the fiber axis (Hamilton et al.). Small angle X-ray scattering by DNA in solution yields the radius of gyration and mass per unit length expected from a Watson–Crick double helix (Luzzati and Nicolaieff). X-ray diffraction studies show that DNA combined with proteins as in reconstituted nucleoprotamine fibers (Feughelman et al.), intact sperm heads of cephalopods (Wilkins and Randall), extracted nucleohistone, and isolated nuclei (Zubay and Wilkins 1962) has the same structure as purified DNA at high humidity (B-form). For oriented sheets of nucleohistone, such findings were confirmed by polarized infrared studies (Bradbury et al. 1962).

The presence of double-stranded DNA in native chromatin has been confirmed by heat denaturation studies. Chamberlain and Walker (1965) demonstrated the hyperchromic effect associated with heat denaturation of double-stranded DNA in single boar sperm nuclei. Nash and Plaut took advantage of the different fluorescence of acridine orange when complexed with single- or double-stranded DNA to demonstrate reversible heat denaturation of DNA in *Drosophila* polytene chromosomes.

The presence of double-stranded DNA in chromatin is thus well established. The great stability of the double helix is, of course, one of the properties that make this molecule especially suitable as genetic material. On the other hand, during DNA replication and, perhaps, during RNA synthesis (transcription) also, the two strands must separate. The conditions which control this localized strand separation in chromosomes at normal temperatures are naturally of great interest. DNA in solution, even under condition of maximal stability, undergoes continuous localized strand separation and rejoining (Printz and Von Hippel). Frenster (1966) compared the heat denaturation of DNA in fractionated inactive and active chromatin. He found that the stability of the double helix in active chromatin was less than in inactive chromatin and that its hyperchromicity was reduced about 60%. The DNAs extracted from the two fractions, however, behaved identically upon heat denaturation. Frenster concluded that in the active chromatin the strands must be separated in a considerable fraction of the DNA.

DNA molecules visualized in the electron microscope (Hall and Litt; Kleinschmidt and Zahn; Beer and Zobel; Lang et al. 1967) appear as unbranched fibers about 20 Å thick. Under certain conditions, single-stranded DNA or partially denatured double helixes can be visualized in electron micrographs (Lang et al. 1964; Freifelder and Kleinschmidt; Inman).

Much effort has been spent in obtaining information on the length of the DNA in chromosomes. One would like to know whether the DNA is covalently linked by continuous 3′-5′-phosphodiester links for the entire length of the chromosomes or whether it consists of subunits which are linked in some other fashion. Unfortunately, the great shear sensitivity of DNA makes it extremely difficult to extract long DNA molecules without breakage. The more carefully the DNA is handled the larger have been the pieces obtained. The values reported in the literature must, therefore, be considered minima rather than true molecular weights. Sedimentation–viscosity studies and light scattering have been used for molecular weight determinations. The most useful methods recently employed, however, are length measurements from either autoradiographs of labeled DNA or electron micrographs. The molecular weight is then calculated on the basis of a mass per length of 196 Daltons per Å, a value obtained from X-ray diffraction studies of the sodium salt of DNA. Table 1 presents some typical values of DNA length from a variety of organisms. It is evident that even these minimal values indicate extremely long molecules. We shall return to the question of DNA subunits later.

TABLE 1

Minimal lengths of DNA from chromosomes

Source	Method	Molecular weight ($\times 10^6$ Daltons)	Length (μ)	Reference
Physarum polycephalum	sedimentation	15	—	McGrath and Williams
Wheat germ	sedimentation	100	—	Hotta and Bassel
Wheat germ	electron microscope (EM)	—	up to 31	Hotta and Bassel
Chironomus tentans	EM	—	8.1–89.4	Wolstenholme et al.
Chironomus thummi	EM	—	5.2–154.5	Wolstenholme et al.
Sea urchin sperm	EM	—	about 100	Solari
Trout sperm	sedimentation	60–200	—	Davison
Boar sperm	EM	—	0.7–17	Hotta and Bassel
Calf thymus	sedimentation viscosity	50	—	Aten and Cohen
Chinese hamster	autoradiography	—	up to 1100	Huberman and Riggs
Mouse lymphoblasts	sedimentation	500	—	Lett

On the basis of the demonstration of closed-circular DNA molecules in many viruses (Ris and Chandler) and bacteria (Cairns 1963; Bode and Morowitz), it has been suggested that chromosomes consist of 'daisy chains' of such circles (Stahl). Hotta and Bassel actually found circular DNA molecules in extracts from boar sperm. However, since mitochondrial DNA from many sources is usually circular (Sinclair and Stevens; Hudson and Vinograd) it remains questionable whether these circles actually represent nuclear DNA. Nuclear DNA has now been prepared from many different animals and plants; generally only open, linear pieces of considerable length have been observed (Table 1). The only other circular DNA was isolated from nucleoli of amphibian oocytes (Miller 1966) and this is known to be extra-chromosomal DNA. It appears very unlikely that chromosomal DNA is normally in closed, circular form.

(b) *RNA*

According to the present concepts of gene function, cellular RNA is synthesized in the nucleus on a DNA template (transcription). (The only exception is the RNA of certain organelles such as chloroplasts and mitochondria, and of intracellular symbionts which have their own DNA transcription mechanism.) Although most of these RNA molecules are eventually transported to the cytoplasm, they must at some time be part of chromosomal structures. They might occur in hydrogen-bonded triple chains with a DNA double helix, in a double helix with only one strand of the DNA, or in DNA–RNA–protein complexes. Double-stranded DNA–RNA hybrids have been isolated from *in vitro* transcription systems and from intact prokaryotic cells (Hayashi; Hayashi and Hayashi) from nuclei of *Neurospora* (Schulman and Bonner) and from *Drosophila* (Mead). X-ray diffraction studies showed that such duplexes closely resemble the A-form of the DNA double helix (Milman et al.).

Kleinschmidt has published an electron micrograph of T_7 phage DNA prepared at the time of transcription: it shows structures which might represent DNA–messenger RNA complexes.

Besides the RNA which is only temporarily associated with chromosomes, other RNA molecules remain part of chromosomal organization. Bonner and co-workers (1966, 1967, 1968) described an RNA consisting of about 40 nucleotides which is bound to a group of histones and complexes with specific regions of DNA. This RNA is particularly interesting because it could provide a means for selective attachment of histones to DNA.

(c) *Histones*

Histones and protamines are defined as relatively small proteins (Mw 8,000–20,000) rich in arginine and lysine and, therefore, highly basic. They are normally associated with DNA; and, like DNA, they are a specific component of chromosomes. Chromosomal DNA, except perhaps in the sperm of the crab *Eupagurus* (Chevaillier), is always associated with histones or protamines.

In recent years, much progress has been made in the preparation and characterization of these chromosomal components (reviews by Johns; Murray; Hnilica). The most striking finding has been that the number of distinct types of histones is small (6–10) and that their relative proportions are remarkably constant from one cell to another. The histone pattern is similar in a wide variety of plants and animals and in different tissues of a given organism. This pattern exhibits no significant differences between embryonic and adult tissue (Lindsay; Kischer and Hnilica), dividing and non-dividing cells (Comings), euchromatin and heterochromatin (Comings), or active and inactive chromatin (Frenster 1965).

Despite this general invariance, certain differences in histone patterns have been observed. The greatest change occurs during spermiogenesis in some animals when histones are replaced by the simpler and more basic protamines. In nucleated erythrocytes and sea urchin sperm, a unique lysine-rich histone has been described (Hnilica and Edwards). Another unique histone has been shown to appear during meiosis in lily and persist into the microspore (Sheridan and Stern). The entire complement of very lysine-rich histones seems to be absent in yeast (Tonino and Rozijn). A very interesting modification of histone patterns was found in the toad *Xenopus* associated with the loss of the nucleolar organizer. In the anucleolate mutant the lysine-rich and moderately lysine-rich fractions are missing (Berlowitz and Birnstiel).

The conformation of the various histone types has been investigated using optical rotary dispersion and infrared and nuclear magnetic resonance spectroscopy (Bradbury et al. 1967). In solution, protamines and the lysine-rich histone fractions, including the unique lysine-rich histone of chicken erythrocytes, exist as largely extended chains irrespective of ionic strength and *p*H. In the native nucleoproteins, protamines and lysine-rich histones are in the same extended conformation. In contrast, the other histone fractions contain varying proportions of α-helix, and the proportion of the molecule in α-helical configuration increases with the ionic strength of the solutions. In combination with DNA, a considerable part of the slightly lysine-rich and arginine-rich histones is in the helical form.

Titration studies of histones and nucleohistones (Bradbury et al. 1967) indicate that positively charged amino acids are grouped closely together, separated by sequences of non-basic amino acids. Peptide analysis also shows that basic amino acids are separated by long stretches of non-basic amino acids (Phillips). In nucleohistones, the amino groups of the basic amino acids are bound to the phosphate groups of the DNA, and the stretches of non-basic amino acids must loop away from the DNA (Walker 1965; Phillips 1966).

(d) *Non-histone protein*

The non-histone proteins of chromatin were first recognized by Stedman and Stedman (chromosomin; 1947) and Mirsky and Ris (residual protein; 1951). A variety of proteins are left after extraction of all the histones from chromatin. Some are bound to DNA, but most seem to be associated with RNA. Certain of the non-histone proteins of chromatin are soluble in dilute alkali (acidic proteins) while others form an insoluble residue. Quantitatively the non-histone protein fraction varies greatly from one tissue to another and seems to be related to the synthetic activity of cells. In certain nuclei it is greatly reduced and in nuclei of certain sperms it is absent (Felix). Therefore, it cannot be considered a constant structural component of chromosomes but seems to be associated mainly with active chromatin. Because these proteins are difficult to solubilize they are still very poorly known. Some of them label more rapidly than any other nuclear fraction and are, therefore, of great interest. Wang has isolated a component that is associated with DNA and is part of a protein-synthesizing system that appears to differ fundamentally from the ribosomal system (Wang).

Certain acidic proteins are of interest because they form complexes with histones. It has been suggested that they may function as 'de-repressors' by removing histones from specific regions of DNA (Busch; Frenster 1965). In this category belong the phosphoproteins studied by Langan.

Other non-histone proteins are chromatin-associated enzymes such as DNA polymerase (Mazia and Hinegardner; Patel et al.), RNA polymerase (Huang and Bonner; Hotta and Stern), DPN pyrophosphorylase and nucleoside triphosphatases (Siebert and Humphrey).

Important for the problem of chromosome structure are proteins or polypeptides that perhaps function as 'linkers' between DNA molecules. Dounce and Hilgartner reported evidence for protein linked covalently to DNA in chromatin from rat liver. A seryl or threonyl oligopeptide linker between nucleic acid molecules was proposed by Bendich and Rosenkranz.

Another acidic chromosomal protein (RNA-binding protein) was recently reported by Bonner (1967) and by Huang. It is thought to join a complex of several histone molecules to the special chromosomal RNA which is in turn base-paired with a definite region of DNA.

Cytochemical studies also provide evidence for non-histone proteins in regions of active chromatin. In the puffs of salivary chromosomes, such proteins accumulate and are apparently part of RNA-containing granules of various sizes (Swift 1959, 1965). On the loops of lampbrush chromosomes, non-histone proteins are combined with RNA in the form of granules and fibers (Miller 1965). These proteins are perhaps synthesized on the loops themselves (Gall and Callan).

In summary, chromosomes contain more or less tightly bound non-histone proteins for which the following roles have been suggested: chromatin-bound enzymes; linkers between DNA molecules; linkers between chromosomal RNA and histones; components of nuclear ribosomes or of a non-ribosomal protein-synthesizing system; protective proteins associated with messenger RNA.

Recent reviews of non-histone proteins of chromatin were published by Busch, by Wang and by Hnilica.

(e) *Metal ions*

The presence of calcium in chromatin was first recognized by Miescher in his pioneering studies on fish sperm. Since that time, numerous investigators have demonstrated the close association of calcium and magnesium ions with interphase chromatin and mitotic chromosomes (Policard and Pillet; Scott; Somers et al.; Cantor and Hearst; Cole; Maio and Schildkraut). In *Drosophila* salivary gland chromosomes, the bulk of these minerals is localized in the band regions (Barigozzi). A detailed study of the magnesium and calcium content of calf thymus nuclei isolated in non-aqueous medium showed that these nuclei contain 0.024% calcium and 0.115% magnesium. The magnesium is bound mainly to DNA and RNA, and about one in twenty phosphates of the DNA is associated with magnesium. The calcium, on the other hand, seems to be complexed with histones (Naora et al.). Radioactive labeling experiments have shown that Ca^{45} is firmly bound to chromosomal material and retains this association through several cell divisions in lilies and in the wasp *Habrobracon* (Steffensen). Divalent cations apparently function in the maintenance of chromosome structure since their removal by the use of chelating agents leads to the dispersal of salivary gland chromosomes and grasshopper spermatocyte chromosomes in media of low ionic strength (Mazia). However, the precise function of metal ions in chromosome structure is still unknown.

3. *Arrangement of molecular components in chromosomes*

In most nuclei, the major constituent of chromosomes is a DNA–histone complex (DNH). Condensed inactive chromatin consists almost exclusively of DNH, and in certain cells such as calf thymocytes, erythrocytes of lower vertebrates and sperm the nuclei contain 90–100% inactive chromatin. Since the DNH is the preponderant nuclear fraction and has a relatively simple composition, it is the best known chromosomal component. In active chromatin, the DNA–histone association is modified in an unknown manner, and other types of molecules are combined with the DNH. Since this fraction is more difficult to prepare in pure form, its molecular organization is still largely undefined.

(a) *The structure of inactive chromatin*

In chromatin, the DNA and histone are combined into a stable complex. Although the molecular structure of DNA is not changed, the association with histones has profound effects on certain properties of DNA: it stabilizes the DNA against heat denaturation, protects it against radiation damage, causes conformational changes and interferes with its template activity in the RNA polymerase system. The specific characteristics of the binding of basic proteins to DNA is therefore of considerable interest.

Despite the relative simplicity of the histones, it has become evident that their association with DNA is rather complex. Therefore, it will be useful to consider first certain model compounds such as DNA-polyamines and DNA-homopolypeptides. Liquori et al. investigated the structure of DNA complexed with spermine and spermidine. These polyamines fit into the narrow groove of the DNA double helix, bound through electrostatic interactions, hydrogen bonding and hydrophobic interactions. The DNA in the complex is considerably more stable than naked DNA as evidenced by its higher melting temperature upon heat denaturation.

The binding of poly-L-ornithine, poly-L-lysine and poly-L-arginine with DNA was studied by Olins et al. They found that the binding is cooperative and depends not only on charge interaction but also on the length and hydrophobicity of the amino acid side chains. Stoichiometric, stable compounds were formed in which the DNA was markedly protected against thermal denaturation. Poly-L-lysine preferentially stabilizes A–T-rich regions (see also Johns and Butler; Leng and Felsenfeld; Ohba 1966b). X-ray diffraction studies indicate that in poly-L-lysine-DNA the polypeptide is situated in the small groove of the extended double helix (Wilkins).

The protamines found in combination with DNA in sperm of certain animals are less complex than histones: they are smaller and contain fewer kinds of amino acids. The structure of the DNA–protamine complexes, nucleoprotamines, is well known from X-ray diffraction studies (Feughelman et al.). The extended polypeptide chain is wrapped around the DNA in the small groove of the helix with the amino groups of the protamine side chains linked to the phosphates on the DNA. Short sequences of non-basic amino acids are thought to loop out from the backbone. The nucleoprotamine, therefore, forms relatively straight fibers with the DNA oriented parallel to the fiber axis. Such fibers can pack closely side-by-side. Unfixed oriented cephalopod sperm gave X-ray diffraction patterns indicating that the same structure is present within the sperm with the DNA oriented in the long axis of the nucleus (Wilkins and Randall). Electron microscopy of developing sperm of octopus revealed fibers 30–40 Å thick oriented in the long axis of the sperm nucleus. These are closely packed in the mature sperm (Ris 1959).

The nucleohistones of somatic nuclei are much more complex than the structures just described. Very little is known about how the individual types of histones are arranged on the DNA. Within the limits of resolution of the available methods, it has not been possible to find any specific association of individual histone fractions with specific regions of the DNA. Removal of histone fractions from sheared nucleohistone particles did not change the distribution of sedimentation coefficients for these particles (Giannoni and Peacocke; Ohba 1966a). It was concluded that the various histone fractions were uniformly distributed in the population of particles. Olivera (quoted by Bonner 1967) investigated the heat denaturation of DNA in nucleohistones during removal of particular histone fractions. He found no evidence for the presence of naked DNA after extraction of any specific histone type. This means that there are no stretches of DNA longer than about 200 nucleotides associated with a single type of histone.

The stable association of DNA and histone is due mainly to charge interaction (Mirsky and Ris; Vendrely et al.; Walker; Bayley et al.). However, hydrogen bonding and hydrophobic interactions also play a role. Akinrimisi et al. found that the affinity for DNA varies from one histone fraction to another and that it is related to the arginine–lysine ratio of the histones. Protamines were bound most strongly, followed by arginine-rich histones. Lysine-rich histones and poly-L-lysine had the lowest affinity. Since the arginine-rich fraction does not have more basic residues, factors other than charge interaction must be involved, for instance hydrophobic interactions between the bases of DNA and non-polar regions of the histones (Bradbury et al. 1967). These differences in the binding of histones to DNA make it possible to extract different histone fractions with increasing salt concentration (Ohlenbush et al.). The greater the arginine–lysine ratio, the higher the salt concentration necessary to dissociate the histone from DNA.

The alteration of certain properties of DNA when combined with histones depends on the nature of the histone fraction. Ohba (1966b) and Fredericq and Houssier showed that the increase in thermal stability of DNA in nucleohistones was due mainly to arginine-rich histones. The lysine-rich histones preferentially stabilized A–T base pairs so that in native nucleohistone these are more stable than G–C pairs. All histone fractions participate to some extent in the suppression of DNA-dependent RNA synthesis (Bonner 1967). The inhibitory effect is not the same for each histone fraction and seems to be related to its binding affinity for DNA (Hurwitz et al.; Huang et al.).

Physicochemical studies have provided some information on the molecular structure of nucleohistones. The tendency of nucleohistones to form gels had made it difficult to study their molecular properties. Zubay and Doty developed a method for preparation of calf thymus nucleohistone that avoids gel formation and yields free particles with an average molecular weight of 18 million. Using light scattering and hydrodynamic methods, they showed that the nucleohistone particle contains a single DNA molecule associated with an equal weight of histones. The average length of the particle is about one tenth of the contour length of its DNA. Flow birefringence and flow dichroism analysis of similar preparations during the progressive removal of histones showed that in the original nucleohistone the apparent length of DNA is greatly shortened with only about 40% of the base pairs of DNA oriented perpendicular to the particle axis (Ohba 1966a). Such studies (see also Giannoni and Peacocke, Lloyd and Peacocke) indicate that the DNA in nucleohistone is highly folded or coiled. The arginine-rich histones seem to be largely responsible for this folding (Ohba 1966a).

The apparent molecular dispersion of the soluble DNH of Zubay and Doty makes it more amenable to study with methods of macromolecular analysis. However, it is questionable that this DNH of about 20 million particle weight represents a native unit of chromosomes. Other workers (Dounce and O'Connell; Itzhaki; Fredericq and Houssier) consider the gel properties of DNH preparations as characteristic of the native state. In view of the susceptibility of nucleohistone to shear and enzymatic degradation, they have judged the free particles of 'soluble DNH' to be artifacts. The isolation of DNA of up to 100 μ in length from many different types of nuclei (Table 1) also makes it very unlikely that the DNH particle of Zubay and Doty represents a native unit of chromosomes.

X-ray diffraction analysis, a technique which can give pertinent information about regular periodic structures, was spectacularly successful in elucidating the structure of DNA. This strengthened hopes that it could also be used to solve the structure of chromosomes (Wilkins et al.). Wilkins and his group have made X-ray diffraction studies of fibers drawn from fowl erythrocyte and calf thymus nuclei, of sea urchin sperm and of isolated nucleohistone from calf thymus. From these studies it can be concluded that the DNA in nucleohistones has the B-structure of the double helix and that it is not well oriented in the fiber axis, but rather folded or coiled in some way. A series of diffraction rings indicate spacings at 110, 55, 35, 27 and 22 Å and suggest a complex tertiary structure which depends on the water content (Pardon et al.). However, no unambiguous information was obtained regarding the conformation of DNA in the nucleohistone fiber or on the arrangement of the histone molecules in the DNA–protein complex. It was postulated that histones were relatively loosely attached and formed bridges at 35 Å intervals between adjacent DNA molecules or adjacent regions of the same folded molecule (Wilkins et al.; Zubay). More recently an alternative model was proposed by Pardon et al. They suggest that a basic 30 Å thick nucleohistone fiber is folded into a superhelix with a diameter of 100 Å and a pitch of 120Å. Luzzati and Nicolaieff, and Nicolaieff have studied small-angle X-ray scattering by solutions of calf thymus and chicken erythrocyte nucleohistones at various concentrations. They concluded that DNH does not exist as discrete macromolecules with protein linked to individual DNA molecules but as characteristic phases depending on the water content. At lowest concentrations, DNH was thought to exist as micelles in which four straight DNA molecules form a core surrounded by histones. At higher concentration, they concluded, DNA molecules are associated in pairs and at highest concentration in a hexagonal packing. Bram recently completed a study involving small angle X-ray scattering analysis and electron microscopic examination of calf thymus DNH. While some of his observations are in agreement with those of Luzzati and Nicolaieff, others are not and lead to quite different conclusions. These results will be discussed in connection with electron microscopic studies of nucleohistones.

Apparently, the organization of nucleohistones is not sufficiently regular to allow the use of the X-ray diffraction analysis alone in solving the problem of chromosome structure. For determination of the structure of individual molecules and irregular complexes, the electron microscope is the instrument of choice. Of course, electron microscopy has its own limitations, and the possibility that artifacts are introduced by the various preparative procedures must be kept in mind. Wherever possible, results should be confirmed by independent techniques.

Various procedures have been used to prepare chromatin for observation in the electron microscope. The most useful has been a modification of Kleinschmidt's monolayer technique. Minced tissue, free cells or isolated nuclei are applied to a clean air–water interface. Cell and nuclear membranes rupture osmotically allowing the chromatin to spread out hanging from a protein monolayer at the water surface. The surface film can be picked up on a grid (Gall 1963). This allows a study of free nucleohistone fibers derived from individual nuclei or chromosomes. In another approach, a drop of dispersed chromatin (e.g. calf thymus nucleohistone) is applied to filmed grids. This method has the advantage that information obtained by the electron microscope can be compared with physicochemical studies of the same preparation. For the investigation of chromatin structure *in situ*, it is necessary to use thin sections of fixed tissues or replicas prepared with the freeze-etching technique (Moore et al.).

The spreading technique has been used to study the chromatin of interphase nuclei from various tissues of plants, animals and protozoa (Gall 1963, 1966; Ris 1963, 1966, 1967; DuPraw 1965a, b; S. Wolfe 1965a, b; J. Wolfe), sperm nuclei (Gall 1966; Ris 1966; Solari), mitotic and meiotic chromosomes (DuPraw 1965a, b, 1966; Wolfe, 1965a, b; Wolfe and John; Wolfe and Hewitt; Gall 1966), salivary gland chromosomes (Rae) and lampbrush chromosomes (Miller 1965). Interphase and mitotic chromosomes dispersed in this manner are always found to consist of chromatin fibers that are about 250 Å thick (Figs. 1 and 2). This is in contrast to the many reports that in sections of fixed cells interphase chromatin and mitotic chromosomes consist of fibers about 100 Å thick (for references, see Kaufmann et al.; Ris 1961, 1966; Kaye and McMaster-Kaye). Similar 100-Å fibers are also observed when nuclei are spread on chelating agents rather than on water (Ris 1966, 1967) or when nucleohistones are extracted in the presence of chelating agents as in the Zubay–Doty procedure (Ris 1961). These observations raise three major questions:

(1) What is the relationship between the 100-Å and the 250-Å fibers revealed by the electron microscope?

(2) What is the native structure inside the intact nucleus?

(3) What is the molecular organization of these fibers?

Most workers have interpreted the 250-Å fiber as a supercoil of a single nucleoprotein fibril (DuPraw 1965b; Wolfe 1965b; Gall 1966). On the other hand I found indications that the 250-Å fiber consists of two 100-Å fibrils lying side-by-side (Ris and Chandler). This doubleness is most clearly demonstrated by treating 250-Å fibers briefly with chelating agents (5 mM sodium citrate or 1 mM EDTA) (Ris 1967). Two knobby 100-Å fibrils are then clearly distinguishable (Fig. 4). If the treatment with chelating agents is prolonged, the two fibrils separate completely. It appears that

---

Fig. 1. Electron micrograph of metaphase chromosome from human liver cell culture spread at air–water interface. (Courtesy of Dr. E. J. DuPraw, University of Maryland School of Medicine.)

Fig. 2. Electron micrograph of nucleohistone fibers from erythrocyte nucleus of the salamander *Triturus viridescens* spread at air–water interface. Fixed in ethanol, dried from amyl acetate. The fibers are about 250 Å thick.

Figs. 3 and 4. Nucleohistone fibers from erythrocyte nucleus of the salamander spread at air–water interface, treated for 10 sec. with 5 mM sodium citrate, fixed with 10% formalin, stained with 1% uranyl acetate and dried from amyl acetate. The 250-Å fibers consist of two 100-Å fibrils which separate when treated with chelating agents.

Fig. 5. Nucleus of erythrocyte in spleen from the salamander. Freeze-etched. Surface of nuclear membrane (N.M.) with two nuclear pores (N.P.). In the fractured portion of the nucleus, one sees chromatin fibers (arrows) about 250 Å thick. Bracket represents 250 Å.

Fig. 6. Nucleus from unidentified cell in spleen of salamander. Freeze-etched. The light discs and short rods (arrows) are interpreted as cross- and oblique fractures of 250-Å chromatin fibers (N.M. = nuclear membrane; brackets represent 250 Å).

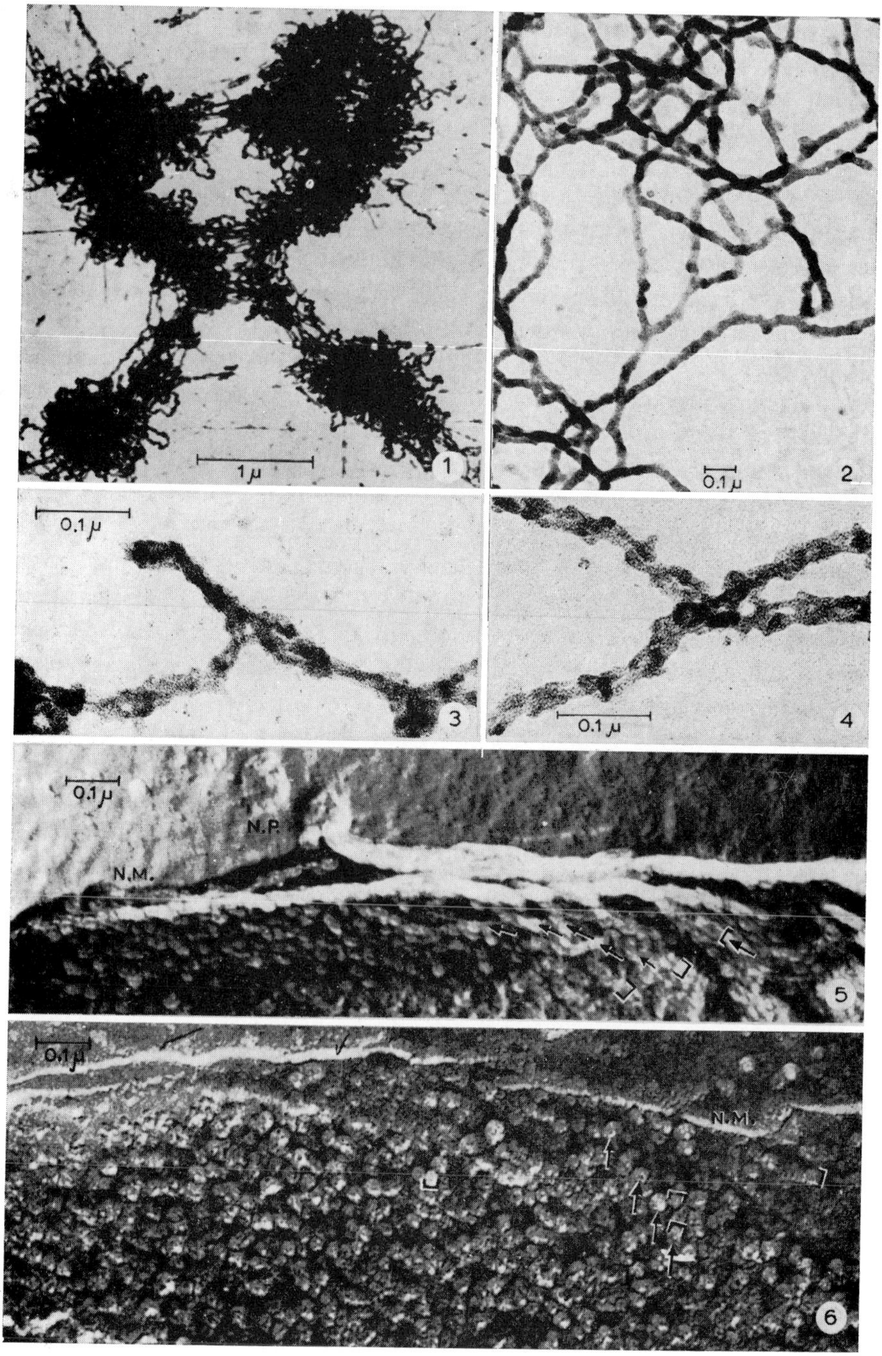
1 μ
1
0.1 μ
2
0.1 μ
3
0.1 μ
4
0.1 μ
N.P.
N.M.
5
0.1 μ
N.M.
6

either two 100-Å fibrils are associated side-by-side or one and the same fibril is folded back on itself. Side branches of the 250-Å fibers are clearly the result of the folding of a single fibril back on itself (Fig. 3). However, side-by-side association of independent fibrils cannot be excluded as an explanation of the doubleness in other regions.

My observations thus suggest that the 250-Å fibers are formed as a result of the folding of 100-Å fibrils under the influence of divalent cations to give a branched system of 250-Å fibers. Free ends tend to stick to other fibers to produce as network-like structure (Figs. 2 and 11). When the metal ions (probably calcium or magnesium) are removed, the fibers unfold into 100-Å fibrils (Ris 1967).

It is now clear that there is a direct relationship between the 100-Å fibrils and 250-Å fibers. However, it remains to be determined which of these is the 'native' configuration of DNH. I mentioned earlier that most investigators have found fibrils with an average thickness of 100 Å in sections of fixed chromosomes and nuclei, while unfixed nuclei or chromosomes spread at an air–water interface yield 250-Å fibers. Wolfe and Grim recently investigated this question and concluded that the 250-Å fiber is an artifact formed by the accretion of extraneous material onto the basic 100-Å fibril during nuclear lysis of unfixed material. Wolfe (1967) showed that the fibrils released from nuclei spread on water after fixation with 2% formalin in 0.05 M phosphate buffer are about 150 Å thick. He concluded that fixation prior to spreading preserved the native structure found in the intact nucleus.

However, an alternative interpretation is possible: since phosphate is known to bind metal ions, Wolfe's 150-Å fibrils may be artifacts produced by an unfolding of 'native' 250-Å fibrils through the action of the buffer. It turns out that this is the correct explanation (Ris, unpublished observations). Unfixed erythrocytes of the salamander *Triturus viridescens* were spread on phosphate buffer, cacodylate buffer, veronal acetate buffer and s-collidine buffer. In every case the fibrils were about 100 Å thick. When erythrocytes were spread on buffers such as N-2-hydroxyethylpiperazine-N′-2-ethane sulfonic acid (HEPES) or N-tris (hydroxymethyl)-methyl-2-aminoethane sulfonic acid (TES) that are known not to bind metals (Good et al.), the fibrils were about 250 Å thick.

One might predict, therefore, that erythrocytes fixed in 0.1 M phosphate-buffered formalin would yield 100-Å fibrils when spread on water, while those fixed in the 0.1 M TES- or HEPES-buffered 2% formalin should yield 250-Å fibrils. Such was found to be the case.

The 250-Å fibrils fixed with formalin retain the ability to dissociate into 100-Å fibrils upon removal of metal ions: 100-Å fibrils are obtained when erythrocytes fixed in TES- or HEPES-buffered formalin are spread on 5 mM sodium citrate. Such experiments provide further evidence that the association of the 100-Å fibrils into 250-Å fibers is accomplished by the metal ions and not through protein links. These findings suggest that the 100-Å fibrils are folded back on themselves to give 250-Å fibers in the intact nucleus and that this structure is preserved when nuclei are ruptured osmotically. It is, however, disrupted when fixed in the presence of metal-binding buffers.

Studies with the freeze-etching technique developed by Moore et al. provide further evidence that the 250-Å fiber is the native structure in the intact nucleus. This method has the advantage that any effect of the fixative or buffer can be avoided. Bullivant and Ames observed a 250-Å granulation in the heterochromatin of mouse intestinal cells prepared with this method. I have used the device designed by McAlear and Kreutziger (available from C. W. French, Weston, Mass.) to freeze-etch spleen from the salamander *Triturus viridescens*. Fig. 5 shows 250-Å fibers in an erythrocyte nucleus and Fig. 6 shows the 250-Å 'granulation' interpreted as cross-fractures of similar fibers in an unidentified cell from the same spleen (Ris, unpublished observations). The organization of the chromatin as it appears when spread at an air–water interface, therefore, seems to represent adequately the chromatin structure in the intact nucleus. In Fig. 5, the chromatin fibers are seen to be oriented more or less parallel along the nuclear membrane. Davies, and Davies and Small have described a similar orientation of chromatin fibers in sections of a variety of nuclei. The fibers, which are said to be 150–200 Å thick, are arranged in layers parallel to the nuclear membrane and separated from each other and from the nuclear membrane by electron-translucent layers about 100 Å thick. The fibers show short lateral projections and often appear hollow in cross section. It is probable that these fibers correspond to our 250-Å fibers. Sheet-like projections of nuclei have been observed which contain one such layer of chromatin fibers (for references see Davies and Small).

Treatment with metal-binding agents unfolds the 250-Å fibers into 100-Å fibrils which may be considered to be the basic unit of organization of the DNH in inactive chromatin. The question of organization of DNH is, therefore, essentially a question of organization of the 100-Å fibril.

The 100-Å fibrils are not uniform in width but have a characteristic knobby appearance due to the many short lateral projections which extend from the fibril axis (Figs. 7, 8). When 100-Å fibrils attached to a formvar substrate are digested with pronase a single 20–30 Å thick strand remains (Fig. 9). Since the 20–30 Å strand stains with uranyl acetate and is sensitive to DNase, it is concluded that it represents the DNA axis of the 100-Å fibril. This supports the view that in nucleohistones a single DNA double helix is associated with histones. The appearance of fibrils that are only partially digested with pronase suggests that when associated with histones the DNA is folded on itself (Fig. 9). Thus, the short lateral projections on the 100-Å fibrils may represent regions where the DNA is looped out and folds back on itself, held in place by histones. Such electron micrographs also suggest that the packing of the DNA involves irregular folding rather than regular supercoiling (Ris 1967).

Bram compared small-angle X-ray scattering by calf thymus nucleohistone (modified Zubay–Doty preparations, saline–versene *p*H 6.5) with electron micrographs obtained from the same preparation and found excellent agreement between the data obtained by these two techniques. At low concentrations of nucleohistone, X-ray scattering analysis indicated the existence of two radii of gyration. The major fraction

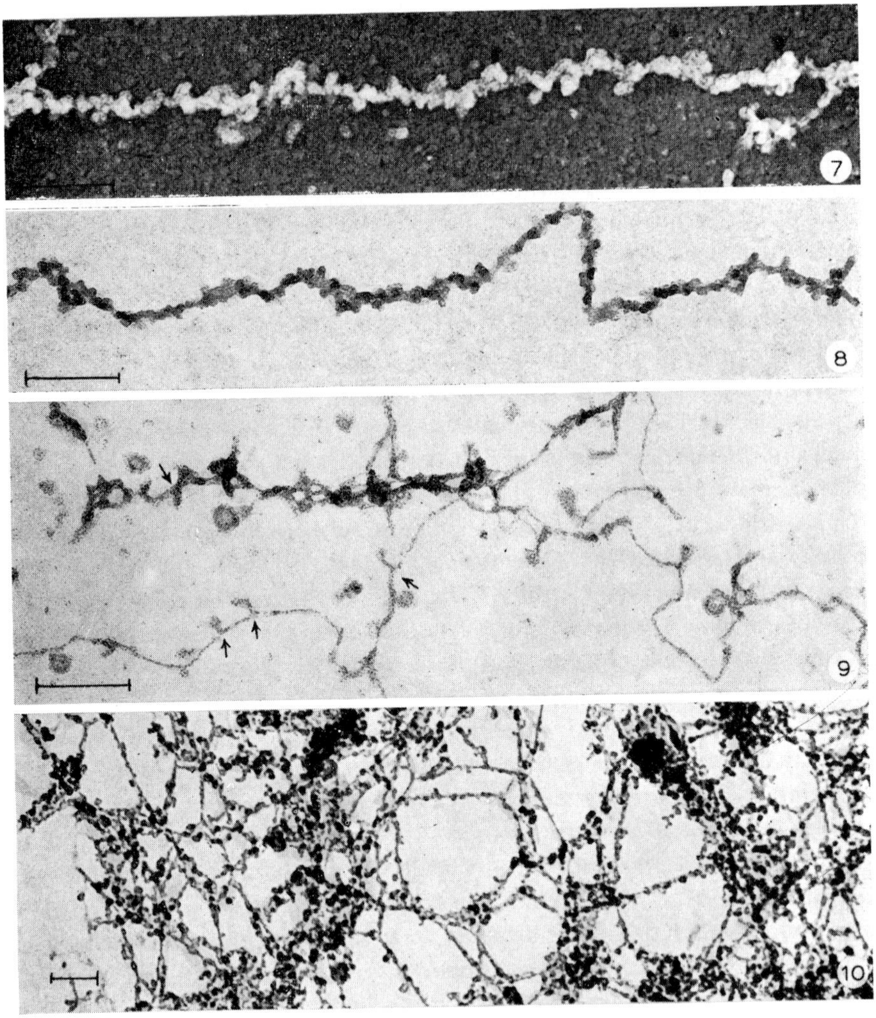

Fig. 7. Nucleohistone fibril from erythrocyte nucleus of salamander spread on 5 mM sodium citrate. Fixed in ethanol, dried from amyl acetate, shadowed with carbon–platinum. The average thickness of the knobby fibril is about 100 Å.

Fig. 8. Same as Fig. 7, but stained with 1% uranyl acetate. Note the many short side branches on the 100-Å fibril.

Fig. 9. Same as Fig. 8, but digested with pronase. A single molecule of DNA about 20 Å thick is left after digestion of the histones. Note the many places where the DNA loops back on itself (arrows). The loops appear to correspond to the short side branches on the nucleohistone fibril.

Fig. 10. Calf thymus nucleohistone prepared according to a modified Zubay–Doty procedure (saline–versene, *p*H 6.5). Fixed in ethanol, dried with critical point method. Note knobby 100-Å fibrils similar to those from salamander erythrocyte.

corresponds to a cross-section radius of 40–50 Å; this agrees well with the average diameter of 100 Å seen in electron micrographs. The minor fraction had a cross-section radius of about 80 Å and could represent the short lateral projections extending from the fibers (Fig. 10). The mass per unit length of the major fraction was 1500 Daltons/Å in agreement with the value given by Luzzati and Nicolaieff. On the other hand, Bram's data, especially the shape of the scattering curve and the average radius of gyration (30 Å), indicate that the fiber is extensively solvated. This contradicts the Luzzati and Nicolaieff model which proposes that nucleohistone exists as a solid cylinder containing four DNA molecules with an equal weight of protein. The observed mass per unit length could also be obtained if the DNH contained a single DNA fiber that is coiled or folded on itself as suggested by electron microscopy and sedimentation data. To give the observed mass per unit length, a DNA molecule associated with equal weight of protein when coiled into a 100-Å fiber would have to have a pitch of about 50 Å. The observed scattering curve, however, excludes any such *regular* structure, including the regular coil of 120 Å pitch proposed by Pardon et al. The model giving a calculated scattering curve closest to the observed includes an *irregular* coil with an average radius of gyration of 30 Å. Such a model is in reasonable agreement with the electron microscopic observations; and electron micrographs such as Fig. 10, therefore, give a reasonably accurate picture of the nucleohistone in solution.

The 30-Å smooth fibril illustrated by Zubay and Doty (1959) as representative for their 'soluble' nucleohistone looks very different from the chromatin fibrils obtained under conditions of minimal shear. This supports the view that the 'soluble' DNH is probably an artifact and does not represent the structure of native DNH. The tendency of the 100-Å fibrils to attach to each other and form networks is in accord with the idea that gel formation is a natural property of DNH.

A characteristic surface structure is evident in the 100-Å nucleohistone fibrils. This is revealed by negative staining, (Fig. 11) or positive staining with uranyl magnesium acetate according to Frasca and Parks (1965; Fig. 14), by tungsten shadowing (Fig. 12) and even in sectioned material (Fig. 14). In negatively stained preparations, the surface appears to have a fibrillar structure with a fibril thickness of 35 Å. Tungsten-shadowed preparations sometimes show a rather regular arrangement with a periodicity of 30–35 Å. When 100-Å fibrils (spread on 0.5 mM sodium citrate) are floated briefly on 2 M NaCl the knobby outline disappears and the fibrils become smooth and approximately 80 Å thick. They still show the fibrillar substructure with regions of 30–35 Å periodicity (Fig. 13). It is tempting to speculate that these structures represent the 35 Å spacing suggested by the X-ray diffraction data of Wilkins et al.).

Several other investigators have reported surface detail on nucleohistone fibers. Gall (1966) described negatively stained nucleohistone fibers with irregular patches about 50 Å in diameter. Barnicot observed fibrillar elements less than 50 Å in diameter on negatively stained, spread newt chromosomes. A pattern of 20–30-Å fibrils was reported by Huxley and Zubay in oriented calf thymus DNH, and such a pattern was described by Wettstein and Sotelo in 100-Å fibrils from meiotic chromosomes of the cricket.

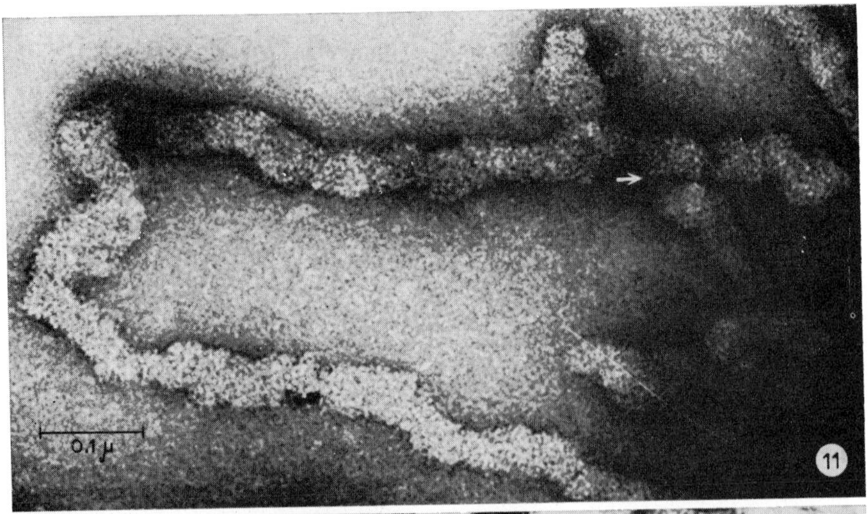
0,1 μ
11

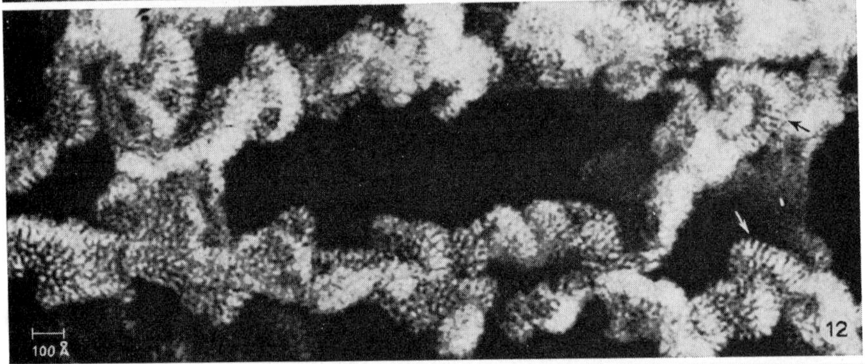
100 Å
12

100 Å
13

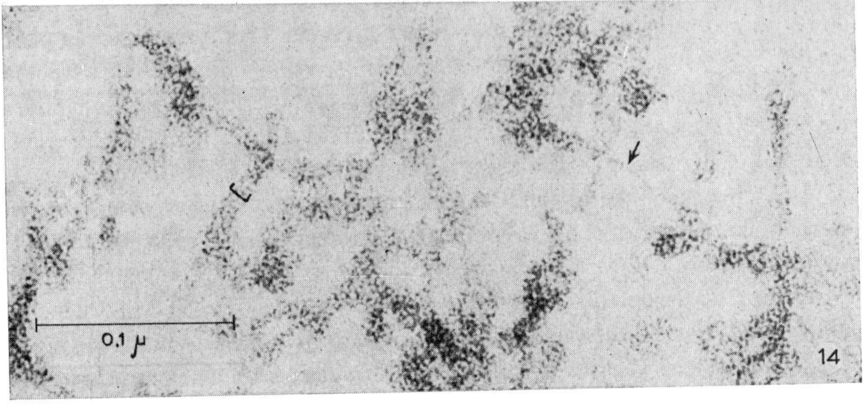
0,1 μ
14

Unfortunately, since there is as yet no means for selective staining of DNA or histone, it is impossible to interpret these electron micrographs with regard to the exact arrangement of DNA and histone in the fiber.

(b) *Molecular complexes in active chromatin*

The structural organization of active chromatin is less well known than that of inactive chromatin. It makes up a smaller fraction of chromatin in most nuclei and also is more complex in composition. For a structural analysis of active chromatin, the lampbrush chromosomes of amphibian oocytes and the polytene chromosomes of dipteran larvae are especially well suited.

During the growth of the oocyte, the chromosomes are in the diplotene stage of meiotic prophase. They increase enormously in size, reaching 1 mm in length. The size increase is accompanied by the appearance of loop-like structures of various but specific length and morphology (cf. chapter by Callan). RNA synthesis and perhaps also protein synthesis was shown to occur on these loops (Gall and Callan). Recent electron microscope studies have to some extent clarified the nature of the lampbrush chromosome loops (Miller 1965; Sapp). Each loop contains a single DNA double helix that appears to have unfolded from the chromomeres in the chromosome axis (Fig. 16). The DNA forms the axis of the loop and is surrounded by granules and a fuzzy mass of fibrils (Fig. 15) some of which may reach 20 μ in length (Miller 1965). These fibrils and granules consist of ribonucleoproteins which are arranged into specific patterns to give each loop a characteristic appearance. Davidson et al. have presented evidence that large amounts of RNA are produced during the lampbrush stage and stored in the oocyte. Though 98% of this RNA consists of ribosomal RNA, the mass of template-RNA accumulated by the end of oogenesis is equivalent to 3900 times the mass of DNA in the oocyte chromosomes. In spite of the extensive activity on these chromosomes only about 3% of the DNA is transcribed in the oocyte (Davidson et al.). According to Gall and Callan about 5% of the chromosomal DNA is present in the

Fig. 11. Nucleohistone fiber from salamander erythrocyte spread on water, fixed in 10% formalin. Negative staining with 1% uranyl acetate. At arrow one fiber touches another. Note short side branch on upper fiber.

Fig. 12. Nucleohistone fibers from salamander erythrocyte spread on water, fixed in 10% formalin, dried by the critical point method and shadowed with tungsten. Note the surface structure which in certain places shows a regular periodicity of about 35 Å (arrows).

Fig 13. Nucleohistone fiber from salamander erythrocyte spread on 5 mM sodium citrate, treated for 15 min with 2 M NaCl fixed in 10% formalin, dried with the critical point method and shadowed with tungsten.

Fig. 14. Calf thymus nucleohistone as in Fig. 10, fixed in 10% formalin in 0.1 M phosphate buffer *p*H 7.2 followed by 1% OsO_4 in the same buffer. Sections stained with uranyl magnesium acetate and lead citrate. The bracket indicates 100 Å. At arrow, the 100-Å fibril tapers into a fibril about 20 Å thick.

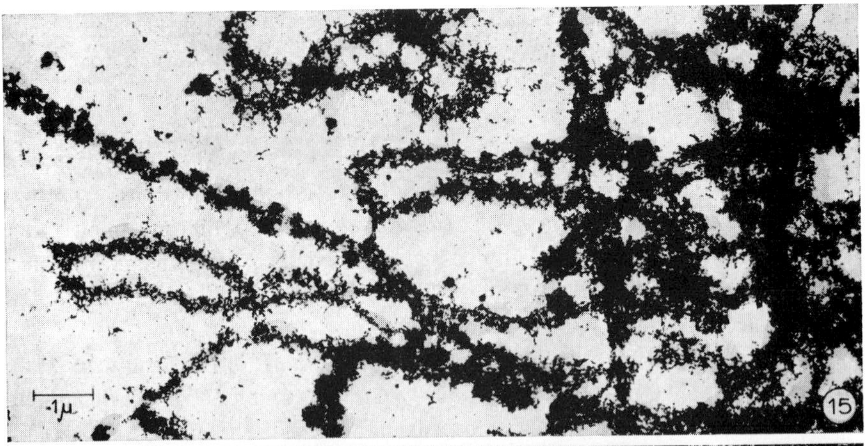

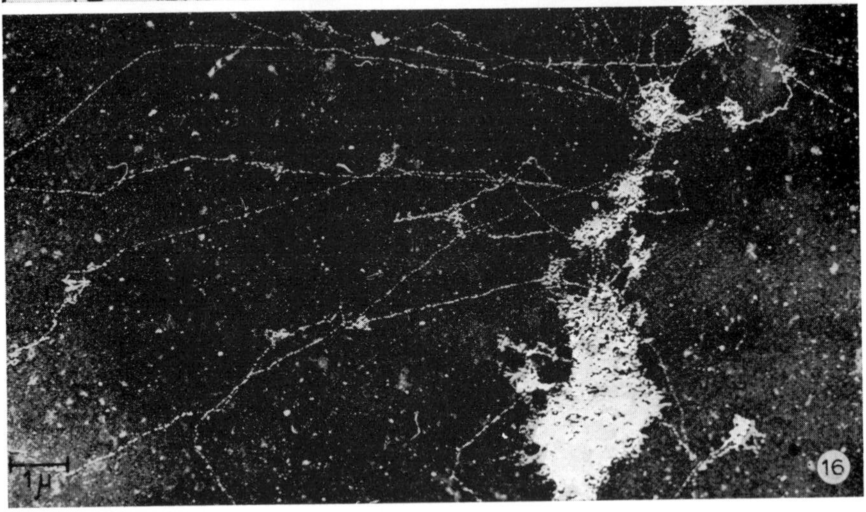

Fig. 15. Several loops from a lampbrush chromosome of *Triturus viridescens*. Chromosome isolated in 0.1 M KCl and 0.1 M NaCl at *p*H 6.7, fixed in 10% formalin and dried by critical point method. (Electron micrograph through courtesy of Dr. W. Sapp, Tuskegee Institute.)

Fig. 16. Lampbrush chromosome prepared as in Fig. 15 but digested with trypsin. The thin fibers which remain are sensitive to DNAse. It appears that a single DNA molecule forms the axis of the loops, connecting one chromomere with the next. (Electron micıograph through courtesy of Dr. W. Sapp, Tuskegee Institute.)

loops at any one time. The findings of Davidson et al., therefore, suggest that only the DNA present in the loops is transcribed during the lampbrush stage. This contradicts the proposal of Gall and Callan that all DNA in a chromomere is used as template as it moves through the loop into the adjacent chromomere.

The giant chromosomes characteristic of many tissues in dipteran larvae are interphase chromosomes that have undergone many cycles of replication without strand separation and have reached such unusual dimensions that they are individually visible. These polytene chromosomes have a characteristic banding pattern and many of the bands are known to represent the loci of specific genes. RNA staining and autoradiography following incorporation of RNA precursors (Pelling) allow one to visualize active regions on these chromosomes. In some of these regions, the chromosome is swollen, forming so-called 'puffs'. Puffs are considered to be individually recognizable chromosome loci that are active in DNA-dependent RNA synthesis (Beermann 1962) and originate from specific bands through unravelling of the chromatin. The fine structure of puffs was first studied by Beermann and Bahr and their findings have been confirmed and expanded by Swift (1962) and Stevens and Swift. Puffs contain strands about 0.2 μ thick which loop out to form the expanded chromosome region. These strands resemble lampbrush chromosome loops in that they are covered with bristle-like 180–270-Å fibers and 300–400-Å granules consisting of RNA-protein. Puff-specific granules of various sizes also fill the space between the threads. Less intense DNA staining in the puff regions suggests that during 'puffing' the DNA unravels and thus becomes diluted. The DNA axis, however, has not yet been demonstrated in these loops of puffs. Granules similar to those seen in puffs are present in the nucleoplasm and in the pores of the nuclear membrane. It was suggested that they represent protein coated messenger RNA on the way from the puffs to the cytoplasm (Stevens and Swift).

A similar type of active chromatin is found in spermatocytes of *Drosophila* (Hess and Meyer). During meiotic prophase, several loci on the Y-chromosome produce large paired structures that resemble lampbrush chromosome loops. They consist of fibrils, granules and tubular structures made of RNA and non-histone protein. Fragmentation of loops with DNase and labeling with H^3-thymidine are evidence that these structures contain a DNA axis (Hennig).

Lampbrush chromosome loops, polytene chromosome puffs and Y-chromosome loops are transitory structures which depend on continued DNA-dependent RNA synthesis for their existence. Actinomycin D has been found to cause all three structures to decrease in size and even disappear (Izawa et al.; Beermann 1965; Meyer and Hess). DNA-dependent RNA synthesis, complexing of the RNA with a protein and temporary storage of the nucleoprotein fibrils and granules on the DNA seem to be the factors leading to the formation of these variants of active chromatin.

In ordinary somatic nuclei where individual chromosomes are not visible, active chromatin is more difficult to localize. Electron-microscope autoradiography, after pulse labeling with RNA precursors, indicates that most RNA synthesis occurs in the diffuse regions of chromatin and very little in the condensed heterochromatic areas

(Granboulan and Granboulan; Littau et al.; Karasaki; Kemp). The labeled chromatin regions correspond to the RNA-rich areas demonstrated by Huxley and Zubay. These areas contain RNA–protein granules associated with fibrils, the interchromatin granules of Bernhard and Granboulan and of Swift (1959). In calf thymus nuclei, the interchromatin granules and fibrils which are seen to be continuous with the condensed chromatin persist after extraction of DNA and histone in 2 M sodium chloride (Ris 1962) and thus correspond to the residual chromatin of Mirsky and Ris. In amphibian embryos the interchromatin granules appear first at gastrulation, the time when DNA-dependent RNA synthesis increases (Karasaki).

Frenster et al. and Bonner (1967) have succeeded in separating active and inactive chromatin by differential centrifugation of fragmented chromatin of pea embryo, calf thymus and rat liver nuclei. This allows a more detailed analysis of the composition of active and inactive chromatin. Inactive chromatin consists almost exclusively of DNA and histone. Active chromatin also contains histones. According to Bonner (1967) active chromatin contains less and qualitatively different histones. Frenster (1965) on the other hand, finds only insignificant differences in histones of active and inactive fractions. His results are supported by histochemical studies on puffs of polytene chromosomes (Gorovsky and Woodard) and by biochemical studies comparing active and inactive chromatin from various sources (Comings). It appears, therefore, that the histones in active chromatin are not basically different but may have undergone some subtle changes which modify their binding to DNA, allowing the DNA to unravel and the RNA polymerase to become functional. Acetylation, methylation and phosphorylation of histones which seem to accompany activation of chromatin may be related to such changes in DNA–histone binding (see Allfrey et al.).

Active chromatin contains a variety of non-histone proteins including phosphoproteins (Langan). It has been suggested that these proteins might act as derepressors by combining with histones. Frenster (1965) has compared the melting temperature and hyperchromicity of DNA in active and inactive chromatin and found indications for partial strand separation of the DNA in active chromatin.

(c) *The nature of structural continuity of chromosomes*

The longitudinal continuity of chromosomes could be due to either protein or DNA. Indirect evidence from the treatment of unfixed chromosomes with enzymes suggests that DNA is largely responsible for this continuity. Lampbrush chromosomes fragment when treated with DNase but not with RNase or proteases (Callan and McGregor; Gall 1963). The same is true for polytene chromosomes of diptera (Lezzi). Though DNA seems to be the major component of the chromosomal 'backbone', the question remains whether there are continuous 3′-5′-phosphodiester linkages from one end of the chromosome to the other or whether a number of DNA molecules are joined by non-DNA material.

Non-DNA linkers were first proposed to allow for several initiation points of DNA replication (Freese). The length of DNA per chromosome is several centimeters and the rate of replication of DNA has been estimated to be from 0.5–1 μ per minute (Cairns 1966). Thus the duration of DNA synthesis in the cell cycle would be too short to allow for doubling of the DNA if the chromosome consisted of a single replicating unit. Autoradiographic studies on mitotic chromosomes and dipteran polytene chromosomes have now clearly shown that chromosomes consist of several independent replicating units or replicons (for references see Huberman; Taylor). Plaut and Nash estimate that there are about 50 replicons in a *Drosophila* salivary chromosome. From the average DNA content of *Drosophila* chromosomes (1.5–7.5 cm), one obtains a length of 0.3–1.5 mm for the average replicating unit (Huberman and Riggs). This agrees well with the longest pieces of DNA measured by autoradiography or the electron microscope (Table 1). Non-histone proteins and peptides have been proposed as linkers between replicating units (references in Josse and Eigner). However, convincing evidence for such linkers covalently bound to the DNA has not been presented.

According to the simplest model, a chromosome would contain a single nucleohistone fibril. However, there are many features of chromosomes that suggest a multistranded structure. At present the controversy between a unineme or multineme chromosome model is still unresolved. The arguments for and against these models are critically reviewed by Swift (1965).

References

AKINRIMISI, E.O., J.BONNER and P.O.TS'O: Binding of basic proteins to DNA. J. Mol. Biol. 11 (1965) 128.

ALLFREY, V.G., B.G.T.POGO, A.O.POGO, L.J.KLEINSMITH and A.E.MIRSKY: The metabolic behaviour of chromatin. In: A.V.S.de Reuck and J.Knight, eds.: Histones. London, J. & A.Churchill, Ltd. (1966) 42.

ATEN, J.B.T. and J.A.COHEN: Sedimentation-viscosity studies of high molecular weight DNA. J. Mol. Biol. 12 (1965) 537.

BARIGOZZI, C.: La signification du spodogramme pour l'étude de la structure des chromosomes. Bull. Histol. Appl. 15 (1938) 213.

BARNICOT, N.A.: A study of newt mitotic chromosomes by negative staining. J. Cell Biol. 32 (1967) 585.

BAYLEY, P.M., B.N.PRESTON and A.R.PEACOCKE: Thymus deoxyribonucleoprotein II. Dissociation in sodium chloride solution. Biochim. Biophys. Acta 66 (1962) 943.

BEER, M. and D.R.ZOBEL: Electron stains II: electron microscopic studies on the visibility of stained DNA molecules. J. Mol. Biol. 3 (1961) 717.

BEERMANN, W.: Riesenchromosomen. Protoplasmatologia, Vol. VI D. Vienna, Springer-Verlag (1962).

BEERMANN, W.: Structure and function of interphase chromosomes. Genetics today, Proc. XI Int. Congr. Genet. Pergamon Press (1965) 375.

BEERMANN, W. and G.F.BAHR: The submicroscopic structure of the Balbiani-ring. Exptl. Cell Res. 6 (1954) 195.

BENDICH, A. and H.S.ROSENKRANZ: Some thoughts on the double-stranded model of deoxyribonucleic acid. Progr. Nucleic Acid Res. 1 (1963) 219.

BERLOWITZ, L. and M.L.BIRNSTIEL: Histones in the wild-type and the anucleolate mutant of *Xenopus laevis*. Science 156 (1967) 78.

BERNHARD, W. and N. GRANBOULAN: The fine structure of the cancer cell nucleus. Exptl. Cell Res. Suppl. 9 (1963) 19.

BODE, H. R. and H. J. MOROWITZ: Size and structure of the Mycoplasma hominis H39 chromosome. J. Mol. Biol. 28 (1967) 191.

BONNER, J.: The role of histones in the regulation of RNA synthesis. In: V. V. Koningsberger and L. Bosch, eds.: BBA Library. Amsterdam, Elsevier Publishing Co. 10 (1967) 211.

BONNER, J.: Control of gene function and development in higher organisms. Biophys. J. 8 (1968) A-5.

BONNER, J. and R. C. HUANG: Histones as specified repressors of chromosomal RNA synthesis. In: A. V. S. de Reuck and J. Knight, eds.: Histones. Ciba Foundation Study Group No. 24. London, J. & A. Churchill, Ltd. (1966) 18.

BONNER, J., M. E. DAHMUS, D. FAMBROUGH, R. C. HUANG, K. MARUSHIGE and D. Y. H. TUAN: The biology of isolated chromatin. Science 159 (1968) 47.

BRADBURY, E. M., W. C. PRICE and G. R. WILKINSON: Polarized infrared studies of nucleoproteins. J. Mol. Biol. 4 (1962) 39.

BRADBURY, E. M., C. CRANE-ROBINSON, H. GOLDMAN, H. W. E. RATTLE and R. M. STEPHENS: Spectroscopic studies of the conformations of histones and protamine. J. Mol. Biol. 29 (1967) 507.

BRAM, S.: A study of the structure of nucleohistone and DNA. Thesis, University of Wisconsin (1968).

BULLIVANT, S. and A. AMES, III: A simple freeze-fracture replication method for electron microscopy. J. Cell Biol. 29 (1966) 435.

BUSCH, H.: Histones and other nuclear proteins. New York, Academic Press, Inc. (1965).

CAIRNS, J.: The chromosome of *Escherichia coli*. Cold Spring Harbor Symp. Quant. Biol. 28 (1963) 43.

CAIRNS, J.: Autoradiography of HeLa cells in DNA. J. Mol. Biol. 15 (1966) 372.

CALLAN, H. G. and H. C. MACGREGOR: Action of deoxyribonuclease on lampbrush chromosomes. Nature 181 (1958) 1479.

CANTOR, K. P. and J. E. HEARST: Isolation and partial characterization of metaphase chromosomes of a mouse ascites tumor. Proc. Natl. Acad. Sci. U.S. 55 (1966) 642.

CHAMBERLAIN, P. J. and P. M. B. WALKER: The thermal denaturation of nucleoprotein in boar sperm. J. Mol. Biol. 11 (1965) 1.

CHEVAILLIER, P.: Contribution a l'étude du complexe ADN-histone dans le spermatozoïde du pagure *Eupagurus bernhardus* L. (crustace decapode). J. Microscopie 5 (1966) 739.

COLE, A.: Chromosome structure. In: A. Cole, ed.: Theoretical and experimental biophysics. New York, Marcel Dekker, Inc. 1 (1967) 305.

COMINGS, E. D.: Histones of genetically active and inactive chromatin. J. Cell Biol. 35 (1967) 699.

DAVIDSON, E. H., M. CRIPPA, F. R. KRAMER and A. E. MIRSKY: Genomic function during the lampbrush chromosome stage of amphibian oogenesis. Proc. Natl. Acad. Sci. U.S. 56 (1966) 856.

DAVIES, H. G.: Fine structure of heterochromatin in certain cell nuclei. Nature 214 (1967) 208.

DAVIES, H. G. and J. V. SMALL: Structural units in chromatin and their orientation on membranes. Nature 217 (1968) 1122.

DAVISON, P. F.: Sedimentation of DNA isolated under low hydrodynamic shear. Nature 185 (1960) 918.

DOUNCE, A. L. and M. O'CONNELL: Composition and properties of the thymus deoxyribonucleoprotein of Doty and Zubay. J. Am. Chem. Soc. 80 (1958) 2013.

DOUNCE, A. L. and C. A. HILGARTNER: A study of the DNA nucleoprotein gels and the residual protein of isolated nuclei. Exptl. Cell Res. 36 (1965) 228.

DU PRAW, E. J.: The organization of nuclei and chromosomes in honeybee embryonic cells. Proc. Natl. Acad. Sci. U.S. 53 (1965a) 161.

DU PRAW, E. J.: Macromolecular organization of nuclei and chromosomes: a folded fibre model based on whole-mount electron microscopy. Nature 206 (1965b) 338.

DU PRAW, E. J.: Evidence for a 'folded-fibre' organization in human chromosomes. Nature 209 (1966) 577.

FELIX, K.: Zur Chemie des Zellkerns. Experientia 8 (1952) 312.

FEUGHELMAN, M., R. LANGRIDGE, W. E. SEEDS, A. R. STOKES, H. R. WILSON, C. W. HOOPER, M. H. WILKINS, R. K. BARCLAY and L. D. HAMILTON: Molecular structure of deoxyribose nucleic acid and nucleoprotein. Nature 179 (1955) 834.

FRASCA, J. M. and V. R. PARKS: A routine technique for doublestaining ultrathin sections using uranyl and lead salts. J. Cell Biol. 25 (1965) 157.

FREDERICQ, E. and C. HOUSSIER: Physico-chemical properties of native and recombined calf thymus nucleohistones. European J. Biochem. 1 (1967) 51.

FREESE, E.: The arrangement of DNA in the chromosome. Cold Spring Harbor Symp. Quant. Biol. 23 (1958) 13.

FREIFELDER, D. and A. K. KLEINSCHMIDT: Single strand breaks in duplex DNA of coliphage T7 as demonstrated by electronmicroscopy. J. Mol. Biol. 14 (1965) 271.

FRENSTER, J. H.: Mechanisms of repression and de-repression within interphase chromatin. In: D. J. Dawe, ed.: In vitro, vol. 1 – The chromosome. Publication of the Tissue Culture Assoc., Inc. 1 (1965) 78.

FRENSTER, J. H.: Control of DNA strand separations during selective transcription and asynchronous replication. In: M. G. Ord, L. A. Stoken, H. M. Klouwen and I. Betel, eds.: The cell nucleus. London, Taylor & Francis, Ltd. (1966) 27.

FRENSTER, J. H., V. B. ALLFREY and A. E. MIRSKY: Repressed and active chromatin isolated from interphase lymphocytes. Proc. Natl. Acad. Sci. U.S. 50 (1963) 1026.

GALL, J. G.: Chromosome fibers from an interphase nucleus. Science 139 (1963) 120.

GALL, J. G.: Chromosome fibers studied by a spreading technique. Chromosoma 20 (1966) 221.

GALL, J. G. and H. G. CALLAN: H^3-uridine incorporation in lampbrush chromosomes. Proc. Natl. Acad. Sci., U.S. 48 (1962) 562.

GIANNONI, G. and A. R. PEACOCKE: Thymus deoxyribonucleoprotein III. Sedimentation behaviour. Biochim. Biophys. Acta 68 (1963) 157.

GOOD, N. E., G. D. WIGNET, W. WINTER, T. N. CONNOLLY, S. IZAWA and R. M. SINGH: Hydrogen ion buffers for biological research. Biochemistry 5 (1966) 467.

GOROVSKY, M. A. and J. WOODARD: Histone content of chromosomal loci active and inactive in RNA synthesis. J. Cell Biol. 33 (1967) 723.

GRANBOULAN, N. and P. GRANBOULAN: Cytochimie ultrastructural du nucléole II. Etude des sites de synthèse du RNA dans le nucléole et le noyau. Exptl. Cell Res. 38 (1965) 604.

HALL, C. E. and M. LITT: Morphological features of DNA macromolecules as seen with the electron microscope. J. Biophys. Biochem. Cytol. 4 (1958) 1.

HAMILTON, L. D., R. K. BARCLAY, M. H. F. WILKINS, G. L. BROWN, H. R. WILSON, D. A. MARVIN, H. EPHRUSSI-TAYLOR and N. S. SIMMONS: Similarity of the structure of DNA from a variety of sources. J. Biophys. Biochem. Cytol. 5 (1959) 397.

HAYASHI, M.: A DNA-RNA complex as an intermediate of *in vitro* genetic transcription. Proc. Natl. Acad. Sci. U.S. 54 (1965) 1736.

HAYASHI, M. N. and M. HAYASHI: Participation of a DNA-RNA hybrid complex in *in vivo* genetic transcription. Proc. Natl. Acad. Sci. U.S. 55 (1966) 635.

HENNIG, W.: Untersuchungen zur Struktur und Funktion des Lampenbürsten-Y-chromosoms in der Spermatogenese von Drosophila. Chromosoma 22 (1967) 294.

HESS, O. and G. F. MEYER: Chromosomal differentiations of the lampbrush type formed by the Y-chromosome in *Drosophila hydei* and *Drosophila neohydei*. J. Cell Biol. 16 (1963) 527.

HNILICA, L. S.: Proteins of the cell nucleus. Progr. Nucleic Acid Res. 7 (1967) 25.

HNILICA, L. S. and L. S. EDWARDS: The evolution of histones. Seventh Int. Congr. Biochem. Tokyo. Colloquium IX. Histones (1967) 513.

HOTTA, Y. and A. BASSEL: Molecular size and circularity of DNA in cells of mammals and higher plants. Proc. Natl. Acad. Sci. U.S. 53 (1965) 356.

HOTTA, Y. and H. STERN: Ribonucleic acid polymerase activity in extended and contracted chromosomes. Nature 210 (1966) 1043.

HUANG, R.C.: Dihydrouridylic acid containing RNA from chick embryo chromatin. Federation Proc. 26 (1967) 603.

HUANG, R.C. and J. BONNER: Histone, a suppressor of chromosomal RNA synthesis. Proc. Natl. Acad. Sci. U.S. 48 (1962) 1216.

HUANG, R.C., J. BONNER and K. MURRAY: Physical and biological properties of soluble nucleohistones. J. Mol. Biol. 8 (1964) 54.

HUBERMAN, J.A.: J. Mol. Biol. 32 (1968) (In press).

HUBERMAN, J.A. and A.D. RIGGS: Autoradiography of chromosomal DNA fibers from Chinese hamster cells. Proc. Natl. Acad. Sci. U.S. 55 (1966) 599.

HUDSON, B. and J. VINOGRAD: Catenated DNA molecules in HeLa cell mitochondria. Nature 216 (1967) 674.

HURWITZ, J., A. EVANS, C. BABINET and A. SKALKA: On the copying of DNA in the RNA polymerase reaction. Cold Spring Harbor Symp. Quant. Biol. 28 (1963) 59.

HUXLEY, H.E. and G. ZUBAY: Preferential staining of nucleic acid-containing structures for electron microscopy. J. Biophys. Biochem. Cytol. 11 (1961) 273.

INMAN, R.B.: A denaturation map of the λ phage DNA molecule determined by electron microscopy. J. Mol. Biol. 18 (1966) 464.

ITZHAKI, R.F.: Structure and properties of rat-thymus deoxyribonucleoprotein. A comparison of the electric birefringence and other properties of deoxyribonucleoprotein prepared by various methods. Biochem. J. 100 (1966) 211.

IZAWA, M., V.G. ALLFREY and A.E. MIRSKY: The relationship between RNA synthesis and loop structure in lampbrush chromosomes. Proc. Natl. Acad. Sci. U.S. 49 (1963) 544.

JOHNS, E.W.: The fractionation and characterization of histones and their interactions with deoxyribonucleic acid. In: M.G. Ord, L.A. Stoken, H.M. Klouwen and I. Betel, eds.: The cell nucleus. London, Taylor & Francis, Ltd. (1966) 115.

JOHNS, E.W. and J.A.V. BUTLER: Specificity of the interactions between histones and deoxyribonucleic acid. Nature 204 (1964) 853.

JOSSE, J. and J. EIGNER: Physical properties of deoxyribonucleic acid. Annual review of biochemistry. 35 (1966) 789.

KARASAKI, S.: Electron microscopic examination of the sites of nuclear RNA synthesis during amphibian embryogenesis. J. Cell Biol. 26 (1965) 937.

KAUFMANN, B.P., H. GAY and M.R. MCDONALD: Organizational patterns within chromosomes. Intern. Rev. Cytol. 9 (1960) 77.

KAYE, J.S. and R. MCMASTER-KAYE: The fine structure and chemical composition of nuclei during spermiogenesis in the house cricket I. Initial stages of differentiation and the loss of nonhistone protein. J. Cell Biol. 31 (1966) 159.

KEMP, D.L.: Electron microscope autoradiographic studies of RNA metabolism in *Trillium erectum* microspores. Chromosoma 19 (1966) 137.

KISCHER, C.W. and L.S. HNILICA: Analysis of histones during organogenesis. Exptl. Cell Res. 48 (1967) 424.

KLEINSCHMIDT, A.K.: Nukleinsäuren. Naturwissenschaften 54 (1967) 417.

KLEINSCHMIDT, A. and R.K. ZAHN: Morphologie gelöster Desoxyribonukleinsäure-Preparate und einige ihrer Eigenschaften in Oberflächen-Mischfilmen. Fourth Int. Conf. Electron Micr., Vol. II. Berlin, Springer-Verlag (1960) 115.

LANG, D., A.K. KLEINSCHMIDT and R.K. ZAHN: Elektronenmikroskopische Darstellung, Längenverteilung und Konfiguration einsträngiger Desoxyribonukleinsäure im Cytochrom-c-film. Biophysik 2 (1964) 73.

LANG, D., H. BUJARD, B. WOLFF and D. RUSSELL: Electron microscopy of size and shape of viral DNA in solutions of different ionic strengths. J. Mol. Biol. 23 (1967) 163.

LANGAN, T. A.: A phosphoprotein preparation from liver nuclei and its effect on the inhibition of RNA synthesis by histones. In: V.V. Koningsberger and L. Bosch, eds.: BBA Library. Amsterdam, Elsevier Publishing Co. 10 (1967) 233.

LENG, M. and G. FELSENFELD: A study of polyadenylic acid at neutral *p*H. J. Mol. Biol. 15 (1966) 455.

LETT, J. T., I. CALDWELL, C. J. DEAN and P. ALEXANDER: Rejoining of X-ray induced breaks in the DNA leukaemia cells. Natuıe 214 (1967) 790.

LEZZI, M.: Die Wirkung von DNAse auf isolierte Polytän-chromosomen. Exptl. Cell Res. 39 (1965) 289.

LINDSAY, D. T.: Histones from developing tissues of the chicken: heterogeneity. Science 144 (1964) 420.

LIQUORI, A. M., L. COSTANTINO, V. CRESCENZI, V. ELLA, E. GIGLIO, R. PULITI, M. D. S. SAVINO and V. VITAGLIANO: Complexes between DNA and polyamines: a molecular model. J. Mol. Biol. 24 (1967) 113.

LITTAU, V. C., V. G. ALLFREY, J. H. FRENSTER and A. E. MIRSKY: Active and inactive regions of nuclear chromatin as revealed by electron microscope autoradiography. Proc. Natl. Acad. Sci. U.S. 52 (1964) 93.

LLOYD, P. H. and A. R. PEACOCKE: The polydispersity of thymus deoxyribonucleohistone. Biochim. Biophys. Acta 95 (1965) 522.

LUZZATI, V. and A. NICOLAÏEFF: The structure of nucleohistones and nucleoprotamines. J. Mol. Biol. 7 (1963) 142.

MAIO, J. J. and C. L. SCHILDKRAUT: Isolated mammalian metaphase chromosomes I. General characteristics of nucleic acids and proteins. J. Mol. Biol. 24 (1967) 29.

MAZIA, D.: The particulate organization of the chromosome. Proc. Natl. Acad. Sci. U.S. 40 (1954) 521.

MAZIA, D. and R. T. HINEGARDNER: Enzymes of DNA synthesis in nuclei of sea urchin embryos. Proc. Natl. Acad. Sci. U.S. 50 (1963) 148.

MCGRATH, R. A. and R. W. WILLIAMS: Interruptions in single strands of the DNA in slime mold and other organisms. Biophys. J. 7 (1967) 309.

MCLEAR, J. H. and G. O. KREUTZIGER: Freeze etching with radiant energy in a simple cold block device. Proc. 25th Annual Meeting, EMSA. Baton Rouge, Arceneaux Ethyl Corp. (1967) 116.

MEAD, C. G.: A deoxyribonucleic acid-associated ribonuleic acid from *Drosophila melanogaster*. J. Biol. Chem. 239 (1964) 550.

MEYER, G. F. and O. HESS: Struktur-differenzierungen im Y-chromosom von *Drosophila hydei* und ihre Beziehungen zu Genaktivitäten. Chromosoma 16 (1965) 18.

MIESCHER, F.: Die histochemischen und physiologischen Arbeiten. Leipzig (1897).

MILLER, O. L.: Fine structure of lampbrush chromosomes. Natl. Cancer Inst. Monograph 18 (1965) 79.

MILLER, O. L., JR.: Structure and composition of peripheral nucleoli of salamander oocytes. Natl. Cancer Inst. Monograph 23 (1966) 53.

MILMAN, G., R. LANGRIDGE and M. J. CHAMBERLIN: The structure of a DNA-RNA hybrid. Proc. Natl. Acad. Sci. U.S. 57 (1967) 1804.

MIRSKY, A. E. and H. RIS: The composition and structure of isolated chromosomes. J. Gen. Physiol. 34 (1951) 475.

MOORE, H., K. MÜHLETHALER, H. WALDNER and A. FREY-WYSSLING: A new freezing-ultramicrotome. J. Biophys. Biochem. Cytol. 10 (1961) 1.

MURRAY, K.: The basic protein of cell nuclei. Ann. Rev. Biochem. 34 (1965) 290.

NAORA, H., H. NAORA, A. E. MIRSKY and V. G. ALLFREY: Magnesium and calcium in isolated cell nuclei. J. Gen. Physiol. 44 (1961) 713.

NASH, D. and W. PLAUT: On the denaturation of chromosomal DNA *in situ*. Proc. Natl. Acad. Sci. U.S. 51 (1964) 731.

NICOLAÏEFF, A.: Structure of nucleoproteins studied by means of small-angle scattering. In: H. Brumberger, ed.: Small angle X-ray scattering. New York, Gordon and Breach (1967) 221.

OHBA, Y.: Structure of nucleohistone I. Hydrodynamic behaviour. Biochim. Biophys. Acta 123 (1966a) 76.

OHBA, Y.: Structure of nucleohistone II. Thermal denaturation. Biochim. Biophys. Acta 123 (1966b) 84.

OHLENBUSCH, H.H., B.M. OLIVERA, D. TUAN and N. DAVIDSON: Selective dissociation of histones from calf thymus nucleoprotein. J. Mol. Biol. 25 (1967) 299.

OLINS, D.E., A.L. OLINS and P.H. VON HIPPEL: Model nucleoprotein complexes: studies on the interaction of cationic homopolypeptides with DNA. J. Mol. Biol. 24 (1967) 151.

PARDON, J.F., M.G.F. WILKINS and B.M. RICHARDS: Super-helical model for nucleohistone. Nature 215 (1967) 508.

PATEL, G., R. HOWK and T.Y. WANG: Partial purification of a DNA-polymerase from the non-histone chromatin proteins of rat liver. Nature 215 (1967) 1488.

PELLING, C.: Ribonukleinsäure-synthese der Riesenchromosomen. Autoradiographische Untersuchungen an *Chironomus tentans*. Chromosoma 15 (1964) 71.

PHILLIPS, D.M.P.: Studies on the primary structure of some histones. Biochem. J. 101 (1966) 23P.

PLAUT, W. and D. NASH: Localized DNA synthesis in polytene chromosomes and its implication. In: The role of chromosomes in development. New York, Academic Press Inc. (1964) 113.

POLICARD, A. and D. PILLET: Sur la richesse du noyau cellulaire en composés calciques. Compt. Rend. Soc. Biol. 98 (1928) 1350.

PRINTZ, M.P. and P.H. VON HIPPEL: Hydrogen exchange studies of DNA structure. Proc. Natl. Acad. Sci. U.S. 53 (1965) 363.

RAE, P.M.: Whole mount electron microscopy of *Drosophila* salivary chromosomes. Nature 212 (1966) 139.

RIS, H.: Die Feinstruktur des Kerns während der Spermiogenese. Chemie der Genetik. Colloquium der Gesellschaft für physiologische Chemie. Berlin, Springer-Verlag (1959) 1.

RIS, H.: Ultrastructure and molecular organization of genetic systems. Can. J. Genet. Cytol. 3 (1961) 95.

RIS, H.: Interpretation of the ultrastructure in the cell nucleus. In: R.J.C. Harris, ed.: The interpretation of ultrastructure. London, Academic Press Inc. 1 (1962) 69.

RIS, H.: Fine structure of chromosomes. Proc. Roy. Soc. (London), Ser. B 164 (1966) 246.

RIS, H.: Ultrastructure of the animal chromosome. In: V.V. Koningsberger and L. Bosch, eds.: Regulation of nucleic acid and protein biosynthesis. Amsterdam, Elsevier Publishing Co. 10 (1967) 11.

RIS, H. and B. CHANDLER: The ultrastructure of genetic systems in prokaryotes and eukaryotes. Cold Spring Harbor Symp. Quant. Biol. 28 (1963) 1.

SAPP, W.: The effect of enzymes on the fine structure of lampbrush chromosomes. J. Cell Biol. 31 (1966) 159A.

SCHULMAN, H. and D.M. BONNER: A naturally occurring DNA-RNA complex from *Neurospora crassa*. Proc. Natl. Acad. Sci. U.S. 48 (1962) 53.

SCOTT, G.H.: The disposition of the fixed mineral salts during mitosis. Bull. Histol. Appl. 7 (1930) 251.

SHERIDAN, W.F. and H. STERN: Histones of meiosis. Exptl. Cell Res. 45 (1967) 323.

SIEBERT, G. and G.B. HUMPHREY: Enzymology of the nucleus. Advan. Enzymol. 27 (1965) 239.

SINCLAIR, J.H. and B.J. STEVENS: Circular DNA filaments from mouse mitochondria. Proc. Natl. Acad. Sci. U.S. 56 (1966) 508.

SOLARI, A.J.: Electron microscopy of native DNA in sea urchin cells. J. Ultrastruct. Res. 17 (1967) 421.

SOMERS, C.E., A. COLE and T.C. HSU: Isolation of chromosomes. Exptl. Cell Res. Suppl. 9 (1963) 220.

STAHL, F.W.: A chain model for chromosomes. Proc. Soc. de Chim. Phys. 11th Ann. Reunion, Pergamon Press (1962) 194.

STEDMAN, E. and E. STEDMAN: The chemical nature and functions of the components of cell nuclei. Cold Spring Harbor Symp. Quant. Biol. 12 (1947) 224.

STEFFENSEN, D.M.: Chromosome structure with special reference to the role of metal ions. Intern. Rev. Cytol. 12 (1961) 163.

STEVENS, B.J. and H. SWIFT: RNA transport from nucleus to cytoplasm in *Chironomus* salivary glands. J. Cell Biol. 31 (1966) 55.

SWIFT, H,: Studies on nuclear fine structure. Brookhaven Symp. in Biol. 12 (1959) 134.

SWIFT, H.: Nucleic acids and cell morphology in dipteran salivary glands. In: M. Allen, ed.: The molecular control of cellular activity. New York, McGraw-Hill Book Co., Inc. (1962) 73.

SWIFT, H.: Molecular morphology of the chromosome. In: D.J. Dawe, ed.: In vitro, Vol. 1: The chromosome. Publication of the Tissue Culture Assoc., Inc. 1 (1965) 26.

TAYLOR, H.: The duplication of chromosomes. In: P. Sitte, ed.: Probleme der biologischen Reduplikation. Berlin, Springer-Verlag (1966) 9.

TONINO, G.J.M. and TH.H. ROZIJN: Studies on the yeast nucleus: II. The histones of yeast. In: M.G. Ord, L.A. Stoken, H.M. Klouwen and I. Betel, eds.: The cell nucleus. London, Taylor & Francis, Ltd. (1966) 125.

VENDRELY, R., A. KNOBLOCH-MAZEN and C. VENDRELY: A comparative biochemical study of nucleohistones and nucleoprotamines in the cell nucleus. In: The cell nucleus. New York, Academic Press (1960) 200.

WALKER, I.O.: Electrometric and spectrophotometric titration of histone and deoxyribonucleohistone. J. Mol. Biol. 14 (1965) 381.

WANG, T.Y.: The chromatin and nucleolar acidic proteins: isolation, characteristics and roles in nuclear metabolism. In: M.G. Ord, L.A. Stoken, H.M. Klouwen and I. Betel, eds.: The cell nucleus. London, Taylor & Francis, Ltd. (1966) 243.

WETTSTEIN, R. and J.R. SOTELO: Fine structure of meiotic chromosomes. J. Ultrastruct. Res. 13 (1965) 367.

WILKINS, M.H.F.: Physical studies of the molecular structure of deoxyribose nucleic acid and nucleoprotein. Cold Spring Harbor Symp. Quant. Biol. 21 (1956) 75.

WILKINS, M.H.F. and J.T. RANDALL: Crystallinity in sperm heads; molecular structure of nucleoprotein *in vivo*. Biochim. Biophys. Acta 10 (1953) 192.

WILKINS, M.H.F., G. ZUBAY and H.R. WILSON: X-ray diffraction studies of the molecular structure of nucleohistone and chromosomes. J. Mol. Biol. 1 (1959) 179.

WOLFE, J.: Structural aspects of amitosis: a light and electron microscope study of the isolated macronuclei of *Paramecium aurelia* and *Tetrahymena pyriformis*. Chromosoma 23 (1967) 59.

WOLFE, S.L.: The fine structure of isolated chromosomes. J. Ultrastruct. Res. 12 (1965) 104.

WOLFE, S.L.: The fine structure of isolated metaphase chromosomes. Exptl. Cell Res. 37 (1965) 45.

WOLFE, S.L.: The effect of fixation on the diameter of chromosome fibers isolated by the Langmuir trough-critical point method. J. Cell Biol. 35 (1967) 145A.

WOLFE, S.L. and J.N. GRIM: The relationship of isolated chromosome fibers to the fibers of the embedded nucleus. J. Ultrastruct. Res. 19 (1967) 382.

WOLFE, S.L. and G.M. HEWITT: The strandedness of meiotic chromosomes from *Oncopeltus*. J. Cell Biol. 31 (1966) 31.

WOLFE, S.L.and B. JOHN: The organization and ultrastructure of male meiotic chromosomes in *Oncopeltus fasciatus*. Chromosoma 17 (1965) 7.

WOLSTENHOLME, D.R., I.B. DAWID and H.J. RISTOW: An electron microscope study of DNA molecules from *Chironomus*. J. Cell Biol. 35 (1967) 145A.

ZUBAY, G.: Nucleohistone structure and function. In: J. Bonner and P. Ts'o, eds.: The nucleohistones. San Francisco, Holden-Day, Inc. (1964) 95.

ZUBAY, G. and P. DOTY: The isolation and properties of deoxyribonucleoprotein particles containing single nucleic acid molecules. J. Mol. Biol. 1 (1959) 1.

ZUBAY, G. and M. H. F. WILKINS: An X-ray diffraction study of histone and protamine in isolation and combination with DNA. J. Mol. Biol. 4 (1962) 444.

CHAPTER 12

Biochemistry and molecular biophysics of heterochromatin and euchromatin

JOHN H. FRENSTER

Division of Oncology, Department of Medicine,
Stanford University School of Medicine, Stanford, California

Contents

1. Introduction
2. History of heterochromatin and euchromatin
3. Isolation of chromatin fractions
4. The DNA within heterochromatin and euchromatin
5. Ligands and counter-ligands to DNA within chromatin
6. Isolated heterochromatin and euchromatin as assay systems
7. Macromolecular interaction within heterochromatin and euchromatin
8. Cellular transitions between heterochromatin and euchromatin

This research was supported by a Scholar award from the Leukemia Society and by a research grant (CA-10174) from the National Cancer Institute of The U.S. Public Health Service.

1. Introduction

Much of the data of modern molecular biology has been obtained from the study of isolated macromolecules in solution or in the crystalline state. Thus, the detailed analysis of enzymatic mechanisms is largely based on methods for studying the reactions of isolated enzymes in solution. Similarly, the mapping of the secondary and tertiary structure of macromolecules has depended to a large degree either on methods of X-ray diffraction analysis applied to isolated macromolecules in the fibrous or crystalline state, or on methods of optical activity analysis applied to isolated macromolecules in solution. Increasingly, it has become evident that both the conformation and the activity of macromolecules are markedly influenced by associated ligand molecules (Frenster 1966). Such ligand molecules are removed during the isolation of the macromolecule, and the native state of the macromolecule, defined as that possessed while within the intact cell, can be lost by such an isolation procedure. Thus, both the act of isolation and the act of transfer from the intracellular state to the soluble or the crystalline state are capable of producing artefacts in macromolecular structure and function.

The aim of molecular cytology has been to determine macromolecular structure and function as it exists within the living cell. In these studies, it has proved to be not only desirable but necessary to modify and combine the techniques of high-resolution electron microscopy, somatic cell genetics, analytic and preparative biochemistry, and conformational probe molecular biophysics. By such combined studies, cell structure and function are kept equally in focus, and the combined findings from the intact cell can be used as criteria of the native state for isolated subcellular organelles and macromolecules.

2. History of heterochromatin and euchromatin

Recent progress in the study of the cell nucleus has heightened the long interest in heterochromatin and euchromatin, and has illustrated the value of combined studies. Heitz originally described as heterochromatin that portion of the nuclear chromatin which demonstrated its allocycly by maintaining a condensed state throughout interphase while the remainder of the nuclear chromatin was extending to what he termed the euchromatin state. Cooper was able to summarize the data from studies on *Drosophila* which suggested that heterochromatin and euchromatin differed in their physical conformation and in the expression of their genes, but not in their overall DNA content. Since that time, the increasingly detailed studies of the heterochromatic X-chromosome of female mammalian cells (Lima-de-Faria, this volume) have revealed that heterochromatin represents repressed portions of the genome (Grumbach et al.; Frenster et al. 1963), and that heterochromatin offers direct cytologic evidence of the degree of nuclear differentiation (Brown and Nur; Mittwoch), and of the regulation of gene expression in higher organisms (Frenster 1965d, 1966).

3. *Isolation of chromatin fractions*

In molecular cytology, the development of techniques for cell fractionation and subcellular organelle isolation have proven particularly important. Isolation of subcellular organelles has permitted a detailed analysis of organelle function in circumstances greatly simplified and defined compared to those within the intact cell. In addition, isolation of subcellular organelles provides a useful first step in the subsequent isolation and analysis of macromolecules confined to particular organelles.

The ultimate criteria of successful subcellular organelle isolation are that the organelles be obtained in high yield, free of other cellular materials, and in a state in which the structures and functions which the organelle displayed while within the intact cell are retained in the isolated state. These criteria preclude conditions of isolation which are markedly removed from the neutral *p*H and isotonicity of the intact cell, and it was within these constraints that the chromatin fractionation procedure was developed.

The gentle isolation of native heterochromatin and native euchromatin from interphase calf thymus lymphocytes (Frenster et al. 1963) depended upon at least three prior developments in molecular cytology. The first of these was the increasing recognition by electron microscopists that osmium-fixed and methacrylate-embedded cells do not reveal the wealth of nuclear detail that can be observed either by light microscopy or by the use of lead or uranyl acetate staining of epon-embedded cells in electron microscopy (Huxley and Zubay; Bernhard and Granboulan). Use of these improved methods of tissue preparation permitted a definition by electron microscopy (Figs. 1–3) of the ultrastructure of heterochromatin and euchromatin within intact cells (Frenster et al. 1963; Frenster 1965a), and provided a morphologic criterium by which to judge the quality of the isolation (Figs. 4, 5) of the chromatin fractions (Frenster et al. 1963).

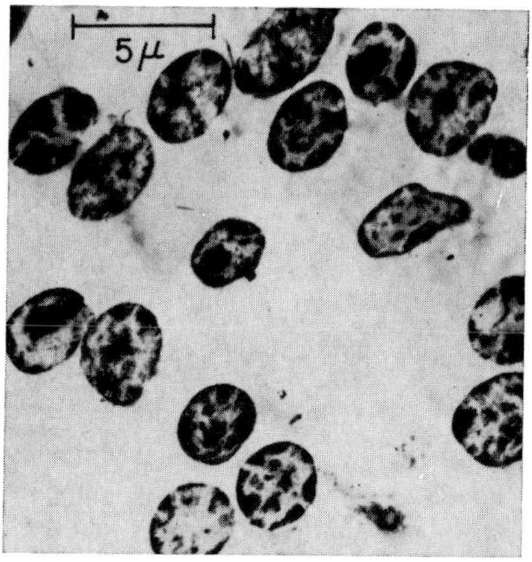

Fig. 1. Isolated nuclei of interphase calf thymus lymphocytes. Details of electron microscopy as previously described (Frenster et al. 1963).

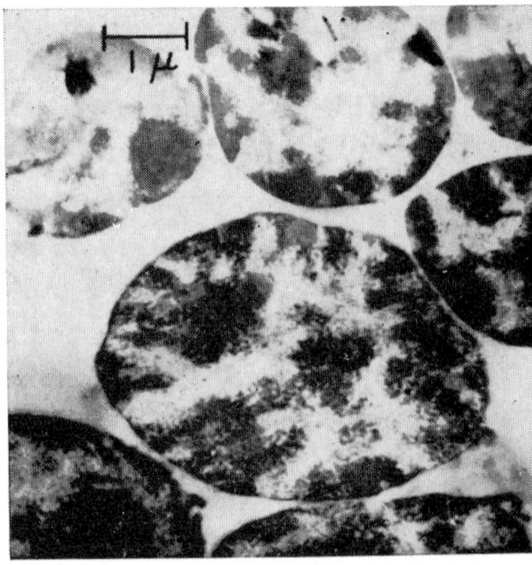

Fig. 2. Higher magnification of Fig. 1, displaying the condensed masses of repressed heterochromatin and the extended microfibrils of active euchromatin (Frenster et al. 1963).

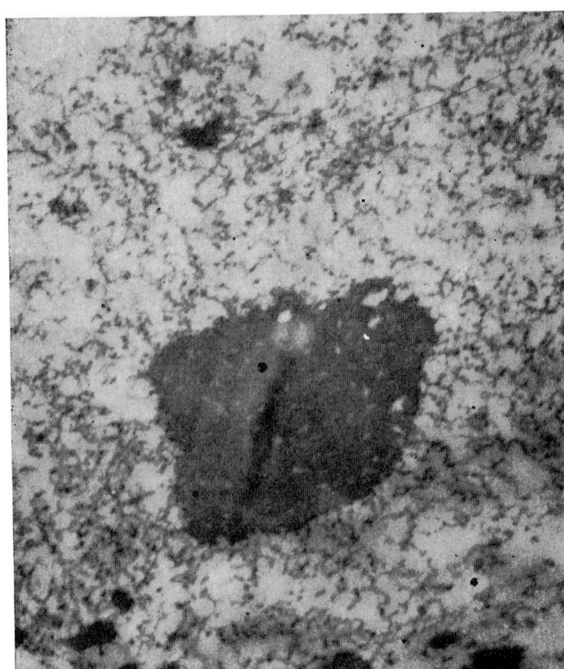

Fig. 3. Detail at higher magnification of the ultrastructural continuity between the extended microfibrils of active euchromatin and the dense reticulum of fibrils within the condensed mass of repressed heterochromatin. The euchromatin microfibrils are of 100 Å diameter, and can be followed for up to 1.0 μ of their length. The sharp zone of transition between euchromatin and heterochromatin is of a fibril length of less than 100 Å. The fibrils within heterochromatin are not resolved. Electron microscopy as previously described (Frenster 1965a). × 30,000.

The second essential development was the increasing indirect data which suggested that much of the DNA of differentiated cells was inactive in RNA synthesis (Allfrey and Mirsky), and that by pre-labelling chromatin *in situ* with radioactive precursors of RNA (Hsu) it might be possible to provide, for attempts at chromatin fractionation, a radioactive marker on those portions of the genome which are active as templates for RNA synthesis *in vivo*.

The third essential development was the recognition that heterochromatin replicated its DNA at a time interval later than that of euchromatin (Lima-de-Faria), and that by pre-labelling chromatin *in situ* with radioactive precursors of DNA (Hay and Revel) it might be possible to provide, for attempts at chromatin fractionation, an additional radioactive marker to distinguish the heterochromatin and euchromatin portions of the genome.

These three developments were then utilized to follow the fate of heterochromatin and euchromatin through the fractionation procedure and to judge the quality of the isolated fractions (Frenster et al. 1963). The yield of the chromatin fractionation was over 80 percent of the starting material, and judging by detailed electron microscopy at each step during fractionation, the chromatin fractions obtained were free of contamination by other cell organelles (Figs. 4, 5). The morphology of heterochromatin and euchromatin as seen within intact cells before fractionation (Huxley and Zubay; Frenster et al. 1963), was preserved within the isolated chromatin fractions, as were the RNA and DNA radioactive labels applied before fractionation. The heterochromatin fraction was contaminated to a minor degree by euchromatin, on both morphologic and radioactive marker evidence, but the euchromatin fraction was free of heterochromatin contamination (Frenster et al. 1963). Interestingly enough, the isotonic and neutral pH conditions of the fractionation procedure proved gentle

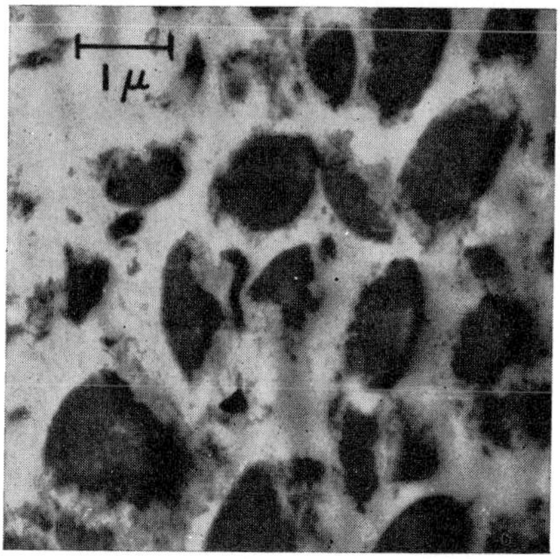

Fig. 4. Fraction of condensed heterochromatin masses isolated from the nuclei of interphase calf thymus lymphocytes (see Figs. 1–3). The ultrastructure of the heterochromatin masses is preserved. A minor degree of contamination by adherent euchromatin microfibrils is evident on some of the masses. Electron microscopy as previously described (Frenster et al. 1963).

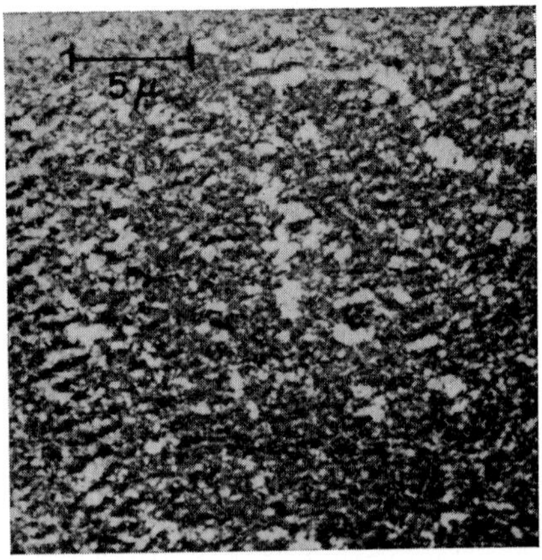

Fig. 5. Fraction of extended euchromatin microfibrils isolated from the same nuclei as in Figs. 1-4. The ultrastructure of the euchromatin microfibrils is preserved. The fraction is free of any contamination by heterochromatin masses. Electron microscopy as previously described (Frenster et al. 1963).

enough so that the chromatin fractions retained the same differential biosynthetic activity as templates for RNA synthesis after isolation which they had displayed before fractionation while still within the intact cell or nucleus (Frenster 1965b).

Thus, on either morphologic, biochemical, or biosynthetic criteria, the isolated heterochromatin and euchromatin fractions preserve the native state of heterochromatin and euchromatin as found within intact cells or nuclei before fractionation (Frenster 1965d, 1966).

4. The DNA within heterochromatin and euchromatin

This isolation of native complexes of heterochromatin and euchromatin prepared in parallel from single tissue samples permitted a direct test of several hypotheses regarding DNA structure and function. These hypotheses included: (1) the possibility that much of the DNA of differentiated cells is inactive in gene transcription; (2) the possibility that the activity of a DNA template during gene transcription closely influences the activity of that same template during gene replication later in the cell cycle; and (3) the possibility that the secondary and tertiary physical conformations of DNA may vary during gene transcription.

In regard to the first hypothesis, Feulgen staining combined with electron microscopy (Huxley and Zubay) had demonstrated that much of the DNA of thymus lymphocytes is contained within condensed heterochromatin complexes. DNase digestion experiments had indirectly suggested that as much as 80 percent of the nuclear DNA is inactive in RNA synthesis (Allfrey and Mirsky). A comparison of the DNA contents of native heterochromatin and euchromatin fractions prepared in parallel from single tissue samples gave the first direct quantitative data (Frenster et al. 1963) confirming these impressions. Up to 80 percent of the recovered nuclear DNA is found within the repressed heterochromatin fraction (Table 1).

TABLE 1

Comparative DNA content and pre-isolation template activity of chromatin fractions (from Frenster et al. 1963)

	DNA content (%)	Thymidine-2-C^{14} incorp. into DNA (%)	Orotic acid-6-C^{14} incorp. into RNA (%)	Specific template activity For DNA synth. (%)	For RNA synth. (%)
Total chromatin	100	100	100	100	100
Heterochromatin	74	19	21	26	28
Intermediate	13	29	18	223	138
Euchromatin	13	52	61	400	470

When the intact interphase lymphocyte nuclei are first pre-incubated with a radioactive precursor of either RNA or early DNA synthesis before chromatin fractionation, it was found (Frenster et al. 1963) that most of the newly synthesized RNA or early DNA is localized within the euchromatin fraction (Table 1). Such localization of early DNA synthesis to euchromatin had been shown previously by electron-microscopic radioautography (Hay and Revel). After the data regarding localization of RNA synthesis to euchromatin had been obtained first by light-microscopic radioautography (Hsu), and then quantitated by chromatin fractionation (Frenster et al. 1963), it was subsequently confirmed (Littau et al. 1964) by electron-microscopic radioautography (Figs. 6, 7).

In regard to the second hypothesis, when a quantitative comparison was made between the *in situ* DNA template specific activities of chromatin which had been prelabeled for early DNA synthesis or for RNA synthesis before chromatin fractionation (Table 1), it was seen that both RNA synthesis and early DNA synthesis is over 15 times as active within euchromatin as within heterochromatin (Frenster et al. 1963). This was the earliest direct data demonstrating a close quantitative correlation within particular portions of the genome between template activity for RNA synthesis in interphase and template activity for DNA synthesis early in the S phase. Since these nuclei are labelled in mid-interphase, DNA synthesis occurring late in the S phase appears as inactivity in these nuclei. This close correlation between sites of RNA synthesis and of early DNA synthesis has been confirmed by chromosome breakage experiments (Klevecz and Hsu), and by cell viability experiments (Mueller and Kajiwara). Such uniform template specific activities suggest a common template control mechanism affecting both RNA synthesis and early DNA synthesis equally (Frenster 1966).

In regard to the third hypothesis, analysis of the DNA isolated from heterochromatin

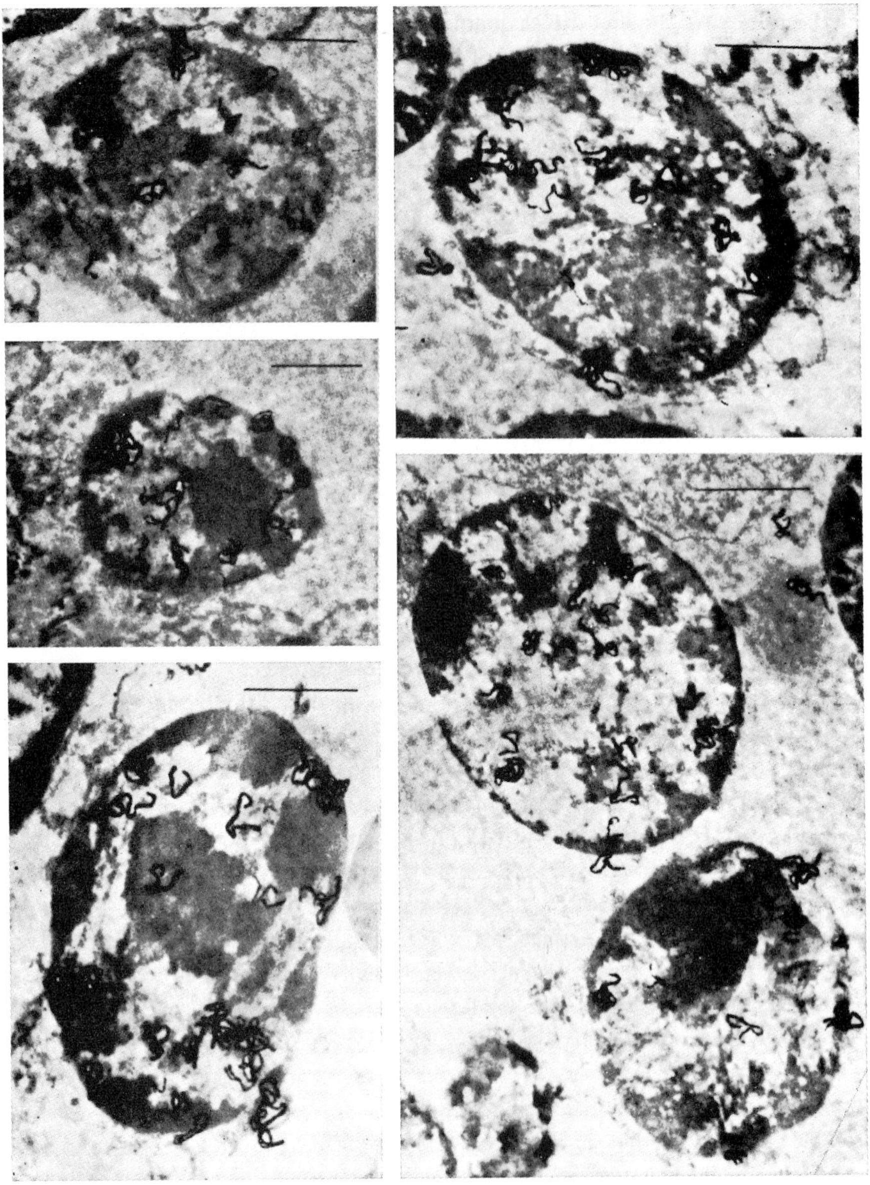

Fig. 6. Electron-microscopic radioautography of RNA synthesis within isolated nuclei of interphase calf thymus lymphocytes, following their incubation with tritiated uridine. Silver tracks overlying sites of newly synthesized RNA are seen to correspond to the extended microfibrils of the euchromatin complexes. The condensed masses of the heterochromatin complexes are strikingly free of new RNA synthesis. Experimental details as previously described (Littau et al. 1964). Magnification marker represents 1.0 μ.

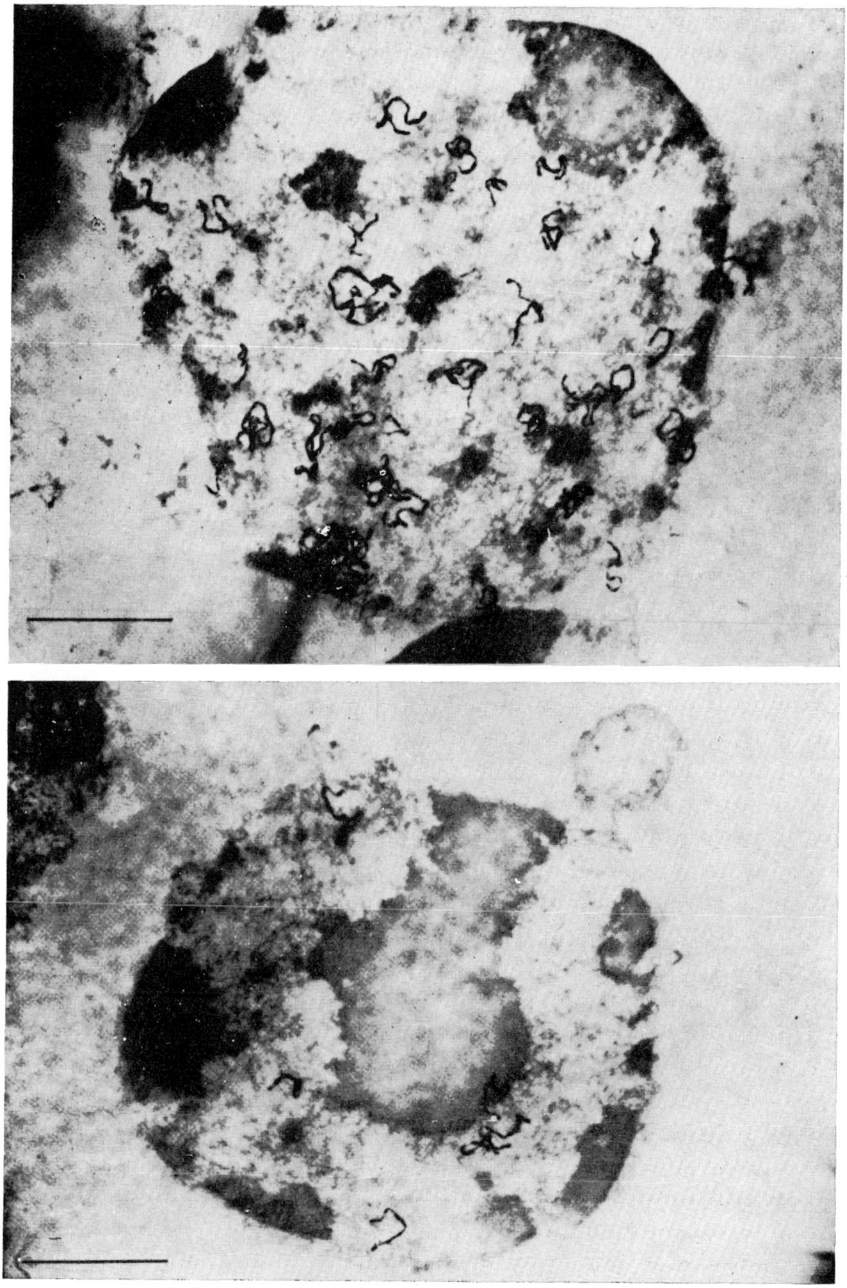

Fig. 7. Electron-microscopic radioautography as in Fig. 6. The nuclei have been allowed to swell in isotonic sucrose to reveal their structural details. Experimental details as previously described (Littau et al. 1964).

or euchromatin complexes (Frenster 1965b, d) revealed no gross differences between the isolated DNAs in overall base composition (Table 2), in thermal denaturation (Fig. 8), or in reactivity with anti-DNA antibodies (Table 3). By contrast, when the DNA was examined while still within the native heterochromatin or euchromatin complexes (Frenster 1965b, d, e), it was found that the DNA within heterochromatin is more stabilized against thermal denaturation (Fig. 8) and against reactivity with anti-DNA antibodies (Table 3) than is the DNA within euchromatin. A similarly reduced stabilization of DNA against thermal denaturation has recently been demonstrated in the active extended Balbiani rings of *Chironomus* as compared to the inactive condensed band regions (MacInnes and Uretz).

In addition, the DNA within euchromatin displays a deficiency of its expected thermal hyperchromicity (Fig. 8) which it regains when the DNA is isolated from the euchromatin complex, suggesting that up to 60 percent of the DNA within native euchromatin complexes is in a partially looped or locally strand-separated state (Frenster 1965c-e), which reverts to the usual double helical state upon isolation of the DNA from the euchromatin complex. Such reversion to the helical state would be expected to occur if some residual portion of each DNA molecule always remained in perfect double helical register while within the euchromatin complex (ibid.). A constant opening and closing ('breathing') of localized portions of the DNA helix has been demonstrated

TABLE 2

Base composition of DNA isolated from chromatin fractions (from Frenster 1965d)

	Moles/100 moles of total bases present as			
	Adenine	Thymine	Guanine	Cytosine
Heterochromatin	27.9	27.7	22.85	21.55
Euchromatin	29.2	27.8	22.15	20.85

TABLE 3

Reactivity with anti-DNA antibodies of DNA before and after isolation from chromatin fractions (from Frenster 1965b)

	Euchromatin	Heterochromatin
Isolated DNA (free of proteins and RNA)	reactive	reactive
Isolated histones	non-reactive	non-reactive
Isolated DNA + isolated histones	non-reactive	non-reactive
DNA within native chromatin complex	reactive	non-reactive

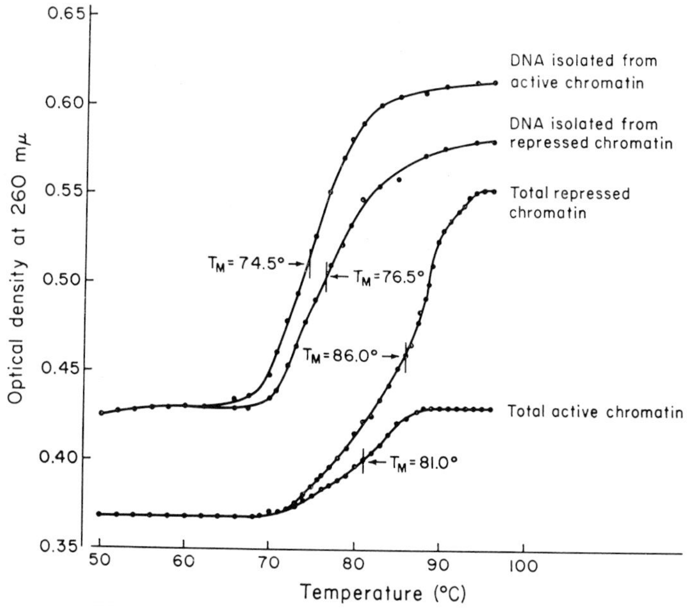

Fig. 8. Thermal hyperchromicity of DNA within native chromatin complexes, and after its isolation from such complexes. The DNA within active euchromatin complexes is less well stabilized by its histones against strand separation than is the DNA within repressed heterochromatin complexes. The DNA within euchromatin also displays a 60 percent reduction of its expected hyperchromicity, which is regained upon isolation of the DNA. Buffer system: 0.015 M NaCl – 0.0015 M Na_3 citrate as described (Frenster 1965b).

within DNA molecules in solution (Printz and Von Hippel), and more recently a localized separation of the DNA strands during *in vivo* RNA synthesis has also been demonstrated in bacteria (Hayashi and Hayashi).

In addition to these changes in the secondary structure of DNA, changes in the tertiary structure of DNA are apparent during RNA synthesis (Frenster 1965a). DNA molecules within native euchromatin are found as extended microfibrils of 100 Å diameter (Fig. 3), while DNA molecules within native heterochromatin are found in a highly condensed state. It is known that for isolated DNA in solution, the extended configuration is induced by a mutual repulsion among the repeating negative changes of the phosphate groups on the exterior of the DNA helix (Kawade; Schildkraut and Lifson). When these negative charges are neutralized, the mutual repulsion is reduced, and the extended DNA helix can collapse to a condensed configuration (ibid.).

Thus, the DNA molecules within native euchromatin complexes differ from the DNA molecules within native heterochromatin complexes both in their secondary and tertiary physical conformations and in the magnitude of their specific activity as templates for RNA synthesis or early DNA synthesis. After isolation from the chromatin complexes, these differences are lost (Fig. 8, Table 3). It thus seemed possible that the observed differences in these DNA properties were not intrinsic to the DNA molecules themselves but rather were stabilized by those macromolecules which are associated with DNA while within the heterochromatin or euchromatin complexes.

5. *Ligands and counter-ligands to DNA within chromatin*

In the native state within higher organisms, DNA is usually found in close physical association with a variety of ligand macromolecules, the chief of which are the polycationic proteins known as histones (Phillips). Histone ligands have been shown to repress the template activity of DNA in a variety of cell-free systems (Frenster et al. 1961; Huang and Bonner 1962), and to inhibit both DNA strand separations (Huang and Bonner 1962; Allfrey et al.) and DNA reactivity with anti-DNA antibodies (Kunkel and Tan). Within isolated native heterochromatin and euchromatin complexes, DNA molecules were found to differ in these very parameters of template activity, thermal denaturation and reactivity with anti-DNA antibodies (Frenster 1965b). It was therefore quite natural to use the availability of such native chromatin complexes to test the hypothesis that modifications or deficiencies of histone repressor ligands accounted for the differences in DNA conformation and template activity observed within active euchromatin as compared to repressed heterochromatin.

When the total histones are extracted from native heterochromatin and euchromatin complexes which have been prepared in parallel from a single tissue sample, it can be seen (Table 4) that the histone–DNA ratios are not significantly different within the two types of chromatin (Frenster 1965b). Furthermore, when the total histones are fractionated by differential extraction or by cellulose polyacetate electrophoresis (Fig. 9), the proportions among the various subcategories of histones are seen to be the same within either repressed heterochromatin or active euchromatin (Frenster 1965b, d).

TABLE 4

Relation of nuclear ligands and counter-ligands to DNA within isolated chromatin fractions (from Frenster 1965b)

	No. of animals	Euchromatin (mg/100 mg DNA)	Heterochromatin (mg/100 mg DNA)	Euchromatin/ heterochromatin
Total histones	10	90.7 ± 7.7	101.1 ± 9.1	0.90 ± 0.07
Non-histone residual proteins	4	109.0 ± 6.1	54.9 ± 5.7	2.00 ± 0.08
Total phospholipids	5	17.0 ± 3.6	3.7 ± 1.3	4.93 ± 1.26
Total RNA	8	9.0 ± 4.7	1.8 ± 0.7	5.15 ± 2.86
Histone N-acetyl	4	0.385 ± 0.035	0.235 ± 0.035	1.64 ± 0.09
Phosphoprotein phosphorous	4	0.418 ± 0.028	0.117 ± 0.019	3.74 ± 0.56

Mean ± S.E.

Finally, when the degree of native N-terminal acetylation of histones is determined (Table 4), again no significant differences are found between heterochromatin and euchromatin. This uniformity of histone quantities and types within both active euchromatin and repressed heterochromatin is consistent with a similar histone uniformity within animal cells of widely varying tissue of origin (Phillips 1962), age and rate of RNA synthesis (Dingman and Sporn) or neoplastic character (Laurence et al.; Busch and Steele). Such histone uniformity has recently been confirmed for the active puffs and the inactive bands of *Drosophila* chromosomes as well (Gorovsky and Woodard).

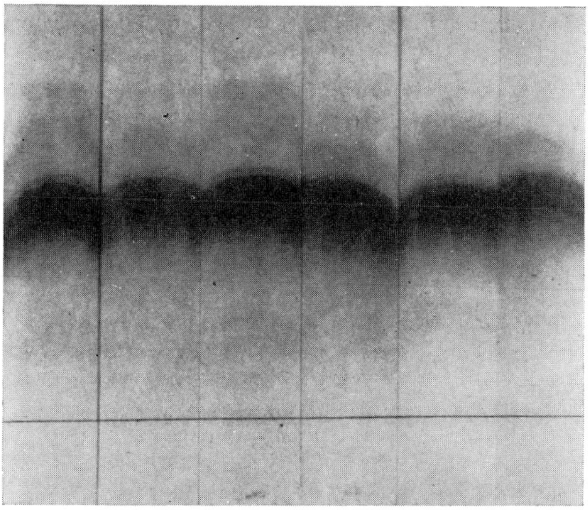

Fig. 9. Electrophoresis of the total histones extracts from repressed heterochromatin (strips 1, 3, and 5 from left) and from active euchromatin (strips 2, 4, and 6 from left) prepared in parallel from single tissue samples. The relative proportion of lysine-rich, moderately lysine-rich and arginine-rich histones are similar in the extracts from either heterochromatin or euchromatin. Similar results are obtained by chemical fractionation of the total histones. Methods as described previously (Frenster 1965d).

Because of the demonstrated uniformity of histone quantities and types within native heterochromatin and euchromatin, histone repressors were judged (Frenster 1965c, d) to be a necessary but not sufficient mechanism to account for those differences in DNA template activity (Table 1), DNA melting temperature (Fig. 8), and DNA reactivity with anti-DNA antibodies (Table 3) which has previously been observed between native heterochromatin and euchromatin complexes (Frenster 1965b). Upon further analysis, it became apparent that other macromolecules of the chromatin complex, functioning as counter-ligand de-repressors, were more influential in determining such differential DNA activity.

In contrast to the uniformity of histones, nuclear polyanions, such as non-histone residual proteins, RNA, phosphoproteins, and phospholipids were found (Table 4) to be present in significant excess within active euchromatin as compared to repressed heterochromatin (Frenster 1965b).

An excess of non-histone residual proteins had been demonstrated previously within the chromatin of active tissues as compared to inactive tissues (Mirsky and Ris; Alfert; Steele and Busch; Dingman and Sporn). Up to 30 percent of the non-histone residual proteins have been shown to consist of phosphoproteins (Johnson and Albert; Sperti et al.; Langan and Lipmann 1968). Such phosphoproteins were found in excess (Table 4) within active euchromatin (Frenster 1965b), and were later shown to exchange their phosphate groups at a rapid rate (Kleinsmith et al.). Phosphoproteins function as counter-ligands by forming polyanion–polycation complexes with repressor histones, which are thereby reduced in effectiveness as ligands to DNA (Frenster 1965b-d; Langan and Smith).

Similar polyanion–polycation complexes are formed within active euchromatin between certain species of nuclear RNA and repressor histones (Frenster 1965b-d), and a type of RNA–histone complex has recently been isolated from nuclei (Huang and Bonner 1965; Benjamin et al.). Phospholipids also present in excess within active euchromatin (Rose and Frenster; Frenster 1965b), have been thought to form lipoprotein complexes with certain of the non-histone residual proteins (Wang et al. 1953). Non-histone residual proteins are also thought to offer binding sites for estrogens (Noteboom and Gorski), for testosterone (Loeb and Wilson), and for aldosterone (Fanestil and Edelman), all of which are concentrated within the cell nucleus during their stimulation of RNA synthesis.

The presence of such nuclear polyanions in significant excess within native euchromatin complexes suggested that they function as antagonists, to the DNA–histone interaction (Frenster 1965b), that is, as counter-ligands to the ligand properties of repressor histones. One consequence of such counter-ligand activities by nuclear polyanions would be to de-repress DNA molecules for template activity in RNA synthesis by reducing the intensity of interaction between DNA templates and histone repressors (Frenster 1965b).

6. *Isolated heterochromatin and euchromatin as assay systems*

In order to test the hypothesis that nuclear polyanions do function as de-repressors of RNA synthesis *in vivo* it was necessary to develop an *in vitro* test system for the assay of molecular de-repressor activity. Ideally, it seemed desirable that such a system should distinguish between those macromolecules which affect only previously repressed DNA templates and those macromolecules which affect all DNA templates indiscriminately. In addition, it seemed desirable that the test system should be capable of assaying for repressor activity as well as for de-repressor activity. Finally, because of the problem of poor penetration of large macromolecules into intact cells, it seemed necessary that the test system should be a cell-free or a sub-cellular system which would be accessible to macromolecules of diverse size, charge, and configuration.

The isolated native fractions of heterochromatin and euchromatin which were prepared in parallel from a single tissue sample seemed to provide the basis for such an assay system with each of these desired characteristics. It was soon demonstrated (Fig. 10) that native euchromatin remained 3 to 8 times as active in RNA synthesis after its isolation, compared to native heterochromatin isolated in parallel from the same tissue sample (Frenster 1965b). Such RNA synthesis within isolated euchromatin requires the addition of all four ribonucleotide triphosphates but utilizes the endogeneous RNA polymerase contained in native configuration within the chromatin complex, thus avoiding artifacts that might arise upon addition of exogenous RNA polymerase. Experiments utilizing either trypsin pre-digestion or the addition of polyethylene sulfonate revealed that both isolated euchromatin and heterochromatin could increase the rates of RNA synthesis to a level 3 to 4 times the basal control level within untreated euchromatin, indicating that endogeneous RNA polymerase is not rate-limiting in the basal control state (Frenster 1965b). Such RNA synthesis is sensitive to a variety of metabolic inhibitors and enzyme pre-treatments (Table 5), and over

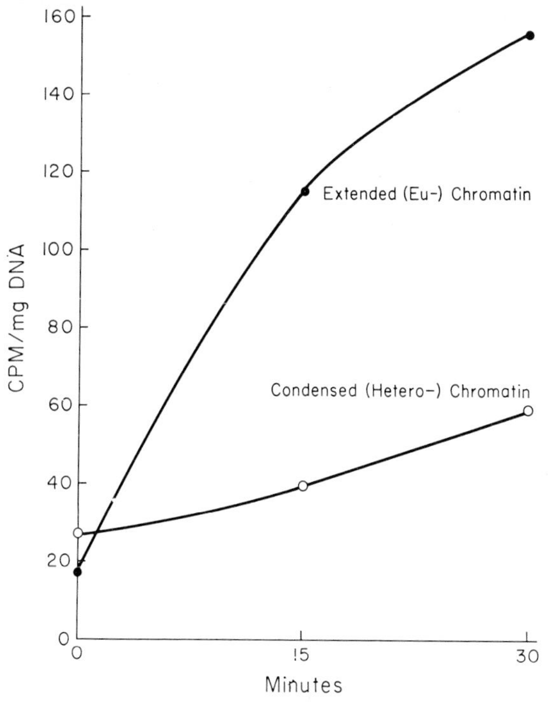

Fig. 10. Incorporation of ATP-8-C^{14} into RNA following the isolation in parallel of the chromatin fractions from a single tissue sample. The isolated chromatin fractions retain the repressed and active states which they displayed before fractionation within the intact nucleus. Materials and methods as described previously (Frenster 1965b).

70% of the newly synthesized RNA can be removed by subsequent RNAse digestion (Frenster 1965b).

When those nuclear polyanions which are found in excess within isolated native euchromatin are added to isolated native heterochromatin (Table 6), they are each found to possess varying degrees of de-repressor activity without having any such effect on already active euchromatin (Frenster 1965b). This suggests that potential binding sites for such de-repressor molecules are already saturated within the active euchromatin complex, but are available within repressed heterochromatin for reaction with de-repressor molecules.

Especially interesting in this regard is the de-repressor activity of nuclear RNA, which is capable of raising the rate of RNA synthesis within repressed heterochromatin to a

TABLE 5

Sensitivity of RNA synthesis within isolated chromatin fractions (from Frenster 1965b)

	Euchromatin (counts/min/mg DNA)	Heterochromatin (counts/min/mg DNA)
Control	51.7 ± 1.1	29.1 ± 1.7
Deoxyribonuclease	25.6 ± 0.2	14.3 ± 0.7
Ribonuclease	38.5 ± 2.1	19.1 ± 0.6
Actinomycin	30.1 ± 0.1	15.4 ± 0.3
Puromycin	65.2 ± 3.1	28.3 ± 0.4
Trypsin	163.0 ± 16.8	104.6 ± 3.5
Acridine orange	43.9 ± 4.9	8.5 ± 1.2

Mean ± S.E.

TABLE 6

Effect of nuclear ligands and counter-ligands on RNA synthesis within isolated chromatin fractions (from Frenster 1965b)

	Euchromatin (counts/min/mg DNA)	Heterochromatin (counts/min/mg DNA)
Control	222.2 ± 13.8	76.2 ± 4.4
Total nuclear RNA	249.5 ± 8.5	185.2 ± 11.8
Soluble nuclear proteins	262.0 ± 1.0	121.7 ± 7.2
Non-histone residual proteins	286.0 ± 1.0	118.4 ± 0.3
Phosphatidyl choline micelles	265.6 ± 9.5	93.6 ± 0.4
Total histones	97.6 ± 4.8	59.9 ± 4.8

Mean ± S.E.

level which is almost as high as the basal control level within the active euchromatin prepared from the same tissue sample, without having any significant effect on the rate within such euchromatin (Table 6). Such a specific de-repressor effect of nuclear RNA on repressed heterochromatin is in marked contrast to the non-specific de-repressor activity of the synthetic polyanion–polyethylene sulfonate which increases the rate of RNA synthesis within both active euchromatin and repressed heterochromatin (Frenster 1965b) despite being a known inhibitor of RNA polymerase (Chambon et al.). In a similar fashion, histones and other polycations are found to be non-specific inhibitors of RNA synthesis within both isolated euchromatin and isolated heterochromatin (Table 6).

When the nuclear RNA of interphase lymphocytes is fractionated and assayed for de-repressor activity (Fig. 11), it can be seen that nuclear S-RNA is only a fair de-repressor while nuclear ribosomal RNA is a poor de-repressor. If it is remembered that nuclear ribosomal RNA constitutes the largest fraction of total nuclear RNA (Sibatani et al.), it can then be inferred that the high de-repressor activity of total RNA (Fig. 11)

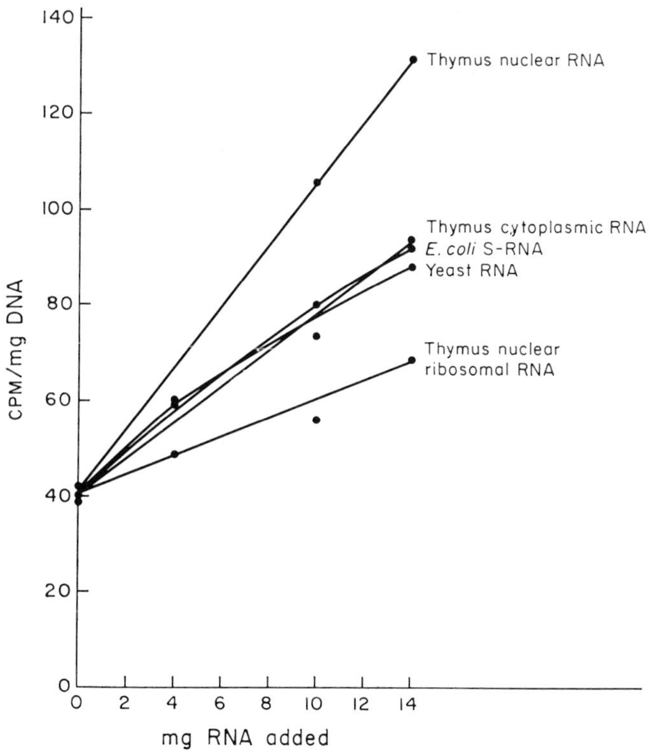

Fig. 11. Assay of de-repressor activity within nuclear RNA species, tested for their effect on incorporation of UTP-2-C^{14} into RNA of isolated repressed heterochromatin. Materials and methods as described previously (Frenster 1965b). A species of de-repressor RNA within the total nuclear RNA fraction accounts for the high de-repressor activity of the total nuclear RNA fraction.

must be due to other nuclear RNA species. Further, since all RNA species have the same polyanionic character (Magasanik), the potency of such nuclear de-repressor RNA species must be due to some property other than their polyanionic character, such as their specific base sequences and/or their molecular conformation (Frenster 1965b, c). New nuclear RNA species distinct from messenger RNA, ribosomal RNA, or S-RNA, have recently been detected within mammalian cell nuclei (Warner et al.; Soeiro et al. Attardi et al.; Houssais and Attardi; Scherrer et al.). Some of these RNA species are apparently in complex formation with histone repressor molecules (Huang and Bonner 1965; Benjamin et al.), and some of these RNA species apparently never leave the cell nucleus (Shearer and McCarthy). The isolation in preparative amounts of nuclear de-repressor RNA will permit a further definition of these interesting actions on isolated heterochromatin complexes.

7. *Macromolecular interaction within heterochromatin and euchromatin*

These diverse data concerning the composition and conformation of DNA templates within native repressed heterochromatin and active euchromatin complexes, concerning the quantitative analysis of the various types of histone repressors and nuclear polyanion de-repressors within each type of chromatin, and concerning the effects of nuclear RNA de-repressor molecules on previously repressed heterochromatin, permitted the construction of a model of selective gene transcription in mammalian cells (Fig. 12), which integrated these diverse data, and which predicted new data which have subsequently been confirmed.

The model has four basic elements which have emerged from the experimental data (Frenster 1965c, d). The first element is that nuclear polyanions can form electrostatic complexes with polycationic histone repressor molecules. As a result of such histone–polyanion complex formation, the histones are partially displaced from their electrostatic bonds with the phosphate groups of DNA template molecules, although the histone–polyanion complexes are losely retained within the chromatin complex so that the overall content of histone within the complex is not altered. Each of the nuclear polyanions so far detected in excess within native euchromatin complexes (RNA, phosphoprotein, phospholipid, non-histone residual proteins) has been found to be capable of effecting such histone displacement by complex formation (Frenster 1965b). The nuclear proteins which can be extracted by neutral buffers (Frenster et al. 1960) have also been found to contain polyanions (Patel and Wang) and are also active in the de-repression of isolated heterochromatin (Frenster 1965b). The direct evidence for such histone displacement within euchromatin is found in the thermal hyperchromicity and anti-DNA–antibody reactivity studies (Frenster 1965b) described earlier.

The second element of the model is that the DNA templates which formerly underlay such displaced histone repressors now become subject to intermittent localized strand

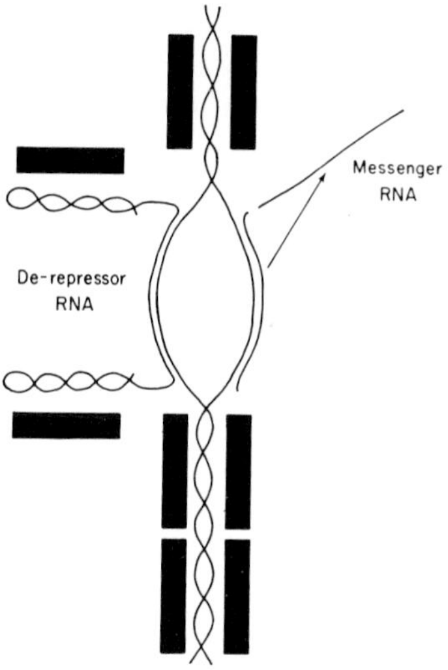

Fig. 12. Strand separation model of selective gene transcription. Polycationic histone repressors interact electrostatically with the negative phosphate groups on the exterior of the DNA helix, stabilizing the helix against strand separation and consequent transcription. Nuclear polyanions form complexes with such histones nonselectively, partially displacing these histones from the underlying DNA helix, permitting accelerated acetylation of the N-terminal groups of the displaced histones, and allowing separation of the strands of the DNA helix in a random fashion. De-repressor RNA species, specific for particular gene loci, hybridize with the anti-coding strand of DNA within such loci, and stabilize the strand separation loop in the open position. The remaining (coding) DNA strand within the stabilized separation loop is then free to serve as a template for gene-specific and strand-specific asymmetric transcription (Frenster 1965c, 1966).

separations of the type described earlier for DNA molecules in solution (Printz and Von Hippel). The forces for such spontaneous localized strand separations apparently lie in the mutual repulsions between adjacent phosphate groups along the exterior of the DNA helix. Prior to histone displacement these phosphate groups had been neutralized in electrostatic bonds with the polycationic histone molecules. The direct evidence for such localized DNA strand separations within euchromatin is found in the thermal hyperchromicity studies (Frenster 1965c–e) described earlier.

The third element of the model is that nuclear RNA de-repressor molecules are capable of DNA–RNA hybrid formation with one strand of DNA within such localized strand separation loops. The formation of such DNA–RNA hybrids is dependent upon complementary base sequences in the DNA and RNA strands, and has the effect of stabilizing the strand separation loop in the open position. The direct evidence for such nuclear RNA de-repressor activity is found in the de-repressor assays (Frenster 1965b) described earlier. By such hybrid formation, particular de-repressor RNA molecules can select both a gene locus and a particular DNA strand for stabilization and thus account for the gene-specific and strand-specific features of selective gene transcription in higher organisms (Frenster 1966).

The fourth element of the model is that the remaining free strand of each DNA strand separation loop is now available to serve as a direct template for messenger RNA synthesis. Increasing data from both micro-organisms and higher organisms suggest that messenger RNA synthesis utilizes only one DNA strand as a template at each gene locus (Frenster 1966). Direct data for such asymmetric transcription at each locus in a higher organism has recently been obtained in rat liver (Marashuge and Bonner) and earlier, by indirect evidence obtained by competitive hybridization studies (McCarthy and Hoyer).

In addition to integrating the existing data regarding molecular interactions within active euchromatin during selective gene transcription, the strand separation model predicted two major types of data which are subsequently being confirmed to an increasing degree.

The first of these predictions concerns ligand molecules which bind to DNA and counter-ligand molecules antagonizing the binding of ligands to DNA. The model predicted that any molecule which bound preferentially to single-stranded DNA would be found to increase the rate of RNA synthesis on such DNA templates during binding (Frenster 1965d–f). Conversely, it predicted that any molecule which bound preferentially to double-stranded DNA would be found to decrease the rate of RNA synthesis on such DNA template molecules during binding (Frenster 1965d-f). An analysis (Frenster 1965f) revealed that direct ligands to DNA were capable of shifting the equilibrium between inactive double-stranded DNA helices and active single-stranded DNA loops by virtue of such preferential binding (Table 7). An extension of this analysis reveals (Fig. 13) that counter-ligands are able to reverse the effects of particular direct ligands

TABLE 7

Correlation of the preferred form of DNA for binding with the effect on RNA synthesis (from Frenster 1965f, 1966)

Ligand	Preferred form of DNA for binding	Effect of ligand on RNA synthesis
Histones	double-stranded	inhibition
Polylysine	double-stranded	inhibition
Actinomycin D	double-stranded	inhibition
Acridine orange	double-stranded	inhibition
Chloroquine	double-stranded	inhibition
Testosterone	single-stranded	stimulation
Estradiol	single-stranded	stimulation
Methylcholanthrene	single-stranded	stimulation
RNA polymerase	single-stranded	stimulation
De-repressor RNA	single-stranded	stimulation
Polyoma viral DNA	single-stranded (of host)	stimulation (of host)

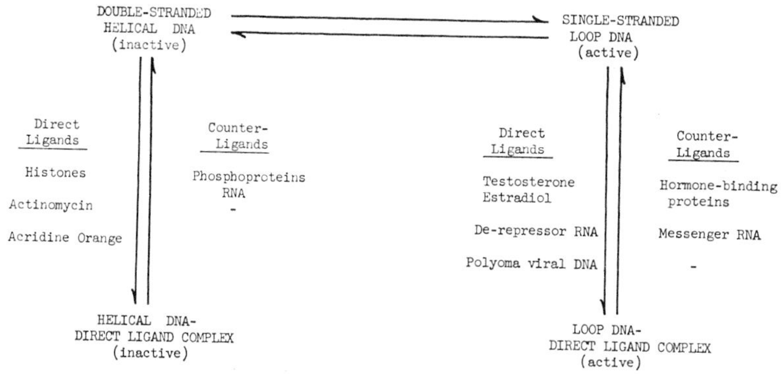

Fig. 13. Stabilization of DNA transcription states by control ligands. Direct ligands can shift the equilibrium between inactive double-stranded helical DNA and active single-stranded loop DNA by means of preferential binding to one of these two conformations of DNA (Frenster 1965f). Counter-ligands can reverse the effects of these direct ligands by competitively forming complexes with the direct ligands. Where no natural counter-ligand exists for a particular direct ligand (actinomycin, methylcholanthrene, polyoma viral DNA) the effects of the direct ligand may be less reversible (Frenster 1966).

by competitively forming complexes with the direct ligands. Where direct ligands do not have natural counter-ligands (actinomycin, methyl-cholanthrene, polyoma viral DNA) the action of the direct ligand may be less reversible.

The second major prediction of the model concerned the natural occurrence of double-stranded RNA–RNA complexes between messenger RNA and de-repressor RNA molecules specific for a given gene locus. This prediction resulted from the recognition that messenger RNA and de-repressor RNA at a given locus are each complementary to one of the two DNA strands at that locus and are thus complementary to each other (Frenster 1965d, 1966). Increasing evidence suggests that certain mammalian nuclear RNA molecules are indeed double-stranded. This evidence includes 10–90 S-RNA molecules in the nucleus, whose base compositions are nearer to that of DNA than are those of messenger RNA (Houssais and Attardi), and from the data indicating that certain nuclear RNA species may compete in DNA hybridization studies by direct RNA–RNA interactions (Birnboim et al.). The significance of such potential RNA–RNA complexes between messenger RNA and de-repressor RNA in a single gene locus is that they offer a molecular mechanism (Frenster 1966) for the interesting gene dosage compensation phenomena based on the heterochromatization of excess X-chromosomes observed in female mammalian cells by Grumbach et al. These authors postulated the presence of an activating episome molecule specific for each gene. They further postulated the inactivation of such an activating episome by an excess of messenger RNA specific for the same gene. Nuclear de-repressor RNA molecules are now thought to function in the role of such activating episomes (Frenster 1965g). The intersecting cycles of molecular associations pictured in Fig. 14 integrate the data of Grumbach et al. with this experimental data, and are now being subjected to further detailed analysis.

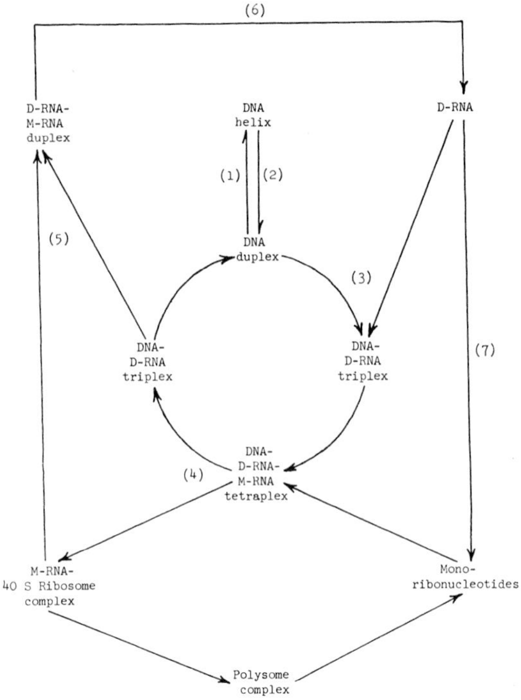

Fig. 14. Nucleic acid interactions during gene dosage compensation in mammals. M-RNA, messenger RNA; D-RNA, de-repressor RNA. (1) Template repression by stabilization of the DNA helix against strand separation. (2) Template labilization by random formation of strand-separation DNA loops. (3) Template selection by triplex formation between labilized DNA templates and de-repressor RNA molecules, specific for the particular gene locus. (4) Template transcription by RNA synthesis on the free copying DNA strand of the selected triplex. (5) Selector inactivation by removal of de-repressor RNA from DNA following the formation of competitively more stable RNA–RNA complexes between M-RNA and D-RNA, each specific for a particular gene locus. (6) Selector liberation by removal of messenger RNA from such RNA–RNA complexes. (7) Selector degradation by hydrolysis of de-repressor RNA molecules (Frenster 1966).

8. *Cellular transitions between heterochromatin and euchromatin*

A variety of cell systems in higher organisms undergo changes which are accompanied by transitions between heterochromatin and euchromatin. These systems include the study of blastogenesis following phytohemagglutinin or antigen stimulation of lymphocytes (Robbins; B. Pogo et al.), the study of regeneration following subtotal hepatic resection (A. O. Pogo et al.), the study of differentiation and senescence during erythropoiesis and granulopoiesis (Anderson), and the study of gene dosage compensation in cells which are polysomic for a particular chromosome (Zakharov et al.).

Each of these systems provides a means whereby further data can be obtained regarding the biochemistry and molecular biophysics of heterochromatin and euchromatin. The methods of chromatin fractionation, high resolution electron microscopy, molecular probe conformation analysis, and biosynthetic assay for de-repressor activity, which have proved so useful in the study of heterochromatin and euchromatin within interphase lymphocytes, promise to be similarly useful in these systems as well (Stanley et al.).

References

ALFERT, M.: Variations in cytochemical properties of cell nuclei. Exptl. Cell Res. Suppl. 6 (1958) 227.

ALLFREY, V.G., R.FAULKNER and A.E.MIRSKY: Acetylation and methylation of histones and their possible role in the regulation of RNA synthesis. Proc. Natl. Acad. Sci., U.S. 51 (1964) 786.

ALLFREY, V.G. and A.E.MIRSKY: Evidence for the complete DNA-dependence of RNA synthesis in isolated thymus nuclei. Proc. Natl. Acad. Sci., U.S. 48 (1962) 1590.

ANDERSON, D.R.: Ultrastructure of normal and leukemic leukocytes in human peripheral blood. J. Ultrastruct. Res., Suppl. 9 (1966) 5.

ATTARDI, G., H.PARNAIS, M.-I.H.HWANG and B.ATTARDI: Giant-size rapidly-labeled nuclear ribonucleic acid and cytoplasmic messenger ribonucleic acid in immature duck erythrocytes. J. Mol. Biol. 20 (1966) 145.

BENJAMIN, W., A.D.LEVANDER, A.GELLHORN and R.H.DE BELLIS: An RNA-histone complex in mammalian cells and the isolation and characterization of a new RNA species. Proc. Natl. Acad. Sci., U.S. 55 (1966) 858.

BERNHARD, W. and N.GRANBOULAN: The fine structure of the cancer cell nucleus. Exptl. Cell Res., Suppl. 9 (1963) 19.

BIRNBOIM, H.C., J.J.PENE and J.E.DARNELL: Studies on HeLa cell nuclear DNA-like RNA by RNA–DNA hybridization. Proc. Natl. Acad. Sci., U.S. 58 (1967) 320.

BROWN, S.W. and V.NUR: Heterochromatic chromosomes in the coccids. Science 145 (1964) 130.

BUSCH, H. and W.J.STEELE: Nuclear proteins of neoplastic cells. Advan. Cancer Res. 8 (1964) 41.

CHAMBON, P., M.RAMUZ, P.MANDEL and J.DOLY: Inhibition of RNA polymerase by sodium polyethylene sulphonate. Biochim. Biophys. Acta. 149 (1967) 584.

COOPER, K.W.: Cytogenetic analysis of major heterochromatic elements (especially X_H and Y) in *Drosophila melanogaster*, and the theory of heterochromatin. Chromosoma 10 (1959) 535.

DINGMAN, C.W. and M.B.SPORN: Studies on chromatin. I. Isolation and characterization of nuclear complexes of DNA, RNA, and protein from embryonic and adult tissues of the chicken. J. Biol. Chem. 239 (1964) 3483.

FANESTIL, D.D. and I.S.EDELMAN: Characteristics of the renal nuclear receptors for aldosterone. Proc. Natl. Acad. Sci., U.S. 56 (1966) 872.

FRENSTER, J.H.: Ultrastructural continuity between active and repressed chromatin. Nature 205 (1965a) 1341.

FRENSTER, J.H.: Nuclear polyanions as de-repressors of synthesis of ribonucleic acid. Nature 206 (1965b) 680.

FRENSTER, J.H.: A model of specific de-repression within interphase chromatin. Nature 206 (1965c) 1269.

FRENSTER, J.H.: Mechanisms of repression and de-repression within interphase chromatin. In: C.J. Dawe and G.Yerganian, eds.: The chromosome – structural and functional aspects. Baltimore, Williams and Wilkens Co., Inc. (1965d) pp. 78–101.

FRENSTER, J.H.: Localized strand separations within deoxyribonucleic acid during selective transcription. Nature 208 (1965e) 894.

FRENSTER, J.H.: Correlation of the binding to DNA loops or to DNA helices with the effect on RNA synthesis. Nature 208 (1965f) 1093.

FRENSTER, J.H.: Control of DNA strand separations during selective transcription and asynchronous replication. In: H.M. Klouwen, ed.: The cell nucleus – metabolism and radiosensitivity. London, Taylor and Francis Ltd, (1966)

FRENSTER, J.H., V.G. ALLFREY and A.E. MIRSKY: Metabolism and morphology of ribonucleo-protein particles from the cell nucleus of lymphocytes. Proc. Nat!. Acad. Sci., U.S. 46 (1960) 432.

FRENSTER, J.H., V.G. ALLFREY and A.E. MIRSKY: In vitro incorporation of amino acids into the proteins of isolated nuclear ribosomes. Biochim. Biophys. Acta. 47 (1961) 130.

FRENSTER, J.H., V.G. ALLFREY and A.E. MIRSKY: Repressed and active chromatin isolated from interphase lymphocytes. Proc. Natl. Acad. Sci., U.S. 50 (1963) 1026.

GOROVSKY, M.A. and J. WOODARD: Histone content of chromosomal loci active and inactive in RNA synthesis. J. Cell Biol. 33 (1967) 723.

GRUMBACH, M.M., A. MORISHIMA and J.H. TAYLOR: Human sex chromosome abnormalities in relation to DNA replication and heterochromatinization. Proc. Natl. Acad. Sci., U.S. 49 (1963) 581.

HAY, E.D. and J.P. REVEL: The fine structure of the DNP component of the nucleus, an electron microscopic study utilizing autoradiography to localize DNA synthesis. J. Cell Biol. 16 (1963) 29.

HAYASHI, M.N. and M. HAYASHI: Participation of a DNA–RNA hybrid complex in in-vivo genetic transcription. Proc. Natl. Acad. Sci., U.S. 55 (1966) 635.

HEITZ, E.: Heterochromatin, Chromocentren, Chromomeren. Ber. Deut. Botan. Ges. 47 (1988) 274.

HOUSSAIS, J.F. and G. ATTARDI: High molecular weight non-ribosomal type nuclear RNA and cytoplasmic messenger RNA in HeLa cells. Proc. Natl. Acad. Sci., U.S. 56 (1966) 616.

HSU, T.C.: Differential rate in RNA synthesis between euchromatin and heterochromatin. Exptl. Cell Res. 27 (1962) 332.

HUANG, R.C. and J. BONNER: Histone, a suppressor of chromosomal RNA synthesis. Proc. Natl. Acad. Sci., U.S. 48 (1962) 1216.

HUANG, R.C. and J. BONNER: Histone-bound RNA, a component of native nucleohistone. Proc. Natl. Acad. Sci., U.S. 54 (1965) 960.

HUXLEY, H.E. and G. ZUBAY: Preferential staining of nucleic acid-containing structures for electron microscopy. J. Biophys. Biochem. Cytol. 11 (1961) 273.

JOHNSON, R.M. and J. ALBERT: Incorporation of P^{32} into the phosphoprotein fraction of mammalian tissue. J. Biol. Chem. 200 (1953) 335.

KAWADE, Y.: Interaction between DNA and histone in strong saline. Biochim. Biophys. Acta 26 (1957) 61.

KLEINSMITH, L.J., V.G. ALLFREY and A.E. MIRSKY: Phosphoprotein metabolism in isolated lymphocyte nuclei. Proc. Natl. Acad. Sci., U.S. 55 (1966) 1182.

KLEVECZ, R.R. and T.C. HSU: The differential capacity for RNA synthesis among chromosomes: A cytological approach. Proc. Natl. Acad. Sci., U.S. 52 (1964) 811.

KUNKEL, H.G. and E.M. TAN: Autoantibodies and disease. Advan. Immunol. 4 (1964) 351.

LANGAN, T.A. and F. LIPMANN: Phosphoproteins isolated from rat liver nuclei. J. Biol. Chem. (1968). In press.

LANGAN, T.A. and L. SMITH: The effect of a phosphoprotein preparation from liver nuclei on the inhibition of RNA synthesis by histones. Federation Proc. 25 (1966) 778.

LAURENCE, D.J.R., P. SIMPSON and J.A.V. BUTLER: Studies on histones. 5. The histones of the Crocker sarcoma and spontaneous tumors of mice. Biochem. J. 87 (1963) 200.

LIMA-DE-FARIA, A.: Differential uptake of tritiated thymidine into hetero- and euchromatin in *Melanoplus* and *Secale*. J. Biophys. Biochem. Cytol. 6 (1959) 457.

LITTAU, V. C., V. G. ALLFREY, J. H. FRENSTER and A. E. MIRSKY: Active and inactive regions of nuclear chromatin as revealed by electron microscope auto-radiography. Proc. Natl. Acad. Sci., U.S. 52 (1964) 93.

LOEB, P. M. and J. D. WILSON: Intranuclear localization of testosterone 1, 2-H^3 in the preen gland of the duck. Clin. Res. 13 (1965) 45.

MACINNES, J. W. and R. B. URETZ: Thermal depolarization of flourescence from polytene chromosomes stained with acridine orange. J. Cell Biol. 33 (1967) 597.

MAGASANIK, B.: Isolation and composition of the pentose nucleic acid and of the corresponding nucleoproteins. In: E. Chargaff, ed.: The nucleic acids, Vol. 1. New York, Academic Press (1955).

MARASHUGE, K. and J. BONNER: Template properties of liver chromatin. J. Mol. Biol. 15 (1966) 160.

MCCARTHY, B. J. and B. H. HOYER: Identity of DNA and diversity of messenger RNA molecules in normal mouse tissues. Proc. Natl. Acad. Sci., U.S. 52 (1964) 915.

MIRSKY, A. E. and H. RIS: The composition and structure of isolated chromosomes. J. Gen. Physiol. 34 (1951) 475.

MITTWOCH, V.: Sex chromosomes. New York, Academic Press, Inc. (1967).

MUELLER, G. C. and K. KAJIWARA: Early- and late-replicating deoxyribonucleic acid complexes in HeLa cell nuclei. Biochim. Biophys. Acta 114 (1966) 108.

NOTEBOOM, W. D. and J. GORSKI: Stereo specific binding of estrogens in the rat uterus. Arch. Biochem. Biophys. 111 (1965) 555.

PATEL, G. and T. Y. WANG: Chromatography and electrophoresis of nuclear soluble proteins. Exptl. Cell Res. 34 (1964) 120.

PHILLIPS, D. M. P.: The histones. Progr. Biophys. Biophys. Chem. 12 (1962) 211.

POGO, A. O., V. G. ALLFREY and A. E. MIRSKY: Evidence for increased DNA template activity in regenerating liver nuclei. Proc. Natl. Acad. Sci., U.S. 56 (1966) 550.

POGO, B. G. T., V. G. ALLFREY and A. E. MIRSKY: RNA synthesis and histone acetylation during the course of gene activation in lymphocytes. Proc. Natl. Acad. Sci., U.S. 55 (1966) 805.

PRINTZ, M. P. and P. H. VON HIPPEL: Hydrogen exchange studies of DNA structure. Proc. Natl. Acad. Sci., U.S. 53 (1965) 363.

ROBBINS, J. H.: Tissue culture studies of the human lymphocyte. Science 146 (1965) 1648.

ROSE, H. G. and J. H. FRENSTER: Composition and metabolism of lipids within repressed and active chromatin of interphase lymphocytes. Biochim. Biophys. Acta 106 (1965) 577.

SCHERRER, K., L. MARCAUD, F. ZAJKELA, I. M. LONDON and F. GROS: Patterns of RNA metabolism in a differentiated cell: A rapidly labeled, unstable 60 sRNA with messenger properties in duck erythrocytes. Proc. Natl. Acad. Sci., U.S. 56 (1966) 1571.

SCHILDKRAUT, C. L. and S. LIFSON: Dependence of the melting temperature of DNA on salt concentration. Biopolymers 3 (1965) 195.

SHEARER, R. W. and B. J. MCCARTHY: Evidence for ribonucleic acid molecules restricted to the cell nucleus. Biochem. 6 (1967) 283.

SIBATANI, A., S. R. DE KLOET, V. G. ALLFREY and A. E. MIRSKY: Isolation of a nuclear RNA fraction resembling DNA in its base composition. Proc. Natl. Acad. Sci., U.S. 48 (1962) 471.

SOEIRO, R., H. C. BIRNBOIM and J. E. DARNELL: Rapidly labelled HeLa cell nuclear RNA. II. Base composition and cellular localization of a heterogenous RNA fraction. J. Mol. Biol. 19 (1966) 362.

SPERTI, S., M. LORINI, L. A. PINNA and V. MORET: Phosphorylserine sequences in phosphoproteins from Ehrlich ascites cells. Biochim. Biophys. Acta 82 (1964) 476.

STANLEY, D. A., J. H. FRENSTER and D. A. RIGAS: Subnuclear localization of H^3-phytohemaglutinin during gene de-repression within human lymphocytes. J. Cell Biol. (1968). In press.

STEELE, W. J. and H. BUSCH: Studies on the acidic nuclear proteins of the Walker tumor and liver. Cancer Res. 23 (1963) 1153.

WANG, T. Y., D. R. MAYER and L. E. THOMAS: A. Lipoprotein of rat liver nuclei. Exptl. Cell Res. 4 (1953) 102.

WARNER, J.R., R.SOEIRO, H.C.BIRNBOIM, M.GIRARD and J.E.DARNELL: Rapidly labeled HeLa cell nuclear RNA. T. Identification by zone sedimentation of a heterogenous fraction separate from ribosomal precursor RNA. J. Mol. Biol. 19 (1966) 349.

ZAKHAROV, A.F., N.A.EGOLINA and E.S.KAKPAKOVA: Late-replicating chromosomal segments in aneuploid chinese hamster cell lines as determined by autoradiography. J. Natl. Cancer Inst. 36 (1966) 215.

CHAPTER 13

DNA replication and gene amplification in heterochromatin

A. LIMA-DE-FARIA

Institute of Molecular Cytogenetics, Tornavägen 13, University of Lund, Sweden

Contents

1. Introduction
2. Late replication of DNA in heterochromatin
   (a) The cytological picture of heterochromatin
   (b) The autoradiographic picture and heterochromatin
   (c) Relation between heterochromatin and late replication
   (d) The rule of chromosome replication
   (e) Relation between late ending and late beginning of DNA synthesis.
3. Replication of human chromosomes studied at mitosis and meiosis
   (a) The heterochromatin of the autosomes of man
   (b) The replicons of human chromosomes
   (c) DNA synthesis in human meiotic chromosomes
4. Gene amplification in heterochromatin
   (a) Tritium autoradiography, ultrastructure and cytochemistry of the heterochromatic DNA body of *Tipula*
   (b) Tritium autoradiography and cytochemistry of the heterochromatic DNA body of *Acheta*
   (c) Biochemical analysis of the DNA of *Acheta* and the location of ribosomal cistrons in heterochromatin
   (d) Ultrastructural analysis of the DNA body of *Acheta* and the presence of multiple synaptonemal complexes in this structure
5. Summary and conclusions

1. Introduction

In the study of the molecular organization of the chromosome of higher organisms heterochromatin has attracted especial attention. This is due to its structural and genetic behaviour.

Of all the structural differentiations of the chromosome this is the one which has been most extensively studied. Heterochromatin is of widespread occurrence in plants and animals and it appears in interphase and early prophase nuclei in the form of relatively well delimited regions which are recognized in the light and electron microscopes. The genes located in the heterochromatin behave differently from those present in euchromatin.

In this chapter will be discussed the following aspects of the molecular organization of heterochromatin: (1) the late replication of DNA in heterochromatin as compared to euchromatin, (2) the change in the time of DNA replication related to tissue differentiation, (3) the relation between late ending of DNA synthesis in heterochromatin and late beginning of DNA synthesis in the same chromosome or chromosome region, (4) the presence of major and minor replicons and the degree of independence between replicons situated in the hetero- and euchromatin, (5) the occurrence of amplification of ribosomal cistrons in the heterochromatic DNA body of the house cricket (*Acheta*), and (6) the finding that multiple synaptonemal complexes are present in the DNA body in a number that seems to be related to the degree of amplification.

2. Late replication of DNA in heterochromatin

Until 1959 heterochromatin was considered to be an elusive chromosome material difficult to approach experimentally at the cytological level (Schultz; Caspersson; Lima-de-Faria 1956). The radioisotope work with P^{32} and H^{3} had not until then yielded any relevant information on this chromosomal material.

The first experimental demonstration that heterochromatin synthesizes its DNA at a different time and later than the euchromatic regions of the chromosome complement was obtained in the grasshopper *Melanoplus differentialis* (Lima-de-Faria 1959a, b). In this species there is at prophase of meiosis a large heterochromatic X-chromosome in the male. The autosomes are mainly euchromatic. The injection of tritiated thymidine into the body cavity of the animals revealed that in the spermatocytes, at zygotene and pachytene, the heterochromatic X was labelled at a different time from the autosomes (Figs. 1–4). In the testicular tubules the spermatocytes are grouped in cysts which are synchronised at a given meiotic stage. The cysts move along the tubule as meiosis progresses, so that from their relative position, it is possible to know which are developmentally the most advanced. In sections of this material it was found that the spermatocytes of the cysts which were later in development were labelled only in the heterochromatic X-chromosome, whereas cysts at an earlier stage of development

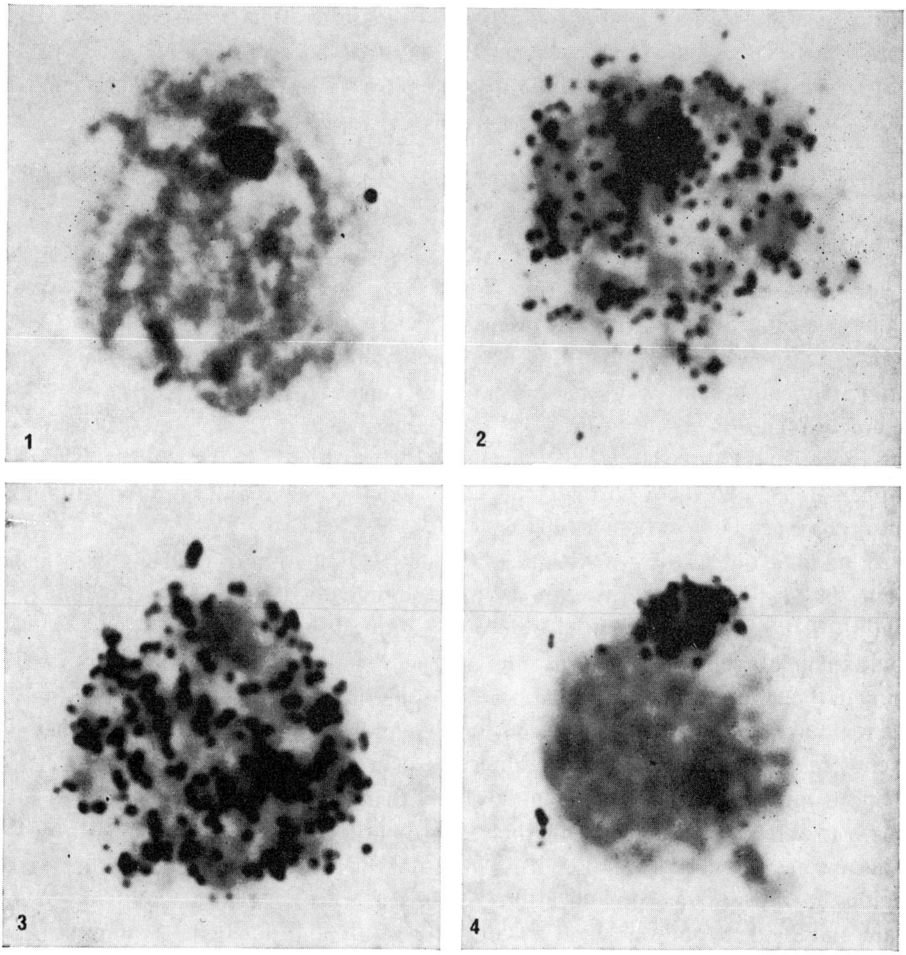

Figs. 1–4. *Melanoplus differentialis* spermatocytes at zygotene–pachytene labelled with H^3-thymidine.

Fig. 1. Unlabelled nucleus showing the heterochromatic sex chromosome (at 12 o'clock, in the four nuclei) surrounded by the enchromatic autosomes.

Fig. 2. Fully labelled nucleus.

Fig. 3. Nucleus labelled in the autosomes but not in the sex chromosome.

Fig. 4. Nucleus showing only the sex chromosome labelled and the autosomes unlabelled. Feulgen stain. (From Lima-de-Faria 1959b.) × 2900.

were only labelled in the autosomes. This result established that heterochromatin in this species, and in this tissue, replicated later than euchromatin.

To find out whether this phenomenon occurred in other organisms, leaves from seedlings of rye (*Secale cereale*) were exposed to H^3-thymidine. In this organism (Lima-de-Faria 1952), all chromosomes are heterochromatic on both sides of the kinetochore and possess heterochromatic 'knobs' at most ends. The autoradiographic picture of interphase nuclei disclosed that in this species heterochromatin also replicated at a different time from euchromatin (Lima-de-Faria 1959b).

Since then many different research workers have studied the same phenomenon in plant, animal and human material by means of H^3-autoradiography.

(a) *The cytological picture of heterochromatin*

Heterochromatin as originally described by Heitz (1928, 1931, 1933, 1934, 1935) represents a differential behaviour of the chromosome phenotype. Heterochromatic regions are characterized, in interphase and early prophase nuclei, as 'chromosome regions that form massive blocks of Feulgen positive material' (Schultz).

Heterochromatin is a state of the chromosome rather than a substance, as is sometimes assumed, because it does not occur at all stages of development. In *Drosophila* heterochromatin is absent in the early embryonic stages of the fly, but it is found at later stages in the three largest chromosomes (Brown 1966). In the male of the grasshopper *Melanoplus* the X-chromosome is not heterochromatic in the spermatogonia, but becomes so later in the spermatocytes.

As pointed out already by Schultz, 'nucleic acid starvation' (Darlington and La Cour) or 'negative heteropycnosis' (White) should not be included in heterochromatin. If it is, every differential state of the chromosome during the division cycle could qualify as heterochromatin. The original definition would break down, everything in the chromosome becoming heterochromatin depending on the appearance of the region used as a standard. Recent results confirm the idea that negative heteropycnosis is a phenomenon distinct from heterochromatin.

Spectrophotometric measurements disclose that the amount of DNA per unit area is two to three times higher in the heterochromatin than in the euchromatin of the same nucleus (Lima-de-Faria 1959b). This is not the case in negatively heteropycnotic regions in which there is no indication of increase or decrease in DNA content (Woodward and Swift; Woodward et al.). Thus, this result contradicts the assumption that negative heteropycnosis is the reverse state of positive heteropycnosis, a term also used for heterochromatin. Moreover, autoradiographic studies in *Trillium* disclose that cold-induced negative heteropycnotic regions can occur in chromosomes which had completed their DNA synthesis before the cold treatment started (Boothroyd and Lima-de-Faria). This result, as well as the spectrophotometric measurements, shows that the designation sometimes given to such chromosomal segments of 'nucleic acid starved regions' does not describe appropriately the actual macromolecular organisation of these regions.

Negative heteropycnosis is thus not necessarily the opposite of heterochromatin, although it is a particular state of the chromosome, and probably an equally significant one. Moreover, it is not in agreement with the available evidence to call heterochromatin 'positive heteropycnosis' as has sometimes been done. One should stick to the original description of this well-defined state of the chromosome which is characterized by the appearance of a massive block of Feulgen positive material at a given stage of development. Other states of the chromosome should be considered as separate phenomena until we have a better knowledge of the macromolecular organization of the chromosome during these states.

(b) *The autoradiographic picture and heterochromatin*

The evidence obtained by the different laboratories on DNA synthesis studied with H^3-autoradiography has varied in the degree of accuracy with which the relation between the autoradiographic picture and the occurrence of heterochromatin has been established in a given tissue. Accordingly these results may be divided into three main groups. (1) Autoradiographic studies were carried out in the same tissue and at the same stage at which heterochromatin has been well established. (2) Tritiated thymidine was administered to tissues where heterochromatin was not recognizable but the chromosomes studied were heterochromatic in another tissue. (3) Tritiated thymidine was added to a given tissue but no exact information was available on the occurrence of heterochromatin in the tissue studied or in other tissues. In this group are some of the results on sex chromosomes, or presumed sex chromosomes.

The experiments of groups (2) and (3) although of interest to this problem, cannot be considered to furnish reliable information on the relation between the occurrence of heterochromatin and the sequence of DNA synthesis. To establish this relation with accuracy it is necessary: (a) that there is clearcut evidence that a given chromosome or chromosome segment is actually heterochromatic; and (b) that the autoradiographic picture be studied in the tissue where heterochromatin is displayed.

A well-known phenomenon, since Heitz's discovery of heterochromatin, is that a given chromosome is not necessarily heterochromatic in all tisues of an organism, and that not all sex chromosomes are heterochromatic.

(c) *Relation between heterochromatin and late replication*

In this chapter we will deal mainly with the evidence from the first group of results where the two conditions just postulated are fulfilled. There are now many results from different laboratories, which belong in this category. These allow us to assess the general validity of the findings originally made in *Melanoplus* and *Secale*.

In plants (Table 1) four species have been found to exhibit this phenomenon: *Secale cereale* (Lima-de-Faria 1959b; Darlington and Haque; Lima-de-Faria and Jaworska 1969), *Fritillaria lanceolata* (Pelc and La Cour), *Vicia faba* (Evans) and *Hordeum vulgare* (Kusanagi). In these species heterochromatin is displayed, among other tissues, in root and leaf nuclei. It shows up at interphase in the form of chromocenters and at prophase as large chromomeres or deeply stained segments. The H^3-thymidine was administered to these tissues and the autoradiographic picture was studied at interphase, prophase and metaphase. In the four species the chromocenters at interphase, the large chromomeres at prophase, and the corresponding regions at metaphase were found to replicate later than the euchromatic regions (Table 1).

Tanaka has claimed that in *Spiranthes sinensis* euchromatin replicated later than heterochromatin but his results have been criticized because: (1) the number of cells labelled was small, (2) the number of silver grains in the autoradiographs was very low, and (3) the large number of chromosomes of *Spiranthes* ($2n = 30$) and their small size did not allow an exact distinction between the euchromatic and heterochromatic regions of the chromosomes.

Among insects (Table 2) four species exhibit the same phenomenon: *Melanoplus differentialis*, *Bombyx mori*, *Pseudococcus obscurus* and *Drosophila melanogaster*. Three of them: *Drosophila*, *Melanoplus* and *Pseudococcus* are classical examples of organisms with heterochromatin. The behaviour of the X-chromosome in *Melanoplus* was mentioned above. In *Drosophila*, where heterochromatin was initially studied by Heitz (1928, 1931, 1933, 1934, 1935) at prophase and metaphase in somatic cells, the whole Y-chromosome, the proximal regions of the X and of chromosomes II and III are heterochromatic. The incorporation of H^3-thymidine into this same tissue where heterochromatin is observed reveals the late replication of the heterochromatic regions relative to the euchromatic ones (Barigozzi et al.). Particularly striking is the case of *Pseudococcus* where a whole set of chromosomes is heterochromatic (Hughes-Schrader). This whole set is later in DNA replication than the euchromatic set found in the same nucleus (Baer). In *Bombyx* (Karnkowska-Gorska), heterochromatin in the spinning glands is also found to be late replicating when H^3-thymidine is administered to this tissue. In the four cases the autoradiographic picture was studied in the same tissue and at the same stage as the heterochromatin.

Mammals, including man, furnish the largest number of examples that confirm the rule of late replication of heterochromatin. We include in Table 3 only the cases where DNA replication has been studied in the chromocenters at interphase. With the exception of a few cases, only such conditions allow an accurate study of the sequence of DNA replication in heterochromatin relative to euchromatin. Only if the information from the chromocenters at interphase, or, from heterochromatic chromosomes at prophase, can be directly related to specific chromosomes at metaphase is one in a position to state that the late DNA replication seen at metaphase is representative of the heterochromatin observed at interphase or prophase. Metaphase chromosomes are seldom heterochromatic.

Man is the species in which the relation between the metaphase and interphase pictures has been best established due to there being individuals with multiple X-chromosomes. The number of chromocenters (Barr bodies) seen at interphase in diploid cells is equal to the number of X-chromosomes minus one (according to the rule of Harnden). Thus, in man the autoradiographic picture of the X-chromosome at metaphase can be considered to furnish reliable information on the late DNA replication of heterochromatin (German; Gilbert et al. 1962; Morishima et al.). Studies of DNA replication in individuals with multiple sex chromosomes have confirmed the relation between the number of Barr bodies seen at interphase and the number of late replicating X-chromosomes present at metaphase (Morishima et al.; Grumbach et al.; Rowley et al. 1963; Atkins et al.; Giannelli; Mukherjee et al. 1964; Hsu and Lockhart; Atkins and Gustavson). Moreover, there have been several studies of the H^3-autoradiographic picture of Barr bodies at interphase confirming the late replication of heterochromatin in man at the chromocenter stage (Atkins et al. 1963; Bishop and Bishop; Comings). In addition to the sex chromatin (Barr bodies), autosomal heterochromatin has also been described at interphase in the human male and female. This has been found to replicate at a different time from the euchromatin (Lima-de-Faria and Reitalu; Lima-de-Faria et al. 1965).

The Chinese hamster (*Cricetulus griseus*) has X- and Y-chromosomes which form distinct chromocenters at interphase (Taylor 1960; Hsu). These were found to replicate later than the euchromatic regions of the autosomes in interphase nuclei and at metaphase (Taylor 1960; Hsu). A similar situation is found in the Syrian hamster (*Mesocricetus auratus*) and in the Guinea pig (*Cavia cobaya*), in which several major and minor chromocenters, present in the interphase nucleus, have been found to be late replicating relative to the euchromatin (Schmid 1967a, b).

In *Microtus agrestis* (Wolf et al.) the sex chromosomes are amongst the largest known in mammals and their heterochromatin can be seen at interphase in the form of very large chromocenters and at prophase. In chinchilla (Galton et al.), the Y- and X-chromosome in the male are heterochromatic at interphase forming two large chromocenters. In these two species the pattern of H^3-thymidine uptake into DNA was studied at metaphase but also at interphase where the distinct chromocenters were found to replicate later than the euchromatin.

In the dog, (Fraccaro et al. 1964) the donkey-grevy zebra hybrid (Benirschke et al. 1964) and in the mouse (Tiepolo et al. 1967b) there are one or several chromocenters at interphase. These represent either one X-chromosome (dog and donkey-grevy zebra hybrid) or they cannot be directly related to sex chromosomes (mouse). In every mammalian species included in Table 3 the autoradiographic picture and the heterochromatin were studied both in the same tissue and at interphase, disclosing the late replication of the chromocentral heterochromatin.

(d) *The rule of chromosome replication*

The results on the 17 species of plants, insects and mammals (Tables 1–3) allow one to formulate the following rule of chromosome replication.

When tritirated thymidine is incorporated into the cells of a given tissue in which massive Feulgen positive chromosome regions are present at interphase or early prophase, the heterochromatic regions replicate their DNA later than the euchromatic segments. This can be seen when the autoradiographic picture is studied in the same tissue and at the same stage in which heterochromatin is displayed. This phenomenon occurs irrespective of the position of the organism in the evolutionary scale and within the organism irrespective of the tissue in which heterochromatin is observed.

If a chromosome is heterochromatic in a given tissue and replicates its DNA later than the euchromatin, it does not follow that it necessarily replicates its DNA later in

TABLE 1

Plant species where the incorporation of H^3-thymidine was studied in the same tissue and at the

Species	Autoradiography		Heterochromatin	
	Tissue	Stage	Tissue	1) Stage 2) Chromosomes
Secale cereale	Leaves Roots	Interphase, prophase, metaphase	Leaves Roots	1) Interphase, prophase 2) Proximal, and medial regions o mosomes and 'knobs'
Fritillaria lanceolata	Roots	Interphase	Roots	1) Interphase 2) Chromocenters
Vicia faba	Roots	Interphase	Roots	1) Inphase, prophase 2) Near centromeres and other re
Hordeum vulgare	Roots	Metaphase	Roots	1) Interphase, prophase 2) Proximal regions of all chromo

TABLE 2

Insect species where the incorporation of H^3-thymidine was studied in the same tissue and at the

Species	Autoradiography		Heterochromatin	
	Tissue	Stage	Tissue	1) Stage 2) Chromosomes
Melanoplus differentialis	Testis	Prophase of meiosis	Testis	1) Prophase of meiosis 2) X-chromosome
Bombyx mori	Spinning glands	Interphase	Spinning glands	1) Interphase 2) Chromocenters
Pseudococcus obscurus	Somatic cells	Interphase, metaphase	Somatic cells	1) Interphase 2) Whole heterochromatic some set
Drosophila melanogaster	Embryonic cells	Prophase, metaphase	Embryonic cells	1) Prophase, metaphase 2) Whole Y, prox. reg. of chrom. II and III

erochromatin has been well established. (From Lima-de-Faria and Jaworska 1968.)

on period of omatin	References: Autoradiography	References: Heterochromatin
n euchromatin	Lima-de-Faria (1959b) Darlington and Haque Lima-de-Faria and Jaworska (1969)	Lima-de-Faria (1950, 1952) Tjio and Levan
n euchromatin	Pelc and Lacour	Pelc and Lacour
n euchromatin	Evans	McLeish
n euchromatin	Kusanagi	Tjio and Levan

erochromatin has been well established. (From Lima-de-Faria and Jaworska 1968.)

tion period of ochromatin	References: Autoradiography	References: Heterochromatin
an euchromatic	Lima-de-Faria (1959a, b, 1961)	Lima-de-Faria (1959a, b, 1961)
euchromatin	Karnkowska-Gorska	Karnkowska-Gorska
euchromatic set	Baer	Hughes-Schrader Brown and Nur
euchromatin	Barigozzi et al.	Heitz (1935)

TABLE 3

Mammalian species where the incorporation of H^3-thymidine was studied in the same tissue and a

Species	Autoradiography		Heterochromatin	
	Tissue	Stage	Tissue	1) Stage 2) Chromosomes
Cricetulus griseus (Chinese hamster)	Embryonic tissues	Interphase, metaphase	Embryonic cells, kidney and nerve cells	1) Interphase 2) Chromocenters i ing X and Y
Chinchilla lanigera (Chinchilla)	Kidney cell cultures	Interphase, metaphase	Kidney cell cultures	1) Interphase 2) Chromocenters i ing X and Y
Microtus agrestis (field vole)	Bone marrow cultures, fibroblast cells	Interphase, metaphase	Bone marrow cultures, fibroblast cells	1) Interphase 2) Chromocenters, and part of X
Mesocricetus auratus (Syrian hamster)	Kidney cell cultures	Interphase, metaphase	Kidney cell cultures, nerve cells	1) Interphase 2) Major and mino centres
Cavia cobaya (Guinea pig)	Kidney cell cultures	Interphase, metaphase	Kidney cell cultures, nerve cells	1) Interphase 2) Large and smal centers
Canis familiaris (dog)	Kidney cell cultures, bone marrow	Interphase, metaphase	Kidney cell cultures, buccal mucosa	1) Interphase 2) Chromocenters, chrom.
Donkey-grevy zebra hybrid	Skin cultures	Interphase, metaphase	Skin cultures	1) Interphase 2) Chromocenters, chrom.
Mus musculus (mouse)	Kidney epithelial cells	Interphase	Kidney epithelial cells	1) Interphase 2) 4 to 20 chromo
Homo sapiens (man)	Various somatic tissues (fibroblasts, blood, skin)	Interphase, metaphase	Various somatic tissues (fibroblasts, blood, skin, nerve cells)	1) Interphase 2) Chromocenters, chromosome (B and autosomes)

e heterochromatin has been well established. (From Lima-de-Faria and Jaworska 1968.)

ion period of romatin	References	
	Autoradiography	Heterochromatin
n euchromatin	Taylor (1960) Hsu	Taylor (1960) Schmid (1967b)
n euchromatin	Galton et al.	Galton et al.
n euchromatin	Wolf et al. Schmid (1967a)	Wolf et al. Schmid (1967a)
n euchromatin	Schmid (1967a)	Schmid (1967a)
n euchromatin	Schmid (1967a)	Schmid (1967a)
n euchromatin	Fraccaro et al.	Fraccaro et al.
n euchromatin	Benirschke et al.	Benirschke et al.
n euchromatin	Tiepolo et al. (1967a, b)	Tiepolo et al. (1967a, b)
n euchromatin	German Gilbert et al. (1962) Morishima, et al. Rowley et al. (1963) Giannelli Lima-de-Faria and Reitalu Bishop and Bishop Mukherhee et al. (1964) Hsu and Lockart Atkins and Gustavson Lima-de-Faria et al. (1965) Comings	Barr Klinger and Schwarzacher Lima-de-Faria and Reitalu Atkins et al.

other tissues where it may be euchromatic. Demonstration of this phenomenon was obtained in the grasshopper (*Melanoplus*). At prophase of meiosis, in spermatocytes, the X-chromosome is heterochromatic in the males, and replicates its DNA later than the autosomes (Lima-de-Faria 1959a, b, 1961). The same chromosome is, however, euchromatic or slightly negatively heteropycnotic in the spermatogonia, and in this last tissue the incorporation of tritiated thymidine takes place at the same time as in the autosomes (Nicklas and Jaqua).

Another example of this phenomenon is found in the female of the golden hamster (*Mesocricetus auratus*). In eight cell embryos only one arm of both X-chromosomes replicates late in the period of DNA synthesis. Mid-gestation embryos and adult fibroblasts show one X-chromosome labelled in one arm but the other X is labelled throughout. Between cleavage and mid-gestation one of the arms of an X-chromosome shifts from an early to a later time of replication resulting in the late replication of one and a half X-chromosomes (Hill and Yunis).

A third case of variation in time of DNA replication with differentiation has been described in the Chinese hamster (*Cricetulus griseus*) by Utakoji and Hsu. In somatic cells in tissue culture and bone marrow cells *in vivo* the long arm of the X and the entire Y replicate in the late S phase. However, in spermatogonia the long arm of the X and the entire Y are not labelled in the late S phase. The three cases just described (Table 4) demonstrate that: (1) there are controlling mechanisms affecting the chromosomes of higher organisms at the molecular level, which shift the time of DNA replication of given chromosomes or chromosome segments from one period to another of the S phase, (2) that this phenomenon is tissue specific, i.e. it is correlated with the differentiation of the organism, and (3) that the shift occurs, at least in one case, in connection with the heterochromatization of the chromosome.

These results are also most significant in demonstrating that it is not valid to study the autoradiographic picture of a given chromosome in a tissue where this chromosome is not known with accuracy to be heterochromatic and from such a result draw conclusions concerning the relation between heterochromatin and the sequence of DNA replication.

In *Microtus oregoni* Hsu et al. described results which they believed contradicted the rule of chromosome replication. In this species Ohno et al. (1963, 1964), had observed a large chromocenter in embryonic liver cells which they interpreted as representing two-thirds of the X-chromosome seen at prophase. Hsu et al. did not administer H^3-thymidine to this tissue but to lung fibroblasts grown *in vitro* in which they then studied the DNA replication at metaphase, a stage at which heterochromatin is not usually visible. They did not find late replication at the segments presumed to be heterochromatic at interphase in the liver, and they concluded that this case represented a departure from the relation between late replication and heterochromatin. Since the autoradiography was done in one tissue and heterochromatin observed in another, such an experiment cannot be used as an example in establishing the relation between late replication and heterochromatin.

TABLE 4

DNA replication in relation to differentiation. Organisms where the time of DNA synthesis of given chromosomes or chromosome regions changes during development.

Taxonomic group	Organism	Type of replication: Early development		Late development		References
		Tissue	Chromosomes	Tissue	Chromosomes	
Insects	*Melanoplus differentialis*	Spermatogonia	X replicating at the same time as autosomes	Spermatocytes	X replicating later than autosomes	Lima-de-Faria, 1959b, 1961 Nicklas and Jaqua
Mammals	*Cricetulus griseus* (Chinese hamster)	Spermatogonia	Long arm of X and entire Y not late repl.	Bone marrow (*in vivo*) Somatic cells (*in vitro*)	Long arm of X and entire Y late repl.	Utakoji and Hsu
	Mesocricetus auratus (golden hamster)	Eight cell embryos	One arm of one X late repl. One arm of other X late repl.	Mid-gestation embryos and adult fibroblasts	One arm of one X late repl. Both arms of other X late repl.	Hill and Yunis

TABLE 5

Relation between late ending and late beginning of DNA synthesis in the same chromosome, or chro

Taxonomic group	Species	Tissue	Chromosome or chromosome regio
Plants	*Secale cereale*	Roots	Euchromatic and heteroch regions of all chromosome
Insects	*Melanoplus differentialis*	Spermatocytes	Heterochromatic X-chrom and euchromatic autosom
Mammals	*Cricetulus griseus* (Chinese hamster)	Cell culture embryonic tissues	Heterochromatic X, Y; ar somes
	Macropus cangaru (Grey kangaroo)	Leucocytes	X-chromosomes and auto
	Protemnodon eugenii (Kangaroo, Island Wallaby)	Leucocytes	X-chromosomes and auto
	Canis familiaris (Dog)	Bone marrow cells *in vitro*	X-chromosomes and auto
	Bos taurus (ox)	Kidney cell cultures	X-, Y-chromosomes and a
	Homo sapiens	Leucocytes	X-chromosomes and auto
		Leucocytes (aminopterin used to synchronize cells)	X-chromosomes and auto
		Fibroblast cultures	subject: XXXXY and au
		Leucocytes	X-chromosomes and auto
		Leucocytes	iso-X chromosome and a
		Fibroblasts (FUdR used to synchronize cells)	XY, XX and XXX versus somes
		Fibroblast cultures	X-chromosomes and auto

…g of DNA synthesis	Ending of DNA synthesis	Late replicating region (or chromosome) heterochromatic	References
…romatic regions …g *after* euchro- …gments by narrow …e	Heterochromatic regions ending *after* euchromatic segments by an appreciable difference	+	Lima-de-Faria and Jaworska (1969)
…ing *after* auto- … narrow difference	X ending *after* autosomes by an appreciable difference	+	Lima-de-Faria (1961)
…n of X and Y begin- …r autosomes	Long arm of X and Y ending *after* autosomes	+	Taylor (1960) Schmid (1967b)
…nosome beginning …osomes	X_2-chromosome ending *after* autosomes	+	Graves
…nosome beginning …osomes	X_2-chromosome ending *after* autosomes	+	Graves
…eginning *after* …nd autosomes	One X ending *after* other X and at the same times as some autosomes	+	Brown et al.
One X beginning …*ously* with autosomes … beginning appre- …*er* than X and …es	Female: One X finishing *later* than autosomes Male: Y ending *later* than X and autosomes	Not known	Gartler and Burt
—	One X ending *after* other X and autosomes	+	Morishima et al. German Gilbert et al. (1962) Klinger and Schwarzacher
…ginning *after* …nd autosomes	—	+	Petersen
…Y ending *later* …osomes	3 X and Y beginning *later* than autosomes	+ (X)	Hsu and Lockhart
…ginning *after* …nd autosomes	One X ending *after* other X and autosomes	+	Cave
…inning *after* auto-	iso-X ending *after* autosomes	+	Ockey et al.
…X and 2 X respec- …inning *after* other …omes	No X, 1 X and 2 X respectively ending *after* other chromosomes	+	Priest et al.
…ginning 2.5 hr …r X and autosomes	One X ending 1.6 hr *after* other X and autosomes	+	Comings

It is not a corollary of the DNA rule, formulated above, that any chromosome or chromosome region that is late replicating is heterochromatic. Thus, within the chromosomes of various species different regions replicate at different times showing no indication of being heterochromatic. When heterochromatin is not present, other factors not yet apparent determine the sequence of replication of various segments within a chromosome and between chromosomes (Taylor 1958; Lima-de-Faria 1961; Lima-de-Faria et al. 1967).

It may be stated at present that what determines the presence of heterochromatin, determines the late replication of a chromosome, or in other terms, what changes the condensation cycle of the chromosome, at the same time shifts its timing of DNA replication. However, what determines the late replication of a chromosome or chromosome region may not necessarily determine the onset of heterochromatin.

It should be recalled that heterochromatin was originally discovered by its expression at the chromosome phenotype, and it is still to-day primarily recognised by the changes that occur at this level. What happens at the gene level or at the molecular level of chromosome organisation, when heterochromatin becomes apparent at the microscopic level – a jump from the Angstrom to the micron level – is mainly unknown.

(e) *Relation between late ending and late beginning of DNA synthesis*

The question arises whether chromosomes which finish their DNA synthesis after all the others also initiate their DNA synthesis later than the other chromosomes. As a rule late replicating chromosomes start later than the other chromosomes, but the difference at the beginning of the S period does not seem to be as dramatic as at the end (Table 5). In the spermatocytes of *Melanoplus*, where this phenomenon was studied in detail (Fig. 5), the heterochromatic X-chromosome starts only slightly later than the euchromatic autosomes, but at the end of the S period the X goes on replicating for an appreciable period of time after the autosomes have finished (Lima-de-Faria 1961). Each of the seven chromosomes of the complement of rye consists of euchromatic and heterochromatic regions. There is a sequence of DNA synthesis in these chromosomes which is related to the degree of heterochromatinization of each segment. The euchromatic regions appear labelled first but are very soon followed by the heterochromatic ones. At the end of DNA synthesis the regions with the highest degree of heterochromatinization go on replicating for an appreciable time after all other regions have finished (Lima-de-Faria and Jaworska 1969). In rye as in *Melanoplus* the time difference at the start is not as great as at the end of the S period. In mammals the same situation seems to prevail (Table 5). In Man where the phenomenon has been studied in several laboratories, and using individuals with chromosome complements containing multiple Xs, it is well established that the heterochromatic X-chromosome begins and ends its replication later than the other chromosomes. The results of Bianchi and Bianchi (1965) are sometimes cited as showing that one X in the human female started simultaneously with the autosomes but the information they produced had to do mainly with the end of the S period. These workers (1966) in a

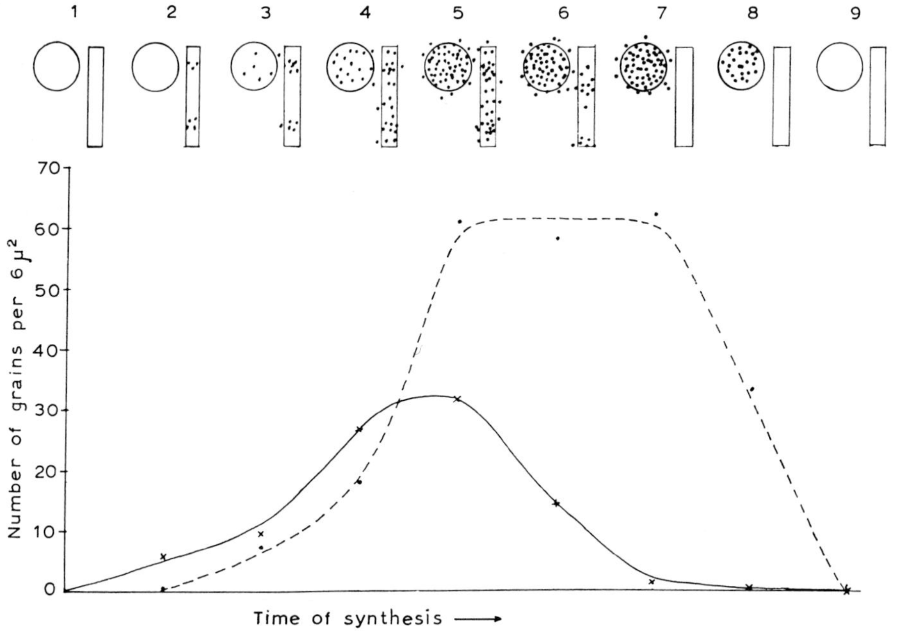

Fig. 5. Sequence of DNA synthesis in *Melanoplus* chromosomes at meiosis. The large circle represents the sex chromosome, the bar a representative segment of the autosomes with an area equal to that of the sex chromosome (6 μ^2). There are nine distinguishable periods from the initiation until the end of the DNA synthesis. Dotted line represents the sex chromosomes; solid line, the autosomes. The time of synthesis is in arbitrary units since meiosis is difficult to time *in vivo*. (From Lima-de-Faria 1961.)

study of the rat mentioned that the X-chromosomes started DNA synthesis at different times in two different tissues, but, as they pointed out, the X-chromosomes cannot be distinguished with accuracy from the others in this species. In Table 5 are assembled only the studies in which the sex chromosomes could be identified with accuracy and where the beginning and end of DNA synthesis were studied in detail. It can be seen that in these cases the heterochromatic regions or heterochromatic chromosomes usually start later and finish later than euchromatic ones. Moreover, as is the case in rye, the more heterochromatic a given region of the chromosome is, the later it starts and the later it finishes DNA synthesis. It should be kept in mind that different genetic or physiological conditions prevailing in different tissues or culture media may affect the exact timing of this phenomenon.

3. Replication of human chromosomes studied at mitosis and meiosis

The study of late DNA replication in heterochromatin leads us to other aspects of DNA replication, viz.: (1) the size of the replicons in the euchromatin and heterochromatin, and (2) the possible interaction between replicons situated in the hetero- and euchromatin. Mammalian chromosomes and especially human chromosomes have been extensively studied in this repect.

(a) *The heterochromatin of the autosomes of man*
Besides the heterochromatic X of the human female, heterochromatin is present in both human males and females in the autosomes (Lima-de-Faria and Reitalu; Lima-de-Faria et al. 1965). In interphase nuclei this heterochromatin replicates at a different time from the surrounding euchromatin. This heterochromatin is located in chromosomes associated with the nucleolus and in other autosomes of the complement, but it is not seen at metaphase because heterochromatin is usually not visible at this stage. Some, but not necessarily all, of the segments showing asynchrony of DNA synthesis at metaphase must represent the heterochromatic ones showing the asynchrony seen at interphase. Thus, a part of the asynchrony we are seeing at metaphase is due to the heterochromatin present at interphase in the autosomes. This does not mean, however, that every segment that replicates differentially at metaphase is a heterochromatic segment.

(b) *The replicons of human chromosomes*
When DNA synthesis was studied in human leucocytes, a complex pattern of chromosome replication was found (Lima-de-Faria et al. 1961). This study revealed: (1) that not all chromosomes synthesize DNA at the same time, (2) that not all segments within a chromosome replicate simultaneously, and (3) that homologous chromosomes replicate at different times. Many other laboratories have made similar contributions to the study of DNA synthesis in human chromosomes.

Today the number of publications in this field is quite large but, in addition to the works cited above in connection with the replication of heterochromatin, the following may be mentioned for their pioneer contribution to our knowledge of DNA synthesis in human mitotic chromosomes: German; Gilbert et al. (1962); Morishima et al.; Stubblefield and Mueller; Bender and Prescott; Moorhead and Defendi; Bader et al.; Grumbach et al.; Schmid (1963); Kikuchi and Sandberg (1963, 1964); Muldal et al.; Rowley et al. (1963); Gilbert et al. (1965); Bianchi and Bianchi (1965); Cave, Büchner et al.

The contributions from many different laboratories have established the following major points. (1) The asynchrony of replication between the chromosomes of the complement as well as between regions of a chromosome has been generally well demonstrated. (2) One of the X-chromosomes of the human female has been found to be late in replication. (3) Homologues seem to have essentially the same labelling features but at times they are out of phase in their replication. This results in a differential labeling of the homologues in the X-chromosomes and in the autosomes. (4) Characteristic patterns of replication have been found for those chromosomes that can be identified with accuracy and for given pairs within a group. (5) Within each chromosome, there are segments which replicate at a different time from others. (6) These segments are well delimited. (7) They can be followed from cell to cell, being present at the same site of a given chromosome, and having the same size. (8) These segments are of different sizes in different chromosomes. They are as large as a whole arm, or they may be as small as one micron, the limit of resolution of tritium. (9) There is no indication of a given sequence of synthesis within each chromosome or within each arm. Evidence that the kinetochore or the telomeres are determinants in the replication sequence is not available. (10) Each chromosome finishes replication at a site or region not related to the others.

It is beyond the scope of this chapter to deal with the study of DNA synthesis in chromosomes involved in structural changes but mention may be made to a few cases. Structural rearrangements which have led to the formation of X-iso-chromosomes and ring X-chromosomes in the human female have not resulted in detectable changes of the pattern of DNA replication in these chromosomes (Miller et al.; Muldal et al.; Grumbach et al.; Rowley et al.; Ockey et al.).

Another case is the Philadelphia chromosome (Ph^1). In a patient with chronic granulocytic leukemia the large deletion in chromosomes 21 or 22 which resulted in the Philadelphia chromosome did not lead to an inhibition of DNA synthesis in the remaining DNA segments of this chromosome, or to a change of its timing or pattern of replication (Figs. 6–9). The Ph^1 was as much or more labeled than the other chromosomes in the group 21–22 and it finished DNA synthesis at the same time as the other chromosomes of this group (Table 6, Lima-de-Faria et al. 1967). This means that in these cases the units of replication present along the human chromosome are to a large extent independent of each other, but the measure of their degree of independence cannot be ascertained at present.

TABLE 6

Number of labeled and unlabeled Philadelphia chromosomes in relation to the labeling of the other chromosomes in group 21–22.

Hours	15		10		5	
	Unlab. Ph^1	Lab. Ph^1	Unlab. Ph^1	Lab. Ph^1	Unlab. Ph^1	Lab. Ph^1
3 chrom. labeled		8		3		
2 labeled 1 unlabeled		1		1		
1 labeled 2 unlabeled		2	1	1	1	
3 chrom. unlabeled			4	2	8	
Total	0	11	5	7	9	0

From Lima-de-Faria et al. (1967).

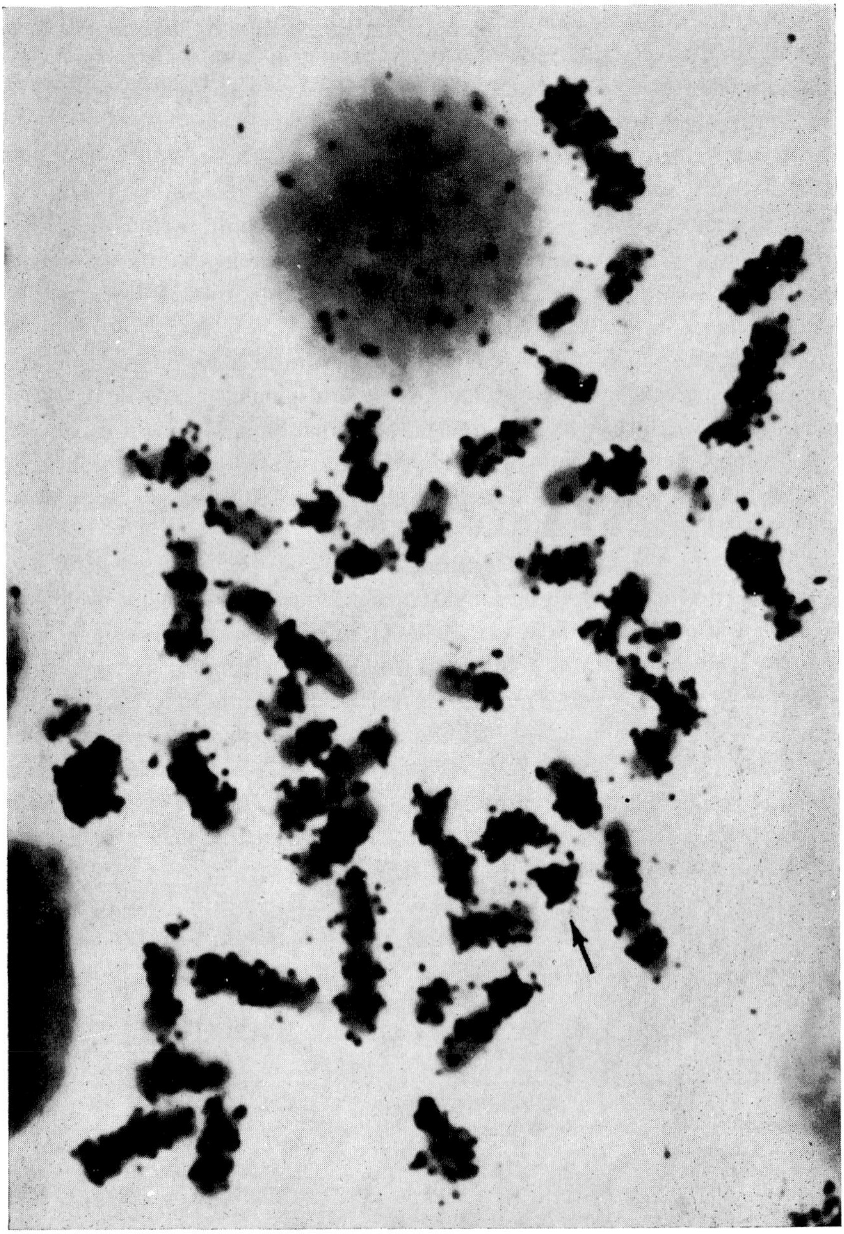

Fig. 6. Female patient with chronic granulocytic leukemia. 20 min H^3-thymidine pulse administered to leucocytes *in vitro* followed by fixation after 15 hr. The Philadelphia chromosome (Ph^1) is indicated by an arrow (compare Fig. 7). A nucleus belonging to another cell is seen at the top. (From Lima-de-Faria et al. 1967.) $\times$ 2,550.

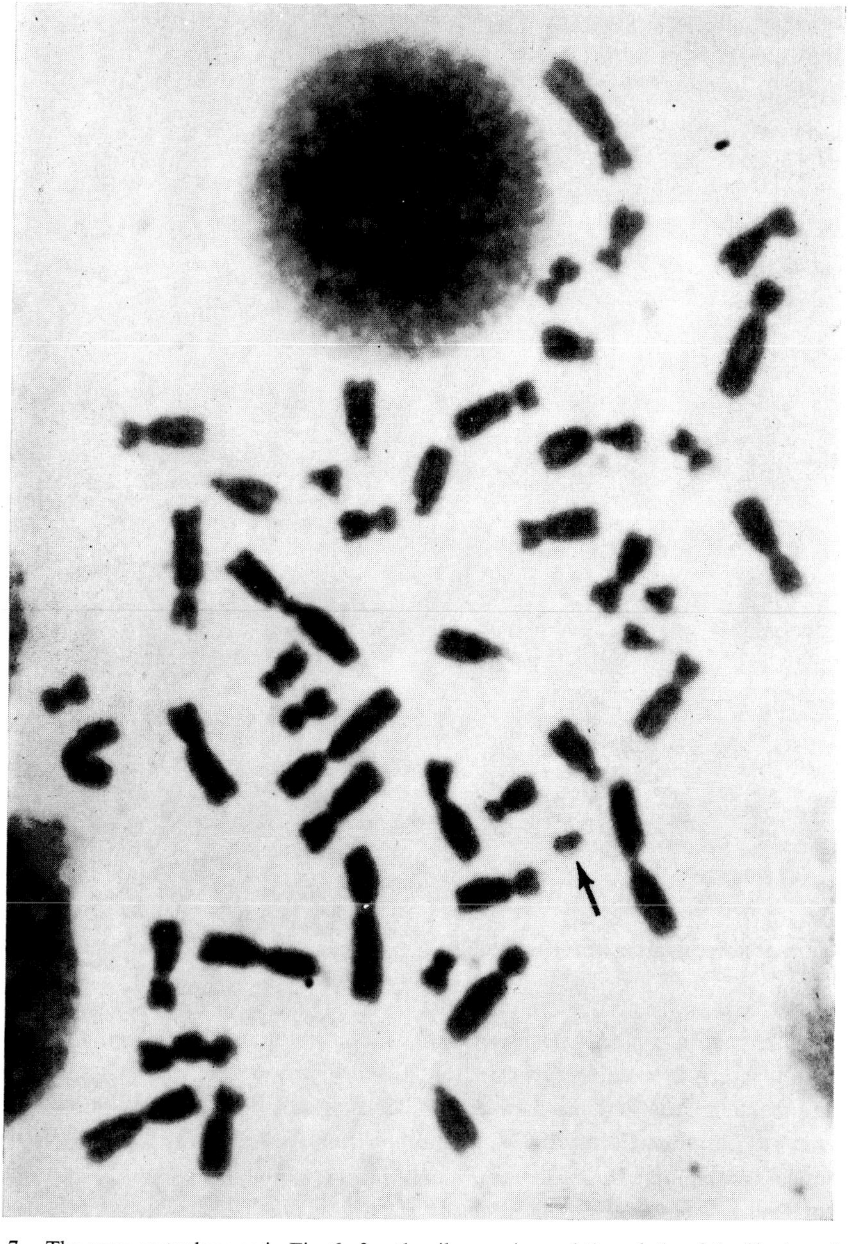

Fig. 7. The same metaphase as in Fig. 6 after the silver grains and the gelatin of the film have been removed. The Philadelphia chromosome is indicated by an arrow (compare Figs. 6, 8 and 9). × 2,550.

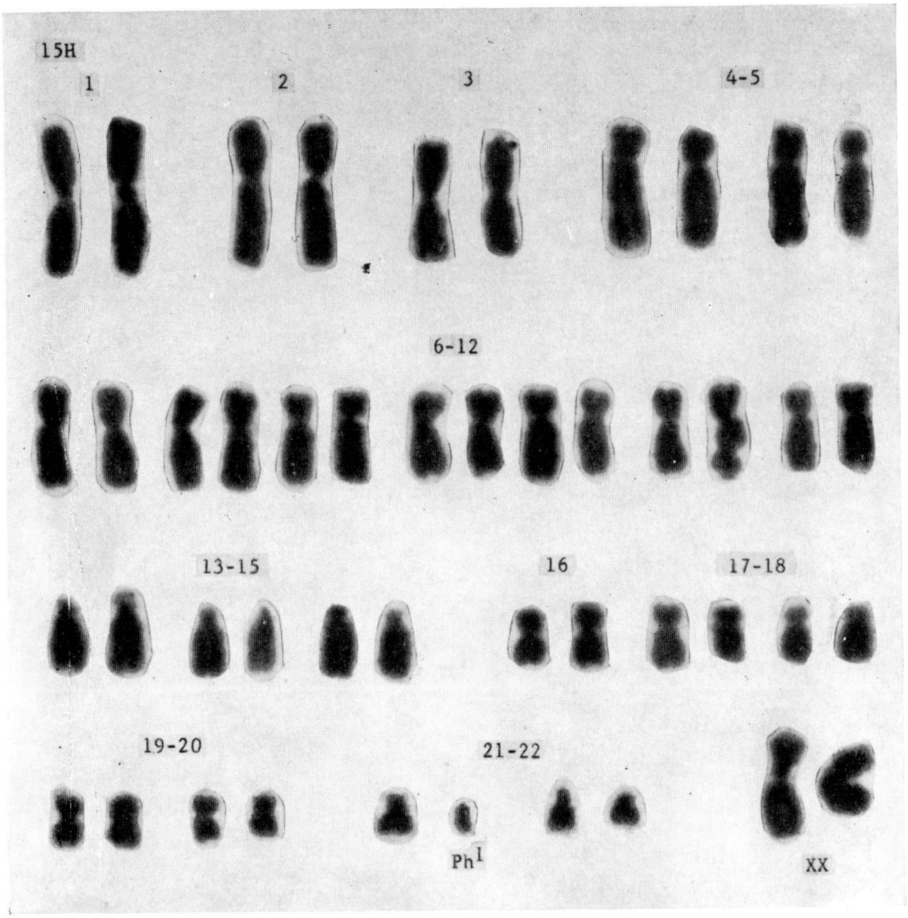

Fig. 8. Karyotype of metaphase shown in Fig. 7. The Philadelphia chromosome is marked as Ph^1.

The information available at present shows that in human chromosomes there is a system by which DNA units are turned on and off in a way that resembles the genetic bacterial system described by Jacob et al. The bacterial chromosome is known to be a circular DNA duplex (Cairns 1963). The replication of the DNA in this closed ring is explained by assuming the existence of an initiator and a replicator within the replicon (Jacob et al.). The use of similar systems for mammalian cells in which operator genes turn on or off structural genes, has been proposed by Ingram, on the basis of his data on the regulation of the synthesis of the hemoglobin molecules in human material. In human chromosomes such a system could also explain the behaviour of the replicons along the chromosome.

In *Drosophila melanogaster* Barigozzi found that in translocations involving the heterochromatic regions of the X- and Y-chromosomes the time of DNA replication of

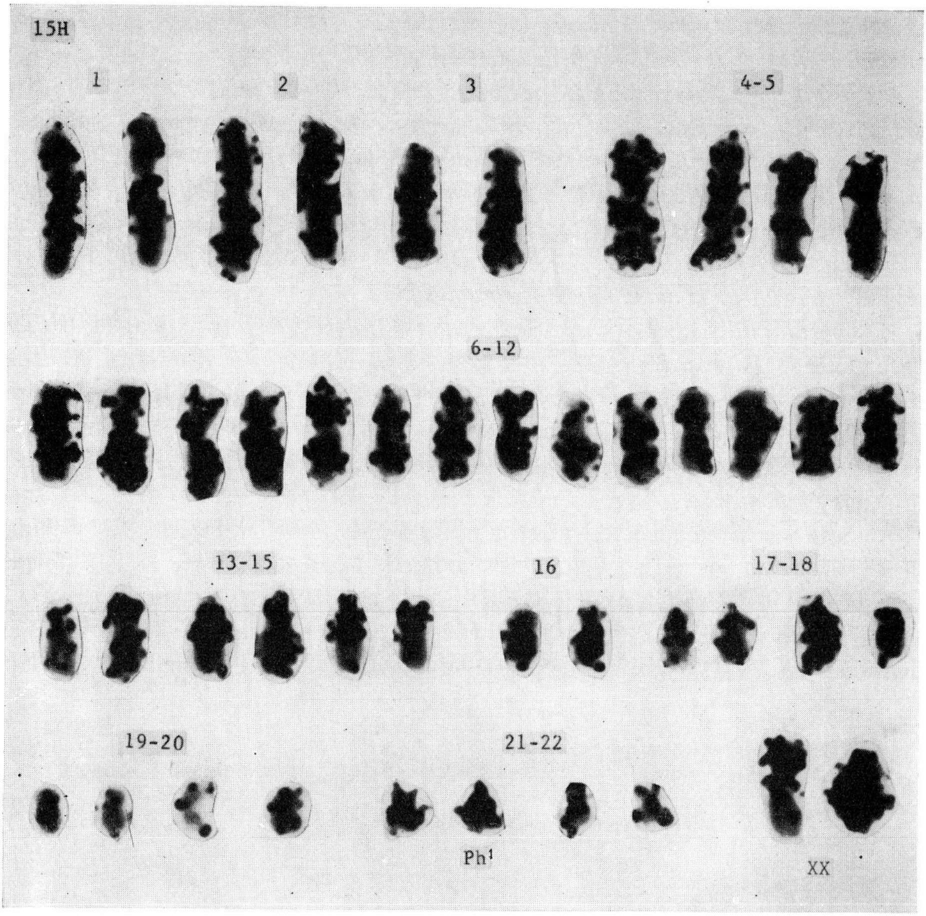

Fig. 9. The same karyotype as in Fig. 8 showing labelled chromosomes. Most chromosomes are heavily labelled including the Ph^1.

the replicons was affected by the presence of the translocated heterochromatic regions. This means that, in this case, the replicons are not fully independent.

It should be noted that the tritium picture obtained in a mitotic metaphase chromosome is quite a crude one. At this stage the chromosome is strongly condensed and the length of one micron in a metaphase chromosome corresponds to several microns in the same chromosome at mitotic prophase or pachytene. Moore and Uren have shown in *Protemndon bicolor* that the late-replicating segments seen with tritium autoradiography at metaphase, are composed of several minor units of replication when the same chromosome is studied at prophase. Thus, the human chromosome is most probably composed of many more minor replicons than those which can be disclosed by a study of mitotic metaphase chromosomes.

What we see in mitotic chromosomes are *major* replicons, which represent sequences of a large number of *minor* replicons, found at the level of the DNA molecule, and which happen to synthesize their DNA with a given degree of synchrony.

According to Pelling, in the giant chromosomes of *Chironomus tentans* there are 300 independently replicating units and these seem to be as many as the chromomeres or bands. In these chromosomes the hypothetical length of the replicating DNA pieces is 30 μ. This figure agrees with the average size of the replicon in mammalian chromosomes (Chinese hamster and HeLa cells) calculated by Hubermann and Riggs.

(c) *DNA synthesis in human meiotic chromosomes*

Due to various difficulties, DNA synthesis in meiotic chromosomes of man has hardly been studied. Human germ cells were labelled by injecting H^3-thymidine into the testes of inmates of penitentiaries by Heller and Clermont, but when such a procedure is used H^3-thymidine is incorporated into other cells of the human body as well. This leads to the permanent irradiation of chromosomes in cells of various somatic tissues of healthy individuals.

We have developed a method which avoids this procedure but permits the labelling of human chromosomes during meiosis (Lima-de-Faria et al. 1966, 1968a) Small specimens of tissue from testicular biopsies can be cultured *in vitro* from the period of DNA synthesis preceding meiosis to near the end of the prophase of the first meiotic division (Figs. 10–11). The meiotic cells and other testicular cells apparently develop

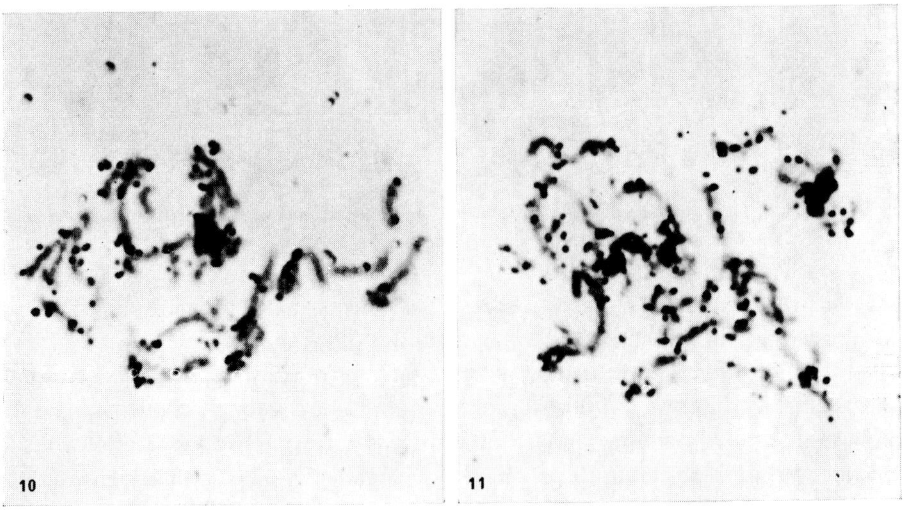

Figs. 10 and 11. Spermatocytes from testes biopsies of man were exposed to H^3-thymidine for 45 min *in vitro* followed by removal of the isotope and washing. The cells were subsequently cultured for 14 days and fixed. This is the space of time necessary for the spermatocytes to develop from interphase of meiosis to late pachytene. Two labelled late pachytene nuclei. The sex vesicle and the 22 autosome bivalents are separated from each other throughout most of their length. Feulgen squash. (From Lima-de-Faria et al. 1968a.) $\times$ 2,900.

normally in culture for periods extending to sixteen days. The *in vitro* incorporation of H^3-thymidine into human chromosomes of cells that may lead to the formation of spermatozoa opens the possibility of interfering with the genetic material of man in a readily accessible form. Mutations may be induced *in vitro* at the time of DNA synthesis. Moreover, this study discloses that, under the conditions of our experiments, DNA synthesis occurs at the interphase preceding meiosis and also at the early stages of the meiotic prophase: leptotene and leptotene-zygotene (Lima-de-Faria et al. 1966, 1968a). This is a finding of significance for the understanding of the mechanism of crossing-over because this phenomenon is known to occur at zygotene-pachytene (see chapter by Henderson).

4. *Gene amplification in heterochromatin*

The results of the study of DNA synthesis with H^3-autoradiography have improved our cytogenetic picture of heterochromatin by bringing our experimental approach to the level of DNA replication, but have not furnished data on the genetic constitution of this material.

Demonstration of gene amplification for ribosomal cistrons in heterochromatin has now been obtained following a biochemical analysis of the DNA-body of *Acheta domesticus*, house cricket (Lima-de-Faria et al. 1969)

In 1901 Giardina described for the first time a chromatin body that was only present in the nuclei of females of *Dytiscus*. This chromatin body was later studied in *Tipula*. The Feulgen reaction showed that it contained DNA and that it was built in contact with the sex chromosomes (Bauer 1931, 1933). The occurrence of the DNA body in several species of the *Tipulidae* was established by Bayreuther (1952, 1956).

(a) *Tritium autoradiography, ultrastructure and cytochemistry of the heterochromatic DNA body of Tipula*

An analysis of the DNA body of *Tipula*, which included incorporation of tritiated thymidine and spectrophotometric measurements, revealed the following (Lima-de-Faria 1960, 1962): (1) The DNA-body synthesised its DNA later than the chromosomes, (2) the body contained about 59% of the DNA of the nucleus, and (3) it disintegrated at the end of prophase of meiosis, the DNA being released into the nuclear sap.

To obtain further information on the nature of the DNA of the body of *Tipula* an ultrastructural and cytochemical analysis was carried out (Lma-de-Faria and Moses). When studied in the electron microscope, the DNA body appeared composed of a tight mass of intertwined fibrils. Demonstration that the main mass of the body was composed of DNA was obtained from cytochemical tests which revealed that the DNA body was Feulgen positive, stained green with azure B, incorporated H^3-thymidine and after digestion with DNase became Feulgen negative (Fig. 12 and Table 7). The DNA of the body is complexed with histone, like the DNA of the chromosomes, as was

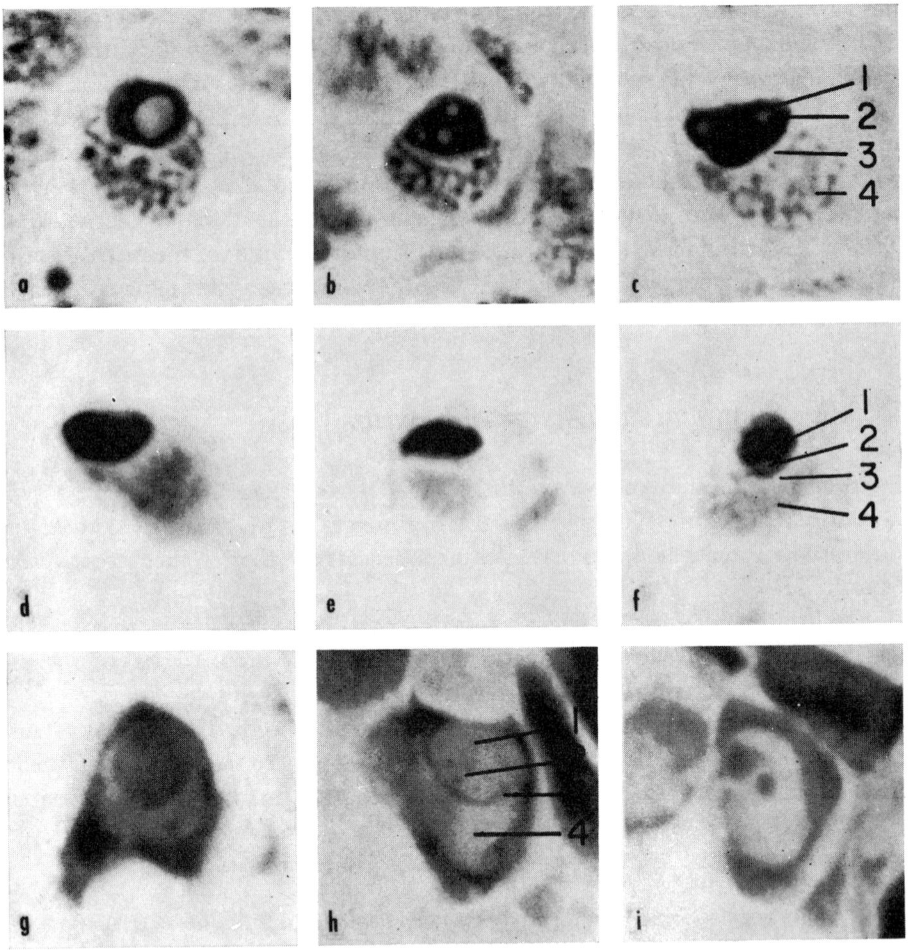

Fig. 12. *Tipula oleracea* oocytes at early prophase of meiosis. Light microscopy, cytochemical tests. *a* to *c*, Feulgen reaction: The Feulgen-positive body (1) contains Feulgen-negative nucleolar areas (2). Between the body and the chromosomes (4) there is a Feulgen-negative band (3). *d* to *f*, Alkaline fast green: the DNA body (1) stains heavily green, whereas the nucleolar areas (2) remain unstained. An alkaline fast green-negative band (3) is seen between the chromosomes (4) and the DNA body. *g* to *i*, azure B; the cytoplasm stains deep violet; the DNA body (1) is bright green; the nucleoli (2) stain violet; the band (3) between the body and the chromosomes stains violet; and the chromosomes (4) are green. Buffered formaldehyde; polyester wax. (From Lima-de-Faria and Moses.) ×2,750.

TABLE 7

Results of cytochemical methods applied to the oocytes of *Tipula oleracea*.

	DNA body		Band between DNA body and chromosomes	Chromosomes	Cytoplasm
	DNA mass	Nucleolar areas			
Feulgen reaction	+	–	–	+	–
Alkaline fast green	+	–	–	+	–
Azure B	Green	Violet	Violet	Green	Violet
DNase plus Feulgen	–	–	–	–	–
RNase plus azure B	Green	–	–	Green	–

From Lima-de-Faria and Moses (1966).

revealed by an intense alkaline fast green staining. Electron microscope examination of oocytes revealed that one side of the DNA body is in close contact with the nuclear envelope and that the other side possesses an outer shell composed mainly of particles 150 to 250 Å in diameter (Fig. 13). Between the outer shell and the chromosomes there is a band of low electron opacity, 4000 to 7000 Å thick. In the light microscope, this light band together with the outer shell is Feulgen negative and stains violet with azure B; this is confirmation of the presence of RNA. In the oocytes the nucleoli are found inside the DNA body. These nucleoli have a nucleolonema composed mainly of particles 150 to 250 Å. The nucleoli are Feulgen negative, alkaline fast green negative, stain violet with azure B, and do not stain with azure B after RNase digestion, thus confirming their RNA content (Fig. 12). The DNA body is indistinguishable from heterochromatin both in the light and electron microscopes. Since the DNA of the body was complexed with histone, as in the chromosomes, the body contained more than half of the DNA of the nucleus, and the nucleoli were located inside the body, the simplest interpretation of the DNA body was that it represented extra copies of the genes of the nucleolar organizing region or neighbouring regions. The situation found in *Tipula* had several basic features in common with the polytene chromosomes of other Diptera and with the hundreds of nucleoli present in *Triturus* oocytes. In all three cases, genes seemed to be copied hundreds of times but were kept in different types of packages.

This interpretation could only be tested biochemically and since *Tipula* is difficult to raise in the laboratory, we searched for another species with a similar body which would be easy to raise in large quantities. Such a species is *Acheta domesticus* (Nilsson).

(b) *Tritium autoradiography and cytochemistry of the heterochromatic DNA body of Acheta*

Tritium labelling and a cytochemical study of the ovaries of *Acheta domesticus* dis-

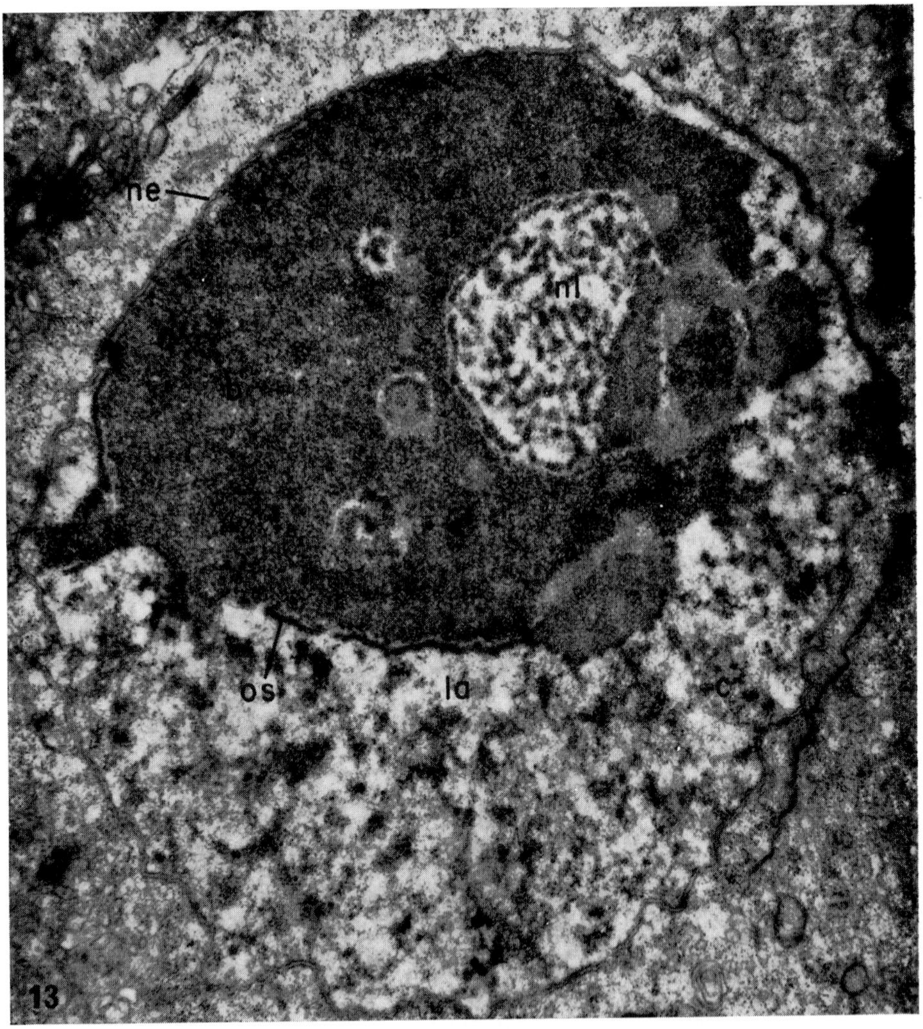

Fig. 13. *Tipula oleracea.* Oocyte at early prophase of meiosis, showing DNA body inside the nucleus. One side of the DNA body (*b*) is in close contact with the nuclear envelope (*ne*), and the other side is surrounded by an outer shell (*os*). A lighter area (*la*) is seen between the outer shell and the chromosome material (c). The circular area with a ramified nucleolonema inside the body is the main nucleolus (*nl*). Three smaller nucleolar islands are found to the left of the large nucleolus in the body. Buffered OsO_4; Epon. (From Lima-de-Faria and Moses.) ×18,000.

closed that the DNA body of this species is essentially similar to that of *Tipula* (Lima-de-Faria et al. 1968b). The body of *Acheta* is also a DNA mass indistinguishable from heterochromatin. The characteristics of the DNA body of *Acheta* were found to be the following; (1) the body is present in the females in the oogonia and oocytes, (2) it attains its largest size at the interphase before meiosis (Figs. 14–16), (3) a similar body is not present in the males at the corresponding stages, (4) the DNA body is active in DNA synthesis at the interphase and early prophase of meiosis, as disclosed by H^3-thymidine incorporation (Figs. 17–19), (5) the DNA of the DNA body is complexed with histone (6) the nucleoli are part of the body at interphase of meiosis, (7) at pachytene and diplotene a large shell of RNA is found around the DNA body (Fig. 20–22), (8) this shell is active in RNA synthesis at diplotene as disclosed by H^3-uridine incorporation, (9) the DNA body disintegrates at late diplotene (Fig. 23) releasing its DNA, RNA and histone into the nuclear sap (Lima-de-Faria et al. 1968b). Some of the properties of the DNA body of *Acheta* have also been studied by Heinonen and Halkka, Bier et al. and by Kunz.

The data just mentioned (Table 8) furnished the basis for planning the biochemical experiments.

TABLE 8

Results of cytochemical tests and tritium labeling in *Acheta* oocytes.

Stage of development of oocytes	Cell structure	Feulgen	Fast green	Azure B	H^3-thymidine	H^3-uridine
Interphase or early prophase of meiosis	DNA body	+	+	Green	+	weak or –
	Nucleoli inside body	–	–	Purple	–	weak
	Chromosomes	+	+	Green	+	weak or –
	Cytoplasm	–	–	Purple	–	weak
Diplotene	Inner DNA zone of body	+	+ or weak	Pale green	–	–
	Outer RNA zone of body	–	–	Purple	–	+
	Chromosomes	+	weak	Pale green	–	+
	Cytoplasm	–	–	Purple	–	–

From Lima-de-Faria et al. (1968b).

(c) *Biochemical analysis of the DNA of Acheta and the location of ribosomal cistrons in heterochromatin*

In *Xenopus laevis* a mutant has been described which does not contain nucleoli. A comparative biochemical analysis of the ribosomal cistrons in the wild type, the

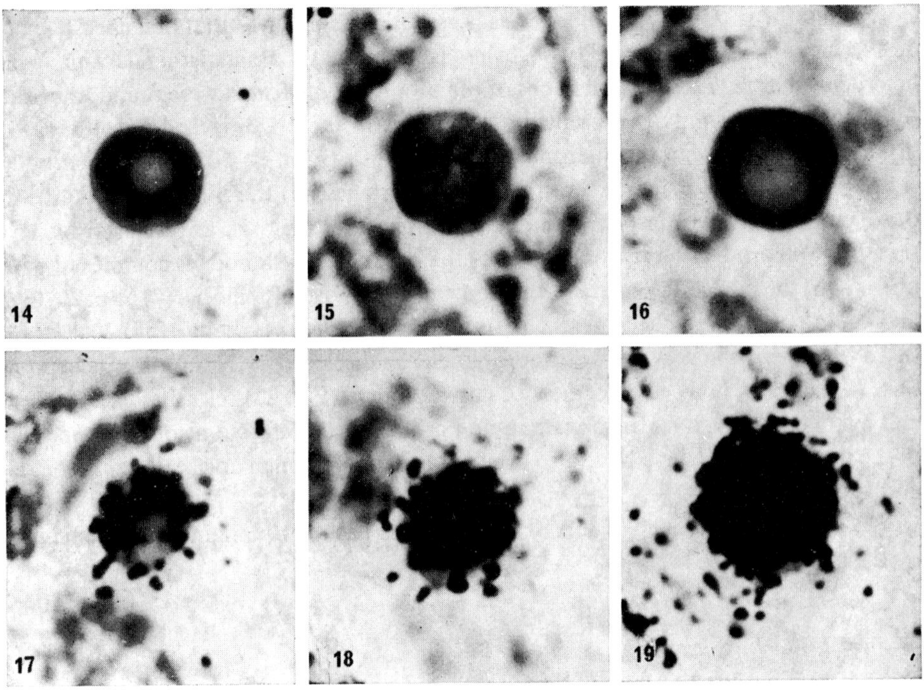

Figs. 14–19. *Acheta domesticus.* The DNA body at interphase or early prophase of meiosis stained with Feulgen (Figs. 14–16) and labeled with H^3-thymidine (Figs. 17–19). 3 μ sections. (From Lima-de-Faria et al. 1968b.) $\times$ 2,550.

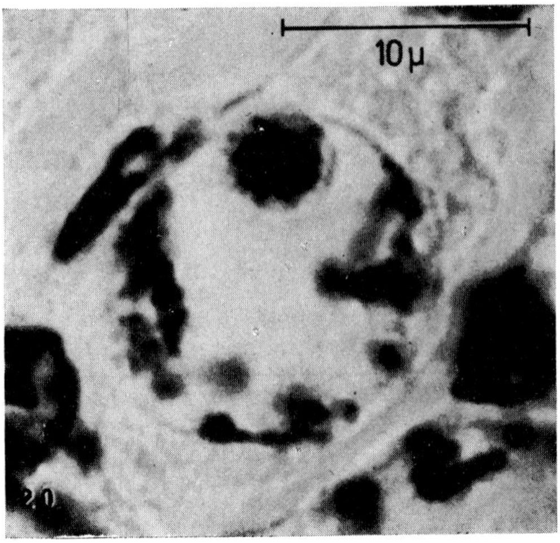

Fig. 20. *Acheta domesticus.* Oocytes. Feulgen staining. The DNA body at late pachytene, showing the inner Feulgen positive DNA core from which fibrils radiate into a Feulgen negative outer shell. 3 μ sections. (From Lima-de-Faria et al. 1968b.) $\times$ 2,400.

heterozygote and the mutant has permitted the allocation of the ribosomal cistrons in or near the nucleolus organizing region (Wallace and Birnstiel 1966; Birnstiel et al. 1966).

In *Acheta* such a mutant is not available but a comparable situation occurs. The females possess a DNA body in the oogonia and oocytes but no DNA body of comparable size is present in the spermatocytes. Moreover, the DNA body is known to synthesize its DNA at the interphase and early prophase of meiosis, but is not active in DNA synthesis at diplotene. Thus, in the biochemical analysis a comparison was made between (1) the DNA extracted from ovaries versus that extracted from testes, and (2) the DNA extracted from ovaries at the time the DNA body is replicating its DNA versus that of ovaries at pachytene-diplotene, when DNA replication is not occurring in the DNA body (Fig. 24).

The experiments of Lima-de-Faria et al. (1969) demonstrate a differential amplification of ribosomal cistrons in the ovaries of *Acheta domesticus*, and locate this differential amplification in the DNA body. The sources of evidence are the following (1) There is a DNA satellite in the analytical centrifuge which has a calculated GC content of 56% (Fig. 25). (2) The ribosomal RNA of *Acheta* has a GC content of the order of 56%. (3) The hybridisation peak between ribosomal RNA and DNA of *Acheta* occurs at the position of the DNA satellite (Figs. 26 and 27). (4) The DNA satellite of ovaries at interphase of meiosis, where the DNA body is largest, contains 14% of the ovarian DNA, whereas the DNA satellite of testes, where no DNA body of comparable size is present contains 0.8% of the testes DNA. (5) The amount of satellite DNA in the ovaries at interphase is 18 times higher than in the testes. (6) Finally, the hybridisation experiments at the saturation level reveal that a similar degree of amplification of ribosomal cistrons exists in the ovaries at interphase when compared with testes.

The fact that the DNA body of *Acheta* contains extra copies of ribosomal cistrons is in agreement with the prediction made for the DNA body of *Tipula* (Lima-de-Faria and Moses 1966) and for the DNA body of *Acheta* (Lima-de-Faria et al. 1968) that this cell structure contained extra copies of the genes of the nucleolar organising region. The same situation occurs in the DNA body of two other insect species, *Dytiscus* and *Colymbetes*, as has been shown by Gall et al. Gene amplification has previously been thoroughly investigated in amphibians, where preferential synthesis and amplification of the DNA in the oocyte is evident (Gall; Brown and Dawid; Evans and Birnstiel).

The DNA body of *Tipula* and *Acheta* is indistinguishable from heterochromatin and is one of the classical examples of heterochromatin.

The evidence is the following. (1) In *Tipula* and *Acheta* the DNA body is a Feulgen positive mass, at interphase of mitosis (oogonia) and at interphase of meiosis (oocytes). (2) In *Tipula* the DNA body is a part of the sex chromosomes and in *Acheta* is part of an autosome. (3) In both species the nucleoli are found inside or around the DNA mass, the DNA mass is the classical example of nucleolus associated heterochromatin described by Heitz (1928, 1931, 1933, 1934, 1935) and later studied by Caspersson and Schultz (Caspersson 1950). One can either describe this structure as a DNA body con-

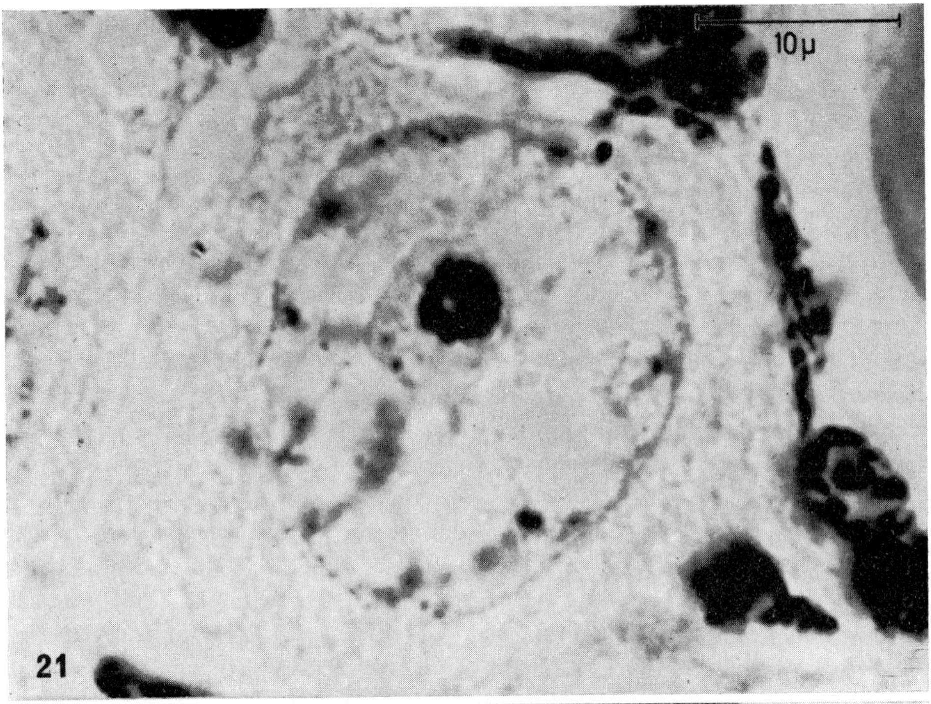

21

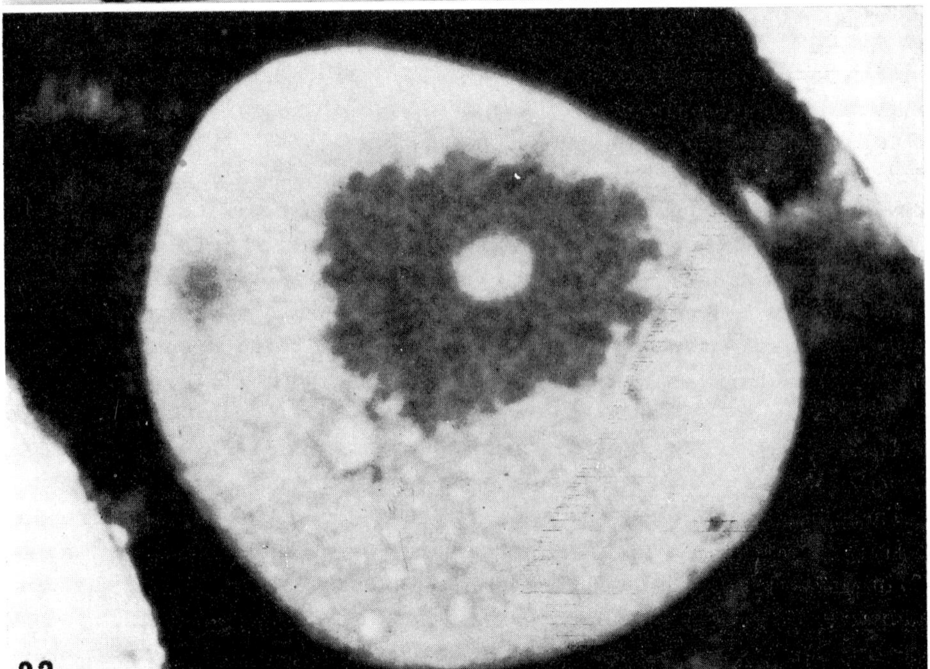

22

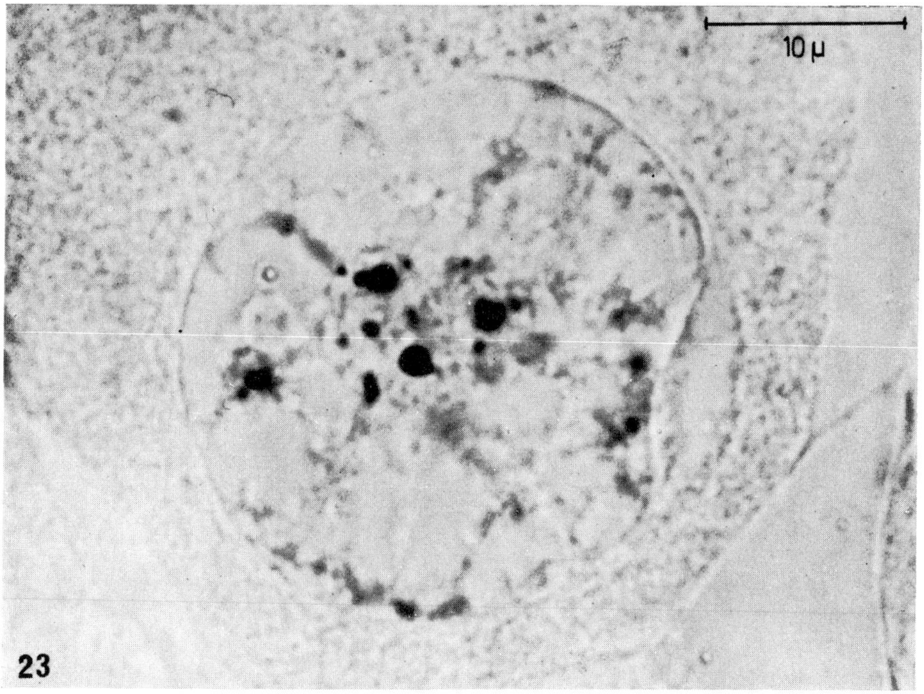

Fig. 23. *Acheta domesticus.* Diplotene. Feulgen staining. The final stage of the disintegration of the DNA body. The body breaks down into a series of minor components and finally vanishes. 3 μ sections. (From Lima-de-Faria et al. 1968b.) $\times$ 2,250.

ORGAN	OVARIES		TESTES
DIAMETER	200 μ	1–2 mm	2 mm
MAIN STAGES OF MEIOSIS	INTERPHASE	PACHYTENE DIPLOTENE	VARIOUS STAGES
DNA BODY	PRESENT	PRESENT	ABSENT
DNA SYNTHESIS IN BODY	ACTIVE	NO SYNTHESIS	——

Fig. 24. Developmental stages of ovaries and testes of *Acheta* used in biochemical experiments. (From Lima-de-Faria et al. 1969.)

Figs. 21 and 22. *Acheta domesticus.* Oocytes at diplotene.

Fig. 21. Feulgen staining. The DNA body consists of a Feulgen positive inner zone from which fibrils protrude into a large Feulgen negative shell. The lampbrush chromosomes are only faintly stained.

Fig. 22. Azure B. The cytoplasm and the outer shell of the DNA body are stained purple-violet (RNA). The inner zone of the DNA body, the fibrils which radiate from it and the chromosomes are pale green (DNA). 3 μ sections. (From Lima-de-Faria et al. 1968b.) $\times$ 2,300.

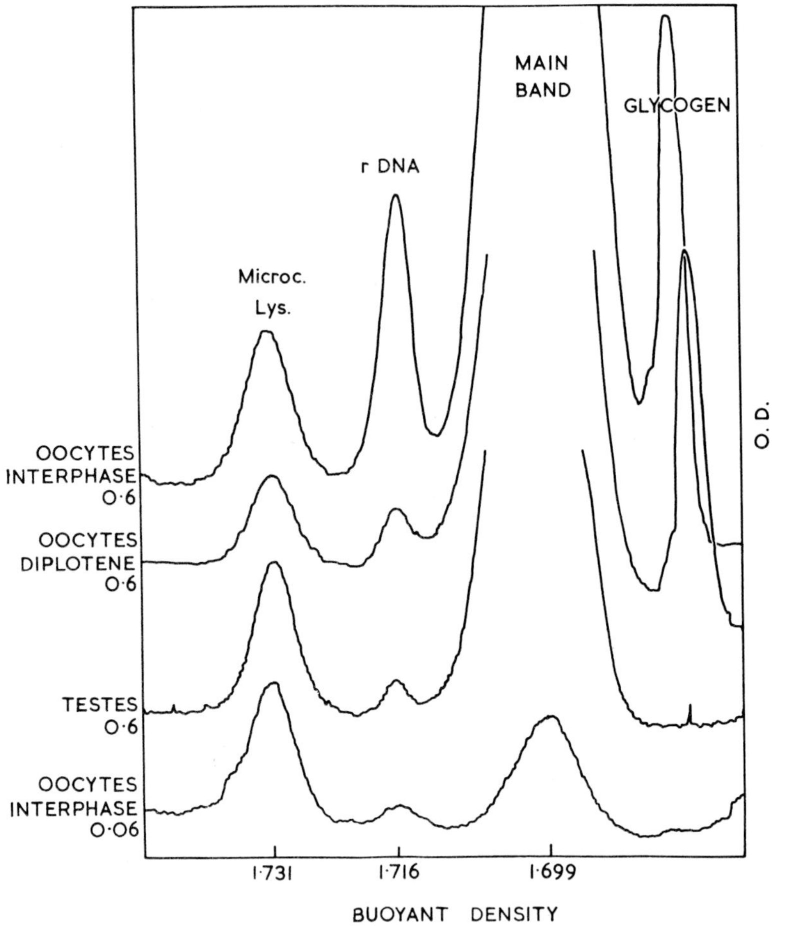

Fig. 25. Analytical centrifugation of the DNA of different tissues of *Acheta*. 0.6 O.D. of DNA from oocytes at interphase of meiosis is compared with the same amount of DNA from oocytes at diplotene and from testes. The relation between the amount of DNA in the satellite and the main band is better seen in the picture given by a ten-times-diluted sample of DNA (0.06 O.D., 2 μg total, bottom curve). No other satellite is present between the main band and the marker DNA from *Micrococcus lysodeikticus*. The buoyant density of the main band is 1.699 g.cm^{-3} and that of the satellite is 1.716 g.cm^{-3}. The amount of DNA contained in the satellite of ovaries at interphase, where the DNA body is largest, is 18 times that found in the satellite of the testes where no DNA body of comparable size is present. rDNA, ribosomal DNA; O.D., optical density. (From Lima-de-Faria et al. 1969.)

taining nucleoli or as nucleoli containing or being surrounded by a large mass of heterochromatin. (4) In the electron microscope the DNA body is indistinguishable from heterochromatin both in *Tipula* (Lima-de-Faria and Moses) and in *Acheta* (Jaworska and Lima-de-Faria).

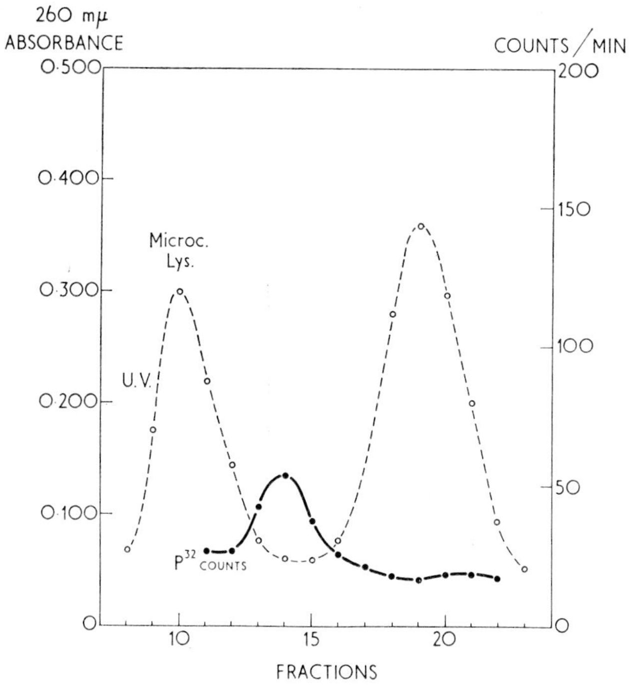

Fig. 26. Hybridisation between unlabelled DNA (ovaries) and P^{32}-labelled ribosomal RNA. The position of the peak of hybridisation relative to the positions of the main DNA band (1.699 $g.cm^{-3}$) of *Acheta* and of the DNA of *Micrococcus lysodeikticus* (1.731 $g.cm^{-3}$). After the optical density of each gradient fraction had been measured, fractions 11–22, between the marker and the end of the main band, were selected for hybridisation and challenged with *Acheta* P^{32}-rRNA. It may be seen that the hybridisation curve peaks at fraction 14. This is the position which corresponds exactly with the location of the DNA satellite seen in the analytical centrifuge (where the DNA of *Micrococcus lysodeikticus* was also used as a marker; from Lima-de-Faria et al. 1969).

Thus, the results of Lima-de-Faria et al. (1969) locate the ribosomal cistrons in the nucleolus associated heterochromatin.

Evidence that ribosomal cistrons are present in the nucleolus organizing region was obtained in *Xenopus* by Wallace and Birnstiel and in *Drosophila melanogaster* by Ritossa and Spiegelman. Redundancy of ribosomal cistrons is also present in this and other *Drosophila* species (Ritossa). The nucleolus organizing region of *Drosophila melanogaster*, situated in the X-chromosome, is a well-known case of heterochromatin.

The presence of cistrons for ribosomal RNA in the heterochromatin shows that this chromosomal material contains genes that participate in one of the basic cellular processes i.e. protein synthesis.

The DNA body of *Acheta* is not particularly active in RNA synthesis at the interphase of meiosis when it is a compact heterochromatic mass. At pachytene and diplotene many Feulgen positive threads untwist and protrude from this heterochromatic mass and are embedded in a shell of RNA. At this stage the DNA body gets the appearance of a large 'puff'. Incorporation of H^3-uridine discloses that the RNA shell is active in RNA synthesis. Thus, the genes present in the DNA body become particularly active as the heterochromatic condition turns into a 'puff' structure where the different copies separate from each other. Finally these copies become free during the disintegration of the DNA body which occurs at late diplotene (Lima-de-Faria et al. 1968b).

Genetic activity associated with the heterochromatin has also been shown to occur in the Y-chromosome of *Drosophila melanogaster* where partially or totally Y deficient males lack functional spermatids. These males seem to possess all structural components of spermatid organelles but their assembly into functional units is partially or totally inhibited in these animals (Meyer).

The presence of amplification of ribosomal cistrons in the nucleolus associated heterochromatin of *Acheta* and other insect species, does not necessarily imply that ribosomal cistrons are present in other heterochromatic regions of these same species or in the heterochromatin of other species. Most probably the bulk ofheterochromatin in most species does not contain ribosomal cistrons. However, it remains to be seen whether other heterochromatic regions or heterochromatin in other organisms contain amplification or redundancy for other types of genes.

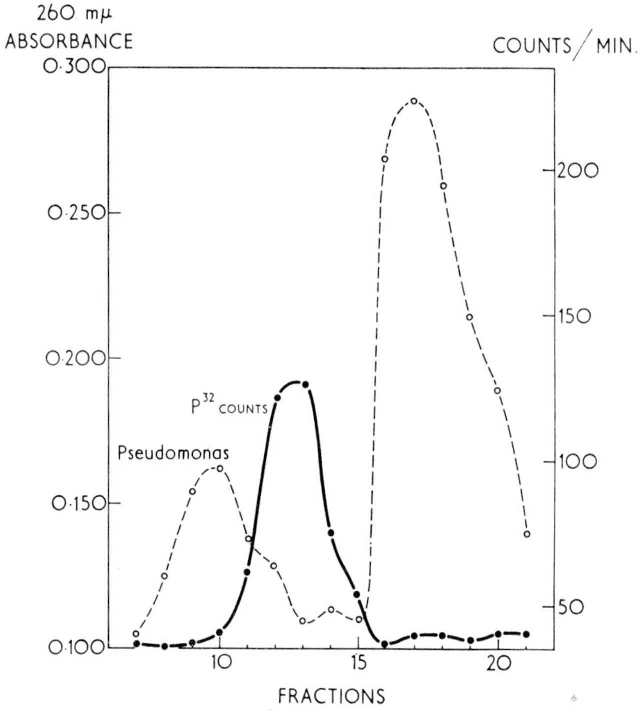

Fig. 27. The hybridisation peak between P^{32} ribosomal RNA (28S+18S) from *Acheta* and the unlabelled ovarian DNA (interphase of meiosis) occurs at the same density position as in the previous experiments. DNA of *Pseudomonas aeruginosa* (1.727 g.cm^{-3}) was added as a marker. (From Lima-de-Faria et al. 1969.)

In our experiments we observed that the efficiency with which *Acheta* satellite DNA annealed to ribosomal RNA was low (Lima-de-Faria et al. 1969). A similar observation has been made by Gall et al. for ribosomal DNA of *Dytiscus* and *Colymbetes*. The fact that only a small percentage of the satellite DNA hybridises in all three cases with ribosomal RNA indicates that the DNA body contains other DNA sequences which do not code for ribosomal RNA, but which are amplified as well. Thus, the heterochromatic mass of the DNA body, contains other DNA sequences which do not code for ribosomal RNA, but which are amplified as well. Thus the heterochromatic mass of the DNA body contains ribosomal cistrons but predominantly other DNA sequences whose function is unknown.

Heterochromatin is a state of the chromosome since, in insects such as coccids, a given chromosome set becomes heterochromatic during embryonic development and at a later stage of development the same chromosome set reverts to the euchromatic state (Nur).

The situation in *Acheta* may not be very different from that in the coccids. The nucleolar heterochromatin is found in large amounts in the oogonia and oocytes (DNA body) and later at diplotene is released from the chromosome as the body disintegrates (Lima-de-Faria et al. 1968b). At the following stages of meiosis the nucleolar region of the chromosome reverts to its euchromatic condition, since the extra copies are no longer attached to the chromosome. What contributes to make the situation in *Acheta* look different, is the fact that the very large number of extra copies that are formed cannot be easily accommodated within the body of the chromosome and are obliged to form the large protuberance that for the sake of simplicity is called the DNA body. The DNA body actually appears in the oogonia where it is only 2 μ in diameter and increases appreciably in size in the oocytes where it becomes 6 μ in diameter (Lima-de-Faria et al. 1968b). Thus, the degree of heterochromatinization at the nucleolar organising region increases first in the oogonia, becomes still larger in the oocytes and by late diplotene diminishes, the chromosome region reverting to its previous state.

The problem that remains is to find out whether heterochromatin in other chromosome regions or other species represents gene redundancy or amplification, as it does in the nucleolus organising region, or whether it represents some other form of molecular organisation or both.

(d) *Ultrastructural analysis of the DNA body of Acheta and the presence of multiple synaptonemal complexes in this structure*

The DNA body of *Acheta* was studied with the electron microscope (Jaworska and Lima-de-Faria). Ovaries were fixed at two stages of development: (1) ovaries containing oocytes mainly at pachytene and diplotene, and (2) ovaries containing mainly oocytes at interphase and early prophase of meiosis.

The electron microscope study was accompanied by two types of controls. (1) Thick sections were cut adjacent to the thin sections used in the E.M., and were ana-

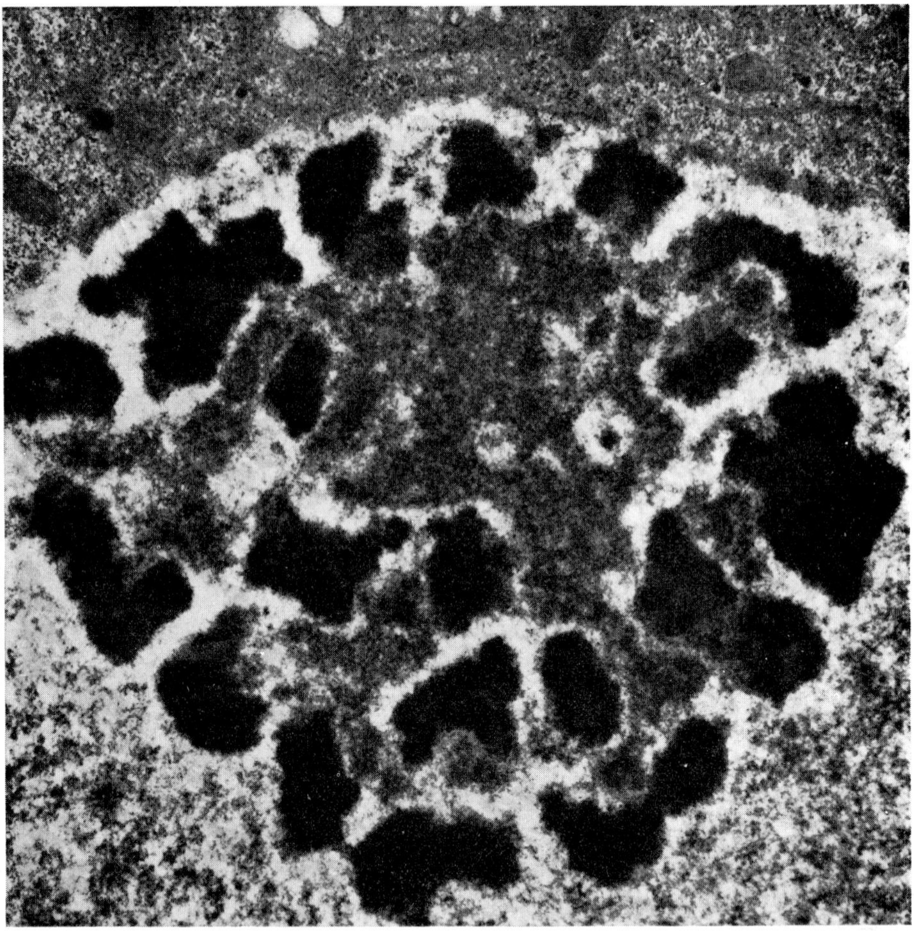

Fig. 28. *Acheta domesticus.* Oocyte at late pachytene showing DNA body. One side of the DNA body is near the nuclear envelope, and the other side faces the chromosome material (lower part of figure). The DNA body consists of an inner zone of fibrillar material (DNA zone, see Figs. 20 and 21) from which stretches of fibrillar material radiate into an outer region composed of islands of dense material (RNA zone, see Fig. 22). Buffered gluteraldehyde plus OsO_4. Epon-araldite. Uranyl acetate plus lead citrate. × 23,500.

lysed in the light microscope after methyl green-pyronin and toluidine blue staining. This permitted us to identify the meiotic stage and the shape of the DNA body. (2) As described above (Table 8), ovaries at comparable stages of development were fixed in acetic-alcohol or 4% formaldehyde and the paraffin sections were subsequently stained with Feulgen, Azure B and alkaline Fast Green for the identification, in different components of the DNA body, of DNA, RNA and histones respectively. Incorporation of H^3-thymidine and H^3-uridine was also used to determine the period of DNA and RNA replication and the location of the incorporation in the body (Table 8).

In the ovaries containing cells mainly at pachytene-diplotene it can be seen in the light microscope that the body consists of an inner DNA zone and an outer RNA zone. From the inner DNA region protrude Feulgen positive fibres which extend into the RNA zone. This gives the body the appearance of a large puff (Figs. 20–22 and Table 8).

The electron microscope picture agrees quite well with that seen in the light microscope. In the DNA body at pachytene there is a central zone consisting of a fibrillar material (the DNA zone) and an outer region formed by small areas of darkly stained

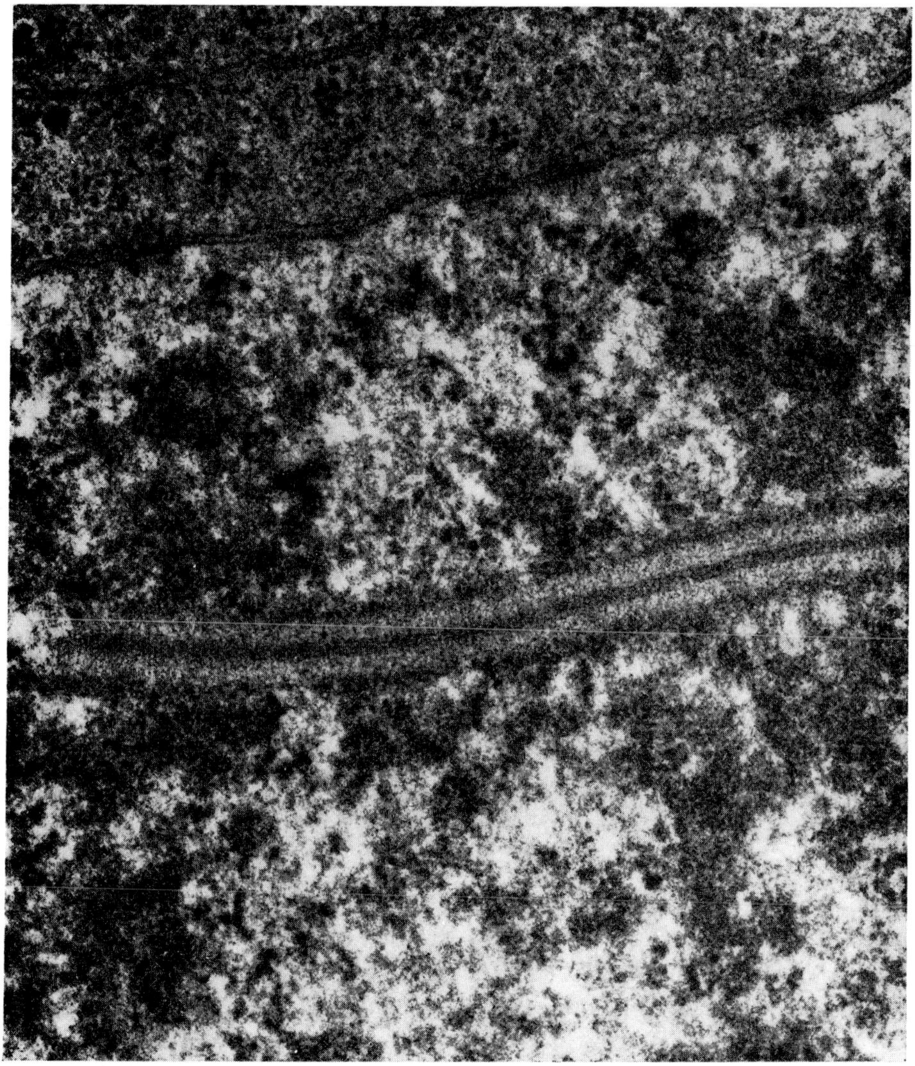

Fig. 29. *Acheta deomesticus*. Oocyte at late pachytene showing a single synaptonemal complex in a region of the nucleus. Buffered gluteraldehyde plus OsO_4. Epon-araldite. Uranyl acetate plus lead citrate. $\times$ 60,000.

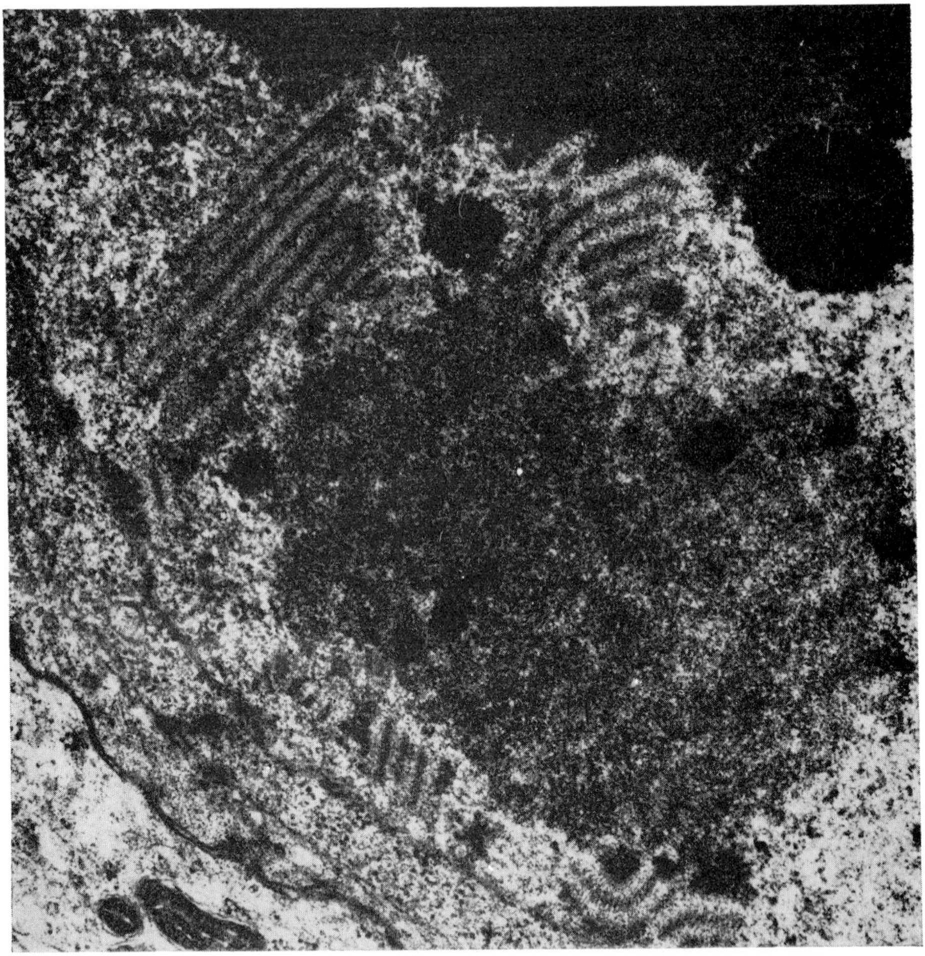

Fig. 30. *Acheta domesticus.* Oocyte at interphase or early prophase of meiosis showing the three components found at this stage in the DNA body: (1) several packages of multiple synaptonemal complexes, (2) a fibrillar chromatin mass in the middle and around the complexes, and (3) small and large areas of dense material, which are usually circular. Buffered formaldehyde. Epon-araldite. Uranyl acetate plus lead citrate. × 34,500.

material (RNA region) which appear as islands located around the central zone. The central fibrillar mass extends into the outer region in the form of many stretches of fibrillar material which occur between the dark masses (Fig. 28). This is the same situation as in the light microscope where the Feulgen positive fibres extend into the RNA area (Figs. 20–21). At this stage synaptonemal complexes are seen in the nucleus, but are seldom associated with the DNA body. They are present as single units in other unspecific nuclear regions (Fig. 29).

In the oocytes at interphase and early prophase of meiosis, where the DNA body is active in DNA replication, the DNA body appears in the light microscope as a large Feulgen positive sphere containing Feulgen negative areas (Figs. 14–16). In the electron microscope, at this stage, it consists of three main components. (1) A fibrillar material which is similar to that seen in the DNA inner zone of the body at pachytene. (2) Islands of dense material which are similar to the islands of the outer RNA region

Fig. 31. *Acheta domesticus.* Oocyte at interphase or early prophase of meiosis. The DNA body contains a package of 12 synaptonemal complexes starting from a centre (at the bottom of figure), oriented in a circular fashion and parallel to each other. Buffered formaldehyde. Epon-araldite. Uranyl acetate plus lead citrate. × 62,000.

seen at pachytene. At interphase these areas are much fewer than at pachytene and are of many different sizes, some of them being quite small. This suggests that they are in the process of formation. (3) At interphase synaptonemal complexes are an integral part of the DNA body and they appear grouped in large numbers (Fig. 30).

This last component deserves special attention since the complexes are known to occur in connection with chromosome pairing, and gene amplification is present in the DNA body.

The synaptonemal complexes show the following features (1) They are packed side by side building large assemblies. (2) This packing starts from one or several centres. (3) The complexes are parallel to each other and are arranged in a circular fashion related to the position of each center. (4) As many as 16 synaptonemal complexes have been found to be packed together in this circular fashion (Fig. 31).

This number of synaptonemal complexes agrees well with the degree of amplification found by biochemical methods at this stage. There are about 18 times more ribosomal cistrons in ovaries at interphase of meiosis than in testes where no DNA body of comparable size is present.

Do the multiple complexes seen in the DNA body represent the amplification process demonstrated biochemically? The evidence available at present does not allow a definite answer to this question for the following reasons. (1) At this stage the chromosomes seem to be in a kind of bouquet stage and the packing of the complexes could be related to the packing of the chromosomes. These would separate at a later stage liberating the complexes from one another. This interpretation is, however, improbable due to the fact that there are only 11 bivalents in *Acheta* and as many as 16 complexes are seen together. (2) The actual process of formation of the complex and its exact relation to the paired chromosomes at pachytene is so far unknown. Moreover, it is not known at present whether the synaptonemal complex contains DNA (see chapter by Sotelo).

Thus, the multiple complexes may be a structure that may reflect the amplification without necessarily being a physical image of the actual process of amplification. They may just be formed in between the extra copies of the nucleolar cistrons, or they may have nothing to do with the amplification as such. However, since the complexes are an integral part of the DNA body they are most probably related in one way or another to the amplification process.

5. *Summary and conclusions*

The following aspects of the molecular organization of heterochromatin were discussed.

(1) Heterochromatin replicates its DNA later than euchromatin. The general occurrence of this phenomenon establishes it as a rule of chromosome replication.

(2) The timing of DNA replication is affected by differentiation. There are organisms where the time of DNA synthesis of given chromosomes or chromosome regions changes

during development. This phenomenon is connected with the change from euchromatin to heterochromatin.

(3) There is a relation between late ending of DNA synthesis in heterochromatin and late beginning of DNA synthesis in the same chromosome or chromosome region. The late beginning of heterochromatic regions seems to be quite a widespread phenomenon, if not of general occurrence, but the difference at the beginning of synthesis between euchromatin and heterochromatin seems to be less pronounced than at the end of the S period.

(4) The replication units of chromosomes, or replicons, have been most extensively studied in mammalian and human chromosomes. Major replicons are the units of replication seen in prophase or metaphase chromosomes. These are composed of minor replicons which are present at the level of the DNA molecule. Structural rearrangements involving euchromatic and heterochromatic regions show that major replicons are to a large extent independent of each other, but that in given cases some replicons may affect the time of replication of other chromosome segments.

(5) Tritium autoradiography, cytochemistry and a biochemical analysis have disclosed the occurrence of gene amplification in the heterochromatic DNA body of *Acheta domesticus*. The DNA body contains extra copies of the cistrons for ribosomal RNA. There are about 18 times more ribosomal cistrons in ovaries at interphase or early prophase of meiosis, where the DNA body is largest, than in the testes where no DNA body of comparable size is present.

(6) The ultrastructural analysis of the heterochromatic DNA body at the interphase or early prophase of meiosis shows the presence of large packages of synaptonemal complexes in this structure. These packages start from one or several centres, the complexes are arranged in a circular fashion and parallel to each other. As many as 16 complexes have been found to be packed together in this circular fashion. This number of complexes agrees well with the degree of amplification for ribosomal cistrons present in the DNA body, but the actual relation between the complexes and the amplification demands further study.

Aknowledgements

This work was supported by research grants from the Swedish Natural Science Research Council.

References

ALLFREY, V.G. and A.E. MIRSKY: Mechanisms of synthesis and control of protein and ribonucleic acid synthesis in the cell nucleus. Cold Spring Harbor Symp. Quant. Biol. 28 (1963) 247.

ATKINS, L., J.A. BÖÖK, K.H. GUSTAVSON, O. HANSSON and H. HJELM: A case of XXXXY sex chromosome anomaly with autoradiographic studies. Cytogenetics 2 (1963) 208.

ATKINS, L. and K. H. GUSTAVSON: The pattern of DNA synthesis in human chromosomes in cells with an XXY sex chromosome constitution. Hereditas 51 (1964) 135.

BADER, S., O. F. MILLER and B. B. MUKHERJEE: Observations on chromosome duplication in cultured human leucocytes. Exptl. Cell Res. 31 (1963) 100.

BAER, D.: Asynchronous replication of DNA in a heterochromatic set of chromosomes in *Pseudococcus obscurus*. Genetics 52 (1965) 275.

BARIGOZZI, C.: DNA replication pattern of somatic chromosomes of *D. melanogaster*. XII Int. Congress of Genetics Tokyo (1968) 71.

BARIGOZZI, C., S. DOLFINI, M. FRACCARO, G. R. RAIMONDI and L. TIEPOLO: In vitro study of the DNA replication patterns of somatic chromosomes of *Drosophila melanogaster*. Exptl. Cell Res. 43 (1966) 231.

BARR, M. L.: Correlations between sex chromatin patterns and sex chromosome complexes in Man. In: K. L. Moore, ed.: The sex chromatin. Saunders Co. (1966) p. 128.

BAUER, H.: Die chromosomen von *Tipula paludosa* meig. in Eibeldung und Spermatogenese. Z. Zellforsch. 14 (1931) 138.

BAUER, H.: Die Wachsende Oocytenkerne einiger Insekten in ihrem Verhalten zur Nucleal Färbung. Z. Zellforsch. 18 (1933) 254.

BAYREUTHER, K.: Extra-chromosomale Feulgen Positive Körper (Nukleinkörper) in der Oogenese des Tipuliden. Naturwissenschaften 39 (1952) 71.

BAYREUTHER, K.: Die Oogenese der Tipuliden. Chromosoma 7 (1956) 508.

BENDER, M. A. and D. M. PRESCOTT: DNA synthesis and mitosis in cultures of human peripheral leucocytes. Exptl. Cell Res. 27 (1962) 221.

BENIRSCHKE, K., R. J. LOW, L. E. BROWNHILL, L. B. CADAY and J. DE VENECIA-FERNANDEZ: Chromosome studies of a donkey-grevy zebra hybrid. Chromosoma 15 (1964) 1.

BERLOWITZ, L.: Correlation of genetic activity, heterochromatinization and RNA metabolism. Proc. Natl. Acad. Sci. 53 (1965) 68.

BIANCHI, N. O. and M. S. A. DE BIANCHI: DNA replication sequence of human chromosomes in blood cultures. Chromosoma 17 (1965) 273.

BIANCHI, N. O. and M. S. A. DE BIANCHI: Shifting in the duplication time of sex chromosomes in the rat. Chromosoma 19 (1966) 286.

BIER, K., W. KUNZ and D. RIBBERT: Struktur und Funktion der Oocyten-chromosomen und Nukleolen sowie der Extra-DNA während der Oogeneses panoistischer und meroistischer Insekten. Chromosoma 23 (1967) 214.

BIRNSTIEL, M. L., J. SPEIRS, I. PURDOM, K. JONES and U. E. LOENING: Properties and composition of the isolated ribosomal DNA satellite of *Xenopus laevis*. Nature 219 (1968) 454.

BIRNSTIEL, M. L., H. WALLACE, J. L. SIRLIN and M. FISCHBERG: Localisation of the ribosomal DNA complements in the nucleolar organiser region of *Xenopus laevis*. In: W. S. Vincent and O. L. Miller, Jr., eds.: International Symp. on the Nucleolus, its structure and function. Natl. Cancer Inst. Monograph 23 (1966) 431.

BISHOP, A. and O. N. BISHOP: Analysis of tritium labelled human chromosomes and sex chromatin. Nature 199 (1963) 930.

BONNER, J.: The molecular biology of development. Oxford, Claredon Press (1965) p. 155.

BOOTHROYD, E. R. and A. LIMA-DE-FARIA: DNA synthesis and differential reactivity in the chromosomes of Trillium at low temperature. Hereditas 52 (1964) 122.

BROWN, D. D. and I. B. DAWID: Specific gene amplification in oocytes. Science 160 (1968) 272.

BROWN, R. C., W. L. K. CASTLE, W. H. HUFFINES and J. B. GRAHAM: Pattern of DNA replication in chromosomes of the dog. Cytogenetics 5 (1966) 206.

BROWN, S. W.: Heterochromatin. Science 151 (1966) 417.

BROWN, S. W. and U. NUR: Heterochromatic chromosomes in the coccids. Science 145 (1964) 130.

BÜCHNER, TH., A. WILKENS and R. A. PFEIFFER: Asynchrone Reduplikation bei Längenunterschied zwischen den homologen Chromosomen Nr. 1 beim Menschen. Exptl. Cell Res. 46 (1967) 58.

CAIRNS, J.: The chromosome of *Escherichia coli*. Cold Spring Harbor Symp. Quant. Biol. 28 (1963) 43.

CAIRNS, J.: Autoradiography of HeLa cell DNA. J. Mol. Biol. 15 (1966) 372.

CASPERSSON, T. O.: Cell growth and cell function. New York, W. W. Norton (1950) p. 185.

CAVE, M. D.: Reverse patterns of thymidine-H^3 incorporation in human chromosomes. Hereditas 54 (1966) 338.

COMINGS, D. E.: The duration of replication of the inactive X-chromosome in humans based on the persistence of the heterochromatic sex chromatin body during DNA synthesis. Cytogenetics 6 (1967) 20.

DARLINGTON, C. D. and A. HAQUE: Organization of DNA synthesis in Rye chromosomes. Heredity, Suppl. 19 (1966) 102.

DARLINGTON, C. D. and L. LA COUR: Nucleic acid starvation of the chromosomes in *Trillium*. J. Genetics 40 (1940) 185.

EVANS, H. J.: Uptake of H^3-thymidine and patterns of DNA replication in nuclei and chromosomes of *Vicia faba*. Exptl. Cell Res. 35 (1964) 381.

EVANS, D. and M. BIRNSTIEL: Localization of amplified ribosomal DNA in the oocyte of *Xenopus laevis* Biochim. Biophys. Acta 166 (1968) 274.

FRACCARO, M., I. GUSTAVSSON, M. HULTEN, J. LINDSTEN, A. MANNINI and L. TIEPOLO: DNA replication patterns of canine chromosomes in vivo and in vitro. Hereditas 52 (1965) 265.

FRENSTER, J. H.: Control of DNA strand separations during selective transcription and asynchronous replication. In: The cell nucleus – metabolism and radiosensitivity. (1966) p. 27.

GALL, J. G.: Differential synthesis of the genes for ribosomal RNA during amphibian oogenesis. Proc. Natl. Acad. Sci. 60 (1968) 553.

GALL, J. G., H. C. MACGREGOR and M. E. KIDSTON: Gene amplification in the oocytes of Dytiscid water beetles. Chromosoma (1969) in the press.

GALTON, M., K. BENIRSCHKE and S. OHNO: Sex chromosomes of the chinchilla: allocycly and duplication sequence in somatic cells and behavior in meiosis. Chromosoma 16 (1965) 668.

GARTLER, S. M. and B. BURT: Replication patterns of bovine sex chromosomes in cell culture. Cytogenetics 3 (1964) 135.

GERMAN, J. L.: III. DNA synthesis in human chromosomes. Trans. N.Y. Acad. Sci. 24 (1962) 395.

GIANNELLI, F.: The pattern of X-chromosome deoxyribonucleic acid synthesis in two women with abnormal sex-chromosome complements. Lancet 1 (1963) 863.

GIANNELLI, F. and R. M. HOWLETT: The identification of the chromosomes of the D group (13–15) Denver: An autoradiographic and measurement study. Cytogenetics 5 (1966) 186.

GIARDINA, A.: Origine del oociti e delle cellule nutrici nel Dytiscus. Inst. Mschr. Anat. Physiol. 18 (1901) 417.

GILBERT, C. W., S. MULDAL and L. G. LAJTHA: Rate of chromosome duplication at the end of the deoxyribonucleic acid synthetic period in human blood cells. Nature 208 (1965) 159.

GILBERT, C. W., S. MULDAL, L. G. LAJTHA and J. ROWLEY: Time-sequence of human chromosome duplication. Nature 195 (1962) 869.

GILLESPIE, D. and S. SPIEGELMAN: A quantitative assay for DNA-RNA hybrids with DNA immobilized on a membrane. J. Mol. Biol. 12 (1965) 829.

GRAVES, J. A. M.: DNA synthesis in chromosomes of cultured leucocytes from two marsupial species. Exptl. Cell Res. 46 (1967) 37.

GRUMBACH, M. M., A. MORISHIMA and J. H. TAYLOR: Human sex chromosome abnormalities in relation to DNA replication and heterochromatinization. Proc. Natl. Acad. Sci. 49 (1963) 581.

HARNDEN, D. G.: Nuclear sex in triploid XXY cells. Lancet 2 (1961) 488.

HEITZ, E.: Das Heterochromatin der Moose I. Jahrb. Wiss. Bot. 69 (1928) 762.

HEITZ, E.: Die Ursache der gesetzmässingen Zahl, Lage, Form und Grösse pflanzlicher Nukleolen. Panta 12 (1931) 775.

HEITZ, E.: Die somatische Heterophyknose bei *Drosophila melanogaster* und ihre genetische Bedeutung. Z. Zellforsch. 20 (1933) 237.

HEITZ, E.: Über - und -heterochromatin sowie Konstanz und Bau der Chromomeren bei *Drosophila.* Biol. Zbl. 54 (1934) 588.

HEITZ, E.: Chromosomenstruktur und Gene. Z. Ind. Abst. Vererbgsl. 70 (1935) 402.

HEINONEN, L. and O. HALKKA: Early stages of oogenesis and metabolic DNA in the oocytes of the house cricket, *Acheta domesticus* (L.). Ann. Med. Exp. Fenn. 45 (1967) 101.

HELLER, C.G. and Y. CLERMONT: Spermatogenesis in man: an estimate of its duration. Science 140 (1963) 184.

HILL, R.N. and J.J. YUNIS: Mammalian X-chromosomes: change in patterns of DNA replication during embryogenesis. Science 155 (1967) 1120.

HORIKAWA, M. and A.S. FOX: Culture and embryonic cells of *Drosophila melanogaster* in vitro. Science 145 (1964) 1437.

HSU, T.C.: Mammalian chromosomes in vitro. XVIII. DNA replication sequence in the Chinese hamster. J. Cell Biol. 23 (1964) 53.

HSU, T.C. and L.H. LOCKHART: The beginning and the terminal stages of DNA synthesis of human cells with an XXXXY constitution. Hereditas 52 (1965) 320.

HSU, T.C., W. SCHMID and E. STUBBLEFIELD: DNA replication sequences in higher animals. In: Role of chromosomes in development. New York, Academic Press (1964) p. 83.

HUBERMAN, J.A. and A.D. RIGGS: On the mechanism of DNA replication in mammalian chromosomes. J. Mol. Biol. 32 (1968) 327.

HUGHES-SCHRADER, S.: Cytology of Coccids (Coccoidea-Homoptera). In: M. Demerec, ed.: Advances in genetics. 2 (1948) 127.

INGRAM, V.M.: The hemoglobins in genetics and evolution. New York, Columbia Univ. Press (1963).

JACOB, F., S. BRENNER and F. CUZIN: On the regulation of DNA replication in bacteria. Cold Spring Harbor Symp. Quant. Biol. 28 (1963) 329.

JAWORSKA, H. and A. LIMA-DE-FARIA: (in preparation).

KARNKOWSKA-GORSKA, Z.: Incorporation of tritium labelled thymidine into the spinning glands of the silk worm *Bombyx mori* L. Bulletin Acad. Pol. Sci. 8 (1960) 353.

KIKUCHI, Y. and A.A. SANDBERG: Chronology and pattern of human chromosome replication. J. Clin. Invest. 42 (1963) 947.

KIKUCHI, Y. and A.A. SANDBERG: Chronology and pattern of human chromosome replication. I. Blood leucocytes of normal subjects. J. Natl. Cancer Inst. 32 (1964) 1109.

KLINGER, H.P. and H.G. SCHWARZACHER: The sex chromatin and heterochromatic bodies in human diploid and polyploid nuclei. J. Biophys. Biochem. Cytol. 8 (1960) 345.

KUNZ, W.: Die Entstehung multipler Oocytennukleolen aus akzessorischen DNS-Körpern bei *Gryllus domesticus.* Chromosoma 26 (1969) 41.

KUSANAGI, A.: Rate of DNA replication in the DNA synthesis period of the barley chromosomes. Chromosoma 20 (1966) 125.

LIMA-DE-FARIA, A.: The chromosomes of *Secale cereale* at pachytene. Proc. Seventh Int. Bot. Congr. (1950) 217.

LIMA-DE-FARIA, A.: Chromomere analysis of the chromosome complement of rye. Chromosoma 5 (1952) 1.

LIMA-DE-FARIA, A.: The role of the kinetochore in chromosome organization. Hereditas 42 (1956) 85.

LIMA-DE-FARIA, A.: Incorporation of tritiated thymidine into meiotic chromosomes. Science 130 (1959a) 503.

LIMA-DE-FARIA, A.: Differential uptake of tritiated thymidine into hetero- and euchromatin in *Melanoplus* and *Secale.* J. Biophys. Biochem. Cytol. 6 (1959b) 457.

LIMA-DE-FARIA, A.: Tritium autoradiography of metabolic DNA in *Tipula*. Reports of 2nd Conference on Cell Research, Lunds Universitets Årsskrift, Lund, Gleerups, 56 (1960) 43.

LIMA-DE-FARIA, A.: Initiation of DNA synthesis at specific segments in the meiotic chromosomes of *Melanoplus*. Hereditas 47 (1961) 674.

LIMA-DE-FARIA, A.: Metabolic DNA in *Tipula oleracea*. Chromosoma 13 (1962) 47.

LIMA-DE-FARIA, A., N. O. BIANCHI and P. C. NOWELL: Patterns of chromosome replication in a patient with chronic granulocytic leukemia. Hereditas 58 (1967) 31.

LIMA-DE-FARIA, A., M. BIRNSTIEL and H. JAWORSKA: Amplification of ribosomal cistrons in the heterochromatin of *Acheta*. Genetics (1969) (in the press).

LIMA-DE-FARIA, A., J. GERMAN, M. GHATNEKAR, J. MCGOVERN and L. ANDERSON: In vitro labelling of human meiotic chromosomes with H^3-thymidine. Hereditas 60 (1968a) 249.

LIMA-DE-FARIA, A. and H. JAWORSKA: Late DNA synthesis in heterochromatin. Nature 217 (1968) 138.

LIMA-DE-FARIA, A. and H. JAWORSKA: (1969) (in preparation).

LIMA-DE-FARIA, A. and M. J. MOSES: Ultrastructure and cytochemistry of metabolic DNA in *Tipula*. J. Cell Biol. 30 (1966) 177.

LIMA-DE-FARIA, A., B. NILSSON, D. CAVE, A. PUGA and H. JAWORSKA: Tritium labelling and cytochemistry of extra DNA in *Acheta*. Chromosoma 25 (1968b) 1.

LIMA-DE-FARIA, A. and J. REITALU: Heterochromatin in human male leukocytes. J. Cell Biol. 16 (1963) 315.

LIMA-DE-FARIA, A., J. REITALU and S. BERGMAN: The pattern of DNA synthesis in the chromosomes of man. Hereditas 47 (1961) 695.

LIMA-DE-FARIA, A., J. REITALU and A. M. O'SULLIVAN: Replication of autosomal heterochromatin in man. Chromosoma 16 (1965) 152.

MARMUR, J.: A procedure for the isolation of deoxyribonucleic acid from micro-organisms. J. Mol. Biol. 3 (1961) 208.

MCLEISH, J.: The action of maleic hydrazide in *Vicia*. Heredity, Suppl. 6 (1953) 125.

MEYER, G. F.: Genetics (1969) in the press.

MILLER, O. J., B. B. MUKHERJEE, S. BADER and A. C. CHRISTAKOS: Autoradiographic studies of X-chromosome duplication in an XO/X-isochromosome X mosaic human female. Nature 200 (1963) 918.

MOORE, R. and J. UREN: The pattern of DNA synthesis in short-term leukocyte cultures of *Protemnodon bicolor*. Exptl. Cell Res. 38 (1965) 341.

MOORHEAD, P. S. and V. DEFENDI: Asynchrony of DNA synthesis in chromosomes of human diploid cells. J. Cell Biol. 16 (1963) 202.

MORISHIMA, A., M. M. GRUMBACH and J. H. TAYLOR: Asynchronous duplication of human chromosomes and the origin of sex chromatin. Proc. Natl. Acad. Sci. 48 (1962) 756.

MUKHERJEE, B. B., G. D. BURKHOLDER, A. K. SINHA and S. K. GHOSAL: Sequence of DNA replication in the iso-X-chromosome from X/iso-X human females during the initial stages of the synthetic period. Can. J. Genet. Cytol. 8 (1966) 631.

MUKHERJEE, B. B., O. J. MILLER, W. R. BREG and S. BADER: Chromosome duplication in cultured leucocytes from presumptive XXX and XXXXY human subjects. Exptl. Cell Res. 34 (1964) 333.

MULDAL, S., C. W. GILBERT, L. G. LAJTHA, J. LINDSTEN, J. ROWLEY and M. FRACCARO: Tritiated thymidine in corporation in an isochromosome for the long arm of the X-chromosome in man. Lancet 20 (1963) 861.

MUKHERJEE, B. B., A. K. SINHA, K. E. MANN, S. K. GHOSAL and W. C. WRIGHT: Replicative behaviour of bovine X-chromosomes during early DNA synthesis. Nature 214 (1967) 710.

NICKLAS, R. B. and R. A. JAQUA: A developmental change in the relative time of X-chromosome DNA replication. J. Cell Biol. 23 (1964) 67A.

NILSSON, B.: DNA-bodies in the germline of *Acheta domesticus* (Orthoptera). Hereditas 56 (1966) 396.

NUR, U.: Reversal of heterochromatinization and activity of the paternal chromosome set in the male mealy bug. Genetics 56 (1967) 375.

OCKEY, CH. H., J. WENNSTRÖM and A. DE LA CHAPELLE: Isochromosome-X in man. Part II. Hereditas 54 (1966) 277.

OHNO, S., W. BEÇAK and M. L. BEÇAK: X-autosome ratio and the behavior pattern of individual X-chromosomes in placental mammals. Chromosoma 15 (1964) 14.

OHNO, S., J. JAINCHILL and C. STENIUS: The creeping vole (*Microtus oregoni*) as a gonosomic mosaic. I. The OY/XY constitution of the male. Cytogenetics 2 (1963) 232.

PELC, S. R. and L. F. LA COUR: Some aspects of replication in chromosomes. In: J. S. Mitchell, ed.: The cell nucleus. London, Butterworth and Co. (1960) p. 232.

PELLING, C.: Giant chromosomes and chromosome structure. XII Int. Congress of Genetics, Tokyo (1968) 74.

PERA, F. and U. WOLF: DNS-Replikation und Morphologie der X-Chromosomen während der Syntheseperiode bei *Microtus agrestis*. Chromosoma 22 (1967) 378.

PETERSEN, A. J.: DNA synthesis and chromosomal asynchrony. J. Cell Biol. 23 (1964) 651.

PRIEST, J. H., J. E. HEADY and R. E. PRIEST: Delayed onset of replication of human X-chromosomes. J. Cell Biol. 35 (1967) 483.

RITOSSA, F. M.: Genetics (1969) in the press.

RITOSSA, F. M. and S. SPIEGELMAN: Localization of DNA complementary to ribosomal RNA in the nucleolus organizer region of *Drosophila melanogaster*. Proc. Natl. Acad. Sci. 53 (1965) 737.

ROWLEY, J., S. MULDAL, C. W. GILBERT, L. G. LAJTHA, J. LINDSTEN, M. FRACCARO and K. KAIJSER: Synthesis of deoxyribonucleic acid on X-chromosomes of an XXXXY male. Nature 197 (1963) 251.

ROWLEY, J., S. MULDAL, J. LINDSTEN and CH. W. GILBERT: H^3-thymidine uptake by a ring X-chromosome in a human female. Proc. Natl. Acad. Sci. 51 (1964) 779.

SCHMID, W.: DNA replication of human chromosomes. Cytogenetics 2 (1963) 175.

SCHMID, W.: Heterochromatin in mammals. Arch. Klaus-Stiff. Vererb. Forsch. 42 (1967a) 1.

SCHMID, W.: Personal information (1967b).

SCHNEIDER, L. K. and W. O. RIEKE: DNA replication patterns and chromosomal protein synthesis in Opossum lymphocytes in vitro. J. Cell Biol. 33 (1967) 497.

SCHULTZ, J.: The nature of heterochromatin. Cold Spring Harbor Symp. Quant. Biol. 12 (1947) 179.

STUBBLEFIELD, E. and G. C. MUELLER: Molecular events in the reproduction of animal cells. II. The focalized synthesis of DNA in the chromosomes of HeLa cells. Cancer Res. 22 (1962) 1091.

TANAKA, R.: H^3-thymidine autoradiographic studies on the heteropycnosis, heterochromatin and euchromatin in *Spiranthes sinensis*. Bot. Mag. Tokyo 78 (1965) 50.

TAYLOR, J. H.: The mode of chromosome duplication in *Crepis capillaris*. Exptl. Cell Res. 15 (1958) 350.

TAYLOR, J. H.: Asynchronous duplication of chromosomes in cultured cells of Chinese hamster. J. Biophys. Biochem. Cytol. 7 (1960) 455.

RIEPOLO, L., M. FRACCARO, M. HULTEN and J. LINDSTEN: Double aneuploidy (46, XXY, D-, D-, t(DqDq)$^+$). Ann. Génét. 10 (1967a) 114.

TIEPOLO, L., M. FRACCARO, M. HULTEN, J. LINDSTÉN, A. MANNINI and L. M. PÉN-MIND: Timing of sex chromosome replication in somatic and germ-line cells of the mouse and the rat. Cytogenetics 6 (1967b) 51.

TJIO, J. H. and A. LEVAN: The use of oxiquinoline in chromosome analysis. An. Estacion Exp. Aula Dei 2 (1950) 21.

UTAKOJI, T. and T. C. HSU: DNA replication patterns in somatic and germ-line cells of the male chinese hamster. Cytogenetics 4 (1965) 295.

WALLACE, H. and M. L. BIRNSTIEL: Ribosomal cistrons and the nucleolar organizer. Biochim. Biophys. Acta 114 (1966) 296.

WHITE, M. J. D.: Animal cytology and evolution. London and New York, Cambridge University Press (1945) p. 375.

WOLF, U., G. FLINSPACH, R. BÖHM and S. OHNO: DNS-Reduplikationsmuster bei den Riesen-Geschlechtschromosomen von *Microtus agrestis*. Chromosoma 16 (1965) 609.

WOODARD, J., M. GOROWSKY and H. SWIFT: DNA content of a chromosome of *Trillium erectum*: effect of cold treatment. Science 151 (1966) 215.

WOODARD, J. and H. SWIFT: The DNA content of cold treated chromosomes. Exptl. Cell Res. 34 (1964) 131.

CHAPTER 14

Chromosome pairing, chiasmata and crossing-over

S. A. HENDERSON

Department of Genetics, University of Cambridge, England

Contents

1. Introduction
2. Chromosome pairing
   (a) Classification
      (1) Primary pairing
      (2) Secondary association
      (3) Non-homologous association
   (b) Functions of pairing
   (c) The environmental and genetic modification of chromosome pairing
      (1) Environmental
      (2) Genetic
   (d) The molecular basis of chromosome pairing
3. Chiasmata and crossing-over
   (a) General
   (b) The autoradiographic demonstration of crossing-over
   (c) The environmental and genetic modification of chiasmata and crossing-over
      (1) Environmental
      (2) Genetic
   (d) The time of chiasma formation and crossing-over during meiotic prophase
   (e) The molecular basis of crossing-over and chiasma formation
4. Conclusion

1. Introduction

The two main topics which form a basis for this chapter, pairing and chiasma formation, are still inexplicable in molecular terms. Although a beginning has been made in thinking about the kinds of molecular processes which may be involved in the mechanism of chiasma formation, it is not possible to formulate hypotheses of comparable plausibility to explain chromosome pairing. The many actions and interactions of environmental and genetic factors which are known to lead to modifications of pairing, chiasma formation or genetic crossing-over, are even further from being understood and expressed in molecular terms. Much of this chapter will therefore be concerned with describing some of the things that we know, and that need to be explained, rather than what they mean at the level of the molecule. However, studies in progress, using a number of different techniques, which include electron microscopy, microspectrophotometry, autoradiography and the labelling of chromosomes with radioactively marked biochemicals, are beginning to elucidate some of the questions which were unanswerable ten years ago. It is to be expected that definite answers to many of the key questions in this particularly difficult field of investigation will be forthcoming within the next decade.

2. Chromosome pairing

(a) *Classification*

During interphase, mitosis or meiosis in those plants or animals which have been studied cytologically, it has been found that whole chromosomes, or chromosome segments, may undergo pairing, lateral association or juxtaposition of one of three main types. These may be termed: (A) primary pairing, (B) secondary association and (C) non-homologous association.

(1) *Primary pairing.* Primary pairing involves the lateral association, or synapsis, of genetically homologous chromosome regions. More than one type of homologous pairing of this type can be recognised, depending on whether it is found at mitosis, meiosis or interphase. The modes of pairing found at mitosis and interphase are probably of the same general type and are likely to involve the same kinds of molecular mechanisms or physical forces. A similar type of pairing is also found at meiosis in a number of organisms, but in the majority of plants and animals the pairing which characterises meiotic prophase is very different and is associated with chiasma formation and genetic crossing-over.

Mitotic pairing. Usually termed *somatic* pairing, this form of chromosome synapsis characterises all mitotic prophases and metaphases in the insect group of two-winged flies, the Diptera. As this behaviour is found in those mitoses involved in the development of the germ-line and gonads, as well as the soma, it is suggested that the term mitotic pairing is more apt. The two sets of homologous chromosomes present in diploid cells, which in most organisms are widely separated at mitosis, are here found closely apposed throughout prophase stages and rather more loosely associated at metaphase. It differs markedly from chiasmate meiotic pairing in one important respect: whereas the latter is invariably restricted to two chromosomes at any one point, mitotic pairing is not. In cells possessing higher multiples than two of either (i) single chromosomes (aneuploids) or (ii) whole chromosome complements (polyploids), all sets of homologues present are found paired throughout their length.

Interphase pairing. It would seem both logical and likely that the pairing seen throughout Dipteran mitotic prophase stages, and even tending to persist at metaphase when chromosomes are mechanically active on a spindle, represents a continuation of a synaptic state found also in interphase nuclei. This has not yet been demonstrated, in normal, diploid nuclei, though it would surprise me if this were shown not to be the case when suitable techniques have been developed to study interphase chromosomes. In many differentiated cell types and tissues in Dipteran larvae and adults, such interphase pairing is readily visible, however, for it is accompanied by the massive endopolyploidisation of the nuclei. The many hundreds or thousands of chromosome strands produced by repeated replication remain closely paired throughout their length, with the production of giant polytene chromosomes. Such chromosomes are, most commonly developmentally stable, but may undergo dissociation, giving rise to numerous oligotene fibrils (Matuszewski; Henderson 1967) and these are even capable of re-associating to give 'secondary' polytene chromosomes (Bier).

Meiotic pairing. At both male and female meiosis in the majority of plants and animals, homologous chromosomes become very intimately paired throughout their length, during the self-descriptive zygotene stage. Such pairing is usually strictly homologous and always involves only two chromosomes at any one point. When more than two chromosomes are present, pairing can lead to the association of all elements in a composite fashion, but, at any one site, only two strands will be found synapsed. It has been suggested by some that pairing may usually be initiated only terminally, and spread along the chromosomes in a manner similar to the closing of a zip. While this zipper-like spread of synapsis is indeed likely to occur from initial contact points (Darlington 1937), these can sometimes be shown to be far more numerous than the two telomeres which terminate each chromosome. Thus, in tetraploid cells of the locust *Schistocerca gregaria*, to produce the complex quadrivalents sometimes found (John and Henderson), there must be, distributed along the length of the longer chromosomes, a minimum of six independent sites at which synapsis can begin (Fig. 1). Different plant and animal species, and different chromosomes within a complement should be expected to differ in the number and distribution of such pairing initiation sites along their chromosomes.

This type of meiotic pairing is usually abruptly terminated at the end of pachytene and chromosome association maintained thereafter by the chiasmata which formed while the chromosomes were intimately associated. In some species, however, chias-

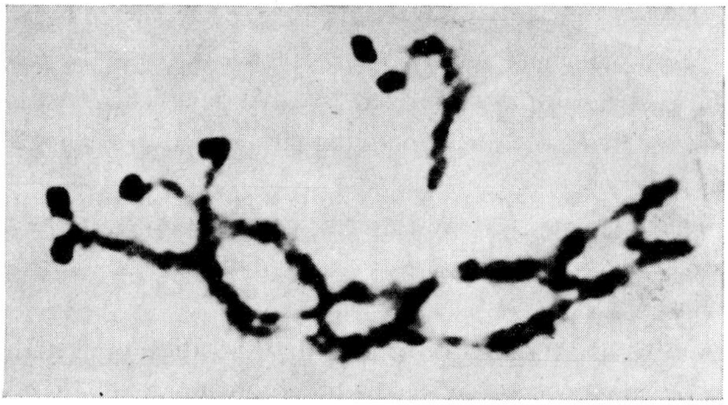

Fig. 1. One of the long quadrivalents from a tetraploid pachytene in a spermatocyte of the locust *Schistocerca gregaria.* It can be seen that pairing was initiated at six independent sites to produce this configuration. The exchanges visible are *not* chiasmata but regions where exchange of pairing partners occurs. A small bivalent is also shown. (Terminal heterochromatic chromomeres mark the positions of the centromeres.) ×1,500

mata do not form and chromosome association is maintained by a persistent pairing force during the spindle stage of metaphase I. In such non-chiasmate meioses (see below) the type of pairing found is not similar to that found in chiasmate meioses. It much more closely resembles that described above as mitotic, though it is not identical: there is greater adhesion between homologous chromosomes at metaphase I, which enables regular co-orientation and reductional segregation to be achieved.

(2) *Secondary association.* At metaphase I in diploid, chiasmate species, primary pairing is usually no longer found, having lapsed at late pachytene and the different bivalents present are usually more or less independently distributed on the equatorial plate. This is unlikely to be completely random, particularly in animals where a 'hollow' spindle is found. But there is, if anything, a tendency for bivalents to be equidistantly spaced and this is often so marked that it has led some to suggest that metaphase chromosomes possess a similar, and therefore repelling, electrical surface charge. At metaphase I in some bivalent-forming polyploid species, the behaviour found is often rather more complex. Genetically dissimilar bivalents show no attraction and are widely spaced, but genetically similar (homoeologous) bivalents are often found in pairs. This behaviour, known as secondary association because of its occurrence after the lapse of primary pairing (Darlington and Moffet; Lawrence 1931), could conceivably reflect merely a continuation of the spatial juxtaposition of homoeologous chromosomes found during pachytene, but its persistence on the metaphase spindle, when bivalents are oscillating under the pulling action of the spindle fibres, does suggest that separate or persistent pairing forces are involved. It has also been shown, using structurally marked chromosomes to facilitate identification, that, even when close apposition of homoeologous bivalents is not immediately apparent down the microscope, genetically similar bivalents may lie close to one another on the

equatorial plate more frequently than would be expected were the distribution completely random (Kempana and Riley 1964). This work has the additional merit of showing that the association does indeed involve genetically similar chromosomes and is not a non-specific attraction depending simply on bivalent size or mass.

(3) *Non-homologous association.* Within this category there are many different types of observation, which, for convenience of description, can be considered to be of two main types:

(1) The first involves the lateral or terminal juxtaposition or even the visible 'fusion' of chromosomes or segments recognised as heterochromatic. This commonly leads to chromocentre formation in interphase nuclei. It is frequently rather variable and haphazard in occurrence, which suggests that, in such cases, it is merely a surface adhesion, or 'stickiness' phenomenon. It is sometimes invariable and regular, as in the centromeric chromocentre formation found in many, though not all, Dipteran polytene nuclei. In these nuclei, pairing forces which do not involve genetically homologous segments must be found.

(2) The second involves the fairly close lateral association of euchromatic chromosome segments, which should, in theory, be non-homologous. This may occur at zygotene and pachytene stages and can sometimes lead to chiasma formation. Thus, haploid plants may sometimes not merely complete a relatively satisfactory development, but actually flower and undergo meiosis. As only one homologue is present in a haploid cell, no pairing would be expected, unless many duplications are present, distributed throughout the complement, but both within- and between-homologue synapsis has been observed in haploid rye and *Antirrhinum* plants (Rieger; Rees, unpublished), with occasional chiasma formation. Intra-haploid pairing and chiasma formation has also been found in maize pollen grains possessing the recessive gene for discordant polymitotic divisions (Beadle 1931, 1933). When structurally heterozygous chromosomes are paired, synapsis may also spread from homologous regions and come to include non-homologous segments. This, however, may merely be torsional or 'non-effective' pairing (McClintock; Darlington 1937).

(b) *Functions of pairing*

The principal functions of the two main types of meiotic pairing are relatively simple to define. The zygotene synapsis found in chiasmate meioses brings homologous chromosomes sufficiently close together, and holds them there for a sufficiently long period of time, for chiasma formation or genetic crossing-over to occur. When this has been achieved, its function is ended and pairing lapses. The persistent pairing found until metaphase I in non-chiasmate meioses is clearly to maintain bivalent association so that co-orientation and segregation are orderly and the sterilising irregularity of univalent behaviour is avoided.

The functions of some of the other types of pairing are not so obvious and may not, in some cases be of very great importance. Thus, the phenomena of secondary association or variable, non-specific chromocentre formation may not serve any useful functions in the cells in which they are found. Regular chromocentre formation of the type found in polytene nuclei is much more likely to owe its regularity to some functional, selective advantage. Perhaps it enables chromosome-limited diffusable substances to pass from one chromosome to another non-homologous chromosome? In the Cecidomyid *Dasyneura crataegi*, the mode of centromeric heterochromatin proliferation observed in two of the chromosomes within the complement suggests that the proliferation pattern of one may be influenced in this way by its association with the centromeric region of the other, in chromocentre formation (Henderson 1967) (compare below).

The possible functions of interphase (polytene) and mitotic (somatic) pairing do not appear to have been discussed very much in the literature. Their widespread maintainance throughout the Diptera implies a strong selective advantage for these states and their functions merit closer attention than they have received in the past. In my opinion the most likely single function of these kinds of pairing is the facilitation of the diffusion and transfer, from one homologue to another, of chromosome-limited substances involved in the regulation of gene activities. That interchromosomal transport of gene products is involved in some position effect phenomena in *Drosophila* was suggested by Lewis who concluded that the intimacy of somatic pairing is of importance in determining the expression of the so-called 'transvection' effect. Similarly, although they do not always act in this way in puff heterozygotes, such substances have recently been shown to be involved in the expression of puffing activity of two polytene chromosome loci in *Drosophila melanogaster* (Ashburner 1967, and unpublished). There is also some evidence that they may sometimes be involved in the control of nucleolar organising activity and even, possibly the heterochromatin proliferation referred to above (Henderson 1967). It is likely that many more examples of these types will come to light in the near future. Indeed, the observations of Berendes on the behaviour of asynapsed chromosomes in *Drosophila hydei* are relevant here. He found that when asynapsis of the two homologous bundles of fibrils comprising a polytene chromosome occurred, the two 'homologues' often differed slightly in their appearance. Such differences included staining properties, distances between bands and the structure or 'functional state' of bands. Berendes concluded that these variations reflected differences in physiological state and implied a certain autonomy and asynchrony of action of each 'homologue'. It is unlikely that these deviations were the cause of asynapsis. They are almost certainly a result of the failure of pairing and hence a limitation in the diffusion of regulatory substances from one 'homologue' to the other, which normally leads to synchronous action at each site.

(c) *The environmental and genetic modification of chromosome pairing*

(1) *Environmental.* The only environmental factor known to lead to gross changes in

the normal mode of pairing is temperature. Extremes of temperature have been shown to affect both the completeness of polytene chromosome interphase pairing (Goldschmidt) and the prophase pairing in chiasmate meioses. Either high or low temperatures can lead to a reduction in zygotene pairing in different plant or animal species (e.g. Sax; Barber 1941, 1942; Pao and Li; Dowrick; Henderson 1962). Such reduction may be extensive and can culminate in complete failure of pairing (asynapsis).

(2) *Genetic.* Some of the most interesting and rewarding work which has been carried out in recent years on chromosome pairing has been concerned with an analysis of its genetic control and its specificity. This work, far from explaining the molecular basis of pairing, however, is showing how very complex are the interactions and controls within the cell and how difficult it will be to provide a molecular explanation of sufficient versatility to accomodate all aspects of chromosome behaviour. In the space available here only a brief resumé is possible. For further information the reader is referred to the recent review of Riley and Law.

It has been shown that the genetic control of chromosome pairing operates at two levels: (i) quantitative and (ii) qualitative.

Quantitative. Major genes which affect either the presence or the efficiency of overall chromosome pairing have been found in a number of organisms. At one extreme, no pairing occurs (asynapsis), while at the other extreme, although visible pairing is found, this is, in some way, inadequate and chiasma formation fails (desynapsis). Between these two extremes many intergrades may be found, which emphasize that one is not dealing with an 'all or none' phenomenon, but a variable process which may be arrested or modified in different ways in different organisms. Most aspects of an organisms phenotype are generally considered to be subject to two different types of genetic control: major gene and polygene control (Mather 1949). Though they are likely to differ less than was once thought (see Thoday), it is still convenient to recognise these two types of gene systems. Workers investigating the genetic control of chromosome behaviour during meiosis have often failed to clarify the relation found in their material between the level of chromosome pairing present at pachytene and the chiasma frequency, or univalent frequency, scored at metaphase I. Although these have sometimes been discussed as if they were synonymous and all under the operation of the same genetic control, it is more correct to say that the distinction between the genetic control of chromosome pairing and the control of chiasma formation has yet to be clarified, though there need be no doubt that both systems are under both modes of genetic control. With this reservation in mind, it has been shown, in the inbreeding plant wheat (*Triticum aestivum*) that the presence of univalents in different varietal lines, and their presence in crosses and backcrosses, is under complex, or polygenic control, with negative heterosis in F_1's (see Riley and Law). As univalents result from either asynapsis or desynapsis, some pairing failure or inadequacy is likely to be involved, though it is possible that the fault may sometimes lie in the chiasma forming processes (see below).

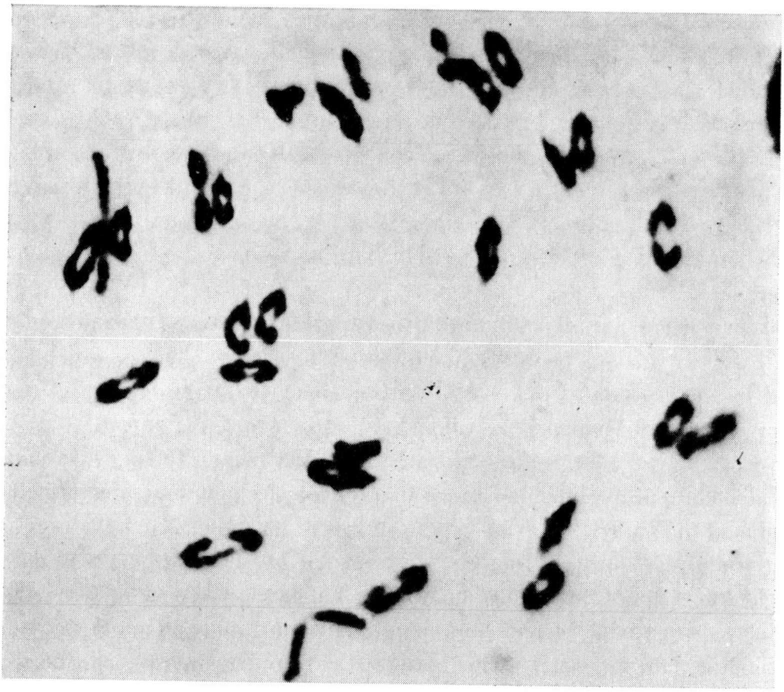

Fig. 2

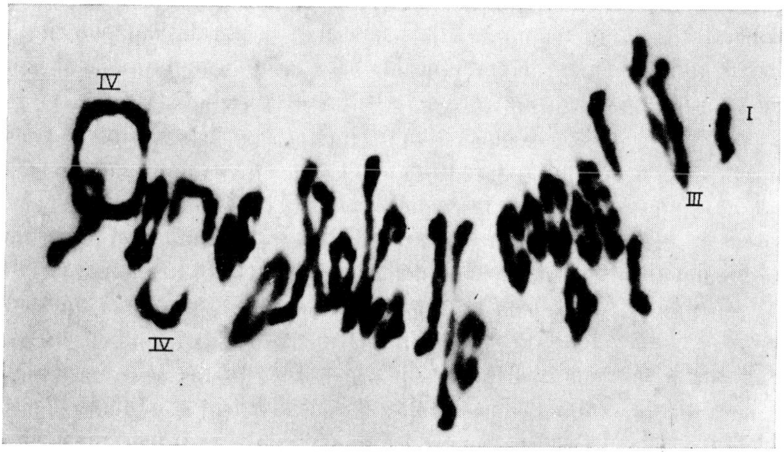

Fig. 3.

Figs. 2 and 3. The genetic control of chromosome pairing in wheat. As in the eudiploid, regular bivalent formation in the synthetic amphiploid from the cross *Triticum aestivum* × *Aegilops longissima* (illustrated) is maintained by the action of chromosome 5B (Fig. 2). When this chromosome pair is absent (Fig. 3) inter-homoeologue pairing occurs and multivalents form. (Photographs kindly provided by Dr. Ralph Riley.)

The presence or absence of whole chromosomes has also been shown to affect univalent frequency and hence, probably, pairing behaviour. Thus, deficiency of chromosome 3B in wheat increases univalent frequency (Kempana) as can the addition to the wheat complement of chromosomes from other species, such as rye (*Secale cereale*) (Riley). Conversely, the wheat genotype can interfere with the efficiency of pairing of rye chromosomes if two rye chromosomes are added to the wheat complement (Riley). The combination of wheat and rye chromosomes may thus lead to a breakdown in the balanced regulation of the pairing behaviour of the chromosomes of either species.

Qualitative. Explanations of quantitative variations in overall chromosome pairing are likely to pose less of a problem than qualitative effects of the type which have been revealed by an analysis of the role of chromosome 5B in the regulation of pairing specificity in wheat. Wheat is an allohexaploid in which the chromosome complements (or genomes) of three species are combined (Sears 1954, 1958; Okamoto). Genetically comparable chromosomes in each of the genomes are termed homoeologous and in synthetic hybrids can be shown to be sufficiently alike genetically to pair and undergo chiasma formation. The regular bivalent formation found in allohexaploid wheat is not due to non-homology, but to the presence of a genetic system restricting pairing to only strictly homologous chromosomes and abolishing it between homoeologous chromosomes. This system was found to involve chromosome 5B: when this chromosome pair is absent, pairing between homoeologues is no longer repressed and multivalents form (Riley et al.; Sears and Okamoto). The 5B system of control operates in synthetic amphiploids as well as in normal euploids and derivatives (Figs. 2 and 3). The gene(s) reponsible have been located on one chromosome arm. Indeed, only one locus may prove to be involved (Kimber).

Many subtleties have been discovered in the interactions between the 5B system and different genotypes or conditions (see Riley and Law). One example may be mentioned because of its interest when mechanisms of the control of pairing are being considered. As stated above, deficiency for chromosome 3B leads to a reduction in chromosome pairing, with univalent formation, while deficiency for 5B leads to an increase. Hybrids from a *T. aestivum* × *Secale montanum* cross deficient for both do not show complete dominance for either condition, nor is an intermediate state found. Cells within an anther fall into a bimodal distribution in which 16% of the cells resemble the 3B deficient pattern, the remainder resembling the 5B deficient condition (Fig. 4). The effects of both deficiencies thus appear to be expressed separately in different cells of the same anther (Kempana and Riley 1962).

(d) *The molecular basis of chromosome pairing*

No satisfactory explanation of the molecular forces or interactions involved in the various types of chromosome pairing recognised, can be advanced at the present state of our knowledge. Many workers, however, have attempted to formulate explanations during the past 50 years and hypotheses have been proposed involving chemical, physical or structural approaches. None of these can explain all that we know of pairing; some involve physical forces which, apparently, operate only over relatively short distances and not the long distances which chromosomes traverse when pairing; and most are untestable. In view of these facts and because they have recently been considered by Serra, Rhoades and Riley and Law, they will not be re-listed here.

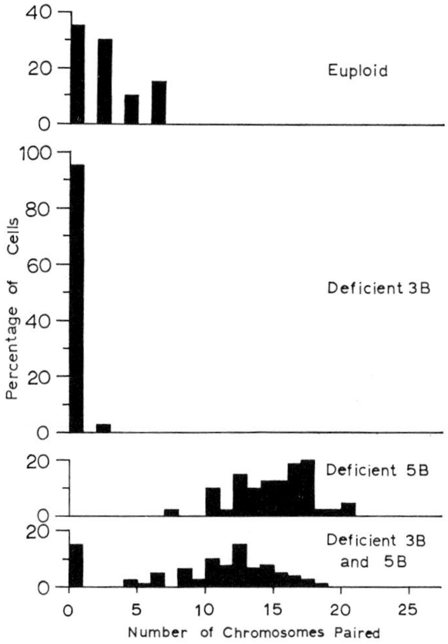

Fig. 4. Histograms showing the numbers of chromosomes paired in hybrids derived from a *Triticum aestivum* (−3B, −5B) × *Secale montanum* cross. (From Kempana and Riley 1962; redrawn.)

A suitable hypothesis must explain many complex factors which includes the following: (1) the linear locus specificity of pairing (2) the long range action of pairing forces (3) the restriction of pairing to two's in meiotic (chiasmate) pairing, but not in mitotic or interphase pairing (4) the infrequency of interlocking despite multiple pairing initiation sites (b) the completeness of pairing (c) the efficiency of visibly paired regions (d) the specificity between homologous, homoeologous or non-homologous chromosomes. It is not surprising, therefore, that no simple chemical or physical mechanism has the versatility to account for such a wide range of points.

The introduction of the electron microscope to biological research opened a new approach to studies of pairing. Moses (1956, 1958) found that, whereas most chromosomes have a diffuse, irresolvable, fibrous appearance when examined with the electron microscope, zygotene and pachytene chromosomes differ in forming highly organised tripartite linear structures which have been termed synaptinemal complexes (see the chapter by Sotello). Between two outer dense axial elements which represent the two paired homologues, a third electron dense zone is found marking the pairing interface between the two chromosomes. This third zone has been termed the synaptic centre by Lu and the medial complex by Roth. Although originally found in spermatocytes of the crayfish, these complexes have since been found at both male and female meiosis in a wide variety of animal, plant and fungal species. Opinions still differ as to the detailed organisation of chromosomes when paired to form a synaptinemal complex. In my own opinion, the most plausible explanation is that the two homologues are of a lampbrush grade of organisation, with lateral loops projecting in all directions (compare Moses and Coleman; Nebel and Coulon). The loops projecting inwards, towards the synaptic centre, would need to be very much shorter than those projecting outwards. The synaptic centre would appear to be mostly protein in nature (Coleman and Moses; Wolstenholme and Meyer) and formed where inwardly directed loop tips meet.

The recent work of Meyer (1960, 1964) has established beyond reasonable doubt, in the Diptera, at least, that the type of pairing which leads to chiasma formation is characterised by complexes of this type, whereas other types of visible pairing are not. The evidence for associating this organisation with chiasmate pairing is summarised in Table 1.

TABLE 1

Evidence for associating synaptinemal complex formation with meiotic recombination in the Diptera

Species and/or condition	Visible pairing	Chiasma formation or genetic cross-over	Synaptinemal complexes
1. All chiasmate meioses so far examined, including *Tipula oleracea* ♂ *Drosophila melanogaster* ♀	+	+	+
2. *Tipula caesia* ♂ *Drosophila melanogaster* ♂ *Phryne fenestralis* ♂	+	–	–
3. *Drosophila melanogaster* ♀:			
(a) triploid	+ (should be in two's)	+	+ (normal two's)
(b) mutant C3G	–	–	–
(c) multiply inverted heterozygote	reduced	reduced	reduced

The synaptinemal complex, or more particularly, the synaptic centre, would appear to be a device which has evolved in chromosomal organisms to bring together and align the DNA molecules from paired homologous chromosomes in order that crossing-over may take place between them. The fact that atypical multiple complexes can be found in mosquito oocyte and nurse cell nuclei (Roth) or cricket spermatids (Sotello and Trujillo-Cenoz; Sotello and Wettstein; Schin 1965a, b; Wolstenholme and Meyer) need in no way detract from the above conclusions. Such atypical complexes may represent associations of persistent molecules of the extrachromosomal material which forms the basis of the synaptinemal complex (Schin 1965b; Roth). Wolstenhome and Meyer are not of this opinion, however.

Roth and Ito have recently shown that both the initial formation of the synaptinemal complex and the 'maturation' of the complex during pachytene, so that homologues may separate in diplotene, appear to involve a small amount of DNA synthesis. Deoxyadenosine, an inhibitor of DNA synthesis, was found to interfere with both the initiation of pairing and diplotene separation if applied to *Lilium* anthers cultured *in vitro*. This DNA synthesis was not considered to be involved in the exchange processes leading to chiasma formation, but to involve some aspect of delayed chromosome replication.

Another approach which may help towards an understanding of the molecular basis of chromosome pairing was initiated by the work of Ansley (1954, 1957). He found differences in the DNA:histone ratios, determined cytophotometrically following Feulgen and fast green staining, in normal and asynaptic spermatocytes of the centipede *Scutigera* and the Hemipteran bug *Loxa*. Although the differences observed may not reflect changes in the actual content of DNA or histone, but in their mode of molecular association (Ansley 1957), the work suggests that chromosomal histone may be of importance in synapsis. However, Hayter and Riley have been unable to detect any differences in the DNA:histone ratios of *Triticum durum* plants which differed in their synaptic behaviour. The normal dominant homozygote, and recessive asynaptic and desynaptic homozygotes, were all found to yield identical DNA:histone values.

In a comparison of normal maize microsporocytes and those from plants homozygous for the gene *ameiotic*, where a non-chiasmate, mitotic, type of division is found, Sinha found differences in the DNA:RNA ratios present, as well as differences in the composition of the precursor pool. RNA is not an important structural component of chromosomes, but serves quite different genetic functions and it is unlikely that the differences observed are the causes of the different patterns of cell division, including the presence or absence of pairing. They are more likely to be consequences of the different modes of division adopted.

3. *Chiasmata and crossing-over*

(a) *General*

Most cytologists and geneticists are prepared to accept a general equation of chiasmata and genetic cross-overs, though not all would accept that there is an invariable 1:1 correspondence of the two. The main lines of evidence for equating chiasmata and cross-overs have been described by others (e.g. Mather 1938; Whitehouse 1965) and will not be re-listed here in detail. The four approaches which have been involved are: (1) evidence that breakage and exchange of chromosome segments must be involved in chiasma formation and this must therefore lead to genetic crossing-over. This includes, for example, the behaviour of heteromorphic bivalents at meiosis (Fig. 5). (2) evidence that cytologically detectable chromosome segment exchange occurs when marker gene exchange occurs. (3) parallels between the behaviour of chiasmata and cross-overs and (4) similarities between chiasma frequencies and cross-over frequencies.

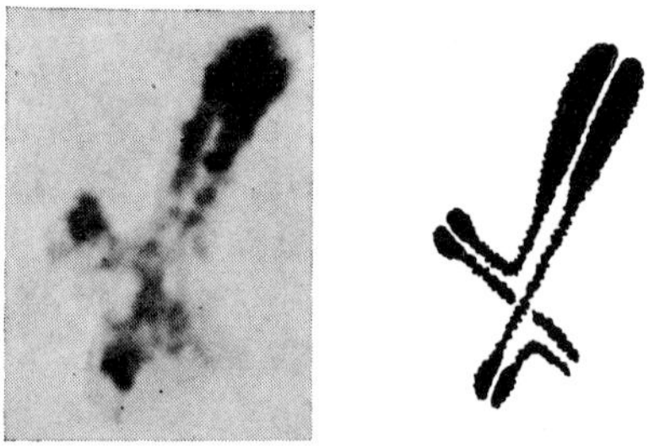

Fig. 5. Heteromorphic bivalent at diplotene, from the grasshopper *Calliptamus barbarus barbarus*. × 2,250

The genetic importance of chiasma formation, enabling intra-chromosomal recombination to supplement the inter-chromosomal recombination which results from random chromosome orientation and segregation at the first meiotic division, cannot be too strongly stressed. It is not the only role of chiasmata, however. In most species they serve the mechanical function of maintaining bivalent association in order that regular segregation may be achieved. This role, long supported by Darlington is in no way discredited by the observation that chiasma formation may be abandoned during meiosis in some species, without sterility ensuing, as it usually does, due to the presence of unpaired chromosomes, or univalents. Such species are exceptional in possessing a persistent, rather special, type of pairing at metaphase I (referred to above) which facilitates regular segregation in a non-chiasmate meiosis. Non-chiasmate association may characterise either male or female meioses (see John and Lewis, Table 4), but in no case has it been found to be present in both sexes simultaneously. Semi-chiasmate meioses may also be recognised, in which some chromosomes (e.g. sex chromosomes) may be maintained as bivalents or multivalents by non-chiasmate pairing forces, while the remaining chromosomes form normal chiasmate bivalents (see Henderson 1968a).

Chiasmata or genetic cross-overs are never random in distribution. The presence of one reduces the chance of a second occurring in the immediate vicinity and this phenomenon of *positive interference* tends to lead to an equidistant spacing of exchanges along the length of paired chromosomes (Müller; Mather 1936a, 1938; Henderson 1963b). The number of chiasmata which a chromosome pair may possess at meiosis is therefore determined both by the magnitude and mode of action of the interference present, themselves under genetic control, and by the relative length of the chromosomes within the complement (Fig. 6). The average number of chiasmata formed by a chromosome pair, cell or individual, termed the *chiasma frequency*, is roughly constant for any given species, but may be modified by genetic or environmental action (see below).

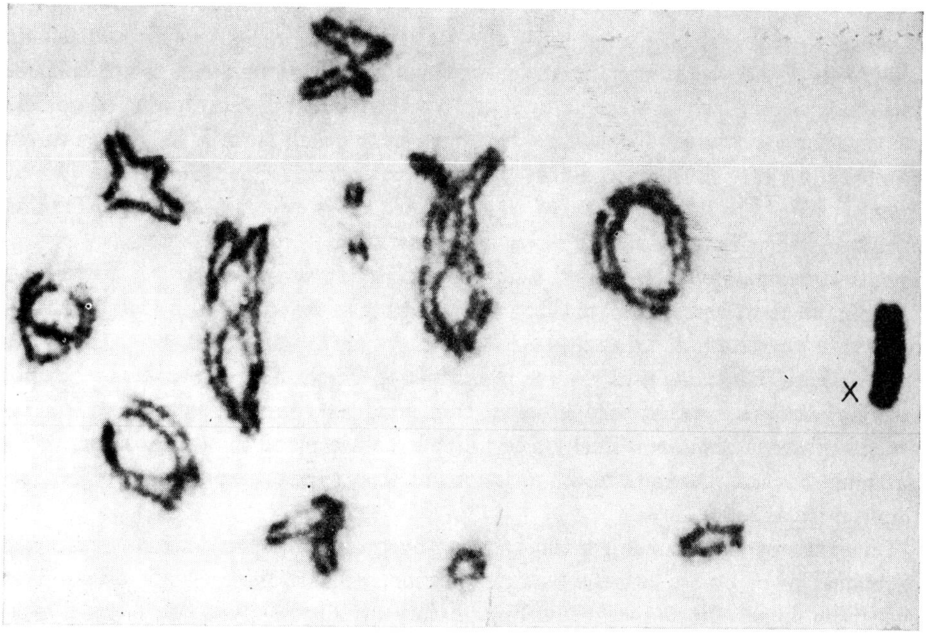

Fig. 6. Chiasma distribution at diplotene in the locust *Locusta migratoria*. The chiasma frequency of this cell (18) is fairly high for this species. Chromatid behaviour in bivalents possessing one, two or three chiasmata is illustrated. × 2,000

Within a cell the control of the chiasma frequencies of different bivalents could, in theory, be brought about in one of two ways: (i) for a limited number of 'potential chiasmata' to be present and for bivalents to 'compete' for them, in which case the chiasma frequencies of different bivalents should be negatively correlated. (ii) for the proportion of chiasmata formed by all bivalents to remain similar and increases or decreases to affect all bivalents in a similar way. In this case, one would expect a positive correlation between the chiasma frequencies of different bivalents within a cell. There is evidence that both types of control may operate in different cases (Mather 1936b; Jain and Maherchandani; Henderson 1963a; Shah), though the second method would seem to be the more common of the two.

It was thought, by some, that the phenomenon of positive cross-over interference could affect chromatids individually and that once one pair of chromatids became involved in an exchange they were less likely to be involved a second time than the other two present. Cross-over data from a number of fungal species now show that this does not appear to be the case (see Whitehouse 1965).

Not all species choose to exploit high recombination frequencies. In a number of plants and animals it has been found that there may be a tendency, which, in some cases, may be an absolute restriction, for chiasmata to form only in certain regions of a bivalent. Three types of chiasma localisation may be recognised; (i) *proximal*, when chiasmata are found only adjacent to the centromere (ii) *distal*, in which chiasmata only form at non-centromeric terminal regions or (iii) *proterminal*. Here chiasma formation occurs only at terminal regions, whether these are centromeric or not. In some instances chiasma localisation can be seen to result from a restriction in the completeness of visible chromosome pairing (Darlington 1935a; Henderson 1969b). Even if visible pairing is completed in some species, however, it is conceivable that chiasma localisation could be achieved by a restriction in the development of synaptinemal complexes between paired homologues (Henderson 1969b).

While, in most cases, a distal siting of chiasmata at diakinesis and metaphase I is due to the operation of localisation, this does not always appear to be the case. In some species chiasmata which were interstitial in origin may slip towards the ends during diakinesis, so that only terminal chiasmata are found at metaphase I. This process of *terminalisation* is likely to be much less widespread than originally thought and many cases of presumed terminalisation are likely to be examples of distal localisation (see Henderson 1969a).

Chiasma formation and genetic crossing-over occur at the 4-strand stage and exchanges involve only 2 of the 4 strands present. One of these usually comes from each homologue, i.e. non-sister chromatids are usually involved. Both cytological and genetical evidence has been presented to support the suggestion that crossing-over can sometimes occur between sister chromatids. At mitosis this has been shown to occur using autoradiography (Taylor 1958), though here the radioactivity from the tritium used may influence the frequency of exchanges observed. At meiosis in ring-rod heterozygotes of maize (Schwarz 1953), the observed frequency of bridges at anaphase stages did not equal that predicted and Schwarz suggests that the occurrence of sister-strand crossing-over may be influencing the bridge frequency observed. Schwarz (1954, 1955) has also involved sister-strand exchanges in the mitotic crossing-over (see below) found in *Drosophila*, but the evidence is not convincing (Brown and Welshons).

Finally, in this general context, one should mention that crossing-over is not an exclusively meiotic phenomenon. In several organisms, including *Drosophila* (Stern) and fungi (Pontecorvo), mitotic, or somatic, crossing-over has been found. The frequency is highest in *Drosophila*, which is not surprising in view of the mitotic pairing present. This mode of crossing-over does not seem to require synaptinemal complex formation for its occurrence, as does meiotic crossing-over, and it is still not clear whether identical molecular mechanisms are involved in the two processes, though it is unlikely that the basic exchange mechanisms will prove to be very different. The chromosomes of the species involved are generally too small to see whether chiasmata are produced from such exchanges, though it is not inconceivable that some of the chiasma-like configurations observed by Cooper could have involved mitotic crossing-over. This was not his interpretation of the figures, however.

(b) *The autoradiographic demonstration of crossing-over*

It is not *necessary* to demonstrate autoradiographically that chiasma formation involves segmental exchange and hence genetic crossing-over. This is adequately demonstrated by heteromorphic bivalents, for example (Fig. 6). Neither would it be necessary to demonstrate a correspondence of chiasma and cross-over frequencies autoradiographically, if sufficiently detailed genetic information were available. Although not essential, this approach has its attraction and a number of workers have begun autoradiographic studies along these lines, with variable success. Thus, in a recent publication Taylor (1965) examined the relationship between the frequencies of exchanges observed between labelled and unlabelled chromosomes and the chiasma frequency at male meiosis in a grasshopper, *Romalea microptera*. Because it did not prove feasable to demonstrate this correspondence at diplotene and metaphase I, Taylor scored the frequency of exchanges between labelled and unlabelled chromatids at metaphase II, in the second wave of labelled cells to pass through meiosis after H^3-labelled thymidine was injected. From the number of labelled/unlabelled switch points recorded at metaphase II for chromosomes in two size groups, an estimate of the chiasma frequency of these groups was made. These were: A group 3.6, B group 2.6. The recorded chiasma frequencies were surprisingly similar: A group 3.67, B group 2.62. As Taylor also points out, this correspondence is not as acceptable as it would at first appear, however, for a number of reasons including the following points: (1) an X-chromosome was present in group A which does not undergo chiasma formation and its presence was not corrected for, (2) the distribution of exchanges throughout the size groups was found to be random, whereas the distribution of chiasmata within these groups is certainly non-random, (3) the presence of sister-chromatid exchanges, expected from Taylor's earlier work with mitotic chromosomes, would tend to confuse relationships and would be expected to increase the frequency of exchanges observed. Some evidence from incompletely labelled diplotene chromosomes showed that sister-chromatid exchange had taken place, though, in Taylor's opinion, the frequency was not high. One is forced to conclude that, whereas, as expected, there is a suggestion that there is some similarity between chiasma and exchange frequencies, a 1:1 correspondence is not demonstrated by the data. Indeed, Taylor himself concludes that because the switch points which he found were randomly distributed, whereas chiasmata are not, there may not be a 1:1 relation between chiasmata and cross-overs.

More recently, Moens attempted to determine the relationship between segmental exchange, as revealed by crossing-over between labelled and unlabelled chromosomes, and the distribution of chiasmata, at diplotene. Here again, no simple correlation was found between the two.

In the experiments which I carried out to determine the time of chiasma formation in relation to the time of DNA synthesis (Henderson 1966), one individual was obtained in which chiasma formation between labelled and unlabelled chromosomes could be seen at methaphase I. The individual's chiasma frequency had been reduced by heat-treatment, but a mean of 8.5 chiasmata per cell was found. Though most chiasmata were distal, some were interstitial. In some bivalents, one of the four chromatids present was originally labelled throughout its length. The label was seen to switch at the point of chiasma formation in the manner expected (Fig. 7), but, as autoradiographic resolution of individual chromatids was not very good in these cells, the bivalents could not be considered to prove the equation of segmental exchange and chiasma formation. Clearly, this is a field where further careful work on a number of different organisms may help to clarify the relationship between chiasmata and cross-overs.

(c) *The environmental and genetic modification of chiasmata and crossing-over*

(1) *Environmental.* The modification of chiasma, or cross-over, frequencies by environmental factors has received a great deal more attention than the effects of these same factors on chromosome pairing. Effective factors include temperature, radiations, chemicals, nutrition, age and sex, though this latter effect could also be considered genetic.

Effects of temperature on chiasma formation fit into a more unified pattern than

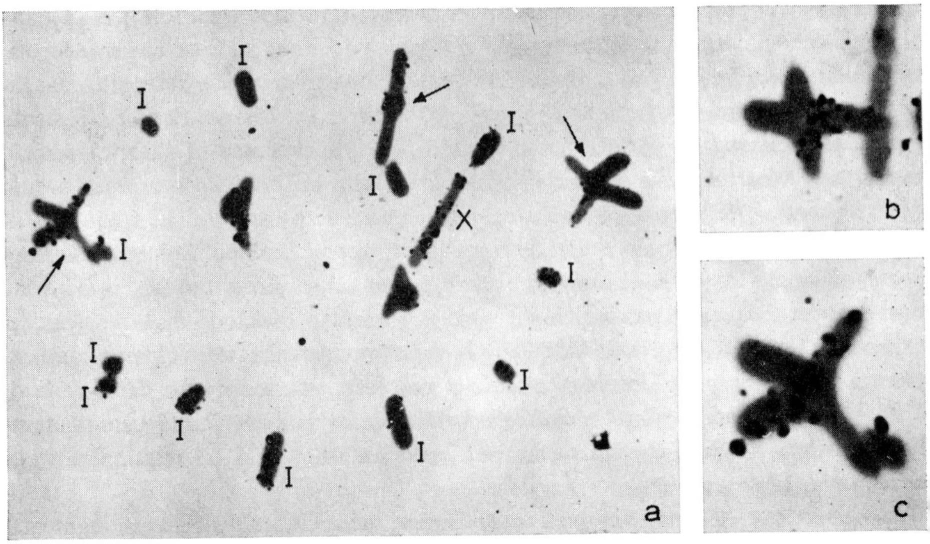

Fig. 7a. Autoradiograph of a metaphase I from a heat-treated individual of *Schistocerca gregaria*, showing chiasma formation between labelled and unlabelled chromosomes (arrows). (I = univalents) ×1,500. Figs. 7b and c. Enlarged metaphase bivalents showing label distribution. × 3,000

effects on recombination. In my opinion, this may, at least in part, prove to be due to differences in the methodology of the genetic and cytological approaches rather than implying that there are fundamental differences in their overall reponse. Typically, chiasma frequency response to temperature treatments is an inverted-U-shaped curve, with reduction in chiasma frequencies at high and low temperatures, which can culminate in asynapsis (Wilson; Elliott 1955, 1958; Dowrick; Henderson 1962, 1963a). The discrepancy between this response and the U-shaped effect on recombination found by Plough in *Drosophila melanogaster*, using proximal genetic markers, can be explained, if, accompanying a genuine overall reduction in cross-over frequency at high and low temperatures in *Drosophila*, there is the tendency for proximal localisation. This would lead to a misleading increase in crossing-over in proximal regions. The behaviour of chiasmata and cross-overs at less extreme temperatures would seem to be more complex and suggest that more subtle redistributions may be involved, without gross changes in overall frequency. The fact that a more careful investigation of the effects of heat-treatments of 40 °C on male meiosis has shown not one, but, apparently, four distinct effects indicates that many other published examples may prove to be more complex on re-investigation.

Ionising radiation treatments have been shown to have two effects on either chiasma or cross-over frequency: (1) irradiation during the premeiotic DNA S-phase decreases, and (2) irradiation during zygotene increases, the numbers of chiasmata or cross-overs found (Lawrence 1961a, b, 1965a). Similar chiasma frequency responses were obtained with *Tradescantia* and *Lilium*. The recombination data was obtained with *Chlamydomonas* and was shown to be dose-rate dependent (Lawrence 1965b). Infra-red radiation was found by Snoad to affect both chiasma frequency and position in *Tradescantia*. The chiasma frequency was increased by the infra-red treatment given and the increase involved the production of interstitial chiasmata.

The effects of drugs which inhibit RNA and DNA synthesis are particularly interesting in view of the suggested possible roles of RNA or DNA synthesis in the molecular exchange process which leads to chiasma formation or recombination. Suzuki (1965a, b) found that both the RNA synthesis inhibitor actinomycin and the DNA synthesis inhibitor mitomycin affected crossing-over in *Drosophila melanogaster* females. Both drugs increased recombination in proximal regions, the effects first being seen some 6–9 days after injection. Mitomycin has also been found to increase mitotic crossing-over in *Ustilago maydis* and *Saccharomyces cerevisiae* (Holliday 1964a). Another DNA synthesis inhibitor, 5-fluorodeoxyuridine, has been found to increase genetic recombination in *Ustilago maydis* (Esposito and Holliday) and *Neurospora crassa* (Wolff and deSerres). Chloramphenicol, a protein synthesis inhibitor was without effect on recombination in *Neurospora*, however (Wolff and deSerres).

Both mono- and bi-functional alkylating agents have been found to depress recombination in *Chlamydomonas reinhardi*. Their effects are not simple to interpret, but Davies is of the opinion that they provide evidence of two distinct periods during which recombination can be affected.

Nutritional factors which have been found to affect recombination, or chiasma, frequencies include the concentration of calcium or potassium in the external milieu (Paliwal and Hyde; Law) or the presence of nutritional gradients within an anther undergoing meiosis (Rees and Naylor). In *D. melanogaster* the effect of maternal age on recombination frequency has been known for many years and the difference between the two sexes of this species was one of the first findings to be noted when the genetics of this organism were initially studied. Sex differences in chiasma frequency or even localisation type are now known in many plants and animals (see John and Lewis: Tables 5 and 6).

(2) *Genetic.* Like chromosome pairing, chiasma formation and crossing-over are under both major and polygenic control (Rees 1961). The control of pairing and recombination can not be considered entirely independently, however, for clearly the initial presence of pairing is a prerequisite of recombination. Thus an asynaptic mutant is also one with no recombination. The distinction is more difficult to draw in desynaptic mutants – is the failure due to an ineffectiveness of the mode of pairing or a fault in the mode of chiasma formation? In no case can we yet draw this distinction, though failure at both levels is theoretically possible.

Illustration of the polygenic control of chiasma frequency comes from a study of the effects of inbreeding, hybridisation and selection. Rye (*Secale cereale*) is normally an outbreeding plant. It can be selfed and inbred lines have been maintained for many years. Due to unconscious selection in establishing the lines, they tend to differ in their mean chiasma frequencies. F_1 hybrids between two inbred lines show marked, positive heterosis, with a reduction in variance, while in F_2's there is a return towards the parental means and variances (Fig. 8). This behaviour is typical for polygenically controlled characters. Selection of high and low chiasma frequency lines in F_3 and subsequent generations also proved possible (Fig. 8). Indeed, in the example figured, recombination led to the establishment of a new genotype characterised by a lower chiasma frequency than either parent.

More precise information about the mode of operation of the polygenic control of chiasma frequency in rye was obtained by the use of the diallel cross analysis (Jinks). Using 4 inbred lines and all possible F_1 combinations it was shown that positive heterosis in F_1 hybrids resulted from non-allelic interactions.

The genetic system of rye, an outbreeder, is adapted to give a high chiasma frequency when genic heterozygosity is high. This is the reverse of the behaviour of wheat (*Triticum aestivum*), an inbreeder. Outcrossing wheat varieties leads to a fall in chiasma frequency and the presence of univalents: heterosis here is negative (Riley and Kimber). In both cases a change in the breeding system leads to a deleterious change in the genetic balance present. A diallel cross analysis of 8 varieties of wheat again revealed that the negative heterosis was largely due to non-allelic interactions (Watanabe).

Modifications to recombination or chiasma frequencies which should also be considered to be genetic include the effects of structural or numerical changes (e.g. Schultz and Redfield; Hewitt and John) and the effects of supernumary (B) chromosomes (e.g. John and Hewitt 1965) or supernumary heterochromatic segments (John and Hewitt 1966). No explanations can be advanced at the moment for most of these effects, but the behaviour of tandem duplication (Green) suggests that here, at least, an effect on the regularity or intimacy of chromosome pairing at the site of the duplication is involved.

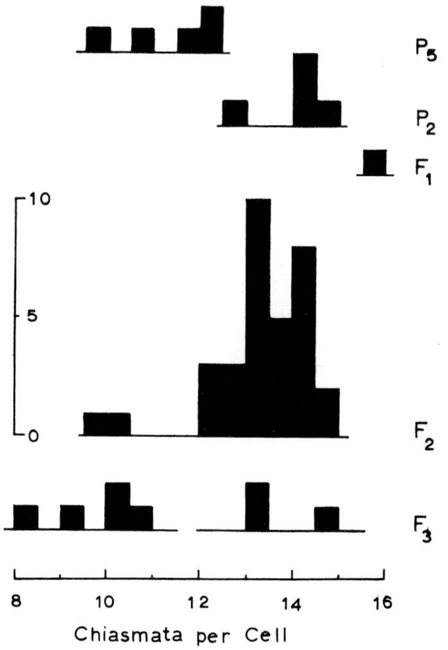

Fig. 8. Histograms of mean chiasma frequencies per cell in two inbred lines of rye, their F_1, F_2 and two families in the F_3. (From Rees 1955; redrawn.)

(d) *The time of chiasma formation and crossing-over during meiotic prophase*

If one is to attempt a useful explanation of chiasma formation or crossing-over in molecular terms it is clearly essential to know exactly when they occur. It is unfortunately not possible to see the event in progress down the light microscope and, until recently its timing was a matter for speculation. As a result, hypotheses have been suggested in the past in which it was proposed that chiasma formation occurred either (a) after chromosome replication, during zygotene or pachytene, when chromosomes are double (b) at the time of chromosome replication or (c) prior to chromosome replication, when chromatids are single. Using a number of different techniques and approaches it has now proved possible to narrow this undesirably wide field of speculation and restrict it to the first of the above three alternatives.

The demonstration by Mitra that the time of chromosome duplication prior to meiosis, as determined by the induction of chromosome and chromatid aberrations by X-rays, coincides with the period of premeiotic DNA synthesis, is not proof that recombination does not occur at the time of DNA synthesis. Those who have suggested that this work does directly illuminate the problem of the time of crossing-over in relation to the time of chromosome duplication are assuming that no chromosome pairing, even between small segments, occurs prior to the cytologically definable zygotene stage of prophase. However, in supporting the copy-choice model of crossing-over (see following section), Pontecorvo and Pritchard (1960a, b) suggested that a certain amount of pairing between small segments of homologous chromosomes may take place prior to and persist through, premeiotic DNA replication, and that genetic exchange might involve these segments alone. Zygotene pairing might be merely a continuation of this early synapsis and not be correlated with crossing-over at all. Possibilities such as this meant that further work was necessary to pin-point more precisely the time of chiasmate pairing and crossing-over during meiotic prophase.

As outlined in the previous section, it has been established that an environmental change, in the form of high temperature treatment, leads to a modification of pairing and chiasma formation in male locusts in a fairly repeatable and predictable fashion (Henderson 1962, 1963a). Use of this fact was made to test the relation between the time of chiasma formation, or synapsis, sensitive to heat-treatment, and the time of the main S-phase of premeiotic DNA synthesis, using this as a marker of chromosome replication. Initially, two experiments involving heat-treatments were carried out, using the locust *Schistocerca gregaria*. Immediately prior to the commencement of each heat-treatment, locusts were injected with H^3-thymidine and the time taken for the effect of heat-treatment to lead to a modification of chiasma frequency compared with the time taken for labelled cells to reach metaphase I. In the first experiment, locusts were kept at a constant 40 °C, which leads to a progressive reduction in chiasma frequency over a period of several days, culminating in widespread asynapsis on day 6. In the second experiment, locusts were subjected to a temperature of 40 °C for only 2 days, followed by a return to the control level of 30 °C. A wave of affected cells passed through meiosis on days 9–12. In both cases, autoradiographs showed that the observed effects on chiasma formation and chromosome pairing took place *after* DNA synthesis was complete (Henderson 1966).

Subsequent experiments, involving heat-treatments of varying durations in *Schistocerca*, have shown that the single major effect, a reduction in chiasma frequency, used as a marker in the above work, is not the only one brought about by heat-shocks. No less than 4 effects can sometimes be obtained, two of which lead to decreases in chiasma frequency and two of which lead to increases (Henderson, unpublished). These are interpreted in the following way: (1) an effect on spermatogonial mitosis, prior to the onset of meiosis (2) an effect on early zygotene synapsis. This is the largest effect, studied before. (3) An effect immediately prior to and (4) an effect at the time of chiasma formation. If these interpretations are correct, they enable one to state that, at male meiosis in *Schistocerca gregaria* maintained at a temperature of approximately 30 °C, the time of chiasma formation is likely to be some 8–9 days after DNA synthesis is complete, in late zygotene nuclei, and some 3–4 days prior to metaphase I.

An effect of heat-treatment on genetic recombination in the liverwort *Sphaerocarpus donnellii* was also used by Abel to deduce that recombination can be affected if such a heat-treatment is applied after DNA synthesis, as determined by radiation-induced mutation studies, is completed. An explanation of the discrepancy between these results and those obtained by Grell and Chandley in *Drosophila melanogaster* has been discussed elsewhere (Henderson 1966).

An entirely different approach, which also leads to the conclusion that chiasma formation and recombination must occur after the completion of DNA synthesis, is provided by the work of Rossen and Westergaard. Using the Ascomycete fungus *Neottiella rutilans*, where the fusion of two haploid nuclei immediately precedes meiosis, they have shown that DNA doubling takes place before nuclear fusion. This was demonstrated cytophotometrically, following Feulgen staining. Clearly recombination cannot occur at the time of DNA synthesis in this material, for at this time the haploid nuclei have not yet fused.

(e) *The molecular basis of crossing-over and chiasma formation*

It has become increasingly apparent in recent years that crossing-over occurs with molecular precision and that purely mechanical models, such as the torsion hypothesis (Darlington 1935b), are unsatisfactory. Until recently the most widely accepted hypothesis, particularly to explain aberrant microbial recombination data, was the copy-choice hypothesis (Lindegren and Lindegren; Lederberg; Pritchard 1960a, b). This involves a synthetic error at the time when new chromatids are being synthesised. Although presented in a far more plausible and sophisticated form than when it was originally proposed by Belling, its theoretical and practical limitations are considerable (see Whitehouse 1965). For example, to accomodate semiconservative DNA replication and the existence of 3- and 4-strand multiple cross-overs, additional events have to be proposed, which must involve more straightforward breakage and reunion. Faith in the copy-choice hypothesis was first shaken by the demonstration that recombination in virus *lambda* of *Escherichia coli* involved 'chromosome' breakage and could, apparently take place in the absence of DNA replication (Meselson and Weigle; Kellenberger, Zichichi and Weigle; Meselson 1964, 1965). The work described above, in the previous section, revealing the time of chiasma formation or crossing-over in relation to the time of DNA synthesis, now shows beyond doubt that segmental exchange does not involve a synthetic error at the time of the main S-phase of DNA replication. Indeed, in *Schistocerca* it appears to take place more than a week after replication is completed.

Any molecular model to explain crossing-over must do more than account for the simple exchange of segments between two paired homologous chromosomes. High resolution microbial genetic analyses have revealed several new phenomena which have proved to be closely associated with recombinational events and which must be accomodated by any satisfactory explanation of crossing-over. These are:

(1) *Gene conversion.* Instead of the expected 2 normal and 2 mutant meiotic products

from the meiosis of a heterozygote, one may sometimes obtain 3:1 or 1:3 ratios. (2) *Post meiotic segregation.* In Ascomycete fungi, meiosis is followed by a mitosis, with the production of 8 ascospores. In addition to aberrant ascospore ratios of the 6:2 or 2:6 type, 5:3 and 3:5 ratios have been obtained, indicating that segregation of conversion products can occur in the postmeiotic mitosis.

(3) *Polarized conversion.* It has been shown in a number of fungi that the relative position of a mutant on the chromosome may influence its conversion behaviour. Conversion may occur in a directional, polarized, fashion. The segment of genetic material showing such polarized recombinational behaviour has been termed a *polaron.*

(4) *Negative interference.* Although 'coarse' genetic analysis and chiasma distribution studies reveal the presence of strong positive interference (see above) high resolution techniques have shown the existence of what has been called localised *negative* interference between very closely linked sites.

These four phenomena are unexpected, and indeed inexplicable, on the classical models of crossing-over. The differences in behaviour which one finds when studying recombination between different genes ('non-allelic' crossing-over) and between different alleles of the same genetic locus ('allelic' crossing-over) has, in fact, led some to suggest that two quite different, independent crossing-over mechanisms are involved (see review by Westergaard). This is no longer necessary, for it is now possible to accomodate both modes of recombinational behaviour within single hypotheses of crossing-over.

In 1962 Holliday suggested that recombination could be achieved, and some of these anomalous patterns of behaviour explained, if breakage and reunion of chromosomal DNA molecules involved the localised separation of component polynucleotide chains and their re-association in hybrid complexes. If this occurred between heterozygous loci differing in base sequence, correction of mis-pairing would lead to gene conversion. Suggestions of this type have since been proposed and modified by a number of workers, including Whitehouse (1963, 1966); Holliday (1964b); Meselson (1964, 1965); Hastings and Whitehouse; and Whitehouse and Hastings. Whitehouse has also pointed out that negative interference may similarly be explained in terms of correction of mis-pairing.

In its simplest form, the *hybrid DNA* hypothesis of Holliday is summarised in Fig. 9. Primary breakage and separation involves polynucleotide chains of identical polarity in the two DNA molecules representing each chromatid (2). This is followed by an exchange of polynucleotide chains, with the formation of segments of 'hybrid' DNA (3). Correction of any mis-pairing which might occur in such segments would lead to gene conversion. Secondary breakage in the other polynucleotide chains leads to a chiasma (4), while secondary breakage in the original strand could lead to gene conversion without crossing-over between outside markers (5).

More complex conversion behaviour is explicable if conversion occurs during a temporary hybrid DNA association which does not persist because of the instability of pairing in heterozygous regions (Fig. 10).

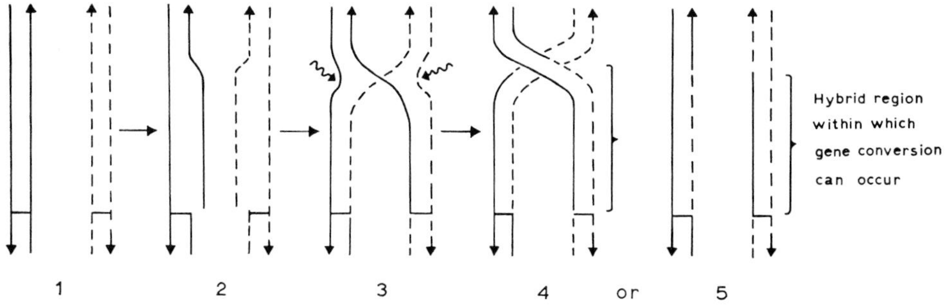

Fig. 9. The hybrid DNA hypothesis of Holliday for crossing-over and gene conversion. (From Holliday 1964b; redrawn). For explanation see text.

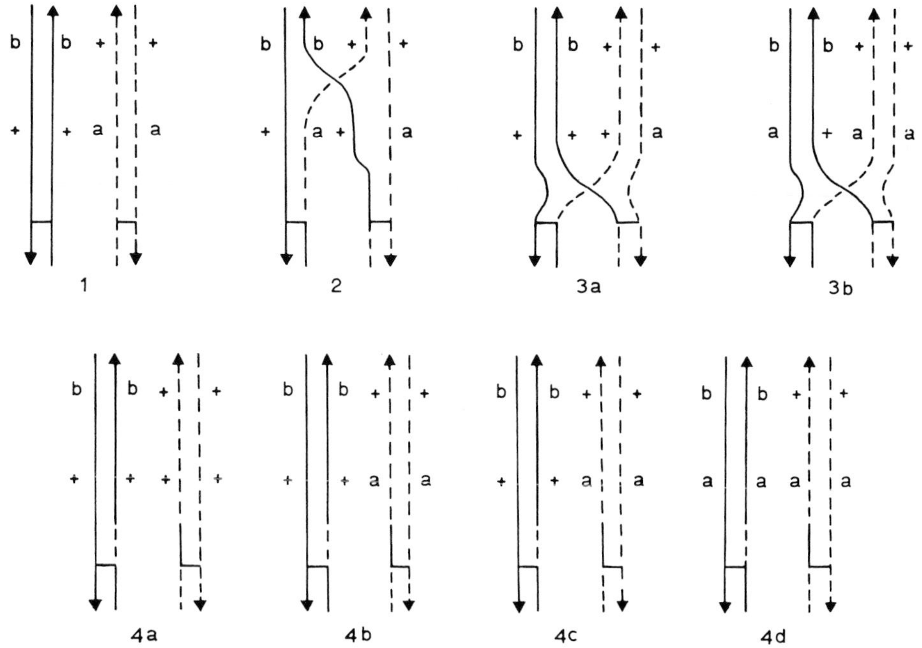

Fig. 10. Conversion without crossing-over, due to temporary polynucleotide chain pairing, on the Holliday model of hybrid DNA formation. Conversion of one or other of the two strands in a heterozygous region (3a or 3b) may be followed by correction in one of two ways to give the four possibilities shown. (From Holliday 1964b; redrawn.)

The hypothesis supported by Whitehouse differs in a number of important respects (Fig. 11): (1) the primary breakage involves polynucleotide chains of opposite polarity (2) synthesis of new polynucleotide chains is envisaged, which are assumed to separate from their templates and pair with the strands which first separated (3) this is followed by correction of mis-pairing and finally, breakdown of the remains of the unpaired polynucleotide chains.

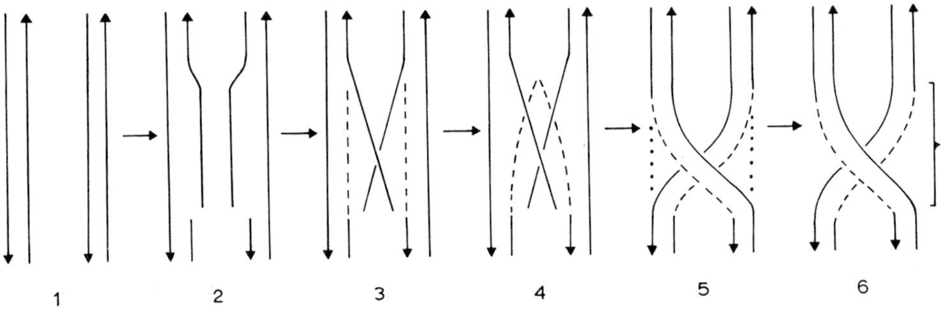

Fig. 11. The hybrid DNA hypothesis of Whitehouse for crossing-over and gene conversion. (Based on Whitehouse 1965; re-drawn and simplified.) For explanation see text.

This hypothesis is clearly far more intricate than that proposed by Holliday and requires a small amount of additional DNA synthesis at zygotene. In support of this, the autoradiographic work of Wimber and Prensky has been quoted. They found a small amount of DNA synthesis at this stage of meiosis in newts. DNA synthesis extending from interphase of meiosis into leptotene-zygotene has also been found in human chromosomes by Lima-de-Faria et al. (1966) (see his chapter). Using chemical extraction techniques, Hotta, Ito and Stern (see also chapter by Stern and Hotta) were able to detect a small amount of DNA synthesis during meiotic prophase which they were unable to demonstrate autoradiographically. This was found during zygotene and the amount of DNA replicated was no more than 0.3% of the total present. Tests showed that it appeared to be double stranded and part of the normal chromosomal DNA, but its base composition was unusually high in C:G and low in A:T bases.

While the presence of this zygotene DNA synthesis might be considered to provide valuable support for the Whitehouse hypothesis of recombination, the interpretation of Hotta et al. is that at least some of this replication which they observe is not associated with recombination, but with the delayed replication of some chromosomal component(s). This is further indicated by the work of Roth and Ito. Using the same system, they found that the DNA synthesis inhibitor deoxyadenosine could modify chromosome behaviour in 3 different ways during first meiotic prophase in *Lilium*, indicating 3 separate short periods of post-S-phase DNA synthesis. These, however, did not appear to modify the process of chiasma formation *itself*, but affect chromosome pairing, synaptinemal complex formation and chromosome separation. For example, if applied when synaptinemal complex formation was just beginning, further development of the complex was arrested.

The fact that a drug which inhibits DNA synthesis, such as mitomycin, is said to *increase* recombination, is certainly unexpected if this involves DNA synthesis, particularly when, as in *Drosophila* (Suzuki 1965b), the drug is not effective at prophase stages but most active when applied at S-phase or even gonial stages. The effect could be much more readily understood if the drug were acting in a similar manner to that described by Roth and Ito – restricting pairing and chiasma formation to initial contact points. This would lead to an effective increase in recombination for the genes located in those segments which did succeed in pairing. This is the interpretation which I also place on the effects of elevated temperature on the recombination of proximal loci in *Drosophila*. The increase in crossing-over brought about by the DNA synthesis inhibitor 5-fluorodeoxyuridine in *Ustilago* (Esposito and Holliday) and *Neurospora* (Wolff and deSerres) are similarly unexpected. Indeed, any substance which either increases or decreases the speed of DNA synthesis should not be expected to affect the frequency of exchanges, only the duration, or completeness, of the processes involved. A true increase in recombination frequency necessitates the production of new breaks and this should be independent of the duration of any subsequent repair synthesis.

The effects of such substances are not easy to explain in terms of existing hybrid DNA hypotheses and a final decision in favour of one is not possible at this stage, though Whitehouse (personal communication) is of the opinion that some of the most complex recombination data is explicable only in terms of his model. A Holliday-type of mechanism is supported by Fogel and Hurst, however, who, to explain conversion in their yeast recombination data, suggest a further model differing from that proposed by Holliday in only a few respects.

In a series of papers elegantly illustrating his extension of logical deduction and argument, Whitehouse has developed a model of crossing-over which explains the events occurring at the level of the gene and chromosome segment. These conclusions are not really affected by the validity or otherwise of his suggested basic hybrid DNA exchange mechanism, and could certainly involve an alternative mode of polynucleotide chain exchange. To accomodate the phenomenon of polarised gene conversion, Hastings and Whitehouse first proposed a polaron hybrid DNA hypothesis in which fixed points of primary breakage were postulated. They pointed out the similarities between such a model and the presumed mode of messenger RNA synthesis. Whitehouse and Hastings found evidence that the polaron coincided with the gene or cistron. Not all recombinational behaviour could be explained, even with this model, however, and Whitehouse (1966) suggested that a better explanation of the observed patterns of recombination could be provided by an operator model. On this model, dissociation of polynucleotide chains, prior to crossing-over can only occur at one particular end of a gene and it extends through the gene and into the neighbouring one. It is suggested that the behaviour of the control mechanism for recombination closely parallels the behaviour of the control mechanism for transcription outlined by Jacob and Monod. Indeed, it is considered that the two systems may prove to be identical.

Callan has proposed that the chromosomes of eukaryotes are organised in such a fashion that 'master' segments are associated with many repeated 'slave' segments. As chromosomes behave genetically as though they were composed only of contiguous 'master' segments, however, Whitehouse (1967) has suggested that prior to the exchange process between masters, excision of 'slaves' must occur, followed by their re-incorporation into the chromosome structure after crossing-over between masters is completed. Both excision and re-incorporation, Whitehouse suggests, may be brought about by cross-over events involving hybrid DNA formation.

4. Conclusion

A simplified summary of the present position is that crossing-over is most likely to involve some form of hybrid DNA association; that this can sometimes occur at mitosis, between unpaired or loosely paired chromosomes, and widely occurs at meiosis, between chromosomes paired to form a synaptinemal complex. Explanations of gene conversion and negative interference may be provided by corrections of base mis-pairing, but explanations of positive interference, or the many subtle interactions between and within chromosomes and genes, or the effects of environmental agencies are not so readily made. Even if much remains to be accounted for, there are good reasons for hoping that the basic mechanism of segmental exchange, which leads to chiasma formation or genetic crossing-over, may soon be fully understood in molecular terms.

References

ABEL, W.O.: Über den Zeitpunkt des Crossing-over und der Chromosomenverdopplung bei *Sphaerocarpus*. Z. Vererbungslehre 96 (1965) 228.

ANSLEY, H.R.: A cytological and cytophotometric study of alternative pathways of meiosis in the house centipede (*Scutigera forceps*. Raffinesque). Chromosoma 6 (1954) 656.

ANSLEY, H.R.: A cytophotometric study of chromosome pairing. Chromosoma 8 (1957) 380.

ASHBURNER, M.: Gene activity dependent on chromosome synapsis in the polytene chromosomes of *Drosophila melanogaster*. Nature 214 (1967) 1159.

BARBER, H.N.: Chromosome behaviour in *Uvularia*. J. Genet. 42 (1941) 223.

BARBER, H.N.: Experimental control of chromosome pairing in *Fritillaria*. J. Genet. 43 (1942) 359.

BEADLE, G.W.: A gene in maize for supernumary cell divisions following meiosis. Cornell Univ., Agr. Expt. Sta. Mem. 135 (1931) 1.

BEADLE, G.W.: Polymitotic maize and the precocity hypothesis of chromosome conjunction. Cytologia (Tokyo) 5 (1933) 118.

BELLING, J.: A working hypothesis for segmental interchange between homologous chromosomes in flowering plants. Univ. Calif. (Berkeley) Publ. Botany 14 (1928) 283.

BERENDES, H.D.: Asynapsis in the salivary gland chromosomes of *Drosophila hydei*. Genet. Iberica 33 (1963) 288.

BIER, K.: Der Karyotyp von *Calliphora erythrocephala* Meigen unter besonderer Berücksichtigung der Närzellkernchromosome in gebundelten und gepaarten Zustand. Chromosoma 11 (1960) 335.

BROWN, S.W. and W. WELSHONS: Maternal aging and somatic crossing-over of the ring X-chromosome of *Drosophila melanogaster*. Proc. Natl. Acad. Sci. U.S. 41 (1955) 209.

CALLAN, H.G.: The organisation of genetic units in chromosomes. J. Cell Sci. 2 (1967) 1.

COLEMAN, J.R. and M.J. MOSES: DNA and the fine structure of synaptic chromosomes in the domestic rooster (*Gallus domesticus*). J. Cell Biol. 23 (1964) 63.

COOPER, K.W.: The cytogenetics of meiosis in *Drosophila*. Mitotic and meiotic autosomal chiasmata without crossing-over in the male. J. Morphol. 84 (1949) 81.

DARLINGTON, C.D.: The internal mechanics of the chromosomes II. Prophase pairing at meiosis in *Fritillaria*. Proc. Roy. Soc. (London), Ser. B. 118 (1935a) 59.

DARLINGTON, C.D.: The time, place and action of crossing-over. J. Genet. 31 (1935b) 185.

DARLINGTON, C.D.: Recent advances in cytology, 2nd ed. London, Churchill (1937).

DARLINGTON, C.D. and A.A.MOFFET: Primary and secondary chromosome balance in *Pyrus*. J. Genet. 22 (1930) 129.

DAVIES, D.R.: The comparative effects of a mono- and a bi-functional alkylating agent on recombination in *Chlamydomonas reinhardi*. Z. Vererbungslehre 98 (1966) 61.

DOWRICK, G.J.: The influence of temperature on meiosis. Heredity 11 (1957) 37.

ELLIOTT, C.G.: The effect of temperature on chiasma frequency. Heredity 9 (1955) 385.

ELLIOTT, C.G.: Environmental effects on the distribution of chiasmata among nuclei and bivalents and correlation between bivalents. Heredity 12 (1958) 429.

ESPOSITO, R.E. and R.HOLLIDAY: The effect of 5-fluorodeoxyuridine on genetic replication and mitotic crossing over in synchronised cultures of *Ustilago maydis*. Genetics 50 (1964) 1009.

FOGEL, S. and D.D.HURST: Meiotic gene conversion in yeast tetrads and the theory of recombination. Genetics 57 (1967) 455.

GOLDSCHMIDT, E.: The influence of temperature on synapsis in hybrid salivary glands. Biol. Bull. 103 (1952) 67.

GREEN, M.M.: The effects of tandem duplications on crossing over in *Drosophila melanogaster*. Genet. Iberica 33 (1962) 154.

GRELL, R.F. and A.C.CHANDLEY: Evidence bearing on the coincidence of exchange and DNA replication in the oocyte of *Drosophila melanogaster*. Proc. Natl. Acad. Sci. U.S. 53 (1965) 1340.

HASTINGS, P.J. and H.L.K.WHITEHOUSE: A polaron model of genetic recombination by the formation of hybrid deoxyribonucleic acid. Nature 201 (1964) 1052.

HAYTER, A.M. and R.RILEY: The significance of DNA:histone ratios in meiotic synapsis. In: Chromosomes today, Vol. 2. Proc. 2nd Oxford Chrom. Conf. Edinburgh, Oliver and Boyd (1968).

HENDERSON, S.A.: Temperature and chiasma formation in *Schistocerca gregaria* II. Cytological effects and the mechanism of heat-induced univalence. Chromosoma 13 (1962) 437.

HENDERSON, S.A.: Temperature and chiasma formation in *Schistocerca gregaria* I. An analysis of the response at a constant 40 °C. Heredity 18 (1963a) 77.

HENDERSON, S.A.: Chiasma distribution at diplotene in a locust. Heredity 18 (1963b) 173.

HENDERSON, S.A.: Time of chiasma formation in relation to the time of deoxyribonucleic acid synthesis. Nature 211 (1966) 1043.

HENDERSON, S.A.: The salivary gland chromosomes of *Dasyneura crataegi* (Diptera: Cecidomyiidae). Chromosoma 23 (1967) 38.

HENDERSON, S.A.: The time and mode of chiasma formation. Advan. Genet. (1969a) (in prep.).

HENDERSON, S.A.: Chiasma localisation and the incompleteness of chromosome pairing. In: Chromosomes today, Vol. 2. Proc. 2nd Oxford Chrom. Conf. Edinburgh, Oliver and Boyd (1969b).

HEWITT, G.M. and B.JOHN: The influence of numerical and structural chromosome mutations on chiasma conditions. Heredity 20 (1965) 123.

HOLLIDAY, R.: Mutation and replication in *Ustilago maydis*. Genet. Res. 3 (1962) 472.

HOLLIDAY, R.: The induction of mitotic recombination by mitomycin C in *Ustilago* and *Saccharomyces*. Genetics 50 (1964a) 323.

HOLLIDAY, R.: A mechanism for gene conversion in fungi. Genet. Res. 5 (1964b) 282.

HOTTA, Y., M.ITO and H.STERN: Synthesis of DNA during meiosis. Proc. Natl. Acad. Sci. U.S. 56 (1966) 1184.

JACOB, F. and J.MONOD: Genetic regulatory mechanisms in the synthesis of proteins. J. Mol. Biol. 3 (1961) 318.

JAIN, H.K. and N.MAHERCHANDANI: The control of intranuclear distribution of chiasmata in *Delphinium*. Heredity 16 (1961) 383.

JINKS, J.L.: The analysis of quantitative inheritance in a diallel cross of *Nicotiana rustica* varieties. Genetics 39 (1954) 767.

JOHN, B. and S.A.HENDERSON: Asynapsis and polyploidy in *Schistocerca paranensis*. Chromosoma 13 (1962) 111.

JOHN, B. and G.M.HEWITT: The B-chromosome system of *Myrmeleotettix maculatus* I. The mechanics. Chromosoma 16 (1965) 548.

JOHN, B. and G.M.HEWITT: A polymorphism for heterochromatic supernumary segments in *Chorthippus parallelus*. Chromosoma 18 (1966) 254.

JOHN, B. and K.R.LEWIS: The meiotic system. Protoplasmatologia 6 (1965) 1.

KELLENBERGER, G., M.L.ZICHICHI and J.WEIGLE: Exchange of DNA in the recombination of bacteriophage λ. Proc. Natl. Acad. Sci. U.S. 47 (1961) 869.

KEMPANA, C.: Investigations into the genetic regulation of meiotic chromosome behaviour in *Triticum aestivum*. Ph.D. Thesis. Cambridge University, England (1963).

KEMPANA, C. and R.RILEY: Relationships between the genetic effects of deficiencies for chromosomes III and V on meiotic pairing in *Triticum aestivum*. Nature 195 (1962) 1270.

KEMPANA, C. and R.RILEY: Secondary association between genetically equivalent bivalents. Heredity 19 (1964) 289.

KIMBER, G.: Estimate of the number of genes involved in the genetic suppression of the cytological diploidisation of polyploid wheat. Nature 212 (1966) 317.

LAW, C.W.: An effect of potassium on chiasma frequency and recombination. Genet. Iberica 33 (1963) 313.

LAWRENCE, C.W.: The effect of irradiation of different stages of microsporogenesis on chiasma frequency. Heredity 16 (1961a) 83.

LAWRENCE, C.W.: The effect of radiation on chiasma formation in *Tradescantia*. Radiation Botany 1 (1961b) 91.

LAWRENCE, C.W.: Influence of non-lethal doses of radiation on recombination in *Chlamydomonas reinhardi*. Nature 206 (1965a) 789.

LAWRENCE, C.W.: The effect of dose duration on the influence of irradiation on recombination in *Chlamydomonas*. Mut. Res. 2 (1965b) 487.

LAWRENCE, W.J.C.: The secondary association of chromosomes. Cytologia (Tokyo) 2 (1931) 352.

LEDERBERG, J.: Recombination mechanisms in bacteria. J. Cellular Comp. Physiol. 45 (1955) 75.

LEWIS, E.B.: The theory and application of a new method of detecting chromosomal rearrangements in *Drosophila melanogaster*. Am. Naturalist 88 (1954) 225.

LINDEGREN, C.C. and G.LINDEGREN: Non-random crossing-over in *Neurospora*. J. Heredity 28 (1937) 105.

LU, B.C.: Meiosis in *Coprinus lagopus*: a comparative study with light and electron microscopy. J. Cell Sci. (1967) (in press).

MATHER, K.M.: The determination of the position in crossing over I. *Drosophila melanogaster*. J. Genet. 33 (1936a) 207.

MATHER, K.M.: Competition between bivalents during chiasma formation. Proc. Roy. Soc. (London), Ser. B. 120 (1936b) 208.

MATHER, K.M.: Crossing over. Biol. Rev. Cambridge Phil. Soc. 13 (1938) 252.

MATHER, K.M.: Biometrical genetics. London, Methuen (1949).

MATUSZEWSKI, B.: Transition from polyteny to polyploidy in salivary glands of *Cecidomyidae*. Chromosoma 16 (1965) 22.

MCCLINTOCK, B.: The association of non-homologous parts of chromosomes in the mid-prophase of meiosis in *Zea mays*. Z. Zellforsch. Mikroskop. Anat. 19 (1933) 191.

MESELSON, M.: On the mechanism of genetic recombination between DNA molecules. J. Mol. Biol. 9 (1964) 734.

MESELSON, M.: The duplication and recombination of genes. Proc. 16th. Int. Congr. Zool. (1963). New York (1965).

MESELSON, M. and J.J. WEIGLE: Chromosome breakage accompanying genetic recombination in bacteriophage. Proc. Natl. Acad. Sci. U.S. 47 (1961) 857.

MEYER, G.F.: The fine structure of the spermatocyte nuclei of *Drosophila melanogaster*. Proc. 2nd. Europ. Reg. Conf. Electron Mic., Delft (1960) 951.

MEYER, G.F.: A possible correlation between the submicroscopic structure of meiotic chromosomes and crossing over. Proc. 3rd. Europ. Reg. Conf. Electron Mic., Prague (1964) 461.

MITRA, S.: Effects of X-rays on chromosomes of *Lilium longiflorum* during meiosis. Genetics 43 (1958) 771.

MOENS, P.B.: Segregation of tritium-labelled DNA at meiosis in *Chorthippus*. Chromosoma 19 (1966) 277.

MOSES, M.J.: Chromosome structures in crayfish spermatocytes. J. Biophys. Biochem. Cytol. 2 (1956) 215.

MOSES, M.J.: The relation between the axial complex of meiotic chromosomes and chromosome pairing in a salamander (*Plethodon cinereus*). J. Biophys. Biochem. Cytol. 4 (1958) 633.

MOSES, M.J. and J.R. COLEMAN: Structural patterns and the functional organisation of chromosomes. In: The role of chromosomes in development. New York, Academic Press (1964).

MÜLLER, H.J.: The mechanism of crossing over. Am. Naturalist 50 (1916) 193, 284, 350, 421.

NEBEL, B.R. and E.M. COULON: Enzyme effects on pachytene chromosomes of the male pigeon evaluated with the electron microscope. Chromosoma 13 (1962) 292.

OKAMOTO, M.: Identification of the chromosomes of common wheat belonging to the A and B genomes. Can. J. Genet. Cytol. 4 (1962) 31.

PALIWAL, R.L. and B.B. HYDE: Effect of calcium and magnesium on chiasma frequency in *Plantago ovata*. Genetics 42 (1957) 387.

PAO, W.K. and H.W. LI: Desynapsis and other abnormalities induced by high temperature. J. Genet. 48 (1948) 297.

PLOUGH, H.H.: The effect of temperature on crossing over in *Drosophila*. J. Exptl. Zool. 24 (1917) 147.

PONTECORVO, G.: Trends in genetic analysis. New York, Columbia University Press (1958).

PRITCHARD, R.H.: Microbial genetics. London, Cambridge University Press (1960a).

PRITCHARD, R.H.: The bearing of recombination analysis at high resolution on genetic fine structure in *Aspergillus nidulans* and the mechanism of recombination in higher organisms. Symp. Soc. Gen. Microbiol. 10 (1960b) 155.

REES, H.: Heterosis in chromosome behaviour. Proc. Roy. Soc. (London), Ser. B 144 (1955) 150.

REES, H.: Genotypic control of chromosome form and behaviour. Botan. Rev. 27 (1961) 288.

REES, H. and B. NAYLOR: Developmental variation in chromosome behaviour. Heredity 15 (1960) 17.

RHOADES, M.M.: Meiosis. In: The cell, Vol. III. New York, Academic Press (1961).

RIEGER, R.: Inhomologenpaarung und Meiose bei haploiden Formen von *Antirrhinum majus* L. Chromosoma 9 (1957) 1.

RILEY, R.: The meiotic behaviour, fertility and stability of wheat-rye chromosome addition lines. Heredity 14 (1960) 89.

RILEY, R., V. CHAPMAN and G. KIMBER: Genetic control of chromosome pairing in intergeneric hybrids with wheat. Nature 186 (1959) 259.

RILEY, R. and G. KIMBER: Aneuploids and the cytogenetic structure of wheat varietal populations. Heredity 16 (1961) 275.

RILEY, R. and C.N. LAW: Genetic variation in chromosome pairing. Advan. Genet. 13 (1965) 57.

ROSSEN, J.M. and M. WESTERGAARD: Studies on the mechanism of crossing over II. Meiosis and the time of chromosome replication in the Ascomycete *Neottiella rutilans* (Fr.) Dennis. Compt. Rend. Trav. Lab. Carlsberg 35 (1966) 233.

ROTH, T.R.: Changes in the synaptinemal complex during meiotic prophase in mosquito oocytes. Protoplasma 61 (1966) 346.

ROTH, T.R. and M.ITO: DNA-dependent formation of the synaptinemal complex at meiotic prophase. J. Cell Biol. 35 (1967) 247.

SAX, K.: Effects of variations in temperature on nuclear and cell division in *Tradescantia*. Am. J. Botany 24 (1937) 218.

SCHIN, K.S.: Meiotische Prophase und Spermatidenreifung bei *Gryllus domesticus* mit besonderer Berücksichtigung der Chromosomenstruktur. Z. Zellforsch. Mikroskop. Anat. 65 (1965a) 481.

SCHIN, K.S.: Core-strukturen in den meiotischen und post-meiotischen Kernen der Spermatogenese von *Gryllus domesticus*. Chromosoma 16 (1965b) 436.

SCHULTZ, J. and H.REDFIELD: Interchromosomal effects on crossing over in *Drosophila*. Cold Spring Harbour Symp. Quant. Biol. 16 (1951) 175.

SCHWARZ, D.: Evidence for sister-strand crossing over in maize. Genetics 38 (1953) 251.

SCHWARZ, D.: Studies on the mechanism of crossing over. Genetics 39 (1954) 692.

SCHWARZ, D.: Studies on crossing over in maize and *Drosophila*. J. Cellular Comp. Physiol. 45 (1955) 171.

SEARS, E.R.: The aneuploids of common wheat. Missouri Univ., Agr. Expt. Sta. Res. Bull. 572 (1954) 59.

SEARS, E.R.: The aneuploids of common wheat. Proc. 1st. Int. Wheat Genet. Symp., Winnipeg (1958) 221.

SEARS, E.R. and M.OKAMOTO: Intergenomic chromosome relationships in hexaploid wheat. Proc. 10th. Int. Genet. Congr., Montreal, Vol. 2 (1959) 258.

SERRA, J.A.: Physical chemistry of the nucleus. In: Encyclopaedia of plant physiology, Vol. 1. Berlin, Springer (1955) 472.

SHAH, S.S.: Inter-relationships of chiasma frequencies in normal set bivalents in presence of extra heterochromatin and euchromatin in *Dactylis glomerata* subsp. *Lusitanica*. Heredity 20 (1965) 470.

SINHA, S.K.: Ph.D. Thesis: Indiana Univ., U.S.A. (1960); referred to by Rhoades, M.M. (1961) (see above).

SNOAD, B.: The action of infra red upon chiasma formation. Chromosoma 7 (1955) 451.

SOTELLO, J.R. and O.TRUJILLO-CENOZ: Electron microscope study on spermatogenesis, chromosome morphogenesis at the onset of meiosis (cyte I) and nuclear structure of early and late spermatids. Z. Zellforsch. Mikroskop. Anat. 51 (1960) 243.

SOTELLO, J.R. and R.WETTSTEIN: Electron microscope study on meiosis. The sex chromosome in spermatocytes, spermatids and oocytes of *Gryllus argentinus*. Chromosoma 15 (1964) 389.

STERN, C.: Somatic crossing over and segregation in *Drosophila melanogaster*. Genetics 21 (1936) 625.

SUZUKI, D.T.: Effects of Actinomycin D on crossing over in *Drosophila melanogaster*. Genetics 51 (1965a) 11.

SUZUKI, D.T.: Effects of Mitomycin C on crossing over in *Drosophila melanogaster*. Genetics 51 (1965b) 635.

TAYLOR, J.H.: Sister chromatid exchanges in tritium-labelled chromosomes. Genetics 43 (1958) 515.

TAYLOR, J.H.: Distribution of tritium-labelled DNA among chromosomes during meiosis I. Spermatogenesis in the grasshopper. J. Cell Biol. 25 (1965) 57.

THODAY, J.M.: Location of polygenes. Nature 191 (1961) 368.

WATANABE, Y.: Meiotic irregularities in intervarietal hybrids of common wheat. Wheat Inform. Service 14 (1962) 5.

WESTERGAARD, M.: Studies on the mechanism of crossing over I. Theoretical considerations. Compt. Rend. Trav. Lab. Carlsberg 34 (1964) 359.

WHITEHOUSE, H. L. K.: A theory of crossing over by means of hybrid deoxyribonucleic acid. Nature 199 (1963) 1034.

WHITEHOUSE, H. L. K: Towards an understanding of The Mechanism of Heredity. London, Edward Arnold (1965).

WHITEHOUSE, H. L. K.: An operator model of crossing over. Nature 211 (1966) 708.

WHITEHOUSE, H. L. K.: A cycloid model for the chromosome. J. Cell Sci. 2 (1967) 9.

WHITEHOUSE, H. L. K. and P. J. HASTINGS: The analysis of genetic recombination on the polaron hybrid DNA model. Genet. Res. 6 (1965) 27.

WILSON, J. Y.: Chiasma frequency in relation to temperature. Genet. Iberica 29 (1959) 290.

WIMBER, D. E. and W. PRENSKY: Autoradiography with meiotic chromosomes of the male newt (*Triturus viridescens*) using H^3-thymidine. Genetics 48 (1963) 1731.

WOLFF, S. and F. J. DESERRES: Chemistry of crossing over. Nature 213 (1967) 1091.

WOLSTENHOLME, D. R. and G. F. MEYER: Some facts concerning the nature and formation of axial core structures in spermatids of *Gryllus domesticus*. Chromosoma 18 (1966) 272.

PART V

Ultrastructure of the interphase nucleus and chromosomes

CHAPTER 15

The ultrastructure of chromatin in nuclei of interphase cells and in spermatids*

JEROME S. KAYE

Department of Biology, University of Rochester, Rochester, N.Y. 14627

Contents

1. Introduction
2. Structure of chromatin in interphase nuclei
3. Structure of chromatin in spermatids

* Some of the work reported here was supported in part by Grant GM-09747 from the United States Public Health Service.

1. Introduction

Chromosomes and nuclei were among the first cellular objects to be studied with the electron microscope. The increased resolution of the electron microscope gave promise of yielding information on such problems as the kind, number, size, and arrangement of component parts of chromosomes, and on changes in components or in their arrangement that presumably underlie the gross changes in morphology during mitosis and meiosis, and might underlie cell differentiation and function. Very little of this information has been obtained. Research on the nucleus seems remarkably unfruitful compared with that on cytoplasmic organelles, when results achieved by similar efforts are considered. The thin contorted fibers which are the generally observed component of chromatin, are at once too small in one dimension for their substructure to be readily determined, and so long and irregularly disposed that any particular arrangement of these fibers that exists in chromatin or in chromosomes is difficult to determine.

Identification of the structural components of chromatin has depended on various methods of determining the localization of DNA. It is sometimes done indirectly by determining the distribution of Feulgen stain in thick sections with the light microscope and comparing it with the distribution of material in thin sections studied with the electron microscope. Sometimes chromatin in the same cell is identified in adjacent thick and thin sections. DNA has also been identified directly in thin sections studied with the electron microscope, with the technique of autoradiography, using H^3-thymidine as a label. The resolution of these methods is no better than about 0.2 μ, and usually worse. Detection of DNA in electron-microscope preparations by staining with heavy metals potentially offers an improvement in resolution of two orders of magnitude. Presently all the available techniques for staining with metals suffer in some degree from lack of specificity, and also from the fact that fixatives which yield the best specificity in staining do not yield excellent preservation of ultrastructure.

2. Structure of chromatin in interphase nuclei

Fibers are consistently present in regions of chromatin. In condensed chromatin, either from mitotic chromosomes or the heterochromatin of interphase nuclei, they are apparently the only structures present. A thin section of condensed chromatin, as seen in the electron microscope, is composed of linear and punctate profiles (Fig. 1). These are best interpreted as being longitudinal and transverse views of fibers. It is unlikely that the dark linear profiles are edge views of sheets because broad gray profiles, which sheets would show in face view, do not occur. The punctate profiles presumably represent fibers seen in transverse section, since they have the same size range as the thickness of the linear profiles. Although it is still impossible to rule out the occurrence of some fine granules, since no one has reported success in tracing a punctate element through successive sections, it is generally assumed that fibers are the sole component of condensed chromatin in somatic nuclei.

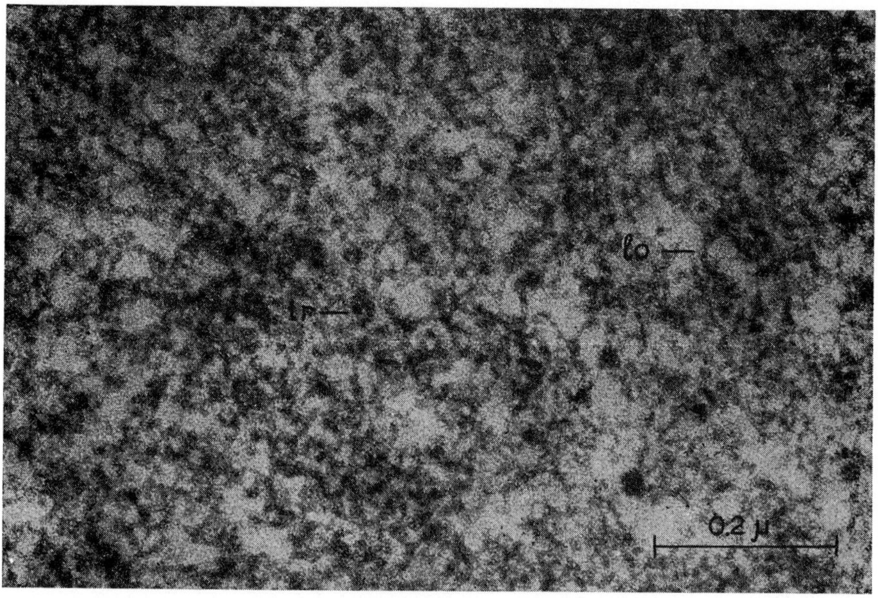

Fig. 1. A section through chromatin in an early spermatid of the house cricket, which has interphase-like chromatin fibers. Fibers seen in longitudinal and transverse views are marked (lo) and (tr) respectively. ×130,000. (From Kaye and McMaster-Kaye.)

Most nuclei contain, in addition to fibers of the type found in condensed chromatin, irregular granules with sizes ranging from about 200 to 800 Å, and some amorphous material which cannot be characterized. These structures are frequently intermingled in the nucleoplasm, but are too small to be resolved from each other by the most reliable methods used to identify chromatin, thus uncertainty exists about the identification of any individual element. Autoradiographic evidence that DNA is restricted to the fibrous elements was given by Hay and Revel, who studied interphase nuclei where clumps of fibrillar material were fairly well segregated from other material; H^3-thymidine labelled DNA was detected only in the fibrillar material. Swift (1963) also concluded that granules are not components of chromatin; he reported that their susceptibility to nucleases indicates that the large irregular granules contain RNA, but not DNA. Granules are still a poorly characterized nuclear fraction, and it is clear that several different types exist. The only type for which there is any evidence of its containing DNA, is the perichromatin granule described by Watson.

Recent reports indicate that the thickness of chromatin fibers in sections falls in the range of about 40 to 150 Å (Ris 1962; Hay and Revel; Kaye and McMaster-Kaye). There are considerable differences among various reports, but the published data do not allow one to conclude whether these differences reflect experimental errors or real variations due to cell type or organism. Fibers are difficult to measure; they are thin and their edges are indistinct. Most workers seem to have made only casual measurements of thickness, and give no indication of their sample size or of the variation within a sample, and only rarely give the extreme ranges found. Data on the accuracy in calibration of magnification of the electron microscope are usually lacking. Detailed study of the diameters of chromatin fibers, in interphase-like nuclei of early spermatids (Kaye and McMaster-Kaye), showed there is considerable variation in the thickness of fibers within a given sample of chromatin. There is variation both among fibers and along the length of a single fiber. The frequency distribution of a typical sample is shown in Fig. 3. Nonetheless, the mean thickness of fibers in chromatin of five different types was nearly constant; the total range of mean diameters was 79 to 84 Å.

Several studies have used surface-spread preparations rather than sectioned material, and have reported observations on the fibers which are obtained from nuclei by this technique (Gall 1966). Surface-spread material can be examined directly, after collecting on a grid and drying, or after additional procedures such as shadowing or staining; the usual fixation, embedding and sectioning of material have been avoided in these studies. Fibers are the only component of the nucleus found in spread preparations (Fig. 2), and they are fairly well separated, hence more exposed to view than

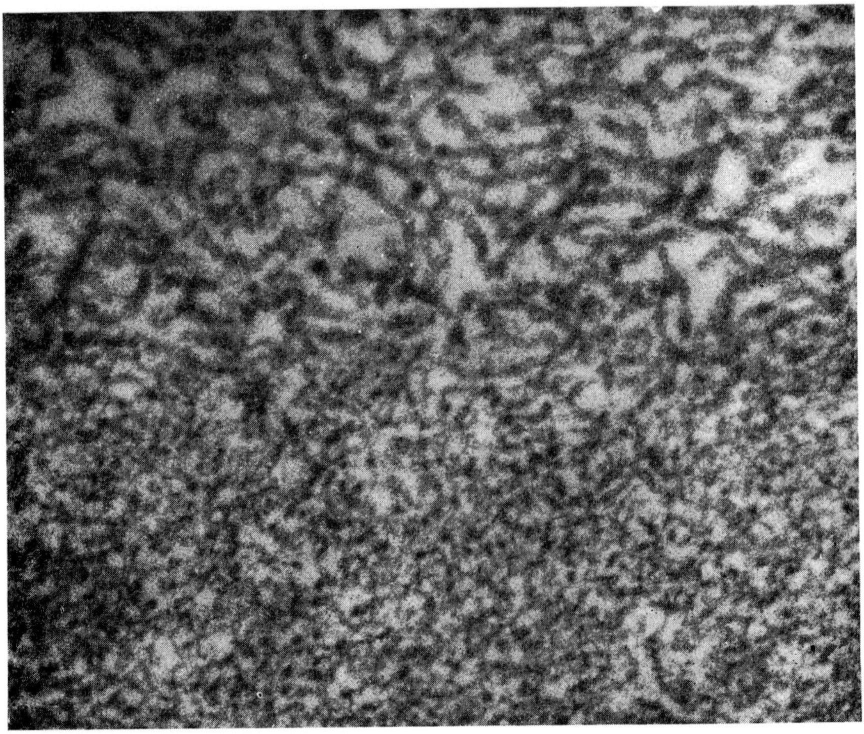

Fig. 2. A portion of a *Triturus* erythrocyte nucleus which was partially spread on a water surface, then was fixed, embedded and sectioned. The portion in the top half of the figure presumably spread on the water surface, the portion in the bottom half did not. The thick fibers in the top half are characteristic of surface spread fibers; the thinner fibers in the bottom half are characteristic of the usual fibers in sectioned nuclei. × 60,000. (From Wolfe and Grim.)

in sections. They appear to be interconnected, forming a network in most preparations. Early studies suggested surface-spread fibers were as thick as 600 Å and were constructed around a longitudinal core of dense material. Recent studies, however, have found no evidence of such a core, and have indicated that the average fiber thickness is somewhat less. The fibers are frequently of variable diameter, a single fiber showing thicknesses of 50 to 250 Å, for example (Gall 1966), and inhomogeneous, with local granularities and also indications of longitudinal splitting (Ris 1967); in other preparations, fibers are relatively homogeneous in appearance and uniform in diameter, with a total range of diameters of about 200 to 300 Å (Wolfe and Grim). In general, the fibers average about 250 Å in diameter, about two to three times as thick as the chromatin fibers of sectioned material. Wolfe and Grim have investigated several factors that might explain the greater thickness of fibers in spread preparations as compared with sections; they have shown that fiber thickness increases, to about 250 Å, when nuclei lyse and release their fibers during the spreading procedure, and that such 250 Å fibers are not decreased in size significantly by fixation and embedding. They have suggested that chromatin fibers, of about 100 Å diameter, are coated with some contaminating substance from the cell during lysis to produce the thickened fiber seen in surface-spread preparations.

The substructure of chromatin fibers is still unsettled with regard to the number and arrangement of DNA molecules with associated histone. A fiber thickness in the range of 100 Å is consistent with quite different possibilities assuming that a 35-Å DNA–histone fiber, of the type reported by Zubay and Doty, exists in chromatin. For example an 80-Å fiber could contain up to five such fibers if they are closely packed. On the other hand, a single supercoiled DNA–histone complex could also be a fiber 80 Å thick.

The thinnest chromatin fibers reported are about 40 Å thick. This is true for sectioned material and surface spread preparations. Such fibers are of special interest because they seem too thin to be made of more than one DNA–histone complex. It has been suggested that the thicker fibers generally observed may be aggregates of the thinnest fibers (Swift 1962). However, the thinnest fibers do not seem to constitute a separate class of fibers, as would be the case if thicker fibers were aggregates of thinner ones. Frequency distributions of fiber thicknesses in chromatin containing such fibers show only one class; the thinnest fibers are simply the low end of a normal distribution curve, as seen in Fig. 3.

Fairly high resolution micrographs of chromatin fibers in thin sections usually show some finer lines within them which may be interpreted as evidence of subfibers. The most convincing report of such structure has been published by Wettstein and Sotelo. Unfortunately the size of this substructure is just about at the limit of resolution that is usually obtained on sections. Phase-contrast background effects in even slightly under-focussed pictures, such as those of Wettstein and Sotelo, give images similar to the supposed substructure of the fibers. Ris (1967) has concluded from a study of surface-spread fibers which were digested with pronase that chromatin fibers contain only a single DNA molecule.

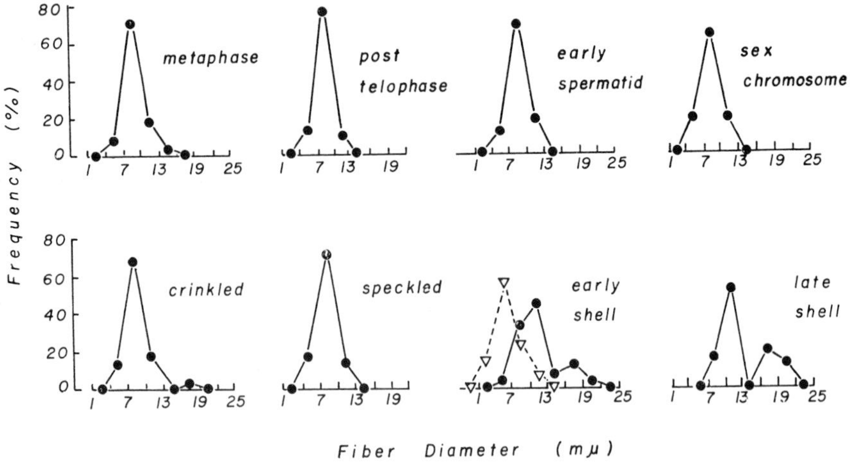

Fig. 3. Frequency distributions of measured diameters of house cricket chromatin fibers in chromosomes of meiotic divisions ('metaphase') and from different stages of early spermatids ('post telophase' through 'speckled'). Mean fiber diameters are constant until the shell stages and only one size class is present. There is considerable spread about the mean. During the shell stage the diameters increase and two classes appear. Non-chromatin fibers in the early shell stage are shown with a broken line. (From Kaye and McMaster-Kaye.)

3. Structure of chromatin in spermatids

It seems likely that most mature sperm have a chromatin structure which is different from the structure typical of somatic nuclei. Only the sea urchin has been reported to have the somatic-type structure, and no detailed study of this organism has been reported. Many studies have been concerned with the development of the sperm nucleus, and a number of unusual nuclear structures, and sequences of structures, have been found to precede the final maturation of the sperm nucleus. Features noted in different organisms are summarized in Table 1.

In most studies, the structure of chromatin at the beginning of spermiogenesis has not been analyzed in detail. Nuclei have been described as generally similar in appearance to somatic nuclei. Although few micrographs have been published, it seems clear that the chromatin can not be strikingly unusual on a gross scale. At second meiotic telophase and in early spermatids of an organism which we examined (Kaye and McMaster-Kaye), the chromatin was found to have the structure that might be expected in an interphase nucleus of a somatic cell; the fibers averaged about 80 Å in diameter, were contorted, and irregularly arranged.

Condensation of material occurs during the differentiation of the sperm nucleus. In the process, nuclei of some organisms go through stages in which apparently random clumping of unorganized material seems to occur, while some organisms show stages in which very well-defined structures, with a very regular arrangement, make up the

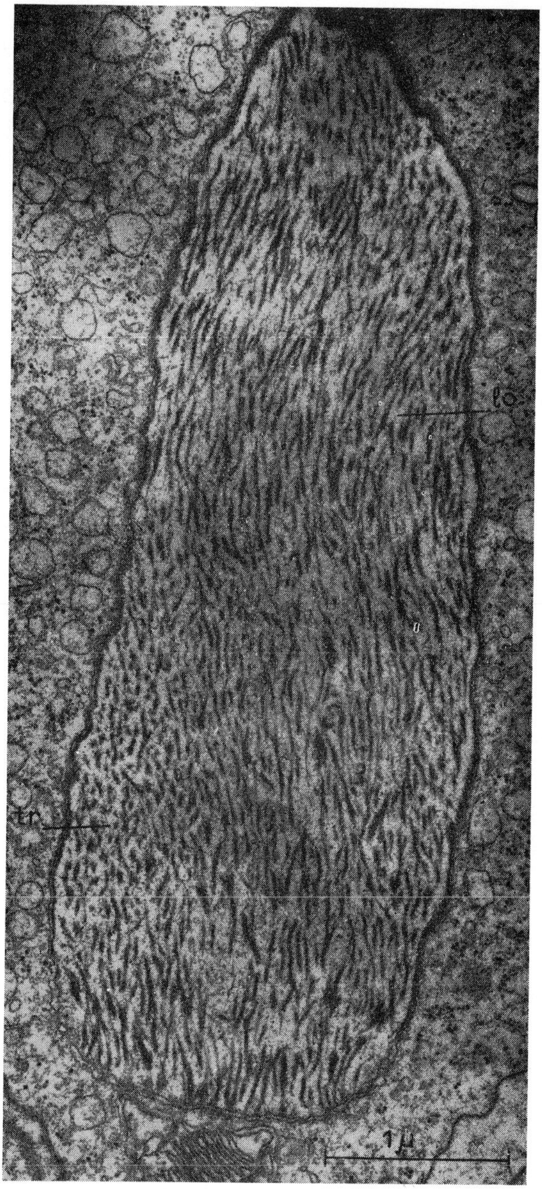

Fig. 4. A nearly longitudinal section through a spermatid nucleus in the snail *Viviparus contectoides* at an early stage of nuclear elongation. The nuclear fibers follow a loose helical path, roughly parallel with the long axis of the nucleus. Most fibers are seen in longitudinal view (lo). Some are seen nearly end-on (tr). × 25,000. Osmic-formalin fixation.

nuclei. Much more attention has been given to organisms of the latter type in studies to date.

In most vertebrates (with the exception of reptiles, as noted below) nuclear differentiation is accomplished without the appearance of well-organized structure. Burgos and Fawcett described the nuclear material of toad spermatids as consisting of small granules which get larger during spermiogenesis. Eventually the granules give way

TABLE 1

Nuclear structure in spermatids of different species

Species	Group	Early spermatids	Later spermatids	Mature sperm	Reference
PLATYHELMINTHES					
Paragonimus miyazakii	Lung, fluke	'diffuse'	1. sheets, 250 Å[a, b, e]	dense[i]	Sato et al.
NEMATHELMINTHES					
Aspicularis tettraptera	Nematode	No nucleus is present in spermatids; chromatin is diffusely spread through the cell.			Lee and Anya
ANNELIDA					
Lumbricus terrestris	Oligochaete	'evenly dispersed'	1. condensed material[d] 2. condensed material[c]	dense[j]	Anderson et al.
Enchytraeus albidus	Oligochaete	n.g.	1. sheets[f], thick 2. sheets[f], thin	dense[j]	Reger (1967)
Spirobis mörchi	Polychaete	'diffuse'	1. condensed material[c] 2. fibers[r]	dense[j]	Potswald
ARTHROPODA					
Oniscus assellus	Isopod	n.g.	1. sheets, 350 Å[b, f]	dense[j]	Reger (1966)
Armidillidium vulgare	Isopod	n.g.	1. condensed material[d] 2. sheets, 250 Å[b, f]	dense[j]	Fain-Mauriel
Procambarus clarkii	Decapod	'interphase-like'	1. fibers[k]	fibers[k] 70–200 Å	Moses (1961a, b)
Thermobia domestica	Insecta, thysanura	n.g.	n.g.	lamellae[b] 60 Å	Bawa
Aeschna grandis	Insecta, odonata	n.g.	1. fibers[r], 600 Å 2. condensed material[j]	dense[j]	Kessel

Gryllus (Acheta) *domestıcus*	Insecta, orthoptera	'interphase-like'	1. condensed material[c] 2. fibers[s], 200 Å 3. dense[c, j, n]	dense[j]	Schin
Acheta domesticus	Insecta, orthoptera	interphase-like	1. fibers[c], ca. 170 Å plus thinner interior fibers 2. fibers[s], 200–1000 Å 3. dense[c, j, n]	dense[j]	Kaye and McMaster-Kaye (1966); also unpublished observations
Locusta migratoria	Insecta, orthoptera	'lacks organization'	1. ribbons[r], 60–100 Å 2. sheets[f], 60–80 Å 3. sheets[g], 60 Å	dense[j]	Gibbons and Bradfield
Chortophaga viridifasciata; *Chorthippus curtipennis*; *Romalea microptera*	Insecta, orthoptera	fibers[p], 200 Å	1. fibers[r], 100–150 Å 2. fibers[r], 40 Å 3. sheets[f] 4. sheets[g]	dense[j]	Dass and Ris
Disostiera carolina; *Melanoplus fermur-rubrum*	Insecta, orthoptera	fibers, 150 Å	1. sheets[r], 150 Å 2. sheets[f], 70Å 3. sheets[g], 70 Å	dense[j]	Gall and Bjork
Oncopeltus fasciatus	Insecta, hemiptera	interphase-like	1. condensed material[c] 2. fibers[r] 3. sheets[f]	dense[j]	Barker and Riess
Drosophila melanogaster	Insecta, diptera	n.g.	1. fibers[k] 2. condensed material	dense[j]	Shoup
Sciara coprophila	Insecta, diptera	n.g.	1. fibers[k, b] 100–200 Å 2. condensed material	dense[j]	Phillips
MOLLUSCA					
Mytilus edulis	Polycepoda	n.g.	progressive condensation[d]	granular	Longo and Dornfeld

TABLE 1, *continued*

Species	Group	Early spermatids	Later spermatids	Mature sperm	Reference
Viviparus contectoides	Gasteropoda	'interphase-like'	1. fibers[r], 100–140 Å 2. fibers[r], 100–300 Å 3. fibers[r], lamellar sub-structure	dense[j]	Kaye
Otala lactea	Gasteropoda	n.g.	1. ribbons[r], 60 Å 2. sheets[r], 60 Å	dense[j]	Rebhun
CHORDATA					
Jenynsia lineata	Teleostei	n.g.	1. fibers[k] 2. condensed fibers or granules[c], plus thinner fibers[m]	dense[j]	Dadone and Narbaitz
Bufo arenarum	Amphibia	n.g.	1. granules, 100–150 Å 2. granules, 600–700 Å 3. conglomerate of granules	n.g.	Burgos and Fawcett
Anolis carolinensis	Reptilia	n.g.	1. fibers[k] 2. fibers[r], 100–180 Å[b] 3. sheets[f], 130–160 Å	dense[j]	Clark
Python sebae	Reptilia	n.g.	1. fibers[r] 2. sheets[f]	dense[j]	Boissin and Mattei
Gallus domesticus	Aves	n.g.	1. undetermined, fine texture 2. granules, 400 Å	dense[j]	McIntosh and Porter
Human	Mammalia	n.g.	1. undetermined, fine texture 2. small granules, 150–250 Å 3. larger and larger granules up to 900 Å	n.g.	Horstmann

Explanation of table. The structural components reported for spermatids and sperm are listed in the table. The arrangement of the components is also indicated, mainly by footnotes. The sequence of stages is indicated by the numbers, i.e. 1, 2, 3 etc. In most cases the complete sequence of stages has not been reported.

[a] Called fibers by the authors; sheets are the interpretation of the present author.
[b] Approximate measurements made by the present author from the published micrographs.
[c] Condensation of nuclear material in a shell at nuclear periphery.
[d] Random clumps of dense material.
[e] Sheets, closely spaced.
[f] Sheets form the walls of tubes of irregular cross section.
[g] Sheets arranged like walls of a honey comb.
[h] Closely packed lamellae.
[i] Perhaps fibrillae.
[j] Uniformly electron opaque.
[k] Fibers, random orientation.
[m] Interior of nucleus has thinner fibers.
[n] Interior of nucleus has sheets.
n.g. Not given.
[p] Made of two 100 Å fibers.
[r] Longitudinal or helical orientation.
[s] Fibers at periphery of nucleus which are oriented perpendicular or oblique to long axis of nucleus, plus thinner fibers in interior of nucleus.

to an electron-opaque nucleus. Nuclei of bird and mammalian spermatids seem to be similar. Nuclear structures in these vertebrate spermatids are difficult to analyze. Close examination of Burgos and Fawcett's pictures shows numerous objects of elongated profile, as well as those with circular outline; they might be interpreted as tightly coiled fibers, rather than granules. Further work on vertebrate spermatids is badly needed.

In some invertebrates, no discrete nuclear structures are formed in spermatids. In earthworms, mussels and some dipterans, for example, the nuclear contents appear to condense in local regions of the nucleus at first; eventually no empty spaces or uncondensed material remains.

A highly organized structure is typical of the spermatid nuclei of certain insects, snails and other invertebrates. Some reptiles have structures that are astonishingly similar. In these organisms, striking patterns result when a regular arrangement of well-defined structural components appears in the nucleus during mid and late spermiogenesis. Clearly, nuclear structure is unusual in these cases. The factors which make the structure unusual may be the arrangement of the structural components, the presence of unusual components, or a combination of both.

Long, nearly straight fibers characterize an early stage of nuclear differentiation in many organisms; they are arranged nearly parallel to each other and, in most cases, to the long axis of the nucleus. A nucleus of this kind is shown in Fig. 4. Such fibers might appear as a result of straightening, and longitudinal orientation, of the contorted interphase-like fibers typical of very early spermatids; their thickness is reportedly similar in some cases, about 100–150 Å, but this is insufficient evidence to prove they are actually identical to the interphase-like fibers.

In most cases of unusual nuclear structure observed in spermatids, it is the structural components which are clearly unusual. Fibers occur which are significantly thicker than the somatic type, ranging from about 300 Å to about 1000 Å in thickness, depending on the organism and the stage of differentiation (Fig. 5). Unusually thin fibers, averaging about 40–60 Å in diameter, also occur; as pointed out below, these are probably not chromatin. Material is also found in the form of thin ribbons, sheets, and lamellae, in many organisms. In the course of differentiation, the larger structural components, whether sheet-like or thick fibers, occur after the earlier stages with the straight fibers of about 100–150 Å. This classification of structural components according to shape is not meant to suggest that components of the same shape are equivalent in other respects. Rather, it should be emphasized that shape is a poor criterion for identification. For example, the sheets of isopods are about 250 to 350 Å thick, and may be quite different from other sheets such as those of 70 Å thickness found in grasshoppers.

Ribbons and sheet-like material seem to follow fairly straight courses along the long axis of the nucleus, but many variations in nuclear structure have been noted depending on the arrangement across the short axes of the nucleus. Material may occur as separate ribbons which seem randomly arranged with respect to the short

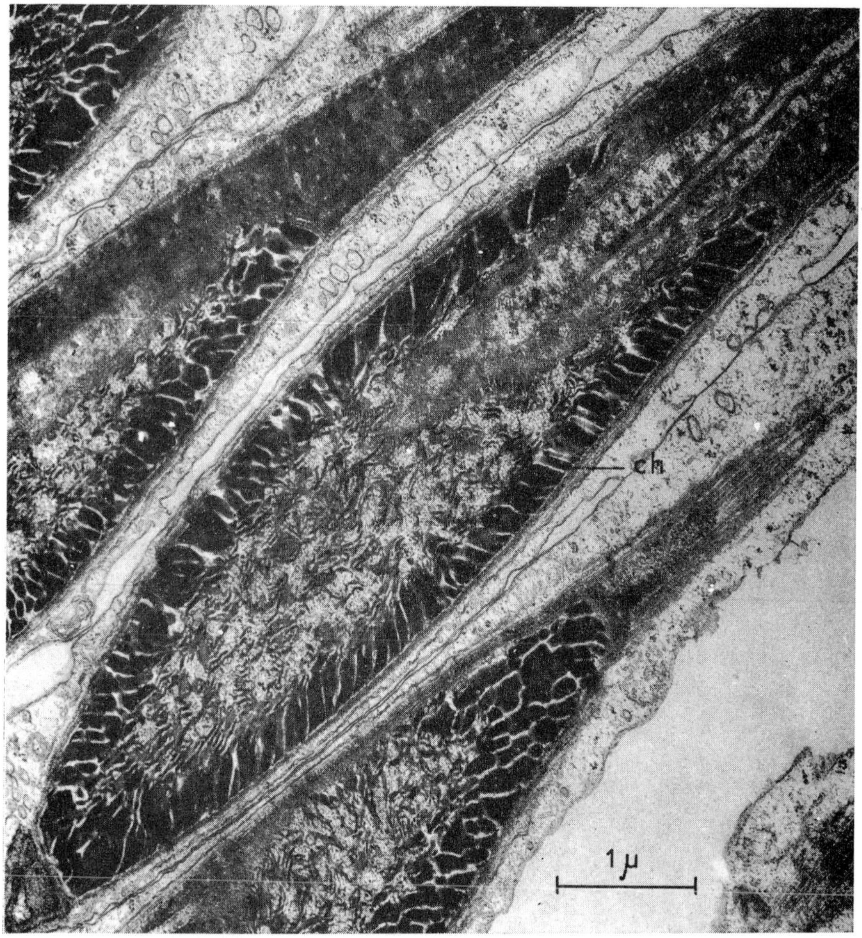

Fig. 5. A longitudinal section through a spermatid nucleus of the house cricket. Chromatin (Ch) is concentrated in the thick fibers at the nuclear periphery. The orientation of these fibers is unusual in that they are perpendicular or oblique to the long axis of the nucleus, rather than parallel with it. Plates of uncertain identification occur in the interior. × 19,000. Osmic-formalin fixation.

axes of the nucleus. In other cases, separate sheets are not visible, but instead the material in cross section has the appearance of a net work and apparently forms the walls of long empty spaces; these spaces are wide and variable in outline in some cases, and so narrow and uniform in others that they suggest the closely packed cells of a honeycomb. Nuclear material is in the form of closely packed lamellae in some cases, with a very regular spacing; lamellae may lie fairly straight across the nucleus or may occur in concentric arrangements. Figs. 6 to 8 show examples of some different structures composed of sheet-like material.

In most cases reported, no structure is discernible in mature sperm nuclei; they are uniformly electron opaque (see Fig. 9). Exceptions are noted in Table 1. The absence of visible structure does not mean that a random arrangement of the nuclear contents has replaced the ordered arrangement of earlier stages. On the contrary, the DNA appears to be highly ordered in mature sperm of many species. Pattri found that sperm heads from a large number of species exhibited negative birefringence which indicated some element of the heads were ordered. Caspersson measured the U.V. dichroism of grasshopper sperm heads, and concluded that longitudinally oriented elements were composed of DNA. Wilkins and Randall found that DNA in squid sperm gave X-ray diffraction patterns characteristic of a crystal or many microcrystals. Probably the reason that structure is not detected in electron micrographs of sperm heads (although other techniques indicate ordered structures), is that the ordered elements are too closely packed to be resolved. Other factors having to do with

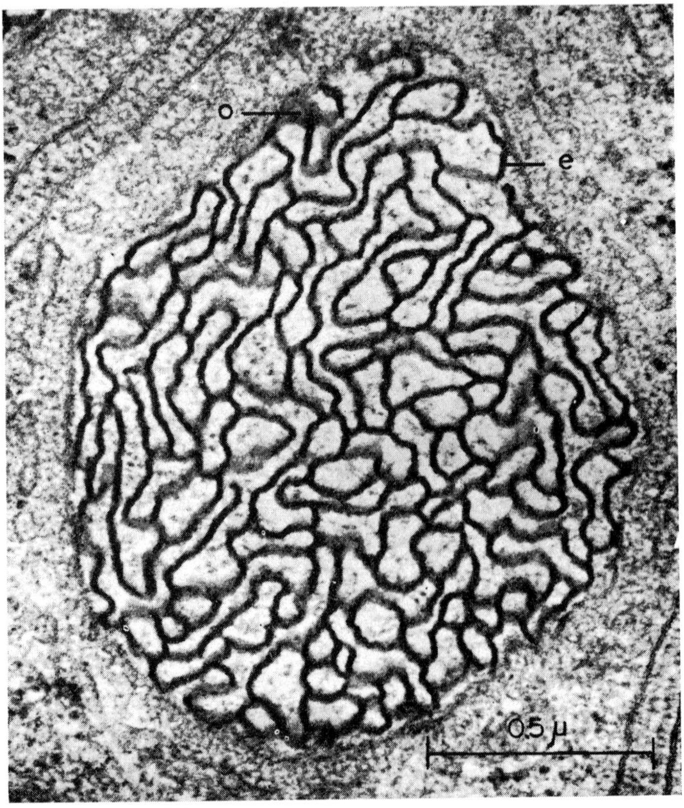

Fig. 6. A transverse section through an elongated grasshopper spermatid nucleus. Sheets occur with their faces nearly parallel with the long axis of the nucleus. They are seen mainly in edge view as dark lines (e). They appear as broader gray areas (O) where they are somewhat oblique to the plane of the section. The sheets form the walls of longitudinal tubes of irregular cross-section. × 65,000. Osmic-formalin fixation.

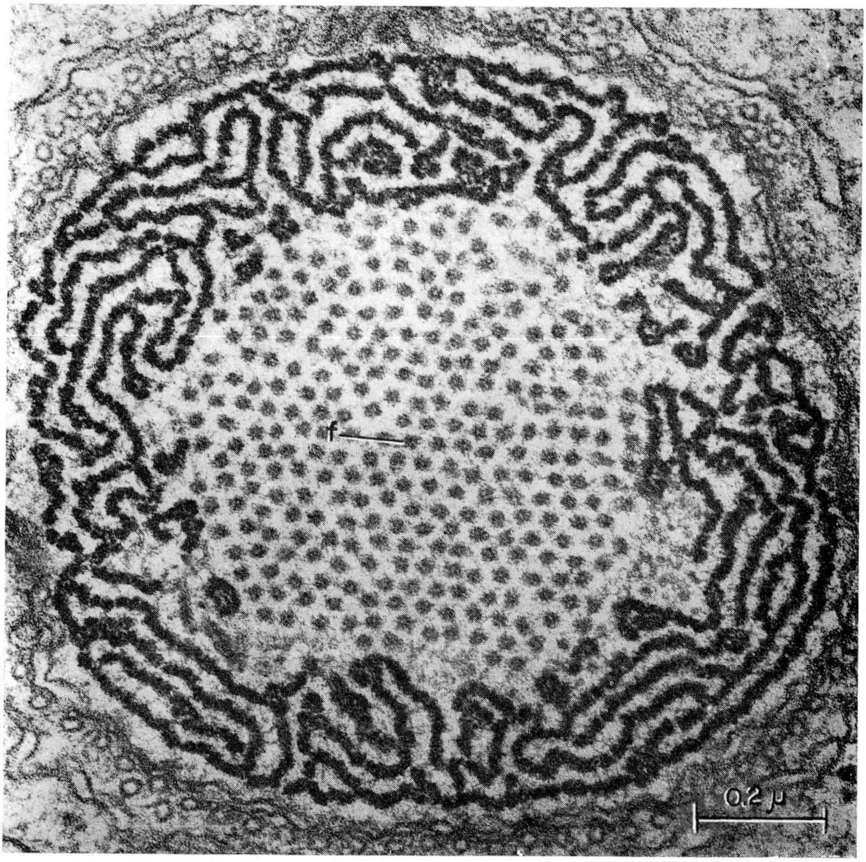

Fig. 7. A transverse section through an elongated spermatid nucleus of the field cricket *Acheta assimilis*. Chromatin sheets about 200 Å thick occur in the peripheral zone; they are seen in edge view as dark lines. Long, straight fibers (f) seen in end-view, occur in the central part of the nucleus where DNA is not detected. × 90,000. Glutaraldehyde-osmic fixation.

specimen preparation may be responsible. Koehler demonstrated lamellae in bull sperm prepared by the freeze-etch method where none have been reported in the usual preparations of sections of osmium fixed nuclei.

Determination of the precise localization of chromatin in spermatid nuclei is difficult, and has not been accomplished. The use of light-microscope cytochemical methods for direct identification of the unusual components seen in spermatid nuclei is hardly feasible, since these structures are generally smaller than the resolving power of the light microscope. In most studies of nuclei which contain well-defined structural components, such as prominent fibers or sheets, only one kind of component has been found in a given nucleus. In these cases it is a reasonable assumption that since chromatin must be somewhere in the nucleus, it must be localized in whatever particular fibers or sheets are present in the spermatid. The study of grasshopper spermatids by Gibbons and Bradfield supports this assumption; they used lanthanum nitrate as an electron stain, which would be expected to have an affinity for DNA, and found it stained the various fibers and sheets which occur in grasshopper nuclei.

In nuclei which contain more than one structural element, DNA cannot be presumed to occur in all of the elements. Just after the early stages of spermiogenesis in the house cricket, a stage occurs where dense material concentrates in a shell at the nuclear periphery, while material in the interior is much less dense. Thin fibers, about 40 to 50 Å thick (indicated by broken lines in Fig. 3), are found in the interior and have the

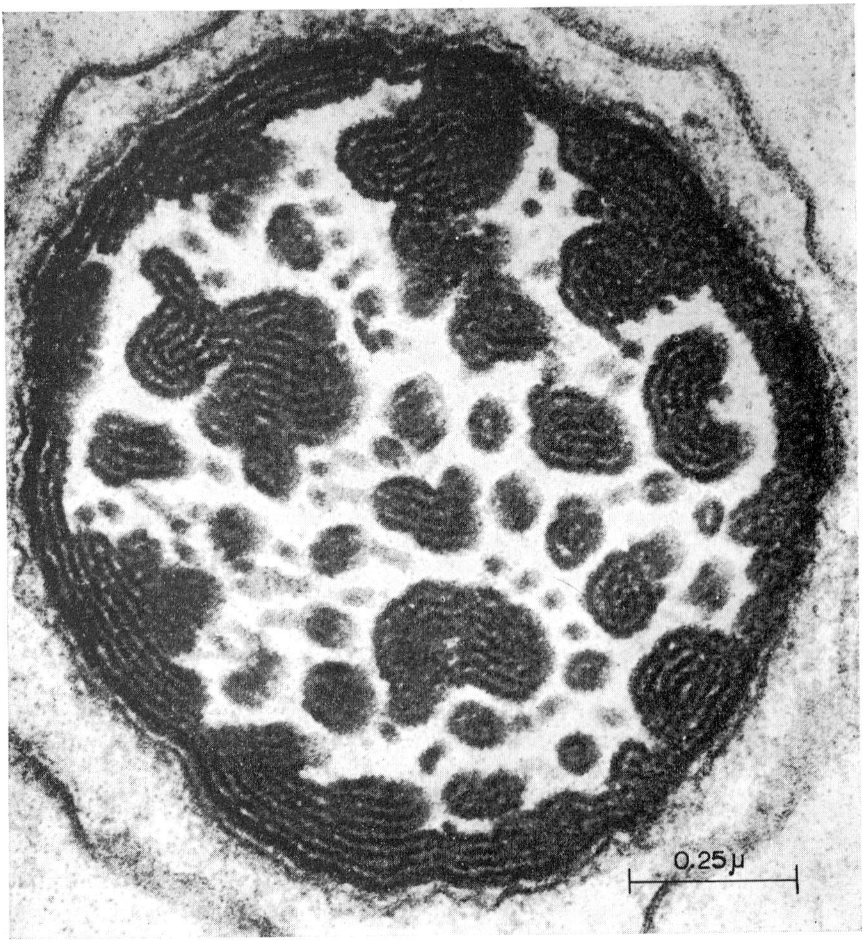

Fig. 8. Transverse section through an elongated nucleus of a late spermatid in the snail *Viviparus contectoides*. Thick fibers of irregular cross-section occur which are seen in end view. They are made of closely packed sheets. Some sheets are also distributed around the periphery of the nucleus, against the nuclear membrane. × 95,000. Osmic-formalin fixation.

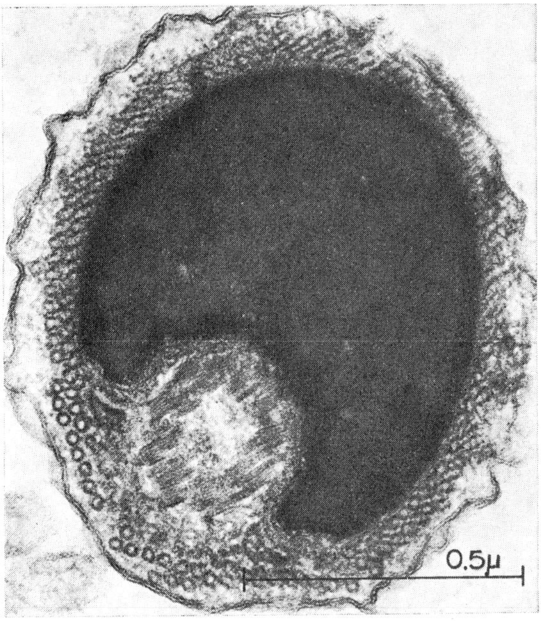

Fig. 9. Transverse section through the anterior end of the head of a mature house cricket sperm The head is uniformly electron-opaque. × 77,000. Osmic-formalin fixation.

appearance expected of chromatin fibers, but no DNA, only non-histone protein was detected where they occur. Chromatin is localized in the peripheral dense material. An analogous situation exists in later spermatids of the field cricket. Feulgen stain for DNA is not detectable in the interior of the nucleus (unpublished observations), where the electron microscope shows that conspicuous, well-organized fibers occur (see Fig. 7). The studies on cricket nuclei do not rule out the possibility that DNA in low concentration may occur in the interior of the nuclei. This work does indicate the real uncertainty that exists in identifying chromatin elements in spermatid nuclei.

There are a number of steps in nuclear differentiation during spermiogenesis. In house cricket spermatids, the initial change in chromatin structure, occurs at the stage mentioned above, where chromatin is concentrated in a peripheral shell. The interphase-type 80-Å fibers are replaced by thicker ones up to 180 Å (Fig. 3). The observation that the fibers increase in diameter gradually, and assume a contorted appearance suggested the change was accomplished by super-coiling. Studies of other organisms are needed to determine whether such a change in structure is typical of the first change in spermiogenesis.

In most cases there is a general tendency for the cross-sectional area of nuclear elements to increase during nuclear differentiation, i.e. when fibers are replaced by thicker fibers or by sheets, while at the same time the total number of nuclear elements decreases. As an explanation of these two events it has been suggested that side by side association of elements of smaller cross section occurs to form the larger ones. This is probably the simplest explanation, though direct evidence for it is limited to a few reports of thick fibers having some thinner branches.

Some sort of association must occur; the number of individual nuclear elements is eventually reduced to one in the compact sperm head. However, a clear distinction must be made between simple aggregation of elements where the identity of the individual elements is retained, and association where the elements undergo an intrinsic change, lose their identity, and become transformed into a new type of structure. Morphological evidence indicates it is the latter process which occurs. No substructure is resolved in nuclear elements which resembles elements that occurred in a previous stage. Thus, sheets are homogeneous in structure when they succeed fibers; they are not made up of rows of fibers. In some cases the dimensions of nuclear fibers rule out the possibility that simple aggregation occurs. In grasshopper spermatids, fibers are about twice as thick as the sheets which follow them. Similarly in *Viviparus*, fibers are from two to three times thicker than the lamellae which follow in a succeeding stage.

It has long been known that protamines replace histones as the basic protein component of chromatin in some mature sperm. Cytochemical studies (Bloch and Hew) have shown the change to protamine occurs late in spermiogenesis, and that it is preceded by a progressive change in the histone component, from histones characteristic of those in somatic cells, to histones that are richer in arginine. Thus, evidence from chemical and electron microscope studies both point to the conclusion that nuclear elements are transformed during differentiation, not simply rearranged. It is reasonable to assume that some causal relationship exists between changes in chemical composition and structure of nuclear elements. A specific structure may be determined in part by the species of basic proteins which are present. For example, the high electron-opacity of mature sperm heads may be the result of the fact that DNA–protamine complexes which occur in them pack in a dense crystalline pattern (Wilkins). The nonhistone proteins of spermatid nuclei have been largely neglected, but there are indications (unpublished observations) that they may be a factor in the formation of sheets in orthopteran spermatids. Future work should yield precise correlations between chemical and structural changes in nuclear elements during nuclear differentiation. It may become clear then, to what extent the structure of nuclear elements is a function of their composition.

References

ANDERSON, W. A., A. A. WEISMAN and R. A. ELLIS: Cytodifferentiation during spermiogenesis in *Lumbricus terrestris*. J. Cell Biol. 32 (1967) 11.

BARKER, K. R. and R. W. RIESS: An electron microscope study of spermateleosis in the hemipteran *Oncopeltus fasciatus*. La Cellule LXVI (1966) 40.

BAWA, S. R.: Electron microscope study of spermiogenesis in a fire-brat insect, *Thermobia domestica* Pack. I. Mature spermatozoon. J. Cell Biol. 23 (1964) 431.

BLOCH, D.P. and H.HEW: Schedule of spermatogenesis in the pulmonate snail *Helix aspersa*, with special reference to histone transition. J. Biophys. Biochem. Cytol. 7 (1960) 515.

BOISSON, C. and X.MATTEI: La spermiogenèse de *Python sabae* Gmelin observée au microscope électronique. Ann. Sc. Nat., Zool. ser. 12, tome 8 (1966) 363.

BURGOS, M.H. and D.W.FAWCETT: An electron microscope study of spermatid differentiation in the toad, *Bufo arenarum* Hansel. J. Biophys. Biochem. Cytol. 2 (1956) 223.

CASPERSSON, T.: Nukleinsäureketten und Genvermehrung. Chromosoma 1 (1940) 605.

CLARK, A.W.: Some aspects of spermiogenesis in a lizard. Am. J. Anat. 121 (1967) 369.

DADONE, L. and R.NARBAITZ: The submicroscopic structure of spermatozoa of a cyprinodontiform teleost, *Jenynsia lineata*. Z. Zellforsch. Mikroskop. Anat. 80 (1967) 214.

DASS, C.M. and H.RIS: Submicroscopic organization of the nucleus during spermiogenesis in a grasshopper. J. Biophys. Biochem. Cytol. 4 (1958) 129.

FAIN-MAUREL, M.A.: Contribution à l'histologie et à la caryologie de quelques isopodes. Spermiogenèse et infrastructure du spermatozoïde des oniscides et des cymothoïdes. Ann. Sc. Nat., Zool. ser. 12, tome 8 (1966) 1.

GALL, J.G.: Chromosome fibers studied by a spreading technique. Chromosoma 20 (1966) 221.

GALL, J.G. and L.B.BJORK: The spermatid nucleus in two species of grasshopper. J. Biophys. Biochem. Cytol. 4 (1958) 479.

GIBBONS, I.R. and J.R.G.BRADFIELD: The fine structure of nuclei during sperm maturation in the locust. J. Biophys. Biochem. Cytol. 3 (1957) 133.

HAY, E.D. and J.P.REVEL: The fine structure of the DNP component of the nucleus. J. Cell Biol. 16 (1963) 29.

HORSTMANN, E.: Elektronenmikroskopische Untersuchungen zur Spermiohistogenese beim Menschen. Z. Zellforsch. Mikroskop. Anat. 54 (1961) 68.

KAYE, J.S.: Changes in the fine structure of nuclei during spermiogenesis. J. Morphol. 103 (1958) 311.

KAYE, J.S. and R.MCMASTER-KAYE: The fine structure and chemical composition of nuclei during spermiogenesis in the house cricket. I. Initial stages of differentiation and the loss of nonhistone protein. J. Cell Biol. 31 (1966) 159.

KESSEL, R.G.: The association between microtubules and nuclei during spermiogenesis in the dragonfly. J. Ultrastruct. Res. 16 (1966) 293.

KOEHLER, J.K.: Fine structure observations in frozen-etched bovine spermatozoa. J. Ultrastruct. Res. 16 (1966) 359.

LEE, D.L. and A.O.ANYA: The structure and development of the spermatozoan of *Aspicularis tetraptera* (nematoda). J. Cell Sci. 2 (1967) 537.

LONGO, F.J. and E.J.DORNFELD: The fine structure of spermatid differentiation in the mussel, *Mytilus edulis*. J. Ultrastruct. Res. 20 (1967) 462.

MCINTOSH, J.R. and K.R.PORTER: Microtubules in the spermatids of the domestic fowl. J. Cell Biol. 35 (1967) 153.

MOSES, M.J.: Spermiogenesis in the Crayfish (*Procambarus clarkii*). I. Structural characterization of the mature sperm. J. Biophys. Biochem. Cytol. 9 (1961a) 222.

MOSES, M.J.: Spermiogenesis in the crayfish (*Procambarus clarkii*). II. Description of stages. J. Biophys. Biochem. Cytol. 9 (1961b) 301.

PATTRI, H.O.E.: Über die Doppelbrechung der Spermien. Z. Zellforsch. Mikroskop. Anat. 16 (1932) 723.

PHILLIPS, D.M.: Observations on spermiogenesis in the fungus gnat *Sciara coprophila*. J. Cell Biol. 30 (1966) 477.

POTSWALD, H.E.: An electron microscope study of spermiogenesis in *Spirorbis* (*Laeospira*) *mörchi* Levinsen (Polychaeta). Z. Zellforsch. Mikroskop. Anat. 83 (1967) 231.

REGER, J.F.: A study on the fine structure of developing spermatozoa from the oligochaete, *Enchytraeus albidus*. Z. Zellforsch. Mikroskop. Anat. 82 (1967) 257.

REGER, J.F.: A comparative study on the fine structure of developing spermatozoa in the isopod, *Oniscus asellus* and the amphipod, *Orchestoidea*. Z. Zellforsch. Mikroskop. Anat. 75 (1966) 579.

RIS, H.: Interpretation of ultrastructure in the cell nucleus. In: R.J.C.Harris, ed.: The interpretation of ultrastructure. New York, Academic Press (1962) 69.

RIS, H.: Ultrastructure of the animal chromosome. In: H.V.Koningsberger and L.Bosch, eds.: Regulation of nucleic acid and protein biosynthesis. Amsterdam, Elsevier Publishing Co. (1967) 20.

SATO, M., M.OH and K.SAKODA: Electron microscope study of spermatogenesis in the lung fluke (*Paragonimus mijazakii*). Z. Zellforsch. Mikroskop. Anat. 77 (1967) 232.

SCHIN, K.S.: Meiotische Prophase und Spermatidenreifung bei *Gryllus domesticus* mit besonderer Berücksichtigung der Chromosomenstruktur. Z. Zellforsch. Mikroskop. Anat. 65 (1965) 33.

SHOUP, J.R.: Spermiogenesis in wild type and in a male mutant of *Drosophila melanogaster*. J. Cell Biol. 32 (1967) 663.

SWIFT, H.: Nucleic acid and cell morphology in Dipteran salivery glands. In: J.M.Allen, ed.: The molecular control of cellular activity. New York, McGraw Hill Book Co. (1962) 73.

SWIFT, H.: Cytochemical studies on nuclear fine structure. Exptl. Cell Res. Suppl. 9 (1963) 54.

WATSON, M.L.: Observations on a granule associated with chromatin in nuclei of cells of rat and mouse. J. Cell Biol. 13 (1962) 162.

WETTSTEIN, R. and R.J.SOTELO: The fine structure of meiotic chromosomes. The elementary components of metaphase chromosomes of *Gryllus agentinus*. J. Ultrastruct. Res. 13 (1965) 367.

WILKINS, M.H.F.: (Physical studies of the molecular structure of deoxyribose nucleic acid and nucleoprotein. Cold Spring Harbor Symp. Quant. Biol. 21 (1956) 75.

WILKINS, M.H.F. and J.T.RANDALL: Crystailinity in sperm heads: Molecular structure of nucleoprotein *in vivo*. Biochem. Biophys. Acta 10 (1953) 192.

WOLFE, S.L. and J.N.GRIM: The relationship of isolated chromosome fibers to the fibers of the embedded nucleus. J. Ultrastruct. Res. 19 (1967) 382.

ZUBAY, G. and P.DOTY: Isolation and properties of deoxyribonucleoprotein particles containing single nucleic acid molecules. J. Mol. Biol. 1 (1959) 1.

CHAPTER 16

Organization of nuclear structures in mitotic cells

J. G. LAFONTAINE and A. LORD

Département de Biologie, Université Laval, Québec, Canada

Contents

1. Structure of the chromosomes at interphase
2. Structure of the chromosomes at mitosis
   (a) Preprophase and prophase chromosomes
   (b) Metaphase and anaphase
      (1) Organization and strandedness of chromosomes
      (2) Centromere and secondary constrictions
   (c) Telophase
3. Organization of puff-like chromosome segments
4. Organization of the nucleolus
   (a) Ultrastructure
   (b) Distribution of RNA and proteins
   (c) Intranucleolar chromatin and the organizer loops
5. Mode of formation of the nucleolus at telophase
   (a) The prenucleolar substance
   (b) Role of the chromosomes in nucleologenesis

* Preparation of this paper was aided by research grants from the National Cancer Institute of Canada and the National Research Council.

1. Structure of the chromosomes at interphase

Studies of the organization of the interphase nucleus have led to much controversy and debate in the past. The living interphase nucleus exhibiting little evidence of the presence of chromosomes as formed structural elements, many authors assumed that the morphological details seen following fixation were artefactual in nature. Such views gained futher support from the wide variety of images produced by classical fixatives. It has been realized since then that the structure of interphase nuclei is most diversified indeed. In plants, for instance, early observations showed that certain interphase nuclei are characterized by irregular and conspicuous chromatin masses often closely associated to the nuclear envelope or to the nucleolus (Fig. 1); other species were found instead to consist of a meshwork of fine convoluted strands (Figs. 2 and 3). More extensive investigations, mainly by the Belgian and French schools of karyologists (reviewed in Delay), uncovered the existence of various intermediates between the above two extreme types which have become known as prochromosomal and reticulate nuclei respectively. The former type of interphase nucleus is also quite commonly observed in animal cells (see Moses for a recent discussion). The following description deals primarily with reticulate nuclei.

From classical accounts, the reticulate interphase nucleus is known to consist of long, tenuous, chromatin strands certain segments of which, the heterochromatic regions, are thicker and more densely stained. Due to the highly unravelled condition of the individual chromosomes and their interlacing throughout the nuclear cavity, the impression is gained that, at many places, the tortuous strands anastomose or branch thus giving rise to an intricate three-dimensional network. Since phase contrast observations likewise reveal a rather close packing of the chromatin strands in living interphase nuclei (Bajer and Molé-Bajer) it may safely be assumed that these apparent anastomoses, in fixed material, correspond to fortituous contacts between neighboring segments of chromosomes. Attempts in our laboratory to resolve this complex organization by means of serial sections (0.5–1 μ) have proved unsuccessful.

Interphase nuclei of the reticulate type (e.g. *Vicia faba*) may be shown by means of the autoradiographic technique to belong to distinct classes (Moses and Lafontaine; Chevalier and Dontigny, unpublished). Following exposure (6–8 hr) to tritiated thymidine, certain nuclei remain completely unlabeled. Such nuclei are often found singly or as linear arrays of two or more cells scattered in regions of the root others than the apex. To all appearances, these nuclei correspond to the quiescent nuclei recently

---

Fig. 1. Interphase nucleus from *Tropaeolum majus* meristematic cell. Except for the irregular dense heterochromatic masses located next to the nuclear envelope, the chromosomes (ch) are in a highly extended state and merge with nucleoplasm material. One of these heterochromatin blobs extends to the nucleolar surface and is seen projecting within its mass. Several small patches (arrows) of chromatin may be recognized throughout the nucleolar body. These are restricted to the fibrillar and more compactly organized portions of the nucleolus. The distribution of these chromatin zones suggests that part of the nucleolar chromosomes meander through the nucleolus. $\times$17,000

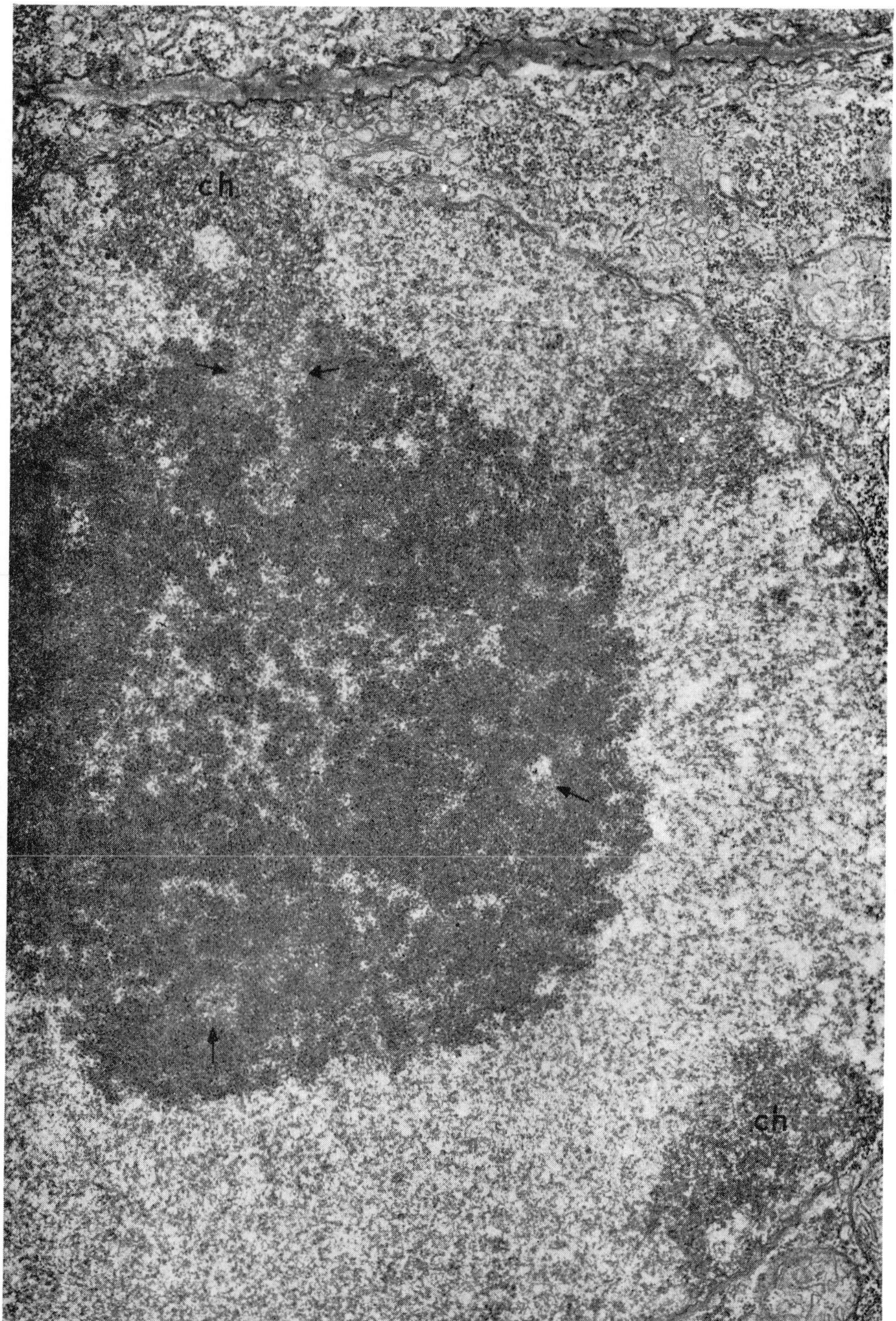

Fig. 1

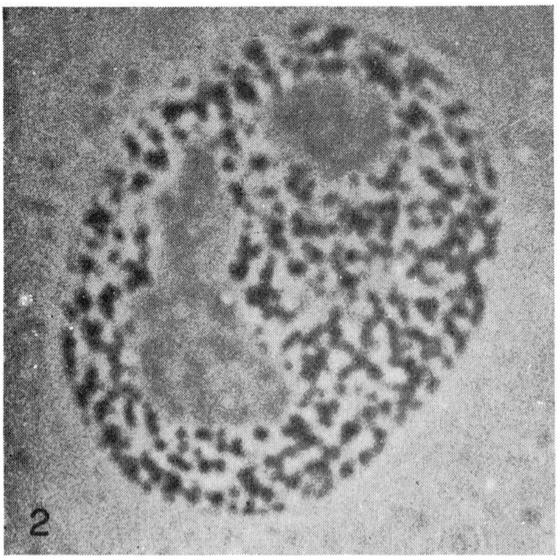

Fig. 2. Early interphase nucleus from *Triticum vulgare* meristematic cell. Note that the chromatin strands are extremely kinky and may therefore be followed for short distances only. A number of small heterochromatin masses are found throughout the nucleus and especially in the upper portion of the figure. The nucleolus appears quite heterogeneous and consists of dense irregular portions intermingled with less compact zones. Root tip fixed in glutaraldehyde and embedded in glycol methacrylate. Phase contrast micrograph of section 0.5 μ thick, stained by means of the Feulgen reaction. $\times$ 3,500

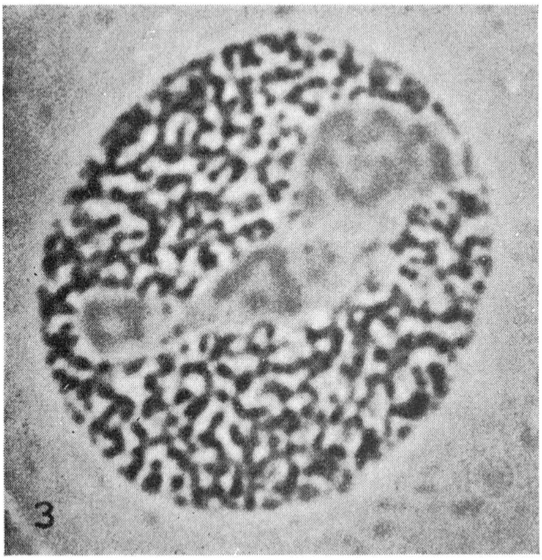

Fig. 3. Same type of preparation as preceeding figure. This interphase nucleus is characterized by chromatin strands of constant diameter which may be followed for longer distances than in the early interphase nucleus above. Note, moreover, that these strands now form an intricate meshwork. This conformation of the chromosomes is typical of nuclei which become heavily labelled following short (30 min–1 hr) exposures to H^3-thymidine. The two types of nucleolar zones are particularly conspicuous in the present preparation. $\times$3,500

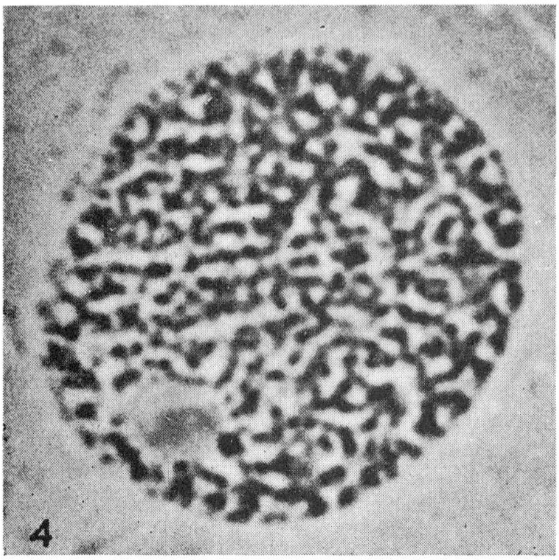

Fig. 4. Same type of preparation as Figs. 2 and 3. This micrograph represents a very early prophase nucleus. The apparent reticulum is beginning to disorganize and at several places there may now be observed parallel segments of slightly coiled strands. These regions presumably correspond to profiles of chromosomes at the unset of condensation. $\times$ 3,500

observed in *Vicia faba* by other workers (Rasch et al.; Webster and Davidson). Under light microscopy, except for numerous heterochromatic lumps of various sizes, these nuclei show little evidence of a chromatin reticulum. At higher magnification, narrow irregular segments of strands 0.1 to 0.15 μ in diameter may be recognized together with a whole spectrum of larger chromatin regions. Some of the latter presumably correspond to kinks of the chromatin strands or to random sections through the heterochromatic masses. On account of the presence of these interphase nuclei which do not become labeled following long exposure to thymidine-H^3, the task of following the morphological evolution of G_1 nuclei turns out to be rather difficult in root meristems. Although posttelophase nuclei can easily be recognized by their still irregular contours, relatively small dimensions, and the size of their nucleoli, such identification becomes more hazardous as they approach the S period. Once nuclei have entered the S period they are, on the contrary, easily singled out by means of a short exposure to thymidine-H^3. These nuclei are characterized by thick (ca. 0.3 μ) strands (Figs. 2, 3 and 5) which now form a quite conspicuous meshwork. Following treatment with uncoiling agents, the narrowest filaments observed are approximately 0.1 μ in diameter (Fig. 6). Other segments some of which appear double are roughly twice as thick. This thickening of the chromatin strands during the S period is undoubtedly related to the DNA-histone synthesis process. However, examination of such replicating nuclei has failed so far to uncover any distinct ultrastructural changes which might accompany these biochemical events. Likewise, no noticeable difference in texture is noted between the heterochromatic lumps and the extended regions of chromatin strands. At high enough magnification, both condensed and extended chromatin regions consist of fine fibrils approximately 100 Å in diameter. Following duplication of their DNA, chromosomes enter a third interphase or G_2 period which lasts for several hours in the majority of animal and plant materials so far studied. In rapidly growing tissues, as is the case of plant meristems, chromosomes then reorganize progressively in preparation for mitosis proper. For ease of presentation, these changes will be described below together with those characterizing early prophase chromosomes.

To our knowledge few data are presently available of the progressive evolution of the gross conformation of chromosomes during the G_1, S and G_2 interphase periods in animal cells. It has been noted, however, that heterochromatic segments of interphase chromosomes duplicate their DNA later than the euchromatic portions (Lima-de-Faria, this volume). The correlated autoradiographic and electron microscopic observations of Hay and Revel on proliferating *Amblystoma* cells have, moreover, clearly demonstrated that replicating chromatin centers exhibit a much more relaxed meshwork-like ultrastructural organization than inert chromosome segments. It has likewise recently been found that, when lymphocytes are stimulated to growth (Tokuyasu et al.), the interphase heterochromatin lumps progressively transform into diffuse chromatin regions. DNA synthesis within these interphase nuclei is observed predominantly in areas characterized by such loosened chromatin. In plant meristematic cells with prochromosomal interphase nuclei (e.g. *Raphanus sativus*, *Tropaeolum majus*), the chromosomes show the following labeling pattern following exposure (40–60 min) to thymidine-H^3. A certain number of nuclei, usually grouped in linear arrays of two, three or more, remain unlabeled as just indicated for plants with reticulate interphase nuclei. Some of the labeled nuclei contain radioautographic grains scattered over diffuse chromatin throughout the nuclear cavity but these are sometimes also concentrated over heterochromatic lumps. In other nuclei, presumably at a more advanced stage of interphase judging from their larger size, most of the silver grains are restricted to the heterochromatic masses. This last observation raises the question as to whether DNA synthesis in these nuclei does take place within the condensed chromatin. This problem appears difficult to settle since thymidine may actually be incorporated, during a certain portion of the S period, within specific euchromatic chromosome segments which soon condense to form the chromocenters under discussion. The chromocenters characterizing nuclei of rapidly dividing meristematic cells may also be quite different, metabolically, from the extensive aggregates of condensed chromatin found in certain differentiated animal cells. This problem remains unresolved.

2. *Structure of the chromosomes at mitosis*

(a) *Preprophase and prophase chromosomes*

In spite of difficulties in following the sequential morphological changes which interphase chromosomes undergo during the G_2 period, the following evolution is thought to take place from late interphase to the unset of prophase. The earliest noticeable modification of the chromatin reticulum characterizing late interphase nuclei consists in a slight loosening of the meshwork presumably due to a reduction in the degree of apparent anastomoses between neighboring chromatin strands (Fig. 4). It is also evident that the unset of coiling is causing filaments previously meandering throughout the nucleus to become confined to more restricted domains. As this disorganization of the reticulum and concomitant redistribution of the strands take place, more individualized segments of filaments are detected and distinct profiles of early prophase chromosomes progressively emerge, here and there, within the nuclear cavity. During this rearrangement process, twin parallel segments of strands become discernible; how

Fig. 5. Electron micrograph of portion of a nucleus (*Allium porrum*) the organizational pattern of which closely corresponds to that of Fig. 3. The appearance of a reticulum at this stage is seen to result from the extreme proximity of neighboring segments of strands which at places even seem to have adhered during fixation. One segment of chromatin strand (arrow) exhibits a much more relaxed conformation and is thought to correspond to a micropuff. ×11,000

Fig. 6. Micrograph of interphase nucleus (*Allium porrum*) depicting the unravelling of chromatin strands induced by a one hour treatment with 10^{-4} M maleic hydrazide. The narrowest segments now range from 0.1 to 0.15 μ in diameter. Two micropuffs are seen in lower right portion of the figure. ×12,500

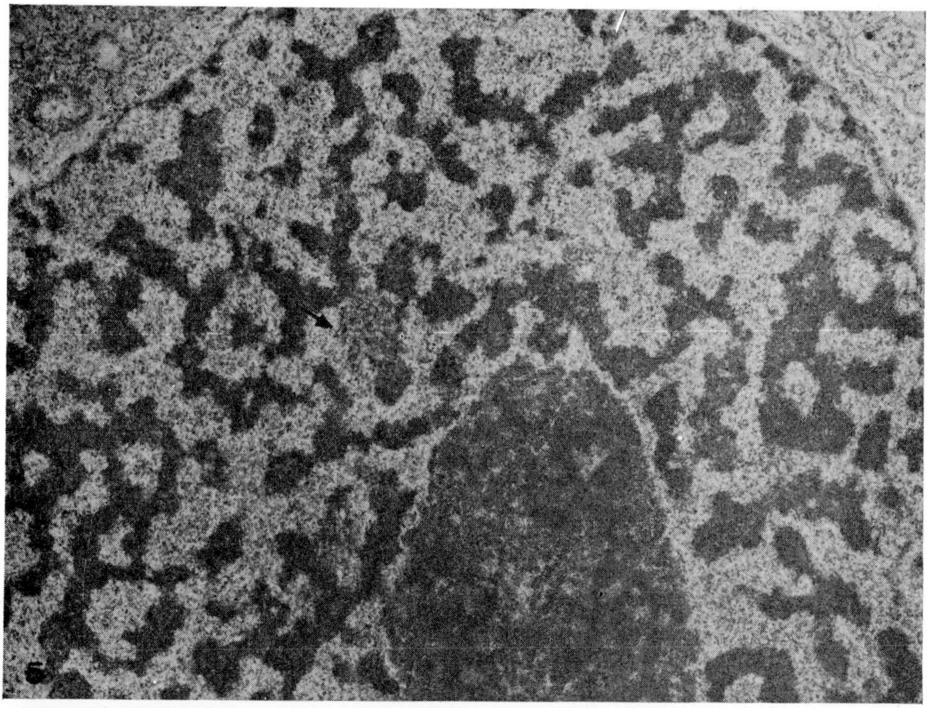
5

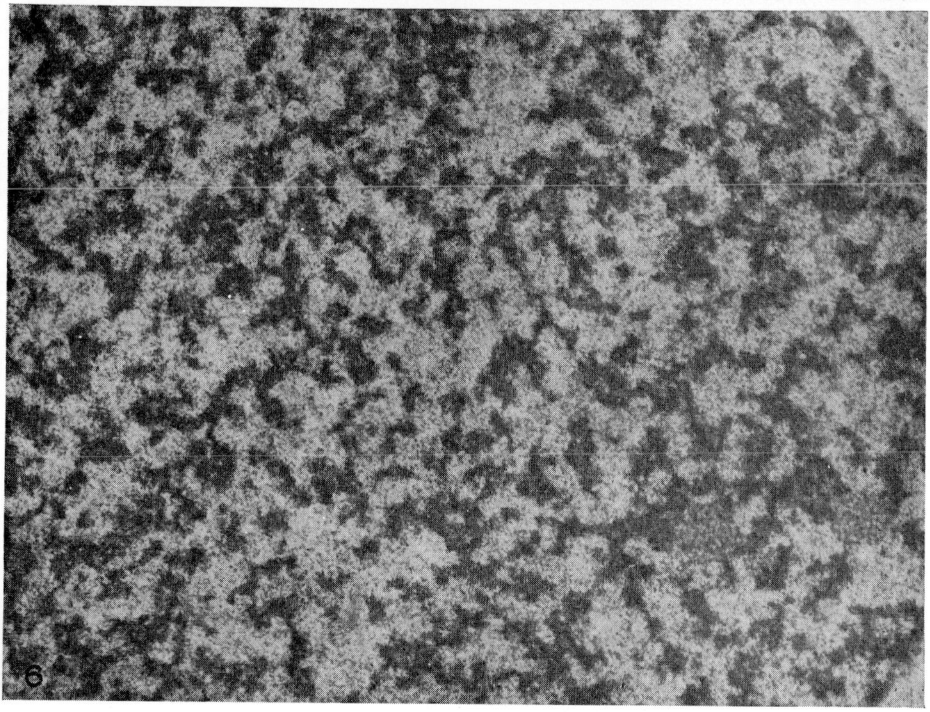
6

these paired elements originate from the filaments characterizing replicating interphase nuclei remains obscure. At any rate, the diameter of the coiled strands forming early prophase chromosomes does not appear significantly different from that of the replicating interphase chromosomes. However, following treatment with uncoiling agents, prophase chromosomes take on a lampbrush appearance under light microscopy, and at higher magnification they then exhibit profiles of twisted filaments certain segments of which are approximately 0.1 μ in diameter. The involvement of these strands precludes any interpretation as to how they might be arranged within the chromosomes.

At early prophase, light irregular spaces filled with fine fibrillar nucleoplasm material may be observed under electron microscopy between the loosely coiled chromonemata. As further spiralization of these strands takes place, the interchromonemal regions disappear and the chromosomes progressively assume a more compact organization. By late prophase their two constituent chromatids have reached such a degree of condensation that, under either phase contrast (0.5 μ sections) or electron microscopy, they no longer show evidence of any internal structure. Such masking of the gyres within late prophase chromatids has given rise to the hypothesis that some sort of matrix material deposits on the chromosomes at that stage. The view, sponsored by classical authors, that this substance is of nucleolar origin has received little support from recent autoradiographic studies. Only restricted amounts of labelled RNA are observed on late prophase chromosomes and by metaphase this labelling has usually disappeared (Prescott and Bender; Davidson). According to similar investigations, nucleolar proteins do not either appear to accumulate noticeably onto the condensing chromosomes. Electron microscopic observations have shown that during dissolution of the late prophase nucleolus both its fibrillar and particulate components disperse throughout the nuclear cavity and pervade zones immediately adjacent to the chromosomes. However, although such a possibility could not be excluded, no clear-cut evidence of association of nucleolar material with the chromosomes was obtained (Lafontaine and Chouinard).

Whether or not a so-called matrix material really exists, there seems little doubt that the increased compactness and density of late prophase, metaphase and anaphase chromosomes mostly reflect the highly spiralized condition of their subunit strands at these stages. This conclusion gains further support from the observation that the internal organization of such condensed chromosomes cannot be more clearly visualized in ultrathin sections extracted with ribonuclease, pepsin, trypsin or combinations of these enzymes. The same situation prevails whether these digested preparations are examined under light, ultraviolet or electron microscopy (Lord, unpublished).

(b) *Metaphase and anaphase*

(1) *Organization and strandedness of chromosomes.* Owing to their great density and complex architecture, metaphase and anaphase chromosomes have proved most difficult to study under the electron microscope. Admittedly, all authors agree that chromosomes consist of similar microfibrillar units at all stages of mitosis (Ris 1966,

1967; also in this volume). However, much uncertainty remains as to how these basic units are arranged within chromosomes to give rise to the familiar organizational patterns observed under light microscopy. Their three dimensional structure with hierarchies of coils is, for example, very poorly reflected in thin sections (Lafontaine and Chouinard; Barnicot and Huxley; Sparvoli et al.; Davies and Tooze). The only indications, in such preparations, suggestive of any helical arrangement of strands within the condensed chromatids are their wavy contours, the frequent presence of finger-like lateral projections and the observation at anaphase of a central light core.

As a result of the rather limited informational content of thin sections, many authors have turned to the examination of whole-mount preparations for studying chromosomes (Barnicot; DuPraw; Gall 1966; Wolfe). Although providing an overall view of chromosomes together with a resolution sufficient to record macromolecular details, this technique has not yet permitted to uncover their three-dimensional architecture. Such visualization, in depth, of the organization of chromosomes can apparently now be achieved from stereo pictures of relatively thick (0.5–1 μ) sections recorded under high voltage electron microscopy (Porter and Hama).

The difficulty in interpreting available ultrastructural data on chromosomes stems not only from their complex organization but also from our persisting ignorance of the number of basic strands they contain. Evidence in favour as well as against a multineme chromosome structure has accumulated from various sources during the last few years.

The examination under light microscopy of isolated mammalian and plant metaphase chromosomes treated with enzymes or uncoiling agents, suggests the presence of at least two subunits within the chromatids. In favorable preparations, up to four such strands may be demonstrated (Gimenez-Martin et al.; Trosko and Wolff; Trosko and Brewen). Some authors believe, from the examination of thin sections, that these latter subunits in turn consist of several microfibrils (refer to Kaufmann et al.), but the evidence gathered from such preparations is far from conclusive, owing to difficulties of interpretation.

Although there thus presently exist much observational data in favour of a certain degree of strandedness in chromosomes, other results appear rather consistent with the unineme concept. The most compelling observations, perhaps, come from autoradiographic and radiation-induced breakage studies (reviewed in Swift 1966). This hypothesis has received additional support from the recent demonstration that, on spreading at an air–water interface, condensed chromosomes unravel considerably and often transform into extended fibers (reviewed in Ris, this volume). The thymidine-H^3 labeling pattern of these filaments suggests that they consist of several tandemly joined replication segments, or replicons (Cairns; Sasaki and Norman; Huberman and Riggs). The extreme length of some of these threads as well as the paucity of free ends in favorable preparations are taken to indicate by some authors that chromosomes possibly contain a single microfibrillar strand only. It is still unclear, however, how such a macromolecular unit, even if folded back on itself according to some complex pattern, could give rise to coiled structures which, as the mitotic chromosomes, also appear multistranded.

(2) *Centromere and secondary constrictions.* In most animal and plant species, chromosomes are characterized by a constriction which also corresponds to the site of attachment of the spindle filaments (refer to Mazia for a review). This region is believed from studies with squash preparations (Lima-de-Faria) or isolated chromosomes (Gall 1954) to contain several small Feulgen-positive chromomeres (however, refer to Ohnuki). Recent observations have corroborated the classical view that centromeres are functionally involved in the movement of chromosomes during mitosis (reviewed in Forer, this volume). It has thus been shown that part of the microtubular elements forming the spindle apparatus are grouped into bundles or chromosome fibers. The latter structures seem to become intimately associated with the centromere regions shortly after dissolution of the nuclear envelope and remain anchored within these chromosomal loci during the following mitotic stages.

Much progress has also been accomplished, of late, in elucidating the fine structure of the centromere proper with the electron microscope. In the majority of materials studied so far, the centromere region appears as a dense structure, sometimes plate-like (Brinkley and Stubblefield; Jokelainen) or dome-shaped (Bajer), located at the surface and in close continuity with the chromosome body. In many instances, this localized region has been reported to exhibit a microfibrillar texture indistinguishable from the remainder of the chromosome but favorable preparations reveal a rather complex architecture. According to some authors (Brinkley and Stubblefield), the centromere is a rounded filament 0.1 to 0.2 μ long which winds around the chromosome. This structure consists of two components, a dense core 200–300 Å in diameter surrounded by a lighter zone. Interestingly enough, the peripheral less-dense zone of these centromeres is found to consist of fibrils 50–80 Å in diameter which form microloops projecting from the central region. These observations seem to confirm therefore that, contrary to the remaining condensed segments of mitotic chromosomes, the centromeres maintain an extended conformation as previously demonstrated with light microscopy (Lima-de-Faria). Other workers (Jokelainen), have furnished evidence that, in certain cell types at least, the organizational pattern of the centromere is still more intricate than believed previously. The sister centromeres often occur at a deep depression on the paired metaphase chromosomes and they consistently display a complex trilaminar organization. Spindle microtubules, according to these observations, are anchored within the centromere and, after piercing its three layers, occasionally project into the underlaying chromosome material. In favorable sections running parallel to the equatorial metaphase plate, the centromere appears circular in structure and is surrounded by a ring of light material. Such tangential preparations show convincing cross-sections of the group of 4 to 7 microtubules which project through the mass of a centromere. Evidence was also obtained by this author that the outer centromere layer condenses during late prophase or at prometaphase within a particular area on the chromosomal surface. Correlation of this particular organization of the centromere to its very specialized activity and function during mitosis is a most interesting problem which still remains to be resolved.

Besides the centromere or primary constriction just discussed, chromosomes also show other differentiated regions known as secondary constrictions. These are usually Feulgen-negative but careful examination reveals a fine chromatin strand bridging the gap (discussed in Moses; Ohnuki). As shown by classical authors, and more recently by several groups of workers studying mutant *Xenopus* embryos (Hay), certain of these constrictions, the nucleolar constrictions, play a decisive role in relation with nucleologenesis (section 5 (b)). In plants such constrictions are quite conspicuous under electron microscopy and correspond to slightly narrower portions of the metaphase and anaphase chromosomes. Following staining with both uranyl acetate and lead hydroxide, these segments are much lighter than other chromosome regions but otherwise exhibit a similar fine fibrillar texture. Although such constrictions have repeatedly been observed in this laboratory no indication was ever detected of a central denser strand corresponding to the Feulgen-positive filament seen in conventional preparations. This particular reaction of the nucleolar constrictions to heavy metal solutions holds true up to early telophase but is slightly modified later on when small nucleolar bodies begin to form in close association with these chromosomal loci (section 4 (c)).

(c) *Telophase*

Telophase nuclei vary greatly in appearance depending on the material examined. In plants with prochromosomal interphase nuclei, as well as in many animal cells, the early telophase chromosomes soon loose their rod-like organization. Certain segments remain quite dense and are thought to give rise to the irregular heterochromatic masses which appear in such nuclei (Fig. 7). Other regions undergo extensive uncoiling and become progressively more difficult to detect as they merge with the surrounding nucleoplasm.

In nuclei of the reticulate type, progress of the telophase chromosomes is much more easily recorded. In certain species (e.g. *Vicia faba*, *Lathyrus odoratus*) the chromosomes remain rather compact till midtelophase by which time they are immersed in large amounts of diffuse material which under electron microscopy exhibits a fibrillogranular texture. In other plants (*Allium cepa*, *Allium porrum*), however, chromosomes begin to uncoil as they reach the cell poles and small spherical bodies and irregular patches of fibrillogranular material soon appear between them. Whatever their particular conformation at early telophase, once chromosomes have sufficiently unravelled, they then exhibit two distinct subunits which are loosely coiled around each other (Fig. 9). Under electron microscopy, corresponding images of early to midtelophase chromosomes appear much more involved (Fig. 10). It seems difficult to imagine that such complex chromosomal profiles reflect the presence of only two coarse strands forming the regular helices seen in 0.5 μ preparations (Fig. 9). One

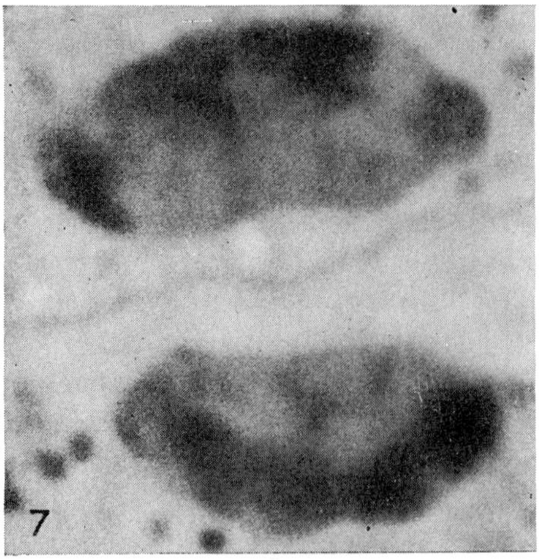

7

Fig. 7. Midtelophase nuclei from *Raphanus sativus* meristematic cell. The chromosomes which are rather small are barely visible owing to the fact that their density closely matches that of the forming nucleoli. The latter structures correspond to the irregular and more intensely stained masses located at the periphery of the nuclei. The remaining portions of the nuclei are pervaded by the less dense prenucleolar material. × 4,700

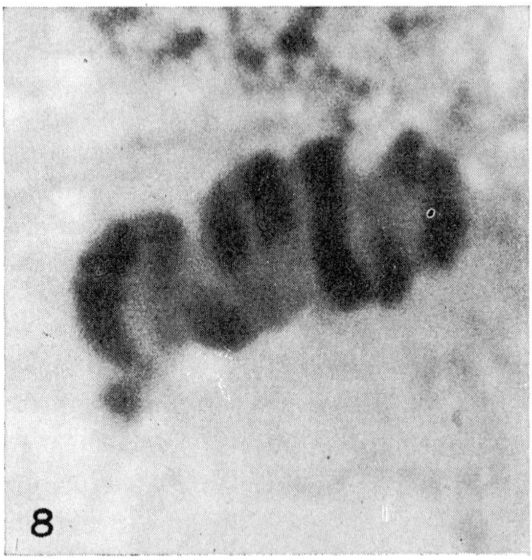

8

Fig. 8. Midtelophase nucleus (*Lathyrus odoratus*) illustrating the still quite compact conformation of the chromosomes at a time when large amounts of prenucleolar substance have accumulated between them. × 4,700

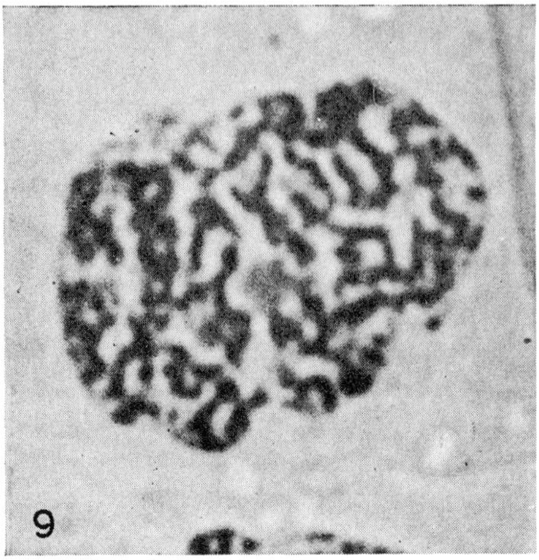

9

Fig. 9. *Allium cepa* midtelophase nucleus. In this species the chromosomes start uncoiling as they reach the cell poles; by the time the nucleolus begins to form the chromosomes exhibit two distinct smaller strands. In certain chromosomes these two subunits are clearly coiled around each other but at other places they appear as two parallel twin strands. × 4,200

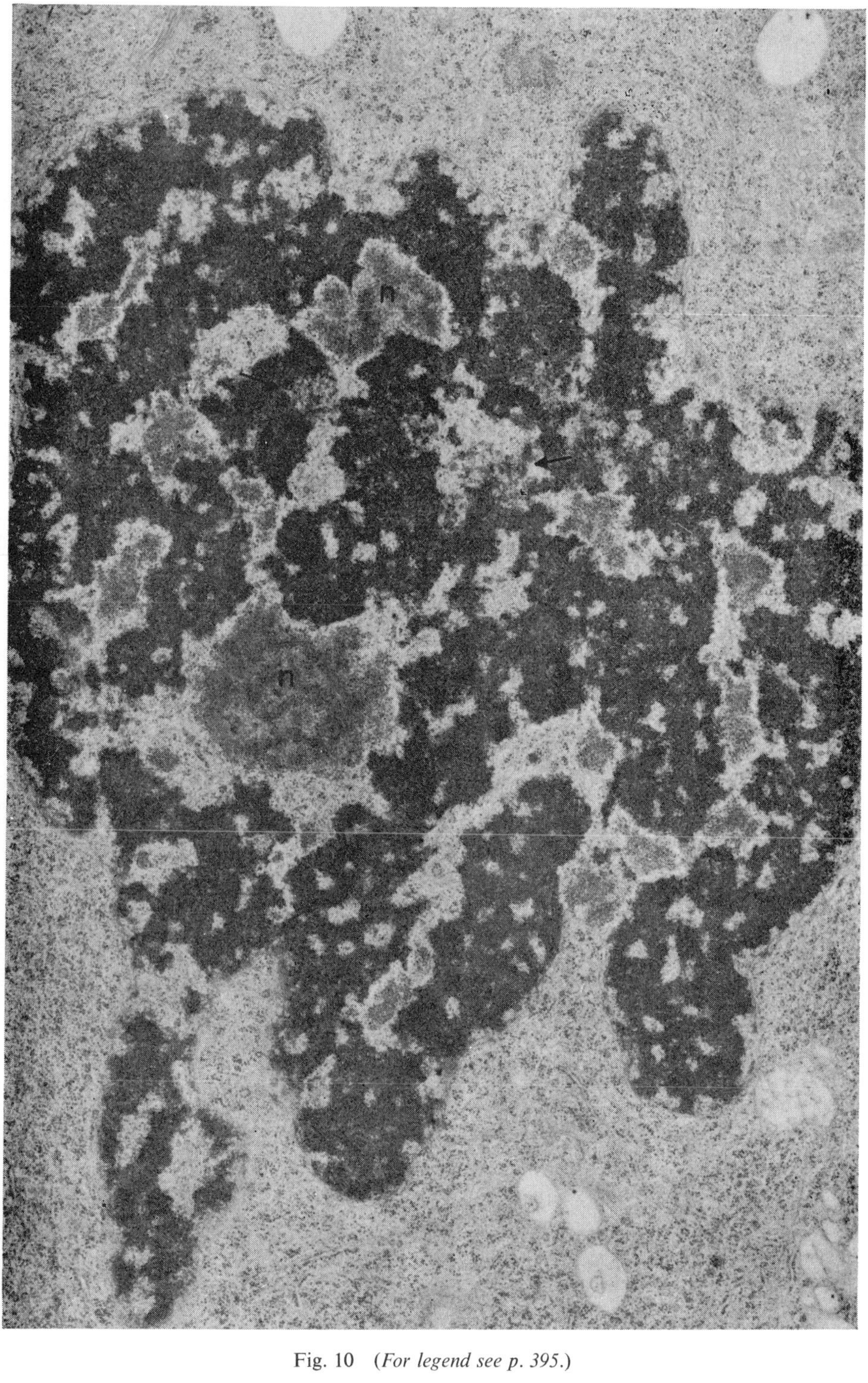

Fig. 10 (*For legend see p. 395.*)

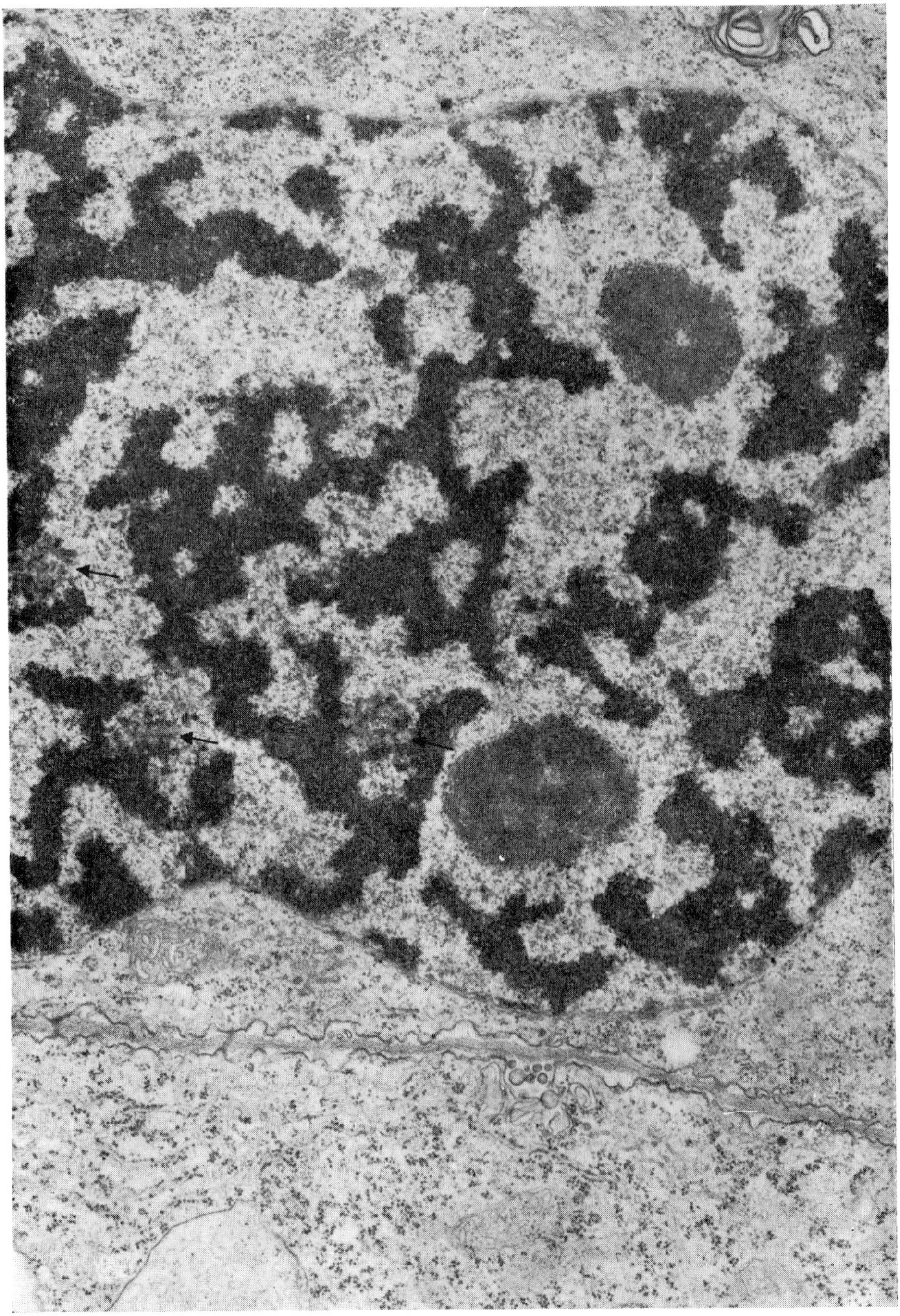

Fig. 11

would therefore tend to assume that the loosely coiled strands observed in the light microscope in turn consist of at least two intertwined smaller units as already suggested by other authors (Sparvoli et al.). The possibility that the narrowest strands recorded at higher magnification (Fig. 10) contain one or more smaller units is strongly suggested by the lampbrush appearance which early telophase chromosomes exhibit under electron microscopy following treatment with uncoiling agents (unpublished observations).

Concurrent with further unravelling, the loosely coiled midtelophase chromosomes gradually transform into a very irregular meshwork of strands the diameter of which varies from place to place (Fig. 11). The largest chromatin masses have very irregular contours and are best interpreted as corresponding to portions of telophase chromosomes which are still partially coiled. Whether such masses of entangled strands correspond to portions of chromosomes which will evolve into the heterochromatin lumps characterizing the interphase nucleus remains to be established. By late telophase, fine chromosomal strands have dispersed throughout the still irregularly shaped nucleus and given rise to the chromatin reticulum described earlier. To summarize, therefore, the morphological evolution of the compact early telophase chromosomes into fine interphase strands can be recorded rather easily under electron microscopy. However, at no time is it possible to ascertain the degree of strandedness of these chromosomes.

Fig. 10. Electron micrograph depicting a midtelophase nucleus (*Allium porum*). Several relatively long segments of chromosomes, still oriented in the pole to pole direction, may be recognized in this figure. Each chromosome is characterized by an alveolated structure indicative of the presence of a number of coiled subunits. Although these smaller strands vary considerably in diameter, many rather regular segments 0.1–0.15 μ wide, are found in all chromosomes. These fine strands, it should be noted, are markedly narrower than those recorded in corresponding nuclei (Fig. 9) under light microscopy.

One of the young nucleoli (n) appears to be located within a gap in a chromosome which corresponds to a secondary constriction. Presumably due to its particular staining characteristics, the chromatin strands from this constriction cannot be recognized within the nucleolar mass. The two young nucleoli already exhibit a quite heterogeneous architecture. Their central and most important portion is predominantly fibrillar in texture and shows a coarse reticulum quite similar to that revealed in mature nucleoli, following digestion with pepsin (Fig. 16). A thin layer of particulate material may also be observed at the periphery of these small nucleolar bodies. Besides the foregoing structures, the nucleus is finally characterized by numerous small irregular masses (arrows) scattered between the chromosomes and sometimes closely associated with their surface. This prenucleolar material, it should be noted, stains identically to the nucleoli and shows a fine particulate texture also strikingly reminiscent of that of the peripheral portion of these organelles. $\times$18,500

Fig. 11. Electron micrograph of portions of a mid- to late-telophase nucleus from *Allium porum* meristematic cell. The chromosomes have unravelled to the extent that they no longer appear as coiled structures. The diameter of the chromatin strands varies greatly. The larger masses would seem to correspond to uncoiled segments of chromosomes or kinks. The narrowest strands range from 0.15 to 0.25 μ in diameter. It is of interest to note that certain segments of these strands (arrows) show a relaxed conformation and form a fine meshwork of threads the interstices of which contain a material markedly denser than the surrounding nucleoplasm. The prenucleolar blobs seen at early telophase (Fig. 10) have disappeared. $\times$ 25,000

3. Organization of puff-like chromosome segments

Interphase and preprophase plant nuclei frequently exhibit, besides the nucleolus, spherical structures possessing rather interesting cytochemical and ultrastructural characteristics. In *Allium cepa* and several other species investigated, these structures are commonly found at points of convergence of two chromatin strands and appear intimately associated with them. A closer examination reveals that such spherules consist of a distinct meshwork of convoluted microfibrils and of a more amorphous material slightly denser than the surrounding nucleoplasm (Figs. 5 and 6). Following double staining with uranyl acetate and lead hydroxyde, the entangled microfibrils match the chromatin in density; stereoscopic electron micrographs then permit to verify that these loose spheres of microfibrils are actually continuous with the immediately adjacent chromosome segments.

Although these bodies are difficult to discern under the light microscope, their metachromatic staining with Azure B indicates the presence of RNA. That these nuclear structures also contain proteins is revealed by their noticeably greater transparency following digestion with pepsin. The interstices of the fibrillar network then match the nucleoplasm in density. When trypsin and pepsin are used sequentially, the chromosomes loose a great deal of their density but still exhibit a fibrillar ultrastructure. Quite similar microfibrils are recognized within the adjoining spherical structures. Preparations of material fixed in glutaraldehyde and embedded in glycol methacrylate are, in our experience at least, difficult to digest with deoxyribonuclease. However, following treatment with both pepsin and desoxyribonuclease in that order, most of the chromosome substance is removed and the bodies under discussion are then no longer recognizable. Considering the mode of action of the above three enzymes, these spherules appear to consist essentially of a meshwork of DNA microfibrils the interstices of which are pervaded by an amorphous material containing RNA and proteins.

The foregoing series of observations are presently best interpreted, we think, by assuming that the spherical structures under discussion correspond to highly unravelled segments of chromosomes and are therefore equivalent, but on a much smaller scale, to the puffs and loops of polytene and lampbrush chromosomes respectively. This assumption is suggested not only by the highly distended organization of the microfibrillar chromatin elements within these micropuffs but also by the presence of RNA and of proteins part of which are extracted by pepsin and, therefore, may possibly be acidic in nature as reported earlier in the case of active loci along giant chromosomes (Gall and Callan; Swift 1962, 1966). Before the nature of these presumed micropuffs is fully understood, more precise data will be required concerning the RNA synthesis pattern of interphase chromosomes. There is general agreement that during the mitotic cycle, RNA synthesis within the nucleus extends from telophase to midprophase. Part of this synthesis was shown to take place on the chromosomes (Das; Hsu; Schiff). According to current concepts (Frenster 1966, and this volume), one should expect that only de-repressed chromatin regions are involved in RNA transcription. Further work should show how the synthetically active loci are distributed along the chromosomes during these stages and permit to verify whether RNA transcription is limited, at a given moment, to discrete chromosome segments analogous in size and macromolecular conformation to the distended spherules described above.

There exists a rather extensive literature (reviewed in Lafontaine) on the occurrence in plant cells of spherical bodies or micronucleoli which, to all appearances, are related to the structures under discussion. Judging from their similarities in size, distribution, cytochemical and ultrastructural characteristics it is indeed conceivable that the spherules often seen at interphase, preprophase and prophase within the nucleoplasm originate from micropuffs. According to this interpretation, hence, the material elaborated by these relaxed chromosomal segments eventually forms free bodies which migrate to the nucleoplasm.

The formation of nuclear spherules at different loci along interphase chromosomes, as postulated here, seems to correspond closely to the situation described by Gabrusewycz-Garcia and Kleinfeld in popytene chromosomes where small chromatin loops are thought to elaborate a whole spectrum of micronucleolarlike bodies.

4. *Organization of the nucleolus*

(a) *Ultrastructure*

The notion is now well established that both animal (Bernhard and Granboulan) and plant (Hyde; Lafontaine; Swift and Stevens) nucleoli consist of different substances some of which are segregated into more or less distinct types of zones. Since other chapters of this volume review the organization of this organelle in animal cells, the following section will deal primarily with plants.

The nucleolar zones just referred to are easily detected in 0.5–1 μ preparations following staining with a variety of cytochemical procedures. In preparations stained with methylene blue, for instance, the nucleolus exhibits dense irregular regions immersed within a lighter substance, and extending throughout its mass in the form of a coarse three-dimensional network. These more compact nucleolar portions, as described later on (section 4 (c)) contain a coarse convoluted thread which is thought to correspond to the nucleolar organizer (LaCour and Wells; Lord and Lafontaine). Under electron microscopy such zones are made up predominantly of fine fibrils some 60–100 Å in diameter. Cytochemical observations described further on indicate that these fibrillar regions consist of at least two components, proteins and RNA. As will also be made clear shortly (section 4 (b)), the fibrillar zones of plant nucleoli also often exhibit patches of chromatin the texture of which can be distinguished from that of the surrounding nucleolar substance.

Besides the zones just described, the mature interphase nucleolus consistently shows other regions composed mostly of particles similar to the cytoplasmic ribosomes. A closer examination of these nucleolar regions as well as enzymatic digestion studies reveal, however, that these RNP particles are immersed in an amorphous substance difficult to characterize under electron microscopy.

(b) *Distribution of RNA and proteins*

Cytochemical, autoradiographic (Woodard et al.; De; Mattingly; Marinozzi; Suskind) and biochemical (Vincent; Stern et al.) studies indicate that the nucleolus of both animal and plant cells consists mainly of proteins and to a lesser extent of RNA. It is presently believed that nucleolar proteins are quite heterogeneous and belong to three or four broad fractions (Birnstiel et al.; Muramatsu and Busch). The nature of the various types of nucleolar RNAs is not elucidated completely (discussed in Hay). There exists, nevertheless, a consensus of opinion that 45 S RNA is transformed within the nucleolus into subunits which subsequently interact with proteins to form subribosomal particles. The mechanisms involved in the elaboration of these particles within certain regions of the nucleolus are being investigated in a number of laboratories (reviewed in Darnell, Perry 1967, and this volume).

Significant progress has been made during recent years towards a better understanding of the cytochemical organization of the nucleolus as a result of the adaptation of radioautography and enzymatic digestion techniques to the field of ultrastructural research. Interesting new information has thus been obtained concerning the distribution of both RNA and proteins throughout the various nucleolar regions. Thus, the well known basophilia of the nucleolus has been shown to reflect the presence of RNA in both fibrillar and granular zones of this organelle (Swift 1963; Marinozzi; Granboulan and Granboulan 1965; Geusken and Bernhard). Studies of the organization of the nucleolus in meristematic plant cells have led to similar conclusions. The young telophase nucleolus stains with azure B from the beginning of its formation and continues to exhibit this cytochemical characteristic during late telophase, as dense and light zones become discernible throughout its mass. This specific metachromatic staining property is also observed in both types of zones of the mature interphase nucleolus and it persists till late prophase, at which time the peripheral zones of this organelle first dissolve. It may thus be concluded from such observations that the presence of RNA is a constant characteristic of these nucleolar zones. No data are presently available, however, as to whether the respective concentrations of RNA within these regions vary from telophase to the unset of nucleolar desintegration.

Following digestion of 1 μ sections with ribonuclease, the nucleolus as a whole no longer stains with azure B (Figs. 12–14). A significant amount of UV absorbing material, presumably proteinaceous in nature, may, however, still be detected in such preparations. Likewise, under electron microscopy, this enzyme is found to disorganize the nucleolar RNP particles and to also remove material from the fibrillar zones, but a good deal of substance remains in these different regions.

In view of the importance and variety of nucleolar proteins, there undoubtedly exists a close relationship between the localization of these protein fractions within the different morphological zones of this organelle and their respective biochemical function. Hopefully, part of the answer to this difficult problem will be forthcoming from ultrastructural cytochemical studies. However, although digestion of fixed material with proteolytic enzymes has long been used by cytochemists, the effect of such hydrolysis on cellular structures sometimes becomes quite difficult to interpret at the electron microscope level. There indeed exist no conclusive data demonstrating that the spectrum of action of these enzymes on fixed tissues is similar to that which has been determined with well known preparations of proteins. It has also recently become evident that the cytochemical localization of proteins within the nucleolus is subject to added uncertainties as a result of the nature of these proteins (discussed in Lord and Lafontaine). From available biochemical data it would thus appear that the various nucleolar protein fractions are characterized by rather similar percentages of the key amino acids involved in the formation of peptide linkages susceptible to specific hydrolysis by either pepsin or trypsin (Birnstiel et al.; Busch et al.; Muramatsu and Busch). As a result, it is presently rather difficult to assess to what extent the material extracted from the nucleolus by pepsin or trypsin corresponds to any one of the different classes of nucleolar proteins isolated by biochemical techniques. In spite of the above reservations concerning the specificity of proteinases in relation to nucleolar proteins, useful information has slowly been accumulating in recent years on their overall distribution within the mass of this organelle.

Available data concerning the effect of pepsin on the nucleolus of both animal and plant material are, for instance, quite convergent. Following hydrolysis of 1 μ sections with this enzyme, plant nucleoli stain intensely with azure B or methylene blue and still contain important amounts of material absorbing in the 260–280 mμ range (Lord and Lafontaine). At the ultrastructural level, the nucleolus as a whole decreases in density, the RNP particles characterizing the granular zones become noticeably more conspicuous, and coarse convoluted threads are revealed within the fibrillar portions of this organelle (Fig. 16). As already observed in the case of animal nucleoli (Marinozzi), pepsin extracts an all pervading amorphous substance or matrix from the nucleolar mass. Double digestion with pepsin and ribonuclease, in that order, completely disorganizes the nucleolar RNP particles as well as the cytoplasmic ribosomes (Marinozzi; Bernhard and Granboulan; Lord and Lafontaine). The granular zones of the nucleolus decrease greatly in density but much amorphous material, presumably proteinaceous in nature, persists. Such preparations exhibit, still more clearly than those extracted with either ribonuclease or pepsin, the coarse skein which is typically found in the fibrillar zones of plant nucleoli (section 4 (c)).

Relevant information on the extent of hydrolysis of nucleolar proteins by trypsin is still rather meager. This enzyme is found to react more slowly with cellular structures than pepsin and its activity also seems to depend on the fixation conditions of the specimens (Leduc and Bernhard). Previous reports concur in the finding that trypsin first affects the morphological integrity of both nucleolar RNP particles and cytoplas-

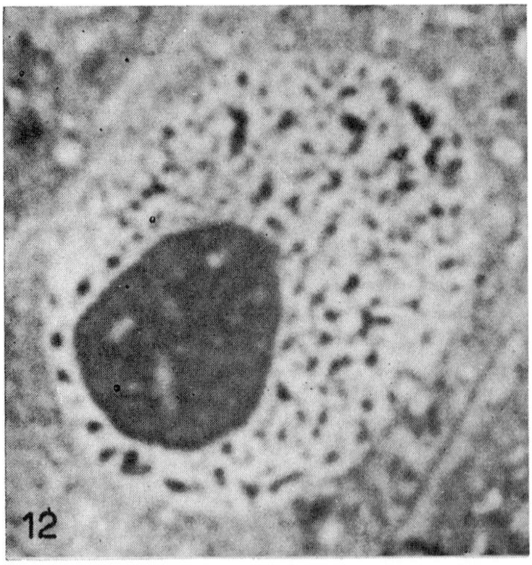

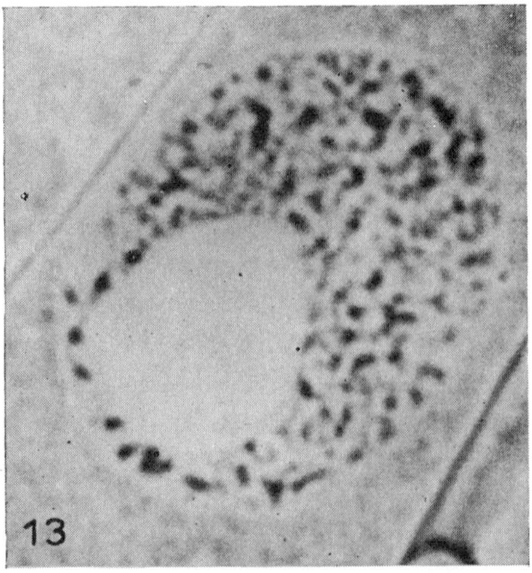

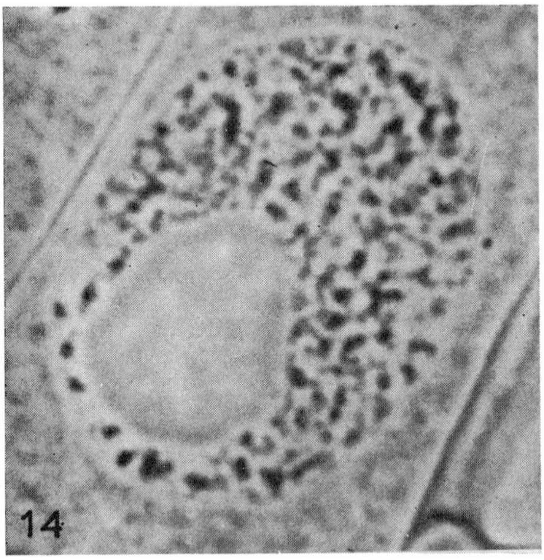

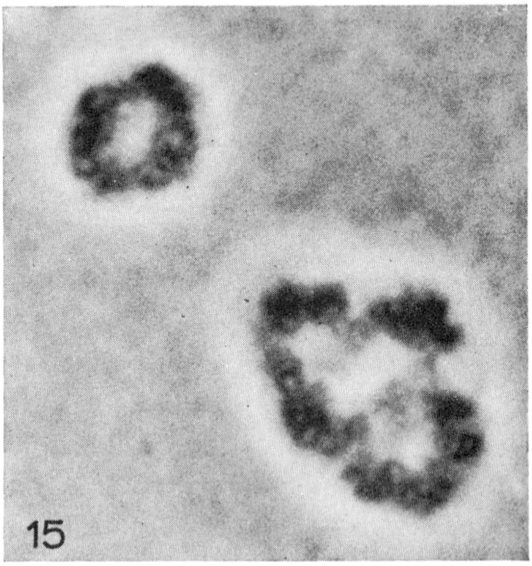

Figs. 12–14. This series of micrographs illustrates the action of ribonuclease on nuclear structures. The material (*Triticum vulgare*) was fixed in 4 per cent formaldehyde adjusted to *p*H 7.2 with sodium cacodylate and embedded in glycol methacrylate. The section (0.7 μ) was stained in 0.25% azure B in McIlvaine's buffer at *p*H 4.0. Digestion with ribonuclease (0.2% in distilled water adjusted to *p*H 6.8 with 0.01 N NaOH) was performed for 2 hr at 37 °C.

Fig. 12 shows the untreated preparation. The nucleolus stains quite intensely with azure B and exhibits denser zones as well as vacuolar regions. Following extraction with ribonuclease (Fig. 13), the chromosomes appear almost as dense as in the untreated preparation but the nucleolus no longer shows any staining. The persistence of material, presumably proteins, within the nucleolar mass following digestion with ribonuclease may, however, be demonstrated under phase contrast microscopy (Fig. 14). A quite similar distribution of persisting nucleolar material may be recorded with ultraviolet microscopy. Note here, that with phase optics, the vacuolar regions correspond closely to those seen in the unextracted preparation. $\times$ 3,500

Fig. 15. Phase contrast micrograph of nucleoli (*Allium porrum*) treated with 'Tween 80' for a few minutes. A coarse filamentous component has become visible following dispersion of most of the surrounding nucleolar material. Compare with loops seen in Fig. 16. $\times$ 3,000.

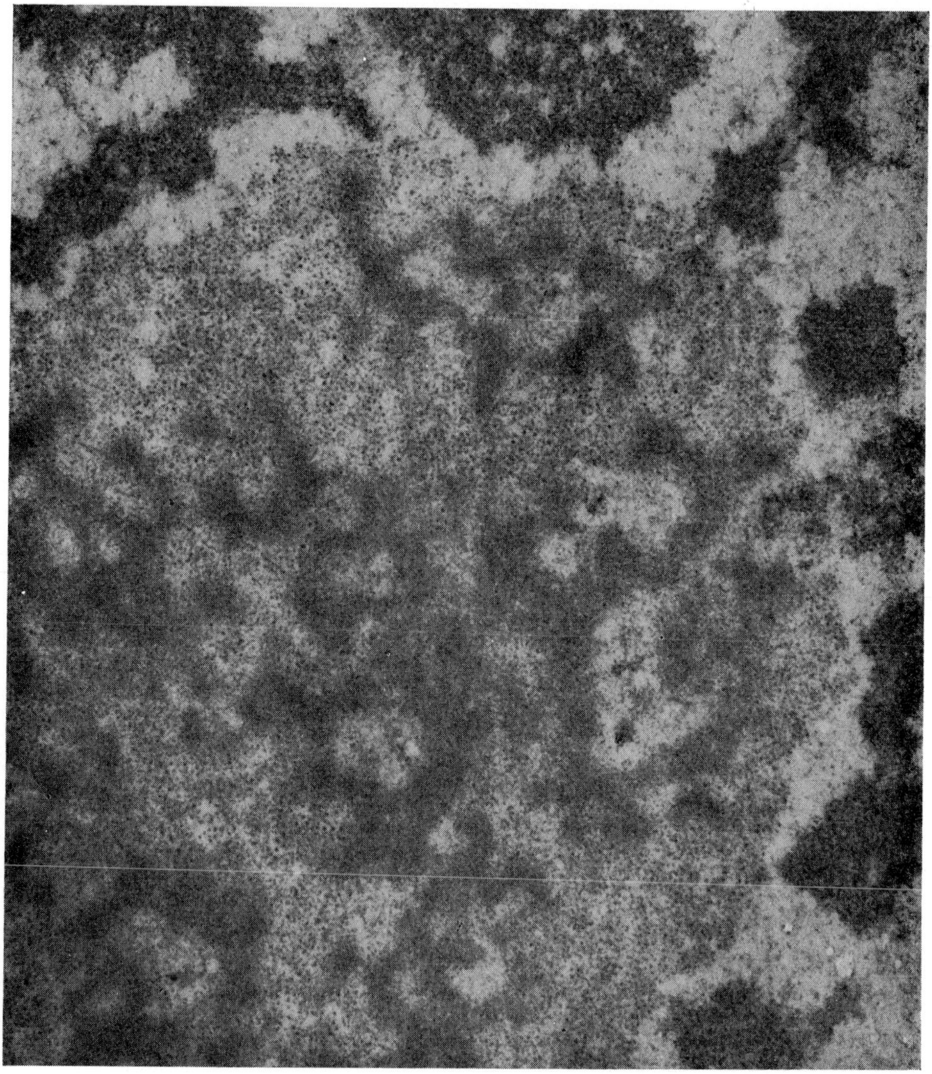

Fig. 16. Electron micrograph of portion of interphase nucleus (*Allium porrum*). The preparation was fixed in glutaraldehyde and embedded in glycol methacrylate. Following digestion in 0.5% pepsin at *p*H 1.2 for 3 hr, the section was stained in 2% uranyl acetate. This enzyme is seen to remove noticeable amounts of material throughout the nucleolar mass. The nucleolus now clearly exhibits a coarse reticulum consisting predominantly of densely packed fibrillar material. The particulate nucleolar portions also appear much more transparent and the RNP granules more conspicuous than in control preparations indicating that the amorphous substance pervading such zones has been partially extracted. The chromosomes stain as intensely as in untreated preparations but show a fine particulate texture which may reflect slight kinks in their constituent microfibrils. ×32,000

mic ribosomes. Following longer extraction periods (4–6 hr), additional material is removed from plant nucleoli which then take on a uniformly amorphous appearance. These observations could be taken to imply that trypsin first attacks basic proteins which, as now seems well established, represent a significant proportion of the proteins found in both the nucleolus and ribosomes (Birnstiel et al.; Low and Wool; Mundell). The rate of extractions of other nucleolar protein fractions would presumably be slower. The recent finding (Tunis) that commercial trypsin contains sufficient ribonuclease for extensive in vitro degradation of RNA may account, partly at least, for our earlier observation that it also removes RNA from the nucleolus in 0.7 μ sections of glycol methacrylate embedded material (Lord and Lafontaine). There nevertheless exist indications from various sources to the effect that RNA is complexed with proteins throughout the nucleolar mass (discussed in Bernhard and Granboulan; Hay).

(c) *Intranucleolar DNA and the organizer loops*

Classical studies (reviewed in Moses; Hay; Lafontaine) have shown that the nucleolus arises at telophase in close association with specific chromosome segments (Figs. 9 and 10). In many instances, parts of telophase and interphase chromosomes are seen projecting within the nucleolus but it is usually difficult to follow these chromatin strands within its mass except for short distances. Animal nucleoli commonly exhibit irregular patches of chromatin and in certain cases concentric lamellae of similar material have also been observed (Swift 1963; Granboulan and Granboulan 1964). In other nucleoli, chromating cannot be recognized morphologically under electron microscopy but the presence of DNA is clearly demonstrated by means of the autoradiographic technique (Hay and Revel).

A rather similar situation prevails for plant nucleoli. In virtually all species examined so far under electron microscopy (Porter; Hyde; Lafontaine and Lord), patches of chromatin material may be recognized throughout the nucleolar mass. These chromatin areas seem to be significantly more numerous in interphase prochromosomal nuclei and are consistently located within the fibrillar portions of the nucleolus (Fig. 1). The degree of association of chromatin with the nucleolus is such in some of these plants that, following 30 min labeling periods, significant incorporation of tritiated thymidine takes place over certain nucleolar areas. Other plants, however, show no such Feulgen positive nucleolar inclusions (McLeish 1964, 1968; LaCour) and incorporation of tritiated thymidine is very limited.

Although intranucleolar chromatin zones are currently often assumed to represent part of the nucleolar organizer, new evidence has come forth which indicates that the organizer proper would rather correspond to convoluted strands exhibiting certain morphological and cytochemical characteristics. These strands or loops were first clearly demonstrated in plant nucleoli following treatment with a detergent (LaCour; LaCour and Wells) (Fig. 15); our observations reveal that they represent an important portion of the irregular dense zones seen in preparations stained with methylene blue and which at the ultrastructural level consist of closely packed fibrillar material. It may be infered from these findings that the typically irregular disposition of the fibrillar zones within the nucleolus closely reflects a corresponding complex arrangement of the underlying skein throughout the mass of this organelle. The foregoing intimate morphological relationship between the nucleolar loops and the fibrillar regions holds true in the case of plants with either reticulate (e.g. *Allium cepa, Allium porrum, Triticum vulgare, Vicia faba*) or chromocentric (e.g. *Raphanus sativus, Tropaeolum majus*) interphase nuclei. As was to be expected if the alledged organizer loops are in fact involved in nucleologenesis, similar structures are already quite evident within the very early telophase nucleolus (Fig. 10). Closer examination of such nucleoli, as they are first recognized in association with certain early or mid-telophase chromosomes, shows that they then consist predominantly of interwoven strands forming a coarse skein which is permeated with fibrillar material. The ultrastructural texture of this latter material is indistinguishable from that of the substance forming the fibrillar zones of mature interphase nuclei. Only a thin peripheral irregular layer of granules may be detected within these early telophase or midtelophase nucleoli (section 5 (b)).

Cytochemical and radioautographic studies under both light and electron microscopy have uncovered some rather unexpected characteristics of these nucleolar loops. They cannot be detected in Feulgen preparations and persist following treatment with deoxyribonuclease, ribonuclease, pepsin, trypsin or combinations of these enzymes (Lord and Lafontaine). These structures, moreover, show very low incorporation of thymidine-H^3 after long exposure to this precursor. Taken together, the above data tend to indicate that these nucleolar loops contain much less DNA than anticipated, considering their relatively coarse dimensions, and, moreover, that this DNA is complexed with substances quite resistant to both nucleases and proteinases. The important fact that this DNA is otherwise involved in intense metabolic processes can be demonstrated by means of pulse labeling experiments with uridine-H^3. Following short exposures (5 min), there can indeed be observed a most striking distribution of radioautographic grains over the irregular and more centrally located zones of the nucleolus which contain the organizer loops. Quite significantly, the remaining nucleolar portions consisting of RNP particles show no evidence of incorporation in these preparations. These results with plant nucleoli closely match, therefore, those reported by other workers investigating the initial site of synthesis of rapidly labeled nucleolar RNA in a variety of animal cells (Karasaki; Geuskens and Bernhard; Gaudecker).

To conclude, the nucleolar organizer must be visualized as a distinct and essential morphological partion of the nucleolus. Its capacity for transcribing 45 S RNA species (discussed in Perry, this volume) is reflected, at the cytological level, by a rapid radioautographic labeling over the fibrillar zones of the nucleolus. According to current thinking, this 45 S RNA then migrate to the adjoining granular nucleolar areas where it is processed and is involved in the elaboration of preribosomal particles. In spite of this encouraging progress towards the elucidation of the specific biochemical function and of the localization of the organizer within the nucleolar body, it is evident that much remains to be learned concerning both its cytochemical make-up and ultrastructure. Further work will also be needed to clearly establish the relation of this coarse filamentous nucleolar component to the Feulgen-positive inclusions often observed within this organelle.

5. *Mode of formation of the nucleolus at telophase*

(a) *The prenucleolar substance*

The problems of the formation of the nucleolus at telophase and that of the nature and origin of the so-called prenucleolar substance have been closely linked, over the years (see Moses; Swift and Stevens; Tandler; Lafontaine, for recent reviews). Although most authors agree that the early telophase nucleus is characterized by the presence of a basophilic substance appearing as a diffuse coating over the chromosomes or forming numerous spheres scattered between them, it is still debated where this substance comes from and, most important, to what extent, if any, it is related to formation of the nucleolus throughout telophase. Concerning the first point three main hypotheses may be considered: (a) the basophilic substance detected at early and midtelophase is shed from the chromosomes and corresponds to the matrix of classical authors; (b) this material originates from the spindle or (c) finally, it is elaborated within the forming nucleus as a result of the synthetic activity of the chromosomes.

In its original form, the first assumption implied that the matrix corresponds to a condensation on late prophase chromosomes of material from the dissolving nucleolus. According to this interpretation part of the nucleolus material is transported to the cell poles by the chromosomes and is therefore continuous from one division cycle to the next. Although certain cytochemical observations later suggested that nucleolar RNA accumulates onto late prophase chromosomes (Kaufmann et al. 1948; Jacobson and Webb), recent autoradiographic investigations have failed to substantiate these findings. It has likewise been impossible, under electron microscopy, to obtain any conclusive evidence that part of the nucleolar substance deposits on the chromosomes. That this problem may be far from settled is, however, suggested by the recent demonstration that metaphase chromosomes contain noticeable amounts of ribosomal RNA part of which is represented by 30 S and 50 S particles (Maio and Schildkraut). Further studies will undoubtedly permit to elucidate the origin of this RNA and verify whether or not it is nucleolar in nature.

Apart from the foregoing data, a number of additional arguments may be invoked against the classical notion that the basophilic substance seen throughout the early and midtelophase nucleus originates in bulk from a chromosomal matrix. In plants with prochromosomal interphase nuclei, for instance, the volume of this substance is comparable to that of the chromosomes themselves (Fig. 7). Moreover, the accumulation of this interchromosomal material, is not accompanied in various species (e.g. *Vicia faba*, *Lathyrus odoratus*) by a corresponding decrease in the density of the chromosomes (Fig. 8). Nonetheless available data do not permit to reject the possibility that some material, but in restricted amount, is indeed contributed by the telophase chromosomes.

According to a second proposal, the basophilic interchromosomal substance under discussion originates from spindle material trapped within the telophase nucleus at the time the nuclear envelope reforms. Again there presently exists little conclusive evidence in favour of such a view. A close examination of published electron micrographs of both animal and plant early telophase nuclei, reveals in fact that the nuclear envelope forms in intimate contact with the outside surface of the chromosomes closely grouped at the cell poles. Only restricted amounts of spindle material are seen within the nucleus at that stage. Even though no clear-cut evidence exists suggesting that material is subsequently transported across the envelope during telophase and interphase, as the chromosomes uncoil and the nucleus enlarges, such a mechanism cannot be ruled out. Recent studies with synchronized cells indeed point to the possibility that part of the interphase nucleolar RNA is synthesized during the preceding cell cycle (Gaffney and Nardone). Moreover, it should be recalled that the origin of the bulk of the nucleolar mass, the various protein fractions, is still a matter for speculation. Part of these may well be synthesized in the cytoplasm and move to the nucleus later on, as has been demonstrated for certain other nuclear proteins (Robbins and Borun).

We now come to the last hypothesis, that the so-called prenucleolar substance is formed as a result of the synthetic activity of the chromosomes. This interpretation needs serious reexamination in the light of recent biochemical and genetic data closely linking the genes of the nucleolar organizer with the formation of nucleolar macromolecules (reviewed in Perry). These elegant observations have in fact clearly established that synthesis of ribosomal RNA is under the direct control of polycistronic loci clustered within chromosomal segments corresponding to the classical nucleolar organizers. Such studies have evidently pinpointed the site of formation of only part of the nucleolar substance, namely the 45 S preribosomal RNA. The problem of the origin of the interchromosomal or prenucleolar material remains, therefore, largely unsettled (Moses; Lafontaine and Lord; Tandler; Swift and Stevens; Hay; Lafontaine).

Finally, to what extent is the so-called prenucleolar substance involved with formation of the nucleolus at telophase? Unfortunately, all of the various lines of evidence brought forth so far are circumstantial in nature and generally rest on certain cytochemical or ultrastructural characteristics which this material shares with the nucleolus. This substance, whether diffused or in the form of small irregular bodies, stains with azure B and is partly digested with ribonuclease; its strong UV absorption at 2800 Å following such extraction indicates that, as the nucleolus, it consists mostly of proteins (Lord, unpublished). Moreover this interchromosomal material and the nucleolus contain a silver-reducing component, presumably proteinaceous in nature (Tandler). At the ultra-structural level, the prenucleolar substance has finally been found to sometimes contain dense doughnut-like particles which are otherwise restricted to the fibrillar zones of the mature nucleolus.

The view, expressed by early authors and a number of recent workers, that the substance under discussion is truly prenucleolar in nature in the sense that it contributes to the formation of the nucleolus, is based not only on the aforementioned properties but also on the consistent observation of its decreasing importance during growth of the nucleolus. The number of prenucleolar bodies, often described as closely attached to the surface of chromosomes, has for instance been reported to diminish during nucleologenesis. Such bodies are generally thought to fuse into larger structures which eventually merge with the forming nucleolus. Likewise, the diffused interchromosomal material seen in certain plant species has been observed to progressively decrease in amount as the nucleolus enlarges. Electron microscopy reveals, furthermore, that this fibrillogranular material is continuous with the surface of the growing nucleolus.

Admittedly, the various cytochemical and ultrastructural characteristics of this so-called prenucleolar substance as well as its particularly suggestive distribution during nucleologenesis, point to a close relationship with the forming nucleolus; they constitute no definitive proof, however, that the material in question is synthesized within the telophase nucleus or, for that matter, that it is directly involved in formation of the nucleolus. Available autoradiographic data on this aspect of the problem are, unfortunately, still rather inconclusive. Both RNA and protein synthesis have been demonstrated at telophase but there remains some uncertainty as to when exactly, relative to the appearance of the prenucleolar substance, such synthesis is initiated (Prescott and Bender; Das; Schiff). Following short (5–20 min) exposures to tritium labeled uridine or cytidine, we have observed incorporation in telophase nuclei (*Allium porrum*) where the chromosomes are still regularly coiled and the prenucleolar bodies quite numerous. Similar incorporation was observed in other species at a stage characterized by the presence of diffused interchromosomal material. Incorporation of basic amino acids does not appear significantly different from that of RNA precursors. In all species we have examined so far, it is evident, however, that the synthesis of both RNA and proteins is considerably more important at interphase than at midtelophase. Recent biochemical studies with synchronous cultures point to the same conclusion (Klevecz and Stubblefield; Gaffney and Nardone). More detailed data will consequently be required before the foregoing results are accepted as evidence that the prenucleolar substance in question is the site of synthetic activities which are relevant to the processes of nucleolar formation.

(b) *Role of the chromosomes in nucleologenesis*

Even though specific chromosome segments, the classical nucleolar organizers, have long been known to participate in formation of the nucleolus, their overall role in the elaboration of the nucleolar substance is not yet fully documented. An impressive body of biochemical, genetic and cytological data has accumulated, of late, closely linking these chromosome loci with transcription of 45 S preribosomal RNA (reviewed in Perry). During the same period much information has likewise been obtained to the effect that the nucleolus consists mostly of proteins of various sorts and of certain species of RNA (discussed in Hay) in addition to the preribosomal RNAs. The problem therefore arises as to the origin of these various other nucleolar constituents. Is their synthesis also controlled by the nucleolar organizer? These questions remain mostly unanswered at the present time. Nevertheless, different types of observations tend to indicate that a number of chromosome sites participate in the elaboration of the various nucleolar constituents. It has been noted, for instance (Heitz), that micronuclei containing no organizer chromosomes still form small nucleolar-like bodies. Electron microscopic evidence (Phillips and Phillips) reveals that these spherical bodies possess both fibrous and granular components similar to those characterizing true nucleoli. Mutants lacking nucleolar organizers are likewise capable of forming nuclear bodies but these are mostly devoid of RNP particles (Hay and Gurdon; Swift and Stevens) and no ribosomes are synthesized in such cells (Brown and Gurdon). These pseudonucleoli nevertheless still contain some RNA and a number of authors have advanced hypotheses on the possible origin of this RNA (Swift and Stevens; Hay). The present consensus of opinion is that an interrelationship of distinct nuclear RNA synthesizing sites is implicated in formation of the nucleolus. The observations that in embryonic cells (Karasaki) and plant oospheres (Camefort) early nucleoli first consist exclusively of fine fibrillar material, the RNP particles appearing later on, could conceivably also be interpreted as an indication that the first activated nucleolar genes are distinct from the nucleolar organizer.

Now, to come back to the nucleolar organizer proper, relevant observational evidence leaves little doubt that it plays a key role in initiating formation of the nucleolus from early to midtelophase. As already pointed out (section 4 (c)), the young nucleolus first appears as a spherical body the mass of which consists predominantly of a coarse skein of loose chromosome loops (Fig. 10). This organization is still more evident in electron micrographs of preparations digested with both pepsin and ribonuclease. At such an early stage of nucleolar development, the small interstices between the convoluted loops contain fine fibrils similar to those characterizing the fibrillar zones of the mature nucleolus. The nucleolus then shows only limited amounts of particles at its surface even though numerous irregular bodies, distinctly particulate in texture, are scattered between the uncoiling chromosomes. Since very few radioautographic grains are detected in such nucleoli, following exposure of the specimens to either uridine-H^3 or lysine-H^3, it is clear that nucleolar synthesis of RNA and proteins is still marginal if not insignificant. By midtelophase, when the chromosomes have uncoiled further, growth of the nucleolus is seen to proceed mostly by the addition of particulate material around the centrally located fibrillar skein. In *Allium porrum*, numerous patches of particulate material, indistinguishable from that of the forming granular nucleolar zones, are still found scattered throughout the nucleus. These patches, it is interesting to note, are frequently closely associated with segments of chromosomes. Midtelophase chromosomes are also already characterized, in this species, by puff-like structures the interstices of which appear to contain a low density fibrillar material (Fig. 11).

It is evident from these observations that, in addition to the nucleolus, the midtelophase nucleus contains different types of bodies the exact nature of which is not known. From a variety of data (section 5 (a)) it would nevertheless appear that, concurrent with growth of the nucleoli at the organizer loci, a number of chromosome segments are also involved in the formation of a variety of other materials. Till more definitive cytochemical and radioautographic data become available one may only conjecture as to the possible role of these bodies in relation to nucleologenesis.

References

BAJER, A.: Behavior and fine structure of spindle fibers during mitosis in endosperm. Chromosoma 25 (1968) 249.

BAJER, A. and J. MOLÉ-BAJER: Cine analysis of some aspects of mitosis in endosperm. In: G. G. Rose, ed.: Cinemicrography in cell biology. New York, Academic Press Inc. (1963).

BARNICOT, N. A.: A study of newt mitotic chromosomes by negative staining. J. Cell Biol. 32 (1967) 585.

BARNICOT, N. A. and H. E. HUXLEY: Electron microscope observations on mitotic chromosomes. Quart. J. Microscop. Sci. 106 (1965) 197.

BERNHARD, W. and N. GRANBOULAN: Electron microscopy of the nucleolus in vertebrate cells. In: A. J. Dalton and F. Haguenau, eds.: Ultrastructure in biological systems: The nucleus. New York, Academic Press Inc. Vol. 3 (1968) 81.

BIRNSTIEL, M. L., M. I. H. CHIPCHASE and W. G. FLAMM: On the chemistry and organisation of nucleolar proteins. Biochim. Biophys. Acta 87 (1964) 111.

BRINKLEY, B. R. and E. STUBBLEFIELD: The fine structure of the kinetochore of a mammalian cell in vitro. Chromosoma 19 (1966) 28.

BROWN, D. D. and J. B. GURDON: Size distribution and stability of DNA-like RNA synthesized during development of anucleolate embryos of *Xenopus laevis*. J. Mol. Biol. 19 (1966) 399.

BUSCH, H., R. DESJARDINS, D. GROGAN, K. HIGASHI, S. T. JACOB, M. MURAMATSU, T. S. RO and W. J. STEELE: Composition of nucleoli isolated from mammalian cells. Natl. Cancer Inst. Monograph 23 (1966) 193.

CAIRNS, J.: Autoradiography of HeLa cell DNA. J. Mol. Biol. 15 (1966) 372.

CAMEFORT, H.: Observations sur la structure des chromosomes et des nucléoles de l'oosphère des Pins. Compt. Rend. 259 (1964) 4335.

DARNELL, J. E.: Ribonucleic acids from animal cells. Bacteriol. Rev. 32 (1968) 262.

DAS, N. K.: Chromosomal and nucleolar RNA synthesis in root tips during mitosis. Science 140 (1963) 1231.

DAVIDSON, D.: RNA synthesis in roots of *Vicia faba*. Exptl. Cell Res. 35 (1964) 317.

DAVIES, H. G. and J. TOOZE: Electron- and light-microscope observations on the spleen of the newt *Triturus cristatus*: The surface topography of the mitotic chromosomes. J. Cell Sci. 1 (1966) 331.

DE, D. N.: Autoradiographic studies of nucleoprotein metabolism during the division cycle. Nucleus (Calcutta) 4 (1961) 1.

DELAY, C.: Recherches sur la structure des noyaux quiescents chez les phanérogames. Rev. Cytol. Biol. Vegetales 10 (1948) 103.

DUPRAW, E.J.: Macromolecular organization of nuclei and chromosomes: A folded fibre model based on whole-mount electron microscopy. Nature 206 (1965) 338.

FRENSTER, J.H.: Control of DNA strand separations during selective transcription and asynchronous replication. In: The cell nucleus: Metabolism and radiosensitivity. London, Taylor and Francis Ltd. (1966) 27.

GABRUSEWYCZ-GARCIA, N. and R.G. KLEINFELD: A study of the nucleolar material in *Sciara coprophila*. J. Cell Biol. 29 (1966) 347.

GAFFNEY, E.B. and R.M. NARDONE: Nucleolar RNA synthesis in synchronous cultures of strain L-929. Exptl. Cell Res. 53 (1968) 410.

GALL, J.G.: Lampbrush chromosomes from oocyte nuclei of the newt. J. Morphol. 94 (1954) 283.

GALL, J.G.: Chromosome fibers studied by a spreading technique. Chromosoma 20 (1966) 221.

GALL, J.G. and H.G. CALLAN: H^3-uridine incorporation in lampbrush chromosomes. Proc. Natl. Acad. Sci. U.S. 48 (1962) 562.

GAUDECKER, B. VON: RNA synthesis in the nucleolus of *Chironomus thummi* as studied by high resolution autoradiography. Z. Zellforsch. Mikrosk. Anat. 82 (1967) 536.

GEUSKENS, M. and W. BERNHARD: Cytochimie ultrastructurale du nucléole III. Action de l'actinomycine D sur le métabolisme du RNA nucléaire. Exptl. Cell Res. 44 (1966) 579.

GIMÉNEZ-MARTIN, G., J.F. LOPEZ-SAEZ and A. GONZALEZ-FERNANDEZ: Somatic chromosome structure. (Observations with the light microscope). Cytologia (Tokyo) 28 (1963) 381.

GRANBOULAN, N. and P. GRANBOULAN: Cytochimie ultrastructurale du nucléole I. Mise en évidence de chromatine à l'intérieur du nucléole. Exptl. Cell Res. 34 (1964) 71.

GRANBOULAN, N. and P. GRANBOULAN: Cytochimie ultrastructurale du nucléole II. Etude des sites de synthèse du RNA dans le nucléole et le noyau. Exptl. Cell Res. 38 (1965) 604.

HAY, E.D.: Structure and function of the nucleolus in developing cells. In: A.J. Dalton and F. Haguenau, eds.: Ultrastructure in biological systems: The nucleus. New York, Academic Press Inc. Vol. 3 (1968) p. 1.

HAY, E.D. and J.B. GURDON: Fine structure of the nucleolus in normal and mutant *Xenopus* embryo. J. Cell Sci. 2 (1967) 151.

HAY, E.D. and J.P. REVEL: The fine structure of the DNP component of the nucleus. J. Cell Biol. 16 (1963) 29.

HEITZ, E.: Die Ursache der gesetzmässigen Zahl, Lage, Form und Grosse pflanzlicher Nukleolen. Planta 12 (1931) 775.

HSU, T.C.: Differential rate in RNA synthesis between euchromatin and heterochromatin. Exptl. Cell Res. 27 (1962) 332.

HUBERMAN, J.A. and A.D. RIGGS: On the mechanism of DNA replication in mammalian chromosomes. J. Mol. Biol. 32 (1968) 327.

HYDE, B.B.: Changes in nucleolar ultrastructure associated with differentiation in the root tip. J. Ultrastruct. Res. 18 (1967) 25.

JACOBSON, W. and M. WEBB: The two types of nucleoproteins during mitosis. Exptl. Cell Res. 3 (1952) 163.

JOKELAINEN, P.T.: The ultrastructure and spatial organization of the metaphase kinetochore in mitotic rat cells. J. Ultrastruct. Res. 19 (1967) 19.

KARASAKI, S.: Electron microscopic examination of the sites of nuclear RNA synthesis during amphibian embryogenesis. J. Cell Biol. 26 (1965) 937.

KAUFMANN, B.P., M. MCDONALD and H. GAY: Enzymatic degradation of ribonucleoproteins of chromosomes, nucleoli and cytoplasm. Nature 162 (1948) 814.

KAUFMANN, B.P., H. GAY and M.R. MCDONALD: Organizational patterns within chromosomes. Intern. Rev. Cytol. 9 (1960) 77.

KLEVECZ, R.R. and E.STUBBLEFIELD: RNA synthesis in relation to DNA replication in synchronized chinese hamster cell cultures. J. Exptl. Zool. 165 (1967) 259.

KRISHAN, A.: Fine structure of the kinetochores in vinblastine sulfatetreated cells. J. Ultrastruct. Res. 23 (1968) 134.

LACOUR, L.F.: The internal structure of nucleoli. In: C.D.Darlington and K.R.Lewis, eds.: Chromosomes today. London, Oliver and Boyd 1 (1966) 150.

LACOUR, L.F. and B.WELLS: The loops and ultrastructure of the nucleolus of *Ipheion uniflorum*. Z. Zellforsch. Mikrosk. Anat. 82 (1967) 25.

LAFONTAINE, J.G.: Structural components of the nucleus in mitotic plant cells. In: A.J.Dalton and F.Haguenau, eds.: Ultrastructure in biological systems: The Nucleus. New York, Academic Press Inc. Vol. 3 (1968) 151.

LAFONTAINE, J.G. and L.A.CHOUINARD: A correlated light and electron microscope study of the nucleolar material during mitosis in *Vicia faba*. J. Cell Biol. 17 (1963) 167.

LAFONTAINE, J.G. and A.LORD: Ultrastructure and mode of formation of the nucleolus in plant cells. Natl. Cancer Inst. Monograph 23 (1966) 67.

LEDUC, E.H. and W.BERNHARD: Water-soluble embedding media for ultrastructural cytochemistry. Digestion with nucleases and proteinases. In: R.J.C.Harris, ed.: The interpretation of ultrastructure. Symp. Intern. Soc. Cell. Biol. New York, Academic Press Inc. Vol. 1 (1962) 21.

LIMA-DE-FARIA, A.: Recent advances in the study of the kinetochore. Intern. Rev. Cytol. 7 (1958) 123.

LORD, A. and J.G.LAFONTAINE: The organization of the nucleolus in meristematic plant cells. A cytochemical study. J. Cell Biol. 40 (1969) No. 3.

MAIO, J.J. and C.L.SCHILDKRAUT: Isolated mammalian metaphase chromosomes I. General characteristics of nucleic acids and proteins. J. Mol. Biol. 24 (1967) 29.

MARINOZZI, V.: Cytochimie ultrastructurale du nucléole – RNA et protéines intranucléolaires. J. Ultrastruct. Res. 10 (1964) 433.

MATTINGLY, SR., A.: Nuclear protein synthesis in *Vicia faba*. Exptl. Cell Res. 29 (1963) 314.

MAZIA, D.: Mitosis and the physiology of cell division. In: J.Brachet and A.E.Mirsky, eds.: The cell. New York, Academic Press Inc. 3 (1961) 77.

MC LEISH, J.: Deoxyribonucleic acid in plant nucleoli. Nature 204 (1964) 36.

MC LEISH, J.: Chemical and autoradiographic studies of intranucleolar DNA in *Vicia faba*. Exptl. Cell Res. 51 (1968) 157.

MOSES, M.J.: The nucleus and chromosomes: A cytological perspective. In: G.H.Bourne, ed.: Cytology and cell physiology, 3rd ed. New York, Academic Press Inc. (1964) 423.

MOSES, M.J. and J.G.LAFONTAINE: Structural components of the nucleus at interphase and during division. In: Recent Advan. Botany 2 (1961) 1053.

MUNDELL, R.D.: Studies on nucleolar and ribosomal basic proteins and their relationship to nucleolar function. Exptl. Cell Res. 53 (1968) 395.

MURAMATSU, M. and H.BUSCH: Isolation, composition, and function of nucleoli of tumors and other tissues. In: H.Busch, ed.: Methods in cancer research. New York, Academic Press Inc. Vol. 2 (1967) p. 303.

OHNUKI, Y.: Structure of chromosomes I. Morphological studies of the spiral structure of human somatic chromosomes. Chromosoma 25 (1968) 402.

PERRY, R.P.: The nucleolus and the synthesis of ribosomes. Progr. Nucl. Acid Res. Mol. Biol. 6 (1967) 219.

PHILLIPS, S.G. and D.M.PHILLIPS: Sites of nucleolus production in cultured chinese hamster cells. J. Cell Biol. 40 (1969) 248.

PORTER, K.R.: Problems in the study of nuclear fine structure. Intern. Kongr. Elektronenmikroskopie, 4, Berlin (1958). (W.Bargmann et al., eds.). Berlin, Springer-Verlag 2 (1960) 186.

PORTER, K.R. and K.HAMA: High-voltage electron microscope study of tissue sections. J. Cell Biol. 39 (1968) 157a.

PRESCOTT, D.M. and M.A.BENDER: Synthesis of RNA and protein during mitosis in mammalian tissue culture cells. Exptl. Cell Res. 26 (1962) 260.

RASCH, R.W., E.M.RASCH and J.W.WOODARD: Heterogeneity of nuclear populations in root meristems. Caryologia 20 (1967) 87.

RIS, H.: Fine structure of chromosomes. Proc. Roy. Soc. (London), Ser. B: 164 (1966) 246.

RIS, H.: Ultrastructure of the animal chromosome. In: V.V.Koningsberger and L.Bosch, eds.: Regulation of nucleic acid and protein biosynthesis. Amsterdam, Elsevier Publishing Company (1967) 11.

ROBBINS, E. and T.W.BORUN: The cytoplasmic synthesis of histones in HeLa cells and its temporal relationship to DNA replication. Proc. Natl. Acad. Sci. U.S. 57 (1967) 409.

SASAKI, M.S. and A.NORMAN: DNA fibres from human lymphocyte nuclei. Exptl. Cell Res. 44 (1966) 642.

SCHIFF, S.O.: Ribonucleic acid synthesis in neuroblasts of *Chortophaga viridifasciata* (De Geer), as determined by observations in individual cells in the mitotic cycle. Exptl. Cell Res. 40 (1965) 264.

SPARVOLI, E., H.GAY and B.P.KAUFMANN: Number and pattern of association of chromonemata in the chromosomes of *Tradescantia*. Chromosoma 16 (1965) 415.

STERN, H., F.B.JOHNSTON and G.SETTERFIELD: Some chemical properties of isolated pea nucleoli. J. Biophys. Biochem. Cytol. 6 (1959) 57.

STEVENS, B.J.: The fine structure of the nucleolus during mitosis in the grasshopper neuroblast cell. J. Cell Biol. 24 (1965) 349.

SUSKIND, R.G.: Autoradiographic and cytochemical evidence for synthesis of a lysine-containing ribonucleoprotein in nucleoli inhibited by actinomycin D. J. Cell Biol. 24 (1965) 309.

SWIFT, H.: Nucleic acids and cell morphology in dipteran salivary glands. In: J.M.Allen, ed.: The molecular control of cellular activity. New York, McGraw-Hill (1962) 73.

SWIFT, H.: Cytochemical studies on nuclear fine structure. Exptl. Cell Res. Suppl. 9 (1963) 54.

SWIFT, H.: Molecular morphology of the chromosome. In: C.J.Dawe, ed.: The Chromosome: Structural and functional aspects. Baltimore, Williams and Wilkins Inc. 1 (1966) 26.

SWIFT, H. and B.J.STEVENS: Nucleolar-chromosomal interaction in microspores of maize. Natl. Cancer Inst. Monograph 23 (1966) 145.

TANDLER, C.J.: Detection and origin of nucleolar components: A model for nucleolar RNA function. Natl. Cancer Inst. Monograph 23 (1966) 181.

THOMAS, P.: Etude, en microscopie électronique, de l'action de la pepsine et de la ribonucléase sur des cellules méristématiques de radis et de courge. Compt. Rend. 262 (1966) 745.

TOKUYASU, K., S.C.MADDEN and L.J.ZELDIS: Fine structural alterations of interphase nuclei of lymphocytes stimulated to growth activity in vitro. J. Cell Biol. 39 (1968) 630.

TROSKO, J.E. and S.WOLFF: Strandedness of *Vicia faba* chromosomes as revealed by enzyme digestion studies. J. Cell Biol. 26 (1965) 125.

TROSKO, J.E. and J.G.BREWEN: Cytological observations on the strandedness of mammalian metaphase chromosomes. Cytologia (Tokyo) 31 (1966) 208.

TUNIS, M.: Ribonuclease activity in commercial crystalline trypsin and a method for removal. Science 162 (1968) 912.

VINCENT, W.S.: The isolation and chemical properties of the nucleoli of starfish oocytes. Proc. Natl. Acad. Sci. U.S. 38 (1952) 139.

VINCENT, W.S., E.BALTUS, A.LOVLIE and R.E.MUNDELL: Proteins and nucleic acids of starfish oocyte nucleoli and ribosomes. Natl. Cancer Inst. Monograph 23 (1966) 235.

WEBSTER, P.L. and D.DAVIDSON: Evidence from thymidine-H^3-labeled meristems of *Vicia faba* of two cell populations. J. Cell Biol. 39 (1968) 332.

WOLFE, S.L.: The fine structure of isolated chromosomes. J. Ultrastruct. Res. 12 (1965) 104.

WOODARD, J., E.RASCH and H.SWIFT: Nucleic acid and protein metabolism during the mitotic cycle in *Vicia faba*. J. Biophys. Biochem. Cytol. 9 (1961) 445.

CHAPTER 17

Ultrastructure of the chromosomes at meiosis

J. ROBERTO SOTELO

Instituto de Investigación de Ciencias Biológicas, Departamento de Ultraestructura Celular, Avda. Italia 3318, Montevideo, Uruguay

Contents

1. Introduction
2. Techniques
3. Morphology and fine structure of prophase chromosomes
   (a) Leptotene stage
   (b) Synaptene – pachytene stages
4. Structure of meiotic chromosomes at division
5. The sex chromosome during the course of meiotic prophase
6. Sinaptonemal-like structures in post-meiotic cells
7. Conclusions

1. Introduction

As early as 1952 Watson studied the spermatogenesis of albino rats with the electron microscope and found two parallel, linear structures in spermatocyte nuclei.

Four years later, Moses (1956a) reported on the chromosomes of crayfish spermatocytes (*Cambarus clarkii*). He described the occurrence of alternate light and dark concentric layers in the chromosome axis (cores). These findings (1956b) were accompanied by analysis of adjacent thick and thin sections using the light and electron microscopes respectively. From this study it was apparent that the chromosome stained areas (Feulgen) were continuous with the electron dense layers recognized in the cores. About the same time Fawcett (1956) studied the spermatocytes of pigeon, cat and man. The images reported by Fawcett, were similar to those shown by Watson in rat spermatocytes, and the same axial structure was found in all three species. It consists of two parallel, helically twisted, ribbon-like dense regions running parallel to the longitudinal axis of an irregularly outlined chromatin mass. Between the two parallel dense regions Fawcett also detected a less dense line.

By 1958 the number of species which had been studied increased to seven: Sotelo and Trujillo-Cenóz investigated spermatocytes of *Cnesterodon decenmaculatus* (fish), *Mus norvegicus albinus* (rat), *Heteropachylloidelus robustus*, at present *Acanthopachylus aculaetus*, (Opilion) and in the same year a careful comparative study of thick and thin sections of salamander spermatocytes was published by Moses (1958). He recognized that the stage in which the triple structure appeared was concomitant with that of chromosome pairing. From this work emerged a new term, 'synaptinemal complex', for the so-called 'cores'. The word synaptonemal has been lately substituted for the original term coined by Moses (Fawcett 1966; Wettstein and Sotelo 1967). Other authors have used the French derivative 'synaptonematique'.

Before 1959 no female specimen of any zoological group had been examined. In that year Sotelo published observations made on the primary oocytes of the albino rat and provided evidence that axial structures occurred in the gonocytes of both males and females of the same species. Insects and plants were also examined and the fine structure of prophase nuclei of *Gryllus argentinus* (cricket), *Blaptica dubia* (cockroach) and *Laplatacris dispar* (grasshopper) were reported (Sotelo and Trujillo-Cenóz 1960). In 1960 Chardard made a detailed analysis of meiotic chromosomes of orchids and Meyer reported his first observations on *Drosophila* gonocytes. In oocytes, in which crossing-over occurs, he found synaptonemal complexes, but in spermatocytes which lack crossing-over and chiasma formation, due to a lack of orthodox chromosome pairing, no synaptonemal complexes were found. Similar facts were collected from other organisms. The results of these investigations indicated: (a) few variants could be expected in the general morphology of synaptonemal complexes; (b) they were not found in somatic divisions. The complexes seemed to occur in all cases where pairing and chromosome reduction were concomitant, but they may also occur in situations independent of orthodox pairing.

Among the contributions published after 1960, the papers by Nebel and Coulon (1962a) and by Coleman and Moses, deserve special mention as these authors introduced histochemical tests for the study of meiosis with the electron microscope. It is also important to mention the investigations by Roth and Ito who used deoxyadenosine to inhibit DNA synthesis. Whereas the work of the authors firstly mentioned contributed to the knowledge of DNA location in relation to the components of the complexes; the investigations of the latter show small bursts of DNA synthesis at different stages of meiosis; the first of these bursts seems to precede the formation of the synaptonemal complex.

Interconnections between the lateral arms and the medial component of synaptonemal complexes were described by several authors after 1960 (Sotelo and Trujillo-Cenóz 1960; Gall 1961; Meyer 1964). Interest in these structures increased by virtue of the higher resolution that could be achieved through technical improvements in electron microscopy, and significant differences in the organization of the pairing space were found when nine species of insects were compared (Sotelo and Wettstein 1965, 1966). Westergaard and von Wettstein studied the synaptonemal complexes of an ascomycete, *Neottiella rutilans* and also found an ordered disposition of components along the pairing space.

Study of spermatogenesis and spermiogenesis brought to light structures which were either unknown or incompletely described by light microscopists. For instance, close association between nucleolus and sex chromatin of *Gryllidae* spermatocytes was well known to Baumgartner and to von Winiwarter, but the synaptonemal-like material involved in this association was disclosed only by electron microscopy (Sotelo and Trujillo-Cenóz 1960, 1961; Sotelo and Wettstein 1964; Schinn 1965a, b; Guenin 1965). Moreover, multiple associations of synaptonemal complexes which may take place at different stages of spermatogenesis and spermiogenesis were also recognized for the first time.

In this chapter, the reader's attention will be directed to certain specific questions (listed below) for which answers have been sought using both light and electron microscopic techniques. These questions are also summarized briefly at the end of the chapter because they represent the core of the morphological studies and seem to be directly related to the molecular basis of heredity in higher organisms.

(1) Light microscopists have considered chromatids and half-chromatids as the smallest units that may be directly or indirectly demonstrated with the light microscope. Does the electron microscope provide evidence for the existence of two chromatids in each member of the bivalent and do the morphological sub-units (fibrils and filaments) depicted in electronmicrographs of meiotic chromosomes exhibit a particular order which would help to understand chromosome organization?

(2) Pairing of homologs has been described as taking place by gradual contact (zipping process). Do findings made with the electron microscope contribute to an understanding of this process?

(3) Genetic interchange (crossing-over) occurs between the homologous chromosomes.

Do images disclosed by high resolution electron microscopy contribute information to the understanding of crossing-over?

(4) In a number of species the material that appears interposed between the two halves of the bivalents was found to be organized in a characteristic and constant pattern. However, in these species the same pattern occurs in situations other than orthodox pairing. Can it be considered the material substratum of effective pairing, or is it an 'epiphenomenum' of the pairing process?

2. *Techniques*

Standard electronmicroscopic techniques in combination with conventional procedures of light microscopy have been the most common method of study. Scanning thin sections with the electron microscope Watson saw the presence of linear structures slightly beyond the limits of resolution of the light microscope. Comparison, of adjacent thick and thin sections, with the light and the electron microscope respectively, helped to identify the stage of meiosis in which these linear structures occur. Embedding tissue in n-butyl methacrylate facilitated this work, since the plastic can easily be removed with acetone from the thick sections, and conventional staining methods can subsequently be applied.

Enzymatic treatment of cells, followed by appropriate electron dense stains, were later used. Sections of methacrylate embedded cells were incubated with enzymes such as ribonuclease, deoxyribonuclease, and trypsin and examined either directly or after staining with uranyl acetate, lead hydroxide or indium trichloride. Certain combinations of these technical procedures permitted the location of DNA in the bivalent fields, and allowed Coleman and Moses to demonstrate that DNAse digestion leaves exposed a chromosomal skeleton which is morphologically identical to the undigested chromosome.

Tridimensional reconstruction of meiotic nuclei and their chromosomes by serial thin sectioning and electron microscopic examination is another recent innovation. Reconstruction of several nuclei can be made from short series of 100 to 120 sections (1000 Å thick). This method is very useful for the study of morphological characteristics of the whole chromosome complement. Although it is laborious and does not permit examination of large quantities of material, it is the only way to combine the high resolution of the electron microscope with a global evaluation of cell components.

Air-water interface spreading of material followed by mounting and drying on electron microscope grids was successfully used to study chromosomes from a variety of organisms (Ris 1961, 1967; Gall 1966), but it has not been used extensively to study meiosis.

The formation of synaptonemal complexes in relation to DNA synthesis was studied by Roth and Ito (1967) by culturing, in vitro, anthers of plants (lily, variety Cinnabar) and treating the cultures with inhibitors of DNA synthesis (deoxyadenosine). The electron microscope is finally used for the recognition of synaptonemal complexes and their time of appearance in relation to the stages of meiosis and incorporation of the inhibitor.

Incorporation of radioactive tracers to complement information already elicited by histochemical methods (DNA location) has begun in this laboratory. Evaluation of the results depends on the degree of resolution that can be obtained.

3. *Morphology and fine structure of prophase chromosomes*

(a) *Leptotene stage*

Besides the light microscope descriptions, little is known about the morphology of chromosomes during the leptotene stage. Electronmicroscopists devoted most of their attention to the structures recognizable in the ensuing synaptene-pachytene stages. Leptotene stage is of short duration in most species while the pachytene stage lasts longer. In a large number of species, spermatogenic waves (leptotene organization) start at considerably separated intervals of time, thus decreasing the possibility of finding cells at this stage in random samples of material. In the electron microscope, leptotene chromosomes were depicted as thin continuous threads. In these cases the stage was recognized, either by determining the stage of meiosis in relation to the animal's life cycle, as in the studies of Franchi and Mandl on rat oocytes, or by determining the location of cells in the testicular tubules or in the sex organs of plants. Most information has come from electronmicrographs of random sections which leave some doubt as to whether all single threads observed are really single or form part of incompletely sampled tripartite complexes.

Clearly identifiable single units were recently found in the course of serial section analysis of spermatocytes from *Periplaneta* prepared by Wettstein (unpublished observations). In this particular case two categories of units were seen: (a) thread-like, well defined loops extending between two separate points of the nuclear envelope and (b) short segments of threads attached by one end to the nuclear envelope and losing individuality on the inside of a chromatin-like condensation of the nucleus. Also, single units are shown at low magnification by Baker and Franchi (1967a) in the polarized nuclei (bouquet) of human oocytes.

Correlation of reported information on leptotene chromosomes makes it seem likely that leptotene threads consist of a dense core, 170–200 Å thick to which microfibrils of ill-defined length are attached (Fig. 1A). It can not be ascertained whether the dense core is formed of a material which is different from the microfibrils or whether it appears dense due to their particular ordering along the chromosome length. No structures like these occur at prophase of diploid divisions of somatic or gonadal cells. Therefore it is evident that a unique, irreversible change has occurred. The essence of this change consists in the ordering of dispersed chromosome material of preceding stages into a definite number of visible strands. Each strand may already contain two

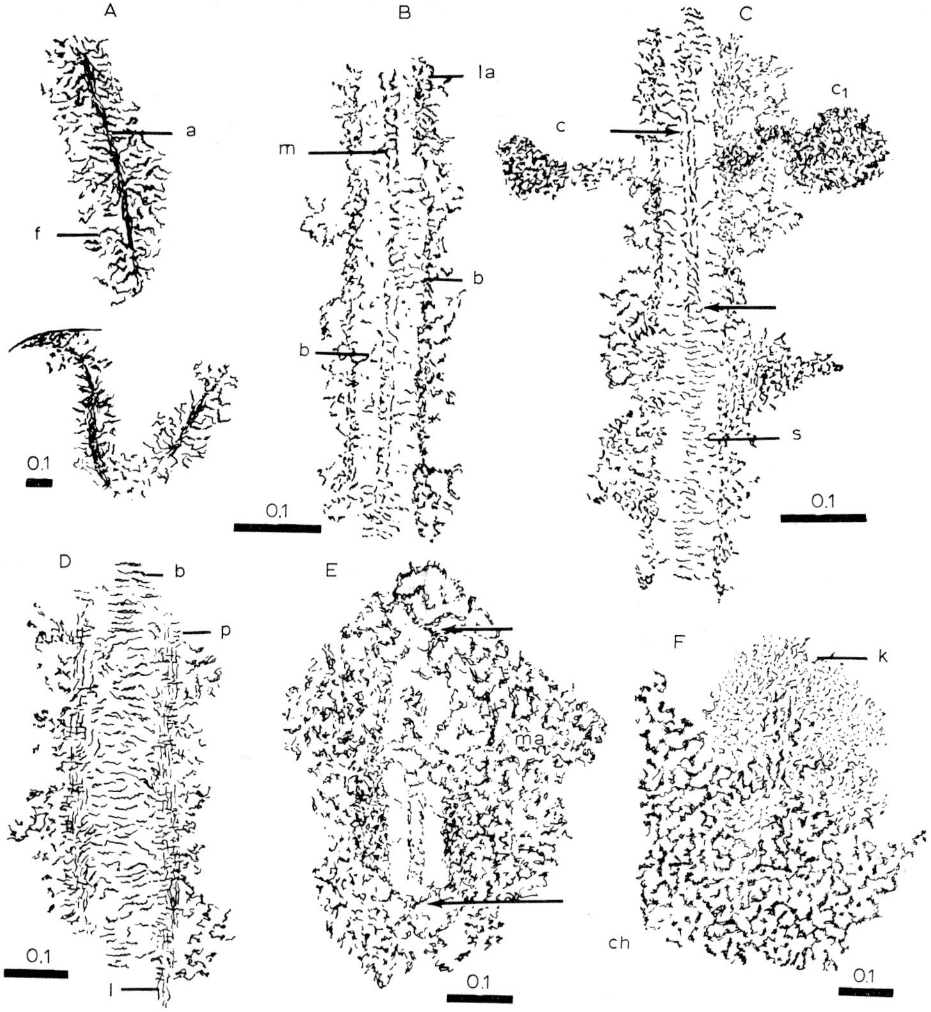

Fig. 1. Semidiagrammatic drawings made by tracing of the more prominent components visible in the electronmicrographs. A: *Leptotene stage* in the cockroach *Periplaneta americana.* The two segments of leptotene threads, belong to the same nucleus. The upper one forms part of a longer chromosome which has one ill-defined extremity ending toward the center of the nucleus and the other is attached to the nuclear envelope. Both extremities are present in other sections of the series. The other thread is a very short chromosome forming a loop between two very close points of the nuclear envelope; only one attachment point is seen in the electronmicrograph; the other is present in the next section of the series. Note the longitudinal array of components in the axis -*a*- and the lateral fibrils -*f*-. 70,000 ×. B: *Synaptene stage* in *Coptoterix gayi* (Mantoidea) (longitudinal-frontal view of the section of the series. Note the longitudinal array of components in the axis -*a*- and the lateral fibrils -*f*-. mal complex. The lateral arms -*la*- are immersed in the loose network of the nuclear background (not traced in the picture). In this species and in cockroaches, the medial density -*m*- is composed of two layers. Crossing filaments (bridges) are indicated at -*b*-. 240,000 ×. C: *Early pachytene* in *Gryllus argentinus.* At this stage the helical turns of the synaptonemal complexes are elongated and of very

linear units which may be recognized or not in the electron microscope. Labelling experiments have supported the hypothesis that duplication has already occurred before leptotene (for literature referring to light microscope on meiosis, see Rhoades). It is also legitimate to assume that prior to the organization of leptotene threads a factor or a group of factors (codified in the DNA molecule) become active, determining the order mentioned above. This activity may be unapparent or repressed in ordinary mitotic prophase. The release of the coded information of chromosome structure is probably followed by the synthesis of the proteins necessary for the construction of the pairing frame. Further ordering of leptotene threads in the nucleus (bouquet and subsequent pairing) may also depend on this chemical process. The trigger for this activity has to be sought among factors which set-up the process of sex maturation at a determined stage in the life of the animal.

Ris (1961) postulated that the leptotene chromosomes of *Tradescantia* and *Lilium* are formed of two bundles (the chromatids) each consisting of approximately eight fibrils. However, extensive exploration of meiocytes at leptonema in this laboratory convinced us that the morphological existence of a double structure cannot be proved in all cases. This does not necessarily invalidate positive observations. It may simply mean that physical separation of DNA strands has not advanced to the point where it can be identified in thin sections with the electron microscope. On the other hand, thin section studies with the electron microscope have not yet progressed far enough to determine which part of the strand is composed of DNA, which is associated protein material, and how they are associated. This intimate interspersion of DNA and associated moieties is perhaps one of the most difficult factors obstructing morphologic analysis.

An attractive solution to the general organization of the chromosomes of higher organisms is to attribute lampbrush-like structures to leptotene (or synaptene) threads. This was proposed by several authors to explain the structure of the lateral arms and adjacent fields of synaptonemal complexes. Baker and Franchi (1967b) have recently shown fibrillar strands projecting laterally from the major strands of the synaptonemal complexes. These authors provide a schematic interpretation of these strands in which lampbrush-like loops are represented. However, the electron microscope

---

small radius. Axis rotation is recognized in this picture because the medial ribbon, which is tri-layered in frontal views, appears striated (above and below the arrows). The striae are marked *-s-*. Two chromomere-like bodies *-c-* and *-c_1-* united to the lateral ribbons by pedicles are seen. 120,000 ×. D: Early pachytene in the grasshopper *Laplatacris dispar*. In this species the lateral ribbons consist of perpendicular filaments *-l-* and *-p-* thus forming a square-like linear pattern. The pairing space is in turn crossed by transverse filaments or bridges *-b*. 170,000 ×. E: Cross section of a bivalent at *advanced pachytene* in *Coptoterix gayi*. The mantle *-ma-* surrounding the complex is very thick and an interchange of fibrils between both halves is seen (arrows). The medial ribbon is two-layered. 170,000 ×. F: Kinetochore region of a *Gryllus argentinus* chromosome at *metaphase I*. Note the contrast between the typical net-like disposition of fibrils in the chromosome area *-ch-* and the kinetochore region components *-k*. Some fibrils are seen penetrating the center of the kinetochore region. 150,000 ×.

evidence does not yet seem conclusive. The main obstacle to this interpretation is to find, in thin sections, complete loops. In addition, the insertion of the lateral projections in the lateral arms of the synaptonemal complexes remains obscure as the intricacy of elements and their thickness makes the analysis at high resolution difficult.

(b) *Synaptene – pachytene stages*

Most knowledge about the structure of prophase chromosomes is based on images corresponding to completely paired chromosomes. There is little information on the events related to the approximation of the homologs. Moses (1958) was the first to show, in *Plethodon cinereus*, two linear parallel units (with an intermediate element between) which diverge and lose their individuality near the nuclear membrane. This represented to him either incomplete pairing or precocious disjunction. Images of this kind are undoubtedly rare in electronmicrographs. In this laboratory two similar structures were fortuitously encountered in *Acanthopachylus aculeatus* spermatocytes and *Forficula sp.* spermatocytes, but without information from serial sections they could not be properly interpreted. It seems that no one, up to now, has made serial electronmicrographs of adequate resolution in which the homologs are in the process of coming together (zipping process).

Sotelo (1959) and Sotelo and Trujillo-Cenóz (1960) attempted an interpretation of the formative process at the time of pairing and postulated that each tripartite group differentiated from a single elementary thread. This assumption was based on the presence of: (a) numerous isolated fragments of medial units and, (b) continuity between the elements of the medial and the lateral ribbons. It was then supposed that each tripartite group represented a member of the diploid complement.

Even though continuity between the elements was recently shown to be the case (bridging), correlation with light microscopic information consistently pointed to the conclusion that each lateral arm represents a homologous chromosome. This means that each nucleus should have a haploid set of tripartite complexes and serial work in this laboratory confirmed this assumption (Wettstein and Sotelo 1967). However, it remains uncertain whether the appearance of the so-called 'medial material' precedes, is concomitant with, or takes place after the meeting of each pair of leptotene strands.

Once synapsis has been completed bivalents are recognized, in panoramic views of nuclei, by the presence of three parallel ribbon-shaped densities each measuring 0.80 to 0.25 μ wide and 200 to 400 Å thick (synaptonemal complexes). They have been referred to as *pairing* or *synaptic ribbons* and the space between as the *pairing* or *synaptic space*. In general, the ribbon located in the middle of the pairing space is less dense than its partners. The majority of bivalents are attached by both ends to the nuclear envelope like leptotene strands. Free ends were rarely found in the species in which serial reconstruction was performed. The ribbons are as long as the bivalent itself and as both homologs are coiled (relational coiling) the ribbons appear twisted around the bivalent axis. At early prophase the helical turns are few, long and wide, but as prophase advances they become more numerous and short. The existence of such coiling and the curved trajectory of the bivalents within the nucleus results in a frequent dissection of the tripartite groups and multiple variations of the images recorded. Fig. 6 shows the geometrical relationship between the three ribbon-like layers, as reconstructed from serially recorded electronmicrographs.

The following terminology has been used to describe synaptonemal complexes; *longitudinal frontal* sections are those in which the three components of the complex are equidistant and show the same thickness along a given segment; *longitudinal lateral* sections show a side view of one lateral arm; *longitudinal sagittal* sections show a side view of the medial component; in *transverse sections* the three components are seen in their smallest dimension; *pairing face* is the inner face of each lateral arm; *pairing space* the distance separating both pairing faces whereas *intermediate spaces* are the clear regions interposed between the lateral arm and the medial density; *bridges* are

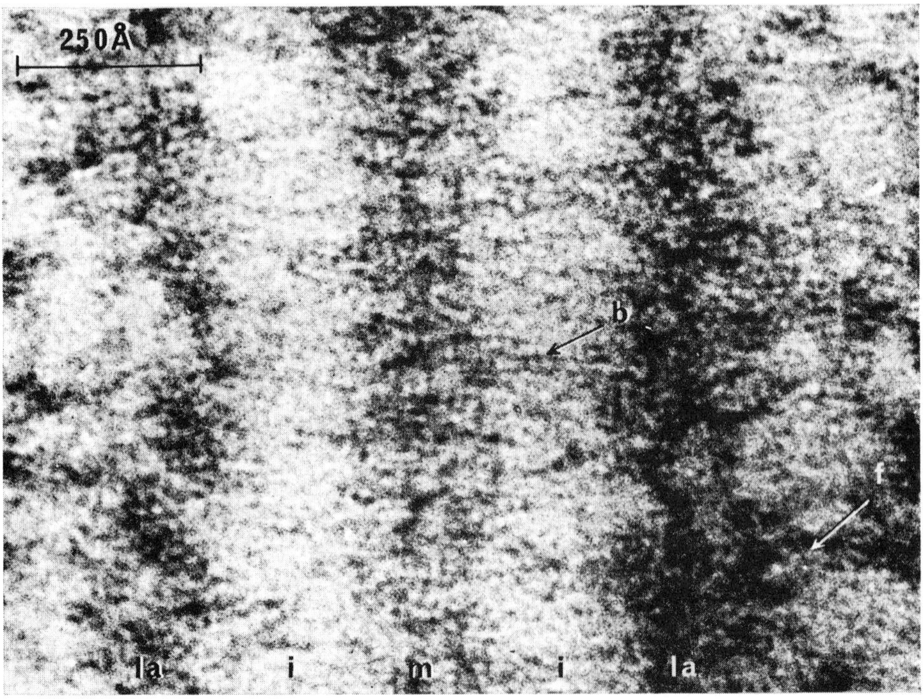

Fig. 2. *Gryllus argentinus. Early pachytene.* This is a high power electronmicrograph of a synaptonemal complex at synaptene stage. The distribution of filaments in the lateral arms *-la-*, the intermediate space *-i-* and the medial ribbon *-m-* are seen. The complex has been cut obliquely so that the trilayered structure of the medial ribbon cannot be distinguished. However, this orientation demonstrates the bridges which are, in general, oblique to the frontal plane. At the place marked *-b-* two filamentous bridges can be clearly depicted. It can also be observed that the filaments are denser in the lateral arms and medial ribbon. On the outer side of the synaptonemal complex the filaments of the lateral arms are continuous with those assembled in fibrils *-f-*. Original magnification 60,000 ×: Enlargement 8 ×.

the interconnecting elements which cross the intermediate spaces; *mantle* is the chromatin layer surrounding the complexes.

Transition between zygotene and pachytene stages occurs gradually. In some species focal condensation of chromatin-like material associated with the ribbons is recognized at the end of synaptene or early pachytene (Figs. 1C and 5). These condensations have been considered to be homologous to chromomeres of classic light microscopy. The analysis of serially cut sections permits a better knowledge of their spatial distribution. Located at various distances from the synaptic ribbons they may have long or short stalks; others on the contrary are sessile. Although chromomeres are said to correspond to one another on each side of the bivalent, these condensations frequently are not. Notwithstanding, a certain number do correspond closely.

No careful examination has been made of these discrete bodies in more advanced

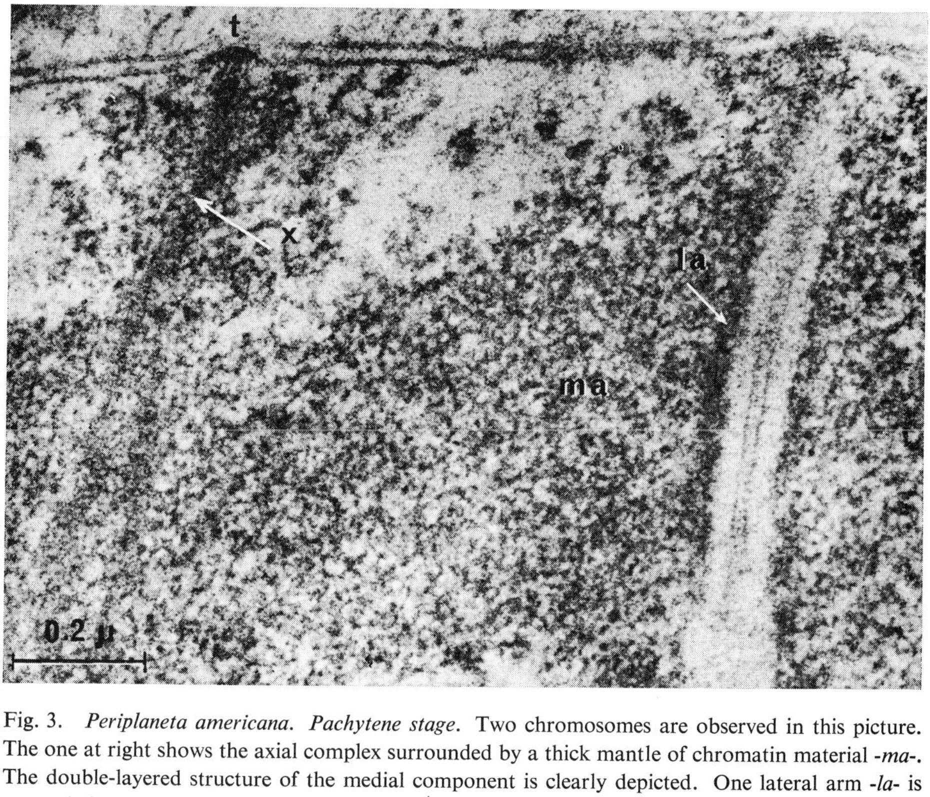

Fig. 3. *Periplaneta americana. Pachytene stage.* Two chromosomes are observed in this picture. The one at right shows the axial complex surrounded by a thick mantle of chromatin material *-ma-*. The double-layered structure of the medial component is clearly depicted. One lateral arm *-la-* is more obvious than its partner because the complex is describing a wide curve and the axis has rotated. At the left side of the picture two crossing chromosome threads are seen *-x*. One of them *-t-* is attached to the inner sheet of the nuclear envelope. The two components are clearly separated in most parts of their trajectory. This photograph is interpreted as a side view of one of the lateral arms of the complex and the two threads may correspond to precociously separated chromatids Original magnification 40,000 ×: Enlargement 2.5 ×.

stages. However, it can be seen that the microfibrillar network surrounding the complex (like a mantle) from mid-pachytene onwards, shows similar structure (Fig. 1E). The mantle itself does not look alike in all cases. In many species it forms a continuous layer all around the tripartite complexes, in others it looks like a thick thread coiled around them (*Acrididae*).

Doubleness of the lateral strands has been described. Some authors have stated that the chromatids of one side face the two of the opposite side. Others located all four chromatids in the same plane so that there would be two internal and two external chromatids. It has to be noted that two helically wound threads may give one or the other image depending on the plane of section. In a recent paper, Baker and Franchi (1967a) clearly show several images of double lateral arms.

Images like the one shown in Fig. 3 are encountered in the electronmicrographs. Here, two elements arising from nearby points of the nuclear envelope are seen; they cross one another within the thickness of the section and remain as separate units. They obviously do not correspond to the two lateral arms of a complex since the distance separating them is unequal and less than normal and since there is no interposed medial fabric (compare with the synaptic complex of the same picture). It can tentatively be suggested that the image is a side view (lateral) of the two chromatids of one member of a bivalent.

Further consideration of this point might lead one to think that calling chromatids the two units observed in the synaptic ribbons is tantamount to attributing to each ribbon full representation of each homologous chromosome. However, the surrounding chromatin fields which are prominent from mid-pachytene onwards must not be disregarded. According to the schematic representation by Moses and Coleman (1964) each lateral ribbon corresponds to the displaced axis of the chromosome and the surrounding fields (including the material of the pairing space), are formed of fibrils attached to the side of each axis. We still do not know whether the synaptic complexes are proper parts of the chromosome and constitute the true substratum of pairing or whether they are simply a mechanical device to facilitate it. High resolution observations of DNA distribution in the different chromosome layers become imperative.

The constancy of the distance separating both lateral ribbons is one of the most characteristic features of the synaptonemal complexes; it remains the same all along the length of the bivalent, within all bivalents of the complement, and varies only a few Å in different species. Fusion or direct contact of the two synaptic ribbons has not been encountered in random samples or in three dimensional reconstruction of chromosomes. This shows that the only interrelation between the ribbons takes place through components of the pairing space. However, intermixing of the peripheral microfibrils is observed frequently at both edges of the ribbons. This offers the possibility for another place of interchange between homologs (Fig. 1E).

In all the examined species a large number of filaments (bridges) emerge from the compact layer, obliquely traverse the intermediate space, and become incorporated into the medial fabric. Part of these filaments occur as isolated elements, and part

4 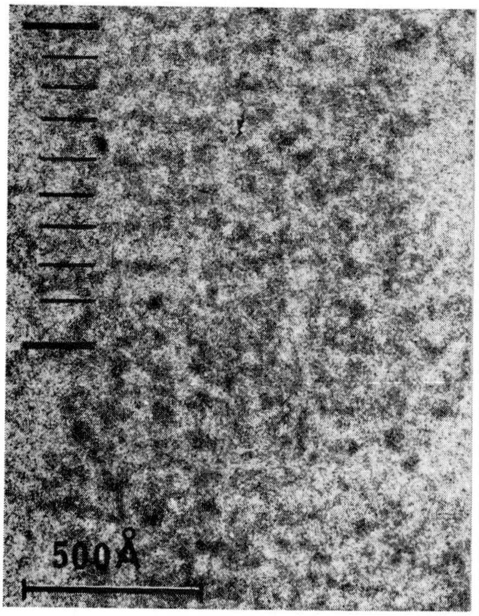

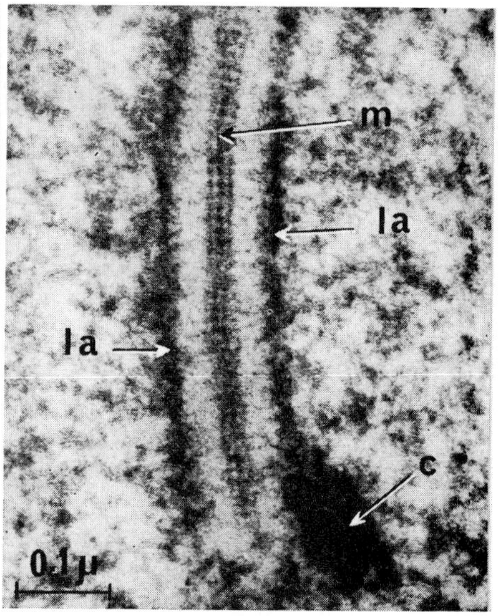 5

Fig. 4. *Gryllus argentinus. Early pachytene.* This figure shows a lateral view of a small area of the medial ribbon. The bars at the left side of the picture indicate segments of parallelly oriented filaments. Original magnification 30,000 ×: Enlargement 15 ×.

Fig. 5. *Gryllus argentinus. Early pachytene.* Low magnification picture of a synaptonemal complex. The following details can be observed: the two dense lateral arms -*la*- the tri-layered medial ribbon -*m*-, and a chromomere-like mass -*c*- attached to the right arm of the complex. Original magnification 30,000 ×: Enlargement 4 ×.

are associated in bundles 70 to 80 Å thick. Their electron density decreases as they leave the compact layer but may increase again in the middle of the pairing space. Within the space of the medial fabric (central or medial density) the filaments may or may not be ordered in a definite pattern. Though few species have been studied up to now, three patterns have been clearly recognized. These three patterns are schematically represented in the diagrams of Figs. 7, 8 and 9 which summarize observations made from high resolution pictures of many synaptonemal complexes cut in a variety of planes.

In electronmicrographs of cricket cells, for instance, frontal longitudinal and cross sections of the synaptonemal complexes show three parallel, longitudinal lines (Figs. 1C and 5). This implies that the medial density is composed of three sagital planes. The same section planes show, in *Coptoterix* (Fig. 1B,E) and in cockroaches (Fig. 3), that the medial density is composed only of two sagittal planes. However, in both groups, lateral views of these planes show periodical antero-posterior striations (Fig. 4), which are fairly regularly spaced (about 10 striae in 0.1 μ). At magnifications above 200,000 × the filamentous composition of the planes is well depicted (Fig. 2).

We have referred to the structural patterns as 'cricket' and 'cockroach pattern', since they were initially found in these animals. This denomination does not imply

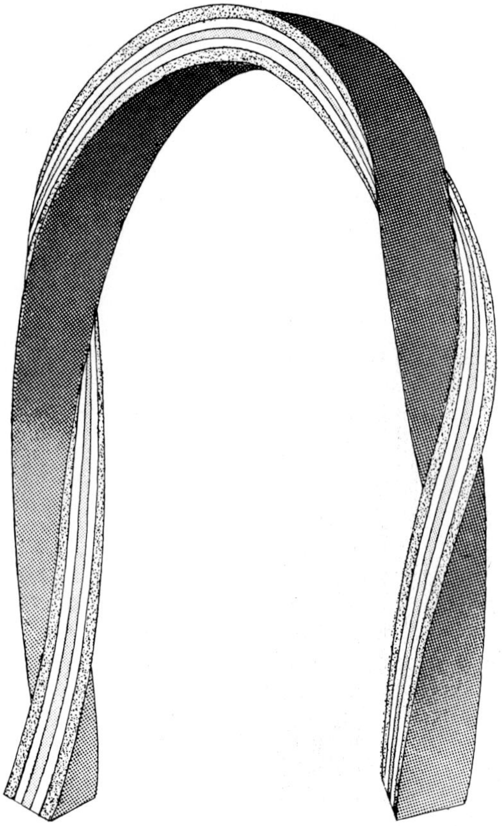

Fig. 6. Schematic representation inferred from the examination of random and serially cut sections of synaptonemal complexes of many species. The diagram shows the long helical turns of the three main components.

that they occur exclusively in these species. We also found the cricket pattern in *Diloboderus abderus* (Coleoptera) and the cockroach pattern in *Coptoterix gayi* (Orthoptera, Mantoidea) (Figs. 1B and E) and is probably the pattern occurring in *Blaps mucronata* (Coleoptera, Guenin and Gautier) and in *Philaenus spumarius* (Homoptera, Maillet and Folliot). A variation of the longitudinal pattern is present in mosquito oocytes where four lines can be counted in the medial density (Roth).

An entirely different arrangement whose main characteristic is the absence of longitudinal planes was found in three Acrididae species (Fig. 1D). Bridging takes place by means of free or associated transverse filaments arranged in a periodic fashion (about 10 transverse planes are counted in 0.1 μ). As in other species, the filaments lose electron density as they emerge from the synaptic ribbon, but are dense again in the middle of the pairing space. The synaptonemal complexes of the *Neottiella rutilans* fungus, studied by Westergaard and von Wettstein, show a similar disposition.

Despite fairly complete data from high resolution electron microscopy of synaptonemal complexes, there are many points for which we have no information. For example, it is easy to trace the crossing filaments where they come out of the synaptic ribbon or where they are incorporated into the medial fabric, but it is impossible to know how they end in these layers because of the superposition of several layers of filaments (less than 25 Å) in the 150–250 Å sections prepared for high resolution work. Furthermore, it is relatively easy to count the number of transverse components, or

Fig. 7

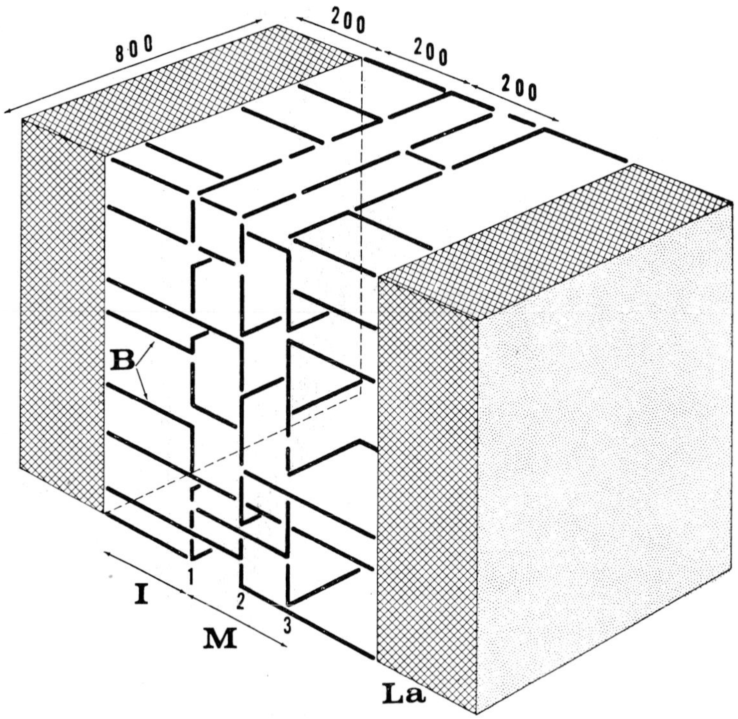

Figs. 7, 8 and 9. Diagrammatic representation of the filaments emerging from the inner face of each lateral ribbon which meet in the pairing space and contribute to the formation of the so-called medial density. In some species the filaments are organized in a constant pattern. In Fig. 7 the pattern found in several species of *Gryllus* is shown. The shadowed area corresponds to the lateral arms -*la*- and the straight lines represent the filaments (bridges -*B*-) in the intermediate space -*I*- and in the medial fabric -*M*-. The latter is composed of three sagittal planes (numbered 1, 2 and 3). It is assumed that filaments coming from both sides incorporate to these planes, change their orientation, and become longitudinal or antero-posterior. In Fig. 8 the structural pattern of the medial ribbon of cockroaches is shown. The pattern is similar to the one observed in *Gryllus* but only two sagittal planes (1 and 2) compose the medial fabric. Fig. 9 corresponds to the pattern observed in *Acrididae*. The transverse planes of filaments extended between both lateral ribbons are represented by broken lines. About 10 planes each 0.1 μ can be counted. However, to avoid overlapping only three separate planes were represented in the diagram. The figures at the top of the drawings indicate in Å the dimensions of the respective layers.

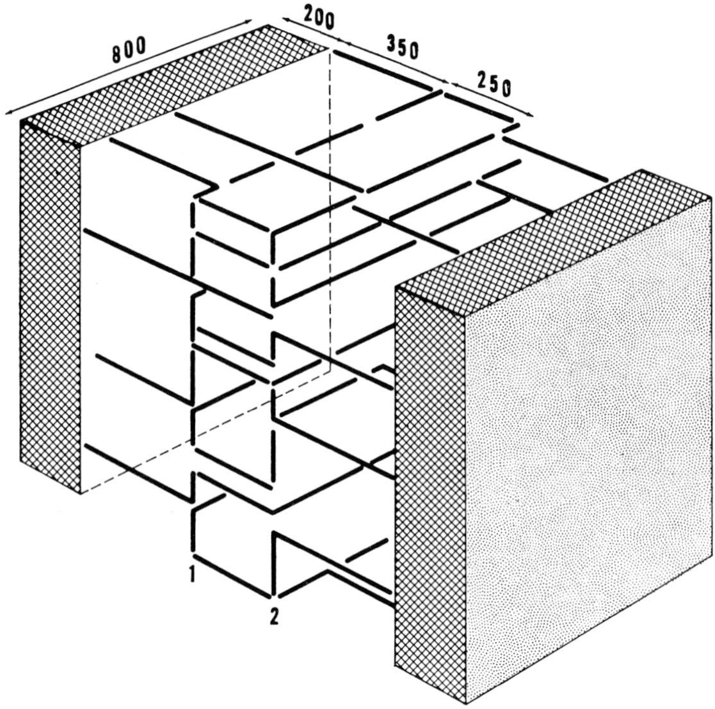

Fig. 8

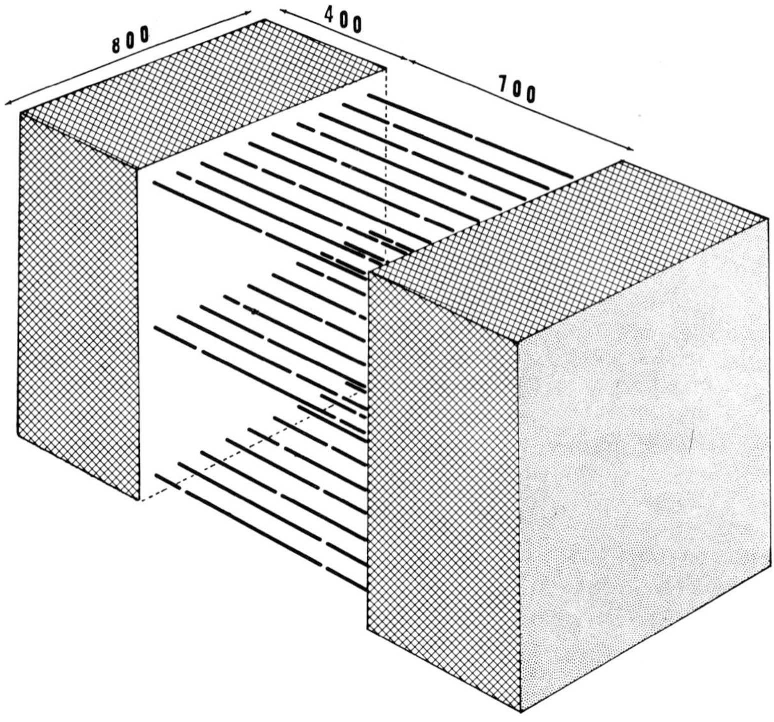

Fig. 9

the antero-posterior striae, in longitudinal planes (about 10 each 0.1 μ) but it is not feasible to count the number of individual filaments in each plane. Obstacles to such an evaluation are: (a) the mentioned disproportion between the thickness of filaments and the thickness of sections (superposition), (b) the varied orientation of the same filaments within the limits of a given layer or plane, and (c) the fact that complexes may be dissected by sectioning and thus leave out considerable portions. In favourable cases, filaments were seen to traverse the whole medial layer, invade the opposite field, and come back to their region of origin. These fortuitous cases do not provide adequate basis for any interpretation of the relations between homologs.

According to the concepts expressed above, it is pertinent to point out that conclusions which are based on a count of crossing elements should be regarded as provisional. On the other hand, the morphological units involved in interchange (filaments or groups of filaments) and the real place of interchange between DNA molecules has not been determined. Coleman and Moses, who employed DNAse digestion and histochemical tests to study synaptonemal complexes, found that little, if any, DNA occurs in the pairing space. According to these findings one would be inclined to think that the material of the pairing space represents part of a structural apparatus to facilitate pairing. However, more definite proof will be necessary since the resolution obtained from histochemical preparations is far from adequate for making a definitive statement.

4. Structure of meiotic chromosomes at division

No special features are found in meiotic chromosomes when they have reached the condensed state characteristic of prometaphase and metaphase, and it is impossible to differentiate them from mitotic chromosomes in the same stages. There is fairly good evidence that the specialized components related to synapsis disappear by the end of pachytene or in diplotene. Baker and Franchi (1967a) were able to see, in human oocytes, dense linear structures in the middle of diplotene chromosomes which they found to be the size of lateral ribbons of pachytene chromosomes. This would mean that synaptonemal complexes dissociate at disjunction. No observations have been reported on the way the bridging material disappears.

The basic structure of dividing chromosomes is quite similar to that observed in the condensed parts of prophase chromosomes (microfibrils of the chromosomes and mantle of the bivalents). Panoramic or high magnification views (above 200,000 $\times$) of metaphase or anaphase figures show chromosomes as homogeneous masses (Fig. 1F) in which only a denser area – the centromere or kinetochore region – can be differentiated. The microfibrils are composed of thinner filaments which thread their way from one fibril to another. The net-like disposition of the chromosome microfibrils changes into a packed mass of filaments inside the centromere region. The change takes place gradually and probably accounts for the greater density of the centromere region or the proximal region of the chromosomes arms (Wettstein and Sotelo 1965b).

We must discuss to what extent the high resolution images of chromosomes represent the natural state of their elementary components. It is known that part of the nuclear material is undoubtedly removed during fixation and dehydration, and as observations are limited by the available fixatives, embedding media, and staining procedures, it is difficult to assess the extent or the nature of the changes which have occurred. Information using other approaches is certainly desirable, such as examination of samples which have not been embedded, particularly those treated with enzymes (Ris 1967).

It is also pertinent to inquire whether dehydration, plastic polymerization and other procedures influence the distribution of components. So far there is no evidence that the embedding does affect their structure as judged from the constancy with which a given structural configuration is present in numerous samples of the same species. Examples are the filamentous patterns shown in the preceding section and the structure of the centromere region in relation to the rest of the chromosome body.

It can be argued that polymerization forces may act differently upon structures of different composition, thus eliciting characteristic images, or that polymerization may induce artificial fragmentation of the filaments composing the fibrils, but there is no factual evidence to support these contentions.

5. *The sex chromosome during the course of meiotic prophase*

It has long been known that sex chromosomes differ from autosomes in shape, behaviour and stainability. Therefore, they can be easily recognized if light microscopy of thick sections, and serial reconstruction with the electron microscope, are parallelly carried out.

Special characteristics of the functional activity of the Y-chromosome of *Drosophila* spermatocytes were investigated by Meyer, Hess and Beermann, and Hess and Meyer. Beermann's group recognized with the light microscope, the presence of four polarized, paired components which they interpreted as lampbrush-type loops of the Y-chromosome. Although in the light microscope (phase contrast of living specimens) these functional structures differ in their general aspect, they are of similar submicroscopic organization and, according to Hess and Meyer, the paired loops are formations of the heterochromatin.

The X-chromosome, of several *Gryllus* species, has been studied in our laboratory for several years. It is the most prominent component of the spermatogonial nuclei, and it behaves during spermatocyte prophase in a way different from sex chromosomes of other species. The nucleolus and the sex chromosome join at synaptene and their association brings about a little later (early pachytene) the formation of several synaptonemal-like complexes within both nuclear components. The complexes do not form part of the regular complement and are provisionally called extra-complexes. They are of two types: (i) short units located either within the nucleolus or the sex chromosome and (ii) short and long units interposed between both bodies – in such a way that one lateral arm is composed of nucleolar material – and the other of chromosome material. The long complexes emerge from the main mass and end on the nuclear envelope at a considerable distance. In random sections this complex cannot be distinguished from regular synaptonemal complexes, but serial sectioning demonstrates its origin. At mid-pachytene a cylindrical, rod-like structure composed of synaptonemal-like material develops within the nucleolar mass and sometimes extends into the nucleoplasm. At advanced pachytene the association has been transformed into an intricate structure from which a multilayered body later forms.

It is unknown how the sex chromosomes and the nucleolus separate as there are no data on the precise relationship between the multilayered bodies and the X-chromosome after completion of prophase. Serial studies recently made by Wettstein (unpublished) indicate that the multilayered bodies found at metaphase (Wettstein and Sotelo 1964) are probably of a very different nature. Schinn (1965b) disagrees with the postulated relationship of the origin of the multilayered bodies (association of nucleolus X-chromosome) and thinks it is not a regular event. He also suggests that multiple extra-complexes may be formed by core material separated from chromosomes at diplotene. However, in *Gryllus argentinus* extra-complexes start to develop at early pachytene.

The evidence reviewed shows that there is a special activity in the prophase nucleus, which is constantly repeated in each meiotic cycle of several species of a given genus. In *Gryllus* this activity appears to involve the X-chromosome but it does not seem to be the same in other species. In mosquito oocytes, Roth found, at the end of diplotene, many parallelly stacked groups of synaptonemal complexes (polycomplexes) and he postulated that they are formed by the synaptonemal complexes discarded at disjunction. Similar aggregations of complexes occur in the Homoptera *Philaenus spumarius*. In other species such as the Opilion *Acanthopachylus aculaetus*, several complexes associate at early prophase, and give rise to two small bodies showing a tridimensional hexagonal pattern (Wettstein and Sotelo 1965a).

6. *Sinaptonemal-like structures in post-meiotic cells*

Under this heading we have included the extra-complexes observed in spermatids of crickets and cockroaches. Their common denominator is that in each case they have the same structural pattern as paired autosomes at prophase. Most of the studies have been made in species of *Gryllidae* in which they are particularly prominent. In the cockroach *Blaptica dubia* they form groups of two or three synaptonemal-like complexes some 0.2–0.4 μ long, each of which is embedded in a large chromatin mass. So far no similar extra-complexes have been observed in the spermatocytes of this species.

In *Gryllus argentinus* extra-complexes start to develop in very young spermatids (just after telophase II) where they only consist of one or two tripartite units located randomly in the nucleus. In later stages they are multilayered and located beneath the nuclear envelope. It seems that the extra-complexes of spermatids cannot be compared with those of spermatocytes, since Wolstenholme and Meyer found them in X and O spermatids.

Since spermiogenesis has been studied in a greater number of species than spermatogenesis it can be assumed that extra-complexes are more frequent in the latter cells. A survey of the cases reported (oocytes, spermatocytes or spermiocytes) leads on to conclude that: (a) they may appear at different phases of the meiotic cycle and may or may not be related to other nuclear components; (b) it seems that their existence is dependent on gene activity, since they appear to be repeated in a similar way in all specimens of the same species.

7. Conclusions

The purpose of this chapter has been to review briefly electron microscopic information about the meiotic process in a variety of organisms, as well as to evaluate its contribution to the understanding of the structural problems of meiosis.

Four questions were asked in the introduction related to the following points namely: (1) chromatid organization and fibrillar structures at early prophase; (2) approximation of homologs at synaptene (zipping process); (3) crossing-over and submicroscopic organization; (4) structural patterns in the bivalents and in other nuclear components. These four points are discussed in the following paragraphs.

Doubleness of chromosomes at different phases of the mitotic cycle was proved by several means in fixed cells and lately demonstrated by observation of living cells (Bajer). In meiosis, the slender appearance of the prophase chromosome makes it difficult to see whether chromosomes are already double at leptotene or synaptene. The electron microscope has demonstrated doubleness only in already paired chromosomes of a few species. Why this state is visible in some cases earlier than in others is not clearly understood.

Chromatid organization is important since it is closely related to the debated point of chromosome multistrandedness. Most of the electron microscopic research on chromosome fine structure reported in this chapter is based on the examination of thin sections. It has to be compared with the electron microscopic information obtained from whole mounts or from the air–water interface spreading method. By using both procedures 250 Å fibrils were depicted in the chromosomes. Furthermore, Ris (1967) digested spread fibrils with pronase and 25 Å filaments sensible to DNAse remained. Therefore the following points need investigation: (1) whether the 250 Å fibrils mentioned above and the 70–150 Å ones observed in embedded material are the same; (2) whether the 15–25 Å filaments seen in sections are similar to those remaining after enzyme digestion of 250 Å fibrils; and (3) whether the segments of fibrils and/or filaments are part of a multifolded single unit or are parts of separate units.

Either single or multiple, it is accepted that fibrils should be longitudinally arranged as it has been shown in whole chromosome mounts (Wolfe and Hewitt). However, embedded samples from a variety of organisms do not show such array. Sectioning limitations (fragmentation) have been invoked to explain this discordance, but this argument is weak because longitudinal views of chromosomes can be frequently found in sections thicker than 250 Å and thin sectioning has not been a handicap in observing fibrillar arrays in other cells. Therefore some kind of folding must be accepted to explain chromosome organization. Lampbrush-like folding has been postulated, although not conclusively demonstrated. Such an organization would provide the suitable array for interaction between the homologs at the time of pairing and the 'zipping process' would be facilitated by the existence of long loops extending in several spatial planes. Unfortunately, no detailed electron microscopic analysis of adequate resolution has yet been made during the phase of approximation of the homologs. Information on the way it takes place would help to clarify other points of chromosome structure among which should be mentioned the mechanism facilitating recombination.

The findings on the synaptonemal complexes and their bridging system – which have been described extensively in this chapter – have opened a promising line in the investigation of the structural basis of crossing-over. Until now the following data have been collected: (a) synaptomenal complexes are typical in meiotic prophase and they are absent when pairing and crossing-over do not occur; (this contention would be contradicted by a finding by Gassner in *Panorpa nuptialis*); (b) their fabric extends all along each bivalent and its organization repeats in successive generations of the same species; (c) several types of the bridging system were found, however, all of them have a common basis: the meeting of chromosome filaments in the pairing space.

The conditions enumerated above are consistent with Meyer's hypothesis (1964) that crossing-over is related to these structures. In spite of this, two findings are found to be in disagreement: (1) it has been claimed that little DNA (or none) is present in the pairing space (Coleman and Moses 1964); (2) similarly organized structures occur in germ cells in circumstances other than orthodox pairing (Sotelo and Wettstein 1967).

Specific interrelations between DNA molecules from both halves of the bivalent may occur: (i) within the pairing space; it implies the existence of DNA among the components referred to above; (ii) in the field surrounding the synaptonemal complex; it would be facilitated by relational coiling of the homologs, and intimate intermixing of the fibrils at the contact area; and (iii) in both sites. Only further investigation of the distribution of DNA in the bivalent layers will help to decide which is the actual site.

A serious obstacle to considering the filamentous apparatus of the pairing space as the material substrate for crossing-over is the presence of similarly built structures in components not related to the bivalents. Synaptonemal-like complexes appear in the association of nucleolus-sex chromosome of *Gryllus argentinus* and in multilayered bodies of spermatocytes and spermiocytes of several species. There is no explanation for these phenomena. We do know that some of them are fixed hereditary characteristics, but why synaptonemal-like complexes appear interrelating dissimilar nuclear components or form multiple associations is an open question. A working hypothesis is that the codified information for the construction of the interconnecting fabric may be transferred to other nuclear components and may result in the formation of varied associations of synaptonemal-like structures at different periods of the germ cell cycle.

The key to this basic problem is to find out whether or not DNA occurs among the molecules of the pairing space. The resolution of the electron microscope is one of the limiting factors when histochemical tests are made. Therefore morphological information has to be complemented with other technical approaches.

Acknowledgements

This work was supported during the years 1962–1965 by the U.S. Public Health Service, Research Grant G.M. 08337, from the Research Grants Branch, Division of Medical Sciences; and during the years 1966, 1967 by the U.S.A. Air Force Office of Scientific Research, Office of Aerospace Research under AFOSR Grant N° 1224–67.

The author is indebted to Dr. and Mrs. Larry Stensaas and to Dr. O. Trujillo-Cenóz for critical comments on the manuscript.

References

BAKER, T.G. and L.L.FRANCHI: The fine structure of oogonia and oocytes in human ovaries. J. Cell Sci. 2 (1967a) 213.

BAKER, T.G. and L.L.FRANCHI: The structure of the chromosomes in human primordial oocytes. Chromosoma (Berl.) 22 (1967b) 358.

CAUMGARTNER, W.J.: Some new evidences for the individuality of the chromosomes. Biol. Bull. 8 (1904) 1.

BHARDARD, R.: Recherches sur les cellules-mères des microspores des Orchidées. Étude au microscope électronique. Rev. Cytol. Biol. Végét. 24 (1962) 1.

COLEMAN, J. and M.MOSES: DNA and the fine structure of synaptic chromosomes in the domestic rooster (Gallus domesticus). J. Cell Biol. 23 (1964) 63.

FAWCETT, D.: The fine structure of chromosomes in the meiotic prophase of vertebrate spermatocytes. J. Biophys. Biochem. Cytol. 2 (1956) 403.

FAWCETT, D.: An atlas of fine structure. The cell its organelles and inclusions. Philadelphia, W.B. Saunder Co. (1966).

FRANCHI, L.L. and A.M.MANDL: The ultrastructure of oogonia and oocytes in the foetal and neonatal rat. Proc. Roy. Soc. (Biol.) 157 (1962) 99.

GALL, J.: Centriole replication. A study of spermatogenesis in the snail Viviparus. J. Biophys. Biochem. Cytol. 10 (1961) 163.

GALL, J.: Chromosome fibers studied by a spreading technique. Chromosoma (Berl.) 20 (1966) 221.

GASSNER, G. III: Synaptinemal complexes: recent findings. Preprinted from The Journal of Cell Biology 35 (1967) 166A.

GUÉNIN, H. A.: Observations sur la structure submicroscopique du complexe axial dans les chromosomes méiotiques chez Gryllus campestris L. et G. bimaculatus De Geer (Orthopt. Gryll.). J. Micros. 4 (1965) 749.

GUÉNIN, H. A. and A. GAUTIER: Observations sur la structure submicroscopique des chromosomes du Blaps mucronata (Latr.) (Col. Tenebr.). Rev. Suisse Zool. 67 (1960) 210.

HESS, O. and G. F. MEYER: Chromosomal differentiations of the lampbrush type formed by the Y-chromosome in *Drosophila hydei* and *Drosophila neohydei*. J. Cell Biol. 16 (1963) 527.

MAILLET, P. L. and R. FOLLIOT: Sur les ultrastructures chromosomiques de la méiose chez 'Philaenus spumarius' L. Male (Homoptere 'Cercopidae'). C.R. Acad. Sc. Paris, 260 (1965) 3486.

MEYER, G. F.: The fine structure of spermatocyte nuclei of Drosophila melanogaster. Proc. Eur. Reg. Conf. on Elect. Microsc. Delft 11 (1960) 951.

MEYER, G. F.: A possible correlation between the submicroscopic structure of meiotic chromosomes and crossing-over. Prague, Publishing House of the Czechoslovak Academy of Sciences (1964) 461.

MEYER, G. F., O. HESS and W. BEERMANN: Phasenspezifische Funktionsstrukturen in Spermatocytenkernen von *Drosophila melanogaster* und ihre Abhängigkeit vom Y-Chromosom. Chromosoma (Berl.) 12 (1961) 676.

MOSES, M. J.: Chromosomal structures in Crayfish spermatocytes. J. Biophys. Biochem. Cytol. 2 (1956a) 215.

MOSES, M. J.: Studies on nuclei using correlated cytochemical, light and electron microscope techniques. J. Biophys. Biochem. Cytol. 2 (1956b) 397 Suppl.

MOSES, M. J.: The relation between the axial complex of meiotic prophase chromosomes and chromosome pairing in a salamander (Plethodon cinereus) J. Biophys. Biochem. Cytol. 4 (1958) 633.

MOSES, M. J. and J. R. COLEMAN: Structural pattern and the functional organization of chromosomes. Reprinted from Role of Chromosomes in Development. New York Acad. Press Inc. (1964) 11.

NEBEL, B. R. and E. M. COULON: The fine structure of chromosomes in pigeon spermatocytes. Chromosoma (Berl.) 13 (1962) 272

RIS, H.: The annual invitation lecture. Ultrastructure and molecular organization of genetic systems. J. Genet. Cytol. 3 (1961) 95.

RIS, H.: Ultrastructure of the animal chromosome. Reprinted from Regulation of Nucleic Acid and Protein Biosynthesis. Amsterdam, Elsevier Pub. Co. (1967) 11.

RHOADES, M. M.: The Cell. New York, Academic Press, 1961.

ROTH, T. F.: Changes in the synaptinemal complex during meiotic prophase in mosquito oocytes. Protoplasma 61 (1966) 346.

ROTH, T. F. and M. ITO: DNA-dependent formation of the synaptinemal complex at meiotic prophase. J. Cell Biol. 35 (1967) 247.

SCHINN, K. S.: Meiotische Prophase und Spermatidenreifung bei Gryllus domesticus mit besonderer Berücksichtigung der Chromosomenstruktur. Z. Zellforsch. 65 (1965) 481.

SCHINN, K. S.: Core-Strukturen in den meiotischen und post-meiotischen Kernen der Spermatogenese von Gryllus domesticus. Chromosoma (Berl.) 16 (1965) 436.

SOTELO, J. R.: An electron microscope study on the cytoplasmic and nuclear components of rat primary oocytes. Z. Zellforsch. 50 (1959) 749.

SOTELO, J. R. and O. TRUJILLO-CENÓZ: Microscopic structure of meiotic chromosomes during prophase. Exp. Cell Res. 14 (1958) 1.

SOTELO, J. R. and O. TRUJILLO-CENÓZ: Electron microscope study on spermatogenesis. Chromosome morphogenesis at the onset of meiosis (Cyte I) and nuclear structure of early and late spermatids. Z. Zellforsch. 51 (1960) 243.

SOTELO, J. R. and O. TRUJILLO-CENÓZ: Electron microscope study on chromosome structure during meiosis. Path. Biol. (Paris) 9 (1961) 762.

SOTELO, J. R. and R. WETTSTEIN: Electron microscope study on meiosis. The sex chromosome in spermatocytes, spermatids and oocytes of Gryllus argentinus. Chromosoma (Berl.) 15 (1964) 389.

SOTELO, J. R. and R. WETTSTEIN: Fine structure of meiotic chromosomes of Gryllus argentinus. Experientia 20 (1964) 1.

SOTELO, J. R. and R. WETTSTEIN: Fine structure of meiotic chromosomes. J. Nat. Cancer Inst. Monogr. 18 (1965) 133.

SOTELO, J. R. and R. WETTSTEIN: Fine structure of meiotic chromosomes. Comparative study of nine species of insects. Chromosoma (Berl.) 20 (1966) 234.

WATSON, M.: Spermatogenesis in the adult albino rat as revealed by tissue section in the electron microscope. The University of Rochester. Atomic Energy Project (1952).

WESTERGAARD, M. and D. VON WETTSTEIN: Studies on the mechanism of crossing-over. III. On the ultrastructure of the chromosomes in Neottiella rutilans (Fr.) Dennis, C. L. Laboratoire Carlsberg 35 (1966) 261.

WETTSTEIN, R. and J. R. SOTELO: Electron microscope study on the meiotic cycle of Acanthopachylus aculeatus (Arachnida, Opiliones). The composite bodies of primary spermatocytes. Chromosoma (Berl.) 17 (1965a) 246.

WETTSTEIN, R. and J. R. SOTELO: Fine structure of meiotic chromosomes. The elementary components of metaphase chromosomes of Gryllus argentinus. J. Ultrastruct. Res. 13 (1965b) 367.

WETTSTEIN, R. and J. R. SOTELO: Electron microscope serial reconstruction of the spermatocyte I nuclei at pachytene. J. Microscopie 6 (1967) 557.

WINIWARTER, H. DE: Étude du cycle chromosomique chez diverses races de Gryllotalpa gryll. (L). Arch. Biol. (Liège) 37 (1927) 515.

WOLFE, S. L. and G. M. HEWITT: The strandness of meiotic chromosomes from Oncopeltus. J. Cell Biol. 31 (1966) 31.

WOLSTENHOLME, D. R. and G. F. MEYER: Some facts concerning the nature and formation of axial core structures in spermatids of Gryllus domesticus. Chromosoma (Berl.) 18 (1966) 272.

PART VI

Biochemistry of the interphase nucleus, chromosomes and spindle

CHAPTER 18

Nuclear protein fractions

DOUGLAS M. FAMBROUGH, JR.

Division of Biology, California Institute of Technology, Pasadena, California

Contents

1. Introduction
2. Classification of nuclear protein fractions
3. Acidic and residual nuclear proteins
4. The nuclear enzymes
   (a) Enzymes soluble in 0.14 M NaCl
   (b) Enzymes soluble in 1 M NaCl
   (c) Enzymes soluble only in detergent solutions
   (d) Validity of enzyme classification
5. Nuclear ribosomal proteins and nuclear protein synthesis
6. The histones and protamines
   (a) Preparation of histones
   (b) Histone nomenclature
   (c) Fractionation of histones
7. Description of histone components
   (a) Lysine-rich histones
   (b) Slightly lysine-rich histones
   (c) Arginine-rich histones
8. Histone heterogeneity and specificity
9. The protamines
10. Primary structure of histones
11. Histone and protamine metabolism
12. The functions of histones
13. Conclusion

1. Introduction

The nucleus is the cellular organelle in which the bulk of each cell's genetic information is stored and processed. Three functional classes of proteins participate in this storage and processing of information: structural proteins, regulatory proteins, and enzymes. Proteins play an essential role in the structural organization of interphase chromatin, metaphase chromosomes, nucleolar elements, and the nuclear membrane. Regulatory proteins insure the availability of only those units of genetic information required for the proper function of each cell type. Nuclear enzymes catalyze such essential reactions as replication, transcription, the chemical and physical modification of nucleic acids, the synthesis of NAD, and possibly even nuclear-specific protein synthesis. The many molecular events in the nucleus must therefore involve a very large number of different proteins.

2. Classification of nuclear protein fractions

Our paucity of knowledge precludes any classification of nuclear proteins based solely upon their functions. For the great bulk of nuclear proteins no function is definitely known, and it is likely that many molecular events in the nucleus remain undiscovered. Current classification schemes such as the one presented in Table 1 are based primarily

TABLE 1

Classification of nuclear proteins

- Nuclear sap proteins
  - Ribosomal proteins
  - Nuclear 'globulins'
    - Enzymes of the total soluble cell space
    - Nuclear-specific soluble enzymes
- Chromosomal proteins
  - Histones
    - Very lysine-rich histone I (f1)
    - Slightly lysine-rich histone IIb2 (f2b)
    - Lysine–arginine-rich histone IIb1 (f2a2)
    - Arginine–glutamic acid-rich histone III (f3)
    - Arginine–glycine-rich histone IV (f2a1)
    - Protamines
  - Acidic and residual chromosomal proteins
    - Chromatin-bound enzymes
- Proteins of the ribonucleoprotein network
- Membrane associated proteins
  - Microsomal and lysozomal enzymes (?)
  - Membrane structural proteins

upon solubility characteristics and location of nuclear proteins with respect to the various nuclear structures.

As techniques for the isolation of nuclei and fractionation of nuclear elements have improved and as new methods for the extraction of proteins have come into use, the classifications based upon these techniques and methods have evolved in a manner which makes comparison of data difficult. Fortunately, numerous chemical analyses of nuclear fractions and in a few cases direct observation of the nuclear residue subsequent to extraction permit identification of the native location of many nuclear protein fractions. Direct observations of nuclei after extraction have been reported by Zbarsky and Georgiev, Georgiev and Chentsov, and Zbarsky et al. Their electron micrographs demonstrate that extraction of nuclei with 0.14 M NaCl removes the nuclear sap; subsequent extraction with 2 M NaCl removes the filamentous deoxyribonucleoprotein (chromatin); extraction with dilute alkali removes nucleoli and extranucleolar ribonucleoprotein fibrils and granules. The residue left after these extractions consists of membranes and lamellar debris.

The chemical composition of rat liver nuclei and of some subnuclear components (taken from Steele and Busch) are presented in Table 2. These data represent only

TABLE 2

Composition of rat liver nuclei and nuclear fractions[a]

Fraction[b]	% Lipid-free[c] dry weight	% Total nuclear protein	Composition of fraction		
			% Protein	% DNA	% RNA
Nuclear sap 0.14 M NaCl	18.1	23.0	95.1	1.5	3.4
Nuclear sap II 0.01 M Tris *p*H 7.6	5.6	6.1	82.3	6.8	10.9
Deoxyribonucleoprotein[d] 2.0 M NaCl	68.0	60.5[e]	66.6	28.2	5.2
Nucleolar and fibrillar ribonucleoprotein 0.05 M NaOH	6.0	7.2	90.8	0.3	8.9
Membrane residue	2.3	3.1	99.4	0.0	0.6
Whole nuclei[f]	100.0	100.0	74.8	19.9	5.3

[a] Calculated from Steele and Busch.

[b] Fractions prepared by successive extraction of whole nuclei with the indicated solvents.

[c] Total recovered material was 94.1% of lipid-free dry weight. Figures here are percentages of the recovered material.

[d] It should be noted that while this fraction is called deoxyribonucleoprotein, it contains over 50% of total nuclear RNA.

[e] Contains the histones as approximately 30% of total nuclear proteins.

[f] Rat liver nuclei were prepared by homogenization of liver in isotonic sucrose solution with or without 5×10^{-3} M $CaCl_2$. The nuclei were sedimented at $600 \times g$ for 10 min and subsequently sedimented from 2.2 M sucrose at $40{,}000 \times g$ for 30 min.

rough approximations since experimental values can be significantly altered by the use of different techniques for the isolation of nuclei and fractionation of nuclear components.

Each nuclear fraction contains a mixture of proteins. Thus nuclear sap contains many or perhaps all of the proteins which occur free in the total soluble space of the cell, such proteins penetrating freely through an apparently porous nuclear membrane. The deoxyribonucleoprotein consists of DNA to which is complexed the acid-soluble histones, alkali-soluble chromosomal 'acidic' proteins and very insoluble residual protein. The nucleolar ribonucleoprotein network consists of acid soluble non-histone proteins, alkali soluble 'acidic' proteins and residual protein.

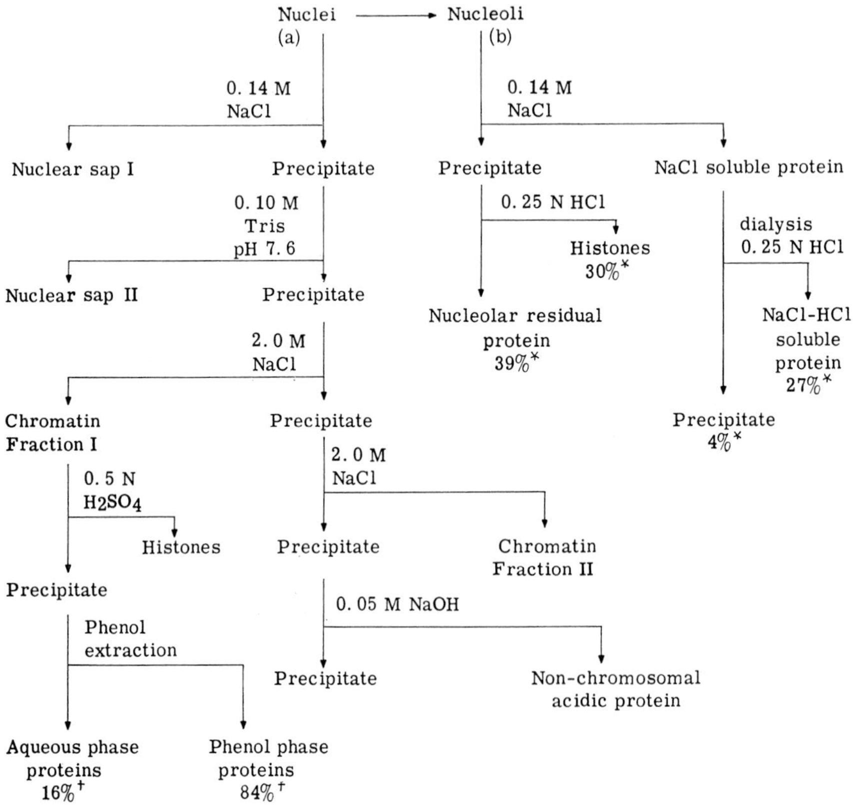

Fig. 1a. Fractionation of nuclear proteins according to the methods of (a) Steele and Busch and (b) Grogan et al. Solvents used in each extraction are indicated. After each centrifugation, the soluble supernatant is removed (indicated by horizontal lines) from the insoluble material. Amino acid compositions of certain fractions are presented in Table 3.

* Values are percentages of total nucleolar protein.

† Values are percentages of total chromosomal non-histone protein.

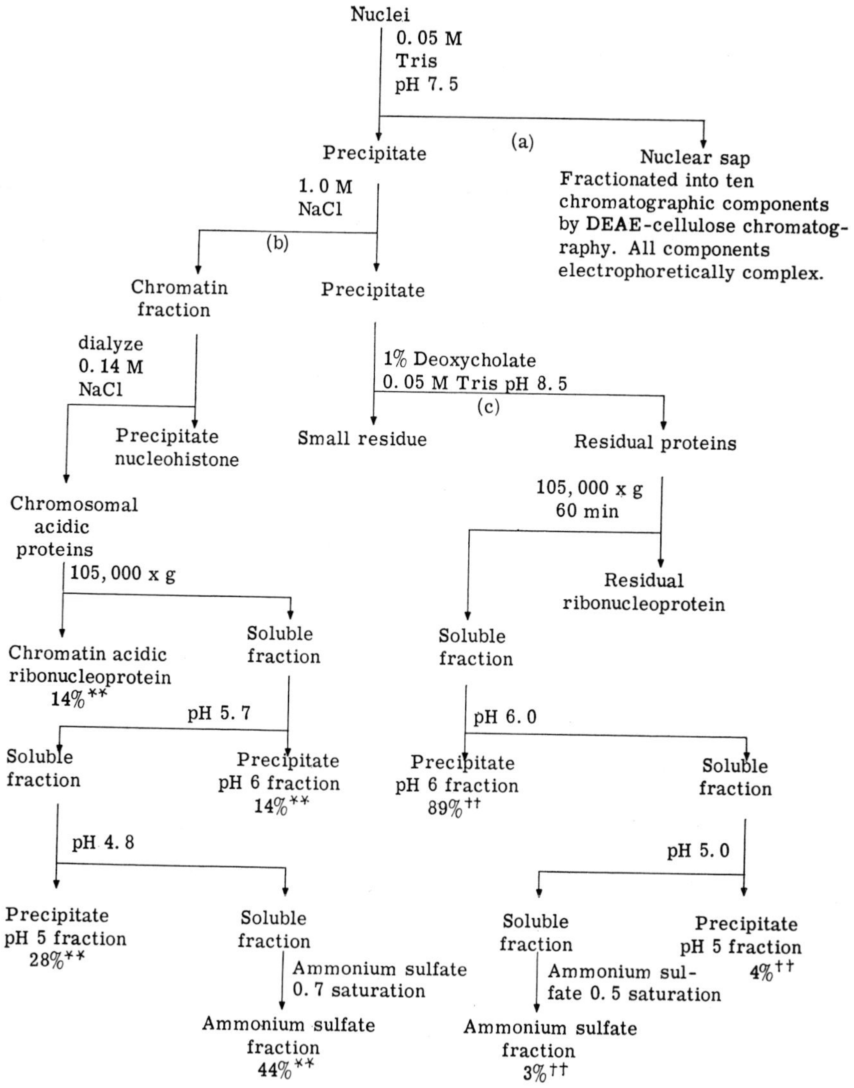

Fig. 1b. Fractionation of nuclear proteins according to the methods of (a) Patel and Wang, (b) Wang (1967) and (c) Wang (1966). Amino acid compositions of certain fractions are presented in Table 3.

** Values are percentages of total chromosomal acidic protein.

†† Values are percentage of total nuclear residual protein.

3. *Acidic and residual nuclear proteins*

This subject has recently been reviewed by Busch. The methods for the preparation and fractionation of the acidic and residual nuclear proteins are undergoing rapid change. This is necessitated by the failure of older methods to yield meaningful separations. Thus the terms 'acidic' and 'residual' protein must be defined anew for each investigation. Generally the term 'acidic proteins' is used for the alkali soluble proteins which remain after extraction of nuclear sap and histones, while 'residual proteins' refers to the alkali-insoluble proteins. Most proteins, including the basic histones, are however soluble in alkali (0.1 M NaOH). Thus solubility under such drastic conditions is not *per se* an indication of overall acidic character. Amino acid analyses usually demonstrate that the molar ratio of acidic to basic amino acids (Glu + Asp/Lys + Arg) in the nuclear acidic proteins is greater than one. However, amide content of the so-called acidic proteins has never satisfactorily been determined and it is even possible that they are in fact basic.

Flow diagrams for the preparation of acidic and residual protein fractions from isolated nuclei are presented in Figs. 1a and b. Amino acid compositions of some of these fractions are presented in Table 3. These compositions reveal few differences

TABLE 3

Amino acid compositions of some rat liver nuclear protein fractions

Amino acid	Nuclear sap[a]	Chromosomal acidic and residual protein $(NH_4)_2SO_4$ precipitate[b]	Chromosomal acidic protein[a]	Non-chromosomal acidic protein[a]	Residual nucleolar protein[c]	Residual ribonucleoprotein[d]	Histone[a]
Lys	8.3	7.7	7.3	6.3	7.8	7.0	15.5
His	4.0	2.1	2.3	2.3	2.1	1.9	1.9
Arg	2.9	4.6	7.7	5.7	5.5	5.4	8.5
Asp	10.5	9.7	9.1	9.3	9.1	7.0	5.8
Thr	5.1	5.3	5.0	5.7	4.4	5.4	6.0
Ser	6.2	5.2	6.9	7.4	7.7	5.2	6.2
Glu	9.2	15.2	12.4	12.1	12.8	8.0	8.8
Pro	5.5	4.8	6.4	5.5	5.8	6.4	5.3
Gly	8.4	8.3	9.0	8.0	8.6	7.9	7.8
Ala	9.8	8.2	6.7	7.4	7.9	10.2	11.6
Val	7.6	7.1	5.1	6.1	6.5	6.5	5.6
Met	1.3	1.9	2.2	2.6	1.4	3.0	1.1
Ile	3.8	4.7	4.4	4.4	4.6	4.8	4.4
Leu	9.9	7.7	8.3	9.4	9.5	10.3	7.4
Tyr	2.2	2.5	3.2	2.8	1.6	4.0	2.5
Phe	4.4	4.2	3.8	4.0	3.5	5.2	2.0
Cys	0.8	0.9	0.4	1.3	1.4	0.6	
Try			1.3	0.9		1.2	0.1

[a] Data from Steele and Busch
[b] Data from Wang (1967)
[c] Data from Grogan et al.
[d] Data from Wang (1966)

between the various non-histone fractions and give no hint as to the heterogeneity of these fractions. Amino-terminal analyses typically demonstrate the presence of many different terminal residues, none representing as much as 30% of the total.

A variety of functions have been suggested for the nuclear acidic and residual proteins. The chromatin acidic and residual proteins seem to be preferentially associated with chromatin active in DNA-dependent RNA synthesis (Frenster), and may include RNA polymerase, as well as proteins involved in stabilization of the extended form of chromatin, and possibly even proteins associated with gene derepression. The chromosomal residual proteins include a fraction containing 4–5 mole % phosphoserine and phosphothreonine (Kleinsmith et al. and unpublished data of Langan and co-workers). This fraction accounts for about 85% of the alkali-liable phosphorus in calf thymus nuclei. There are interesting correlations between the occurrence of this protein fraction and a high rate of DNA-dependent RNA synthesis. All of the chromatin acidic proteins show rather rapid turnover.

The non-chromosomal acidic and residual proteins may include unassembled elements of the mitotic apparatus, regulatory proteins in dynamic equilibrium with chromatin, proteins involved in the transport of messenger RNA from chromatin to cytoplasm, proteins involved in the production of ribosomal RNA, and proteins related to the cytoplasmic ribosomal proteins. These proteins also exhibit a high rate of turnover.

The nuclear acidic and residual proteins, because of their solubility characteristics and apparent complexity have received pitifully little attention. A definitive fractionation and characterization of these proteins has yet to be accomplished. The presumed importance of these proteins in nuclear functions together with rapid technological advances in the field of protein chemistry should stimulate new approaches to the task. The solubility problems might be overcome by the use of solvents containing detergents, formic acid, and/or denaturing agents such as urea and guanidinium chloride. Exclusion chromatography in the presence of such solvents has not been reported. Solubility properties might be altered by complete removal of lipids and nucleic acids. Resolution of these proteins by electrophoresis in systems designed for the analytical and preparative fractionation of membrane proteins (Neville) might well succeed. A somewhat different approach to the problem of characterizing these proteins could take advantage of enzymatic properties. No nucleus-specific enzyme has been purified and chemically and physically characterized. In the accomplishment of this much more limited objective a great deal of information on the characteristics of nuclear proteins would surely be generated.

4. The nuclear enzymes

Recent progress in the study of nuclear enzymes owes much to advances in techniques for the isolation of nuclei and evaluation of cytoplasmic contamination. Critical reviews of methods used for the isolation of nuclei are those of Siebert and Smellie, Mirsky and Osawa, and Roodyn. A thoughtful review of nuclear enzymes, including a list of exacting criteria which would be employed for determining the natural cellular locations of enzymes, is that of Siebert and Humphrey. Nuclei are most commonly isolated by methods involving homogenization of tissue in isotonic sucrose or saline solution, followed by differential centrifugation. When such methods are used, considerable redistribution of cellular material is possible. To avoid such redistribution, very different methods must be employed: the cellular components of fresh tissue are immobilized by rapid freezing and nuclei isolated by the non-aqueous method of Behrens. This method involves lyophilization of the tissue followed by repeated homogenization and centrifugation in a hydrophobic solvent such as carbon tetrachloride, toluene, petroleum ether or their mixtures. These procedures are not only essential to the maintenance of proper cellular distribution of enzymes during isolation, but also appear to minimize proteolysis (Umana and Dounce).

Criteria for the purity of isolated nyclei include failure to demonstrate adherent cytoplasmic debris by electron microscopy, low RNA–DNA ratio, absence of cytochromes b, a and a_3, and the absence of other enzymes known to be confined specifically to other cellular organelles. A list of some enzymes used as 'markers' for cellular organelles is presented in Table 4. In assessing the occurrence of an enzyme in the nucleus, the analysis of enzyme activity on nuclear fractions in several stages of purification provides valuable help.

Nuclear enzymes, just like bulk nuclear proteins, may be classified according to their solubility properties. Three solubility groups have been described.

TABLE 4

Activity of marker enzymes in rat liver and in rat liver nuclei[a]

		Activity	
Enzyme	Cellular fraction	Solvent-treated rat liver	Nuclei (non-aqueous)
NAD pyrophosphorylase[b]	nucleus	10	80
Glutamic dehydrogenase[c]	mitochondria	0.2	0.01
Catalase[c]	microbodies	422[d]	22[d]
Acid phosphatase[c]	lysozomes	0.7	0.3
Glucose-6-phosphatase[c]	microsomes	0.8	0.2
Glycolytic enzymes[e]	soluble cell space	1.0	1.3

[a] Taken from Siebert and Humphrey
[b] μmoles NAD/hr/g dry weight
[c] μmoles substrate/min/mg protein
[d] Perborate as substrate
[e] Average of 16 enzymes, whole tissue activity arbitrarily taken as 1.0.

(a) *Enzymes soluble in 0.14 M NaCl*

Many enzymes can be solubilized almost completely by a single extraction of nuclei with 0.14 M NaCl in 2×10^{-3} M EDTA. Under these conditions the chromatin and ribonucleoprotein network are completely insoluble. Thus the solubilized enzymes are those which occur in the soluble space of the nucleus – the nuclear sap. These include all of the glycolytic enzymes. Since there appear to be no major permeability barriers between nucleus and cytoplasm, it is thought that the enzymes of this fraction are those which also occur in the soluble space of the cytoplasm. In support of this view is the finding that the isozymes of lactic dehydrogenase isolated from nucleus and cytoplasm are physically and chemically alike (Siebert and Hannover).

DNA polymerase is an important enzyme of this solubility class. When nuclei are isolated by aqueous methods, DNA polymerase is found in the soluble supernatant, rather than in the nucleus. However, when non-aqueous methods are used, this enzyme is found preferentially located in the nucleus. The behavior of DNA polymerase during isolation of nuclei provides strong support for the superiority of non-aqueous isolation methods.

(b) *Enzymes soluble in 1 M NaCl*

After extraction of nuclei with 0.14 M NaCl, extraction with 1 M NaCl can be used to effect solubilization of deoxyribonucleoprotein. This treatment partially dissociates deoxyribonucleoprotein into free histone, some free non-histone protein and DNA still complexed with some slightly lysine-rich and arginine-rich histones and with a portion of the non-histone protein (Ohlenbusch et al.). The enzymes of this solubility group are not solubilized by extraction with weak detergent solution, sonication or enzymatic hydrolysis of nucleic acids. They are precipitated together with DNA and histone when the NaCl concentration is lowered to 0.14 M NaCl. Thus the 1 M NaCl-soluble, 0.14 NaCl-insoluble enzymes are apparently lost in the preparation of 'chromatin acidic proteins' by the method of Wang (see Fig. 1b). Enzymes of this category also include RNA polymerase. An RNA polymerase bound to DNA and known as 'aggregate enzyme' can be prepared by extraction of chromatin with 1 M NaCl, precipitation from 0.4 M KCl and winding out of the fibrous aggregate (Weiss). Huang and Bonner have found that 50% of the RNA polymerase activity of pea bud chromatin is still bound to DNA after dissociation of chromatin in 4 M CsCl. Only about 3% of the chromosomal protein remains bound to DNA under these conditions (Bonner, personal communication 1967).

Another important enzyme of this category is NAD pyrophosphorylase. This enzyme is exclusively located in the chromatin fraction of mammalian nuclei. NAD is thus the only known cofactor synthesized exclusively in the nucleus. The pertinence of the nuclear localization of NAD pyrophosphorylase to regulation of metabolism is a matter of speculation. Its nuclear localization is of great practical value in assessing the contamination of cytoplasmic fractions by nuclei or chromatin fragments. Isolation and characterization of NAD pyrophosphorylase and studies of the interaction of this enzyme with DNA should greatly increase our understanding of the nature of chromosomal non-histone proteins.

Two sets of nucleoside triphosphatases (termed A and B) are also associated with chromatin. These two sets possess different *p*H optima and apparently contain enzymes specific to each of the commonly occurring riboside- and deoxyriboside triphosphates.

Recent studies have further localized many of the nuclear enzymes of this solubility group (Seibert et al.). With the help of a method for the preparation of nucleoli from nuclei, it was found that RNA polymerase and RNAse and to a lesser extent NAD pyrophosphorylase and nucleoside triphosphatase A are preferentially located in the nucleolar fraction. The same fraction does, however, contain roughly 5% of total nuclear DNA, and it is not known which enzymes are located in the RNA-rich portions of the nucleolar fraction and which are preferentially located in the surrounding chromatin or whether the surrounding chromatin is in any way biologically related to nucleolar functions.

(c) *Enzymes soluble only in detergent solutions*

The third group of enzymes is characterized by solubility only in detergents such as 1% digitonin. These enzymes include glucose-6-phosphatase and acid phosphatase, enzymes otherwise used as markers for lysozomes and microsomes. The importance of their occurrence in nuclei is difficult to assess. In theory this group of enzymes contains those which are associated with membranes in the native state. Non-aqueous isolation procedures destroy membranes and may liberate membrane fragments with which these enzymes are associated. For the study of enzymes of this category, aqueous methods for the isolation of nuclei will have to be used. Enzymes associated with both inner and outer nuclear membranes are to be included in this category.

(d) *Validity of enzyme classification*

Many of the nuclear enzymes are recovered in excellent yield in a single solubility group. This is true both of enzymes of the soluble space and of some enzymes of the chromatin fraction. Other enzymes, however, show less pronounced solubility behavior. These include the 'microsomal enzymes' which are approximately 50% solubilized by 0.14 M or 1 M NaCl as well as perhaps RNA polymerase. Furthermore the solubility characteristics of many nuclear enzymes have not been determined.

Estimates place the quantity of protein represented by nuclear enzymes at between 0.5 and 15% of total nuclear protein. These estimates could all be low. It has been estimated that if all of the RNA polymerase binding sites on bacterial DNA were filled, the complex would contain about equal weights of polymerase and DNA (Sted and Jones). A similar situation is conceivable for the template-active portions of chromatin of higher organisms. On this basis, RNA polymerase alone might make up 3–30% of nuclear protein.

The properties of nuclear enzymes are quite relevant to analysis of data concerning bulk nuclear protein. First, much of nuclear protein in each solubility category may be enzyme. Second, analysis of enzyme activities might prove valuable in assessing attempts to fractionate the presumably complex mixtures of nuclear proteins. The fact that some enzymes are only partially solubilized in the fractionation procedures now available indicates that gross cross-contamination of nuclear protein fractions is likely.

5. Nuclear ribosomal proteins and nuclear protein synthesis

There have been many reports of the occurrence of ribosomes and of the synthesis of proteins in the nucleus. This work has been partially summarized by Allfrey, Wang (1963), and Murray (1965). Particles resembling ribosomes and polysomes can be seen in electron micrographs of the nuclei of many mammalian tissues. Such particles have been isolated from calf thymus nuclei by extraction of nuclei with 0.05 M Tris buffer *p*H 7.5 and thus constitute part of the nuclear sap. The nuclear ribonucleoprotein particles have been shown to grossly resemble cytoplasmic ribosomes in appearance in the electron microscope, in chemical composition, and in sedimentation behavior as well as in sensitivity of sedimentation values to magnesium ion concentration. Since aqueous methods for the isolation of calf thymus nuclei were used in these experiments and since the purity of isolated nuclei was not established it is difficult to preclude contamination by cytoplasmic ribosomes. The occurrence of ribonucleoprotein particles in the nucleus which are not ribosomes (Samariva et al.) further complicates appraisal of these experiments. The nucleoli are the sites of synthesis of ribosomal RNA and nucleoli are surrounded by large numbers of ribonucleoprotein granules. It is possible that these granules are ribosomal subunits or precursors of them. Characterization of the proteins associated with granules and comparison with cytoplasmic ribosomal proteins should clarify the relationships if any between the two. The observations of ribonucleoprotein granules and of incorporation of amino acids into macromolecules in the puff regions of polytene chromosomes (Lezzi) suggests the presence of ribosomes in some Dipteran nuclei. This example may be atypical and so may be that of calf thymus. The nucleus–cytoplasm ratio for calf thymus cells is roughly 3/2 (an extremely large value), and many normally cytoplasmic reactions, including protein synthesis, may occur in calf thymus nuclei.

The amino acid composition of the total protein of calf thymus nuclear ribosomes is quite similar to that of cytoplasmic ribosomal protein. The proteins of ribosomes are extremely heterogeneous, representing probably more than thirty molecular species. The acid soluble proteins of chromatin contaminated by ribosomes include both histones and basic ribosomal proteins. While amino acid analysis indicates some similarity between whole acid soluble ribosomal protein and whole histone, these two classes of proteins are quite distinct biologically and physically. They can be distinguished easily by electrophoresis and can be well separated by ion exchange chromatography on Amberlite CG-50 by the method of Luck et al. Ribosomal proteins are not retained by this resin in the presence of 0.8 M guanidinium chloride at *p*H 6.8 while all of the histones are retained.

It has been repeatedly suggested that many nuclear proteins and possibly ribosomal proteins as well are synthesized in the nucleus. The strongest evidence is that of Reid and Cole, which demonstrates the *in vitro* synthesis of lysine-rich histone in a preparation of isolated calf thymus nuclei. Allfrey et al. (1964) have demonstrated *in vitro* incorporation of tritiated amino acids into isolated calf thymus nuclei by high resolution autoradiography. Since histone synthesis is inhibited by puromycin and by actinomycin D (which block protein synthesis and RNA synthesis respectively) the mechanism of histone synthesis, regardless of the site of histone synthesis, is typical of all protein synthesis. Rigorous proof of the nuclear synthesis of protein is needed. Even if nuclear protein synthesis is a common phenomenon, it still remains to be determined whether the proteins so synthesized are specifically related to nuclear function or whether ribosomes are merely sometime inhabitants of the soluble space in the nucleus as well as the cytoplasm.

6. *The histones and protamines*

Histones are basic proteins which are natively complexed with DNA in the chromosomes of higher organisms. This definition is intentionally vague, for it is not known whether histones are natively complexed with the DNA of cytoplasmic organelles such as mitochondria or only with nuclear DNA, and although it is clear that histones are not found in bacteria (Zubay and Watson; Burlet 1964; Raaf), it is not known whether the protozoa and all the metazoa contain histones or only those organisms which are phylogenetically advanced. The protamines are a special class of histones which occur only in the mature spermatids of some animals. Histones are a popular subject of biological research. Reviews by Felix, Phillips (1961), Murray (1965), Busch, Vendrely and Vendrely, Bloch, and Bonner et al. (1968) emphasize different aspects of the subject and together contain a rather complete bibliography through 1965.

(a) *Preparation of histones*

For the preparation of histones minimally contaminated by ribosomal and other basic proteins, it is first necessary to prepare highly purified deoxyribonucleoprotein. The 0.05 M Tris buffer and 0.14 M NaCl extracts of isolated nuclei contain considerable acid-soluble protein, perhaps largely in association with ribosomes or other ribonucleoprotein granules. Thus repeated extraction of nuclei with these solutions prior to isolation of histones is highly desirable. The extracted nuclei contain deoxyribonucleoprotein which is still highly contaminated and can be substantially purified by sedimentation through 1.7 M sucrose. Additional non-histone protein can be removed by shearing purified chromatin and sedimentation of non-histone protein aggregates. The 'soluble nucleohistone' can then be recovered by high-speed centrifugation (Bonner et al. 1967). Compositions of pea bud and calf thymus nucleohistone are presented in Table 5. Finally some non-histone protein can be extracted from nucleohistone by 0.3 M NaCl without removal of any histone. When large quantities of histone are being prepared, it is generally impractical to perform so many purification steps. However, one may use histone prepared from such pure material as a standard against which to compare histone isolated from less purified starting materials. Acid-soluble proteins found in crude deoxyribonucleoprotein but not in highly purified nucleohistone are not histones.

TABLE 5

Chemical composition of calf thymus and pea bud nucleohistone

	DNA	RNA	Acid-soluble protein	Non-histone protein
Calf thymus	1.00	0.01	1.15	0.50
Pea bud	1.00	0.05	1.35	0.25

For the large scale preparation of histones, isolated nuclei can be extracted with 0.05 M Tris, 0.14 M NaCl and 0.3 M NaCl to maximally remove impurities. The deoxyribonucleoprotein can next be treated in three ways. One, histone can be solubilized by repeated extraction with 0.25 N or 0.50 N H_2SO_4 and precipitated by the addition of three volumes of ethanol. Extraction with HCl of the same concentrations is less selective and recovery of histones more difficult. Lower concentrations of acid result in only partial removal of histones from DNA. Two, histones can also be prepared by dissociation of nucleohistone in high concentrations of salt, followed by sedimentation of the DNA through dense sucrose solution. In this case, some non-histone protein accompanies the histone, but under these circumstances histone denaturation is minimized. Two molar NaCl dissociates more than 99% of all histone from DNA. Selective dissociation of histone components is possible by the use of different salts and salt concentrations. Three, histones can be sequentially removed from nucleohistone and further fractionated by chemical extraction and precipitation methods developed by Johns, and by Phillips and Butler (described below).

(b) *Histone nomenclature*

When highly purified histone components are subjected to amino acid analysis, N-terminal and C-terminal analysis, tryptic peptide mapping, exclusion chromatography, and electrophoresis, all of these criteria usually indicate molecular homogeneity. Thus it is useful to think of histone components as unique molecular species and to apply the nomenclature formerly used for crude histone components to the major molecular species in such crude histone fractions. Table 6 summarizes several popular nomenclatures and describes the histone components. This text will use a nomenclature based largely upon that of Luck et al. In view of the growing realization of the limited molecular heterogeneity and extremely limited phylogenetic variability of histones, a new nomenclature of histones should be forthcoming.

(c) *Fractionation of histones*

Most methods of histone fractionation yield fractions which contain mixtures of histones. Such methods are still quite useful as initial steps in histone purification. These methods include selective dissociation of histones from DNA by salts and by acids, chemical fractionations, and ion chromatography.

Different salts may be used to selectively dissociate different histones. Extraction of plant or animal deoxyribonucleoprotein with 0.5 or 0.6 M NaCl results in the selective extraction of lysine-rich histone, extraction with 0.3 M guanidinium chloride removes some lysine-rich and most arginine-rich histones; extraction with 0.05 M DOC selectively removes slightly lysine-rich histone. Nucleohistone selectively stripped of various histones is currently being studied to determine the contribution of each histone to nucleohistone structure and biological properties (Bonner et al. 1968; Palau et al.). Murray (1966) has studied dissociation of histones from chromatin by H_2SO_4. Extraction at *p*H 2.6 to 1.8 solubilizes only lysine-rich histone I. At lower *p*H all histones are removed but the slightly lysine-rich histones are more readily extracted than are the arginine-rich. In the method of De Nooij and Westerbrink, the lysine-rich histone can be selectively solubilized by 5% trichloroacetic or perchloric acid. This extraction may depend more upon solubility than dissociation. It has been used in studies of lysine-rich histone by Kinkade and Cole, who extract whole calf thymus gland. The extraction is also fairly effective for preparation of plant lysine-rich histone (Sheridan and Stern).

In methods developed by Johns and Phillips and Butler for chemical fractionation of calf thymus histones extraction of lysine-rich histones from deoxyribonucleoprotein by 5% perchloric acid is sometimes the initial step. One popular method is outlined in Fig. 2. Several investigators have reported poor results, using such methods to fractionate histones from sources other than calf thymus. These methods evidently depend upon subtle factors and must be adjusted to suit the histones of various organisms.

Several cation exchange resins combined with various *p*H and salt gradients have been used for fractionation of histones. Those resins most commonly used are carboxymethyl-cellulose and Amberlite CG-50 (IRC-50). A particularly successful and generally applicable chromatographic procedure is that developed by Luck et al. Histones are fractionated on Amberlite CG-50, using a gradient of guanidinium chloride from 8% to 13% followed by 40%. Recovery of histone is 100% and high

TABLE 6

Major similarities and differences between homologous calf thymus and pea bud histone components[a]

Histone component[b]	Synonyms[c, d]	Relative electrophoretic mobility[e]	N-terminal amino acid[f]	C-terminal amino acid	Major compositional similarities and other features[g, h]
Calf Iab Pea Iabc	f1, *α*	slow slow	blocked blocked	Lys Lys	Lysine-rich histone containing 25–28% Lys, 22–24% Ala, 8–10% Pro, <1% Tyr and Phe, no Met. Microheterogeneity. Pea contains His.
Calf IIb2 Pea IIa1, 2	f2b, *γ*	intermediate intermediate	Pro Pro	Lys Ser, Ala	Slightly lysine-rich histones containing 16–17% Lys and 6–7% Arg. Calf is serine-rich. Pea is two components.
Calf IIb1 Pea IIb	f2a2, *β*	intermediate intermediate	blocked blocked	Lys Ala	Slightly lysine-rich histones containing 10–11% Leu and 11% Gly. Lys/Arg ratio about 1.2. All amino acids present to comparable extent in pea and calf.
Calf III Pea III	f3, *β*	complex [i] complex [i]	Ala Ala	Ala Ala	Arginine-rich histones containing *ε*-methyl Lys, Cys, 11% Glu. All amino acids present to comparable extent in pea and calf. Extremely similar peptide maps.
Calf IV Pea IV	f2a1, *β*	fast fast	blocked blocked	Gly Gly	Arginine-rich histones containing 15–17% Gly, <2% Pro. All amino acids present to comparable extent. Extremely similar peptide maps.

[a] Data from Fambrough

[b] Calf thymus histone nomenclature based largely upon Luck et al. Pea histone nomenclature is that of Fambrough and Bonner.

[c] Nomenclature of Johns, Phillips, and Butler. See Butler (1965).

[d] Nomenclature of Cruft, Hindley, Mauritzen and Stedman (1957).

[e] Electrophoresis in polyacrylamide gel at *p*H 4.3.

[f] Blocked N-terminal groups are presumably N-acetylated. This is known to be the case for calf thymus histone IIb1 (Phillips 1966) and Iab.

[g] Values for amino acid composition are in mole per cent.

[h] In addition, all histone fractions lack tryptophan. This has been demonstrated by fluorometric analysis (R. Jensen, unpublished data) and by negative results from staining peptide maps with Ehrlich's reagent. All histone fractions except histone III also lack cysteine.

[i] The complex electrophoretic patterns of calf and pea histone III are due to the formation of histone III complexes by interpeptide chain disulfide bridges. Pea histone III, containing one cysteine per molecule, can exist as monomer and dimer. Calf histone III, containing two cysteines per molecule, can exist as monomer and various sized multimers.

resolution of some components is achieved. Ion exchange chromatography of histones in the presence of 6 M urea (a technique used so successfully for resolution of the ribosomal proteins) has not yet been reported, but should yield good results. A tendency of histones to aggregate makes all chromatographic separations thus far attempted subject to some artifacts. The use of urea in chromatography should greatly diminish such interactions.

A particularly useful secondary method of fractionation is exclusion chromatography. Fractionation of arginine-rich histones on Sephadex (Mauritzen et al.) and Bio-Gel (Hnilica and Bess) have resulted in complete separation of histone IIb1, III and IV.

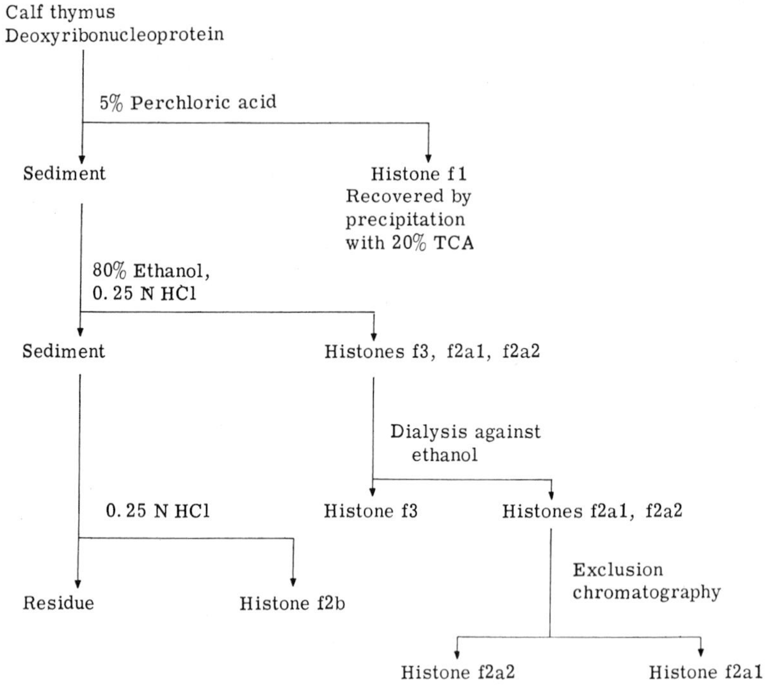

Fig. 2. Fractionation of calf thymus histones by the method of Johns (1964a) and Phillips and Johns. Fractions f1, f2a and f3, and f2b are sequentially solubilized and then removed from calf thymus nucleoprotein by centrifugation. Fractions f2a and f3 are separated by selective precipitation of f3 from ethanolic HCl. Fraction f2a is separated into components f2a1 and f2a2 by stepwise precipitation with acetone from acidified solution or by ion exchange or exclusion chromatography.

For the analysis of small amounts of histone, chromatography of histones on Amberlite CG-50 can be scaled down for the fractionation of sub-milligram quantities and material can be recovered by precipitation with trichloroacetic acid. The most elegant separations of histone components are achieved by electrophoresis. Starch gel electrophoresis has been used extensively in analysis of histones, but it is rapidly being replaced by disc electrophoresis in polyacrylamide gels. Numerous modifications of the original method of Reisfeld et al. have been reported. Those providing highest resolution of histone components use low *p*H gels containing 6 M urea (Bonner et al. 1967; Johns 1967). Single gels 5 mm in diameter are suitable for resolution of 5–30 μg of whole histone. An electrophoretic fractionation of whole pea bud histone is presented in Fig. 3. Both starch gel and acrylamide gel electrophoresis have been quantified for histones, using spectrophotometry of dissolved gel slices (Hnilica et al. 1966; Johns 1967) or densitometry of whole gels (Fambrough et al.).

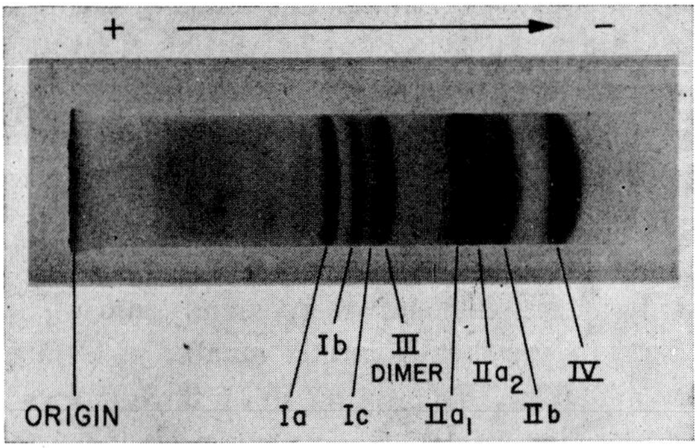

Fig. 3. Fractionation of pea bud histones by disc electrophoresis in polyacrylamide gel. Twenty μg of whole pea bud histones, prepared by acid extraction of purified chromatin, were dissolved in 8 M urea at 1 mg/ml and applied to a 7.5% acrylamide gel containing 6 M urea. Electrophoresis was performed at 4 mA for 90 min (*p*H 4.3, β-alanine buffer). Explanation of histone nomenclature is presented in Table 6. Faint bands of low electrophoretic mobility are lost in preparation of nucleohistone or ion exchange chromatography and are not considered histone components.

Preparative disc electrophoresis has only recently become practical, but limited results are extremely encouraging. A direct scale-up of analytical disc electrophoresis has proven most suitable, and the use of histone fractions rather than whole histone contributes substantially to purity of the fractions.

7. *Description of histone components*

(a) *Lysine-rich histones*

The lysine-rich histones are apparently the largest histone molecules. They are most excluded in gel filtration chromatography, have the lowest electrophoretic mobilities (despite being the histones with highest density of positive charges), and yield the largest number of tryptic peptides. Both as native histone in nucleohistone complexes and as isolated histones, the lysine-rich histones possess little or no alpha helix. Lysine-rich histones are relatively weakly bound to DNA (as judged by ease of extraction with NaCl and H_2SO_4) and are especially prone to proteolysis during preparation. Proteolysis is probably responsible for the low molecular weights reported in the older literature and for the apparent heterogeneity of lysine-rich histones.

Calf thymus lysine-rich histones were successfully fractionated into two fractions by Rasmussen et al. and shown to be identical in electrophoretic behavior but to differ slightly in composition, histone Ia having more arginine than histone Ib. Peptide maps of these two fractions, prepared by the author, demonstrate that Ia and Ib possess extremely similar primary structures (Fig. 4). Calf thymus lysine-rich histones have been studied in detail by Kinkade and Cole, who succeeded in obtaining four fractions which again differ primarily in arginine content. Amino acid compositions of the purified fractions are presented in Table 7. Analysis of tryptic peptides provides proof of extensive sequence identity between the components. These studies suggest a content of one tyrosine, one phenylalanine and three or four arginines per molecule and thus a molecular weight of about 21,000, in agreement with values obtained by sedimentation equilibrium (Teller et al.).

Studies by the author on the lysine-rich histones of the pea plant have yielded similar results. Plant lysine-rich histones are apparently somewhat larger than those of vertebrates as judged by the slightly greater number of tryptic peptides and by lower electrophoretic mobility. There appear to be three molecular species of pea

TABLE 7

Amino acid compositions of lysine-rich histones[a]

		Calf thymus histone I[b]		
	Pea bud histone I	I	II	IIIa, b
Lys	25.5	29.1	30.6	30.4
His	1.1	0	0	0
Arg	2.8	1.9	1.4	1.7
Asp	2.3	1.9	1.8	1.9
Thr	4.0	5.2	5.5	5.2
Ser	4.9	6.0	6.2	6.2
Glu	7.3	3.1	3.1	3.2
Pro	9.9	9.3	9.9	9.5
Gly	2.3	6.2	6.7	6.6
Ala	22.8	26.5	24.3	26.0
Val	5.3	5.0	4.8	3.8
Met	0	0	0	0
Ile	1.9	0.9	0.8	0.8
Leu	4.1	4.0	3.9	3.9
Tyr	0.4	0.5	0.5	0.4
Phe	0.4	0.5	0.5	0.4

[a] Values are in moles per hundred moles of amino acids

[b] Calculated from Kinkade and Cole

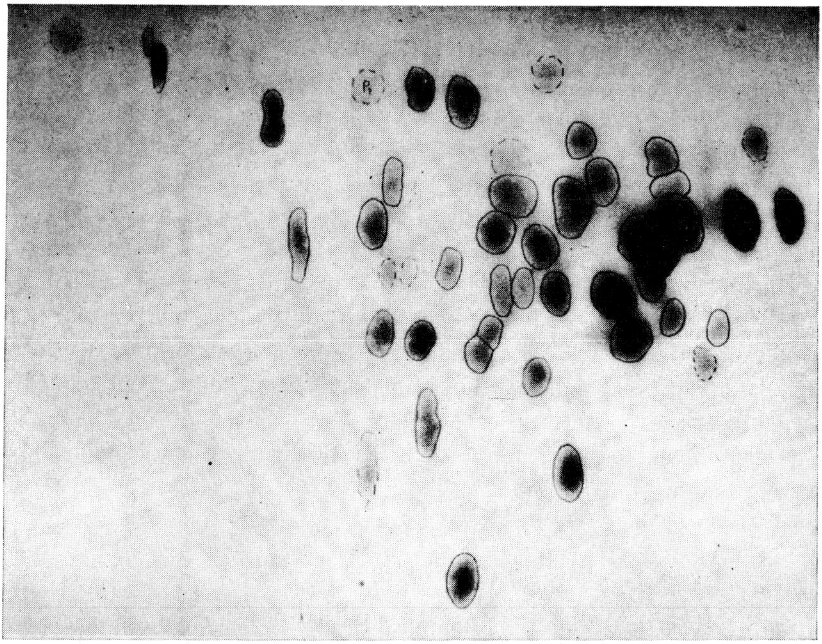

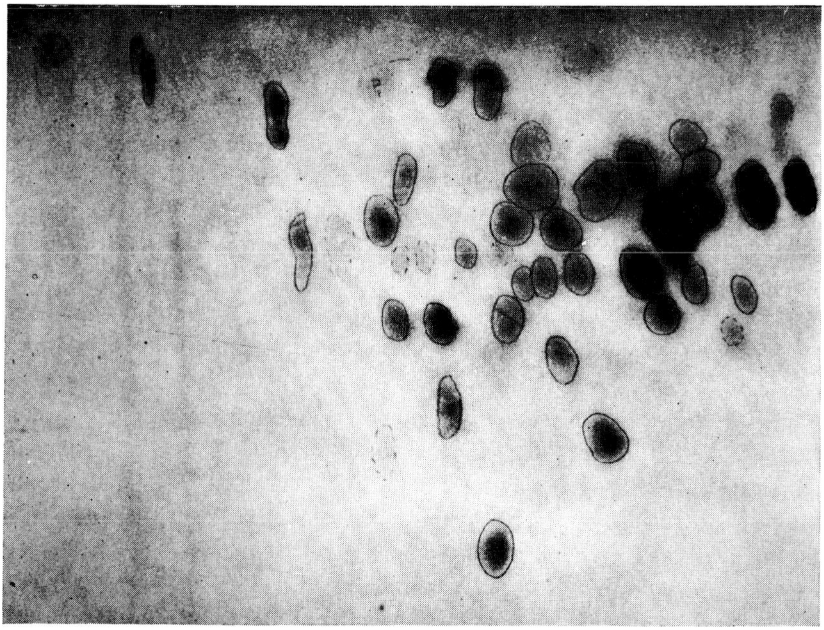

Fig. 4. Peptide maps of tryptic peptides of calf thymus histones Ia (above) and Ib (below). Chromatography: n-propanol. ammonium hydroxide 7:3. Electrophoresis: pyridine acetate buffer, *p*H 3.5.

lysine-rich histones, which differ slightly in electrophoretic mobility but contain much common primary sequence. The amino acid composition of whole pea bud lysine-rich histone is included in Table 7. It differs distinctly from the composition of calf thymus lysine-rich histones by containing histidine and a larger amount of glutamic acid, but is similar in other gross respects, including high lysine and alanine content, high proline content and lack of methionine.

Both calf thymus and pea bud histone I have blocked N-terminal, the single N-terminal region for all calf thymus lysine-rich histones is acetyl-Ser-Glu-Thr-Ala-Pro- and for pea bud acetyl-(Ser, Glu, Thr, Ala, Pro), the peptides being obtained by pronase digestion and Dowex-50 chromatography. Both calf thymus and pea bud histone I have C-terminal lysine. The microheterogeneity of lysine-rich histones probably had its origin in duplications of the gene for lysine-rich histone followed by limited evolutionary divergence.

Lysine-rich histones account for 20–25% of calf thymus whole histone and about 15% of pea bud histone.

(b) *Slightly lysine-rich histones*

There are two principal slightly lysine-rich histones in calf thymus. These two are separated only with difficulty, yet the two components have little in common. One component (IIb2) accounts for about 30% of total histone. It has a Lys–Arg ratio of 2.5 and is rich in serine. The other (IIb1) has a Lys–Arg ratio of only 1.2, represents only 10% of total histone, and has been termed 'lysine–arginine-rich'. There is lingering uncertainty as to the homogeneity of these two components. The most elegant study of histone IIb2 (Hnilica 1966) demonstrates only about twenty-five tryptic peptides separated in peptide maps. Phillips (1967), however, reports isolation of two N-terminal proline peptides. Thus slight heterogeneity is possible. Amino acid compositions of histones IIb2 and IIb1 are presented in Table 8. Calf thymus histone IIb2 contains N-terminal proline, IIb1 has acetylated N-terminal and the sequence acetyl-Ser-Gly-Arg has been reported. Both components have C-terminal lysine.

Three slightly lysine-rich histone components are found in pea plants accounting for about 50% of total pea bud histone. Two of these, IIa1 and IIa2, have not been cleanly separated. They can, however, be partially resolved by disc electrophoresis and can be distinguished on the basis of C-terminal amino acids: IIa1 has C-terminal serine while IIa2 has C-terminal Ala. Only proline is found as N-terminal and it is not known whether or not one of the two components has its terminal amino group acetylated. Since seventy peptides can be distinguished by finger-printing pea histone IIa it is thought that the two components are probably not similar in primary structure.

The third pea slightly lysine-rich histone (IIb) is homologous with calf thymus histone IIb1. It differs in having C-terminal alanine, but like IIb1 has blocked N-terminus and is quite similar in amino acid composition. Also like calf thymus IIb1

TABLE 8

Amino acid compositions of slightly lysine-rich histones

	Pea bud histone IIa	Calf thymus histone IIb2[a]	Pea bud histone IIb	Calf thymus histone IIb1[b]
Lys	16.1	16.4	10.6	11.9
His	1.1	2.5	1.6	2.8
Arg	6.5	6.6	9.0	9.8
Asp	6.0	4.9	6.1	5.8
Thr	4.8	6.2	4.1	4.9
Ser	6.7	11.0	5.6	5.0
Glu	8.0	8.0	6.6	9.3
Pro	6.7	4.6	7.1	4.5
Gly	8.8	5.7	11.4	9.6
Ala	12.3	10.5	12.8	12.0
Val	6.7	7.0	7.9	5.9
Met	0.5	1.4	—	0.7
Ile	4.5	4.8	3.1	4.6
Leu	7.9	5.0	10.6	10.5
Tyr	1.7	3.8	1.9	1.7
Phe	1.9	1.5	1.6	1.2

[a] Taken from Hnilica et al. (1966)
[b] Taken from Mauritzen et al.

it accounts for only about 10% of total histone. Amino acid compositions of pea slightly lysine-rich histones are presented in Table 8.

(c) *Arginine-rich histones*

There are two molecular species of arginine-rich histones in calf, pea and related higher animals and plants. These two species (III and IV) are very dissimilar and are represented by homologous components in all higher organisms.

Histone III is the larger and electrophoretically slower arginine-rich histone, having a molecular weight close to 20,000. It is distinguished by having N-terminal and C-terminal alanine and by containing cysteine, an amino acid not found in other histone fractions. Pea bud and calf thymus histone III are extremely similar in amino acid composition (Table 9); each has the unusual amino acid ε-N-methyl lysine (Murray 1964). Tryptic peptide maps of pea and calf thymus histone III demonstrate the strikingly similar primary structures (Fig. 5).

Histone III is unique among histones due to the presence of cysteine. Calf thymus histone III contains two cysteines per molecule. During preparation, sulfhydryl groups may oxidatively interact, forming disulfide bridges between histone monomers and thus producing a complex mixture of histone III multimers. Treatment with

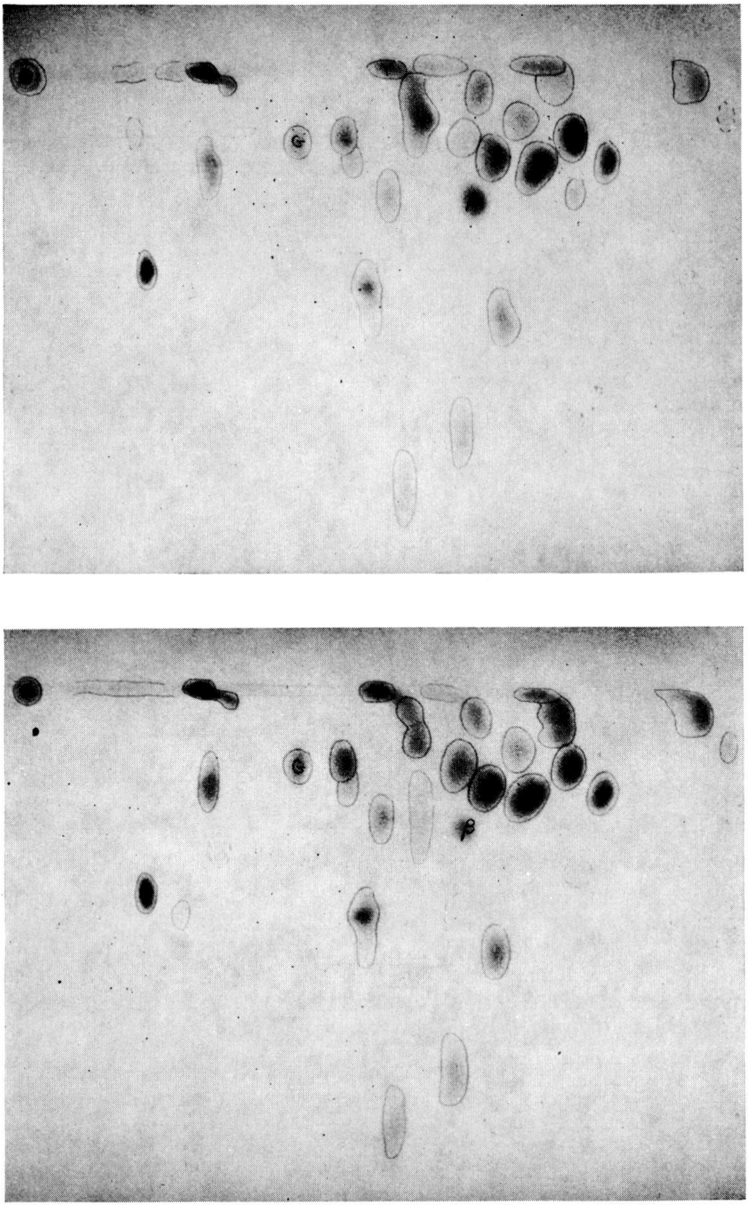

Fig. 5. Peptide maps of the tryptic peptides of calf thymus (above) and Pea bud (below) histone III. The uncircled spot marked 'β' is a trace of β-alanine from the electrophoresis buffer. 'G' gray and 'Y' yellow peptides (staining with collidine–ninhydrin reagent).

TABLE 9

Amino acid compositions of arginine-rich histones

	Pea bus histone III	Calf thymus histone III	Pea bud histone IV	Calf thymus histone IV
Lys	8.6(1.6)*	8.8(1.4)	8.5	9.7(1.1)
His	2.1	1.4	2.4	1.7
Arg	13.1	13.4	15.6	14.1
Asp	4.5	4.5	5.6	5.9
Thr	6.6	7.4	7.3	7.2
Ser	4.1	4.1	2.2	3.2
Glu	10.8	11.6	6.2	6.6
Pro	4.5	4.1	1.4	1.2
Gly	6.6	6.0	17.2	15.3
Ala	12.9	14.0	7.5	7.7
Val	5.2	4.4	6.6	7.4
Met	trace	trace	trace	trace
Ile	5.1	4.7	6.3	5.3
Leu	9.4	8.9	7.6	8.1
Tyr	1.0	1.7	3.0	3.5
Phe	3.9	2.8	2.7	1.9

Values are in moles per 100 moles amino acids.

* Values in parentheses are mole per cent ε-N-methyl lysine in addition to lysine.

β-mercaptoethanol reduces all components to a single electrophoretic species of high electrophoretic mobility. The various multimers have been shown to resemble one another in amino acid composition and in primary structure (Mauritzen et al.; Hnilica and Bess) and dimers can be converted to monomers and repolymerized into high order multimers. Pea bud histone III differs from calf thymus histone III in containing only one cysteine per molecule. Thus pea histone III can exist only as monomer and as dimer, and therefore its electrophoretic pattern is quite simple. The pea and calf monomers have identical electrophoretic mobility. Some investigators have attributed special importance to the cysteine residues in this histone. Since pea histone III possesses only one cysteine per molecule but is otherwise structurally like calf thymus histone III, it must be concluded that only one cysteine is required for the biological functioning of histone III and that multimers of higher order than dimer are not biologically meaningful entities. When histones are isolated by the most rapid techniques and quickly analyzed by electrophoresis, only monomers are found. The apparent heterogeneity of polymerized histone III is largely responsible for the erroneous belief that the histones are extremely heterogeneous. The phenomena described above are illustrated in Fig. 6.

Histone IV is the smallest and electrophoretically fastest of the somatic histones.

It has an acetylated N-terminal amino acid and C-terminal glycine. Its molecular weight is about 11.000 based upon one methionine per molecule. Pea and calf thymus histone IV are virtually identical in primary structure. Peptide maps of pea and calf thymus histone IV illustrate the amazing homology between the two (Fig. 7). Amino acid compositions are presented in Table 9.

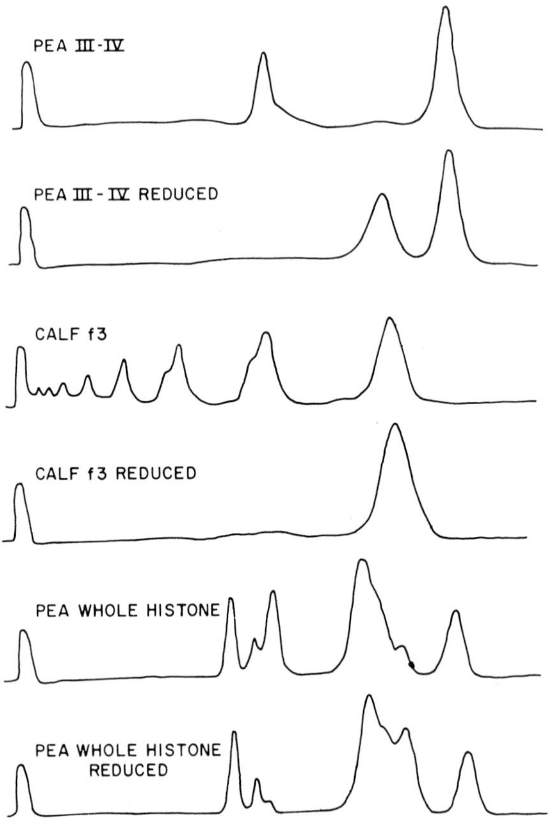

Fig. 6. Densitometric tracings of the electrophoretic patterns of pea bud and calf thymus histone fractions containing histone III in reduced and oxidized forms. From top to bottom they are: (a) Pea bud histone III-IV as isolated by column chromatography (histone III in oxidized form). (b) Pea bud histone III-IV prepared by column chromatography and subsequently treated with 0.1 M β-mercaptoethanol (8 M urea, 37 °C, 30 min) (histone III in reduced form). (c) Calf thymus histone f3 prepared by the method of Johns (1964a) and further purified by column chromatography (histone III in both reduced and oxidized forms). (d) Same material as in (c) except reduced with β-mercaptoethanol (histone III all in reduced form). (e) Whole pea bud histone after prolonged storage in 8 M urea solution (histone III in oxidized form). (f) Same material as in (e) except reduced with β-mercaptoethanol (histone III in reduced form).

8. *Histone heterogeneity and specificity*

A popular theory of histone function proposes that histones are genetic repressors. Thus it was imagined that histones are extremely heterogeneous, each molecular component specifically controlling the expression of only one or a few genes. However, as more accurate studies of histone chemistry are reported, it becomes increasingly clear that the histones are not very heterogeneous.

The apparent heterogeneity of histones can be traced to six sources: (1) contamination of histones by ribosomal or other acid-soluble proteins, (2) proteolysis of histones during preparation (Crampton et al.; Johns 1964b; Kinkade and Cole), (3) aggregation between different histones or between histones and non-histone proteins (Cruft et al. 1958; Hnilica and Bess), (4) formation of histone III multimers by disulfide bridging, (5) formation of histone III–non-histone protein complexes by disulfide bridging, and (6) the occurrence of microheterogeneity in lysine-rich histones.

While a few reports have emphasized the cell and species specificity of histones, more refined methods of analysis have failed to demonstrate either. The same histone components have been demonstrated in many vertebrate and higher plant tissues. The most elegant demonstration is that of Hnilica (1966). Histone IIb2 from various tissues of several vertebrate species was compared by separation and analysis of tryptic peptides. No tissue or species specificity was found. The demonstration of extensive similarities including common elements of primary sequence between calf thymus and pea bud histones (Table 6) further suggests an absence of histone specificity. It appears far more reasonable that a limited number of histone molecular species present as homologous molecules perform the same functions in all higher creatures.

Two examples of histone specificity remain. First, a special histone fraction containing 25 mole % lysine and 11 mole % arginine has been reported to occur specifically in erythrocyte nuclei of birds, amphibians and reptiles (see Hnilica 1965). However, Bellair and Mauritzen have apparently identified this component in all chicken tissues and even in calf thymus (Bellair, personal communication 1967), and it remains to be determined whether it is an additional histone species or whether it is an artifact of degradation as the reported multiplicity of terminal amino acids suggests.

The second example is the basic proteins occurring complexed with DNA in the sperm of certain vertebrate and invertebrate animals. These small, very basic proteins, found only in sperm, constitute a special class of molecules which fall into our loose definition of histones but are usually considered separately as the 'protamines'.

9. *The protamines*

Protamines are very basic proteins of molecular weight about 5000, generally composed largely of arginine and containing relatively few sorts of amino acids. They

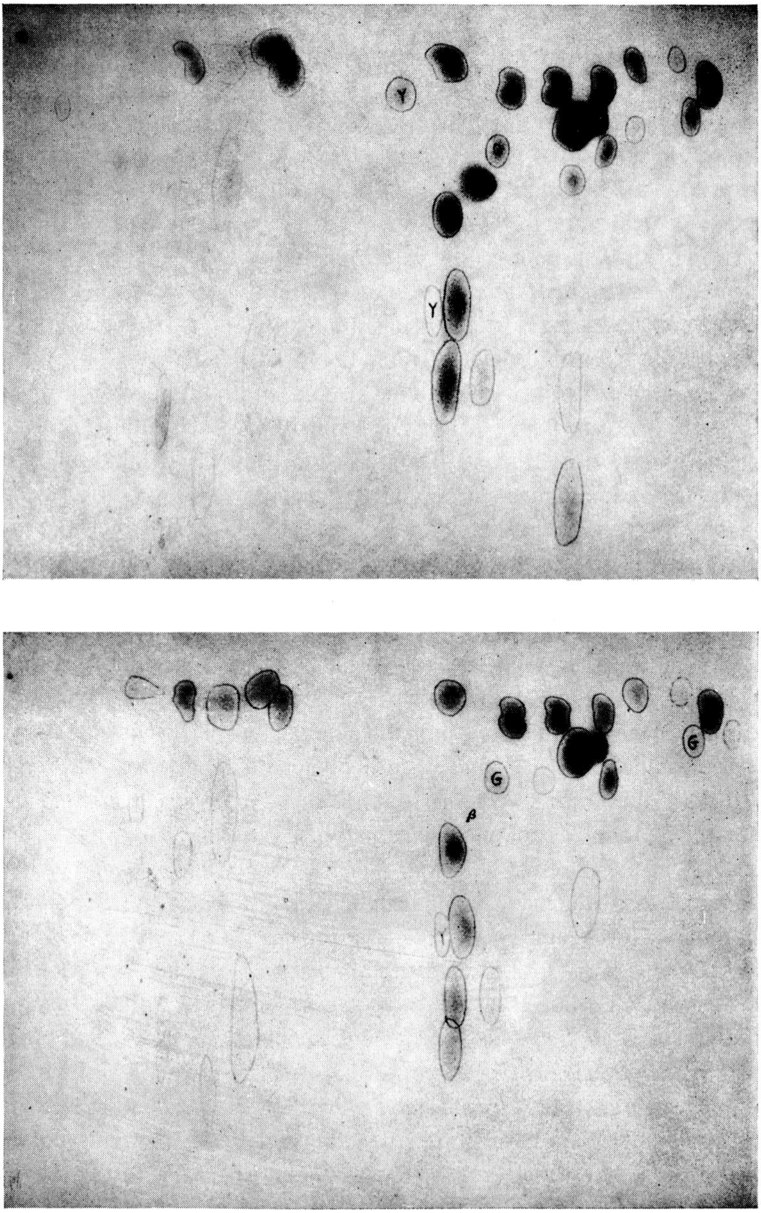

Fig. 7. Peptide maps of the tryptic peptides of calf thymus (above) and pea bud (below) histone IV. The uncircled spot marked '*β*' is a trace of *β*-alanine from the electrophoresis buffer. 'G' gray and 'Y' yellow peptides (staining with collidine–ninhydrin reagent).

have been found in sperm of some birds, of many fish and of many invertebrates. They have not been sought in motile plant gametes. Sperm of many organisms, however, including some fish, frog and echinoderms and the pollen of angiosperms apparently contain typical somatic histones, although little direct molecular information is available.

Protamines are prepared either by direct acid extraction from sperm heads, or by extraction from isolated nucleoprotamine. Nucleoprotamine is prepared by 1 M NaCl extraction of sperm or sperm nuclei. The DNA and protamines are dissociated in 1 M NaCl and can be separated by dialysis, the small protamines slowly passing through dialysis tubing. A more common method of recovery of protamines is precipitation as picrate salts, conversion to sulfates with sulfuric acid and reprecipitation in ethanol. Fractionation procedures include countercurrent distribution, electrophoresis, and chromatography on paper, ion exchange resins, and alumina.

Virtually all chemical studies of protamines have employed clupeine, the protamines from herring sperm. However, limited studies suggest that protamines from other fish are of comparable heterogeneity and nature. Clupeine from the Pacific herring *Clupea pallasii* has been extensively studied by Ando and co-workers. It consists of three major components present in nearly equal quantities. These components are separated by chromatography on alumina and subsequent countercurrent distribution or by trinitrophenylation and chromatography on carboxymethylcellulose. The amino acid sequences of all three components have been determined and are presented in Table 10. The general sequence similarities are obvious, and clustering of arginines in twos and fours at certain positions is a most striking feature. The elucidation of these primary structures represents a major advance in our understanding of nuclear proteins.

At present there is too little information on basic proteins in other sperm to draw many general conclusions. Vendrely has suggested that Arg–phosphate ratio greater than 1 in sperm may be a useful although crude criterion for the presence of protamines. The ratio for bovine sperm is 1.21. However, no protamine-like material has been prepared from this source despite many efforts; an arginine-rich, cysteine-rich 'keratin-like' protein has been partially described by Henricks and Mayer.

TABLE 10

Amino acid sequences of the three components of *Clupea pallasii* protamine

I	H-Ala-Arg$_3$-Arg-Ser- Ser-Arg-Pro-Ile- Arg$_4$-Pro-Arg$_2$-Arg-Thr-Thr-Arg$_4$-Ala-Gly-Arg$_4$-OH
II	H-Pro-Arg$_3$- Thr-Arg$_2$-Ala-Ser-Arg-Pro-Val-Arg$_4$-Pro-Arg$_2$- -Val-Ser-Arg$_4$-Ala- Arg$_4$-OH
	H-Ala-Arg$_3$-Arg-Ser-Arg$_2$-Ala-Ser-Arg-Pro-Val-Arg$_4$-Pro-Arg$_2$- -Val-Ser-Arg$_4$-Ala- Arg$_4$-OH

aken from Ando et al. and Ando and Suzuki (1966, 1967).

10. *Primary structure of histones*

Although it is expected that the complete sequence of some histone components will soon be known, no complete primary sequence of a somatic histone has thus far been reported. Fragmentary sequence work (see Bonner and T'so) is sufficient to demonstrate that no regular order of basic amino acids occurs in any histone fraction. On the basis of composition and terminal analysis of tryptic peptides, it has been estimated that up to half of the lysines in lysine-rich histone and the arginines in other histone fractions occur in pairs, but the distance between adjacent basic amino acids may vary from zero to at least eight. Thus in the ionic interaction of histones and DNA, irregularly distributed positively charged amino acids complex with regularly distributed negative phosphates, perhaps forming loops of polypeptide chains extending out from the nucleohistone axis. This model is a gross oversimplification. We can infer from studies on selective removal of different histones with NaCl, guanidinium chloride, and deoxycholate that specific hydrogen bonding and hydrophobic interactions also occur between individual histones and nucleohistone. For a detailed exposition of nucleohistone and nucleoprotamine structure the reader is referred to chapters by Ris and Kaye.

11. *Histone and protamine metabolism*

Four metabolic phenomena involve histone metabolism: (1) modification of histone structure by methylation, acetylation and phosphorylation (Allfrey et al. 1966), (2) histone synthesis during cell proliferation, (3) histone turnover in differentiated tissues, and (4) replacement of histones by protamines or other proteins during spermiogenesis and oogenesis (Bloch).

Acetylation of histones probably reflects turnover of N-terminal acetyl groups of histones I, IIb1, and IV, and methylation, the turnover of methyl groups of ε-N-methyl lysine in histones III and IV. Relatively rapid acetylation and methylation in template active euchromatin may simply reflect the proximity of substrates and enzymes in the more extended euchromatin. Phosphoserine and phosphothreonine have been identified in calf thymus histone I and III, representing on the order of 1–3 phosphates per molecule. Phosphorylation of these histones is also more rapid in euchromatin than in heterochromatin. Ingles and Dixon have shown that newly synthesized trout protamine has all of its serine residues phosphorylated. They postulate that phosphorylation, by decreasing net positive charge, may decrease interaction of newly synthesized protamines with RNA and facilitate transport of protamines through the nucleus to binding sites on chromatin.

During cell proliferation in regenerating rat liver (Irvin et al.) a burst of histone synthesis precedes DNA synthesis, although the two overlap. Histone turnover independent of DNA synthesis is indicated both by inhibitor studies and by isotopic labelling of histones in synchronized cell cultures (Sadgopal).

The conversion of nucleohistone to nucleoprotamine during spermiogenesis in some creatures and the changes in basic nuclear proteins during early embryogenesis are surely crucial processes in the proper functioning of the genetic material. Unfortunately these processes have been studied almost exclusively by cytochemical methods. A complete summary and critical evaluation of such methods has recently been published (Bloch).

A popular staining procedure fairly specific for somatic histones is the alkaline fast green method (Alfert and Geschwind), involving fixation in 10% formalin, hydrolysis of nucleic acids in 5% trichloroacetic acid, and staining of histones with a solution of fast green FCF at *p*H 8.1–8.3. To stain protamines, two methods developed by Bloch and Hew involve similar fixation, hydrolysis of nucleic acids in saturated picric acid, and staining with eosin Y at *p*H 8.1–8.3 or with bromphenol blue at *p*H 2.3. The value of these staining procedures is enhanced when they are used in conjunction with deamination or acetylation to remove or block lysine amino groups and thus to permit specific staining of very arginine-rich histones and protamines.

These cytochemical stains have been applied by Alfert and by Bloch and co-workers and Kaufman and co-workers (summarized in Bloch) to spermiogenesis and development in various arthropods, molluscs, and vertebrates. In a majority of cases, typified by salmon, squid and snail, early spermatids stain with alkaline fast green as do somatic cell nuclei and this staining can be abolished by prior acetylation of lysine amino groups; later spermatids show intense staining which is not affected by acetylation; and finally mature sperm are not stained with alkaline fast green but can be stained by protamine stains. Starch gel electrophoresis of basic proteins and amino acid analysis in the case of squid, indicate that the somatic histones are replaced by an 'arginine-rich histone' which is in turn replaced by typical protamines. A more complex sequence of alternations in basic proteins is observed during spermiogenesis in the mollusc *Mytilus edulis*. In other organisms such as the grasshopper *Chortophaga viridifasciata* the transition in basic proteins is incomplete and an 'arginine-rich histone' rather than protamine is found in mature sperm. In the sperm of many other organisms proteins apparently intermediate between typical histones and protamines are believed to be present, and typical histones may also occur in sperm.

Changes in basic nuclear proteins during oogenesis have not been studied. After fertilization, protamines are not demonstrable in the zygote, apparently being replaced by regulatory and structural proteins from the egg. No histones can be detected by staining techniques in the zygotes of *Drosophila*, the snail *Helix aspera*, and the mouse. During later stages in development typical somatic histones again appear. The interpretation of the cytochemical studies may not be so straight-forward. Permeability barriers to stain may exist in the zygote and early embryo. Detailed chemical studies of the nuclear basic proteins during spermiogenesis and embryogenesis are badly needed.

12. The functions of histones

The biological functions of the histones are still not well understood. A large body of data has been amassed to support the hypothesis that histones are directly involved in repression of genetic information (reviewed in Bonner et al. 1968). It is clear that histones lack the specificity required to serve as the total means of gene repression. Thus gene recognition by some auxiliary mechanism must be imagined, and, in principle, only a single histone species might be required for the task of repression.

It is also apparent that at least some components of histone confer special structural properties on native nucleohistone (Zubay and Doty; Wilkins et al.; Peacocke and Preston; Giannoni and Peacocke; Ohba; Palau et al.). However, there is strong evidence that histones are not directly involved in determining the structural differences between template active euchromatin and template inactive heterochromatin (Frenster; Grogan et al.; Maio and Schildkraut; Comings). The impressive conservation of primary structure of the arginine-rich histones suggests that these histones interact in a specific way with the sugar–phosphate backbone of the DNA and may well be an integral part of the structure of nucleohistone. The more variable lysine-rich and slightly lysine-rich histone components seem to be better candidates for the role of repressors. It seems most likely that each histone component has its own particular function, which may in one case be repression and in another stabilization of structure. Or it may be that the distinction between structural and repressor components is not completely valid.

13. Conclusion

Molecular information on nuclear enzymes and other non-histone proteins is still meager. The fractionation, purification and characterization of these components are important and challenging problems. Information on somatic histones, on the other hand, is already substantial: the primary structures of all of the histones will soon be known and the biological role of each histone fraction identified. Due to technological advances in separation and characterization of basic proteins, molecular information of the histone–protamine transition during spermiogenesis and the basic proteins present in early embryogenesis should be readily obtainable.

The vast majority of nuclear proteins are present as macromolecular complexes, involving both proteins and nucleic acids. We must try now to understand not only the nature of the separated components but also the molecular details of their interactions and the nature of the resulting complexes.

Addendum

Since the completion of the literature survey for this chapter, several papers have appeared which provide important new information and contain many references to the recent literature. Two reports present somewhat divergent views on the roles of chromosomal acidic proteins (MARUSHIGE, K., D. BRUTLAG and J. BONNER: Properties of chromosomal nonhistone protein of rat liver, Biochemistry 7 (1968) 3149; PAUL, J. and R. S. GILMOUR: Organ-specific restriction of transcription in mammalian chromatin, J. Mol. Biol. 34 (1968) 305).

There have been two additional reviews concerning histones and protamines (HNILICA, L. S.: Proteins of the cell nucleus, Progr. Nucleic Acid Res. Mol. Biol. 7 (1967) 25; DIXON, G. H. and M. SMITH: Nucleic acids and protamine in salmon testes, Progr. Nucleic Acid Res. Mol. Biol. 8 (1968) 9). Further evidence for the synthesis of lysine-rich histones in calf thymus nuclei has been reported (REID, B. R., R. H. STELLWAGEN and R. D. COLE: Further studies on the biosynthesis of very lysine-rich histones in isolated nuclei, Biochim. Biophys. Acta 155 (1968) 593). Additional microheterogeneity has been detected in the lysine-rich histone fraction (BUSTIN, M. and R. D. COLE: Species and organ specificity in very lysine-rich histones, J. Biol. Chem. 243 (1968) 4500). It is now apparent that histone acetylation includes N-acetylation of the lysine in histone IV (GERSHEY, E. L., G. VIDALI and V. G. ALLFREY: Chemical studies of histone acetylation, J. Biol. Chem. 243 (1968) 5018). However, the meaning of histone acetylation remains obscure. The complete amino acid sequences of pea bud and calf thymus histone IV are now known (DELANGE, R. J., D. M. FAMBROUGH, E. L. SMITH and J. BONNER: J. Biol. Chem. (1968) papers in press). Pea bud and calf thymus histone IV are each molecules of 102 amino acid residues. Their amino acid sequences are identical except for an Ile-Val interchange at position 60 and an Arg-Lys interchange at position 77. Both contain N-acetyl lysine as less as one mole per mole protein. These sequences reveal an unusual distribution of basic and acidic amino acid residues: the N-terminal 45 residues possess a net positive charge of 16 while the C-terminal portion has a net positive charge of only 3. The distribution of both charged and other amino acid residues suggests that the N-terminal region is the primary DNA binding site while the C-terminal region may be highly folded. Structural studies on the very lysine-rich histones (personal communication from R. David Cole's laboratory to James Bonner) suggest that the reverse situation pertains: the basic amino acids are clustered in the C-terminal region of histone I.

References

ALFERT, M. and I. I. GESCHWIND: A selective staining method for the basic proteins of cell nuclei. Proc. Natl. Acad. Sci. U.S. 39 (1953) 991.

ALLFREY, V. G.: Nuclear ribosomes. Exptl. Cell Res., Suppl. 9 (1963) 183.

ALLFREY, V. G., V. C. LITTAU and A. E. MIRSKY: Methods for the purification of thymus nuclei and their application to studies of nuclear protein synthesis. J. Cell Biol. 21 (1964) 213.

ALLFREY, V. G., B. G. T. POGO, A. O. POGO, L. J. KLEINSMITH and A. E. MIRSKY: The metabolic behavior of chromatin. In: Histones – their role in the transfer of genetic information. Ciba Found. Study Group No. 24. Boston, Little, Brown and Co. (1966) 42.

ANDO, T., K. IWAI, S. ISHII, M. AZEGAMI and C. NAKAHARA: The chemical structure of one component of clupeine. Biochim. Biophys. Acta 56 (1962) 628.

ANDO, T. and K. SUZUKI: The amino acid sequence of the second component of clupeine. Biochim. Biophys. Acta 121 (1966) 427.

ANDO, T. and K. SUZUKI: The amino acid sequence of the third component of clupeine. Biochim. Biophys. Acta 140 (1967) 375.

BLOCH, D. P.: Cytochemistry of histones. Protoplasmatologia V 3d (1966).

BLOCH, D. P. and H. Y. C. HEW: Changes in nuclear histones during fertilization and early embryonic development in the pulmonate snail *Helix aspera*. J. Biophys. Biochem. Cytol. 8 (1960) 69.

BONNER, J., G. R. CHALKLEY, M. DAHMUS, D. FAMBROUGH, R. C. HUANG, J. HUBERMAN, R. JENSEN, K. MARUSHIGE, H. OHLENBUSCH, B. M. OLIVERA, and J. WIDHOLM: Isolation and characterization of chromosomal nucleoproteins. In: S. Colowick and N. Kaplan, eds.: Methods in enzymology, vol. XII: The nucleic acids. New York, Academic Press (1967).

BONNER, J., M. DAHMUS, D. FAMBROUGH, R. C. HUANG, K. MARUSHIGE and D. TUAN: The biology of isolated chromatin. Science 159 (1968) 47.

BONNER, J. and P. O. P. T'SO: The nucleohistones. San Francisco, Holden Day (1964).

BUSCH, H.: The histones and other basic proteins. New York, Academic Press (1965).

BUTLER, J. A. V.: Fractionation and characteristics of histones. In: J. Bonner and P. O. P. T'so, eds.: The nucleohistones. San Francisco, Holden Day (1964) 36.

BUTLER, J. A. V.: Complexity and specificity of histones. In: Histones – their role in the transfer of genetic information. Ciba Found. Study Group No. 24. Boston, Little, Brown and Co. (1966) 4.

COMINGS, D.: Histones of genetically active and inactive chromatin. J. Cell Biol. 35 (1967) 699.

CRAMPTON, C. F., W. H. STEIN and S. MOORE: Comparative studies on chromatographically purified histone. J. Biol. Chem. 225 (1957) 363.

CRUFT, H. J., J. H. HINDLEY, C. M. MAURITZEN and E. STEDMAN: Amino acid composition of the six histones of calf thymocytes. Nature 180 (1957) 1107.

CRUFT, H. J., C. M. MAURITZEN and E. STEDMAN: Isolation of β-histone from calf thymocytes and the factors affecting its aggregation. Proc. Roy. Soc. (London), Ser. B 149 (1958) 21.

DE NOOIJ, E. H. and H. G. K. WESTERBRINK: Isolation of a homogeneous lysine-rich histone from calf thymus. Biochim. Biophys. Acta 62 (1962) 608.

FAMBROUGH, D.: Studies on plant and animal histones. Ph.D. Thesis. Pasadena, California Institute of Technology (1968).

FAMBROUGH, D. and J. BONNER: On the similarity of plant and animal histones. Biochemistry 5 (1966) 2563.

FAMBROUGH, D., F. FUJIMURA and J. BONNER: The quantitative distribution of histones in various organs of the pea plant. Biochemistry 7 (1968) 575.

FELIX, K.: Protamines. Advan. Protein Chem. 15 (1960) 1.

FRENSTER, J. H.: Nuclear polyanions as de-repressors of synthesis of ribonucleic acid. Nature 206 (1965) 680.

GEORGIEV, G. P. and J. S. CHENTSOV: On the structural organization of nucleochromosomal ribonucleoproteins. Exptl. Cell Res. 27 (1962) 570.

GIANNONI, G. and A. R. PEACOCKE: Thymus deoxyribonucleoprotein III. Sedimentation behavior. Biochim. Biophys. Acta 68 (1963) 157.

GROGAN, D. E., R. DESJARDINS and H. BUSCH: Nucleolar proteins of rat liver and Walker tumor. Cancer Res. 26 (1966) 775.

HENDRICKS, D. M. and D. T. MAYER: Isolation and characterization of a basic keratin-like protein from mammalian spermatozoa. Exptl. Cell Res. 40 (1965) 402.

HNILICA, L. S.: The role of nuclear proteins in genetic regulation. Developmental and metabolic control mechanisms and neoplasia. Baltimore, The Williams and Wilkins Co. (1965) 273.

HNILICA, L. S.: Observations on the tissue and species specificity of the moderately lysine-rich histone fraction 2b. Biochim. Biophys. Acta 117 (1966) 163.

HNILICA, L. S. and L. G. BESS: The heterogeneity of arginine-rich histones. Anal. Biochem. 12 (1965) 421.

HNILICA, L. S., L. J. EDWARDS and A. E. HEY: Studies on nuclear proteins II. Quantitative distribution of histone fractions in various tissues. Biochim. Biophys. Acta 124 (1966) 109.

INGLES, C. J. and G. H. DIXON: Phosphorylation of protamine during spermatogenesis in trout testes. Proc. Natl. Acad. Sci. U.S. 58 (1967) 1011.

IRVIN, J. L., D. J. HOLBROOK, J. H. EVANS, H. C. MCALLISTER and E. P. STILES: Possible role of histones in regulation of nucleic acid synthesis. Exptl. Cell Res., Suppl. 9 (1963) 359.

JOHNS, E. W.: A degradation product of lysine-rich histone. Biochem. J. 93 (1964) 161.

JOHNS, E. W.: The electrophoresis of histones in polyacrylamide gel and their quantitative determination. Biochem. J. 104 (1967) 78.

KINKADE, J. M. and R. D. COLE: The resolution of four lysine-rich histones derived from calf thymus. J. Biol. Chem. 241 (1966) 5790.

KINKADE, J. M. and R. D. COLE: A structural comparison of different lysine-rich histones of calf thymus. J. Biol. Chem. 241 (1966) 5798.

KLEINSMITH, L. J., V. G. ALLFREY and A. E. MIRSKY: Phosphoprotein metabolism in isolated lymphocyte nuclei. Proc. Natl. Acad. Sci. U.S. 55 (1966) 1182.

LEZZI, M.: RNA- und Protein-Synthese in Puffs isolierter Speicheldrüsenchromosomen von *Chironomus*. Chromosoma 21 (1967) 72.

LUCK, J. M., P. S. RASMUSSEN, K. SATAKE and A. N. TSVETIKOV: Further studies on the fractionation of calf thymus histone. J. Biol. Chem. 233 (1958) 140.

MAIO, J. J. and C. L. SCHILDKRAUT: Isolated mammalian metaphase chromosomes: General characteristics of nucleic acids and proteins. J. Mol. Biol. 24 (1967) 29.

MAURITZEN, C. M., W. C. STARBUCK, I. S. SAROJA, C. W. TAYLOR and H. BUSCH: The fractionation of arginine-rich histones from fetal calf thymus by exclusion chromatography. J. Biol. Chem. 242 (1967) 2240.

MIRSKY, A. E. and S. OSAWA: The interphase nucleus. In: J. Brachet and A. E. Mirsky, eds.: The cell, vol. II. New York, Academic Press (1961) 677.

MURRAY, K.: The occurrence of ε-N-methyl lysine in histones. Biochemistry 3 (1964) 10.

MURRAY, K.: Basic proteins of cell nuclei. Ann. Rev. Biochem. 34 (1965) 209.

MURRAY, K.: The acid extraction of histones from calf thymus deoxyribonucleoprotein. J. Mol. Biol. 15 (1966) 409.

NEVILLE, D. M.: Fractionation of cell membrane proteins by disc electrophoresis. Biochim. Biophys. Acta 133 (1967) 168.

OHBA, Y.: Structure of nucleohistone I. Hydrodynamic behavior. Biochim. Biophys. Acta 123 (1966) 76.

OHLENBUSCH, H. H., B. M. OLIVERA, D. TUAN and N. DAVIDSON: Selective dissociation of histones from calf thymus nucleoprotein. J. Mol. Biol. 25 (1967) 299.

PALAU, J., J. F. PARDON and B. M. RICHARDS: The reversibility of dissociation of nucleohistone by salt. Biochim. Biophys. Acta 138 (1967) 633.

PATEL, G. and T. Y. WANG: Chromatography and electrophoresis of nuclear soluble proteins. Exptl. Cell Res. 34 (1964) 120.

PEACOCKE, A. R. and B. N. PRESTON: Effect of gamma-rays on thymus nucleoprotein in solution. Nature 192 (1961) 228.

PHILLIPS, D. M. P.: The histones. Progr. Biophys. Biophys. Chem. 12 (1961) 211.

PHILLIPS, D. M. P.: Studies on the primary structure of some histones. Biochem. J. 101 (1966) 23P.

PHILLIPS, D. M. P. and E. W. JOHNS: A fractionation of the histones of group f2a from calf thymus. Biochem J. 94 (1967) 127.

RAAF, J.: Studies on the biochemistry of genetic repression. D. Phil. Ph.D. Thesis. Oxford, Oxford University (1966).

RASMUSSEN, P. S., K. MURRAY and J. M. LUCK: On the complexity of calf thymus histone. Biochemistry 1 (1962) 79.

REID, B. R. and R. D. COLE: Biosynthesis of lysine-rich histone in isolated calf thymus nuclei. Proc. Natl. Acad. Sci. U.S. 51 (1964) 1044.

REISFELD, R. A., U. J. LEWIS and D. E. WILLIAMS: Disc electrophoresis of basic proteins and peptides on polyacrylamide gels. Nature 195 (1962) 281.

ROODYN, D. B.: A comparative account of methods for the isolation of nuclei. Biochem. Soc. Symp. 23 (1963) 20.

SADGOPAL, A.: Histone metabolism in synchronized HeLa cell cultures. Ph.D. Thesis. Pasadena, California Institute of Technology (1968).

SAMARINA, O. P., E. M. LUKANIDIN and G. P. GEORGIEV: On the structural organization of the nuclear complexes containing messenger RNA. Biochim. Biophys. Acta 142 (1967) 561.

SHERIDAN, W. F. and H. STERN: Histones of meiosis. Exptl. Cell Res. 45 (1967) 323.

SIEBERT, G. and R. HANNOVER: Lactatdehydrogenase-Studien an isolierten Zellkernen. Biochem. Z. 339 (1963) 162.

SIEBERT, G. and G. B. HUMPHREY: Enzymology of the nucleus. Advan. Enzymol. 27 (1965) 239.

SIEBERT, G. and R. M. S. SMELLIE: Enzymatic and metabolic studies on isolated nuclei. Intern. Rev. Cytol. 6 (1957) 383.

SIEBERT, G., J. VILLILOBOS, T. S. RO, W. J. STEELE, G. LINDERMAYER, H. ADAMS and H. BUSCH: Enzymatic studies on isolated nucleoli of rat liver. J. Biol. Chem. 241 (1966) 71.

STED, N. W. and O. W. JONES: Stability of RNA polymerase-DNA complexes. J. Mol. Biol. 26 (1967) 131.

STEELE, W. J. and H. BUSCH: Studies on acidic nuclear proteins of the Walker tumor cell nuclei. Cancer Res. 23 (1963) 1153.

TELLER, D. C., J. M. KINKADE and R. D. COLE: The molecular weight of lysine-rich histone. Biochem. Biophys. Res. Commun. 20 (1965) 739.

UMANA, R. and A. L. DOUNCE: Relation of rat liver cathepsins to autolytic degradation of proteins in the liver cell nucleus. Exptl. Cell Res. 35 (1964) 277.

VENDRELY, R. and C. VENDRELY: Biochemistry of histones and protamines. Protoplasmatologia V 3c (1966).

WANG, T. Y.: Physico-chemical and metabolic properties of nuclear ribosomes. Exptl. Cell Res., Suppl. 9 (1963) 213.

WANG, T. Y.: Solubilization and characterization of the residual proteins of the cell nucleus. J. Biol. Chem. 241 (1966) 2913.

WANG, T. Y.: The isolation properties, and possible functions of chromatin acidic proteins. J. Biol. Chem. 242 (1967) 1220.

WEISS, S. B.: Enzymatic incorporation of ribonucleoside triphosphatates into the interpolynucleotide linkages of ribonucleic acid. Proc. Natl. Acad. Sci. U.S. 46 (1960) 1020.

WILKINS, M.H.F., G.ZUBAY and H.R.WILSON: X-ray diffraction studies of the molecular structure of nucleohistone and chromosomes. J. Mol. Biol. 1 (1959) 179.

ZBARSKY, I.B., N.P.DMITRIEVA and L.P.YERMOLAYEVA: On the structure of tumor cell nuclei. Exptl. Cell Res. 27 (1962) 573.

ZBARSKY, I.B. and G.P.GEORGIEV: Cytological characteristics of protein and nucleoprotein fractions of cell nuclei. Biochem. Biophys. Acta 32 (1959) 301.

ZUBAY, G. and P.DOTY: Isolation and properties of deoxyribonucleoprotein particles containing single nucleic acid molecules. J. Mol. Biol. 1 (1959) 1.

ZUBAY, G. and M.R.WATSON: The absence of histone in the bacterium *Escherichia coli*. J. Biophys. Biochem. Cytol. 5 (1959) 51.

CHAPTER 19

DNA, RNA, and protein synthesis during the mitotic cell cycle

VALERIO MONESI

Institute of Histology and Embryology of the University of Roma, and Laboratory of Animal Radiobiology, C.S.N.-Casaccia, Roma

Contents

1. Introduction
2. The period of DNA synthesis preceding mitosis
   (a) Cell cycle analysis in cells of higher organisms
   (b) Constancy in duration of the S and G_2 periods
   (c) Change in duration of the S period during differentiation
   (d) Asynchrony of DNA replication in cells of higher organisms
   (e) DNA replication and segregation in chromosomes of higher organisms. Stage of chromosome splitting during the cell cycle
   (f) Regulation of DNA synthesis and control of cell division
3. RNA and protein synthesis during the cell cycle
   (a) Cellular sites of RNA synthesis
   (b) Pattern of synthesis of RNA and protein during the cell cycle
   (c) Histone synthesis during interphase and mitosis
   (d) Nucleocytoplasmic interactions during the cell cycle

* Supported by PHS grant No. RH-00304 from the Division of Radiological Health, U.S.A.

1. Introduction

There are a large number of biochemical events in the reproductive cycle of cells. These include the replication and segregation of the genetic material; the interaction of DNA with histone and other proteins; the arrangement of macromolecules in the chromosome and chemical changes of chromosomes during the coiling and uncoiling processes; the synthesis and dissemination of informational molecules from the chromosomes; the regulative processes of the sequence of gene replication and gene transcription during the cell life cycle; the synthesis and assembly of the molecular components of the mitotic apparatus and of other structures (endoplasmic reticulum, Golgi complex, cell and nuclear membranes, centrioles, nucleolus, etc.); the provision of energy sources for division; the synthesis of precursors and enzymes concerned with replication of macromolecules, gene transcription and energetic metabolism, etc.

Only a few of these biochemical processes will be discussed in this chapter. Other facets of the general problem of biochemical regulation of cell division are covered in other chapters of this book or in previous reviews and articles (Bullough; Swift 1954, 1962; Ris 1957, 1961, 1966; Swann 1957, 1958; Zeuthen 1960, 1961; Zimmerman; Mazia 1961a,b; Mirsky and Osawa; Prescott 1961; Lark; Stern and Hotta; and others).

2. The period of DNA synthesis preceding mitosis

(a) *Cell cycle analysis in cells of higher organisms*

It is now well established that the doubling of DNA in cells that divide by mitosis takes place during an appreciable interval of the interphase period, and not during division. In many bacteria, on the other hand, DNA synthesis is a continuous process through the cell life cycle (Schaechter et al.; Abbo and Pardee; Cummings). The conclusion that DNA doubles during interphase in cells of higher organisms had already been reached many years ago from experiments employing measurements of UV-absorption or Feulgen-histophotometry (Walker and Yates; Patau and Swift; see also the review by Bloch 1958). However, the conclusive evidence has come from the use of radioactive isotopes and radioautographic techniques. The earlier findings by Howard and Pelc (1951), Taylor and McMaster, and others, obtained by studying P^{32} incorporation into DNA, have been later confirmed and extended by the use of a specific DNA precursor (thymidine) labeled with tritium (Hughes et al.; Cronkite et al.; Painter and Drew; Quastler and Sherman; Stanners and Till; Taylor 1960; Wimber; Monesi 1962). Even though cells normally synthesize the thymidilic acid *via* deoxyuridylic acid, thymidine is effectively incorporated into DNA. It has also been shown that, with few exceptions, thymidine is incorporated exclusively into DNA and may therefore be considered as a specific precursor of deoxyribonucleic acid (Reichard and Estborn; Friedkin et al.).

Autoradiographic experiments with ^{3}H-thymidine have shown that in cells of higher organisms dividing by mitosis, DNA is synthesized during the middle part of the interphase interval which is called the S period. The portions of interphase preceding and following DNA synthesis are called the G_1 and G_2 periods respectively. Cells move along the cycle from G_1 to S to G_2, then divide and the daughter cells enter a new cycle of division (Fig. 1). This terminology, G_1, S, G_2, has been proposed by Howard and Pelc (1953) and is now currently used by most workers.

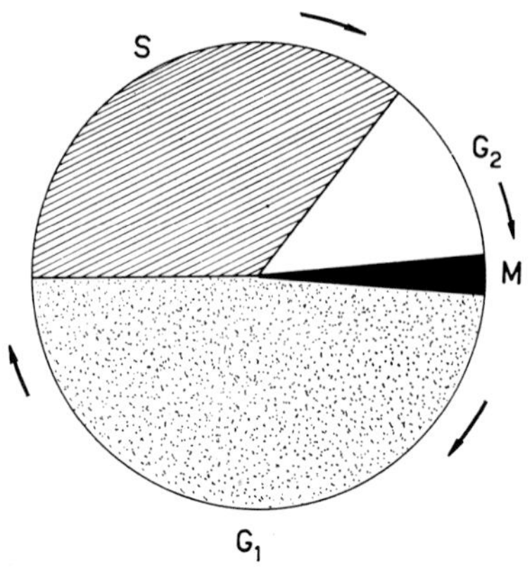

Fig. 1. Diagram of the cell cycle of a cell population in exponential growth. In any given moment, a small portion of cells is in mitosis (M), while interphase cells are either in the pre-synthetic interval (G_1), in the period for DNA synthesis (S) or in the post-synthetic interval (G_2). Cells proceed along the cycle clockwise from G_1 through S to G_2, then divide and the daughter cells enter a new cycle.

An example of a typical experiment designed to study the time of DNA synthesis and the duration of the various phases of the cell division cycle in a homogeneous and asynchronous population of cells in logarithmic growth cultured *in vitro* is shown in Fig. 2 (Monesi et al. 1967). The cells were incubated for a short period (15 min) with the radioactive DNA precursor ^{3}H-thymidine, then the radioactive medium was withdrawn, the cells were washed, reincubated again in a non-radioactive medium and examined for the presence of the label over the chromosomes at various intervals after labeling, as they moved into the metaphase stage. During the incubation with the radioactive precursor, only those cells which were synthesizing DNA, namely the cells which were in the S period, incorporated ^{3}H-thymidine into the newly synthesized DNA and became labeled. Following further incubation in a non-radioactive medium, the labeled cells proceeded through G_2 into mitosis and there appeared the first labeled metaphase figures, that rapidly increased in frequency up to almost 100 per cent. The interval between the time of labeling (time zero) and the time when 50 per cent of the metaphase figures appeared labeled represents therefore the average duration of G_2. By this method, G_2 includes the portion of interphase between the end of DNA synthesis and prophase and metaphase stages. After the initial rise, the frequency of labeled metaphase figures formed a plateau, as the labeled cells which were in earlier

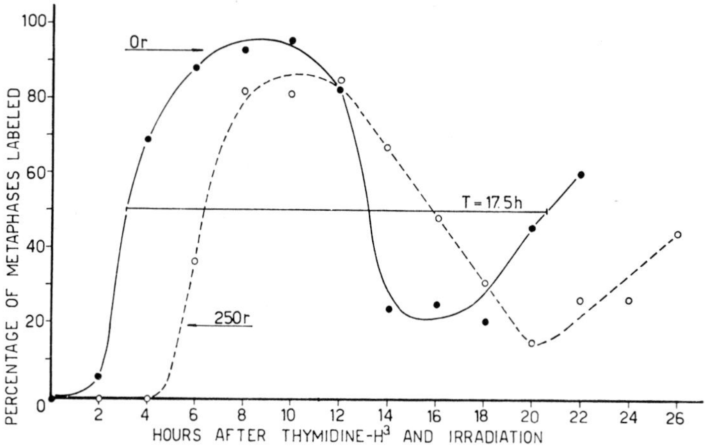

Fig. 2. Frequency of metaphase figures labeled, at various intervals after a 15-min incubation with ^{3}H-thymidine. Chinese hamster cells cultured *in vitro*. Continuous line, control cultures. Broken line, cultures irradiated with 250 R of X-rays immediately after labeling. In the unirradiated population, the average time-parameters of the cell cycle are as follows: G_1, including anaphase and telophase, about 4.5 hr, S about 10 hr, G_2 until metaphase about 3 hr. Irradiation with 250 R has caused a reversible mitotic lag in G_2 of the progression of the cells through the cycle, of about 3 hr, with the consequent lengthening of G_2 from 3 to 6 hr. (From Monesi et al.)

intervals of the phase of synthesis, at the time of labeling, moved into metaphase, and then dropped to zero or almost to zero, as the unlabeled cells in G_1 came to the metaphase stage. As the labeled cells proceeded through the subsequent cycle into the second metaphase after labeling, a second rise of frequency of labeled metaphase figures appeared. The average generation time ($G_1 + S + G_2 + M$) is estimated as the interval between the 50 per cent points on two successive ascending curves. The average duration of the period for DNA replication (S) may be estimated by any one of the following three methods:

(a) By multiplying the frequency of cells labeled after a short thymidine pulse (time zero) by the average generation time. This method of determination is based on the criterion that in an asynchronous cell population growing exponentially, the proportion of cells which become labeled after a very short contact with ^{3}H-thymidine is a direct measure of the fraction of the cell cycle during which DNA is synthesized. This concept, however, is valid only when the cell population is homogeneous and all cells divide (Monesi 1962). This method of determining the duration of the S period has recently been criticized by Cleaver (1965) on theoretical grounds.

(b) By determining the time required for the cell population to become 100 per cent labeled in the continuous presence of ^{3}H-thymidine. This time is a measure of the interval between the end of the S phase and the onset of DNA synthesis of the next cycle, and includes therefore the length of G_2, M and G_1. If this time is subtracted from the generation time, the duration of the S period is obtained.

(c) By measuring the interval between the 50 per cent points on the ascending and descending curve of frequency of labeled metaphase figures (Fig. 2). This last method is that most frequently used to estimate the duration of the S period.

The average duration of the G_1 interval is estimated by subtracting the sum of the two intervals G_2 and S from the average generation time. With this method of determination, the G_1 interval thus includes anaphase, telophase and the portion of interphase preceding DNA synthesis.

The duration of the true pre-synthetic interphase and post-synthetic interphase may be estimated by computing the duration of the various phases of mitosis from the mitotic index and the generation time, and subtracting these values from the lengths of G_1 and G_2 as estimated above.

In the cell population shown in Fig. 2, G_1 lasts, on the average, about 4.5 hr, S 10 hr and G_2 3 hr.

The slopes of the upward and downward portions of the curve of frequency of labeled mitotic figures (Fig. 2) indicate the variability between cells in the duration of the G_2 and S periods, respectively. If the ascending curve rises rapidly, there is little variability in the post-synthetic period; if the curve rises slowly, cells take different times to proceed from the end of DNA synthesis into mitosis. Accordingly, if the descending curve is symmetrical with the ascending one, there is little or no variability in the period for DNA synthesis; if the curve is asymmetrical, cells take different times to complete the synthesis of DNA.

(b) *Constancy of duration of S and G_2 periods*

The length of the generation time varies considerably in mammalian cells depending on the cell type and, within the same cell population, on the function and conditions of the cells. The evidence available shows that in a given cell population the duration of the S and G_2 periods is little affected by the physiological or environmental conditions of the cells, and may be considered as a constant characteristic of the cell type. Moreover, there is also general evidence that, with a few exceptions, the length of the S and G_2 periods is of the same order of magnitude in different mammalian cell types, whether growing *in vitro* or *in vivo* (see discussion in: Defendi and Manson; Cameron; Monesi 1967). For most cell types thus far investigated, the duration of the DNA synthesis period is between 6 and 10 hr, with most of the values distributed around 7–8 hr, and that of the G_2 period about 2 to 5 hr (Painter and Drew; Quastler and Sherman; Mendelsohn et al.; Stanners and Till; Defendi and Manson; Cameron; Monesi et al. 1967). Apart from the cases discussed below, the only apparent exceptions to this generalization are: (1) the ear epidermis of the mouse with an average synthetic period of 30 hr (Sherman et al.), (2) a special class of cells of the epidermis of the mouse which remain in G_2 for an indefinite period of time acting as a reservoir of cells immediately ready to undergo mitosis (Gelfant 1962, 1966), and (3) the cells of the mammary gland of the mouse which exhibit an S period ranging from 9 to about 30 hr (Bresciani).

Unlike the cells of higher organisms, in many bacteria (Schaechter et al.; Abbo and

Pardee) and in the synchronous yeast cultures (Mitchison 1966), DNA synthesis is a continuous process through the cycle with no measurable G_1 and G_2 periods. The cell cycle has been analyzed also in some protozoa and insects. For instance, in the macronucleus of the protozoan *Euplotes eurystomus* DNA synthesis lasts about 8 hr, is preceded by a G_1 period of about 4 hr and ends just before macronuclear division without measurable G_2 period (Prescott 1966). In *Tetrahymena pyriformis*, the S period is about 40 to 60 min, and the G_1 and G_2 periods vary between 40 and 100 min, depending on the medium and temperature of incubation (Cameron and Nachtwey). In grasshopper neuroblasts, DNA synthesis is continuous from telophase to prophase with no measurable G_1 or G_2 (Gaulden).

In contrast to the S and G_2 periods, the duration of the G_1 period is affected to a great extent by physiological or environmental factors, and varies considerably among different cell types and it also varies within the same cell population (from 3–4 hr to a few days), thus accounting for the differences of the generation time encountered within a given cell population and in different cell types (Mendelsohn et al.; Sherman et al.; Defendi and Manson; Tobey et al. 1967). For instance, in mammary tumors of the mouse the G_1 period varies from a few hours up to 3 days (Mendelsohn et al.). The very long pre-synthetic interval, found in tumor cells (Mendelsohn et al.) and in the stem cells of the epidermis (Sherman et al.), of the testis (Monesi 1962) and of the bone marrow (Lajtha), is now preferentially referred to as G_0 stage, as opposed to the true G_1 stage which is a period of intense metabolic activity of preparation to the replication of DNA and cell division.

The length of the S and G_2 periods is not apparently related to chromosome ploidy in mammalian cells cultured *in vitro*. We have observed that in two lines of Chinese hamster cells cultured *in vitro* (a diploid with 22 chromosomes and a tetraploid with 44 chromosomes and a double amount of DNA per cell) the time parameters of the cell cycle are essentially identical (G_1 about 4.5 hr; S about 8 hr and G_2 about 3 hr) (Monesi and Zito Bignami, unpublished). This implies that the rate of DNA synthesis per cell is twice as high in the tetraploid clone. In plants, the S period of root meristem cells of several species has been shown to be related to the amount of DNA per cell (Van 't Hof 1965), but the length of the S period is apparently the same in diploid and colchicin-induced tetraploid cells within a given tissue (Van 't Hof 1966).

(c) *Change of duration of the S period during differentiation*

Apart from the cases mentioned above (ear epidermis and mammary gland of the mouse), there are a few exceptions to the principle of the constancy of the period of DNA synthesis. These exceptions may, however, be explained on the basis that the altered S phase results from a process of cell differentiation.

Monesi (1962) has observed that in spermatogonia of the mouse the process of differentiation from the stem cell (type AI spermatogonium) to the mature (type B) spermatogonium is characterized by a progressive lengthening of the S period, from 7 to 14.5 hr, and a parallel shortening of the G_2 and prophase period, from 14 to

4.5 hr. The total duration of the cell cycle (27 to 30.5 hr) and that of the G_1 period (6.5 to 9.5 hr) remains approximately constant. Similar findings have been obtained more recently in other mammals (Hilscher 1967; Hochereau 1967). This progressive increase of the S period during differentiation of the spermatogonia may possibly be related to the progressive condensation of the chromosomes which characterizes the process of development of spermatogonia in most animal species (Monesi 1964, 1967). It has indeed been shown that in many cases the condensed chromosomal segments (heterochromatin) complete DNA replication after the dispersed chromatin (euchromatin) (Lima-de-Faria; Lima-de-Faria and Jaworska).

Bresciani has observed that the duration of the period of DNA synthesis in the alveolar cells of the mammary gland of the mouse, which in normal conditions varies between 14.8 and 27.6 hr with 20.1 hr as an average, diminishes to 9.5–11.9 hr following treatment for 3–4 days with 17-β-estradiol and progesterone.

A few observations appear to indicate that the period of DNA synthesis is shorter in embryonic cells, where the chromosomes are less condensed than in adult tissues. For instance, in male and female pronuclei of rabbit eggs the S period is 3–4 hr, followed by a long G_2 period of 10–12 hr (Szollosi). In the neural tube of the 10-day mouse embryo the S period is 4 hr, with a G_2 period (until metaphase) of 1.5 hr and a G_1 period of about 3 hr (Kaufman). The S period is 5 hr in the 6-day chick embryo (Fujita).

(d) *Asynchrony of DNA replication in cells of higher organisms*

The cell-specificity and constancy of the duration of the S period depends probably on the fact that, in most cell systems thus far investigated, the process of DNA replication in the various chromosomal loci of the complement follows a well defined temporal sequence which is specific of the cell type.

I shall only summarize the basic principles of the asynchrony of DNA replication, since this problem is discussed in Lima-de-Faria's chapter in this book. The main conclusions that can be drawn from the papers published on this subject are the following.

(1) The replication of DNA is a typical asynchronous process in most organisms and cell types thus far investigated. The asynchrony consists in the fact that different chromosomes of the complement and different loci within the same chromosome synthesize their DNA at different intervals during the cell S period, following a well defined and regular temporal sequence which is specific of the cell type, suggesting the existence of a genetic control of the sequence of replication.

(2) The sequence of replication is probably correlated with the genetic constitution of the chromosomal loci. For instance, the heterochromatic sex chromosomes, and often also the heteropycnotic segments of some autosomes, have repeatedly been demonstrated to complete DNA replication after the euchromatic chromosomes. As a general rule, those chromosomes or chromosome parts which are heteropycnotic during interphase exhibit a late DNA-replication pattern and genetic inactivity. The

typical example is that concerning one of the two X-chromosomes of the female cells in most mammalian species (see also as review articles: Sonneborn; Brown; Monesi 1967; Lima-de-Faria and Jaworska).

(3) The length of the period that the cell spends in the phase of synthesis depends to a large extent on the asynchrony of replication; in other words, the duration of the S period results from the sum of the times that the individual asynchronous chromosomal loci take to duplicate their DNA. A a result of the asynchrony of DNA replication between chromosomes, the period of synthesis for specific chromosomes (or for specific portions of a chromosome) may be only a fraction of the total S period of the cell, and the G_2 period may begin at different intervals for different chromosomes.

(4) The pattern of gene replication during the cell cycle seems to be consistent from cell generation to cell generation in mammalian cells in culture (Mueller and Kajiwara 1966a), but a particular sector of a chromosome may change its replication pattern (and presumably its pattern of DNA condensation and rate of transcription) during cellular differentiation. In this context, heterochromatin and euchromatin may be regarded as states, rather than as substances, and their distribution through the complement may vary in the various differentiated tissues (see Brown for review). Since differentiation is at present interpreted in terms of differential inactivation of the individual genes, the implication of the above considerations is that the process of heterochromatization may be considered as a mechanism for differentiation.

(e) *DNA replication and segregation in chromosomes of higher organisms. Stage of chromosome splitting during the cell cycle*

In 1957, Taylor et al. conducted an experiment designed to study the mechanism of replication and segregation of the DNA in chromosomes during division. Root cells of *Vicia faba* were labeled during the S period with ^{3}H-thymidine, and then allowed to develop in the absence of the radioactive precursor until the first, second and third metaphase following the incorporation of the isotope. The authors observed that at the first metaphase after exposure to ^{3}H-thymidine both chromatids were labeled in all chromosomes. At the second metaphase only one sister chromatid was labeled (except at points where an exchange between sister chromatids had occurred), and at the third metaphase approximately only half of the chromosomes was labeled over one chromatid (Fig. 3). These results were interpreted to demonstrate (Fig. 3) that the chromosome in G_1 consists of two complementary subunits of replication which remain intact during successive replications (except at points of sister chromatid exchanges, Taylor 1958a). When the cell enters the S period the two subunits separate and each of them synthesizes a new subunit. Each chromatid would then receive an original or parental subunit (continuous line) and a new subunit (broken line). This mechanism of replication and segregation of the chromosome appears to be identical to the 'semiconservative' model of replication and segregation of the two complementary chains of the DNA molecule in *Escherichia coli* (Meselson and Stahl).

The experiments of Taylor and coworkers have led to controversy (LaCour and

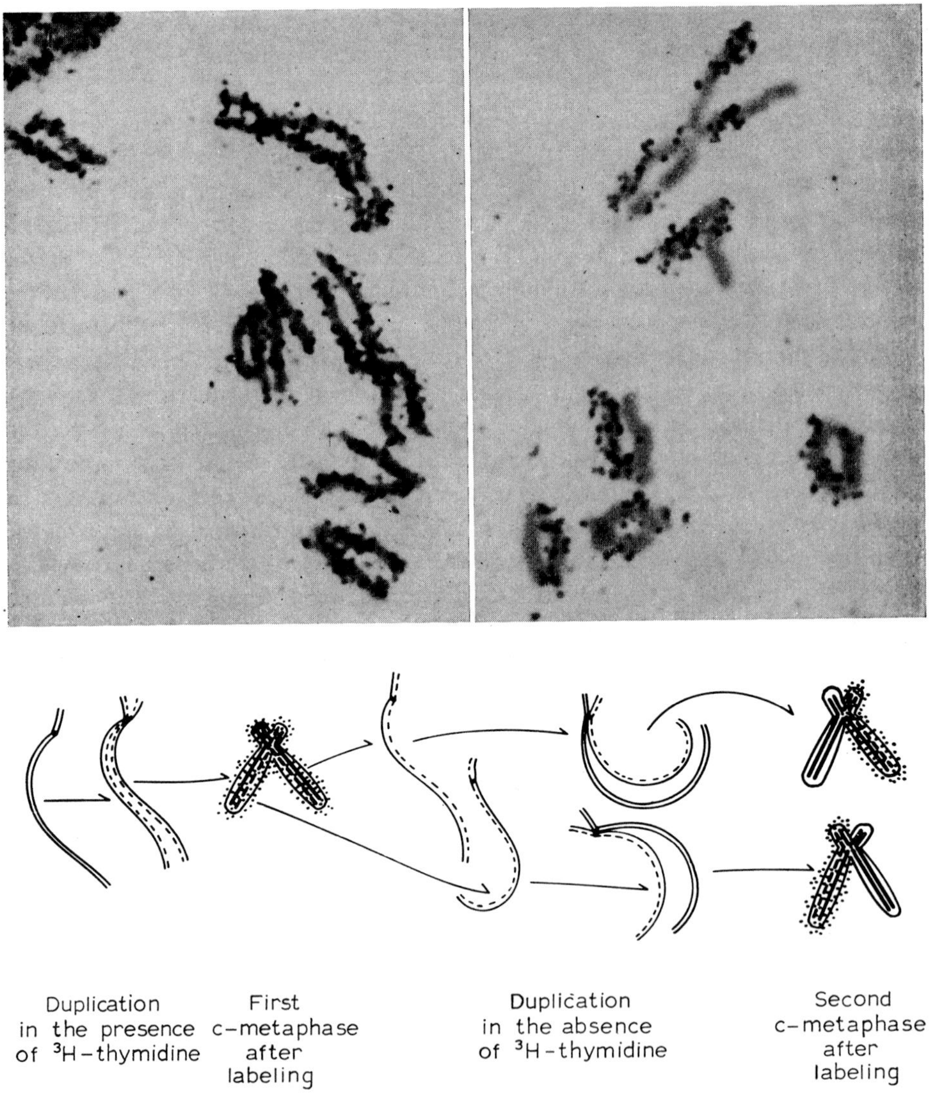

Fig. 3. *Above*, autoradiographs of *Vicia faba* chromosomes at the first (left) and the second (right) metaphase after the interphase incorporation of ^{3}H-thymidine into DNA. Sister chromatid exchanges are visible in second metaphase-chromosomes (figure on the right).

Below, diagrammatic representation of replication and segregation of the subunits of the chromosome during division. Broken line represent labeled subunits and unbroken lines indicate unlabeled subunits. The dots represent silver grains in the autoradiograms. See text for interpretation of the figure. (Taylor et al.)

Pelc 1958, 1959; Woods and Schairer). At present, the conclusion can be drawn that, although frequent exceptions to the pattern of segregation of label described by Taylor have been found by several authors (see below), the experiments of Taylor have received substantial confirmation in various organisms and cell types. These organisms and cell types are the following: *Bellevalia romana* (Taylor 1958a); *Crepis capillaris* (Taylor 1958b), *Allium cepa* and *Tradescantia paludosa* (Taylor 1962), HeLa cells in culture (Taylor 1962), Chinese hamster and human cells in culture (Prescott and Bender 1963a), *Potorus tridactylis*, a marsupial (Walen). Similar findings were also obtained in meiosis (Taylor 1965). From these results it seems to be well established that the mechanism of chromosome replication and segregation is semiconservative in chromosomes of higher organisms, as it is in bacteria.

The semiconservative scheme of replication and segregation of chromosomes may suggest that the chromatid consists of just one DNA molecule, or several DNA molecules joined linearly end-to-end. However, one can easily envisage a model by which a semiconservative segregation could also yield similar results from a multistranded chromosome (Peacock 1963; see also Fig. 4).

Support for the idea that the chromosome of higher organisms consists of several separate units along its length, comes from the general observation in autoradiographic experiments that DNA replication is initiated simultaneously at more than one point along a chromosome at any given time. On the assumption that a DNA molecule replicates sequentially from a given starting point (as it occurs in bacteria), these observations indicate that there are several separate replicating units (called 'replicons' by Jacob and Brenner) distributed along a chromosome, which are possibly joined together by some kind of linkers (see for example the model of Taylor 1963).

Recently, Cairns has calculated from autoradiographic experiments on the DNA from HeLa cells, that the process of DNA duplication moves at a speed of 0.5 μ per min, or less. Assuming that the average human chromosome contains about 3 cm of DNA double helix, and knowing that each round of DNA duplication in human cells takes about 6 hr (Painter and Drew), one can calculate that to duplicate 3 cm of DNA in 6 hr, at least 100 sites of duplication are required, if all sites operate simultaneously at the rate of 0.5 μ min (Cairns). This figure is certainly an underestimate of the true number of replicating sites, since it is based on the assumption that all sites duplicate simultaneously. In fact, using a different approach which takes into account the asynchrony of DNA replication, Painter et al. have estimated that the number of replicating units is 10^3 to 10^4 in HeLa cells.

Several lines of evidence seem to indicate that the chromosome of higher organisms, besides being made up of a longitudinal array of several replicating units arranged lengthwise, is multi-stranded in the sense that it is constituted by more than one such array of replicons, arranged laterally. The evidence in support of this conclusion is as follows: (a) the cytological observation of half-chromatid or even quarter-chromatid structures in many plant chromosomes (Trosko and Wolff; see also discussion in Peacock 1965 and in Wolff 1965); (b) the electron microscopic observation of 100 Å 'elementary fibrils' which are associated laterally in thicker entities in chromosomes of both animals and plants (Kaufmann et al.; Ris 1961, 1966; Sotelo and Wettstein); (c) the evidence from radiation experiments that half-chromatids may act as units of breakage and reunion in prophase cells (see discussion in Peacock 1965 and in Wolff 1965); and finally (d) the demonstration that, at variance with Taylor's results, a significant proportion of chromosomes at the second metaphase after ^{3}H-thymidine labeling display silver grains over homologous regions of sister chromatids in *Vicia faba* (Peacock 1963) and other organisms. This condition was termed 'isolabeling'. Isolabeling is certainly not due to an incorporation from a residual pool of radioactive thymidine occurring during the second interphase after labeling. In many cases it was also possible to exclude that it arose from interchromosomal exchanges, as was suggested by Wolff (1964), or that it was an artifact due to the occurrence of many chromatid exchanges over a small region of the chromosome (Peacock 1965). Peacock (1963, 1965) has stressed the idea that the most probable interpretation of the isolabeling is that the chromatid is made up of at least two DNA 'pieces' arranged laterally, which at the second cycle after incorporation of the isotope, can segregate in two

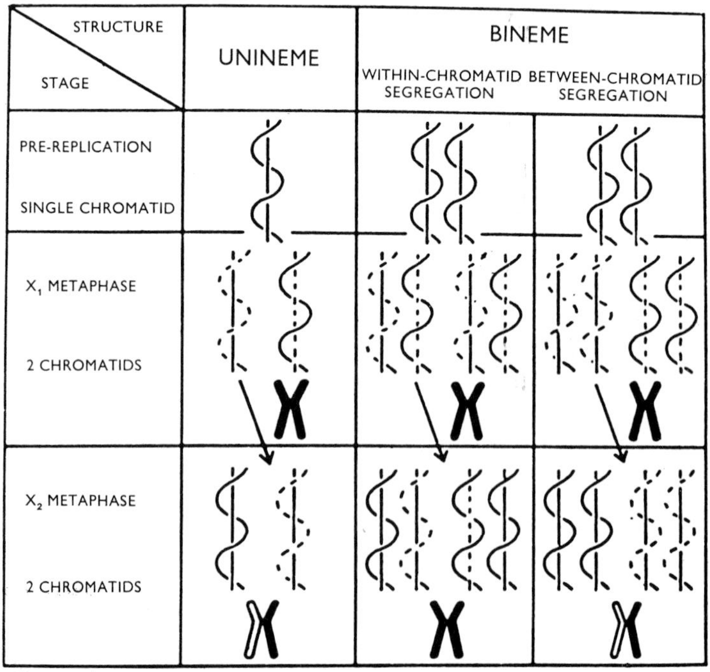

Fig. 4. Possible distribution of DNA helices during mitosis in a mono-stranded (unineme) and in a double-stranded (bineme) model of the chromosome. Two successive cycles of chromosome replication are represented, the first (X_1) in the presence and the second (X_2) in the absence of ^{3}H-thymidine. X_1, X_2 metaphase: first and second metaphase after interphase incorporation of the isotope. The presence of ^{3}H-thymidine is indicated by a broken line in DNA helices and by a blocked line in chromatids. (Peacock 1963.)

possible ways, to give either just one sister chromatid labeled or an isolabeling (Fig. 4).

Recently, by means of experiments combining X-irradiation and ^{3}H-thymidine labeling of the chromosomes during the S phase, several authors (Hsu et al.; Evans and Savage; Wolff and Luippold; Monesi et al. 1967) have shown that the chromosome changes its reponse to radiation from single (chromosome type aberrations) to double (chromatid type aberrations) in late G_1. These results were interpreted to indicate that the chromosome splits into two chromatids in G_1, before DNA synthesis.

The effective doubling of the chromosome before DNA synthesis has been interpreted as being the result of a physical separation of the replicating strands of the chromosome, whatever they are, occurring before the actual process of replication (Evans and Savage; Monesi et al. 1967). Wolff and Luippold put forward the alternative interpretation that the protein moiety of the chromosome duplicates before the DNA moiety, so that the doubling of the chromosome before DNA synthesis would reflect the earlier replication of the protein moiety. This second hypothesis implies that the protein component of the chromosome as well as the DNA contributes to its linear continuity, and that the protein moiety rather than the DNA is the unit of breakage of the chromosome, as it was indeed proposed by Wolff (1959, 1965).

(f) *Regulation of DNA synthesis and control of cell division*

The problem of how DNA synthesis is initiated and regulated and how cell division is controlled, is one of the most interesting problems facing molecular cytology, but in spite of the great attention focussed on this problem very little is known (see chapter by McLaren). Sequential gene activation during the cycle plays probably a major role in the regulation of the reproductive cycle of cells, but this problem has scarcely been studied.

The G_1 period of the cell cycle is certainly most important in this respect, since in this interval the cell must fulfill specific requirements needed for the initiation of replication and for division. The primary importance of the G_1 stage in controlling cell division stems from the general observation that when cells cease proliferative activity, they come to rest in G_1. Exceptions to this generalization are those already reported, viz., the cells of the epidermis in the mouse (Gelfant 1962, 1966), and the apical cells of the root of *Marsilea strigosa* (D'Amato and Avanzi) which may come to rest in G_2. The fact that the S and G_2 periods, in mammalian cells, have a fairly uniform duration also suggests that, under normal conditions, once DNA synthesis is initiated, it proceeds through and is followed by G_2 and mitosis at a constant rate until the next G_1. The general implication of this concept is that cellular growth cannot be the direct trigger for division, as suggested by Swann (1957), but that this trigger may act further back in the cycle at the time of transition from G_1 to the S phase.

Several hypotheses have been proposed to explain how DNA synthesis is initiated but most of them have proved to be unsatisfactory. For instance, neither the attainment of a critical level of the nucleotide pools in the cell, nor the induction of synthesis of DNA polymerase, can be regarded as controlling mechanisms for the initiation of DNA synthesis, since the nucleotide pools (Stone et al.) and the DNA polymerase activity (Littlefield et al.) have been shown to be present throughout the cell cycle. The role of DNA precursors in controlling DNA synthesis has been reviewed by Lark.

It has been demonstrated in bacteria, protozoa and in animal and plant cells, that the initiation of DNA replication requires the synthesis of specific proteins and RNA. In some bacteria, the inhibition of protein synthesis by amino acid starvation allows DNA replication to be completed in those cells which were synthesizing DNA but prevents the initiation of a new round of replication (Maaløe and Hanawalt; Pritchard and Lark). Similar conclusions were reached by various workers: (a) Stone and Prescott in synchronous cultures of *Tetrahymena pyriformis* utilizing starvation of essential amino acids to prevent protein synthesis; (b) Hotta and Stern (1963a) in microspores of *Lilium longiflorum* with various inhibitory agents, and (c) Baserga et al. in mammalian cell systems studied *in vivo* and Lieberman et al., E.W.Taylor (1965) and Mueller and Kajiwara (1966b) in mammalian cells studied *in vitro* (using actinomycin D, puromycin or p-fluorophenylalanine treatments). All these workers have shown that the maximum effect of depression of DNA synthesis (and subsequent cell division) is obtained when the inhibition is applied during G_1. Once a cell has begun DNA synthesis it becomes relatively insensitive to the inhibitory effect. However, higher doses of puromycin also inhibit the continuation of DNA synthesis (Littlefield and Jacobs; Bloch et al.). This is possibly due to a toxic effect of the drug. Stone and Prescott have reported circumstantial evidence suggesting that the protein involved in the initiation of DNA replication is probably thymidine kinase. They have shown that the activity of this enzyme (and probably of other enzymes concerned with the production of deoxyribonucleoside triphosphate pools) appears at the very beginning of DNA synthesis, remains throughout S, and it disappears when DNA synthesis is finished. This interpretation is in agreement with other reports describing the cyclic appearance of the activity of thymidine kinase in relation to DNA synthesis in other cell systems (Bollum and Potter; Weissman et al.; Mittermayer et al.). Also in support of this idea is the observation that *Tetrahymena* does not take up ^{3}H-thymidine into a soluble pool during G_2, mitosis and G_1, although such a pool exists throughout the division cycle (Stone et al.). On the contrary, in animal cells E.W.Taylor (1965) and Baserga et al. have reported that the inhibition of thymidine kinase and DNA polymerase activities cannot be implicated in the observed depression of DNA synthesis, since in their experiments the activity of these enzymes was not depressed by puromycin or actinomycin treatment. In Baserga's experiments, the sucrose gradient analysis has shown that the RNA class which was most inhibited by very low doses of actinomycin was ribosomal RNA.

In mammalian cells *in vitro* it has also been shown that the inhibition of RNA and protein synthesis during the S period, even though it does not prevent the continuation of DNA synthesis, blocks cell progression to G_2, preventing cell division. These findings suggest that protein synthesis is not needed for the continuation of DNA synthesis, but is required for the completion of cell division (Kishimoto and Lieberman; Arrighi and Hsu; E.W.Taylor 1965; Mueller and Kajiwara 1966b; Tobey et al. 1966; Sisken and Wilkes).

E.W.Taylor (1965) and Kishimoto and Lieberman have concluded, from experiments with actinomycin D, that the synthesis of RNA needed for division is completed about 3 hr before metaphase (i.e., at about the end of S) in mammalian cells in culture. These and other workers (Arrighi and Hsu; Tobey et al. 1966; Sisken and Wilkes) have, however, pointed out, from experiments with inhibitors of protein synthesis, that the synthesis of protein required for division continues after the time of completion of DNA synthesis until a few minutes prior to metaphase in mammalian cells in culture. According to these results the G_2 period is a time when the cell must finally fulfill specific metabolic requirements to sustain division. At variance with these findings are those of Mueller and Kajiwara (1966b), who worked with the metabolic inhibitor p-fluorophenylalanine. They claimed that in HeLa cells in culture the end point for the synthesis of a protein essential for cell division is at about the end of the S period.

3. *RNA and protein synthesis during the cell cycle*

(a) *Cellular sites of RNA synthesis*

Experiments of various kinds have established that the ribonucleic acids are synthesized in the nucleus and then continuously released into the cytoplasm (reviews by Monesi and Crippa, and Mitchison 1966). Most of these experiments do not, however, exclude the possibility that some RNA fraction of low turnover rate might be synthesized independently in the cytoplasm, on the cytoplasmic DNA for instance (discussion in Mitchison 1966). Not all the RNA which is synthesized in the nucleus moves, however, to the cytoplasm. There is evidence that there is a rapidly labeled RNA synthesized in the nucleus which is degraded *in situ*. Harris (1959, 1963) has favored the view that most rapidly labeled RNA is degraded *in situ* and cannot then be regarded as the precursor of the cytoplasmic RNA. Shearer and McCarthy, by means of DNA-RNA hybridization experiments on L mouse cells cultured *in vitro*, have shown that, although cytoplasmic RNA originates in the nucleus, there is a distinct class of nuclear RNA which is degraded within the nucleus without ever entering the cytoplasm; this RNA restricted to the nucleus represents, according to these authors, a product transcribed from a major portion (about 80 per cent) of the genome. This last finding has been interpreted to indicate that the RNAs restricted to the nucleus cannot be concerned solely with the production of nuclear proteins (histones and other chromosomal proteins, proteins of the mitotic apparatus, nucleic acid polymerases, etc.) or of the ribosomal protein, but might possibly be engaged in gene activation and repression. For instance these RNAs could code for specific activating proteins which may act as gene derepressors according to the model proposed by Frenster (1965a, b).

During the last few years, conclusive evidence has been obtained that the nucleolus is the major site of synthesis of ribosomal RNA and that the genes which code for ribosomal RNA are localized in the nucleolar organizing region of the nucleolar chromosomes. This conclusion has been reached through many different experimental approaches: (a) autoradiographic observations (Sirlin 1960, 1962; Fujita and Takamoto; Pelling); (b) studies on actinomycin D inhibition of synthesis of ribosomal RNA (Perry 1962, 1965); (c) microelectrophoretic studies (Edström; Edström et al. 1961; Edström and Gall 1963); (d) electron microscopy and density gradient sedimentation (Birnstiel and Hyde; Birnstiel et al. 1963; Jones 1965; Perry 1965, 1966); (e) DNA–RNA hybridization experiments (McConkey and Hopkins; Perry et al.; Perry 1965; Ritossa and Spiegelman); (f) investigations on the anucleolate mutant of *Xenopus laevis* (Brown and Gurdon; Gurdon and Brown; Wallace and Birnstiel). Some results have suggested that the nucleolus might also be the site of synthesis of transfer RNA or of methylation of transfer RNA (Swift 1962; Birnstiel et al. 1963; Sirlin et al.; Comb and Katz; Ozban et al.), of synthesis of histones (Birnstiel and Flamm; Flamm and Birnstiel 1964b), and of the ribosomal protein (Birnstiel and Hyde).

(b) *Pattern of synthesis of RNA and protein during the cell cycle*

One of the problems of the cell cycle is how the different genes involved in cell division are transcribed during the reproductive cycle. Is there a sequence of gene transcription similar to that found for gene replication and, if so, how is gene transcription temporarily linked to gene duplication? It is apparent that the sequence of gene transcription during the cell division cycle might play a major role in the regulation of the cycle. Recently, it has been shown that in synchronous cultures of some bacteria (Masters et al.) and of the budding yeast (Gorman et al.) the activity of specific enzymes increases in steps, in most cases one step for each cell cycle, and that the position of the step in each cycle remains the same for each enzyme, suggesting that the synthesis of specific protein and the transcription process from the individual genes are ordered in the cycle. Masters et al. have also suggested that the synthesis associated with a particular gene takes place soon after the gene has doubled.

Little information on this problem is available in higher cells, except the evidence of a sudden synthesis of thymidine kinase at the beginning of DNA synthesis (Bollum and Potter; Weissman et al.; Hotta and Stern 1963a; Mittermayer et al.). Klevecz and Ruddle have recently shown that the activity of the enzymes glucose-6-phosphate dehydrogenase and lactate dehydrogenase increases intermittently in synchronous cultures of Chinese hamster cells, with three sharp peaks, during the G_1 phase, midway through the S phase and again in late S.

The rate of RNA and protein synthesis along the cell cycle has been recently studied in many cell systems, often using various synchronization procedures. In cells of higher organisms there are several lines of evidence which indicate that the rate of RNA synthesis increases continuously from G_1 through S into G_2, and then suddenly drops to zero at metaphase to resume again at telophase (Taylor 1960; Prescott and

Bender 1962; Feinendegen and Bond; Seed; Monesi 1964, 1965; Monesi and Crippa; Scharff and Robbins 1965; Crippa; Klevecz and Stubblefield; Showacre et al.). Other authors have shown a more complicated picture with two peaks of incorporation of ^{3}H-uridine in G_1 and G_2 (Kim and Perez). Klevecz and Stubblefield have reported a sudden increase of RNA synthesis at the very beginning of DNA synthesis. It has been shown that the RNA synthesized on the chromosomes during interphase and prophase does not remain associated with the chromosomes throughout division but is suddenly shed to the cytoplasm as the cell enters prometaphase (Taylor 1960; Prescott and Bender 1962; Feinendegen and Bond; Monesi and Crippa; Monesi 1965). A complicating factor which should be taken into account in these experiments, is the possibility of a change of the size of the RNA precursors pool during the cycle. This would affect the intracellular specific activity and thereby the rate of incorporation.

Protein synthesis in the cell follows a general pattern similar to that of RNA. There is, in mammalian cells, a continuous increase in rate during the cycle from G_1 to G_2 (Zetterberg and Killander). Unlike RNA synthesis, however, protein synthesis continues during metaphase and anaphase but at a much lower rate than in interphase and prophase (Taylor 1960; Prescott and Bender 1962; Mattingly; Monesi 1965; Salb and Marcus; Scharff and Robbins 1966). By means of sedimentation analysis and electron microscopy, Scharff and Robbins (1966) have shown that partially synchronized HeLa cells exhibit a complete disaggregation of polyribosomes and a compensatory increase of single ribosomes during metaphase. These workers have pointed out that the breakdown of polyribosomes and the drop in protein synthesis in metaphase cannot be explained solely by the arrest of RNA synthesis during this stage, since messenger RNA from HeLa cells has an average half-life of about 3 to 4 hr (Penman et al.), as compared to the 15 min duration of metaphase. This observation suggests that in metaphase there is a regulatory mechanism for inhibiting protein synthesis. Salb and Marcus (1965) have observed, in partially synchronized HeLa cells, that, while ribosomes from metaphase cells are incapable of supporting the synthesis of polyphenylalanine in the presence of poly-U and supernatant from either interphase or metaphase cells, they become able to do so when trypsin is added to the system. They concluded that ribosomes of mitotic cells are prevented from supporting protein synthesis (and associating in polyribosome complexes) by the presence of a trypsin sensitive substance possibly localized on their surface. Salb and Marcus have speculated that this substance might be a histone, possibly released from the nucleus upon breakdown of the nuclear membrane.

Kasten and Strasser have reported that in synchronized human tumor cells *in vitro* there is a G_1 burst of incorporation of amino acids in nucleoli and a second peak of incorporation of lysine in nucleoli and chromatin, at the end of S. These authors have speculated that the G_1 peak of incorporation might be concerned with the synthesis and accumulation of arginine-rich histones in the nucleolus and the late S peak with the synthesis of lysine-rich protein necessary for triggering mitosis.

Several reports have been published on the pattern of synthesis of chromosomal proteins during the division cycle. These studies have been carried out by labeling cells with ^{3}H-amino acids and observing the distribution of the label on the chromosomes, as interphase and prophase cells reach metaphase. Most of these experiments have shown that, unlike DNA, chromosomal proteins are synthesized throughout the cycle in mammalian cells *in vitro* (Cave; Schneider and Rieke) and in *Vicia faba* root meristem cells (Prensky and Smith). This finding is not in contrast with the growing evidence that histone proteins are synthesized during the S period in association with DNA synthesis, since it is known that chromosomes contain other proteins beside histones. At variance with the above results are those of Bloch et al. These authors have observed in *Allium cepa* root cells, labeled with ^{3}H-lysine and ^{3}H-arginine, that most of the chromosomal protein is synthesized during the S period and during a G_2 interval of short duration. Extraction procedures have indicated that most of the protein labeled during the S period is histone. These authors have also found, contrary to the observations of Prescott and Bender (1963b) and Prensky and Smith, that most of the chromosomal protein is conserved from one division to the next. An interesting feature of chromosomal proteins is that, unlike DNA, they do not appear to be distributed semiconservatively to the chromosomes of daughter cells (Prescott and Bender 1963b; Cave). The pattern of synthesis of the histone protein associated with the DNA in chromosomes of higher organisms is more extensively discussed in a separate paragraph (see below).

The synthesis of DNA, RNA and protein during meiosis has been studied in plants by Hotta and Stern (1963b,c), Stern and Hotta and Hotta et al.; in the mouse by Monesi (1962, 1964, 1965); and in the grasshopper by Henderson and by Muckenthaler.

Unlike in higher cells, in microorganisms, both protein and RNA syntheses continue unaffected through nuclear division (Abbo and Pardee; Mitchison 1963; Gorman et al.; Cummings). This might be expected in view of their lack of condensed chromosomes during division. The pattern of synthesis of RNA, protein and carbohydrate in yeast cells has been extensively studied by Mitchison (1963).

An interesting pattern correlating RNA and protein synthesis with DNA synthesis, during the cell cycle, is that described in the protozoan *Euplotes eurystomus*. In the macronucleus of this protozoan DNA synthesis begins at the tips of the long ribbon-like nucleus and proceeds toward the center in the form of two darkly stainable replicating bands, and terminates when the two bands meet in the center (Gall; Prescott and Kimball). Prescott and Kimball have observed that no RNA synthesis is detectable in the regions of DNA synthesis and that all RNA is eliminated from the nucleus just ahead of the advancing wave of DNA synthesis. In a subsequent paper, Prescott (1966), by using synchronized cultures and both autoradiography and gas flow counter determination of the tritium incorporation, found that in the macronucleus of *Euplotes* ^{3}H-amino acids are incorporated in total protein at a constant rate during G_1 and during S throughout the macronucleus, whereas incorporation into histone protein (acid-soluble fraction) occurs exclusively during the S period, probably in a band fashion like the DNA replication pattern. This last observation indicates that the syntheses of histone and DNA are closely coupled events (see below).

For the differential pattern of RNA synthesis between euchromatin and heterochromatin, see the chapter by Frenster.

(c) *Histone synthesis during interphase and mitosis*

It is well known that histone proteins (as well as other proteins) are present in fixed quantities in chromosomes of higher cells in some association with the DNA. Problems related to histone composition and metabolism, molecular association with the DNA, histone function and distribution in chromosomes are discussed in other chapters of this book.

There have been many attempts to establish the temporal relationship of histone and DNA synthesis. The earlier histochemical demonstration, of parallel increase in staining of DNA with the Feulgen reaction and of histone with alkaline-fast green during interphase, has been interpreted to show that histones are synthesized during the S period simultaneously with the DNA (Alfert; Bloch and Godman). These conclusions were later confirmed using histochemical procedures (Gall; McLeish). They have however been criticized on the ground that the change of the alkaline fast-green staining during the cell cycle might reflect a change of the chemical composition of histone rather than an increase in amount. It has also been pointed out that this reaction reveals only the histone associated with the DNA, leaving open the possibility that histones are synthesized before DNA synthesis and become complexed with the DNA during DNA replication. The observation of a low but appreciable histone synthesis in non-proliferating tissues (see Busch; Chalkley and Maurer) seemed to substantiate the idea that the synthesis of histone may be dissociated from that of the DNA.

Biochemical analysis of histone synthesis in synchronized cells has furnished conflicting evidence. This may reflect the different techniques used for synchronization, the different degrees of synchronization, the various cell systems used and the frequently inadequate means to identify histones. The synthesis of histone has been reported to be dissociated from that of DNA in regenerating rat liver (Irvin et al.; Umana et al.). It has been reported that in regenerating liver, the DNA-histone ratio fluctuates considerably during the cell cycle (Irvin et al.; Umana et al.). This has been interpreted as a mechanism for the initiation and termination of DNA synthesis (Irvin et al.). Umana et al. have found that the ratio of histone to DNA is higher for non-dividing cells (close to 2) than for dividing cells (close to 1), and that in regenerating liver there are two classes of histones, a stable one, which is presumably wound around the major groove of the DNA double helix, and a metabolically labile class, which is presumably more loosely associated with the DNA molecule. In mouse fibroblasts partially synchronized with 5-fluorodeoxyuridine, it was reported that some histone synthesis begins prior to DNA synthesis, although most of the histone is synthesized concurrently with the DNA (Littlefield and Jacobs). In other studies with HeLa cells synchronized with thymidine or amethopterin, synthesis of histones was detected throughout interphase but markedly increased during DNA replication (Spalding et al).

Recently a few papers have appeared which strengthen the early idea that histones are synthesized simultaneously with the DNA. Robbins and Borun studied HeLa cells synchronized by the shaking procedure. They used a quantitative analysis of ^{3}H-lysine and ^{3}H-arginine incorporation into the various acrylamide gel electrophoresis fractions of the extracted acid soluble material, and compared the incorporation curve with the ^{3}H-thymidine incorporation curve. By this method, they were able to show that the incorporation of lysine into the electrophoretic fractions characteristic of histone coincides with the initiation of DNA synthesis and is maintained through late S, but is absent in G_1. Little or no incorporation of ^{3}H-tryptophan was detected in these 'histone' fractions.

In the macronucleus of the protozoan *Euplotes eurystomus* incorporation of ^{3}H-amino acids into histone protein (acid soluble fraction) occurs exclusively during the S period concomitantly with the synthesis of DNA, while the incorporation in total protein takes place throughout the cell cycle (Prescott 1966). In these studies it was also possible to exclude the possibility that the histone labeling in the macronucleus could arise from a synthesis occurring during other phases of the cell cycle, followed by the association of the newly synthesized histone with the DNA during the S phase. Bloch et al., by determining with autoradiography the time interval between the incorporation of ^{3}H-lysine and ^{3}H-arginine in interphase cells and the appearance of labeling in mitotic figures, have reported that in *Allium cepa* root cells, most of the chromosomal protein is synthesized during the period of DNA synthesis and during an additional period of short duration in G_2. Extraction procedures have indicated that most of the protein labeled during the S period is histone. Similar evidence of association of DNA and histone syntheses was obtained with biochemical procedures by Niehaus and Barnum in the regenerating rat liver.

Although DNA and histone syntheses seem to be associated events in the cell cycle, it seems that the two processes are not necessarily dependent on each other. Histone synthesis can proceed at a normal rate under conditions in which the synthesis of DNA is completely blocked by the DNA inhibitor 5-fluorodeoxyuridine or by other treatments (Flamm and Birnstiel 1964a; Ontko and Moorehead; Bloch et al.). Conversely, as mentioned above, the inhibition of protein synthesis by low doses of puromycin or actinomycin has little or no effect on the progression of DNA synthesis once this has begun (Baserga et al.; E.W.Taylor 1965; Mueller and Kajiwara 1966b), with the possible exception of *Allium cepa* (Bloch et al.).

During differentiation of the germ line it is a well known phenomenon that the two processes of DNA and histone synthesis may be uncoupled. In many animal species arginine-rich histones have repeatedly been demonstrated to be synthesized in late spermatids without a concurrent synthesis of DNA (Bloch and Hew; Bloch 1962; Das et al. 1964a, b; Monesi 1965). Conversely, in some plants (*Lilium longiflorum* and

Tulipa gesneriana) the meiotic histone, which is synthesized during the premeiotic interphase, persists through meiosis, microsporogenesis and pollen maturation; during this interval two DNA replications take place which are not accompanied by histone synthesis (Sheridan and Stern).

The cellular site of histone synthesis during mitosis and meiosis is still an open question. Conflicting evidence has been reported. Reid and Cole have described histone synthesis in isolated calf thymus nuclei, whereas Robbins and Borun have presented evidence that in HeLa cells histones are synthesized in the cytoplasm on small polysomes and soon after transferred to the nucleus. Bloch and Brack have also favored the idea based on circumstantial evidence, that in grasshopper spermatids the arginine-rich histone is synthesized in the cytoplasm and then transferred to the nucleus where it combines with the DNA, thus becoming detectable with the alkaline-fast green reaction. Monesi (1965) has, on the contrary, favored the opposite view that an intranuclear synthesis of the arginine-rich histone takes place in mouse spermatids. Birnstiel and Flamm, on the basis of the kinetics of amino acid incorporation into protein of cytoplasmic and nuclear fractions, have reported that in cells of pea seedlings histones are synthesized in the nucleolus and then transferred to the chromosomes.

(d) *Nucleocytoplasmic interactions during the cell cycle*

Since the pioneer work of Caspersson, which indicated that the cell nucleus is the controlling center of cellular activities, the role of the nucleus in the regulation of protein synthesis has been well established.

There is, however, growing evidence that the cytoplasm might also influence the activity of the nucleus, through the synthesis and transfer into the nucleus of specific proteins which are thought to mediate feedback information from the cytoplasm to the nucleus. This work has been carried out mainly in amoeba using labeling and nuclear transplantation experiments (Byers et al.; Goldstein; Goldstein and Prescott), but recently it has been extended to mammalian cells by Zetterberg.

Prescott and Bender (1963b) have reported that in *Amoeba proteus* nucleus-specific proteins are released to the cytoplasm during mitosis and then rapidly return to the nucleus in late telophase and early interphase. Nuclei labeled with ^{3}H-amino acids were transplanted to unlabeled cells and then an analysis was made of distribution of the label between the grafted nucleus, the host cell nucleus and the host cytoplasm (Byers et al.; Goldstein; Goldstein and Prescott). These authors have demonstrated by this technique the presence of two fractions of nuclear proteins in *Amoeba proteus*. One fraction, which accounts for about 40 per cent of the proteins in the nucleus, migrates continuously back and forth between the nucleus and the cytoplasm (rapidly migrating proteins, RMP). The other fraction which is about 60 per cent of nuclear proteins is, on the contrary, relatively non-migratory (slow turnover proteins, STP). Both these classes of proteins are synthesized, at least in part, in the cytoplasm. Since STP show a greater solubility in acetic acid than RMP, histones probably belong to the

STP class together with structural proteins of the nucleus. Recently, similar findings were obtained by Zetterberg in mouse fibroblasts cultured *in vitro*. In these cells most of protein synthesis occurs in the cytoplasm. During interphase, and mainly during the S phase, a migration (and an accumulation) of labeled proteins takes place from the site of synthesis in the cytoplasm to the nucleus.

References

ABBO, F.E. and A.B. PARDEE: Synthesis of macromolecules in synchronously dividing bacteria. Biochim. Biophys. Acta 39 (1960) 478.

ALFERT, M.: Quantitative cytochemical studies on patterns of nuclear growth. In: Fine structure of cells. New York, Interscience Publ. Inc. (1955) 137.

ARRIGHI, F.E. and T.C. HSU: Experimental alteration of metaphase chromosome morphology. Effect of actinomycin D. Exptl. Cell Res. 39 (1965) 305.

BASERGA, R., R.D. ESTENSEN and R.O. PETERSEN: Inhibition of DNA synthesis in Ehrlich ascites cells by actinomycin D II. The presynthetic block in the cell cycle. Proc. Natl. Acad. Sci. U.S. 54 (1965) 1411.

BIRNSTIEL, M.L., M.I.H. CHIPCHASE and B.B. HYDE: The nucleolus, a source of ribosomes. Biochim. Biophys. Acta 76 (1963) 454.

BIRNSTIEL, M.L. and W.G. FLAMM: Intranuclear site of histone synthesis. Science 145 (1964) 1435.

BIRNSTIEL, M.L., E. FLEISSNER and E. BOREK: Nucleolus: a center of RNA methylation. Science 142 (1963) 1577.

BIRNSTIEL, M.L. and B.B. HYDE: Protein synthesis by isolated pea nucleoli. J. Cell Biol. 18 (1963) 41.

BLOCH, D.P.: Changes in the desoxyribonucleoprotein complex during the cell cycle. In: S.L. Palay, ed.: Frontiers in cytology. New Haven, Yale University Press (1958) 113.

BLOCH, D.P.: Symposium: synthetic processes in the cell nucleus I. Histone synthesis in non-replicating chromosomes. J. Histochem. Cytochem. 10 (1962) 137.

BLOCH, D.P. and S.D. BRACK: Evidence for the cytoplasmic synthesis of nuclear histone during spermiogenesis in the grasshopper *Chortophaga viridifasciata* (De Geer). J. Cell Biol. 22 (1964) 327.

BLOCH, D.P. and G.C. GODMAN: A microphotometric study of the synthesis of desoxyribonucleic acid and nuclear histone. J. Biophys. Biochem. Cytol. 1 (1955) 17.

BLOCH, D.P. and H.Y.C. HEW: Schedule of spermatogenesis in the pulmonate snail *Helix aspersa*, with special reference to histone transition. J. Biophys. Biochem. Cytol. 7 (1960) 515.

BLOCH, D.P., R.A. MACQUIGG, S.D. BRACK and J.-R. WU: The syntheses of deoxyribonucleic acid and histone in the onion root meristem. J. Cell Biol. 33 (1967) 451.

BOLLUM, F.J. and V.R. POTTER: Nucleic acid metabolism in regenerating rat liver VI. Soluble enzymes which convert thymidine to thymidine phosphates and DNA. Cancer Res. 19 (1959) 561.

BRESCIANI, F.: Effect of ovarian hormones on duration of DNA synthesis in cells of the C3H mouse mammary gland. Exptl. Cell Res. 38 (1965) 13.

BROWN, D.D. and J.B. GURDON: Absence of ribosomal RNA synthesis in the anucleolate mutant of *Xenopus laevis*. Proc. Natl. Acad. Sci. U.S. 51 (1964) 139.

BROWN, S.W.: Heterochromatin. Science 151 (1966) 417.

BULLOUGH, W.S.: The energy relationships of mitotic activity. Biol. Rev. Cambridge Phil. Soc. 27 (1952) 133.

BUSCH, H.: Histones and other nuclear proteins. New York, Academic Press (1965).

BYERS, T.J., D.B. PLATT and L. GOLDSTEIN: The cytonucleoproteins of Amoebae I. Some chemical properties and intracellular distribution. J. Cell Biol. 19 (1963) 453.

CAIRNS, J.: Autoradiography of HeLa cell DNA. J. Mol. Biol. 15 (1966) 372.

CAMERON, I.L.: Is the duration of DNA synthesis in somatic cells of mammals and birds a constant? J. Cell Biol. 20 (1964) 185.

CAMERON, I.L. and D.S. NACHTWEY: DNA synthesis in relation to cell division in *Tetrahymena pyriformis*. Exptl. Cell Res. 46 (1967) 385.

CASPERSSON, T.: Cell growth and cell function. New York, Norton (1950).

CAVE, MAC D.: Incorporation of tritium-labeled thymidine and lysine into chromosomes of cultured human leukocytes. J. Cell Biol. 29 (1966) 209.

CHALKLEY, G.R. and H.R. MAURER: Turnover of template bound histone. Proc. Natl. Acad. Sci. U.S. 54 (1966) 498.

CLEAVER, J.E.: The relationship between the duration of the S phase and the fraction of cells which incorporate ^{3}H-thymidine during exponential growth. Exptl. Cell Res. 39 (1965) 697.

COMB, D.G. and S. KATZ: Studies on the biosynthesis and methylation of transfer RNA. J. Mol. Biol. 8 (1964) 790.

CRIPPA, M.: The rate of ribonucleic acid synthesis during the cell cycle. Exptl. Cell Res. 42 (1966) 371.

CRONKITE, E.P., V.P. BOND, T.M. FLIEDNER and J.R. RUBINI: The use of tritiated thymidine in the study of DNA synthesis and cell turnover in hemopoietic tissues. Lab. Invest. 8 (1959) 263.

CUMMINGS, D.J.: Macromolecular synthesis during synchronous growth of *E. coli* B/r. Biochim. Biophys. Acta 95 (1965) 341.

D'AMATO, F. and S. AVANZI: DNA content, DNA synthesis and mitosis in the root apical cells of *Marsilea strigosa*. Caryologia 18 (1965) 383.

DAS, C.C., B.P. KAUFMANN and H. GAY: Histone-protein transition in *Drosophila melanogaster* I. Changes during spermatogenesis. Exptl. Cell Res. 35 (1964a) 507.

DAS, C.C., B.P. KAUFMANN and H. GAY: Autoradiographic evidence of synthesis of an arginine-rich histone during spermiogenesis in *Drosophila melanogaster*. Nature 204 (1964b) 1008.

DEFENDI, V. and L.A. MANSON: Analysis of the life-cycle in mammalian cells. Nature 198 (1963) 359.

EDSTRÖM, J.-E.: Composition of ribonucleic acid from various parts of spider oocytes. J. Biophys. Biochem. Cytol. 8 (1960) 47.

EDSTRÖM, J.-E. and J.G. GALL: The base composition of ribonucleic acid in lampbrush chromosomes, nucleoli, nuclear sap, and cytoplasm of *Triturus* oocytes. J. Cell Biol. 19 (1963) 279.

EDSTRÖM, J.-E., W. GRAMPP and N. SCHOR: The intracellular distribution and hererogeneity of ribonucleic acid in starfish oocytes. J. Biophys. Biochem. Cytol. 11 (1961) 549.

EVANS, H.J. and J.R.K. SAVAGE: The relation between DNA synthesis and chromosome structure as resolved by X-ray damage. J. Cell Biol. 18 (1963) 525.

FEINENDEGEN, L.E. and V.P. BOND: Observations on nuclear RNA during mitosis in human cancer cells in culture (HeLa-S_3), studied with tritiated cytidine. Exptl. Cell Res. 30 (1963) 393.

FLAMM, W.G. and M.L. BIRNSTIEL: Inhibition of DNA replication and its effect on histone synthesis. Exptl. Cell Res. 33 (1964a) 616.

FLAMM, W.G. and M.L. BIRNSTIEL: Studies on the metabolism of nuclear basic proteins. In: J. Bonner and P. Ts'o, eds.: The nucleohistones. San Francisco, Holden-Day Inc. (1964b) 230.

FRENSTER, J.H.: Nuclear polyanions as derepressors of synthesis of ribonucleic acid. Nature 206 (1965a) 680.

FRENSTER, J.H.: A model of specific derepression within interphase chromatin. Nature 206 (1965b) 1269.

FRIEDKIN, M.D., D. TILSON and D. ROBERTS: Studies on deoxyribonucleic acid biosynthesis in embryonic tissues with thymidine-C^{14}. J. Biol. Chem. 220 (1956) 627.

FUJITA, S.: Kinetics of cellular proliferation. Exptl. Cell Res. 28 (1962) 52.

FUJITA, S. and K. TAKAMOTO: Synthesis of messenger RNA on the polytene chromosomes of dipteran salivary cells. Nature 200 (1963) 494.

GALL, J.G.: Macronuclear duplication in the ciliated protozoan *Euplotes*. J. Biophys. Biochem. Cytol. 5 (1959) 295.

GAULDEN, M.E.: DNA synthesis and X-ray effects at different mitotic stages in grasshopper neuroblasts. Genetics 41 (1956) 645.

GELFANT, S.: Initiation of mitosis in relation to the cell division cycle. Exptl. Cell Res. 26 (1962) 395.

GELFANT, S.: Patterns of cell division: the demonstration of discrete cell populations. In: Methods in cell physiology, Vol. II. New York, Academic Press (1966) 359.

GOLDSTEIN, L.: Interchange of protein between nucleus and cytoplasm. In: C.P. Leblond and K.B. Warren, eds.: Symp. Internat. Soc. Cell Biol., Vol. 4: The use of radioautography in investigating protein synthesis. New York, Academic Press (1965) 79.

GOLDSTEIN, L. and D.M. PRESCOTT: Proteins in nucleocytoplasmic interactions I. The fundamental characteristics of the rapidly migrating proteins and the slow turnover proteins of the *Amoeba proteus* nucleus. J. Cell Biol. 33 (1967) 637.

GORMAN, J., P. TAURO, M. LABERGE and H. HALVORSON: Timing of enzyme synthesis during synchronous division in yeast. Biochem. Biophys. Res. Commun. 15 (1964) 43.

GURDON, J.B. and D.D. BROWN: Cytoplasmic regulation of RNA synthesis and nucleolus formation in developing embryos of *Xenopus laevis*. J. Mol. Biol. 12 (1965) 27.

HARRIS, H.: Turnover of nuclear and cytoplasmic ribonucleic acid in two types of animal cells, with some further observations on the nucleolus. Biochem. J. 73 (1959) 362.

HARRIS, H.: Rapidly labelled ribonucleic acid in the cell nucleus. Nature 198 (1963) 184.

HENDERSON, S.A.: RNA synthesis during male meiosis and spermiogenesis. Chromosoma 15 (1964) 345.

HILSCHER, W.: DNA synthesis, proliferation and regeneration of the spermatogonia in the rat. Arch. Anat. Micr. 56, Suppl. (1967) 75.

HOCHEREAU, M.T.: Synthèse de l'ADN; multiplication et renouvellement des spermatogonies chez le taureau. Arch. Anat. Micr. 56, Suppl. (1967) 85.

HOTTA, Y., M. ITO and H. STERN: Synthesis of DNA during meiosis. Proc. Natl. Acad. Sci. U.S. 56 (1966) 1184.

HOTTA, Y. and H. STERN: Molecular facets of mitotic regulation I. Synthesis of thymidine kinase. Proc. Natl. Acad. Sci. U.S. 49 (1963a) 648.

HOTTA, Y. and H. STERN: Inhibition of protein synthesis during meiosis and its bearing on intracellular regulation. J. Cell Biol. 16 (1963b) 259.

HOTTA, Y. and H. STERN: Synthesis of messenger-like ribonucleic acid and protein during meiosis in isolated cells of *Trillium erectum*. J. Cell Biol. 19 (1963c) 45.

HOWARD, A. and S.R. PELC: Nuclear incorporation of P^{32} as demonstrated by autoradiographs. Exptl. Cell Res. 2 (1951) 178.

HOWARD, A. and S.R. PELC: Synthesis of deoxyribonucleic acid in normal and irradiated cells and its relation to chromosome breakage. Heredity 6 Suppl. (1953) 261.

HSU, T.C., W.C. DEWEY and R.M. HUMPHREY: Radiosensitivity of cells of Chinese hamster in vitro in relation to the cell cycle. Exptl. Cell Res. 27 (1962) 441.

HUGHES, L., V.P. BOND, G. BRECHER, E.P. CRONKITE, R.B. PAINTER, H. QUASTLER and F.G. SHERMAN: Cellular proliferation in the mouse as revealed by autoradiography with tritiated thymidine. Proc. Natl. Acad. Sci. U.S. 44 (1958) 476.

IRVIN, J.L., D.J. HOLBROOK JR., J.H. EVANS, H.C. MC ALLISTER and E.P. STILES: Possible role of histones in regulation of nucleic acid synthesis. Exptl. Cell Res. Suppl. 9 (1963) 359.

JACOB, F. and S. BRENNER: Sur la régulation de la synthèse du DNA chez les bactéries: l'hypothèse du réplicon. Compt. Rend. 256 (1963) 298.

JONES, K.W.: The role of the nucleolus in the formation of ribosomes. J. Ultrastruct. Res. 13 (1965) 257.

KASTEN, F.H. and F.F. STRASSER: Amino acid incorporation patterns during the cell cycle of synchronized human tumor cells. In: Internat. symp. the nucleolus, its structure and function. Natl. Cancer Inst. Monograph 23 (1966) 353.

KAUFFMAN, S.L.: An autoradiographic study of the generation cycle in the ten-day mouse embryo neural tube. Exptl. Cell Res. 42 (1966) 67.

KAUFMANN, B.P., H.GAY and M.R.MC DONALD: Organizational patterns within chromosomes. Intern. Rev. Cytol. 9 (1960) 77.

KIM, J.H. and A.G.PEREZ: Ribonucleic acid synthesis in synchronously dividing populations of HeLa cells. Nature 207 (1965) 974.

KISHIMOTO, S. and I.LIEBERMAN: Synthesis of RNA and protein required for the mitosis of mammalian cells. Exptl. Cell Res. 36 (1964) 92.

KLEVECZ, R.R. and F.H.RUDDLE: Cyclic changes in synchronized mammalian cell cultures. Science 159 (1968) 634.

KLEVECZ, R.F. and E.STUBBLEFIELD: RNA synthesis in relation to DNA replication in synchronized Chinese hamster cell cultures. J. Exptl. Zool. 165 (1967) 259.

LA COUR, L.F. and S.R.PELC: Effect of colchicine on the utilization of labelled thymidine during chromosomal reproduction. Nature 182 (1958) 506.

LA COUR, L.F. and S.R.PELC: Effect of colchicine on the utilization of thymidine labelled with tritium during chromosomal reproduction. Nature 183 (1959) 1455.

LAJTHA, L.G.: Cytokinetics and regulation of progenitor cells. J. Cell Physiol. 67, Suppl. 1 (1966) 133.

LARK, K.G.: Cellular control of DNA biosynthesis. In: J.H.Taylor, ed.: Molecular genetics. New York, Academic Press (1963) 153.

LIEBERMAN, I., R.ABRAMS and P.OVE: Changes in the metabolism of ribonucleic acid preceding the synthesis of deoxyribonucleic acid in mammalian cells cultured from the animal. J. Biol. Chem. 238 (1963) 2141.

LIMA-DE-FARIA, A.: Progress in tritium autoradiography. In: J.A.V.Butler, H.E.Huxley and R.E Zirkle, eds.: Progress in biophysics and biophysical chemistry, Vol. 12. Oxford, Pergamon Press (1962) 282.

LIMA-DE-FARIA, A. and H.JAWORSKA: Late DNA synthesis in heterochromatin. Nature 217 (1968) 138.

LITTLEFIELD, J.W. and P.S.JACOBS: The relation between DNA and protein synthesis in mouse fibroblasts. Biochim. Biophys. Acta 108 (1965) 652.

LITTLEFIELD, J.W., A.P.MCGOVERN and K.B.MARGESON: Changes in the distribution of polymerase activity during DNA synthesis in mouse fibroblasts. Proc. Natl. Acad. Sci. U.S. 49 (1963) 102.

MAALØE, O. and P.C.HANAWALT: Thymine deficiency and the normal DNA replication cycle I. J. Mol. Biol. 3 (1961) 144.

MASTERS, M., P.L.KUEMPEL and A.B.PARDEE: Enzyme synthesis in synchronous cultures of bacteria. Biochem. Biophys. Res. Commun. 15 (1964) 38.

MATTINGLY, SISTER A.: Nuclear protein synthesis in *Vicia faba*. Exptl. Cell Res. 29 (1963) 314.

MAZIA, D.: Biochemistry of the dividing cell. Ann. Rev. Biochem. 30 (1961a) 669.

MAZIA, D.: Mitosis and the physiology of cell division. In: J.Brachet and A.E.Mirsky, eds.: The Cell, Vol. 3. New York, Academic Press (1961b) 77.

MCCONKEY, E.H. and J.W.HOPKINS: The relationship of the nucleolus to the synthesis of ribosomal RNA in HeLa cells. Proc. Natl. Acad. Sci. U.S. 51 (1964) 1197.

MCLEISH, J.: Comparative microphotometric studies of DNA and arginine in plant nuclei. Chromosome 10 (1959) 686.

MENDELSOHN, M.L., F.C.DOHAN JR. and H.A.MOORE JR.: Autoradiographic analysis of cell proliferation in spontaneous breast cancer of C3H mouse I. Typical cell cycle and timing of DNA synthesis. J. Natl. Cancer Inst. 25 (1960) 477.

MESELSON, M. and F.W.STAHL: The replication of DNA in *Escherichia coli*. Proc. Natl. Acad. Sci. U.S. 44 (1958) 671.

MIRSKY, A.E. and S.OSAWA: The interphase nucleus. In: J.Brachet and A.E.Mirsky, eds.: The cell, Vol. 2. New York, Academic Press (1961) 677.

MITCHISON, J.M.: The cell cycle of a fission yeast. In: R.J.C.Harris, ed.: Symp. Internat. Soc. Cell Biology, Vol. 2: Cell growth and cell division. New York, Academic Press (1963) 57.

MITCHISON, J.M.: Some functions of the nucleus. Intern. Rev. Cytol. 19 (1966) 97.

MITTERMAYER, C., R.BOSSELMANN and V.BREMERSKOV: Initiation of DNA synthesis in a system of synchronized L-cells: rhythmicity of thymidine kinase activity. European J. Biochem. 4 (1968) 487.

MONESI, V.: Autoradiographic study of DNA synthesis and the cell cycle in spermatogonia and spermatocytes of mouse testis using tritiated thymidine. J. Cell Biol. 14 (1962) 1.

MONESI, V.: Ribonucleic acid synthesis during mitosis and meiosis in the mouse testis. J. Cell Biol. 22 (1964) 521.

MONESI, V.: Synthetic activities during spermatogenesis in the mouse. RNA and protein. Exptl. Cell Res. 39 (1965) 197.

MONESI, V.: L'autoradiografia con i precursori degli acidi nucleici e delle proteine. Riv. Istochim. Norm. Patol. 13 (1967) 5.

MONESI, V. and M.CRIPPA: Ribonucleic acid transfer from nucleus to cytoplasm during interphase and mitosis in mouse somatic cells cultured in vitro. Z. Zellforsch. Mikroskop. Anat. Abt. Histochem. 62 (1964) 807.

MONESI, V., M.CRIPPA and R.ZITO BIGNAMI: The stage of chromosome duplication in the cell cycle as revealed by X-ray breakage and ^{3}H-thymidine labeling. Chromosoma 21 (1967) 369.

MUCKENTHALER, F.A.: Autoradiographic study of nucleic acid synthesis during spermatogenesis in the grasshopper, *Melanoplus differentialis*. Exptl. Cell Res. 35 (1964) 531.

MUELLER, G.C. and K.KAJIWARA: Early- and late replicating deoxyribonucleic acid complexes in HeLa nuclei. Biochim. Biophys. Acta 114 (1966a) 108.

MUELLER, G.C. and K.KAJIWARA: Actinomycin D and p-fluorophenylalanine, inhibitors of nuclear replication in HeLa cells. Biochim. Biophys. Acta 119 (1966b) 557.

NIEHAUS, W.G. JR. and C.P.BARNUM: Incorporation of radioisotope *in vivo* into ribonucleic acid and histone of a fraction of nuclei preparing for mitosis. Exptl. Cell Res. 39 (1965) 435.

ONTKO, J.A. and W.R.MOOREHEAD: Histone synthesis after inhibition of deoxyribonucleic acid replication. Biochim. Biophys. Acta 91 (1964) 658.

OZBAN, N., C.J.TANDLER and J.L.SIRLIN: Methylation of nucleolar RNA during development of the amphibian oocyte. J. Embryol. Exptl. Morphol. 12 (1964) 373.

PAINTER, R.B. and R.M.DREW: Studies on deoxyribonucleic acid metabolism in human cancer cell culture (HeLa) I. The temporal relationship of deoxyribonucleic acid synthesis to mitosis and turnover time. Lab. Invest. 8 (1959) 278.

PAINTER, R.B., D.A.JERMANY and R.E.RASMUSSEN: A method to determine the number of DNA replicating units in cultured mammalian cells. J. Mol. Biol. 17 (1966) 47.

PATAU, K. and H.SWIFT: The DNA content during mitosis in a root tip of onion. Chromosoma 6 (1953) 149.

PEACOCK, W.J.: Chromosome duplication and structure as determined by autoradiography. Proc. Natl. Acad. Sci. U.S. 49 (1963) 793.

PEACOCK, W.J.: Chromosome replication. In: Internat. Symp. Genes and Chromosomes Structure and Function. Natl. Cancer Inst. Monograph 18 (1965) 101.

PELLING, C.: Ribonukleinsäure-Synthese der Riesenchromosomen. Autoradiographische Untersuchungen an *Chironomus tentans*. Chromosoma 15 (1964) 71.

PENMAN, S., K.SCHERRER, Y.BECKER and J.E.DARNELL: Polyribosomes in normal and poliovirus-infected HeLa cells and their relationship to messenger-RNA. Proc. Natl. Acad. Sci. U.S. 49 (1963) 654.

PERRY, R.P.: The cellular sites of synthesis of ribosomal and 4SRNA. Proc. Natl. Acad. Sci. U.S. 48 (1962) 2179.

PERRY, R.P.: The nucleolus and the synthesis of ribosomes. In: Internat. Symp. Genes and Chromosomes Structure and Function. Natl. Cancer Inst. Monograph 18 (1965) 325.

PERRY, R.P.: On ribosome biogenesis. In: Internat. Symp. The Nucleolus, Its Structure and Function. Natl. Cancer Inst. Monograph 23 (1966) 527.

PERRY, R.P., P.R.SRINIVISAN and D.E.KELLEY: Hybridization of rapidly labeled nuclear ribonucleic acids. Science 145 (1964) 504.

PRENSKY, W. and H.H.SMITH: Incorporation of ^{3}H-arginine in chromosomes of *Vicia faba*. Exptl. Cell Res. 34 (1964) 525.

PRESCOTT, D.M.: The growth-duplication cycle of the cell. Intern. Rev. Cytol. 11 (1961) 255.

PRESCOTT, D.M.: The synthesis of total macronuclear protein, histone, and DNA during the cell cycle in *Euplotes eurystomus*. J. Cell Biol. 31 (1966) 1.

PRESCOTT, D.M. and M.A.BENDER: Synthesis of RNA and protein during mitosis in mammalian tissue culture cells. Exptl. Cell Res. 26 (1962) 260.

PRESCOTT, D.M. and M.A.BENDER: Autoradiographic study of chromatid distribution of labeled DNA in two types of mammalian cells *in vitro*. Exptl. Cell Res. 29 (1963a) 430.

PRESCOTT, D.M. and M.A.BENDER: Synthesis and behaviour of nuclear proteins during the cell life cycle. J. Cellular Comp. Physiol. 62, Suppl. 1 (1963b) 175.

PRESCOTT, D.M. and R.F.KIMBALL: Relation between RNA, DNA, and protein syntheses in the replicating nucleus of *Euplotes*. Proc. Natl. Acad. Sci. U.S. 47 (1961) 686.

PRITCHARD, R.H. and K.G.LARK: Induction of replication by thymine starvation at the chromosome origin in *Escherichia coli*. J. Mol. Biol. 9 (1964) 288.

QUASTLER, H. and F.G.SHERMAN: Cell population kinetics in the intestinal epithelium of the mouse. Exptl. Cell Res. 17 (1959) 420.

REICHARD, J.S. and B.ESTBORN: Utilization of deoxyribosides in the synthesis of polynucleotides. J. Biol. Chem. 188 (1951) 839.

REID, B.R. and R.D.COLE: Biosynthesis of a lysine-rich histone in isolated calf thymus nuclei. Proc. Natl. Acad. Sci. U.S. 51 (1964) 1044.

RIS, H.: Chromosome structure. In: W.D. McElroy and B.Glass, eds.: The chemical basis of heredity. Baltimore, Johns Hopkins Press (1957) 23.

RIS, H.: Ultrastructure and molecular organization of genetic systems. Can. J. Genet. Cytol. 3 (1961) 95.

RIS, H.: Fine structure of chromosomes. Proc. Roy. Soc. (London), Ser. B: 164 (1966) 245.

RITOSSA, F.M. and S.SPIEGELMAN: Localization of DNA complementary to ribosomal RNA in the nucleolus organizer of *Drosophila melanogaster*. Proc. Natl. Acad. Sci. U.S. 53 (1965) 737.

ROBBINS, E. and T.W.BORUN: The cytoplasmic synthesis of histones in HeLa cells and its temporal relationship to DNA replication. Proc. Natl. Acad. Sci. U.S. 57 (1967) 409.

SALB, J.M. and P.I.MARCUS: Translation inhibition in mitotic HeLa cells. Proc. Natl. Acad. Sci. U.S. 54 (1965) 1353.

SCHAECHTER, M., M.W.BENTZON and O.MAALØE: Synthesis of deoxyribonucleic acid during the division cycle of bacteria. Nature 183 (1959) 1207.

SCHARFF, M.D. and E.ROBBINS: Synthesis of ribosomal RNA in synchronized HeLa cells. Nature 208 (1965) 464.

SCHARFF, M.D. and E.ROBBINS: Polyribosome disaggregation during metaphase. Science 151 (1966) 992.

SCHNEIDER, K. and W.O.RIEKE: DNA replication patterns and chromosomal protein synthesis in opossum lymphocytes *in vitro*. J. Cell Biol. 33 (1967) 497.

SEED, J.: Studies of biochemistry and physiology of normal and tumour strain cells. Nature 198 (1963) 147.

SHEARER, R. and B.MCCARTHY: Evidence for RNA molecules restricted to the cell nucleus. Biochemistry 6 (1967) 283.

SHERIDAN, W.F. and H.STERN: Histones of meiosis. Exptl. Cell Res. 45 (1967) 323.

SHERMAN, F.G., H.QUASTLER and D.R.WIMBER: Cell population kinetics in the ear epidermis of mice. Exptl. Cell Res. 25 (1961) 114.

SHOWACRE, J.L., W.G.COOPER and D.M.PRESCOTT: Nucleolar and nuclear RNA synthesis during the cell life cycle in monkey and pig kidney cells *in vitro*. J. Cell Biol. 33 (1967) 273.

SIRLIN, J.L.: Facts and speculation on the functions of nuclear components. In: The cell nucleus. London, Butterworths (1960) 35.

SIRLIN, J.L.: The nucleolus. In: J.A.V.Butler, H.E.Huxley and R.E.Zirkle, eds.: Progress in biophysics and biophysical chemistry, Vol. 12. Oxford, Pergamon Press (1962) 25.

SIRLIN, J.L., J.JACOB and C.J.TANDLER: Transfer of [^{14}C-methyl] methionine to nucleolar ribonucleic acid. Biochem. J. 87 (1963) 37P.

SISKEN, J.E. and E.WILKES: The time of synthesis and the conservation of mitosis-related proteins in cultured human amnion cells. J. Cell Biol. 34 (1967) 97.

SONNEBORN, T.M.: The differentiation of cells. Proc. Natl. Acad. Sci. U.S. 51 (1964) 915.

SOTELO, J.R. and R.WETTSTEIN: Fine structure of meiotic chromosomes. In: Internat. Symp. Genes and Chromosomes Structure and Function. Natl. Cancer Inst. Monograph 18 (1965) 133.

SPALDING, J., K.KAJIWARA and G.C.MUELLER: The metabolism of basic proteins in HeLa cell nuclei. Proc. Natl. Acad. Sci. U.S. 56 (1966) 1535.

STANNERS, C.P. and J.E.TILL: DNA synthesis in individual L-strain mouse cells. Biochim. Biophys. Acta 37 (1960) 406.

STERN, H. and Y.HOTTA: Facets of intracellular regulation of meiosis and mitosis. In: R.J.C.Harris, ed.: Symp. Internat. Soc. Cell Biology, Vol. 2: Cell growth and cell division. New York, Academic Press (1963) 57.

STONE, G.E., O.L.MILLER JR. and D.M.PRESCOTT: H^3-thymidine derivative pools in relation to macronuclear DNA synthesis in *Tetrahymena pyriformis*. J. Cell Biol. 25 (1965) 171.

STONE, G.E. and D.M.PRESCOTT: Cell division and DNA synthesis in *Tetrahymena pyriformis* deprived of essential amino acids. J. Cell Biol. 21 (1964) 275.

SWANN, M.M.: The control of cell division: A review I. General mechanisms. Cancer Res. 17 (1957) 727.

SWANN, M.M.: The control of cell division: A review II. Special mechanisms. Cancer Res. 18 (1958) 1118.

SWIFT, H.: Nucleoproteins in the mitotic cycle. Texas Rept. Biol. Med. 11 (1954) 755.

SWIFT, H.: Nucleic acids and cell morphology in dipteran salivary glands. In: J.M.Allen, ed.: The molecular control of cellular activity. New York, McGraw-Hill (1962) 73.

SZOLLOSI, D.: Time and duration of DNA synthesis in rabbit eggs after sperm penetration. Anat. Record 154 (1966) 209.

TAYLOR, E.W.: Control of DNA synthesis in mammalian cells in culture. Exptl. Cell Res. 40 (1965) 316.

TAYLOR, J.H.: Sister chromatid exchanges in tritium-labeled chromosomes. Genetics 43 (1958a) 515.

TAYLOR, J.H.: The mode of chromosome duplication in *Crepis capillaris*. Exptl. Cell Res. 15 (1958b) 350.

TAYLOR, J.H.: Nucleic acid synthesis in relation to the cell division cycle. Ann. N.Y. Acad. Sci. 90 (1960) 409.

TAYLOR, J.H.: Chromosome reproduction. Intern. J. Cytol. 13 (1962) 39.

TAYLOR, J.H.: The replication and organization of DNA in chromosomes. In: J.H.Taylor, ed.: Molecular genetics. New York, Academic Press (1963) 65.

TAYLOR, J.H.: Distribution of tritium-labeled DNA among chromosomes during meiosis I. Spermatogenesis in the grasshopper. J. Cell Biol. 25 (1965) 57.

TAYLOR, J.H. and R.D.MCMASTER: Autoradiographic and microphotometric studies of desoxyribonucleic acid during microgametogenesis in *Lilium longiflorum*. Chromosoma 6 (1954) 489.

TAYLOR, J. H., P. S. WOODS and W. L. HUGHES: The organization and duplication of chromosomes as revealed by autoradiographic studies using tritium-labeled thymidine. Proc. Natl. Acad. Sci. U.S. 43 (1957) 122.

TOBEY, R. A., E. C. ANDERSON and D. F. PETERSEN: The effect of thymidine on the duration of G_1 in Chinese hamster cells. J. Cell Biol. 35 (1967) 53.

TOBEY, R. A., D. F. PETERSEN, E. C. ANDERSON and T. T. PUCK: Life cycle analysis of mammalian cells III. The inhibition of division in Chinese hamster cells by puromycin and actinomycin. Biophys. J. 6 (1966) 567.

TROSKO, J. E. and S. WOLFF: Strandedness of *Vicia faba* chromosomes as revealed by enzyme digestion studies. J. Cell Biol. 26 (1965) 125.

UMANA, R., S. UPDIKE, J. RANDALL and A. L. DOUNCE: Histone metabolism. In: J. Bonner and P. O. P. Ts'o, eds.: The nucleohistones. San Francisco, Holden-Day Inc. (1964) 200.

VAN'T HOF, J.: Relationships between mitotic cycle duration, S period duration and the average rate of DNA synthesis in the root meristem cells of several plants. Exptl. Cell Res. 39 (1965) 48.

VAN 'T HOF, J.: Comparative cell population kinetics of tritiated thymidine labeled diploid and colchicine-induced tetraploid cells in the same tissue of *Pisum*. Exptl. Cell Res. 41 (1966) 274.

WALEN, K.: The pattern of DNA synthesis in the chromosomes of the marsupial *Potorus tridactylis*. In: Genetics today. Proc. XI Internat. Congress of Genetics, Vol. I. (1963) 106.

WALKER, P. M. B. and H. B. YATES: Ultraviolet absorption of living cell nuclei during growth and division. Symp. Soc. Exptl. Biol. 6 (1952) 265.

WALLACE, H. and M. BIRNSTIEL: Ribosomal cistrons and the nucleolar organizer. Biochim. Biophys. Acta 114 (1966) 296.

WEISSMAN, S. M., R. M. S. SMELLIE and J. PAUL: Studies on the biosynthesis of deoxyribonucleic acid by extracts of mammalian cells IV. The phosphorylation of thymidine. Biochim. Biophys. Acta 45 (1960) 101.

WIMBER, D. E.: Duration of the nuclear cycle in *Tradescantia paludosa* root tips as measured with H^3-thymidine. Am. J. Botany 47 (1960) 828.

WOLFF, S.: Interpretation of induced chromosome breakage and rejoining. Radiation Res. Suppl. 1 (1959) 453.

WOLFF, S.: Are sister strand exchanges sister strand crossovers or radiation-induced exchanges? Mutation Res. 1 (1964) 337.

WOLFF, S.: On the chemistry of chromosome continuity. In: Internat. Symp. Genes and Chromosomes Structure and Function. Natl. Cancer Inst. Monograph 18 (1965) 155.

WOLFF, S. and H. E. LUIPPOLD: Chromosome splitting as revealed by combined X-ray and labeling experiments. Exptl. Cell Res. 34 (1964) 548.

WOODS, P. S. and M. U. SCHAIRER: Distribution of newly synthesized deoxyribonucleic acid in dividing chromosomes. Nature 183 (1959) 303.

ZETTERBERG, A.: Protein migration between cytoplasm and cell nucleus during interphase in mouse fibroblasts *in vitro*. Exptl. Cell Res. 43 (1966) 526.

ZETTERBERG, A. and D. KILLANDER: Quantitative cytophotometric and autoradiographic studies on the rate of protein synthesis during interphase in mouse fibroblasts *in vitro*. Exptl. Cell Res. 40 (1965) 1.

ZEUTHEN, E.: Cycling in oxygen consumption in cleaving eggs. Exptl. Cell Res. 19 (1960) 1.

ZEUTHEN, E.: Cell division and protein synthesis. Proc. I. IUB/IUBS Symp., Vol. 2. New York, Academic Press (1961).

ZIMMERMAN, A. M.: Physico-chemical analysis of the isolated mitotic apparatus. Exptl. Cell Res. 20 (1960) 529.

CHAPTER 20

Biochemical activity of interphase chromosomes (polytene chromosomes)

H. D. BERENDES and W. BEERMANN

Max-Planck-Institut für Biologie, Abt. Beermann, Tübingen

Contents

1. Introduction
2. Chemical components and their relation to chromosome structure
3. Patterns of macromolecular synthesis
   (a) DNA synthesis
   (b) RNA synthesis
   (c) Protein synthesis
   (d) Control of chromosomal activity (puffing)

1. Introduction

Giant polytene chromosomes are typically found in the giant cells of Dipteran larvae, but they have also been described for several other organisms, animals as well as plants, in a variety of cell types (see Beermann 1962). They represent bundles of extended interphase chromosomes. Many details with respect to the macromolecular organization of chromosomes in the most active phase of the chromosome cycle, the interphase, have been ascertained by investigations on giant chromosomes. The relationship between structure and function of the chromosome, the occurrence of local structural changes which affect chromosome morphology and coincide with particular developmental processes or with the appearance of particular cell products, and the establishment of defined patterns of macromolecular synthesis have provided new insights into chromosome metabolism and regulational systems in metazoan cells.

The polytene chromosomes in salivary gland cells of Dipteran larvae have contributed most to our knowledge. The development and differentiation of these chromosomes can be studied throughout larval life. The number of cells in each of the larval tissues of Diptera becomes established at an early embryonic stage. For example, in the salivary gland anlage of *Drosophila melanogaster* mitotic activity ceases after 18 hours of embryonic development (Ross 1939), and further development takes place by cell growth while the chromosomal complement reduplicates a number of times. Cytophotometric DNA measurements on prepupal salivary glands of *D. melanogaster* revealed that the chromosome complement has undergone 8 to 9 successive duplications during larval development (Rodman 1967).

The chromatid is the basic unit from which the giant chromosome develops. The typical morphology of the chromosomes results from the intimate association of the newly synthesized chromatids with the parental chromatids after each duplication. The basic unit has been demonstrated by the administration of tritiated thymidine to *Chironomus* embryos at a stage during which the last mitotic divisions of the salivary

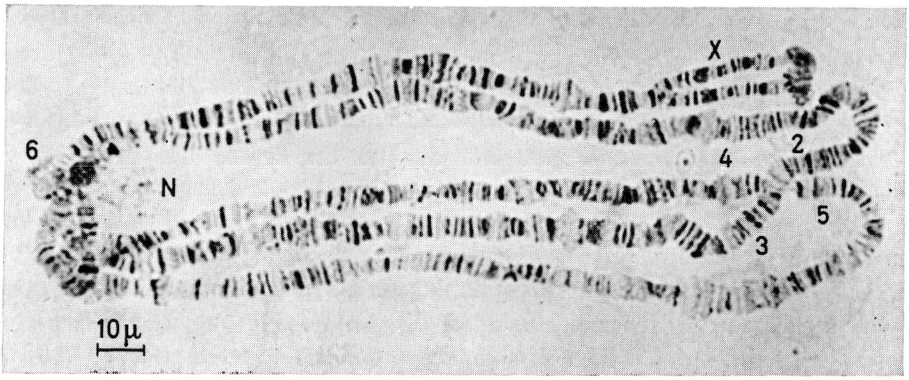

Fig. 1. Squashed salivary gland nucleus of *Drosophila hydei* showing 6 polytene chromosomes. N = nucleolus.

gland anlage cells take place. Autoradiographs, made from fully developed salivary gland chromosomes, show that the interphase chromosomes labelled during the last mitotic divisions before polytenization are present as continuously labelled strands along the entire length of the polytene chromosome (Beermann and Pelling 1965).

The pattern of bands and interbands, characterizing each element of the karyotype (cf. Fig. 1) is assumed to reflect an alternating sequence of condensed, folded or spiralized and extended portions of the DNA chain which is thought to constitute the individual chromatid. The idea that this 'chromomeric' subdivision, which is genetically fixed, also reflects the linear arrangement of the genes, is at least partly supported by combined cytological and genetical localization experiments.

2. *Chemical components and their relation to chromosomal structure*

It is generally accepted that the structural integrity of chromosomes in metazoan cells depends on DNA associated with protein. RNA and acidic proteins represent molecular species which occur in the chromosome during periods of metabolic activity. These macromolecules appear either as metabolic products which are synthesized at particular chromosomal sites (RNA), or accumulate in metabolically active regions (acidic protein). Thus, these components may only be temporarily present.

DNA constitutes the basic structural element of the chromosomes. Its presence in the band regions of polytene chromosomes is demonstrated by a positive Feulgen reaction. The presence of DNA in the interband regions cannot directly be demonstrated by the usual cytochemical staining methods, nor by autoradiographic techniques, but there is a number of arguments in favor of the continuity of DNA through the interbands. In enzyme digestion experiments on 'living' chromosomes with DNAse, Lezzi (1965) found that the interband regions were preferably attacked by the enzyme. The above-mentioned observations on the presence of single labelled chromatids in polytene chromosomes also speak for the preservation of structural continuity by means of DNA alone.

The structural continuity of the DNA in each individual chromatid does not conflict with the idea that the DNA shows a chain-like subdivision into units which, at least during DNA replication, exhibit some individuality. This concept has been discussed in relation to the chromomeric pattern of the chromosomes (Beermann 1966; S. Beermann 1966; Pelling 1966), and it has been assumed that each individual chromomere represents one particular DNA segment. This assumption finds strong support in the pattern of thymidine incorporation in giant polytene chromosomes.

Further support for the individuality of the chromomere DNA is obtained from observations on the DNA content of homologous bands in two subspecies of *Chironomus thummi* (Keyl 1965). In hybrid nuclei it is found that some bands of the *Ch. th. thummi* genome exhibit a DNA content which is an exact geometric multiple of that of the homologous bands in the genome of *Ch. th. piger*. The finding that exact geometric multiplications of the DNA content occur only in particular bands of the genome, and the fact that different bands of the group showing this type of variation do not all reach the same level of multiplication, demonstrates that at least during evolution these bands behaved as individual units (Keyl 1965).

Inferences on a possible subdivision of the chromosomal DNA may also be drawn from recent experiments in which DNA, prepared from isolated salivary gland nuclei of *D. melanogaster*, was spread on an air-water interface and studied by electron microscopy. Preparations, made from the surface film, showed DNA strands with a length varying from 5 μ to 114 μ. The mean length calculated is 37 μ. A comparison of these data with cytophotometric and chemical DNA determinations on salivary gland nuclei of the same species reveals striking similarities.

The mean DNA content of a single nucleus of *D. melanogaster* salivary glands at a prepupal stage is 284 $\mu\mu$g (Patterson and Dackerman 1952). At this stage the nuclei have undergone 8 to 9 replication cycles (1024C; Rodman 1967). The chromosomal complement of the species contains certainly not more than 3.000 bands on account of electron microscopic mapping data (Berendes, in prep.). The mean DNA content of a single chromomere thus would be 0.9×10^{-4} $\mu\mu$g. The length of a DNA strand of this weight is 29 μ. This calculated value is very close to the value found for electron microscopical preparations of nuclear DNA. Another similarity between cytophotometric data and the length of spread DNA strands is the difference in DNA content between the thickest and thinnest band of the genome and the longest and shortest DNA strand; both differ by a factor of 10 to 15.

Other techniques used to study nuclear DNA of higher organisms permit the visualization of much longer DNA strands. By using a modified autoradiographic technique originally developed by Cairns (1963) for bacterial DNA, Huberman and Riggs (1966) found labelled DNA strands (autoradiograms) of various sizes from Chinese hamster cells. Although the most frequent strands seen in autoradiographs were shorter than 100 μ, 6 percent were longer than 800 μ, the longest being 1900 μ. Strands of similar length (1200 μ) were observed after applying this technique to isolated nuclei of *D. hydei* salivary glands (Berendes, unpublished). Assuming that DNA segments of these sizes are derived from polytene chromosomes, one can almost be certain that these segments represent more than one single chromomeric unit. These data do not conflict with the idea of a functional subdivision of chromosomal DNA, but do indicate a structural continuity of the DNA throughout bands and interbands. A similar conclusion might be drawn from the data presented by Plaut et al. (1966), who found that within 15 percent of the cumulative length of the genome of *D. melanogaster* at least 30 replication units can be distinguished. With a total of 3,000 chromomeres in this species, one single replication unit would then include maximally 15 chromomeres. Taking the average DNA content of chromomeres to be 0.9×10^{-4} $\mu\mu$g, the maximum length of the replication unit would be of the order of 500 μ. However, since other data favor the idea of much shorter replication units (one chromomere – one replication unit) (see also: Huberman and Riggs 1968), and since the existence of interstitial heterochromatin poses additional problems (Arcos, unpublished), these calculations have to be regarded with some reservations. In addition, it cannot be excluded that the rare, very long, autoradiograms are derived from heterochromatic chromosomes or chromosome arms which may behave as one replication unit.

Other components of the chromosome may bear on the problem of the molecular organization of the DNA. The basic proteins (histones), which are known to be intimately associated with the DNA do not, however, seem to be responsible for DNA continuity within each chromatid. From enzymatic studies with trypsin and pronase, no evidence is obtained for such a role, since these enzymes do not affect the length distribution of the observed DNA strands. This has been observed in electron microscopic and in autoradiographic studies.

Histochemical methods have shown that histones closely follow the DNA distribution in the chromosome. The correspondence in distribution and the fact that chromosomes after fixation retained their structural organization following treatment with DNAse suggested that the DNA itself could not be responsible for the structural integrity of the chromosomes (Mazia and Jaeger 1939). This hypothesis has been supported by data of many other authors (see Alfert 1954). However, native chromosomes can be disintegrated by DNAse. Disintegration primarily occurs in the interbands as would be expected, since in these regions the DNA must be more exposed than in the bands, indicating that components other than DNA which may be present are not able to maintain the structural integrity when the DNA is removed (Lezzi 1965). It would also be inferred from Lezzi's experiments that histones are partially, or totally absent from interband regions. This would provide a basis for differentiation of a continuous chromosomal DNA chain into chromomeric and interchromomeric regions, the former being segments in which DNA is associated with histone and, therefore, condensed; the latter being segments devoid of histone. The absence of histones in interband regions might also be concluded from the fact that after treatment with hydrochloric acid and pepsin the interband regions show a much stronger contraction than the band regions possibly owing to the removal of a non-histone protein (Mazia et al. 1947; Beermann 1962).

The presence of a globulin type of 'higher' protein in the chromosomes has been concluded from UV-absorption studies (Caspersson 1940). This type of protein which may be described as acidic protein on account of its Fast Green binding capacity at low *p*H, shows an overall distribution similar to that of the basic proteins. This is no surprise in view of the distribution of dry mass along the chromosome. In contrast to the reaction of basic protein with alkaline Fast Green, acidic proteins can be observed without prior removal of the DNA. The general correspondence of the chromosomal acidic protein banding pattern with that of the DNA banding pattern is also indicated by the pattern of label distribution after short pulses with H^3-tryptophane, an amino acid certainly absent in histones. The labelling pattern very often corresponds exactly with the DNA banding pattern.

A characteristic difference in the distribution of basic and acidic proteins is found in the 'active' regions (puffs and Balbiani rings). The quantity of basic protein measured by densitometry is not changed when a particular chromosome region becomes active (Swift 1964). In striking contrast, the amount of acidic protein increases strongly during the puffing of a chromosomal locus (Rudkin 1962). Since the application of labelled amino acids has consistently failed to demonstrate a specific incorporation in regions that are active, and since protein accumulation in active regions occurs also when protein synthesis is inhibited (Clever 1964), it is virtually certain that the acidic proteins are taken up by the chromosomes from the nuclear sap. When an active region becomes inactive again the extra acidic protein is also lost. Thus, the acidic proteins may be divided into at least two classes, those which are permanently bound to the chromosomes and those which are only temporarily incorporated.

3. *Patterns of macromolecular synthesis*

Autoradiographic studies on the pattern of synthesis of macromolecules, DNA, RNA, and protein, in combination with cytophotometric analyses of the quantitative distribution of these macromolecules, particularly of DNA, have provided detailed information with respect to the macromolecular organization of the chromosome. The interrelation of these components in chromosome metabolism has also been clarified by these studies.

(a) *DNA synthesis*

Cytophotometric measurements on nuclear DNA content of fully developed salivary gland cells of different *Drosophila* species indicate that these nuclei contain 128 (2^7C) to 512 (2^9C) times as much as 2C interphase nuclei of the same species (Swift 1962; Rodman 1967).

In *D. melanogaster* 8 or 9 duplications of the genome occur within the 120-hour-period of larval development. Assuming that each duplication of the giant chromosomes has the same duration, a single duplication must be completed within 15 hours. Autoradiographical studies on DNA synthesis in salivary gland chromosomes reveals that certainly during the last instar a number of cells is not in a replication phase. This indicates that the replication cycle may have a duration of less than 15 hours. An attempt was made to determine the duration of the replication of mid-third instar chromosomes of *D. hydei*, with double labelling experiments in which C^{14}-thymidine injection was followed after various incubation periods by H^3-thymidine. The results indicated a duration of 7–8 hours for a replication cycle in the third instar.

It is difficult to ascertain whether or not the duration of one complete replication cycle is the same in all cells. It seems that with increasing polyteny more time is needed to complete replication (Keyl and Pelling 1963). Another question of interest is whether replication regularly includes all parts of the genome throughout polytenization. A comparison of the karyotype observed in diploid mitoses, with that of polytene nuclei clearly shows that some chromosomes, or specific chromosome sections, do not have a polytenic organization. Heitz (1934) in his report on the heterochromatin in *D. virilis* pointed to this discrepancy and related it to those portions of the genome which are composed of '*α*'-heterochromatin, such as the entire Y-chromosome and some proximal sections of the X and the autosomes. Heitz concluded from careful cytological studies that *α*-heterochromatic sections do not 'grow' during polytenization and that this accounts for their virtual absence in polytenic nuclei. In modern terms this would constitute an exception to the rule of genomic, or DNA, constancy. Recent cytophotometric investigations show that this is the case.

Rudkin (1965) was the first to present evidence that the polytene nuclei in the salivary glands of *D. melanogaster* do not contain an exact geometric multiple of the DNA content of mitotic interphase nuclei. He concluded that the chromocentral DNA, made up of the complete heterochromatic Y-chromosome, the heterochromatic arm of the X-chromosome and the centromeric regions of the autosomes, stop replication soon after the nuclei begin to become polytene. Likewise, the nuclei of the brain ganglion of *D. hydei*, which contain either diploid, tetraploid, and octoploid chromosome complements or polytene chromosomes, do not render DNA–Feulgen absorbancy values which can be arranged into a geometric series (Berendes and Keyl 1967). If, however, the absorbancy values for the compact chromocenter and those for the rest of the nuclear DNA (euchromatin) are taken separately, it is found that the chromocenter values as well as those for the euchromatin can be arranged into geometric series. Different nuclei, showing the same 'euchromatin' value, can however display different values of their heterochromatin (Fig. 2). In addition, it is obvious that in most of the polytene nuclei, heterochromatin has completed fewer replication cycles than the euchromatic portions of the DNA.

Replications in polytene nuclei may also be locally out of step in the forward direction. Pavan and Breuer (1955) described disproportionate DNA synthesis occurring at particular regions of *Rhynchosciara* polytene chromosomes. In contrast to the labelling of the rest of the chromosomal complement, tritiated thymidine is incorporated at a very high rate in these regions at particular developmental stages (Fig. 3; Pavan 1965; Gabrusewycz-Garcia 1964). The expected strong increase of DNA in these regions ('DNA puffs') was cytophotometrically confirmed by Rudkin and Corlette (1957). Keyl and Crouse (in press) studied the origin of DNA puffs in *Sciara coprophila*. The relative DNA value of the puff region was measured using the relative DNA value of a particular band in its neighborhood as reference. Various stages of puff development were studied. During a given period, the reference band underwent 3 replication cycles. During the same period the DNA 'puff' completed 4–5 replication cycles (Fig. 4). In each cycle the DNA of the 'puff' region was duplicated exactly, indicating that a particular segment of the DNA in those puffs can replicate independently from the rest of the genome. Apart from being an additional illustration of the individuality of chromosomal DNA segments, these data clearly demonstrate that, at least in polytene (and polyploid) cells, the concept of DNA constancy is not valid.

Detailed insight into the topography of DNA replication along the polytene chromosome is obtained by means of autoradiography (Plaut 1963; Keyl and Pelling 1963; Gabrusewycz-Garcia 1964). After administration of H^3-thymidine over a short period, two types of chromosomal label distribution can be distinguished in the nuclei of salivary glands of *Drosophila*. Some of the nuclei show continuous labelling over the whole chromosome complement. Other nuclei show a discontinuous labelling pattern. The discontinuous labelling pattern shows a clear correspondence with the banding pattern of the chromosomes. The number of labelled bands per chromosome varies in the different nuclei. In some nuclei only very few bands are labelled, in others almost all the bands are labelled. The various patterns of labelled bands can be arranged into a series displaying either an increasing number or a decreasing number of bands. From the observation that most of the nuclei of prepupal glands (which are assumed to finish their last replication cycle, Rodman 1967), show a discontinuous

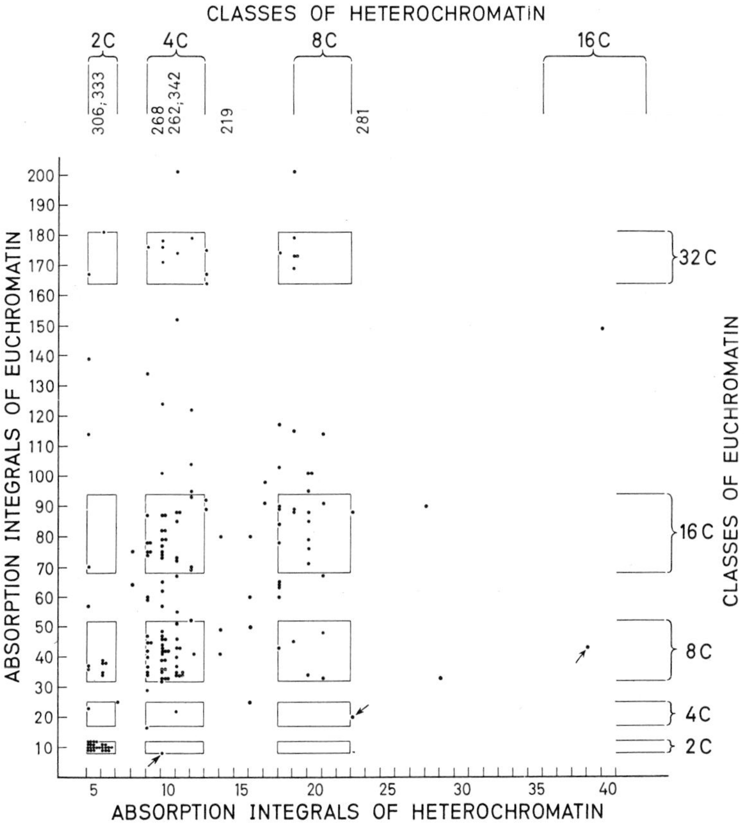

Fig. 2. Diagram of the distribution of DNA in heterochromatin and euchromatin of polytene brain ganglion nuclei of *Drosophila hydei*. This diagram clearly illustrates that the DNA in the euchromatic part of the chromosome complement has completed more duplications than the DNA in the heterochromatic part. (From Berendes and Keyl 1967.)

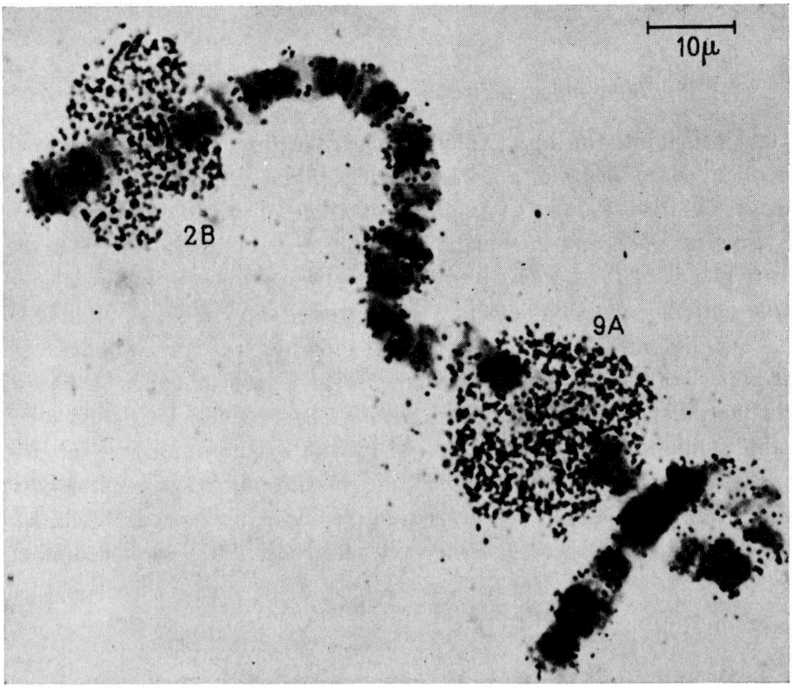

Fig. 3. DNA puffs (2B and 9A) in chromosome 2 of *Sciara coprophila* at a stage of DNA synthesis. The strong incorporation of H^3-thymidine into these regions is correlated in this particular nucleus with a duplication phase of the entire nucleus. (Courtesy Dr. N. Gabrusewycz-Garcia.)

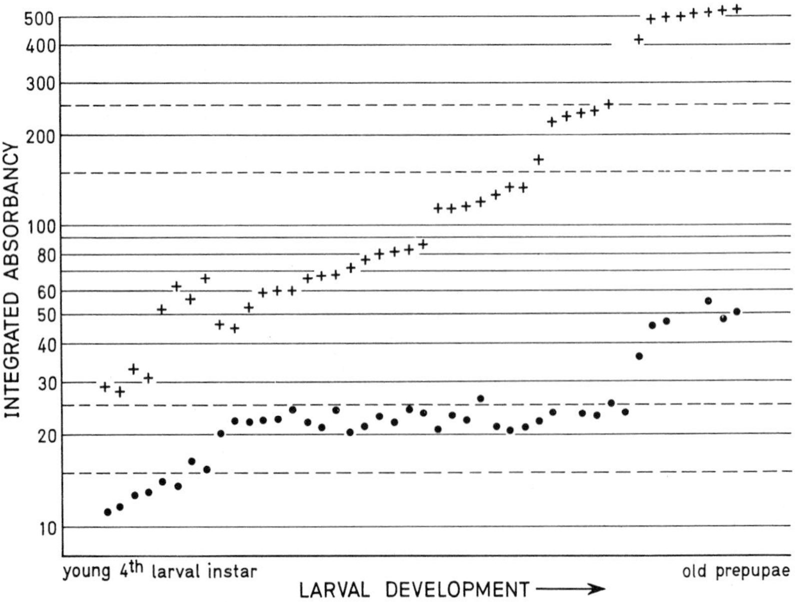

Fig. 4. Diagram illustrating the relation between the increase in DNA content of a DNA-puff region, II-2B (++) and that of a region following orthodox chromosomal replication, II-1C2 (..) during the 4th larval instar of *Sciara coprophila*. During the same period in which the region representative for normal replication performs three replication cycles, the DNA-puff region completes five replication cycles. (Courtesy Dr. H.-G. Keyl.)

labelling pattern, it is concluded that this pattern occurs frequently at the end of a replication cycle. This idea is supported by double labelling experiments with C^{14}- and H^3-thymidine on *Chironomus* chromosomes which showed that replication starts with a continuous labelling pattern (Keyl and Pelling 1963). The data of these experiments suggest that the various banding patterns of discontinuously labelled chromosomes should be arranged into a series displaying a decreasing number of labelled bands. Investigation of the discontinuous labelling pattern in *D. melanogaster* chromosomes revealed that the various sequences of labelled bands can indeed be arranged into a particular and constant order (Plaut et al. 1966). Thus, with respect to replication, the chromosome appears to be subdivided into discrete pieces which correspond to chromomeres or groups of chromomeres and which complete duplication at specifically different times.

In the data presented above, there was no indication that different chromomeres might also have different starting times for replication. However, this is mainly a matter of the temporal resolution which can be achieved in labelling studies. A careful study of the replication of *Sciara* chromosomes has shown that, in addition to the continuous labelling pattern, two complementary kinds of discontinuous patterns are present one of which is observed much less often than the other (Gabrusewycz-Garcia 1964). It is likely that this latter type of discontinuous labelling is due to particular regions which start their DNA replication later than the rest of the chromosomes. These regions are mainly those which also complete their replication later. The continuous labelling pattern would then represent an intermediate phase of the replication of the chromosome complement. This conclusion is supported by recent observations on the replication of *Chironomus* chromosomes (Hägele, unpublished).

The length of the period of DNA synthesis of individual DNA segments (chromomeres) is related at least to some extent to their DNA content and, presumably, reflects the length of the DNA segment involved. Those bands which are among the last ones to finish replication generally belong to the thickest class of bands of the chromosome complement. Some further evidence in this direction is provided by the study of Keyl and Pelling (1963) on giant chromosomes of *Ch. th. thummi* × *Ch. th. piger* hybrids. In asynapsed sections of the hybrid chromosomes, there is a complete linear correspondence of the banding of the two homologues. The replication period of two homologous bands, situated on the two unsynapsed chromosomes, is different in those cases in which the band on the chromosome derived from the *Ch. th. thummi* parent contains a multiple of the DNA content of the homologous band situated on the *Ch. th. piger* chromosome. In these cases the band on the *Ch. th. piger* homologue finishes its replication earlier than the homologous band on the *Ch. th. thummi* element.

The DNA content of individual chromomeres may not be the only factor influencing the duration of replication. It has been found that X-chromosomes of male and female larvae of *D. hydei* and *D. melanogaster* are different in their replication behavior (Berendes 1966). Although the relative DNA content per chromomere has been found to be the same in male and female X-chromosomes (Aronson et al. 1954), the latter complete their replication later than the male ones, if the autosomes are taken as standard. The male X-chromosome, present in a haploid state, shows an increased diameter if compared with a haploid element of an asynapsed female X-chromosome. The increase in diameter of the male X-chromosome may be due to a less compact state of the individual chromomeres. This may not only have some bearing on the rate of RNA synthesis (Mukherjee and Beermann 1965), but could also influence DNA synthesis in the direction observed.

(b) *RNA synthesis*

Polytene chromosomes provide an excellent tool for the investigation of metabolic activity in interphase chromosomes. They permit a detailed analysis of the location and biochemical characteristics of RNA synthesis. With relatively simple staining methods, viz. the metachromatic staining reaction with toluidine blue (Fig. 5) and the reaction with pyronin, followed by control by RNAse, the distribution of RNA along the polytene chromosomes can be determined. The pattern of local RNA concentrations is found to be different from that of the DNA but similar to that of one class of acidic proteins. In places of high RNA concentration chromosomal structure appears locally modified in a typical fashion. The 'active' site is swollen and the original banding is no longer recognizable. These regions are known as puffs and bulbs.

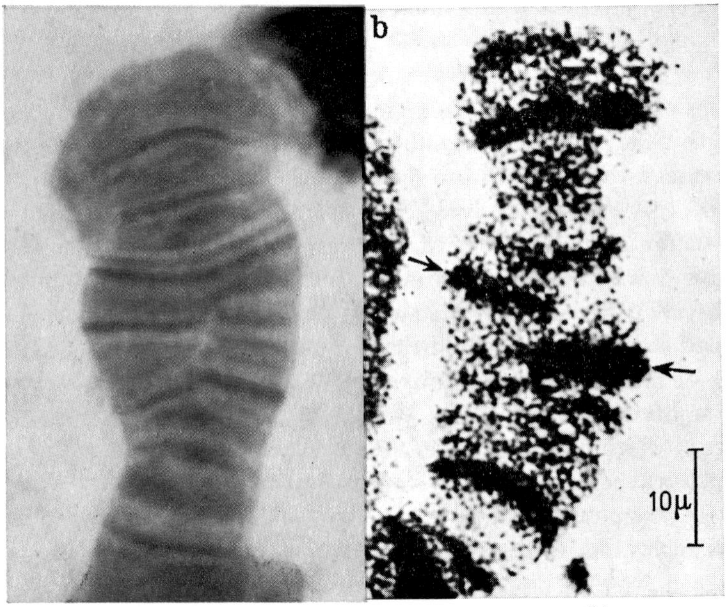

(a) (b)

Fig. 5. Part of chromosome 3 of *Chironomus tentans* showing evident correspondence of the pattern of toluidine blue staining (RNA) (a) and H^3-uridine incorporation (b). Arrows indicate puff III-14C2. (Courtesy Dr. C. Pelling.)

Extremely large, ring-like puffed structures (Balbiani rings) containing high quantities of RNA ($\sim 10^{-11}$ g) can be observed at particular sites of the giant chromosomes in *Chironomids*, *Sciarids*, and *Collemboles* (Fig. 6). In these regions, the chromosome is split into numerous strands. The separation of the individual chromatids reaches its maximum in the peripheral zones with the highest concentration of ribonucleoprotein. It seems that the ring is formed by loops of completely stretched chromatids radiating from the chromosome axis. The constant location of these Balbiani rings and the fact that they never arise from typical puffs in *Drosophila* and *Chironomus* suggests that Balbiani rings, though functionally analogous to puffs, are structurally somewhat different. As has been suggested earlier (Beermann 1952), a prerequisite for the formation of Balbiani rings seems to be the continuous presence of puffing at the locus in question from the beginning of polytenization.

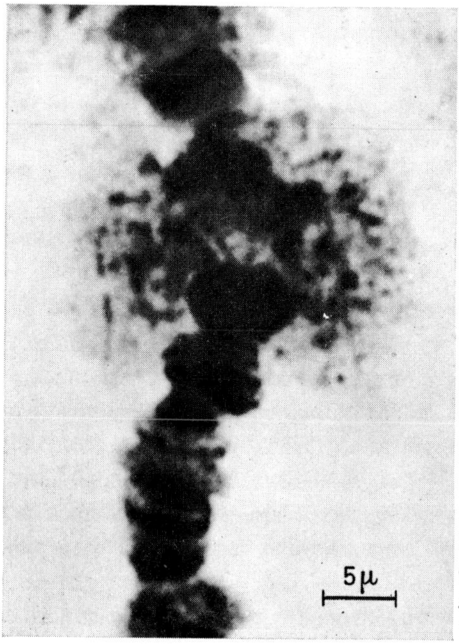

Fig. 6. Balbiani ring in the chromosomes of *Neanura grassei* (Collemboles). Courtesy Prof. P. Cassagnau.

The nucleolus is a special RNA-containing structure. This nuclear organelle can be present at many locations on the chromosome complement but always at definite positions, the nucleolar organizing regions. These may be situated within heterochromatic, or within euchromatic, regions where they appear as a special class of 'bands' (cf. Beermann 1960).

Autoradiographic experiments with the RNA precursor uridine have shown that regions with intensive RNA staining generally display high incorporation rates of labelled precursor (Fig. 5b). Therefore, the three types of structures just described may be interpreted as sites of active RNA synthesis. *In vivo* as well as *in vitro* administration of the antibiotic actinomycin D results in a complete inhibition of the incorporation of labelled precursors into puffs, Balbiani rings and nucleoli, indicating that RNA synthesis is suppressed. These experiments further indicate that the newly formed RNA in the active regions is the product of transcription of a particular segment of the chromosomal DNA. The antibiotic is a well known specific inhibitor of DNA-dependent RNA synthesis that binds to the guanine residues of the DNA. The question whether or not the RNA present in a particular puff consists only of locally synthesized RNA is as yet unclear. Recent studies on the nature of puff RNA provide some indication of its molecular composition. Edström and Beermann (1962) isolated RNA from particular chromosome regions (mainly Balbiani rings) of *Chironomus tentans* and determined its base composition. The base composition of different RNA samples obtained from different Balbiani rings was compared with the base composition of total chromosomal DNA. It was found that the RNA of different Balbiani rings has an asymmetric base composition. The A–U ratio in one of the Balbiani ring RNA fractions was 2.2, in others a ratio of 1.5 and 1.7 was found. The asymmetric base composition is assumed to be the consequence of the transcription of one of the DNA strands only (Beermann 1963). Moreover, the base compositions of the Balbiani ring RNA's was significantly different from that of ribosomal RNA. These facts indicate that most of the RNA in Balbiani rings is synthesized at the locus itself and that they are not involved in the synthesis, or accumulation, of a ribosomal precursor. It is probable, therefore, that the Balbiani rings produce other types of RNA, including messenger and/or transfer RNA. Recently, Pelling developed a method to characterize pulse labelled RNA extracted from isolated *Chironomus* chromosomes. These experiments show that each of the chromosomes yields a characteristic sedimentation pattern of RNA. Chromosomes with active Balbiani rings show radioactive fractions of particularly high molecular weight RNA (35–45S) as well as a low molecular weight component of approximately 4S. It is suggested that the high molecular weight polydisperse RNA represents messenger-type RNA and the 4S fraction transfer RNA, both synthesized in the Balbiani rings. Similar results have been published by Edström and Daneholt (1967).

After prolonged incubation periods the sedimentation pattern shows a shift of the main radioactive peaks from higher to lower molecular weight components. This indicates that at the chromosomal level definite changes in the newly synthesized RNA can occur.

Unfolding, or despiralization, of the DNA is thought to be a prerequisite for transcription. No data are available which show whether or not all of the chromomere DNA becomes despiralized, when forming a puff. In Balbiani rings of *Chironomus*, no clear indication of differential condensation of the DNA along the individual loops has been found. In all likelihood, these loops are completely stretched deoxyribonucleoprotein strands, approximately 5 μ long (Beermann and Bahr 1954). DNA isolated from salivary gland nuclei of *Chironomus*, spread on a water–air interphase and studied electron microscopically, shows a mean strand length of approximately 50 μ (Wolstenhome, in press). If this is taken as a measure for the DNA length, which is present in the average chromomere, then Balbiani ring loops might only represent part of a longer DNA segment. Even so, if the total information of a 5 μ long DNA strand were transcribed, it would suffice to code for 25–30 proteins of an average size of 200 amino acids. In case of a complete transcription of this DNA, it should be considered that different RNA species might be synthesized which differ in their base sequences. However, it is also possible that only one species of RNA is formed. This could mean that the same information is sequentially repeated many times along the puffed DNA segments. The occurrence of such a redundancy in particular chromosomal elements is illustrated by RNA–DNA hybridization experiments for the nucleolar organizer region of *D. melanogaster* (Ritossa and Spiegelman 1965). On the other hand, it is possible that only a short initial DNA segment is really active in transcription.

(c) *Protein synthesis*

In contrast to our knowledge of DNA and RNA synthesis of polytene chromosomes, little information concerning protein synthesis is available. Autoradiographic experiments with labelled amino acids, tryptophan, histidine, arginine, lysine, leucine, proline, and glutamic acid, reveal that these amino acids all become incorporated into the chromosomes, after *in vivo* as well as after *in vitro* administration. In these experiments the cytoplasm is more strongly labelled than the nuclear components. Therefore, it is difficult to exclude the possibility that the chromosomal labelling is in fact derived from proteins synthesized in the cytoplasm and transported to the chromosome. The distribution of silver grains after short incubation periods (5 min) seems to follow the pattern of bands. This may simply be a reflection of the mass distribution of protein in the polytene chromosome.

Pulse labelling experiments further reveal that particularly during the end of the last larval instar of *Drosophila* all nuclei show a strong incorporation of amino acids. By feeding young larvae tritiated histidine for 2 hr, and preparing autoradiographs at 2 days after the larvae have been placed on non-radioactive food, it has been demonstrated that the chromosomal label acquired during the short application period is retained in the chromosomes. This indicates that the newly synthesized protein is a stable component of the chromosome (Petit and Rasch 1966).

In order to determine the time of synthesis of the different types of protein in the polytene chromosomes, in relation to the time of DNA synthesis, the incorporation of tryptophane (which is absent in histones) and of histidine was studied in combination with extraction of histones. No evident relationship between DNA synthesis and the synthesis of tryptophan-containing proteins could be detected. Microdensitometric measurements performed on alkaline Fast Green stained chromosomes, from which the DNA had been extracted subsequent to Feulgen spectrophotometry, revealed in all instances a constant quantitative relation between the DNA and the histones (Gorovsky and Woodard 1967). These studies indicate that in the giant chromosomes the synthesis, or accumulation, of histones occurs simultaneously with DNA synthesis. In contrast to histone synthesis or accumulation, it seems that other proteins are synthesized, or accumulated, without any particular relationship to DNA synthesis. This is clearly demonstrated by the fact that within the same pair of glands almost all nuclei become labelled with H^3-tryptophane, whereas only part of the nuclei show incorporation of H^3-thymidine.

Recent studies on the pattern of histidine incorporation correlated with protein staining on the polytene chromosomes of *D. virilis* show that particularly during the last part of the third instar chromosomal protein content raises considerably. It is during this period that many new puffs arise. The formation of new puffs is always accompanied by a strong local increase in acidic protein (Fig. 7). The increase in

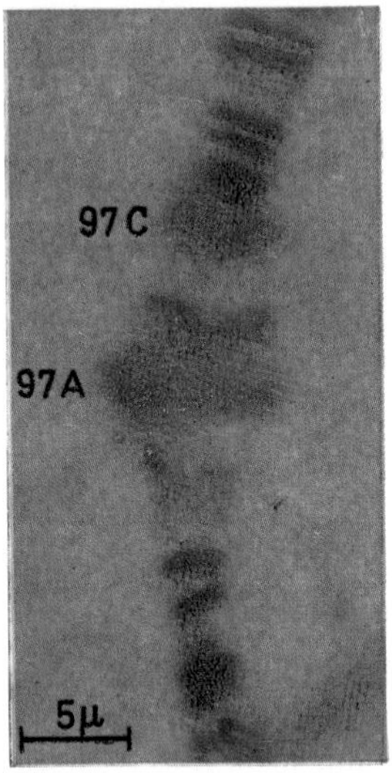

Fig. 7. Fast Green staining of acidic proteins in two puffs in the 5th chromosome of *Drosophila hydei*. These puffs were experimentally induced by the molting hormone ecdysone.

chromosomal proteins at this stage thus could be explained by the occurrence of many new puffs which are specifically related with the process of puparium formation. However, these puffs, although enormously increasing their binding capacity to acid fast green, do not show a preferential uptake of labelled amino acids. Moreover, when puromycin, or cycloheximide, are applied in concentrations which almost completely suppress cellular protein synthesis, the appearance of the specific puffs is not inhibited (Clever 1966). Therefore, *de novo* synthesis of protein does not seem to be correlated with puff formation. On the contrary, there are indications that specific local incorporation of amino acids into puffed regions occurs at a stage of puff regression (Petit and Rasch 1966).

Clever (1966) found that the regression of one ecdysone-sensitive puff in *Chironomus tentans* is dependent on protein synthesis. Application of inhibitors of protein synthesis during the active period of this puff prevented its regression. In this case, however, we are dealing with a presumed case of feedback inhibition involving an unknown number of intermediate links in the regulatory system.

The chemical composition and the quantitative relationships of the different types of proteins in puffs have to be elucidated further before definite conclusions can be drawn with respect to their significance for local metabolic activity and their bearing on the maintenance of the structural integrity of the polytene chromosome.

(d) *Control of chromosomal activity (puffing)*

Well-established correlations between local chromosomal activity and particular cell properties indicate the significance of chromosomal puffing for cell metabolism. The activity of a particular Balbiani ring in the salivary glands of *Chironomus* is correlated with the presence of a particular granular cell product (Beermann 1961). Although other correlations between puff activity at particular chromosomal loci and the presence of certain cell products have been suggested, this is the only one supported by genetical experiments. The combination of genetical research and the study of local metabolic activity in the giant chromosomes is a promising approach to detect more specific correlations. Particularly the location of genes responsible for the production of certain proteins, e.g., enzymes specifically found in only some cell types, combined with a study of changes in metabolic activity at the particular chromosome locus might improve our knowledge, not only with respect to the significance of the puffing phenomenon for cell metabolism, but also with respect to the problem of regulation mechanisms involved.

Studies on the differences of puffing patterns in closely related species, or different mutant stocks, of the same species can also be used to obtain better insight in the regulation and the mechanism of puffing, particularly by the study of hybrids differing in puffing pattern (Ashburner 1967).

It is well known that within the same chromosomal component different puffing patterns can be observed at various developmental periods. Furthermore, different tissues or cell types can show characteristic differences in their puffing pattern. These variations must have a correlation on the level of cellular function. In *Chironomus* some relations between tissue-specific puffing differences and the pattern of protein synthesis begin to become elucidated in recent studies (Grossbach, unpublished; see Beermann 1967; Baudisch and Panitz 1967). The latter authors have found that the presence of a Balbiani ring in the main lobe of the salivary gland of *Acricotopus* is correlated with the incorporation of radioactive proline, in the form of hydroxyproline, into the lobe-specific secretion.

Studies on the relationship between the induction of gene activity and the specific inductive stimulus are also in the beginning stage. Only few agents have been detected which produce a specific and constant effect on the pattern of gene activity. However, the mechanism of their action is still largely unknown.

In particular, the studies on the experimental induction of puffing changes by hormones such as ecdysone have provided information on those processes involved in changes of the metabolism of particular loci. Clever (1961) as well as Berendes (1967) observed a complex pattern of local changes in chromosomal activity in *Chironomus tentans* and *Drosophila hydei* respectively, after the experimental administration of ecdysone. Both authors found that ecdysone-induced changes in the puffing pattern are similar, if not identical, to those occurring during normal development before puparium formation. Depending on the experimental conditions, some time relations may be disturbed as compared to the normal development.

The experimental administration of ecdysone provides the possibility to perform a detailed analysis of the various processes which occur during the development of a puff. The first recognizable change in all regions activated by ecdysone is the appearance of an acidic protein. This conclusion is supported by the finding that in animals in which RNA synthesis is completely suppressed by a 1-hour pretreatment with actinomycin D, puffing of ecdysone-sensitive sites could still be induced partially. These sites show intensive protein staining but no RNA synthesis. The occurrence of acidic protein precedes actual puffing. At 5 min after administration of the hormone, acidic protein can be demonstrated, but no visible increase in chromosomal diameter has occurred. Since the demonstration of acidic proteins is performed by staining, it could be supposed that the protein is already present at the activated region, and becomes changed in its molecular configuration during the period of activation. However, Rudkin (1962) proved by means of UV spectrophotometry that the protein content of active regions has indeed increased if compared with their inactive state. It thus can be assumed that during the activation of a chromosome region (gene?) one of the first steps is the accumulation of acidic proteins. The process of accumulation of proteins in the puff region seems to precede the onset of RNA synthesis. Tritiated uridine was administered to *Drosophila* at various times after a raise in temperature. The radioautography revealed that RNA synthesis, in temperature-induced puffs, starts only after a definite accumulation of acidic proteins. The local increase in acidic protein, at a time when no evident morphological change can be observed, may simply be related with the process of despiralization of the DNA, or it may indicate the attachment of a large quantity of polymerase molecules to the activated site. One the other hand, the presence of distinct ribonucleoprotein particles in some puffs (Beermann and Bahr 1954; Swift 1962; Stevens and Swift 1966) indicates that the newly formed RNA is transported to the nuclear membrane in association with protein (Beermann 1967). However, the protein staining intensity of newly induced puffs is clearly stronger than that of steady state puffs. This indicates that the 'early' puff proteins are more specifically related to the process of activation rather than being carrier proteins. It has recently been shown that in other systems, in which the specific action of steroid hormones was studied, the hormone becomes associated with proteins at different cellular levels. Acceptor proteins for hormones have been found to be located in the nucleus, and hormone-bound protein has been isolated (Lippert et al. 1967; Maurer and Chalkley 1967; Jungblut et al. 1967).

Although similar experiments have not yet been performed on Diptera with the hormone ecdysone, these results suggest a specific relationship between the steroids and particular proteins rather than a direct relation of the steroid to particular segments of the chromosomal DNA.

Summarizing the available data on the process of puffing, it is likely that the first step in activation of a particular chromosome region is the accumulation of acidic protein which is followed by a despiralization of a DNA segment that will be transcribed. Then RNA synthesis is started. The newly synthesized RNA is presumably transformed into the final messenger form within the puff region and combined with protein in the form of discrete particles which become transported to the nuclear membrane. Puff activity could be repressed either by the disappearance of the inducing stimulus, or actively by means of specific repressor proteins.

References

ALFERT, M.: Composition and structure of giant chromosomes. Int. Rev. Cytol. 3 (1954) 131.

ARONSON, J.F., G.T.RUDKIN and J.SCHULTZ: A comparison of giant X-chromosomes in male and female *Drosophila melanogaster* by cytophotometry in the ultraviolet. J. Histochem. Cytochem. 2 (1954) 458.

ASHBURNER, M.: The genetic control of puffing in polytene chromosomes. Genetics Today 2 (in press).

BAUDISCH, W. and R.PANITZ: Kontrolle eines biochemischen Merkmals in den Speicheldrüsen von *Acricotopus lucidus* durch einen Balbiani ring. Exptl. Cell Res. 49 (1968) 470.

BEERMANN, S.: A quantitative study of chromatin diminution in *Cyclops furcifer*. Genetics 54 (1966) 567.

BEERMANN, W.: Chromomerenkonstanz und spezifische Modifikationen der Chromosomenstruktur in der Entwicklung und Organdifferenzierung von *Chironomus tentans*. Chromosoma 5 (1952) 139.

BEERMANN, W.: Der Nukleolus als wichtiger Bestandteil des Zellkernes. Chromosoma 11 (1960) 263.

BEERMANN, W.: Ein Balbianiring als Locus einer Speicheldrüsenmutation. Chromosoma 12 (1961) 1.

BEERMANN, W.: Riesenchromosomen, Protoplasmatologia IVD. Berlin, Springer Verlag (1962).

BEERMANN, W.: Cytological aspects of information transfer in cellular differentiation. Am. Zool. 3 (1963) 23.

BEERMANN, W.: Differentiation at the level of chromosomes. In: Cell differentiation and morphogenesis. Amsterdam, North-Holland Publ. Co (1966) 24.

BEERMANN, W.: Gen-Regulation in Chromosomen höherer Organismen. Jahrb. 1966 der Max Planck Gesellsch. (1967) 69.

BEERMANN, W. and G.F.BAHR: The submicroscopic structure of the Balbianiring. Exp. Cell Res. 6 (1954) 195.

BEERMANN, W. and C.PELLING: H^3-Thymidin-Markierung einzelner Chromatiden in Riesenchromosomen. Chromosoma 16 (1965) 1.

BERENDES, H.D.: Differential replication of male and female X-chromosomes. Chromosoma 20 (1966) 32.

BERENDES, H.D.: The hormone ecdysone as effector of specific changes in the pattern of gene activities of *Drosophila hydei*. Chromosoma 22 (1967) 274.

BERENDES, H.D. and H.-G.KEYL: Distribution of DNA in heterochromatin and euchromatin of polytene nuclei of *Drosophila hydei*. Genetics 57 (1967) 1.

CAIRNS, J.: The bacterial chromosome and its manner of replication as seen by autoradiography. J. mol. Biol. 6 (1963) 208.

CASPERSSON, T.: Die Eiweissverteilung in den Strukturen des Zellkerns. Chromosoma 1 (1940) 562.

CLEVER, U.: Genaktivitäten in den Riesenchromosomen von *Chironomus tentans* und ihre Beziehungen zur Entwicklung. I. Genaktivierungen durch Ecdyson. Chromosoma 12 (1961) 607.

CLEVER, U.: Von der Ecdysonkonzentration abhängige Genaktivitätsmuster in den Speicheldrüsenchromosomen von Chironomus tentans. Develop. Biol. 6 (1963) 73.

CLEVER, U.: Induction and repression of a puff in *Chironomus tentans*. Develop. Biol. 14 (1966) 421.

EDSTRÖM, J.-E. and W. BEERMANN: The base composition of nucleic acids in chromosomes, puffs, nucleoli, and cytoplasm of *Chironomus* salivary gland cells. J. Cell. Biol. 14 (1962) 371.

EDSTRÖM, J.-E. and B. DANEHOLT: Sedimentation properties of the newly synthesized RNA from isolated nuclear components of *Chironomus tentans* salivary gland cells. J. Mol. Biol. 28 (1967) 331

GABRUSEWYCZ-GARCIA, N.: Cytological and autoradiographic studies in *Sciara coprophila* salivary gland chromosomes. Chromosoma 15 (1964) 312.

GOROVSKY, M.A. and J. WOODARD: Histone content of chromosomal loci active and inactive in RNA synthesis. J. Cell. Biol. 33 (1967) 723.

HEITZ, E.: Über α und β Heterochromatin sowie Konstanz und Bau der Chromomeren bei *Drosophila*. Biol. Zbl. 54 (1934) 588.

HUBERMAN, J.A. and A.D. RIGGS: Autoradiography of chromosomal DNA fibers from Chinese hamster cells. Proc. Nat. Acad. Sci. 55 (1966) 599.

HUBERMAN, J.A. and A.D. RIGGS: On the mechanism of DNA replication in mammalian chromosomes. J. Mol. Biol. 32 (1968) 327.

JUNGBLUT, P.W., J. HÄTZEL, E.R. DESOMBRE und E.V. JENSEN: Über Hormon-'Receptoren'. Die oestrogenbindenden Prinzipien der Erfolgsorgane. In: Wirkungsmechanismen der Hormone. Berlin, Springer Verlag (1967).

KEYL, H.-G.: Duplikationen von Untereinheiten der chromosomalen DNS während der Evolution von *Chironomus thummi*. Chromosoma 17 (1965) 139.

KEYL, H.-G. and C. PELLING: Differentielle DNS-Replikation in den Speicheldrüsenchromosomen von *Chironomus thummi*. Chromosoma 14 (1963) 347.

LEZZI, M.: Die Wirkung von DNAse auf isolierte Polytän-Chromosomen. Exptl. Cell Res. 39 (1965) 289.

LIPPERT, U., K.-O. MOSEBACH and G. KRAMPITZ: Cell proteins as primary hormone acceptors after injection of testosterone-4-C^{14} into immature rats. Nature 214 (1967) 917.

MAURER, H.R. and G.R. CHALKLEY: Some properties of a nuclear binding site of estradiol. J. mol. Biol. 27 (1967) 431.

MAZIA, D., T. HAYASHI and K. YUDOWITCH: Fiber structure in chromosomes. Cold Spring Harbor Symp. Quant. Biol. 12 (1947) 122.

MAZIA, D. and L. JAEGER: Nuclease action, protease action and histochemical tests on salivary chromosomes of *Drosophila melanogaster*. Proc. Nat. Acad. Sci. 25 (1939) 456.

MUKHERJEE, A.S. and W. BEERMANN: Synthesis of ribonucleic acid by the X-chromosomes of *Drosophila melanogaster* and the problem of dosage compensation. Nature 207 (1965) 785.

PATTERSON, E.K. and M.E. DACKERMAN: Nucleic acid content in relation to cell size in the mature larval salivary gland of *Drosophila melanogaster*. Arch. Biochem. Biophys. 36 (1952) 97.

PAVAN, C.: Synthesis. Genetics Today 2 (1965) 335.

PAVAN, C. and M.E. BREUER: Differences in nucleic acid content of the loci in polytene chromosomes of *Rhynchosciara angelae* according to tissues and larval stages. Symposium on cell secretion. Belo Horizonte. (1955) 90.

PELLING, C.: A replicative and synthetic chromosomal unit. The modern concept of the chromomere. Proc. Roy. Soc. B. 164 (1966) 279.

PETTIT, B.J. and R.W. RASCH: Tritiated-histidine incorporation into *Drosophila* salivary chromosomes. J. Cell. Comp. Phys. 68 (1966) 325.

PLAUT, W.: On the replicative organization of DNA in the polytene chromosome of *Drosophila melanogaster*. J. Mol. Biol. 7 (1963) 632.

PLAUT, W., D. NASH and T. FANNING: Ordered replication of DNA in polytene chromosomes of *Drosophila melanogaster*. J. Mol. Biol. 16 (1966) 85.

RITOSSA, F. M. and S. SPIEGELMAN: Localization of DNA complementary to ribosomal RNA in the nucleolus organizer region of *Drosophila melanogaster*. Proc. Nat. Acad. Sci. 53 (1965) 737.

RODMAN, T. C.: DNA replication in salivary gland nuclei of *Drosophila melanogaster* at successive larval and prepupal stages. Genetics 55 (1967) 375.

ROSS, E. B.: The postembryonic development of the salivary glands of *Drosophila melanogaster*. J. Morphol. 65 (1939) 471.

RUDKIN, G. T.: Nucleic acid metabolism in giant chromosomes of *Drosophila melanogaster*. Ann. Histochim. Suppl. 2 (1962) 77.

RUDKIN, G. T.: Nonreplicating DNA in giant chromosomes. Genetics 52 (1965) 470.

RUDKIN, G. T. and S. L. CORLETTE: Disproportionate synthesis of DNA in a polytene chromosome region. Proc. Nat. Acad. Sci. 43 (1957) 964.

STEVENS, B. J. and H. SWIFT: RNA transport from nucleus to cytoplasm in *Chironomus* salivary glands. J. Cell Biol. 31 (1966) 55.

SWIFT, H.: Nucleic acids and cell metabolism in Dipteran salivary glands. In: J. M. Allen. The molecular control of cellular activity. New York, McGraw-Hill Book Co. (1962) p. 73.

SWIFT, H.: The histones of polytene chromosomes. In: J. Bonner and P. Ts'o. The nucleohistones. San Francisco, Holden Day Inc. 1964.

CHAPTER 21

Biochemistry of meiosis

HERBERT STERN and YASUO HOTTA

Department of Biology, University of California, San Diego, La Jolla, California 92037

Contents

1. Introduction
2. A physiological description of meiosis
   (a) Time span of cytological stages
   (b) Metabolic activities
   (c) Enzymatic equipment of meiotic cells
3. Molecular events during chromosome pairing
   (a) DNA synthesis
   (b) Protein synthesis
   (c) RNA synthesis
4. Molecular events during chiasma formation
   (a) DNA synthesis
   (b) Protein synthesis
5. Coordination of events. Achiasmatic meiosis.
6. Differentiation of meiotic cells
   (a) The G_2 interval
   (b) A model

This work was supported by a grant from the National Science Foundation (GB-5173X).

1. Introduction

The pairing and crossing-over of chromosomes are characteristic events of meiosis. Their occurrence in somatic cells is rare and may be properly regarded as exceptions which prove the rule. Thus, no better objective could be set for a biochemical approach to meiosis than the elucidation of those mechanisms which are responsible for pairing and crossing-over. And, inasmuch as meiotic cells are products of mitotic divisions, no better companion problem could be chosen than the identification of those processes which lead to the differentiation of meiotic cells from their mitotic progenitors. Undoubtedly, if these two problems were solved, the general resolution of the meiotic process would be within easy reach. The two problems have, of course, not been solved. The most this article can provide is a limited clarification of some of the mechanisms which are associated with these two characteristic events.

The classical cytological description of pairing and crossing-over provides the basis for all subsequent discussions. Despite some finer points of dispute among cytologists, this description coupled with genetic correlations furnishes the most lucid conceptual account of the process. The prophase of meiosis may be divided into several cytologically distinguishable stages. The first of these is 'leptonema' and, by most accounts, the chromosomes at this stage are identifiable as single threads. This is in contrast with mitotic prophase in which identifiable chromosome threads appear to be double. In meiotic cells, doubleness of chromosome threads becomes evident at the second prophase stage, 'zygonema'. This doubleness, however, is not a manifestation of prior chromosome reproduction, but is a consequence of pairing between homologous chromosomes. The zygotene stage is thus characterized by a progressive pairing of homologs. When zygotene cells are viewed under the electron microscope, the presence of a complex structure between homologs, the 'synaptinemal complex', is evident. 'Pachynema' follows zygonema and during this third prophase stage, the chromosomes remain paired and contract progressively. At the termination of pachynema homologs fall apart and chiasmata become apparent. Generally, chiasmata are regarded as the physical counterparts of genetic crossing-over. A great deal of evidence has been adduced in favor of this interpretation, but rigorous proof that this is actually so is still lacking. In this article chiasma formation will be assumed to be identical with crossing-over, but the assumption is made in order to facilitate discussion and not to exclude other possibilities.

The completion of pachynema marks the termination of a distinctive physiological phase of meiosis. With very few exceptions, cytological events from leptonema through pachynema are the same in all meiotic cells. Beyond pachynema, however, cells may follow one of several developmental patterns. In the microsporocytes of higher plants, diplonema, diakinesis, metaphase I, anaphase I and division II follow in quick succession. By contrast oocytes of various animal species frequently remain at diplonema for extended periods during which extensive macromolecular syntheses occur. Ribosome synthesis has been intensively studied in such cells. Mammalian oocytes do not complete meiosis until after fertilization when three of the haploid nuclei are eliminated from the egg as 'polar bodies' and the fourth one fuses with the sperm nucleus to form the zygote. From these and similar observations one may draw the tentative conclusion that once chiasma formation is completed, meiotic cells may engage in various physiological activities which are neither necessary for nor antagonistic to the consummation of meiosis. At what point in pachynema the completion occurs is not clear. The termination of pachynema is identified cytologically by the separation of homologs which is most probably a consequence of the disruption of the synaptinemal complex. We do not yet know whether such disruption is immediately triggered by the completion of chiasma formation and, indeed, we need not assume on *a priori* grounds that a quick succession of events is obligatory. The behavior of cells in late pachynema may thus reflect processes which need not be tied to pairing and chiasma formation.

The analysis of meiosis which is presented in this article is based almost entirely on studies conducted in our laboratory. The narrow experimental base is compensated for by the many other articles in this volume and is justified by the paucity of biochemical studies of meiosis in the literature. All of our experiments have been performed with the microsporocytes of a few species of liliaceous plants. These microsporocytes can be cultured *in vitro* and most of the biochemical and cytological studies have been done with cultured cells during the past two to three years. The reader may consult the following references for detailed accounts: Hotta and Stern (1963a, b, 1965a, b); Hotta et al., Ito and Stern, Ito et al., Roth and Ito, Stern (1963a, b), Stern and Hotta (1967a, b).

In addition, we are including a number of results for which manuscripts are now in preparation. The inclusion is made only because they appear to have a major significance to the problems dicussed here and are not minor addenda to published work. We wish to note that Dr. L.G. Parchman is principally responsible for studies of protein behavior and that Drs. Y. Hayashi and H. Ninnemann have collaborated in the studies of RNA metabolism. References to work outside this laboratory will be indicated at appropriate places in the text.

2. *A physiological description of meiosis*

(a) *Time span of cytological stages*

A major and characteristic difference between mitosis and meiosis is in the duration of the division cycle. Commonly, the duration of the cell cycle in mitotic tissues is of the order of 10–20 hours, whereas that in meiotic tissues extends for days, weeks or even months. Cells in the root tip of lilies, for example, undergo a full division cycle in about 24 hours, whereas those in the germinal tissue of the anther take about two weeks to progress through DNA synthesis and meiosis. The longer duration of meiosis is largely due to the prophase interval. Mitotic prophase is usually $\frac{1}{2}$–1 hour long; meiotic prophase is frequently 4–5 days. The difference is nicely illustrated by cultured cells of *Trillium erectum*. Following the premeiotic S-phase, explanted cells may be induced to enter either a mitotic or meiotic type of division (See part 6). As shown in Table 1, the population of cells which undergoes mitosis completes its full division long before the meiotic cells have completed prophase. This comparison is particularly significant because at the time of explantation the two populations of cells are virtually identical. Except for the fact that the premeiotic cells were more advanced in their development by a few days at the time of explantation, the two types of cells have identical developmental histories and undergo division in identical environments. The observed difference in time spans of prophase can only be attributed to the physiological properties which cells acquire after they have entered either meiosis or mitosis. The obvious conclusion which can be drawn is that the metabolic events underlying meiotic prophase are far more extensive than those underlying mitotic prophase. The problem, of course, is to identify the nature and significance of the metabolic events in question.

(b) *Metabolic activities*

The evidence that RNA and protein synthesis occur during meiotic prophase is unequivocal. Autoradiography has been used to advantage in showing that radioactive precursors of proteins and RNA are incorporated by cells during the prophase of meiosis. Similar results have been obtained by biochemical analyses of meiotic cells. Thus, despite the fact that chromosomes are undergoing a progressive contraction during

TABLE 1

Duration of cell cycle in cultured microsporocytes of *Lilium* (var. Cinnabar)

Stage of explantation	Type of division	Prophase duration (days)	Time to maximum metaphase count (days)
1. Premeiotic interphase	mitosis		3
2. Premeiotic interphase	achiasmatic meiosis	10	12
3. Late interphase-leptonema	achiasmatic meiosis	8	9

Cells were cultured at approximately 22 °C. No duration is given for mitotic prophase because it was too short to be measured by the procedure used. Samples were removed from culture at 1-day intervals. In the case of 'mitotic revertants' 10% of the cells in the first sample were in metaphase. No metaphase figures were seen in meiotic cells for the first 7–9 days. Cells in group 2 were approximately 1 day ahead of group 1 in their development. Data are taken from studies of Ito, Hotta and Stern (manuscript in preparation).

meiotic prophase, the cells retain biosynthetic activity. Such activity falls sharply as the cells enter metaphase and, in this respect, meiotic and mitotic cells are identical.

One issue which has remained in doubt is the question of DNA synthesis during meiotic prophase. This question too has now been resolved and the general statement may therefore be made that at least three categories of macromolecules are synthesized during meiotic prophase. In the case of liliaceous plants, polysaccharides may be added as a fourth category. Microsporocytes characteristically synthesize an extracellular layer of polysaccharide material called 'callose' during the latter stages of prophase.

(c) *Enzymatic equipment of meiotic cells*

With the exception of proteins, the synthesis of macromolecules during meiotic prophase has been found to be periodic. Were it possible to identify the types of protein made during this interval, a periodic formation of specific proteins would undoubtedly become apparent. To the extent that a relationship is sought between biosynthetic activities and enzymatic equipment the problem is to identify the mechanisms by which such activities are regulated. Thus far, only RNA and DNA synthesis have been examined, but the results shed little light on the mechanism of regulation. Both RNA and DNA polymerases have been identified in meiotic nuclei and the activities of these enzymes as measured *in vitro* are approximately constant during the entire cycle (Hotta and Stern 1965b; Stern and Hotta 1967b). The pyrimidine ribotide kinases are also approximately constant in activity throughout the cycle. The one striking correlation which has been observed between enzyme activity and rate of biosynthesis *in situ* relates to the riboside and deoxyriboside kinases. The level of cytidine and uridine kinase in cell extracts parallels the level of RNA synthesis *in situ*. A similar relationship has been found between thymidine kinase and DNA synthesis (Hotta and Stern 1965a). The significance of these correlations is unclear. Conceivably, the increased activities of these enzymes at appropriate intervals permit the cells to utilize efficiently the ribosides and deoxyribosides which are present within the anther. However, even if this is actually so, it is doubtful that these enzymes control the rates and timing of nucleic acid synthesis.

Most of these problems concerning metabolic regulation are not unique to meiotic cells. Most probably, meiotic cells furnish excellent material for resolving some of these regulatory problems, but the problems as such do not touch upon the unique features of the meiotic process. Clearly, meiotic cells, like all other cells, are programmed with respect to their metabolic activities. Our immediate objective is to define those activities which have a specific relevance to the progression of cytological events during the cycle. As already stated, the two events with which we are primarily concerned are chromosome pairing and crossing-over.

3. Molecular events during chromosome pairing

(a) *DNA synthesis*

The DNA of meiotic chromosomes is replicated during premeiotic interphase. The evidence for this has been obtained by autoradiographic (Taylor and McMaster; Lima-de-Faria and Borum) and also by biochemical techniques (Stern and Hotta 1967a). Thus, despite the distinctive behavior of chromosomes during meiotic prophase, the temporal pattern of chromosome reproduction appears to be similar to that characterizing mitotic cells. The interval between completion of the S-phase and the beginning of leptonema may vary considerably between different organisms. In *Trillium erectum* the interval is of the order of several weeks; in some species of *Lilium*, it is of the order of several days. In at least certain microorganisms, where meiosis follows zygote formation, the interval extends from the time of the last DNA synthesis in the gametic tissue to the initiation of meiosis following the fusion of gametes. DNA synthesis does not occur between the time of fusion and that of meiosis (Rossen and Westergaard). The fact that chromosome replication precedes meiosis has generated numerous discussions and speculations about the timing and mechanisms of crossing-over. On the basis of cytological data crossing-over would be expected to occur during pachynema and if so, it should be accompanied by some DNA synthesis. Although Wimber and Prensky had reported some autoradiographic evidence for DNA synthesis during meiotic prophase, their conclusion has not been generally accepted. Recent studies, however, no longer leave this conclusion in doubt.

The equivocal nature of the autoradiographic evidence for DNA synthesis during meiotic prophase can be attributed to the fact that the total amount of such synthesis is exceedingly small. If, however, biochemical techniques are used the evidence obtained is unambiguous. The period of major DNA synthesis occurs during premeiotic interphase and a second period of synthesis occurs during meiotic prophase. The amount of DNA synthesized during this second period is no more than 0.3–0.4% of the total DNA. A central fact about prophase DNA synthesis is that the composition of the product does not mirror the average composition of the total DNA (Table 2). The prophase product has a much higher content of guanine-cytosine residues. The significance of this compositional difference is not immediately apparent even though it serves as a convenient identifying mark for various other experiments. If, however, prophase-labeled DNA is resolved on a CsCl gradient a much broader basis is provided for speculation (Fig. 1). The peak position of the label corresponds closely to a composition of DNA which is similar to that obtained by direct chemical analysis. The composition of the newly formed DNA is thus virtually identical with that of the DNA molecules which band in the denser region of the gradient. Regardless of whether all or part of the molecules in that region are labeled, the discreteness of the band reflects the presence of a population of molecules with distinctive composition. A replication of short but randomly located stretches of DNA would result in a label which tracked

TABLE 2

Base composition of total DNA and of DNA labeled during meiotic prophase

	C	G	T	A
Total DNA (moles %)	20.2	21.4	29.6	28.9
Labeled DNA				
Premeiosis (% radioactivity)	20	22.8	30.2	27.0
Meiotic prophase	25.6	25.3	24.3	24.8
Zygonema	26.1	27.0	25.0	22.7
Zygonema-pachynema	25.3	25.3	25.3	24.1

The data shown above are similar to those previously published (Hotta et al.). Note that labeling of cells during the premeiotic S-phase yields a distribution of radioactivity among the deoxynucleotides which is very similar to the molar composition of total DNA obtained by chemical analysis.

Data on prophase label were obtained by exposing cells to P^{32} from zygonema to completion of meiosis. The zygonema–pachynema data were obtained from a mixture of zygotene and pachytene cells. The higher G–C content of the zygotene label is evident.

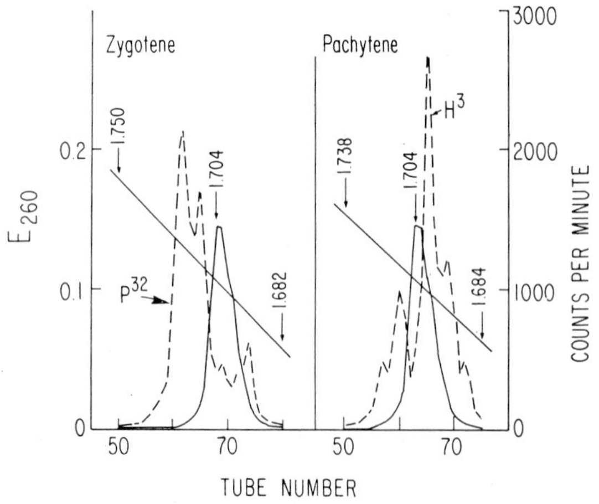

Fig. 1. Patterns of DNA synthesis during meiotic prophase. Meiotic cells were cultured in the presence of P^{32}-phosphate during the zygotene stage and another group of cells was cultured in the presence of H^3-thymidine during the pachytene stage. The buoyant densities of the nuclear DNA from each group of cells were resolved by centrifugation in a solution of CsCl. Solid curves indicate the distribution of optical density readings and broken lines indicate radioactivities. The regression lines represent the density of the CsCl solution (g/cc) in the eluted fractions. Values are included for three of the tubes. The mean density of total DNA extracted from these cells is 1.704. The plots are intended to show that the buoyant density of DNA synthesized during meiotic prophase differs from that of total nuclear DNA.

the optical density profile even though the stretches were rich in G–C residues. The average molecular weight of the labeled DNA is in the neighborhood of 6×10^6. Since the DNA is subjected to shearing forces in the course of preparation this value represents a lower limit. We may infer from these results that the material synthesized during meiotic prophase represents coherent regions of DNA with distinctive composition. The DNA has been shown to be nuclear, but whether or not it is an integral part of the chromosomes cannot be resolved by these biochemical experiments.

Closer inspection of the temporal character of the synthesis reveals that the composition of the DNA labeled is not constant over the entire prophase period. The several peaks of radioactivity shown in Fig. 1 do not appear simultaneously if the labeling period is limited to different intervals of the prophase. Although a sharp characterization of the labeling at each of the different prophase stages has not yet been achieved it is already clear that the heaviest peak is more or less characteristic of the zygotene stage whereas the lighter peaks are formed during pachynema. Thus, the cytological differences between zygotene and pachytene cells are matched by differences in the composition of the DNA synthesized. Such matching would suggest, but by no means prove, that meiotic DNA synthesis reflects more than one physiological function. If so, the different physiological functions must be associated with DNA regions of different composition.

The main question which arises from this speculative conclusion is the location of these regions with respect to the chromosomes. Thus far, no direct answer has been obtained. The possibility therefore remains that some extra-chromosomal but intranuclear structure is the site of prophase DNA synthesis. Circumstantial evidence, however, does not favor this possibility. The thrust of such evidence is in the direction of a very intimate association between the sites of prophase DNA synthesis and the integrity of chromosome structure.

A clear temporal correlation has been found between the initiation of DNA synthesis and the initiation of chromosome pairing. To be sure, a very precise identification of the respective cytological stages at which each of these processes begins is impossible with present experimental techniques. Nevertheless, despite the imprecision in timing, there is little doubt that the first phase of DNA synthesis extends through zygonema and that it begins somewhere between leptonema and zygonema. The significance of the temporal correlation is given more meaning by experiments in which DNA synthesis is inhibited by appropriate agents. If inhibition is effected in early zygonema the cells fail to proceed through zygonema. Cells thus inhibited show no evidence of synaptinemal complexes under the electron microscope (Roth and Ito). Moreover, the progressive formation of the synaptinemal complex during zygonema is arrested from the time at which the inhibitor is applied. A necessary relationship thus appears to exist between zygotene synthesis of DNA and the progression of chromosome pairing. Tentatively at least, the conclusion may be drawn that one function of DNA synthesis during meiotic prophase is to make possible chromosome pairing.

Models could be easily constructed in which this DNA is an integral part of chromosome structure in order to rationalize the observed relationship between DNA synthesis and chromosome pairing. Despite the attractiveness of such models, they are not justified by the data. Other pieces of cytological evidence, however, do have a more direct bearing on this issue. The most general effect of partially inhibiting DNA synthesis in zygotene cells is the appearance of aberrations in chromosome structure. Depending to some extent upon the species tested, these aberrations may be manifest as an extreme fragmentation of all chromosomes or as an extensive stickiness between chromosomes together with a fragmentation. Other properties of the chromosome such as contraction, metaphase alignment, or anaphase separation are not directly affected by inhibition of DNA synthesis. In those cells which have not suffered extensive chromosome fragmentation, the progression of the chromosomes through subsequent stages of division can be observed.

Leaving aside the particulars of the process which leads to chromosome fragmentation, the important conclusion which can be drawn is that interference with DNA synthesis during zygonema results in structural lesions along the entire length of each of the chromosomes. In some way, therefore, the maintenance of structural integrity depends upon completion of DNA synthesis during zygonema. The pattern of aberrations is characteristic for zygotene cells. Pachytene cells respond differently to DNA inhibition and cells at other stages of the meiotic cycle in which no DNA synthesis has been detected show no effect of DNA inhibitors. One may therefore reasonably speculate that the DNA which is replicated during zygotene is distinctive not only with respect to its chemical composition but also with respect to its functional role in chromosome organization. The pairing of chromosomes during meiosis appears to be directly tied to a simultaneous replication of distinctive regions within the chromosomes.

(b) *Protein synthesis*

The structure which lies between the paired homologs during zygonema is certainly not composed of DNA alone and most probably contains a large amount of protein (Moses and Coleman). This much seems reasonable to infer from EM studies. Thus, even though the DNA synthesized during zygonema is necessary for pairing, it is insufficient to account for the pairing structure. One might suppose that the protein of the synaptinemal complex is synthesized during zygonema and that the initiation of its synthesis is tied to the initiation of DNA synthesis. This supposition is not easily tested for proteins mediate many more types of cellular events than does DNA. Proteins are ubiquitously distributed within the cell whereas DNA is highly localized.

One generalization may be confidently made about proteins in relation to meiosis. They are synthesized through most of the meiotic cycle. Evidence for this has been obtained by both autoradiographic and biochemical analysis (Taylor; Hotta and Stern 1963a). If meiotic cells are cultured during any of the prophase stages in the presence of radioactive amino acids, they become heavily labeled in their acid-insoluble components. The cytoplasm is predominantly labeled in cells exposed to isotope for no longer than one hour. After 4–5 hours of exposure, the label is equally concentrated in nucleus and cytoplasm. No clear evidence has been obtained for a migration of label from cytoplasm to nucleus. In pulse-labeled cells which have been transferred to an isotope-free culture medium, the distribution and concentration of label remain approximately constant during several days of culture. Thus, apart from the general conclusion that proteins are synthesized during meiotic prophase, little can be said about the site of synthesis of nuclear proteins or about the precise location of the proteins formed.

The generalized occurrence of protein synthesis as measured by amino acid incorporation is matched by the generalized effect of inhibitors of protein synthesis on meiosis. Cells exposed to 1 μg/ml of cycloheximide, a concentration which inhibits amino acid incorporation by 80–90%, become arrested in their meiotic development. A less severe but equally pronounced arrest occurs at a concentration of 0.5 μg/ml. The effect of cycloheximide is observed at all meiotic stages up to metaphase. Although inhibitory, the drug is not toxic and cells which are maintained in culture in presence of the drug gradually resume their progress through division after 20–30 days. The rate and degree of progress depend upon the stage at which the cells were first exposed and the concentration of inhibitor used. A much more rapid recovery, of the order of 2–3 days, is obtained if the cells are transferred to an inhibitor-free medium. The principal conclusion which may be drawn from these experiments is that protein synthesis during the prophase interval is essential to meiotic development. Whether all the proteins synthesized are thus essential or whether the essential proteins are directly involved in chromosomal behavior cannot be inferred from these experiments.

Pointers to a specific role of certain proteins in prophase events come from biochemical analyses. The analyses are still at a preliminary stage and are restricted to the nuclear fraction of the cells. As would be expected from autoradiographic data, nuclei isolated from cells which had been exposed to radioactive amino acids during zygonema or pachynema contain radioactive protein. The highest specific activity is found in proteins which have been extracted from mechanically disrupted nuclei with 0.01 M K–Na phosphate buffer at a *p*H of 8.0–8.5. If this extract is resolved on a DEAE column, a major peak of radioactivity elutes ahead of the major peak of optical density. This peak of radioactivity, which is abolished by protease treatment, accounts for a very small proportion of the total protein in the extract. Cells labeled either prior to zygonema or after pachynema have no appreciable amount of radioactivity in this peak even though other fractions on the column are as radioactive as those obtained from zygotene or pachytene cells (Fig. 2). The only basis for selecting this particular peak of radioactivity from all the others is its temporal correlation with zygonema–pachynema stages. This correlation, coupled with the fact that the protein is nuclear, has prompted further studies.

Circumstantial evidence has been obtained for a more or less direct involvement of this protein fraction in prophase events. Radioactivity in the selected peak, but not in the others, is abolished in zygotene–pachytene cells exposed to 0.5 μg/ml of cycloheximide, a concentration which arrests meiotic development. Concentrations of cycloheximide in the range of 2–5 μg/ml abolish all radioactivity, but cells thus treated become necrotic. The selective inhibitory effect of low cycloheximide concentrations of protein synthesis is matched by a selective inhibitory effect of meiotic development. The basis for this selective inhibition is not at all clear but the fact that synthesis of a particular group of nuclear proteins is essential to meiotic development but not to cell viability points to a distinctive role for these proteins in the meiotic process.

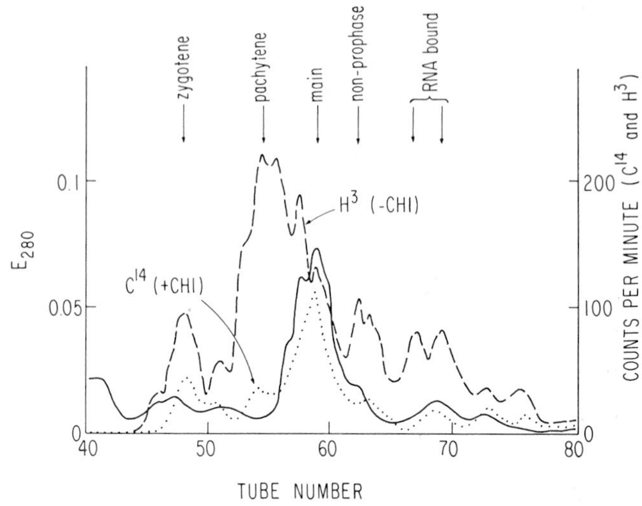

Fig. 2. Chromatographic profile of a nuclear protein fraction prepared from cells in meiotic prophase. The protein fraction was obtained by a slightly alkaline extraction of fragmented nuclei (see text). Cells were exposed to labeled leucine in the presence or absence of cycloheximide (CHI). The protein extract was resolved on a DEAE column using a linear gradient of increasing sodium chloride concentrations for elution. The solid line represents optical density. Notations in the upper part of the figure indicate the following: Peaks marked zygotene and pachytene do not become labeled at other stages. The 'non-prophase' peak is labeled at most meiotic stages. The RNA peaks represent a mixture of RNA and protein. As discussed in the text, zygotene and pachytene peaks contain DNA. The profile of labeled protein does not track that of optical density. However, in the presence of cycloheximide (0.5 μg/ml) inhibition is selective and the residual labeling more or less tracks the optical density profile. The figure is based on data from Hotta, Parchman and Stern.

The circumstantial evidence is further strengthened by the chemical relationship between this arbitrarily selected protein group and the DNA replicated during meiotic prophase. Under the conditions used for extracting protein, negligible amounts of DNA are extracted from the nuclei. However, the very small amounts of DNA thus extracted represent 50–70% of prophase-labeled material. The partial extraction of labeled DNA may be due to an incomplete breakage of nuclei but, whether or not this is so, the significant feature is the selective extraction of prophase-labeled DNA. The basis for this selective extraction is revealed by experiments in which prophase cells are doubly labeled with radioactive thymidine and leucine. If the alkaline extract from the nuclei of such cells is resolved on a DEAE column, the DNA–thymidine and the protein leucine-peaks coincide. The appearent protein–DNA complex bands as a single peak in a cesium chloride gradient. The complex is unaffected by high salt concentrations but is disrupted by heat or alkaline denaturation. Both components are precipitated in acid solutions. To the extent that these experiments reveal a natural complex between specific components of DNA and protein respectively, the conclusion may be drawn that the distinctive role which has been assigned to DNA with respect to chromosome pairing must be broadened to include a specific group of proteins. Since we do not know how this presumed nucleoprotein complex relates to chromosome structure, the nature of that distinctive role must remain undefined.

Despite the absence of information about structural relationships between the DNA and protein synthesized during meiotic prophase, some evidence has been obtained about functional relationships. Inhibition of protein synthesis results in an inhibition of DNA synthesis. This secondary inhibitory effect appears to be restricted to DNA; RNA synthesis is unaffected. If cells exposed to cycloheximide are transferred to an inhibitor-free medium, DNA synthesis is resumed. The synthesis of DNA during meiotic prophase thus requires the concomitant synthesis of a structurally associated protein. Since formation of the synaptinemal complex does not proceed in the absence of prophase DNA synthesis, we must conclude that it cannot proceed in the absence of this specific protein synthesis.

(c) *RNA synthesis*

Information about the nature of RNA synthesis during meiotic prophase is very limited. As is the case for proteins, evidence from a variety of studies indicates that RNA is synthesized during one or more stages of meiotic prophase (Das; Taylor; Monesi). Moreover, the synthesis during zygonema and at least the earlier half of pachynema is mainly restricted to the nuclei. Autoradiographic analyses of cells in the male germ line also show the exclusion of label from the nucleoli. In light of the evidence that ribosomal RNA is synthesized in the nucleoli, the conclusion may be drawn that such RNA is not synthesized to any detectable degree during the early stages of meiosis. Meiotic cells are nevertheless capable of synthesizing ribosomal RNA. When oocytes of *Amphibia*, for example, reach diplonema they begin to synthesize very large amounts of ribosomal RNA (Gall). The synthesis is clearly related to the special needs of oocyte development and does not appear to have a specific relevance to the meiotic process *per se*.

The important question concerning RNA synthesis is whether it has one or more functional roles in early stages of meiosis. The studies of Hayashi and Ninnemann in our laboratory indicate that the kind of RNA synthesized during zygonema and up to mid or late pachynema is different from that synthesized during subsequent stages. At the later stages, most of the RNA formed is similar to if not identical with ribosomal RNA. At earlier stages synthesis is predominantly of the non-ribosomal type. A sharp transition thus occurs at some time during the late pachytene stage. The apparent absence of ribosomal RNA synthesis during meiotic prophase has been interpreted as evidence of message RNA synthesis (Hotta and Stern 1963b; Rossen and Westergaard). This interpretation must be considered as speculative since message RNA has not been definitively demonstrated.

4. *Molecular events during chiasma formation*

Chiasmata become cytologically evident at diplonema and are assumed to be formed during pachynema. Although no direct evidence has been obtained to support this assumption, the argument for it is unusually strong. The fact that chiasmata are interchanges between homologous chromosomes requires that homologs be in close association at the time of interchange. Since pairing occurs during zygonema, it is reasonable to infer that chiasmata are formed upon completion of pairing. An objection can be raised to this argument on the grounds that chiasmata might already be present in leptotene chromosomes and that pairing follows rather than precedes chiasma formation. As will be discussed below, the objection is untenable since it can be shown that leptotene chromosomes are not chiasmatic. The more difficult question which has already been raised, and to which we have no definitive answer, is whether genetic crossing-over and chiasmata are different aspects of the same process.

(a) *DNA synthesis*

DNA synthesis occurs during pachynema just as it does during zygonema. The relative amounts of DNA synthesized during the respective intervals have not been precisely determined, but mention has already been made of the evidence that the composition of the DNA formed changes with the progression of prophase. It is attractive to suppose that these changes reflect the cytologically observable changes in chromosome behavior. Direct evidence in support of this supposition is lacking. Circumstantial evidence, on the other hand, does point to some distinctive function for pachytene DNA synthesis.

The occurrence of DNA synthesis during pachynema is consistent with the assumption that crossing-over occurs during this same interval. The critical question, however, is whether pachynema DNA synthesis exclusively reflects this one process. Were this so, meiotic cells would be model systems for studying the molecular mechanisms of crossing-over. The evidence, limited though it is, does not support this simple conclusion. As yet, we have been unable to detect any major differences in DNA patterns between chiasmatic and achiasmatic cells. Thus, although certain differences probably do exist between chiasmatic and achiasmatic cells, it would appear as though the bulk of prophase DNA synthesis is not a reflection of crossing-over. A question which remains unanswered is whether pachynema synthesis is essential to crossing-over even though it might not be a part of the immediate process.

Inhibition of DNA synthesis during pachynema does not lead to the same pattern of structural lesions as inhibition during zygonema. Generally, pachynema cells exposed to inhibitor progress through the first meiotic division more or less normally. Chiasmata are evident at diplonema, at least under conditions which lead to a 60% inhibition of DNA synthesis. Lesions are nevertheless produced in the chromosomes and these become evident during the second meiotic division. Although some chromatid breaks may be seen in first anaphase chromosomes, the frequency is about one tenth of that observed during metaphse II and anaphase II. The differences between the respective responses of zygotene and pachytene cells to DNA inhibition may be trivial or profound. At present, we have no experimental basis for making a choice. In either case, there can be little doubt about the principal conclusion that pachynema synthesis, like zygonema synthesis, occurs in regions of the chromosome which are essential to its structural integrity.

(b) *Protein synthesis*

The biochemical patterns of protein synthesis shown in Fig. 2 cover both the zygotene and pachytene stages. A resolution of protein synthesis with respect to each of the stages has not yet been performed. That cells require protein synthesis in order to progress through pachynema is demonstrated by the fact that cycloheximide arrests such progress. A more revealing result is obtained, however, by exposing cells to cycloheximide for 2–3 days and tracing their subsequent behavior upon being returned to an inhibitor-free medium. Directly pertinent to the phenomenon of chiasma formation is the behavior of cells which have been exposed to cycloheximide during late zygonema. Cells thus treated resume their progress through meiosis in normal medium but show no chiasmata when they reach what might be considered the equivalent of diplonema. The timing of inhibitor treatment is critical; mid or late pachynema cells similarly treated do show chiasmata at diplonema even though they manifest other aberrations at a later stage.

One important conclusion which may be drawn from these observations is that chiasmata are not formed during zygonema, a conclusion which is identical with that generally made on cytological grounds. This conclusion, however, does not touch upon the most interesting feature of the experiment, namely, that a temporary block in protein synthesis during late zygonema results in a by-passing of chiasma formation during pachynema. The result implies that certain chromosomal changes have occurred in the presence of cycloheximide so that upon resumption of protein synthesis the chromosomes have already progressed beyond the stage at which chiasma formation is possible. The implication is clarified by cytological observations. Arrest of protein synthesis results in desynapsis so that the 'pachytene' chromosomes are poorly paired. The failure to form chiasmata may thus be a consequence of a failure to maintain pairing. If so, the conclusion would be reinforced that the persistence of pairing through pachynema is essential to the formation of chiasmata. These results do not, of course, exclude the possibility that some specific protein synthesis is directly involved in chiasma formation.

5. *Coordination of events. Achiasmatic meiosis*

A question which has been given prominence with respect to meiotic mechanisms is the relationship of zygotene pairing to chiasma formation. This question, which has already been raised in preceding sections, lends itself better to analysis if considered under two headings. One problem is to define the time of chiasma formation in order to determine whether chiasmata are formed prior to zygotene pairing or whether they are formed after the completion of pairing. Given an answer to this first problem it is then possible to examine the factors which might be responsible for a coordination of the two processes if such coordination appears to exist.

On the question of whether chiasmata are formed during the premeiotic S-phase or during meiotic prophase, an unambiguous answer can now be given. If chiasmata are defined as durable exchanges between chromosome pairs, formation must be assigned to meiotic prophase. If, on the other hand, the criterion of durability is regarded as superfluous and the position is taken that chiasmata form during the premeiotic S-phase but may or may not persist as such through meiotic prophase, no answer can be given until the occurrence of genetic crossing-over, or the lack of it, can be demonstrated in achiasmatic cells. For reasons already given, we will assume the identity of chiasmata with crossing-over. On this basis the evidence for the timing of chiasma formation is formidable. In several organisms, achiasmatic cells have been induced by subjecting meiotic tissue to elevated temperatures at various stages of the meiotic cycle. In general, the results have led to the conclusion that heat effectively reduces chiasma frequency if applied at the zygotene–pachytene stages (Henderson). One exception which assigns the heat-sensitive period to the premeiotic S-phase could be explained by the uncertainty in the method used to determine stage of treatment. The reasoning used to interpret the temperature experiments is that if chiasmata were already present at zygonema they would not be abolished by the treatment. This reasoning has been supported by evidence that elevated temperatures do not reduce chiasma frequency if applied during the premeiotic S-phase or at stages later than the sensitive interval.

Our own studies have been of a similar nature although more direct with respect to stage of treatment. Achiasmatic meioses are readily induced in cells by explanting them into culture media after the premeiotic S-phase but prior to mid-leptonema. Under the appropriate conditions, virtually all cells are rendered achiasmatic. However, if cells at mid-leptonema or later are explanted under identical conditions, they enter chiasmatic meiosis. Moreover, two forms of behavior may be observed in cells explanted at the leptonema stage. At one temperature (e.g., 20 °C) cells enter a normal meiosis; at a higher temperature (27 °C) a substantial proportion of the cells becomes achiasmatic. No effect of temperature on production of achiasmatics has been observed in cells at stages later than leptonema. These results and those reported by others all point to the fact that chiasma formation can be suppressed by relatively mild environmental disturbances during an interval of development between the premeiotic S-phase and diplonema. On the assumption that chiasmata, once formed, would be evident at diplonema, the results must be interpreted as indicating that their formation has not yet occurred during the interval of sensitivity to environmental perturbations.

The evidence obtained in our laboratory indicates that the interval of sensitivity does not coincide with that of pairing but precedes it. Such behavior cannot, however, be explained on the basis of an interference with the pairing process. Cells explanted in late premeiotic interphase or in early leptonema show a typical pattern of zygotene pairing under the light microscope. Although we may presume that pairing is essential to chiasma formation, it is clear that pairing does not assure such formation. Certain processes must therefore be disturbed prior to the initiation of pairing which do not interfere with pairing itself but which do interfere with chiasma formation following pairing. The identity of these processes is unknown, but their relationship to the production of achiasmatics may depend upon one of two possibilities. The processes may normally occur either prior to zygonema or after it. In the first case, environmental disturbances such as explantation or elevated temperature would be viewed as inhibiting or deranging the processes. In the second case the disturbances would be viewed as inducing them precociously. Our own preference is for the second alternative because of the attractiveness of the simple explanation that the processes in question are prophasic DNA synthesis and that this synthesis is induced precociously by explantation or heat treatment.

6. *Differentiation of meiotic cells*

(a) *The G_2 interval*

The technique of explanting premeiotic cells at various intervals between the S-phase and leptonema provides the experimental basis for a few conclusions which can be drawn concerning the physiological characteristics of the G_2 interval. Immediately following completion of premeiotic DNA synthesis, cells are still capable of reverting to a normal mitotic division. If, therefore, certain processes which are unique to meiosis do occur during the S-period, they do not commit the cells to meiosis. The duration of the interval following S-phase which permits complete reversion is short but its limits have not been precisely determined. In *Trillium erectum* the phenomenon is easily demonstrated whereas in various species of *Lilium* it is difficult to obtain an explant in which the response is uniform.

Following this interval, two characteristics of meiotic cells become determined prior to their entry into leptonema – delayed centromere division and pairing. The first of these characteristics becomes evident in explanted cells which enter a mitotic type of division. Progress is normal up to and including metaphase, but anaphase separations do not occur and, instead, the chromosomes revert to an interphase morphology. The second characteristic is apparent in cells which are explanted shortly before leptonema. Such cells enter into a typical meiotic prophase but, as already pointed out, give rise to achiasmatic cells.

Against this background of cytological evidence, the only molecular evidence now available relates to DNA synthesis. In all cases of 'revertants' thus far studied, the explanted cells show a pattern of DNA synthesis similar to that found during meiotic prophase. We can only speculate that part or all of the DNA synthesized during normal meiotic prophase represents a delayed synthesis. The speculation may be extended to a generalization that this DNA represents a unique structural part of the chromosome and that in mitotic cells it is replicated at the termination of the S-phase or in the G_2 interval. To the extent that this speculation is correct, the conclusion may be drawn that among the immediate changes associated with the entry of a cell into meiosis, a suppression of the replication of this critical structural element is the first.

(b) *A model*

So many models of chromosome structure have been devised to rationalize cytogenetic data that additional ones are almost certain to be superfluous. A diagrammatic representation of the essential findings discussed here would, nevertheless, be useful to the reader. This is the purpose of the model shown in Fig. 3. It has kinships with many other models and, originality, if there appears to be any, is accidental.

The critical feature of the model is the designation of relatively small segments of the DNA filament as 'axial elements.' Whether the axial elements form a continuous chain subtending large filaments of DNA, or whether they link large DNA loops is irrelevant to our immediate purpose. Two functional properties are assigned to these elements: (1) They are located along the entire length of the chromosome; (2) Their replication in meiotic cells is delayed until zygonema. The pattern of their distribution has been chosen in order to support the speculation that the axial regions are the primary sites of pairing between homologs. The timing of their replication has been chosen in order to provide a simplified account of the pairing process.

Our model for the mechanism of pairing avoids the difficult question of how homologs are initially aligned. We begin with the assumption that pairing between homologs is due to a pairing between single DNA filaments of each of the respective homologs. Since such pairing would first require a disruption of base pairing within the unreplicated portion of the chromosome, we imagine that the initiation of DNA synthesis in the axial regions is sufficient to disrupt the original pairing. This mechanism is attractive from the energetic standpoint. Since the bulk of chromosomal DNA is assumed to have replicated in the S-phase, the total energy of hydrogen bonding in the axial regions is relatively small, and if junction points are spread apart upon initiation of axial replication, the remainder of the axial elements could be readily disengaged. Homologous strands of opposite polarity could then bond to one another. Since such bonding would be destroyed as the strands replicate we suppose that formation of the synaptinemal complex occurs simultaneously with replication. The complex is thus imagined as a mechanism to stabilize the pairing.

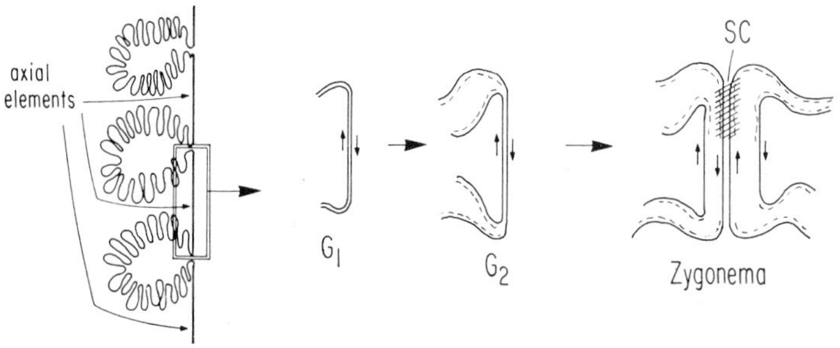

Fig. 3. A model of chromosome pairing which is consistent with the studies reported here. The critical structure in this model is the axial element which ties together the very large loops of DNA. The loops may or may not be circles but, regardless of their configuration, they are presumed to account for 99% or more of the DNA. The critical event in this diagram is the suppression of axial replication during the premeiotic S-phase. Thus, the axial elements are still unreplicated at G_2. Replication of the axial element is presumed to begin at zygonema. The initiation of axial replication permits a separation of complementary strands within a chromatid thus facilitating pairing between strands of homologous chromatids. Such pairing would not persist in regions where replication has occurred. The coordinated initiation of protein synthesis with DNA synthesis in zygonema is presumed to be the mechanism whereby the synaptinemal complex (SC) is formed as replication proceeds. The complex would thus account for the stabilization of pairing. The data now available do not permit any realistic speculation about the relationship of this model to crossing-over.

Our present experimental data on events at pachynema do not justify any further elaboration of this speculative scheme. Moreover, the limited scheme provides for more than enough inferences which need to be tested. These inferences may be listed as follows: (1) The persistence of pairing, but not pairing as such, is the function of the synaptinemal complex. If axial elements are replicated under conditions where the mechanisms for synaptinemal complex formation are turned off, the result would be a mitotic division. Since replication of the axial elements would represent the critical event in the reproduction of a chromosome into two chromatids, it is attractive to suppose that such replication occurs in the G_2 phase of mitotic divisions. However, it would be equally logical to suppose that the replication occurs in early S-phase. In meiotic cells the timing of the axial replication is critical and the speculative scheme would not have to be altered if the premeiotic S-phase extended into leptonema (Lima-de-Faria et al.). On the other hand, the scheme would have to be discarded if it were shown that no axial replication occurs in post-zygotic meiosis where bulk DNA synthesis is absent between fusion and initiation of meiosis. (2) Prematurely initiated DNA synthesis in meiotic cells would lead to incomplete synaptinemal complexes and hence to their instability. (3) Stabilized pairing is an essential condition for chiasma formation. Premature dissolution of the pairing complex should lead to a failure in chiasma formation.

If schemes such as this one appear to be reasonable, more tribute must be paid to our ignorance than to our understanding. If any part of the scheme turns out to be correct, luck rather than prescience will be the responsible agent. Hopefully, the errors in the scheme will help uncover a few areas of ignorance.

References

DAS, N.K.: Inactivation of the nucleolar apparatus during meiotic prophase in corn anthers. Exptl. Cell Res. 40 (1965) 360–364.

GALL, J.G.: Nuclear RNA of the salamander oocyte. Natl. Cancer Inst. Monograph 23 (1966) 475–488.

HENDERSON, S.A.: Time of chiasma formation in relation to the time of deoxyribonucleic acid synthesis. Nature 211 (1966) 1043–1047.

HOTTA, Y., M.ITO and H.STERN: Synthesis of DNA during meiosis. Proc. Natl. Acad. Sci. U.S. 56 (1966) 1184–1191.

HOTTA, Y., L.G.PARCHMAN and H.STERN: Protein synthesis during meiosis. Proc. Natl. Acad. Sci. U.S. 60 (1968) 575–582.

HOTTA, Y. and H.STERN: Inhibition of protein synthesis during meiotic development and its bearing on intracellular regulation. J. Cell Biol. 16 (1963a) 259–279.

HOTTA, Y. and H.STERN: Synthesis of messenger-like ribonucleic acid and protein during meiosis in isolated cells of *Trillium erectum*. J. Cell Biol. 19 (1963b) 45–58.

HOTTA, Y. and H.STERN: Inducibility of thymidine kinase by thymidine as a function of interphase stage. J. Cell Biol. 25 (1965a) 99–108.

HOTTA, Y. and H.STERN: Polymerase and kinase activities in relation to RNA synthesis during meiosis. Protoplasma 60 (1965b) 218–232.

ITO, M., Y.HOTTA and H.STERN: Studies of meiosis *in vitro* II. Effect of inhibiting DNA synthesis during meiotic prophase on chromosome structure and behavior. Develop. Biol. 16 (1967) 36–53.

ITO, M. and H.STERN: Studies of meiosis *in vitro* I. *In vitro* culture of meiotic cells. Develop. Biol. 16 (1967) 54–77.

LIMA-DE-FARIA, A. and K.BORUM: The period of DNA synthesis prior to meiosis in the mouse. J. Cell Biol. 14 (1962) 381–388.

LIMA-DE-FARIA, A., J.GERMAN, M.GHATNEKAR and L.ANDERSON: DNA synthesis in the meiotic chromosomes of man. A preliminary report. Hereditas 56 (1966) 398–399.

MONESI, V.: Ribonucleic acid synthesis during mitosis and meiosis in the mouse testis. J. Cell Biol. 22 (1964) 521–532.

MOSES, M.J. and J.R.COLEMAN: Structural patterns and the functional organization of chromosomes. In: M.Locke, ed.: The role of chromosomes in development. New York, Academic Press (1964) 11–50.

ROSSEN, J.M. and M.WESTERGAARD: Studies on the mechanism of crossing-over. II. Meiosis and the time of meiotic chromosome replication in the Ascomycete *Neotitella rutilans*. Compt. Rend. Trav. Lab. Carlsberg 35 (1966) 233–260.

ROTH, T.F. and M.ITO: DNA dependent formation of the synaptinemal complex at meiotic prophase. J. Cell Biol. 35 (1967) 247–255.

STERN, H.: Intracellular regulatory mechanisms in chromosome replication and segregation. Federation Proc. 22 (1963) 1097–1102.

STERN, H. and Y.HOTTA: Regulated synthesis of RNA and protein in the control of cell division. Brookhaven Symposia in Biology 16 (1963) 59–72.

STERN, H. and Y.HOTTA: Chromosome behavior during development of meiotic tissue. In: L.Goldstein, ed.: The control of nuclear activity. Englewood Cliffs, N.Y., Prentice-Hall (1967a) 47–67.

STERN, H. and Y.HOTTA: Biochemical studies of male gametogenesis in liliaceous plants. Topics in Devel. Biology III, New York, Academic Press (1967b) (in press).

TAYLOR, J.H.: Autoradiographic studies of nucleic acids and proteins during meiosis in *Lilium longiflorum*. Am. J. Botany 46 (1959) 477–484.

TAYLOR, J.H. and R.D.MCMASTER: Autoradiographic and microspectrophotometric studies of desoxyribosenucleic acid during microgametogenesis in *Lilium longiflorum*. Chromosoma 6 (1954) 489–521.

WINBER, D.E. and W.PRENSKY: Autoradiography with meiotic chromosomes of the male newt (*Triturus viridescens*) using H^3-thymidine. Genetics 48 (1963) 1731–1738.

CHAPTER 22

Biochemical activities of chromosomes during the prophase of meiosis

H. G. CALLAN

Department of Zoology, The University, St. Andrews, Scotland

Contents

1. Introduction
2. DNA synthesis during prophase of meiosis
3. RNA and protein synthesis during female meiotic prophase
4. RNA and protein synthesis during male meiotic prophase
5. Oocyte regulators of gene activity

1. Introduction

The gross morphology of chromosomes during the complex sequence of events which constitutes meiosis has been well documented; and in view of the universality of Mendelian genetic laws it is not surprising that these events, responsible for the production of cells containing nuclei with variously recombined haploid gene complexes, are in general terms similar in diploid plants and animals, similar on the male and female side, and similar in haploid organisms where meiosis follows, rather than precedes, syngamy. The sequence begins with leptotene, when chromosomes resolvable with the light microscope appear within nuclei previously at interphase. Chromosomes at leptotene have a characteristic chromomeric organization, and during this and the following two stages they contract in length. Concurrent with contraction in length, axial cores of protein are laid down along each chromosome, structures which later appear as the lateral components of the synaptinemal complex. Synapsis of homologous chromosomes occurs during zygotene; in some organisms, e.g. *Amphibia*, synapsis progresses from the free ends of the chromosomes towards middle regions, leading to a characteristic 'bouquet' arrangement. In such organisms the contraction in chromosome length as synapsis progresses is especially evident. With synapsis the middle component of the synaptinemal complex makes its appearance. In other organisms, e.g. *Zea mays*, a synizetic knot is formed during synapsis, and the progression of homologous chromosome pairing is obscure.

It is during the next two stages of first meiotic prophase, pachytene and diplotene, that great variation in chromosome morphology is encountered, between organisms, and between sexes. At one extreme we have grasshopper male meiosis; lateral extensions project from the chromosome axes, but the chromosomes as a whole progressively shorten, reaching their most contracted state and ultimately withdrawing their lateral projections at first meiotic metaphase (Henderson). At the other extreme we have urodele amphibian female meiosis; lateral 'lampbrush' loops extend from the chromosomes during pachytene and a prolonged diplotene, and this process is accompanied by an enormous elongation of chromosome axes, with the reappearance of chromomeric organization. Just prior to first metaphase the lateral loops are withdrawn, and rapid contraction of chromosome axes leads to the obliteration of chromomeres and the production of short, compact chromosomes with smooth outlines (Callan and Lloyd). In this chapter the rest of the meiotic process will not be considered; my concern here is to discuss what is known about the biochemical activities of meiotic prophase, particularly lampbrush, chromosomes.

2. DNA synthesis during prophase of meiosis

It seems likely that the lampbrush organization of chromosomes at pachytene–diplotene is universal. Admittedly for plants the evidence for this statement is extremely meagre (it rests on the mere observation that pachytene–diplotene chromosomes often have fuzzy outlines; see Grun) but for animals more and more evidence has been accumulating that lampbrush chromosomes are widespread both in male and female meiosis (Callan 1957; and for a more recent demonstration see Kunz).

It has been firmly established that DNA synthesis precedes meiosis (Swift; Taylor 1953, 1959), though in material where the beginning of leptotene can be clearly identified, e.g. *Tradescantia* and urodele male meiosis, the end of the premeiotic DNA synthesis laps over into leptotene. According to Lima-de-Faria et al. premeiotic DNA synthesis in humans even extends to zygotene. There is no unequivocal evidence for further chromosomal DNA synthesis during meiosis, though there has been at least one such claim (Wimber and Prensky), and a recently proposed theory in explanation of crossing-over (Whitehouse) requires that DNA synthesis on a limited scale should occur after synapsis. In the oocyte nuclei of *Xenopus laevis*, which contain multiple detached nucleoli, the synthesis of nucleolar DNA occurs during pachytene (Gall 1968; Macgregor 1968). Although the pachytene–diplotene lampbrush phase may involve enormous elongation of the chromosomes, no chromosomal DNA synthesis accompanies this process.

3. *RNA and protein synthesis during female meiotic prophase*

Studies on dipteran polytene chromosomes have shown that RNA synthesis is restricted to those regions of the chromosomes (puffs and Balbiani rings) where the DNA is in an extended state. This being so it might seem logical to consider the extension of lateral loops from chromomeres in lampbrush chromosomes as meeting a direct functional requirement for RNA synthesis, i.e. that the lampbrush organization exists to provide for such synthesis during meiotic prophase. The validity of this conclusion may be doubted. There is plenty of evidence that RNA synthesis does take place on the lateral loops of lampbrush chromosomes, evidence to be considered later, but it is incorrect to assume that the lampbrush phase of meiosis is always coincident in time with particularly intense synthesis of RNA. Thus, for example, spermatocytes of the plethodont salamander *Batrachoseps attenuatus* have exceedingly 'whiskery' chromosomes during pachytene–diplotene, yet these spermatocytes show a progressively diminishing rate of RNA synthesis as they pass from pre-leptotene, through a lampbrush phase, to first meiotic metaphase (Callan, unpublished).

The lampbrush pattern of organization may have quite another significance. If, as proposed by Callan (1967), genetic units in the chromosomes of higher organisms consist of serially repeated code sequences, each series comprising a 'master' sequence followed by 'slave' sequences, then the extension of lateral loops from chromosome axes may result from a progressive base-pair matching of slave sequences against the master sequence, one-way (master → slave) correction of incongruous base pairs, followed by the lateral extension of corrected slaves. After slave sequence correction at this crucial moment in the life cycle (immediately post-synapsis, when recombination between homologous master sequences may have occurred), the slave sequences become available for coding RNA if the nature of the gene and of the gametocyte, male or female, so requires. It should be noted that in the ovaries of some insects, e.g. *Diptera*, the post-synaptic oocyte nucleus appears not to engage in any RNA synthesis (Bier); it would be particularly interesting to have more information about chromosome organization in such genuinely resting nuclei.

Autoradiographic studies on urodele lampbrush chromosomes show that the overwhelming majority of the lateral loops engage in RNA synthesis, different loops at different rates, and that (with a few notable exceptions) there are equal rates of accumulation of labelled RNA on different portions of any given loop (Fig 5). In other words the morphological differentiation along a typical lateral loop, thin at one end and progressively thicker towards the other end, which reflects the quantity of RNP matrix attached to the DNA-containing loop axis (Fig. 4) is not correlated with differential rates of RNA synthesis. Gall (unpublished) broke lampbrush loops with X-rays, yet found post-irradiation incorporation of H^3-uridine into RNA on both sides of breaks. This conclusively establishes that RNA synthesis occurs simultaneously along the entire lengths of normal loops (see also Miller).

In the newt *Triturus cristatus cristatus* there is an exceptional lateral loop, the giant granular loop on the smallest (XIIth) chromosome (Fig. 1), where short-term incorporation of H^3-uridine only labels RNA in the dense tip at this loop's thinner end (Fig. 2) (Gall and Callan 1962). A similar exceptional loop occurs in *T. viridescens* (Gall 1963). With the passage of time the labelled RNA moves towards the thicker end of this loop, and since for longer term observations H^3-uridine must be injected into the female newt, and since the injected labelled uridine enters a pool in the oocyte and hence remains available for incorporation into newly synthesized RNA for a matter of weeks, autoradiographs of the giant granular loop made from oocytes fixed at progressively longer time intervals after injection show progressively greater lengths of labelled loop matrix (Fig. 3). Under ordinary conditions the giant granular loop becomes labelled throughout its length about 10 days after H^3-uridine injection (the process can be accelerated by gonadotrophic hormone stimulation) and there is no indication that labelled RNP matrix is discharged from the giant granular loop until it arrives at the thick end, where the loop axis inserts into the chromomere. This means that the RNA synthesized by the giant granular loop remains for a remarkably long time physically attached to the chromosome, and during this time there is a massive increase in bulk of loop matrix protein associated with that RNA. Is this protein synthesized *in situ*, inside the nucleus? This is an important, as yet unanswered question. Another unanswered question is whether the DNA-containing loop axis moves along with the loop matrix, or whether the matrix moves over a stationary loop axis.

The asymmetrical distribution of matrix is a feature of lateral loops generally, not merely of the giant granular loop, and this has prompted the speculation that movement occurs in all. Direct evidence for such movement has not yet been obtained. If the speculation is correct, it is likely that in normal circumstances matrix RNP is

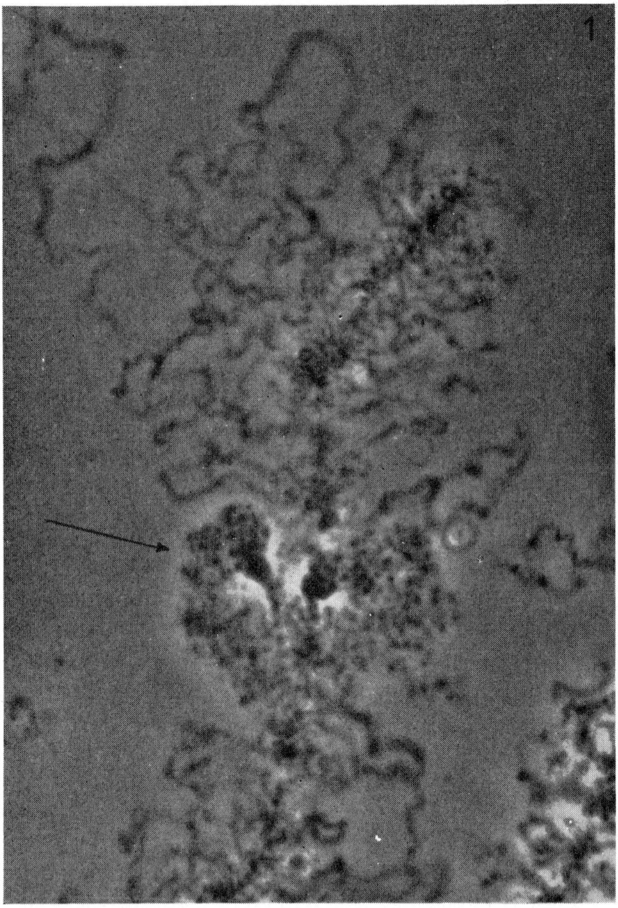
1

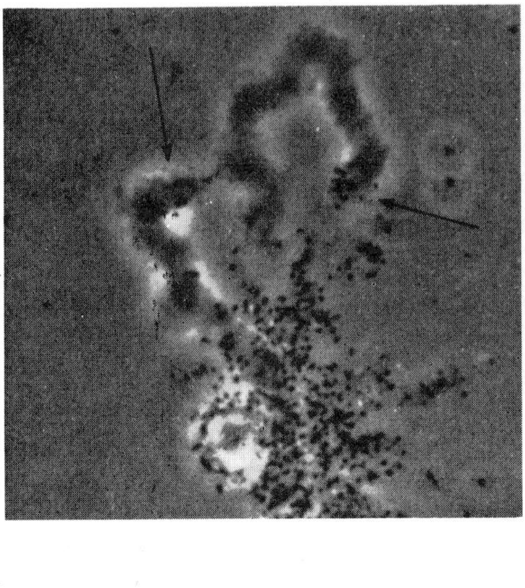

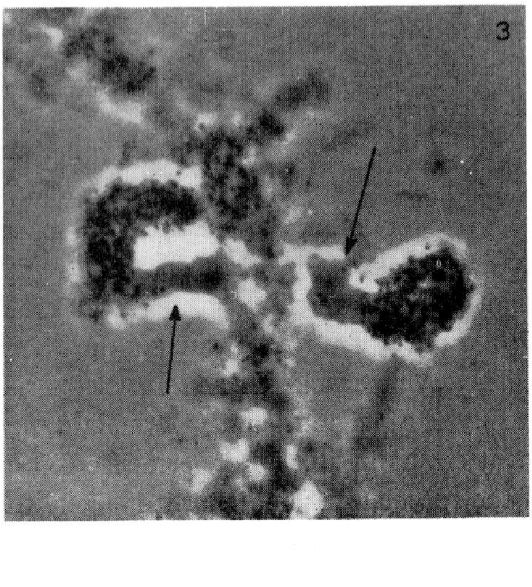
3

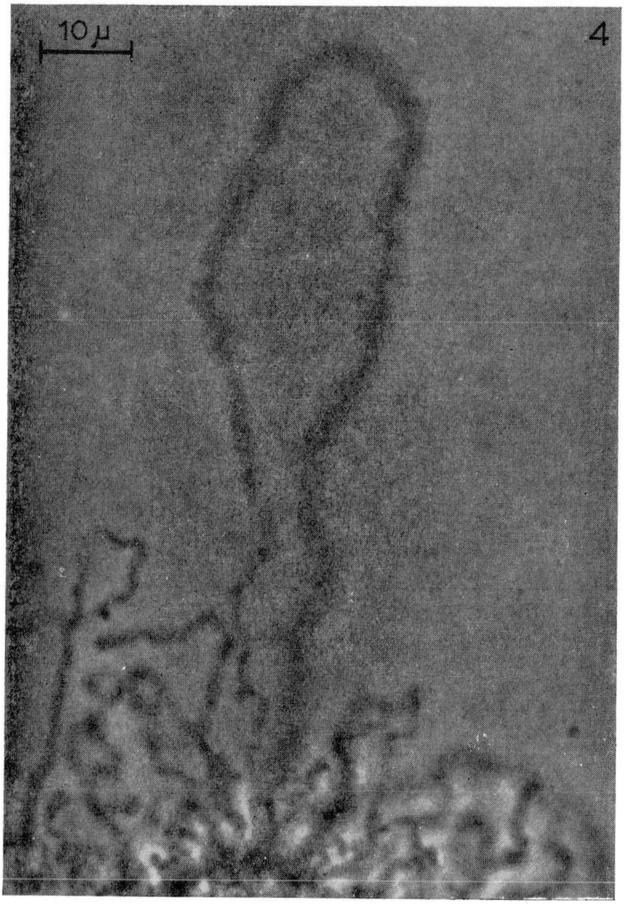

not discharged throughout a loop's length but is similarly limited to the region adjacent to its thicker insertion. It would then follow that for ordinary loops as well as the giant granular loop, much of the RNA has a lengthy period of association with the

Fig. 1. End of left arm of chromosome XII of *T.c. cristatus*, unfixed, phase contrast. An arrow points to the pair of giant granular loops.

Fig. 2. Autoradiograph from an oocyte incubated for 4 hr with H^3-uridine, phase contrast. Arrows point to silver grains over the dense tips of the giant granular loops, the rest of these loops being unlabelled.

Fig. 3. Autoradiograph from an oocyte removed from a newt 6 days after injection of H^3-uridine, phase contrast. Arrows point to the unlabelled thick ends of the giant granular loops, the rest of these loops being labelled.

Fig. 4. A large but otherwise 'normal' loop projecting from the left arm of chromosome I of *T.c. cristatus*, unfixed, phase contrast. Progressive increase in the width of this loop, from the thin to the thick ends inserting in the chromomere, is evident. An axis within the loop is also visible.

loop axis on which it was synthesized, and this again may imply that it is concerned *locally* with protein synthesis.

Such a proposal seems to be warranted by the time course of nuclear and cytoplasmic RNA labelling as observed in autoradiographs of sections of small, non-yolky newt oocytes. Interpretation of such autoradiographs is complicated by the fact that it has not proved possible to pulse-label oocytes; after injection there is a progressive increase in total labelled RNA until all labelled free uridine has been exhausted. The significant feature, however, is that there is a long interval (about a day) between the presentation of labelled uridine and the first appearance of any labelled RNA in the cytoplasm (or in the nuclear sap), even though the chromosomes are heavily labelled by this time. This situation is to be contrasted with that in larger, yolky oocytes, where an hour's incubation with H^3-uridine results in detectable labelling of cytoplasmic as well as nuclear RNA. Yolky amphibian oocytes have large, multiple nucleoli which are actively engaged in RNA synthesis, at an overall rate much higher (according to Davidson and Mirsky, nearly 50 times higher) than the overall rate of chromosomal RNA synthesis. In small, non-yolky oocytes, on the contrary, the preponderant RNA synthesis is chromosomal, not nucleolar. Hence the possibility should be borne in mind that virtually all of the cytoplasmic RNA in newt oocytes is ribosomal, derived from nucleolar synthesis (direct evidence that this is so will be mentioned later) whilst the involvement of chromosomal RNA, other than that perhaps concerned with yolk protein synthesis, may be restricted to the oocyte's germinal vesicle nucleus and concerned there with the synthesis of loop matrix proteins specifically different in character from one loop to another. The fact that ultimately all labelled RNA is discharged from the oocyte nucleus, even in non-yolky oocytes, need not be held as an argument against this proposal. Breakdown of chromosomal RNA within the nucleus following discharge from the loops would release uridine available for ribosomal as well as chromosomal RNA synthesis, i.e. once it has been trapped by the nucleoli, labelled uridine will necessarily end up in labelled cytoplasmic RNA, thus depleting the pool. Speculation along such tenuous lines may be objectionable, but the unusually long attachment of RNA to the lampbrush chromosomes on which it has been synthesized is a peculiar feature, and it merits emphasis.

Davidson et al., from studies on *Xenopus*, offer an alternative proposal. On the basis of template-activity determinations carried out on oocyte RNA of high molecular weight they claim that, like ribosomal RNA, chromosome-synthesized RNA accumulates throughout oogenesis, that it constitutes about 2 % of the total RNA in a mature oocyte, and that it is protected from degradation by locally synthesized loop matrix proteins. In other words the long period of physical association between RNA and its site of synthesis is held to be a requirement for some kind of packaging operation in progress on the loops. Slater and Spiegelman have similarly shown that 4 to 5 per cent of the RNA extracted from unfertilised eggs of the echinoderm *Lytechinus* is template-active, and they discuss two further lines of evidence supporting the notion that unfertilised eggs accumulate 'masked' messenger RNA during oogenesis, messenger which is

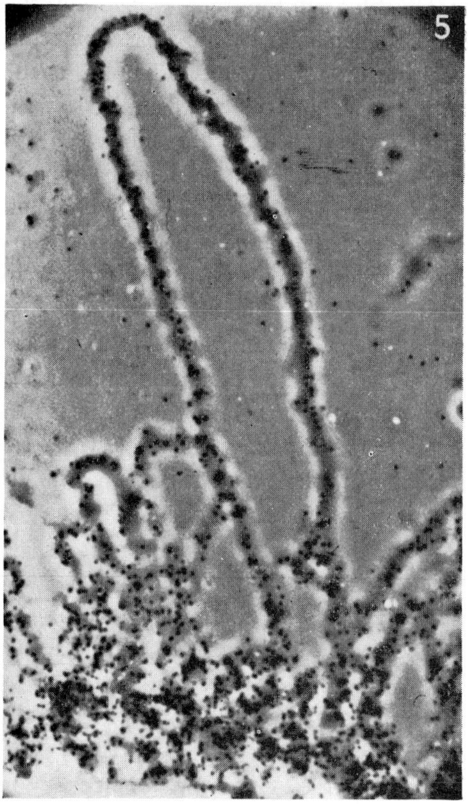

Fig. 5. Autoradiograph from an oocyte removed from a newt 18 hr after injection of H^3-uridine, phase contrast. The large loop is comparable to that shown in Fig. 4 and is labelled throughout its length. All these photographs are at the magnification indicated by the scale on Fig. 4.

unmasked at fertilization: the several demonstrations that the onset of protein synthesis when eggs are fertilised is not sensitive to actinomycin, nor dependent on the presence of nuclear DNA.

It is necessary to mention here that there is as yet no incontrovertible evidence that protein synthesis does occur within newt or other oocyte nuclei. For various reasons autoradiographic evidence of incorporation of labelled amino acids into lampbrush chromosome proteins *in situ* is suspect (D. Milne, unpublished). The most that can be said for the present is that autoradiographs of sectioned oocytes show about equal labelling of protein in nucleus and cytoplasm regardless of the length of time of incubation of oocytes with a labelled amino acid, overall labelling rising linearly with time. Taken at its face value this certainly suggests concurrent protein synthesis in nucleus and cytoplasm, but synthesis in the cytoplasm alone, with rapid transfer of a standard proportion of this protein to the nycleus, is not excluded. Morphological, entirely circumstantial evidence for protein synthesis *in situ* on lampbrush chromosomes will be mentioned later.

Edström and Gall studied the base composition of RNAs extracted from various components of newt oocytes. A feature of the chromosomal RNA is its relatively low guanine plus cytosine content, about 45% and close to that of newt DNA but without base complementarity (too little adenine and guanine, too much uracil and cytosine). Nucleolar RNA, on the other hand, proved to have a high guanine plus cytosine content, approaching 60% and similar to that of RNA extracted from oocyte cytoplasm. This information therefore supports the view that at least most of the cytoplasmic RNA is synthesized by the nucleoli.

Gall (1966) has studied the sedimentation patterns of nuclear and cytoplasmic RNAS extracted from newt oocytes, and the distribution of radioactivity in the various RNA fractions resulting from H^3-uridine incorporation during short- and long-term experiments. His general conclusion is that the original ribosomal precursor is made in the nucleoli, as material sedimenting at 40S; thereafter this is converted to an 18S fraction which migrates rapidly, and a 28S fraction, derived from a 30S fraction, which migrates more slowly to the cytoplasm. The sedimentation properties of oocyte chromosomal RNA have not yet been determined, owing to the great preponderance of nucleolar over chromosomal RNA synthesis in the yolky oocytes studied.

Izawa et al. incubated portions of newt ovary with actinomycin D before testing the capacity of such oocytes to incorporate RNA precursors. They showed not only that actinomycin D can inhibit RNA synthesis by lampbrush chromosomes and nucleoli, but that conditions of treatment which are effective result in lampbrush chromosomes whose lateral loops have 'disappeared'. These observations have been substantiated by Callan and Gall, but Izawa et al. also claimed that the stripping effect can be observed when lampbrush chromosomes are directly isolated into saline containing actinomycin D. If proper attention is paid to saline *p*H and concentration, however, (and if *p*H and saline concentration are not appropriately arranged, loss of loop matrix with retraction of loop axes will occur anyway (Macgregor and Callan)) actinomycin D does not strip loop matrix from isolated chromosome preparations. The detachment of loop matrix consequent on actinomycin treatment is in some way dependent on oocyte metabolism. Extensive matrix stripping occurs if excised oocytes are kept for an hour or two in physiological saline containing 10 μg actinomycin D per ml, but anaesthetised whole newts, with their ovaries drawn out through slits made in the body wall, and submerged for 4 hours in saline containing 100 μg actinomycin D per ml, show little or no sign of loop matrix stripping. However if the ovarian blood circulation is shut off with a ligature, essentially total stripping of matrix occurs within an hour of exposure to actinomycin D at 100 μg per ml. If thereafter the ligature is released, the newt washed in saline and its ovaries returned to the body cavity, there is progressive restoration of matrix and most loops are back to their normal appearance within five days (Callan, unpublished). It has yet to be demonstrated that this dramatic recovery represents synthesis of new protein; it is certainly accompanied by re-acquisition of RNA-synthesizing capacity.

4. RNA and protein synthesis during male meiotic prophase

Substantial evidence that chromosomes pass through a lampbrush stage during male meiotic prophase comes from recent work on *Drosophila* species, notably *D. hydei* and *D. neohydei* (Meyer 1963; Hess and Meyer). By ingenious genetical experiments the Y-chromosome in spermatocytes has been shown to generate several morphologically distinguishable lampbrush loops which extend during prophase and regress before metaphase; the order of these loops along the Y is now known (Hess 1965). The materials which accumulate on these loops, rendering them visible in the light microscope, consist of RNP. Just as in newt oocytes, it is the texture and distribution of these materials which permit the various loops to be identified. The Y-chromosome loops are sites of intense RNA synthesis (Hennig) and if actinomycin C or D is injected into *Drosophila* larvae, disintegration of the loop RNP follows. The maximum state of disaggregation is reached within 24 to 30 hours of injection, but there follows a regeneration of the loops which is complete by 100 to 120 hours (Meyer and Hess). The situation in *Drosophila* spermatocytes therefore shows a remarkable comparability to that in newt oocytes.

Hess (1964) induced heritable mutant Y-chromosome loops in *D. hydei* by X-irradiation, the mutant loops being morphologically distinct from wild-type. Meyer and Hess worked with males possessing two Y-chromosomes, one carrying the wild-type loops, the other the mutant. Actinomycin injection leads to the disappearance of both wild-type and mutant loops, but subsequently these regenerate, conserving to the full their morphological distinction. Meyer and Hess hold this as evidence that each Y-chromosome autonomously determines its specific type of loop, that not only RNA but specific protein is synthesized *in situ*, for if the regeneration process were merely re-attachment of already synthesized but shed loop matrix, the regeneration of loops which maintain their distinctive morphology would scarcely be anticipated.

Hess (1965) has shown that *D. hydei* males lacking any one of the Y-chromosome loops are sterile, spermiogenesis being arrested at different stages depending on which loop is absent. This suggests very strongly indeed that specifically distinct loop materials, perhaps protein, shed into the cytoplasm at first meiotic metaphase, are immediately and directly involved in sperm differentiation. Meyer (1963) points out that the nuclei of secondary spermatocytes and spermatids show little sign of physiological activity, and indeed it should be recalled that first meiotic prophase is the last occasion in *Drosophila* when materials can be synthesized by the Y-chromosome and made available to cells which, after the meiotic division, possess no Y-chromosome. When one considers *Drosophila* spermatocytes it is difficult to see justification for the claim by Davidson that loop matrix proteins are substances whose function it is to protect chromosomal RNA from degradation; for unlike the egg cell, whose differentiation to produce an embryo normally awaits activation at fertilization, the more limited differentiation of the sperm cell is the *immediate* follow-up to meiosis.

5. Oocyte regulators of gene activity

In eggs which show mosaic development there is plenty of evidence, at a biological (though not chemical) level of analysis, that a variety of specific materials have accumulated during the growth of the oocyte ready to act as regulators of gene activity during early embryogenesis. In such eggs these regulator substances are rapidly segregated, and allocated to particular blastomeres at cleavage. In regulation eggs the evidence is all against an early segregation of organ-determining substances, yet we may certainly surmise that the cytoplasms of regulation eggs nevertheless contain some remarkably specific materials. The universal breakdown of hybrid merogons, even when the species involved are so closely related that they produce viable diploid hybrids, and in particular of diploid hybrid merogons (Hennen) produced by nuclear transplantation, is clear evidence of nucleocytoplasmic incompatibility and therefore of cytoplasmic specificity. Hennen has argued convincingly from her experimental results that such cytoplasmic specificity largely resides in substances capable of regulating the activities of a genome of one species, incapable of regulating that of another.

Recent work carried out on the axolotl gives a clear indication as to the origin of one such substance. A female axolotl homozygous for the recessive gene ○, offspring from the mating of two heterozygotes +/○, produces eggs which fail to neurulate regardless of the genetic constitution of the fertilizing sperm (Humphrey). A cytoplasmic deficiency is responsible for this failure; it can be made good by injection of cytoplasm from a normal mature egg, either +/+ or +/○, or of germinal vesicle material taken from a normal large ovarian oocyte (Briggs and Cassens). By comparing volumes of injected material needed to correct the deficiency, Briggs and Cassens have demonstrated that the supplementary factor is present at much higher concentration in the germinal vesicle nucleus than in mature egg cytoplasm, and that it is barely detectable in ovarian oocyte cytoplasm. Briggs and Cassens suggest that the corrective factor may be the direct product of the normal allele of gene ○, namely an RNA, but whereas RNAs do not accumulate in the germinal vesicle nucleus, proteins certainly do. It is very possible that this corrective factor is a protein and that it, and other specific regulatory substances, are synthesized via chromosomal RNA on the loops of the lampbrush chromosomes, stored in the germinal vesicle nucleus, and released to the cytoplasm when they are required, just prior to embryogenesis.

References

BIER, K.: Die Kern-Plasma-Relation und das Riesenwachstum der Eizellen. Verh. Dtsch. Zool. Ges., Zool. Anz., Suppl. 26 (1964) 84.

BRIGGS, R. and G. CASSENS: Accumulation in the oocyte nucleus of a gene product essential for embryonic development beyond gastrulation. Proc. Natl. Acad. Sci. U.S. 55 (1966) 1103.

CALLAN, H. G.: The lampbrush chromosomes of *Sepia officinalis*, *Anilocra physodes* and *Scyllium catulus* and their structural relationship to the lampbrush chromosomes of Amphibia. Pubbl. Staz. Zool. Napoli 29 (1957) 329.

CALLAN, H.G.: The organization of genetic units in chromosomes. J. Cell Sci. 2 (1967) 1.

CALLAN, H.G. and L.LLOYD: Lampbrush chromosomes of crested newts *Triturus cristatus*. Phil. Trans. Roy. Soc., London, Ser. B 243 (1960) 135.

DAVIDSON, E.H., M.CRIPPA, F.R.KRAMER and A.E.MIRSKY: Genomic function during the lampbrush chromosome stage of amphibian oogenesis. Proc. Natl. Acad. Sci. U.S. 56 (1966) 856.

DAVIDSON, E.H. and A.E.MIRSKY: Gene activity in oogenesis. In: Genetic control of differentiation. Brookhaven Symposia in Biology no. 18 (1965) 77.

EDSTRÖM, J.-E. and J.G.GALL: The base composition of ribonucleic acid in lampbrush chromosomes, nucleoli, nuclear sap and cytoplasm of *Triturus* oocytes. J. Cell Biol. 19 (1963) 279.

GALL, J.G.: Chromosomes and cytodifferentiation. In: M.Lock, ed.: Cytodifferentiation and macromolecular synthesis. New York, Academic Press (1963) 119.

GALL, J.G.: Nuclear RNA of the salamander oocyte. Natl. Cancer Inst. Monograph 23 (1966) 475.

GALL, J.G.: Differential synthesis of the genes for ribosomal RNA during amphibian oogenesis. Proc. Natl. Acad. Sci. U.S. 60 (1968) 553.

GALL, J.G. and H.G.CALLAN: H^3-uridine incorporation in lampbrush chromosomes. Proc. Natl. Acad. Sci. U.S. 48 (1962) 562.

GRUN, P.: Plant lampbrush chromosomes. Exptl. Cell Res. 14 (1958) 619.

HENDERSON, S.A.: RNA synthesis during male meiosis and spermiogenesis. Chromosoma 15 (1964) 345.

HENNEN, S.: Nucleocytoplasmic hybrids between *Rana pipiens* and *Rana palustris* I. Analysis of the developmental properties of the nuclei by means of nuclear transplantation. Develop. Biol. 11 (1965) 243.

HENNIG, W.: Untersuchungen zur Struktur und Funktion des Lampenbürsten-Y-Chromosoms in der Spermatogenese von *Drosophila*. Chromosoma 22 (1967) 294.

HESS, O.: Struktur-differenzierungen im Y-Chromosom von *Drosophila hydei* und ihre Beziehungen zu Gen-Aktivitäten I. Mutanten der Funktionsstrukture. Verh. Dtsch. Zool. Ges., Zool. Anz., Suppl. 28 (1964) 156.

HESS, O.: Struktur-Differenzierungen im Y-Chromosom von *Drosophila hydei* und ihre Beziehungen zu Gen-Aktivitäten III. Sequenz und Lokalisation der Schleifenbildungsorte. Chromosoma 16 (1965) 222.

HESS, O. and G.F.MEYER: Chromosomal differentiations of the lampbrush type formed by the Y-chromosome in *Drosophila hydei* and *Drosophila neohydei*. J. Cell Biol. 16 (1963) 527.

HUMPHREY, R.R.: A recessive factor (o, for ova deficient) determining a complex of abnormalities in the Mexican axolotl (*Ambystoma mexicanum*). Develop. Biol. (1966) 57.

IZAWA, M., V.G.ALLFREY and A.E.MIRSKY: The relationship between RNA synthesis and loop structure in lampbrush chromosomes. Proc. Natl. Acad. Sci. U.S. 49 (1963) 544.

KUNZ, W.: Lampenbürstenchromosomen und multiple Nukleolen bei Orthopteren. Chromosoma 21 (1967) 446.

LIMA-DE-FARIA, A., J.GERMAN, M.GHATNEKAR, J.MCGOVERN and L.ANDERSON: In vitro labelling of human meiotic chromosomes with H^3-thymidine. Hereditas 60 (1968) 249.

MACGREGOR, H.C.: Nucleolar DNA in oocytes of *Xenopus laevis*. J. Cell Sci. 3 (1968) 437.

MACGREGOR, H.C. and H.G.CALLAN: The actions of enzymes on lampbrush chromosomes. Quart. J. Microscop. Sci. 103 (1962) 173.

MEYER, G.F.: Die Funktionsstrukturen des Y-Chromosoms in den Spermatocytenkernen von *Drosophila hydei*, *D. neohydei*, *D. repleta* und einigen anderen *Drosophila*-Arten. Chromosoma 14 (1963) 207.

MEYER, G.F. and O.HESS: Struktur-Differenzierungen in Y-Chromosom von *Drosophila hydei* und ihre

Beziehungen zu Gen-Aktivitäten II. Effekt der RNS-synthese-Hemmung durch Actinomycin. Chromosoma 16 (1965) 249.

MILLER, O. L.: Fine structure of lampbrush chromosomes. Natl. Cancer Inst. Monograph 18 (1965) 79.

SLATER, D. W. and S. SPIEGELMAN: An estimation of genetic messages in the unfertilized echinoid egg. Proc. Natl. Acad. Sci. U.S. 56 (1966) 164.

SWIFT, H. H.: The desoxyribose nucleic acid content of animal nuclei. Physiol. Zool. 23 (1950) 169,

TAYLOR, J. H.: Autoradiographic detection of incorporation of P^{32} into chromosomes during meiosis and mitosis. Exptl. Cell Res. 4 (1953) 164.

TAYLOR, J. H.: Autoradiographic studies of nucleic acids and proteins during meiosis in *Lilium longiflorum*. Am. J. Botany 46 (1959) 477.

WHITEHOUSE, H. L. K.: A theory of crossing-over by means of hybrid deoxyribonucleic acid. Nature 199 (1963) 1034.

WIMBER, D. E. and W. PRENSKY: Autoradiography with meiotic chromosomes of the male newt (*Triturus viridescens*) using H^3-thymidine. Genetics, Princeton 48 (1963) 1731.

CHAPTER 23

Chromosome movements during cell-division

ARTHUR FORER*

Zoology Department, Downing Street, University of Cambridge, England

Contents

1. Introduction
2. Description of normal cell-division
3. Studies using light microscopy
   (a) The chemical nature of spindles
   (b) The organization and physical nature of spindles
   (c) The forces and energies for chromosome movement
   (d) General characteristics of the force system
   (e) The identity and function of the elements causing chromosome movements
4. Studies using electron microscopy
   (a) Electron microscopy compared with light microscopy
   (b) Functional aspects
5. Biochemical analyses of isolated spindles
   (a) Isolated MA compared with *in vivo* MA
   (b) Components present in isolated MA
6. Summary

* Helen Hay Whitney Foundation Fellow.

1. Introduction

This chapter is concerned with chromosome movements during anaphase of cell-division. It deals with such problems as the morphological identification of the material(s) which transmit force to the chromosomes, and the composition and function of this material. At the present time very little is known about such problems, but I hope that this survey will point out some of the questions which need be, and can now be, asked.

The material will be discussed in the following order: (a) the time course of cell-division as seen in living and fixed cells, defining the terms to be used, and defining the problem: chromosome movements during anaphase; (b) the morphological and chemical nature of the materials controlling chromosome movement as deduced from light microscopic observations and experiments; (c) electron microscopic observations and their relation to the light microscopic observations; and finally, (d) biochemical analyses of the spindle as studied by isolation techniques.

In all four sections I touch on many problems which are discussed in more detail in the following general reviews: Wilson; Cornman; Hughes; Schrader; and Mazia (1961).

2. Description of normal cell-division

The course of cell-division is as follows (see general reviews, above, for details and references).

Chromosomes are not seen within interphase nuclei, but become distinguishable in prophase nuclei. After nuclear membrane breakdown the chromosomes are seen inside a spindle-shaped region called the spindle. All or some of the chromosomes move within the spindle (toward and away from the poles) during prometaphase, and generally all chromosomes are at the equator during metaphase. The mitotic chromosomes divide (or meiotic chromosomes disjoin into half-bivalents) and move poleward during anaphase. This poleward movement can be primarily a shortening of the chromosome-to-pole distance while the pole-to-pole distance is constant, or it can be primarily an increase in the pole-to-pole distance while the chromosome-to-pole distance is constant, or it can be a mixture of the two. In this article I shall be concerned primarily with the first case.

Generally, all the chromosomes in one cell begin anaphase at the same time, and move poleward with about the same velocity. But in some cells various chromosomes regularly move poleward at different times; in some cells different chromosomes regularly have different velocities.

Chromosome velocities during anaphase range from 0.2 to 5.0 μ per minute, and each chromosome's velocity is approximately constant throughout anaphase. Pole-to-pole distances are of the order of 10–30 μ, and, as expected, the time between chromosome separation (start of anaphase) and chromosome arrival at the poles (end of anaphase) is in the range 2–60 min, depending on the conditions and the cell in question.

The chromosomes reach the poles (telophase), and cell cleavage then ensues.

Cell-division is illustrated in Figs. 1 and 2, which show living crane fly spermatocytes photographed using a phase-contrast microscope. These cells are particularly favorable for studies of cell-division, for the pole-to-pole distances are of the order of 20–30 μ and there are only five chromosomes, usually less than 4–5 μ long; further, the chromosomal velocities in anaphase are of the order of 0.5 μ per minute, and anaphase lasts 30–40 min. As is seen in the photographs, the 2 sex-chromosomes do not form a bivalent, and do not move poleward at the same time as the autosomes.

The spindle area is not structureless in fixed and stained cells, but contains spindle fibres. The spindle fibres are of two kinds: *chromosomal spindle fibres* (or, for short, chromosomal fibres), which extend between individual chromosomes and the poles, and *continuous* (spindle) *fibres*, which extend from pole-to-pole, without connection with chromosomes. The chromosomal fibres can be from 0.2 to 1.5 μ in diameter, and often appear to be made up of many units of smaller diameter. The continuous fibres are of the order of 0.2 μ in diameter.

The chromosomal fibres attach to the chromosomes at specialised regions called kinetochores, chromosomes either having one localized kinetochore, or having a diffuse kinetochore spread throughout the length of the chromosome. During anaphase, chromosomes with localized kinetochores move poleward with the kinetochore in front and with the chromosomal arms trailing, while chromosomes with diffuse kinetochores move poleward as one straight unit.

In animal cells astral fibres extend radially from each pole, forming the asters.

The region between the chromosomes and the pole is the half-spindle, and the region between the separating anaphase chromosomes is the interzonal region. Ex-

---

The photographs are all of *Nephrotoma suturalis* (Loew) primary spermatocytes. Fig. 1–7 are of living cells; Figs. 1 and 2 were taken through a phase-contrast microscope (objective-lens NA = 1.25), and Figs. 3–7 through a polarizing microscope (objective-lens NA = 0.6). Figs. 8–13 are electron micrographs, of which Figs. 8, 9, and 11 were generously provided by Dr. O. Behnke. Details of the techniques are given elsewhere (Forer 1964, 1965, 1966; Behnke and Forer 1966, 1967).

In Figs. 1–5 the times are given relative to the time of nuclear membrane breakdown, and in Figs. 6 and 7 the times are given relative to the time at which the irradiation took place.

In the phase-contrast microscope micrographs the chromosomes are dark (e.g., *b* in Fig. 1) and the spindle appears in large part structureless. In the polarizing microscope micrographs the spindle fibres appear bright (e.g., *sf* in Fig. 4), and the chromosomes (*b*) have little contrast; for those not familiar with polarizing microscope images, the amount of birefringence is roughly proportional to the brightness relative to the background.

Fig. 1 (overleaf) shows one cell progressing from before nuclear membrane breakdown to late anaphase. At 90 min after nuclear membrane breakdown 2 bivalents are illustrated, and one is labelled *b*; the third bivalent is in a different plane of focus. The sex-chromosomes (one of which is labelled *u*) do not move poleward until the autosomal half-bivalents have reached the poles. × 2,050.

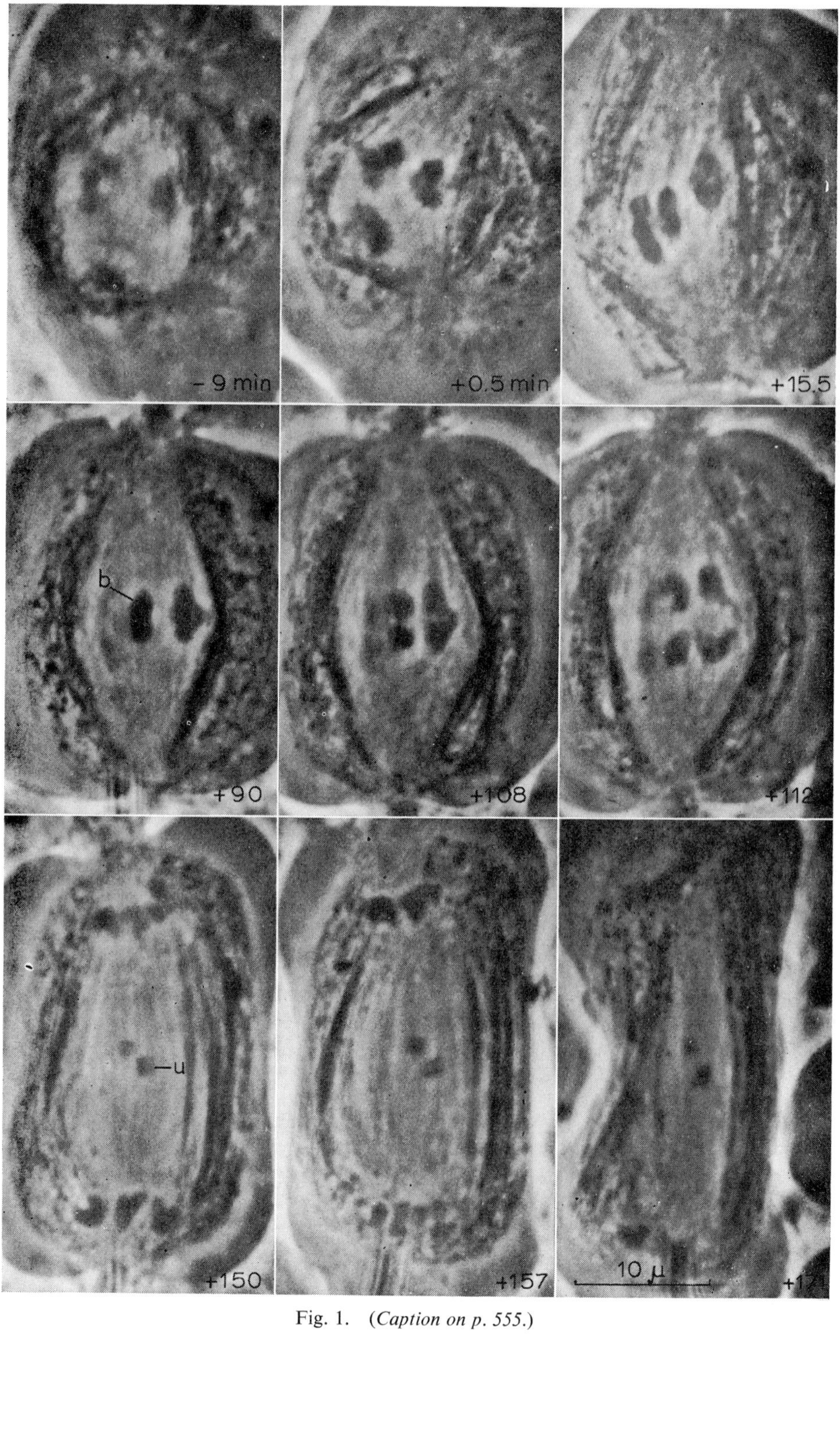

Fig. 1. (*Caption on p. 555.*)

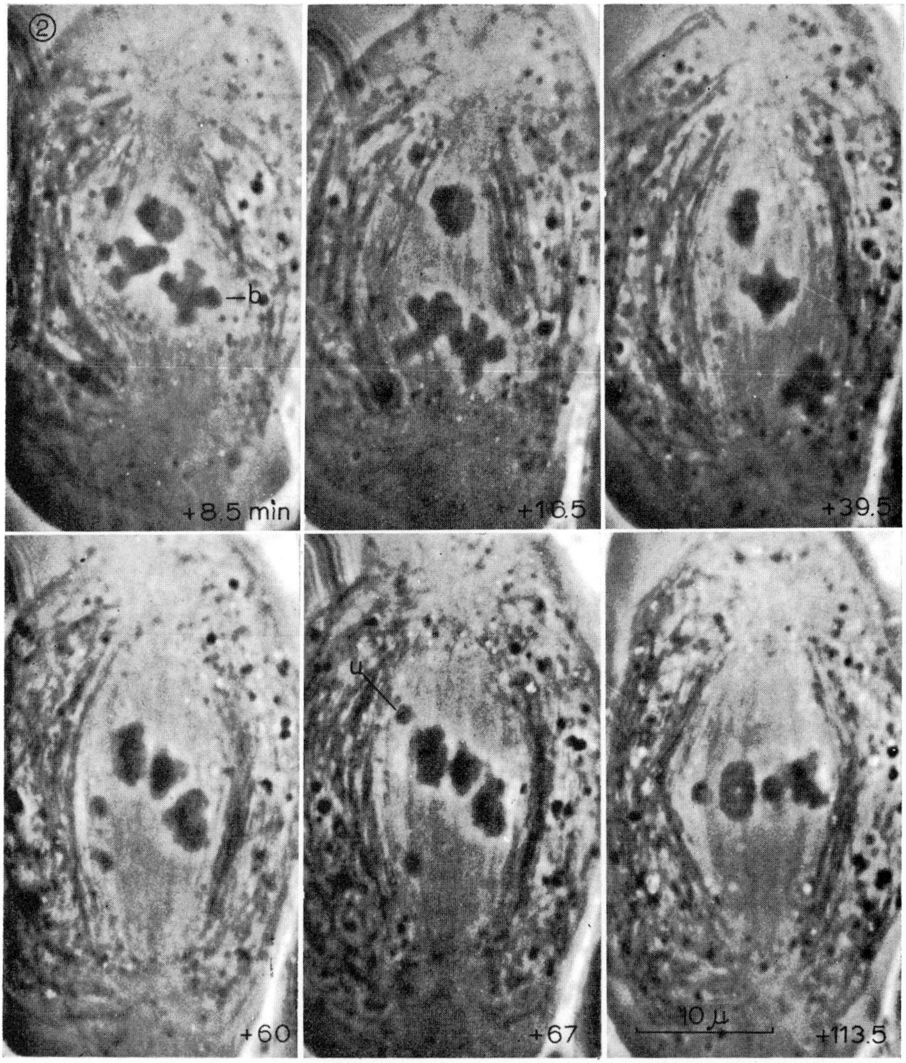

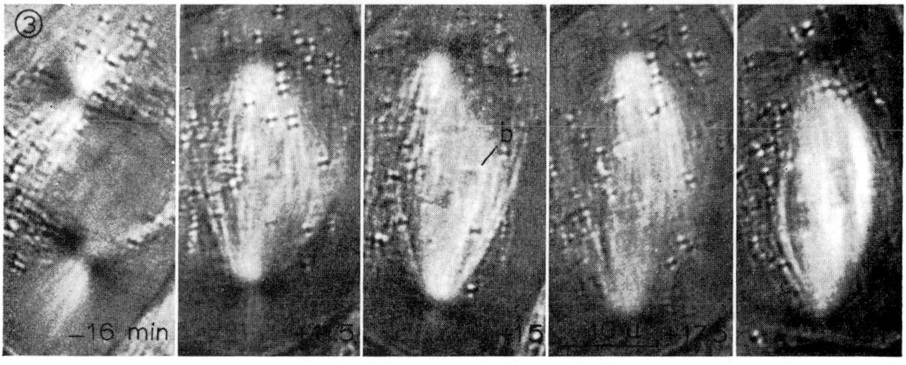

Figs. 2 and 3. (*Capitions on p. 558.*)

tending across the interzonal region are often found fibres which stain differently from spindle fibres; since these fibres appear to connect the separating chromosomes, they are called interzonal connections.

Collectively all of these structures constitute the 'mitotic apparatus', abbreviated MA, which, as defined by Mazia and Dan, is "the ensemble of structures constituting the 'chromatic' and 'achromatic' figures in the classical descriptions of mitosis".

Generally, spindle fibres can not be seen in *living cells* with bright-field microscopy, phase-contrast microscopy, dark-field (dark-ground) microscopy, ultraviolet absorption microscopy, or interference microscopy. Spindle fibres can be seen with these microscopes in fixed cells, in moribund cells, or in cells treated with acid (in the latter case the effect is reversible), but spindle fibres are not seen with these microscopes in healthy, living cells.

Spindle fibres can be demonstrated in living cells, however, with a sensitive polarizing microscope, and these fibres appear morphologically the same as in fixed and stained cells (reviewed by Inoué and Sato). This is illustrated in Figs. 3–5, in crane fly spermatocytes. Spindle fibres are weakly birefringent (generally of the order of 1 mμ) and the birefringence is positive with respect to the length of the fibre. (I use the term 'birefringence' to mean (thickness) *times* (difference of refractive indices), and use the term 'coefficient of birefringence' to refer to the difference of refractive indices, both referring to measurements with light of wavelength 5460 Å.) In animal cells the chromosomal spindle fibre birefringence is strongest near the kinetochores and near the poles, and weakest in the region in between. This condition applies in metaphase, and prevails throughout most of anaphase. In plant cells the chromosomal fibre birefringence is strongest near the kinetochores and gradually becomes weaker toward the poles, being weakest at the poles. This, too, applies to metaphase and most of anaphase.

Continuous fibre birefringence generally is strongest in early prometaphase, and is very weak during metaphase and early and middle anaphase. Continuous fibre birefringence generally increases during late anaphase.

Polarizing microscope photographs of living crane fly spermatocytes are presented in Figs. 3–5, for comparison with phase-contrast photographs of the same cell type (Figs. 1, 2). In these cells, at metaphase and anaphase each chromosomal spindle fibre is visible, there are 5 chromosomal fibres going to each pole, and each fibre is

---

Fig. 2 (overleaf) shows one cell progressing from early prometaphase to metaphase, illustrating the prometaphase movements of the bivalents (one of which is labelled *b*) and the sex-chromosome univalents (one of which is labelled *u*). ×1,850.

Fig. 3 (overleaf) shows one cell progressing from prophase to early prometaphase. In these stages continuous fibre birefringence predominates and the chromosomes are difficult to see clearly (one bivalent is labelled *b*). ×1,350.

about 1 μ in diameter, with strongest birefringence (3–4 mμ) near the kinetochore and weakest birefringence near the pole. Continuous fibre birefringence predominates in early prometaphase (Fig. 3), but there is very little or no continuous fibre birefringence during metaphase and anaphase (Figs. 4, 5).

Fig. 4

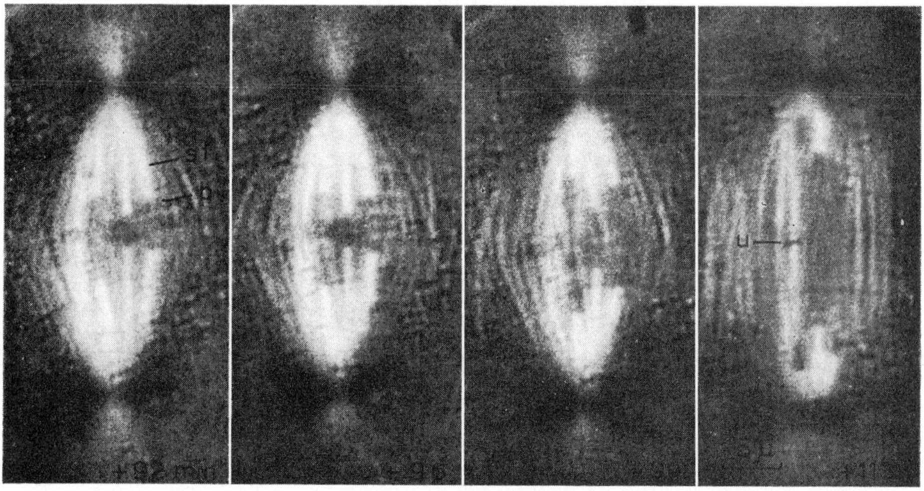

Fig. 5

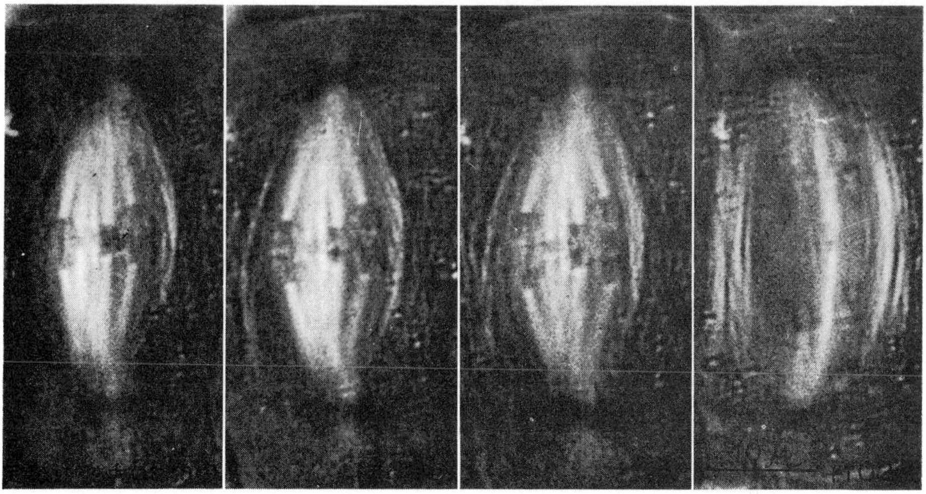

Figs. 4 and 5 each illustrate individual cells progressing from metaphase to middle or late anaphase. In these stages there is very little continuous fibre birefringence, and though the bivalents are of low contrast (one is labelled *b*), they are easily identified at the termination of the clearly visible chromosomal fibres (one of which is labelled *sf*). Each univalent (one is labelled *u*) has a chromosomal spindle fibre extending to each pole. Fig. 4: ×1,590; Fig. 5: ×1,380.

TABLE 1

Chemicals present in half-spindle region

Cell	Protein	RNA	Lipi
Various cell types	Present, and constitutes most of the material in isolated MA	Present (cytochemically); about 5% by weight of isolated MA	Present in isol
Primary spermatocytes of grasshopper (*Podisma sapporense*)	Present, even after RNAase removes RNA staining. Strongest staining near poles	Strongly staining and strongest near chromosomes	Present
Lilium pollen mother cells *Allium* root tip cells *Lilium*, *Pisum*, *Zea*, and *Vigna* root tips	Present; strongly staining	Strongly staining	—
Tradescantia pollen mother cells, and *Spirogyra* cells	Present. Spindle fibres stain differently from 'ground substance of the spindle'	—	—
Vicia faba root tip cells. *Tradescentia* pollen mother cells	—	—	Present in spi
HeLa cells; Ehrlich ascites tumor cells	Present. Spindle fibres stain strongly for tyrosine	— —	Present in spi 'background'; most strongly chromosomes
HeLa	—	Present	—
Various sea urchin eggs	Present	—	—
Various plant cells, meiotic and mitotic	—	—	Present in spi
Meiosis and mitosis in *Artemia salina* eggs	—	—	—
Sea urchin eggs *Acanthocidaris crassispina* and *Pseudocentrotus depressus*		—	—

arbohydrate	ATPase	Remarks	References
cytochemically. st staining near d equator	Present in isolated MA	ATPase is Mg^{2+} activated. Zinc and SH groups are also present. Phosphatase is not present	Mazia (1961)
	—	Studied cytochemically	Kobayashi and Makino
staining staining ntly staining – none	— — —	Studied cytochemically	Shimamura and Ôta
	—	Studied cytochemically	Shinke and Shigenage
	—		
	—	Studied cytochemically	Love and Suskind
	—	Detected by incorporation of radioactive RNA precursors	Errera and Brunfaut
	—	Detected by incorporation of radioactive amino acids	Stafford and Iverson; Gross and Cousineau; Bibring and Cousineau
	—	Detected cytochemically	Serra and Seixas
More intensely near the chromo- nd the poles; in between. fibres stain	—	Detected cytochemically	Fautrez and Fautrez-Firlefijn
	Present, functional at *p*H 6.2 and *p*H 8.2	Detected cytochemically. Neither acid phosphatase nor alkaline phosphatase are present in spindle	Miki (1963); Miki (1964)

TABLE 2

Dry mass of *in vivo* spindles and cytoplasm

Cell	g dry mass per 100 cm^3 of spindle	g dry mass per 100 cm^3 of cytoplasm	Method	Remarks	References
Endosperm cells: *Leucojum aestiveum*	$\geqslant 11$ (metaphase) $\geqslant 22$ (anaphase)	$\geqslant 8$–9	Interference microscopy	These values are calculated from the stated values of phase retardations, and are *minimum* estimates, assuming spindle refractive index increment of 0.20, and assuming that the spindle occupies the entire 5 μ thickness of the cell	Ambrose and Bajer
Sea urchin eggs: *Psammechinus miliaris*	23	25.5	Interference microscopy	The spindle concentration is calculated from the stated cytoplasm concentration, and the statement that spindle concentration is 0.89 times cytoplasm concentration	Mitchison and Swann
Grasshopper spermatocytes: *Chortippus parallelus*	$\geqslant 11$	~ 11	Immersion refractometry with phase contrast and interference microscopes	The spindle value is deduced from the stated cytoplasm concentration and the appearance of spindle fibres as slightly darker than the cytoplasm in the published photographs	Barer and Joseph
Fixed eggs of *Cyclops strenuus*	50	?	X-ray absorption	This value is calculated from the stated dry mass and volume of spindle	Stich and McIntyre

Chick fibroblasts	Optical density is 0.28	Optical density is 0.3	Ultraviolet microscopy at wavelength 2650 Å	—	Davies
Grasshopper spermatocyte: *Podisma sapporense*	Spindle proteins stain more strongly than cytoplasmic proteins		Cytochemical staining for protein	—	Kobayashi and Makino
Various plant root tip cells, and pollen mother cells	Spindle proteins stain with about the same intensity as cytoplasmic proteins		Cytochemical staining for protein	—	Shimamura and Ôta
Various animal cells	The spindle absorbs ultraviolet light to about the same extent as does the cytoplasm		Ultraviolet microscopy at wavelength 2537, 2650 or 2750 Å	This is stated by authors, or is inferred from the lack of contrast between spindle and cytoplasm, in published micrographs	Bradfield; Lucas and Stark; Wyckoff, Ebeling and TerLouw; Wyckoff; Harvey and Lavin;
Carnoy fixed microsporocytes of *Zea mays*	The spindle has a higher concentration of dry matter than the cytoplasm		Interference microscopy	—	Longwell and Mota

In summary, spindle fibres seen in fixed and stained preparations can be seen in living cells only with a sensitive polarizing microscope. In general, the birefringent spindle fibres have their strongest birefringence near the kinetochores and near the poles, and this pattern is maintained throughout anaphase. During anaphase, chromosomes move poleward with a constant velocity, of the order of 0.2–5.0 μ per minute, moving with the kinetochores leading the way to the poles.

3. Studies using light microscopy

I have briefly described the course of cell-division as seen using light microscopes. The remainder of this article is concerned mainly with identifying the cause of chromosome movement, and discerning how this movement is controlled. This section deals with evidence from light microscopy. I approach the problem by discussing: (a) the chemical nature of spindles (kinds and amounts of materials); (b) the organization and physical nature of spindles; (c) the forces and energies needed for chromosome movement; and (d) characteristics of the force system which can be specified independently of any particular theory of chromosome movement. Using this information as background, I then discuss (e) the identity and function of the component(s) causing chromosomes to move.

(a) *The chemical nature of spindles*

Chemicals which have been found in spindles include: protein, RNA, lipid, carbohydrate, and zinc; enzymes present include ATPase (Table 1). Phosphatase has not been found (Table 1). This information derives mostly from cytochemical studies, and, in a few cases, from autoradiographic detection of precursor incorporation.

Various reports agree that there are differences in stainability within individual spindles: proteins, RNA, carbohydrate, and -SH groups stain strongly near the kinetochores and near the poles, and less strongly in between (Table 1). This is similar to the birefringence pattern discussed in the previous section.

These techniques give only qualitative results, however, of strong or weak staining, and of presence or absence. Quantitative data have been obtained as well, using a variety of techniques, and some results are listed in Table 2.

These results show, firstly, that the concentration of dry matter in the spindle is about the same as that in the cytoplasm. This is true for both quantitative and qualitative estimates, using a variety of techniques. Thus, the fraction of the cell's dry mass which is in the spindle is about the same as the fraction of the cell's volume which is occupied by the spindle. If, e.g., MAs in *Arbacia* eggs are 10% of the volume of the egg (Kane 1967), then these MAs are 10% of the mass of the egg.

Secondly, spindles contain of the order of 10–20 g of dry matter per 100 cm^3 of spindle volume (Table 2). While the data give concentration of material, the exact composition of this material can not be specified, because interference microscopy does not distinguish between proteins, nucleic acids, carbohydrates, etc. (see Davies and Wilkins).

Thus, spindles contain protein, RNA, carbohydrate, and lipid totalling to a concentration of 10–20 g of material per 100 cm^3 of spindle; this is about the same concentration of dry matter as the cytoplasm. Spindle material is not evenly distributed throughout the spindle, but stains more strongly near the kinetochores and near the poles.

(b) *The organization and physical nature of spindles*

Spindles are in some senses *stable*, for they remain intact as a unit after being taken out of cells (see last section), and they can be pushed *en masse* through the cytoplasm by applying a microneedle to any point on the spindle (Carlson). The mechanical rigidity of a spindle fibre is more than enough to support the stretching of attached chromosomes. This is shown by micromanipulation experiments (Nicklas and Staehly): metaphase meiotic chromosomes can be stretched to more than 3 or 4 times their original length while the attached spindle fibres do not change in length.

While in some respects stable, spindle fibres are nonetheless quite *labile*, as follows. A chromosome can be detached from the spindle by micromanipulation, and the chromosome reforms a spindle fibre; this operation can be repeated many times (Nicklas 1967). Similarly, some chromosomes regularly break their connection with one pole, turn around, and make a connection with the other pole; this too may occur several times during the course of one division (reviewed by Nicklas 1967). Many other factors can cause changes in spindle volume and birefringence (reviewed by Inoué and Sato). These include changes in external *p*H, temperature, and pressure; application of chemicals; substitution of D_2O for H_2O; and stretching of spindles. With many of these agents spindle fibre birefringence can be made to disappear reversibly, such that upon return to the original conditions the birefringent fibres reappear.

Because of this lability, and because of changes in spindle birefringence during the division cycle, Inoué suggested that spindle fibres are in 'dynamic equilibrium' between a non-birefringent state, (A), of non-oriented material, and a birefringent state, (B), of oriented material (reviewed in Inoué 1964). This is written as (A) $\rightleftarrows$ (B).

To further characterize this equilibrium, Inoué and co-workers subjected some of their data to thermodynamic analysis (reviewed in Inoué and Sato). Below a certain temperature the birefringence is zero, and as the temperature is raised the birefringence increases to a maximum value, and may decrease again with further increase in temperature. Values for enthalpy changes (ΔH), free energy changes (ΔF), and entropy changes (ΔS) were calculated from the data of birefringence vs. temperature. The calculated parameters seem similar to those measured during tobacco mosaic virus polymerization and other polymerizations involving water displacement, so Inoué and co-workers inferred that water displacement is involved in the polymerization of (A) to form the birefringent spindle, (B). I shall now consider the assumptions made in performing the calculation, and suggest other possible interpretations.

Besides the basic assumption of one-to-one stoichiometry in the reaction (A) ⇄ (B), the following four assumptions are made:

(1) *The amount of oriented material (B) is directly proportional to the birefringence.* While this seems a reasonable assumption, it is also possible that some of the change in birefringence is due to change in other parameters, such as orientation, stress and intrinsic birefringence, etc. Further, I argue in the following section that more than one component contributes to spindle fibre birefringence. If this is true, the thermodynamic treatment might be greatly affected, depending on the relationships of the contributing materials, and the temperature sensitivities of their chemical reactions.

(2) '*Only the equilibrium constant between oriented and nonoriented material is influenced by temperature*' (Inoué 1959). But entire cells are treated, and the temperature change could affect all reactions in the cell. It is possible, for example, that the birefringence reaction, (A) ⇄ (B), is a temperature-insensitive link in a series of reactions (X) ⇄ (Y) ⇄ (A) ⇄ (B) ⇄ (C) ...; if so, the temperature could primarily affect another reaction, and birefringence would be changed via the effects on the other reactions in the series. Thus, while *some* temperature sensitive reaction might have ΔS, ΔF, and ΔH values as calculated, this would not be the reaction (A) ⇄ (B). The following results favor this possibility.

Temperature changes affect the birefringence of *in vivo* spindles within a period of seconds, or minutes, yet temperature changes do not affect the birefringence of isolated spindles (i.e., spindles released from cells) during such small time periods (e.g., Kane and Forer). Temperature changes do affect the birefringence of isolated spindles as measured over time periods of hours, but this effect is *opposite* to that found *in vivo*: with isolated MA, cold temperatures *retard* the loss of birefringence which occurs at higher temperatures (Kane and Forer; Rebhun and Sander). Though these data are open to more than one interpretation, one distinct possibility is the one under discussion. Thus, it seems quite possible that the effect of temperature *in vivo* is not directly on the equilibrium between oriented and unoriented states, but rather on another reaction, and birefringence is affected via a coupled reaction (or reaction series) which is not present in isolated spindles. (I argue in the last section that there is indeed loss of material when MA are isolated.)

(3) *The maximum amount of unoriented (pool) material is fixed.* Inoué and Sato give supporting evidence for this, using protein inhibitors.

(4) *The maximum amount of unoriented material, called (A_0), is given by the plateau of the curve of birefringence vs. temperature.* If this is true, the plateau birefringence should never be exceeded. However, in the same cells for which the calculations were made, birefringence does exceed (A_0) when spindles are stretched by flattening (Inoué 1952), or when spindles are treated with D_2O (Carolan, Sato, Inoué 1965, 1966). One might try to avoid this internal inconsistency by arguing that some (A) material is in equilibrium with (B) while other (A) material is in an inaccessible compartment, and that these treatments cause (A_0) to be exceeded merely be opening this compartment

and making *all* (A) material accessible. But it is difficult to imagine that two such different treatments would unlock the same compartment. Thus the plateau can be exceeded and assumption 4 is not valid.

The use of the original (A_0) produces a straight line of (log $B/(A_0-B)$) versus (1/temperature) which is quite striking compared with curves obtained using other values for (A_0). Nonetheless since (A_0) can clearly be exceeded, (A_0) is not the maximum amount of material present, and the interpretation of the calculation is not clear.

I should make it quite explicit that this discussion of the above 4 assumptions does not affect the idea of a 'dynamic equilibrium', but rather affects only the interpretation of the thermodynamic analysis.

I should also point out that the thermodynamic analysis is based solely on data from non-functional spindles, i.e., spindles which are arrested in metaphase and which will not cause chromosome movement unless they are further activated. Low temperature does cause reversible disappearance of birefringence from both arrested and functional spindles (Inoué 1964), but neither temperature vs. birefringence curves nor thermodynamic analyses have yet been published on functional spindles. Thus non-functional spindles may be different from functional spindles.

Summarizing the conclusions to this point: Spindle fibres are attached to chromosomes, and are mechanically rigid enough to support the stretching of attached chromosomes. On the other hand spindle fibres are labile and can be reversibly made to disappear. Birefringent spindle component(s) are in equilibrium with non-oriented component(s), but it is not clear if the agents causing spindle disappearance affect the birefringence reaction directly, or through coupled reactions. The molecular interpretation of this equilibrium is as yet uncertain.

I now consider how the birefringent material becomes organized.

It has been argued that spindle fibres are organized by kinetochores and spindle poles (centrioles). Mazia (1955), for example, suggested this because isolated spindles were least soluble near the poles. Such an idea might also account for the manner of formation of spindles, and for the differences in staining properties within spindles.

The regions responsible for the organization of spindle fibres were termed 'orienting centres' by Inoué (1964), and Inoué (1959) suggested that the birefringence is stronger adjacent to an orienting centre than it is in the rest of the structure. Orienting centres, then, can be detected in living cells using this criterion, and for spindle fibres the orienting centres would be kinetochores (in all cases) and spindle poles (in some cases). This criterion is tested in the following way.

Consider a chromosomal spindle fibre with strongest birefringence near the chromosome, and weakest birefringence near the pole. The kinetochore, then, would be the sole orienting centre. If the birefringence were locally destroyed on a portion of the fibre poleward from the kinetochore, the repair of this fibre should occur in the poleward direction, i.e., away from the orienting centre (kinetochore). Thus if ultraviolet light were focused on a portion of a spindle fibre, the birefringence of that portion would be expected to disappear and the regeneration of new fibre should occur from

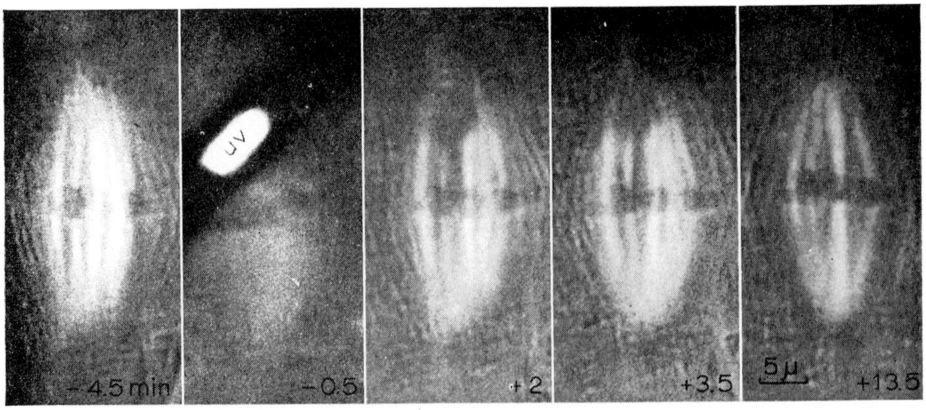

Fig. 6

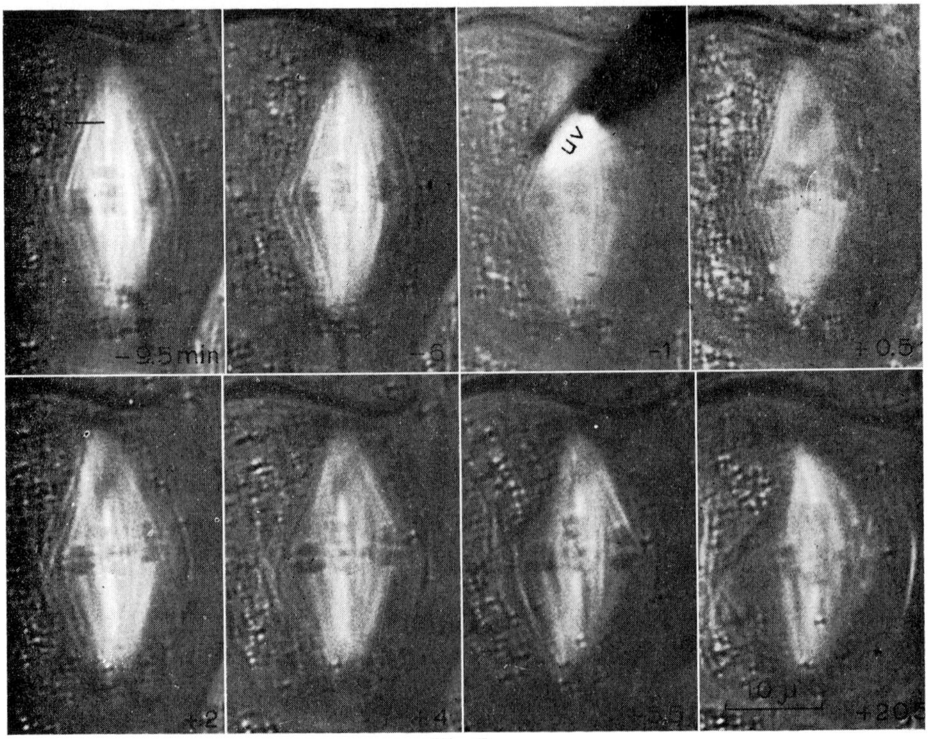

Fig. 7

Figs. 6 and 7 each illustrate the effect of ultraviolet microbeam irradiation on metaphase spindle fibres. The image of the ultraviolet source is labelled *UV*. Irradiation produces an area of reduced birefringence, and this area moves to the pole while the metaphase chromosomes remain at the equator. (Fig. 7 is the exceptional case cited in Forer (1966): all half-bivalents disjoined shortly after irradiation, and the half-bivalent associated with the irradiated chromosomal fibre moved poleward when the 'lesion' moved poleward, while the other 5 half-bivalents remained at the equator until the 'lesion' reached the pole.) Fig. 6: ×1,310; Fig. 7: ×1,300. (Fig. 6 from Forer 1965.)

the kinetochore poleward. (The portion of the fibre poleward from the irradiated region might be expected to retain or to lose birefringence, depending on what exactly the ultraviolet radiation does, and on how the orienting centre works.) In fact, that is what is found when the experiment is done.

When ultraviolet light is focused to a portion of a spindle fibre in metaphase crane fly spermatocytes, the birefringence disappears in the irradiated portion and is unaffected on both sides of this area (Figs. 6 and 7; Forer 1965). The irradiation-induced 'lesion' immediately moves poleward and a normal-looking spindle fibre is formed; the metaphase chromosomes remain at the equator during this process (Figs. 6 and 7; Forer 1965). Similar results are obtained with *Haemanthus* endosperm cells (Inoué 1964), in which spindle fibre birefringence is weak near the poles.

Thus, birefringent spindle fibres are organized by (and outward from) 'orienting centres' and stronger birefringence is diagnostic for 'orienting centres' in living cells.

I should point out that in discussing the general properties of spindles and their organization, I have not distinguished between stages of cell-division; yet there are distinct differences between metaphase and anaphase spindles. While anaphase spindles are sensitive to some of the same agents as are metaphase spindles, and can be reformed after having been made to disappear (e.g., Inoué 1964; Forer 1965, 1966), distinct differences are seen with micromanipulation (Nicklas and Staehly), D_2O-induced volume changes (Inoué and Sato), spindle reformation after cold treatment (Inoué 1964), effects of ultraviolet microbeam irradiation (Forer 1966), and effects of chemical agents (Mazia 1961); many of the latter destroy spindles during metaphase but are no longer effective during anaphase, "as though the structure 'locks'" (Mazia 1961). These dramatic differences between metaphase and anaphase are detected only physiologically, however, and as of yet have not been seen as differences in staining, or in amount of birefringence, or in distribution of birefringence within the spindle. This might be because with the polarizing microscope and the staining techniques we do not observe the component(s) which change.

(c) *The forces and energies for chromosome movement*

The force needed to move a chromosome from the equator to the pole is estimated as 10^{-8} dynes, applied during the entire movement period (Table 3). This calculation is based on the measured chromosome velocities and sizes, and on an estimate of viscous drag on the chromosome. (The force needed to overcome chromosomal inertia is negligible compared to the force needed to overcome frictional resistance.) There is some uncertainty in the calculation because the spindle viscosity may be non-Newtonian (i.e. the viscosity coefficient may vary with velocity), but high values of viscosity were chosen, and thus the force estimates are upper limits, with order-of-magnitude accuracy (Nicklas 1965; Taylor).

A force of 10^{-8} dynes is very small relative to the capacity of a cell. The energy expenditure is (force) *times* (distance), and if this energy arises from terminal phosphates of ATP, at 7 kilocalories per mole, it is seen that dephosphorylation of around

TABLE 3

Forces and energies for various movements

Cell	Factor	Calculated value	Remarks	References
Grasshopper spermatocyte	Force per chromosome (applied throughout anaphase) to move the chromosome to the pole	$\sim 10^{-8}$ dynes	—	Nicklas (1965)
Newt fibroblast			This value is my extrapolation from the stated values of work and distance	Taylor
Grasshopper spermatocyte	Number of ATP molecules needed to move one chromosome to the pole	~ 13	—	Nicklas (1965)
Newt fibroblast		~ 36	This value is my extrapolation from the stated values of total energy, total chromosome number and kcal. per mole of ATP	Taylor
Pea root tip		~ 4	This value is my extrapolation from the stated values of chromosome velocity, number of chromosomes, and total power required, assuming a total distance of 20 μ	Amoore
Frog sartorius muscle	Force exerted by a muscle	$\sim 3 \times 10^{-2}$ dynes per μ^2 cross-sectional area	This is a measured value	Lowy et al.
Large abfrontal gill cilium of *Mytilus edilus*	Force exerted by one cilium	$\sim 2 \times 10^{-4}$ dynes	This is a measured value, for a cilium 1 μ in diameter	Yoneda
		$\sim 10^{-5}$ dynes	This value is for force per 9+2 group of tubules, assuming that the large abfrontal cilium is composed of 20 groups of 9+2 tubules	
Frog sartorius muscle	Force exerted by one thick filament (cross-sectional area 10^4 Å^2) and associated thin filaments	3–5 $\times 10^{-5}$ dynes	—	Lowy et al.; Wolpert

30 ATP molecules could suffice to move one chromosome to the pole (Table 3). This is a small number of ATP molecules: 30 ATP molecules could be dephosphorylated in *one second* by *one molecule* of dynein (the ATPase from cilia; see the data of Gibbons). In fact the number of ATP molecules required to move the entire set of chromosomes to the poles is of the order of 10^9 times smaller than is required to synthesize spindle protein, assuming one ATP per peptide bond (Taylor).

As further comparison, it is seen that the force for chromosome movement is much smaller than that exerted by one cilium or by one myofibril (Table 3). In skeletal muscle, one thick filament (and associated thin filaments) bears a force 10^3 larger than that required to move a chromosome to a pole (Table 3). Thus, even if the actual force required to move a chromosome were 100 times larger than estimated, the force generated by one thick filament (and associated thin filaments) is still 30 times larger than needed. It is concluded, then, that the force necessary to move a chromosome against viscous resistance is very small, and could be accounted for by one thick filament (and associated thin filaments) from skeletal muscle.

The force produced may be quite a bit larger than that calculated, however, for it is possible that the chromosomal frictional resistance is negligible compared to other factors (Taylor; Nicklas (1965) termed this model 'force insignificance'). If this were true, chromosome velocity would not decrease when there is an increase in frictional resistance to motion; indeed, chromosome velocity is unchanged when this resistance is increased (a) by a factor of 10, due to variations in spindle viscosity (Taylor), (b) by a factor of more than 2, due to variations in chromosome size (Nicklas 1965), and (c) by a factor of more than 2, due to late disjunction of meiotic chromosomes (Nicklas 1963). However, none of these demonstrations are in themselves foolproof; for example, Taylor assumed that the measured cytoplasmic viscosity was a direct measure of spindle viscosity, and, as pointed out by Nicklas (1965), this assumption needs not be valid. But while one might argue against each conclusion separately, the 3 different arguments taken together make a reasonably convincing case that velocity is independent of load, for each of the 3 relies on a different set of assumptions.

The independence of velocity and load does not prove that frictional resistance is negligible compared to other factors, however. It is possible, for example, that a constant velocity is obtained, independent of load, because the applied force changes as the load changes, that is, the force for chromosome movement is adjusted continuously to give exactly that which is needed to overcome viscous resistance (Nicklas (1965) termed this model 'force compensation'). There are arguments which favor force compensation (Forer 1966), but there is no conclusive evidence to rule out either force insignificance or force compensation.

It is worth noting that 'force insignificance' still requires relatively small forces. Even allowing a tolerance of 10^2 to account for inefficiency in spindle 'thick filaments' and errors in estimates of viscous resistance, 2 or 3 thick filaments still produce 100 times the necessary force. With forces this large, increases in viscous load by factors of 10 are still 'insignificant'. Since such a small amount of material *could* cause chromosome movement, this suggests that much of the spindle material is not involved in force production *per se*, but has some other role(s).

In conclusion: the viscous resistance to chromosome movement is very small ($\sim 10^{-8}$ dynes). But chromosome velocity is independent of load and thus viscous resistance might be negligible compared to the force actually available (force insignificance). Alternatively, the force is continually adjusted to account for different loads (force-compensation). In either case only a few thick filaments could account for the force, suggesting that a large part of the spindle material has some role(s) other than force production.

(d) *General characteristics of the force system*

Other factors as well must be accounted for by theories of anaphase chromosome movement and Mazia (1961) has listed and given evidence for several 'criteria for a theory of chromosome movement'. I shall not repeat his evidence, but I shall give further evidence relating to some of these same points, and shall discuss additional criteria. Theories for anaphase chromosome movement can be rejected if they run counter to these criteria.

(1) The force for chromosome movement acts at the kinetochore, and directs the chromosome toward the pole (i.e., along the length of the chromosomal fibre) (see Mazia 1961).

(2) The force causes chromosomes to move with approximately constant velocities in the range 0.2–5.0 μ per minute.

(3) The initial separation of single metaphase chromosomes into two anaphase chromosomes is independent of subsequent anaphase movement (Mazia 1961, p. 267; Forer 1966).

(4) Of the chromosomes moving toward one pole, the forces act on each chromosome individually, and independently of others moving to the same pole.

The evidence for this is: (a) In some cells, different chromosomes regularly move at different times from others (e.g., Hughes-Schrader; Dietz 1956, 1958, 1959; Mazia 1961; Bauer et al.; Forer 1966). (b) In some cells some chromosomes regularly move poleward with a velocity different from other chromosomes (Hughes and Preston; Dietz 1956; Bauer et al.; Nicklas 1965). (c) Micromanipulation of one anaphase chromosome (half-bivalent) moving to a pole has no effect on the movement of other chromosomes going to the same pole (Nicklas and Staehly). (d) Individual metaphase and anaphase chromosomes can be moved laterally across the spindle (i.e., perpendicular to its length) yet the movements of other chromosomes are not affected (Nicklas and Staehly). (e) Chromosomes moving to one pole are affected independently by ultraviolet microbeam irradiation of spindle fibres: some half-bivalents continue to move normally while others temporarily stop moving; and of those that stop moving, different chromosomes resume movement at different times, and with different velocities relative to the pre-irradiation velocities (Forer 1966).

(5) The forces act *individually* on separating chromosomes, but under some circum-

stances the force on one chromosome is *not independent* of the partner moving to the opposite pole.

The evidence for this is: (a) *Individuality.* Chromosomes moving to opposite poles do not necessarily move with the same velocity (Mazia 1961; Dietz 1956; Bauer et al.; Izutsu; Forer 1964). (b) *Not independence.* When irradiation of a chromosomal fibre stops the anaphase movement of the associated chromosome (half-bivalent), the partner chromosome moving to the opposite pole also stops moving; both partners resume movement at the same time (Forer 1966).

(6) In meiosis, pairing is not a prerequisite for coordinated movement to opposite poles (Schrader; Mazia 1961; Dietz 1956).

(7) No theory can be incompatible with the chemical and physical nature of the spindle and the independence of velocity and load described in the previous three sections.

With these criteria in mind, I now discuss the morphological entities which cause chromosomes to move during anaphase.

(e) *The identity and function of the elements causing chromosome movement*

What causes the chromosomes to move poleward during anaphase? It is thought that each chromosome is somehow pulled to a pole by its chromosomal spindle fibre; the chromosomal fibre transmits the force to the kinetochore, in any case, even if the force is produced elsewhere. Detailed arguments for this conclusion are presented in the general reviews cited in the Introduction, in Inoué (1964) and in Inoué and Sato. These arguments are all indirect ones, however, being based either on treatments of whole cells or on the elimination of other theories.

More direct evidence is supplied by ultraviolet microbeam irradiation of various parts of the cell: irradiation with a given dose stops movement only when chromosomal fibres are irradiated, but not when the interzonal region or cytoplasm are irradiated (Forer 1966). While this does not prove that chromosomal fibres *cause* movement, it at least shows that chromosomal fibres are *necessary* elements for chromosome movement.

The experiments also provide evidence about the *length* of chromosomal fibre that is necessary for normal movement. This is shown by irradiating at different positions between the kinetochore and the pole and seeing if chromosome movement is blocked. The results are for positions up to 8 μ out of a fibre length of 10 μ, and they indicate that at least 80% of the fibre length is necessary for chromosome movement (Forer 1966, and unpublished).

Though these results directly implicate *something* associated with the chromosomal fibre, this something is not the birefringent material. This conclusion is based on the following observations (Forer, 1966): (1) Chromosomes can move normally after irradiation of the chromosomal spindle fibre adjacent to the kinetochore has caused spindle fibre birefringence to be greatly reduced or to disappear; (2) the chromosome and the irradiated fibre region move poleward with velocities which can differ by as much as a factor of 3, the chromosomes moving faster, at the same rate as, or slower than the irradiated fibre region; (3) when irradiation of the fibre causes the associated chromosome to stop moving, the irradiated region on the fibre nonetheless moves to the pole; (4) chromosomes which have stopped moving may resume movement before the irradiated region reaches the pole; and (5) ultraviolet microbeam irradiation can block chromosome movement without affecting spindle fibre birefringence.

These results suggest that chromosomal spindle fibres contain: (a) a force-transmitting component and (b) a birefringent component, and that these components are independent and can be affected independently (detailed arguments are presented in Forer (1966).

This argument and these 5 points refer solely to irradiations during anaphase. None of the first 4 points is valid for irradiations prior to anaphase. After irradiation of spindle fibres during metaphase (Forer 1966), (1) chromosomes do not move poleward when the irradiated region is present on a spindle fibre: even if the half-bivalents disjoin before the irradiated region reaches the pole, poleward movement is delayed until normal-looking chromosomal fibres are formed; and (2) when the half-bivalents finally move poleward, their velocity is related to the previous movement of the irradiated region, always being less than the velocity of the irradiated region. Using the same argument as above, one arrives at the opposite conclusion, namely that the birefringent material *is* necessary for chromosome movement. Thus, *before anaphase* the birefringent material is necessary for something related to anaphase chromosome movement, but *during anaphase* the birefringent material is *not* necessary for chromosome movement. It might be that before anaphase the birefringent fibre is necessary because it helps to form and make functional the force transmitting element, i.e., it helps in the completion of Mazia's 'motor mechanism' (Mazia 1961, p. 268).

Thus, my explanation involves two hypotheses, (1) there are two components, and (2) the two components become independent at anaphase (Forer 1966). These hypotheses are testable, they are consistent with the various components in spindles, with the various criteria for theories of movement, and with the idea that only a small portion of the fibre produces force for movement while most of the fibre has some other role (see above). Furthermore, the hypotheses suggest that we do not observe the 'locking' of the spindle at anaphase because we do not as yet observe the force transmitting component. As pointed out above, the temperature effect on spindle birefringence might be indirect, and due to its effect on the force element (the 'motor mechanism'). Little can be said about possible mechanisms until these two components are further identified.

Because of its relevance to theories of anaphase chromosome movement I should point out that removal of material from chromosomal fibres must take place at the pole; the evidence for this is that the irradiated region on the fibre moves to the pole without changing shape (Forer 1965; Inoué and Sato). This is true for *Nephrotoma suturalis* spermatocytes, but it is not yet tested for other materials. It will be recalled that spindle fibres in crane fly spermatocytes have weakest birefringence at the poles, and strongest birefringence at the kinetochores, so it is not surprising that the poles act as 'disorienting centres'. But if stronger birefringence is a valid criterion for orienting centres, the poles would be orienting centres in cells in which the chromosomal fibre birefringence was strong at the poles. In such cells the repair of the irradiation-induced lesion should be away from both orienting centres, and thus the irradiated spindle fibre region should not move poleward, as in crane fly spermatocytes, but rather the two ends should grow together. This experiment has not yet been done, however.

In summary, some material associated with the chromosomal spindle fibre is necessary for anaphase chromosome movement, and the necessary length of this material is at least 80 % of the length of the chromosomal spindle fibre, both conclusions being deduced from ultraviolet microbeam irradiations of spindle fibres. The results strongly suggest that in anaphase the spindle fibre component necessary for chromosome movement functions independently of the birefringent material, though in metaphase this is not true. It is suggested that the 'locking' of the spindle at anaphase is due to completion of the functional form of the non-birefringent, force-producing material.

4. *Studies using electron microscopy*

I have discussed several aspects of cell-division as viewed with light microscopes, and have presented evidence that the force for chromosome movement comes from some chromosomal spindle fibre component separate from the birefringent component. Studies of cell-division using the electron microscope should in theory provide evidence at a different level of organization, near the molecular. I shall now discuss some electron microscope studies, firstly to see which structures in the electron microscope correspond to the structures seen with the light microscope, and secondly to consider the functions of these structures.

(a) *Electron microscopy compared with light microscopy*

The term 'microtubule' (Slautterback; Ledbetter and Porter) is used to designate cellular structures which with usual fixation and staining procedures appear cylindrical, of outer diameter in the range 180–300 Å. Microtubules have electron-dense walls about 50–60 Å thick, and are present in spindles fixed with glutaraldehyde, and, in some cases, fixed with osmium (e.g., Harris 1965).

It is generally assumed that the light microscopic chromosomal and continuous fibres are groups of microtubules. This idea is based on (1) the observations that spindle microtubules are oriented in the pole-to-pole direction, and are often found in 'bundles', (2) the idea that protein oriented in this way would give rise to positive birefringence, and hence would give rise to the observed birefringence of spindle fibres, and (3) the observations that some microtubules appear to be attached to chromosomes.

The arrangement and number of spindle microtubules has not been compared quantitatively with the birefringence and morphology of *in vivo* spindle fibres, however, and fixation for electron microscopy seems to alter the spindle fibre birefringence. Spindle birefringence is reduced by more than 50% after glutaraldehyde fixation and osmium tetroxide post-fixation of *Pectinaria* eggs (Inoué and Sato), and spindle fibre birefringence is reduced by about 30% after osmium tetroxide fixation of isolated sea urchin egg MA and isolated clam egg MA (Rebhun and Sander). Dehydration, as well, can cause loss of birefringence (Forer, unpublished). In most cases birefringence has not been measured, but if this loss of birefringence is a general phenomenon with glutaraldehyde and osmium fixations, it is not clear how the electron microscopic image of spindles corresponds to the *in vivo* situation. Quantitative comparison needs be made between the amount of birefringence and the electron microscopic image at various portions of the same spindle, under conditions where the birefringence is preserved. Until something like this is done, uncertainty must attend any presumed correlation of spindle microtubules with spindle fibre birefringence.

Furthermore, microtubules might not necessarily give rise to form birefringence. It is possible, for example, that the microtubule 'wall' is not protein at all, but rather a phase boundary which is selectively stained; or the wall could be lipoprotein, or other

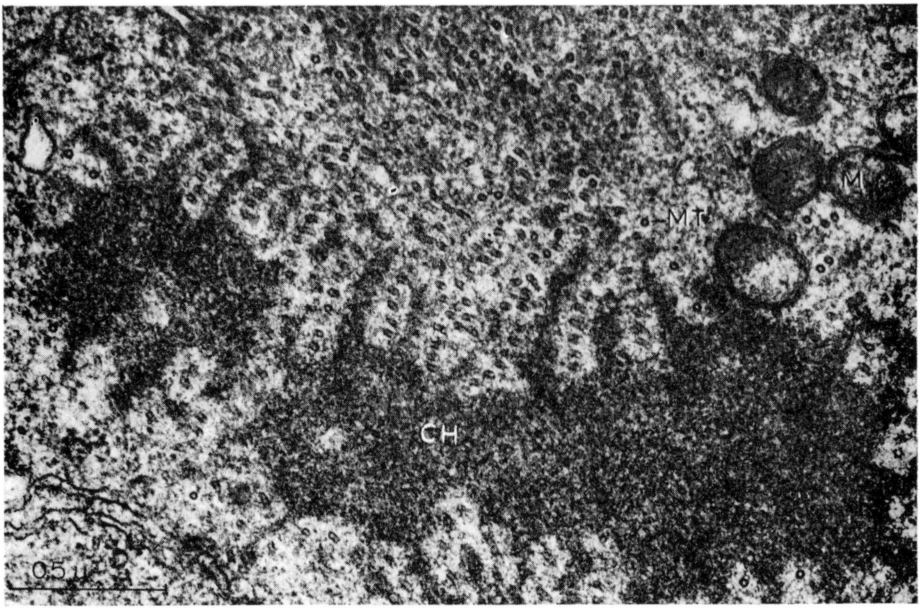

Fig. 8 illustrates an individual chromosome (CH) in a primary spermatocyte. This figure shows primarily cross-sectioned microtubules (MT). M: mitochondria. × 42,500.

substances; or even if microtubules were protein, a microtubule could be of the same refractive index as its surrounds, and hence cause no form birefringence; or, if microtubules are protein, in a medium of different refractive index, the form birefringence of microtubules might not be measurable, or might be masked or added to by the intrinsic and form birefringence of other materials which are present and which are oriented by the microtubules. While there is some evidence that microtubules give rise to at least some birefringence (discussed in Rebhun and Sander; and Inoué and Sato), this evidence is open to other interpretations as well. Thus, it is not clear how much, if any, of the spindle birefringence is due to microtubules.

Despite the uncertainties stressed above, there are some positive conclusions which can be drawn, as follows.

(1) *Spindle fibre birefringence is probably not due solely to microtubules.* This conclusion is based on the observation that no microtubules are seen when 30–50% of the spindle birefringence remains (and is preserved through fixation). This occurs after isolated MA are stored at *p*H 6.1, or are washed several times (Goldman; Rebhun, Sander, Goldman and Bernstein). Using the same techniques, microtubules are present in abundance in freshly isolated MA. In this case, then, at least 30–50% of the birefringence of isolated MA is due to non-microtubular material. The converse experiment implies the same conclusion, as follows: addition of basic protein to glutaraldehyde-fixed isolated MA causes the birefringence to double, without a change in the number of microtubules (Goldman).

These experiments do not *conclusively* demonstrate the proposition stated above, for, in the absence of further data, counter arguments are possible. Furthermore, extrapolation to *in vivo* MA is uncertain, since it is not known how the birefringence of isolated MA is related to that of *in vivo* MA (see last section, and discussion of Rebhun and Sander). Nonetheless, these data are at least as convincing as those from which the opposite conclusion is drawn and thus I state the conclusion as above and reiterate that we need careful experimental analysis of microtubules and other spindle components and how they contribute to the observed spindle birefringence.

(2) *Spindles contain more than microtubules.* Published reports and electron micrographs show that besides microtubules, spindles contain vesicles (smooth and granular); membranes; ribosome-like particles; endoplasmic reticulum; amorphous or greyish 'background' material; filamentous material associated with microtubules; lamellae; dense material associated with microtubules; 'small circular bodies' (Whaley et al.); and non-staining 'clear areas' around microtubules. Figs. 11–13 show microtubules in spindles in crane fly spermatocytes, illustrating 'clear areas' around many of the spindle microtubules, and illustrating the large amount of non-microtubule material. Other illustrations of this latter point can be seen in papers of Robbins and Gonatas; George et al.; Roth et al.; Krishan and Buck (1965a, b); de Thé; Jokelainen; and Brinkley et al. These articles and the discussion below provide references to other studies.

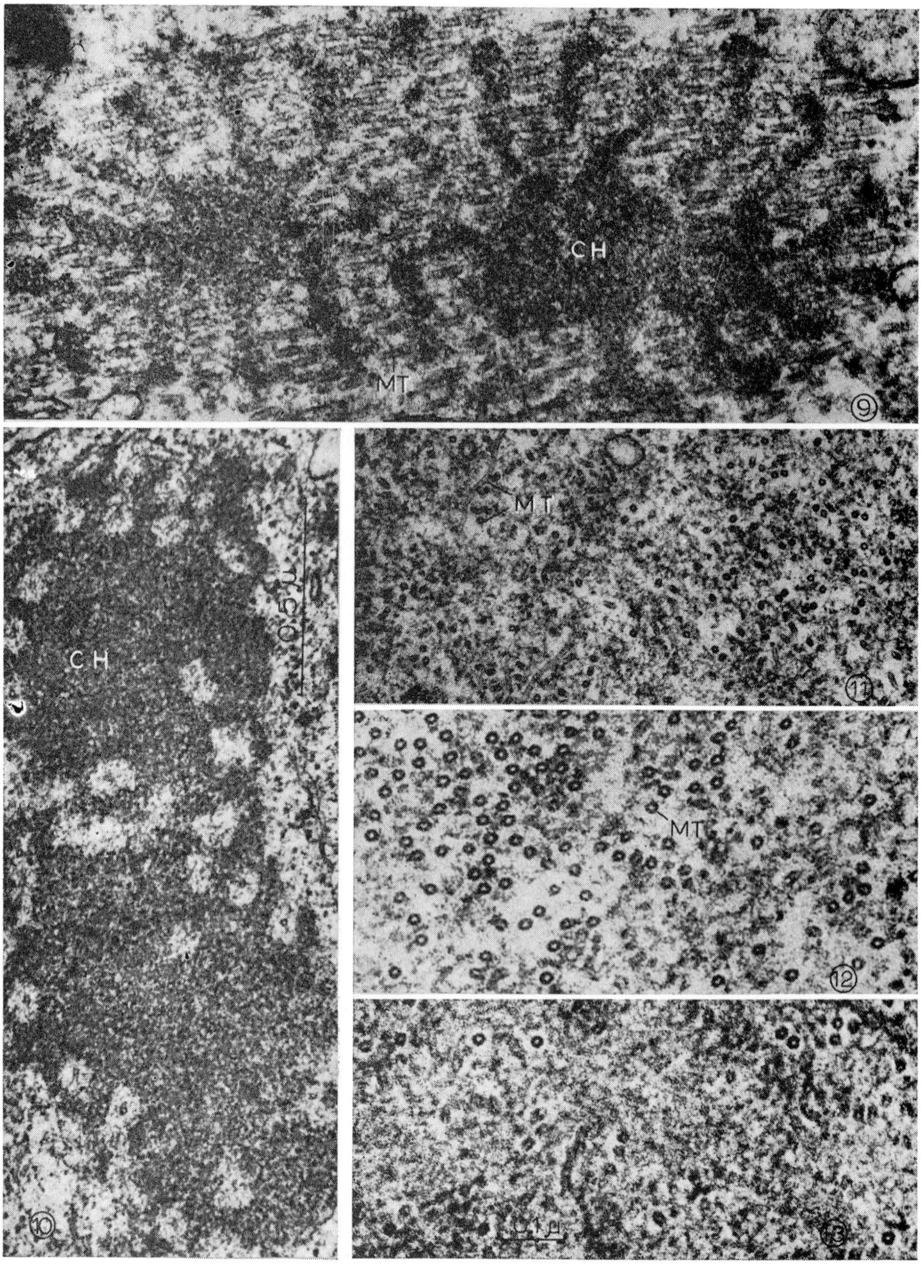
CH
MT
9
CH
0.5μ
10
MT
11
MT
12
0.1μ
13

That the non-microtubule components might have an important role in spindle structure is suggested by the finding that isolated MAs are stable even when the microtubules have been extracted (Kane and Forer; Goldman; Borisy and Taylor; Bibring and Baxandall).

(3) *A minority portion of the spindle mass and volume is in the form of microtubules.* There are of the order of 0.1–2.0 ml of microtubules per 100 ml of spindles (i.e. 0.1–2.0% by volume). These are maximum values estimated from published counts of microtubules per cross-section of spindle, and estimated from published micrographs by direct measurement over regions of at least 1 μ^2 (Table 4). As seen in Table 5, one can estimate the mass fraction of microtubules as about 9 times the volume fraction, and thus volume fractions of 0.1–2.0% correspond to 0.9–18.0 g of microtubules per 100 g of spindle (i.e., 0.9–18.0% by weight). In this calculation I assume that a microtubule is a solid cylinder of protein, of density 1.37 g/cm^3 (Mahler and Cordes), and that the spindle is 15% dry matter (Table 2). For 'hollow' cylinders of such protein, the corresponding factor is seven and the mass fractions are 0.7–14.0%. The mass estimates, too, are estimates of maximum values.

Spindle microtubules can occupy 4–5% of the spindle volume, however, in rather small regions of the spindle, of the order of 0.1 μ^2 (Table 4). In a few cases they occupy 10% of the volume (Table 4). These values are yet higher in protozoans. Again, this is based on a few published counts of numbers of microtubules, and on direct measurement from published micrographs. One can not have as much confidence in estimates of mass fractions over small areas, though, because the spindle masses have been measured as averages over the entire spindles, and it is not known if small regions may have smaller or larger mass than average. Nonetheless, applying the calculation as above, volume fractions of 5% correspond to mass fractions of no more than 45% (or 34%, for 'hollow' microtubules). Even in the few cases with 10% of microtubules by volume, the micrographs show that materials other than microtubules are present in the microtubule bundles.

It should be emphasized that conclusion (3) is solely for material in the form of microtubules. The estimates do not include microtubule precursors which might be present, for it is not known how much, if any, of the non-microtubule material is precursor. One can say, however, that at least *some* of the non-microtubule material

---

Figs. 9 and 10 illustrate individual chromosomes (CH) in primary spermatocytes. Fig. 9 shows primarily obliquely sectioned microtubules and Fig. 10 shows primarily cross-sectioned microtubules (MT). Microtubules are associated with chromosomes over a large area. M: mitochondria. Fig. 9: $\times$ 61,500; Fig. 10: $\times$ 51,750.

Figs. 11–13 illustrate cross-sections of spindles, showing microtubules (MT), large amounts of non-microtubule material, and non-staining 'clear areas' surrounding many of the microtubules. Some regions show microtubules in both cross-section and longitudinal section (Fig. 11). Fig. 11: $\times$35,000; Fig. 12: $\times$ 87,000; Fig. 13: $\times$ 89,500.

TABLE 4

Volume fractions occupied by spindle microtubules

Cell	Volume fraction of microtubules	Type of section, and *cross-sectional areas* for measurement	Remarks	References
		A. Larger areas		
Haemanthus endosperm cells	⩽ 0.035 (metaphase)	Longitudinal sections, over areas of ∼1 μ^2	The authors estimate 50–100 microtubules per metaphase kinetochore. The volume fraction is a maximum estimate, using the maximum number of microtubules, the minimum kinetochore size in light micrographs (1 μ) and maximum size of microtubules (200 Å)	Harris and Bajer
Nephrotoma spermatocytes	0.01	Cross-sections, over areas of ∼75 μ^2	The authors count ∼1700 microtubules per spindle cross-section	Behnke and Forer (1966)
	0.02–0.05	Cross-sections over areas ranging from 1 μ^2 to 12 μ^2	These volume fractions are measured from unpublished photographs	Behnke and Forer (unpublished)
Isolated MA, from *S. purpuratus* eggs	0.001	Cross-sections, over areas of ∼200 μ^2	The authors count on the average 465 microtubules per spindle cross-section (in metaphase)	Bibring and Baxandall (personal communication)
Isolated MA, from *A. punctulata* eggs	0.005	Cross-sections, over areas of ∼200 μ^2	The authors count approximately 2000 microtubules per spindle cross-section (in metaphase)	Cohen and Rebhun (personal communication)
S. purpuratus eggs	0.02	Longitudinal section, over an area of ∼1 μ^2	My estimate, from published micrographs	Harris and Mazia
	0.005–0.01	Longitudinal sections, over areas of ∼4–9 μ^2	My estimate, from published micrographs	Harris (1962) and Harris (1965)
HeLa cells	0.025	Longitudinal section, over an area of ∼1 μ^2	My estimate, from published micrographs	George et al.

Isolated MA, from *A. punctulata* eggs	0.005–0.015	Longitudinal sections and cross-section, over areas of ∼1 μ^2–36 μ^2	My estimate, from published micrographs	Kane (1962b); Kane and Forer
Isolated MA, from *Spisula* eggs	0.01–0.02	Longitudinal sections and cross-sections, over areas ranging from ∼7 μ^2 to 16 μ^2	My estimate, from published micrographs	Rebhun and Sander
Isolated MA, from *S. purpuratus* eggs	0.003–0.02	Longitudinal sections and cross-sections, over areas ranging from 1 μ^2 to 15 μ^2	My estimate, from published micrographs	

B. Smaller areas

Pelomyxa (Giant amebae)	0.025	Longitudinal section, over an area ∼0.2 μ^2	My estimate, from published micrograph	Roth et al.
Ostrinia nubilalis spermatocytes	0.04–0.05	Cross-sections, over areas ∼0.09–0.13 μ^2		
HeLa cells	0.045	Longitudinal sections, over areas of ∼0.3 μ^2	My estimate, from published micrographs	Robbins and Gonatas
L-strain fibroblasts	0.05–0.055	Longitudinal sections, over areas of ∼0.2–0.5 μ^2	My estimate, from published micrographs	Krishan and Buck (1965a)
Ascites tumor cells	0.055	Cross-section, over an area of ∼0.06 μ^2	My estimate, from published micrograph	de Thé
Mitotic cells in fetal rats	0.055	Cross-section, over an area of ∼0.03 μ^2	Jokelainen counted 7 microtubules per 2000 Å diameter kinetochore	Jokelainen
	0.025	Cross-section, over an area of ∼0.12 μ^2	My estimate, from published micrographs	
S. purpuratus eggs	0.065	Longitudinal section, over an area of ∼0.05 μ^2	My estimate, from published micrograph	Harris and Mazia
	0.035–0.10	Longitudinal sections, over areas of ∼0.04–0.09 μ^2	My estimate, from published micrographs	Harris (1962, 1965)
Blatoides germanica spermatocytes	0.09	Longitudinal section, over an area of ∼0.2 μ^2	My estimate, from published micrographs	Krishan and Buck (1965b)
Campanella umbellaria (macronuclei)	0.13–0.17	Cross-section, over areas of ∼0.04–0.06 μ^2	My estimate, from published micrographs	Carasso and Favard
Nassula sp. (micronuclei)	0.12–0.13	Longitudinal sections and cross-sections, over areas of ∼0.8 μ^2	My estimate, from published cross-sections of 'separation spindles'	Tucker

TABLE 5

Volume and mass fractions of microtubules

Diameter of microtubule	180 Å	200 Å	240 Å	250 Å
Number of microtubules per μ^2 cross-sectional area giving rise to the volume fraction below	4	3.2	2.2	2
Volume fraction of microtubules (ml of microtubules per ml of MA)		0.001		
Mass of microtubules (g of microtubules per ml of MA)		0.00137		
Expected g dry mass per ml of MA (Table 2)		0.15		
Mass fraction of microtubules in MA (g microtubules per g MA)		0.009		

is not microtubule precursor. The evidence for this is: (a) chemical analyses show at least three different components (discussed below), and (b) spindles remain structurally intact after microtubules have been chemically extracted (Borisy and Taylor; Bibring and Baxandal).

(4) *Spindle microtubules are not evenly distributed throughout the spindle area.* Inspection of micrographs and estimates of microtubule density show that in some areas of the spindles microtubules are closer together than in other areas of the same spindles.

Taken together the evidence leads us to conclude that a considerable portion of the spindle birefringence is probably due to non-microtubule material, and that more than 50% of the spindle mass and more than 95% of the spindle volume is not in the form microtubule. Non-microtubule components are seen in all regions of the spindle.

These conclusions are relevant to observations of crane fly spermatocytes (Behnke and Forer 1966), which will now be briefly discussed.

Behnke and Forer found no correlation between the positions of microtubules and the positions of birefringent spindle fibres. (The birefringent spindle fibres of these cells are illustrated in Figs. 3–5, and discussed above.) This statement is based on the following: we do not see 5 bundles of microtubules in cross-sectioned spindles, but rather microtubules throughout the entire spindle, and even outside the spindle area; we do not see microtubules attached to the chromosomes, but rather microtubules passing through and around the chromosomes; spindle microtubules are not all oriented in the same direction (e.g., Fig. 11); in anaphase we see microtubules in the not birefringent interzonal region as well as between the chromosomes and the pole; and, finally, spindle microtubules are associated with individual chromosomes over a region of up to 3–4 μ in length and 1.5–2 μ in width (Figs. 8–10), while the kinetochore region as seen with the light microscope is only 1 μ in diameter (compare the electron micrographs of Figs. 8–10 with the light micrographs of Figs. 4–7).

Why are these results different from the results reported by others? We have not yet sectioned cells in predetermined regions, so it is possible that we never have seen a proper cross-section of an anaphase spindle. However, we have looked at many cells, and have used secondary criteria for identifying stages, so this is probably not the main difference. In line with the previous discussion, I suggest the following as more likely possibilities.

(A) It is possible that there are different kinds of spindle microtubules, different either in themselves, or by virtue of some intimately associated material, some microtubules giving rise to birefringent spindle fibres and other microtubules not. In crane fly spermatocytes 'bundles' of 'birefringent microtubules' are masked by the presence of the other, morphologically identical microtubules, while in other cells the fixative preserves only the microtubules in the birefringent bundle. This explanation implies that these different microtubules exhibit differences in fixation and other properties; indeed, when spermatids are treated in various ways, different microtubules respond differently to the same treatment, and 4 classes of microtubules can be distinguished in individual cells (Behnke and Forer 1967). This lends credence to the postulated different kinds of spindle microtubules. Furthermore, chromosome-associated microtubules respond differently from other spindle microtubules when crane fly spermatocytes are treated experimentally (Behnke and Forer, in preparation), suggesting that there may indeed be different kinds of spindle microtubules.

(B) It is possible that the main contribution to spindle fibre birefringence is not from microtubules, but from some as yet unidentified material, which the microtubules might help to orient (see conclusion 1, above).

(C) It is possible that the birefringence was not preserved throughout the preparatory procedures for the electron microscope. While there was no change of birefringence during the first 2–3 min in glutaraldehyde (Behnke and Forer 1966), longer fixation causes loss of birefringence in other cells (discussed above), so on this point our results may be in doubt.

In summary: spindles contain various components, including microtubules; microtubule-associated filaments, clear areas, and dense material; amorphous or greyish 'background' material; membranes; endoplasmic reticulum; ribosome-like particles; and smooth and granular vesicles. The exact contribution of spindle microtubules to spindle birefringence is unknown, but it is probable that at least 30–50% of the spindle birefringence is due to non-microtubule material. More than 50% of the spindle mass and 94% of the spindle volume is non-microtubule in form, and at least some of this non-microtubule material is not microtubule precursor. It is suggested that there may be different kinds of spindle microtubules. Because of these considerations and because in crane fly spermatocytes spindle microtubules are associated with chromosomes over a larger area than represented by the light microscopic kinetochore, there is considerable uncertainty regarding the exact relationship between the light microscopic and electron microscopic components.

(b) *Functional aspects*

If one considers the functions of the various components seen in the electron microscope, it seems clear from the previous uncertainties and discussion that many problems need be clarified before one can begin to speculate on what these components might be doing. Furthermore, while it is known that the spindle properties change dramatically between metaphase and anaphase, electron microscopy has not yet provided indications of any corresponding morphological changes between metaphase and anaphase. This fact, plus the previous conclusion that only a few thick filaments could provide 100 times enough force for chromosome movements, suggest that as of yet we might not be looking at the material responsible for transmitting the force to the chromosomes.

5. *Biochemical analyses of isolated spindles*

We have pointed out that chromosomes are pulled to the pole by a spindle fibre component different from the birefringent component. From electron microscopic observations it is not clear which components give rise to birefringence, or to the force for chromosome movement, but the observations do show that spindle microtubules are a minority component of spindles, by volume and by mass. We will now consider biochemical analyses of isolated MAS; firstly the correspondence between isolated MAS and *in vivo* MAS, and secondly biochemical studies on isolated MAS. The methods for isolation of MAS will not be considered, for these can be obtained from the references discussed below. There are several different methods for isolating MAS from sea urchin eggs (references below), and methods for isolating MAS from clam eggs (Rebhun and Sander) and from HeLa cells (Sisken et al.). The biochemical data derive primarily from MA isolated from sea urchin eggs.

(a) *Isolated MA compared with in vivo MA*

There are some *similarities* between isolated and *in vivo* MA. Firstly, the effect of *p*H is similar (Kane 1962a), acid *p*H accentuating the fibrillar structure. Secondly, the polar regions of isolated MA are least soluble (Table 6), reminiscent of the *in vivo* staining and birefringence patterns. Thirdly, direct chemical analyses of isolated MA (Table 7) reveal most kinds of material detected cytochemically (Table 1). Finally, isolated MA contain microtubules and other structures seen electron microscopically in *in situ* MA (cf. Kane 1962b; Harris 1962, 1965).

Some points are not yet clear. Isolated MA are birefringent (Kane and Forer), but these birefringence values have not been compared quantitatively with those of *in vivo* MA. And there have been no reports of differences between isolated metaphase and anaphase MA, though perhaps this has not been looked for carefully.

There are some *clear differences* between isolated and *in vivo* MA. Firstly, chromosome movement has not yet occurred in isolated MA. Secondly, with isolated MA

TABLE 6

Solubility of regions of isolated MA

Isolation method	Solubility	Solvent	Reference
Ethanol-digitonin	First the peripheral asters and the equator dissolve, and then dissolution progresses toward the poles	Thioglycollate, *p*H 11	Mazia (1955)
		Salyrgan	Zimmerman
	The same as above, but the regions around the poles (centrospheres) remain undissolved	Parachloro-mercuri-benzoate or sulfite	Sakai
Dithiodiglycol or dithiodipropanol	First the spindles dissolve, then the asters. The centrospheres remain undissolved	0.53 M KCl, *p*H 7–8.5	Sakai; Kiefer et al.
Hexylene glycol, *p*H 6.4	First the spindles dissolve, and then the asters	H_2O, at *p*H 7.5	Kane and Forer

neither colchicine nor low temperature cause loss of spindle fibre birefringence or dissolution of structure (e.g., Borisy and Taylor; Inoué and Sato; Kane and Forer). In fact, the temperature effect on isolated MA is the reverse of that on *in vivo* MA, as has been discussed previously.

Finally, there is quite a big difference in the amount of material present. Sea urchin egg MA *in vivo* contain about 23 g of dry matter per 100 ml of MA (Table 2), while sea urchin egg MA when isolated contain about 1 g protein per 100 ml of MA (Table 8), i.e., 95% *less than expected.* (As seen in Table 8, this is true for all isolation methods for which this measurement is available.) It is unlikely that interference microscope measurements on *in vivo* MA are wrong by more than a few per cent in dry mass, and indeed interference microscope estimates of cytoplasmic dry mass agree reasonably well with chemical analyses: interference microscopy of *Psammechinus miliaris* egg cytoplasm (Table 2) shows 25 g of dry matter per 100 ml of cytoplasm, while biochemical analysis of *Arbacia punctulata* eggs shows about 26 g dry matter per 100 ml of eggs (Harvey). Furthermore, interference microscope measurements in various cells and by various workers all give *in vivo* concentrations in the range of 10–20 g of dry matter per 100 ml of MA (Table 2). Therefore I conclude that the discrepancy between the masses of *in vivo* and isolated MA represents a real difference, and that MAs lose of the order of 95% of their mass during the isolation procedure.

There is one important qualification, however: since interference microscopy does not distinguish between different materials, it is in theory possible that the entire MA dry mass is indeed isolated, but that 95% of it is not protein, and has not been analyzed. This is not the case for ethanol-digitonin isolated MA, for measurements of dry weight (Zimmerman) indicate that isolated MA contain 1.55 g of dry matter per 100 ml

TABLE 7

Materials present in MA isolated from sea urchin eggs

(as % of total weight)

Isolation method	Protein	RNA	Lipid	Carbo-hydrate	ATPase	Species	Remarks	Reference
Ethanol-digitonin	> 95%	2–3%	—	Some	—	*Strongylocentrotus purpuratus*	These are the percentages of materials present in the thyo-glycollate soluble fraction	Mazia (1955)
Ethanol-digitonin	94–95%	5–6%	—	—	—	*Strongylocentrotus purpuratus*	These are the materials present in the Salyrgan soluble fraction	Zimmerman
Dithiodiglycol	—	—	—	—	Present	*S. purpuratus*	ATPase was present in KCl soluble fraction	Mazia et al.
Dithiodipropanol	—	4–5%	Present	—	—	*S. purpuratus*	These are materials present in the KCl soluble fraction. The lipid is noted, and discarded	Sakai
Ethanol-sonication	—	—	—	—	Present	*Anthocidaris crassispina*	—	Miki (1963)
20% Hexylene glycol-sonication	—	—	—	—	Present	*Pseudocentrotus depressus*	ATPase is present, in 2.3S material found after solubilization with KCl, and treatment with NaOH	Miki-Noumara
Hexylene glycol (*p*H 6.4)	90%	5–10%	None	6%	None	*S. purpuratus*, *S. droebachiensis* and *Arbacia punctulata*	These are the percentages of material present in the 22S fraction of KCl soluble material	Stephens (1967)

Amount of protein in MA isolated from sea urchin eggs

Isolation method	g protein per 100 ml of MA	ml per MA	g protein per MA	Species	Remarks	References
Ethanol-duponol	1.1	—	$\sim 2.4 \times 10^{-9}$	*Strongylocentrotus franciscanus*	—	Mazia and Dan
Ethanol-digitonin	<1.46	—	<1.2–3.1 $\times 10^{-10}$	*Strongylocentrotus purpuratus*	The value 1.46 is an upper limit, obtained by subtracting the measured amount of RNA from the measured dry weight. The other value was calculated from the value 1.46, and the volume of the MA, using the 2 different volume estimates of Kane (1967) and Bibring and Baxandall	Zimmerman
Hexanediol, *p*H 6.3	∾1.0	—	2×10^{-10}	*Arbacia punctulata*	The value 2×10^{-10} was calculated from the measured value 1.0 using the volume of the MA given by Kane (1967)	Mangan et al.
Hexylene glycol, *p*H 6.4	0.75	2.7×10^{-8}	2×10^{-10}	*S. purpuratus*	The ml per MA was calculated from the stated yield of MA (0.1 ml) from 1 ml of eggs, and from the volume of the eggs (Harvey)	Kane (1967)
		2.1×10^{-8}	1.6×10^{-10}	*A. punctulata*		
Hexylene glycol, *p*H 6.4	0.9	—	7.5×10^{-11}–2.4×10^{-10}	*S. purpuratus*	These values were calculated from data given in authors' Table III (protein in various fractions of MA), and methods given on p. 541 (MA gave 'about 0.1 ml packed volume'), assuming these methods were used to obtain the data in Table III	Borisy and Taylor
Hexylene glycol *p*H 6.4	0.9	8.3×10^{-9}	7.5×10^{-11}	*S. purpuratus*	The authors calculated MA volume from measurements of dimensions	Bibring and Baxandall (personal communication)

TABLE 9

Protein components solubilized from sea urchin egg MA after isolation (as % of total weight in the solub

Isolation method	Solubility		Components in soluble fr	
		2.3–2.5S	3.2–5S	6S
Ethanol-duponol	Not soluble in salts. Soluble in 0.5 N NaOH	—	All	—
Ethanol-digitonin	Soluble in thioglycollate, Salyrgan, performic acid, and parachloro-mercurobenzoate	—	83%	—
Dithiodipropanol	85% soluble in 0.53 M KCl	—	50%	—
Dithiodipropanol	70% soluble in 0.6 M KCl	75%	—	—
Dithiodipropanol	70% soluble in 0.6 M KCl	—	60%	—
Hexylene glycol, *p*H 6.4	60% soluble in 0.6 M KCl, *p*H 7.5	—	20%	—
Hexylene glycol, *p*H 6.4	80% soluble in 0.6 M KCl	—	Some	Some
Hexylene glycol *p*H 6.4	8% soluble after 75 min in HCl, *p*H 3	—	85%	—

22S	28S	S > 28	Species	Remarks	References
—	—	—	*Strongylocentrotus purpuratus* and *S. franciscanus*	—	Mazia and Dan
—	—	—	*S. purpuratus*	Data are for material soluble in Salyrgan, using Salyrgan at a concentration of $>10^3$ moles Salyrgan per 6×10^5 g of MA protein (cf. Stephens 1968), and are my estimates of areas under published curves	Zimmerman
13%	10%	—	*S. purpuratus*	The percentages of the various S components are my estimates of areas under published optical density curves	Wilt et al.
5%	—	—	*S. purpuratus*	The data are of sulfite treated material, and are my estimates of areas under published curves	Sakai
5%	—	—	*S. purpuratus*	The value 60% is calculated from the stated KCl solubility and the statement that the 3.5S component of Sakai is 40% of all the protein in the MA. The other values are calculated from this 60% value and the data of Sakai, for sulfite-treated material, knowing that sulfite does not affect the amount of 22S material (Sakai)	Kiefer et al.
80%	—	—	*S. purpuratus* and *A. punctulata*	The 20% fraction is 'heterogenous 4–5S material'	Kane (1967)
Most	—	—	*S. purpuratus*	The solubility is deduced from their Table 3	Borisy and Taylor
15%	—	—	*S. purpuratus*	—	Bibring and Baxandall

of isolated MA, i.e., still 93% less than expected. This possibility should be tested for the other isolation methods as well.

In conclusion, while there are some similarities between *in vivo* and isolated MA, there are striking differences as well, notably in the effect of temperature, and in the loss of 95% of the *in vivo* mass.

I now discuss analyses of the components present in isolated MA, and try to relate these components to structural and functional properties of spindles in cells, realizing that this latter correlation is severely restricted by the loss of material during isolation.

(b) *Components present in isolated MA*

Biochemical analyses of isolated MA are summarized in Table 9. It is seen that different workers obtain different results.

Chemical studies have been performed on various of the components, studying their behaviour at different *p*H, their dissociation and reassociation reactions, etc. (e.g., Zimmermann; Sakai; Stephens 1967). Stephens purified 22S material, and carefully studied its dissociation into subunits, and reassociation into various larger units; on the basis of the conditions under which units of certain S values were stable, Stephens concluded that 'the 4S component of Mazia (1955), the 8.6S material of Zimmerman, and the 13–14S particles of Sakai correspond to subunits obtained from the 22S protein' while the 2.5S and 3.5S components of Sakai and the 3.7S component of Zimmerman 'may more likely correspond to some component in the 4–5S heterogeneous mixture reported by Kane (1967)'. However, as Stephens admits, the arguments are somewhat circumstantial. Also, there are still unresolved differences. Nonetheless, it is tentatively concluded that there are at least two chemically different MA components in the soluble fraction, plus at least one other component in the insoluble fraction.

Other chemical data support this conclusion. Bibring and Baxandall show that the 22S material is antigenically different from the 4–5S material (in hexylene glycol isolated MA) and the 4–5S material is precipitated by calcium whereas the 22S material is not; furthermore, the 4–5S material is similar to the 3.5S material of Zimmerman, in that at *p*H 7 the 4–5S units do not associate to form 13S or 22S units, as do subunits of 22S material. Finally, Stephens (1968) reports that the molecular weight of the 22S subunit is significantly different from that of the 4–5S material, and, preliminarily, that the amino acid composition of 'sub-optimal amounts' of 4–5S material (from hexylene glycol preparations) is different from the amino acid composition of 22S material.

Cumulatively, then, this is reasonably strong evidence that isolated MA contain at least two different components in the soluble fraction. The possibility of a third component is suggested by the work of Borisy and Taylor, who showed that colchicine binds to only a small fraction of the 4–5S material in hexylene glycol preparations. But at present it is too early to be certain of more than two components in the soluble fraction.

While isolated MAS contain at least two different components in the soluble fraction, MAS isolated by different methods have different proportions of the two components. For the purposes of discussion, I consider the 13.5S and 21S components of Sakai, and the 8.6S component of Zimmerman as 22S material; and I consider the 4–5S material of Kane and Stephens as 3.5S material. It is seen in Table 10 that the proportions of the two components are reversed when one compares hexylene glycol MA *vs.* dithiodipropanol MA or ethanol-digitonin MA. But MA prepared with different methods all have about the same total mass (Table 8). One might account for the different proportions of the same material found in about the same total mass by assuming that there is an MA 'skeleton', which comprises a small fraction of the MA mass; if this skeleton can bind only a limited amount of material the total mass would remain constant, but the bound material would be different depending on how the skeleton and various bound components change with different isolation conditions. Such an idea might also explain the observation of Goldman, cited above, that the birefringence of glutaraldehyde-fixed isolated MA can be doubled by the addition of basic protein.

TABLE 10

(derived from Table 9)

Soluble components present in MA isolated using different isolation procedures

Method of isolation	Amount of component 22S	3.5S	Ratio of amounts 22S:3.5S
Hexylene glycol	80%	20%	4:1
Dithiodipropanol	25%	75%	1:3
Ethanol-digitonin	17%	83%	1:5

Summarizing, I conclude that isolated MAS contain at least two different components in the soluble fraction, plus insoluble component(s), and that under different conditions of isolation MAS have the same total mass but different proportions of the soluble components. This may arise by differential binding to a limited number of sites on an MA 'skeleton'.

But what do these different components do?

MAS exist as stable structures with only 5% of their *in vivo* mass. Thus it is reasonable to think that this 5% contains skeletal elements responsible for holding the MA together. While it is tempting to consider that the spindle microtubules are these skeletal elements, one should remember that MAS stay together even when microtubules have broken down (Kane and Forer; Goldman) or when microtubules have been selectively extracted (Goldman; Borisy and Taylor; Bibring and Baxandall). But perhaps the microtubules are the initial supports on which the skeletal structure is cast.

Even though it is not clear what the spindle microtubules do, there is some evidence that the 3.5S material derives from microtubules. This evidence is that microtubules disappear when 8 % of the MA mass is extracted, and this extracted material is mostly 3.5S material with properties similar to those of material extracted from the outer doublet tubules of sperm tails (Bibring and Baxandall).

Other than structural aspects, it is difficult to discuss the biochemistry of MAs in functional terms, because isolated MAs are not functional, and because most of the MA material is lost during isolation. Because of this loss of material it is not even certain that isolated MAs contain the force producing machinery.

It should be emphasized that in these studies, the solubility properties, the birefringence, and the fine-structure of isolated MAs are not invariant. The solubility decreases with storage (Zimmerman; Kane and Forer; Sakai), and both birefringence and fine-structure change with storage (Kane and Forer; Rebhun and Sander; Goldman), with conditions of isolation (Kane 1962b), and with washing of isolated MAs in the absence of salts (Goldman; Rebhun, Sander, Goldman and Bernstein). Since small and perhaps yet unknown differences do matter, solubility, birefringence, and fine-structure should not be taken for granted, but should be measured as controls during the isolation and subsequent experimental procedures.

In summary, MAs isolated by various techniques are mostly protein, with some RNA (about 6 % by weight), and some carbohydrate and lipid. There are at least two different protein components in the soluble fraction of isolated MAs, though the concentration of material in isolated MAs is about 95 % lower than the concentration *in vivo*. It is suggested that the 3.5S material derives from microtubules, and it is argued that isolated MAs consist of various proteins bound to a 'skeleton', the proportion of different proteins being different with different isolation methods. But it is not known which chemical elements comprise the structural element which holds MAs together.

6. *Summary*

This chapter deals with the movements of chromosomes during cell-division, and the role of the spindle in these movements. It is concluded that some component associated with the chromosomal spindle fibre causes the chromosome to move. The force for chromosome movement is either continually adjusted or is large compared to the viscous drag on the chromosome, the latter being $\sim 10^{-8}$ dynes. In either case a few thick filaments from skeletal muscle produce enough force to account for chromosome movement; this suggests that much of the spindle fibre material is not involved in force production but has some other role. Similar conclusions are drawn from experiments in which spindle fibres are irradiated with an ultraviolet microbeam. These experiments suggest (a) that spindle fibres contain two separate components, a birefringent component and a force-producing component; (b) that during anaphase the birefringent component is independent of the force-producing component; and (c) that during metaphase the birefringent component is not independent of the force-producing component, and may even be necessary for the formation of the force-producing component.

These conclusions are compatible with the physical and chemical nature of the spindle. There are about 15 g of dry matter per 100 ml of spindle (*in vivo*), and this dry matter includes protein, nucleic acid, carbohydrate, lipid, ATPase, free -SH groups, and zinc, but not phosphatase. The staining and birefringence are different in different regions of the spindle, being strongest near the chromosomes and the poles, and weakest in between. The birefringent spindle fibres are labile throughout all stages of cell-division; they are probably in equilibrium with non-birefringent material; and they are probably organized by kinetochores (and, in some cases, poles). Physiologically, there are striking differences between metaphase and anaphase spindles, though both appear identical morphologically.

Electron microscopic observations agree with the light microscopic observations in that they show several spindle components. It is not certain how these components relate to the birefringent chromosomal and continuous fibres of light microscopy because spindle fibre birefringence may not be preserved by electron microscope fixatives, and because spindle microtubules are associated with chromosomes over an area much larger than that of the light microscopic kinetochore. It is concluded that 30–50% of the spindle fibre birefringence is probably due to some non-microtubule component; that spindle microtubules as seen to date are a minority fraction of the spindle fibre volume and mass; and that spindle microtubules are not distributed evenly throughout the spindle region. It is not known which, if any, of the described components causes chromosome movement.

Spindles (MA) lose 95% of their mass when they are isolated from sea urchin eggs with present techniques. There is about 1 g of protein per 100 ml of isolated MA, and this corresponds to about 5% of the material present in *in vivo* MA.

Isolated MAs contain at least two components in the soluble fraction, plus insoluble material. The relative proportions of the soluble components are different with different isolation techniques, but the total mass is about the same with all techniques. To account for this it is suggested that there is an MA 'skeleton', comprising a small fraction of the mass of the isolated MA, and that only a limited amount of material can adhere to this skeleton.

Acknowledgements

I would like to thank Drs. T. Bibring and J. Baxandall, R. Goldman, J. Mangan, and R. Stephens for allowing me to see reports of their work prior to publication; and I would like to thank Drs. Bibring and Baxandall, and W. Cohen and L. Rebhun for allowing me to cite their unpublished results. I am especially grateful to Dr. O. Behnke for the unpublished electron micrographs in Figures 8, 9, and 11, and for invaluable discussion and collaboration (some of it in conjunction with F. B. T. Birkes-Børge). I am grateful to Dr. V. A. Parsegian for discussion of various portions of this review, and I would like to thank Drs. A. Mullinger and R. Bruce Nicklas for valuable critical comments on a draft manuscript. This work was supported by a Helen Hay Whitney

Foundation research fellowship. Portions were supported by the European Office of Aerospace Research contract F6 1052 67 C0012 to Prof. T. Weis-Fogh.

Note added in proof

Light microscopic cytochemical studies on spindle components relevant to Table 1 of this review can be found in the articles by Fautrez-Firlefyn and Roels; Shifrin and Levine; and Goldman and Rebhun; and in that of Hartmann which I had overlooked. No change is required in Table 1 except that the exact localization of spindle ATPase is not clear (discussed by Shifrin and Levine).

Electron microscopically, several spindle components are seen in *Haemanthus* endosperm cells (Bajer 1968a, b, c) and isolated sea urchin MA (Goldman and Rebhun). The volume fractions of microtubules seen in the electron micrographs are all in the same range as summarized in Table 4 of this review.

In section 4a I discussed birefringence with no microtubules present, and loss of microtubules during the washing of isolated MA; Goldman and Rebhun present these data and detailed discussion of them. I should point out one discrepancy not discussed by them: whereas Goldman and Rebhun found that all microtubules were lost aftei isolated MA were washed in Mg^{++}-free hexylene glycol at *p*H 6.4, electron micrographs of Bibring and Baxandall, and Kane and Forer show similarly washed MA which do indeed contain microtubules. Some technical differences which might account for this discrepancy include speed of centrifugation, cation of the phosphate buffer, amount of shaking, etc., and since Goldman and Rebhun found loss of microtubules only at *p*H 6.4, and not at *p*H 6.3, *p*H might need to be controlled to within several hundredths of a *p*H unit. This emphasizes the point made at the end of section 5, above, that the fine-structure (and other parameters) of isolated MA should not be taken for granted but should be measured routinely.

Comparison of the electron microscopic results of Bajer (1968a, b, c) with previous studies of birefringence in the same endosperm cells (Inoué and Bajer; Inoué 1964) substantiates the discussion in section 4a on the lack of one-to-one correspondence between microtubules and spindle birefringence. For example, Bajer found microtubules associated with many regions of the chromosomes and not just the kinetochores. Photographs in Inoué and Bajer, and in Inoué (1964) show that the birefringent chromosomal fibres are at least 1.0–1.5 μ in diameter at the kinetochores, whereas electron microscopically the microtubule bundles are only 0.5–0.6 μ in diameter at the 'kinetochores'. The continuous fibres are very weakly birefringent at metaphase and anaphase while the chromosomal fibres are strongly birefringent, yet, when the same stages are studied electron microscopically, the bundles of 'continuous fibre microtubules' in both the half-spindle and interzonal regions are of the same volume fraction of microtubules and overall diameter as the bundles of 'chromosomal fibre microtubules'. Furthermore, Bajer observed that 'continuous fibre microtubules' and 'chromosomal fibre microtubules' *intermingle* a short distance from the 'kinetochore'. If microtubules were the sole contributor to birefringence, such intermingling would obscure the chromosomal fibre birefringence. But since it is not obscured (Inoué and Bajer; Inoué 1964), the microtubules are not the sole contributors to birefringence.

These results are quite relevant to my discussion of Behnke and Forer (1966) at the end of section 4a, and they support the possibilities suggested there. But I must restate the point made in section 4, that any correlation of electron microscopic structure and birefringent spindle fibres will be tentative until one measures birefringence throughout the entire electron microscopic preparation procedure, and quantitatively compares this birefringence with the electron microscopic image. In this regard, Cassim et al. discuss several theoretical difficulties inherent in predicting birefringence from known orientations of macromolecules and filaments.

Burton gives further evidence that all microtubules are not the same (discussed in section 4). Comparison of Burton's data with those of Behnke and Forer (1967) suggests the possibility of even more than 4 classes of microtubules.

With regard to the functional aspects of ultrastructural components (section 4b), Girbardt gives convincing evidence that microtubules are not responsible for nuclear oscillations and stretching in the basidiomycete *Polystictus versicolor*. In these cells, nuclear stretchings and oscillations arise from forces applied to 'activity centres', or 'kinetochore equivalents', found at the two ends of the nucleus. Microtubules are associated with the nuclear 'kinetochore equivalents' much as they are with chromosomal 'kinetochores', but because of their specific arrangement and changes of arrangement during the movements (see Girbardt's Fig. 2) microtubules can not be responsible for the force. Microtubules are also not responsible for the polyelectrolyte-gel properties of isolated MA. Cohen demonstrated that isolated MA which were stored for up to 2 months swelled and shrank like polyelectrolyte gels. This property is not due to microtubules, for such stored MA do not contain visible microtubules (Goldman and Rebhun). The stored MA are birefringent (Goldman and Rebhun), though, and this non-microtubular birefringent material may be responsible for, or at least necessary for, the polyelectrolyte-gel properties.

Data on isolated MA relevant to Table 6 are given by Hartmann and Zimmerman, and Miki-Noumara. Data relevant to Table 9 are given by Miki-Noumara, who studied *Hemicentrotus pulcherrimus* egg MA isolated using 1 M hexylene glycol at *p*H 6.3, and found that such MA were 60% soluble in 0.5 M KCl, and that the soluble material was at least 25% 2.3S material and contained no 22S component. The discrepancy between these results and those in Table 9 is probably methodological, for there are many differences in methods. Further, there are differences in species, and, as discussed below, MA isolated from eggs of different sea urchin species sometimes have different properties at the same *p*H and equivalent properties only at different *p*Hs (Forer and Goldman).

Sakai provides further evidence that the 4–5S material of hexylene glycol isolated MA is different than the 22S material (section 5b). He used hexanediol isolated MA, and showed that sulfite converted 4S material to 2.8S material while having no effect on the 22S component. Data of Hartmann and Zimmerman show *four* different soluble components, all with sedimentation values $\geqslant$74S, when hexylene glycol isolated MA are dissolved in solutions of KCl plus Mg^{++}. This is different from the 22S and 4–5S material found after solubilization with KCl only (Table 9), so it is likely that some of these heavier components are polymerized from 22S and 4–5S material. While one can not exclude the possibility that three of these compounds arise from such polymerization, the 74S material can not have arisen simply in this way, for it has much more RNA than either the 4–5S or 22S material. This suggests that there is at least one more soluble component besides those discussed in section 5b.

Cohen showed that isolated MA contain divalent cation. This ties in with the results of Goldman and Rebhun that addition of divalent cation retards ultrastructural changes during washing and storage of isolated MA. Both these results, together with the result that solubilization in KCl plus Mg^{++} yields different components than solubilization in KCl alone (discussed above), suggest that the chemical components in *in vivo* or in intact MA exist as polymers stabilized (or induced) by divalent cations.

Finally, I summarize some recent results which bear on several sections of this review (Forer and Goldman; and Goldman and Forer, in preparation; and Forer and Goldman, in preparation).

Goldman and I studied *in vivo* and isolated MA of eggs of the British sea urchins *Echinus esculentus* and *Psammechinus miliaris.* We compared these isolated MA with previous studies of MA isolated from the eggs of the American sea urchin *Arbacia punctulata*, and found that the MA of the different species have different properties with the same *p*H hexylene glycol isolation medium. They had equivalent properties only at different *p*Hs, and we concluded that *Arbacia* egg MA isolated at *p*H 6.4 are equivalent to *Echinus* egg MA isolated at *p*Hs > 6.8 and to *Psammechinus* egg MA isolated at *p*Hs > 7.0 (the data are summarized in Forer and Goldman). Thus one can not directly compare MA isolated from eggs of different species until one is certain of the properties of the different MA at the *p*Hs in question.

We measured MA mass and birefringence, both *in vivo* and after isolation, and found that at the usual *p*H (equivalent to *Arbacia* egg MA at *p*H 6.4) MAs lost 85–90% of their mass during the isolation (as deduced in section 5a), and lost about 40% of their birefringence. At lower *p*Hs 100% of the birefringence and up to 60% of the mass were preserved during the isolation (summarized in Forer and Goldman). Chemical analyses showed that more than half of the 60% was non-protein.

Though there was 5 times more mass in high-mass MA than in low-mass MA, preliminary electron microscopic observations showed no differences (Goldman), and thus most of the material is either lost during the electron microscopic preparatory procedure or is not stained.

Analyses of the isolated MA gave strong evidence that the birefringence derives from at least 2 components. One reason is that the birefringence was fractionated both by varying the *p*H of the isolation medium and by adding different solvents. Low *p*Hs preserved 100% of the birefringence, and high *p*Hs 60%, implying that there might be two components of different solubilities. This was substantiated by taking MAs with 100% of the *in vivo* birefringence, adding a solvent which removed 40% of the birefringence, adding a second solvent which removed the rest of the birefringence (without dissolving the MA), and seeing that different chemicals were extracted with the two different solvents. This substantiates the discussion in section 4a, and provides strong evidence that the thermodynamic treatment of spindle birefringence (section 3b) is based on a faulty assumption.

It might be of interest to note that when the MA birefringence was extracted with the two solvents, one of the extracted proteins had bound nucleotide.

References

AMBROSE, E.J. and A.BAJER: The analyses of mitoses in single living cells by interference microscopy. Proc. Roy. Soc. (London) Ser. B 153 (1961) 357.

AMOORE, J.E.: Non-identical mechanisms of mitotic arrest by respiratory inhibitors in pea root tips and sea urchin eggs. J. Cell Biol. 18 (1963) 555.

BAJER, A.: Chromosome movement and fine structure of the mitotic spindle. Symp. Soc. Exptl. Biol. 22 (1968a) 285.

BAJER, A.: Fine structure studies on phragmoplast and cell plate formation. Chromosoma 24 (1968b) 383.

BAJER, A.: Behavior and fine structure of spindle fibers during mitosis in endosperm. Chromosoma 25 (1968c) 249.

BARER, R. and S.JOSEPH: Phase-contrast and interference microscopy in the study of cell structure. Symp. Soc. Exptl. Biol. 10 (1957) 160.

BAUER, H., R.DIETZ and C.RÖBBELEN: Die Spermatocytenteilungen der Tipuliden. III. Das Bewegungverhalten der Chromosomen in Translokationsheterozygoten von *Tipula oleracea*. Chromosoma 12 (1961) 116.

BEHNKE, O. and A.FORER: Some aspects of microtubules in spermatocyte meiosis in a crane fly (*Nephrotoma suturalis*, Loew): intranuclear and intrachromosomal microtubules. Compt. Rend. Trav. Lab. Carlsberg 35 (1966) 437.

BEHNKE, O. and A.FORER: Evidence for four classes of microtubules in individual cells. J. Cell Sci. 2 (1967) 169.

BEHNKE, O. and A.FORER: see review (1966) and (1967).

BIBRING, T. and J.BAXANDALL: Mitotic apparatus: the selective extraction of protein with mild acid. Science 161 (1968) 377.

BIBRING, T. and J.BAXANDALL: see review.

BIBRING, T. and G.H.COUSINEAU: Percentage incorporation of leucine labelled with Carbon-14 into isolated mitotic apparatus during early development of sea urchin eggs. Nature 204 (1964) 805.

BORISY, G. and E.W.TAYLOR: The mechanism of action of colchicine. II. Colchicine binding to sea urchin eggs and the mitotic apparatus. J. Cell Biol. 34 (1967) 535.

BRADFIELD, J.R.G.: The ultra-violet absorption of living cells. Discussions Faraday Soc. 9 (1950) 481.

BRINKLEY, B.R., P.MURPHY and L.C.RICHARDSON: Procedure for embedding *in situ* selected cells cultured *in vitro*. J. Cell Biol. 35 (1967) 279.

BURTON, P.R.: Effects of various treatments on microtubules and axial units of lung-fluke spermatozoa. Z. Zellforsch. 87 (1968) 226.

CARASSO, N. and P.FAVARD: Microtubules fusoriaux dans les micro- et macronucleus de ciliés péritriches en division. J. Microscopie 4 (1965) 395.

CARLSON, J.G.: Microdissection studies of the dividing neuroblast of the grasshopper *Chortophaga viridifasciata* (De Geer). Chromosoma 5 (1952) 199.

CAROLAN, R.M., H.SATO and S.INOUÉ: A thermodynamic analysis of the effect of D_2O and H_2O on the mitotic spindle. Biol. Bull. 129 (1965) 402.

CAROLAN, R.M., H.SATO, and S.INOUÉ: Further observations on the thermodynamics of the living mitotic spindle. Biol. Bull. 131 (1966) 385.

CASSIM, J.Y., P.S.TOBIAS and E.W.TAYLOR: Birefringence of muscle proteins and the problem of structural birefringence. Biochim. Biophys. Acta 168 (1968) 463.

COHEN, W.D.: Polyelectrolyte properties of the isolated mitotic apparatus. Exptl. Cell Res. 51 (1968) 221.

CORNMAN, I.: A summary of evidence in favor of the traction fiber in mitosis. Am. Naturalist 78 (1944) 410.

DAVIES, H.G.: The ultra-violet absorption of living chick fibroblasts during mitosis. Exptl. Cell Res. 3 (1952) 453.

DAVIES, H.G. and M.H.F.WILKINS: Interference microscopy and mass determination. Nature 169 (1952) 541.

DIETZ, R.: Die Spermatocytenteilungen der Tipuliden II. Graphische Analyse der Chromosomenbewegung während der Prometaphase I im Leben. Chromosoma 8 (1956) 183.

DIETZ, R.: Multiple Geschlechtschromosomen bei den cypriden Ostracoden, ihre Evolution und ihr Teilungsverhalten. Chromosoma 9 (1958) 359.

DIETZ, R.: Centrosomenfreie Spindelpole in Tipuliden-Spermatocyten. Z. Naturforsch. 14b (1959) 749.

ERRERA, M. and M.BRUNFAUT: Observations of mitotic figures in pulse labelled HeLa cells. Exptl. Cell Res. 33 (1964) 105.

FAUTREZ, J. and N.FAUTREZ-FIRLEFIJN: Les polysaccharides au cours de mitoses pendant la maturation et la segmentation de l'oeuf d'*Artemia salina*. Arch. Biol. (Liège) 70 (1959) 133.

FAUTREZ-FIRLEFYN, N. and F.ROELS: Liaison entre fibres fusoriales et chromosomes au cours de la méiose. Compt. Rend. 267 (1968) 1521.

FORER, A.: Evidence for two spindle fiber components: a study of chromosome movement in living crane fly (*Nephrotoma suturalis*) spermatocytes, using polarization microscopy and an ultraviolet microbeam. Ph.D. Thesis, Dartmouth College, U.S. (1964).

FORER, A.: Local reduction of spindle fiber birefringence in living *Nephrotoma suturalis* (Loew) spermatocytes induced by ultraviolet microbeam irradiation. J. Cell Biol. 25, No. 1, Pt. 2 (1965) 95.

FORER, A.: Characterization of the mitotic traction system, and evidence that birefringent spindle fibers neither produce nor transmit force for chromosome movement. Chromosoma 19 (1966) 44.

FORER, A. and R.D.GOLDMAN: Some comparisons of *in vivo* and isolated mitotic apparatuses. Nature 222 (1969) 689.

GEORGE, P., L.J.JOURNEY and M.N.GOLDSTEIN: Effect of vincristine on the fine structure of HeLa cells during mitosis. J. Natl. Cancer Inst. 35 (1965) 355.

GIBBONS, I.R.: Studies on the adenosine triphosphatase activity of 14S and 30S dynein from cilia of *Tetrahymena*. J. Biol. Chem. 241 (1966) 5590.

GIRBARDT, M.: Ultrastructure and dynamics of the moving nucleus. Symp. Soc. Exptl. Biol. 22 (1968) 249.

GOLDMAN, R.D.: The structure and some properties of the isolated MA. Ph.D. Thesis, Princeton University, U.S. (1967).

GOLDMAN, R.D. and L.I.REBHUN: The structure and some properties of the isolated mitotic apparatus. J. Cell Sci. 4 (1969) 179.

GROSS, P.R. and G.H.COUSINEAU: Synthesis of spindle-associated proteins in early cleavage. J. Cell Biol. 19 (1963) 260.

HARRIS, P.: Some structural and functional aspects of the mitotic apparatus in sea urchin embryos. J. Cell Biol. 14 (1962) 475.

HARRIS, P.: Some observations concerning metakinesis in sea urchin eggs. J. Cell Biol. 25, No. 1, Pt. 2 (1965) 73.

HARRIS, P. and A. BAJER: Fine structure studies on mitosis in endosperm metaphase of *Haemanthus katherinae* Bak. Chromosoma 16 (1965) 624.

HARRIS, P. and D. MAZIA: The finer structure of the mitotic apparatus. In: R.J.C. Harris, ed.: The interpretation of ultrastructure. Symp. Intern. Soc. Cell Biol. Vol. 1. New York, Academic Press (1962).

HARTMANN, J. F.: Cytochemical localization of adenosine triphosphatase in the mitotic apparatus of HeLa and Sarcoma 180 tissue culture cells. J. Cell Biol. 23 (1964) 363.

HARTMANN, J. F. and A. M. ZIMMERMAN: The isolated mitotic apparatus. Studies on nucleoproteins. Exptl. Cell Res. 50 (1968) 403.

HARVEY, E. B.: The American *Arbacia* and other sea urchins. Princeton, Princeton University Press (1956).

HARVEY, E. B. and G. I. LAVIN: The chromatin in the living *Arbacia punctulata* egg, and the cytoplasm of the centrifuged egg as photographed with ultra-violet light. Biol. Bull. 86 (1944) 163.

HUGHES, A.: The mitotic cycle. London, Butterworths Scientific Publications (1952).

HUGHES, A. F. W. and M. M'E. PRESTON: Mitosis in living cells of amphibian tissue cultures. J. Roy. Microscop. Soc. 69 (1949) 121.

HUGHES-SCHRADER, S.: Expulsion of the sex chromosome from the spindle in spermatocytes of a mantid. Chromosoma 3 (1948) 257.

INOUÉ, S.: The effect of colchicine on the microscopic and submicroscopic structure of the mitotic spindle. Exptl. Cell Res. Suppl. 2 (1952) 305.

INOUÉ, S.: Motility of cilia and the mechanism of mitosis. Rev. Mod. Phys. 31 (1959) 402.

INOUÉ, S.: Organization and function of the mitotic spindle. In: R.D. Allen and N. Kamiya, eds.: Primitive motile systems in cell biology. New York, Academic Press (1964).

INOUÉ, S.: see review (1964).

INOUÉ, S. and A. BAJER: Birefringence in endosperm mitosis. Chromosoma 12 (1961) 48.

INOUÉ, S. and H. SATO: Cell motility by labile association of molecules. J. Gen. Physiol. 50, No. 6, Pt. 2 (1967) 259.

IZUTSU, K.: Effects of ultraviolet microbeam irradiation upon division in grasshopper spermatocytes. II. Results of irradiation during metaphase and anaphase I. Mie Med. J. 11 (1961) 213.

JOKELAINEN, P. T.: The ultrastructure and spatial organization of the metaphase kinetochore in mitotic rat cells. J. Ultrastruct. Res. 19 (1967) 19.

KANE, R. E.: The mitotic apparatus: isolation by controlled *p*H. J. Cell Biol. 12 (1962a) 47.

KANE, R. E.: The mitotic apparatus. Fine structure of the isolated unit. J. Cell Biol. 15 (1962b) 279.

KANE, R. E.: The mitotic apparatus. Identification of the major soluble component of the glycol-isolated mitotic apparatus. J. Cell Biol. 32 (1967) 243.

KANE, R. E. and A. FORER: The mitotic apparatus. Structural changes after isolation. J. Cell Biol. 25, No. 3, Pt. 2 (1965) 31.

KANE, R. E. and A. FORER: see review.

KIEFER, B., H. SAKAI, A. SOLARI and D. MAZIA: The molecular unit of the microtubules of the mitotic apparatus. J. Mol. Biol. 20 (1966) 75.

KOBAYASHI, J. and S. MAKINO: Some preliminary observations on the cytochemical nature of the spindle body of grasshopper spermatocytes under normal and water-treated conditions. Nucleus (Calcutta) 5 (1962) 29.

KRISHAN, A. and R. C. BUCK: Structure of the mitotic spindle in L strain fibroblasts. J. Cell Biol. 24 (1965a) 433.

KRISHAN, A. and R.C.BUCK: Ultrastructure of cell division in insect spermatogenesis. J. Ultrastruct. Res. 13 (1965b) 444.

LEDBETTER, M.C. and K.R.PORTER: A 'microtubule' in plant cell fine structure. J. Cell Biol. 19 (1963) 239.

LONGWELL, A. and M.MOTA: The distribution of cellular matter during meiosis. Endeavour 19 (1960) 100.

LOVE, R. and R.G.SUSKIND: Further observations on ribonucleoproteins of mitotically dividing mammalian cells. Exptl. Cell Res. 22 (1961) 193.

LOWY, J., B.M.MILLMAN and J.HANSON: Structure and function in smooth tonic muscles of lamellibranch molluscs. Proc. Roy. Soc. (London) Ser. B 160 (1964) 525.

LUCAS, F.F. and M.B.STARK: A study of living sperm cells of certain grasshoppers by means of the ultraviolet microscope. J. Morphol. 52 (1931) 91.

MAHLER, H.R. and E.H.CORDES: Biological chemistry. London, Harper and Row (1966).

MANGAN, J., T.MIKI-NOUMARA and P.R.GROSS: Protein synthesis and the mitotic apparatus. Science 147 (1965) 1575.

MAZIA, D.: The organization of the mitotic apparatus. Symp. Soc. Exptl. Biol. 9 (1955) 335.

MAZIA, D.: Mitosis and the physiology of cell division. In: J.Brachet and A.E.Mirsky, eds.: The cell, Vol. 3. New York, Academic Press (1961).

MAZIA, D., R.R.CHAFFEE and R.IVERSON: Adenosine triphosphatase in the mitotic apparatus. Proc. Natl. Acad. Sci. U.S. 47 (1961) 788.

MAZIA, D. and K.DAN: The isolation and biochemical characterization of the mitotic apparatus of dividing cells. Proc. Natl. Acad. Sci. U.S. 38 (1952) 826.

MIKI, T.: The ATPase activity of the mitotic apparatus of the sea urchin egg. Exptl. Cell Res. 29 (1963) 92.

MIKI, T.: ATPase staining of sea urchin eggs during the first cleavage. Embryologia (Nagoya) 8 (1964) 158.

MIKI-NOUMARA, T.: Isolation of fine filaments from the mitotic apparatus of sea urchin eggs. Embryologia (Nagoya) 9 (1965) 98.

MIKI-NOUMARA, T.: Purification of the mitotic apparatus protein of sea urchin eggs. Exptl. Cell Res. 50 (1968) 54.

MITCHISON, J.M. and M.M.SWANN: Measurements on sea-urchin eggs with an interference microscope. Quart. J. Microscop. Sci. 94 (1953) 381.

NICKLAS, R.B.: A quantitative study of chromosomal elasticity and its influence on chromosome movement. Chromosoma 14 (1963) 276.

NICKLAS, R.B.: Chromosome velocity during mitosis as a function of chromosome size and position. J. Cell Biol. 25, No. 1, Pt. 2 (1965) 119.

NICKLAS, R.B.: Chromosome micromanipulation II. Induced reorientation and the experimental control of segregation in meiosis. Chromosoma 21 (1967) 17.

NICKLAS, R.B. and C.A.STAEHLY: Chromosome micromanipulation I. The mechanics of chromosome attachment to the spindle. Chromosoma 21 (1967) 1.

REBHUN, L.I. and G.SANDER: Ultrastructure and birefringence of the isolated mitotic apparatus of marine eggs. J. Cell Biol. 34 (1967) 859.

REBHUN, L.I., G.SANDER, R.D.GOLDMAN and L.BERNSTEIN: The organization of the mitotic apparatus. In: Abstracts volume of Seventh International Congress of Biochemistry, Tokyo, August 19–25 (1967) Symp. VI – 4, 6.

ROBBINS, E. and N.K.GONATAS: The ultrastructure of a mammalian cell during the mitotic cycle. J. Cell Biol. 21 (1964) 429.

ROTH, L.E., H.J.WILSON and J.CHAKRABORTY: Anaphase structure in mitotic cells typified by spindle elongation. J. Ultrastruct. Res. 14 (1966) 460.

SAKAI, H.: Studies on sulfhydryl groups during cell division of sea-urchin eggs VIII. Some properties of mitotic apparatus proteins. Biochim. Biophys. Acta 112 (1966) 132.

SAKAI, H.: Contractile properties of threads from sea urchin eggs in relation to cell division. Intern. Rev. Cytol. 23 (1968) 89.

SCHRADER, F.: Mitosis: the movements of chromosomes in cell division. New York, Columbia University Press (1953).

SERRA, J.A. and M.P.SEIXAS: On the existence of lipids in the centromere and the spindle. Rev. Port. Zool. Biol. Ger. 3 (1962) 263.

SHIFRIN, N. and L.LEVINE: Cytochemical adenosinetriphosphatase in plant root meristem. J. Cell Sci. 3 (1968) 423.

SHIMAMURA, T. and T.ÔTA: Cytochemical studies on the mitotic spindle and the phragmoplast of plant cells. Exptl. Cell Res. 11 (1956) 346.

SHINKE, N. and M.SHIGENAGE: A histochemical study of plant nuclei in rest and mitosis. Cytologia (Tokyo) 4 (1933) 189.

SISKEN, J.E., E.WILKES, G.M.DONNELY and T.KAFEKUDA: The isolation of the mitotic apparatus from mammalian cells in culture. J. Cell Biol. 32 (1967) 212.

SLAUTTERBACK, D.: Cytoplasmic microtubules I. *Hydra.* J. Cell Biol. 18 (1963) 367.

STAFFORD, D.W. and R.M.IVERSON: Radioautographic evidence for the incorporation of leucine-carbon-14 into the mitotic apparatus. Science 143 (1964) 580.

STEPHENS, R.E.: The mitotic apparatus. Physical chemical characterization of the 22S protein component and its subunits. J. Cell Biol. 32 (1967) 255.

STEPHENS, R.E.: On the structural protein of flaggellar outer fibers. J. Mol. Biol. 32 (1968) 277.

STICH, H.F. and J.MCINTYRE: X-Ray absorption studies on the nuclear protein and RNA content during the development of the mitotic apparatus. Exptl. Cell Res. 14 (1958) 635.

TAYLOR, E.W.: Brownian and saltatory movements of cytoplasmic granules and the movement of anaphase chromosomes. In: E.H.Lee, ed.: Proceedings Fourth International Congress of Rheology, Brown University. New York, Interscience Publishers (1965).

THÉ, G. de: Cytoplasmic microtubules in different animal cells. J. Cell Biol. 23 (1964) 265.

TUCKER, J.B.: Changes in nuclear structure during binary fission in the ciliate *Nassula.* J. Cell Sci. 2 (1967) 481.

WHALEY, W.G., M.DAUWALDER and J.E.KEPHART: The Golgi apparatus and an early stage in cell plate formation. J. Ultrastruct. Res. 15 (1966) 169.

WILSON, E.B.: The cell in development and heredity. New York, The Macmillan Company (1928).

WILT, F.H., H.SAKAI and D.MAZIA: Old and new protein in the formation of the mitotic apparatus in cleaving sea urchin eggs. J. Mol. Biol. 27 (1967) 1.

WOLPERT, L.: Cytoplasmic streaming and amoeboid movement. Symp. Soc. Gen. Microbiol. 15 (1965) 270.

WYCKOFF, R.W.G.: Ultraviolet microscopy as a means of studying cell structure. Cold Spring Harbor Symp. Quant. Biol. 2 (1934) 39.

WYCKOFF, R.W.G., A.H.EBELING and A.L.TERLOUW: A comparison between the ultraviolet microscopy and the Feulgen staining of certain cells. J. Morphol. 53 (1932) 189.

YONEDA, M.: Force exerted by a single cilium of *Mytilus edulis.* J. Exptl. Biol. 37 (1960) 461.

ZIMMERMAN, A.M.: Physico-chemical analysis of the isolated mitotic apparatus. Exptl. Cell Res. 20 (1960) 529.

PART VII

Ultrastructure and biochemistry of the nucleolus

CHAPTER 24

Nucleolar structure and function

O. L. MILLER, JR. and BARBARA R. BEATTY

*Biology Division, Oak Ridge National Laboratory, Oak Ridge, Tennessee**

Contents

1. Introduction
2. Nucleolar composition and general fine structure
   (a) Composition of isolated nucleolar fractions
   (b) General fine structure
3. Structure and nucleolar metabolism
   (a) Fibrous nucleolar component (core)
   (b) Granular nucleolar component (cortex)
4. Conclusions

* Operated by Union Carbide Corporation for the U.S. Atomic Energy Commission.

1. Introduction

A primary role for the nucleolus in ribosome biogenesis is now well documented (see reviews by Birnstiel; Perry; and Perry, this volume). Although the steps in nucleolar RNA metabolism have been most precisely detailed for mammalian tissue culture cells, evidence from other organisms (amphibia – Brown and Gurdon, Gall; insects – Edström and Daneholt, Applebaum et al.; an echinoderm – Vincent et al.; and a plant – Waters and Dure) strongly suggests that the events in nucleolar RNA metabolism are similar in all eukaryotic cell types.

Even though the major constituent of the nucleolus is protein, the steps in protein metabolism and the protein–RNA relationships within the nucleolus are not as well defined as the RNA metabolism. Recent evidence, however, indicates that most of the proteins of cytoplasmic ribosomes are represented in the nucleolus (Warner and Soeiro; Mundell).

The relationships of the structural features of the nucleolus to the known sequences in its RNA and protein metabolism are not clear. The purpose of this chapter is to review the more pertinent observations correlating the known metabolic events to nucleolar composition and ultrastructure, as observed in sections of intact cells and in isolated nucleoli. Emphasis is placed on structure and metabolism in the extrachromosomal nucleoli of amphibian oocytes. With this cell type the nucleus and nucleoli can be isolated easily by manual techniques, and the nucleolar components can be separated while maintaining microscopical identification of the parts to be examined on the fine structure level (Miller 1966).

2. Nucleolar composition and general fine structure

Information on nucleolar composition, ultrastructure, and cytochemistry has recently been reviewed in detail (Birnstiel). Some selected observations relative to the correlation of structure and function in the nucleolus are presented in this section.

(a) *Composition of isolated nucleolar fractions*

Although the chemical constituents of nucleoli vary in amount depending on cell type and physiological state, generally three main components are present in isolated nucleolar fractions – DNA, RNA, and protein (Vincent et al., tables 4 and 5). In some cases, relatively high amounts of DNA (3–18%) have been reported. It is probable that most of this DNA is not active in nucleolar RNA metabolism, but rather consists of portions of chromosomes adjacent to the nucleolar organizing regions. This is supported by the fact that DNA is not detectable in some amphibian oocyte nucleoli by the usual biochemical tests (Finamore) or by Feulgen cytochemistry (Brown and Ris), although experiments using DNase digestion (Miller 1966) and labeling with actinomycin D (Ebstein) of similar isolated nucleoli show DNA to be present.

Kinetic analyses of nucleolar fractions show that a number of species of nucleolar RNAS are involved in the biogenesis of ribosomal RNA (rRNA) (Weinberg et al.). This is further supported by similarity between base ratios of total nucleolar RNA and cytoplasmic rRNA in several cell types, including amphibian oocytes (Edström). The molecular species of nucleolar RNA are considered in detail in the section on nucleolar metabolism.

Most nucleolar proteins have neutral or slightly acidic isoelectric points; the remainder consists primarily of basic proteins (Busch et al.; Vincent et al.). In nucleoli from starfish oocytes, RNA appears to be associated with both types of proteins.

If the composition of isolated nucleolar fractions is calculated excluding DNA and its associated histone (Vincent et al.), the RNA content ranges between 3% and 13% of the dry weight, averaging 8%. The protein content ranges between 82% and 97%, averaging 92%. These figures show that protein to RNA ratios vary between 30:1 and 5:1, with an average of about 11.5:1.

A portion of the protein content of nucleoli must necessarily consist of the enzymes involved in the various metabolic events catalysed within the nucleolus. The proportion of the nucleolar protein that falls in this category and the locations of enzymes within the nucleolus are unknown at present (Siebert).

The presence of trace amounts of lipids in nucleolar fractions has been reported (Finamore).

(b) *General fine structure*

Although nucleolar shape and size vary widely depending on the organism, cell type, and physiological state of the cell, nucleoli that are active in RNA synthesis typically exhibit two distinct structural regions, one fibrous and one granular in appearance. In many nucleoli these two components are more or less intermixed. However, in some cell types, including amphibian oocytes, the granular element usually forms a cortical shell around a compact fibrous component (Fig. 1). Again depending on the cell type or stage, either the fibrous material or the granular component or both may be arranged in coarse threads 0.1–0.2 μ in diameter (Fig. 2). Staining, enzymatic digestion, and autoradiographic techniques show that both components contain RNA and protein, and that DNA active in RNA synthesis is finely dispersed in the fibrous component.

In thin section, the granular region appears to contain numerous particles 150–200 Å in diameter (Fig. 3). Some investigators, however, have interpreted these as coiled regions of thin ribonucleoprotein (RNP) fibrils rather than as discrete granules (Kalnins et al.; Shankarnarayan et al.). The fibrous component is generally interpreted as consisting mainly of thin RNP fibrils, but devoid of granules. The presence of an amorphous proteinaceous matrix in both nucleolar constituents has been reported (Marinozzi).

'Core' and 'cortex' are brief terms which have been used to describe the fibrous and granular appearing areas, respectively, of amphibian oocyte nucleoli (Miller 1966;

MacGregor). Since all of the micrographs presented in this chapter are concerned with this nucleolar type, these terms are used in the following discussion.

3. Structure and nucleolar metabolism

The steps in nucleolar RNA metabolism have been most precisely defined by using HeLa tissue culture cells (Weinberg et al.). This sequence can be briefly outlined as follows: (1) transcription and concurrent methylation of large rRNA precursor molecules (45S RNA) on the nucleolar DNA cistrons (rDNA); (2) cleavage of each 45S RNA molecule through several intermediate steps involving loss of nonmethylated portions to give one 32S molecule and one 18S molecule, the latter being rapidly transferred from the nucleolus to the small ribosomal subunit in the cytoplasm; and (3) cleavage of the 32S molecule with further loss of nonmethylated RNA to form a 28S RNA molecule that remains in the nucleolus for a short time before transfer to the large ribosomal subunit in the cytoplasm. The molecular weights of the various nucleolar RNA species have been reported as approximately 4.5×10^6 for 45S RNA, 2.2×10^6 for 32S RNA, 1.6×10^6 for 28S RNA, and 0.6×10^6 for 18S RNA (Weinberg et al.). On the assumption that RNA molecules occur in RNP complexes, and that when these complexes are extended, each RNA molecule retains the same weight to length ratio as the DNA polynucleotide chain on which it was transcribed, one can translate the above molecular weights into approximate linear measurements by the factor $1 \times 10^6 = 1\ \mu$ (Peacocke and Drysdale). In this case, an extended RNP complex containing a 45S RNA molecule would be $\sim 4.5\ \mu$ long, one with 32S RNA $\sim 2.2\ \mu$, one with 28S RNA $\sim 1.6\ \mu$, and one with 18S RNA $\sim 0.6\ \mu$. Approximately half of the 45S molecule appears to be discarded during the formation of the 18S and 28S RNA molecules.

Based on sedimentation values, the sizes of the RNA molecules involved in this sequence vary a little in different organisms. The precursor RNA molecules in amphibians have slightly lower sedimentation values (Gall) than those given above for HeLa cells, and therefore may actually be somewhat shorter molecules. However, because estimates of the molecular weights of the RNA species involved in ribosome biogenesis have been made only for mammalian material, these estimates as they relate to the lengths of the RNA molecules involved are used throughout this chapter on nucleolar structure and function.

The synthesis and movement of RNA within the two major components of the nucleolus have been studied in several organisms by autoradiography. Synthesis of RNA is first detected in the fibrous DNA-containing component, and label subsequently appears over the granular area. Although not rigorously shown, labeling of the granular region correlates reasonably well with the apperance of the precursor to the larger rRNA molecule in nucleolar fractions of cells of mammals (Granboulan and Granboulan; Simard and Bernhard; Weinberg et al.), amphibians (MacGregor; Lane; Gall), and insects (Von Gaudecker; Edström and Daneholt).

(a) *Fibrous nucleolar component (core)*

Evidence has been presented that the portion of the genome coding for rRNA consists of multiple rDNA cistrons and that these cistrons are clustered in one segment of the genome, i.e., the nucleolar organizer (Birnstiel et al.; Ritossa et al.). The kinetics of nucleolar RNA metabolism (Weinberg et al.) suggest that each cistron coding for a 45S RNA molecule contains one each of the DNA segments coding for the 28S and 18S rRNA. In addition, studies on fractionated rDNA (Brown et al.) indicate that these segments are strictly alternating within the cluster of rDNA cistrons.

The evidence that other genetic loci also may be arranged in polycistronic clusters has recently been reviewed (Callan). The possibility that such clusters are read as single units to produce extremely long RNP molecules (greater than 20 μ) is suggested by fine structure observations of the lateral loops of isolated lampbrush chromosomes (Miller 1965). On the other hand, analysis of RNA from nucleolar fractions indicates that the largest RNA species present is the 45S molecule (approximately 4.5 μ long), which suggests that each rDNA cistron in the nucleolar locus is transcribed as a single unit.

The question of whether the rDNA cistrons are read as single or as polycistronic units can be approached in isolated amphibian oocyte nucleoli by using media which disperse the two nucleolar components to varying degrees (Fig. 4). In preparations in which the nucleolar cores unwind, each core can be seen to consist of a long, coarsely coated filament. Enzymatic digestion experiments and fine structure observations indicate that the continuity of the filament is maintained by a single DNA molecule irregularly coated with RNP matrix (Miller 1966). When such core filaments are stretched, the DNA axis exhibits a periodicity which consists of alternating lengths of matrix-free and matrix-covered segments, with the latter exhibiting a thin to thick gradation (Fig. 5). Essentially all of the DNA axis within the nucleolar core appears to be involved in this periodicity; i.e., most of the axis is covered with matrix when not stretched (Fig. 6).

When the core axis appears maximally stretched, the periodic unit is 7 to 8μ in length, with the matrix-covered portion ranging from 4.3 to 5μ and the matrix-free length ranging from 2.7 to 3μ. The length of the matrix-covered segment corresponds reasonably well to the approximate 4.5 μ length of DNA necessary to code for the 45S RNA molecule. This indicates that the clustered nucleolar rDNA cistrons are read singly rather than in polycistronic units. In the latter case, matrix-covered segments much longer than 4.5 μ would be expected. It also appears that each rDNA cistron coding for a 45S molecule is separated from its neighboring cistrons by nontranscribed DNA segments. In partially unwound nucleolar cores, several of the matrix-free segments are occasionally found in parallel register. This alignment suggests that the nontranscribed DNA may have a role in the orientation of the rDNA cistrons within the nucleolar core *in vivo*.

Under certain isolation conditions, the matrix covering the DNA axis is revealed to consist of numerous individual fibers, each connected by one end to the DNA axis

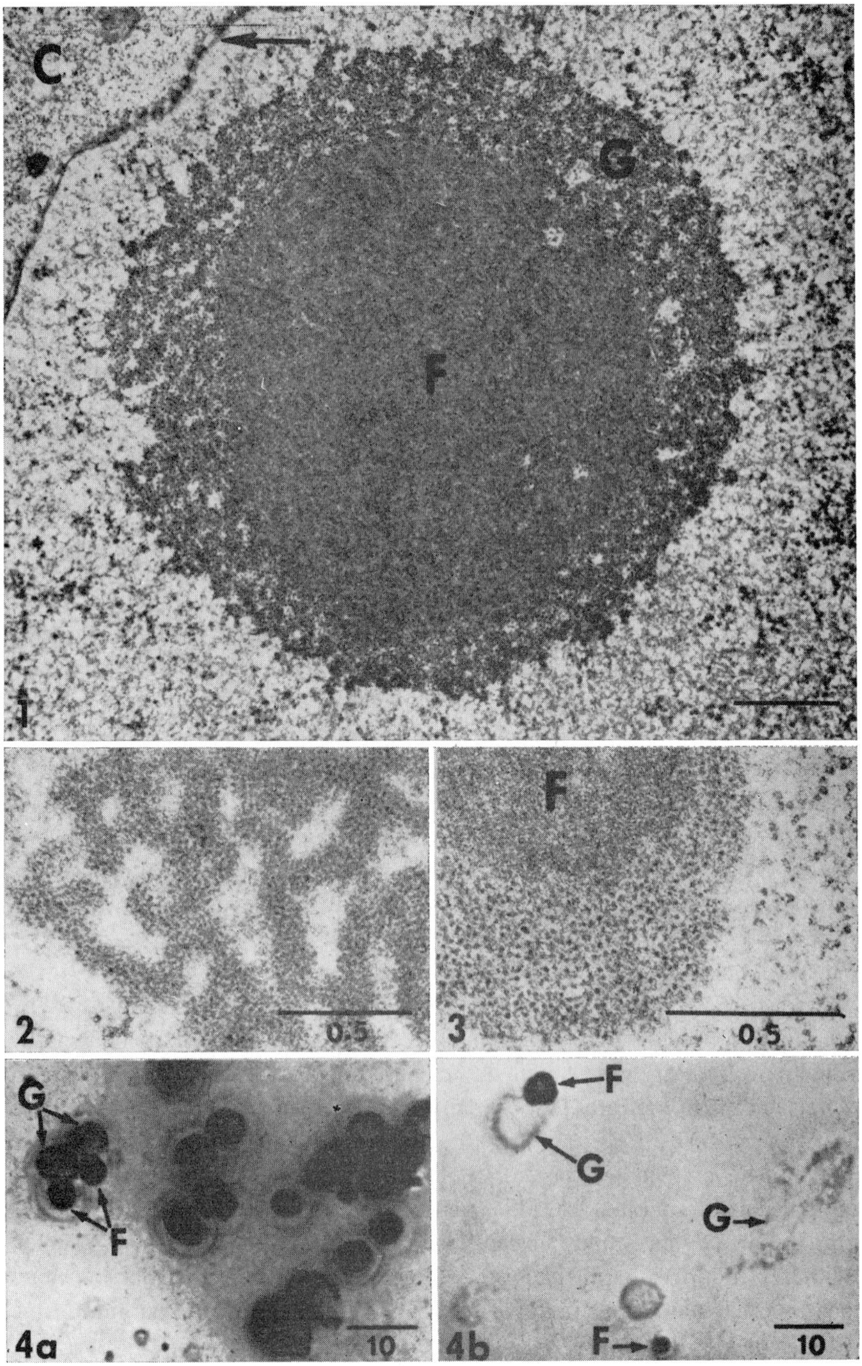
C
G
F
1
2
0.5
F
3
0.5
G
F
4a
10
F
G
G
4b
F
10

(Fig. 7). The high protein to RNA ratio in the nucleolus and the fact that either ribonuclease or protease digestion completely removes the fibers from the core axis suggest that each fiber consists of an RNA axis coated with protein. The fact that RNP matrix fibers (Figs. 8 and 9) longer than lengths expected for 45S RNA ($\sim$4.5 μ) have not been observed, further supports the conclusion that the rDNA cistrons are read as single units.

The rate of synthesis of the 45S molecule appears to be very rapid in all cell types actively engaged in rRNA synthesis. The question of whether a small number of rapidly transcribing RNA polymerases per cistron are involved in this process, as opposed to a large number of more slowly transcribing polymerases, can also be approached through unwound nucleolar core preparations. If the axis of each attached matrix fibril represents a maturing 45S RNA molecule being transcribed by one polymerase, then at least 100 RNA polymerases are present on each rDNA cistron (Fig. 7) in amphibian oocyte nucleoli. In the case of *Xenopus laevis*, it has been estimated (Birnstiel et al.; Brown et al.) that the nucleolar organizer locus contains 800 rDNA cistrons. If the entire nucleolar organizer locus is involved in synthesizing RNA, these two estimates suggest that there are at least 80,000 polymerases simultaneously transcribing 45S RNA molecules within the nucleolus of this organism.

On the assumption that the axes of the matrix fibrils consist of single RNA molecules, the diameters of stretched fibrils ($\sim$ 50 Å, Fig. 8) suggest that the protein to RNA ratio is on the order of 5 to 10:1. This is near the protein to RNA ratio found by biochemical analysis of whole amphibian oocyte nucleoli (Finamore). It appears that the protein is combined with the RNA at the transcription junction.

Particles containing 45S RNA with a protein to RNA ratio similar to that of ribosomes (approximately 1:1) have recently been isolated from HeLa cell nucleoli by the use of detergent extraction techniques (Warner and Soeiro). In the amphibian oocyte nucleolus the 45S RNA of the core is seen only in an extended fibrillar form with a protein to

---

Fig. 1. Thin section of peripheral nucleolus of *Triturus viridescens* oocyte. The granular component (G) forms a shell around a compact fibrous core (F). Portions of the nuclear envelope (arrow) and cytoplasm (C) are visible at the upper left. (Electron micrograph – OsO_4 fixation, uranyl acetate stain.)

Fig. 2. Thin section of the granular component of peripheral nucleolus of *Rana clamitans* oocyte showing arrangement in coarse threads approximately 0.15 μ in diameter. (Electron micrograph – OsO_4 fixation, uranyl acetate stain.)

Fig. 3. Thin section of a portion of peripheral nucleolus of *Rana clamitans* oocyte. The cortical region surrounding the fibrous core (F) appears to contain granules approximately 150 Å in diameter. Granules in the nucleoplasm to the right of the nucleolus are about 200 Å in diameter. (Electron micrograph – OsO_4 fixation, uranyl acetate stain.)

Fig. 4. (a) Peripheral nucleoli of *Triturus viridescens* oocyte isolated into 0.1 M veronal acetate–HCl buffer. The nucleolar cores (F), which comprise the fibrous component in thin section, and the cortices (G), which appear granular in thin section, have separated to varying degrees. (b) Preparation made as in 4(a) and then treated with 1 M KCl. The cores (F) have remained intact, whereas the cortices (G) have been partially dispersed. (Phase contrast micrographs.)

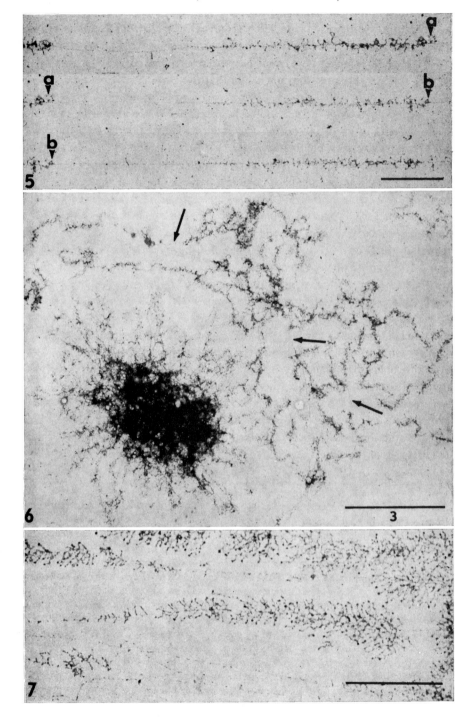
a
a
b
b
5

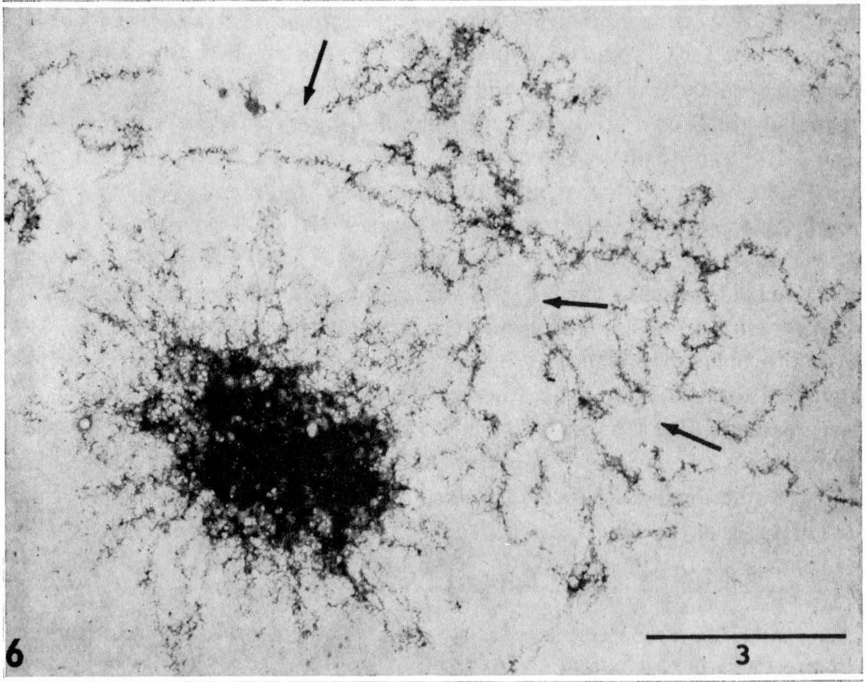
6
3

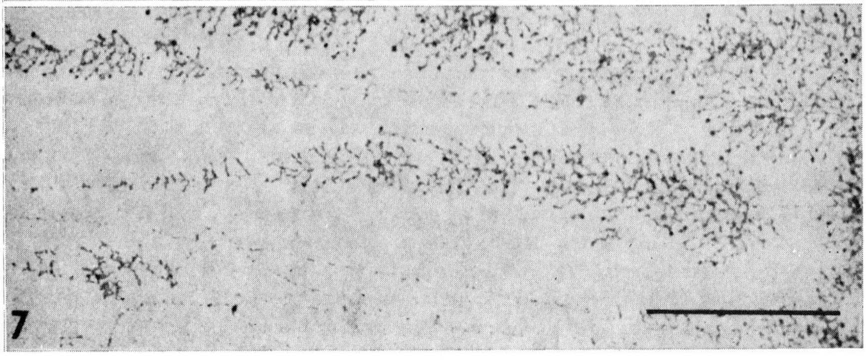
7

RNA ratio that appears to be much higher than the 1:1 ratio of these isolated particles. If the structure of mammalian nucleoli is similar to that of amphibian oocyte nucleoli, it seems likely that the detergent extraction is eliminating a portion of the RNA-associated protein and allowing the extracted fibrils containing 45S RNA to assume a particulate configuration.

The presence of a membranous component (Fig. 10) attached to the DNA-containing core of the amphibian oocyte nucleolus has been reported (Miller, 1966 1967). This structure has been reported only for amphibian oocytes, and its function is unknown at this time. The membranous component may account for the small amount of lipid detected in isolated nucleolar fractions from amphibian oocytes (Finamore).

(b) *Granular nucleolar component (cortex)*

The ultrastructural organization of the granular portion can be observed in isolated amphibian oocyte nucleoli in which the granular component is only partially dispersed. Observations of such preparations show that this region consists of a well-defined fibrillar element to which granules are irregularly attached (Fig. 11–13). Whether or not the granules represent coiled regions of a continuous RNP fiber, as has been suggested, has not been resolved.

The correlation of autoradiographic and biochemical data indicates that the 32S RNA is located in the granular region of the nucleolus. In this case RNA molecules in the nucleolar cortex should be no longer than 2.2 μ. Fiber segments slightly longer than 2 μ have been observed both free of granules and with granules attached. The size and intensity of electron staining of the granules are similar to those of ribosomes, suggesting that the amount of RNA in a granule is similar to the amount of RNA in a ribosome ($\sim$2.2 μ long). If each granule contains as much RNA as a ribosome and is a coiled region of a continuous RNP fiber, then the length of the RNA present in the granule plus the associated fiber would be longer than that expected for the 32S RNA. The fact that particles containing 32S RNA can be isolated from the nucleolus by relatively gentle methods suggests that the fibers and granules of the cortex are not

---

Fig. 5. Stretched portion of an unwound isolated nucleolar core from *Xenopus laevis* oocyte. The micrograph shows three adjacent periodic units along the DNA axis. Identical parts of adjoining periods are indicated (a, b). Each period ($\sim$6.25 μ long) consists of a matrix-free ($\sim$2.50 μ) and a matrix-covered segment ($\sim$3.75 μ). (Electron micrograph – isolated into 10^{-4} M magnesium acetate at *p*H 7.5, formalin fixation, ethyl alcohol–uranyl acetate stain.)

Fig. 6. Two nucleolar cores isolated from *Xenopus laevis* oocyte. The core at lower left is partially unwound; the other has been largely dispersed showing that most of the core axis exhibits periodicity. Several matrix-free segments of periodic units are indicated (arrows). (Electron micrograph – preparation similar to Fig. 5.)

Fig. 7. Portion of nucleolar core isolated from *Xenopus laevis* oocyte, showing matrix-covered and matrix-free regions of core axis. The RNP matrix is composed of individual fibrils approximately 100 Å in diameter, and displays a gradient from short to long fibrils. A least 100 fibrils appear to be present on each matrix-covered segment. (Electron micrograph – preparation similar to Fig. 5.)

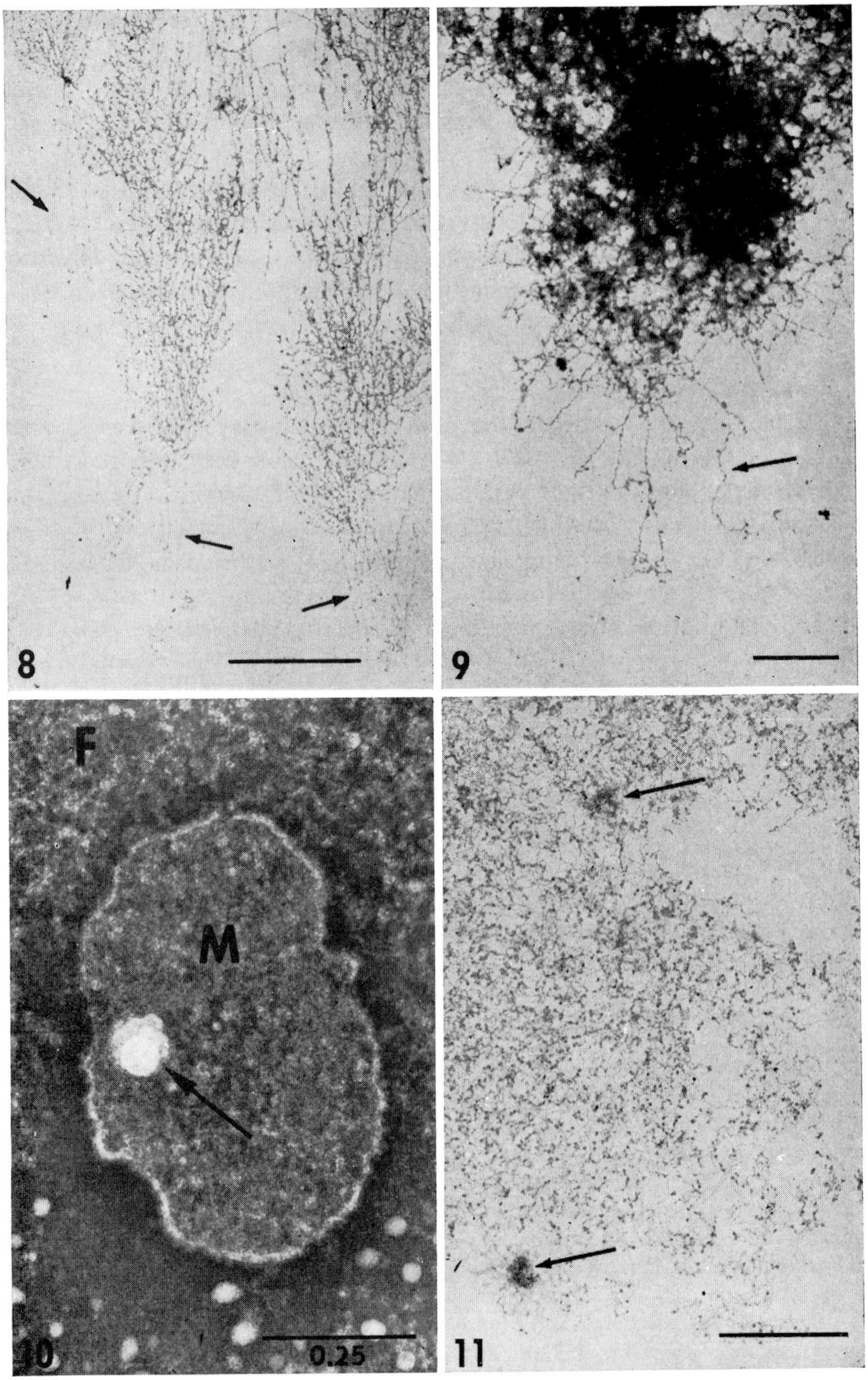
8
9
F
M
10
0.25
11

composed of the same continuous fiber (Warner and Soeiro). Such isolated particles also are reported to contain a 5S RNA. However, kinetics of labeling of the 5S RNA relative to the 28S RNA indicates that these molecules are not synthesized on the same cistrons (Knight and Darnell). The time at which the 5S RNA becomes associated with the 32S and their structural relationship within the nucleolus are unknown.

It has been suggested from observations on thin sections (Marinozzi and Bernhard) that the granular component is formed by fibers from the core coiling up at the core–cortex interface. If this occurs over the entire interface, it should be difficult to separate the core and cortex. The fact that they can be separated easily in amphibian oocyte nucleoli indicates that the attachment between the two components is relatively labile (Fig. 4). Partially dispersed cortices sometimes exhibit a number of more tightly coiled differentiated points (Fig. 11). These possibly could be sites involved in the processing of the larger RNA molecules in the core to the smaller RNA species of the cortex. In this case, a limited number of transition sites on the core–cortex interface would explain the relative ease with which the cores and cortices can be separated.

The labeling kinetics of cytoplasmic ribosomal proteins (Warner and Soeiro) suggest the presence of pools of precursor protein in the nucleolus. Observations on both isolated cores and cortices of amphibian oocyte nucleoli indicate that essentially all the protein present is associated with RNA. If preformed protein pools exist in the nucleolus *in vivo* then either they are attached to RNA or are leached out in the preparations of amphibian oocyte nucleoli described here.

The sequence of nucleolar RNA metabolism shows that the 18S RNA molecule leaves the nucleolus at essentially the time that the 45S molecule is cleaved in the formation of the 32S RNA. Autoradiographic studies suggest that this cleavage occurs at the core–cortex interface. If so, the 18S molecule must pass through the cortex during its

---

Fig. 8. Portion of an isolated nucleolar core from *Xenopus laevis* oocyte showing stretched RNP fibers approximately 50 Å in diameter (arrows). The longest of these is close to 2 μ long and presumably contains a half mature RNA molecule near the center of a rDNA cistron. (Electron micrograph – isolated into 10^{-4} M EDTA at *p*H 7.5, formalin fixation, ethyl alcohol–uranyl acetate stain.)

Fig. 9. Portion of an isolated nucleolar core from *Xenopus laevis* oocyte in which the RNP fibrils have not been stretched. The designated fiber (arrow) is $\sim$2.5 μ long. (Electron micrograph – isolated into 0.05 M veronal acetate buffer + 10^{-4} M EDTA at *p*H 7.5, formalin fixation, ethyl alcohol–uranyl acetate stain.)

Fig. 10. Membranous component (M) attached to a core (F) isolated from a peripheral nucleolus of *Triturus viridescens* oocyte. This component appears to be surrounded by a membrane $\sim$100 Å thick and often contains a relatively electron transparent element (arrow). Granularity present at bottom of micrograph is a staining artifact. (Electron micrograph – isolated into 0.025 M KCl + 0.025 M sucrose at *p*H 7.5, formalin fixation, negatively stained with phosphotungstic acid.)

Fig. 11. Portion of a partially dispersed nucleolar cortex isolated from *Xenopus laevis* oocyte. Most of the cortex consists of a fibrous network to which granules are irregularly attached. Several differentiated regions (arrows) can be seen in each isolated cortex in such preparations. (Electron micrograph – isolated into 0.05 M veronal acetate–HCl buffer at *p*H 7.5, formalin fixation, ethyl alcohol–uranyl acetate stain.)

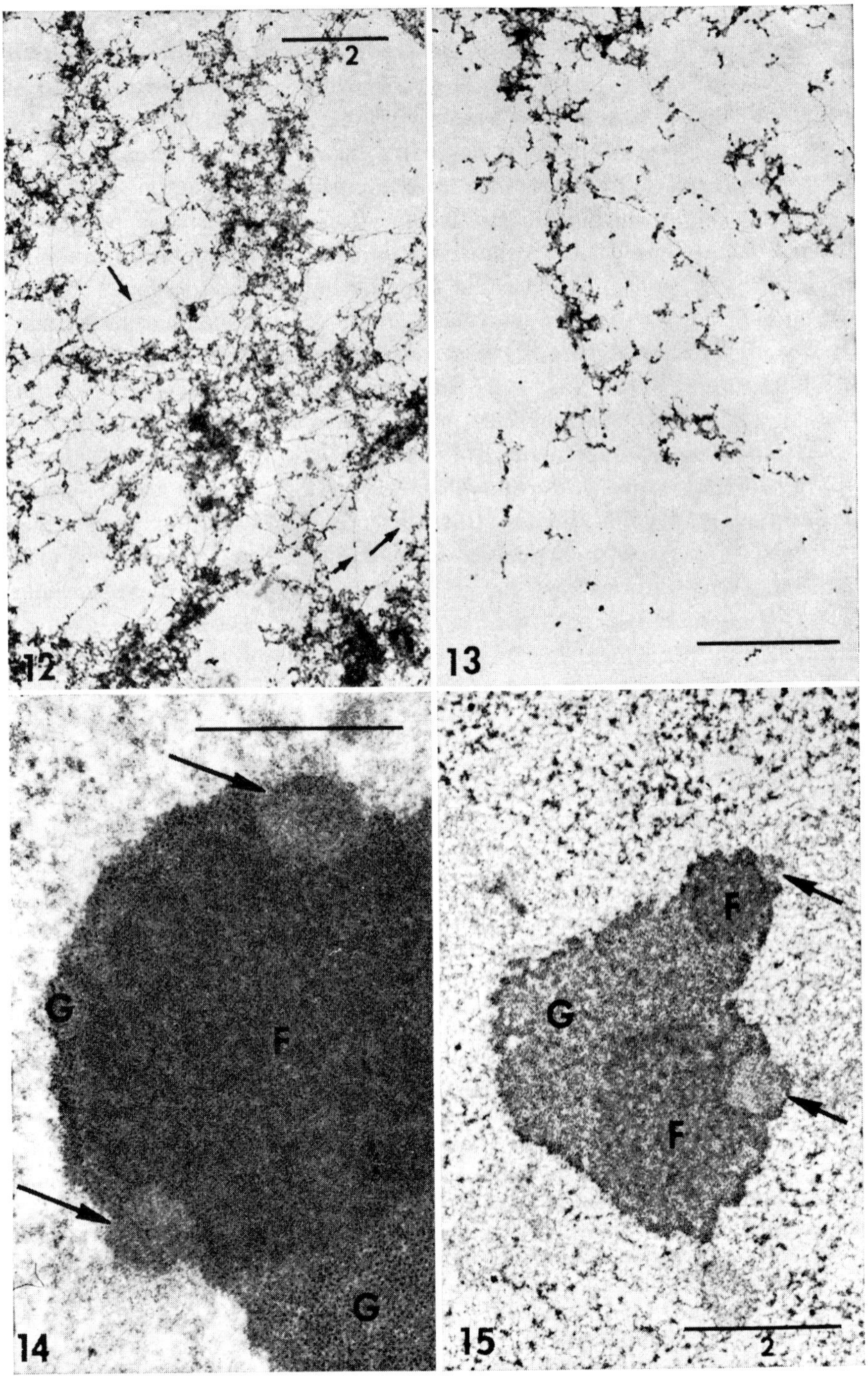
2
12
13
G
F
G
14
F
G
F
15
2

rapid exit from the nucleolus. In thin sections of some amphibian oocyte nucleoli, differentiated channels passing through the cortex from the core are observed (Figs. 14 and 15). It is suggested that these sites may represent the migration of 18S molecules from the nucleolus to the nucleoplasm.

Observations of thin sections of the nucleolar-nucleoplasm boundary show granule-free fibers surrounding the nucleolus (Figs. 14 and 15). This suggests that the precursor to the 28S RNA of the large ribosomal subunit leaves the nucleolus in a fibrous rather than a granular configuration. This is also supported by the fact that the granules observed in the nucleoplasm are somewhat larger than those observed in the nucleolus (Figs. 1 and 3).

4. *Conclusions*

It is well established that the nucleolus has a primary role in ribosome biogenesis. It also appears that the major events of nucleolar metabolism are similar in all eukaryotic cell types, even though the details may differ.

The typical nucleolus is divided into two structurally distinct components. One appears fibrous in thin section and contains the ribosomal RNA genes on which the initial large precursor molecule is synthesized. The second is a granular-appearing component containing RNA molecules that are precursors to the RNA of the large ribosomal subunit. In both cases, the RNA is present in the form of RNP molecules.

Fine structure observations and estimates of the sizes of RNA molecules in the nucleolus indicate that the rDNA cistrons are read as single units by RNA polymerase molecules rather than as polycistronic units. The high number of RNP fibrils attached to the rDNA cistrons indicates that each cistron is essentially coated with RNA polymerases.

Observations on amphibian oocyte nucleoli suggest that the rDNA cistrons are separated by segments of DNA which are not used in transcription. If this arrangement is universal, the presence of such segments, plus the fact that half of the initial rRNA precursor molecule is discarded in the formation of rRNA, indicates that the portion of

---

Fig. 12. Portion of a partially dispersed nucleolar cortex isolated from *Xenopus laevis* oocyte. This component is composed of a fibrogranular network. Stretches of fibrils approximately 2 μ long with and without attached granules can be observed (arrows). (Electron micrograph – isolated in 0.05 M veronal acetate–HCl buffer at *p*H 7.5, formalin fixation, uranyl acetate stain.)

Fig. 13. Portion of a partially dispersed nucleolar cortex isolated from *Xenopus laevis* oocyte. Granules ranging from ~150 Å to ~400 Å in diameter are irregularly spaced on fibrils approximately 50 Å in diameter. (Electron micrograph – isolated into 0.5% formalin + 10^{-4} magnesium acetate at *p*H 7.4, uranyl acetate stain.)

Figs. 14 and 15. Thin sections of peripheral nucleoli of *Rana clamitans* oocytes. Differentiated channels (arrows) passing from core (F) through the cortex (G) may represent exit sites of the 18S RNA molecules of the nucleolus. The nucleoplasm immediately surrounding the nucleoli contains fibers and is relatively free of granules. (Electron micrographs – Fig. 14, OsO_4 fixation, uranyl acetate stain; Fig. 15, formalin–OsO_4 fixation, uranyl acetate stain.)

the genome contained in the nucleolar organizer locus is considerably underestimated by rRNA–DNA hybridization experiments.

The granular-appearing nucleolar component consists of a fibrous network to which granules are irregularly attached. The structure of this component indicates that the cleavage of the large RNA precursor molecules giving rise to the smaller RNA molecules of the granular region is considerably more complex than a simple formation of discrete RNP granules.

In summary, biochemical, autoradiographic, cytochemical, and fine structure studies of the nucleolus have been combined to describe the number and location of the rDNA cistrons within the nucleolus as well as the sizes and probable locations of the various nucleolar RNA molecules involved in ribosome biogenesis. However, many important aspects of nucleolar metabolism and structure remain to be clarified. The location of the enzymes involved in the RNA cleavages and the number of such processing sites in the nucleolus have not been determined. An interpretation of the fibrogranular network found in the granular nucleolar component relative to the steps in nucleolar RNA metabolism cannot be made at present. The sites of synthesis of nucleolar proteins and the precise molecular relationships of both the ribosomal-like proteins and non-ribosomal proteins to the various nucleolar RNA species are also unknown. Finally, the structural basis of the mechanisms by which the nucleolar genes, as well as other genetic loci, are turned on and off for RNA synthesis during cell cycles and during development remains to be ascertained.

References

APPLEBAUM, S. W., R. P. EBSTEIN and G. R. WYATT: Dissociation of ribosomal ribonucleic acid from silkmoth pupae by heat and dimethysulfoxide: Evidence for specific cleavage points. J. Mol. Biol. 21 (1966) 29.

BIRNSTIEL, M.: The nucleolus in cell metabolism. Ann. Rev. Plant Physiol. 18 (1967) 25.

BIRNSTIEL, M., H. WALLACE, J. L. SIRLIN and M. FISCHBERG: Localization of the ribosomal DNA complements in the nucleolar organizer region of *Xenopus laevis*. Natl. Cancer Inst. Monograph 23 (1966) 431.

BROWN, C. A. and H. RIS: Amphibian oocyte nucleoli. J. Morphol. 104 (1959) 377.

BROWN, D. D. and J. B. GURDON: Absence of ribosomal RNA synthesis in the anucleolate mutant of *Xenopus laevis*. Proc. Natl. Acad. Sci. U.S. 51 (1964) 139.

BROWN, D. D., C. S. WEBER and J. H. SINCLAIR: Ribosomal RNA and its genes during oogenesis and development. Carnegie Inst. Wash. Year Book 66 (1966–67) 580.

BUSCH, H., R. DESJARDINS, D. GROGAN, K. HIGASHI, S. T. JACOB, M. MARAMATSU, T. S. RO and W. J. STEELE: Composition of nucleoli isolated from mammalian cells. Natl. Cancer Inst. Monograph 23 (1966) 193.

CALLAN, H. G.: The organization of genetic units in chromosomes. J. Cell Sci. 2 (1967) 1.

EBSTEIN, B. S.: Tritiated actinomycin D as a cytochemical label for small amounts of DNA. J. Cell Biol. 35 (1967) 709.

EDSTRÖM, J.-E.: Composition of the nucleolus as a basis for views on its function. Natl. Cancer Inst. Monograph 23 (1966) 223.

EDSTRÖM, J.-E. and B. DANEHOLT: Sedimentation properties of the newly synthesized RNA from isolated nuclear components of *Chironomus tentans* salivary gland cells. J. Mol. Biol. 28 (1967) 331.

FINAMORE, F. J.: The nucleic acids – metabolic key to development? Quart. Rev. Biol. 36 (1961) 117.

GALL, J. G.: Nuclear RNA of the salamander oocyte. Natl. Cancer Inst. Monograph 23 (1966) 475.

GRANBOULAN, N. and PH. GRANBOULAN: Cytochimie ultrastructurale du nucléole II. Etude des sites de synthèse de RNA dans le nucléole et le noyau. Exptl. Cell Res. 38 (1965) 604.

KALNINS, V. I., H. F. STICH and S. A. BENCOSME: Fine structure of nucleoli and RNA-containing chromosome regions of salivary gland chromosomes of chironomids and their interrelationship. Can. J. Zool. 42 (1964) 1147.

KNIGHT, E., JR. and J. E. DARNELL: Distribution of 5s RNA in HeLa cells. J. Mol. Biol. 28 (1967) 491.

LANE, N. J.: Spheroidal and ring nucleoli in amphibian oocytes. J. Cell Biol. 35 (1967) 421.

MACGREGOR, H. C.: Pattern of incorporation of H^3-uridine into RNA of amphibian oocyte nucleoli. J. Cell Sci. 2 (1967) 145.

MARINOZZI, V.: Cytochimie ultrastructurale du nucléole – RNA et protéines intranucléolaires. J. Ultrastruct. Res. 10 (1964) 433.

MARINOZZI, V. and W. BERNHARD: Présence dans le nucléole de deux types de ribonucleoprotéines morphologiquement distinctes. Exptl. Cell Res. 32 (1963) 595.

MILLER, O. L., JR.: Fine structure of lampbrush chromosomes. Natl. Cancer Inst. Monograph 18 (1965) 79.

MILLER, O. L., JR.: Structure and composition of peripheral nucleoli of salamander oocytes. Natl. Cancer Inst. Monograph 23 (1966) 53.

MILLER, O. L., JR.: Observations on isolated components of amphibian oocyte nucleoli. J. Cell Biol. 35 (1967) 94A.

MUNDELL, R. D.: The occurrence of ribosomal proteins in nucleoli of starfish oocytes. Biochem. Biophys. Res. Commun. 28 (1967) 117.

PEACOCKE, A. R. and R. B. DRYSDALE: The molecular basis of heredity. Washington, Butterworths (1965).

PERRY, R. P.: The nucleolus and the synthesis of ribosomes. Progr. Nucleic Acid Res. Mol. Biol. 6 (1967) 219.

RITOSSA, R. M., K. C. ATWOOD, D. L. LINDSLEY and S. SPIEGELMAN: On the chromosomal distribution of DNA complementary to ribosomal and soluble RNA. Natl. Cancer Inst. Monograph 23 (1966) 449.

SHANKARNARAYAN, K., M. MURAMATSU, K. SMETANA and H. BUSCH: Ultrastructural studies on RNA and DNA components of isolated nucleoli of Walker 256 carcinosarcoma. Exptl. Cell Res. 41 (1966) 81.

SIEBERT, G.: Nucleolar enzymes of isolated rat liver nucleoli. Natl. Cancer Inst. Monograph 23 (1966) 285.

SIMARD, R. and W. BERNHARD: A heat-sensitive cellular function located in the nucleolus. J. Cell Biol. 34 (1967) 61.

VINCENT, W. S., E. BALTUS, A. LØVLIE and R. E. MUNDELL: Proteins and nucleic acids of starfish oocyte nucleoli and ribosomes. Natl. Cancer Inst. Monograph 23 (1966) 235.

VON GAUDECKER, B.: RNA synthesis in the nucleolus of *Chironomus thummi* as studied by high resolution autoradiography. Z. Zellforsch. Mikroskop. Anat. 82 (1967) 536.

WARNER, J. R. and R. SOEIRO: Nascent ribosomes from HeLa cells. Proc. Natl. Acad. Sci. U.S. 58 (1967) 1984.

WATERS, L. and L. DURE, III: Ribosomal-RNA synthesis in the absence of ribosome synthesis in germinating cotton seeds. Science 149 (1965) 188.

WEINBERG, R. A., U. LOENING, M. WILLEMS and S. PENMAN: Acrylamide gel electrophoresis of HeLa cell nucleolar RNA. Proc. Natl. Acad. Sci. U.S. 58 (1967) 1088.

CHAPTER 25

Nucleoli: the cellular sites of ribosome production

ROBERT P. PERRY

The Institute for Cancer Research, 7701 Burholme Avenue, Philadelphia, Pennsylvania 19111

Contents

1. Introduction
2. Characterization of the genes coding for ribosomal RNA
   (a) Relation to nucleolar organizer
   (b) Properties of the rRNA cistrons
   (c) Amplification of the rRNA cistrons
3. Synthesis of the precursor of ribosomal RNA
   (a) The nucleolus as the site of synthesis
   (b) Molecular properties of the precursor
   (c) Association of precursor with protein
4. Subsequent events in the formation of ribosomes
   (a) Cleavage of the 45S component
   (b) Synthesis of ribosomal protein
   (c) Assembly of ribosomes and export to cytoplasm
5. Summary

The author would like to acknowledge support during the preparation of this material from the National Science Foundation (GB 4137) and the National Institutes of Health (CA 06927 and FR 05539) and an appropriation from the Commonwealth of Pennsylvania.

1. Introduction

The central role of ribosomes in protein biosynthesis is well established (see chapter on ribosomes in this volume), and although many of the details concerning their function are still obscure, it is clear that they are indispensible constituents of all living organisms. In eukaryotes the production of these complex particles* occurs at well defined cellular sites: the nucleoli**, which have been observed by cytologists for over a century (Montgomery). The nucleoli may be thought of as chromosomal locations containing the genes coding for ribosomal RNA, the primary gene products, derivatives of these products and their associated proteins, and some, if not all, of the enzymatic machinery required for the synthetic, conversion, and assembly processes.

In this chapter I wish to summarize our current concepts regarding the nature of the ribosomal genes and their mode of expression, and, insofar as is possible, to describe the stages of ribosome biosynthesis that are believed to occur within the nucleolus. For more details of much of the material presented here the reader should consult the proceedings of The International Symposium on The Nucleolus – Its Structure and Function (Natl. Cancer Inst. Monog. 23 (1966), obtainable from the Superintendent of Documents, U.S. Govt. Printing Office, Washington, D.C., U.S.A.).

2. Characterization of the genes coding for ribosomal RNA

(a) *Relation to nucleolar organizer*

Direct evidence linking the genetic material responsible for nucleolus formation with that responsible for the synthesis of ribosomal RNA (rRNA) was provided by the finding of Brown and Gurdon that embryos of the mutant of *Xenopus laevis* that lack the ability to form nucleoli are also incapable of synthesizing rRNA. Homozygotes of this mutant die at the tail-bud stage, whereas heterozygotes develop and synthesize rRNA at the same rate as normal embryos.

Further elucidation of the relationship between the DNA that codes for rRNA and the DNA associated with the nucleolus or belonging to the nucleolar organizing regions of the genome has been achieved using the technique of DNA–RNA hybridization (Hall and Spiegelman). In these experiments, isotopically labeled rRNA is allowed to anneal with DNA from various sources. Determination of the maximal amount of rRNA that can form specific duplexes with a given quantity of DNA allows an estimate of the number of cistrons or DNA complements coding for rRNA in the particular DNA sample.

* I am ignoring here the ribosomes of DNA-containing organelles such as chloroplasts and mitochondria. These ribosomes, which usually comprise only a very small portion of the total cell complement, have a different size and composition from the bulk of the ribosomes (Stutz and Noll; Rifkin et al.), and undoubtedly are synthesized by a separate pathway.

** The word *nucleolus* is a diminutive of *nucleus*, which is itself a diminutive of the latin *nuc-*, *nux*: nut.

Utilizing this method and the anucleolate *Xenopus* mutant, Wallace and Birnstiel compared the saturation plateaus obtained when rRNA was hybridized with DNA from wild-type, homozygous mutant, and heterozygote embryos. Their results indicated that in *Xenopus* each nucleolar organizer contains on the order of 1000 rRNA cistrons, and that the anucleolate mutation is a total deletion of these genes.

In a similar type of experiment Ritossa and Spiegelman determined the number of DNA complements of rRNA in stocks of *Drosophila melanogaster* containing X-chromosomes either deficient or duplicated for a short piece of heterochromatin containing the nucleolar organizer. Appropriate choice of material supplied genomes possessing one, two, three and four organizers. The data indicated a complement of about 260 rRNA cistrons per organizer and a direct proportionality between the number of cistrons and the number of nucleolar organizers.

Both of the above experiments provide convincing evidence for the assertion that the DNA complementary to rRNA is confined to a region of the genome encompassing the organizer.

In *Drosophila* it appears that the 'bobbed' locus, which maps within the aforementioned heterochromatic region of the X-chromosome, is the site of the organizer (Ritossa et al.). Examination of the DNA from a series of 'bobbed' mutants has revealed a varying number of rRNA cistrons, all less than that characteristic of the wild-type genome. These mutants are characterized by abnormally short bristles. Since bristles are produced rapidly and therefore require an especially intense protein synthesis, one might suppose that the 'bobbed' condition arises as the result of a ribosome deficiency.

(b) *Properties of the rRNA cistrons*

Isolation of the rRNA cistrons was achieved with the *Xenopus* system by banding the DNA in CsCl density gradients (Birnstiel et al. 1966). A satellite band of buoyant density about 0.025 g/cm^3 greater than the major band and comprising roughly 0.15–0.2% of the total DNA was demonstrable. This satellite, which was not found in the DNA of the anucleolate mutant, was many times more active in forming hybrids with rRNA than the major DNA component. The practicability of isolating the satellite is itself indicative that the rRNA cistrons exist in extended clusters. From molecular weight estimates it is apparent that these clusters can contain as many as ten rRNA cistrons, thus indicating that the cistrons occur in a repetitive linear sequence within the genome.

The cistrons complementary to the large (28S) rRNA component are distinct from those responsible for the small (18S) rRNA component; no evidence of competition is found and hybridizations with both components are completely additive (Ritossa et al.; Wallace and Birnstiel). The question naturally arises: are the multicistrons for each rRNA component completely redundant or is there some degree of uniqueness within each population? A definite answer cannot yet be given. The existence of the 'bobbed' *Drosophila* mutants and of a mutant *chironomid* with a 'split nucleolar organizer' (Beermann; Pelling and Beermann) suggests that the degree of redundancy is probably high. This follows from the fact that in these instances the deletion of a major portion of organizer DNA, directly shown to be equivalent to a deletion of rRNA cistrons in *Drosophila*, does not necessarily constitute a lethal event. Moreover, there is no measurable difference in the RNA base composition of nucleoli formed by organizers located on two different chromosomes in *chironomous* (Edström 1964). On the other hand, analyses of the terminal bases of the large and small rRNAs suggest that each component consists of a major species with characteristic end groups, but that some minor species with other termini may also exist (Lane and Tomaoki; McIlreavy and Midgley). If this is correct, it would imply that there is a certain degree of heterogeneity within the rRNA population.

The above mentioned genetic data on insects suggest a rather high degree of interspersion of the genes for the two rRNA components; they do not seem to be located on blocks of DNA on opposite sides of the organizer. Are the cistrons for the two components in an exactly alternating sequence? Recent evidence suggests that this is probably the case. Brown and Weber have detected linkage between the 28S and 18S rRNA cistrons with fragments of *Xenopus* DNA having an average doublestranded molecular weight of about seven million. Fragmentation of the DNA to about one half million daltons destroyed the linkage. DNA of molecular weight seven million would consist of an appreciable proportion of linked cistrons only if they were in an alternating sequence of ones or pairs. However this amount of DNA could code for less than one of the large 45S rRNA precursor molecules (see section 3b) and there is some indication that in mammalian cells the 45S precursor contains stretches which are not converted to rRNA (Weinberg et al.). Thus, if one assumes that the general characteristics of the rRNA genes and the precursor molecules are similar in these two biological systems, it follows that the cistrons are strictly alternating but intermingled with the stretches coding for the nonconserved part of the rRNA precursor.

The genes coding for the small 5S RNA component that is associated with the large ribosomal subunit (Rosset et al.; Galibert et al.) are probably not linked to those coding for the 18S and 28S rRNA components (Brown). Although the genes seem to be clustered they are apparently not part of the nucleolar organizer since they are present in the anucleolate mutant. In spite of this, however, the mutant does not accumulate any detectable quantity of 5S RNA.

(c) *Amplification of the rRNA cistrons*

The numerous extrachromosomal nucleoli that are present in immature amphibian oocytes contain over half of the total DNA of the nucleus. This large increase in the proportion of nucleolar DNA over that found in somatic cells has recently been shown to represent an amplification of roughly 3000-fold in the number of rRNA cistrons relative to the rest of the genome (Brown; Gall). A preferential duplication of rRNA genes has also been observed in *Urechis* oocytes, which do not possess extra-chromosomal nucleoli, and a similar situation may exist in the fly, *Tipula oleracea* (Lima-de-Faria and Moses). Such a gene amplification may help the oocyte accomplish its intense rRNA synthesis: per genome about 10^5 times that of a liver cell (Brown). On the other hand, among different types of somatic cells of the chicken, the same proportion of genes coding for rRNA were found, even though the rates of rRNA synthesis in these cell types varied by orders of magnitude (Ritossa et al.). Gene amplification is obviously not the only way by which cells control the output of rRNA.

3. *Synthesis of the precursor of ribosomal RNA*

(a) *The nucleolus as the site of synthesis*

Realization that RNA synthesized in the nucleolar region of the nucleus might be a precursor to rRNA came initially as a result of studies designed to clarify the relationship between nuclear and cytoplasmic RNA (see Prescott for refs.). Once it became evident that the bulk of the cytoplasmic RNA is ribosomal, then the demonstrations of nucleolar dependence of cytoplasmic RNA synthesis (Perry 1960; Perry et al. 1961; Perry and Errera), or close similarity in base composition between nucleolar and cytoplasmic RNA (Edström 1960), were readily interpretable in terms of a nucleolar origin for rRNA. Early attempts at cellular fractionation by the phenol method and separation of the RNA into high and low molecular weight fractions also pointed towards this conclusion (Georgiev and Samarina). Strong confirmation for this hypothesis was the demonstration that low doses of actinomycin D, which selectively inhibit nucleolar RNA synthesis, also selectively inhibit the synthesis of the precursor to rRNA (Perry 1962; 1963). That the nucleolus contains the necessary enzymatic apparatus for the polymerization of RNA and its subsequent methylation has also been shown (Siebert et al.; Liau and Hurlbert; Birnstiel et al. 1963).

(b) *Molecular properties of the precursor*

Characterization of the precursor of rRNA in several cell types became possible as methods were developed for the extraction of rapidly labeled nuclear RNAs in an undegraded form (Sherrer and Darnell). When pulse-labeled RNA from a wide variety of sources is submitted to zonal centrifugation on sucrose gradients, the radioactivity profile is readily distinguishable from the 28 and 18S rRNA components. Under favorable circumstances, the rapidly labeled RNA can be seen to consist of a 45S component, some polydisperse components which appear to be the most rapidly synthesized of all, and a 4S component. After slightly longer periods of labeling, a clearly defined 32S component is visible as well. Several lines of evidence, including actinomycin-chase kinetics (Perry 1962; Rake and Graham; Sherrer et al.; Georgiev et al.; Tamaoki; Kempf and Mandel), selective inhibition of the formation of the 45S component with low doses of actinomycin D (Perry 1962; 1964), diminished synthesis of 45S RNA in the anucleolate mutants of *Xenopus*, which are incapable of rRNA synthesis (Brown and Gurdon), and studies of the methylation pattern (Wagner et al.) combine to indicate that the 45S component* is the early precursor of rRNA. In HeLa cells the estimated time for transcription of a 45S molecule is 2.3 minutes (Greenberg and Penman).

With the advent of techniques for isolating pure nucleoli (Penman et al.; Busch et al.) and the introduction of acrylamide gel electrophoresis for characterization of RNA (Loening) it is now possible to obtain 45S RNA relatively free from contamination with other RNA components in sufficient quantities for molecular weight determinations and other physical analyses. From the mobility on acrylamide gels (Weinberg et al.) and calculations based on equilibrium ultracentrifugation data (McConkey) it is concluded that the molecular weight of the 45S component is between 4.0 and 4.5×10^6. An estimation made on the basis of the sedimentation coefficient yields a molecular weight of 4.4×10^6.

It has not been possible to dissociate the 45S component into smaller pieces under conditions favoring hydrogen bond breakage, e.g., heating in the presence of formaldehyde or treatment with high concentrations of urea or dimethylsulfoxide (Kempf and Mandel; McConkey; Katz and Penman). Thus it seems probable that the 45S precursor is a covalently continuous molecule containing the two rRNA components. This would be compatible with the concept of alternating rRNA cistrons discussed in section 2b.

The combined molecular weight of the 18S and 28S rRNA components is about 2.2 to 2.5×10^6. Therefore, one might imagine either that the 45S component contains more than one of each of the rRNAs, or that it contains other stretches of different composition which are lost during its maturation. The latter seems more likely in view of the intermediate size and degree of methylation of the 32S component and the possible existence of still other conversion products of intermediate size (see below).

A certain fraction of the ribose moieties in rRNA have O-methyl groups at the 2′-position (Brown and Attardi). Detailed kinetic studies indicate that these methyl groups are derived from methionine by a transmethylation which occurs in the nucleolus during the transcription of the 45S component, and that little or no further methylation of rRNA occurs beyond the 45S stage (Greenberg and Penman; Muramatsu; Zimmerman and Holler). In spite of this, the 45S component seems to have a lower proportion of methylated nucleotides than either of the rRNA components suggesting that the elements of the 45S component which are not conserved are relatively deficient in methyl groups (Weinberg et al.).

(c) *Association of precursor with protein*

Tamaoki and Mueller (1965) and Tamaoki (1966) used a combination of deoxycholate,

* As used here, the term '45S component' refers to the relatively monodisperse RNA component that can be observed in the 45S region of a sucrose gradient. It should not be confused with that portion of the rapidly labeled heterogeneous RNA sedimenting in the 45S region. These two species can be readily distinguished under conditions where rRNA synthesis is selectively depressed (Perry et al. 1964) or by further fractionation of nuclei prior to extraction of the RNA (Penman et al.).

DNase, and dextran sulfate to isolate the 45S component as part of a heterogeneous group of ribonucleoprotein complexes sedimenting between 60 and 100S. These complexes had the same effective charge density as ribosomes and contained some newly synthesized protein. It was proposed that they might represent early stages in the formation of the ribosome particles. More recently 45S RNA has been found in a more homogenous class of particles sedimenting at about 80S (Warner and Soeiro). These particles were extracted from nucleolar preparations along with 55S particles which contained exclusively 32S RNA.

4. *Subsequent events in the formation of ribosomes*

(a) *Cleavage of the 45S component*

Details concerning the conversion of the 45S precursor molecule to the 28 and 18S rRNA components have been obtained from the following types of studies: (a) kinetics of incorporation of nucleosides into the various RNA components (Perry 1965; Rake and Graham; Sherrer et al.; Georgiev et al.; Girard et al. 1964); (b) alteration of the pattern of incorporation with analogs and inhibitors, e.g., 8-azaguanine (Perry 1964, 1965), thioacetamide (Kleinfeld; Busch et al.), or puromycin (Perry 1964; Tamaoki and Mueller; Holland), which block specific stages in the transformation sequence; and (c) use of refined cellular fractionation techniques to separate cellular structures containing different intermediates (Gall 1966; Penman et al.; Busch et al.; Weinberg et al.).

In pulse-chase experiments, including those in which continued incorporation from nonexchangeable nucleotide pools is prevented with actinomycin D, one observes a sequential labeling of 45S then 32 and 18S, and finally 28 and 18S components (Rake and Graham; Sherrer et al.). When part of the RNA guanine is replaced by 8-azaguanine, the early step in this conversion can still occur, but the later step is greatly retarded. Since under these conditions much of the labeled RNA accumulates in the nucleolus rather than the cytoplasm, it was concluded that the early step in the conversion of 45S component occurs in the nucleolus (Perry 1965).

Rather convincing evidence for this point was obtained by analysis of the labeling of RNAs from isolated nucleolar, nucleoplasmic, and cytoplasmic fractions (Gall 1966; Penman et al.; Busch et al.). In these cases, sequential labeling of the 45 and 32S RNA could be observed in a series of nucleolar fractions prepared from cells labeled for different periods or chased in the presence of actinomycin. Moreover, in some cases, very little 18S RNA appears to be associated with the nuclei, indicating that upon cleavage of the 45S molecule there is a rapid exit of the 18S component to the cytoplasm (Gall 1966; Penman et al.). This is in accord with the early appearance of labeled 18S RNA (Perry 1964; Girard et al. 1964) or, more specifically, particles bearing 18S RNA (Perry 1965; Girard et al. 1965), in the cytoplasm.

The improved resolution obtainable with the acrylamide gel electrophoresis technique has revealed the presence in nucleolar preparations of two minor RNA components of molecular weight intermediate between the 45S and 32S component and another component slightly larger than the 18S component (Weinberg et al.). These minor components may represent short-lived intermediate stages in the conversion process, although more work will be required before this point is completely clear.

A later stage of processing involves the transition from 32S to the 28S component. Penman et al. (1965) observed that, whereas the major RNA component in the nucleoplasm of HeLa cells sediments at 28S, the bulk of the RNA from nucleoli sediments at 32S. Similarly, Busch and co-workers extracted 28S RNA from both nucleoli and nucleoplasm of Walker tumor cells and 35S RNA exclusively from the nucleolar fractions (Busch et al.). Furthermore, it is possible that some of the 28S RNA found in the nucleoplasm comes from the particulate rim of the nucleolus, which is frequently lost during isolation procedures (Birnstiel, Panel on Ribosome Biogenesis, 1966). Thus one might suspect that the transition to 28S occurs in the nucleolus and that release into the nucleoplasm is concomitant with, or immediately follows, this conversion.

From acrylamide gel (Weinberg et al.) and equilibrium ultracentrifuge analyses (McConkey) it has been estimated that the molecular weight of the 32S component is about 2.1 to 2.3×10^6. This would imply that the 32S → 28S conversion involves a splitting off of RNA amounting to about one-half million molecular weight.

If the conclusions discussed in the preceding paragraphs are correct in that the production of rRNA entails the splitting of a small number of the approximately 7000 diester bonds in the 45S molecule, one must seriously consider what types of mechanism could possess the necessary specificity to mediate such a cleavage. Since all the methylation of rRNA appears to take place on the 45S molecule during its synthesis, it is considered unlikely that methylation could be directly responsible for the cleavage, especially for the 32S → 28S transformation. However, methylation could be indirectly implicated by creating specific sites for a couple of nuclease-catalyzed hydrolyses (Comb, Panel on Ribosome Biogenesis, 1966). Alternatively, one could derive the necessary specificity from appropriate protein ligands, since both the 45S and the 32S components apparently exist *in vivo* as complexes with protein (cf. section 3c).

(b) *Synthesis of ribosomal protein*

Compared to our knowledge of rRNA, much less is known concerning the synthesis and properties of the protein elements of the ribosome. In part this is because ribosomal proteins belong to a much larger and diverse class of cellular macromolecules than does the rRNA, and consequently the task of sorting and characterizing them is considerably more difficult. Also, the techniques for isolating, preserving, and analyzing ribonucleoproteins have not been developed to the extent of those used in RNA studies, so that there is a much greater possibility of working with structures that are modified from the native state in different ways by different procedures.

From sedimentation–diffusion studies and analyses using gel electrophoresis, it appears that the mature ribosome contains twenty to thirty-five different proteins, having an average molecular weight of about 25,000 (Leboy et al.; Warner). Not more than a few of these are common to the two subunits. In gross features, the ribosomal proteins from higher organisms seem sufficiently similar to those of bacteria (Peterman), so that initially, at least, one is encouraged to extrapolate from one system to the other when attempting to elucidate the mechanism of ribosomal protein synthesis. We can suppose that the structural proteins of the ribosome are those tightly bound to the rRNA and not readily dissociable in solutions of relatively high ionic strength (0.5 M) (Peterman; Peterman and Pavlovec; Gavrilova et al.). These proteins appear to be linked to a particular rRNA component so as to form a 'ribonucleoprotein strand', which can apparently fold in discrete stages into a ribosome subunit by means of Mg^{2+}-dependent protein–protein interactions (Gavrilova et al.; Spirin). At least 30% of the protein can be dissociated from the ribosome by treatment with concentrated CsCl and then reassociated *nonenzymatically* with a precision sufficient to restore the protein synthesizing capacity of the particle (Hosokawa et al.; Spirin and Belitsina; Staehelin and Meselson).

The questions concerning us here are: Where is this protein synthesized, and where and how is it assembled into the ribosomal structure? One could imagine that the sites of synthesis and assembly might be different. The ribosomal protein could be synthesized in the cytoplasm and assembled together with the rRNA in the nucleolus. Conversely, both synthesis and assembly could occur in the nucleolus or in the cytoplasm. Let us consider some of the available data that might be useful in formulating an hypothesis.

Among the more detailed studies of the sites of synthesis of ribosomal protein have been those by Birnstiel, Flamm, and collaborators on pea and tobacco cells. These studies featured a mechanical separation of nuclei, nuclear subfractions, and cytoplasm, followed by differential extraction of several distinct protein fractions. Ribonucleoprotein particles with an RNA–protein ratio of 0.5 and of sizes corresponding to monoribosomes and their subunits were obtained from nucleolar fractions considered to be free of cytoplasmic contamination (Birnstiel et al. 1963). The protein of these particles comprises less than one quarter of the total nucleolar protein* and is not labeled when cells are given short pulses of C^{14} amino acids. In contrast the protein associated with a residual nucleolar fraction not solubilized by deoxycholate or 1–2 M NaCl (Flamm and Birnstiel; Birnstiel et al. 1964) is rapidly labeled. The amino acid composition of the protein from the 'residue' fraction strongly resembles

* The over-all ratio of protein to RNA in these nucleoli is about 8 to 1. The high proportion of protein in nucleoli has also been noted by Vincent (1952) in studies of nucleoli isolated from starfish oocytes. It implies that in such cells a considerable portion of nucleolar protein is probably not complexed with RNA, certainly not in proportions characteristic of ribosomes. The bulk of this protein is nonhistonelike and extractable at high ionic strength or with deoxycholate (Birnstiel et al. 1964). Its abundance compared to ribosomal protein may well depend on the physiological state of the cell.

that of the cytoplasmic ribosomes (Birnstiel et al. 1964). From these and other results, it was suggested that ribosomal protein is produced according to the following sequence: protein of 'residue' fraction → protein of nuclear ribonucleoprotein particles → protein of cytoplasmic ribosomes. However, because of the relatively great amount of protein synthesis occurring simultaneously in the cytoplasm, it is difficult to exclude the possibility that the protein of the residue fraction is originally synthesized in the cytoplasm and rapidly transferred to the nucleolus.

Efforts to resolve this problem by autoradiographic means have also been inconclusive, essentially for the same reason. In virtually all cell types studied by this method, there is no preferential labeling of nucleolar protein, even after short pulses of radioactive amino acids (Prescott and Bender; Zalokar; Errera et al.). After administration of actinomycin D in doses that selectively block ribosomal RNA synthesis, some depression of amino acid incorporation into nucleolar protein was noted (Suskind; Stenram). However, this was considerably less than the inhibition of nucleoside incorporation into nucleolar RNA, and furthermore it was observed when a sufficiently long time had elapsed after actinomycin treatment so that there was a measurable decrease in nucleolar volume. Thus, these results could equally well be explained if the nucleolus were an assembly site, but not a synthetic site for ribosomal protein.

One might pose the question in a slightly different way and ask whether nucleoli are indeed capable of protein synthesis. Beginning with the work of Allfrey, Mirsky, and co-workers (see Allfrey for refs.) there have been numerous reports of a protein synthetic capacity of isolated nuclei that does not appear to be attributable to a contamination with remnants of cytoplasm (Ficq and Errera). In some cases, this activity could be further ascribed to ribosomal particles isolated from nuclei (Frenster et al.; Pogo et al.). There is some indication that these ribosomes can utilize DNA as well as RNA as a direct template for protein synthesis (Frenster et al.; Naora), but as yet there is no evidence implicating them in the synthesis of ribosomal protein. Isolated nucleoli supplied with appropriate supplements are also capable of supporting polypeptide synthesis (Vincent 1964; Maggio), but no one has yet succeeded in localizing this activity in a particulate fraction. Indeed, in the case of plant material, those particles that can be liberated from nucleoli appear to be relatively inactive in protein synthesis (Flamm and Birnstiel). Therefore it is reasonable to suppose that, if the ribosomal proteins are actually synthesized in the nucleolus, the mechanism may be entirely different from that operative in the synthesis of cytoplasmic protein. Recently a search for such an unconventional mechanism has been stimulated by the finding that certain highly purified nuclei contain very few small ribosome subunits (cf. section 4a).

Another consideration of some relevance here is whether cells contain any preformed pools of ribosomal protein. Studies of this problem in cultured mammalian cells (Warner) and yeast (Vincent, Panel on Ribosome Biogenesis, 1966) suggest that there is a pool of preformed protein capable of combining with newly synthesized rRNA and consequently responsible for the fact that an inhibitor of protein synthesis such as cycloheximide does not inhibit the effective chase of 45S RNA radioactivity into the 18 and 28S RNA of cytoplasmic particles. In mammalian cells, the pool is believed to comprise on the order of 5 to 10% of the total ribosomal protein.

In summary, most of the data discussed in this section are consistent with the idea that at least part of the ribosomal protein is synthesized prior to its association with rRNA in the nucleolus. Whether the protein is synthesized in the cytoplasm and rapidly transported to the nucleolus, or in the nucleolus by some rather unique mechanism remains to be determined.

(c) *Assembly of ribosomes and export to cytoplasm*

Consideration of the nucleolus as the site of ribosome assembly was inferred from the observation that 18 and 28S RNA are observable in the cytoplasm only as ribonucleoprotein complexes having properties of ribosome subunits, and not as free RNA, or as complexes having a reduced proportion of protein to RNA (Perry 1965; Girard et al. 1965).

Recently Warner and Soeiro (1964) have extracted particles containing the 45S and 32S rRNA precursors from isolated HeLa cell nucleoli. The particles containing 32S RNA sediment at 55S under conditions where the large ribosomal subunit sediments at 50S or at about 65S when isolated under conditions where the large subunit sediments at 60S (Liau and Perry). They also contain 5S RNA. Their protein constituents exhibit an electrophoretic pattern on acrylamide gels almost identical to that of the large subunit.

The nucleolar 55S or 65S particles have buoyant densities in CsCl in the range 1.50 to 1.54 g/cm^3 (Liau and Perry). Such densities are significantly *lower* than the density of mature (1.57 g/cm^3) or of newly formed (1.55 g/cm^3) large cytoplasmic subunits (Perry and Kelley 1966a; Perry 1967). In the latter case, the difference in buoyant density was traced to the presence in new subunits of supplementary protein components, termed accessory proteins (Perry and Kelley 1966b, 1968). The still lower buoyant density of the nucleolar particles may be related to their possession of additional accessory proteins.

One interpretation of the above observations is that there is a progressive conformational change during maturation of ribosome subunits from a large extended ribonucleoprotein strand into relatively compact particles. Concomitant with the processing of the rRNA from a 45S precursor to the 18 and 28S components there might be a stepwise dispensation of accessory proteins and a folding of the derivative nucleoproteins. These ideas are currently being tested by a more detailed study of the physical-chemical properties of nucleolar particulates.

The quantity of subunits, especially small subunits, which exist in the nucleus outside of the nucleolus is very small, suggesting that when newly formed subunits exit from the nucleoli they spend very little time in the nucleoplasm. Upon reaching the cytoplasm the subunits are rapidly combined with messenger RNA and incorporated into polyribosomes (Perry and Kelley 1968).

After a pulse of radioactive RNA precursor, labeled small subunits appear in the

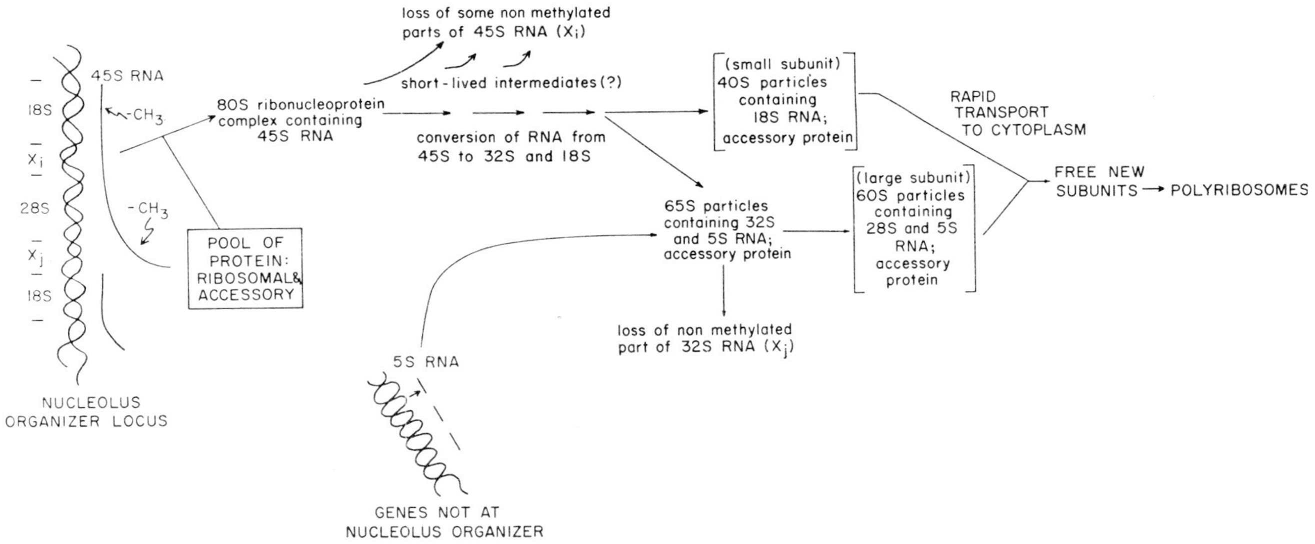

Fig. 1. Schematic representation of the biosynthesis of ribosomes in a typical eukaryotic cell. See text, Section 5, for detailed explanation.

cytoplasm before labeled large subunits, probably because of the longer time required for maturation of the large subunit (Perry 1965; Girard et al. 1965). It was also observed in studies of rat liver cells that the cytoplasmic pool of 'free' newly formed small subunits is larger than the pool of 'free' newly formed large subunits (Kleinfeld and Perry, in preparation). This suggests that large subunits, once they reach the cytoplasm, are more quickly incorporated into polyribosomes than are small subunits.

5. Summary

The data discussed in the preceding sections are summarized diagrammatically in Fig. 1. The synthesis and maturation of ribosomal RNA and its combination with protein to form ribosomal subunits can be described in the following steps:
(1) Synthesis of 45S RNA directed by a set of ribosomal genes existing in an alternating sequence of 18S and 28S cistrons interspersed with stretches coding for the non-conserved parts of the 45S molecule (X_i, X_j).
(2) Methylation (primarily 2′-O-methyl) of the 18S and 28S regions of the 45S molecule occurring during its transcription.
(3) Combination of 45S RNA with proteins to form a complex sedimenting at about 80S. Protein constituents of these complexes may include ribosomal and other (accessory) types.
(4) Conversion of 45S RNA to 18 and 32S pieces by cleavage and loss of non-methylated parts. RNA transitions are accompanied by changes in protein constitution, the loss of some of the accessory proteins and alterations in the conformation of the particle. This process probably involves several short-lived intermediate stages.
(5) Incorporation of 5S RNA (transcribed from nonnucleolar genes) into the nascent large subunit (65S nucleolar particle).
(6) Cleavage of the 32S RNA to yield 28S RNA; concomitant change in ribonucleoprotein particle from 65S to 60S.
(7) Rapid transport of subunits to cytoplasm, their combination with messenger RNA to form polyribosomes and their separation from residual accessory proteins.

References

ALLFREY, V.G.: Observations on the mechanism and control of protein synthesis in the cell nucleus. Proc. 5th Intern. Congr. Biochemistry, Moscow 2 (1961) 127.

BEERMANN, W.: Der Nukleolus als lebenswichtiger Bestandteil des Zellkernes. Chromosoma 11 (1960) 263.

BIRNSTIEL, M.L., M.I.H.CHIPCHASE and W.G.FLAMM: On the chemistry and organization of nucleolar proteins. Biochim. Biophys. Acta 87 (1964) 111.

BIRNSTIEL, M.L., M.I.H.CHIPCHASE and B.B.HYDE: The nucleolus, a source of ribosomes. Biochim. Biophys. Acta 76 (1963) 454.

BIRNSTIEL, M.L., E.FLEISSNER and E.BOREK: Nucleolus: A center of RNA methylation. Science 142 (1963) 1577.

BIRNSTIEL, M.L., H.WALLACE, J.L.SIRLIN and M.FISCHBERG: Localization of the ribosomal DNA complements in the nucleolar organizer region of *Xenopus laevis*. Natl. Cancer Inst. Monograph 23 (1966) 431.

BROWN, D.D.: In: A. Monroy and A.A. Moscona, eds.: Current topics in developmental biology, Vol. II. New York, Academic Press (1966).

BROWN, D.D. and J.B.GURDON: Absence of ribosomal RNA synthesis in the anucleolate mutant of *Xenopus laevis*. Proc. Natl. Acad. Sci., U.S. 51 (1964) 139.

BROWN, D.D. and C.S.WEBER: Gene linkage by RNA–DNA hybridization. II Arrangement of redundant gene sequences for 28S and 18S ribosomal RNA. J. Mol. Biol. 34 (1968) 681.

BROWN, G.M. and G.ATTARDI: Methylation of nucleic acids in HeLa cells. Biochem. Biophys. Res. Commun. 20 (1965) 298.

BUSCH, H., R.DESJARDINS, D.GROGAN, K.HIGASHI, S.JACOB, M.MURAMATSU, T.S.RO and W.J.STEELE: Composition of nucleoli isolated from mammalian cells. Natl. Cancer Inst. Monograph 23 (1966) 193.

COX, E.C., J.R.WHITE and J.G.FLAKS: Streptomycin action and the ribosome. Proc. Natl. Acad. Sci. U.S. 51 (1964) 703.

EDSTRÖM, J.E.: Composition of ribonucleic acid from various parts of spider oocytes. J. Biophys. Biochem. Cytol. 8 (1960) 47.

EDSTRÖM, J.E.: Chromosomal RNA and other nuclear RNA fractions. In: Role of chromosomes in development. New York, Academic Press (1964) 137.

ERRERA, M., A.HELL and R.P.PERRY: The role of the nucleolus in ribonucleic acid and protein synthesis. II. Amino acid incorporation into normal and nucleolar inactivated HeLa cells. Biochim. Biophys. Acta 49 (1961) 58.

FICQ, A. and M.ERRERA: Metabolic processes in cell nuclei. Exptl. Cell Res. Suppl. 7 (1959) 145.

FLAMM, W.G. and M.L.BIRNSTIEL: The nuclear synthesis of ribosomes in cell cultures. Biochim. Biophys. Acta 87 (1964) 101.

FRENSTER, J.H., V.G.ALLFREY and A.E.MIRSKY: In vitro incorporation of amino acids into the proteins of isolated nuclear ribosomes. Biochim. Biophys. Acta 47 (1961) 130.

GALIBERT, F., C.J.LARSEN, J.C.LELONG and M.BOIRON: A ribosomal ribonucleic acid of low molecular weight isolated from mammalian cells. Bull. Soc. Chim. Biol. 48 (1966) 21.

GALL, J.G.: Nuclear RNA of the salamander oocyte. Natl. Cancer Inst. Monograph 23 (1966) 475.

GALL, J.G.: Differential synthesis of the genes for ribosomal RNA during amphibian oögenesis. Proc. Natl. Acad. Sci. U.S. 60 (1968) 553.

GAVRILOVA, L.P., D.A.IVANOV and A.S.SPIRIN: The structure of ribosomes. III. Stepwise unfolding of the 50S particles without loss of ribosomal protein. J. Mol. Biol. 16 (1966) 473.

GEORGIEV, G.P. and O.P.SAMARINA: Metabolic activity of components of the nuclear sap. Biokhimiya 26 (1961) 401.

GEORGIEV, G.P., O.P.SAMARINA, M.I.LERMAN, M.N.SMIRNOV and A. N.SEVERTZOV: Biosynthesis of messenger and ribosomal ribonucleic acids in the nucleolochromosomal apparatus of animal cells. Nature 200 (1963) 1291.

GIRARD, M., H.LATHAM, S.PENMAN and J.E.DARNELL: Entrance of newly formed messenger RNA and ribosomes into HeLa cell cytoplasm. J. Mol. Biol. 11 (1965) 187.

GIRARD, M., S.PENMAN and J.E.DARNELL: The effects of Actinomycin on ribosome formation in HeLa cells. Proc. Natl. Acad. Sci. U.S. 51 (1964) 205.

GREENBERG, H. and S.PENMAN: Methylation and processing of ribosomal RNA in HeLa cells. J. Mol. Biol. 21 (1966) 527.

HALL, B.D. and S.SPIEGELMAN: Sequence complementary of T2-DNA and T2-specific RNA. Proc. Natl. Acad. Sci. U.S. 47 (1961) 137.

HOLLAND, J.J.: Effects of puromycin on RNA synthesis in mammalian cells. Proc. Natl. Acad. Sci. U.S. 50 (1963) 436.

HOSOKAWA, K., R.FUJIMURA and M.NOMURA: Reconstitution of functionally active ribosomes from inactive subparticles and proteins. Proc. Natl. Acad. Sci. U.S. 55 (1966) 198.

KATZ, L. and S.PENMAN: Personal communication.

KEMPF, J. and P.MANDEL: RNA de haut poids moleculaire, rapidement marqué, des sarcomes plasmocytaires de la souris. Bull. Soc. Chim. Biol. 48 (1966) 211.

KLEINFELD, R.: Altered patterns of RNA metabolism in liver cells following partial hepatectomy and thioacetamide treatment. Natl. Cancer Inst. Monograph 23 (1966) 369.

LANE, B.G. and T.TAMAOKI: Studies of the chain termini and alkali-stable dinucleotide sequences in 16S and 28S ribosomal RNA from L cells. J. Mol. Biol. 27 (1967) 335.

LEBOY, P., E.C.COX and J.G.FLAKS: The chromosomal site specifying a ribosomal protein in *Escherichia coli*. Proc. Natl. Acad. Sci., U.S. 52 (1964) 1367.

LIAU, M.C. and R.B.HURLBERT: Comparative studies of RNA synthesis in isolated nucleoli from rat novikoff tumor and rat liver. Proc. Am. Ass. Cancer Res. 7 (1966) 42.

LIAU, M.C. and R.P.PERRY: Ribosome precursor particles in nucleoli. J. Cell Biol. 39 (1968) 81A.

LOENING, U.: The fractionation of high-molecular weight ribonucleic acid by polyacrylamide-gel electrophoresis. Biochem. J. 102 (1967) 251.

MCCONKEY, E.H.: Personal communication.

MCILREAVY, D.J. and J.E.M.MIDGLEY: The chemical structure of bacterial ribosomal RNA. I. Terminal nucleotide sequences of *Escherichia coli* ribosomal RNA. Biochim. Biophys. Acta 142 (1967) 47.

MAGGIO, R.: Progress report on the characterization of nucleoli from guinea pig liver. Natl. Cancer Inst. Monograph 23 (1966) 213.

MONTGOMERY, T.H.: Comparative cytological studies. I. A special regard to the morphology of the nucleolus. J. Morphol. 15 (1898) 265.

MURAMATSU, M.: Methylation of 45 sRNA in the nucleolus. Personal communication. Info. Exchange Group #7, Memo #776.

NAORA, H.: Deoxyribonucleic acid-dependent protein synthesis in nuclear ribosome system *in vitro*. Biochim. Biophys. Acta 123 (1966) 151.

PANEL ON RIBOSOME BIOGENESIS. Natl. Cancer Inst. Monograph 23 (1966) 547.

PELLING, C. and W.BEERMANN: Diversity and variation of the nucleolar organizing regions in *Chironomids*. Natl. Cancer Inst. Monograph 23 (1966) 393.

PENMAN, S., I.SMITH, E.HOLTZMAN and H.GREENBERG: RNA metabolism in the HeLa cell nucleus and nucleolus. Natl. Cancer Inst. Monograph 23 (1966) 489.

PERRY, R.P.: On the nucleolar and nuclear dependence of cytoplasmic RNA synthesis in HeLa cells. Exptl. Cell Res. 20 (1960) 216.

PERRY, R.P.: The cellular sites of synthesis of ribosomal and 4 sRNA. Proc. Natl. Acad. Sci. U.S. 48 (1962) 2179.

PERRY, R.P.: Selective effects of actinomycin D on the intracellular distribution of RNA synthesis in tissue culture cells. Exptl. Cell Res. 29 (1963) 400.

PERRY, R.P.: Role of the nucleolus in ribonucleic acid metabolism and other cellular processes. Natl. Cancer Inst. Monograph 14 (1964) 73.

PERRY, R.P.: The nucleolus and the synthesis of ribosomes. Natl. Cancer Inst. Monograph 18 (1965) 325.

PERRY, R.P.: The nucleolus and the synthesis of ribosomes. In: J.N.Davidson and W.E.Cohn, eds.: Progress in nucleic acid research and molecular biology, Vol. 6. New York, Academic Press (1967) 219.

PERRY, R.P. and M.ERRERA: The influence of nucleolar ribonucleic acid metabolism on that of the nucleus and cytoplasm. In: J.S.Mitchell, ed.: The cell nucleus. London, Butterworth & Co. (1960) 24.

PERRY, R.P., A. HELL and M. ERRERA: The role of the nucleolus in ribonucleic acid and protein synthesis. I. Incorporation of cytidine into normal and nucleolar inactivated HeLa cells. Biochim. Biophys. Acta 49 (1961) 47.

PERRY, R.P. and D.E. KELLEY: Buoyant densities of cytoplasmic ribonucleoprotein particles of mammalian cells: Distinctive character of ribosome subunits and the rapidly labeled components. J. Mol. Biol. 16 (1966a) 255.

PERRY, R.P. and D.E. KELLEY: Evidence for specific association of protein with newly formed ribosomal subunits. Biochem. Biophys. Res. Commun. 24 (1966b) 459.

PERRY, R.P. and D.E. KELLEY: Messenger RNA-protein complexes and newly synthesized ribosomal subunits: analysis of free particles and components of polyribosomes. J. Mol. Biol. 35 (1968) 37.

PERRY, R.P., P.R. SRINIVASAN, D. KELLEY: Hybridization of rapidly labeled nuclear ribonucleic acids. Science 145 (1964) 504.

PETERMAN, M.L.: The physical and chemical properties of ribosomes. Amsterdam, Elsevier (1964).

PETERMAN, M.L. and A. PAVLOVEC: Ribonucleoprotein from a rat tumor, the Jensen sarcoma. J. Biol. Chem. 236 (1961) 3235.

POGO, A.O., B.G.T. POGO, V.C. LITTAU, V.G. ALLFREY, A.E. MIRSKY and M.G. HAMILTON: The purification and properties of ribosomes from the thymus nucleus. Biochim. Biophys. Acta 55 (1962) 849.

PRESCOTT, D.M.: Cellular sites of RNA synthesis. In: J.N. Davidson and W.E. Cohn, eds.: Progress in nucleic acid research and molecular biology, Vol. 3. New York, Academic Press (1964) 33.

PRESCOTT, D.M. and M.A. BENDER: Synthesis of RNA and protein during mitosis in mammalian tissue culture cells. Exptl. Cell Res. 26 (1962) 260.

RAKE, A.V. and A.F. GRAHAM: Kinetics of incorporation of uridine-^{14}C into L-cell RNA (ribonucleic acid). Biophys. J. 4 (1964) 267.

RIFKIN, M.R., D.D. WOOD and D.J.L. LUCK: Ribosomal RNA and ribosomes from mitochondria of *Neurospora crassa*. Proc. Natl. Acad. Sci. U.S. 58 (1967) 1025.

RITOSSA, F.M., K.C. ATWOOD, D.L. LINDSLEY and S. SPIEGELMAN: On the chromosomal distribution of DNA complementary to ribosomal and soluble RNA. Natl. Cancer Inst. Monograph 23 (1966) 449.

RITOSSA, F.M. and S. SPIEGELMAN: Localization of DNA complementary to ribosomal RNA in the nucleolus organizer region of *Drosophila melanogaster*. Proc. Natl. Acad. Sci. U.S. 53 (1965) 737.

ROSSET, R., R. MONIER and J. JULIEN: Ribosomes of *Escherichia coli*. I. Detection of ribosomic ribonucleic acid (RNA) of low molecular weight. Bull. Soc. Chim. Biol. 46 (1964) 87.

SHERRER, K. and J.E. DARNELL: Sedimentation characteristics of rapidly labelled RNA from HeLa cells. Biochem. Biophys. Res. Commun. 7 (1962) 486.

SHERRER, K., H. LATHAM and J.E. DARNELL: Demonstration of an unstable RNA and of a precursor to ribosomal RNA in HeLa cells. Proc. Natl. Acad. Sci. U.S. 49 (1963) 240.

SIEBERT, G., J. VILLALOBOS, T.S. RO, W.J. STEELE, G. LINDENMAYER, H. ADAMS and H. BUSCH: Enzymatic studies on isolated nucleoli of rat liver. J. Biol. Chem. 241 (1966) 71.

SPIRIN, A.S.: In: Struktur und Funktion des genetischen Materials. Berlin, Akademie-Verlag, III (1964) 163, Erwin-Baur-Gedachtnisvorlesungen.

SPIRIN, A.S. and N.V. BELITSINA: Biological activity of the re-assembled ribosome-like particles. J. Mol. Biol. 15 (1966) 282.

STAEHELIN, T. and M. MESELSON: In vitro recovery of ribosomes and of synthetic activity from synthetically inactive ribosomal subunits. J. Mol. Biol. 16 (1966) 245.

STENRAM, V.: Radioautographic RNA and protein labeling and the nucleolar volume in rats following administration of moderate doses of actinomycin D. Exptl. Cell Res. 36 (1964) 242.

STUTZ, E. and H. NOLL: Characterization of cytoplasmic and chloroplast polysomes in plants: Evidence for three classes of ribosomal RNA in nature. Proc. Natl. Acad. Sci. U.S. 57 (1967) 774.

SUSKIND, R.G.: Autoradiographic and cytochemical evidence for synthesis of a lysine-containing ribonucleoprotein in nucleoli inhibited by actinomycin D. J. Cell Biol. 24 (1965) 309.

TAMAOKI, T.: The particulate fraction containing 45 sRNA in L-cell nuclei. J. Mol. Biol. 15 (1966) 624.

TAMAOKI, T. and G.C. MUELLER: The effects of actinomycin D and puromycin on the formation of ribosomes in HeLa cells. Biochim. Biophys. Acta 108 (1965) 73.

VINCENT, W.S.: The isolation and chemical properties of the nucleoli of starfish oocytes. Proc. Natl. Acad. Sci. U.S. 38 (1952) 139.

VINCENT, W.S.: The nucleolus. In: Genetics today. Proc. XI Intern. Congr. of Genet. (1964) 343.

WAGNER, E., S. PENMAN and V. INGRAM: Methylation patterns of HeLa cell ribosomal RNA and its nucleolar precursors. J. Mol. Biol. 3 (1967) 29.

WALLACE, H. and M.L. BIRNSTIEL: Ribosomal cistrons and the nucleolar organizer. Biochim. Biophys. Acta 114 (1966) 296.

WARNER, J.: The assembly of ribosomes in HeLa cells. J. Mol. Biol. 19 (1966) 383.

WARNER, J.R. and R. SOEIRO: Nascent ribosomes from HeLa cells. Proc. Natl. Acad. Sci. U.S. 58 (1967) 1984.

WEINBERG, R.A., V. LOENING, M. WILLEMS and S. PENMAN: Acrylamide gel electrophoresis of HeLa cell nucleolar RNA. Proc. Natl. Acad. Sci. U.S. 58 (1967) 1088.

ZALOKAR, M.: Sites of protein and ribonucleic acid synthesis in the cell. Exptl. Cell Res. 19 (1960) 559.

ZIMMERMAN, E.F. and B.W. HOLLER: Methylation of 45S ribosomal RNA precursor in HeLa cells. J. Mol. Biol. 23 (1967) 149.

PART VIII

Control mechanisms of cellular differentation

CHAPTER 26

Recent studies on developmental regulation in vertebrates

ANNE McLAREN

Institute of Animal Genetics, University of Edinburgh

Contents

1. Regulation of nucleic acid synthesis in eggs
2. Differentiation of the inner cell mass in early embryos
3. The effect of embryo fusion on differentiation
   (a) Sexual differentiation
   (b) Distribution of cells
   (c) Human chimaeras
4. Summary

This chapter will describe three fields of research which the author considers are at present making an active contribution to our understanding of developmental regulation, namely: (1) Regulation of nucleic acid synthesis in eggs. (2) Differentiation of the inner cell mass in early embryos. (3) The effect of embryo fusion on differentiation. These topics are concerned respectively with regulation within the cell (gamete or zygote), regulation between cells in the early embryo, and regulation between cells and tissues in the more complex system of the later embryo.

1. Regulation of nucleic acid synthesis in eggs

Throughout most of oogenesis, the eggs of vertebrates show active synthesis of ribosomal RNA, but no nuclear DNA synthesis. After ovulation, the unfertilized egg synthesizes no DNA and little if any RNA. After fertilization, intense DNA synthesis occurs, but little RNA synthesis.

Some of the factors responsible for the control of DNA synthesis in the egg of the frog (*Xenopus laevis*) have recently been elucidated by Gurdon and his colleagues. Cells from an adult frog's brain very rarely synthesize DNA; if, however, their nuclei are injected into the cytoplasm of an unfertilized egg together with a solution of tritiated thymidine, within an hour they begin to incorporate the radioactive isotope, showing that DNA synthesis has been stimulated. The effect is not very specific: frog egg cytoplasm will also induce DNA synthesis in over 90% of mouse liver nuclei. Removal of the egg nucleus has no effect (Graham et al.). The DNA in the injected frog brain nuclei is replicated much more rapidly than is normal for a somatic cell, though less rapidly than that in the nucleus of a fertilized egg. Brain nuclei are not induced to synthesize DNA by injection into early oocytes, whether into the cytoplasm or into the germinal vesicle (nucleus) or into a mixture of both. It is only when the nuclear envelope has disappeared, which normally occurs under the influence of luteinizing hormone from the pituitary, that the injected nuclei begin to incorporate tritiated thymidine (Gurdon). At this stage of maturation the oocyte's own chromosomes are condensed, and therefore do not synthesize DNA; not until after fertilization or activation does DNA synthesis take place in the pronuclei.

Conversely, if nuclei from a frog blastula, actively synthesizing DNA but little if any RNA, are injected into early oocytes, DNA synthesis is inhibited within 1–2 hours; at this time RNA synthesis commences and continues for up to 3 days (Gurdon and Woodland).

There seems little doubt that, in this instance, nuclear activity (DNA synthesis) depends on the cytoplasmic environment. The exact nature of the DNA-synthesis initiator is not known. It cannot be present in either germinal vesicle or oocyte cytoplasm before maturation; yet once induced, it persists for at least an hour. The pituitary hormone does not act directly on the injected nuclei: *in vitro* incubation of brain nuclei with luteinizing hormone does not stimulate DNA synthesis, nor does injection of nuclei and hormone into oocytes with an intact germinal vesicle (Gurdon). Nuclei injected into the unfertilized egg undergo a marked swelling before DNA synthesis begins: there is some evidence that this is accompanied by the uptake of pre-existing cytoplasmic protein into the nuclei. Suppression of almost all protein synthesis by puromycin, and RNA synthesis by actinomycin D, apparently does not affect the stimulation of DNA synthesis (Gurdon and Woodland).

The state of the cytoplasm appears to determine not only nuclear DNA synthesis, but also RNA synthesis. Intestine nuclei from *Xenopus* tadpoles actively synthesize ribosomal RNA; when they are transplanted to enucleated eggs ribosomal synthesis stops, and only begins again at the gastrula stage, as in normal embryos (Gurdon and Brown). Within an hour of transplantation they undergo a 40-fold increase in volume, reaching the same size as zygote nuclei during this stage, and their definitive nucleoli disappear. In this experiment the genes controlling the synthesis of ribosomal RNA must have undergone transient inactivation, during the period of cleavage. If blastula nuclei are injected into oocytes, not only is DNA synthesis inhibited, as described above, but RNA synthesis is stimulated. Here again the nuclei swell, to a hundred times their normal volume within 12 hours (Gurdon and Woodland). This swelling seems to be characteristic of any change in nuclear synthetic activity, including, for instance, the stimulation of lymphocyte nuclei by phytohaemagglutinin.

The low level of protein synthesis in the unfertilized egg, and its rapid increase after fertilization, seems not to be a consequence of the regulation of nucleic acid synthesis. The unfertilized eggs of sea-urchins (Gross and Cousineau) and amphibia (Brown and Littna) have been found to contain messenger RNA (mRNA) which was presumably produced during oogenesis, but this is thought to be stored in some masked inactive form until fertilization. In early embryos of the loach, Spirin has shown that mRNA is actively synthesized, but that this RNA is not used in protein synthesis until the blastula or gastrula stage. During cleavage, the ribosomes are apparently equipped with the previously inactive maternal mRNA synthesized during oogenesis. A similar situation is found in amphibia (Brown and Littna). Spirin suggests that, both in the unfertilized egg and in the early embryo, mRNA is complexed with protein to form particles somewhat lighter than ribosomes, which he has termed 'informosomes'.

In the mammalian embryo, developing in a protected environment, the synthesis of what is almost certainly ribosomal RNA begins, though at a low level, immediately after fertilization. There is some evidence that paternal genes may be active during cleavage, suggesting that even at this early stage new mRNA is not only being produced, but is actually being used in protein synthesis.

2. *Differentiation of the inner cell mass in early embryos*

The distinction between inner cell mass and trophoblast is the earliest clear-cut evidence of differentiation which can be detected in the mammalian embryo. It arises at the blastocyst stage; in the mouse, a normal embryo contains some 30–60 cells at this time. The trophoblast develops into the foetal placenta and extra-embryonic membranes, while the inner cell mass gives rise to the embryo proper.

The developmental basis of this distinction is still a matter of debate. If chemically different regions of cytoplasm are spatially localized in the fertilized egg, then cytoplasmic segregation during cleavage might be sufficient to account for subsequent differentiation. Dalcq and his colleagues have carried out extensive cytochemical investigations on rodent eggs, and have reported differences between cells in the early cleavage stages (for reviews, see Dalcq; Mulnard 1961). They suggest that the uncleaved egg possesses both polarity and bilateral symmetry, and that the 'dorsal' and 'ventral' cytoplasm is segregated during cleavage so as to produce differentiation into inner cell mass and trophoblast cells respectively. However, conclusions as to causation cannot safely be drawn from descriptive studies alone, and it is therefore necessary to consider experimental evidence as to the developmental potentialities of single blastomeres in early embryos,

If one blastomere of a 2-celled embryo is destroyed, the other may continue developing to produce a normal individual. Seidel (1952, 1960) succeeded in bringing to term rabbits derived from single blastomeres. In mice, Tarkowski (1959a, b; 1965) found that the majority of single blastomeres from the 2-celled stage would develop into blastocysts. These were often normal in size, but the inner cell mass tended to be only about half the size of that in control blastocysts. Embryonic size continued to be approximately halved until about the 10th day of gestation, but by full-term, regulation was complete and birth weight was normal. Sometimes, however, the inner cell mass was very small indeed, or even non-existent, so that the remaining blastomere developed into a so-called 'trophoblastic vesicle', completely devoid of inner cell mass and incapable of further development.

The variation in the results obtained could only be explained on the 'cytoplasmic segregation' hypothesis if the plane of first cleavage bore no constant relation to the plane of bilateral symmetry, so that 'dorsal' and 'ventral' cytoplasm was distributed in a variable manner to the daughter blastomeres.

Moore et al. (personal communication) have tried by similar means to produce identical twins in rabbits (Table 1). In their experiments rabbits have been born from

TABLE 1

Survival of single blastomeres of rabbit embryos, after destruction of all other blastomeres in zona at various cell stages. (From Moore et al., unpublished.)

Cell stage	Number of embryos: Transferred	Survived to 10 days	Percent survival
2	70	26	37
4	72	19	26
8	72	11	15

a single blastomere surviving from the 2-cell, 4-cell or even 8-cell stage. Unfortunately their attempts to induce development of both blastomeres, separated at the 2-celled stage, were unsuccessful because the rabbit embryo, unlike the mouse, is apparently unable to develop without a zona pellucida. They tried transferring one blastomere to a previously evacuated zona, but this also was unsuccessful.

In order to test the hypothesis that potential trophoblastic and inner cell mass material was spatially localized in the fertilized egg, Mulnard (1965) separated the blastomeres at the 2-celled stage in mice, and obtained 16 cases in which both partners continued to develop in culture. If the first cleavage resulted in segregation of such cytoplasmic material, the two partners should have developed in a complementary fashion, so that if inner cell mass material were strongly represented in one, it should have been weak or absent in the other. But no complementarity was apparent. In some pairs both members showed some inner cell mass material, while in others, both developed into trophoblastic vesicles (Table 2). In fact the data are exactly as would be expected if the probability of developing inner cell mass material were equal for each blastomere.

The development *in vitro* of single blastomeres from disaggregated 4- and 8-cell mouse embryos has been studied by Tarkowski and Wróblewska. Cleavage rate appeared unaffected by disaggregation, so that 8-cell embryos cultured for 36–48 hours contained eight times as many cells as did single blastomeres from 8-cell stages, cultured for the same period of time. The incidence of blastocysts, as opposed to trophoblastic vesicles, was lower when pairs of blastomeres were isolated from 8-cell stages (31 %) than when single blastomeres were isolated from 4-cell embryos (45 %), although in terms of cytoplasmic constitution, these two forms should be equivalent. The difference may reflect a different reaction of the older stages to *in vitro* culture. When single blastomeres from 8-cell stages were isolated the incidence of blastocysts was still lower (18 %).

The material includes 17 embryos where the fate of every blastomere was observed: in some of these cases up to three of the sister blastomeres gave rise to blastocysts, but in a number of others, only forms lacking an inner cell mass were produced (e.g. trophoblastic vesicles).

TABLE 2

Presence (+) or absence (−) of 'positive' cells (i.e. those showing the presence of inner cell mass material) in paired embryos developing from separated blastomeres. (Data from Mulnard 1965.)

Embryo 1	Embryo 2	No. of pairs
+	+	4
+	−	8
−	−	4

These data are hard to explain on any preformationist theory of the cytoplasmic segregation type, but agree well with the epigenetic hypothesis proposed by Tarkowski and Wróblewska. According to this, the fate of a blastomere is still labile at the 8-cell stage, and is determined at the morula stage (which contains 20–30 cells in the mouse), by whether it is on the outside of the embryo, surrounded by the external medium, or on the inside, surrounded by other cells. The outer cells develop into trophoblast, the inner ones into inner cell mass. If, at the time that the blastocoele fluid begins to be secreted, the ball of cells is not large enough to contain any members isolated from the external medium, then a trophoblastic vesicle will be produced, devoid of inner cell mass. The arrangement as well as the number of cells is presumably important: Tarkowski and Wróblewska illustrate a 4-cell 'morula', in which one blastomere is completely enclosed by the other three. Some of their blastocysts contain only 8 cells, 2 in the inner cell mass and the remaining 6 trophoblastic.

A comparison of the results of Moore et al. with those of Tarkowski and Wróblewska suggests that single blastomeres from the 8-cell stage are more likely to develop normally (implying the differentiation of an inner cell mass) in rabbits than in mice. This is to be expected on the 'enclosure' hypothesis, since mouse eggs are already cavitating at the 5th cleavage division (32 cells), while rabbit eggs probably do not begin to cavitate till the 6th or 7th cleavage division (Adams, personal communication). The $\frac{1}{8}$ rabbit can therefore amass more cells before cavitation starts.

The secretion of blastocoele fluid at a certain time after fertilization seems, from Tarkowski and Wróbleska's observations, to be an inherent property of the cells of the egg, which appears irrespective of its developmental fate, even if cleavage is suppressed.

3. The effect of embryo fusion on differentiation

When mouse embryos are deprived of the zona pellucida at the 8-cell stage, they will fuse together, and continue their development as a single chimaeric individual. The first report of mice born as a result of this ingenious technique was from Tarkowski (1961). The following year Mintz published an abstract (Mintz 1962), showing that she had independently been working along very similar lines, and in 1964 she described results of various studies in which chimaeras were allowed to develop to the blastocyst stage, fusing lethal with normal, and radioactively labelled with unlabelled embryos (Mintz 1964, 1965a). Her technique is more convenient than Tarkowski's in at least two respects, namely enzymatic rather than mechanical removal of the zona, and aggregation of blastomeres at 37 °C rather than at room temperature.

The technique of embryo fusion has been slow to spread to species other than the mouse, but recently J.L. Hancock and Eleanor Pighills (personal communication) have attempted to fuse sheep embryos. The zona pellucida had to be removed mechanically, as it was resistant to treatment with pronase, and total fusion between pairs of embryos proved hard to obtain. After transfer to pseudopregnant ewes, several embryos in the experimental series developed to term. Where the transferrin types of the animals were known, it is possible to compare the supposedly chimaeric lamb with its four putative parents (Table 3). In one case, where the lamb died late in gestation, there is good evidence that chimaerism had in fact been obtained.

TABLE 3

Parentage of 3 lambs born to ewes receiving fused eggs. (From Hancock and Pighills, unpublished.)

Recipient ewe	Eggs transferred after fusion	Lambs born
Blackface (BD)	Blackface (AC × AB) Blackface (AC × CE)	Blackface ♂ (AC)
Blackface (CD)	Blackface (AC × CE) Blackface (AC × AB)	Blackface ♂ (BCE)
Blackface (CD)	Blackface (AC × DD) Welsh (BC × BB or BC)	Blackface ♀ (AD)

Transferrin types are given in parenthesis; for the transferred eggs, the mother's and father's types are given for both of the fused partners. Normally, an individual is characterized by two transferrin types only; the supposed chimaeric lamb showed three.

The two major fields of study which have been illuminated by Tarkowski's and Mintz' experiments are first, sexual differentiation and the fate of sex chimaeras, and second, the distribution of cells in the developing embryo, and the differentiation of pattern.

(a) *Sexual differentiation*

Tarkowski's original series contained 3 hermaphrodites out of a total of 14 presumed chimaeras (Tarkowski 1961, 1964b). The remaining mice consisted of 9 males and only 2 females. Mintz (1965b) confirmed the rare occurrence of hermaphrodites, and also the preponderance of males. Her most recent data are described in Mintz (1968)*. On *a priori* grounds, 50% of all embryo fusions should be between male and female embryos, and one might expect all these to show some evidence of hermaphroditism

* This paper was not available to the author when the present chapter was written.

in their later development. At least four explanations can be put forward to account for the low incidence of hermaphrodites. (1) All the cells derived from one component may often be concentrated in the trophoblast, so that the embryo proper would be non-chimaeric. In this case not only would no hermaphroditism develop, but genetic and chromosomal analysis would yield no evidence of chimaerism. (2) The sex of an individual may be determined by the sex of a relatively small number of cells (e.g. in the primitive gonad) at a particular stage of embryonic development, small enough to have a good chance of all stemming from either one component or the other. (3) Sexual development may be so highly canalized that a very small overall majority of male or female cells in the body may be enough to switch sexual development into the male or female channel respectively. (4) The majority of potentially hermaphrodite chimaeras may develop in a phenotypically male direction. This, which was Tarkowski's original hypothesis, would account not only for the scarcity of hermaphrodites, but also for the predominantly male sex ratio.

This last hypothesis has been confirmed by the recent work of Mystkowska and Tarkowski, in which the chromosomes of mice developing from fused embryos were analysed for evidence of chimaerism and also to determine the karyotypic sex of the chimaera components. Of 8 mice examined 6 proved to be cell chimaeras: one of these had arisen from the fusion of female embryos, and two from male embryos. Of the remaining three, each of which developed from fusion of a female with a male embryo, one was a hermaphrodite (testis on one side, ovotestis on the other), but the other two were normal, fully fertile males. In the bone marrow, the hermaphrodite showed 96%, and the two males 51% and 19%, of cells of female origin. If these percentages are typical, one may conclude that the majority, perhaps the overwhelming majority, of cells in a mammalian embryo have to be of XX constitution before development is shifted in the female direction.

Among female cattle, twins to males, the degree of masculinization of the reproductive tract was found by Herschler and Fechheimer to be positively correlated with the percentage of XY cells (ranging from 3–100%) in cultures of peripheral blood.

The occurrence of fertile male mice, chimaeric for XX and XY cells, enables one to look for sex reversal in the germ cells. In amphibia, the type of gametogenesis of germ cells does not depend on their genetic sex but on the type of somatic differentiation of the gonads (see Burns 1961, for references). If the same were true in mammals, it might be possible to get XX cells undergoing spermatogenesis: mating with a normal female would then give entirely female progeny. This intriguing possibility (of potential economic importance) is not supported by Mystkowska and Tarkowski's results. XX/XX and XY/XY chimaeras produced germ cells of both genetic types, but the two fertile XX/XY males only produced sperm corresponding to the genotype of the XY component. The data given in Table 4 can be used to test the null hypothesis that, in an XX/XY chimaera, both cell types are equally likely to undergo spermatogenesis. By Fisher's exact test, a distribution similar to that observed would be expected by chance on only 1 in 10 occasions; when account is taken of the fact that the deviation

TABLE 4

Results of breeding tests and chromosomal analysis on 5 fertile chimaeric mice. (From Mystkowska and Tarkowski.)

	Chimaeras producing progeny of one genetic type	Chimaeras producing progeny of two genetic types
XX/XY chimaeras	2	0
XX/XX and XY/XY chimaeras	0	3

is in the expected direction, and further, that for each of the two chimaeras producing only one type of progeny there is only a 50% probability that the progeny observed would correspond to the XY component, it can be seen that the data indicate a considerably higher probability level. It therefore seems unlikely (though not yet excluded) that XX cells can be induced to undergo spermatogenesis in mice.

Whether this conclusion holds also for other mammals is not clear. XX cells have been reported in the testes of adult male marmosets born from heterosexual twin pregnancies and showing sex-chromosome chimaerism in the bone marrow (Benirschke and Burnhill). XX cells have also been detected in the testes of newborn bulls from twin pregnancies with a free-martin (Ohno et al.); on the other hand serological examination of 17 progeny from one such bull failed to prove that any spermatozoa had developed from XX germ cells (Stone et al.). Turner and Asakawa have observed secondary spermatocytes in the sex cords of masculinized mouse ovaries; conversely, XY germ cells in the transformed testis of an opposum were apparently not subject to the first reduction division (Burns 1956).

Further evidence that the type of gametogenesis may be under genetic rather than environmental control comes from Mystkowska and Tarkowski's observations of oocytes growing within the otherwise normal testis of a 5-day-old chimaeric mouse.

(b) *Distribution of cells*

The chimaeric nature of mice developed from fused embryos was established first by an examination of the retinas of pink-eyed/agouti chimaeras (Tarkowski 1961, 1964a). More recent evidence comes from the variegation in coat colour often shown by chimaeric individuals differing for coat colour markers (Mintz 1965a, b, 1967; Mystkowska and Tarkowski), from the breeding behaviour of presumed chimaeras (Mystkowska and Tarkowski), from chromosomal analyses of bone marrow cells (Mystkowska and Tarkowski) and from electrophoretic analyses of isocitrate dehydrogenase isozymes (Mintz and Baker).

Mice homozygous for allelic variants at the autosomal *isocitrate dehydrogenase-1* locus produce only a single isozyme band each upon electrophoresis; the heterozygote produces the two parental enzymes, and also a third, hybrid enzyme. When pure-strain embryos differing at this locus were fused, the hybrid enzyme could be demonstrated in skeletal muscle of the resulting chimaeras, though not in cardiac muscle, nor in non-muscular tissue (Mintz and Baker). This finding confirms the origin of syncytial skeletal muscle by myoblast fusion, rather than by repeated nuclear division without cell division. It also suggests that the monomeric polypeptides making up this enzyme are synthesized separately, and then assembled into the complete protein in the cytoplasm. Since diffusion of monomers between cells apparently does not occur, the alleles on both chromosomes must be functioning in F_1 hybrid cells.

Of the various lines of evidence outlined above, only the bone marrow and the breeding analyses give accurate quantitative evidence as to the relative frequency of cells from the two chimaera components. Some individuals have been found with more or less equal amounts of the two components, while in others, one component is in the overwhelming majority. The two components are not necessarily present in the same relative proportions in different tissues.

As to the spatial distribution of the genetically differing cell types within the chimaeric individual, only the retinas and the coat bear witness. In the retinas (Tarkowski 1961, 1964a), the chimaerism is astonishingly fine-grained, with patches of pigmented and non-pigmented cells containing not more than a hundred or so cells in each. This must imply an enormous amount of cell mixing in the course of ontogeny. A very similar mosaic appearance of the retina is seen in the mottled mice which develop when an autosomal segment of chromosome heterozygous for a colour marker is translocated onto the X-chromosome, and hence, according to the Lyon hypothesis, becomes involved in X-chromosome inactivation (Cattanach, personal communication).

The characteristic striped markings often found in mice derived from the fusion of embryos differing in coat colour genes was first commented on by Mintz (1965a, b). In a recent paper (Mintz 1967), she describes what she terms the 'standard pattern', consisting of 3 transverse bands on the head, 6 on the body and 8 on the tail; other patterns, derived from this basic plan, were also seen. To explain the existence of these bands, Mintz postulates that each consists of a clone of melanoblasts, descended by cell division from a single primordial melanoblast. Thus two longitudinal mid-dorsal chains of 17 melanoblasts each would exist in the neural crest. According to this hypothesis, the 17 aligned melanoblasts 'seem first to take up alternating rather than random position in the chains', i.e. alternating according to the chimaera component of origin (coloured versus albino, for example).

Mystkowska and Tarkowski also report variegation in the coat colour of some (though not all) of the individuals proved in other ways to be chimaeric, developed from fused 'agouti' and 'pink-eyed' embryos. Although they observed transverse banding in some animals, they failed to detect any definite or constant pattern of pigmentation. The light and dark areas are reported as showing mixed composition of hair, and being irregular in outline and variable in size.

The possibility that the striped pattern of some coat colour chimaeras reflects major embryological cell movements seems unlikely in view of the fine-grained nature of the retinal chimaerism. Further, the relative proportions of the two chimaera components will be expected to vary from individual to individual from the very outset of embryonic development, according to how many cells each partner contributes to the inner cell mass rather than to the trophoblast. It should follow from Mintz' clonal hypothesis that, when one partner is represented considerably less than the other, fewer than 17 of the 34 'primordial melanocytes' will belong to the minority genotype. One would then expect to find fewer bands of the corresponding coat colour, but those bands that do develop should be of normal size. This 'all-or-none' result is not borne out by the published photographs; those chimaeric animals with a preponderance of one coat colour appear to show several small and irregular bands of the minority colour, rather than one or two large bands.

How then does the pattern come about? The problem is similar to the one that Grüneberg has discussed in relation to the ordered pattern shown by heterozygotes for coat colour markers (e.g. *tabby*) located on the X-chromosome, though tabby mice show thinner and much more regular striping than do chimaeras. Grüneberg is puzzled by how *random* inactivation of one X-chromosome per cell (the Lyon or 'inactive-X' hypothesis) could bring about an *ordered* coat colour pattern, and suggests that the transverse striping may have its developmental basis in the transverse skin wrinkling shown by mouse foetuses, or the transverse skin folds which arise postnatally. This seems plausible for tabby mice, but less so for chimaeras. Grüneberg goes further, and argues that the inactive-X hypothesis is untenable. I would suggest that, both in experimental chimaeras and in X-chromosome heterozygotes, one is dealing with an underlying fine-grained mosaicism of the type demonstrated in the retina of both types of mice; and that this enables a genetically determined 'pre-pattern' to be manifested through secondary shifts in cell distribution and/or gene expression. In other words, the existence of more than one genetically distinct cell population, whether due to embryo fusion or to X-chromosome inactivation, is a *necessary* condition for the manifestation of the pattern, but it may not, by itself, be a sufficient condition.

In the case of embryo fusion, one possible type of shift of cell distribution which could be causally related to the development of coat colour pattern is specific cell aggregation within the neural crest. The retina seems to be one of the most reliably chimaeric regions of the body: in the animals so far examined, if chimaerism could be demonstrated anywhere, it was seen in the retina. Yet the retina is derived, embryologically, from a relatively small area of the neural plate. If this small area has a mixed cell population, fine-grained cellular mixing must surely be present throughout the neural crest at the same stage of development. The appearance of transverse markings could then be due to a tendency for aggregation of like cells with like within the neural crest, at a stage before ventral migration of the neural crest cells takes place. If one cell type were in the minority, it would form smaller, but not necessarily fewer, stripes.

As we have seen, this agrees well with observation. Different combinations of genotypes might differ in the degree of aggregation which the components showed: this would lead to different coat colour markings in the chimaeric individual. In particular, Mystkowska and Tarkowski's animals, where the two cell types were very closely related (CBA-p and CBA-T6T6), would be expected to show less striking aggregation patterns than Mintz', where embryos from two different inbred strains were fused; this might explain the more regular and definite coat colour patterns reported by Mintz.

(c) *Human chimaeras*

In our own species, numerous reports exist of individuals containing cells of more than one genotype. Many of these are doubtless cases of mosaicism, arising through non-disjunction or somatic mutation, but some are hard to interpret as other than chimaeras. (The term 'mosaic' is applied to individuals derived from two gametes only, in contrast to a chimaera, which is the product of more than two gametes.)

In particular, there have been a number of cases documented in which two chromosomally distinct cell populations exist, one with an apparently normal female complement (XX) and the other with an apparently normal male complement (XY), or in one case one with 46 chromosomes and the other with 47 (trisomy G), differing from one another in respect of one or more genetically determined characters (e.g. blood groups). The XX/XY individuals are usually phenotypically male, with varying degrees of hermaphroditism. The presence of two cell lines differing at a number of loci for which the parents are allelic suggests strongly that here we are dealing with chimaerism. Indeed, one of the cases (Zuelzer et al.), which occurred in a boy of mixed Negro-Amerindian-Caucasian ancestry, shows a pattern of patchy skin pigmentation somewhat reminiscent of Mintz' mice. The darker skin (XX) constituted only about 10% of the total body surface, and grew more slowly in culture than did the lighter (XY) skin.

By analysis of blood groups and genetically determined biochemical variants, it is often possible to show that each parent has contributed two sets of genes, one to each cell line. As an example, I shall cite a recent unpublished case, kindly made available by Dr. Ferguson-Smith, of a 15-year-old true hermaphrodite with bilateral ovotestes, and rudimentary uterus and tubes. 5% of his lymphocyte mitoses and 73% of his fibroblast mitoses were XX, the remainder XY. He secreted both A and H substance in his saliva, his serum contained no anti-A antibodies, and 3% of his red cells belonged to group A_2, the remainder to group O. The two classes of red cells were separated by ABO agglutination, and typed for the acid phosphatase (A, B, C) and phosphoglucomutase (1, 2) loci. The results in Table 5 show that the patient must have received a double genetic contribution from each of his parents (Ferguson-Smith, Renwick, Izatt, Marian and Mack, unpublished observations).

Whether any of these cases of apparent chimaerism are a consequence of embryonic

TABLE 5

Genetic constitutions at 3 loci of the two distinct red cell populations in an XX/XY true hermaphrodite, and of his parents. (From Ferguson-Smith, Renwick, Izatt, Marian and Mack, unpublished observations.)

	ABO	Acid phosphatase	Phosphoglucomutase
Mother	O	AB	2:1
Father	A_2	BC	1:1
Patient			
Red-cell population 1 (97%)	O	BB	1:1
Presumed genotype of egg	O	B	1
Presumed genotype of sperm	O	B	1
Red-cell population 2 (3%)	A_2	AC	2:1
Presumed genotype of egg	O	A	2
Presumed genotype of sperm	A_2	C	1

fusion has not been established. In the mouse, fusion has only been induced experimentally in embryos up to the blastocyst stage. Since mouse embryos do not lose the zona spontaneously at this stage, it seems unlikely that, in this species at least, embryonic fusion could take place *in vivo*. But no information exists as to the timing or mode of loss of the zona in our own species.

An alternative interpretation which may account for some of the observations is double fertilization, i.e. fertilization of the egg by one spermatozoon and the first or second polar body by another, with subsequent incorporation of the cleavage products of both into the developing embryo. This may not be so unlikely as it sounds: Braden has shown, again in the mouse, that either the first or, more often, the second meiotic division occasionally results in the formation of two almost equally sized cells ('immediate cleavage'), instead of one large oocyte and a smaller polar body. It has also been suggested that a mitotic division of the haploid female pronucleus might occur, with again each product fertilized by a different sperm.

These various suggested mechanisms give rise to differing genetic expectations. All involve two spermatozoa, so there should be a 50% chance of demonstrating a double genetic contribution at any locus for which the father is heterozygous. The evidence summarized in Table 6 shows that at 9 out of 10 such loci, a double genetic contribution from the father could be demonstrated. (The significant departure from expectation may be an artefact, since presumably the parents would be more likely to be examined for those characters for which the two cell lines of the patient had already been shown to differ.) If chimaera formation is by embryo fusion, or by double fertilization of products of the first meiotic division, there should equally be a 50% chance of demonstrating a double genetic contribution at any locus for which the mother is heterozygous. Double fertilization of products of the second meiotic division would reduce this probability to below 25%, with genes nearest the centromere being least likely to show any further segregation, while double fertilization of mitotic products should give identical maternal contributions. Unfortunately the evidence (Table 6) is inconclusive: in 3 cases, the two diploid cell lines were identical with respect to each of several independently segregating traits identifiable as maternal in origin, suggesting that the two fertilized egg nuclei were mitotic products of a post-meiotic nucleus, while in the remainder, the maternal contribution must have consisted of two dissimilar egg nuclei.

TABLE 6

Evidence as to the double genetic contribution from each parent in 7 human chimaeras

	Father		Mother	
Reference	No. of loci 'at risk'	No. showing evidence of double contribution	No. of loci 'at risk'	No. showing evidence of double contribution
Gartler et al.	2	2	4	0
De Grouchy et al.	1	1	2	0
Zuelzer et al.	2	2	4	1
Myhre et al.	2	1	5	0
Brøgger and Gudersen	0	–	2	2
Corey et al.	1	1	3	3
Ferguson-Smith et al. (unpublished)	2	2	2	2

All were XX/XY chimaeras, except that described by Brøgger et al. in which one of the two cell lines was distinguished by showing trisomy G. Loci 'at risk' are those loci (a) at which the father or mother is heterozygous, and so has an equal chance of contributing each allele to any one gamete, and (b) at which the other parent does not possess the same two alleles, since it would then be impossible to tell from which parent the double contribution came.

If a single mechanism is to be invoked, then double fertilization of products of the second meiotic division would be the most likely, but it may be that different individuals owe their chimaerism to different developmental anomalies.

4. Summary

(1) Experiments involving nuclear transplantation into amphibian eggs suggest that nuclear RNA and DNA synthesis are under cytoplasmic control. The DNA-synthesis initiator develops during the course of oocyte maturation, under the influence of pituitary hormones.
(2) Differentiation of the early embryo into trophoblast and inner cell mass has been investigated by isolating single blastomeres of mouse and rabbit embryos at the 2-cell,

4-cell and 8-cell stage. The results do not support the view that cytoplasmic regions corresponding to future trophoblast and inner cell mass material exist in the fertilized egg, but indicate that the fate of the cells is determined epigenetically, by their position in the ball of cells comprising the morula.

(3) The technique of fusing pairs of 8-cell mouse embryos has added to our understanding of development in the following ways:

(a) The fine-grained nature of the chimaerism at the neural plate stage implies a remarkable amount of cell mixing during early embryogenesis. At least some chimaeric individuals subsequently develop fairly regular large-scale coat patterns; the developmental mechanism underlying this has not yet been satisfactorily established.

(b) The development of multinucleate myotubes in skeletal muscle has been proved to be by cell fusion rather than by nuclear division.

(c) Fusion between male and female embryos results in XX/XY chimaeras. Most of these develop as apparently normal, fertile males; probably only when XX cells are in a considerable majority does the individual develop as a hermaphrodite.

(d) The available evidence suggests that XX cells in XX/XY male chimaeras do not undergo spermatogenesis.

(4) A few chromosomal chimaeras (usually XX/XY individuals) have been reported in our own species. Analysis of blood groups and biochemical traits establishes that they must have received a double genetic contribution from the father and sometimes also from the mother. Although some of these human chimaeras may have arisen through the fusion of embryos, a more likely explanation would seem to be double fertilization of some form of binucleate egg.

Acknowledgements

I am grateful to Dr. Gurdon (Dept. of Zoology, University of Oxford), Drs. Moore, Adams and Rowson (Agricultural Research Council Unit of Reproductive Physiology and Biochemistry, Cambridge), Dr. Hancock and Miss Pighills (Animal Breeding Research Organization, Edinburgh), Drs. Mystkowska and Tarkowski (Dept. of Embryology, University of Warsaw) and Dr. Ferguson-Smith (Dept. of Genetics, University of Glasgow), for generously making their experimental results available to me before publication.

References

BENIRSCHKE, K. and L.E. BROWNHILL: Heterosexual cells in testes of chimeric marmoset monkeys. Cytogenetics 2 (1963) 331.

BRADEN, A.W.H.: Variation between strains in the incidence of various abnormalities of egg maturation and fertilization. J. Genet. 55 (1957) 476.

BRØGGER, A. and S.K. GUDERSEN: Double fertilization in Down's syndrome. Lancet 1 (1966) 1270.

BROWN, D.D. and E.LITTNA: RNA synthesis during the development of *Xenopus laevis*, the South African clawed toad. J. Mol. Biol. 8 (1964) 669.

BURNS, R.K.: Transformation du testicule embryonnaire de l'opossum en ovotestis ou en 'ovaire' sous l'action de l'hormone femelle, le dipropionate d'oestradiol. Arch. Anat. Microscop. Morphol. Exp. 45 (1956) 173.

BURNS, R.K.: Role of hormones in the differentiation of sex. In: W.C.Young, ed.: Sex and internal secretions, vol. 1, 3rd edition. Baltimore, Williams and Wilkins Co. (1961).

COREY, M.J., J.R.MILLER, J.R.MACLEAN and BRUCE CHOWN: A case of XX/XY mosaicism. Am. J. Human Genet. 19 (1967) 378.

DALCQ, A.M.: Introduction to general embryology. London, Oxford University Press (1957) pp. 103–128.

DE GROUCHY, J., J.MOULLEC, C.SALMON, N.JOSSO, J.FREZAL and M.LAMY: Hermaphrodisme avec caryotype XX/XY. Etude génétique d'un cas. Ann. Génét. 7 (1964) 25.

GARTLER, S.M., S.H.WAXMAN and E.R.GIBLETT: An XX/XY human hermaphrodite resulting from double fertilization. Proc. Natl. Acad. Sci. U.S. 48 (1962) 332.

GRAHAM, C.F., K.ARMS and J.B.GURDON: The induction of DNA synthesis by frog egg cytoplasm. Develop. Biol. 14 (1966) 349.

GROSS, P.R. and G.H.COUSINEAU: Macromolecule synthesis and the influence of actinomycin on early development. Exptl. Cell Res. 33 (1964) 368.

GRÜNEBERG, H.: More about the tabby mouse and about the Lyon hypothesis. J. Embryol. Exptl. Morphol. 16 (1966) 569.

GURDON, J.B.: On the origin and persistence of a cytoplasmic state inducing nuclear DNA synthesis in frogs' eggs. Proc. Natl. Acad. Sci. U.S. 58 (1967) 545.

GURDON, J.B. and D.D.BROWN: Cytoplasmic regulation of RNA synthesis and nucleolus formation in developing embryos of *Xenopus laevis*. J. Mol. Biol. 12 (1965) 27.

GURDON, J.B. and H.R.WOODLAND: The cytoplasmic control of nuclear activity in animal development. Biol. Rev. 43 (1968) 233.

HERSCHLER, M.S. and N.S.FECHHEIMER: The role of sex chromosome chimaerism in altering sexual development of mammals. Cytogenetics 6 (1967) 204.

MINTZ, B.: Formation of genotypically mosaic mouse embryos. Amer. Zool. 2 (1962) Abstr. No. 310.

MINTZ, B.: Formation of genetically mosaic mouse embryos, and early development of 'lethal (t^{12}/t^{12}) – normal' mosaics. J. Exptl. Zool. 157 (1964) 273.

MINTZ, B.: Genetic mosaicism in adult mice of quadriparental lineage. Science 148 (1965a) 1232.

MINTZ, B.: Experimental genetic mosaicism in the mouse. In: G.E.W.Wolstenholme and M. O'Connor, eds.: Ciba Fndn. symp. on Preimplantation stages of pregnancy. London, Churchill (1965b) 194.

MINTZ, B.: Gene control of mammalian pigmentary differentiation. 1. Clonal origin of melanocytes. Proc. Natl. Acad. Sci., U.S. 58 (1967) 344.

MINTZ, B.: In: A.Nalbandov, ed.: Proc. 8th Bienn. Symp. Anim. Repr., Urbana. (1968). In press.

MINTZ, B. and W.W.BAKER: Normal mammalian muscle differentiation and gene control of isocitrate dehydrogenase synthesis. Proc. Natl. Acad. Sci., U.S. 58 (1967) 592.

MULNARD, J.G.: Problèmes de structure et d'organisation morphogénétique de l'oeuf des Mammifères. In: Symposium on The germ cells and earliest stages of development. Milan, Fondazione A. Baselli, Instituto Lombardo (1961) 639.

MULNARD, J.G.: Studies of regulation of mouse ova *in vitro*. In: G.E.W.Wolstenholme and M. O'Connor, eds.: Ciba Fndn. symp. on Preimplantation stages of pregnancy. London, Churchill (1965) 123.

MYHRE, B.A., T.MEYER, J.M.OPITZ, R.R.RACE, R.SANGER and T.J.GREENWALT: Two populations of erythrocytes associated with XX/XY mosaicism. Transfusion (Philad.) 5 (1965) 501.

MYSTKOWSKA, E.T. and A.K.TARKOWSKI: Observations on CBA-p/CBA-T6 T6 mouse chimaeras. J. Embryol. Exptl. Morphol. 19 (1968) in press.

OHNO, S., J.M.TRUJILLO, C.STENIUS, L.C.CHRISTIAN and R.L.TEPLITZ: Possible germ cell chimeras among newborn dizygotic twin calves (*Bos taurus*). Cytogenetics 1 (1962) 258.

SEIDEL, F.: Die Entwicklungspotenzen einen isolierten Blastomere des Zweizellenstadiums im Säugetiere. Naturwissenschaften 39 (1952) 355.

SEIDEL, F.: Die Entwicklungsfähigkeiten isolierter Furchungszellen aus dem Ei des Kaninchens *Oryctolagus cuniculus*. Arch. Entwicklungsmech. Org. 152 (1960) 43.

SPIRIN, A.S.: On 'masked' forms of messenger RNA in early embryogenesis and in other differentiating systems. Curr. Top. Develop. Biol. 1 (1966) 1.

STONE, W.H., D.T.BERMAN, W.J.TYLER and M.R.IRWIN: Blood types of the progeny of a pair of cattle twins showing erythrocyte mosaicism. J. Hered. 51 (1960) 136.

TARKOWSKI, A.K.: Experiments on the development of isolated blastomeres of mouse eggs. Nature 184 (1959a) 1286.

TARKOWSKI, A.K.: Experimental studies on regulation in the development of isolated blastomeres of mouse egg. Acta Theriol. 3 (1959b) 191.

TARKOWSKI, A.K.: Mouse chimaeras developed from fused eggs. Nature 190 (1961) 857.

TARKOWSKI, A.K.: Studies on mouse chimaeras developed from eggs fused *in vitro*. Natl. Cancer Inst. Monograph 11 (1963) 51.

TARKOWSKI, A.K.: Patterns of pigmentation in experimentally produced mouse chimaerae. J. Embryol. Exptl. Morphol. 12 (1964a) 575.

TARKOWSKI, A.K.: True hermaphroditism in chimaeric mice. J. Embryol. Exptl. Morphol. 12 (1964b) 735.

TARKOWSKI, A.K.: Embryonic and postnatal development of mouse chimaeras. In: G.E.W.Wolstenholme and M.O'Connor, eds.: Ciba Fndn. symp. on Preimplantation stages of pregnancy. London, Churchill (1965) 183.

TARKOWSKI, A.K. and J.WROBLEWSKA: Development of blastomeres of mouse eggs isolated at the 4- and 8-cell stage. J. Embryol. Exptl. Morphol. 18 (1967) 155.

TURNER, C.D. and H.ASAKAWA: Experimental reversal of germ cells in ovaries of fetal mice. Science 143 (1964) 1344.

ZUELZER, W.W., K.M.BEATTIE and L.E.REISMAN: Generalized unbalanced mosaicism attributable to dispermy and probable fertilization of a polar body. Am. J. Human Genet. 16 (1964) 38.

CHAPTER 27

Cytochemical properties of nuclear proteins and deoxyribonucleoprotein complexes in relation to nuclear function

NILS R. RINGERTZ

Institute for Medical Cell Research and Genetics, Karolinska Institutet, Stockholm

Contents

1. Introduction
2. Methodological aspects
   (a) The Feulgen reaction
   (b) UV absorption
   (c) Dye binding
   (d) Melting profile of DNP
   (e) Actinomycin binding
3. Nuclear proteins and the cell growth cycle
   (a) Nuclear dry mass
   (b) Histones
   (c) Deoxyribonucleoprotein complexes
4. Nuclear proteins and cell differentiation
   (a) General
   (b) Spermiogenesis
   (c) Reactivation of hen erythrocyte nuclei
   (d) Cell hybridization experiments with hen erythrocytes
   (e) Reactivation of the erythrocyte nucleus and the role of cell membranes
   (f) Phytohemagglutinin (PHA) stimulation
5. Some aspects on the regulation of gene expression during nuclear activation
   (a) Early DNP changes
   (b) Enzymatic modifications of DNA-bound proteins
   (c) Synthesis of rapidly labelled RNA
   (d) Increase in nuclear dry mass and volume
   (e) DNA synthesis
   (f) Nucleolus and ribosomal RNA synthesis
   (g) Specific protein synthesis
6. Conclusions

1. Introduction

Very little is known about the mechanisms regulating the synthesis of RNA in animal and plant cell nuclei. It seems likely, however, that regulatory mechanisms similar to those discovered in bacteria may also be operating in higher cells.

Animal and plant cells differ from bacteria in that histones and other proteins are bound to their nuclear DNA. To the deoxyribonucleoprotein (DNP) are also bound divalent metal ions and other low molecular substances which may modify the functional properties of the DNP. Several years ago Stedman and Stedman suggested that histones may be involved in the regulation of gene activity. At the time there was very little evidence in support of this theory. Work during the last decade has established that histones block the ability of DNA to function as a template for RNA synthesis. Furthermore, these proteins seem to be important in stabilizing the double helical structure of DNA, in the packing of nucleoprotein helices into superhelices and in the maintenance of chromatin and chromosome structures. (For reviews see Bonner et al., and Busch.) It now seems quite reasonable in the light of these observations to hypothesize that the DNA-linked histones may be part of a system regulating genetic activity at the transcription level. The evolution of new control mechanisms in addition to those found in bacteria may very well be the basis for such complex phenomena as e.g. cell differentiation in higher organisms.

The main purpose of this review is to correlate changes in nuclear proteins and deoxynucleoprotein complexes with changes in nuclear function. The first part of the review deals with changes during the normal cell growth cycle and the second part discusses nuclear changes during cell differentiation. It is concluded that major changes in nuclear function are associated with alterations in the stability and dye binding properties of deoxynucleoprotein complexes present in chromatin. The existence of a *chromatin activation reaction* is suggested. Through this reaction inactive (condensed) chromatin regions are decondensed and dispersed. The reaction would be one of perhaps several steps, necessary in turning inactive chromatin into an active template for RNA synthesis. The role of membranes, cytoplasmic and nuclear ionic environments and the migration of protein in the control of genetic expression is briefly discussed.

2. Methodological aspects

The cytochemical investigations into the state and composition of nuclear chromatin in differentiated, single cells, have been made possible through the development of new biophysical instruments and techniques which permit the analysis of very small objects (Caspersson and Lomakka). In spite of these improvements the results obtained by cytochemical methods are, however, often very difficult to interpret in biochemical terms. It is therefore necessary to comment on the methods which are now available for the cytochemical analysis of deoxynucleoprotein (DNP) complexes and to evaluate critically the information which can be collected with these methods.

(a) *The Feulgen reaction*

The Feulgen reaction is generally considered as a reasonably specific and quantitative method for demonstrating DNA. This is probably true if the method is rigourously standardized and comparisons are restricted to cells which are actively multiplying. Non-growing and highly differentiated cells do, however, show a Feulgen reactivity which differs from that of rapidly multiplying cells. Within the individual cell nucleus heterochromatin and euchromatin may differ in the amount of Feulgen stain obtained per unit amount of DNA. These 'artefacts' which reduce very much the value of the Feulgen reaction for quantitative determinations of DNA are, however, interesting phenomena and may reflect such factors as the state of the DNP complex and the degree of chromatin condensation.

It is quite difficult to evaluate in each specific situation what the background is for these 'Feulgen artefacts'. Already in 1932 Caspersson pointed out that proteins interfere with the Feulgen reactivity of DNA and later work has revealed that changes in Feulgen reactivity occur simultaneously with changes in the basicity of the DNA-linked proteins (histones) and/or the degree of chromatin condensation. The two most likely steps where proteins may interfere with the Feulgen reaction are the acid hydrolysis step and the Schiff staining.

Using low temperature–long time acid hydrolysis Sandritter et al. (1965) have studied the loss of purines, the creation of Schiff reactive sites and the liberation of free phosphate groups in various types of nuclei. The hydrolysis patterns obtained differ considerably for nuclei containing different proportions of hetero- and euchromatin.

These observations and those of Agrell and Bergqvist and of Brachet et al. suggest that the Feulgen reaction, or more specifically, the acid hydrolysis step in this reaction may be used as a tool in demonstrating differences in chromatin and nucleoprotein composition between different types of cell nuclei.

(b) *UV absorption*

In order to determine DNA separately by UV microspectrophotometry it is necessary to remove RNA by extraction or enzyme digestions. Unfortunately it is difficult or impossible to make the removal of RNA complete. In tissues where the quantity of DNA-bound RNA is very small it may be possible to calculate the amount of DNA from the light absorption at 260 mμ. In this calculation the total extinction is corrected for the contribution of protein absorption and for unspecific light losses. Lindström et al. have determined the extinction coefficients for RNA and DNA at concentrations approaching those found in cells. This, in principle, makes it possible to figure out absolute amounts of nucleic acid from the corrected 260 mμ absorption of the cell.

(c) *Dye binding*

A number of different dyes have been used in attempts to quantitate intracellular amounts of DNA. Of these methyl green, toluidine blue and chromalum-gallocyanin have been used most widely. For a detailed review of this work recent articles by Deitsch, Sandritter et al. (1966) and Scott should be consulted.

More recently, fluorescent dyes have been introduced. Among these acridine orange (AO) seems to offer advantages in the analysis of small quantities of nucleic acids in cells. The fluorescence emitted by AO–DNA complexes appears green to the eye, whereas AO–RNA complexes show a red fluorescence. The red fluorescence of AO–RNA is due to dye aggregation phenomena which shift the emission maximum of acridine orange (monomer form $\lambda_{max} = 530$ mμ) to higher wavelengths (RNA $\lambda_{max} = 650$ mμ). Rigler has suggested that the ratio between the fluorescence intensities at 590 mμ and 530 mμ ($F_{590}/F_{530} = a$) can be used for determinations of the relative amounts of helix and random coil regions in nucleic acids.

When applied to fixed cells AO-binding to DNA and RNA yields fluorescence spectra similar to those recorded in model systems (Rigler). Quantitative measurements of intracellular nucleic acids are, however, complicated by basic protein groups and cations competing with dye molecules for binding sites. The differences in AO-binding of different types of fixed cells appear to reflect variations in the composition and physical chemical properties of the deoxyribonucleoprotein complex which have not been discovered by other methods.

(d) *Melting profile of DNP*

Denaturation of DNA by heat treatment brings about strand separation and an increase in UV absorption. The temperatures at which strand separation is brought about is higher for DNP complexes than for pure DNA because of the stabilizing influence of proteins and divalent metal ions. Chamberlain and Walker have used UV microspectrometry to study the increase in UV absorption during heat denaturation of bull spermatozoa. We have used a slightly modified technique in analysing the 'melting profile' of erythrocyte and lymphocyte nuclei. In these experiments renaturation is prevented by the addition of formaldehyde and by rapid cooling of the slides. Strand separation is studied by UV absorption measurements or by acridine orange microfluorimetry (Rigler et al.). Results obtained with these new techniques are illustrated in Fig. 7 and will be discussed further in connection with studies on the reactivation of human lymphocytes and hen erythrocytes.

(e) *Actinomycin binding*

Actinomycin under certain conditions has the ability to block specifically the DNA-dependent RNA synthesis. The mechanism of action seems to be that actinomycin binds to DNA and interferes with its template activity (reviews by Reich and Goldberg; Gellert et al.). The ability to bind specifically to DNA has been used by Brachet and Ficq for the cytochemical demonstration of small quantities of DNA.

In model experiments Ringertz and Bolund have found that native nucleoprotein isolated according to Zubay and Doty binds less actinomycin D (AMD) than DNA. Whereas DNA binds one molecule of AMD per 14–20 nucleotides (depending on base composition), DNP only binds one molecule of AMD per 35–140 nucleotides. Since the AMD binding sites in DNP have properties similar to those in DNA, these observations suggest that directly or indirectly, proteins block a number of potential AMD binding sites in DNP. Divalent metal ions (Ca^{++}, Mg^{++} and Mn^{++}) were also found to block AMD binding to DNA *in vitro*. The chromatin of the intact cell nucleus is made up of DNA, DNA linked proteins, divalent metal ions and other low molecular substances, and it is obvious therefore that the actinomycin binding to DNA *in vivo* can vary depending on physiological variations in the composition and properties of chromatin. In experiments which will be discussed below we have used staining with H^3-actinomycin as a technique for demonstrating changes in the chromatin of human lymphocytes upon stimulation with phytohemagglutinin. The results obtained suggest that the amount of actinomycin bound to nuclear chromatin may reflect the amount of template available for transcription by RNA synthesis.

3. *Nuclear proteins and the cell growth cycle*

(a) *Nuclear dry mass*

During normal exponential cell multiplication the nucleus undergoes a doubling in volume and in dry mass. Most of the nuclear dry mass (> 70 %) is made up of protein. RNA and DNA together only account for approximately 20–25 per cent of the total nuclear dry mass. Microinterferometric measurements of nuclei in cells representing known stages of the cell growth cycle show that a doubling in nuclear dry mass occurs during the DNA replication phase (Kimball et al.; Ringertz and Hoskins; Zetterberg 1966). The synchrony between the accumulation of nuclear proteins and the DNA replication is especially striking in the macronucleus of the ciliate *Euplotes* (Prescott and Kimball; Ringertz and Hoskins). In this nucleus, DNA synthesis starts at the two extreme ends of the elongated nucleus (Gall) and proceeds towards the centre of the macronucleus. The narrow zones where DNA replication is going on are visible as refractile transverse bands referred to as 'reorganization bands'. Microinterferometric measurements of the dry mass of macronuclei (Fig. 1) isolated by microdissection show that the nuclear dry mass doubles at the same time as the DNA amount (Ringertz and Hoskins). Autoradiography after amino acid labelling of macronuclei showed that labelled protein accumulates distal to the reorganization bands. Some protein labelling could also be observed during G1 and in those parts of S-phase nuclei which are not affected by DNA replication during the labelling period. Thus amino acids are incorporated into protein also in the absence of DNA replication and under conditions where no major increase in the amount of nuclear protein can be detected.

Whether the proteins accumulating in the nucleus are synthesized in the nucleus is uncertain. Work by Byers et al. and by Prescott and Bender on amoebae has clearly demonstrated that nuclear proteins are in fact synthesized in the cytoplasm and migrate into the nucleus.

The observations made on protozoan nuclei have to a great extent been confirmed by studies of mammalian cells. Zetterberg (1966) found that in fibroblasts the nuclear dry mass increases in good synchrony with DNA replication. His results also suggest that at least 70% of the total amount of protein accumulating in the nucleus during S-phase must be material which was synthesized in the cytoplasm.

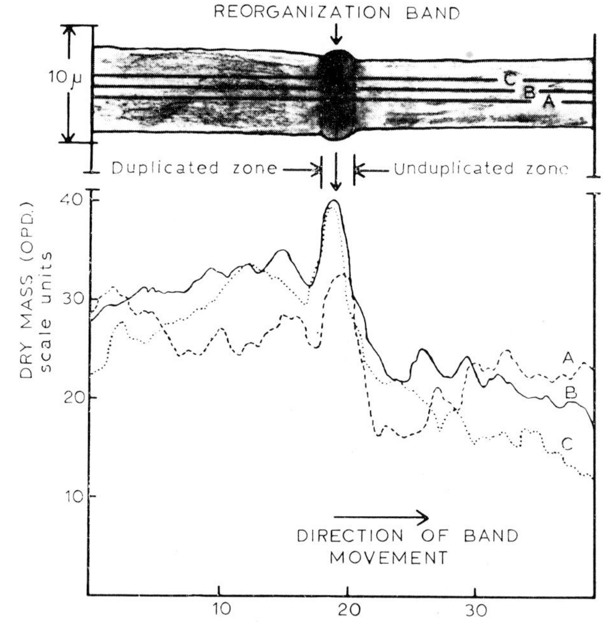

Fig. 1. Increase in nuclear dry mass during DNA replication in the macronucleus of *Euplotes*. DNA synthesis takes place in narrow zones ('reorganization bands') which move over the threadlike nucleus. Dry mass was measured by scanning microinterferometry using a narrow measuring beam. (From Ringertz and Hoskins.)

Though the increase in nuclear dry mass and nuclear protein is fairly well synchronized with DNA replication, the accumulation of nuclear protein can take place also in the absence of DNA replication. Thus in Ehrlich ascites tumours accumulation of nuclear protein takes place also if the nuclei have been blocked in G2 phase by a dose of X-radiation which prevents mitosis (Killander et al.). If the G1 period in fibroblasts is prolonged by blocking DNA synthesis with fluorodeoxyuridin, some increase in nuclear dry mass can still take place (Zetterberg, personal communication). The rate of dry mass accumulation is, however, much slower than during normal S-phase. Part of the nuclear protein accumulation may therefore be dependent on DNA synthesis.

An attempt to summarize the situation is made in Fig. 2. During the G1 period,

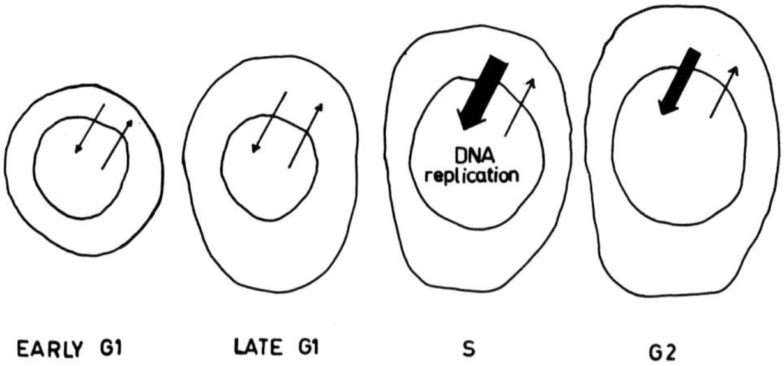

Fig. 2. Migration of protein across the nuclear membrane at different stages of the cell growth cycle.

non-histone proteins are synthesized in the cytoplasm and possibly also in the nucleus. This causes some protein labelling also in the absence of DNA replication. Since the nuclear dry mass does not increase, the inward migration of protein into the nucleus must be compensated by protein degradation or protein migration out of the nucleus. During S-phase the amount of protein entering the nucleus is much greater than the amount leaving the nucleus. Histone synthesis is initiated at the same time as DNA replication and histones migrate into the nucleus throughout the S-phase. The result is a net increase in histone and other nuclear proteins. During G2 nuclear proteins other than histone continue to accumulate in the nucleus also after DNA replication has been completed and if the normal initiation of cell division is prevented, the result is giant G2 nuclei.

There are several possible explanations for the synchronous increase in DNA and nuclear protein during S-phase. The increased amount of negatively charged nucleic acid in the nucleus will in itself tend to bind basic proteins and low-molecular cations which migrate into the nucleus. This explanation alone does not, however, account for the increase in dry mass which is seen in nuclei arrested in G2 by irradiation. Another explanation may be that the initiation of DNA replication coincides with a change in the properties of the nuclear membrane. This change would permit new types of nuclear protein or a greater quantity of protein to cross the nuclear membrane and accumulate in the nuclear compartment. It would be the membrane change rather than the DNA replication itself which causes the relatively good correlation between nuclear dry mass and DNA increase during S-phase. The altered membrane would also permit accumulation of protein in the nucleus after the cessation of DNA synthesis, i.e., during G2. After division, a new nuclear membrane is formed and this membrane would again be less permeable to nuclear proteins.

Another but only partial explanation is that net synthesis of proteins specific for the nucleus, only occurs during S and G2. Evidence suggesting that specific types of nuclear proteins are synthesized only during part of the cell cycle exists for thymidine kinase (Littlefield) and for histones (Prescott; Robbins and Borun).

In order to evaluate these possibilities further, new data on the relative importance of cytoplasmic *versus* nuclear synthesis of nuclear proteins is required. It is clear, however, that the extensive migration of proteins in and out of the cell nucleus may be an important factor in transmitting signals from the cytoplasm to the nucleus and the other way round.

(b) *Histones*

Early cytochemical data revealed a parallelism between the amount of basic protein as demonstrated by the alkaline fast green reaction and the amount of DNA as demonstrated by the Feulgen reaction (Bloch and Godman). Experiments where cells were arrested in G2 by X-radiation showed that the amount of histone (as determined by cytochemical techniques) did not increase beyond the normal G2 level even though the total nuclear dry mass continued to grow (Ringertz). These results suggested that the amount of histone increases in good synchrony with DNA replication during the cell growth cycle, and that the accumulation of histone might in fact be dependent on DNA replication.

Recent biochemical data seem to support this conclusion. Gall and Prescott have found that in the macronucleus of *Euplotes* the synthesis of histone is very well synchronized with DNA replication whereas labelled amino acids are incorporated into other nuclear proteins throughout the cell cycle. Similar results have been obtained by Robbins and Borun and others in studies on mammalian cells.

Biochemical experiments have also demonstrated that fluorodeoxyuridine blocks the increase in nuclear histone accumulation at the same time as DNA synthesis is blocked. Some incorporation of labelled amino acids into histone fractions can, however, be observed also in the absence of any net increase in histone amount (Littlefield and Jacobs).

Autoradiographic studies on spermiogenesis by Bloch and Brack suggest that some special histones ('protamines') are synthesized in the cytoplasm and migrate into the nucleus. In HeLa cells Robbins and Borun find that histones are synthesized in the cytoplasm during the DNA replication period. Consequently, the evidence available suggests that like the majority of nuclear proteins, histones are synthesized in the cytoplasm and migrate into the nucleus.

(c) *Deoxyribonucleoprotein complexes*

The state of condensation and staining properties of nuclear chromatin varies considerably from one cell type to another. Within one and the same cell nucleus hetero- and euchromatin differ in their staining properties. The biochemical background for these differences is as yet incompletely investigated but can probably be traced back to differences in the state of condensation of the DNP component.

At the end of the normal cell growth cycle interphase chromatin condenses into chromosomes. The condensation process is sensitive to actinomycin treatment (Arrighi and Hsu). The effect is not an immediate one, suggesting that the cells complete the actinomycin-sensitive processes some time before division. Under certain conditions cells are capable of entering mitosis in spite of actinomycin treatment. In such cells the chromosomes remain extended and incompletely condensed suggesting that actinomycin may be competing with histones involved in chromosome condensation.

The condensation of interphase chromatin into chromosomes causes a decrease in the green (F_{530}) fluorescence of ethanol:acetone fixed, acridine orange stained fibroblast chromatin by only 20–30 per cent (Ringertz, unpublished observation). This effect probably does not reflect a decreased acridine orange binding since at the same time a shift towards a more reddish fluorescence is observed. The F_{590}/F_{530} ratio for metaphase equatorial plates was found to be 0.61 as compared to 0.35 for telophase chromatin. It is interesting that the condensation of interphase chromatin into chromosomes does not seem to be associated with any major depression of the ability to bind acridine orange.

As will be discussed in more detail below, the chromatin condensation which takes place during the inactivation of the cell nucleus during spermiogenesis, erythropoesis and lymphopoesis is characterized by a marked decrease in the ability of DNP to bind acridine orange. It may be, therefore, that the mechanisms causing chromosome condensation are basically different from the mechanisms responsible for the more long-term condensation and inactivation of interphase chromatin.

4. *Nuclear proteins and cell differentiation*

(a) *General*

The nuclear volume and nuclear protein content varies considerably from one cell type to another. Schultze and Maurer have demonstrated that the rate of RNA synthesis is proportional to the nuclear volume in a number of different tissues. Large nuclei normally have a greater protein content and also a more dispersed, less condensed chromatin structure. The chromatin of cells undergoing rapid growth binds greater amounts of basic dyes per unit amount of DNA than does the chromatin of slow-growing, differentiating cells (Alfert; Bloch and Godman 1955b). The reason for this qualitative difference in the chromatin has been thought to reside in the binding of basic proteins to DNA-phosphate groups and in the state of condensation of the nuclear chromatin. In our work on chromatin changes during cell differentiation *in vitro* we have tried to explore these questions further. Our central aim has been to relate major changes in nuclear function with changes in the cytochemical properties of the DNP component of nuclear chromatin.

(b) *Spermiogenesis*

In fish, spermiogenesis is associated with a change in the composition of nuclear proteins and nuclear DNP complexes. The histones characteristic of somatic tissues are substituted with more low-molecular and more arginine-rich histones referred to as protamines. With the aid of the alkaline fast green reaction combined with acetylation of lysine-amino groups it has been possible to obtain evidence suggesting that a similar phenomenon also occurs in snails (Bloch and Hew) and insects (Das et al.).

In higher animals, biochemical studies on sperm nucleoprotein have met with technical problems. Though some investigators have referred to the basic proteins of mammalian sperm as being 'histone'-like, cytochemical work by Monesi suggests that DNP changes occur also during mammalian spermiogenesis. Thus Monesi demonstrated that the alkaline fast green reaction of cells representing the early stages of spermiogenesis could be blocked by acetylation, whereas the later cell stages still bound fast green. These observations can be interpreted as a change from a more lysine-rich to a more arginine-rich type of protein.

We have examined by quantitative cytochemical methods the changes which take place in the nuclear proteins and deoxyribonucleoprotein complexes during spermiogenesis in the bull (Gledhill et al. 1966a). As the early spermatids mature into testicular spermatozoa the ability of the DNP complex to bind acridine orange and methyl green decreases by a factor of more than 50 (Fig. 3). At the same time the amount of

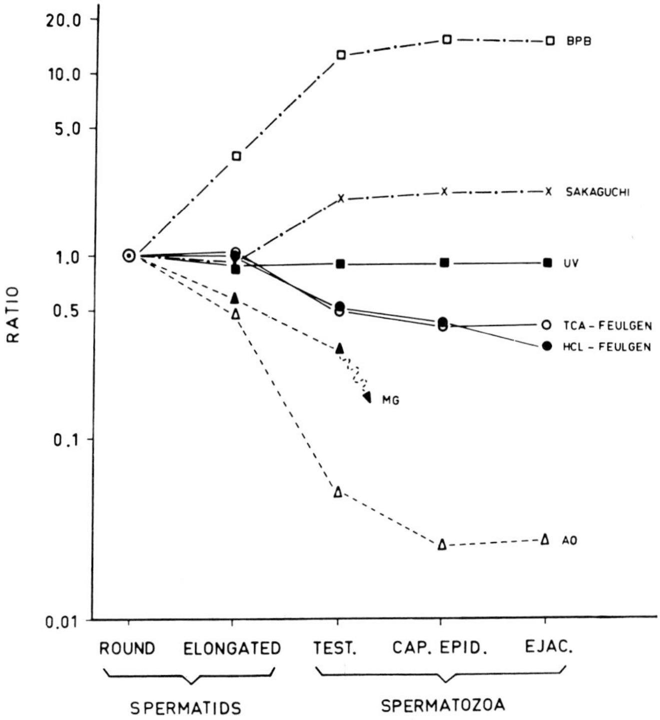

Fig. 3. Cytochemical properties of nuclear proteins and deoxyribonucleoprotein complexes during spermiogenesis in the bull (round spermatids = 1.0). (From Gledhill et al. 1966a.)

protein-bound arginine (Sakaguchi reaction) and the overall basicity of the DNA-linked proteins (alkaline bromphenol blue reaction, see Ringertz and Zetterberg) increase markedly. These changes take place at the same time as there is a decrease in the Feulgen reactivity of the DNP. Together these data suggest that DNA–phosphate groups in the DNP become progressively more firmly bound to protein. Whether the decrease in binding sites for basic dyes reflects a direct blocking of negatively charged groups by proteins or whether it is secondary consequence of the condensed state of the DNP is difficult to decide. The increased ability of the protein component in DNP to bind acid dyes at alkaline *p*H and the increase in the total amount of protein-bound arginine in the nucleus most likely reflect a qualitative change from the somatic types of histones towards more basic, protamine-like proteins.

Thus it seems that a histone–protamine transition occurs also during spermiogenesis in higher animals. The biological importance of this phenomenon may be that it allows the genetic material to be packed into a smaller volume at the same time as the DNA molecules are stabilized against different forms of denaturation.

The Feulgen artefact is interesting since in certain types of infertility in cattle and in man (Leuchtenberger et al. 1953, 1956) the ejaculated spermatozoa give higher Feulgen-DNA values than do spermatozoa from fertile individuals. The previous interpretation, namely that the infertile spermatozoa contain abnormal amounts of DNA may very well be wrong. In a group of infertile bulls examined in this laboratory the sperm heads were found to give Feulgen values which were higher than normal, whereas the UV absorption was normal. Examination of the AO and methyl green binding capacity of the nucleoprotein were also found to be pathological whereas the reactions for basic proteins only revealed slightly abnormal values. For these reasons we have suggested (Gledhill et al. 1966b) that a defect in the histone protamine transition may be the cause of certain types of male infertility.

(c) *Reactivation of hen erythrocyte nuclei*

Erythrocytes are highly specialized cells and constitute the final product of a long differentiation process. In mammals this process is terminated by the degradation and expulsion of the cell nucleus. In birds and certain other species the nucleus persists but assumes an inactive form with a tightly condensed nuclear chromatin. The synthesis of protein is very much reduced and the synthesis of RNA and DNA is blocked (Cameron and Prescott).

Recently Harris has shown that the nuclei of hen erythrocytes can be reactivated by cell hybridization techniques. Using quantitative cytochemical techniques Bolund, Ringertz and Harris have investigated changes in the composition of the erythrocyte nucleus and its DNP complexes during this reactivation process. In other experiments we have found that similar chromatin changes are also induced by phytohemagglutinin (PHA) treatment and by washing the cell surface free from serum proteins (Ringertz and Bolund). It seems possible to use the hen erythrocyte system as an experimental model in studying the interrelationship between the state of the cell membranes and the state of the nuclear chromatin.

(d) *Cell hybridization experiments with hen erythrocytes*

Hen erythrocytes have been fused with rapidly multiplying HeLa cells by the method developed by Harris (1965). This technique is illustrated in Fig. 4. In the heterokaryons, the two different types of nuclei can easily be identified on the basis of their size, form and chromatin structure (Fig. 5a and b). When the heterokaryons are kept in tissue culture for 2–3 days one can observe how the erythrocyte nuclei gradually increase in volume. Soon after the erythrocyte nuclei have come into contact with HeLa cytoplasm, RNA synthesis is initiated and as the nuclei grow in size the rate of RNA synthesis accelerates (Harris 1967). Maximum enlargement is obtained approximately 48 hours after cell fusion. Microinterferometry on erythrocyte nuclei *in situ* and on erythrocyte nuclei isolated from heterokaryons (Bolund et al.) shows that the enlargement in nuclear size is not merely due to swelling but to an increase in dry mass (Fig. 6). Part of this dry mass increase occurs simultaneously with DNA replication and may represent the increase in nuclear proteins which accompanies DNA synthesis

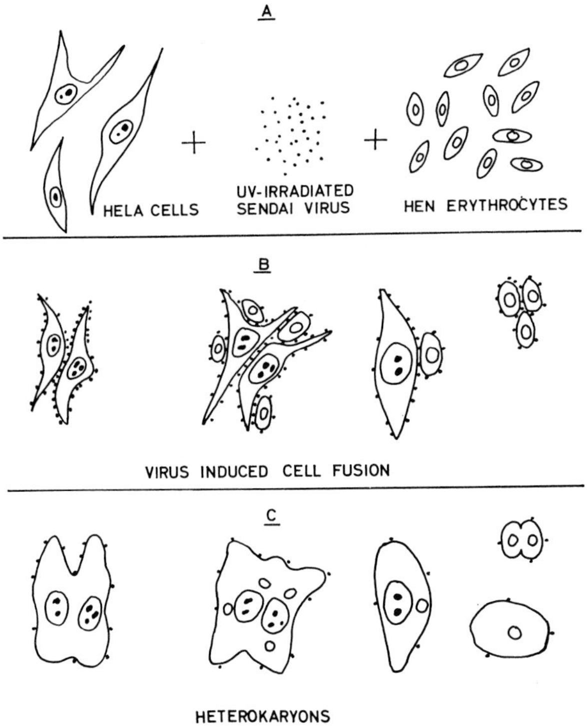

Fig. 4. Fusion of HeLa cells and hen erythrocytes with UV-irradiated Sendai virus. The killed virus binds to cell surfaces and induces an increased 'stickiness'. Various combinations of cells fuse.

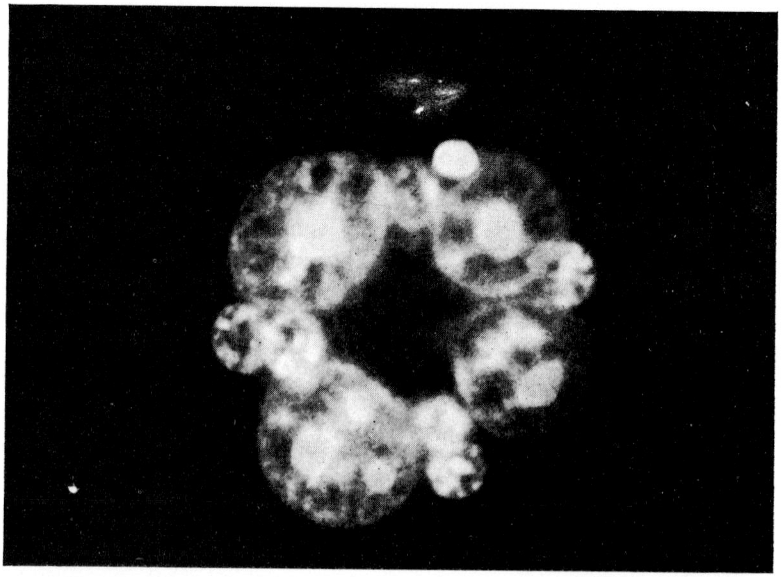

a

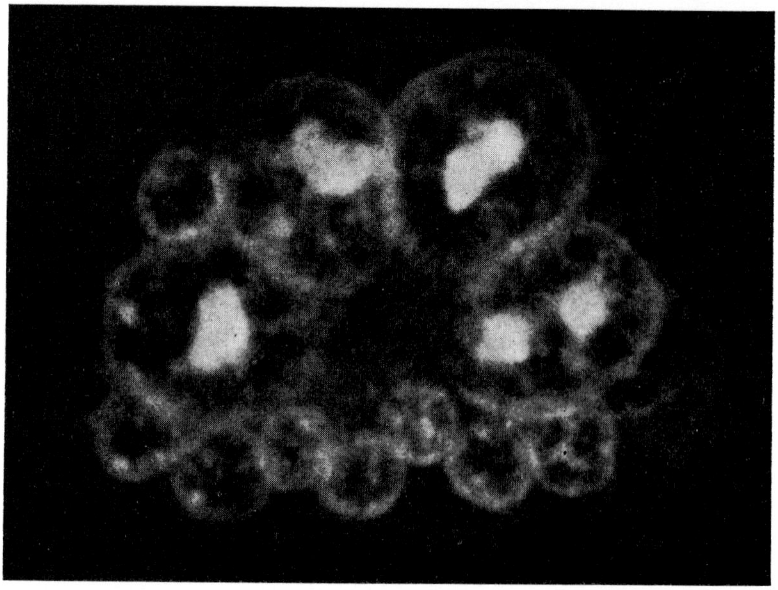

b

Fig. 5. (a) Acridine orange-stained heterokaryon containing 4 HeLa nuclei and 7 erythrocyte nuclei. The HeLa nuclei have large nucleoli. The erythrocyte nuclei are considerably smaller than the HeLa nuclei. Sixteen hours after cell fusion. × 2,000. (b) Ethidium-stained heterokaryon containing 4 HeLa nuclei and 8 erythrocyte nuclei; 74 hr after cell fusion. × 3,000.

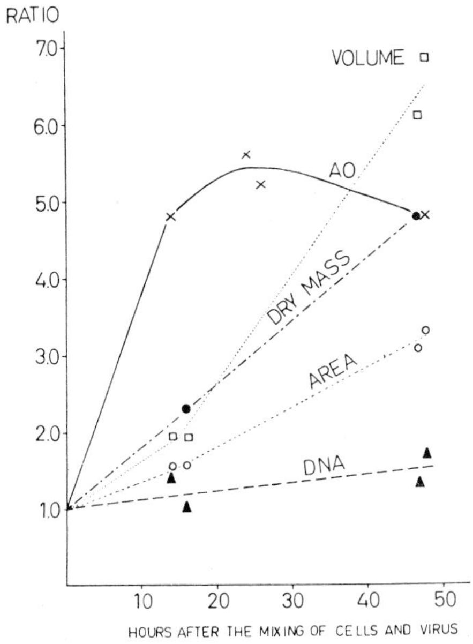

Fig. 6. Nuclear changes during reactivation of erythrocyte nuclei in heterokaryons. The earliest change is an increased ability of the nuclear DNP to bind acridine orange (AO). RNA synthesis and an increase in nuclear dry mass follow soon after. DNA synthesis starts approximately 16–20 hr after cell fusion.

during the normal cell growth cycle. Part of the dry mass increase, however, occurs before DNA replication is initiated and may represent protein accumulation necessary for the transition from a G0 to a G1 state.

It is interesting that an increase in nuclear dry mass takes place during the first 48 hours after cell fusion also if RNA synthesis in the erythrocyte nucleus is blocked by irradiating the erythrocytes with UV-light before the cells are fused (Bolund, Darzynkiewicz and Ringertz, unpubl. observations). This suggests that the increase in nuclear dry mass may be due to the migration of HeLa i.e. human proteins into the hen nucleus. This interpretation also receives support from the observation by Harris et al., that hen specific antigens are not synthesized till after nucleoli have developed in the erythrocyte nuclei i.e. on the fourth to eighth day after cell fusion.

The reactivation of the hen erythrocyte nuclei in these heterokaryons is also associated with qualitative changes in the properties of the DNP complexes (Bolund et al.). The binding of acridine orange and ethidium bromide to the DNA-phosphate groups of the complex is increased by a factor of more than four already a short time after cell fusion, i.e. before any DNA replication has started. The melting profiles i.e. the curves which describe the temperature dependence of the F_{590}/F_{530} ratio of acridine orange stained nuclei, indicate that the DNP complex of 'activated' nuclei reisolated from heterokaryons melts at a lower temperature than does the DNP complex of nuclei isolated with the same method from normal erythrocytes (Fig. 7a).

It is quite interesting that the activation of the erythrocyte nuclei in heterokaryons is also accompanied by an altered Feulgen reactivity. We have previously demonstrated that the repression and condensation of nuclear chromatin during spermiogenesis is associated with a decrease in Feulgen reactivity. These Feulgen artefacts may be due to changes in the susceptibility of the DNP complex to acid hydrolysis (as will be discussed further below). It is not possible yet to explain these Feulgen artefacts but there are strong reasons to believe that these artefacts reflect changes in protein and ion binding to the DNA as well as the state of condensation of the entire DNP complex.

(e) *Reactivation of the erythrocyte nucleus and the role of cell membranes*

In some experiments, Ringertz and Bolund have observed that if hen erythrocytes are washed and incubated at 37 °C for 60 min in salt solutions or tissue culture media, which do not contain serum proteins, the ability of the nuclear chromatin to bind acridine orange is increased to levels approaching those recorded in cell hybridization experiments and in PHA stimulation experiments. The same effect can also be obtained by washing ghosts isolated after lysis with Nonidet P40.

In this type of experiments the intact cells or ghosts are allowed to sediment and attach to glass slides placed on the bottom of a Petri dish. After fixation in ethanol–acetone (1:1) the nuclei of the cells or ghosts are analyzed by quantitative cytochemical techniques. In the absence of serum proteins virtually all cells and ghosts attach to the slides. In the presence of serum proteins the attachment varies from 1–20% of the total number of cells/ghosts which sedimented on to the slides.

Ghost nuclei which have been washed and incubated in serum free media show the same UV absorption at 265 mμ and the same dry mass as control nuclei exposed to the same solutions containing 0.05 per cent serum proteins. The 'serum free' nuclei do, however, differ from the control nuclei with respect to the properties of the DNP component. Since our evidence suggests that the DNP component has been altered in the same direction as seen during reactivation in heterokaryons the DNP change is tentatively referred to as an 'activation'.

The DNP component of the activated nuclei binds 3–4 times as much acridine orange and 5–10 times as much ethidium bromide as does the DNP of control nuclei. Furthermore when isolated nuclei are examined by the AO melting technique (Fig. 7a) or the UV melting technique (Fig. 7b), the 'activated' DNP melts at a lower temperature than control DNP. Using optimum hydrolysis time the Feulgen reactivity of the activated nuclei is increased beyond the level represented by control nuclei. A closer examination of the Feulgen hydrolysis curve revealed marked differences in shape which may explain this Feulgen 'artefact'.

The chromatin 'activation' is inhibited or prevented if dialyzed serum or human serum proteins from Cohn fractions III and IV are present at concentrations of 0.01–

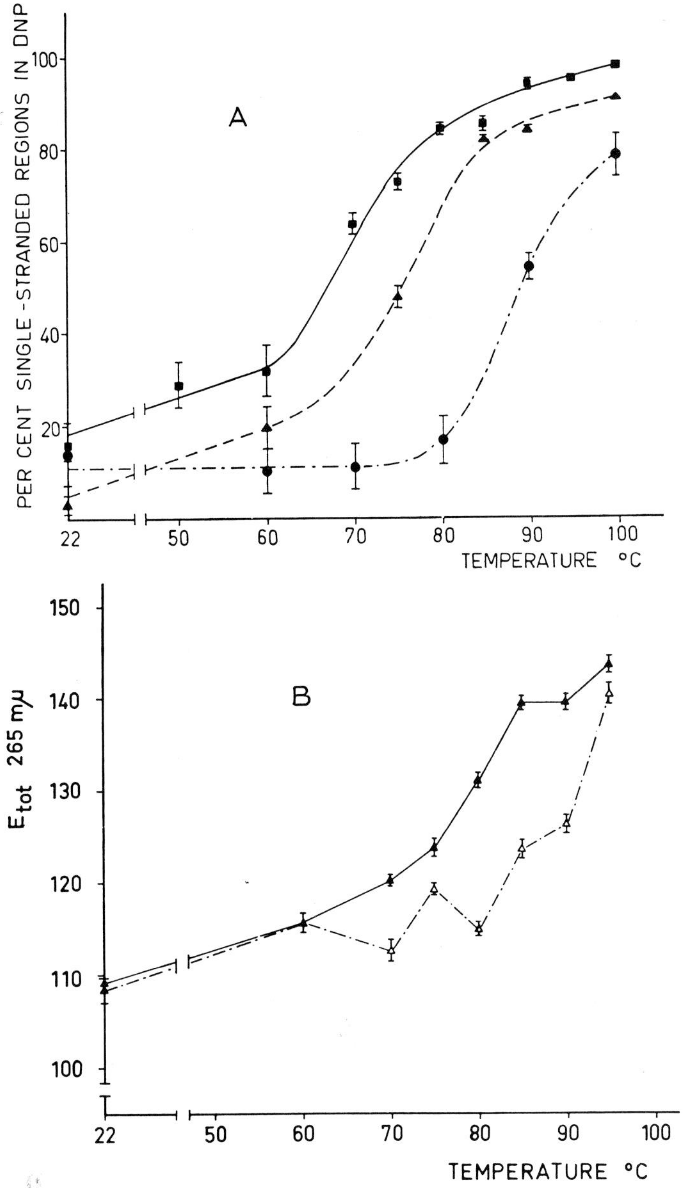

Fig. 7. Cytochemical heat denaturation curves obtained on 'activated' and control nuclei. (A) DNP denaturation as studied by acridine orange microfluorimetry on nuclei of ghosts washed and incubated in the absence of serum proteins (— ■ — ■ —), nuclei isolated from HeLa–hen erythrocyte heterokaryons 41 hr after cell fusion (– –▲– – – –▲– –) and nuclei of ghosts washed and incubated in the presence of serum proteins (–.●–.–.–●–.–.). (B) DNP denaturation studied by UV-microspectrophotometry on ghost nuclei 'activated' by washing and incubating in the absence of serum proteins (—— ▲—▲—) and control nuclei as represented by ghosts washed in the presence of serum proteins (–.△–.–.△–.) (Ringertz and Bolund.)

0.05 per cent in the washing and incubation media. The activation cannot be prevented, however by adding neutral polysaccharides (Ficoll, Pharmacia), bovine serum albumin or human γ-globulin. Nor can the activation be prevented by 10^{-3} M iodoacetic acid or 2×10^{-4} M paranitrophenol or by lowering the incubation temperature to 0 °C. Divalent metal ions such as Mn^{2+} (0.06 mM) and Mg^{2+} (0.01 M) do, however, inhibit the increase in AO binding induced by washing and incubation in serum free salt solutions. These observations and the fact that versene is capable of increasing the AO binding capacity also in the presence of serum proteins suggest that divalent metal ions are important in the activation phenomenon.

It is possible that the DNP changes reflect a removal of divalent metal ions from the DNP complex. This effect could be due to an altered ionic environment resulting from changes in the properties of cell membranes. Some observations indicate, however, that the situation is more complicated than this. If ghosts are washed and then incubated in the absence of serum proteins at concentrations higher than 3.000 ghosts/mm^3 (= 5.000 ghosts/mm^2) the DNP changes are regularly induced. If, however, the ghost concentration during incubation is lower than this no increase in acridine orange binding occurs and the nuclei retain the properties of serum treated ghost nuclei with respect to their sensitivity to thermal denaturation. This shows that the induction of the DNP changes is dependent not only upon the washing of the ghosts and upon their attachment to glass, but also on some form of 'cell-to-cell' interaction. It is interesting in this context that the DNP changes can be induced at low concentrations of hen erythrocyte ghosts if washed human erythrocytes are mixed in to give a total cell concentration of more than 10.000 cells/mm^3. This suggests that the 'cell-to-cell' interaction is a relatively unspecific phenomenon and it cannot be excluded that the interaction is mediated by membrane material in the medium. In view of these results it seems possible that the ability of serum proteins to prevent the induction of the DNP changes may be due to some form of stabilizing or 'shielding' effect on the cell membranes so that no cell-to-cell interaction takes place.

We do not yet know with certainty whether the nucleoprotein changes induced in the model experiments are actually the same as those found during the reactivation of hen erythrocytes in heterokaryons. They do resemble each other with respect to (a) the increased ability to bind acridine orange, (b) the increased ability to bind ethidium bromide, (c) the changes in melting profile and (d) the appearance of a Feulgen 'artefact'.

(f) *Phytohemagglutinin (PHA) stimulation*

When added to human lymphocytes *in vitro*, phytohemagglutinin induces part of the cell population to start RNA synthesis and to undergo blast transformation. During the earliest stages of this gene activation process the cytochemical properties of the chromatin undergo marked changes. Killander and Rigler (1965) have demonstrated that the ability of the DNP complex to bind acridine orange increases more than five-fold and that the DNP becomes much more sensitive to thermal denaturation (Rigler and Killander). Other evidence indicating early DNP-changes during lymphocyte activation has been obtained by Black and Ansley who noted that antigen stimulation of lymphoid cells results in changes in the ammoniacal-silver reaction and alkaline fast green reactions for histone. Similar observations have also been made by Burton and by Zetterberg and Auer on lymphoid cells stimulated by PHA. From the data of Killander and Rigler on acridine orange binding and of Zetterberg and Auer on the binding of bromphenol blue to histones it appears that the DNP change involves not only 100 per cent of the lymphocytes but also all of the polymorphonuclear leucocytes present in these cultures. This is somewhat surprising in view of the fact that only part of the lymphocyte population and no or only very few leucocytes initiate RNA synthesis and undergo blast transformation.

PHA stimulation of human lymphocytes also results in an increased ability of the chromatin to bind H^3-actinomycin (Darzynkiewicz, Ringertz and Bolund, to be published). In some of these experiments we saturated the lymphocytes with non-radioactive actinomycin before the cells were stimulated. After washing away excess free actinomycin the cells were then stimulated with PHA at the same time as H^3-actinomycin was added. Autoradiography on preparations fixed after 2 hr of incubation showed that about half the population of PHA-stimulated lymphocytes were labelled whereas in the non-stimulated cultures only very few cells were labelled. In both control preparations and PHA-stimulated preparations only a very small number of labelled leucocytes could be found.

Results obtained by Pogo et al. suggest that histone acetylation may be an important early step in the activation of lymphocytes by PHA. Their observations as well as those of Mukherjee and Cohen show that this phenomenon affects only part of the lymphocyte population, and that polymorphonuclear leucocytes are not affected. Double emulsion autoradiography using C^{14}-acetate and H^3-uridine indicates that the fraction of the lymphocyte population which responds to PHA by an increased acetate incorporation is identical with the fraction initiating RNA synthesis (Darzynkiewicz, Ringertz and Bolund, to be published). During the later stages of the activation process the nucleus of the PHA-stimulated lymphocytes increases in volume and dry mass (Sörén, personal communication), synthesizes DNA (Bender and Prescott) and undergoes the morphological changes referred to as ‘blast transformation’.

RNA synthesis is initiated within the first hours after the addition of PHA (Darzynkiewicz et al. 1965; Cooper and Rubin) i.e. at the same time or shortly after one can observe the altered cytochemical properties of the DNP complex. The earliest RNA synthesis represents non-ribosomal RNA (Cooper and Rubin) which is rapidly labelled and rapidly degraded (Darzynkiewicz and Pienkowski).

Though the PHA-stimulation of lymphocytes obviously must derepress a great number of genes, it is as yet not clear what the exact relationship is between the DNP changes observed by cytochemical methods and the derepression phenomenon. It seems likely, however, that the altered DNP properties reflect a dispersion and stretching out of previously condensed DNP molecules.

The mechanisms by which PHA and antigens induce DNP changes in lymphocytes may be similar to those which trigger DNP changes in the hen erythrocytes. PHA binds to the cell membranes of the lymphocytes and induces membrane changes which manifest themselves as an increased tendency to stick to glass (Killander and Rigler 1965) and an altered phospholipid metabolism (Fisher and Mueller; Kay). It is also known that the extent to which lymphocytes are stimulated by PHA and antigens *in vitro* is highly dependent on cell density (Moorhead et al.; Valentine and Lawrence) and on the concentration of serum proteins in the medium (Forsdyke). From other types of cell cultures we know that growth of small number of cells in a new medium is greatly stimulated if the cells are crowded together on the glass surface (Rein and Rubin). The dependency of lymphocyte stimulation on the concentration of serum in the medium, on cell density and on attachment to glass is interesting in view of the results obtained with the model system based on hen erythrocytes. In this model system these are factors which seem to control the initiation of the early DNP changes characteristic of nuclear activation.

It is also of some interest in this connection that when hen erythrocytes are treated with PHA *in vitro* the acridine orange binding capacity of the nuclear chromatin is increased by a factor of three (Bolund, Killander and Ringertz, unpublished observations). At 37 °C this effect is attained within approximately one hour (Fig. 8). In a series of 16 experiments this reaction was observed in 5 cases. The reason why no reaction is recorded in so many experiments is unknown. It appears to be due to variations among individual animals rather than to variation among the PHA preparations or other experimental conditions. Though difficult to reproduce this observation is interesting in view of the growth-stimulating effect of PHA in other cell

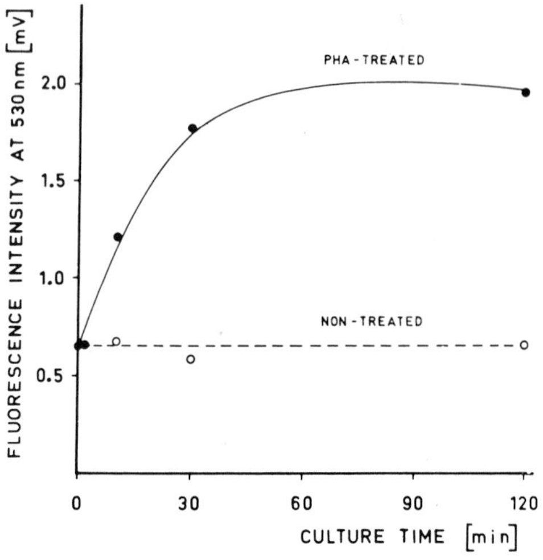

Fig. 8. Phytohemagglutinin-induced increase in the binding of acridine orange to hen erythrocyte nuclei. (From Bolund, Killander and Ringertz, unpublished observations.)

systems and the similarity of the phenomenon to the effects recorded in the cell hybridization studies.

5. *Some aspects on the regulation of gene expression during nuclear activation*

From the information summarized in this review it is evident that the cytochemical properties of nuclear proteins and deoxyribonucleoprotein complexes vary considerably with the functional properties of the cell nucleus. It appears, therefore, that it may be useful to consider these observations in relation to the mechanisms which regulate gene expression in animal cells. Practically all which is known about the regulation of gene expression in the individual cells derives from studies of microorganisms. In bacteria gene expression is regulated at the transcription level (DNA → RNA), at the translational level (RNA → polypeptide), and possibly also at the assembly level (polypeptide → protein). The greatest emphasis has been put on regulation at the transcription level. It seems possible and probable that mechanisms similar to those suggested by the Jacob-Monod model are operating in the 'point control' of specific genes also in animal cells. It is also probable that as these more complex cells evolved and acquired the ability to live in multicellular aggregates, to undergo cell differentiation and interact with each other, new and additional mechanisms for the regulation of gene activity evolved. The cytochemical data accumulated in studies on the activation of the red cell nucleus and the lymphocyte nucleus indicate that this may be so.

In both the erythrocyte and the lymphocyte system nuclear activation appears to be a multistep process. Similar steps seem to be involved in both systems though the rate at which the nucleus passes through the different steps may be different. The following stages can be discerned:

(a) Early changes in the physicochemical properties of DNP;
(b) Enzymatic modification of histones and other nuclear proteins;
(c) Formation of rapidly labelled, rapidly degraded RNA;
(d) Increase in nuclear dry mass and volume;
(e) Initiation of DNA synthesis and further increase in nuclear dry mass;
(f) Ribosomal RNA synthesis and nucleolus formation;
(g) Initiation of specific protein synthesis.

These stages will be briefly discussed as to their possible importance in the regulation of gene expression.

(a) *Early DNP changes*

The nucleoprotein changes observed during the reactivation of hen erythrocyte nuclei in heterokaryons and PHA-activation of lymphocytes may reflect the existence of a phenomenon which we would like to label a *chromatin activation reaction.* It would represent an early step, perhaps only one of several steps necessary in transforming inactive chromatin segments into active templates for RNA synthesis. The chromatin activation reaction would be part of a course genetic control mechanism operating by opening up or closing down a large number of genes or entire nuclei. Rather simple signals such as an altered ionic environment around the deoxynucleoprotein complex may be capable of inducing the reaction. From this follows that the transport of ions and other low-molecular material across nuclear and cell membranes will be important factors in controlling the reaction. Changes in the local microenvironment surrounding the cell, cell to cell contacts, binding and removal of macromolecules to and from the cell membrane would in their turn be important. The chromatin activation reaction would not require any synthesis of RNA and it may be an altogether non-enzymatic phenomenon.

The basic change which the chromatin activation reaction induces affects the DNP component. Phosphate groups which were previously inaccesible to dye binding are exposed, the DNP complex changes from a well neutralized random coil which can be packed in a small volume into a more charged structure which tends to stretch out. The stability of the DNP complex to heat denaturation is lowered. The altered DNP structure may also cause changes in Feulgen reactivity and Feulgen hydrolysis curves of the chromatin.

The exact mechanism by which phosphate groups become available for the increased dye binding is not known. The phosphate groups of the DNA molecules are bound to basic protein groups and to ions. The unmasking of phosphate groups could be due to a change in either or both types of counter ions.

Changes in the binding of ions to DNA–phosphate groups can probably explain both the altered dye binding properties (Lawley), the lowered stability to heat denaturation (Dove and Davidson) and the Feulgen artefacts (Cerroni and Neff). Divalent ions are also known to be very important in the maintenance of a condensed chromatin and DNP structure (Mazia). It is therefore conceivable that the decondensation of chromatin observed during the activation of a large number of genes can be explained by assuming a change in the counter ion environment around the DNP–phosphate groups. That such a change could be of great importance for the control of genetic activity is suggested by Kroegers finding that the activation of a specific gene loci in giant insect chromosomes is controlled by the Na^+–K^+ balance in the nuclear compartment.

At the moment it is not possible to decide whether the unmasking of phosphate groups in the DNP complex are due to changes in the binding of histone or in the binding of low-molecular counter ions.

(b) *Enzymatic modifications of DNA-bound proteins*

Pogo et al. have demonstrated that gene activation in lymphocytes is accompanied by an early acetylation of some histone amino groups. The kinetics of the reaction is similar to the increase in acridine orange binding observed by Killander and Rigler (1965). Acetylation would be one possibility for rendering histones incapable of binding to DNA phosphate groups. However, so far it has not been demonstrated that histone acetylation is of such quantitative importance that it can explain the large number of dye binding sites exposed. Furthermore, the increased acetylation of nuclear proteins which can be detected by C^{14}-acetate incorporation into PHA stimulated buffy coat cells only affects part of the lymphocyte population whereas the increased acridine orange binding and the altered staining properties for histones apparently affect the entire lymphocyte population and in addition the polymorphonuclear leucocytes. The increased acetate incorporation, however, appears to be well correlated with the initiation of RNA synthesis. It is interesting that the increased ability to bind H^3-actinomycin also seems to affect only a part of the lymphocyte population. It seems therefore that the modification of the template which occurs during the early stages of gene activation may be a multistep phenomenon. The early 'physicochemical' changes in the DNP component may not be enough in producing an active template. Other and later steps involving enzymatic and other modifications of the DNA-bound proteins may be necessary in conserving the DNP in an 'activated', extended state and in producing an active template. It also appears that a physicochemical change affecting a large part of the DNP is too crude a mechanism to be involved in the point regulation of individual operons. Enzymatic modification of histones and changes in the type of protein bound to DNA are more likely to be involved in this form of regulation.

Other enzymatic reactions which can lead to a modification in the proteins bound to DNA is methylation (Tidwell et al.), thiolation (Hilton and Stocken), and phosphorylation of histones (Kleinschmidt et al.; Ord and Stocken).

(c) *Synthesis of rapidly labelled RNA*

In both the PHA-lymphocyte (Cooper and Rubin; Kay and Korner) and the erythrocyte-heterokaryon systems (Harris et al.) the early stages of gene activation are characterized by a synthesis of polydisperse, rapidly labelled RNA. Compared to later stages the synthesis of ribosomal RNA is insignificant. Harris et al. have demonstrated that very little if any of the RNA synthesized at the earliest stage of nuclear activation is transferred to the cytoplasm. It is not till the fourth or fifth day after cell fusion i.e. after the nucleolus has formed that transfer of RNA from the erythrocyte nucleus to the cytoplasm can be demonstrated.

(d) *Increase in nuclear dry mass and volume*

The marked increase in nuclear dry mass which occurs during the activation of the erythrocyte and lymphocyte nuclei are apparently due to the accumulation of proteins in the nuclear compartment. The increase in dry mass occurs to a great extent before DNA replication has begun and before any significant amounts of RNA have accumulated. In the lymphocytes most of this increase must be due to the net synthesis of new proteins specified by the lymphocyte nuclei. In the erythrocyte-heretokaryons it appears, however, that HeLa proteins may move from the cytoplasm into the erythrocyte nucleus. In this system both the induction of DNP changes and the increase in dry mass can take place in the absence of any significant RNA synthesis in the erythrocyte nucleus. That proteins move from the cytoplasm into the erythrocyte nucleus is hardly surprising as such since most if not all the nuclear proteins are normally synthesized in the cytoplasm and migrate into the nucleus. More remarkable would be the low degree of specificity in protein migration into the nucleus.

It is difficult to decide what causes the shift in protein distribution between the cytoplasm and the erythrocyte nuclei. One possibility is that the initial DNP change results in a more 'charged' DNP which is capable of binding and retaining more of the proteins which enter the nuclear compartment. It seems probable that the type of protein available for binding to the DNA can be of great importance for the regulation of gene expression at the transcription level. Results obtained by Bonner et al., Paul and Gilmour and other groups indicate that histones and other DNA linked proteins modulate the template properties of the chromatin. (For reviews see Bonner et al. and Hnilica.)

(e) *DNA synthesis*

In both the hen erythrocyte-heterokaryon system and PHA-lymphocyte systems DNA synthesis is initiated at a relatively late stage in the activation process. The increase in DNA quantity is of importance in the regulation of over-all RNA synthesis since more template becomes available for transcription. That under normal circumstances an increase in the amount of template also results in an increase in transcription is indicated by the results of Zetterberg and Killander. These authors found that in fibroblasts the rate of RNA synthesis is proportional to the amount of DNA.

(f) *Nucleolus and ribosomal RNA synthesis*

In both the hen erythrocyte and lymphocyte nuclei the formation of a nucleolus and the appearance of 16 and 28 S RNA constitute later steps in the nuclear activation process. Harris et al. have suggested that the formation of the nucleolus and the 28 S ribosomal subunit is important for the transfer of RNA containing genetic information to the cytoplasm. It appears that the 28 S ribosomal subunit synthesized in the nucleolus may engage the polydisperse RNA which carries the genetic information and ferry this RNA to the cytoplasm of the cell (Harris et al.). If the nucleolus has not yet been formed and no 28 S subunits are present the polydisperse RNA is rapidly degraded. If the 28 S subunits are available they may help protect the polydisperse RNA from degradation in the nucleus.

It seems likely on the basis of Harris results that the nucleolus and the 28 S ribosomal subunit may play an important role in the regulation of gene expression at a level intermediate between the transcription and translation levels. The genes controlling the production of 28 S RNA may regulate the total volume of genetic information which reaches the cytoplasm.

(g) *Specific protein synthesis*
In the PHA stimulated lymphocytes it is obvious from the marked increase in cellular dry mass that a marked increase in protein synthesis follows upon nuclear activation (Darzynkiewicz et al. 1967; Steffen and Sören). This appears to be the case also in the hen erythrocyte/HeLa cell heterokaryons where Harris et al. find a marked increase in hen specific antigens. This begins on the fourth to eighth day after cell fusion i.e. after the erythrocyte nuclei have formed their nucleoli.

6. *Conclusions*

The cytochemical properties of nuclear proteins and deoxyribonucleoproteins (DNP) complexes vary markedly during the cell growth cycle and during differentiation. Such variations are reviewed and discussed with special reference to the mechanisms which regulate gene expression in animal cells.

From cytochemical studies on nuclei undergoing large-scale activation, it appears that gene expression is controlled at many different levels.

(1) Nuclear activation is accompanied by striking changes in the properties of the DNP complex. Experiments with HeLa cell–hen erythrocyte heterokaryons and a model system based on hen erythrocyte ghosts indicate that the first step in nuclear activation involves changes in the physicochemical properties of DNP triggered by changes in the ionic environment and by membrane phenomena. This chromatin activation reaction may serve as one step in the transformation of inactive chromatin into an active template for RNA synthesis.

(2) The DNP is probably further modified by enzymatic modifications of the proteins bound to DNA. It seems possible that acetylation of histones may represent a second step in the nuclear activation process. Among lymphocytes stimulated by phytohemagglutinin all cells undergo the first step involving changes in the physicochemical properties. The second step as measured by C^{14}-acetate incorporation into intact lymphocytes appears to affect only that portion of the lymphocyte population which actually initiates RNA synthesis. It is also only a part of the lymphocyte population which acquires an increased ability to bind H^3-actinomycin. This suggests that the transformation of inactive chromatin into an active template may involve several steps and that some cells which undergo the first step are 'switched off' by their inability to undergo later steps.

(3) Following the initial DNP-changes, the nuclear protein content increases markedly. In the case of the hen erythrocyte nucleus undergoing reactivation in HeLa–hen erythrocyte heterokaryons, this process appears to be a passive phenomenon which is

independent of RNA synthesis in the hen erythrocyte nucleus. The results obtained indicate that HeLa proteins migrate into the erythrocyte nucleus from the cytoplasm. It is proposed that the shift in protein distribution between the cytoplasmic and nuclear compartments is caused by the altered properties of the DNP complex. The unmasking of negatively charged groups in the DNP complex may serve to retain more protein and water in the nucleus. On the basis of previous chemical work on isolated chromatin it seems logical to assume that such a change in the binding of proteins to DNA can be very important in regulating gene expression at the transcription level.

(4) The DNA synthesis which is initiated later in the activation process is of importance for the regulation of gene expression since it makes more template available for transcription.

(5) During the activation of erythrocyte and lymphocyte nuclei there is a marked change in the type of RNA produced. At the earliest stage, polydisperse, rapidly labelled and rapidly degraded RNA is produced. At a later stage of the activation process more stable 28 S and 16 S RNA fractions appear and nucleoli are formed. Evidence obtained by Harris using cell hybrids suggests that the formation of a nucleolus and the appearance of the 28 S ribosomal subunit may be steps necessary for the transfer of genetic information from the nucleus to the cytoplasm. The 28 S ribosomal subunit may act as an adaptor engaging rapidly labelled RNA, thereby protecting this RNA from degradation by intranuclear enzymes or facilitating its passage across the nuclear membrane. It is possible that in animal cells the genes and factors which control the production of the 28 S ribosomal subunit also act as regulators for the total volume of genetic information transferred to the cytoplasm. This would represent a level of control which would be intermediate to the transcription and translation levels.

References

AGRELL, I. and H. A. BERGQVIST: Cytochemical evidence for varied DNA complexes of undifferentiated cells. J. Cell Biol. 15 (1962) 604.

ALFERT, M.: Variations in cytochemical properties of cell nuclei. Exptl. Cell Res., Suppl. 6 (1958) 227.

ARRIGHI, F. E. and T. C. HSU: Experimental alteration of metaphase chromosome morphology. Effect of Actinomycin D. Exptl. Cell Res. 39 (1965) 305.

BENDER, M. A. and D. M. PRESCOTT: DNA synthesis and mitosis in cultures of human peripheral leucocytes. Exptl. Cell Res. 27 (1962) 221.

BLACK, M. M. and H. R. ANSLEY: Antigen induced changes in lymphoid cell histones. I. Thymus. J. Cell Biol. 26 (1965) 201

BLOCH, D P. and S. D. BRACK: Evidence for the cytoplasmic synthesis of nuclear histone during spermiogenesis in the grasshopper *Chortophaga viridifasciata* (De Geer). J. Cell Biol. 22 (1964) 327.

BLOCH, D. P. and G. C. GODMAN: A microphotometric study of the synthesis of desoxyribonucleic acid and nuclear histone. J. Biophys. Biochem. Cytol. 1 (1955a) 17.

BLOCH, D. and G. GODMAN: Evidence of differences in the desoxyribonucleoprotein complex of rapidly proliferating and non-dividing cells. J. Biophys. Biochem. Cytol. 1 (1955b) 531.

BLOCH, D. P. and H. Y. C. HEW: Schedule of spermatogenesis in the pulmonate snail *Helix aspersa* with special reference to histone transition. J. Biophys. Biochem. Cytol. 7 (1960) 515.

BOLUND, L., N. R. RINGERTZ and H. HARRIS: Changes in the cytochemical properties of erythrocyte nuclei reactivated by cell fusion. J. Cell Sci. In print.

BONNER, J., M. E. DAHMUS, D. FAMBROUGH, R. C. HUANG, K. MARUSHIGE and D. Y. H. TUAN: The biology of isolated chromatin. Science 159 (1968) 47.

BRACHET, J. and A. FICQ: Binding sites of ^{14}C-Actinomycin in amphibian ovocytes and an autoradiography technique for the detection of cytoplasmic DNA. Exptl. Cell Res. 38 (1965) 153.

BRACHET, J., N. HULIN and J. GUERMONT: Acid lability of deoxyribonucleic acids and cell differentiation. Exptl. Cell Res. 51 (1968) 509.

BURTON, D. W.: Initial changes in the DNP-complexes of kangaroo lymphocytes stimulated with phytohemagglutinin. Exptl. Cell Res. 53 (1968) 329.

BUSCH, H.: Histones and other nuclear proteins. New York, Academic Press (1965).

BYERS, T. S., B. PLATT and L. GOLDSTEIN: The cytonucleoproteins of Amoebae. I. Some chemical properties and intracellular distribution. II. Some aspects of cytonucleoprotein behaviour and synthesis. J. Cell Biol. 19 (1963) 453 and 467.

CAMERON, I. L. and D. M. PRESCOTT: RNA and protein metabolism in the maturation of the nucleated chicken erythrocyte. Exptl. Cell Res. 30 (1963) 609.

CASPERSSON, T. O.: Die quantitative Bestimmung von Thymonukleinsäure mittels fuchsinschwefliger Säure. Biochem. Z. 253 (1932) 97.

CASPERSSON, T. O. and G. M. LOMAKKA: Scanning microscopy techniques for high-resolution quantitative cytochemistry. Ann. N.Y. Acad. Sci. 97 (1962) 449.

CERRONI, R. E. and R. J. NEFF: Inhibition of the Feulgen reaction by ions. Exptl. Cell Res. 16 (1959) 465.

CHAMBERLAIN, P. J. and P. WALKER: The thermal denaturation of nucleoprotein in boar sperm. J. Mol. Biol. 11 (1965) 1.

COOPER, H. L. and A. D. RUBIN: Synthesis of nonribosomal RNA by lymphocytes: A response to phytohemagglutinin treatment. Science 152 (1966) 516.

DARZYNKIEWICZ, Z., V. K. DOKOV and M. PIENKOWSKI: Dry mass of lymphocytes during transformation after stimulation by phytohaemagglutinin. Nature 214 (1967) 1265.

DARZYNKIEWICZ, Z., T. KRASSOWSKI and E. SKOPINSKA: Effect of phytohemagglutinin on synthesis of 'rapidly labelled' ribonucleic acid in human lymphocytes. Nature 207 (1965) 1402.

DARZYNKIEWICZ, Z. and M. PIENKOWSKI: Autoradiographic studies on the stability of ribonucleic acid in phytohemagglutinin stimulated lymphocytes. Exptl. Cell Res. In print.

DAS, C. C., B. P. KAUFMANN and H. GAY: Histone-protein transition in *Drosophila melanogaster*. Exptl. Cell Res. 35 (1964) 507.

DEITCH, A. D.: Cytophotometry of nucleic acids. In: G. L. Wied, ed.: Introduction to quantitative cytochemistry. New York, Academic Press (1966).

DOVE, W. F. and N. DAVIDSON: Cation effects on the denaturation of DNA. J. Mol. Biol. 5 (1962) 467.

FISHER, D. B. and G. C. MUELLER: An early alteration in the phospholipid metabolism of lymphocytes by phytohemagglutinin. Proc. Natl. Acad. Sci. 60 (1968) 1369.

FORSDYKE, D. R.: Association of attachment to glass with activation of cultured lymphocytes by phytohemagglutinin. Biochem. J. 104 (1967) 68P.

GALL, J. G.: Macronuclear duplication in the ciliated protozoan *Euplotes*. J. Biophys. Biochem. Cytol. 5 (1959) 295.

GELLERT, M., C. E. SMITH, D. NEVILLE and G. FELSENFELD: Actinomycin binding to DNA. Mechanism and specificity. J. Mol. Biol. 11 (1965) 445.

GLEDHILL, B. L., M. P. GLEDHILL, R. RIGLER, JR. and N. R. RINGERTZ: Changes in deoxyribonucleoprotein during spermiogenesis in the bull. Exptl. Cell Res. 41 (1966a) 652.

GLEDHILL, B. L., M. P. GLEDHILL, R. RIGLER, JR. and N. R. RINGERTZ: Atypical changes of deoxyribonucleoprotein during spermiogenesis associated with a case of infertility in the bull. J. Reprod. Fertility 12 (1966b) 575.

HARRIS, H.: Behaviour of differentiated nuclei in heterokaryons of animal cells from different species. Nature 206 (1965) 583.

HARRIS, H.: The reactivation of the red cell nucleus. J. Cell Sci. 2 (1967) 23.

HARRIS, H., E. SIDEBOTTOM, D. M. GRACE and M. E. BRAMWELL: The expression of genetic information. A study with hybrid animal cells. J. Cell Sci. In print.

HILTON, J. and L. A. STOCKEN: The role of thiol groups in the modification of the template activity of histone-deoxyribonucleic acid complexes. Biochem. J. 100 (1966) 21C.

HNILICA, L. S.: Proteins of the cell nucleus. In: J. N. Davidson and W. E. Cohn, eds.: Progress in nucleic acid research and molecular biology. 7 (1967) 25. Academic Press, New York.

KAY, J. E.: Early effects of phytohemagglutinin on lymphocyte RNA synthesis. European J. Biochem. 4 (1968) 225.

KAY, J. E. and A. KORNER: Effect of cycloheximide on protein and ribonucleic acid synthesis in cultured human lymphocytes. Biochem. J. 100 (1966) 815.

KILLANDER, D., C. RIBBING, N. R. RINGERTZ and B. M. RICHARDS: The effect of X-radiation on nuclear synthesis of protein and DNA. Exptl. Cell Res. 27 (1962) 63.

KILLANDER, D. and R. RIGLER, JR.: Initial changes of deoxyribonucleoprotein and synthesis of nucleic acid in phytohemagglutinin-stimulated human leukocytes *in vitro*. Exptl. Cell Res. 39 (1965) 701.

KIMBALL, R. F., L. VOGT-KÖHNE and T. O. CASPERSSON: Quantitative cytochemical studies on *Paramecium aurelia*. III. Dry weight and ultraviolet absorption of isolated macronuclei during various stages of the interdivision interval. Exptl. Cell Res. 20 (1960) 368.

KLEINSMITH, L. J., V. G. ALLFREY and A. E. MIRSKY: Phosphoprotein metabolism in isolated lymphocyte nuclei. Proc. Natl. Acad. Sci. 55 (1966) 1182.

KROEGER, H.: Potentialdifferenz und Puff-muster. Exptl. Cell Res. 41 (1966) 64.

LAWLEY, P. D.: Interaction studies with DNA. IV. The binding of 5-aminoacridine studied fluorimetrically and its comparison with the binding of rosaniline. Biochim. Biophys. Acta 22 (1956) 451.

LEUCHTENBERGER, C., I. MURMANIS, L. MURMANIS, S. ITO and D. R. WEIR: Interferometric dry mass and microspectrophotometric arginine determinations on bull sperm nuclei with dry mass and microspectrophotometric arginine determinations on bull sperm nuclei with normal and abnormal DNA content. Chromosoma 8 (1956) 73.

LEUCHTENBERGER, C., F. SCHRADER, D. R. WEIR and D. P. GENTILE: The deoxyribonucleic acid (DNA) content in spermatozoa of fertile and infertile human males. Chromosoma 6 (1953) 61.

LINDSTRÖM, M., A. ZETTERBERG and L. CARLSSON: Quantitative microspectrophotometric analysis of nucleic acids in concentrated solutions, in solid droplets and in lymphocytes. Exptl. Cell Res. 43 (1966) 537.

LITTLEFIELD, J. W.: The periodic synthesis of thymidine kinase in mouse fibroblasts. Biochim. Biophys. Acta 114 (1966) 398.

LITTLEFIELD, J. W. and P. S. JACOBS: The relation between DNA and protein synthesis in mouse fibroblasts. Biochim. Biophys. Acta 108 (1965) 652.

MAZIA, D.: The particulate organization of the chromosome. Proc. Natl. Acad. Sci. U.S. 40 (1954) 521.

MONESI, V.: Synthetic activities during spermatogenesis in the mouse. Exptl. Cell Res. 39 (1965) 197.

MOORHEAD, J. F., J. J. CONNOLLY and W. MCFARLAND: Factors affecting the reactivity of human lymphocytes in vitro. I. Cell number, duration of culture and surface area. J. Immunol. 99 (1967) 413.

MUKHERJEE, A. B. and M. M. COHEN: Histone acetylation: cytological evidence in human lymphocytes. Exptl. Cell Res. In press.

ORD, M. G. and L. A. STOCKEN: Metabolic properties of histones from rat liver and thymus gland. Biochem. J. 98 (1966) 888.

PAUL, J. and R. S. GILMOUR: Template activity of DNA is restricted in chromatin. J. Mol. Biol. 16 (1966) 242.

POGO, B.G.T., V.G.ALLFREY and A.E.MIRKSY: RNA synthesis and histone acetylation during the course of gene activation in lymphocytes. Proc. Natl. Acad. Sci., U.S. 55 (1966) 805.

PRESCOTT, D.M.: The synthesis of total macronuclear protein, histone and DNA during the cell cycle in *Euplotes eurystomus*. J. Cell Biol. 31 (1966) 1.

PRESCOTT, D.M. and M.A.BENDER: Synthesis and behaviour of nuclear proteins during the cell life cycle. J. Cellular. Comp. Physiol. 62 (1963) 175.

PRESCOTT, D.M. and R.F.KIMBALL: Relation between RNA, DNA and protein synthesis in the replicating nucleus of *Euplotes*. Proc. Natl. Acad. Sci., U.S. 47 (1961) 686.

REICH, E. and I.H.GOLDBERG: Actinomycin and nucleic acid function. In: J.N.Davidson and W.E. Cohn, eds.: Progress in nucleic acid research and molecular biology. New York, Academic Press (1964).

REIN, A. and H.RUBIN: Effects of local cell concentrations upon the growth of chick embryo cells in tissue culture. Exptl. Cell Res. 49 (1968) 666.

RIGLER, R., JR.: Microfluorometric chracterization of intracellular nucleic acids and nucleoproteins by acridine orange. Acta Physiol. Suppl. 267, vol. 64 (1966).

RIGLER, R. and D.KILLANDER: Activation of deoxyribonucleoprotein in human leucocytes stimulated by phytohemagglutinin. Exptl. Cell Res. In print.

RIGLER, R., D.KILLANDER, L.BOLUND and N.R.RINGERTZ: Cytochemical characterization of deoxyribonucleoprotein in individual cell nuclei. Techniques for obtaining heat denaturation curves with the aid of acridine orange microfluorimetry and ultraviolet microspectrophotometry. Exptl. Cell Res. In press.

RINGERTZ, N.R.: The effect of X-radiation on nuclear histone content. Exptl. Cell Res. 32 (1963) 401.

RINGERTZ, N.R. and L.BOLUND: Actinomycin binding to deoxyribonucleoprotein. Biochim. Biophys. Acta. In print.

RINGERTZ, N.R. and L.BOLUND: 'Activation' of hen erythrocyte deoxyribonucleoprotein. Exptl. Cell Res. In press.

RINGERTZ, N.R. and G.C.HOSKINS: Cytochemistry of macronuclear reorganization. Exptl. Cell Res. 38 (1965) 160.

RINGERTZ, N.R. and A.ZETTERBERG: Cytochemical demonstration of histones and protamines. Mechanism and specificity of the alkaline bromphenol blue binding reaction. Exptl. Cell Res. 42 (1966) 243.

ROBBINS, E. and T.BORUN: The cytoplasmic synthesis of histone in HeLa cells and its temporal relationship to DNA replication. Proc. Natl. Acad. Sci. 57 (1967) 409.

SANDRITTER, W., K.JOBST, L.RAKOW and K.BOSSELMANN: Zur Kinetik der Feulgenreaktion bei verlängerter Hydrolysezeit. Histochemie 4 (1965) 420.

SANDRITTER, W., G.KIEFER and W.RICK: Gallocyanin chrome alum. In: G.L.Wied, ed.: Introduction to quantitative cytochemistry. New York, Academic Press (1966).

SCHULTZE, B. and W.MAURER: In: Tritium in the physical and biological sciences. Vol. II. p. 229 (1900) International Atomic Energy Agency, Vienna.

SCOTT, J.E.: On the mechanism of the methylgreen pyronin stain for nucleic acids. Histochemie 9 (1967) 30.

STEDMAN, E. and E.STEDMAN: Probable function of histone as a regulator of mitosis. Nature 152 (1943) 556.

STEFFEN, J. and L.SÖREN: Changes in dry mass of PHA stimulated human lymphocytes during blast transformation. Exptl. Cell Res. 53 (1968) 626.

TIDWELL, T., V.G.ALLFREY and A.E.MIRSKY: The methylation of histones during regeneration of the liver. J. Biol. Chem. 243 (1968) 707.

VALENTINE, F.T. and H.S.LAWRENCE: Role of cell density in response of lymphocyte cultures to antigenic stimulation. Fed. Proc. 27 (1968) 265.

ZETTERBERG, A.: Synthesis and accumulation of nuclear and cytoplasmic proteins during interphase in mouse fibroblasts in vitro. Exptl. Cell Res. 42 (1966) 500.

ZETTERBERG, A. and G. AUER: The effect of phytohemagglutinin on histone stainability of human lymphocytes. Exptl. Cell Res. In print.

ZETTERBERG, A. and D. KILLANDER: Quantitative cytochemical studies on interphase growth. Exptl. Cell Res. 39 (1965) 22.

PART IX

Chromosome abnormalities and other pathological conditions

CHAPTER 28

Ultrastructure of the cancer cell

W. BERNHARD

Institut de Recherches sur le Cancer, 94-Villejuif, France

Contents

1. Introduction

2. Ultrastructural variations of cancer cells from spontaneous or experimentally induced tumors
   (a) The nucleus
      (1) The nuclear membrane
      (2) The nucleoplasm
      (3) The nucleolus
      (4) Chromosomes and mitosis
   (b) The cytoplasm
      (1) Mitochondria
      (2) Ribosomes and ergastoplasm
      (3) The Golgi apparatus
      (4) Other cytoplasmic organelles
      (5) Pathological inclusions
      (6) The cell membrane
      (7) Intercellular connections
   (c) The problem of anaplasia

3. Early ultrastructural changes induced by chemical carcinogens

4. The significance of virus particles in tumor cells
   (a) DNA viruses
   (b) RNA viruses

5. Model systems of *in vitro* transformed cells

6. Summary

1. Introduction

The title of this chapter indicates that we are considering the rather abstract concept of 'the' cancer cell, as if there were a characteristic ultrastructural feature of malignancy, easily distinguishable from the normal cell. In fact, the fine structure of tumor cells is as variable as that of their normal homologues and no specific and universally present pattern of cancer has ever been found in spite of 15 years of electron microscopical research. The routine diagnosis of cancer remains based on histological rather than on cytological or even fine structural criteria and it is certainly more appropriate to speak of cancer cells in the plural (Fig. 1). Nevertheless, in spite of their bewildering polymorphism, an attempt will be made to present the most characteristic lesions, frequently encountered in tumor cells, whatever their histological origin may be. The definition of malignancy is still dependent on clinical criteria i.e., whether or not a cell invades other tissues and thus no longer follows the laws of growth regulation in a normal organism.

If the pathogenetical problem of cancer is still unsolved, it is precisely due to the fact that the differences between the normal cell and the cancer cell – at least before it outgrows to a tumor tissue – are minute. Looking at the morphological and physiological characteristics of the malignant cell, we can speak of *tendencies* or *rules*, not of strict laws. Thus, the ultrastructural features of the malignant cell in the early stages of its transformation are similar to those of the homologous normal cells. Only after a certain number of cell divisions and under the influence of complex nutritional or immunological factors will the initial differences, probably already present on the molecular level, be amplified and become visible on the ultrastructural and, finally, on the light microscopical level. It would be impossible to give a complete bibliography on this subject, which would have to include several thousands of papers. Previous reviews should be consulted (Oberling and Bernhard; Bernhard 1961, 1963; Dalton 1959; Luse).

2. Ultrastructural variations of cancer cells from spontaneous or experimentally induced tumors

It has to be remembered that a solid tumor is not homogeneous from the cytological point of view. Blood vessels and blood cells, accompanied by fibroblasts and collagen belong to the common scaffold of tumor tissue. Grinding of such specimens for biochemical or immunological use will necessarily include an uncertain amount of non-malignant cells. Furthermore, necrobiotic phenomena are extremely frequent in solid tumors. Such areas are difficult to recognize, as those cells are still functioning, but under poor physiological conditions. The ultrastructural pattern will be changed accordingly with clumping of the chromatin, swelling of the mitochondria and the ergastoplasmic cisternae and the appearance of lipid inclusions as the most common

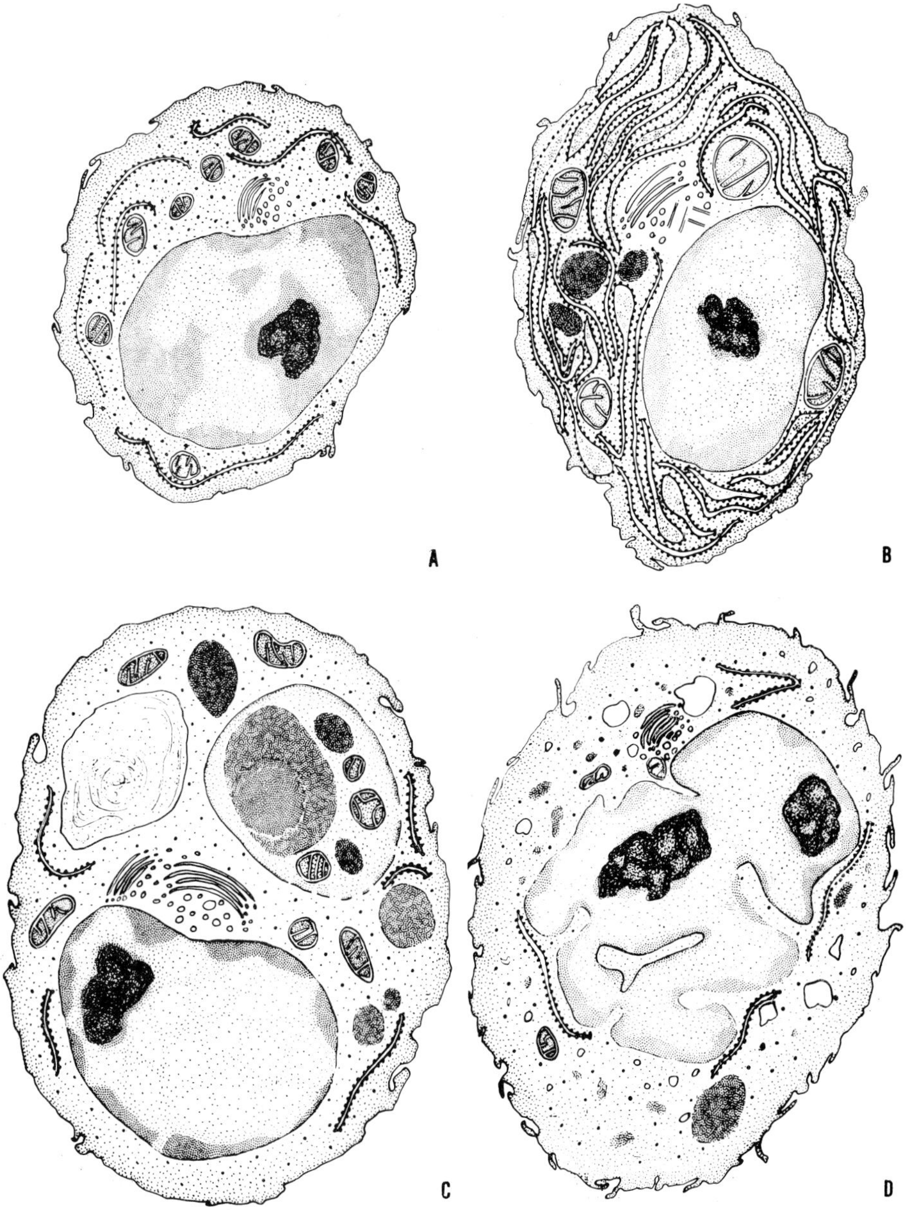

Fig. 1. Polymorphism of cancer cells. Schematic representation of four different types. A. Malignant human lymphoblast from a human lymphosarcoma. No fine structural difference compared with normal lymphoblasts. B. Plasmoblast-like cell from malignant human reticulum cell sarcoma, abundant ergastoplasmic lamellae. C. Cytoplasmic inclusions revealing strong phagocytic activity of a tumor cell in a reticulosarcoma. D. Sternberg–Reed cell from a case of Hodgkin's disease. Large nucleoli, deep invaginations of the nuclear membrane. Anaplastic cytoplasm with lysosomes. (From Bernhard and Leplus.)

non-specific changes. Electron micrographs representing tumor tissues have always to be checked for such alterations which are not directly linked with the malignant process, but are frequently present in tumor tissue.

(a) *The nucleus*

The interphase nucleus of cancer cells is usually enlarged and shows an irregular outline. The nucleo-cytoplasmic ratio is increased. The large size of the nucleus is probably in many cases linked with the increased ploidy of the chromosome set, frequently encountered in cancer cells. But the nuclear size may also be enlarged by swelling under unphysiological conditions ('nuclear edema'). Ultrastructural changes of the nuclear components in cancer cells are observed as follows (Fig. 2).

(1) *The nuclear membrane.* As far as its fine structure is concerned, there dose not seem to be any difference between normal and malignant cells. Tangential sections occasionally reveal groups of nuclear pores of the same size and spacing as in normal cells. The only unusual features which are frequently found are deep invaginations of the membrane into the nucleoplasm, leading to narrow clefts which may be single or multiple and which are frequently in contact with a nucleolus. These infoldings are responsible for the irregular outline of many cancer cell nuclei. One may speculate that they are associated with a regulatory mechanism which could facilitate nucleo-cytoplasmic exchange. It also seems probable that some of these deep clefts may lead to total segregation of portions of nuclei, thus inducing nuclear fragmentation ('amitosis'). The more irregular the surface of the nucleus, the more likely are tangential sections of the nuclear membrane. This is the reason why pictures representing nuclear pores are more frequently encountered in certain tumor cells. Other types of malformations of the nuclear membrane which lead either to infolding or to cytoplasmic projections are called *nuclear blebs*, described by Achong and Epstein in Burkitt tumors and by McDuffie in human leukemic cells.

(2) *The nucleoplasm.* It is here defined as the whole nuclear content with the exception of the nucleolus, but including both hetero- and euchromatin and the inter-chromatinic substance of the interphase nucleus. It is obvious that changes of the karyotype will induce more or less important changes in the interphase. Irregular distribution or increase of chromatin are often observed. No ultrastructural changes are visible in the twisted nucleohistone filaments on thin sections. Margination of chromatin may simply be more accentuated but it is probably a non-specific reaction of the tumor cell to environmental factors. It is very pronounced in dying cells (Yasuzumi et al.). *Perichromatin granules* have been observed in increased numbers in various tumors, e.g., in human mammary scirrhus (Murad and Scarpelli). Their size is similar to that described in normal nuclei. The significance of these granules which probably contain RNA and protein altogether is still completely unknown.

The *interchromatinic area* is predominantly filled with proteins, but also contains some uncoiled DNA and various types of RNP granules, among which the *interchroma-*

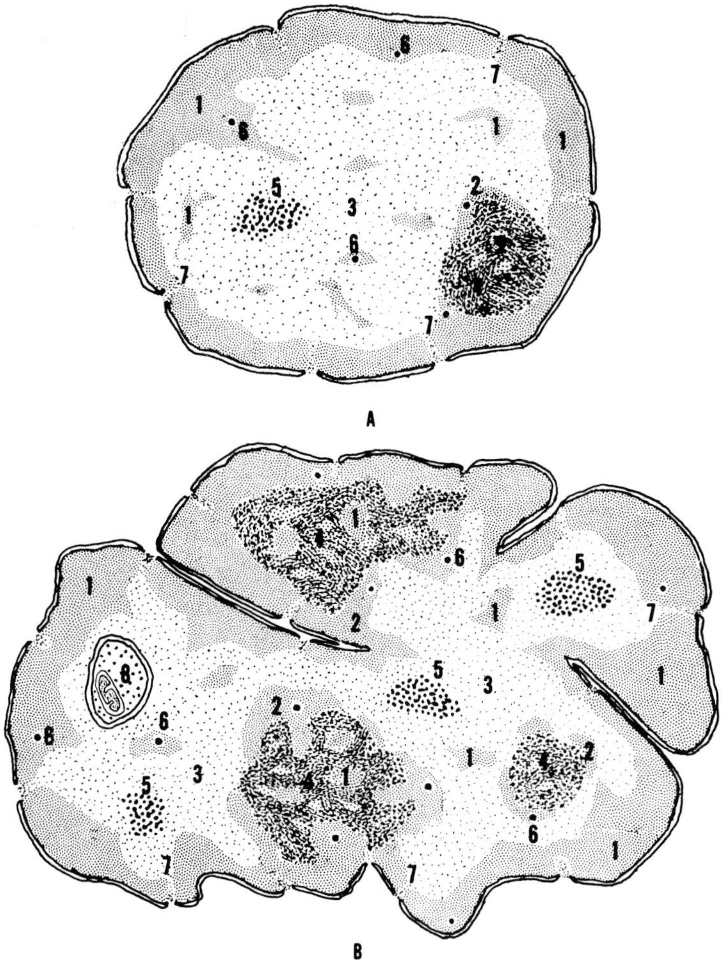

Fig. 2. Schematic representation of a normal (A) and a cancer cell nucleus (B). (1) chromatin; (2) nucleolus-associated chromatin; (3) interchromatinic substance; (4) nucleolus; (5) interchromatin granules; (6) perichromatin granules; (7) nuclear pores; (8) invagination of the nuclear membrane (pseudo-inclusion). The morphological features of cancer cell nuclei vary considerably from case to case. (From Bernhard and Granboulan 1963.)

tin granules are the most easily visible and best defined. Interchromatin granules are mostly present as clusters in which they can be found in linear arrays as elements of small chains. In cancer cells, the number of these granules may be increased, the clusters may appear denser and their form may be more irregular. However, there is no indication that they show any *constant* specific feature compared to normal cells (Bernhard and Granboulan 1963). Finally, it should be mentioned that 'nuclear bodies' (0.2–2 μ in diameter) characterized by concentric fibrillar or lamellar structures which may include small dense granules in their center, were first described in carcinoma cell nuclei by De Thé et al. Such inclusions have since been found in many normal or pathological tissues, but seem to be particularly frequent in tumor cells or any type of activated cells (Bouteille et al. 1967).

(3) *The nucleolus.* The most typical feature of the cancer cell nucleolus is its hypertrophy. The increased size of this organelle, together with the enlarged and irregularly shaped nucleus, are considered as characteristic, although non-specific signs of malignancy. The shape of the nucleolus is often more irregular than in normal cells and quite frequently there are several nucleoli present within one nucleus. This is likely to be a consequence of polyploidy, leading to multiple nucleolar organizers. Concerning the fine structure, it may either be unchanged or show any type of abnormality, leading to extremes (Bernhard and Granboulan 1963, 1968). The chromatin associated with the nucleolus may be prominent or sparse; it may be localized as usual, mainly on the periphery, or penetrate deeply into the nucleolar body. The proportion of macromolecular components of the nucleolus is equally extremely variable: cancer cell nucleoli may contain almost exclusively RNP granules or, on the contrary, RNP fibrils. The nucleolonema may form the usual spongy network, or it may be reduced to small condensed and isolated fibrillar areas. The nucleolar body may be extremely dense and spherical, or it may have the appearance of a loose reticulum with very irregular outlines or be ring-shaped (Smetana et al.). Besides the usual components, various types of intranucleolar pathological inclusions may be found. Single or multiple vacuoles within the nucleolar body are very common. They may have a very low electron density or, on the contrary, be filled with a precipitate of proteins. The most intriguing inclusions appear as multiple dense coarse granules, 0.1–0.3 μ in diameter, attached to the threads of the nucleolonema. Such granules have been found in nucleoli of Sternberg–Reed cells in Hodgkin's disease (Leplus et al.). Much attention has been paid to such lesions because of the fact that similar granules appear in cells infected with viruses, such as polyoma, herpes simplex, Molluscum contagiosum, etc. (see Bernhard 1963). Although the origin of such granules might also be viral in the mentioned human tumor cells, these observations do not prove the presence of a latent virus.

Many of the variations in size, shape and composition of the cancer cell nucleolus may simply be due to increased growth, nutritional factors or necrobiotic phenomena. Rapidly growing embryonic cells also have large nucleoli. A diet with either excessive or deficient protein will strongly influence the nucleolar fine structure as will autolytic processes. It is, therefore, very difficult to distinguish between primary nucleolar lesions which would be directly linked with the phenomenon of malignant growth and those which are the consequence of it.

(4) *Chromosomes and mitosis.* The study of chromosomes and mitosis in ultrathin sections with the present-day techniques of electron microscopy is unrewarding and has given much less information than has light microscopy. The practically two-

dimensional electron microscopical cytology cannot reveal within one section, the whole number of chromosomes and the highly twisted chromosomal fine structural elements. Coarse chromosomal abnormalities are therefore better detected by the light microscope and fine structural changes, if they really do exist, are unlikely to be revealed. Up to now, no difference in the ultrastructure of chromosomes of normal and malignant cells has been shown. Furthermore, cancer cells seem to have normal centrioles and spindle fibres, with the rare exception of myeloma cells, where the centriole may be much longer than usual (Bessis et al. 1958; Maldonado et al.). The mitotic apparatus, though leading frequently to atypical mitosis ('laggards', aberrant chromosomes, stickiness of chromosomes, tripolar mitoses, etc.) does not, as a rule, have any pathological feature visible with the electron microscope.

(b) *The cytoplasm*

(1) *Mitochondria.* Among all fine structural changes in tumor cells, mitochondrial alterations are the most frequent and striking ones. However they are not constant. Many tumor cells do have mitochondria whose number, shape, and fine structure cannot be distinguished from those of homologous normal cells. But more often than in normal tissue, cancer cell mitochondria are swollen and have structural deficiencies: fewer irregular or parallel tubular cristae (Leduc and Wilson), concentric cristae (Seljelid and Ericsson 1965a), unhomogeneous matrix, myelin figures and irregular shapes of the mitochondrial body, e.g., cup-shaped mitochondria (Trotter). Their size may be larger or, on the contrary, smaller. Some cancer cells may have more mitochondria than usual, others less. The less differentiated a tumor, the less mitochondria are present. On the other hand, there are tumors with an unusually high number of mitochondria e.g., hypernephromas of the kidney (Oberling et al. 1959; Ericsson et al.) and, especially, the so-called oncocytomas, where the whole cytoplasm is packed with mitochondria (Tandler and Shipkey 1964a; Becher; McGavran; Hübner et al). Tumor cell mitochondria may have various kinds of inclusions: glycogen (Tandler and Shipkey 1966a), protein crystals (Hruban et al. 1965), dense irregular bodies (Svoboda 1964).

The origin of mitochondrial deficiencies is uncertain. They may frequently be explained by the lack of adequate nutritional conditions especially in solid tumors If such tumors are cultivated *in vitro* in a suitable medium, swollen and irregular mitochondria may become elongated and have a normal appearance.

There are, however, exceptions. In the case of hamster tumors induced with adenovirus 12, the unusually large, swollen and irregularly shaped mitochondria visible in primary tumors persist through many tissue culture passages, whereas normal controls or hamster cells transformed by polyoma and SV_{40} virus do not show the same feature in identical culture media. Some of these atypical mitochondria have an unusually high amount of DNA fibres (Bernhard and Tournier). The morphology of these mitochondria is influenced by the age of the culture. The lesions are pronounced during exponential growth (Fig. 3). In stationary cultures, mitochondria tend to elongate

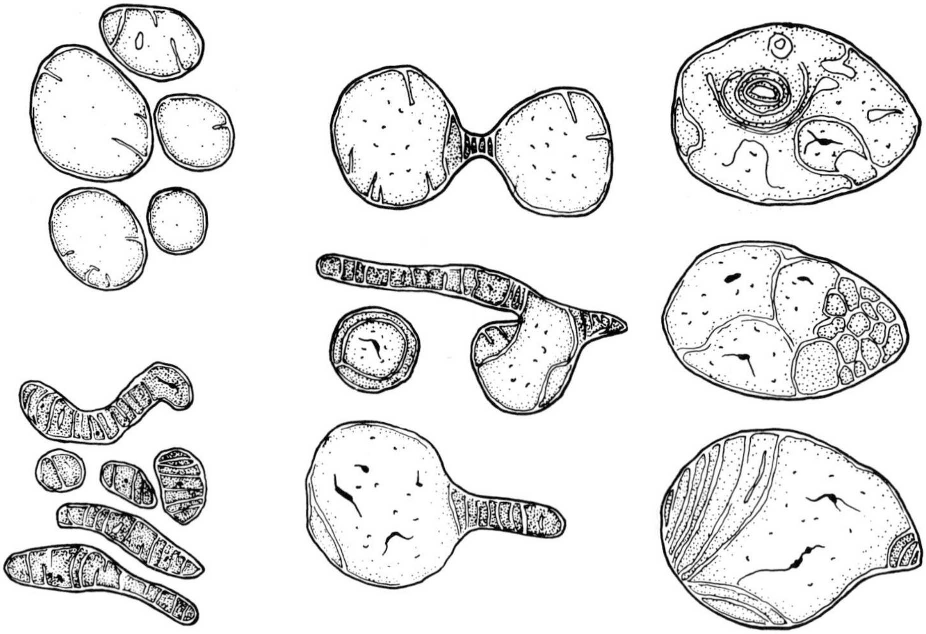

Fig. 3. Normal, swollen and atypical mitochondria in adenovirus 12-induced hamster tumor cells. Similar alterations may be found in other types of cancer cells. Intramitochondrial DNA fibres are frequently observed. (From Bernhard and Tournier.)

and to become normal (Leduc et al. 1966). There is no doubt that in this system some particular transmissible changes of mitochondria occur, but unfortunately the phenotype is subject to too many non-specific changes for these organelles to be used as genetic markers. Morphological alterations of mitochondria, similar to those observed in adenovirus-transformed cells, were also shown in methylcholanthrene-induced tumors, but the transmission of deficient mitochondria was more irregular.

Structural mitochondrial abnormalities in malignant cells are of course of particular importance in view of the fact that cancer tissues may show abnormal glycolysis, observations which led to Warburg's well-known theory of cancer. From the fine structural point of view it is impossible to decide if altered mitochondria in tumor cells are somehow directly linked with the phenomenon of malignant growth or if the alterations are only the consequence of it, depending on karyotypic variations, vascularisation of the tumor, induced microenvironmental changes. However, we have to stress the fact that atypical mitochondria are certainly more frequently observed in cancer tissues than in normal cells.

(2) *Ribosomes and ergastoplasm.* No constant and specific feature can be detected for the ultrastructural substrate of protein synthesis. As a rule, cancer cells grow rapidly and therefore have to produce an increased amount of proteins comparable to

embryonic cells. As already mentioned, the nucleolar apparatus producing ribosomal precursors displays an almost constant hypertrophy. In the cytoplasm, polysomal formations are more frequent. The development of ergastoplasmic lamellae depends upon the degree of differentiation (Figs. 4, 5). In benign adenoma or even cancer cells (e.g., from liver (Dalton 1964) or glandular tissue) the cytoplasm may be packed with ergastoplasm which may even be functional e.g., in milk-producing mouse mammary tumors (Oberling and Bernhard), thyroid tumors (Dmitriyeva; Lupulescu and Petrovici), myeloma cells (Bessis et al. 1963; Maldonado et al. 1966).

However, even cell lines of mesenchymal tumors maintained during many passages *in vitro* may have a considerable amount of ergastoplasmic lamellae, e.g., Rous sarcoma cells, and a methylcholanthrene-induced tumor cell line. In the case of adenovirus 12-induced tumors cultivated *in vitro* there is very little ergastoplasm visible, but many free ribosomes appear. The degree of differentiation in this case is very low, although the conditions of tissue culture are similar (Bernhard and Tournier). The viral genome may influence the architecture of the tumor cell as it was shown by Haguenau and

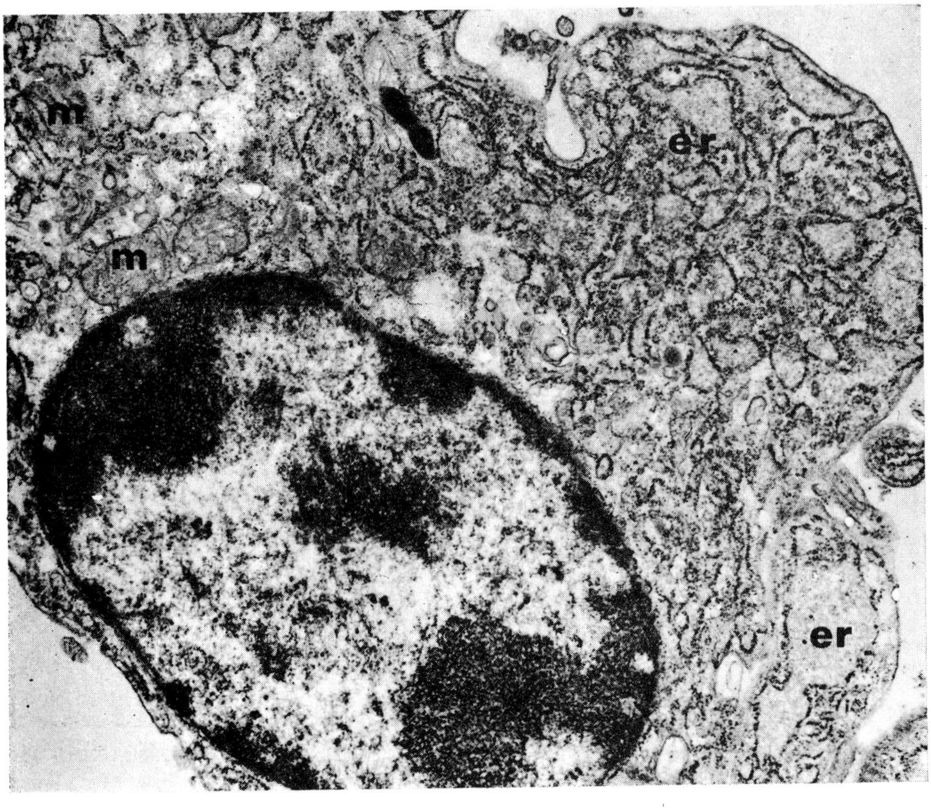

Fig. 4. Epidermoid carcinoma of a bronchus (human). Highly organized ergastoplasm (er) in a tumor cell with glandular appearance. × 15,000.

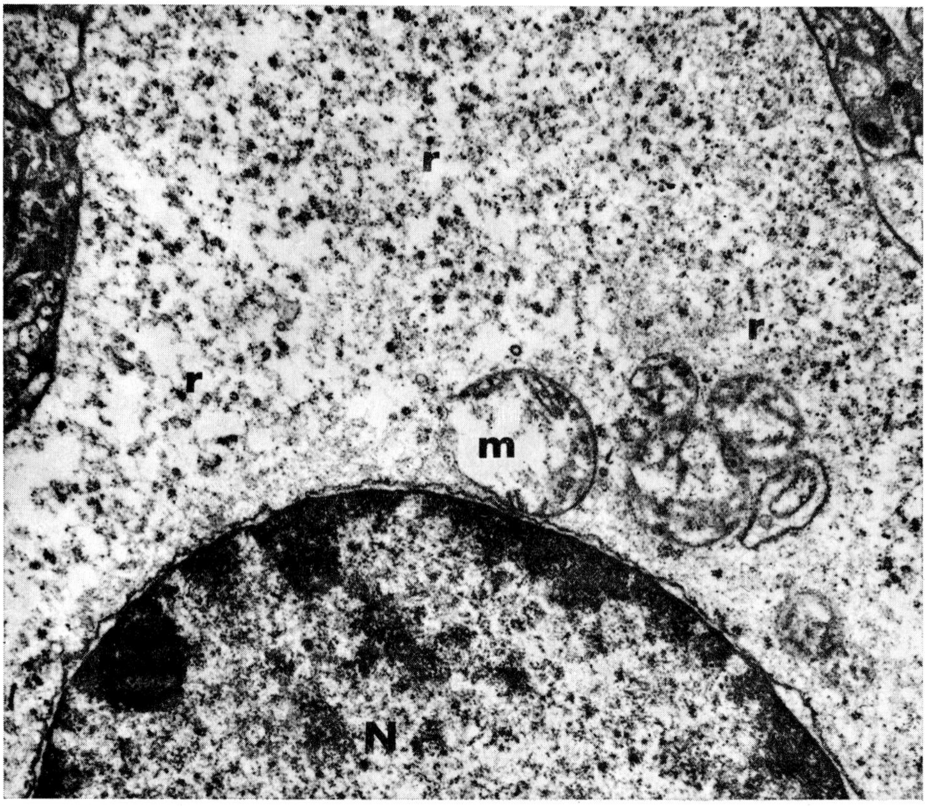

Fig. 5. Epidermoid carcinoma of a bronchus. Same case as Fig. 4. Example of a highly anaplastic tumor cell. Poorly organized cytoplasm. Free ribosomes (r) mostly grouped in rosettes. A few swollen mitochondria (m), and a nucleus (N). × 15,000.

Hanafusa for RAV and Rous virus infected chicken fibroblasts. RAV virus maintains many ergastoplasmic lamellae. Rous virus induces partial disorganization. The growth rate and the age of the tumor cell lines is also important. Very rapidly growing cells have less ergastoplasm than slowly growing ones. Therefore, as for mitochondria, both intrinsic and extrinsic factors influence the degree of development of the ergastoplasm. This is equally true for its shape. The cisternae may be flat with ramifications forming a continuous system, or they may be swollen and disrupted into vesicles. No conclusion whatsoever can be drawn with relation to the malignant process.

(3) *The Golgi apparatus.* This organelle may be considerably developed in tumor cells from exocrine organs, following more or less the degree of organization of the ergastoplasm. Typical examples are mouse mammary tumors which may have a large juxtanuclear Golgi area in which quite frequently virus particles may be found. Spontaneous or experimentally induced hepatomas have a larger Golgi area than normal

liver cells (Dalton 1964; Hruban et al. 1965; Novikoff and Biempica). Rous sarcoma cells may also have a very large Golgi zone. But as a rule the cancer cells have a poorly developed Golgi system. The more the tumors are dedifferentiated, the less it is developed. In frequently cultivated tumor cell lines (e.g., HeLa, Kb, or BHK transformed *in vitro* by polyoma and SV_{40} virus) this organelle is poorly developed and rarely seen on ultrathin sections. Its ultrastructure may undergo considerable variations between the predominantly vesicular or lamellar type, but nothing has been found which could be considered as specific for tumor cells or malignancy. The so-called *multivesicular bodies*, which are related to increased pinocytosis and are often localized in the vicinity of the Golgi area, have been found extremely hypertrophic in some tumors, e.g., in reticulosarcoma cells (Vasquez et al.) and in myelomas (Sorensen). Such formations may be quite similar to viral inclusions.

(4) *Other cytoplasmic organelles. Microbodies* with uricase crystals usually scattered among mitochondria in normal liver cells have also been found frequently in experimentally induced hepatomas (Hruban et al. 1965; Novikoff and Biempica; Ma and Webber).

Annulate lamellae are more frequently encountered in tumor cells than in normal tissues, except in oocytes where they have been described by various authors. Schulz (1957) found similar organelles in a mammary tumor of the rat and since they have been found in many other types of tumor cells (see Chambers and Weiser). Their ultrastructure is similar to that of the nuclear membrane and it has been suggested that they may represent an abnormality in the reconstitution of this membrane after cell division. Another type of membrane structure which is also quite frequently seen in tumor cells is the *paired cisterna* shown by Epstein in HeLa cells and observed in various other tumor tissues, e.g., in a fibromyxosarcoma by Leak et al. 'Paired cisternae' consist of two pairs of closely applied membranes, and are found to be linked with the endoplasmic reticulum.

Unusual organelles, which may be considered as a rather rare accident in tumor cells, are single *cilia* at the cell surface e.g., in Rous sarcoma cells. These organelles are induced during interphase by centrioles which migrate to the vicinity of the cell membrane. Centrioles may thus function as basal corpuscles. Single cilia are also detected in many normal cells within the organ or in tissue culture. An unusually high frequency of cilia has once been observed in an experimental renal hamster tumor (Mannweiler and Bernhard).

(5) *Pathological inclusions.* Cytoplasmic or nuclear inclusions, visible in tumor cells in the light microscope, have played an important role in classical pathology ever since oncologists were looking for etiological agents responsible for cancer, such as parasites, fungi or viruses. One of the important contributions of electron microscopy has been the identification of all these unusual structures.

(5a) *Cytoplasmic inclusions.* We have first to mention various inclusions which are due to persistent cellular activity of the malignant cell, e.g., milk droplets in mammary tumors, mucus in gastric cancer (Fig. 6), colloidal substance in thyroid tumors, secretion granules in intestinal carcinoids (Luse and Lacy; Schumacher and Schulz) and bronchial carcinoids (Bouteille et al. 1964; Verley), in insulinomas (Lazarus and Volk; Bencosme et al.; Greider and Elliott) and in phaeochromocytomas (Bässler and Habighorst). Melanin pigment is found in melanomas (Rappaport et al.) (Fig. 7), mast cell granules in mastocytomas (Mengel and Trier; Christensen et al.), eosinophilic granules in certain human leukemias (De Harven et al.), lipids and glycogen in hypernephromas (Oberling et al.), mucopolysaccharides in myxosarcomas, large protein droplets in hepatomas (Hruban et al. 1966) or protein crystals in oncocytomas (Tandler and Shipkey 1966b). Bundles of tiny cytoplasmic fibrils may be seen in leukemia cells (Bessis and Breton-Gorius) in reticulo-sarcomas (Matsui), gliomas (Bucciarelli et al. 1967b) or in ascites tumors (Bergstrand and Ringertz). Myofilaments may persist in myoepithelial cells from mammary tumors (Haguenau 1959a; David and Mangakis) or in rhabdomyosarcomas (Friedmann et al. 1965). Chordomas

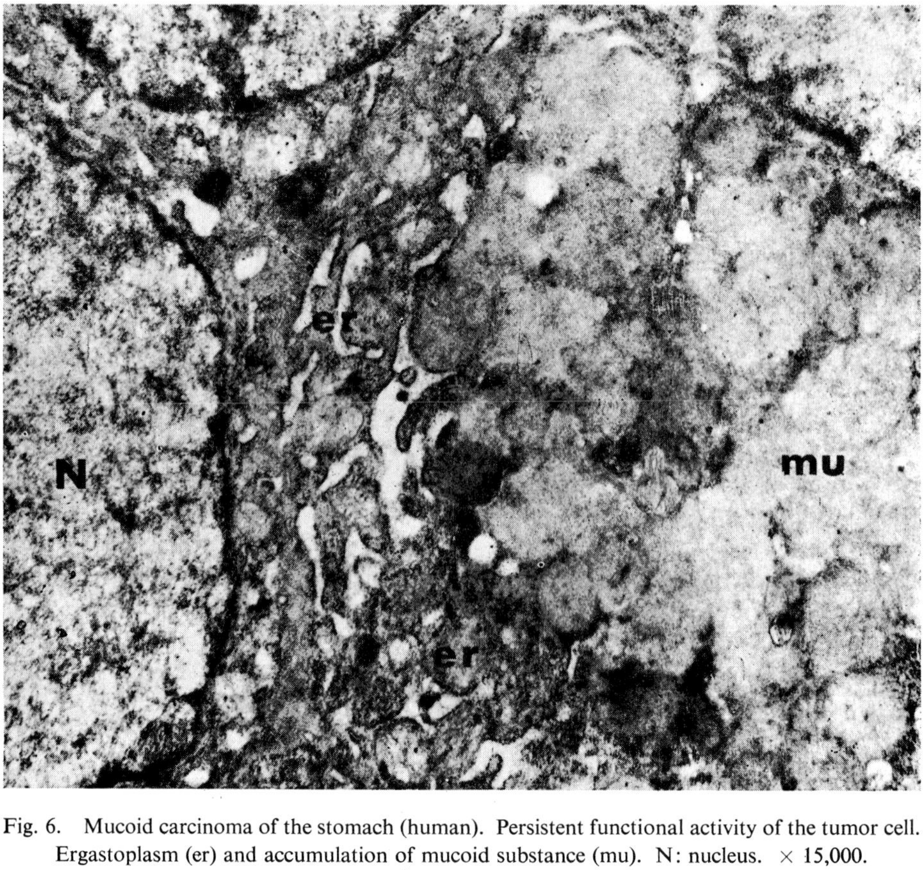

Fig. 6. Mucoid carcinoma of the stomach (human). Persistent functional activity of the tumor cell. Ergastoplasm (er) and accumulation of mucoid substance (mu). N: nucleus. × 15,000.

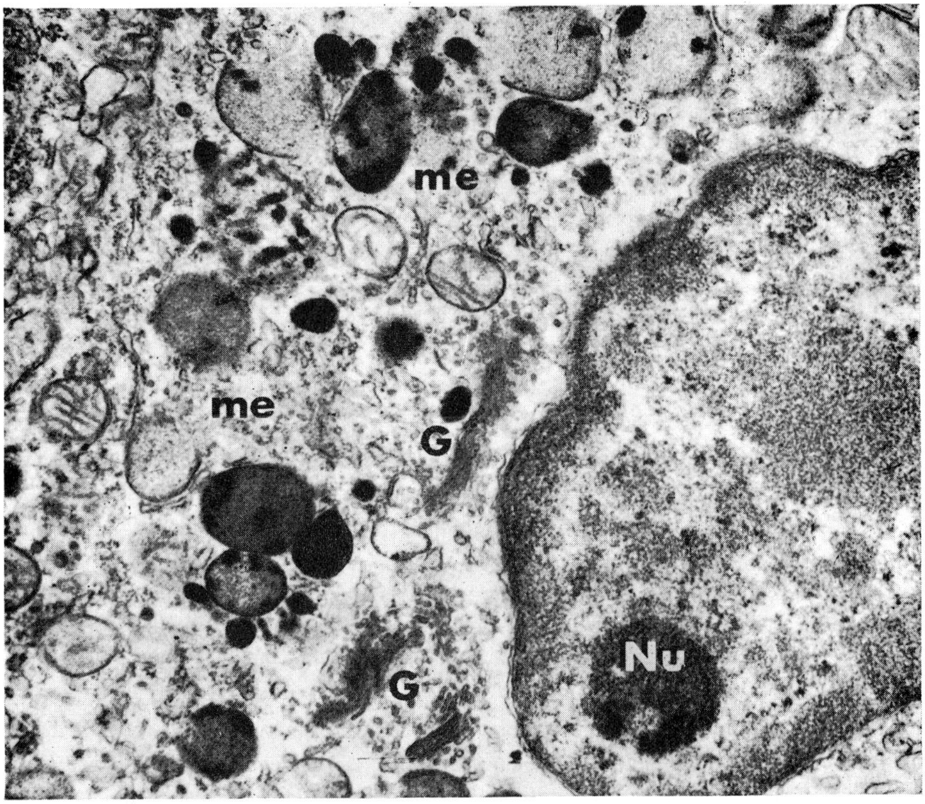

Fig. 7. Malignant melanoblastoma (human). Portion of a tumor cell producing melanin granules (me). Golgi apparatus (G); nucleolus (Nu). × 10,000.

are characterized by large cytoplasmic vacuoles (Friedmann et al. 1962; Spjut and Luse).

Many tumor cells have phagocytic activity. Cell debris of all kinds may be found in the cytoplasm in various stages of disintegration and digestion. In Hodgkin's disease Sternberg–Reed cells may engulf lymphocytes or erythrocytes: phagocytozed nuclei may explain most of the Feulgen-positive cytoplasmic inclusion (Sobin; Fisher and Sharkey). Similar inclusions are observed in reticulum cell sarcomas (Bernhard and Leplus) (Fig. 1). They are found within membrane-bound phagocytic vacuoles which are as usual transformed into lysosomes. Lysosomes with positive acid phosphatase reaction may be extremely numerous in certain tumors (e.g., Takahashi and Mottet). On the other hand, it is possible to observe local cytoplasmic sequestration which leads to autophagic vacuoles (Mao and Molnar; Novikoff and Biempica). Myelin figures as well as fat droplets are also encountered. Many of the light microscopically visible inclusions may be explained by the presence of such non-specific material.

Parasites have not been found, but in the case of mammary tumors of mice, the light microscopically visible 'Guérin bodies' have been revealed as viral inclusions, composed of many so called A-particles (see below). The PAS-positive paranuclear inclusions described by Klärner and Gieseking in pulmonary adenomas of mice are not viral (Svoboda 1962; Hattori et al.).

(5b) *Nuclear inclusions*. The most frequently found nuclear 'inclusions' in tumor cell nuclei are in fact 'pseudo-inclusions', i.e., invaginations of the nuclear membrane, including cytoplasmic material: mitochondria, fat droplets, Golgi material, myelin figures. Such 'pseudo-inclusions' have been observed in many tumors, but similar invaginations also occur under different pathological conditions. However, there also exist pathological inclusions in nuclei without connection with the nuclear membrane. Important glycogen deposits have been shown by Friedlaender-Binggeli in a chemically induced chicken sarcoma. Similar glycogen inclusions have been observed by Gusek in human meningiomas. Vacuoles have been seen by Klärner and Gieseking in pulmonary adenomas of mice. Spherical protein bodies may be found in human mammary tumor nuclei (Haguenau 1959b) and in myeloma cells (Frühling and Porte; Maldonado et al.).

Nuclear viral inclusions in tumor cells have hitherto only been found in the case of the frog adenocarcinoma carrying the Lucké virus, and in cultivated Burkitt tumor cells where a virus similar to herpes appears after several weeks of culture (see below).

(6) *The cell membrane*. Until recently, the electron microscope did not reveal any difference between cell membranes of normal and tumor cells. The classical techniques of double fixation and uranium–lead stain have shown the double leaflets of the unit membrane of total thickness of about 75 Å. Its molecular composition is therefore supposed to be basically similar to that of normal cell membranes. However, the loss of contact inhibition of certain strains of cancer cells observed in tissue culture (see review by Abercrombie and Ambrose) has to be explained by a change of the molecular cell membrane structure. These authors admitted that a generalized diminution of adhesiveness might be an important part of malignant transformation. They also observed an increase of the negative charge of certain cancer strains, perhaps linked with mucopolysaccharide production at the cell surface. It has been demonstrated that normal cells indeed have a very thin layer of mucopolysaccharides on their surface which can be visualized in the electron microscope by means of special cytochemical reactions. Concerning cancer cells, Defendi and Gasic have shown in the light microscope that hamster fibroblasts, transformed *in vitro* by polyoma virus, produce considerably more sialic acid than the normal control cells. This observation was confirmed in detail in electron microscopy for SV_{40} virus and adenovirus 12-transformed hamster cells (Martinez-Palomo and Brailovsky). Using the ruthenium red method by Luft, these authors could demonstrate regular increase of the thickness of the mucopolysaccharide layer in the virus induced tumor cells. Increased mucopolysaccharide production *in vitro* of Rous virus transformed chicken

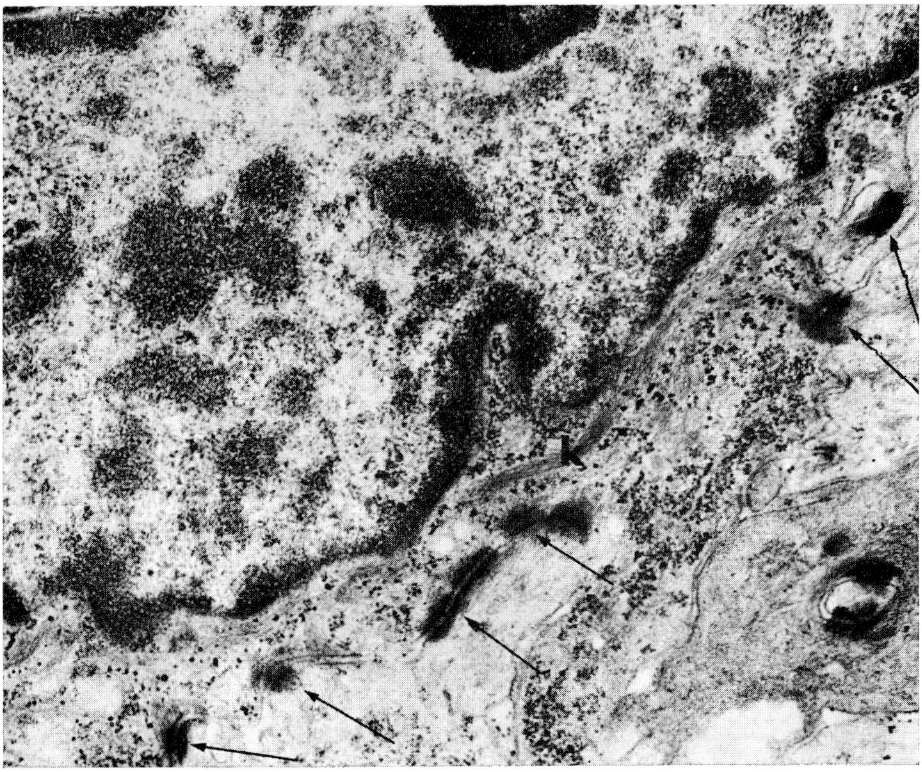

Fig. 8. Epithelial cancer of the tongue (human). The highly differentiated tumor cells form many desmosomes (arrows) and keratin fibrils in the cytoplasm (k). × 15,000.

fibroblast was also observed with the ruthenium method (Morgan).

The cell surface of tumor cells also undergoes immunological changes. It has been shown by Sjoegren et al. and Habel that in virus-induced tumors, specific transplantation antigens appear which are supposed to be localized at the cell surface. Such foreign proteins are also likely to influence the surface properties of the cell. They have not yet been visualized in the electron microscope.

An important observation on the change of the molecular pattern of cancer cell membranes was made by Emmelot and Benedetti (1967): they could show on isolated and negatively stained cell membranes of chemically induced rat hepatomas that the geometrical pattern of globular subunits appearing in the membrane was changed. Instead of the usually hexagonal arrangement an irregular layer of fluffy material was observed. No other tumors have been examined so far with this technique, and one does not know if this observation has a more general significance.

(7) *Intercellular connections.* All pathologists know about the reduced mutual adhesion of fresh tumor tissue before fixation. Coman in particular has studied this

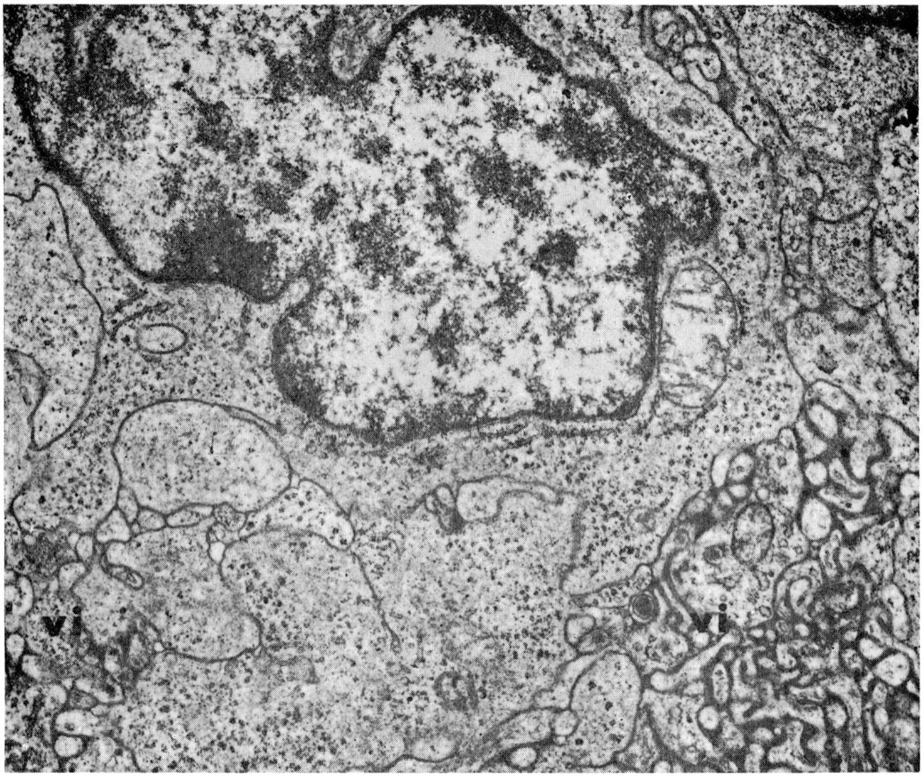

Fig. 9. Bronchial carcinoma (human). Cell surface of an anaplastic tumor cell with cell processes or villi (vi) forming a complex entangled system with the neighbor cells. ×10,000.

phenomenon in a series of papers. The surface charge, the presence of Ca^{++} ions, intercellular 'cement' and the existence of cell contacts are factors responsible for the cohesion of normal or malignant tissues. If the cancer tissue is usually more friable than the normal homologous tissue, one has to assume that these factors are somehow changed. Electron microscopy has frequently shown desmosomes in epithelial cancers (Fig. 8). Their number as well as cytoplasmic keratin fibrils are very much increased in keratinizing epithelial tumors (Fasske and Themann; Hinglais-Guillaud et al.; Schulz 1961; Haguenau et al.). In other cases, their number may be decreased (Easty and Mercer). In cell cultures, Martinez-Palomo et al. have shown that adenovirus 12- and SV_{40} virus-transformed cells form desmosomes as usual, but no tight junctions when the cells form multilayered foci, whereas the normal cells under similar conditions frequently form both desmosomes and tight junctions. Emmelot and Benedetti (1967) have made a similar observation in rat hepatomas. Other types of cell connections are interdigitated microvilli or multifolded, entangled cell processes (Fig. 9). Such connections may also be strongly increased in various tumor tissues: human mammary tumors (Haguenau 1959b), rectal polyps (Hollmann), renal carcinomas (Seljelid and Ericsson 1965b), meningeal tumors (Napolitano et al.; Bucciarelli et al. 1967a). In strongly dedifferentiated cells, the surface tends to be flat.

As well as normal cells, mesenchymal tumor cells are also able to synthesie collagen which accumulates in the intercellular spaces. Epithelial tumors may be limited by basal membranes which are locally disrupted by some enzymatic process. Tiny cytoplasmic pseudopods are then observed to penetrate across the small holes (Hinglais-Guillaud et al.; Frei; Birbeck and Wheatley; Schrodt and Foreman; Mao et al.; Fasske and Morgenroth; Sugar).

(c) *The problem of anaplasia*

Little can be added to our previous discussion of this problem (Oberling and Bernhard; Bernhard 1963). Anaplasia is characterized by the very low degree of differentiation of rapidly growing tumors. Malignant tissues gradually lose the architecture of the normal homologous tissue. Their growth form tends to become chaotic. On the cellular level, the fine structure of cytoplasm is much less organized. The polarization of cells may be inverted, or is gradually lost. The number of mitochondria varies, but has the tendency to decrease. Ergastoplasmic lamellae are rare or disappear completely, as well as the Golgi apparatus (Fig. 5). The cytoplasm may have a hydropic appearance similar to cellular changes associated with tumor regression (Scott et al.). The nucleus has very irregular outlines. The important question to be discussed is whether this lack of organization on the histological and cellular level is directly linked with the malignant process, or if anaplasia is at least partially the expression of increased growth rate. Rapidly dividing cells may not have enough time to build up the complete cellular architecture which would enable the tumor cell to function normally. Normal tissues, when grown in tissue culture and incited to rapid cell division, also dedifferentiate. On the other hand, it is well known that slowly growing tumors have as a rule a more complex histological and cytological organization. But the growth rate alone certainly does not explain the phenomenon of anaplasia. It is likely that the loss of organization is also due to different functioning of genes responsible for the regulation of cellular metabolism. The frequent aneuploidy of cancer cells is expected to produce biochemical disturbances, but even small variations of gene activity of a 'normal' chromosome would of course be enough to change the cellular phenotype.

3. Early ultrastructural changes induced by chemical carcinogens

The difficulties of ultrastructural studies on the action of carcinogens are due to the fact that, besides the possible specific ultrastructural lesion which is searched for, many other non-specific lesions, produced by the toxicity of the compound, are observed. Furthermore, nothing proves that the early ultrastructural changes have anything to do with carcinogenesis. Porter and Bruni studied the action of butter yellow on rat liver and clearly showed that after 2 days of feeding the endoplasmic reticulum gradually lost its ribosomes and thus became 'smooth'. Glycogen also disappeared. The smooth membranes got aggregated and formed hyaline inclusions. Pintchouk et al. have shown in the same system that lysosomes are very rare during the first 3 days, but become more numerous afterwards. In combined biochemical and electron microscopical investigations, Emmelot and Benedetti (1960) also showed degranulation of the liver ergastoplasm after the early action of dimethylnitrosamine (DMNA). In parallel to these morphological changes, inhibition of amino acid incorporation in the microsomal fraction was observed. Later, smooth lipid membranes were synthesized in excess and produced large cytoplasmic myelin figures. Similar observations were reported by Mölbert et al. and by Mukherjee et al. Aminofluorenes also produce detachment of the ribosomes from ergastoplasmic cisternae and hypertrophy of the smooth membranes (Kobayashi; Hartmann). Another liver carcinogen, thioacetamide (TAA), leads to slight degranulation of the ER, but in addition, induces different lesions. The earliest observable changes are visible in the nucleolus which becomes giant after several weeks of treatment (Kleinfeld; Salomon et al.). The cytoplasm first contains less ribosomes, but later has an increased amount of ergastoplasm and mitochondria in the precancerous adenoma stage. Finally, the most potent liver carcinogen, Aflatoxin, induces nucleolar segregation similar to actinomycin D, but the doses used were very much higher than those producing liver tumors after regular administration (Bernhard et al. 1965). It can be concluded that five different liver carcinogens induce different ultrastructural lesions. On the other hand, liver poisons such as carbon tetrachloride also leads to degranulation of the endoplasmic reticulum (Oberling and Rouiller).

The early lesions induced with benzanthracene or methylcholanthrene to produce skin cancers are scarcely more instructive. Besides non-specific mitochondrial swelling and the appearance of dense intramitochondrial granules and fat deposits, the intercellular spaces of the epithelial cells become enlarged; however, comparable pictures are also produced with various non-carcinogenic agents (Setälä et al. 1960a, b; Pillai and Gautier; Nakai et al.). Tarin describes pronounced changes at the dermo-epidermal junction and final disappearance of the basal membrane after methylcholanthrene application.

4. The significance of virus particles in tumor cells

An abundant literature covers this broad field. Review articles should be consulted for the general morphology and development of oncogenic viruses (Bernhard 1960; Gross; Dalton and Haguenau; Dmochowski; Howatson; Haguenau 1966, 1967). Only a very brief survey of the main oncogenic viruses can be given here, without further references, taking into account the new virus classification proposed by Lwoff and Tournier.

(a) *DNA viruses*

The group of *poxviruses* has several representatives which are, as a rule, only weakly oncogenic: The Shope fibroma virus of the rabbit, the Yaba virus of the monkey and Molluscum contagiosum virus of man. However, when the fibroma virus is injected into new born or cortisonized animals, it may give rise to malignant tumors which metastasize. Virus inclusions are constantly visible in the cytoplasm where all stages of viral development are embedded in a diffuse matrix. The virions of the pox group are of extreme complexity with various membranes. Their nucleocapsids have helicoidal symmetry and the double-stranded DNA molecule has an estimated molecular weight of more than 200 million. The length of this molecule would therefore be more than 100 μ.

Among the *papilloviridae*, the most potent and frequently used oncogenic viruses are found: polyoma virus of the mouse, SV_{40} virus of the monkey, Shope papilloma virus of the rabbit and a whole series of papilloma viruses of various animals, but also the common wart virus of man. These viruses either produce a lytic cycle, where many virus particles measuring about 35 mμ in thin sections can be found in the nucleus, or they may induce malignant transformation *in vivo* or *in vitro*, where the virus particles as a rule totally disappear. The virions have no membrane. The protein capsid is composed of 72 capsomeres, arranged in cubic symmetry. The double-stranded DNA molecules of these viruses have a molecular weight varying between 3 to 5 million with the corresponding length of 1.5 to 2.5 μ. The DNA is present either in supercoiled, ring, or in open forms.

Among the human *adenoviridae*, various types are either highly or weakly oncogenic: type (3), (5), (7), 12, 18, 21, and 31. They also induce either a lytic cycle or transform cells without synthesis of virions. The virions have no membrane. Their diameter is 65 mμ and their protein capsid has 252 capsomeres in cubic symmetry. The molecular weight of their double-stranded DNA is between 20 to 22 million, corresponding to a length of the molecules of about 10 μ.

The *herpes group* has two members whose oncogenicity is not absolutely certain, but, at least in the first case, quite probable: the Lucké tumor virus which is present in adenocarcinoma of the kidney of the leopard frog, where it forms nuclear and cytoplasmic inclusions. A second virus of the herpes group has recently been visualized in Burkitt tumor cell lines from African children (Epstein et al.). It is possible, but not proven, that this agent has a causal relationship with the disease. Herpes viruses measure about 180 mμ, have an outer envelope, a protein capsid with 162 capsomeres and double-stranded DNA estimated to have a molecular weight varying between 50 to 80 million. The length of the DNA molecule is therefore likely to measure between 25 and 40 μ.

(b) *RNA viruses*

There are three sub-groups for which the name *thylaxoviridae* has been proposed (anonymous). They are morphologically similar and can be classified in the vicinity of the myxoviruses, although they have their particular features. The first subgroup concerns the Rous sarcoma virus and the leukemia viruses of the chicken and the second is represented by the murine leukemia and sarcoma viruses. Finally, the Bittner virus, inducing mammary tumors of mice, can be considered as a third representative of the group. All virions have an outer envelope and a second inner coat surrounding a nucleoid of RNA. Their diameter is between 90 to 100 mμ. The symmetry of their nucleocapsid seems to be helicoidal, although there is no strict experimental proof for it. The molecular weight of the single-stranded RNA molecules is around 10 million and their length around 9 μ. The virions are assembled by a budding process either on the membrane of the endoplasmic reticulum in the cytoplasm, or at the cell surface. Cells which undergo malignant transformation still can produce infectious virions by a continuous budding process which does not lead to a cytopathic effect.

Concerning the presence of virus particles in tumor cells, they are highly significant in the case of well-known classical RNA virus tumors, such as Rous sarcoma, chicken leukemia and mammary tumors of the mouse. DNA viruses (with the exception of the pox group) disappear in the malignant cells, where only a few genes of the viral genome are functioning. If tumors of unknown origin are examined in the electron microscope and no virus particles can be found, we therefore cannot conclude that the origin of this tumor is not viral. On the other hand, the presence of virions in a cancer cell does not necessarily mean that they represent the causal agent. They may simply represent some non-specific passenger virus.

5. *Model systems of in vitro transformed cells*

One of the most important contributions to experimental cancer research in the last 10 years is certainly the demonstration that single cells can be transformed *in vitro* by oncogenic viruses. Such model systems have many advantages for the study of carcinogenesis. They exclude the complex influence of the organism and the time sequence of events can be studied with genetically well-defined viruses and stabilized pure cell lines. The transforming agents which are most frequently used at present are the polyoma, SV_{40} virus, adenovirus 12 and, as representatives of the RNA viruses, the Rous agent and Rauscher, and Moloney leukemia viruses.

The general ultrastructural pattern of the *in vitro* transformed cells is very close to the organization of the normal cells (Figs. 10, 11). The features of cancer cells in general may also be found in this case, but extreme variations in number or shape of cell organelles do not occur as observed in solid tumors. As already mentioned above, the pattern of organization is on the one hand determined by the origin of the cell line but, on the other hand, influenced by the viral genome. Finally, the degree of differentiation is increased if the growth rate is slow. No fine structural feature shown by classical techniques can be considered as constant and specific for *in vitro* transformed

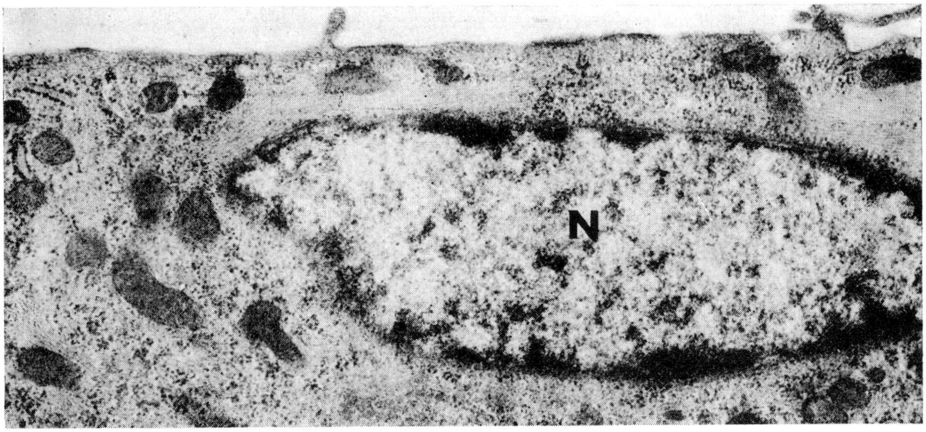

Fig. 10. Culture of normal hamster embryo cell. Vertical section showing a flattened cell with an oval nucleus (N), in the cytoplasm several rod-shaped mitochondria and numerous ribonucleoprotein granules. A few digitations are seen at the cell surface. Glutaraldehyde and osmium tetroxide fixation. × 24,000.

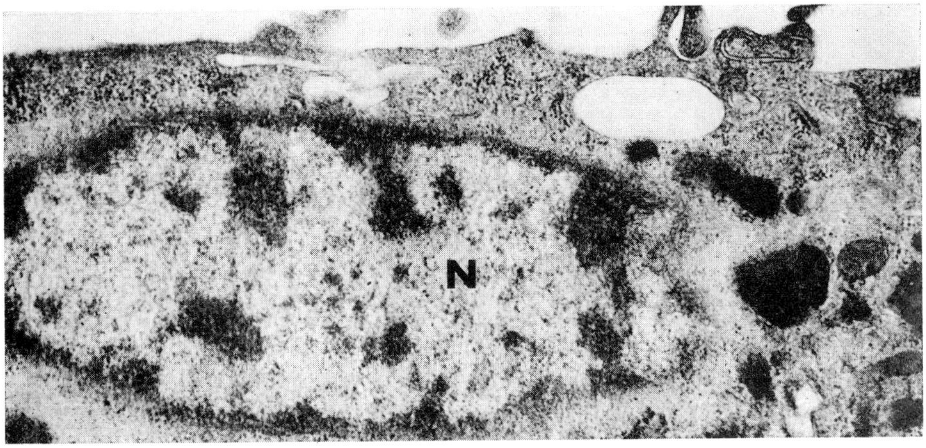

Fig. 11. Culture of hamster embryo cell transformed *in vitro* with oncogenic adenovirus type 12, fixed with glutaraldehyde and osmium. The ultrastructure is basically similar to that of normal controls. × 24,000. (Courtesy of Dr. A. Martinez-Palomo.)

tumor cells. The mitochondrial abnormalities observed in adenovirus 12-transformed cells are quite characteristic for this system, but this phenotypic change is influenced by external factors and cannot be considered as being linked with malignancy (Bernhard and Tournier; Leduc et al.).

There is, however, one phenomenon which is very particular for virus-induced malignancy: the presence of the socalled tumor or T-antigens. Originally shown by

Pope and Rowe by immunofluorescence in the light microscope, they can now also be visualized in the electron microscope by the immunoferritin technique. In the case of the SV_{40} agent, virus-specific tumor antigens are localized in clusters of granules in the nucleus (Oshiro et al.; Levinthal et al. 1967b) and in adenovirus 12 infection, these T-antigens are both nuclear and cytoplasmic and appear as bundles of tiny fibrils (Kalnins et al.; Levinthal et al. 1967a). These antigens are identical with the 'early proteins', appearing in the lytic cycle as the expression of some viral genes which do not contribute to the production of virions. The possible function of such proteins, originally supposed to be enzymatic, is still unknown. As already mentioned, another peculiarity of *in vitro* transformed cells is the loss of contact inhibition. The transformed cells, instead of growing in oriented monolayers, are piled up and form foci of 'criss-cross' growth. The reasons of this changed growth pattern must somehow be linked with the surface properties of the cell membrane e.g., with mucopolysaccharide production and cell connections (Figs. 12, 13).

Combined biochemical, immunological and ultrastructural studies of such membranes, in particular of the *in vitro* transformed cell in general, remains a most rewarding subject for the study of molecular events taking place during carcinogenesis.

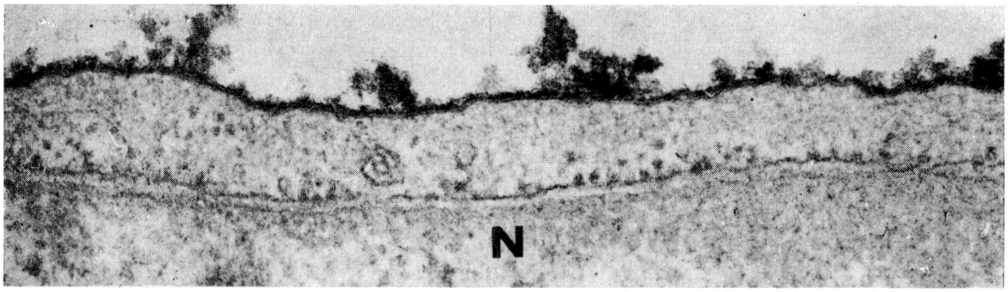

Fig. 12. Normal hamster embryo cell. When ruthenium red is added to the fixatives, a thin dense layer is seen at the surface of the cell, revealing mucopolysaccharides. × 60,000.

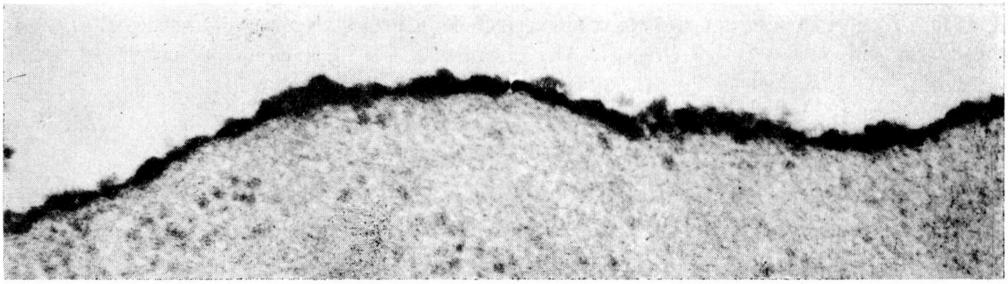

Fig. 13. Same hamster embryo cell transformed with adenovirus 12. Ruthenium red was added to the fixatives; the surface layer is much thicker than in normal cells. × 60,000. (Courtesy of Dr. A. Martinez-Palomo.)

6. *Summary*

Electron microscopy of cancer tissues and cancer cells has visualized many fine structural variations or abnormalities of cellular organelles, but none of the hitherto observed changes can be considered as constant and specifically linked with the malignant process. The fine structure of cancer cells may either be undistinguishable from the normal homologous cell or sometimes it may exaggerate or lose certain structural features. One can speak of tendencies, not of laws. In this sense, the changes in the various cell organelles occurring in tumor cells can be summarized as follows.

The nucleus has a more irregular outline and is usually enlarged. Irregularities in the distribution of chromatin are frequent. Interchromatin- and perichromatin granules may be more numerous or undergo no change. Nuclear bodies are often present. The nuclear membrane is characterized by deep infolding or by bleb formation. Most light microscopically visible nuclear inclusions originate from such invaginations and contain cytoplasmic material. Other nuclear inclusions may contain proteins, glycogen, lipids, or, in rare cases, viruses. Nucleoli are more frequent and generally greatly enlarged. Their molecular population is more irregular and oscillates between extremes. Vacuoles or granular inclusions may be found. No fine structural changes have so far been observed in cancer chromosomes or in the achromatic apparatus.

Concerning the *cytoplasm*, the following alterations are frequently found: mitochondria are often swollen and have various structural abnormalities. Their number may be increased, or, on the contrary, decreased.

The ergastoplasm is less prominent and has the tendency to be replaced by free ribosomes. Polysomal formations are frequent. The Golgi apparatus may be well developed in tumor cells from glandular tissue, but, as a rule, is poorly developed. Annulate lamellae and paired cisternae are more frequently found in cancer cells. Among the pathological inclusions, many are due to phagocytic activity of tumor cells. Lysosomes, fat droplets, glycogen, protein bodies, fibrils of various origin, are also found.

The *cell membrane* does not seem to be different from that of normal cells when shown with the usual techniques, but in certain experimental tumors, mucopolysaccharide production is increased at the cell surface. Intercellular connections may be normal or desmosomes may be more numerous in keratinizing epitheliomas. In certain cases, there are fewer tight junctions than usual, which might partially explain the decreased cohesion of cancer tissue.

The problem of *anaplasia*, frequently found in tumor cells, is considered as a complex phenomenon due to increased growth rate but also to a deficient organizing principle.

Early ultrastructural lesions occurring in cells after applications of various chemical carcinogens, may concern mitochondria, ergastoplasm, the nucleolus or cellular junctions. The specificity of these alterations is doubtful.

The morphology and development of tumor viruses is briefly mentioned. Most of them belong to various groups of classically known viruses and are not a separate entity. They contain either DNA or RNA and may develop in the nucleus, the cytoplasm or at the cell membrane. Cells transformed *in vitro* by means of oncogenic viruses are considered an excellent model system for the molecular analysis of carcinogenesis.

References

ABERCROMBIE, M. and E.J. AMBROSE: The surface properties of cancer cells: a review. Cancer Res. 22 (1962) 525.

ACHONG, B.G. and M.A. EPSTEIN: Fine structure of the Burkitt tumor. J. Natl. Cancer Inst. 36 (1966) 887.

Anonymous. Suggestions for the classification of oncogenic RNA viruses. J. Natl. Cancer Inst. 37 (1966) 395.

BÄSSLER, R. and L.V. HABIGHORST: Vergleichende licht- und elektronenmikroskopische Untersuchungen am Nebennierenmark und Phäochromocytom. Beitr. Pathol. Anat. Allgem. Pathol. 130 (1964) 446.

BECHER, M.: Elektronenmikroskopische Untersuchungen an Onkozyten eines Adenolymphoms. Acta Biol. Med. Ger. 13 (1964) 615.

BENCOSME, S.A., R.A. ALLEN and H. LATTA: Functioning pancreatic islet cell tumors studied electron microscopically. Am. J. Pathol. 42 (1963) 1.

BERGSTRAND, A. and N. RINGERTZ: Electron microscopic examination of the MC1M tumor I. The tumor in ascites form. J. Natl. Cancer Inst. 25 (1960) 501.

BERNHARD, W.: The detection and study of tumor viruses with the electron microscope. Cancer Res. 20 (1960) 712.

BERNHARD, W.: Elektronenmikroskopischer Beitrag zum Studium der Kanzerisierung und der malignen Zustände der Zelle. Verhandl. Deut. Ges. Pathol. 45 (1961) 8.

BERNHARD, W.: Some problems of fine structure in tumor cells. Progr. Exptl. Tumor Res. 3 (1963) 1.

BERNHARD, W., CH. FRAYSSINET, CH. LAFARGE and E. LEBRETON: Lésions nucléolaires précoces provoquées par l'aflatoxine dans les cellules hépatiques de Rat. Compt. Rend. Acad. Sci. 261 (1965) 1785.

BERNHARD, W. and N. GRANBOULAN: The fine structure of the cancer cell nucleus. Exptl. Cell Res. suppl. 9 (1963) 19.

BERNHARD, W. and N. GRANBOULAN: Electron microscopy of the nucleolus in vertebrate cells. In: Dalton and Haguenau, eds.: The nucleus. Academic Press 2 (1968) 87.

BERNHARD, W. and R. LEPLUS: Fine structure of the normal and malignant human lymph node. Pergamon, Gauthier-Villars, McMillan (1964) pp. 1–101.

BERNHARD, W. and P. TOURNIER: Modification persistante des mitochondries dans des cellules tumorales de hamster transformées par l'adénovirus 12. Intern. J. Cancer 1 (1966) 61.

BESSIS, M. and J. BRETON-GORIUS: Examen des cellules leucémiques au microscope électronique par la méthode des coupes. Presse Méd. 63 (1955) 189.

BESSIS, M., J. BRETON-GORIUS and J.L. BINET: Etude comparée du plasmocytome et du syndrome de Waldenström – examen au microscope électronique. Nouvelle Rev. Franç. Hématol. 3 (1963) 159.

BESSIS, M., J. BRETON-GORIUS and J.P. THIERY: Centriole, corps de Golgi et aster des leucocytes. Etude au microscope électronique. Rev. Hématol. 13 (1958) 363.

BIRBECK, M.S.C. and D.N. WHEATLEY: An electron microscopic study of the invasion of ascites tumor cells into the abdominal wall. Cancer Res. 25 (1965) 490.

BOUTEILLE, M., R. ABELANET and J. DELARUE: Etude au microscope électronique des caractères de sécrétion dans les carcinoïdes bronchiques. Ann. Anat. Pathol. 9 (1964) 389.

BOUTEILLE, M., R.R. KALIFAT and J. DELARUE: Ultrastructural variations of nuclear bodies in human diseases. J. Ultrastruct. Res. 19 (1967) 474.

BUCCIARELLI, E., G.F. RABOTTI and A.J. DALTON: Ultrastructure of meningeal tumors induced in dogs with Rous sarcoma virus. J. Natl. Cancer Inst. 38 (1967a) 359.

BUCCIARELLI, E., G.F. RABOTTI and A.J. DALTON: Ultrastructure of gliomas induced in hamsters with Rous sarcoma virus. J. Natl. Cancer Inst. 38 (1967b) 865.

CHAMBERS, V.C. and R.S. WEISER: Annulate lamellae in sarcoma I cells. J. Cell Biol. 21 (1964) 133.

CHRISTENSEN, H.E., O.H. IVERSEN and R. RASK-NIELSEN: Studies on a transplantable mastocytoma in mice II. Electron microscopic observations. J. Natl. Cancer Inst. 30 (1963) 763.

COMAN, D.R.: Mechanisms responsible for the origin and distribution of blood-borne tumor metastases: a review. Cancer Res. 13 (1953) 397.

DALTON, J.A.: Organization in benign and malignant cells. Lab. Invest. 8 (1959) 510.

DALTON, J.A.: An electron microscopical study of a series of chemically induced hepatomas. In: P. Emmelot and O. Mühlbock, eds.: Cellular control mechanisms and cancer. Elsevier (1964) 211.

DALTON, J.A. and FR. HAGUENAU, eds.: Ultrastructure in biological systems, vol. 1: Tumors induced by viruses. Ultrastructural studies. Academic Press (1962) pp. 1–229.

DAVID, H. and N. MANGAKIS: Zur Frage des invasiv-infiltrativen Wachstums von Krebszellen. Arch. Geschwulstforsch. 22 (1963) 92.

DEFENDI, V. and G. GASIC: Surface mucopolysaccharides of polyoma virus transformed cells. J. Cellular Comp. Physiol. 62 (1963) 23.

DE HARVEN, E., B. CLARKSON and A. STRIFE: Electron microscopic study of human leukemic cells in tissue culture. Cancer 20 (1967) 911.

DE THÉ, G., M. RIVIERE and W. BERNHARD: Examen au microscope électronique de la tumeur VX_2 du lapin domestique dérivée du papillome de Shope. Bull. Cancer 47 (1960) 569.

DIMITRIYEVA, N.P.: Cell ultrastructure of the transplantable thyroid tumour. J. Gen. Biol. Acad. Sci. URSS 25 (1964) 277.

DMOCHOWSKI, L.: The electron microscopic view of virus-host relationship in neoplasia. Exptl. Tumor Res. 3 (1963) 35.

EASTY, G.C. and E.H. MERCER: An electron microscope study of the surface of normal and malignant cells in culture. Cancer Res. 20 (1960) 1608.

EMMELOT, P. and E.L. BENEDETTI: Some observations on the effect of liver carcinogens on the fine structure and function of the endoplasmic reticulum of rat liver cells. In: Harris, ed.: Protein biosynthesis. Academic Press (1960) p. 99.

EMMELOT, P. and E.L. BENEDETTI: On the possible involvement of the plasma membrane in the carcinogenis process. In: Carcinogenesis, a broad critique. University of Texas (1967) 471.

EPSTEIN, M.A.: Some unusual features of fine structure observed in HeLa cells. J. Biophys. Biochem. Cytol. 10 (1961) 153.

EPSTEIN, M.A., G. HENLE, B.G. ACHONG and Y.M. BARR: Morphological and biological studies on a virus in cultured lymphoblasts from Burkitt lymphoma. J. exptl. Med. 121 (1965) 761.

ERICSSON, J.L.E., R. SELJELID and S. ORRENIUS: Comparative light and electron microscopic observations of the cytoplasmic matrix in renal carcinomas. Virchows Arch. Pathol. Anat. Physiol. Klin. Med. 341 (1966) 204.

FASSKE, E. and K. MORGENROTH, JR.: Electron microscopic studies on the relation of the basement membrane to the squamous cell carcinomas in animals. Oncologia 20 (1966) 113.

FASSKE, E. and H. THEMANN: Die elektronenmikroskopische Struktur menschlicher Carcinome. Beitr. Pathol. Anat. Allgem. Pathol. 122 (1960) 313.

FISHER, E.R. and D.A. SHARKEY: The ultrastructure of colonic polyps and cancer with special reference to the epithelial inclusion bodies of Leuchtenberger. Cancer 15 (1962) 160.

FREI, J.V.: The fine structure of the basement membrane in epidermal tumors. J. Cell Biol. 15 (1962) 335.

FRIEDLAENDER-BINGGELI, M.: Abnormal intranuclear and cytoplasmic formations associated with a chemically induced, transplantable chicken sarcoma. J. Biophys. Biochem. Cytol. 5 (1959) 143.

FRIEDMANN, I., D.F.N.HARRISON and E.S.BIRD: The fine structure of chordoma with particular reference to the physaliphorous cell. J. Clin. Pathol. 15 (1962) 116.

FRIEDMAN, I., D.F.N.HARRISON, W.N.TUCKER and E.S.BIRD: Electron microscopy of a rhabdomyosarcoma of the ear. J. Clin. Pathol. 18 (1965) 63.

FRUHLING, L. and A.PORTE: Contribution de la microscopie électronique à l'étude d'un sarcome plasmocytaire. Ann. Anat. Pathol. 3 (1958) 538.

GREIDER, M.H. and D.W.ELLIOTT: Electron microscopy of human pancreatic tumors of islet cell origin. Am. J. Pathol. 44 (1964) 663.

GROSS, L.: Oncogenic viruses. Pergamon Press (1961) pp. 1–393.

GUERIN, M.: Corps d'inclusion dans les adénocarcinomes mammaires de la souris. Bull. Cancer 42 (1955) 14.

GUSEK, W.: Submikroskopische Untersuchungen als Beitrag zur Struktur und Onkologie der Meningiome. Beitr. Pathol. Anat. Allgem. Pathol. 127 (1962) 274.

HABEL, K.: Immunological determinants of polyoma virus oncogenesis. J. Exptl. Med. 115 (1962) 181.

HAGUENAU, FR.: Le cancer du sein chez la femme. Etude comparative au microscope électronique et au microscope optique. Bull. Cancer 46 (1959a) 177.

HAGUENAU, FR.: Le cancer mammaire de la souris et de la femme. Etude comparative au microscope électronique. Pathol. Biol. Semaine Hôp. 7 (1959b) 989.

HAGUENAU, FR.: Morphologie des virus oncogènes. Introduction. Virus oncogènes à acide ribonucléique (RNA). Rev. Fr. Etudes Clin. Biol. 11 (1966) 969.

HAGUENAU, FR.: Morphologie des virus oncogènes. II – Virus à acide désoxyribonucléique. Rev. Fr. Etudes Clin. Biol. 12 (1967) 114.

HAGUENAU, FR. and H.HANAFUSA: Personal communication (1967).

HAGUENAU, FR., K.H.HOLLMANN and M.ALBOT-PARTURIER: Ultrastructure des cancers du rectum. Bull. Cancer 51 (1964) 55.

HARTMANN, H.A.: Rat liver after N-hydroxy-2-acetylaminofluorene. Arch. Pathol. 79 (1965) 126.

HATTORI, S., M.MATSUDA and A.WADA: An electron microscopic study of pulmonary adenomas in mice. Gann 56 (1965) 275.

HINGLAIS-GUILLAUD, N., R.MORICARD and W.BERNHARD: Ultrastructure des cancers pavimenteux invasifs du col utérin chez la femme. Bull. Cancer 48 (1961) 283.

HOLLMANN, K.H.: Tumeurs rectales chez l'homme au microscope électronique. Arch. Maladies Appar. Digest. Mal. Nutrit. 53 (1964) 975.

HOWATSON, A.F.: The structure of tumor viruses and its bearing on their relation to viruses in general. Advan. Cancer Res. 8 (1964) 1.

HRUBAN, Z., W.H.KIRSTEN and A.SLESERS: Fine structure of spontaneous hepatic tumors of male C3H/fGs mice. Lab. Invest. 15 (1966) 576.

HRUBAN, Z., H.SWIFT and M.RECHCIGL: Fine structure of transplantable hepatomas of the rat. J. Natl. Cancer Inst. 35 (1965) 459.

HÜBNER, G., H.J.KLEIN and N.SCHÜMMELFEDER: Zur Ultrastruktur der Onkocytome. Klin. Wochschr. 43 (1965) 798.

KALNINS, V.I., H.F.STICH and D.S.YOHN: Electron microscopic localization of virus-associated antigens in human amnion cells (AV-3) infected with human adenovirus, type 12. Virology 28 (1966) 751.

KLÄRNER, P. and R.GIESEKING: Zur Ultrastruktur des Lungentumors der Maus. Z. Krebsforsch. 64 (1960) 7.

KLEINFELD, R.G.: Early changes in the rat liver and kidney cells induced by thioacetamide. Cancer 17 (1957) 954.

KOBAYASHI, E.: Electron microscope study on 2-amino-fluorene carcinogenesis. Sapporo Med. J. 23 (1963) 1.

LAZARUS, S.S. and B.W.VOLK: Histochemical and electron microscopic studies of a functioning insulinoma. Lab. Invest. 11 (1962) 1279.

LEAK, L.V., J.B.CAULFIELD, J.F.BURKE and C.F.MCKHANN: Electron microscopic studies on a human fibromyxosarcoma. Cancer Res. 27 (1967) 261.

LEDUC, E.H., W.BERNHARD and P.TOURNIER: Cyclic appearance of atypical mitochondria containing DNA fibres in cultures of an adenovirus 12 induced tumor. Exptl. Cell Res. 42 (1966) 597.

LEDUC, E.H. and J.W.WILSON: Effect of essential fatty acid deficiency on ultrastructure and growth of transplantable mouse hepatoma BRL. J. Natl. Cancer Inst. 33 (1964) 721.

LEPLUS, R., J.DEBRAY, J.PINET and W.BERNHARD: Lésions nucléaires décelées au microscope électronique dans des cellules de lymphomes malins, chez l'homme. Compt. Rend. Acad. Sci. 253 (1961) 2788.

LEVINTHAL, J.D., J.C.CEROTTINI, C.AHMAD-ZADEH and R.WICKER: The detection of intracellular adenovirus type 12 antigens by indirect immunoferritin technique. Intern. J. Cancer 2 (1967) 85.

LEVINTHAL, J.D., R.WICKER and J.C.CEROTTINI: Study of intracellular SV_{40} antigens by indirect immunoferritin technique. Virology 31 (1967) 555.

LUFT, J.H.: Fine structure of capillary and endocapillary layer as revealed by ruthenium red. Federation Proc. 25 (1966) 1773.

LUPULESCOU, A. and AL.PETROVICI: Ultrastructure des tumeurs thyroïdiennes expérimentales. Acta Biol. Med. Ger. 11 (1963) 409.

LUSE, S.: Ultrastructural characteristics of normal and neoplastic cells. Progr. Exptl. Tumor Res. Basel Karger, 2 (1961) 1.

LUSE, S. and P.E.LACY: Electron microscopy of a malignant argentaffin tumor. Cancer 13 (1960) 334.

LWOFF, A. and P.TOURNIER: The classification of viruses. Ann. Rev. Microbiol. 20 (1966) 45.

MA, M.H. and A.J.WEBBER: Fine structure of liver tumors induced in the rat by 3′-methyl-4-dimethylaminoazobenzene. Cancer Res. 26 (1966) 935.

MALDONADO, J.F., A.L.BROWN, E.D.BAYRD and G.L.PEASE: Ultrastructure of the myeloma cell. Cancer 19 (1966) 1613.

MANNWEILLER, K. and W.BERNHARD: Recherches ultrastructurales sur une tumeur rénale expérimentale du hamster. J. Ultrastruct. Res. 1 (1957) 158.

MAO, P. and J.J.MOLNAR: The fine structure and histochemistry of lead-induced renal tumors in rats. Am. J. Pathol. 50 (1967) 571.

MAO, P., K.NAKAO and A.ANGRIST: Human prostatic carcinoma: an electron microscope study. Cancer Res. 26 (1966) 955.

MARTINEZ-PALOMO, A. and C.BRAILOWSKY: Surface layer in tumor cells transformed by adeno 12 and VS_{40} virus. Virology 34 (1968) 379.

MARTINEZ-PALOMO, A., C.BRAILOWSKY and W.BERNHARD: Ultrastructural modifications of the cell surface and intercellular contacts of some transformed cell strains. Cancer Research, April 1969 (in press).

MATSUI, K.: Ultrastructure of reticulosarcoma. Proc. 4th Intern. Symp. R.E.S. Kyoto, Japan (1964).

MCDUFFIE, N.G.: Nuclear blebs in human leukaemic cells. Nature 214 (1967) 1341.

MCGAVRAN, M.H.: The ultrastructure of papillary cystadenoma lymphomatosum of the parotid gland. Virchows Arch. Pathol. Anat. Physiol. Klin. Med. 338 (1965) 195.

MENGEL, C.E. and J.S.TRIER: Biochemical and morphologic heterogeneity in a transplantable mast-cell neoplasm. J. Natl. Cancer Inst. 27 (1961) 1341.

MÖLBERT, E., K.HILL and F.BÜCHNER: Die Kanzerisierung der Leberparenchymzelle durch Diaethylnitrosamin im elektronenmikroskopischen Bild. Beitr. Pathol. Anat. Allgem. Pathol. 126 (1962) 218.

MORGAN, H.: Ultrastructure of the surfaces of cells infected with avian leukosis-sarcoma viruses. J. Virology 2 (1968) 1133.

MUKHERJEE, T., R.G.GUSTAFSSON, B.A.AFZELIUS and E.ARRHENIUS: Effects of carcinogenic amines on amino acid incorporation by liver systems II. A morphological and biochemical study on the effect of dimethylnitrosamine. Cancer Res. 23 (1963) 944.

MURAD, T.M. and D.G.SCARPELLI: The ultrastructure of medullary and scirrhous mammary duct carcinoma. Am. J. Pathol. 50 (1967) 335.

NAKAI, T., P.SHUBIK and R.FELDMAN: An electronmicroscopic study of skin carcinogenesis in the mouse with special reference to the intramitochondrial body. Exptl. Cell Res. 27 (1962) 608.

NAPOLITANO, L., R.KYLE and E.FISHER: Ultrastructure of meningiomas and the derivation and nature of their cellular components. Cancer 17 (1963) 233.

NOVIKOFF, A.B. and L.BIEMPICA: Cytochemical and electron microscopic examination of Morris 5123 and Reuber H-35 hepatomas after several years of transplantation. Gann Monograph 1 (1966) 65.

OBERLING, CH. and W.BERNHARD: The morphology of the cancer cell. In: J. Brachet and A.E. Mirsky, eds.: The cell, vol. V, Academic Press (1961) p. 405.

OBERLING, CH., M.RIVIERE and FR.HAGUENAU: Ultrastructure des épithéliomas à cellules claires du rein (hypernéphromes ou tumeurs de Grawitz et son implication pour l'histogénèse de ces tumeurs). Bull. Cancer 46 (1959) 356.

OBERLING, CH. and CH.ROUILLER: Les effets de l'intoxication aiguë au tetrachlorure de carbone sur le foie de rat. Ann. Anat. Pathol. 1 (1956) 401.

OSHIRO, L.S., H.M.ROSE, C.MORGAN and K.C.HSU: The localization of SV_{40} induced neoantigens with ferritin-labeled antibody. Virology 31 (1967) 183.

PILLAI, P.A. and A.GAUTIER: A preliminary note on the electron microscopy of induced epidermal hyperplasia in the newt. Oncologia 13 (1960) 303.

PINCHOUK, V.G., L.A.ZOTIKOV and B.D.MONASTYRSKAYA: Ultrastructural cytochemistry of acid phosphatase during the development of experimental hepatoma. Cytologia (Tokyo) 8 (1966) 523.

POPE, J.H. and W.P.ROWE: Immunofluorescent studies of adenovirus 12 tumors and of cells transformed or infected by adenoviruses. J. Exptl. Med. 120 (1964) 577.

PORTER, K.R. and C.BRUNI: An electron microscope study of the early effects of 3′-Me-DAB on rat liver cells. Cancer Res. 19 (1959) 997.

RAPPAPORT, H., T.NAKAI and H.SWIFT: The fine structure of normal and neoplastic melanocytes in the syrian hamster, with particular reference to carcinogen-induced melanotic tumors. J. Cell. Biol. 16 (1963) 171.

SALOMON, J.C., M.SALOMON and W.BERNHARD: Modifications des cellules du parenchyme hépatique du rat sous l'effet de la thioacétamide. Bull. Cancer 49 (1962) 139.

SCHRODT, G.R. and C.D.FOREMAN: Methylcholanthrene-induced carcinoma of the mouse cervix: an electron microscope study. Cancer Res. 25 (1965) 802.

SCHUMACHER, A. and H.SCHULZ: Licht- und elektronenmikroskopische Untersuchungen an einem metastasierenden Dünndarmcarcinoid mit Serotoninbestimmungen an Tumorzellfraktionen. Klin. Wochschr. 41 (1963) 1188.

SCHULZ, H.: Elektronenmikroskopische Untersuchungen eines Mammakarzinoms der Ratte. Oncologia 10 (1957) 307.

SCHULZ, H.: Beitrag zur submikroskopischen Morphologie menschlicher Tumoren. Symposium über Krebsprobleme. Berlin, Springer Verlag (1961).

SCOTT, G.B., H.J.CHRISTIAN and A.R.CURRIE: The Huggins rat mammary tumors: cellular changes associated with regression. In: R.W. Wissler, T.L. Dao and S. Wood, eds.: Endogenous factors influencing host-tumor balance. University of Chicago (1967) p. 99.

SELJELID, R. and J.L.E.ERICSSON: An electron microscopic study of mitochondria, in renal clear cell carcinoma. J. Microscopie 4 (1965a) 759.

SELJELID, R. and J.L.E.ERICSSON: Electron microscopic observations on specializations of the cell surface in renal clear cell carcinoma. Lab. Invest. 14 (1965b) 435.

SETÄLÄ, K., L.MERENMIES, E.E.NISKANEN, M.NYHOLM and L.STJERNVALL: Mechanism of experimental tumorigenesis VI. Ultrastructural alterations in mouse epidermis caused by locally applied carcinogen and dipole-type tumor promoter. J. Natl. Cancer Inst. 25 (1960b) 1155.

SETÄLÄ, K., L. MERENMIES, L. STJERNVALL, M. NYHOLM and Y. AHO: Mechanism of experimental tumorigenesis V. Ultrastructural alterations in mouse epidermis caused by Span 60 and Tween 60-type agents. J. Natl. Cancer Inst. 24 (1960a) 355.

SJOEGREN, H. O., I. HELLSTROM and G. KLEIN: Transplantation of polyoma virus-induced tumors in mice. Cancer Res. 21 (1961) 329.

SMETANA, K., E. J. FREIREICH and H. BUSCH: Chromatin structures in ring-shaped nucleoli of human lymphocytes. Exptl. Cell Res. 52 (1968) 112.

SOBIN, L. H.: Cytoplasmic inclusions in cells of lymphosarcoma 6C3HED II. Electron microscopic observations. Exptl. Cell Res. 26 (1962) 280.

SORENSEN, G. D.: Electron microscopic observation of viral particles within myeloma cells of man. Exptl. Cell Res. 25 (1961) 219.

SPJUT, H. J. and S. A. LUSE: Chordoma: an electron microscopic study. Cancer 17 (1964) 643.

SUGAR, J.: A electron study of early microscopic invasive growth in human skin tumours and laryngeal carcinoma. Europ. J. Cancer 4 (1968) 33.

SVOBODA, D. J.: Ultrastructure of pulmonary adenomas in mice. Cancer Res. 2 (1962) 1197.

SVOBODA, D. J.: Fine structure of hepatomas induced in rats with p-dimethylaminoazobenzene. J. Natl. Cancer Inst. 33 (1964) 315.

TAKAHASHI, N. and N. K. MOTTET: Further observations on the cytoplasmic spherical bodies in HEP-3 carcinoma cells. Lab. Invest. 11 (1962) 743.

TANDLER, B. and F. H. SHIPKEY: Ultrastructure of Warthin's tumor I. Mitochondria. J. Ultrastruct. Res. 11 (1964a) 292.

TANDLER, B. and F. H. SHIPKEY: Ultrastructure of Warthin's tumor II. Crystalloids. J. Ultrastruct. Res. 11 (1964b) 306.

TARIN, D.: Sequential electron microscopical study of experimental mouse skin carcinogenesis. Intern. J. Cancer 2 (1967) 195.

TROTTER, N. L.: Electron microscopic observations on cytoplasmic components of transplantable hepatomas in mice. J. Natl. Cancer Inst. 30 (1963) 113.

VASQUEZ, C., A. PAVLOVSKY and W. BERNHARD: Lésions nucléaires et inclusions cytoplasmiques particulières dans deux cas de lymphoréticulo-sarcomes humains. Compt. Rend. Acad. Sci. 256 (1963) 2261.

VERLEY, J. M.: Les tumeurs carcinoïdes bronchiques et digestives de l'homme. Z. Krebsforsch. 66 (1965) 35.

YASUZUMI, G., R. SUGIHARA S. NAKANO, T. KISE and H. TAKEUCHI: Submicroscopic structure of cell necrobiosis of Yoshida sarcoma as revealed by electron microscopy. Cancer Res. 20 (1960) 339.

CHAPTER 29

Chromosome abnormalities and carcinogenesis

ALBERT LEVAN

Institute of Genetics, University of Lund, Lund, Sweden

Contents

1. Introduction
2. Normal cells
3. Tumor progression
4. Primary tumors
5. Conclusion

1. Introduction

It has long been known that chromosome abnormalities are more frequent in cancer tissues than in comparable samples of normal tissue. Opinions as to the significance of the chromosome abnormalities in cancer have varied widely: whereas some workers have considered the abnormalities as causative factors in the malignancy, others have dismissed them as comparatively uninteresting consequences of the disease.

Although some very fundamental studies of chromosomes in cancer were made long ago, as those of Winge (1927, 1930), technical difficulties in the handling of mammalian chromosomes prevented a detailed and meaningful analysis of chromosomal events associated with malignancy, until new methods in mammalian cytogenetics started coming into use in the early 1950's. Since that time, however, progress has been more rapid and more definite in other fields of mammalian cytogenetics than in cancer. This has been partly because no uniform and simple standard technique, as the leukocyte technique, has become available in cancer, and partly because correlations between karyotype and disease, as in many clinical malformation syndromes, have been vague and obscure in cancer. The one exception to the latter, the Philadelphia chromosome in chronic myelogenous leukemia (CML), has actually contributed to confusion of the general issue, by its very clarity. If one malignancy exhibits an absolute and almost diagrammatical correlation with a certain chromosomal change, why do most other malignancies studied lack every sign of such correlations?

Wherever chromosomal changes take place, they will have a fundamental effect on the cells in which they occur. Thus, there can be no doubt that the incidence of chromosomal deviations in cancer contributes to the characteristics of malignancy. The fact that chromosome deviations have been found in every type of cancer, in which an intensive enough search for them has been made, and the fact that at least in one case a specific chromosome change is associated with a certain disease, make the study of chromosomes in cancer an urgent and promising enterprise. Even though there is still no direct evidence that chromosomal and genetic changes are involved in the primary change starting off a normal cell on its way to malignancy, it seems to be worth while to recall some of the developments in this area of research and to consider their possible bearing on the problem of carcinogenesis.

2. Normal cells

In the early days of mammalian chromosome analysis, claims were often made that chromosome aberrations were of frequent occurrence in normal mammalian cells in their natural environment. A great body of evidence has shown that these claims were often erroneous or exaggerated. Chromosomal deviations in normal cells in their natural surroundings are rare.

It should be observed, however, that chromosomal deviations have been found in normal cells in connection with embryogenesis and aging, thus in both cases under natural conditions. Melander has directed attention to a specific type of chromosome behavior, found during embryogenesis of various groups of animals, including insects, worms and mammals. This is the appearance of anaphase bridges, usually resulting from pseudochiasmata, localized to specific chromosome regions, and it is especially intriguing that Melander has found such events at predetermined stages of differentiation, apparently triggering new pathways of the differentiation pattern. Thus, in the female rabbit, the first appearance of sex chromatin is associated with a temporary adhesion between the chromatids of one of the X-chromosomes, the future late-replicating X. In the present context, it is especially interesting that the course of normal differentiation is accompanied by a chromosomal mechanism of the same kind as the delayed isolocus breakage, which has been shown to play a role in viral carcinogenesis (Nichols 1966). The delayed isolocus breaks were described by Östergren and Wakonig and interpreted as masked chromatid aberrations, which could appear as pseudochiasmata during anaphase, a view corroborated recently by Kihlman and Hartley. The pseudochiasma mechanism studied by Melander does not lead to open chromosome breakage during normal embryogenesis in mammals, and except for the case of chromosomal soma-germline mosaicism of *Microtus oregoni* (Ohno et al.), evidently resulting from predetermined nondisjunction mechanisms, no gross differences in chromosome constitution are known among different tissues in this group. On the other hand, changes in the heterochromatic pattern, and thus presumably in the functioning genetic information of the nucleus, may result from the specific chromosome behavior described by Melander.

Another type of chromosomal irregularity during embryo development has been demonstrated in connection with physiologically occurring cell degeneration, as in the neural epithelium of the chicken (Källén) and in the müllerian epithelium of the mouse (Forsberg; Forsberg and Lannerstad). By changing experimentally the environment of such tissues, cell degeneration may be prevented with the result that the further development of the tissue becomes abnormal, hyperplastic, or even tending to cancerous growth (Forsberg and Källén). As pointed out in this latter paper, these observations imply a possible connection between the artificially induced survival of cells with chromosomal abnormalities and malignancy.

The findings of chromosome variation associated with tissue degeneration during embryogenesis lead over to adult tissues which normally undergo phases of degeneration, as the endometrium. This was one of the tissues, in which a very high incidence of extreme chromosome number variation was early claimed by Therman and Timonen. Even though probably some of the variation described by them was artificial, it is reasonable to assume that chromosomal deviations may occur in tissues predetermined to degeneration, and it is tempting to speculate, in line with the above observations by Källén and Forsberg, that changes in the hormonal environment of such tissues, with resulting survival of cells with chromosome variation, may lead to atypical growth and cancer. In recent investigations, opinions have been divided as to the occurrence of chromosome variation in the endometrium: Hughes and Csermely found a very pronounced variation, whereas other workers (Bowey and Spriggs; Katayama and Jones) found the normal chromosome number of 46 in the normal proliferative endometrium and in benign (cystic) hyperplasia of the endometrium.

All data available indicate that the majority of normally functioning tissues contain only cells with normal karyotype, and in this concept of normal cells are included cells with double or multiple chromosome numbers, which occur in many tissues as a normal part of the differentiation pattern. Disregarding the polyploid cells, most counts in normal tissues give exactly diploid numbers, as in the samples analyzed by Tjio of five different tissues of four mammalian species, in which 1800 exact counts gave no single deviation from the normal diploid numbers (Levan 1959). Just as influences from the outside, with c-mitotic and mutagenic agents, may induce numerical and structural changes into cells of normal tissues, internal changes of hormonal and metabolic factors may lead to the same result. When chromosomal changes take place in a multicellular organism, they do not immediately endanger the survival of the individual. The cells affected may either become eliminated and substituted by normal cells or survive and continue to function as less efficient members of the cellular community. Which of these two courses will be taken, is largely dependent on whether the cells enter mitosis or not. During mitosis, chromosome abnormalities will cause mechanical disturbances that often lead to the death of one or both of the daughter cells. Cells remaining in interphase escape this test and may therefore survive and conserve the chromosomal handicap in the tissue. It is known both from plants (Levan and Lotfy) and animals (Curtis) that chromosomal aberrations tend to accumulate in aging tissues. In the case of animals such observations form the basis of a reasonable hypothesis of aging.

In this connection it is relevant to recall that normal cells in long-term tissue culture normally enter a degenerative phase with increased incidence of chromosomal disturbances (Hayflick and Moorhead). The fact that viral transformation of such tissue cultures into permanent cell lines takes place more readily during the degenerative phase (Jensen et al.) is an interesting parallel *in vitro* to the increased tendency to cancer transformation *in vivo* during higher ages. In both systems there is a correlation between chromosomal variation and increased tendency to cellular adaptation to permanent and uncontrolled growth patterns.

The discussion so far may be summarized, as follows: Normal cells in their natural surroundings rarely show any chromosomal variation. Deviating chromosome behavior may act as a normal factor of differentiation, inducing changes in the interphase heterochromatic pattern. In mammals, this mechanism is not associated with the survival of cells with gross karyotypic changes. Chromosome variation is also found in degenerating tissues and cell populations, associated with an increased tendency to cancer and to permanent *in vitro* growth. Conversely, changes in the normal environment, including aging, may induce an increased incidence of chromosome changes.

3. Tumor progression

In the preceding section it was shown that all organisms on one occasion or another are liable to chromosomal variation. Evidently, most chromosomal disturbances do not lead to cancer. The question arises: are chromosome changes at all involved in cancer development? The experiences of pathologists from as far back as the 1890's all agree that, histopathologically, the one common denominator in cancer is the occurrence of chromosomal and mitotic irregularities. This fact stimulated the proposal of the mutation theory of cancer at an early date.

After the technical improvements in mammalian cytogenetics, the old results were confirmed and the chromosomal abnormalities in cancer were recorded and classified. It was found that although every kind of chromosomal aberration, ever described in normal cells, was seen again in cancer, often in a remarkably high frequency, no really new types were found; no chromosomal behavior could be labelled as specific of cancer cells. The conclusion was that the change from normal cell to cancer cell somehow involved a loss of chromosomal stability and that the laxity thus resulting brings about the appearance of cells with new functional properties, including the capacity of uncontrolled growth.

The aspect of the chromosomal variation as a tool of genetic adaptation of cells to new modes of life gained a great deal in plausibility during the 1950's, when a variety of old tumors, maintained in serial *in vivo* transplantation, was taken up for detailed chromosome study. It was found that the characteristic course of events, by which such tumors became increasingly independent in relation to the environment, that is the so-called tumor progression, was often accompanied by stepwise karyotypic changes. One of the first materials, in which this was clearly ascertained, was murine ascites tumors. It was soon realized that, although individual tumors could vary a great deal in their behavior, there was a common trend in the karyotypic development during progression. Thus, most murine tumors, after a period in the diploid region, shifted into tetraploidy, and this shift was usually associated with an improved capacity of the tumors to withstand environmental strains. This phenomenon was already noticed by Winge (1930) and interpreted in line with the observations gathering at that time that polyploid plants exhibited improved viability and gigantism in comparison with their diploid relations. It was realized later, in tumors as in plants, that chromosome doubling did not usually by itself warrant higher viability but rather provides possibilities to increased chromosomal variation and consequently to selective adaptation. Thus, in the experiments of Hauschka and Levan, the strict host specificity of diploid murine ascites tumors was relieved in tetraploid tumors, in which evidently cells with a decreased degree of histoincompatibility could be provided when needed. Furthermore, tetraploid mouse tumors were able to gradually improve their adaptation to hostile environments, as allogeneic hosts, and the mechanism by which this was achieved was by shedding chromosome segments or entire chromosomes, presumably carrying cumbersome genic material. This, the so-called Ising effect (Ising

1955, 1958), was possible in polyploid stemlines because in them each chromosome type was represented more than twice.

After these early studies, a convincing number of similar observations in several species, including man, have proven that tumor progression is generally accompanied by karyotypic changes. Tumors, as well as established tissue culture cell lines, represent cellular populations, in which the individual cells have become transformed into cells with the life habit of microorganisms. In such populations the genetic adaptation to the environment is never concluded: periods of relative stability, in which the stemline of the population is at ease with the environment, alternate with periods of upheaval, when the utmost chromosomal variability of the population is mustered to overcome the threat. These processes are truly analogous to events in natural evolution, and the sequence of stemline karyotypes in a tumor may form identifiable evolutionary series (Hansen-Melander; Ford and Clarke; Lejeune et al.). One main difference between the two types of evolution, in cellular populations *versus* natural evolution, lies in the time factor: evolution in cell populations is immensely accelerated as compared with evolution in natural organisms. This is understandable, since any change resulting in improved propagative capacity of single cells may be acceptable in a tumor cell population, whereas in natural evolution of multicellular organisms every change has to pass two other tests: (1) for capacity of building up the multicellular soma, and (2) for capacity of going through meiosis and fertilization. Conversely, tumor progression may be regarded as a model system of natural evolution and may help visualizing evolutionary events that are inaccessible in organisms. Thus, the origin of accessory minute chromosomes in tumors may elucidate the unknown evolutionary processes by which accessory chromosomes ('B chromosomes') happened to enter into the karyotypes of many plants and animals (Levan et al. iu press).

If just chromosome numbers are considered, it has been found that stemlines of advanced tumors tend to gather in a certain region of chromosome numbers, called the chromosome number optimum (Ising and Levan). This region is usually wide, and differences in its location are found between species. In man, it has been shown that tumors of widely different origin may tend to converge during progression towards a common karyotypic pattern, inasfar as some of the normal chromosome types have a tendency to increase in number, while others tend to decrease, as compared with their participation in the normal human karyotype. These patterns were detected in material from the literature, consisting of mainly ascitic forms of gastric, mammary, uterine and ovarian carcinomas (Steenis; Levan 1966). It is interesting that a definitively deviating pattern was demonstrated in a similarly compiled material of leukemias (Levan 1967).

In summary, there is good evidence that chromosome changes are involved in the normal development of tumors already established. Tumor progression can be seen as a counterpart on the cellular level to natural evolution on the level of organisms and species.

4. Primary tumors

The confusing variety of karyotypes in advanced tumors seems at first to refute any possibility that specific chromosome changes are associated with specific types of malignancy, and the Philadelphia chromosome of CML stands out as an unintelligible exception. A scanning of the literature, however, reveals quite a few tumors, in which certain signs exist that chromosome picture and disease are correlated, even though the correlation is less obvious than in the CML. Thus a considerable number of primary mouse leukemias, both spontaneous (Wakonig and Stich) and carcinogen-induced (Stich), had trisomic stemlines with 41 instead of 40 chromosomes, and the majority of bovine lymphosarcomas studied by Hare et al. (1967) had hyperdiploid stemlines. In both mice and cattle, however, individual identification of the extra chromosomes is impossible because of the uniform chromosome morphology. Wald et al. demonstrated a consistent karyotypic abnormality in a granulocytic leukemia in the mouse after serial propagation with cell-free ultracentrifugates. A suggestive situation is found in the venereal sarcoma of the dog, in which the same deviating karyotype has been found in 17 distantly separated localities in Japan (Makino), in 2 in Pennsylvania (Weber et al.) and in 3 in France (Barski and Cornefert-Jensen). Also in human tumors, several indications have been found that certain tumor types are associated with vague chromosome patterns. Thus, a characteristic marker chromosome has been seen in several primary Burkitt tumors (Jacobs et al.; Stewart et al.), and another type of marker in several cell lines established from Burkitt tumors (Kohn et al.), and eight human meningiomas all had hypodiploid stemlines or sidelines with one missing G chromosome (Zang and Singer). Many more similar instances can be found, and there is a tendency for such cases to increase in number lately.

Consideration of available facts points at the following possibility: the case of the CML may be unique just because the characteristic Philadelphia chromosome remains identifiable through the progressive karyotypic changes; it may well be that other malignancies, too, have their 'Philadelphia chromosomes', only they become mutilated at an early stage by secondary chromosomal rearrangements. The early and decisive chromosome changes are perhaps very insignificant morphologically, or sometimes even submicroscopic. If that were so, the chromosomal changes we observe in the microscope and classify must necessarily give a distorted and inaccurate representation of the original changes. Still, if in a certain malignancy, largely the same constellation of submicroscopic changes were always formed, this would predetermine the subsequent chromosomal changes to take roughly similar course, viz. towards restitution of optimal viability of the cells which had become disturbed by the early changes. In view of the immense variety of malignancies, it would be expected that a continuous series of transitions exist between the one extreme, the CML case, in which the original change is maintained through all secondary changes, and the other extreme, in which the original changes are immediately blurred by the progressive variation.

Most cases would be expected to be intermediate, that is to show vague but undisputable patterns.

In order to facilitate the discovery of any such patterns, the materials studied and the procedures employed must fulfil certain conditions, as (1) the chromosomes of the host species must be individually recognizable; (2) as early tumor stages as possible should be studied; (3) comparable stages should be studied of different tumors, or preferably a sequence of stages in each tumor; (4) a fair number of individual tumors should be studied of each tumor type; if the pattern is vague and variable it may materialize only after many stemline karyotypes have been characterized.

With these ideas in mind, our group in Lund and Camden has concentrated during the last few years on chromosome studies in a tumor material in several different rodent species but with uniform etiology, viz. sarcomas induced by the Schmidt–Ruppin strain of the Rous virus. In the following, some results relevant to the present problem will be mentioned.

In the rat, some 15 primary tumors were analyzed (Levan 1961 and unpublished; Nichols 1963). About half of them had normal diploid stemline, one had hypodiploid, and the rest had trisomic stemline. In all of the latter, the extra chromosome was a telocentric of medium size. Although this extra chromosome could not be distinguished from the other telocentric chromosomes, the results are compatible with the presence of a pattern.

Two broad investigations within this project have recently been concluded, as far as chromosomes of primary tumors are concerned: the study by Mark (1967) of 91 tumors in the mouse and by Kato (1968) of 42 tumors in the Chinese hamster. These two studies, which are probably so far the most comprehensive chromosome analyses

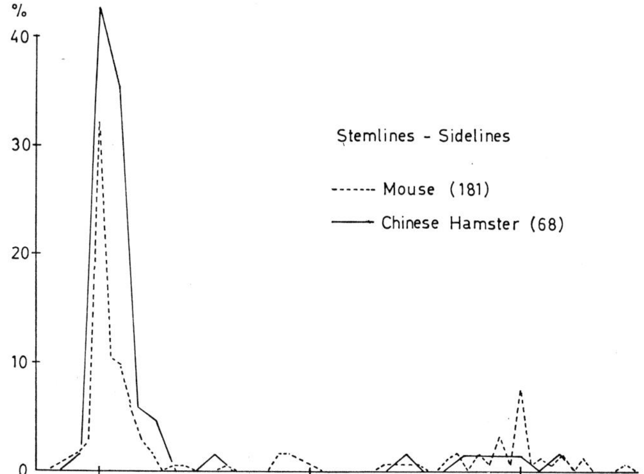

Fig. 1. Comparison between percentage distributions of chromosome numbers of stem- and sidelines in primary RSV-SR-induced sarcomas of the mouse and of the Chinese hamster (Kato 1968).

S	Sex	K	1	2	X	Y	4	5	6	7	8	9	10	11	Marker
			Chromosome types												
21	M	1						−							
22	F	2													
	M	3													
	F	4		−											+
	M	5				+					−				
23	F	6						+++ ++							
	M	7			+			+							
	M	8				+									
	M	9					−						+		+
	F	10							+++ +++						
	M	11							+++						
	F	12											++		
	M	13											+++		
	M	14													+
24	F	15					+	+							
	M	16						+			+				
	M	17											+	+	
	M	18													++
25	F	19					+	+	+						
	M	20						+			+		+		
	F	21						+					+	+	
28	M	22						+		+	+	+	+	+	
37-8	M	23	−−	−	−	−	−		−−	−−	−−		+		++ ++
41	F	24	−	−				−							
43	F	25	−												
	M	26	−−												+
	M	27	−	−					−	−−	−−				+++ +++
45-6	M	28				++	−	−					+	+	

Fig. 2. Gains (+) and losses (−) of individual chromosome types in deviating karyotypes of stem- and sidelines. On diploid level, note clusters of trisomic Nos. 5, 6 and 10 and frequent involvement of No. 5 in higher hyperdiploid classes. On tetraploid level, conversely, losses of Nos. 1 and 2 and gains of marker chromosomes are the most common changes (Kato 1968).
S = chromosome number of stem- or sideline; K = karyotype No.; Marker = presence of one or more structurally changed chromosomes.

in primary tumors of identical etiology, give suggestive evidence of chromosomal similarities, not only within the tumors of each host species but also between the tumors of the two hosts. In Fig. 1, a summary is given of chromosome numbers in stemlines and sidelines of the two materials. The agreement between the two curves is striking: in both, the diploid number predominates, the trisomic class is second in frequency, and a small proportion of tumors have stemlines or sidelines in the tetraploid region.

In the mouse, it was impossible, because of the uniform chromosome morphology, to carry the analysis further. In the Chinese hamster, however, each stemline and sideline karyotype could be characterized in relation to the normal diploid or tetraploid karyotypes in terms of gains or losses of individual chromosomes. In the entire material of the 42 Chinese hamster tumors, 26 sidelines occurred, and the chart of Fig. 2 surveys the distribution of these 68 stem- and sidelines on 28 different karyotypes. Of these karyotypes, 22 were in the diploid region, and 6 in the tetraploid. It is seen that most of the variation on the diploid level was by addition of chromosomes with normal morphology, while on the tetraploid level, much more structural variation with consequent appearance of marker chromosomes was found. For the present purpose, it is enough to focus on the trisomic class of stem- and sidelines. This class is second in frequency after the normal diploid class. It is striking that the extra chromosomes in the 22 stem- and sidelines of this class that had a normal extra chromosome were distributed far from randomly:

Chromosome No.	X, Y	5	6	10	Total
Incidence	2	6	9	5	22

Thus, only 3 of the 10 possible autosome types were represented.

Some other observations from the study of Kato (1968) should be mentioned, since they may help to elucidate some early chromosomal events in these tumors. Thus a correlation was demonstrated between the occurrence of normal diploid cells in these tumors and tumor age (= time from virus inoculation to fixation of the cells). In young tumors, the proportion of normal diploid cells was higher than in old tumors. It was also found that the diploid tumors formed two groups, each with about the same number of cases: (1) tumors without any sidelines; (2) tumors with one or more sidelines. In both groups a certain chromosomal background variation was found, both numerical and structural. It was noticed that this variation was considerably heavier in group (2) with sidelines, than in group (1) without sidelines, indicating that the balance of the population was more upset in group (2). Again, the stemlines of the trisomic tumors showed no more background variation than the diploid group (1), and in them evidently good balance had been restituted.

From these observations, the following course of events may be visualized: Disregarding tumors that may take their origin from pre-existing tetraploid cells, these tumors start out with mainly diploid cells in their population. Mitotic and chromosomal disturbances occur, however, and single cells with deviating karyotypes appear. In the present material, trisomic cells were most frequent among the deviating ones. Next step is the development of a sideline, usually trisomic, meaning that at least 10% of the cells belong to one deviating karyotype. Now the entire population shows signs of increased imbalance. Eventually a trisomic sideline increases in importance and becomes the new stemline. After that step has been taken, the signs of imbalance subside: the tumor has reached a new equilibrium. The fact that in the present material, 91% of the trisomic stemlines had 1 of 3 autosomal types as their extra chromosome, while the other 7 types were not represented, shows that the development is predetermined and nonrandom. The findings in the Rous virus induced tumors of the Chinese hamster undoubtedly support the idea that the karyotypic development in tumors is dependent on underlying genetic changes. The establishment of nonrandom patterns in the karyotypes, indicates that also the submicroscopic variation is nonrandom.

Studies during recent years on the action of viruses on chromosomes of normal cells in tissue culture have made it possible to form some idea about still earlier chromosomal events in primary tumors, viz. the immediate response of chromosomes of the first, second etc. mitosis after exposure to the virus. This aspect has been covered by Dr. Nichols in his article in the present volume. He points out that among the chromosomal responses to viral action, it is especially one response which may be considered significant in connection with cancer development, viz. the appearance of chromosome breaks of the delayed isolocus type. Several circumstances, as the incidence of this type of breaks together with true gene mutations in *Drosophila* after exposure to the Rous virus (Burdette and Yoon), make it probable that this type of chromosome breaks, ubiquitous in all kinds of virus infections, can be regarded as an indicator system of mutagenic activity on the submicroscopic level. It is suggestive that the work with Rous virus in this area has demonstrated clear nonrandom patterns of the isolocus breaks both in man (Nichols et al.) and in the Chinese hamster (Kato 1967).

As a summary of the present section, it may be said that in the few primary tumors, which have been investigated in a sufficiently large scale to permit any general conclusions, chromosomal disturbances occur in a much higher frequency than in normal cells *in situ*. This is true of the earliest stages that have been approachable for direct study. That even still earlier stages, all the way back to the first mitosis after virus infection, are liable to chromosome variation may be inferred from *in vitro* experiments.

5. *Conclusion*

Cytogenetically, the phenomenon of malignancy may be regarded as genetic adaptation of cells to a new mode of life. Malignant cells represent the entire scale of transitional stages from normal cells filling their place in tissues of multicellular organisms to cells living as parasites in these multicellular organisms. The only comparable phenomenon so far known is the adaptation of the same type of original cells to life outside the body, in tissue culture. These two adaptations both mean gain of independence to the individual cell in relation to the host organism, and both comprise an indefinite number of genetic steps, analogous to the events during natural evolution of organisms.

The present article focuses on the possible role of chromosomal irregularities in carcinogenesis. Even though we know less about carcinogenesis so far than about other phases of cancer development, there is safe evidence that carcinogenesis, as well as all other stages of malignancy, is accompanied by chromosomal irregularities; nothing is known, however, as to the significance of these chromosome irregularities in relation to the carcinogenic transformation.

The chromosome variation in malignancy is of a specific kind: it generally oscillates around average karyotypes, and each cancer cell population is characterized by one predominant karyotype, the stemline karyotype, and in addition often one or more sideline karyotypes. It is true that during certain periods, the stemline may become less predominant, for instance after drastic environmental changes, as after explantation in tissue culture of a tumor cell population firmly adapted to the conditions of *in vivo* environment (Hsu and Klatt; Nielsén), but if the population survives long enough, a definitive stemline will again form. The fact that the chromosome variation in tumors is never haphazard but gathers around stemlines and sidelines is compatible with the idea that the development in each tumor takes place according to an evolutionary pattern: the most viable karyotype prevails at all times.

An important question is whether specific types of tumors are correlated to specific karyotypic patterns. Since the properties of each tumor, its phenotype, must be determined by the interplay between its genotype and its environment, and since the tumor genotype is reflected in its stemline karyotype, it would be reasonable to expect *a priori* that each tumor type would be characterized by one karyotype, just as in natural evolution a species is characterized by its karyotype. Such is the situation, as far as known, only in CML. In all other cases, conditions are more complex.

It has been pointed out above that even though obvious correlations do not usually exist between karyotype and tumor type, it has been ascertained, in some materials intensively studied, that predetermined chromosome patterns occur. Such patterns have been demonstrated at three different levels: (1) in the mitoses immediately following the exposure of normal cells to carcinogenic agents; (2) in the mitoses of the developing primary tumor; (3) during advanced stages of tumor progression.

(1) The relations between the first type of pattern and the other two are not yet clear, since so far the immediate response to carcinogenic viruses and chemicals has been approachable only in tissue culture systems. However, highly clarifying studies on the relations between the original open isolocus breaks, the subsequent structural and numerical variation and the eventual appearance of sidelines and new stemlines have been made in the experiments of Moorhead and Saksela on human cell strains exposed to SV_{40} virus, and it is reasonable to assume that essentially similar sequences may occur *in vivo*.

(2) The presence in some primary tumors of a variety of stemline karyotypes together forming a pattern, rather than one single stemline karyotype, reflects the well-known condition that two tumors, even though of the same etiology and the same tissue origin, are rarely identical. Thus, a well-defined tumor type, as the Rous

sarcomas of the Chinese hamster, comprises a spectrum of different variants. In the work of Kato (1968) referred to above, this is well illustrated by the observation that within the stemline pattern found, one specific karyotype – trisomy No. 6 – was correlated with a specific histopathologic type, a highly differentiated fibro-sarcoma. It may be expected that such observations will gradually form interesting additions to the histopathologic diagnostics and even become of clinical value. Thus, Tjio et al. observed that CML patients without the Philadelphia chromosome form a clinically recognizable entity with a prognosis different from the Philadelphia chromosome positive cases.

(3) After long periods of progression, tumors of many different kinds tend to converge towards a vaguely uniform karyotypic pattern. This long-term tendency of the karyotypes is parallelled by the development of the cells towards anaplasia. A somewhat different collective karyotype pattern was found in some human ascites tumors of varying origin, as compared with human leukemias.

In summary: Chromosome variation is an integrated part of tumor development from the earliest beginning of carcinogenesis to the latest progressive stages. Even before any malignancy has started chromosome variation in a normal tissue is generally associated with an increased tendency to cancer. There is good reason to assume that the visible chromosome variation is an indicator system of invisible genetic changes, which may actually play a more important role in cancer than the visible changes. Although apparently haphazard, the chromosome variation in cancer has been demonstrated in all carefully analyzed instances to be governed by strict rules. The only immediately evident case of correlation between chromosomes and malignancy, so far known, is the CML, but less obvious correlations are found in other types of tumors.

Although recent work in the field of chromosomes and cancer has gone a long way towards supporting the mutation theory of cancer, there is still no evidence that any chromosomal changes are directly involved in the unknown change which starts off normal cell towards malignancy. It seems that the question whether chromosome changes are, or are not, causative factors in carcinogenesis is still premature. Much more information is needed concerning the nature of the cellular mechanisms leading up to the chromosome changes during carcinogenesis. This is an area of research which is intensely worked on at present, and it is to be expected that continued collaboration of, among others, cytogenetics, biochemistry, virology and electron microscopy will help to put meaningful questions and, eventually, to elucidate the role of chromosomes in carcinogenesis.

Acknowledgements

The present work has been supported by U.S. Public Health Service Research Grant No. CA-06415-06 from the National Cancer Institute and by grants from the Swedish

Cancer Society, the Swedish Medical and Natural Science Research Councils. I also wish to thank Drs. J.-G. Forsberg, Bengt Källén, Yngve Melander and Warren W. Nichols for constructive criticism.

References

BARSKI, G. and F. CORNEFERT-JENSEN: Cytogenetic study of Sticker venereal sarcoma in European dogs. J. Natl. Cancer Inst. 37 (1966) 787.

BOWEY, C.E. and A.I. SPRIGGS: Chromosomes of human endometrium. J. Med. Genet. 4 (1967) 91.

BURDETTE, J.M. and J.S. YOON: Mutations, chromosomal aberrations, and tumors in insects treated with oncogenic virus. Science 154 (1967) 340.

CURTIS, H.J.: Biological mechanisms underlying the aging process. Science 141 (1963) 686.

FORD, C.E. and C.M. CLARKE: Cytogenetic evidence of clonal proliferation in primary reticular neoplasms. Canad. Cancer Conf. 5 (1963) 129.

FORSBERG, J.-G.: The occurrence of mitotic irregularities during a normal epithelial proliferation. Experientia 23 (1967) 841.

FORSBERG, J.-G. and B. KÄLLÉN: Cell death during embryogenesis. Rev. Roum. Embryol. Cytol., Sér. Embryol. (1968) in press.

FORSBERG, J.-G. and B. LANNERSTAD: Chromosome aberrations during normal epithelial proliferation. Nature 217 (1968) 568.

HANSEN-MELANDER, E.: Accelerated evolution of cancer stemlines following environmental changes. Hereditas 44 (1958) 471.

HARE, W.C.D., T.-J. YANG and R.A. MCFEELY: A survey of chromosome findings in 47 cases of bovine lymphosarcoma (leukemia). J. Natl. Cancer Inst. 38 (1967) 383.

HAUSCHKA, T.S. and A. LEVAN: Inverse relationship between chromosome ploidy and host-specificity of sixteen transplantable tumors. Exptl. Cell Res. 4 (1953) 457.

HAYFLICK, L. and P.S. MOORHEAD: The serial cultivation of human diploid cell strains. Exptl. Cell Res. 25 (1961) 585.

HSU, T.C. and O. KLATT: Mammalian chromosomes *in vitro*. X. Heteroploid transformation in neoplastic cells. J. Natl. Cancer Inst. 22 (1959) 313.

HUGHES, E.C. and T.V. CSERMELY: Chromosomal constitution of human endometrium. Nature 209 (1966) 326.

ISING, U.: Chromosome studies in Ehrlich mouse ascites cancer after heterologous transplantation through hamsters. Brit. J. Cancer 9 (1955) 592.

ISING, U.: Effect of heterologous transplantation on chromosomes of ascites tumours: A contribution to our knowledge of environmental influence on tumour cells. Acta Pathol. Microbiol. Scand., Suppl. 127 (1958) 102 pp.

ISING, U. and A. LEVAN: The chromosomes of two highly malignant human tumours. Acta Pathol. Microbiol. Scand. 40 (1957) 13.

JACOBS, P.A., I.M. TOUGH and D.H. WRIGHT: Cytogenetic studies in Burkitt's lymphoma. Lancet 2 (1963) 1144.

JENSEN, F., H. KOPROWSKI and J. PONTÉN: Rapid transformation of human fibroblast cultures by simian virus 40. Proc. Natl. Acad. Sci. U.S. 50 (1963) 343.

KÄLLÉN, B.: Degeneration and regeneration in the vertebrate central nervous system during embryogenesis. Progr. Brain Res. 14 (1965) 77.

KATAYAMA, K.P. and H.W. JONES JR.: Chromosomes of atypical (adenomatous) hyperplasia and carcinoma of the endometrium. Am. J. Obstet. Gynecol. 97 (1967) 978.

KATO, R.: Localization of 'spontaneous' and Rous sarcoma virus-induced breakage in specific regions of the chromosomes of the Chinese hamster. Hereditas 58 (1967) 221.

KATO, R.: The chromosomes of forty-two primary Rous sarcomas of the Chinese hamster. Hereditas 59 (1968) 63.

KIHLMAN, B. A. and B. HARTLEY: 'Sub-chromatid' exchanges and the 'folded fibre' model of chromosome structure. Hereditas 57 (1967) 289.

KOHN, G., W. J. MELLMAN, P. S. MOORHEAD, J. LOFTUS and G. HENLE: Involvement of C group chromosomes in five Burkitt lymphoma cell lines. J. Natl. Cancer Inst. 38 (1967) 209.

LEJEUNE, J., R. BERGER, M. HAINES, J. LAFOURCADE, J. VIALETTE, P. SATGE and R. TURPIN: Constitution d'un clone à 54 chromosomes au cours d'une leucoblastose congénitale chez une enfant mongolienne. C.R. Acad. Sci. 256 (1963) 1195.

LEVAN, A.: Relation of chromosome status to the origin and progression of tumors: The evidence of chromosome numbers. Ann. Symp. Fundam. Cancer Research 13 (1959) 151.

LEVAN, A.: Preliminary chromosome data on Rous sarcoma in rats. Symp. carcinogenesis, Oslo (1961).

LEVAN, A.: Non-random representation of chromosome types in human tumor stemlines. Hereditas 55 (1966) 28.

LEVAN, A.: Some current problems of cancer cytogenetics. Hereditas 57 (1967) 343.

LEVAN, A. and T. LOTFY: Naphthalene acetic acid in the *Allium* test. Hereditas 35 (1949) 337.

LEVAN, A., G. MANOLOV and P. CLIFFORD: The chromosomes of a human neuroblastoma. A new case with accessory minute chromosomes. J. Natl. Cancer Inst. 41 (1968) in press.

MAKINO, S.: Some epidemiologic aspects of venereal tumors of dogs as revealed by chromosome and DNA studies. Ann. N.Y. Acad. Sci. 108 (1963) 1106.

MELANDER, Y.: Cell differentiation and delayed separation of anaphase chromosomes. Hereditas 49 (1963) 277.

MOORHEAD, P.S. and E. SAKSELA: The sequence of chromosome aberrations during SV_{40} transformation of a human diploid cell line. Hereditas 52 (1965) 271.

NICHOLS, W. W.: Relationships of viruses, chromosomes and carcinogenesis. Hereditas 50 (1963) 53.

NICHOLS, W. W.: Studies on the role of viruses in somatic mutation. Hereditas 55 (1966) 1.

NICHOLS, W. W., A. LEVAN and B. KIHLMAN: Chromosome breakage associated with viruses and DNA inhibitors. Symp. Int. Soc. Cell Biol. 3 (1964) 255.

NIELSÉN, K.: Chromosome studies in the Ehrlich ascites tumor of the mouse grown *in vitro*. Hereditas 58 (1967) 73.

OHNO, S., J. JAINCHILL and C. STENIUS: The creeping vole (*Microtus oregoni*) as a gonosomic mosaic I. The OY/XY constitution of the male. Cytogenetics 2 (1963) 232.

ÖSTERGREN, G. and T. WAKONIG: True or apparent sub-chromatid breakage and the induction of labile states in cytological chromosome loci. Botan. Notiser (1954) 357.

STEENIS, H. VAN: Chromosomes and cancer. Nature 209 (1966) 819.

STEWART, S. E., E. LOVELACE, J. J. WHANG and V. A. NGU: Burkitt tumor: Tissue culture cytogenetic and virus studies. J. Natl. Cancer Inst. 34 (1965) 319.

STICH, H. F.: Chromosomes of tumor cells. I. Murine leukemias induced by one or two injections of 7,12-dimethylbenz(a)anthracene. J. Natl. Cancer Inst. 25 (1960) 649.

THERMAN, E. and S. TIMONEN: Inconstancy of the human somatic chromosome complement. Hereditas 37 (1951) 266.

TJIO, J. H., P. P. CARBONE, J. WHANG and E. FREI III: The Philadelphia chromosome and chronic myelogenous leukemia. J. Natl. Cancer Inst. 36 (1966) 567.

WAKONIG, R. and H. F. STICH: Chromosomes in primary and transplanted leukemias of AKR mice. J. Natl. Cancer Inst. 25 (1960) 295.

WALD, N., A. C. UPTON, V. K. JENKINS and W. H. BORGES: Radiation-induced mouse leukemia: Consistent occurrence of an extra and a marker chromosome. Science 143 (1964) 810.

WEBER, W. T., P. C. NOWELL and W. C. D. HARE: Chromosome studies of a transplanted and primary canine venereal sarcoma J. Natl. Cancer Inst. 35 (1965) 537.

WINGE, Ö.: Zytologische Untersuchungen uber die Natur maligner Tumoren I. 'Crown gall' der Zuckerrübe. Z. Zellforsch. Mikroskop. Anat. 6 (1927) 397.

WINGE, Ö.: Zytologische Untersuchungen über die Natur maligner Tumoren II. Teerkarzinome bei Mäusen. Z. Zellforsch. Mikroskop. Anat. 10 (1930) 683.

ZANG, K. D. and H. SINGER: Chromosomal constitution of meningiomas. Nature 216 (1967) 84.

CHAPTER 30

Interactions between viruses and chromosomes

WARREN W. NICHOLS

Institute for Medical Research, Camden, New Jersey

Contents

1. Introduction
2. Observations on virus-induced chromosome abnormalities
3. Mechanisms of virus-induced chromosome change
4. Summary

This work was supported by U.S. Public Health Service research grants CA 03845 and Career Development Award 5-K3-16,749 from the National Institutes of Health.

1. *Introduction*

The interaction between viruses and chromosomes is receiving a great deal of attention and is stimulating many investigations. This is primarily because of the potential importance of these interactions in the production of somatic mutations, which in turn could hold part or all of the key to cancer and aging. Most observations in this field have dealt with virus-induced chromosome abnormalities, but some studies have also been designed to detect the incorporation of the virus genome into the chromosome, nucleus or cytoplasm of the host cell. This chapter will review the observations on virus-induced chromosome abnormalities initially, and then discuss some of the possible mechanisms of virus-induced chromosome abnormalities.

2. *Observations on virus-induced chromosome abnormalities*

In recent years it has been established beyond a reasonable doubt that some viruses are capable of producing abnormalities that involve the chromosomes. These include at least three types of change: single chromosome breaks, chromosome pulverizations and cell fusion with spindle abnormalities. 'Single breaks' in this context signify the chromatid and chromosome breaks that fit the morphologic description of 'delayed isolocus breaks' (Östergren and Wakonig). In this description these authors described a range of abnormalities from an induced secondary constriction or gap in only one chromatid – or, as in the typical example, a secondary constriction in one chromatid with a corresponding break in the other, to a complete break in both chromatids (Fig. 1). Besides the morphologic description, these authors put forth a proposed mechanism of the delayed isolocus break. There is no evidence at present that this mechanism holds for virus induced breaks but the morphology is certainly the same. As is evident from this morphologic description, the changes encompass both gaps, defined as an achromatic area in a chromatid without loss of alignment and assuming unstained material between the two stained pieces; and true breaks in which there is true disruption of continuity between the two stained pieces of the chromatid or chromosome, which is confirmed by displacement of the fragment. Since all variations between gaps and true breaks occur in the same virus-infected material, cell, or even chromosome, it is probable that they represent different stages or degrees of the same process in this case. Multiple single breaks may occur in a cell, but these are easily differentiated from the extreme chromosome fragmentation termed *pulverization*, in which all or most of the chromosome material is finely fragmented and in a state of coiling with almost complete loss of chromosome morphology.

These changes have been demonstrated with a large variety of viruses in both *in vitro* and *in vivo* systems. Studies in which chromosome breaks of either the single variety or pulverizations have been reported and are summarized in Table 1.

The single chromosome break associated with virus infection was first described by Hampar and Ellison in 1961, in a heteroploid cell line originating from Chinese ham-

TABLE 1

Virus-induced chromosome breaks

Virus	Cell system	Type defect	Reference
Herpes simplex	Chinese hamster *in vitro*	Single breaks	Hampar and Ellison (1961, 1963)
,, ,,	,, ,, ,, ,,	,, ,,	Mazzone and Yerganian (1963)
,, ,,	,, ,, ,, ,,	,, ,,	Rapp and Hsu (1965)
,, ,,	,, ,, ,, ,,	,, ,,	Stich et al. (1964)
,, ,,	Human lung *in vitro*	Pulverization and single breaks	Stich et al. (1964)
,, ,,	Monkey kidney cells *in vitro*	Single breaks and pulverization	Boiron et al. (1966)
Herpes zoster	Human lung *in vitro*	Single breaks and pulverization	Benyesh-Melnick et al. (1964)
Adenovirus type 12	Chinese hamster *in vitro*	Single breaks and pulverization	Stich et al. (1964)
,, ,, ,,	Syrian hamster *in vitro*	,, ,, ,, ,,	MacKinnon et al. (1966)
,, ,, ,,	Syrian hamster *in vivo* (tumors)	,, ,, ,, ,,	Stoltz et al. (1967)
,, ,, ,,	Human leukocytes *in vitro*	Single breaks	Nichols (1966)
Adenovirus type 5 and 7	Syrian hamster *in vitro*	,, ,,	Utsumi (1965)
SV_{40}	Human fibroblast *in vitro*	Single breaks	Koprowski et al. (1962)
,,	Human kidney *in vitro*	,, ,,	Yerganian et al. (1962)
,,	Hamster kidney cells *in vitro*	,, ,,	Cooper and Black (1963, 1964)
,,	Human fibroblast	,, ,,	Moorhead and Saksela (1963)
,,	,, ,,	,, ,,	Todaro et al. (1963)
,,	,, ,,	,, ,,	Moorhead and Saksela (1965)
,,	,, ,,	,, ,,	Weinstein and Moorhead (1965)
,,	,, ,,	,, ,,	Wolman et al. (1964)
,,	Monkey kidney	,, ,,	Fernandes and Moorhead (1965)
,,	Human fibroblast	,, ,,	Girardi et al. (1966)

Polyoma	Hamster fibroblast	Single breaks	Vogt and Dulbecco (1963)
,,	Chinese hamster *in vitro*	,, ,,	Yerganian et al. (1964)
Schmidt-Ruppin Rous sarcoma virus	Rat embryo fibroblasts	Single breaks	Nichols (1963)
,, ,, ,, ,,	Rat tumor *in vitro*	,, ,,	,, ,,
,, ,, ,, ,,	Human leukocytes	,, ,,	Nichols et al. (1964)
,, ,, ,, ,,	Mouse tumors *in vivo*	,, ,, (low incidence)	Mark (1967a, b)
,, ,, ,, ,,	,, ,, ,, ,,	,, ,, (double minute)	Mark (1967a, b)
Rous sarcoma virus	Rat cells	Single breaks	Vrba and Donner (1964a, b)
,, ,, ,,	*Drosophila in vivo*	,, ,,	Burdette and Yoon (1967)
Shope papilloma virus	Rabbit kidney *in vitro*	Single breaks	Prunieras et al. (1966)
Rubeola (measles)	Human leukocytes *in vivo*	Single breaks	Nichols et al. (1962) Nichols (1963)
,, ,,	Rabbit kidney *in vitro*	,, ,,	Mauler and Hennessen (1965)
,, ,,	Human leukocytes *in vivo* Human fibroblasts *in vitro*	,, ,,	Aula (1965)
,, ,,	Human tissue cultures	Pulverization	Nichols et al. (1964, 1965)
,, ,,	HEp-2 tissue culture	Single breaks	Fjelde and Holterman (1962)
Chickenpox	Human leukocytes *in vivo*	Single breaks	Aula (1963, 1965)
Yellow fever vaccine	Human leukocytes *in vivo*	Pulverization	Harnden (1964)
Sendai virus	Human heteroploid and diploid cells *in vitro*	Pulverization	Saksela et al. (1965)
,, ,, (mumps, measles, Newcastle disease virus)	HeLa cells *in vitro*	,,	Cantell et al. (1966)

TABLE 1, *continued*

Virus	Cell system	Type defect	Reference
Tumor virus	*R. angelae* (Diptera Sciaridae) *in vivo*	Single breaks	Diaz and Pavan (1965)
Rubella (German measles)	Human diploid cells *in vitro*	Single breaks	Boué et al. (1964)
,, ,, ,,	Human diploid cells *in vivo* and *in vitro*	,, ,,	Chang et al. (1966)
,, ,, ,,	Leukocytes	,, ,,	Nusbacher et al. (1967)
,, ,, ,,	Leukocytes *in vivo*	,, ,,	Kuroki et al. (1966)
Infectious hepatitis	Leukocytes *in vivo*	Single breaks	Mella and Lang (1967)
,, ,,	Bone marrow *in vivo*	,, ,,	Matsaniotis et al. (1966)
,, ,,	Leukocytes *in vivo*	,, ,,	El-Alfi et al. (1965)
Mumps (measles, chickenpox)	Leukocytes *in vivo*	Single breaks	Gripenberg (1965)
Aseptic meningitis	Leukocytes *in vivo*	Single breaks	Makino et al. (1965)
ECHO 10 virus Columbia SK	HeLa *in vitro*	Single breaks	Nachtigal et al. (1966)

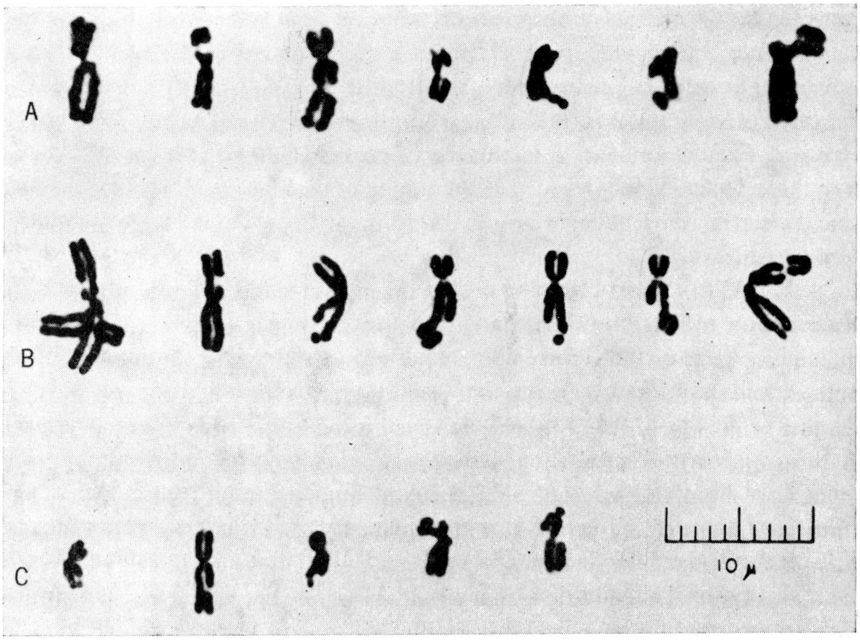

Fig. 1. Chromosomes demonstrating various stages of morphology of the delayed isolocus break. (a) Chromosomes from several cells from clinical measles. (b, c) Chromosomes from single cells treated with deoxyadenosine (AdR).

ster infected with herpes simplex virus. In the first division after the addition of virus the cells exhibited a significantly higher number of chromosome and chromatid breaks than control cultures. The initial studies did not show cytopathogenic effects or mitotic inhibition, but later work by these authors (1963) demonstrated early cell kill as well as chromosomal changes in infected cells. Following this, similar observations were made by several workers in a variety of virus-cell systems, including diploid as well as heteroploid cell lines (Table 1).

In vivo studies on patients with clinical viral syndromes have included both positive and negative observations. In 1962 Nichols et al. reported chromosome breaks in leukocyte cultures from patients with clinical measles. The occurrence of these breaks was of short duration as revealed by a series of 4 to 5 bleedings on alternate days from each patient. Chromosome breakage was seen to a lesser extent in patients receiving live attenuated measles vaccine, and this breakage could be reduced to control levels by active or passive immunization. The broken chromosomes remained open with little tendency for reunions or rearrangement. The measles observations were confirmed by Aula and by Gripenberg, and chromosome breakage has also been observed in leukocyte cultures from patients with chickenpox, after yellow fever vaccination, and in patients with aseptic meningitis, mumps, and infectious hepatitis. Chromosome breaks were searched for in measles and not found by Harnden, and Tanzer et al. The reasons for the differences in observations have not been determined, but may be due to the presence of a second virus that can act either as an enhancing agent or produce interference. It may also be because of different strains of virus in different epidemics or selection of viral mutants by passage from patient to patient as any given epidemic progresses. Factors influencing restitution of breaks could also play a role. In addition to these, technical factors such as the timing of bleedings and whether the first or second division of the leukocyte culture was examined could make large differences in observed results.

Single breaks have been observed during the phenomenon of viral-induced cellular transformation or alteration. Although transformation is a somewhat ambiguous term, it has come to include loss of contact inhibition of the cells, continuing mitosis in a confluent cell sheet, change in cellular morphology, chromosomal change, and change in the rate of growth of the cells. Where tested it has also frequently been associated with the capability of producing malignancy when injected into animals. These changes have been studied with SV_{40} virus in human diploid cell cultures, mouse cultures, and hamster cell cultures; with polyoma virus in hamster cells and mouse cells; with Rous sarcoma virus in chicken, rat, simian and human cell cultures; and with various types of adenoviruses in hamster cells. The sequential cytogenetic events in viral transformation have been especially well studied by Saksela and Moorhead and Moorhead and Weinstein in a human diploid fibroblast system with SV_{40} as the transforming agent. After the addition of virus several weeks elapsed before the first observable changes, which consisted of continued mitosis in a confluent sheet and chromatid breaks that occurred almost simultaneously. These are followed by changes in cell morphology and growth rate, and finally by changes in chromosome structure and an increase in aneuploid and tetraploid cells. The time from infection to the onset of the changes is related to the tissue culture passage of the diploid cells used (Todaro et al.; Jensen et al.). The later the passage, the more rapidly the changes are seen. An increase in spontaneous chromosome abnormalities has been observed with increasing passage numbers in human diploid cells by Saksela and Moorhead and Yoshida and Makino.

Diaz and Pavan reported very interesting observations in the polytene chromosomes of cells of *Rhynchosciara angelae* (Diptera, Sciardiae) infected by either a protozoan or a virus. In protozoan infection they observed an increase in chromosome size and a change in the heterochromatic blocks to a structure that had characteristics of both a large puff and a nucleolus. The increase in chromosome size was also seen in virus infected cells and was accompanied by specific changes in banding pattern. In more severely affected cells there was degeneration of chromosomes, bridges between fragments and some vacuolation of chromosomes.

The type of chromosome abnormality discussed up to this point and termed *single chromosome break* is the one believed most likely to serve as a bridge between viral and somatic mutation theories of carcinogenesis. It is likely that damage to the genetic material of the cell severe enough to be visualized microscopically would

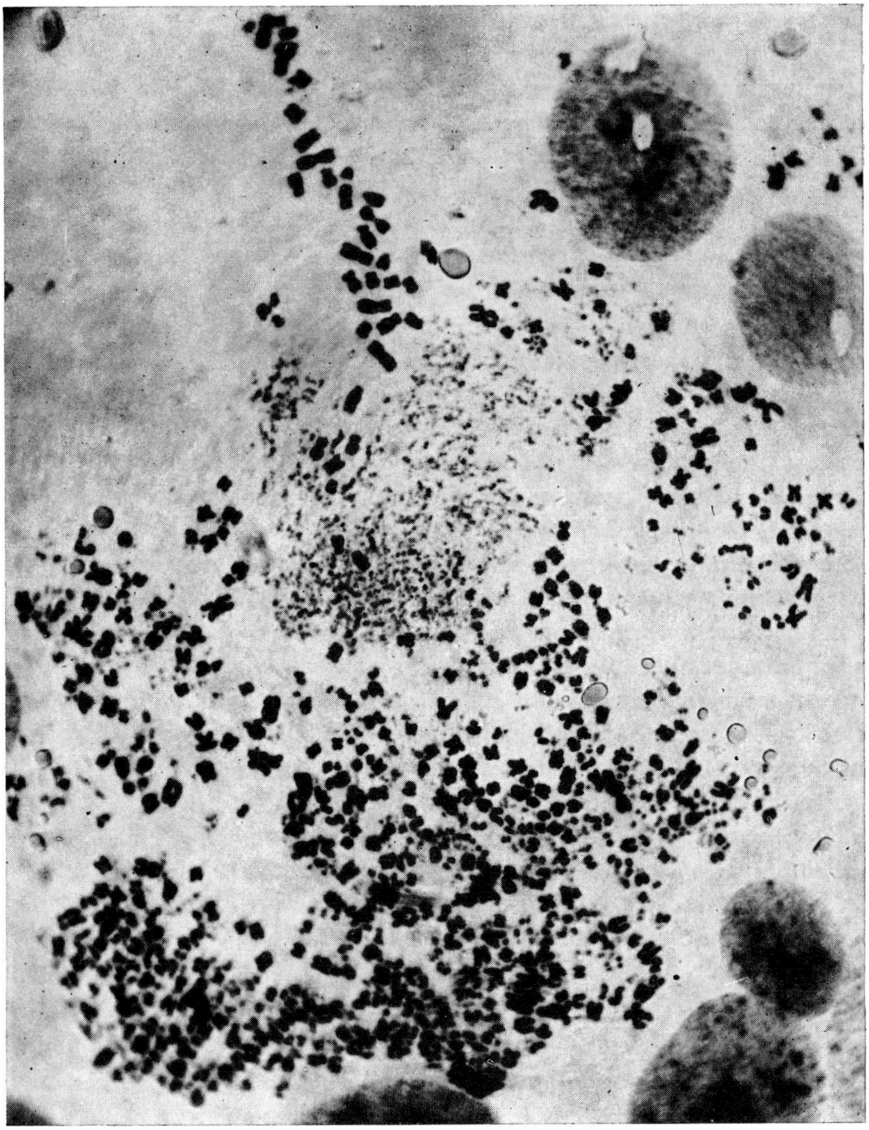

Fig. 2. Pulverization in a syncytium in LU 106 tissue culture cells produced by exposure to measles virus. The various nuclear chromosome groups demonstrate different stages of fragmentation and contraction. (From Nichols et al. 1964.)

often result in the death of the cell. However, it is possible that these breaks are an indicator system for submicroscopic mutagenic activity similar to that seen in X-ray, in which the number of microscopically visible breaks reflects the incidence of mutation. On this basis the possible role of viruses in a somatic mutation theory of carcinogenesis has been discussed by Nichols (1963). Here it was pointed out that chromosome breaks are a common denominator for the three known types of carcinogen (irradiation, chemicals and viruses) in their interaction with cells. If these breaks do reflect submicroscopic mutagenic events they may occasionally be capable of producing a growth advantage and malignancy. In this perspective other changes as aneuploidy and polyploidy, frequently observed in malignant tumors, could also be manifestations of associated mutations that affect nondisjunction and the mitotic mechanism as has long been known in *Drosophila* and plants. Burdette and Yoon have placed *Drosophila* in medium containing Rous sarcoma virus and found an increase in lethal mutation, visible mutations, chromosomal nondisjunctions and losses, as well as tumors.

A second type of chromosomal change associated with virus infection has been termed *chromosome pulverization* (Nichols et al. 1964). This consists of extreme fragmentation of chromosomal material and is seen most commonly with viruses that produce cell fusion and syncytia such as measles, Sendai, mumps, Newcastle, herpes zoster and herpes simplex. The same or a similar process in single cells of leukocyte cultures from patients receiving yellow fever vaccine was reported by Harnden. Pulverizations occur typically but not exclusively in syncytia. Usually chromosome sets and nuclei making up the syncytium retain a certain degree of individuality and vary in the degree of damage from apparently intact chromosome sets to completely powdered or pulverized material (Fig. 2). Originally the pulverized material was considered to be fragmented and despiralized metaphase chromosomes. However, recent work by Nichols et al. (1967) has demonstrated with autoradiography that these pulverized nuclei are actually S or synthesis period material that is fragmented and exhibits increased spiralizations (Fig. 3a, b).

The third type of chromosome change associated with virus infection is also associated with cell fusion and syncytia formation; especially the sharing of common centrosomes. These changes have been studied especially by Heneen and can lead to increasing degrees of polyploidy, changes in gene dose and possibilities of genetic recombinations. This viral-induced fusion has many similarities to the process termed *cell hybridization* by Barski et al. and Ephrussi et al. In this work two mouse cell lines, each with specific marker chromosomes, were cultured in the same bottle and were found in some instances to fuse forming cells with both types of chromosome marker and the additive number of chromosomes of the two parent cells. Hybridization occurs more readily if at least one of the parent cell cultures is malignant. Harris has utilized the fusion effect of ultraviolet-inactivated Sendai virus to produce cell fusions between a variety of cell types.

3. *Mechanisms of virus-induced chromosome change*

The mechanisms of virus-induced chromosome change are not established, but many

3b

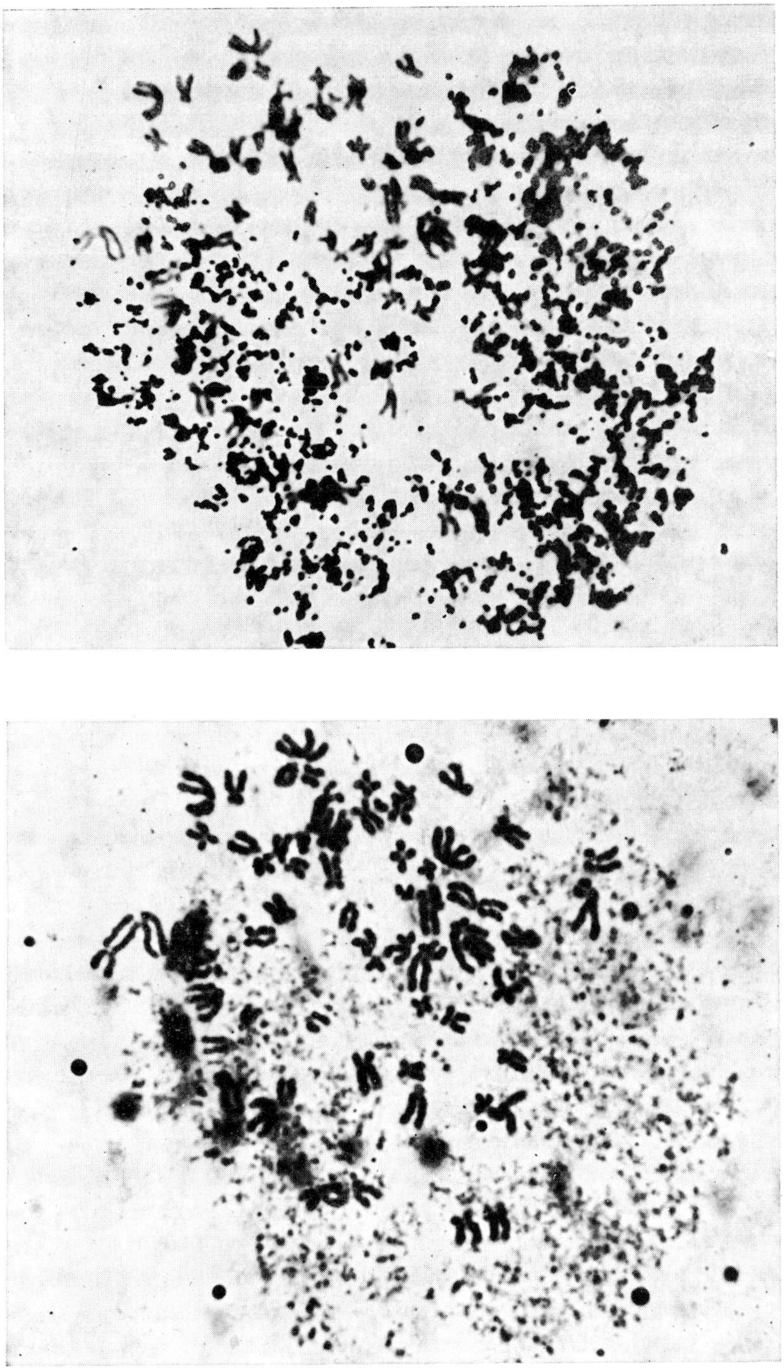

3a

Fig. 3. (a) A syncytium with intact and pulverized chromosomes after treatment with hemolytic fraction of measles virus that had been preceded by a pulse of tritiated thymidine. (b) The same syncytium after application of photographic emulsion and exposure for two weeks, showing silver grains over the pulverized portion of the chromosomes. (From Nichols et al. 1967.)

hypotheses and much interesting work is in progress in this field. Possible mechanisms include interference with cellular DNA synthesis, either by inhibiting cellular enzymes or competing for nucleic acid building blocks; an indirect effect mediated through a cellular organelle as the lysosome, and a direct virus 'attack' or a combination of viral and cellular DNA in the chromosomes.

Interest in interference with DNA synthesis as a possible mechanism of virus-induced chromosome change arose as a result of morphologic similarities between the virus-induced chromosome breaks and the breaks produced by a group of nucleosides and nucleotides that inhibit DNA synthesis. As was mentioned in the section on observations, virus-induced chromosome breaks usually remain open and fit the morphologic description of the delayed isolocus break in contrast to breaks produced by irradiation and radiomimetic chemicals in which reunions and recombinations are frequent.

It was observed that 5′-fluorodeoxyuridine (FUdR) (Taylor et al.; Kihlman 1962) and deoxyadenosine (AdR) (Kihlman 1963) produced chromosomal defects in plant cells morphologically indistinguishable from the virus induced defects. Similar observations were made with mammalian cells using arabinosylcytosine (araC) and AdR (Kihlman et al.) and arabinosyladenine (Nichols 1964) (see Fig. 1). All of these nucleosides are known to inhibit DNA synthesis, and it was hypothesized that the chromosome breaking effect was on this basis (Taylor et al.; Taylor; Kihlman 1962). Because of the morphologic similarities of the chromosomal defects other comparisons between effects of these inhibitors of DNA synthesis and viruses were made. It was determined that both produce mitotic inhibition (Kihlman et al.; Nichols 1964; Nichols and Heneen), both produce defects very shortly after exposure (Kihlman et al.; Nichols and Heneen), and both had similarities in localizations of the chromosome breaks (Nichols et al. 1964, 1965b).

It was reasoned that if these similar breaks had similar mechanisms, perhaps the inhibitors of DNA synthesis might be capable of producing somatic mutations or cellular transformation, as is seen with certain viruses. If this were so it could offer a method to separate mutations produced by the addition of viral genetic material and those due to alterations in the cell's genetic material. The capability of these inhibitors of DNA synthesis to produce cellular transformation was tested using araC in human diploid fibroblasts (WI-38) (Nichols and Heneen; Heneen and Nichols) and comparing the immediate and long-term changes with those seen with SV_{40} transformations of the same cell type. Immediately after the araC was added a high incidence of open breaks was found. After a recovery period, changes in cell morphology and growth pattern were noted, and when chromosomes were studied at this time, changes similar to those seen in virus transformed cells were observed. These consisted of new chromosome types, dicentrics, and rearrangements. Continuing mitosis in a confluent sheet and increased growth rate were not seen. While these changes are similar to several of the changes seen with viral transformed cells, they also resemble the senescent stage of diploid cultures with chromosome abnormalities and decreased growth rate.

An indication of the importance of DNA synthesis in transformation was supplied by Todaro and Green when they showed that non-growing 3T3 cells were not susceptible to transformation by SV_{40} virus. They felt this was probably because of a necessity for the cell to be synthesizing DNA in order to be affected by the virus, either because integration of the viral DNA is involved or because only replicating cellular DNA is susceptible to virus-induced change.

A further similarity between the changes produced by inhibitors of DNA synthesis and viruses was revealed in studies with cytidine triphosphate (CTP). While it has not been definitely established that CTP is an inhibitor of DNA synthesis, it produces changes similar to the known inhibitors and there is some indirect evidence that it fits into the same category (Nichols et al. 1965). When CTP is used in conjunction with the Schmidt–Ruppin strain of Rous sarcoma virus it acts synergistically in the production of breaks in human leukocytes.

Before proceeding from the discussion of the comparisons between the effects of the inhibitors of DNA synthesis and viruses, it should be pointed out that while there is agreement that these nucleosides inhibit DNA synthesis and that they do produce chromosomal abnormalities, there is not agreement that the mechanism of the breakage is the inhibition of DNA synthesis. Bell and Wolff, and Brewen feel that these two effects are not related. Some of the pros and cons of these arguments are discussed in Nichols and Heneen (1965) and Nichols (1966). Perhaps the most persuasive argument for a relationship between the inhibition of DNA synthesis and the chromosome breaks is the ability to prevent the breaks in the presence of an inhibitor of synthesis, like FUdR or araC, by the addition of excess of the specific normal deoxyriboside as TdR and CdR, respectively.

Ahnstrom and Natarajan have put forth a theory of breakage for viruses and inhibitors of DNA synthesis that attributes only partial responsibility for the chromosome damage to inhibition of DNA synthesis. The remainder of the effect is attributed to a reversal of the DNA polymerease reaction by an accumulation of pyrophosphate or an upset in the equilibrium of the nucleotides, resulting in an active removal of the nucleotide material from already formed DNA. Experimentally they added excess pyrophosphates to lateral roots of *Vicia faba* and observed chromosome breaks. Acceptance of this interesting possibility must await the exclusion of other actions of pyrophosphate.

Another interesting hypothesis on the mechanism of chromosome breakage was presented by Allison and Paton. These authors attribute the primary event to the breakdown of lysosome membranes and the chromosomal damage to the hydrolytic enzymes released from the lysosomes. This was based on the induction of chromosome breaks in human diploid fibroblast cells after treatment with vital dyes such as acridine orange and neutral red, which bind to lysosomal membranes, followed by illumination with visible light in order to break down the lysosomal membranes. Aula and Nichols investigated the role of lysosomes in virus-induced chromosome breakage, using cytochemical stains for acid phosphatase to detect lysosomal breakdown in various virus–cell systems. Adenovirus type 12 in human diploid cells produced single chromosome breaks but no increase in acid phosphatase staining, and measles virus that produced chromosome pulverization in heteroploid cell lines caused no increase in acid phosphatase staining. In contrast to this, diploid and heteroploid cells infected with poliovirus showed marked increases in the acid phosphatase staining but lacked chromosome breakage. Also cortisone, which is said to have a lysosomal stabilizing action, did not reduce the single breaks of adenovirus type 12 in diploid cells, nor the pulverizations of measles in heteroploid cells. This indicates that the lysosomal enzymes do not play a major role in the mechanism of virus-induced chromosome breaks.

Mycoplasma organisms (PPLO) have been reported to produce chromosome breaks (Fogh and Fogh; Paton et al.) in tissue culture systems. Aula and Nichols (1967) showed an indirect chemical effect of three human strains of mycoplasma, *M. salivarium*, *M. hominis type 2* and *M. fermentans*, in human leukocyte cultures. All three produced mitotic inhibition of varying degree, and *M. salivarium* produced chromosome breaks after five days in culture. Since these organisms are known to deplete arginine, the effect of added arginine on the breaks and mitotic inhibition was tested. Arginine was capable of preventing both the mitotic inhibition and the chromosome breaks. Further studies on this mechanism revealed that when the same cells were grown in arginine-deficient medium without PPLO, chromosomal changes and mitotic inhibition of the same type were produced.

It is known that virus multiplication is not necessary for the induction of chromosome abnormalities. This has been demonstrated for some virus transformation systems and also with measles virus in rabbit kidney cells by Mauler and Hennessen, and for Schmidt–Ruppin strain of Rous sarcoma virus in human leukocytes by Nichols et al. (1964). After infection these cells show no evidence of virus multiplication or release of virus. The pulverization phenomenon can be produced by non-infectious virus fractions. Norrby et al. reported pulverizations with the intact measles virus and the hemolytic fraction of the measles virus, but not by the hemagglutinating fraction or heat killed virus. Similar studies with Sendai virus demonstrated that noninfectious virus particles produced by ultraviolet irradiation could induce pulverizations (Cantell et al.).

By means of radioactive label in the virus, attempts are being made to trace the viral nucleic acid within the cell. This has been approached by Rapp and Hsu, by adding tritiated thymidine to herpes simplex infected diploid Chinese hamster cells not in the synthesis period. Any tritiated thymidine incorporated is believed to be incorporated into synthesizing virus particles. When this was tested, radioactivity was found in the nucleus, but none was localized to chromosomal regions. In work by Nichols et al. (1967) the nucleic acid of adenovirus type 12 was labeled with tritiated thymidine. This labeled virus was then used to infect leukocyte cultures and localization studied by autoradiographs. In non-dividing cells, label was found limited to the nucleus in some cells and over nucleus and cytoplasm in others (Fig. 4a, b). In dividing cells label was found associated with chromosomes (Fig. 4c). The number of grains over individual chromosomes was compared to the relative chromo-

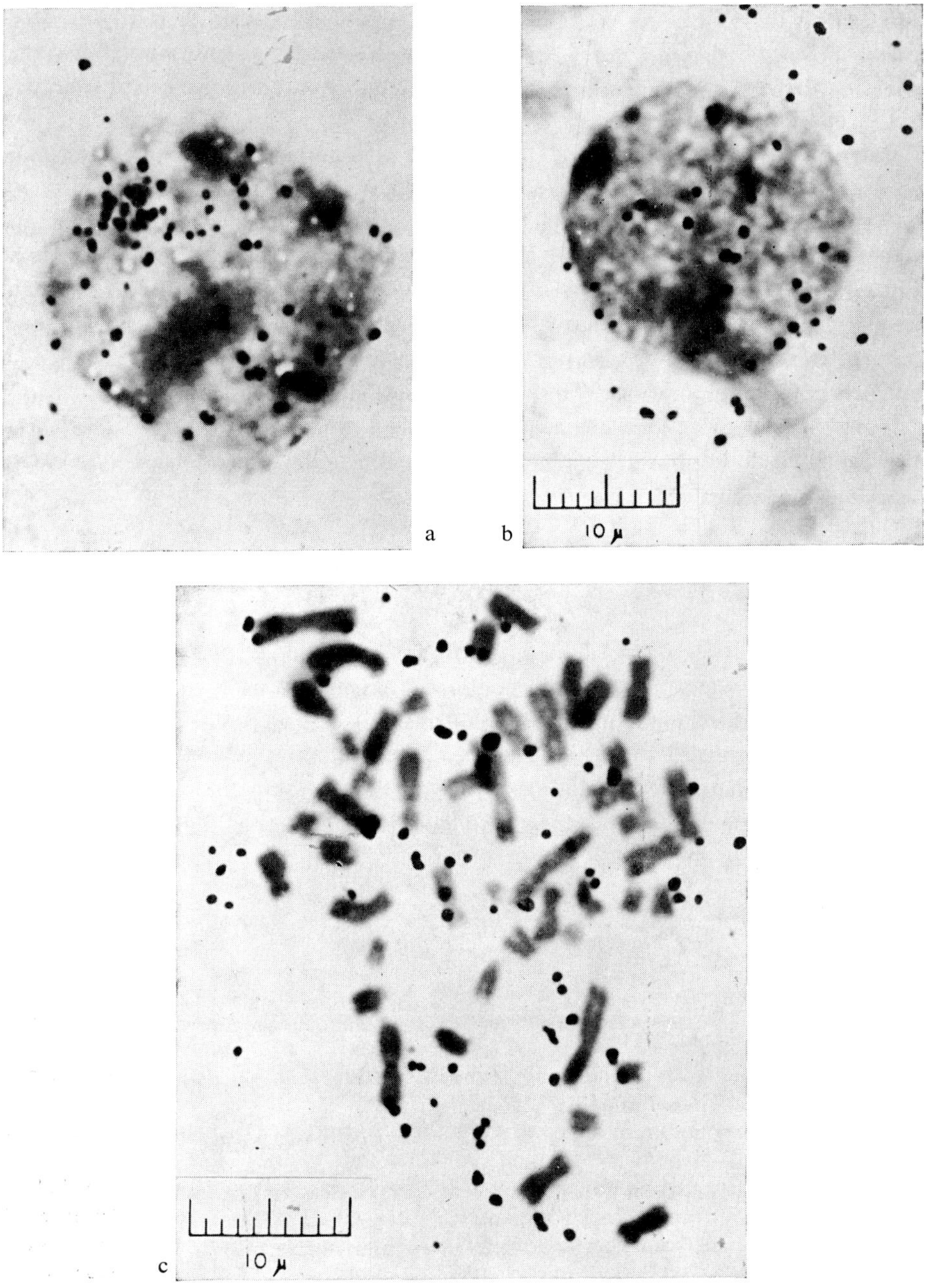

Fig. 4. (a) Autoradiograph of leukocytes treated with H^3-labeled adeno type 12 virus with silver grains limited to nucleus. (b) Autoradiograph of leukocyte treated with H^3-labeled adeno type 12 virus with silver grains over cytoplasm and nucleus. (c) Autoradiograph of metaphase plate from leukocyte treated with H^3-labeled adeno type 12 virus demonstrating label associated with chromosomes. (From Nichols et al. 1967)

some length and revealed a random grain distribution. However, there was an occasional chromosome with a heavy grouping of grains. Label was not limited to metaphases with chromosome breaks, and in cells exhibiting chromosome breaks label was not localized to these areas.

Polyoma virus labeled with H^3 valine and thymidine has been used to follow viral protein and nucleic acid, respectively (Khare and Consigli). When primary mouse embryo cultures were infected and the polyoma nucleic acid followed, grains were observed in the cytoplasm at 3 hr post infection, at the nuclear membrane at 6 hr on to 18 hr, when the greatest numbers were found. After 24 hr grains were again seen to appear in the cytoplasm. When the viral protein was followed in the same culture, grains were observed over the cytoplasm from 3 to 15 hr after infection, but never inside the nucleus. Chromosomes were not studied in these experiments.

None of the work up to this time has supplied a definitive answer to the mechanism of virus-induced chromosome damage. The present indications suggest that several mechanisms are involved.

4. Summary

In summary, viruses are associated with chromosome damage *in vivo*, *in vitro*, and in transformation systems. At least three types of change are recognized. The first is the single break, the second, pulverization of chromosomes, and the third is cell fusion and spindle abnormalities. Current studies on the mechanism of breaks include direct and indirect chemical effects and direct virus attack or combination with the chromosome. While these studies are not yet conclusive, they suggest that more than one mechanism may be involved.

References

AHNSTRÖM, G. and A.T. NATARAJAN: Mechanism of chromosome breakage. A new theory. Hereditas 54 (1966) 380.

ALLISON, A.C. and G.R. PATON: Chromosome damage in human diploid cells following activation of lysosomal enzymes. Nature 207 (1965) 1170.

AULA, P.: Chromosome breaks in leukocytes of chickenpox patients. Preliminary communication. Hereditas 49 (1963) 451.

AULA, P.: Chromosome breaks in leukocytes of chickenpox, measles and mumps patients and of cell cultures infected with measles virus. Ann. Acad. Sci. Fennicae, Ser. A, IV Biologica 89 (1965) 78.

AULA, P.: Virus-associated chromosome breakage. A cytogenetic study of chickenpox, measles and mumps patients and of cell cultures infected with measles virus. Ann. Acad. Sci. Fennicae, Ser. A, IV. Biologica 89 (1965).

AULA, P. and W.W. NICHOLS: The cytogenetic effects of mycoplasma in human leukocyte cultures J. Cell Physiol. Vol. 70, No. 3 (1967) 281.

AULA, P. and W.W. NICHOLS: Lysosomes and virus induced chromosome breakage. Exptl. Cell Res. 51 (1968) 595.

BARSKI, G., S. SORIEUL and F. CORNEFERT: 'Hybrid' type cells in combined cultures of two different mammalian cell strains. J. Natl. Cancer Inst. 26 (1961) 1269.

BELL, S. and S. WOLFF: Studies on the mechanism of the effect of fluorodeoxyuridine on chromosomes. Proc. Natl. Acad. Sci. U.S. 51 (1964) 195.

BENYISH-MELNICK, M., H. STICH, F. RAPP and T. C. HSU: Viruses and mammalian chromosomes III. Effect of herpes zoster virus on human embryonal lung cultures. Proc. Exptl. Biol. Med. 117 (1964) 546.

BOIRON, M., J. TANZER, M. THOMAS and A. HAMPE: Early diffuse chromosomal alterations in monkey kidney cells infected in vitro with herpes simplex virus. Nature 209, 5024 (1966) 737.

BOUÉ, J. G., A. BOUÉ, P. S. MOORHEAD and S. A. PLOTKIN: Altérations chromosomiques induites par le virus de la rubéole dans les cellules embryonnaires diploïdes humaines cultivées in vitro. C.R. Acad. Sci. Paris 259 (1964) 687.

BREWEN, J. G.: The induction of chromatid lesions by cytosine arabinoside in post-DNA-synthetic human leukocytes. Cytogenetics 4 (1965) 28.

BREWEN, J. G. and N. T. CHRISTIE: Studies on the induction of chromosomal aberrations in human leukocytes by cytosine arabinoside. Exptl. Cell Res. 46 (1967) 276.

BURDETTE, W. J. and J. S. YOON: Mutations, chromosomal aberrations, and tumors in insects treated with oncogenic virus. Science 154 (1967) 340.

CANTELL, K., E. SAKSELA and P. AULA: Virological studies on chromosome damage of HeLa cells induced by myxoviruses. Ann. Med. Exptl. Biol. Fennicae 44 (1966) 255.

CHANG, T. H., P. S. MOORHEAD, J. BOUÉ, S. A. PLOTKIN and J. M. HOSKINS: Chromosome studies of human cells infected in utero and in vitro with rubella virus. Proc. Soc. Exptl. Biol. Med. 122 (1966) 236.

COOPER, H. L. and P. H. BLACK: Cytogenetic studies of hamster kidney cell cultures transformed by the simian vacuolating virus (SV_{40}). J. Natl. Cancer Inst. 30 (1963) 1015.

COOPER, H. L. and P. H. BLACK: Cytogenetic studies of three clones derived from a permanent line of hamster cells transformed by SV_{40}. J. Cellular Comp. Physiol. 64 (1964) 220.

DIAZ, M. and C. PAVAN: Changes in chromosomes induced by microorganism infection. Proc. Natl. Acad. Sci., U.S. 54 (1965) 1321.

EL-ALFI, O. S., P. M. SMITH and J. J. BIESELE: Chromosomal breaks in human leukocyte cultures induced by an agent in the plasma of infectious hepatitis patients. Hereditas 52 (1965) 285.

EPHRUSSI, B. and S. SORIEUL: Nouvelles observations sur l'hybridation in vitro de cellules de souris. C.R. Acad. Sci. 254 (1962) 181.

FERNANDES, M. V. and P. S. MOORHEAD: Transformation of African green monkey kidney cultures infected with simian vacuolating virus (SV_{40}). Texas Rep. Biol. Med. Vol. 23 (1965) 242.

FJELDE, A. and D. A. HOLTERMANN: Chromosome studies in the HEp 2 tissue culture cell line during infection with measles virus. Life Sciences 12 (1962) 683.

FOGH, J. and H. FOGH: Chromosome changes in PPLO-infected FL human amnion cells. Proc. Soc. Exptl. Biol. Med. 119 (1965) 233.

GIRARDI, A. J., D. WEINSTEIN and P. S. MOORHEAD: SV_{40} transformation of human diploid cells. Ann. Med. Exptl. Biol. Fennicae 44 (1966) 242.

GRIPENBERG, U.: Chromosome studies in some virus infections. Hereditas 54 (1965) 1.

HAMPAR, B. and S. A. ELLISON: Chromosomal aberrations induced by an animal virus. Nature 192 (1961) 145.

HAMPAR, B. and S. A. ELLISON: Cellular alterations in the MCH line of Chinese hamster cells following infection with herpes simplex virus. Proc. Natl. Acad. Sci., U.S. 49 (1963) 474.

HARNDEN, D. G.: Cytogenetic studies on patients with virus infections and subjects vaccinated against yellow fever. Am. J. Human Genet. 16 (1964) 201.

HARRIS, H.: Behavior of differentiated nuclei in heterokaryons of animal cells from different species. Nature 206, 4984 (1965) 583.

HENEEN, W.K.: Studies in syncytia formation after treatment of human cells (Lu 106) with measles virus. Presented, Fjärde Nordiska Genetikermötet, Lund, June 15–17, 1966.

HENEEN, W.K. and W.W.NICHOLS: Cell morphology of a human diploid cell strain (WI-38) after treatment with arabinosylcytosine. Cancer Res. 27 (1967) 242.

JENSEN, F.C., A.J.GIRARDI, R.N.GILDEN and H.KOPROWSKI: Infection of human and simian tissue cultures with Rous sarcoma virus. Proc. Natl. Acad. Sci. U.S. 52 (1964) 53.

JENSEN, F., H.KOPROWSKI and J.A.PONTEN: Rapid transformation of human fibroblast cultures by simian virus 40. Proc. Natl. Acad. Sci. U.S. 52 (1964) 53.

KHARE, G.P. and R.A.CONSIGLI: Multiplication of polyoma virus I. Use of selectively labeled (H^3) virus to follow the course of infection. J. Bacteriol. 90 (1965) 819.

KIHLMAN, B.: The production of chromatid aberrations by 5-fluorodeoxyuridine alone and in combination with X-ray and 8-ethoxycaffeine. Caryologia 15 (1962) 261.

KIHLMAN, B.: Deoxyadenosine as an inducer of chromosomal aberrations in Vicia Faba. J. Cellular Comp. Physiol. 62 (1963) 267.

KIHLMAN, B.A., W.W.NICHOLS and A.LEVAN: The effect of deoxyadenosine and cytosine arabinoside on the chromosomes of human leukocytes in vitro. Hereditas 50 (1963) 139.

KIT, S., D.R.DUBBS, L.J.PIEKARSKI, R.A.DE TORRES and J.L.MELNICK: Acquisition of enzyme function by mouse kidney cells abortively infected with papovavirus SV_{40}. Proc. Natl. Acad. Sci. U.S. 56, 2 (1966) 463.

KOPROWSKI, H., J.A.PONTEN, F.JENSEN, R.G.RAVDIN, P.S.MOORHEAD and E.SAKSELA: Transformation of cultures of human tissue infected with simian virus SV_{40}. J. Cellular Comp. Physiol. 59 (1962) 381.

KUROKI, Y., S.MAKINO, T.AYA and T.NAYAGAMA: Chromosome abnormalities in cultured leukocytes from rubella patients. Jap. J. Hum. Genet. 11 (1966) 17.

MACKINNON, E., V.I.KALNINS, H.F.STICH and D.S.YOHN: Viruses and mammalian chromosomes. VI. Comparative karyologic and immunofluorescent studies on syrian hamster and human amnion cells infected with adenovirus type 12. Cancer Res. 26 (1966) 612.

MAKINO, S., K.YAMADA and T.KAJII: Chromosome aberrations in leukocytes of patients with aseptic meningitis. Chromosoma 16 (1965) 372.

MARK, J.: Chromosomal analysis of ninety-one primary Rous sarcomas in the mouse. Hereditas 57 (1967a) 23.

MARK, J.: Double-minutes – a chromosomal aberration in Rous sarcomas in mice. Hereditas 57 (1967b) 1.

MATSANIOTIS, N., K.A.KIOSSOGLOU, F.MADUNIS and D.E.ANAGNOSTAKIS: Chromosomes in infectious hepatitis. Lancet II (1966) 1421.

MAULER, R. and W.HENNESSEN: Virus-induced alterations of chromosomes. Arch. Ges. Virusforsch. 16 (1965) 175.

MAZZONE, H.M. and G.YERGANIAN: Gross and chromosomal cytology of virus infected Chinese hamster cells. Exptl. Cell Res. 30 (1963) 591.

MELLA, B. and D.LANG: Leukocyte mitosis: Suppression in vitro associated with acute infectious hepatitis. Science 155 (1967) 80.

MOORHEAD, P.S. and E.SAKSELA: Non-random chromosomal aberrations in SV_{40}-transformed human cells. J. Cellular Comp. Physiol. 62 (1963) 57.

MOORHEAD, P.S. and E.SAKSELA: The sequence of chromosome aberrations during SV_{40} transformation of a human diploid cell strain. Hereditas 52 (1965) 271.

MOORHEAD, P.S. and D.WEINSTEIN: Recent results in cancer research: Malignant transformation by viruses. New York, Springer-Verlag Publ. Co. (1966).

NACHTIGAL, M., I.ADERCA, M.AGRIPINA and M.IFTIMOVICI: Chronic infections with RNA viruses in cell cultures. III. Chromosomal changes in normal and chronically infected cell cultures. Rev. Roum. Inframicrobiol. 3 (1966) 43.

NICHOLS, W.W.: Relationships of viruses, chromosomes and carcinogenesis. Hereditas 50 (1963) 53.

NICHOLS, W.W.: In vitro chromosome breakage induced by arabinosyladenine in human leukocytes. Cancer Res. 24 (1964) 1502.

NICHOLS, W.W.: Studies on the role of viruses in somatic mutation. Hereditas 55 (1966) 1.

NICHOLS, W.W., P.AULA, A.LEVAN, W.HENEEN and E.NORRBY: Radioautography with tritiated thymidine in measles and Sendai virus induced pulverization. J. Cell Biol. 35 (1967) 257.

NICHOLS, W.W. and W.K.HENEEN: Chromosomal effects of arabinosylcytosine in a human diploid cell strain. Hereditas 52 (1965) 402.

NICHOLS, W.W., A.LEVAN, P.AULA and E.NORRBY: Extreme chromosome breakage induced by measles virus in different in vitro systems. Preliminary communication. Hereditas 51 (1964) 380.

NICHOLS, W.W., A.LEVAN, P.AULA and E.NORRBY: Chromosome damage associated with measles virus in vitro. Hereditas 54 (1965) 101.

NICHOLS, W.W., A.LEVAN, L.L.CORIELL, H.GOLDNER and C.G.AHLSTROM: In vitro chromosome abnormalities in human leukocytes associated with Smidt-Ruppin Rous sarcoma virus. Science 146 (1964 248.

NICHOLS, W.W., A.LEVAN, B.HALL and G.ÖSTERGREN: Measles-associated chromosome breakage. Preliminary communication. Hereditas 48 (1962) 367.

NICHOLS, W.W., A.LEVAN, W.K.HENEEN and M.PELUSE: Synergism of the Schmidt-Ruppin strain of the Rous sarcoma virus and cytidine triphosphate in the induction of chromosome breaks in human leukocytes. Hereditas 54 (1965) 213.

NICHOLS, W.W., M.PELUSE, C.GOODHEART, R.MC ALLISTER and C.BRADT: Autoradiographic studies on nuclei and chromosomes of cultured leukocytes after infection with tritium labeled adenovirus type 12. Virology 34 (1968) 303.

NORRBY, E., A.LEVAN and W.W.NICHOLS: The correlation between the chromosome pulverization effect and other biologic activities of measles virus preparations. Exptl. Cell Res. 41 (1966) 483.

NUSBACHER, J., K.HIRSCHHORN and L.COOPER: Chromosomal abnormalities in congenital rubella. New Engl. J. Med. 25 (1967) 1409.

ÖSTERGREN, G. and T.WAKONIG: True or apparent sub-chromatid breakage and the induction of labile states in cytological chromosome loci. Botan. Notiser (1954) 357.

PATON, G.R., J.P.JACOBS and F.T.PERKINS: Chromosome changes in human diploid cell cultures infected with mycoplasma. Nature 207 (1965) 43.

PRUNIERAS, M., M.JACQUEMONT, Y.CHARDONNET and L.GAZZOLO: Etudes sur les rapports virus-chromosomes VI. Etude caryotypique du papillome de Shope. Ann. Inst. Pasteur Lille Extrait Fevrier 11 (1966) 145.

RAPP, F. and T.C.HSU: Viruses and mammalian chromosomes IV. Replication of herpes simplex virus in diploid Chinese hamster cells. Virology 25 (1965) 401.

RUBIN, H.: Virus defectiveness and cell transformation in the Rous sarcoma. J. Cellular Comp. Physiol. 64, Suppl. 1 (1964) 173.

SAKSELA, E., P.AULA and K.CANTELL: Chromosomal damage of human cells induced by Sendai virus. Ann. Med. Exptl. Biol. Fenniae 43 (1965) 132.

SAKSELA, E. and P.S.MOORHEAD: Aneuploidy in the degenerative phase of serial cultivation of human cell strains. Proc. Natl. Acad. Sci. U.S. 50 (1963) 390.

STICH, H.F., T.C.HSU and F.RAPP: Viruses and mammalian chromosomes. I. Localization of chromosome aberrations after infection with herpes simplex virus. Virology 22 (1964) 439.

STICH, H.F., G.L.VAN HOOSIER and J.J.TRENTIN: Viruses and mammalian chromosomes. Chromosome aberrations by human adenovirus type 12. Exptl. Cell Res. 34 (1964) 400.

STOLTZ, D.B., H.F.STICH and D.S.YOHN: Viruses and mammalian chromosomes. VII. The persistence of a chromosomal instability in regenerating, transplanted, and cultured neoplasms induced by human adenovirus type 12 in Syrian hamsters. Cancer Res. 27 (1967) 587.

TANZER, J., Y.STOITCHKOV, P.HAREL and M.BOIRON: Chromosomal abnormalities in measles. Lancet 2 (1963) 1070.

TAYLOR. J.H.: DNA synthesis in relation to chromosome reproduction and the reunion of breaks. J. Cellular Comp. Physiol. 62 (1963) 73.

TAYLOR, J.H., W.F.HAUT and J.TUNG: Effects of fluorodeoxyuridine on DNA replication, chromosome breakage, and reunion. Proc. Natl. Acad. Sci. U.S. 48 (1962) 190.

TEMIN, H.M.: Separation of morphological conversion and virus production in Rous sarcoma virus infection. Cold Spring Harbor Symp. Quant. Biol. 27 (1962) 407.

TODARO, G.J. and H.GREEN: Cell growth and the initiation of transformation by SV_{40}. Proc. Natl. Acad. Sci. U.S. 55 (1966) 302.

TODARO, G.J., S.R.WOLMAN and H.GREEN: Rapid transformation of human fibroblasts with low growth potential into established cell lines by SV_{40}. J. Cellular Comp. Physiol. 62 (1963) 257.

UTSUMI, K.R.: Recent studies on chromosome aberrations induced by viruses. Japan. J. Genetics 40 (1965) 241.

VOGT, M. and R.DULBECCO: Steps in the neoplastic transformation of hamster embryo cells by polyoma virus. Proc. Natl. Acad. Sci. U.S. 49 (1963) 171.

VRBA, M. and L.DONNER: Chromosome numbers and karyotypes of two rat tumors induced by Rous sarcoma in vitro. Folia Biol. 10 (1964a) 373.

VRBA, M. and L.DONNER: Summary findings on the rat karyotype and on the chromosomal characteristics of rat tumours induced by the Rous sarcoma virus in vitro. Neoplasma 12 (1964b) 265.

WEINSTEIN, D. and P.S.MOORHEAD: Karyology of permanent human cell line W-18 VA2, originated by SV_{40} transformation. J. Cellular Comp. Physiol. 65 (1965) 85.

WOLMAN, S.R., K.HIRSCHHORN and G.J.TODARO: Early chromosomal changes in SV_{40}-infected human fibroblast cultures. Cytogenetics 3 (1964) 45.

YERGANIAN, G., T.HO and S.S.CHO: Retention of euploidy and mutagenicity of heterochromatin in culture. In: R.J.C.Harris, ed.: Cytogenetics of cells in culture. New York & London, Academic Press 3 (1964) 79.

YERGANIAN, G., H.M.SHEIN and J.F.ENDERS: Chromosomal disturbances observed in human fetal renal cells transformed in vitro by Simian virus 40 and carried in culture. Cytogenetics 1 (1966) 314.

YOSHIDA, M.C. and S.MAKINO: A chromosome study of a non-treated and an irradiated human in vitro cell line. Jap. J. Hum. Genet. 5 (1963) 39.

CHAPTER 31

Sex chromosomes and their abnormalities in man and mammals

JOHN L. HAMERTON

Pediatric Research Unit, Guy's Hospital Medical School, London

Contents

1. Introduction
2. The normal human chromosomes
3. The sex chromatin
   (a) Introduction
   (b) Morphology
   (c) Frequency
   (d) Single X derivation of the sex chromatin
   (e) Clinical significance of the sex chromatin
4. Single active X hypothesis of dosage compensation in mammals
5. The sex chromosomes and sex determination in mammals
   (a) The XO condition
   (b) Autosomal modification of sex determination in mammals
   (c) Sex determination
6. The origin of chromosome abnormalities
7. Sex chromosome abnormalities
   (a) Phenotypic males with two or more X-chromosomes
      47,XXY
      46,XX
      48,XXXY and 49,XXXXY
   (b) Phenotypic males with one or more X-chromosomes and at least two Y-chromosomes
      48,XXYY and 47,XYY
   (c) Phenotypic females
      Females with one X-chromosome or structural abnormalities of the second X including some mixoploids
      Females with multiple X-chromosomes
         47,XXX
         48,XXXX

8. Origin of the abnormalities
   (a) Males: The maternal or paternal occurrence of sex chromosome non-disjunction
   (b) Females
       45,X
       46,XXqi

9. The somatic effect of loss or gain of sex chromosomes
   (a) Stature
       Males
       Females
   (b) Psychosocial disorder and mental defect

10. Discussion
    (a) Sex chromosome control of somatic characters
        Stature
        Psychosocial characters
        Variability of phenotype and karyotype in ovarian dysgenesis
    (b) Control mechanism

    Appendix

1. Introduction

The study of the chromosomes and their abnormalities is playing an ever increasing part in the study of disease in mammals, particularly in man. This trend has developed since 1959 when the first condition specifically known to be caused by a chromosome abnormality was described. This was Down's syndrome (mongolism), which is due to the presence of one of the small autosomes in triplicate (*trisomy*) (Lejeune et al.) In the same year, both the 45,X and 47,XXY sex chromosome abnormalities were described (Ford et al.; Jacobs and Strong).

Three years prior to these discoveries, Tjio and Levan published a report which indicated that the diploid chromosome number of man was 46 and not, as previously thought, 48 (Painter 1921, 1923). This observation was rapidly confirmed (Ford and Hamerton). These discoveries were pre-dated by technical developments throughout the fifties, which culminated in the development of diploid cell culture techniques suitable for the study of human chromosomes. These utilised fibroblasts, bone marrow and finally, the peripheral blood lymphocyte (Reviews: Clarke; Mellman), which when combined with preparative techniques using Colcemid, hypotonic solutions and air drying, give preparations of extremely high quality (Table 1). The

TABLE 1

Developments in human cytogenetics

Date	Diploid no.	Sex chromosomes	Author
1891	18, 24 >40	—	Hansemann
1912	47♂, 48♀	XO–XX	Von Winiwarter
1921	46 or 48	XY–XX	Painter
1923	48	XY–XX	Painter
1936	48	XY–XX	Koller
1949	Sex chromatin discovered in mammals		Barr and Bertram
1951–55	Technical developments hypotonic pretreatment, colchicine, simple fixatives. Tissue culture.		Various
1956	46 (Tissue culture) XY–XX		Tjio and Levan
1956	46 (n = 23) Testis XY (2n = 46)		Ford and Hamerton
1958	Bone marrow culture, sex chromosome anomalies.		Ford, Jacobs and Lathja
1959	Down's syndrome (47,XXorXY,G+)		Lejeune et al.
1960	Blood Culture		Moorhead et al.
1960–64	Clinical cytogenetics		
1964–68	Population cytogenetics		

development of the lymphocyte culture techniques (Hungerford et al.; Moorhead et al.) and the development of 'micro-techniques', utilising very small quantities of blood (Froland) have enabled cytogenetic studies to be carried out on a population scale which was at one time unthinkable (Court Brown et al. 1966; Court Brown). A study of the sex chromatin, originally observed in the neurones of female cats (Barr and Bertram), has proved of great value in the study of sex chromosome abnormalities found in human populations. The value of this sex specific chromocentre as a clinical tool was recognised soon after its discovery (Moore et al.; Polani et al.; Plunkett and Barr), and its study has now been extended to cover not only man, but also the majority of other animal groups (Barr; Moore 1966b). Davidson and Smith demonstrated that the sexual dimorphism of the neutrophil leucocytes in peripheral blood could also be used in clinical practice. The method is however more time consuming and more subjective and has never been utilised to the same degree as the sex chromatin test.

Technical developments which have been stimulated by a study of human cytogenetics have also been utilised for the study of mammalian karyotypes, and several significant observations have been made in relation to the evolution of mammalian karyotypes (Hamerton et al. 1963; Benirschke) and more recently, chromosome studies are proving of interest in the study of congenital malformations and intersexuality in domestic mammals (Biggers and McFeely; Hamerton et al. 1968).

The present chapter deals firstly with the normal human chromosome complement, the sex chromatin and sex chromosomes in mammals. Sex determination is considered in some detail in this section. The last part deals with the phenotype of sex chromosome abnormalities in man. The nomenclature used throughout this chapter is that recommended by the Chicago Conference (see appendix at the end of this chapter).

2. *The normal human chromosomes*

The internationally accepted classification of the human karyotype is given in Fig. 1 (Denver; London). This shows that, despite considerable progress during the past eleven years, on the basis of chromosome morphology alone we are still only able to recognise four pairs of homologous chromosomes, Nos. 1, 2, 3, 16 and the Y-chromosome in males. The remainder of the chromosome set can be classified into seven groups, and some of these can be sorted further, on the basis of terminal DNA replication patterns and measurement. In particular this applies to the D group, the E group and the B group (Giannelli and Howlett 1966, 1967; Miller et al.; Warburton et al.). Attempts have also been made to separate the chromosomes which comprise the F and G groups with limited success.

Chromosomes 4 and 5 (Group B) can be separated into a shorter early replicating pair of chromosomes, and a longer late replicating pair. The short early replicator is defined as No. 5 (Denver) while the longer pair is considered to be No. 4. In Group E,

(a)

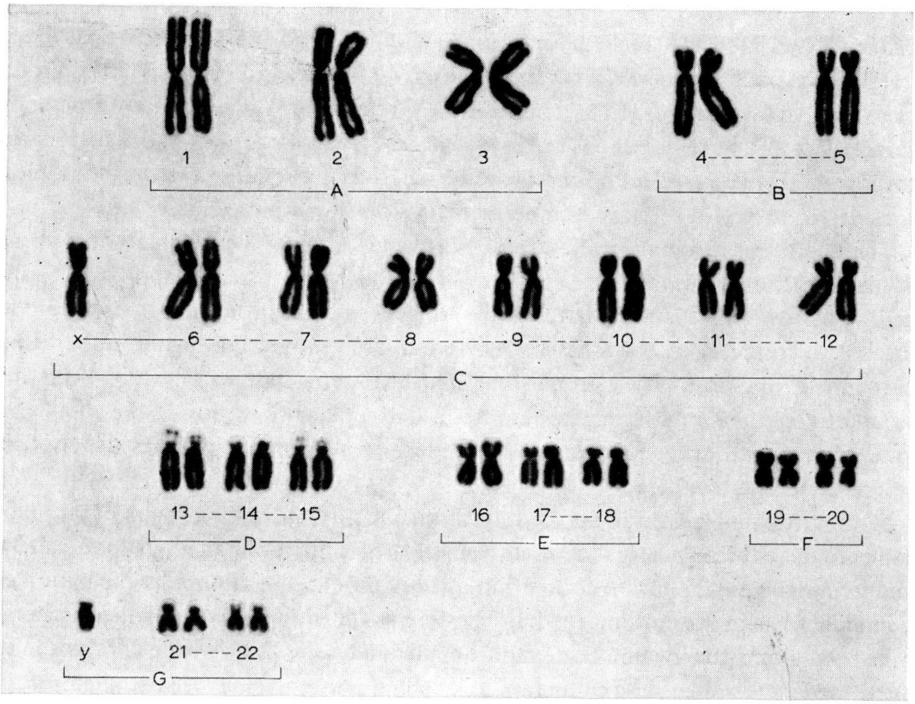

(b)

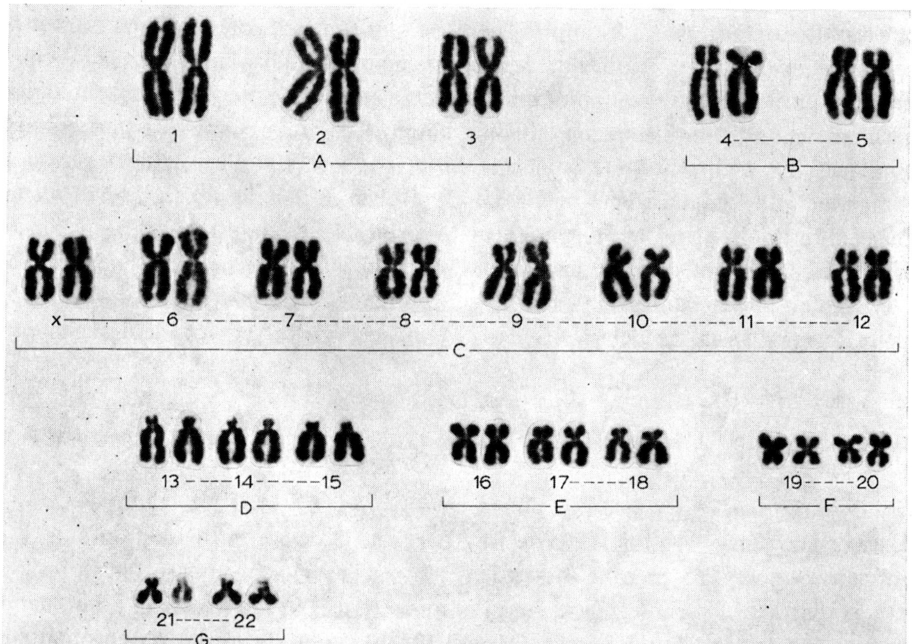

Fig. 1. The human chromosomes. (a) male; (b) female. Arranged to show the Denver (numbers) and London (letters) classifications. (Aceto-orcein, ×1,400).

Giannelli and Howlett (1967) have used grain counts and the morphological index (total length of chromosome/arm ratio) to separate the six chromosomes in this group into three pairs. Pair No. 16 has a high index and can be recognised by its morphology alone. Two of the remaining four chromosomes have a low index and a high grain count, and this late replicating chromosome is No. 18. The other two chromosomes, considered to be No. 17, have an intermediate index and a low grain count.

The D group, chromosome Numbers 13, 14, and 15, present even greater problems of identification by means of morphology alone, but using a similar approach, Giannelli and Howlett (1966) showed that the longest pair of chromosomes, No. 13, are the last to complete DNA synthesis, and have a late synthesising region in the distal part of the long arm. The chromosome pair of intermediate length (No. 14) is the second to complete DNA synthesis and has a late replicating region in the short arm and proximal part of the long arm. The shortest chromosome (No. 15) is also the first to complete DNA synthesis.

Four criteria have been used to establish the identity of the eight pairs of chromosomes in these three groups. These are: length, arm ratio, terminal replication pattern and terminal grain count. In each group this has produced a meaningful definition of homologous pairs, according to the Denver classification, whereas if these criteria were used alone, they would not enable an adequate separation of the chromosomes to be made. Terminal autoradiographic labelling patterns have been studied for all the remaining chromosome groups, but have unfortunately not given the same clear cut results for Groups C, F, and G, and the autosomes in these groups cannot be separated in this way. In Group A, chromosome No. 1 has a distinctive labelling pattern, but within this group the chromosomes can be separated on a morphological basis alone, and for this reason labelling patterns or grain counts are unnecessary. Similarly, the Y-chromosome replicates during the terminal part of the S period as compared with the autosomes of Group G. However, usually it can also be distinguished on the basis of its morphology. In Group C, the late replicating X can be distinguished, but apart from this, autoradiography is of little value in separating the very similar chromosomes of this large group (Schmid; German). Autoradiography may also be of use in the identification of chromosomes involved in structural changes.

3. The sex chromatin

(a) *Introduction*

The sex chromatin was first described by Barr and Bertram in the neurones of cats. Subsequent observations have shown that this sex specific chromocentre can be seen in a proportion of the interphase nuclei of many tissues in the female of a number of mammalian species including man (Moore 1966b). A study of the sex chromatin in human populations enables the rapid selection of individuals with an abnormal number of X-chromosomes without the necessity for time-consuming chromosome studies of whole populations, most of whom have normal chromosomes. Sex chromatin analysis is routinely carried out on smears, usually from the oral mucosa, although it can be detected in most human tissues with a greater or lesser frequency (Barr; Klinger).

(b) *Morphology*

A recent review of sex chromatin morphology (Klinger) covered the essential points, and the salient features only will be discussed here.

Sex chromatin can be seen in living cells (De Mars; Schwarzacher). In living fibroblast cells of human origin these authors found a dense intranuclear particle in the cells of female origin, but no similar particle in the cells of male origin. Schwarzacher reports that sex chromatin is visible in 46% of living human female nuclei and that a further 10% contain a similar but less contrasty particle, also seen at the periphery of the nucleus, adjacent to the nuclear membrane (Fig. 2). Both these authors were able

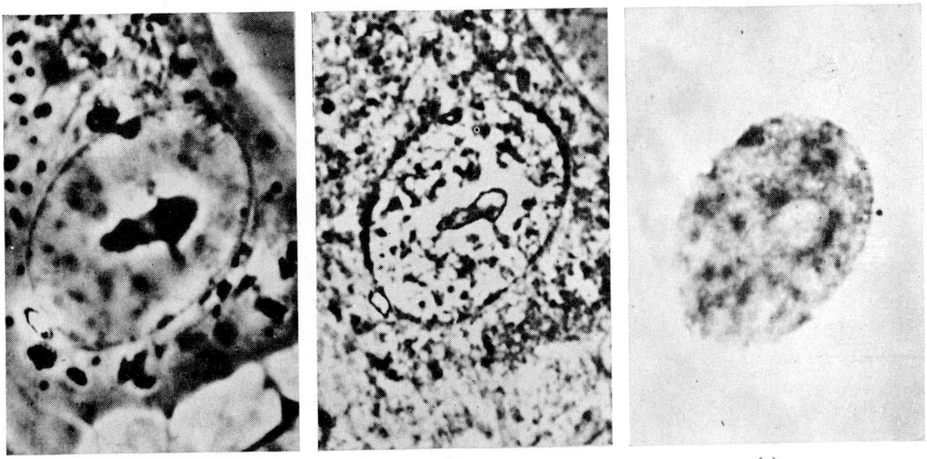

(a) (b) (c)

Fig. 2. Sex chromatin in living and fixed cells. A cultured cell from an adult female. (a) In the living state; (b) after fixation with 96% ethyl alcohol; (c) after thionin staining. (a and b phase contrast, c bright field). (From Schwarzacher.)

to show that this dense mass was Feulgen-positive, and formed the sex chromatin in fixed and stained nuclei.

Under these conditions, the sex chromatin is often seen as a plano-convex body, lying adjacent to the inner surface of the nuclear membrane. More detailed examination often reveals this to be a V or U shaped structure with its apex pointing to the centre of the nucleus (Figs. 3–5). In nerve cells the sex chromatin, when not adjacent to the nuclear membrane, may be spherical in shape. The size of the sex chromatin is relatively constant between different tissues and frequently between different mammalian species, measuring 0.8 $\times$1.1 μ with a range of 0.7 $\times$1.0 μ to 1.0 $\times$1.4 μ. This correlates well with the approximately constant size of the X-chromosome in many mammals (Ohno 1967). The DNA content of the sex chromatin is also constant between different human tissues, as well as between different primate species, again showing a

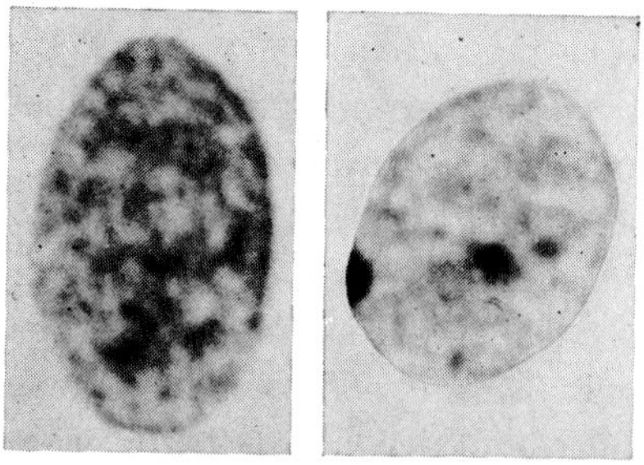

(a) (b)

Fig. 3. Sex chromatin in oral smears. (a) negative; (b) positive. (Feulgen, $\times$ 2,000.)

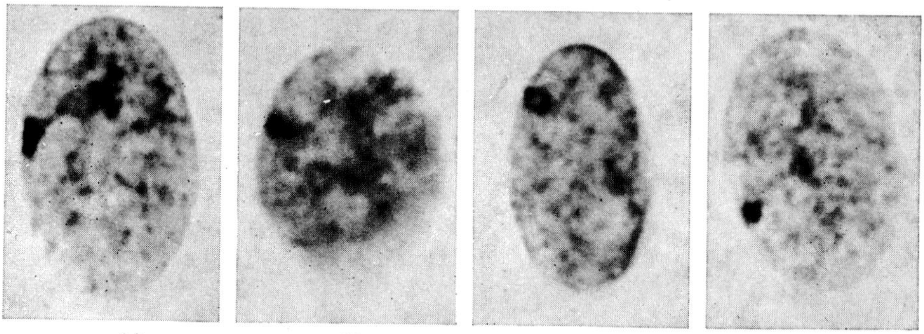

(a) (b) (c) (d)

Fig. 4. Sex chromatin in oral smears. Various morphological appearances. (a) U-shaped; (b) triangular; (c) vacuolated; (d) circular. (Feulgen, $\times$ 2,000).

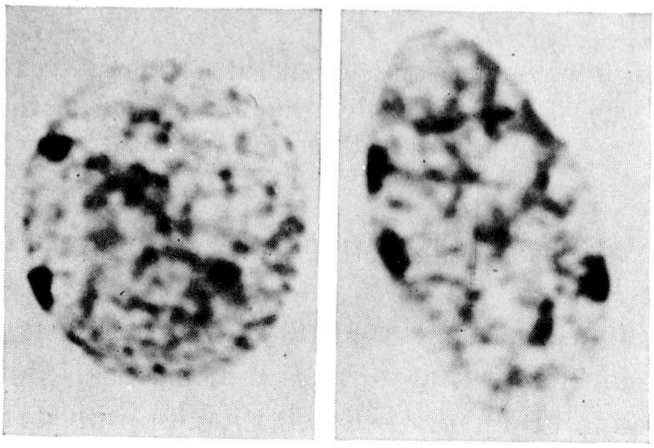

(a) (b)

Fig. 5. Sex chromatin in oral smears. (a) Nucleus with two sex chromatin masses, (b) nucleus with three sex chromatin masses. (Aceto-orcein, $\times$ 2,000).

correlation between size and DNA constancy of the X-chromosome within the mammals. Exceptions to this rule are found in species with exceptionally large X-chromosomes, and in man in subjects with deleted or duplicated X-chromosomes.

(c) *Frequency*

It is now clear that not all nuclei in mammalian females, even within a single tissue, have a visible sex chromatin body and that the frequency of sex chromatin positive cells varies from tissue to tissue within one species. Technical factors may influence the sex chromatin frequency, and for this reason observations between different laboratories may be difficult to compare. Under optimum technical conditions (Klinger; Culling) there is still considerable variation between tissues. In nervous tissue, frequencies of the order of 85% have been found (Moore and Barr; Thompson et al.) while in whole mounts of amnion epithelium or chorion, the frequency of chromatin positive nuclei may be as high as 96%. At the other extreme, the frequency of chromatin positive nuclei in oral smears usually varies between 20 and 50% and rarely rises as high as 60 to 70% in normal females. Frequencies of less than 10 to 15% are suspect, and the observation should be repeated. If similar low frequencies are found in subsequent smears, then this may be suggestive of mixoploidy (chromosome mosaicism) and chromosome studies are indicated. Low frequencies have been found in newborn infants during the first few days of life (Smith et al.; Taylor). Taylor also reported a temporary decrease in sex chromatin frequency after treatment with ACTH and hydrocortisone. Other authors have failed to show this increase in sex chromatin frequency during the immediate postnatal period (Robinson and Puck 1965, 1967; Moore 1959; MacLean), although none of these studies were specially designed to test this. Hsu et al., using extremely rigid selection criteria, failed to show this steep rise in sex chromatin frequency in the immediate postnatal period; instead, they showed a much less steep rise during the first three days of life. The same authors were, however, able to show a much increased rise during the immediate postnatal period, if less stringent cell selection criteria were employed. They also showed a higher frequency of nuclei unsuitable for sex chromatin analysis during the immediate postnatal periods, and concluded that if even a proportion of these nuclei were included in the counts as chromatin negative, this would artificially lower the frequency and might therefore account for the steep rise observed by some authors.

The frequency of chromatin positive nuclei has been observed to vary during different phases of the cell cycle. In particular, several authors have shown a decrease in frequency during the log phase of growth in culture (Miles; Therkelsen and Petersen). Klinger reports increased sex chromatin frequencies in monolayer cultures as the cell density increases. This could correlate with a reduction in mitotic index, which also decreases as density increases. However, in further experiments in which the mitotic index was kept constant while cell density increased, there was still some reduction in sex chromatin frequency, so that the reduction was not only related to the mitotic index. Mittwoch and Mittwoch et al. have studied the effect of nuclear size on the sex chromatin frequency and have found that chromatin negative nuclei are larger than positive nuclei. The opposite result however was found by Klinger et al. (1967) who observed that in general the area of positive nuclei was larger than the area of negative ones. Various studies using brief pulse labelling with H^3-thymidine have shown that a morphologically distinct sex chromatin body can be recognised in cells even while they are replicating their DNA. Wolf et al. showed that under these conditions the sex chromatin body itself takes up H^3-thymidine when pulse labelled. Furthermore, Comings (1967a), using a similar pulse labelling technique, has shown clearly that the sex chromatin body retains its heterochromatic form during DNA synthesis. Comings (1967b) has shown that if nuclei immediately following division which tend to be small and resting, or G_0 nuclei, which are hypoactive and tend to be large, are excluded, then there was no significant difference between the size of chromatin positive as opposed to chromatin negative nuclei. Klinger et al. (1968) have shown that the sex chromatin frequency increases with cell density *in vitro* monolayer culture but is not directly related to the mitotic index. They suggest that sex chromatin frequency may be related to the metabolic state of the cell.

These results have still not answered the question why some female nuclei do not show a sex chromatin mass. They are apparently not cells in any particular phase of the cell cycle, and neither is there any clear cut size difference between positive and negative cells or nuclei, nor is there a direct relationship to the cellular growth phase *in vitro*. There may be, however, some relationship to the cell cycle or mitotic index. It is possible that in the log phase of cell growth a higher proportion of nuclei have just concluded division and that these may not show sex chromatin. Comings (1967b) suggests that negative cells are those lacking heterochromatic coiling. In the log phase of growth, rapid cell division with a relatively short interphase may result in a higher proportion of interphase cells, which lack heterochromatic coiling, whereas in the stationary phase this proportion may increase as cells cease to divide rapidly. At this time there is also a reduction in cell size and perhaps an increase in the coiling density of heterochromatin resulting in a higher sex chromatin frequency.

(d) *Single X derivation of the sex chromatin*

Until 1961 it was generally thought that the sex chromatin was derived from the heterochromatic regions of both X-chromosomes which fuse during interphase (Barr). There is now, however, no doubt that the sex chromatin is derived from the condensation of a single heterochromatic X during interphase. Evidence for this statement is based first on observations of a single heterochromatic X during early prophase of mammalian somatic cells (Ohno 1966); second, on the fact that in normal females with two X-chromosomes, only *one* of these shows late synthesis of DNA during the S period, the so-called 'hot-X'; and finally, on the correlation between the total number of X-chromosomes, the number of late replicating X-chromosomes and the number of sex chromatin bodies in subjects with X-chromosome polysomy (Table 2). Subjects with three or four X-chromosomes have respectively a maximum of two

TABLE 2

Phenotype, sex chromatin and X-chromosomes in man

Chromosome constitution	Phenotype	Maximum number of sex chromatin masses	Maximum number of late replicating X-chromosomes
46,XX	♀ normal	1	1
46,XY	♂ normal	Nil	Nil
45,X	♀ T.S./O.D.	Nil	Nil
46,XXqi	♀ T.S./O.D.	1 (large)	1 (invariably Xqi)
46,XXq-	♀ T.S./O.D.	1 (small)	1 (invariably Xq-)
46,XXr	♀ T.S./O.D.	1 (small)	1 (invariably Xr)
46,XXpi	♀T.S./O.D.	1 (small)	1 (invariably Xpi)
46,XXp-	♀ T.S./O.D.	1 (small)	1 (invariably Xp-)
47,XXX	♀ normal → mentally deficient	2	2
48,XXXX	♀ mentally deficient	3	3
49,XXXXX	♀ mentally deficient	4	4
47,XXY	♂ Klinefelter's syndrome	1	1
48,XXXY	♂ Klinefelter's syndrome	2	2
49,XXXXY	♂ infertile various somatic anomalies	3	3
47,XYY	♂ fertile, tall, aggressive	Nil	Nil
48,XXYY	♂ Klinefelter's syndrome, tall, aggressive	1	1
49,XXXYY	♂ Klinefelter's syndrome, tall, aggressive	2	2
46,XX	♂ or ♂ K.S. or intersex	1	1
46,XY	♂ or ♂ testicular feminisation or intersex	Nil	Nil

T.S. = Turner's syndrome; O.D. = ovarian dysgenesis. See appendix at the end of this chapter for other abbreviations.

or three sex chromatin bodies and a maximum of two or three late replicating X-chromosomes. Females with two X-chromosomes and males with XXY sex chromosomes have only one. XY and XO subjects are chromatin negative. This relationship applies to diploid cells in which it can be stated unequivocally that the maximum number of sex chromatin bodies is equal to the number of X-chromosomes minus 1, or equal to the number of late replicating X-chromosomes.

Evidence from polyploids, however, indicates that the number of haploid autosome complements influences the number of late replicating X-chromosomes. In tetraploid cells with four X-chromosomes (92,XXXX), only two sex chromatin bodies are found. Harnden has expressed the overall relationships as follows:

$$B = x - p/2$$

(where B = the number of sex chromatin bodies, x = the number of X-chromosomes and p = the number of haploid autosome sets). In diploid cells $p/2 = 1$ so that the number of sex chromatin bodies is one less than the number of X-chromosomes; in tetraploid cells it is two less, so that 92,XXXX cells have two sex chromatin bodies and 92,XXYY cells are chromatin negative. This relationship holds for all even degrees of ploidy (2*n*, 4*n*, 6*n*, 8*n*, etc.). Triploids should have 1.5 sex chromatin bodies in XXX and none in XXY cells. In fact, some XXX triploids have one, and some have two sex chromatin bodies (Carr). If we equate the sex chromatin and late replicating X with the genetically inactive X of the Lyon hypothesis, then the biological significance of these observations becomes apparent. In diploid somatic cells one X always remains active, whereas in tetraploid cells two X-chromosomes are active. It can therefore be argued that the number of haploid autosome sets affects the number of genetically active euchromatic X-chromosomes, one active X-chromosome being required to balance each pair of haploid autosome complements. This argument can be extended. In the majority of mammalian species, including man, the X-chromosome represents 5% of the genome. Duplicate type X-chromosomes representing 10% of the genome have been found in the eurasian hamsters, for instance *Cricetulus griseus*, as well as in various other rodents. A triplicate type X representing 15% of the genome is found in the rodent *Microtus oregoni*, while a quadruplicate X representing 20% of the genome is found in the field vole (*Microtus agrestis*). In each instance facultative heterochromatinisation acts so that only X-chromosome material representing 5% of the genome remains euchromatic and active, the remainder is heterochromatic, shows interphase condensation and is late labelling (Fig. 6) (Ohno 1967). In man, as we shall see, when a structurally abnormal X is present, it is always this X which becomes late labelling, heterochromatic and inactive, again leaving a single active normal X.

It seems very clear from this evidence that for the normal somatic functioning of cells in mammals, X-chromosome material representing about 5% of the genome is required, and it can be suggested that the process of inactivation must be under autosomal control and must ensure a balanced genome. It may be that the requirement differs during different stages of development and it must differ in the primordial gonad at the time of differentiation. This may require a switching mechanism controlling the process of heterochromatinisation operating at different times in different tissues (see below).

(e) *Clinical significance of the sex chromatin*

The clinical value of the sex chromatin has been recognised since 1954, when Polani and his co-workers recognised that a proportion of females with ovarian dysgenesis were chromatin negative, while at the same time males with Klinefelter's syndrome were shown to be chromatin positive (Plunkett and Barr). In the past ten years a wide range of anomalous sex chromatin findings have been observed and correlated with the chromosome findings (Table 2). It can be seen that in both males and females the maximum number of sex chromatin masses correlates directly with the number of X-chromosomes, and that the Y-chromosomes have no influence on sex chromatin formation. The sex chromatin can therefore be used in diploid cells as a direct clinical test in order to establish the number of X-chromosomes present, and this can be used irrespective of the phenotypic sex, or the number of Y-chromosomes present. Moore (1966a).

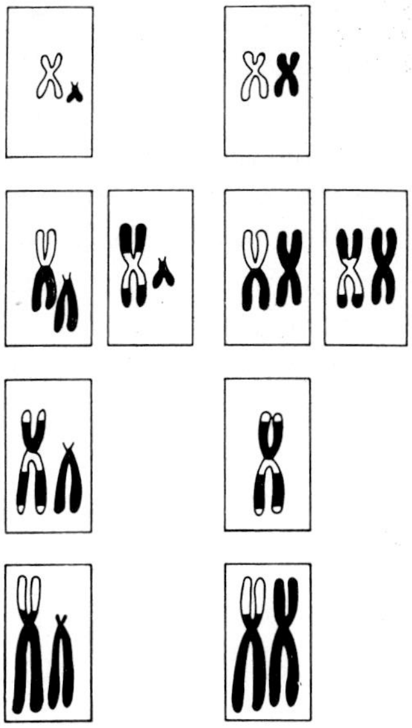

Fig. 6. Schematic representation of the behaviour pattern of various types of X-chromosomes in male and female somatic cells of mammals; the males are represented on the left and the females on the right. Euchromatic parts of the X are outlined while the heterochromatic parts of the X, as well as the Y are black.
Top row: The original-type X, comprising 5% of the genome, is found in a great majority of mammals including man, the mouse, and the cat. In the male (left), only the minute Y is heterochromatic, while in the female, one entire X is heterochromatic.
2nd row: The duplicate-type X found in Eurasian hamsters, *Mastomys* and *Chinchilla*. In the male, one-half of the X and the entire Y are heterochromatic while in the female one entire X and one-half of the other X are heterochromatic. Because the Chinchilla is exceptional in two aspects, the pattern of inactivation of the X of this species is shown to the right in both columns.
3rd row: The triplicate-type X found in the creeping vole (*Microtus oregoni*). In the male, two-thirds of the X, as well as the entire Y are heterochromatic. The female of this species is normally XO, yet two-thirds of a single X is heterochromatic.
Bottom row: The quadruplicate-type X of the field vole (*Microtus agrestis*). In the male, three-fourths of the X and the entire Y are heterochromatic, while in the female, one entire X as well as three-fourths of the other X are heterochromatic. (From Ohno 1967).

4. Single active X hypothesis of dosage compensation in mammals

The differential behaviour of the two X-chromosomes in mammalian females described above and the fact that 39,X female mice were normal and fertile led Lyon (1961, 1962, 1963, 1966) to consider that the heteropycnotic X in mammals was also genetically inactive, and to put forward the inactive X hypothesis, which can be stated:
(a) that one of the two X-chromosomes in cells of normal female mammals is genetically inactive;

(b) the inactive X can either be the maternal or paternal one in different cells of the same animal, and the decision which X becomes inactive is taken at random;
(c) the inactivation occurs early in embryonic development and once it has occurred, remains fixed throughout the further development of each cell line.

The main genetic evidence for this hypothesis was the mosaic phenotype observed to be characteristic of female mice heterozygous for sex-linked recessive genes affecting the coat. Furthermore the inactivation of at least three major sex-linked gene loci has been unequivocally demonstrated at the cellular level in man. These are G-6-PD (Beutler et al.; Davidson et al.), the Hunter–Hurler syndrome (Danes and Bearn) and juvenile hyperuricaemia (Migeon et al.; De Mars, personal communication). Evidence for inactivation of other gene loci in man and other mammals is summarised in Table 3.

TABLE 3

X-linked genes showing a mosaic phenotype in the heterozygous state in mammals (after Lyon 1966)

Mouse		Man	
Coat colour	Skin and hair texture	Cell or tissue	Gene locus
Mottled	Tabby	Skin	Incontinentia pigmenti
Brindled	Striated		Anhydrotic ectodermal dysplasia
Tortoise-shell	Greasy	Eye	Choroidermia
Dappled		Teeth	Sex-linked enamel
Dappled-2		Erythrocytes	G-6-PD deficiency
Blotchy		Cultured fibroblasts	G-6-PD deficiency, juvenile hyperuricaemia, Hunter-Hurler syndrome
		Cultured leucocytes	Agammaglobulinaemia

Other mammals

Species	Gene locus	Effect
Golden hamster	Mottled white tortoise-shell	Coat
Cat	Yellow	Coat
Cow	Streaked hairlessness	Coat

Genes showing incomplete penetrance or an intermediate effect

Mouse	Man	Others
Bent tail	Christmas disease	
Jimpy	Haemophilia A	Haemophilia A (dog)
Sex-linked anaemia	Duchenne muscular dystrophy	
X-linked antigen		
Gyro		

This hypothesis is important when considering the biological significance of the cytological observations discussed above. It is well known that heterochromatic regions synthesise DNA late in the S period. There is therefore a clear correlation in mammalian females, between inactivation of *major* gene loci on all but one X and the heterochromatinisation of all but one X-chromosome.

We may conclude therefore that the sex chromatin seen in interphase nuclei represents the late replicating heterochromatic X-chromosome which, at least so far as major gene loci are concerned, is inactive. Grüneberg (1965, 1966a, b, 1967) has criticised the genetic evidence for gene inactivation in mice, but has failed to explain the extensive cytological data which are now available, and it seems likely that although the single active X hypothesis put forward by Lyon and in a modified form by Russell (1963, 1964) may require some alteration with regard to the totality of inactivation, and to the function of the heterochromatic X, in essentials it is likely to be correct.

5. *The sex chromosomes and sex determination in mammals*

The evolution of the heteromorphic XY pair in mammals from a primitive homomorphic pair seen in lower organisms has been discussed recently (Ohno 1967). In mammals the male is the heterogametic sex and carries the heteromorphic XY pair, whilst the female carries the two homomorphic X-chromosomes. Until recently it was considered that sex determination in mammals followed closely the pattern observed in *Drosophila* in which the sex is determined by a balance between the number of X-chromosomes and the number of sets of autosomes (Bridges). The Y-chromosome in *Drosophila* is heterochromatic, and required not for determination of the male sex, but for its fertility. XO diploid flies are sterile males, (Table 4) the Y-chromosome being required for the production of functional spermatozoa (Stern; Meyer 1963, 1968). Thus, in *Drosophila* the Y-chromosome, which is heterochromatic and inert in somatic cells and throughout development, becomes 'switched on' in the secondary spermatocyte or spermatids in order to produce functional sperm. Examination of Table 4 compares the findings on sex determination in *Drosophila*, the mouse and man. It can be seen that the Y-chromosome in man, and generally in mammals, is strongly male determining; XXY and even XXXXY individuals having male phenotypes.

This statement, however, says little, and we need to know how the Y determines maleness and the X femaleness, what the significance of the heterochromatic X is, and why if it is completely inactivated do 45,X and 46,XX subjects differ in phenotype. We also need to examine the problems raised by the exceptions, the XX males and XY females in man, XO as the normal female karyotype in *Microtus oregoni*, and the sterile XX male pseudohermaphrodites in the goat (*Capra hirca*).

TABLE 4

Sex determination in *Drosophila* and man

Drosophila						*Man*	
No. of X-chromosomes	No. of haploid autosome sets	X/A	Y-chromosome	Chromosome complement	Phenotype	Chromosome complement	Phenotype
3	2	1.5	–	2A+XXX	Super ♀	–	–
4	4	1.0	–	4A+XXXX		–	–
3	3	1.0	–	3A+XXX		3A+XXX	♀
2	2	1.0	–	2A+XX	Normal ♀	2A+XX	Normal ♀
1	1	1.0	–	1A+X		–	–
2	2	1.0	+	2A+XXY		2A+XXY	Sterile ♂
2	3	0.67	–	3A+XX	Intersex	3A+XXY	♂
1	2	0.5	+	2A+XY	Normal ♂	2A+XY	Normal ♂
1	2	0.5	–	2A+X	Sterile ♂	2A+X	Sterile ♀
1	3	0.33	+	3A+XXY	Super ♂	–	–
						2A+XXXY	Sterile ♂
						2A+XXX	Fertile ♀
						2A+XXXXY	Sterile ♂
						2A+XXXX	?Fertile ♀
						Mouse	
						2A+X	Fertile ♀
						2A+XXY	Sterile ♂

(a) *The XO condition*

In man, 45,X females are usually sterile girls of short stature with variable somatic anomalies and ovarian dysgenesis. A study of 45,X fetuses has shown that there is little difference between 45,X and 46,XX gonads up to the third month of gestation and that both contain germ cells in approximately equal numbers (Singh and Carr). However, after the third month there is a proportionally greater increase in the amount of stromal tissue in 45,X gonads. At birth and up to one year post partum there are still some germ cells present in these gonads (Polani, personal communication). The number of germ cells in 45,X gonads at this stage is, however, considerably reduced compared to the gonads of normal females. Baker has estimated that there are about 0.7–2.0 $\times 10^6$ germ cells present in normal ovaries at six months post partum which can be compared with Polani's estimate of 30,000 in two 45,X females, one at one month, and one at one year post partum. In these females it is rare to find any germ cells in the streak gonads after puberty. It is therefore clear that the absence of a second X-chromosome does not prevent either cortical stimulation and the development of an ovary or the formation of germ cells and their migration to the germinal ridge (Fig. 7). Their degeneration may be due to a deficiency of follicle cells and failure of organisation of primordial follicles (Singh and Carr). However, the finding of

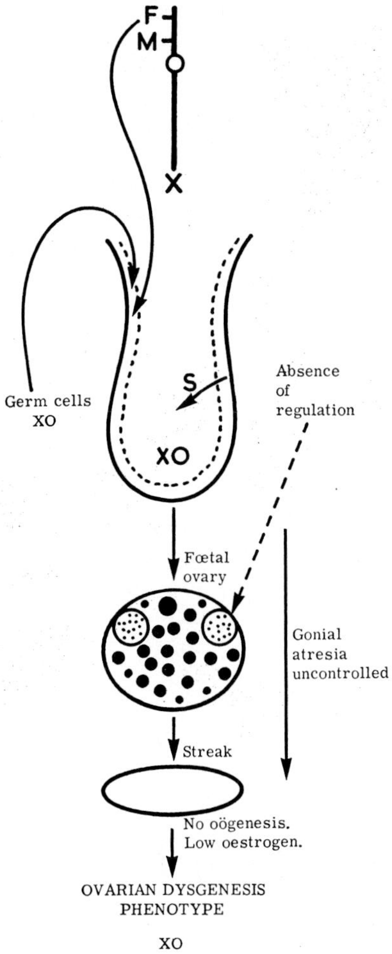

Fig. 7. Diagram to illustrate that only one X-chromosome is required for cortical stimulation in a 45,X female (see Fig. 12).

well organised follicles in 45,X infants at one month and one year post partum (Fig. 8) does not support this. It is probable that in man the normal process of germ cell atresia is regulated by the herochromatic X. In the absence of this chromosome atresia is unregulated and accelerated, so that by the time puberty is reached all the germ cells have degenerated (Fig. 9). Variation in the rate of atresia would account for the rare 45,X female who is fertile or has secondary amenorrhoea. The heterochromatic X-chromosome may also control oestrogen production which is invariably reduced in 45,X females, and results in the sexual infantilism observed. 45,X females also show raised or normal levels of F.S.H. (follicle stimulating hormone) after puberty (Hauser) suggesting that the hypophysis is not affected despite the absence at this time of germinal epithelium. Abnormal levels of F.S.H. or other gonadotrophins at critical periods may be one cause of the more rapid follicular degeneration observed. Finally, abnormalities of somatic development so often observed in 45,X human females may result from abnormal rates of development which might normally be controlled by X-heterochromatin. In the mouse, 39,X females are normal and fertile, although the observed reduction in litter size suggests either that there are fewer germ cells present than in normal females, or that the 39,Y fetuses which would be produced are lethal and therefore resorbed.

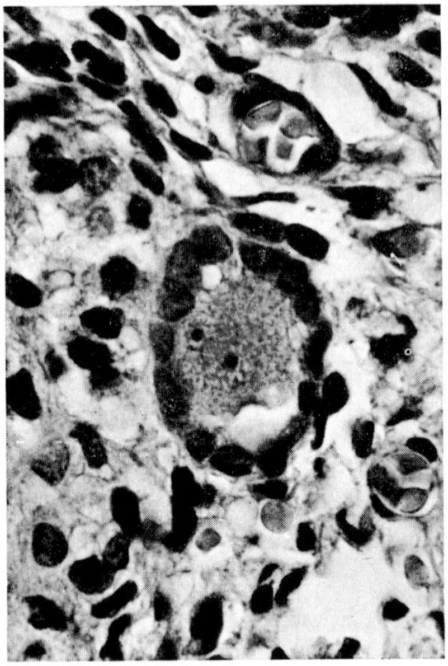

Fig. 8. Primordial follicle from the ovary of a 45,X female one month after birth (haematoxylin and eosin, ×1,800).

In *Microtus oregoni* the normal female somatic chromosome complement is 17,X. Males are 18,XY. The mechanism here is predirected non-disjunction of the X in the primordial germ cells in the testis, so that XXY and OY germ cells are produced. The XXY germ cells fail to develop, and the OY germ cells produce gametes containing on the one hand no sex chromosome and on the other a Y. Similar non-disjunction during the formation of the gonad in females produces an 18,XX gonad (Fig. 10). In this way the species survives, avoids the production of two types of heterogamety and also demonstrates the ultimate dosage compensation in the female somatic tissues, the loss of one unnecessary X-chromosome. It does, however, also show that even in this species, two X-chromosomes are necessary for the development of a normal ovary, and at least a Y for the normal development of the testis.

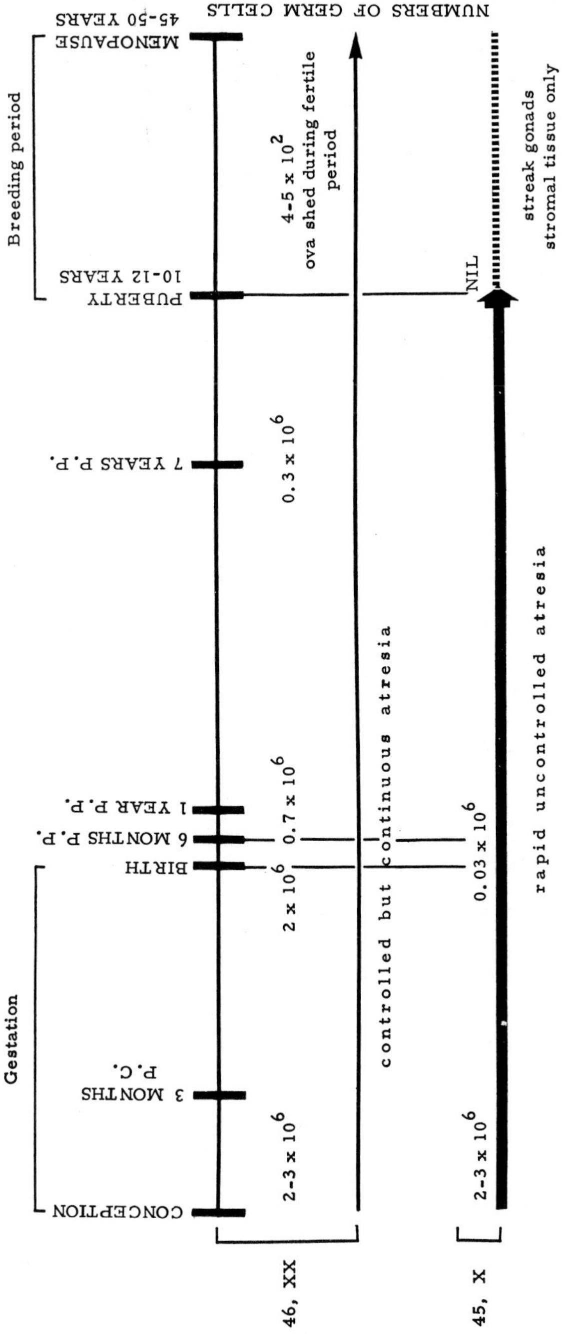

Fig. 9. Diagram to show the proposed differential rates of germ cell atresia in normal 46,XX females as compared to 45,X females.

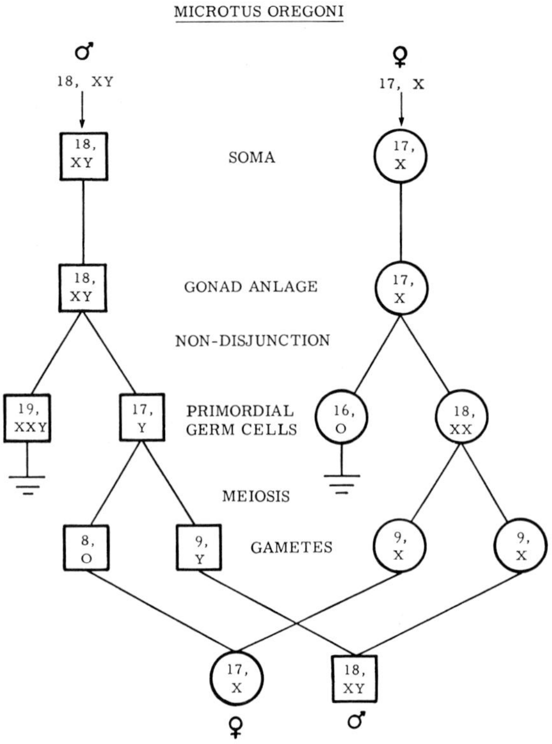

Fig. 10. A diagram to illustrate the course of oogenesis and spermatogenesis in *Microtus oregoni*

(b) *Autosomal modification of sex determination in mammals*

There are a number of autosomal genes which modify gonadal development. In the mouse, the *W* series of alleles (*W*, W^v and W^j) cause sterility in both sexes in the homozygous state and affect the number of germ cells but not the type of gonad. In the W^jW^j genotype, very few primordial germ cells reach the gonadal ridge; and the deficiency of germ cells is even more severe in the *WW* state, and in this condition no germ cells are seen in newborn embryos of that genotype. This gene does not however affect the development of the gonads and each individual develops a testis or an ovary according to its sex chromosome constitution (Mintz) which supports Ohno's hypothesis that the primary act of sex determination is at the somatic level and not the level of the germ cells.

In the goat (*Capra hirca*), the autosomal dominant gene for polled (*P*) leads to sterility of all (*PP*) homozygous XX females which develop testes. These usually lack germ cells at birth and may be intra-abdominal, inguinal or scrotal in position. The same gene in the homozygous state in the male may cause sterility, due to an epididymal blockage. In homozygous (*PP*) female goats degenerating germ cells which are found in the testis at four months gestation have disappeared completely by birth

(Hamerton et al. 1969). This is conclusive evidence of the somatic nature of sex decision, for in this instance we are dealing with a gene, which, in genetic females, results in testicular development, despite the presence of XX sex chromosomes. It has, however, no effect on the formation or migration of the germ cells which are female, but despite their genotype are apparently unable to prevent the formation of a

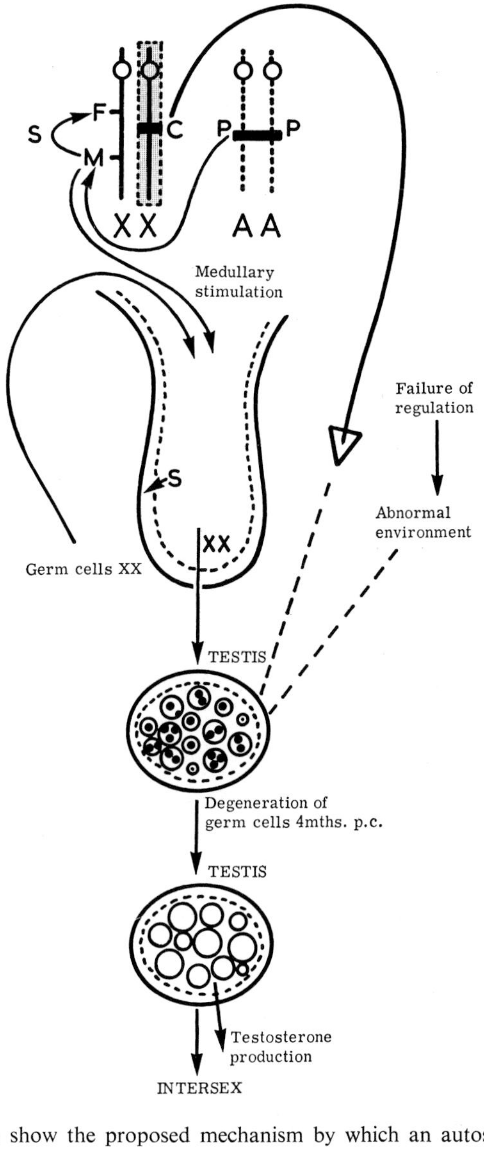

Fig. 11. A diagram to show the proposed mechanism by which an autosomal gene *PP* acts by controlling the 'Medullary Stimulating' gene (M) carried by the X-chromosome, resulting in the formation of a testis in genetic females in the goat (*Capra hirca*). (For full key see Fig. 12.)

testis. They are also apparently unable to survive in a testicular environment; despite the fact that the testis seems to behave normally and to produce adequate amounts of testosterone (Fig. 11).

In man apart from the intersexes, two exceptions occur: XX males with testes and features of Klinefelter's syndrome, and XY 'females' with testes and the syndrome of testicular feminisation. These 'females' are in fact, sex reversed genetic males, as a result of the action of either a sex-linked recessive or, more probably, a sex-limited autosomal dominant gene, which acts on the target organs making them insensitive to testosterone, so that a female phenotype develops. Human XX males, if they are not mixoploid, 46,XX/47,XXY, or result from an XXY zygote in which the Y has been lost, could be the result of an autosomal gene acting in a similar manner to the 'polled' gene in the goat.

(c) *Sex determination*

The sex of an individual is determined very early in embryonic life, in man by about two months, and there is considerable evidence, which is outlined above, that the primary act of sex decision is on the somatic elements of the indifferent gonad and that the genetic constitution of the germ cells does not affect or control the type of gonad produced. The act of sex decision may be the simple inhibition of cortical development in the male, allowing the primary sex cords of the medulla to develop into a testis. In the female the cortex is stimulated allowing the secondary sex cords to develop into an ovary while the primary sex cords degenerate. This hypothesis (Fig. 12) suggests that in the normal mammalian female the single euchromatic X carries both the structural gene for female determination and its operator and that this structural gene mediates the production of a 'cortical stimulating substance'. In the normal male, it is suggested that the Y-chromosome acts as a 'controlling centre' for the male structural gene or its operator which are themselves situated elsewhere in the complement. In the presence of a Y-chromosome these become 'switched on' and mediate the production of a medullary stimulating substance or cortical inhibitor. It is further suggested that autosomal modifiers such as *P* in the goat, and probably a similar gene in the pig, act in the same way as the 'Y controlling centre' by 'switching on' the male gene or its operator. The most likely site for both the 'male' and 'female' structural genes is on the X-chromosome, if we remember that the heteromorphic XY-chromosomes originally evolved from a homomorphic pair and that the two genes are likely to be situated fairly close to each other, particularly if the activity of one leads to suppression of the other (McFeeley et al.; Hamerton 1968b).

In males with multiple X-chromosomes there is imbalance in the amount of X- and Y-heterochromatin. On the hypotheses outlined above, an XXY male has both normal male and female heterochromatin. The Y-heterochromatin is dominant so that the X-borne male determiners produce a testis which becomes hypertrophied after puberty. These males also have increased gonadotrophin and reduced androgen secretion. The result, as expected, is a male with certain feminine features such as are found in

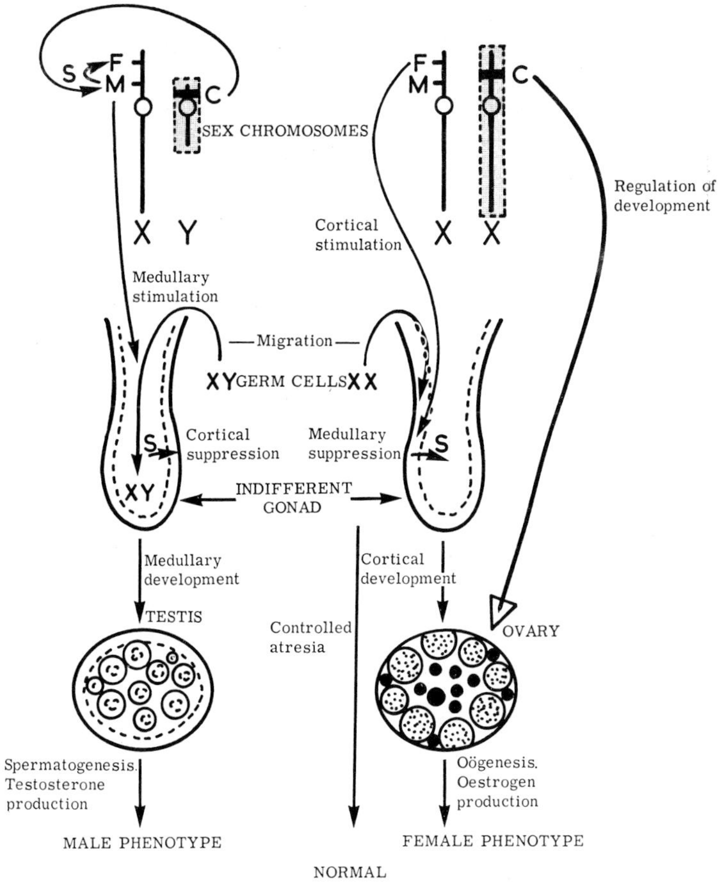

Fig. 12. Diagram to illustrate the proposed scheme for sex determination in mammals. M: gene for medullary stimulation. F: gene for cortical stimulation. C: controlling elements on X and Y. S: suppression; hatched chromosomes are heterochromatic.

Klinefelter's syndrome (see below). Increasing imbalance, in 48,XXXY and 49, XXXXY demonstrates the dominance of the Y. Both these classes of subjects are male, but with an even more abnormal phenotype than the XXY subjects.

6. *The origin of chromosome abnormalities*

The normal course and the biochemistry of mitosis and meiosis have been described in other chapters of this Handbook, and we now turn to the errors which may occur during these processes and their results. Errors in cell division may be either numerical or structural. Numerical errors are caused by non-disjunction which leads to the gain or loss of whole chromosomes. This results in an aneuploid cell, which may be either

TABLE 5

Oogenesis

Spermatogenesis		Normal disjunction	Non-disjunction MI (MII normal)		Non-disjunction MII (MI normal)		Non-disjunction MI and MII			
		X	XX	O	XX	O	XXX	XXXX	X	O
Normal disjunction	X	XX	XXX	X	XXX	X	XXXX	XXXXX	XX	X
	Y	XY	XXY	Y	XXY	Y	XXXY	XXXXY	XY	Y
Non-disjunction MI (MII normal)	XY	XXY	XXXY	XY	XXXY	XY	XXXXY	XXXXXY	XXY	XY
	O	X	XX	OO	XX	OO	XXX	XXXX	X	OO
Non-disjunction MII (MI normal)	XX	XXX	XXXX	XX	XXXX	XX	XXXXX	XXXXXX	XXX	XX
	YY	XYY	XXYY	YY	XXYY	YY	XXXYY	XXXXYY	XYY	YY
Non-disjunction MI and MII	XXY	XXXY	XXXXY	XXY	XXXXY	XXY	XXXXXY	XXXXXXY	XXXY	XXY
	XXYY	XXXYY	XXXXYY	XXYY	XXXXYY	XXYY	XXXXXYY	XXXXXXYY	XXXYY	XXYY
	XYY	XXYY	XXXY	XYY	XXXYY	XYY	XXXXYY	XXXXXYY	XXYY	XYY
	O	X	XX	OO	XX	OO	XXX	XXXX	X	OO

trisomic or monosomic. Non-disjunction can be most simply defined as 'the failure of two homologous chromosomes in the first division of meiosis, or two chromatids in mitosis, or the second division of meiosis, to pass to opposite poles of the spindle'. Non-disjunction during meiosis results in the formation of chromosomally abnormal gametes which if concerned in fertilisation will result in an abnormal zygote. During mitosis, it usually results in either a developmental or proliferative mixoploid (Ford 1960, 1961). The results of non-disjunction during gametogenesis can best be illustrated by its effect on the sex chromosome complement (Table 5). Non-disjunction may occur at the first division of meiosis, at the second division of meiosis after a normal first division, or at both the first and second divisions. Examination of Table 5 shows that a number of the commoner sex chromosome complements can result from non-disjunction occurring at various meiotic stages, for instance, a 47,XXY zygote can be produced by non-disjunction, either at the first or second division in the female and fertilisation of an XX ova by a Y bearing sperm, or non-disjunction at first division in the male, so that an XY sperm fertilises a normal X ova.

Non-disjunction or anaphase lagging which occurs during an early cleavage division of a normal or an abnormal zygote will result in a developmental mixoploid if both cell lines are viable. If not, and one cell line is lethal, than a non-mixoploid fetus may be formed (Fig. 13). Non-disjunction, after organogenesis is complete, may result in

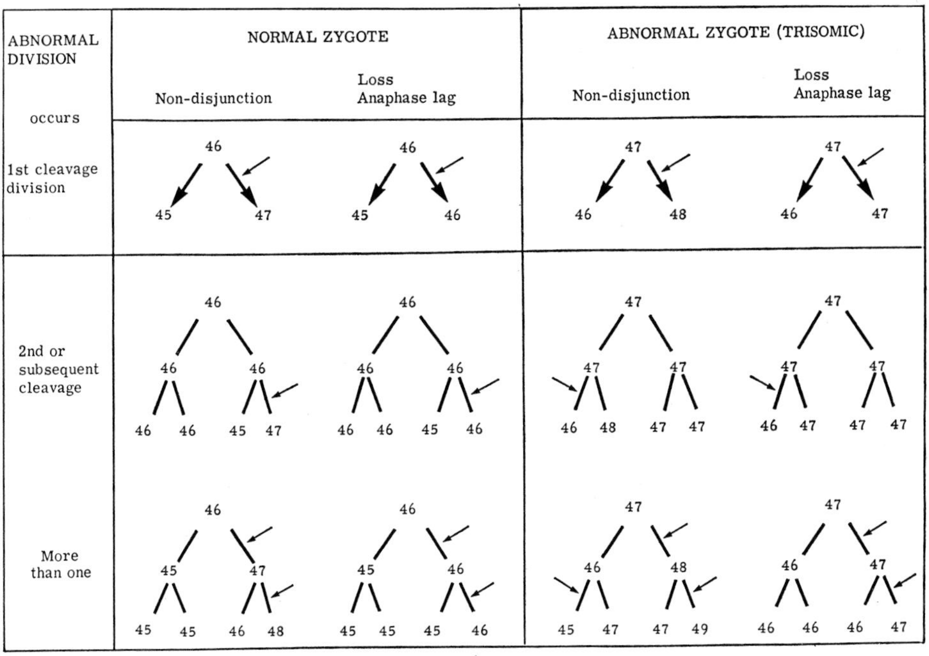

Fig. 13. The results of non-disjunction and anaphase lagging during cleavage in either a chromosomally normal or trisomic zygote. The small arrows indicate the division in which the error occurs.

chromosomally abnormal clones of cells occurring in particular tissues. Such proliferative mixoploids might be expected to occur more frequently in rapidly dividing tissues and with increasing age.

Chromosome structural rearrangements result from transverse chromosome breakage and reunion of the broken ends in an abnormal manner. An individual carrying such a rearranged chromosome complement is a structural heterozygote, and unless some chromosome imbalance has resulted from the rearrangement, usually has a normal phenotype. The major types of chromosome structural change are summarised in Fig. 14. Transverse breakage and reunion of chromatids can also result in abnormal chromosomes. This mechanism, if it occurs during gametogenesis, could account for the finding of some morphologically abnormal chromosome complements. For instance, chromatid inter- or intra-change may result in both deletion and duplication (Fig. 15).

The commonest type of structural rearrangement detectable in human populations by means of a study of somatic chromosomes is the reciprocal translocation (Court Brown et al. 1966; Court Brown; Hamerton 1966, 1968a, 1969). A few families with

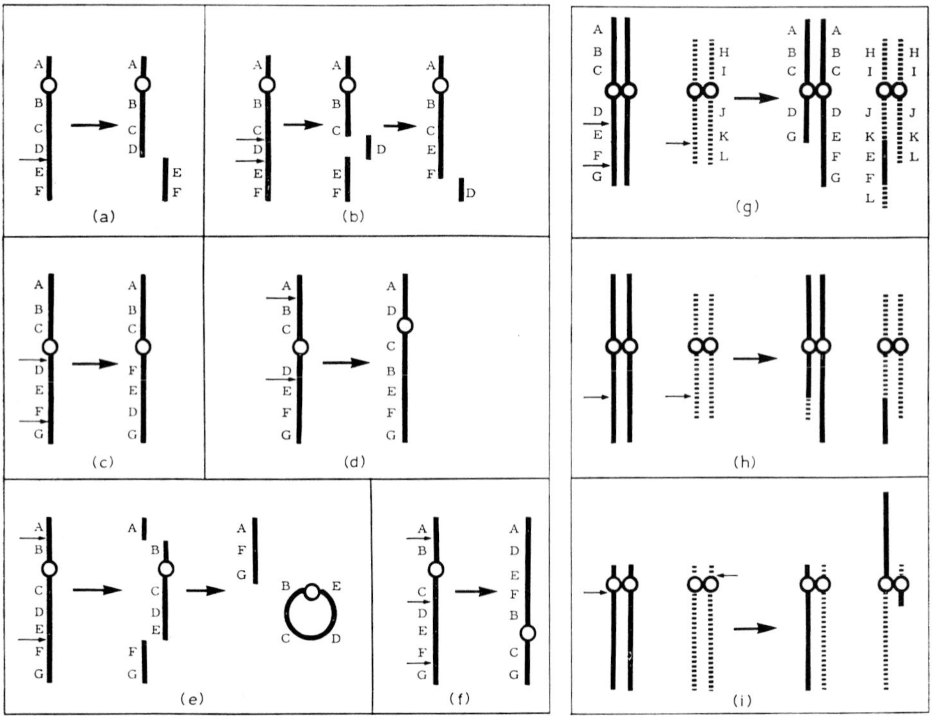

Fig. 14. Diagram to illustrate the types of chromosome rearrangement: (a-f): intrachromosome rearrangements; (g-i): interchromosome rearrangements. (a) terminal deletion; (b) interstitial deletion; (c) paracentric inversion; (d) pericentric inversion; (e) ring chromosome formation; (f) shift; (g) transposition; (h) reciprocal translocation; (i) Robertsonian translocation.

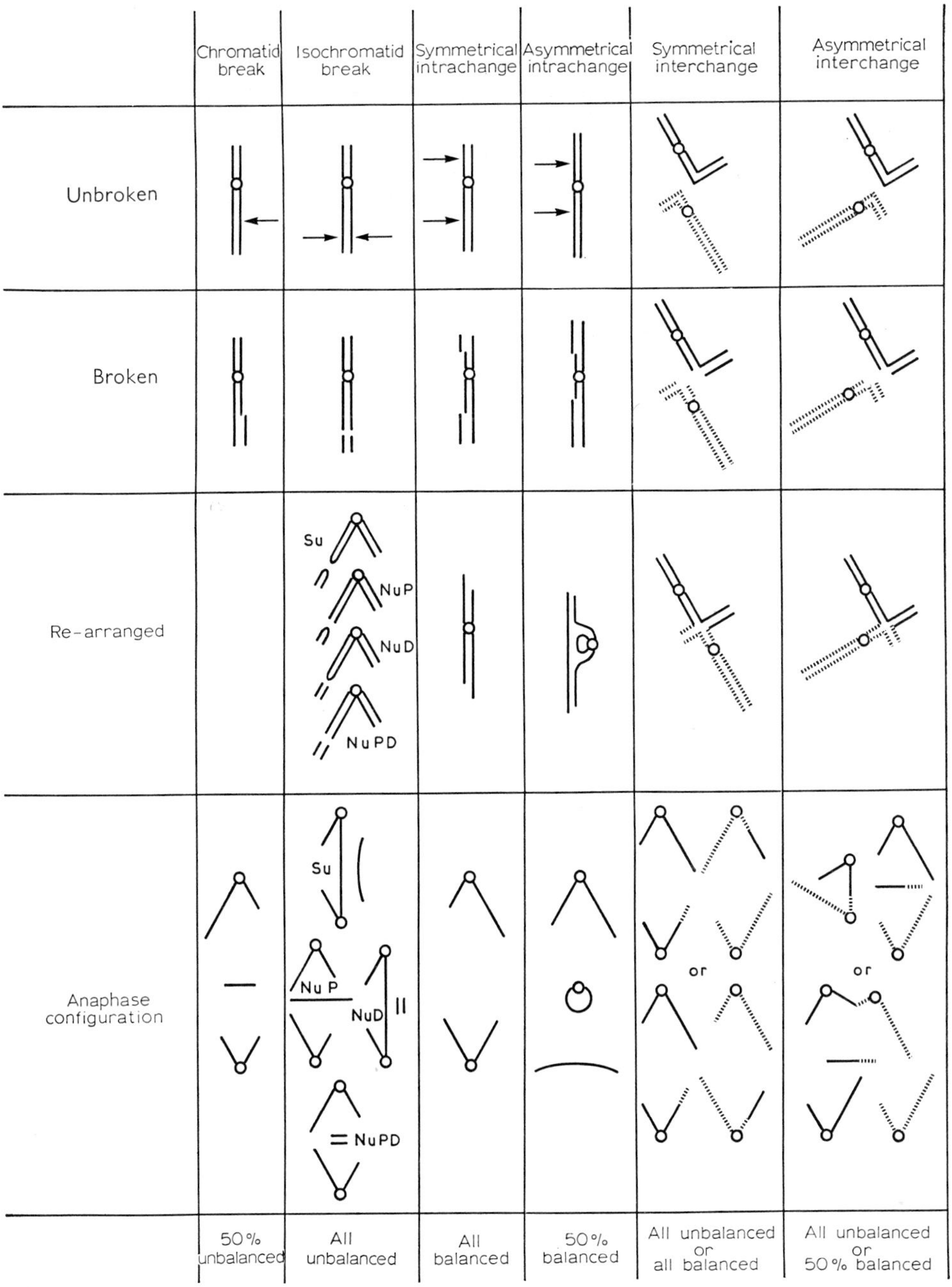

Fig. 15. Diagram to illustrate chromatid rearrangement (redrawn from Lea).

Su = Sister union

NuP = No union proximal

NuD = No union distal

NuPD = No union proximal or distal

segregating pericentric inversions have been located (Court Brown; Jacobs et al. 1968a), and these usually show a very low frequency of subjects with chromosome imbalance. This may be due to a suppression of crossing over within the inverted region and hence a low frequency of recombinant chromatids. It may also be the reason for the low frequency with which these families are ascertained, as the chromosomally balanced subjects show little or no phenotypic effect. Studies on the general population may reveal a higher frequency of this type of structural change than is at present thought. Other types of rearrangement are likely to be much more difficult to detect without the help of meiotic studies, and in this group is included in particular the paracentric inversion. Deletions, duplication and shifts may be detectable by means of studies of somatic chromosome morphology, but if family studies are uninformative, then it is probable that only meiotic studies will enable the exact origin of the rearrangements to be determined. For instance, an apparently deleted chromosome could have resulted from one of several mechanisms (Fig. 16) each of which would give rise to a chromosome of similar morphology, but carrying totally different genetic material.

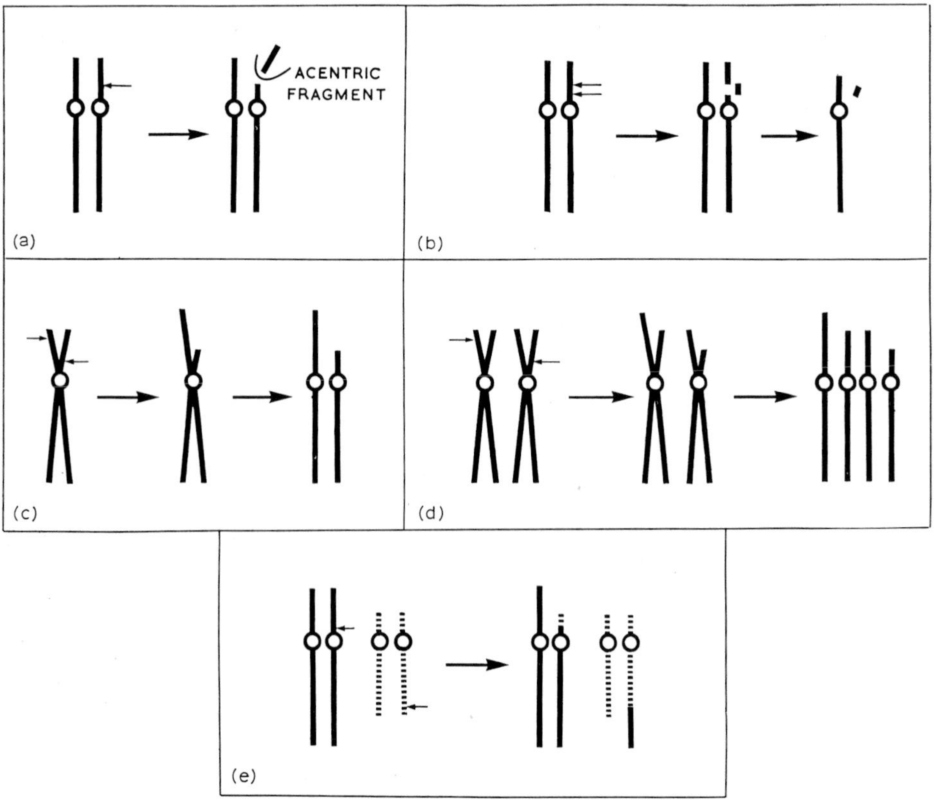

Fig. 16. Various types of chromosome and chromatid rearrangements which can result in a morphologically identical end-product which is genetically different (a) terminal deletion; (b) interstitial deletion; (c) chromatid intra-change; (d) chromatid inter-change; (e) reciprocal translocation.

TABLE 6

Abnormal sex chromosomes and phenotype in the male

Chromosome complement	Eponym	Sex chromatin	Phenotype	Mean age of parents at birth*	
				Mother	Father
47,XXY	Klinefelter's syndrome	Positive	Often tall eunuchoid males with hypogonadism, feminine distribution of hair, gynecomastia testicular atrophy after puberty with hyalinised tubules, leydig cell hyperplasia, often low I.Q., psychosocial difficulties.	30.13 (167)	34.60 (90)
48,XXXY	Klinefelter's syndrome	Double positive	As 47,XXY males, features usually more pronounced, invariably mentally defective, low I.Q.	28.90 (8)	33.00 (8)
49,XXXXY	—	Treble positive	Characteristic facies; skeletal anomalies including radio-ulnar synostosis; hypogenitalism with small penis and scrotum, testes small or very small, partial or complete cryptorchidism, defective prepubertal testicular development, abnormal dermatoglyphics low grade mental defectives.	27.90 (14)	30.38 (13)
46,XX	Klinefelter's syndrome	Positive	Rare typical Klinefelter's syndrome. No evidence of Y in seven males.	—	—
48,XXYY	Klinefelter's syndrome	Positive	Typical features of Klinefelter's syndrome; usually very tall, eunuchoid, frequently aggressive.	27.45 (11)	31.33 (9)
47,XYY	—	Negative	Often no phenotypic abnormalities, usually tall to very tall, aggressive, I.Q. usually in low normal range, often with criminal tendencies.	27.71 (24)	31.01 (23)

* Numbers in brackets refer to numbers of cases.

7. *Sex chromosome abnormalities*

(a) *Phenotypic males with two or more X-chromosomes*

47,XXY males. The major clinical features, sex chromatin findings and mean maternal and paternal ages are given in Table 6. Data on the frequency of these chromatin positive males of 1.98 per 1,000 live births, and of double-positive males of less than summarised recently by Taylor and Moores. In six surveys, 46 single positive and one double positive male were found in 23,229 newborn children, an incidence of single-positive males of 1.98 per 1,000 live births, and of double-positive males of less than 1 in 20,000 newborns. The frequency among mentally retarded, mentally diseased and psychotic patients is about four times higher than in general newborn populations (Table 7), single positive males having a frequency of about 8.8 per 1,000 males. Among severely defective individuals about 1.33 per 1,000 have double masses and are probably 48,XXXY. Among males attending sterility or subfertility clinics, between 10 and 20% are chromatin positive. In the newborn population about two-thirds of chromatin positive males are 47,XXY and the remaining one-third 48,XXYY, or mixoploids (Maclean et al.).

46,XX males. Seven males with an apparently normal female chromosome complement and the major features of Klinefelter's syndrome have been reported. Extensive chromosome studies have in each case failed to detect a Y-chromosome. The frequency in the general population is extremely low, and they have never been detected in routine surveys, but have always been referred for clinical reasons. They invariably have testes with a very similar histological appearance to the testes of 47,XXY subjects. There are three possible explanations to account for the presence of a testis in the absence of a Y-chromosome. First, they may be potential mixoploids 46,XX/47,XXY in which the 47,XXY line was lost after sex determination. Second, assuming

TABLE 7

Frequency of chromatin positive males and double positive females in various populations

	Males			Females		
Population	Total no.	Chromatin + ve	+ ve per 1,000	Total no.	Chromatin ++ ve	++ ve per 1,000
Newborn babies*	25,050	51	2.4	23,718	15	1.6
Mental hospital patients**	6,000	30	5.0	7,207	17	2.4
Mental deficiency institute patients**	4,178	41	9.8	3,384	20	5.9

* From Taylor and Moores; Maclean et al.

** From Maclean et al.

ve = Sex chromatin double positive.

that the Y acts as a male determiner and not simply as a controlling element, the male determining factors on the Y may have become transferred to one X as a result of structural change. Third, an autosomal sex reversal gene is operating and that these subjects are in fact sex reversed females (see above).

48,XXXY and *49,XXXXY.* These males are rare in the general population, having an incidence of perhaps less than 1 in 20,000. 48,XXXY males have all been found among populations of severely mentally subnormal subjects and in these populations the frequency is about 1 in 1,000. 49,XXXXY males are usually ascertained on the basis of clinical observation and about 40 males with this chromosome complement are known. They are all severely retarded with a hypoplastic penis, usually a hypoplastic scrotum, small or very small testes, and sometimes partial or complete cryptorchidism. They have a characteristic facies (Fig. 17) and often skeletal anomalies.

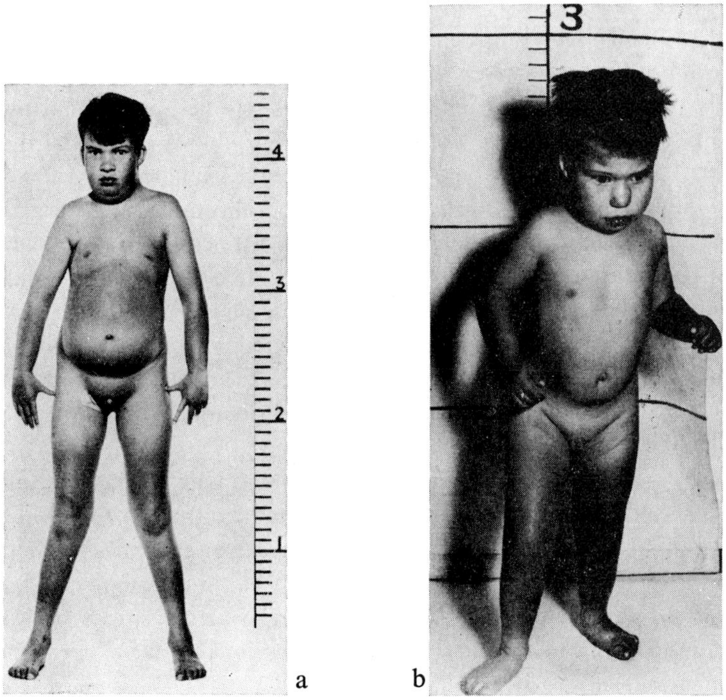

Fig. 17. The 49,XXXXY phenotype. (a) No. H4198 aged 9 years; (b) No. H5842, aged 5 years.

(b) *Phenotypic males with one or more X-chromosomes and at least two Y-chromosomes*
48,XXYY and 47,XYY males. Males with a 48,XXYY chromosome complement are chromatin positive men with the major features of Klinefelter's syndrome and until 1965 about fifteen had been reported in the world literature. They are usually

extremely tall even before puberty, and show an excess of limb over trunk growth, but apart from this and the fact that the majority had been found in surveys of mentally deficient or mentally diseased patients, no specific significance was attached to the presence of the additional Y-chromosome. The clue to the significance of this second Y-chromosome came from a sex chromatin survey of two special security institutions for the mentally subnormal (Casey et al.). 21 chromatin positive males were found among 942 male inmates (2.2%); of these seven were 48,XXYY, twelve were 47,XXY, while two were mixoploids, 46,XY/47,XXY. The seven 48,XXYY subjects were significantly taller than the twelve men with a 47,XXY chromosome complement; this difference being entirely accounted for by a greater pubis-sole measurement (94.8 cm) in the 48,XXYY compared with 89.4 cm for the 47,XXY men. This finding of such a high frequency of men with two Y-chromosomes led Jacobs and her colleagues (1965, 1968b) to investigate the chromosomes of male patients in the Scottish State Institution at Carstairs. Of 315 men studied, sixteen had a chromosome abnormality, nine were 47,XYY, one 47, XXY, and one a mixoploid. The remaining four had autosomal abnormalities. In this group therefore, the frequency of men with two Y-chromosomes was also extremely high (3.14%) compared with probably less than 0.05% in the general population. Until these studies, only about twelve XYY males had been reported in the world literature (Balodimos et al.) and these had all been referred for various reasons, including mental subnormality, abnormality of sexual phenotype, and as a relative of a patient with a chromosome abnormality. None of these males, therefore, can be said to have had a distinctive phenotype which can be related to the additional Y-chromosome, and the same applies to nine males in the Carstairs survey with two Y-chromosomes. These males are, however, all tall, the mean height for this group being 181.2 cm compared with the 305 men with one Y-chromosome only, those mean height is 170.7 cm. The tallest man in the population was the 48,XXYY subject who was 196.0 cm tall. Price and Whatmore have analysed the behaviour of these nine men and found that:

(a) they had a severe personality disorder associated with intellectual impairment;
(b) they displayed less violence against persons than did the control group;
(c) they began their criminal activities on an average five years earlier than the control group;
(d) they had no significant family history of crime or mental illness;
(e) their criminal behaviour was resistant to conventional forms of corrective training and treatment.

Recently Court Brown et al. (1968) have summarised the data on a further fifteen of these males, only one of whom was ascertained in a survey of the newborn. Of the remaining fourteen, eight were identified in hospitals for the mentally subnormal or mentally diseased, one in an epileptic colony, three in prison, Borstal or young offenders institutions, and one in a psychiatric clinic. The one remaining patient was identified in a survey of patients receiving intra-arterial thorotrast. Of the fourteen patients ranging in age from 13 to 62 years, eight had been convicted by the courts for largely

TABLE 8

Classification of females with ovarian dysgenesis (O.D.) (after Polani)

Name of condition	Turner's syndrome	Ovarian dysgenesis	Pure gonadal dysgenesis
Features	O.D. with webbing of neck, short stature (>153 cm), often congenital heart disease, skeletal defects, renal anomalies.	O.D. without webbing of neck. Less frequent somatic anomalies, invariable short stature (>153 cm).	Primary gonadal failure, no associated somatic anomalies, normal stature.
Sex chromatin	Usually negative	50% negative	Negative or positive.
Chromosomes	45,X (rare 45,X/46XY) occasional mixoploids and structurally abnormal X.	45,X(−ve) Mixoploid or X-structurally abnormal (+ve) e.g. 46,XXqi, 46,XXq-, 46,XXp-, 46,XXpi, 46,XXr.	46,XX or 46,XY

petty offences. With the exception of two of these patients, all were over 180 cm tall, the tallest being a prepubertal boy of 202 cm height.

(c) *Phenotypic females*

Females with one X-chromosome or structural abnormalities of the second X including some mixoploids. Turner first described a syndrome in females in which the major features are primary amenorrhoea, infantile or absent ovaries, little or no pubic or axillary hair, infantile external genitalia and short stature, with often certain somatic anomalies including webbing of the neck, cubitus valgus and shield chest. A simplified classification and summary of sex chromatin and chromosome findings are given in Table 8. Chromosome studies on this group of females was stimulated by the observation by Polani and his co-workers that a proportion of affected girls were chromatin negative.

These data show that the chromosome findings are extremely variable. Among girls with Turner's syndrome a high proportion are chromatin negative compared with only about 50% of the girls with ovarian dysgenesis. In both groups however, the 45,X chromosome complement is by far the commonest. Thus, of all the patients with ovarian dysgenesis in these series just over 50% have the 45,X chromosome complement, while the remainder are either mixoploids (30%) or have a structurally abnormal X-chromosome.

Females with multiple X-chromosomes. *(a) 47,XXX females.* The absence of a distinctive phenotype caused by the presence of an additional X-chromosome has meant that these women have been ascertained either by chance or during sex chromatin surveys of the newborn, or mental hospital populations. The incidence of double positive females in sex chromatin surveys of the newborn is about 0.67 per 1,000 births (15/22,068) (Taylor and Moores) a frequency considerably less than that found for XXY males (1.98/1,000). The incidence in mentally defective or subnormal population is much higher than in the newborn population, a frequency of 3.95 per 1,000 (21/5308) defective females being obtained. In a group of psychotic patients, three women with 47,XXX chromosomes were located in a total of 837 female psychotics, an incidence of 3.58 per 1,000 which is not significantly different from the 3.95/1,000 found among defective females.

The available evidence suggests that the majority of these 47,XXX females are fertile. Four 47,XXX women are known to have produced children, twelve boys and five girls, all of whom are phenotypically normal and have normal sex chromatin (Fraser et al.; Stewart and Sanderson). The finding is unexpected as with random disjunction, 50% of the ova would be expected to be disomic while 50% would be normal, so that half of these sons should be XXY and half of the daughters XXX. The explanation is probably directed segregation during oogenesis, so that the disomic complement is regularly included in one of the polar bodies and not in the ova. A few 47,XXX females have primary or secondary amenorrhoea. Of the 33 cases summarised by Court Brown et al. (1964), nine were prepubertal and 24 postpubertal, of whom fourteen menstruated regularly, three irregularly, one had a primary and one a secondary amenorrhoea, and in five instances no details of menstrual history were available. The phenotype of 47,XXX females is not distinctive and the vast majority have no congenital malformations, nor is there any evidence of any increase in stature.

Kidd et al. have carried out a detailed psychiatric investigation into 22 47,XXX women. Eleven are mentally subnormal (I.Q. $>$ 69), the remaining eleven have normal I.Q.'s but are psychotic. The major difficulties seem to be behavioural, 77% have inter-personal difficulties (control: 52%) while 81% show social withdrawal (control: 59%). The major psychiatric diagnosis was shown to be schizophrenia and paraphrenia (7 cases), while mental subnormality with psychosis accounted for four cases. In the mentally normal group the diagnosis was typical of the population from which they were derived. This is not so however, for the mentally subnormal group, in whom the most outstanding feature was a superimposed psychosis. In institutions, primary subnormality (feeble-mindedness) normally accounts for 80% of the population, however, in the 47,XXX group only two (16%) were so diagnosed. It can therefore be concluded that genetically predisposed mental subnormality is not a primary feature of the triplo-X condition.

(b) 48,XXXX females. The frequency of this chromosome constitution in the newborn population is much lower, and none have been located in the surveys. However, among mental defectives Day et al. found one such female in 1,088 female defectives. In the same population these authors found 3 47,XXX females, thus giving a maximum estimate of probably less than about one third of the number of triplo-X females, or about 1.0 per 1,000 defectives.

8. *Origin of the abnormalities*

(a) *Males. The maternal or paternal occurrence of sex chromosome non-disjunction* The maternal or paternal occurrence of sex chromosome non-disjunction has been studied, using three X-linked genetic markers, Xg(a), red-green colour blindness and G-6-PD. The greater part of these data refers to the 47,XXY state in which 16 informative families are known (Nowakowski et al.; Ferguson Smith et al.; Frøland et al.). 10 of these males are $X^M X^M Y$ whilst 6 are $X^M X^P Y$. In 10 of these subjects (Frøland et al.) maternal age is known and there seems little difference between those with maternal and those with paternal non-disjunction (Table 9). In general maternal ages in 47,XXY Klinefelter's syndrome are increased above the age for the general

TABLE 9

Parental ages of subjects with Klinefelter's syndrome in whom the origin of the X-chromosomes is known. (From Frøland et al.)

Sex chromosome constitution	Age at birth of patient	
	Father	Mother
$X^M X^P Y$	22	16
	30	32
	44	36
	30	27
Mean	31.5	27.8
$X^M X^M Y$	39	42
	36	31
	30	19
	32	30
	36	30
	30	27
Mean	33.8	29.7
$X^M X^M X^M X^M Y$	40	32

population as a whole (Table 6). There is, however, no evidence of an increase in parental ages in the 48,XXXY, 48,XXYY or 49,XXXXY males. Examination of Table 5 shows that there are a number of mechanisms by which these chromosome complements could have arisen. Xg(a) studies on one male with 48,XXYY chromosomes who was the Xg(a+) son of an Xg(a+) father and an Xg(a−) mother suggests fertilisation of an X-bearing ovum by an XYY sperm. 48,XXXY males show no increase in maternal or paternal ages (Table 6). In one case, colour vision studies suggested that successive non-disjunctional events occurred during oogenesis resulting in an XXX ovum being fertilised by a Y-bearing sperm (Breakey). Table 5 indicates several other possible mechanisms. There is very little evidence concerning the origin of the 49,XXXXY state. There is no increase in parental ages and little genetic marker data. Xg(a) studies on 4 49,XXXXY males suggest that in one instance the origin of all the X-chromosomes is maternal, the result of successive non-disjunction at events at first and second division of meiosis in the mother (Lewis et al.; Frøland et al.). The most likely origin of XYY subjects is the fertilisation of an X ovum by a YY sperm.

In conclusion therefore, both Xg(a) studies and increased maternal age suggest that the 47,XXY condition more often results from a non-disjunctional error during oogenesis rather than spermatogenesis. However, the origin of the more complex sex chromosome aneuploids is by no means so clear and there is very little data available. Failure to find any increase in maternal or paternal age suggests at least that oocyte ageing is not the only mechanism involved, but without further data, speculation is profitless.

(b) *Females*

45,X females. The lack of any increase in parental ages in subjects with a 45,X karyotype suggests that ageing of the oocyte is not the primary cause of this monosomic condition. Russell (1963) has suggested that the majority of X-monosomic zygotes in mice result from a post fertilisation error and loss of the paternal X- or Y-chromosome and the same may apply to man. If this is so then it might be expected that the majority of 45,X subjects would carry a maternally derived $X(X^{M})$. Evidence from Xg(a) and colour blindness studies on 24 families show that the single X is maternally derived in 20 families and paternally derived in four (Lindsten et al. 1963a; Turpin et al.), which at first sight seems to support the above hypotheses. However, Lindsten et al. (1963a), taking into consideration the fact that maternal origin of the X, using Xg(a), can be much more readily demonstrated than paternal origin, do not consider the above figures conclusive and consider the paternal X as likely to contribute to the 45,X state as the maternal.

46,XXqi (see appendix for nomenclature symbols). Analysis of the Xg(a) data from eight families showed the isochromosome to be paternally derived in two and probably paternally derived in the other six, provided that the Xg(a) locus was genetically inactivated or was to be found on the short arm of the X (Lindsten et al. 1963b). The majority of subjects with a structurally abnormal X are mixoploids suggesting either a post zygotic origin of the structurally abnormal X-chromosome or loss of this chromosome from one cell line during an early cleavage division. The non-mixoploid Xqi subjects seem to be largely paternally derived and the isochromosome is presumably formed during meiosis perhaps as a result of misdivision of the centromere due to synaptic failure of the X and Y. In this case the isochromosome would be paternal and Lindsten et al. (1963b) have shown a paternal origin in eight out of fourteen families.

47,XXX. Both maternal and paternal ages are increased; in forty subjects the mean maternal age is 31.98 ±1.39 years, while the paternal age is 35.83 ±1.38, a difference of 3.8. This level of increase is clearly not as high as that found in the autosomal trisomies (see chapter by Taylor), but is on a level with the findings in Klinefelter's syndrome and suggests that non-disjunction may be more frequently maternal than paternal. There is no informative data on genetic markers in this condition. Examination of Table 5 shows that the condition could arise as a result of non-disjunction of several different stages of gametogenesis.

9. *The somatic effect of loss or gain of sex chromosomes*

(a) *Stature*

Males. The effect of sex chromosome abnormalities on stature is shown in Fig. 18 and the progression is clear. Males with 46,XY chromosomes are, on average, shorter than those with 47,XXY and 48,XXXY, whilst the 47,XYY and 48,XXYY subjects are, on average, considerably taller than any of the preceding groups. There may be however, a difference in growth between the multiple-X and multiple-Y males, although the evidence for this is by no means conclusive. In general the presence of multiple-X chromosomes leads to a greater excess of limb than of trunk growth, while excess Y-chromosomes seems to result in a greater than usual size throughout childhood. 48,XXYY males are extremely tall, often well over 180 cm and usually have extremely long legs. The single 49,XXXYY male reported is 193 cm tall with a pubis-sole measurement of 102 cm (Bray and Josephine).

Females. 45,X females with ovarian dysgenesis are invariably short and this applies to all the various chromosome complements which cause ovarian dygenesis including the mixoploids (Fig. 17), and including those with structurally abnormal X-chromosomes (46,XXqi; 46,XXp−; 46,XXr). Girls with 46,XXq− and 46,XXpi may, however, be of more normal stature. Finally there is no evidence of any increase in stature among 47,XXX females. 45,X females fail to respond to growth hormone perhaps due to a defect in the target tissues at the peripheral level.

(b) *Psychosocial disorder and mental defect*

The data discussed here indicate clearly that many males with sex chromosome anomalies suffer from some form of mental disease or mental defect and have difficulty in adjusting themselves to a normal social existence. Subjects with 48,XXXY and 49,XXXXY sex chromosomes are invariably low grade mental defectives. 47,XXY males may be mental defectives, but are frequently in the more normal I.Q. or E.S.N. (educationally subnormal) range. They frequently have difficulties in adjusting themselves to a normal social existence and may come up against society for acts of a criminal nature. A proportion of the double Y subjects have greater problems, the

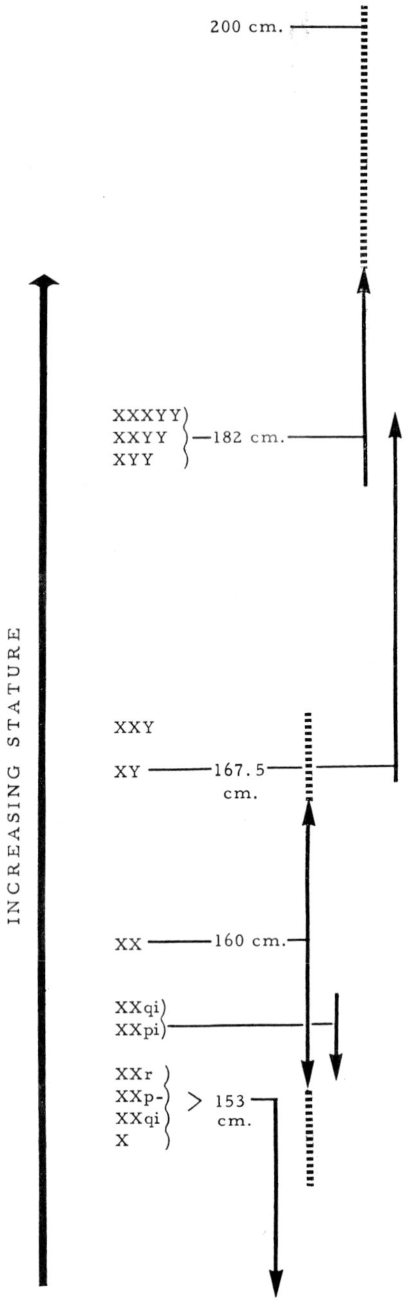

Fig. 18. Diagram to illustrate the effect of sex chromosome abnormalities on stature.

highest concentrations of such males being found in institutions for mentally defective subjects requiring special security. They are frequently aggressive, often appear in court or a child guidance centre at a very early age for aggressiveness and crimes against property and the person. However, by no means all XYY subjects come to this at an early age, and many may drift along in the lower strata of society until quite late in life before finally falling foul of the law, often for petty offences (Court Brown et al. 1968).

The data presented by Kidd et al. taken together with the finding of a significantly higher frequency of 47,XXX females among mental defective and psychotic groups suggest that among females as well as males, the additional X has a deleterious effect on the mental processes leading to difficulties of social adjustment as well as to mental and psychological abnormality.

10. Discussion

(a) *Sex chromosome control of somatic characters*

Stature. The data presented here suggest the following hypothesis. That growth controlling centres are located in the heterochromatic X- and Y-chromosomes, and that when there is an increase in the number of heterochromatic X-chromosomes and a normal or increased complement of Y-chromosomes, the increase in height results from increased limb, rather than trunk growth, but that when there is a normal complement of X-chromosomes and an increased complement of heterochromatic Y-chromosomes, there is an increase in size throughout childhood. It is suggested that centres located in heterochromatic X- and Y-chromosomes act as regulators and that an increased dose of these centres results in an increased growth rate. 48,XXYY males might therefore be expected to be tall throughout life but also to show the characteristic increase in limb as compared with trunk growth seen in XXY subjects, whereas 47,XYY subjects would be expected to be tall throughout life and this is supported by the extreme height of the few prepubertal 47,XYY boys who have been detected (Court Brown et al. 1968; Cowie and Kahn).

This argument, in relation to stature, is supported by data on 45,X females, who are invariably short. Short stature is also a characteristic of most of the other chromosome complements found in ovarian dysgenesis. Finally, in man it is invariably the abnormal X-chromosome which becomes heterochromatic, and presumably therefore, genetically inactive. The evidence suggests that the controlling centres located in the heterochromatic X only operate correctly when both X-chromosomes are of normal structure. Deletion or duplication of the second X-chromosome which then becomes heterochromatic results in an abnormal amount of heterochromatin and abnormal control. The invariable short stature of 45,X girls with ovarian dysgenesis but not those with pure gonadal dysgenesis, or to a lesser extent those with a normal or duplicated short arm, suggests that at least some of the controlling centres are located on the short arm of the X. On this hypotheses, 47,XXX females should be tall. This however, is not found to be so. This would seem to suggest that whereas in the male the interaction of a normal or excess amount of Y-heterochromatin with a normal or excess of X-heterochromatin leads to excessive height, in the female a single structurally normal heterochromatic X is necessary for the attainment of normal stature. Excess of X-heterochromatin alone, however, does not apparently lead to an increase in height.

Psychosocial characters. It is clear that no single gene controls intelligence or mental capacity but rather that, like stature, they result from the effects of a number of interacting genes or chromosome regions (controlling centres). The data therefore suggest that controlling genes are located on the heterochromatic X and Y, and imbalance in these chromosomes leads to abnormal psychosocial development, possibly aggressiveness and possibly mental defect, as well as leading to abnormalities of height. In females the effect of an additional X-chromosome apparently leads to similar though less severe disturbances, to those observed in males. The excess of X-heterochromatin in 47,XXX females affects in some cases at least their potentiality for social adjustment and many such women are psychotic and are frequently found to commit petty offences against the law. This failure to adjust is very similar to that found among males with 47,XXY chromosomes, but considerably less severe than the maladjustment observed in groups of 47,XYY males. The excess of X-heterochromatin is not so deleterious as the excess of Y-heterochromatin, at least in respect to psychosocial development.

Variability of phenotype and karyotype in ovarian dysgenesis. An interesting feature of ovarian dysgenesis is the extreme variability of the chromosome complement relative to the phenotypic similarity of the clinical features within the three main groups. Of the two groups with ovarian dysgenesis (Table 9) there are 229 girls who can be classified clearly as having either Turner's syndrome or ovarian dysgenesis, and of these, 152 have 45,X chromosomes. 71 have the full clinical features of Turner's syndrome, whilst 81 have only ovarian dysgenesis without major associated somatic abnormalities. Furthermore, about 5% of spontaneous abortions also have a 45,X chromosome complement. What then is the significance of this phenotypic variability?

The primary failure in ovarian dysgenesis is gonadal; it is not however, a failure of germ cell formation or migration, but is apparently a failure to regulate the rate of germ cell atresia and it has been argued above that this is the main function of the second heterochromatic X-chromosome. The finding therefore, of a variety of chromosome complements in ovarian dysgenesis besides 45,X and the fact that structurally abnormal X-chromosomes are invariably heterochromatic argues that this control is so carefully balanced, that loss or gain of heterochromatin leads to imbalance and resulting phenotypic abnormality. This, however, does not apply to the 47,XXX or 47,XYY states, both of which usually result in potentially fertile subjects, of normal or relatively normal phenotype.

The variability of the 45,X phenotype is much more difficult to account for, and may be related to the degree of development attained by the gonad, (see also above). It has been suggested that the heterochromatic X may regulate the rate of germ cell atresia, and oestrogen production by the ovary. In somatic tissues absence of the heterochromatic X could result in abnormalities in various developmental processes which are normally regulated by this heterochromatin; leading to the variable somatic phenotype observed in 45,X females, and to a lesser extent in females with a structurally abnormal X-chromosome. Finally, why are the majority of 45,X zygotes lost prior to birth? It is thought that the majority of liveborn 45,X females carry the maternally derived X-chromosome, and it is suggested that many of these result from loss of the paternal sex chromosome at a very early cleavage division. Perhaps there are in fact two classes of 45,X zygotes, one class resulting from meiotic non-disjunction (primary) and a second class resulting from early mitotic non-disjunction (secondary) in which the original zygote was XX or XY and in which the paternal X or Y was lost. If so, it may well be that the primary 45,X zygotes are deficient in some essential and lost during foetal life, whilst the secondary 45,X zygotes may be more viable. These may have started with a normal 46,XX or XY chromosome complement and lost an X or Y during early cleavage. Alternatively non-disjunction and mixoploidy followed by overgrowth by the 45,X cell line, could result in the development of a 45,X foetus, and it might be expected that these zygotes would be more viable than those resulting from meiotic non-disjunction.

(b) *Control mechanism*

Commoner has suggested that DNA acts in two ways. First as the mediator of typical Mendelian inheritance through the nucleotide sequence which makes up the genetic code, and that this code relates to the production of proteins, and is confined to the euchromatic chromosome regions. Second, DNA acts as a powerful agent of nucleotide sequestration giving rise thereby to genetic regulation of certain metabolic processes and that the genetic effects of heterochromatic DNA appear to be exclusively mediated through this system. These effects determine cell size, total rate of oxidative metabolism and probably more specific regulation of metabolic pathways which are affected by free nucleotide concentration. The phenotypic effects of this nucleotide sequestration system are related to the total amount of DNA and probably to the nucleotide composition of the DNA synthesised during particular times in the development of the cell. The effects are typically quantitative in contrast with the qualitative all or none effects of the Mendelian euchromatic system.

Recently Cattanach and Isaacson have reported the existence of 'controlling elements' in heterochromatic X-chromosomes in the mouse which control the spread of genetic inactivation to associated autosomal structural genes introduced into the X by translocation. In maize, McClintock (1956, 1965) has identified elements which control and regulate the function of associated structural genes and act as a 'switching' mechanism at precise times in development and with precise frequencies. This system may involve two elements, one controlling the action of the structural gene and the other regulating the action of the controller, and both of these elements may undergo 'changes in state' which result in altered expressions of the structural gene.

It is becoming clear that there are similarities between position effect variegation in *Drosophila* and the mouse and the mechanism of genetic instability in maize and it is reasonable to assume that similar mechanisms will be found to exist in man. At least one of these systems in maize, the Spm-type element can be independently located to the gene it controls, and the control exercised is affected by the dose of the controlling elements. Finally, controlling elements in *Drosophila* and the mouse are mediated through heterochromatin while in maize this is probably so although direct cytological evidence is not available. In man, control of sex determination and some somatic characters is also heterochromatin mediated and is affected both by the dose of heterochromatin and interaction between X- and Y-heterochromatin, and it is therefore reasonable to postulate controlling elements or controlling centres situated in the heterochromatic X and Y. These controlling elements might act through nucleotide sequestration, although there is at present no evidence for the existence of this mechanism. If so they could act by directly controlling m-RNA formation on the DNA template by blocking polynucleotides required or by blocking the action of the RNA polymerase. If this is not an all or none effect but the amount of structural gene product depends on the dose of the controlling element, then an hypothesis is available to account for the effect of varying doses of heterochromatin, both on the germ line and soma. An alternative hypothesis expressed in more conventional terms would require decondensation of the controlling elements, thus exposing the DNA template, at specific times and in specific cells, to RNA-polymerase so that the appropriate m-RNA required could be made. A close control over the pulse length and amount of messenger produced could equally well exercise the type of quantitative control required.

The somatic characters principally affected by an excess or decrease of sex chromosome heterochromatin in man are quantitative, in particular height and psychosocial development, and these could well be the type of characters regulated by such systems, and variation in the amount of heterochromatin might therefore be expected to affect them. Sex determination, which although basically controlled by Mendelian genes which determine whether the primitive gonad develops into a testis or an ovary may be controlled by such a system. It has been suggested above, moreover, that these Mendelian genes are located on the X-chromosome only, and that their action depends on the regulatory effect of either the heterochromatic X or Y so that imbalance in the amount of heterochromatin might well affect the action of these sex determining genes. Such conditions as pure gonadal dysgenesis and various forms of intersexuality in which the sex chromosome complement is either 46,XX or XY might well be accounted for by autosomal modifiers superimposing their effects on the sex determining mechanism. Examples of this are known in other mammals and may well occur in man.

The effect of Y-heterochromatin is clearly stronger than the effect of X-heterochromatin both as regards sex determination and the somatic effects. Subjects from 47,XXY to 49,XXXXY are male, although their maleness is modified by excessive X-heterochromatin. The somatic effects too, such as height and psychotic disturbances are more pronounced when a Y is present, and even more so when two Y-chromosomes are found. This can be contrasted with the effect of three or even rarely four X-chromosomes alone, which have little effect on height or sex determination and have a lesser psychotic effect, and suggests an interaction between controlling elements on the X and Y.

It may be concluded therefore that the X and Y act primarily through their heterochromatin and that despite the fact that the major gene loci are inactive on all but one X, both the X and Y as a result of heterochromatinisation, have an extremely powerful regulatory function.

Acknowledgements

I am grateful to Professor P. E. Polani for reading the manuscript, and for providing Fig. 7; to Dr. S. Ohno for permission to reproduce Fig. 6 from Ohno (1967); to Professor H. G. Schwarzacher for permission to reproduce Fig. 2 from Schwarzacher; to the editor of Nature for permission to use Figs. 7, 11 and 12. I am grateful to Dr. M.C. Joseph for referring the patients illustrated. The figures were kindly prepared by Miss D. A. Baker. Mr. L. Kelberman carried out some of the photography.

Appendix

The system of nomenclature outlined below is taken from the report of the Chicago Conference (1966).

Numerical aberrations

In a description of karyotype findings the first item to be recorded is the total number of chromosomes, including the sex chromosomes, followed by a comma (,). The sex chromosome constitution is given next, e.g.,

45,X	45 chromosomes, one X-chromosome.
47,XXY	47 chromosomes, XXY sex chromosomes.
49,XXXXY	49 chromosomes, XXXXY sex chromosomes.

The autosomes are specified only when there is an abnormality present. Thus, if there is a numerical aberration of the autosomes, the group letter of the extra or missing autosome, followed by a plus (+) or minus (—) sign, succeeds the sex chromosome designation, e.g.,

45,XX,C—	45 chromosomes, XX sex chromosomes, a missing C group chromosome.
48,XXY,G+	48 chromosomes, XXY sex chromosomes, an additional G group chromosome.

The plus or minus sign after a chromosome letter or number indicates that the *entire* autosome is extra or missing. When the extra or missing chromosome or chromosomes have been identified with certainty, the chromosome number may be used, e.g.,

45,XX,16—	45 chromosomes, two X-chromosomes, a missing No. 16 chromosome.
47,XY,21+	47 chromosomes, XY sex chromosomes, an additional No. 21 chromosome.
46,XY,18+,21—	46 chromosomes, XY sex chromosomes, an extra No. 18 and missing a No. 21.

A question mark (?) is used in the normal way to indicate uncertainty. If it is suspected that a missing or extra chromosome belongs to a particular group, but this is not certain, the question mark may *precede* the group designation or in some cases the chromosome number, e.g.,

45,XX,?C—	45 chromosomes, XX sex chromosomes, a missing chromosome which probably belongs in group C.

Another example would describe the karyotype of a sex chromatin positive female with an additional small acrocentric chromosome; this could be written, depending on the amount of available information, as: 47,XX,?G+; 47,XX,G+; 47,XX,?21+ or 47,XX,21+.

A *triploid* or *polyploid* cell should be evident from the chromosome number and from the further designations, e.g., 69,XXY; 70,XXY,G+. An *endoreduplicated* metaphase can be indicated by preceding the karyotype designation with the abbrevation 'end', e.g., end46,XX. If multiplicity of endoreduplications is to be indicated, an Arabic numeral can be used before 'end' to indicate this, e.g., 2end46,XX; 4end-46,XX.

The method for describing chromosome complements containing structurally rearranged chromosomes, such as dicentrics, acentric fragments and markers, is given on page 5.

Chromosome mosaics. The chromosome constitution of the different cell lines are listed in numerical or alphabetical order, *irrespective of the frequencies of the cell types in the individual studied.* The karyotype designations are separated by a diagonal (/), e.g.,

45,X/46,XY	A chromosome mosaic with two cell types, one with 45 chromosomes and a single X, the other with 46 chromosomes and XY sex chromosomes.
46,XX/46,XY	A chromosome mosaic with both XX and XY cell lines.
46,XY/47,XY,G+	A chromosome mosaic with a normal male cell line and a cell line with an extra G group chromosome.
45,X/46,XX/47,XXX	A triple cell line mosaic.

Structural alterations

The *short arm* of a chromosome is designated by the lower-case letter 'p', the *long arm* by the letter 'q', a *satellite* by the letter 's', a secondary constriction by the letter 'h' and the *centromere* by the abbreviation 'cen'.

Increase in length of a chromosome arm is indicated by placing a plus sign (+) and *decrease in length* by placing a minus sign (—) *after* the arm designation, e.g., 2p+; Bp—; Gq—. When one arm of a mediocentric chromosome, viz., Nos. 1, 3, 19 and 20, is changed this is indicated by placing a question mark *between* the chromosome designation and the plus or minus sign. For example, a No. 3 chromosome with an elongated arm would be designated as 3?+.

The result of a *pericentric inversion* is indicated by p+q— or p—q+, which is enclosed in parentheses and preceded by the abbreviation 'inv', e.g., inv(Dp+q—).

A translocation is indicated by the letter 't' followed by parentheses which include the chromosomes involved, e.g.,

46,XY,t(Bp—;Dq+) or 46,XY,t(Bp+;Dq—)	A balanced reciprocal translocation between the short arm of a B and the long arm of a D group chromosome.

Translocations involving a sex chromosome and an autosome would be designated as, e.g.,

46,X,t(Xq+;16p—)	A reciprocal translocation between the long arm of an X and the short arm of a No. 16 in a female.
46,Y,t(Xq+;16p—)	The same translocation in a male.
46,X,t(Yp+;16p—)	A reciprocal translocation between the short arm of a Y and the short arm of a No. 16.

The remaining normal sex chromosome is written in its usual position after the chromosome number, and the other sex chromosome which is involved in the translocation is included in parentheses preceding the autosome concerned.

The separation of the chromosomes within the parentheses by a semicolon(;) indicates that two structurally altered chromosomes are present and that the translocation is balanced. In a 'centric fusion' type of translocation, in which only one translocation chromosome is present, the semicolon is omitted, e.g.,

45,XX,D—,G—,t(DqGq)+	45 chromosomes, XX sex chromosomes, one chromosome missing from the D group and one from the G

group, their long arms having united to form a DG translocation chromosome.

If, as rarely happens, a small centric fragment is present as well, implying a reciprocal translocation, it could be written as, e.g., 46,XX,D−,G−,t(DpGp)+,t(DqGq)+.

Where a 'centric fusion type of translocation results in duplication of part of one of the chromosomes involved, this could be written as, e.g.,

46,XX,D−,t(DqGq)+	46 chromosomes, XX sex chromosomes, one chromosome missing from the D group; the long arm of this chromosome is united with the long arm of a G group chromosome. Since there are four normal G group chromosomes, part of a G is present in triplicate.

When family studies clearly show that a particular chromosome has been inherited from the mother or the father, this may be indicated by the abbreviations 'mat' or 'pat'. For instance, in a family in which a father is carrying a balanced reciprocal translocation, 46,XY,t(Bp−;Dq+), and in which his malformed son has inherited only one of the two abnormal chromosomes, the son's complement would be written as 46,XY,Bp−pat or 46,XY,Dq+pat, depending on which abnormal chromosome had been transmitted. If the son had inherited both chromosomes involved in the translocation, his complement would be expressed as 46,XY,t(Bp−;Dq+)pat.

Duplicated chromosome structures are indicated by repeating the appropriate designation. Thus, 46,XX,Gpss would describe the karyotype of a female in which one of the G group chromosomes has double satellites on the short arm. If satellites appear on a chromosome arm where they are not usually found, this arm should be designated, e.g., 46,XY,18ps, indicating a No. 18 with satellited short arms; 46,XX, Gpsqs, indicating a G group chromosome with both long and short arms satellited. Enlarged satellites are indicated, for instance, by Gs+.

Isochromosomes are designated by the lower-case letter 'i' placed after the chromosome arm involved, e.g., 46,XXqi; or if this is presumptive, then 46,XXq?i. This would indicate an isochromosome or a presumptive isochromosome for the long arm of one X-chromosome.

Ring chromosomes are indicated by the letter 'r' placed after the chromosome involved; e.g., 46,XXr would indicate a ring X, and a ring B would be written 46,XY,Br.

In describing cells damaged by ionizing radiation, chemicals, viruses, etc., the system of nomenclature that has been described should be used where applicable. This may not be possible where the cell contains a grossly unbalanced chromosome complement. In such instances the following convention is suggested. The chromosome count in a given cell should include all centric chromosome structures present in that cell regardless of the number of centromeres. Unidentified chromosomes are indicated by 'mar' (marker). *Acentric* fragments are *not* included in the count but may be indicated by 'ace'. *Dicentric* and *tricentric* chromosomes are counted as one body and indicated by 'dic' and 'tri'. As an example, a cell derived from a normal female with a total of 48 centric chromosome structures, one missing F group chromosome, a *dicentric* and an *acentric* fragment, as well as two unidentified marker chromosomes would be written as: 48,?X?X,F−,dic+,mar1+,mar2+,ace*. If necessary, an asterisk (*) following a chromosome designation may be used to draw attention to an explanation in the text.

If *other designations* are needed for special conditions, they should, whenever possible, be taken from the first three letters of the word required, used in lower-case, clearly defined and placed immediately before or after the chromosome symbol or the bracketed chromosome designation to which they refer. If single letters are to be used for special designations, they should be in lower-case and should not duplicate the capital letters A to G, X and Y or those lower-case letters representing other structures. Lower-case letters which are easily confused with numerals, such as 'l' or 'o', should not be used. Subscripts and superscripts should be avoided since they are easily written incorrectly, not readily handled by computers and difficult to set in type.

In regard to *abnormal chromosomes described for the first time*, it was suggested in the Denver Report that such chromosomes be named after the laboratory of origin. Instead, it is now proposed that the chromosome be described according to its morphology, by use of the shorthand nomenclature recommended. The only exception to this, for historical reasons, is to be the Ph^1 chromosome first described by Nowell and Hungerford.

The terms describing abnormalities of chromosome number, such as aneuploid, heteroploid, etc., are often used in a variety of ways. Levan and Müntzing have restated the original definitions of these and other terms and commented on usage.

A further problem that often arises in chromosome nomenclature is that of defining the position of the centromere. Such terms as telocentric and submetacentric are sometimes misused. Levan et al. have proposed a standardized nomenclature defining the centromeric position in terms of the arm ratio.

TABLE OF NOMENCLATURE SYMBOLS

A–G	the chromosome groups
1–22	the autosome numbers (Denver System)
X,Y	the sex chromosomes
diagonal (/)	separates cell lines in describing mosaicism
plus sign (+) or minus sign (−)	when placed immediately after the autosome number or group letter designation indicates that the particular chromosome is extra or missing; when placed immediately after the arm or structural designation indicates that the particular arm or structure is larger or smaller than normal
question mark (?)	indicates questionable identification of chromosome or chromosome structure

asterisk (*)	designates a chromosome or chromosome structure explained in text or footnote
ace	acentric
cen	centromere
dic	dicentric
end	endoreduplication
h	secondary constriction or negatively staining region
i	isochromosome
inv	inversion
inv(p+q−) or inv(p−q+)	pericentric inversion
mar	marker chromosome
mat	maternal origin
p	short arm of chromosome
pat	paternal origin
q	long arm of chromosome
r	ring chromosome
t	satellite
s	translocation
tri	tricentric
repeated symbols	duplication of chromosome structure

References

BAKER, T.G.: A quantitative and cytological study of germ cells in human ovaries. Proc. Roy. Soc. (London), Ser. B 158 (1963) 417.

BALODIMOS, M.C., H.LISCO, I.IRWIN, W.MERRILL and J.F.DINGMAN: XYY karyotype in a case of familial hypogonadism. J. Clin. Endocrinol. Metab. 26 (1966) 443.

BARR, M.L.: The sex chromatin. In: C.Overzier, ed.: Intersexuality. London and New York, Academic Press (1963) p. 48.

BARR, M.L. and E.G.BERTRAM: A morphological distinction between neurones of the male and female, and the behaviour of the nucleolar satellite during accelerated nucleoprotein synthesis. Nature 163 (1949) 676.

BENIRSCHKE, K.: Sterility and fertility of interspecific mammalian hybrids. In: K.Benirschke, ed.: Comparative aspects of reproductive failure. New York, Springer-Verlag (1967) p. 218.

BEUTLER, E., M.YEH and V.F.FAIRBANKS: The normal human female as a mosaic of X-chromosome activity: studies using the gene for G-6-PD deficiency as a marker. Proc. Natl. Acad. Sci. U.S. 48 (1962) 9.

BIGGERS, J.D. and R.A.MCFEELY: Intersexuality in domestic mammals. In: A.McLaren, ed.: Advances in reproductive physiology, Vol. 1. London and New York, Logos and Academic Press (1966) p. 129.

BRAY, P. and SISTER ANN JOSEPHINE: An XXXYY sex chromosome anomaly. J. Am. Med. Assoc. 184 (1963) 179.

BREAKEY, W.R.: Sex chromatin analyses in a mentally defective population. J. Anat. 95 (1961) 618.

BRIDGES, C.B.: The genetics of sex in *Drosophila*. In: E.Allen, ed.: Sex and internal secretions, 1st ed. Baltimore, Williams and Wilkins Co. (1932) p. 55.

CARR, D.H.: Chromosome studies in spontaneous abortions. Obstet. Gynecol. 26 (1965) 308.

CASEY, M.D., L.J.SEGALL, D.R.K.STREET and C.E.BLANK: Sex chromosome abnormalities in two State hospitals for patients requiring special security. Nature 209 (1966) 641.

CATTANACH, B.M. and J.H.ISAACSON: Controlling elements in the mouse X-chromosome. Genetics 57 (1967) 331.

CHICAGO CONFERENCE: Standardization in human cytogenetics. Birth defects: Original Article Series, Vol. 2, No. 2. New York, The National Foundation (1966).

CLARKE, C.M.: Techniques in the study of human chromosomes. In: J.L.Hamerton, ed.: Chromosomes in medicine. London, Heinemann Medical Books Ltd. (1962) p. 232.

COMINGS, D.E.: The duration of replication of the inactive X-chromosome in humans based on the persistence of the heterochromatic sex chromatin body during DNA synthesis. Cytogenetics 6 (1967a) 20.

COMINGS, D.E.: Sex chromatin, nuclear size and the cell cycle. Cytogenetics 6 (1967b) 120.

COMMONER, B.: Roles of deoxyribonucleic acid in inheritance. Nature 202 (1964) 960.

COURT BROWN, W.M.: Human population cytogenetics. Amsterdam, North-Holland Publishing Co. (1967).

COURT BROWN, W.M., D.G.HARNDEN, P.A.JACOBS, N.MACLEAN and D.J.MANTLE: Abnormalities of the sex chromosome complement in man. Medical Research Council Spec. Rep. Ser. No. 305. London, Her Majesty's Stationery Office (1964).

COURT BROWN, W.M., K.E.BUCKTON, P.A.JACOBS, I.M.TOUGH, E.V.KUENSSBERG and J.D.E.KNOX: Chromosome studies on adults. Eugenics Laboratory Memoirs XLII, Galton Laboratory, University College, London. Cambridge University Press (1966).

COURT BROWN, W.M., W.H.PRICE and P.A.JACOBS: Further information on the identity of 47, XYY males. Brit. Med. J. 2 (1968) 325.

COWIE, J. and J.KAHN: The XYY constitution in a prepubertal child. Brit. Med. J. 1 (1968) 748.

CULLING, C.F.A.: Staining affinities and cytochemical properties of the sex chromatin. In: K.L. Moore, ed.: The sex chromatin. Philadelphia, W.B.Saunders Co. (1966) p. 91.

DANES, B.D. and A.G.BEARN: Hurler's syndrome. A genetic study in cell culture. J. Exptl. Med. 123 (1966) 1.

DAVIDSON, R.G., H.M.NITOWSKY and B.CHILDS: Demonstration of two populations of cells in the human female heterozygous for glucose-6-phosphate dehydrogenase variants. Proc. Natl. Acad. Sci. U.S. 50 (1963) 481.

DAVIDSON, W.M. and D.R.SMITH: A morphological sex difference in the polymorphonuclear neutrophil leucocytes. Brit. Med. J. 2 (1954) 6.

DAY, R.W., W.LARSON and S.W.WRIGHT: Clinical and cytogenetic studies on a group of females with XXX sex chromosome complement. J. Pediat. 64 (1964) 24.

DE MARS, R.: Sex chromatin mass in living, cultivated human cells. Science 138 (1962) 980.

DENVER CONFERENCE: A proposed standard system of nomenclature of human mitotic chromosomes. Lancet 1 (1960) 1063.

FERGUSON-SMITH, M.A., W.S.MACK, P.M.ELLIS, M.DICKSON, R.SANGER and R.R.RACE: Parental age and the source of the X-chromosomes in XXY Klinefelter's syndrome. Lancet 1 (1964) 46.

FORD, C.E.: Human cytogenetics: Its present place and future possibilities. Am. J. Human Genet. 12 (1960) 104.

FORD, C.E.: Human chromosome mosaics. In: Human chromosomal abnormalities. London, Staples Press (1961) p. 23.

FORD, C.E. and J.L.HAMERTON: The chromosomes of man. Nature 178 (1956) 1020.

FORD, C.E., P.A.JACOBS and L.G.LAJHTA: Human somatic chromosomes. Nature 181 (1958) 1565.

FORD, C.E., K.W.JONES, P.E.POLANI, J.C.DE ALMEIDA and J.H.BRIGGS: A sex-chromosome anomaly in a case of gonadal dysgenesis (Turner's syndrome). Lancet 1 (1959) 711.

FRASER, J.H., J.CAMPBELL, R.C.MACGILLIVRAY, E.BOYD and B.LENNOX: The XXX syndrome: Frequency among mental defectives and fertility. Lancet 2 (1960) 626.

FRØLAND, A.: A micromethod for chromosome analysis on peripheral blood-cultures. Lancet 2 (1962) 1281.

FRØLAND, A., R.SANGER and R.R.RACE: Xg blood groups of 78 patients with Klinefelter's syndrome and of some of their parents. J. Med. Genet. (1968) in press.

GERMAN, J.: Autoradiographic studies of human chromosomes 1. A review. In: Proc. 3rd. Int. Congr. of Hum. Genet. Chicago, 1966. Baltimore, Johns Hopkins Press (1967) p. 123.

GIANNELLI, F. and R.M.HOWLETT: The identification of the chromosomes of the D group (13–15) Denver: An autoradiographic and measurement study. Cytogenetics 5 (1966) 186.

GIANNELLI, F. and R.M.HOWLETT: The identification of the chromosomes of the E group (16–18) Denver: An autoradiographic and measurement study. Cytogenetics 6 (1967) 420.

GRÜNEBERG, H.: Genes and genotypes affecting the teeth of the mouse. J. Embryol. Exptl. Morphol. 14 (1965) 137.

GRÜNEBERG, H.: The molars of the tabby mouse and a test of the 'single-active' X-chromosome hypothesis. J. Embryol. Exptl. Morphol. 15 (1966a) 223.

GRÜNEBERG, H.: More about the tabby mouse and about the Lyon hypothesis. J. Embryol. Exptl. Morphol. 16 (1966b) 569.

GRÜNEBERG, H.: Sex linked genes in man and the Lyon hypothesis. Ann. Hum. Genet. 30 (1967) 239.

HAMERTON, J.L.: Chromosome segregation in three human interchanges. In: C.D.Darlington and K.R.Lewis, eds.: Chromosomes today, Vol. 1. Proc. 1st Oxford Chromosome Conference, 1964. Edinburgh and London, Oliver and Boyd (1966) p. 237.

HAMERTON, J.L.: Robertsonian translocations in man: evidence for prezygotic selection. Cytogenetics 7 (1968a) 260.

HAMERTON, J.L.: The significance of sex chromosome derived heterochromatin in mammals. Nature 219 (1968b).

HAMERTON, J.L.: Reciprocal translocations in man. In: C.D.Darlington and K.R.Lewis, eds.: Chromosomes today, Vol. 2. Proc. 2nd. Oxford Chromosome Conference, 1967. Edinburgh and London, Oliver and Boyd (1969) in press.

HAMERTON, J.L., H.P.KLINGER, D.E.MUTTON and E.M.LANG: The somatic chromosomes of the Hominoidea. Cytogenetics 2 (1963) 240.

HAMERTON, J.L., J.DICKSON, C.E.POLLARD, S.A.GRIEVES and R.V.SHORT: Genetic intersexuality in goats. J. Reprod. Fertility (1968) in press.

HANSEMANN, D.: Ueber pathologische Mitosen. Virchows Arch. Pathol. Anat. Physiol. Klin. Med. 123 (1891) 356.

HARNDEN, D.G.: Nuclear sex in triploid XXY human cells. Lancet 2 (1961) 488.

HAUSER, G.A.: Gonadal dysgenesis. In: C.Overzier, ed.: Intersexuality. London and New York, Academic Press (1963) p. 298.

HSU, L.Y.F., H.P.KLINGER and J.WEISS: Influence of nuclear selection criteria on sex chromatin frequency in oral mucosa cells of newborn females. Cytogenetics 6 (1967) 371.

HUNGERFORD, D.A., A.J.DONNELLY, P.C.NOWELL and S.BECK: The chromosome constitution of a human phenotypic intersex. Am. J. Human Genet. 11 (1959) 215.

JACOBS, P.A. and J.A.STRONG: A case of human intersexuality having a possible XXY sex-determining mechanism. Nature 183 (1959) 302.

JACOBS, P.A., M.BRUNTON, M.M.MELVILLE, R.P.BRITTAIN and W.F.MCCLEMONT: Aggressive behaviour, mental subnormality and the XYY male. Nature 208 (1965) 1351.

JACOBS, P.A., G.CRUIKSHANK, M.J.W.FAED, A.FRACKIEWICZ, E.B.ROBSON, H.HARRIS and I.SUTHERLAND: Pericentric inversion of a group C autosome: a study of three families. Ann. Human Genet. 31 (1968a) 219.

JACOBS, P.A., W.H.PRICE, W.M.COURT BROWN, R.P.BRITTAIN and P.B.WHATMORE: Chromosome studies on men in a Maximum Security Hospital. Ann. Human Genet. 31 (1968b) 339.

KIDD, C. B., R. S. KNOX and D. J. MANTLE: A psychiatric investigation of triple-X chromosome females. Brit. J. Psychiat. 109 (1963) 90.

KLINGER, H. P.: Morphological characteristics of the sex chromatin. In: K. L. Moore, ed.: The sex chromatin. Philadelphia, W. B. Saunders Co. (1966) p. 76.

KLINGER, H. P., H. G. SCHWARZACHER and J. WEISS: DNA content and size of sex chromatin positive and negative nuclei during the cell cycle. Cytogenetics 6 (1967) 1.

KLINGER, H. P., J. DAVIS, P. GOLDHUBER and T. DITTA: Factors influencing mammalian X-chromosome condensation and sex chromatin formation I. The effect of *in vitro* cell density on sex chromatin frequency. Cytogenetics 7 (1968) 39.

KOLLER, P. C.: Genetical and mechanical properties of sex chromosomes. III Man. Proc. Roy. Soc. B 57 (1937) 194.

LEA, D. E.: Actions of radiations on living cells, 2nd ed. Cambridge, University Press (1955).

LEJEUNE, J., M. GAUTIER and R. TURPIN: Etude des chromosomes somatiques de neuf enfants mongoliens. Compt. Rend. 248 (1959) 1721.

LEWIS, F. J. W., A. FRØLAND, R. SANGER and R. R. RACE: Source of the X-chromosomes in two XXXXY males. Lancet 2 (1964) 589.

LINDSTEN, J., P. BOWEN, C. S. N. LEE, V. A. MCKUSICK, P. E. POLANI, M. WINGATE, J. H. EDWARDS, J. HAMPER, P. TIPPETT, R. SANGER and R. R. RACE: Source of the X in XO females: The evidence of Xg. Lancet 1 (1963a) 558.

LINDSTEN, J., M. FRACCARO, P. E. POLANI, J. L. HAMERTON, R. SANGER and R. R. RACE: Evidence that the Xg blood group genes are on the short arm of the X-chromosome. Nature 197 (1963b) 648.

LONDON CONFERENCE: The normal human karyotype. Ann. Hum. Genet. 27 (1963) 295.

LYON, M. F.: Gene action in the X-chromosome of the mouse (*Mus musculus L.*) Nature 190 (1961) 372.

LYON, M. F.: Sex chromatin and gene action in the mammalian X-chromosome. Am. J. Human Genet. 14 (1962) 135.

LYON, M. F.: Attempts to test the inactive-X theory of dosage compensation in mammals. Genet. Res. 4 (1963) 93.

LYON, M. R.: X-chromosome inactivation in mammals. In: D. H. M. Woollam, ed.: Advances in teratology, Vol. 1. London, Logos Press (1966) p. 25.

MCCLINTOCK, B.: Controlling elements and the gene. Cold Spring Harbor Symposia on Quantitative Biology, Vol. XXI. New York, Cold Spring Harbor (1956) p. 197.

MCCLINTOCK, B.: The control of gene action in maize. Brookhaven Symposia in Biology, No. 18., Upton. New York, Brookhaven National Laboratory (1965) p. 162.

MCFEELEY, R. A., W. C. D. HARE and J. D. BIGGERS: Chromosome studies in 14 cases of intersex in domestic mammals. Cytogenetics 6 (1967) 242.

MACLEAN, N.: Sex chromatin surveys of new born babies. In: K. L. Moore, ed.: The sex chromatin. Philadelphia, W. B. Saunders Co. (1966) p. 202.

MACLEAN, N., D. G. HARNDEN, W. M. COURT BROWN, J. BOND and D. J. MANTLE: Sex chromosome abnormalities in newborn babies. Lancet 1 (1964) 286.

MATHER, K.: The genetical activity of heterochromatin. Proc. Roy. Soc. (London) B 132 (1944) 308.

MELLMAN, W. J.: Human peripheral blood leucocyte cultures. In: J. J. Yunis, ed.: Human chromosome methodology. New York, Academic Press (1965) p. 22.

MEYER, G. F.: Die Funktionsstrukturen des Y-Chromosoms in den Spermatocytenkernen von *Drosophila hydei*, *D. neohydei*, *D. repleta*, und einigen anderen *Drosophila*-arten. Chromosoma 14 (1963) 207.

MEYER, G. F.: Spermiogenese in normalen und Y-defizienten Männchen von *Drosophila melanogaster* und *D. hydei*. Z. Zellforsch. Mikroskop. Anat. 84 (1968) 141.

MIGEON, B. R., V. M. DER KALOUSTIAN, W. L. NYHAN, W. J. YOUNG and B. CHILDS: X-linked hypoxanthine guanine phosphoribosyl transferase deficiency; heterozygote has two clonal populations. Science 160 (1968) 425.

MILES, C.P.: Morphology and functional relations of sex chromatin in cultured amnion cells. Exptl. Cell Res. 20 (1960) 324.

MILLER, O.J., W.R.BREG, D.WARBURTON, D.A.MILLER, I.L.FIRSCHEIN and K.HIRSCHHORN: Alternative DNA replication patterns associated with long arm length of chromosomes 4 and 5 in the cri du chat syndrome. Cytogenetics 5 (1966) 137.

MINTZ, B.: Interaction between two allelic series modifying primordial germ cell development in the mouse embryo. Anat. Record 128 (1957) 591.

MITTWOCH, U.: Barr bodies and their relation to nuclear size. Cytogenetics 3 (1964) 62.

MITTWOCH, U., K.P.LELE and W.S.WEBSTER: Relationship of Barr bodies, nuclear size and deoxyribonucleic acid value in cultured human cells. Nature 205 (1965) 477.

MOORE, K.L.: Sex reversal in newborn babies. Lancet 1 (1959) 217.

MOORE, K.L.: The development of clinical sex chromatin tests. In: K.L.Moore, ed.: The sex chromatin. Philadelphia, W.B.Saunders Co. (1966a) p. 173.

MOORE, K.L.: Sex chromatin patterns in various animals. In: K.L.Moore, ed.: The sex chromatin. Philadelphia, W.B.Saunders Co. (1966b) p. 16.

MOORE, K.L. and M.L.BARR: Morphology of the nerve cell nucleus in mammals, with special reference to the sex chromatin. J. Comp. Neurol. 98 (1953) 213.

MOORE, K.L., M.A.GRAHAM and M.L.BARR: The detection of chromosomal sex in hermaphrodites from a skin biopsy. Surg. Gynecol. Obstet. 96 (1953) 641.

MOORHEAD, P.S., P.C.NOWELL, W.J.MELLMAN, D.M.BATTIPS and D.A.HUNGERFORD: Chromosome preparations of leukocytes cultured from human peripheral blood. Exptl. Cell Res. 20 (1960) 613.

NOWAKOWSKI, H., W.LENZ, S.BERGMAN and J.REITALU: Chromosomenbefunde beim echten Klinefelter-syndrom. Acta Endocrinol. 34 (1960) 483.

OHNO, S.: Single-X derivation of sex chromatin. In: K.L.Moore, ed.: The sex chromatin. Philadelphia, W.B.Saunders Co. (1966) p. 113.

OHNO, S.: Sex chromosomes and sex-linked genes. Berlin, Heidelberg, New York, Springer-Verlag (1967).

PAINTER, T.S.: The Y-chromosome in mammals. Science 53 (1921) 503.

PAINTER, T.S.: Studies in mammalian spermatogenesis II. The spermatogenesis of man. J. Exptl. Zool. 37 (1923) 291.

PLUNKETT, E.R. and M.L.BARR: Testicular dysgenesis affecting the seminiferous tubules principally, with chromatin positive nuclei. Lancet 2 (1956) 853.

POLANI, P.E.: Sex chromosome anomalies in man. In: J.L.Hamerton, ed.: Chromosomes in medicine. London, Heinemann Medical Books Ltd. (1962) p. 73.

POLANI, P.E., W.R.HUNTER and B.LENNOX: Chromosomal sex in Turner's syndrome with coarctation of the aorta. Lancet 2 (1954) 120.

PRICE, W.H. and P.B.WHATMORE: Behaviour disorders and pattern of crime among XYY males identified at a maximum security hospital. Brit. Med. J. 1 (1967) 533.

ROBINSON, A. and T.T.PUCK: Chromatin studies in newborns: evidence for nonrandom factors affecting nondisjunction in man. J. Pediat. 67 (1965) 1054.

ROBINSON, A. and T.T.PUCK: Studies on chromosomal nondisjunction in man II. Am. J. Human Genet. 19 (1967) 112.

RUSSELL, L.B.: Mammalian X-chromosome action: Inactivation limited in spread and in region of origin. Science 140 (1963) 976.

RUSSELL, L.B.: Another look at the single-active-X-hypothesis. Trans. N.Y. Acad. Sci. 26 (1964) 726.

SCHMID, W.: DNA replication patterns of human chromosomes. Cytogenetics 2 (1963) 175.

SCHWARZACHER, H.G.: Sex chromatin in living human cells *in vitro*. Cytogenetics 2 (1963) 117.

SINGH, R.P. and D.H.CARR: The anatomy and histology of XO human embryos and fetuses. Anat. Record 155 (1966) 369.

SMITH, D.W., P.M.MARDEN, M.J.MCDONALD and M.SPECKHARD: Lower incidence of sex chromatin in buccal smears of newborn females. Pediatrics 30 (1962) 707.

STERN, C.: Untersuchungen über Aberrationen des Y-Chromosoms von *Drosophila melanogaster.* Z. Vererbungslehre 51 (1927) 253.

STEWART, J.S.S. and A.R.SANDERSON: Fertility and oligophrenia in an apparent triplo-X female. Lancet 2 (1960) 21.

TAYLOR, A.I.: Sex chromatin in the newborn. Lancet 1 (1963) 912.

TAYLOR, A.I. and E.C.MOORES: A sex chromatin survey of newborn children in two London hospitals. J. Med. Genet. 4 (1967) 258.

THERKELSEN, A.J. and G.B.PETERSEN: Frequency of sex-chromatin positive cells in the logarithmic and postlogarithmic growth phases of human cells in tissue cultures. Exptl. Cell Res. 28 (1962) 588.

THOMPSON, B.K., R.A.HAGGAR and M.L.BARR: The accessory body of Cajal in nerve cell nuclei of the cat. J. Comp. Neurol. 108 (1957) 253.

TJIO, J.H. and A.LEVAN: The chromosome number of man. Hereditas 42 (1956) 1.

TURNER, H.H.: A syndrome of infantilism, congenital webbed neck and cubitus valgus. Endocrinology 23 (1938) 566.

TURPIN, R., J.LEJEUNE and C.SALMON: Discussion de l'origine paternelle de l'X d'un S de Turner XO, protanope et XG(a-). Compt. Rend. 260 (1965) 369.

VON WINIWARTER, H.: Etudes sur la spermatogenèse humaine. Arch. Biol. 27 (1912) 97.

WARBURTON, D., D.A.MILLER, O.J.MILLER, W.R.BREG, A.DE CAPOA and M.W.SHAW: Distinction between chromosome 4 and chromosome 5 by replication pattern and length of long and short arms. Am. J. Human Genet. 19 (1967) 399.

WOLF, U., G.FLINSPACH, R.BÖHM and S.OHNO: DNS Reduplikationsmuster bei den Rüsen-Geschlechtschromosomen von *Microtus agrestis*. Chromosoma 16 (1965) 609.

CHAPTER 32

Autosomal abnormalities

ANGELA I. TAYLOR

Paediatric Research Unit, Guy's Hospital Medical School, London

Contents

1. Introduction
2. Numerical abnormalities
   (a) Down's syndrome
   (b) Edwards' syndrome
   (c) Patau's syndrome
   (d) Autosomal trisomy not associated with syndromes
3. Structural abnormalities
   (a) Short arm deletion – chromosome 4
   (b) Cri du chat syndrome
   (c) Long arm deletion – D chromosome
   (d) Short arm deletion – chromosome 18
   (e) Long arm deletion – chromosome 18
   (f) 'Antimongolism'
   (g) Structural anomalies not associated with syndromes
4. Comments and conclusions

1. Introduction

Man has 22 pairs of autosomes; thus 22 different single primary autosomal trisomies and a vast number of other autosomal abnormalities are theoretically possible. This theoretical expectation is not met, yet autosomal abnormalities are relatively numerous, and can be divided into two major groups – numerical and structural, with the first group the more familiar and well documented. Nine autosomal abnormalities each have a consistent phenotype and a discussion of these nine syndromes will form the major part of this chapter. Other anomalies will be considered briefly.

2. Numerical abnormalities

These comprise three trisomic syndromes, Down's syndrome (trisomy 21) was the first autosomal abnormality to be described in man (Lejeune et al. 1959). Edwards' syndrome (trisomy 18) and Patau's syndrome (trisomy 13) were described simultaneously in 1960 by Edwards and his colleagues in England, and Patau and his colleagues in the U.S.A.

The single human autosomal monosomy – G monosomy – is associated with features described by its discoverers (Lejeune et al. 1964), as 'le contre-type du mongolisme'. It is, however, associated with a variety of cytogenetic findings and will be discussed in the section on structural abnormalities.

(a) *Down's syndrome (47,XXorXY,G+, for nomenclature see Appendix in Hamerton's chapter)*

Down's syndrome, or mongolism, was recognised as a clinical entity in 1866 by Langdon Down in his paper 'Observations on an ethnic classification of idiots'. Gradually, however, the genetic nature of the condition became apparent, with occurrence of rare families with two affected sibs and the birth of an affected child to an affected mother. The association of Down's syndrome with raised maternal age has been known for some time (Jenkins). Clinical findings in Down's syndrome include mental retardation, certain somatic anomalies, characteristic facies and dermal ridge patterns on hands and feet (Table 1). The problems of diagnosis and prevalence of features in the newborn have been discussed recently (Carter and MacCarthy; Hall) while the condition as a whole has been reviewed very fully (Penrose and Smith), so that only a brief description will be given.

The population incidence is approximately 1 in 600 live births. Birth weight is low and birth is at term. The face is round or pear shaped with a clustering of facial features (Fig. 1). The palpebral fissures slant upwards and outwards and epicanthic folds are present. The nose is short from root to tip. The iris often has peripheral speckles known as Brushfield's spots. The ears are usually small, squarish and rather primitive with rolled helices, but not low set. In babies muscular hypotonia is very

TABLE 1

Findings in Down's syndrome. (Data from Levinson et al., Oster et al., Hall, and unpublished.)

Mean maternal age at birth	32.5 yr
Mean gestation age	37.9 wk
Mean birth weight	2832.0 g = 6 lbs. 4 oz.
Mean survival (1963)	18 yr
Sex ratio	Normal
Feature	*% Recorded*
Developmental retardation	100
Muscular hypotonia	79
Oblique palpebral fissures	83
Epicanthic folds	59
Speckled irises	57
Flat nasal bridge	75
Abnormal external ears	68
Frequently protruded tongue	57
Flat occiput	75
Excessive nape skin	80
Single palmar crease	48
Short little finger	66
Incurved little finger	57
Absent flexion crease on little finger	23
Widespread first and second toes	56
Hyperabduction of hip joints	84
Absent Moro reflex	82
Cardiac defects	56

marked, but this lessens in severity as the child ages. Cardiac defects may be severe, and are responsible for most of the deaths in infancy (Evans); oesophageal or duodenal atresia are rarer causes of death. Children with Down's syndrome are unusually susceptible to infections and the coming of antibiotics has greatly increased their life expectancy. In 1929 the mean survival age for London children with the syndrome was 9 years, whereas the most recent estimate for Australia in 1963, was 18 years (Penrose 1932; Collman and Stoller).

Affected children are invariably mentally retarded with an I.Q. rarely exceeding 50, except in a few mixoploids (see below). The intellectual capacity of these children is, however, quite variable, and a recent study shows that a proportion of these children can profitably attend schools for the educationally sub-normal (Dunsdon et al.). Since Lejeune et al. (1959) demonstrated that Down's syndrome was caused by trisomy G, chromosome studies to confirm the diagnosis and to detect translocations have become routine. There are four cytogenetic variants: primary G trisomy (47,XXorXY, G+); two types of Robertsonian translocations (46,XXorXY,D−t(DqGq)+; 46, XXorXY,G−,t(GqGq)+), and a particularly interesting group of mixoploids who have both normal and trisomic cell lines (46,XXorXY/47,XXorXY,G+). Richards has collected data on 1,103 cases and has calculated that frequencies of the different types are G+/94.4%,t(DqGq/1.7%,t(GqGq)/1.4%, mixoploids/2.5%. These figures are probably valid although the frequency of mixoploids may be too low, as most routine chromosome examinations would fail to detect all but the most obvious. Down's syndrome with normal chromosomes is unknown. Double aneuploids are relatively rare in Down's syndrome. The commonest is 48,XXY,G+ which occurs with a frequency of 1 in 11,000 live male births (Taylor and Moores). 48,XXX,G+ is very rare and 48,XYY,G+ was described by Uchida et al. (1966). Various double autosomal aneuploids, usually mixoploid, are known (Zellweger and Abbo).

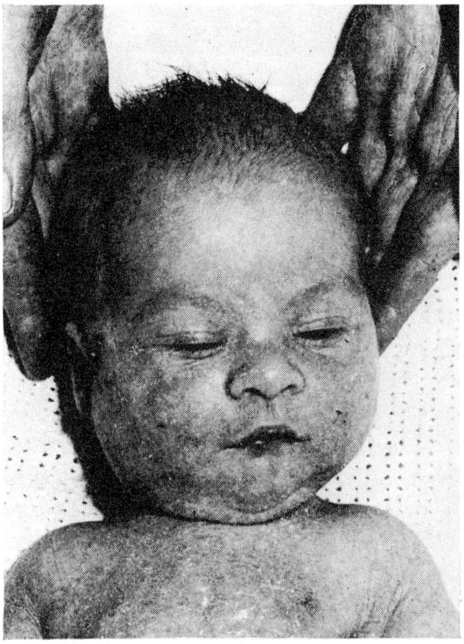

Fig. 1. Newborn boy with Down's syndrome. Note slanting palpebral fissures, epicanthic folds, short nose and cupid's bow mouth. The skin texture is coarse and dry, a frequent finding in newborn Down's 47,XY,G+.

The Robertsonian translocations are of particular importance as they may produce familial Down's syndrome (Hamerton 1968a). However, the majority would appear to be sporadic, the parents of the affected children usually having normal chromosomes (Polani et al.).

Another mechanism for direct transmission by secondary nondisjunction is mixoploidy in one parent. Penrose and Smith, from the evidence of dermatoglyphic microsigns in mothers of affected children, estimate that 10% of mothers are mixoploids. Mixoploid individuals are ascertained as doubtful cases with a 'diluted' phenotype or as phenotypically normal mothers or fathers of affected children.

A longitudinal cytogenetic study of a group of young babies with normal and trisomic cell lines shows that vigorous cell selection is taking place in the stem cells of the peripheral blood lymphocytes of young mixoploids (Taylor 1968a). In each child either the normal or trisomic cell lines may increase in proportion as the result of selection and once the direction of increase is established, this appears to be maintained (Fig. 2). A control group of 4 adult mixoploids shows no change in cell pıo-portions with time, presumably because an equilibrium has been reached.

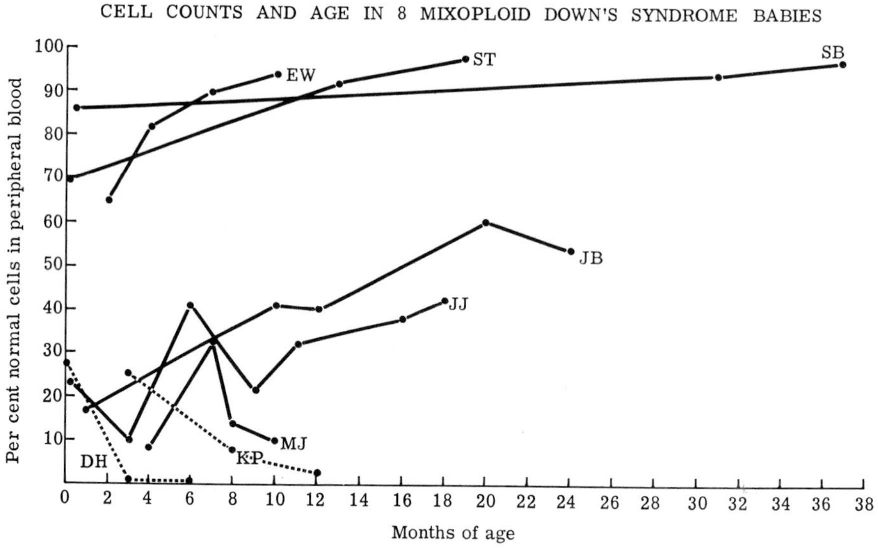

Fig. 2. Percentage of normal cells in peripheral blood with age in 8 normal/primary G trisomic mixoploid babies.

Since the extra chromosome 'G' was detected there have been numerous attempts to locate genes on it by biochemical, blood group and other studies on affected children and controls. There is much conflicting data, which has been summarised by Penrose and Smith. Leucocyte alkaline phosphatase, galactose 1-phosphate uridyl transferase and glucose-6-phosphate dehydrogenase values are all elevated in Down's syndrome, although as one of these is sex linked (G6PD) this is probably a non-specific effect.

Association between Down's syndrome and leukemia within families and in the same individuals has often been observed. The death rate from leukemia, among affected children, has been found by Holland et al. to be eighteen times that in the general population.

The dermatoglyphic features of Down's syndrome are very characteristic. There is distal t triradius on the palm resulting in a raised atd angle, an excess of ulnar loops on finger tips and often a tibial arch on the hallucal area of the sole. The frequencies of the different fingertip patterns, high atd angles and single transverse palmar creases in Down's syndrome, Edwards' syndrome, Patau's syndrome and controls are compared in Table 2. Fig. 3 shows a normal hand with the a,b,c,d and t triradii, and the four types of fingertip pattern are shown in Fig. 4. A single transverse palmar crease on one or both hands is found in 48.2% of subjects with Down's syndrome.

Trisomy of a G autosome is observed in 2.6% of spontaneous abortions (Carr). It

TABLE 2

Frequencies of fingertip patterns, a distal t-triradius and a single transverse palmar crease in the 3 autosomal trisomic syndromes and controls. (Data on Down's syndrome (DS) and controls (C) from Holt and Penrose and Smith; on Edwards' (ES) and Patau's (PS) syndromes from Taylor (unpublished).)

Fingertip patterns	Frequency %			
	ES	PS	DS	C
Arches	87.0	38.4	2.74	4.98
Ulnar loops	8.0	40.1	82.76	63.54
Radial loops	4.0	11.1	1.77	5.36
Whorls	1.0	10.2	12.13	26.12
Palms				
Distal t with atd > 57°	62.4	90.4	82.9	8.5
Single palmar crease (one or both hands)	44.6	56.2	48.2	9.3

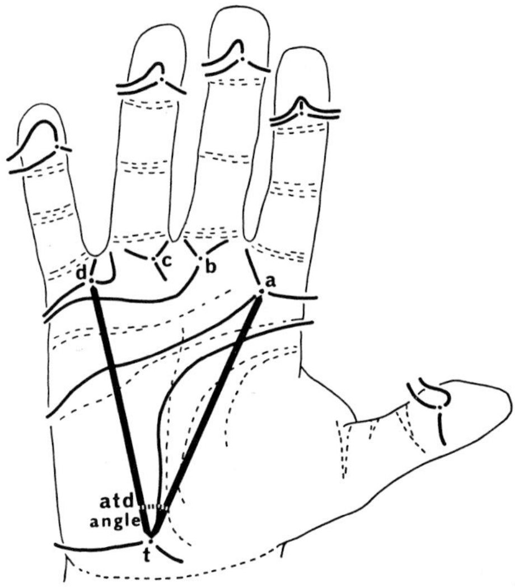

Fig. 3

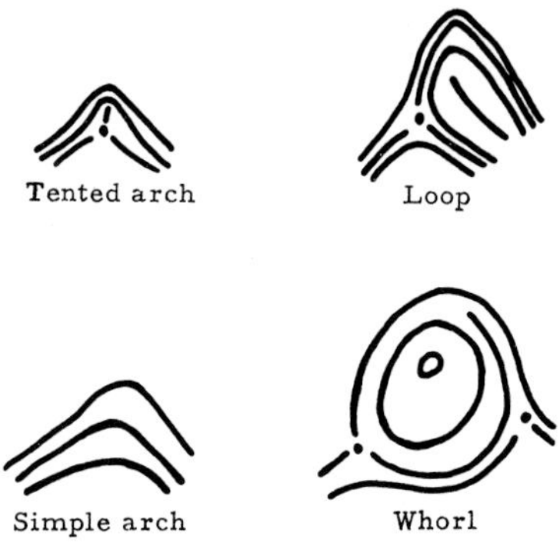

Fig. 4

Fig. 3. Diagram of a normal hand showing the a,b,c,d and t triradii.

Fig. 4. The four types of finger tip pattern, simple arch, tented arch, loop and whorl.

is not, however, certain whether this is the same chromosome which causes Down's syndrome, and if it is, why such a high proportion abort while others survive to term.

The major component in the aetiology of Down's syndrome is advanced maternal age. The mean maternal age is 32.5, but the distribution is bimodal (Fig. 5). In the maternal age dependent group there is presumably an increased frequency of non-disjunction due to ageing of the oocytes. The majority of familial Robertsonian translocations occur in the maternal age independent group. Viral infections have been implicated in the aetiology of Down's syndrome (Stoller and Collman), and clustering of Down's syndrome and sex chromosomal and other autosomal anomalies in families has often been noticed. It may be that recessive rare genes cause a predisposition to non-disjunction.

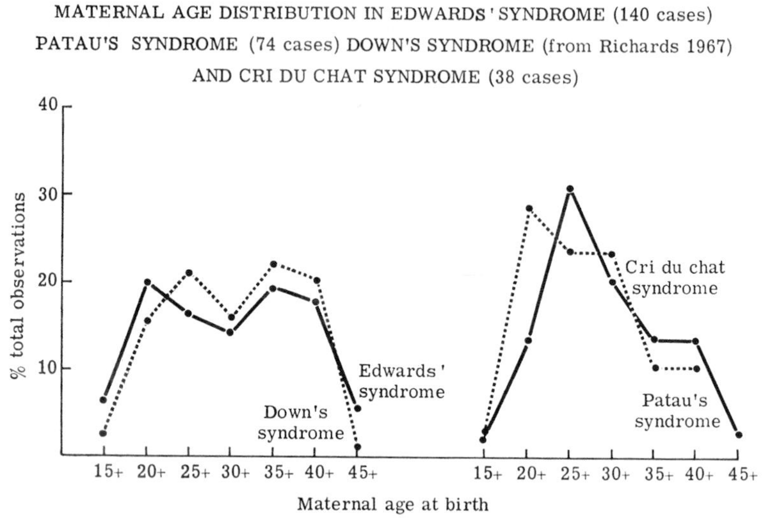

Fig. 5. Maternal age distributions in Down's syndrome, Edwards' syndrome, Patau's syndrome and cri du chat syndrome.

(b) *Edwards' syndrome: (47,XXorXY,18+)*

This condition was first described by Edwards et al., and since then some 200 cases have been reported (Weiss et al.; Taylor and Polani; Butler et al.; and Taylor 1968b). The clinical and post mortem findings in 29 cases of Edwards' and 29 cases of Patau's syndrome are compared in Table 3, and birth and survival data in Table 4 (for references see Taylor 1968b).

The birth weight is low, the infant looks premature and there may be a single umbilical artery. The main features of Edwards' syndrome are developmental retardation, serious multiple somatic anomalies, a characteristic facies and characteristic dermal ridge patterns. Survival longer than 3 months is unusual, although a few older individuals with gross physical and mental retardation, and trisomy 18, are

TABLE 3

Clinical and post mortem findings in 29 cases of Edwards' syndrome and 29 cases of Patau's syndrome (20 cases of ES and 24 cases of PS autopsied; Data from Taylor (1968b) and unpublished.)

Feature (clinical)	% ES	% PS	Feature (post mortem)	% Recorded ES	% Recorded PS
Feeding difficulty	97	92	Short dorsiflexed hallux	77	26
Jaundice	21	42	Calcaneo-valgus feet	48	7
Failure to thrive	97	88	Equino-varus feet	7	23
Retardation	97	100	Prominent calcaneus	75	33
Hypertonia	46	28	Fibular S-shaped hallucal arch	5	37
Hypotonia	41	48	Limited hip abduction	67	18
Apnoea	48	63	Abnormal shoulder abduction	12	5
Seizures	25	28	Short sternum	71	15
Presumptive deafness	29	53	Inguinal/umbilical hernia	21	39
High pitched cry	32	4	Congenital heart disease	86	76
Microcephaly	11	59	Undescended testis	100	93
Elongated skull	90	15			
Ocular hypertelorism	82	93	Ventricular septal defect	50	52
Epicanthic folds	45	52	Major atrial septal defect	39	87
Microphthalmos	32	78	Patent ductus arteriosus	59	67
Eye defect	32	86	Coarctation of the aorta	11	9
Iris colobomata	—	35	Dextraposed heart	12	17
Lowset malformed ears	89	81	Normal heart	26	22
Lowset normal ears	4	11	Horseshoe kidney	27	—
Hare lip	3	55	Pyelon duplex	7	13
Cleft palate	10	65	Polycystic renal cortex	20	30
Micrognathia	93	86	Renal anomaly	67	52
Extra nape skin	59	63	Hydronephrosis/ureter	20	17
Webbed neck	29	—	Normal renal tract	33	44
Short neck	65	81	Malrotation of intestine	21	17
Capillary haemangioma	21	73	Oesophageal atresia	—	—
Polydactyly	7	78	Tracheo-oesophageal fistula	5	—
Partial syndactyly	37	15	Thin diaphragm/eventration	33	59
Distally implanted thumb	56	15	Meckel's diverticulum	33	9
Retroflexible thumbs	50	27	Imperforate anus	—	—
Flexion deformity of fingers	93	70	Biseptate uterus	—	43
Hypoplastic toenails	67	38	Cerebral holosphere	—	—
Long hyperconvex nails	15	71	Superficially normal brain	93	25
Single palmar creases	60	64	Absent olfactory bulbs	—	71
Distal t triradius	52	77	Meningomyelocoele	10	—
Simple arches	96	29			

known. The facies is rounded or squarish with wide spaced eyes, microstomia, micrognathia and low set, often malformed ears (Fig. 6). Eye defects, particularly microphthalmia, are common. The skull may be elongated anteroposteriorly with prominence of the occipital region. There are multiple skeletal anomalies including a

TABLE 4

Birth and survival findings in Edwards' and Patau's syndromes. (Data from the literature and unpublished.)

Edwards' syndrome (trisomy 18) (153 cases)	
Mean maternal age at birth	31.7 yr
Mean paternal age at birth	34.9 yr
Mean gestation age	42.2 wk
Mean birth weight	2242.6 g = 4 lbs. 15 oz.
Mean survival in days	70.85 (variance exceeds mean)
Sex 113 ♀; 30 ♂ Actually 109,XX; 4,XXX; 27,XY; 3,XXY	
Patau's syndrome (trisomy 13) (74 cases)	
Mean maternal age at birth	31.6 yr
Mean paternal age at birth	31.9 yr
Mean gestation age	39.0 wk
Mean birth weight	2609.9 g = 5 lbs. 12 oz.
Mean survival in days	89.2 (variance exceeds mean)
Sex: 35 ♀; 29 ♂	

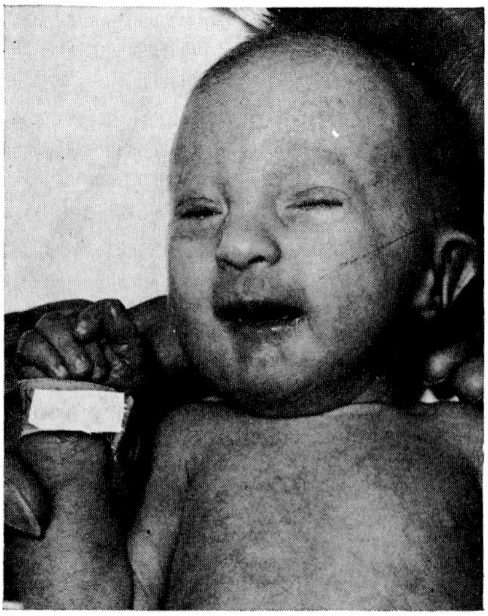

Fig. 6. Newborn girl with Edwards' syndrome. Note round face, microphthalmia, micrognathia and low set malformed ear. The hand shows the characteristic flexion deformity with axial deviation of fingers and short, distally implanted thumb. 47,XX,18+.

short sternum, and flexion contractures and deformities of joints. Severe congenital heart and renal anomalies are common. Muscle tone is abnormal.

The majority of cases are primary trisomics (47,XXorXY,18+). The identity of the trisomic chromosome was established autoradiographically by Yunis et al. A minority of cases have reciprocal translocations usually involving chromosomes of the D and E groups, and in a few families one of the parents has been shown to be a balanced heterozygote. Double sex chromosome/autosome aneuploids occur with an unexpectedly high frequency in Edwards' syndrome; out of 29 cases, one was 48,XXX, 18+ and one 48,XXY,18+. Double autosomal trisomies are known, with trisomy of E and D, or E and G chromosomes, these are rare, and are usually mixoploids (Zellweger and Abbo). Normal/trisomic mixoploids are fairly frequent – two in 29 of the author's cases, including a child who survived unusually long ($4\frac{1}{2}$ years). Rare individuals with Edwards' syndrome and with apparently normal chromosomes are presumably phenocopies. Numerous attempts to locate genes on chromosome 18 have met with no success – it appears that the major effect of the trisomic genotype is a non specific retardation of development.

The incidence of Edwards' syndrome among live births has yet to be established, however, a minimal estimate of about 1 in 7,000 live births has been obtained (Conen and Erkman 1966b; Taylor 1968b). 17–18 trisomy occurs in 0.44% of spontaneous abortions (Carr).

An unexplained anomaly in Edwards' syndrome is the abnormal sex ratio – 78% of recorded cases are female. Affected females also survive longer than males (Conen and Erkman 1966a; Taylor 1968b).

The dermatoglyphic findings in Edwards' syndrome are very characteristic, and reported cases all have simple arches on three or more digits. The percentage of digits with dermal ridge dysplasia of the finger tips is 11.5%. The frequencies of the different fingertip patterns, high atd angles and a single transverse palmar crease are presented in Table 2. A single transverse palmar crease on one or both hands occurs in 44.4% of affected children (Taylor 1968b).

The aetiology of Edwards' syndrome is unknown. A proportion of cases are born to older mothers but the maternal age independent group is larger than in Down's syndrome (Fig. 5). A seasonal incidence of births has been reported by Conen and Erkman (1966a) and by Taylor (1968b) but the condition is so rare that the data are inadequate for analysis. Mixoploidy in a parent has not been described but is a possible minor factor.

(c) *Patau's syndrome: (47,XXorXY,13+)*

This syndrome was described simultaneously with Edwards' syndrome in 1960 by Patau and his collaborators. About 80 cases have been reported including several series of cases (Taylor and Polani; Snodgrass et al.; Taylor 1968b).

Clinical, post mortem, birth and survival findings are presented in Tables 3 and 4.

The birth weight is low, birth being slightly before term. The main features are developmental retardation, very severe somatic anomalies with emphasis upon 'mid-line' defects, a characteristic facies and unusual dermatoglyphic findings. Survival beyond 3 months is rare.

The face is trapezium shaped with hypertelorism, epicanthic folds, a large flat triangular nose, a long thin mouth and micrognathia (Fig. 7). About half the cases have a hare lip and two thirds have a cleft palate. Eye defects are very common, usually microphthalmia with iris colobomata, sometimes anophthalmia which is usually associated with absence of the optic nerves. The ears are low set and malformed.

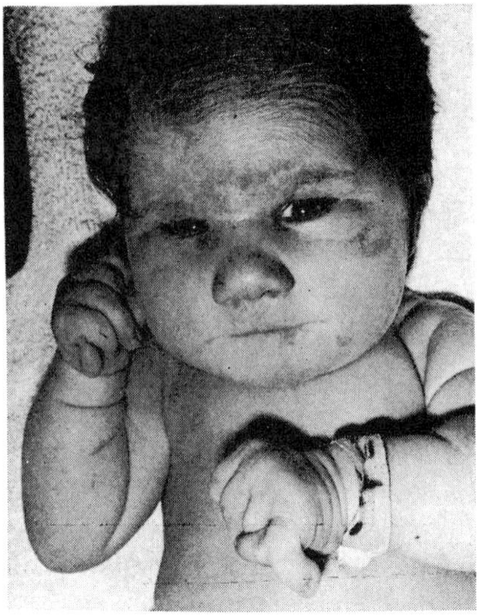

Fig. 7. Newborn girl with Patau's syndrome. Note squarish face, right microphthalmia and hypertelorism, capillary haemangiomas on face and eyelids. The mouth is long and thin. The hands show long hyperconvex fingernails and ulnar polydactyly. This patient was a mixoploid 46,XX/47,XX, 13+/48,XX,13+,13+.

Skeletal and joint anomalies are rarer than in Edwards' syndrome. Polydactyly is common and inguinal and umbilical hernias are a fairly frequent finding. Neurological studies indicate that most affected infants are deaf and probably also blind. Seizures and breath holding spells are frequent. Muscle tone is abnormal. Severe cardiac and renal anomalies are common. Arhinencephaly is a characteristic finding at post mortem, and rarely a cerebral holosphere is observed.

The majority of cases are 47,XXorXY,13+. The identity of the trisomic chromosome was first established by Buchner et al. and by Giannelli, in 1965, by autoradiographic studies. Sporadic translocations of the t(DqDq) type in which the parents have normal chromosomes occur in 4 out of 29 of the author's series of cases and with an even higher frequency (4 out of 9) in Conen and Erkman's (1966b) series. Mixoploids appear to be rarer than in Edwards' syndrome (1 in 29 in the author's series). Double aneuploids with XXY,13+;13+;G+;13+;E+ occur very rarely (Zellweger and Abbo). Occasional cases with normal chromosomes occur but these are presumptive phenocopies. No genes on chromosome 13 have been located, and abnormal findings such as persistence of embryonic and foetal haemoglobins may be attributed to retarded development in utero (Huehns et al.)

A detailed analysis of the somatic anomalies in Patau's syndrome suggests that they are established during the 5th and 6th weeks of embryogenesis (Mottet and Jensen).

The population incidence is similar to that of Edwards' syndrome (Conen and Erkman 1966b; Taylor 1968b) with a minimum estimate of about 1 in 7,000 live births. The incidence of D trisomy in spontaneous abortions is the same as G trisomy, 2.6% (Carr), but anatomic studies in some of the D trisomic foetuses do not suggest features of Patau's syndrome (Singh and Carr).

Like the other two autosomal trisomic syndromes, Patau's syndrome has characteristic dermatoglyphics. The most striking finding is that 36.7% of digits have dermal ridge dysplasia (Taylor 1968b). Among the remainder, simple arches and ulnar loops predominate (Table 2). An extremely distal t-triradius is very common and a single transverse palmar crease occurs in 66.2% of the author's series. A fibular S-shaped arch on the hallucal region of the sole is a common finding but the most typical pattern on the sole is a tibial loop in the proximal thenar region associated with an f-triradius (Penrose 1966). There is a slight excess of females among the cases reported.

The aetiology of Patau's syndrome is largely unknown. Very rarely familial transmission of the t(DqDq) translocations may lead to production of a chromosomally unbalanced child with Patau's syndrome (Hamerton 1968a). The maternal age distribution is slightly bimodal with the larger of the two groups being maternal age independent (Fig. 5). Mixoploidy in the father of an affected child is known in one case (Taylor unpublished), and is a possible minor factor in the aetiology.

(d) *Autosomal trisomy not associated with syndromes*

There are occasional reports of malformed or phenotypically normal individuals with extra chromosomes which do not appear to be structurally abnormal, but the majority of autosomal trisomies other than 13, 18, or 21 are found only in spontaneous abortions. A,B,C-group trisomies are all reported among spontaneous abortions (W.H.O. Memorandum), and have not yet been described in living patients. Normal/C trisomic mixoploids have variable malformations and occasionally survive and have also been reported in certain myeloproliferative disorders, presumably as a secondary change (Lawler et al.).

One surviving 16-trisomic has multiple congenital anomalies, and 16-trisomy occurs in 3.5% of spontaneous abortions (Carr).

Two surviving normal/F trisomic mixoploids are reported (Gagnon et al.; Mosanyi et al.) and F trisomy is also reported in spontaneous abortions.

Trisomy G (without Down's syndrome) occurs rarely among living births.

3. *Structural abnormalities*

There are six syndromes which are associated with presumptive autosomal deletions.

TABLE 5

Findings in presumptive deletion of the short arm of chromosome 4 (7 cases – 2 with autopsies; data from the literature.)

Mean maternal age at birth	26.4 yr
Mean paternal age at birth	30.4 yr
Mean gestation age	38.4 wk
Mean birth weight	1959.2 g = 4 lbs. 5 oz.
Survival: ranges from 1 day to alive at 13 yr	
Sex: 4 ♀; 3 ♂	

Feature	*% Recorded*
Feeding difficulty	67
Failure to thrive	100
Developmental retardation	100
Hypotonia	100
Apnoeic spells	33
Seizures	57
High pitched cry	20
Microcephaly	100
Ocular hypertelorism	100
Epicanthic folds	17
Iris colobomata	43
Strabismus	60
Low set malformed ears	100
Hare lip	43
Cleft palate	71
Micrognathia	67
Extra skin of nape	80
Haemangioma	60
Flexion deformity of fingers	33
Hypoplastic nails	50
Long hyperconvex nails	50
Retroflexible thumbs	20
Single palmar crease	40
Distal t-triradius	60
Simple arches on fingers	25
Dermal ridge dysplasia	75
Short dorsiflexed hallux	80
Equino-varus feet	50
Limited hip abduction	50
Congenital heart disease	50
Undescended testes	50 ♂
Hypospadias	100 ♂
Hydrocephalus	66
Ventricular septal defect	50
Atrial septal defect	50
Dextrocardia	50
Abnormal lungs	100
Renal anomaly	100
Absent kidney	50
Common mesentery	50
Superficially normal brain	100

Only two of these have names – the cri du chat syndrome, and antimongolism. The others will be described according to the chromosome groups involved. Reference to Fig. 16 in the chapter by Hamerton, indicates that each of these may have arisen from one of a number of different cytological mechanisms which may explain the variable phenotype observed. In general the mechanism of origin cannot be determined unless either the parental chromosomes are informative or meiotic studies are possible.

(a) *Short arm deletion – chromosome 4 (46,XXorXY,4p−)*

This condition was first described by Sidbury et al., and the identity of the deleted chromosome was established by autoradiography in 1965 (Wolf et al.).

Seven cases are known (Taylor 1968b). Clinical features, post mortem findings, and birth and survival data are presented in Table 5.

The birth weight is low and the impression is of prematurity. Developmental retardation and severe somatic anomalies are universal. The facies resembles that of Patau's syndrome, or of a 'midline' syndrome (Fig. 8). Survival varies from a few minutes to 13 years.

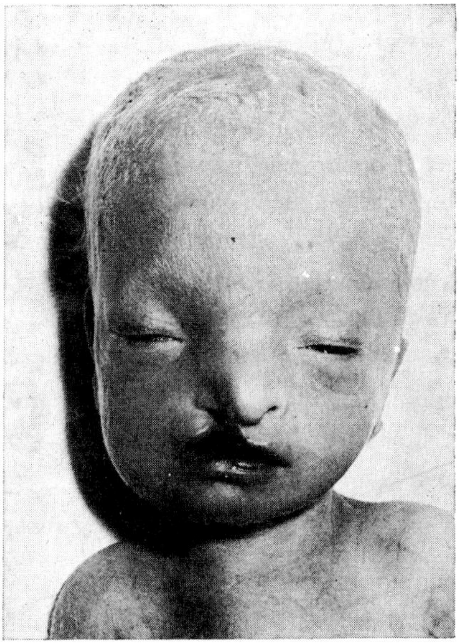

Fig. 8. Newborn boy with 4p− syndrome. Note extreme hypertelorism, very broad flat nose an unilateral hare lip. 46,XY,4p−.

Dermatoglyphic features are a raised frequency of simple arches, a distal t triradius and a single transverse palmar crease. Partial dermal ridge dysplasia occurred in 75% of affected subjects. The only estimate of population incidence is 1 in 165,000 live births (Fraser Roberts and Taylor unpublished). There is no evidence of increased maternal age, but this may not be significant in view of the small number of cases. There are no other indications as to the aetiology.

(b) *Cri du chat syndrome (46,XXorXY,5p−).*

This condition was first described by Lejeune et al. (1963), and since then about 50 cases have been published (Lejeune et al. 1964; Taylor 1967).

Clinical features and birth and survival data are presented in Table 6.

TABLE 6

Findings in cri du chat syndrome. (Presumptive deletion of the short arm of chromosome 5; 38 cases; data from the literature and unpublished.)

Mean maternal age at birth	28.50 yr
Mean paternal age at birth	31.32 yr
Mean gestation age	39.90 wk
Mean birth weight	2680.0 g = 5 lbs. 14 oz.
Survival: one case died at 23/12. Oldest survivor 13 yr	
Sex: 23 ♀; 14 ♂	

Features	*% Recorded*
Round face	71
Hypertelorism	89
Epicanthic folds	86
Antimongoloid slant to eyes	64
Strabismus	32
Eye defect	13
Malformed ears	37
Low set ears	77
Rotated ears	11
Accessory auricles	9
Microcephaly	92
Flat occiput	46
Broad nasal bridge	53
Micrognathia	67
Cleft palate	—
High pitched cry	95
Abnormal larynx	32
Feeding difficulty	45
Syndactyly	19
Hypertonia	10
Hypotonia	50
Skeletal anomalies	22
Congenital heart disease	35
Retarded growth	95
Failure to thrive	88
Oligophrenia	94 or 97
Jaundice	9
Single palmar crease	45
Distal t triradius	62
Absent c triradius	7

The major features are physical and mental retardation, an unusual high pitched cry due to laryngeal abnormalities and a characteristic facies. The birth weight is low and gestation time is normal. The face (Fig. 9) is rounded with hypertelorism, epicanthic folds and low set ears. There are a variety of minor somatic anomalies (Table 6). Muscular hypotonia is common. This condition is not incompatible with survival, and there is a report of only one death, at 23 months, from pneumonia, and the oldest survivor is 13 years old.

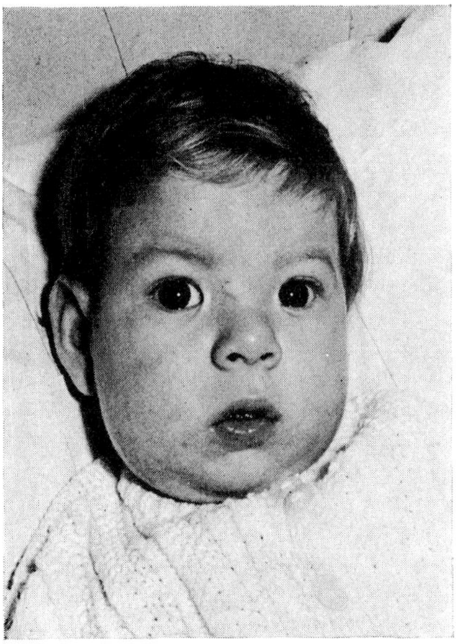

Fig. 9. Nine-month-old boy with cri du chat syndrome. Note the oval face, wide spaced eyes and epicanthic folds. Not a particularly abnormal face. 46,XY,5p−.

In most cases both parents have normal chromosomes but in a few, the effective deletion results from the segregation of a reciprocal translocation identified in one parent (Lejeune et al. 1965; Laurent and Robert). In the family described by Laurent and Robert, there are three affected sibs (46, XY, Bp−mat) and another abnormal sib with a presumptive partial trisomy of the B short arm (46,XX,Cq+mat). The mother has a balanced reciprocal translocation, 46,XX,t(Bp−;Cq+).

The population incidence of cri du chat syndrome is unknown. It appears to be considerably rarer than the autosomal trisomies. No cases have been identified in an attempted total ascertainment of about 165,000 live births in South East England (Fraser Roberts and Taylor unpublished).

The sex proportion is abnormal with 62% of cases being females. Abnormal dermatoglyphic findings include a distal t triradius in about two thirds of the cases and a single transverse palmar crease in about one half. The aetiology of the cri du chat syndrome is unknown. Maternal age is not raised (mean 28.5 years) (Fig. 5).

(c) *Long arm deletion – D chromosome (46,XXorXY,Dq−)*

This was originally described by Laurent et al.; 2 further cases were reported by Mikelsaar and by Taylor (1968b). The three affected infants resemble Patau's syndrome. Clinical features and birth and survival data are presented in Table 7. Birth weight is low, with birth just before term. The face is similar to that of a child with Patau's syndrome, but without a hare lip or cleft palate. Microphthalmia, skeletal abnormalities and congenital heart disease were present in all three infants. The longest survivor lived 3½ months. Two of the three cases had a single palmar crease and all three had a distal t triradius. The two cases in whom finger prints were recorded had an excess of whorls. All the cases had parents with normal chromosomes. Aetiology is unknown and maternal age is not raised but the data is too small for significant assessment. Mikelsaar's case was a mixoploid with a normal cell line, so presumably the origin of the deletion was post-zygotic in this instance.

TABLE 7

Findings in presumptive deletion of the long arm of a D chromosome (3 cases; data from the literature.)

Mean maternal age at birth	27.5 yr
Mean paternal age at birth (1 case)	35.0 yr
Mean gestation age	37.3 wk
Mean birth weight	2473.0 g = 5 lbs. 7 oz.

Survival: stillborn, 17 days and 3½ months respectively.
Sex: 2 ♀; 1 ♂

Feature	*% Recorded*
Hypertelorism	67
Epicanthic folds	33
Microphthalmos	100
Iris colobomata	33
Malformed ear pinnae	67
Low set ears	33
High arched palate	33
Micrognathia	100
Skeletal anomalies	100
Equino-varus feet	67
Congenital heart disease	100
Failure to thrive	100
Developmental retardation	100
Single palmar crease	67
Distal t triradius	100
Excess whorls on fingertips	100

(d) *Short arm deletion – chromosome 18 (46,XXorXY,18p−)*

This syndrome was first described by de Grouchy et al. (1963). Fourteen cases are now known, with excellent summaries by de Grouchy et al. (1966) and Migeon.

The main features are mental retardation, retarded growth and relatively minor somatic anomalies. Clinical features and birth and survival data are summarised in Table 8. The oldest survivor is 33 years of age. There are no characteristic dermatoglyphic findings. Many of the cases have clinical features of the Status Bonnevie-Ullrich. As with many other autosomal syndromes there is an excess of females (64 %).

TABLE 8

Findings in presumptive deletion of the short arm of chromosome 18 (14 cases; data from the literature.)

Mean maternal age at birth	33.2 yr
Mean paternal age at birth	36.0 yr
Mean gestation age	39.0 wk
Mean birth weight	2823.3 g = 6 lbs. 4 oz.
Survival: range from 25 min to alive at 33 yr	
Sex: 9 ♀; 5 ♂	
Feature	*% Recorded*
Hypertelorism	38
Epicanthic folds	38
Strabismus	21
Ptosis	21
Cyclopia	7
Eye defects	36
Malformed ear pinnae	36
Low set ears	28
Micrognathia	28
Microcephaly	23
Abnormal limbs	43
Webbed neck	31
Retarded growth	91
Mental retardation	92

All the cases are sporadic in origin except those reported by Uchida et al. (1965), who described a mixoploid (46,XX/46,XX,18p—) affected mother with two affected children.

Maternal age at birth is raised with a mean value of 33.2 years.

(e) *Long arm deletion – chromosome 18 (46,XXorXY,18q—)*
This condition was first described by de Grouchy et al. (1964). Eleven cases are now known (Wertelecki et al.). Clinical features and birth and survival data are presented in Table 9. The main features are mental retardation, microcephaly, dysplasia of the mid-facial region, eye defects and retarded growth. Birth weight is low and birth is at term. Muscular hypotonia and congenital heart defects are frequent findings. The condition is not incompatible with life, the oldest patient surviving is 10 years of age.

TABLE 9

Findings in presumptive deletion of part of the long arm of chromosome 18 (11 cases).

Mean maternal age at birth	29.8 yr
Mean paternal age at birth	34.0 yr
Mean gestation age	38.0 wk
Mean birth weight	2688.0 g = 5 lbs. 15 oz.
Survival: oldest alive at 10 yr	
Sex: 7 ♀; 4 ♂	
Feature	*% Recorded*
Mid-facial dysplasia	82
Microcephaly	100
Eye defect	82
Nystagmus	70
Malformed ear pinnae	100
Hearing defect	50
Long thumbs	29
Hypotonia	64
Mental retardation	100
Growth retardation	90
Congenital heart disease	50
Excess of whorls on fingertips (>25%)	89

The only consistent dermatoglyphic finding is an excess of whorls on fingertips – a finding only paralleled in the Dq—syndrome (see above).

All the cases are sporadic in origin, except one in which the mother of the proband is a balanced translocation heterozygote (46,XX,t(18q—;Gq+) (Law and Masterson). Maternal age at birth is slightly raised, otherwise the aetiology is unknown.

(f) *'Antimongolism' (46,XXorXY,Gq—orGr;or45,XXorXY,G—)*

This condition was first described by Lejeune et al. in 1964. Seven cases are now known, and have been summarised by Al-Aish et al. Clinical findings and birth data are given in Table 10.

The birth weight is low and birth is at term. Major findings are developmental retardation, failure to thrive and multiple somatic anomalies. The face is abnormal (Fig. 10), with eye defects, low set malformed ears and micrognathia. The nasal bridge is unusually prominent. Skeletal anomalies, pyloric stenosis and cardiac defects are common. None of the cases described has normal muscle tone, all but one have hypertonia. Thrombocytopaenia occurs in about half the cases. The oldest survivor is 6 years old.

There are several cytogenetic variants: Gq—, Reisman et al., Gr, Hoefnagel et al., Gr/G—mixoploids, Lejeune et al. (1964), Challacombe and Taylor, and apparent monosomics, G—, Thorburn and Johnson, Hall et al. and Al-Aish et al.

Until recently autosomal monosomy in man was thought to be incompatible with

TABLE 10

Findings in 'antimongolism' (7 cases; data from the literature).

Mean maternal age at birth	23.4 yr
Mean paternal age at birth	28.8 yr
Mean gestation age	40.1 wk
Mean birth weight	2479.68 g = 5 lbs. 7 oz.
Survival: oldest alive at 6 yr	
Sex: 3 ♀; 4 ♂	
Feature	*% Recorded*
Feeding difficulty	86
Jaundice	14
Failure to thrive	100
Developmental retardation	100
Hypertonia	86
Hypotonia	14
Cataracts/other eye defects	57
Hypertelorism	71
Cleft palate	14
High arched palate	43
Low set malformed ears	86
Micrognathia	72
Prominent nasal bridge	72
Flexion deformity of fingers	50
Rocker bottom feet	29
Inguinal hernia	43
Undescended testes	100 ♂
Hypospadias	75 ♂
Nail dystrophia	28
'Spoon' nails	14
Skeletal abnormalities	86
Pyloric stenosis	43
Congenital heart disease	57
Distal t triradius	14
Single palmar crease	14
Thrombocytopaenia	43

life and had not even been reported in spontaneous abortions. Three cases of antimongolism appear to be fully monosomic but the possibility of mixoploidy with the other line containing an unstable ring chromosome must be entertained, although in the study of Al-Aish et al. the authors failed to demonstrate mixoploidy in blood, skin or bone marrow.

It is rather surprising that there are no characteristic dermatoglyphic findings. The chromosome involved cannot be identified with certainty as the same one as in Down's syndrome although the impression is that the clinical features are antithetic to those seen in Down's syndrome.

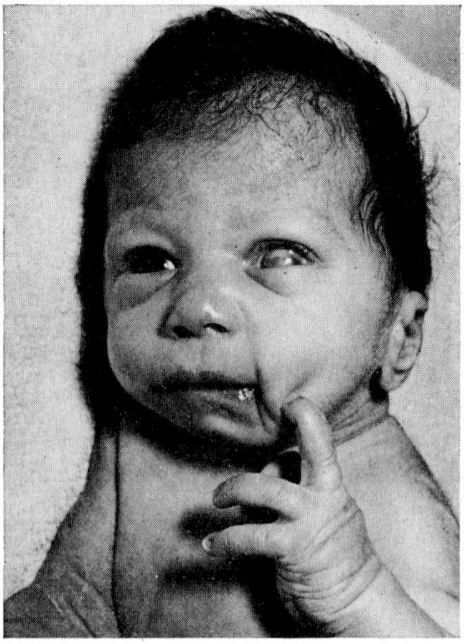

Fig. 10. Three-week-old boy with antimongolism. Note the wide spaced eyes with bilateral corneal opacities, prominent nasal bridge, low set malformed ear and marked micrognathia. This patient was a mixoploid. 45,XY,G−/46,XY,Gr.

All the cases were sporadic in origin. Maternal age is not raised and there are no other indications as to the aetiology.

TABLE 11

Chromosomes involved in 55 reciprocal translocations in man, according to group

Chromosome group	Proportion total length*	Number of chromosomes involved Obs.	Exp.[f]	X^2
A (1–3)	0.246	15	27.06	5.37
B (4–5)	0.127	20	13.97	2.60
C (6–12)	0.347	31	38.17	1.35
D (13–15)	0.106	22**	11.66	9.16
E (16–18)	0.091	13	10.01	0.89
F (19–20)	0.049	1	5.39	3.58
G (21–22)	0.035	8**	3.85	4.47
	Total	110	110.11	27.42
			d.f. = 6 $P < 0.0005$	

* Based on combined Denver and London figures.

** Excluding Robertsonian translocations.

[f] Calculated on assumption of random breakage and rearrangement distributed according to relative length of the chromosome group (column 2).

(g) *Structural anomalies not associated with syndromes*

There is a great variety of structural anomalies, usually associated with multiple congenital abnormalities, including ring chromosomes, deletions and additional atypical monocentric chromosomes. Translocations occur in the general population with a frequency of 0.5% (Court Brown et al.), and many of the abnormal individuals with structural chromosome anomalies are the unbalanced progeny of balanced heterozygotes, or the result of sporadic events during gametogenesis. Hamerton (1968b) has collected and analysed data on 55 familial reciprocal translocations. Their distribution within the chromosome groups is summarised in Table 11 (from Hamerton 1968b). The phenotype of the 55 probands and distribution of chromosomally balanced and unbalanced relatives is presented in Table 12.

4. *Comments and conclusions*

In some plant and animal species the theoretical complement of trisomics is realised, for example in *Datura* where all twelve possible trisomics are viable, phenotypically distinct and fertile (Blakeslee). In man trisomy of the smallest chromosome causes Down's syndrome, in which condition the life expectancy is considerably reduced and proven fertility extremely rare. Trisomy 18 and trisomy 13 are virtually lethal and full trisomy of F, C, B, and A group chromosomes, with the exception of the X-chromosome, occurs only among spontaneous abortions. Finally, even small presumptive deletions which are probably duplication-deletion complexes produce mental retardation and severe somatic anomalies which may prove lethal.

The frequency of balanced reciprocal translocations in the general population is about 3 per 1,000 adults, and these rearrangements provide a mechanism for karyotypic change. The stability of the human karyotype results probably not from a lower frequency of rearrangements than those which are found in other mammalian groups but more likely from the extremely low level of inbreeding which occurs in human populations, which Darlington has termed the 'incest taboo', and which effectively prevents the establishment of rearranged homozygotes.

The phenotype of any individual is produced by the genotype and its interaction with the intra-uterine environment. The majority of individuals with chromosome abnormalities have an abnormal phenotype, presumably largely as a result of their abnormal genotype. The data on the intra-uterine environment in such cases is small but there are indications that it may be abnormal. There is a raised frequency of abnormal pregnancies, threatened abortions, abnormal placentae and single umbilical arteries associated with these conditions.

Data on the genotype are also limited, but a number of loci, mainly blood groups and blood or tissue enzymes, have been tested. Anomalous inheritance of Xg in a child with Edwards' syndrome and a child with Patau's syndrome has been described (Noades et al.) but there are no other reports of anomalous inheritance in the autosomal abnormalities.

TABLE 12

A summary of cytogenetic and family data, and phenotypic effects of 55 reciprocal translocations. For Hamerton (1968b)

No.	Translocation	Chromosome imbalance in proband	Balanced heterozygote relati
62	t(2p−;3?+)	2pdup;3?del	M, MGF, S
33	t(2q−;3?+)	2qdup;3?del	M, A, U, MGM, MGA
13	t(2p+;Bq−)	?Balanced	F
64	t(3?−;Bp+)	3?dup;Bpdel	13 confirmed herozygote
14	t(2p−;Bp+)	?Balanced	M.S
10, 11	t(1?−;Cq+)	Balanced	F, A, PGM
16	t(1?−;Cp+)	1?dup;Cpdel	F
66	t(1?−;Cq+)	Balanced	M, 2S
6	t(3?−;Cq+)	3?dup;Cqdel	M, S
20	t(3?+;Cq−	Balanced	M, A, MGF
25	t(2p−;?C?+)	Balanced	F, S, N
17	t(3?−;Gp+)		M.2A, 2U, S, Co.
29	t(1?−;Gq+	Balanced	M. MGM, MGA, MGGM
60	t(4p+;5q−	?4pdel;?5qdup	M,2A, Co.
16	t(Bq+;Cp−)	Bqdel;Cpdup	F
34	t(Bp+;Cq−)	Balanced	F, U, PGF, S
45	t(Bq+;Cq−)	Balanced	Ch.
10, 11	t(Bq+;Cq−)	Bqdel;Cqdup	M
44	t(Bp−;Cp+)	Bpdel;Cpdup	F
31	t(Bp−;Cq+)	1.Bpdel;Cqdup(3) 2.Bpdup;Cqdel(1)	M
49	t(Bq+;Dq−)	Bqdup;Dqdup	M, S
37	t(Bp−;Dq+)	1.(Bpdel;Dqdup) 2.(Bpdup;Dqdel)	M, A, MGF
23	t(Bq−;Dq+)	Balanced	M
1	t(Bp−;Dp+)	Bpdup;Dpsdel	M, MGM, 3MGA, 2U, 3A
30	t(Bp−;Dp+)	Bpdel;Dpdup	F
53	t(Bq−;Ep+)	Balanced	M, U, MGM, S
18	t(Bq−;Eq+)	Bqdup;Eqdel	F, PGF, S
10	t(Bq−;Eq+)	Balanced	2Ch.
21	t(Bp−;Gp+)	Bpdup;Gpdel	M
40	t(Cq−;Cp+)	Cdup;Cdel	F, PGM, A, S
34	t(Cq−;Cq+)	Balanced	M
58	t(Cq−;Cq+)	Cqdup;Cqdel	M
15	t(Cq−;Dq+)	Cqdup;Dqdel	M, S
10, 11	t(Cp−;Dq+)	Balanced	M

...tives with imbalance	Phenotype of proband
	Upslanted eyes, micrognathia, small nose, cardiac murmur, umbilical hernia, hypertonia, 8/10 simple arches on fingertips
	Cebocephaly, malformed ears, micrognathia, cleft palate, heart murmur, 6/10 simple arches
	Retardation, hypertonia, microcephaly seizures, normal dermatoglyphics
...eral abnormal infants studied	Hare lip, cleft palate, eye defects, low set ears, polydactyly, heart murmur, renal abnormality
	Normal
	Normal except for carcinoma
	Multiple skeletal anomalies, severe mental retardation
	Syndactyly, polydactyly, asymmetry, mental retardation
	Retarded growth, mental retardation, cardiac anomaly
	Von Recklinghausen's disease, kyphoscoliosis
	Normal
...Co.	Deep set eyes, pug nose, mental retardation, features of gargoylism
	Down's syndrome
	Microcephaly, malformed ears, joint abnormalities, single kidney
	Minor somatic anomalies, mental retardation
	Minor somatic anomalies, mental retardation
	Normal
	Severe congenital malformations, growth and mental retardation
	Cri du chat syndrome
	3 sibs with cri du chat syndrome, 1 sib with mental retardation
	Choanal atresia, cardiac anomaly, growth and mental retardation
	Retarded growth, mental retardation, microphthalmia in proband and one sib, 2 sibs with cri du chat syndrome
	Normal
	Facial asymmetry, eye defects, talipes, pyloric stenosis
	Cri du chat syndrome
	Coloboma, micrognathia, and dental abnormalities
	Minor somatic anomalies, odd facies
	Normal
	Omphalocoele, anal atresia, odd facies, eye defects, skeletal abnormalities, hypotonia, failure to thrive
	Hare lip, cleft palate, microcephaly, heart and renal abnormalities
...band has had 4 2/12 ...rtions	Normal
	Eye defects, skeletal anomalies, simian creases, juvenile hypothyroidism
	Eye defects, flat nasal bridge, low set ears, renal anomaly, mental retardation
	Normal

TABLE 12 (*cont.*)

No.	Translocation	Chromosome imbalance in proband	Balanced heterozygote relati[v
61	t(Cp+;Dq−)	Cpdel;Dqdup	F, U, PGF, S
50	t(Cp+;Dq−)	Cpdup;Dpqdup	M
26	t(Cq−;Dq+)	Cqdup;Dqdup	M, A, MGF, MGA, Co.
59	t(Cp+;Dq−)	Balanced	F
57	t(Cq−s+;Dp+s−)	Cpdup;Dpdup	M
48	t(Cp−;Dq+)	Balanced	M
52	t(Cp−;Eq+)	Cpdup;Eqdel	F
56	t(Cq−;18q+)	Cpdup;18qdel	F, A, PGM, S
35	t(Cp−;F?+)	Cpdup;F?del	M, S
54	t(Cq−;Gp+)	Cqdup;Gpsdel	M, S
41	t(Cq−;Gq+)	Gpqdup;Gqdel	M, U, A, MGM
27	t(Dq+;Dq−)	Dpqdup	M, 2A, 2U, MGF
55	t(Dp+;16q−)	Dpdup;16pqdup	M(mosaic)
11	t(Dp−s−;18p+s+)	Balanced	2S
2	t(Dq−;17q+)	Dpqdup;Eqdup	M, MGF
24	t(Dq−;Ep+)	1. Dpqdup;Eqdup 2. Dqdup;Eqdel	M, S
46	t(Dp+;Ep−)	Dpsdel;Epdup	F, PGM, S
32	G−t(Dq+)	Dqdel;Gqdup	M, 2U, MGM
12	t(Dp−;Gp+)	Balanced	M, U, S
36	t(17p+;18p−)	17p?dup;18pdel	M, A, MGF
63	t(18q−;Gq+)	18qdup;−Gqdel	M, A, MGF, MGA, Co.,2

tives with imbalance	Phenotype of proband
	Retarded growth, haemangiomata of face, polydactyly, V.S.D., mental retardation
	Deepset eyes, toe syndactyly, mental retardation
	Congenital malformations, mental retardation
	Down's syndrome
	No details
	Aplasia of corpus callosum, aortic atresia, aplasia of radius, polycystic kidneys, odd facies
	Features resembling Edwards' syndrome
orted and 1 mal- ed sib	Optic atrophy, iris heterochromia, over-riding 4th toes, hernia, cardiac murmur, and mental retardation
	Growth and mental retardation, skeletal abnormalities, odd facies
	Abnormal face and hands
	No details
eral abortions in y	Seizures, minor somatic anomalies, mental retardation, 10 simple arches on fingertips
ther spontaneous tions	Spontaneously aborted foetus
	Normal
	Seizures, dolicocephaly, minor somatic anomalies, mental retardation
	1. Microcephaly, haemangiomata, hernias, mental retardation
	2. Retardation, odd facies, multiple anomalies
	Odd facies, low set ears, hydronephrosis, V.S.D., coarctation of the aorta, agenesis of most of corpus callosum and absent olfactory nerves
	Down's syndrome
	Congenital heart disease
	18p−syndrome
	Failure to thrive, hypertonia, odd facies, skeletal, renal and cardiac anomalies, mental retardation

ions: M = mother; F = father; PGM, MGM = paternal/maternal grandmother; PGF, MGF = naternal grandfather; MGA = maternal great aunt; A = aunt; U = uncle; MGGM = maternal ndmother; Co. = cousin; Ch = child; S = sib.

The most obvious effect of the trisomic and the other abnormal genotypes is interference in the timing of embryogenesis. There is a tendency to a low birth weight associated with a normal or increased gestation time resulting in infants who are 'small for dates'. They appear premature, and suffer from some of the illnesses often found in premature normal infants such as respiratory distress syndrome and neonatal jaundice. Mottet and Jensen have studied infants with Patau's syndrome, and conclude that the somatic anomalies are initiated during the 5th and 6th weeks of embryogenesis. Naeye has studied prenatal organ and cellular growth in Down's, Edwards' and Patau's syndromes and controls. He concludes that in all three trisomic syndromes infants are reduced in size at birth due to retarded intra-uterine growth and that the basis of this growth retardation is a subnormal number of cells in many body organs.

Haemoglobin studies in Edwards' and Patau's syndromes show rare persistence of embryonic haemoglobin to the time of birth. Foetal haemoglobin levels are high in all newborns, so persistence of foetal haemoglobin can only be demonstrated in babies who survive the neo-natal period. In two children with Edwards' syndrome, both 3 months old, foetal haemoglobin values were 20% and 54%, and in a child with Patau's syndrome sampled at 2 months and 3 months, the values were 50% and 31%. These results are presumably due to delay in the switching off of the syntheses of embryonic and foetal haemoglobins and in the switching on of adult haemoglobin synthesis.

It is difficult to compare phenotypes between and even within the chromosome abnormalities as many cases resemble children with multiple congenital abnormalities of different or unknown aetiology. Down's, Edwards' and Patau's syndromes are sufficiently distinctive to be valid syndromes, but some if not all of the presumptive deletion syndromes may disappear with greater knowledge.

In Edwards', Patau's and the cri du chat syndromes there is an excess of females amongst cases reported and in the two former conditions females survive longer than males. Furthermore, there is also an excess of females among aborted 17–18 trisomic foetuses. It is possible that male foetuses with certain abnormal chromosome complements selectively fail to implant. Another possible mechanism is gametic selection; work on the T-locus of the mouse has shown that the genotype of the egg may influence the sex of the sperm which is able to fertilise it (Braden and Weiler). If gametic selection is to be implicated, this presupposes that the egg is the chromosomally abnormal gamete and the tendency to a raised maternal age in these conditions offers some evidence for this. It is interesting that in Down's syndrome the sex ratio is normal.

With the exception of those instances in which one parent is a mixoploid or a balanced translocation heterozygote, the only indication as to aetiology is raised maternal age. Jacobs et al. and Hamerton et al. have demonstrated reduced mitotic efficiency with age and although there is no evidence of reduced meiotic efficiency with age in man, recently Henderson and Edwards have shown a reduction in chiasma frequency with age in female mice.

A variety of other agents such as ionising radiation, viral infection and social class have been implicated in the aetiology of chromosome abnormalities but the role of none of these has been established (Day).

A large number of autosomal genetic markers are known, many of them polymorphic, thus detailed studies of increasing numbers of cases and type of chromosome abnormality will eventually enable the location of some of the autosomal genes.

Acknowledgements

I am grateful to Professor P.E.Polani for reading the manuscript and to the following clinicians for referring the patients illustrated: Dr. M.Dynski-Klein, Dr. O.D. Fisher, Dr. T.P.Mann, Dr. T.E.Oppé, Dr. A.Robinson, and Dr. I.G.Wickes. The Medical Illustration Department, Guy's Hospital, prepared Figs. 2 and 5.

References

AL-AISH, M.S., F.DE LA CRUZ, L.A.GOLDSMITH, J.VOLPE, G.MELLA and J.C.ROBINSON: Autosomal monosomy in man – complete monosomy G (21–22) in a four and one half year old mentally retarded girl. New Engl. J. Med. 277 (1967) 777.

BLAKESLEE, A.F.: Genetics of *Datura*. Verh. V. Internat. Kong. Vererb. 1 (1928) 117.

BRUSHFIELD, T.: Mongolism. Brit. J. Child. Dis. 21 (1924) 241.

BRADEN, A.W.H. and H.WEILER: Transmission ratios at the T-locus in the mouse; inter- and intra-male heterogeneity Australian J. Biol. Sci. 17 (1964) 921.

BUCHNER, T., R.A.PFEIFFER and E.STUPPERICH: Reduplikationsverhalten der Chromosomen der Gruppe D (13–15) und Identifikation des Extrachromosoms bei Trisomie D. Klin. Wochschr. 43 (1965) 1062.

BUTLER, L.J., G.J.A.I.SNODGRASS, N.E.FRANCE, L.SINCLAIR and A.RUSSELL: E (16–18) trisomy syndrome: Analysis of 13 cases. Arch. Disease Childhood 40 (1965) 600.

CARR, D.H.: Chromosome anomalies as a cause of spontaneous abortion. Am. J. Obstet. Gynecol. 97 (1967) 283.

CARTER, C.O. and D.MACCARTHY: Incidence of mongolism and its diagnosis in the newborn. Brit. J. Soc. Med. 5 (1951) 83.

CHALLACOMBE, D.N. and A.I.TAYLOR: Monosomy for a G autosome. Arch. Disease Childhood 44 (1969) 113.

CHICAGO CONFERENCE: Standardisation in human cytogenetics. Birth Defects Original Article Series II. National Foundation New York (1966).

COLLMAN, R.D. and A.STOLLER: A life table for mongols in Victoria, Australia. J. Mental Deficiency Res. 7 (1963) 53.

CONEN, P.E. and B.ERKMAN: Frequency and occurrence of chromosomal syndromes II. E-trisomy. Am. J. Human. Genet. 18 (1966a) 387.

CONEN, P.E. and B.ERKMAN: Frequency and occurrence of chromosomal syndromes. I D-trisomy. Am. J. Human Genet. 18 (1966b) 374.

CONEN, P.E., B.ERKMAN and C.METAXOTOU: The 'D' syndrome. Report of 4 trisomic and one D/D translocation case. Amer. J. Diseases Children 111 (1966) 236.

COURT BROWN, W.M., K.E.BUCKTON, P.A.JACOBS, I.M.TOUGH, E.V.KUENSSBERG and J.D.E.KNOX: Chromosome studies on adults. Eugenics Lab. Memoirs (1966) 42.

DAY, R.W.: The epidemiology of chromosome aberrations. Am. J. Human Genet. 18 (1966) 70.

DUNSDON, M.I., C.O.CARTER and R.M.C.HUNTLEY: Upper end of range of intelligence in mongolism. Lancet 1 (1960) 565.

EDWARDS, J.H., D.G.HARNDEN, A.H.CAMERON, V.M.CROSSE and O.H.WOLFFE: A new trisomic syndrome. Lancet 1 (1960) 787.

EVANS, P.R.: Cardiac anomalies in mongolism Brit. Heart J. 12 (1950) 258.

GAGNON, J., L.ARCHAMBAULT, J.R.DUCHARNIE and N.KATYK-LONGTIN: Résultats preliminaires sur une étude cytogénétique d'une famille affectée de nephropathie. Rev. Can. Biol. 22 (1963) 133.

GIANNELLI, F.: Autoradiographic identification of the D (13–15) chromosome responsible for D_1 trisomic Patau's syndrome. Nature 208 (1965) 669.

DE GROUCHY, J., J.BONNETTE and CH.SALMON: Délétion du bras court du chromosome 18. Ann. Génét. 9 (1966) 19.

DE GROUCHY, J., M.LAMY, S.THIEFFRY, M.ARTHUIS and CH.SALMON: Compt. Rend. 256 (1963) 1028.

DE GROUCHY, J., P.ROYER, CH.SALMON, and M.LAMY: Délétion partielle des bras longs du chromosome 18. Pathol. Biol. Semaine Hôp. 12 (1964) 579.

HALL, B.: Mongolism in newborns; a clinical and cytogenetic study. Lund, Berlingska Baktryckeriet (1964).

HALL, B., K.FREDGA and N.SVENNINGSEN: A case of monosomy G? Hereditas 57 (1967) 356.

HAMERTON, J.L.: Robertsonian translocations in man: Evidence for prezygotic selection. Cytogenetics 7 (1968a) (in press).

HAMERTON, J.L.: Reciprocal translocations in man. In: C.D.Darlington and K.R.Lewis, eds.: Chromosomes today, Vol. 2. (1968b) (in press).

HAMERTON, J.L., A.I.TAYLOR, R.ANGELL and V.M.MCGUIRE: Chromosome investigations of a small isolated human population; chromosome abnormalities and distribution of chromosome counts according to age and sex among the population of Tristan da Cunha. Nature 206 (1965) 1232.

HAYWARD, M.D. and B.D.BOWER: The chromosomal constitution of the Sturge-Weber syndrome. Lancet 1 (1961) 558.

HENDERSON, S.A. and R.G.EDWARDS: Chiasma frequency and maternal age in mammals. Nature 218 (1968) 22.

HOEFNAGEL, D., T.M.SCHROEDER, K.BENIRSCHKE and F.H.ALLEN, JR.: A child with a group G ring chromosome. Humangenetik 4 (1967) 52.

HOLLAND, W.W., R.DOLL and C.O.CARTER: Mortality from leukaemia and other cancers among patients with Down's syndrome (mongols) and among their parents. Brit. J. Cancer 16 (1962) 177.

HOLT, S.B.: Fingerprint patterns in mongolism. Ann. Hum. Genet. 27 (1964) 279.

HUENS, E.R., F.HECHT, J.V.KEIL and A.G.MOTULSKY: Developmental haemoglobin anomalies in a chromosomal triplication: D_1 trisomy syndrome. Proc. Natl. Acad. Sci. U.S. 51 (1964) 89.

JACOBS, P.A., M.BRUNTON, W.M.COURT BROWN, R.DOLL and H.GOLDSTEIN: Change of human chromosome count distributions with age: evidence for a sex difference. Nature 197 (1963) 1080.

JENKINS, R.L.: Etiology of mongolism. Am. J. Diseases Children 45 (1933) 506.

LANGDON DOWN, J.: Observations on an ethnic classification of idiots. Clin. Lectures and Reports, London Hospital 3 (1866) 259.

LAURENT, C., J.B.COTTON, Z.NIVELEN and M.TH.FREYCEN: Délétion partielle du bras long d'un chromosome du group (13–15)Dq–. Ann. Génét. 10 (1967) 25.

LAURENT, C. and J.M.ROBERT: Étude génétique et clinique d'une famille de sept enfants dans laquelle trois sujets sont atteint de la 'maladie du cri du chat'. Ann. Génét. 9 (1966) 113.

LAW, E.M. and J.G.MASTERSON: Partial deletion of chromosome 18. Lancet 2 (1966) 1137.

LAWLER, S.D., H.E.M.KAY and M.S.C.BIRBECK: Marrow dysplasia with C trisomy and anomalies of the granulocyte nuclei. J. Clin. Pathol. 19 (1966) 214.

LEWIS, F.J.W., J.M.HYMAN, J.MACTAGGART and R.H.POULDING: Trisomy of autosome 16. Nature 199 (1963) 1404.

LEJEUNE, J., R.BERGER, M.RETHORE, L.ARCHAMBAULT, H.JÉRÔME, S.THIEFFRY, J.AICARDI, M.BROYER, J.LAFOURCADE, J.CRUVEILLIER and R.TURPIN: Monosomie partielle pour un petit acrocentrique. Compt. Rend. 259 (1964) 4187.

LEJEUNE, J., M.GAUTIER, J.LAFOURCADE, B.BERGER and R.TURPIN: Délétion partielle du bras court du chromosome 5 – cinquième cas de syndrome du cri du chat. Ann. Génét. 7 (1964) 7.

LEJEUNE, J., M.GAUTIER and R.TURPIN: Les chromosomes humains en culture de tissus. Compt. Rend. 256 (1959) 602.

LEJEUNE J., J.LAFOURCADE, R.BERGER and M.O.RETHORE: Maladie du cri du chat et sa reciproque. Ann. Génét. 8 (1965) 11.

LEJEUNE, J., J.LAFOURCADE, R.BERGER, J.VIALATTE, M.BOESWILLWALD, P.SEVINGE and R.TURPIN: Trois cas de délétion partielle du bras court d'un chromosome 5. Compt. Rend. 257 (1963) 3098.

LEVINSON, A., A.FRIEDMAN and F.STAMPS: Variability of mongolism. Pediatrics 16 (1955) 43.

MIGEON, B.R.: Short arm deletions in group E and chromosomal 'deletion' syndromes. J. Pediat. 69 (1966) 432.

MIKELSAAR, A.V.N.: The mosaicity with respect to the deletion of part of the long arm of one of the chromosomes in group D (in man). Genetika 10 (1967) 142.

MOSONYI, L., D.SCHULER, E.ACS and S.KISS: 19-20 (hereditary?) trisomy in a family with multiple congenital malformations. Acta Med. Acad. Sci. Hung. 23 (1966) 41.

MOTTET, N.K. and H.JENSEN: The anomalous embryonic development associated with trisomy 13–15. Am. J. Clin. Pathol. 43 (1965) 334.

ØSTER, J.: Mongolism. Copenhagen, Danish Science Press Ltd. (1953).

NAEYE, R.L.: Prenatal organ and cellular growth with various chromosomal disorders. Biol. Neonatorum 11 (1967) 248.

NOADES, J., J.GAVIN, P.TIPPETT, R.SANGER and R.R.RACE: The X-linked blood group system Xg. Tests on British, Northern American and Northern European unrelated people and families. J. Med. Genet. 3 (1966) 162.

PATAU, K., D.W.SMITH, E.THERMANN, S.L.INHORN and H.P.WAGNER: Multiple congenital anomaly caused by an extra autosome. Lancet 1 (1960) 790.

PENROSE, L.S.: Dermatoglyphic patterns in large acrocentric trisomy. J. Mental. Deficiency Res. 10 (1966) 1.

PENROSE, L.S.: On the interaction of heredity and environment in the study of human genetics, with special reference to mongolian imbecility. J. Genet. 25 (1932) 407.

PENROSE, L.S. and G.F.SMITH: Down's Anomaly. London, J. and A.Churchill Ltd. (1966).

POLANI, P.E., J.L.HAMERTON, F.GIANNELLI and C.O.CARTER: Cytogenetics of Down's syndrome II. Frequency of interchange trisomics and mutation rate of chromosome interchanges. Cytogenetics 4 (1965) 193.

REISMAN, L.E., S.KASAHARA, C-YCHUNG, A.DARNELL and B.HALL: Antimongolism: studies in an infant with partial monosomy of chromosome 21. Lancet 1 (1966) 394.

RICHARDS, B.W.: Mongolism, the effect of trends in age at childbirth on incidence and chromosomal type. J. Ment. Subnormality 13 (1967) 3.

SIDBURY, J.B., JR., R.D.SCHMICKEL and M.GRAY: Findings in a patient with apparent deletion of short arms on one of the B group chromosomes. Soc. Ped. Res. 34th Ann. Meeting, Seattle, 1964. Abstr. J. Pediat. 65 (1964) 1098.

SINGH, R.P. and D.H.CARR: Anatomic findings in human abortions of known chromosomal constitution. Obstet. Gynecol. 29 (1967) 806.

SNODGRASS, G.J.A.I., L.J.BUTLER, N.E.FRANCE, L.CROME and A.RUSSELL: The 'D' (13–15) trisomy syndrome; an analysis of 7 examples. Arch. Disease Childhood 41 (1966) 250.

STOLLER, A. and R. D. COLLMAN: Incidence of infective hepatitis followed by Down's syndrome nine months later. Lancet 2 (1965) 1221.

TAYLOR, A. I.: Patau's, Edwards' and cri du chat syndromes; a tabulated summary of current findings. Dev. Med. Child Neurol. 9 (1967) 78.

TAYLOR, A. I.: Cell selection *in vivo* in normal/G trisomic mosaics. Nature 219 (1968a) 1028.

TAYLOR, A. I.: Autosomal trisomy syndromes: a detailed study of 27 cases of Edwards' syndrome and 27 cases of Patau's syndrome. J. Med. Genet. 5 (1968b) 227.

TAYLOR, A. I. and E. C. MOORES: A sex chromatin survey of newborn children in 2 London hospitals. J. Med. Genet. 4 (1967) 258.

TAYLOR, A. I. and P. E. POLANI: Autosomal trisomy syndromes, excluding Down's. Guy's Hosp. Rep. 113 (1964) 231.

THORBURN, M. J. and B. E. JOHNSON: Apparent monosomy of G autosome in a Jamaican infant. J. Med. Genet. 3 (1966) 290.

UCHIDA, I. A., K. N. MCRAE, H. C. WANG and M. RAY: Familial short arm deficiency of chromosome 18 concomitant with arhinencephaly and alopecia congenita. Am. J. Human Genet. 17 (1965) 410.

UCHIDA, I. A., M. RAY and B. P. DUNCAN: 21 trisomy with an XYY sex chromosome complement. J. Pediat. 69 (1966) 295.

WEISS, L., A. M. DIGEORGE and H. W. BAIRD: Four infants with the trisomy-18 syndrome and one with trisomy-18 mosaicism. Am. J. Disease Children 104 (1962) 533.

WERTELECKI, W., A. M. SCHINDLER and P. S. GERALD: Partial deletion of chromosome 18. Lancet 2 (1966) 641.

WOLF, U., R. REINWEIN, R. PORSCH, R. SCHROTER and H. BARTSCH: Defizienzen des kurzen Armen eines Chromosoms nr. 4. Humangenetik 1 (1965) 397.

WORLD HEALTH ORGANISATION MEMORANDUM: Standardisation of procedures for chromosome studies in abortions. Bull. World Health Organ. 34 (1966) 765.

YUNIS, J. J., E. B. HOOK and M. MAYER: DNA replication pattern of trisomy 18. Lancet 2 (1964) 286.

ZELLWEGER, H. and G. ABBO: Double trisomy and double trisomic mosaicism. Am. J. Disease Children 113 (1967) 329.

PART X

The nuclear envelope

CHAPTER 33

The nuclear envelope

BARBARA J. STEVENS and JEAN ANDRÉ*

Laboratoire de Biologie Cellulaire 4, Faculté des Sciences, Orsay, France

Contents

1. Introduction

2. Structure
   (a) Inner and outer membranes
   (b) Perinuclear space
   (c) Pores
   (d) Annular material
   (e) Internal dense lamella

3. Function
   (a) Behavior in mitosis
   (b) Dynamic character of the nuclear envelope
      Evolution of pores
      Relationships with nuclear components
      Relationships with cytoplasmic organelles
      Annulate lamellae
   (c) Permeability and nucleocytoplasmic exchange
      Selective passage of ions and molecules
      Electrophysiological properties
      Enzymatic activity
      Nucleocytoplasmic exchanges

4. Conclusions

* The authors wish to thank Madame Monique Balmefrézol for excellent technical assistance
This work received financial support from the C.N.R.S. (L.A. 86).

1. Introduction

One of the essential features which distinguishes the higher organisms or *eukaryotes* from the *prokaryotes* (bacteria and blue-green algae) is the presence of a membranous envelope enclosing the nuclear material. While the structure of the *nuclear envelope* remained unknown prior to electron microscopic studies, its existence was already evident from observations made both on living cells and cytological preparations. Microdissection experiments had demonstrated that the nuclear envelope is elastic and has tensile strength. Physiological studies indicated that it is permeable to a variety of ions and molecules (see reviews by Callan; Baud; Anderson; Mirsky and Osawa; Feldherr and Harding).

2. Structure

From the numerous electron microscope studies on the nuclear envelope, initiated by Callan and Tomlin in 1950, it can be stated that this cellular component has the same fundamental fine structure in all eukaryotic cells (see reviews by Baud; Watson 1955, 1959; Moses; Gall 1964). The few exceptions noted to the fundamental scheme involve variations of the elements rather than major deviations from the scheme. No doubt this reflects an underlying molecular basis common to all nuclear envelopes.

What appeared to light microscopists as a 'membrane' (in the old sense of this term) separating the nucleus from the cytoplasm, has been revealed by the electron microscope as a complex, double membraned structure. In consequence of its complexity, the term *nuclear envelope* (after Anderson) is employed to describe the ensemble of the following constituents: inner and outer nuclear membranes, perinuclear space, pores, annular material and internal dense lamella (Fig. 1).

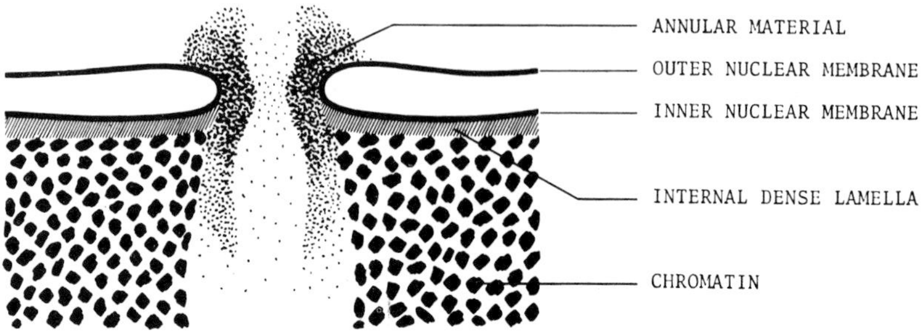

Fig. 1. Diagram of a nuclear pore as viewed in a section normal to the nuclear surface. This diagram summarizes observations from a variety of cell types.

(a) *Inner and outer membranes*

The inner and outer nuclear membranes lie in concentric and more or less parallel array at the nuclear periphery. The outer membrane is in direct contact with the cytoplasm; the inner membrane borders the nuclear side. The membranes resemble most of the other lipoprotein membranes of the cell, having a thickness of about 70 to 80 Å. In certain preparations, it is possible to demonstrate the typical so-called unit membrane structure (Robertson, see chapter on membranes in this book) consisting of two opaque layers about 30 Å thick, separated by a transparent space of about 30 Å (Vivier; André and Rouiller; Moor and Mühlethaler). However, the rarity of this image in preparations where it is clearly visible at the cell surface suggests that some fundamental difference at the molecular level exists between the membranes of the nuclear envelope and the plasma membrane.

(b) *Perinuclear space*

The two membranes are separated by an electron transparent area, generally about 150 to 300 Å wide, termed the *perinuclear space* (Policard and Bessis; Watson 1959). The width of the perinuclear space is subject to considerable variation and is not usually constant along the entire nuclear periphery. Some of the variation can result from the fixation or embedding methods, but it can also reflect the physiological state of the cell (Baud). In particular, plasma cells and fibroblasts often demonstrate considerable enlargements of this space and obvious connections with the cisternae of the endoplasmic reticulum. The contents of the space generally have no discernible substructure, although this does not imply that the space is void of organic material and ions. As we shall see below, the perinuclear space provides one of the available pathways for nucleo-cytoplasmic exchanges.

(c) *Pores*

The nuclear envelope does not form an uninterrupted, continous sheath around the nucleus. At intervals along the surface of the envelope, the two membranes are joined together to form a circular discontinuity or *pore*.*

In thin sections where the nuclear envelope is cut normally to its surface, the inner and outer membranes are directly continous with each other and form a rounded lip around the perinuclear space on either side of the pore (Figs. 2 and 6). In sections tangential to the nuclear surface (Figs. 3 and 10), in whole mounts of isolated nuclear envelopes (Fig. 7) and in frozen-etched preparations (Fig. 8), nuclear pores appear as

* The term 'pore' is not entirely satisfactory for the description of this entity, since it implies an open foramen and easy transport. Such is not the case here. However, the term has been firmly implanted in the literature and it is more familiar than others: discontinuity, gap, interruption, opening, fenestration, etc.... We shall therefore continue to make use of the term, without any implication as to openness or patency.

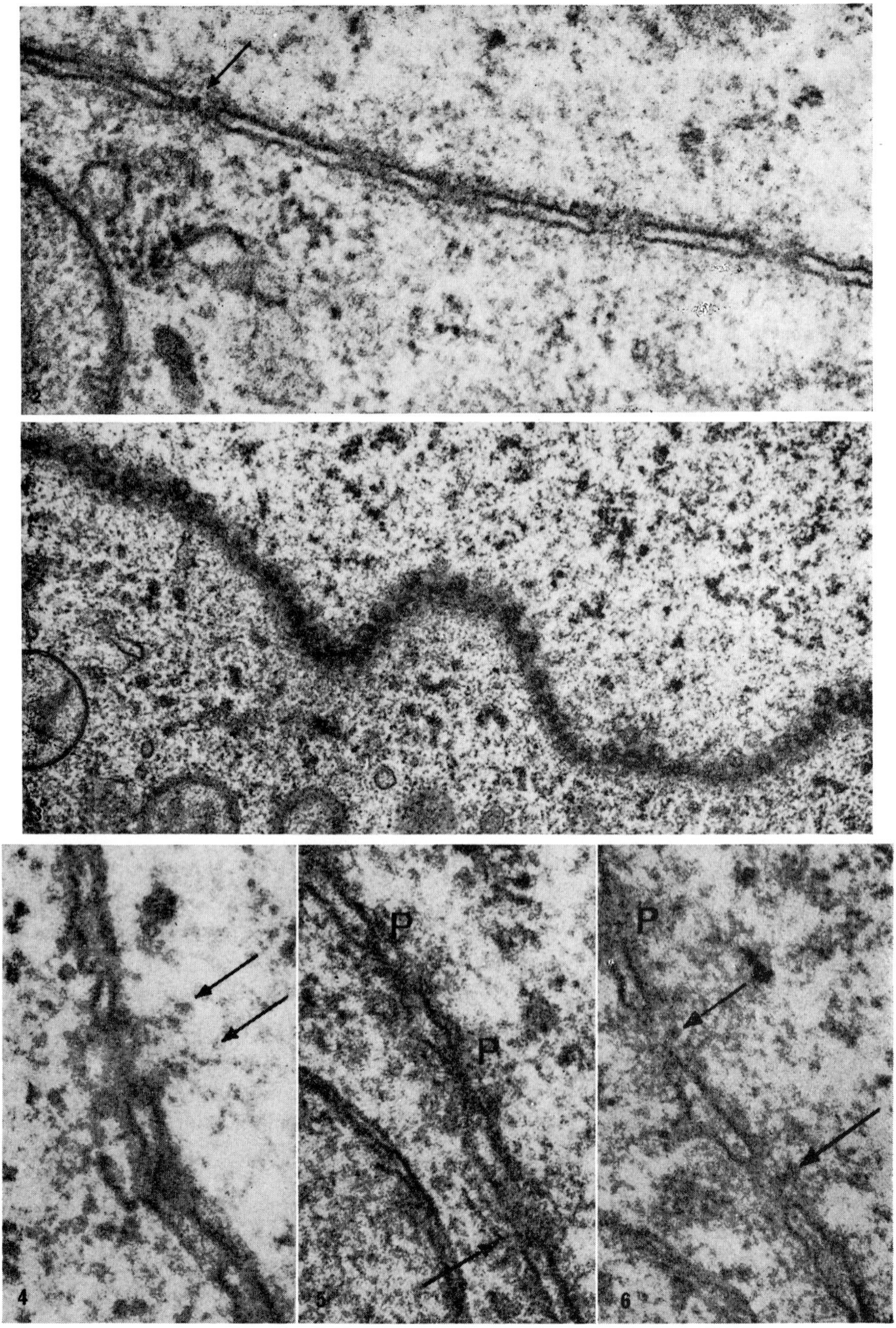
2
4
P
P
5
P
6

more or less regular arrays of identical rings. This aspect of a nuclear pore in face-on view has been termed the *annulus* by Callan and Tomlin. An annulus then represents the perimeter of the pore formed by the junction of the two membranes. This definition is complicated by the presence of diffuse, finely divided material within the pore at the membrane level and in an encircling halo on either side. Thus, the image of the annulus includes the membrane limited periphery of the pore as well as the *annular material* within and about it. In our description, we shall employ the term 'pore' to indicate the circular junction of the two membranes. The pore and its associated annular material together will be termed the 'pore complex' (after Watson 1959). The term 'annulus' shall be reserved for the appearance of the pore complex in face-on view (Fig. 12).

Nuclear pores are a basic feature of the nuclear envelope and have been observed in all eukaryotes so far examined with the electron microscope. They are visible in thin sections after all the fixations commonly used. They have equally been demonstrated by such diverse techniques as freeze-etching (Fig. 8), negative staining (Fig. 7) and shadowing (Callan and Tomlin; Gall 1964). As evident below, a synthesis of results from these various techniques can aid us in the interpretation of the pore and pore complex.

One of the first problems encountered in the description of the nuclear pore is its actual diameter. From the multiple observations on nuclear pores, the diameter has been estimated from about 300 Å up to 1000 Å. Much of this uncertainty about a structure that is of such universal occurrence may be resolved by a consideration of the limitations of the fixation and thin sectioning techniques.

It was first pointed out by Barnes and Davis that the thickness of the section could

---

Figs. 2–6. Fine structure of the nuclear envelope in oocytes of the spider, *Tegenaria sp.* Cytoplasm at lower left; nucleus at upper right in all figures.

Fig. 2. The thin section passes transversely to the nuclear surface and includes several pores sectioned in their median plane, as in Fig. 13 B. The arrow points to a dense granule possibly in transit through a pore. Osmium. × 86,000.

Fig. 3. An oblique section of the nuclear envelope showing a number of dense rings or annuli, which represent face-on views of the nuclear pores. Glutaraldehyde–osmium. × 28,500.

Fig 4. Normal section of a nuclear pore which demonstrates the annular material in the shape of a cylinder (arrows) as diagrammed in Fig. 1. The material projects more deeply into the nucleoplasm than into the cytoplasm. It is more prominent after double fixation than after osmium alone (compare with Figs. 2 and 6). Glutaraldehyde–osmium. × 120,000.

Fig. 5. Normal section of two nuclear pores (P) in which a portion of the front (or back) plane is included, producing the image of a diaphragm across the opening, as in Fig. 13 C. A third pore (arrow) does not exhibit a distinct margin due to the position of the section, as in Fig. 13 A. Osmium. × 120,000.

Fig. 6. Two pores which each show a dense rod or granule near the center (arrows), possibly representing material in transit from nucleus to cytoplasm. Pore at P is sectioned as in Fig. 13 A. Osmium. × 120,000.

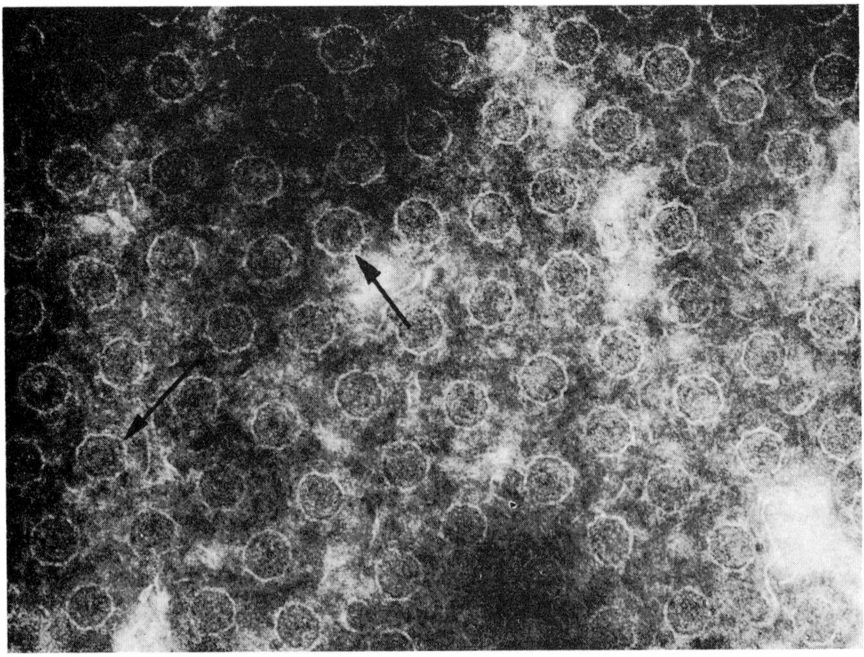

Fig. 7. Isolated nuclear envelope from an oocyte of the newt, *Triturus viridescens*, negatively stained with phosphotungstic acid. The white lines represent the pore margins. Some of them (arrows) tend to show an octagonal symmetry. $\times$ 85,000. (From J. G. Gall 1967.)

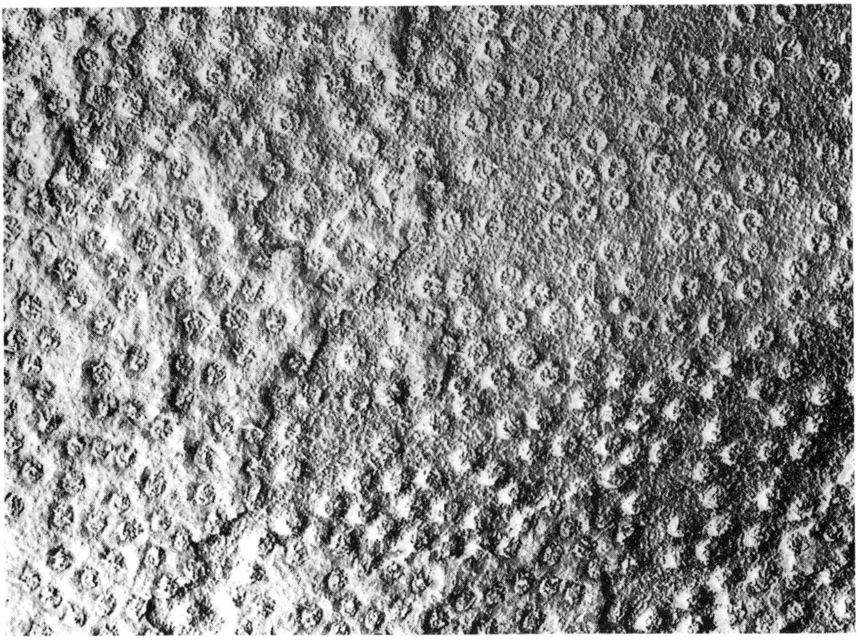

Fig. 8. Frozen-etched preparation of a salivary gland cell from *Drosophila hydei*, showing the nuclear envelope. The outer surface of the inner nuclear membrane is visible in the main portion of the micrograph (center and right); at the left, the outer surface of the outer membrane is seen. The surface of the inner membrane is dotted with fine particles while that of the outer membrane is much smoother. The pores appear filled with granular or fibrillar material. Annular material is not seen with this technique. $\times$ 35,000. (From H. Moor 1967.)

greatly influence our perception of the pore. The estimated diameter range of 300 to 1000 Å is about the same as that of the thickness of thin sections. In a section exactly normal to the nuclear envelope, the images of pores will depend not only on the section thickness, but also on the portion of the pore included in the section. Recalling that the entire thickness of a section is in focus in the electron microscope, a true picture of the pore at its diameter will be obtained in a very thin section ($\sim$400 Å) which includes only a narrow zone around the diameter (Figs. 2 and 13B). Such sections are rather rare. Most of the usual sections include a portion of the nuclear membrane in their front or back plane or a larger zone around the diameter. In the former case, superpositions render the image more opaque, mostly in the median plane and create the appearance of a membranous diaphragm (Figs. 5 and 13C); in the latter case, the image of the pore can portray a smaller diameter and an apparent fuzziness of pore lips (Figs. 5, 6 and 13A). Finally, the decision as to the exact limits of the pore is highly subjective and the measurements are affected to a large degree by these factors.

A number of investigators have used the inner diameter of the annulus in tangential sections or whole mounts to indicate the pore diameter. A dense, narrow line, which represents the membrane limit of the pore can sometimes be distinguished in the annulus (Watson 1959; Vivier; Fig. 12). In general, though, the inner margin of the annulus is blurred and inexact due to the presence of annular material, and such measurements may be more inaccurate than those of normal sections.

The role of the fixative as an influence on pore diameter has been demonstrated by Merriam (1961) and Gall (1964) who compared measurements after osmium and permanganate fixation. They concluded that permanganate fixation results in pore diameters up to 2 times greater than after osmium fixation.

In spite of the improvements and standardization in fixation and sectioning techniques since the beginning years of electron microscopy, more recent measurements of pore diameter still fall within a wide range. A lower limit of about 450 Å (Wiener et al.) and an upper limit of 1000 Å (Vivier) do not allow a comprehensive and precise figure. Perhaps the most accurate measurements of pore diameter have been made by Gall (1967) on negatively stained, isolated nuclear envelopes of amphibian and sea urchin oocytes. Here, the stain appears to penetrate into the pore and also into the perinuclear space up to the merger of the membranes at the pore limit. The result is a negative image of the membrane at the pore periphery (Fig. 7). Measurements of the inner pore diameter fall within a narrow limit: 663 ± 5 Å. These measurements are from two widely separated groups of animals, but all have been made on oocytes. It is not known whether this measurement is applicable to other cells; we cannot be sure to what extent the nuclear pore diameter is constant for all cell types and organisms.

The shape of the nuclear pore has consistently been described as circular, but the study cited above by Gall has demonstrated a regular octagonal outline. The negatively stained unit membrane at the pore perimeter is revealed to have an 8-sided symmetry. An 8-fold symmetry had previously been reported for the annulus by a

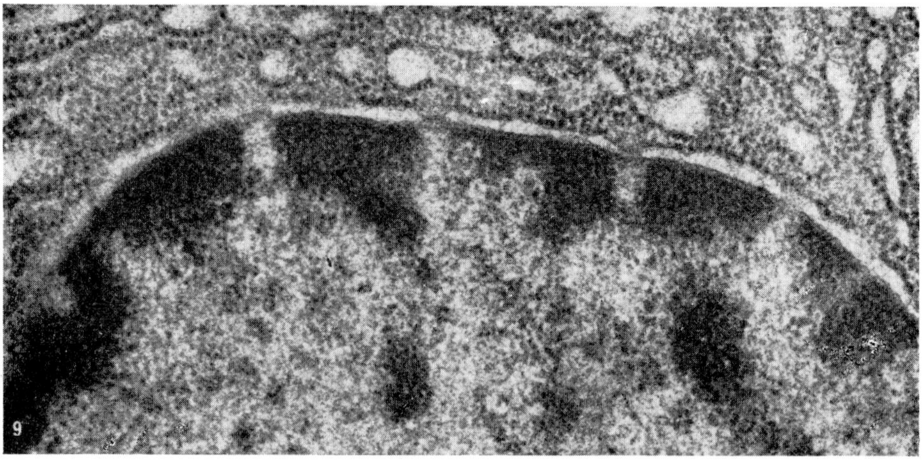

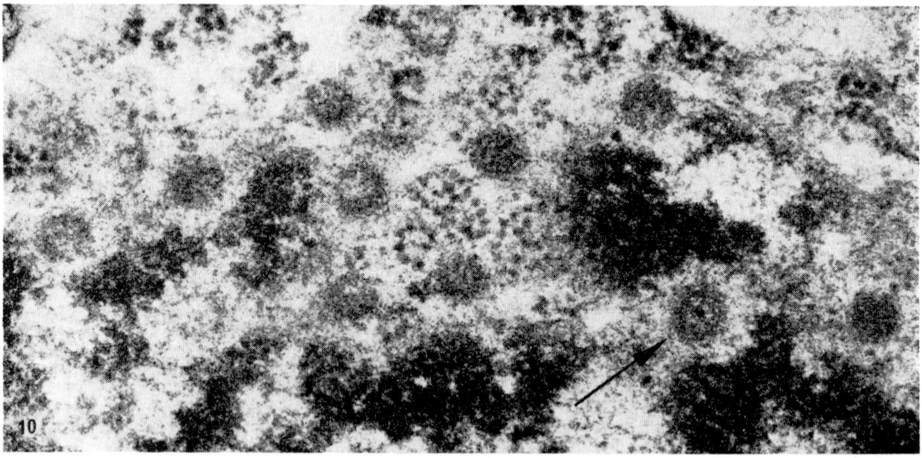

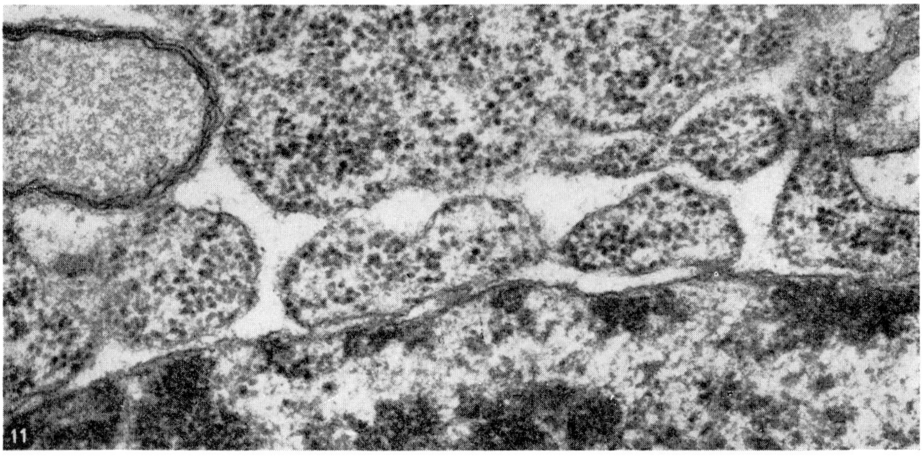

number of investigators all of whom attributed the 8 units to the annular material, either within the pore itself in the form of hollow tubules (Wischnitzer; Vivier) or lying around the periphery on the cytoplasmic side (Watson 1959; Merriam 1961). Franke has likewise found an 8-fold symmetry in negatively stained isolated envelopes, but concluded that this is due to 8 globular subunits arranged in a circular pattern in the annulus. It is difficult indeed to find a demonstration more convincing than that of Gall's (Fig. 7), and we therefore suggest that the underlying octagonal pattern is an integral part of the pore margin. It seems likely that an 8-fold symmetry could be imposed upon the annular material in the annulus as a consequence of the octagonal shape of the pore.

For a number of years following the original descriptions of the nuclear envelope, a controversy existed over the existence of a thin membranous diaphragm stretched across the pore and effecting a more complete barrier between the nucleus and cytoplasm. For questions of permeability and nucleocytoplasmic exchange, the presence or absence of such a barrier was a vital point to establish.

A rational explanation can be found for most images of transversely sectioned envelopes, such as Fig. 5, where the double membranes of the envelope seem to fuse into a single thin membrane extending across the pore. By using again the consideration of section thickness and Fig. 13, it becomes obvious that sections passing through one side of the pore will contain a small thickness of one or both membranes at the edge. This material will appear in the image as a thinner single or sometimes double membrane extending across the middle of the pore.

Nevertheless, there are some images of pores that appear to be 'plugged' or filled with material of greater density than that on either side. The best example of this is the erythroblast where a septum thicker than a membrane is frequently observed in the pore. These cases cannot be explained by an effect of the section, but it is possible to state that the diaphragm or plug in question is not a membrane comparable to others in the cell. The problem of identifying this material directs our attention to another basic component of the nuclear envelope: the *annular material.*

Fig. 9. Portion of the nucleus from a mouse pancreatic cell. Several intranuclear channels through the dense, marginated chromatin are shown. Each channel abuts on a nuclear pore. Glutaraldehyde–osmium. × 43,000.

Fig. 10. A grazing section of the nuclear surface of a tapetal cell from a young anther of *Zea mays*. A number of dense annuli are observed between dark masses of chromatin. The arrow points to an annulus situated above (or below) the center of an intranuclear channel; this annulus contains a dense central granule. Scattered between the annuli are several polysomes (center). Glutaraldehyde–osmium. × 77,500.

Fig. 11. A section normal to the nuclear surface of a tapetal cell, as in Fig. 10. Extensive communications between the perinuclear space and the endoplasmic reticulum cisternae are observed. Plastid at upper left. Glutaraldehyde–osmium. × 51,500.

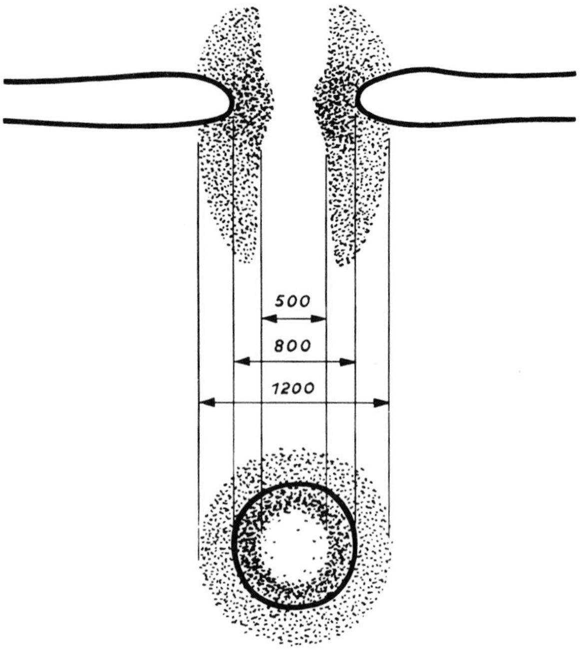

Fig. 12. Diagram of the correspondence between the image of a pore complex in a normal section (top) and that in a tangential section (bottom). In most preparations, the inner and outer diameters of the annulus in tangential section blur the true pore margin. The measurements are mean values obtained from the literature.

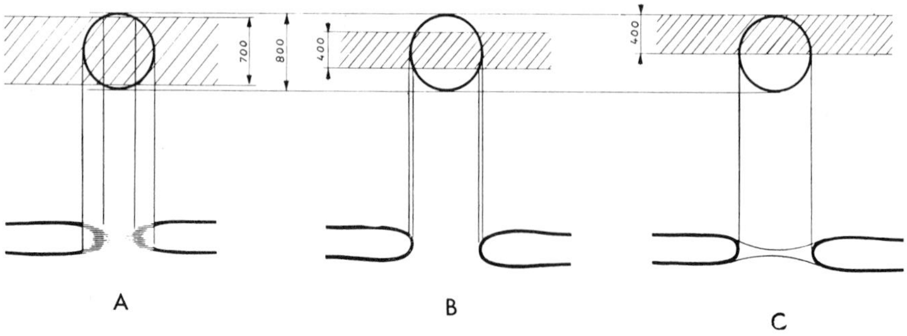

Fig. 13. Effect of section thickness and position on the resulting image of a pore: three typical cases of the appearance of pores in normal sections. The hatched areas of the upper figures represent the part included in the sections. (A) represents a thick section which includes a large zone around the pore diameter and portrays a pore with fuzzy and ill-defined edges (cf. Figs. 5, arrow and 6, P). (B) represents a thin section which passes through a narrow zone around the diameter and presents a well-defined image of the pore (cf. Fig. 2). (C) represents a section in which a portion of the front (or back) plane of the pore is included, creating the appearance of a membranous diaphragm (cf. Fig. 5, P).

(d) *Annular material*

Attempts to describe the arrangement and form of the annular material of the pore complex suffer from a lack of discernible organization and constancy from one cell type to another. In osmium fixed tissue, particularly after prefixation by glutaraldehyde, the nuclear pores never have an 'empty' appearance but they contain diffuse material filling the pore at the membrane level and extending into the cytoplasm and nucleus in the form of a short cuff. Most, if not all, of this material is lost after permanganate fixation (Gall 1964; Merriam 1961).

Thin transverse sections of osmium fixed nuclei show delicate tufts of annular material projecting from both sides of the nuclear envelope, vaguely resembling a cylinder. It is this material, superimposed upon the image of the membrane limit of the pore, which creates the dense annulus seen in surface views. Attempts to correlate these two aspects of the annular material have resulted in the conception of various models of the pore complex. Afzelius (1955) imagined an 'encircling wall', 240 Å thick, whose inner boundary coincides with the pore limit and which projects 200 Å into the cytoplasm and 600 Å into the nucleus. Wischnitzer placed a 'cylinder' completely inside the pore and extending 600 Å on both sides of the envelope. Vivier has also represented the annular material as a sleeve-like structure within the pore, but less regular in form than that of Wischnitzer. André and Rouiller, Watson (1959) and Gall (1964) have visualized a less organized arrangement of the annular material which penetrates to a greater or lesser extent into the pore and on either side of the envelope.

Several observations suggest that the arrangement of this component cannot be diagrammed with precise dimensions and outlines, at least not as a general representation of the pore complex. Measurements of the outside diameter of the annulus show that the annular material is disposed in a circular area larger than that of the pore margin (Fig. 12). The outlines of the annulus are diffuse and the outer limit is dependent upon the thickness and level of the section. The density and amount of the material depend greatly on the fixative. The annulus is not visible in frozen-etched preparations (Fig. 8), indicating that the substance is not firmly attached to the envelope and probably does not have a compact organization. Variations in the component are also a function of the cell type: oocytes and spermatocytes demonstrate the most prominent arrangements (Fig. 4); embryonic cells are also well endowed in general; secretory cells having cisternae of the endoplasmic reticulum closely applied to the nuclear envelope show less evidence of projecting annular material (Fig. 9). A large variety of cells with dense chromatin in contact with most of the inner nuclear membrane tend to contain only little of the material on the nuclear side (Fig. 9).

These rather subjective appreciations lead us to propose the diffuse, unordered arrangement of the annular material schematized in Fig. 1. A layer of the finely granular material is present within the pore at the level of the nuclear envelope. This same material extends around the membranes at the pore periphery and projects in a diffuse tubular form on either side of the envelope. In general, the annular material extends more deeply and more irregularly into the nucleoplasm than into the cytoplasm.

Our knowledge of the composition of the annular material is sparse. Some experiments by Merriam (1961) indicate that the material within the pore is removable by trypsin digestion. Treatment of thin Epon sections with pepsin specifically removes the annular material of the pores and leaves a clear area (Beaulaton). These results and the observation that the annular material is lost after permanganate fixation suggest that the material is mainly protein in nature.

(e) *Internal dense lamella*

The remaining structural element of the nuclear envelope, the internal dense lamella, has become recognized only very recently as an often occurring feature. Early studies had shown a prominent thick layer (about 2800 Å) of homogeneous and compact material closely apposed to the inner surface of the inner nuclear membrane in a few cells: *Amoeba proteus* and *Gregarina melanopli* (see Gall 1964). The arrangement of this material in the form of closely packed hexagonal prisms about 1400 Å wide gave it the name of 'honeycomb layer'; each cell of the honeycomb was shown to abut on a nuclear pore. A similar honeycomb layer (1800 Å thick) was subsequently observed in the glial cells of the leech ventral nerve cord and a thinner layer (600 Å) in the neurones (Grey and Guillery).

For a number of years these isolated cases were considered as peculiar variations of the otherwise uniform structure of the nuclear envelope throughout the eukaryotes. Fawcett, Patrizi and Poger, Kalifat et al., and Mazanec, however, have recently reported the existence of a thinner, regular layer in a number of vertebrate cell types: endothelial, connective tissue, smooth muscle, epithelial and tissue culture. These authors have attributed the clear demonstration of this layer to improved preservation of the tissues by glutaraldehyde–osmium fixation. Nevertheless, they show that the layer still can be identified after osmium fixation alone (phosphate- or collidine-buffered). These recent observations, along with the frequent mention in earlier studies (e.g., Watson 1955; Bernhard) that the inner nuclear membrane appears thicker than the outer, lead us to propose that the internal dense lamella is a common constituent of the nuclear envelope (Fig. 14).

The intimate structure of the thickened internal lamella in *Amoeba proteus* or leech glial cells clearly can be described as finely filamentous. For this reason, the layer has been termed the 'fibrous lamina' by Fawcett, who has extended the term to the corresponding layer in vertebrate cells although its fibrous nature there has not been fully demonstrated. Patrizi and Poger have proposed the term *Zonula nucleum limitans* or nuclear limiting zone. Mazanec has employed this same term to describe the finely granular or fibrillar layer in some human cells and has noted the resemblance to the basement membrane. Kalifat et al. describe the layer as homogeneous or granular and use the term 'dense lamella'. For the sake of simplicity, we shall adopt the latter terminology.

These reports have described the lamella in vertebrate cells as less opaque than both

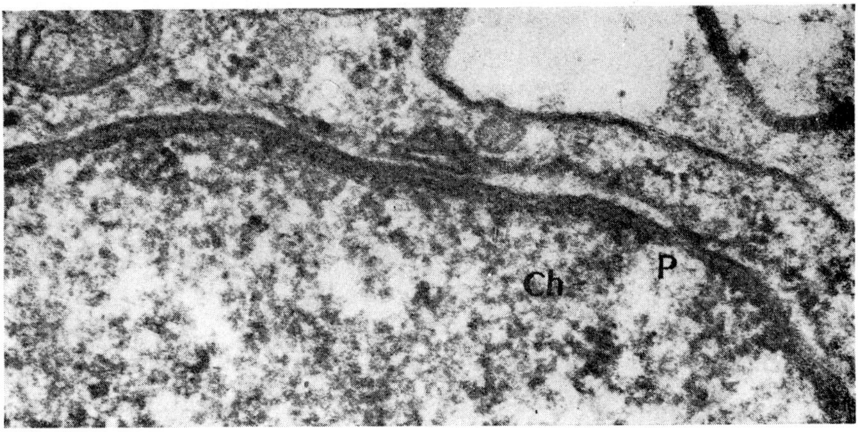

Fig. 14. Section of a mouse fibroblast cell. The inner nuclear membrane is coated by the so-called internal dense lamella. At the pore (P) the lamella seems to be interrupted. Chromatin (Ch) lies in close contact with the lamella. Glutaraldehyde–osmium. × 72,000.

the chromatin and the inner membrane after standard fixation and staining techniques. It is directly applied to the inner membrane and no separation has been observed between the two elements. On the inner or nuclear face, the lamella is generally bordered by clumps of chromatin, the surface of which forms a regular beaded row along the line of contact with the lamella. After double fixation, the thickness of the lamella varies from 200 up to 800 Å according to the cell type and, after osmium alone, it is usually 200 Å or less. At the level of the nuclear pores, the lamella generally seems to become thinner and to merge imperceptibly with the annular material (Patrizi and Poger; Kalifat et al.; Mazanec). Fawcett, however, finds that the lamella continues almost unchanged across the pore.

It is not yet possible to make a general rule about the presence and structure of the lamella according to cell type and organism, but certain tendencies can be cited. The lamella is prominent in those vertebrate cells already noted. It seems to be absent or very thin in spermatocytes (Fawcett) and oocytes (Figs. 2 and 4), and so far has not been reported in other invertebrate somatic cells nor in plant cells. It has been observed in another gregarine, *Lecudina* (Vivier), in the dinoflagellate *Noctiluca* (Afzelius 1962), and in other amoebae, *A. terricola* (Fauré-Fremiet and André, unpublished observations) and *Hyalosphenia papilio* (Joyon and Charret). In addition, in *Entamoeba blattae* (see Gall 1964) and in *A. terricola*, there is an external lamella situated on the outer side of the nuclear envelope.

At present, we have no indication as to the chemical composition of the lamella, nor if we can consider it to be similar to that of the annular material. Its fine structure and staining properties clearly distinguish the lamella from the chromatin. Preliminary investigations in our laboratory using digestion methods on thin sections of Araldite-Epon embedded tissues indicate that the internal lamella of mouse cells is resistant to pepsin and pronase treatment. Fawcett has suggested that the lamella may have a supporting function. In fact, in those cases where the lamella is evident, the inner membrane of the envelope has a straight course, compared to the more wavy course of the outer membrane (Fig. 15); the lamella appears to act as a stiff substratum for the inner membrane and to support it against deformation by cytoplasmic movements and fixation artifacts. Fawcett has also considered a physiological role for the lamella, acting in nuclear permeability, and Mazanec believed that it may be formed during certain nuclear syntheses. The other authors suggest a chemical role, such as the site of enzymatic processes.

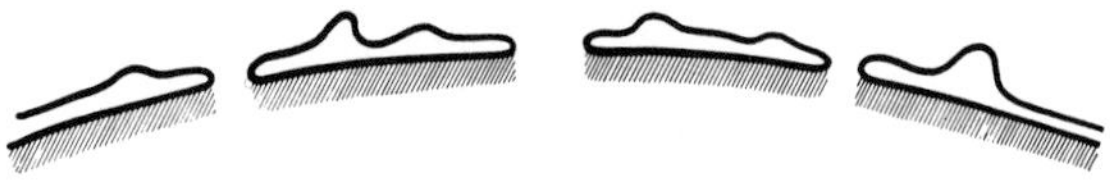

Fig. 15. Schematic representation of the 'stabilizing' effect of the internal dense lamella on the inner nuclear membrane. The outer membrane often seems flexible, in contrast to the more rigid appearance of the inner.

3. *Function*

(a) *Behavior in mitosis*

In most cells, the nuclear envelope undergoes a cyclic breakdown and reformation during mitosis. Its disappearance precisely marks the end of prophase and the beginning of prometaphase in living cells. The process, as viewed in the electron microscope, seems not to involve an actual dissociation of the envelope at the molecular level, but rather a fragmentation and dispersal of small, double membrane units. The envelope first shows local irregularities and then becomes interrupted by the release of small vesicles or larger sheets (Moses). It is not clear whether the pores act as points of rupture. The free ends of the fragments are always closed around the perinuclear space showing that local molecular rearrangements occur at the ruptured points, so as to join the two membranes. Such reparations are usual each time that membranes are naturally or artificially fragmented. Once scattered in the cytoplasm, the envelope fragments rapidly lose their identity and become indistinguishable from elements of the endoplasmic reticulum. Nothing in their morphology recalls the pores, annular material and internal lamella. The fate of these fragments is unknown, and it is generally assumed that they do not retain any specificity (Porter and Machado), becoming part of the membrane pool of the cell.

During metaphase and anaphase, double membrane profiles are observed surrounding the spindle and often interspersed with the spindle fibers in the pole regions. In a number of cells, such as onion root tip (Porter and Machado), HeLa cells (Robbins and Gonatas), and grasshopper neuroblasts (personal observations), there appears to be a proliferation of such membranes encircling the mitotic apparatus. It is suggested that this membrane sheath can serve to maintain a partial isolation of the mitotic apparatus from the rest of the cell.

The degree of disruption of the envelope can vary with the cell type. The nuclear envelopes of ciliate micronuclei and many fungal cells, including yeast, do not undergo breakdown, but simply increase in surface area and remain intact around an intranuclear spindle. In amoebae (Roth and Daniels) and rat thymocytes (Murray et al.) the nuclear envelope is only partially dispersed and the majority of the fragments closely surround the mitotic spindle. In these cells where there are few other cytoplasmic membranes, fragments of the original envelope are no doubt reutilized for the daughter nuclei. The complete disappearance of the envelope then is not a universal event and it must be concluded that, although in most metaphase cells the nuclear components are not separated from the cytoplasm, an intermixing of these two cellular compartments is not essential to the mitotic cycle in all cells.

Reformation of the nuclear envelope begins toward the end of anaphase and is concluded during telophase. The mechanism is basically a reversal of the fragmentation process (Moses; Gall 1964). Small vesicles and flattened cisternae appear at the surface of the condensed chromosomes; gradual deposition and fusion produces a continuous envelope. Most of the newly formed nuclear envelope appears to be acquired from the membranes surrounding the mitotic apparatus during mid-mitosis. Membrane profiles can be observed with one end closely apposed to a chromosome and the other free in the cytoplasm. It is therefore generally agreed that the origin of the nuclear envelope is from elements of the cytoplasmic membrane system (Porter and Machado; Moses). A strictly *de novo* formation of the envelope can be excluded but it

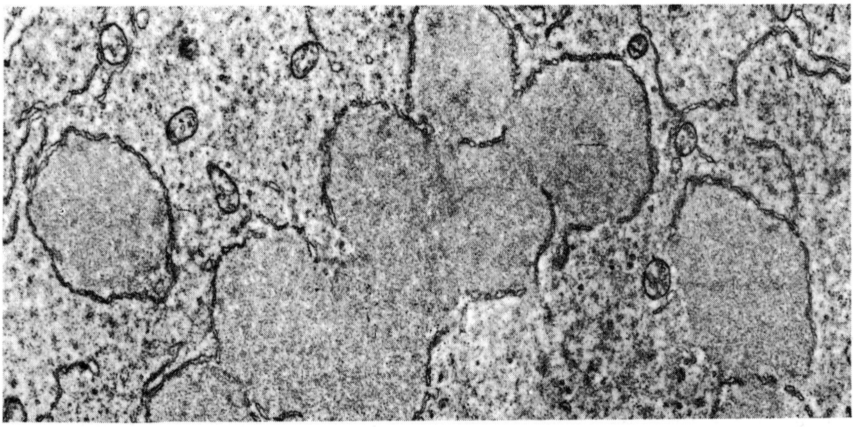

Fig. 16. A group of anaphase chromosomes in a neuroblast cell of the grasshopper embryo, *Chortophaga viridifasciata*. Individual chromosomes are more or less separately enclosed by the reforming nuclear envelope. Pores are already visible. The new envelope is closely applied to the chromosomal surface and some fragments are trapped between chromosomes as the partial karyomeres fuse to form the nucleus. Osmium vapor–$KMnO_4$. ×15,000.

remains entirely possible that initial vesicles may act to 'seed' the synthesis of new membrane along the chromosome surface.

It has been noted that the individual chromosomes of many cells tend to form their own envelope before a continuous envelope enclosing the entire nucleus is produced (Moses; Murray et al.; Fig. 16). Subsequent fusion of the individual membranes often traps free segments inside the nucleus which may persist into interphase. This partial karyomere condition suggests a specific interaction of the membranes with the chromosomal surface rather than with the nucleus as a whole.

Neither fragmentation nor reformation is an instantaneous process. Some evidence points to a preferential region where the fragmentation is initiated. Observations in the light microscope showed that the nuclear limits vanish first in the vicinity of the developing spindle and electron microscope studies support this indication. In HeLa cells at prophase (Robbins and Gonatas), the centrioles lie in an indentation of the nuclear envelope whose numerous infoldings in the area precede the first disruptions. Gaps in the envelope first appear near the centriolar region in thymocytes (Murray et al.) and in grasshopper neuroblasts (personal observations). Reconstruction appears to follow a converse pattern in which the centromere regions are the last to be endowed with an envelope (Robbins and Gonatas), even though envelope formation begins along the polar surfaces of the chromosomes, around the centromeres (Murray et al.).

The acquisition of the specific features of the nuclear envelope – pores, annular material and internal lamella – occurs rapidly during reformation. The short segments of double membranes adhering to anaphase chromosomes already are interrupted by regular pores (Robbins and Gonatas; Murray et al.; Fig. 16) which show evidence of annular material. The appearance of pores is a rapid process whose modalities have not been observed. It is not known if they appear at particular sites on the constituting fragments, for example at their points of junction, or if their formation is determined by the underlying chromatin. The lamella is reformed later than the pores. In *Amoeba proteus* (Stevens) and in some vertebrate cells (Patrizi), it appears only after the entire reconstitution of the nuclear envelope.

(b) *Dynamic character of the nuclear envelope*

Evolution of pores. A variation in the number of nuclear pores according to the metabolic state of the cell can be remarked. Among those cells which demonstrate the highest number of pores per surface area are oocytes (40 to $80/\mu^2$, Afzelius 1955), dipteran salivary gland cells (about $40/\mu^2$, from Fig. 8; 25% surface area, Wiener et al.), and protozoa (95 to $135/\mu^2$, Franke). A considerably lower number of pores has been noted for example in acidophil cells of the pituitary (3%, Barnes and Davis), late erythroblasts (Grasso et al.), and yeast cells (10 to $15/\mu^2$, Moor and Mühlethaler). Finally, in many mature sperm nuclei, pores appear to be entirely absent. These examples disclose a general tendency for undifferentiated cells and/or cells engaged in active synthesis to possess numerous pores, whereas some specialized cells have many fewer.

A transition in the number of pores during cellular differentiation has been followed in a few cells. Merriam (1962) noted a significant decrease from $35/\mu^2$ in immature to $25/\mu^2$ in mature amphibian oocytes. In the development of mammalian erythrocytes, Grasso et al. have shown a marked loss of pores by the normoblast stage. The disappearance of the numerous pores found in spermatocytes continues during the long spermatid stage and the metabolically inactive nucleus which emerges in the sperm cell is devoid of pores. It is furthermore noted that the disappearance of pores follows a constant pattern: the first area to lack pores is the region covered by the developing acrosome or nuclear cap, whereas the last is the posterior end of the nucleus. A comparable observation has been made in differentiated normoblasts and in old yeast cells (Moor and Mühlethaler): the distribution of pores becomes uneven and some areas of the nuclear surface may be barren. This evidence, however scant, suggests a direct correlation between a high frequency of pores and an actively functioning nucleus provided with large nucleoli and much diffuse chromatin.

Relationships with nuclear components. A dense layer of marginated chromatin lines the inner surface of the nuclear envelope in most vertebrate somatic cells but is characteristically absent in nuclei of oocytes, spermatocytes, protozoa and embryonic cells in general. When present, it is regularly interrupted at the level of each pore by an area of low density (Watson 1959; Swift 1958; Barnes and Davis). These areas are continuous with similar areas (interchromatin regions) in the nuclear interior and establish an apparent passage from the pores to central parts of the nucleus (Fig. 9). The term 'intranuclear channel' has been proposed by Watson (1959) for these regions. At the nuclear surface, the intranuclear channels are roughly cylindrical and measure about 1000 to 1500 Å in diameter; deeper into the nucleus, their diameter becomes greater and their shape more irregular. In tangential views just inside the nucleus, a channel appears as a well-defined circular area bordered by dense chromatin, within which the smaller image of the associated annulus is frequently seen (Fig. 10).

The intimate relationship of the intranuclear channels to the pores is particularly evident at mitosis. At the moment of the reformation of the nuclear envelope, the first observable pores are always accompanied by a clarification of the condensed chromatin at the pore site (Swift 1958).

The marginated chromatin layer in somatic nuclei so far has not been shown to involve specific chromosome attachment sites on the envelope. A particular case in which the ends of chromosomes terminate on the nuclear envelope is encountered during meiotic prophase in many animal gametocytes. Throughout most of the synaptic period, the paired chromosomes have a polarized orientation (the bouquet formation) as a consequence of the fixation of their ends on the envelope near the centrosome region. A modification of the nuclear envelope is observed at the attachment sites of the synaptic chromosomes, or synaptinemal complexes (Moses): both membranes show an increase in opacity and apparent rigidity; the inner membrane appears slightly thickened and the outer membrane develops a tuft of fine fibrils on the cytoplasmic side; the perinuclear space is more even and narrower than usual and pores are excluded (Moses; Fig. 17). There is no evidence to explain the role of this close association. It may support the often postulated hypothesis that chromosomes are attached to the nuclear envelope, a situation analogous to the DNA–membrane attachment demonstrated in bacteria.

Nucleoli frequently appear to be in contact with the nuclear envelope. Closer examination, however, generally shows a narrow, interposing layer of chromatin between the nucleolus and the envelope. There are usually pores present in the region. Light microcinematography has shown that the nucleolus–envelope association may be transitory and it is likely that it involves transfer of material of nucleolar origin through the nuclear envelope (see reviews by Bernhard; Baud).

Relationships with cytoplasmic organelles. A direct continuity of the outer nuclear membrane with the membranes of the endoplasmic reticulum is frequently observed in a large variety of interphase cells (e.g. Watson 1955; Bernhard; Whaley et al.; Fig. 11). This situation, which is of general occurrence, brings the perinuclear space into communication with the cavities of the endoplasmic reticulum and provides a membrane-enclosed pathway for rapid exchange, an example of which is given later. In addition to evidence that the nuclear envelope is derived from the endoplasmic reticulum after mitosis, the direct connection of these membranes is further proof of their closely related origin. The nuclear envelope can be considered as a specialized part of the cytoplasmic membrane system, which, conversely, can give rise to endoplasmic reticulum cisternae by blebbing of its outer membrane (Swift 1958).

One of the morphologic features of the endoplasmic reticulum, the presence of chains, rosettes and spirals of ribosomes (polysomes) on the external surface, is also found on the nuclear envelope. In many cell types, particularly embryonic and active protein synthesizing cells, the outer surface of the outer nuclear membrane is dotted with similar arrays of polysomes (Fig. 10). There is no evidence to show if these polysomes are newly-formed or otherwise distinguishable from those in the cytoplasm, nor is it demonstrated that their placement bears any relation to the nuclear pores. The arrays of ribosomes seem merely to be scattered at random among the pores.

Mitochondria are often seen in close vicinity to the nuclear envelope (see review by Moses). The association is generally transitory and no doubt closely linked with exchanges of energetic intermediates, metabolites or basic constituants. A striking example of one such association is described later.

The centriolar apparatus sometimes assumes a particular orientation with the nuclear envelope. In large lymphocytes, for example, the diplosome typically lies in the concavity of the reniform nucleus. In rapidly dividing cells, such as spermatogonia, one of the centrioles is directed at right angles to the nuclear envelope with its distal end near it. In some spermatids, the centriole moves centripetally toward the nucleus, creating a dome-shaped concavity at its base, opposite to the acrosome. In the nucleus, the nucleoprotein filaments converge toward the centriole. Thus, the nuclear membrane, which is devoid of pores at this stage, seems permeable to the polarizing action of the centriole.

Annulate lamellae. The unique fine structure of the nuclear envelope with its pores and annular material is repeated in an unusual class of cytoplasmic membranes first observed by Afzelius (1955) and known as 'annulate lamellae' (after Swift 1956). A recent, extensive review of this cytomembrane system can be found in Kessel (1968). The annulate lamellae occur as stacks of parallel, double-membraned elements, each having the same dimensions as the nuclear envelope and containing pore complexes identical to those in the nuclear envelope. The elements are arranged in a highly ordered fashion with a regular spacing between them (Fig. 18). The pores and annular projections of adjacent layers may be in perfect alignment with each other and the annular material often appears to join the elements together by a series of diffuse cylinders traversing the pores and producing a three-dimensional lattice (Swift 1956, 1958; Rebhun; see also reviews by Gall 1964; Moses; Kessel 1963, 1968). In tangential view, the pores are more numerous and more regularly spaced than in the nuclear envelope, giving a hexagonal pattern (Rebhun; Merriam 1962). The center of each annulus frequently contains a dense granule, but typical ribosomes are not usually found on the membranes. Single or unorganized lamellae may also occur in the nuclear interior.

Annulate lamellae are commonly observed in oocytes and spermatocytes, and in a variety of somatic cells and some cancer cells (see Kessel 1963). They are not constant features in these cells and in oocytes, for example, have been found to form during maturation (Merriam 1962; Moses). A striking generation of up to 100 layers is reported during experimentally provoked maturation of *Nereis* oocytes (Durchon and Boilly). In general, the presence of annulate lamellae is indicative of actively growing cells.

The close resemblance of the annulate lamellae to the nuclear envelope and the fact that single elements are frequently observed in the close vicinity of and parallel to the nuclear envelope have suggested that the lamellae arise in some manner from the envelope. Among possible modes of formation, two mechanisms have received some support from morphological evidence. One of these proposes that single, small vesicles are formed from the outer nuclear membrane by an active blebbing process; the vesicles are released into the cytoplasm in groups where they partially fuse to form flattened, annulated lamellae. Addition of further layers produces the characteristic stacks (Kessel 1963). The other mechanism proposes that single lamellae arise by a duplication of the nuclear envelope due to some template action. Some images suggest such a mechanism and show an alignment of the pores of the apposed lamella with those of the nucleus (Rebhun; Swift 1956, 1958).

The close kinship of these cytoplasmic membranes with the nuclear envelope, in form and origin, suggests a closely associated function. Evidence that the annulate lamellae are basophilic and contain RNA (Rebhun) has led Swift (1956, 1958) to

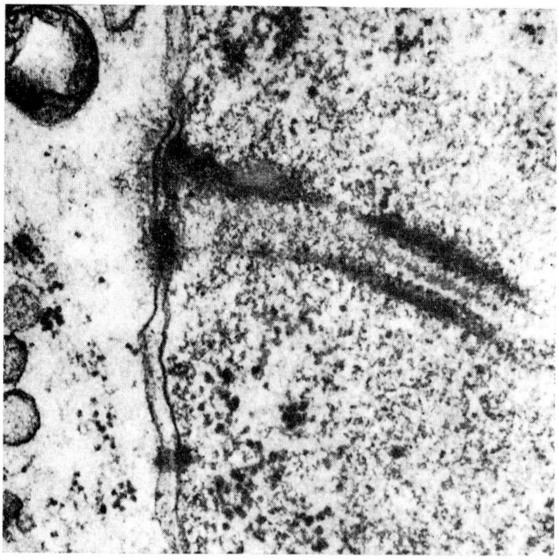

Fig. 17. Rat spermatocyte showing the attachment of a meiotic prophase chromosome (synaptinemal complex) to the nuclear envelope. At the point of attachment both membranes appear thicker and more rigid, and the perinuclear space is reduced. Tufts of fine fibrils project externally from the outer membrane. Osmium. × 32,000.

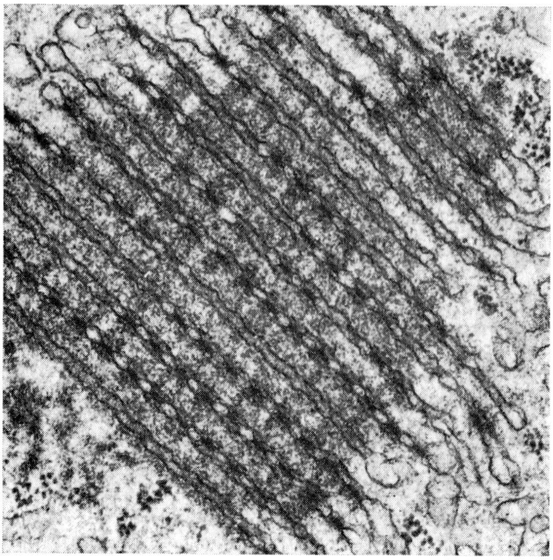

Fig. 18. A stack of annulate lamellae in the cytoplasm of a crayfish spermatocyte, *Cambarus sp.* Glutaraldehyde–osmium. × 30,000. (From W. A. Anderson and R. A. Ellis.)

propose that this system functions in the transmission and storage of genetic information from the nucleus and that the abundant annular material has an important role in its realization. Further biochemical studies are likely to shed light on the significance of this system, particularly in relation to cellular differentiation.

(c) *Permeability and nucleocytoplasmic exchange*

The foregoing account of the structure and comportment of the nuclear envelope poses a fundamental problem: What is its role in the constant flow of enzymes, nucleoproteins, metabolites, etc.... between the nucleus and cytoplasm? Does the envelope regulate the passage of these substances and therefore have a part in the control of gene expression? If there is a selective passage of ions and macromolecules across the envelope, how does it operate and does the same mechanism serve for all substances exchanged? The present theories of the regulation of cellular metabolism require a rapid interchange of precursors and products, enzymes and energetic intermediates. How can we explain the presence of the complex nuclear envelope interposed between the genetic material and the rest of the machinery for cellular function when the bacteria, for example, successfully manage without such a structure?

Our possibilities for studying these questions are fairly restricted at present. A large part of investigations of the permeability of the nuclear envelope has been performed on isolated nuclei or has employed non-biological substances as markers. Investigations at the fine structural level lack means of demonstrating many of the molecules important in cell metabolism. Finally, we are limited in our understanding of the molecular structure of membranes and their ability to transport ions and molecules across.

Selective passage of ions and molecules. Long before our present knowledge of the structure of the nuclear envelope was acquired, many physiological studies had been carried out on the permeability characteristics of both isolated and intact nuclei. Some of the principal reviews of this work can be found in Anderson, Baud, Feldherr and Harding, Mirsky and Osawa, and Goldstein. Most of the experimental conditions permitted observations of permeability in only one direction, that of cytoplasm to nucleus, and perhaps should not be interpreted to indicate a two-way passage.

Studies on isolated nuclei provide ample evidence for permeability to water, various cations and anions, and low molecular weight molecules such as mono- and disaccharides, amino acids, and nitrogenous bases (Callan; Feldherr and Harding; Mirsky and Osawa). They show that the nuclear envelope does not act as a semipermeable membrane between nucleus and cytoplasm. Furthermore, measurements of nuclear swelling in response to the salt concentration of the medium indicate a non-osmotic character of the volume changes. Swelling is observed at both high and low salt concentrations (Callan). An explanation of this phenomenon by the entrance into the nuclei of osmotically-active substances which then cause swelling is insufficient and overly simplified. The colloidal properties of the nucleoprotein content of the nucleus have been stressed by Anderson as an important factor in the nuclear volume changes The fact that different cations result in marked variations of nuclear swelling also suggests an effect of the ions on envelope permeability (Callan). There is substantial evidence for a sodium-dependent transport of amino acids into isolated nuclei (Mirsky and Osawa).

A list of macromolecules capable of penetrating isolated nuclei has also been established. Trypsin, chymotrypsin, RNase and DNase can readily pass across the nuclear envelope, as evidenced by their rapid effect on nuclear structures. In the case of histones, protamines and highly anionic macromolecules such as heparin, their passage into the nucleus may be accompanied by a displacement of the DNA or histone. Hemoglobin may also penetrate, but the nuclear envelope appears to be impermeable to such substances as egg albumin and glycogen (Feldherr and Harding; Anderson).

The brief summary given above of nuclear envelope permeability comes from preparations of isolated nuclei, and we cannot ignore the unphysiological aspects of these studies. The nuclear envelope, while remaining unbroken in good nuclear preparations, may be drastically altered at the molecular level and various parameters, as ionic strength, *p*H, etc. ... of the isolation medium may further influence its biophysical properties as well as those of the nuclear components. In spite of these reservations, the studies do demonstrate that ions, small molecules and some macromolecules above 15,000 molecular weight can pass into the nucleus but that the nuclear envelope exercises some selectivity over the passage.

Permeability studies on intact nuclei likewise show the ability of ions and small molecules to enter the nucleus. Experiments using frog oocytes exposed to solutions containing labeled sodium, potassium, phosphate and sulfate ions and several amino acids have demonstrated an accumulation of these substances in the nucleus. The radioactive sodium ions entering the nuclei replace 15 to 20% of the total nuclear sodium. Upon subsequent incubation in cold buffer, labeled ions are released from the nuclei, indicating a reverse passage (Naora et al.). Determinations of sodium and potassium in the oocytes demonstrate that both ions are 2–3 times more concentrated in nuclei than cytoplasm. The movement of these ions across the envelope against a gradient implicates a process more complex than diffusion which may involve transporter molecules or so-called active transport.

The penetration of larger molecules into the nucleus *in vivo* has been followed using fluorescein labeled proteins placed in the extracellular medium. Some results show that after intravenous injection of serum albumin and gamma globulin, the markers are found to enter the nucleus (Baud), but in other experiments (Feldherrr and Harding) these proteins injected into the cytoplasm of oocytes were not able to penetrate the nucleus.

The most instructive experiments on nuclear membrane permeability have been accomplished by Feldherr (1965; Feldherr and Harding). Following injection of colloidal gold particles coated with polyvinylpyrrolidone into the cytoplasm of amoebae, the cells were fixed at various times and the location of the electron-opaque particles was determined with the electron microscope. Some gold particles were found inside nuclei after 10 min, and by 24 hr the number of particles within nuclei was equal to or in some cases greater than that in the cytoplasm. More significant was the distribution of particles within the first few minutes after injection. Particles were located in high concentrations adjacent to and within the nuclear pores; those particles within the pores were located specifically in the centers (Fig. 19). Feldherr also noted a maximum size of 125 to 145 Å for the particles able to enter nuclei and speculated that the passage involved an attachment of the particles to the annular material. We can conclude from this sequence of the spatial distribution of gold particles that macromolecules can pass into nuclei through the nuclear pores. A limitation to entrance of macromolecules, however, exists within the pores and passage is restricted to a central channel. These results clearly point to the diffuse annular material associated with pores as playing an active role in the exchange mechanism.

Fig. 19. Diagrammatic representation showing the distribution of gold particles in relation to the pores, after injection of colloidal gold in *Amoeba proteus*. Cytoplasmic surface at top. (After C. M. Feldherr.)

The varying and often conflicting results of the permeability studies briefly outlined here certainly depend in part on variations in the experimental conditions. More important to recognize, however, is that nuclear envelope permeability should not be treated as an isolated phenomenon but probably is intimately bound up with the cell type and its activity.

Electrophysiological properties. By means of fine microelectrodes inserted into nuclei, the electrophysiological properties of several different nuclear envelopes have been examined by Loewenstein and colleagues (1964; Wiener et al.; Ito and Loewenstein). One electrode serves to pass current between the nuclear interior and the grounded extracellular fluid. Two other electrodes, inserted into nucleus and cytoplasm respectively, record the resulting voltage drops across the nuclear envelope and plasma membrane. The resistance of the envelope is directly determined and thus its relative ionic conductance is known.

Studies on dipteran salivary gland nuclei reveal an average potential difference of 15 mV between the nucleus and cytoplasm that is associated with the nuclear envelope. The inside of the nucleus is negative relative to the cytoplasm. The nuclear envelope in these cells has a high electrical resistance, of the order of 1 to 2 Ω cm^2, and so maintains an effective barrier to ion flow. Oocyte nuclei, on the other hand, demonstrate almost negligible potential difference between nucleoplasm and cytoplasm. The envelope in this case appears to offer no resistance to free ion flow.

The high order of resistance in gland nuclear envelopes was compared to the theoretical resistance presented by an envelope of the same structure in which the pores were assumed to be free communications between nucleus and cytoplasm and filled with material having a resistivity similar to that of the nucleoplasm, about 100 Ω cm. The resistance of such a hypothetical porous envelope approaches that of the nucleoplasm, or 10^{-3} Ω cm^2, and would be three orders of magnitude lower than that observed. The envelope of salivary gland cells then cannot be a freely porous structure nor can the pores be open throughout their diameter. Loewenstein and colleagues suggest that the electron-opaque annular material may present a diffusion barrier within the pore.

The marked dissimilarity in membrane resistance between oocyte and salivary gland nuclear envelopes has not been satisfactorily explained by a comparison of their fine structure (Wiener et al.). However, as Loewenstein has mentioned, a variation in the organization or composition of the material within the pores may be responsible for the difference in permeability. Along the same line, the study by Ito and Loewenstein on salivary gland nuclear envelope permeability during development in *Chironomus* reveals an increase followed by a decrease during the latter stages of larval development. The same trend can be produced by an injection of the growth hormone ecdysone. It is not known whether an actual change in the number of pores accompanies the permeability changes, nor if any observable difference can be found in the annular material during the period. Nevertheless, these studies indicate that permeability of the nuclear envelope can vary according to cell type and presumably with cellular activity

Enzymatic activity. Continuing our investigation of the role of the nuclear envelope in nucleocytoplasmic exchange, we can ask ourselves what, if any, enzymatic activity has been localized in this protoplasmic partition? It is not certain whether transfer across the envelope is an energy-dependent process (Georgiev), although this author has postulated that the penetration of some low molecular weight substances involves enzymatic reactions and has suggested that permeases attached to the envelope may be responsible for the transport of precursor molecules into the nucleus. Mirsky and Osawa state that there are some indications that the sodium-dependent amino acid transport into the nucleus requires ATP or a similar energy carrier. Finally, if the penetration and accumulation of such substances as sodium ions are insured by a mechanism of active transport, or the accelerated transfer of molecules and ions through membranes against either an electrochemical or a concentration gradient, energy sources probably in the form of high-energy phosphates would be required.

Histochemical methods for enzyme localization do not, for the most part, permit the resolution of the narrow region of the nuclear envelope. At the ultrastructural level, reaction products from a number of dephosphorylating enzymes have been shown to have a membranous location. Among these, glucose-6-phosphatase has been demonstrated on the nuclear envelope in kidney and liver cells (Goldfischer et al.

1964). Several nucleoside diphosphatases having a narrow substrate range – hydrolyzing the diphosphates of guanosine, inosine and uridine – have been localized on the nuclear envelope in a variety of cell types. Some of these cells also show thiamine pyrophosphatase activity on the envelope (Novikoff et al. 1962). Acid phosphatase activity has been localized in the perinuclear space in a ciliate (Goldfischer et al. 1963), in plant cells (Catesson and Czaninski), and in snail spermatids (W. A. Anderson, unpublished observations). One report (Yasuzumi and Tsubo) has shown ATPase activity in the pores of the nuclear envelope but the significance of the observation remains uncertain. Finally, acetylcholinesterase activity has been demonstrated by several investigators in the perinuclear space of neurons from sympathetic and dorsal root ganglia of several species (Novikoff et al. 1966; Brzin et al.). The latter authors have suggested the possibility that the enzyme may be linked to a permeability mechanism controlling ion movements in the perikaryon membranes.

As can be seen, the positive reactions for specific enzyme localizations are limited and few concentrated efforts have been made to examine specifically the nuclear envelope. It is hoped that future refinements in electron microscope cytochemical methods for enzyme detection will increase our knowledge of nuclear envelope components and thus of the machinery for its permeability.

Nucleocytoplasmic exchanges. Although our knowledge of the permeability properties and mechanisms residing in the nuclear envelope is far from complete, there is a growing assortment of clear biochemical and morphological evidence for nucleocytoplasmic exchanges in living cells. The most important body of facts deals with RNA. Based on substantial autoradiographic and biochemical data, it is now universally agreed that the main bulk of cellular RNA in eukaryotic cells is synthesized in the nucleus and irreversibly translocated to the cytoplasm. The kinetics of the transfer vary according to the class of RNA and the cell type. It is generally assumed that the RNA is complexed with protein, but the exact form of the molecules in transit is unknown. The 18S and 28S components of ribosomal RNA emerge separately from the nucleus in the form of ribonucleoprotein particles, identical to the small and large ribosomal subunits (Perry, see chapter on nucleolar function in this book). The form of messenger and transfer RNA molecules in transit to the cytoplasm remains undefined at present. Studies on nucleocytoplasmic movements of protein and other molecules offer serious technical problems and almost no data are available. In one case, the migration of a particular protein species, this time from cytoplasm to nucleus, has been shown in some autoradiographic studies (Goldstein).

In considering possible mechanisms for exchanges across the nuclear envelope, several different pathways are conceivable. On a large scale, transport could occur by the extrusion of important amounts of nuclear material in the form of emission bodies, or by the release of nuclear material during envelope breakdown in mitosis. Another possibility is the formation of annulate lamellae, which may insure the passage of some nuclear products. At the scale of individual molecules or molecular complexes, three principal routes for traversing an intact nuclear envelope can be visualized: across both membranes to the cytoplasmic ground substance (Fig. 20, B and E), across the inner membrane to the perinuclear space and cavities of the endoplasmic reticulum (A and F), and through the nuclear pores (C and D). These pathways are discussed below with regard to the available evidence and the relative importance of each.

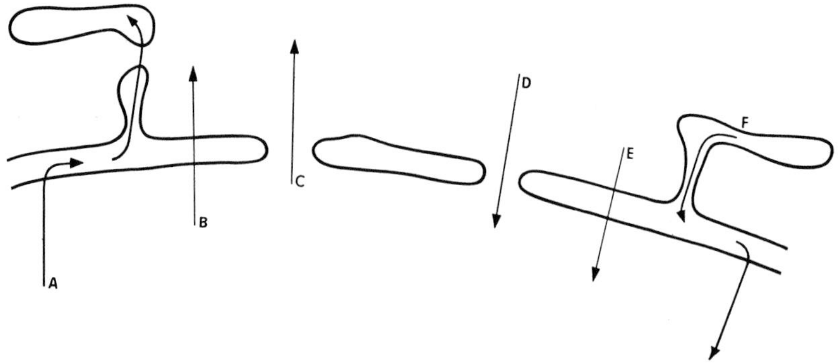

Fig. 20. Diagram showing possible pathways traversing the nuclear envelope (cytoplasm at top). Morphological evidence has been obtained for route C and the route indicated by the second of the two arrows in A. Route D has been demonstrated for gold particles injected into amoebae (Feldherr). No evidence is available for routes B, E and F, but it is postulated that route E is important for the entry of ions and small molecules.

At the light microscope level, there are a number of examples of the release of nuclear substances by the formation of nuclear blebs. Electron microscope observations disclose that such blebs are surrounded by a portion of the nuclear envelope which detaches from the nucleus and carries the material into the cytoplasm where it eventually breaks down. Examples of this process have been described in which chromosomal material or small nucleoli are transferred to the cytoplasm (see reviews by Bernhard; Baud; Kessel 1966). Such occasions are rare, however, and nucleocytoplasmic transport by means of large scale blebbing cannot be recognized as a general activity of cells. At variance from a true blebbing, Afzelius (1962) has described a unique process in *Noctiluca* in which intranuclear 'annulated vesicles' are pressed against the nuclear envelope and release their contents into the cytoplasm after rupture of the envelope.

Diffusion of some nuclear substances into the cytoplasm following the breakdown of the nuclear envelope in mitosis no doubt does occur. However, the facts that nuclear synthetic processes are almost completely arrested by mid-mitosis and that many specialized cells in adult tissues do not divide for long periods of time suggest that this mechanism is of limited importance. A reverse passage, by trapping of cytoplasm within the telophase nucleus, is probably negligible since the nuclear envelope reforms in direct contact with the chromosomal surface (Fig. 16).

In the proposed mechanism for exchange involving the formation of annulate lamellae (Swift 1956), nuclear information may be carried in the membranes and pores of the lamellae, or the lamellae may enclose some material derived from the nucleus, as in the case of 'heavy bodies' in sea urchin eggs (Harris). The presence of a non-particulate form of RNA associated with annulate lamellae and their occurrence in rapidly growing cells point to a specialized type of transfer. Annulate lamellae may act to remove, store and later release a specific RNA product of the nucleus.

Of the three pathways across an intact nuclear envelope, the one passing directly through both membranes (Fig. 20, B and E) has received no supporting evidence. Nevertheless, by correlation with other cellular membranes, it must be assumed that this route is practicable and probably important for small molecules.

A striking instance of the utilization of the nucleocytoplasmic pathway via the perinuclear space and endoplasmic reticulum cisternae (Fig. 20, A) has been shown in a study of antibody location in differentiating plasma cells by Leduc et al. Antibody to peroxidase was demonstrated by coupling it with its antigen and revealing the complex histochemically. In primitive hemocytoblast cells, antibody appears first in the perinuclear space (Fig. 21). In differentiating plasmablasts, antibody continues to be present in the perinuclear space and now fills the ergastoplasmic cisternae (Fig. 22). Later, in immature plasma cells, antibody is more irregularly distributed in these cavities whose continuity is clearly shown (Fig. 23). Finally, in mature plasma cells it is located only in cytoplasmic vesicles or distributed throughout the cytoplasm. This series of images denotes a sequence in the synthesis and transport of antibody, and strongly suggests that antibody formation is initiated in the perinuclear space. It is not known whether some components of the antibody are derived from the nucleus, but it is likely that at least some nuclear component participates in the initial antibody synthesis. It is conceivable that this pathway is utilized in other cells.

The pathway from nucleus to cytoplasm via the nuclear pores has been most clearly demonstrated (Fig. 20, C). This route appears to be of major importance. Although cell physiologists have asserted that nuclear pores are large enough for any biological macromolecule to pass through (Mirsky and Osawa; Goldstein), images clearly evoking the process are rare. The difficulty to observe material in transit through pores may be due, on the one hand, to the rapidity of the movement and, on the other, to the low electron-opacity and lack of clearly defined structure for many proteins and other macromolecules, including RNAS.

The first and often cited example at the fine structural level of transit through pores was demonstrated in nurse cells of the hemipteran *Rhodnius* by Anderson and Beams. In this case and in a number of oocytes studied since (see Kessel 1966), nuclear material appears to be directly continuous across the nuclear envelope with large, electron-opaque amorphous masses in the cytoplasm. In tunicate oocytes (Kessel 1966), the nuclear component which apparently contributes to the cytoplasmic masses is amorphous, but in amphibian oocytes and spermatocytes (Clérot), groups of well-defined granules about 350 Å in diameter are localized in the nucleus opposite to the promi-

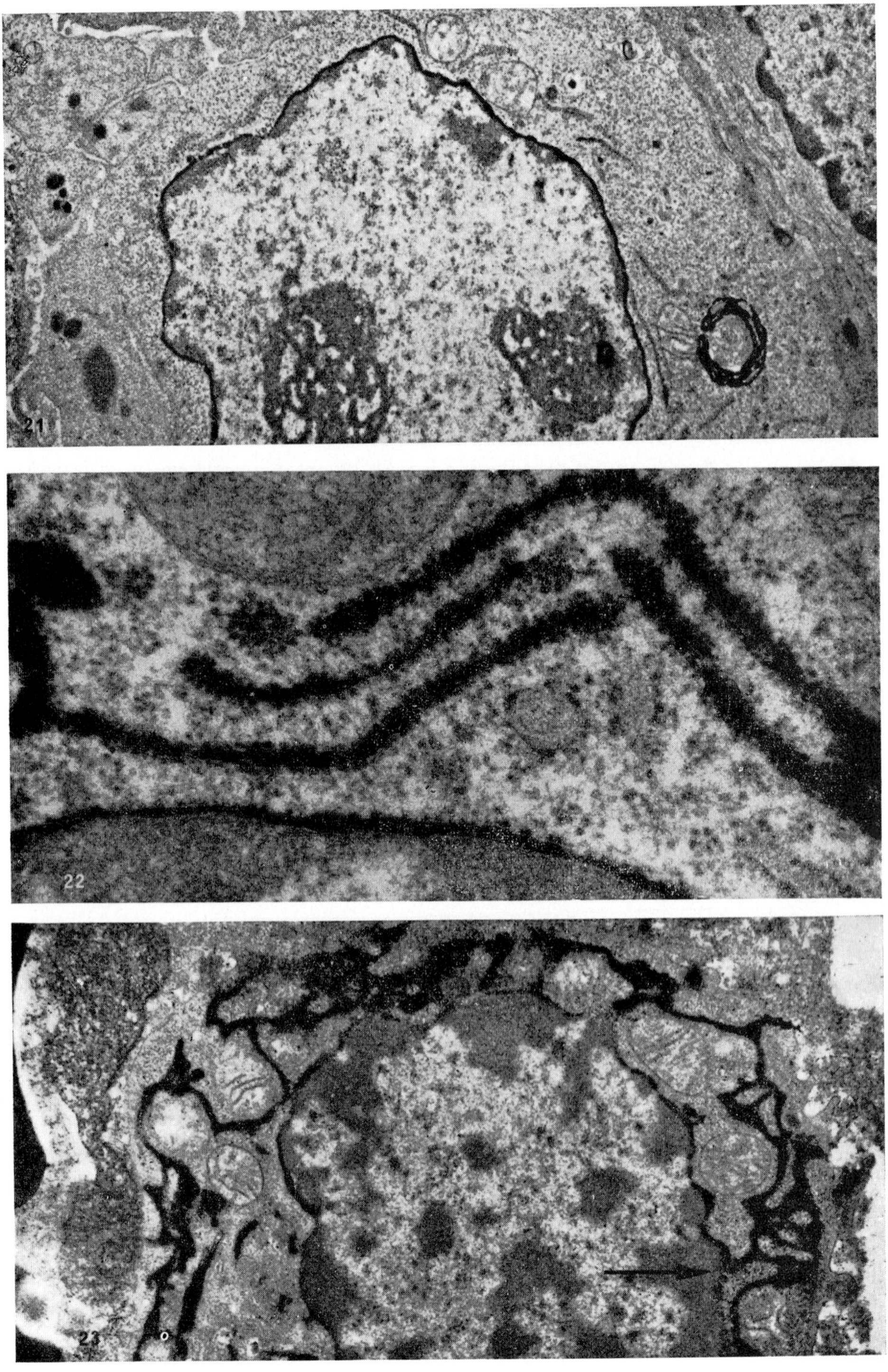
21
22
23

nent extrusions in the cytoplasm (Fig. 24). Individual granules may be directly linked to the material engaged in the pores. An important characteristic of most of these cases is the form of the material at the level of the pore. Only a narrow strand less than 200 Å wide penetrates the pore center, while a short distance on the other side of the envelope in the cytoplasm, the material collects into large masses (Fig. 24). The nature of the amorphous material accumulating on the cytoplasmic side of the envelope has often been claimed to be ribonucleoprotein, but a recent study in our laboratory (Clérot) indicates that the major portion is composed of non-histone protein and that the presence of RNA is uncertain.

Another feature of the nucleocytoplasmic exchange in oocytes and spermatocytes is the intimate relationship of mitochondria with the cytoplasmic accumulations. Large numbers of mitochondria surround and are partially embedded in the electron-opaque material. These large groups are particularly prominent at the time of an important increase in mitochondrial numbers; a nuclear participation in this process is implied.

Two other examples of passage through pores involve characteristic ribonucleoprotein particles of the nucleus. In *Chironomus* salivary gland nuclei (Stevens and Swift), quantities of spherical, RNA-containing granules about 400 Å in diameter are produced at particular chromosomal loci, the Balbiani rings, and become distributed throughout the nucleoplasm. At the nuclear envelope, many granules have been observed partially or completely within the nuclear pores where they undergo a constriction and an elongation and pass through the pore center in a narrow rodlike form about 200 Å wide (Fig. 25). The granules generally are not visible in the cytoplasm where they are rapidly transformed. The other example concerns the RNA-containing helices in *Amoeba proteus* nuclei (Stevens). These unusual structures occur in clusters in the nucleus; single helices have been observed within the honeycomb layer and in contact with nuclear pores (Fig. 26). Occasional helices are also found in the cytoplasm near the envelope where they appear to be distintegrating. Thus, there is suggestive evidence that helices pass from nucleus to cytoplasm via the pores. It is not certain whether the helix uncoils at the pore level, but the 130 Å wide filament could conceivably pass through the center of the pore. In both cases it is suggested that the particles represent a packaged form of RNA molecules complexed with protein.

The examples cited so far of passage through pores all concern cells active in protein synthesis and/or containing large and characteristic nuclear particles. What

---

Figs. 21–23. Formation of antibody against peroxidase in rabbit spleen. The antibody is revealed histochemically as the black areas in the micrographs. (From E. H. Leduc et al.)

Fig. 21. In hemocytoblasts, the antibody appears first in the perinuclear space. The cisternae of the endoplasmic reticulum show little or no reaction product. ×12,000.

Fig. 22. In differentiating plasmablasts, antibody continues to be present in the perinuclear space and also fills the ergastoplasmic cisternae. × 51,500.

Fig. 23. In plasma cells, antibody is less abundant in the perinuclear space and has completely invaded the enlarged cavities of the ergastoplasm. Several communications of the perinuclear space with the ergastoplasmic cavities are seen (arrow). ×12,000.

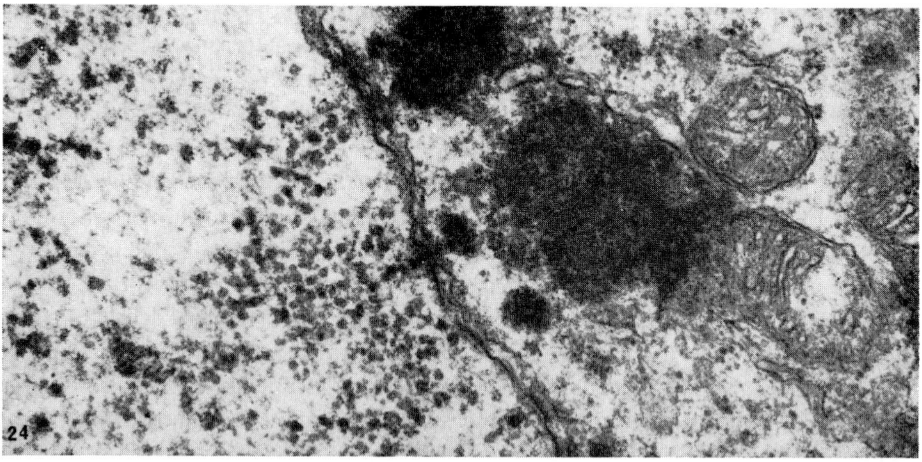
24

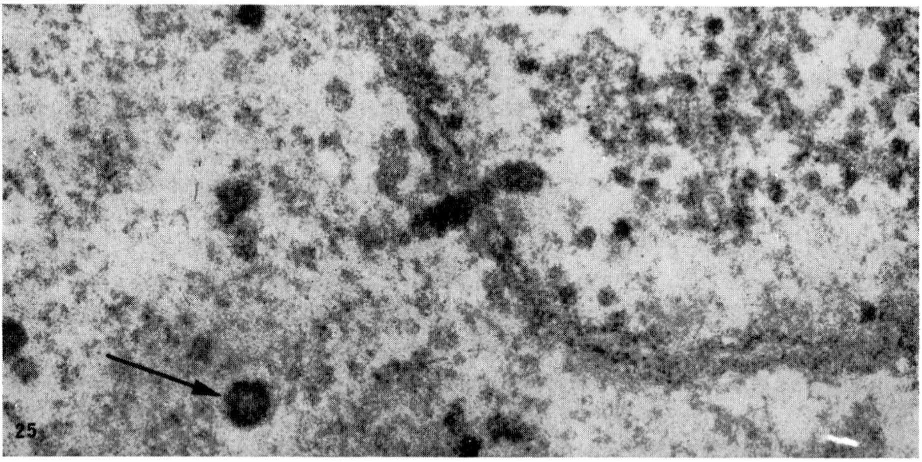
25

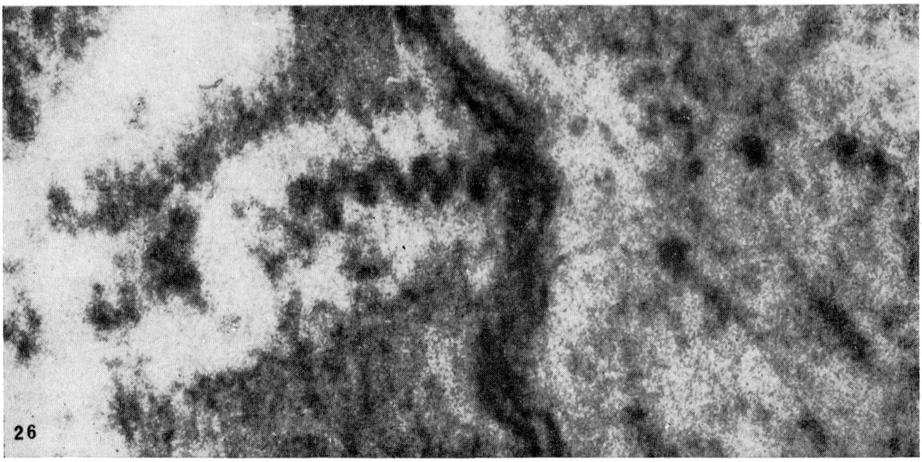
26

evidence is there for a similar passage in other cells? In our observations on spider oocytes, very thin sections showed faint but distinct figures of electron-opaque granules or rods in the center of normally sectioned pores (Figs. 2 and 6). The granules and rods are presumed to be of nuclear origin, and they probably represent another example of material in transit through pores. This example is much less striking than the others and we use it to illustrate the diversity and range of visibility among images demonstrating transport via pores. There are surely many other cases like this one and no doubt many more which remain imperceptible with present electron microscope techniques.

One other observation which has frequently been made strengthens the postulate that the nuclear pores serve as a principal route in nucleocytoplasmic transport. Sections tangential to the envelope very often show an electron-opaque granule, about 150 to 200 Å in diameter, located in the center of annuli (Fig. 10). The 'central granule' was first pointed out by Afzelius (1955), and since has been noted in many studies (e.g., Swift 1958; Watson 1959; Vivier). It is not observed after permanganate fixation. We interpret these granules as representing material in transit through the pores. Their diameter and central location coincides with images of material engaged in pores viewed in normal sections. While it is puzzling that observations of the central granule are frequent in tangential sections and relatively rare in normal sections, the fact can be satisfactorily explained by an effect of electron optics. In normal sections, the low electron-opacity of a granule easily could be masked by an overlying portion of the pore margin. In tangential sections, the electron-opacity of the material to the contrary would be increased, due to the fact that its entire elongated form within the pore would be included in the section thickness. It appears unlikely that the central granule represents a stable, structural component of the pore complex. Its occurrence and size suggest rather that it represents a transitory structure, that of material traversing the envelope via the pores.

A significant observation in these cases is the constricted or 'strangled' form of the

---

Figs. 24–26. Evidence for passage from nucleus to cytoplasm through the nuclear pores.

Fig. 24. Oocyte of the frog, *Rana temporaria*. A narrow strand of electron-opaque material traverses the nuclear envelope through the center of a pore, from a cluster of granules on the nuclear side to an amorphous, dark mass on the cytoplasmic side. Some granules appear to be continuous with the material in transit. Mitochondria accumulate around the dark cytoplasmic masses. Glutaraldehyde–osmium. × 51,500. (From J.-C. Clérot.)

Fig. 25. Salivary gland cell from *Chironomus thummi* larva. Arrow points to an RNA-rich granule formed at another site in the nucleus, on a particular puff, the Balbiani ring. Another granule is in the process of traversing the nuclear envelope through the center of a pore. The granule has become elongated and appears to be constricted at the level of the envelope. Acrolein + formalin–osmium. × 130,000. (From B. J. Stevens and H. Swift.)

Fig. 26. Pore in the nuclear envelope of *Amoeba proteus*. An RNA-containing nuclear helix touches the nuclear envelope in the region of a pore. Such helices are at times encountered on the cytoplasmic side. Nucleus at left. × 95,000. (From A. R. Stevens.)

material within the pore. The nuclear components passing through pores appear to be transformed into elongated structures which fill only a narrow channel in the pore center. The transformation is particularly evident in the passage of Balbiani ring granules in *Chironomus* (Fig. 27). The central channel diagrammed here is exactly similar to that portrayed in the passage of gold particles (Fig. 19). Both series of observations indicate that the arrangement of the annular material limits the pathway within the pore and creates the diffusion barrier suggested in other studies. How this material effects the transformation of substances in transit, and whether the substances become attached to it, as Feldherr has proposed, remain to be answered.

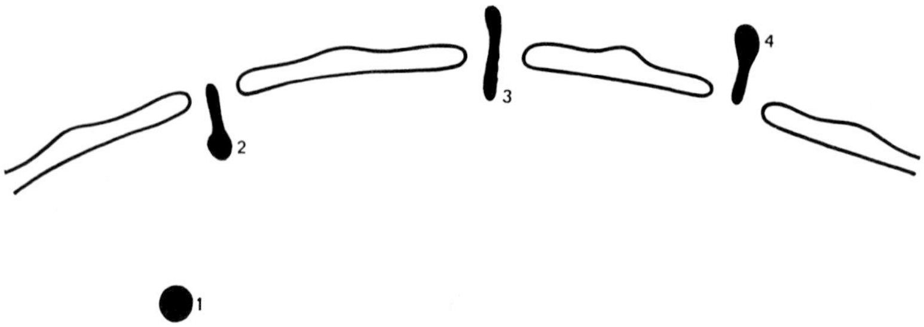

Fig. 27. Schematic interpretation of the transit of Balbiani ring granules through the nuclear pores from nucleus to cytoplasm in *Chironomus* salivary gland cells. Numbers 1 to 4 indicate the successive steps as observed by electron microscopy. The granules become greatly constricted and appear to pass through a narrow channel in the center of the pore.

4. Conclusions

From a general point of view, the nuclear envelope appears as a highly specialized partition between the protoplasmic volumes where transcription and translation of the genetic information are respectively operated. This partition controls the numerous, rapid and constant exchanges between the two protoplasmic compartments. For the main part, the exchanges can be understood as an entrance of small molecules and ions, and an exit of macromolecules synthesized inside the nucleus. We have seen that under normal conditions, direct visualization of material entering the nucleus has not been realized, whereas the reverse movement can be demonstrated in a variety of actively synthesizing cells. Possibly, entrance of small molecules and ions occurs across both membranes, over the whole surface (route E in Fig. 20), while exit of macromolecules operates through specialized loci, the pores (route C). Membrane permeability in general is still poorly understood and controversial, and that of the nuclear membranes can be explained neither at the molecular nor at the energetic level. The passage of macromolecules through pores is beginning to be understood, at least on morphological grounds. Our present knowledge places emphasis on the annular material as of prime importance in the control of pore permeability. This material, mostly proteinaceous, is probably endowed with enzymatic activities which determine the physiological 'openness' or 'closedness' of the pores.

As a whole, the 'permeability' of the nuclear envelope is no doubt much more complicated than that of any other cellular membrane. The nuclear envelope specifically controls the movement of many molecules in a unidirectional and irreversible manner. Its complex organization reflects the complexity of its roles. Its acquisition by eukaryotic cells seems to have constituted a decisive evolutionary advantage.

References

AFZELIUS, B. A.: The ultrastructure of the nuclear membrane of the sea urchin oocyte as studied with the electron microscope. Exptl. Cell Res. 8 (1955) 147.

AFZELIUS, B. A.: The nucleus of *Noctiluca scintillans*. Aspects of nucleocytoplasmic exchanges and the formation of nuclear membrane. J. Cell Biol. 19 (1962) 229.

ANDERSON, E. and H. W. BEAMS: Evidence from electron micrographs for the passage of material through pores of the nuclear membrane. J. Biophys. Biochem. Cytol., Suppl. 2 (1956) 439.

ANDERSON, N. G.: On the nuclear envelope. Science 117 (1953) 517.

ANDERSON, W. A. and R. A. ELLIS: Cytodifferentiation of the crayfish spermatozoon: Acrosome formation, transformation of mitochondria and development of microtubules. Z. Zellforsch. Mikroskop. Anat. 77 (1967) 80.

ANDRÉ, J. and C. ROUILLER: L'ultrastructure de la membrane nucléaire des ovocytes de l'Araignée (*Tegenaria domestica* Clerk). In: F.S. Sjöstrand and J. Rhodin, eds.: Electron microscopy, Proceedings of the Stockholm conference. Uppsala, Almqvist and Wiksells (1956) 162.

BARNES, B. G. and J. M. DAVIS: The structure of nuclear pores in mammalian tissue. J. Ultrastruct. Res. 3 (1959) 131.

BAUD, C. A.: Ultrastructure et fonctions de la membrane nucléaire. In: J. A. Thomas, ed.: Problèmes d'ultrastructures et de fonctions nucléaires. Paris, Masson et Cie (1959) 1.

BEAULATON, J.: Sur l'action d'enzymes au niveau des pores nucléaires et d'autres structures de cellules sécrétrices prothoraciques inclusés en épon. Z. Zellforsch. Mikroskop. Anat. 89 (1968) 453.

BERNHARD, W.: Ultrastructural aspects of nucleocytoplasmic relationship. Exptl. Cell Res., Suppl. 6 (1958) 17.

BRZIN, M., V. M. TENNYSON and P. E. DUFFY: Acetylcholinesterase in frog sympathetic and dorsal root ganglia. A study by electron microscope cytochemistry and microgasometric analysis with the magnetic diver. J. Cell Biol. 31 (1966) 215.

CALLAN, H. G.: A general account of experimental work on amphibian oocyte nuclei. Symp. Soc. Exptl. Biol. 6 (1952) 243.

CALLAN, H. G. and S. G. TOMLIN: Experimental studies on amphibian oocyte nuclei. I. Investigation of the structure of the nuclear membrane by means of the electron microsocpe. Proc. Roy. Soc. (London), Ser. B 137 (1950) 367.

CATESSON, A.-M. and Y. CZANINSKI: Mise en évidence d'une activité phosphatasique acide dans le réticulum endoplasmique des tissus conducteurs de Robinier et de Sycomore. J. Microscopie 6 (1967) 509.

CLÉROT, J.-C.: Mise en évidence par cytochimie ultrastructurale de l'émission de protéines par le noyau d'auxocytes de Batraciens. J. Microscopie. In press.

DURCHON, M. and B. BOILLY: Etude ultrastructurale de l'influence de l'hormone cérébrale des Néréidiens sur le développement des ovocytes de *Nereis diversicolor* O. F. Müller (Annélide Polychète) en culture organotypique. Compt. Rend. Acad. Sci. 259 (1964) 1245.

FAWCETT, D.W.: On the occurrence of a fibrous lamina on the inner aspect of the nuclear envelope in certain cells of vertebrates. Am. J. Anat. 119 (1966) 129.

FELDHERR, C.M.: The effect of the electron-opaque pore material on exchanges through the nuclear annuli. J. Cell Biol. 25 (1965) 43.

FELDHERR, C.M. and C.V.HARDING: The permeability characteristics of the nuclear envelope at interphase. Protoplasmatologia 5 (1964) 35.

FRANKE, W.W.: Zur Feinstruktur isolierter Kernmembranen aus tierischen Zellen. Z. Zellforsch. Mikroskop. Anat. 80 (1967) 585.

GALL, J.G.: Electron microscopy of the nuclear envelope. Protoplasmatologia 5 (1964) 4.

GALL, J.G.: Octagonal nuclear pores. J. Cell Biol. 32 (1967) 391.

GEORGIEV, G.P.: The nucleus. In: D.B.Roodyn, ed.: Enzyme cytology. London, Academic Press Inc. (1967) 27.

GOLDFISCHER, S., N.CARASSO and P.FAVARD: The demonstration of acid phosphatase activity by electron microscopy in the ergastoplasm of the ciliate *Campanella umbellaria*. J. Microscopie 2 (1963) 621.

GOLDFISCHER, S., E.ESSNER and A.B.NOVIKOFF: The localization of phosphatase activities at the level of ultrastructure. J. Histochem. Cytochem. 12 (1964) 72.

GOLDSTEIN, L.: Nucleocytoplasmic relationships. In: G.H.Bourne, ed.: Cytology and cell physiology, third ed. New York, Academic Press Inc. (1964) 559.

GRASSO, J.A., H.SWIFT and G.A.ACKERMAN: Observations on the development of erythrocytes in mammalian fetal liver. J. Cell Biol. 14 (1962) 235.

GREY, E.G. and R.W.GUILLERY: On nuclear structure in the ventral nerve cord of the leech *Hirudo medicinalis*. Z. Zellforsch. Mikroskop. Anat. 59 (1963) 738.

HARRIS, P.: Structural changes following fertilization in the sea urchin egg. Formation and dissolution of heavy bodies. Exptl. Cell Res. 48 (1967) 569.

ITO, S. and W.R.LOEWENSTEIN: Permeability of a nuclear membrane: Changes during normal development and changes induced by growth hormone. Science 150 (1965) 909.

JOYON, L. and R.CHARRET: Sur l'ultrastructure du Thécamoebien *Hyalosphenia papilio* (Leidy). Compt. Rend. Acad. Sci. 255 (1962) 2661.

KALIFAT, S.R., M.BOUTEILLE and J.DELARUE: Etude ultrastructurale de la lamelle dense observée au contact de la membrane nucléaire interne. J. Microscopie 6 (1967) 1019.

KESSEL, R.G.: Electron microscope studies on the origin of annulate lamellae in oocytes of *Necturus*. J. Cell Biol. 19 (1963) 391.

KESSEL, R.G.: An electron microscope study of nuclear-cytoplasmic exchange in oocytes of *Ciona intestinalis*. J. Ultrastruct. Res. 15 (1966) 181.

KESSEL, R.G.: Annulate lamellae. J. Ultrastruct. Res., Suppl. 10 (1968).

LEDUC, E.H., S.AVREMEAS and M.BOUTEILLE: Ultrastructural localization of antibody in differentiating plasma cells. J. Exptl. Med. 127 (1968) 109.

LOEWENSTEIN, W.R.: Permeability of the nuclear membrane as determined with electrical methods. Protoplasmatologia 5 (1964) 26.

MAZANEC, K.: Présence de la '*zonula nucleum limitans*' dans quelques cellules humaines. J. Microscopie 6 (1967) 1027.

MERRIAM, R.W.: On the fine structure and composition of the nuclear envelope. J. Biophys. Biochem. Cytol. 11 (1961) 559.

MERRIAM, R.W.: Some dynamic aspects of the nuclear envelope. J. Cell Biol. 12 (1962) 79.

MIRSKY, A.E. and S.OSAWA: The interphase nucleus. In: J.Brachet and A.E.Mirsky, eds.: The cell, vol. II. New York, Academic Press Inc. (1961) 677.

MOOR, H.: In: N.Higashi, ed.: The world through the electron microscope, Biology, Vol. III. JEOL Co. (1967) 88.

MOOR, H. and K.MÜHLETHALER: Fine structure in frozen-etched yeast cells. J. Cell Biol. 17 (1963) 609.

MOSES, M.J.: The nucleus and chromosomes: A cytological perspective. In: G.H.Bourne, ed.: Cytology and cell physiology, third ed. New York, Academic Press Inc. (1964) 423.

MURRAY, R.G., A.S.MURRAY and A.PIZZO: The fine structure of mitosis in rat thymic lymphocytes. J. Cell Biol. 26 (1965) 601.

NAORA, H., H.NAORA, M.IZAWA, V.G.ALLFREY and A.E.MIRSKY: Some observations on differences in composition between the nucleus and cytoplasm of the frog oocyte. Proc. Natl. Acad. Sci. U.S. 48 (1962) 853.

NOVIKOFF, A.B., E.ESSNER, S.GOLDFISCHER and M.HEUS: Nucleosidephosphatase activities of cytomembranes. In: R.J.C.Harris, ed.: The interpretation of ultrastructure. New York, Academic Press Inc. (1962) 149.

NOVIKOFF, A.B., N.QUINTANA, H.VILLAVERDE and R.FORSCHIRM: Nucleoside phosphatase and cholinesterase activities in dorsal root ganglia and peripheral nerve. J. Cell Biol. 29 (1966) 525.

PATRIZI, G.: Further considerations on the ultrastructure of the nuclear periphery with observations on human plasma cells. J. Microscopie 7 (1968) 293.

PATRIZI, G. and M.POGER: The ultrastructure of the nuclear periphery. The *Zonula Nucleum Limitans*. J. Ultrastruct. Res. 17 (1967) 127.

POLICARD, A. and M.BESSIS: Sur l'espace périnucléaire. Compt. Rend. Acad. Sci. 242 (1956) 2496.

PORTER, K.R. and R.D.MACHADO: Studies on the endoplasmic reticulum. IV. Its form and distribution during mitosis in cells of onion root tip. J. Biophys. Biochem. Cytol. 7 (1960) 167.

REBHUN, L.I.: Some electron microscope observations on membranous basophilic elements of invertebrate eggs. J. Ultrastruct. Res. 5 (1961) 208.

ROBBINS, E. and N.K.GONATAS: The ultrastructure of a mammalian cell during the mitotic cycle. J. Cell Biol. 21 (1964) 429.

ROTH, L.E. and E.W.DANIELS: Electron microscopic studies of mitosis in amebae. II. The giant ameba *Pelomyxa carolinensis*. J. Cell Biol. 12 (1962) 57.

STEVENS, A.R.: Machinery for exchange across the nuclear membrane. In: L.Goldstein, ed.: The control of nuclear activity. Englewood Cliffs, N.J., Prentice-Hall, Inc. (1967) 189.

STEVENS, B.J. and H.SWIFT: RNA transport from nucleus to cytoplasm in *Chironomus* salivary glands. J. Cell Biol. 31 (1966) 55.

SWIFT, H.: The fine structure of annulate lamellae. J. Biophys. Biochem. Cytol., Suppl. 2 (1956) 415.

SWIFT, H.: Cytoplasmic particulates and basophilia. In: W.D.McElroy and B.Glass, eds.: A symposium on the chemical basis of development. Baltimore, Johns Hopkins Press (1958) 174.

VIVIER, E.: Observations ultrastructurales sur l'enveloppe nucléaire et ses 'pores' chez des Sporozoaires. J. Microscopie 6 (1967) 371.

WATSON, M.L.: The nuclear envelope. Its structure and relation to cytoplasmic membranes. J. Biophys. Biochem. Cytol. 1 (1955) 257.

WATSON, M.L.: Further observations on the nuclear envelope of the animal cell. J. Biophys. Biochem. Cytol. 6 (1959) 147.

WHALEY, W.G., H.H.MOLLENHAUER and J.H.LEECH: Some observations on the nuclear envelope. J. Biophys. Biochem. Cytol. 8 (1960) 233.

WIENER, J., D.SPIRO and W.R.LOEWENSTEIN: Ultrastructure and permeability of nuclear membranes. J. Cell Biol. 27 (1965) 107.

WISCHNITZER, S.: An electron microscope study of the nuclear envelope of amphibian oocytes. J. Ultrastruct. Res. 1 (1958) 201.

YASUZUMI, G. and I.TSUBO: The fine structure of nuclei as revealed by electron microscopy. III. Adenosine triphosphate activity in the pores of nuclear envelope of mouse choroid plexus epithelial cells. Exptl. Cell Res. 43 (1966) 281.

PART XI

Ultrastructure and biochemistry of mitochondria and chloroplasts

CHAPTER 34

Ultrastructure of mitochondria

E. A. MUNN

Biochemistry Department, Agricultural Research Council Institute of Animal Physiology, Babraham, Cambridge

Contents

1. Introduction
2. Methods of study
3. Structure revealed by thin sectioning
4. Structure revealed by negative staining
5. Structure revealed by freeze-etching
6. Composition of mitochondrial membranes
7. Interpretations of membrane structure seen in thin sections
8. Native situation of the stalked particles
9. Nature of the stalked particles
10. Organization of the cristae
11. Continuity of the intracristal and peripheral spaces, compartmentation
12. Changes associated with large amplitude swelling and contraction
13. Changes associated with different metabolic steady states
14. The matrix
15. Mitochondrial inclusions
16. Mitochondrial DNA

1. Introduction

The study of the ultrastructure of mitochondria began in 1952 with observations by Palade and Sjöstrand on the electron microscopic appearance of finely sectioned tissues. The data on both structure and function of mitochondria available up to 1960 was reviewed by Novikoff. This correlative approach was developed extensively by Lehninger. Since then significant advances have been made in this area.

Virtually all aerobic cells contain mitochondria. There may be only one per cell, as in the case of the minute flagellate, *Chromulina pussilla*, (Manton) or some hundreds of thousands, as in the giant amoeba *Chaos chaos* (Andresen). The mitochondria may appear to lie randomly as in a hepatic cell, or they may be characteristically orientated and/or localised in one area of the cell, as are the mitochondria in the mid-piece of mammalian sperm. Mitochondria which are localised or specifically orientated are probably fairly static. Phase contrast microscopy of live cells, however, shows that mitochondria which are not so localised move freely through the cell. The movements are accompanied by changes in shape and apparently in size, and the mitochondria also appear to divide and coalesce. This plasticity of form should be borne in mind when considering the studies of the ultrastructure of mitochondria described below.

2. Methods of study

Our knowledge of mitochondrial ultrastructure is derived from two main methods of study: electron microscopy and biochemical analyses. The techniques of electron microscopy which have provided most information on mitochondrial structure are thin sectioning, negative staining and, most recently, freeze-etching. For sectioning specimens have first to be 'fixed' and then embedded in a supporting medium. Because of the lack of inherent electron density in biological specimens they have to be 'stained' with electron dense molecules. This is done during fixation by the use of osmium tetroxide or potassium permanganate, or subsequently by treating the fixed specimen with a solution of heavy metal salt (lead, uranium, vanadium). The stain accumulates in some parts of the specimen which are thus distinguished from the other parts. In negative staining the specimen is surrounded by an aqueous solution of an electron-dense salt (e.g. potassium phosphotungstate, ammonium molybdate) which is allowed to dry in a thin film around the specimen and is thought to preserve it in a hydrated state, or at least one resembling the hydrated state (Bangham and Horne). The negative stain penetrates more or less into the hydrophilic parts of specimens and the resulting image in the electron microscope reveals the unpenetrated regions as relatively electron transparent structures against an electron-dense background. The specimen may be treated with a fixative before negative staining. In the freeze-etching technique the specimen is rapidly frozen to about −190 °C; under vacuum the frozen material, now at about −100 °C, is fractured to expose a surface which is frozen-dried to a depth of a few hundred Ångstroms (etching) and then shadowed with platinum-carbon to form a replica which can be examined in the electron microscope.

In general the techniques of negative staining and chemical analysis are restricted to isolated mitochondria although negative staining can be applied to the study of mitochondria in certain specialised cells, e.g. spermatozoa, and in pinched off fragments of cells (Whittaker and Sheridan). Sectioning and freeze-etching can equally well be used in the study of isolated mitochondria or of mitochondria *in situ*.

3. *Structure revealed by thin sectioning*

On historical grounds and also in consideration of the large amount of information which the technique has provided, it is appropriate to consider the data derived from the study of thin sections first. The apparent structure of mitochondria *in situ* examined by thin-sectioning depends on the type of cell in which the mitochondria occur, the physiological state of the cell, and, not least, on the procedure to which the cell is subjected in its preparation for examination in the electron microscope. The apparent structure of isolated mitochondria further depends on their treatment during isolation and prior to preparation for sectioning. Within these limits all mitochondria can be referred to a general basic pattern as first described by Palade (1952, 1953), Sjöstrand (1953) and Sjöstrand and Rhodin. Each mitochondrion consists of a limiting or *outer membrane* within which is an *inner membrane* which in turn encloses an inner space called the *matrix* (Fig. 1). Lying in the matrix are a variable number of membranous

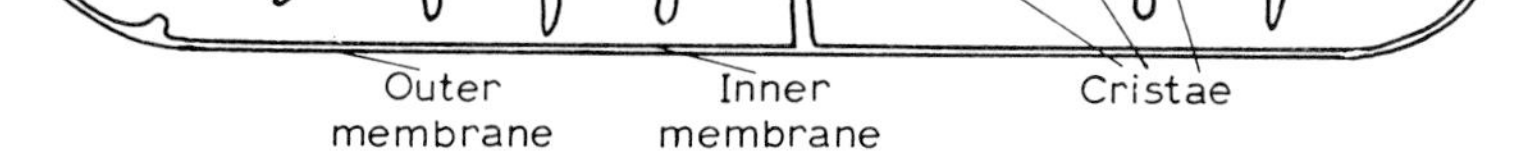

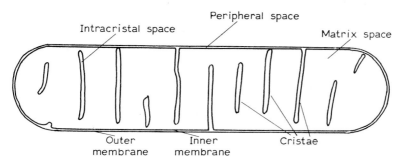

Fig. 1. Diagram of section of mitochondrion; compare with electron micrographs in Figs. 8 and 10.

structures called *cristae* which appear either to lie free, or are associated with the inner membrane. The cristae are sometimes seen to contain a space, the *intracristal space*, and in mitochondria which have this appearance there is also usually a space between the outer and inner membranes, the *peripheral space*. Occasionally the inner membrane and the cristae membranes are seem to be continuous so that there is continuity between the intracristal and the peripheral spaces. The intracristal and peripheral spaces, when present, usually appear to be empty – that is they contain no material which reacts with the electron dense stains. The matrix, however, appears more or less electron dense and finely granular. The matrix may contain discrete electron dense granular, crystalline or fibrous inclusions.

Although Chandra has published electron micrographs of the liver and adrenal cortex of 2- to 4-day old hamsters which appear to demonstrate continuities between inner and outer membranes of mitochondria it is generally held that these are two separate entities. Most studies utilizing thin sectioning reveal no difference in their fine structure, but in all mitochondria which have been examined by negative staining, and in mitochondria of human endometrial cells (Claude) and abdominal ganglia of adults and pupae of the wax moth, *Galleria mellonella*, (Ashhurst) examined by thin sectioning they are seen to be structurally distinct. Furthermore, they can be isolated and they have been shown to have different physical and chemical properties (see below).

The apparent fine structure of mitochondrial membranes in sections depends primarily on the fixative employed. In mitochondria fixed in buffered osmium tetroxide each membrane appears as an osmiophilic (electron dense) band 50 Å or more in width. This can sometimes be resolved into three separate layers each about 15 Å in width, the outer layers being electron dense, sandwiching a relatively electron transparent layer which may appear to be bridged by strands of stained material (Sjöstrand 1963). In mitochondria fixed in potassium permanganate each membrane appears as an electron dense band 50–60 Å wide and with a central row of globular electron lucid regions 30 Å across and about 40 Å centre to centre. The membranes of each crista and the inner and outer membranes at the periphery of the mitochondria are frequently closely apposed in this fixative. Malhotra compared the structure of mitochondria in mouse pancreatic and central nervous tissues fixed in osmium tetroxide or formaldehyde with and without cooling to about −200 °C. Frozen tissues were fixed in osmium tetroxide by a process called freeze-substitution which was thought to produce a more accurate representation of the *in vivo* distribution of water than direct chemical fixation. Non-frozen tissues were fixed in aqueous formaldehyde *p*H 6.4 and some were subsequently post-osmicated. In tissues frozen within 30 seconds after decapitation of the animals and then freeze-substituted the cristal and peripheral membranes had a 5-layered appearance and generally there was no evidence of intracristal or peripheral spaces (Fig. 2a). Some mitochondria, particularly in freshly frozen cerebral cortex, however, showed an intracristal space formed by the separation of the central opaque layer (Fig. 2b) giving an appearance similar to that commonly seen in material fixed directly in osmium tetroxide. The 5-layered pattern of mitochondrial membranes is also seen in tissues which have been fixed in permanganate (Sjöstrand 1963), or in glutaraldehyde (without subsequent treatment with osmium tetroxide). In mitochondria fixed in formaldehyde (without post-osmication) the cristae appear as electron transparent layers about 140 Å wide in an electron-dense matrix; each layer is bisected by an electron-dense line about 35 Å wide. The cristae of rat-liver mitochondria fixed in formaldehyde have a very similar appearance (Pease). Mitochondria fixed in

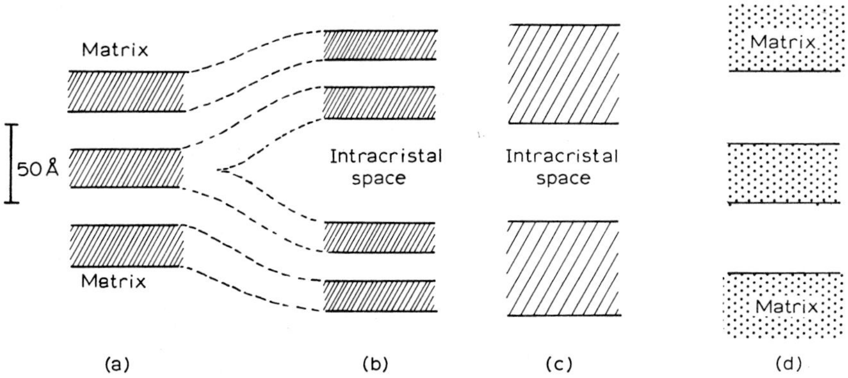

Fig. 2. Diagrams to show appearance of sections of cristal membranes after treatment with various fixatives. (a) and (b): osmium tetroxide by freeze-substitution (see text); (c): osmium tetroxide, or formaldehyde followed by osmium tetroxide; (d): formaldehyde alone.

formaldehyde and then post-osmicated have the same appearance as mitochondria in tissues fixed directly in osmium tetroxide. In general, the outer, inner and cristal membranes have the same apparent fine structure and dimensions in sections. However, Claude and Ashhurst using conventionally fixed material have observed that the surface of the cristal membranes facing the matrix is studded with electron-dense globular particles. These particles have been equated with similar structures (called elementary particles or inner membrane subunits) which have been observed associated with the inner membranes of virtually all disrupted mitochondria which have been examined by the negative staining technique.

4. *Structure revealed by negative staining*

Intact mitochondria examined by the negative staining technique after fixation with formaldehyde or osmium tetroxide have an appearance which is directly referable to the characteristic structure deduced from the study of thin sections (Horne and Whittaker; Whittaker 1963, 1966). The negative stain (potassium phosphotungstate) penetrates between the outer and inner membranes to reveal a space which is clearly seen to be continuous with the intracristal spaces. The stain does not penetrate into the matrix space in these pre-fixed intact mitochondria (Whittaker 1966). There is a marked difference in appearance between these preparations and mitochondria negatively stained with phosphotungstate without prior fixation. In the latter case the mitochondria appear more or less disrupted (e.g. Fig. 3) with the bulk of the inner membranes in the form of ribbon-like tubules and vesicles (Fernández-Morán 1962; Greville, Munn and Smith; Parsons 1963a, b; Smith). Disruption of the mitochondria may be due to surface tension effects (Parsons 1963b) or to the hypotonic conditions to which the mitochondria are subjected during the negative staining procedure (Greville

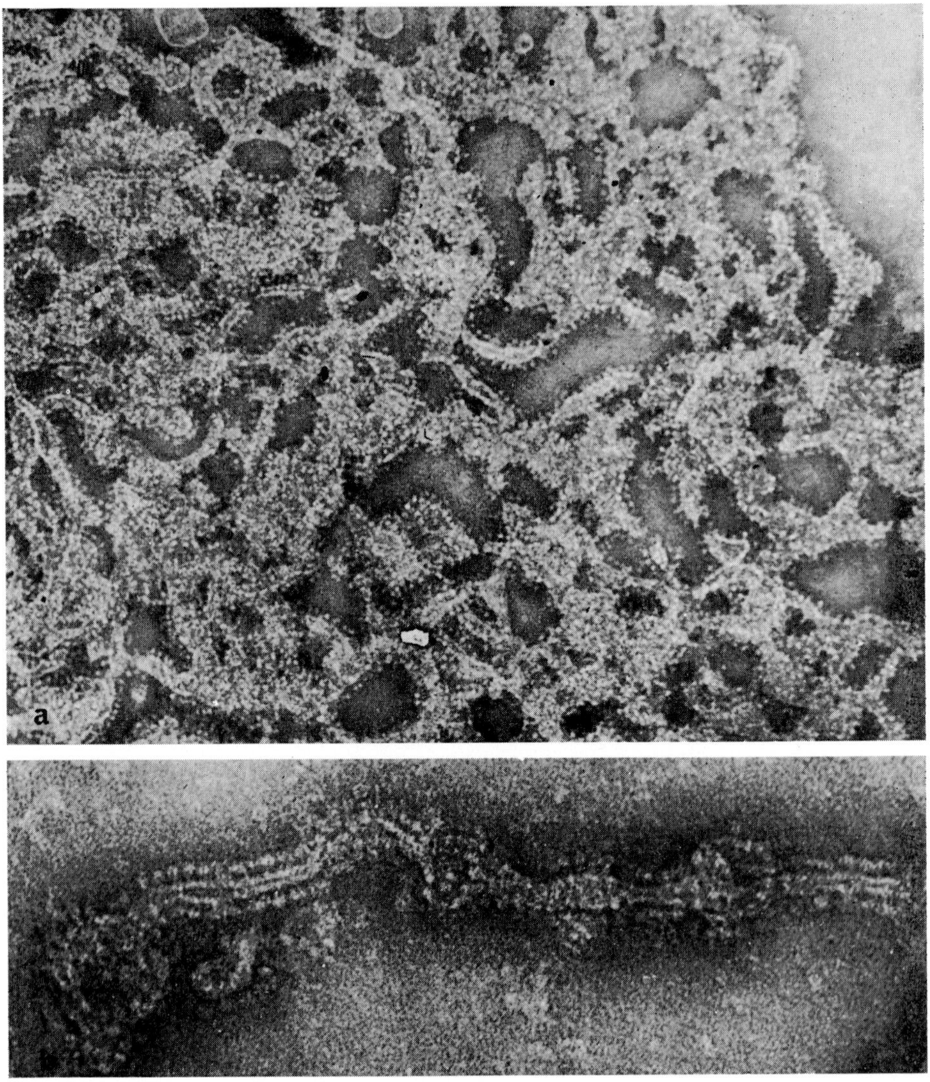

Fig. 3. Electron micrographs of (a): partially disrupted cristal membrane from *Calliphora* flight muscle mitochondrion negatively stained with sodium tungstosilicate; (b): tubular fragment derived from cristal membrane of artichoke mitochondrion, negatively stained with ammonium molybdate. (a): × 75,000; (b): ×150,000.

et al.; Whittaker 1966). Most negative stains are hypo-osmotic but the negative stain ammonium molybdate at concentrations at which other negative stains are normally used is isosmotic with the media commonly employed in the isolation of mitochondria. The majority of mitochondria negatively stained with ammonium molybdate are preserved intact without fixation. The negative stain penetrates the outer membrane but does not penetrate the intact inner membrane (Fig. 4).

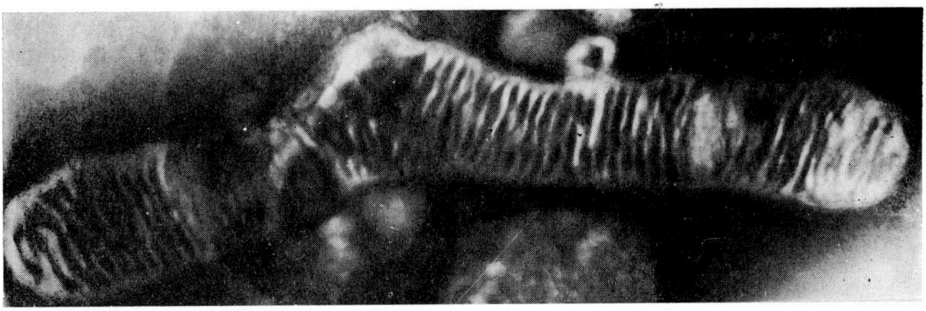

Fig. 4. Electron micrograph of mitochondrion isolated from rabbit brown adipose tissue in 0.44 M sucrose, negatively stained with 5% ammonium molybdate. × 23,500.

The exposed inner membranes of disrupted mitochondria are studded with large numbers of the particulate components, about 90 Å in diameter, first described by Fernández-Morán. In blowfly flight muscle there are about 4,000 particles per μ^2, in ox heart, 2,000 to 4,000, and in *Neurospora crassa*, about 3,000 per μ^2. Parsons and Chance have reported that the centre to centre spacing of the particles in rat-liver mitochondria is 100 Å. In mitochondria from the flight muscles of emergent bees the spacing is 174 Å and in adult bees 115 Å. The particles are attached by a stalk (Fernández-Morán 1963; Parsons 1963a, b; Stoeckenius 1963; Smith) to a base-piece (Smith). The reported dimensions of these components are set out in Table 1.

TABLE 1

Dimensions (in Å) of the components of the inner membranes revealed by negative staining

Source of mitochondria	Head	Stalk		Base	Ref.
		Height	Width		
Ox heart	80–100	50	—	45 × 114	1,2
Blowfly flight muscle	80–95	45–50	—	~ 50 (diam)	3,4
Bee flight muscle	60–150 (Av. 90)	—	—	40 × 70	5,6
Rodent liver	75–80	45–50	30–35	—	7
Neurospora crassa	~ 85	40–50	~ 30	—	8
Castor bean	75–95 (Av. 85)	40–60	~ 40	—	9
Mung bean (and others)	90–110	45	35–40	—	10
Yeast	80 × 60	40–50	—	—	11
Ascaris	40–120 (Av. 80)	—	—	—	6

References: 1, Fernández-Morán (1962, 1963); 2, Fernández-Morán et al.; 3, Smith; 4, Greville et al.; 5, Parsons (1965); 6, Chance and Parsons; 7, Parsons (1963a, b); 8, Stoeckenius (1963); 9, Nadakavukaren; 10, Parsons et al. (1965); 11, Shingawa et al.

The base-piece has been described as either spherical (in blowfly flight muscle mitochondria), cylindrical (in ox heart mitochondria) or rectangular (in bee flight muscle mitochondria). Frequently it requires the eye of faith to distinguish the base-pieces since they form a continuous layer from which the heads project on stalks. This layer is probably the same as the membrane revealed in sections, the base-pieces accounting for the bulk of the membrane thickness. The inner membranes of mitochondria from brown adipose tissue are the only ones so far described which lack the stalked particles (Lindberg et al.).

The outer mitochondrial membrane of all tissues (except possibly blowfly flight muscle) can be distinguished from the inner membranes by its lack of projecting 90 Å-diameter particles. Parsons has shown that parts of the outer membrane of rat, guinea pig and ox liver mitochondria show arrays of hollow cylinders, 60 Å high, 60 Å in diameter with a central hole penetrated by negative stain 20 Å in diameter. The centre to centre spacing of the cylinders is 80 Å. Parsons has also reported that the outer membrane of some plant mitochondria is penetrated by numerous pits 25–30 Å across, spaced somewhat irregularly but with an average centre to centre spacing of 45 Å (Fig. 5). It is not clear whether the pits are true perforations of the membrane or just surface depressions.

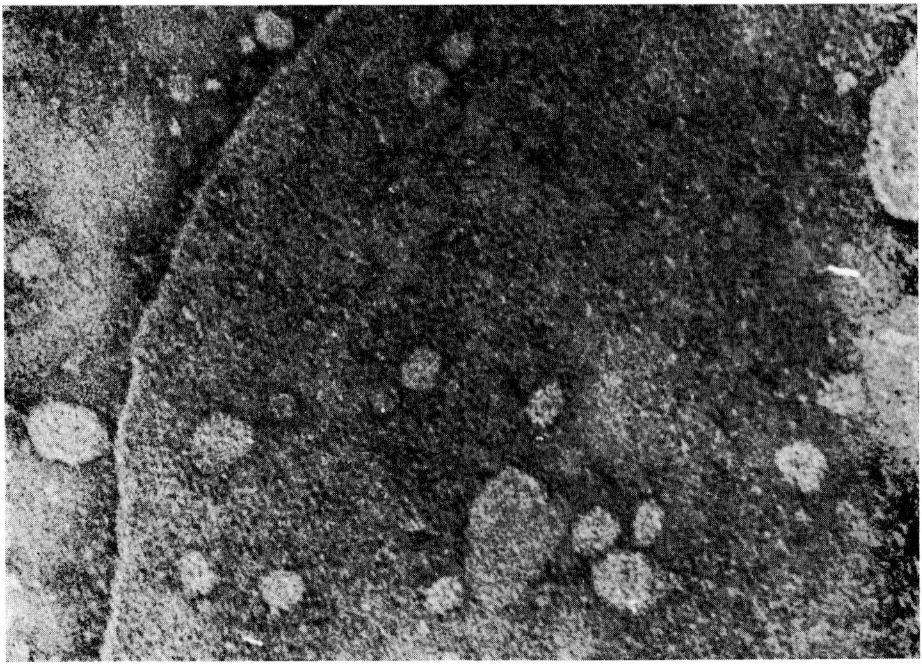

Fig. 5. Part of outer membrane of artichoke mitochondrion, negatively stained (with ammonium molybdate) to show the pitted appearance described by Parsons (Parsons 1965; Parsons et al. 1965). × 380,000.

5. *Structure revealed by freeze-etching*

Outer, inner and cristal membranes can be distinguished in mitochondria examined by the freeze-etching technique and these appear to be arranged in the same way as seen in sectioned material (Moor and Mühlethaler). In some micrographs globular particles apparently associated with the surface of the membranes facing the matrix can be discerned (Moor et al.). Although it is thought that the freeze-etching technique reveals the structure of the inside of some membranes (Branton) no data of this kind are yet available for mitochondrial membranes.

6. *Composition of mitochondrial membranes*

The mitochondrial membranes contain some 60–65% by weight protein and 35–40% lipid. The lipids, of which the bulk are phospholipids, are distributed unequally between the inner and outer membranes (Table 2). About half of the protein is so-called structural protein(s) and the rest consists of a number of enzymes. Some of these enzymes, notably the components of the respiratory chain and those bringing about oxidative phosphorylation are specifically associated with the inner membrane. D.E. Green and his colleagues have isolated the respiratory chain in the form of four complexes. The complexes are thought to represent natural groupings of their components (except for the cytochrome *b* found in complex II). The particle weights of the complexes, some of their components and related enzymes are set out in Table 3.

TABLE 2

Lipid content (mg per g protein) of whole mitochondria and inner and outer membranes. (Data from Fleischer, Rouser, Fleischer, Casu and Kritchevsky; Parsons et al. (1967); and Parsons and Yano.)

				Guinea pig liver		
	Ox heart	Ox kidney	Ox liver	Whole mitochondria	Inner membrane	Outer membrane
Total lipid	320	240	180	—	—	—
Neutral lipid	18	17	16	—	—	—
Cholesterol	4	11	4	2	5	30
Phospholipid	283	190	145	159	301	878
Phosphatidylcholine*	41	40	43	40	44.5	55.2
Phosphatidylethanolamine*	37	38	35	28	25.3	27.7
Cardiolipin*	19	19	17	22.5	21.5	3.2
Phosphatidyl inositol (and others)*	3	4	5	7	4.2	13.5

* % of total phospholipid.

TABLE 3

Particle weights of electron transport complexes, their components and some associated enzymes.

Component	Source	Particle weight (daltons)	Ref.
Complex I (Non-haem iron protein, structural protein, acid-extractable flavin, lipid)	Ox heart	117×10^4	1
Complex II (Non-haem iron protein, cytochrome *b*, acid-extractable flavin, lipid)	Ox heart	20×10^4	2
Complex III (Non-haem iron protein, cytochrome *b*, cytochrome *c*, core protein, lipid)	Ox heart	30×10^4	3
Complex IV (Cytochrome a, a_3, copper protein, lipid)	Ox heart	$26–36 \times 10^4$	1, 4
Cytochrome *a* (monomer)	Ox heart	7.2×10^4	11
Cytochrome *c*	Horse heart	1.2×10^4	5
Cytochrome c_1	Ox heart	$3.6–3.8 \times 10^4$	6, 11
Cytochrome *b*	Ox heart	$2.0–2.8 \times 10^4$	7
	Ox heart, *Musca* flight muscle	$2.5–3.0 \times 10^4$	8
Non-heam iron protein	Ox heart	$2.5–3.0 \times 10^4$	9
Core protein	Complex III	$4–5 \times 10^4$	10
Structural protein	Ox heart	2.2×10^4	11
	Neurospora	2.3×10^4	12
Copper protein	Complex IV	1.2×10^4	17
NADH dehydrogenase	Yeast	$5–6 \times 10^4$	13
	Heart	$7–9 \times 10^4$	13
	Ox heart	7.8×10^4	14
	Heart	$\sim 10 \times 10^4$	15
Succinate dehydrogenase	Ox heart	$2–3 \times 10^4$	16

References: 1, Green and Tzagoloff; 2, Ziegler and Doeg; 3, Baum et al.; 4, Tzagoloff et al.; 5, Margoliash et al.; 6, Bomstein et al.; 7, Goldberger et al.; 8, Ohnishi (1966a, b, c); 9, Rieske et al.; 10, Silman et al.; 11, Criddle et al.; 12, Woodward and Munkres; 13, Mackler; 14, Mahler; 15, King et al.; 16, Basford et al.; 17, MacLennan and Tzagoloff.

7. *Interpretations of membrane structure seen in thin sections*

The appearance of the mitochondrial membranes has most frequently been interpreted in terms of a bimolecular lipid leaflet structure sandwiched between layers of protein (e.g. Fig. 6). This view has had to be modified in attempts to account for the globular pattern observed in permanganate-fixed material. Sjöstrand (1963) has suggested that this represents globular micelles of lipid (30 Å in diameter) enclosed by protein. Lucy has proposed a structure for biological membranes in general involving lipid both in globular and lamellar (bimolecular leaflet) forms which are interchangeable.

One major difficulty in the interpretation of the appearance of the mitochondrial membranes in sections is the lack of knowledge of the sites of deposition of stain and the possibility that the agents used as fixatives bring about changes in the molecular organization of the membranes. Criegee established that osmium tetroxide reacted stoichiometrically with olefines to form relatively stable osmic acid esters and more recently Korn and co-workers have shown that under conditions frequently used for fixation (2% osmium tetroxide in water at 0 °C) methyl oleate is quantitatively converted to the stable bis(methyl-9,10-dihydroxystearate)osmate. This substance has also been isolated from biological material following fixation with osmium tetroxide. In the model reactions, approximately half of the osmium was recovered as uncharacterized products, presumed to be lower oxides; it is possible therefore that osmium

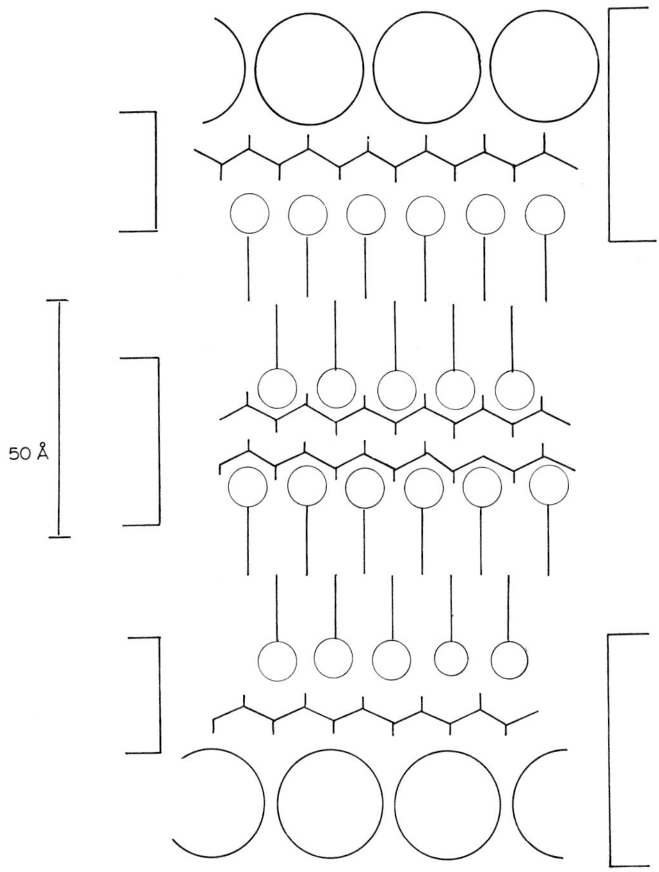

Fig. 6. Diagram to show organisation of proteins and phospholipids in cristal membranes as proposed by Sjöstrand (1960). The position of the electron dense layers observed in material fixed in osmium tetroxide is shown at the right, and those of material fixed in potassium permanganate at the left. (⚲): phospholipid molecule; (○): protein molecules.

other than that bound at the hydrocarbon portions of fatty acids may be deposited in the membrane. Stoeckenius (1959) showed that when bimolecular lipid leaflets were fixed in osmium tetroxide a triple layered structure consisting of two outer electron-dense lines each approximately 18 Å wide and about 25 Å apart was obtained. The width of the outer dense lines increased to 25 Å or more when protein was adsorbed on to the lipid but it is not established whether this represents reaction of the osmium with the protein as such or whether the adsorption of protein increases the thickness of a layer of charged groups reacting with osmium (Curtis). It has long been appreciated that phospholipids in tissues are complexed with proteins, being largely unextractable with diethyl ether until released by polar solvents such as ethanol (Dawson). Benson has proposed a model for biological membranes in which the lipids are bound by hydrophobic association of their hydrocarbon chains with complementary hydrophobic regions within the interior of the proteins. The resulting two-dimensional lipoprotein aggregates would possess the strongly anionic charged groups of the phospholipids on the surface. It is these groups which Benson suggests take up osmium to give the characteristic triple-layered appearance to the membranes. A similar arrangement of phospholipid and protein has been proposed on the basis of studies of membrane formation by proteins obtained from mitochondrial inner membranes (Green and Perdue). It would appear that in the mitochondrial inner membrane at least, osmium tetroxide reacts with some component(s) other than lipids since it has been shown that the appearance of this membrane fixed with osmium tetroxide after extraction of over 95% of the lipids is essentially similar to that of non-extracted membranes (Fleischer et al.).

A clear limitation of the thin sectioning technique is that the apparent fine structure of the inner and outer membranes is in general identical despite the pronounced differences in their composition. Although the negative staining technique demonstrates clear structural differences between the two membranes some doubt has been cast on the validity of the images obtained in this way.

8. *Native situation of the stalked particles*

The use of negative staining in the study of biological membranes in general and mitochondrial membranes in particular has been criticized by Finean and Rumsby and Sjöstrand et al. respectively. Sjöstrand et al. carried out a series of experiments designed to test for the artefactual nature of the globular structures seen on the inner membranes by negative staining using mitochondria obtained from rat heart and kidney in 0.44 M sucrose media. In fresh preparations of the mitochondria fragmented in a Lourdes Microwaring blendor and negatively stained with 'phosphotungstic acid' only a few of the particles could be seen. In preparations kept for 15 min before negative staining there were even fewer particles, after 30 min the number had approximately doubled, but after one hour had attained a new minimum; after two hours the numbers had again risen and after one day virtually all the fragments of membrane appeared to bear particles. In preparations in which the sucrose was diluted to 0.044 M with Tyrode's solution no particles could be seen after 15 min, but they then steadily increased in numbers over the next two hours. On the other hand, in preparations 15 min after dilution with distilled water there were approximately three times the number of particles, after one hour there were fewer particles than observed initially and after two hours there were somewhat more than at 15 min. Sjöstrand et al. found it more diffcult to see the edge-bound particles on fragments of mitochondria from heart than on those from kidney. They concluded that the particles represented a myelin figure-like transformation of the membrane lipoproteins during deterioration of the mitochondrial structure, and that they did not represent the normal *in vivo* structural organization. However, by teasing out blowfly flight muscles into negative stain the disrupted mitochondria can be ready for examination in the electron microscope very quickly. Similarly, by the surface-spreading technique of Parsons (1963) the mitochondrial membranes can be examined rapidly and without being subjected to the influence of isolation media. In both cases the membranes are found to have their full complement of particles. The observations of Sjöstrand et al. indicate that negative staining as such does not lead to the appearance of the stalked particles. Furthermore, several workers have observed that the particles are present on mitochondrial membranes treated with fixatives before negative staining although the evidence is equivocal. After treatment with osmium tetroxide the particles are present on the membranes of blowfly flight muscle mitochondria (Smith) and in reduced numbers on those of liver and heart mitochondria (Parsons 1965). The particles are not visible on membrane fragments from mitochondria of *Neurospora crassa* treated with osmium tetroxide or potassium permanganate (Stoeckenius 1963), but they are well preserved by fixation with aldehydes. It can be argued (Sjöstrand et al.) that those fixatives which allow the visualization of the stalked particles by negative staining are poor fixatives for the mitochondrial membranes. Alternatively the formation of the stalked particles may be attributed to disorganization of the membrane when it becomes broken into tubules or vesicles (before fixation). It should be noted that preparations of this type examined by the thin-sectioning technique still do not show the particles. It has been concluded that, in general, dehydration and embedding of mitochondrial material fixed with osmium tetroxide results in disappearance of the particles.

Although the particles, in negatively stained preparations, appear to be on stalks, it is by no means certain that this is their native situation. In *Calliphora* flight muscle mitochondria the intercristal space (matrix) seems scarcely wide enough to accommodate particles and stalks (Smith) and possibly the stalks arise as the result of the subjection of the membranes to unaccustomed media. Oda and Nishi have suggested that the situation of the particles may depend on the functional state of the mitochondria.

9. Nature of the stalked particles

The group led by D. E. Green originally proposed that the stalked particles each embodied one complete mechanism for electron transport (Fernández-Morán et al.), but calculation of the minimal total weight (about 9×10^5 daltons) of the proteins of the respiratory chain from their estimated molecular weights and molar proportions indicated that the complex was too large to be accommodated by the observed structures. Subsequently it was suggested that the base-pieces also were required; this of course means the whole of the inner membranes. Most recently the base-pieces alone have been equated with components of the electron transfer chain.

The work of E. Racker and his colleagues indicates that the headpieces are molecules of ATPase. Oxidative phosphorylation and ATPase activity in mitochondria and vesicular fragments of mitochondrial membranes are inhibited by oligomycin (and rutamycin). Purified ATPase (F_1) which is required for oxidative phosphorylation in F_1-deficient membrane fragments, however, is insensitive to oligomycin. When F_1 is added to membrane fragments from which ATPase activity has been removed by sequential treatment with trypsin and urea (TU-particles), or by passage down a Sephadex-50 column and then treatment with urea (SU-particles), the ATPase activity again becomes sensitive to oligomycin. The loss of ATPase activity in the preparation of TU- or SU-particles is accompanied by loss of their stalked particles (or at least the head-pieces) (Fig. 7a, b). The addition of F_1 leads to restoration of the original particle-covered appearance of the vesicular membranes (Fig. 7c) (Racker and Horstman). The isolated ATPase has been examined in the ultracentrifuge and has a $S^{\circ}_{20,w}$ of 12.9S and appears to be a compact symmetrical molecule with an estimated molecular weight of 284,000. It consists of about 10 subunits, each having a molecular weight of about 26,000. The isolated enzyme is cold-labile, at 0 °C it dissociates into smaller components and a concentration-dependent equilibrium develops between subunits of 11.9S, 9.1S and 3.5S (Penefsky and Warner). The hydrodynamic data agree well with the appearance of the enzyme when examined in the electron microscope by the negative staining technique (Fig. 7d). It appears very similar to the head-pieces, and there is some evidence of substructure (Schatz et al.).

Kopaczyk et al. have extended these observations using a preparation of inner membranes (R_4) obtained from ox heart mitochondria. When treated with potassium cholate, ammonium sulphate, and dithiothreitol, R_4 could be separated into a sedimentable portion and a supernatant. The supernatant was fractionated by addition of further amounts of ammonium sulphate to obtain a preparation of a rutamycin-

---

Fig. 7. Electron micrographs of (a): vesicular fragments of mitochondrial membranes, (b): SU-particles obtained by treatment of material shown in (a) with Sephadex-50 and urea, (c): membranous fragments resembling those in (a), formed by addition of F_1 to SU-particles; (d) purified yeast ATPase. All negatively stained with potassium phosphotungstate. (a–c) from Racker and Horstmann. $\times$ 280,000. (d) from Schatz et al. $\times$ 300,000.

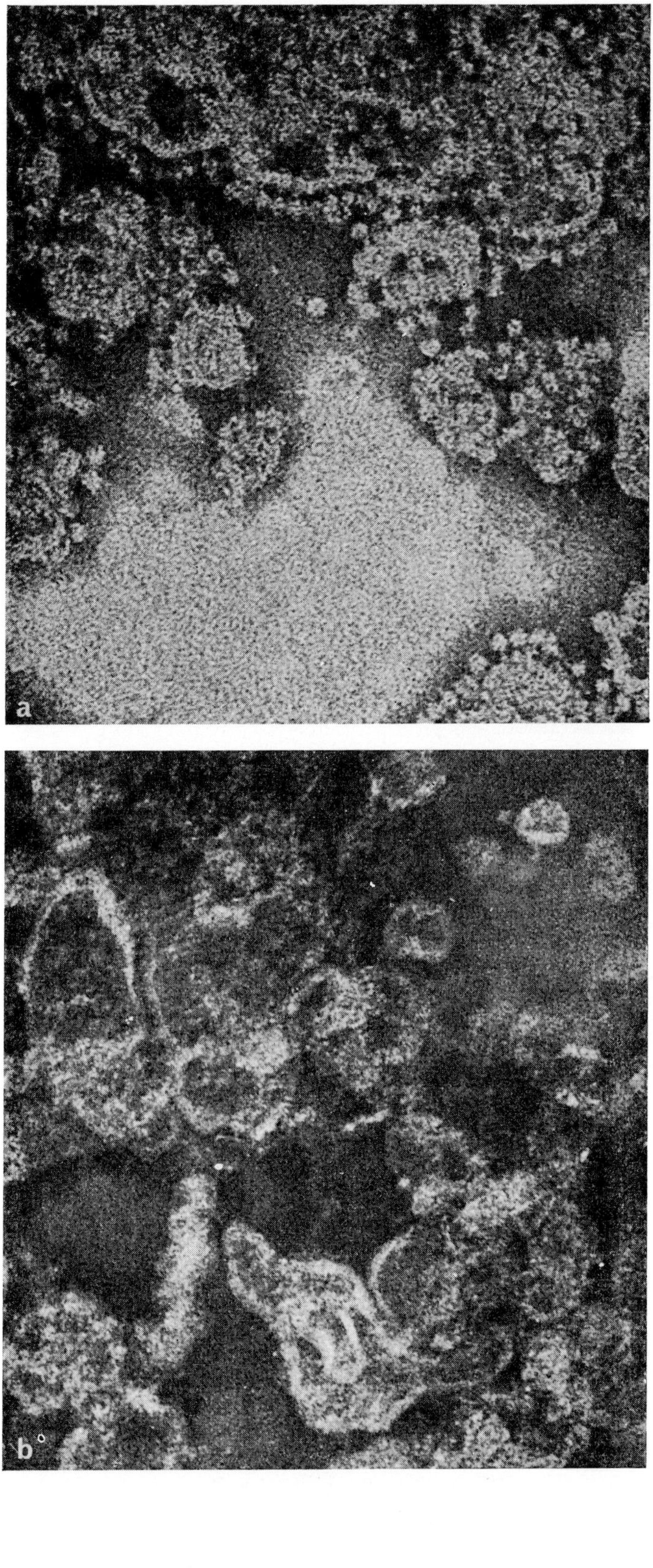

Fig. 7 (a, b)

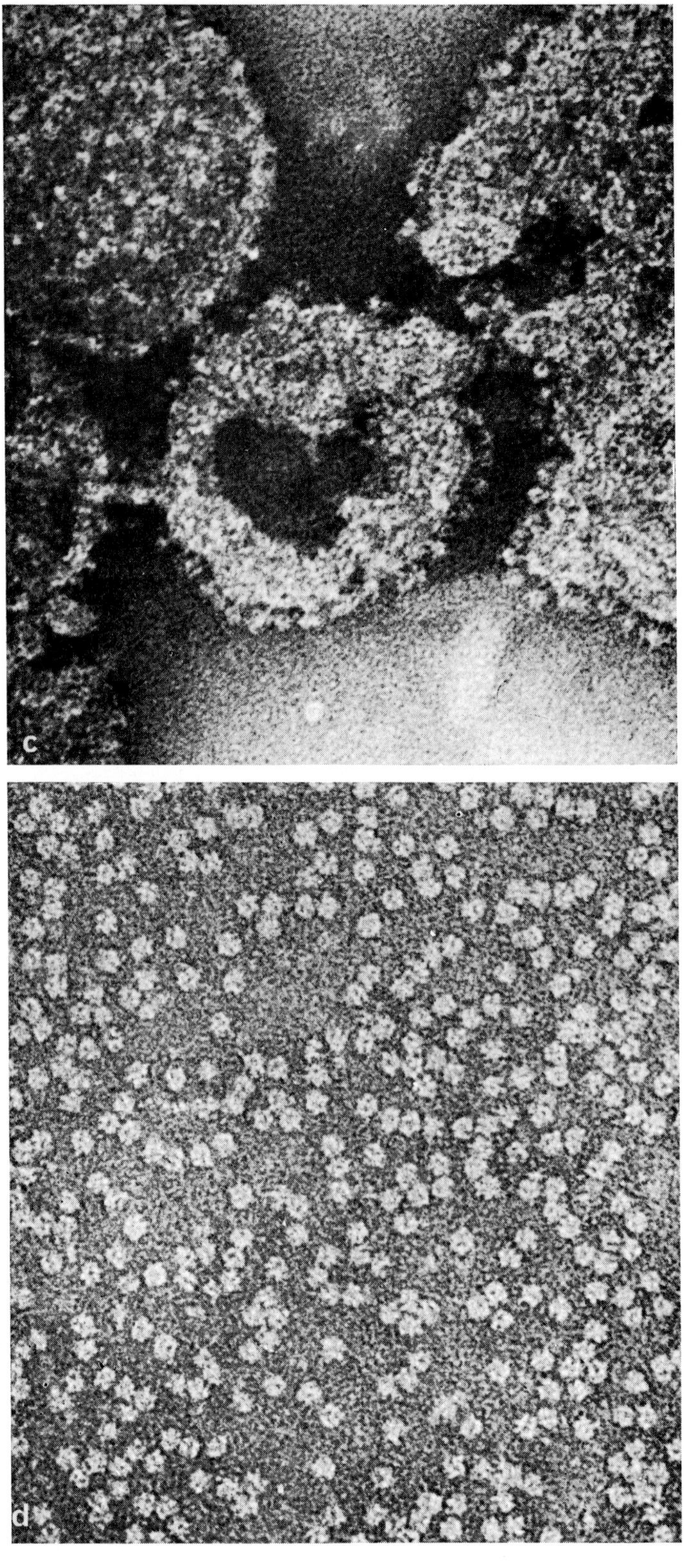

Fig. 7 (c, d)

sensitive ATPase (P_2) which was strongly dependent on the addition of phospholipid for activity. P_2 could be rendered rutamycin-insensitive by heating, part of the material becoming insoluble, the insensitive part (S_3) remaining soluble. In the electron microscope, P_2 negatively stained with phosphotungstate appeared as aggregates of particles similar in size and shape to the head-pieces. In the presence of phospholipid these reveal stalks with which they become associated with the phospholipid to give arrays similar to that seen in R_4. The rutamycin-insensitive ATPase preparation (S_3) does not interact with phospholipid and Dr. Green and his colleagues conclude that the stalks contain a component which confers rutamycin-sensitivity on the ATPase in the head-pieces and that they associate hydrophobically with the base-pieces (or, in the model system described, with phospholipids).

10. Organization of the cristae

Based on their appearance in mitochondria fixed *in situ* cristae may be classified broadly as either lamellar or tubular (villous). In the lamellar form the sides of each crista generally appear more or less parallel in section, the most common departure from this being the occurrence of clearly defined angular indentations in one or other of the membranes (Fig. 8). A variety of shapes and sizes of lamellar cristae have been described. They may be irregularly disposed (as in mammalian liver mitochondria), or regularly arrayed, usually at right angles to the long axis of the mitochondria (as in mammalian kidney), or arranged in whorls (as in tree shrew retina, Samorajski et al.). In some mitochondria (such as those of mammalian kidney or brown adipose tissue) the cristae appear to form complete septa and if this is so the matrix space is thus divided into a number of separate compartments. In the majority of cases, however, it is clear that there is continuity throughout the matrix space.

Tubular cristae may be circular in cross-section and of uniform internal diameter (Fig. 9) or have irregular dimensions, or, rarely, they are triangular (prismatic) in cross-section (Revel et al.; Blinzinger et al.; Suzuki and Mostofi). They may be coiled apparently at random, as in many protozoa, or very precisely arrayed as in some of the mitochondria of *Pelomyxa carolinensis* (Pappas and Brandt) in which there is also fusion of some of the tubules to form a reticulum. A similar arrangement is present in the mitochondria of canary heart (Slautterback), but not in the mitochondria of sparrow or zebra finch hearts. Adult blowfly flight muscle mitochondria have fenestrated lamelliform cristae which are intermediate in appearance between reticuliform tubules and complete lamellae (Smith).

It is possible that cristae do not have a fixed shape *in vivo* (André; Rouiller) and considerable changes in their appearance can be induced *in vitro* (see below). There are numerous examples of changes in mitochondrial structure associated with development of cells. The most striking changes are those associated with spermatogenesis (e.g. rat, *Testacella*, *Pieris*; André). Similarly changes are associated with development of the mitochondria themselves (Berger).

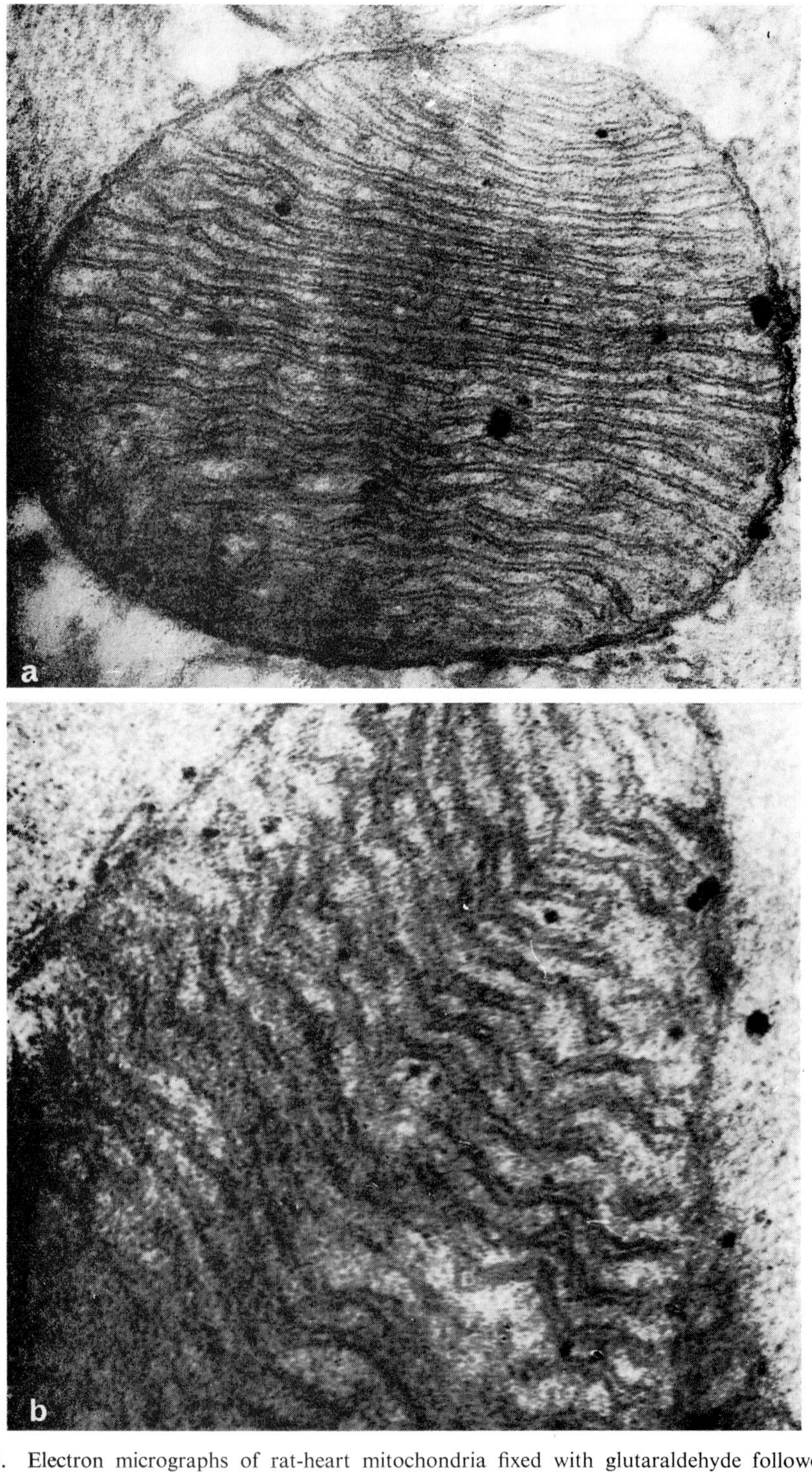

Fig. 8. Electron micrographs of rat-heart mitochondria fixed with glutaraldehyde followed by osmium tetroxide. A few of the cristae in the mitochondrion in (a), and all the cristae in the mitochondrion in (b), show angular indentations. Electron micrographs generously provided by Mrs. P. Tegerdine. (a): × 71,000; (b): × 112,000.

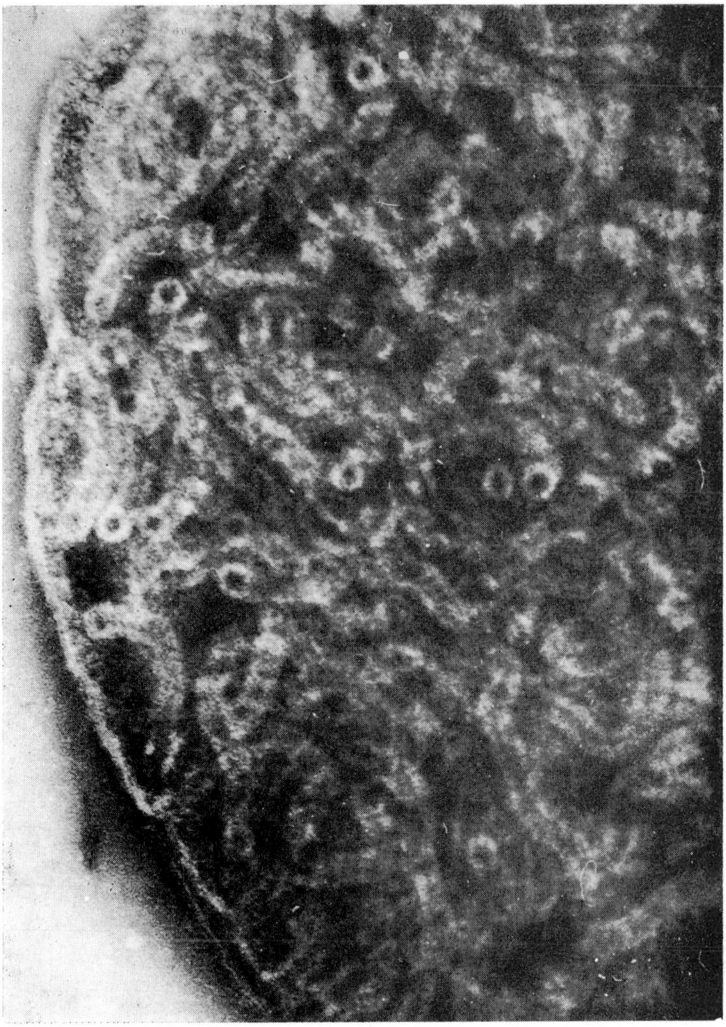

Fig. 9. Electron micrograph of part of mitochondrion from *Paramecium*, negatively stained with ammonium molybdate, to show uniform circular cross-sections of cristae. (From Munn.) × 125,000.

Although cristae showing angular indentations (Fig. 8) are usually found in only a small number of mitochondria in a given cell at any one time, they may well be forms which all the mitochondria are capable of adopting under certain physiological conditions. Thus, the regular arrays of tubular cristae observed in a few of the mitochondria of *Pelomyxa* by Pappas and Brandt can be induced in up to 79 % of the mitochondria by starvation (Daniels and Breyer).

The mitochondria of the proximal tubular cells of the frog, *Rana pipiens* (examined during the summer when feeding) have fairly regularly orientated, transverse cristae.

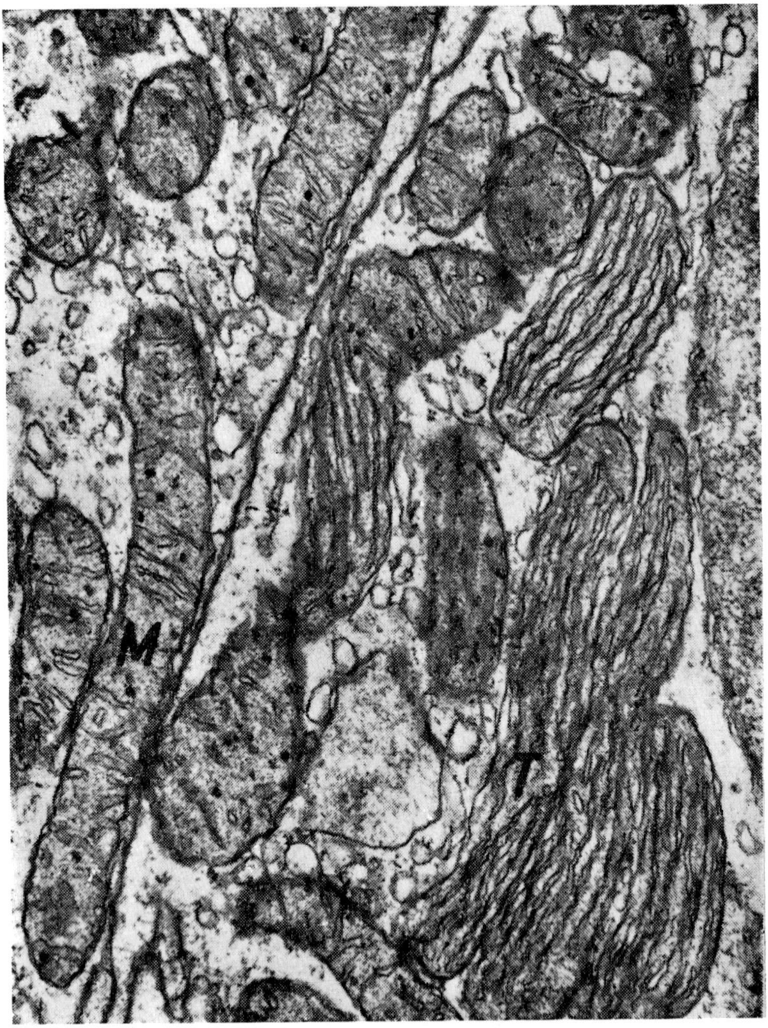

Fig. 10. Section of proximal kidney tubule of a starved summer frog showing mitochondria (M) with transversely orientated cristae, and (T) with longitudinally orientated cristae. (From Karnovsky.) ×14,000.

On starvation the cristae of many of the mitochondria become arranged longitudinally (Fig. 10). This structural change is correlated with a loss of cytochrome oxidase activity (Karnovsky). The mitochondria of the round worm, *Ascaris*, examined by negative staining, have cristae which are of normal appearance but lack both cytochrome oxidase and cytochrome *c* (Chance and Parsons). These cases apart, there is in general a correlation between the cristal area and the amount of cytochrome ***a*** (and other respiratory pigments) which the mitochondria contain (Table 4). The total surface area of the cristal membranes, which is determined by the number of cristae and their extent, is related to the type of cell in which they occur. In general mitochondria in the cells which have the greatest sustained demands for ATP have the greatest cristal membrane surface. Accurate comparisons are difficult because of the problem of estimating the area of the cristae in mitochondria in which they are irregularly arranged and/or tubular.

TABLE 4

Cytochrome *a* content of mitochondria.

Source of mitochondria		μ mols cyt. *a* per g protein	Ref.
Musca domestica	flight muscle	0.61	1
Rat	heart	0.56	1
		0.42	2
Pigeon	heart	0.50	2
Pigeon	breast muscle	0.43	2
Rat	kidney	0.27	2
Guinea pig	kidney	0.24	1
Rat	skeletal muscle	0.23	2
Rat	liver	0.25	2
		0.19	1
Mouse	liver	0.20	1
Guinea pig	liver	0.08	1

References: 1, Estabrook and Holowinsky; 2, Schollmeyer and Klingenberg.

Although there is no direct evidence indicating whether or not the inner membrane is identical with the cristae membranes, they have both been reported to bear stalked particles; the two are sometimes seen to be continuous; and the former seems able to extend by incorporating the latter (during large amplitude swelling), so it is most probable that they are one and the same thing.

11. Continuity of the intracristal and peripheral spaces, compartmentation

There has been considerable discussion as to the extent to which the membranes of the cristae and the inner membrane are continuous, and to the extent to which the intracristal and peripheral spaces are continuous. In a study utilizing serial sections of mouse skeletal muscle mitochondria Andersson-Cedergren observed that of seventeen clear contacts between cristal membranes and inner peripheral membrane only two showed continuity of the spaces. Daems and Wisse have more recently concluded that in mitochondria in mouse liver the cristae are attached to the inner membranes through tubes (called pediculus cristae) of varying length and about 300Å in external diameter. Because of the narrowness of the tubes in many sections it would appear that the cristae were not attached to the inner membranes, or that there was no continuity of the spaces. As indicated above, the procedures employed in the preparation of specimens for electron microscopy determine the apparent presence or absence of the intracristal and peripheral spaces of mitochondria fixed *in situ*. The cristal membranes and the peripheral membranes are frequently closely apposed in mitochondria in tissues fixed with potassium permanganate, aldehydes without subsequent treatment with osmium tetroxide, or with osmium tetroxide by the freeze-substitution technique. Malhotra argued that the absence of a pronounced intracristal space is typical of the *in vivo* state at least for rat pancreatic exocrine cells, cerebellar cortex, medulla oblongata and liver. In mitochondria in tissues examined by freeze-etching the peripheral membranes usually touch each other, but the membranes of the cristae are 50–100 Å apart. In intact isolated mitochondria examined in the electron microscope by sectioning or by negative staining the intracristal and peripheral spaces are always present, they are sometimes extremely large, and the connections between intracristal and peripheral spaces are usually obvious. Thus isolated mitochondria which by a variety of biochemical criteria (high respiratory control, latency of enzymes, retention of co-factors) are deemed intact (see however Klingenberg) usually appear different from control preparations fixed *in situ* (e.g. Deshpande et al.; Burgos et al.). The major differences can be attributed to the metabolic state of the mitochondria or the nature of the media in which they are isolated and suspended (Chappell and Greville). In 0.25 M sucrose, which is the most frequently employed isolation medium, mitochondria which *in situ* appear elongated become spherical. In 0.44 M sucrose, or in 0.25 M sucrose containing substances of high molecular weight (e.g. polyvinylpyrrolidone, Novikoff 1957) the elongated form is retained, but mitochondria which have become rounded by suspension in 0.25 M sucrose media will not recover their rod-like form if transferred to 0.44 M sucrose (Whittaker 1966). Although these changes in shape are not necessarily accompanied by changes in volume isolated mitochondria do undergo volume changes in response to changes in their osmotic environment and under the influence of so-called swelling agents. The mitochondria behave as two-compartment systems with one compartment accessible to sucrose and a number of other relatively small molecules such as sodium and potassium chloride (Amoore and Bartley), coenzyme A, acetyl-CoA, carnitine and acetyl carnitine (Garland and Yates), fumarate and oxaloacetate (Chappell and Haarhoff), and the other compartment inaccessible to these substances. Part of the water in the sucrose-

TABLE 5

Properties of rat liver mitochondria in 272 milliosmols sucrose medium. (Data of Bentzel and Solomon.)

Wet/dry weight	2.91 $\pm$ 0.10
Water in sucrose accessible space	0.462 $\pm$ 0.001 μl/μl mitochondria
Water in sucrose inaccessible space	0.210 $\pm$ 0.008 μl/μl mitochondria
Nonsolvent water in sucrose inaccessible space	0.103 $\pm$ 0.013 μl/μl mitochondria
Volume of membranes and solutes	0.301 $\pm$ 0.009 μl/μl mitochondria

inaccessible space (Table 5) does not participate in osmotic phenomena and it is thought that this corresponds to the water of hydration of the mitochondrial macromolecules (Bentzel and Solomon). The volume of the remainder of the water in the sucrose-inaccessible space varies inversely with the osmolality of the medium. The sucrose-inaccessible space has been equated with the matrix space (Klingenberg and Pfaff) and the permeability barrier to sucrose has been equated with the inner membrane (which, incidentally, is also impermeable to negative stains). The outer membrane appears to be impermeable to a number of relatively large molecules.

12. Changes associated with large amplitude swelling and contraction

When mitochondria are subjected to markedly hypotonic conditions or undergo so-called large amplitude swelling induced by swelling agents they accumulate quite massive amounts of water. Pronounced structural changes associated with this process have been described for mitochondria from rodent liver (Neubert; Parsons et al.; Wlodawer et al.; and Hackenbrock), rat kidney and mung bean (Parsons et al.) and ox heart (Munn and Blair). Fig. 11 shows the changes undergone by ox heart mitochondria. The changes have been explained as follows. The outer membrane is flexible and possibly slightly elastic. In isotonic or hypertonic media it is not fully distended. The mitochondria are therefore able to undergo shape and small volume changes without change in surface area. In hypotonic media water passes through the outer and inner membranes into the matrix space which enlarges. The inner membrane presses against the outer membrane which because of its limited elasticity becomes

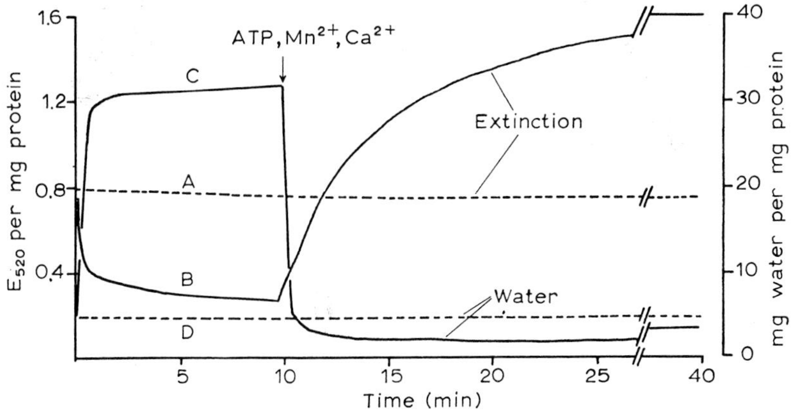

Fig. 11. Extinction and water content of isolated ox-heart mitochondria undergoing hypotonic swelling and ATP-induced contraction. Curves A and B: extinction at 520 mμ expressed per mg protein. Curves C and D: water content expressed as mg water per mg protein. Curves A and D are controls. (From Munn and Blair.)

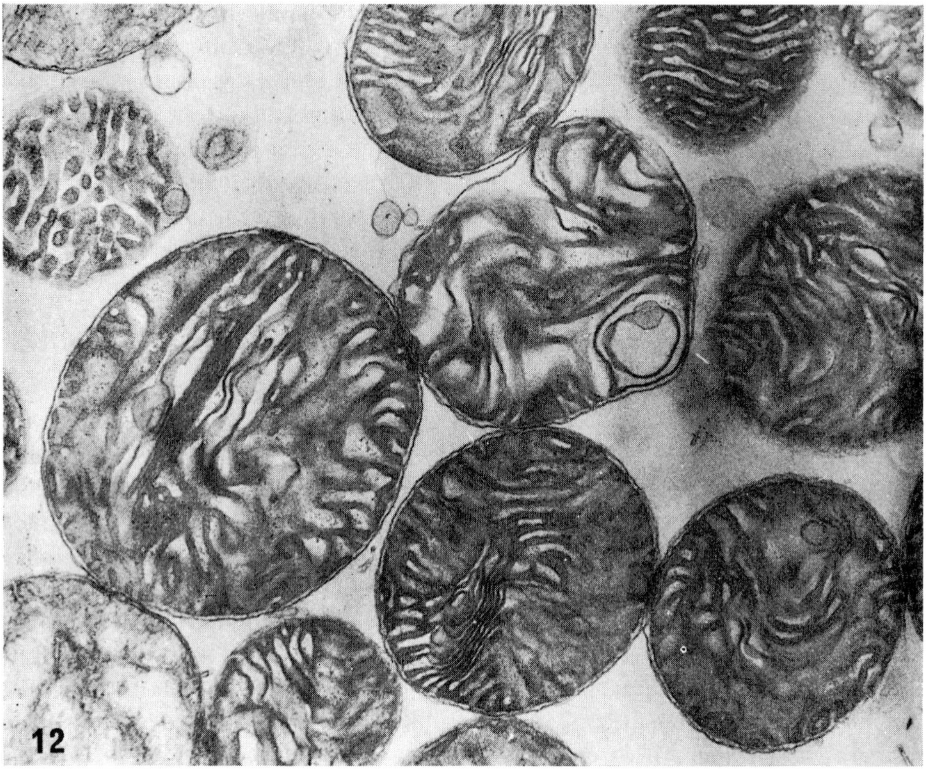

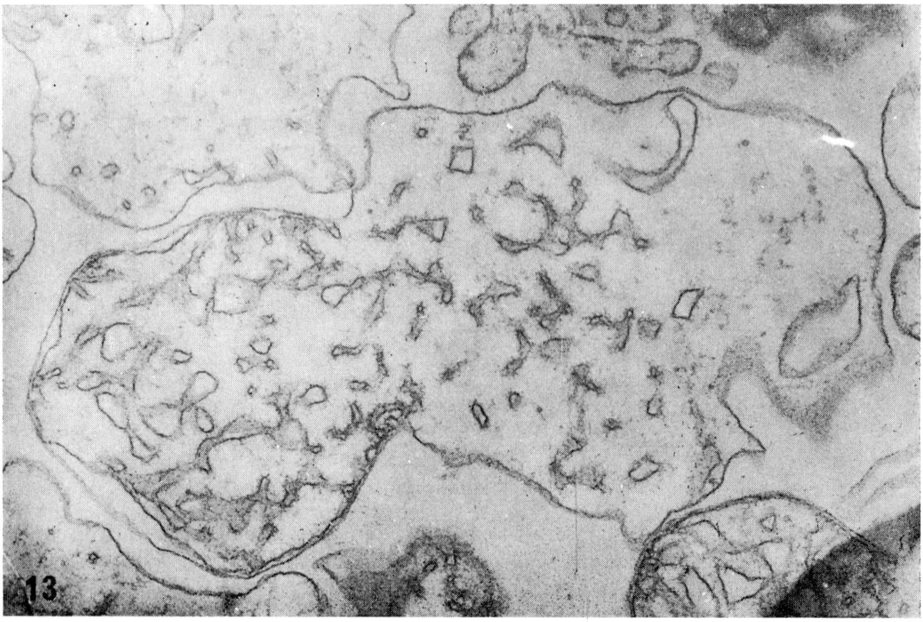

Fig. 12. Electron micrograph of ox-heart mitochondria in 0.25 M sucrose, 0.02 M imidazole acetate *p*H 7.2. Fixed in glutaraldehyde and postosmicated. Compare with Fig. 13. (From Munn and Blair.) × 34,000.

Fig. 13. Electron micrograph of ox-heart mitochondria swollen for 10 min in 0.02 M imidazole acetate *p*H 7.2. Fixed in glutaraldehyde and postosmicated. Compare with Fig. 12. × 31,000.

ruptured (Fig. 13). The inner membrane is able to extend with material derived from the unfolding cristae (Malamed) some of which however become more or less vacuolated and are seen to be in the form of tubules and/or vesicles. The extension of the inner membrane may be a passive process due solely to the increased pressure in the matrix space associated with the accumulation of water, or it is a special property of the inner membrane that on dilution of some unknown factor or factors on the matrix side of the membrane it takes up an extended configuration. The extended inner membrane does not appear taut (Fig. 13) as might be expected if the process were due to internal pressure along. On addition of ATP and divalent cations to the swollen ox heart mitochondria the inner membrane immediately contracts around the remnants of the cristae. In the case of mouse liver mitochondria the addition of ATP causes the membranes to break up into small vesicles which subsequently aggregate and fuse (Neubert). This process is accompanied by extrusion of water (Fig. 11) but the cristae do not become reorganized into their original form.

13. Changes associated with different metabolic steady states

Hackenbrock has described a number of dramatic but completely reversible changes in the organization of the inner membrane of mouse liver mitochondria (see also Weinbach et al.). The changes studied by Hackenbrock are associated with transitions between the various metabolic steady states defined by Chance and Williams on the basis of characteristic respiratory rates and oxidation-reduction levels of the carriers in the electron transport chain (Table 6). The mitochondria as isolated in 0.25 M

TABLE 6

Characteristics of metabolic steady states, defined by Chance and Williams.

State	1	2	3	4	5
ADP level	Low	High	High	Low	High
Substrate level	Low	Approaching 0	High	High	High
Respiration rate	Slow	Slow	Fast	Slow	Zero

sucrose have a very electron-dense matrix which is reduced in volume compared to that of mitochondria examined *in situ*. The intracristal spaces are enlarged, tortuous and frequently they anastomose. The peripheral space is very large. These mitochondria are said to be in the condensed form. The condensed form is retained by mitochondria incubated in 0.25 M sucrose at 30 °C (Fig. 14a) but on incubation in State 1 the mitochondria change in appearance until after 7 min they resemble mitochondria examined *in situ* (the so-called orthodox form, Fig. 14b). Mitochondria in State 4 show the orthodox form, but change to the condensed form within 40 sec of

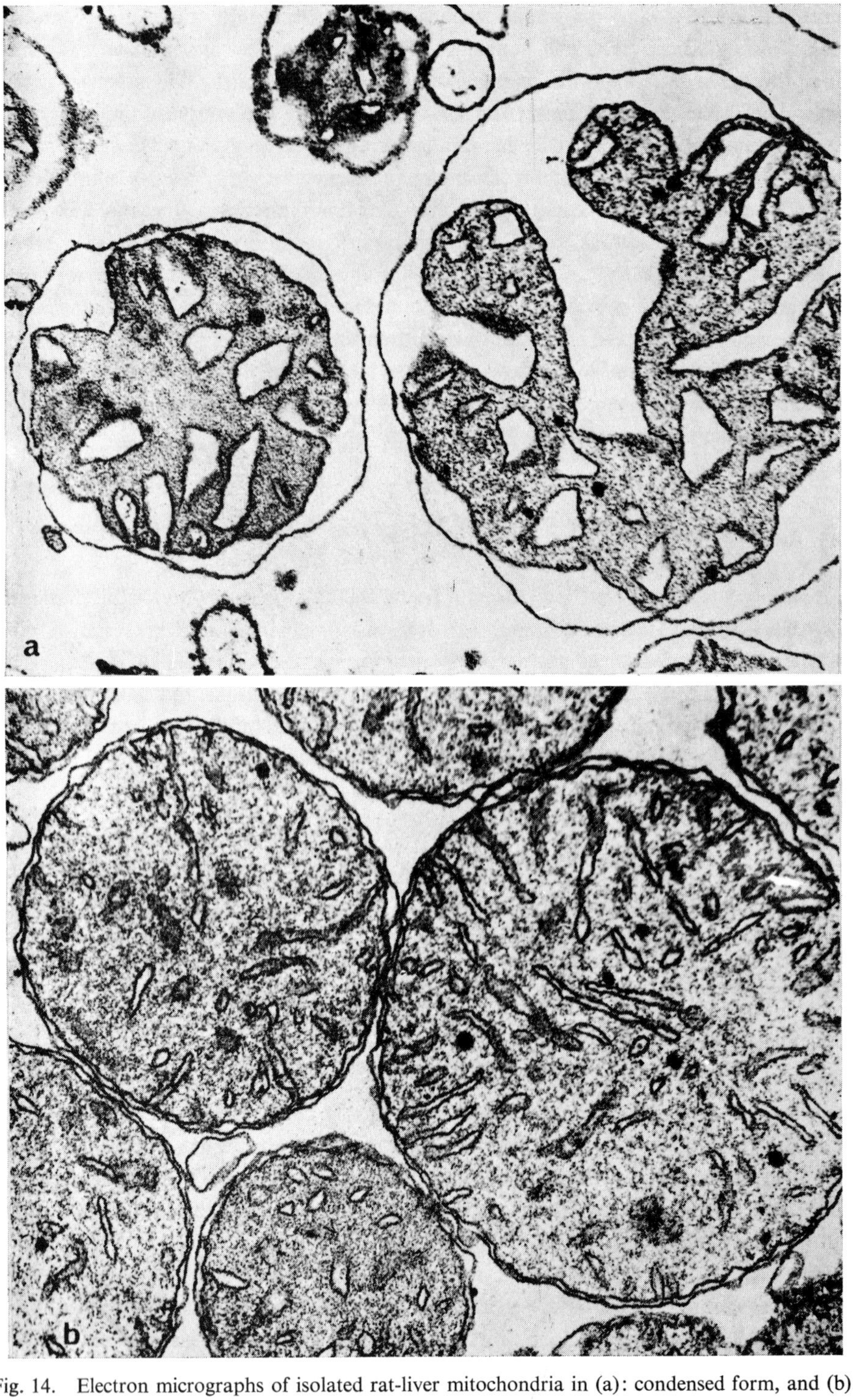

Fig. 14. Electron micrographs of isolated rat-liver mitochondria in (a): condensed form, and (b): orthodox form (see text). (From Hackenbrock.) $\times$ 75,000.

addition of ADP (State 3). This change is reversed when phosphorylation of the ADP is completed. Mitochondria in State 2 are in the condensed form. Mitochondria incubated up to 27 min in State 1 and State 4 gradually increase in total volume by about 20% – this increase occurs during and after the change from condensed to the orthodox form. When phosphorylation is initiated by the addition of succinate followed by ADP to mitochondria incubated in State 1 for 15 min and the mitochondria examined after phosphorylation ceases, they show dilution of the matrix and a volume increase of up to 50% compared to the mitochondria examined just prior to phosphorylation.

Deamer et al. have more recently carried out a similar study on the structure of rat-liver mitochondria exhibiting synchronised (but out of phase) oscillatory changes in light scattering, oxidation-reduction levels of the respiratory carriers and ion transport induced by succinate and phosphate. These changes have a period of about 2 min and become attenuated as the system becomes anaerobic. Examination in the electron microscope shows that the mitochondria undergo structural changes between a condensed form and one similar to the orthodox form described by Hackenbrock. As the oscillations become smaller more of the mitochondria remain in the condensed form. The change from condensed to orthodox forms is associated with an increase in mass of the fixed mitochondrial pellet.

Clearly there are two degrees of swelling. One is relatively small and is determined by the amount to which the outer membrane can be extended without rupturing. Associated with this there may be large changes in the distribution of the water inside the outer membrane, i.e. between the peripheral-intracristal spaces and the matrix space. The other is relatively large and begins when the restraint imposed by the intact outer membrane is lost when it ruptures.

The nature of the molecular mechanism underlying these changes in the inner membrane is one of the most important problems in the study of mitochondrial ultrastructure. Several models for the mechanisms have been proposed by Lehninger and depend primarily on changes in the arrangement of respiratory carriers in relation to one another; it is implied that these changes depend on conformational changes in the component molecules. Chance et al. and Urry et al. have presented evidence for conformational changes in the electron carriers.

Penniston et al. have recently proposed changes in the conformation of the repeating units to account for the variety of appearances of the cristae membranes of canary heart mitochondria *in situ* and ox heart mitochondria *in vitro*.

14. The matrix

When isolated mitochondria are disrupted by sonication a portion of their protein is rendered soluble. For blowfly flight muscle mitochondria it is 18% of the total protein (Greville et al.), for ox heart mitochondria 15% (Green and Ziegler), and for liver about 50% (Schneider). Although some of this protein may be derived from the membranes the bulk is thought to be protein which is in solution in the intact mitochondria. A number of mitochondrial enzymes are soluble after extraction or disruption of the organelles and on the basis of their latency or otherwise, and the extent to which they can be extracted under progressively harsher conditions, are thought to be present in either the intracristal and/or peripheral spaces and the matrix space. The relatively larger amount of soluble protein in the mitochondria with relatively larger matrix space (liver compared to flight muscle and heart) suggests that the bulk of the soluble enzymes and other soluble protein is present in the matrix space.

In thin sections in most mitochondria fixed *in situ* the matrix space appears to contain fine (about 40–50 Å across), moderately electron-dense granules. In isolated mitochondria, as described above, the matrix space often appears reduced in size and has correspondingly greater electron density. Some of the enzymes and enzyme complexes which have been assigned to the matrix have been examined in the electron microscope: L-glutamate dehydrogenase (EC 1.4.1.3) (Hall; Horne and Greville), 2-oxoglutarate dehydrogenase complex and pyruvate dehydrogenase complex and some of their component enzymes (Ishikawa et al.). Some structural features of these are summarised in Table 7.

TABLE 7

Hydrodynamic properties of glutamate dehydrogenase, a-keto acid dehydrogenase complexes and their components, and malate dehydrogenase

	Source	$S_{20,w}$ (s)	$D_{20,w}$ ($cm^2 sec^{-1}$)	Approx. wt. (daltons)	Ref.
Glutamate dehydrogenase	Ox liver	26.6	2.54×10^{-7}	1×10^6	1
	Ox liver	31.2	1.52×10^{-7}	2×10^6	2
Pyruvate complex	Pigeon breast muscle	58	1.4×10^{-7}	4×10^6	3
	Pig heart	67.5	0.6×10^{-7}	10×10^6	4
	Ox kidney	62,80	—	—	5
Pyruvate decarboxylase	Pig heart	7.8	—	—	6
Lipoyl reductase transacetylase	Pig heart	27.6	—	—	6
Lipoamide dehydrogenase	Pig heart	5.7	—	—	6
	Ox liver	5.6	—	1×10^5	7
Oxoglutarate complex	Pig heart	30	—	—	8
	Pig heart	36	1.2×10^{-7}	3×10^6	9
	Ox kidney	51	—	—	5
Malate dehydrogenase	Ox heart	4.6	6.6×10^{-7}	6.5×10^4	10
	Neurospora	4.8	8.3×10^{-7}	5.4×10^4	11
	Various	—	—	$\sim 6.7 \times 10^4$	12

References: 1, Olson and Anfinsen; 2, Sund; 3, Schweet et al.; 4, Hayakawa et al.; 5, Ishikawa et al.; 6, Hayakawa and Koike; 7, Lusty; 8, Massey; 9, Hirashima et al.; 10, Grimm and Doherty; 11, Munkres and Richards; 12, Murphey et al.

Glutamate dehydrogenase dissociates in dilute solution into four or five subunits. By the use of shadow casting Hall obtained particles 145 Å wide and 80 Å high from dilute enzyme solutions. By negative staining Horne and Greville have observed particles, the predominant shape of which was that of an equilateral triangle with sides averaging 104 Å, thought to represent views of the subunit of glutamate dehydrogenase. The subunit is envisaged as a tetrahedron formed from six rods, each 104 Å long and about 27 Å wide, lying parallel to the edges. The components of the *a*-keto acid dehydrogenase complexes, on the other hand, are globular. The complexes tend to partially dissociate when negatively stained with phosphotungstate *p*H 7. The relatively intact complex of 2-oxoglutarate dehydrogenase from ox kidney mitochondria has the appearance of a polyhedron with a diameter of about 250 Å. It consists of a number of peripheral globular components (presumed to be molecules of 2-oxoglutarate decarboxylase and dihydrolipoyl dehydrogenase) and a core which resembles isolated dihydrolipoyl transsuccinylase: 8 globular units arranged at the vertices of a cube with sides about 150 Å long overall. The appearance of the intact complex is similar to that of both pyruvate dehydrogenase and 2-oxoglutarate dehydrogenase complexes obtained from *E. coli* (Fig. 15). The intact mammalian (ox kidney) pyruvate dehydrogenase complex is about 400 Å in diameter and consists of a number

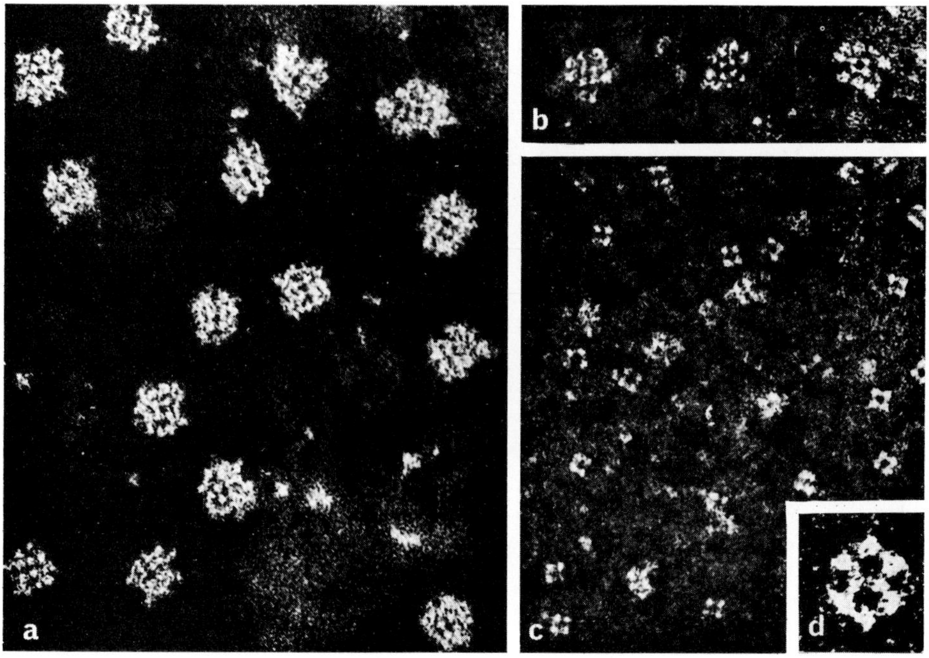

Fig. 15. Electron micrographs of (a): 2-oxoglutarate dehydrogenase complexes from *E. coli*; (b): 2-oxoglutarate dehydrogenase complexes from ox kidney mitochondria; (c): dihydrolipoyl transsuccinylase and (d): dihydrolipoyl transacetylase from ox kidney. All negatively stained with phosphotungstate. Electron micrographs generously provided by Dr. Lester J. Reed. × 210,000 approx.

of particles (presumed to be pyruvate decarboxylase and dihydrolipoyl dehydrogenase) surrounding the dihydrolipoyl transacetylase which appears to consist of subunits situated at the 20 vertices of a pentagonal dodecahedron about 210 Å in diameter.

15. Mitochondrial inclusions

A large number of mitochondrial inclusions have been described; most of them occur in the matrix. The inclusions may be either granular, filamentous or crystalline (Table 8). Some of the granular inclusions have been shown to be ribosomes. O'Brien

TABLE 8

Examples of mitochondrial inclusions.

Type	Site	Nature	Tissue	Comment	Ref.
Granular	Matrix	250–300 Å particles of calcium and phosphate	most	can be deposited excessively *in vitro*	1, 2
	Intracristal	glycogen	rat retinal receptors		3
	Unspecified		*Testacella* sperm, tumour cells		4, 5
	Matrix	ribosomes	rat and chicken		6
			Beta vulgaris		7
			Neurospora		8
			rat liver	have been isolated	9
	Matrix	precursor of aldosterone	adrenal of Na^+-deprived rats		10
Crystalline	Matrix	crystals	frog oocyte		11
			Peregrinus sperm, epitheliomuscular cells of *Hydra*		12,13
	Modified cristae		goldfish hypothalamus		14
	Matrix	crystalline arrays of tubules	rat adrenal cortex		15
	Matrix	crystalline arrays of fibres	human liver, snake renal tubules		16 17
Fibrous	Matrix	filaments of DNA	many – see text		
	Matrix	bundles of filaments	rat kidney		18
	Intracristal and/or peripheral space	helical filaments	rat corpus striatum		19

References: 1, Palade (1952, 1953); 2, Greenawalt et al.; 3, Ishikawa and Pei; 4, Personne and André; 5, Tandler and Shipkey; 6, André and Marinozzi; 7, Kislev et al.; 8, Luck; 9, O'Brien and Kalf; 10, Giacomelli et al.; 11, Ward; 12, Herold and Munz; 13, Davis; 14, Braak; 15, Kjaerheim; 16, Wills; 17, Kurosumi et al.; 18, Suzuki and Mostofi; 19, Mugnaini.

and Kalf have isolated the ribosomes from highly purified rat liver mitochondria. The ribosomes have a sedimentation coefficient of 55S. When examined by negative staining after fixation with glutaraldehyde they have an average diameter of 145 Å. 78S ribosomes isolated from microsomes have an average diameter of 190 Å. There is a similar disparity in the sizes of mitochondrial and microsomal ribosomes when they are examined in thin sections.

16. Mitochondrial DNA

Suzuki and Mostofi list a wide variety of filamentous inclusions observed by themselves and other workers. At the present time the most interesting of these are the ones which have been shown to be DNA. The occurrence of DNA in mitochondria was first demonstrated by Chèvremont et al. (1959, 1961) using a combination of autoradiography and Feulgen staining. The first demonstration of mitochondrial DNA in the electron microscope was that of Nass and Nass and this stimulated a great deal of research on its nature and role in mitochondria. Nass et al. have demonstrated DNA in mitochondria from some twenty different organisms. The DNA fibrils appear to lie predominantly in the matrix, but connections to the cristae or inner membrane are also seen. Nass also observed that during its isolation DNA was often attached to fragments of membranes, and Kroon reported that digitonin particles from ox heart mitochondria were enriched in DNA (which was involved in amino acid incorporation by the particles).

DNA has been isolated from the mitochondria of a number of microorganisms, plants and animals. The buoyant densities of mitochondrial DNA isolated from a number of mammalian tissues are all very similar, within the range 1.699–1.704. The buoyant densities of mitochondrial DNA from a number of plants were all found to be 1.706 (Suyama and Bonner). Mitochondrial DNA from a number of sources has been shown to be doublestranded. It has a very rapid rate of renaturation after thermal denaturation which indicates that it is relatively homogeneous in its base composition (Borst and Ruttenberg). Characteristically mitochondrial DNA is circular (Van Bruggen et al.; Sinclair and Stevens; Nass; Kroon et al.), but after isolation it may be in one or other of a variety of conformations (Kroon et al.). Mitochondrial DNA isolated from yeast is non-circular under conditions which preserve circular molecules of nuclear DNA (Sinclair et al.). The mean contour lengths of the circular molecules from different sources range from 4.74–5.45 μ. The molecular weight of a DNA molecule about 5 μ long is about 10 million (assuming 1.92 daltons per μ; Wilkins), which corresponds to some 15,000 base pairs. Sinclair and Stevens estimate that this would provide information enabling the synthesis of about 600,000 daltons of protein (about 5,000 amino acids). Although Nass reported that there may be two to six rings of DNA per mitochondrion, Borst et al. conclude that the maximum coding capacity for the DNA in each mitochondrion is still only for about 5,000 amino acids. It is suggested that duplication of the DNA may account for the presence of several molecules per mitochondrion (see also Edelman et al.). DNA-polymerase activity has been demonstrated in isolated yeast mitochondria (Wintersberger 1966a).

DNA-dependent RNA polymerase activity has been demonstrated in mitochondria isolated from yeast (Wintersberger 1966b; Wintersberger and Tuppy), rat liver (Wintersberger 1964), lamb heart (Kalf) and *Neurospora crassa* (Luck and Reich). A number of species of RNA with differing sedimentation coefficients have been isolated from yeast mitochondria: 23S, 16S, 4S (Wintersberger 1966b); 22.4S, 17.8S and 12.7S (Rogers et al.). The two larger components in each case are presumed to derive from mitochondrial ribosomes. Wintersberger demonstrated an RNA species similar to messenger RNA, and showed that the 4S RNA was similar to transfer RNA (tRNA). tRNA's for fifteen amino acids and the corresponding aminoacyl-RNA synthetases have been demonstrated in mitochondria isolated from *Neurospora crassa* (Barnett et al.). For aspartate, phenylalanine and leucine at least, the mitochondria contain unique enzymes and tRNA's.

It is established that isolated mitochondria can synthesise protein the bulk of which is incorporated into the substance of the mitochondrion. It appears likely that all mitochondria will be found to have complete mechanisms for transcription and translation of the genetic information carried in mitochondrial DNA. The relationship of this mechanism and that controlled by the nucleus to the formation of the molecules unique to mitochondria, and the organization of these molecules in ways characteristic of cell-type, remains to be elucidated.

References

AMOORE, J. E. and W. BARTLEY: The permeability of isolated rat-liver mitochondria to sucrose, sodium chloride and potassium chloride at 0°. Biochem. J. 69 (1958) 223.

ANDERSSON-CEDERGREN, E.: Ultrastructure of motor end plate and sarcoplasmic components of mouse skeletal muscle fibre as revealed by three-dimensional reconstructions from serial sections. J. Ultrastruct. Res. Suppl. 1 (1959) 1.

ANDRÉ, J.: Étude au microscope électronique de l'évolution du chondriome pendant la spermatogénèse du scorpion *Euscorpius flavicaudis*. J. Ultrastruct. Res. 2 (1959) 288.

ANDRÉ, J.: Contribution à la connaissance du chondriome. Étude de ses modifications ultrastructurales pendant la spermatogénèse. J. Ultrastruct. Res. Suppl. 3 (1962) 7.

ANDRÉ, J. and V. MARINOZZI: Présence dans les mitochondries de particules ressemblant aux ribosomes. J. Microscopie 4 (1965) 615.

ANDRESEN, N.: Cytological investigations on the giant amoeba *Chaos chaos* L. Compt. Rend. Trav. Lab. Carlsberg 29 (1956) 435.

ASHHURST, D. E.: Mitochondrial particles seen in sections. J. Cell Biol. 24 (1965) 497.

BANGHAM, A. D. and R. W. HORNE: Negative staining of phospholipids and their structural modification by surface-active agents as observed in the electron microscope. J. Mol. Biol. 8 (1964) 660.

BARNETT, W. E., D. H. BROWN and J. L. EPLER: Mitochondrial-specific aminoacyl-RNA synthetases. Proc. Natl. Acad. Sci. U.S. 57 (1967) 1775.

BASFORD, R. E., H. D. TISDALE and D. E. GREEN: Studies on the terminal electron transport system VIII.

Conversion of succinic dehydrogenase complex to soluble succinic dehydrogenase. Biochim. Biophys. Acta 24 (1957) 290.

BAUM, H., H. I. SILMAN, J. S. RIESKE and S. H. LIPTON: On the composition and structural organization of complex III of the mitochondrial electron transfer chain. J. Biol. Chem. 242 (1967) 4876.

BENSON, A. A.: On the orientation of lipids in chloroplast and cell membranes. J. Am. Oil Chemists' Soc. 43 (1966) 265.

BENTZEL, C. J. and A. K. SOLOMON: Osmotic properties of mitochondria. J. Gen. Physiol. 50 (1967) 1547.

BERGER, E. R.: Mitochondria genesis in the retinal photoreceptor inner segment. J. Ultrastruct. Res. 11 (1964) 90.

BLINZINGER, K., N. B. NEWCASTLE and H. HAGER: Observations on prismatic-type mitochondria within astrocytes of the syrian hamster brain. J. Cell Biol. 25 (1965) 293.

BOMSTEIN, R., R. GOLDBERGER and H. TISDALE: Studies on the electron transport system XXXIV. Isolation and properties of mammalian cytochrome c_1. Biochim. Biophys. Acta 50 (1961) 527.

BORST, P. and G. J. C. M. RUTTENBERG: Renaturation of mitochondrial DNA. Biochim. Biophys. Acta 114 (1966) 645.

BORST, P., E. F. J. VAN BRUGGEN, G. J. C. M. RUTTENBERG and A. M. KROON: Mitochondrial DNA II. Sedimentation analysis and electron microscopy of mitochondrial DNA from chick liver. Biochim. Biophys. Acta 149 (1967) 156.

BRAAK, H.: Electronenmikroskopische Untersuchungen an Catecholaminkernen im Hypothalamus vom Goldfisch (*Carassius auratus*). Z. Zellforsch. Mikroskop. Anat. 83 (1967) 398.

BRANTON, D.: Fracture faces of frozen membranes. Proc. Natl. Acad. Sci. U.S. 55 (1966) 1048.

BURGOS, M. H., A. AOKI and F. L. SACERDOTE: Ultrastructure of isolated kidney mitochondria with phlorizin and ATP. J. Cell Biol. 23 (1964) 207.

CHANCE, B., C.-P. LEE and L. MELA: Control and conservation of energy in the cytochrome chain. Federation Proc. 26 (1967) 1341.

CHANCE, B. and D. F. PARSONS: Cytochrome function in relation to inner membrane structure of mitochondria. Science 142 (1963) 1176.

CHANCE, B. and G. R. WILLIAMS: Respiratory enzymes in oxidative phosphorylation III. The steady state. J. Biol. Chem. 217 (1955) 409.

CHANDRA, S.: The reversal of mitochondrial membrane. J. Cell Biol. 12 (1962) 503.

CHAPPELL, J. B. and G. D. GREVILLE: The influence of the composition of the suspending medium on the properties of mitochondria. In: J. K. Grant, ed.: Methods of separation of subcellular structural components. Cambridge, University Press (1963) p. 39.

CHAPPELL, J. B. and K. N. HAARHOFF: The penetration of mitochondrial membrane by anions and cations. In: E. C. Slater, Z. Kanivea and L. Wojtczak, eds.: Biochemistry of mitochondria. London and Warsaw, Academic Press and PWN (1967) p. 75.

CHÈVREMONT, M., R. BASSLEER and E. BAECKELAND: Nouvelles recherches sur les acides désoxyribonucléiques dans des cultures de fibroblastes refroidies puis réchauffées. Études cytophotométrique et histoautoradiographique. Localisation cytoplasmique d'ADN. Arch. Biol. (Liège) 72 (1961) 501.

CHÈVREMONT, M., S. CHÈVREMONT-COMHAIRE and E. BAECKELAND: Action de désoxyribonucléases neutre et acide sur des cellules somatiques vivantes cultivées *in vitro*. Arch. Biol. (Liège) 70 (1959) 811.

CLAUDE, A.: Microscopy, differential centrifugation and biochemistry in the exploration of the cell. In: P. Buffa, ed.: Symposium on Electron Microscopy, Modena. Rome, Consiglio Nazionale delle Ricerche (1964) p. 49.

CRIDDLE, R. S., R. M. BOCK, D. E. GREEN and H. D. TISDALE: Physical characteristics of proteins of the electron transfer system and interpretation of the structure of the mitochondrion. Biochemistry 1 (1962) 827.

CRIEGEE, R.: Osmiumsäure-ester als Zwischenprodukte bei Oxydationen. Ann. Chem. 522 (1936) 75.

CURTIS, A.S.G.: The cell surface: its molecular role in morphogenesis. London, Logos and Academic Press (1967).

DAEMS, W.TH. and E.WISSE: Shape and attachment of the cristae mitochondriales in mouse hepatic cell mitochondria. J. Ultrastruct. Res. 16 (1966) 123.

DANIELS, E.W. and E.P.BREYER: Starvation effects on the ultrastructure of Amoeba mitochondria. Z. Zellforsch. Mikroskop. Anat. 80 (1968) 159.

DAVIS, L.E.: Intramitochondrial crystals in *Hydra*. J. Ultrastruct. Res. 21 (1967) 125.

DAWSON, R.M.C.: The metabolism of animal phospholipids and their turnover in cell membranes. In: P.N.Campbell and G.D.Greville, eds.: Essays in biochemistry, Vol. 2. London, Academic Press (1966) p. 69.

DEAMER, D.W., K.UTSUMI and L.PACKER: Oscillatory states of mitochondria III. Ultrastructure of trapped conformational states. Arch. Biochem. Biophys. 121 (1967) 641.

DESHPANDE, P.D., D.D.HICKMAN and R.W.VON KORFF: Morphology of isolated rabbit heart muscle mitochondria and the oxidation of extramitochondrial reduced diphosphopyridine nucleotide. J. Biophys. Biochem. Cytol. 11 (1961) 77.

EDELMAN, M., H.T.EPSTEIN and J.A.SCHIFF: Isolation and characterization of DNA from the mitochondrial fraction of *Euglena*. J. Mol. Biol. 17 (1966) 463.

ESTABROOK, R.W. and A.HOLOWINSKY: Studies on the content and organization of the respiratory enzymes of mitochondria. J. Biophys. Biochem. Cytol. 9 (1961) 19.

FERNÁNDEZ-MORÁN, H.: Cell-membrane ultrastructure. Low-temperature electron microscopy and X-ray diffraction studies of lipoprotein components in lamellar systems. Circulation 26 (1962) 1039.

FERNÁNDEZ-MORÁN, H.: Subunit organization of mitochondrial membranes. Science 140 (1963) 381.

FERNÁNDEZ-MORÁN, H., T.ODA, P.V.BLAIR and D.E.GREEN: A macromolecular repeating unit of mitochondrial structure and function. J. Cell Biol. 22 (1964) 63.

FINEAN, J.B. and M.G.RUMSBY: Negatively stained lipoprotein membranes: the validity of the image. Nature 197 (1963) 1326.

FLEISCHER, S., B.FLEISCHER and W.STOECKENIUS: Fine structure of lipid-depleted mitochondria. J. Cell Biol. 32 (1967) 193.

FLEISCHER, S., G.ROUSER, B.FLEISCHER, A.CASU and G.KRITCHEVSKY: Lipid composition of mitochondria from bovine heart, liver and kidney. J. Lipid Res. 8 (1967) 170.

GARLAND, P.B. and D.W.YATES: Fatty-acid oxidation and mitochondrial structure and compartmentation. In: E.Quagliariello, S.Papa, E.C.Slater and J.M.Tager, eds.: Mitochondrial structure and compartmentation. Bari, Adriatica Editrice (1967) p. 385.

GIACOMELLI, F., J.WIENER and D.SPIRO: Cytological alterations related to stimulation of the zona glomerulosa of the adrenal gland. J. Cell Biol. 26 (1965) 499.

GOLDBERGER, R., A.L.SMITH, H.TISDALE and R.BOMSTEIN: Studies of the electron transport system XXXVII. Isolation and properties of mammalian cytochrome *b*. J. Biol. Chem. 236 (1961) 2788.

GREENAWALT, J.W., C.S.ROSSI and A.L.LEHNINGER: Effect of active accumulation of calcium and phosphate ions on the structure of rat liver mitochondria. J. Cell Biol. 23 (1964) 21.

GREEN, D.E. and J.F.PERDUE: Correlation of mitochondrial structure and function. Ann. N.Y. Acad. Sci. 137 (1966) 667.

GREEN, D.E. and A.TZAGOLOFF: The mitochondrial electron transfer chain. Arch. Biochem. Biophys. 116 (1966) 293.

GREEN, D.E. and D.M.ZIEGLER: Electron transport particles. In: S.P.Conowick and N.O.Kaplan, eds.: Methods in enzymology, Vol. 6. New York, Academic Press (1963) p. 416.

GREVILLE, G.D., E.A.MUNN and D.S.SMITH: Observations on the fragmentation of isolated flight-muscle mitochondria from *Calliphora erythrocephala* (Diptera). Proc. Roy. Soc. (London) Ser. B 161 (1965) 403.

GRIMM, F.C. and D.G.DOHERTY: Properties of the two forms of malic dehydrogenase from beef heart. J. Biol. Chem. 236 (1962) 1980.

HACKENBROCK, C.R.: Ultrastructural bases for metabolically linked mechanical activity in mitochondria II. Electron transport-linked ultrastructural transformations in mitochondria. J. Cell Biol. 37 (1968) 345.

HALL, C.E.: Measurement of globular protein molecules by electron microscopy. J. Biophys. Biochem. Cytol. 7 (1960) 613.

HAYAKAWA, T., M.HIRASHIMA, S.IDE, M.HAMADA, K.OKABE and M.KOIKE: Mammalian α-keto acid dehydrogenase complexes I. Isolation, purification and properties of pyruvate dehydrogenase complex of pig heart muscle. J. Biol. Chem. 241 (1966) 4694.

HAYAKAWA, T. and M.KOIKE: Resolution and reconstitution of the mammalian pyruvate dehydrogenase complex. Abstr. 7th Int. Congr. Biochem., Tokyo (1967) 772.

HEROLD, F. and K.MUNZ: Ultrastructure of spermatozoa of *Peregrinus maidus* (Homoptera, Delphacidae). Z. Zellforsch. Mikroskop. Anat. 83 (1967) 364.

HIRASHIMA, M., T.HAYAKAWA and M.KOIKE: Mammalian α-keto acid dehydrogenase complexes II. An improved procedure for the preparation of 2-oxoglutarate dehydrogenase complex from pig heart muscle. J. Biol. Chem. 242 (1967) 902.

HORNE, R.W. and G.D.GREVILLE: Observations on ox-liver L-glutamate dehydrogenase with the electron microscope. J. Mol. Biol. 6 (1963) 506.

HORNE, R.W. and V.P.WHITTAKER: The use of the negative staining method for the electron-microscopic study of subcellular particles from animal tissues. Z. Zellforsch. Mikroskop. Anat. 58 (1962) 1.

ISHIKAWA, E., R.M.OLIVER and L.J.REED: α-Keto acid dehydrogenase complexes V, Macromolecular organization of pyruvate and α-ketoglutarate dehydrogenase complexes isolated from beef kidney mitochondria. Proc. Natl. Acad. Sci. U.S. 56 (1966) 534.

ISHIKAWA, T. and Y.F.PEI: Intramitochondrial glycogen particles in rat retinal receptor cells. J. Cell Biol. 25 (1965) 402.

KALF, G.F.: Deoxyribonucleic acid in mitochondria and its role in protein synthesis. Biochemistry 3 (1964) 1702.

KARNOVSKY, M.J.: Mitochondrial changes and cytochrome oxidase in the frog nephron. 5th Int. Congr. Electron Microscopy 2 (1962) Q-9.

KING, T.E., R.L.HOWARD, J.KETTMAN, B.M.HEGDEKAR, M.KUBOYAMA, K.S.NICKEL and E.A.POSSEHL: Comparison of soluble NADH dehydrogenases from the respiratory chain of cardiac mitochondria. In: E.C.Slater, ed.: Flavins and flavoproteins. Amsterdam, Elsevier Publishing Co. (1966) p. 441.

KISLEV, N., H.SWIFT and L.BOGORAD: Nucleic acids of chloroplasts and mitochondria in Swiss Chord. J. Cell Biol. 25 (1965) 327.

KJAERHEIM, A.: Crystrallized tubules in the mitochondrial matrix of adrenal cortical cells. Exptl. Cell Res. 45 (1967) 236.

KLINGENBERG, M.: Enzyme profiles in mitochondria. In: R.W.Estabrook and M.E.Pullman, eds.: Methods in enzymology, Vol. VI. New York, Academic Press (1967) p. 3.

KLINGENBERG, M. and E.PFAFF: Structural and functional compartmentation in mitochondria. In: J.M.Tager, S.Papa, E.Quagliariello and E.C.Slater, eds.: Regulation of metabolic processes in mitochondria. Amsterdam, Elsevier Publishing Co. (1966) p. 180.

KOPACZYK, K., J.ASAI, D.W.ALLMANN, T.ODA and D.E.GREEN: Resolution of the repeating unit of the inner mitochondrial membrane. Arch. Biochem. Biophys. 123 (1968) 602.

KORN, E.D.: Structure of biological membranes. Science 153 (1966) 1492.

KROON, A.M.: Protein synthesis in mitochondria III. On the effects of inhibitors on the incorporation of amino acids into protein by intact mitochondria and digitonin fractions. Biochim. Biophys. Acta 108 (1965) 275.

KROON, A.M., P.BORST, E.F.J.VAN BRUGGEN and G.J.C.M.RUTTENBERG: Mitochondrial DNA from sheep heart. Proc. Natl. Acad. Sci. U.S. 56 (1966) 1836.

KUROSUMI, K., T. MATSUZAWA and N. WATARI: Mitochondrial inclusions in the snake renal tubules. J. Ultrastruct. Res. 16 (1966) 269.

LEHNINGER, A. L.: The mitochondrion. New York, W. A. Benjamin Inc. (1964).

LINDBERG, O., J. DE PIERRE, E. RYLANDER and B. A. AFZELIUS: Studies of the mitochondrial energy-transfer system of brown adipose tissue. J. Cell Biol. 34 (1967) 293.

LUCK, D. J.: The influence of precursor pool size on mitochondrial composition in *Neurospora crassa.* J. Cell Biol. 24 (1964) 445.

LUCK, D. J. and E. REICH: DNA in mitochondria of *Neurospora crassa.* Proc. Natl. Acad. Sci. U.S. 52 (1964) 931.

LUCY, J. A.: Globular lipid micelles and cell membranes. J. Theoret. Biol. 7 (1964) 360.

LUSTY, C. J.: Lipoyl dehydrogenase from beef liver mitochondria. J. Biol. Chem. 238 (1963) 3443.

MACKLER, B.: The DPNH dehydrogenases of the electron-transport systems of heart muscle and yeast. In: E. C. Slater, ed.: Flavins and flavoproteins. Amsterdam, Elsevier Publishing Co. (1966) p. 427.

MACLENNAN, D. H. and TZAGOLOFF, A.: The isolation of a copper protein from cytochrome oxidase. Biochim. Biophys. Acta 96 (1965) 166.

MAHLER, H. R., N. K. SARKAR and L. P. VERNON: Studies on diphosphopyridine nucleotide-cytochrome c reductase II. Purification and properties. J. Biol. Chem. 199 (1952) 585.

MALAMED, S.: Structural changes during swelling of isolated rat mitochondria. Z. Zellforsch. Mikroskop. Anat. 65 (1965) 10.

MALHOTRA, S. K.: A study of the structure of the mitochondrial membrane system. J. Ultrastruct. Res. 15 (1966) 14.

MANTON, I.: Electron microscopical observations on a very small flagellate: the problem of *Chromulina pusilla* Butcher. J. Marine Biol. Assoc. U.K. 38 (1959) 319.

MARGOLIASH, E., E. L. SMITH, G. KREIL and H. TUPPY: Amino-acid sequence of horse heart cytochrome c. The complete amino-acid sequence. Nature 192 (1961) 1125.

MASSEY, V.: The composition of the ketoglutarate dehydrogenase complex. Biochim. Biophys. Acta 38 (1960) 447.

MOOR, H. and K. MÜHLETHALER: Fine structure in frozen-etched yeast cells. J. Cell Biol. 17 (1963) 609.

MOOR, H., C. RUSKA and H. RUSKA: Elektronenmikroskopische Darstellung tierischer Zellen mit der Gefrierätztechnik. Z. Zellforsch. Mikroskop. Anat. 62 (1964) 581.

MUGNAINI, E.: Helical filaments in astrocytic mitochondria of the corpus striatum in the rat. J. Cell Biol. 23 (1964) 173.

MUNKRES, K. D. and F. M. RICHARDS: The purification and properties of *Neurospora* malate dehydrogenase. Arch. Biochem. Biophys. 109 (1965) 466.

MUNN, E. A.: On the structure of mitochondria and the value of ammonium molybdate as a negative stain for osmotically sensitive structures. J. Ultrastruct. Res. 25 (1968) 362.

MUNN, E. A. and P. V. BLAIR: An electron microscopic study of structural changes during the large amplitude swelling and contraction of isolated beef-heart mitochondria. Z. Zellforsch. Mikroskop. Anat. 80 (1967) 205.

MURPHEY, W. H., G. B. KITTO, J. EVERSE and N. O. KAPLAN: Malate dehydrogenases I. A survey of molecular size measured by gel filtration. Biochemistry 6 (1967) 603.

NADAKAVUKAREN, M. J.: Fine structure of negatively stained plant mitochondria. J. Cell Biol. 23 (1964) 193.

NASS, M. M. K.: The circularity of mitochondrial DNA. Proc. Natl. Acad. Sci. U.S. 56 (1966) 1215.

NASS, M. M. K., S. NASS and B. A. AFZELIUS: The general occurrence of mitochondrial DNA. Exptl. Cell Res. 37 (1965) 516.

NASS, S. and M. M. K. NASS: An electron histochemical study of mitochondrial fibrous inclusions. J. Roy. Microscop. Soc. 81 (1963) 209.

NEUBERT, D.: Studies on swelling and contraction of mitochondria and the significance of factors with peroxidase activity in these reactions. In: J. M. Tager, S. Papa, E. Quagliariello and E. C. Slater, eds.: Regulation of metabolic processes in mitochondria. Amsterdam, Elsevier Publishing Co. (1966) p. 351.

NOVIKOFF, A.B.: Biochemical heterogeneity of the cytoplasmic particles of rat liver. Symp. Soc. Exptl. Biol. 10 (1957) 92.

NOVIKOFF, A.B.: Mitochondria (chondriosomes). In: J.Brachet and A.E.Mirsky, eds.: The cell, Vol. II. London, Academic Press (1961) p. 299.

O'BRIEN, T.W. and G.F.KALF: Ribosomes from rat liver mitochondria II. Partial characterization. J. Biol. Chem. 242 (1967) 2180.

ODA, T. and Y.NISHI: Fundamental structure and function of mitochondrial membrane. J. Electron-microscopy (Tokyo) 12 (1963) 290.

OHNISHI, K.: Studies on cytochrome *b* I. Isolation, purification and some properties of cytochrome *b* from beef heart muscle. J. Biochem. (Tokyo) 59 (1966) 1.

OHNISHI, K.: Studies on cytochrome *b* II. Crystallization and some properties of cytochrome *b* from larvae of the housefly, *Musca domestica* L. J. Biochem. (Tokyo) 59 (1966) 9.

OHNISHI, K.: Studies on cytochrome *b* III. Comparison of cytochrome *b*'s from beef heart muscle and larvae of the housefly. J. Biochem. (Tokyo) 59 (1966) 17.

OLSON, J.A. and C.B.ANFINSEN: The crystallization and characterization of L-glutamic acid dehydrogenase. J. Biol. Chem. 197 (1952) 67.

PALADE, G.E.: The fine structure of mitochondria. Anat. Record 114 (1952) 427.

PALADE, G.E.: An electron microscope study of the mitochondrial structure. J. Histochem. Cytochem. 1(1953) 188.

PAPPAS, G.D. and P.W.BRANDT: Mitochondria I. Fine structure of the complex patterns in the mitochondria of *Pelomyxa carolinensis* Wilson (*Chaos chaos* L.). J. Biophys. Biochem. Cytol. 6 (1959) 85.

PARSONS, D.F.: Negative staining of thinly spread cells and associated virus. J. Cell Biol. 16 (1963) 620.

PARSONS, D.F.: Mitochondrial structure: Two types of subunits on negatively stained mitochondrial membranes. Science 140 (1963) 985.

PARSONS, D.F.: Recent advances correlating structure and function in mitochondria. Intern. Rev. Exptl. Pathol. 4 (1965) 1.

PARSONS, D.F. and Y.YANO: The cholesterol content of the outer and inner membranes of guinea-pig liver mitochondria. Biochim. Biophys. Acta 135 (1967) 362.

PARSONS, D.F., W.D.BONNER and J.G.VERBOON: Electron microscopy of isolated plant mitochondria and plastids using both the thin-section and negative-staining techniques. Can. J. Botany 43 (1965) 647.

PARSONS, D.F., G.R.WILLIAMS and B.CHANCE: Characteristics of isolated and purified preparations of the outer and inner membranes of mitochondria. Ann. N.Y. Acad. Sci. 137 (1966) 643.

PARSONS, D.F., G.R.WILLIAMS, W.THOMPSON, D.WILSON and B.CHANCE: Improvements in the procedure for the purification of mitochondrial outer and inner membrane. Comparison of the outer membrane with smooth endoplasmic reticulum. In: E.Quagliariello, S.Papa, E.C.Slater and J.M. Tager, eds.: Mitochondrial structure and compartmentation. Bari, Adriatica Editrice (1967) p. 29.

PEASE, D.C.: A unique structural component of mitochondrial cristae. 5th Int. Congr. Electron Microscopy, Q-1 (1962).

PENEFSKY, H.S. and R.C.WARNER: Partial resolution of the enzymes catalyzing oxidative phosphorylation VI. Studies on the mechanism of cold inactivation of mitochondrial adenosine triphosphatase. J. Biol. Chem. 240 (1965) 4694.

PENNISTON, J.T., R.A.HARRIS, J.ASAI and D.E.GREEN: The conformational basis of energy transformations in membrane systems I. Conformational changes in mitochondria. Proc. Natl. Acad. Sci. U.S. 59 (1968) 624.

PERSONNE, P. and J.ANDRÉ: Existence de glycogène mitochondrial dans le spermatozoide de la Testacelle. J. Microscopie 3 (1964) 643.

RACKER, E. and L.L.HORSTMAN: Partial resolution of the enzymes catalyzing oxidative phosphorylation

XIII. Structure and function of submitochondrial particles completely resolved with respect to coupling factor 1. J. Biol. Chem. 242 (1967) 2547.

REVEL, J.P., D.W.FAWCETT and C.W.PHILPOTT: Observations on mitochondrial structure. Angular configurations of the cristae. J. Cell Biol. 16 (1963) 187.

RIESKE, J.S., D.H.MACLENNAN and R.COLEMAN: Isolation and properties of an iron-protein from the (reduced coenzyme Q-)cytochrome c reductase complex of the respiratory chain. Biochem. Biophys. Res. Commun. 15 (1964) 338.

ROGERS, P.J., B.N.PRESTON, E.B.TITCHENER and A.W.LINNANE: Differences between the sedimentation characteristics of the ribonucleic acids prepared from yeast cytoplasmic ribosomes and mitochondria. Biochem. Biophys. Res. Commun. 27 (1967) 405.

ROUILLER, C.: Physiological and pathological changes in mitochondrial morphology. Intern. Rev. Cytol. 9 (1960) 227.

SAMORAJSKI, T., J.M.ORDY and J.R.KEEFE: Structural organization of the retina of the tree shrew (*Tupaia glis*). J. Cell Biol. 28 (1966) 489.

SCHATZ, G., H.S.PENEFSKY and E.RACKER: Partial resolution of the enzymes catalyzing oxidative phosphorylation XIV. Interaction of purified mitochondrial adenosine triphosphatase from baker's yeast with submitochondrial particles from beef heart. J. Biol. Chem. 242 (1967) 2552.

SCHNEIDER, W.C.: Mitochondrial metabolism. Advan. Enzymol. 21 (1959) 1.

SCHOLLMEYER, P. and M.KLINGENBERG: Über den Cytochrom-Gehalt tierischer Gewebe. Biochem. Z. 335 (1961) 426.

SCHWEET, R.S., B.KATCHMAN, R.M.BOCK and V.JAGANNATHAN: Pyruvic oxidase of pigeon breast muscle II. Physicochemical studies. J. Biol. Chem. 196 (1952) 563.

SHINGAWA, Y., A.INOUYE, T.OHNISHI and B.HAGIHARA: Electron microscope studies of isolated yeast mitochondria with negative staining and thin sectioning methods. Exptl. Cell Res. 43 (1966) 301.

SILMAN, H.I., J.S.RIESKE, S.H.PILTON and H.BAUM: A new protein component of complex III of the mitochondrial electron transfer chain. J. Biol. Chem. 242 (1967) 4867.

SINCLAIR, J.H. and B.J.STEVENS: Circular DNA filaments from mouse mitochondria. Proc. Natl. Acad. Sci. U.S. 56 (1966) 508.

SINCLAIR, J.H., B.J.STEVENS, P.SANGHAVI and M.RABINOWITZ: Mitochondrial-satellite and circular DNA filaments in yeast. Science 156 (1967) 1234.

SJÖSTRAND, F.S.: Electron microscopy of mitochondria and cytoplasmic double membranes. Nature 171 (1953) 30.

SJÖSTRAND, F.S.: Morphology of ordered biological structures. Radiation Res. Suppl. 2 (1960) 349.

SJÖSTRAND, F.S.: A new ultrastructural element of the membranes in mitochondria and some cytoplasmic membranes. J. Ultrastruct. Res. 9 (1963) 340.

SJÖSTRAND, F.S., E.ANDERSSON-CEDERGREN and U.KARLSSON: Myelin-like figures formed from mitochondrial material. Nature 202 (1964) 1075.

SJÖSTRAND, F.S. and J.RHODIN: The ultrastructure of the proximal convoluted tubules of the mouse kidney as revealed by high resolution electron microscopy. Exptl. Cell Res. 4 (1953) 426.

SLAUTTERBACK, D.B.: Mitochondria in cardiac muscle cells of the canary and some other birds. J. Cell Biol. 24 (1965) 1.

SMITH, D.S.: The structure of flight muscle sarcosomes in the blowfly *Calliphora erythrocephala* (Diptera). J. Cell Biol. 19 (1963) 115.

STOECKENIUS, W.: An electron microscope study of myelin figures. J. Biophys. Biochem. Cytol. 5 (1959) 491.

STOECKENIUS, W.: Some observations on negatively stained mitochondria. J. Cell Biol. 17 (1963) 443.

SUND, H.: Struktur und Wirkungsweise der Glutaminsäuredehydrogenase I. Grösse und Gestalt der Glu-DH aus Rinderleber. Acta Chem. Scand. 17, Suppl. 1 (1963) 102.

SUYAMA, Y. and W.D.BONNER: DNA from plant mitochondria. Plant Physiol. 41 (1966) 383.

SUZUKI, T. and F. K. MOSTOFI: Intramitochondrial filamentous bodies in the thick limb of Heule of the rat kidney. J. Cell Biol. 33 (1967) 605.

TANDLER, B. and F. H. SHIPKEY: Ultrastructure of Warthin's tumor I. Mitochondria. J. Ultrastruct. Res. 11 (1964) 292.

TZAGOLOFF, A., P. C. YANG, D. C. WHARTON and J. S. RIESKE: Studies on the electron-transfer system LX. Molecular weights of some components of the electron-transfer chain in beef-heart mitochondria. Biochim. Biophys. Acta 96 (1965) 1.

URRY, D. W., W. W. WAINIO and D. GREBNER: Evidence for conformational differences between oxidized and reduced cytochrome oxidase. Biochem. Biophys. Res. Commun. 27 (1967) 625.

VAN BRUGGEN, E. F. J., P. BORST, G. J. C. M. RUTTENBERG, M. GRUBER and A. M. KROON: Circular mitochondrial DNA. Biochim. Biophys. Acta 119 (1966) 437.

WARD, R. T.: The origin of protein and fatty yolk in *Rana pipiens* II. Electron microscopical and cytochemical observations of young and mature oocytes. J. Cell Biol. 14 (1962) 309.

WEINBACH, E. C., J. GARBUS and H. G. SHEFFIELD: Morphology of mitochondria in the coupled, uncoupled and recoupled states. Exptl. Cell Res. 46 (1967) 129.

WHITTAKER, V. P.: The separation of subcellular structures from brain tissue. In: J. K. Grant, ed.: Methods of separation of subcellular structural components. Cambridge, University Press (1963) p. 109.

WHITTAKER, V. P.: The ultrastructure of mitochondria. In: J. M. Tager, S. Papa, E. Quagliariello and E. C. Slater, eds.: Regulation of metabolic processes in mitochondria. Amsterdam, Elsevier Publishing Co. (1966) p. 1.

WHITTAKER, V. P. and M. N. SHERIDAN: The morphology and acetylcholine content of isolated cerebral cortical synaptic vesicles. J. Neurochem. 12 (1965) 363.

WILKINS, M. H. F.: Molecular configuration of nucleic acids. Science 140 (1963) 941.

WILLS, E. J.: Crystalline structures in the mitochondria of normal human liver parenchymal cells. J. Cell Biol. 24 (1965) 511.

WINTERSBERGER, E.: DNA-abhäuige RNA-synthese in Rattenleber-mitochondrien. Hoppe-Seylers Z. Physiol. Chem. 336 (1964) 285.

WINTERSBERGER, E.: Occurrence of a DNA-polymerase in isolated yeast mitochondria. Biochem. Biophys. Res. Commun. 25 (1966) 1.

WINTERSBERGER, E.: Synthesis and function of mitochondrial ribonucleic acid. In: J. M. Tager, S. Papa, E. Quagliariello and E. C. Slater, eds.: Regulation of metabolic processes in mitochondria. Amsterdam, Elsevier Publishing Co. (1966) p. 439.

WINTERSBERGER, E. and H. TUPPY: DNA-abhäuige RNA-synthese in isolierten Hefe-Mitochondrien. Biochem. Z. 341 (1965) 399.

WLODAWER, P., D. F. PARSONS, G. R. WILLIAMS and L. WOJTCZAK: Morphological changes in isolated rat-liver mitochondria during swelling and contraction. Biochim. Biophys. Acta 128 (1966) 34.

WOODWARD, D. O. and K. D. MUNKRES: Alterations of a maternally inherited mitochondrial structural protein in respiratory-deficient strains of *Neurospora*. Proc. Natl. Acad. Sci. U.S. 55 (1966) 872.

ZIEGLER, D. M. and P. A. DOEG: Studies on the electron transport system XLIII. The isolation of a succinic-coenzyme Q reductase from beef heart mitochondria. Arch. Biochem. Biophys. 97 (1962) 41.

CHAPTER 35

Biochemistry and function of mitochondria

P. BORST

Department of Medical Enzymology, Laboratory of Biochemistry, University of Amsterdam, The Netherlands

Contents

1. Introduction
2. Chemical composition of mitochondria
3. Oxidative phosphorylation and related reactions
4. The transport of molecules through the mitrochondrial membranes
   (a) Transport of divalent cations
   (b) Transport of monovalent cations
   (c) Transport of anions
   (d) Transport of nucleotides
   (e) Transport of fatty acids
   (f) Physiological importance of translocases
5. Swelling and shrinking of mitochondria
6. Fractionation of the respiratory-chain phosphorylation system and attempts at reconstitution of the system from purified components
   (a) Respiratory chain preparations
   (b) Respiratory chain fragments
   (c) Components of the phosphorylating machinery
7. Drugs used by mitochondriacs
8. Intra-mitochondrial localization of mitochondrial enzymes
9. Organization of the mitochondrial membrane
10. The role of mitochondria in carbohydrate metabolism and haem synthesis
11. Involvement of mitochondria in lipid metabolism
12. The contribution of mitochondria to amino acid metabolism
13. Mitochondria with unusual properties

1. *Introduction**

The primary function of mitochondria in the cell is to synthesize ATP from ADP and P_i. Under aerobic conditions over 80% of the ATP requirement of cells lacking chloroplasts is met by the mitochondria, with the possible exception of some tumour cells and yeast strains with a very high rate of aerobic glycolysis (Racker). The energy required for the synthesis of ATP is derived from the aerobic oxidation of a variety of substrates. Therefore, all mitochondria, whether present in yeast, plants, protozoa, insects or other animal tissues, contain the following basic enzymatic equipment: dehydrogenases to extract hydrogens from substrates; a chain of hydrogen and electron carriers, carrying the reducing equivalents to O_2 (the respiratory chain); and phosphorylating enzymes, utilizing the energy liberated in the oxidation reactions for the synthesis of ATP. In addition, it is likely that all mitochondria contain carrier systems (often called translocases) mediating the transport of substrates, products, nucleotides, etc. through the mitochondrial inner membrane, and enzymes involved in the biosynthesis and turn-over of mitochondrial constituents. A summary of the enzymes involved in these basic mitochondrial reactions is given in Table 1.

In addition to the primary function of providing the cell with ATP, the mitochondrion fulfills many secondary functions. The most important of these are listed in Table 2. The quantitative importance of these secondary functions varies greatly in mito-

TABLE 1

Enzyme systems involved in basic mitochondrial functions.

Enzyme system	Reference	Exclusively present in mitochondria
Respiratory chain and respiratory-chain phosphorylation	Sections 3 and 6	+
NAD(P) transhydrogenase	Section 3	+
Pyruvate dehydrogenase complex	Roodyn	+
Krebs tricarboxylic acid cycle	Krebs and Lowenstein	+[a]
Fatty acid oxidation system[b] and acetyl and palmityl carnitine transferases[b]	Section 11	+
Inner membrane translocases	Section 4	
Haem synthesis (in part)	Section 10	+?
Enzyme systems involved in the biosynthesis and turnover of mitochondrial constituents	Chapters 36, 37	

[a] Some of the individual reactions contributing to the cycle can also take place in the cell sap (Greville in reference II).

[b] Not present in the flight-muscle mitochondria of carbohydrate-utilizing insects.

* *Non-standard abbreviations*: Mitochondriac: A person spending his life studying isolated mitochondria. P_i: Inorganic phosphate. Q: Ubiquinone (coenzyme Q).

chondria of different sources and some of the enzyme systems listed in Table 2 are only found in specialized mitochondria, e.g. the capacity for citrulline synthesis is only found in liver mitochondria of ureotelic animals. As indicated in Table 2, many enzymes found in mitochondria are also present in other cell fractions (Greville, in reference II). Often the intra- and extra-mitochondrial enzymes differ in properties and it is likely that in most cases of a double intra-cellular localization the enzymes will turn out to have different amino acid sequences.

TABLE 2

Enzyme systems involved in secondary mitochondrial functions

Enzyme systems	Reference	Exclusively present in mitochondria
Carbohydrate metabolism	Section 10	
Gluconeogenesis from pyruvate (in part)		(+)
Lipid metabolism	Section 11	
Fatty acid oxidation (see also Table 1)		
GTP-dependent fatty-acyl CoA synthetase		+
Enzymes involved in oxidation of uneven and branched-chain fatty acids		+?
Ketone body metabolism		+
Provision of citrate for extra-mitochondrial fatty acid synthesis		
Amino acid metabolism	Section 12	
Glutamate dehydrogenase		+
P_i-activated glutaminase		+
Transaminases (in part):		
Aspartate transaminase		−
Alanine transaminase		−
Ornithine-δ-transaminase		?
Branched-chain amino acid-oxoglutarate transaminase		−
Proline oxidation:		
Proline dehydrogenase		+
Pyrroline-5-carboxylate dehydrogenase		−
Ornithine → glutamate conversion		−
Enzymes involved in glycine metabolism		
Gamma-aminobutyrate → glutamate conversion		+
Synthesis of citrulline from ornithine		+
Miscellaneous		
Nucleoside diphosphate kinase	Sections 3 and 8	−
Adenylate kinase	Sections 3 and 8	−
GTP-AMP phosphotransferase	Sections 3 and 8	?
Monoamine oxidase	Section 8	+
Thiosulphate sulfur transferase	Greville	−
NADH-cytochrome b_5 reductase	Section 8	−
Cytochrome b_5	Section 8	−

In this chapter the main functions and properties of mitochondria will be considered. The limitations of the discussion may be listed at the outset: Firstly, the comparative enzymology of mitochondria has received little attention up till now and the generalizations about 'the' mitochondrion presented in Table 1 and throughout this chapter, are based on limited experimental evidence. For instance, localization of the enzymes involved in haem synthesis has only been ascertained in liver and avian erythrocytes (Lascelles), but it seems reasonable to assume that in this case the localization will be the same in all cells containing mitochondria (see section 10). Similar considerations hold for the recently discovered inner-membrane translocases. Notwithstanding this basic similarity, mitochondria of some sources are known to deviate in essential respects from the general picture drawn in this chapter. A few examples are discussed in section 13. Secondly, it is clear from Tables 1 and 2 that the biochemistry of the mitochondrion is essentially the biochemistry of intermediary metabolism, which is treated *in extenso* in all elementary biochemistry textbooks. A major part of this chapter will therefore deal with some of the problems which are currently most intensively studied by cytologists and biochemists and which are hardly mentioned in textbooks. Thirdly, the interpretation of many of the basic facts about the biochemistry of the mitochondrion is still highly controversial. To present a coherent picture of basic principles it was necessary for the author to cut some of the Gordian knots and to choose between alternatives. The choice made will not please everybody, but a more extensive and balanced discussion of the doubts and contradictory experimental findings plaguing mitochondriacs can be found in the reviews and papers quoted.

Various aspects of mitochondrial biochemistry and function are discussed in detail in the books of Lehninger and Racker, the reviews by Pullman and Schatz and Roodyn, the proceedings of several recent symposia and volume X of the Methods in Enzymology (1967). To save space, the symposia and the Methods volume will be indicated in the text by Roman numerals, specified in the reference list.

2. *Chemical composition of mitochondria*

The organic matter of mitochondria consists predominantly of protein and lipid. The lipid/protein ratio shows a positive correlation with respiratory activity and the development of the cristae (cf. chapter by Munn). More than 90% of mitochondrial lipid is phospholipid (Table 3) and recent work (Fleischer and Rouser, in I; Parsons, in III and 1968) suggests that the phospholipid composition of animal mitochondria is both highly characteristic and simple (Tables 3 and 4). The bulk of the cellular diphosphatidyl glycerol (cardiolipin) is concentrated in the mitochondrial inner membrane and the 3 major classes of phospholipids are present as 1:2:2 on a weight basis, which is equivalent to 1:4:4 on a molar basis. Mitochondrial phospholipids are highly unsaturated and have a high plasmalogen content.

The relative amounts of components of the respiratory chain and phosphorylating

TABLE 3
Lipid composition of bovine mitochondria. (From Fleischer et al.)

Lipid class	Heart	Kidney	Liver
Total lipid (mg/mg protein)	0.32	0.24	0.18
Neutral lipid (% of total lipid)	5.7	7.2	9.0
Cholesterol (% of total lipid)	1.1	4.7	2.3
Ubiquinone (% of total lipid)	1.06	0.57	0.43
Ubiquinone (μmoles/g protein)	3.94	1.58	0.89
Lipid P (μg/mg protein)	11.3	7.6	5.8
Lipid P (μg/mg lipid)	33	31	33
Diphosphatidyl glycerol[a] (cardiolipin)	19	19	17
Phosphatidyl ethanolamine[a]	37	38	35
Phosphatidyl choline[a]	41	40	43
Minor components[a] (mainly phosphatidyl inositol)	3	4	5
[Cytochrome aa_3[b] (μmoles/g protein)	0.5		0.14]

[a] % of total phospholipid.
[b] from Table 5.

TABLE 4
Comparison of mitochondrial and microsomal membranes. (After Parsons).

	Mitochondria		Smooth endoplasmic reticulum
	Inner membrane	Outer membrane	
Density	1.21	1.13	1.13
Protein:lipid (w:w)	1:0.275	1:0.829	1:0.385
Diphosphatidyl glycerol*	21.5	3.2	0.5
Phosphatidyl inositol*	4.2	13.5	13.4
Phosphatidyl serine*	Not detected	Not detected	4.5

* % of total phospholipid.

TABLE 5
Metal content of rat-liver mitochondria. (From Lehninger et al.)

Metal	μmoles/g protein
K	100–300
Mg	76.5
Na	15.3
Ca	10.8
Fe	6.0
Zn	0.85
Mn	0.29
Cu	0.40

TABLE 6

Concentration (μmoles/g protein) of components of the respiratory chain and of phosphorylating systems in mitochondria. (From Heldt and Klingenberg; Slater, in reference V; Ohnishi et al.)

	Beef heart	Rat liver	Yeast
Cytochrome aa_3	0.5	0.14	0.15
Cytochrome c	0.5		} 0.65
Cytochrome c_1	0.25		
Cytochrome b	0.5		0.28
Flavin non-extractable by acid	0.2		
Flavin extractable by acid	0.5		
Non-haem iron	3		
Ubiquinone	4	2.5	5.4
NAD (total)	6	4	7
NADP (total)	1	5	1
Adenine nucleotides[a]		14	6
Guanine nucleotides[a,b]		0.2	0.3
Cytosine nucleotides[a,b]		0.1	0.2
Uracil nucleotides[a,b]		0.1	0.6

[a] All values are minimum values obtained after a brief incubation with substrate and not corrected for leakage of nucleotides during incubation.
[b] Based on indirect determinations or incomplete data.

systems in mitochondria are presented in Table 6, and Table 5 shows that K^+ and Mg^{2+} are the major metal ions present in rat-liver mitochondria. The adenine nucleotides and the nicotinamide-adenine-dinucleotides make up the bulk of mitochondrial non-lipid organic phosphate compounds (Table 6). The NADP content of mitochondria from different sources varies considerably (cf. Table 6). The function of the various nucleotides in mitochondria is discussed by Heldt and Klingenberg.

3. *Oxidative phosphorylation and related reactions*

Present knowledge about the structure of the respiratory chain is summarized in Fig. 1. Reducing equivalents enter the chain at NAD or Q and are carried by a chain of carriers of decreasing redox potential (Slater 1966 and in V) to cytochrome aa_3, where in a complex reaction involving two haem *a* molecules and two copper molecules, four protons and a molecule of O_2, two molecules of H_2O are formed. There is still some controversy whether all the Q is directly involved in the main chain (Klingenberg and Kröger, in V), while non-haem iron may function as an additional electron carrier (Slater, in V; Pullman and Schatz).

Part of the energy liberated by the oxidation of substrates is used for the synthesis of ATP from ADP and P_i. The stoicheiometry of this process is expressed as the P/O ratio (= μmoles of phosphate esterified per μatom of oxygen consumed). It is now generally accepted that there are three phosphorylation steps associated with the

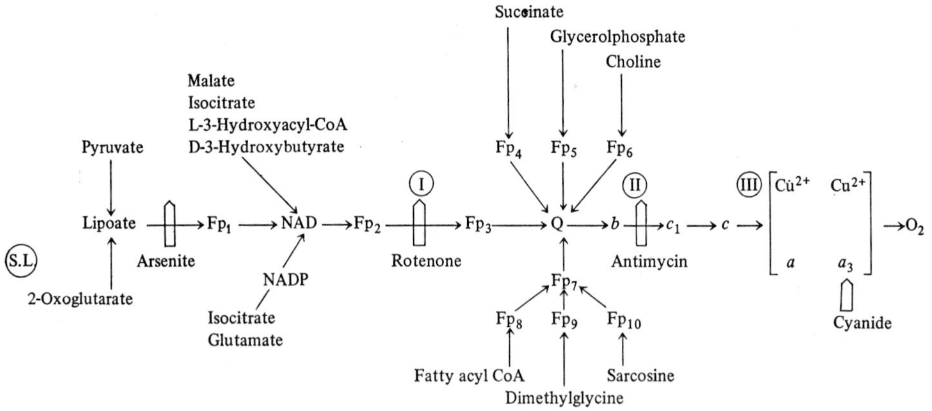

Fig. 1. Schematic diagram of the respiratory chain. (After Lehninger; Slater 1966; Garland et al.; Pullman and Schatz; Biggs et al.; and refs. I and IV.)
Q: ubiquinone (= coenzyme Q), b, c_1, c, a, a_3, cytochrome b, c_1, c, a, a_3; Fp_1: lipoamide dehydrogenase (EC 1.6.4.3); Fp_2: NADH dehydrogenase (EC 1.6.99.3); Fp_3: Fp_{D_2} of Garland et al.; Fp_4: succinate dehydrogenase (EC 1.3.99.1); Fp_5: glycerolphosphate dehydrogenase (EC 1.1.99.5); Fp_6: choline dehydrogenase (EC 1.1.99.1); Fp_7: electron transfer flavoprotein; Fp_8: fatty acyl-CoA dehydrogenase (EC 1.3.2.2); Fp_9: dimethylglycine dehydrogenase; Fp_{10}: sarcosine dehydrogenase; S.L.: site of substrate-linked phosphorylation; I: site I respiratory chain phosphorylation; II: site II respiratory chain phosphorylation; III: site III respiratory chain phosphorylation; ⌂: site of action of inhibitors indicated.

respiratory chain, as indicated in Fig. 1, and one additional substrate-linked phosphorylation step in the oxidation of 2-oxoglutarate (Slater 1966). Therefore, the maximal P/O ratio for the one-step oxidation of 2-oxoglutarate to succinate is 4. The P/O ratio found in experiments with isolated mitochondria is usually somewhat lower because of side reactions (for a discussion of technical problems involved in the determination of P/O ratio's, see Slater, in I and Estabrook, in I).

The mechanism of the substrate-linked phosphorylation step is in principle understood, if not in detail (Cha, Cha and Parks). Part of the energy liberated by the oxidative decarboxylation of 2-oxoglutarate is conserved in the high-energy thiol ester bond of succinyl-CoA. The energy of this thiol ester bond is utilized to make ATP according to reactions 1+2a or 1+2b+2a:

$$\text{succinyl-CoA} + \text{GDP} + P_i \rightleftharpoons \text{succinate} + \text{GTP} + \text{CoA} \quad (1)$$

$$\text{GTP} + \text{ADP} \rightleftharpoons \text{GDP} + \text{ATP} \quad (2a)$$

$$\text{GTP} + \text{AMP} \rightleftharpoons \text{GDP} + \text{ADP} \quad (2b)$$

Reaction (1) is catalyzed by succinyl-CoA synthetase (EC 6.2.1.4) and it involves a phosphorylated form of the enzyme, the phosphate being bound to a histidine residue. Reaction (2a) is catalyzed by the matrix-space nucleoside diphosphate kinase (EC 2.7.4.6); the alternative reaction (2b) catalyzed by the GTP–AMP phosphotransferase (EC 2.7.4.10) is apparently the only enzyme available in the matrix space to phosphorylate AMP, since adenylate kinase (EC 2.7.4.3) is exclusively present in the intermembrane space (Van den Bergh, in III; Heldt and Schwalbach).

Despite 20 years of intensive research in many laboratories, the details of oxidative phosphorylation are still not understood. A general scheme used to interpret experimental findings is presented in Fig. 2. In this scheme AH_2 and B represent adjacent carriers of the respiratory chain, $A \sim C$ and $C \sim P$ are hypothetical intermediates. The evidence for the formation of a phosphorylated intermediate and for ADP as primary phosphate acceptor (and not AMP) has been reviewed by Slater (1966) and Hill and Boyer. This scheme accounts for some of the main features of oxidative phosphorylation, to wit:

$$AH_2 + B + C \rightleftharpoons A{\sim}C + BH_2 \quad (3)$$

$$A{\sim}C + P_i \rightleftharpoons A + C{\sim}P_i \quad (4)$$

$$C{\sim}P_i + ADP \rightleftharpoons C + ATP \quad (5)$$

$$A{\sim}C + H_2O \xrightarrow{\text{uncoupler}} A + C \quad (6)$$

Fig. 2. Schematic representation of respiratory chain phosphorylation. (After Slater 1966.)

All reactions are readily reversible. When the ratio $\frac{[ATP]}{[ADP]\,[P_i]}$ (the phosphate potential) is low and BH_2 is rapidly reoxidized by the next component in the chain' ATP is synthesized. When oxidation of BH_2 by the next component in the chain is slow and the phosphate potential is high, A is reduced by BH_2. A possible exception to this rule is electron transport in the region cytochrome $aa_3 \rightarrow O_2$, since the reduction of cytochrome *c* with concomitant O_2 production from H_2O has not been demonstrated experimentally.

In intact mitochondria respiration and phosphorylation are tightly coupled and the rate of respiration is controlled by the supply of ADP and phosphate. The ADP-dependent respiratory control (usually abbreviated as R.C.) is of fundamental importance in cell physiology, because by this control the rate of energy production by the mitochondria is adapted to the energy demand by the cell. An experiment demonstrating respiratory control with isolated mitochondria is given in Fig. 3. The experiment also presents the definitions of metabolic states introduced by Chance and Williams.

The compulsory coupling between respiration and phosphorylation can be broken either by damage to the mitochondria or by *uncoupling* agents. As shown in Fig. 2, uncoupling agents are usually thought to bring about hydrolysis of the intermediate $A \sim C$, thereby allowing respiration to proceed in the absence of phosphorylation. Damage to the mitochondrial membranes leads to the same result. In addition, any reaction involving the use of $A \sim C$ for synthetic purposes without the intervention of ATP synthesis (see below) also leads to an activation of respiration. The term uncoupler is, therefore, reserved for substances which have a catalytic effect (contrast effect Ca^{2+}, section 4).

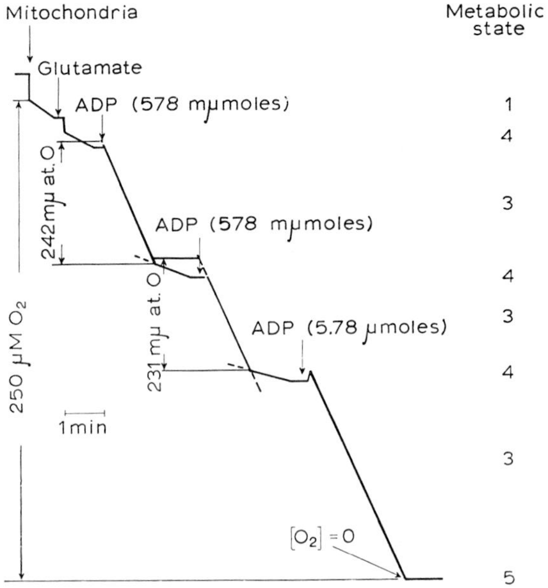

Fig. 3. Determination of the P/O ratio and respiratory control ratio by the method of Chance and Williams. The figure represents the trace of an oxygen polarograph, measuring O_2 concentration as a function of time. At the first arrow, 0.05 ml rat-liver mitochondria (1.5 mg protein) in 0.25 M sucrose were added to 1.75 ml of a reaction mixture containing 60 μmoles phosphate buffer (*p*H 7.3), 30 μmoles KCl, 2 μmoles EDTA, 100 μmoles Tris-HCl buffer (*p*H 7.3) and 10 μmoles $MgCl_2$, 0.02 ml L-glutamate (10 μmoles) were added at the second arrow followed by 0.06 ml of ADP (0.578 μmole) at the third arrow. A further addition of 0.06 ml of ADP (0.578 μmole) was made as shown. Finally, 0.06 ml of a more concentrated solution of ADP was added to allow the suspension to go anaerobic ($[O_2] = 0$). The P/O ratios calculated from the two experiments are 0.578/0.242 = 2.39 and 0.578/0.232 = 2.50, respectively. (The short horizontal traces during the additions were caused by the fact that the polarograph was turned off during this period.)

Definition of metabolic states (Chance and Williams):
State 1: $[O_2] > 0$, [ADP] = low, no added substrate.
State 2 (not shown): $[O_2] > 0$, [ADP] = high, no added substrate.
State 3: $[O_2] > 0$, [ADP] = high, added substrate present.
State 4: $[O_2] > 0$, [ADP] = low, added substrate present.
State 5: $[O_2] = 0$, [ADP] = high, added substrate present.
(From Slater 1966.)

The complex oxidative phosphorylation system can be studied in a number of partial reactions. The most useful are:
(a) Respiration without phosphorylation (e.g. in the presence of uncouplers);
(b) Reversed electron transport (e.g. the energy-linked reduction of NAD^+ by succinate, Ernster and Lee, in I);
(c) P_i-ATP exchange (reaction (4) + (5) in Fig. 2);
(d) ADP–ATP exchange (reaction (5) in Fig. 2);
(e) ATPase activity (reaction (6) + (4) + (5) in Fig. 2).

Intact mitochondria display an active P_i–ATP and ADP–ATP exchange and hardly any ATPase activity. Addition of uncoupling agents abolishes reaction (b), (c) and (d) and activates the ATPase. As long as the mitochondria are reasonably intact no added Mg^{2+} is necessary for these reactions, presumably because sufficient endogenous bound Mg^{2+} is present. Fragmentation of the mitochondria also abolishes reactions (b) and (c), but in this case ATPase activity can only be measured in the presence of added Mg^{2+} (Slater 1966).

Numerous attempts have been made to identify the postulated high-energy intermediates of oxidative phosphorylation and many proposals as to their chemical nature can be found in the literature (see Pullman and Schatz). This lack of success has led Mitchell to formulate an entirely different hypothesis for the mechanism of oxidative phosphorylation. According to the Mitchell hypothesis or chemi-osmotic theory the respiratory chain transports H^+ from the matrix space through the inner membrane into the inter-membrane space. The resulting electrochemical potential over the inner membrane is used to drive an ATPase in the direction of ATP synthesis. A full discussion of this ingenious and stimulating hypothesis is given by Mitchell (in V, 1966 and 1967) and some of the basic objections against it are pointed out by Slater (1967).

The oxidation of NADPH in mitochondria involves a NAD(P) transhydrogenase (EC 1.6.1.1) catalyzing reaction (7):

$$\text{NADPH} + \text{NAD}^+ \rightleftharpoons \text{NADP}^+ + \text{NADH} \quad (7)$$

The equilibrium constant of the isolated enzyme is 1, but in intact mitochondria and sub-mitochondrial particles the transhydrogenase reaction is energy-linked, so that values up to 480 (Ernster and Lee in I and II) for the quotient $\frac{[\text{NAD}^+]\,[\text{NADPH}]}{[\text{NADH}]\,[\text{NADP}^+]}$ have been measured. Under these conditions the reduction of $NADP^+$ by NADH involves the expenditure of one high-energy bond per NADP reduced according to reaction (8):

$$\text{NADH} + \text{NADP}^+ + \text{A} \sim \text{C} \rightarrow \text{NAD}^+ + \text{NADPH} + \text{A} + \text{C} \quad (8)$$

The reversibility of reaction (8) has not been demonstrated. Apparently mitochondrial NADPH is either reoxidized in synthetic reactions or by a transhydrogenase not involving $A \sim C$.

The wide distribution of the energy-linked transhydrogenase suggests that it plays an important role in keeping the intramitochondrial $NADPH/NADP^+$ ratio high to provide reducing equivalents for synthetic reactions (Klingenberg and Bücher). The only other two enzymes of high activity which react with NADP in mitochondria are glutamate dehydrogenase (EC 1.4.1.3) and the NADP-linked isocitrate dehydrogenase (EC 1.1.1.42). The sum of the activities of these two enzymes in mitochondria of various sources correlates well with the NADP content (Pette, in II) and mitochondrial NADPH may, therefore, be mainly used for the provision of citrate for extra-mitochondrial fatty acid synthesis (see section 11) and the temporary fixation of NH_4^+.

The energy-linked transhydrogenase is one of the three cases where high-energy intermediates of oxidative phosphorylation are directly used for energy-requiring reactions without the intervention of ATP synthesis. The other two cases are energy-linked ion uptake (section 4) and reversed electron transport at one site of the respiratory chain driven by high-energy intermediates generated at another site, e.g. reduction of NAD^+ by QH_2 driven by high-energy intermediates generated at site III (cf. Fig. 1).

4. The transport of molecules through the mitrochondrial membranes

The outer membrane of mitochondria is freely permeable to molecules up to the size of inulin. Diffusion of most molecules through the inner membrane is restricted and mediated by carrier systems or translocases. The following transport systems have been characterized.

(a) *Transport of divalent cations*
Isolated mitochondria from a variety of sources are able to concentrate divalent cations, like Ca^{2+}, Mg^{2+}, Mn^{2+}, Ba^{2+} and Sr^{2+} against a concentration gradient by an energy-requiring process (Chance; Chance and Mela, in V; Chappell and Crofts, in II; Chappell and Haarhoff, in V; Lehninger et al.). If care is taken to prevent damage to the mitochondria induced by massive Ca^{2+} loading, uptake of two Ca^{2+} ions is accompanied by the hydrolysis of one energy-rich bond and by the ejection of two protons, or less in the presence of certain permeant anions. Under some conditions the ratio of Ca^{2+} taken up per energy-rich bond hydrolyzed may exceed 2 (Lehninger et al.). It is likely that this is due to binding of Ca^{2+} to the mitochondrial membrane outside the cation barrier. The uptake of Ca^{2+} is reversible and lowering of the external Ca^{2+} concentration or addition of uncoupling agents leads to an outflux of accumulated Ca^{2+}. Respiration-supported Ca^{2+} uptake is blocked by dinitrophenol, but is not affected by oligomycin, while Ca^{2+} uptake supported by external ATP is abolished both by oligomycin and dinitrophenol. Therefore, Ca^{2+} uptake is directly coupled to the utilization of an energy-rich intermediate of the $A \sim C$ type (cf. Fig. 2), without the prior synthesis of ATP. The affinity of mitochondria for Ca^{2+} is not very high ($K_m = 45\ \mu M$), but the rate at which it interacts with the oxidative phosphorylation system is exceptionally high and it competes effectively with ADP and P_i for $A \sim C$. This explains why Ca^{2+} was originally known as an uncoupler. In the absence of a permeant anion, Ca^{2+} uptake by mitochondria is limited and the Ca^{2+} is apparently mainly bound to the internal membrane, possibly to phospholipid. In the presence of a permeant anion larger amounts of Ca^{2+} may be taken up and if the anion is P_i, calcium phosphate deposits may become conspicuous in the matrix space in electron micrographs of the mitochondria.

While the uptake of Sr^{2+} and Mn^{2+} has similar characteristics to Ca^{2+} uptake by mitochondria, Mg^{2+} uptake in liver (but not in heart) requires the presence of an inducing agent, like parathyroid hormone (Rasmussen et al.) or Zn^{2+} (Brierley and Settlemire). It is possible that the transport of all 4 divalent cations involves a common 'cation pump'.

(b) *Transport of monovalent cations*

The inner membrane of intact liver mitochondria is relatively impermeable to monovalent cations, like K^+, Na^+, NH_4^+, Cs^+ and Rb^+ and it shares this property with artificial lipid membranes (Chappell and Crofts, in II; Chappell and Haarhoff, in V; Harris et al. 1966, 1967; Lehninger et al.). Permeability of both the artificial membranes and the mitochondrial membranes is strikingly enhanced by certain antibiotics of the macrolide group. Valinomycin mainly enhances permeability to K^+ while gramicidin is less specific. The increased uptake of K^+ is accompanied by a 500-fold increase in K^+ exchange. At low K^+ concentration, valinomycin-induced K^+ transport leads to an intra-mitochondrial K^+ concentration which can exceed the extra-mitochondrial concentration by a factor of 20, and this uphill transport requires energy. Apparently, at least seven K^+ ions can be transported per energy-rich bond hydrolyzed. The accumulated K^+ is rapidly discharged by another antibiotic, nigericin (Harris et al. 1967). However, nigericin does not affect the valinomycin-induced K^+ exchange.

The interpretation of these results is less clear than in the case of divalent cation transport. A reasonable hypothesis is that the mitochondrial inner membrane contains an energy-requiring cation pump enabling mitochondria to concentrate monovalent cations from the medium. Valinomycin specifically facilitates access of K^+ to the pump, while nigericin allows equilibration of intra- and extra-mitochondrial K^+.

A facilitation of monovalent ion transport through the mitochondrial membrane (though less specific or spectacular as with the antibiotics) is also obtained by adding Zn^{2+} (Brierley and Settlemire), EDTA (Azzone and Azzi, in II), or low molecular weight basic proteins, like histones and parathyroid hormone, to mitochondria (Harris et al.). These substances apparently act by removing Mg^{2+} which blocks access to the cation pump. Probably, the low, but measurable permeability of intact mitochondria to cations in the absence of permeability-increasing substances, is adequate to ensure an optimal cation content in the intact cell.

(c) *Transport of anions*

In 1962 Van den Bergh and Slater discovered that intact mitochondria from the flight muscle of flies (Van den Bergh, in I) are impermeable to Krebs-cycle intermediates. The only respiratory substrates that penetrate are pyruvate and glycerolphosphate, the end products of glycolysis in flight muscle. Flight-muscle mitochondria are highly specialized to carry out ATP synthesis and presumably do not require transport of Krebs-cycle intermediates through the mitochondrial membrane. However, in mitochondria with important secondary functions, carrier systems should be present to mediate anion transport.

On the basis of experiments with rat-liver mitochondria, summarized in Table 7, Chappell has postulated the presence of three anion carrier systems: A system carrying phosphate and arsenate, a dicarboxylic acid carrier, and a tricarboxylic carrier requiring activation by L-malate. More recently, the presence of three additional carriers has been postulated in rat-liver mitochondria: A 2-oxoglutarate carrier activated by L-malate or malonate (De Haan and Tager); a glutamate carrier, and an aspartate carrier activated by glutamate (Azzi et al.).

Mitochondria from several sources are able to concentrate Krebs-cycle intermediates and other substrate anions against a concentration gradient. To explain this phenomenon, Van Dam and Slater have proposed the existence in mitochondria of relatively non-specific energy-linked anion carriers or pumps, which transport the anions selected by the specific anion translocases mentioned above, through the mitochondrial membrane.

TABLE 7

Penetration of the mitochondrial membrane by anions, aldoses and polyhydroxylic compounds. (From Chappell and Haarhoff, in reference V)

		With P_i present	With P_i and L-malate present
Penetrants			
	Phosphate	D-malate	Citrate
	Arsenate	L-malate	*cis*-aconitate
	Formate	Malonate	D-tartrate
	Acetate	Succinate	L-tartrate
	Propionate	Methylsuccinate	
	Butyrate	*meso*-tartrate	
	Glycerol		
	D-erythrose		
Non-penetrants			
	Chloride	Fumarate	*trans*-aconitate
	Bromide	D-malate	
	Bicarbonate	Methylmalate	
	Sulphate	Methylfumarate	
	D-ribitol		
	D-sorbitol		
	D-glucose		

(d) *Transport of nucleotides*

The mitochondrial inner membrane has a very low permeability for ribo- and deoxyribonucleotides and related compounds like NAD$^+$ and CoA, with the sole exception of ADP and ATP, which are rapidly transported in and out by an adenine nucleotide translocase or permease (Klingenberg, Pfaff and Heldt, in II and III). This carrier system has been found in all mitochondria investigated, including mitochondria from yeast (Ohnishi et al.) and *Neurospora* (Greenawalt et al., in I). Rather than catalyzing the accumulation of adenine nucleotides from the medium the enzyme catalyzes a rapid exchange between internal and external nucleotides. It is very specific for ribo-ADP and -ATP, it is competitively inhibited by low concentrations of atractyloside, it has a K_m for ADP of $< 50\ \mu M$ and, in mitochondria of higher organisms, it has an unusually high Q_{10}. The presence of this enzyme is responsible for the apparent specificity for adenine nucleotides of oxidative phosphorylation and the very low rate of oxidative phosphorylation below 5° in intact mitochondria, since ADP has to be transported by the translocase to reach the site of oxidative phosphorylation.

(e) *Transport of fatty acids*

See section on lipid metabolism.

(f) *Physiological importance of translocases*

The discovery of carrier systems depends on finding specific inhibitors or activators of the transport process and undoubtedly the recent discovery of the carrier systems described above will be supplemented by others in the years to come. Nonetheless, it is already clear that for all studies involving the function of the intact isolated mitochondrion consideration of permeability factors is of paramount importance, while the existence of energy-linked transport systems has intimately linked ion transport to oxidative phosphorylation. This is illustrated by the fact that the primary site of action of several compounds affecting oxidative phosphorylation (like Ca^{2+} or valinomycin) is actually on ion transport and it is underlined by recent ideas about the mechanism of uncoupling, worked out in a detailed theory by Van Dam and Slater. Most good uncouplers are relatively lipophilic weak acids and Van Dam and Slater propose that the anionic form of the uncoupler is transported (together with a cation) on the non-specific energy-linked anion carrier, mentioned above, into the mitochondria; inside it picks up a proton and the undissociated form of the uncoupler diffuses out. The proton exchanges against a cation by an exchange-diffusion system (Mittchell 1967) and the net result is the hydrolysis of an energy-rich bond. Competition for a common nonspecific anion carrier may also explain why uncoupling by anionic uncouplers can be reversed in part by high concentrations of an anionic substrate or why the inhibition of respiration by anionic respiratory-chain inhibitors can be partially released in several cases by anionic uncouplers (Van Dam and Slater).

Clearly the permeability characteristics of mitochondria could be of great importance in the cell as one of the factors determining the distribution of substrates and small ions between mitochondria and cell sap (Lehninger et al.). The possible role of the mitochondria in regulating muscle contraction in heart by the reversible sequestration of Ca^{2+} has been discussed by Chance while Rasmussen et al. have studied the possible physiological significance of the effect of parathyroid hormone on the cation transport of isolated mitochondria. In both cases, the evidence is inconclusive.

5. *Swelling and shrinking of mitochondria*

In the intact cell mitochondria are highly mobile and they may undergo extensive and reversible changes in form and possibly also in volume. Swelling of mitochondria *in vitro* was discovered by Kölliker in 1888 and in the last 15 years it has been the subject of numerous experimental studies, reviewed by Lehninger. It has been known for some time that the mitochondrial matrix space behaves as a perfect osmometer within certain limits of osmolarity (Klingenberg and Pfaff, in II; Chappell and Crofts, in II). The matrix space can expand considerably without rupture of the inner membrane, because the surface area of the inner membrane can increase by taking up some of the unfolded cristae. The outer membrane on the other hand ruptures in high-amplitude swelling as indicated schematically in Fig. 4 (B → C).

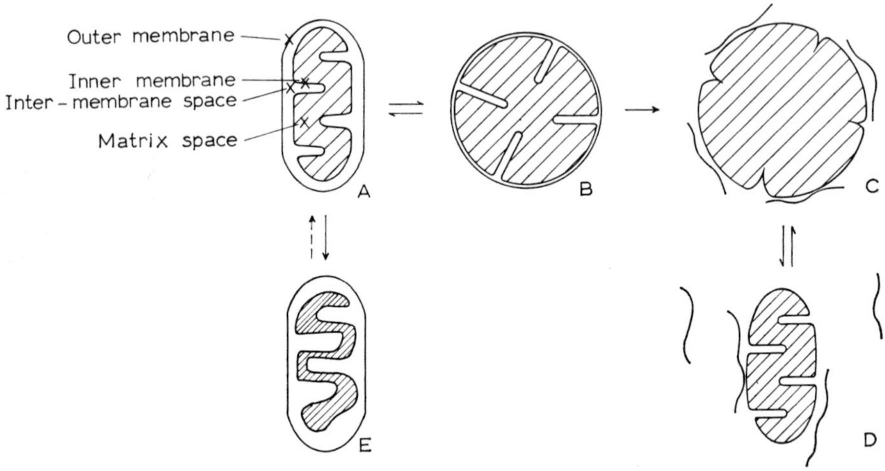

Fig. 4. Schematic diagram of mitochondrial swelling. (Modified after Wlodawer et al.) A ⇌ B, reversible, small-amplitude swelling of matrix space; B → C, high-amplitude swelling of matrix space, outer membrane broken; C → D, contraction; outer membrane remains broken; A ⇄ E, contraction of matrix space with intact outer membrane. If induced by hyperosmotic non-penetrants, the contraction is reversible; if induced by leakage of osmotically active components from the matrix space, it is probably irreversible.

On the basis of the known permeability characteristics of the mitochondrial membrane, three types of osmotic swelling can be expected: (1) Swelling due to a decrease of the concentration of a non-permeant solute in the suspending medium, for instance sucrose. (2) Swelling due to the active uptake of permeant solutes (in an osmotically active form). The swelling accompanying the uptake of calcium acetate or the valinomycin-induced uptake of potassium acetate is of this type. (3) Swelling caused by damage to the mitochondrial membrane, leading to penetration of solutes like sucrose, that do not penetrate the intact inner membrane.

In the literature, swelling studies have usually been divided in low-amplitude and high-amplitude swelling, but the distinction between the two is arbitrary. Low-amplitude swelling (Packer, in I) is usually defined as the energy-dependent, rapid volume changes associated with changes in the metabolic state of the mitochondria. These changes concern probably less than 5% of the matrix volume, they are completely reversible, and the similarity in the requirements for low-amplitude swelling and energy-linked ion uptake strongly suggests that low-amplitude swelling is of type 2. High-amplitude swelling (Hunter and Smith, in I) is not only caused by a decrease in the osmolarity of the mitochondrial suspending medium, but also by a large number of compounds including Ca^{2+}, fatty acids, thyroxin, ascorbate, glutathione, several peptide hormones, heavy metals, gramicidin and phlorizin (see Lehninger). The fact that this swelling could be reversed by ATP in some cases, suggested that the mitochondrial membrane can actively control mitochondrial volume by the presence of ATP-activated 'mechano-enzymes', a concept eloquently set forth by Lehninger. In the last 2 years evidence is increasing, however, that the term large-amplitude swelling covers a series of different processes, none of which is truly reversible, because contraction (Fig. 4, C → D) never leads to reformation of an intact outer membrane (Whittaker, in II; Wlodawer et al.), while in some cases apparent contraction is due to vesiculation of the mitochondria and aggregation of the vesicles (Neubert, in II). Large-amplitude swelling induced by some agents, e.g. by Ca^{2+} and gramicidin, is primarily type 2 swelling (Chappell and Crofts, in II; Azzone and Azzi, in II; Lehninger et al.). There is suggestive evidence that many of the agents enumerated above can lead to type 3 swelling. Ascorbate and glutathione, for instance, can lead to peroxidation of mitochondrial lipids and under extreme conditions to comlpete lysis of the mitochondria. High concentrations of Ca^{2+} lead to release of fatty acids from mitochondrial preparations and in the presence of ATP reincorporation of the fatty acids may take place. Repair of membrane damage may also be responsible for the restoration of contraction ability in aged mitochondria by phosphatidyl inositol and activated fatty acids (Vignais and Vignais, in II), while the effect of some protein factors affecting the ability of aged mitochondria to contract (so-called contraction or C-factors) may be connected with their ability to remove peroxides (Neubert, in II).

In view of the apparent tendency of the inner membrane passively to follow the volume of the matrix space, it is not unexpected that drastic damage to the inner membrane leading to virtually complete loss of osmotically active solutes, will lead to a collapse of the matrix space and an increase of the intermembrane space as shown in Fig. 4, Stage E (Neubert, in II). A similar picture (Whittaker, in II; Klingenberg and Pfaff, in II) may be obtained for liver mitochondria freshly isolated in isotonic sucrose, in which the matrix space is only 20–30% of the total mitochondrial H_2O (Harris and Van Dam). However, in this case the shrinking of the matrix space is readily reversible.

In summary, most, if not all, volume changes of mitochondria *in vitro* can be explained by one of the 3 types of osmotic swelling discussed in this chapter. Whether mitochondria can also undergo active contraction and relaxation by conformation changes in a contractile protein, is not established (however, see Lehninger; and Harris and Van Dam for a different opinion).

6. *Fractionation of the respiratory-chain phosphorylation system and attempts at reconstitution of the system from purified components*

Mitochondria can be fragmented by a variety of mechanical or chemical procedures. The sub-mitochondrial particles obtained essentially consist of inner membrane fragments, mainly present as vesicles owing to the strong tendency of the mitochondrial membrane to vesiculate. They may contain an intact respiratory chain, but up till now even the mildest fractionation procedures devised are accompanied by some decrease in the integrity of the phosphorylating system, e.g. a partial or complete loss of respiratory control. With more drastic fractionation procedures, the energy-linked functions are partially or completely lost, the enzymes involved in phosphorylation may be solubilized and the respiratory chain may break up.

(a) *Respiratory chain preparations*

Sub-mitochondrial particles containing an intact respiratory chain can be made with detergents like digitonin, by mechanical disruption or by sonication. Although digitonin particles have lost most of their complement of matrix enzymes (cf. section 8), some respiratory control and energy-dependent ion accumulation can still be demonstrated, while part of the adenine nucleotide translocase is still functional (Lehninger et al.; Elliott and Haas, in I). Many procedures are available for the preparation of sub-mitochondrial particles by sonication, differing in reaction medium, intensity of sonic treatment and the degree of fragmentation achieved (see ref. I). These particles lack respiratory control, P/O ratio's are substantially lower than those obtained with intact mitochondria and ion translocases cannot be demonstrated any more with the exception of active Ca^{2+} transport. It has been suggested that sonic particles consist of 'inside-out' vesicles of the inner membrane, with the matrix side of the membrane on the outside (Mitchell 1966). Lastly, mitochondria can be fragmented by shaking with glass beads (Schatz, in I), or by grinding with sand under hypotonic conditions (King, in I). The famous Keilin and Hartree heart-muscle preparation made by sand grinding of heart muscle washed with tap water, was long thought to lack the phosphorylating machinery completely. However, in the presence of low concentrations of oligomycin, which block hydrolytic side reactions (section 7), these heart-muscle preparations both synthesize ATP with a maximal P/O ratio of 0.1 and catalyze the energy-linked transhydrogenase reaction (Van Dam and Ter Welle, in II).

(b) *Respiratory chain fragments*

Many components of the respiratory chain have been prepared in a highly purified form (cf. ref. I) and in the case of cytochrome *c* even the complete amino acid sequence is known (Margoliash and Walasek, in I). In analogy with the present concepts about the assembly of complex viruses, it is likely that the correct assembly of the respiratory chain *in vivo* is governed only by the interaction between the component proteins and lipids. Reconstruction of the respiratory chain *in vitro* from purified components should, therefore, be possible in principle. In practice difficulties are encountered, but partial reconstruction has been achieved in a number of cases: succinate dehydrogenase can be specifically dissociated by alkali from a respiratory-chain preparation and such a deficient preparation will specifically and stoicheiometrically bind purified succinate dehydrogenase in functionally active form: the reconstituted succinate oxidase system is identical with the unfractionated system (King, in I). Mitochondria from yeast mutants which completely lack cytochrome *c* will in a similar way stoicheiometrically bind purified yeast cytochrome *c* (Mattoon and Sherman). Fleischer and coworkers (see Fleischer and Fleischer, in I) have developed methods to deplete respiratory chain preparation of lipids by treatment either with aqueous acetone or with phospholipase A. This has allowed the demonstration of the specific requirement for Q in the oxidation of NADH and succinate by O_2 and for phospholipid in the spans NADH → cytochrome *c*, succinate → cytochrome *c* and cytochrome *c* → O_2. Lastly, the respiratory chain breaks up into several large fragments in the presence of cholate or deoxycholate + high salt concentrations. In this way, Green and coworkers have split the respiratory chain in 4 fragments (NADH → Q; succinate → Q; QH_2 → cytochrome *c*; cytochrome *c* → O_2), which can recombine to form a functional respiratory chain (Green and Fleischer). The preparation of such fragments is discussed in ref. I.

(c) *Components of the phosphorylating machinery*

Numerous claims for the isolation of the postulated high-energy intermediates of respiratory-chain phosphorylation can be found in the literature, but none of these claims have survived a critical examination in other laboratories (Slater 1966; Pullman and Schatz). Attempts to isolate protein components involved in phosphorylation have been more successful, even though the interpretation of experiments in this field is complicated by the non-specific protection of energy-conserving reactions in submitochondrial particles by a variety of compounds like serum albumin or oligomycin, which have nothing to do with the phosphorylating machinery *per se*. Racker and coworkers have isolated from beef heart a series of protein 'coupling' factors, which will increase the P/O ratio of respiratory chain preparations prepared by drastic sonication. Factor 1 (F_1) is identical with the inner-membrane spheres and it catalyzes the Mg^{2+}-dependent hydrolysis of ATP (Racker and Horstman, in I). The F_1 ATPase has a molecular weight of 284,000, it is cold labile and it is not inhibited by oligomycin (Penefsky, in I). The enzyme specifically recombines with F_1-deficient mitochondrial sonic fragments and after recombination the enzyme is inhibited by oligomycin and is cold-stable. By treatment with cholate a factor CF_0 can be obtained from sonic fragments. Factor CF_0 lacks a functional respiratory chain; it also specifically recombines with F_1 rendering it sensitive to oligomycin and cold stable, but in this case phospholipid is required for ATPase activity (Kagawa, in I). Similar cold-stable ATPases have been obtained from mitochondria of liver, yeast and *Neurospora* (Schatz et al.). Oxidative phosphorylation by F_1-depleted fragments has an absolute and specific requirement for homologous F_1 and phosphorylation in reconstituted preparations is completely blocked by an antibody against F_1. There is little doubt, therefore, that F_1 is involved in the terminal phosphorylation step of oxidative phosphorylation. Optimal phosphorylation in mitochondrial fragments prepared by sonication in the presence of ammonia (A-particles) or a phospholipid mixture (P-particles) requires, in addition to F_1, the coupling factors F_2 and F_3, which have not yet been extensively purified or characterized (Fessenden and Racker, in I; Fessenden et al., in I; Conover and Zalkin, in I). Coupling factors similar to those of Racker and coworkers, have been described by Lam et al. and Vallejos et al.

Protein-bound phosphohistidine was proposed as an intermediate in oxidative phosphorylation by Boyer and coworkers, but they subsequently showed that the rapidly labelled protein-bound phosphohistidine in mitochondria is present in succinyl coenzyme A synthetase (EC 6.2.1.4) (Slater 1966). Wadkins and coworkers (Wadkins and Glaze, in I) have purified an ADP–ATP exchange enzyme from mitochondria. They have proposed that this is the enzyme which catalyzes the terminal transphosphorylation step of oxidative phosphorylation and that this enzyme is responsible for the ADP–ATP exchange reaction of intact mitochondria (section 3). It is now clear however, that the enzyme is a nucleoside diphosphate kinase (EC 2.7.4.6) unrelated to oxidative phosphorylation and probably extracted from the inter-membrane space (Groot and Van den Bergh).

7. *Drugs used by mitochondriacs*

The difficulties encountered in fractionating the oxidative phosphorylation system into its constituent enzymes have forced mitochondriacs to attack the problem by indirect routes and much of our present knowledge about oxidative phosphorylation and ion translocation is derived from the judicious use of appropriate inhibitors. A list of the most important compounds affecting mitochondrial metabolism is given in Table 8. Some of these compounds have more than one effect, but they are listed according to their most conspicuous property, e.g. oligomycin is an inhibitor of respiratory-chain phosphorylation, but in low concentrations it also blocks hydrolytic side reactions. Low concentrations of oligomycin which partly inhibit the P_i-ATP exchange reaction of intact mitochondria will therefore *increase* the P/O ratio of sub-mitochondrial particles (Lee and Ernster, in II). In addition, it should be obvious that the close coupling of respiration, phosphorylation and ion translocation in intact mitochondria has as a result that an inhibitor of one of these processes also affects the others.

TABLE 8

Commonly used chemicals affecting mitochondrial metabolism (After Slater, in reference I)

Compound	Main site of action and comments
Inhibitors of respiration	
Malonate	Competitive inhibitor of succinate dehydrogenase
Arsenite	Pyruvate and α-oxoglutarate dehydrogenase complex
Rotenone	Respiratory chain between NADH and cytochrome *b*
Amytal	As rotenone
Antimycin	Respiratory chain between cytochromes *b* and *c*
Cyanide	Respiratory chain at cytochrome oxidase
Sulfide	As cyanide
Inhibitors of phosphorylation	Reaction (4) of Fig. 2
Oligomycin	
Aurovertin	As oligomycin?
Alkylguanidines	Site I phosphorylation
Uncoupling agents	Reaction (6) of Fig. 2
Dinitrophenols (DNP)	
Fatty acids	
Dicoumarol	
Carbonyl-cyanide *m*-chlorophenyl hydrazone (Cl-CCP)	
Arsenate	Also uncouples substrate-linked phosphorylation
Drugs affecting active transport	
Atractyloside	Inhibits translocation of ADP and ATP through the inner mitochondrial membrane
Valinomycin	Increases permeability of inner membrane to K^+
Gramicidin	Increases permeability of inner membrane to Na^+, K^+ and H^+. Also uncouples
Nigericin	Increases permeability of inner membrane to K^+

8. *Intra-mitochondrial localization of mitochondrial enzymes*

Three procedures have been used to determine the intra-mitochondrial localization of enzymes. The first is fractional extraction, separating enzymes tightly bound to the mitochondrial membranes from those that are readily released. Some of these enzymes (presumably in the inter-membrane space) can already be largely released by simple incubation with 0.1 M phosphate buffer, which leads to breakage of the outer membrane, e.g. adenylate kinase, creatine kinase, nucleoside diphosphate kinase; others, like malate, citrate and glutamate dehydrogenase and the transaminases, require mechanical disruption for release (Klingenberg and Pfaff, in II; Pette, in II).

The second procedure is based on the determination of enzymes present in purified outer and inner membrane fractions. The outer membrane may be rather specifically stripped off with digitonin (Schnaitman et al.) or by drastic swelling of the mitochondria (cf. Fig. 4) followed by equilibrium density centrifugation in sucrose (Parsons and Williams, in I and III; Sottocasa et al., in I and III), which separates the inner and outer membranes, because of their marked difference in lipid content (Table 4). The enzymes indicated in the first part of Table 9 are highly concentrated in the outer membrane fraction.

Thirdly, the localization of mitochondrial enzymes may sometimes be inferred from other data: the mitochondrial ATPase was tentatively identified by Racker et al. with the inner-membrane 'spheres'. Mitochondrial DNA and RNA polymerase must be in the same space as mitochondrial DNA, the matrix space; and several indirect arguments point to the location of the enzymes involved in fatty acid oxidation within the con-

TABLE 9

Tentative intra-mitochondrial localization of some mitochondrial enzymes. (After Klingenberg and Pfaff, in reference II; Pette, in II; Sottocasa et al., in I; Okamoto et al.)

Outer membrane
NADH-cytochrome b_5 reductase (EC 1.6.2.2)
Cytochrome b_5
Monoamine oxidase (EC 1.4.3.4)
Fatty acyl-CoA synthetase (ATP-dependent) (EC 6.2.1.3)
Kynurenine-3-hydroxylase (EC 1.14.1.2)
Inter-membrane space
Adenylate kinase (EC 2.7.4.3)
Creatine kinase (EC 2.7.3.2)
Nucleoside diphosphate kinase (EC 2.7.4.6)
Inner membrane
Respiratory chain and phosphorylating enzymes
NAD–NADP transhydrogenase (EC 1.6.1.1)
NADH dehydrogenase (EC 1.6.99.3)
Succinate dehydrogenase (EC 1.3.99.1)
Glycerolphosphate dehydrogenase (EC 1.1.99.5)
Choline dehydrogenase (EC 1.1.99.1)
β-Hydroxybutyrate dehydrogenase (EC 1.1.1.30)
Citrate synthase (EC 4.1.3.7)
ADP/ATP translocase
Carnitine acetyl and palmityl transferases (EC 2.3.1.7)
Matrix
Malate dehydrogenase (EC 1.1.1.37)
NAD-linked isocitrate dehydrogenase (EC 1.1.1.41)
NADP-linked isocitrate dehydrogenase (EC 1.1.1.42)
2-Oxoglutarate and pyruvate dehydrogenase complexes
GTP–AMP phosphotransferase (EC 2.7.4.10)
Nucleoside diphosphate kinase (EC 2.7.4.6)
Aconitate hydratase (EC 4.2.1.3)
Fumarate hydratase (EC 4.2.1.2)
Glutamate dehydrogenase (EC 1.4.1.3)
Enzymes involved in protein and nucleic acid synthesis
Enzymes involved in fatty acid oxidation

fines of the inner mitochondrial membrane and matrix space (Van den Bergh, in III; Garland et al.).

The results obtained by these three methods, which agree quite well, are summarized in Table 9. The main conclusion to be drawn from Table 9 (and Table 4) is that the inner and the outer membrane of liver mitochondria are completely different not only in permeability properties and lipid composition, but also in enzymic make up. It should be noted that the methods employed do not distinguish between enzymes loosely bound and enzymes free in suspension. Therefore, the enzymes located in the inter-membrane space according to Table 9, may be loosely bound to the inner or the outer membrane while the matrix enzymes may be loosely bound to the inner membrane. The fact that cytochrome *c* is partly released from mitochondria under conditions which lead to release of inter-membrane enzymes suggests that it is bound to the outside of the inner membrane. Evidence for a loose association of mitochondrial malate dehydrogenase with the mitochondrial membrane has been presented by Woodward and Munkres.

The study of the intra-mitochondrial enzyme localization was initiated only recently and the distribution shown in Table 9 is mainly based on work with liver mitochondria. The fact that a completely different enzyme localization has been proposed by Green and coworkers (Green, in III; Allmann and Bachmann, in I) underlines the difficulties encountered in subfractionating mitochondria and identifying the fractions obtained.

9. *Organization of the mitochondrial membrane*

Two models for the macromolecular structure of the mitochondrial inner membrane have been proposed: according to the first proposal, based on the unit membrane model of Robertson, the membrane is thought to consist of a phospholipid bilayer sandwiched between two protein layers, consisting of structural protein. The respiratory chain and ancillary enzymes are hooked up to this membrane structure (Lehninger). Structural protein is a hydrophobic protein with a molecular weight of 22,000–23,000. It has no enzymatic activity, but it readily combines with purified cytochromes and phospholipids. It makes up 35–45% of mitochondrial protein (Allmann et al., in I). Two objections have been raised against this model (Green and Perdue): in the first place it is possible almost quantitatively to extract mitochondrial phospholipids with very little change in the appearance of the membrane in electron micrographs. Secondly, isolated fragments of the respiratory chain, dissociated by bile salts, will spontaneously reaggregate into vesicles when the bile salts are removed. The formation of membranes under these conditions requires the presence of mitochondrial phospholipids, but an active respiratory chain can be reconstituted in the absence of structural protein. On this basis Green and Perdue propose another model in which the mitochondrial membrane is built up from ten different repeating lipoprotein units with a molecular weight of about 1.2×10^6. The respiratory chain and the phosphorylating enzymes are distributed over several of these units. The role of structural protein in this model is not clear.

The relative merits of these and other models are discussed in ref. III. Detailed calculations for the spacing of membrane-bound enzymes in the mitochondrial inner membrane have been presented by Estabrook and Holowinsky; Lehninger; and Klingenberg (in III).

10. The role of mitochondria in carbohydrate metabolism and haem synthesis

All mitochondria can oxidize pyruvate to CO_2 and H_2O by means of the Krebs tricarboxylic acid cycle. Intact mitochondria (except yeast mitochondria, section 13) are unable to oxidize added NADH, because NADH is unable to penetrate the inner membrane (Lehninger; Greville, in II). Therefore the NADH formed in glycolysis must be reoxidized in an indirect way. The only indirect pathway that is well established is the glycerolphosphate cycle, illustrated in Fig. 5. The operation of this cycle has

Cell sap:	$NADH + H^+ +$ dihydroxyacetone-P	$\rightleftharpoons$	$NAD^+ +$ glycerol-P
Mitochondria:	Glycerol-P $+ \frac{1}{2} O_2$	$\longrightarrow$	dihydroxyacetone-P $+ H_2O$
Sum:	$NADH + H^+ + \frac{1}{2} O_2$	$\longrightarrow$	$NAD^+ + H_2O$

Fig. 5. The glycerolphosphate cycle for oxidation of extra-mitochondrial NADH by mitochondria. (From Borst.)

been demonstrated *in vitro* and its importance in some tissues, e.g. insect flight muscle, is well established (Klingenberg and Bücher; Borst). Since the mitochondrial glycerolphosphate dehydrogenase activity is very low in some tissues, however, the glycerolphosphate cycle cannot account for the mitochondrial oxidation of glycolytic NADH in all tissues (Borst). Other substrate cycles involving the mitochondrial and the cell-sap malate dehydrogenases or the malate dehydrogenases together with the aspartate transaminase of both cell compartments, have been considered, but their functional significance remains to be established (Borst; Greville, in II).

Mitochondria play a vital role in gluconeogenesis from pyruvate, because they contain the bulk of cellular pyruvate carboxylase (EC 4.1.1.1.) (Mehlman et al.). The importance of the mitochondria in providing the reducing equivalents for gluconeogenesis has been stressed by Krebs (in V).

The enzyme δ-aminolevulinate synthetase, which catalyzes the synthesis of δ-aminolevulinate from succinyl-CoA and glycine, the rate-controlling step in porphyrin synthesis, is present in the mitochondrial fraction of rat liver and avian erythrocytes (Lascelles; Granick). Nothing is known about the distribution of this enzyme in other tissues or organisms, but in view of the absolute requirement of porphyrins for mitochondrial functions, the exclusive presence of succinyl-CoA synthetase within the mitochondrial inner membrane and the impermeability of the inner membrane to CoA esters, it is probable that the enzyme will turn out to be present in all mitochondria. While conversion of δ-aminolevulinate to coproporphyrinogen takes place outside the mitochondria, the conversion of coproporphyrinogen to haem is again a mitochondrial process (Lascelles).

11. Involvement of mitochondria in lipid metabolism

All mitochondria, with the exception of the flight-muscle mitochondria of carbohydrate-utilizing insects, are able to oxidize fatty acids (Van den Bergh, in I). In many tissues carnitine is required to transport the fatty acids into the matrix space, because the acyl-CoA synthetases are only present in the microsomes and in the outer mitochondrial membrane (Bremer, in III), while the inner membrane is impermeable to acyl-CoA esters. The inner membrane carnitine acetyl transferase (EC 2.3.1.7) and carnitine palmityl transferase can convert the fatty acyl-CoA esters into corresponding carnitine esters, which are able to enter the mitochondrion (Bremer et al., in III). Mitochondria of some tissues do not require carnitine, probably because they contain an additional acyl-CoA synthetase in the matrix space, while in liver and kidney mitochondria the matrix space also contains a GTP-linked acyl-CoA synthetase (Van den Bergh, in I). Continued fatty acid oxidation requires the complete oxidation of acetyl-CoA to CO_2 and H_2O in the Krebs cycle to regenerate free CoA. In liver and kidney CoA can also be regenerated by condensing acetyl units to acetoacetate, and the enzymes for ketone body formation and utilization, including 3-hydroxybutyrate dehydrogenase (EC 1.1.1.30) and 3-ketoacid CoA-transferase (EC 2.8.3.5) are all located in the mitochondria. 3-Hydroxybutyrate dehydrogenase is very firmly bound to the mitochondrial membrane. For a long time, the enzyme withstood all attempts at purification, until Sekuzu and coworkers discovered that the solubilized enzyme is completely dependent on the addition of lecithin for activity. The complete oxidation of odd-numbered fatty acids and the carbon skeleton of the branched-chain amino acids by mitochondria of some tissues is possible, because of the presence in mitochondria of propionyl-CoA carboxylase (EC 6.4.1.3) and methylmalonyl-CoA mutase (EC 5.4.99.2).

Synthesis of fatty acids takes place in isolated mitochondria of many different tissues. The available evidence suggests that this is due to the reversal of the fatty acid oxidation pathway at high NADH/NAD^+ ratios, although the existence of a pathway involving malonyl-CoA for fatty acid synthesis in mitochondria has not been definitely excluded (Hülsmann et al., in II; Whereat et al.). In addition, transfer of mitochondrial citrate to the cell sap is probably important in providing reducing equivalents and acetyl-CoA for extra-mitochondrial fatty acid synthesis (Ball). Little is known about the biosynthesis and breakdown of mitochondrial phospholipids. Wojtczak and coworkers (in II) have reported that rat-liver mitochondria incorporate both fatty acids and glycerolphosphate into the phospholipids of the mitochondrial outer membrane (Wojtczak and Zborowski). A Ca^{2+}-requiring phospholipase A (EC 3.1.1.4) was found in rat-liver mitochondria by Scherphof and Van Deenen. This enzyme may be responsible for the Ca^{2+}-stimulated release of fatty acids from mitochondria *in vitro*.

12. The contribution of mitochondria to amino acid metabolism

The important role of mitochondria in amino acid metabolism is clear from Table 2. Mitochondria contain all cellular glutamate dehydrogenase, the major enzyme in animal tissues for the oxidative deamination of amino acids or the reductive amination of 2-oxo acids. In liver, up to 5% of all mitochondrial protein can be glutamate dehydrogenase (Klingenberg). In other tissues the activity is often very low, but the enzyme has been detected in nearly all mitochondria studied.

Transaminases are found associated with the mitochondrial fraction in some tissues (De Duve et al.) and one of these, the ornithine-δ-transaminase (EC 2.6.1.13) of mammalian liver, is inducible by dietary amino acids. Mitochondria of various sources contain the enzymes for the conversion of ornithine into glutamate. Degradation of proline to glutamate by means of an essentially irreversible pathway can take place by the consecutive action of proline dehydrogenase, a flavoprotein probably feeding in reducing equivalents into the respiratory chain at Q (see Fig. 1), and Δ'-pyrroline-5-carboxylate dehydrogenase, an NAD-linked enzyme (Borst). Synthesis of proline from ornithine, however, requires an extra-mitochondrial enzyme converting Δ'-pyrroline-5-carboxylate into proline (Strecker; Meister 1965).

Mitochondria are also involved in glycine metabolism since they contain dimethylglycine and sarcosine dehydrogenases, δ-aminolevulinate synthetase (section 10) and enzymes involved in the degradation of glyoxylate (Stewart and Quayle) and the synthesis of benzoylglycine (hippurate) (De Duve et al.).

The enzymes converting 4-aminobutyrate to succinate, 4-aminobutyrate transaminase (EC 2.6.1.19) and succinate semialdehyde dehydrogenase (EC 1.2.1.16) are concentrated in the mitochondrial fractions of brain (Salganicoff and Robertis; Van Kempen et al.) and the quantitative importance of this pathway follows from the fact that 4-aminobutyrate is a good substrate for brain mitochondria.

The enzymes responsible for the synthesis of citrulline from ornithine, CO_2 and NH_3, carbamoylphosphate synthetase (EC 2.7.2.5) and ornithine carbamoyltransferase (EC 2.1.3.3), are exclusively found in the liver mitochondria of ureotelic animals (De Duve et al.). This quantitatively major metabolic pathway (Charles et al.) is a good example of specialized secondary functions that mitochondria may acquire and which lead to the metabolic diversity of mitochondria from different sources.

13. Mitochondria with unusual properties

Mitochondria from a number of sources are known to deviate substantially from the general picture given in this chapter. A few examples follow:

(1) Mitochondria from *Saccharomyces* (yeast) strains lack the site I respiratory-chain phosphorylation, and oxidation of NADH-linked substrates is not inhibited by rotenone or Amytal. Mitochondria from another yeast, *Torulopsis*, are normal in both respects. In addition, *Saccharomyces* mitochondria have two other unusual characteristics: tightly coupled mitochondria can oxidize external NADH at maximal rates and yeast mitochondria contain L- and D-lactate dehydrogenases (EC 1.1.2.3 and 1.1.2.4, respectively), which feed in electrons into the respiratory chain at cytochrome *c* (Ohnishi et al.).

(2) House fly flight-muscle mitochondria lack the anion carriers for Krebs-cycle intermediates (section 4).

(3) Mitochondria of *Ascaris lumbricoides* muscle lack both cytochrome c_1 and cytochrome aa_3 and aerobic oxidation of succinate and NADH by the amputated respiratory chains of these organisms leads to formation of H_2O_2 instead of H_2O (Kmetec and Bueding; Chance and Parsons).

(4) The properties of mitochondria from higher plants differ in several aspects from those of animal and insect tissues: the respiratory chain contains two additional *b* type cytochromes (which could be concerned in hydroxylation reactions) and cytochrome c_1 is replaced by another *c* type cytochrome; it is claimed that plant mitochondria do not behave as osmometers indicating a profound difference in properties of the internal membrane and although K^+ uptake can be induced by valinomycin, plant mitochondria do not accumulate Ca^{2+} (Bonner). The enzymes of the glyoxylate cycle, first reported to be present in plant mitochondria, appear to be localized in a separate peroxisome-like particle (see chapter by Baudhuin).

(5) Mitochondria from ox adrenal cortex are unusual in that they contain a very active system for steroid hydroxylation, involving NADPH, NADPH-adrenodoxin reductase, a non-haem iron protein and cytochrome P-450. In addition, the energy-transfer reactions for ATP formation are deficient in these mitochondria relative to the respiratory capacity and this leads to a channeling of reducing equivalents *via* the energy-linked transhydrogenase and also possibly *via* malic enzyme into hydroxylation reactions (Cammer and Estabrook). In liver the same hydroxylation system is exclusively localized in the microsomes (see also chapter by Goldblatt).

(6) Although there are numerous reports in the literature that tumour mitochondria are abnormal in one way or another, none of these claims has been confirmed (Wenner).

Acknowledgements

I am indebted to my colleagues S. G. Van den Bergh, E. C. Slater and J. M. Tager for many helpful suggestions during the preparation of this chapter.

References

I Methods in Enzymology, Vol. X. Ed. by Estabrook, R.W. and Pullman, M.E. New York and London, Academic Press Inc. (1967).

II Regulation of Metabolic Processes in Mitochondria, Bari (1965). Ed. by Tager, J.M., Papa, S., Quagliariello, E. and Slater, E.C. Amsterdam, Elsevier Publishing Comp. (1966).

III Mitochondrial Structure and Compartmentation, Polignano a Mare (1966). Ed. by Quagliariello, E., Papa, S., Slater, E.C. and Tager, J.M. Bari, Adriatica Editrice (1967).

IV Flavins and Flavoproteins: Proceedings of a Symposium of the International Union of Biochemistry, Amsterdam (1965). Ed. by Slater, E.C. Amsterdam, Elsevier Publishing Comp. (1966).

V Biochemistry of Mitochondria: Colloquium held on occasion of the 3rd Meeting of the Federation of European Biochemical Societies, organized by the Polish Biochemical Society, Warsaw, April (1966). Ed. by Slater, E.C., Kaniuga, Z. and Wojtczak, L. London and New York, Academic Press Inc. and Warsaw, P.W.N. (1967).

AZZI, A., J.B. CHAPPELL and B.H. ROBINSON: Penetration of the mitochondrial membrane by glutamate and aspartate. Biochem. Biophys. Res. Commun. 29 (1967) 148.

BALL, E.G.: Regulation of fatty acid synthesis in adipose tissue. In: G.Weber, ed.: Advances in enzyme regulation, Vol. 4, Part 3. New York, Pergamon Press (1966).

BIGGS, D.R., J.HAUBER and T.P.SINGER: Studies on the respiratory chain-linked NADH dehydrogenase XII. Interrelations of NADH-cytochrome *c* reductase and NADH-CoQ reductase. J. Biol. Chem. 242 (1967) 4563.

BONNER, W.D., JR.: Mitochondria and electron transport. In: J.Bonner and J.E.Varner, eds.: Plant Biochemistry. New York, Academic Press (1965) p. 89.

BORST, P.: Hydrogen transport and transport metabolites. In: P.Karlson, ed.: Funktionelle und morphologische Organisation der Zelle. Berlin, Springer Verlag (1963) p. 137.

BRIERLEY, G.P. and C.T. SETTLEMIRE: Ion transport by heart mitochondria IX. Induction of the energy-linked uptake of K^+ by Zn^{2+}. J. Biol. Chem. 242 (1967) 4324.

CAMMER, W. and R.W. ESTABROOK: Respiratory activity of adrenal cortex mitochondria during steroid hydroxylation. Arch. Biochem. Biophys. 122 (1967) 721.

CHA, S., C.J.M.CHA and R.E.PARKS: Succinic thiokinase V. Preparation of labelled substrates, their bindings to the enzyme, and isotope exchange studies. J. Biol. Chem. 242 (1967) 2582.

CHANCE, B.: The energy-linked reaction of Ca^{2+} with mitochondria. J. Biol. Chem. 240 (1965) 2729.

CHANCE, B. and D.F.PARSONS: Cytochrome function in relation to inner membrane structure of mitochondria. Science 142 (1963) 1176.

CHANCE, B. and G.R.WILLIAMS: The respiratory chain and oxidative phosphorylation. Advan. Enzymol. 17 (1956) 65.

CHARLES, R., J.M.TAGER and E.C.SLATER: Citrulline synthesis in rat-liver mitochondria. Biochim. Biophys. Acta 131 (1967) 29.

DE DUVE, C., R.WATTIAUX and P.BAUDHUIN: Distribution of enzymes between subcellular fractions in animal tissues. Advan. Enzymol. 24 (1962) 291.

ESTABROOK, R.W. and A.HOLOWINSKY: Studies on the content and organization of the respiratory enzymes of mitochondria. J. Biophys. Biochem. Cytol. 9 (1961) 19.

FLEISCHER, S., G.ROUSER, B.FLEISCHER, A.CASU and G.KRITCHEVSKY: Lipid composition of mitochondria from bovine heart, liver and kidney. J. Lipid Res. 8 (1967) 170.

GARLAND, P.B., B.CHANCE, L.ERNSTER, C.-P.LEE and D.WONG: Flavoproteins of mitochondrial fatty acid oxidation. Proc. Natl. Acad. Sci. U.S. 58 (1967) 1696.

GRANICK, S.: The induction *in vitro* of the synthesis of δ-ALA synthetase in chemical porphyria: a response to certain drugs, sex hormones and foreign chemicals. J. Biol. Chem. 241 (1966) 1359.

GREEN, D.E. and S.FLEISCHER: The role of lipids in mitochondrial electron transfer and oxidative phosphorylation. Biochim. Biophys. Acta 70 (1963) 554.

GREEN, D.E. and J.F.PERDUE: Membranes as expressions of repeating units. Proc. Natl. Acad. Sci. U.S. 55 (1966) 1295.

GROOT, G.S.P. and S.G.VAN DEN BERGH: The role of the ADP-ATP exchange enzyme in oxidative phosphorylation. Biochim. Biophys. Acta 153 (1968) 22.

HAAN, E.J. DE and J.M.TAGER: Evidence for a permeability barrier for α-oxoglutarate in rat-liver mitochondria. Biochim. Biophys. Acta 153 (1968) 98.

HARRIS, E.J., G.CATLIN and B.C.PRESSMAN: Effect of transport-inducing antibiotics and other agents on K^+ flux in mitochondria. Biochemistry 6 (1967) 1360.

HARRIS, E.J. and K.VAN DAM: Changes of total H_2O and sucrose space accompanying induced ion uptake by or P_i swelling of rat-liver mitochondria. Biochem. J. 106 (1968) 759.

HARRIS, E.J., J.D.JUDAH and K.AHMED: Ion transport in mitochondria. In: D.R.Sanadi, ed.: Current topics in bioenergetics, Vol. 1. New York, Academic Press Inc. (1966) p. 255.

HELDT, H.W. and M.KLINGENBERG: Endogenous nucleotides of mitochondria participating in phosphate transfer reactions as studied with ^{32}P-labelled orthophosphate and ultramicro scale ion exchange chromatography. Biochem. Z. 343 (1965) 433.

HELDT, H.W. and K.SCHWALBACH: The participation of GTP-AMP-P transferase in substrate-level phosphate transfer of rat-liver mitochondria. European J. Biochem. 1 (1967) 199.

HILL, R.D. and P.D.BOYER: Inorganic orthophosphate activation and ADP as the primary phosphoryl acceptor in oxidative phosphorylation. J. Biol. Chem. 242 (1967) 4320.

KLINGENBERG, M. and TH.BÜCHER: Biological oxidations. Ann. Rev. Biochem. 29 (1960) 669.

KLINGENBERG, M.: Hydrogen transfer in mitochondria III. Energetic aspects of the NH_3 incorporation into amino acids. Biochem. Z. 343 (1965) 479.

KMETEC, E. and E.BUEDING: Succinic and DPNH oxidase systems of ascaris muscle. J. Biol. Chem. 236 (1961) 584.

KREBS, H.A. and J.M.LOWENSTEIN: The tricarboxylic acid cycle. In: D.M.Greenberg, ed.: Metabolic pathways, Vol. I. New York, Academic Press (1960) p. 129.

LAM, K.W., J.B.WARSHAW and D.R.SANADI: The mechanism of oxidative phosphorylation XIV. Purification and properties of a second energy-transfer factor. Arch. Biochem. Biophys. 119 (1967) 477.

LASCELLES, J.: Tetrapyrrole biosynthesis and its regulation. New York, Benjamin Inc. (1964).

LEHNINGER, A.L.: The mitochondrion. New York, Benjamin Inc. (1964).

LEHNINGER, A.L., E.CARAFOLI and C.S.ROSSI: Energy-linked ion movements in mitochondrial systems. Advan. Enzymol. 29 (1967) 259.

MATTOON, J.R. and F.SHERMAN: Reconstitution of phosphorylating electron transport in mitochondria from a cytochrome *c*-deficient yeast mutant. J. Biol. Chem. 241 (1966) 4330.

MEHLMAN, M.A., P.WALTER and H.A.LARDY: Paths of carbon in gluconeogenesis and lipogenesis VII. The synthesis of precursors for gluconeogenesis from pyruvate and bicarbonate by rat-kidney mitochondria. J. Biol. Chem. 242 (1967) 4594.

MEISTER, A.: Biochemistry of the amino acids, 2nd. Ed. New York, Academic Press Inc. (1965).

MITCHELL, P.: Chemiosmotic coupling in oxidative and photosynthetic phosphorylation. Biol. Rev. Cambridge Phil. Soc. 41 (1966) 445.

MITCHELL, P.: Translocation through natural membranes. Advan. Enzymol. 29 (1967) 33.

OHNISHI, T., A.KRÖGER, H.W.HELDT, E.PFAFF and M.KLINGENBERG: The response of the respiratory chain and adenine nucleotide system to oxidative phosphorylation in yeast mitochondria. European J. Biochem. 1 (1967) 301.

OKAMOTO, H., S.YAMAMOTO, M.NOZAKI and O.HAYAISHI: On the sub-mitochondrial localization of L-kynurenine-3-hydroxylase. Biochem. Biophys. Res. Commun. 26 (1967) 309.

PARSONS, D.F.: Ultrastructural and molecular aspects of cell membranes. Proc. 7th Canad. Cancer Res. Conf. Honey Harbour, Ontario (1966), Oxford etc., Pergamon (1967) p. 193.

PULLMAN, M.E. and G.SCHATZ: Mitochondrial oxidations and energy coupling. Ann. Rev. Biochem. 36 (1967) 539.

RACKER, E.: Mechanisms in bioenergetics. New York, Academic Press Inc. (1965).

RACKER, E. and L.L.HORSTMAN: Partial resolution of the enzymes catalyzing oxidative phosphorylation XIII. Structure and function of sub-mitochondrial particles completely resolved with respect to coupling factor 1. J. Biol. Chem. 242 (1967) 2547.

RASMUSSEN, H., H.SHIRASU, E.OGATA and C.HAWKER: Parathyroid hormone and mitochondrial metabolism. Specificity, sensitivity and physiological correlates. J. Biol. Chem. 242 (1967) 4669.

ROODYN, D.B.: The mitochondrion. In: D.B.Roodyn, ed.: Enzyme cytology. New York, Academic Press Inc. (1967) p. 103.

SALGANICOFF, L. and E.DE ROBERTIS: Subcellular distribution of the enzymes of the glutamic acid, glutamine and γ-aminobutyric acid cycles in rat brain. J. Neurochem. 12 (1965) 287.

SCHATZ, G., H.S.PENEFSKY and E.RACKER: Partial resolution of the enzymes catalyzing oxidative phosphorylation XIV. Interaction of purified mitochondrial ATPase from baker's yeast with submitochondrial particles from beef heart. J. Biol. Chem. 242 (1967) 2552.

SCHERPHOF, G.L. and L.L.M.VAN DEENEN: Phospholipase A activity of rat-liver mitochondria. Biochim. Biophys. Acta 98 (1965) 204.

SCHNAITMAN, C., V.G.ERWIN and J.W.GREENAWALT: The sub-mitochondrial localization of monoamine oxidase. J. Cell Biol. 32 (1967) 719.

SEKUZU, I., P.JURTSHUK, JR. and D.E.GREEN: Studies on the electron transfer system LI. Isolation and characterization of the D-(−)-β-hydroxybutyric apodehydrogenase from beef-heart mitochondria. J. Biol. Chem. 238 (1963) 975.

SLATER, E.C.: Oxidative phosphorylation. In: M.Florkin and E.H.Stotz, eds.: Comprehensive Biochemistry, Vol. 14. Amsterdam, Elsevier Publishing Comp. (1966) p. 327.

SLATER, E.C.: An evaluation of the Mitchell hypothesis of chemiosmotic coupling in oxidative and photosynthetic phosphorylation. European J. Biochem. 1 (1967) 317.

STEWART, P.R. and J.R.QUAYLE: The synergistic decarboxylation of glyoxylate and 2-oxoglutarate by an enzyme system from pig-liver mitochondria. Biochem. J. 102 (1967) 885.

STRECKER, H.J.: Purification and properties of rat-liver ornithine δ-transaminase. J. Biol. Chem. 240 (1965) 1225.

VALLEJOS, R.H., S.G.VAN DEN BERGH and E.C.SLATER: On coupling factors of oxidative phosphorylation. Biochim. Biophys. Acta 153 (1968) 509.

VAN DAM, K. and E.C.SLATER: A suggested mechanism of uncoupling of respiratory-chain phosphorylation. Proc. Natl. Acad. Sci. U.S. 58 (1967) 2015.

VAN KEMPEN, G.M.J., C.J.VAN DEN BERG, H.J.VAN DER HELM and H.VELDSTRA: Intracellular localization of glutamate decarboxylase, γ-aminobutyrate transaminase and some other enzymes in brain tissue. J. Neurochem. 12 (1965) 581.

WENNER, C.E.: Progress in tumour enzymology. Advan. Enzymol. 29 (1967) 321.

WHEREAT, A.F., F.E.HULL, M.W.ORISHIMO and J.L.RABINOWITZ: The role of succinate in the regulation of fatty acid synthesis by heart mitochondria. J. Biol. Chem. 242 (1967) 4013.

WLODAWER, P., D.F.PARSONS, G.R.WILLIAMS and L.WOJTCZAK: Morphological changes in isolated rat-liver mitochondria during swelling and contraction. Biochim. Biophys. Acta 128 (1966) 34.

WOJTCZAK, L. and J.ZBOROWSKI: Synthesis of phospholipids in isolated liver mitochondria. Proc. 4th Meeting Fed. European Biochem. Socs., Oslo (1967) Abstr. no. 361, p. 91.

WOODWARD, D.O. and K.D.MUNKRES: Alterations of maternally inherited mitochondrial structural protein in respiratory-deficient strains of *Neurospora*. Proc. Natl. Acad. Sci. U.S. 55 (1966) 872.

CHAPTER 36

DNA and RNA from mitochondria and chloroplasts (biochemistry)

A. M. KROON*

Department of Medical Enzymology, Laboratory of Biochemistry, University of Amsterdam, Amsterdam, The Netherlands

Contents

1. Introduction
2. Properties of DNA from mitochondria and chloroplasts
3. DNA from mitochondria of animal tissues
4. Properties of RNA and ribosomes from mitochondria and chloroplasts
5. Replication, transcription and translation activities of isolated mitochondria and chloroplasts
6. The information content and genetic function of mitochondrial DNA
7. Information content and genetic function of chloroplast DNA
8. The evolutionary origin of mitochondria and chloroplasts
9. The biogenesis of mitochondria and chloroplasts

* Present address: Laboratory of Physiological Chemistry, State University, Groningen, the Netherlands.

1. Introduction

The evolutionary origin and biogenesis of mitochondria and chloroplasts has fascinated a growing number of scientists since the beginning of the 20th century. Although for a long time this interest could be satisfied mainly by poorly documented evidence, the rapid development of molecular biology has put today's electron microscopists, geneticists and biochemists in a position that enables them to approach the problems of the biogenesis of mitochondria and chloroplasts more systematically and on a sounder experimental basis.

Much is now known about the properties of the nucleic acids from mitochondria and chloroplasts and about their functional activity in replication, transcription and translation. During the last few years many different experiments have been designed to unravel the genetics of organelle DNA. In spite of this, many links in the chain of our knowledge are still missing. It is the aim of this chapter to give a critical survey of the recent developments in the field of mitochondrion and chloroplast biosynthesis. Many aspects of the biogenesis of mitochondria have recently been discussed in the proceedings of a symposium on this subject (reference I) and in reviews by Borst et al. (1967a), Roodyn and Wilkie, and Borst and Kroon. For more detailed information about the biosynthetic aspects of chloroplasts one may consult the reviews by Iwamura, Granick and Gibor, and Borst et al. (1967a).

2. Properties of DNA from mitochondria and chloroplasts

The presence of DNA within mitochondria and chloroplasts has been a matter of discussion for a long time. The first clear evidence that DNA is an intrinsic component of these organelles came from morphological, cytochemical and autoradiographic studies (reviewed by Swift et al., in I, and Borst et al. 1967a). Biochemically it has been shown subsequently that the DNA associated with mitochondria and chloroplasts of a great variety of organisms differed from their corresponding nuclear DNAs by one or more of the following criteria:

(a) base composition as calculated from the buoyant density in equilibrium density gradients, from T_m determinations or in a limited number of cases from direct base analysis;

(b) homogeneity as measured either by the degree of renaturability or the width and unimodality of bands formed in equilibrium density gradients;

(c) structural conformation as based on sedimentation analysis or on direct examination with the electron microscope.

Table 1 gives a comprehensive summary of the available literature. An extensive and detailed survey with references to the original experimental work has recently been given by Borst and Kroon. It can be seen that there is a high variability in base composition between mitochondrial DNAs from different origins, the range for closely related organisms being relatively small. The same holds for the base composition of chloroplast DNAs. The base compositions were calculated from the equilibrium densities, using the relation $\rho = 0.098\,(\%\text{GC}) + 1.660\ \text{g/cm}^3$ (Schildkraut et al.) and assuming that no odd bases were present in substantial amounts. In cases where the base composition was determined by an independent method, e.g. by direct analysis or from melting curves, no evidence for the presence of unusual bases was obtained. For *Euglena gracilis* it has been shown that the chloroplast DNA does not contain any methylcytosine. This base is present to the extent of 2.3 mole % in total *Euglena* DNA (Brawerman and Eisenstadt).

An exception to the homogeneity of mitochondrial DNA is that found by Reich and Luck, who showed that the mitochondria of *Neurospora crassa* and *Neurospora sitophila* contain 2, respectively 3 DNA components, distinguishable by their equilibrium density. The cause and biological significance of this phenomenon are unknown.

Another difficulty is encountered in the equilibrium densities reported for mitochondrial DNA from human leucocytes of patients with leukaemia (1.705 g/cm^3, corresponding to a % GC of 46; Clayton and Vinograd) and from cultured human Chang liver-cells (1.688 g/cm^3, corresponding to a % GC of 29; Koch and Stokstad). Since for both DNAs some of the other criteria for their mitochondrial origin (see below) are met, it is very difficult to rate these experiments at their true value as yet and it seems wise not to draw any conclusion about the base composition of human mitochondrial DNA before data obtained with normal human tissues become available.

In general one may conclude that a difference in base composition between organelle DNA and nuclear DNA is not the law of Medes and Persians. In some organisms, e.g. yeasts of the genus *Saccharomyces* a clear difference exists; in others, e.g. mammals no or only small differences can be measured. If existing, a major difference in base composition (i.e. equilibrium density) provides a very nice criterion for measuring cross contamination of organelle DNA preparations with nuclear DNA. As indicated in Table 1, in the higher plants analyzed up till now there is a significant difference in base composition between mitochondrial DNA and nuclear DNA on the one hand and between mitochondrial DNA and chloroplast DNA on the other. However, there is no general agreement about which DNA in chloroplast preparations has to be considered as true chloroplast DNA and which as nuclear, c.q. mitochondrial contamination (Chun et al.; Shipp et al.; Tewari and Wildman 1966; Wells and Birnstiel; Whitfeld and Spencer).

Attempts have been made to estimate the molecular weight of organelle DNA by:
(a) length measurements on electron micrographs of DNA molecules from isolated mitochondria and chloroplasts, spread according to different modifications of the Kleinschmidt technique (Borst et al. 1967b; Woodcock and Fernández-Morán);
(b) sedimentation analysis of these DNAs on sucrose gradients or by analytical band and boundary centrifugation.

Table 1 shows the extreme variability in length of all organelle DNAs studied except

TABLE 1
Some physicochemical characteristics of DNA from mitochondria and chloroplasts.

	Source of organelle DNA: Mitochondria from a
Base composition (%GC) [a]	Mammals: 42–44 (2 Birds: 48–52 Amphibia: 44 Fish: 44 Echinoderms: 44
Difference in base composition between organelle DNA and corresponding nuclear DNA	in some cases
Difference in base composition between mitochondrial DNA and corresponding chloroplast DNA	—
Length of DNA molecules as measured from electron micrographs (μ)	4.5–5.6
Conformation of DNA molecules as based on electron microscopical evidence	circular
Minimal molecular weight calculated from electron microscopical length measurements [i]	$\pm 10 \times 10^6$
Maximal molecular weight calculated from electron microscopical length measurements [i]	$\pm 10 \times 10^6$
Molecular weight based on sedimentation analysis	$\pm 10 \times 10^6$
Conformation of DNA molecules as based on sedimentation analysis	circular
Maximal molecular weight based on quantitative renaturation experiments	$\pm 10 \times 10^6$
g organelle DNA/organelle	$0.5–2 \times 10^{-16}$

a: The data on base composition in this table summarize the available literature to date. The base comp calculated from the equilibrium densities and T_ms and in a limited number of cases from direct base The experimental details and all references to the original literature are given by Borst and Kroon; b: T between brackets represent the range in base composition of mammalian mitochondrial DNA if data on cell lines and human leucemic cells are included; c: The experimental data summarized concern t *Saccharomyces* only; d: Data summarized by Sinclair; e: Swift, in I; f: Van Bruggen, Borst and Talen lished observations. For discussion see Borst and Kroon; g: Woodcock and Fernández-Morán; h: and Miura; i: 1 μ equals 1.96×10^6 daltons (Thomas); j: Ray and Hanawalt; k: Suyama (1966); l: V Birnstiel; m: Borst et al. (1967a); n: Granick and Gibor; o: Schatz et al.

ıondria from higher plants	Mitochondria from unicellular organisms	Chloroplasts
57	*Euglena*: 32 Yeast [c]: 23–24 *Neurospora*: see text *Paramecium*: 47 *Tetrahymena*: 23–26	Higher plants: 36–47 Unicellular organisms: 26–36 [d]
	in most cases	in some cases
	yes	—
ɔ 7 [e] [f]	Yeast [c]: 5–20 *Neurospora*: 7 *Tetrahymena*: 17.6 [h]	Spinach: 5–20 [g]
ır	Yeast [c]: linear *Neurospora*: linear *Tetrahymena*: linear	linear
4 $\times 10^6$	$\pm$ 10 $\times 10^6$	$\pm$ 10 $\times 10^6$
0 $\times 10^6$	$\pm$ 40 $\times 10^6$	$\pm$ 40 $\times 10^6$
xperimental data available	*Euglena*: 3–4 $\times 10^6$ [j] *Tetrahymena*: $\pm$ 40 $\times 10^6$ [k]	*Euglena*: 20–40 $\times 10^6$ [j]
xperimental data available	*Euglena*: no indication for circularity Yeast [c]: idem *Tetrahymena*: idem [k]	no experimental data available
xperimental data available	no experimental data available	higher plants: $\pm$ 80 $\times 10^6$ [l]
gbean: 10^{-16}	Yeast [c]: 1–3 $\times 10^{-16}$ *Tetrahymena*: 3.7 $\times 10^{-16}$ [o]	1–100 $\times 10^{-16}$ [m,n]

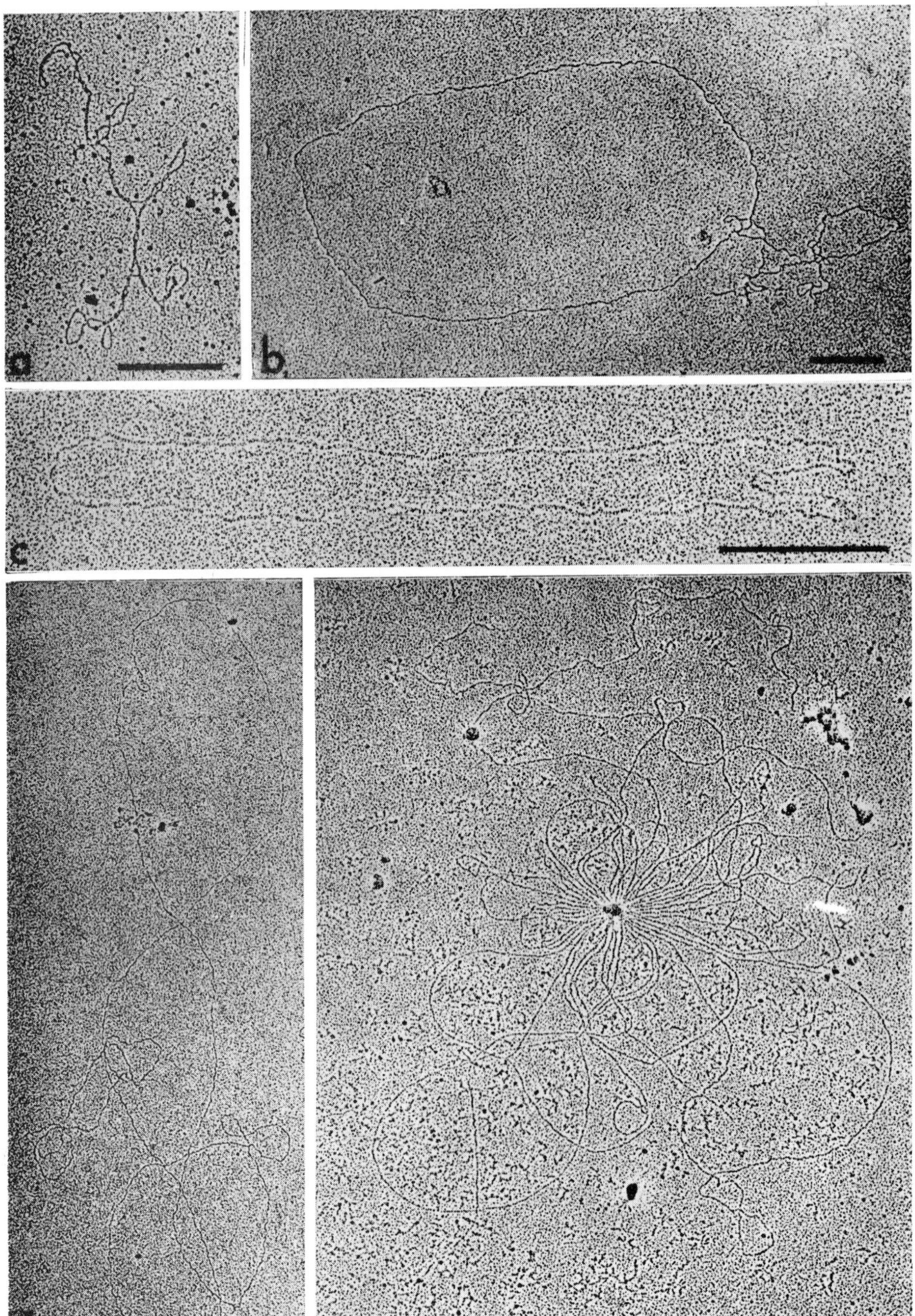

for those from animal tissues. Especially for mitochondria and chloroplasts from higher plants, however, the experimental data are limited. By electron microscopy Van Bruggen et al. and independently Sinclair and Stevens were the first who showed that the mitochondrial DNA of chick liver, mouse liver and ox heart consists of a homogeneous population of circular molecules. In the meantime this observation has been confirmed for many other animals (Van Bruggen et al.). The circumference of all animal mitochondrial DNAs studied so far is about 5 μ, thus putting the lower and upper limit of the molecular weight of this DNA at about 10.10^6 daltons. With DNA from mitochondria of higher plants and unicellular organisms and from chloroplasts the situation is less clear, since only linear fragments have been observed in these cases. We favour the idea that the smaller fragments present in these organelle DNA preparations are derived from the larger ones, but there is no indication as yet that these larger molecules really do represent the intact organelle DNA molecules. They may well be themselves fragments of still larger, possibly circular molecules. Electron microscopical examination of the DNA molecules released from yeast mitochondria (Swift, Sinclair, Stevens, Rabinowitz and Gross, in I; Borst, in I; Slonimski, in I; Van Bruggen et al.) and spinach chloroplasts (Woodcock and Fernández-Morán) after osmotic shock has revealed discontinuous, flowerlike structures with total lengths of about 50 μ for yeast mitochondria (Fig. 1e) and complex meshworks of measurable total lengths up to 150 μ for fully dispersed chloroplasts. It remains to be established, however, whether these larger structures are chemically continuous under conditions that exclude any enzymatic or shear degradation.

Two reports have appeared claiming that yeast mitochondrial DNA consists of circular molecules. In the report of Avers it is suggested that the majority of mitochondrial DNA molecules from *Saccharomyces cerevisiae* are circles with a contour length ranging from 0.5 to 10 μ (mean 3–4 μ). According to Shapiro et al. a minority of the mitochondrial DNA molecules from the same yeast is present as circles with a contour length of 4.5 μ. Because it is difficult to visualize how linear molecules up to 20 μ can arise from 4 μ circles and because of the possibility that the circles seen by these authors are of nuclear origin (cf. Sinclair et al.), the problem of the characterization of yeast mitochondrial DNA remains unsolved.

With the exception of the mitochondrial DNA from animal tissues, there is only scanty information available about the molecular weight of organelle DNA from sedimentation analysis. There are a few and inconclusive data for mitochondria and

---

Fig. 1. Electron micrographs of mitochondrial DNA from chick liver and yeast. 1a: chick-liver mitochondrial DNA, component I, a hypertwisted circular molecule (released by osmotic shock); 1b: chick-liver mitochondrial DNA, a catenated dimer, an open circular molecule, interlocked with a hypertwisted molecule (isolated with the dye-buoyant density method); 1c: chick-liver mitochondrial DNA, component II, an open circular molecule (isolated according to standard procedures); 1d: chick-liver mitochondrial DNA, a tetramer (isolated with the dye-buoyant density method); 1e: yeast mitochondrial DNA (released by osmotic shock). All bars are 0.40 μ.

chloroplasts of *Euglena* (Ray and Hanawalt) and for mitochondria from *Tetrahymena pyriformis* (Suyama 1966).

A further criterion to distinguish between organelle DNA and nuclear DNA is found in the renaturability of organelle DNA after denaturation by heat or alkali, a property due to the homogeneity of the molecules in organelle DNA preparations. It has indeed been shown by qualitative renaturation methods that mitochondrial DNA from animal tissues renatures completely under conditions in which the bulk of nuclear DNA does not renature at all. This renaturation follows second-order kinetics, thus showing that the two strands separate during denaturation (for review, see Borst and Kroon).

An important tool in the search for the maximal molecular weight of the DNA from cell organelles, is the fact that the complexity of DNA (i.e. the number of basepairs in the total genome, redundant sequences excluded) and the second-order constant of renaturation are linearly related, as shown by Britten and Waring; Britten and Kohne, and Wetmur and Davidson. Quantitative renaturation of organelle DNA may, therefore, give the final answer to the problem of the extent of autonomy of mitochondria and chloroplasts from different sources, since the rate of renaturation puts the unequivocal limit of maximal genetic information comprised in a cell organelle. Borst et al. (1967c) have shown that the renaturation rate of chick-liver mitochondrial DNA reveals a complexity of about 12.10^3 basepairs or 8.10^6 daltons. This value lies close to that of the molecular weight calculated from the contour length and the sedimentation behaviour. Similarly, Wells and Birnstiel have obtained a renaturation rate equivalent to 80.10^6 daltons for chloroplast DNA from higher plants. If we assume that these 80.10^6 daltons are present in only one DNA molecule, the length of this molecule should be about 40 μ, being the minimal size recorded by Woodcock and Fernández-Morán for DNA associated with one osmotically shocked chloroplast.

The renaturation rate and not the DNA content is the most reliable measure for the total genetic potential of mitochondria and chloroplasts and any theory about the degree of autonomy of cell organelles or about the contribution of DNA from mitochondria and chloroplasts to their own biosynthesis should be based on the limitations of this potential. For this reason there is an obvious need for more detailed renaturation studies, specially with those organelle DNAs for which no estimates of their molecular weights are available.

3. *DNA from mitochondria of animal tissues*

As has been discussed in paragraph 2 mitochondrial DNA from animal tissues has a circular conformation and a total length of 5 μ. The immediate cause to investigate mitochondrial DNA by electron microscopy was the observation by Borst and Ruttenberg that DNA from purified chick-liver mitochondria showed up as two distinct components with sedimentation constants ($s_{20,w}$) of 39S and 27S, if analyzed by sedimentation velocity centrifugation. By electron microscopy the 39S DNA (component I) was shown to contain mainly highly twisted circular molecules, whereas the 27S DNA (component II) consisted of mainly open circular molecules. Fig. 1a shows an example of an electron micrograph of a highly twisted circle in the typical 'dachshund' configuration, Fig. 1c an open circular molecule. It is now well established that the mitochondrial DNA in tissues of a great variety of animals is present in the form of this closed circular duplex molecule that appears as the hypertwisted molecule after extraction from the mitochondria. The contour length as well as the sedimentation constants are compatible with a molecular weight of about 10.10^6 daltons.

In the last few years it has been shown that mitochondrial DNA from animal tissues shares most of the physicochemical characteristics of the viral closed circular duplex DNAs (see Vinograd and Lebowitz). Fig. 2 gives a schematic representation of the different forms to which mitochondrial DNA can be converted. Component I, 39S, is the native DNA that is characterized by the presence of superhelical twists. These superhelical twists are right-handed and from electron micrographs a ballpark estimate of the number of twists, about 35, has been made (Van Bruggen et al.; Borst et al., in I). Component I can be converted to the open circle (= component II, 27S) by one or more single-strand breaks. The single-strand breaks can be introduced either by shear or by treatment with pancreatic deoxyribonuclease. Due to such a break the two strands can freely rotate around each other. This leads to the release of the superhelical twists, a lowering of the rigidity of the molecule and therewith to a decrease of the sedimentation constant to 27S. Similarly a double-strand break converts component I to a linear molecule of the same molecular weight, but with a sedimentation constant of 24S.

Since denaturation of DNA leads to an increase of the number of base pairs per turn

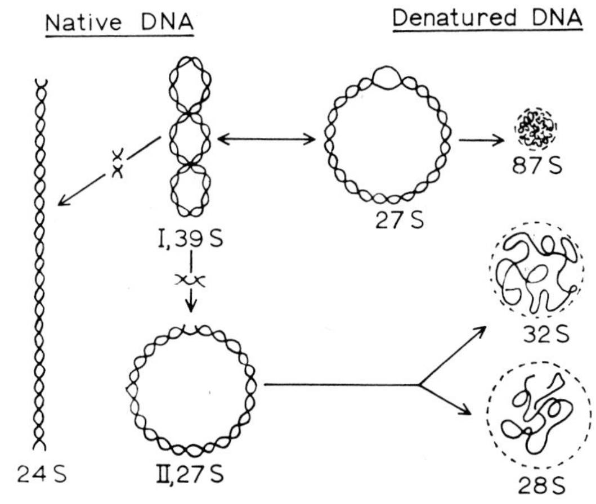

Fig. 2. Diagrammatic representation of the various forms of DNA from animal mitochondria (from Borst and Kroon).

of the Watson-Crick helix, one may expect that on gradual denaturation the right-handed superhelical twists will disappear first and that on further unwinding of the double helix left-handed twists will be introduced. At the stage of denaturation that all right-handed twists have disappeared and yet no left-handed twists have been introduced, the molecule will have an open circular configuration and a lower sedimentation constant, comparable with component II. The final denaturation product of component I is composed of the two interlocked, single-stranded circles which are highly convoluted by the left-handed twists and which accordingly have a very high sedimentation constant. Denaturation of component II gives rise to the appearance of circular and linear single-stranded molecules. All the components mentioned above have been tentatively characterized by either heat denaturation in the presence of formaldehyde or by denaturation with alkali. Furthermore, it has been shown that the T_m as well as the pH_m are higher for component I than for component II, as is the case for other closed circular duplex DNAS.

An interesting feature is the difference between components I and II in their capacity for binding intercalating dyes as ethidium bromide. Intercalation between the base-pairs of double-stranded DNA causes unwinding of the Watson and Crick helix. As has been shown by Radloff et al., Crawford and Waring, and Bauer and Vinograd, the degree of unwinding is a function of the dye concentration. In component I a gradual increase of ethidium bromide concentration will – just as in the case of denaturation – bring about the disappearance of the right-handed superhelical twists and the formation of left-handed twists. The sedimentation constant will also in this case be lowest at the stage that no superhelical twists are present in the molecule. Since it is known (Crawford and Waring) that intercalation of 1 molecule of ethidium bromide unwinds the helix by 12°, it is possible to calculate the number of superhelical twists of component I from the ethidium bromide concentration necessary for complete unwinding, i.e. for reaching the minimal sedimentation constant. Using this technique Ruttenberg et al. arrived at a value of 40 right-handed twists per molecule for chick-liver mitochondrial DNA. In view of the limitations of the techniques this value and the value of 35 obtained by electron microscopy are not considered to be significantly different. The number of superhelical twists per unit length found for other closed circular duplex DNAS are of the same order (Crawford and Waring; Van Bruggen et al.). It is, furthermore, known that the pitch of the DNA double helix may vary with changes in temperature or ionic environment. For these reasons many people favour the idea that the twists in component I found *in vitro* do not exist as such *in vivo*. They may arise as the consequence of a difference in helix configuration between isolated DNA and the DNA within the intact cell.

Because the two strands of closed circular duplex DNAS lack the possibility to rotate freely around each other, their capacity to intercalate ethidium bromide is limited as compared to open circular and linear molecules (Radloff et al.; Bauer and Vinograd). The specific gravity of closed circular duplex DNAS is much higher than of open circular and linear DNAS at saturating concentrations of ethidium bromide. A method to separate closed circular duplex DNA from open circular and linear DNA based on this property was introduced by Radloff et al. as the dye-buoyant density method. This method may be an attractive tool in the search for circular molecules in mitochondria from other than animal sources and in chloroplasts.

Radloff et al., and Hudson and Vinograd, using the dye-buoyant density method, have observed that HeLa cells contain closed circular duplex molecules of 2–4 times the length of the mitochondrial DNA. In a subsequent study with leucocytes of patients with leukemia these multimers were found in a high percentage and it was shown that they are indeed mitochondrial in origin (Clayton and Vinograd). Besides the circular multimers with a contour length of a multiple of 5 μ, also catenated multimers were observed, consisting of one or more independent circular duplex molecules, interlocked as links in a chain. It has been shown by Borst and Van Bruggen (unpublished) that catenated multimers are also present (although infrequent: about 1 %) in mitochondrial DNA from chick- and rat liver. Circular multimers are even less frequent. Fig. 1b shows 2 interlocked monomers, one as component I, the other as component II; Fig. 1d is an example of a tetramer. Apparently the appearance of these multimeric forms is not exclusively bound to malignancy. However, as yet neither the origin of the multimers nor the significance of their high frequency in malignant cells is understood. They may arise from symmetric crossing-over during recombination (Hudson and Vinograd). If this suggestion is correct, the presence of multimers is the only indication to date that recombination occurs in animal mitochondrial DNA.

For a further discussion on different aspects of mitochondrial DNA from animal tissues and for an extensive list of references to the literature, see Borst and Kroon.

4. *Properties of RNA and ribosomes from mitochondria and chloroplasts*

The presence of ribosomes in mitochondria and chloroplasts has been shown by morphological means (André and Marinozzi; Swift, Rabinowitz and Getz, in I; Bogorad). The size of these ribosomes as reported by different authors varies from 100–150 Å. This variation may be due, however, to limitations of the fixation techniques (Swift, in discussion after Swift, Rabinowitz and Getz, in I) and for this reason it seems impossible to draw any conclusion about the expected sedimentation characteristics of organelle ribosomes by morphological comparison with either bacterial or cytoplasmic ribosomes. (Throughout this chapter the designation cytoplasmic is used for the ribosomes bound to the endoplasmic reticulum or freely present in the cytosol.)

In Table 2 we have summarized the sedimentation characteristics of the ribosomes from mitochondria and chloroplasts and of the RNA components of these ribosomes. Only the results of those investigations in which the organelle RNAs and ribosomes were compared to similar components with well-established characteristics, have been

TABLE 2

Sedimentation characteristics of RNA and ribosomes from mitochondria and chloroplasts.

Component	Sedimentation coefficient		
	Animals	Higher plants	Unicellular organisms
Mitochondrial ribosomes	(55S) [a]	no experimental data available	*Neurospora*: 73S [j]
Chloroplast ribosomes	—	70S [c,f-h]	*Euglena*: 60S [k]
Cytoplasmic ribosomes *sensu stricto*	80S [b,c]	80S [f-h]	*Neurospora*: 77S [j] Yeast: 80S [b,l,m] *Euglena*: 70S [k]
RNA from mitochondrial ribosomes	23S; 16S [d]	no experimental data available	*Neurospora*: 23.0S; 16.2S [j,n] Yeast: 22.4S; 17.8S; 12.7S [l,m] *Tetrahymena*: 18S; 14S [o]
RNA from chloroplast ribosomes	—	23S; 16S [c,g,i]	*Euglena*: 19S; 14S [k]
RNA from cytoplasmic ribosomes *sensu stricto*	29S; 18S [b-e]	25S; 16S (18S) [b,c,e,g]	*Neurospora*: 25S; 17S [j,n] Yeast: 24.6S; 16.2S [l,m] *Euglena*: 19S [k]

a: O'Brien and Kalf; b: Peterman; c: Stutz and Noll; d: Kroon and Aaij, in I; e: Click and Tint; f: Iwamura; g: Loening and Ingle; h: Svetailo et al.; i: Spencer and Whitfeld (1966); j: Küntzel and Noll; k: Brawerman and Eisenstadt; l: Rogers et al.; m: Linnane, in I; n: Dure et al.; o: Suyama (1967).

taken into consideration. This comparison is of paramount importance because it is impossible to obtain organelle preparations completely free of contamination with other cell constituents. Especially in the case of animal tissues the problem of contamination is a serious one, because in most animal cells the mitochondrial RNA content is low and the endoplasmic reticulum highly developed. We have recently related the RNA content of mitochondrial preparations from rat liver to the glucose-6-phosphatase activity as measure for microsomal contamination. Assuming a linear relationship between the amount of ribosomes present on these contaminating microsomes and their glucose-6-phosphatase activity, we have calculated that the content of true mitochondrial RNA is about 1 μg per mg of protein in preparations of normal liver and about 3 μg per mg protein in preparations from regenerating liver (Kroon, De Vries and Smit). If our assumption is correct, this would mean that the RNA content of rat-liver mitochondria has been overestimated by a factor of 10 (Kroon 1966; Roodyn and Wilkie). Therefore, biochemical characterization of the organelle preparations used seems a compelling requirement. The RNA content of mitochondria from lower organisms and of chloroplasts is in the order of 50 μg/mg protein and thus considerably higher than that of animal mitochondria.

O'Brien and Kalf have concluded that mitochondrial ribosomes from rat liver have a sedimentation constant of 55S. However, the RNA/protein ratio of these ribosomes was very low, they were neither shown to be built up of ribosomal subunits nor to contain high-molecular-weight RNA and finally they were not tested for protein synthetic activity in a reconstituted system. Specially this last criterion seems vital in our opinion. Since mitochondrial protein synthesis is sensitive to a number of antibiotics to which cytoplasmic ribosomes are resistant (see paragraph 5) only those particles should be designated mitochondrial ribosomes that have typical ribosomal characteristics on the one hand and that are active in protein synthesis sensitive to these antibiotics on the other hand. Of course these stipulations can be taken with a pinch of salt in cases that unique physico-chemical properties of these ribosomes are proven unequivocally, e.g. as in *Neurospora* (see Table 2).

According to the criteria put above, there is no doubt that chloroplasts contain ribosomes distinguishable from the cytoplasmic ribosomes. Also polysomal structures have been isolated (Boardman et al; Stutz and Noll). Only the characteristics reported by Brawerman and Eisenstadt for *Euglena* chloroplast ribosomes do not fit into the general picture. Since the sedimentation constants have been obtained in a comparative study with ribosomes and ribosomal subunits from *Escherichia coli*, there is no obvious reason why these values should be incorrect. However, some reserve seems advisable, because the data reported for the ribosomal RNAs of *Euglena* are difficult to interpret (see Loening and Ingle; Stutz and Noll).

For mitochondria there is much less evidence for the presence of unique ribosomes. Only in the the case of *Neurospora* both ribosomes and ribosomal RNAs have been characterized. Also polysomes have been identified (Küntzel and Noll). For yeast and rat liver only data for ribosomal RNAs are available. There is some disagreement in the literature as to whether ribosomal RNAs from animal mitochondria are characterized by sedimentation values of 23S and 16S (Kroon and Aaij, in I) or of 27S and 17S (Dubin and Brown). The cytoplasmic origin of the 27S and 17S RNA components is insufficiently excluded, in our opinion, especially for the 27S RNA. Dubin and Brown have also measured the degree of methylation of these 27S and 17S RNAs. From the degree of methylation they concluded that the 27S RNA was of the mammalian type and only the 17S RNA of the bacterial type. However, also the characterization of 23S and 16S RNAs isolated by Kroon and Aaij awaits further verification.

Some of the organelle ribosomal RNAs have been shown to differ significantly from their cytoplasmic counterparts in base composition (Brawerman and Eisenstadt; Küntzel and Noll).

At the present experimental stage it seems justified to conclude that mitochondria and chloroplasts contain ribosomes which are smaller than the corresponding cytoplasmic ribosomes and similar to bacterial ribosomes. However, the evidence supporting this conclusion for mitochondria is still scanty. The expectation that also mitochondrial ribosomes and ribosomal RNAs will be characterized in a wide variety of organisms in spite of problems of low content and high contamination seems warranted the more so as high resolution of RNAs with different molecular weights can be achieved by polyacrylamide gel electrophoresis (Loening and Ingle; Bishop et al.) and by constant velocity centrifugation (Noll).

TABLE 3

Factors involved in replication, transcription and translation; their presence within mitochondria and chloroplasts.

Factors	Type of evidence for localization within organelle	Differences from corresponding factors outside the organelle[a]	
		Mito-chondria	Chloro-plasts
DNA	Electron microscopy: presence of DNase sensitive fibrils within organelles	+ [b]	+ [c]
	Autoradiography after thymidine incorporation	— [b]	— [c]
	Concentration of DNA with unique properties in isolated organelles	+ [d]	+ [d]
	Concentration of DNA with unique properties in anucleate fragments	+ [e]	+ [e]
DNA polymerase	Incorporation of deoxyribonucleotides into DNA by isolated organelles	— [f-h]	— [i,j]
	Identification of product of *in vitro* incorporation as organelle DNA	+ [f,h]	+ [i,j]
Polynucleotide ligase	Incorporation of deoxyribonucleotides into closed circular duplex molecules of mitochondrial DNA by isolated chick-liver mitochondria	○ [f]	○
RNA polymerase	Incorporation of ribonucleotides into RNA by isolated organelles	— [k]	— [l,m]
Messenger RNA	Deduced from the incorporation of aminoacids into protein and from ribonucleotides into RNA	○ [k,n,o]	○ [l,m]
Ribosomes	Presented in paragraph 4 of this paper	+ [p]	+ [p]
Transfer factors	Puromycin-sensitive incorporation of aminoacids into protein by intact organelles	○ [q]	○ [l]
Transfer RNA	Isolation of tRNA with special coding properties from mitochondrial extracts	+ [r-u]	○
	Deduced from aminoacid dependent exchange reactions in organelle extracts, independence of aminoacid incorporation by intact, isolated organelles of added transfer RNA, etc.	— [n,o,u]	— [v,w]
Aminoacyl-transfer RNA synthetases	Purification of aminoacyl-tRNA synthetases from mitochondrial extracts	+ [t,u,x]	○
	Deduced from aminoacid dependent exchange reactions in organelle extracts, independence of aminoacid incorporation by intact, isolated organelles of added aminoacyl-tRNA synthetase, etc.	— [n,o]	— [l,w]
Energy generation	Complete dependence of all incorporation activities in isolated organelles on either oxidative phosphorylation or photophosphorylation or exogenous ATP-generating systems	○ [n,v]	○ [l,w]

a: + = difference, — = no difference, ○ = either not relevant or no experimental data available; b: Swift, Rabinowitz and Getz, in I; c: Granick and Gibor; d: paragraphs 2 and 3 of this paper; e: Green et al.; f: Ter Schegget and Borst, unpublished experiments; g: Neubert, Oberdisse and Bass, in I; h: Parsons and Simpson, in I; Wintersberger, in I; i: Spencer and Whitfeld 1967a; j: Tewari and Wildman 1967; k: Neubert, Helge and Merker, in I; Saccone et al., in I; l: Iwamura; m: Spencer and Whitfeld (1967b); n: Roodyn and Wilkie, o: Kroon (1966); p: paragraph 4 of this paper; q: Borst et al. (1967a); r: Epler and Barnett; s: Barnett and Brown; t: Suyama and Eyer (1967); u: Fournier and Simpson, in I; v: Kroon, in discussion after Neupert et al., in I; w: Ramirez et al.; x: Barnett et al.

5. Replication, transcription and translation activities of isolated mitochondria and chloroplasts

Isolated mitochondria and chloroplasts contain all factors necessary for the incorporation of nucleotides into DNA and RNA and for the incorporation of aminoacids into protein. The evidence for the localization of these factors within mitochondria and chloroplasts is summarized in Table 3. A few additional remarks should be made.

The replication of DNA in chloroplasts of *Chlamydomonas* (Chang and Sueoka) follows a semi-conservative mechanism. This has been inferred from experiments with synchronized cells in which the [^{15}N]-density labeling technique was used. After one replication cycle of the chloroplast DNA all of this DNA was present in the expected [^{15}N]:[^{14}N] hybrid form. Reich and Luck have arrived at a similar conclusion for mitochondria of *Neurospora*. However, in the latter case the experimental data are less clearcut because incorporation of [^{15}N] nucleotides into mitochondrial DNA continued after the shift to [^{14}N] medium.

On the basis of the inhibition of aminoacid incorporation in isolated mitochondria by actinomycin D it has been proposed that the translation process of these isolated organelles is continuously dependent on transcription (Kroon 1963). The same argument holds for chloroplasts (Iwamura). The strong inhibition of mitochondrial protein synthesis (Kroon, Botman and Saccone, in I) and mitochondrial RNA synthesis (Saccone et al., in I) by low concentrations of acriflavin is in agreement with this hypothesis. As a consequence one would expect active messenger-RNA synthesis within mitochondria. However, there are as yet very few direct indications that messenger-RNA is indeed formed. With the exception of the report on spinach chloroplasts of Spencer and Whitfeld (1967b) no RNA-labeling patterns suggestive for the synthesis of messenger-RNA have been obtained, nor has any organelle RNA fraction been shown convincingly to stimulate aminoacid incorporation in a reconstituted protein synthesizing system.

During the last years a number of papers have appeared in which serious doubt is cast on the physiological significance of the incorporation activities in isolated organelles. Bacterial contamination was suggested to be responsible for all synthetic activities measured. It may be stressed, however, that the incorporation activities in germ-free mitochondrial preparations from rat liver (Kroon, Botman and Saccone, in I) and yeast (Grivell) are the same as in standard preparations.

In Table 4 the inhibitors of protein synthesis in isolated organelles are listed. The effects of actinomycin D and acriflavin have already been discussed. The fungicide cycloheximide, an inhibitor of protein synthesis on cytoplasmic = 80S ribosomes, has no effect on protein synthesis in mitochondria. On the other hand a great number of antibiotics which are known to interfere with protein synthesis in bacterial = 70S ribosomes have been shown to be potent inhibitors of organelle protein synthesis. Specially in the case of yeast (Linnane, in I) the effects of these antibiotics are studied intensively. For chloroplasts and chloroplast ribosomes in a reconstituted system the

TABLE 4
Inhibitors of organelle protein synthesis.

Inhibitor	Rat-liver mitochondria	Yeast mitochondria	Intact chloroplasts	Chloroplast ribosomes
Actinomycin D	±	+	+	−
Acriflavin (2 μg/ml)	++	+	○	○
Cycloheximide	−	−	○	○
Puromycin	++	++	++	++
Chloramphenicol	++	++	++	++
Oxytetracycline	++	++	○	○
Streptomycin	+	+	+	○
Erythromycin	±	++	○	○
Lincomycin	−	++	○	○
Oleandomycin	−	++	○	○
Spiramycin	○	++	○	○
Carbomycin	○	++	○	○

+ = partial inhibition; ++ = strong inhibition; ± no inhibition in intact mitochondria, inhibition after altering the permeability; − = no inhibition; ○ = no experimental data available. Literature: Kroon (1963); Iwamura; Borst et al. (1967a); Gnanam and Kahn; Roodyn and Wilkie; Linnane, in I; Kroon, Botman and Saccone, in I; Kroon, De Vries and Smit.

experimental data are limited in number. From Table 4 a clear difference between mitochondria from rat liver and yeast is apparent with respect to their response to the antibiotics of the group of macrolides (lines 8–12). Whereas protein synthesis in intact isolated mitochondria from rat liver was resistant to erythromycin, we have been able to show that hypotonic treatment of the mitochondria renders the incorporation sensitive to this antibiotic (Kroon, De Vries and Smit). This has been interpreted to mean that the mitochondrial ribosomes themselves are erythromycin-sensitive. The differential sensitivity of organelle protein synthesis has been used successfully to trace the genetic function of organelle DNA at the level of translation (see paragraphs 6 and 7). Furthermore, it gives strong additional evidence, that the organelle-ribosomes are of the bacterial type.

6. The information content and genetic function of mitochondrial DNA

In paragraph 2 we have discussed the importance of quantitative renaturation studies for delimiting the maximal genetic information of organelle DNA. For mitochondria from animal tissues these studies have revealed that the genetic information is equal to the coding capacity comprised in a single mitochondrial DNA molecule of 10.10^6 daltons, i.e. to 15,000 basepairs or 5,000 aminoacids. For mitochondria from other sources no such data are available. A rough calculation of the genome capacity required for all components known to be present within mitochondria, gives rise to a much higher molecular weight. Most mitochondrial components must, therefore, be coded for by nuclear DNA.

The intriguing question as to which components are genetically determined by mitochondrial DNA and which by nuclear DNA has been attacked from various angles. The tentative results obtained by different experimental approaches are summarized in Table 5. The general pattern emerging from this table points to a genetic function for mitochondrial DNA in coding for structural components while the structural genes for the mitochondrial enzymes appear to be localized on the nuclear genome. An apparent exception in this respect concerns the results obtained with method 5. This method is based on the fact that mitochondrial protein synthesis is sensitive to antibiotics to which cytoplasmic protein synthesis is completely resistant. If yeast cells or animal cells are cultured in the presence of e.g. chloramphenicol it has been observed that the synthesis of cytochrome aa_3, and for yeast also b and c_1, is completely blocked. This proves, therefore, that the mitochondrial translation machinery is necessary for the synthesis of these cytochromes. Since mitochondrial protein synthesis is continuously dependent on RNA synthesis (see paragraph 5) this can be explained easiest by assuming that the message for these cytochromes is actually transcribed from mitochondrial DNA. However, alternative explanations are obvious:

(a) messenger RNA for these cytochromes is actually transcribed from nuclear DNA, in one or another way transported to the mitochondria and translated on the mitochondrial ribosomes (Borst et al. 1967a);

(b) the synthesis of these cytochromes occurs in the cytoplasm, but is strongly controlled by a regulatory protein synthesized in the mitochondria.

In principle, the latter possibility can be tested by looking for a differential inhibition with cycloheximide. Cycloheximide has no effect on mitochondrial protein synthesis but is a strong inhibitor of protein synthesis mediated by the cytoplasmic (= 80S) ribosomes. One would expect, therefore, that the synthesis of proteins within the mitochondria is not affected by the presence of cycloheximide. Experiments with cycloheximide have been done for yeast (Rabinowitz, Getz and Swift, in I; Yu et al., in I; Mahler et al.). It appears that cycloheximide inhibits the synthesis of cytochrome c oxidase either partially or completely. As long as this cycloheximide inhibition is not satisfactorily explained, the involvement of both mitochondrial and cytoplasmic ribosomes in the synthesis of cytochromes b, c_1 and aa_3 remains to be considered. *A fortiori* these experiments at the level of translation do not lend themselves to final conclusions about the localization of the structural genes of the enzymes involved. For this reason we have put the question marks in Table 5.

The interpretation of the results obtained with some of the other methods is further hampered by the fact that in some experiments the designation mitochondrial 'structural protein' is used as the collective name for all native and denatured proteins that cannot be solubilized. But even in the experiments in which the term 'structural

TABLE 5
Experimental approaches to the localization of the genetic information for different mitochondrial co

Method	Description	Mit
		by mitocho
1	DNA–RNA hybridization	ribosomal R
		ribosomal R
2	Characterization of the products of *in vitro* mitochondrial protein synthesis	'structural
		F_1 ATPase
		Coupling fa
3	Pulse-chase experiments *in vivo*	
		'structural p
4	Specific transfer of radioactive mitochondrial enzymes from microsomes to mitochondria	
5	Differential inhibition of the *in vivo* synthesis of mitochondrial proteins with antibacterial antibiotics	cytochrome
		cytochrome
		cytochrome
		cytochrome
6	Correlation of aminoacid replacement in mitochondrial proteins with mutational changes in mitochondrial DNA	'structural
7	Correlation of mutations affecting mitochondrial processes with mutational changes in mitochondrial DNA	ribosomal c
8	Localization of the structural genes of mitochondrial proteins on nuclear DNA	
9	Search for mitochondrial enzymes in cells lacking functionally active mitochondrial DNA	

a: Suyama 1967; Suyama and Eyer 1968; b: Fukuhara, in I; c: Roodyn and Wilkie; d: Neupert
e: Work, in I; f: Work; g: Borst, chapter 35 of this Handbook; h: González-Cadavid and Ca
Beattie et al.; j: Kadenbach, in I; k: Clark-Walker and Linnane; l: Kroon and Jansen; m: Wo
Munkres; n: Thomas and Wilkie (1968a, b); o: Sherman et al.; p: for detailed references to the lit
discussion, see Borst and Kroon.

s coded for by nuclear DNA	Organism	Reference
:r RNA	*Tetrahymena*	a
	yeast	b
	rat liver	c, d, e
	rat liver	f, g
	rat liver	e
rome c	rat liver	e, h
	Krebs ascites tumour cells	c
: protein	rat liver; rat kidney	i
rome c	rat liver	j
rome c ite hydratase ite dehydrogenase dehydrogenase	yeast	k
	beating rat-heart cells	l
	Neurospora	m
	yeast	c, n
rome c	yeast	o
ite dehydrogenase :ytochrome c reductase mycin-sensitive) ite cytochrome c reductase ite cytochrome c reductase ate hydratase ite hydratase (malate dehydrogenase)	yeast	k, p

protein' has a more restricted sense, the fraction has been poorly characterized. The difficulties encountered can be illustrated by the recent observations of Tuppy and Swetly, that mitochondrial structural protein from wild-type yeast consisted of several components, only one of which was missing in a cytoplasmic 'petite'. This protein lacking in the structural protein fraction of the 'petite' mutant has been tentatively related to the absence in mutated yeast of a factor necessary to provide cold-stability of the atractyloside sensitive binding of ATP. The heterogeneity of structural protein is clearly shown by these observations. Furthermore, as will be discussed below, we are to conclude that the 'structural proteins' present in the 'petite' mutants are genetically determined by nuclear DNA. As a consequence the suggestion by Woodward and Munkres that all cellular structural proteins are identical and coded for by mitochondrial DNA becomes rather unlikely.

The most reliable conclusions with respect to the localization of genetic information on either nuclear or mitochondrial DNA, can be drawn from genetic analyses. Unfortunately, these analyses are not applicable to all organisms, and the information available concerns mainly yeasts. The nuclear localization of the structural gene of cytochrome *c* is beyond doubt (Sherman et al.). From physico-chemical characterization of the mitochondrial DNAs from cytoplasmic 'petite' mutants it is clear that the 'petite' mutation may result in gross alterations in the base composition, although it is not at all clear how these arise (Roodyn and Wilkie; discussion after Mounolou et al., in I). In some mutants the mitochondrial DNA was found to consist of nearly pure dAT, implying the loss of all mitochondrial genetic information though not of mitochondrial DNA (Tecce, personal communication). It is not unreasonable to assume that the genetic information of mitochondrial DNA is also lost already if the alterations of the base composition are somewhat less pronounced. This means (method 9) that all mitochondrial enzymes present in such 'petite' mutants have to be coded for by nuclear DNA, including the DNA polymerase responsible for the perpetuation of these non-sensical DNAs through thousands of generations.

It is clear that the 'petite' mutants with their complete loss of all cytoplasmic information do not represent a sensitive tool for the genetic mapping of the mitochondrial 'gene'. However, Wilkie and coworkers have developed an ingenious method for relating phenotypical changes to alterations at the level of mitochondrial DNA (Roodyn and Wilkie; Thomas and Wilkie 1968a, b). These experimental approaches were again based on the sensitivity of mitochondrial protein synthesis to antibacterial antibiotics. They have isolated yeast strains resistant to several of these antibiotics. For erythromycin two types of resistant mutants were obtained: nuclear gene mutants and cytoplasmic mutants (Thomas and Wilkie 1968b). In the former resistance was shown to be due to a permeability barrier for erythromycin presumably of the inner mitochondrial membrane, in the latter indirect evidence strongly indicated that the mitochondrial ribosomes themselves had gained resistance, most likely due to a mutational change in one of the ribosomal proteins. The cytoplasmic segregation pattern of this resistance is, therefore, a strong indication that ribosomal proteins are coded for by mitochondrial DNA. This together with the still limited evidence for complementarity between mitochondrial DNA and RNA from mitochondrial ribosomes (method 1, Table 5), make these ribosomes the favourite candidates for the genetic representation on mitochondrial DNA.

Thomas and Wilkie (1968a) also isolated mutants resistant to other antibiotics. Under carefully chosen conditions recombinants were obtained from crosses between strains with different drug resistance markers. The general occurrence and significance of recombination between mitochondrial DNAs awaits further experimentation.

In summary, it seems reasonable to assume, that mitochondrial DNA most likely codes for the RNA and protein components of mitochondrial ribosomes and for some of the structural proteins, whereas probably the genetic information for mitochondrial enzymes resides within the nucleus. Further experiments will be necessary to show whether this generalization is justified.

7. *Information content and genetic function of chloroplast DNA*

According to the results of the quantitative renaturation experiments of Wells and Birnstiel the total information content of higher plant chloroplasts is 80.10^6 daltons. If we assume that this value has general validity, the coding capacity of chloroplasts amounts to 120,000 basepairs. This seems not enough for an independent subsistence within the cell. It is, furthermore, well known that plastid development and chlorophyll formation depend on the activity of nuclear genes. Direct indications that also chloroplast DNA is genetically active are:

(a) the maternal type of inheritance of plastid anomalies;

(b) the localization of the DNA targets for U.V. mutations (mainly involved in the differentiation of the proplastid to chloroplast) in the cytoplasm (Gibor and Granick; Granick and Gibor).

As in the case of mitochondria, experiments have been undertaken to explore the genetic function of chloroplast DNA by characterizing its transcription and translation products. By DNA–RNA hybridization it has been shown that the RNA components of chloroplast ribosomes are complementary to the chloroplast DNA (Scott and Smillie; Tewari and Wildman 1968). If one starts from the assumption that also in chloroplast DNA only one strand is informative and that the cistrons for the ribosomal RNAs are non-redundantly present on the organelle genome, the information content of chloroplasts can be calculated to be $4–8 \times 10^8$ daltons on the basis of these hybridization experiments. The large discrepancy between the results of quantitative renaturation and hybridization experiments has not yet been elucidated.

Very little is known about the products of *in vitro* incorporation of aminoacids by chloroplasts. After lysis most of the newly synthesized proteins are found in the fraction containing the chloroplast membranes (Gnanam and Kahn). These proteins are, therefore, often called structural proteins, a designation that lacks precise chemical or functional definition.

The differential inhibition of organelle protein synthesis by chloramphenicol and other anti-bacterial antibiotics, as discussed for mitochondria in the preceding paragraph, has also been applied to chloroplasts. From experiments with *Phaseolus vulgaris* (Margulies) and *Euglena* (Aaronson et al.; Linnane and Stewart; Smillie et al.) it may be concluded that the protein synthetic machinery of chloroplasts is involved in the development of chloroplast structure and photosynthetic phosphorylation activities. It cannot yet be decided, however, whether the inhibitions observed for the synthesis of soluble and membrane bound chloroplast proteins really mean that the messages of these proteins are translated within the chloroplast or that alternative mechanisms are responsible for the inhibition.

8. *The evolutionary origin of mitochondria and chloroplasts*

It is generally believed that mitochondria and chloroplasts in eukaryotic cells find their origin in the symbiosis with formerly independent prokaryotes. In a detailed and well-documented hypothesis Sagan has treated this problem. According to this hypothesis the eukaryotic cell itself has evolved from a number of symbiotic events between different prokaryotic organisms early in evolution. Firstly a heterotrophic anaerobe ingested an aerobic prokaryotic microbe (proto-mitochondrion) resulting in the evolution of aerobic amitotic amoeboid organisms. Some of these in turn ingested motile prokaryotes, which became symbiotic, thus giving rise to primitive amoeboflagellates, in which the characteristic features of mitosis developed. Furthermore, the presence of chloroplasts in eukaryotic algae and higher plants is thought to be the result of a similar symbiosis between protoplastids of the blue-green algae type and these primitive amoeboflagellates.

The evidence brought forward in support of the endosymbiont theory concerns mainly striking similarities between mitochondria and bacteria (Roodyn and Wilkie), c.q. chloroplasts and blue-green algae (Sagan). An example of such a similarity is found in the sedimentation studies of Küntzel and Noll with ribosomes. These authors noticed that the size range within the class of 70S ribosomes is such, that the chloroplast ribosomes group together with the ribosomes from photosynthetic bacteria at the lower limit and the mitochondrial ribosomes with those of obligatory aerobic bacteria at the upper limit.

Sagan predicted that it might be possible to find the prokaryotic equivalents of mitochondria and chloroplasts as free-living cells co-descended with the eukaryotic organelles. She suggests that the DNAs of these counterparts might contain homologous sequences. This point of view seems rather optimistic. In the first place this suggestion implies the assumption that the mutation rate and the selective pressure during evolution have been the same or at least comparable for the free-living proto-organelles and the organelles symbiotically embodied in the eukaryotic cells. Secondly, as outlined in paragraphs 6 and 7, the genetic potential of mitochondria and chloroplasts is too moderate to govern all functions necessary for independent propagation of any organism whatsoever. Since the larger part of the original genome of the symbiont might have been inserted into the nuclear genome, one would expect homology (if any) of proto-organelle DNA with nuclear DNA rather than with mitochondrial or chloroplast DNA.

The reason that, in our opinion, searches for homologies in base sequences cannot contribute to an understanding of the evolutionary origin of cell organelles is also based on the observation by Dawid and Wolstenholme (in I) that no sequence complementarity exists between mitochondrial DNA from yeast and frog. It seems doubtful, therefore, that sequence homology will be found between the DNAs of phylogenetically much less related organisms.

In conclusion one may say that the endosymbiont theory for the origin of mitochondria and chloroplasts is attractive though difficult to prove at the molecular level. In view of the many alterations the original symbiont has undergone, and due to the complex relationships between nuclei and organelles that have evolved, the evolutionary origin stands in fact apart from the complicated problems of propagation and origination of fully equipped organelles within the eukaryotic cells.

9. *The biogenesis of mitochondria and chloroplasts*

If one surveys our present-day knowledge of the activities involved in the biosynthesis of mitochondria and chloroplasts, it is clear that many details are elucidated but that the precise mechanism of the concerted action of different cell constituents can only be guessed at. The two biosynthetic pathways that can partially be substantiated by experimental facts involve:

(a) growth and division of preexisting organelles
(b) development from pro-organelles.

Especially in the case of facultative aerobes these two pathways are not mutually exclusive. In anaerobic yeast for example promitochondria have been observed. These are vesicular structures containing mitochondrial DNA and associated with certain mitochondrial enzyme activities. On aeration these promitochondria develop into normal adult mitochondria with normal cristae and a full enzymic equipment. The propagation of these mitochondria may take place by growth and division. For *Neurospora* Luck has shown that new mitochondria arise by growth and division of the preexisting ones. These elegant experiments have been discussed at length by Borst et al. (1967a) and Roodyn and Wilkie.

The following mainly hypothetical mechanism for the perpetuation of cell organelles within eukaryotic cells may be envisaged. In the first stage of the multiplication of cell organelles, replication of the organelle genome occurs, followed by the organelle-DNA directed synthesis of the components of the organelle ribosomes. This process may take place either in proplastids and promitochondria or in the fully developed mitochondria. Each type of particle is surrounded by a double membrane.

The lipid components of the organelle membranes and most of the structural proteins are synthesized (most likely in the cytoplasm) under the direction of nuclear genes. These membrane components may coalesce with the preexisting membranes, thus extending the total lipid surface, the amount of mitochondrial cristae, c.q. the chloroplast lamellae. It is conceivable that some additional and specific membrane proteins are synthesized within the organelles. The direct and spontaneous assembly of the basic membrane structure with the latter specific structural proteins and special lipid components, e.g. cardiolipin (see the chapter by Borst in this Handbook) will subsequently confer the unique properties to the inner membranes, cristae and lamellae.

Although there is no strong experimental evidence for the proposed mechanism, the hypothesis furnishes an explanation for the presence of DNA, ribosomes, etc. within mitochondria and chloroplasts. Since apparently many proteins coded for by nuclear genes can be transferred to the organelle matrix by one or another mechanism, there is no obvious need for the extra protein synthetic machinery within the organelles. If one assumes, however, that the assembly of the membranes is a spontaneous process, the differentiation of membranes with special intracellular localization and properties could be achieved by compartmentation of at least some of the characteristic components of these membranes. Exclusive synthesis at the place where these membranes have to be assembled offers an elegant solution to this problem of compartmentation.

The final enzymic equipment of the organelles will be either specifically transferred from the endoplasmic reticulum to the organelles or synthesized within the organelles themselves. In the latter case two possible origins of the messages should be considered. Both organelle and nuclear messenger-RNAs may be concerned. If nuclear messages are indeed involved, a special device for the transport through the organelle membranes of these polynucleotides should be present (Borst et al. 1967a).

Most of the experimental data that have been discussed in this paper fit into this model. Many details, however, are speculative although open to experimental verification. It is, therefore, to be hoped that in the forthcoming years some progress will be made in the elucidation of the different aspects of this fascinating problem.

Acknowledgements

I wish to thank Dr. P. Borst for the many discussions during the last 3 years and for his critical comments on the manuscript. I am further indebted to Professor E. C. Slater for his interest and advice and to Dr. E. F. J. van Bruggen for providing the electron micrographs.

Abbreviations

% GC mole percentage guanine plus cytosine

T_m midpoint of the 260 nm transition profile of DNA melted out by a gradual increase in temperature

pH_m the pH at which the change in A_{260} nm or sedimentation coefficient is half of that observed at complete alkaline denaturation.

References

I Biochemical Aspects of the Biogenesis of Mitochondria. Ed. by E.C. Slater, J.M. Tager, S. Papa and E. Quagliariello. Bari, Italy, Adriatica Editrice.

AARONSON, S., B.B. ELLENBOGEN, L.K. YELLEN and S.H. HUTNER: *In vivo* differentiation of *Euglena* cytoplasmic and chloroplast protein synthesis with chloramphenicol and DL-ethionine. Biochem. Biophys. Res. Commun. 27 (1967) 535.

ANDRÉ, J. and V. MARINOZZI: Présence, dans les mitochondries, de particles ressemblant aux ribosomes. J. Microscopie 4 (1965) 615.

AVERS, C.J.: Heterogeneous length distribution of circular DNA filaments from yeast mitochondria. Proc. Natl. Acad. Sci. U.S. 58 (1967) 620.

BARNETT, W.E. and D.H. BROWN: Mitochondrial transfer ribonucleic acids. Proc. Natl. Acad. Sci. U.S. 57 (1967) 452.

BARNETT, W.E., D.H. BROWN and J.L. EPLER: Mitochondrial-specific aminoacyl-RNA synthetases. Proc. Natl. Acad. Sci. U.S. 57 (1967) 1775.

BAUER, W. and J. VINOGRAD: The interaction of closed circular DNA with intercalative dyes I. The superhelix density of SV40 DNA in the presence and absence of dye. J. Mol. Biol. 33 (1968) 141.

BEATTIE, D.S., R.E. BASFORD and S.B. KORITZ: Studies on the biosynthesis of mitochondrial protein components. Biochemistry 5 (1966) 926.

BISHOP, D.H.L., J.R. CLAYBROOK and S. SPIEGELMAN: Electrophoretic separation of viral nucleic acid on polyacrylamide gels. J. Mol. Biol. 26 (1967) 373.

BOARDMAN, N.K., R.I.B. FRANCKI and S.G. WILDMAN: Protein synthesis by cell-free extracts of Tobacco leaves III. Comparison of physical properties and protein synthesizing activities of 70S chloroplast and 80S cytoplasmic ribosomes. J. Mol. Biol. 17 (1966) 470.

BOGORAD, L.: Biosynthesis and morphogenesis in plastids. In: T.W. Goodwin, ed.: Biochemistry of chloroplasts, Vol. II. London, Academic Press (1967) 615.

BORST, P. and A.M. KROON: Mitochondrial DNA: physico-chemical properties, replication and genetic function. Intern. Rev. Cytol. (1968) in press.

BORST, P. and G.J.C.M. RUTTENBERG: Renaturation of mitochondrial DNA. Biochim. Biophys. Acta 114 (1966) 645.

BORST, P., A.M. KROON and G.J.C.M. RUTTENBERG: Mitochondrial DNA and other forms of cytoplasmic DNA. In: D. Shugar, ed.: Genetic elements, properties and function. London and Warsaw, Academic Press and PWN (1967a) 81.

BORST, P., E.F.J. VAN BRUGGEN, G.J.C.M. RUTTENBERG and A.M. KROON: Mitochondrial DNA II. Sedimentation analysis and electron microscopy of mitochondrial DNA from chick liver. Biochim. Biophys. Acta 149 (1967b) 156.

BORST, P., G.J.C.M.RUTTENBERG and A.M.KROON: Mitochondrial DNA I. Preparation and properties of mitochondrial DNA from chick liver. Biochim. Biophys. Acta 149 (1967c) 140.

BRAWERMAN, G. and J.M.EISENSTADT: The nucleic acids associated with the chloroplasts of *Euglena gracilis* and their role in protein synthesis. In: C.Sironval, ed.: Le Chloroplaste, croissance et vieilissement. Paris, Masson et Cie. (1967) 162.

BRITTEN, R.J. and M.WARING: Renaturation of the DNA of higher organisms. Carnegie Inst. Wash. Publ. 64 (1965) 316.

BRITTEN, R.J. and D.E.KOHNE: Nucleotide sequence repetition in DNA. Carnegie Inst. Wash. Publ. 65 (1966) 78.

CHIANG, K.S. and N.SUEOKA: Replication of chloroplast DNA of *Chlamydomonas reinhardi* during vegetative cell cycle: its mode and regulation. Proc. Natl. Acad. Sci. U.S. 57 (1967) 1506.

CHUN, E.H.L., N.H.VAUGHAN, JR. and A.RICH: The isolation and characterization of DNA associated with chloroplast preparations. J. Mol. Biol. 7 (1963) 130.

CLARK-WALKER, G.D. and A.W.LINNANE: The biogenesis of mitochondria in *Saccharomyces cerevisiae*. J. Cell Biol. 34 (1967) 1.

CLAYTON, D.A. and J.VINOGRAD: Circular dimer and catanane forms of mitochondrial DNA in human leukaemic leucocytes. Nature 216 (1967) 652.

CLICK, R.E. and B.L.TINT: Comparative sedimentation rates of plant, bacterial and animal ribosomal RNA. J. Mol. Biol. 25 (1967) 111.

CRAWFORD, L.V. and M.J.WARING: Supercoiling of Polyoma virus DNA measured by its interaction with ethidium bromide. J. Mol. Biol. 25 (1967) 23.

DAWID, I.B. and D.R.WOLSTENHOLME: Renaturation and hybridization studies of mitochondrial DNA. Biophys. J. 8 (1968) 65.

DUBIN, D.T. and R.E.BROWN: A novel ribosomal RNA in hamster cell mitochondria. Biochim. Biophys. Acta 145 (1967) 538.

DURE, L.S., J.L.EPLER and W.E.BARNETT: Sedimentation properties of mitochondrial and cytoplasmic ribosomal RNAs from *Neurospora*. Proc. Natl. Acad. Sci. U.S. 58 (1967) 1883.

EPLER, J.L. and W.E.BARNETT: Coding properties of *Neurospora* mitochondrial and cytoplasmic leucine-transfer RNAs. Biochem. Biophys. Res. Commun. 28 (1967) 328.

GIBOR, A. and S.GRANICK: Plastids and mitochondria: inheritable systems. Science 145 (1964) 890.

GNANAM, A. and J.S.KAHN: Biochemical studies on the induction of chloroplast development in *Euglena gracilis*. Biochim. Biophys. Acta 142 (1967) 475, 486, 493.

GONZÀLEZ-CADAVID, N.F. and P.N.CAMPBELL: Sequence of incorporation *in vivo* of [^{14}C]lysine into cytochrome *c* and total proteins of rat-liver subcellular fractions. Biochem. J. 105 (1967) 443.

GRANICK, S. and A.GIBOR: The DNA of chloroplasts, mitochondria and centrioles. Progr. Nucl. Acid Res. Mol. Biol. 6 (1967) 143.

GREEN, B., V.HEILPORN, S.LIMBOSCH, M.BOLOUKHERE and J.BRACHET: The cytoplasmic DNAs of *Acetabularia mediterranea*. Proc. Natl. Acad. Sci. U.S. 58 (1967) 1351.

GRIVELL, L.A.: Aminoacid incorporation by mitochondria isolated, essentially free of micro-organisms, from *Saccharomyces carlsbergensis*. Biochem. J. 105 (1967) 44C.

HUDSON, B. and J.VINOGRAD: Catenated circular DNA molecules in HeLa cell mitochondria. Nature 216 (1967) 647.

IWAMURA, T.: Nucleic acids in chloroplasts and metabolic DNA. Progr. Nucl. Acid Res. Mol. Biol. 5 (1966) 133.

KOCH, J. and E.L.R.STOKSTAD: Incorporation of [^{3}H]thymidine into nuclear and mitochondrial DNA in synchronized mammalian cells. European J. Biochem. 3 (1967) 1.

KROON, A.M.: Inhibitors of mitochondrial protein synthesis. Biochim. Biophys. Acta 76 (1963) 165.

KROON, A.M.: Aminoacid incorporation by isolated mitochondria. The relationship to oxidative phosphorylation and the role of nucleic acids. In: J.M.Tager, S.Papa, E.Quagliariello and E.C. Slater, eds.: Regulation of metabolic processes in mitochondria, BBA Library, Vol. 7. Amsterdam,

Elsevier (1966) 397.

KROON, A.M. and R.J.JANSEN: The effect of low concentrations of chloramphenicol on beating rat-heart cells in tissue culture. Biochim. Biophys. Acta 155 (1968) 629.

KROON, A.M., I.J.DE VRIES and J.L.J.SMIT: (in press).

KÜNTZEL, H. and H.NOLL: Mitochondrial and cytoplasmic polysomes from *Neurospora crassa*. Nature 215 (1967) 1340.

LINNANE, A.W. and P.R.STEWART: The inhibition of chlorophyll formation in *Euglena* by antibiotics which inhibit bacterial and mitochondrial protein synthesis. Biochem. Biophys. Res. Commun. 27 (1967) 511.

LINNANE, A.W., G.W.SAUNDERS, E.B.GINGOLD and H.B.LUKINS: The biogenesis of mitochondria V. Cytoplasmic inheritance of erythromycin resistance in *Saccharomyces cerevisiae*. Proc. Natl. Acad. Sci. U.S. 59 (1968) 903.

LOENING, U.E. and J.INGLE: Diversity of RNA components in green plant tissues. Nature 215 (1967) 363.

MAHLER, H.R., PH.PERLMAN, C.HENSON and C.WEBER: Selective effects of chloramphenicol, cycloheximide and nalidixic acid on the biosynthesis of respiratory enzymes in yeast. Biochem. Biophys. Res. Commun. 31 (1968) 474.

MARGULIES, M.: Effect of chloramphenicol on light-dependent formation of structure and protein of chloroplasts of *Phaseolus vulgaris*. In: C.Sironval, ed.: Le chloroplaste. Paris, Masson et Cie. (1967) 191.

NOLL, H.: Characterization of macromolecules by constant velocity sedimentation. Nature 215 (1967) 360.

O'BRIEN, TH.W. and G.F.KALF: Ribosomes from rat-liver mitochondria I. Isolation procedure and contamination studies II. Partial characterization. J. Biol. Chem. 242 (1967) 2172, 2180.

PETERMAN, M.L.: The physical and chemical properties of ribosomes. New York, Elsevier Publishing Company, Inc. (1964).

RADLOFF, R., W.BAUER and J.VINOGRAD: A dye-buoyant-density method for the detection and isolation of closed circular duplex DNA: the closed circular DNA in HeLa cells. Proc. Natl. Acad. Sci. U.S. 57 (1967) 1514.

RAMIREZ, J.M., F.F.DEL CAMP and D.I.ARNON: Photosynthetic phosphorylation as energy source for protein synthesis and carbon dioxide assimilation by chloroplasts. Proc. Natl. Acad. Sci. U.S. 59 (1968) 606.

RAY, D.S. and P.C.HANAWALT: Satellite DNA components in *Euglena gracilis* cells lacking chloroplasts. J. Mol. Biol. 11 (1965) 760.

REICH, E. and D.J.L.LUCK: Replication and inheritance of mitochondrial DNA. Proc. Natl. Acad. Sci. U.S. 55 (1966) 1600.

ROGERS, P.J., B.N.PRESTON, E.B.TITCHENER and A.W.LINNANE: Differences between the sedimentation characteristics of the ribonucleic acids prepared from yeast cytoplasmic ribosomes and mitochondria. Biochem. Biophys. Res. Commun. 27 (1967) 405.

ROODYN, D.B. and D.WILKIE: The biogenesis of mitochondria. London, Methuen and Co., Ltd. (1968).

RUTTENBERG, G.J.C.M., E.M.SMIT, P.BORST and E.F.J.VAN BRUGGEN: The number of superhelical turns in mitochondrial DNA. Biochim. Biophys. Acta 157 (1968) 429.

SAGAN, L.: On the origin of mitosing cells. J. Theoret. Biol. 14 (1967) 225.

SCHILDKRAUT, C.L., J.MARMUR and P.DOTY: Determination of the base composition of deoxyribonucleic acid from its buoyant density in CsCl. J. Mol. Biol. 4 (1962) 430.

SCHATZ, G., E.HASLBRUNNER and H.TUPPY: Deoxyribonucleic acid associated with yeast mitochondria. Biochem. Biophys. Res. Commun. 15 (1964) 127.

SCOTT, N.S. and R.M.SMILLIE: Evidence for the direction of chloroplast ribosomal RNA synthesis by chloroplast DNA. Biochem. Biophys. Res. Commun. 28 (1967) 598.

SHAPIRO, L., L. I. GROSSMAN, J. MARMUR and A. K. KLEINSCHMIDT: Physical studies on the structure of yeast mitochondrial DNA. J. Mol. Biol. 33 (1968) 907.

SHERMAN, F., J. W. STEWART, E. MARGOLIASH, J. PARKER and W. CAMPBELL: The structural gene for yeast cytochrome *c*. Proc. Natl. Acad. Sci. U.S. 55 (1966) 1498.

SHIPP, W. S., K. J. KIERAS and R. HASELKORN: DNA associated with tobacco chloroplasts. Proc. Natl. Acad. Sci. U.S. 54 (1965) 207.

SINCLAIR, J. H.: Mitochondrial DNA and other low molecular weight cellular DNAs. Ph.D. Thesis, Chicago (1966).

SINCLAIR, J. H. and B. J. STEVENS: Circular DNA filaments from mouse mitochondria. Proc. Natl. Acad. Sci. U.S. 56 (1966) 508.

SINCLAIR, J. H., B. J. STEVENS, P. SANGHAVI and M. RABINOWITZ: Mitochondrial satellite and circular DNA filaments in yeast. Science 156 (1967) 1234.

SMILLIE, R. M., D. GRAHAM, M. R. DWYER, A. GRIEVE and N. F. TOBIN: Evidence for the synthesis *in vivo* of proteins of the Calvin cycle and of the photosynthetic electrontransfer pathway on chloroplast ribosomes. Biochem. Biophys. Res. Commun. 28 (1967) 604.

SPENCER, D. and P. R. WHITFELD: The nature of the ribonucleic acid of isolated chloroplasts. Arch. Biochem. Biophys. 117 (1966) 337.

SPENCER, D. and P. R. WHITFELD: DNA synthesis in isolated chloroplasts. Biochem. Biophys. Res. Commun. 28 (1967a) 538.

SPENCER, D. and P. R. WHITFELD: Ribonucleic acid synthesizing activity of spinach chloroplasts and nuclei. Arch. Biochem. Biophys. 121 (1967b) 336.

STUTZ, E. and H. NOLL: Characterization of cytoplasmic and chloroplast ribosomes in plants: evidence for three classes of ribosomal RNA in nature. Proc. Natl. Acad. Sci. U.S. 57 (1967) 774.

SUYAMA, Y.: Mitochondrial deoxyribonucleic acid of *Tetrahymena*. Its partial physical characterization. Biochemistry 5 (1966) 2214.

SUYAMA, Y.: The origins of mitochondrial ribonucleic acids in *Tetrahymena pyriformis*. Biochemistry 6 (1967) 2829.

SUYAMA, Y. and J. EYER: Leucyl tRNA and leucyl tRNA synthetase in mitochondria of *Tetrahymena pyriformis*. Biochem. Biophys. Res. Commun. 28 (1967) 746.

SUYAMA, Y. and J. EYER: Ribonucleic acid synthesis in isolated mitochondria from *Tetrahymena*. J. Biol. Chem. 243 (1968) 320.

SUYAMA, Y. and K. MIURA: Size and structural variations of mitochondrial DNA. Proc. Natl. Acad. Sci. U.S. 60 (1968) 235.

SVETAILO, E. N., I. I. PHILIPPOVICH and N. M. SISSAKIAN: Differences in sedimentation properties of chloroplast and cytoplasmic ribosomes from pea seedlings. J. Mol. Biol. 24 (1967) 405.

TEWARI, K. K. and S. G. WILDMAN: Chloroplast DNA from tobacco leaves. Science 153 (1966) 1269.

TEWARI, K. K. and S. G. WILDMAN: DNA polymerase in isolated tobacco chloroplasts and nature of the polymerized product. Proc. Natl. Acad. Sci. U.S. 58 (1967) 689.

TEWARI, K. K. and S. G. WILDMAN: Function of chloroplast DNA I. Hybridization studies involving nuclear and chloroplast DNA with RNA from cytoplasmic (80S) and chloroplast (70S) ribosomes. Proc. Natl. Acad. Sci. U.S. 59 (1968) 569.

THOMAS, C. A., JR.: The arrangement of information in DNA molecules. J. Gen. Physiol. 49 (1966) Proc. Symp. 143.

THOMAS, D. Y. and D. WILKIE: Recombination of mitochondrial drug-resistance factors in *Saccharomyces cerevisiae*. Biochem. Biophys. Res. Commun. 30 (1968a) 368.

THOMAS, D. Y. and D. WILKIE: Inhibition of mitochondrial synthesis in yeast by erythromycin: cytoplasmic and nuclear factors controlling resistance. Genet. Res. 11 (1968b) 33.

TUPPY, H. and P. SWETLY: Binding of nucleotides to 'structural protein' of wild-type and respiration-deficient yeast mitochondria. Biochim. Biophys. Acta 153 (1968) 293.

VAN BRUGGEN, E. F. J., C. M. RUNNER, P. BORST, G. J. C. M. RUTTENBERG, A. M. KROON and F. M. A. H. SCHUURMANS STEKHOVEN: Mitochondrial DNA III. Electron microscopy of DNA released from mitochondria by osmotic shock. Biochim. Biophys. Acta 161 (1968) 402.

VINOGRAD, J. and J. LEBOWITZ: Physical and topological properties of circular DNA. J. Gen. Physiol. 49 (1966) Proc. Symp. 103.

WELLS, R. and M. L. BIRNSTIEL: A rapidly renaturing deoxyribonucleic acid component associated with chloroplast preparations. Biochem. J. 105 (1967) 53P.

WETMUR, J. G. and N. DAVIDSON: Kinetics of renaturation of DNA. J. Mol. Biol. 31 (1968) 349.

WHITFELD, P. R. and D. SPENCER: Buoyant density of tobacco and spinach chloroplast DNA. Biochim. Biophys. Acta 157 (1968) 333.

WOODCOCK, C. L. F. and H. FERNÀNDEZ-MORÀN: Electron microscopy of DNA conformations in spinach chloroplasts. J. Mol. Biol. 31 (1968) 627.

WOODWARD, D. O. and K. D. MUNKRES: Genetic control, function and assembly of a structural protein in *Neurospora*. In: H. J. Vogel, J. O. Lampen and V. Bryson, eds.: Organizational biosynthesis. New York, Academic Press (1967) 489.

WORK, T. S.: The function of mitochondrial nucleic acids in protein synthesis. Biochem. J. 105 (1967) 38P.

CHAPTER 37

Mitochondria and chloroplasts: nucleic acids and the problem of biogenesis (genetics and biology)*

HEWSON SWIFT and DAVID R. WOLSTENHOLME

Whitman Laboratory, University of Chicago, Chicago, Ill.

Contents

1. Introduction
2. Mitochondria
   (a) Mitochondria of trypanosomes
   (b) Yeast mitochondria
      Genetic analysis
      Mitochondrial DNA
      Mitochondrial RNA
      Protein synthesis
      Conclusions
   (c) Neurospora mitochondria
      Genetic analysis
      Mitochondrial DNA
      Mitochondrial RNA
      Structure proteins
      Conclusions
   (d) Mitochondria of other organisms
      Mitochondrial continuity
      Mitochondrial DNA – Cytochemistry
      Mitochondrial DNA – Molecular studies
      Mitochondrial RNA
      Protein synthesis
3. Chloroplasts
   Genetic analysis
   Nucleic acids
4. Conclusions

* The authors would like to dedicate this chapter to Arthur W. Pollister, pioneering investigator of the cellular role of nucleic acids, on the occasion of his retirement.

1. Introduction

Mitochondria and chloroplasts can be distinguished from most, if not all, other cytoplasmic organelles by their property of genetic continuity and the now well established presence of DNA. It is now apparent that the eukaryote cell must be considered in some respects as an ecological unit, where two (for animals) or three (for plants) different genotypes have been balanced and inter-related through selection to form an integrated biological system. The hypothesis that this situation arose through symbiosis, as stated in contemporary terms by Ris (1961, 1962), seems intellectually satisfying, but evidence for an event that must have occurred at the dawn of eukaryote evolution should be difficult if not impossible to obtain.

The concept that chloroplasts arise primarily by division from pre-existing plastids or proplastids has been largely accepted since the late nineteenth century. The helical ribbon-shaped chloroplast of *Spirogyra* was seen by Strasburger in the living algal cell to be divided in two at cell division, and Chmielevsky described how the chloroplast in the male *Spirogyra* zygospore degenerated following fertilization, so that subsequent propagation was entirely from the chloroplast of the female gamete. An even more striking indication of chloroplast continuity was reported by von Wisselingh, who found a cell of *Spirogyra* with one normal and one abnormal chloroplast, both of which divided at cell division to produce a clone of cells, each bearing a normal and abnormal chloroplast. Schimper in 1883 figured chloroplasts in the process of division, and similar extensive observations by Meyer strongly supported the general concept of chloroplast continuity in cell division and gamete formation. Such evidence led Mereschkowsky and Famintizin to postulate that chloroplasts derived from symbiotic microorganisms similar to blue-green algae.

Evidence for mitochondrial continuity has been far less conclusive. This is doubtless because of technical difficulties in the observation of mitochondria in living cells, related to their small size and great lability, and from the problems of their fixation and staining. Altmann in 1890 considered that both mitochondria and free-living bacteria were 'elementary organisms' or 'biosomes', the mitochondria living within the cytoplasm somewhat as some slime bacteria live within a secreted gelatinous mass. But there were comparatively few proponents of the biosome hypothesis in subsequent years. Among them were Meves, who not only postulated the ability of mitochondria to propagate, but also to metamorphose into myofibrils, neurofibrils, and secretion granules; Portier, whose book 'Les Symbiotes' described similarities between mitochondria, *Rickettsia*, and intracellular bacterial parasites, and Wallin, who cultivated pieces of rabbit liver *in vitro* and considered that the mitochondria left the tissue and invaded the medium. Among the stronger proponents of mitochondrial continuity was Guillermond whose observations on plant tissues led him to the conclusion that mitochondria, like chloroplasts 'must be considered as permanent entities of the cell, incapable of arising *de novo* and capable of being trasmitted from cell to cell by division'. He was also convinced, however, that mitochondria gave rise to plastids in the course of plant development.

Many early workers were impressed with the extreme variability of mitochondria, and felt that these structures could readily arise *de novo*, or even merely constituted a 'gel phase' of the hyaloplasm (Giroud). Beckwith and later Harvey centrifuged coelenterate or echinoderm eggs to produce small hyaline fragments. In many cases these fragments would undergo development on fertilization, even though they were thought to contain no mitochondria. Beckwith concluded that mitochondria 'arise *de novo* throughout the egg', a conclusion not confirmed by later studies with the electron microscope; several investigators (Lansing et al.; P. Gross et al. 1960) reported that some mitochondria always remained after centrifugation amid lipid droplets at the centripetal pole.

Numerous other descriptions of *de novo* mitochondrial origin are in the cytological literature. Hirsch reported that X-rays destroyed all mitochondria in mouse pancreas, and that secretion resumed only after new mitochondria arose. Bensley described a marked loss and fragmentation of mitochondria in guinea pig liver following starvation, an observation that led him to the opinion that mitochondria 'were simply temporary aggregates of complex composition'. These and other studies were obviously hampered by the limitations of cytological techniques. Conclusive evidence on the nature of mitochondria awaited development of cell fractionation methods, pioneered by Bensley, Hoerr and Claude and the concise definition of mitochondrial fine structure first provided by Palade and Sjöstrand. For reviews of the classical literature on the formation of mitochondria see Duesberg; Cowdry (1918, 1924); Takagi; Guillermond; Newcomer (1940, 1951); and Novikoff (1961).

In recent years an impressive mass of literature has accumulated relating to the biogenesis of mitochondria. For reviews on various aspects of mitochondrial biogenesis see Gibor and Granick (1964); Wilkie; Swift; Luck (1965); Roodyn (1967); Borst et al. (1967); Rabinowitz; Deanin; Roodyn and Wilkie; and the Symposium on Biochemical aspects of mitochondrial biogenesis (Slater et al.). See also ch. 36.

2. *Mitochondria*

Our concepts of mitochondrial continuity have been considerably strengthened with a better understanding of the biosynthetic processes of which mitochondria are capable. Recognition of the presence of mitochondrial nucleic acids is comparatively recent. It was possible, for example, for Novikoff to write in 1961 that 'mitochondria lack DNA and possess little, if any RNA'. Somewhat prophetically, however, he added 'although the concentration of RNA in mitochondria may be low its significance may be great'. During the past five years we have progressed from indirect indications and speculation on mitochondrial nucleic acids, with biochemical determinations subject to suspicions of contamination, to the present clear evidence for the existence of specific kinds of RNA and DNA unique to mitochondria. These findings, together with the demonstration of independent polymerases, activating enzymes, and amino acid incorporation, now provide exceedingly strong if not incontrovertible evidence that an independent genetic system and its transcription mechanism exist in mitochondria.

We are unfortunately still confronted with the task of attributing a biological significance to this machinery of sufficient importance to have assured its separate survival throughout evolution. The realization that mitochondria, and plastids as well, contain their own DNA, together with much fragmentary evidence for their role in cytoplasmic inheritance, suggests that these organelles possess a considerable degree of genetic autonomy. Other evidence, however, demonstrates a close dependence upon the environment provided by the cell. A number of nuclear genes are known that directly or indirectly affect the enzyme content of mitochondria. Some mitochondrial proteins are probably manufactured *in situ,* but there is evidence that others may be appropriated from the surrounding cytoplasm. The manner in which mitochondria are thus assembled as the product of spatially different genotypes and two separate but doubtless interacting protein-forming mechanisms would seem to form a basic problem that must be explored in the future before the biological role of mitochondrial biosynthesis is understood. In the pages that follow we have tried to stress the biological aspects of mitochondrial and chloroplast biosynthesis. The field is now too vast for a comprehensive review in the allotted space, and the inclusion of many conflicting and inconclusive observations seems of little current value. Biochemical aspects are discussed in the chapter by Borst.

(a) *Mitochondria of trypanosomes*

The first clear indication of mitochondrial DNA (M-DNA) was long considered to be an unusual special case, although striking parallels with mitochondrial systems in other cells are now apparent. Immediately following the development of the Feulgen reaction for DNA (Feulgen and Rossenbeck) it was shown by Bresslau and Scremin that the kinetoplast of trypanosome flagellates was Feulgen-positive. The mitochondrial nature of this structure, which lies adjacent to the basal granule of the flagellum, was long suspected, particularly because of its intense stainability with Janus green B (Shipley), but it remained for electron microscopy to demonstrate that the Feulgen-positive body, here called the kinetoplast, but also termed the kinetonucleus or parabasal body by some authors, is located within the matrix area of a modified mitochondrion, to which other more typical mitochondria are attached (Meyer; Clark and Wallace; Steinert 1960; Ris 1962). The DNA-containing kinetoplast has been shown in several trypanosomid species to be strap- or disc-shaped, with fibers traversing its short axis, as shown in Fig. 1. Although it clearly contains much more DNA than the mitochondria of other cell types, under the electron microscope it possesses much the same filamentous structure. It seems likely that its prominence is associated with the extensive changes in mitochondrial morphology which accompany stages in the complex life cycle of these parasitic organisms. For example, trypanosomes of the *Trypanosoma brucei* group possess a restricted mitochondrial morphology in the blood

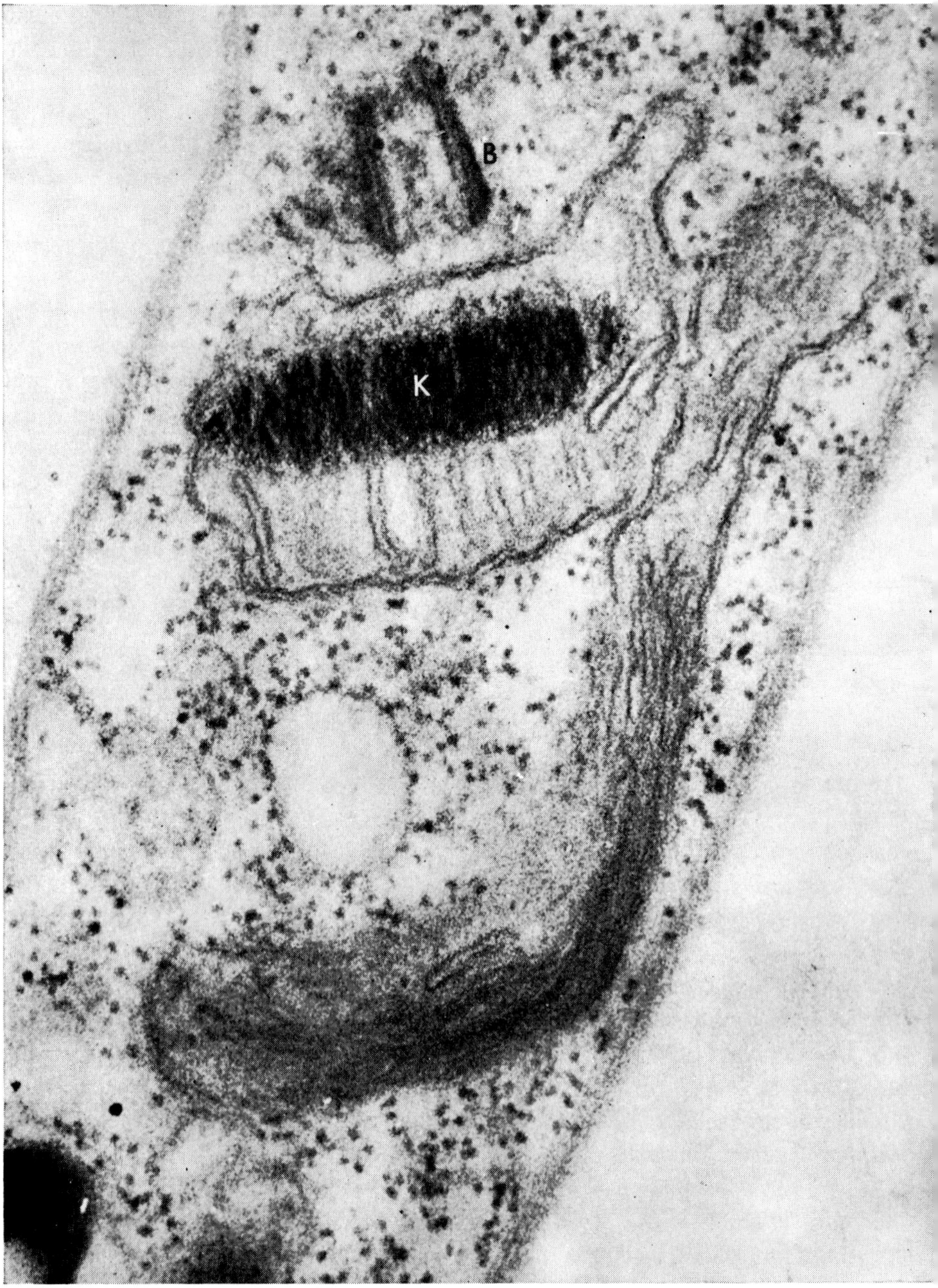

Fig. 1. Kinetoplast region of *Trypanosoma lewisi* showing the fibrous kinetoplast (K) within the matrix of a modified mitochondrion. Also visible is an attached mitochondrial branch on the right, and the basal granule (B) of the flagellum. (From Ris 1962.) × 70,000

stream of the mammalian host, and some cells may lack cytochrome proteins and mitochondrial cristae. In the gut of the tsetse fly vector, however, the mitochondria become greatly enlarged. The tetrazolium reaction for NAD diaphorase demonstrates a prominent anastomosing complex of mitochondrial branches emanating from the kinetoplast and ramifying throughout the cell (Vickerman). A similar budding of mitochondrial branches from the lateral edges of the kinetoplast has been followed *in vitro* in cultures of *Leishmania tarentolae* during induced transformation from leishmania to leptomonad stages (Rudzinska et al.). Although the specific role of the kinetoplast in this process is obscure, the mitochondrial transformation, and the accompanying 5- to 7-fold increase in QO_2, were inhibited by actinomycin D, and also by puromycin and mitomycin C (Simpson 1968b).

Radioautographic studies have demonstrated that the kinetoplast incorporates tritiated thymidine into its DNA in most cases during a time coincident with the nuclear S period (Steinert and Steinert; Simpson 1968c). It can clearly be seen to divide prior to cell division. The mitochondrial branches apparently remain attached during division, and appear to be passively segregated. Immediately before division, electron microscopy of *L. conorhini* showed the kinetoplast disc to be transversely split into two parallel plates, the two portions apparently later moving apart, always surrounded by the characteristic inner and outer mitochondrial membranes (Milder and Deane). The alkaline fast green reaction was found to be negative for *T. mega* kinetoplasts, an indication that no demonstrable histone protein is associated with the DNA (Steinert 1965).

Feulgen-positive kinetoplasts are apparently universal in hemoflagellate parasites, and in related protomonads such as *Bodo* and *Cryptobia*. Stainable DNA is characteristically absent only in one hemoflagellate species, *T. equinum*, although occasional strains lacking kinetoplast DNA have been found in nature in *T. equiperdum* and *T. evansi*. The loss of kinetoplast DNA apparently is irreversible. It has been known for many years that loss of demonstrable kinetoplast DNA could be experimentally induced in up to 80% of the trypanosomes in a culture by treatment with acriflavin, trypflavin, and related dyes (Werbitzki; Robertson; Mühlpfordt). The first noticeable change on acriflavin treatment involves a clumping of the kinetoplast DNA fibers (Trager and Rudzinska). DNA synthesis is selectively inhibited, apparently as the result of a greater sensitivity to acriflavin of kinetoplast than nuclear DNA or a greater dye uptake by the mitochondria. Although the kinetoplast may continue to divide a few times, it was seen to decrease in size in cultures of *L. tarentolae* through lack of DNA synthesis, and eventually the entire detectable DNA passed to only one daughter cell (Simpson 1968c). Cells lacking stainable DNA also failed to stain for mitochondrial respiratory activity with Janus green B or tetrazolium (Vickerman). Electron microscopy of acriflavin-treated *L. tarentolae* demonstrated that the kinetoplast region may still contain a dense amorphous band, although evidence of DNA fibers was lacking. Since some vestige of the kinetoplast may still be present, it was suggested that these cultures should be termed 'dyskinetoplastic', instead of akinetoplastic.

It is an important fact that mitochondrial morphology in these dyskinetoplastic strains appeared abnormal, with cristae swollen and reduced in number, or replaced by whorls of membranous material. The QO_2 of *L. tarentolae* was also progressively reduced with continuous treatment in acriflavin over a 4-day period. Although the degree of QO_2 inhibition was not strictly proportional to the number of dyskinetoplastic cells produced, the implication seems clear that acriflavin affects cell respiration by suppressing the synthesis of kinetoplast DNA needed to maintain normal mitochondrial structure and function.

Dyskinetoplastic strains grow poorly or not at all in culture media (Trager and Rudzinska; Simpson 1968c) and are incapable of infecting the invertebrate host (Vickerman). At least in some cases in the genus *Trypanosoma* they are still capable of passage in the vertebrate blood stream. It is of interest that in the naturally occurring strains which apparently lack kinetoplast DNA (the horse parasites *T. equinum*, and strains of *T. equiperdum* and *T. evansi*) the invertebrate host stage is also absent, transmission being either by intercourse or by direct hypodermic action of horse flies. Trager and Vickerman thus have postulated that kinetoplast DNA is responsible for the production of normal mitochondria required in the environment of the invertebrate host or laboratory culture, but not essential for growth in the richer environment of the vertebrate vascular system, where respiration apparently involves a specialized flavoprotein oxidase system occurring outside of the mitochondria (Ryley).

Few biochemical studies on isolated kinetoplasts have yet been published, although methods for kinetoplast isolation have been described (DuBuy et al.; Simpson 1968a). Whole cell DNA has been extracted from six different species of hemoflagellates and studied by ultracentrifugation in cesium chloride. All showed the presence of a satellite band of lower buoyant density than the major band, and thus of an estimated lower GC content (Schildkraut et al.; Marmur et al.; Schiff and Epstein). In three species, isolated kinetoplast preparations showed enrichment for the satellite, and no satellite band was demonstrable in DNA from cultures of dyskinetoplastic cells (DuBuy et al.; Simpson 1965; Riou et al). In normal cells of *L. tarentolae* the satellite DNA was estimated to comprise 5 to 10% of the total. It thus is evident that kinetoplast DNA resembles the M-DNA of many other but not all cell types in possessing a base ratio statistically different from that of nuclear DNA. The fact that the *Leishmania* satellite DNA banded more rapidly than nuclear DNA in cesium chloride, and dispersed more rapidly when the rotor was stopped, suggested to DuBuy et al. that it possessed a lower molecular weight, and a shape more favorable to banding. When DNA from whole cell *T. equiperdum* was spread by the Kleinschmidt method and shadowed for electron microscopy, a number of circular DNA molecules were observed which averaged approximately 7 and 14 μ in length (Sinclair and Stevens 1966b). Measurements on DNA molecules from preparations of isolated kinetoplasts are needed. See also Riou and Paoletti, and Riou and Delain.

That kinetoplast DNA codes for certain proteins needed in functional respiratory assemblies of the trypanosome mitochondrial system seems strongly suggested if not yet established. The close relationship between the kinetoplast and the basal granule of the flagellum (sometimes called the blepharoplast or kinetosome) has also suggested that a functional relationship may exist with locomotor function. As seen in Fig. 1 there is no obvious continuity of structure between kinetoplast and basal granule, but in isolated kinetoplasts, even when artificially swollen, an attachment between the flagellum and Feulgen-positive body is maintained, presumably through adhesion between material at the proximal end of the basal granule and the outer kinetoplast membrane (Simpson 1968a). Acriflavin treatment of *L. tarentolae* cells in culture also frequently produced a loss in flagella, but since dyskinetoplastic cells occur in which demonstrable DNA is absent but flagella are still maintained, there appears to be no specific dependency for structural integrity of the flagellum upon the kinetoplast.

In summary, the kinetoplast of trypanosomes and related forms contains DNA of a GC content lower than the nucleus. It probably is not associated with histone protein. It is located within a specialized region of the single large mitochondrial complex characteristic of these cells. Irreversible loss of kinetoplast DNA can be induced in cultures of hemoflagellates by acriflavin, in which case oxidative metabolism is inhibited and the cells may grow slowly or not at all. Mitochondrial morphology is also disrupted in cells lacking kinetoplast DNA. A marked enlargement of mitochondria into an anastomosing complex ramifying throughout the cell occurs during the transformation induced by transfer of trypanosomes from the mammalian blood stream to the invertebrate host, or from leishmania to leptomonad stages as induced *in vitro*. This transformation, and the accompanying increase in QO_2, is inhibited by actinomycin D, and fails to occur in cells in which the kinetoplast is lacking. It seems likely that kinetoplast DNA carries some of the genetic information necessary to direct this change.

(b) *Yeast mitochondria*

Genetic analysis. Cells of baker's yeast, *Saccharomyces cerevisiae*, have been particularly important to our understanding of mitochondrial biogenesis. In every haploid or diploid culture a small number of cells are found which grow more slowly, and thus form smaller 'petite' colonies on glucose agar plates. In the classical studies of Ephrussi it was shown that mitochondria of petite cells stained poorly with the G-Nadi reaction for cytochrome oxidase, and thus it was suspected that a mitochondrial defect was involved. This supposition was later confirmed. Petite cells were found to lack cytochromes $a+a_3$ and b entirely (although cytochrome c was present), and thus grow only by the fermentation of glucose or other fermentable substrates (Ephrussi and Slonimski). Studies by electron microscopy showed that the mitochondrial morphology of petites is also abnormal, the cristae being replaced by irregular whorls of membranes, much as in the mitochondria of dyskinetoplastic trypanosomes (Yotsuyanagi 1962). Influenced by the work on trypanosomes, Ephrussi and collaborators tried the effects of acriflavin on yeast. The results were striking. Up to 99% of the cells could be transformed to petites on a single application of the dye. The change was heritable and completely stable; petite strains showed no reversions to the wild type, or grande condition. Later studies have shown a similar induction with other DNA-intercalating molecules such as ethidium bromide (Slonimski et al.), ultraviolet light (Wilkie), and the pyrimidine analogue, 5-fluorouracil (Moustacci and Markovitch).

Genetic analysis of petite strains is restricted, partly because diploid petite cells cannot sporulate. Crosses need to be made by somatic recombination between two haploid strains. Such crosses between petite and grande cells demonstrate the presence of three kinds of petites: (1) In a few cases progeny show a typical Mendelian 1:1 segregation, two of the haploid spores in an ascus being petite and two grande. The petite character in these strains thus appears related to a typical chromosomal gene. These are called *segregational* petites; they are least common, and unlike other petites, are not produced by acriflavin. (2) Progeny are all grande and the petite character is lost. This indicates that although cell fusion resulted in a mixture of two types of non-chromosomal determinants, the defective petite component was subsequently lost. These are called *neutral* petites. (3) Progeny are all petite, and the normal grande character is lost. This also indicates the presence of non-chromosomal determinants, with the mutant (petite) determinant retained and the wild type determinant lost. These are called *suppressive* petites. The suppressive characteristic occurs in all degrees. Some strongly suppressive strains produce 99% petites when crossed with grandes, while in others the suppressive character is typically weaker.

A formal indication that the suppressive petite character is indeed non-nuclear was obtained by Wright and Lederberg on strains of yeast (var. ellipsoideus) where haploid cell fusion occurs without nuclear fusion. This produces heterokaryons where nuclei of each parental strain exist together in a common cytoplasm. During subsequent vegetative growth homokaryon cells may again be produced, bearing the haploid nuclei of the original parental strains. In crosses between strains marked with wild type and mutant nuclei, the suppressive petite character was successfully transferred from association with one genetically marked nucleus to another, an indication that the suppressive character was transferable even where transmission of nuclear genes did not take place.

These crosses demonstrate the presence of a non-chromosomal factor in yeast heredity, which is markedly influenced by acriflavin, and which is somehow linked both to cell respiration and mitochondrial morphology. On the other hand they also demonstrate that certain aspects of mitochondrial function are under *nuclear* control, since one class of cells, segregational petites, shows normal Mendelian segregation. Thus it can be concluded that the presence of cytochromes $a + a_3$ and b in the cell is dependent upon a combination of chromosomal and non-chromosomal factors. Analysis of segregational petites has indicated the presence of nine independent chromosomal alleles, each one capable of producing mitochondria deficient in cytochromes a and b (Hawthorne and Mortimer; Sherman and Ephrussi; Sherman). Three of these are of particular interest, since when segregational petites bearing them are crossed with neutral petites, instead of the suspected 1:1 segregation, all progeny are petite. Products of these three loci thus appear to be necessary for the maintenance of the cytoplasmic factors involved. It is also of interest that mitochondrial morphology in segregational petites is relatively normal (Yotsuyanagi 1962).

One additional fact concerning the nuclear control of mitochondrial enzymes should be stressed. In yeast, as in other cells, cytochrome c is a major component of mitochondria, and cytochrome c is equally present in mitochondria of normal grande as well as petite cultures. Six different chromosomal loci are known which produce various degrees of cytochrome c deficiency. Although some of these loci apparently influence cytochrome synthesis indirectly, one locus (cy_1) appears to represent the structural gene for iso-1-cytochrome c, the principal cytochrome c component of the yeast mitochondrion (Sherman et al. 1965, 1966). This provides a clear indication that the structural gene for at least one major mitochondrial protein resides in the nucleus.

Mitochondrial DNA. Normal yeast mitochondria as viewed by electron microscopy, following adequate fixation, contain a prominent filamentous component within the matrix areas (Fig. 2). The filaments are removable when DNase extraction is carried out on fixed cells prior to embedding, and show the uranyl acetate binding characteristic of DNA (Yotsuyanagi and Guerrier; Swift et al. 1968). Under certain conditions (anaerobiosis or glucose repression) the DNA filaments appear to be attached to an osmiophilic membranous body (Fig. 3); see also Yotsuyanagi (1966).

DNA extracted from isolated yeast mitochondria (Schatz et al.; Tewari et al.; Corneo et al.) possesses a buoyant density lighter than the nuclear DNA, as shown by ultracentrifugation in cesium chloride (Fig. 4). In our determinations, nuclear DNA possessed a density of 1.698 and M-DNA of 1.683, characteristic of a lower GC content (nuclear: 38%; mitochondrial 23%). This M-DNA showed the increase in density following heat denaturation (100 °C for 10 min in standard saline-citrate) of 0.014 g/cc, characteristic of double-stranded DNA. It differed from nuclear DNA, however, in its ability to renature and return to the original density when incubated for 5 hr at 65 °C (Corneo et al.; Sinclair). This property of renaturation would obviously be expected of DNA possessing a high degree of molecular homogeneity, where the likelihood of contact between reciprocal single stranded partners was increased. Rapid renaturation appears to be a basic property of M-DNA from many sources (see Borst et al. 1967). The amount of M-DNA per yeast cell varies greatly between different strains and under different conditions of growth. It may reach 20% of the total cell DNA in strain R_1 or may be reduced to levels below 1% in anaerobic cells. In normal cells it may average between 10 to 14% (Mounolou et al.; Shapiro et al.), an amount roughly comparable to M-DNA levels in trypanosomes.

M-DNA spread on surface films by the Kleinschmidt method mostly contained double-stranded linear molecules averaging 4 to 4.5 μ long (Shapiro et al.). A small number of molecules were 2 or 3 times this length, and about 3% were in the form of open or twisted circles, also 4 to 4.5 μ (rarely 8 to 9 μ) long (Fig. 14). Similar circular molecules,

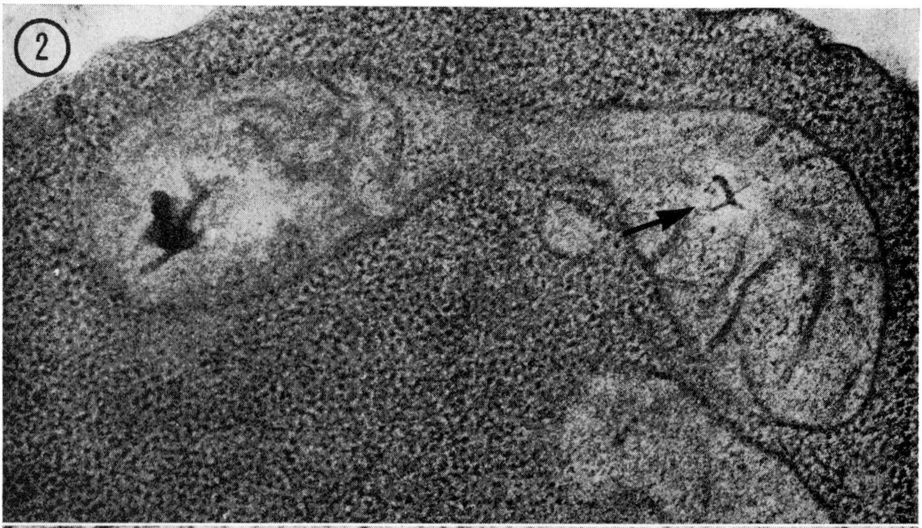

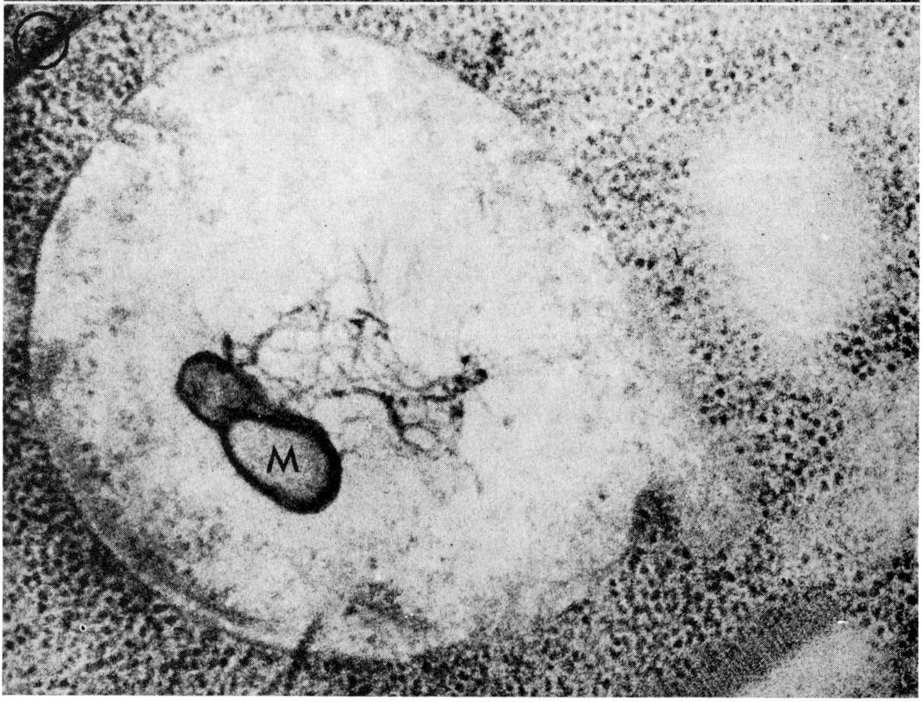

Fig. 2. Mitochondrion of a yeast cell grown aerobically, showing DNA filaments (arrow). ×90,000

Fig. 3. Mitochondrion of a yeast cell grown anaerobically followed by 60 min aerobic adaptation. DNA filaments are associated with an osmiophilic membranous component (M). ×110,500

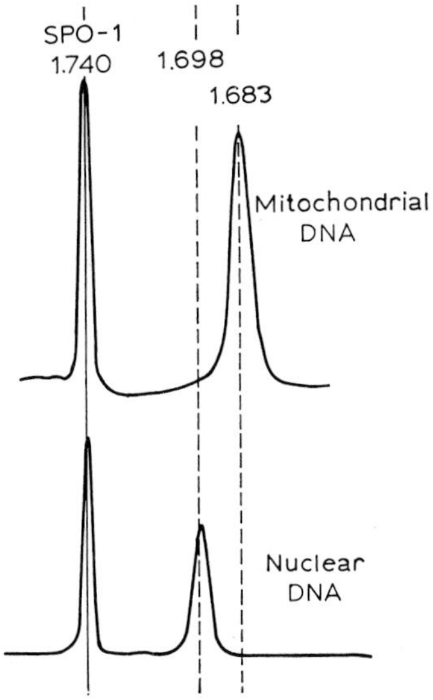

Fig. 4. Distribution of optical density of nuclear and mitochondrial DNA from ρ^+ yeast foam 237 (Data from M. Rabinowitz et al., unpubl.)

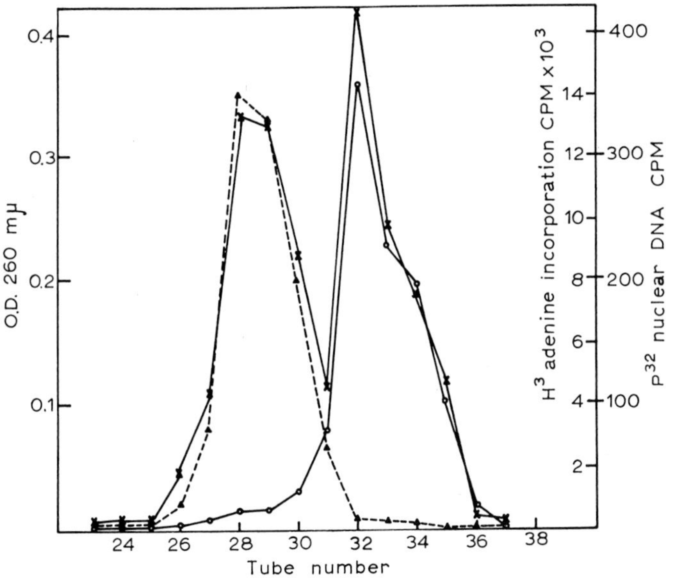

Fig. 5. A comparison of the incorporation of H^3 adenine into yeast nuclear and mitochondrial DNA during adaptation. Cells were grown anaerobically, and allowed to adapt in an aerated medium for 1 hr in the presence of H^3 adenine. Mitochondria were isolated in a manner sufficient to provide roughly equal parts of nuclear and mitochondrial DNAs, as determined on preparative cesium chloride gradients. Closed circles: optical density at 260 mμ, showing the separation of nuclear DNA (left peak) and mitochondrial DNA (right peak). Open circles: H^3 adenine incorporation, demonstrating a large amount of incorporation into M-DNA, but only slight incorporation into nuclear DNA. Dotted line: added P^{32}-labeled nuclear DNA. (Data from M. Rabinowitz et al., unpubl.)

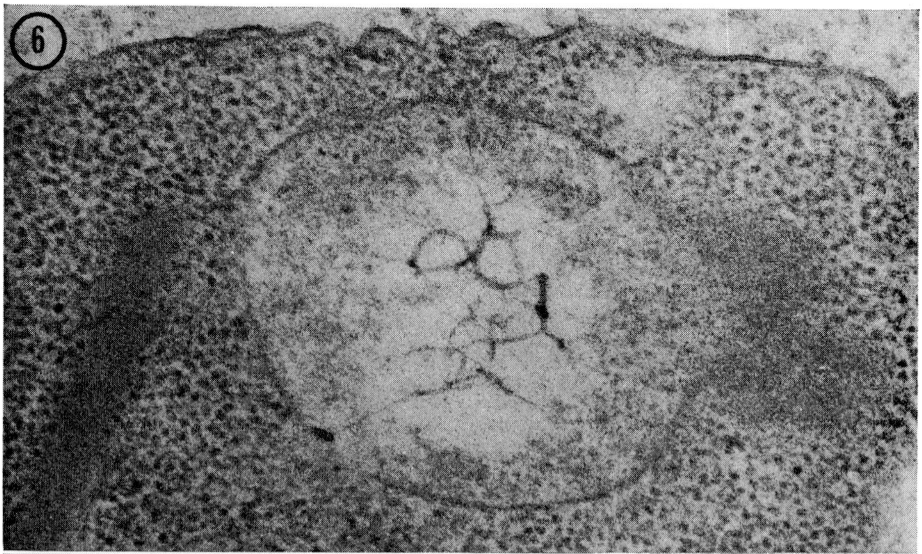

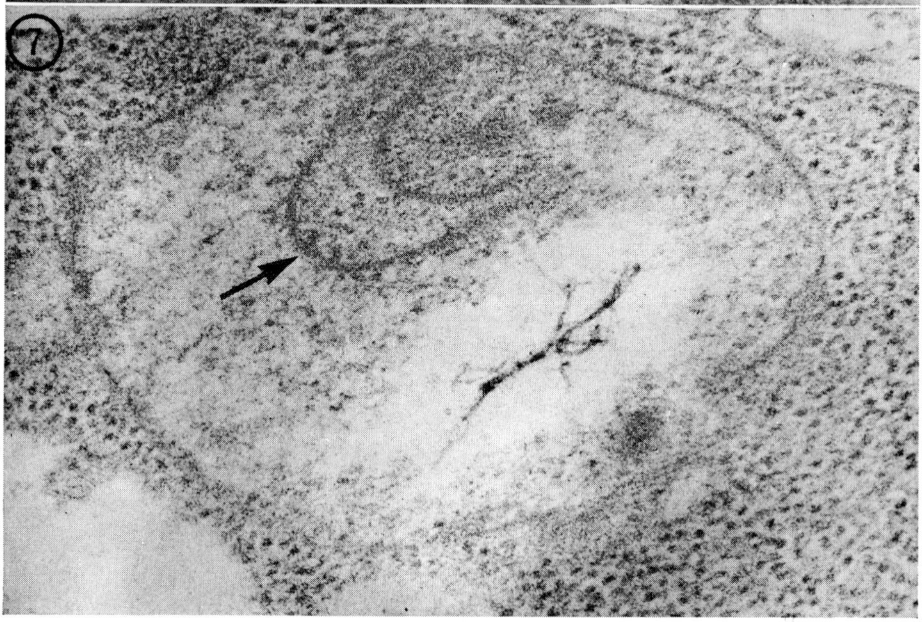

Fig. 6. Mitochondrion of a yeast cell grown anaerobically. The mitochondrion lacks cristae but DNA filaments are evident. ×110,500

Fig. 7. Mitochondrion of a yeast cell grown anaerobically followed by 60 min aerobic adaptation. Reforming cristae are visible (arrow). ×110,500 from vertebrate mitochondria, are shown in Figs. 6 and 7. Sedimentation of yeast M-DNA in sucrose gradients showed three components, sedimenting in the ratios 1:1.19:1.9. The slowest component was considered to be the lineara tolecules, the intermediate component the open circles, and the heaviest component the twisted or super-coiled circular molecules. Open circles could be experimentally converted to linear molecules by heating to 70 °C for 5 min. Linear molecules could be transformed, up to 25%, to open circles by incubation at 50 °C for 2 hr. Such effects parallel the behavior of λ bacteriophage DNA which has been shown to form circles by the hydrogen bonding of complementary single-stranded ends of the molecule (Hershey et al.; Ogawa and Tomizawa). These 'sticky' ends could thus convert a linear molecule to a circle at 50 °C, under conditions favorable to renaturation, but would break apart at 70 °C to change circular to linear molecules.

The nature of the heaviest M-DNA component, the twisted circles, is best understood by its similarity to another viral DNA molecule, the 1.7 μ long circular DNA of polyoma mouse tumor virus (Vinograd and Lebowitz). Polyoma DNA characteristically exists as a covalently closed circular double-stranded DNA molecule, twisted back on itself in a small number of tertiary coils, or supercoils. These supercoiled molecules can be recognized by their faster sedimentation rate in sucrose gradients. On gentle treatment of these molecules with DNase, to produce an average of only one single break per molecule, one strand of the DNA duplex is broken and the supercoil can then unwind on the phosphodiester bond swivel into an open circle. DNA ligase enzyme, isolated from *E. coli*, is capable of repairing such single-strand nicks in the DNA. It can, for example, change hydrogen-bonded phage λ circles into covalently bonded circles (Gellert; Gefter et al.). Shapiro et al. were able to show that M-DNA of intermediate density (closed circles) could be converted to the rapidly sedimenting component upon treatment with ligase.

From these studies it appears that M-DNA of yeast can be isolated as molecules 4 to 4.5 μ long, with single-stranded sticky ends, capable of forming hydrogen-bonded circular molecules, or dimers and trimers. Some molecules also can be obtained as supercoiled covalently bonded circles. The presence of polymer molecules makes it seem likely that the single-stranded ends are not formed by random breaks, but instead represent a specific aspect of the M-DNA molecule.

The M-DNA composition of petite yeast has been studied by Mounolou et al., who have reported wide differences in base ratios between different strains. A normal grande strain showed the expected density of 1.687, and a segregational petite also possessed a density of 1.687. A neutral petite, however, had an M-DNA density of 1.683 (an estimated 5% GC content *lower* than the normal grande) and a suppressive petite of 1.695 (an estimated 8% *higher* content of GC). Such wide shifts in DNA content are presently difficult to explain. Any normal mutation, representing an alteration in a single base pair, would obviously produce an undetectable change in base ratio. These major shifts indicate cataclysmic alteration in the M-DNAs of vegetative petites, as might possibly be produced by drastic deletion and duplication of specific highly asymmetrical portions of the molecule, or the 'infection' by episomal DNAS, or some major error in replication associated with a possibly abnormal DNA polymerase. These data, together with the high spontaneous incidence of cytoplasmic petites, and the almost complete transformation produced by acriflavin, indicate that petite strains cannot be considered as point mutations in the usual sense. Such gross alterations would be expected to accompany drastic variations in mitochondrial physiology, as would also be expected from the acriflavin-induced major deletions in kinetoplast DNA in trypanosomes.

Yeast mitochondria have been thought to disappear entirely under conditions of anaerobic growth and where levels of ergosterol and unsaturated fatty acids in the growth medium are reduced to very low levels (Vitols et al.; Linnane et al.; Wallace et al.; Jollow et al.). Certainly under anaerobic conditions many respiratory enzymes are no longer demonstrable. The presence of oxygen is necessary for the synthesis of cytochromes (Slonimski; Somlo and Fukahara) and also for cytochrome c oxidase and succinate cytochrome c reductase. Where anaerobic cells were cultured in media with only very low levels of ergosterol and unsaturated fatty acids, electron microscopy of permanganate-fixed cells failed to show characteristic mitochondrial profiles. It was reported by Linnane and collaborators that mitochondria rapidly reappear upon aeration of the medium, or with the addition of ergosterol and Tween 80. The *de novo* formation of mitochondria, possibly from other membranes of the cell, was thus postulated.

Anaerobic cells can still be shown to possess the DNA component with a density of 1.682 characteristic of mitochondria (Fig. 5) (Rabinowitz et al. 1969). When anaerobic cells, grown in Linnane medium, are fixed for electron microscopy in glutaraldehyde, mitochondria are still evident in yeast cells, although they are markedly different in morphology from those of aerobic cells. DNA filaments are evident, and amorphous electron-dense material is present in the matrix areas, but cristae are usually absent altogether. Upon the addition of oxygen the cristae rapidly reform, and the respiratory enzymes are resynthesized (Figs. 6, 7 and 8). It seems likely that the apparent total loss of mitochondria in anaerobic cells reported by Linnane, rather represents a change in the composition of mitochondrial membranes such that they no longer contain sufficient unsaturated fatty acids necessary for permanganate reduction and consequent visibility in the electron microscope.

The addition of oxygen to anaerobically grown yeast cells not only induces the synthesis of respiratory enzymes and the reappearance of mitochondrial cristae, but also produces a rapid and marked increase in the synthesis of M-DNA. As shown in Fig. 8, incorporation of H^3 adenine into M-DNA was stimulated by the addition of oxygen, reaching a peak after the first 15 min when M-DNA possessed a specific activity 22 times that of the nuclear DNA. M-DNA and nuclear DNA thus did not show parallel patterns of incorporation, a finding that stressed the relative independence of nuclear and cytoplasmic DNA. Also, the most rapid M-DNA incorporation occurred before the synthesis of appreciable cytochrome c oxidase, and at a time when mitochondrial

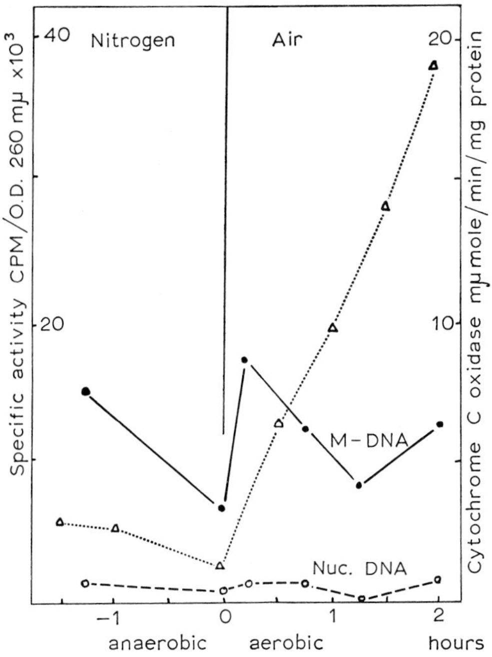

Fig. 8. A comparison of H^3 adenine incorporation into ρ^+ yeast M-DNA and nuclear DNA during adaptation from anaerobic to aerobic growth. Yeast cells were grown in a nitrogen atmosphere, were transferred to air at time 0, and vigorously shaken in a medium containing 0.1% glucose, 2% ethanol and 0.05 M succinate. Incorporation into M-DNA showed a marked increase at 15 min adaptation, while nuclear DNA incorporation increased only slightly. The activity of mitochondrial cytochrome c oxidase (dotted line) showed the characteristic rapid increase during adaptation. (Data from M. Rabinowitz et al., 1969)

number apparently remained constant. Mitochondrial divisions were not observed until 6 hr after addition of oxygen (Rabinowitz et al. 1969). M-DNA synthesis thus preceded both the formation of appreciable respiratory enzymes, and mitochondrial propagation. Oxygen thus stimulates M-DNA synthesis through some relatively direct mechanism, and not indirectly by its effect on respiratory enzyme synthesis. This was further shown by the fact that O_2 still induced DNA synthesis in the presence of inhibitors of protein synthesis, chloramphenicol and cycloheximide, as well as in a respiratory deficient petite incapable of synthesizing respiratory enzymes. Also of interest was the fact that acriflavin inhibited the oxygen-induced incorporation of H^3 adenine into M-DNA, a finding consistent with its effects on kinetoplast DNA synthesis.

DNA synthesis can still take place in isolated yeast mitochondria. Preparations may be freed of nuclear DNA contamination by treatment with DNAse, which fails to penetrate the mitochondrial membranes. Incubation of isolated mitochondria in the presence of deoxynucleoside triphosphates and magnesium ions demonstrated incorporation of labeled dATP into acid insoluble M-DNA. The rate of incorporation was maximal at 15 min, and later declined to lower levels. The incorporation was inhibited by actinomycin D and mitomycin C (Wintersberger 1966a). These studies indicate that a DNA polymerase exists in yeast mitochondria, as also shown in rat liver mitochondria by Neubert et al. and Parsons and Simpson; it also strongly suggests that M-DNA is synthesized *in situ* and not elsewhere in the cell, although the possibility that incorporation only represented repair, not synthesis, was not ruled out (see below).

To summarize the above discussion, yeast M-DNA comprises roughly 10% of the total DNA of normal cells. It has a GC content lower than nuclear DNA, and is visible in electron micrographs of intact cells as a filamentous component in the mitochondrial matrix, in some cases in contact with a membranous body. In surface-spread preparations, M-DNA molecules are 4 to 4.5 μ in length, capable of existing either in linear or circular form because of the presence of sticky single-stranded ends. Petite strains show cytoplasmic inheritance of slow growth and deficient respiration; they lack cytochromes a and b, and their mitochondria are abnormal in structure. Petites arise spontaneously, but can be induced with nearly 100% efficiency with acriflavin. DNA base ratios of cytoplasmic petites may differ markedly from those of normal cells; this fact, plus the high induction rate, indicate that petites are not the result of point mutations of M-DNA, but rather involve a much more drastic alteration. When grown under anaerobic conditions, mitochondria of normal yeast lose their cristae and respiratory enzymes. Return to an O_2-rich environment induces a rapid synthesis of M-DNA, followed by synthesis of respiratory enzymes, and reappearance of cristae. Isolated mitochondria incorporate labeled deoxynucleoside triphosphates into DNA, an observation which strongly suggests M-DNA is made *in situ*, rather than merely being appropriated from elsewhere in the cell.

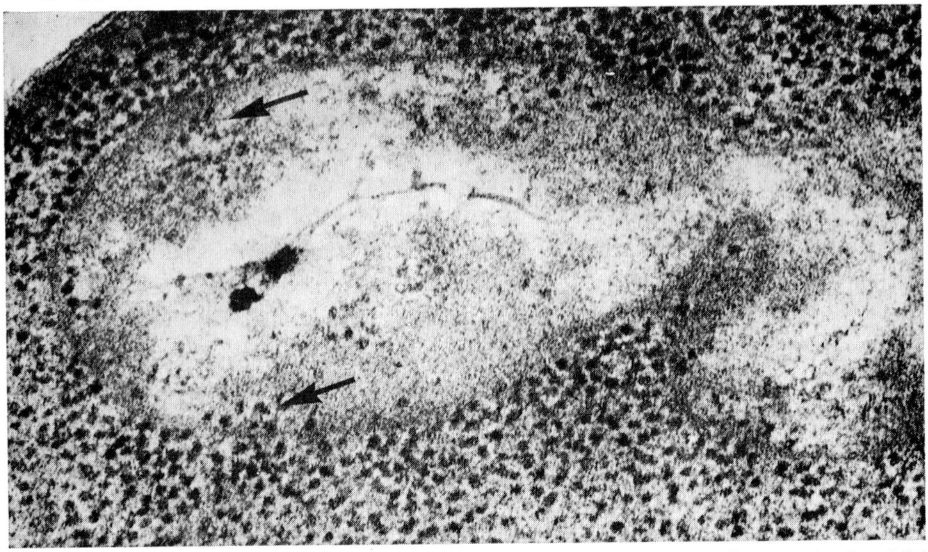

Fig. 9. Mitochondrion of a yeast cell grown aerobically. The arrows point to mitochondrial ribosomes. ×140,500

Mitochondrial RNA. Electron microscopy of yeast mitochondria demonstrates a small-particle component in the matrix area, slightly smaller than cytoplasmic ribosomes, but resembling them in the ability to bind uranyl ions. They are less regular than cytoplasmic ribosomes, possibly as a result of fixation difficulties (Fig. 9). They were apparently first seen in frozen-dried yeast preparations by Mundkur, and are now known to exist in the mitochondria of a wide variety of animals and plants (Swift; André and Marinozzi). Their ability to bind uranyl ions is removable by RNase (Swift et al. 1964).

RNA extracted from yeast mitochondria by Wintersberger (1966b) and run on sucrose gradients, showed the presence of three molecular species, sedimenting at about 23S, 16S and 4S. Somewhat similar values (22.4S, and 17.8S) were found by Rogers et al., although the presence of an additional peak at 12.7S was also reported. The distribution of S values for mitochondrial RNAs is also shown in Fig. 10, taken from recent work by Fauman and Rabinowitz. The mitochondrial RNA is clearly distinguishable from the RNA of yeast ribosomes, which peak at about 26S and 17.5S, and thus cannot be due to ribosome contamination. It is interesting that the S values for yeast mitochondria closely resemble those for *E. coli*, when RNAs from the two sources are cosedimented (Fig. 11). The possibility that bacterial contamination is responsible for these components seems unlikely, however, as no bacteria were detected in electron micrographs of mitochondrial pellets. The possible role of bacterial contamination in studies of mitochondrial protein synthesis is discussed below. Mitochondrial RNA from *Neurospora* (Rifkin et al.), rat liver (Kroon 1968), and hamster cell cultures (Dubin) has also been shown to contain similar fractions attributable to mitochondrial ribosomes and distinguishable by their S values from the cytoplasmic ribosomes of the same cells.

Evidence for the presence of RNA synthesis in isolated yeast mitochondria was obtained by Wintersberger (1966b). Mitochondria were incubated for 1 hr in a medium containing sucrose, EDTA, magnesium ions, and nucleoside triphosphates. H^3-labeled ATP was incorporated into RNA sedimenting in the regions of the mitochondrial ribosomal RNAs, and also prominently in the 4S region. These studies indicated the presence of RNA polymerase enzymes in yeast mitochondria capable of incorporating nucleoside triphosphates into 23S, 16S and 4S RNAs. It is also of interest that when mitochondria were pulse labeled for only 15 min, the distribution of labeled RNAs was not in the ribosome region, but instead was largely distributed between the 16S and 4S peaks. This rapidly labeled heterogeneous RNA also differed from the fraction labeled for 1 hr, in that its synthesis was more strongly inhibited by actinomycin C. It was also much less stable, possessing a half life, in the presence of actinomycin, of only about 15 min. This rapidly labeled and unstable RNA component thus bears some similarity to messenger RNA from bacterial cells, but more work is obviously needed before its role is clear.

Yeast mitochondrial RNA has also been shown to contain the amino acid acceptor activity characteristic of transfer RNAs. When mitochondrial RNA was incubated with

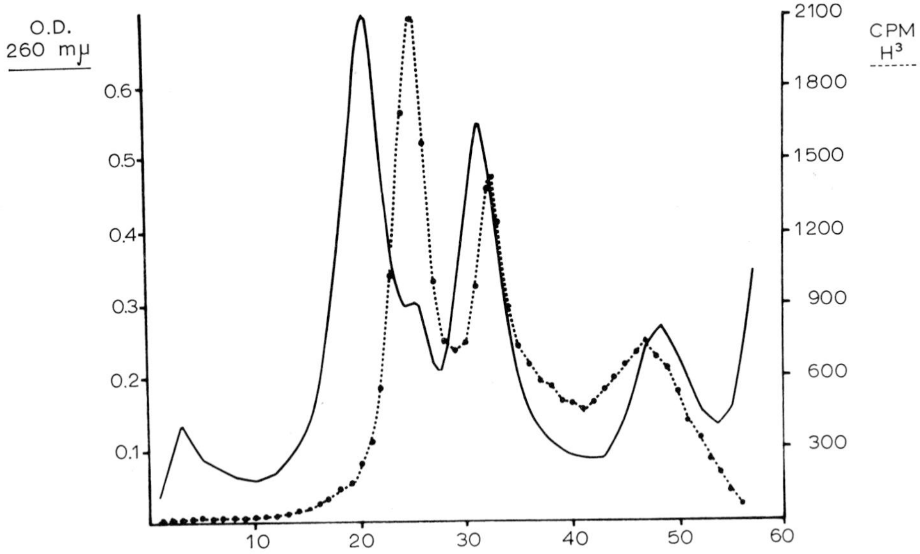

Fig. 10. Sedimentation profiles of yeast mitochondrial RNA and whole cell RNA. Dotted line: RNA isolated from mitochondria of H^3 adenine-labeled cells, showing 22S, 15S and 4S components. Solid line: whole cell RNA showing 26S, 17S and 4S components. A 4.8 ml gradient was centrifuged for 10 hr at 39,000 rpm, at 4 °C in a 15–30% sucrose gradient. (Data from Fauman et al.)

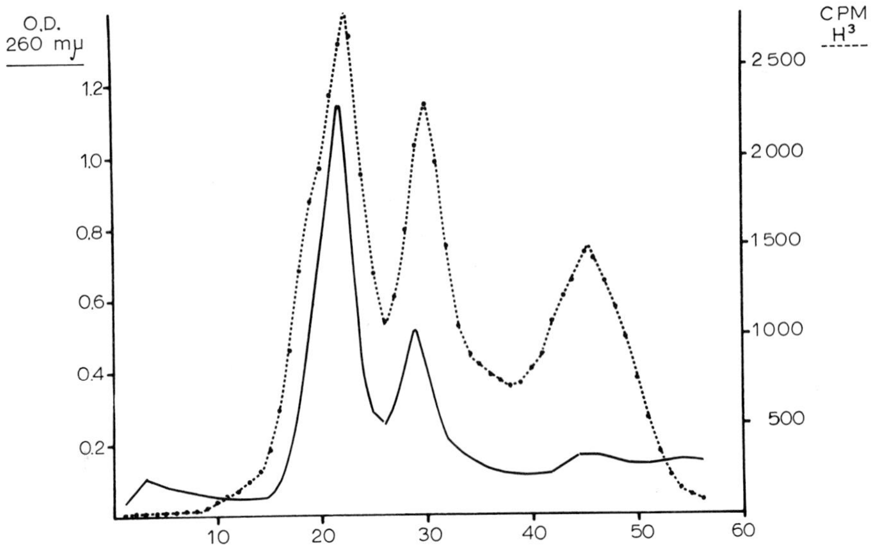

Fig. 11. Cosedimentation of H^3 adenine-labeled yeast mitochondrial RNA (dotted line) and whole ribosomal RNA from bacterial (*E. coli*) RNA (solid line). Note the similarity between sedimentation characteristics of mitochondrial and bacterial RNAs, as compared with those of cytoplasmic ribosomes of yeast (Fig. 10). Conditions similar to those for Fig. 10. (Data from Fauman et al.)

C^{14}-labeled leucine or phenylalanine, in the presence of added yeast aminoacyl-RNA synthetase, both amino acids were bound to the RNA but were removable in 1.9 M Tris buffer at *p*H 8, and glycine buffer at *p*H 10.5. This lability is characteristic of the aminoacyl bond. The amino acid acceptor activity was further shown to reside in RNA from the 4S region of the gradient, and not in 23S or 16S RNA. Wintersberger (1966b) concluded that 'all these data show unequivocally that mitochondria contain an RNA fraction with physical and chemical properties similar to those of hyaloplasmic transfer-RNA'. Other studies (Wintersberger 1965) showed the presence of aminoacyl-RNA synthetase enzymes within the soluble proteins of yeast mitochondria, as also shown in *Neurospora* by Barnett et al.

A question of obvious importance concerns the origin of these mitochondrial RNA fractions: whether they are synthesized on M-DNA templates, or, as seems likely for some mitochondrial proteins, are derived from the surrounding cytoplasm. Studies on the extent of DNA-RNA hybridization between mitochondrial and extramitochondrial nucleic acids were made by Fukuhara, using the nitrocellulose filter method of Gillespie and Spiegelman. Whole cell DNA was separated into two fractions, M-DNA and nuclear DNA, on the basis of buoyant density in cesium sulfate.

Yeast cells were given P^{32} phosphate and then for additional hybridization experiments the $P^{32}O_4$-labeled cultures were 'chased' for 3 hr with cold phosphate, so that only stable RNA was labeled. The cytoplasmic components were divided by centrifugation into two fractions, one containing cytoplasmic ribosomes, and the other the mitochondria plus contaminating cell membrane material. M-DNA showed no significant hybridization with cytoplasmic ribosomal RNA, but RNA from the mitochondria-plus-membrane fraction was bound in significant amounts. Nuclear DNA hybridized with both fractions about equally. These experiments show that stable ribosome-like RNA from the mitochondrial fraction forms significant hybridization to M-DNA. They also indicate that M-DNA has no detectable homology with the RNA of cytoplasmic ribosomes. The fact that nuclear DNA showed significant binding to the mitochondria-plus-membrane fraction may be due either to the membrane contaminants, or to real homologies between mitochondrial and nuclear DNA. Better separation methods for mitochondrial RNA are required.

Studies on yeast mitochondrial RNA have so far demonstrated the clear presence of ribosomal RNAs with sedimentation values of about 24S and 17S. Evidence for transfer RNA has also been provided, as well as indications of a rapidly labeled, unstable fraction of intermediate size that thus possesses some characteristics of messenger RNA. Other RNA fractions in the region between 17S and 4S have been reported from sucrose gradients of whole mitochondrial RNA, but the nature of these components has yet to be determined. Hybridization experiments have clearly implied that M-DNA does not code for the RNA of cytoplasmic ribosomes, but does code for RNAs that probably derive from mitochondrial ribosomes. Isolated yeast mitochondria incorporate labeled ATP into RNA in the presence of riboside triphosphates. They thus contain an RNA polymerase. The formation of aminoacyl-RNA in isolated mitochondria also indicates the presence of synthetase enzymes. Similar enzymes have been extensively studied in *Neurospora*, as discussed below.

Protein synthesis. Isolated yeast mitochondria were shown to incorporate C^{14} leucine and phenylalanine into their proteins (Wintersberger 1965). Mitochondria were incubated for 1 hr at 37 °C in a medium containing saccharose, Tris buffer, EDTA, magnesium chloride and potassium chloride in addition to the labeled amino acid. When mitochondrial proteins were fractionated, almost all of the radioactivity was found in fractions insoluble in 9% Triton X 100 (so-called 'structure protein'). A very few counts were in the soluble proteins of the mitochondrial matrix. The incorporation was inhibited by anaerobic conditions or the addition of KCN, and thus appeared to be dependent upon functional oxidative metabolism. It was also inhibited by acriflavin, chloramphenicol, puromycin, and actinomycin, but unlike the usual cytoplasmic protein forming system, was not inhibited by RNase, presumably because it failed to penetrate the mitochondrial membranes.

Distinction between cytoplasmic and mitochondrial protein synthesis in intact cells has also been demonstrated with chloramphenicol. Amino acid incorporation into yeast cytoplasmic ribosomal systems is relatively unaffected (So and Davie) while mitochondrial protein synthesis, like bacterial systems, is markedly inhibited by the antibiotic (Clark-Walker and Linnane). Chloramphenicol and several other antibiotics known to inhibit bacterial protein synthesis (tetracycline, erythromycin, carbomycin, spiramycin, oleandomycin, lincomycin) were found also to induce the partial or total loss of cytochromes $a+a_3$ in yeast cultures, although the cells could continue to grow and synthesize cytoplasmic proteins if they were provided with glucose as a source for fermentation. These findings, like those of Wintersberger, are interpreted as demonstrating the presence of two distinct protein-forming systems in the cell, cytoplasmic and mitochondrial, distinguishable by their respective insensitivity and sensitivity to antibiotic inhibition.

Thomas and Wilkie have isolated several spontaneously occurring mutants where the sensitivity to particular antibiotics has been lost. That these mutations involve mitochondria is indicated by the fact that petite mutants arising from resistant strains often show a concomitant loss in the resistance character. This is presumably because a portion of the M-DNA is deleted which influences both the synthesis of cytochrome proteins and antibiotic resistance. Strains of normal yeast, sensititive and resistant to erythromycin, spiramycin, and puramycin have been isolated. Two and three character crosses were made, and the zygotes grown into diploid clones, which were tested for their antibiotic sensitivity. The presence of large numbers of stable recombinants was reported. In nearly all cases, cells in one clone were phenotypically homogeneous. The authors conclude that the stability of recombinant strains produced implies there has been true recombination of genetic material between mitochondria from different parental strains. This seems an intriguing finding, suggesting that a genuine genetic analysis of the mitochondrial protein forming system may be conceivable provided suitable genetic markers are obtainable. As discussed below, evidence for similar recombination in *Neurospora* heterokaryons is lacking, but this may be attributable to the absence of suitable markers. Thomas and Wilkie postulate that recombination in yeast may be facilitated by changes in membrane structure induced by anaerobiosis.

Conclusions. Yeast cells, which have supplied one of the first clear indications of cytoplasmic inheritance, continue to provide important material for the exploration of genetic and biosynthetic properties of mitochondria. The following points have been discussed above: (1) Yeast mitochondria contain an endogenous protein forming system, including unique species of DNA, ribosomes, transfer RNA and possibly also specific messenger RNAS. M-DNA codes for at least some of the mitochondrial RNA, but not for the extramitochondrial RNA of the ribosomes or transfer RNA of the cytoplasm. The presence within mitochondria of RNA and DNA polymerases and synthetases has also been described. (2) Because of their active fermentative abilities, yeast cells are well suited to studies of factors controlling the cytochrome system. Alterations in M-DNA, induced by acriflavin, ethidium bromide, 5-fluorouracil, or UV irradiation, produce slow growing 'petite' colonies, lacking cytochromes $a + a_3$ and b, but not cytochrome c, which possesses a structural gene in the nucleus. The petite characters show cytoplasmic inheritance; they are associated with major shifts in base ratios of M-DNA and thus are not simple point mutations. Mitochondrial structure in petite cells is abnormal. (3) Readily reversible changes in all cytochromes and other respiratory enzymes are induced by subjecting normal yeast to conditions of strict anaerobic growth. Mitochondria are reduced in number, lose cristae, and their limiting membranes may no longer 'stain' with permanganate if exogenous fatty acids are not provided in the medium. Restoration of oxygen results in an immediate acceleration of M-DNA synthesis, and the rapid formation of respiratory enzymes and return of normal mitochondrial morphology. (4) Chloramphenicol and other antibiotics selectively inhibit mitochondrial protein synthesis, but do not suppress cell growth. They may induce a temporary loss of mitochondrial cristae and in cytochromes $a + a_3$. Strains of yeast cells that are resistant to certain antibiotics have been isolated, the factors for sensitivity and resistance are thought to occur in M-DNA. These factors show patterns of segregation suggestive of recombination events within M-DNA.

(c) *Neurospora mitochondria*

Genetic analysis. From genetic analysis over the past twenty-five years, over 200 chromosomal genes for biochemical and morphological characters are now known for *Neurospora crassa.* A very few traits, mostly involving slow growth and defective respiration, show patterns of non-chromosomal inheritance. *Neurospora* is haploid, except for the zygote nucleus, and is heterothallic, so that reciprocal crosses are possible between the small asexual spores (conidia) and larger female protoperithecia, provided they are of opposite mating type. Cell fusion of conidia and protoperithecia is followed by nuclear fusion to form the zygote. Subsequent meiosis produces the well-known arrays of eight haploid ascospores in the perithecia, bearing the ordered products of chromosomal segregation. Asexual reproduction can take place by direct germination of conidia. Also, two haploid hyphae can fuse to form a heterokaryon where the haploid nuclei of the two parental types exist side by side in a common cytoplasm but do not fuse. Heterokaryons can again give rise to homokaryons via conidia, where nuclei are again all of one kind.

In a study of spontaneous slow-growing mutants, Mitchell and Mitchell isolated three strains (mi-1 or 'poky', mi-3, mi-4) that were deficient in cytochromes a and b, with cytochrome c markedly increased, and which often possessed depressed levels of succinic oxidase and cytochrome oxidase. When reciprocal crosses were made with poky, the trait was transmitted to all progeny where poky was the protoperithecial (maternal) parent, but when poky was the conidial parent, no transmission was obtained. Similar results were found by Srb in a strain (SG) isolated after acriflavin treatment, where spores, both conidia and ascospores, germinated more slowly, although later growth was apparently normal. The SG character was passed on to 100% of the progeny, provided it was the protoperithecial parent. Extensive analysis with nuclear marker genes showed normal 2:2 segregation in meiosis for all seven linkage groups so that the SG character was unmappable on any chromosome. When heterokaryons were produced by hyphal fusion with genetically marked normal strains and homokaryons later isolated, the SG character could be recovered in association with either nuclear type. These results are thus similar to those obtained with suppressive petites by Wright and Lederberg. In other hyphal fusion experiments SG could even be passed into other species of *Neurospora*, *N. sitophila* and *N. tetrasperma*. In hyphal fusion experiments between mi strains, Pittenger found that poky/mi-3 crosses still maintained slow growth and the phenotype of either parent. Poky/mi-4 crosses at first grew at normal rates, but later resumed the mutant characters indicating that no stable recombinant had been produced.

The consistent maternal inheritance patterns shown by poky and SG are of interest, since they imply that mitochondria from the conidia may not survive once they have been incorporated into the protoperithecium. Electron micrographs of microconidia clearly demonstrate the presence of mitochondria (Lowry et al.).

Two additional spontaneously arising strains (abn-1 and abn-2), one derived from an inositol requiring culture, the other from wild type, were characterized by poor viability and slow growth, finer hyphae, absence of aerial branches, and the presence of needle-like intracellular protein crystals (Garnjobst et al.). The cytochrome pattern was also abnormal, with cytochrome b low or absent, and cytochrome c markedly elevated. In spite of the altered levels in respiratory pigments, oxygen consumption was about normal, as has also been described for mi-3. The mitochondria of abn-1 were atypical; electron micrographs showed few cristae (Tatum and Luck). Conidia from abn-1 and abn-2, crossed with wild type protoperithecia produced all normal progeny. The reciprocal cross could not be made, since the abnormal strains, as also in mi-4, could not produce functional protoperithecia. Heterokaryons were made, however, by hyphal fusion, with a microconidial strain bearing nutritional markers. Results were variable, but in a few cases it was possible to isolate microconidial strains bearing growth characteristics of abn-1, demonstrating non-nuclear transference of the character.

The most direct indication that mitochondrial defects were responsible for the slow growth and characteristic cytochrome imbalance of these strains, came from microinjection experiments. Utilizing methods developed by Wilson, cell fractions isolated from abn-1 were injected into single hyphae of wild type strains. Mitochondria were purified on sucrose density gradients, and small aliquots were injected by micropipette and micromanipulator, into a hyphal cell compartment close to a septum, so that material could be forced through the septal pore into an adjacent undamaged cell. In a number of cases this procedure resulted in the successful transfer of abn-1 characters, including slow growth and abnormal cytochrome patterns, into the wild type strain. The transfer of nuclei bearing nutritional markers complementary to the host cells produced no effect, nor did injections of isolated DNA. These experiments obviously do not conclusively prove that the genetic system within the mitochondria is responsible for the transferred characters, since it is possible that another infective agent could be present in mitochondrial suspensions. But the assumption that mitochondria themselves are responsible for the transmission of the abn-1 phenotype seems fully consistent with other studies on cytoplasmic transmission of mitochondrial characters.

Mitochondrial DNA. The DNA associated with mitochondria of *Neurospora crassa* contains a major component in cesium chloride gradients with a buoyant density of 1.702 and a minor component of 1.698. Nuclear DNA has a higher GC ratio, with a buoyant density of 1.713 (Luck and Reich; Reich and Luck). Preparations of M-DNA spread for electron microscopy showed only linear molecules, one of which was 6.6 μ in length. Attempts to follow M-DNA replication by N^{15}-labeling and ultracentrifugation after the method of Meselson and Stahl were not entirely successful. Synthesis of M-DNA was not synchronized and the large pool size of N^{15} in relation to the amount of M-DNA present made it impossible to chase heavy isotope with N^{14} at a specific time. Nevertheless, evidence for hybrid N^{14}-N^{15} DNA was obtained and also indications that heavy DNA molecules remained intact during cell growth. The physical continuity of DNA molecules during mitochondrial replication was thus established. Also, it was evident that the N^{15} pool size for nuclear DNA was much more restricted, so that M-DNA and nuclear DNA are clearly metabolically independent, and the possibility of any simple precursor-product relationship between them is excluded.

M-DNA of *Neurospora sitophila* was shown to have a major density peak at 1.692, with a minor peak at 1.701, thus readily distinguishable from the 1.702 and 1.698 peaks of *N. crassa* M-DNA. It was also shown that the poky mutant possessed the characteristic 1.702 and 1.698 densities of *N. crassa*. In crosses between poky as the protoperithecial parent and conidia from *N. sitophila* all progeny were poky, with DNA densities characteristic of *N. crassa*. However, when protoperithecia were from *N. sitophila* and conidia from *N. crassa*, all progeny showed the 1.692 and 1.701 peaks characteristic of the maternal parent (Reich and Luck). These observations show that M-DNA follows the same patterns of maternal inheritance shown for poky and other mi mutants, and also for SG and abn-1 and -2.

Mitochondrial RNA. Ribosome-like particles within matrix areas of *Neurospora* mitochondria are clearly visible in electron micrographs of both normal (Luck 1965) and abn-1 strains (Tatum and Luck). The RNA components of the mitochondrial ribosomes were further characterized by Rifkin et al. Mitochondria were purified on sucrose gradients, and sedimentation characteristics of the phenol-cresol extracted RNA were determined. Mitochondrial RNA showed three clear peaks on sucrose density gradients at 25S, 19S and 4S, when run at low salt concentrations, somewhat resembling the yeast sedimentation profile shown in Fig. 10. Cytoplasmic ribosomes showed peaks at 28S and 18S under similar conditions. Base ratios were determined (Table 1),

TABLE 1

Nucleotide composition of ribosomal RNAs from mitochondria and cytoplasm of *Neurospora* (Data from Rifkin et al.).

Source of RNA	Moles per cent				
	C	A	U	G	G+C
Mitochondria					
Fast component (25S)	15.0 ± 0.4*	33.9 ± 0.1	31.9 ± 0.4	19.1 ± 0.4	34.1 ± 0.5
Slow component (19S)	16.0 ± 0.1	31.8 ± 0.1	31.7 ± 0.3	20.4 ± 0.5	36.4 ± 0.5
Cytoplasm					
Fast component (28S)	21.9 ± 0.2	24.8 ± 0.1	23.9 ± 0.1	29.4 ± 0.2	51.3 ± 0.3
Slow component (18S)	21.6 ± 0.1	25.3 ± 0.1	25.4 ± 0.3	27.7 ± 0.4	49.3 ± 0.4

* Mean and standard error of 4 to 6 determinations.

and demonstrate that both slow and fast components of mitochondrial ribosomal RNA were significantly lower in GC content than in the ribosomal RNA of the cytoplasm. Somewhat similar sedimentation characteristics for *Neurospora* mitochondrial ribosomes were found by Dure et al. and also by Kuntzel and Noll, who reported the presence of polysome peaks in sucrose gradients, corresponding to groups of from 2 to 5 ribosomes. When isolated mitochondria were incubated in medium with C^{14} leucine, and the ribonucleoproteins separated on sucrose gradients, incorporation into protein occurred primarily in the polysome region, an indication that mitochondrial polysomes are active in protein synthesis.

The sedimentation characteristics of ribosome subunits were also studied. Mitochondria were lysed with deoxycholate, and the ribonucleoprotein particles were analyzed on sucrose gradients. Mitochondrial ribosome preparations showed three peaks with S values calculated to be 81S, 61S, and 47S, representing the intact ribosome monomer, and subunits containing the 25S and 19S RNAS, respectively. The values obtained were close to the 81.9S value obtained for cytoplasmic ribosomes, but mitochondrial ribosomes were distinguishable by the fact that subunits dissociated at concentrations of $MgCl_2$ of 2 mM, as compared with 0.1 mM for cytoplasmic ribosomes (Rifkin et al.).

The presence of RNA polymerase enzymes in *Neurospora* mitochondria was demonstrated by Luck and Reich. Isolated mitochondria, when incubated with riboside triphosphates in a medium containing Tris buffer, magnesium sulfate, manganese chloride, mercaptoethanol, phosphoenol-pyruvate and pyruvate kinase, were found to incorporate H^3-labeled GTP into RNA. The incorporation was maximal at 5 min, and showed a gradual decline in acid insoluble counts over the subsequent 25 min. Incorporation of GTP into intact mitochondria was unaffected by DNase or RNase in the incubating medium, doubtless because the enzymes could not penetrate the mitochondrial membranes. The reaction was completely suppressed, however, by actinomycin D or by disruption of mitochondria by deoxycholate. Analysis of the labeled RNA by venom phosphodiesterase and alkaline phosphatase showed GMP distributed throughout the molecule.

In studies on the transfer RNAS and aminocecyl-RNA synthetases of *Neurospora*, the presence of two distinct synthetase enzymes was found for aspartic acid, and also for phenylalanine. This led to the discovery that mitochondria possess a full complement of transfer RNAS and synthetases, forming aminoacyl-transfer RNA with all 18 amino acids tested, and that at least in three cases, both the transfer RNA and its synthetase are clearly unique to mitochondria and different from the corresponding components of the cytoplasm (Barnett and Brown; Barnett et al.). *Neurospora* mitochondria were isolated in large numbers by zonal sucrose gradient centrifugation, disrupted by sonication, and the soluble proteins purified by precipitation in ammonium sulfate. Soluble cytoplasmic proteins were separated from nucleic acids on DEAE-cellulose columns, and similarly prepared. Both cytoplasmic and mitochondrial proteins were fractionated on hydroxylapatite columns, and the C^{14} amino acid acceptor activity was tested in the presence of preparations of transfer RNA from mitochondria and cytoplasm. Two synthetase enzymes for each of the three amino acids tested (phenylalanine, aspartic acid, and leucine) were clearly demonstrated, as determined by their distinctly different elution patterns. Thus in these cases mitochondrial synthetases obviously involve quite different proteins from their counterparts in the cytoplasm. In addition, the mitochondrial synthetases for aspartic acid and phenylalanine showed a marked preference for transfer RNA preparations from mitochondria as compared to transfer RNAS of cytoplasmic origin. This indicates that the transfer RNAS of mitochondria and cytoplasm are also different. It was further determined that added exogenous mitochondrial transfer RNA was not selectively bound or taken up by mitochondria under the conditions of isolation, and that the transfer RNAS in intact isolated mitochondria were not susceptible to enzymatic digestion by phosphodiesterase. The transfer RNAs thus appear to be contained inside the mitochondria as an integral part of the organelle.

The coding properties of leucine transfer RNAs from mitochondria and cytoplasm were also determined, in a study of binding affinities between transfer RNAs and ribosomes in the presence of synthetic nucleotide polymers (Epler and Barnett). The leucyl-transfer RNA prepared from the cytoplasm showed binding affinities to UG and UC copolymers, and also to poly U. *Neurospora* cytoplasm thus contains multiple leucine transfer RNAs, with coding properties similar to those reported for *E. coli.* Leucyl-transfer RNA prepared from mitochondria, however, responded only to poly UC. This affords yet another indication of RNA differences between mitochondria and cytoplasm.

Structure proteins. When isolated mitochondria of yeast, rat liver, or beef heart, have been incubated with labeled amino acids, most incorporation has been found to occur in the so-called 'structure protein' fraction, consisting of membrane lipoproteins with little or no enzyme activity (Chatterjee et al.; Roodyn 1966; Wintersberger 1965). It thus seems a logical assumption that the protein-forming system of mitochondria may be largely directed towards the formation of mitochondrial membrane, upon which the respiratory enzymes, possibly synthesized outside the mitochondrion, may be regularly arranged. The studies of Woodward and Munkres (1966, 1967) and Munkres and Woodward have been directed towards this concept.

Because of their insolubility, structure proteins are difficult to characterize. They may be solubilized at neutral *p*H in 8 M urea, or in highly basic (about *p*H 10.5) or acidic (below *p*H 3) solutions. They readily complex with other compounds; binding with phosphates can reduce solubility, but when bound to other proteins such as myoglobin solubility may be increased. Woodward and Munkres (1967) calculated a molecular weight of about 23,000 as determined by equilibrium sedimentation, and amino acid or tryptic peptide composition. S values in the ultracentrifuge were 2.1 or 2.2, although boundaries were often heterogeneous. Polyacrylamide gels also gave variable results, but usually showed a diffuse pattern. Amino acid analyses showed no unusual features, and in fact structure proteins isolated from nuclei, microsomes, and soluble protein fractions were indistinguishable from those of mitochondria.

Amino acid analyses of structure proteins from poky mitochondria were compared with wild type, and consistently showed lower values for tryptophan and elevated values for cysteine, suggestive of a single amino acid replacement of one residue of tryptophan by one of cysteine per structure protein molecule. Interestingly enough, the same substitution was observed in proteins of nuclei, microsomes, and supernatant fractions.

These findings demonstrate that poky mutants possess altered extramitochondrial as well as mitochondrial proteins. This has suggested to Woodward and Munkres that M-DNA may code for protein that plays an essential role in all membrane systems of the cell, and also exists in a soluble form in the ground cytoplasm. This theory attributes an entirely new role to the mitochondrion, in addition to its accepted function in cell respiration. Verification of this concept presently awaits improved techniques for the isolation and characterization of cell lipoproteins. The interesting recent finding that a fraction of membrane bound RNA isolated from HeLa cell cultures shows specific hybridization to M-DNA, has been interpreted as possibly supporting the concept of Woodward and Munkres (Attardi and Attardi). No amino acid differences were found in comparisons between structure proteins of grande and cytoplasmic petite yeast (Katoh and Sanukida).

Studies on the lipid component of mitochondrial lipoproteins have been conducted by Luck (1963a, b). Mitochondria of a choline-requiring strain of *Neurospora* were labeled by addition of H^3 or C^{14} choline to the medium in logarithmically growing cultures. Logarithmic growth was continued on nonradioactive medium and the mitochondria were isolated at intervals for biochemical analysis or spread on slides for autoradiography. Under these conditions the incorporation was stable during later cell growth, and the radioactivity always showed a random distribution throughout the mitochondrial population. This distribution apparently was not the result of isolation procedures. Pulse labeling experiments for 10 min also provided a random distribution of silver grains among mitochondria. These results are all consistent with an increase in mitochondrial mass in growing cells by growth and division of pre-existing mitochondria. *De novo* formation of mitochondria under these conditions would be expected to produce an unlabeled population, which was not found; the data also do not support the presence of any structural mitochondrial precursors. Further studies (Luck 1965) showed that the phospholipid levels in mitochondrial membranes could be markedly altered by controlling the amount of choline or amino acids in the culture medium. Rates of phospholipid and protein incorporation thus show a partial independence, although the protein components of mitochondrial membranes showed far less variation when measured in terms of enzyme activity. Similar marked alterations in lipid components of mitochondrial membranes occur when anaerobic yeast cells are grown with limiting levels of ergosterol and fatty acids, as discussed above.

Conclusions. Studies on *Neurospora* have added considerable additional evidence for the unique character of the mitochondrial protein forming system. Mitochondrial ribosomes, transfer RNAs and synthetase enzymes all appear specific and unlike those in the cytoplasm. The sophisticated genetic analysis, as well as direct injection experiments, conducted with *Neurospora* leave little doubt that the mitochondrial genetic system is responsible for the handful of traits that show cytoplasmic inheritance of slow growth and defective respiration. But the specific role of M-DNA in producing these abnormal phenotypes is still, as in yeast, unclear.

(d) *Mitochondria of other organisms*

Mitochondrial continuity. Although the studies of yeast and *Neurospora* described above clearly show that mitochondria are conserved from one cell generation to another, there are a number of reports of *de novo* origin of mitochondria from the cell membrane (Gey et al.) or other membrane systems (Robertson; Berger) or in blebs from the nuclear envelope (Brandt and Pappas; Linnane et al.; Bell and Muhlethaler; Pannese). In no case has the origin of mitochondria either *de novo* or from other organelles been adequately demonstrated. The theory that a chromosomal locus for M-DNA may exist, containing a so-called master copy, capable on occasion of producing copies which are then free to invade the cytoplasm and form mitochondria (Wilkie), is presently without any substantial evidence. No evidence for sequence homology between M-DNA and nuclear DNA was obtained with agar hybridization (Humm and Humm) but the technique is so insensitive that roughly a thousand copies of M-DNA would be needed for detection. Indeed, if future hybridization experiments do indicate the presence of M-DNA sequences in nuclear DNA, their function in biogenesis would also need to be established, since their occurrence could be equally explained by chance intercalation. Mitochondria are not infrequently taken into nuclei, either during telophase or as invaginations of cytoplasm which may later rupture, spilling their contents into the nucleoplasm. It is not inconceivable that pieces of M-DNA thus released in the nucleus, might on rare occasions be incorporated into the chromosomes.

The apparent division of mitochondria has been frequently observed in time-lapse motion pictures of mammalian cells (Lewis and Lewis; Chevremont and Frederic), but since mitochondria are also observed to fuse, whether or not such division represents true fission or merely the resolution of an earlier fusion cannot readily be determined. Mitochondrial fission can be followed in certain microorganisms, for example in *Micromonas*, a small chrysophyte flagellate with a single mitochondrion and a single plastid, both of which undergo fission shortly before cell division (Manton 1959; Manton and Parke). Kinetoplast division can also clearly be followed in trypanosomes, as discussed above.

Electron micrographs of mitochondria occasionally show a partitioning, where two inner membranes form a complete septum across the width of the organelle. This was described by Fawcett in rat liver, with the suggestion that the partition might represent a stage in either fusion or division. That this almost certainly is a stage in mitochondrial division has been indicated by Tandler et al. After prolonged riboflavin deficiency, mouse hepatocytes contained mitochondria that were reduced in number and greatly enlarged, in some cases nearly equal in size to the nucleus. On supplemental feeding of riboflavin, the normal mitochondrial number and size was restored within 48 hr. During this period, where mitochondrial number was known to be increasing, numerous profiles of the kind shown in Fig. 12 and 13 were seen. In some cases morphological studies have suggested a more complex form of mitochondrial replication than simple fission. Mitochondrial 'clusters' suggesting stages of mitochondrial growth have been described in liverwort meristems and flagellates (Manton 1961), amphibian oocytes (Ornstein; Massover) and in rat spermatocytes (André). The dramatic changes in mitochondrial morphology that occur during spermiogenesis in many insects deserve detailed consideration with problems of mitochondrial reproduction and biosynthesis in mind (see Bowen; André; Personne; Phillips; Pratt).

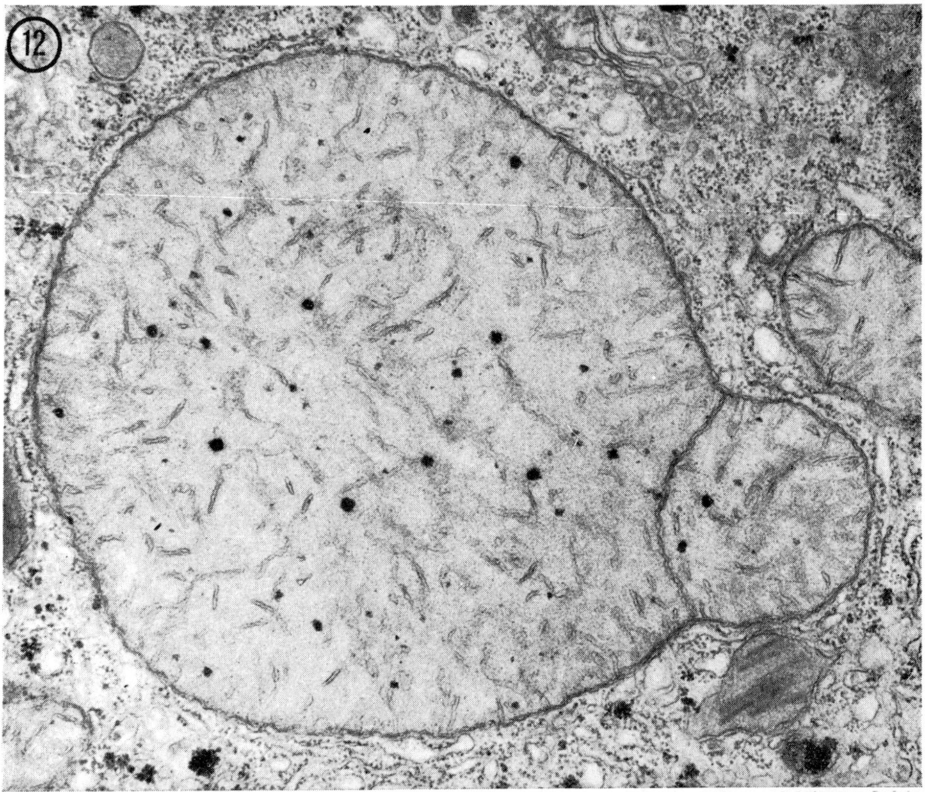

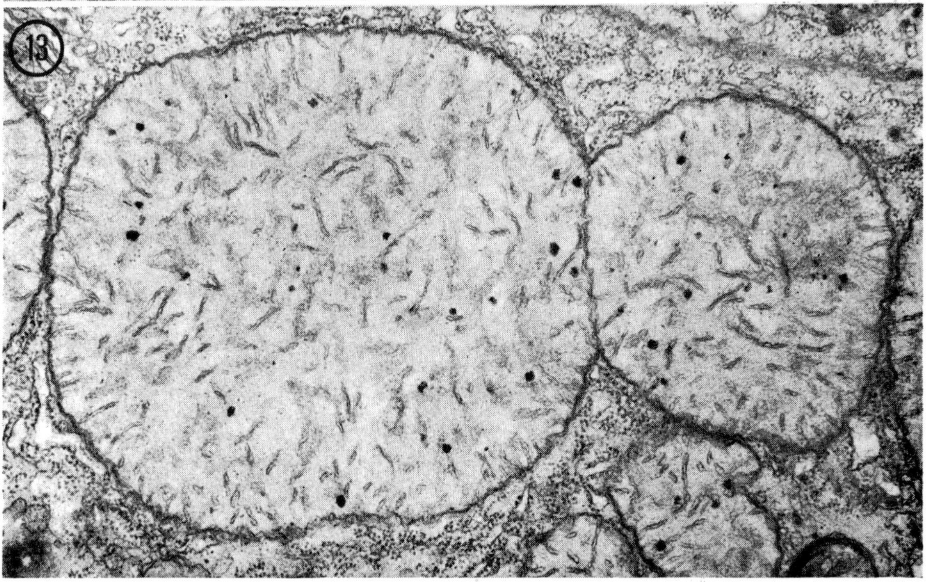

Figs. 12 and 13. Mitochondria from the liver of a mouse fed on a riboflavin-free, high fat diet, followed by 24 hr of supplemental feeding with riboflavin. Enlarged mitochondria, formed as a result of vitamin deficiency, return to normal size following return to standard diet. Mitochondria with partitions are probably dividing. (Micrographs by Tandler et al.). Fig. 12: $\times$ 32,000; Fig. 13: $\times$ 28,500.

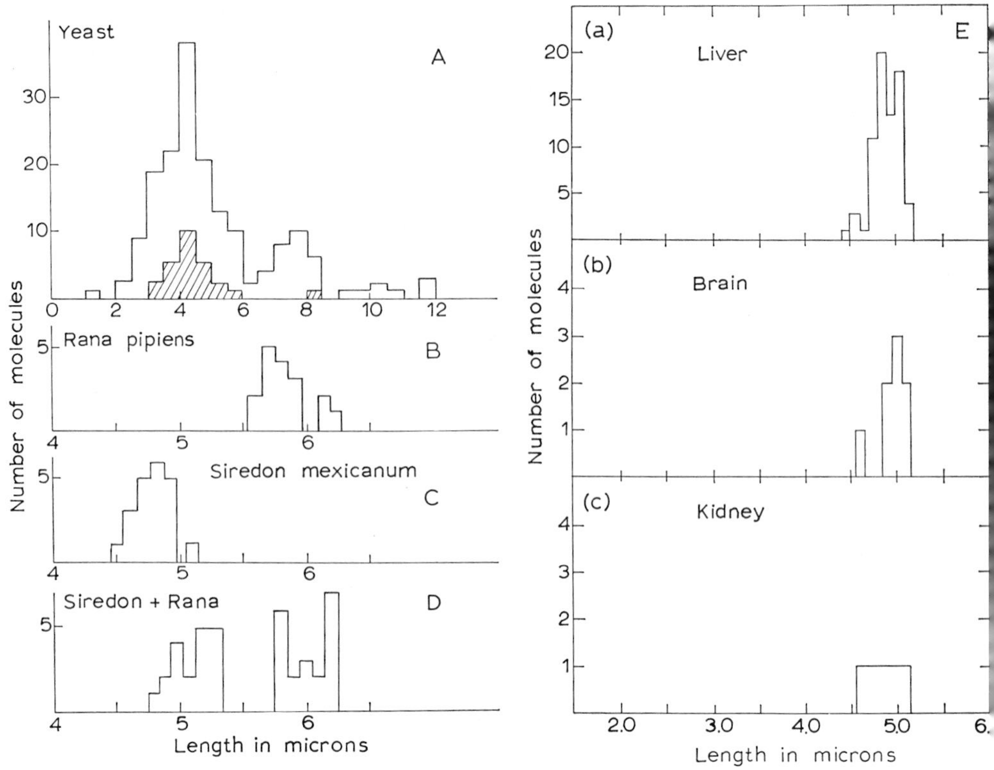

Fig. 14. Lengths of M-DNA molecules as determined on electron micrographs of surface spread preparations. A: Yeast M-DNA as determined by Shapiro et al. Open bars, linear molecules. Shaded bars, circular molecules. B: *Rana pipiens* oocyte M-DNA. C: *Siredon mexicanum* oocyte M-DNA. D: A mixed preparation of *R. pipiens* and *S. mexicanum* oocyte M-DNA. (B, C and D from Wolstenholme and Dawid, 1968). E: M-DNA circles from liver, brain and kidney of mouse. F: M-DNA circles from chick liver, rat liver and beef heart. (E and F from Sinclair and Stevens 1967.)

Most sperm contain mitochondria in the midpiece, associated with the flagellar apparatus, although certain aflagellate sperm lack mitochondria altogether (e.g. in crayfish and crabs; Moses; Langreth). In many cases sperm mitochondria clearly enter the egg cytoplasm (see Cowdry 1924 for review), but they remain attached to the midpiece as a unit, and enter only one blastomere of the cleaving egg. In a few cases, e.g. nereid worms, the midpiece does not enter the egg at all. There is also the possibility that sperm mitochondria may degenerate in the egg cytoplasm, as suggested in the electron micrographs of fertilized rat ova by Szollosi. Continuity of mitochondria during fertilization in plants was reported by Guillermond, but no distinction was made between mitochondria and proplastids. The generalization that fertilization involves a mixing of paternal with maternal mitochondria thus cannot be made. Even where mitochondrial transfer with sperm is established, maternal effects might still be expected because of the vastly unequal numbers of mitochondria in sperm and

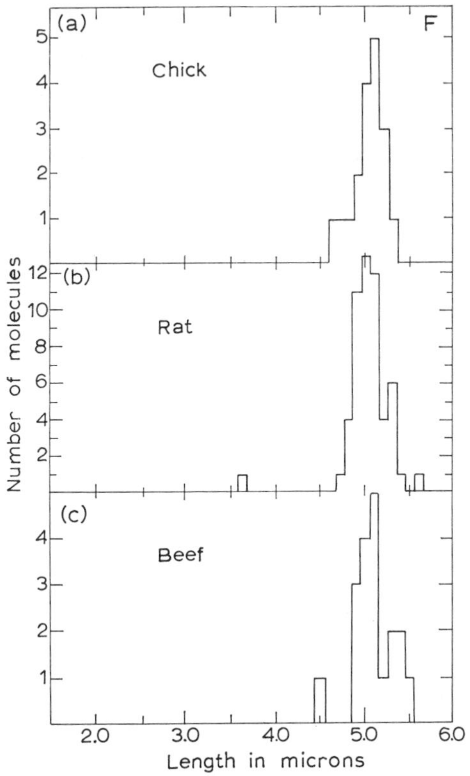

Fig. 14 F

egg.

In summary, morphological evidence for mitochondrial fission is not extensive, but apparently clear in the case of a few microorganisms and in mouse hepatocytes on recovery from vitamin deficiency. Also, sperm mitochondria are transferred to the egg on fertilization in most, but not all, organisms, since in a few cases the midpiece is left outside the egg, or sperm mitochondria may degenerate in the oocyte, or may even be absent altogether. Evidence for mitochondrial origin from cell membranes or from other vesicles or organelles is weak and cannot be considered convincing. The related problem of whether M-DNA is synthesized in the nucleus or cytoplasm is discussed below.

Mitochondrial DNA – Cytochemistry. The first clear demonstration of mitochondrial DNA in higher cells is often attributed to Chèvremont and collaborators (see Chèvremont for review), yet it is hard to equate these interesting findings with our present knowledge of M-DNA. Feulgen-positive bodies, which also incorporated tritiated thymidine and were DNase extractable, were induced in the cytoplasm of chick fibroblasts in culture by a variety of methods. Most effective were 24–48 hr treatments with high concentrations of acid DNase, but similar results were obtained by keeping the cultures at 16 °C for 5 days, and with a mitotic inhibitor, trihydroxy-N-methylindole. No DNA-containing bodies were seen in untreated cells. During the treatment some, but not necessarily all, mitochondria could be observed in time-lapse motion pictures to round up. Such 'transformed' mitochondria could then be shown to be Feulgen-positive but had lost their ability to stain with Janus green B. These events were reversible, with loss of demonstrable DNA, if the cultures were returned to normal media. Results of the treatments were somewhat variable, the transformation not being obtained in all cases, but when present was obvious throughout the culture and thus could not be attributed to an occasional micronucleus or extruded chromosome. Also, unlike nuclear DNA, special fixatives, osmium-dichromate or osmium tetroxide vapor, were required for preservation. Because of its induction by rather drastic means, its instability and the need for special methods of preservation, this DNA component is rather unlike M-DNA studied by other workers. Biochemical and electron microscopic analyses of these treated cultures would be of interest, and the possibility that the transformed mitochondria might be lysosomal in nature needs to be excluded. The presence of DNA in lysosomes may occur through phagocytosis of cell fragments or infecting microorganisms (Swift) and mitochondria can also be incorporated into lysosomes via autophagic vacuoles, a process often enhanced by toxic agents (Swift and Hruban).

In a paper on the structure of genetic elements, Ris (1961) published electron micrographs of fine filaments of 25 to 30 Å in thickness present in certain regions of *Chlamydomonas* chloroplasts. These regions were also shown by Ris and Plaut to be Feulgen-positive. Similar fine filaments were also shown to be characteristic of DNA-containing nucleoid areas of blue green algae and Kappa particles of *Paramecium*. In a subsequent paper (Ris 1962) similar filaments were demonstrated in a mitochondrion of the alga *Micromonas*, leading Ris to suggest that 'the self-dependence of plastids, the kinetoplast and perhaps mitochondria ... is based on their possession of a genetic system (DNA) which determines some of their properties'.

These observations were extended to mitochondria of embryonic chick tissues by Nass and Nass (1963) who showed that the filaments, somewhat like the DNA component of certain bacteria (Ryter et al.) occurred in regions of lower electron density in the matrix areas. They further reported that, if the osmium fixed tissues were subjected to DNase prior to embedding under conditions where much, if not all, nuclear DNA was extracted, the filaments were no longer evident. Similar observations were made on mitochondria and chloroplasts of Swiss chard by Kislev et al. The presence of organelle DNA could be defined cytochemically on tissues fixed for the electron microscope with formaldehyde, and thus possessing little inherent electron density, as that component which bound uranyl ions but was extractable with DNase prior to embedding under conditions known effectively to remove DNA from the tissues. Additional evidence for the DNA nature of this component came from Yotsuyanagi and Guerrier who showed that the mitochondrial filaments, and also nuclear chromatin, stained intensely in onion tissues fixed in potassium permanganate, treated in thin methacrylate sections with RNase, and then stained with uranyl acetate. This staining reaction utilized the property of RNase to form complexes with DNA.

This evidence from electron microscope cytochemistry is consistent, although the techniques of nuclease extraction and electron staining are apt to be capricious and must be subject to careful interpretation. There is general agreement, however, that the mitochondrial filaments on morphological grounds closely resemble prokaryote nuclei, and also that they are extractable with DNase under appropriate conditions.

The presence of filaments has been noted in a wide variety of other plant and animal mitochondria (Figs. 15 and 16). Nass et al. reported fibers from eight animal phyla, and concluded that 'DNA is an integral part of most and probably all mitochondria, although the fibers in some cases are difficult to visualize'. It has been pointed out by several workers (Nass and Nass 1963; Swift; Swift et al. 1968) that filaments were more evident, and probably also more numerous, in embryonic or meristematic cells than in differentiated or slowly growing tissues. This may, in some cases, be a matter of demonstrability. The filaments are difficult to find, for example, in mitochondria of skeletal muscle among densely packed cristae or amid the electron dense matrix characteristic of adult liver, but stand out clearly in the more open mitochondria characteristic of many embryonic cells. The filaments often show most clearly in mitochondria swollen or leached in fixation. Since careful analysis of almost any tissue will usually indicate the presence of filaments, it is very likely a universal component of mitochondria, but because it is often small and relatively inconspicuous, and subject to variations of tissue preparation, its quantitative aspects are difficult to study by electron microscopy.

The number of separate filaments per mitochondrion is difficult to determine. Elongate mitochondria clearly have several areas of clumped fibers (Nass et al.; Rabinowitz et al. 1965; Swift et al. 1968). Surface spread preparations (Nass) have demonstrated up to five separate pieces of DNA in one mitochondrion.

In mitochondria of the slime mold *Didymium* Schuster observed that fibers about 40 Å in diameter, considered to be DNA, occurred in longitudinal bundles within a dense, elongate core 110 to 180 mμ in diameter, arranged parallel to the long axis of the mitochondrion. A variety of other inclusions occur within mitochondria (see Haust for review), but for most of them no relation to M-DNA has been demonstrated. Filaments about 40 Å thick, arranged in tight, even spirals of about 140 Å diameter have been observed in a number of rat tissues, including hepatocytes (Behnke; Blecher; Svoboda and Higginson), astrocytes (Mugnaini) and ameloblasts (Jensen). Somewhat similar spirals, but larger and very electron-dense, have been reported from slime mold (*Didymium*) mitochondria (Schuster). These spirals have been considered as possibly protein (Mugnaini and Walberg) or phospholipid (Svoboda and Higginson) in nature, although Blecher reported their loss from some mitochondria following DNase extraction, and suggested they contain DNA. The spirals are, however, located within cristae and are thus separated from the matrix area by the inner mitochondrial

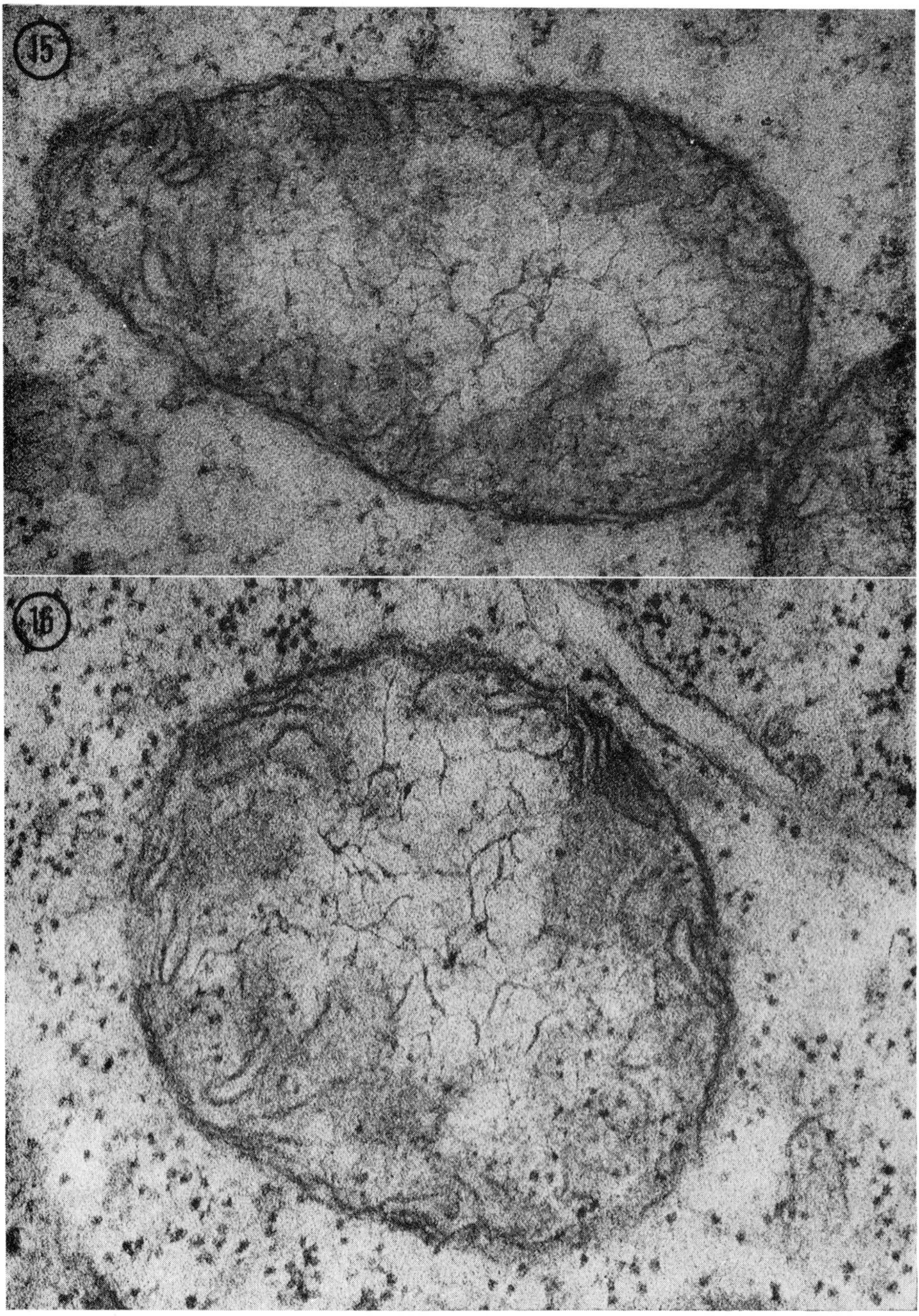

Fig. 15 and 16. Mitochondria from root tip of the broad bean, *Vicia faba*, showing the prominent DNA filaments and mitochondrial ribosomes characteristic of rapidly growing plant tissues. Both micrographs × 65,000.

membrane. They are relatively rare in occurrence, and highly variable in amounts per mitochondrion. Also, at least in some cases such as *Didymium*, membrane bound spirals and DNA filaments in the matrix are both evident in the same mitochondrion. This together with the fact that their dimensions are difficult to reconcile with DNA molecules, makes it seem unlikely that the spirals represent DNA.

Autoradiographs with tritiated thymidine have shown a cytoplasmic label in a small number of protozoan and plant tissues. These studies have been of necessity limited to cells which could be made available to high concentrations of labeled precursor, a situation usually unobtainable for most *in vivo* systems in higher animals. In some cases, for example in amoebae, cytoplasmic endosymbiotes seemed to be involved (Plaut and Sagan; Rabinovitch and Plaut; Wolstenholme and Plaut). In other cases, the label was not removable with DNase, so that incorporation of labeled breakdown products into tissue proteins seemed likely (Takats and Smellie; Lima-de-Faria; Lima-de-Faria and Moses; Steffensen and Sheridan; Muckenthaler and Mahowald).

Autoradiographic evidence for cytoplasmic DNA in higher plants was obtained for fern oogonia by Bell (1959) and Bell and Mulethaler, and for leaves of Swiss chard by Kislev et al. and Swift. In all cases DNase extraction removed some or all of the cytoplasmic label. Bell and Mulethaler demonstrated that the label was associated with cell particulates, but it was difficult to distinguish between mitochondria and proplastids in the permanganate-fixed tissues used. Much of the label in all three studies on higher plants was probably attributable to plastids. In a study on the slime mold *Physarum*, Guttes and Guttes demonstrated a clear acid insoluble, DNase extractable, label over mitochondria.

The most complete autoradiographic studies of M-DNA have been made on the ciliate *Tetrahymena*. Strains of *T. pyriformis* possess a pyrimidine requirement, and are efficient at absorbing labeled thymidine from the medium. Furthermore, they may be grown in sterile culture. A cytoplasmic, DNase extractable label was shown by Scherbaum. Electron microscope autoradiography by Stone and Miller demonstrated a DNase removable cytoplasmic label, with 73% of the silver grains located directly over mitochondria, and 97% within 1 micron following a 4-hr labeling period (see Fig. 9). Individual animals were followed through three consecutive divisions in cold medium with no detectable loss in cytoplasmic label. The M-DNA was thus shown to be stable over the period of study (about 24 hr). Similar results were obtained on spread cells studied with the light microscope, by Parsons, and Parsons and Rustad. On long presentation time (one population doubling time) silver grains over mitochondria occurred in a Poisson distribution, indicating all mitochondria had participated in DNA synthesis. Short labeling times (15 min) showed a non-random grain distribution indicating DNA synthesis in a small number of mitochondria. Incorporation occurred at all times of the cell cycle, but the rate of incorporation into M-DNA was twice as large during the period of macronuclear DNA synthesis. M-DNA was shown to be stable during four consecutive generations of logarithmic growth. Under the conditions of the formalin fixation used, there was no evidence of label elsewhere in the cytoplasm, for example over the basal granules.

In summary, cytochemical techniques have demonstrated fibers with DNA-like characteristics (uranyl ion binding, DNAse extraction) in mitochondria of a wide spectrum of plants and animals. Mitochondria of a few organisms have been shown to incorporate tritiated thymidine into a stabile, DNase removable component. Incorporation patterns in *Tetrahymena* mitochondria have been shown to differ from those of the nucleus.

Mitochondrial DNA – Molecular studies. M-DNA has now been isolated from a wide variety of animal and plant cells, and its buoyant density determined in cesium chloride gradients. In the great majority of cells, mitochondria possess buoyant densities distinguishable from nuclear DNA, although in a few cases, (*Xenopus*, mouse) the values are almost identical. A collection of characteristic values is given in Table 2. These are only roughly comparable, because of differences in technique and computation. One can conclude, however, that in most cases values are roughly similar within major taxonomic groups, and also that nuclear DNA and M-DNA appear to vary independently. Thus fungi (yeast, slime mold, *Neurospora*) show density values for M-DNA below that of nuclear DNA, while in higher plants (onion, bean, turnip, sweet potato) they are considerably higher. Also, amphibia and mammals possess values for M-DNA and nuclear DNA of roughly equal density, whereas values for birds (chick, duck, pigeon) all show M-DNA of higher GC content than nuclear DNA. Such patterns would be expected from conservative evolutionary changes in base ratio possibly occurring as slow random drift, in two independent genetic systems. It is thus in accord with the concept that nuclei and mitochondria contain separate although interdependent DNA replicating systems.

Sequence homologies may be detected between two different DNA samples by the technique of co-renaturation (Britten and Waring). If two samples of different buoyant densities are melted and renatured together, homology is indicated by formation of a DNA hybrid of intermediate density. Such hybrids were obtained between M-DNAS of *Xenopus* and chick (Dawid and Wolstenholme 1968), and *Xenopus* and axolotl (Dawid and Wolstenholme, unpubl.). Hybrids were not obtained between M-DNA and nuclear DNA of *Xenopus*, or between M-DNAS of *Xenopus* and yeast.

M-DNA from all cells of higher animals so far studied is in the form of circles, 4.5 to 6 μ in contour length. This has been observed in Kleinschmidt preparations from nematodes (Wolstenholme, unpubl.), insects (van Bruggen et al. 1967), echinoderms (Pikó et al. 1967) amphibia (Wolstenholme and Dawid 1967, 1968), reptiles (Wolstenholme, unpubl.), birds (Kroon et al.), and mammals (Sinclair and Stevens 1966; Nass; Kroon et al.; Radloff et al.; Clayton and Vinograd). Fresh preparations of M-DNA contain varying proportions of highly twisted or supercoiled molecules, and open circles (Figs. 17, 18 and 19). In the supercoiled form, the two strands of the DNA double helix are topologically interlocked (Kroon et al.; Dawid and Wolstenholme 1967; Clayton

TABLE 2

Buoyant densities of mitochondrial and chloroplast DNAS.

	Nuclear	Mitochondrial	Chloroplast	Ref.
Protista				
Paramecium aurelia	1.689	1.702	—	1
Tetrahymena pyriformis	1.688	1.682	—	1
Trypanosoma equiperdum	1.713	1.690	—	2
Leishmania tarentolae	1.716	1.703	—	3
Euglena gracilis	1.707	1.691	1.686	1
Chlamydomonas reinhardi	1.723	1.712(?)	1.695	9
Chlorella ellipsoida	1.716	—	1.695	1
Amphibia				
Rana pipiens	1.702	1.702	—	4
Xenopus laevis	1.700	1.702	—	4
Siredon mexicanum	1.704	1.695	—	5
Necturus maculosus	1.707	1.695	—	5
Birds				
Duck	1.700	1.711	—	1
Pigeon	1.700	1.707	—	1
Chick	1.701	1.708	—	1
Mammals				
Rat	1.703	1.701	—	1
Mouse	1.701	1.701	—	1
Guinea pig	1.700	1.702	—	1
Rabbit	1.701	1.703	—	1
Beef	1.704	1.703	—	1
Lamb	1.703	1.703	—	6
Fungi				
Yeast	1.700	1.685	—	1
Neurospora crassa	1.712	1.701	—	1
Higher plants				
Onion	1.688	1.706	(1.718)	7
Sweet potato	1.692	1.706	—	7
Cabbage	1.692	1.706	1.695	7
Mung bean	1.691	1.706	—	7
Red bean	1.693	1.707	—	8
Beet	1.695	(1.705)	1.719	1
Swiss chard	1.689	—	1.700	1
Tobacco	1.690	—	1.703	1

1. See Borst, Kroon and Ruttenberg for original references; 2. Sinclair; 3. Simpson, L. (1968c); 4. Dawid; 5. Wolstenholme and Dawid (1968); 6. Kroon et al.; 7. Suyama and Bonner; 8. Wolstenholme and Gross; Sueoka et al.

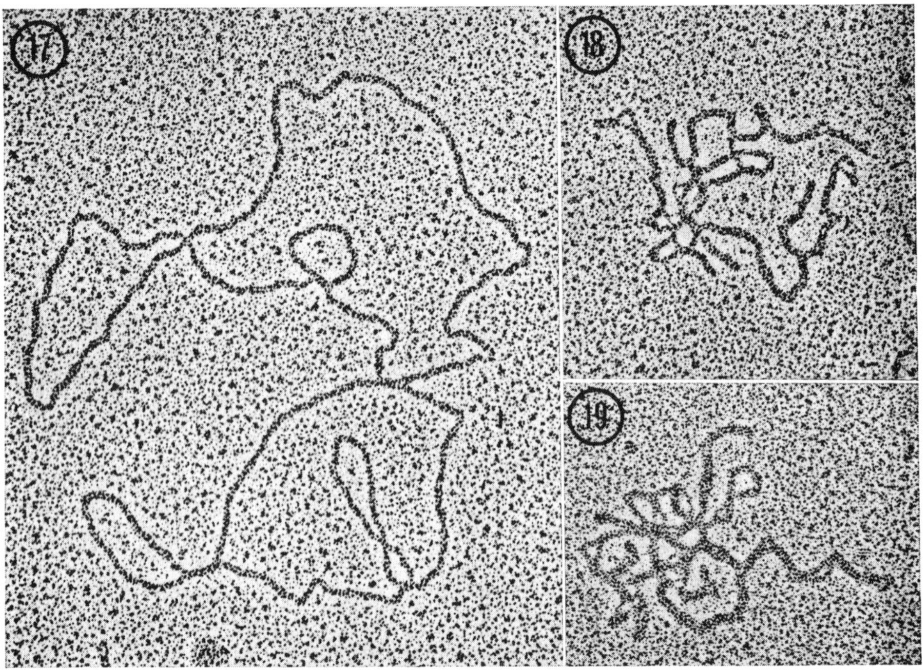

Figs. 17, 18 and 19. Molecules of native DNA from oocyte mitochondria of *Xenopus laevis*, × 78,000. Fig. 17, an open circle of contour length 5.6 μ. Fig. 18 and 19, twisted circles. (From Dawid and Wolstenholme 1967.)

and Vinograd; Pikó et al. 1968). The supercoiling is apparently brought about by a deficiency of turns in the closed molecule such that, in order to complete base pairing, the molecule must twist on itself. As mentioned above for the covalently bonded circles of yeast M-DNA, the supercoiled molecule may be converted to the open circular form by breakage of a single phosphodiester bond in one of the strands, for example by gentle treatment with DNase. The molecule can then swivel about the phosphodiester bond, so that the supercoil is relaxed (see the chapter by Kroon, Fig. 2).

Circular M-DNA molecules which are catenated or topologically interlocked like links in a chain have been isolated from HeLa cells (Hudson and Vinograd), leukemic leucocytes (Clayton and Vinograd) and unfertilized sea urchin eggs (Pikó et al. 1968). The most common form consists of two interlocked molecules, but higher oligomers comprising as many as 7 circles have been recorded. Catenanes account for about 10% of the M-DNA molecules. Double-sized molecules have been found with a frequency of 26% (59% by weight) in DNA extracted from leukemic leucocyte mitochondria; similar forms, however, were not found in M-DNA of HeLa cells or in sea urchin eggs. Double sized circles occur with a frequency of only about 0.1% in M-DNA from rat liver (Kirschner et al., unpubl.).

At present, molecular structure of M-DNA has been studied in comparatively few plants and microorganisms. DNA isolated from *Tetrahymena pyriformis* was found to be linear, the longer molecules having a modal value of about 17 μ (Suyama and Mira). *Neurospora* molecules were also linear. Yeast M-DNA, as discussed above, occurred both as linear molecules 4.5 to 5 μ in length, and as circles formed by hydrogen bonding between sticky ends. M-DNA molecules from the red bean, *Phaseolus vulgaris*, were found to be all linear, varying in length from 1 to 62 μ, having a mean length of 19.5 μ (Wolstenholme and Gross). Mitochondria were isolated from etiolated hypocotyl tissues, and were freed of contaminating nuclear and plastid DNA with DNase. The M-DNA had a buoyant density of 1.707, distinct from nuclear and plastid DNA with DNase. The M-DNA had a buoyant density of 1.707, distinct from nuclear and plastid DNA, and showed the rapid renaturation characteristic of M-DNA.

Both the circular animal M-DNAS and linear M-DNA molecules of yeast and higher plants can be readily reannealed after heat denaturation to native density or to values close to native density (Borst and Ruttenberg; Corneo et al.; Sinclair et al.; Dawid and Wolstenholme 1967; Wolstenholme and Dawid 1968; Wolstenholme and Gross). This behavior has also been found for viral DNAS (Kozinski and Bier; Subirana), but does not occur with nuclear DNA. It is primarily a function of the homogeneity of the M-DNA molecules. However, the topological interlocking of the two intact polynucleotide chains of the supercoiled circles facilitates instant 'snap back' of separated strands of this form of molecule upon removal of the denaturating agent (Dawid and Wolstenholme 1967), i.e. molecules indistinguishable from native supercoiled forms were found immediately after neutralization following alkali denaturation.

The biological importance of circular DNA molecules in animal mitochondria is not clear. The added stability that the circular configuration adds to the molecule was pointed out by Vinograd and Lebowitz. The genetic information that could be carried by a single circular DNA molecule of 5 μ is obviously limited. This length corresponds to a molecular weight of about 10^7 (MacHattie and Thomas). A DNA molecule this size could code for about 25 proteins with an average molecular weight of 20,000 or the equivalent of about 3 sets of both ribosomal RNAS. It is, of course, possible that the DNA molecules in mitochondria are not all identical. As mentioned above, several areas of DNA filaments may be evident in one mitochondrion. Nass ruptured mitochondria on a surface film by osmotic shock, and demonstrated as many as five circles in association with one mitochondrion of rat liver. It is evident, however, that circles within one animal species are all of one size class, when circles from a single tissue or several different tissues are compared (Sinclair et al.). Although differences in circle size between different animal species are slight, a real length difference of 10 to 20% has been demonstrated between anuran and urodele amphibian M-DNA (Wolstenholme and Dawid 1968) (see Fig. 14). If M-DNA circles represent more than one molecular species, then equal size changes would have had to occur during evolution in all the molecules involved.

It is also possible that one circle can contain less than the possible genetic information because of the presence of tandem sequence repeats. Since denaturation-rean-

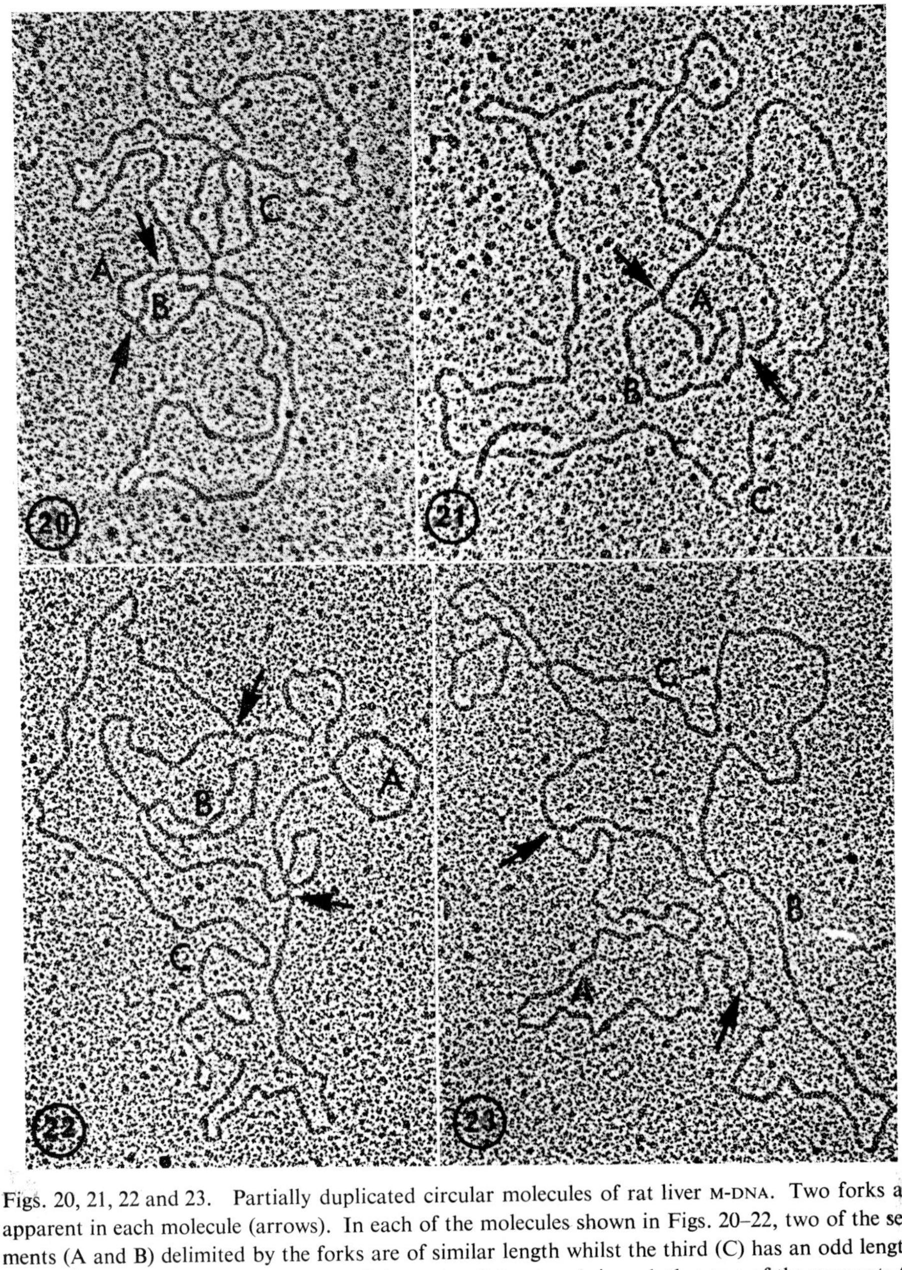

Figs. 20, 21, 22 and 23. Partially duplicated circular molecules of rat liver M-DNA. Two forks are apparent in each molecule (arrows). In each of the molecules shown in Figs. 20–22, two of the segments (A and B) delimited by the forks are of similar length whilst the third (C) has an odd length. In Fig. 23 one possible interpretation of the paths of the strands is such that two of the segments (A and B) are also similar in length whilst the third (C) has an odd length. In each molecule the sum of the lengths of either A or B, plus C equals a length which is within the range of lengths of non-duplicated molecules. The sum of the lengths of A and B, however, always gives molecules which are too short. Figure 20: $A = B = 0.2\ \mu$, $C = 5.0\ \mu$, $A + C = 5.2\ \mu$. Fig. 21: $A = B = 0.5\ \mu$, $C = 4.8\ \mu$, $A + C = 5.3\ \mu$. Fig. 22: $A = B = 1.7\ \mu$, $C = 3.5\ \mu$, $A + C = 5.2\ \mu$. Fig. 23: $A = B = 1.8\ \mu$, $C = 3.3\ \mu$, $A + C = 5.1\ \mu$. All micrographs $\times$ 69,500. (From Kirschner et al.)

nealing experiments on *Xenopus* M-DNA produced double stranded circles with contour lengths indistinguishable from the original preparation (Dawid and Wolstenholme 1968), the presence of tandem repeats seems unlikely, since these would enable smaller circles to form on renaturation. It thus seems likely that in any one animal, the characteristic 5 μ M-DNA circles are genetically identical, and capable of carrying an extremely limited quantity of genetic information.

Since 15 min pulse labeling with DNA precursors in *Tetrahymena* demonstrates a substantial number of mitochondria labeled, and since isolated mitochondria also incorporate DNA precursors, it seems clear that M-DNA must be synthesized *in situ*, rather than be manufactured elsewhere in the cell for transfer to the mitochondrion. A direct indication of DNA synthesis in mitochondria is the finding of open circular molecules apparently in the process of replication. Examination of DNA isolated from rat liver mitochondria showed one molecule in approximately 500 in which two forked regions were apparent (Figs. 20–23). Two of the segments of the filament delimited by the forks were equal in length while the third was either longer or shorter. The length of the duplicated segment differed from molecule to molecule but in each case the sum of the length of one of the similar segments and the length of the odd segment always equaled a length which was within the range of lengths of the unforked circular molecules. Addition of the lengths of the similar segments always gave molecules which were either too long or too short. This is precisely the configuration expected if DNA synthesis proceeded in M-DNA as suggested by Cairns for the large circular DNA molecule of *E. coli*.

Turnover studies on M-DNA have been made on seven rat tissues by Naupert et al. and Gross et al. (see Rabinowitz). In autoradiographic studies on *Tetrahymena*,

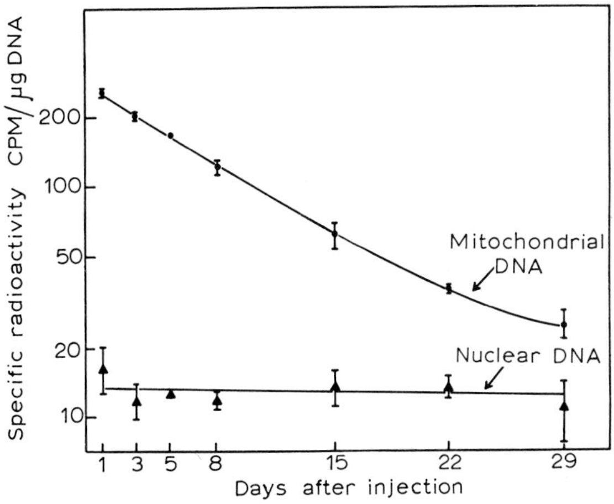

Fig. 24. Relative turnover rates of mitochondrial and nuclear DNA in rat liver. Rats weighing between 200 and 230 g were each injected with 200 μc H^3 thymidine on day 0, and sacrificed at intervals during the next 29 days. The half-life estimate for mitochondrial DNA was 9.4 days; nuclear turnover was negligible during the experimental period. (Data from Gross et al.)

Stone and Miller, and Parsons and Rustad, showed that M-DNA was stable over 3 or 4 cell generations (about 24 hr). It is possible to study retention of label for longer periods in mammalian tissues. Rats were given three hourly intraperitoneal injections of H^3 thymidine and P^{32}, and were then sacrificed at intervals during the next month. The turnover of nuclear DNA in rat liver was found to be negligible during the experimental period. M-DNA, on the other hand, showed an initial specific activity 15 to 20 times that of nuclear DNA, and possessed a much more rapid turnover, with a half-life at approximately 9.4 days (Fig. 24). By comparison, the half-life of M-DNA from heart muscle was 6.7 days, kidney 10.4 days, and brain 31 days. One may conclude that M-DNA has turnover characteristics significantly different from DNA of cell nuclei, and also that M-DNAs from various tissues may possess markedly different turnover times. It is of interest that when the turnover of liver M-DNA is compared with that of mitochondrial cardiolipin, lecithin, and phosphatidyl ethanolamine, nearly parallel values are obtained (Fig. 25). This provides an indication that these components are metabolized at much the same rate, as would be expected if mitochondria were made and

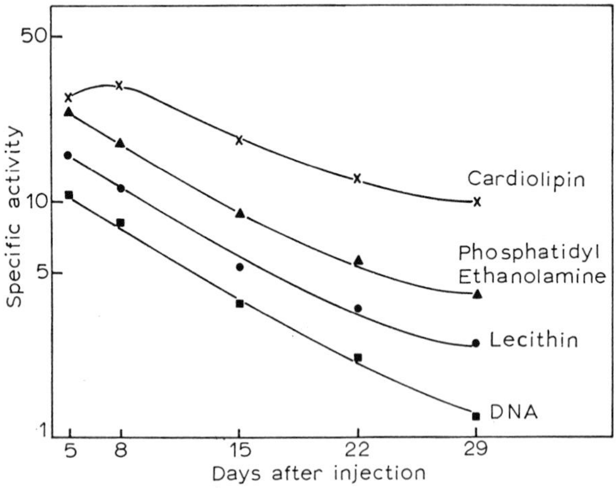

Fig. 25. The turnover of mitochondrial components in rat liver. Animals received simultaneous intraperitoneal injections of H^3 thymidine, P^{32} phosphate and C^{14} glycerol and were sacrificed at intervals over the next 29 days. After the first 8 days, the turnover rates of mitochondrial cardiolipin, phosphatidyl ethanolamine and lecithin are about equal, and similar to that of mitochondrial DNA. (Data from Gross et al.)

lost as specific organized entities, a conclusion also reached by Fletcher and Sanadi, who estimated that liver mitochondria possessed a half-life of 8 days, as compared with estimates for liver nuclei of 350 days or more (Fresco and Bendich; MacDonald). Lysosomes in rat liver and other tissues frequently can be seen to contain mitochondria in varying stages of degeneration (Ashford and Porter; Swift and Hruban). Lysosomes must thus afford a route for the removal and autophagic digestion of mitochondria.

The lack of dependence of *in vivo* incorporation of M-DNA upon the mitotic index and age of the tissue was also stressed by Neubert et al. Rates of *in vivo* thymidine incorporation into liver nuclear DNA and M-DNA were compared for young (60 g) and old (350 g) rats. Although nuclear specific activity decreased with age by a factor of 20, incorporation into M-DNA showed little difference. Thus although nuclear turnover rates seem strongly age dependent, this apparently does not hold true for mitochondria (Table 3).

Evidence for DNA synthesis in isolated mitochondria, in addition to the studies of Wintersberger (1965) on yeast discussed above, has been demonstrated in mitochondria from slime mold *Physarum* (Brewer et al.) and rat liver (Haldar et al.; Parsons and Simpson). In the studies of Parsons and Simpson, mitochondria were isolated from rat liver homogenates on sucrose gradients, washed in 0.25 M sucrose, and suspended in a medium containing deoxynucleoside triphosphates, ATP, nicotinamide, pyruvate, succinate, malate, potassium chloride, magnesium chloride, and potassium acid phosphate. Maximum incorporation of C^{14}-labeled ATP or dATP was dependent on all four triphosphates, the reaction showing a decline in rate after two hours. The system was only very slightly inhibited by DNase, which presumably was unable to penetrate mitochondrial membranes. It was completely inhibited, however, by treatment with strongly hypertonic (1.5 M) sucrose. The DNA was labeled throughout the molecule, as indicated by analysis with micrococcal nuclease and spleen phosphodiesterase. That the incorporation was indeed into DNA, and not into contaminating fractions from nuclei or bacteria, was shown by the ability of the isolated labeled DNA (original density in cesium chloride was 1.701) to melt to a density of 1.715, and to renature to nearly the original density (1.703).

TABLE 3

Incorporation of H^3 thymidine into DNA of mitochondria and nuclei in rats of different ages. (Data from Neubert et al.)*

Animal weight (g)	Organ	Specific activity (cpm/μg DNA) Mitochondria	Nuclei	Ratio mitochondria/nuclei
60	Liver	140	86	1.6
140	Liver	191	71	2.7
	Kidney	87	25	3.5
250	Liver	169	19	9
	Kidney	94	8	12
350	Liver	128	4	32
	Kidney	78	3	26

* Each animal received an intravenous injection of 500 μc H^3 thymidine (6000 μc/μM) 4 hr before sacrifice.

In summary, electron microscopy has demonstrated DNA-like filaments in enough plant and animal species to justify the general conclusion that they are a universal component. They appear in greatest amounts, however, in rapidly growing cells. In a few cases (*Tetrahymena*, *Physarum*) M-DNA has also been demonstrable by radioautography. Studies on base ratios of M-DNA from many sources demonstrate broad evolutionary trends, independent of shifts in DNA. M-DNA exists as circular supercoiled molecules in all higher invertebrates and vertebrates studied, with a total contour length of 4.5 to 6 μ. There may be several circles per mitochondrion, but they are all of one size class per species, and thus there is no evidence for genetic heterogeneity between the molecules of one species. One 5 μ circle could code for about 25 different protein molecules. M-DNA from *Tetrahymena* and bean is linear and apparently of higher molecular weight. Forked molecules, presumably replication stages, have been found in rat liver. Rat liver M-DNA also shows incorporation rates 15 to 20 times that of nuclear DNA, and a much more rapid rate of turnover, with a half-life of 9.4 days as compared to 350 days for nuclear DNA. Incorporation rates of nuclear DNA decrease markedly with age, but no such age dependence occurs with M-DNA. M-DNA turnover is more rapid (6.7 days) in heart muscle, and slower (31 days) in brain. Mitochondria isolated from yeast, slime mold (*Physarum*) or rat liver show *in vitro* incorporation of labeled deoxyriboside triphosphates, and thus contain DNA polymerase. All of these characteristics serve to emphasize the fundamental independence of M-DNA, in metabolic, spatial, and evolutionary terms, from DNA of the nucleus.

Mitochondrial RNA. The presence of RNA in mitochondria has been suspected for many years. A number of workers have pointed out the existence of ribosome-like particles in the matrix areas (Dalton et al.; Mundkur; Luck 1965; Bernhard and Tournier). The RNA content of these particles has been demonstrated by their stainability with nucleic acid stains and sensitivity to RNase or cold perchloric acid extraction (Swift et al. 1964; Swift; Watson and Aldridge; André and Marinozzi). They are clearly more abundant in mitochondria in rapidly growing tissues, such as embryos and plant meristems. They occasionally appear clustered or in rows, but most frequently are sparsely distributed between cristae (Fig. 9; see also Figs. 15 and 16). Electron microscope radioautographs of mitochondrial RNA in the flagellate *Ochromonas*, utilizing H^3 uridine incorporation, have been reported (Gibbs).

Isolated mitochondrial preparations contain variable amounts of RNA (Schneider and Hogeboom; Siekevitz and Watson; Novikoff 1957), and in the absence of any distinguishing features (Rendi; Rendi and Warner; Truman; Elaev 1964) the possibility of ribosome contamination could not be eliminated. The first suggestive evidence for RNAS specific to mitochondria comes from the demonstration of protein synthesis in isolated mitochondria independent of added *p*H 5 enzymes from the supernatant, and susceptible to chloramphenicol and actinomycin D. These findings, as discussed below, strongly implied the presence of an intramitochondrial protein synthesis system different from the cytoplasm (McLean et al.; Roodyn et al. 1961; Kroon 1963). With improved techniques of isolation and purification, the existence of mitochondrial RNAs has now been firmly established. Mitochondrial ribosomal RNAs are slightly smaller, and bacteria-like in their sedimentation characteristics (Fig. 11), and possess distinctive base ratios, as discussed above for yeast and *Neurospora*. Mitochondrial ribosomes from rat liver were described as containing a 55S ribonucleoprotein particle, as compared with 78S of cytoplasmic ribosomes. When isolated mitochondria were incubated *in vitro* with C^{14} leucine, proteins of the 55S particles were labeled; under similar conditions the cytoplasmic ribosomes showed no incorporation (O'Brien and Kalf). This component could not be dissociated into subunits. It is possibly comparable to the larger of the 61 and 47S subunits isolated by Rifkin et al. from *Neurospora* mitochondria, which contained 25S and 19S RNAs, respectively. Mitochondrial RNA sedimenting at 27S, 17S, and 4S has been isolated from hamster cell cultures by Dubin and Brown. These peaks are slightly lighter than the analogous 28S and 18S RNAs of the cytoplasmic ribosomes. Actinomycin D was found selectively to depress incorporation of C^{14} uridine into the 27S component, when added to cultures of intact cells, leading Dubin to suggest that the 17S but not the 27S component is manufactured within the mitochondrion. Ribosomes from rat heart mitochondria were studied by Elaev (1966), who found monosome values of 83S, with 63S and 46S subunits. *Tetrahymena* mitochondria were found to contain only 18S and 14S peaks (Suyama), although the author states that these unusual values may be the result of RNA degradation during isolation. In spite of probable degradation, the 18S to 14S RNA fractions were found selectively to hybridize with M-DNA up to 6.8%, whereas no hybridization was obtained with lighter (4S) mitochondrial RNAs. The presence of mitochondrial transfer RNAs for leucine and phenylalanine, distinct from those in the cytoplasm, have been reported for rat liver (Meyer et al.; Buck and Nass). These reports are thus in agreement with the extensive studies on *Neurospora* transfer RNAs by Barnett and Brown.

The presence of RNA polymerase enzymes has been demonstrated in preparations of isolated mitochondria, by the incorporation of labeled nucleoside triphosphate into RNA. The reaction is dependent on the presence of all four triphosphates. Reports on *Neurospora* (Luck and Reich) and yeast (Wintersberger 1966) are discussed above; essentially similar findings have been obtained with mitochondria of lamb heart (Kalf), pigeon heart and breast muscle, and rat liver, heart, kidney, brain, and Jensen sarcoma (Neubert et al.). That the polymerase was DNA dependent was indicated by the inhibitory effects of actinomycin D, acriflavin, and DNase. Similar results were obtained for ciliate (*Tetrahymena*) mitochondria, where sucrose gradient analysis of the RNA synthesized *in vitro* showed a broad peak with a maximum between 14S and 18S, but little activity in the 4S region (Suyama and Eyer). One cannot conclude from these studies that M-DNA does not code for the transfer RNAs of mitochondria, since limitations may reside in the conditions of incubation. A large incorporation into RNA in the 4S region was obtained by Wintersberger (1966) in isolated yeast mitochondria.

It seems clear from DNA–RNA hybridization studies (Fukuhara; Suyama and Eyer) that M-DNA codes for at least part of the RNA components of mitochondria. That some mitochondrial RNA of mouse tissues hybridizes with nuclear DNA has been reported by Humm and Humm but the methods used have been criticized (Borst et al. 1967). Since actinomycin D differentially inhibited incorporation into mitochondrial 27S but not 17S RNA in intact cultured hamster cells. Dubin suggested that the larger component of the mitochondrial ribosomal RNA but not the smaller, might be of nuclear origin. Evidence that M-DNA might even code for extramitochondrial RNA has been presented by Attardi and Attardi, since membrane-bound polysomes isolated from the cytoplasm of HeLa cells contained a messenger-like RNA which hybridized with M-DNA. It was suggested that these hybrid polysomes composed of mitochondrial message, attached to cytoplasmic ribosomes, might direct the synthesis of structure proteins similar to those described both for mitochondria and cytoplasmic membranes by Woodward and Munkres. Although such indication that a kind of complementation in protein synthesis may exist between mitochondrial and extramitochondrial components are of great interest, the evidence on which they are based is presently too fragmentary to be properly evaluated.

Protein synthesis. There have been numerous studies on protein synthesis in mitochondria, since the early indications obtained by Hultin and Siekevitz that incorporation of amino acids into mitochondrial proteins was an energy dependent process, inhibited, for example, by dinitrophenol. For reviews see Simpson (1962), Roodyn (1965); Kroon (1966); Wheeldon and Lehninger; Haldar et al.; Pullman and Schatz and Roodyn and Wilkie. There have been a number of conflicting reports, particularly concerning the role of contaminating bacteria during *in vitro* incubation (Von der Decken et al.). But the fact that mitochondrial protein synthesis in rat liver is influenced by the physiological state of the animal, e.g. is stimulated by triiodotyrosine following thyroidectomy, or by hepatectomy (Roodyn et al. 1965; Braun et al.), strongly indicates that incorporation is an inherent property of mitochondria. In addition, bacterial contamination with care may be reduced to exceedingly low levels (Beattie et al. 1967a) without interfering with levels of mitochondrial incorporation. Also, incorporation rates are highly reproducible, depending upon the number of mitochondria present, show no lag phase, and are not influenced by penicillin (Kroon 1966; Wheeldon). The ability to synthesize proteins is clearly an endogenous property of mitochondria. It has been reported for isolated mitochondria of rat liver (McLean et al.; Rendi; Truman and Korner; Kroon 1964; Roodyn 1965) as well as rat spleen, kidney, lung, heart, and skeletal muscle. Other tissues studied include frog liver (Roodyn 1965), locust flight muscle (Bronsert and Neupert), sea urchin embryos (Guidice), *Tetrahymena* (Mager), yeast (Wintersberger 1965), and the cow pea, *Vigna* (Das et al.).

Mechanisms of amino acid incorporation into mitochondrial proteins are complex, and not fully understood. They obviously depend upon the intactness of the organelle, as well as the relative concentration of all the endogenous RNA components discussed above. The synthesis and maintenance of mitochondrial ribosomes, transfer RNAS and messenger RNAS requires the presence of nucleoside triphosphate pools, involving the active phosphorylation of different nucleoside mono- and diphosphates. In addition, the transport of amino acids across the mitochondrial membranes is an energy requiring process, as is also the ATP-dependent activation of amino acids, and presumably the GTP-associated formation of peptide bonds as well. These are in turn effected by ion concentration, the balance between internal and external ATP and ADP, and all of the complex interacting processes of mitochondrial phosphorylation, and oxidative metabolism. The specific requirement for oxidizable substrates such as succinate to provide an energy source for protein synthesis, was reported by Roodyn (1965), but Wheeldon and Lehninger found maximal incorporation only required external ATP. It is evident that the mitochondrion approaches in complexity the organization of an intact organism.

Mitochondrial protein synthesis differs from cytoplasmic protein synthesis in its relative independence from soluble components of the cytoplasm and its response to certain inhibitors. Unlike microsomal systems, isolated mitochondria incorporate amino acids into protein in the absence of added *p*H 5 enzymes and ATP. Reasons for this are obvious. As discussed above, intact mitochondria contain their own synthetases, and often also possess endogenous substrates, although added succinate or ATP may be necessary for more prolonged incorporation. Similarly, dinitrophenol at 5×10^{-5} M has no effect on microsomal protein synthesis, but inhibits mitochondrial synthesis through uncoupling of oxidative phosphorylation, thus effecting endogenous energy supplies required for protein synthesis. In some cases, such as the effects of RNase on living cells, the greater sensitivity of cytoplasmic protein synthesis seems to be because the mitochondrial system is protected by membranes through which the enzymes cannot penetrate. Haldar et al. treated Krebs ascites tumor cells with hypotonic media to increase their permeability, and RNase was added to the media. Cytoplasmic protein synthesis was disrupted by the process, but incorporation of H^3 leucine into mitochondrial proteins continued. RNase was similarly ineffective *in vitro* on isolated mitochondria of yeast (Wintersberger 1965). Effects of actinomycin D on intact cells (Dubin) were also reported to produce greater effects on nuclear RNA synthesis than in mitochondria, presumably because of relatively lower permeability to mitochondria. On the other hand, actinomycin D has little or no effect on isolated microsomal protein-forming systems, but can rapidly inhibit protein synthesis in isolated mitochondria of rat liver (Kroon 1963; Wheeldon and Lehninger), presumably because it interferes with DNA-dependent RNA polymerase necessary for the production of short-lived mitochondrial messenger RNAS. Acriflavin, as discussed above, appears to effect M-DNA synthesis in trypanosomes and yeast, and shows a selective uptake by kinetoplast DNA. It also produces a rapid inhibition of protein synthesis in mitochondria of yeast (Wintersberger 1965) and rat liver (Borst et al. 1967) presumably because like actinomycin D it interferes with mitochondrial RNA synthesis.

Of particular interest are the effects of chloramphenicol, which appears to interfere with the formation of functional ribosomes, and of cycloheximide, which apparently disrupts the attachment of ribosomes to messenger RNA. Bacterial ribosomes are known to be sensitive to chloramphenicol, and not to cycloheximide, whereas in eukaryote cells, the reverse is true. When intact yeast cells were treated with cycloheximide, their growth rate was reduced or blocked, but the cytochrome a and a_3 content of mitochondria was normal. Similar treatment with chloramphenicol, as mentioned above, produced a total absence of cytochromes a and a_3 but cell growth continued (Clark-Walker and Linnane). It was concluded that chloramphenicol also inhibited protein synthesis in isolated mitochondria of yeast (Wintersberger 1965) and rat liver (Wheeldon and Lehninger). Mitochondrial protein-forming systems can thus be considered similar to bacteria in their response to these inhibitors.

When isolated rat liver mitochondria are incubated with labeled amino acids, the incorporation is limited almost entirely to the insoluble proteins. Virtually no activity is in soluble proteins, presumably of the matrix, that are liberated into the medium by sonication (Roodyn 1962; Wheeldon and Lehninger). Soluble enzymes isolated from mitochondria (cytochrome c, malate dehydrogenase, and catalase) were unlabeled (Roodyn 1966). Almost all radioactivity has been consistently found in the 'structure protein' fraction, which can be separated from other proteins of the insoluble membrane fraction by solubilizing in deoxycholate, and precipitating with 11–12% saturated ammonium sulfate (Criddle et al.). Some incorporation was also obtained with heart muscle mitochondria into an insoluble lipoprotein with ATPase activity (Kalf and Grece).

Although there is little doubt that structure proteins are major components of mitochondrial membranes, the fraction undoubtedly contains a crude mixture of a number of different constituents. When structure proteins from rat liver mitochondria were studied by polyacrylamide gel electrophoresis, a large number of bands were obtained, several of which were labeled when isolated mitochondria were incubated for 1 hr with a C^{14} protein hydrolysate as amino acid source (Haldar et al.). It has been possible to fractionate structure proteins further, into those of inner and outer membranes. Since the two limiting membranes of mitochondria show different permeabilities, the outer membrane can thus be swollen and separated from the inner membranes and cristae, and then isolated by differential centrifugation (Parsons et al.). Other techniques for separating inner and outer membranes include controlled osmotic lysis, and treatment with digitonin in isotonic media (Schnaitman and Greenawalt). When isolated mitochondria from rat liver were incubated in C^{14} leucine, and inner and outer membranes isolated, incorporation was almost exclusively into the inner membrane fraction. Activity of outer membrane protein was calculated to be less than 5% of the inner membrane, when corrected for contamination utilizing levels of succinate cytochrome c reductase and monoamine oxidase as markers for inner and outer membranes respectively (Neupert et al.). These findings support the suggestion of Parsons et al. that the inner membrane may represent the product of mitochondrial protein synthesis, while the outer membrane may be contributed by cytoplasmic synthesis, related to the formation of smooth endoplasmic reticulum. In addition to the fact that both the morphology and enzyme content of inner and outer membranes show marked differences (Parsons et al.; Schnaitman and Greenawalt), it is also of interest that cardiolipin may be an exclusive component of lipoproteins of the inner membrane.

Since endogenous protein synthesis provides only a small fraction of total mitochondrial proteins, it is obvious that the surrounding cytoplasm must contribute the remainder. The clear evidence that the structural gene for yeast cytochrome c resides in the nucleus is discussed above. In studies on intact ascites tumor cells, Haldar et al. showed that RNase strongly inhibited protein synthesis in the cytoplasm. The inhibition also extended to the cytochrome c of mitochondria, although the synthesis of mitochondrial structure protein was much less affected, as mentioned above. These findings provide an indication that cytochrome c is manufactured by the RNase-sensitive cytoplasmic system, and then transferred to the mitochondria. A much more direct indication of the transfer process was obtained by Kadenbach. Microsome fractions from rat liver were labeled *in vitro* with C^{14} leucine. The labeled microsomes were then incubated with unlabeled mitochondria for 20-min periods. During this time labeled proteins were released from the microsomes and were selectively taken up into both the soluble and insoluble protein fractions of the mitochondria. The reaction required intact microsomes. When microsomal proteins alone were added to mitochondria, there was no uptake. The reaction was energy dependent, requiring an ATP generating system, and apparently also the presence of GTP. It was inhibited by dinitrophenol and KCN.

Indications that soluble and insoluble mitochondrial protein come from two different sources has also been obtained in intact animals by Beattie et al. (1966). C^{14} leucine was administered to rats, and at intervals from 2 min to 8 hr, mitochondria of liver and kidney were isolated and their proteins analyzed. As would be expected from their presumed endogenous site of synthesis, insoluble proteins had the highest activities during the first few minutes, but later the soluble protein fractions increased in activity. Clear evidence that cytochrome c in liver is manufactured first in the endoplasmic reticulum (microsomes) and later transferred to mitochondria has been presented by Gonzalez-Cadavid and Campbell. C^{14} lysine was injected into rats, and the animals were sacrificed after 7.5, 15, 30 and 60 min, and the cytochrome c was isolated from microsomes and mitochondria. Cytochrome c was present in the microsomal fraction in two states, either weakly bound (water-extractable) or strongly bound (extractable with 0.15 M sodium chloride). Specific activity in the strongly bound fraction reached a maximum at 15 min, and then fell to about 50% of maximum by 30 min, while activity of the water extractable cytochrome c increased. Cytochrome c activity in mitochondria rose gradually, reaching a plateau by 30 min. These results suggest that cytochrome c is first tightly bound to ribosomes in the microsomal fraction, and then is held more loosely, possibly because it is released to the cisternal contents. It is then presumably transferred to mitochondria, by a mechanism as yet unknown.

Future research on mitochondrial proteins must concern itself with such mechanisms for the rapid uptake of specific soluble enzymes and other components of the complex respiratory assemblies, and for their ordered arrangement into the structure of mitochondrial membranes. It is evident that in at least some of the mitochondrial mutants of *Neurospora* and yeast, defects in either the uptake or assembly of soluble proteins are involved. Cytoplasmic petites in yeast and the mi mutants in *Neurospora* all have elevated levels of cytochrome c, and yet this component is apparently non-functional because it is not part of a properly ordered mitochondrial array. Another soluble protein of *Neurospora* mitochondria, malate dehydrogenase, has been investigated by Mundkres and Woodward, who have concluded that although the enzyme from poky mutants has normal characteristics when extracted, its function *in situ* is markedly altered by a defective attachment to mutant structure protein. At present it seems as if such complex interaction will ultimately be understood only by a sophisticated combination of biochemical, genetic, and structural analysis, in which the functional integrity of both the cytoplasm and the mitochondrion must be considered.

In summary, the ability to conduct protein synthesis is clearly a property of intact mitochondria. With proper precautions, interference from contaminating bacteria can be eliminated. Protein synthesis entails many energy requiring steps, such as the maintenance and synthesis of mitochondrial nucleic acids, the transport of amino acids across the mitochondrial membranes, amino acid activation, and GTP-linked peptide bond formation. The ultilization of oxidizable substrates or of exogenous ATP is thus required. Mitochondrial protein synthesis is relatively resistant to inhibitors such as RNase which do not penetrate mitochondrial membranes. It is suppressed by actinomycin D and acriflavin, presumably through inhibition of DNA-dependent synthesis of short-lived RNAs. It is selectively inhibited by chloramphenicol, and relatively insensitive to cycloheximide. In these respects it more closely resembles protein synthesis in bacteria than in eukaryotes. Mitochondrial protein synthesis involves the formation of insoluble proteins, presumably primarily of the inner mitochondrial membranes. Most soluble proteins of mitochondria, including cytochrome c, appear to be made on the endoplasmic reticulum, and transferred to the mitochondria by a specific energy requiring process. The formation of endogenous and exogenous proteins of mitochondria thus appears to involve two quite different but equally complex processes. Certain broad outlines are now evident, but many aspects are still unclear.

3. *Chloroplasts*

Chloroplasts appear to have many aspects in common with mitochondria. They are surrounded by two membranes, the inner membrane being continuous with the lamellar system during its formation, somewhat as the inner mitochondrial membrane is continuous with the cristae. They clearly possess genetic continuity, as mentioned in the introduction. The most dramatic recent demonstration of chloroplast division has been provided by time-lapse motion pictures of *Nitella* where repeated binary fission of chloroplasts has been shown (Green). Plastids, like mitochondria, contain DNA, in many cases with a buoyant density different from the nucleus, ribosomes distinguishable in size and composition from those in the cytoplasm, and the ability *in vitro* to incorporate amino acids into protein. Chloroplasts are, unlike mitochondria, of larger size and greater biochemical complexity. They occur in embryonic and meristematic tissues as small, undifferentiated proplastids, which are capable of a number of different paths of development. In higher plants, for example, proplastids enlarge in root tissues into colorless leucoplasts, which may later develop into starch-accumulating amyloplasts. Oil-containing plastids, elaioplasts, are characteristic of some epidermal cells of leaves, and pigment bearing chromoplasts give color to fruit and flowers. Chloroplasts are often of two kinds within one plant, typically with grana in the mesophyll cells of the leaf, but without grana in vascular associated cells. If higher plants are grown in the dark, chloroplast development is arrested at a specific stage which Kirk and Tilney-Basset have called the etioplast. Etioplasts contain prominent crystalloid prolamellar bodies, which possess the red fluorescence characteristic of protochlorophyll (Boardman and Wildman), and may also contain large quantities of RNA (Jacobson et al.). They are capable of a rapid greening process in the presence of light. For a detailed analysis of chloroplast inheritance and biochemistry, see Kirk and Tilney-Basset and various papers in the volumes edited by Goodwin. For other reviews on chloroplast biogenesis see Rhoades (1955), Granick (1955, 1961), Gibor and Granick (1964), Wilkie, Jinks, Schiff and Epstein, Bogorad (1967), Granick and Gibor, and Brawerman and Eisenstadt.

Genetic analysis. It is clear that many of the components of chloroplasts, as in mitochondria, are under nuclear control. Nuclear genes that block the normal development of barley plastids have been studied by Von Wettstein (1959, 1961) utilizing electron microscopy. In the albino-20 mutant, for example, abnormal plastids are produced which, like etioplasts, contain a prolamellar body but develop no further, even though the plants are capable of chlorophyll synthesis. In other mutants mature chloroplasts are formed but their morphology is abnormal. Mutant xantha-15 contains enlarged grana, and in xantha-3 the grana are lacking entirely, in spite of the fact that the ability to synthesize chlorophylls and carotenoids is maintained. In still other mutants the synthesis of chlorophylls or carotenoids is blocked at specific steps. The xantha-10 mutant of barley was totally unable to synthesize protochlorophyll or chlorophyll, and thus the step from protoporphyrin appeared to be blocked. In another barley mutant, chlorophyll a was manufactured but not chlorophyll b (Hirono and Redei). In yet another mutant, albino-12, vesicles and lamellae formed from the inner membrane, but appeared to be unstable, and continuously broken down. Such instability of chlorophyll is thought to be due to the absence of carotenoids (Stanier).

Numerous other examples of chromosomal mutants affecting morphological characteristics of plastids, or chlorophyll or carotenoid synthesis, have been described (see Kirk 1966). Over one hundred different genetic loci that produce plastid variegation are known from maize alone. Such mutants can provide a clear indication that controlling genes for major components of chloroplasts, reside in the nucleus. It is evident, however, that in some cases a mutation may affect chloroplasts by altering the physiology of the plant. Chlorophyll synthesis was greatly impaired, for example, in a thiamine-less mutant of tomato, but normal synthesis could be restored with added thiamine (Langridge and Brock).

A great many species of plants show variegation, where leaf regions may be yellow or white, and contain defective plastids. Variegation is of several kinds (see Kirk and Tilney-Basset for classification), but often the affected areas of tissue reflect the cell lineages of the growing leaf. In such cases some mutational event has taken place in a growing cell that has been transmitted to its progeny. This event can be due to mutation of an unstable nuclear gene, or in some cases to repeated loss of an unstable chromosome. In many cases, however, cell-line variegation apparently involves the sorting out of two kinds of cytoplasmic factors. The inheritance of plastid variegation was described by Correns in 1909, in his classical studies of four-o-clocks (*Mirabilis jalapa*). (1) Inheritance of plastid differences was strictly maternal; the kind of pollen did not influence the progeny. (2) Flowers on normal green branches provided normal offspring. (3) Flowers on white or pale branches produced only white lethal seedlings. (4) Flowers from variegated branches yielded normal green, white, or variegated progeny. Similar results on 33 other species are listed by Kirk and Tilney-Basset. In maize, Demerec found patterns of variegation depended on the position of the kernel on the ear. Green plants came from green regions, white plants from white regions, and variegated plants from borderline areas between white and green tissue.

Variegated plants often show 'sorting out' effects, where new shoots may be all green or all white. That this may involve segregation of two genetically distinct plastid types was concluded by Gregory. In the primrose, *Primula sinensis albomaculata*, he could detect both small yellow and large green plastids in cells from variegated leaves, but only large green plastids in green leaves, and only the small yellow plastids in chlorotic leaves. Although such experiments do not prove that the plastid itself contains the heritable defective character (Correns believed in the presence of 'diseased cytoplasm'), such an hypothesis certainly seems a likely possibility.

Many cases of variegation have arisen spontaneously. One case, that of iojap maize, was shown by Rhoades (1943) to be produced in interaction with a specific gene on chromosome 7. Plants homozygous for the iojap gene produced white striped seedlings. Once formed, such variegation continued in further crosses, showing exactly the maternal inheritance pattern described for *Mirabilis*, even in plants crossed repeatedly with wild type, so that the iojap gene was no longer present.

Other cases of nucleus-chloroplast interaction occur in the evening primrose, *Oenothera* and *Euoenothera*, as demonstrated in the extensive studies of Renner and

Stubbe. Because of the peculiar structural heterozygosity of the chromosomes, it is possible to produce 'hybrid' plants with ease, in which certain stable combinations of nuclear genes can be combined with specific cytoplasms. Renner showed that when certain nuclei were combined with other cytoplasms chloroplasts were affected, becoming pale green, yellow, or white. That this was a temporary influence of the nucleus upon the plastids, and not an induced cytoplasmic mutation as in iojap, was indicated since with a recombination of the affected cytoplasm with its original nucleus, normal chloroplast morphology was regained. Stubbe investigated such interactions in 14 species of *Euoenothera*, and concluded that the plastids could be divided into five types, each of which was normal with its own nucleus but produced various degrees of abnormality in hybrids. Evidence was also obtained by Renner that certain crosses resulted in variegated plants, which were green with small yellow flecks. These small areas of yellow tissue he attributed to leakage of incompatible plastids through the pollen, where they were diluted by the much larger number of normal chloroplasts, but later were segregated out during development of the plant.

The loss of green pigments may be induced in the flagellate *Euglena* by treatment with ultraviolet light or streptomycin. Colorless cells are formed, which then must depend upon an exogenous carbon source for their metabolism. Such changes are stable and irreversible. The ultraviolet action spectrum for the bleaching process was shown to have peaks at wavelengths of 260 and 280 mμ, suggesting the involvement of nucleoproteins. That the bleaching effect was cytoplasmic and not nuclear was shown by Gibor and Granick (1961), ultilizing ultraviolet microbeam irradiation. Treatment of the nucleus alone was ineffective, but the irradiation of cytoplasm, with the nucleus shielded, produced the bleaching effect. In an electron microscope investigation of *Euglena* clones made colorless by treatment with ultraviolet light, the total absence of plastids was reported (Schiff and Epstein). This finding has been questioned by Granick and Gibor who feel that plastids may still be present, in spite of the fact that their ability to become green has been lost, as discussed below.

A series of nonchromosomal mutants of the flagellate *Chlamydomonas* have been induced by treatment with streptomycin (see Sager). These include acetate-requiring strains, where acetate can be replaced by yeast extract, and strains resistant to streptomycin, or with a dependence on streptomycin. Although the species used (*C. reinhardi*) had morphologically similar male and female gametes (was isogamous), the transmission of the characters was maternal, in almost all cases the phenotype of the + mating type being transferred to all offspring. In a very few cases (less than 1%) exceptional zygotes were produced bearing characteristics of both parents, which later segregated out when the four haploid products of meiosis (zygospores) were grown. When a two-factor cross was made, with cells bearing both streptomycin dependency and acetate requirement, then the zoospores from exceptional zygotes at first showed characteristics of both parental types. When progeny of the cross were grown for several generations the acetate and streptomycin characters segregated into pure clones, in a rather haphazard manner. Although recombination occurred, the segregations were not reciprocal, and sometimes occurred early and sometimes after several divisions. Once a pure type segregated out, however, all the progeny were similar.

In summary, it is evident that genetic analysis of plastid heredity, as in the case of mitochondria, is in a rather unsatisfactory state. Nevertheless a few generalizations can be made. Numerous nuclear genes appear to be important in the control of chloroplast structure and composition. On the other hand stable mutations which show non-Mendelian heredity, presumably located in the chloroplast (although this has nowhere been unequivocally demonstrated) produce rather general and poorly defined abnormalities. Inheritance patterns of leaf variegation in higher plants, or nutritional mutants and streptomycin resistance in *Chlamydomonas*, are usually entirely maternal, with a few examples where characteristics of both parents appear in the offspring. Attempts at quantitative genetic analysis of nonchromosomal characters are largely inconclusive. Although evidence for recombination of cytoplasmic characters has been presented, the apparently unpredictable patterns obtained indicate the extreme difficulties encountered in genetic analysis where biologically controlled events of recombination and segregation appear to be lacking.

Nucleic acids. Most early reports on the presence of nucleic acids in chloroplasts were unconvincing, because of the likelihood of contamination in biochemical isolations, and the vagaries of cytochemical methods. Nevertheless, the presence of DNA and RNA was considered likely; for example Rhoades made the categorical statement in 1946 that plastids contain nucleoproteins. Cytochemical evidence for chloroplast nucleic acids has been reviewed in the chapter by Lefort-Tran, and will not be considered here.

The presence of small amounts of DNA in chloroplasts of tobacco was reported by Jagendorf and Wildman in a study on methods of plastid isolation. Chiba and Sugahara found that the DNA associated with spinach and tobacco chloroplasts was more readily extracted by perchloric acid than the DNA of the nucleus. An adenine to guanine ratio for DNA of broad bean chloroplasts significantly higher than nuclear DNA was reported by Kirk (1963). With the development of cesium chloride centrifugation methods for DNA analysis, the presence of chloroplast-associated satellite bands was reported for *Chlamydomonas*, *Chlorella*, and spinach by Chun et al., for *Euglena* by Leff et al., and by Sager and Ishida for *Chlamydomonas*. It was usually not possible to obtain chloroplast DNA entirely free from nuclear contamination. In mitochondrial preparations, the presence of nuclear DNA can be virtually eliminated by DNase, which does not penetrate the mitochondrial membrane, but chloroplast membranes were generally found to be DNase permeable. Analysis of *Euglena* DNA demonstrated the presence of two satellite bands, one of which (density 1.686 g/cc) was associated with chloroplasts, and the other (density 1.691 g/cc) with cytochrome-containing particles, probably mitochondria; buoyant density of nuclear DNA was 1.707 g/cc (Edelman et al. 1964, 1965). Also, 2.3 moles % of 5 methylcytosine were found in *Euglena* nuclear DNA, whereas this rare base was absent from the chloroplast satellite (Ray and Hanawalt). A similar absence of 5-methylcytosine in chloroplast DNA, but its presence in nuclear DNA, was found for tobacco (Tewari and Wildman).

Base ratios of chloroplast DNA, as for M-DNA, show broad evolutionary differences, which do not parallel similar broad shifts in nuclear DNA (Table 2). In general, algal chloroplast DNAS from *Euglena*, *Chlamydomonas*, *Chlorella*, and *Acetabularia*, are all of lower estimated GC content than the corresponding nuclear DNA, while chloroplast DNAS from higher plants (wheat, onion, tobacco, Swiss chard, mung bean, turnip, sweet potato) all possess higher GC ratios than nuclear DNA (see Schiff and Epstein, Iwamura; Granick and Gibor).

Chloroplast DNA molecules are clearly larger than circular molecules of animal M-DNA, but their exact extent has not been determined. Estimates of the DNA per chloroplast in *Euglena* vary from 12×10^{-16} g (Edelman et al. 1964) to 110×10^{-16} g (Brawerman and Eisenstadt). As single molecules in the β-form this amount of DNA would be 360 μ to 3300 μ long. Plastid DNA in *Chlamydomonas* was found to occur in amounts sufficient to make it clearly visible in the light microscope with the Feulgen reaction or acridine orange binding (Ris and Plaut). Tewari and Wildman estimated the DNA per tobacco chloroplast to be 47×10^{-16} g, and to comprise about 9% of total leaf DNA. In preparations of tobacco chloroplasts ruptured on surface films, Woodcock and Fernandez-Moran found linear and looped DNA molecules up to 150 μ long emanating from plastid membranes. In preparations of *Acetabularia* DNA, where the possibility of nuclear contamination was adequately eliminated by enucleation, Wolstenholme and Shephard (unpubl.) found long filaments, many of which were up to 50 μ in length, and Woodcock and Bogorad estimated that one plastid may contain up to 1 mm of DNA. No evidence for circular molecules was obtained. Estimates of the DNA per chloroplast in *Acetabularia* vary between 1 and 10×10^{-16} g (Gibor and Izawa).

Chloroplast DNA from tobacco, like M-DNA, showed the property of renaturing to original or nearly original buoyant density following heat denaturation (Tewari and Wildman). Under similar conditions nuclear DNA showed no evidence of renaturation. Also like M-DNA, chloroplast DNA in some cases may show a more rapid rate of replication than DNA of the nucleus. In young tobacco seedlings, incorporation of P^{32} into chloroplast DNA was several times higher than into nuclear DNA (Green and Gordon). Much more marked differences in incorporation rates between chloroplast DNA and nuclear DNA were found by Shipp et al. Small secondary tobacco leaves were grown in nutrient solutions with P^{32}, at a stage in which nuclear DNA synthesis was largely completed, but cell growth was continuing. Ratios of chloroplast to nuclear DNA incorporation of nearly 1000 to 1 were obtained. Such studies serve to demonstrate the relative independence of DNA synthesis in nuclei and chloroplasts.

As mentioned above, treatment of *Euglena* with heat, streptomycin, or ultraviolet light, can result in the production of colorless clones, where the ability to produce chlorophyll has apparently been permanently lost. A number of such colorless forms may still contain plastid-like inclusions when examined under the electron microscope, but in some strains no structure resembling a proplastid or leucoplast is observed (Moriber et al.). Four strains reportedly capable of forming a 'partial chloroplast' were found to possess chloroplast DNA, while five mutants 'incapable of making even a partial chloroplast' were found to lack chloroplast satellite DNA altogether (Edelman et al. 1965). The conclusion that plastids are completely absent in these strains has been questioned by Granick and Gibor and Kirk and Tilney Basset. Satellite DNA of chloroplast density was also described as absent in *Polytoma*, a colorless flagellate somewhat similar morphologically to *Chlamydomonas* (Leff et al.). However, *Polytoma* clearly possesses plastids, which, though colorless, are capable of storing starch (Lang). The problem thus seems analogous to that of diskinetoplastic strains of trypanosomes, where most, if not all, DNA appears to be lost, and yet an abnormal kinetoplast and mitochondrial complex is still formed. The question as to whether or not clones still capable of forming abnormal plastids or mitochondria may retain small but undetected amounts of satellite DNA has yet to be answered.

Bleaching of *Euglena* by low levels of ultraviolet light apparently effects the cytoplasm but may leave the nucleus undamaged. The fact that such bleaching is always irreversible can be used as one argument against the *de novo* origin of plastids from DNA-containing blebs from the nucleus, as postulated by Bell and Muhlethaler. Nevertheless, some evidence has been presented, through DNA–RNA hybridization techniques on membrane filters, that sequence homologies exist between *Euglena* nuclear and chloroplast DNA (Richards). It was estimated that approximately 15 to 17% of the chloroplast DNA sequences are found in the nuclear genome, and conversely between 2 and 4.5% of the nuclear DNA in the chloroplast genome. Any biological reason why a small portion, but not all, of the chloroplast DNA should be represented in the nucleus seems presently obscure. It seems remotely possible, however, as mentioned above, that if two kinds of DNA exist in the same cell, rare recombination events might occur between them, comparable to chromosomal translocations.

The ability of isolated spinach chloroplasts to incorporate H^3 thymidine triphosphate into chloroplast DNA has been reported by Spencer and Whitfeld. The incorporation required the presence of all four deoxynucleoside triphosphates, and was inhibited by actinomycin D and DNase, but not by RNase. The presence in chloroplasts of a DNA polymerase thus seems established.

The presence of ribosomes in plastids was first indicated by Lyttleton, who found two different ribonucleoprotein particles, as determined by their sedimentation properties in sucrose gradients, associated with spinach leaves, but only one component in the root. Only the smaller slowly sedimenting component was found in preparations of chloroplasts. Similar results were obtained for Chinese cabbage leaves by Clark et al., who reported 68S ribosomes in preparations of chloroplasts, and 85S ribosomes associated with the cytoplasm, and also for tobacco (Boardman et al.), spinach (Spencer) and *Chlamydomonas*, maize and bean (Stutz and Noll). Chloroplast ribosomes of pea seedlings had a sedimentation constant of 62S, which dissociated in low magnesium ion concentrations into 46S and 32S subunits, as compared to the 76S

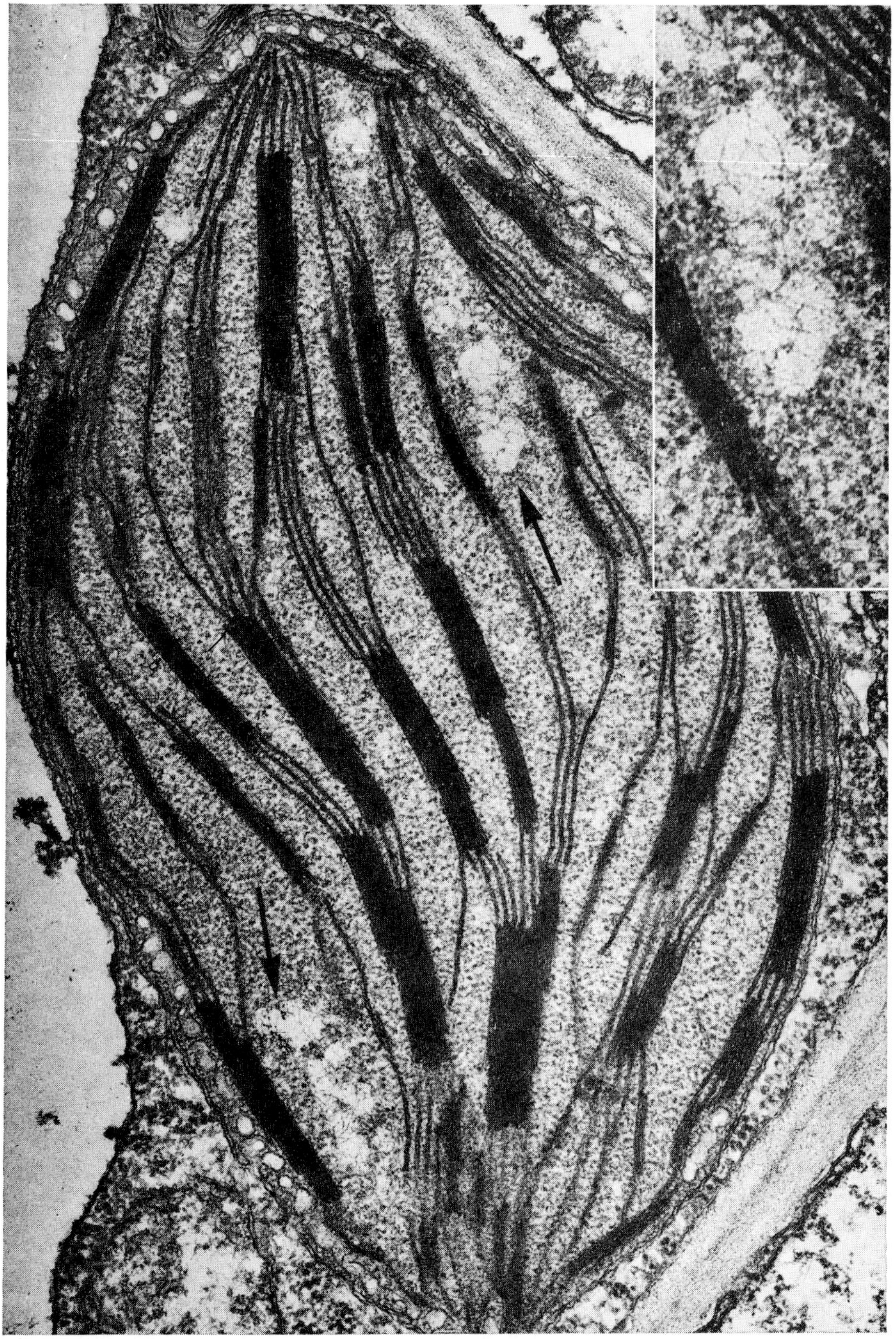

Fig. 26. Chloroplast of leaf tissue of a 7 day maize seedling. Areas between lamellae are filled with large numbers of chloroplast ribosomes except in regions containing DNA filaments (arrows). × 36,500. Inset × 91,500. (Micrograph by James A. Lauretis and Elliot Kitajima, unpubl.)

cytoplasmic ribosomes, with subunits of 54S and 38S (Sissakian et al.). Etiolated corn leaves, as studied under the electron microscope, also showed large numbers of ribosomes, somewhat smaller than those in surrounding cytoplasm (Jacobson et al.) (see Fig. 27). RNA isolated from chloroplast ribosomes of *Euglena* showed 19S and 14S components (see Eisenstadt), while cytoplasmic 80S ribosomes have been shown to contain 24S and 20S RNAS (Rawson and Stutz). The RNA base ratios of chloroplast and cytoplasmic ribosomes showed significant differences (see reviews by Brawerman and Eisenstadt; Eisenstadt). The presence of polysomes in bean chloroplasts was shown by Stutz and Noll. Evidence that chloroplast DNA codes for the RNA of chloroplast ribosomes was presented by Scott and Smillie. Using membrane filter methods for DNA–RNA hybridization, specific binding was found between chloroplast DNA and P^{32}-labeled RNA of chloroplast ribosomes. Uptake of whole cell RNA from dark-grown cells, largely cytoplasmic ribosomal RNA, was negligible. It was calculated that at saturation, about 1% of the total sites on chloroplast DNA was occupied by chloroplast ribosomal RNA.

Isolated chloroplasts of broad bean and spinach have been shown to incorporate C^{14} ATP into RNase sensitive, perchloric acid or ethanol precipitable material, presumably RNA. The reactions failed to occur in the presence of actinomycin D or DNase (Kirk 1964; Semal et al.). Similar results were obtained with isolated chloroplasts of *Euglena* by Shah and Lyman.

When dark grown leaves of maize were exposed to light for 30 to 120 min, a marked increase in P^{32} incorporation into RNA was obtained. Both the increase in rates of RNA synthesis and chlorophyll synthesis could be blocked by actinomycin D. When the P^{32}-labeled leaves were fractionated, and the RNAS from chloroplasts and cytoplasm were compared, it was apparent that most of the light-induced increase in RNA synthesis was attributable to the plastids. Substantial incorporation was found not only in the 22S and 17S fractions of the chloroplast ribosomes, but also in the 4S region, and to a lesser extent throughout the gradient. A concomitant light-induced rise in the plastid RNA polymerase was also found, which was strongly inhibited if the leaves were treated with chloramphenicol prior to exposure to light (Bogorad 1967).

There have been many studies on the ability of isolated chloroplasts to incorporate labeled amino acids into proteins, since the first report on tobacco chloroplasts by Stephenson et al. As also found for mitochondrial protein synthesis, the incorporation of C^{14} leucine was not inhibited by RNase, presumably because it failed to penetrate the limiting membrane. Unlike mitochondria, incorporation was stimulated by light. Similar reports for *Euglena* and several higher plants are reviewed by Brawerman and Eisenstadt, and Kirk and Tilney-Basset. It is of particular interest that protein synthesis in isolated chloroplasts is inhibited by chloramphenicol at concentrations not affecting synthesis in cytoplasmic ribosomes (Eisenstadt and Brawerman). A similar differential sensitivity between chloroplast and cytoplasmic protein synthesis in intact *Euglena* cells has been reported by Aaronson et al. Chlorophyll synthesis in dark grown cells was inhibited by concentrations of chloramphenicol which did not inhibit cell growth and multiplication. This finding has obvious parallels to that of Clark-Walker and Linnane, who found chloramphenicol could suppress the synthesis of cytochromes a and a_3 in yeast, while cell growth continued.

In summary, nucleic acids of chloroplasts show certain similarities to but also certain differences from the nucleic acids of mitochondria. Chloroplast DNAs are often distinguishable from nuclear DNA by differences in base ratios, the absence of 5-methylcytosine, and the capacity for rapid renaturation. Amounts of DNA per chloroplast are probably somewhat larger than amounts of DNA per mitochondrion. No circular molecules have been reported. The ribosomes of chloroplasts, like mitochondrial ribosomes, appear to be somewhat smaller than ribosomes of the cytoplasm, resembling bacterial ribosomes in size. They also contain the characteristic two subunits. Ribosomal RNAs are, at least in part, homologous to regions of chloroplast DNA. As in both mitochondria and bacteria, chloroplast ribosomes are sensitive to chloramphenicol at concentrations which leave protein synthesis in the cytoplasm unimpaired. Isolated chloroplasts, like mitochondria, are known to synthesize DNA, RNA, and proteins, and thus possess a complete endogenous protein forming system, but unlike mitochondria, the system is stimulated by illumination. One of the specific proteins stimulated by light treatment in intact cells is an RNA polymerase.

4. Conclusions

Through the studies of many interested workers, our knowledge of the biogenesis of mitochondria and chloroplasts has increased remarkably in a very short period of time. The fact that both mitochondrial and chloroplast protein synthetic systems are more prokaryote-like than eukaryote-like seems clearly established, particularly in terms of ribosome size, magnesium ion dependency, and sensitivity to chloramphenicol. Thus the theories of Altmann, Schimper, and Famintzen for the origin of these organelles from symbiotic microorganisms, are given new support.

Our knowledge of the various specific aspects of organelle DNA, the three classes of RNA, and protein synthesis is now considerable, with new details being added at a rapid rate. But probably the most evasive aspect of the complex patterns of protein synthesis in mitochondria and chloroplasts concerns the nature of the product formed. As yet, in spite of many promising directions of research, not one single protein has been adequately characterized that is clearly the product of these synthetic systems. This is doubtless because the category of structure lipoproteins of chloroplast and mitochondrial membranes, which are the most likely products, currently present many problems of preparation and characterization. But the careful analysis of this class of proteins seems clearly necessary to a further understanding of the nature of known abnormal organelles: the petite and poky mitochondria, the dyskinetoplastic kinetoplasts, and the ultraviolet or streptomycin bleached proplastids. Another promising field for future research concerns the acquisition by mitochondria and chloroplasts of proteins from the cytoplasm, and the exploration of the specific mechanisms of transport probably required for this process. How many components of the organelle are the product of the internal system, and how much the product of the surrounding cell? Such information would obviously provide new evidence for or against the theory of symbiotic origin. Can we suppose that the complex mutual interdependence of cell and organelle arose in evolution through progressive modification from a remote bacteria-like or alga-like ancestor?

Wishful thinking would indicate another much needed approach, that of improved techniques for genetic analysis. Clonal inheritance of noninterbreeding individuals at best provides limited material for studies on gene action and control. Our knowledge of any genetic system depends heavily upon analysis of recombination. In this respect the reported recombinants obtained in yeast and in *Chlamydomonas* would seem to offer hope for the future, but one is struck by the tremendous operational difficulties in obtaining as yet a comparatively small amount of information, in organelles where recombination is at best fitful and no mechanism for orderly segregation seems to be present. We need the good fortune to find Hfr^+ strains of mitochondria and chloroplasts.

Acknowledgements

The authors wish to express their sincere appreciation to a number of colleagues for permission to quote from their recent unpublished work. These include Dr. Murray Rabinowitz, Dr. Godfrey S. Getz, Mr. James S. Casey, Dr. Nicholas J. Gross, Mr. Michael Fauman, Dr. James A. Lauretis, and Dr. Elliot Kitajima. We also much appreciate the opportunity to reproduce micrographs from a study of mouse liver mitochondria during vitamin deficiency by Drs. B. Tandler and R. A. Erlandson. Thanks are also due to Dr. Hans Ris for the micrograph of *Trypanosoma lewisi*. The valuable secretarial help of Miss Laura Chapman is gratefully acknowledged. Research from this laboratory included here has been supported by Grants HD-1242, and Training Grant HD-174 from the U.S. Public Health Service and Grant No. GB-5908 from the National Science Foundation.

References

AARONSON, S., B. B. ELLENBOGEN, L. K. YELLEN and S. H. HUTNER: *In vivo* differentiation of *Euglena* cytoplasmic and chloroplast protein synthesis with chloramphenicol and DL-ethionine. Biochem. Biophys. Res. Commun. 27 (1967) 535.

ALTMAN, R.: Die Elementarorganismen. Leipzig, Veit and Comp. (1890).

ANDRÉ, J.: Contribution à la connaissance du chondriome. Étude de ses modifications ultrastructurales pendant la spermatogenèse. J. Ultrastruct. Res. Suppl. 3 (1962) 1.

ANDRÉ, J. and V. MARINOZZI: Présence dans les mitochondries, de particules ressemblant aux ribosomes. J. Microscopie 4 (1965) 615.

ASHFORD, T.P. and K.R.PORTER: Cytoplasmic components in hepatic cell lysosomes. J. Cell Biol. 12 (1962) 198.

ATTARDI, B. and G.ATTARDI: A membrane-associated RNA of cytoplasmic origin in HeLa cells. Proc. Natl. Acad. Sci. U.S. 58 (1967) 1051.

BARNETT, W.E. and D.H.BROWN: Mitochondrial transfer ribonucleic acid. Proc. Natl. Acad. Sci. U.S. 57 (1967) 452.

BARNETT, W.E., D.H.BROWN and J.C.EPLER: Mitochondrial-specific aminoacyl-RNA synthetases. Proc. Natl. Acad. Sci. U.S. 57 (1967) 1775.

BEATTIE, D.S., R.E.BASFORD and S.B.KORITZ: Studies on the biosynthesis of mitochondrial protein components. Biochemistry 5 (1966) 926.

BEATTIE, D.S., R.E.BASFORD and S.B.KORITZ: Bacterial contamination and amino acid incorporation by isolated mitochondria. J. Biol. Chem. 242 (1967) 3366.

BECKWITH, C.J.: The genesis of the plasma-structure in the egg of *Hydractinia echinata*. J. Morphol. 25 (1914) 189.

BEHNKE, O.: Helical filaments in rat liver mitochondria. Exptl. Cell Res. 37 (1965) 687.

BELL, P.R.: Deoxyribonucleic acid in eggs of the Polypodiaceous ferns. Nature 184 (1959) 1664.

BELL, P.R. and K.MUHLETHALER: Evidence for the presence of deoxyribonucleic acid in the organelles of the egg cells of *Pteridium aquilinum*. J. Mol. Biol. 8 (1964) 853.

BENSLEY, R.R.: On the nature of the pigment of mitochondria and of submicroscopic particles in the hepatic cell of the guinea pig. Anat. Record 98 (1947) 609.

BENSLEY, R.R. and N.L.HOERR: Studies on cell structure by the freezing drying method VI. The preparation and properties of mitochondria. Anat. Record 60 (1934) 449.

BERGER, E.R.: Mitochondria genesis in the retinal photo receptor inner segment. J. Ultrastruct. Res. 11 (1964) 90.

BERNHARD, W. and P.TOURNIER: Modification persistante des mitochondries dans les cellules tumorales de hamster transformées par l'adenovirus 12. Intern. J. Cancer 1 (1966) 61.

BLECHER, S.R.: Mitochondrial chromosomes. Currents Modern Biol. 1 (1967) 249.

BOARDMAN, N.K., R.I.B.FRANCK and S.G.WILDMAN: Protein synthesis by cell-free extracts from tobacco leaves II. Association of activity with chloroplast ribosomes. Biochemistry 4 (1965) 872.

BOARDMAN, N.K. and S.G.WILDMAN: Identification of proplastids by fluorescence microscopy and their isolation and purification. Biochem. Biophys. Acta 59 (1956) 222.

BOGORAD, L.: Aspects of chloroplast assembly. In: H.J.Vogel, J.O.Campen and V.Bryson, eds.: Organizational biosynthesis. New York, Academic Press (1967) p. 395.

BOGORAD, L.: The organization and development of chloroplasts. In: J.M.Allen, ed.: Molecular organization and biological function. New York, Harper and Row (1967) p. 134.

BOLTON, E.T., R.J.BRITTEN, D.B.COWIE, R.B.ROBERTS, P.SZAFRANSKI and M.J.WARING: Biophysics: Interactions of nucleic acids. Carnegie Inst. Wash. Publ. 64 (1965) 313.

BORST, P., A.M.KROON and G.J.C.M.RUTTENBERG: Mitochondrial DNA and other forms of cytoplasmic DNA. In: D.Shugar, ed.: Genetic Elements: Properties and function. London and Warsaw, Academic Press and P.W.N. (1967) p. 81.

BORST, P. and G.J.C.M.RUTTENBERG: Renaturation of mitochondrial DNA. Biochim. Biophys. Acta 114 (1966) 645.

BORST, P., E.F.J. VAN BRUGGEN, G.J.C.M.RUTTENBERG and A.M.KROON: Mitochondrial DNA II. Sedimentation analysis and electron microscopy of mitochondrial DNA from chick liver. Biochim. Biophys. Acta 149 (1967) 156.

BOWEN, R.H.: Studies on insect spermatogenesis III. On the structure of the nebenkern in the insect spermatid and the origin of nebenkern patterns. Biol. Bull. 42 (1922) 53.

BRANDT, P.W. and G.D.PAPPAS: Mitochondria II. The nuclear mitochondrial relationship in *Pelomyxa carolinensis* Wilson. J. Biophys. Biochem. Cytol. 6 (1959) 91.

BRAUN, C.A., J.B.MARSH and D.L.DRABKIN: Amino acid incorporation into protein by liver mitochondria from nephrotic and partially hepatectomized rats. Biochim. Biophys. Acta 72 (1963) 645.

BRAWERMAN, G. and J.M.EISENSTADT: The nucleic acids associated with the chloroplasts of *Euglena gracilis* and their role in protein synthesis. In: H.J.Vogel, J.O.Lampen and V.Bryson, eds.: Organizational biosynthesis. New York, Academic Press (1967) p. 419.

BRESSLAU, E. and L.SCREMIN: Die Kerne der Trypanosomen und ihr Verhalten zur Nuclealreaktion. Arch. Protistenk. 48 (1924) 509.

BREWER, E.N., A.DEVRIES and H.P.RUSCH: DNA synthesis by isolated mitochondria of *Physarum polycephalum*. Biochim. Biophys. Acta 145 (1967) 686.

BRONSERT, U. and W.NEUPERT: Protein synthesis in locust flight-muscle sarcomes. In: J.M.Tager, S.Papa, E.Quagliariello and E.C.Slater, eds.: Regulation of metabolic processes in mitochondria. Amsterdam, Elsevier Publishing Company (1966) p. 426.

BUCK, C. and M.M.K.NASS: Chromatographic differences between cytoplasmic and mitochondrial transfer RNA. Federation Proc. 27 (1968) 342.

CAIRNS, J.: The chromosome of *Escherichia coli*. Cold Spring Harbor Symp. Quant. Biol. 28 (1963) 43.

CHATTERJEE, S.K., H.K.DAS and S.C.RAY: Deoxyribonucleic acid and the synthesis of protein in plant mitochondria IV. Biochim. Biophys. Acta 114 (1966) 349.

CHÈVREMONT, M.: Cytoplasmic deoxyribonucleic acids: Their mitochondrial localization and synthesis in somatic cells under experimental conditions and during the normal cell cycle in relation to the preparation for mitosis. In: R.Harris, ed.: Cell Division and Growth. Symp. Int. Soc. Cell Biol. 2 (1963) 323.

CHÈVREMONT, M. and J.FREDERIC: Contributions à l'étude des chondriosomes vivantes. In: Fine structure of cells. Symp. 8th Cong. Cell Biology, Leiden. New York, Interscience (1954) 33.

CHIBA, V. and K.SUGAHARA: The nucleic acid content of chloroplasts isolated from spinach and tobacco leaves. Arch. Biochem. Biophys. 71 (1957) 367.

CHMIELEVSKY, V.: Eine Notiz über das Verhalten der Chlorophyll-bänder in den Zygoten der Spirogyraarten. Botan. Zh. 48 (1890) 773.

CHUN, E.H.L., M.N.VAUGHAN and A.RICH: The isolation and characterization of DNA associated with chloroplast preparations. J. Mol. Biol. 7 (1963) 130.

CLARK, M.F., R.E.F.MATTHEWS and R.K.RALPH: Ribosomes and polyribosomes in *Brassica pekinensis*. Biochim. Biophys. Acta 91 (1964) 289.

CLARK, T.B. and F.G.WALLACE: A comparative study of kinetoplast ultrastructure in the Trypanosomatidae. J. Protozool. 7 (1960) 115.

CLARK-WALKER, G.D. and A.LINNANE: *In vivo* differentiation of yeast cytoplasmic and mitochondrial protein synthesis with antibiotics. Biochem. Biophys. Res. Commun. 25 (1966) 8.

CLAUDE, A.: The constitution of protoplasm. Science 97 (1943) 451.

CLAYTON, D.A. and J.VINOGRAD: Circular dimer and catenate forms of mitochondrial DNA in human leukaemic leucocytes. Nature 216 (1967) 652.

CORNEO, G., C.MOORE, D.R.SANADI, L.I.GROSSMAN and J.MARMUR: Mitochondrial DNA in yeast and some mammalian species. Science 151 (1966) 687.

CORRENS, C.: Vererbungsversuche mit blass (gelb) grünen und bluntblättrigen Sippen bei *Mirabilis*, *Urtica*, and *Lunaria*. Z. Vererbungslehre 1 (1909) 291.

COWDRY, E.V.: The mitochondrial constituents of protoplasm. Contrib. Embryol. (Carnegie Inst.) Wash. 8 (1918) 39.

COWDRY, E.V.: General cytology. Chicago, The University of Chicago Press (1924).

CRIDDLE, R.S., R.M.BOCK, D.E.GREEN and H.TISDALE: Physical characteristics of proteins of the electron transfer system and interpretation of the structure of the mitochondrion. Biochemistry 1 (1962) 827.

DALTON, A.J., M.POTTER and R.MERWIN: Some ultrastructural characteristics of a series of primary and transplanted plasma cell tumors of the mouse. J. Natl. Cancer Inst. 26 (1961) 122.

DAS, H.K., S.K.CHATTERJEE and S.C.ROY: Protein synthesis in plant mitochondria I. Incorporation of amino acid in peptide linkage. J. Biol. Chem. 239 (1964) 1126.

DAWID, I.B.: Evidence for the mitochondrial origin of frog egg cytoplasmic DNA. Proc. Natl. Acad. Sci. U.S. 56 (1966) 269.

DAWID, I.B. and D.R.WOLSTENHOLME: Ultracentrifuge and electron microscope studies on the structure of mitochondrial DNA. J. Mol. Biol. 28 (1967) 233.

DAWID, I.B. and D.R.WOLSTENHOLME: Renaturation and hybridization studies of mitochondrial DNA. Biophys. J. 8 (1968) 65.

DEANIN, G.G.: Mitochondrial protein synthesis in cell free systems. Bull. Inst. Cellular Biol. Univ. Connecticut 9 (1968) 9.

DEMEREC, M.: A second case of maternal inheritance of chlorophyll in maize. Botan. Gaz. 84 (1927) 139.

DUBIN, D.T.: The effect of actinomycin on the synthesis of mitochondrial RNA in hamster cells. Biochem. Biophys. Res. Commun. 29 (1967) 655.

DUBIN, D.T. and R.E.BROWN: A novel ribosomal RNA in hamster cell mitochondria. Biochim. Biophys. Acta 145 (1967) 538.

DUBUY, H.G., C.F.T.MATTERN and F.L.RILEY: Isolation and characterization of DNA from kinetoplasts of *Leishmania enriettii*. Science 147 (1965) 754.

DUESBERG, J.: Plastosomen, 'apparato reticulare interno' und Chromidialapparat. Ergebn. Anat. Entwicklungsgesch. 20 (1912) 567.

DURE, S.L., J.L.EPLER and W.E.BARNETT: Sedimentation properties of mitochondrial and cytoplasmic ribosomal RNAs from *Neurospora*. Proc. Natl. Acad. Sci. U.S. 58 (1967) 1883.

EDELMAN, M., C.A.COWAN, H.T.EPSTEIN and J.A.SCHIFF: Studies of chloroplast development in *Euglena* VIII. Chloroplast-associated DNA. Proc. Natl. Acad. Sci. U.S. 52 (1964) 1214.

EDELMAN, M., J.A.SCHIFF and H.T.EPSTEIN: Studies of chloroplast development in *Euglena* XII. Two types of satellite DNA. J. Mol. Biol. 11 (1965) 769.

EISENSTADT, J.M. and G.BRAWERMAN: The protein-synthesizing systems from the cytoplasm and the chloroplasts of *Euglena gracilis*. J. Mol. Biol. 10 (1964) 392.

ELAEV, I.R.: An investigation into the metabolic activity of cytoplasmic, nuclear and mitochondrial ribosomes. Biokhimiya 29 (1964) 413.

ELAEV, I.R.: The isolation and some properties of ribosomes from a highly purified mitochondria fraction. Biokhimiya 31 (1966) 234.

EPHRUSSI, B.: Nucleo-cytoplasmic relations in microorganisms. Oxford, Clarendon Press (1953).

EPHRUSSI, B. and P.P.SLONIMSKI: Subcellular units involved in the synthesis of respiratory enzymes in yeast. Nature 176 (1955) 1207.

EPLER, J.L. and W.E.BARNETT: Coding properties of *Neurospora* mitochondrial and cytoplasmic leucine transfer RNA's. Biochem. Biophys. Res. Commun. 28 (1967) 328.

FAMINTIZIN, A.: Die Symbiose als Mittel der Synthese von Organismen. Biol. Zentralbl. 27 (1907) 353.

FAUMAN, M., M.RABINOWITZ and G.GETZ: Base composition and sedimentation properties of mitochondrial RNA of *Saccharomyces cerevisiae*. Biophys. Biochim. Acta 182 (1969) 355.

FAWCETT, D.W.: Observations on the cytology and electron microscopy of hepatic cells. J. Natl. Cancer Inst. 15 (1955) 1475.

FEULGEN, R. and H.ROSSENBECK: Mikroskopisch-chemischer Nachweis einer Nucleinsäure vom Typus de-Thymonucleinsäure und die darauf beruhende elektiv Färbung von Zellkernen in mikroskopischen Präparaten. Z. Physiol. Chem. 135 (1924) 203–248.

FLETCHER, M.J and D.R.SANADI: Turnover of rat liver mitochondria. Biochim. Biophys. Acta 51 (1961) 356.

FREIFELDER, D. and A.K.KLEINSCHMIDT: Single strand breaks in duplex DNA of coliphage T_7 as demonstrated by electron microscopy. J. Mol. Biol. 14 (1965) 271.

FRESCO, J.R. and A.BENDICH: The metabolic stability of rat liver deoxyribonucleic acid: A turnover study. J. Biol. Chem. 235 (1960) 1124.

FUKUHARA, H.: Informational role of mitochondrial DNA studied by hybridization with different classes of RNA in yeast. Proc. Natl. Acad. Sci. U.S. 58 (1967) 1065.

GARNJOBST, L., WILSON, J. F. and E. L. TATUM: Studies on a cytoplasmic character in *Neurospora crassa.* J. Cell Biol. 26 (1965) 413.

GEFTER, M. L., A. BECKER and J. NURWITZ: The enzymatic repair of DNA I. Formation of circular λ DNA. Proc. Natl. Acad. Sci. U.S. 58 (1967) 240.

GELLERT, M.: Formation of covalent circles of lambda DNA by *E. coli* extracts. Proc. Natl. Acad. Sci. U.S. 57 (1967) 148.

GEY, G.O., P. SHARRAS, F.B. BANG and M.K. GEY: Some relations of inclusion droplets (pinocytosis, Lewis) and mitochondrial behavior in normal and malignant cells. In: Fine structure of cells. Groningen, P. Noordholt (1955) p. 38.

GIBBS, S. P.: Radioautographic evidence for the *in situ* synthesis of chloroplast and mitochondrial RNA in *Ochromonas danica.* J. Cell Biol. 35 (1967) 45A.

GIBOR, A. and S. GRANICK: The plastid system of normal and bleached *Euglena gracilis.* J. Protozool. 9 (1962) 327.

GIBOR, A. and S. GRANICK: Plastids and mitochondria: Inheritable systems. Science 145 (1964) 890.

GIBOR, A. and M. IZAWA: The DNA content of the chloroplasts of *Acetabularia.* Proc. Natl. Acad. Sci. U.S. 50 (1963) 1164.

GILLESPIE, D. and S. SPIEGELMAN: A quantitative assay for DNA–RNA hybrids with DNA immobilized on a membrane. J. Mol. Biol. 12 (1965) 829.

GIROUD, A.: Recherches sur la nature chimique du chondriome. Protoplasma 7 (1929) 72.

GIUDICE, G.: Incorporation of labelled amino-acids into the proteins of the mitochondria isolated from the unfertilized eggs and developmental stages of *Paracentroles lividus.* Exptl. Cell Res. 21 (1960) 222.

GONZALEZ-CADAVID, N.F. and P.N. CAMPBELL: The biosynthesis of cytochrome c. Biochem. J. 105 (1967) 443.

GOODWIN, T.W., ed.: Biochemistry of chloroplasts. London, Academic Press, Vol. I (1966) and Vol. II (1967).

GRANICK, S.: Plastid structure, development and inheritance. In: W. Ruhland, ed.: Encyclopedia of Plant Physiology, Vol. 1. Berlin, Springer (1955) 507.

GRANICK, S.: The chloroplasts inheritance, structure and function. In: J. Brachet and A.E. Mirsky, eds.: The cell, Vol. II. New York, Academic Press (1961).

GRANICK, S. and A. GIBOR: The DNA of chloroplasts, mitochondria, and centrioles. In: J.N. Davidson and W.E. Cohn, eds.: Progress in nucleic acid research and molecular biology, Vol. 6. New York, Academic Press (1967) p. 143.

GREEN, B.R. and M.P. GORDON: Replication of chloroplast DNA of tobacco. Science 152 (1966) 1071.

GREEN, P.B.: Cinematic observations on the growth and division of chloroplasts in *Nitella.* Am. J. Botany 51 (1964) 334.

GREGORY, R.P.: On variegation in *Primula sinensis.* J. Genet. 4 (1915) 305.

GROSS, N.J., G.S. GETZ and M. RABINOWITZ: Apparent turnover of mitochondrial deoxyribonucleic acid and mitochondrial phospholipids in the tissues of the rat. J. Biol. Chem. 244 (1969) 1552.

GROSS, P.R., D.E. PHILPOTT and S. NASS: Electron microscopy of the centrifuged sea urchin egg, with a note on the structure of the ground cytoplasm. J. Biophys. Biochem. Cytol. 7 (1960) 135.

GUILLERMOND, A.: The cytoplasm of the plant cell. Waltham, Mass., Chronica Botanica Company (1941).

GUTTES, E. and S. GUTTES: Thymidine incorporation by mitochondria in *Physarum polycephalum.* Science 145 (1964) 1057.

HALDAR, D., K. FREEMAN and T.S. WORK: Biogenesis of mitochondria. Nature 211 (1966) 9.

HARVEY, E.B.: Structure and development of the clear quarter of the *Arbacia punctulata* egg. J. Exptl.

Zool. 102 (1946) 253.

HAUST, M.D.: Crystalloid structures of hepatic mitochondria in children with heparitin sulfate muco-poly-saccharidosis (Sanfilippo type). Exptl. Mol. Pathol. 8 (1968) 123.

HAWTHORNE, D.C. and R.K.MORTIMER: Chromosome mapping in *Saccharomyces*: centromere-linked genes. Genetics 45 (1960) 1085.

HERSHEY, A.D., E.BURGI and L.INGRAHAM: Cohesion of DNA molecules isolated from phage lambda. Proc. Natl. Acad. Sci. U.S. 49 (1963) 748.

HIRONO, Y. and G.D.RÉDEI: Multiple allelic control of chlorophyll b level in *Arabidopsis thaliana*. Nature 197 (1963) 1324.

HIRSCH, G.C.: Analyse der Restitution des Sekretmaterials in Pankreas mittels Röntgenstrahlen. Roux Arch. 123 (1931) 792.

HUDSON, B. and J.VINOGRAD: Catenated circular DNA molecules in HeLa cell mitochondria. Nature 216 (1967) 647.

HULTIN, T.: Incorporation in vivo of ^{15}M-labeled glycine into liver fractions of newly hatched chicks. Exptl. Cell Res. 1 (1950) 376.

HUMM, D.G. and J.H.HUMM: Hybridization of mitochondrial RNA with mitochondrial and nuclear DNA in agar. Proc. Natl. Acad. Sci. U.S. 55 (1966) 114.

IWAMURA, T.: Nucleic acids in chloroplasts and metabolic DNA. Progr. Nucl. Acid Res. Mol. Biol. 5 (1966) 133.

JAGENDORF, A.T. and S.G.WILDMAN: The proteins of green leaves VI. Centrifugal fractionation of tobacco leaf homogenates and some properties of isolated chloroplasts. Plant Physiol. 29 (1954) 270.

JENSEN, H.: The morphology and distribution of mitochondria in ameloblasts with special reference to a helix-containing type. J. Ultrastruct. Res. 22 (1968) 120.

JINKS, J.L.: Extrachromosomal inheritance. Englewood Cliffs, New Jersey, Prentice Hall (1964).

JOLLOW, D., G.M.KELLERMAN and A.W.LINNANE: The biogenesis of mitochondria III. The lipid composition of aerobically and anaerobically grown *Saccharomyces cerevisiae* as related to the membrane system of cells. J. Cell Biol. 37 (1968) 221.

KADENBACH, B.: Synthesis of mitochondrial proteins: Demonstration of a transfer of proteins from microsomes into mitochondria. Biochim. Biophys. Acta 134 (1967) 430.

KALF, G.F.: Deoxyribonucleic acid in mitochondria and its role in protein synthesis. Biochemistry 3 (1964) 1702.

KALF, G.F. and M.A.GRECE: The isolation of deoxyribonucleic acid from lamb heart mitochondria. J. Biol. Chem. 241 (1966) 1019.

KATOH, T. and S.SANUKIDA: The mitochondrial structural proteins from wild-type and respiratory-deficient yeasts. Biochem. Biophys. Res. Commun. 21 (1965) 373.

KIRK, J.T.O.: The deoxyribonucleic acid of broad bean chloroplasts. Biochim. Biophys. Acta 76 (1963) 417.

KIRK, J.T.O.: DNA-dependent RNA synthesis in chloroplast preparations. Biochem. Biophys. Res. Commun. 14 (1964) 393.

KIRK, J.T.O.: Nature and function of chloroplast DNA. In: T.W.Goodwin, ed.: Biochemistry of chloroplasts. New York, Academic Press 1 (1966) 319.

KIRK, J.T.O. and R.A.E.TILNEY-BASSETT: The plastids, their chemistry, structure, growth, and inheritance, London, W.H.Freeman (1967).

KIRSCHNER, R.H., D.R.WOLSTENHOLME and N.J.GROSS: Replicating molecules of circular mitochondrial DNA. Proc. Natl. Acad. Sci. U.S. 60 (1968) 1466.

KISLEV, N., H.SWIFT and L.BOGORAD: Nucleic acids of chloroplasts and mitochondria of Swiss chard. J. Cell Biol. 25 (1965) 327.

KLEINSCHMIDT, A.K., D.LANG, D.JACHERTS and R.K.ZAHN: Darstellung und Langenmessungen des gesamten Desoxyribonucleinsäure-inhaltes von T_2-Bacteriophagen. Biochim. Biophys. Acta 61 (1962) 857.

KOZINSKI, A.W. and M.BEER: Effect of concentration on the formation of molecular hybrids from T_4 DNA. Biophys. J. 2 (1962) 129.

KROON, A.M.: Inhibitors of mitochondrial protein synthesis. Biochim. Biophys. Acta 76 (1963) 165.

KROON, A.M.: Protein synthesis in mitochondria II. A comparison of mitochondria from liver and heart with special reference to the role of oxidative phosphorylation. Biochim. Biophys. Acta 91 (1964) 145.

KROON, A.M.: Amino acid incorporation by isolated mitochondria. In: J.M.Tager, S.Papa, E.Quagliariello and E.C.Slater, eds.: Regulation of metabolic processes in mitochondria. Amsterdam, Elsevier (1966) 396.

KROON, A.M.: On the evolution of ribosomal RNA from rat-liver mitochondria. In: E.C.Slater, J.M. Tager, S.Papa and E.Quagliarriello, eds.: Biochemical aspects of the biogenesis of mitochondria. Bari, Adriatica Editrice (in press).

KROON, A.M., P.BORST, E.F.J. VAN BRUGGEN and G.J.C.M.RUTTENBERG: Mitochondrial DNA from sheep heart. Proc. Natl. Acad. Sci. U.S. 56 (1966) 1836.

KUNTZEL, H. and H.NOLL: Mitochondrial and cytoplasmic polysomes from *Neurospora crassa.* Nature 215 (1967) 1340.

LANG, N.J.: Electron microscope demonstration of plastids in *Polytoma*. J. Protozool. 10 (1963) 333.

LANGRETH, S.G.: Ultrastructural observations on the sperm of the crab, *Cancer borealis*. J. Cell Biol. 27 (1965) 56A.

LANGRIDGE, J and R.D.BROCK: A thiamine-requiring mutant of the tomato. Australian J. Biol. Sci. 14 (1961) 66.

LANSING, A.I., J.HILLIER and T.B.ROSENTHAL: Electron microscopy of some marine egg inclusions. Biol. Bull. 103 (1952) 294.

LEFF, J., M.MANDEL, H.T.EPSTEIN and J.A.SCHIFF: DNA satellites from cells of green and aplastidic algae. Biochim. Biophys. Res. Commun. 13 (1963) 126.

LEWIS, W.H. and M.R.LEWIS: Mitochondria and other cytoplasmic structures in tissue cultures. Am. J. Anat. 17 (1915) 339.

LIMA-DE-FARIA, A. and M.J.MOSES: Labeling of *Zea mays* chloroplasts with H^3-thymidine. Hereditas 52 (1964) 367.

LIMA-DE-FARIA, A.: Labeling of the cytoplasm and the meiotic chromosomes of *Agapanthus* with H^3-thymidine. Hereditas 53 (1965) 1.

LINNANE, A.W., E.VITOLS and P.G.NOWLAND: Studies on the origin of yeast mitochondria. J. Cell Biol. 13 (1962) 345.

LOWRY, R.J., T.L.DURKEE and A.S.SUSSMAN: Ultrastructural studies of microconidium formation in *Neurospora crassa*. J. Bacteriol. (in press).

LUCK, D.J.L.: Genesis of mitochondria in *Neurospora crassa*. Proc. Natl. Acad. Sci. U.S. 49 (1963a) 233.

LUCK, D.J.L.: Formation of mitochondria in *Neurospora crassa*. A quantitative radioautographic study. J. Cell Biol. 16 (1963b) 483.

LUCK, D.J.L.: The influence of precursor pool size on mitochondrial composition in *Neurospora crassa*. J. Cell Biol. 24 (1965a) 445.

LUCK, D.J.L.: Formation of mitochondria in *Neurospora crassa*. A study based on mitochondrial density changes. J. Cell Biol. 24 (1965b) 461.

LUCK, D.J.L.: Formation of mitochondria in *Neurospora crassa*. Am. Naturalist 99 (1965c) 241.

LUCK, D.J.L. and E.REICH: DNA in mitochondria of *Neurospora crassa*. Proc. Natl. Acad. Sci. U.S. 52 (1964) 931.

LYTTLETON, J.W.: DNA synthesis in partially synchronized L cells. Exptl. Cell Res. 26 (1962) 312.

MACDONALD, R.A.: 'Lifespan' of liver cells. Autoradiographic study using tritiated thymidine in normal cirrhotic and partially hepatectomized rats. Arch. Intern. Med. 107 (1961) 335.

MACHATTIE, L.A. and C.A.THOMAS: DNA from bacteriophage lambda: Molecular length and conformation. Science 144 (1964) 1142.

MAGER, J.: Chloramphenicol and chlortetracycline inhibition of amino acid incorporation into proteins in a cell-free system from *Tetrahymena pyriformis.* Biochim. Biophys. Acta 38 (1960) 150.

MANTON, I.: Electron microscopical observations on a very small flagellate: The problem of *Chromulina pusilla* Butcher. J. Marine Biol. Assoc. U.K. 38 (1959) 319.

MANTON, I.: Some problems of mitochondrial growth. J. Exptl. Botany 12 (1961) 421.

MANTON, I. and M.PARKE: Further observations on small green flagellates with special reference to possible relatives of *Chromulina pusilla* Butcher. J. Marine Biol. Assoc. U.K. 39 (1960) 275.

MARMUR, J., M.E.CAHOON, Y.SHIMURA and H.J.VOGEL: Deoxyribonucleic acid type attributable to a bacterial endosymbiote in the protozoan *Crithidia* (*Strigomonas*) *oncopelti.* Nature 197 (1963) 1228.

MASSOVER, W.H.: Cytoplasmic cylinders in bullfrog oocytes. J. Ultrastruct. Res. 22 (1968) 159.

MCLEAN, J.R., G.L.COHN, I.K.BRANDT and M.V.SIMPSON: Incorporation of labeled amino acids into the protein of muscle and liver mitochondria. J. Biol. Chem. 233 (1958) 657.

MERESCHKOWSKY, C.: Über Natur und Ursprung der Chromatophoren in Pflanzenreiche. Biol. Zentralbl. 25 (1905) 593.

MESELSON, M. and F.W.STAHL: The replication of DNA in *Escherichia coli.* Proc. Natl. Acad. Sci. U.S. 44 (1958) 671.

MEVES, F.: Die Plastosomentheorie der Vererbung. Arch. Mikroskop. Anat. 92 (1918) 41.

MEYER, A.: Das Chlorophyllkorn in chemischer, morphologischer und biologischer Beziehung. Leipzig, A. Felix (1883).

MEYER, H.: Electron microscope study of *Trypanosoma cruzi* in thin sections of infected tissue cultures and of blood agar ferns. Parasitology 48 (1958) 1.

MEYER, R.R., M.J.FOURNIER and M.V.SIMPSON: DNA polymerase, aminoacyl-sRNA synthetases and sRNA from rat liver mitochondria. Federation Proc. 27 (1968) 802.

MILDER, R. and M.P.DEANE: Ultrastructure of *Trypanosoma conorhini* in the crithidial phase. J. Protozool. 14 (1967) 65.

MITCHELL, M.B. and H.K.MITCHELL: A nuclear gene suppressor of a cytoplasmically inherited character in *Neurospora crassa.* J. Gen. Microbiol. 14 (1956) 84.

MORIBER, L.G., B.HERSHENOY, S.AARONSON and B.BENSKY: Teratological chloroplast structures in *Euglena gracilis* permanently bleached by exogenous physical and chemical agents. J. Protozool. 10 (1963) 80.

MOSES, M.J.: Spermiogenesis in the crayfish (*Procambarus clarkii*) I. Structural characterization of the mature sperm. J. Biophys. Biochem. Cytol. 9 (1961) 222.

MOUNOLOU, J.C., H.JACOB and P.P.SLONIMSKI: Mitochondrial DNA from yeast 'petite' mutants specific changes of buoyant density corresponding to different cytoplasmic mutation. Biochem. Biophys. Res. Commun. 24 (1966) 218.

MOUSTACCHI, E. and H.MARCOVITCH: Induction de la mutation 'petite colonies' chez la levure par le 5-fluorouracile. Compt. Rend. Acad. Sci. Paris 256 (1963) 5646.

MUCKENTHALER, F.A. and A.P.MAHOWALD: DNA synthesis in the ooplasm of *Drosophila melanogaster.* J. Cell Biol. 28 (1966) 199.

MUGNAINI, E.: Helical filaments in astrocytic mitochondria of the corpus striatum in the rat. J. Cell Biol. 13 (1964) 173.

MUGNAINI, E. and F.WALBERG: Ultrastructure of neuroglia. Ergeb. Anat. Entwickl. Ges. 37 (1964) 193.

MÜHLPFORDT, H.: Über die Bedeutung und Feinstruktur des Blepharoplasten bei parasitischen Flagellaten. 1 (1963) 14; 2 (1963) 357, 476.

MUNDKUR, B.: Electron microscopical studies of frozen dried yeast II. The nature of basophile particles and vesicular nuclei in *Saccharomyces.* Exptl. Cell Res. 25 (1961) 1.

MUNKRES, K.D. and D.O.WOODWARD: On the genetics of enzyme locational specificity. Proc. Natl. Acad. Sci. U.S. 55 (1966) 1217.

NASS, M.M.K.: The circularity of mitochondrial DNA. Proc. Natl. Acad. Sci. U.S. 56 (1966) 1215.

NASS, M.M.K. and S.NASS: Intramitochondrial fibers with DNA characteristics I. Fixation and electron staining reactions. J. Cell Biol. 19 (1963) 593.

NASS, M.M.K., S.NASS and B.A.AFZELIUS: The general occurrence of mitochondrial DNA. Exptl. Cell Res. 37 (1965) 516.

NASS, S. and M.M.K.NASS: Intramitochondrial fibers with DNA characteristics II. Enzymatic and other hydrolytic treatments. J. Cell Biol. 19 (1963) 613.

NEUBERT, D., H.HELGE and R.BASS: Einbau von Thymidin in die Deoxyribonucleinsäure von Mitochondrien. Naunyn-Schmiedeberg's Arch. Exptl. Pathol. Pharmakol. 252 (1965) 258.

NEUPERT, W., D.BRDICZKA and TH.BÜCHER: Incorporation of amino acids into the outer and inner membrane of isolated rat liver mitochondria. Biochem. Biophys. Res. Commun. 27 (1967) 488.

NEWCOMER, E.H.: Mitochondria in plants. Botan. Rev. 6 (1940) 85.

NEWCOMER, E.H.: Mitochondria in plants II. Botan. Rev. 17 (1951) 53.

NOVIKOFF, A.B.: Biochemical heterogeneity of the cytoplasmic particles of rat liver. Symp. Soc. Exptl. Biol. 10 (1957) 92.

NOVIKOFF, A.B.: Mitochondria (chondriosomes). In: J.Brachet and A.Mirsky, eds.: The cell, Vol. 2. New York, Academic Press (1961) 299.

O'BRIEN, T.W. and G.F.KALF: Ribosomes from rat liver mitochondria I. Isolation procedure and contamination studies. J. Biol. Chem. 242 (1967) 2172.

OGAWA, H. and J.TOMIZAWA: Bacteriophage lambda DNA with different structures found in infected cells. J. Mol. Biol. 23 (1967) 265.

ORNSTEIN, L.: Mitochondrial and nuclear interaction. J. Biophys. Biochem. Cytol. Suppl. 2 (1956) 351.

PALADE, G.E.: The fine structure of mitochondria. Anat. Record 114 (1952) 427.

PANNESE, E.: Expansive growth of the nuclear envelope and formation of mitochondria in ganglionic neuroblasts. Z. Zellforsch. 72 (1966) 295.

PARSONS, D., G.WILLIAMS and B.CHANCE: Characteristics of isolated and purified preparations of the outer and inner membranes of mitochondria. Ann. N.Y. Acad. Sci. U.S. 137 (1966) 643.

PARSONS, J.A.: Mitochondrial incorporation of tritiated thymidine in *Tetrahymena pyriformis*. J. Cell Biol. 25 (1965) 641.

PARSONS, J.A. and R.C.RUSTAD: The distribution of DNA among dividing mitochondria of *Tetrahymena pyriformis*. J. Cell Biol. 37 (1968) 683.

PARSONS, P. and M.V.SIMPSON: Biosynthesis of DNA by isolated mitochondria: incorporation of thymidine triphosphate-2-C^{14}. Science 155 (1967) 91.

PERSONNE, P.: Etude cytochimique du derivé mitochondrial du spermatozoïde de la testacelle. J. Microscopie 4 (1965) 627.

PHILLIPS, D.M.: Observations on spermiogenesis in the fungus gnat *Sciara*. J. Cell Biol. 30 (1966) 477.

PIKÓ, L., D.G.BLAIR, A.TYLER and J.VINOGRAD: Cytoplasmic DNA in the unfertilized sea urchin egg: physical properties of circular mitochondrial DNA and the occurrence of catenated forms. Proc. Natl. Acad. Sci. U.S. 59 (1968) 838.

PIKÓ, L., A.TYLER and J.VINOGRAD: Amount, location, priming, capacity, circularity and other properties of cytoplasmic DNA in sea urchin egg. Biol. Bull. 132 (1967) 68.

PITTENGER, T.H.: Synergism of two cytochemically inherited mutants in *Neurospora crassa*. Proc. Natl. Acad. Sci. U.S. 42 (1956) 747.

PLAUT, W. and L.A.SAGAN: Incorporation of thymidine in the cytoplasm of *Amoeba proteus*. J. Biophys. Biochem. Cytol. 4 (1958) 843.

PORTIER, P.: Les Symbiotes. Paris, Masson et Cie (1918).

PRATT, S.A.: An electron microscope study of nebenkern formation and differentiation in spermatids of *Murgantia histrionica* (Hemiptera, Pentatomidae). J. Morph. 126 (1968) 31.

PULLMAN, M.E. and G.SCHATZ: Mitochondrial oxidations and energy coupling. Ann. Rev. Biochem. 36 (1967) 539.

RABINOVITCH, M. and W.PLAUT: Cytoplasmic DNA synthesis in *Amoeba proteus* I. On the particulate nature of the DNA-containing elements. J. Cell Biol. 15 (1962) 525.

RABINOWITZ, M.: Extranuclear DNA. Bull. Soc. Chim. Biol. 50 (1968) 311.

RABINOWITZ, M., G.GETZ, J.CASEY and H.SWIFT: Synthesis of mitochondrial and nuclear DNA in anaerobically grown yeast during the development of mitochondrial function in response to oxygen. Submitted for publication.

RABINOWITZ, M., J.SINCLAIR, L.DESALLE, R.HASELKORN and H.H.SWIFT: Isolation of deoxyribonucleic acid from mitochondria of chick embryo heart and liver. Proc. Natl. Acad. Sci. U.S. 53 (1965) 1126.

RADLOFF, R., W.BAUER and J.VINOGRAD: A dye-buoyant-density method for the detection and isolation of closed circular duplex DNA: The closed circular DNA of HeLa cells. Proc. Natl. Acad. Sci. U.S. 57 (1967) 1514.

RAWSON, J.R. and E.STUTZ: Characterization of *Euglena* cytoplasmic ribosomes and ribosomal RNA by zone velocity sedimentation in sucrose gradients. J. Mol. Biol. 33 (1968) 309.

RAY, D.S. and HANAWALT: Properties of the satallite DNA associated with chloroplasts of *Euglena gracilis*. J. Mol. Biol. 9 (1964) 812.

REICH, E. and D.J.L.LUCK: Replication and importance of mitochondrial DNA. Proc. Natl. Acad. Sci. U.S. 55 (1966) 1600.

RENDI, R.: On the occurrence of intramitochondrial ribonucleoprotein particles. Exptl. Cell Res. 17 (1959) 585.

RENDI, R. and R.C.WARNER: Intracellular sites for amino acid incorporation into proteins. Ann. N.Y. Acad. Sci. 88 (1960) 741.

RENNER, O.: Zur Kenntnis der nichtmendelnden Buntheit der Laubblätter. Flora (Jena) 30 (1936) 218.

RHOADES, M.M.: Genic induction of an inherited cytoplasmic difference. Proc. Natl. Acad. Sci. U.S. 29 (1943) 327.

RHOADES, M.M.: Plastid mutations. Cold Spring Harbor Symp. Quant. Biol. 11 (1946) 202.

RHOADES, M.M.: Interaction of genic and non-genic hereditary units and the physiology of non-genic inheritance. Encycl. Plant Physiol. Berlin, Springer 1 (1955) 19.

RICHARDS, O.C.: Hybridization of *Euglena gracilis* chloroplast and nuclear DNA. Proc. Natl. Acad. Sci. U.S. 57 (1967) 156.

RIFKIN, M.R., D.D.WOOD and D.J.L.LUCK: Ribosomal RNA and ribosomes from mitochondria of *Neurospora crassa*. Proc. Natl. Acad. Sci. U.S. 58 (1967) 1025.

RIOU, G. and E.DELAIN: Electron microscopy of the circular kinetoplastic DNA from *Trypanosoma cruzi*: Occurrence of catenated forms. Proc. Natl. Acad. Sci. U.S. 62 (1969) 210.

RIOU, G. and C.PAOLETTI: Preparation and properties of nuclear and satellite DNA of *Trypanosoma cruzi*. J. Mol. Biol. 28 (1967) 377.

RIOU, G., R.PAUTRIZEL and A.PAOLETTI: Fractionnement et caractérisation de l'ADN de Trypanosome (*T. equiperdum*). Compt. Rend. Acad. Sci. 262 (1966) D2376.

RIS, H.: Ultrastructure and molecular organization of genetic systems. Can. J. Genet. Cytol. 3 (1961) 95.

RIS, H.: Ultrastructure of certain self dependent cytoplasmic organelles. Fifth Intern. Congr. Electron Micros. New York, Academic Press p. xx–1.

RIS, H. and W.PLAUT: Ultrastructure of DNA-containing areas in the chloroplast of *Chlamydomonas*. J. Cell Biol. 13 (1962) 383.

ROBERTSON, J.D.: The ultrastructure of cell membranes and their derivatives. Biochem. Soc. Symp. (Cambridge, Engl.) 16 (1959) 3.

ROBERTSON, M.: The action of acriflavin upon *Bodo candutus*. Parasitology 21 (1929) 375.

ROGERS, P.J., B.N.PRESTON, E.B.TITCHENER and A.W.LINNANE: Differences between the sedimentation characteristics of the ribonucleic acids prepared from yeast cytoplasmic ribosomes and mitochondria. Biochem. Biophys. Res. Commun. 27 (1967) 405.

ROODYN, D.B.: Protein synthesis in mitochondria III. The controlled disruption and subfractionation of mitochondria labelled *in vitro* with radioactive valine. Biochem. J. 85 (1962) 177.

ROODYN, D.B.: Further study of factors affecting amino acid incorporation into protein by isolated mitochondria. Biochem. J. 97 (1965) 782.

ROODYN, D.B.: Factors affecting the incorporation of amino acids into protein by isolated mitochondria. In: J.M.Tager, S.Papa, E.Quagliariello and E.C.Slater, eds.: Regulation of metabolic processes in mitochondria. Amsterdam, Elsevier Publishing Company (1966) p. 383.

ROODYN, D.B.: The mitochondrion. In: Enzyme cytology. New York, Academic Press (1967).

ROODYN, D.B., K.B.FREEMAN and J.R.TATA: The stimulation by treatment *in vivo* with tri-iodotyrosine of amino acid incorporation into protein by isolated rat liver mitochondria. Biochem. J. 94 (1965) 628.

ROODYN, D.B., P.J.REIS and T.S.WORK: Protein synthesis in mitochondria; requirements for the incorporation of radioactive amino acids into mitochondrial protein. Biochem. J. 80 (1961) 9.

ROODYN, D.B. and D.WILKIE: The biogenesis of mitochondria. London, Methuen and Co. (1968).

RUDZINSKA, M.A., P.A.D'ALESANDRO and W.TRAGER: The fine structure of *Leishmania donovani* and the role of the kinetoplast in the leishmania-leptomonad transformation. J. Protozool. 11 (1964) 166.

RYLEY, J.F.: Comparative metabolism of blood stream and culture forms of *Trypanosoma rhodesiense*. Biochem. J. 85 (1962) 211.

RYTER, A., E.KELLENBERGER, A.BIRCH-ANDERSEN and O.MAALØE: Étude au microscope électronique de plasmas contenant de l'acide désoxyribonucléique I. Les nucléoides des bactéries en croissance active. Z. Naturforsch. 13b (1958) 597.

SAGER, R.: Non-chromosomal genes in *Chlamydomonas*. In: S.J.Geerts, ed.: Genetics today. Proc. XI Int. Cong. Genetics, Vol. 3. Oxford, Pergamon Press (1965) p. 479.

SAGER, R. and M.R.ISHIDA: Chloroplast DNA in *Chlamydomonas*. Proc. Natl. Acad. Sci. U.S. 50 (1963) 725.

SCHATZ, G., E.HASELBRUNNER and H.TUPPY: Deoxyribonucleic acid associated with yeast mitochondria. Biochem. Biophys. Res. Commun. 15 (1964) 127.

SCHERBAUM, O.: Possible sites of metabolic control during the induction of synchronous cell division. Ann. N.Y. Acad. Sci. 90 (1960) 565.

SCHIFF, J.A. and H.T.EPSTEIN: The continuity of the chloroplast in *Euglena*. In: M.Locke, ed.: Reproduction: molecular, subcellular and cellular. Symp. Soc. Develop. Biol. 24 (1965) 131.

SCHILDKRAUT, C.L., M.MANDEL, S.LEVISOHN, J.E.SMITH-SONNEBORN and J.MARMUR: Deoxyribonucleic acid base composition and taxonomy of some protozoa. Nature 196 (1962) 795.

SCHIMPER, A.F.W.: Ueber die Entwickelung der Chlorophyllkörper und Farbkörper. Botan. Ztg. 41 (1883) 105, 121, 137, 153.

SCHNAITMAN, C. and J.W.GREENAWALT: Enzymatic properties of the inner and outer membranes of rat liver mitochondria. J. Cell Biol. 38 (1968) 158.

SCHNEIDER, W.C. and G.H.HOGEBOOM: Cytochemical studies of mammalian tissues: The isolation of cell components by differential centrifugation: A review. Cancer Res. 11 (1951) 1.

SCHUSTER, F.L.: A deoxyribose nucleic acid component in mitochondria of *Didymium nigripes*, a slime mold. Exptl. Cell Res. 39 (1965) 329.

SCOTT, N.S. and R.M.SMILLIE: Evidence for the direction of chloroplast ribosomal RNA synthesis by chloroplast DNA. Biochem. Biophys. Res. Commun. 28 (1967) 598.

SEMAL, J., D.SPENCER, Y.T.KIM and S.G.WILDMAN: Properties of a ribonucleic acid synthesizing system in cell-free extracts of tobacco leaves. Biochim. Biophys. Acta 91 (1964) 205.

SHAH, V.C. and H.LYMAN: DNA dependent RNA synthesis in chloroplasts of *Euglena gracilis*. J. Cell Biol. 29 (1966) 174.

SHAPIRO, L., L.I.GROSSMANN, J.MARMUR and A.K.KLEINSCHMIDT: Physical studies on the structure of yeast mitochondrial DNA. J. Mol. Biol. 33 (1968) 907.

SHERMAN, F.: Respiration-deficient mutants of yeast I. Genetics. Genetics 48 (1963) 375.

SHERMAN, F. and B. EPHRUSSI: The relationship between respiratory deficiency and suppressiveness in yeast as determined with segregational mutants. Genetics 47 (1962) 695.

SHERMAN, F., J. W. STEWART, E. MARGOLIASH, J. PARKER and W. CAMPBELL: The structural gene for yeast cytochrome c. Proc. Natl. Acad. Sci. U.S. 55 (1966) 1498.

SHERMAN, F., H. TABER and W. CAMPBELL: Genetic determination of iso-cytochromes c in yeast. J. Mol. Biol. 13 (1965) 21.

SHIPLEY, P. G.: The vital staining of mitochondria in *Trypanosoma lewisi* with Janus green. Anat. Record 10 (1916) 439.

SHIPP, W. S., F. J. KIERAS and R. HASELKORN: DNA associated with tobacco chloroplasts. Proc. Natl. Acad. Sci. U.S. 54 (1965) 207.

SIEKEVITZ, P.: Uptake of radioactive alanine in vitro into the proteins of rat liver fractions. J. Biol. Chem. 195 (1952) 549.

SIEKEVITZ, P. and M. WATSON: Cytochemical studies of mitochondria II. Enzymes associated with a mitochondrial membrane fraction. J. Biophys. Biochem. Cytol. 2 (1956) 653.

SIMPSON, L.: The kinetoplast and transformation in *Leishmania*. Intern. Conf. Protozool. 2 (1965) 30.

SIMPSON, L.: Behavior of the kinetoplast of *Leishmania tarentolae* upon cell rupture. J. Protozool. 15 (1968a) 132.

SIMPSON, L.: The leishmania-leptomonad transformation of *Leishmania donovani*: Nutritional requirements, respiration changes and antigenic changes. J. Protozool. 15 (1968b) 201.

SIMPSON, L.: Effect of acriflavin on the kinetoplast of *Leishmania tarentolae*. Mode of action and physiological correlates in the loss of kinetoplast DNA. J. Cell Biol. 37 (1968c) 66.

SIMPSON, M. V.: Protein biosynthesis. Ann. Rev. Biochem. 31 (1962) 333.

SINCLAIR, J. H.: Mitochondrial DNA and other low molecular weight cellular DNAs. Ph.D. Thesis, University of Chicago (1966).

SINCLAIR, J. H. and B. J. STEVENS: Circular DNA filaments from mouse mitochondria. Proc. Natl. Acad. Sci. U.S. 56 (1966a) 508.

SINCLAIR, J. H. and B. J. STEVENS: Circular mitochondrial DNA. J. Cell Biol. 31 (1966a) 108A (Abstr.).

SINCLAIR, J. H., B. J. STEVENS, N. GROSS and M. RABINOWITZ: The constant size of circular mitochondrial DNA in several organisms and different organs. Biochim. Biophys. Acta 145 (1967) 528.

SINCLAIR, J. H., B. J. STEVENS, P. SANGHAVI and M. RABINOWITZ: Mitochondrial-satellite and circular DNA filaments in yeast. Science 156 (1967) 1234.

SISSAKIAN, N. M., I. I. FILIPPOVITCH, E. N. SVETAILO and R. A. ALIYEV: On the protein-synthesizing system of chloroplasts. Biochim. Biophys. Acta 95 (1965) 474.

SJÖSTRAND, F. S.: Electron microscopy of mitochondria and cytoplasmic double membranes. Nature 171 (1953) 30.

SLATER, E. C., J. M. TAGER, S. PAPA and E. QUAGLIARIELLO: Biochemical aspects of the biogenesis of mitochondria. Bari, Italy, Adriatica Editrice (in press).

SLONIMSKI, P. P.: Formation des enzymes respiratoires chez la levure. Paris, Masson (1953).

SLONIMSKI, P. P., G. PERRODIN and J. H. CROFT: Ethidium bromide induced mutation of yeast mitochondria: Complete transformation of cells into respiratory deficient non-chromosomal 'petites'. Biochem. Biophys. Res. Commun. 30 (1968) 232.

SO, A. G. and E. W. DAVIE: The incorporation of amino acids into protein in a cell-free system from yeast. Biochemistry 2 (1963) 132.

SOMLO, M. and H. FUKUHARA: On the necessity of molecular oxygen for the synthesis of respiratory enzymes in yeast. Biochem. Biophys. Res. Commun. 19 (1965) 587.

SPENCER, D.: Protein synthesis by isolated spinach chloroplasts. Arch. Biochem. Biophys. 111 (1965) 381.

SRB, A.M.: Extrachromosomal factors in the genetic differentiation of *Neurospora*. Symp. Soc. Exptl. Biol. 17 (1963) 175.

STANIER, R.Y.: Formation and function of the photosynthetic pigment system in purple bacteria. Brookhaven Symp. Biol. 11 (1958) 43.

STEFFENSEN, D.M. and W.F.SHERIDAN: Incorporation of H^3-thymidine into chloroplast DNA of marine algae. J. Cell Biol. 25 (1965) 619.

STEPHENSON, M.L., K.V.THIMANN and P.C.ZAMECNIK: Incorporation of C^{14}-amino acids into proteins of leaf disks and cell-free fractions of tobacco leaves. Arch. Biochem. Biophys. 65 (1965) 194.

STEINERT, M.: Mitochondria associated with the kinetonucleus of *Trypanosoma meger*. J. Biophys. Biochem. Cytol. 8 (1960) 542.

STEINERT, M.: L'absence d'histone dans le kinétonucléus des trypanosomes. Exptl. Cell Res. 39 (1965) 69.

STEINERT, M. and G.STEINERT: Inhibition de la synthèse de l'acide désoxyribonucléique de *Trypanosoma mega* par l'urée à faible concentration. Exptl. Cell Res. 19 (1960) 421.

STONE, G.E. and O.L.MILLER: A stable mitochondrial DNA in *Tetrahymena pyriformis*. J. Exptl. Zool. 159 (1965) 33.

STRASBURGER, E.: Ueber den Theilungsvorgang der Zellkerne und das Verhaltniss der Kerntheilung zur Zelltheilung. Arch. Mikroskop. Anat. 21 (1882) 476.

STUBBE, W.: Der Role des Plastoms in der Evolution der Oenotheren. Ber. Deut. Botan. Ges. 76 (1963) 154.

STUTZ, E. and H. NOLL: Characterization of cytoplasmic and chloroplast polysomes in plants: Evidence for three classes of ribosomal RNA in nature. Proc. Natl. Acad. Sci. U.S. 57 (1967) 774.

SUBIRANA, J.A.: Kinetics of renaturation of denatured DNA II. Products of the reaction. Biopolymers 4 (1966) 189.

SUEOKA, N., K.S.CHIANG and J.R.KATES: Deoxyribonucleic acid replication in meiosis of *Chlamydomonas reinhardi*. I. Isotopic transfer experiments with a strain producing eight zoopoires. J. Mol. Biol. 25 (1967) 47.

SUYAMA, Y.: The origins of mitochondrial ribonucleic acids in *Tetrahymena pyriformis*. Biochemistry 6 (1967) 2829.

SUYAMA, Y. and W.D.BONNER: DNA from plant mitochondria. Plant Physiol. 41 (1966) 383.

SUYAMA, Y. and J.EYER: Ribonucleic acid synthesis in isolated mitochondria from *Tetrahymena*. J. Biol. Chem. 243 (1968) 320.

SUYAMA, Y. and K.MIURA: Size and structural variation of mitochondrial DNA. Proc. Natl. Acad. Sci. U.S. 60 (1968) 235.

SUYAMA, Y. and J.R.PREER: Mitochondrial DNA from protozoa. Genetics 52 (1965) 1051.

SVOBODA, D. and J.HIGGINSON: Ultrastructural changes produced by protein and related deficiencies in the rat liver. Am. J. Pathol. 45 (1964) 353.

SWIFT, H.: Nucleic acids of mitochondria and chloroplasts. Am. Naturalist 99 (1965) 201.

SWIFT, H., B.J.ADAMS and K.LARSEN: Electron microscope cytochemistry of nucleic acids in *Drosophila* salivary glands and *Tetrahymena*. J. Roy. Microscop. Soc. 83 (1964) 161.

SWIFT, H. and Z.HRUBAN: Focal degradation as a biological process. Federation Proc. 23 (1964) 1026.

SWIFT, H., M.RABINOWITZ and G.GETZ: Cytochemical studies on mitochondrial nucleic acids. In: E.C.Slater, J.M.Tager, S.Papa and E.Quagliarriello, eds.: Biochemical aspects of biogenesis of mitochondria. Bari, Italy, Adriatica Editrice.

SZOLLOSI, D.: The fate of sperm middle-piece mitochondria in the rat egg. J. Exptl. Zool. 159 (1965) 367.

TAKAGI, S.: Contribution to the study of mitochondria. Mem. Coll. Sci., Univ. Kyoto, Ser. B 15 (1939) 167.

TAKATS, S.T. and R.M.S.SMELLIE: Thymidine degradation products in plant tissues labelled with tritiated thymidine. J. Cell Biol. 17 (1963) 59.

TANDLER, B., R.A.ERLANDSON, A.L.SMITH and E.L.WYNDER: Riboflavin and mouse hepatic cell structure and function. II. Division of mitochondria during recovery from simple deficiency. J. Cell Biol. 41 (1969) 477.

TATUM, E.L. and D.J.L.LUCK: Nuclear morphology and cytoplasmic control of morphology in *Neurospora*. In: M.Locke, ed.: Control mechanisms in developmental processes. Develop. Biol. Suppl. 1 (1967) 32.

TEWARI, K.K., W.VÖTSCH and H.R.MAHLER: Biochemical correlates of respiratory deficiency VI. Mitochondrial DNA. J. Mol. Biol. 20 (1966) 453.

TEWARI, K.K. and S.G.WILDMAN: Chloroplast DNA from tobacco leaves. Science 153 (1966) 1269.

THOMAS, D.Y. and D.WILKIE: Recombination of mitochondrial drug-resistance factors in *Saccharomyces cerevisiae*. Biochem. Biophys. Res. Commun. 30 (1968) 368.

TRAGER, W.: The kinetoplast and differentiation in certain protozoa. Am. Naturalist 99 (1965) 255.

TRAGER, W. and M.A.RUDZINSKA: The riboflavin requirement and the effects of acriflavin on the fine structure of the kinetoplast of *Leishmania tarentolae*. J. Protozool. 11 (1964) 133.

TRUMAN, D.E.S.: Incorporation of amino acids into the proteins of sub-mitochondrial particles. Exptl. Cell Res. 31 (1963) 313.

TRUMAN, D.E.S. and A.KORNER: Incorporation of amino acids into the protein of isolated mitochondria. Biochem. J. 83 (1962) 588.

VAN BRUGGEN, E.F.J., P.BORST, G.J.C.M.RUTTENBERG, M.GRUBER and A.M.KROON: Circular mitochondrial DNA. Biochim. Biophys. Acta 119 (1966) 437.

VAN BRUGGEN, E.F.J., M.M.C.LEURS, P.BORST, A.M.KROON and G.J.C.M.RUTTENBERG: quoted by Borst et al. (1967).

VAN WISSELINGH, C.: Über Variabilität und Erblichkeit. Z. Vererbungslehre 22 (1920) 65.

VICKERMAN, K.: Polymorphism and mitochondrial activity in sleeping sickness trypanosomes. Nature 208 (1965) 762.

VINOGRAD, J. and J.LEBOWITZ: Physical and topological properties of circular DNA. J. Gen. Physiol. 49 (1966) 103.

VITOLS, E., R.J.NORTH and A.W.LINNANE: Studies on the oxidative metabolism of *Saccharomyces cerevisiae*. J. Biophys. Biochem. Cytol. 9 (1961) 689.

VON WETTSTEIN, D.: The formation of plastid structures. Brookhaven Symp. Biol. 11 (1958) 138.

VON WETTSTEIN, D.: Nuclear and cytoplasmic factors in development of chloroplast structure and function. Can. J. Botany 39 (1961) 1537.

WALLACE, P.G., M.HUANG and A.W.LINNANE: The biogenesis of mitochondria II. The influence of medium composition on the cytology of anaerobically grown *Saccharomyces cerevisiae*. J. Cell Biol. 37 (1968) 207.

WALLIN, I.E.: The independent growth of mitochondria in artificial culture medium VII. Anat. Record 25 (1922) 152.

WATSON, M.L. and W.G.ALDRIDGE: Selective electron staining of nucleic acids. J. Histochem. Cytochem. 12 (1964) 96.

WERBITZKI, F.W.: Über blepharophastlose Trypanosomen. Zentr. Bakteriol. Parasitenk., Abt. I. Orig. 53 (1910) 303.

WHEELDON, L.: The problem of bacterial contamination in studies of protein synthesis by isolated mitochondria. Biochem. Biophys. Res. Commun. 24 (1966) 407.

WHEELDON, L.W. and A.L.LEHNINGER: Energy-linked synthesis and decay of membrane proteins in isolated rat liver mitochondria. Biochemistry 5 (1966) 3533.

WILKIE, D.: The cytoplasm in heredity. London, Methuen and Co. (1964).

WILSON, J.F.: Micrurgical techniques for *Neurospora*. Am. J. Botany 48 (1961) 46.

WINTERSBERGER, E.: Proteinsynthese in isolierten Hefe-Mitochondrien. Biochem. Z. 341 (1965) 409.

WINTERSBERGER, E.: Occurrence of a DNA-polymerase in isolated yeast mitochondria. Biochem. Biophys. Res. Commun. 25 (1966) 1.

WINTERSBERGER, E.: Synthesis and function of mitochondrial ribonucleic acid. In: J. M. Tager, S. Papa and E. Quagliariello, eds.: Regulation of metabolic processes in mitochondria. Amsterdam, Elsevier Publ. Co. (1966) p. 437.

WOLSTENHOLME, D. R. and I. B. DAWID: Circular mitochondrial DNA from *Xenopus laevis* and *Rana pipiens*. Chromosoma 20 (1967) 445.

WOLSTENHOLME, D. R. and I. B. DAWID: A size difference between mitochondrial DNA molecules of urodele and anuran amphibia. J. Cell Biol. 39 (1968) 222.

WOLSTENHOLME, D. R. and N. J. GROSS: The form and size of mitochondrial DNA of the red bean *Phaseolus vulgaris*. Proc. Natl. Acad. Sci. U.S. 61 (1968) 245.

WOLSTENHOLME, D. R. and W. PLAUT: Cytoplasmic DNA synthesis in *Amoeba proteus* III. Further studies on the nature of the DNA-containing elements. J. Cell Biol. 22 (1964) 505.

WOODCOCK, C. L. F. and H. FERNÁNDEZ-MORÁN: Electron microscopy of DNA conformations in spinach chloroplasts. J. Mol. Biol. 31 (1968) 627.

WOODWARD, D. O. and K. D. MUNKRES: Alterations of a maternally inherited mitochondrial structural protein in respiratory-deficient strains of *Neurospora*. Proc. Natl. Acad. Sci. U.S. 55 (1966) 872.

WOODWARD, D. O. and K. D. MUNKRES: Genetic control, function, and assembly of a structural protein in *Neurospora*. In: H. J. Vogel, J. O. Lampen and V. Bryson, eds.: Organizational biosynthesis. New York, Academic Press p. 489.

WRIGHT, R. E. and J. LEDERBERG: Extranuclear transmission in yeast heterokaryons. Proc. Natl. Acad. Sci. U.S. 43 (1957) 919.

YOTSUYANAGI, Y.: Études sur le chondriome de la levure II. Chondriomes des mutants à deficience respiratoire. J. Ultrastruct. Res. 7 (1962) 141.

YOTSUYANAGI, Y.: Un mode de différentiation de la membrane mitochondriale evoquant le mésosome bactérien. Compt. Rend. Acad. Sci. 262 (1966) 1348.

YOTSUYANAGI, Y. and C. GUERRIER: Mise en évidence par des techniques cytochimiques et la microscopie électronique d'acide désoxyribonucléique dans les mitochondries et les proplastes d'*Allium cepa*. Compt. Rend. Acad. Sci. 260 (1965) 2344.

CHAPTER 38

Cytochemistry and ultrastructure of chloroplasts

MARCELLE LEFORT-TRAN

Laboratoire de Cytobiologie Expérimentale associé au C.N.R.S., Faculté des Sciences, Orsay 91, France

Contents

1. Introduction

2. Structural and pigment molecules
   (a) Structural molecules
      Lamellar structures
      Particulate structures
      Enzyme treatments
      Discussion
   (b) Pigment molecules
      Chlorophylls
      Phycobiliproteins

3. Nucleic acids of chloroplasts
   (a) Historical review
      Specific staining
      Autoradiography
   (b) Ultrastructural studies
      Deoxyribonucleic acid – *in situ*
      Isolated DNA of plastids
      Plastid RNA
   (c) Genetic implications

4. Conclusions

1. Introduction

By their structure, function, and mechanism of inheritance, chloroplasts occupy in the cell a unique place which distinguishes them from other cellular organelles. They are the seat of photosynthetic phenomena: light reactions (absorption of photons and electron transport), dark reactions (fixation of CO_2 to give highly polymerised compounds such as starch), and synthesis of the energy-rich adenine nucleotide (ATP) molecule by photophosphorylation. Thus, it is at the level of the chloroplast that the bio-energetic phenomena take place which, starting with solar energy, go on to permit animals and men to assimilate and utilise that energy.

It has long been observed that chloroplasts appear to have a means of inheritance different from that of the cells which contain them. The discovery by cytological and biochemical means of DNA and RNA in the plastids, and the fact that these nucleic acids appear to differ from those of the rest of the cell in their density and nucleotide sequence, confirm forcefully the idea that plastids have some degree of genetic independence. Since the chloroplast is considered as the photosynthetic unit, the analysis of its structure can not be dissociated from an analysis of its characteristic function. Moreover, an analysis of the molecules endowed with the information which directs its replication ought to be considered in this context.

To the classical techniques cytology, which relied essentially on staining reactions specific for certain structures or molecules (e.g. the Feulgen reaction for DNA, or the double stain methyl green pyronine), have been added a number of specific techniques. Techniques involving enzymatic digestion are the following: digestion of nucleic acids by DNAse and RNAse, Brachet's test; protein digestion by proteolytic enzymes (Leduc and Bernhard 1962) and lipid digestion by specific lipases (Park et al.). To these enzymatic methods have been added other techniques: (1) autoradiography combined with electron microscopy (Caro, Granboulan and Droz), (2) freeze-etching (Moor) and (3) negative staining in association with other treatments or with chemical and enzymatic reactions.

2. Structural and pigment molecules

(a) *Structural molecules*

Lamellar structures. Fig. 1 represents a sagittal section of a chloroplast from a cell of *Zea mays*. One can distinguish within the double limiting membrane (Me) the co-existence of two distinct systems: (1) a granular matrix (Ma) composed of ribosomes and soluble proteins, and (2) in the midst of this matrix, a lamellar system which is differentiated into (a) *grana lamellae* or *thylakoids* (thy) (Menke), the stacking of which into piles constitutes the *grana* and (b) into finer *intergrana lamellae* or *stroma lamellae*, which join *grana* together (thy. s, see Figs. 1 and 3). These intergrana lamellae, of a thickness of about 70 Å, also constitute the marginal membrane of the

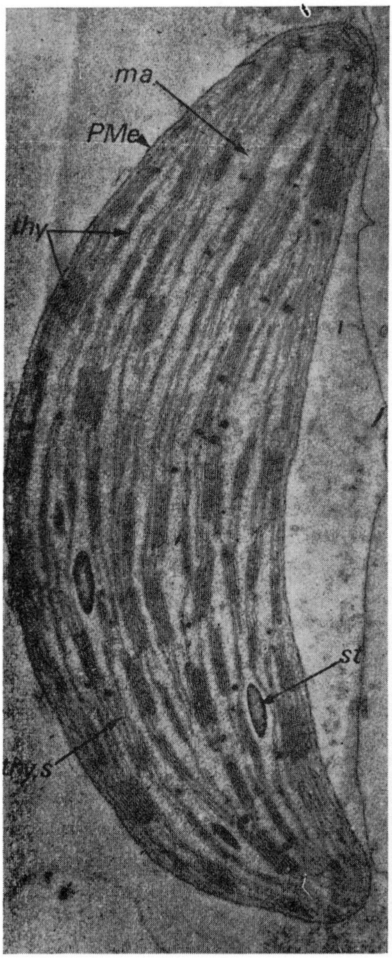

Fig. 1

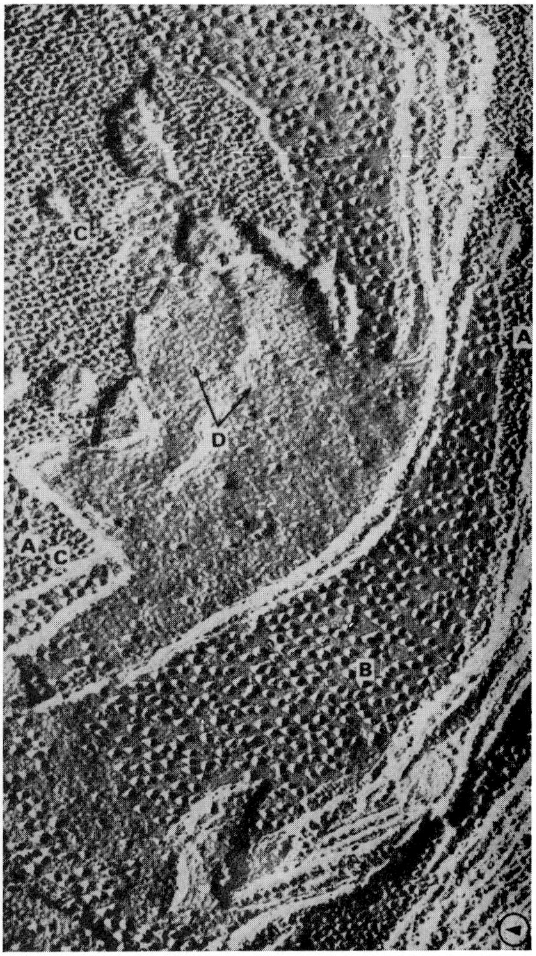

Fig. 2

Fig. 1. Chloroplast of *Zea mays* in sagittal section. Lamellar system characterised by thylakoids (thy) stacked to form grana and by intergrana lamellae (thy.s.); grains of starch (st) in the granular matrix (ma). PMe = double plastid membrane. (Glutaraldehyde–osmium ×17,500.)

Fig. 2. Lamellar surfaces after freeze-etching. Three types of surface are revealed, they have been arbitrarily labeled A, B, and C. Face A is a rough surface devoid of discrete particles. Face B is formed of a relatively smooth surface on which are distributed particles of 160 to 200 Å in diameter. Arrows indicate the depressions (D) from which particles have been pulled away during fracture. Face C consists primarily of small particles 100 to 130 Å (occasionally larger particles up to 200 Å). Isolated spinach chloroplasts resuspended in glycerol (10%). (Courtesy of R.B. Park; × 78,000.)

grana. Within the grana the fusion of two adjacent membranes (or lamellae) gives the appearance of a leaflet (thy) of a thickness of about 150 Å (Fig. 3). The stacking of these leaflets corresponds to the picture of 'a pile of falling coins' which was shown first by Steinmann in 1952 on shadowed membranes of isolated chloroplasts. Each of the 70-Å membranes may correspond to what is conventionally called a 'unit membrane'. The concept of a unit membrane, defined by Robertson (1957), has been a very useful working model for understanding the importance of membrane structures in the cell and for making structural interpretations of membranes at the molecular level. According to this concept, the 70-Å intergrana lamellae, which resolve into two dark lines of 20 Å each enclosing a clear zone of 30 Å, are made up of two layers of oriented lipids each covered with a layer of hydrophilic protein which is in direct contact with the highly hydrated matrix of the chloroplast. The idea of a leaflet structure for the chloroplast, according to the 'unit membrane' model, has almost become a dogma for some researchers. (See the chapter by Robertson.)

Particulate structures. In the shadowed preparations of Steinmann (1952), as in those of Park and Pon (1961), one discerns, on the surface of the membrane, a certain granularity which sometimes appears to be regular. The presence of globular subunits, considered as integral parts of the membrane (Weier and Benson 1966, 1967) or as particles bound to the inner or outer surfaces of the membranes (Fig. 5), seems to

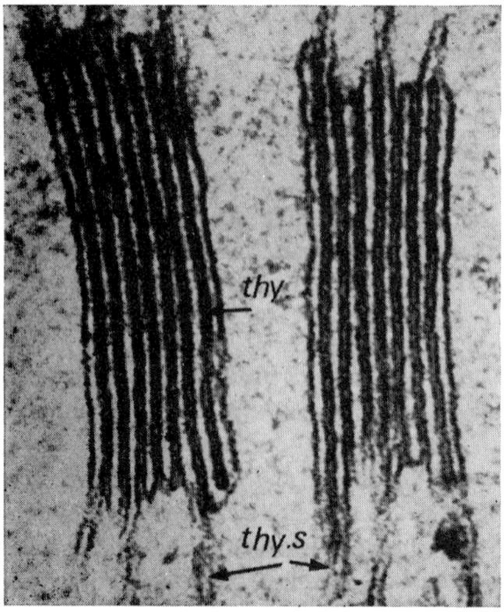

Fig. 3

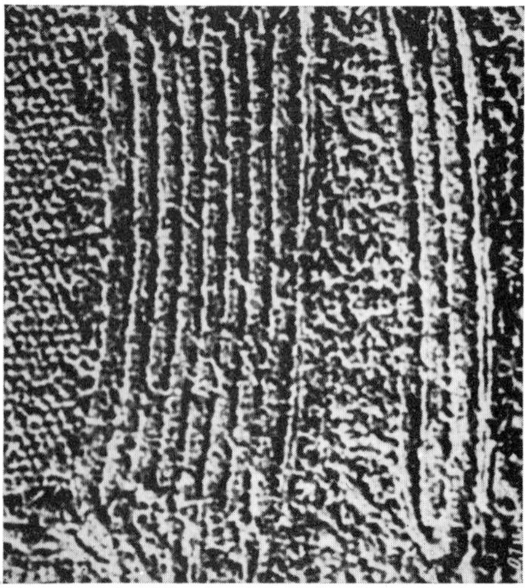

Fig. 4

Fig. 3. Detail of grana; the marginal membranes are 70 Å thick and correspond to the single unit membrane. Two membranes joined side by side form a thylakoid or 'partition' (Weier, see Fig. 6) of 150 Å thickness. (Courtesy of Mühlethaler; Glutaraldehyde–osmium tetroxide fixation, ×124,000.)

Fig. 4. Section of grana after freeze-etching. The two marginal grana thylakoids consist of a triple-layered membrane. (Courtesy of Mühlethaler; ×114,000.)

be confirmed by numerous studies: (1) negative staining (Park and Pon; Oda and Huzisige; Bronchart; Wessels), (2) shadowing techniques (Menke and Park), and (3) freeze-etching (Mühlethaler; Frey-Wyssling; Park et al.). Particles 185 Å long, 155 Å wide and 100 Å thick (Branton 1967) usually appear randomly scattered. These isolated particles, with a part of the membrane, constitute the units able to carry out the Hill reaction. Park and Pon have suggested that these units represent *the smallest morphological expression of the photosynthetic unit* as it was formulated by Emerson and Arnold in 1932 and redetermined by Kok and Businger in 1957. They gave it the name of 'quantasome'. According to the first schema of Park and Pon (1961) the quantasomes are flattened spheres arranged between two osmophilic layers of a lipid nature.

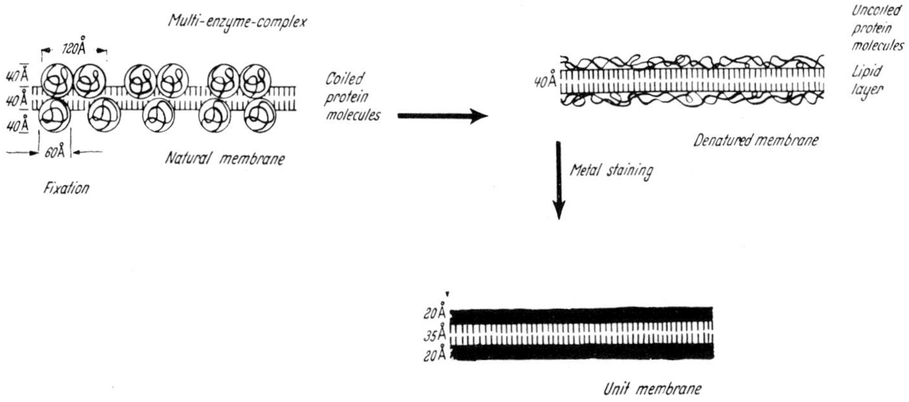

Fig. 5. Structure of a thylakoid according to Mühlethaler, showing the formation of the 'unit membrane' during fixation. The globular particles are thought to be uncoiled and spread over the surface of the lipid layer. After metal staining, the uncoiled protein molecules appear as dark lines in sections.

The new techniques of 'freeze-etching' introduced by Mühlethaler and Moor reveal particles on the fracture surfaces of the chloroplasts. These particles, which are thought to be globular proteins, have a diameter of 60 Å, appear isolated or in groups of four, and are thought to be arranged in a bimolecular lipid layer (Fig. 5). According to Mühlethaler et al. the globular proteins are denatured by fixation, i.e. their tertiary structure is disorganised. The uncoiled protein molecules are spread over the surface of the lipid layer, and after metal staining the protein films appear as dark lines on either side of the central lipid layer, giving rise to the tripartite image in agreement with the concept of the 'unit membrane'. According to this model, the membrane is symmetrical.

In contrast, according to Branton, Park and Branton, the membranes are essentially *asymmetric*. Assuming that the fractures disclosed by freeze-etching are not the outer faces of the membrane but the internal faces, since they are produced at the level of the hydrophobic lipid zone, Branton et al. distinguish three aspects of a thylakoid (see Fig. 2 and Fig. 6). (1) Face B appears as a relatively smooth surface upon which are randomly distributed particles 160 to 200 Å in diameter which may correspond to quantasomes. (2) Face A is seen only when thylakoids are stacked to form a granum, but never when only individual thylakoids are seen. This face is often compound and appears as an embedding matrix which perhaps surrounds and covers the large discrete particles of surface B. (3) Face C is made up of both 175-Å and smaller particles and corresponds to the opposite side of face A (Branton).

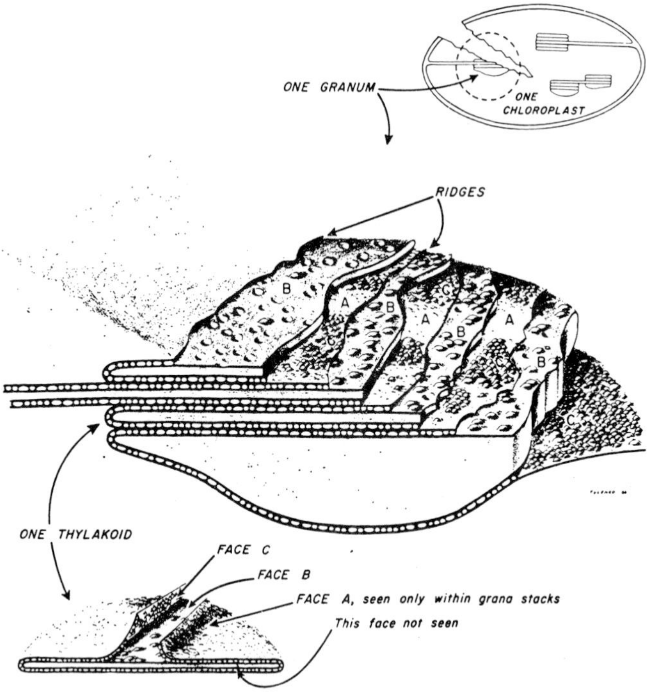

Fig. 6. Interpretation of the surface of the thylakoids according to Branton and Park (1967).

Enzyme treatments. Bamberger and Park treated the lamellae of isolated chloroplasts with lipases (extracted from runner bean leaves) which break down galactolipids to fatty acids, glycerol, and galactose, and with protease-pronase extracts which hydrolyse most peptide bonds to amino acids.

On examining the freeze-etched replicas after these treatments, they concluded that the substrate of face B consists of galactolipids and that it is devoid of chlorophyll. The particles of face A consist partly of lipid and partly of protein. Chlorophyll appears to be associated exclusively with the large 175-Å particles and their embedding matrix and not with the galactolipid layer of face B. The 175-Å particles may correspond to the 'quantasomes' seen in shadowed preparations.

Discussion. There are a number of objections to the results obtained with freeze-etching. It is possible that the particles appearing on the fracture planes are micelles formed on the lipid layers during the freezing. It is also possible that the surfaces exposed during etching were contaminated with particulate material. In addition, the pictures obtained after freeze-etching are not comparable to those obtained either by negative staining or by shadowed preparations of isolated lamellae.

We will now consider the validity of these objections. If the particles were due to micelle formation or to contamination of the fractured membrane surfaces, one would not expect to find the presence, on the same membrane, of depressions with a diameter equal to that of the particles. These depressions probably represent spaces from which particles were torn. Also, if the particles were artifacts, one would expect to find them on all membranes treated by the same method. However, freeze-etching methods show that myelinated membranes are smooth and almost devoid of particles, that nuclear membranes have some particles, and that chloroplast lamellae are highly particulate (Branton; Park) (Fig. 2).

The negative-staining method, with which one can observe only the outside of the membrane, reveals particles which in the past had been identified as a membrane component. In size and structure, many of these particles resemble carboxydismutase, a soluble protein of the plastid matrix. Thus the particles seen with the negative-staining method may not even be associated with the membrane: These results thus do not contradict those obtained with freeze-etching, which suggested that the particulate structures of the thylakoid were embedded within the membrane (Park and Branton 1967).

Freeze-etching preparations might very well be expected to differ from shadowed preparations, for shadowed preparations reveal the external surfaces of membranes while freeze-etching is believed to split membranes to expose their inner surfaces. Freeze-etching replicas of chloroplasts from both glutaraldehyde treated and untreated material give the same surface images. Since glutaraldehyde is known to affect cross linkage of the hydrophilic portions of proteins, it must be admitted that freeze-etched membrane faces are views of inner hydrophobic areas and not of the outer hydrophilic glutaraldehyde susceptible surfaces of these membranes. On the other hand, a replica of chloroplasts from which the lipids have been removed does not show any surface membrane. However, the shape of the chloroplast and the disposition of its starch grains are preserved. Thus, the lipids appear to be necessary to establish planes of weakness in the frozen membranes.

Both observations are consistent with a membrane whose external surface, in contact with the aqueous phase, consists primarily of the polar ends of lipids which in turn are bound to non-polar micelles in the membrane. Though lipids are of prime importance in determining the fracture planes in frozen membranes (Figs. 5 and 6) it is unnecessary to assume that all chloroplast lamellar lipids are disposed as a smectic mesophase, which is a relatively stable disposition of lipids. Other conformations may be imagined which also lead to the presence of hydrophobic bonds in the plane of the membrane. Branton has suggested that the membrane components may exist in part as extended bilayers and in part as globular or micellar subunits.

The models proposed (Figs. 5 and 6) can evidently serve only as approximations to the molecular complexity found within photosynthetic membranes. The chemical and enzymatic extractions performed by Park et al. represent promising tests for the elucidation of the molecular structure of these membranes, especially when they are supplemented by immunological methods which will localize more precisely the structural molecules. Results of antigen-antibody reactions with the proteins of the membrane (Berzhorn 1968) seem to confirm the external location of protein.

(b) *The pigment molecules*

Chlorophylls. There is much evidence that chlorophyll is localized at the level of the membranous structures of the photosynthetic apparatus. Fractionation of the chloroplasts of algae, of those of higher plants, and of the chromatophores of photosynthetic bacteria (*Rhodospirillum*), demonstrates that the chlorophyll pigments are always bound to the lamellar or vesicular fractions. It is also known that etiolated plastids, which show neither green colour in white light nor fluorescence in U.V. light, are devoid of lamellar structure and all trace of chlorophyll. After exposure of etiolated plastids to light, chlorophyll appears at the same time as lamellar differentiation.

1. *Reduction of silver salts (Molisch's reaction).* Molisch's reaction is an *in vivo* reduction of silver nitrate by light at the chloroplast level. It was thought that it could be used as a 'marker' for the localisation of chlorophyll molecules at the level of the lamellar system. With the electron microscope, Brown, Mollenhauer and Johnson noted an absence of reduced silver precipitate in the grana of angiosperm chloroplasts but the presence of numerous silver grains localised on the intergrana lamellae (Fig. 7). In the red algae, where the lamellar system of the plastid consists of an aggregation of double membranes aligned along its long axis, the precipitate is regularly distributed along these lamellae (Giraud; Fig. 8). Thus, even though Molisch's reaction is photo-inducible and has an action spectrum resembling that of the absorption spectrum of chlorophyll (Thomas, Post and Vertregt 1954), it appears that it can not be used for the precise localisation of the chlorophyll pigments.

2. *Reduction of tetrazolium salts: in chloroplasts 'in situ'.* This reaction relies on the same principle as that which uses TTNB (tetrazole tetranitroblue or 'nitro BT') for the localisation of enzymatic reduction reactions in mitochondrial cristae. In both cases a diformazan salt is formed at the sites of reduction.

In studies of chloroplasts, the electron dense tetrazolium salt is used as a Hill's oxidant to localize the sites of *photoreduction.* Weier et al. (1966) have attempted to localise chlorophyll cytochemically with TTNB at the level of certain regions of the chloroplast's lamellar system. It is their hypothesis that if chlorophyll exists mainly, if not exclusively, at the level of the membranes in contact with the grana (the 'parti-

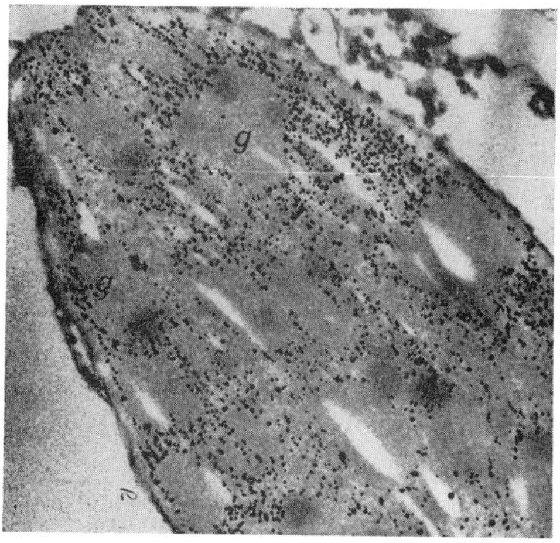

Fig. 7

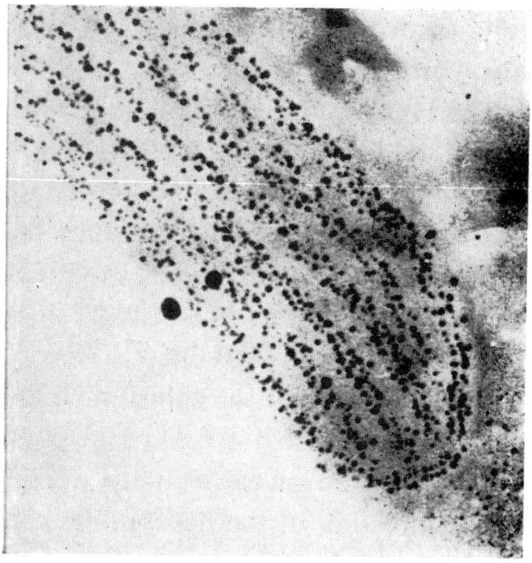

Fig. 8

Fig. 7. Molisch's reaction on chloroplasts from maize. Note that the silver grains are outside the grana (g) and follow the path of the intergrana lamellae. (× 32,000.)

Fig. 8. Molisch's reaction on the rhodoplasts of *Rhodosorus marinus*. ($AgNO_3$, 0.5% in an isotonic sucrose solution in the culture medium, postfixation with osmium tetroxide 0.2%). The coupled membrane appears underlined by the silver precipitate which borders it. (Courtesy of Giraud; × 70,000.)

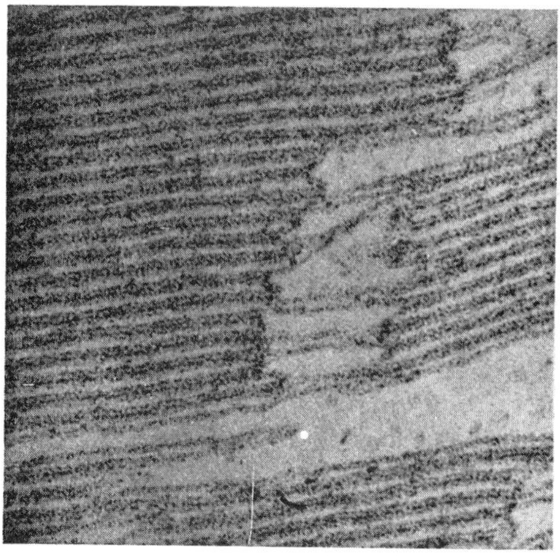

Fig. 9

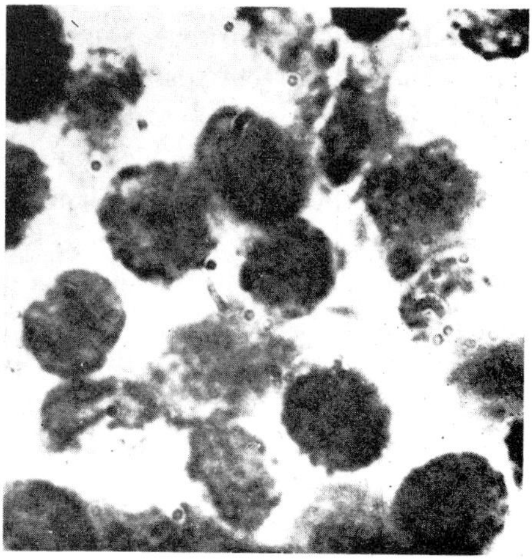

Fig. 10

Fig. 9. The site of deposition of TTNB reduced by light to diformazan. It appears at the point of contact of two thylakoids ('partition' according to Weier). (× 131,400)

Fig. 10. Molisch's reaction on isolated chloroplasts (light microscopy). TTNB has been used as an acceptor for the Hill reaction. Note the black deposit of diformazan on the surface of the chloroplasts. (Weier et al.; × 2,000.)

tion' according to Weier), the initial reaction of photoreduction should take place at this 'partition'.

The Hill reaction is carried out with isolated chloroplasts using TTNB as a proton-acceptor. Reduction in the presence of light of TTNB to diformazan blue is evident around the chloroplasts, as observed with the light microscope (Fig. 10). The contrast of the diformazan salt deposit may be intensified by staining the section before performing electron microscopic examinations. A dense line, which is absent in control chloroplasts, appears in the midst of the 'partition' in those chloroplasts which have been treated with TTNB (Fig. 9). According to Weier et al. this dense deposit coincides with the location of the chlorophyll molecules. He and his colleagues suggest that in chloroplasts *in vivo*, the part of the photoreaction which involves chlorophyll produces in the 'partition' an electron flux which should occur along the length of the 'partition' in the direction of the hydrophilic zone of the stroma. However, this conclusion is weakened by the observation that some fragments of the chloroplast membrane are still capable of reducing NADP and of phosphorylating ADP. One wonders if it is necessary to conclude that the reducing capacity is localised at the level of discrete units of the 'quantasome' type and that, after fragmentation of the membranes, each of the smallest fragments still retains one of these units and thus the ability to reduce. In other words, is photoreduction exclusively localised in units provisionally called 'quantasomes' or is the entire chloroplast membrane endowed with this power?

3. *Reduction of tetrazolium salts in isolated lamellae.* Howell and Moudrianakis (1967) tried to solve this question by studying isolated chloroplast membranes. They also used tetrazolium salts as an indicator of the reducing sites, but substituted INT (2-p-iodopheny-3-p-nitrophenyl-monotetrazole chloride) for TTNB. Their preliminary studies showed: (1) that 'quantasome'-like particles existed in their preparations of the chloroplast membrane, (2) that the INT tetrazolium salt would serve as a Hill reactant and (3) that the diformazan deposit is specifically bound to the membranes. In later experiments, the kinetics of the deposition of reduced diformazan in isolated chloroplast membranes was followed for 5, 15, and 45 min. This was achieved by integrating on a microdensitometer the micrographic negatives of these isolated membranes (Fig. 11).

This kinetic study demonstrated that photoreduction is a phenomenon which involves *the entire membrane*. Since photoreduction did not appear to be confined to particles bound to the membranes, it is natural to ask whether a membrane preparation without 'quantasome'-like particles is still capable of photoreduction. According to Howel and Moudrianakis the smooth membranes have a reductive activity equal to, if not superior to, that of membranes with granules.

In conclusion: The reduction of tetrazolium salts to diformazan salts which are visible in the electron microscope, can be used to show that photoreduction in the chloroplast is not confined to particles such as those known as 'quantasomes' but that the *entire membrane is functional*. One is led to conclude that either the sites of photoreduction are much smaller than quantasomes and that present techniques do not allow their resolution or that the particles are transitory or are destroyed by the treatments (Howell, Moudrianakis). One could also ask if this reaction is not exclusively allied to a form of chlorophyll which absorbs at wavelengths below 680 mμ (system II) and which is bound, according to Vernon's results (1968), to the lamellae and not to the particles.

Phycobiliproteins. 1. *Localisation 'in situ'*. In addition to chlorophyll, which appears to be entirely situated in the membranes, there are, in certain organisms, photosynthetic pigments which actively participate in photosynthesis as primary photon acceptors, and whose energy of excitation is later transferred to chlorophyll *a*. These water soluble pigments are chromoproteins whose prosthetic groups are phycobilins (similar to biliary pigments), and are found only in the red algea and in the *Cyanophyceae*. Until 1966 their localisation was, if not unknown, at least strongly controversial. While Brody and Vatter (1959) supported a lamellar location for these supplementary hydrophylic pigments, Giraud supported the idea that they were distributed in the stroma, *between* the lamellae.

A study of the mutants of *Cyanidium caldarium* (Bogorad et al. 1963) which are devoid of phycobilins did not allow the detection of any difference between the thickness of lamellae of control cells with phycobilins, and those of the mutants. These results suggest that the phycobilins do not form an integral part of the photosynthetic lamellae.

Simultaneously, Gantt and Conti (1965) using *Porphyridium cruentum*, a unicellular red alga, and Lefort using *Glaucocystis nostochinearum*, a symbiotic species of the *Cyanophaceae*, demonstrated some granules of about 400 Å at the photosynthetic lamellar level of these organisms. These granules were electron dense, protein in nature, and regularly spaced at 500-Å intervals on the outer edges of the membrane pairs (Figs. 12 and 13). Observation of various tangential, longitudinal, and transverse planes of the sections, such as those of replicas after freeze-etching (Bourdu and Lefort 1967; Fig. 14) demonstrated that these 400-Å granules are the ends of rows separated by a distance of about 500 Å and arranged parallel to the surface of the leaflets. In *Porphyridium* these granulations remain firmly attached to the membrane when the cells are prefixed in glutaraldehyde, whereas they are readily liberated in the isolating medium (buffer) if they are not submitted to any pre-treatment. After separation of

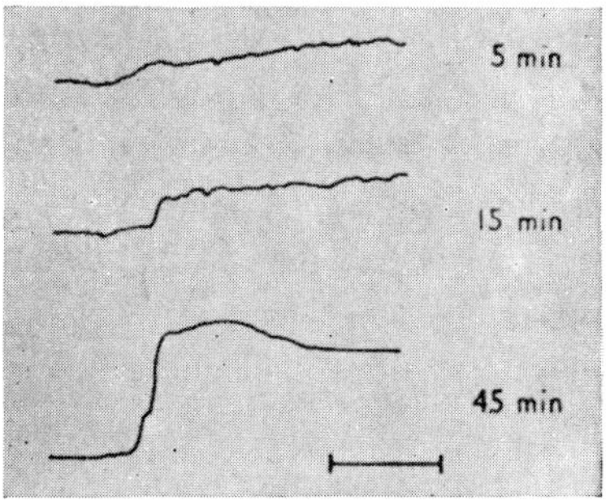

Fig. 11. Microdensitometric curves integrated from micrographs. The colour intensity of photo-reduced INT increases with time. The bar corresponds to 50 Å on the photographic plate (Howell and Moudrianakis).

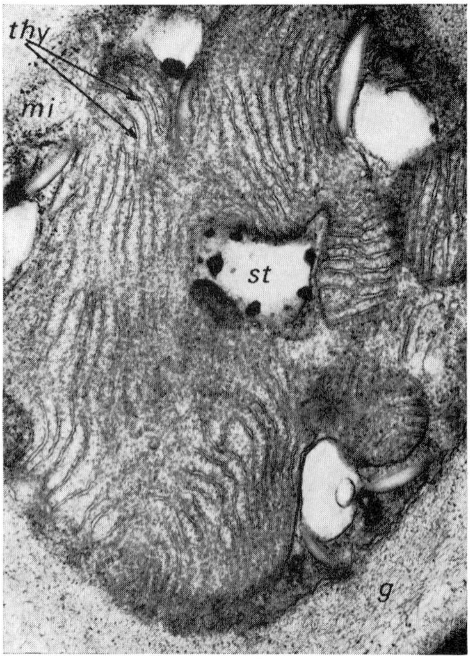

Fig. 12

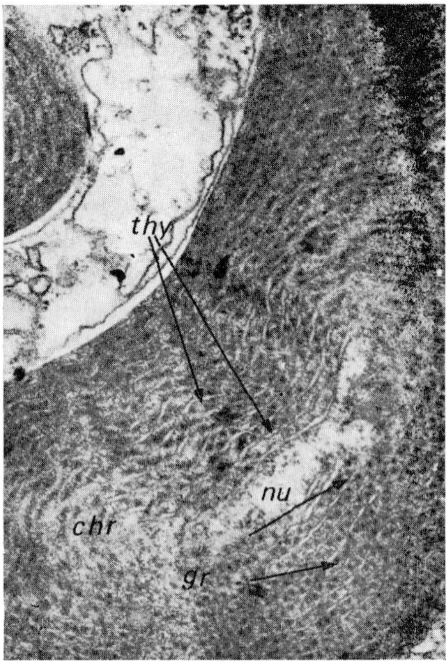

Fig. 13

Fig. 12. *Porphyridium cruentum*. Glutaraldehyde–osmium. The diverticulated chloroplast consists of a lamellar system formed from paired membranes (thy) to which 400-Å granules are attached, (g) a mucilaginous matrix around the cell, (mi) mitochondria, (st) floridean starch (× 24,800).

Fig. 13. *Glaucocystis nostochinearum*. Osmium tetroxide. A symbiotic *Cyanophyceae* whose photosynthetic chromatoplasma system (chr) consists of double membranes (thy) to which 400-Å contrast particles (gr) are bound. The organisation and structure are identical to the chloroplasts of *Porphyridium*. (nu) nuclear area not separated from the chromatoplasma and in which fine filaments of DNA may be seen. (× 27,000.)

these granules from the membrane it is seen that the red colour characteristic of phycoerythrin is found in the light granular fraction whilst the green deposit exhibits a spectrum characteristic of chlorophyll *a* (Fig. 17). It therefore appears to be easy to separate chlorophyll pigments from phycobilin pigments. Gantt and Conti (1966) treated whole cells with deoxycholate. After fixation, embedding and sectioning by the usual techniques for electron microscopy, a complete absence of granules at the rhodoplastid level is observed and only lipoprotein plates, to which chlorophyll *a* is bound, remain (Lefort and Pouphile 1967). (Fig. 16 illustrates the same results obtained with *Glaucocystis*).

The reverse experiment is possible; it involves the treatment of the glutaraldehyde pre-treated cells with an 80:20 mixture of methanol and acetone. In this solvent mixture, chlorophyll and many of the carotenoids but not the phycobilins, are removed, as shown by the spectrum. After the extraction, the cells are rose-purple. Under electron microscopy (Fig. 15) the lamellar structure has disappeared while the large granules, whose regular arrangement is preserved remain in place. The results are the same in sections (Gantt and Conti) and in replicas after freeze-etching (Bourdu and Lefort 1967). Thus, it is possible by differential treatments to separate chlorophyll, which is well attached to lamellar structures, from phycobilins, which appear to be localised in the granular structures observed in sections.

2. *Methods of isolation.* The isolation of phycobiliproteins may be obtained by fractionating the cells in the presence or absence of glutaraldehyde. This method facilitates the study of the role of these granules and of their mechanism of attachment to the membrane (Cohen-Bazire and Lefort). In a sucrose gradient two fractions can be separated in the control cells. The light fraction has a spectrum which corresponds to that of phycobilins (T_3, Fig. 17) and contains only 400-Å granules, like those which are arranged quincuncially on the borders of the lamellar discs (Fig. 15). The other fraction is green and is composed of the debris of *smooth* membranes in the form of vesicles, its spectrum is that of chlorophyll *a* and carotenoids. (T6, Fig. 17).

On the other hand, after fractionation of glutaraldehyde-pretreated cells only a single band is observed in the gradient. This band corresponds spectrophotometrically to the three principal categories of pigments: carotenoids, phycoerythrin and chlorophyll *a* (G7, Fig. 18). Negative staining reveals that this fraction, which is brown, is composed of short membrane fragments to which the granules are still attached.

Thus, the results of the glutaraldehyde treatment have established that the binding between the membrane and the granules is sufficiently strong to resist fractionation, even though rupture is produced in the membranous area between the granules. The

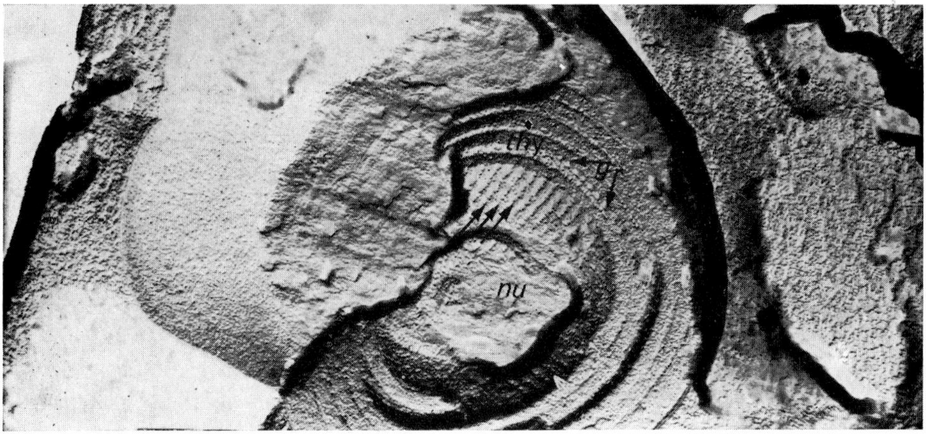

Fig. 14. *Glaucocystis nostochinearum.* Replica after freeze-etching. The double membranes (thy) may appear in transverse section with granules distributed on their external edges (g) as in sections or in polar view; note the parallel alignments, the extremities of which correspond to the 400-Å grains. Nu: nuclear area. Compare the rows on the surface of the membranes and the equivalent zone (al) in the oblique section in Fig. 13. × 24,300.

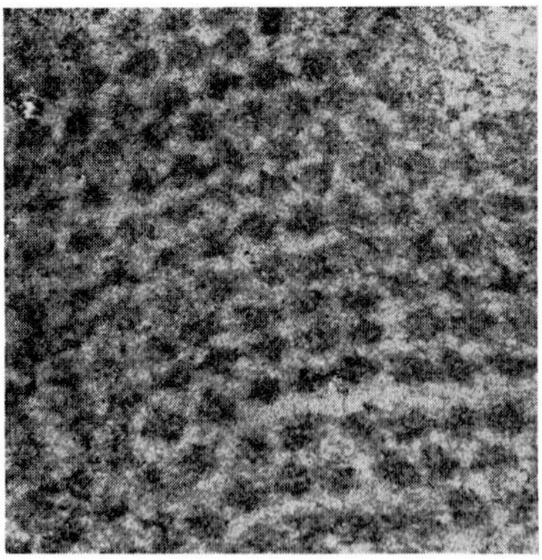

Fig. 15

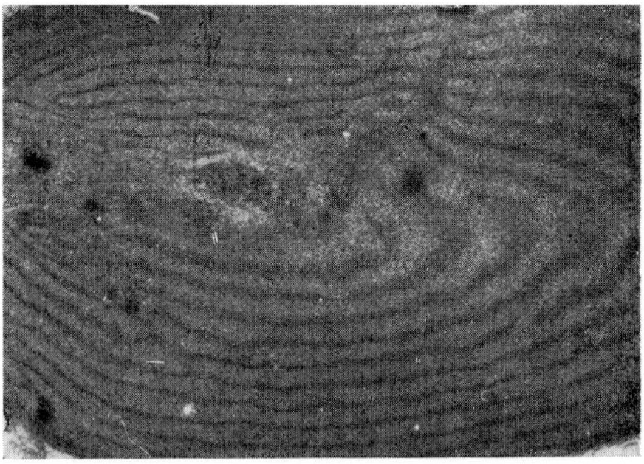

Fig. 16

Fig. 15. *Porphyridium cruentum* treated with methanol-acetone, fixed in glutaraldehyde and contrasted with osmium. The membranes have disappeared, only the grains seen in Figs. 13 and 21 remain in place. These cells appear red. (Courtesy of Gantt; ×103,500.)

Fig. 16. *Glaucocystis nostochinearum* treated with deoxycholate, fixed in glutaraldehyde–osmium. The granules have disappeared, only the double membranes have remained in place. These cells appear green. (×36,300)

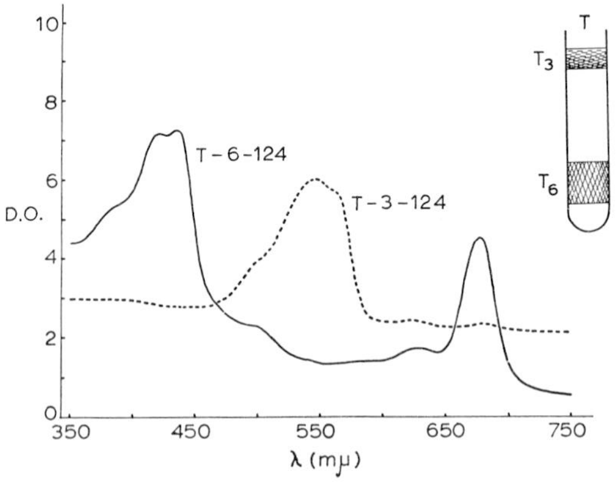

Fig. 17. Spectra of fractions from *Porphyridium cruentum* control isolated on a sucrose gradient. T_3: colon spectrum of the red, light granular fraction corresponding to phycoerythrin. T_6: colon heavy fraction, the spectrum of which corresponds to chlorophyll *a* and carotenoids. In negative staining, these lamellar fractions are deprived of grains.

knowledge that we have of the lability of these granular structures, to which the phycobiliproteins are bound *in vivo*, and in particular of the sensitivity of their attachment to osmotic shocks, suggests that in the living cell these granules are not strongly incorporated into the lamellae and that they can be removed in a reversible manner or detached completely. Glutaraldehyde allows the establishment of bonds between the hydrophilic portions of proteins. The fact that after fixation by glutaraldehyde it

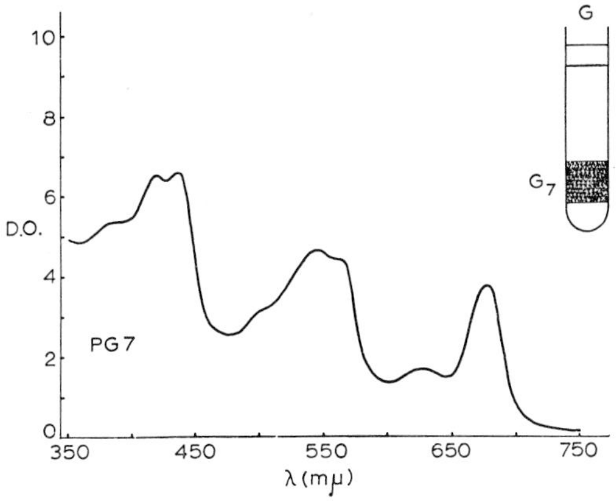

Fig. 18. Spectra of fractions from *Porphyridium cruentum* isolated on sucrose gradients, prefixed in glutaraldehyde before grinding. Under these conditions only one fraction (brown in colour) is obtained in the gradient, the spectrum corresponds to pG7 where the three types of pigment are represented; from short to long wavelength: carotenoids, phycoerythrin and chlorophyll. This spectrum is analogous to that of the whole organism before performing the sucrose gradient.

becomes impossible to detach the granules from the lamellae suggests that the distances between the granules and the membranous structures are of molecular order and the attachment involves protein molecules.

3. *Nucleic acids of chloroplasts*

If chloroplasts are considered as cytoplasmic entities endowed with genetic continuity, it is to be expected that they contain, in the form of nucleic acids, the necessary information for their replication and differentiation.

(a) *Historical review*

Specific staining. Certain authors have occasionally indicated that chloroplasts give a positive Feulgen reaction (Milovidov 1936; Yuasa 1938). Whereas Milovidov attributed the colour to the presence of aldehyde groups in starch precursors, Yuasa thought it was simply an artifact.

Chiba (1951) was the first to demonstrate, by cytochemical methods, the presence of nucleic acids in chloroplasts. He obtained a positive reaction with both the Feulgen reagent and with methyl green, while treatment with trichloroacetic acid prevented both reactions. With pyronine he obtained an equally positive response. Even though he was unable to do the necessary controls, involving specific enzymatic digestions (which were difficult to perform at that time) he came to the conclusion that chloroplasts contained DNA (in polymerised and depolymerised forms) and possibly also RNA.

These experiments were repeated by other workers (Metzner 1952; Littau) but contradictory results were obtained.

Autoradiography. After this early period experiments using radioisotopes were carried out. Tritiated thymidine was used by Stocking and Gifford studying *Spyrogyra*, and by Brachet studying *Acetabularia.* Brachet wrote that this molecule is also incorporated 'into the cytoplasm, apparently in the chloroplast'. Thus in 1961, the presence of nucleic acids in plastids was still a contested problem.

(b) *Ultrastructural studies*

Using cytochemical tests, light microscopy (Feulgen and acridine orange), and electron microscopy, Ris and Plaut (1962) were the first to demonstrate that in the chloroplasts of *Chlamydomonas* there were particles of 150–200 Å in diameter 'which resemble the ribosomes in the cytoplasm outside the chloroplast'. In addition they could distinguish clear areas containing fine fibrils of 25–30 Å in thickness (Fig. 19) which disappeared after treatment with DNAse. These fibrils can also be found in the plastids of *Anthoceros*, *Elodea* and *Zhea mays* and resemble those which are observed in the nucleoplasm of bacteria by Ryter and Kellenberger (Fig. 20), and of *Cyanophyceae* (Fig. 21). They concluded that the presence of DNA and the similarity in ultrastructure with the chromatin bodies of Monera (bacteria and blue green algae) suggest that these areas with 25 Å fibrils are the genetic system of plastids. Ris used this finding to develop the endosymbiotic theory of plastids to which we shall return later.

Deoxyribonucleic acid – in situ. Kislev, Swift and Bogorad (1965) and Swift (1965), using various cytochemical techniques including autoradiography with ^{3}H-thymidine,

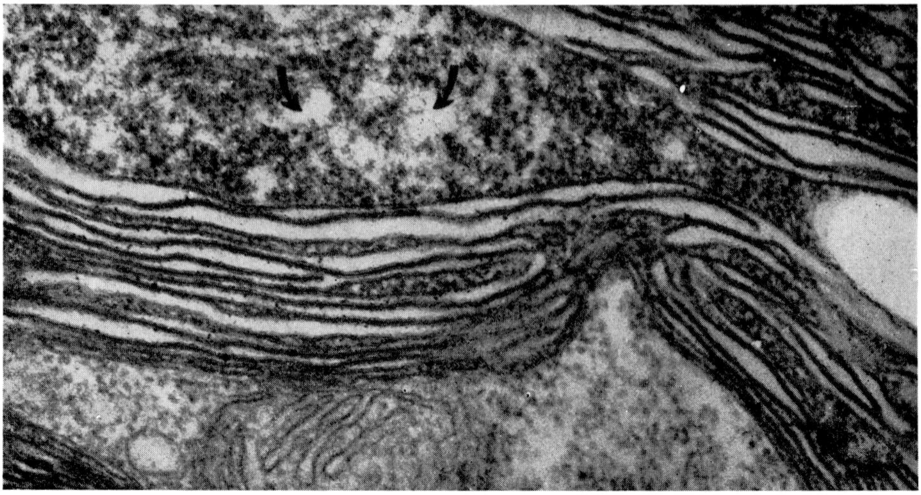

Fig. 19. The arrows indicate the DNA fibrils in a chloroplast from *Chlamydomonas reinhardii.* (Courtesy of Ris; × 72,000.)

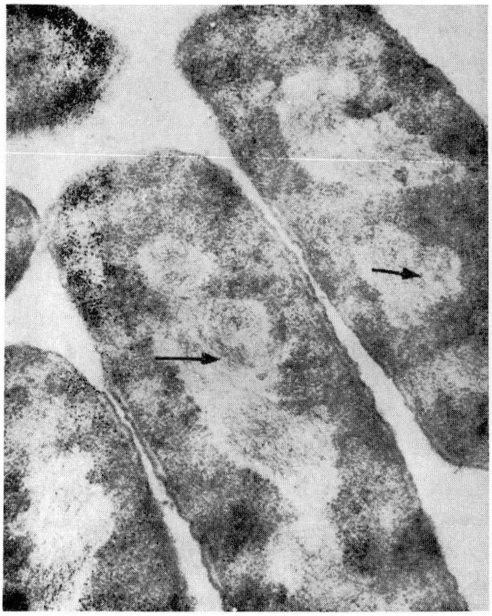

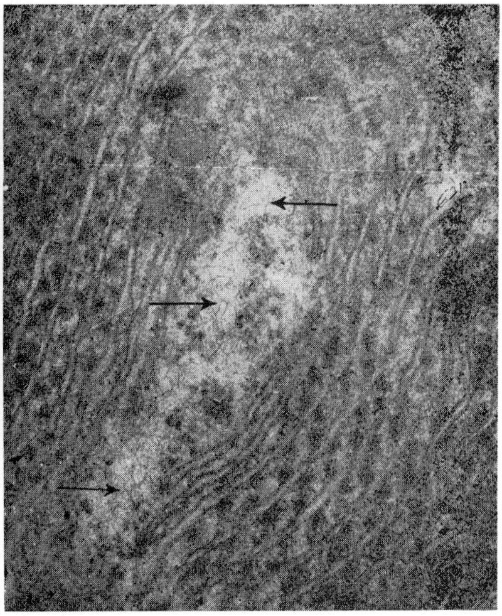

Fig. 20 Fig. 21

Fig. 20. Bacterial *nuclear body* DNA fibrils. (Courtesy of A. Ryter; × 47,000.)

Fig. 21. Nuclear area of a symbiotic *Cyanophyceae*: *Glaucocystis nostochinearum*. The arrows indicate the 25-Å fibrils of DNA. (× 60,000.)

uranyl staining for electron microscopy, and DNAse extractions (Figs. 26 and 27), confirmed Ris' (1961) first observations in a comparative study of chloroplasts and mitochondria. DNA exists in these cellular organelles in the form of approximately 25 Å fibrils after fixation by the method of Ryter and Kellenberger. This method of fixation involves complexing DNA with uranyl ions before dehydration and causes the DNA to appear in a filamentous form as in bacterial nuclear bodies (Fig. 20). It so happens that after osmium or formalin fixation but without uranyl treatment, the filaments collapse during dehydration into a compact structure (Figs. 22 and 25). This artifact only serves to stress the analogy between chloroplast DNA and the DNA of bacterial nuclear bodies (Ryter and Kellenberger) which is distinguished from that of higher organisms by the absence of histone. However, discussions were lively as the results did not appear convincing to everyone.

In fact, the incorporation of ^{3}H-thymidine appears to be possible only in the young leaves and in the actively elongating roots of *Nicotinia rustica* (Wollgiehn and Mothes 1964). These results were confirmed by DeVitry (1965) for the chloroplasts of *Acetabularia*. In addition, the work of Lima-de-Faria and Moses (1964) has shown that the radioactivity of tritiated thymidine absorbed by the leaves of *Zea mays* is not always susceptible to treatment with DNAse. Their experiments have alerted researchers to the danger of localising DNA by thymidine labelling only. The same warning was issued by Sagan (1965). Her work on *Euglena* shows that the incorporation of ^{3}H-

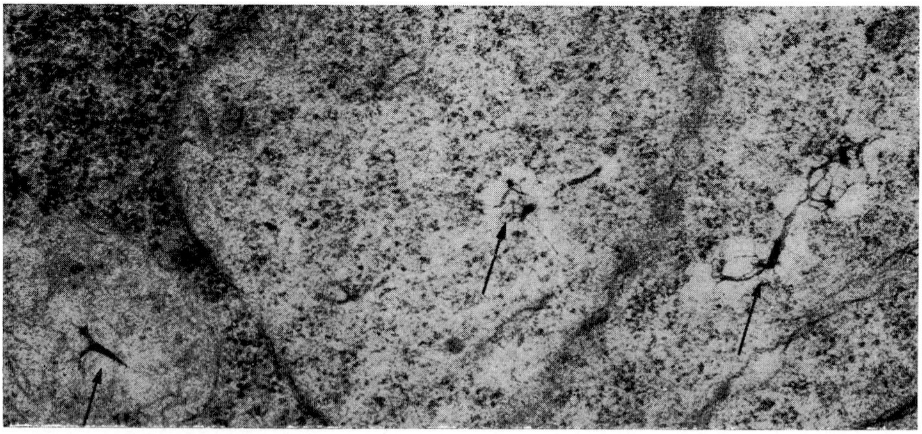

Fig. 22. Parts of a chloroplast (to the right) and of a mitochondrion (to the left) in an etiolated bean leaf. Note the coagulated filaments (arrowed) corresponding to DNA in these organelles. The granulation of the chloroplast is less dense and finer than that of the cytoplasm (cy). (Courtesy of Swift; × 43,200.)

Fig. 23. Part of a completely dispersed chloroplast showing the typical conformations of DNA. Platinum shadowing on a carbon-mica substrate. (Courtesy of Woodcock and Fernández-Morán; × 20,000.)

label into the cytoplasm following administration of ^{3}H-thymidine is not a proof of the presence of DNA unless the label is shown to be specifically removable with DNAse. Sagan showed that *Euglena* did not possess the necessary enzymes for the metabolism of exogenous pyrimidines whilst purines are metabolised. In fact she succeeded in labelling *Euglena* with ^{3}H-guanine. After treatment with RNAse the radioactivity found in the nucleus and chloroplasts could only be interpreted as an incorporation of nucleic acid precursors into the DNA of these cellular organelles.

By using an elegant staining technique based on the formation of DNA-RNAse complexes, Yotsuyanagi (1965) succeeded in showing that DNA exists at several sites in the same organelle (Fig. 25). In addition his pictures suggest a form of DNA replication.

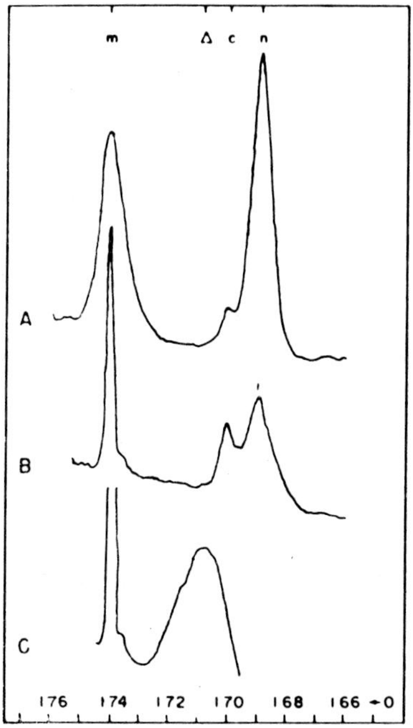

Fig. 24. DNA preparation from Swiss Chard photographed at equilibrium on an analytical ultracentrifuge. A: Coarse particulate fraction. B: Chloroplast fraction; C: Chloroplast fraction after heating for 10 min at 100 °C; m: marker band of DNA from phage SPO1 (ρ = 1,740 g/cm^3); c: minor band, presumably chloroplast band; n: major band, presumably nuclear band; Δ: position of heated DNA (maximum). (Courtesy of Kislev, Swift and Bogorad.)

Isolated DNA of plastids. Woodcock and Fernández-Morán (1968), working with chloroplasts isolated from spinach, succeeded in observing filaments of DNA similar to those already seen in mitochondria. By osmotic shock they spread the organelle onto a protein layer and succeeded in liberating DNA. After rotational shadowing they showed the relationship of the DNA to the membrane constituents (Fig. 23). The maximum length of DNA from a single chloroplast was about 150 μ. According to biochemical estimations the total DNA in one chloroplast would be 10^{-15} to 10^{-16} g, which corresponds to a molecular weight of 5×10^7 to 5×10^8. If one assumes the double helical form, this molecular weight corresponds to a length of 30 to 300 μ.

The value of 150 μ, which was obtained from the measurements made on the rotated shadowed preparations appears to be within this order of magnitude.

It is not yet possible to say whether the chloroplast DNA is a single molecule if it is composed of a number of smaller entities. It does possess in any case a highly organised spatial structure whose complexity is in proportion to that of the chloroplast itself.

Buoyant density analysis permits the demonstration of the existence of satellite bands in the distribution of the total cellular DNA (Fig. 24). In Swiss chard this satellite peak at about 1.707 g/cm^3 corresponds to the chloroplast DNA (the major peak of nuclear DNA is at 1.689). Thermal denaturation studies indicate that the chloroplast DNA exists in the form of a double strand. Its estimated GC content is greater than that of the nuclear DNA [GC = 42 % for the chloroplast DNA instead of 31 % for the nuclear DNA, as determined by Kislev, Swift and Bogorad (1965)]. Similar results have been obtained in other higher plants (Edelman et al. 1968) and are discussed in the chapter by Swift and Wolstenholme.

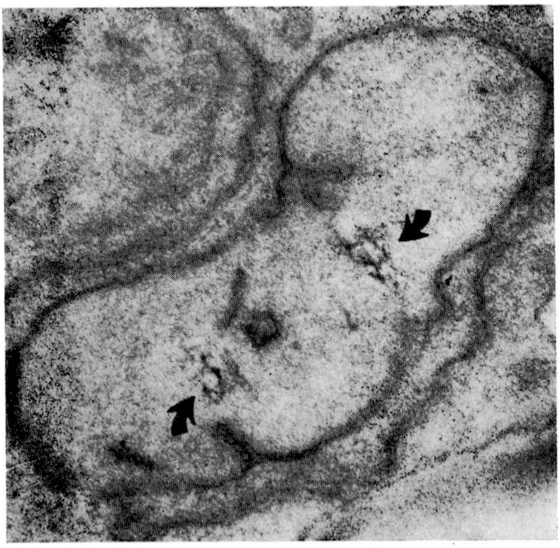

Fig. 25. Proplastid apparently dividing in a root of *Allium cepa*: specific staining enables the demonstration of two masses of DNA which simulate a mitotic division. (Courtesy of Yotsuyanagi; × 40,000.)

Plastid RNA. 1. *Chloroplast ribosomes.* Etiolated plastids in the process of turning green show intense protein synthesis. Considering the role of ribosomes in protein synthesis (Jacob and Monod 1961), these plastids should be particularly well suited to demonstrate RNA in the form of ribosomal particles.

Etiolated plastids of *Zea mays* seedlings which have germinated in the dark possess at their centre a pseudocrystalline structure which is called the prolamellar body and which is composed of lipoprotein vesicles (Fig. 28). After exposure to the light the plastid rapidly acquires (within 3 hr) a typical lamellar system (Fig. 1).

The etiolated plastids stain intensively with azure B and show numerous silver grains after the seedling has incorporated ^{3}H-cytidine (Jacobson, Swift and Bogorad). The fact that basophilia and radioactivity disappear completely after digestion with

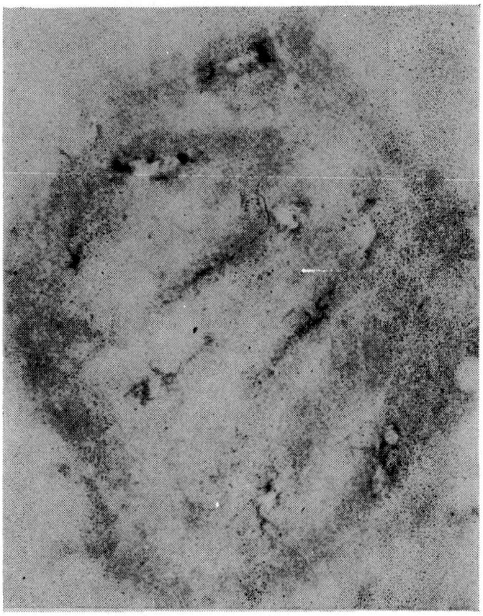

Fig. 26. Chloroplast from a young leaf of Swiss Chard treated with RNAse. The identifiable filamentous component of DNA is evident in the matrix. The particulate component has disappeared. (Courtesy of Kislev, Swift and Bogorad; × 38,000.)

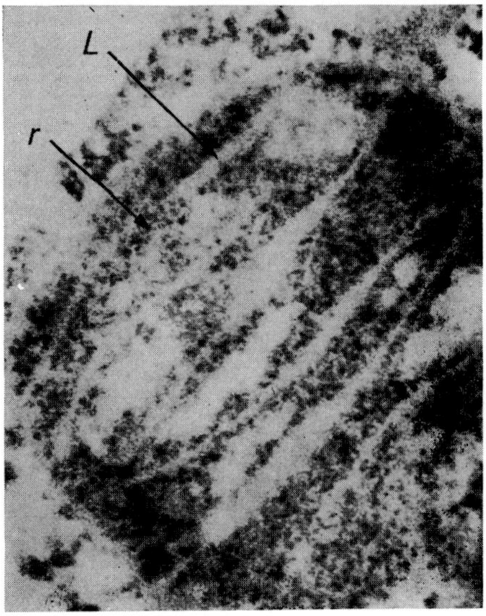

Fig. 27. Similar chloroplast treated with DNAse. The filamentous component has disappeared; the ribosomal particles (r) are still evident between the plastid lamellae (L). (Courtesy of Kislev, Swift and Bogorad; × 40,000.)

ribonuclease, shows that the etiolated plastids contain ribonucleoproteins. After prefixation in aldehyde followed by an osmic post-fixation a characteristic particulate structure is observed in etiolated plastids (Figs. 22 and 28). The observed particles are about 120 to 170 Å and are sensitive to treatment with RNAse (Fig. 26). They therefore appear to be comparable to ribosomes. These ribosomal particles can be seen also in the adult chloroplasts, but they are often less numerous.

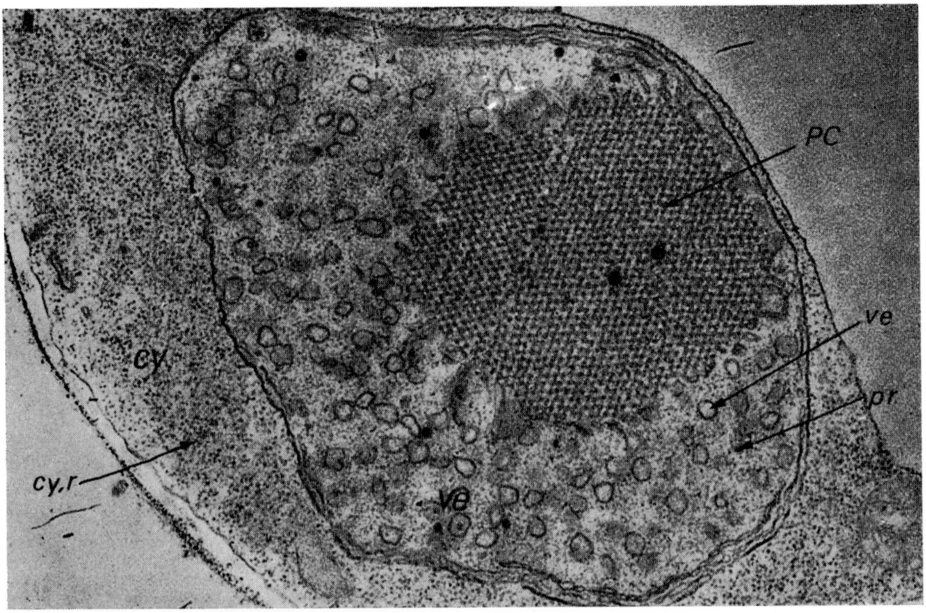

Fig. 28. Etiolated plastids in a seedling of *Zea mays*; PC: pseudocrystalline prolamellar body; ve: numerous vesicles; pr: plastid ribosomes; cy,r: cytoplasmic ribosomes. (Glutaraldehyde–osmium; × 40,500.)

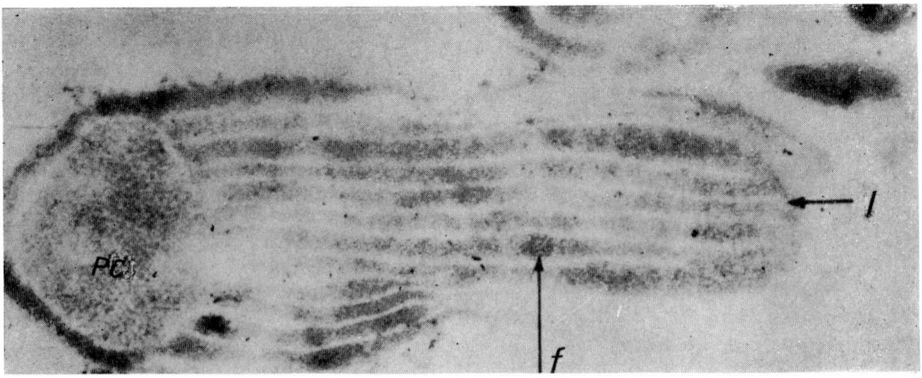

Fig. 29. Proplastids of *Zea mays* treated with ribonuclease. The prolamellar body (PC) and the lamellae (L) are still visible; ribosomes and particles of the plastid matrix have been destroyed. F: phytoferritin granules. (Courtesy of Jacobson, Swift and Bogorad; × 23,400.)

Another biological material which has proved useful for the demonstration of ribosomes of chloroplasts is *Euglena*. *Euglena* is a green flagellate which can live in the dark as a heterotroph. Under these conditions it possesses only regressed plastid structures, often less than 1 μ in size. Exposure to light induces intense protein synthesis accompanied by chloroplast differentiation. The chloroplasts are 5 to 6 μ in size and possess a characteristic lamellar structure. Sagan, Ben-Shaul and Schiff (1964) were able to demonstrate in *Euglena*, which were in the process of turning green, that the radioactivity from ^{3}H-guanine and ^{3}H-adenine incorporated in the chloroplasts is removed by ribonuclease. Therefore, the differentiation of the chloroplasts in the light is accompanied by RNA synthesis probably associated with an increase in the number of ribosomes. These results leave no doubt as to the existence of ribosomes in chloroplasts.

2. *Characteristics.* It was soon noted that the ribosomal particles of chloroplasts differ from those of the cytoplasm by their size, (100 to 150 instead of 150 to 200 Å) and by their sedimentation coefficient [62 S (Svetailo et al. 1967) or 70 S (Stutz and Noll 1966) instead of 80 S]. Thus, they appear to belong to the class of bacterial ribonucleoproteins whereas the cytoplasmic ribosomes belong to a class with a sedimentation coefficient of 80 S (characteristic of plants and higher animals as well as of yeasts and algae).

We shall not dwell upon these studies, which are treated in chapter 36 of this book, but merely point out that the existence of fundamental differences between chloroplasts and cytoplasmic ribosomes is confirmed by examinations of sections (Fig. 28) and of positively or negatively stained preparations (Bruskov and Odintsova 1968, Figs. 30 and 31). In summary, numerous cytological studies using staining techniques and specific enzyme digestions of nucleic acids, together with autoradiographic methods, have permitted the demonstration that chloroplasts contain DNA and RNA and that these two nucleic acids are of the bacterial type.

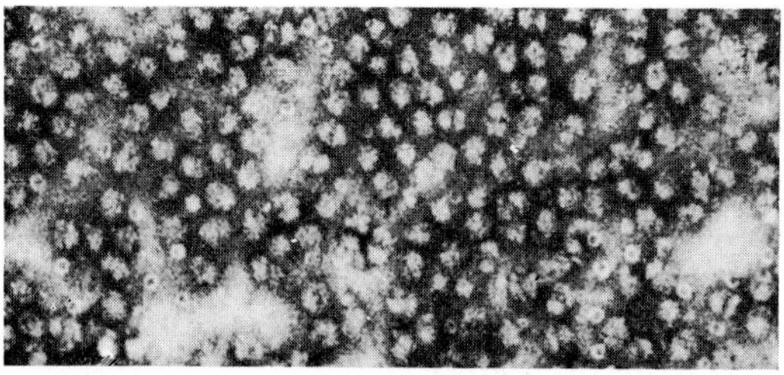

Fig. 30. Chloroplast ribosomes from bean leaves. Phosphotungstic acid. (Courtesy of Bruskov and Odintsova; ×107,000.)

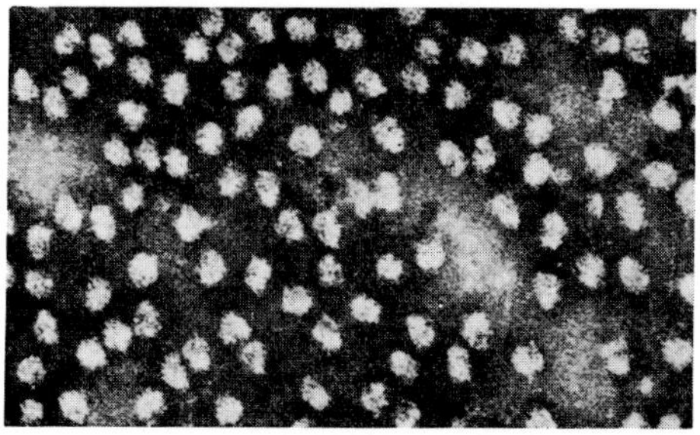

Fig. 31. Cytoplasmic ribosomes from the same bean leaves. Phosphotungstic acid. (Courtesy of Bruskov and Odintsova; ×107,000.)

(c) *Genetic implications*

All the evidence accumulated to date supports the idea of the autonomy of plastids. 'The chloroplast resembles a cell within another cell with all the apparatus necessary to assure it a large degree of autonomy' (Schiff and Epstein 1965).

In principle three situations are possible. In the first situation, the genetic information necessary for the differentiation of the plastids resides exclusively in the nucleus. According to this hypothesis, it is necessary to assume that the chloroplasts form *de novo* at each generation. The chloroplast DNA would be deprived of a genetic role and all the ribosomal RNA and messenger systems would be non-functional. On the basis of this hypothesis it is difficult to explain protein synthesis in chloroplast preparations *in vitro* (Spencer 1965). It is also difficult to explain how chloramphenicol inhibits the differentiation of chloroplasts, since it is known that this drug acts only at the level of 70 S ribosomes (i.e. chloroplast ribosomes) and has no effect on the 80 S or cytoplasmic ribosomes. In fact, there is much evidence for genetic continuity and often genetic determination of morphology of the plastids (Manton 1959). The U.V. inactivation curves obtained by Schiff and Epstein in etiolated *Euglena* lead to the estimate that at least 30 targets are present in each cell. Since one can observe 30 proplastids in etiolated *Euglena*, while there are only twelve in green *Euglena*, one may assume one target per proplastid, each proplastid representing a chloroplast unit. There are in an adult chloroplast three units sensitive to U.V. and thought to correspond to three DNA units. One is therefore led to formulate a reverse hypothesis. This is the second situation. In this hypothesis the plastid is considered to be a genetically autoreproductive entity which divides synchronously with the cell. Assuming that the chloroplasts possess a complete genetic system to carry out their own protein syntheses it still remains to be shown that the system is functional. In order to do this, normal cells may be examined, but then it is difficult to determine the influence of the nucleus. Alternatively, isolated chloroplasts may be examined but the fractions employed must be shown to be free of nuclear contaminants. Furthermore it is difficult to relate activity *in vitro* to that of the living cell.

Acetabularia represents an ideal material for this type of study for in this organism it is possible to avoid the difficulties discussed above. Since the nucleus of this giant alga is situated in the rhizoid, it is possible to cut off this cellular region and obtain a chloroplast fraction without nuclear contamination. The alga can continue to grow and cellular and chloroplast proteins and pigments can continue to accumulate long after enucleation. A number of explanations for these phenomena have been proposed. It was thought that a messenger RNA of nuclear origin was present and that, due to its slow turnover, it persisted in the cytoplasm deprived of nucleus. It was also thought that the chloroplasts were capable of carrying out their own replication independently of the nucleus. Starting with this latter hypothesis Shephard (1965) studied by autoradiography the separate and combined effects of enucleation and of actinomycin D (a presumed inhibitor of the transcription of genetic material in the chloroplast and the nucleus) on the incorporation of radioactive thymidine, uridine and leucine. His technique consisted in observing microscopically the labelling of chloroplasts which had been deposited 'in toto' on a slide by crushing an *Acetabularia* cell. In this autoradiographic study it was assumed that the specificity of the labelling was a function of the *specific extractability* of the label in the final product and not simply of the precursors used. The counts of the labelled chloroplasts demonstrated that enucleation did not prevent the incorporation of thymidine into the chloroplast DNA even a week after the operation. Five weeks after enucleation there was still incorporation of uridine into the RNA. In contrast actinomycin prevented this incorporation both in the normal plants and in the enucleated algae. Finally, while enucleation has only a minor effect on the incorporation of leucine by the chloroplasts, actinomycin D greatly reduces (75% in 6 hr) the incorporation of this amino acid into the plastids. These results lead to the conclusion that plastid DNA and some of the RNA are synthesized in the chloroplast. Most messenger RNA from the nucleus would be expected to decay during enucleation. These results are compatible with the hypothesis of an almost complete autonomy of the chloroplasts, whose replication and biosynthetic activity appear to proceed without the coded information of nuclear origin (Shephard 1965). If this is so, at least two modalities can be distinguished; either one considers this organelle is endowed with genetic continuity as an *episome* of the cell, or one considers it as an *endosymbiont*. In both cases, while allowing for some degree of autonomy of the chloroplast, nuclear control may be assumed. This is the third, intermediate situation. According to the episomic theory, at a given time in evolution in the primitive eucaryotic cell, or perhaps in the procaryotic, a part of the cell's genetic information was detached to form the genetic information of the plastids and undoubtedly also that of the mitochondria (Sagan 1967). One would therefore expect to find a certain similarity in base composition and perhaps common sequences with nuclear DNA (see the recent work of Edelman et al. 1967). In order to determine the degree of relationship between the nucleic acids of the nucleus and those of the chloroplasts, Tewari and Wildman (1968) tested the degree of hybridization between DNA (nuclear and chloroplast) and RNA purified from chloroplast ribosomes (70 S) or cytoplasmic ribosomes (80 S). Their results seem to show that chloroplast ribosomal RNA and chloroplast DNA hybridize (0.5%) but that the latter did not have any sequences in common with cytoplasmic ribosomal RNA. On the other hand, nuclear DNA hybridized with cytoplasmic ribosomal RNA (0.25%) and also chloroplast RNA (0.1%). The question remains as to whether the codons in nuclear DNA complementary to the RNA in 70 S ribosomes are functional in the formation of the chloroplast ribosomes or represent a non-functional relic of past evolution. Tewari and Wildman suggest that the chloroplast DNA could code for a small number of specific ribosomes while most of the other chloroplast ribosomes would be derived from information contained in the nucleus; this would support the episomic theory. The effects of hybridization artifacts should also be considered.

The arguments that can be put forward in favour of the symbiotic theory are those which furnish proof of convergence between plastids and *Cyanophyceae* for example, like those between mitochondria and bacteria (see Sagan's review 1967). If chloroplasts are considered as symbiont procaryotic organisms, the symbiosis became so powerful that the organisms became integrated organelles which divide synchronously with the cell and whose specialised metabolic functions have become indispensable to the host. It would therefore be necessary that a regulatory system between the host cell and its symbiont be established.

According to Gibor and Granick one can assume that each plastid contains one unit of DNA or a multiple of these units (Ben-Shaul; Schiff and Epstein (1967) and Yotsuyanagi and Guerrier). The unit is undoubtedly long enough to code several hundred genes. If one assumes a circular unit analogous to that of bacteria and mitochondria, one could assume that two types of genes exist. One type, called *constitutive* genes, which are responsible for the duplication of the organelles which are sensitive to U.V., and their inactivation leads to the formation of 100% white *Euglena.* When irradiated *Euglena* in which the genes of constitution have been inactivated are placed in conditions favouring cellular division, 100% white *Euglena* are formed. The other type of gene, called *inducible*, would be responsible for the differentiation of the organelles which would be under the control of a regulatory gene. Light could act either directly on these genes, or by the intermediate activation of nuclear genes. It is certain that nuclear genes can directly affect the expression of the plastid genes; such is the case with chlorophyll mutations of nuclear origin in higher plants and in some *Chlorophyceae.*

Studies *in vivo* and *in vitro* indicate that chloroplasts carry out the synthesis of at least some of their proteins. This synthetic process involves activating enzymes, transfer RNA, ribosomes and messenger RNA of the chloroplast type. Whichever hypothesis is adopted, symbiosis or episomy, the chloroplast appears to possess, to a very high degree, a genetic and biochemical autonomy.

4. Conclusions

Cytochemical methods have allowed us to acquire a more complete view of the structure and function of the chloroplast. We may assume that the pigments and the electron trasporter components are associated with the three dimensional systems of ramified thylakoids, while the plastid matrix contains the enzymes of the Calvin cycle. Work carried out in different laboratories may soon provide results on the chemical nature and distribution of different components of the membranous structures, which may resolve present contradictory interpretations.

Finally, the demonstration in the chloroplasts of molecules endowed with information (DNA and different types of RNA), and the proof that these molecules are functional, allows speculation about the evolution of the chloroplasts, not only from the biochemical or morphological points of view, but also on the distribution within the cell of genes which determine and regulate the formation of these cellular organelles.

References

BAMBERGER, E.S. and B.PARK: Effect of hydrolytic enzymes on the photosynthetic efficiency and morphology of chloroplasts. Plant Physiol. 41 (1966) 1591.

BEN-SHAUL, Y., H.T.EPSTEIN and S.A.SCHIFF: Studies of chloroplast development in *Euglena.* Can. J. Botany 43 (1965) 129.

BERZBORN, R.: Demonstration of ferredoxin-NADP reductase in the surface of the lamellar system of chloroplasts by specific antibodies. Intern. Congr. Photosynth. Freudenstadt, June 1968.

BOGORAD, L., F.V.MERCER and R.MULLENS: Studies with *Cyanidium caldarium* II. The fine structure of pigment-deficient mutants. Photosynthetic mechanisms in green plants. Natl. Acad. Sci.-Natl. Res. Council, Publ. 1145. (1963) 560.

BOURDU, R. and M.LEFORT: Structure fine, observée en cryodécapage, des lamelles photosynthétiques des cyanophycées endosymbiotiques: *Glaucocystis nostochinearum* (Itzigs) et *Cyanophora paradoxa* (Korschikoff). Compt. Rend. 265 (1967) 37.

BRACHET, J.: New observations on biochemical interactions between nucleus and cytoplasm in *Amoeba* and *Acetabularia.* Exptl. Cell Res. Suppl. 6 (1959) 78.

BRANTON, D.: Structural units of chloroplast membranes. In: C.Sironval, ed.: Le chloroplaste. Paris, Masson et Cie (1967) 48.

BRANTON, D. and R.B.PARK: Subunits in chloroplast lamellae. J. Ultrastruct. Res. 19 (1967) 283.

BRODY, M. and A.E.VATTER: Observations on cellular structures of *Porphyridium cruentum.* J. Biophys. Biochem. Cytol. 5 (1959) 289.

BRONCHART, R.: Structure de la membrane des thylakoïdes. In: C.Sironval, ed.: Le chloroplaste. Paris, Masson et Cie (1967) 55.

BROWN, W.V., H.MOLLENHAUER and C.JOHNSON: An electron microscope study of silver nitrate reduction in leaf cells. Am. J. Botany 49 (1962) 57.

BRUSKOV, V.I. and M.S.ODINTSOVA: Comparative electron microscopic studies of chloroplast and cytoplasmic ribosomes. J. Mol. Biol. 32 (1968) 471.

CARO, L.G.: High resolution autoradiography II. The problem of resolution. J. Cell Biol. 15 (1962) 189.

CHIBA, Y.: Cytochemical studies on chloroplasts, cytologic demonstration of nucleic acids in chloroplasts. Cytologia (Tokyo) 16 (1951) 259.

COHEN-BAZIRE, G. and M.LEFORT-TRAN: Analyse de la localisation des phycobilines chez *Gleocapsa alpicola* et *Porphyridium cruentum.* J. Bacteriol. (in press).

DROZ, B.: Synthèse et transfert de protéines cellulaires dans les neurones ganglionaires. Radioautographie quantitative. J. Microscopie 6 (1967) 201.

EDELMAN, M., D.SWINTON, J.A.SCHIFF, H.T.EPSTEIN and B.ZELDIN: The DNA of the blue green algae. Bacteriol. Rev. 31 (1967) 315.

EMERSON, R. and A.ARNOLD: Photosynthesis in flashing light. J. Gen. Physiol. 16 (1932) 191.

GANTT, E. and S.F.CONTI: The ultrastructure of *Porphyridium cruentum.* J. Cell Biol. 26 (1965) 365.

GANTT, E. and S.F.CONTI: Granules associated with the chloroplast lamellae of *Porphyridium cruentum.* J. Cell Biol. 29 (1966) 423.

GANTT, E. and S.F.CONTI: Phycobiliprotein localization in algae. Energy conversion by the photosynthetic apparatus. Brookhaven Symp. Biol. 19 (1967) 393.

GIBOR, A. and S.GRANICK: Plastids and mitochondria: Inheritable systems. Science 145 (1964) 890.

GIRAUD, G.: La structure des pigments et les caractéristiques fonctionnelles de l'appareil photosynthétique de diverses algues. Physiol. Vég. 1 (1963) 203.

GRANBOULAN, P.: Comparison of emulsion and techniques of radioautography. In: C.Leblond and K.B.Warren, eds.: The use of radioautography in investigating protein synthesis. New York, Academic Press (1965) 43.

HOWELL, S.H. and E.N.MOUDRIANAKIS: Hill reaction site in chloroplast membranes: Non participation of the quantasome particle in photoreduction. J. Mol. Biol. 27 (1967) 323.

HOWELL, S.H. and E.N.MOUDRIANAKIS: Function of the 'quantasome' in photosynthesis: structure and properties of membrane bound particle active in the dark reactions of photophosphorylation. Proc. Natl. Acad. Sci. U.S. 58 (1967) 1261.

KISLEV, N., H.SWIFT and L.BOGORAD: Studies of nucleic acids in chloroplasts and mitochondria in Swiss Chard. J. Cell Biol. 25 (1965) 327.

KOK, B. and J.A.BUSINGER: Report on some recent results at Wageningen III. Photoinhibition. Res. Photosyn. New York, Interscience (1957) 357.

JACOB, F. and J.MONOD: Genetic regulatory mechanisms in the synthesis of proteins. J. Mol. Biol. 3 (1961) 318.

JACOBSON, A.B., H.SWIFT and L.BOGORAD: Cytochemical studies concerning the occurrence and distribution of RNA in plastids of *Zea mays*. J. Cell Biol. 17 (1963) 557.

LEDUC, E.H. and W.BERNHARD: Water soluble embedding media for ultrastructural cytochemistry. Digestion with nucleases and proteinases. In: R.J.C.Harris, ed.: The interpretation of ultrastructure. New York, Academic Press (1962) 21.

LEFORT, M.: Sur le chromatoplasma d'un cyanophycée endosymbiotique: *Glaucocystis nostochinearum* (Itzigs). Compt. Rend. 261 (1965) 223.

LEFORT, M. and M.POUPHILE: Données cytochimiques sur l'organisation structurale du chromatoplasma de *Glaucocystis nostochinearum* (Itzigs). Compt. Rend. Soc. Biol. 161 (1967) 992.

LIMA-DE-FARIA, A. and M.J.MOSES: Labeling of *Zea mays* chloroplasts with H^3-thymidine. Hereditas 52 (1964) 367.

LITTAU, C.V.: A cytochemical study of the chloroplasts in some higher plants. Am. J. Botany 45 (1958) 45.

MANTON, I.: Electronmicroscopic observations on a very small flagellate; the problem of *Chromulina pusilla* (Butcher). J. Marine Biol. Assoc. U.K. 38 (1959) 319.

MENKE, W.: The molecular structure of photosynthetic lamellar systems. Energy conversion by the photosynthetic apparatus. Brookhaven Symp. Biol. 19 (1966) 328.

MENKE, W.: The structure of the chloroplasts. In: T.W.Goodwin, ed.: Biochemistry of chloroplasts. London, Academic Press (1966) 3.

METZNER, H.: Über den Nachweis von Nukleinsäuren in den Chloroplasten höherer Pflanzen. Naturwissenschaften 39 (1952) 64.

METZNER, H.: Cytochemische Untersuchungen über das Vorkommen von Nukleinsäuren in Chloroplasten. Biol. Zentralbl. 71 (1952) 257.

MILOVIDOV, P.F.: Zur Theorie und Technik der Nuclealfärbung. Protoplasma 25 (1936) 570.

MOOR, H.: Die Gefrier-Fixation lebender Zellen und ihre Anwendung in der Elektronenmikroskopie. Z. Zellforsch. Mikroskop. Anat., Abt. Histochem. 62 (1964) 546.

MOOR, H., K.MÜHLETHALER, H.WALDNER and A.FREY-WYSSLING: A new freezing ultramicrotome. J. Biophys. Biochem. Cytol. 10 (1961) 1.

MÜHLETHALER, K.: L'ultrastructure de la lamelle des chloroplastes. In: C.Sironval, ed.: Le chloroplaste; croissance et vieillissement. Paris, Masson et Cie (1967) 42.

ODA, T. and M.HUZISIGE: Macromolecular repeating particles in the chloroplast membrane. Exptl. Cell Res. 37 (1965) 481.

PARK, R.B.: Substructure of chloroplast lamellae. J. Cell Biol. 27 (1965) 151.

PARK, R.B. and J.BIGGINGS: Quantasome: size and composition. Science 144 (1964) 1009.

PARK, R.B. and D.BRANTON: Freeze-etching of chloroplasts from glutaraldehyde fixed leaves. Brookhaven Symp. Biol. 19 (1967) 341.

PARK, R.B. and N.G.PON: Correlation of structure with function in *Spinacea oleracea* chloroplasts. J. Mol. Biol. 3 (1961) 1.

PARK, R.B. and N.G.PON: Chemical composition and the substructure of lamellae isolated from *Spinacea oleracea* chloroplasts. J. Mol. Biol. 6 (1963) 105.

RIS, H.: Ultrastructure and molecular organization of genetic systems. Can. J. Genet. Cytol. 3 (1961) 95.

RIS, H. and W. PLAUT: Ultrastructure of DNA-containing areas in the chloroplast of *Chlamydomonas*. J. Cell Biol. 13 (1962) 383.

ROBERTSON, J. D.: New observations on the ultrastructure of the membranes of frog peripheral nerve fibers. J. Biophys. Biochem. Cytol. 3 (1957) 1043.

RYTER, A. and E. KELLENBERGER: Etude au microscope électronique de plasmas contenant de l'ADN. Z. Naturforsch. 13 (1958) 597.

SAGAN, L.: An unusual pattern of tritiated thymidine incorporation in *Euglena*. J. Protozool. 12, 1 (1965) 105.

SAGAN, L.: On the origin of mitosing cells. J. Theoret. Biol. 14 (1967) 225.

SAGAN, L., Y. BEN-SHAUL and J. A. SCHIFF: Radiographic localization of DNA in the chloroplasts of *Euglena*. Abstr. 4th Ann. Meeting of the American Soc. for Cell Biol., Cleveland, Ohio, 1964.

SCHIFF, J. A. and H. T. EPSTEIN: The continuity of the chloroplast in *Euglena*. In: M. Locke, ed.: Reproduction: molecular, subcellular and cellular. New York, Academic Press (1965) p. 131.

SHEPHARD, D. C.: An autoradiographic comparison of the effects of enucleation and actinomycin D on the incorporation of nucleic acid and protein precursors by *Acetabularia* chloroplasts. Biochim. Biophys. Acta 108 (1965) 635.

SPENCER, D.: Protein synthesis by isolated spinach chloroplast. Arch. Biochem. Biophys. 111 (1965) 381.

STEINMANN, E.: An electron microscope study of the lamellar structure of chloroplast. Exptl. Cell Res. 3 (1952) 367.

STOCKING, C. and E. GIFFORD: Incorporation of thymidine into chloroplasts of *Spirogyra*. Biochem. Biophys. Res. Commun. 1 (1959) 159.

STUTZ, E. and H. NOLL: Characterization of cytoplasmic and chloroplast polysomes in plants: evidence for three classes of ribosomal RNA in nature. Proc. Natl. Acad. Sci. U.S. 57 (1966) 774.

SVETAILO, E. N., I. I. PHILIPPOVICH and N. M. SISSAKIAN: Differences in sedimentation properties of chloroplast and cytoplasmic ribosomes from pea seedlings. J. Mol. Biol. 24 (1967) 405.

SWIFT, H.: Nucleic acids of mitochondria and chloroplasts. Am. Naturalist 99 (1965) 201.

TEWARI, K. K. and S. G. WILDMAN: Function of chloroplast DNA I. Hybridization studies involving nuclear and chloroplast DNA with RNA from cytoplasmic (80 S) and chloroplast (70 S) ribosomes. Proc. Natl. Acad. Sci. U.S. 59 (1968) 569.

THOMAS, J. B., L. C. POST and N. VERTREGT: Localization of chlorophyll within the chloroplast. Biochim. Biophys. Acta 13 (1954) 20.

VERNON, L. P., E. SHAW and H. H. MOLLENHAUER: Biochemical and structural properties of photosystems I and II of chloroplasts. Intern. Congr. Photosynth. Res., Freudenstadt, June 1968.

DE VITRY, F.: Etude du métabolisme des acides nucléiques chez *Acetabularia mediterranea*. Bull. Soc. Chim. Biol. 47 (1965) 1353.

WEIER, T. E., C. R. STOCKING and L. K. SHUMWAY: The photosynthetic apparatus in chloroplasts of higher plants. Brookhaven Symp. Biol. 19 (1966) 353.

WEIER, T. E. and A. A. BENSON: The molecular organization of chloroplast membranes. Am. J. Botany 54 (1967) 389.

WESSELS, J. S. C.: Separation of the two photochemical systems of photosynthesis by digitonin fragmentation of spinach chloroplasts. Proc. Roy. Soc. (London), Ser. B: 157 (1963) 345.

WESSELS, J. S. C., A. DORSMAN and A. J. LUITINGH: Digitonin particles of chloroplast lamellae. In: C. Sironval, ed.: Le chloroplaste; croissance et vieillissement. Paris, Masson et Cie (1967) 60.

WOLLGIEHN, R. and K. MOTHES: Über die Inkorporation von ^{3}H Thymidin in die chloroplasten DNS von *Nicotiana rustica*. Exptl. Cell Res. 35 (1964) 52.

WOODCOCK, C. L. F. and H. FERNÁNDEZ-MORÁN: Electron microscopy of DNA conformations in spinach chloroplasts. J. Mol. Biol. 31, 3 (1968) 627.

YOTSUYANAGI, Y. and C. GUERRIER: Mise en évidence par des techniques cytochimiques et la microscopie électronique d'acide désoxyribonucléique dans les mitochondries et les proplastes d'*Allium cepa*. Compt. Rend. 260 (1965) 2344.

YUASA, A.: Studies on the cytology of *Pteridophyta* XV. A critical consideration of the cytological fixation and staining in the *Sporophyta* cells, prothallium cells and spermatozoids of *Dryopteris uniformis* (Makino). Japan J. Bot. 9 (1938) 145.

PART XII

Ultrastructure and biochemistry of ribosomes, endoplasmic reticulum and Golgi apparatus

CHAPTER 39

Ribosomes: properties and function

J. C. H. DE MAN and N. J. A. NOORDUYN

Department of Submicroscopical Pathology, Pathological Laboratory, University of Leiden, The Netherlands

Contents

1. Introduction

2. Properties
   (a) General
   (b) Classes of ribosomes occurring in nature
   (c) Morphology of polyribosomes, ribosomes, and ribosomal subunits
   (d) Composition and structure of the ribosome

3. Function
   (a) General
   (b) Chain initiation, chain elongation and chain termination in protein synthesis
   (c) Protein synthesis and antibiotics
   (d) Concluding remarks

1. Introduction

In the middle fifties the molecular basis for protein synthesis was elucidated by the discovery that the microsomal fraction from a cell homogenate plus an energy-providing system would incorporate radioactively labeled amino acids. Ribosomes, the particles containing RNA and protein, have been identified as the fundamental units of this microsomal fraction, by means of the electron microscope and by the study of protein synthesis in cell-free systems (Palade and Siekevitz; Zamecnik et al.).

At about that time it was generally believed that RNA might be the intermediate molecule between the genetic code residing in DNA and protein synthesis. However, an RNA molecule did not appear to have the steric properties to polymerize amino acids directly into a characteristic sequence. Therefore, it seemed likely that amino acids were first individually attached to adaptor molecules which could then form hydrogen bonds with the intermediate template RNA. The existence of such adaptor molecules, which became known as transfer RNA, was demonstrated by Hoagland et al., but the ribosome was still assumed to contain the template RNA molecule. However, three main objections were raised to this assumption: firstly, the base ratio of the ribosomal RNA differed from that of the DNA providing the template; secondly, the stability of the ribosomal RNA was in conflict with the hypothesis that the RNA intermediate must be very labile (Jacob and Monod); and thirdly, the assumption of a template, coiled inside the ribosome, posed topological problems. Therefore, in addition to ribosomal and transfer RNA, the occurrence of a third species now called messenger RNA had to be assumed. In 1961 Brenner et al. provided support for this concept in the form of evidence that bacterial ribosomes attach to newly formed phage messenger RNA to make the proteins required for phage reproduction. Thus, ribosomes appeared to be structures that synthesize the protein dictated by the messenger with which they happen to become associated.

About 1962 Warner et al. put forward the hypothesis that the protein factories of the cell are not single ribosomes working in isolation but collections of ribosomes, *polyribosomes*, working together in orderly fashion. The basis for this hypothesis was their discovery that incorporation of radioactively labeled leucine occurred only in association with polyribosomes, whereas single ribosomes from the same population were inactive (Warner et al. 1963). By both measurement of isolated reticulocyte polyribosomes as seen in the electron microscope and sucrose gradient analysis, a relation was demonstrated between the calculated length of the messenger RNA, the number of the ribosomes in polyribosomes, and the length of the polypeptide chain expressed in the number of amino acids (Warner et al. 1962). It was assumed then that in polyribosomes the ribosomes move relative to the messenger RNA molecule and that each one makes a complete polypeptide chain. Although it has since been found that the relation between the length of the messenger RNA and that of the polypeptide chain cannot be generalized for all types of polyribosomes, the general concept of ribosomes moving relative to the messenger RNA is still valid.

In this chapter we will discuss the various types of ribosomes, their morphology and composition and their function in the protein-synthesizing mechanism.

2. *Properties*

(a) *General*

Ribosomes occur in all living cells as highly hydrated structures. They consist of two subunits, a large and a small one, both containing RNA and protein. The complete ribosome, the subunits, and the RNA molecules found in the subunits, are generally defined by their sedimentation coefficient or S values.

Biological properties of the ribosome can be tested in a cell-free system consisting of ribosomes, a supernatant fluid obtained by centrifugation of cell homogenate containing tRNA and enzymes, an energy-providing system, and Mg^{2+}. After the addition of amino acids and a synthetic (polyuridylic acid or poly-U) or naturally occurring (virus) messenger, polypeptides are formed (Nirenberg and Matthaei). The polyceptide-synthesizing capacity of the system can be estimated by the amount of radiopatively labeled amino acids incorporated into the peptide chain.

Some general properties of the ribosome are summarized in Table 1 (Petermann; Arnstein 1963).

TABLE 1

General properties of ribosomes

	70 S ribosomes		80 S ribosomes	
1. M.W.	2.7×10^6		4×10^6	
2. RNA content	65%		45%	
3. Protein content	35%		55%	
4. Basic proteins with M.W.	25,000		12,000–25,000	
5. Diameter	140–270 Å		220–300 Å	
6. Optimum Mg^{2+} concentration for maximum amino acid incorporation	10–15 mM		1.5 mM	
7. Inhibition of protein synthesis by antibiotics	Inhibition		No inhibition	
8. Subunits	30 S	50 S	40 S	60 S
M.W.	0.9×10^6	1.8×10^6	1.3×10^6	2.6×10^6
M.W. RNA	0.6×10^6	1.2×10^6	0.6×10^6	1.7×10^6
S value RNA	16	23	18	28

(b) *Classes of ribosomes occurring in nature*

The sedimentation coefficients reported for ribosomes from several species of microorganisms, plants, and animals, indicate that ribosomes fall into two distinct classes (Taylor and Storck). Ribosomes from bacteria, blue-green algae, mitochondria, and chloroplasts belong to the 70 S class, whereas cytoplasmic ribosomes from green plants, animals, yeast, and a number of fungi are characterized by sedimentation coefficients of approximately 80 S. The S values in the 70 S and 80 S ribosomal classes show a rather wide range, i.e., from 67 S to 73 S and from 77 S to 81 S, respectively (Küntzel and Noll; see Table 2). Various other systematic differences between the two classes of ribosomes are listed in Table 1.

TABLE 2

Sedimentation rate of ribosomal RNA from different species of ribosomes

	Ribosomal RNA		Ribosomes
Rat liver cytoplasm	29.5	17.8	81
Bean cytoplasm	25.9	17.0	78
Neurospora cytoplasm	25.0	17.4	77
E. coli	21.2	16.0	70
Mitochondria	20.5	16.4	73
Chloroplasts	20.8	15.7	67

There are indications that, besides similar physical characteristics, ribosomes within each class also have similarities with respect to their biological properties. In poly-U directed cell-free systems, combination of ribosomes of one class with the supernatant enzymes from cells of the other kind does not lead to the incorporation of amino acids, whereas the mixing of enzymes and ribosomes of two different species within one class gives substantial incorporation (Parisi). It even appears that mixing of 50 S *B. subtilis* and 30 S *E. coli* subunits gives good amino acid incorporating activity (Takeda and Lipmann). It thus seems to be possible to prepare active hybrids with ribosomal subunits from different species belonging to the same class. Another interesting aspect of the difference between the 70 S and 80 S ribosomal classes also related to function, is the influence of some antibiotics such as streptomycin on the translating mechanism of ribosomes of the 70 S class as contrasted with the absence of such an influence on ribosomes belonging to the 80 S class.

(c) *Morphology of polyribosomes, ribosomes, and ribosomal subunits*

In the electron microscope, isolated polyribosomes, prepared with positive staining techniques, have been described as 'extended arrays of ribosomes connected by a strand approximately 10 Å in width' (Slayter et al.). Because the strand stains positively with uranyl acetate, which is known to react with nucleic acids, it is believed that the connecting strand represents the messenger RNA molecule (Fig. 1b). Furthermore, it has been shown that under the action of very small quantities of ribonuclease, polyribosomes are converted to single ribosomes (Warner et al. 1963). Polyribosomes

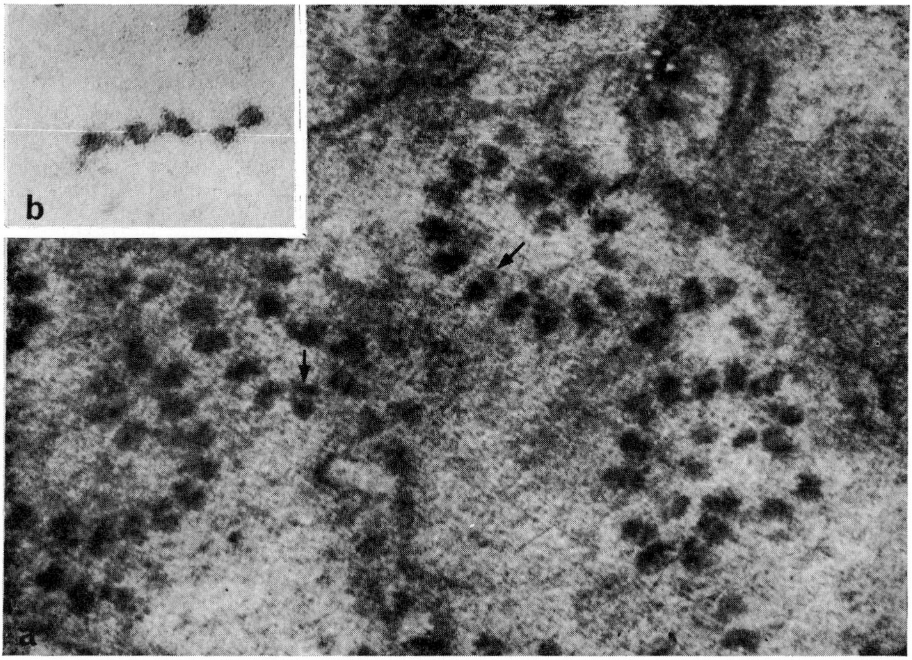

Fig. 1. (a) Rosette-like polyribosomes in a section of a rat liver cell. Note division by a cleft into a smaller elongated component (arrows) measuring 150 × 80 Å at the inner side of the rosette, and a larger component with a maximum diameter of 220 Å at the periphery. × 210,000. (b) Positively stained (uranyl acetate) rat liver polyribosome. Note connecting strand between ribosomes. × 150,000.

are often seen as rosettes and sometimes in the form of a helix (Behnke; Waddington and Perry; Benedetti et al.; Pfuderer et al.), the small subunit facing towards the centre of the spiral (Shelton and Kuff; see Fig. 1a).

Cytoplasmic polyribosomes occur in two forms: membrane-attached and free cytoplasmic (Benedetti et al.). In cells synthesizing protein for secretion the majority of the ribosomes are attached to membranes of the endoplasmic reticulum (Porter). There is reason to believe that the presence of Mg^{2+} and of nascent protein on the ribosome may have an effect on the attachment of the large ribosomal subunit to the microsomal membrane (Sabatini et al.; Siekevitz).

As can be seen from Table 1, there is a difference in size between the two classes of ribosomes which amounts to about 270 × 210 Å for the chloroplast ribosome as a member of the 70 S class and about 280 × 220 Å for plant cytoplasmic ribosomes as members of the 80 S class (Miller et al.). For *E. coli* ribosomes, diameters are given as 140 × 180 Å (Huxley and Zubay) and for animal cell cytoplasmic ribosomes 260 × 300 Å (Shelton and Kuff).

The 70 S ribosomes of *E. coli* have been described by Huxley and Zubay as being built up 'of two unequal subunits; the larger subunit somewhat flattened on the side which faces the smaller one and the smaller one often appears slightly concave on the side which faces the larger one so that it gives the impression of fitting onto it like an overlapping cap'. A distinct cleft is visible between the two subunits. The chloroplast ribosomes strikingly resemble those of *E. coli.* Although in animal cytoplasmic ribosomes a general fuzziness may obscure a division into a small and large subunit (Mathias et al.), clefts between the two have been observed in several types of mammalian ribosomes (Benedetti et al.; Shelton and Kuff; Sabatini et al.; see Fig. 2b).

The large subunit (50 S bacterial ribosomal unit) has been described as an approximately spherical subunit when observed in association with the cap-like smaller subunit. However, isolated large subunits of *E. coli* have been described by Huxley and Zubay as 'having a diameter of 140–160 Å and sometimes appearing very approximately pentagonal'. Angular appearances of ribosomes or large ribosomal subunits have been reported (Lubin; Kisselev and Spirin). Isolated small ribosomal subunits have been described as elongated particles with a somewhat variable shape and meas-

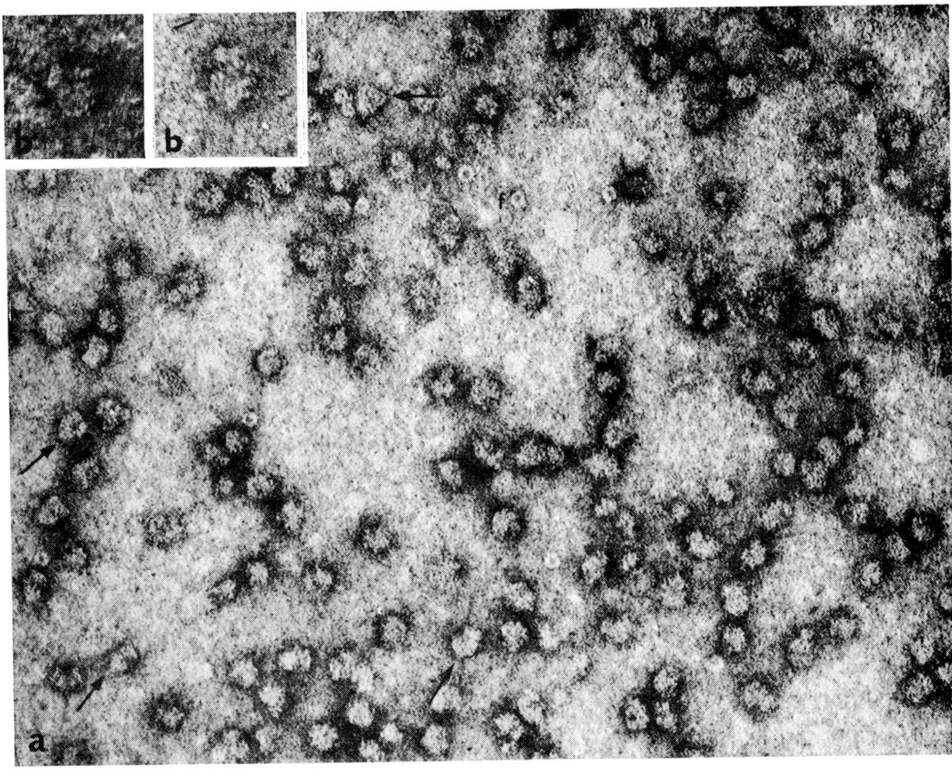

Fig. 2. (a) Negatively stained (uranyl acetate) isolated rat liver ribosomes showing angular outlines (arrows). f = ferritin particles. × 180,000. (b) Negatively stained (uranyl acetate) rat liver ribosomes showing a division into a large and a bipartite small subunit. × 320,000.

uring 180 × 70 Å. Plant cytoplasmic, chloroplast and mammalian ribosomal small subunits appear as bipartite structures (Fig. 2b; Miller et al.; Shelton and Kuff).

An interesting form of ribosomal aggregation was reported in 1966 by Byers, who discovered that hypothermia of chick embryo cells induces the formation of crystallized curved sheets of ribosomes (Fig. 3). In mitotic cells these sheets are stacked, forming three-dimensional crystals. Crystalline ribosomes also occur in the cysts of *Entamoeba invadens*, forming helical structures (Fig. 4). This latter type of crystallized collections of ribosomes is light microscopically known as the so-called chromatoid body (Barker 1963a, b; Morgan et al.).

(d) *Composition and structure of the ribosome*

Ribosomal RNA reveals a characteristic asymmetrical base composition. For instance in *E. coli* it is: 25% A (adenine), 22% U (uracil), 32% G (guanine) and 21% C (cytosine). The 16 S RNA molecule in the small subunit (30 S) differs from the 23 S RNA molecule in the large subunit (50 S) in its base composition and sequence. Therefore, these two types of ribosomal RNA should be regarded as distinct molecular species. In general, the base composition of ribosomal RNA varies much less than that of DNA. Only a small portion of the cell DNA has a base sequence complementary to the ribosomal RNA. The percentage of total DNA comprising rRNA cistrons varies from 0.005–0.02 in HeLa cells to 0.42–0.65 in *E. coli* (Perry). In addition to the 16 S and 23 S

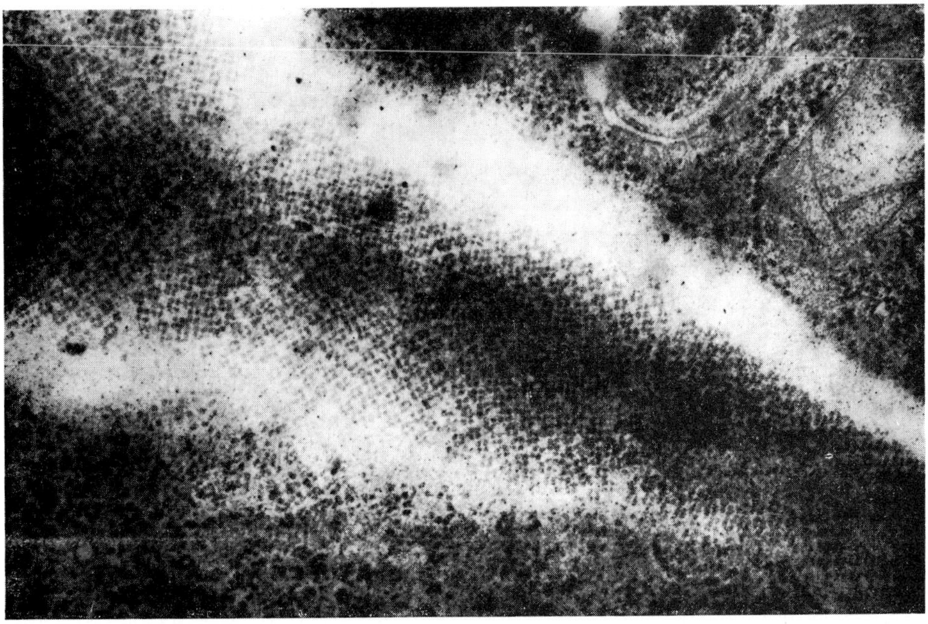

Fig. 3. Frontal section of a sheet of crystalline ribosomes in hypothermic chick-embryo cells. Ribosomes are arranged in a tetrameral configuration. × 33,000.

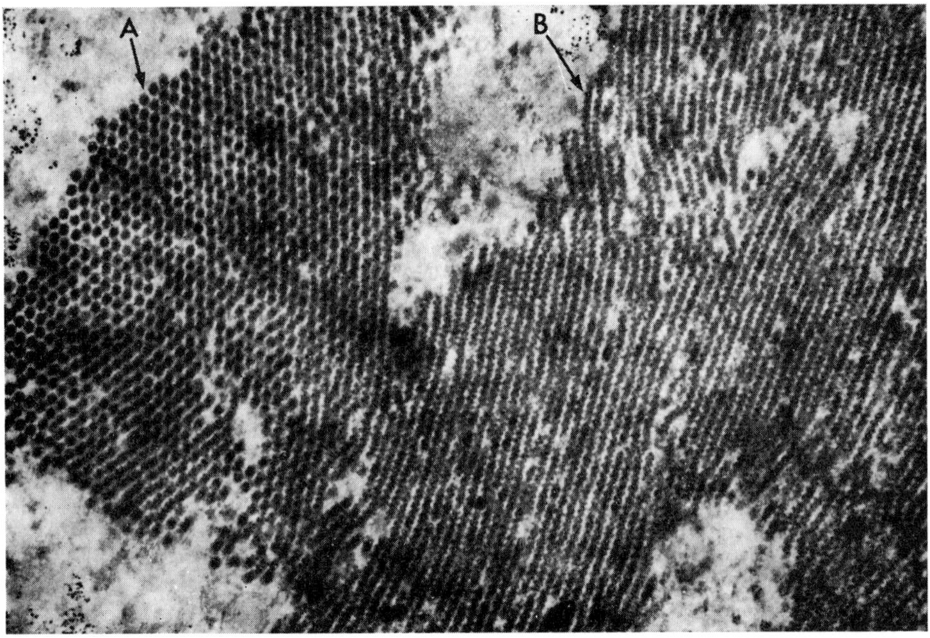

Fig. 4. Section of chromatoid body in a cyst of *Entamoeba invadens* (strain Rodhain, cultured by Dr. J.J. Laarman, Institute of Tropical Medicine, University of Leiden). Ribosomes are arranged in helical configurations (A = transversely, B = longitudinally sectioned helices). × 25,000.

RNA, a low molecular weight ribonucleic acid (5 S RNA) has been demonstrated in the 50 S ribosomal subunit of *E. coli* (Rosset et al.). This RNA differs from tRNA in having a length of 120 nucleotides as compared to about 75 nucleotides in tRNA and lacks any unusual bases (Brownlee et al.).

The currently accepted model of the ribosome is based on the idea that ribosomal RNA has a partially double helical structure (Fresco et al.; Langridge; Cotter et al.). However, Furano et al., in their report of a study on the conformation of the RNA in the ribosome, state that 'the most judicious conclusion at this point would be that the experimental evidence available cannot be viewed as sufficiently discriminatory to completely eliminate either a double-helical or single-stranded conformation of the RNA in the intact ribosome'. There is general agreement that the surface of the ribosome consists chiefly of RNA and that protein is located internally.

Although in general all the ribosomal proteins are alike in being rich in the amino acids lysine and arginine and in aspartic- and glutaminic acid, the ribosomal proteins on the other hand show a remarkable multiplicity. Gesteland and Staehelin studied *E. coli* ribosomal proteins isolated from 70 S, 50 S, and 30 S particles by acrylamide gel electrophoresis and found at least fifteen 30 S ribosomal components and twenty 50 S protein components. The 50 S and 30 S patterns are additive producing the 70 S pattern, making thirty-one distinguishable components in all. Immunological analysis of *E. coli* ribosomes indicated that they contain at least seven different proteins and that at least two proteins of the 50 S ribosomal subunit are homologous to two proteins in the 30 S ribosomal subunit (Estrup and Santer). It is believed that ribosomal proteins are partly α-helical (McPhie and Gratzer), globular in character and have a diameter of the order of 30 Å (Cotter et al.; Hart).

The proteins appear to be differently attached to the ribosomes. This seems to be related to the structure and function of the ribosome:

(1) Some of the protein is loosely attached to the ribosome. By chromatography on diethylaminoethylcellulose (DEAE), biologically active ribosomes can be purified. With this procedure, about 30% of the protein is lost as compared to the result of washing by repeated centrifugation. However, in spite of this protein loss, the purified ribosomes have the same sedimentation values and are active in amino acid incorporation (Furano).

(2) Some of the protein appears to be rather strongly bound to the ribosome, but can be reversibly dissociated from normal *E. coli* 50 S and 30 S ribosomal subunits. By density gradient centrifugation in a solution of cesium chloride in the presence of an appropriate concentration of Mg^{2+}, a discrete amount of protein (called 'split' protein) dissociates from the ribosomal subunits, turning these into protein-deficient 43 S and 28 S so-called 'core' particles (Staehelin and Meselson). These 'core' particles can be converted into even more protein-deficient 28 S and 22 S particles containing 20% protein (Lerman et al.). This dissociation of protein appears to be fully reversible. Reassociation of the dissociated protein and the particles leads via 43 S and 28 S to the formation of 50 S and 30 S ribosomal subunits, which may combine to give 70 S ribosomes active in protein synthesis. By fractionating the 'split' protein in subgroups and by reassociation of subgroups with the 'core' particles, it is possible to determine which ribosomal protein groups are essential for protein synthesis (Traub et al.).

(3) Some of the protein remains irreversibly bound to the 'core' particles. These are structural proteins probably having a supporting function for the RNA strand, thereby helping to determine the shape of the ribosome.

Current work on the structure and function of the ribosome is aimed at the identification of the molecular components and the relation of their properties to the function of the organelle in protein synthesis. The above-mentioned dissociation of 'split' proteins from the ribosomes is one of the approaches by which an attempt can be made to determine the function of the individual components.

Another approach to the determination of the function of the individual components concerns the study of the biosynthesis of ribosomes. There are several ways to inhibit the formation of complete ribosomes in bacteria. When chloromycetin-sensitive bacteria are treated with this drug during growth, protein synthesis is inhibited but the rate of RNA synthesis is not depressed. In these cells ribonucleoproteins are accumulated which are distinct from 50 S and 30 S ribosomal subunits because they are richer in RNA (76%). These particles are called 'CM' particles and they have sedimentation coefficients of 25 S and 18 S, containing 23 S and 16 S RNA respectively (Osawa). Similar particles can be obtained by culturing *E. coli* in Mg^{2+}-deficient media (Mg^{2+} particles) and also by culturing one of the amino acid-requiring mutants of *E. coli* that can synthesize RNA in the absence of the amino acid (relaxed mutants). Unlike the other mutants of this group (stringent mutants), in which both protein and RNA synthesis is stopped in the absence of the required amino acid, the relaxed mutants show continuation of RNA synthesis while protein synthesis is inhibited. The ribonucleoprotein ('RC' particles) accumulated in these cells consists of two components; 23 S and 20 S containing RNA of 23 S and 16 S, respectively. These particles have a protein content of 30 per cent (Nakada). 'CM' particles, 'MG' particles and 'RC' particles are inactive in protein synthesis, but their amino acid-incorporating activity is restored by removal of the inhibitory factor from the medium, after which the particles are completed by a preferential ribosomal protein synthesis. Contrary to this, the addition of 5-fluorouracil to *E. coli* cultures, is followed by an accumulation of 30 S particles that cannot be completed after removal of the 5-fluorouracil and are distinct from 30 S ribosomal subunits, since they contain both 23 S and 16 S RNA components having incorporated fluorouracil (Osawa).

The results of experiments involving dissociation of protein from ribosomes and of studies on ribosomal biosynthesis *in vivo* suggest the existence within ribosomes of groups of cooperatively organized protein molecules.

Much remains to be learned about the surface structure of the ribosome in physicochemical terms (Moore). Until precise information on the exact structure of the ribosome becomes available, our knowledge of the ribosomal binding sites of mRNA and other factors involved in protein synthesis will continue to be vague.

3. *Function*

(a) *General*

It is now well established that ribosomes play their fundamental role in protein synthesis in the form of aggregates of several ribosomes to which is attached the messenger RNA. This RNA carries the genetic information from DNA. Thus, the polyribosome is the smallest functional unit in protein synthesis. Protein synthesis involves the following sequence (Arnstein 1965):

(1) Amino acids are activated by reacting with adenosine triphosphate (ATP) to give aminoacyl adenylate and pyrophosphate. The enzymes that catalyse this reaction are specific for each of the 20 amino acids occurring in proteins (Fig. 5).

(2) Aminoacyl adenylates are intermediates that react with the appropriate transfer RNA to give aminoacyl tRNA, a reaction catalyzed by the same specific enzymes (aminoacyl tRNA synthetase) as those involved in the formation of the aminoacyl adenylate. Transfer RNAs are polynucleotides containing about 75 nucleotides which

apart from the four commonly present in RNA (A, G, C, U), include some unusual nucleotides such as pseudouridylic acid. The tRNA molecules terminate at the free 3′-hydroxyl end with the sequence pCpCpA and at the 5′-hydroxyl end with pG. Each tRNA carries a specific triplet of bases (referred to as anticodon) comprising complementary bases to a messenger RNA codon that specifies the appropriate amino acid (Holley et al.) (Fig. 6).

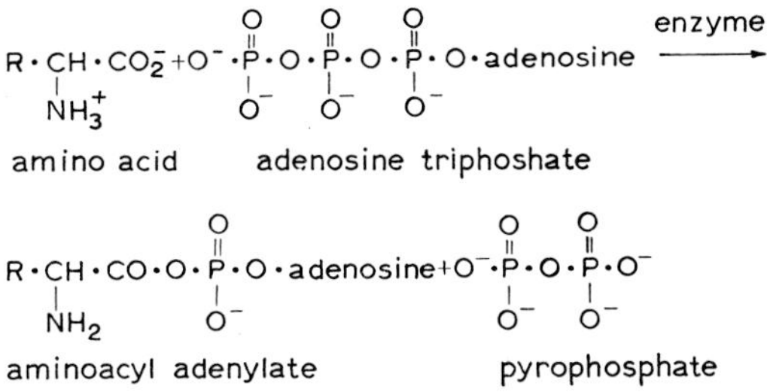

Fig. 5. Diagram of amino acid activation by adenosine triphosphate.

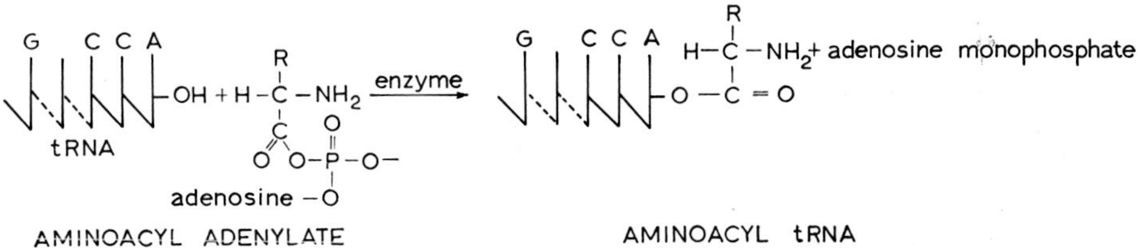

Fig. 6. Diagram of biosynthesis of aminoacyl tRNA.

(3) Ribosomes attach to the 5′-hydroxyl end of the messenger molecule (Smith et al. 1966) and move relative to the messenger RNA. The role of the aminoacyl-tRNA molecule is to deliver a specific amino acid to the site at which messenger RNA and a ribosome collaborate in the synthesis of a polypeptide. The correctly charged tRNA is selected by the binding to the codon of the messenger RNA of an anticodon on the tRNA molecule.

(4) Peptide bond synthesis involves the reaction of the carboxyl group of a peptidyl tRNA with the amino group of an incoming aminoacyl tRNA. While the peptide chain grows, the carboxyl group always remains attached to a tRNA molecule carrying the last-incorporated amino acid.

(b) *Chain initiation, chain elongation and chain termination in protein synthesis*

It has been known for some time that at any moment two tRNA molecules are attached to the functioning ribosome (Warner and Rich; Arlinghaus et al.). These molecules have been correlated with two specific sites on the ribosome: one site capable of binding the peptidyl tRNA and the other binding the correct incoming aminoacyl tRNA as directed by the messenger RNA (Bretscher and Marcker). It follows that an incoming aminoacyl tRNA can only form a peptide bond when the peptidyl site is occupied by a tRNA charged with at least one amino acid. From this arises the stringent question of how the system starts.

This problem was elucidated by the finding of a unique species of tRNA (Marcker and Sanger) capable of binding to the peptidyl site, whereas the other aminoacyl-tRNAs bind to the aminoacyl site of the ribosome and as a second step switch during peptide bond formation to the peptidyl site of the ribosome. The base sequence of this species of tRNA (called $tRNA_f$) shows several interesting features which may be related to its role in initiation (Dube et al.). Formylmethionine, the amino acid that can be accepted by this tRNA, also shows a unique characteristic in that the formyl group attached to the amino group prevents peptide bond formation. As a consequence, formylated methionine must occupy a special position in the peptide molecule, i.e., it must constitute the initial unit of the polypeptide. Since the discovery of the occurrence of formylmethionine at the N-terminal end of the polypeptides propagated in a cell-free system directed by natural viral messenger RNA (Adams and Capecchi), the F-met-$tRNA_f$ molecule has been recognized as an initiator of peptide synthesis.

It should be stressed that in cell-free protein-synthesizing systems polypeptide synthesis can occur without a $tRNA_f$ molecule if the ribosome–messenger association is sufficiently stable. A high concentration of magnesium (0.02–0.03 M) appears to stabilize the messenger–ribosome complex sufficiently for the alignment of two amino-acyl tRNAs to take place (Nakamoto and Kolakofsky). Therefore, these systems can initiate in a non-specific manner at high Mg^{2+} concentrations, whereas F-met-$tRNA_f$ does not require such high levels (0.01 M), making it a suitable initiator in the living cell.

Evidence for the preferential binding of F-met-$tRNA_f$ to the peptidyl site of the ribosome has come from experiments with the antibiotic puromycin. This peptide-formation blocking agent is known to have a molecular structure similar to that of

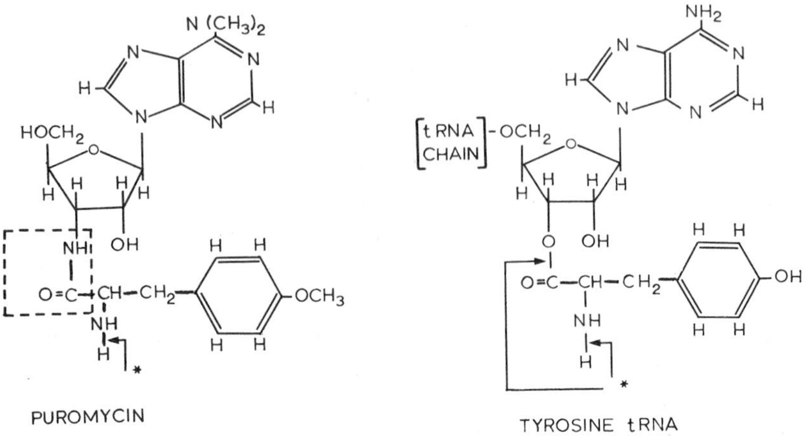

Fig. 7. Structure of puromycin showing the close resemblance to the structure of the terminal end of tyrosine tRNA. Asterisk denotes site for peptide binding.

the end of a tRNA molecule that attaches to an amino acid (Yarmolinsky and De La Haba). It can form a peptide bond with an amino acid, but it lacks the free COOH group of a normal amino acid and therefore cannot form a second peptide bond (Smith et al. 1965; see Fig. 7). Consequently it cannot participate in chain elongation. Experiments indicate that puromycin reacts with F-met-$tRNA_f$ and not with other aminoacyl-tRNAs. These facts can be explained by assuming that puromycin and F-met-$tRNA_f$ bind to the ribosome at different sites, i.e., puromycin to the aminoacyl site and F-met-$tRNA_f$ to the peptidyl site of the ribosome.

Further light has been shed on the problem of protein chain initiation by: (1) The recognition of the specific role of the 30 S ribosomal subunit. (2) The discovery of initiating factors F_1 and F_2, which stimulate F-met-$tRNA_f$ binding to ribosomes. (3) the finding that this binding is GTP (guanosine triphosphate)-dependent. (4) The deciphering of the initiating codons AUG and GUG recognized by the anticodon of F-met-$tRNA_f$.

By means of a schematic representation (Fig. 8) protein chain initiation, elongation and termination can be described as follows. First, messenger RNA binds to the 30 S ribosomal subunit, stimulated by a specific protein factor F_3 (Brown and Doty). Then, initiating factors F_1 and F_2 stimulate F-met-$tRNA_f$ binding to the peptidyl site of the 30 S ribosomal subunit (Stanley et al.; Salas et al.; Eisenstadt and Brawerman 1966, 1967; Brawerman and Eisenstadt; Revel and Gros 1966; Hille et al.). It is known that for this binding the presence of GTP is necessary, although it is not hydrolysed at this stage (Arlinghaus et al.; Ohta et al.; Anderson et al.; Allende and Weissbach). The initiation complex consisting of mRNA programmed with AUG or GUG at the 5′-terminal end, a 30 S ribosomal subunit, initiating factors F_1 and F_2, and F-met-$tRNA_f$, is an obligatory intermediate of initiation (Clark and Marcker; Ghosh et al.; Nomura et al.).

Once the initiation complex is formed, it binds a 50 S ribosomal subunit to produce a 70 S ribosome attached to the messenger molecule, after which another aminoacyl tRNA molecule can bind at the aminoacyl site. The binding of the aminoacyl tRNA is stimulated by GTP and a supernatant factor T (transferase separated as a heat-labile T_u and a stable T_s factor) which are thought to complex in the presence of aminoacyl tRNA (Lucas-Lenard and Lipmann; Rao and Moldave; Lucas-Lenard and Haenni; Allende et al.; Gordon). At this stage the first peptide bond can be formed. Evidence has been presented that peptide binding is catalysed by the enzyme peptide synthetase residing in the 50 S subunit and that GTP and factor T are not necessary for this reaction (Monro). It is generally agreed that GTP plays a role in bringing amino acid polymerization further and that it is hydrolyzed in this process (Thach et al.). There are indications that one phosphate is liberated for every amino acid condensed into peptide bonds (Nishizuka and Lipmann). It is assumed that GTP as well as supernatant factor T and a factor G are needed to complete the cycle of peptide bond formation by promoting translocation of the newly formed peptidyl-tRNA to the peptidyl site of the ribosome, after which $tRNA_f$ is released.

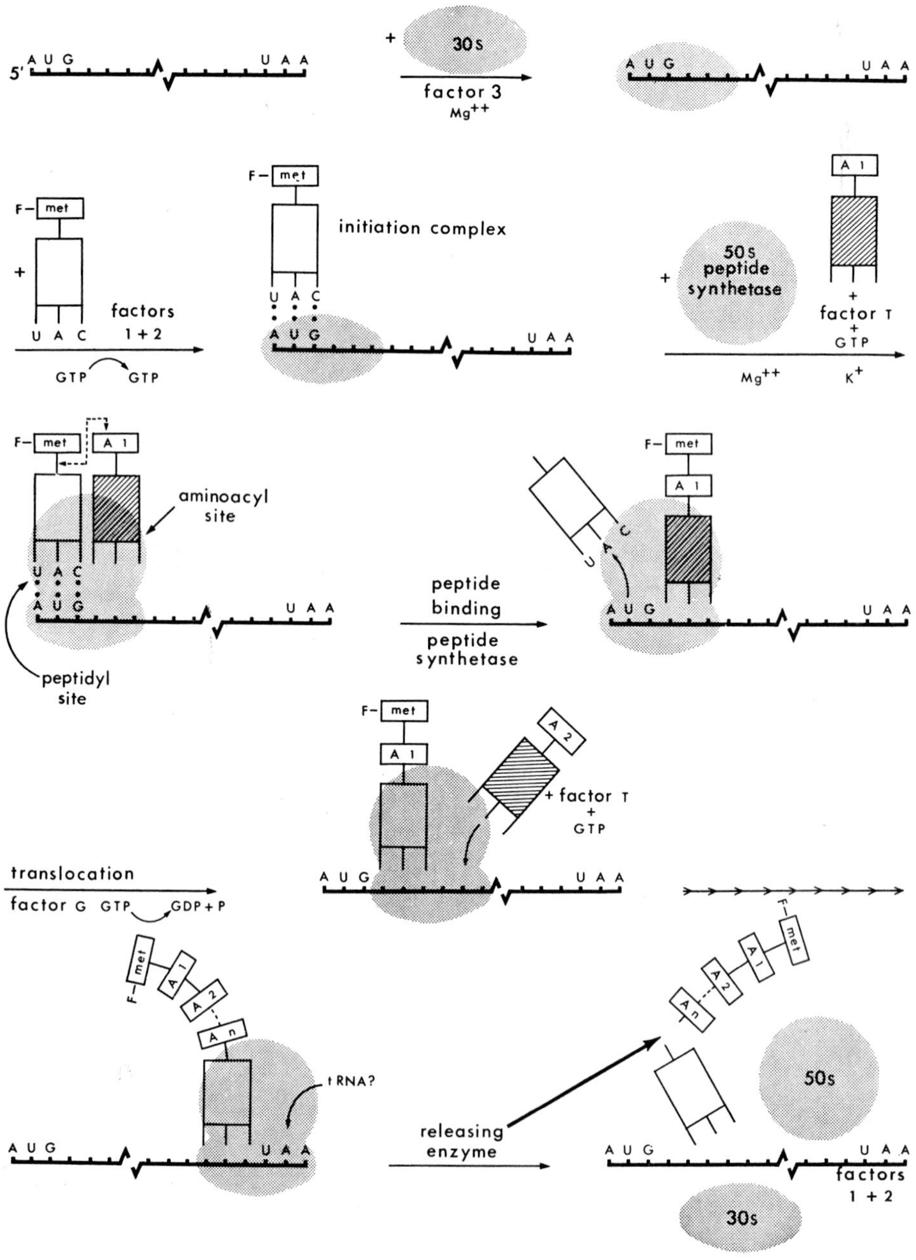

Fig. 8. Schematic representation of the mechanism of protein synthesis. AUG or GUG: initiating codons. UAA, UGA or UAG: terminating codons.

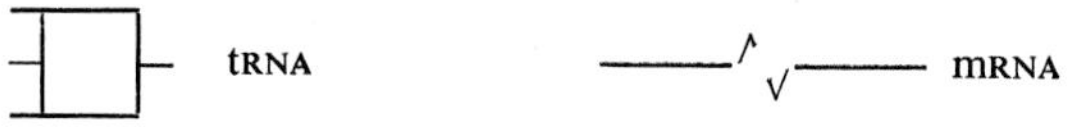

It has been shown that in *E. coli* protein, the great majority of N-terminal groups are either methionine or alanine. There is reason to believe that the majority of these *E. coli* proteins start with the sequence N-formylmethionyl-alanine and that either the formyl moiety or formylmethionine is removed enzymatically (Adams and Capecchi).

For chain termination it is assumed that the messenger RNA strand includes signals for ending the polypeptide chain during translation of the genetic message. These codons, called terminating codons, have been deciphered as UAA, UAG and UGA (Brenner et al.; Takanami and Yan). The hydrolysis of the ester bond between polypeptide and the final tRNA could be catalyzed by a specific releasing enzyme (Cuzin et al.). Recently, evidence has been presented that a tRNA molecule for chain termination does not exist (Bretscher), but that a protein factor is implicated which is separable into two components, called R_1 and R_2. The first component is believed to hydrolyse peptidyl tRNA in the presence of the terminating codons UAA or UAG, whereas R_2 will do this in the presence of the codons UAA or UGA (Capecchi; Caskey et al.; Scolnick et al.). These processes described for protein synthesis concern bacterial cells and little is known about these in higher organisms.

(c) *Protein synthesis and antibiotics*

Some antibiotics inhibit bacterial protein synthesis both *in vivo* and *in vitro* (Collins). They may be classified according to whether they (a) block synthesis (chloramphenicol), (b) misdirect it (streptomycin), or (c) interrupt it (puromycin).

(a) A number of antibiotics blocks protein synthesis by binding to the 50 S ribosomal subunit. Chloramphenicol, sparsomycin, gougerotin and aureomycin belong to this group. It has been suggested that aureomycin may combine with ribosomes in such a way as to obstruct the binding site for aminoacyl-tRNA (Suarez and Nathans; Hierowski). The other mentioned antibiotics do not interfere with the binding of aminoacyl-tRNA to the ribosome. Sparsomycin and gougerotin are blocking agents having features in common with chloramphenicol, although sparsomycin does not compete with chloramphenicol in binding to ribosomes. All three antibiotics interfere with the peptide-bond-forming step, probably by inhibiting the peptide synthetase, because they are inhibitors of the puromycin-induced release of polypeptide from ribosomes (Monro and Vazquez; Goldberg and Mitsugi 1967a, b). Unlike chloramphenicol, sparsomycin is a potent inhibitor of mammalian cell-free polypeptide synthesis.

Another group of antibiotics inhibits protein synthesis by binding to the 30 S ribosomal subunit. Erythromycin and spectinomycin are examples of this group (Oleinick and Corcoran; Davies et al.).

(b) Streptomycin is an interesting antibiotic in that it causes misreading of the genetic message (Spotts and Stanier). From the results of genetic experiments with *E. coli* and experiments with cell-free *E. coli* systems, the action of streptomycin on translation can be explained by assuming that streptomycin binds at the 30 S subunit of the ribosome (Cox et al.; Davies et al.). It alters in some manner the conformation of the 30 S subunit, thus leading to improper codon-anticodon alignment (Leon and Brock). Alteration of the conformation of the ribosome by the action of streptomycin seems likely, because of differences in physical properties between streptomycin-sensitive and -resistant ribosomes. Neomycin acts in a similar way on the translation mechanism, but there are indications that it requires a different specific recognition site on the ribosome. The biological activity of streptomycin is primarily related to its cationic group. The antibiotic can replace part of the Mg^{2+} required to stabilize the 70 S ribosome.

(c) The antibiotic puromycin has already been dealt with in connection with peptide bond formation. Puromycin interrupts protein synthesis and induces the release of a growing peptide chain from the ribosome. Its mode of action can be understood from its molecular structure (Yarmolinsky and De La Haba; see Fig. 7). Because it resembles the structure formed by the amino acid tyrosine and the terminal base of tRNA, it can bind to the aminoacyl site of the ribosome and form a peptide bond through its amino group to the carboxyl end of the polypeptide on the peptidyl site of the ribosome. However, the CONH linkage in puromycin is less reactive than the -COO- linkage in tyrosine tRNA. Therefore, translocated to the peptidyl site of the ribosome, puromycin cannot form a peptide bond with a newly incoming aminoacyl tRNA. This results in interruption and release of the growing polypeptide (Nathans; Gilbert).

(d) *Concluding remarks*

Some interesting and important problems related to the function of ribosomes have not been discussed, because it was felt that in this chapter the description of ribosomal properties and function should be restricted to a discussion of factors and mechanisms involved in protein synthesis. To complete the picture of our knowledge of ribosomal function at the present time, a few other interesting functional aspects will be briefly outlined.

Ribosomes are known to be involved in the regulation of the information flow from DNA to the polyribosomes and this is one of the aspects that is becoming increasingly important. For instance, it has been discovered that ribosomes, at least in bacteria, participate in the control of the rate of DNA-mRNA transcription and that *in vitro* they probably have some direct effect on the release of mRNA from the DNA template (Bladen et al.; Shin and Moldave 1966, 1967; Naono et al.; Brown and Doty; Revel and Gros 1967).

It is not known whether such a direct releasing effect of ribosomes or ribosomal subunits on mRNA from the template also exists in animal cells, but there is some evidence indicating that in such cells the 40 S ribosomal subunit possibly plays a role in the transport of mRNA from the nucleus to the cytoplasm (Joklik and Becker; Henshaw et al.; McConkey and Hopkins). However, the evidence related to the problem of 40 S subunits carrying mRNA is still controversial (Perry and Kelley).

Thus, the chain of events by which mRNA and ribosomal subunits are assembled to a functional unit awaits further elucidation.

This problem is possibly related to the disaggregation of host-cell polyribosomes in virus infection and the subsequent association of virus mRNA and host-cell ribosomes (Joklik and Merigan). But a discussion of the factors involved in the interaction between infecting virus and host-cell polyribosomes goes beyond the functional aspects of ribosomes in the normal living cell and belongs to the field of pathology.

References

ADAMS, J.M. and M.R.CAPECCHI: N-formylmethionyl-sRNA as the initiator of protein synthesis. Proc. Natl. Acad. Sci. 55 (1966) 147.

ALLENDE, J.E., N.W.SEEDS, T.W.CONWAY and H.WEISSBACH: Guanosine triphosphate interaction with an amino acid polymerization factor from *E. coli.* Proc. Natl. Acad. Sci. 58 (1967) 1566.

ALLENDE, J.E. and H.WEISSBACH: GTP interaction with a protein synthesis initiation factor preparation from *Escherichia coli.* Biochem. Biophys. Res. Commun. 28 (1967) 82.

ANDERSON, J.S., M.S.BRETSCHER, B.F.C.CLARK and K.A.MARCKER: A GTP requirement for binding initiator tRNA to ribosomes. Nature 215 (1967) 490.

ARLINGHAUS, R., J.SHAEFFER and R.SCHWEET: Mechanism of peptide bond formation in polypeptide synthesis. Proc. Natl. Acad. Sci. 51 (1964) 1291.

ARNSTEIN, H.R.V.: The structure and function of ribosomes. Rept. Progr. Appl. Chem. 60 (1963) 512.

ARNSTEIN, H.R.V.: Mechanism of protein biosynthesis. Brit. Med. Bull. 21 (1965) 217.

BARKER, D.C.: Ribosome structures revealed by negative staining subcellular fractions from a crystalline ribonucleoprotein body. Exptl. Cell Res. 32 (1963) 272.

BARKER, D.C.: A ribonucleoprotein inclusion body in *Entamoeba invadens.* Z. Zellforsch. Mikroskop. Anat. 58 (1963) 641.

BEHNKE, O.: Helical arrangement of ribosomes in the cytoplasm of differentiating cells of the small intestine of rat foetuses. Exptl. Cell Res. 30 (1965) 597.

BENEDETTI, E.L., W.S.BONT and H.BLOEMENDAL: Electron microscopic observation on polyribosomes and endoplasmic reticulum fragments isolated from rat liver. Lab. Invest. 15 (1966) 196.

BLADEN, H.A., R.BYRNE, J.G.LEVIN and M.W.NIRENBERG: An electron microscopic study of a DNA-ribosome complex formed *in vitro.* J. Mol. Biol. 11 (1965) 78.

BRAWERMAN, G. and J.M.EISENSTADT: A factor from *Escherichia coli* concerned with the stimulation of cell-free polypeptide synthesis by exogenous ribonucleic acid II. Characteristics of the reaction promoted by the stimulation factor. Biochemistry 5 (1966) 2784.

BRENNER, S., F.JACOB and M.MESELSON: An unstable intermediate carrying information from genes to ribosomes for protein synthesis. Nature 190 (1961) 576.

BRENNER, S., L.BARNETT, E.R.KATZ and F.H.C.CRICK: UGA: a third nonsense triplet in the genetic code. Nature 213 (1967) 449.

BRETSCHER, M.S. and K.A.MARCKER: Polypeptidyl-sribonucleic acid and amino-acyl-sribonucleic acid binding sites on ribosomes. Nature 211 (1966) 380.

BRETSCHER, M.S.: Polypeptide chain termination: an active process. J. Mol. Biol. 34 (1968) 131.

BROWN, J.C. and P.DOTY: Protein factor requirement for binding of messenger RNA to ribosomes. Biochem. Biophys. Res. Commun. 30 (1968) 284.

BROWNLEE, G.G., F.SANGER and B.G.BARRELL: Nucleotide sequence of 5 S-ribosomal RNA from *Escherichia coli.* Nature 215 (1967) 735.

BYERS, B.: Structure and formation of ribosome crystals in hypothermic chick embryo cells. J. Mol. Biol. 26 (1967) 155.

CAPECCHI, M.R.: Polypeptide chain termination *in vitro*: isolation of a release factor. Proc. Natl. Acad. Sci. 58 (1967) 1144.

CASKEY, C.T., R.TOMPKINS, E.SCOLNICK, T.CARYK and M.NIRENBERG: Sequential translation of trinucleotide codons for the initiation and termination of protein synthesis. Science 162 (1968) 135.

CLARK, B.F.C. and K.A.MARCKER: The role of N-formyl-methionyl-sRNA in protein biosynthesis. J. Mol. Biol. 17 (1966) 394.

COLLINS, J.F.: Antibiotics, proteins and nucleic acids. Brit. Med. Bull. 21 (1965) 223.

COTTER, R.I., P.MCPHIE and W.B.GRATZER: Internal organization of the ribosome. Nature 216 (1967) 864.

COX, E.C., J.R.WHITE and J.G.FLAKS: Streptomycin action and the ribosome. Proc. Natl. Acad. Sci. 51 (1964) 703.

CUZIN, F., N.KRETCHMER, R.E.GREENBERG, R.HURWITZ and F.CHAPEVILLE: Enzymatic hydrolysis of N-substituted aminoacyl-tRNA. Proc. Natl. Acad. Sci. 58 (1967) 2079.

DAVIES, J., W.GILBERT and L.GORINI: Streptomycin, suppression, and the code. Proc. Natl. Acad. Sci. 51 (1964) 883.

DAVIES, J., P.ANDERSON and B.D.DAVIS: Inhibition of protein synthesis by spectinomycin. Science 149 (1965) 1096.

DUBE, S.K., K.A.MARCKER, B.F.C.CLARK and S.CORY: Nucleotide sequence of N-formyl-methionyl-transfer RNA. Nature 218 (1968) 232.

EISENSTADT, J.M. and G.BRAWERMAN: A factor from *Escherichia coli* concerned with the stimulation of cell-free polypeptide synthesis by exogenous ribonucleic acid. I. Evidence for the occurrence of a stimulation factor. Biochemistry 5 (1966) 2777.

EISENSTADT, J.M. and G.BRAWERMAN: The role of the native subribosomal particles of *Escherichia coli* in polypeptide chain initiation. Proc. Natl. Acad. Sci. 58 (1967) 1560.

ESTRUP, F. and M.SANTER: Immunological analysis of the proteins of *Escherichia coli* ribosomes. J. Mol. Biol. 20 (1966) 447.

FRESCO, J.R., B.M.ALBERTS and P.DOTY: Some molecular details of the secondary structure of ribonucleic acid. Nature 188 (1960) 98.

FURANO, A.V.: Chromatography of *Escherichia coli* ribosomes on diethylaminoethyl cellulose. J. Biol. Chem. 241 (1966) 2237.

FURANO, A.V., D.F.BRADLEY and L.G.CHILDERS: The conformation of the ribonucleic acid in ribosomes. Dye stacking studies. Biochemistry 5 (1966) 3044.

GESTELAND, R.F. and T.STAEHELIN: Electrophoretic analysis of proteins from normal and cesium chloride-treated *Escherichia coli* ribosomes. J. Mol. Biol. 24 (1967) 149.

GHOSH, H.P., D.SÖLL and H.G.KHORANA: Studies on polynucleotides LXVII. Initiation of protein synthesis *in vitro* as studied by using ribopolynucleotides with repeating nucleotide sequences as messengers. J. Mol. Biol. 25 (1967) 275.

GILBERT, W.: Polypeptide synthesis in *Escherichia coli*. II. The polypeptide chain and s-RNA. J. Mol. Biol. 6 (1963) 389.

GOLDBERG, I.H. and K.MITSUGI: Sparsomycin inhibition of polypeptide synthesis promoted by synthetic and natural polynucleotides. Biochemistry 6 (1967) 372.

GOLDBERG, I.H. and K.MITSUGI: Inhibition by sparsomycin and other antibiotics of the puromycin-induced release of polypeptide from ribosomes. Biochemistry 6 (1967) 383.

GORDON, J.: A stepwise reaction yielding a complex between a supernatant fraction from *E. coli*, guanosine 5′-triphosphate, and aminoacyl-sRNA. Proc. Natl. Acad. Sci. 59 (1968) 179.

HART, R.G.: Surface features of the 50 S ribosomal component of *Escherichia coli*. Proc. Natl. Acad. Sci. 53 (1965) 1415.

HENSHAW, E.C., M.REVEL and H.H.HIATT: A cytoplasmic particle bearing messenger ribonucleic acid in rat liver. J. Mol. Biol. 14 (1965) 241.

HIEROWSKI, M.: Inhibition of protein synthesis by chlortetracycline in the *E. coli in vitro* system. Proc. Natl. Acad. Sci. 53 (1965) 594.

HILLE, M.B., M.J.MILLER, K.IWASAKI and A.J.WAHBA: Translation of the genetic message VI. The role of ribosomal subunits in binding of formylmethionyl-tRNA and its reaction with puromycin. Proc. Natl. Acad. Sci. 58 (1967) 1652.

HOAGLAND, M.B., M.L.STEPHENSON, J.F.SCOTT, L.I.HECHT and P.C.ZAMECNIK: A soluble ribonucleic acid intermediate in protein synthesis. J. Biol. Chem. 231 (1958) 241.

HOLLEY, R.W., J.APGAR, G.A.EVERETT, J.T.MADISON, M.MARQUISEE, S.H.MERILL, J.R.PENSWICK and A.ZAMIR: Structure of a ribonucleic acid. Science 147 (1965) 1462.

HUXLEY, H.E. and G.ZUBAY: Electron microscope observations on the structure of microsomal particles from *Escherichia coli*. J. Mol. Biol. 2 (1960) 10.

JACOB, F. and J.MONOD: Genetic regulatory mechanisms in the synthesis of proteins. J. Mol. Biol. 3 (1961) 318.

JOKLIK, W.K. and Y.BECKER: Studies in the genesis of polyribosomes II. The association of nascent messenger RNA with the 40 S subribosomal particle. J. Mol. Biol. 13 (1965) 511.

JOKLIK, W.K. and T.C.MERIGAN: Concerning the mechanism of action of interferon. Proc. Natl. Acad. Sci. 56 (1966) 558.

KISSELEV, N.A. and A.S.SPIRIN: Structure of ribosomes as revealed by electron microscopy. In: M.Titlbach, ed.: Proceedings of the third European regional conference on electron microscopy, vol. B. Prague, Publishing House of the Czechoslovak Academy of Sciences (1964) p. 39.

KÜNTZEL, H. and H.NOLL: Mitochondrial and cytoplasmic polysomes from *Neurospora crassa*. Nature 215 (1967) 1340.

LANGRIDGE, R.: Ribosomes: a common structural feature. Science 140 (1963) 1000.

LEON, S.A. and T.D.BROCK: Effect of streptomycin and neomycin on physical properties of the ribosome. J. Mol. Biol. 24 (1967) 291.

LERMAN, M.I., A.S.SPIRIN, L.P.GAVRILOVA and V.F.GOLOV: Studies on the structure of ribosomes II. Stepwise dissociation of protein from ribosomes by caesium chloride and the re-assembly of ribosome-like particles. J. Mol. Biol. 15 (1966) 268.

LUBIN, M.: Observations on the structure of *E. coli* ribosomes by electron microscopy. Federation Proc. 26 (1967) 285.

LUCAS-LENARD, J. and F.LIPMANN: Separation of three microbial amino acid polymerization factors. Proc. Natl. Acad. Sci. 55 (1966) 1562.

LUCAS-LENARD, J. and A.L.HAENNI: Requirement of guanosine 5′-triphosphate for ribosomal binding of aminoacyl-sRNA. Proc. Natl. Acad. Sci. 59 (1968) 554.

MARCKER, K. and F.SANGER: N-formyl-methionyl-s RNA. J. Mol. Biol. 8 (1964) 835.

MATHIAS, A.P., R.WILLIAMSON, H.E.HUXLEY and S.PAGE: Occurrence and function of polysomes in rabbit reticulocytes. J. Mol. Biol. 9 (1964) 154.

MCCONKEY, E.H. and J.W.HOPKINS: Subribosomal particles and the transport of messenger RNA in HeLa cells. J. Mol. Biol. 14 (1965) 257.

MCPHIE, P. and W.B.GRATZER: The optical rotatory dispersion of ribosomes and their constituents. Biochemistry 5 (1966) 1310.

MILLER, A., W.KARLSSON and N.K.BOARDMAN: Electron microscopy of ribosomes isolated from tobacco leaves. J. Mol. Biol. 17 (1966) 487.

MONRO, R.E.: Catalysis of peptide bond formation by 50 S ribosomal subunits from *Escherichia coli*. J. Mol. Biol. 26 (1967) 147.

MONRO, R.E. and D.VAZQUEZ: Ribosome-catalyzed peptidyl transfer: effects of some inhibitors of protein synthesis. J. Mol. Biol. 28 (1967) 161.

MOORE, P.B.: Studies on the mechanism of messenger ribonucleic acid attachment to ribosomes. J. Mol. Biol. 22 (1966) 145.

MORGAN, R.S., H.S. SLAYTER and D.L. WELLER: Isolation of ribosomes from cysts of *Entamoeba invadens*. J. Cell Biol. 36 (1968) 45.

NAKADA, D.: Formation of ribosomes by a 'relaxed' mutant of *Escherichia coli*. J. Mol. Biol. 12 (1965) 695.

NAKAMOTO, T. and D. KOLAKOFSKY: A possible mechanism for initiation of protein synthesis. Proc. Natl. Acad. Sci. 55 (1966) 606.

NAONO, S., J. ROUVIÈRE and F. GROS: Messenger RNA forming capacity in ribosome-depleted bacteria. Biochim. Biophys. Acta 129 (1966) 271.

NATHANS, D.: Puromycin inhibition of protein synthesis: incorporation of puromycin into peptide chains. Proc. Natl. Acad. Sci. 51 (1964) 585.

NIRENBERG, M.W. and J.H. MATTHAEI: The dependence of cell free protein synthesis in *E. coli* upon naturally occurring or synthetic polyribonucleotides. Proc. Natl. Acad. Sci. 47 (1961) 1588.

NISHIZUKA, Y. and F. LIPMANN: Comparison of guanosine triphosphate split and polypeptide synthesis with a purified *E. coli* system. Proc. Natl. Acad. Sci. 55 (1966) 212.

NOMURA, M., C.V. LOWRY and C. GUTHRIE: The initiation of protein synthesis: joining of the 50 S ribosomal subunit to the initiation complex. Proc. Natl. Acad. Sci. 58 (1967) 1487.

OHTA, T., S. SARKAR and R.E. THACH: The role of guanosine 5′-triphosphate in the initiation of peptide synthesis III. Binding of formylmethionyl-tRNA to ribosomes. Proc. Natl. Acad. Sci. 58 (1967) 1638.

OLEINICK, N.L. and J.W. CORCORAN: Two types of erythromycin binding to ribosomes of *Bacillus subtilis*. Federation Proc. 26 (1967) 285.

OSAWA, S.: Biosynthesis of ribosomes in bacterial cells. In: J.N. Davidson and W.E. Cohn, ed.: Progress in nucleic acid research and molecular biology, IV. New York/London, Academic Press (1965) p. 161.

PALADE, G.E. and P. SIEKEVITZ: Liver microsomes. An integrated morphological and biochemical study. J. Biophys. Biochem. Cytol. 2 (1956) 171.

PARISI, B., G. MILANESI, J.L. VAN ETTEN, A. PERANI and O. CIFERRI: Species specificity in protein synthesis. J. Mol. Biol. 28 (1967) 295.

PERRY, R.P.: The nucleolus and the synthesis of ribosomes. In: J.N. Davidson and W.E. Cohn, ed.: Progress in nucleic acid research and molecular biology, VI. New York/London, Academic Press (1967) p. 219.

PERRY, R.P. and D.E. KELLEY: Buoyant densities of cytoplasmic ribonucleoprotein particles of mammalian cells: distinctive character of ribosome subunits and the rapidly labeled components. J. Mol. Biol. 16 (1966) 255.

PETERMANN, M.L.: The physical and chemical properties of ribosomes. Amsterdam/London/New York, Elsevier Publishing Company (1964).

PFUDERER, P., P. CAMMARANO, D.R. HOLLADAY and G.D. NOVELLI: A helical polysome model. Biochim. Biophys. Acta 109 (1965) 595.

PORTER, K.R.: The ground substance; observations from electron microscopy. In: J. Brachet and A.E. Mirsky, ed.: The cell, II. New York/London, Academic Press (1961) p. 621.

RAO, P. and K. MOLDAVE: The binding of aminoacyl sRNA and GTP to transferase I. Biochem. Biophys. Res. Commun. 28 (1967) 909.

REVEL, M. and F. GROS: A factor from *E. coli* required for the translation of natural messenger RNA. Biochem. Biophys. Res. Commun. 25 (1966) 124.

REVEL, M. and F. GROS: The stimulation by ribosomes of DNA transcription: requirement for a translation factor. Biochem. Biophys. Res. Commun. 27 (1967) 12.

ROSSET, R., R. MONIER and J. JULIEN: Les ribosomes d'*Escherichia coli* I. Mise en évidence d'un RNA ribosomique de faible poids moléculaire. Bull. Soc. Chim. Biol. 46 (1964) 87.

SABATINI, D.D., Y. TASHIRO and G.E. PALADE: On the attachment of ribosomes to microsomal membranes. J. Mol. Biol. 19 (1966) 503.

SALAS, M., M.B.HILLE, J.A.LAST, A.J.WAHBA and S.OCHOA: Translation of the genetic message II. Effect of initiation factors on the binding of formyl-methionyl-tRNA to ribosomes. Proc. Natl. Acad. Sci. 57 (1967) 387.

SCOLNICK, E., R.TOMPKINS, T.CASKEY and M.NIRENBERG: Release factors differing in specificity for terminator codons. Proc. Natl. Acad. Sci. 61 (1968) 768.

SHELTON, E. and E.L.KUFF: Substructure and configuration of ribosomes isolated from mammalian cells. J. Mol. Biol. 22 (1966) 23.

SHIN, D.H. and K.MOLDAVE: Effect of ribosomes on the biosynthesis of ribonucleic acid *in vitro*. J. Mol. Biol. 21 (1966) 231.

SHIN, D.H. and K.MOLDAVE: Effect of ribosomes, sRNA, aminoacyl sRNA and soluble protein on RNA synthesis *in vitro*. Federation Proc. 26 (1967) 285.

SIEKEVITZ, P.: Distribution of nascent amylase in microsomal sub-fractions of guinea pig pancreas. Federation Proc. 24 (1965) 293.

SLAYTER, H.S., J.R.WARNER, A.RICH and C.E.HALL: The visualization of polyribosomal structure. J. Mol. Biol. 7 (1963) 652.

SMITH, J.D., R.R.TRAUT, G.M.BLACKBURN and R.E.MONRO: Action of puromycin in polyadenylic acid-directed polylysine synthesis. J. Mol. Biol. 13 (1965) 617.

SMITH, M.A., M.SALAS, W.M.STANLEY, A.J.WAHBA and S.OCHOA: Direction of reading of the genetic message II. Proc. Natl. Acad. Sci. 55 (1966) 141.

SPOTTS, C.R. and R.Y.STANIER: Mechanism of streptomycin action on bacteria: a unitary hypothesis. Nature 192 (1961) 633.

STAEHELIN, T. and M.MESELSON: *In vitro* recovery of ribosomes and of synthetic activity from synthetically inactive ribosomal subunits. J. Mol. Biol. 15 (1966) 245.

STANLEY, W.M., M.SALAS, A.J.WAHBA and S.OCHOA: Translation of the genetic message: factors involved in the initiation of protein synthesis. Proc. Natl. Acad. Sci. 56 (1966) 290.

SUAREZ, G. and D.NATHANS: Inhibition of aminoacyl-sRNA binding to ribosomes by tetracycline. Biochem. Biophys. Res. Commun. 18 (1965) 743.

TAKANAMI, M. and Y.YAN: The release of polypeptide chains from ribosomes in cell-free amino acid-incorporating systems by specific combinations of bases in synthetic polyribonucleotides. Proc. Natl. Acad. Sci. 54 (1965) 1450.

TAKEDA, M. and F.LIPMANN: Comparison of amino acid polymerization in *B. subtilis* and *E. coli* cell-free systems; hybridization of their ribosomes. Proc. Natl. Acad. Sci. 56 (1966) 1875.

TAYLOR, M.M. and R.STORCK: Uniqueness of bacterial ribosomes. Proc. Natl. Acad. Sci. 52 (1964) 958.

THACH, R.E., K.F.DEWEY and N.MYKOLAJEWYCZ: Role of guanosine 5′-triphosphate in the initiation of peptide synthesis II. Synthesis of dipeptides. Proc. Natl. Acad. Sci. 57 (1967) 1103.

TRAUB, P., K.HOSOKAWA, G.R.CRAVEN and M.NOMURA: Structure and function of *E. coli* ribosomes IV. Isolation and characterization of functionally active ribosomal proteins. Proc. Natl. Acad. Sci. 58 (1967) 2430.

WADDINGTON, C.H. and M.M.PERRY: Helical arrangement of ribosomes in differentiating muscle cells. Exptl. Cell Res. 30 (1963) 599.

WARNER, J.R., A.RICH and C.E.HALL: Electron microscope studies of ribosomal clusters synthesizing hemoglobin. Science 138 (1962) 1399.

WARNER, J.R., P.M.KNOPF and A.RICH: A multiple ribosomal structure in protein synthesis. Proc. Natl. Acad. Sci. 49 (1963) 122.

WARNER, J.R. and A.RICH: The number of soluble RNA molecules on reticulocyte polyribosomes. Proc. Natl. Acad. Sci. 51 (1964) 1134.

YARMOLINSKY, M.B. and G.L.DE LA HABA: Inhibition by puromycin of amino acid incorporation into proteins. Proc. Natl. Acad. Sci. 45 (1959) 1721.

ZAMECNIK, P.C., E.B.KELLER, M.B.HOAGLAND, J.W.LITTLEFIELD and R.B.LOFTFIELD: Studies on the mechanism of protein synthesis. In: G.E.W.Wolstenholme and C.M.O'Connor, eds.: Ciba Foundation Symposium on ionizing radiations and cell metabolism. London, Churchill Ltd. (1956) p. 161.

CHAPTER 40

The endoplasmic reticulum

PETER J. GOLDBLATT*

Dept. of Pathology, University of Pittsburgh School of Medicine, Pittsburgh, Pennsylvania 15213

Contents

1. Introduction
2. The rough-surfaced endoplasmic reticulum
3. The smooth-surfaced endoplasmic reticulum
4. Specializations of the endoplasmic reticulum
5. Modulations of the endoplasmic reticulum in cell function and cell injury
6. Comments and conclusions

* Post-doctoral Scholar of the American Cancer Society, Inc. Grant PRS-23. This work was supported in part by Grant 10629 and GM 135 NIH, Bethesda, Maryland 20014.

1. Introduction

The development of the electron microscope and cell fraction techniques refocused the attention of cytologists on the structure of the cytoplasm of plant and animal cells, which could only be dimly defined by the preexisting techniques of biochemistry and microscopy. Investigation of the areas of cytoplasmic basophilia, termed 'ergastoplasm' by Garnier and described extensively at the turn of the century (see Haguenau), revealed an interlacing network of tubules concentrated in the more central areas (endoplasm) of the cytoplasm of whole cells, viewed in the electron microscope (Porter et al.). The components of this tubular reticulum were rapidly delineated, and their association with ribonucleoprotein particles (Palade 1955) and with the microsomes isolated by Claude was firmly established (Palade and Siekevitz). Some of the structural and functional modulations of this reticulum in physiologic and pathologic states, and particularly those that may reveal the molecular organization of this system, are the subject of this chapter.

It is difficult to separate the discussion of the endoplasmic reticulum (ER) from that of the ribosome and protein synthesis, the Golgi complex, the nuclear envelope and membranes in general. However, since these topics are presented elsewhere in this handbook, this presentation will be limited to features of the rough (ribosome studded) and smooth reticulum (membranes devoid of ribosomes) and some of their more distinctive modifications. It is impossible to catalogue exhaustively, in the space allotted, the vast literature available on even these more limited topics. An arbitrary selection of reference material has therefore been made, which hopefully will introduce certain important concepts. For further details, and investigations which could not be included, the more extensive reviews of Haguenau, Porter (1961a, b), Siekevitz, Moule and Sjöstrand (1964) are recommended.

2. The rough-surfaced endoplasmic reticulum

In a preliminary report in 1897, Garnier drew attention to filamentous areas of cytoplasmic basophilia which were evident in the basal portions of acinar cells of human submaxillary gland and pancreas as well as many other cells. He reported that in animals, they disappeared after fasting and formed on refeeding, and suggested that this 'ergastoplasm' played a definite part in the preparation of zymogen granules for secretion. The function as well as the existence of these structures was debated and investigated by cytologists for the succeeding half century (see Haguenau). Early investigations with the electron microscope revealed a lace-like net of tubules in the inner (endoplasmic) zone of the cytoplasm (Porter 1953) of whole mounts of several cell types. Though the reticular nature of these endoplasmic tubules was obvious in whole cells shadowed with heavy metals, their three dimensional relationships were lost in thin sections. Palade and Porter were able to resolve some of the confusion over the identity of the membrane-bounded oval or tubular profiles by comparing thin sections with shadowed whole mounts of macrophages derived from peripheral blood. The designation of oval profiles as vesicles, and elongated membrane-bounded spaces as cisternae, indicates the investigators' (Porter and Kallman; Porter 1953) feeling that this endoplasmic reticulum (ER) is a fluid-filled system whose watery contents, of low electron density, were held in these little bladders, or larger reservoirs, by the limiting membrane. The subsequent observations of Watson, Epstein, and Copeland and

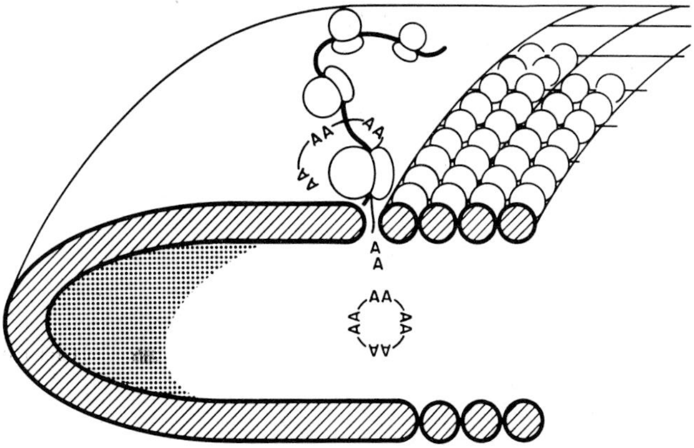

Fig. 1. Schematic cross section of end of cisterna of rough endoplasmic reticulum. The membrane is composed both of lamellar and globular areas. The squares indicate that portions of the membrane may perform as functional units. The polysomal chain lying on a triple layered portion of the membrane is composed of ribosomes along a strand of RNA, oriented with their smaller subunits toward the inside of the helix. A growing chain of amino acids (AA) is indicated as passing through a 'hole' between globular and lamellar portions of the membrane to form a secretion granule in the lumen.

Dalton established connection between the nuclear envelope and smooth and rough tubular profiles, as well as close approximation of ER to plasma membrane, and regular association with cytoplasmic organelles such as mitochondria and Golgi complex. This led naturally to the concept that the ER represents an intracellular waterway conducting materials from organelle to organelle, and possibly from nucleus to extracellular environment, or the reverse. It became evident from the investigations of Palade (1955) that many of these membranes were associated with a particle or granule on their hyaloplasmic surface, while others were devoid of granules or smooth-surfaced (Figs. 2 to 5). These two types of images represent the major subdivisions of the system, but were noted, in many cells, to be interconnected (Fig. 5) (Porter 1961a). They are associated with the Golgi complex, and connect directly to other membranous structures with rather distinctive morphologic features to be detailed below. As pointed out by Porter (1961a) and described by Haguenau, the rough and smooth ER are seen in virtually every cell, with the exception of the mature mammalian erythrocyte, and assume conformations and distributions which are rather characteristic of the

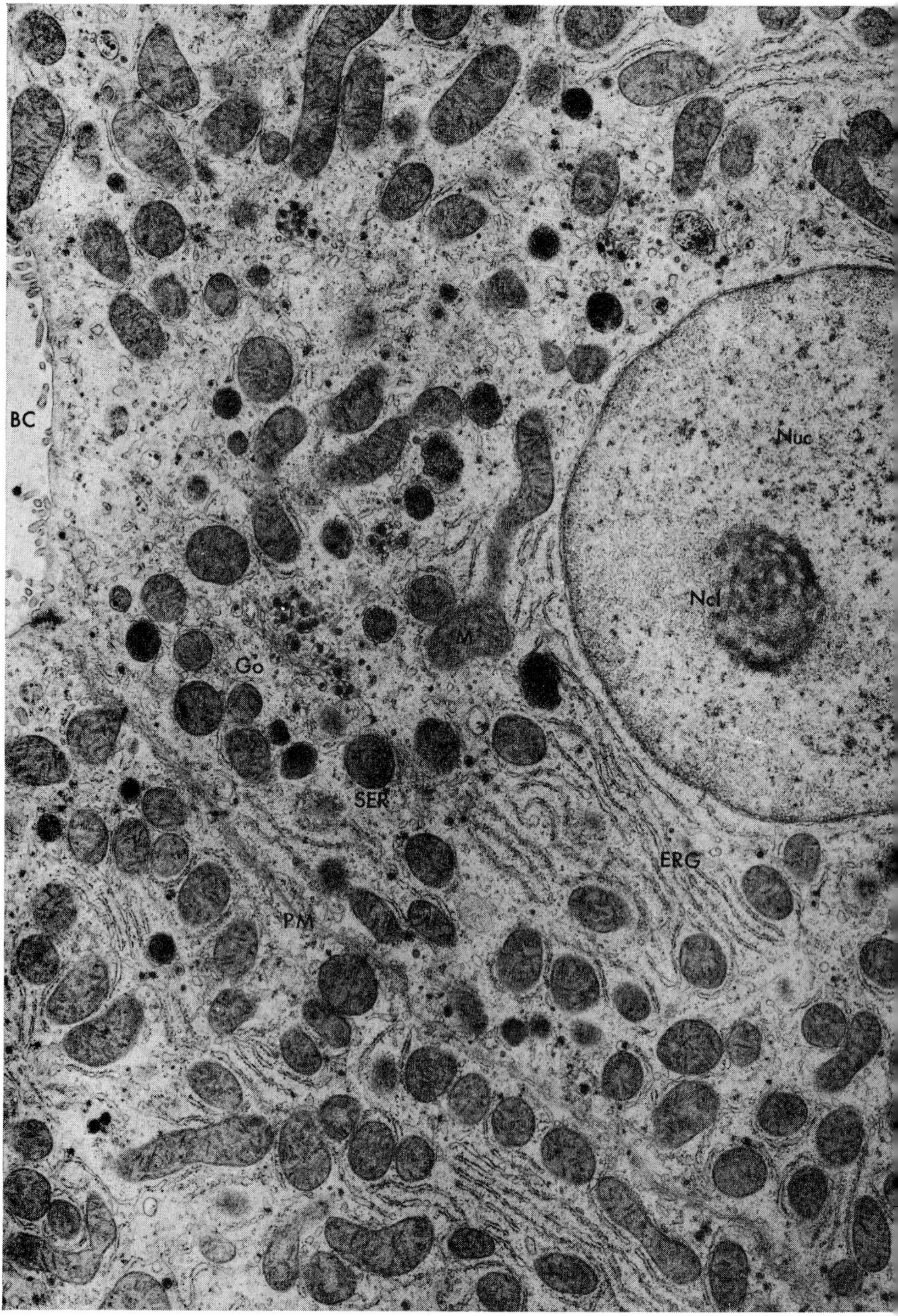

Fig. 2. Portions of two hepatic parenchymal cells of a fasted rat. The nucleus (Nuc) and nucleolus (Ncl) one cell are seen at the right and a bile canaliculus (BC) is present at left. The plasmalemma (PM) of each c runs diagonally from left to right. Stacks of rough-surfaced endoplasmic reticulum (ERG) and small areas smooth-surfaced reticulum (SER) are present in both cells. A Golgi zone (Go) filled with dense lipid droplet present near the bile canaliculus, and numerous mitochondria (M) and microbodies (Mb) are scatte through the hyaloplasm. ×9,100

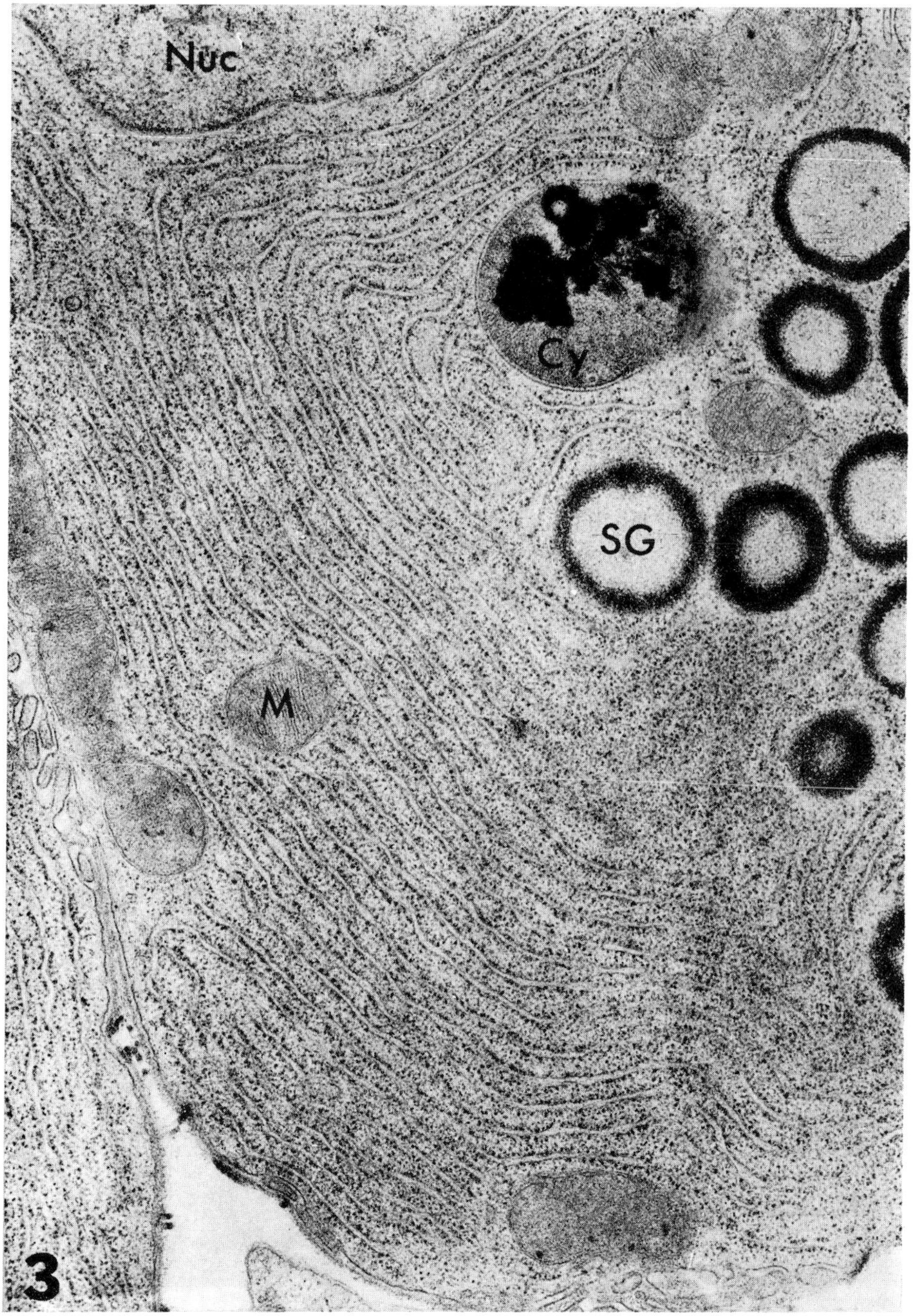

Fig. 3. Basal portion of acinar cell of submaxillary gland of mouse. Cell border with microvillae is seen at left and the nucleus (Nuc) at the top. Secretion granules (SG) showing extraction of internal contents, and a large cytosome (Cy) are seen at upper right. There are scattered mitochondria (M). The cytoplasm is filled with an orderly array of rough-surfaced membranes. This is the electron microscopic appearance of the classical ergastoplasm. ×26,600

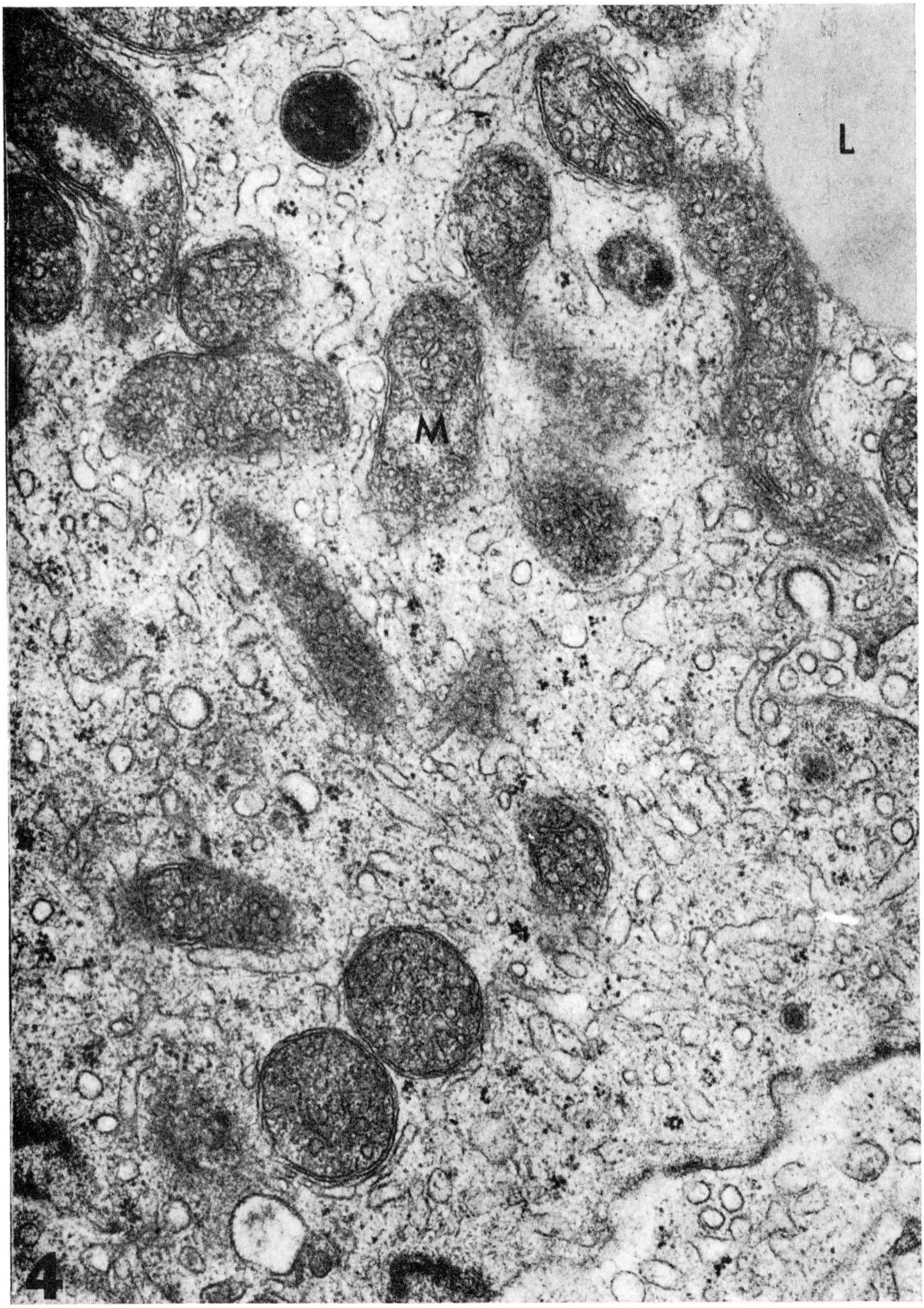

Fig. 4. Portion of cytoplasm of cell from adrenal cortex of dog. A large lipid inclusion (L) is at right, and there are numerous mitochondria (M) showing tubular arrangement of the cristae. The hyaloplasm is filled with tubular membranous profiles predominantly of the smooth variety. ×31,800

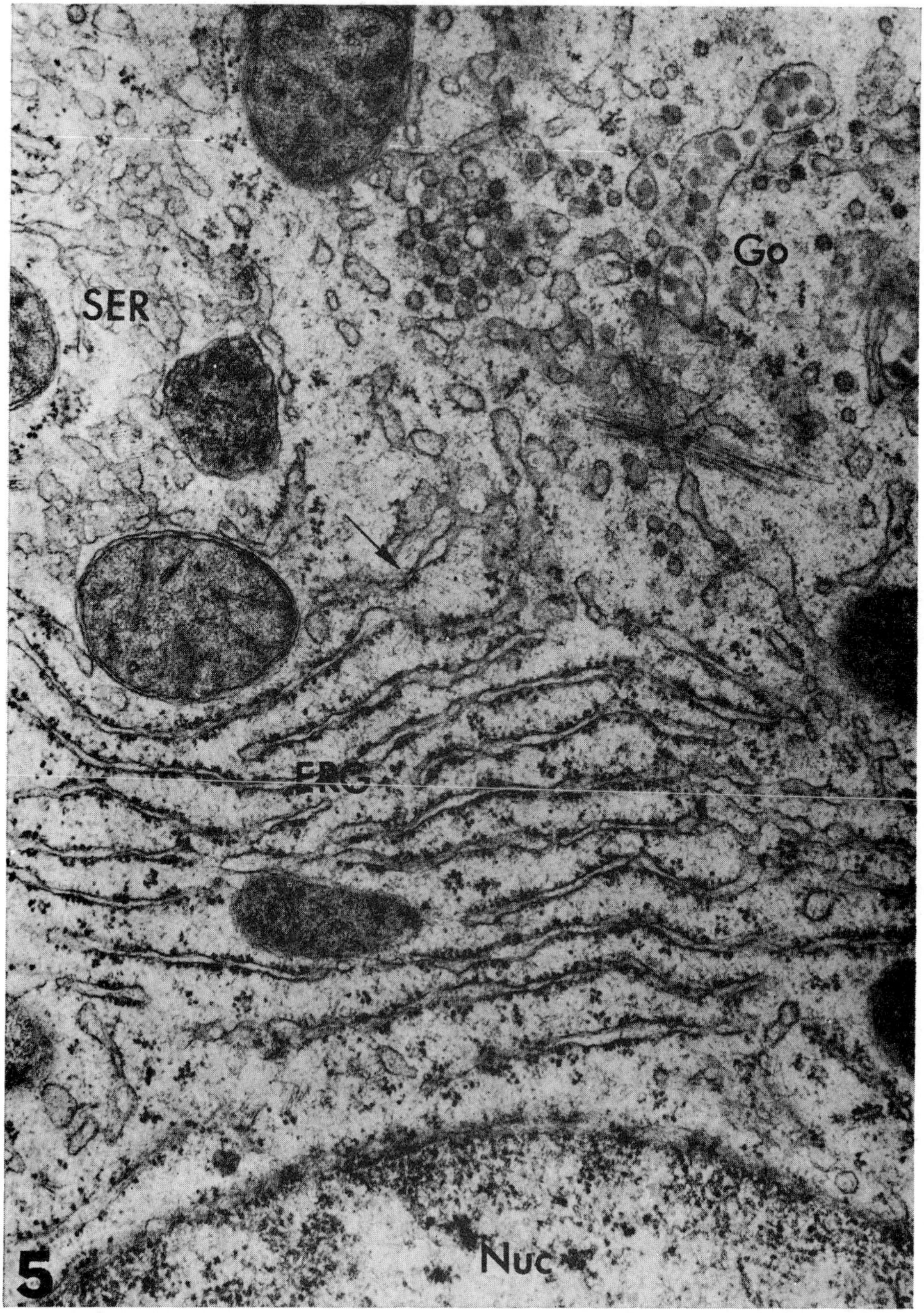

Fig. 5. Portion of hepatic parenchymal cell of fasted rat. The nucleus (Nuc) is at the bottom, and part of a Golgi zone (Go) is at upper right. An aggregate of smooth tubules (SER) is seen at upper left, and stacks of rough-surfaced cisternae (ERG) in the middle. The arrows indicate an area of anastomosis between rough and smooth tubules. ×25,400

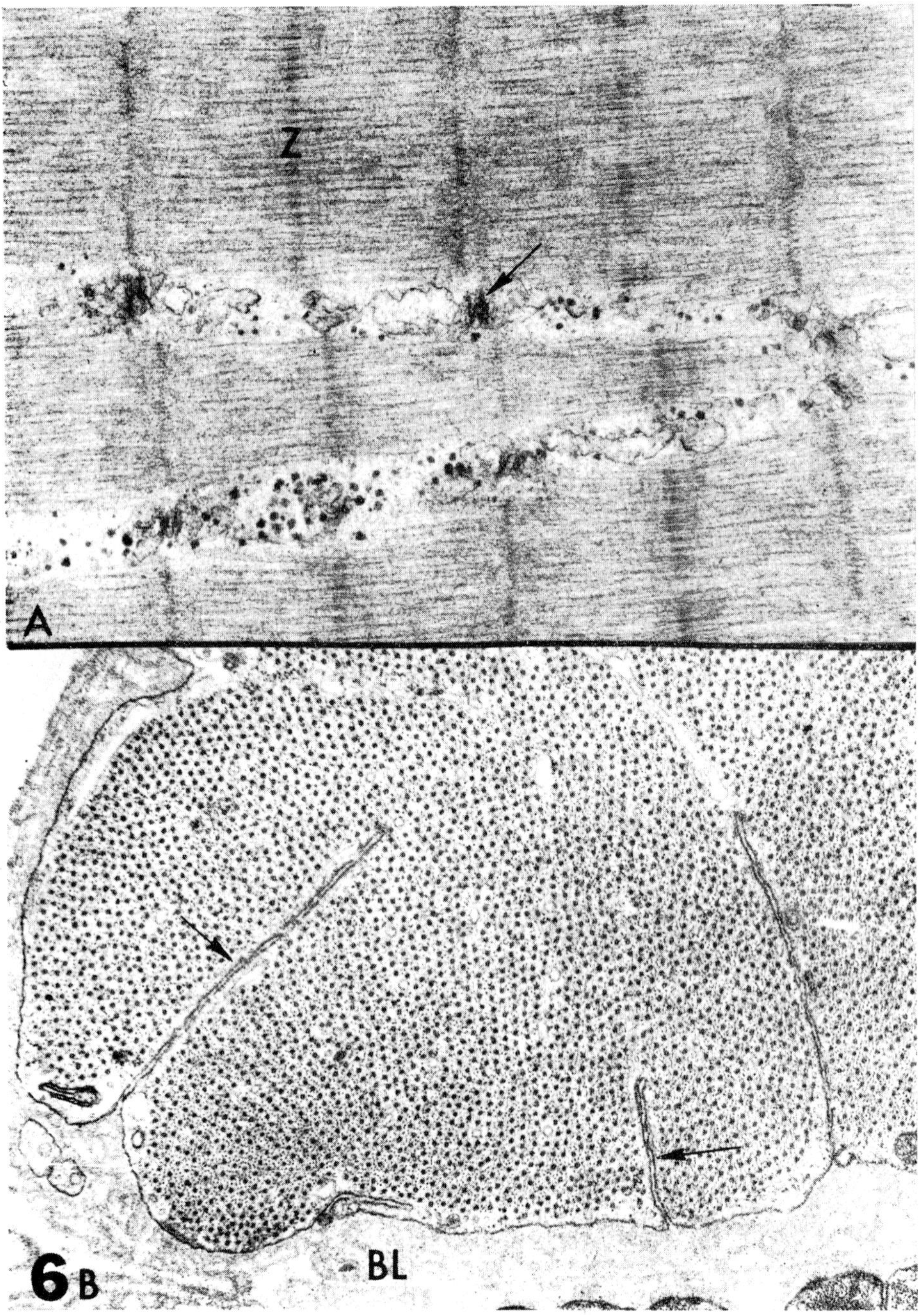

Fig. 6. (A) Sartorius muscle of frog. Sarcoplasmic reticulum is present between myofibrils. The dense Z lines (Z) are separated by narrow A bands, and surrounded by faint I bands. The T-system is not well seen, but there are triads (arrow). Dense glycogen granules obscure parts of the reticulum. (B) Cross section of muscle fiber from body of silver fish (*Lepisma, sp.*). The fiber is encased in a basal lamina (BL). The T-system is seen arising as a deep invagination of the plasma membrane (arrows). (6B courtesy of Dr. Howard Scalzi.) (A) ×28,900. (B) ×21,200

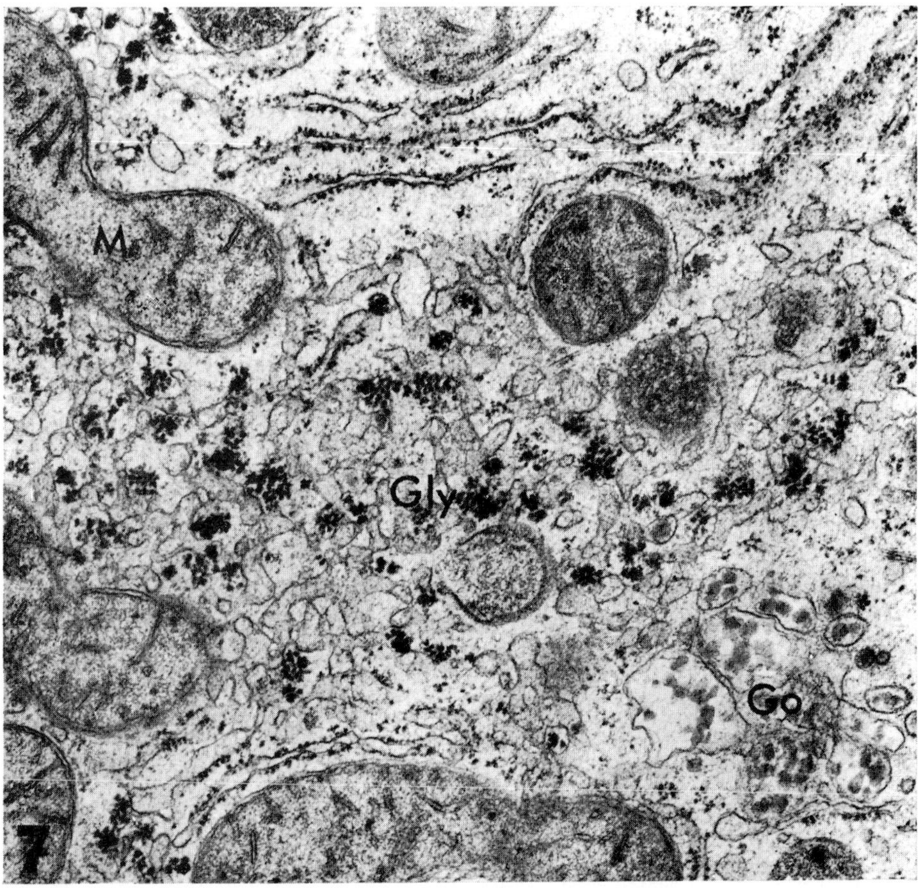

Fig. 7. Portion of cytoplasm of hepatic parenchymal cell of fasted rat. Scattered mitochondria (M) and a Golgi zone (Go) containing lipid droplets are seen. Dense glycogen deposits (Gly) are seen in the center in close association with anastomosing smooth-surfaced tubules. ×27,700

individual cell type. However, Porter (1961a) has also emphasized the plasticity of the system: within the same or similar cells there may be individual vesicles ranging from 25 to 500 mμ in diameter, and tubular and cisternal profiles 30 to 300 mμ in cross section. The latter are usually separated by 150 mμ from each other when they occur in stacks, and maintain approximately this distance from organelles such as mitochondria. This pleomorphism makes it difficult to define the endoplasmic reticulum exactly; however, Porter and Machado have suggested, on the basis of studies of the onion-root tip, that the ER is best defined as a membranous system arising from, or based upon, the nuclear envelope. It seems reasonable, however, to use criteria such as those mentioned above, and with the addition of the 150 to 200 Å ribosomal particle, which is spaced at approximately 150 Å intervals, to define the rough endoplasmic reticulum as an anastomosing intracytoplasmic system consisting, in thin sections, of

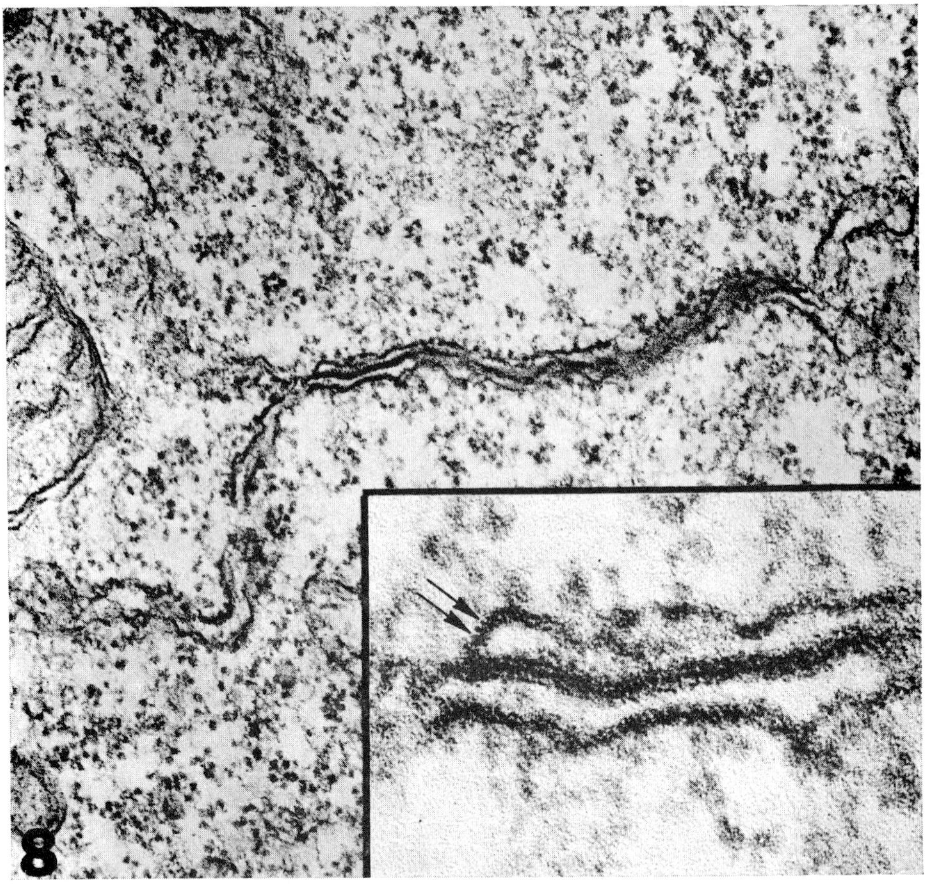

Fig. 8. Cytoplasm of Yoshida ascites hepatoma cell. Small aggregates of ribosomes are scattered through the hyaloplasm. In the center two rough-surfaced tubules are seen to have come into close apposition and their adjacent membranes, which have lost their ribosomal particles, have fused to form a median raphé. This portion is seen at high magnification in the inset. The upper and lower membranes show electron dense cross-bridges (arrows) suggesting a globular configuration. The central membrane is lamellar, with a somewhat thicker internal dense layer. Such a configuration is similar to a tight junction (zonula occludens). Material courtesy of Mr. Joseph Locker. ×58,700. Inset ×269,200

vesicular, tubular, and broad cisternal profiles, often arranged in regular arrays. These contain variable, but usually electron-lucent contents, bounded by a dense (adielectronic) membrane which is thinner (50 Å) and less distinctly trilaminar than the plasma membrane. On the outer (hyaloplasmic) surface of this membrane, in fixed material, electron-dense ribonucleoprotein particles appear at regular intervals. These ribosomes serve as a 'marker' making identification of rough ER relatively easy and certain. No such distinctive structural feature exists for smooth reticulum, and Sjöstrand (1964) and Fawcett (1963) suggest that what is presently grouped under the designa-

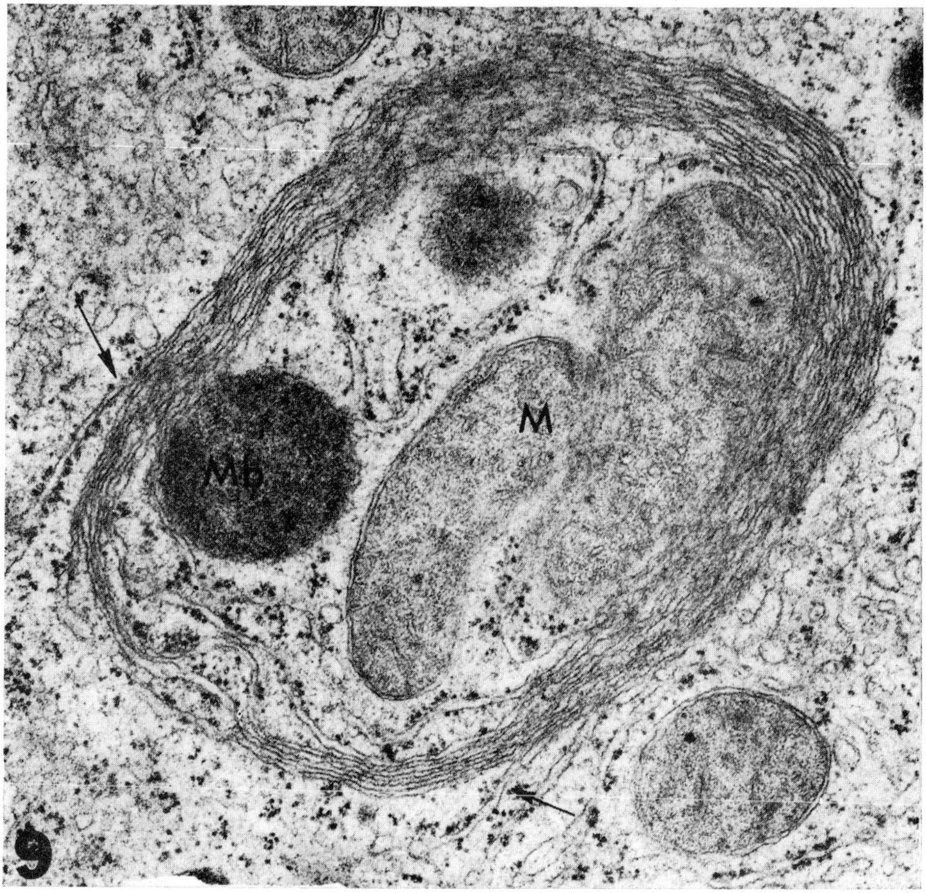

Fig. 9. Cytoplasm of hepatic cell of rat given 0.25 mg of cyclohexamide three hours before sacrifice. A membranous whorl largely devoid of ribosomes surrounds mitochondria (M) and a microbody (Mb). The membranes are clearly connected to rough-surfaced endoplasmic reticulum at arrows. Such whorls (finger prints, Nebenkerne) have been seen under a variety of conditions of cellular injury. Material courtesy of Dr. Robert Verbin. ×34,000

tion of smooth ER may well prove to be membrane bounded structures of great diversity, when methods of greater discrimination are developed.

The adaptability of this system, and indeed its existence, which can only be inferred from static observation on fixed material, has been beautifully illustrated by phase contrast studies of living cells, such as those of Buckley. In time lapse cinematographic observations, the fusion and movement of the tubular profiles can be amply illustrated. Buckley has postulated that transformations of form of the lipid components of the membrane may, in fact, be important in the movement of the internal contents of the tubular system.

An important contribution, which allowed rapid advances in the chemical charac-

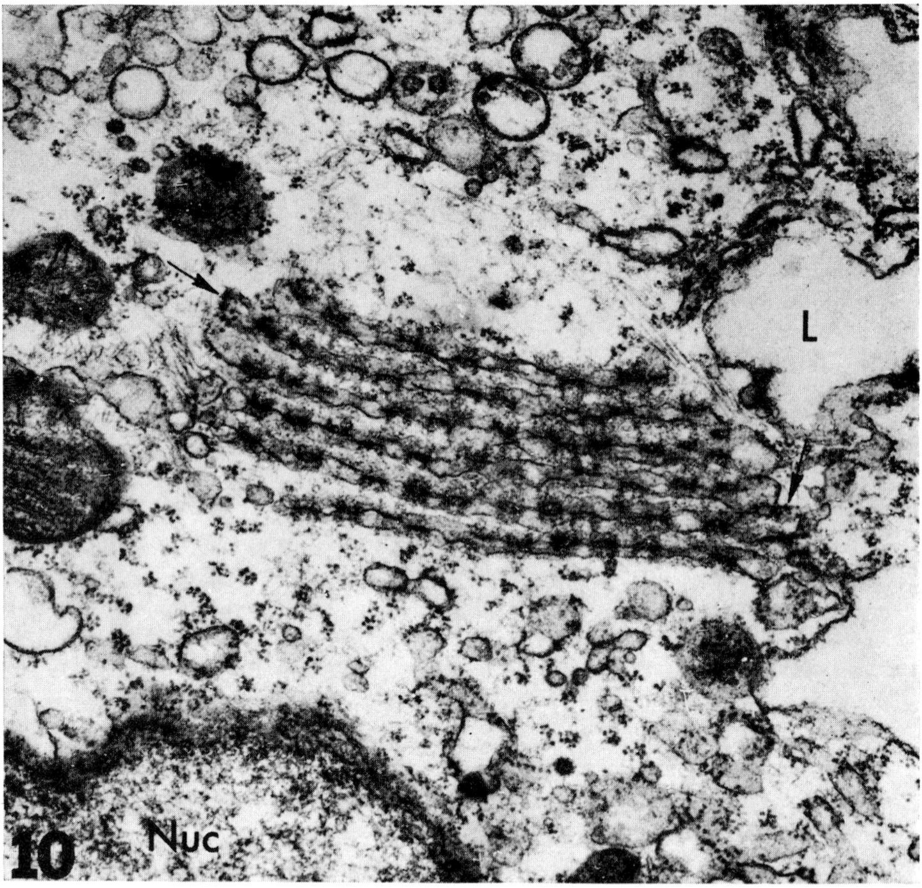

Fig. 10. Portion of Yoshida ascites hepatoma cell. The nucleus (Nuc) is at lower left and lipid vacuoles (L) are present on the right. Lamellar arrays of membranes with tangentially cut pores, annulate lamellae, occupy the center of the picture. These lamellae communicate with ribosome studded membranes at the periphery (arrows). Picture courtesy of Mr. Joseph Locker. ×33,000

terization of the ER, was the documentation by Palade and Siekevitz that the 'microsomal' fraction first isolated by differential centrifugation by Claude consisted in large part of tubular and vesicular membranous structures, some of which retained the dense granules on their external surfaces, and therefore corresponded to the endoplasmic reticulum (ergastoplasm) of the intact cell. This melding of structural and chemical information has provided the basis for our understanding of the molecular organization of cells, and truly represents one of the fundamental approaches of the science of molecular biology. We may assume, for the moment, that the microsomal fraction consisting of free ribosomes, and membranes with and without attached ribosomes, sedimenting at approximately 105,000 times gravity for thirty minutes (after previous removal of nuclear, mitochondrial and lysosomal fractions) can operationally

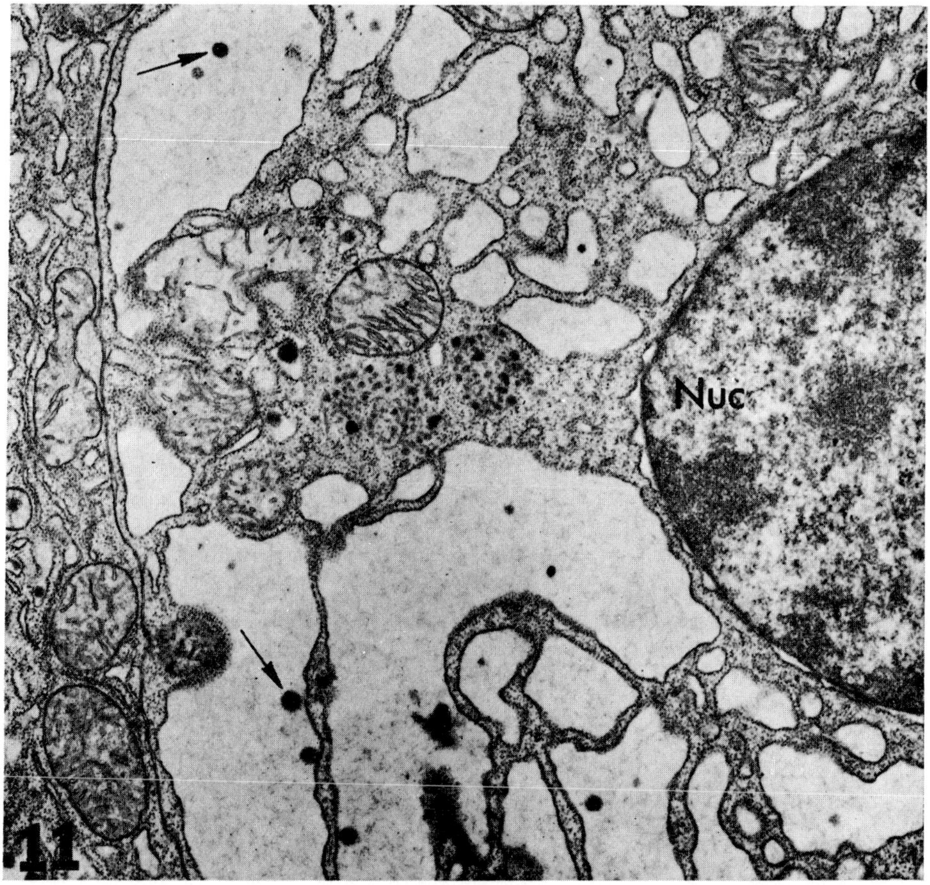

Fig. 11. Acinar cells of pancreas of rat given 6 subcutaneous doses of puromycin (40 mg/kg) and killed 24 hours after the first injection. Nucleus (Nuc) of cell with greatly dilated cisternae of ribosome studded endoplasmic reticulum is at right. Small granules (arrows) are seen in lumen of some cisternae. Picture contributed by Dr. H. Shinozuka. ×17,000

be considered to represent the endoplasmic reticulum. Therefore, the data available for enzymic and chemical constitution of this fraction may be used to describe the molecular make-up of the ER. However, relatively few studies of microsomes have made an attempt to separate smooth from rough reticulum, or, in fact, made an attempt to characterize the structural components of the fraction (see Rothschild; Dallner; Manganiello and Phillips). Then too, the most extensive studies have been carried out on one tissue, liver, usually of the rat (see Moulé), and it would seem hazardous to generalize from such restricted data. Another objection to too strict extrapolation from the chemical data is that raised by Wallach. He points out that the shearing forces employed in homogenization and centrifugation favor the transformation of membrane sheets, notably the plasmalemma, into small vesicles which

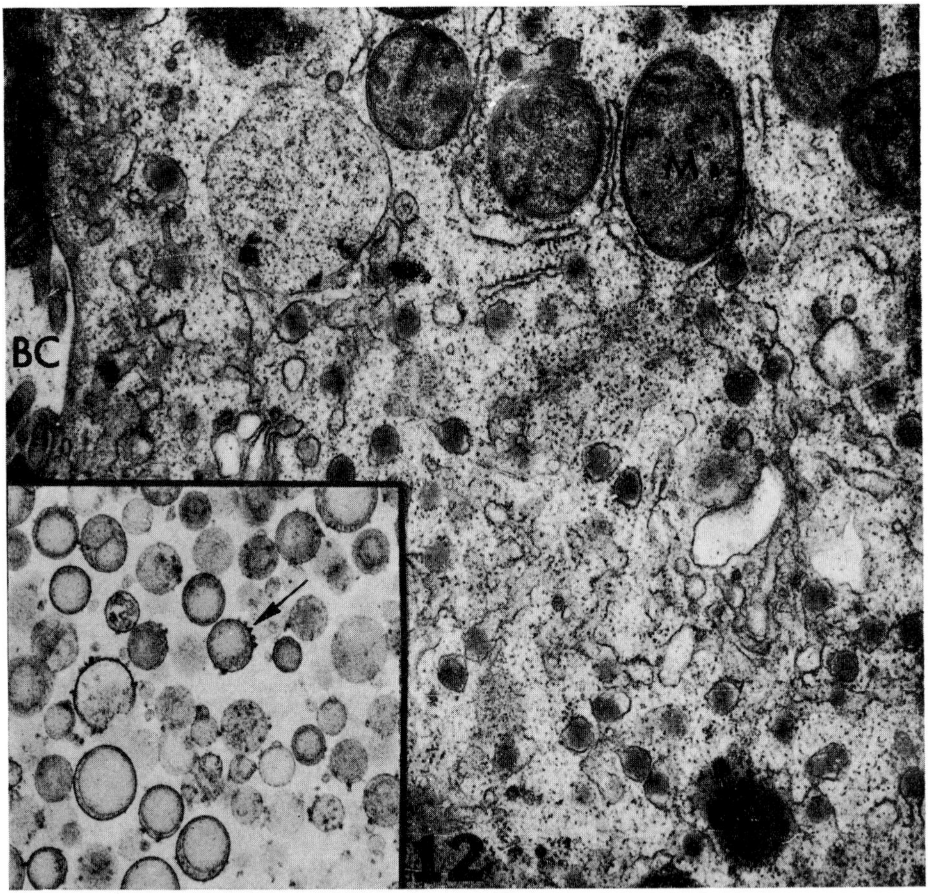

Fig. 12. Hepatic parenchymal cell of female rat given an intraperitoneal injection of 1 mg of ethionine per gram body weight 6 hours prior to being killed. A bile canaliculus (BC) is at left and some dilated Golgi saccules at the right. Numerous smooth and rough-surfaced vesicles contain dense lipid granules. The hyaloplasm is filled with individual ribosomes and no organized arrays (polysomes) are seen. This degranulation is not entirely uniform, membrane-bound ribosomes being visible on cisternae surrounding mitochondria (M) at the top. The inset shows 'liposomes' isolated from an ethionine treated rat. Dense lipid granules similar to those seen *in situ* are seen within membranous vesicles, some of which are studded with ribosomes (arrow). Material for inset provided by Dr. F. Schlunk. ×23,800. Inset ×28,400

would undoubtedly sediment with the microsomal fraction. In fact, the finding of significant concentrations of ion-dependent ATPase and other plasma membrane constituents, such as sialic acid, in the microsomal fraction, would tend to substantiate this criticism (Wallach). Suitable methods for overcoming these difficulties, and for separating smooth from rough ER are discussed by Rothschild.

With these reservations, it is still profitable to accept as a gross estimate of the molecular constitution of the endoplasmic reticulum those components which are

TABLE 1

Partial list of constituents and enzyme activities of microsomes*

Composition
- RNA
  - ribosomal, other
- Protein (variable)
  - enzymes, structural
- Lipids (30–50%)
  - phospholipids (70% of total)
    - lecithin, phosphatidylethanolamine
    - phosphatidylserine (slight)
    - phosphatidyl inositol
  - cholesterol and cholesterol esters (3–6%), less than plasmalemma
  - Fatty acids (tend to be unsaturated)
- Sialic acid
- Acid soluble:
  - inosine, cytidylic 3′-phosphate
  - NAD, NADP

Carbohydrate metabolism
- Glucose-6-phosphatase
- L-ascorbic acid synthesis
- YDP-glucose dephosphorylation
- UDP-glucuronic acid metabolism

Protein metabolism
- Protein synthesis, variety of peptidases, amidases
- Incorporation of iodine into amino acids and protein

Drug detoxication
- N- and O-dealylations
- Hydroxylation of Azo dyes, various aromatic carcinogens, others
- N-demethylation, glucuronosidation
- Side-chain and thio-ether oxidation, deamination, desulphuration, deiodination

Fatty acid metabolism
- Reductive synthesis of short-chain fatty acids
- Acylation with acyl-CoA (ligase)
- Neutral glyceride synthesis

Phospholipid metabolism
- Phosphatidic acid synthesis
- Phosphatidylcholine synthesis
- Decarboxylation of phosphatidylserine
- Transmethylation and deacylation of phosphatides
- Redistribution of phosphatides in membranes

Steroid metabolism
- Synthesis of cholesterol from acetate
- Interconversion and degradation of steroids: hydroxylations, aromatization, variety of steroid dehydrogenases and hydroxylases

Other lipids
- Synthesis of glycolipids and plasmalogens

Nucleotide metabolism
- Nucleoside diphosphatases, 5′-nucleotidase, NAD and NADH pyrophosphatase, NADase

Binding properties
- Azo dyes, K^+, Na^+, Ca^{++}, iodide (*in vitro*), epinephrine and norepinephrine

Oxidation-reduction
- NADH and NADPH cytochrome-C-reductase activity, pyridine nucleotides,
- Nonspecific and NADP diaphorase, cytochromes B_3, B_5 and p-450, coenzyme Q

Transport and transmission
- Sarcoplasmic AMPases, cholinesterase
- Ion stimulated (Mg^{++}, K^+, Na^+) AMPases

* Compiled largely from Rothschild; Siekevitz; and Fouts. This is intended to reflect the diversity of activities, rather than representing a complete list. Some constituents, like sialic acid, may reflect plasma membrane contamination.

consistently found in the microsomal fraction, a partial list of which is shown in Table 1 (see also Siekevitz; Rothschild; Fouts). There is little doubt that the majority of cytoplasmic RNA is associated with the endoplasmic reticulum (Blobel and Potter 1967a), and that this is preponderantly ribosomal (28S and 18S) in type. Several studies suggest that other species of RNA are intimately associated with the microsomal membrane (see Siekevitz; Pitot). It is evident from work such as that of Ernster et al., that some enzymes such as glucose-6-phosphatase and NADH-cytochrome C reductase, are firmly bound to the microsomal membranes, whereas others are more loosely associated, being released by treatment with detergent. It is well to keep in mind, as pointed out by Rothschild, that many constituents of the so-called soluble fraction may ultimately be shown to have been released from ER, or other membranes, during the isolation procedure. The converse, that many enzymic activities currently ascribed to the microsomes may be subsequently shown to reside in other cellular constituents, has also been emphasized (see Siekevitz; Wallach). It seems established that the membranes consist in large part of lipoproteins and phospholipids, and that these are specific for different membrane types (Ernster and associates; Fleisher and Rouser). It has also been established that enzymes of an electron transport system (NAD- and NADP-cytochrome C reductases; a diaphorase; cytochromes B_5 and p-450), some enzymes of glycogen metabolism (glucose-6-phosphatase) and those of sterol metabolism (almost the entire complement of enzymes for formation of cholesterol from acetate) as well as various enzymes of detoxication (methylases) and hydroxylation (hydroxylation of a number of steroid hormones) are consistently associated with the microsomal fractions of a variety of tissues (see Siekevitz; Rothschild; Fouts). Several studies (Rothschild; Dallner; Manganiello and Phillips) employing differential and gradient centrifugation, coupled with electron microscope examination of the fractions, have succeeded in giving partial separation of smooth vesicles from rough-surfaced membranes and free ribosomal particles. Whether this represents true separation of rough endoplasmic reticulum from smooth, or simply separation of ribosomes from membranes, cannot be answered, except that it appears to be rather difficult to remove bound ribosomes (Blobel and Potter 1967a, b). Such an approach does promise to give more exact localization and definition to the enzymic content and molecular constitution of this reticular system. The association of the membranes with ribosomal particles will be commented upon below, but the role of the ribosome in protein synthesis is the subject of another chapter.

The 'unit membrane' concept (Robertson) has been brought into question (Korn) particularly on the basis of high resolution examination of the endoplasmic reticulum. Karrer was unable to demonstrate triple layered structure in membranes of rough endoplasmic reticulum, and found that they were thinner than the plasma membrane. Sjöstrand (1963a, b) demonstrated not only that the rough ER membranes and outer membranes of mitochondria were thinner (50 Å in osmium fixed material) than the plasmalemma, but that the α cytomembranes (ER) showed electron dense cross-bridges, giving them a globular rather than a lamellar appearance (see Fig. 8 inset). He suggested (Sjöstrand 1963a, b, 1964), that these membranes consist of lipoprotein micelles in which the protein cross-bridges prevent the coalescence of the lipid globules (see also Glauert). He further pointed out that the α cytomembranes were symmetrical, whereas the plasmalemma shows distinct asymmetry. Examination of isolated mitochondrial membranes by the negative staining technique revealed a globular-projection approximately 90 Å in diameter (Fernández-Morán). Negatively stained preparations of microsomes from rabbit and rat liver and beef heart (Cunningham and associates) disclosed vesicles 100–300 mμ in diameter of two types: some with 50–60 Å projections and those which appeared to be composed of granules 25 to 30 Å wide, but did not show projections. It has subsequently been shown that the plasma membrane has small surface projections, but that ER membranes are devoid of such projections (Benedetti and Emmelot). Several studies, among them that of Perlmann and Morgan, indicate that microsomes have antigens distinct from those of the cell membrane, further demonstrating a constitutive difference between them. It therefore seems established that the membranes of the ER are distinct from the plasma membrane, being symmetrical, thinner, and showing a globular rather than a laminar substructure. They are devoid of surface projections, and antigenically distinct from other membranes.

3. *The smooth-surfaced endoplasmic reticulum*

The association of dense particles with intracytoplasmic membranes (Palade 1955) was not recognized until several years after the initial descriptions of the endoplasmic tubular system, and therefore, in a strict sense, the smooth reticulum was described first. At any rate, the existence of a network of anastomosing tubules devoid of particles, particularly in cells involved in sterol metabolism was soon established (Palade 1956). In fact, Palade (1956) proposed that the smooth and rough-surfaced profiles merely represent modifications of a single interconnected (Fig. 5) vesicular, tubular and cisternal system exhibiting wide variations in its degree of organization. The difficulty in defining the smooth reticulum, however, is immediately obvious: no distinctive marker, like the ribosome, is associated with these membranes. For some time the Golgi region as well as a variety of cytoplasmic membrane-bounded spaces probably more closely related to the cell membrane were included in the general category of smooth reticulum. Sjöstrand (1964) and Fawcett (1963) have emphasized the obvious over-simplification of such a classification of the diverse membrane-bounded images whose only obvious association is their predominant disposition in the 'endoplasm'. There is little doubt that many vesicular and tubular profiles, particularly in the apical portion of absorptive cells such as the intestinal epithelium, should in reality be classified as invaginations of plasma membrane or pinocytotic vesicles. As emphasized by Sjöstrand (1964), the reticular nature of the majority of cytoplasmic vesicles seen in thin sections is highly speculative. It seems evident, however, that a smooth-surfaced tubular system interconnected with ribosome studded cisternae, does exist within cells adapted for secretion of protein or fatty substances. A similar system is prominent in cells which function primarily in absorption, or in endocrine cells, particularly those which synthesize steroid hormones (Fig. 4). Biochemical identity of the membranes of these two systems is being established (Manganiello and Phillips) and the interconversion of rough-surfaced membranes to smooth-surfaced reticulum in cytodifferentiation has recently been postulated (Dallner et al. 1966a, b). Aggregates of smooth tubular profiles are seen in areas of hepatic parenchymal cells depleted of glycogen by fasting (Figs. 5 and 7), and many of these can be seen to connect with rough surfaced cisternae. Recognizing the complexity of the interrelationships of these tubules, it seems legitimate to retain the designation of smooth ER, until a functional classification is practicable.

The exact mechanism of participation of the rough and smooth reticulum in absorptive and secretory activities is still under active investigation. In a number of investigations, Palade and associates have shown a functional connection between rough and smooth tubules, as well as Golgi cisternae and ultimately plasma membrane in the synthesis and secretion of zymogen granules in the pancreas. The absorption and secretion of lipid in the small intestine has similarly been extensively studied. Palay and Karlin concluded that lipid is taken up by pinocytosis at the base of microvillae and that these vesicles traverse the terminal web and fuse with the smooth reticulum which can be seen to contain large numbers of lipid droplets. In a recent reexamination of this mechanism, Cardell and associates conclude that pinocytosis plays little or no part in absorption of lipids. They propose that monoglycerides and fatty acid micelles are selectively absorbed through the microvillae. Resynthesis into triglycerides occurs in the smooth ER and droplets are secreted as chylomicra into the lateral cell space. They conclude that this secretion may involve fusion of vesicles of smooth ER with the plasmalemma, and that the role of the Golgi is still open to question. Droplets of similar size and electron opacity are seen in cisternae of rough and smooth ER of the liver under a variety of conditions such as fasting (Trump et al. 1962; Bruni and Porter) and treatment with agents which produce fatty liver (Lombardi). Since the liver is the principle source of serum lipoproteins, these droplets have been postulated to contain lipid. The histochemical experiments of Novikoff and associates (1966) indicate the probable lipid nature of these granules. The recent autoradiographic studies of Stein and Stein show clearly that these droplets contain lipid, and they, as well as others, suggest that the lipid is probably absorbed from chylomicra in the plasma, synthesized into lipoproteins, and assembled within cisternae of rough and smooth ER. The lipoproteins are repackaged in the Golgi zone and secreted, perhaps via Golgi vesicles, into the space of Dissé of the sinusoids. The exact point at which lipid and protein are conjugated is not established. It would therefore seem that a functional connection between rough and smooth ER exists in many cells, and that these tubules participate in the absorption, transport, and secretion of a variety of lipid and protein substances.

Evidence is accumulating that the smooth reticulum is important in drug detoxication reactions (Fouts; Rothschild) and masses of smooth membranes have been observed following administration of agents such as barbiturates (Remmer and Merker) and carcinogens (Emmelot and Benedetti) as well as in response to hormone stimulation. These instances have thus far been associated predominantly with increases in enzymes of hydroxylation or methylation. A further role in electrolyte metabolism, particularly of cations, is suggested by the fact that microsomes bind Na^+ and K^+ (Siekevitz). However, the abundant smooth tubules seen in such cells as the oxyntic cells of gastric mucosa and salt glands of fish and birds, and felt to be important in electrolyte transport, may represent complex plasma membrane infoldings, rather than endoplasmic reticulum. The role of the sarcoplasmic reticulum in Ca^{++} transport will be discussed below.

It seems clear then, that the smooth reticulum is actively involved in transport within and perhaps out of cells, and that it plays a major role in fatty acid and sterol synthesis. It also appears to participate in a number of drug detoxication reactions. Although glucose-6-phosphatase activity appears to be a constant component of microsomal membranes (Ernster et al.; Manganiello and Phillips), and smooth membranes are frequently seen in areas of glycogen deposition (Fig. 7), the exact relationship of the ER to glycogen metabolism is a matter of debate (see Philips et al.).

The work of Omura and associates, Mason, and others, seems to elucidate the role of the nonmitochondrial electron transport system described first by Strittmatter and Ball. It has been suggested (Omura et al.) that this system functions as a 'mixed function oxidase' (see Mason), transporting electrons from reduced NAD or NADP ultimately to cytochrome p-450 (a cytochrome sensitive to light and carbon monoxide). Though this cytochrome may function in other reactions such as oxidative N-demethylation (Ziegler and Pettit) it can react with molecular oxygen and, in turn, can hydroxylate steroids or various drugs, including carcinogens (Omura et al.). This represents a plausible explanation for the presence of this electron transport system in the microsomes, which even a few years ago represented a major unsolved problem of biochemistry (Siekevitz).

4. *Specializations of the endoplasmic reticulum*

Besides the two major subdivisions described above, several morphologically, and perhaps functionally distinct entities which seem to represent specializations of the ER deserve comment.

The Nissl's body or chromophil substance of neurons has been a subject of intense interest for many years. These areas of basophilia occupy the majority of the cell body of large neurons, extending into the dendrites, but not into the axon or axon hillock. The affinity for basic dyes disappears after ribonuclease digestion. In the electron microscope, they consist of stacks of rough ER and interspersed ribosomes. Their extreme responsiveness to stimulation of the neuron or injury to the cell body or axon (chromatolysis) has led to the supposition that they must play an important part in the synthesis of secretory products of neurons.

At the turn of the century, Veratti demonstrated a delicate reticulum surrounding myofibrils of skeletal muscle. This was rediscovered by Bennett and Porter, who delineated a smooth tubular system between and surrounding myofibrils. Anderson-Cedergren then noted that this system consisted of two major divisions: the sarcoplasmic reticulum (Fig. 6a), which runs between myofibrils, and a transverse tubular system (T system) which appears in some species to connect directly with the extracellular space (Fig. 6b). This anatomic connection is confirmed by experiments showing penetration of tracers from extracellular fluid into the reticulum between the fibers (Huxley). Direct continuities between the T system and the sarcoplasmic reticulum have not been demonstrated, but the T system intercepts the reticulum at regular intervals (at the junction of A-1 bands in mammals and at the Z line in fish) forming *triads* with dilated *terminal cisternae* of the sarcoplasmic reticulum. At these sites, a junctional complex sometimes resembling a tight junction is formed. The possible importance of this system in coordinating contraction of muscle fibrils has recently been summarized by Smith. Following depolarization of the plasma membrane, the excitation is conducted along the T system and transferred across the triadic junction, releasing calcium ions from the sarcoplasmic reticulum. Calcium diffuses to the actinmyosin cross links and activates the dephosphorylation of ATP, with resultant muscle contractions. Finally, reaccumulation of calcium within the sarcoplasmic tubules allows for relaxation. It must be pointed out, however, that Sjöstrand (1964) has questioned the propriety of including the sarcoplasmic reticulum in the category of endoplasmic reticulum at all.

Another specialization, of as yet undefined significance, is the annulate lamellae (Fig. 10), first clearly delineated by Swift, and seen predominantly in embryonic, germinal, or neoplastic cells. These arrays have been suggested to be involved in protein synthesis, formation of endoplasmic reticulum, or, because of the resemblance, may be analogous to nuclear pores. The 'pores' are hexagonally packed (Swift), but the individual pores show variable symmetry. They definitely connect with rough cisternae, and some authors have asserted that they are RNA containing, because they occur in sites of cytoplasmic basophilia (Swift). Another structural modification of the rough ER, also seen more frequently in embryonic, germinal, or neoplastic cells, is 'pairing' of cisternae (Fig. 8). Parallel cisternae appear to lose their ribosomal particles along apposing surfaces and then fuse or become closely associated. The significance of this formation in not known. At times several paired cisternae may be seen in ordered arrays in a single cell (Leake et al.).

A distinctive modification of the ER seen in retinal cells, is a complex array of tightly packed membranes clearly attached proximally to the endoplasmic reticulum. These 'myeloid bodies' are seen frequently in retinal pigment epithelium (Porter and Yamada) and the possibility that they are photosensitive has been considered (Porter 1961a).

5. *Modulations of the endoplasmic reticulum in cell function and cell injury*

The malleability of the endoplasmic reticulum is amply illustrated by its reaction to agents which induce cell damage or death. Several reaction patterns are evident: vesiculation and fragmentation, dilatation, degranulation, abnormal accumulation of cisternal contents and proliferation. With the obvious exception of degranulation, these reactions are common to both major types of reticulum under both pathologic and physiologic circumstances.

Vesiculation and fragmentation represent one of the commonest reactions of the ER, but should be viewed with caution, since they may be found frequently in poorly fixed tissue. They are seen in the process of cell death (Trump et al. 1965; Smuckler and Trump). The small vesicles seen in the microsomal fraction may arise through a similar membrane transformation, and thus be analogous to vesiculation *in vivo* (Trump and Ericsson).

Extreme dilatation of the ER is one phenomenon recognized as 'hydropic degeneration' at the light microscopic level. It may be seen following administration of puromycin (Longnecker and Shinozuka), chloroform, carbon tetrachloride, and other injurious agents, presumably reflecting alterations in the membrane or accumulation of water and electrolytes in the lumen (Fig. 11).

Degranulation, that is, loss of attachment of ribosomal particles to the membrane, has been observed following carbon tetrachloride (Smuckler et al.), dimethylnitrosamine (Emmelot and Benedetti) and ethionine (Baglio and Farber) administration, among other compounds. Though some of these (ethionine, carbon tetrachloride, puromycin) inhibit protein synthesis, this does not seem invariably to cause degranulation, since cyclohexamide does not, despite its marked inhibition of protein formation (Verbin et al.). Unfortunately, the exact nature of the forces binding ribosomes to the membrane is unknown. It must be pointed out, that what has been designated degranulation may not, in all instances, reflect loss of ribosomes from membranes. The increase in individual ribosomes in the hyaloplasm and decrease of polysomes and increase in monomers found biochemically (Villa-Trevino et al.) may indicate breakdown of ordered arrays in the hyaloplasm, rather than detachment of individual ribosomes from membranes, which appears to be more difficult (Blobel and Potter 1967a, b).

Accumulation of electron dense droplets within cisternae and vesicles of endoplasmic reticulum has been seen in a number of physiologic and pathologic situations. Prozymogen droplets appear in the ER of the pancreas after fasting and refeeding (Palade et al.). Similar droplets, of unknown composition, have been seen in pancreatic ER following puromycin inhibition of protein synthesis (Longnecker and Shinozuka). Fasting is accompanied by the appearance of electron dense granules within ER and Golgi cisternae (Trump and associates 1962; Bruni and Porter). The most extensively studied instance of droplet accumulation is the formation of numerous lipid or lipoprotein droplets in rough and smooth endoplasmic reticulum in the development of fatty liver (Lombardi; Novikoff et al. 1966). As pointed out previously, the ER of the intestine and liver is actively involved in the processes of absorption and transport of lipids (Cardell et al.; Stein and Stein). The mechanism of development of fatty liver has recently been reviewed by Lombardi. Fatty liver results from imbalance in the rate of synthesis versus the rate of utilization (secretion) of hepatic triglyceride (TG). Although both triglyceride and phospholipid are synthesized within the microsomes of the liver (Stein and Stein) the accumulation of fat in the liver is very largely or exclusively as TG. Increase in hepatic triglyceride can result from (a) block in utilization, (b) increased synthesis, (c) increase in synthesis and block in utilization. A fourth possibility is that synthesis takes place in a cell compartment other than ER where it normally occurs (Lombardi). An example of block of normal secretion is the fatty liver of ethionine intoxication. In this condition triglyceride accumulates due, presumably, to a block in protein synthesis occasioned by trapping of ATP as S-adenosyl ethionine. The condition is largely reversed by adenine administration. Baglio and Farber noted numerous dense lipid droplets in cisternae of rough and smooth ER within 4 hours after ethionine administration (Fig. 12). These lipid droplets, termed liposomes, are mobilized within two hours after adenine administration and appear in the space of Dissé. Recently, Schlunk and Lombardi have isolated these liposomes within microsomal vesicles, (insert, Fig. 12) and have confirmed their lipid nature.

Masses of tubular smooth membranes accompanying enzyme induction have been noted after administration of phenobarbital (Ernster and Orrenius; Orrenius and Ericsson) and a wide variety of other agents. Apparent increase in smooth membranes has also been noted after fasting, dimethylnitrosamine feeding (Emmelot and Benedetti) and following hormone stimulation of steroid synthesis in many endocrine organs. Rough surfaced arrays increase in the pancreas following fasting and refeeding (Palade 1956), but this may reflect merely a reorientation of preexisting cisternae.

Another response of the ER, to a growing list of stimuli, is close application to, and enwrapping of cytoplasmic organelles. In its most fully developed form, this may result in complex whorls which have been called 'finger print' configurations (Fig. 9) (see Verbin et al.). Though the term 'Nebenkerne' has also been used for these formations, this designation has been applied to other cytoplasmic structures and should probably not be retained (see Haguenau). The origin and significance of these structures is not yet clear. They may reflect rearrangements in the phospholipid or protein components of the membrane in response to changes in the intracellular environment (see Fawcett 1961). They might also be an exaggerated instance of cytoplasmic segregation or autophagia (Ericsson et al.). Recent investigations of this latter phenomenon by Arstila and Trump following glucagon administration, suggest active participation of the endoplasmic reticulum in the formation of cytoplasmic inclusions. In these investigations, wrapping of cytoplasmic organelles by ER membranes to form first double, then single membrane limited bodies, is energy dependent, but not dependent on RNA or protein synthesis. In the maturation of these inclusions the inner membrane disappears, the outer one thickens, and acid phosphatase activity concurrently appears within them. Participation of a specialized Golgi associated region of the ER (GERL) in lysosome formation has been suggested previously by Novikoff and associates (1964). They have also suggested that the microbody (peroxisome) forms within the ER, acquiring its single membrane by budding from a cisterna. It is evident, then, that the endoplasmic reticulum is a system of great responsiveness which participates in numerous degenerative and regenerative phenomena, as well as in various aspects of physiologic cellular response.

6. *Comments and conclusions*

Information about the molecular arrangement of the membranes, internal content, and associated enzymes, transport systems, and even the structural arrangement of the ribosomes on the endoplasmic reticulum, is largely lacking, or so fragmentary that speculation is extremely hazardous. Nevertheless, it is interesting to try to advance some hypotheses about the possible molecular arrangement of this extremely variegated system.

From recent investigations it seems clear that membranes of the rough ER differ from the plasma membrane in a number of ways. The ER membranes measure approximately 50 to 60 Å in width, in osmium fixed material, whereas the plasmalemma is 75 to 100 Å wide. Membranes of the ER are symmetrical, but show dense cross bridges which have been interpreted to represent protein bands separating lipid micelles. Thus, they have a globular appearance, while plasma membranes show a more typical trilaminar or 'unit' structure (Robertson), though they tend to be asymmetrically thickened on the inner lamina (Sjöstrand 1963a, b). In negatively stained preparations no globular surface projections either such as those seen on plasmalemma or those on the inner mitochondrial membrane are found in ER membranes. Chemical analysis indicates that microsomal membranes are more similar to mitochondrial membranes than the plasmalemma. Like mitochondria they contain little cholesterol (3–6 %), predominantly unsaturated fatty acids, and high amounts of lecithins and phosphatidyl ethanolamine. They differ from mitochondria in that they contain little or no cardiolipin, and their low cholesterol content sets them apart from the plasma membrane (Fleisher and Rouser). Antigenically, the major membrane types appear distinct (Pearlmann and Morgan) (see also Sjöstrand 1964; Glauert; Benedetti and Emmelot). Wallach and associates have shown that fragments of ER membrane, from Ehrlich ascites tumor, differ in density, turbidity, and refractive index from fragments of plasma membrane. The affinity of the two membranes for calcium and magnesium ions, and their 'isoelectric' points differ. The visible asymmetry of plasma membrane (Sjöstrand 1963a, b) is reflected in its ionically distinct surfaces, while ER does not show this lack of ionic symmetry (Wallach et al.). The

ER membranes show much larger increases in density and turbidity with addition of Mg^{++} and Ca^{++}, which may be related to the recognized dependence of ribosome-membrane association on Mg^{++} concentration.

It has been seriously questioned whether the particulate representation of ribosomes, gained from electron micrographs, is accurate (Sjöstrand 1964; Kavanau). There seems, however, to be little debate about the association of ribosomal RNA with membranes, and another species of RNA seems also to be frequently a component of microsomes (Siekevitz; Wallach et al.). Ernster and associates have shown that some enzymes appear to be tightly bound, or to be an integral part of the membrane, while others are easily made soluble by detergent treatment. Such observations have given rise to various hypotheses linking the membrane, its enzymes and its associated RNA, into a synthetic unit. One possibility proposed recently by Pitot, is that a molecule of messenger RNA is associated with a specific area of the membrane, and operates with ribosomes and transfer RNA as a cytoplasmic 'operon' regulating synthesis. He terms this unit the 'membron'.

How the ER functions to determine which products of synthesis will be secreted or retained is still unclear. The 30S subunit is always oriented toward the center of the helix of the polysome (Sheldon and Kuff). Thus, the direction of growth (into the membrane or into the hyaloplasm) of the peptide chain might depend on the internal end of the helix being 3′ or 5′-hydroxyl (Pitot). Redmann and Sabatini have proposed that the growing peptide chain is vectorially directed toward (or we assume, away from) the ER lumen, based on *in vitro* observations of hepatic and pancreatic microsomes. They state that channels within the large ribosomal subunit have been observed and that there are discontinuities in the ER membranes. They propose that the unidirectional transfer of peptides to the lumen might occur passively through the channel and the 'holes' in the membrane. A corollary might be that ribosomes synthesizing constitutive proteins are bound over 'closed' areas of the membrane. If such 'holes' occurred between globular subunits, it would seem probable tnat the closed areas could represent lamellar portions of the membrane. Some of these concepts are depicted in Fig. 1. Redman and Sabatini also suggest that the growing peptide chains aid in the attachment of the ribosome to the membrane. Another mode of attachment of ribosomal aggregates to the membrane was depicted by Benedetti and associates who visualized long filaments containing RNA (messenger?), studded with ribosomes, and attached to microsomal membranes apparently by a single ribosome. All of these concepts suppose that the particulate conformation of the ribosome is accurate.

That the plasticity of the endoplasmic reticulum, repeatedly mentioned and illustrated, must reflect its molecular organization, is self evident. Kavanau has extensively discussed models for transformations of membranes, including fragmentation, growth, degrowth and fusion. Each of these must involve complex molecular rearrangements in which the breaking of hydrophobic bonds between lipid and protein, the reorganization of the hydration shell, and the 'globulation' of proteins and lipid of the membrane must play a role (see Kavanau, chapter 9). That these molecular rearrangements may be important in propelling the luminal contents has also been suggested (Buckley; Siekevitz). The globular nature of the ER membranes has been pointed out repeatedly (Sjöstrand 1963a, b; Wallach; Glauert) and undoubtedly plays a role in their complex absorptive and secretory functions. It serves also to functionally differentiate them from the plasma membrane, which must maintain a more highly lamellar structure to preserve its semi-permeability (Glauert). In a recent review Rosenberg has pointed out the importance of phase transitions in the growth and development of cell membranes, and the possibility that membranes are assembled from lipoprotein or glycolipoprotein subunits. He cites evidence that the smooth endoplasmic reticulum originates by budding of the nuclear envelope. Leduc and co-workers have demonstrated the formation of antibody within the nuclear envelope and ER of differentiating plasma cells. Their studies further indicate the functional connection between nuclear envelope and ER and demonstrate that antibody production occurs first in the nuclear envelope, extending successively in a centripedal fashion and finally occurring only in the outer ER lamellae as 'maturation' of the ER progresses (Leduc et al.). Such studies would seem to indicate functional specializations and transitions in developing endoplasmic reticulum. Dallner and associates (1966a, b) have concluded that smooth ER arises from differentiation of the rough ER. Their studies of ER development in rat liver during late prenatal and early antenatal growth indicate little change in phospholipid to protein ratios, but a drastic change in fatty acid composition of phosphatides after birth. They conclude that the enzymic pattern was not greatly influenced by the fatty acid or phospholipid composition of the ER membranes during antenatal growth (Dallner et al. 1966b). Porter and Machado have presented morphologic evidence supporting the notion that the ER participates in the reformation of the lateral cell membrane after cell division in plants. That the ER membranes can transform to more 'plasma membrane-like' seems to be substantiated by the observations of Arstila and Trump, showing participation of the ER in the formation of autophagic vacuoles, and the demonstration that transformation from ER-like membrane to membrane of plasma membrane type takes place in the Golgi lamellae (Grove et al.).

Thus, the endoplasmic reticulum represents a complex, interwoven, tubular system, the lumina of which appear to convey metabolites, macromolecules, and perhaps electrolytes into, out of, and within the cytoplasm. The lumina are bounded by lipoprotein membranes which differ in configuration and constitution from the plasmalemma, but which bring the nuclear envelope into close association to, if not into contiguity with, the Golgi apparatus and the cell membrane. Many of these membranes are associated with ribonucleoprotein and they may well participate intimately with these ribosomes in protein synthesis. Other, smooth-surfaced, membranes probably are more intimately concerned with various reactions in drug detoxication and sterol metabolism. As our exact knowledge grows, some structures currently grouped with the endoplasmic reticulum will be separated from it; others will be shown to constitute a part of this complex system. In the more than half a century since it was first visualized, the role of the endoplasmic reticulum in glandular secretion, first suggested in 1897 (Garnier) seems firmly established; the multiplicity of other actions ascribed to this most evanescent of cellular organelles still entices investigation.

Acknowledgements

The author is grateful to Miss Gloria Diluiso for excellent technical assistance; to Drs. R. Verbin and F. Schlunk and Mr. Joseph Locker for contributing material; to Drs. H. Scalzi and H. Shinozuka and Mr. J. Locker for providing electron micrographs, and to Drs. E. L. Benedetti, E. Farber, D. Goldblatt, H. Goldblatt, E. A. Smuckler and B. F. Trump for helpful criticism of the manuscript.

References

ANDERSON-CEDERGREN, E.: Ultrastructure of motor end plate and sarcoplasmic components of mouse skeletal muscle fiber. J. Ultrastruct. Res. Suppl. 1 (1959) 126.

ARSTILA, A. U. and B. F. TRUMP: Studies on cellular autophagocytosis. The formation of autophagic vacuoles in the liver after glucagon administration. Am. J. Pathol. 53 (1968) 687.

BAGLIO, C. M. and E. FARBER: Reversal by adenine of the ethionine-induced lipid accumulation in the endoplasmic reticulum of the rat liver. J. Cell Biol. 27 (1965) 591.

BENEDETTI, E. L., W. S. BONT and H. BLOEMENDAL: Electron microscopic observation on polyribosomes and endoplasmic reticulum fibers isolated from rat liver. Lab. Invest. 15 (1966) 196.

BENEDETTI, E. L. and P. EMMELOT: Electron microscopic observations on negatively stained plasma membranes isolated from rat liver. J. Cell Biol. 26 (1965) 299.

BENNETT, H. S. and K. R. PORTER: An electron microscope study of sectioned breast muscle of the domestic fowl. Am. J. Anat. 93 (1953) 61.

BLOBEL, G. and V. R. POTTER: Studies on free and membrane bound ribosomes in rat liver I. Distribution as related to total cellular RNA. J. Mol. Biol. 26 (1967) 279.

BLOBEL, G. and V. R. POTTER: Studies on free and membrane bound ribosomes in rat liver II. Interaction of ribosomes and membranes. J. Mol. Biol. 26 (1967) 293.

BRUNI, C. and K. R. PORTER: The fine structure of the parenchymal cell of the normal rat liver I. General observations. Am. J. Pathol. 46 (1965) 691.

BUCKLEY, I. K.: Phase contrast observations on the endoplasmic reticulum of living cells in culture. Protoplasma 59 (1964) 569.

CARDELL, R. R., JR., S. BADENHAUSEN and K. R. PORTER: Intestinal triglyceride absorption in the rat. J. Cell Biol. 34 (1967) 123.

CLAUDE, A.: The constitution of protoplasm. Science 97 (1943) 451.

COPELAND, D. E. and A. J. DALTON: An association between mitochondria and the endoplasmic reticulum in cells of the pseudobranch gland of a teleost. J. Biophys. Biochem. Cytol. 5 (1958) 393.

CUNNINGHAM, W. P., J. W. STILES and F. L. CRANE: Surface structure of negatively stained membranes. Exptl. Cell Res. 40 (1965) 171.

DALLNER, G.: Studies on the structural and enzymic organization of the membranous elements of liver microsomes. Acta Pathol. Microbiol. Scand., Suppl. 166 (1963) 1.

DALLNER, G., P. SIEKEVITZ and G. E. PALADE: Biogenesis of endoplasmic reticulum membranes I. Structural and chemical differentiation in developing rat hepatocyte. J. Cell Biol. 30 (1966) 73.

DALLNER, G., P. SIEKEVITZ and G. E. PALADE: Biogenesis of endoplasmic reticulum membranes II. Synthesis of constitutive microsomal enzymes in developing rat hepatocyte. J. Cell Biol. 30 (1966) 97.

EMMELOT, P. and E. L. BENEDETTI: Changes in the fine structure of rat liver cells brought about by dimethylnitrosamine. J. Biophys. Biochem. Cytol. 7 (1960) 393.

EPSTEIN, M. A.: The fine structural organization of Rous tumor cells. J. Biophys. Biochem. Cytol. 3 (1957) 851.

ERICSSON, J. L. E., B. F. TRUMP and J. WEIBEL: Electron microscopic studies of the proximal tubule of the rat kidney II. Cytosegresomes and cytosomes: Their relationship to each other and to the lysosome concept. Lab. Invest. 14 (1965) 1341.

ERNSTER, L. and S. ORRENIUS: Substrate-induced synthesis of the hydroxylating enzyme system of liver microsomes. Federation Proc. 24 (1965) 1190.

ERNSTER, L., P. SIEKEVITZ and G. E. PALADE: Enzyme-structure relationships in the endoplasmic reticulum of rat liver. A morphological and biochemical study. J. Cell Biol. 15 (1962) 541.

FAWCETT, D. W.: The membranes of the cytoplasm. Lab. Invest. 10 (1961) 1162.

FAWCETT, D. W.: Morphological and functional variations in the endoplasmic reticulum. J. Cell Biol. 19 (1963) 80A.

FERNÁNDEZ-MORÁN, H.: Cell-membrane ultrastructure. Low-temperature electron microscopy and X-ray diffraction studies of lipoprotein components in lamellar systems. Circulation 26 (1962) 1039.

FLEISHER, S. and G. ROUSER: Lipids of subcellular particles. J. Am. Chem. Soc. 42 (1965) 588.

FOUTS, J. R.: Interaction of drugs and hepatic microsomes. Federation Proc. 21 (1962) 1107.

GARNIER, C.: Les filaments basaux des cellules glandulaires. Note préliminaire. Bibliogr. Anat. 5 (1897) 278.

GLAUERT, A. M.: Electron microscopy of lipids and membranes. J. Roy. Microscop. Soc. 88 (1968) 49.

GROVE, S. N., C. E. BRACKER and J. D. MORRÉ: Cytomembrane differentiation in the endoplasmic reticulum-Golgi apparatus-vesicle complex. Science 161 (1968) 171.

HAGUENAU, F.: The ergastoplasm: its history, ultrastructure and biochemistry. Intern. Rev. Cytol. 7 (1958) 425.

HUXLEY H. E.: Evidence for continuity between the central elements of the triads and extracellular space in frog sartorius muscle. Nature 202 (1964) 1067.

KARRER, H. E.: Electron microscopic study of the phagocytosis process in the lung. J. Biophys. Biochem. Cytol. 7 (1960) 357.

KAVANAU, J. L.: Structure and function in biological membranes, Vol. 2. San Francisco, Holden-Day, Inc. (1965).

KORN, E. D.: Structure of biological membranes. Science 153 (1966) 1491.

LEAKE, L. V., J. B. CAULFIELD, J. F. BURKE and C. F. MCKHANN: Electron microscopic studies on a human fibromyxosarcoma. Cancer Res. 27 (1967) 261.

LEDUC, E. H., S. AVRAMEAS and M. BOUTEILLE: Ultrastructural localization of antibody in differentiating plasma cell. J. Exptl. Med. 127 (1968) 109.

LOMBARDI, B.: Considerations on the pathogenesis of fatty liver. Lab. Invest. 15 (1966) 1.

LONGNECKER, D. S. and H. SHINOZUKA: Molecular pathology of in-vivo inhibition of protein synthesis. Electron microscopy of rat pancreatic acinar cells in puromycin-induced necrosis. Am. J. Pathol. 52 (1968) 891.

MANGANIELLO, V. C. and A. H. PHILLIPS: The relationship between ribosomes and the endoplasmic reticulum during protein synthesis. J. Biol. Chem. 240 (1965) 3951.

MASON, H. S., J. C. NORTH and M. VANNESTA: Microsomal mixed function oxidation: the metabolism of xenobiotics. Federation Proc. 24 (1965) 1172.

MOULÉ, Y.: Endoplasmic reticulum and microsomes of rat liver. In: M. Locke, ed.: Cellular membranes in development. New York, Academic Press, Inc. (1964) p. 97.

NOVIKOFF, A.B., E.ESSNER and N.QUINTANA: Golgi apparatus and lysosomes. Federation Proc. 23 (1964) 1010.

NOVIKOFF, A.B., P.S.ROHEIM and N.QUINTANA: Changes in rat liver cells induced by orotic acid feeding. Lab. Invest. 15 (1966) 27.

OMURA, T., R.SATO, D.Y.COOPER, O.ROSENTHAL and R.W.ESTABROOK: Function of cytochrome p-450 of microsomes. Federation Proc. 24 (1965) 1181.

ORRENIUS, S. and J.L.E.ERICSSON: On the relationship of liver glucose-6-phosphatase to the proliferation of endoplasmic reticulum in phenobarbitol induction. J. Cell Biol. 31 (1966) 243.

PALADE, G.E.: A small particulate component of the cytoplasm. J. Biophys. Biochem. Cytol. 1 (1955) 567.

PALADE, G.E.: The endoplasmic reticulum. J. Biophys. Biochem. Cytol. Suppl. 2 (1956) 85.

PALADE, G.E. and K.R.PORTER: Studies on the endoplasmic reticulum I. Its identification in cells *in situ*. J. Exptl. Med. 100 (1954) 641.

PALADE, G.E. and P.SIEKEVITZ: Liver microsomes. An integrated morphological and biochemical study. J. Biophys. Biochem. Cytol. 2 (1956) 171.

PALADE, G.E., P.SIEKEVITZ and L.G.CARO: Structure, chemistry and function of the pancreatic exocrine cell. In: A.V.S.De Reuck and M.P.Cameron, eds.: CIBA Foundation Symposium on the Exocrine Pancreas. London, J. and A.Churchill, Ltd. (1962) p. 23.

PALAY, S.L. and L.J.KARLIN: An electron microscopic study of the intestinal villus II. The pathway of fat absorption. J. Biophys. Biochem. Cytol. 5 (1959) 373.

PERLMANN, P. and W.S.MORGAN: Immunological studies of microsomal structure and function, Vol. 1. In: T.W.Goodwin and O.Lindberg, eds. New York, Academic Press, Inc. (1961) p. 209.

PHILIPS, M.J., N.J.UNAKAR, G.DOORNEWAARD and J.W.STEINER: Glycogen depletion in the newborn rat liver. An electron microscopic and electron histochemical study. J. Ultrastruct. Res. 18 (1967) 142.

PITOT, H.C.: The endoplasmic reticulum and phenotypic variability in normal and neoplastic liver. Arch. Pathol. (in press).

PORTER, K.R.: Observations on a submicroscopic basophilic component of the cytoplasm. J. Exptl. Med. 97 (1953) 727.

PORTER, K.R.: The ground substance: Observations from electron microscopy. In: J.Brachet and A.E.Mirsky, eds.: The cell, Vol. 2. New York, Academic Press, Inc. (1961) p. 621.

PORTER, K.R.: The endoplasmic reticulum: Some current interpretations of its forms and functions, In: T.W.Goodwin and O.Lindbert, eds.: Biological structure and function, Vol. 1. New York. Academic Press, Inc. (1961) p. 127.

PORTER, K.R., A.CLAUDE and E.F.FULLAM: A study of tissue culture cells by electron microscopy. Methods and preliminary observation. J. Exptl. Med. 81 (1945) 233.

PORTER, K.R. and F.L.KALLMAN: Significance of cell particulates as seen by electron microscopy. Ann. N.Y. Acad. Sci. 54 (1952) 882.

PORTER, K.R. and E.A.MACHADO: Studies on the endoplasmic reticulum IV. Its form and distribution during mitosis in cells of onion root tip. J. Biophys. Biochem. Cytol. 7 (1960) 167.

PORTER, K.R. and E.YAMADA: Studies on the endoplasmic reticulum V. Its form and differentiation in pigment epithelial cells of the frog retina. J. Biophys. Biochem. Cytol. 8 (1960) 181.

REDMAN, C.M. and D.D.SABATINI: Vectorial discharge of peptides released by puromycin from attached ribosomes. Proc. Natl. Acad. Sci. U.S. 56 (1966) 608.

REMMER, H. and H.J.MERKER: Drug-induced changes in the liver endoplasmic reticulum; association with drug-metabolizing enzymes. Science 142 (1963) 1657.

ROBERTSON, J.D.: The ultrastructure of cell membranes and their derivatives. Biochem. Soc. Symp. (Cambridge, Engl.) 16 (1959) 3.

ROSENBERG, M.D.: Single cell properties – membrane development. In: A.V.S. De Reuck and J.

Knight, eds.: Cell differentiation. CIBA Foundation Symposium. Boston, Little Brown and Co. (1967) p. 18.

ROTHSCHILD, J.: The isolation of microsomal membranes. Biochem. Soc. Symp. (Cambridge, Engl.) 22 (1963) 4.

SCHLUNK, F.F. and B.LOMBARDI: Liver liposomes I. Isolation and chemical characterization. Lab. Invest. 17 (1967) 30.

SHELTON, E. and E.L.KUFF: Substructure and configuration of ribosomes isolated from mammalian cells. J. Mol. Biol. 22 (1966) 23.

SIEKEVITZ, P.: Protoplasm: Endoplasmic reticulum and microsomes and their properties. Ann. Rev. Physiol. 25 (1963) 15.

SJÖSTRAND, F.S.: A new ultrastructural element of the membranes in mitochondria and of some cytoplasmic membranes. J. Ultrastruct. Res. 9 (1963) 340.

SJÖSTRAND, F.S.: A comparison of plasma membrane, cyto-membranes, and mitochondrial membrane elements with respect to ultrastructural features. J. Ultrastruct. Res. 9 (1963) 561.

SJÖSTRAND, F.S.: The endoplasmic reticulum. In: G.H.Bourne, ed.: Cytology and cell physiology, 3rd ed. New York, Academic Press, Inc. (1964) p. 311.

SMITH, D.S.: The organization and function of the sarcoplasmic reticulum and T-system of muscle cells. Progr. Biophys. Mol. Biol. 16 (1966) 109.

SMUCKLER, E.A., O.ISERI and E.P.BENDITT: An intracellular defect in protein synthesis induced by carbon tetrachloride. J. Exptl. Med. 166 (1962) 55.

SMUCKLER, E.A. and B.F.TRUMP: Alterations in the structure and function of the rough-surfaced endoplasmic reticulum during necrosis in vitro. Am. J. Pathol. 53 (1968) 315.

STEIN, O. and Y.STEIN: Lipid synthesis, intracellular transport, storage and secretion I. Electron microscopic radioautographic study of liver after injection of tritiated palmitate of glycerols in fasted and ethanol-treated rats. J. Cell Biol. 33 (1967) 319.

STRITTMATTER, C.F. and E.G.BALL: The intracellular distribution of cytochrome components and of oxidative enzyme activity in rat liver. J. Cellular Comp. Physiol. 43 (1954) 57.

SWIFT, H.: The fine structure of annulate lamellae. J. Biophys. Biochem. Cytol. Suppl. 2 (1956) 415.

TRUMP, B.F. and J.L.E.ERICSSON: Some ultrastructural and biochemical characteristics of cell injury. In: B.W.Zweifach, R.T.McCluskey and L.H.Grant, eds.: The inflammatory process. New York, Academic Press, Inc. (1965) p. 35.

TRUMP, B.F., P.J.GOLDBLATT and R.E.STOWELL: An electron microscopic study of early cytoplasmic alterations in hepatic parenchymal cells of mouse liver during necrosis *in vitro* (autolysis). Lab. Invest. 11 (1962) 986.

TRUMP, B.F., P.J.GOLDBLATT and R.E.STOWELL: Studies of necrosis *in vitro* of mouse hepatic parenchymal cells. Ultrastructural alterations in endoplasmic reticulum, Golgi apparatus, plasma membrane and lipid droplets. Lab. Invest. 14 (1965) 2000.

VERATTI, E.: Richerche sulle fine structura della fibra musculare striata. Mem. Reale Inst. Lombardo 19 (1902) 87.

VERBIN, R.S., P.J.GOLDBLATT and E.FARBER: The molecular pathology of inhibition of protein synthesis *in vivo*. The effects of cycloheximide on hepatic parenchymal cell ultrastructure. Lab. Invest. (in press).

VILLA-TREVINO, S., E.FARBER, T.STAEHELIN, F.O.WETTSTEIN and H.NOLL: Breakdown and reassembly of rat liver ergosomes after administration of ethionine or puromycin. J. Biol. Chem. 239 (1964) 3826.

WALLACH, D.F.H.: Isolation of plasma membranes of animal cells. In: B.D.Davis and L.Warren, eds.: The specificity of cell surfaces. Englewood-Cliffs, New Jersey, Prentice-Hall, Inc. (1967).

WALLACH, D.F.H., V.B.KAMAT and M.A.GAIL: Physicochemical differences between fragments of plasma membrane and endoplasmic reticulum. J. Cell Biol. 30 (1966) 601.

WATSON, M.L.: The nuclear envelope. Its structure and relation to cytoplasmic membranes. J. Biophys. Biochem. Cytol. 1 (1955) 257.

ZIEGLER, D.M. and F.H.PETTIT: Microsomal oxidases I. The isolation and dialkylarylamine oxygenase activity of pork liver microsomes. Biochemistry 5 (1966) 2932.

CHAPTER 41

The Golgi apparatus

PIERRE FAVARD

Laboratoire de Biologie Cellulaire, Faculté des Sciences, Université de Paris

Contents

1. Introduction

2. Ultrastructure
   (a) Description
   (b) Value of the observations

3. Chemical composition
   (a) Study *in situ* by cytochemical methods
   (b) Chemical analysis of the Golgi fraction

4. Physiology
   (a) Formation of secretion granules
      Morphology
      Chemical nature of the secretion granules
   (b) Biochemical activities
      Synthesis of polysaccharides
      Transfer of proteins and their coupling to other molecules
   (c) Relationships between the Golgi apparatus and the endoplasmic reticulum

5. Origin

6. Conclusion

1. Introduction

This cell organelle owes its name to the Italian cytologist, Golgi, who described it for the first time in 1898 (a and b). After impregnation of a nervous tissue with a mixture of osmium tetroxide and rubidium bichromate during several days, Golgi brought to light a network around the nucleus taking a dark yellow colour which he named the internal reticular apparatus, now known as the Golgi apparatus. Following Golgi, a number of cytologists using other methods of impregnation, showed that heavy metals like osmium or silver revealed the same apparatus not only in nervous cells, but in a great number of other cellular types.

The impregnation with osmium (according to the methods of Mann–Kopsch or Kolatchev–Nassanov) is carried out in the following manner: the tissues fixed in Champy's mixture (chromic acid, potassium bichromate and osmium tetroxide), are post-osmicated during a period of 3 to 7 days at 37 °C in a 2% solution of osmium tetroxide. The silver impregnation methods are used for tissues previously fixed in a mixture of cobalt nitrate and formalin. The impregnation is carried out in a solution of silver nitrate for 24 to 48 hr.

In vertebrate somatic cells, the methods of impregnation result in deposits of heavy metals which have the appearance of a continuous network; in invertebrate cells and in vertebrate embryonic and germ cells, the deposits have the appearance of isolated scales. These scale-like structures were called dictyosomes (from the Greek *díctyon* = net) by Perroncito in 1910. In fact, the appearance as a network often corresponds to a very close grouping of scales and it can be considered that the Golgi apparatus of vertebrate somatic cells is formed of a group of dictyosomes.

A dictyosome observed with the light microscope after heavy metal impregnation seems to be composed of two regions: a region on which the deposit is formed, the chromophilic region which borders a lighter region where no deposits are formed, named the chromophobic region.

It should be noted that the Golgi apparatus, as it is revealed by the impregnations, has a characteristic morphology and localization for a given cellular type, and moreover, in cells having secretory activity, its development depends on the physiological condition of the cells. The methods of impregnation seem therefore to show that there is a particular organelle in the cells on which the osmium or silver is deposited. However, these results are obtained on previously fixed cells. In living cells, observation with a light microscope does not permit the identification of this organelle at the site where the deposits of heavy metals are formed in fixed cells. This is why, from the first descriptions of Golgi, the existence of this organelle has been questioned; the controversies on this subject lasted until 1954. The reader interested in the details of this argument may consult the reviews of Hibbard, Palay, or the more recent one of Bourne and Tewari. This is a typical case where progress on a particular point has been halted for half a century, due to the lack of technical means to answer the question. The answer to this question was obtained only after observing the ultrastructure of cells in thin sections with the electron microscope. In fact, the descriptions of Dalton and Felix (1954, 1955) proved the existence of the Golgi apparatus which, as we will now see, is a cellular organelle with its own individuality in the cell, from the morphological as well as the physiological point of view.

2. *Ultrastructure*

(a) *Description*

The Golgi apparatus, like the endoplasmic reticulum, is formed by a group of cavities each limited by a membrane, and situated in the cytoplasm of the cell. Unlike the endoplasmic reticulum which is polymorphous, the Golgi apparatus can be recognized by the far more organized arrangement of the membrane-bound cavities which form it. In the cellular regions where the deposits of heavy metals can be observed after impregnation, the examination of thin sections in the electron microscope shows the presence of stacks of flattened saccules or cisternae, each stack forming a dictyosome (Fig. 1).

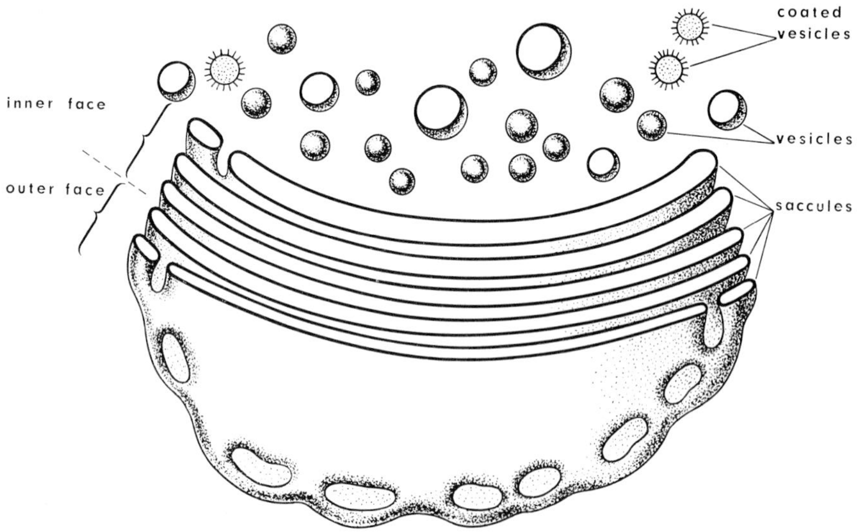

Fig. 1. Diagram illustrating the ultrastructure of a dictyosome. The dictyosome consists of a stack of flattened saccules. Numerous smooth vesicles and occasional coated vesicles are found in the vicinity of the inner or concave face of the stack.

Each saccule has the form of a disk, which is generally slightly concave, and whose edges are fenestrated. The saccules lie in parallel array and are separated from each other by about 200 Å. The number of saccules per dictyosome averages from 4 to 8. Each saccule is surrounded by a smooth membrane without ribosomes about 75 Å thick, which has a characteristic unit membrane structure with its three layers

(Sjöstrand 1963; Robertson; see also the chapter on the cell membrane in this book). The membrane of the saccule encloses a cavity about 150 Å wide whose edges are often dilated.

All the saccules of one particular dictyosome are not identical in their morphology; those on the outer or convex face are very flat whereas those on the inner or concave face are more dilated. Moreover, the electron opacity of these two categories of saccules is often different. On its outer face the dictyosome is often bordered by a cisterna of the endoplasmic reticulum.

On the inner face of the dictyosome and around its periphery as well, many vesicles 200 to 1000 Å in diameter can be seen. These vesicles are also limited by a membrane 75 Å thick, and their contents resemble those of the saccules. This group of vesicles is often formed by two populations: vesicles with smooth membranes which make up the greater part and coated vesicles which are generally less numerous (Bruni and Porter; Cunningham et al.; Holtzman et al.; Friend and Farquhar). As we will see further on, the Golgi vesicles are formed by the activity of the dictyosome and arise by budding of the saccules.

The stack of saccules forming a dictyosome is the characteristic morphological element of the Golgi apparatus. However, the numerous vesicles which occur in its vicinity and result from its functioning also must be included in the description. It should be stressed that the morphological studies show that the dictyosome has a polarity: its two faces, inner and outer, are formed of saccules differing in their aspect and their environment (Fig. 2).

Although no universal terminology has been adopted yet, the nomenclature that we use here is the most common. Moreover, we shall define a certain number of terms which occur in the literature. The group of dictyosomes and the vesicles in their vicinity are sometimes given the name of Golgi complex or Golgi component. Some authors, following the example of Sjöstrand (1956) use the name of gamma-cyto-membrane to indicate the membranes limiting the saccules of dictyosomes; others, like Grassé, use the term 'pôle distal' to speak of the outer face of the dictyosome and 'pôle proximal' for the inner face.

This typical structure of the Golgi apparatus, composed of stacks of saccules and vesicles, can be found in all the cells of the eukaryotes. The Golgi apparatus does not exist in the protokaryotes (bacteria and blue-green algae). In animal cells, the dictyosomes are often grouped around centrioles (see reviews in Carasso and Favard; Fawcett 1966). In plant cells, light microscopy was unable to prove the existence of a Golgi apparatus; with the electron microscope numerous dictyosomes can be seen scattered in the cytoplasm (see reviews in Buvat; Sievers; Mollenhauer and Morré).

The number of dictyosomes per cell depends on the cellular type; on an average it can be estimated at 20. In giant cells, for example the synergid cells of cotton (Jensen) or the salivary gland cells of diptera (Phillips and Swift), there may be several thousand dictyosomes. In certain unicellular organisms, on the other hand, there sometimes exists only one dictyosome.

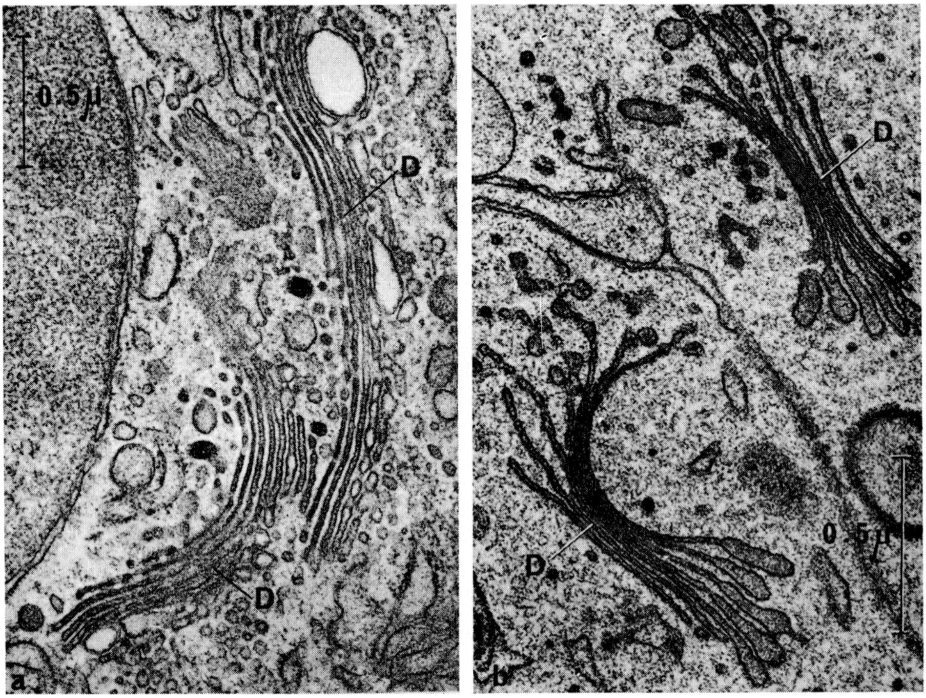

Fig. 2. Ultrastructure of dictyosomes (D) observed in thin sections of cells with the electron microscope. (a) Animal cell: rat plasma cell fixed with osmium tetroxide (micrograph by courtesy of J.P. Thiéry); (b) plant cell: corn root tip cell fixed with potassium permanganate (micrograph by courtesy of H.H. Mollenhauer, J. Leech and W.G. Whaley).

The morphological variations of the Golgi apparatus also involve the size of the dictyosomes whose diameter may vary, as well as the number of saccules which compose them. There are many saccules in certain brown algae for instance (Berkaloff), or in certain protozoa like the symbiotic flagellates (Grassé and Carasso; Grimstone; also see review in Anderson). Finally, the appearance of the contents of the saccules can vary according to the cellular types. The existence of crystalline structures has been pointed out (Linder; Barajas; Souza-Santos).

All that have been mentioned above are but minor variations on the same structure. Indeed, for a certain cellular type of a given organism, the Golgi apparatus has a very characteristic morphology.

(b) *Value of the observations*

The descriptions which have just been given are from micrographs of thin sections of cells fixed with osmium tetroxide and observed with the electron microscope. We must ask ourselves whether the structures described correspond to those which were observed in the past by the impregnation methods and if they really exist in the living cell.

The observation of cells, after impregnation with osmium, with the electron microscope shows that the deposits of osmium are formed on the dictyosomes in the most external saccules; but we still do not know the chemical nature of the constituent responsible for the reduction of the osmium tetroxide (Dalton and Felix 1955; Friend and Murray). The external saccules which reduce osmium tetroxide correspond to the chromophilic substance of the traditional cytology and the more dilated internal saccules correspond to the chromophobic substance. Thus we find once more, the polarized character of the dictyosomes.

There can be no doubt therefore, that the piles of saccules do represent the traditional Golgi apparatus. Do they exist in the living cell? It is noted, first of all, that the ultrastructure of the dictyosomes is unchanged when a fixative other than osmium is used (potassium permanganate or glutaraldehyde). However, glutaraldehyde preserves the contents of the saccules better than osmium and in certain cases it reveals the existence of fibers between the saccules (Mollenhauer; Turner and Whaley). Furthermore, when we freeze cells either by the method of freeze-substitution (Bullivant; Rebhun) or by freeze-etching (Fig. 3) (Moor; Moor et al.; Branton and Moor; Bullivant and Ames) we still observe the same ultrastructure of the Golgi apparatus. The evidence from this latter method, which least modifies the cellular structures, demonstrates the existence of the stacks of saccules in the living cell and shows they are not an artifact due to the techniques of preparation.

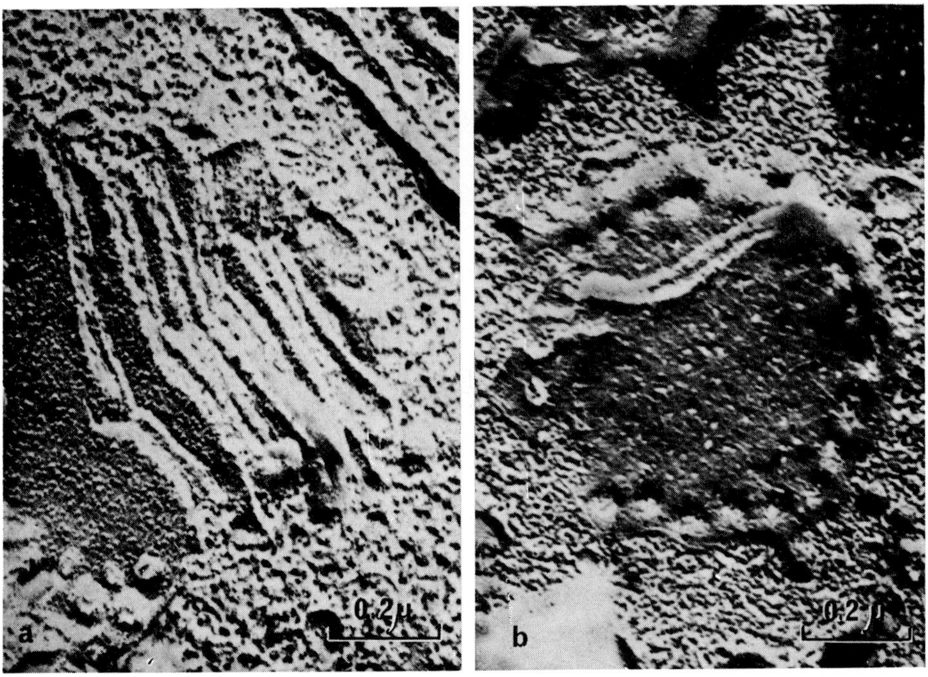

Fig. 3. Ultrastructure of dictyosomes of *Allium cepa* root tips, observed after freeze-etching. (a) Fractured dictyosome showing the stack of saccules; (b) face-on view showing the fenestrated appearance of the edge of the saccules (micrographs by courtesy of D. Branton and H. Moor).

In support of these converging observations, obtained after various processes of fixation using chemical or physical agents, it should be recalled that Monné in 1939 showed the existence of a positive birefringence in the cytoplasm of the living mollusc spermatocytes, observed in the polarizing microscope. This birefringence exists in the region of the spermatocytes where impregnation methods reveal dictyosomes and it is due to the organization of the saccules in piles which form an oriented structure. Observations in the phase-contrast microscope also demonstrate that in the living cell the contrast of the dictyosome region is different from that of the rest of the cytoplasm (Ludford and Smiles; Ludford et al.). In conclusion, we can say that the existence of the Golgi apparatus with its piles of saccules can no longer be questioned today.

3. *Chemical composition*

The study of the chemical composition of the Golgi apparatus can be carried out *in situ* by cytochemical methods, or on isolated Golgi apparatuses.

(a) *Study in situ by cytochemical methods*

At the light microscope level cytochemical methods give uncertain results since the thickness of the dictyosomes and the diameter of the vesicles are at the limit of resolution of this microscope and a precise localization is not possible. On the other hand, cytochemical methods at the ultrastructural level can give precise information. How-

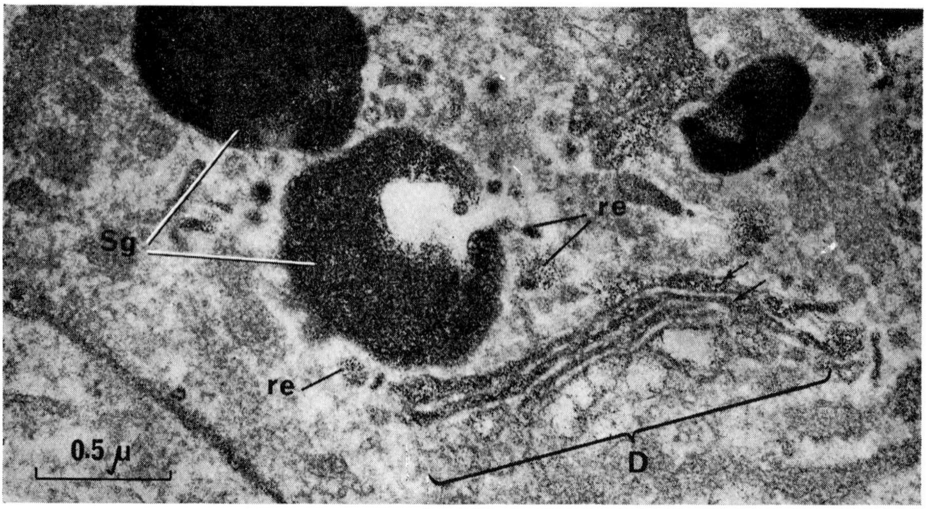

Fig. 4. Demonstration of polysaccharides in a dictyosome of a goblet cell of rat duodenum. The thiocarbohydrazide method produces the formation of electron-dense precipitates in regions of polysaccharide localization. The micrograph shows precipitate located in the outer saccules (arrows) of the dictyosome (D), in the vesicles (re) nearby and in the secretion granules (Sg) (micrograph by courtesy of J.P. Thiéry).

ever, there are few results so far and our knowledge in this field remains very fragmentary.

The presence of polysaccharides – sulfo- and sialomucins (Wetzel et al.) and mucopolysaccharides (Berlin; Thiéry) (Fig. 4) has been revealed in the cavities of the dictyosomes. These polysaccharides are especially abundant in the saccules of the inner face and also in the Golgi vesicles.

The existence of various enzymes has been demonstrated at the level of the dictyosome, in particular the phosphatases: nucleoside diphosphatases, thiamine pyrophosphatase or cocarboxylase, acid phosphatase (Novikoff et al. 1962; Goldfischer et al.; Novikoff 1965; Poux 1963, 1967) and peroxidase (Bainton and Farquhar 1967). These enzymatic activities are revealed on the saccules and vesicles but the precision of the localization is not fine enough to determine whether the corresponding enzymes are situated in the membrane or inside the cavities of the saccules and vesicles (Fig. 5).

A recent study has shown that the coated vesicles budded from the Golgi apparatus contain hydrolases which are characteristic of lysosomes; these vesicles are no doubt small primary lysosomes (Friend and Farquhar; also see review by Straus and the chapter on lysosomes in this book) which carry enzymes to the secondary lysosomes (multivesicular bodies, for instance).

It must be pointed out again that the study of enzymatic activities shows that the saccules are not all equivalent – thiamine pyrophosphatase, for example, only exists in the two or three saccules situated on the inner face of the dictyosome.

(b) *Chemical analysis of the Golgi fraction*

The preparation of Golgi fractions is very difficult to achieve and up to now only two research groups have succeeded in this experimental approach. The control of the purity of the fraction obtained must be carried out with the electron microscope. This test is indispensable as there is yet no biochemical criterion to distinguish the Golgi apparatus (Schneider and Kuff 1964).

The first relatively pure fractions were prepared from rat epididymis (Schneider and Kuff 1954; Kuff and Dalton). More recently, fractions have been prepared from plant cells (Morré and Mollenhauer; Morré et al. 1965a, b; Cunningham et al.) and from liver cells (Hamilton et al. 1967a). It was shown that it is important to stabilize the structures in the homogenate by a pre-fixation with glutaraldehyde before carrying out the gradient centrifugations. The fractions contain piles of saccules and vesicles. The fenestrated structure of the edges of the saccules is particularly well visible when the isolated dictyosomes are observed after negative staining.

The chemical analysis of these fractions is still at its beginning. Kuff and Dalton showed that these fractions contained phospholipids, proteins and acid phosphatase. Morré et al. (1965b) have determined the quantity of phospholipids, sterols and neutral lipids. The presence of phospholipids in these fractions corresponds to the presence of unit membranes in the dictyosomes.

Although the chemical nature of the constituents of the Golgi apparatus is little known, the physiology of this organelle is gradually coming to light.

4. *Physiology*

The morphological and radioautographic studies carried out at the ultrastructural level allow us to understand the role of the Golgi apparatus in the physiology of the cell.

(a) *Formation of secretion granules*

Morphology. In the study of thin sections of secretory cells it is possible to follow the

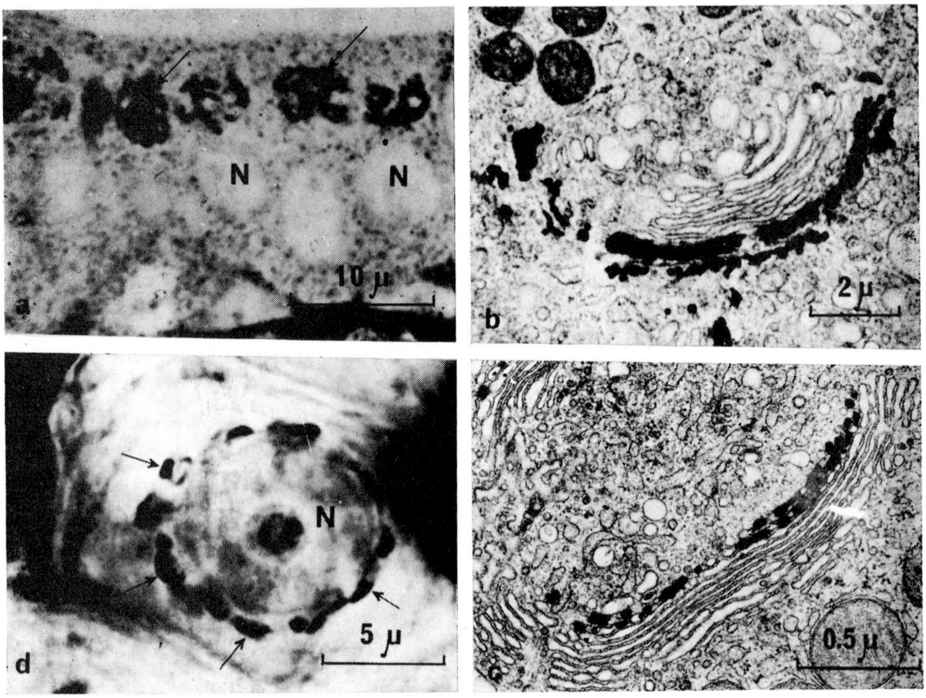

Fig. 5. Structure of the Golgi apparatus and polarity of the dictyosome. (a) and (b): Sections of mouse epididymis after osmium impregnation. (a) Light micrograph of a semi-thick section showing the Golgi apparatus (arrow) located near the nucleus (N) (micrograph by courtesy of K.R.Porter). (b) Electron micrograph of a thin section showing that the osmium is deposited in the outer saccules of the dictyosome. (c) In the same tissue, on the other hand, thiamine pyrophosphatase activity is demonstrated at the ultrastructural level by lead phosphate deposits located in the inner saccules of the dictyosome (micrographs b and c by courtesy of D.S.Friend). (d) Nerve cell showing the location of thiamine pyrophosphatase by precipitates of lead sulfate which are visible in the light microscope. This enzyme activity is located on the dictyosomes which can be distinguished in the form of scales disposed around the nucleus (N) (micrograph by courtesy of A.B.Novikoff).

formation of secretion granules by the dictyosomes. The saccules of the dictyosomes behave like cellular compartments in which the various substances are segregated and then released in the form of vesicles budded from the saccules. These vesicles fuse together to form secretion granules of ever increasing size. The secretion granules are generally transported outside of the cell. During their discharge the membrane which surrounds them fuses with the plasma membrane and we witness a sort of pinocytosis in reverse. It must be underlined that, from the moment when it is accumulated in the dictyosome until the moment when it is discharged, the product of secretion is always separated from the cytoplasm by a membrane. From the morphological point of view, the Golgi apparatus seems to play a role in the packing of the secretory products of the cell, for exportation or as storage for ulterior use.

This functioning of the Golgi apparatus has been observed in many animal and plant cells (Fig. 6). The reader can find many examples in the reviews by Palay; Kurosumi; Dalton; de Robertis et al.; Helander; Sievers; Mollenhauer and Morré

Chemical nature of the secretion granules. While it is difficult to specify the chemical constituents of the saccules, it is much easier to determine the chemical nature of the secretory products which are packaged by the Golgi apparatus to form the secretion granules. Indeed, the size of these granules makes their histochemical study possible with the light microscope and in some cases it has even been possible to isolate them by differential centrifugation for biochemical analysis.

The products of secretion are of a varied nature. Polysaccharides are found among them in the goblet cells of the intestine, for example (Palay), in the cells of Brunner's gland (Friend), in the mucous gland of the snail (Ovtracht) and in spermatids where the Golgi apparatus produces the acrosome (Burgos and Fawcett; Fawcett 1958, 1966; see also the review in Idelman). It must be noted that in general these polysaccharides are associated with proteins to form mucoprotein secretory granules.

In plant cells, the Golgi apparatus participates in the formation of the primary cell wall and the cell plate during mitosis (Leech et al.; Whaley and Mollenhauer; Whaley et al.). In this case, secretion granules contain acid polysaccharides belonging to the family of pectic substances. Slime and mucilages are also secreted by the Golgi apparatus (Schnepf 1964).

The secretion granules originating in the Golgi apparatus can also have a protein nature. We can cite the example of the zymogen granules in pancreatic acinar cells whose chemical analysis has been performed in detail after isolation (Palade et al.; Greene et al.). We can also cite, among others, the pituitary granules (Farquhar; Hymer and McShan; Smith and Farquhar), the azurophilic granules and eosinophilic granules of the polymorphonuclear leucocytes (Bainton and Farquhar 1966), and the protein granules of the mammary gland cells (Wellings and Philp). Finally, lipoprotein granules can be secreted by the dictyosomes in the hepatic cells, for example (Jones et al.; Hamilton et al. 1967b).

We have just seen that substances which differ greatly in their chemical nature and

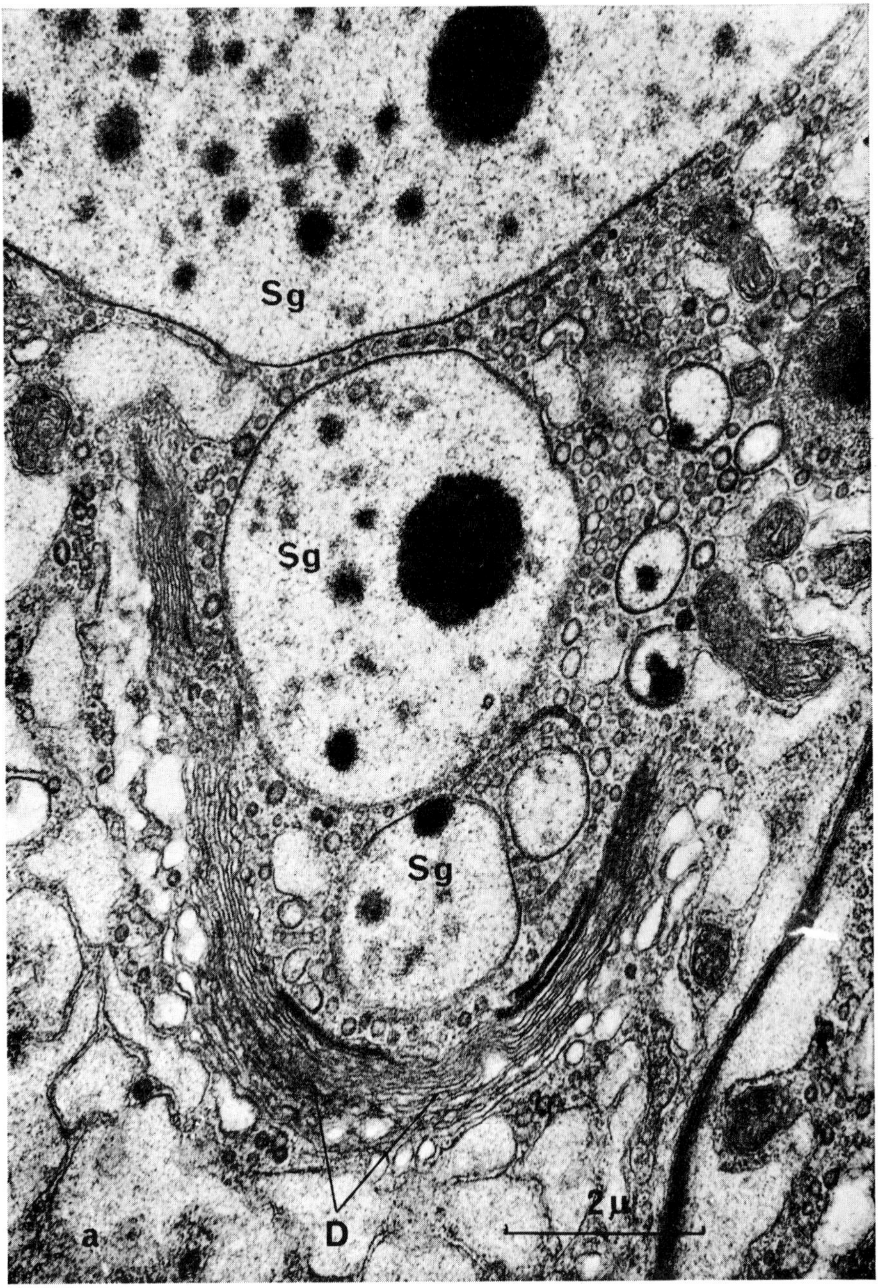

Fig. 6. Formation of secretion granules by the Golgi apparatus.
(a) In a cell from the snail mucous gland, numerous small vesicles on the inner face of a dictoysome (D) fuse to form the secretion granules (Sg) (micrograph by courtesy of L. Ovtracht).

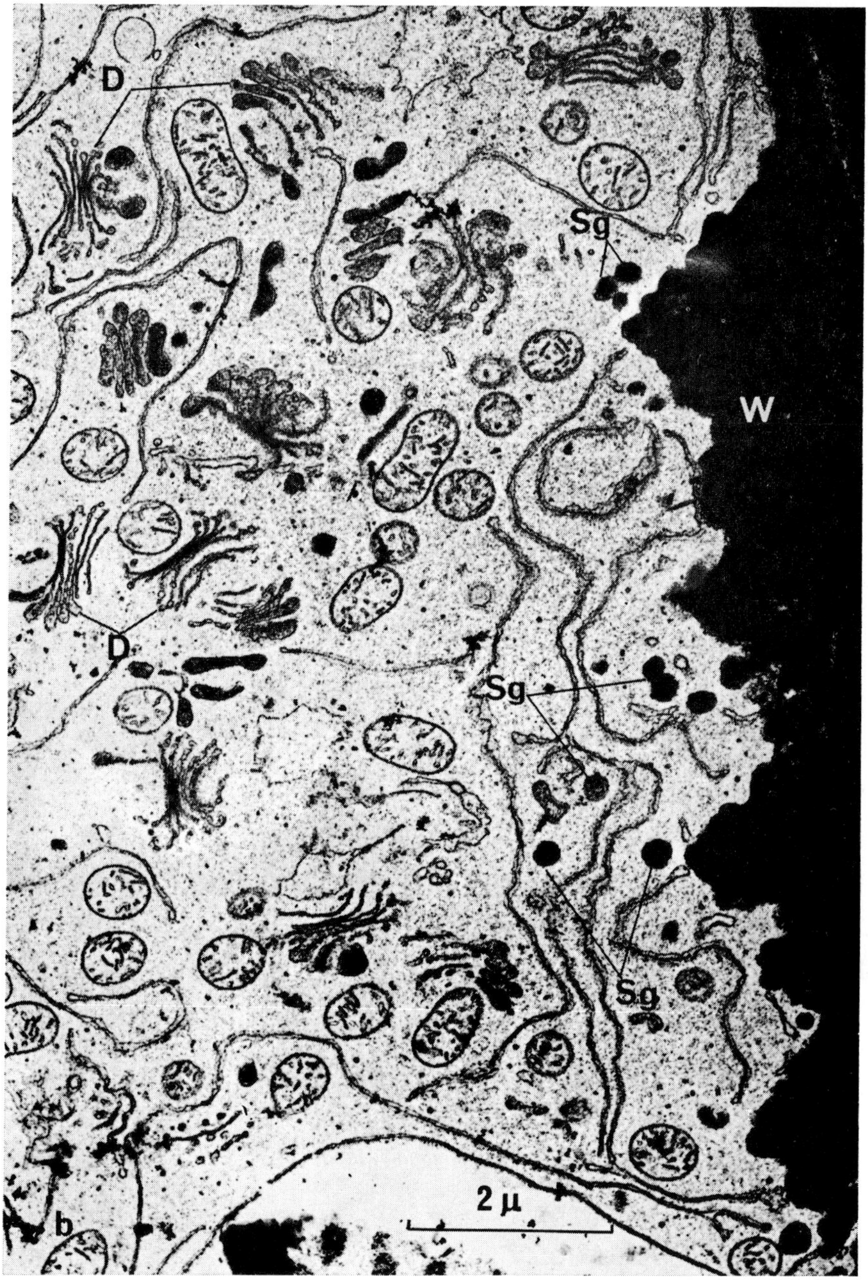

(b) The dictyosomes (D) in a corn root cell give rise to secretion granules (Sg) which move out of the cell; their content of polysaccharides contributes to the formation of the cell wall (W) (micrograph by courtesy of W.G. Whaley, J.E. Kephart and H.H. Mollenhauer).

which are most often polysaccharide or protein macromolecules, or a combination of the two, can be concentrated in the Golgi saccules. We must now investigate where the synthesis of these macromolecules occurs and what is the biochemical role played by the Golgi apparatus in the fabrication of these substances.

(b) *Biochemical activities*

Concerning the proteins found in the Golgi saccules, it is known that they are synthesized by the ribosomes (see chapter on the ribosomes in this book); the Golgi apparatus here plays the role of a collecting organelle only. We shall discuss this phenomenon further on. Conversely, radioautographic studies have shown that it is indeed in the dictyosomes that polysaccharide synthesis and possible subsequent coupling with proteins take place.

Synthesis of polysaccharides. The synthesis of polysaccharides has been followed in the goblet cells of the rat colon by Neutra and Leblond (1966a, b) using radioautographic methods. At 5 min after an intraperitoneal injection of glucose-6-^{3}H, the

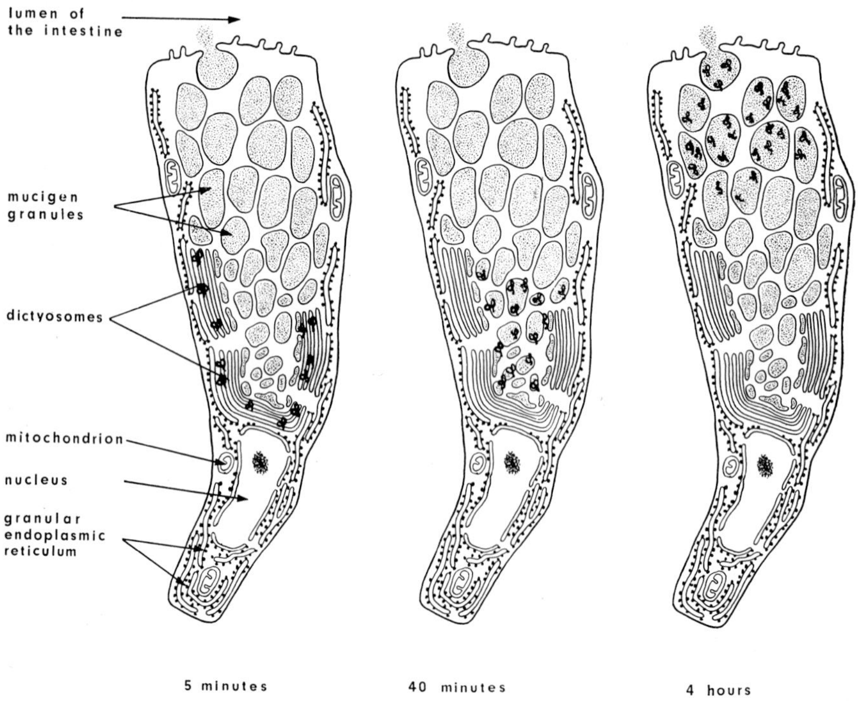

Fig. 7. Diagrams showing the organization of a goblet cell from rat colon and the localization of radioactivity after injection of ^{3}H-glucose. (a) At 5 min after injection, the radioactivity is located in the dictyosomes; (b) At 40 min, the radioactivity is found in the mucous granules near the dictyosomes; (c) At 4 hr, the mucous granules situated near the lumen are radioactive (after M. Neutra and C. P. Leblond).

radioactivity is concentrated in the dictyosomes; at 20 min after injection of the tracer, the silver grains are located on the dictyosomes and on the mucous droplets nearest the Golgi apparatus. At 40 min after injection, the radioactivity has completely disappeared from the Golgi saccules and only the mucous droplets situated close to the dictyosomes are labeled; at 4 hr after injection, the mucous droplets of the apical cell region alone are radioactive (Fig. 7). This experiment shows that the polysaccharides of the mucous droplets are synthesized in the Golgi saccules and carried to the apical region of the cell; their contents are finally discharged into the intestinal lumen. This synthesis of polysaccharides by the Golgi apparatus can be carried out either from glucose or from galactose, or again from both precursors according to the different cellular types, as shown by radioautographic studies at the light microscope level (Peterson and Leblond; Neutra and Leblond 1966b).

In the Golgi apparatus of certain cellular types, the goblet cells for instance, there is not only a polymerization of the glucose units but also a sulfatation of sugars (Jennings and Florey; Lane et al.). Here again, the radioautographic method makes it possible to observe the evolution of the labeling after injection of $^{35}SO_4$. The radioactivity is first of all located in the Golgi apparatus, then, a little later in the mucous granules. The sulfatation of sugars in the Golgi apparatus has also been shown in chondrocytes (Fewer et al.; Godman and Lane).

In plant cells, the Golgi apparatus also synthesizes certain polysaccharides of the cell wall. After incubation of wheat root tips in a medium containing D [1- or 6-H^3] glucose, radioactivity is first detected in the dictyosomes, later in the Golgi vesicles and finally in the cell wall (Northcote and Pickett-Heaps; Pickett-Heaps). Biochemical analysis shows that the polysaccharides are of the hemi-cellulose and pectic groups, radioactivity is mainly linked to galactose and arabinose. In these cells, it seems that the dictyosomes contain a pool of precursors for the synthesis of certain polysaccharides of the cell wall, but they are certainly not involved in the synthesis of the cellulose itself.

Transfer of proteins and their coupling to other molecules. In cells where the Golgi apparatus produces protein secretion granules, the proteins arise in the granular endoplasmic reticulum. It can be stated that following synthesis by the ribosomes, the proteins pass into the cavities of the endoplasmic reticulum and then into the Golgi apparatus which plays a collecting role, before being discharged from the cell.

This phenomenon has been well studied by biochemical and radioautographic methods in the guinea pig and in the pigeon pancreas by Palade and Siekevitz's group (Palade 1959; Siekevitz and Palade 1960a and b; Caro; Palade et al.; Caro and Palade; Redman and Sabatini; Redman et al.; Jamieson and Palade 1965, 1967); and by Leblond's group (Warshawsky et al.; Nadler). After injection of tritiated leucine radioautography indicates that the granular endoplasmic reticulum is labeled in 5 min; after 20 min only the reticulum near the Golgi apparatus is labeled as well as the dictyosomes. One hour after the injection, only the young zymogen granules which also can be called condensing vacuoles, as well as the typical zymogen granules are labeled. The discharge of the labeled zymogen granules occurs 4 hr after injection of the radioactive precursor (Fig. 8). From these experiments and from the biochemical

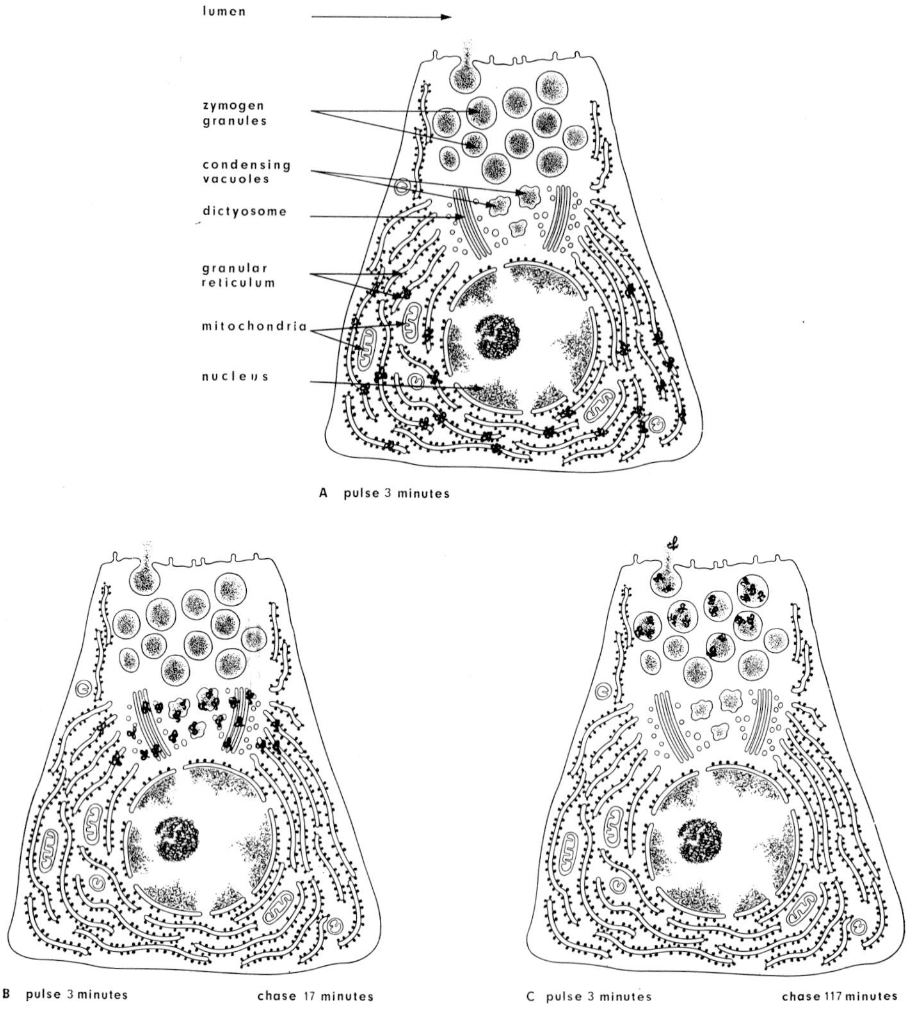

Fig. 8. Diagrams showing the organization of a guinea pig pancreatic acinar cell and the localization of radioactivity after injection of ^{3}H-leucine. (a) After a 3 min pulse, the rough endoplasmic reticulum is labeled. (b) After a 3 min pulse and 17 min chase, the rough endoplasmic reticulum near the dictyosomes, the Golgi apparatus and the condensing vacuoles are labeled. (c) After a 3 min pulse and 117 min chase, only the zymogen granules at the apical pole are labeled (after J. D. Jamieson and G. E. Palade).

analysis of fractions of granular and agranular reticulum and zymogen granules, we can present the following scheme of events:

(a) the enzymic proteins of the pancreatic juice are synthesized by the ribosomes which are attached to the membranes of the endoplasmic reticulum.
(b) these proteins are then transferred into and segregated in the cavities of the endoplasmic reticulum.
(c) they are subsequently carried into the cavities of the dictyosomes which collect and pack them to form the zymogen granules.
(d) the zymogen granules migrate to the apical cytoplasm and are discharged.

A similar sequence of events has been described for other cells in which the Golgi apparatus acts in the transfer of proteins (Fig. 9): in the mammary gland, for example (Wellings and Philp), in chondrocytes (Revel and Hay) and in myelocytes (Fedorko and Hirsch; also see reviews by Porter and Leblond). It must be noted that not all proteins which are segregated in the cavities of the endoplasmic reticulum are transferred through the Golgi apparatus. Thus, in fibroblasts, the collagen precursors after their segregation in the endoplasmic reticulum are discharged directly into the extracellular environment without passing through the dictyosomes (Ross; Ross and Benditt). In the same way, in the spinal ganglion cells (Droz 1965, 1967) and in the secretory cells of carnivorous plants (Schnepf 1963), the Golgi apparatus is not involved in the transition of all the proteins which accumulate in the endoplasmic reticulum.

It appears that the proteins which will be coupled in varying proportions to polysaccharides to form muco- or glycoproteins pass through the Golgi saccules. We already know that the polysaccharides which are used in this coupling are synthesized in the Golgi apparatus. The coupling of proteins with lipids can also occur in the dictyosomes, but our present knowledge on this subject is still very scarce. We can mention here the case of lipoproteins produced by the hepatic cell (Stein and Stein).

(c) *Relationships between the Golgi apparatus and the endoplasmic reticulum*

It has just been seen that the proteins accumulated in the cavities of the endoplasmic reticulum are transferred to the Golgi saccules. We can ask ourselves by what procedure this transfer from one system of cavities to another is accomplished. Two methods can be considered: either the proteins leave the cavities of the endoplasmic reticulum and pass into the hyaloplasm before they are segregated in the Golgi saccules, or the passage from one compartment to the other occurs without liberation of protein in the hyaloplasm. In the latter case, we must look for the means of transport.

The morphological observations on the ultrastructural level enable us to establish the presence of numerous vesicles in the space included between the most external Golgi saccules and the endoplasmic reticulum. Close observation of the endoplasmic reticulum in this zone reveals that the cisternae nearest the dictyosomes are agranular and seem to bud off small vesicles. These static images suggest that the transfer of proteins occurs within the vesicles which arise from the endoplasmic reticulum and then open into the most external Golgi saccule. These vesicles which form what has been called the transition elements (Zeigel and Dalton) can be seen in many types of cells (Fig. 10a) (Palade 1961; Fauré-Fremiet et al.; Mollenhauer and Whaley; Novikoff and Shin; Bouck; Friend; Kessel; Ovtracht).

Transfer by these vesicles has been demonstrated by Jamieson and Palade (1965, 1967). From slices of pancreas incubated in leucine-^{14}C, the authors have isolated several fractions: (1) a smooth microsomal fraction, which corresponds mainly to the

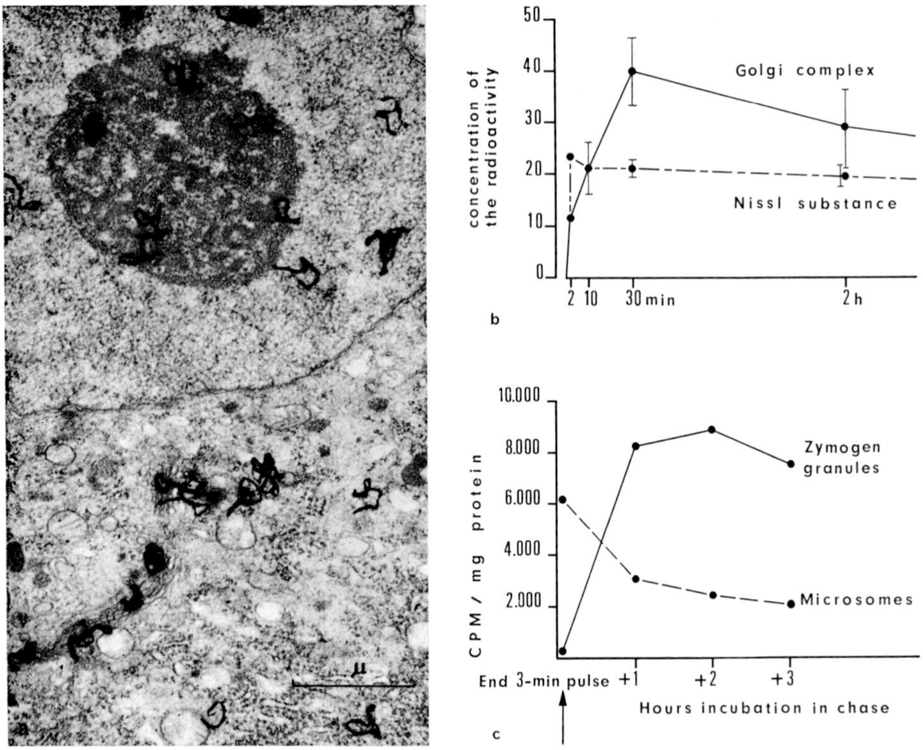

Fig. 9. (a) Autoradiograph of a ganglion nerve cell of a rat having received an injection of ^{3}H-leucine. At 30 min after injection, silver grains are located on the Golgi apparatus and on the nucleus and nucleolus (micrograph by courtesy of B. Droz). (b) Evolution of the concentration of radioactivity in the Golgi apparatus and the rough endoplasmic reticulum (Nissl substance) in neurones. The concentration is measured by counting the number of silver grains associated with each structure on a number of autoradiographs comparable to Fig. 9a. At first located in the reticulum, the activity moves toward the Golgi apparatus (after B. Droz). (c) Evolution of the radioactivity in the microsome and zymogen granule fractions prepared from slices of guinea pig pancreas incubated in medium containing ^{14}C-leucine. After a 3 min pulse, the radioactivity is chased during a variable period. The radioactivity is first concentrated in the microsome fraction, then it diminishes. This is simultaneous with an increase of activity in the zymogen granule fraction (after J. D. Jamieson and G. E. Palade).

transition elements and to the Golgi saccules, which have been more or less fragmented during the preparation, (2) a rough microsomal fraction containing elements

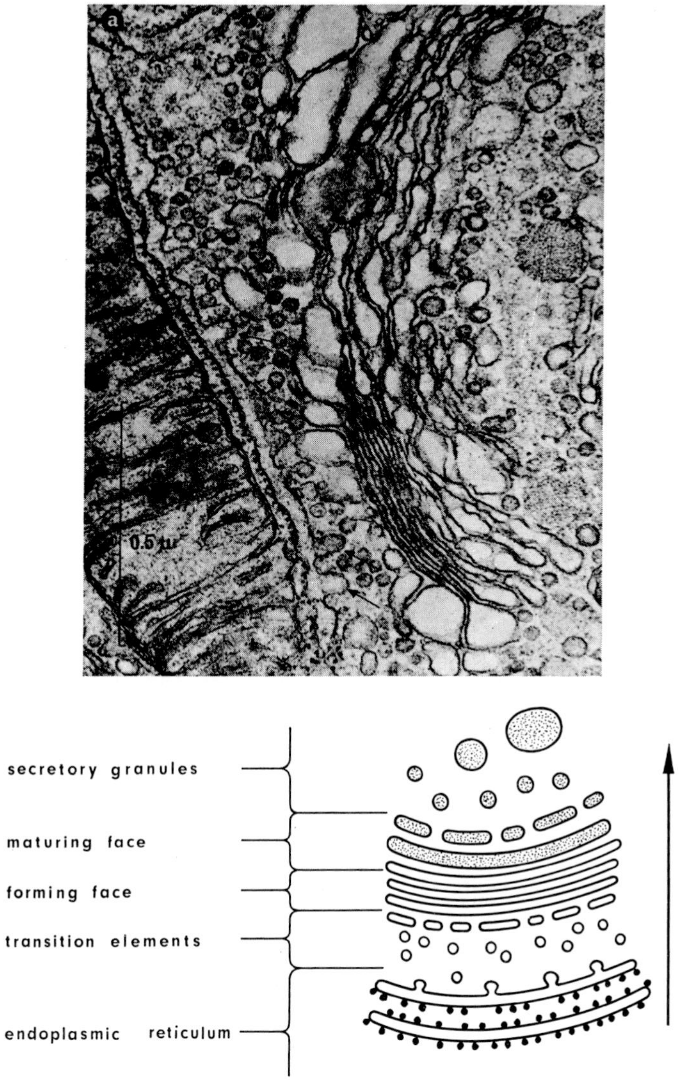

b

Fig. 10. Relations between the endoplasmic reticulum and the Golgi apparatus. (a) Micrograph of a Brunner's gland cell showing vesicles (arrows) which bud from the endoplasmic reticulum and transport protein toward the Golgi apparatus; M, mitochondrion (micrograph by courtesy of D.S. Friend). (b) Diagram illustrating the relation between the endoplasmic reticulum and a dictyosome via the transition elements. New saccules are built on the forming face while those on the maturing face fragment to form secretion granules.

of the granular reticulum, and (3) a zymogen granule fraction. After 3 min incubation the rough microsomal fraction only is labeled. After a 7 min chase, they note that the labeling has decreased in the rough microsomal fraction, while the smooth microsomal fraction has become radioactive. After a longer chase, the radioactivity decreases in the smooth microsomal fraction and appears in the zymogen granules. The labeling observed in the microsomal fractions corresponds to that of the proteins contained in the vesicles; indeed, after an alkaline extraction, which retains the membranes of the microsomes but empties them of their proteins, the radioactivity disappears. From these experiments we can conclude that the proteins are carried from the endoplasmic reticulum toward the Golgi apparatus inside the vesicles whose membrane isolates them from the hyaloplasm.

In the same way it appears that proteins having passed through the Golgi apparatus can then pass into the cavities of the smooth endoplasmic reticulum. Such is the case for the hydrolases which are probably carried by the coated vesicles. Indeed, the existence of a smooth endoplasmic reticulum on the inner face of the dictyosomes where lysosomes can also be formed, has been described in certain cells. This region where the Golgi apparatus, endoplasmic reticulum and lysosomes are found together has been called GERL by Novikoff in order to emphasize the functional association of these organelles (Novikoff 1964; Novikoff et al. 1964; Holtzman et al.).

5. *Origin*

From what we have just seen in the dictyosomes of the cells which secrete proteins, there is a continual contribution of membrane from the vesicles budding off the endoplasmic reticulum. This contribution compensates for the loss of membrane due to the budding of the vesicles that form the secretion granules. Furthermore, one often observes that the vesicles budded by the endoplasmic reticulum align themselves in a row along the most external Golgi saccule. This suggests that the new saccules are formed on the outer face of the dictyosome by the fusion of the aligned vesicles, whereas the most internal saccule appears to break up into vesicles which go to form the secretion granules. This hypothesis, put forward by Grassé in 1957, has been taken up since by many authors and in particular by Mollenhauer and Whaley who call the outer face of the dictyosome, situated near the endoplasmic reticulum, the 'forming face', and the inner face of the dictyosome against which the secretion granules appear, the 'maturing face' (Fig. 10b).

This formation of dictyosomes from the vesicles arising from the endoplasmic reticulum is the hypothesis which is at the moment the most compatible with the morphological, physiological and biochemical results obtained. This hypothesis is consistent with the studies showing that the number of saccules: (1) changes according to the physiological conditions, (2) decreases in the starving cell (Grimstone), and (3) increases when the formation of secretion granules is blocked (Whaley et al.; Schnepf

1964). It is also known that the dictyosomes completely disappear in the enucleated cell (Flickinger). The same hypothesis partly accounts for the turnover of phospholipids during secretion (Hokin and Hokin). In the goblet cells of the intestine, it is possible to estimate that a new Golgi saccule is formed every 3 min (Neutra and Leblond 1966a).

Other hypotheses concerning the origin of the Golgi apparatus which have been put forward can be found in a report by Whaley; they are interesting but are not backed up with as much proof as the one we have developed above.

6. *Conclusion*

As we have just seen, the Golgi apparatus is an organelle which has its own individuality in the cell. It synthesizes polysaccharides which can be exported directly or coupled in the Golgi saccules with proteins coming from the cavities of the endoplasmic reticulum (Fig. 11). Although the physiological study of the Golgi apparatus is just beginning, its functional aspects as we know them at present, are perhaps the most important.

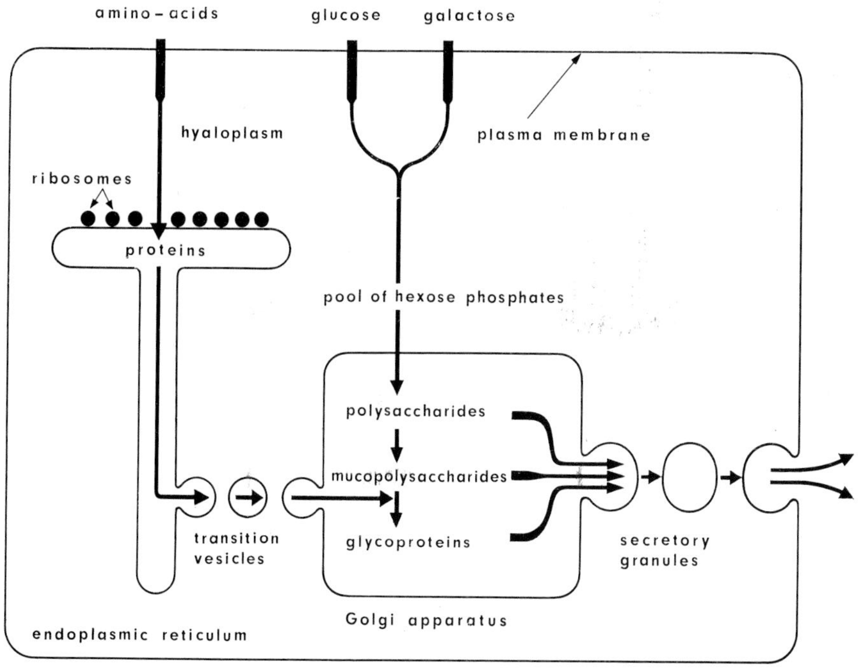

Fig. 11. Diagram summarizing the role of the Golgi apparatus in the cell.

References

ANDERSON, E.: Cytoplasmic organelles and inclusions of protozoa. In: Tze-Tuan Chen, ed.: Research in Protozoology, Vol. 1. (1967) p. 1.

BAINTON, D.F. and M.G.FARQUHAR: Origin of granules in polymorphonuclear leukocytes. J. Cell Biol. 28 (1966) 277.

BAINTON, D.F. and M.G.FARQUHAR: Segregation and packaging of granule enzymes in eosinophils. J. Cell Biol. 35 (1967) 6A.

BARAJAS, L.: The development and ultrastructure of the juxtaglomerular cell granule. J. Ultrastruct. Res. 15 (1966) 400.

BERKALOFF, C.: Les cellules méristématiques d'*Himanthalia lorea* (L.) SF. Gray. Etude au microscope électronique. J. Microscopie 2 (1963) 213.

BERLIN, J.D.: The localization of acid mucopolysaccharides in the Golgi complex of intestinal goblet cells. J. Cell Biol. 32 (1967) 760.

BOUCK, G.B.: Fine structure and organelle associations in brown algae. J. Cell Biol. 26 (1965) 523.

BOURNE, G.H. and H.B.TEWARI: Mitochondria and the Golgi complex. In: G.H.Bourne, ed.: Cytology and cell physiology. New York, Academic Press (1964) p. 377.

BRANTON, D. and H.MOOR: Fine structure in freeze-etched *Allium cepa* L. root tips. J. Ultrastruct. Res. 11 (1964) 401.

BRUNI, C. and K.R.PORTER: The fine structure of the parenchymal cell of the normal rat liver. Am. J. Pathol. 46 (1965) 691.

BULLIVANT, S.: The staining of thin sections of mouse pancreas prepared by the Fernández-Morán helium II freeze-substitution method. J. Biophys. Biochem. Cytol. 8 (1960) 639.

BULLIVANT, S. and A.AMES: A simple freeze-fracture replication method for electron microscopy. J. Cell Biol. 29 (1966) 435.

BURGOS, M.H. and D.W.FAWCETT: Studies on the fine structure of the mammalian testis I. Differentiation of the spermatids in the cat (*Felis domestica*). J. Biophys. Biochem. Cytol. 1 (1955) 287.

BUVAT, R.: Electron microscopy of plant protoplasm. Intern. Rev. Cytol. 14 (1963) 41.

CARASSO, N. and P.FAVARD: L'appareil de Golgi. In: C.Magnan, ed.: Traité de Microscopie électronique. Paris, Hermann 2 (1961) 963.

CARO, L.G.: Electron microscopic radioautography of thin sections: the Golgi zone as site of protein concentration in pancreatic acinar cells. J. Biophys. Biochem. Cytol. 10 (1961) 37.

CARO, L.G. and G.E.PALADE: Protein synthesis, storage and discharge in the pancreatic exocrine cell. J. Cell Biol. 20 (1964) 473.

CUNNINGHAM, W.P., D.J.MORRÉ and H.H.MOLLENHAUER: Structure of isolated plant Golgi apparatus revealed by negative staining. J. Cell Biol. 28 (1966) 169.

DALTON, A.J.: Golgi apparatus and secretion granules. In: J.Brachet and A.E.Mirsky, eds.: The cell, Vol. 2. New York, Academic Press (1961) p. 603.

DALTON, A.J. and M.D.FELIX: Cytological and cytochemical characteristics of the Golgi substance of epithelial cells of the epididymis *in situ*, in homogenates and after isolation. Am. J. Anat. 94 (1954) 171.

DALTON, A.J. and M.D.FELIX: A study of the Golgi substance and ergastoplasm in a series of mammalian cell types. In: Fine structure of cells. Groningen, Noordhoff (1955) p. 274.

DROZ, B.: Fate of newly synthesized proteins in neurons. In: C.P.Leblond and K.B.Warren, eds.: The use of radioautography in investigating protein synthesis. New York, Academic Press (1965) p. 159.

DROZ, B.: Synthèse et transfert des protéines cellulaires dans les neurones ganglionnaires; étude radioautographique quantitative en microscopie électronique. J. Microscopie 6 (1967) 201.

FARQUHAR, M.G.: Origin and fate of secretory granules in cells of the anterior pituitary gland. Trans. N.Y. Acad. Sci. 23 (1961) 346.

FAURÉ-FREMIET, E., P. FAVARD and N. CARASSO: Etude au microscope électronique des ultrastructures d'*Epistylis anastatica*. J. Microscopie 1 (1962) 287.

FAWCETT, D. W.: Changes in the fine structure of the cytoplasmic organelles during differentiation. In: D. Rudnick, ed.: Developmental cytology. New York, The Ronald Press Co. (1958) p. 161.

FAWCETT, D. W.: The cell, its organelles and inclusions. An atlas of fine structure. Philadelphia, W. B. Saunders Co. (1966).

FEDORKO, M. E. and J. G. HIRSCH: Cytoplasmic granule formation in myelocytes. An electron microscope radioautographic study on the mechanism of formation of cytoplasmic granules in rabbit heterophilic myelocytes. J. Cell Biol. 29 (1966) 307.

FEWER, P., J. THREADGOLD and H. SHELDON: Studies on cartilage: electron microscopic observations on the autoradiographic localization of S^{35} in cells and matrix. J. Ultrastruct. Res. 11 (1964) 166.

FLICKINGER, C. J.: Electron microscope study of enucleated *Amoeba proteus*. J. Cell Biol. 35 (1967) 40A.

FRIEND, D. S.: The fine structure of Brunner's glands in the mouse. J. Cell Biol. 25 (1965) 563.

FRIEND, D. S. and M. G. FARQUHAR: Functions of coated vesicles during protein absorption in the rat vas deferens. J. Cell Biol. 35 (1967) 357.

FRIEND, D. S. and M. J. MURRAY: Osmium impregnation of the Golgi apparatus. Am. J. Anat. 117 (1965) 135.

GODMAN, G. C. and N. LANE: On the site of sulfation in the chondrocyte. J. Cell Biol. 21 (1964) 353.

GOLDFISCHER, S., E. ESSNER and A. B. NOVIKOFF: The localization of phosphatase activities at the level of ultrastructure. J. Histochem. Cytochem. 12 (1964) 72.

GOLGI, C.: Sur la structure des cellules nerveuses. Arch. Ital. Biol. 30 (1898a) 60.

GOLGI, C.: Sur la structure des cellules nerveuses des ganglions spinaux. Arch. Ital. Biol. 30 (1898b) 278.

GRASSÉ, P. P.: Ultrastructure, polarité et réproduction de l'appareil de Golgi. Compt. Rend. Acad. Sci. 245 (1957) 1278.

GRASSÉ, P. P. and N. CARASSO: Ultrastructure of the Golgi apparatus in protozoa and metazoa (somatic and germinal cells). Nature 179 (1956) 31.

GREENE, L. J., C. H. W. HIRS and G. E. PALADE: On the protein composition of bovine pancreatic zymogen granules. J. Biol. Chem. 238 (1963) 2054.

GRIMSTONE, A. V.: Cytoplasmic membrane and the nuclear membrane in the flagellate *Trichonympha*. J. Biophys. Biochem. Cytol. 6 (1959) 369.

HAMILTON, R. L., D. J. MORRÉ, R. MAHLEY and V. S. LE QUIRE: Morphologic studies of a Golgi apparatus-rich cell fraction isolated from rat liver. J. Cell Biol. 35 (1967a) 53A.

HAMILTON, R. L., D. M. REGEN, M. E. GRAY and V. S. LE QUIRE: Lipid transport in liver I. Electron microscopic identification of very low density lipoproteins in perfused rat liver. Lab. Invest. 16 (1967b) 305.

HELANDER, H. F.: Morphology of animal secretory cells. In: Funktionelle und morphologische Organisation der Zelle. Sekretion und Exkretion. Berlin, Springer-Verlag (1965) p. 2.

HIBBARD, H.: Current status of our knowledge of the Golgi apparatus in the animal cell. Quart. Rev. Biol. 20 (1945) 1.

HOKIN, L. E. and M. R. HOKIN: Biochemical aspects of excitation of protein secretion in pancreas. In: Funktionelle und morphologische Organisation der Zelle. Sekretion und Exkretion. Berlin, Springer-Verlag (1965) p. 49.

HOLTZMAN, E., A. B. NOVIKOFF and H. VILLAVERDE: Lysosomes and GERL in normal and chromatolytic neurons of the rat ganglion nodosum. J. Cell Biol. 33 (1967) 419.

HYMER, W. C. and W. H. MCSHAN: Isolation of rat pituitary granules and the study of their biochemical properties and hormonal activities. J. Cell Biol. 17 (1963) 67.

IDELMAN, S.: Données récentes sur l'infrastructure du spermatozoïde. Ann. Biol. Animale, Biochim. Biophys. 6 (1967) 113.

JAMIESON, J.D. and G.E.PALADE: Role of the Golgi complex in the intracellular transport of secretory proteins. Proc. Natl. Acad. Sci. U.S. 55 (1965) 424.

JAMIESON, J.D. and G.E.PALADE: Intracellular transport of secretory proteins in the pancreatic exocrine cell I. Role of the peripheral elements of the Golgi complex. II. Transport to condensing vacuoles and zymogen granules. J. Cell Biol. 34 (1967) 577.

JENNINGS, M. and H.W.FLOREY: Autoradiographic observations on the mucous cell of the stomach and intestine. Quart. J. Exptl. Physiol. 41 (1956) 131.

JENSEN, W.W.: The ultrastructure and histochemistry of the synergids of cotton. Am. J. Botany 52 (1965) 238.

JONES, A.L., N.B.RUDERMAN and M.G.HERRERA: An electron microscopic study of lipoprotein production and release by the isolated perfused rat liver. Proc. Soc. Exptl. Biol. Med. 123 (1966) 4.

KESSEL, R.G.: Some observations on the ultrastructure of the oocyte of *Thyone briareus* with special reference to the relationship of the Golgi complex and endoplasmic reticulum in the formation of yolk. J. Ultrastruct. Res. 16 (1966) 305.

KUFF, E.L. and A.J.DALTON: Biochemical studies of isolated Golgi membranes. In: T.Hayashi, ed.: Subcellular particles. New York, The Ronald Press Co. (1959) p. 114.

KUROSUMI, K.: Electron microscopic analysis of the secretion mechanism. Intern. Rev. Cytol. 11 (1961) 1.

LANE, N., L.CARO, R.OTERO-VILARDEBO and G.C.GODMAN: On the site of sulfatation in colonic goblet cells. J. Cell Biol. 21 (1964) 339.

LEBLOND, C.P.: What radioautography has added to protein lore. In: C.P.Leblond and K.B.Warren, eds.: The use of radioautography in investigating protein synthesis. New York, Academic Press (1965) p. 321.

LEECH, J.H., H.H.MOLLENHAUER and W.G.WHALEY: Ultrastructural changes in the root apex. Symp. Soc. Exptl. Biol. 17 (1963) 74.

LINDER, E.: Ueber Struktur, Bildung und Sekretion der Bakteroidkristalle von Lumbriciden. Z. Zellforsch. Mikroskop. Anat. 64 (1964) 338.

LUDFORD, R.J. and J.SMILES: Cytological characteristics of fibroblasts and sarcoma cells demonstrable by phase-contrast microscopy. J. Roy. Microscop. Soc. 70 (1950) 186.

LUDFORD, R.J., J.SMILES and F.V.WELCH: The study of living malignant cells by phase-contrast and ultra-violet microscopy. J. Roy. Microscop. Soc. 68 (1948) 1.

MOLLENHAUER, H.H.: An intercisternal structure in the Golgi apparatus. J. Cell Biol. 24 (1965) 504.

MOLLENHAUER, H.H. and D.J.MORRÉ: Golgi apparatus and plant secretion. Ann. Rev. Plant. Physiol. 17 (1966) 27.

MOLLENHAUER, H.H. and W.G.WHALEY: An observation on the functioning of the Golgi apparatus. J. Cell Biol. 17 (1963) 222.

MONNÉ, L.: Polarisationsoptische Untersuchungen über den Golgi Apparat und die Mitochondrien männlicher Geschlechtszellen einiger Pulmonaten Arten. Protoplasma 32 (1939) 184.

MOOR, H.: Die Gefrier-fixation lebender Zellen und ihre Anwendung in der Elektronenmikroskopie. Z. Zellforsch. Mikroskop. Anat. 62 (1964) 546.

MOOR, H., C.RUSKA and H.RUSKA: Elektronenmikroskopische Darstellung tierischer Zellen mit der Gefrierätztechnik. Z. Zellforsch. Mikroskop. Anat. 62 (1964) 581.

MORRÉ, D.J. and H.H.MOLLENHAUER: Isolation of the Golgi apparatus from plants cells. J. Cell Biol. 23 (1964) 295.

MORRÉ, D.J., H.H.MOLLENHAUER and J.E.CHAMBERS: Glutaraldehyde stabilization as an aid to Golgi apparatus isolation. Exptl. Cell Res. 38 (1965a) 672.

MORRÉ, D.J., H.H.MOLLENHAUER and W.P.CUNNINGHAM: Chemical and structural analysis of dialdehyde stabilized Golgi apparatus. Plant Physiol. Suppl. 40 (1965b) XXIX.

NADLER, N.J.: Calculations of the turnover times of proteins in each region of the acinar cells of the pancreas. J. Cell Biol. 16 (1963) 24.

NEUTRA, M. and C.P. LEBLOND: Synthesis of the carbohydrate of mucus in the Golgi complex as shown by electron microscope radioautography of goblet cells from rats injected with glucose-H^3. J. Cell Biol. 30 (1966a) 119.

NEUTRA, M. and C.P. LEBLOND: Radioautographic comparison of the uptake of galactose-H^3 and glucose-H^3 in the Golgi region of various cells secreting glycoproteins or mucopolysaccharides. J. Cell Biol. 30 (1966b) 137.

NORTHCOTE, D.H. and J.P. PICKETT-HEAPS: A function of the Golgi apparatus in polysaccharide synthesis and transport in the root-cap cells of wheat. Biochem. J. 98 (1966) 159.

NOVIKOFF, A.B.: GERL, its form and function in neurons of rat spinal ganglia. Biol. Bull. 127 (1964) 358.

NOVIKOFF, A.B.: Enzymic activities and functional interrelations of cytomembranes. In: S. Seno and E.V. Cowdry, eds.: Intracellular membranous structure. Okayama, Japan Society for Cell Biology (1965) p. 277.

NOVIKOFF, A.B., E. ESSNER, S. GOLDFISCHER and M. HEUS: Nucleosidephosphatase activities of cytomembranes. In: R.J.C. Harris, ed.: The interpretation of ultrastructure. New York, Academic Press (1962) 149.

NOVIKOFF, A.B., E. ESSNER and N. QUINTANA: Golgi apparatus and lysosomes. Federation Proc. 23 (1964) 1010.

NOVIKOFF, A.B. and W.Y. SHIN: The endoplasmic reticulum in the Golgi zone and its relations to microbodies, Golgi apparatus and autophagic vacuoles in rat liver cells. J. Microscopie 3 (1964) 187.

OVTRACHT, L.: Ultrastructure des cellules sécrétrices de la glande multifide de l'escargot. J. Microscopie 6 (1967) 773.

PALADE, G.E.: Functional changes in the structure of cell components. In: T. Hayashi, ed.: Subcellular particles. New York, The Ronald Press Co. (1959) p. 64.

PALADE, G.E.: Secretory process of the pancreatic exocrine cell. In: J.D. Boyd, F.R. Johnson and J.D. Lever, eds.: Electron microscopy in anatomy. Baltimore, Williams and Wilkins Co. (1961) p. 176.

PALADE, G.E., P. SIEKEVITZ and L.G. CARO: Structure, chemistry and function of the pancreatic exocrine cell. In: Ciba foundation symposium on the exocrine pancreas. London, J. and A. Churchill (1962) p. 23.

PALAY, S.L.: Morphology of secretion. In: Frontiers in cytology. New Haven, Yale University Press (1958) p. 303.

PERRONCITO, A.: Contribution à l'étude de la biologie cellulaire. Mitochondries, chromidies et appareil réticulaire interne dans les cellules spermatiques. Arch. Ital. Biol. 54 (1910) 307.

PETERSON, M. and C.P. LEBLOND: Synthesis of complex carbohydrates in the Golgi region, as shown by radioautography after injection of labeled glucose. J. Cell Biol. 21 (1964) 143.

PHILLIPS, D.M. and H. SWIFT: Cytoplasmic fine structure of Sciara salivary gland I. Secretion. J. Cell Biol. 27 (1965) 395.

PICKETT-HEAPS, J.D.: Further observations on the Golgi apparatus and its functions in cells of the wheat seedling. J. Ultrastruct. Res. 18 (1967) 287.

PORTER, K.R.: Cell fine structure and biosynthesis of intercellular macromolecules. In: The New-York heart association. Connective tissue: intercellular macromolecules. London, J. and A. Churchill (1964) p. 167.

POUX, N.: Localisation de la phosphatase acide dans les cellules méristématiques de Blé (*Triticum vulgare* Vill.). J. Microscopie 2 (1963) 485.

POUX, N.: Localisation d'activités enzymatiques dans les cellules du méristème radiculaire de *Cucumis sativus* L. I. Activités phosphatasiques neutres dans les cellules du protoderme. J. Microscopie 6 (1967) 1043.

REBHUN, L.I.: Application of freeze-substitution to electron microscope studies of invertebrate oocytes. J. Biophys. Biochem. Cytol. 9 (1961) 785.

REDMAN, C.M. and D.D.SABATINI: Tectorial discharge of peptides released by puromycin from attached ribosomes. Proc. Natl. Acad. Sci. U.S. 56 (1966) 608.

REDMAN, C.M., P.SIEKEVITZ and G.E.PALADE: Synthesis and transfer of amylase in pigeon pancreatic microsomes. J. Biol. Chem. 241 (1966) 1150.

REVEL, J.P. and E.D.HAY: An autoradiographic and electron microscopic study of collagen synthesis in differentiating cartilage. Z. Zellforsch. Mikroskop. Anat. 61 (1963) 110.

DE ROBERTIS, E., W.NOWINSKI and F.SAETZ: Cell Biology. Philadelphia, W.B.Saunders Co. (1965) 427.

ROBERTSON, J.D.: Unit membrane: a review with recent new studies of experimental alterations and a new subunit structure in synaptic membranes. In: M.Locke, ed.: Cellular basis in development. New York, Academic Press (1964) p. 1.

ROSS, R.: Synthesis and secretion of collagen by fibroblasts in healing wounds. In: C.P.Leblond and K.B.Warren, eds.: The use of radioautography in investigating protein synthesis. New York, Academic Press (1965) p. 273.

ROSS, R. and E.P.BENDITT: Wound healing and collagen formation V. Quantitative electron microscope radioautographic observations of proline-H^3 utilization by fibroblasts. J. Cell Biol. 27 (1965) 83.

SCHNEIDER, W.C. and E.L.KUFF: On the isolation and some biochemical properties of the Golgi substance. Am. J. Anat. 94 (1954) 209.

SCHNEIDER, W.C. and E.L.KUFF: Centrifugal isolation of subcellular components. In: G.H.Bourne, ed.: Cytology and cell physiology. New York, Academic Press (1964) p. 19.

SCHNEPF, E.: Zur Cytologie und Physiologie planzlicher Drüsen III. Cytologische Veränderungen in der Drüsen von *Drosophyllum* während der Verdauung. Planta 59 (1963) 351.

SCHNEPF, E.: Physiologie und Morphologie sekretorischer Pflanzenzellen. In: Funktionelle und morphologische Organization der Zelle. Sekretion und Exkretion. Berlin, Springer-Verlag (1964) p. 72

SIEKEVITZ, P. and G.E.PALADE: A cytochemical study on the pancreas of the guinea pig V. *In vivo* incorporation of leucine-1-^{14}C into the chymotrypsinogen of various cell fractions. J. Biophys. Biochem. Cytol. 7 (1960a) 619.

SIEKEVITZ, P. and G.E.PALADE: A cytochemical study on the pancreas of the guinea pig VI. Release of enzymes and ribonucleic acid from ribonucleoprotein particles. J. Biophys. Biochem. Cytol. 7 (1960b) 631.

SIEVERS, A.: Funktion des Golgi-Apparates in pflanzlichen und tierischen Zellen. In: Funktionelle und morphologische Organisation der Zelle. Sekretion und Exkretion. Berlin, Springer-Verlag (1965) p. 89.

SJÖSTRAND, F.S.: Ultrastructure of cells as revealed by the electron microscope. Intern. Rev. Cytol. 5 (1956) 455.

SJÖSTRAND, F.S.: A comparison of plasma membranes, cytomembranes and mitochondrial membranes with respect to ultrastructural features. J. Ultrastruct. Res. 9 (1963) 561.

SMITH, R.E. and M.G.FARQUHAR: Lysosome function in the regulation of the secretory process in cells of anterior pituitary gland. J. Cell Biol. 31 (1966) 319.

SOUZA-SANTOS, H. de: The ultrastructure of the mucous granules from starfish tube feet. J. Ultrastruct. Res. 16 (1966) 259.

STEIN, O. and Y.STEIN: Lipid synthesis, intracellular transport, storage and secretion I. Electron microscopic radioautographic study of liver after injection of tritiated palmitate or glycerol in fasted and ethanol treated rats. J. Cell Biol. 33 (1967) 319.

STRAUS, W.: Lysosomes, phagosomes and related particles. In: D.B.Roodyn, ed.: Enzyme cytology. New York, Academic Press (1967) p. 239.

THIÉRY, J.P.: Mise en évidence des polysaccharides sur coupes fines au microscope électronique. J. Microscopie 6 (1967) 987.

TURNER, F.R. and W.G.WHALEY: Intercisternal elements of the Golgi apparatus. Science 147 (1965) 1303.

WARSHAWSKY, H., C.P.LEBLOND and B.DROZ: Synthesis and migration of proteins in the cells of the exocrine pancreas as revealed by specific activity determination from radioautographs. J. Cell Biol. 16 (1963) 1.

WELLINGS, S.R. and J.R.PHILP: The function of the Golgi apparatus in lactating cells of the BALB/c Crgl mouse. An electron microscopic and autoradiographic study. Z. Zellforsch. Mikroskop. Anat. 61 (1964) 871.

WETZEL, M.G., B.K.WETZEL and S.S.SPICER: Ultrastructural localization of acid mucosubstances in the mouse colon with iron containing stains. J. Cell Biol. 30 (1966) 299.

WHALEY, W.G.: Proposals concerning replication of the Golgi apparatus. In: Funktionelle und morphologische Organisation der Zelle. Sekretion und Exkretion. Berlin, Springer-Verlag (1965) p. 340.

WHALEY, W.G., J.E.KEPHART and H.H.MOLLENHAUER: The dynamic of cytoplasmic membranes during development. In: M.Locke, ed.: Cellular membranes in development. New York, Academic Press (1964) p. 135.

WHALEY, W.G. and H.H.MOLLENHAUER: The Golgi apparatus and cell plate formation: a postulate. J. Cell Biol. 17 (1963) 216.

ZEIGEL, R.F. and A.J.DALTON: Speculations based on the morphology of the Golgi systems in several types of protein-secreting cells. J. Cell Biol. 15 (1962) 45.

Note added in proof

Since this chapter was written a number of papers have appeared, of which the following are selected:

AMOS, W.B. and A.V.GRIMSTONE: Intercisternal material in the Golgi body of *Trichomonas*. J. Cell Biol. 38 (1968) 466.

ANDERSON, E.: Oocyte differentiation in the sea urchin, *Arbacia panetulata*, with particular reference to the origin of cortical granules and their participation in the cortical reaction. J. Cell Biol. 37 (1968) 514.

BEAMS, H.W. and R.G.KESSEL: The Golgi apparatus: structure and function. Intern. Rev. Cytol. 23 (1968) 209.

FLICKINGER, C.J.: The effect of enucleation on the cytoplasmic membranes of *Amoeba proteus*. J. Cell Biol. 37 (1968) 300.

FRANCK, A.L. and A.K.CHRISTENSEN: Localization of acid phosphatase in lipofuscin granules and possible antophagic vacuoles in interstitial cells of the guinea pig testis. J. Cell Biol. 36 (1968) 1.

JAMIESON, J.D. and G.E.PALADE: Intracellular transport of secretory proteins in the pancreatic exocrine cell. III – Dissociation of intracellular transport from protein synthesis. J. Cell Biol. 39 (1968) 580.

JAMIESON, J.D. and G.E.PALADE: Intracellular transport of secretory proteins in the pancreatic exocrine cell. IV – Metabolic requirements. J. Cell Biol. 39 (1968) 589.

YOUNG, R.W. and B.DROZ: The renewal of protein in retinal rods and cones. J. Cell Biol. 39 (1968) 169.

PART XIII

Ultrastructure and biochemistry of lysosomes and peroxisomes

CHAPTER 42

Biochemistry and function of lysosomes

R. WATTIAUX

Facultés Universitaires Notre Dame de la Paix, Namur, Belgium

Contents

1. Introduction
2. General biochemical properties of lysosomes
   (a) Nature and specificity of lysosomal enzymes
   (b) Structure-linked latency of lysosomal enzymes
   (c) Some physical properties of lysosomes
3. Functions of lysosomes
   (a) Heterophagic function
   (b) Autophagic function
   (c) Role of lysosomes in physiological processes
   (d) Inadequate function of lysosomes
4. Biochemical methods of study of lysosomes
   (a) Identification of acid hydrolases in tissue homogenates
   (b) Analysis of the distribution pattern of acid hydrolases after differential and isopycnic centrifugation
   (c) Isolation of lysosomes in a pure state
5. Morphology of lysosomes
   (a) Morphologic heterogeneity of lysosomes in living cells
   (b) Identification of lysosomes in subcellular fractions

1. Introduction

Lysosomes are cytoplasmic particles discovered in rat liver tissue about 14 years ago by de Duve and his coworkers. Since then, they have been found in many other animal tissues and there is some evidence that they also exist in plants. These organelles are characterized by their polymorphism, so they cannot easily be distinguished by any typical size or structure. Only their biochemical properties, principally their enzyme content, and the structure-linked latency of these enzymes, define them individually. The intracellular functions of lysosomes depend on their lytic potential; these organelles are involved both in physiological and in some pathological processes.

Papers on lysosomes are getting more and more numerous and it is not possible in this chapter to refer to all that has been published in this field. The reader who is interested in a more exhaustive coverage of some particular aspect of the subject is referred to the following earlier reviews. The discovery and mode of study of lysosomes are described in: de Duve (1959, 1963a, 1965); Novikoff (1961, 1963), and the Ciba Foundation Symposium on Lysosomes (1963).

A discussion of their functions and pathology appears in: de Duve and Wattiaux; de Duve (1964); Weissmann; and the Pathology Symposium on Lysosomes.

2. General biochemical properties of lysosomes

(a) *Nature and specificity of lysosomal enzymes*

All the enzymes which have been localized unambiguously in lysosomes have been found to be hydrolases. All these, already identified in rat liver lysosomes, are reported in Table 1. As has been shown, these granules seem to be deficient in lipolytic enzymes. Until now, only a sphingomyelinase could be found in hepatic lysosomes. However, one cannot be certain that this is a real deficiency because not enough experimental work has yet been done in this field. Very recent results of Stoffel and Greten, obtained on purified rat liver lysosomes, seem to indicate that these granules are endowed with a significant hydrolytic activity towards phosphatidyl choline, triglycerides and cholesteryl linoleate. Moreover, in a short communication, Blaschko et al. have recently described the presence of a phospholipase A in bovine surrenal lysosomes.

The optimum *p*H of lysosomal hydrolases is acid (between 3 and 6); their specificities are various, and thus these enzymes seem to be able to degrade practically all biological macromolecules: proteins, polysaccharides, nucleic acids. However, we have little information about the chemistry of these degradations: the degree of hydrolysis of the polymer substrate, the exact nature of the digestion products, and other processes. It should be realized how very important a good knowledge of these processes is for an adequate understanding of the mechanism of the intracellular digestion performed by the lysosomes.

According to the recent work of Hutterer, and that of Aronson and Davidson,

TABLE 1

Acid hydrolases which have been found in rat liver lysosomes.

Biological substrates	Enzymes
Phosphate esters	Acid phosphatase
Proteins	Cathepsin
	Collagenase
	Phosphoprotein phosphatase
	Arylamidase
Nucleic acids	Acid ribonuclease
	Acid deoxyribonuclease
Polysaccharides and mucopolysaccharides	α-glucosidase
	β-N-acetylglucosaminidase
	β-glucuronidase
	β-galactosidase
	α-mannosidase
	β-xylosidase
	Aryl-sulphatase
	Hyaluronidase
	Neuraminidase
Lipids	Sphingomyelinase
	Esterase*

* As indicated by cytochemical techniques. For a discussion of this problem see Holt.

lysosomal hyaluronidase of rat liver is able to hydrolyse highly polymerized hyaluronic acid into small oligosaccharides. Coffey, in a preliminary note, has reported that hepatic lysosomal cathepsin can digest human globin into small peptides and amino-acids; thus, in these two cases, an extensive hydrolysis of the macromolecular substrate occurs following the action of lysosomal enzymes.

Little is known also about the special physicochemical properties of purified lysosomal hydrolases. In this connection may be cited the work already referred to of Aronson and Davidson on rat liver hyaluronidase, that of Bernardi and his coworkers on pig spleen acid nucleases and acid phosphomonoesterase, and that of Robinson and his coworkers on several rat kidney acid glycosidases.

(b) *Structure-linked latency of lysosomal enzymes*

The lysosomal membrane acts as an effective barrier between the enzymes enclosed in the granule and the external substrates. This phenomenon was demonstrated on granule preparations isolated in an isotonic medium, 0.25 M sucrose. The activity of the acid hydrolases of the preparation is markedly enhanced by treatment with detergents, by repeated freezing and thawing, and other agents (Fig. 1). The responses of the different hydrolases are simultaneous without being necessarily of the same amplitude for each enzyme. The increase in activity is usually accompanied by liberation of part of the enzymes in a soluble form into the suspension medium. This property has led to lysosomes being regarded as sac-like granules containing acid hydrolases in solution and surrounded by a membrane impermeable to several substances, particularly to the substrates of these hydrolases. Little information exists as to the composition of the membrane, which is probably of lipoprotein nature. Information obtained from the physiology of lysosomes (see below) suggests that striking structural analogies exist between the lysosomal membrane and the cell membrane.

The experimental characterization of the latency of lysosomal enzymes is based on a double determination of the activity of acid hydrolases: the *free activity* and the *total activity*. The free activity is measured in an appropriate isotonic medium (usually 0.25 M sucrose) using a short incubation time to minimize the effect of temperature, and of acid *p*H, on the lysosomal membrane. In the case of the rat liver, for example, the incubation time does not exceed 10 min at 37 °C and *p*H 5. Total activity can be

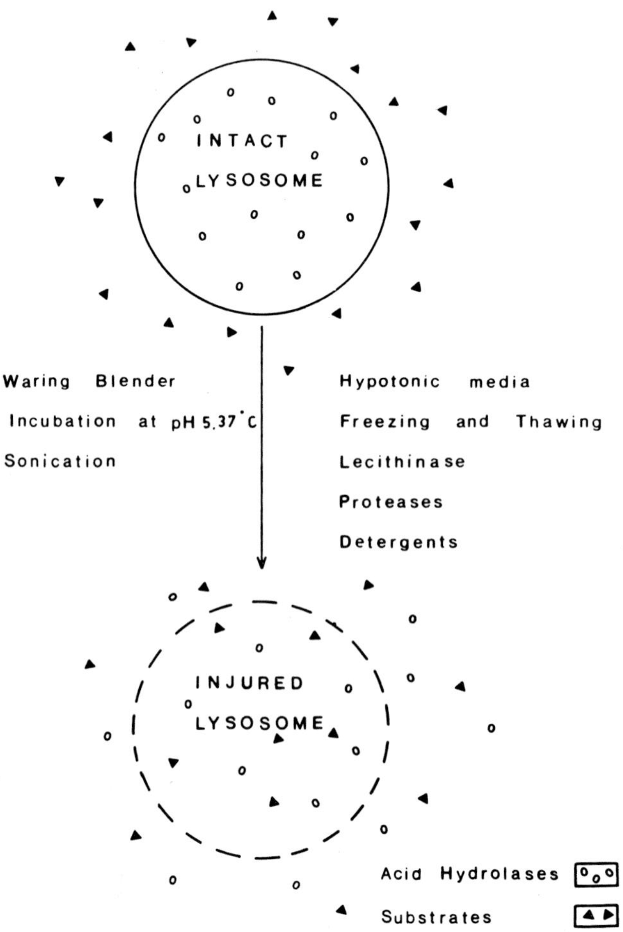

Fig. 1. Schematic representation of the structure-linked latency of lysosomal hydrolases.

obtained after submitting the granules to a treatment sufficient to disrupt the membrane. A commonly used method consists in adding a given concentration of Triton X-100, a non-ionic detergent, to the incubation medium (Wattiaux and de Duve). Some difficulties arise from the experimental determinations of free activity. It is assumed that the granule preparation has been isolated by mild procedures in order to keep the membrane of the lysosomes intact. In fact, a major problem lies in the homogenisation of the tissue which needs relatively drastic procedures. This may be very difficult in some cases (muscle, for example). This, surely, mainly accounts for the important differences existing between the free activities of lysosomal enzymes in homogenates of different tissues.

(c) *Some physical properties of lysosomes*

The information given in this section has been obtained as a result of extensive investigations on rat liver lysosomes by de Duve and coworkers.

According to these authors, rat liver lysosomes behave like granules consisting of an osmotic space, a space freely accessible to sucrose, and a hydrated matrix. The results which have led to these assumptions come from centrifugation experiments. Some quantitative characteristics of these spaces, together with other physical properties of rat liver lysosomes, are given in Table 2. Values have been calculated by de Duve (1965) taking into account the behaviour of two reference enzymes of lysosomes, acid phosphatase and acid deoxyribonuclease. Very significant differences appear when one compares the results obtained using one or the other reference enzyme alone. This is explained chiefly by the great heterogeneity of the lysosomal population.

Little information on this problem is available from lysosomes from other tissues. Some results obtained on rat kidney (Wattiaux-de Coninck et al.) and, more recently,

TABLE 2

Physical properties of rat liver lysosomes.*

	Acid phosphatase	Acid DNase
Dry weight (μg)	2.7×10^{-8}	3.6×10^{-8}
Dry density	1.300	1.331
Osmotically active solutes (milliosmoles/g dry weight)	0.128	0.334
Water compartments (cm^3/g dry weight)		
Hydration	0.256	0.212
Sucrose space	1.075	0.330
Osmotic space in 0.25 M sucrose	0.485	1.265
Total in 0.25 M sucrose	1.816	1.807
Sedimentation coefficient in 0.25 M sucrose (Svedberg units)	4.4×10^3	5×10^3
Diameter in 0.25 M sucrose (μ)	0.51	0.56
Density in 0.25 M sucrose	1.103	1.100

* According to de Duve (1965).

on a transplanted hepatoma (Wattiaux and Wattiaux-de Coninck) seem to indicate that lysosomes of these tissues exhibit similar physical properties to those of lysosomes found in rat liver.

3. *Functions of lysosomes*

Lysosomes take part in intracellular digestion phenomena involving both exogenous materials taken up by the cell, and cellular components. The former process is called the *heterophagic function*, and the latter the *autophagic function* of lysosomes.

(a) *Heterophagic function*

The first indication of the biological role of lysosomes was found in the tubular reabsorption of proteins by the kidney. Straus studied the hyaline droplets found in rat kidney and observed that these droplets contain proteins which have been pinocytosed by the cells of the proximal tubule. They were found to be rich in acid hydrolases and comparable to lysosomes. This observation led to the hypothesis that lysosomes were the site of the intracellular digestion of substances taken up by the cell. This hypothesis has been confirmed by numerous studies on different kinds of cells (liver, kidney thyroid cells, polynuclears, macrophages, protozoa, etc.) and with different substances such as proteins, polysaccharides, etc. (de Duve and Wattiaux).

The results obtained allow us to schematize the heterophagic function of lysosomes in the following way (Fig. 2). The extracellular component: macromolecule, virus or bacteria, is taken in by 'endocytosis' i.e. within a vacuole or *phagosome* arising from invagination of the cell membrane. A phagosome can fuse with another phagosome or it may divide into smaller vacuoles, but its ultimate fate is to fuse with a lysosome. That lysosome may be a *primary lysosome* i.e. a newly synthesised granule which has not yet been involved in digestion phenomena, or a *secondary lysosome*, i.e. a digestive vacuole which has already been the site of hydrolytic events.

In this way exogenous substances are exposed to lysosomal hydrolases and will be degraded to the extent that they are susceptible to hydrolytic attack by these enzymes. Micromolecular degradation products will probably diffuse through the membrane into the cytoplasm. Undigested residues will be confined inside the lysosomes where they are sometimes visible in the electron microscope, as membranous remnants, for example. Lysosomes which have taken part in a digestive process can fuse with other phagosomes and so be engaged in new digestive events. Finally, residues are either eliminated by exocytosis, as is seen in many protozoa, or they may accumulate, if the cell is unable to excrete them in this way.

It is important to note that the heterophagic function of lysosomes is performed in a closed space made of vacuoles isolated from the cytoplasm and surrounded by a membrane related to the cell membrane. Phagosomes and secondary lysosomes can be considered as portions of the extracellular medium enclosed in the cell, and into which primary lysosomes secrete digestive enzymes. The term *vacuolar apparatus* has been proposed for this set of vacuoles; it may be compared to a discontinuous digestive tract in which circulation of material is made possible as a result of fusion and separation processes (de Duve and Wattiaux).

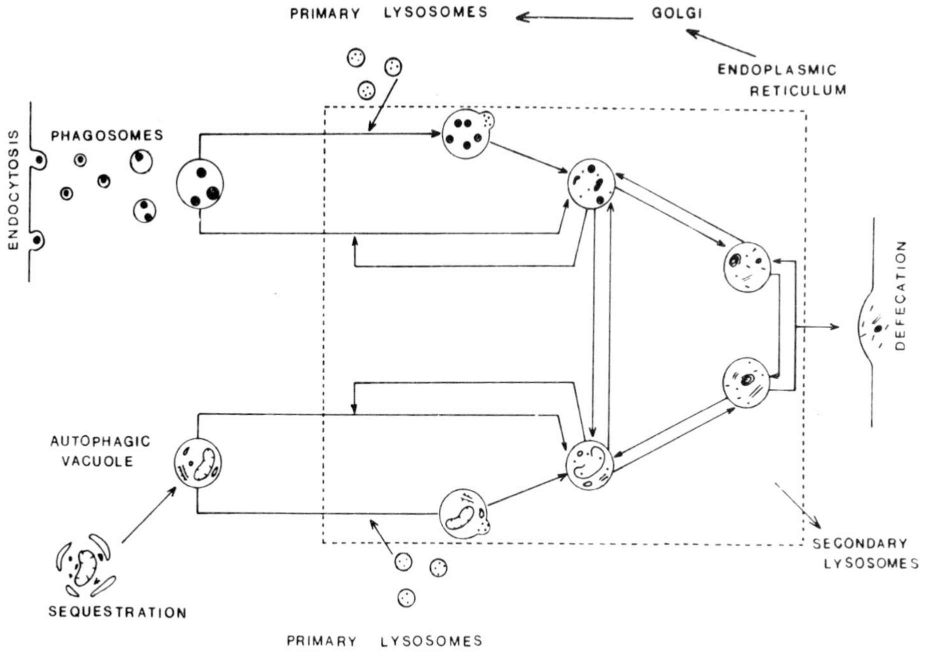

Fig. 2. Schematic representation of the heterophagic and autophagic functions of lysosomes.

It should be pointed out that the origin of primary lysosomes is by no means clear. Several results, principally those of Cohn and his coworkers, suggest that lysosomes are built in a manner similar to that used by the cell to make secretion granules. Acid hydrolases would be synthesized in the rough endoplasmic reticulum and finally liberated from that apparatus into vesicles which become detached and give primary lysosomes. However, more experimental work is needed to determine whether this is a general mechanism which could account for the formation of lysosomes in each kind of cell.

(b) *Autophagic function*

Numerous morphological works have described, in different kinds of cell, the presence of circumscribed cytoplasmic areas in various states of degradation. These zones can be depicted as vacuoles surrounded by a membrane, often unique and containing debris of mitochondria, endoplasmic reticulum, etc. (Figs. 7 and 9). They are known as cytolysomes (Novikoff 1959; Novikoff and Essner) cytosegresomes (Ericsson) or autophagic vacuoles (de Duve 1963b). They are encountered under normal conditions of cellular life but are often more common in differentiating cells or in cells undergoing some metabolic stress, such as starvation, hormonal stimulus or aging. They also appear to be more numerous in cells exhibiting high endocytic activity.

It seems very probable that this focal autolysis is carried out by lysosomal enzymes; indeed, various morphological observations have clearly demonstrated a positive reaction of acid phosphatase in the autolyzing regions (Fig. 7). Moreover, biochemical changes affecting rat liver lysosomes have been reported in conjunction with an increase of autophagic vacuoles in this organ when the animal has been injected with glucagon (Deter and de Duve).

The mechanism of focal autolysis raises some problems which chiefly concern the origin of the membranes surrounding the autophagic vacuoles and the manner in which acid hydrolases reach the vacuoles. An extensive discussion of these problems can be found in the review of de Duve and Wattiaux. To conclude, a plausible hypothesis seems to be that which supposes a coalescence of membranous vesicles (pinocytosis vesicles or endoplasmic reticulum vesicles?) leading to a kind of 'autophagosome' which would acquire acid hydrolases by fusion with a lysosome.

(c) *Role of lysosomes in physiological processes*

Unicellular organisms and, to some extent, even metazoan cells, make use of the heterophagic function of lysosomes in nutrition processes. Moreover, thanks to the autophagic function, endogenous components may be utilizable when exogenous food is not available. With this nutritive role of the lysosomes are associated more specialized functions, mainly in the metazoan cells. The granules take an active part in cell defence against various pathogenic bodies, such as bacteria, viruses and toxic macromolecules. Numerous works illustrate the role of lysosomes in lytic phenomena, leading to the disappearance of intracellular organelles or structures, during differentiation, metamorphosis or organ regression. It has been suggested that, because of its autophagic function, the lysosomal system plays a role in the catabolic phase of the turnover of cellular components.

These functions associated with autonomous cell life, can be integrated in various physiological events: fertilization, immunity reactions, developmental processes. Lysosomes could be specially concerned with the degradation of secreted macromolecules in epithelial, mesothelial and endothelial cells. In some cases, that degradation would account for the liberation of products endowed with special biological properties: thus thyroid hormones seem to be released from a protein which is pinocytosed in the lumen of follicles and digested in the lysosomes (Wetzel et al.).

(d) *Inadequate function of lysosomes*

At the cellular level, lysosomes can produce changes by performing their lytic functions inadequately or in such a way as to damage the cell components. An inadequate lytic activity of the lysosomes will lead to a weakening of the cellular defence against infection. A disequilibrium between the rate of entry of a substance into the lysosomal system and its rate of digestion will cause the system to become overloaded, especially if cellular excretion is hindered or becomes impossible. Various instances of this situation have been found. Either the substance which has been picked up by the cell cannot be digested by the lysosomal hydrolases, or the lysosomes have an abnormal enzymatic equipment. Following either of these situations, the congestive enlargement of the lysosomes may greatly affect their functional state and, consequently, the behaviour of the cell (de Duve and Wattiaux).

Disorders associated with injurious lytic activity of the lysosomal enzymes may be of various kinds. The hydrolases may act upon a precursor of a noxious agent and thereby render it toxic. For example, there is some evidence that the uncoating of some viruses, which is a prerequisite for infectivity, is brought about by lysosomal cathepsin (see, for example, Dales, David-Ferreira and Manaker). Production of cellular and tissue lesions by direct action of lysosomal enzymes has also to be considered. Numerous studies have been devoted to that aspect of lysosomal pathology. In short, the cell may be suffering from excessive autophagic action or from autolysis due to a lysosome rupture. It appears that in some cases lysosomes may also act harmfully on extracellular structures.

Finally, some substances of biological interest such as steroids and liposoluble vitamins, have a labilizing or stabilizing action *in vitro* and sometimes *in vivo* on the lysosomal membrane. Although still poorly understood, the mechanism of action of action of these components merits attention because it is probably related to their physiological or pharmacological role.

4. *Biochemical methods of study of lysosomes*

Comparative studies of lysosomes have shown that these granules cannot easily be characterized by a well defined size or by a typical internal structure. Thus, lysosomes have to be identified chiefly by their biochemical properties. The classical methodology which is followed in the study of these organelles is the following:

(1) Identification of acid hydrolases in tissue homogenates; determination of their latency and sedimentation.

(2) Analysis of the distribution patterns of acid hydrolases after differential and isopycnic centrifugation.

(3) Isolation of lysosomes in a pure state.

(a) *Identification of acid hydrolases in tissue homogenates*

The presence of lysosomes in a tissue presupposes the presence of acid hydrolases in homogenates of the tissue. It is very useful to look for several acid hydrolases in the homogenates, in order to compare their behaviour in different experimental conditions.

We have already drawn attention to problems raised by the determination of the free activity of the enzymes. The tissue homogenization and the conditions in which the enzyme tests are carried out, have to be carefully controlled. As for the sedimentation of acid hydrolases, it is simplest to establish first the proportion of active material which sediments in a cellular extract, after a centrifugation adequate to spin down all the particular components.

(b) *Analysis of the distribution pattern of acid hydrolases after differential and isopycnic centrifugation*

Results obtained from centrifugation experiments make it possible to demonstrate that acid hydrolases are associated with granules which are distinct from mitochondria and other known cytoplasmic constituents. From these results, one can establish some physical characteristics of the granules. The behaviour of the lysosomes will actually depend on the composition of the medium in which they are centrifuged (Beaufay et al.; Beaufay and Berthet).

Differential centrifugation in a homogeneous medium (0.25 M sucrose) and in a stabilizing density gradient may be used. It is better to carry out isopycnic centrifugation in gradients of various kinds. In their work on lysosomes of rat liver tissue, de Duve and his group have successfully made use of sucrose gradients in H_2O and in D_2O, and of a glycogen gradient with aqueous sucrose as a solvent. In general, distribution curves of acid hydrolases are relatively flattened and illustrate the great heterogeneity of lysosomes (Fig. 3 and Table 2). That heterogeneity is mainly the result of the granules' intracellular function but will also show up morphologically as pointed out below.

(c) *Isolation of lysosomes in a pure state*

The purification of lysosomes is a difficult technical problem. So great is the heterogeneity of the granules that it leads to an important overlapping of their distribution pattern with that of mitochondria and other cytoplasmic granules. Tappel and his coworkers have described a method of purification of rat liver lysosomes but the yield obtained by these authors seems to be very poor and makes one fear that their sample was not representative. The same considerations apply to the highly purified preparation isolated, after centrifugation in a glycogen gradient, by Beaufay and coworkers, and analysed in the electron microscope by Baudhuin et al. (1965). The method which currently seems the most promising, at least for rat liver lysosomes, consists in utilizing animals which have been injected with Triton WR-1339, a non-ionic detergent. This substance is taken up by the liver and accumulates in the lysosomes of that organ (Wattiaux et al.). This accumulation causes a great reduction in their density in a sucrose gradient (Fig. 3). In such a gradient, the lysosomes can easily be separated from other cytoplasmic granules. The preparations of lysosomes obtained by this technique are very pure and the yield is satisfactory. It is to be noted that lysosomes isolated by such a method are not in a natural state, since they contain Triton WR-1339 which has certainly modified some of their properties. However, the method may

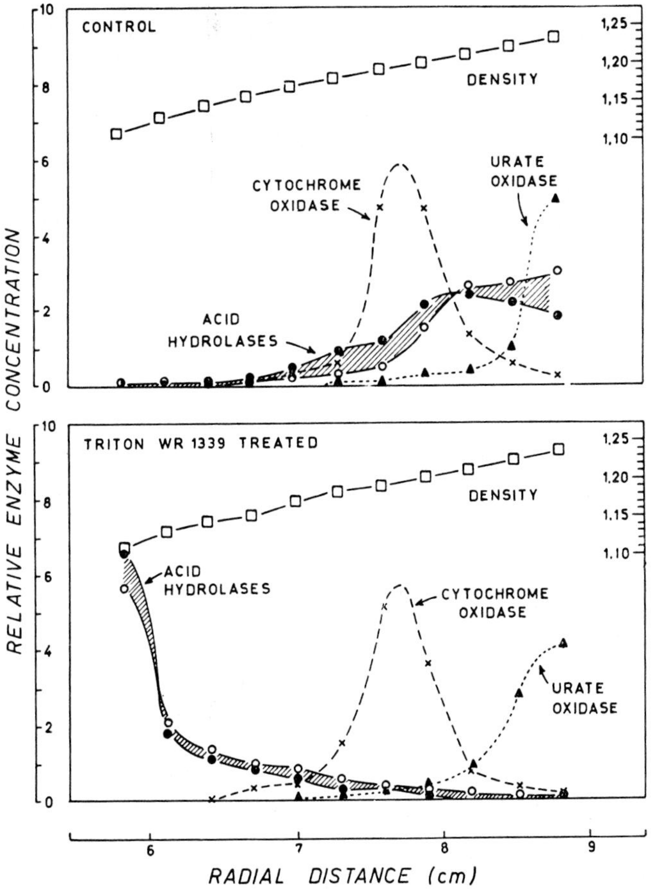

Fig. 3. Influence of the injection of Triton WR-1339 on the equilibrium density of rat liver lysosomes in a sucrose gradient. The treatment of the animal causes a marked shift of the distribution curves of the acid hydrolases (lysosomes) towards the regions of low density. The lysosomes are thus clearly separated from other special components of the mitochondrial fraction: mitochondria (cytochrome oxidase) and microbodies (urate oxidase). According to Wattiaux et al.

be very useful, for example, in analysing in detail the enzyme content of the granules and their digestive capacities. It could perhaps be applied, to some extent, to the study of lysosomes in other tissues.

5. *Morphology of lysosomes*

(a) *Morphologic heterogeneity of lysosomes in living cells*

The heterogeneity of lysosomes is manifested in their morphological appearance. As was pointed out in the previous section, the physiological functions of lysosomes imply that the granules exist in various forms in the cell. This variety is illustrated by the

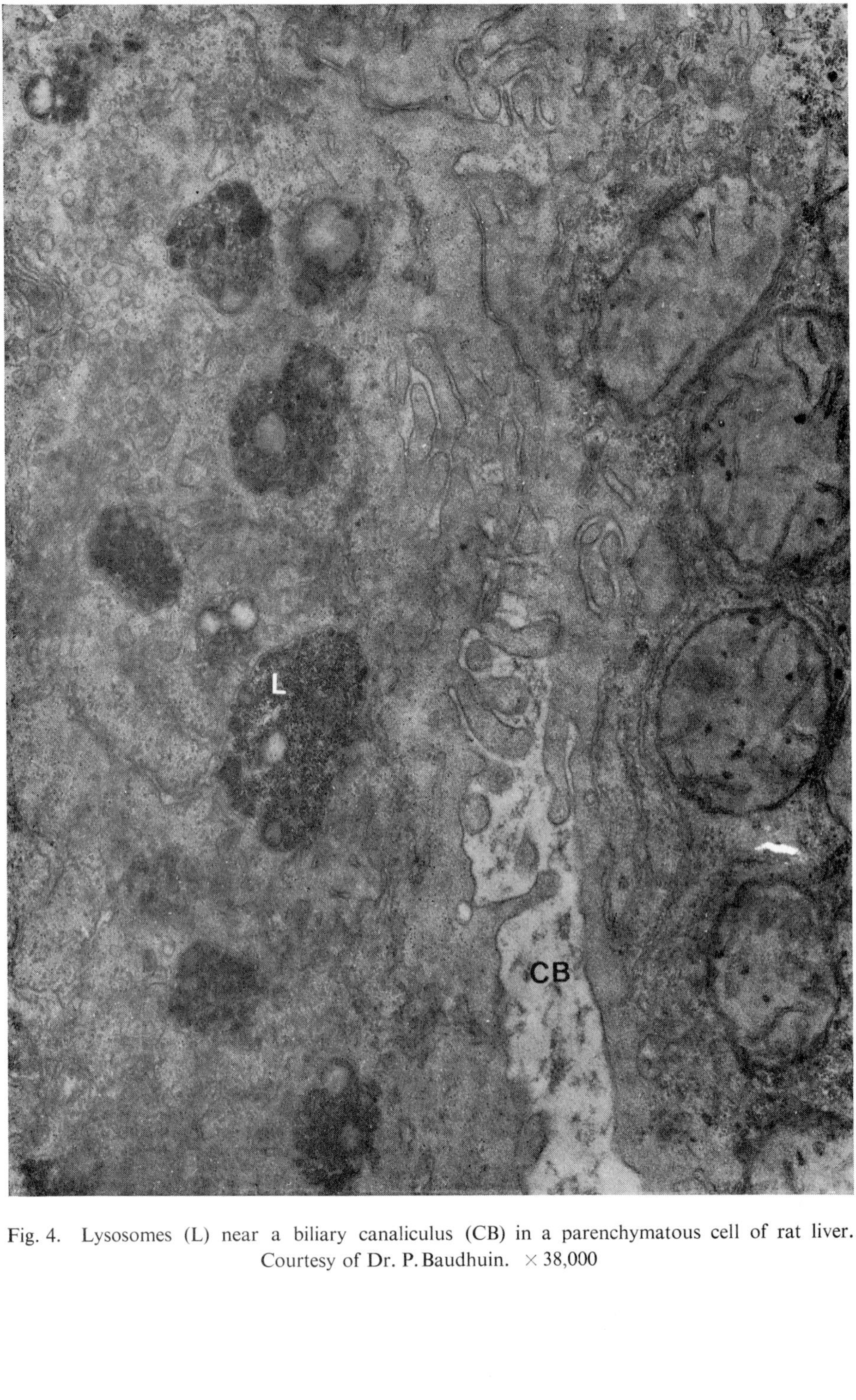

Fig. 4. Lysosomes (L) near a biliary canaliculus (CB) in a parenchymatous cell of rat liver. Courtesy of Dr. P. Baudhuin. × 38,000

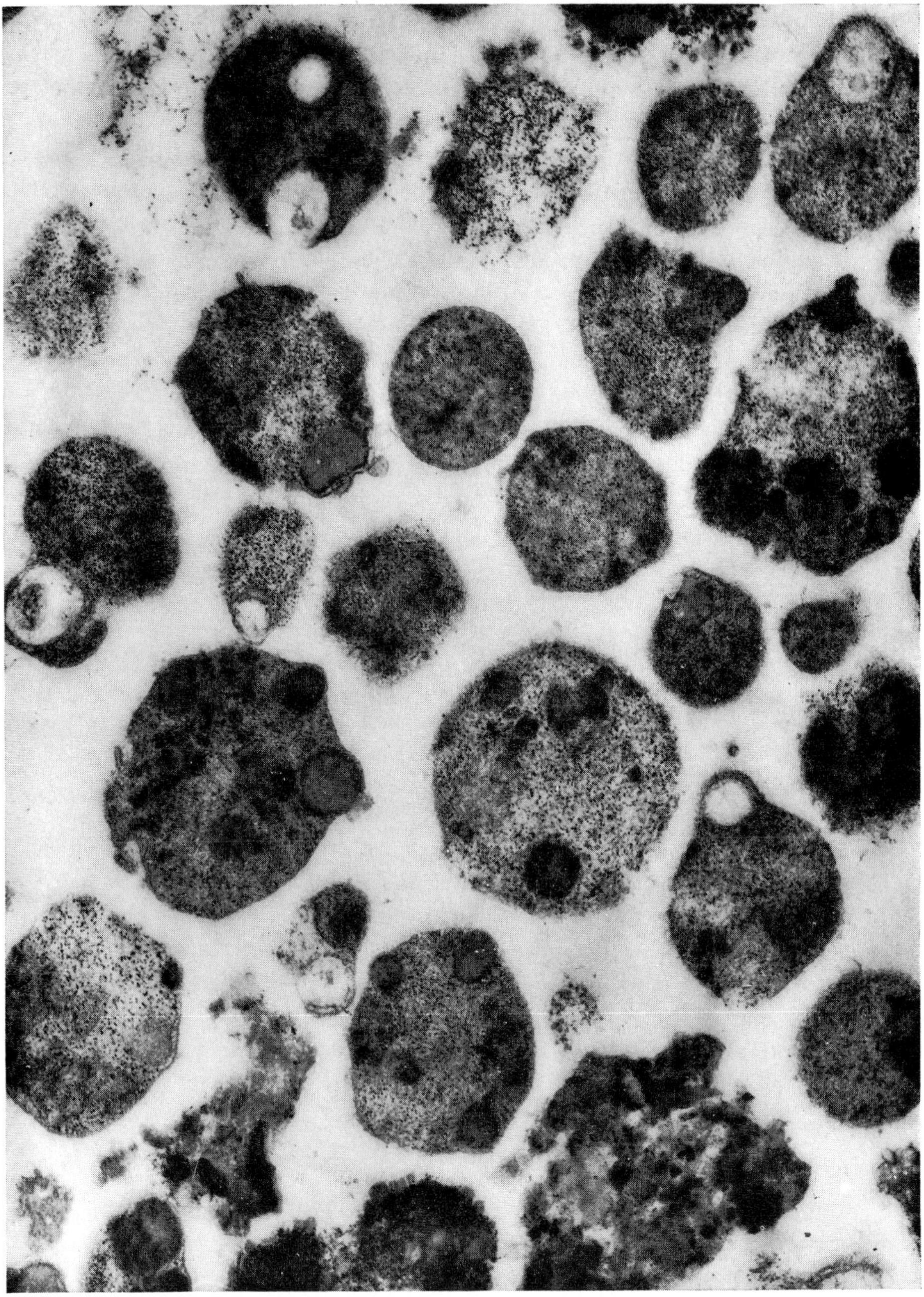

Fig. 5. Rat liver lysosomes isolated by centrifugation in a density gradient. (From Baudhuin et al. 1965.) × 44,500

terminology applied to the components of the lysosomal system: primary lysosomes, heterolysosomes, autolysosomes, etc. (de Duve and Wattiaux). Essentially, all the components of the vacuolar apparatus which are endowed with acid hydrolases may be considered as lysosomes.

Therefore, cytochemistry and especially cytochemical localisation of acid hydrolases are of prime importance in the morphological identification of lysosomes. The detection of acid phosphatase is the most widely utilized procedure because of the easy recognition of the reaction product by light and electron microscopy. Techniques are also available for the detection of the reaction products of thioacetate esterase (Miller and Palade) and of sulfatase, (Goldfischer) by electron microscopy. Other acid hydrolases, like β-glucuronidase (Hayashi et al.) and β-N-acetyl amino deoxyglucosidase (Hayashi) can only be demonstrated by light microscopy.

Finally, it is sometimes possible to identify lysosomes by indirect criteria, such as the presence of exogenous or endogenous material being digested inside the granules.

The micrographs of Figs. 4 to 9 illustrate the morphology of lysosomes.

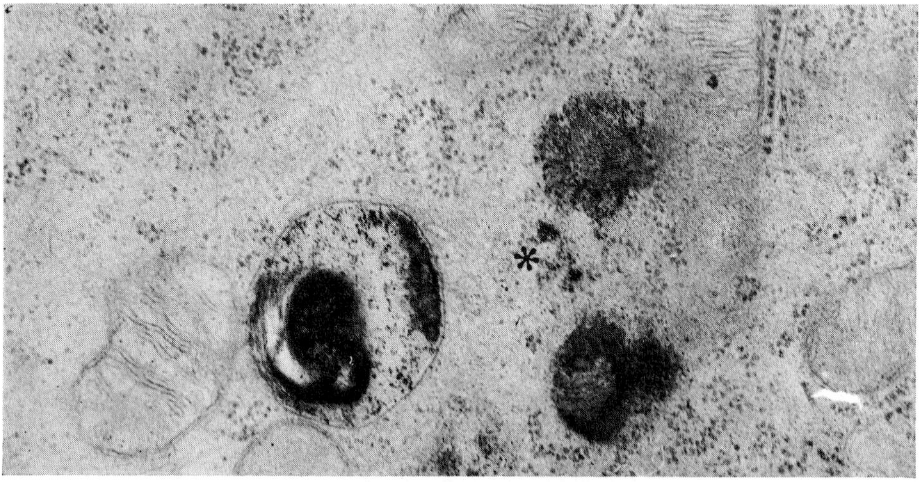

Fig. 6. Part of a stem cell of the duodenal crypt of a mouse, showing acid phosphatase activity as detected by the Gomori reaction. The precipitate of lead phosphate is seen in two dense bodies and in a vacuole with membrane whorls. At the asterisk, a small vesicle with the reaction product. Courtesy of Dr. J. Hugon. × 38,000

(b) *Identification of lysosomes in subcellular fractions*

Very valuable information can be supplied by a combination of the techniques of centrifugation and electron microscopy. Such a method allowed Novikoff, Beaufay and de Duve to propose the hypothesis that rat liver lysosomes were analogous to peribiliary dense bodies. This hypothesis was later confirmed by several authors. Recently Baudhuin and coworkers (1967) have described an interesting method allowing the preparation of representative samples from a particular suspension; this method has been applied with success to morphological analysis of rat liver lysosomes.

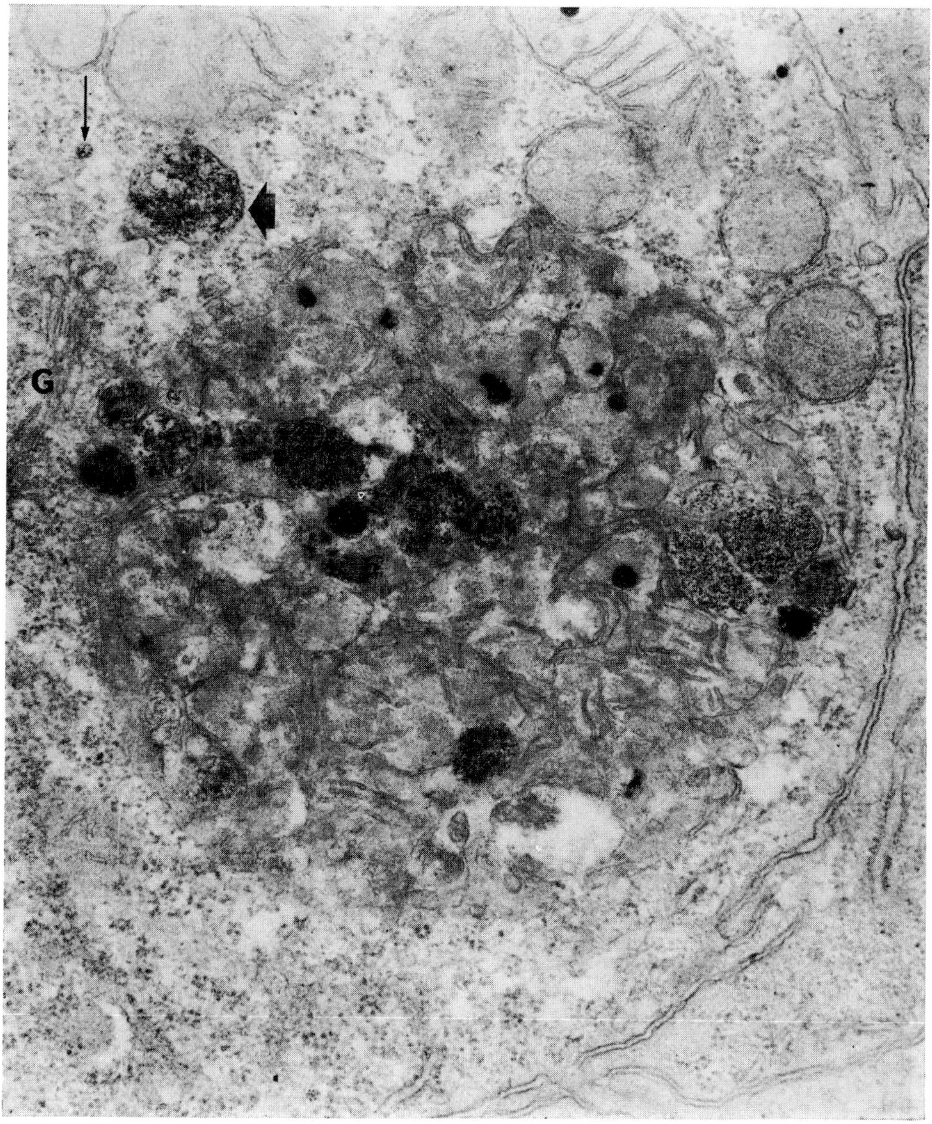

Fig. 7. Duodenal crypt of a mouse, three hours after irradiation with 1,350 r (X-rays). Acid phosphatase activity. A big cytolysome is in the process of formation in a stem cell. Numerous altered mitochondria, large and small vesicles, and dense bodies are gathered near a Golgi zone (G). The precipitate of lead phosphate is abundant on the dense bodies and on some large vesicles. At the thick arrow: a positive dense body is seen near the zone of lysis. At the small arrow: a Golgi vesicle with reaction product. Courtesy of Dr. J. Hugon. ×34,500

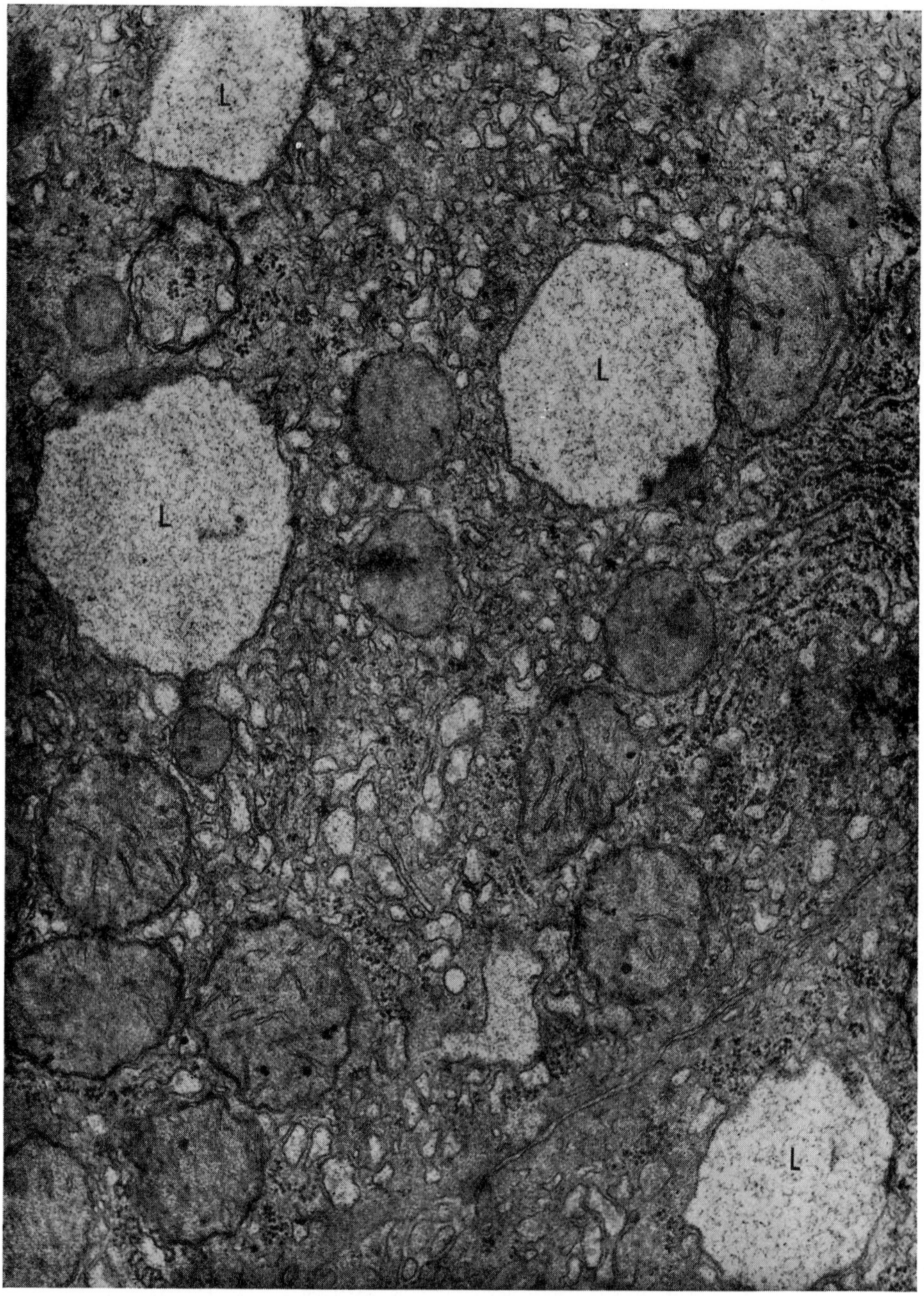

Fig. 8. Heterophagic picture of lysosomes in rat liver parenchymatous cell after injection of the animal with Triton WR-1339. The granules are strikingly enlarged following accumulation of the detergent after pinocytosis. Courtesy of Dr. P. Baudhuin. × 28,750

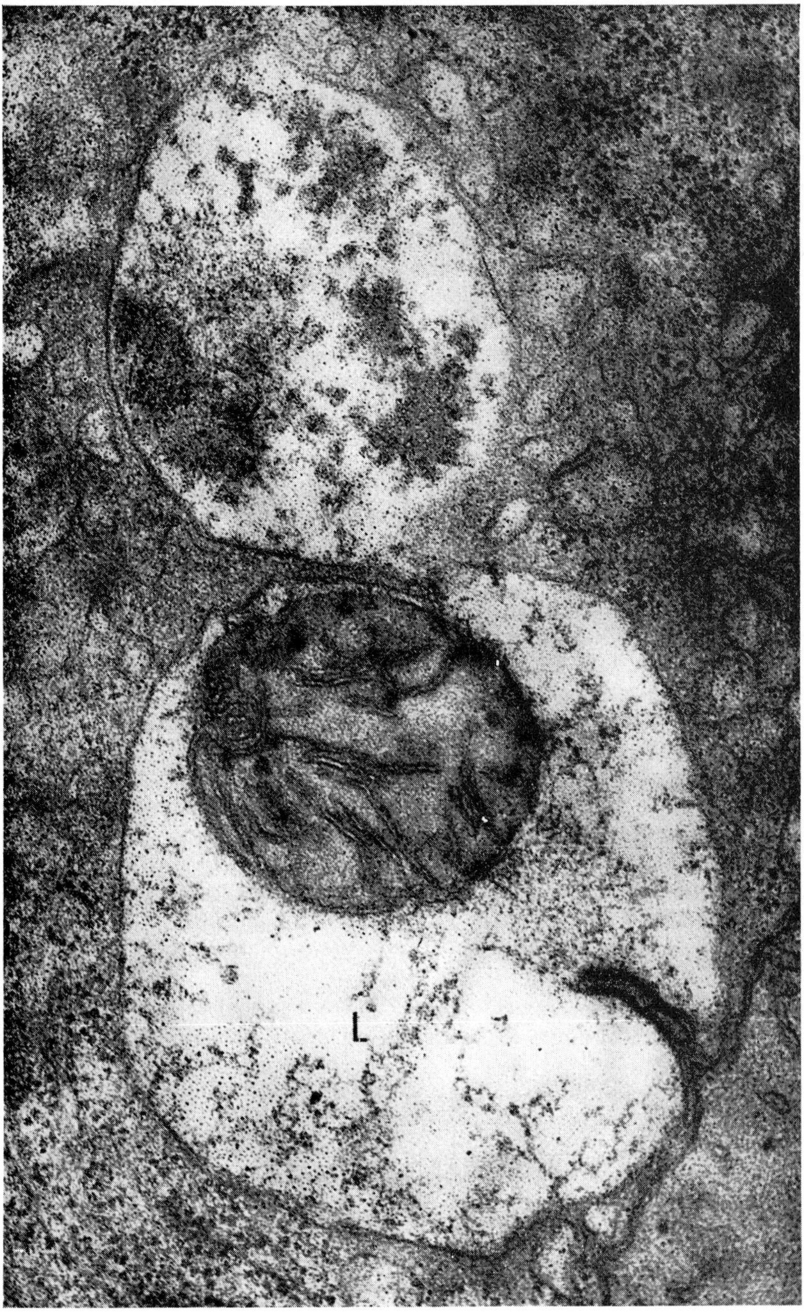

Fig. 9. Heterophagy and autophagy may be seen within the same lysosome (L) in rat liver, after injection of the animal with Triton WR-1339. The granule is enlarged due to the accumulation of the detergent and it contains a mitochondrion which has been trapped by the autophagy mechanism. Courtesy of Dr. P. Baudhuin. × 65,000

References

Ciba Foundation Symposium on Lysosomes. A.V.S.de Reuck and M.P.Cameron, eds. London, J. and A. Churchill Ltd. (1963).

Pathology Symposium on Lysosomes. Federation Proc. 23 (1964) 1009.

ARONSON, N.A. and E.A.DAVIDSON: Lysosomal hyaluronidase from rat liver. J. Biol. Chem. 242 (1967) 437.

BAUDHUIN, P., H.BEAUFAY and C.DE DUVE: Combined biochemical and morphological study of particulate fractions from rat liver. J. Cell Biol. 26 (1965) 219.

BAUDHUIN, P., P.EVRARD and J.BERTHET: Electron microscopic examination of subcellular fractions I. The preparation of representative samples from suspensions of particles. J. Cell Biol. 32 (1967) 181.

BEAUFAY, H. and J.BERTHET: Medium composition and equilibrium density of subcellular particles from rat liver. Biochem. Soc. Symp. (Cambridge, Engl.) 23 (1963) 66.

BEAUFAY, H., P.JACQUES, P.BAUDHUIN, O.Z.SELLINGER, J.BERTHET and C.DE DUVE: Tissue fractionation studies XVIII. Resolution of mitochondrial fractions from rat liver into three distinct populations of cytoplasmic particles by means of density equilibration in various gradients. Biochem. J. 92 (1964) 184.

BERNARDI, A. and G.BERNARDI: Studies on acid hydrolases III. Isolation and properties of spleen acid ribonuclease. Biochim. Biophys. Acta 129 (1966) 23.

BERNARDI, G., A.BERNARDI and A.CHERSI: Studies on acid hydrolases I. A procedure for the preparation of deoxyribonuclease and other acid hydrolases. Biochim. Biophys. Acta 129 (1966) 1.

BLASCHKO, H., A.D.SMITH, H.WINKLER, H.VAN DEN BOSCH and L.L.M.VAN DEENEN: Acid phospholipase A in lysosomes of the bovine adrenal medulla. Biochem. J. 103 (1967) 30c.

CHERSI, A., A.BERNARDI and G.BERNARDI: Studies on acid hydrolases II. Isolation and properties of spleen acid phosphomonoesterase. Biochim. Biophys. Acta 129 (1966) 12.

COFFEY, J.W.: Protein digestion by hepatic lysosomes. J. Cell Biol. 31 (1966) 21A.

COHN, Z.A. and B.BENSON: The differentiation of mononuclear phagocytes. Morphology, cytochemistry and biochemistry. J. Exptl. Med. 121 (1965) 153.

COHN, Z.A. and B.BENSON: The *in vitro* differentiation of mononuclear phagocytes I. The influence of inhibitors and the results of autoradiography. J. Exptl. Med. 121 (1965) 279.

COHN, Z.A. and B.BENSON: The *in vitro* differentiation of mononuclear phagocytes II. The influence of serum on granule formation, hydrolase production and pinocytosis. J. Exptl. Med. 121 (1965) 835.

COHN, Z.A. and B.BENSON: The *in vitro* differentiation of mononuclear phagocytes III. The reversibility of granule and hydrolytic enzyme formation and the turnover of granule constituents. J. Exptl. Med. 122 (1965) 455.

COHN, Z.A., M.FEDORKO and J.G.HIRSCH: The *in vitro* differentiation of mononuclear phagocytes V. The formation of macrophage lysosomes. J. Exptl. Med. 123 (1966) 757.

COHN, Z.A., J.G.HIRSCH and M.E.FEDORKO: The *in vitro* differentiation of mononuclear phagocytes IV. The ultrastructure of macrophage differentiation in the peritoneal cavity and in culture. J. Exptl. Med. 123 (1966) 747.

DALES, S.: The uptake and development of vaccinia virus in strain L cells followed with labelled viral deoxyribonucleic acid. J. Cell Biol. 18 (1963) 51.

DAVID-FERREIRA, J.F. and R.A.MANAKER: An electron microscope study of the development of a mouse hepatitis virus in tissue culture cells. J. Cell Biol. 24 (1965) 57.

DE DUVE, C.: Lysosomes, a new group of cytoplasmic particles. In: T.Hayashi, ed.: Subcellular particles. New York, Ronald Press (1959) p. 128.

DE DUVE, C.: The lysosome concept. Ciba Found. Symp. Lysosomes (1963a) 1.

DE DUVE, C.: The lysosomes. Sci. Am. 208 (1963b) 64.

DE DUVE, C.: Lysosomes and cell injury. In: L. Thomas, J. W. Urh and L. Grant, eds.: Injury, inflammation and immunity. Baltimore, William and Wilkins (1964) 283.

DE DUVE, C.: The separation and characterization of sub-cellular particles. Harvey Lectures Ser. 59 (1965) 49.

DE DUVE, C. and R. WATTIAUX: Functions of lysosomes. Ann. Rev. Physiol. 28 (1966) 435.

DETER, R. L. and C. DE DUVE: Influence of glucagon, an inducer of cellular autophagy, on some physical properties of rat liver lysosomes. J. Cell Biol. 33 (1967) 437.

ERICSSON, J. L. E.: Absorption and decomposition of homologous haemoglobin in renal proximal tubule cells. An experimental light and electron microscopic study. Acta Pathol. Microbiol. Scand. Suppl. 168 (1964) 1.

GOLDFISCHER, S.: The cytochemical demonstration of lysosomal aryl sulfatase activity by light and electron microscopy. J. Histochem. Cytochem. 13 (1965) 520.

HAYASHI, M.: Histochemical demonstration of N-acetyl-β-glucosaminidase employing naphthol AS-BI N-acetyl-β-glucosaminide as substrate. J. Histochem. Cytochem. 13 (1965) 355.

HAYASHI, M., N. NAKAJIMA and W. FISHMAN: The cytologic demonstration of β-glucuronidase employing naphthol AS-BI glucuronide and hexazonium pararosanilin. J. Histochem. Cytochem. 12 (1964) 293.

HELLER, M. and B. SHAPIRO: Enzymic hydrolysis of sphingomyelin by rat liver. Biochem. J. 98 (1966) 763.

HOLT, S. J.: Some observations on the occurrence and nature of esterases in lysosomes. Ciba Found. Symp. Lysosomes (1963) 114.

HUTTERER, F.: Degradation of mucopolysaccharides by hepatic lysosomes. Biochim. Biophys. Acta 115 (1966) 312.

MILLER, F. and G. E. PALADE: Lytic activities in renal protein absorption droplets. J. Cell Biol. 23 (1964) 519.

NOVIKOFF, A. B.: The proximal tubule cell in experimental hydronephrosis. J. Biophys. Biochem. Cytol. 6 (1959) 136.

NOVIKOFF, A. B.: Lysosomes and related particles. In: J. Brachet and A. E. Mirsky, eds.: The cell, Vol. II. New York and London, Academic Press (1961) 423.

NOVIKOFF, A. B.: Lysosomes in the physiology and pathology of cells; contributions of staining methods. Ciba Found. Symp. Lysosomes (1963) 36.

NOVIKOFF, A. B., H. BEAUFAY and C. DE DUVE: Electron microscopy of lysosome-rich fractions from rat liver. J. Biophys. Biochem. Cytol. Suppl. 2 (1956) 179.

NOVIKOFF, A. B. and E. ESSNER: Cytolysomes and mitochondrial degeneration. J. Cell Biol. 15 (1962) 140.

ROBINSON, D., R. G. PRICE and N. DANCE: Separation and properties of β-galactosidase, β-glucosidase, β-glucuronidase and N-acetyl-β-glucosaminidase from rat kidney. Biochem. J. 102 (1967) 525.

STOFFEL, W. and H. GRETEN: Studies on lipolytic activities of rat liver lysosomes. Hoppe-Seylers Z. Physiol. Chem. 348 (1967) 1145.

STRAUS, W.: Isolation and biochemical properties of droplets from the cells of rat kidney. J. Biol. Chem. 207 (1954) 745.

STRAUS, W.: Concentration of acid phosphatase, ribonuclease, deoxyribonuclease, β-glucosaminidase and cathepsin in 'droplets' isolated from the kidney cells of normal rats. J. Biophys. Biochem. Cytol. 2 (1956) 513.

TAPPEL, A. L., P. L. SAWANT and S. SHIBKO: Lysosomes: distribution in animals, hydrolytic capacity and other properties. Ciba Found. Symp. Lysosomes (1963) 78.

WATTIAUX, R. and C. DE DUVE: Tissue fractionation studies VII. Release of bound hydrolases by means of Triton X-100. Biochem. J. 63 (1956) 606.

WATTIAUX, R. and S. WATTIAUX-DE CONINCK: Particules subcellulaires dans les tumeurs II. Analyse de fractions mitochondriales at microsomiales de l'hépatome HW par centrifugation isopycnique. European J. Cancer 4 (1968) 201.

WATTIAUX, R., M. WIBO and P. BAUDHUIN: Influence of the injection of Triton WR-1339 on the properties of rat-liver lysosomes. Ciba Found. Symp. Lysosomes (1963) 176.

WATTIAUX-DE CONINCK, S., M. J. RUTGEERTS and R. WATTIAUX: Lysosomes in rat kidney tissue. Biochim. Biophys. Acta 105 (1965) 446.

WEISSMANN, G.: The role of lysosomes in inflammation and disease. Ann. Rev. Med. 18 (1967) 97.

WETZEL, B. K., S. S. SPICER and S. H. WOLLMAN: Changes in fine structure and acid phosphatase localization in rat thyroid cells following thyrotropin administration. J. Cell Biol. 25 Pt1 (1965) 593.

Note added in proof

Since the present paper was written, the list of hydrolases present in rat liver lysosomes has become longer; there are increasing indications that lysosomes are endowed with an adequate lipolytic activity. More information is also available concerning the chemistry of the degradation of proteins (Coffey, J.W. and de Duve, C., J. Biol. Chem. 243 (1968) 3255), macromolecular carbohydrates (Aronson, N.A. and de Duve, C., J. Biol. Chem. 243 (1968) 4564), and DNA (Van Dyck, J.M. and Wattiaux, R., European J. Bioch. 7 (1968) 15). On the other hand, Leighton et al. (J. Cell Biol. 37 (1968) 482) have described a method of preparation of lysosomes on a large scale from the livers of rats injected with Triton WR 1339.

CHAPTER 43

Peroxisomes (microbodies, glyoxysomes)

PIERRE BAUDHUIN*

Université de Louvain, Laboratoire de Chimie Physiologique, Louvain, Belgium

Contents

1. Introduction
2. Properties of peroxisomes
   - (a) Liver
     - Enzymes
     - Purification
     - Morphology
     - Physical properties
     - Turnover
   - (b) Kidney
   - (c) Protozoa
   - (d) Plant cells
   - (e) Other cell types
3. Physiological role

* Chercheur qualifié of the Belgian Fonds National de la Recherche Scientifique.

1. Introduction

The name 'peroxisome' (de Duve 1965a; de Duve and Baudhuin) designates a special type of respiratory particle characterized by the association of one or more hydrogen peroxide-generating oxidases with large amounts of catalase. As shown in Fig. 1, peroxisomes have the ability of reducing oxygen to water by a two-step mechanism involving hydrogen peroxide as an intermediate. The electron donors in the first step are the oxidase substrates RH_2, which may include uric acid, D-amino acids, L-amino acids, glycolic acid and L-α-hydroxy acids, depending on the cell type. The electron donors in the second step are either a second molecule of hydrogen peroxide, which is oxidized back to oxygen in the typical catalatic reaction, or one of the substrates $R'H_2$, such as methanol, ethanol, formate, formaldehyde, phenols or nitrite ions, that can be oxidized peroxidatically by catalase (for a review of this subject, see Nicholls and Schonbaum). According to the limited data available at the present time, peroxisomes appear to be widely distributed in nature, occurring both in the animal and in the plant kingdom, but to be present only in certain selected cell types of which all representatives known so far are actively concerned with the formation of carbohydrate from non-carbohydrate precursors. Early results in this field have been surveyed by de Duve and Baudhuin.

Breidenbach and Beevers have given the name 'glyoxysome' to a new cytoplasmic particle which they have discovered in germinating castor bean seedlings. The glyoxysomes contain an apparently complete glyoxylate cycle which converts the acetyl groups of acetyl-coenzyme A to succinate. They are clearly involved in the synthesis of carbohydrate from fat. A relationship between glyoxysomes and peroxisomes was first suggested by the results of Müller and Hogg who found the two key enzymes of the glyoxylate bypass, isocitrate lyase and malate synthase, to be constituents of peroxisomes in *Tetrahymena pyriformis*. This relationship has now been confirmed by the finding that the castor bean glyoxysomes contain the bulk of the particulate catalase and glycolate oxidase of the cells (Beevers, personal communication). Thus it appears that glyoxysomes belong to the peroxisome family. The converse may not always be true, since the glyoxylate cycle enzymes appear to be absent in mammalian peroxisomes.

The name 'microbody' was first used by Rhodin to designate a special type of particulate structure present in the convoluted tubule cells of the mouse kidney. Sub-

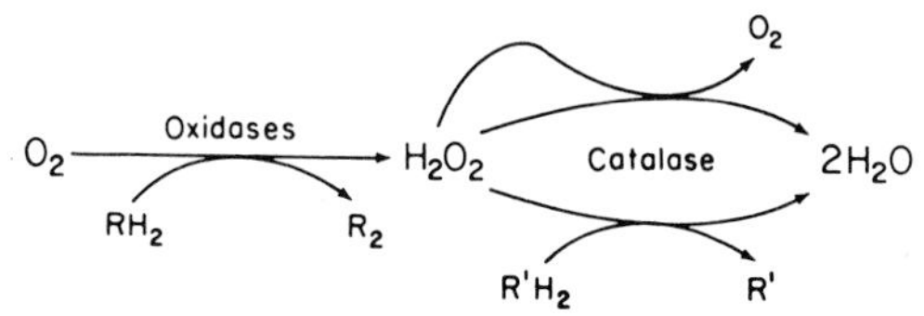

Fig. 1. Enzymic reactions in peroxisomes. (From de Duve and Baudhuin.)

sequently, Gänsler and Rouiller adopted the same name for granules resembling the kidney microbodies which they found in the parenchymal cells of rat liver. It has now been established conclusively that the hepatic microbodies are identical with the peroxisomes (Baudhuin et al. 1965a). The same is probably also true for the kidney microbodies, but caution is required in the biochemical identification of the particles that have been described under the name 'microbody' in other biological materials. Unfortunately, there is as yet no cytochemical staining reaction for the detection of peroxisomes at the electron microscope level. Methods for the visualization of oxidases at the light microscope level have been described by Graham and Karnovsky and by Allen and Beard.

2. *Properties of peroxisomes*

(a) *Liver*

Enzymes. Liver peroxisomes are the bearers of three oxidases, acting respectively on L-α-hydroxyacids, D-aminoacids and urate. Table 1 shows the relative activities on various substrates of these enzymes. In liver, glycolate and L-lactate are most readily oxidized by the peroxisomal L-α-hydroxyacid oxidase. This enzyme is probably also responsible for the slight activity found on L-leucine. Urate oxidase is the most active oxidase in rat liver peroxisomes; it is however not a constant component of these granules since it is absent from the liver of several species. Catalase represents a major component of the granules in rat liver.

Leighton et al. (1968a) have recently found that rat liver peroxisomes also contain a small amount of isocitrate dehydrogenase (NADP). About 80% of the enzyme occurs

TABLE 1

Activity of rat liver peroxisomal oxidases on various substrates. (From Baudhuin et al. 1965b.)

Substrates	Percent of the activity on L-lactate
Glycolate	173
L-lactate	100
DL-α-hydroxybutyrate	60
DL-α-glycerate	27
L-leucine	3
L-alanine	0
D-alanine	330
Urate	750

in the soluble fraction, the remaining 20% being associated partly with mitochondria, partly with peroxisomes.

Purification. Fractionation of rat liver by classical differential centrifugation in 0.25 M sucrose yields only a 5- to 10-fold purification of peroxisomes, with respect to the homogenate. Peroxisomes behave like lysosomes in such experiments; the median sedimentation constant is similar for both types of granules.

As first shown by Beaufay et al. a better purification can be obtained by using density equilibration in a gradient. Even so it is presently not possible to separate completely peroxisomes from lysosomes in normal liver. For the preparation of very pure peroxisomal fractions, advantage is taken of the finding by Wattiaux et al. (1963) that the equilibrium density of lysosomes is drastically reduced by the injection into the animal of Triton WR-1339, 4 days before sacrifice. Leighton et al. (1968a) have recently improved and scaled up this isolation technique, using the automatic rotor assembly designed by Beaufay. Density equilibration is performed on a so-called 'lambda' fraction, prepared by differential centrifugation. This preliminary step yields, starting from 80–100 g of liver, a preparation containing less than 10% of the homogenate protein, with about 40% of the liver catalase. Nuclei and soluble protein are eliminated, together with a substantial part of mitochondria and microsomes. Fig. 2 illustrates the separation obtained by density equilibration of this 'lambda' fraction in a sucrose gradient. The median equilibrium densities observed in these experiments for the Triton-filled lysosomes, mitochondria and peroxisomes, are 1.12, 1.18 and 1.23, respectively. A fraction containing peroxisomes purified approximately 40 times with respect to the homogenate can be isolated by the procedure of Leighton et al. The overall yield is about 20% and the fraction contains roughly 100 mg peroxisomal protein per 100 g liver fractionated. It has a greenish color, due to its high catalase content. Its purity is of the order of 95% according to both the biochemical and the morphological data (see below).

Morphology. The morphological examination of isolated fractions has identified conclusively the hepatic peroxisomes with the particles described under the name of 'microbodies' in the morphological literature (Baudhuin et al. 1965a). This is illustrated in Fig. 3 which shows an electron micrograph of a peroxisomal fraction isolated from rat liver by the procedure of Leighton et al. (1968a).

Liver microbodies (Fig. 4) are corpuscules of approximately 0.5 μ in diameter, bounded by a single, well-contrasted membrane and containing a granular matrix. The latter displays, at least in some species, a more dense part, the core or nucleoid, which often has a regular structure. Considerable variation from species to species seems to exist in the fine structure of the microbody core. In general, it is formed by closely packed tubules. In rat liver, two kinds of tubules are encountered: large ones, with a diameter of 9.5–11.5 mμ, surrounded each by ten smaller ones (Hruban and Swift). Although a few micrographs of suitably oriented sections do show such a

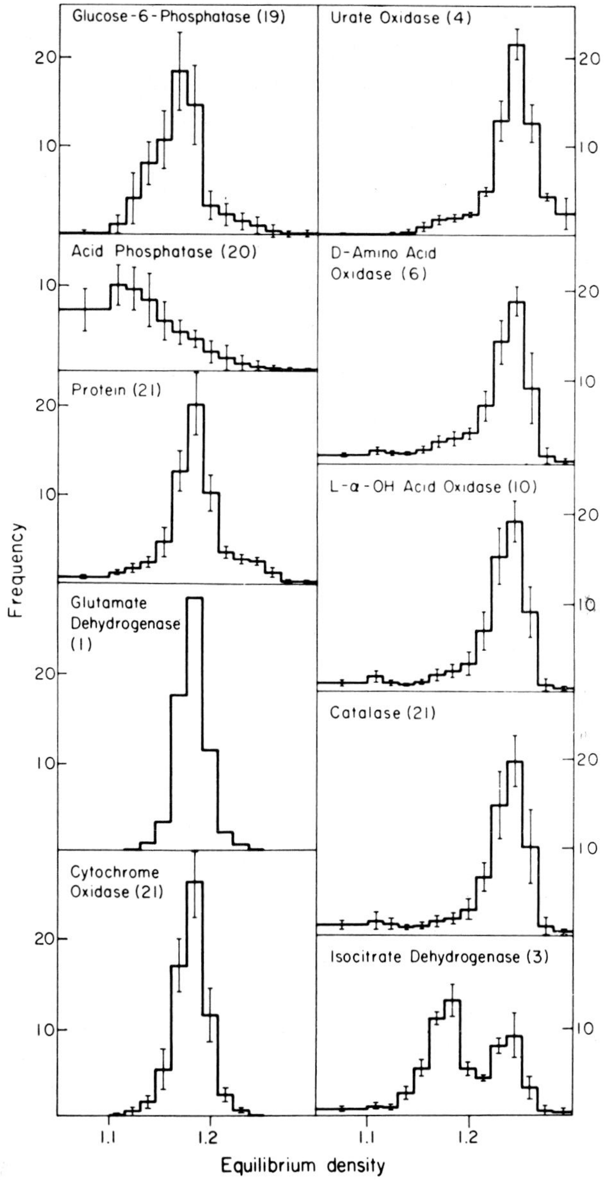

Fig. 2. Purification of rat liver peroxisomes. The animals are injected with 85 mg of Triton WR-1339 per 100 g body weight, four days before sacrifice. Density equilibration is performed on a 'lambda' fraction (see text). The following enzymes are used as markers for the various particle populations: glucose-6-phosphatase for microsomes; cytochrome oxidase and glutamate dehydrogenase for mitochondria; acid phosphatase for lysosomes; catalase and D-aminoacid, α-hydroxyacid and urate oxidases for peroxisomes. Note the bimodal distribution of isocitrate dehydrogenase which is bound partly to mitochondria, partly to peroxisomes. Between parentheses, number of experiments; vertical bars represent standard deviations. (Reproduced from Leighton et al. 1968a.)

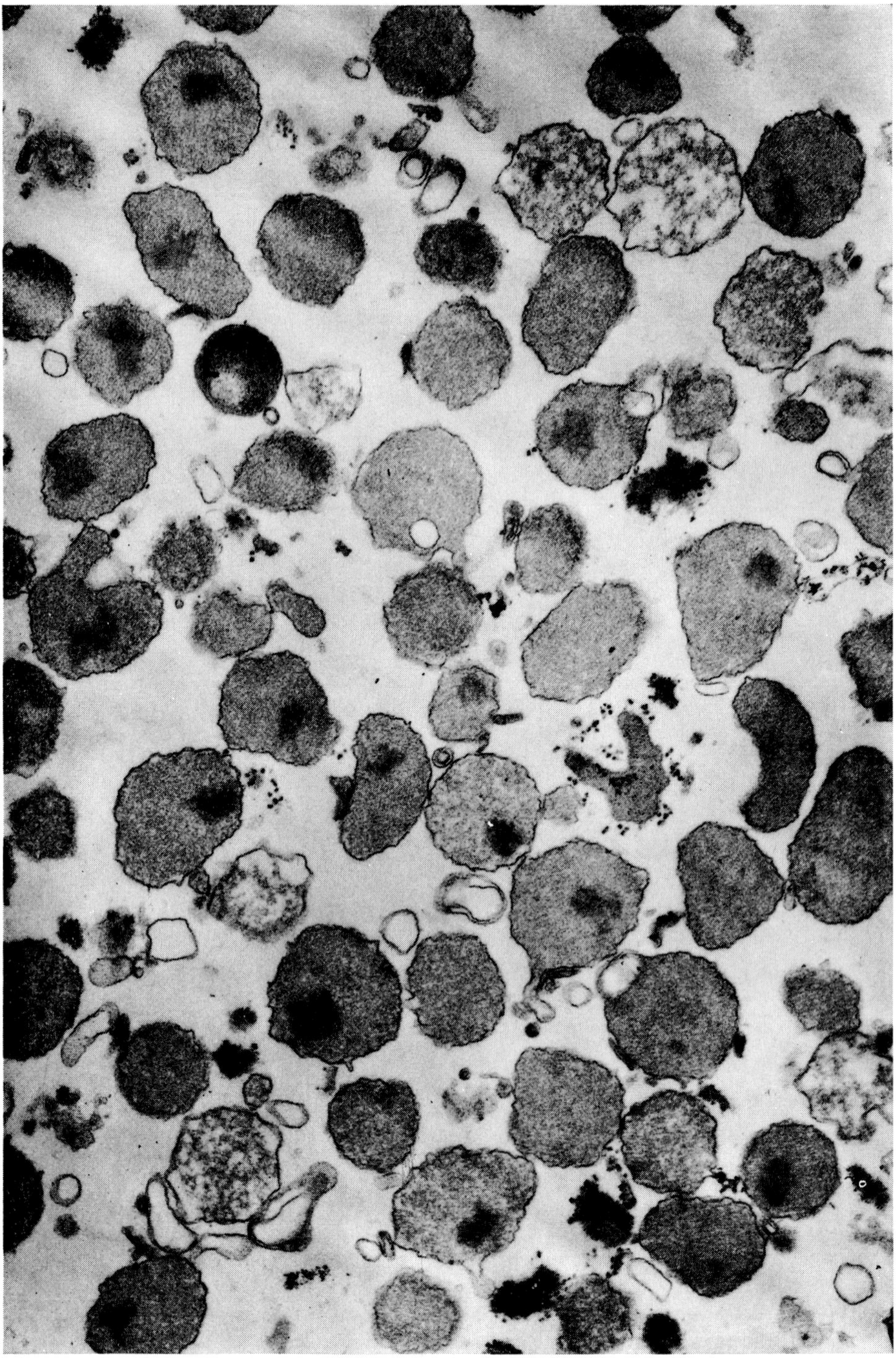

Fig. 3. Purified peroxisomal fraction obtained by the procedure of Leighton et al. (1968a). A lysosome (L) (which has not accumulated Triton WR-1339) can be seen in this field. ×40,000

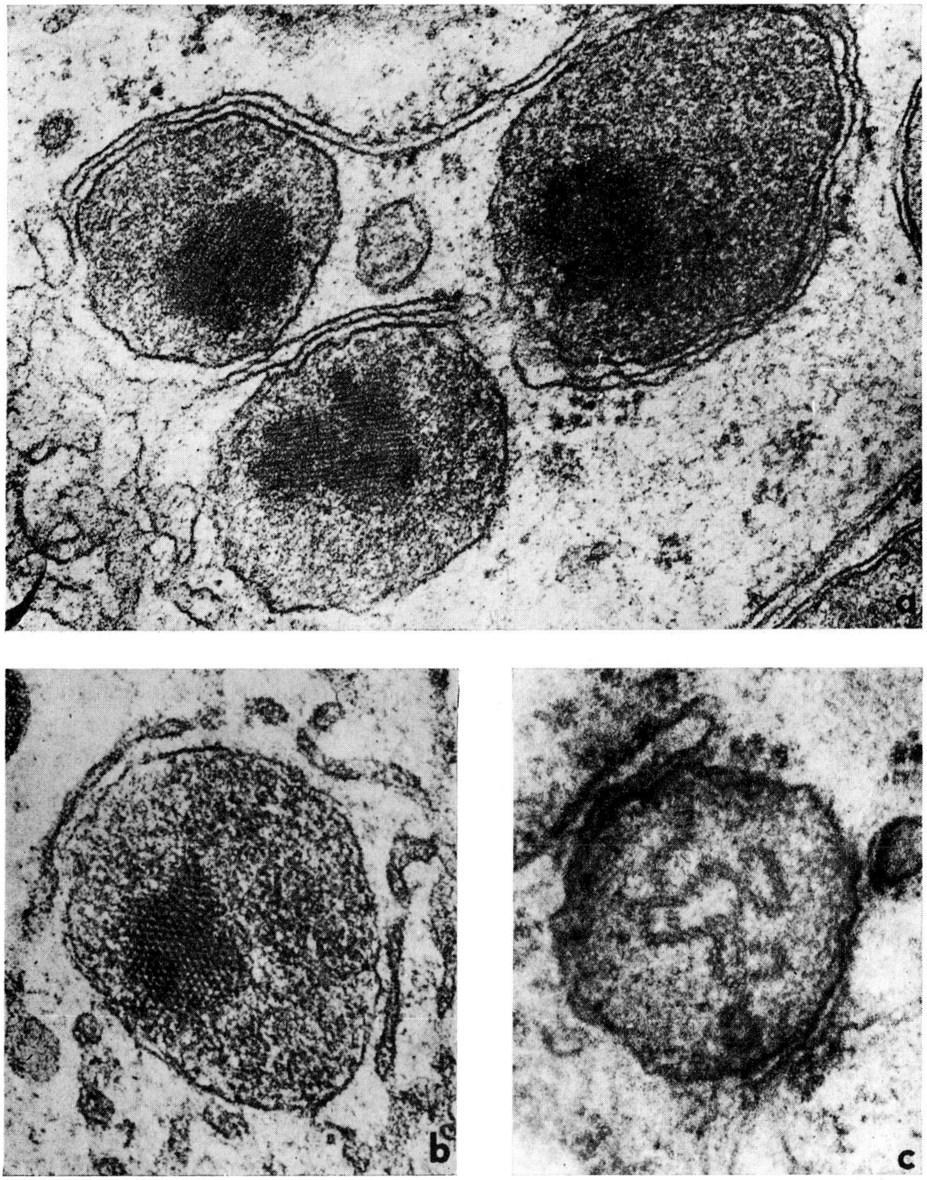

Fig. 4. Liver microbodies. 4a: rat. In two granules, the laminated aspect of the core is apparent. The tubular nature of this structure is visible in the granule on the right, although the incidence of the section does not clearly reveal the regular pattern described by Hruban and Swift. Note the close association of microbodies with endoplasmic reticulum (× 72,000). 4b: guinea pig. The lower part of the core shows a regular hexagonal arrangement (× 75,000). 4c: mouse. In this species, tubules are assembled side by side in a 'palisade' which is seen here in cross-section (× 100,000). (Fig. 4a and 4b from Shnitka, and Fig. 4c from Daems.)

structure (for an example, see Fig. 5a in de Duve and Baudhuin), a laminated aspect is the most commonly encountered (Fig. 4a). In guinea pig, the tubules all have the same diameter and are arranged in a regular hexagonal pattern when viewed in cross-section (Fig. 4b). Nucleoids have a serpentine, thread-like appearance in mouse liver (Daems); they are made of a single row of tubules linked side by side. The resulting 'palisade' may adopt an irregular conformation, with infoldings or branching points (Fig. 4c). Hamster nucleoids are narrow (40–60 mμ wide, up to 1 μ long) and do not display an internal lattice; in cows two structural patterns seem to occur: one is similar to the structure observed in rat liver, but with fewer lamellae, the other is formed by a single plate approximately 13.5 mμ thick, applied to the inner surface of the microbody membrane (Shnitka).

Close spatial relationships between liver microbodies and the endoplasmic reticulum (see Fig. 3a) have often been noted. Novikoff and Shin and more recently Essner have observed narrow attachments between these two types of structures. The former authors even consider it possible that all microbodies are attached to the endoplasmic reticulum. These observations suggest that microbodies originate from the endoplasmic reticulum.

Urate oxidase is firmly attached to the microbody core, whereas the other known peroxisomal enzymes are easily solubilized upon disruption of the particles and are probably localized in their matrix (Hruban and Swift; Baudhuin et al. 1965a; Tsukada et al.; Leighton et al. 1968a). It has been found that commercial preparations of highly purified urate oxidase from hog liver contain structures identical with microbody cores, and it has been claimed on the basis of this finding that the core represents some crystalline form of urate oxidase (Hruban and Swift). This theory recieved some measure of support from comparative studies indicating that well-defined cores are present in all microbodies containing urate oxidase, and are generally absent in the particles lacking this enzyme (Afzelius; Shnitka), although an exception to this rule has been reported by Biempica in a human liver biopsy. However, as pointed out by Baudhuin et al. 1965a, preparations of urate oxidase, about ten times more active on a protein basis than purified cores, have been obtained by Mahler et al. From this result, it would appear that the peroxisome core must contain other proteins besides urate oxidase.

Physical Properties. From their behavior in density gradient experiments, the median dry weight of peroxisomes may be estimated at 2.4×10^{-14} g and their dry density at 1.32. In isotonic sucrose, they contain in weight about 75% of water. A detailed table of their physical properties, with comparative data for mitochondria and lysosomes, can be found in the article of de Duve (1965b). Most strikingly, peroxisomes are devoid of osmotic space in sucrose solutions and their membrane is thus permeable to this molecule. The median sedimentation constant for particulate catalase in 0.25 M sucrose is 5,000 Svedberg units. In normal rat liver, peroxisomes are relatively numerous; there is at least one peroxisome for every five mitochondria (Baudhuin and Berthet, unpublished results). Their abundance in liver may however be subject to large variations: for example, an important increase in the frequency of liver microbodies occurs in rats after injection of ethyldichlorophenoxyisobutyrate (Hess et al.; Svoboda et al. 1966, 1967).

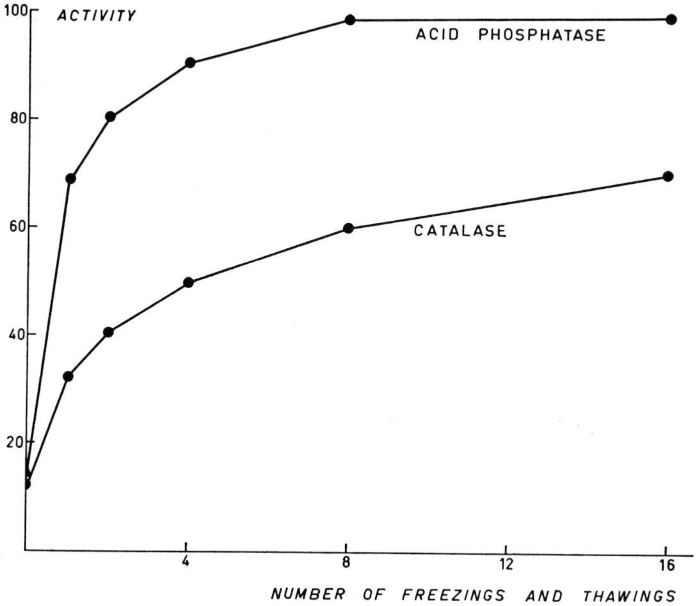

Fig. 5. Activation of rat liver catalase and acid phosphatase, in a large granule fraction, by repeated freezing (acetone–CO_2 mixture) and thawing. Activities are expressed in percent of the maximal activity observed after treatment with a detergent.

The activity of peroxisomal oxidases toward exogenous substrates is not increased when the granules are disrupted. Like sucrose, substrates thus seem to have free access through the membrane to the interior of the particles. However, catalase displays a considerable latency: its activity on exogenous H_2O_2 is small in intact granules and disruption of the particles causes a large increase of the enzymatic activity. Fig. 5 shows the activation of catalase as a result of repeated freezing and thawing. That the effect on enzyme activity is due to damage of the particles is indicated by the fact that catalase is released in soluble form concomitantly with the activation.

The latency of catalase appeared at first very puzzling, since H_2O_2 is a much smaller molecule than sucrose or the substrates for the oxidases. It has been shown (de Duve 1965b) that the latency can be explained on the basis of the very high concentration of the enzyme inside the particle and of the first order kinetics of the reaction catalyzed. As a consequence, although the peroxisomal membrane is very permeable to hydrogen peroxide, diffusion is nevertheless rate-limiting for the activity of particulate catalase.

This interpretation has been confirmed experimentally: progressive inhibition of catalase by KCN is accompanied by the disappearance of the latency phenomenon. The permeability coefficient of H_2O_2 through the peroxisome membrane has been estimated at 0.2 cm.min^{-1} from such inhibition experiments. Such a value may be considered quite high; in the case of the red cell membrane Nicholls found by the same method a value 5.5 times smaller.

The latency of catalase provided a possibility of investigating the effect of various treatments *in vitro* on peroxisomes and of comparing the stability of these granules with that of mitochondria and of lysosomes. Such a comparison is presented in Table 2. As can be seen, marked differences exist between the three types of particles. Particularly striking is the resistance of the particles to osmotic shock, which confirms the permeability of the membrane to sucrose. The lower sensitivity of peroxisomes compared with lysosomes, to detergents and to repeated freezing and thawing (see also Fig. 5) is another characteristic feature.

TABLE 2

Sensitivity of rat liver peroxisomes to various treatments, as compared to lysosomes and mitochondria.

Treatment	Peroxisomes (Catalase)	Lysosomes (Ac. Phosphatase)	Mitochondria (Glutamate-dehydrog.)
M.S.E. Blendor (min)	2	5 (1)	2 (1)
Repeated freezing and thawing (number)	7	<1	8 (1)
Hypotonicity (osmolarity)	Not effective	0.10–0.15 (1)	0.02–0.03 (1)
Detergents (g/l)			
Digitonin	0.8	<0.1	2.8 (3)
Triton X-100	2.5	<0.35 (2)	<1 (1)

Figures refer to the treatment necessary to unmask half of the initially latent enzyme activity. The enzyme given in parentheses is used as reference. (1) From Bendall and de Duve; (2) From Wattiaux and de Duve; (3) Beaufay (unpublished results).

Turnover. Price et al. have studied by different methods the rate of catalase synthesis and breakdown in rat liver and have shown that 2.25% of the total liver enzyme is renewed per hour. This corresponds to a half-life of 1.3 days. The rate of renewal of another major soluble protein component of the peroxisomes and that of the core have recently been determined and found comparable to that of catalase, indicating that peroxisomes are synthesized and destroyed as a whole (Leighton et al. 1968b).

Isotopic experiments (Higashi and Peters) show that catalase is synthesized in the endoplasmic reticulum, from which it is transferred to peroxisomes. This finding is in good agreement with the electron microscopic observation of peroxisomes attached to the endoplasmic reticulum. The final fate of peroxisomes in the cell is unknown.

(b) *Kidney*

Wattiaux-De Coninck et al. first produced evidence that kidney particulate catalase behaves very much like the liver enzyme in fractionation experiments. As can be seen from Table 3, where the enzymic content of peroxisomes in various cell types has been summarized, rat kidney peroxisomes lack urate oxidase. The specificity of L-α-hydroxyacid oxidase is different from that of the liver enzyme: the highest oxidation rate is obtained with α-hydroxybutyrate. The activity on L-leucine is higher than in liver.

It has also been shown by Wattiaux-De Coninck and coworkers that kidney catalase is latent and can be activated by detergents or by repeated freezing and thawing, but not by osmotic shock. Kidney contains microbodies, which were in fact first discovered in this organ (Rhodin), and it is very likely that those particles represent the peroxisomes in kidney, as in liver (Allen and Beard). No core is found in mouse kidney microbodies; in rat kidney, where no urate oxidase is detectable, Ericsson has, however, found a denser zone in the microbodies.

TABLE 3

Enzymes localized in peroxisomes from various cell types.

	Rat liver (1)	Rat kidney (2)	*Tetrahymena pyr.* (3)	*Acanthamoeba* (4)	Castor bean (glyoxysomes) (5)
Catalase	+	+	+	+	+
Oxidases					
D-aminoacid oxidase	+	+	+	−	−
Urate oxidase	+	−	−	+	
L-α-OH acid oxidase	+	+	+	−	+ (glycolate)
Unrelated to H_2O_2 metabolism					
Isocitrate lyase	−	−	+		+
Malate synthase	−	−	+		+
Citrate synthase					×
Malate dehydrogenase					×
Isocitrate dehydrogenase (NADP)	×		×		

+: unique peroxisomal location of particulate enzyme; ×: particulate enzyme also present in mitochondria; −: no appreciable activity in the homogenate. (1) Leighton et al. (1968a); (2) Allen and Beard; Baudhuin et al. (1965b); (3) Baudhuin et al. (1965b); Müller and Hogg; (4) Müller and Max Möller; Müller (personal communication); (5) Beevers (personal communication); Breidenbach and Beevers.

(c) *Protozoa*

The occurrence of peroxisomes has also been demonstrated in *Tetrahymena pyriformis*. *Tetrahymena* peroxisomes are the bearers of D-amino-acid oxidase and of L-*α*-hydroxyacid oxidase (Baudhuin et al. 1965b). The specificity of the latter enzyme is similar to that of the kidney enzyme. Besides catalase and oxidases, Müller and Hogg have found in the peroxisomes of *T. pyriformis* enzymes unrelated to H_2O_2 metabolism, which, although absent in higher organisms, may provide an important clue to the elucidation of the physiological function of peroxisomes (Table 3). The isocitrate lyase and malate synthase found in *Tetrahymena* peroxisomes are the two key enzymes of the glyoxylate bypass (Krebs–Kornberg cycle) present in lower organisms. This reaction sequence bypasses the CO_2 producing steps of the tricarboxylic acid cycle and shares several enzymes with this metabolic pathway (Fig. 6). The main result of the glyoxylate bypass is the formation of C_4 compounds from acetate, thus providing a possibility of converting fat into carbohydrate. *Tetrahymena* peroxisomes are however unable to carry out the complete sequence of the Krebs–Kornberg cycle, since virtually all of the citrate synthase, aconitase, succinic dehydrogenase, fumarase and malate dehydrogenase activities of the cells are located in the mitochondria (Müller and Hogg; de Duve 1967). *Tetrahymena* peroxisomes also contain a dehydrogenase acting on isocitrate. This enzyme requires NADP; it occurs also in the soluble fraction (55%) and in mitochondria (5%).

Peroxisomes have also been found in *Acanthamoeba* (Müller and Max Möller). They contain catalase and urate oxidase; D-aminoacid and L-*α*-hydroxyacid oxidases are absent in this protozoon, or display too small an activity to be measured in fractionation experiments.

(d) *Plant cells*

Breidenbach and Beevers have recently shown that in castor bean (*Ricinus communis*

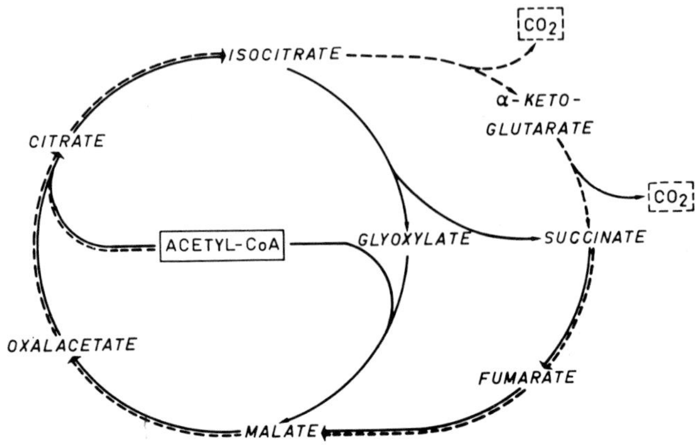

Fig. 6. The glyoxylate cycle. Interrupted lines represent the tricarboxylic acid cycle, continuous lines the glyoxylate pathway.

L.) germinating seedlings the nutritive endosperm contains particles, referred to as glyoxysomes, that contain enzymes of the glyoxylate bypass. These authors have also found similar particles in watermelon cotyledons. With the possible exception of aconitase, which could not be measured because of its instability, all the enzymes needed for conversion of acetyl-CoA into succinate (isocitrate lyase, malate synthase, malate dehydrogenase and citrate synthase) are present in castor bean glyoxysomes. The last two enzymes also occur in mitochondria. Malate synthase and isocitrate lyase levels increase markedly during germination and decrease when all the fat has been metabolized (Beevers). Catalase and an oxidase acting on glycolate are localized in the same particles; but no appreciable D-aminoacid oxidase activity has been found (Beevers, personal communication). Therefore glyoxysomes appear similar in nature to the *Tetrahymena pyriformis* peroxisomes, but are apparently the site of the complete glyoxylate cycle reaction sequence.

When examined with the electron microscope, glyoxysomes appear as particles with a diameter of about one micron, bounded by a single membrane (Beevers, personal communication). It is of interest to note that Mollenhauer et al. have found granules resembling animal microbodies in several plant species.

(e) *Other cell types*

In two transplantable rat tumors (a hepatoma and a radio-induced kidney adenocarcinoma), Wattiaux et al. (1967) have found that catalase is associated with granules sedimenting with the microsomal fraction. Whereas the peroxisomes from all sources described so far have in common a high equilibrium density, of the order of 1.23–1.25, the catalase-bearing particles of these tumors equilibrate at a density between 1.17 and 1.18 in such a gradient. Their distribution differs from that of glucose-6-phosphatase, a marker enzyme for the endoplasmic reticulum fragments which are the main component of the microsomal fraction. Catalase is latent in the homogenates of these tumors; it can be activated by Triton X-100 or a Blendor treatment, but not by osmotic shock or repeated freezing and thawing. Obviously the tumor particles differ greatly in their physical properties from the peroxisomes of the normal organ from which they originate. The presence in these particles of hydrogen peroxide producing oxidases has not yet been investigated.

In bone, part of the catalase of the homogenate is particulate and latent (Vaes; Vaes and Jacques). The particles containing this enzyme have a smaller sedimentation constant than mitochondria; they are not affected by exposure to hypotonic media. No information on the presence of oxidases in bone tissue is presently available.

3. *Physiological role*

The function of peroxisomes in the cell economy is not yet fully understood. The presence of the glyoxylate bypass enzymes in peroxisomes of at least some lower organisms suggests that these particles have an important role in gluconeogenesis. Whereas in castor bean endosperm peroxisomes can most probably handle the complete glyoxylate cycle reaction sequence, complex relationships must exist between mitochondria and peroxisomes in *Tetrahymena pyriformis*, where the glyoxylate cycle requires the participation of enzymes localized in both types of particles. The functional significance of these enzymes in the peroxisomes is not clear. The occurrence of peroxisomes in liver and kidney, which are the main sites of gluconeogenesis, suggests a similar role for the peroxisomes of higher organisms, although no enzymes participating directly in the synthesis of carbohydrate have been localized in liver or kidney peroxisomes. However, the α-ketoacids produced by peroxisomal oxidases may serve as building blocks for the formation of carbohydrate.

Much more difficult to assess is the possible role of catalase and of the peroxisomal oxidases. At first sight, the segregation of these enzymes together in a special particle seems to offer a protection for the cytoplasm against the highly toxic hydrogen peroxide. However, as pointed out by de Duve and Baudhuin, whose review should be consulted for a more detailed discussion of peroxisome functions, such a protection would be very incomplete, since some hydrogen peroxide-producing enzymes, like xanthine and monoamine oxidases, are localized outside the peroxisomes. A purely protective role for peroxisomes thus appears rather improbable.

Several products of the oxidations catalyzed by peroxisomal enzymes (acetaldehyde, α-ketoacids) can be reduced again by dehydrogenases occurring in the cell sap. It has consequently been suggested that peroxisomes may play a role in the reoxidation of extramitochondrial NADH. This coenzyme has no access to the electron transport chain since it cannot penetrate through the mitochondrial membrane. Several systems have been described for the removal of excess electrons from the cell sap. Best known is the α-glycerophosphate cycle: electrons are transferred by a cell sap dehydrogenase from NADH to α-glycerophosphate; the latter substance penetrates into the mitochondria, where phosphodihydroxyacetone is regenerated by an oxidase. The peroxisomal L-α-hydroxyacid oxidase, or catalase by its peroxidatic action on ethanol, could form similar electron shuttle systems together with cell sap dehydrogenases (Fig. 7). To what extent such a mechanism is operative in cells under physiological conditions is impossible to state at the present time. In liver, Kadenbach has brought forth evidence that the α-glycerophosphate cycle alone cannot reoxidize the totality of the NADH that can be produced by oxidation of glucose to pyruvate.

In rat liver, the activity of peroxisomal oxidases is strongly influenced by oxygen concentration and these enzymes show a relatively low affinity for oxygen, which could possibly act as a regulator (de Duve and Baudhuin). It has been suggested that peroxisomal respiration may be activated whenever the oxygen tension rises in the cells as a result of insufficient mitochondrial respiration due, for instance, to a lack of oxidizable substrates. Glycolysis would then be stimulated by the shuttle mechanism shown in Fig. 7, thus providing the mitochondria with new fuel in the the form of pyruvate. Such a control may provide a necessary flexibility for cells

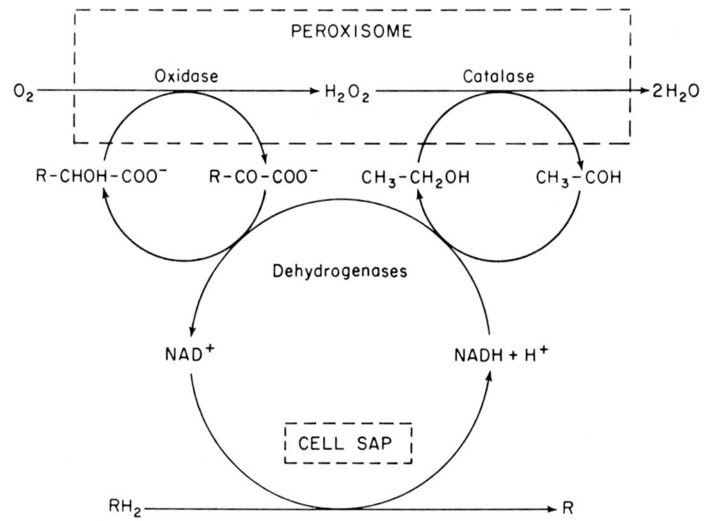

Fig. 7. Possible role of peroxisomes in the reoxidation of the cell sap NADH. (From de Duve and Baudhuin.)

normally oriented toward sparing their carbohydrates.

There is no indication that the energy liberated by peroxisomal oxidations can be reutilized by the cell. It has been estimated that in liver the peroxisome oxidases can account for approximately 20% of the total oxygen consumption of the organ.

No satisfactory explanation for the presence of isocitrate dehydrogenase activity in liver (and *Tetrahymena*) peroxisomes has yet been proposed. The very unusual distribution of this enzyme in liver (80% soluble, 15% mitochondrial and 5% peroxisomal) requires in itself more extended investigations. One would like to know whether one is dealing with a single or with several enzymes.

Note added in proof

In a recent paper (Tolbert, N. E., A. Oeser, T. Kisaki, R. H. Hageman and R. K. Yamazaki; J. Biol. Chem. 243 (1968) 5179) peroxisomes have been shown to be present in plant leaves. Tolbert et al. were able to obtain purified preparations of granules containing catalase, glycolate oxidase and glyoxylate reductase (NAD), from spinach leaves homogenates. When examined with the electron microscope, peroxisome-rich fractions contain particles 0.5–1.0 μ in diameter, bounded by a single membrane.

References

AFZELIUS, B. A.: The occurrence and structure of microbodies. J. Cell Biol. 26 (1965) 835.

ALLEN, J. M. and M. E. BEARD: α-Hydroxy acid oxidase: localization in renal microbodies. Science 149 (1965) 1507.

BAUDHUIN, P., H. BEAUFAY and C. DE DUVE: Combined biochemical and morphological study of particulate fractions from rat liver. J. Cell Biol. 26 (1965a) 219.

BAUDHUIN, P., M. MÜLLER, B. POOLE and C. DE DUVE: Non-mitochondrial oxidizing particles (microbodies) in rat liver, kidney and in *Tetrahymena pyriformis*. Biochem. Biophys. Res. Commun. 20 (1965b) 53.

BEAUFAY, H.: La centrifugation en gradient de densité (Thèse d'agrégation à l'enseignement supérieur, Université Catholique de Louvain). Louvain, Ceuterick (1966).

BEAUFAY, H., P. JACQUES, P. BAUDHUIN, O. Z. SELLINGER, J. BERTHET and C. DE DUVE: Tissue fractionation studies 18. Resolution of mitochondrial fractions from rat liver into three distinct populations of cytoplasmic particles by means of density equilibration in various gradients. Biochem. J. 92 (1964) 184.

BEEVERS, H.: Control of the glyoxylate cycle in germinating seedlings: Abstr. 7th Intern. Congr. Biochem., Tokyo (1967) 1033.

BENDALL, D. S. and C. DE DUVE: The activation of latent dehydrogenases in mitochondria from rat liver. Biochem. J. 74 (1960) 444.

BIEMPICA, L.: Human hepatic microbodies with cristalloid cores. J. Cell Biol. 29 (1966) 383.

BREIDENBACH, R. W. and H. BEEVERS: Association of the glyoxylate cycle enzymes in a novel subcellular particle from castor bean endosperm. Biochem. Biophys. Res. Commun. 27 (1967) 462.

DAEMS, W. T.: The fine structure of mouse-liver microbodies. J. Microscopie 5 (1966) 295.

DE DUVE, C.: Functions of microbodies (peroxisomes). J. Cell Biol. 27 (1965a) 25A.

DE DUVE, C.: The separation and characterization of subcellular particles. Harvey Lectures Ser. 59 (1965b) 49.

DE DUVE, C.: Properties and functions of peroxisomes. Abstr. 7th Intern. Congr. Biochem., Tokyo (1967) 211.

DE DUVE, C. and P. BAUDHUIN: Peroxisomes. (Microbodies and related particles). Physiol. Rev. 46 (1966) 323.

ERICSSON, J. L. E.: Absorption and decomposition of homologous hemoglobin in renal proximal tubular cells. Acta Pathol. Microbiol. Scand. Suppl. 168 (1964) 1.

ESSNER, E.: Endoplasmic reticulum and the origin of microbodies in fetal mouse liver. Lab. Invest. 17 (1967) 71.

GÄNSLER, H. and C. ROUILLER: Modifications physiologiques et pathologiques du chondriome. Schweiz. Z. Allgem. Pathol. Bacteriol. 19 (1956) 217.

GRAHAM, R. C. and M. J. KARNOVSKY: The histochemical demonstration of uricase activity. J. Histochem. Cytochem. 13 (1965) 448.

HESS, R., W. STÄUBLI and W. RIESS: Nature of the hepatomegalic effect produced by ethyl-chlorophenoxy-isobutyrate in the rat. Nature 208 (1965) 856.

HIGASHI, T. and T. PETERS, JR.: Studies on rat liver catalase I. Combined immunochemical and enzymatic determination of catalase in liver cell fractions. J. Biol. Chem. 238 (1963) 3945.

HRUBAN, Z. and H. SWIFT: Uricase: Localization in hepatic microbodies. Science 146 (1964) 1316.

KADENBACH, B.: Der Einfluss von Thyreoidhormonen *in vitro* auf die oxydative Phosphorylierung und Enzymaktivitäten in Mitochondrien. Inaugural-Dissertation, Philipps-Universität, Marburg/Lahn (1964).

LEIGHTON, F., B. POOLE, H. BEAUFAY, P. BAUDHUIN, J. W. COFFEY, S. D. FOWLER and C. DE DUVE: The large-scale separations of peroxisomes mitochondria and lysosomes from the liver of rats injected with Triton WR-1339. J. Cell Biol. 37 (1968a) 482.

LEIGHTON, F., B. POOLE and C. DE DUVE: (1968b) in preparation.

MAHLER, H. R., G. HÜBSCHER and H. BAUM: Studies on uricase I. Preparation, purification, and properties of a cuproprotein. J. Biol. Chem. 216 (1955) 625.

MOLLENHAUER, H. H., D. J. MORRÉ and A. G. KELLEY: The widespread occurrence of plant cytosomes resembling animal microbodies. Protoplasma 62 (1966) 44.

MÜLLER, M. and J. F. HOGG: Occurrence of protozoal isocitrate lyase and malate synthase in the peroxisomes. Federation Proc. 26 (1967) 284.

MÜLLER, M. and K. MAX MÖLLER: Peroxisomes in Acanthamoeba sp. J. Protozool. Suppl. 14 (1967) 12.

NICHOLLS, P.: Activity of catalase in the red cell. Biochim. Biophys. Acta 99 (1965) 286.

NICHOLLS, P. and G. R. SCHONBAUM: Catalases. In: P. D. Boyer, H. Lardy and K. Myrbäck, eds.: The enzymes, Vol. 8. London, Academic Press (1963) 147.

NOVIKOFF, A. B. and W. Y. SHIN: The endoplasmic reticulum in the Golgi zone and its relations to microbodies, Golgi apparatus and autophagic vacuoles in rat liver cells. J. Microscopie 3 (1964) 187.

PRICE, V. E., W. R. STERLING, V. A. TARANTOLA, R. W. HARTLEY, JR. and M. RECHCIGL, JR.: The kinetics of catalase synthesis and destruction *in vivo*. J. Biol. Chem. 237 (1962) 3468.

RHODIN, J.: Correlation of ultrastructural organization and function in normal and experimentally changed proximal convoluted tubule cells of the mouse kidney. Stockholm, Aktiebolaget Godvil (1954).

SHNITKA, T. K.: Comparative ultrastructure of hepatic microbodies in some mammals and birds in relation to species differences in uricase activity. J. Ultrastruct. Res. 16 (1966) 598.

SVOBODA, D. J. and D. L. AZARNOFF: Response of hepatic microbodies to a hypolipidemic agent, ethyl chlorophenoxyisobutyrate (CPIB). J. Cell Biol. 30 (1966) 442.

SVOBODA, D., H. GRADY and D. AZARNOFF: Microbodies in experimentally altered cells. J. Cell Biol. 35 (1967) 127.

TSUKADA, H., Y. MOCHIZUKI and S. FUJIWARA: The nucleoids of rat liver cell microbodies. Fine structure and enzymes. J. Cell Biol. 28 (1966) 449.

VAES, G.: Studies on bone enzymes. The activation and release of latent acid hydrolases and catalase in bone tissue homogenates. Biochem. J. 97 (1965) 393.

VAES, G. and P. JACQUES: Studies on bone enzymes. Distribution of acid hydrolases, alkaline phenylphosphatase, cytochrome oxidase and catalase in subcellular fractions of bone tissue homogenates. Biochem. J. 97 (1965) 389.

WATTIAUX, R. and C. DE DUVE: Tissue fractionation studies 7. Release of bound hydrolases by means of Triton X-100. Biochem. J. 63 (1956) 606.

WATTIAUX, R., S. WATTIAUX-DE CONINCK and J. P. SQUIFFLET: Distribution intracellulaire de la catalase dans deux tumeurs transplantables chez le rat. Arch. Intern. Physiol. Biochim. 75 (1967) 379.

WATTIAUX, R., M. WIBO and P. BAUDHUIN: Influence of the injection of Triton WR-1339 on the properties of rat-liver lysosomes. In: A. V. S. de Reuck and M. P. Cameron, eds.: Lysosomes. London, J. and A. Churchill Ltd (1963) 176.

WATTIAUX-DE CONINCK, S., M.-J. RUTGEERTS and R. WATTIAUX: Lysosomes in rat-kidney tissue. Biochim. Biophys. Acta 105 (1965) 446.

PART XIV

Ultrastructure and biochemistry of centrioles, flagella and cilia

CHAPTER 44

Centriole replication

DOROTHY R. PITELKA

Cancer Research Genetics Laboratory, University of California, Berkeley, Calif.

Contents

1. Introduction
2. Centriole ultrastructure
3. Centriole replication: the modal pattern
4. The centriole–kinetosome transition
5. Ultrastructure and replication of atypical centrioles
6. *De novo* formation of centrioles
7. Composition of centrioles

1. *Introduction*

A centriole is a minute, stainable body occupying the center of each pole of the division figure of most animal cells and many protistan and plant cells. During interphase it persists and duplicates in the cytoplasm; at prophase the two bodies separate to opposite sides of the nucleus, and the next achromatic figure is organized around and between them. Often a centriole moves to the surface and becomes the kinetosome (basal body) of a flagellum or cilium, and at least occasionally a kinetosome functions as a division center.

This description could have been written and elaborated at any time in the past 50 years or so. Most of what we presently know or suspect about the behavior of centrioles was revealed by classical methods of morphological and experimental cytology. Contemporary biophysical and biochemical techniques have amplified both the picture and its uncertainties; in particular electron microscopy has revealed a notably consistent pattern of centriole structure. This chapter will survey the contemporary picture and problems without attempting to recount the older observations upon which they are ultimately founded. Recent, extensive reviews by Went and Mazia furnish copious documentation of studies from the discovery of centrioles by van Beneden in 1876 through the early 1960's, and authority for some of the general statements to follow may be found there. Current ultrastructural information is a synthesis of the work of many investigators over the last 15 years; the descriptions given here are largely based on representative recent accounts by Fawcett, Gall, Gibbons and Grimstone, Murray and collaborators, Robbins and collaborators, and others to be cited.

Centrioles excite attention and controversy because they appear to possess two remarkable capacities: (1) to replicate and (2) to generate other organized structures in the surrounding cytoplasm.

There can be no disputing the observation that the great majority of centrioles and kinetosomes first appear in the immediate vicinity of preexisting ones – so close in fact that light microscopy suggests the division of the parent organelle into two like daughters. Where extra-large or extra-long centrioles are more readily observed, this division is usually unequal, a mature centriole producing a lateral bud that subsequently enlarges to become a replica of its parent. It is also unarguable that the centriole, when present, is the locus of organization of asters and spindles, and the kinetosome is the locus of organization of cilia and flagella, cilium-derived sensory structures (found in most animals), and a variety of intracytoplasmic fibers. That the origin of a new centriole from or near its parent is highly significant if not inevitable is implied by the long migrations that daughter organelles undertake after their formation, merely to reach opposite sides of the nucleus or else to assume appropriate positions for the construction in particular sites of cilia and related structures.

As visible bodies, limited and predictable in number and position, centrioles offer unique advantages for the study of these morphogenetic capacities. Along with the advantages go two long-standing enigmas. First, whereas most centrioles and kinetosomes appear to be self-replicating bodies, there are nonetheless a few outstanding cases where all evidence points to *de novo* formation. The paradox has long defied rational interpretation and, as we shall see, still does. Second, centrioles appear, when present, to control the mechanics of nuclear division, yet they cannot be found in many cells whose nuclei divide quite competently. Biologists have long been haunted by the possibility that the primary significance of centrioles has escaped them. Chatton (whose views are presented and expanded by Lwoff) has argued that kinetosomes, *always* necessary for the development of cilia and flagella in eukaryotic cells, are the primary organelles, whose structure-organizing capacity has been secondarily exploited in many ways, including the organization of the division figure, by organisms fortunate enough to have inherited them.

In dividing cells of higher plants, spindle fibrils as a rule converge on a cytoplasmic pole that is devoid of distinct structure. These polar zones are functional centers for the events of nuclear reproduction, but they probably lack the capacity to organize other cytoplasmic structures and they are not traceable through interphase. Centrioles likewise have not been seen in some animal cells and in many non-flagellated protozoa. Thus there is a spectrum of observed phenomena, ranging from the distinct centriole defined by its ultrastructure, through a variety of objects that behave more or less like centrioles but either have not shown centriolar structure in electron micrographs or have not been examined, to the morphologically centriole-less mitotic centers of certain cells. In this chapter, we will restrict consideration to morphologically demonstrable centrioles.

Where relations and functions are imperfectly known, terminology becomes slippery and over-precise definitions are hazardous. Certain flexible terms will be used here in ways that are convenient without implying absolute definitions. We will speak of 'parents' and 'daughters' and of the 'production' or 'generation' of new organelles by old ones because this is how it looks. 'Centriole' will be used for the organelle whether or not it is known to participate in nuclear division; those centrioles that are temporarily or permanently in a position to produce flagella or cilia will usually be called kinetosomes. The next sections will describe the modal morphology and visible behavior of the most commonly observed (typical, conventional, or orthodox) centrioles and their replication, followed by a consideration of some illuminating departures from the mode. Finally, the scant but provocative data on centriole composition will be presented, and some of their implications discussed.

2. *Centriole ultrastructure*

A typical centriole is a cylinder about 200 mμ in outside diameter and 300 to 500 mμ long. In its wall are nine evenly spaced fibrils running the length of the centriole; each fibril appears in cross section as a band of three microtubules so closely apposed that they seem to share common walls (Figs. 1 and 2). The band of three is inclined at an angle of 30–40° from a tangent to the circumference of the cylinder. The component microtubules of each triplet fibril are about 20 mμ in diameter and are designated, starting with the innermost, the A-, B- and C-subfibrils. A fine filamentous, granular, or amorphous material forms a wall matrix embedding the fibrils and extending to embrace the cylinder in a sleeve of variable extent and density. Surrounding the whole may be a spherical zone of cytoplasm, corresponding in many cases to the centrosome of light microscopy, from which ribosomes, mitochondria, and Golgi elements are excluded.

At one end of the centriole, to be identified as the proximal or old end, the lumen is often occupied by a characteristic cartwheel structure consisting of a central cylindri-

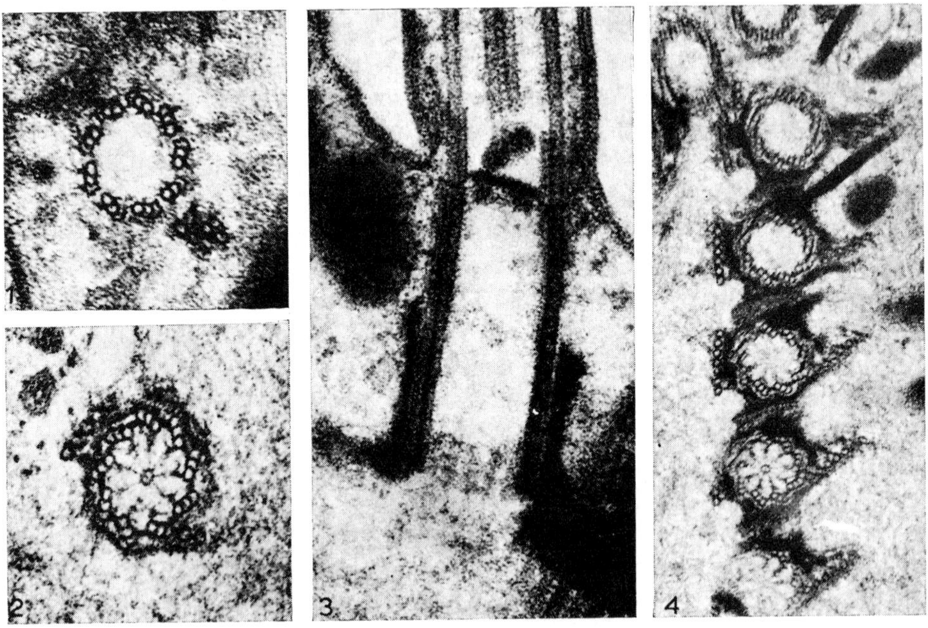

Fig. 1–4 are electron micrographs of thin sections of the ciliate *Didinium nasutum* from unpublished work by D. R. Pitelka and R. V. Dippell.

Fig. 1. A kinetosome cross-sectioned near its distal end. Nine triplet fibrils are clearly visible, with only a small amount of matrix material. The section is viewed from the proximal side, hence the triplet fibrils are skewed inward in the clockwise direction. Some of the C-subfibrils (the outermost fibril of each triplet) appear incomplete. One of the microtubular appendages of this kinetosome appears as a cluster of circular profiles at the lower right. × 71,000

Fig. 2. A kinetosome cross-sectioned at its proximal end. The nine triplet fibrils are peripherally enclosed by dense, amorphous material. Each A-subfibril is connected to its nearest neighboring C-subfibril by a filament. From an axial cylindrical structure, nine delicate spokes radiate outward to connect *via* branching filaments and small densities to the nine A-subfibrils; this central complex is a typical cartwheel. Two microtubule sections appear on an extension of the axis of one of the triplets at the lower right; five additional ones appear in a row at the upper left. These are standard microtubular appendages of most ciliate kinetosomes. × 71,000 *(Cont'd. on p. 1202.)*

cal hub and nine delicate, slightly swirled spokes extending toward the peripheral fibrils (Fig. 2). The distal end may be partly or completely closed by a thin, dense annulus or terminal plate (Fig. 3). A fine filament commonly connects each A-subfibril with its nearest neighboring C.

The structure of the centriole thus is inherently polarized, most evidently by the skewing of the triplet fibrils seen in cross section: if one views the centriole from the proximal end the triplets are skewed inward in the clockwise direction, and anticlockwise inward skewing means that the cross section is being viewed from the distal end. The presence of cartwheel and terminal plate identify proximal and distal ends in longitudinal section.

Reliable demonstration of these structural details requires a favorable plane of section and good contrast and resolution in the electron micrograph, but the diameter and fibrillar nature of the cylinder are so diagnostic that centrioles are readily recognized in oblique section and at low magnification. Within the range of conventional appearances, variations most commonly observed include the partial absence or distortion of the C-subfibrils, the absence of the cartwheel or terminal plate, the presence of dense rods or granules within the centriole's lumen, and modulations in centriole length between about 150 mμ and several microns. It often appears that the amount and density of the wall matrix – always variable – increase to the point of obscuring fine structure just at the times when the most interesting things are happening to the centriole.

This nine-membered cylinder represents the basic design of the centriole, but few are found without appendages of some kind. Most frequently encountered is a dense material, resembling the wall matrix but usually more condensed, in the form of indistinctly bounded, small masses protruding from the matrix or connected to it by filamentous bridges. The amount and manner of organization of this material vary widely in different cell types. Roughly spherical masses (typically around 100 mμ in diameter) generally known as pericentriolar bodies or satellites (Fig. 5) were first recognized by Bessis, Breton-Gorius and Thiéry and by Bernhard and de Harven. Their arrangement varies from a few masses, situated near but connected tenuously if at all to the centriole, to one or more rings of nine radially attached satellites. In

---

Fig. 3. A kinetosome and part of its cilium sectioned longitudinally. The delicate structures occupying about the proximal one-fifth of the lumen of the kinetosome are longitudinally cut elements of the cartwheel; distally the kinetosome is closed by the terminal plate. A sleeve of dense material surrounds the proximal half of the kinetosomal cylinder, and accessory microtubules originate in a heavy band of dense material at the right. ×79,000

Fig. 4. An example of the extreme geometric precision in position of fibrous centriolar appendages characteristic of many ciliated and flagellated cells. Here the same microtubular appendages seen in Fig. 1 and 2 appear in the same relationship to every kinetosome along a longitudinal row. In addition a very dense, solid fiber that extends to the right and anteriorly from each kinetosome is visible except where the plane of section passes below its level of origin. Dense material surrounds and links the kinetosomes. ×47,000

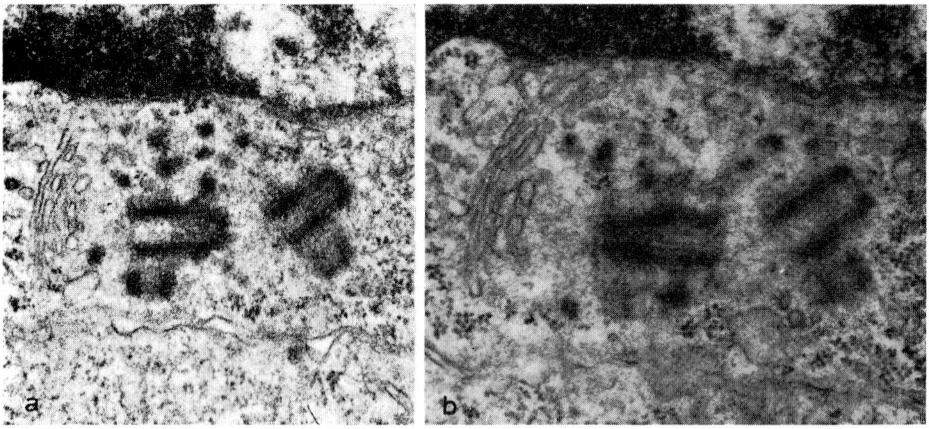

Fig. 5 a and b. Two sections through the same pair of mature centrioles with young procentrioles, in a thymocyte of a young rat. The cell is in very early prophase and the centrioles lie between the nucleus and the cell surface. Each procentriole stands perpendicular to one end of its parent and about 60 mμ from its wall. Clustered around the centriole on the left in both micrographs are numerous small satellites, most of them showing no connection to the centriole wall. Fig. 5b barely grazes the left procentriole but includes nearby a large, attached satellite not present in Fig. 5a. (From Murray et al.) 5a: $\times$ 32,000; 5b: $\times$ 40,000

many instances, the dense substance of longer or larger projections is arranged in repeating bands or segments that may be connected by fine filaments.

Kinetosomes typically bear appendages, some of which may be special developments of this dense material. A blunt, more or less distinctly striated projection known as a basal foot extends in a constant direction from every kinetosome in many metazoan ciliated epithelia. Nine fibrous strands, called transitional fibers by Gibbons and Grimstone, extend from near one end of a kinetosome out toward the plasma membrane in many ciliated and flagellated cells. Unlike most satellites, transitional fibers characteristically slant or curve outward like the blades of a pinwheel; they may occasionally be present on non-ciliated kinetosomes and centrioles, where no relationship to the cell membrane is detected. Also characteristic of many kinetosomes is the presence of one or more discrete, striated fibrils of various dimensions (apart from and more distinctly banded than the basal foot) arising in association with dense material near the base of the kinetosome. In plant and animal flagellates and metazoan epithelia and sensory cells, these root fibrils usually proceed toward the nucleus or cell base; in ciliates they typically extend to the right and anteriorly, parallel to the cell surface (Fig. 4).

Sakaguchi has demonstrated rather complex, striated, filamentous structures radiating from any position on the interphase centrioles of several kinds of non-ciliated cells in vertebrates. In some of these, three segments with different, characteristic, striation patterns are identifiable, and Sakaguchi suggests that satellites, basal feet, and striated root fibrils are all special developments of various segments of these pericentriolar bodies. Although this is by no means certain, the relatively amorphous, dense components of all of these structures, and of the wall matrix, are distinguishable only by their configurations.

Microtubules (relatively straight, hollow-appearing fibrils with reported diameters of 13–30 mμ) are found at some time in association with all centrioles. The nine peripheral, doublet microtubules of the axonemes of cilia and flagella (see chapter by Afzelius in this Handbook) are directly continuous with the A- and B-subfibrils of the kinetosomal triplets; the central axonemal microtubules arise in a dense granule or plate just distal to the kinetosome (Fig. 3). It is reasonably certain that all other associated microtubules connect with the dense material of matrix or satellites and are not continuations of centriolar microtubules. These include the microtubules of the mitotic apparatus; similar, but fewer, diverging cytoplasmic microtubules detectable in most cells in interphase; and a spectrum of more or less precisely organised, microtubular organelles in a variety of cell types. It is characteristic of most of these that they appear and disappear at particular times in the cell's cycle, and some of them, especially in flagellate and ciliate protozoa, arise at fixed points on the kinetosome's circumference (Fig. 4) and diverge from it in geometrically defined, asymmetric patterns. Many examples showing the constancy and intricacy of these patterns are reviewed by Pitelka. It should be pointed out here that in some of these same cell types, as well as in cells that lack centrioles, spindle or cytoplasmic microtubules may be present that have no known centriolar association.

3. *Centriole replication: the modal pattern*

The centrioles of interphase cells typically are paired, the sister organelles lying near one another and with their long axes often at approximately right angles, although tandem, parallel, and various oblique orientations also are observed. During late interphase or before, the two centrioles move slightly apart, and at about the same time a short new centriole, as little as 70 mμ long and frequently more slender than the old one, appears near one end of each mature centriole (Fig. 5). The new organelle, called by Gall the procentriole, is separated from the old one by a distance of about 70 mμ and is perpendicular to it. Cross sections of some procentrioles, perhaps the youngest, show rather indistinct tubular profiles in a dense wall matrix. During prophase the procentriole elongates while maintaining its orientation perpendicular to its parent. By metaphase the two are of equal size and form a pair at the spindle pole. For as long as the original perpendicular orientation of the new centriole is maintained, it remains possible to distinguish new from old: the centriole whose end abuts the wall of its companion, like the stem of an asymmetric T, is the young, or secondary, one. Centrioles, even when fully elongated, have not been seen to bear procentrioles until they have moved away from this initial perpendicular position.

Observation of the behavior of mitotic centers in living sea-urchin embryos after blockage of mitosis by mercaptoethanol led Mazia et al. to conclusions that parallel to a gratifying degree the ultrastructural sequence. Because mercaptoethanol inhibits an early event in the duplication of centers but not their maturation and separation, the authors were able to distinguish these three phenomena. They found the primary reproductive event to occur in late telophase, long before they could see any morphological evidence of duplication. The new center remains experimentally inseparable from its parent through a period that lasts almost a full cell cycle. This maturation period culminates in the splitting apart of parent and daughter that apparently permits each to initiate another duplication, although they still remain close together for a time, and also permits each to act independently as a mitotic center when mercaptoethanol prohibits duplication. Normally the splitting is followed in early prophase by further physical separation, the beginning of the poleward migration of the two mature centers bearing their attached infants. The occurrence of centrioles in pairs thus is a consequence of a one-cycle overlap in centriole generations.

This chronology accords well with the ultrastructural picture, where the first visible evidence of replication is the appearance late in interphase of the short procentriole (the discrepancy in timing may reflect the short cell cycles of the cleaving echinoderm egg), which then grows to full size but remains closely associated with its parent until some time in the next interphase.

The evidence from both sources implies that duplication is achieved not by the division of a parent into two like daughters but by the production of a small element that subsequently determines the growth of a copy of the parent. The Mazia group's conclusion that centriole replication follows a generative, rather than a fission, model has furnished a working hypothesis for most subsequent investigations. Molecular events invisible in electron micrographs of sectioned cells must be assumed to precede the assembly of visible structure, and both the identity and the source of the *initial* small element, the 'germ', remain unknown.

If a cartwheel is present at one end of a mature centriole, it is near this end that the procentriole lies; a cartwheel also is often seen in the short procentriole. Cartwheels are commonly present in kinetosomes, always at the inner or proximal end; the kinetosomal cross section viewed from this end always has the triplet fibrils skewed inward in the clockwise direction. Both structurally and functionally, then, the centriole is polarized from its earliest appearance. A procentriole consists of a proximal end only and appears next to the proximal end of a mature centriole; it grows distally as it matures and, if it becomes a kinetosome, produces a cilium from its distal end.

Although early ultrastructural studies of centriole replication suggested that satellite material might represent the earliest visible precursor of a daughter centriole, more recent evidence has offered little to substantiate this. Robbins et al., studying synchronized HeLa cells, find that satellites and a generally dense, expanded matrix zone, first appear in late interphase, well *after* procentriole formation in these cells, and tend to disappear as spindle fibrils are organized. Murray et al. note that in rat thymocytes satellites may be restricted to one member of a pair of mature centrioles, whereas both members produce procentrioles (Fig. 5). The very abundance, at various times in a centriole's cycle, of satellites, wall matrix, associated microtubules, fine filaments, and vesicles makes it almost impossible to determine whether any of these consistently presage the appearance of a recognizable procentriole.

4. The centriole–kinetosome transition

In metazoan tissues, cells capable of continued division generally show a repetition of the cycle of procentriole formation and maturation just described. One or two centrioles are commonly observable in differentiated cells not destined to divide again. Centrioles that produce cilia in the normal course of events, for example in presumptive photoreceptor cells and in sparsely ciliated epithelia, usually appear to be conventional products of conventional centriolar replicative cycles. In fact, the frequent finding of cilia (numerous reports are summarized by Scherft and Daems) sprouting from centrioles in cells where cilia had not previously been known to occur, and where no function is known for them, suggests that *any* centriole may become a kinetosome if experimentally or fortuitously stimulated to do so. Stubblefield and Brinkley have found, for example, that fibroblasts in cell culture produce extraordinary numbers of cilia after treatment with colcemid. In these normal and abnormal cases the distal end of a centriole becomes attached to the membrane of either an intracytoplasmic vesicle or the cell surface and proceeds to grow a cilium. The processes of flagellar development in animal sperm and fungal reproductive cells are variations on the same theme.

5. Ultrastructure and replication of atypical centrioles

Of all of the reported deviations from the conventional mode of centriolar structure and multiplication, most have been found in ciliated or flagellated cells or their near progenitors in animals, plants, and protists. Because of the light they shed on how centrioles *can* behave, some of these must be examined here.

Centrioles in the somatic tissues of the fungus gnat *Sciara*, studied by Phillips (1967), differ from typical centrioles only in being composed apparently of nine doublet rather than triplet fibrils. Germ-line tissues contain some of these nine-membered centrioles and in addition giant ones consisting of up to 90 singlet fibrils, about 0.5 μ long and disposed around an oval or rectangle that may reach 1 μ in width (Fig. 6). Paired centrioles in early spermatogonia often include a nine-membered old centriole and a giant new one with 20 or more singlet (or occasional doublet) fibrils. In later spermatogonia the number of fibrils per centriole increases; counts made on published micrographs indicate that the number is not necessarily a multiple of nine. That the giant is a true, functional centriole is amply demonstrated by its behavior as a center in mitosis and meiosis and by its subsequent continuity with the numerous axial fibrils of a motile sperm tail. The evidence available does not indicate what becomes of the

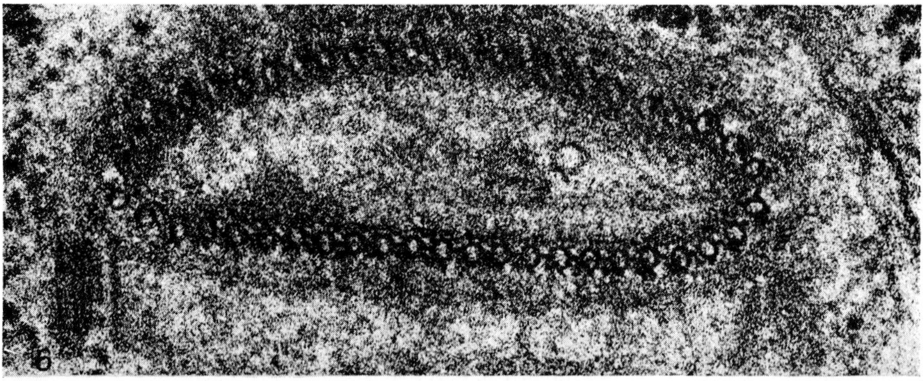

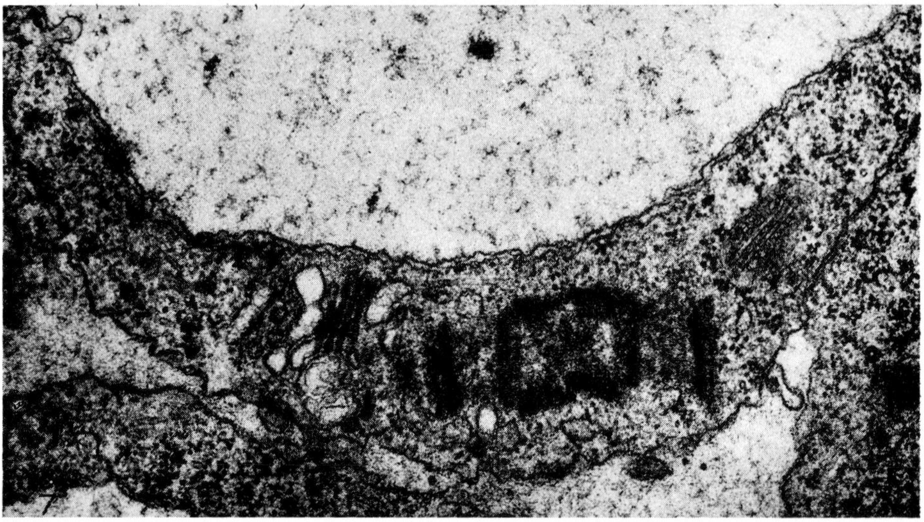

Fig. 6 and 7. Giant centrioles in spermatogonia of *Sciara*. (From Phillips 1967.)

Fig. 6. The parent centriole, cut transversely, consists of about 46 singlet microtubules, linked by fine bridges, in a matrix of moderate density. The daughter, perpendicular and cut longitudinally, is broader than its parent and presumably would contain more microtubules. Just within its wall is visible, on the left side, the band of material distinguishing daughter centrioles in these cells. × 122,000

Fig. 7. Two pairs of longitudinally cut, giant centrioles in an interphase cell. The daughter centrioles are wider than their parents are long, but are conventional in their orientation. × 42,000

conserved, nine-membered centrioles or the early, small giants; only 50- to 90- membered centrioles are found in late spermatogonia.

'Replication' is conventional in that paired centrioles separate during interphase and a new one appears perpendicular to each old one (Fig. 7). The new one shortly develops a distinctive band of dense material just within its fibrillar wall, permitting ready identification of old and young members of each pair. In every instance where centrioles of unequal size are paired, it is the one with this band that contains the larger number of fibrils and that is oriented with its end facing the wall of its companion. The conclusion is inescapable that a mature centriole in this tissue generates a daughter that is unlike itself. The presence of giant centrioles – sometimes two pairs of them – in oocytes and nurse cells suggests that the mature ova of *Sciara* also contain giants, in which case the origin of the nine-membered centrioles of the embryonic somatic tissues is another puzzle.

In several instances, departures from orthodox replication patterns are associated with the rapid production of numerous kinetosomes in ciliated cells. Gall's study of atypical spermatogenesis in the snail *Viviparus* showed that the process parallels normal centriole replication except that numerous – perhaps 15 or more – procentrioles develop simultaneously in a cluster around the proximal end of a normal mature one. Centriole production thus is not limited to a 1:1 ratio of old to new. Each procentriole subsequently elongates and sprouts a flagellum.

A different sort of multiple centriole production occurs in the differentiation of ciliated epithelia in the young mouse and rat, studied by Dirksen and Crocker. A single pair of conventional centrioles is inherited by each cell at the final cytokinesis; some 300 kinetosomes are present in the same cell a few days later, the bulk of morphogenetic activity occurring during a single day. The clearest developmental stages seen are clusters of short procentrioles (probably a maximum of six per cluster) arranged radially about a spherical dense body, about 150 mμ in diameter, that may

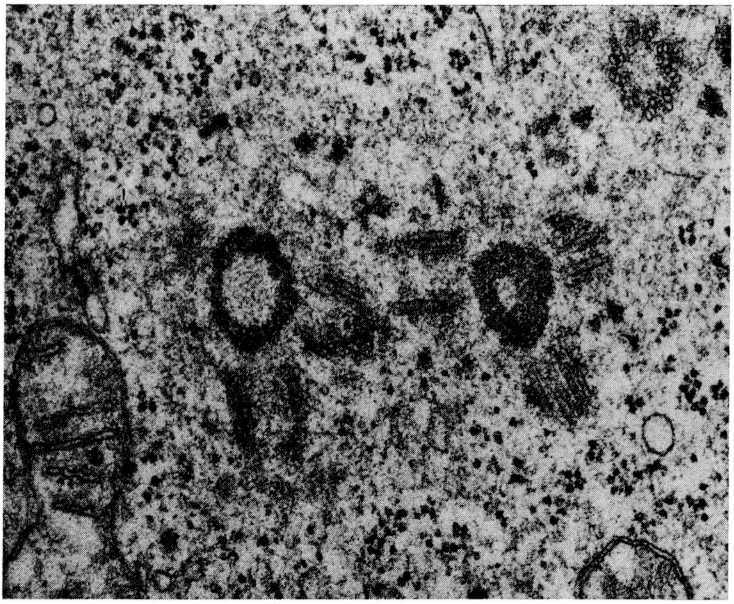

Fig. 8. Two procentriole clusters in oviduct epithelium of a five-day-old suckling mouse. In each cluster three procentrioles (one at the left barely grazed by the section) radiate from a spherical dense body. Such bodies may appear solid or may have central cavities of varying sizes, like those shown here. (From unpublished work of E.R. Dirksen and T.T. Crocker.) $\times$ 62,000

be solid or may have a low-density center (Fig. 8). Similar solid or hollow dense bodies lie free in the cytoplasm. Full-length centrioles are scattered without evident orientation through the cytoplasm, and high-resolution micrographs show very fine filamentous material emanating from them and often merging with larger masses of similar material within which are embedded numerous small dense bodies. The authors suggest that mature centrioles generate these diffuse fibrogranular masses, some of whose substance then condenses into the dense bodies that in turn generate new procentrioles, the whole process being repeatable. Regardless of whether this postulated sequence is verified in further study, the facts are significant. Under these circumstances, when the cell is in a veritable ferment of centriole-synthesis-and-assembly, the embodiment of a procentriole does not require the close physical proximity of a mature centriole, although recently matured ones are present in numbers. However, it evidently does require the presence of something that may be derived from them. Random assembly of presynthesized ingredients in the cytoplasm does not occur.

Multiple kinetosome production has been examined by Mizukami and Gall in the male gametophyte of the fern *Marsilea*. During the final spermatogenous cell generations, spherical structures called blepharoplasts occupy the poles of the mitotic apparatus and are visible near the nuclear membrane in interphase. They range in diameter from 0.3 to 1 μ and consist of densely packed, radially arranged tubules in a dense matrix. Each tubule is about 100 mμ in diameter and shows evidence of a nine-part radial structure. By the last mitotic metaphase the blepharoplast has become a hollow sphere, as if by the dissolution of the inner ends of the tubules; its wall now is made up of radially arranged procentrioles, about 100 mμ in diameter and 80 mμ long and containing distinct central cartwheels. Subsequently the sphere breaks up, and the procentrioles elongate and become the typical kinetosomes of the multiflagellate sperm. A similar kind of blepharoplast was found at comparable stages in the cycad *Zamia*. In these cases the functional mitotic center consists of an aggregate of incipient, nine-membered centrioles without any typical mature ones. The origin of the aggregate could not be traced; no centriolar structures were found in earlier cells of the germ line or elsewhere, and no indications of replication were seen.

In contrast to these examples, where multiple kinetosomes are produced rapidly in a cell that previously has contained only one pair of centrioles at most, is the situation in ciliate protozoa, where a large complement of preexisting kinetosomes is duplicated with each cytokinesis. The duplication affects not only the number of kinetosomes but their topographic arrangement in specific patterns. This replication process in ciliates is of basic importance to the general problem of cell-surface differentiation; Sonneborn, Tartar, and others have shown unequivocally that inheritance of highly asymmetric and polarized cortical pattern is independent of immediate nuclear or endoplasmic control. Whether the new kinetosome population arises by replication of old ones all over the body surface or only in certain locations, one preexisting kinetosome, so far as is known, produces only one new one at a time. Ehret and De Haller, Dippell (1965), and Bradbury and Pitelka have been able to identify with certainty new-formed kinetosomes, but stages in their formation have been notably elusive.

In *Paramecium*, as in many other ciliates, kinetosomes may occur in pairs over the body surface, each pair surrounded by an orderly, asymmetric set of fibrillar appendages and membranes that delineate the repeating unit of cortical pattern. Prior to nuclear division, cortical units in the presumptive fission zone begin to elongate and a new, non-ciliated kinetosome appears anterior and at a slight angle to each of the old ones. The two newly assorted pairs move apart as the unit continues to elongate, cilia and intracellular fibrils grow out from the new kinetosomes, and a partition separates the old unit transversely into two. Repeated duplication leads to the formation of many new units and the elongation of the whole cell. New kinetosomes are readily identifiable by their position when a single unit contains four kinetosomes instead of the usual two; they look just like the old ones. In young cells of the apostome ciliate *Hyalophysa*, newly formed kinetosomes alternate with old ones along a close-set longitudinal row (Fig. 9); they are elliptical instead of circular in cross section, are set deeper in the cortex than the old ones, lack cilia, and, as in *Paramecium*, stand initially at a slight angle to their older neighbors.

In both *Paramecium* and *Hyalophysa* one can identify in electron micrographs sites where a new kinetosome would soon have appeared had the organism not been fixed, but until recently no distinctive structure had been seen there consistently enough to be meaningful. Dippell (1967), however, reports finding thin plaques of dense material,

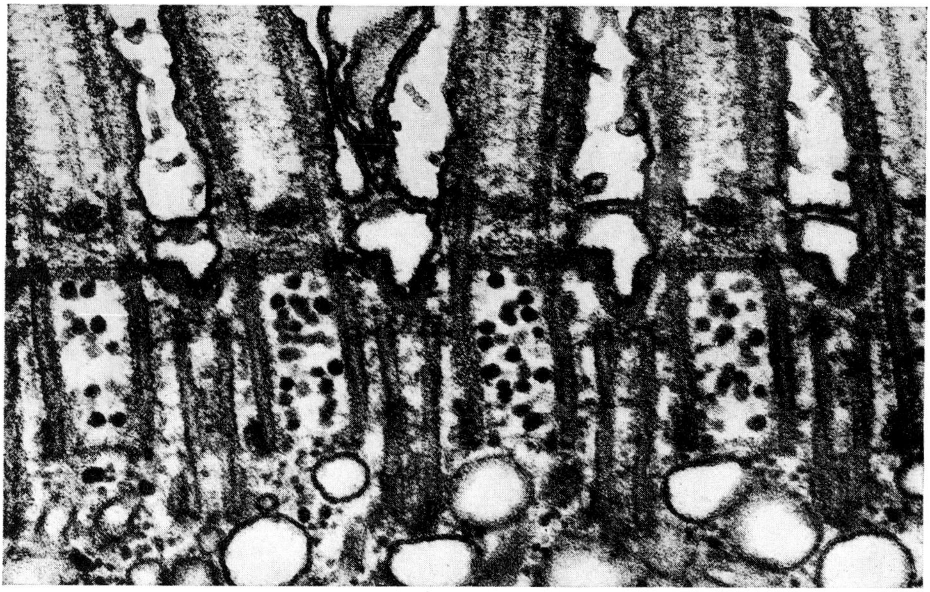

Fig. 9. A row of longitudinally sectioned kinetosomes from a young cell of the ciliate *Hyalophysa chattoni*. Mature, cilium-bearing kinetosomes of conventional structure (but lacking distinct cartwheels) alternate with new, non-ciliated ones. The new ones, elliptical in cross section, are cut on their narrower diameters and appear much more slender than the mature ones; they also are set deeper in the cell cortex. (From unpublished work of P.C. Bradbury and D.R. Pitelka.) × 72,000

at the periphery of which microtubular profiles progressively take shape, first as singlets, then as doublets and triplets, finally coming to resemble a procentriole lying perpendicular to its parent. Allen has found a very few bodies that resemble perpendicular procentrioles in *Tetrahymena*, where replication of body kinetosomes occurs unpredictably during the cell's growth phase. The implication of all these observations is that the kinetosome's morphogenesis is abrupt, and when a procentriole appears at all it must endure only briefly, elongating and tilting so that the formed kinetosome soon is almost parallel to its parent and can promptly sprout a cilium. The prolonged maturation period of conventional procentrioles is clearly not required here.

The centrioles of certain complex flagellate protozoa are large and clearly visible in life. Cleveland has succeeded in following them through complete cycles of sexual and asexual cell reproduction. They differ conspicuously from other known types in that the large bodies that are functional centrioles are at all times distinct from the kinetosomes that produce flagella at the cell surface. The varieties of structure and behavior described and photographed by Cleveland are far too complex to be reviewed here, but his simplified diagram of the centriolar cycle in the genus *Trichonympha* (Fig.

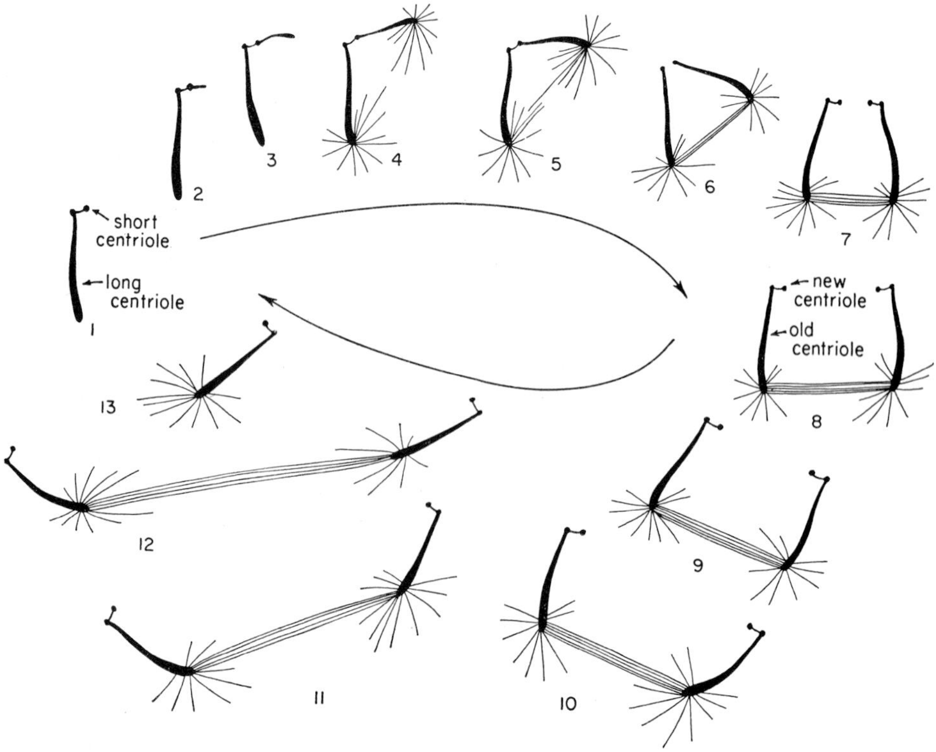

Fig. 10. Diagrammatic representation of the life cycle of centrioles in *Trichonympha*. Explanation in text. (Redrawn from Cleveland 1957.)

10) is a good example, and these centrioles have been examined in the electron microscope by Grimstone and Gibbons.

A slender rod, several microns long, occupies an axial position in the conical apex of the large, multiflagellate cell; this is a long, mature centriole. Its tapering anterior end terminates in a tiny swelling, which in the interphase cell is paired with a short centriole (Fig. 10, stage 1). With the onset of prophase, the short centriole begins to elongate (stages 2–3), while the cell apex broadens, ultimately partitioning its flagellar coat into two fields and permitting the two centrioles to diverge. At the posterior, or distal, ends of both elongate centrioles, asters appear and between them is formed a spindle, which participates with the intact nucleus in mitotic events (stages 4–12). Meanwhile a new short centriole appears next to the proximal swelling of each old one (stage 7). A new half-set of organelles (kinetosomes and a complex of fibrillar structures not shown on the diagram) grows out from the region of the new centriole during stages 7 to 12. Variations from this scheme found in other genera include the resorption of the entire distal length of the old centrioles after cytokinesis and persistence of only short centrioles during interphase; and the severing during prophase of the distal ends of both centrioles, which together migrate posteriorly, proceed to serve their mitotic function, and then disappear.

In electron micrographs of non-dividing *Trichonympha*, what is clearly identifiable as the long, distal portion of the centriole is a rod of dense, spongy, filamentous material, in the center of which is embedded a stack or whorl of long, narrow, very dense lamellae. Above the anterior end of this rod and connected to it only by fine strands is a hemispherical cap of similar, spongy, filamentous structure, surmounting two half-discs of striated or lamellar substance; the latter are perhaps the short centrioles of light microscopy. Within the spongy cap is embedded a long, but otherwise typical, nine-membered centriole, and posterior and at an angle to it – but still anterior to the massed rows of kinetosomes – is a single, flagellum-bearing kinetosome. One can imagine that these two represent a conventional pair of centrioles and that the dense, spongy material of the hemispherical cap and central rod is greatly hypertrophied satellite or matrix material. It would follow that here, as in orthodox mitosis, spindle and astral microtubules originate in satellites or matrix. In only a very few cells, Grimstone and Gibbons found an elongate centriole in an axial position posterior to the centriolar rod; whether these might represent possible division stages or misplaced kinetosomes could not be determined. In the related genus *Pseudotrichonympha*, the same authors found no nine-membered centriole in any appropriate region, although a distribution of spongy material reconcilable with the light-microscope picture of centrioles in this genus was present. Cells of both genera possess thousands of kinetosomes and, separating the latter more or less completely from the centriolar region, a fibrous tube of astonishing complexity. Until these flagellates are examined by electron microscopy during division and reorganization, correlation of ultrastructure with the visible events of morphogenesis is simply not possible.

6. *De novo formation of centrioles*

The composite blepharoplast of *Marsilea* and *Zamia* is the only one of the centriolar structures described above for which no progenitor is known; as in other higher plants, the cells of the sporophyte lack morphologically identified centrioles. Other cases of apparent *de novo* formation, reported by light microscopists, have been reexamined by electron microscopy in the ameboflagellates *Naegleria* by Schuster and by Dingle and Fulton and *Tetramitus* by Outka and Kluss, and in parthenogenetically activated eggs of a sea-urchin by Dirksen. Intensive search of ameboid cells of *Naegleria* from log-phase cultures failed to reveal any trace of a centriole, yet fully-formed, typical kinetosomes are present less than an hour after initiation of ameba-to-flagellate transformation. Flagella and a characteristic set of intracellular fibrils promptly grow out from them.

Transformation is similar in *Tetramitus*, but in this genus the flagellate, as well as the centriole-less ameba, can live and multiply indefinitely without reverse transformation. Outka and Kluss found during the ameba-to-flagellate transition masses of moderately dense material enclosing or adjoining bands of microtubules that presumably were going to contribute to the complex cytoskeleton of the mature flagellate. In flagellates from continuous culture, spherical masses of similar dense material lie proximal to and even invade the lumina of what appear to be young kinetosomes. The latter bear short flagellar stubs or none and often seem to have incompletely formed microtubules. A long, slender, nuclear process frequently extends at this stage to the kinetosome base. The evidence as it relates to kinetosome production is difficult to interpret: while the case for *de novo* formation in the transforming cell is strong, one would on principle expect the flagellate's four kinetosomes to be cyclically self-replicating. But stages in the generation of daughters by flagellum-bearing kinetosomes have not been demonstrated satisfactorily in any other flagellate, and we have for comparison only the scant evidence for the existence of a relatively orthodox, if abbreviated, procentriole stage in ciliates.

The sea-urchin egg is a classical example of a female gamete that appears somehow to lose its centrioles during or after meiosis; when such an egg is fertilized the sperm provides centrioles of zygotic mitosis. If, however, the egg, or even an enucleate fragment of it, is artificially activated, asters appear in the cytoplasm and the cell or fragment may cleave. Dirksen showed that centrioles, typical even to the presence of satellites, are present at the centers of such cytasters.

7. *Composition of centrioles*

Essentially no direct information is available concerning the chemical composition of centrioles or the molecular bases of their formation. Efforts to isolate them in sufficient quantity for chemical analysis have been made, most frequently with *Tetrahymena* as a rich source of kinetosomes. Satir and Rosenbaum, in general agreement with other workers, have shown that isolates thus far achieved are significantly contaminated with adherent membranes and fibrillar appendages, and furthermore that even under these circumstances the kinetosomes themselves have begun to lose structure such as matrix and cartwheels, so that not all of their components may be represented in the bulk analyses.

By selective extraction procedures it may ultimately be possible to accomplish a chemical dissection of centrioles in much the same way as Gibbons has degraded and analysed cilia. It is to be expected that the microtubules of the centriole skeleton will prove similar to those of cilia. Considerable morphological evidence, summarized in recent reports by Barnicot, Phillips (1966), and Ringo, suggests that spindle, cytoplasmic, and ciliary microtubules all are composed of longitudinal filaments, each of which is a linear arrangement of globular units about 40 Å in diameter. The number of filaments counted is most frequently 13 in a singlet microtubule from any source and probably in the A-subfibril of the cilium or kinetosome, and less than 13 in the B- and C-subfibrils. Analyses of purified proteins extracted by Gibbons, Shelanski and Taylor, and others from various kinds of microtubular structures suggest that the main protein subunit may be similar in all cases. But consistent differences in reaction to chemical fixatives have been known for a long time, and recently Behnke and Forer have presented evidence of differential susceptibility of cytoplasmic microtubules, central ciliary microtubules, and A- and B-subfibrils, all in the same cell, to cold, heat, colchicine, and pepsin. It seems likely that a fundamental chemical relationship exists in the protein skeleton and that added components account for some differences in properties. The composition and significance of microtubules in cilia are discussed by Sleigh and by Afzelius in this Handbook, and those of the mitotic apparatus by Forer.

Interest in centrioles as self-replicating bodies has led naturally to a search for a replicating molecule in them, a search intensified since the demonstration of DNA in chloroplasts and mitochondria. Detection of DNA in kinetosome fractions has not been conclusive because of the possibility of contamination; evidence for RNA is even less certain because ribosomal contamination is probable. Hufnagel extracted from well-washed, kinetosome-carrying pellicular ghosts of *Paramecium* a quantity of DNA equal to about 1–2 per cent of total cellular DNA. However, its density was indistinguishable from that of nuclear DNA and she found some evidence of selective binding of extraneous DNA to pellicles.

Cytochemical methods of DNA detection in ciliate pellicles are perhaps more promising, since they permit visual correlation of DNA sites with the precise and specific pattern of kinetosome distribution and with morphogenetic states in individual cells. Using acridine-orange fluorescence and light-microscope autoradiography, Randall and Disbrey found evidence of DNA at kinetosome sites in *Tetrahymena* ghosts, and Smith-Sonneborn and Plaut obtained similar results with *Paramecium*. Both groups report DNase-sensitive fluorescent staining of all kinetosomes but only during part of the interfission period; uncoiling of the DNA molecule or masking by histones might explain its apparent absence during the rest of the cycle. Within the limits of observation, the incorporation of tritiated thymidine into pellicular structures followed the topographic pattern to be expected in each if semi-conservative replication is assumed. The time of maximum incorporation of label into pellicular structures coincided approximately with the peak of fluorescence staining. In other words, new and old kinetosomes contain DNA detectable by fluorescence staining primarily during the latter part of the growth phase, and incorporation of newly synthesized DNA into cortical structures is demonstrable at about the same time.

Randall and Disbrey estimated the amount of DNA per kinetosome at about 2×10^{-16} g. The minuteness of this quantity could account for the failure of numerous efforts to detect DNA in centrioles and kinetosomes of other cells or by other methods, but it also leaves open, to a degree, the possibility that the DNA measured is a contaminant from other cellular sources and makes further verification necessary. Granted that the presence of DNA at least in ciliate kinetosomes seems likely, the data do not tell us whether it resides and replicates in the kinetosome or migrates there periodically from the nucleus.

Although Sonneborn's genetic analyses of *Paramecium* have demonstrated that inheritance of cortical *pattern* in these ciliates is locally determined through many hundreds of generations, we have no evidence in this or any other material of mutation in centrioles or kinetosomes. Mutant strains of *Chlamydomonas* with non-motile flagella are known and nuclear genes that control them have been identified. Warr et al. found 14 of these mutations to effect a marked structural disorganization of the central pair of microtubules in the paralyzed flagella. Thus not all centriolar derivatives are controlled by centriolar DNA alone.

The differentiation of a centriole has to involve at least the following: (1) the synthesis of required polypeptides, (2) the assembly of these into microtubules, dense material, and cartwheel substance (assuming the latter two to be protein), (3) the elaboration from these of the polarized, nine-membered cylinder, and (4) the synthesis and assembly of the proteins of fibrous appendages at specified times and places. Step 3 may be simultaneous with parts of step 2 but is clearly more complex than the mere assembly of microtubules, for example. Satir and Satir offer the ingenious proposition that an alpha-helical protein, perhaps located in the cartwheel inside a procentriole, could generate nine-fold symmetry around its axis by an appropriate periodic repetition of a structurally important amino acid.

It is a necessary premise of the generative model of centriole reproduction that assembly is not random, and the bulk of ultrastructural evidence confirms that either the old centriole is a direct source or its immediate environment is an exclusive site of something essential to procentriole assembly. In some instances the old organelle is replaced, at the moment of assembly, by a sphere of dense material (the Dirksen-Crocker epithelia) or by something so small and unremarkable that it has not been recognized (*Naegleria*, sea-urchin cytasters, *Marsilea*). It is conceivable that Mazia's postulated germ – DNA or no – is concealed in the ubiquitous dense material, often unrecognizable among the morphological miscellany lying about in any cytoplasm.

To extend this hypothesis to cases of apparent *de novo* formation would require that the germ survive and act at great distance, in time and space, from its parent.

The question of how a germ or a genetic message from whatever source determines the structure of a full-blown centriole does not differ in kind from the same question asked for any other complex organelle. The processes of precise assembly from indistinct precursors at sites removed from the parent organelle and at specifically controlled times, the instances of multiple assembly, the possibility of endogenous genetic control, and even the morphology of replication as far as it is understood are reminiscent of viral replication within cells. The centriole is several steps up from a virus in order of complexity, but the brightest promise for understanding its morphogenesis may lie in treating it experimentally as a similar phenomenon.

References

ALLEN, R. D.: Fine structure, reconstruction and possible functions of various components of the cortex of *Tetrahymena*. J. Protozool. 14 (1967) 553.

BARNICOT, N. A.: A note on the structure of spindle fibres. J. Cell Sci. 1 (1966) 217.

BEHNKE, O. and A. FORER: Evidence for four classes of microtubules in individual cells. J. Cell Sci. 2 (1967) 169.

BERNHARD, W. and E. DE HARVEN: L'ultrastructure du centriole et d'autres éléments de l'appareil achromatique. In: W. Bargmann et al., eds.: Proc. 4th Internat. Conf. Electron Microscopy 1958, Vol. 2. Berlin, Springer-Verlag (1960) 217.

BESSIS, M., J. BRETON-GORIUS and J. P. THIÉRY: Centriole, corps de Golgi et aster des leucocytes. Étude au microscope électronique. Rev. Hématol. 13 (1958) 363.

BRADBURY, P. C. and D. R. PITELKA: Observations on kinetosome formation in an apostome ciliate. J. Microscopie 4 (1965) 805.

CLEVELAND, L. R.: Types and life cycles of centrioles of flagellates. J. Protozool. 4 (1957) 230.

CLEVELAND, L. R.: Function of flagellate and other centrioles in cell reproduction. In: L. Levine, ed.: The cell in mitosis. New York, Academic Press (1963) 3.

DINGLE, A. D. and C. FULTON: Development of the flagellar apparatus of *Naegleria*. J. Cell Biol. 31 (1966) 43.

DIPPELL, R. V.: Reproduction of surface structure in *Paramecium*. In: Progress in protozoology. Internat. Congr. Ser. 91. London, Excerpta Medica Foundation (1965) 65.

DIPPELL, R. V.: How ciliary basal bodies develop. Science 158 (1967) 527.

DIRKSEN, E. R.: The presence of centrioles in artificially activated sea urchin eggs. J. Biophys. Biochem. Cytol. 11 (1961) 244.

DIRKSEN, E. R. and T. T. CROCKER: Centriole replication in differentiating ciliated cells of mammalian respiratory epithelium. An electron microscopic study. J. Microscopie 5 (1966) 629.

EHRET, C. F. and G. DE HALLER: Origin, development and maturation of organelles and organelle systems of the cell surface in *Paramecium*. J. Ultrastruct. Res. Suppl. 6 (1963) 1.

FAWCETT, D. W.: The cell. Its organelles and inclusions. Philadelphia, W. B. Saunders Co. (1966).

GALL, J. G.: Centriole replication. A study of spermatogenesis in the snail *Viviparus*. J. Biophys. Biochem. Cytol. 10 (1961) 163.

GIBBONS, I. R.: Chemical dissection of cilia. Arch. Biol. 76 (1965) 317.

GIBBONS, I. R. and A. V. GRIMSTONE: On flagellar structure in certain flagellates. J. Biophys. Biochem. Cytol. 7 (1960) 697.

GRIMSTONE, A. V. and I. R. GIBBONS: The fine structure of the centriolar apparatus and associated structures in the complex flagellates *Trichonympha* and *Pseudotrichonympha*. Phil. Trans. Roy. Soc. London Ser. B 250 (1966) 215.

HUFNAGEL, L. A.: Fine structure and DNA of pellicles isolated from *Paramecium aurelia*. In: R. Uyeda, ed.: Electron microscopy. Proc. 6th Internat. Congr., Kyoto, 1966, Vol. 2. Tokyo, Maruzen Co. (1966) 239.

LWOFF, A.: Problems of morphogenesis in ciliates. New York, John Wiley and Sons (1950).

MAZIA, D.: Mitosis and the physiology of cell division. In: J. Brachet and A. E. Mirsky, eds.: The cell, Vol. 3. New York, Academic Press (1961) 77.

MAZIA, D., P. J. HARRIS and T. BIBRING: The multiplicity of the mitotic centers and the time-course of their duplication and separation. J. Biophys. Biochem. Cytol. 7 (1960) 1.

MIZUKAMI, I. and J. GALL: Centriole replication II. Sperm formation in the fern, *Marsilea*, and the cycad, *Zamia*. J. Cell Biol. 29 (1966) 97.

MURRAY, R. G., A. S. MURRAY and A. PIZZO: The fine structure of mitosis in rat thymic lymphocytes. J. Cell Biol. 26 (1965) 601.

OUTKA, D. E. and B. C. KLUSS: The ameba-to-flagellate transformation in *Tetramitus rostratus* II. Microtubular morphogenesis. J. Cell Biol. 35 (1967) 323.

PHILLIPS, D. M.: Substructure of flagellar tubules. J. Cell Biol. 31 (1966) 635.

PHILLIPS, D. M.: Giant centriole formation in *Sciara*. J. Cell Biol. 33 (1967) 73.

PITELKA, D. R.: Fibrillar systems in flagellates and ciliates. In: T. T. Chen, ed.: Research in protozoology, Vol. 3. Oxford, Pergamon Press (1969) p. 279.

RANDALL, J. T. and C. DISBREY: Evidence for the presence of DNA at basal body sites in *Tetrahymena pyriformis*. Proc. Roy. Soc. (London), Ser. B 162 (1965) 473.

RINGO, D. L.: The arrangement of subunits in flagellar fibers. J. Ultrastruct. Res. 17 (1967) 266.

ROBBINS, E. and N. K. GONATAS: The ultrastructure of a mammalian cell during the mitotic cycle. J. Cell Biol. 21 (1964) 429.

ROBBINS, E., G. JENTZCH and A. MICALI: The centriole cycle in synchronized HeLa cells. J. Cell Biol. 36 (1968) 329.

SAKAGUCHI, H.: Pericentriolar filamentous bodies. J. Ultrastruct. Res. 12 (1965) 13.

SATIR, B. and J. L. ROSENBAUM: The isolation and identification of kinetosome-rich fractions from *Tetrahymena pyriformis*. J. Protozool. 12 (1965) 397.

SATIR, P. and B. SATIR: A model for ninefold symmetry in alpha-keratin and cilia. J. Theoret. Biol. 7 (1964) 123.

SCHERFT, J. P. and W. T. DAEMS: Single cilia in chondrocytes. J. Ultrastruct. Res. 19 (1967) 546.

SCHUSTER, F. L.: An electron-microscope study of the ameba-flagellate, *Naegleria gruberi* (Schardinger) I. The ameboid and flagellate stages. J. Protozool. 10 (1963) 297.

SHELANSKI, M. L. and E. W. TAYLOR: Isolation of a protein subunit from microtubules. J. Cell Biol. 34 (1967) 549.

SMITH-SONNEBORN, J. and W. PLAUT: Evidence for the presence of DNA in the pellicle of *Paramecium*. J. Cell Sci. 2 (1967) 225.

SONNEBORN, T. M.: The differentiation of cells. Proc. Natl. Acad. Sci. U.S. 51 (1964) 915.

STUBBLEFIELD, E. and B. R. BRINKLEY: Cilia formation in Chinese hamster fibroblasts *in vitro* as a response to colcemid treatment. J. Cell Biol. 30 (1966) 645.

TARTAR, V.: The biology of *Stentor*. Oxford, Pergamon Press (1961).

WARR, J. R., A. MCVITTIE, J. RANDALL and J. M. HOPKINS: Genetic control of flagellar structure in *Chlamydomonas reinhardii*. Genet. Res. 7 (1966) 335.

WENT, H. A.: The behavior of centrioles and the structure and formation of the achromatic figure. Protoplasmatologia 6, Gl (1966) 1.

CHAPTER 45

Ultrastructure of cilia and flagella

BJÖRN A. AFZELIUS

The Wenner-Gren Institute, University of Stockholm

Contents

1. Introduction

2. Structure of cilia
   (a) Size of cilia
   (b) Axoneme structure
   (c) Ciliary membrane
   (d) Basal bodies
   (e) Ciliary rootlets

3. Specialized types of cilia
   (a) Compound cilia
   (b) Macrocilia
   (c) Sperm tails
   (d) Protozoan flagella
   (e) Flimmer-flagella
   (f) Flagella with a 9 + 1 pattern
   (g) Flagella with a 9 + 0 pattern
   (h) Flagella with a 9 + 7 or 9 + 9 pattern
   (i) The *Sciara*-type flagellum
   (j) Sensory hairs
   (k) The nematode sensory hair
   (l) Cilia with an 8 + 1 pattern
   (m) Cnidocils

4. Phylogenetic aspects of the ciliary structure

5. Genetic control of ciliary structure

6. Developmental changes in cilia
   (a) Forming cilia
   (b) Disappearing cilia

1. Introduction

A definition of a cilium, based on observations made with the light microscope, has been given by Abercrombie et al. as a 'fine cytoplasmic thread projecting along with many others from the surface of a cell. Cilia of a cell or of a whole epithelium lash with orderly beat in a constant direction. Each cilium moves the fluid surrounding it by lashing stiffly through it like an oar, and then bending on its recovery stroke so as to offer less resistance'. The flagellum is defined by the same authors as 'fine long threads having sinuous movement, projecting from a cell'. A definition of both cilia and flagella based on the structure seen in the electron microscope can read as follows: 'A cylinder consisting of nine peripheral double filaments, two central single filaments and a surrounding membrane'. Modifications of this pattern may occur, as exemplified in section 3. Given these definitions there can hardly be any confusion with other cell components, and in fact cilia and flagella are the most easily recognizable organelles of the cell. Border cases between cilia and flagella can be encountered, and will be exemplified below; as a consequence, the term cilium is nowadays usually used both for cilia proper and flagella, particularly for terms like 'ciliary filament', 'ciliary membrane', etc.

The locomotory apparatus of bacteria consists of projecting fibrous strands with an appearance quite different from that of cilia. The strands are usually referred to as flagella although differing in important respects from ordinary flagella. These 'bacterial flagella' will not be treated in this chapter.

Cilia constitute a homogeneous group of organelles and are widely distributed among protista, plants and animals. They have well defined functions in the life of the cell. It is not surprising that they have been the subject of several review articles and some monographs.

The classical treatise on cilia is the monograph by Gray in 1928. In 1962 Sleigh published a monograph on the biology of cilia and flagella. These two publications contain a wealth of valuable information and so do more recent reviews by Burge and Holwill; Holwill (1966, 1967); Jahn and Bovee (1965, 1967); Kinosita and Murakami; Newton and Kerridge; Pitelka and Child; Parducz; Satir (1965, 1967); and Sleigh (1966). A symposium on the structure and function of respiratory cilia was published in the American Review of Respiratory Diseases, 93 (1966) Suppl., 1–184.

2. Structure of cilia

(a) *Size of cilia*

Whereas the width of different cilia and flagella is remarkably uniform, their length is not. Flagella as short as 1 μ have been described (Manton 1959). At the other extreme is the flagellum of the spermatozoon of *Notonecta* which is about 10 mm long, (Pantel and Sinéty). The sperm flagella of the toad *Discoglossus* (Favard) and of the fruit fly

Drosophila (Meyer) are respectively 1 and several mm long. The compound cilia constituting the swimmingplates of the comb-jellies or ctenophores may also be a few mm long (Fig. 3).

The diameter of cilia is around 0.20 μ. Manton (1959) listed values ranging from 0.14 μ in the flagellate *Chromulina* to 0.25 μ in the moss *Sphagnum*, and measurements on other cilia and by other authors usually fall within these limits. There may, however, be additional components between the cylinder of 9 + 2 filaments and the limiting membrane which makes the diameter considerably bigger. This is often the case in sperm tails and in flagella of protista.

(b) *Axoneme structure*

Fig. 1 summarizes some of the structural features of the cilium as they can be seen in cross-sections. The profiles of the two central filaments are circular, those of the nine peripheral filaments are shaped like figures of eight. The complex of 9 + 2 filaments is called the *axoneme*. It is surrounded by a membrane which is the cell membrane, although often referred to as the ciliary membrane.

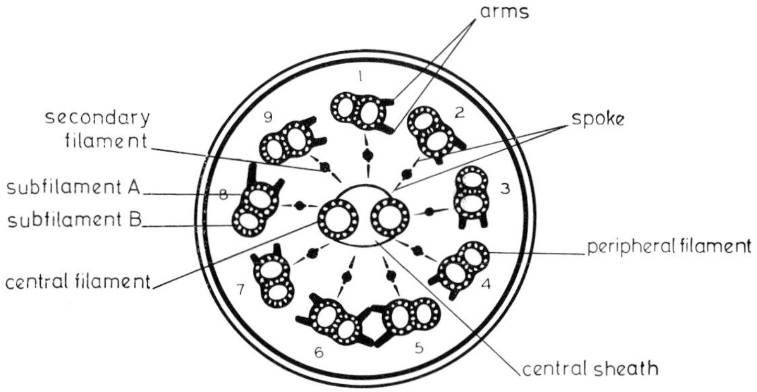

Fig. 1. Terminology of ciliary components.

Between the central and peripheral filaments are slender radial threads which have been called spokes. The peripheral filaments have short dense protrusions extending from their one side, the *arms*. The presence of arms on the peripheral filaments gives the cilium an asymmetrical shape in a cross-section. This asymmetry makes it possible to assign an index number to each of the peripheral filaments (Afzelius 1959). Filament 1 is the filament that is located at an equal distance from the centers of the two inner filaments and the numbers are assigned to the filaments progressing from no. 1 in the direction of the arms. The system of numbering is based on the premise that the 9 + 2 filaments run straight throughout the length of the cilium retaining their mutual relationships and providing it with an absolute structural axis. This premise seems to be borne out by investigations on whole mounts.

In many types of cilia a bridge is found between filaments 5 and 6, and occasionally also to the ciliary membrane. The bridge involves the arms of filament 5 and extensions from filament 6 (Afzelius 1959; Gibbons 1961). The two components of a peripheral filament differ in several respects. One part carries the arms and has been called *subfiber A* (Gibbons and Grimstone), tubule A, or subfilament A. The spoke is also connected to subfilament A. It often appears electron dense and compact whereas subfilament B appears hollow (Telkkä et al.; Gibbons 1961). The impression of one compact and one hollow subunit in the ciliary filament has been strengthened by observations on axonemes studied by the negative staining technique (André and Thiery; Behnke and Forer; Mohri et al.). Meyer (personal communication) has confirmed, by applying the freeze-etch technique on the fruit-fly sperm tail that the subfilaments which appear tubular in electron micrographs are indeed hollow. All arms are oriented in such a fashion that an observer in the cell viewing towards the tip of the cilium would find them pointing clockwise (Gibbons 1963).

High-resolution electron microscopy has enabled Phillips (1966b) and Ringo to resolve subunits in the walls of the ciliary filaments. Phillips considers the partition wall between the two subfilaments to be double and hence to consist of the fused walls of two distinct tubules. Close to the tip the two subfilaments may part. In the flagella described by Ringo the partition wall appears single rather than double. The subunits can also be studied by the negative staining technique. Treated by this method they appear as granules, 35 Å in diameter and arranged in a regular fashion. The most detailed account comes from a study by Grimstone and Klug who subjected their electron micrographs to analysis with an optical diffractometer.

At a level between the inner 2 and the outer 9 filaments an extra set of 9 thin filaments is sometimes seen. These *secondary filaments* have been described by Gibbons and Grimstone, who also have shown that links join them to the central and peripheral ones, in a configuration which reminds one of the spokes. When studied in longitudinal sections the spacing between arms along the filaments has been seen to be 170 Å (André) or 130 Å (Gibbons and Grimstone). Grimstone and Klug have later produced evidence for the periodicity being 160 Å.

The two central filaments are enveloped by what is called the *central sheath* (Gibbons and Grimstone). In cross-sectioned cilia the sheath is more prominent between, rather than around, the central filaments. It hence appears as two arcs, one directed towards filament 1 and a less conspicuous one towards filaments 5–6. In the longitudinal sections the central sheath can be seen to have a spiral composition with an estimated pitch of 120 Å (André).

Nicander and Bane described a further differentiation in the axoneme, namely *stays* which join neighboring spokes. The material within the ciliary membrane, which does not comprise: filaments, arms, spokes, stays, central sheath, and other formed elements, is by definition the *ciliary matrix*.

Some of the components described above are represented diagrammatically in Figs. 1 and 2.

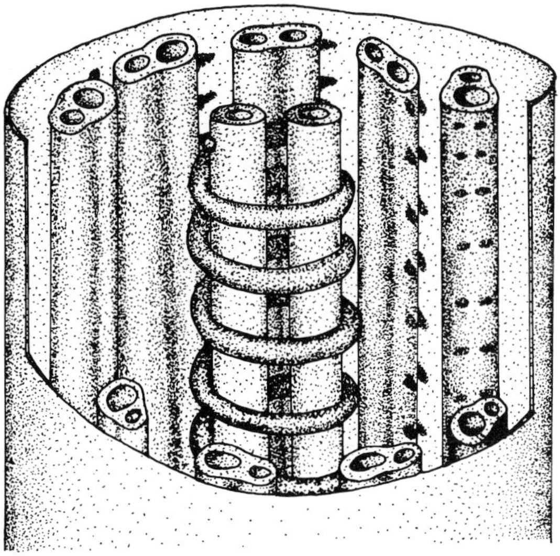

Fig. 2. Three-dimensional reconstruction of a portion of a cilium.

(c) *Ciliary membrane*

The ciliary membrane is just an extension of the plasma membrane or cell membrane covering the rest of the cell. There are no reports on structural specializations of the ciliary membrane which do not also exist in the rest of the cell membrane. Thus, the cell membrane in general (Robertson) and the ciliary membrane (Afzelius 1959) have been reported to be triple-layered and asymmetrical, the inner dense stratum being thicker than the outer one. Later the cell membrane has been reported to have a globular substructure which gives it a rope-ladder like appearance in sections (Sjöstrand). The same structure is seen in the ciliary membrane (Ringo). Flagellates which have the cell membrane covered by scales or fine hairs, may also have scaly and hairy *flagella* (Manton 1966).

Isolated *Tetrahymena* cilia have been subjected to analysis by X-ray diffraction (Silvester). The spots found are believed to be due to the structure of the ciliary membrane. This membrane was, after the myelin sheath and the rod outer segment, the third type of cell membrane to be analyzed by X-ray diffraction. The rod outer segment is a ciliary derivative, although highly specialized in form and function.

(d) *Basal bodies*

The base of the cilium has received many designations: basal body, basal granule, basal corpuscle, kinetosome, centriole, blepharoplast, etc. The first one of these terms seems to be the simplest one and will be used here. It can be defined as the specialized part of the cilium which is located within the cell. The structural variation of the basal body, from one species to another, is much greater than that of the axo-

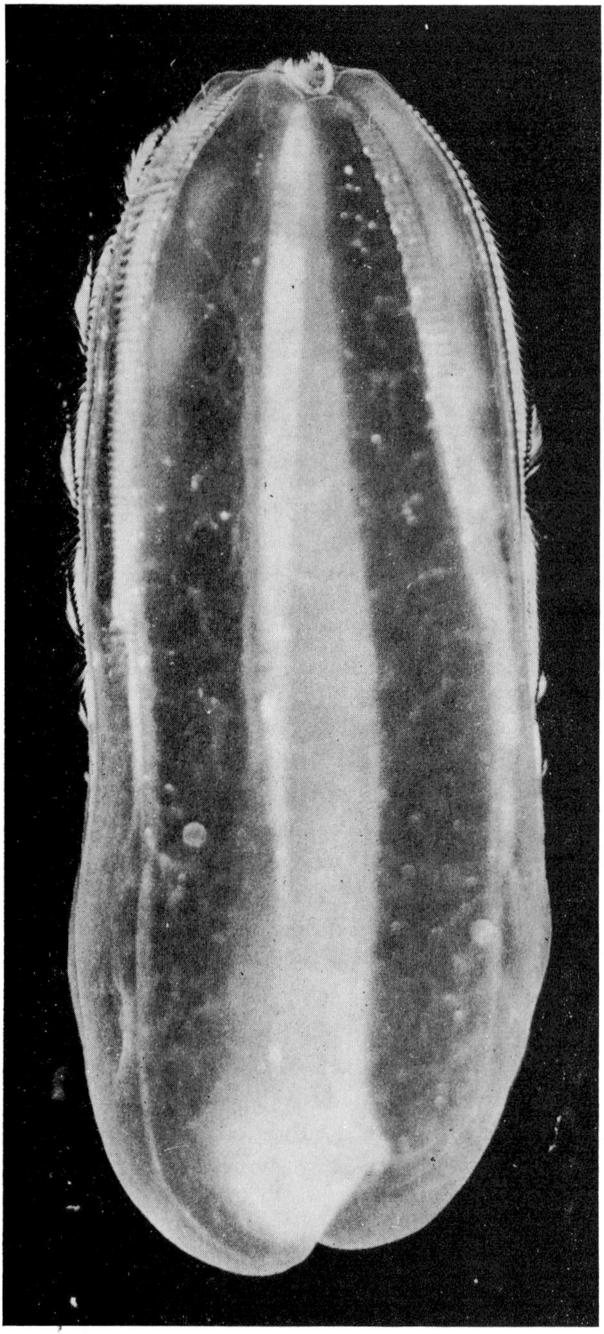

Fig. 3. A specimen of the ctenophore *Beroë ovata*. The metachronal wave in the swimming-plate row on the left side is visible. Natural size 6 cm. (Photograph by M. Laverack.)

Fig. 4. Portion of the flagellar bundle of the flame cell in the tapeworm excretory duct. The flagella are hexagonally tight-packed. (Electron micrograph by von Bonsdorff and Telkkä.) × 200,000

neme. In a review article on cilia Fawcett illustrates six different types of basal bodies and so do Randall and Hopkins. The most consistent structural features of the basal body seem to be that the 9 peripheral filaments appear triple rather than double and that the two central filaments are missing. The basal body may appear short and simple as in the sea urchin sperm (Afzelius 1959) or 5 μ long and complex as in the flagellate *Pseudotrichonympha* (Gibbons and Grimstone).

Whereas some types of basal bodies are radially symmetrical, others are not. Cilia with deviations from the simple cylindrical form may have: (1) a bent shape of the basal body, (2) unilateral extensions called basal feet or spurs, etc., and (3) attachments connected to various other structures. In some cases a correlation can be made between the direction of the spur and the direction of the ciliary beat. Other cilia have the ability to beat in any direction and also have an open cylindrical basal body. However, it is not possible to predict the direction of beating of a given cilium merely from an inspection of its basal body.

(e) *Ciliary rootlets*

The basal bodies of most types of cilia bear fibrous structures extending into the cell, the ciliary roots or rootlets. These constitute the most variable part of the ciliary structure. They frequently resemble collagen in being striated with a periodicity of

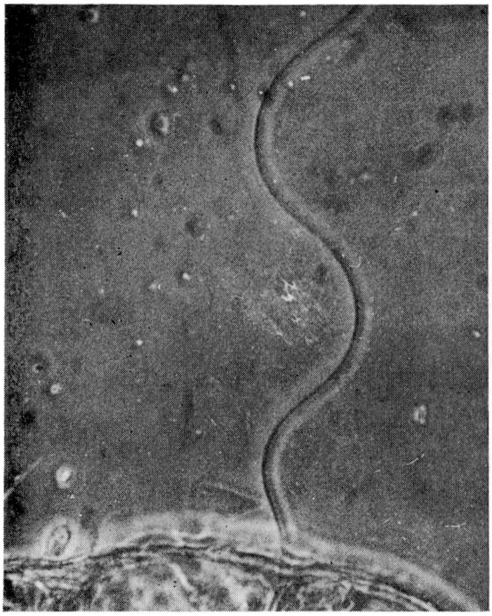

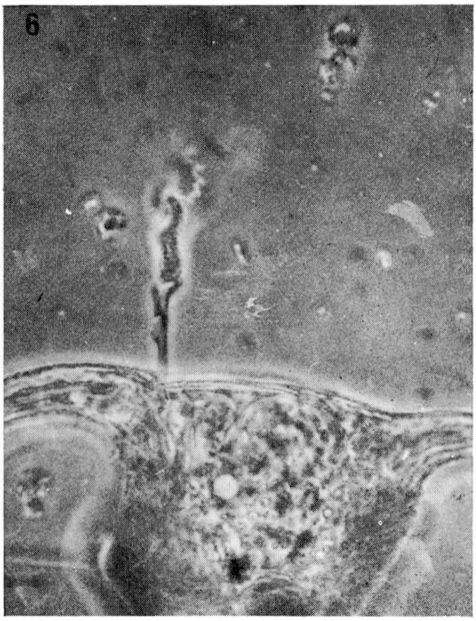

Fig. 5. The anterior flagellum of the dinoflagellate *Ceratium tripos* undulates in one plane when the organism is left undisturbed. $\times$ 500

Fig. 6. The flagellum of *Ceratium* is withdrawn when the animal is disturbed. The flagellum then takes a helical shape, which is retained for a few seconds after extension of the flagellum and before it regains its undulations. $\times$ 660

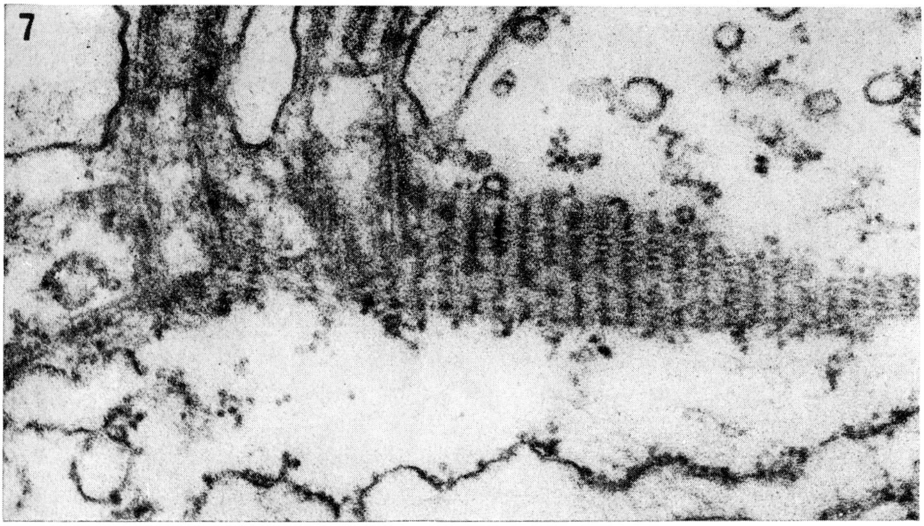

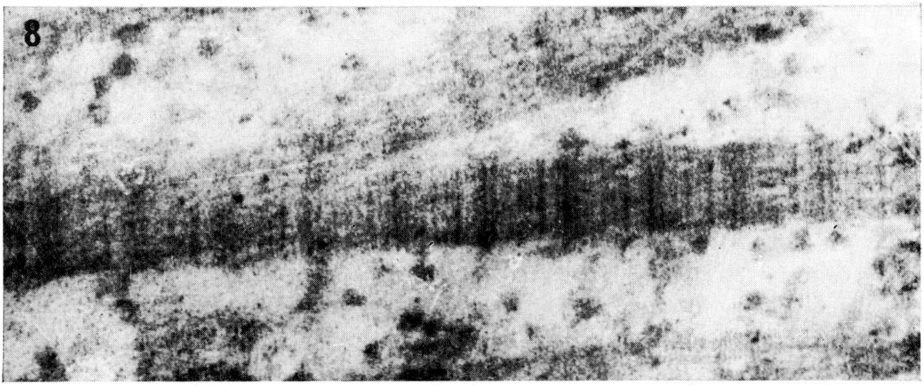

Fig. 7. The prominent rootlet of certain cilia near the apical organ of *Mnemiopsis leideyi* is perpendicular to the axis of the cilium rather than parallel to it. × 66,000

Fig. 8. Rootlet from the gill epithelium of the mussel *Mytilus edulis*. The periodicity is about 700 Å. × 170,000

the order of 700 Å (Figs. 8 and 9). Usually the rootlets form a small angle to the axis of the cilium, but in some types, this angle may increase so that the root runs parallel to the cell surface (Fig. 7). Microtubules (Gibbons 1961) or thin cytoplasmic filaments (Gibbons and Grimstone) may also be connected with the basal bodies. Pitelka has proposed a classification of the different types of fibrous structures, including the various forms of ciliary rootlets, in protozoa.

It has often been suggested that fibrous connections between the cilia in a ciliate, or a ciliated epithelium, constitute the morphological basis of the propagation of the metachronal ciliary waves. The earliest report, on such a fibrous 'silverline system' from an epithelium, seems to be that by Luther in 1904. The variability in beat direc-

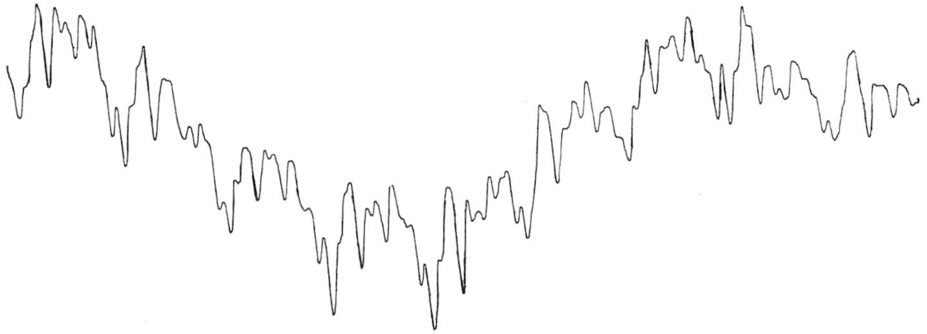

Fig. 9. Photometric tracing revealing the complexity of the periods of the ciliary rootlet shown in Fig. 8.

tion in ciliates is incompatible with this role of the silverline system (Parducz). The discontinuity of the silverline system over cell borders in epithelia also makes a coordinative function unlikely.

3. *Specialized types of cilia*

(a) *Compound cilia*

Cilia which are grouped in a bundle and beat in unison, as if fused, are known as compound cilia. Among the ciliates the term *cirrus* has been used for rod-like compound cilia and the term *membranella* for cilia 'fused' into a plate. By microdissection the individual cilia of cirri and membranellae can be separated out.

Ctenophore swimming-plates are the largest compound cilia, consisting of as many as 100,000 cilia. The orientation of the filaments is the same throughout the swimming-plate. Filaments 3 and 8 are connected to the ciliary membrane by means of slender lamellae, which may cement the cilia together in rows, arranged perpendicular to the beat direction (Afzelius 1961a).

The laterofrontal cilia of the mussel gill are also compound and so are the flagella on the flame cell in platyhelminth excretory ducts. The swimming-plates possess typical ciliary movement, the flame cell flagella undulate in typical flagellar fashion and the protozoan cirri can direct their beat in any direction. The orientation of the $9+2$ filaments is not the same in all flagella of the flame cell of the tapeworm (Fig. 4) (von Bonsdorff and Telkkä 1966).

(b) *Macrocilia*

The ctenophores show a rich variety of types of ciliary organization. Not only is the swimming-plate unique, but there are also: (1) the apical organ with its ciliary field, (2) the cupola, (3) the statocyst pillars and (4) the presumed photoreceptor cilia. Horridge further described a 'macrocilium on the lips of the ctenophore *Beroë*'. It is an organelle, about 6–10 μ thick and 30 μ long, and having a beat frequency of $\frac{1}{2}$–4 per second. Electron microscopy showed the macrocilium to consist of about 3,500 axonemes, which were all joined by the same type of lamellae as had been found in the swimming-plate cilia, but which in this case occurred in several planes around each axoneme. However, all these shafts were within a common ciliary membrane. The ciliary membrane invaginates to form an internal system of tubules at the level of the base of the macrocilium. The resemblance to the transverse sarcotubules of striated muscles is striking.

(c) *Sperm tails*

In many animal and plant species the sperm tail conforms to the description given in section 2. In other species the axoneme is modified (see below), or there are additional components in the tail. The sperm tails of mammals, birds and snakes have 9 dense fibrils, one immediately outside each of the peripheral doublets. Since these 9 dense fibrils are unequal in size and shape, they give the sperm tail a pronounced asymmetry. This is particularly true of the marsupial sperm (Cleland and Rothschild). There are also small dense fibrils in the lamprey and in many invertebrates (insects, snails and the squid). Accessory rods are often found alongside the flagellum, as for instance, in some insects (André, Meyer). Many amphibians have sperm tails with an 'undulatory membrane'. This may be a rod running parallel with the axoneme. In some species the axoneme itself forms an undulating margin of the thick tail. The movements of the spermatozoa with an undulating membrane are quite complex, like an endless screw (Picheral) or a wave which 'may originate at any part of the flagellum and pass either proximally or distally or, in some cases, in both directions at once' (Baker).

(d) *Protozoan flagella*

Flagella from protozoa may have the appearance of unmodified cilia or carry additional components: scales, hairs, flimmer, a crystalline rod, or other 'paraflagellar bodies' of unknown significance (Mignot) (Fig. 12). According to the definition in section 1, flagella have sinuous movement. Although this is often true (Fig. 5) the same flagella may at other times move in other ways (Fig. 6).

(e) *Flimmer-flagella*

In many protozoa, and some multicellular plants, the flagellum bears one or two rows of hair-like appendages called *flimmer* or *mastigonemes*. Such flimmer-flagella have been of interest to investigators in systematic botany, since the appearance of the flimmer seems to be a very reliable phylogenetic character. The different forms of flimmer-flagella and their distribution in the plant flagellates have been described by light microscopists such as Vlk, or electron microscopists such as Pitelka and Kole. The only demonstration of a flimmer-flagellum in a multicellular animal, is from the sponge (Afzelius 1961b). This finding supports the notion of a relationship between sponges and choanoflagellates.

The flimmer is made up of filaments, 20–200 Å wide and 0.2–4 μ long. In some types of flagella, it has been noted that the flimmer is connected to the ciliary peripheral filaments (Manton 1959), in other flagella the flimmer seems to emerge from the ciliary membrane or a helical band just under it (Mignot) (Fig. 13).

The presence of flimmer on the flagellum may affect its mode of creating water currents. In a smooth flagellum a wave transmitted from base to tip will push the water towards the tip. In an undulating flimmer-flagellum the stiff flimmer on the crests of the wave will swing in the direction opposite the transmitted wave, and the net effect of the undulation is to push the water towards the base of a flagellum. The flimmer will hence cause a reversal in the water current. This will occur only if the flimmer is placed in the plane of the undulation and if stiff and long enough. A more detailed explanation of this phenomenon can be found in reviews by Jahn and Bovee and by Holwill.

(f) *Flagella with a 9+1 pattern*

Flatworm spermatozoa have two *flagella* and both have a 9+1 pattern, rather than the common 9+2. This has been described in turbellaria (Silveira and Porter), trematodes (Shapiro et al.), and cestodes (von Bonsdorff and Telkkä 1965). The central filament is in all cases more complex than the two central filaments in ordinary cilia and consists of three concentric zones (Fig. 10). The axoneme is radially symmetrical and suited for the rotational reinforcement technique of Markham et al. Such a reinforcement (Fig. 11) shows the spokes to be curved rather than straight, a feature which can also be discerned in the un-rotated original micrograph, as well as in some 9+2 cilia (text Fig. 1 in Afzelius 1959 and Fig. 1 in Behnke and Forer).

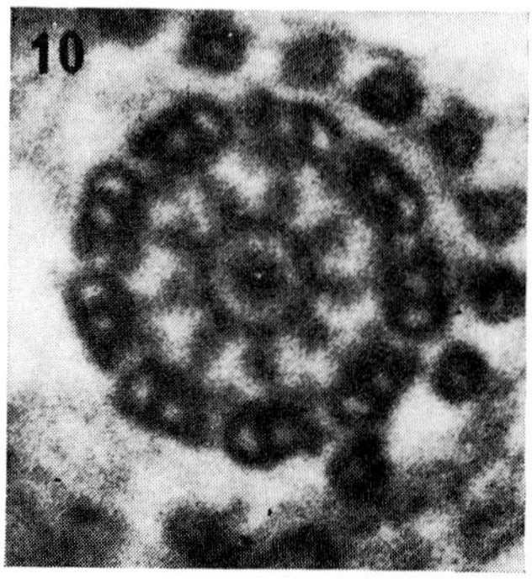

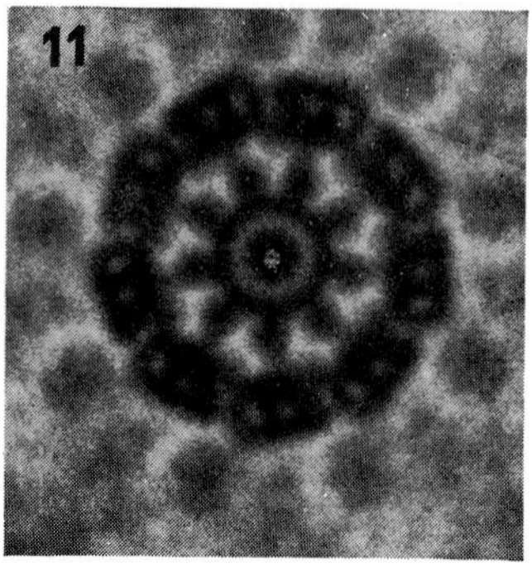

Fig. 10. Cross-section of flagellum from the turbellarian flatworm *Mecynostomum auritum*. Nine peripheral double filaments surround a single central one. ×190,000

Fig. 11. The same micrograph after printing using the rotational reinforcement technique of Markham et al.

Silveira and Porter described different types of 9 + 1 flagella, some having 9 spokes and others having 18 secondary filaments.

Most flatworm spermatozoa that have been examined have 9 + 1 flagella whereas sperm tails from some acoelous turbellarians (Hendelberg, personal communication) and all examined somatic cilia of flatworms are of the ordinary 9 + 2 type. Outside the flatworm group, sperm tails of this appearance, have not been found. Sperm tails of nemerteans, rotifers, annelids, etc. are all typical. Dr. T. Semba of the Kyushu University (personal communication) and Breland et al. have shown that the sperm tail of the Japanese respective a Canadian mosquito may have just one central filament which is simpler than that of the flatworm sperm.

Hendelberg described the movements of the turbellarian spermatozoon as three-dimensional and with waves which may move towards the posterior or anterior end. The spermatozoa thereby move forward or backward.

12

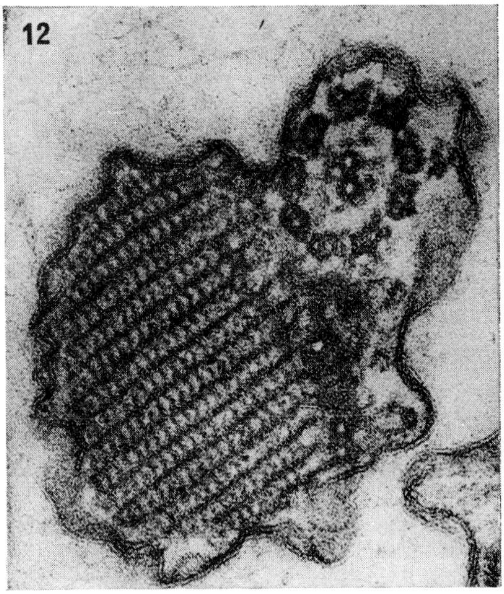

13

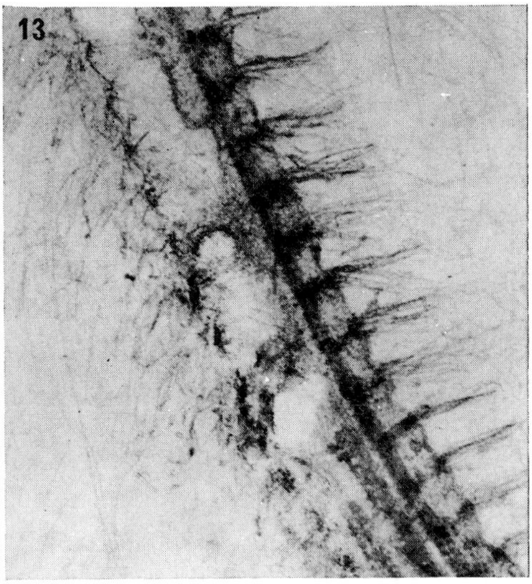

Fig. 12. Cross-section of the trailing filament of the euglenoid flagellate *Entosiphon sulcatum* cut in the region of the reservoir. The crystalline structure of the paraflagellar rod is plainly evident. (Electron micrograph by J.-P. Mignot.) × 91,000

Fig. 13. Tangential section of the anterior flagellum of *Entosiphon sulcatum*. The flimmer is arranged helically in this species. (Electron micrograph by J.-P. Mignot.) × 46,000

(g) *Flagella with a 9 + 0 pattern*

This pattern is found in the sperm tail of the worm *Myzostomum*, the fish *Lycodontis afer* (Boisson et al.), the mayfly Chloën (Baccetti, personal communication), the flagellum of the male gamete of the diatom *Lithodesmium*, and of the gregarine *Stylocephalus longicollis* (Desportes). *Myzostomum* has a mobile flagellum with 9 peripheral and 9 secondary filaments, but without central filaments (Afzelius 1962). The spermatozoa move head-first or tail-first, may show a reversal of the flagellar

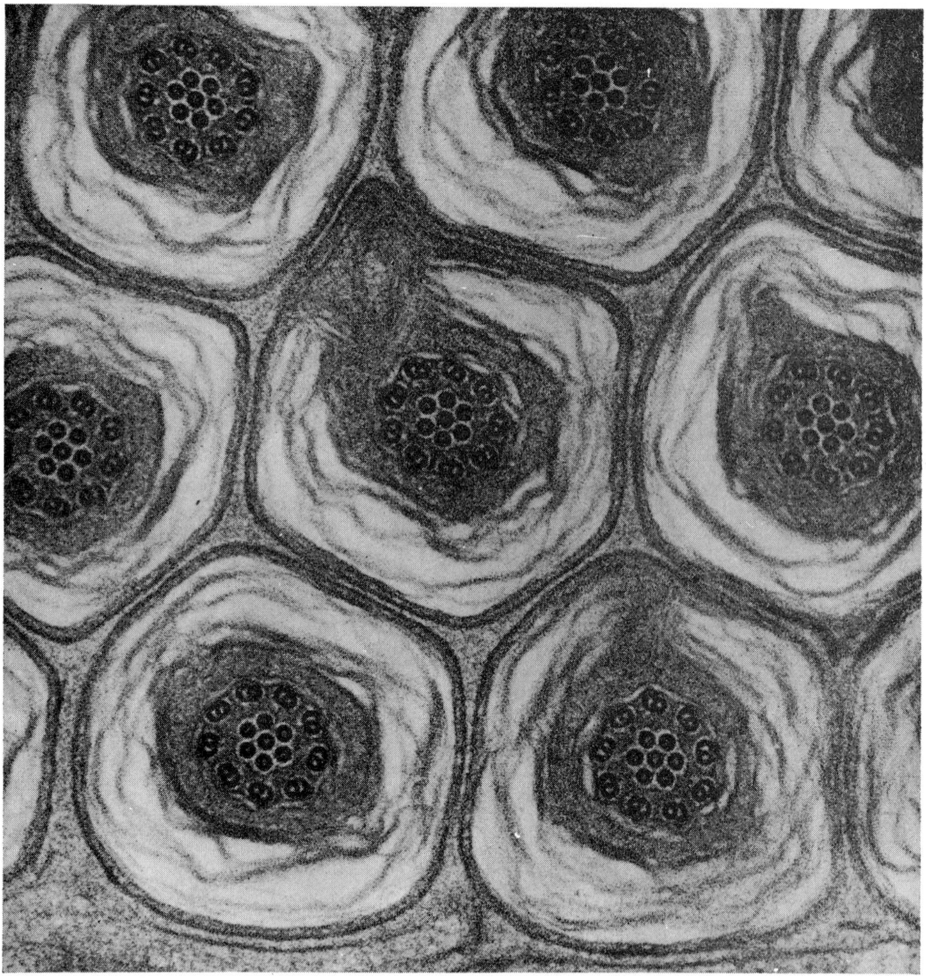

Fig. 14. Cross-sectioned sperm tails from spermatids of a caddis-fly (family Goeridae) show a regular 9 + 7 pattern. (Electron micrograph by D. M. Phillips.) × 87,000

waves, and may beat in three dimensions. The movement of the flagellum of the gregarine gamete similarly is threedimensional, but the undulations of the diatom sperm are of the planar type (Manton and Stosch).

In section 3(j) other cilia will be described which lack the central filaments and hence are of the 9 + 0 type, but these cilia evidently show no motility.

(h) *Flagella with a 9 + 7 or 9 + 9 pattern*

Fig. 14 shows a sperm tail which has to be classified as a 9 + 7 flagellum. This micrograph is reproduced here by courtesy of Dr. David M. Phillips of the Harvard Medical School. It shows the sperm tail of a caddisfly of the family Goeridae (order Trichop-

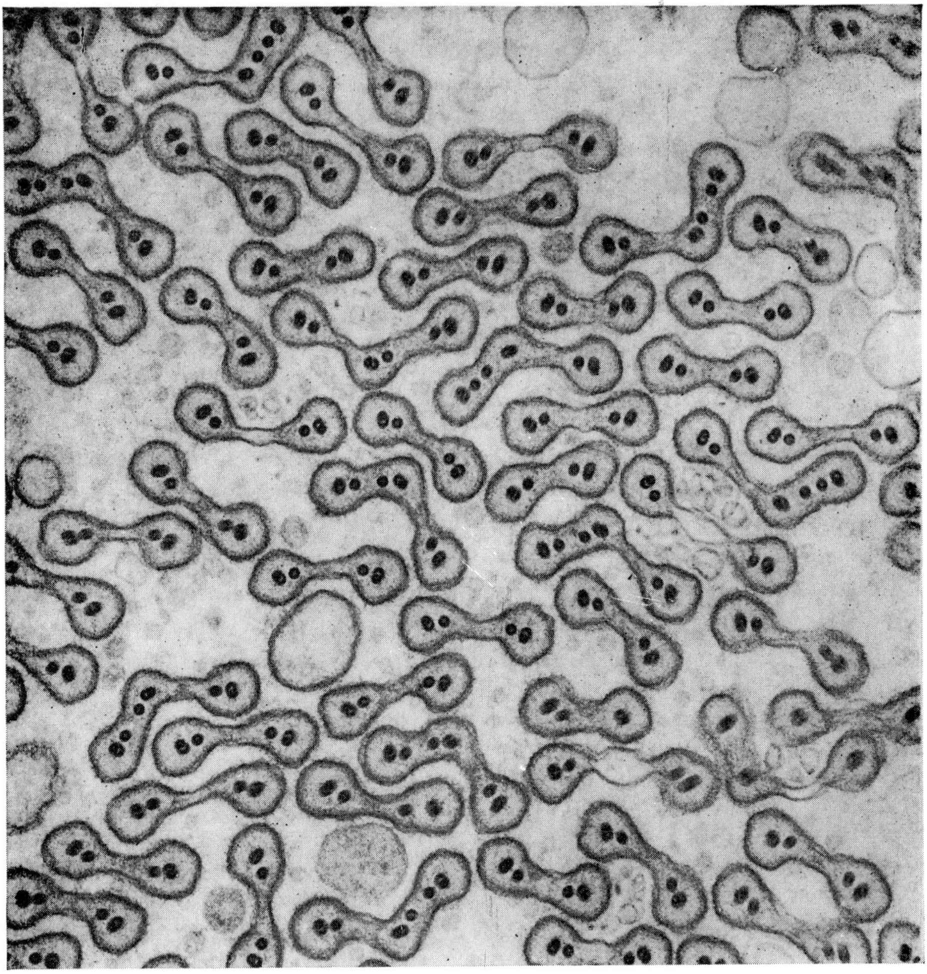

Fig. 15. The flagellum of a tree-hopper sperm is subdivided into four parts: three with two doublets and two singlets and one with three doublets and three singlets; i.e. a modification of a 9 + 9 arrangement. (Electron micrograph by D. M. Phillips.) × 44,000

tera). There are seven central filaments all of which appear single.

The sperm of several species of treehoppers (Family Membracidae, Hemiptera) have also been studied by Dr. Phillips. He found the flagellum to be subdivided, along much of its length, into four parts. Three of these parts possess two double and two single filaments, and one of them has three double and three single filaments. This type of flagellum seems to be a modification of a 9 + 9 type (Fig. 15).

(i) *The Sciara-type flagellum*

In the flagellum of the fungus gnat, *Sciara coprophila*, Phillips (1966a) found that the axial filament complex consists of approximately 70 double filaments, each with an associated single filament. The filaments have the shape and associated dense fibril which are characteristic of the peripheral filaments in an ordinary insect sperm tail. The *Sciara* filament complex arises from a body which acts as a centriole in the spermatocyte division. It can hence be regarded as a strongly modified cilium.

The movements of this unusual sperm tail could not be characterized, as the period of active movement is short, and the actual movements rapid.

Fig. 16 shows a transverse section of the posterior part of a sperm cell where the single fibrils have terminated, and the row of filament doublets are coiled in a spiral arrangement.

(j) *Sensory hairs*

Under this heading are grouped several structures which belong morphologically to $9+2$, $9+0$ or other patterns, but which have related functions in the life of the organism. These structures detect stimuli which may be mechanical, chemical, electrical, or visual.

The sensory cells in the inner ear are examples of *mechanoreceptors*. As described by Lowenstein and Wersäll among others, the hair cells of the inner ear each carry a 'kinocilium' and a bundle of 'stereocilia'. The kinocilium has the structure of an ordinary $9+2$ cilium in which the arms are clearly visible. It is of interest to find that the orientation of the kinocilium and its $9+2$ filament has been correlated with a directional sensitivity of the sensory cell. The asymmetric location of the kinocilium at one side of the bundle of stereocilia coincides with the direction of excitatory stimulation. 'Stereocilia' are microvilli rather than cilia.

The chordotonal organ of the shore crab contains mechanoreceptor cells carrying sensory hairs. One of these has a proximal portion which contains nine double filaments with arms, arranged as $9+2$. More distally there are about 50 single filaments (Whitear).

Other mechanoreceptors with cilia-like sensory hairs have been described. The vibration receptor in the spider is exceptional in having a sensory hair with a homogeneous inner structure, thus revealing no relationship to cilia or basal bodies (Salpeter and Walcott).

Olfactory cilia may exemplify sensory hairs of *chemoreceptor* organs. Those in the frog nostril have been described as having $9+2$ filaments in their proximal parts. Distally single filaments are found in varying number. In the proximal region, which can be induced to beat, the outer filaments carry arms (Reese).

The fine structure of *photoreceptors* has recently been reviewed (Eakin). In the coelenterate, ctenophore, and deuterostome branches of the metazoa the visual cells carry a sensory hair, which at least in its basal parts, appears as a cilium of the $9+0$ type (rarely $9+2$ or $8+1$). There are no arms. Distally the variation is great. The photoreceptor of a protozoan may similarly be associated with the flagellar locomotor

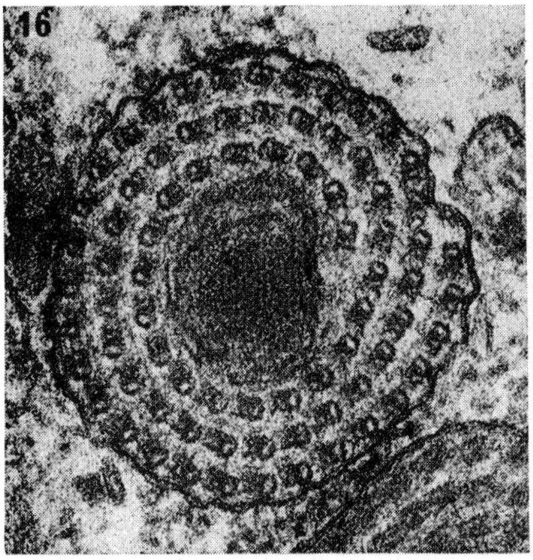

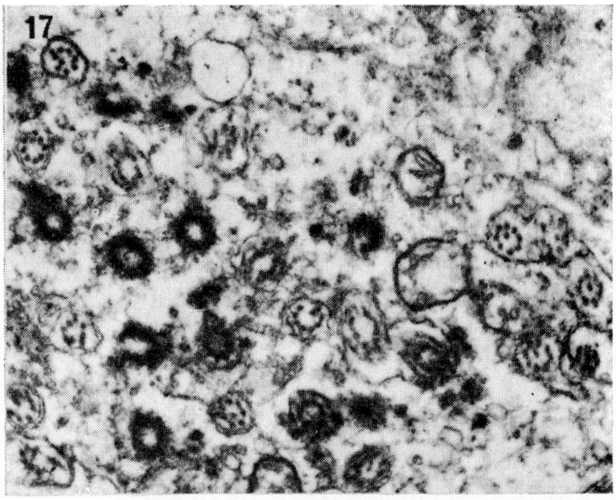

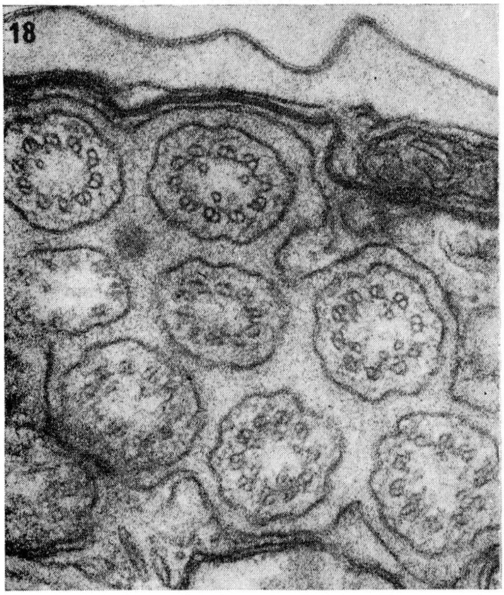

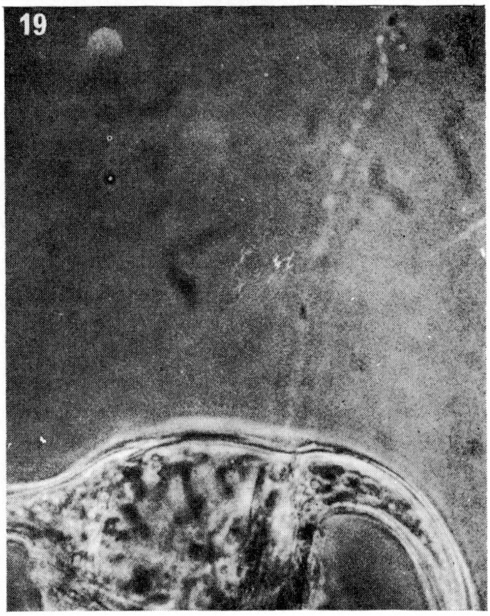

Fig. 16. The axial complex of filaments in the sperm from the fungus gnat, *Sciara coprophila*, is highly aberrant in having approximately 70 double filaments. In the posterior part of the cell the filaments are disposed in a single spiral. (Electron micrograph by D. M. Phillips.) × 66,000

Fig. 17. Some neurons in the neural tube of the ray *Raia batis* carry cilia of the 8 + 1 type. × 31,000

Fig. 18. Modified cilia in a sensory organ from the fourth-stage juvenile larva of the nematode *Haemonchus contortus*. There are 10 outer double filaments. (Electron micrograph by M. M. R. Ross.) × 62,000

Fig. 19. The anterior flagellum of *Ceratium tripos* photographed just after breaking up into a string of small beads. × 460 apparatus (Manton and Harris). This flagellum like other motile ones has arms on the outer filaments.

The sensory cells in the ampullae of Lorenzini of the rays have in all probability an *electroreceptive* function (Waltman). Each receptor cell bears a cilium which contains nine double filaments without arms, either in a 9 + 0 or in an 8 + 1 pattern.

In conclusion, the sensory hairs can have a variety of axonemal patterns. Arms are present in most mechanoreceptors and chemoreceptors, but absent in the metazoan photoreceptors and in the examined electroreceptor. If this generalization is true it may be useful in identifying the role of newly discovered receptors.

(k) *The nematode sensory hair*

Sensory hairs in nematodes are of interest for several reasons. Nematodes lack ciliated epithelia, and ciliary structures in nematode cells have only recently been discovered.

Ross has described the sensory hair as lacking basal body and having 10 rather than 9 outer double filaments in a ring containing none or a few central single filaments (Fig. 18).

(l) *Cilia with an 8 + 1 pattern*

Dahl has described the fine structure of cilia in rat cerebral cortex. He found that each granular neuron or astroglia cell carried one cilium which proximally had a 9 + 0 pattern but along most of its length appeared as an 8 + 1 cilium due to the inflection towards the center of one of the double filaments which takes an axial position. Fig. 17 is a micrograph of the neural tube tissue of the ray and shows a cell carrying several cilia of this type. In discussing the possible functions of these cilia Dahl finds it unlikely that they have a motor or have a receptor role. He concludes that they may be 'vestigial, i.e. formed because of an inherent tendency by the cells to form cilia'.

(m) *Cnidocils*

Nematocysts from the coelenterates have a cilium, the cnidocil. Its function is evident from the synonymous term, the trigger hair. It is a stiff cilium with 9 double filaments surrounding several single filaments (Slautterback).

4. *Phylogenetic aspects of the ciliary structure*

As the foregoing pages have shown there exist a number of modifications of the ciliary structure. However, these modifications can be regarded only as variations of a general pattern, and the constancy of the geometry is more striking than its variations. Indeed, the stability of the 9 + 2 pattern is probably without parallel in cytology.

Such variations of the ciliary structure and distribution have been eminently useful in systematics and in the establishment of phylogenetic relations. The presence of scales on the flagella were used as the basis for the classification of certain algae (Manton and Parke). Flimmer-flagella of different types characterize certain branches of the evolutionary tree as exemplified in section 3(e).

Sagan has published a report, on the origin of mitosis in cells. This study contains a hypothetical account of the mechanisms leading to the evolution of cells dividing by mitosis (eukaryotic cells). The basal bodies of flagella are regarded by him as descendants of once free-living bacteria-like organisms (prokaryotic cells), as are the mitochondria and the chloroplasts.

In most metazoan ciliated epithelia, the cilia are arranged in two geometrically well defined series of rows at right angles to each other. *Orthoplectic* rows are those coinciding with the direction of the ciliary beat; *diaplectic* rows are those perpendicular to the beating direction. Cilia arranged in one of these rows beat synchronously, in the other metachronally . In ciliated epithelia there are four alternative patterns of relationship between beating direction and direction of wave transmission: symplectic, antiplectic, dexioplectic, and laeoplectic metachrony (Knight-Jones). In the ciliates the relationships are more complicated (Parducz). Knight-Jones has shown that dexioplectic and laeoplectic metachrony characterize different groups of metazoa respectively and that these characters seem to be very stable and hence useful for phylogenetic considerations.

5. *Genetic control of ciliary structure*

Cilia lacking one or several filaments or containing extra ones have been reported (e.g. Afzelius 1963) (Fig. 20). It is not known whether such modifications have a genetic background or are due to environmental factors. Nagano found that experimental cryptorchidism provoked changes in the fine structure of the sperm tail, and hence it can be surmised that many of the other described modifications will be shown to be phenotypic.

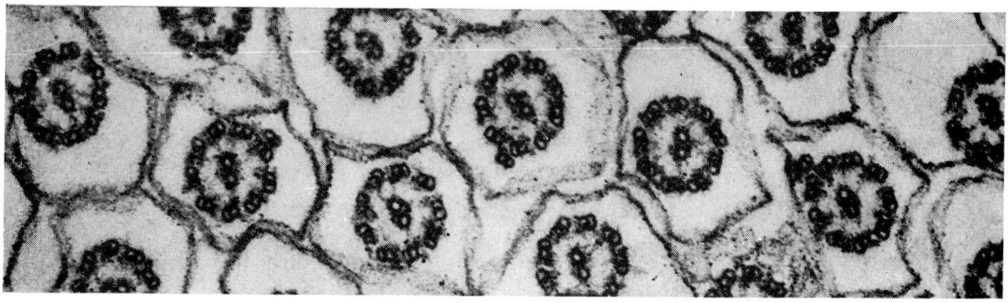

Fig. 20. Cilia from the coelomic lining of the polychaet *Tomopteris helgolandica*. Three cilia have an extra filament and are of a 1+9+2 pattern. ×74,000

However, some clear-cut cases of genotypic variations have been reported. One of the simplest cases is afforded by the experiment of Wolley and Beatty, who bred mice having long or short midpiece lengths in their spermatozoa. Meyer (1968) and Kiefer described abnormal axonemes in immobile spermatozoa from XO *Drosophila* flies. Warr, McVittie, Randall and Hopkins studied the genetic control of the ciliary structure in the green flagellate *Chlamydomonas* treated with mutagenic agents or ultraviolet light. In several isolated mutants the flagellar movement and structure were modified. The outer nine filaments were never visibly affected but in some clones one or both of the inner filaments were missing. They concluded that the mutations either were closely linked to or were at a known locus. A suppressor gene to the mutation was also found which gave rise to a phenotypical reversion.

6. *Developmental changes in cilia*

(a) *Forming cilia*

The development of cilia and flagella has been investigated in a variety of tissues and in protozoa. The first part of a cilium to appear is the basal body. Usually it derives from the centrioles at the mitotic poles or at any rate is formed near preexisting centrioles (Dirksen and Crocker). The amoeboflagellates *Tetramitus* and *Naegleria* are exceptional in that basal bodies appear in cells devoid of centrioles during the transformation to the flagellate state (Outka and Kluss; and Schuster).

Developing cilia may elongate at a maximal rate of 1 μ per min and may be completed in 10–15 min (Rouiller and Fauré-Fremiet). In a detailed study of the kinetics of flagellar development, Tamm found the elongation rate to be deceleratory, and concluded that at least part of the control over changes in flagellar length resides in the flagellum itself. In another study on protozoan flagella, Rosenbaum and Child distinguished between a phase of synthesis of ciliary proteins and a phase of assembly of the protein molecules to form filaments. Results from isotope experiments showed that assembly of the filaments takes place at the tip of the flagellum.

(b) *Disappearing cilia*

Cells have different ways of disposing of their cilia. The flagellum of the euglenoid flagellates is withdrawn into the cell body as a preparatory step to mitosis. The cell can make use of the ciliary breakdown products for the assembly of new flagella (Tamm). Alternatively, a cell may throw off its cilia. Thus the fungus zoospore sheds its flagellum when entering a sessile phase. The shed flagellum swims a short distance (300 μ) before coming to rest (McKeen).

In other cases it has been found that the cilium decomposes when still attached to the cell. Fig. 19 shows the anterior flagellum of *Ceratium* photographed just after breaking up in a string of small beads. This phenomenon is rare but has occasionally been observed by the author. The break-up and dissolution of the flagellum takes a few seconds.

Acknowledgements

Some of the work reported here was supported by the Swedish Natural Science Research Council. Mrs. Eva Fjellstedt has skillfully assisted in the preparation techniques and by making the drawings of Figs. 1 and 2. Fig. 4 has been obtained from Dr. von Bonsdorff, Figs. 12 and 13 from Dr. J.-P. Mignot, Figs. 14–16 from Dr. D. M. Phillips and Fig. 18 from Dr. M. M. R. Ross. The author acknowledges their help with gratitude.

References

ABERCROMBIE, M., C. J. HICKMAN and M. L. JOHNSON: A dictionary of biology. Harmondsworth, Penguin Books (1951).

AFZELIUS, B.: Electron microscopy of the sperm tail. J. Biophys. Biochem. Cytol. 5 (1959) 269.

AFZELIUS, B. A.: The fine structure of the cilia from ctenophore swimming-plates. J. Biophys. Biochem. Cytol. 9 (1961) 383.

AFZELIUS, B. A.: Flimmer-flagellum of the sponge. Nature 191 (1961) 1318.

AFZELIUS, B. A.: The contractile apparatus in some invertebrate muscles and spermatozoa. Proc. 5th Internat. Congr. Electron Microscopy, Philadelphia (1962).

AFZELIUS, B. A.: Cilia and flagella that do not conform to the 9 + 2 pattern. J. Ultrastruct. Res. 9 (1963) 381.

ANDRÉ, J.: Sur quelques détails nouvellement connus de l'ultrastructure des organites vibratiles. J. Ultrastruct. Res. 5 (1961) 86.

ANDRÉ, J. and J. P. THIERY: Mise en evidence d'une sous-structure fibrillaire dans les filaments axonématiques des flagelles. J. Microscopie 2 (1963) 71.

BAKER, C. L.: Spermatozoa and spermateleosis in the Salamandridae with electron microscopy of *Diemictylus*. J. Tenn. Acad. Sci. 41 (1966) 2.

BEHNKE, O. and A. FORER: Evidence for four classes of microtubules in individual cells. J. Cell Sci. 2 (1967) 169.

BOISSON, C., X. MATTEI and C. MATTEI: Le flagelle de type 9 + 0 et la remarquable extension du centriole proximal dans les spermatides de *Lycodontis afer* (Bloch 1795) (Poisson Muraenidae). Compt. Rend. Acad. Sci. (Paris) 264 (1967) 2909.

BONSDORFF, C.-H. VON and A. TELKKA: The spermatozoon flagella in *Diphyllobothrium latum*. Z. Zellforsch. 66 (1965) 643.

BONSDORFF, C.-H. VON and A. TELKKA: The flagellar structure of the flame cell in fish tapeworm (*Diphyllobothrium latum*). Z. Zellforsch. 70 (1966) 169.

BRELAND, O. P., G. GESSNER III, R. W. RIESS and J. J. BIESELE: Certain aspects of the centriole adjunct, spermiogenesis, and the mature sperm of insect. Canad. J. Genet. Cytol. 8 (1966) 759.

BURGE, R. E. and M. E. J. HOLWILL: Hydrodynamic aspects of microbial movement. Symp. Soc. Gen. Microbiol. 15 (1965) 250.

CLELAND, K. W. and LORD ROTHSCHILD: The bandicoot spermatozoon: an electron microscope study of the tail. Proc. Roy. Soc. (London), Ser. B 150 (1959) 24.

DAHL, H. A.: Fine structure of cilia in rat cerebral cortex. Z. Zellforsch. 60 (1963) 369.

DESPORTES, I.: L'ultrastructure du gamète mâle de l'Eugrégarine *Stylocephalus longicollis*. Compt. Rend. Acad. Sci. (Paris) 263 (1966) 517.

DIRKSEN, E. R. and T. T. CROCKER: Centriole replication in differentiating ciliated cells of mammalian respiratory epithelium. J. Microscopie 5 (1965) 629.

EAKIN, R.: Evolution of photoreceptors. Cold Spring Harbor Symp. Quant. Biol. 30 (1965) 363.

FAVARD, P.: Spermatogenèse de *Discoglossus pictus* Otth. Ann. Sci. Natl. Zool. 17 (1955) 370.

FAWCETT, D.W.: Cilia and flagella. In: J. Brachet and A.E. Mirsky, eds.: The cell, Vol. 2. New York, Academic Press (1961) p. 217.

GIBBONS, I.R.: The relationship between the fine structure and direction of beat in gill cilia of a lamellibranch mollusc. J. Biophys. Biochem. Cytol. 11 (1961) 179.

GIBBONS, I.R.: A method for obtaining serial sections of known orientation from single spermatozoa. J. Cell Biol. 16 (1963) 626.

GIBBONS, I.R. and A. GRIMSTONE: On flagellar structure in certain flagellates. J. Biophys. Biochem. Cytol. 7 (1960) 697.

GRAY, J.: Ciliary movement. Cambridge, Cambridge Univ. Press (1928).

GRIMSTONE, A.V. and A. KLUG: Observations on the substructure of flagellar fibres. J. Cell Sci. 1 (1966) 351.

HENDELBERG, J.: On different types of spermatozoa in Polycladida, Turbellaria. Arkiv Zool. 18 (1965) 267.

HOLWILL, M.E.J.: Physical aspects of flagellar movement. Physiol. Rev. 46 (1966) 696.

HOLWILL, M.E.J.: Contractile mechanisms in cilia and flagella. In: D.R. Sanadi, ed.: Current topics in Bioenergetics, Vol. 2. New York, Academic Press (1967).

HORRIDGE, G.A.: Macrocilia with numerous shafts from the lips of the ctenophore *Beroë*. Proc. Roy. Soc. (London), Ser. B 162 (1965) 351.

JAHN, T.L. and E.C. BOVEE: Movement and locomotion of microorganisms. Ann. Rev. Microbiol. 19 (1965) 21.

JAHN, T.L. and E.C. BOVEE: Motile behavior of protozoa. In: T.T. Chen, ed.: Research in Protozoology, Vol. 1. Oxford, Pergamon Press (1967).

KIEFER, B.I.: Ultrastructural abnormalities in developing sperm of X/O Drosophila melanogaster. Genetics 54 (1966) 1441.

KINOSITA, H. and A. MURAKAMI: Control of ciliary motion. Physiol. Rev. 47 (1967) 53.

KNIGHT-JONES, E.W.: Relations between metachronism and the direction of ciliary beat in metazoa. Quart. J. Microscop. Sci. 95 (1954) 503.

KOLE, A.P.: Flagella. In: G.C. Ainsworth and A.S. Sussman, eds.: The fungi. An advanced treatise. New York, Academic Press (1965) p. 77.

LOWENSTEIN, O. and J. WERSALL: A functional interpretation of the electron microscopic structure of the sensory hairs in the cristae of the elasmobranch *Raja clavata* in terms of directional sensitivity. Nature 184 (1959) 1807.

LUTHER, A.: Die Eumesostominen. Z. Wiss. Zool. 77 (1904) 1.

MEYER, G.F.: Spermiogenese in normalen und Y defizienten Männchen von *Drosophila melanogaster* und *D. hydei*. Z. Zellforsch. 84 (1968) 141.

MIGNOT, J.P.: Structure et ultrastructure de quelques euglénomonadines. Protistologica 2 (1966) 51.

MCKEEN, W.E.: The flagellation, movement, and encystment of some phycomycetous zoospores. Can. J. Microbiol. 8 (1962) 897.

MANTON, I.: Electron microscopical observations on a very small flagellate: the problem of *Chromulina pusilla* Butcher. J. Marine Biol. Assoc. U.K. 38 (1959) 319.

MANTON, I.: Observations on scale production in *Pyramimonas amylifera* Conrad. J. Cell Sci. 1 (1966) 429.

MANTON, I. and K. HARRIS: Observations on the microanatomy of the brown flagellate *Sphaleromantis tetragona* Skuja with special reference to the flagellar apparatus and scales. J. Linn. Soc. (Bot) 59 (1966) 397.

MANTON, I. and M. PARKE: Observations on the fine structure of two species of *Platymonas* with special reference to flagellar scales and the mode of origin of the theca. J. Marine Biol. Assoc. U.K. 45 (1965) 743.

MANTON, I. and H.A. VON STOSCH: Observations on the fine structure of the male gamete of the marine centric diatom *Lithodesmium undulatum*. J. Roy. Microscop. Soc. 85 (1966) 119.

MARKHAM, R., S. FREY and G.J. HILLS: Methods for the enhancement of image detail and accentuation of structure in electron microscopy. Virology 20 (1963) 88.

MEYER, G.F.: Die Funktionsstrukturen des Y-Chromosoms in den Spermatocytenkernen von *Drosophila hydei, D. neohydei, D. repleta* und einigen anderen *Drosophila*-arten. Chromosoma 14 (1963) 207.

OUTKA, D.E. and B. KLUSS: The ameba-to-flagellate transformation in *Tetramitus rostratus* II Microtubular morphogenesis. J. Cell Biol. 35 (1967) 323.

MOHRI, H., S. MURAKAMI and K. MARUYAMA: On the protein constituting 9 + 2 fibers of the tail of sea-urchin spermatozoa. J. Biochem. (Tokyo) 61 (1967) 518.

NAGANO, T.: Fine structural changes on the flagella of the spermatid in experimental cryptorchidism of the rat. J. Cell Biol. 18 (1963) 337.

NEWTON, B.A. and D. KERRIDGE: Flagellar and ciliary movement in micro-organisms. Symp. Soc. Gen. Microbiol. 15 (1965) 220.

NICANDER, L. and A. BANE: Fine structure of boar spermatozoa. Z. Zellforsch. 57 (1962) 390.

PANTEL, J. and R. DE SINÉTY: Les cellules de lignée male chez le *Notonecta glauca* L. avec des détails plus étendus sur la periode d'accroissement et sur celle de transformation. Cellule 23 (1906) 87.

PARDUCZ, B.: Ciliary movement and coordination in ciliates. Intern. Rev. Cytol. 21 (1967) 91.

PHILLIPS, D.M.: Fine structure of *Sciara coprophila* sperm. J. Cell Biol. 30 (1966) 499.

PHILLIPS, D.M.: Substructure of flagellar tubules. J. Cell Biol. 31 (1966) 635.

PICHERAL, B.: Structure et organisation du spermatozoïde de *Pleurodeles waltlii* Michah. (Amphibien Urodèle). Arch. Biol. (Liège) 78 (1967) 193.

PITELKA, D.R.: Electron-microscopic structure of protozoa. Oxford, Pergamon Press (1963).

PITELKA, D.R. and F.M. CHILD: The locomotor apparatus of ciliates and flagellates. In: S.H. Hutner, ed.: Relations between structure and function. Biochemistry and physiology of protozoa, Vol. 3. New York, Academic Press (1964).

RANDALL, J.T. and J.M. HOPKINS: On the stalks of certain peritrichs. Phil. Trans. Roy. Soc. London, Ser. B 245 (1962) 59.

REESE, T.S.: Olfactory cilia in the frog. J. Cell Biol. 25:2 (1965) 209.

RINGO, D.L.: The arrangement of subunits in flagellar fibers. J. Ultrastruct. Res. 17 (1967) 266.

ROBERTSON, J.D.: The ultrastructure of cell membrane and their derivates. Biochem. Soc. Symp. (Cambridge, Engl.) 16 (1959) 3.

ROSENBAUM, J.L. and F.M. CHILD: Flagellar regeneration in protozoan flagellates. J. Cell Biol. 34 (1967) 345.

ROSS, M.M.R.: Modified cilia in sensory organs of juvenile stages of a parasitic nematode. Science 156 (1967) 1494.

ROUILLER, C. and E. FAURÉ-FREMIET: Ultrastructure des cinétosomes à l'etat cilière chez un cilié péritriche. J. Ultrastruct. Res. 1 (1958) 289.

SAGAN, L.: On the origin of mitosing cells. J. Theoret. Biol. 14 (1967) 225.

SALPETER, M.M. and C. WALCOTT: An electron microscopical study of a vibration receptor in the spider. Exptl. Neurol. 2 (1960) 232.

SATIR, P.: Structure and function in cilia and flagella – facts and problems. Protoplasmatologia 3 (1965) 1.

SATIR, P.: Morphological aspects of ciliary motility. J. Gen. Physiol. 50 (1967) 241.

SCHUSTER, F.: An electron microscope study of the amoebo-flagellate, *Naegleria gruberi* (Schardinger). J. Protozool. 10 (1963) 297.

SHAPIRO, J.E., B.R. HERSHENOV and G.S. TULLOCH: The fine st ucture of *Haematolaechus* spermatozoon tail. J. Biophys. Biochem. Cytol. 9 (1961) 211.

SILVEIRA, M. and K. R. PORTER: The spermatozoids of flatworms and their microtubular systems. Protoplasma 59 (1964) 240.

SILVESTER, N. R.: The cilia of *Tetrahymena pyriformis*: X-ray diffraction by the ciliary membrane. J. Mol. Biol. 8 (1964) 11.

SLAUTTERBACK, D. B.: The cnidoblast-musculoepithelial cell complex in the tentacles of *Hydra*. Z. Zellforsch. 79 (1967) 296.

SLEIGH, M. A.: The biology of cilia and flagella. Oxford, Pergamon Press (1962).

SLEIGH, M. A.: The co-ordination and control of cilia. Symp. Soc. Exptl. Biol. 20 (1966) 11.

SJÖSTRAND, F. S.: A new ultrastructural element of the membranes in mitochondria and of some cytoplasmic membranes. J. Ultrastruct. Res. 9 (1963) 340.

TAMM, S. L.: Flagellar development in the protozoan *Peranema trichophorum*. J. Exptl. Zool. 164 (1967) 163.

TELKKÄ, A., D. W. FAWCETT and A. K. CHRISTENSEN: Further observations on the structure of the mammalian sperm tail. Anat. Record 141 (1961) 231.

VLK, W.: Ueber den Bau der Geissel. Arch. Protistenk. 90 (1938) 448.

WALTMAN, B.: Electrical properties and fine structure of the ampullary canals of Lorenzini. Acta Physiol. Scand., 66 Suppl. 264 (1966) 1.

WARR, J. R., A. MC VITTIE, J. T. RANDALL and J. M. HOPKINS: Genetic control of flagellar structure in *Chlamydomonas reinhardii*. Genet. Res. 7 (1966) 335.

WHITEAR, M.: The fine structure of crustacean proprioceptors. Phil. Trans. Roy. Soc. London Ser. B 245 (1962) 291.

WOOLLEY, D. M. and R. A. BEATTY: Inheritance of midpiece length in mouse spermatozoa. Nature 215 (1967) 94.

CHAPTER 46

The physiology and biochemistry of cilia and flagella

MICHAEL A. SLEIGH

Department of Zoology, University of Bristol, Bristol 8, England

Contents

1. Introduction
2. Movements of cilia and flagella
3. The molecular organisation of cilia and flagella
4. Mechanisms involved in the movement of cilia and flagella

1. Introduction

This chapter surveys our present knowledge of the biochemical organisation and the functioning of cilia and flagella. Our knowledge of the structure and physiology of these organelles has advanced very rapidly in the last 15 years, and much of the information content of this chapter comes from papers written since the publication of the author's comprehensive review on cilia and flagella (Sleigh 1962). Particularly significant have been the biochemical studies of Gibbons (1965, 1968), which are giving an insight into the structure of cilia at the molecular level. The movement of flagella has been discussed in a review by Holwill and papers by Brokaw, and the movement of cilia in a paper by Sleigh (1968). Recent reviews on the coordination of cilia have been written by Sleigh (1966) and by Kinosita and Murakami.

2. Movements of cilia and flagella

The characteristic 9 + 2 arrangement of fibrils is found in both cilia and flagella, so that the distinction that is made between the two classes of organelle can only be a functional one. A flagellar organelle is typified by the propagation along its axis of a symmetrical undulation which produces a force on the water, the resultant movement of which is along the long axis of the organelle; a ciliary organelle typically has a unilateral beat and exerts a sideways force on the water to move it in a direction perpendicular to the organelle. The production of movement by a flagellum is roughly analogous to that by the screw of a ship, while a cilium produces movement by a swing which has analogies with the stroke of an oar. Between these two typical patterns of movement lie intermediates forming a more or less continuous series which make it impossible to separate the two classes of organelle completely. Clearly, this is a single type of structure whose machinery may be utilised in slightly different ways in order to produce different patterns of beat.

Where these organelles occur singly, on spermatozoa for example, their beat is usually of the flagellar type. Because the flagellum tends to be a solitary functional unit, it may be subject to considerable modifications both of form and of function which are mainly directed at increasing the propulsive efficiency of the structure. Some flagellar sperm tails contain only a 9 + 2 fibrillar axoneme, but in many cases there are additional mitochondrial strands and fibrous material in diverse configurations which may modify the pattern of movement. Comparable variations may also be found in protozoan flagella, where structural modifications include flagellar hairs and undulating membranes as well as additional fibrous material within the flagellar membrane. It is likely that the original flagellar organelle caused movement by propagating planar undulations along its length; in the majority of flagella the undulations appear to be basically if not entirely planar, but in a number of cases the passage of helical waves along flagella has been described. In almost all cases these undulations are passed along the flagellum from the base towards the tip, but cases are known where tip-to-base propagation of undulations occurs. Where flagella occur in large numbers on a cell they tend to have an unmodified structure and a simple pattern of beating.

It is characteristic of cilia that they tend to lack structural modification of the 9+2 fibrillar axis; this may be correlated with the fact that structural modifications comparable with those found in flagella would not be of value in a unilateral beat, and with the fact that increased functional effect is easily achieved by the coordinated activity of a large number of cilia. Cilia are frequently aggregated into compound structures within which the units act in synchrony, and almost invariably, whether simple or compound, the cilia of a group or tract show coordination in the form of metachronal waves of beating. Solitary cilia are subject to a variety of adaptive modifications of the basic pattern of ciliary beating, but the variations found in cilia which occur in tracts where they are coordinated metachronally are only of a minor nature (Sleigh 1968).

In those flagella where planar undulations are propagated from base to tip, the movements originate as flexures of the basal region of the flagellar axis, which is bent first to one side and then to the other in strict alternation (Fig. 1). The flagellar bend-

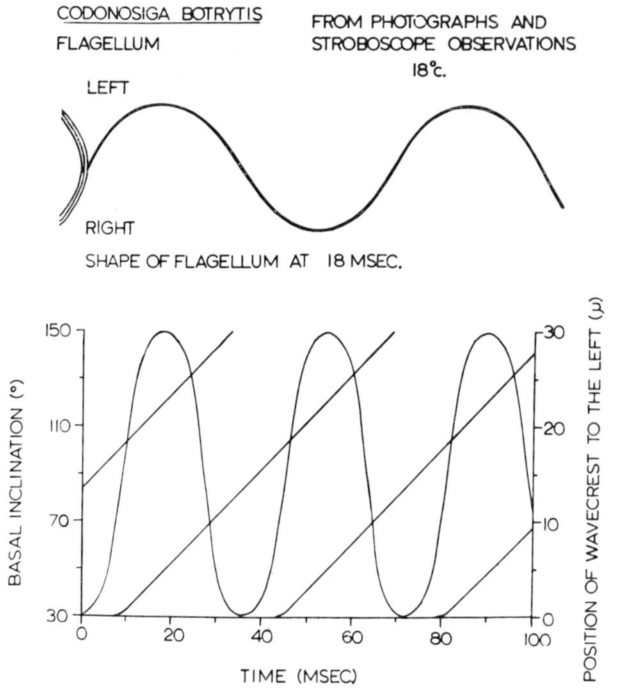

Fig. 1. The movement of the flagellum of the flagellate *Codonosiga*. Above, an instantaneous profile of the flagellum. Below, the angular inclination of the extreme basal region of the flagellum varies between 30° and 150° to the cell surface with a cycle time of 36 msec; waves are propagated up the flagellum at a constant rate. (From Sleigh 1968.)

ing waves which result are found on detailed examination to be made up of circular arcs and straight regions (Brokaw), and are not sinusoidal as has generally been assumed; bending waves are usually symmetrical in healthy flagella. The rate of propagation of the bending waves may be constant or may increase along the flagellar length, in which case the amplitude of the waves usually increases also; the average number of waves within the flagellar length varies in different species. The symmetry of the beat permits a quantitative description of the flagellar activity in terms of readily measurable parameters, viz. the frequency of beat, the flagellar length, the amplitude of the waves and the rate of propagation of the bending wave along the flagellum.

The beat of a cilium involves unilateral bending in an asymmetrical movement which is less easy to describe quantitatively than the movement of a flagellum; a full description of a ciliary beat requires information on the motion of each part of the cilium throughout the cycle. Most cilia can rest in a more or less extended position between the recovery and effective strokes. From this position the cycle of beat starts with a swing of the ciliary axis – the effective stroke – around a bending region near its base (Fig. 2, upper part), and the bend to one side in the basal region is quickly followed by

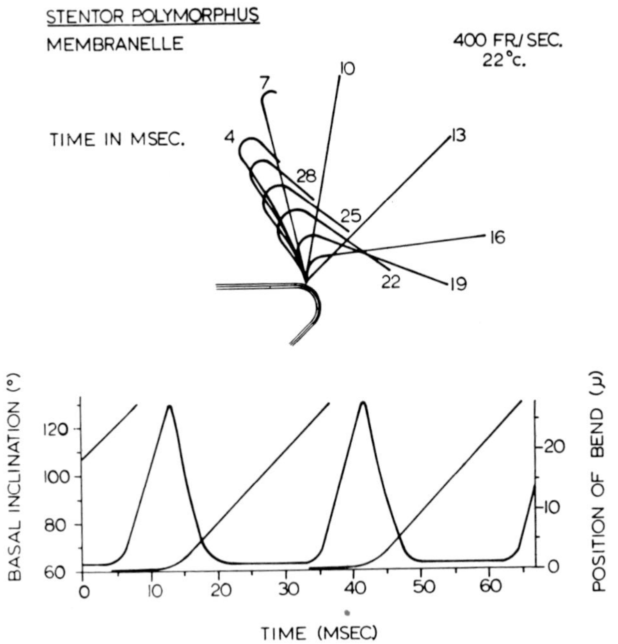

Fig. 2. The movement of membranelles (compound cilia) of the ciliate protozoan *Stentor*, analysed from high-speed cine film. The timing of the profiles in the diagram above corresponds with that of points on the graph below. The line relating the angular inclination of the basal region of the ciliary shaft with time shows the asymmetry of the beat; the bend is propagated up the cilium at a constant rate in the recovery stroke. (From Sleigh 1968.)

a bend to the other side at the extreme base of the cilium, while the distal part of the ciliary axis is continuing to move in the direction followed during the effective stroke. The ciliary flexure produced at the base by these two bending movements is then propagated up the ciliary axis towards the tip during the recovery stroke of the cilium. Many of the measurable features of such a beat are shown in Fig. 2 (lower part), although it is also useful to have a sequence of ciliary profiles to show the position of the region of the ciliary shaft distal to the flexure. From graphs of this type drawn from data on a variety of cilia it was found that (1) the basal bending movement at the start of the recovery stroke is generally quicker than the bending movement in the effective stroke; (2) the duration of the recovery stroke is longer than that of the effective stroke, except in some solitary cilia; (3) in some cilia there is a pause between the recovery stroke of one beat and the effective stroke of the next, and in other cases there is an overlap of adjacent beats; (4) the rate of propagation of the flexure up the ciliary axis often increases towards the tip – it ranges from a few hundred μ/sec in simple cilia and flagella to more than 15 mm/sec in ctenophore comb plates, and shows a rough correlation with the number of component cilia in compound organelles. Considerable variations occur in the timing and angular extent of the movement of cilia from different sources, but the basic form of the movement of cilia from metachronally coordinated groups is broadly similar to that shown in Fig. 2.

The movements described for both types of organelle require some internal mechanism to produce bending of the 9+2 fibril bundle, a means of exciting this bending, and the propagation of the region of bending along the axis of the organelle. It will be necessary to review recent advances in our understanding of the organisation and biochemical nature of the components of cilia and flagella before consideration of hypotheses concerning the mechanisms of ciliary bending, excitation and propagation.

3. *The molecular organisation of cilia and flagella*

There is an almost universal conformity of motile cilia and flagella to the 9+2 fibril pattern, and until more is known of the exceptional cases it is probably not worth considering them further. The components seen in a transverse section, Fig. 3, consist of the major, longitudinal elements, the tubular fibrils at the centre and forming the peripheral doublets, and minor elements, including the arms on the peripheral fibrils, the central sheath which may be a spiral filament, and the radial links with medial thickenings which may be continuous as longitudinal secondary filaments, all of which are enclosed in a membrane which is continuous with the cell membrane. The arms and radial links both project from the peripheral doublets at intervals of about 170 Å along the length of the fibrils.

The tubular fibrils can be seen in high resolution micrographs to be made up of globular molecules arranged in approximately longitudinal rows. Grimstone and Klug studied these fibrils by negative staining and found that the tubular fibrils filled with stain, so that they are presumed to be hollow, and that the longitudinal rows of globular molecules had a lateral spacing of ~50 Å and a longitudinal spacing within the rows of ~40 Å. The occurrence of longer periodicities than 40 Å along the longitudinal axis led to the suggestion that the subunits might not be packed in a parallel array but in a more complex pattern. The number of longitudinal rows of molecules in each tubule appeared in this study to be at least 12; in transverse sections of *Chlamydomonas* flagella Ringo has found that his observations are best fitted by an arrangement with 13 subunits per central fibril, and in the peripheral doublets the pair of fibrils appear to share 3–4 subunits in the common wall so that the entire doublet probably has 23 subunits. A similar substructure has been observed in both central and peripheral fibrils, but the central fibrils disintegrate more easily than the peripherals and are evidently not of identical constitution. Indeed, considerable evidence has been collected by Behnke and Forer to show that not only are the central and peripheral fibrils of different nature, but also that the A and B subfibrils of the peripheral doublets are different, at least to the extent that they show different susceptibility to enzymes. It is clear from the presence of arms on only one subfibril, and the finding of Gibbons that the arm proteins recombined with the A subfibril in specific positions, that there is specificity of different regions of the doublet structure. The possibility is raised later that the arms of subfibril A of one doublet might form links

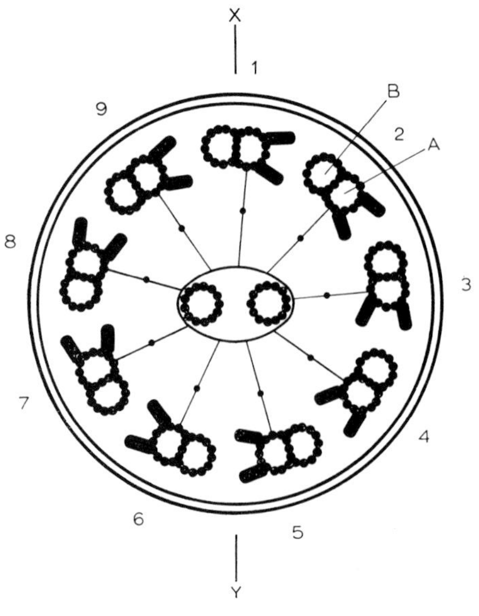

Fig. 3. A diagrammatic transverse section of the shaft of a cilium or flagellum showing the relationships of the parts to one another, and incorporating details of molecular arrangements mentioned in the text. The line XY indicates the normal plane of beating. The conventional numbering scheme for the peripheral doublets is shown, and the two subfibrils (A and B) of doublet number 2 are labelled.

with subfibril B of the adjacent doublet, and this again would be expected to require specific characteristics in part of the doublet structure.

Most of our knowledge of the biochemical structure and properties of the components of cilia and flagella has come from work on the cilia of the protozoon *Tetrahymena*, and studies have also been made on the flagella of flagellate protozoa and sperm tails of echinoderms. These studies depend in the first instance on the separation of cilia or flagella from cell bodies; most studies on *Tetrahymena* cilia have used methods based on the ethanol–EDTA technique of Watson et al., but flagella are often broken from sperm heads by mechanical means. Earlier biochemical work on these organelles was based on analysis of whole isolated cilia or flagella, and by this means it was possible to estimate the proportions of the major chemical constituents (Table 1). It was also possible to demonstrate ATPase activity of isolated cilia and flagella and to show that the relative proportions of amino acids were roughly comparable with those of actin (Watson and Hopkins; Jones and Lewin). However, it was not possible to characterise any of the different components of the organelles, so that the results obtained were inadequate. The elegant 'chemical dissections' of *Tetrahymena* cilia by Gibbons (1965), and his further exploitation of similar techniques (Gibbons 1968), have given a much clearer picture of some of the protein components of cilia separated by fractionation. In these studies the components of isolated cilia were selectively dissolved, with periodic examination of the insoluble parts under the electron microscope to determine which structure was dissolved by a particular treatment, and with studies of the physical and chemical properties of the soluble proteins.

By the use of several different fractionation procedures Gibbons was able to isolate most of the ciliary proteins and to characterise several of them. One technique involved first the extraction of the isolated cilia with digitonin so that on centrifugation the complete $9+2$ axoneme complex was found in the pellet and the membrane and matrix components were in the supernatant; dialysis of the pellet material against a chelating agent at low ionic strength (tris-EDTA) followed by centrifugation separated the 9 outer doublet fibrils of the axoneme in the pellet from the other axoneme proteins – mainly the proteins of the central fibrils and the arms from the peripheral fibrils –

TABLE 1

The proportions of the major constituents of flagella and cilia

Organism Organelles	*Polytoma* Flagella	*Chlamydomonas* Flagella	*Tetrahymena* Cilia	*Tetrahymena* Cilia
Total dry weight	100	100	100	100
Protein	~75	60–65	~80	73–77
Lipid	20	'appreciable'	13–23	17–30
Carbohydrate	5	6–8	1	2–6
Reference	Tibbs	Jones and Lewin	Watson and Hopkins	Culbertson

in the supernatant. In a second technique the whole isolated cilia were dialysed against tris-EDTA directly; the pellet obtained on centrifugation consisted of the membranes and outer fibril doublets and the supernatant contained the other axoneme proteins and the matrix proteins; separation of the membranes from the fibril doublets was achieved by dissolving the latter in KCl or KI solution. In either procedure a fraction was obtained which contained axonemal proteins (other than those of the 9 doublets) dissolved by treatment with a chelating agent. The proteins in these fractions consisted of two major components, a lower molecular weight protein without ATPase activity with a sedimentation coefficient of 4S, and a higher molecular weight protein with ATPase activity sedimenting in two fractions with similar chemical properties at 14S and 30S. The latter component could be identified as the protein forming the arms on the peripheral fibrils and was named dynein. The 4S protein which was dissolved in the chelating agent after digitonin treatment was mainly derived from the central fibrils, while that isolated after the direct dialysis treatment comprised the central fibril protein and matrix proteins.

Five protein components can be recognised by these fractionation treatments; their relative proportions and their ability to hydrolyse ATP are listed in Table 2. The properties of the ATPase from the membrane and dynein fractions are different, e.g. dynein ATPase is activated by both Ca^{2+} and Mg^{2+}, while the membrane ATPase is activated by Mg^{2+} but not by Ca^{2+}. Most attention has so far been directed towards the study of dynein and the protein of the outer fibril doublets.

The axoneme ATPase protein, dynein, appears in the ultracentrifuge as two fractions which sediment at 14S and 30S. The 14S dynein is the monomeric form and is a globular molecule about 140 Å long and 70 to 90 Å in diameter with a molecular weight of about 540,000; it can be broken with 5 M guanidine hydrochloride into large subunits of molecular weight about 220,000 and a fraction of low molecular weight. The 30S dynein has a molecular weight of about 5,000,000, and occurs as short filaments, 70 to 90 Å in diameter and with a 140 Å periodicity, which are linear

TABLE 2

The proportions of protein components and ATPase activity of *Tetrahymena* cilia

	Total protein (%)	Total ATPase activity (%)
Whole cilia	100	100
Membrane protein	22	10–30
Matrix protein	28	—
Central fibril protein	5	—
Dynein (arm protein)	10	70–90
Outer fibril protein	32	—
Other axoneme structures	3	—

Data derived from Gibbons 1965.

polymers of 14S dynein. This protein will recombine with isolated outer fibrils in such a way that the arms reappear in the correct position on one of the subfibrils of each doublet; the presence or absence of arms is correlated with the presence or absence of 30S dynein, and in this respect the 30S dynein appears to be the physiologically active form since 14S dynein recombines only weakly in comparison with the polymer. Gibbons concludes that, since the periodicity of subunits of 30S dynein is of the same order as the distance between the arms along the outer fibrils, the dynein monomers represent the individual arm units and that these are linked in longitudinal polymeric filaments which are bound to the outer fibrils. The ATPase activity of dynein assayed under approximately physiological conditions is equivalent to the hydrolysis of 11 to 35 molecules of ATP per dynein molecule per second, which would correspond to about 1 molecule of ATP hydrolysed by each dynein molecule in each beat of the cilium; Brokaw has found that the utilisation of ATP by glycerinated sperm tails corresponds approximately to 1 molecule of ATP hydrolysed per dynein molecule per beat, although not all of the flagella in the preparation were motile. The similarity of dynein to myosin invites comparison of the two proteins (Table 3): they may well be performing similar functions, but their physical and chemical properties are different. Gibbons and Rowe suggest that dynein is more closely related to myxomyosin, the ATPase protein of slime moulds, than to muscle myosin.

The outer fibril protein is a globular molecule with a molecular weight of about 55,000, which sediments at 4S; this exists as a dimer sedimenting at 6S in the aqueous solution made by dissolving outer fibrils in 0.6 M KCl. In terms of amino acid composition and behaviour on electrophoresis, this protein is very much like actin from muscle; in fact, the differences between outer fibril protein and muscle actin are of the same order as the differences between actins from the muscles of different species of animal. However, the outer fibril protein is different from muscle actin in two respects: (1) the polymerisation conditions are different, i.e. actin molecules form filaments which are arranged to form a double helix, while the outer fibril protein

TABLE 3

Comparison of the properties of myosin and dynein

	Myosin	Dynein
Molecular weight	~ 500,000	~ 540,000
Shape (length/diameter)	~ 60	< 2
Solubility at low ionic strength	insoluble	soluble
ATPase activation by Mg^{2+}	–	+
ATPase activation by Ca^{2+}	+	+
ATPase inhibition by EDTA	–	+
Nucleoside phosphate specificity of the ATPase	unspecific	specific for ATP

forms filaments which are aligned to form the walls of tubular fibrils; (2) the bound nucleotide is different, i.e. muscle actin binds ADP, but outer fibril protein binds guanosine nucleotides: there is also evidence that the manner of binding of the nucleotides is different, since the guanosine nucleotide may be phosphorylated or dephosphorylated while the ciliary protein is in the polymerised state, but phosphorylation or dephosphorylation of ADP only takes place when actin is depolymerised (Stevens et al.).

The molecules of central fibril protein appear in electron micrographs to be about the same size as those of the outer fibrils. Shelanski and Taylor were able to extract the central fibrils of sea urchin sperm flagella selectively, and found a single protein component with a molecular weight of about 100,000 sedimenting at 6S. On the basis of Gibbons' studies on outer fibril proteins, one might expect these molecules of central fibril protein to be dimers.

4. Mechanisms involved in the movement of cilia and flagella

Authorities on both cilia and flagella agree that the movements performed by these organelles must be the result of active processes along the length of the structure and not passive movements resulting from movement of the base within the cell. The discovery of the fibrillar organisation of these organelles provided a basis for several theories of ciliary bending which relied upon a shortening of the fibrils, and in most cases it was assumed that a contraction of the outer nine fibril doublets was involved. These theories mostly required that the fibrils on the inside of a bend in a cilium or flagellum could shorten and produce a contractile force acting against the stiffness of the fibrillar axis of the organelle to distort it, and that the region of shortening was propagated along the organelle to produce flagellar waves or the recovery stroke of the cilium (Bradfield; Sleigh 1962; Silvester and Holwill).

More recently, hypotheses based upon the sliding of the ciliary fibrils have found favour. There is an increasing body of evidence (summarised by Satir) that the ciliary fibrils do not change in length during movement, but merely change their relative positions by sliding along one another. The most convincing evidence was obtained by Satir himself; it is that in electron micrographs of cilia fixed instantaneously at various stages in their beat the terminations of the fibril doublets at the ciliary tips always conform to a pattern in which the fibrils which end first are those which have traversed the longest arc length in the bent part of the cilium, and those which protrude furthest have traversed the shortest arc length. In addition to evidence of this type, the occurrence of the ciliary fibrillar ATPase on arms between the fibrils makes a theory based upon the relative movement of fibrils attractive, especially in view of the similarity of the dynein and outer fibril components of the ciliary axis to the myosin and actin of muscle, and the wide acceptance of the sliding fibril theory of contraction in striated muscle. On present evidence it seems reasonable to believe that the bending of cilia and flagella depends on the sliding along one another of peripheral fibril doublets of constant length, that the force required to perform the movement is derived from the formation by the arms of links between adjacent doublets, and that energy for the formation of links is made available by ATPase activity of the dynein which forms the arms.

The following hypothesis based on this belief has recently been put forward (Sleigh 1968). In an erect cilium at the beginning of a beat fibrils of uniform length will end at the same level (Fig. 4A); when the cilium bends to one side in the effective stroke the peripheral fibrils slide on one another, and, since the fibrils are anchored together in the basal body, changes in the positions of fibrils will be seen as changes in their level of termination (Fig. 4B). During this movement each peripheral fibril doublet of the cilium is thought to move relative to each of its neighbours throughout the full length of the cilium (except perhaps fibrils 5 and 6 in Fig. 3, assuming movement in the plane X–Y). In the region of the bend the amount of sliding between fibrils increases from the base upwards, and from the end of the bend to the ciliary tip the amount of sliding will remain constant at a maximal value. The changes of position which take place allow the formation of new links between fibril doublets throughout the full length and diameter of the cilium during the effective stroke. Each doublet can exert a longitudinal pull on a neighbouring doublet in such a way that the force acts in the region of the attachment of fibrils at the base of the cilium, and the resultant of these forces causes a bending of the shaft.

In the recovery stroke the fibrils would be required to slip back to their original positions as the cilium straightens out from the base upwards (Fig. 4C). Sliding of fibrils along one another is restricted to the region of the ciliary bend during the recov-

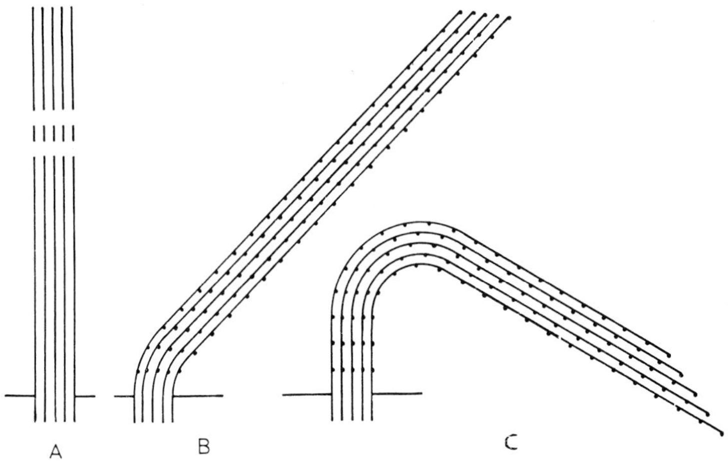

Fig. 4. The position of ciliary fibrils at various stages in the beat according to the sliding fibril hypothesis described in the text. A, the cilium in the erect position; B, during the effective stroke; C, during the recovery stroke. The dots on the fibrils occur at equal intervals and indicate the amount of sliding of the fibrils.

ery stroke, but it allows the formation of new links between fibrils in their original positions in the erect cilium; it is necessary that some chemical energy should be utilised in the recovery stroke since the return movement is believed not to be an entirely elastic one.

The explanation of fibril movements shown in Fig. 4 assumes that in the effective stroke of a cilium the rate of sliding of fibrils throughout the part of the cilium distal to the region of bending would be uniform, and therefore that this part of the cilium would remain straight during its effective stroke. Most cilia do remain almost straight in their distal regions during the effective stroke, but some certainly do not; in these latter cases it appears that the region of sliding of fibrils in the effective stroke extends more slowly up the ciliary shaft, so that the cilium bends backwards to accommodate those fibrils that have slipped, and gradually straightens out as the backward bend travels towards the tip (Sleigh 1968, Figs. 7 and 13). The occurrence of limited regions of sliding is also seen in the movement of flagella, where the sliding of doublets involved in the flexion of the flagellum to one side and then to the other would result in regions of the flagellar axis where the sliding in one direction is maximal alternating with regions where sliding in the other direction is maximal (Fig. 5). The regions of maximal sliding are the straight parts of the flagellum, and the very short regions of no sliding occur at the crests of the waves where the flagellar axis is parallel with the axis of the basal body. The form of the waves would be expected to conform to a sequence of circular arcs and straight regions.

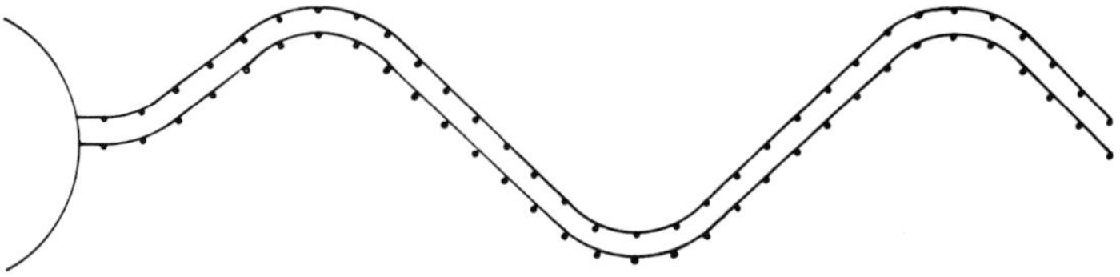

Fig. 5. Two adjacent fibrils of a flagellum showing how the fibrils are believed to slide along one another to bend the flagellar axis. The dots occur at equal intervals along each fibril.

One attraction of this idea is that it allows the entire energetic machinery of the cilium to be used during the effective stroke; it is also simpler than the contraction theories. The amount of sliding between adjacent fibril doublets around the periphery of the cilium would be about 100 Å for every 10° of bending, if one assumes that bending can take place between each pair of adjacent doublets (except 5 and 6) and that the amount of sliding along each of the four lines of movement is about the same. A bend of about 120° is involved in the movement of many cilia, and in some cases bends of up to 180° occur – the latter would involve a total sliding of a doublet at one side of a cilium relative to a doublet at the other side of about 0.63 μ (in an average cilium the diameter of the fibril bundle is 0.2 μ). It is interesting that the rate of sliding between adjacent fibrils required by this hypothesis is about 1–10 μ/sec, which is of the same order as that between the actin and myosin filaments of muscle.

The sliding fibril hypothesis proposed here has so far invoked no functions for the central fibrils and the elements which immediately surround them; indeed, if the radial links rigidly connect the peripheral and central fibrils, sliding movements of the size required by the hypothesis would not be possible. It is believed that the radial links are connected to the sheath around the central fibrils, rather than to the central fibrils themselves, and it is possible that the sheath is constructed in such a way that longitudinal movements are possible; this might still allow the radial links and central structures to act in the maintenance of the integrity of the cylinder of outer fibrils.

The manner in which the arms might form links between adjacent peripheral doublets will also require explanation, since the space between adjacent doublets is about 250 Å and the 14S dynein molecule is only about 140 Å long. It is interesting to speculate on the possibility that there may be specialised regions of the B subfibril to which the arms may link, especially in view of the fact that in the basal body the C subfibril is joined to the B subfibril along lines which could be used as sites for arm linkage in the shaft. Quite a large proportion of the protein content of the cilium appears to come from the matrix and some of this could be involved with the arms in link formations which are too labile to be preserved for electron microscopy, although they must presumably persist in a functional form in glycerinated preparations.

Published suggestions concerning the mechanism of propagation of bending waves along cilia and flagella are based on hypotheses of bending by localised fibrillar shortening and not on a sliding fibril system; problems of the propagation of bending waves have recently been considered in detail by Brokaw. In the propagation along a flagellum of waves of fibrillar shortening there would be bending regions and unbending regions which must travel along the flagellum at the same speed to maintain equal spacing. The propagation of a bending wave could be achieved by a passive mechanical distortion which is transmitted progressively to the relaxed region immediately in front of the wave, but suggested mechanisms for causing the unbending with correct timing to fit observations made under a variety of experimental conditions do not seem to be realistic.

The full implications of the sliding fibril hypothesis advanced above, with regard to bend propagation along organelles, have not been considered. Clearly, the propagation of regions of sliding could result from a passive mechanical movement, because the sliding of a fibril in one part of the cilium is bound to cause a movement in an adjacent region. In a cilium the propagation of the extent of sliding is fast in the effective stroke (unless there is a slow-moving backward bend of the cilium) and slow in the recovery stroke, but the conditions for sliding are quite different in the two parts of the beat. The conditions for sliding in successive half waves of a flagellar beat would appear to be identical, provided that the timing of movements to the two sides is strictly alternate, so that symmetrical waves propagated at similar rates would be expected to occur. It is not quite clear whether one can justifiably regard the complete sliding movement of one half wave as a single process, or whether one has to consider the equivalent of Brokaw's bending and unbending regions in each half wave and to propose solutions of the problems involved in the control of the timing of two processes which must move at the same rate.

The excitation of bending in these organelles has two important aspects, neither of which has been very extensively studied. They are: (1) the regular excitations that give rise to the rhythmical beating of cilia and flagella, and (2) the control mechanism by which the cell may activate or inhibit the movement of the organelle.

The rhythm of the symmetrical flagellar beat is a regular oscillation with equal time intervals between movements towards the two sides, but the asymmetrical ciliary beat has a more complex rhythm of alternate long and short time intervals between movements towards the two sides. The situation in a flagellum would appear to be a simple one; in Fig. 5 it is clear that the flagellum moves without a pause from a position of maximum sliding at one side to a position of maximum sliding at the other side. The duration of maximum sliding on one side (and hence the frequency of oscillation) could be related to physicochemical processes such as the rate of supply of ATP, e.g. if slipping to one side uses up ATP and the release of tension depends on the presence of ATP, then as soon after bending as more ATP is available the fibrils will begin to slide back towards their original position and initiate the sliding movement towards the other side (cf. Silvester and Holwill). The relaxation following one active movement could directly start the next active phase. The beating of two or more flagella lying close together is influenced by viscous forces acting between the moving shafts which modify the frequency and phase of the oscillations of the individual flagella until the mutual interaction is minimal. The activity of a flagellum may be thought of as having analogies with an electronic oscillator which functions spontaneously at a frequency which depends on the details of its construction, but whose frequency and phase may be modified by external influences.

The beat of a cilium also seems to be spontaneously excited at regular intervals in most cases, but here the mechanism would appear to be more complex. The timing interval between the bend in the effective stroke and the basal bend at the beginning of the recovery stroke could normally depend on some process such as the supply of ATP, as in the mechanism suggested for flagella, but the possibility for control of the time interval must be built into the system since some cilia can show a resting pause of variable duration in the fully flexed position. The mechanism responsible for the initiation of each effective stroke is more of a problem. The idea that the beginning of an effective stroke is controlled by feedback from the ciliary tip, so that a new beat starts when the previous bend reaches the tip, can hardly be reconciled with the finding that in some cilia there is a pause between beats and in other cilia an overlap of adjacent beats. It seems more likely that ciliary excitation is an ionic phenomenon (probably tied up with the supply or breakdown of ATP) comparable with that which is implicated in the excitation of muscle; this has a little support from present evidence concerning the excitation of cilia in certain types of metachronal coordination. The explanation may be that electrochemical events which occur when a cilium beats modify the ionic environment so that a new spontaneous beat will not occur until a favourable ionic balance has been restored. This idea is also of interest because the control of ciliary activity is often mediated by nerves or hormones which could act through an influence on the ionic environment. The existence of the phenomenon of metachronal coordination of cilia does not remove the requirement for spontaneous excitation of cilia since the rhythms shown by metachronally coordinated groups of cilia always seem to depend on the spontaneous beating of cilia which may or may not act as pacemakers controlling the rate of beat of other cilia; it is also found that isolated motile cilia of any type may show spontaneous rhythmical activity.

Coordinated movement of cilia may involve synchrony of beating, e.g. of the component cilia of compound organelles, or of cilia which occur in rows parallel with the wave crests in a field of cilia that are metachronally coordinated. Such synchrony appears normally to be the result of mechanical forces between the moving cilia comparable with those between flagella which beat in phase because they lie close together. A more striking form of ciliary coordination is metachronism in which cilia beat in waves, each member of the sequence being somewhat out of phase in comparison with its neighbours (Fig. 6). Metachronal coordination of cilia is based on different mechanisms in different tracts of cilia, and is of two major types. (1) Where cilia are very close together in a group, the resultant rate of beating of the group is the average of the intrinsic frequencies of all of the individuals, because of the mutual constraint caused by the large amount of viscous-mechanical coupling between the moving cilia; some cilia are accelerated and others slowed down, but all are constrained to beat in a particular phase relationship with their neighbours. The theory explaining this type of metachronism is referred to as the 'mechanical interference theory' by Kinosita and Murakami. It is probably the most common type of metachronism, and is well shown by cilia of *Opalina*. (2) Where the beat of the cilia is triggered in some way by the beat of the previous cilium in the metachronal sequence, so that the first cilium of the sequence is a pacemaker cilium which determines the rate of beat of those cilia which follow it. The triggering may be either (a) mechanical, through viscous forces in the water or by actual contact, e.g. the reverse waves of the comb plates of *Pleurobrachia* (Sleigh 1968), or (b) by some form of internal (neuroid) conduction mechanism, which in the forward waves of ctenophore comb plates

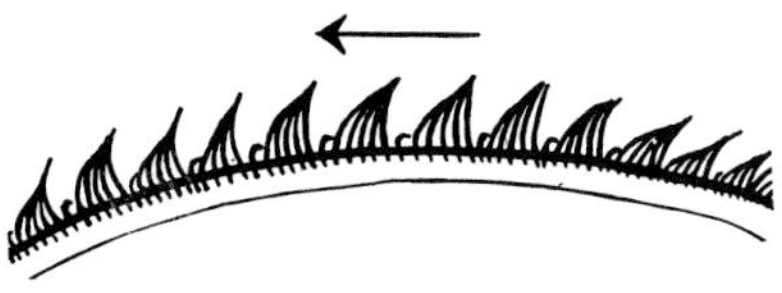

Fig. 6. Metachronal waves of cilia. In this case the cilia beat in a plane at right angles to the direction of wave propagation (arrow). In other cases waves may move in the plane of beat of the cilia, and may be propagated in the direction of the effective stroke or in the opposite direction.

appears to involve the electrotonic spread of an electrical depolarisation (Horridge; Sleigh 1968). Mechanical triggering fits the sliding fibril hypothesis well because it could involve the initiation of a sliding movement between the fibrils of the ciliary axis sufficient to give rise to the propagation of a wave of sliding along the cilium. The triggering of ciliary bending by an electrical change could involve ionic movements associated with the cell membrane which may be related with the provision of a suitable ionic environment for ATP breakdown. In some protozoa, e.g. *Opalina*, *Paramecium*, the direction of ciliary beating is variable and can be related to electrical and ionic conditions (Kinosita and Murakami; Sleigh 1966); these observations, and those on nervous and hormonal control of ciliary beating in metazoa, will have to be accommodated in any theory concerning excitation.

References

BEHNKE, O. and A. FORER: Evidence for four classes of microtubules in individual cells. J. Cell Sci. 2 (1967) 169.

BRADFIELD, J. R. G.: Fibre patterns in animal flagella and cilia. Symp. Soc. Exptl. Biol. 9 (1955) 306.

BROKAW, C. J.: Mechanisms of sperm movement. Symp. Soc. Exptl. Biol. 22 (1968) 101.

CULBERTSON, J. R.: Physical and chemical properties of cilia isolated from *Tetrahymena pyriformis*. J. Protozool. 13 (1966) 397.

GIBBONS, I. R.: Chemical dissection of cilia. Arch. Biol. (Liège) 76 (1965) 317.

GIBBONS, I. R.: The structure and composition of cilia. Symp. Internat. Soc. Cell Biol. 6 (1968) 99.

GIBBONS, I. R. and A. J. ROWE: Dynein: a protein with adenosine triphosphatase activity from cilia. Science, 149 (1965) 424.

GRIMSTONE, A. V. and A. KLUG: Observations on the substructure of flagellar fibres. J. Cell Sci. 1 (1966) 351.

HOLWILL, M. E. J.: Physical aspects of flagellar movement. Physiol. Rev. 46 (1966) 696.

HORRIDGE, G. A.: Pathways of coordination in ctenophores. Symp. Zool. Soc. Lond. 16 (1966) 247.

JONES, R. F. and R. A. LEWIN: The chemical nature of the flagella of *Chlamydomonas moewusii*. Exptl. Cell Res. 19 (1960) 408.

KINOSITA, H. and A. MURAKAMI: Control of ciliary motion. Physiol. Rev. 47 (1967) 53.

RINGO, D. L.: The arrangement of subunits in flagellar fibers. J. Ultrastruct. Res. 17 (1967) 266.

SATIR, P.: Morphological aspects of ciliary motility. J. Gen. Physiol. 50, Suppl. 1 (1967) 241.

SHELANSKI, M. L. and E. W. TAYLOR: Isolation of a protein subunit from microtubules. J. Cell Biol. 34 (1967) 549.

SILVESTER, N. R. and M. E. J. HOLWILL: Molecular hypothesis of flagellar activity. Nature 205 (1965) 665.

SLEIGH, M. A.: The biology of cilia and flagella. Oxford, Pergamon Press (1962).

SLEIGH, M. A.: The coordination and control of cilia. Symp. Soc. exp. Biol. 20 (1966) 11.

SLEIGH, M. A.: Metachronal coordination of the comb plates of the ctenophore *Pleurobrachia*. J. Exptl. Biol. 48 (1967) 111.

SLEIGH, M. A.: Patterns of ciliary beating. Symp. Soc. Exptl. Biol. 22 (1968) 131.

STEVENS, R. E., F. L. RENAUD and I. R. GIBBONS: Guanine nucleotides associated with the protein of the outer fibres of flagella and cilia. Science 156 (1967) 1606.

TIBBS, J.: The properties of algal and sperm flagella obtained by sedimentation. Biochem. Biophys. Acta 28 (1958) 636.

WATSON, M. R. and J. M. HOPKINS: Isolated cilia from *Tetrahymena pyriformis*. Exptl. Cell Res. 28 (1962) 280.

WATSON, M. R., J. M. HOPKINS and J. T. RANDALL: Isolated cilia from *Tetrahymena pyriformis*. Exptl. Cell Res. 23 (1961) 629.

PART XV

Cell surface and function

CHAPTER 47

The cell surface: components and configurations

H. STANLEY BENNETT

Laboratories for Cell Biology, University of Chicago, Chicago, Ill.

Contents

1. Introduction
2. Components of cell surface
   (a) The cell membrane
   (b) The glycocalyx
3. Geometrical configurations of cell surfaces
   (a) Microvilli and cilia
   (b) Caveolae
   (c) Folds and plications
4. Variants and functions of glycocalyx
   (a) Relationship to cell membrane
      Attached glycocalyces
      Unattached glycocalyces
   (b) Mechanical functions of glycocalyces
      Cell walls
      Intercellular matrices
      Basement membranes or basal laminae
      Mucous coats
   (c) Filtering action of glycocalyces
5. Enzymatic activities associated with cell surfaces
6. Attachment areas, or desmosomes
   (a) Classifications of desmosomes
      According to shape
      According to the structure to which the cell surface is bound at the desmosome

According to the similarity or dissimilarity of the structure to which the desmosome binds
According to some important functions attributed to the desmosomes
According to the relations between the membranes of two cell surface areas involved in the desmosomes of a pair
According to the relations of the cytoplasm of the two participating cells
According to the relations of cytoplasmic structures to the membrane of the desmosome

(b) Properties of desmosomes

7. Plasmodesmata

Legend for all figures

A antennula
B basement membrane
C cytoplasm
D secretion caveola
E extracellular space
F fat droplet
G glycocalyx
H desmosome
I microvillus
J virus
K caveola
L lumen
M cell membrane
N virus nucleon
P particle
Q membrane particle
R protein molecule
S secretion vesicle, or lysosome
T bacterium
U mucous coat
V vesicle
W cell wall
X tonofilament
Y collagen
Z plasmodesma

1. Introduction

This chapter and the following one comprise a unit. The components and configurations of the cell surface are described in the first chapter. The second one deals with the movements and recombinations of the cell surface which enable cells to perform many important physiological fuctions.

Units of length used in the text correspond to the Système Internationale d'Unités (SI) (see Nature 216 (1967) 1272). In accordance with this system, the terms 'Ångström units' and 'microns' are avoided. Examples of preferred units used are micrometers (μm, or 10^{-6} m), and nanometers (nm, or 10^{-9} m). 1 nm = 10 Ångström units.

2. Components of cell surface

Two components are recognized as participating in the structure and function of the cell surface (Bennett 1963). The inner one has lipid and protein as its main components and is designated as the 'cell membrane' or 'plasma membrane'. A second component can usually be demonstrated outside the cell membrane. It is rich in saccharides, though always containing other components as well. It is here termed the 'glycocalyx'. In special cases, it has been recognized in forms to which other terms, for example, 'cell wall', 'cell coat', 'basement membrane', 'mucous coat', 'extraneous coat', or 'zona pellucida' have been applied.

(a) *The cell membrane*

The cell membrane or plasma membrane can be accurately traced in electron micrographs of sections of cells. It has been described by Robertson (1959). When viewed in cross section after osmium or permanganate fixation, it often displays a tri-laminate structure, with two dense lines spaced 4 to 6 nm apart on each side of an intervening element of lesser density. It usually appears to be 8 to 10 nm thick over-all (see Fig. 1). This characteristic feature has been named the 'unit membrane' by Robertson (1964). Its molecular structure is presented in his chapter in this Handbook.

The morphological features of membranes of all cells show a considerable similarity. Yet some differences in thickness, in symmetry, and in spacings of the two dense laminae have been described, as the cell membranes of many cell types have come under detailed scrutiny (see Yamamoto). Moreover, varying physiological properties have been detected in membranes of cells of various types. This conveys the information that there are a number of significant molecular variations in structure which are not revealed by present techniques for morphological study.

Functionally, the cell or plasma membrane is usually thought of as limiting the cytoplasm of the cell from extracellular space. It provides the principal barrier separating the special ionic and protein content of the cell cytoplasm from the differing media outside. It has a large role in mediating and regulating active and passive movements of materials between the inside and the outside of the cell. To some of its molecular constituents the specific ionic and molecular pumps are attributed which function in active transport and which are described in the chapter of this Handbook by Professor E. Schoffeniels. In general, the cell membrane resists the passage of water, ions and hydrophilic molecules, but permits the rapid passage by diffusion of oxygen, nitrogen and carbon dioxide. It has a high electric resistance to direct current, a high dielectric constant, and is capable of withstanding voltage gradients of 10^6–10^7 volts per meter (see Cole 1962, 1968; Eccles; Tasaki).

The plasma or cell membrane is sometimes spoken of as the 'cell wall', though such a usage for this term engenders confusion, as the term 'cell wall' is used by botanists and bacteriologists in referring to an entirely different structure, with different properties, discussed later in this chapter under the heading 'Glycocalyx', and described in detail in the chapter of this Handbook by Professor Kreger.

The cell membrane is flexible and easily distorted. It assumes a wide variety of geometric configurations, depending on the type of cell and its physiological state. In many cases, the membrane participates in important movements, changing its configuration from time to time. Under certain circumstances, portions of cell membrane may fuse and recombine with membrane areas in another cell or in other portions of the same cell, thus leading to the coalescence of fluid compartments which previously were separated, or to the division of a fluid compartment into two. These movements and translocations are described in detail in the following chapter.

In some cells, such as nerve, muscle, and electric organ, the cell membrane is excitable, by which we mean that it is capable of undergoing a transient localized molecular instability, which permits momentary surges of ions to traverse it, the surge being driven by the ionic concentration gradients across the membrane. Such a localized disturbance is quickly healed, but prompts a similar disturbance in neighboring regions of the membrane, which in turn triggers off nearby areas, so that the disturbance is propagated over wide regions of the cell surface. Such a propagated but reversible instability is characteristic of the action potential of nerve or muscle (see Cole 1968; Eccles; Tasaki). Excitation of a propagated action potential may occur from spontaneous, oscillatory cell reactions, as in heart muscle, or may be engendered by electrical or chemical membrane disturbances, or in response to a wide variety of special events, such as light, sound, insertion of foreign molecules (as in odor or taste), mechanical displacement, temperature changes, or the like. Special molecular structural features are attributed to excitable membranes, but these are neither well characterized nor understood.

Transient alterations of structure and function of longer duration are known to occur in the membranes of some cells. Brandt and Freeman have described an example in the ameba. In this animal, salt solutions or proteins capable of inducing pinocytosis (encytosis) reversibly produced decreases in membrane resistance up to $^1/_{50}$ the original value, accompanied by increases in thickness of the cell membrane of about 20 per cent.

In many cases, variations in properties can be attributed to different portions of the cell membrane of a single cell. For example, in many vertebrate striated muscle cells, the cell membrane underlying the motor nerve ending is capable of engendering a propagated action potential in response to the localized presence of acetylcholine, but does not initiate such a potential when subjected to modest localized electrical transients. In contrast, other areas of cell membrane along the fiber can be excited by electrical transients, but not by acetylcholine (see Grundfest). Still a third type of membrane specialization is represented at the myotendinal junction, where tendon filaments are bound to the membrane on the external surface and 'tonofilaments', or intracellular, non-contractile, keratin-like filaments connected to Z bands of contractile myofibrils insert on the inner side of the membrane, forming a specialized kind of desmosome (see below). Thus, on a single muscle fiber we recognize one portion of the cell membrane to be specialized in the transmission of mechanical tension to tendon, a second portion specialized in the sensitivity to acetylcholine and a third portion well adapted to the rapid propagation of the action potential impulse and to selective active transport of ions. Each of these recognized special functions conveys that the respective areas of membrane displaying them have special and distinct molecular features. But our knowledge of structural detail is insufficient to permit plausible detailed postulates as to the molecular variations associated with these variant physiological properties.

(b) *The glycocalyx*

The glycocalyx, or cell coat, is the second important component of the cell surface. It lies outside the cell membrane, but is, in many instances, attached wholly or in part to its outer surface. The glycocalyx seems to be more variable in structure than the unit membrane. So far as is known, it always contains sugars of some sort as important components, though these sugars are in the company of, and often covalently bound to, other species of substance, such as amino acids, lipids, lignins, proteins, nucleotides, or other polymers (see Martin; Sharon).

In special cases, the glycocalyx may be impregnated with inorganic crystals, such as calcium phosphate or carbonate. Since the glycocalyx lies outside the lipoprotein membrane of the cell, it can be regarded as an extracellular element. The 'glycocalyx', meaning 'sweet husk', was recognized as a general component of cell surfaces by Bennett (1963). Because of its extracellular nature, Brandt spoke of it as an 'extraneous coat' and Rambourg et al. and Rambourg and Leblond suggested that it be called the 'cell coat'. In contrast to the cell membrane, glycocalyx components are readily pervaded by water, ions and small molecules and show low electrical resistance. From the position occupied by the glycocalyx, these components can exert selective influences on substances in the extracellular medium and thus play a regulating role on the materials which come into contact with the cell membrane itself.

The structural characteristics of glycocalyces show enormous variations (see Fig. 1). Some familiar glycocalyces are robust, rigid and mechanically strong. The cell walls of woody plants and the calcified matrix of bone exemplify these features. At another extreme, the representation of the glycocalyx on the surface of the mammalian red cell is so tenuous that it has not been recognized in ordinary electron micrographs, but has been demonstrated clearly by immunological, biochemical and cytochemical techniques (see Kabat; Lee and Feldman).

Glycocalyces can be classified in several ways: as attached or unattached to the cell membrane; or as antennular, chitinous, mucous, calcified, woody, or otherwise. Several of these types of glycocalyces are described and exemplified later in this chapter.

The range of chemical substances represented in glycocalyces is similarly broad (see Martin; Sharon). Those in plant cell walls are described further in the chapter by Kreger. In vertebrates, sialic acid, hyaluronate and chondroitin sulfates, all associated with proteins, are evident amongst the sugars of the glycocalyx. On amebae and microvilli, the antennular glycocalyx has the properties of mucous coats, and displays strong ion exchange properties, behaving like an anionic polymer (see Marshall and Nachmias; Brandt and Pappas 1960, 1962; Ito).

Fig. 1. I. Diagram of cell surface as displayed on the ameba. The lipoprotein cell membrane (M) is shown as if cut in cross section and lying in a vertical plane normal to the plane of the page. It is represented as showing the trilaminate 'unit membrane' appearance. To its left is the cytoplasm (C). The glycocalyx (G) projects to the right from the membrane. The glycocalyx is represented as attached to the membrane and as displaying a continuous juxtamembranal layer from which numerous antennulae extend towards the right. The entire glycocalyx contains strongly anionic polysaccharides and is capable of binding cations and many proteins and particles. (Drawn from Brandt and Pappas 1960, 1962.)

II. Diagram of cell surface of a fungus, *Neurospora*. The cell membrane (M) in this form is extensively folded and plicated and appears to be capable of movements and configurational changes in which the glycocalyx (G), often called the cell wall (W), does not participate as a whole. The cytoplasm (C) is represented under the membrane. (Drawn from Luck 1963, 1964.)

III. Internal and external surfaces of a vertebrate blood capillary endothelial cell. The cytoplasm of the cell is shown as a light stippling. The endothelial cell membrane (M) is shown bounding the cytoplasm, separating it from extracellular space (E) and invaginated on both surfaces to form numerous caveolae (K). Similar membrane bounds intracytoplasmic vesicles (V). Glycocalyx (G), or basement membrane (or basal lamina) (B), is shown as a dense stippling on both surfaces of the cell. The glycocalyx is less thick over the inner, or lumenal, surface of the endothelial cell, which is here the upper surface. The glycocalyx does not follow intimately every irregularity in configuration of the cell membrane, but bridges or covers over the ostia leading into the caveolae. However, the lumena (L) of the caveolae contain material less dense than that of the basal lamina. This material is also seen in the lumena of the vesicles and may be derived from the glycocalyx. The outer basal lamina (B), shown under the cell, contains collagen in a fine, fibrillar, aperiodic form. (Drawn after Luft 1965 and Fawcett 1966.)

IV. Diagram of the surface of an erythrocyte, as seen in section by electron microscopy. The membrane (M) separates the cytoplasm (C) from extracellular space (E). The membrane shows the characteristic trilaminate 'unit membrane' appearance. No glycocalyx component on the outer surface of the membrane can be recognized clearly in electron micrographs, though sialic acid and polysaccharides can be detected on the external surface by chemical and immunological methods.

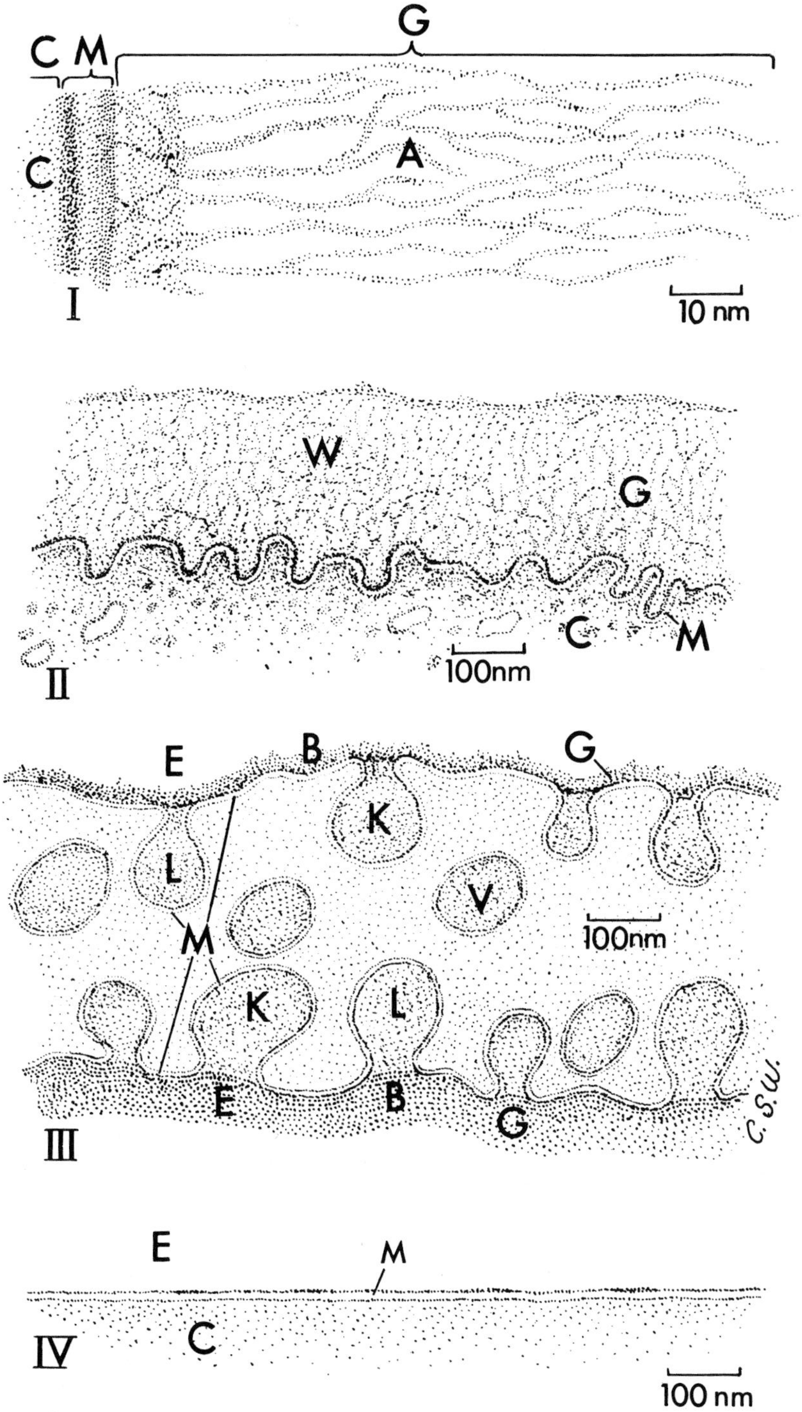
G
C M
C
A
I
10 nm
W
G
C
M
100nm
II
E
B
G
K
L
V
M
100nm
K
L
E
B
G
C.S.W.
III
E
M
C
IV
100 nm

Fig. 1

The selective, regulatory and protective properties of the cell surface are not determined by the cell membrane alone, but depend on the combination of cell membrane and glycocalyx. Many of the carbohydrate components of glycocalyces are strongly acidic and create a layer of anionic groups immediately adjacent to the cell membrane itself, which has a different charge distribution. Such a combination of two layers close together, each with a different charge distribution, has properties different from either alone. Katchalsky and Kedem, and Richardson have pointed out that combinations of this kind have electrical rectifying properties. The calculated theoretical curves of Richardson are remarkably similar to the experimentally determined resistance curves of the ameba as measured by Bruce and Marshall.

3. *Geometrical configurations of cell surfaces*

In early cytological studies, when the light microscope comprised the principal instrument for acquiring structural information about cells, an incomplete picture emerged because of the limitations in resolving power of that instrument. Oversimplified models of configurations of cell surfaces were then formulated (see Wilson). The electron microscope has adequate resolving power for recording configurational details of biological membranes. With the achievements of techniques for preserving and recognizing cell surface components, it became possible to trace them accurately in sectioned material examined in the electron microscope and hence to determine their geometric configurations at the moment of fixation. The electron microscope cannot record movements of membranes directly. Movements and changes in configuration of cell surfaces can be detected by observation and motion pictures of living cells studied with a light microscope, and by electron microscope studies involving the recording of changes in position of recognizable labels bound to or associated with cell surfaces or interior membranes. Movements of components of the cell surface will be discussed in the next chapter. Here we confine our presentation to some of the most common geometric variations in cell surface configurations.

(a) *Microvilli and cilia*

Microvilli and cilia are two types of specialized projections from cell surfaces. Cilia and flagellae are described in the chapters of this Handbook by Professors Afzelius and Sleigh. Here they will be dealt with briefly only as they may be modified for sensory functions.

Microvilli are finger-like projections varying in length from 0.2 to several μm. They lack the internal filaments or tubules characterizing cilia. Examples are shown in diagrammatic form in Figs. 2 and 3. On the apical surfaces of absorbing columnar cells of the vertebrate intestine, finger-like microvilli are seen in great abundance, displaying impressive regularity in size and in geometric arrangement (Ito). On gall bladder epithelial cells, microvilli are more sparse and show less uniformity in length

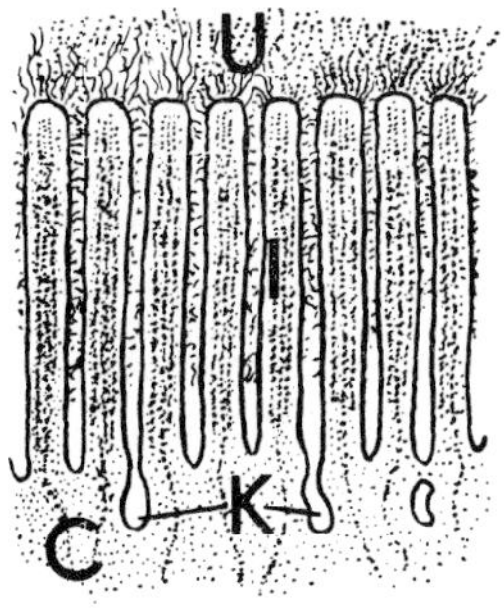

Fig. 2. Diagram of microvilli such as are found on the lumenal surface of intestinal absorbing cells. The stippled cytoplasm (C) is separated from extracellular space above by a cell membrane represented as a single continuous dense black line. The membrane extends over eight finger-like microvilli (I), at the base of which are shown two small caveolae (K). The microvilli are about 1 μm long. Axial filaments can be seen running longitudinally in each microvillus and continuing on into the general cytoplasm of the cell. The glycocalyx in this instance takes the form of a mucous coat (U) which overlies the tips of the microvilli and which shows some antennular projections from tips of microvilli. (Drawn after Ito, and Palay and Revel.)

and regularity in arrangement (Yamada 1955a). Similar projections, often called microvilli, are encountered singly, in small regular or irregular groups or in scattered array on surfaces of a great variety of cells. Microvilli are by no means confined to epithelial cells.

Many microvilli are round in cross section and cylindrical in over-all shape, except for a domed distal extremity. However, microvilli of less regular geometrical configuration are well known, as in the case of the so-called 'stereocilia' of the epididymis or the 'clavate' or club-shaped processes of the choroid plexus and of sensory cells in taste buds (see Fawcett 1966, p. 421; Farbman). Microvilli are invested by membrane continuous with the plasma membrane of the cell, and comprising part of it. Outside is found a representation of the glycocalyx, frequently in antennular form (see Figs. 2 and 3) or as a coating of mucus, forming a layer in which the tips of the microvilli are embedded (Ito; see Fig. 2). Inside the membrane is cytoplasm which is continuous with that of the rest of the cell and which frequently displays ill-defined axial longitudinal filaments.

Functional specializations represented in many microvilli are not well understood and it seems reasonable to reserve the view that all microvilli may not function identically. Since microvilli are found in abundance on the apical surfaces of some cells specialized for absorbing substances from a hollow organ, as are the epithelial cells of intestine (Ito), gall bladder (Yamada 1955a) and proximal tubules of the nephron (Bulger), one infers that the microvilli adorning these cells may have some important role in the absorptive function exercised by these cells. But microvilli are also abundant on the surfaces of the secretory canaliculi of the parietal cells of the stomach (see Ito and Winchester) and on sensory cells. These cells have no known absorptive function. Microvilli do increase substantially the surface area of cells on which they occur. One presumes that the membrane surfaces of microvilli have molecular specializations appropriate for their respective functions, but available knowledge is insufficient to permit characterization. Microvilli of the intestine have specialized, enzymatically active particles attached to the outer surface of the plasma membrane (see Fig. 3). These particles, described by Oda and Seki (1965, 1966), are dealt with more fully in a later section of this chapter.

Specializations of the cell surface for sensory reception are known. Frequently these specialized functions are associated with projections from the surface, such as modified cilia or microvilli. As pointed out by De Robertis (1956a, b) and De Robertis and Lasansky, important examples of cilia modified for sensory function are the rods and cones of the vertebrate eye. Modified cilia associated with highly specialized microvilli also serve as essential sensory components in the lateral line organ (see Flock and Wersäll; Flock 1965; Hama 1965) in acoustic and vestibular receptors (see Flock 1964; Wersäll, Flock and Lundquist) and in olfactory receptor cells (Reese). Sensory cells in taste buds show specialized, clavate projections (De Lorenzo; Gray and Watkins; Farbman).

In each case, the specialized sensitivities of the modified cilia or microvilli betoken special chemical provisions in the cell surface. In retinal photoreceptors, the chemical

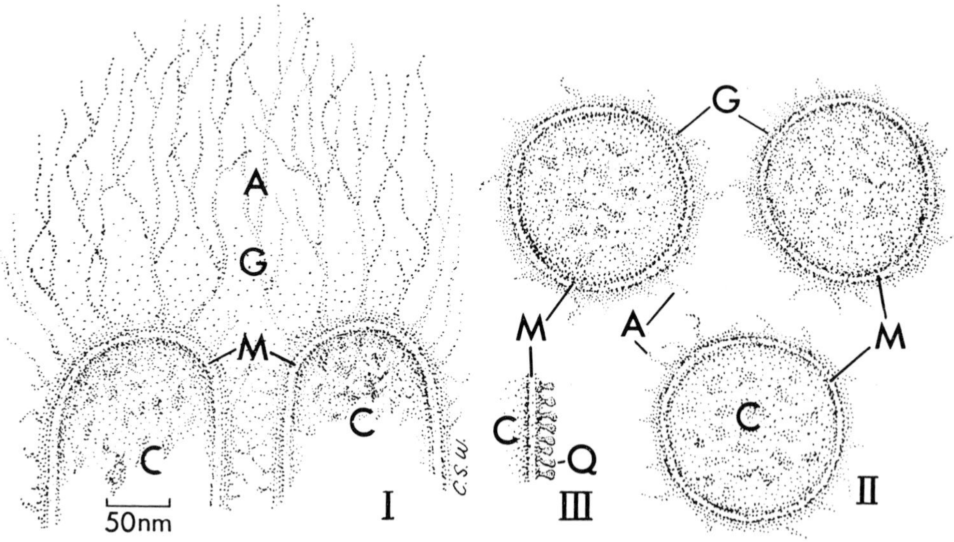

Fig. 3. I. Diagram of a longitudinal section through the tips of two microvilli. The trilaminate 'unit membrane' appearance of the cell membrane (M) is shown bounding the cytoplasm (C) of the microvilli. An attached, antennular glycocalyx (G) appears, with short antennulae along the side of the microvilli and with long antennulae (A) extending into the lumen of the intestine. A continuous basal layer of the glycocalyx merges with the outer surface of the cell membrane. (Drawn after Ito.)
II. Diagram of cross sections of microvilli transected about midway along their length. Cell membrane (M), cytoplasm (C) and glycocalyx (G) with short antennulae (A) are represented. (Drawn from Palay, in Fawcett 1966, p. 419.)
III. A representation of a concept of the cell surface of microvilli after stripping off the glycocalyx. The cytoplasm (C) is faced with a cell membrane (M), the outer layer of which is studded with small particles (Q) called 'elementary particles' by Oda. It is possible to shear these particles from the membrane and to harvest and characterize them. They show dissaccharidase and other hydrolase activities. They probably represent active agents in membrane contact digestion, much studied by Ugolev. (Drawn after Oda and Seki 1965, 1966.)

specialization has been characterized to some extent and can be attributed to a change in shape in a photosensitive molecular membrane component when it absorbs energy from a light quantum (see Wald). In olfactory, taste and other chemoreceptors, one or more molecules from the environment enter into close relation with component molecules of the cell surface, probably in the cell membrane of the cilium or microvillus itself. Specificity of olfactory response, according to Amoore (1964, 1965), Amoore et al., and Rosenberg et al., appears to depend largely on the steric and binding properties of the incident, entering molecule and its interaction with molecules native to the cell surface. Thus, both in photo- and in chemoreceptors, specific molecular configurational changes occurring within the membrane are implicated in initiating the response, which is conveyed elsewhere by propagated action potentials sweeping along the surfaces of receptor and nerve cells.

(b) *Caveolae*

These are cave-like indentations or invaginations of the cell surface (see Fig. 1, III), first named by Yamada (1955a). In a caveola, the unit cell membrane is seen as forming a blind, cave-like or tubular pouch opening to the extracellular space. The dimensions of caveolae vary over a wide range. Small caveolae 40–80 nm in diameter are found in vertebrate capillary endothelial cells (Palade 1953, 1956; Bennett et al.; Karnovsky), in chemical synaptic nerve terminals (De Robertis and Bennett; De Robertis 1964) and in many other locations. The sarcotubular invaginations of the cell membrane of striated muscle cells can be regarded as special examples of caveolae. These have diameters of about 20–100 nm and are of indefinite length, extending into and ramifying extensively in the diameter of the muscle fiber. According to Peachey, in frog sartorius muscle the combined surface area of all the sarcotubules in one fiber is about seven times the exterior surface area of the fiber. Caveolae of considerably larger diameters are encountered in phagocytic cells during the invagination stages of phagocytosis and in certain secretory cells (such as pancreatic acinar cells) during the secretory process (see Zucker-Franklin and Hirsch; Ichikawa). At these larger extremes, caveolae of diameters of several to ten or more μm have been encountered.

Caveolae, like microvilli, serve to increase the surface area of the cell, but more definite functional attributes can be assigned to many caveolae. The sarcotubular invaginations, for example, provide in their long, attenuated cylindrical lumina pathways through which diffusible components of extracellular fluid can penetrate far into the interior of the fiber (Endo; H. E. Huxley; Page). The membrane lining and forming these sarcotubular invaginations appears to be capable of conducting excitatory impulses from the external membrane of the fiber to its interior (Huxley and Taylor), there inducing membranous members of the sarcoplasmic reticulum to release calcium ions and to actuate the contractile mechanisms residing in the myofibrils (Ebashi and Lipmann; Ebashi; Weber et al.).

A large number of caveolae are recognized as transient membrane configurations associated with secretion (eccytosis) and with uptake of materials into the cell by encytosis. These are described further in the next chapter.

Caveolae, particularly small ones, are found in great abundance in electron micrographs of cells. Since they are frequently associated with vesicles morphologically similar to those formed in pinocytosis, many authors have assumed that all small caveolae are encytotic in function, and have somewhat indiscriminately called them 'micropinocytotic' vesicles or invaginations. Such a term implies a physiological function which cannot, in general, be determined from morphological evidence alone. It is reasonable to suspect that many small caveolae and vesicles may be secretory in nature. One is moved to caution against using a terminology which implies a function when speaking of a morphological entity, unless evidence is available to support the view that the function implied is actually served by the structure in question.

(c) *Folds and plications*

Foldings of the cell surface are very commonly encountered, often on such a delicate scale as to escape detection with the light microscope. For example, in the fungus *Neurospora* (see Luck 1963, 1964), the glycocalyx (in this case, the cell wall) displays a smooth surface which defines the general geometric limits of the cell, but underneath it, the plasma membrane is extensively folded and plicated. In these cases, the surface area of the plasma membrane is actually considerably greater than that which would be inferred from a measurement of the geometric parameters of the cell wall and an assumption that the plasma membrane parallels it closely.

Folds and plications on a much coarser scale are seen in certain other types of cells, of which those of the proximal and distal convoluted tubules of the vertebrate kidney are examples (see Pease; Bulger). In these instances, the folds of one cell interdigitate with those of its immediate neighbor in the epithelial layer, with only a thin (about 20 nm) layer of glycocalyx material intervening. The plasma membrane of a striated muscle cell is extensively folded under the motor nerve endings. These folds are associated with high activities of the enzyme choline esterase (see Couteaux; Zacks).

Folds in the cell surface increase the surface area of the cell and, when interleaved with the folds of a neighboring cell, increase considerably the area of mutual contact between the two cells. Since such interleaved or interdigitating folds are often found in epithelia engaged in fluid or electrolyte transport, it is suspected that these geometric configurations of the cell surface may have an important role in transport functions (see Pease). Supporting this idea is the finding that mitochondria are often closely associated with such folds, suggesting that ATP is abundantly produced in the neighborhood and may be extensively utilized by energy-consuming activities in the vicinity, of which active transport is an attractive example.

4. Variants and functions of glycocalyx

(a) *Relationship to cell membrane*

If one takes a general view of the cell surface and attempts to formulate concepts which will be of broad usefulness in characterizing relationships between components of the cell surface, one comes to appreciate that there are some cells in which the extramembranous, polysaccharide-rich component, the glycocalyx, is intimately bound to or attached to the cell membrane and follows closely its every bend and movement, whereas in other cases, the glycocalyx, or an important part of it, is sufficiently separate from the cell membrane so that the latter can undergo movements or display configurational manifestations which are not reflected in large portions of the extracellular coat. This permits a classification of relationships between glycocalyx and cell membrane in accordance with the categories: attached or unattached.

A. *Attached glycocalyces* are characteristically encountered on the vertebrate red cell, on the ameba, on the microvilli of the gall bladder, on the vascular surface of liver parenchymal cells, on a great variety of phagocytotic cells and on many protozoa. In all of these examples, as the plasma or cell membrane moves, indents, bends, folds, forms caveolae, invaginates, or sends out processes, it carries with it in all its geometric variations the entire glycocalyx represented on that portion of the cell.

These features are well illustrated in the ameba, which has been extensively studied from this point of view by Brandt and Pappas (1960, 1962), Brandt, Marshall and Nachmias, and others. In the ameba, the entire surface of the cell is covered with a fringe-like glycocalyx, called by Brandt the 'extraneous coat'. This glycocalyx is composed of a forest of closely spaced parallel antennulae arranged so as to resemble the nap of a rug (see Fig. 1, I). This glycocalyx is rich in acid mucopolysaccharide, behaves like an ion exchange resin with anionic groups on the polymer, is readily detected with the light microscope, and has been called a 'mucous coat' or 'slime coat'. It has an important role in pinocytosis. Features of this participation are presented in the chapter by Professors Stockhem and Wohlfarth-Bottermann. Let it suffice here to say that, as the cell membrane of the ameba invaginates, flows and pinches off, forming vesicles and vacuoles in the course of these activities, the fringe-like antennular glycocalyx is carried closely attached to the plasma membrane through all these evolutions, carrying with it ions, proteins, or other particles or materials bound to it and delivering these bound materials to whatever location it may be carried to by the translocations of the patch of cell membrane to which the overlying glycocalyx may be attached.

In the case of the vertebrate red cell, the glycocalyx, which is exceedingly tenuous, is represented, in part at least, by sialic acid (see Cook; Cook et al.; Ohkuma and Ikemoto) and by other genetically determined mucopolysaccharides which characterize the antigenic blood type of the cell (see Kabat). The surface of the red cell is exceedingly flexible and is easily distorted and moved about by external forces. Cell membrane and glycocalyx participate in unison in the movements. Rambourg and

Leblond showed that the outer surface of rat erythrocytes bound colloidal thorium and attributed this binding to acid sugars, including sialic acid. Benedetti and Emmelot (1967) found evidence for sialic acid attached to the external surface of cell membranes of rat liver cells and considered this to be part, at least, of the representation of the glycocalyx on these cells.

B. *Unattached glycocalyces* are encountered in bacteria, fungi, plants, and in a wide variety of other cells, including muscle cells of vertebrates, and a host of varied animal epithelial cell surfaces presenting to 'basement membranes', or 'basal laminae'.

Examples of unattached glycocalyces can be found on both faces of vertebrate capillary endothelial cells. Luft (1966) has shown that these coverings can be usefully delineated by ruthenium red (see Fig. 1, III). The inner, or lumenal surface of these cells, which presents to the blood plasma, possesses a very delicate glycocalyx, whereas the plasma membrane on the external surface of the endothelial cell is adjacent to a more robust glycocalyx, represented by the capillary basement membrane (or basal lamina). On both surfaces, the endothelial cell membrane is indented to form many caveolae accompanied by vesicles. Neither glycocalyx layer follows closely the smaller geometric irregularities of the external cell surface, such as the caveolae, but each extends as a smooth sleeve or cuff, conforming to the gross, general external surface configuration of the capillary and covering or bridging the orifices or mouths of the caveolae. Luft's study reveals that the endothelial caveolae on both surfaces contain material which binds ruthenium red, but less densely than does the material in the overlying layers of glycocalyx. This suggests that some portion of the glycocalyx of these cells may be free to move with movements of the cell membrane.

A second example of an unattached glycocalyx is recognized in the cell wall of fungi, of which *Neurospora* is a typical case (see Fig. 1, II). As Luck (1963, 1964) has shown in *Neurospora*, the glycocalyx, or cell wall, appears in electron micrographs as a smooth, sleeve-like investment or capsule about 200 nm thick, displaying a fine, fibrillar sub-structure. The cell membrane, as has already been explained, is extensively folded and plicated, so that its surface area is greater than that of the external cell wall. These convolutions and folds of the unit cell membrane are independent of the contour of the cell wall, which passes smoothly over the plications, like a blanket. Thus, the plasma membrane of this cell is capable of moving independently and of assuming varying configurations underneath its rather thick glycocalyx blanket, most of which is not attached to the cell membrane and which does not, as a whole, participate in the cell membrane's geometric variations.

Plasma membranes which are capable of assuming configurations which are not paralleled by an overlying, less pliable glycocalyx are found in cells of many plants, in bacteria and in a great variety of animal cells, including the external surfaces of many epithelial cells.

(b) *Mechanical functions of glycocalyces*

A. *Cell walls* contribute to the mechanical strength of plants and to the ability of the cells to withstand turgor and osmotic variations. Since Professor Kreger's chapter on 'cell walls' in this Handbook conveys much information about these variants of the glycocalyx, they will not be dealt with further here.

B. *Intercellular matrices* can be regarded as extensions of glycocalyces which serve special mechanical functions. In multicellular plants, the cell walls of mutually adjacent cells tend to merge with an intervening matrix which joins the two cell walls together externally and which contains materials similar to those characterizing the cell walls closer to the cells. In animal cells also one frequently encounters situations where the glycocalyx of one cell fuses with that of its neighbor, or merges without sharp boundary with an extensive intercellular matrix which is shared with other cells and which contains chemical components similar to those encountered in members of the glycocalyx in the immediate vicinity of the cells. The intercellular matrices of metazoan connective tissue, of cartilage and of bone, are good examples. The varying physical properties of these matrices can reasonably be attributed to variations in the macromolecular constituents, including collagen. In the case of bone, the deposition of hydroxy-apatite crystals in the matrix is, of course, a variant of the basic connective tissue matrix structure and is an important determinant of some of its mechanical properties.

C. *Basement membranes or basal laminae* can also be regarded as special representations of the glycocalyx. In the classical histological literature, the term 'basement membrane' has been applied to a variety of thin structures closely apposed to the basal surfaces of epithelial cells. With the application of the electron microscope, it came to be understood that some of the light microscopists' 'basement membranes', such as, for example, the membrane surrounding the seminiferous tubules of the mammalian testis, contained cellular elements (see Clermont), whereas others were wholly extracellular and appeared as condensations of extracellular material just outside the cell membrane. It is only the latter variety which are of interest in this chapter. Because of the confusion in the literature, Fawcett (1968) has proposed that the structure we are here considering be called a 'basal lamina'. Here the terms 'basal lamina' and 'basement membrane' will be used as if synonymous.

Typical examples of a basement membrane or basal lamina are seen on the outer surfaces of capillary endothelial cells (see Bennett et al.; Luft 1965, 1966). Fig. 1, III shows a diagram of this basal lamina. Basement membranes or laminae, entirely analogous to those surrounding capillaries, have been demonstrated by electron microscopy around many non-epithelial cells, such as muscle cells (Bennett 1960) and Schwann cells (Robertson 1964). Kefalides and Kefalides and Winzler analyzed basement membrane material from mammalian kidney and reported that the principal constituents include collagen (0.6%), and carbohydrates (10%), such as sialic acid (2.1%), hexosamines (1.4%), fucose (0.75%) and hexose (5.52%). Thus, the components of basal laminae resemble those of intercellular matrices. The basal laminae here described, though containing collagen upon chemical analysis, do not, when examined in electron micrographs, display fibrils with a periodicity of about

65 nm, as do collagen fibers in tendon and skin. Micrographs of basal laminae often show evidence of a fine fibrillar structure, appearing like a network or mesh of slender threads less than 10 nm in diameter, with no periodic repeating pattern. Gross et al. and Schmitt have reported conditions under which solubilized tropocollagen can be precipitated *in vitro* in the form of fine filaments without detectable periodicity.

Attention has already been called to Luft's (1966) demonstration of a delicate coating on the inner or lumenal surface of vertebrate capillary endothelial cells. This inner coating, like the more robust outer one, represents the glycocalyx and can legitimately be termed an example of a basal lamina or basement membrane. Analytical data on its composition are lacking. There is no evidence that it contains collagen and many may deem it reasonable to think of it as an example of a mucous coat. A much more robust, conspicuous internal glycocalyx has been found on the inner surface of certain invertebrate blood vessels by Hama (1960). He found the large blood vessels of the earthworm *Eisenia foetida* to be lined with an extracellular coating which he termed an 'internal basement membrane'. Hama also found an even more highly developed external basal lamina lining a large blood vessel of a prawn (for illustration, see Fig. 1 in Bennett 1963). These two invertebrate endovascular basal laminae resemble the cell walls of plants as much as they do the capillary basement membranes of vertebrate blood vessels.

Many basement membranes clearly serve a mechanical function, utilizing the collagen or other fibrous proteins in them to form a strong reinforcing investment or layer which contributes to the ability of the structure in which they participate to withstand tensile forces without rupture. Some also serve as filters, as will be set forth in a later passage of this chapter.

D. *Mucous coats* are special representations of glycocalyces seen on free surfaces of cells, such as the lumenal surfaces of mucous membranes, the external surfaces of some protozoa (e.g., the ameba) on the skin of frogs, hagfish, salamanders and many other chordate, vertebrate and invertebrate forms, on the gills of clams and fish and in many other situations. Mucous coats are frequently antennular in aspects (see Figs. 1 and 3) and, as in the case of ameba, may be firmly attached to the cell membrane. However, many glycocalyces of the mucous coat variety are unattached and can be rather easily removed from the cell surface, or moved along it by ciliary action.

Chemically, mucous coats are comprised predominantly of mucoproteins, usually with highly anionic sugar groupings, in which carboxylic acids, sulfate esters or sulfamides dominate the ion exchange pattern. For representative analyses of mucous coats, see Horowitz.

It is often realized that mucous coats serve a lubricating function, but in many cases, the specific binding capacities of a mucous glycocalyx are of great physiological importance. Thus, in the case of the ameba, the mucous or slime glycocalyx can bind to a solid substrate, providing purchase which facilitates movements of the organism along the surface. Holter (1959, 1963, 1965), Brandt and Pappas (1960, 1962), and Marshall and Nachmias have reported on the importance of the complementary chemical binding properties of the ameba's glycocalyx in uptake of prey, of proteins and of ions by encytosis. It is also well known that the mucous coating over ciliated surfaces of many aquatic organisms serves to bind nutrients and convey them by means of ciliary action to digestive organs of the animal.

(c) *Filtering action of glycocalyces*

Glycocalyces are porous. Many are sufficiently robust and permeable to act as effective filters (see Bennett 1963). A filtering capacity has been demonstrated for the glycocalyces of the mammalian kidney glomerular endothelial and epithelial cells. This glycocalyx is often called the 'basement membrane' of the glomerulus (see Yamada 1955b). Over the large pores in the endothelial cells and between the foot processes of the epithelial cells, this structure comprises one of the barriers between blood plasma and urinary space. The selective filtration properties of the glomerular membranes have been demonstrated by morphological techniques (see Farquhar and Palade 1960; Palade 1961; Graham and Karnovsky). The 'basement membrane' proper of the glomerulus serves to exercise a certain selection as to size, but Graham and Karnovsky bring forth evidence to support the view that the interstices between the foot processes of the epithelial cells (podocytes) may determine ultimately the limits of the sizes of particles traversing the glomerular barrier. Yamada (1955b) showed that these slits are bridged by a slender 'filtration slit membrane', which represents the glycocalyx of the epithelial cells. This glycocalyx membrane may have an important role in determining the filtration action of the mammalian glomerulus.

Similar filtration properties have been ascribed to the external basement membrane of capillaries such as are found in muscle (see Palade 1961; Bennett et al.), but a quantitative evaluation of the filtering action of this element is difficult because of the problem of separating the action of the endothelial layer from that of the basal lamina.

The thick 'internal basement membranes' seen by Hama (1960) lining the internal surface of blood vessels of earthworm and prawn (see Bennett 1963, Fig. 1), have interstices sufficiently small to prevent the large oxygen-carrying molecules (erythrocruorin in the earthworm; hemocyanin in the prawn) in the blood plasma from coming into direct contact with the cell membrane of the endothelium.

The glycocalyces of many other cells, for example, the cell walls of plants, fungi and bacteria and the basal laminae of vertebrate muscle cells are so disposed and constructed as to serve as filters or as molecular sieves which can retard the passage of particles above a certain size. This filtering action can serve to prevent the access to the cell membrane of large components in the surrounding medium, or can retain in the vicinity of the cell membrane soluble products, such as enzymes, produced by the cell and secreted or expelled into the space outside the cell membrane, but inside the glycocalyx. A glycocalyx capable of retarding the passage of small ions could serve to reduce the demands on ion pumps associated with the plasma membrane by impeding the escape into distant regions of ions preferentially pumped into the cell (such as K^+) and impairing the access to the cell membrane of ions preferentially pumped out of the cell (such as Na^+). Such a function, however, must be regarded as hypothetical.

5. *Enzymatic activities associated with cell surfaces*

Numerous observations have led to the realization that the surfaces of some cells have enzymatically active molecules bound to them, or very closely associated with them. Ugolev has reviewed many of these findings, pointing out that one must conclude that many of these enzymatically active molecules must be integral protein components of the outer surface of the cell membrane itself.

In 1962, Fernández-Morán discovered a dense array of particles studding the membranes of the cristae of mitochondria. Shortly afterward, Benedetti and Emmelot (1965) discovered morphologically similar particles on the external surface of cell membranes from liver and Oda and Seki (1965, 1966) and Johnson found similar particles on the external surface of the cell membrane over the microvilli of intestinal epithelial cells. A diagram representing the appearance of these particles is presented in Fig. 3, III.

Oda and Seki (1966) and Johnson found that these particles were indeed firmly bound to the exterior surface of the cell membrane, but could be brought to separate from the membrane under the influence of trypsin. After separation, the particles were collected, purified and found to be associated with hydrolytic enzymatic activity. The particles were particularly active as disaccharidases, displaying maltase and invertase activity. These observations substantiate and extend the general thesis advanced by Ugolev. It appears clear that in some cases, at least, protein molecules which are bound to or are integral parts of the molecular architecture of the cell surface have enzymatic capabilities.

Further evidence of enzymatic capabilities of cell surfaces derive from cytochemical observations (see Novikoff). For example, Marchesi and Palade showed that ATPase activity is associated with red cell membranes and that its reaction product appears on the inner surface of the membrane. ATPases have frequently been reported as localized on cell surfaces. It is often surmised that these membrane ATPases may be associated with active transport, encytosis or other energy-consuming activities of the cell membrane. Marchesi and Barrnett also found nucleotide hydrolase activities associated with the surface of endothelial cells.

6. *Attachment areas, or desmosomes*

Fine structure and physiological studies of multicellular organisms have shown that it is possible to recognize cell surface areas which have special bonding relationships with an adjacent cell surface or extracellular structure. In contrast, other areas of the cell surface may be in simple apposition to the surface of an adjacent cell or extracellular structure, free to move in relation to it, without any special bonds between them, but often with a discernible layer of glycocalyx intervening between the two cell membranes.

Specialized areas of cell surface serving to bind that surface to another structure are called 'desmosomes', the Greek roots of which signify a 'fastening body', or a 'bonding' or 'binding body'. The term 'desmosome' is sometimes used more narrowly, to refer only to attachment surfaces with some restricted type of shape or configuration (Farquhar and Palade 1963; Kelly), but these restricted definitions have led to ambiguities and inconsistencies. For present purposes as used in cell biology, the term 'desmosome' is used in its literal and broadest sense, to refer to any specialized area of a cell surface which serves to bind preferentially that area or surface to some adjacent structure, which may be another area of cell surface, or some extracellular structure. Note that, as defined here, the term 'desmosome' refers to a single, specialized area of the surface of a cell, rather than to a pair of such areas. The term is sometimes used by others to refer to a pair.

Desmosomes can be classified in several ways. For example, they can be classified as to geometrical shape, or on the basis of symmetry, or on the basis of the relationships of the cell membranes participating in the desmosome, or on the basis of the relations of the desmosome to cytoplasmic structure in the cell. Several ways of classifying desmosomes are now cited.

(a) *Classifications of desmosomes*

A. According to shape.

(1) Macular desmosomes: those which have a discrete, spot-like shape; often called 'maculae adherentes'.

(2) Zonular desmosomes: those which encircle a cell like a belt or zone and bind it to its neighbors all around its circumference at the level of the zonular desmosome. Zonular desmosomes are often called 'terminal bars' or 'zonulae adherentes'.

B. According to the structure to which the cell surface is bound at the desmosome.

(1) Autodesmosomes: those which bind an area of cell surface to another desmosome on another area of the surface of the same cell.

(2) Homodesmosomes: those which bind an area of cell surface of one cell to a desmosome on the cell surface of another cell. Homodesmosomes may be either (a) isodesmosomes, binding one cell to another of the same type, or (b) allodesmosomes, binding one cell to another cell of a different type.

(3) Heterodesmosomes: those which bind an area of cell surface to some non-cellular structure, such as an area of basement membrane, an area of tooth surface, or an area of some artificial substrate, such as a plastic membrane used in tissue culture (see Flaxman et al.). These are often called 'hemidesmosomes' (see Fig. 4, I).

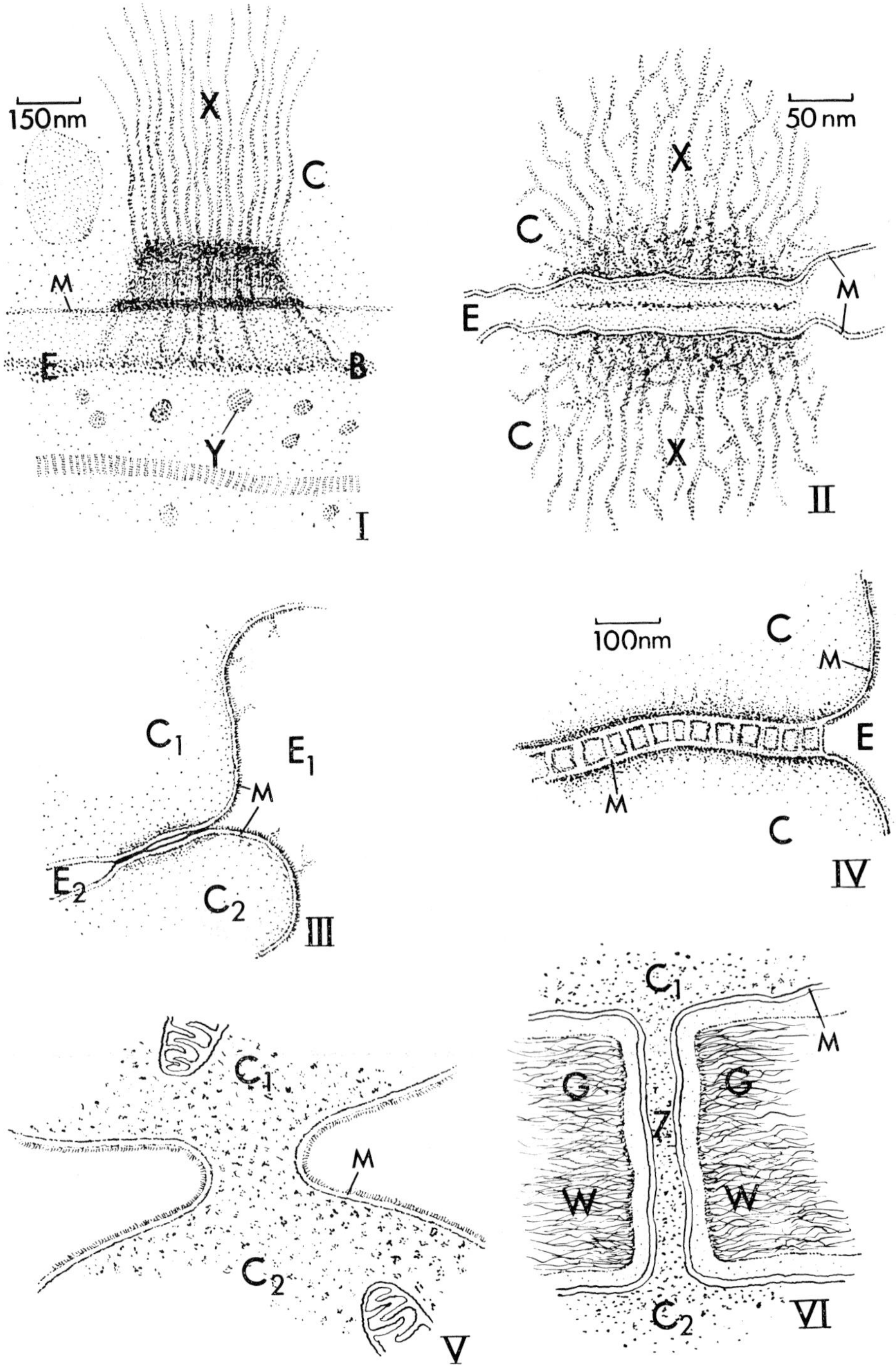
150nm
X
C
M
E
B
Y
I
50 nm
X
C
M
E
C
X
II
C1
E1
M
M
E2
C2
III
100nm
C
M
E
M
C
IV
C1
M
C2
V
C1
M
G
G
Z
W
W
C2
VI

Fig. 4

Fig. 4. Special modifications of cell surfaces characterizing several kinds of desmosomes, or attachments between a cell surface area and another structure.

I. An heterodesmosome, binding a cell to connective tissue. Such a structure is often called a 'hemidesmosome'. The upper portion of the figure represents the cytoplasm (C) of a cell containing many keratinous tonofilaments (X) which run in bundles called tonofibrils. The cell membrane (M) separates the cytoplasm above from the extracellular space (E) below. The stippling in the extracellular regions represents glycocalyx and intercellular matrix. A basement membrane or basal lamina (B) and collagen fibers (Y) cut in cross and in longitudinal section are represented. A tonofibril, or bundle of tonofilaments (X) is shown as anchoring in the cell membrane (M), which is thickened and reinforced at the regions of attachment. Vaguely understood extracellular fibrous structures are seen, extending from cell membrane to basal lamina. In this localized, thickened region, the cell membrane is firmly attached to the underlying connective tissue and is anchored in turn to the cytoplasm of the cell by the strong, keratinous tonofilaments. Where the cell membrane is unspecialized and shows no thickening or special relation with filaments, it merely lies in contact with the extracellular connective tissue components, without being bound very strongly to them. Heterodesmosomes are characteristically macular, that is, they are localized spots of attachment of cell surface to connective tissue or other underlying substrate. (Drawn after Hay, and Kelly.)

II. A pair of dismembranal homo- or autodesmosomes serving the function of binding two cell membrane areas together so as to permit them to withstand strong tensile forces tending to pull them apart. Most desmosomes of this character bind two cells together (homodesmosomes), but the figure also presents features of some autodesmosomes, which bind together two separate cell membrane areas of the same cell. The desmosomes are represented as cut at an angle approximately normal to the planes of the constituent membranes. The configuration is typical in many macular and zonal adherent dismembranal homo- and autodesmosomes, but others show density profiles and features which differ somewhat from those shown here.

The two membranes (M) which are bound together by this pair of desmosomes are represented as separated by a narrow intercellular space (E). The intercellular space is of greater density in the desmosomal region than elsewhere and, in the example here, a layer of increased density lies midway between the two desmosomal membranes. The cell membranes in dismembranal desmosomal regions are increased in thickness and density and are associated with dense cytoplasmic juxtamembranal material into which insert numerous tonofilaments (X) lying in the cytoplasm (C) of the regions of the cells bound together by the desmosomes. (Drawn after Kelly.)

III. Juxtamembranal desmosome, forming a 'tight junction' or 'nexus'. The stippled cytoplasm (C) of two cells is separated from extracellular space (E) by two cell membranes (M). In the desmosomal region, the respective membranes of the two cells become very closely and intimately apposed. Desmosomes of this type are often zonular: that is, they extend around the circumference of each cell like a belt, as if sealing each cell to its neighbor, though macular examples are present in heart muscle. No great mechanical strength is attributed to juxtamembranal desmosomes and they are usually reinforced nearby by parallel zonular dysmembranal desmosomes resembling the one shown in II. Juxtamembranal desmosomes or 'tight junctions' have been associated with two special physiological features. First, when zonular, they are thought to form a seal which resists diffusion or flow of water and water soluble solutes from an extracellular fluid compartment on one side, such as the lumen of a hollow viscus (E_1), to the intercellular space on the other side of the desmosome, which may represent general intercellular space (E_2). Second, juxtamembranal desmosomes have sometimes been implicated as membrane areas of low electrical resistance separating the cytoplasm of two adjacent cells and, hence, serving as an area of reduced resistance to the passage of ions from one cell cytoplasm to that of the adjacent cell. (Drawn after Saito.)

IV. Septate desmosomes. The cytoplasmic domains (C) of two cells are shown, each bounded by a membrane (M) and facing extracellular space (E). Where the two cells are in close relationship, the membrane of each cell is joined to that of its neighbor by a series of septa whose thicknesses and

C. According to the similarity or dissimilarity of the structure to which the desmosome binds.

(1) Symmetrical desmosomes: those which are coupled to another desmosome which is nearly a mirror image of itself and where there is a plane of symmetry between two very similar desmosomes (Fig. 4, II, III, IV, V and VI).

(2) Asymmetrical desmosomes: those which are coupled to another structure not closely similar to the desmosome itself. Heterodesmosomes, or 'hemidesmosomes', are asymmetrical (Fig. 4, I).

D. According to some important functions attributed to the desmosomes.

(1) Adherent desmosomes: those which are highly specialized for resisting tensile forces. Of course, all desmosomes are adherent to some degree, but in conformity with the terminology of Farquhar and Palade (1964), who use the terms 'macula adherens' and 'zonula adherens', one can restrict this class to desmosomes thought to be highly specialized for mechanical strength in bonding a cell membrane area to another structure. Adherent desmosomes are filamentous. Examples are seen in Fig. 4, I and II.

(2) Occluding desmosomes: those that serve to seal one cell membrane to another in such a way as to form a barrier to diffusion and fluid exchanges between one extracellular fluid compartment and another. Septate desmosomes (Fig. 4, IV) and many juxtamembranal desmosomes (Fig. 4, III) are in this class. This terminology conforms to the term 'zonula occludens', used by Farquhar and Palade (1964).

(3) Synaptic desmosomes: those juxtamembranal desmosomes which have the property of providing low resistance to passage of ions between the cytoplasms of two otherwise separated cells joined by the desmosome. These desmosomes hence serve as electrical synapses coupling the two cells together. Many juxtamembranal desmosomes appear to have this property, which is discussed further in a later section of this chapter. Fig. 4, III, represents the appearance of desmosomes

---

density profiles resemble closely those of the cell membranes themselves. The septa appear as if cut in cross section. They are envisioned as passing around each cell like a series of shelves or baffles, each joining each cell to its neighbor, the whole set forming a zonular structure. Septate desmosomes are found on certain epithelial cells and are thought of as forming barriers to the passage of water and solutes between the extracellular space (E) facing the free surface of the epithelial cells and the intercellular spaces between the cells and around their bases. (Drawn after Wood.)

V. Syncytial synmembranal desmosomes, or intercellular bridge. The cytoplasm of two cells (C_1 and C_2), is shown as joined together through a narrow neck, with the cell membrane (M) of each cell fused with and continuous with that of the other. Intercellular connections of this type have been described as linking spermatocytes and spermatids. (Drawn from Nagano.)

VI. A plasmodesma: a syncytial synmembranal desmosome linking two cells (C_1 and C_2) to each other by means of a narrow tube (Z) of cytoplasm, piercing a tunnel in the glycocalyx (G) or cell wall (W). The membrane (M) and the cytoplasm of each cell is continuous with that of the other. This displays the intercellular relationships represented in the plasmodesmata (Z) which connect one plant cell to another, as conceived by Spanswick and Costerton.

thought to have electrical synaptic properties. Chemical synapses are different in structure and do not belong to this class (see De Robertis 1964). Though desmosomes are sometimes associated closely with chemical synapses, there seems to be no reason to include chemical synapses in a classification of desmosomes. Syncytial desmosomes (Fig. 4, V and VI) couple two cells together electrically, but the coupling does not have the character of electrical synapses.

Autodesmosomes and homodesmosomes can be further classified as follows:

E. According to the relations between the membranes of two cell surface areas involved in the desmosomes of a pair.

(1) Dismembranal desmosomes: those in which the participating cell membranes are separated by an appreciable intercellular interval which, nevertheless, contains materials bonding the two cell surfaces together (Fig. 4, II).

(2) Juxtamembranal desmosomes: those in which the two participating cell membranes are very closely and intimately apposed in a parallel array, but yet are not fused with each other. These are often called 'tight junctions' or 'zonulae occludentes' or 'nexus' (Fig. 4, III).

(3) Synmembranal desmosomes: those in which the participating cell membranes are fused (Fig. 4, IV, V and VI; Fig. 1, II of the next chapter).

Three types of synmembranal desmosomes have been recognized. These are:

(a) Septate desmosomes: those in which the cell membranes of the two participating cells extend in a series of baffles or walls or septa which fuse with and are continuous with the other participating cell membrane (Fig. 4, IV).

(b) Syncytial desmosomes: those in which the cell membrane of one participating cell is directly and linearly continuous with that of the other and in which the cytoplasm of one cell is directly continuous with that of another, without any intervening membrane (Fig. 4, V, VI).

(c) Juxtalaminar desmosomes: those in which cell membranes of two adjacent cells lie parallel and side by side, with the outer dense laminae of each membrane missing over the desmosomal area and with the two middle pale laminae of each membrane in intimate, lateral, parallel side by side contact, as if fused. These desmosomes have the appearance of Fig. 1, II of the next chapter, and have been recognized as stable entities in zonular occluding desmosomes of mammalian capillary endothelial cells by Bruns and Palade. In unstable form, desmosomes of this type are envisioned as forming momentarily before recombination of membranes in encytosis (see next chapter). Juxtalaminar desmosomes have been recognized as parts of more extensive juxtamembranal desmosomes.

F. According to the relations of the cytoplasm of the two participating cells.

(1) Apocytial desmosomes: those in which the cytoplasms of the two participating cells are completely separated by membranes of high electrical resistance and are not electrically coupled (Fig. 4, II).

(2) Haptocytial desmosomes: those in which the cytoplasm of the two participating cells is completely separated by membrane, but wherein the separating membranes are of low electrical resistance, permitting some flow of ions between the two cells and thus providing for electrical coupling between the two cells. Electrical synapses belong to this category. Many juxtamembranal desmosomes belong to this class (Fig. 4, III). Those that do can be called synaptic desmosomes.

(3) Syncytial desmosomes: those specified in a preceding passage under E, 3b wherein the cytoplasm of the two participating cells is completely continuous without any intervening membrane. Some plasmodesmata represent syncytial desmosomes (Fig. 4, V, VI).

G. According to the relations of cytoplasmic structures to the membrane of the desmosome:

(1) Filamentous desmosomes: those which are characterized by cytoplasmic tonofilaments of a keratinous nature which insert into and are bound firmly to the cell membrane of the desmosome, which is locally thickened and specialized to accommodate the filaments. These filaments serve to anchor and reinforce the cytoplasm in relation to the desmosome and often extend from one desmosomal area to another in the same cell (Fig. 4, I, II).

(2) Afilamentous desmosomes: those which lack any special relationship to cytoplasmic tonofilaments (Fig. 4, III, IV, V and VI).

(b) *Properties of desmosomes*

Special comment is appropriate in relation to adherent auto-, homo- and heterodesmosomes of apocytial and filamentous character, such as are pictured in Fig. 4, I and II. These desmosomes are the ones which are most highly specialized for withstanding mechanical tensions. The molecular nature of the forces bonding one cell surface to another at these desmosomes is not well understood, but in many cases, desmosomes of this kind can be greatly weakened by treatment with trypsin or by removal of calcium and magnesium (Moscona). One supposes, therefore, that the chain of molecular configurations bonding the two desmosomes together contains links which are joined by calcium bridges and others which are ester or amide linkages adjacent to arginine or lysine and hence accessible to tryptic digestion. The intercellular material between two desmosomes, or between an heterodesmosome and the extracellular structures to which it is bound, is often denser than the usual intercellular matrix and may present inhomogeneities of density which suggest filaments (Fig. 4, I) or layers (Fig. 4, II). In the case of auto- and homodesmosomes, the intercellular inhomogeneities in density usually suggest layers parallel to the cell surface and symmetrically disposed on each side of a plane midway between the two desmosomes. These density patterns of desmosomes are not constant, vary a good deal from case to case and do not give reliable or definite clues as to the molecular configurations participating in the strong bonds linking the two cell surfaces together.

All the heterodesmosomes and homodesmosomes from all the cells in a single stratified epithelium, together with the tonofilaments anchored in the desmosomes, are so arranged as to act together to form an extensive, mechanical reinforcement for the entire, large epithelial layer. Thus, in vertebrate epidermis, the keratinous tonofilaments are arranged in bundles called tonofibrils which criss-cross the cytoplasm of each cell in many directions, providing a three-dimensional reinforcement and anchoring in desmosomes at the cell surfaces. Each desmosome is in turn bound to its opposite fellow in a neighboring cell or to the underlying basement membrane. The whole complex of tonofilaments and desmosomes makes for a mechanically robust epithelium, extensively cross-linked and well adapted to withstand tensile and shearing forces.

A variant of this plan is often found in many simple epithelia one cell thick, such as simple squamous, cuboidal, or columnar epithelia. Every cell in such an epithelium displays one or more zonal desmosomes which surround each cell completely as a zone or belt at a level corresponding to that occupied by the zonal desmosome of the next adjacent cell. Each cell is thus bound to its neighbor all around its circumference. Such an arrangement, standing by itself, would not lead to a very strong structure, as the cytoplasm inside the cells is poorly adapted to withstand tensile forces and would provide vulnerable weak points in the over-all structure. In fact, however, in these epithelia, the cytoplasm of each participating cell is strongly reinforced by a web of criss-crossing keratinous tonofilaments which insert in the zonular desmosome and which traverse the cell in a plane at the level of the zonular desmosome. Such a web is called a 'terminal web' (Leblond et al.). With each cell thus reinforced by a terminal web of strong filaments so arranged as to be capable of transmitting tensile forces to their counterparts in adjacent cells through the zonular desmosomes, the entire system of desmosomes and terminal webs comprises an effective mechanical reinforcement of the whole epithelial structure.

Sometimes several desmosomes of one or more types may be located close together and may exercise complementary functions. Such groupings of desmosomes have been called 'junctional complexes' (Farquhar and Palade 1963). Excellent examples of junctional complexes are seen near the apical ends of columnar epithelial cells of the vertebrate intestine. Here the cells separate the fluid compartment of the lumen of the gut from the fluid compartment of the intercellular space around the bases of the epithelial cells and around the blood and lymphatic vessels of the intestinal wall. One sees on electron microscopy that each cell is sealed to its neighbor by a zonular, occluding, juxtamembranal, afibrillar desmosome (or 'tight junction') just at the apical end of the lateral borders of the cells (Fig. 4, III). The membrane of one cell may not be actually fused to that of its neighbor, but yet apposed to it so intimately and tightly as to make an effective seal which extends around the circumference of each cell and which defends successfully the intercellular spaces from encroachment by the liquid contents of the intestinal lumen. Such a desmosome, though comprising an effective hydraulic seal, is not strong mechanically. In the intestinal epithelium, the weak but hydraulically impermeable juxtamembranal desmosomes are reinforced by one or more zonular, fibrillar, adherent, dismembranal desmosomes of the type previously described, which lie close to and parallel to the zonular seals or 'tight junctions', and which provide the necessary mechanical reinforcement to enable the epithelium to withstand tensile assault without endangering the integrity of the intercellular hydraulic seals provided by the juxtamembranal desmosomes. The whole system of parallel, zonular desmosomes comprises a 'junctional complex'.

The example of the juxtamembranal zonular desmosome just described was cited as functioning to provide a hydraulic seal between two fluid compartments. In some cases, another function has been attributed to juxtamembranal desmosomes. Electrophysiological studies have shown that in heart muscle (Woodbury and Crill) and in certain epithelia (Sheridan) each cell is electrically coupled to its neighbor in the sense that a low resistance pathway for flow of ions appears to exist between two adjacent cells, or between two cells in the same structure separated by a number of intervening cells. Fine structure studies have usually revealed juxtamembranal desmosomes connecting each cell to its neighbor in multicellular structures displaying these physiological properties (see Dewey and Barr; Trelstad et al.). Thus, the idea has been engendered that some juxtamembranal desmosomes may be characterized by specialized molecular membranal structure which permits ionic currents to flow with low resistance from one cell cytoplasm to that of its neighbor, so that the two adjacent cells can be regarded as in electrical synaptic communication. In this way, one heart muscle cell makes juxtamembranal contact with its neighbor over a portion of each intercalated disc (see Dewey and Barr). It is surmised that these areas provide for the electrical transmission of the excitatory cardiac impulse from cell to cell. Other regions of the intercalated discs are characterized by symmetrical dismembranal filamentous desmosomes. The filaments anchoring in the cell surfaces at these desmosomes are connected to the cardiac actin myofilaments at the next adjacent Z band. These desmosomes comprise portions of intercalated discs well adapted to transmit mechanical tension from one cell to its neighbor – a service essential for proper cardiac activity. Thus the intercalated discs of heart muscle are good examples of junctional complexes.

Septate desmosomes are diagrammed in Fig. 4, IV. Their structure is not completely understood and the model used for the diagram may prove to be inaccurate. Septate desmosomes appear to be zonular in configuration and, like many occluding, juxtamembranal desmosomes, have been found in epithelia which separate two fluid compartments. They were first discovered by Wood in the endodermal epithelium of Hydra, where their arrangement and structure suggested that the constituent septa were so disposed as to form a series of membranal barriers to the encroachment of fluid from the endocoele cavity into the intercellular spaces of the Hydra. The density profiles of the septa and of the adjacent desmosomal cell membranes suggested that the lipoid component of the cell membrane extends continuously into the core of the septa. However, definitive evidence as to the molecular structure of the septa in septate desmosomes is not available.

The syncytial desmosomes, diagrammed in Fig. 4, V and VI, include a type of intercellular connection usually called an 'intercellular bridge'. Such connections were described between avian spermatocytes and spermatids by Burgos and Fawcett, Fawcett (1961) and Nagano. Similar but more attenuated connections between adjacent cells of *Nitella*, called plasmodesmata, have been described by Spanswick and Costerton. Broadening the interconnecting cytoplasmic bridge brings the desmosome to approach a complete fusion of cells, such as characterizes many extensive syncytial masses as exemplified by a striated muscle fiber, a phagocytic foreign body giant cell, or the syncytial trophoblast of the primate placenta (see Wislocki and Bennett). The term 'syncytial desmosome' is appropriate only when the cytoplasmic bridge between two cells or cell masses is narrow and constricted enough to make it convenient to think of it as connecting and binding together two cells or cell masses. The term loses its significance if two or more cells are fused in a single mass.

7. *Plasmodesmata*

These are specialized slender projections of cell surfaces, connecting one cell to another, found in many multicellular plants with heavy cell walls. Analogous counterparts are known in animal tissues. In these cases, cells are separated from each other by intervening extracellular material such as cell wall or connective tissue matrix, but communicate with each other through small narrow tunnels several tens of nm in diameter, which pierce the material intervening between the cells. Into these tunnels pass extensions of cells and their surface membranes, so that a cell makes direct contact with its neighbors through such tunnels (see Fig. 4, VI). In plants, the term plasmodesmata is applied to these slender, membrane-covered, communicating process traversing intervening cell walls and extending from one cell to another. They can mediate transfer of fluid and other substances from cell to cell and, hence, through a succession of cells and plasmodesmata, to distant parts of the plant. Spanswick and Costerton point out that the electrical resistance of plasmodesmata in *Nitella* is so low that it evidences continuity of membrane and cytoplasm from cell to cell along the plasmodesma. This relationship would characterize these plasmodesmata as types of slender, elongated syncytial desmosomes.

Although the term plasmodesmata has not been used in connection with animal cells, very closely similar structures are known in the mammalian ovary and in bone. The ovum, a single cell, is surrounded by a representative of the glycocalyx called the *zona pellucida*, which is analogous to a cell wall, being an extracellular structure 2–5 μm thick, composed primarily of glycoprotein, of which a prominent polysaccharide component is hyaluronate. This zona pellucida, or cell wall, is pierced at many places by narrow tunnels 80–200 nm in diameter (see Anderson and Beams; Merker; Adams and Hertig). These tunnels tend to be somewhat tortuous and to branch. Into these tunnels pass slender processes from the surface of the ovum on the one hand, and from the surface of the innermost follicular cells which surround the zona pellucida on the other hand. These two sets of slender processes come into contact with each other in the tunnels.

As described by Dudley and Spiro, bone cells in their lacunae communicate with their neighbors by sending slender cell processes into the canaliculi traversing the intercellular matrix. All such communicating cell processes passing through tunnels piercing a robust layer of glycocalyx separating one cell from another can be called plasmodesmata.

In the case of the plasmodesmata of zona pellucida and of bone, information is scanty as to details of membrane relationships between the surfaces of the slender processes from the two cells which meet in the tunnels or canaliculi. It is not known if a desmosome type of relationship forms where the two processes meet. It is possible that the surfaces of the two processes may merely come into close mutual contact of a simple sort, though there is good reason to believe that one cell communicates with its neighbor through such channels and that nutrients may be passed from cell to cell through such processes.

References

ADAMS, E.C. and A.T.HERTIG: Studies on guinea pig oocytes I. Electron microscopic observations on the development of cytoplasmic organelles in oocytes of primordial and primary follicles. J. Cell Biol. 21 (1964) 397.

AMOORE, J.E.: Current status of the steric theory of odor. Ann. N.Y. Acad. Sci. 116 (1964) 457.

AMOORE, J.E.: Psychophysics of odor. Cold Spring Harbor Symp. Quant. Biol. 30 (1965) 623.

AMOORE, J.E., G.PALMIERI and E.WANKE: Molecular shape and odour: pattern analysis by PAPA. Nature 216 (1967) 1084.

ANDERSON, E. and H.W.BEAMS: Cytological observations on the fine structure of the guinea pig ovary with special reference to the oogonium, primary oocyte and associated follicle cells. J. Ultrastruct. Res. 3 (1960) 432.

BENEDETTI, E.L. and P.EMMELOT: Electron microscopic observations on negatively stained plasma membranes isolated from rat liver. J. Cell Biol. 26 (1965) 299.

BENEDETTI, E.L. and P.EMMELOT: Studies on plasma membranes IV. The ultrastructural localization and content of sialic acid in plasma membranes isolated from rat liver and hepatoma. J. Cell Sci. 2 (1967) 499.

BENNETT, H.S., J.H.LUFT and J.C.HAMPTON: Morphological classifications of vertebrate blood capillaries. Am. J. Physiol. 196 (1959) 381.

BENNETT, H.S.: The structure of striated muscle as seen by the electron microscope. In: G.H.Bourne, ed.: The structure and function of muscle, vol. I. New York and London, Academic Press (1960) p. 137.

BENNETT, H.S.: Morphological aspects of extracellular polysaccharides. J. Histochem. Cytochem. 11 (1963) 14.

BRANDT, P.W.: A consideration of the extraneous coats of the plasma membrane. Circulation 26 (1962) 1075.

BRANDT, P.W. and A.R.FREEMAN: Plasma membrane: substructural changes correlated with electrical resistance and pinocytosis. Science 155 (1967) 582.

BRANDT, P.W. and G.D.PAPPAS: An electron microscopic study of pinocytosis in ameba I. The surface attachment phase. J. Biophys. Biochem. Cytol. 8 (1960) 675.

BRANDT, P.W. and G.D.PAPPAS: An electron microscopic study of pinocytosis in ameba II. The cytoplasmic uptake phase. J. Cell Biol. 15 (1962) 55.

BRUCE, D.L. and J.M.MARSHALL, JR.: Some ionic and bioelectric properties of the ameba, *Chaos chaos*. J. Gen. Physiol. 49 (1965) 151.

BRUNS, R.R. and G.E.PALADE: Studies on blood capillaries I. General organization of blood capillaries in muscle. J. Cell Biol. 37 (1968) 244.

BULGER, R.E.: The shape of rat kidney tubular cells. Am. J. Anat. 116 (1965) 237.

BURGOS, M.H. and D.W.FAWCETT: Studies on the fine structure of the mammalian testis I. Differentiation of the spermatids in the cat (*Felis domestica*). J. Biophys. Biochem. Cytol. 1 (1955) 287.

CLERMONT, Y.: Contractile elements in the limiting membrane of the seminiferous tubules of the rat. Exptl. Cell Res. 15 (1958) 438.

COLE, K.S.: The advance of electrical models for cells and axons. Biophys. J. Suppl. 2 (1962) 101.

COLE, K.S.: Membranes, ions and impulses. Berkeley, University of California Press (1968).

COOK, G.M.W.: Linkage of sialic acid in the human erythrocyte ultra-structure. Nature 195 (1962) 159.

COOK, G.M.W., D.H.HEARD and G.V.F.SEAMAN: Sialic acids and the electrokinetic charge of the human erythrocyte. Nature 191 (1961) 44.

COUTEAUX, R.: Motor end-plate structure. In: G.Bourne, ed.: Structure and function of muscle, vol. 1. New York and London, Academic Press (1960) 337.

DE LORENZO, A.J.: Electron microscopic observations on the taste buds of the rabbit. J. Biophys. Biochem. Cytol. 4 (1958) 143.

DE ROBERTIS, E.: Electron microscope observations on the submicroscopic organization of the retinal rods. J. Biophys. Biochem. Cytol. 2 (1956a) 319.

DE ROBERTIS, E.: Morphogenesis of the retinal rods. An electron microscope study. J. Biophys. Biochem. Cytol. Suppl. 2 (1956b) 209.

DE ROBERTIS, E.: Histophysiology of synapses and neurosecretion. Oxford, Pergamon Press (1964).

DE ROBERTIS, E. and A.LASANSKY: Submicroscopic organization of retinal cones of the rabbit. J. Biophys. Biochem. Cytol. 4 (1958) 743.

DE ROBERTIS, E.D.P. and H.S.BENNETT: Some features of the submicroscopic morphology of synapses in frog and earthworm. J. Biophys. Biochem. Cytol. 1 (1955) 47.

DEWEY, M.M. and L.BARR: A study of the structure and distribution of the nexus. J. Cell Biol. 23 (1964) 553.

DUDLEY, H.R. and D.SPIRO: The fine structure of bone cells. J. Biophys. Biochem. Cytol. 11 (1961) 627.

EBASHI, S.: The role of 'relaxing factor' in contraction-relaxation cycle of muscle. Progr. Theoret. Phys. (Kyoto) Suppl. 17 (1961) 35.

EBASHI, S. and F.LIPMANN: Adenosine triphosphate-linked concentration of calcium ions in a particulate fraction of rabbit muscle. J. Cell Biol. 14 (1962) 389.

ECCLES, J.C.: Neuron physiology. Introduction. In: J. Field, H.W.Magoun and V.E.Hall, eds.: Handbook of Physiology, Sec. I: Neurophysiology. Washington, D.C., Am. Physiol. Soc., vol. 1, chap. II (1959) 959.

ENDO, M.: Entry of a dye into the sarcotubular system of muscle. Nature 202 (1964) 1115.

FARBMAN, A.I.: Fine structure of the taste bud. J. Ultrastruct. Res. 12 (1965) 328.

FARQUHAR, M.G. and G.E.PALADE: Segregation of ferritin in glomerular protein absorption droplets. J. Biophys. Biochem. Cytol. 7 (1960) 297.

FARQUHAR, M.G. and G.E.PALADE: Junctional complexes in various epithelia. J. Cell Biol. 17 (1963) 375.

FARQUHAR, M.G. and G.E.PALADE: Functional organization of amphibian skin. Proc. Natl. Acad. Sci. 51 (1964) 569.

FAWCETT, D.W.: Intercellular bridges. Exptl. Cell Res. Suppl. 8 (1961) 174.

FAWCETT, D.W.: An atlas of fine structure. The cell. Its organelles and inclusions. Philadelphia and London, W.B.Saunders Company (1966).

FAWCETT, D.W.: In: W.Bloom and D.W.Fawcett: A textbook of histology. Philadelphia and London, W.B.Saunders Company (1968) p. 88.

FERNÁNDEZ-MORÁN, H.: Cell membrane ultrastructure: low-temperature electron microscopy and X-ray diffraction studies of lipoprotein components in lamellar systems. In: Ultrastructure and metabolism of the nervous system, vol. 40. Research Publications, Association for Research in Nervous and Mental Disease (1962) p. 235.

FLAXMAN, B.A., M.A.LUTZNER and E.J.VAN SCOTT: Ultrastructure of cell attachment to substratum *in vitro*. J. Cell Biol. 36 (1968) 406.

FLOCK, Å.: Structure of the macula utriculi with special reference to directional interplay of sensory responses as revealed by morphological polarization. J. Cell Biol. 22 (1964) 413.

FLOCK, Å.: Transducing mechanisms in the lateral line canal organ receptors. Cold Spring Harbor Symp. Quant. Biol. 30 (1965) 133.

FLOCK, Å. and J.WERSÄLL: A study of the orientation of the sensory hairs of the receptor cells in the lateral line organ of fish, with special reference to the function of the receptors. J. Cell Biol. 15 (1962) 19.

GRAHAM, R.C. and M.J.KARNOVSKY: Glomerular permeability. Ultrastructural cytochemical studies using peroxidases as protein tracers. J. Exptl. Med. 124 (1966) 1123.

GRAY, E.G. and K.C.WATKINS: Electron microscopy of taste buds of the rat. Z. Zellforsch. mikrosk. Anat. 66 (1965) 583.

GROSS, J., J.H.HIGHBERGER and F.O.SCHMITT: Some factors involved in the fibrogenesis of collagen *in vitro*. Proc. Soc. Exptl. Biol. Med. 80 (1952) 462.

GRUNDFEST, H.: Synaptic and ephaptic transmission. In: J.Field, H.W.Magoun and V.E.Hall, eds.: Handbook of Physiology, Sec. I: Neurophysiology. Washington, D.C., Am. Physiol. Soc., vol. I chap. V (1959) p. 147.

HAMA, K.: The fine structure of some blood vessels of the earthworm, *Eisenia foetida*. J. Biophys. Biochem. Cytol. 7 (1960) 717.

HAMA, K.: Some observations on the fine structure of the lateral line organ of the Japanese sea eel, *Lyncozymba nystromi*. J. Cell Biol. 24 (1965) 193.

HAY, E.: In: D.W.Fawcett: An atlas of fine structure. The cell. Its organelles and inclusions. Philadelphia and London, W.B.Saunders Company (1966) p. 371.

HOLTER, H.: Problems of pinocytosis, with special regard to amoebae. Ann. N.Y. Acad. Sci. 78 (1959) 524.

HOLTER, H.: Pinocytosis. Proc. 5th Intern. Congr. Biochem. II. Oxford, Pergamon Press (1963) p. 248.

HOLTER, H.: Membrane in correlation with pinocytosis. In: S.Seno and E.V.Cowdry, eds.: Intracellular membraneous structure. Proc. 1st Intern. Symp. Cellular Chem. Okayama, Japan, Japan Society for Cell Biology, The Chugoku Press, Ltd. (1965) p. 451.

HOROWITZ, M.I.: Mucopolysaccharides and glycoproteins of the alimentary tract. In: C.F.Code and W.Heidel, eds.: Handbook of Physiology, Sec. 6: Alimentary canal. Washington, D.C., Am. Physiol. Soc., vol. II, chap. 60 (1967) p. 1063.

HUXLEY, A.F. and R.E.TAYLOR: Local activation of striated muscle fibres. J. Physiol. (London) 144 (1958) 426.

HUXLEY, H.E.: Evidence for continuity between the central elements of the triads and extracellular space in frog sartorius muscle. Nature 202 (1964) 1067.

ICHIKAWA, A.: Fine structure changes in response to hormonal stimulation of the perfused canine pancreas. J. Cell Biol. 24 (1965) 369.

ITO, S. and R.J.WINCHESTER: The fine structure of the gastric mucosa in the bat. J. Cell Biol. 16 (1963) 541.

ITO, S.: The enteric surface coat on cat intestinal microvilli. J. Cell Biol. 27 (1965) 475.

JOHNSON, C.F.: Intestinal invertase activity and a macromolecular repeating unit of hamster brush border plasma membrane. In: R. Uyeda, ed.: Electron Microscopy, vol. II: Biology. Tokyo, Maruzen Co., Ltd. (1966) p. 389.

KABAT, E.A.: Blood group substances. Their chemistry and immunochemistry. New York and London, Academic Press (1956).

KARNOVSKY, M.J.: The ultrastructural basis of capillary permeability studied with peroxidase as a tracer. J. Cell Biol. 35 (1967) 213.

KATCHALSKY, A. and O. KEDEM: Thermodynamics of flow processes in biological systems. Biophys. J. Suppl. 2 (1962) 53.

KEFALIDES, N.A.: A collagen of unusual composition and a glycoprotein isolated from canine glomerular basement membrane. Biochem. Biophys. Res. Commun. 22 (1966) 26.

KEFALIDES, N.A. and R.J. WINZLER: The chemistry of glomerular basement membrane and its relation to collagen. Biochemistry 5 (1966) 702.

KELLY, D.E.: Fine structure of desmosomes, hemidesmosomes and an adepidermal globular layer in developing newt epidermis. J. Cell Biol. 28 (1966) 51.

LEBLOND, C.P., H. PUCHTLER and Y. CLERMONT: Structures corresponding to terminal bars and terminal web in many types of cells. Nature 186 (1960) 784.

LEE, R.E. and J.D. FELDMAN: Visualization of antigenic sites of human erythrocytes with ferritin-antibody conjugates. J. Cell Biol. 23 (1964) 396.

LUCK, D.J.L.: Formation of mitochondria in *Neurospora crassa*. A quantitative radioautographic study. J. Cell Biol. 16 (1963) 483.

LUCK, D.J.L.: The influence of precursor pool size on mitochondrial composition in *Neurospora crassa*. J. Cell Biol. 24 (1964) 445.

LUFT, J.H.: The ultrastructural basis of capillary permeability. In: B. W. Zweifach, L. Grant and R. T. McCluskey, eds.: The Inflammatory Process. New York and London, Academic Press (1965) p. 121.

LUFT, J.H.: Fine structure of capillary and endocapillary layer as revealed by ruthenium red. Federation Proc. 25 (1966) 1773.

MARCHESI, V.T. and R.J. BARRNETT: The demonstration of enzymatic activity in pinocytic vesicles of blood capillaries with the electron microscope. J. Cell Biol. 17 (1963) 547.

MARCHESI, V.T. and G.E. PALADE: The localization of Mg-Na-K-activated adenosine triphosphatase on red cell ghost membranes. J. Cell Biol. 35 (1967) 385.

MARSHALL, J.M. and V.T. NACHMIAS: Cell surface and pinocytosis. J. Histochem. Cytochem. 13 (1965) 92.

MARTIN, H.H.: Biochemistry of bacterial cell walls. Ann. Rev. Biochem. 35, II (1966) 457.

MERKER, H.J.: Elektronenmikroskopische Untersuchungen über die Bildung der Zona pellucida in den Follikeln des Kaninchenovars. Z. Zellforsch. mikrosk. Anat. 54 (1961) 677.

MOSCONA, A.: Cell suspensions from organ rudiments of chick embryo. Exptl. Cell Res. 3 (1952) 535.

NAGANO, T.: The structure of cytoplasmic bridges in dividing spermatocytes of the rooster. Anat. Record 141 (1961) 73.

NOVIKOFF, A.B.: Enzymatic activities and functional interrelations of cytomembranes. In: S. Seno and E. V. Cowdry, eds.: Intracellular membraneous structure. Proc. 1st Intern. Symp. Cellular Chem. Okayama, Japan, Japan Society for Cell Biology, The Chugoku Press, Ltd. (1965) p. 277.

ODA, T. and S. SEKI: Molecular structure and biochemical function of the microvilli membrane of intestinal epithelial cells with special emphasis on the elementary particles. J. Electron Microscopy (Tokyo) 14 (1965) 210.

ODA, T. and S. SEKI: Molecular basis of structure and function of the plasma membrane of the microvilli of intestinal epithelial cells. In: R. Uyeda, ed.: Electron Microscopy, vol. II: Biology. Tokyo, Maruzen Co., Ltd. (1966) p. 387.

OHKUMA, S. and S. IKEMOTO: A sialoglycopeptide liberated from human red cells by treatment with trypsin. Nature 212 (1966) 198.

PAGE, S. G.: A comparison of the fine structures of frog slow and twitch muscle fibres. J. Cell Biol. 26 (1965) 477.

PALADE, G. E.: Fine structure of blood capillaries. J. Appl. Phys. 24 (1953) 1424.

PALADE, G. E.: The endoplasmic reticulum. J. Biophys. Biochem. Cytol. Suppl. 2 (1956) 85.

PALADE, G. E.: Blood capillaries of the heart and other organs. Circulation 24 (1961) 368.

PALAY, S. L. and J. P. REVEL: The morphology of fat absorption. In: H. C. Meng, ed.: Lipid transport. Springfield, Ill., Charles C. Thomas (1964) p. 33.

PEACHEY, L. D.: The sarcoplasmic reticulum and transverse tubules of the frog's sartorius. J. Cell Biol. 25 (3, Pt. 2) (1965) 209.

PEASE, D. C.: Infolded basal plasma membranes found in epithelia noted for their water transport. J. Biophys. Biochem. Cytol. Suppl. 2 (1956) 203.

RAMBOURG, A. and C. P. LEBLOND: Electron microscope observations on the carbohydrate-rich cell coat present at the surface of cells in the rat. J. Cell Biol. 32 (1967) 27.

RAMBOURG, A., M. NEUTRA and C. P. LEBLOND: Presence of a 'cell coat' rich in carbohydrate at the surface of cells in the rat. Anat. Record 154 (1966) 41.

REESE, T. S.: Olfactory cilia in the frog. J. Cell Biol. 25 (2, Pt. 2) (1965) 209.

RICHARDSON, I. W.: Multiple membrane systems as analogues for biological membranes. Thesis. The Weizmann Institute, Rehoveth, Israel (1967).

ROBERTSON, J. D.: The ultrastructure of cell membranes and their derivatives. Biochem. Soc. Symp. (Cambridge, Engl.) 16 (1959) 3.

ROBERTSON, J. D.: Unit membranes. A review with recent new studies of experimental alterations and a new subunit structure in synaptic membranes. In: M. Locke, ed.: Cellular membranes in development. 22nd Symposium for the Study of Development and Growth. New York, Academic Press (1964) 1.

ROSENBERG, B., T. N. MISRA and R. SWITZER: Mechanism of olfactory transduction. Nature 217 (1968) 423.

SAITO, A.: Epithelial cells of the distal convoluted tubule of the rat kidney. In: E. Yamada, K. Fukai and Y. Watanabe, eds.: Electron micrographs, Biology 2. Tokyo, Hitachi Printing Co., Ltd. (1966) p. 46.

SCHMITT, F. O.: Macromolecular interaction patterns in biological systems. Proc. Am. Phil. Soc. 100 (1956) 476.

SHARON, N.: Polysaccharides. Ann. Rev. Biochem. 35 II (1966) 485.

SHERIDAN, J. D.: Electrophysiological study of special connections between cells in the early chick embryo. J. Cell Biol. 31 (1966) Cl.

SPANSWICK, R. M. and J. W. F. COSTERTON: Plasmodesmata in *Nitella translucens*: structure and electrical resistance. J. Cell Sci. 2 (1967) 451.

TASAKI, I.: Conduction of the nerve impulse. In: J. Field, H. W. Magoun and V. E. Hall, eds.: Handbook of Physiology, Sec. 1: Neurophysiology. Washington, D.C., Am. Physiol. Soc., vol. 1, chap. III (1959) 75.

TRELSTAD, R. L., J. P. REVEL and E. D. HAY: Tight junctions between cells in the early chick embryo as visualized with the electron microscope. J. Cell Biol. 31 (1966) C6.

UGOLEV, A. M.: Membrane (contact) digestion. Physiol. Rev. 45 (1965) 555.

WALD, G.: The molecular organization of visual systems. In: W. D. McElroy and B. Glass, eds.: A symposium on light and life. Baltimore, The Johns Hopkins Press (1961) p. 724.

WEBER, A., R. HERZ and I. REISS: The regulation of myofibrillar activity by calcium. Proc. Roy. Soc. (London), Ser. B. 160 (1964) 489.

WERSÄLL, J., Å. FLOCK and P. G. LUNDQUIST: Structural basis for directional sensitivity in cochlear and vestibular sensory receptors. Cold Spring Harbor Symp. Quant. Biol. 30 (1965) 115.

WILSON, E.B.: The cell in development and heredity. New York, The Macmillan Company (1925).

WISLOCKI, G.B. and H.S.BENNETT: The histology and cytology of the human and monkey placenta, with special reference to the trophoblast. Am. J. Anat. 73 (1943) 335.

WOOD, R.L.: Intercellular attachment in the epithelium of Hydra as revealed by electron microscopy. J. Biophys. Biochem. Cytol. 6 (1959) 343.

WOODBURY, J.W. and W.E.CRILL: On the problem of impulse conduction in the atrium. In: E. Florey, ed.: Nervous inhibition. Proc. 2nd Friday Harbor Symp. New York and Oxford, Pergamon Press (1961) p.124.

YAMADA, E.: The fine structure of the gall bladder epithelium of the mouse. J. Biophys. Biochem. Cytol. 1 (1955a) 445.

YAMADA, E.: The fine structure of the renal glomerulus of the mouse. J. Biophys. Biochem. Cytol. 1 (1955b) 551.

YAMAMOTO, T.: On the thickness of the unit membrane. J. Cell Biol. 17 (1963) 413.

ZACKS, S.I.: The motor endplate. Philadelphia and London, W.B.Saunders Co. (1964).

ZUCKER-FRANKLIN, D. and J.G.HIRSCH: Electron microscope studies on the degranulation of rabbit peritoneal leucocytes during phagocytosis. J. Exptl. Med. 120 (1964) 569.

CHAPTER 48

The cell surface: movements and recombinations*

H. STANLEY BENNETT

Laboratories for Cell Biology, University of Chicago, Chicago, Ill.

Contents

1. Introduction
2. Fundamental considerations in membrane fusions and recombinations
3. Eccytosis and encytosis
   (a) Eccytosis
      Secretion by pancreatic acinar cells
      Secretion by mammary gland cells
      Liberation of viruses
      Other forms of eccytosis
   (b) Encytosis
      Specific binding at the cell surface
      Membrane flow
      Vesiculation
      Phagocytosis and pinocytosis
      Uptake of viruses
      Cell fusion
   (c) Transport in bulk

* This chapter uses the SI (see Nature 216 (1967) 1272) as a guide for units of measure.

1. Introduction

Many important properties of cell surfaces cannot be understood adequately on the basis of data derived from observation of surface configurations, chemical analyses, characterization of components of membrane and glycocalyx, and measurements of electrical potentials and fluxes of ions and sugars across the cell surface. Required also is understanding of the complex capabilities of components of the cell surface for specific binding, and of the capacity of cell membranes to flow, move, fuse, recombine, and exchange with membrane areas within the cell, or with membranes of other parts of the cell surface, or of the surface of other cells. This chapter deals with these properties of the cell surface, which enable cells to perform many important physiological functions.

The cell surface functions of principal concern here can be divided into two broad groups. The first comprises those which liberate large quantities of material from cells, as in secretion of digestive enzymes, in liberation of some viruses from animal cells, in cell division, in production of blood platelets from megakaryocytes and in the shedding of the erythroblast nucleus in red cell formation. This process we call *eccytosis.* The second group of processes involves the uptake in bulk of large amounts of chemical material by cells, or the fusion of two cells, utilizing the properties of membranes here considered. This process we call *encytosis.* Phagocytosis and pinocytosis are examples of encytosis. This chapter is mainly concerned with the properties of cell surfaces which are displayed in encytosis and eccytosis, with descriptions of the fundamental processes, and with the presentation of a number of illustrative examples of the principal variants of the two.

2. Fundamental considerations in membrane fusions and recombinations

Since the electron microscope came to be applied to studies of cell structure and function, it has come to be realized that membranes similar in structure to the cell membrane are extensively represented around the nucleus and throughout the cytoplasm of many cells. These intracellular membranous components are dealt with in other chapters of this Handbook. Many of the internal membranes and those on the cell surface can move, fuse, recombine and exchange with each other.

All these membrane fusion and recombination phenomena, as seen in eccytosis and encytosis, involve lipoprotein membrane structures which display the basic 'unit membrane' appearance and embody the fundamental architectural plan of the cell or plasma membrane. Similar fusion events are known to characterize membrane structures within the cytoplasm of the cell, without implicating the cell surface itself (see Jamieson and Palade).

The movements, translations, fusions, exchanges, and recombinations of cell surface treated here are similar in some respects to those which can be observed in thin films comprising soap bubbles and on monomolecular films of polar lipid molecules spread on a water surface. Thus, some features of the behavior of the cell surface can be ascribed to properties of the lipid component of the cell membrane. Polar lipid monofilms and soap bubble films behave like two-dimensional liquids and are capable of flow. Soap bubbles, in addition, are capable of fusion, recombination and pinching off. Thus, these two model systems can duplicate some of the properties of cell membranes.

An hypothesis representing some of the relationships involved in membrane fusion and recombination is represented in Figs. 1 and 2. This hypothesis holds that, in order for fusion to occur, the oriented lipid components of two closely apposed membranes must somehow make contact with each other (Figs. 1 and 2, II). The hypothe-

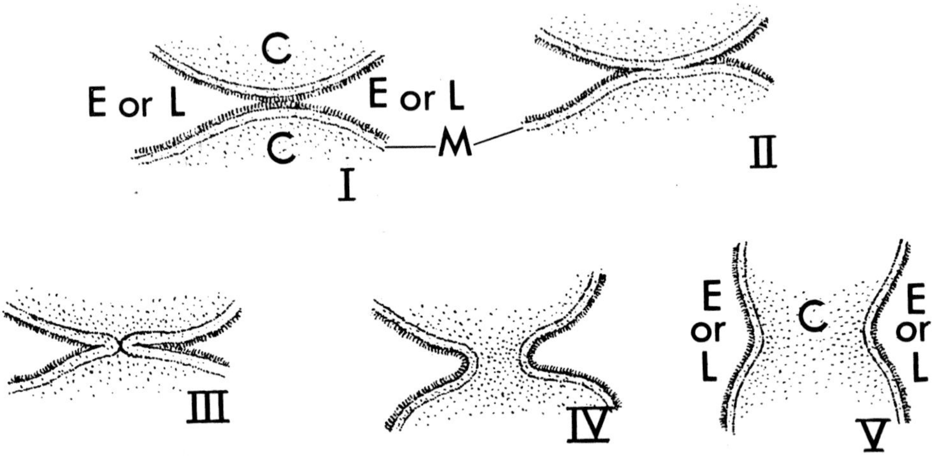

Fig. 1

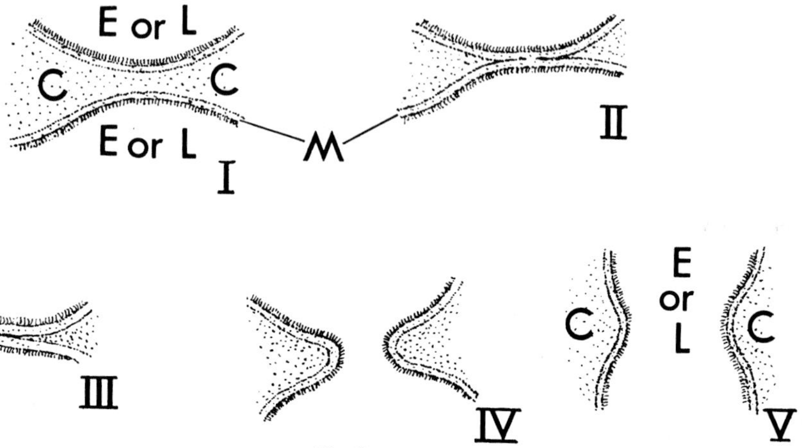

Fig. 2

sis requires further that, upon this direct contact of the lipid components of the two membranes, the original geometric configuration of two membranes becomes less stable than an alternative one, which involves a breaking of the continuity of the two original membranes, a rearrangement of their molecular components and the formation of a recombination wherein two different membranes separate from the area of fusion, each formally oriented in planes, normal to those of the original fusing membranes and each new one composed of membrane material derived from each of the two original membranes (see Figs. 1 and 2, III and IV).

As stated in the previous chapter, there is reason to believe that cell membranes may not be symmetrical with respect to planes parallel to their surfaces and extending down their centers. Moreover, further asymmetries derive from the differences between the glycocalyx on one surface of the membrane and the juxtamembranal cytoplasmic components on the other. These asymmetries are such that a single series

---

Figs. 1 and 2 represent hypothetical stages in the process of membrane fusion and recombination as it occurs in encytosis and eccytosis. In both figures, the cytoplasm (C) is stippled and the extracellular space (E) or lumen (L) of a vesicle or caveola is clear. The cell or vesicle membrane (M) is shown as an asymmetrical trilaminate 'unit membrane'. The cytoplasmic surface of the membrane lies against the stippled area, whereas the external or lumenal surface of the membrane is shown with a fringe-like character which can represent the glycocalyx.

Fig. 1 shows the sequence of events when two membrane areas fuse and recombine after approaching each other and making contact by the apoplasmic, glycocalyx, external or lumenal surfaces, as in endocytosis, which is represented in the fusion of two cells, the pinching off of a caveola to form a vesicle, or the pinching off of an intracytoplasmic vesicle or membranous sac into two.

Fig. 2 shows the sequence of events when two membrane areas fuse and recombine after approaching each other and making contact by the cytoplasmic surfaces, as in eccytosis, which is represented in cell division, or in the fusion of two intracytoplasmic vesicles or vacuoles, or in the liberation of secretion by fusion of membranes of secretion vesicles or lysosomes with the cell membrane, or in the liberation of viruses or fat droplets by fusion and recombination of two areas of cell membrane of the same cell.

In both Figs. 1 and 2, section I represents the two membranes approaching each other. Section II shows the two membranes fusing as the lipid layers of the lipoprotein membrane come into contact and merge with each other. This condition is envisioned as unstable, with a probability of leading to a more stable configuration represented in section III, which shows the fused membranes as recombining to form two new membrane portions, each consisting of a part derived from each of the two original membrane areas. In sections IV and V, the newly recombined membranes are represented as drawing apart, leaving a widening gap between them, filled with cytoplasm in Fig. 1 and extracellular space or lumen of vesicle in Fig. 2.

Fig. 1, II also represents the configuration of a stable form of synmembranal desmosomes with a juxtalaminar portion imbedded in it (see previous chapter). Profiles displaying this appearance have been described by Bruns and Palade in the junctions between adjacent endothelial cells in blood capillaries in vertebrate muscle. They interpret this appearance as representing a fusion of membranes of two adjacent cells in a belt or zone around the circumference of each cell. Such zones form occluding seals resisting the passage of substances between blood plasma and extracellular space. In this context, the fusing membranes form a stable juxtalaminar configuration and do not go on to recombination, as they do in encytosis.

of diagrams cannot be used to represent all fusion events. One can classify these fusions and recombinations on the basis of the polarity of membrane surfaces which come into contact.

The apoplasmic, or glycocalyx, surfaces of two membrane areas come into contact when two cells fuse, or when a caveola is pinched off to form a vesicle (see Figs. 6–9). This can be called fusion and recombination after apoplasmic surface apposition (see Fig. 1), and is characteristic of encytosis.

The cytoplasmic surfaces of two membrane areas come into contact when a secretion vesicle fuses with the plasma membrane to release its secretion material (see Figs. 3 and 4); or when a virus is pinched off from a microvillus tip or bulge from the cell surface (see Figs. 4 and 5); or when a new cell membrane forms to separate two dividing cells in telophase. This process can be called fusion and recombination after cytoplasmic surface apposition (see Fig. 2) and is characteristic of eccytosis.

Note that some ambiguities can arise if the terms 'internal' and 'external' cell surfaces are used. For example, the geometric external surface of a cell presents to glycocalyx and extracellular space, whereas the geometric external surface of a lysosome presents to the cytoplasmic matrix.

3. *Eccytosis and encytosis*

(a) *Eccytosis*

In all cases of eccytosis, membranes, destined to fuse and recombine, make contact with each other at their cytoplasmic surfaces (see Fig. 2). The cytoplasmic surface of the cell membrane is the inner or prosplasmic surface, but the corresponding surface of an intracellular membrane-bound vesicle, such as a secretion vesicle or granule, is geometrically the exterior surface of the membrane bounding the vesicle. Fusion of vesicles within the cytoplasm frequently occurs. This is analogous to eccytosis, and likewise follows apposition of cytoplasmic surfaces of two intracytoplasmic vesicle membranes.

A. *Secretion by pancreatic acinar cells.* A very large variety of cells have capabilities for eccytosis. An excellent example is the mammalian pancreatic acinar cell, which has been much studied by Siekevitz and Palade and by Ichikawa. The products of synthesis of interest here are hydrolytic enzymes and enzyme precursors which become active as proteases, esterases, amylases and nucleases. After synthesis in the pancreas cell, these products are packaged in membrane-bounded vesicles, long known to light microscopists as 'secretion granules'. These come to be stored in the apical portion of the acinar cell until the cell receives a stimulus to release the secretion. Pancreozymin serves as a physiological stimulus for pancreatic secretion, though pilocarpine and other drugs can produce a similar pharmacologic effect.

When the loaded cell receives a suitable stimulus, the secretion granules, which, to repeat, are really membrane-bound vesicles, each enclosing a large number of molecules of enzymes and zymogens, move to the apical surface of the cell where, one by one, the membrane of each vesicle touches and then fuses and combines with the membrane of the cell surface (see Fig. 3). With fusion, the membrane of the vesicle becomes part of the cell surface membrane. The fusion and recombination of cell and vesicle membrane are such as to cause the lumen of the vesicle to form a transient secretion caveola open to the outside. The contents of the caveola are then liberated into the lumen of the acinus, which is continuous with the lumen of the pancreatic ducts. Under vigorous stimulation, several secretion vesicles can fuse with each other and with the cell membrane in such a way as to form a continuous chain of two or more vesicles, their lumina opening into each other and to the outside (Fig. 3, III).

This membrane fusion and recombination adds new areas of membrane to the cell surface. It seems, however, that the surface area of the cell is not very greatly in-

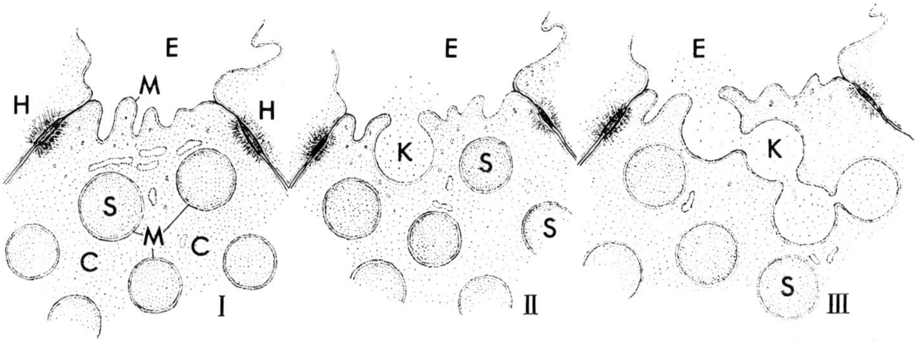

Fig. 3. Cell surface configurations seen in eccytosis (secretion) as represented in the vertebrate pancreatic acinar cell. The apical portion of one cell and parts of the apices of two adjacent cells are shown as bound to each other by zonular homodesmosomes (H), or terminal bars, and as presenting their apical surface membranes (M) to the extracellular space (E) of the lumen of a pancreatic acinus. Section I shows a cell prior to receiving a stimulus for secretion, and displaying in its apical cytoplasm (C) a number of 'secretion granules' (S), which are really a kind of a lysosome and which are vesicles or sacs bound by membrane (M) and loaded with many millions of molecules of pancreatic hydrolytic enzymes and enzyme precursors such as trypsinogen, chymotrypsinogen, pancreatic amylase, lipase and nucleases. These zymogens were synthesized earlier in other portions of the cell. Section II shows the cell as in an early stage of response to a stimulus to secretion, such as pancreozymin. One of the secretion vesicles has moved to the apical surface membrane of the cell. There, the membrane of the vesicle has fused and recombined with the membrane of the cell surface in such a way as to cause the lumen of the previous vesicle to become the lumen of a secretory or eccytosis caveola (K) open to the lumen of the acinus (E). The membrane formerly around the secretory vesicle has now become part of the apical surface membrane of the cell. The contents of the former lysosome or secretion granule or vesicle are represented as flowing or being discharged or liberated into the acinar lumen. Section III shows a more advanced or active stage of secretion. Several secretion vesicles are shown as having fused with each other and with a secretion caveola in such a way as to create an elongated eccytosis caveola (K) derived from four secretion granules. The membranes of all these granules now are part of the cell surface membrane, whose area is considerably augmented by these acquisitions. One must hypothesize a mechanism, so far not identified, for removing membrane from the surface in order to restore normal cell surface area after secretion. (Drawn after Ichikawa.)

creased by the fusions occurring in secretion. This suggests that the cell may have a concomitant and compensatory surface membrane uptake mechanism capable of reducing the cell surface area as or after it is augmented by the acquisition of fresh membrane from the vesicles. Such a membrane uptake mechanism, however, has not been specifically recognized as an accompanying phenomenon in secretion by pancreatic acinar cells.

B. *Secretion by mammary gland cells.* Secretion of milk by the mammary gland displays interesting variants of the eccytosis process. According to Bargmann and Knoop, the principal protein constituents of milk are synthesized and segregated in casein-containing vesicles and liberated into the ducts by fusion and recombination of vesicle and cell membrane and secretory caveola formation (see Fig. 4). This process does not differ from that involved in eccytosis of pancreatic secretory products.

The liberation of fat in the milk, however, takes place by a variant form of eccytosis. Bargmann and Knoop bring forth evidence that fat in mammary gland epithelial cells is segregated in membrane-lined vesicles (fat droplets). During secretion, the fat vesicles move to positions close to the cell membrane on the apical surface (Fig. 4). There a short pseudopod or blunt microvillus or cell projection forms and the fat droplet takes a position close to the distal tip of the protuberance. The cell membrane bounding the protuberance then forms a constriction near the base, tending to cut off the more distal fat droplet from the main body of the cell. Most of the residual cytoplasm around the fat droplet escapes from the vicinity. The cell membrane at the constriction makes contact, fuses and recombines so as to liberate the fat droplet from the cell and permit it to join the other secretory products of the milk, where it can contribute to the cream. According to the concept proposed by Bargmann and Knoop and related here, the secreted fat vesicle possesses two concentric and closely apposed membranes: an outer one derived from the cell surface and an inner one corresponding to that which originally surrounded the fat droplet.

C. *Liberation of viruses.* The liberation of mammary tumor viruses from mammary gland epithelial cells by eccytosis has been studied by Bernhard. The mechanism involves a form of eccytosis very similar to that seen in the discharge of fat in milk secretion. Some features of the sequence of events are diagrammed in Fig. 4. Tumor virus particles made in deep portions of the cell move towards the surface and take positions at the distal tips of microvilli. The membrane of the microvillus then constricts, fuses and recombines just adjacent to and under the virus particle, so that the virus is liberated into the lumen of the gland invested in a spheroidal envelope or capsule consisting of membrane and glycocalyx derived from the surface of the mammary epithelial cell microvillus.

Some viruses appear to be able to stimulate the cell to modify its cell surface locally to produce a microvillus, in the tip of which a virus particle forms. The virus is then liberated in a capsule or envelope constructed of modified cell surface. Cases in point are the influenza myxovirus (Ané) and the Sendai virus. The essential features are shown in Fig. 5, which represents the findings of Berkaloff, who studied the process of liberation of Sendai virus from mammalian cells. According to these reports, material containing the viral nucleic acid, after synthesis in the cell, moves to the superficial regions of cytoplasm and takes a position just adjacent to the cell membrane. The overlying area of cell surface then changes, apparently in response to the local influences of the virus. The changes are characterized by a thickening of the cell membrane and the appearance of a specially luxuriant glycocalyx over this localized area. The changes resemble in some respects those associated with the formation of 'coated vesicles' in encytosis (see Roth and Porter), but in the case of virus liberation, the local area of specialized membrane everts rather than invaginates, forming a small blunt microvillus (see Fig. 5). The viral material is carried into this blunt protuberance, the membrane of which narrows down to a narrow neck, constricting like the orifice of a purse and then fusing, recombining and pinching off, liberating by eccytosis the viral material embedded in a residual mass of cytoplasm and enveloped in membrane and glycocalyx derived from the cell surface, but modified locally by the virus, which utilizes the modified cell surface for its capsule.

D. *Other forms of eccytosis.* The liberation of the nucleus from the late erythroblast in mammalian red cell formation also represents an interesting example of eccytosis. Skutelsky and Danon, and Simpson and Kling have shown that in the late erythroblast, the nucleus is moved to a side position just adjacent to the interior surface of the cell membrane. Near the cytoplasmic surface of the nucleus, a series of vesicles form, which flatten, enlarge, fuse and come to form a nearly continuous layer of flattened cisternae which tend to imprison the nucleus against the plasma membrane. Most of the cytoplasm escapes into the general region of the cell from the enclosure around the nucleus, whereupon fusion of vesicle membrane continues to completion and to fusion with cell membrane all around. The nucleus is thus liberated from the red cell, escaping whilst enclosed rather snugly in cell membrane derived in part from the vesicle and in part from the original erythroblast membrane. The mature red cell itself has a cell surface derived likewise from these two sources.

Another variant of eccytosis is seen in the megakaryocyte of mammalian bone marrow, as it matures to liberate blood platelets. Yamada observed that the maturing megakaryocyte develops an extensive system of smooth cytoplasmic vesicles which arrange themselves along curving intersection planes or sheets, which come to demarcate the future platelets. These platelet demarcation vesicles enlarge and fuse to form a dense network of interconnecting tubules which lie in the interplatelet demarcation planes. These tubules enlarge, fuse and recombine so as to lead to a complete separation of numerous individual platelets from a single megakaryocyte, each platelet surrounded by membrane derived from the demarcation vesicles. Nakao and Angrist have shown that the demarcation vesicles and tubules contain polysaccharide material which later appears as the glycocalyx of the platelet surface.

Cell division itself is an example of eccytosis. In some examples of cell division, the cell at telophase constricts and fusion and recombination of membranes occurs between the two telophase nuclei. In other examples, a series of demarcation vesicles

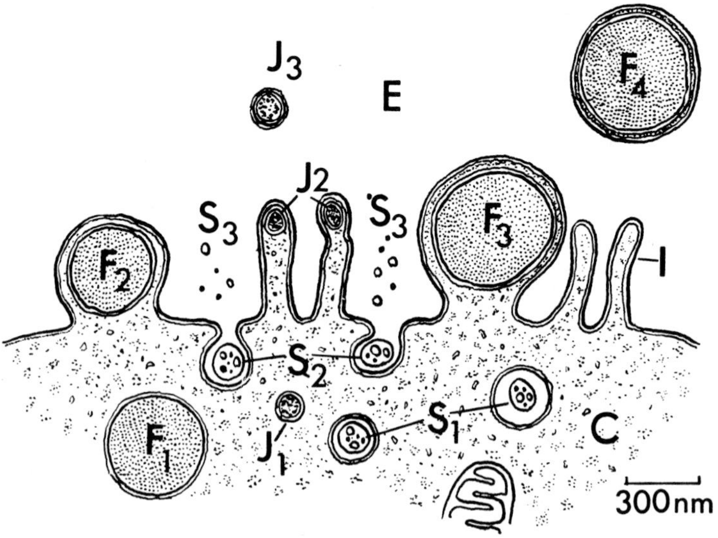
J3
E
F4
J2
S3
S3
F3
F2
I
S2
S1
F1
J1
C
300nm

Fig. 4

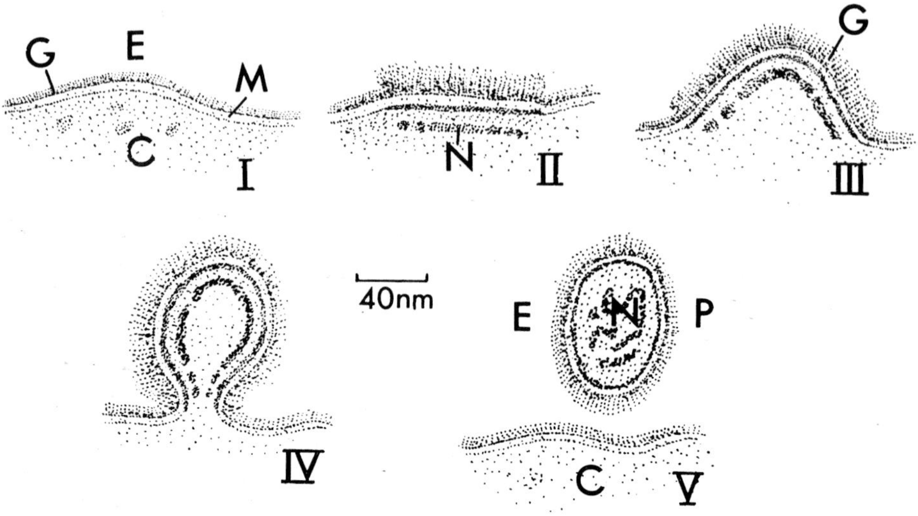
G
E
M
C
I
N
II
G
III
40nm
E
N
P
IV
C
V

Fig. 5

Fig. 4. A composite diagram of cell surface maneuvers in the apical portion of a mammary gland acinar cell, representing eccytosis in various stages of secretion of milk protein, of milk fat, and of liberation of mammary gland tumor virus. The cytoplasm (C) is represented as containing three kinds of bodies, each characterized by material of a different kind made in the cell. F shows a vesicle containing fat, destined to become cream. The vesicle is bound by endoplasmic membrane. J indicates a mammary tumor virus particle which has been synthesized in an infected cell and which is approaching the cell surface prior to liberation into the milk. S represents two membrane-bound vesicles containing casein and other protein constituents of milk. These are true protein-containing secretion granules and resemble lysosomes except that the proteins in the vesicles are not enzymatically active. I indicates two normal microvilli, such as are seen sparsely distributed on the apical surface of normal mammary gland cells.

In secretion of milk protein, the vesicles containing protein (S_1) move to the cell surface, where the membrane of each vesicle fuses and recombines with that of the cell surface to form secretory or eccytosis caveolae (S_2), whence the protein contents are liberated (S_3) into the lumen of the gland (E). This process is the same as secretion in pancreas, as shown in Fig. 3.

In secretion of milk fat, the fat droplet or vesicle (F_1) approaches the cell surface closely. The surface forms a short, broad, rounded pseudopod or projection in which the fat droplet comes to be situated (F_2). This pseudopod or projection extends further and a narrow neck forms at its base, tending to constrict the cytoplasmic connection between the pseudopod and the main body of the cell (F_3). This constriction gets narrower. Most of the cytoplasm is expressed from around the fat droplet and the base of the pseudopod. The cell membrane at its base constricts to closure like the mouth of a purse. Upon contact of apposed surfaces, membrane fusion and recombination takes place and the fat vacuole or droplet is pinched off and liberated into the extracellular lumen of the gland (F_4), surrounded completely by membrane derived from the cell surface.

The virus particles (J_1) are not found, of course, in normal cells. In infected cells they move into the tips of microvilli (J_2). After the virus particles reach these positions, the cell membrane of the microvilli constricts just under the particle (J_2, right). This constriction proceeds to contact, fusion, recombination of membrane and pinching off of the tip of the microvillus to form a vesicle or particle surrounded by membrane derived from the cell surface and containing a virus particle (J_3). Thus the liberation of mammary tumor virus particles is very similar to the secretion of the fatty portion of milk. (Drawn after Bargmann and Knoop, and Bernhard.)

Fig. 5. Diagram showing cell surface behavior occurring in the process of liberation of Sendai virus from chick embryo allantoic cells, as described by Berkaloff. Section I shows the cell surface region of an allantoic cell. The cytoplasm (C) is separated from the extracellular space (E) by the cell membrane (M), on the external surface of which is a glycocalyx (G) of modest proportions. Three dense spots in the cytoplasm under the membrane represent beginning of accumulation of viral material previously synthesized in the cell. Section II shows a later stage, when more viral material (N) has appeared. This material is exerting an influence on the cell surface constituents, which are responding by accumulating a more luxuriant display of glycocalyx and a thickening of the cytoplasmic surface of the cell membrane. In III, the cell surface changes have progressed further and the cell is forming a blunt pseudopod or microvillus, which contains some cell cytoplasm and the viral material. Section IV shows further stages, representing the blunt microvillus as now displaying a constriction at the neck. The membrane areas of the cell surface at the site of constriction are approaching each other prior to contact, fusion and recombination. V shows the situation after fusion and recombination at the constricted neck of the microvillus, leading to pinching off of the tip of the projection to form a vesicular particle (P) lying in extracellular space (E) and enclosing viral material (N). The surface coating of the particle (P) is derived from the cell surface as modified under the influence of the adjacent viral material. The cell surface is restored to a normal membrane and glycocalyx overlying the cytoplasm (C). (Drawn after Berkaloff.)

appears along the line of cleavage. This array of vesicles is often called the cell plate. The cell plate vesicles contain membrane destined to become part of the external cell membrane of the two product cells. The vesicles enlarge and become confluent as their respective membranes fuse and recombine. Final fusion with the external dividing cell membrane serves to free the two cells from each other.

Neurosecretion and the liberation of chemical mediator substance from synaptic vesicles at chemical synapses involves eccytosis (see De Robertis).

The last example to be cited here refers to the sperm cell during the process of fertilization of the ovum. Mature sperm usually possess an acrosomal vesicle, which characteristically appears as a large, flat, curved, membrane-lined cisterna filled with protein material, capping the sperm head and lying immediately under the anterior portion of the cell membrane of the sperm head. Colwin and Colwin (1961a, b, c; 1963a, b) have shown that in *Hydroides* and in *Saccoglossus* sperm, as the spermatozoan makes contact with the glycocalyx of the ovum, the anterior membrane of the acrosomal vesicle fuses with the cell membrane of the anterior tip of the sperm head in such a way as to open the vesicle to the extracellular space, forming a large transient caveola, from which the proteinaceous acrosomal vesicular contents escape into the region just in front of the head of the spermatozoan. At the same moment, the membrane formerly bounding the acrosomal vesicle, becomes a part of the external cell membrane of the spermatozoan. The area of sperm head cell membrane is considerably increased by this acquisition, whereupon one or more membrane-bounded cytoplasmic processes resembling microvilli evert anteriorly through the glycocalyx and approach the cell membrane of the ovum. Thus, penetration of the glycocalyx of the ovum by the spermatozoan is preceded by liberation of the contents of a single secretion vesicle, the acrosomal vesicle, by a process of eccytosis, the formal topology of which is identical to that displayed in secretion of pancreatic enzymes.

(b) *Encytosis*

Upon completion of the foregoing discussion of eccytosis, one is prepared to deal with the concepts of encytosis. Membrane fusions and recombinations occur in both processes. In the case of contact and fusion of plasma or cell membrane in encytosis, the surfaces coming into apposition always represent the apoplasmic, or the external or glycocalyx surfaces of the cell membrane. Intracytoplasmic membrane-bound vesicles and cisternae often pinch off and divide into two compartments by entirely analogous membrane fusion and recombination sequences. These intracytoplasmic vesicle divisions also always involve apposition prior to fusion of the apoplasmic vesicle membrane surface, which, in these cases, represents geometrically the inner surface of the membrane defining the vesicle.

Specific binding reactions at the cell surface can render encytosis highly selective. Membrane flow and vesiculation are important phenomena in encytosis. Brief attention will be devoted to characterizing these terms before proceeding further with descriptions of encytosis.

A. *Specific binding at the cell surface.* In the previous chapter, one finds several references to capacities of glycocalyx components to bind ions, molecules and particles by virtue of strong anionic groups associated with the acidic sugars found in many glycocalyces. Of course, even neutral polysaccharides, such as cellulose, are capable of binding water and other polar molecules by hydrogen bonds. However, greater versatility and selectivity can be expected from glycocalyx saccharides with substituted groupings. Sialic acid, uronic acids, hexosamines and amides and sulfate esters figure importantly amongst the carbohydrate components of glycocalyces. Variations in spacings, geometric arrangements and charge in the side chains of sugar rings can engender selective binding capacities of considerable specificity.

Molecular components which are part of the external surface of the unit cell membrane itself must also be considered as available for specific binding reactions in many cases, but these cell surface components are not as well known as are those of the glycocalyx and are somewhat less accessible to substances in the surrounding medium than are glycocalyx elements, which occupy exposed forward positions favorable for engaging and binding extracellular materials.

Current concepts of uptake of ions and of active transport invoke the idea of specific selective binding groups on the cell surface (see the chapter of this Handbook, by Professor Schoffeniels). Moreover, in encytosis, specific binding of materials to the cell surface provides for selectivity and constitutes an important part of the uptake mechanism (see Bennett 1956, 1965). Components of the glycocalyx, such as sialic acid, are candidates for consideration as important binding groups in these physiological processes.

B. *Membrane flow.* Parks, Parks and Peachey showed that it was possible to label local areas of cell surface membrane by permitting surface components of cells to bind particles which could be recognized and traced in electron micrographs. Through such methods, membrane areas labeled at one time at a certain location on the surface of the cell can be followed and found later in another location on the surface, or in association with membranes inside the cell. Movements of tracer particles bound to the surface of the cell gave rise to the realization that, in some cases, membrane flow occurred on the surfaces of cells, carrying attached or bound material with the moving membrane components (see Bennett 1956). Membrane flow is elegantly represented in the ameba during pinocytosis (see Holter 1963, 1965) when tracer particles bound to the cell surface can be seen, carried by moving membrane into and down the pinocytosis channels. Cell membrane flow often involves mechanisms whereby the membrane is removed from the cell surface in one place and added to it at another. The pinching off and moving away of membrane vesicles from the recesses of pinocytosis channels is a process which creates membrane sinks. Turnover and flow of membrane during pinocytosis suggests that the ameba has mechanisms for feeding membrane material into the cell membrane at other sites, thus providing membrane sources. Marshall and Nachmias have studied the turnover rate of ameba membrane components and have found that the turnover is considerably more rapid in an ameba active in pinocytosis than in an ameba at rest. They postulate that new membrane material is fed into the cell surface directly from the underlying ground cytoplasm.

C. *Vesiculation.* The term 'membrane vesiculation' has been used to apply to the process whereby an indentation of the cell surface or some other tube-like or cave-like membrane structure (a caveola) pinches off by membrane fusion and recombination in such a way as to produce one or more balloon-like, fully enclosed membrane-bounded sacs or vesicles or 'vacuoles', as in encytosis (see Figs. 6–9). Familiar examples are known in the pinching off of recesses of caveolae in pinocytosis and phagocytosis. Less well known examples are described in the process of transfer of protein products of cell synthesis from the cisternae of the endoplasmic reticulum to the Golgi membrane system (see Jamieson and Palade). However, these do not involve the cell surface directly and hence will not be dealt with further in this chapter. The pinching off of viruses from tips of microvilli, or of fat droplets in milk secretion (see Fig. 4), as in eccytosis, also involves membrane fusion and recombination and can be called 'vesiculation', but in these cases, the 'vesicle' so formed contains cytoplasmic matrix derivatives and is extracellular. It is covered by membrane derived from the cell surface.

D. *Phagocytosis and pinocytosis.* Pinocytosis and phagocytosis are selective, energy-consuming, physiological processes which involve uptake of material by the cell from the surrounding medium, utilizing the capacities of the cell surface for specific binding, membrane flow, configurational change, caveola formation, membrane fusion, recombination and vesiculation. They are special examples of encytosis. Although many variants of the basic process have been recognized, the essential topology of membrane configurational sequences is the same in all cases, so that one is justified in considering the two phenomena together. Karnovsky has reviewed many features of the process.

Phagocytosis was described by Metchnikoff in 1882 (see Hirsch 1965a, b). Pinocytosis was discovered by Lewis in 1931 and extended to the ameba by Mast and Doyle in 1934. Originally, phagocytosis was envisioned as the uptake of particles by cells, whereas pinocytosis was defined as the uptake of fluid.

Pinocytosis and phagocytosis were both originally described on the basis of light microscope observations. When particles resolvable with the light microscope were seen to enter the cell, the term phagocytosis was applied. When the process observed showed no detectable particulate component, the phenomenon was called pinocytosis and the impression was reflected that the cell was then taking up fluid, or 'drinking'. Later, with the electron microscope, particles such as protein molecules, which were not resolvable with the light microscope, could be observed entering cells in pinocytosis. Moreover, it came to be realized that one can assign no sharp boundary between 'particulate' and 'non-particulate' uptake, as all matter is particulate; indeed, water and sugar molecules, simple ions and proteins of solution can all be regarded as particulate in nature. Moreover, the mechanisms involved in the two processes proved to be identical. Thus, the original distinction attributed to pinocytosis and phagocytosis was seen to derive from the limits of resolving power of the light microscope and to have no physiological importance.

Since the work of Palade (1953, 1956), Parks and Peachey, Parks, and Odor, it has been evident that many kinds of cells can take up material into the cytoplasm, the uptake being associated with membrane movements. These observations led Bennett (1956) to formulate an hypothesis which proposed that material to be taken up by such membrane movements is first bound to the cell surface, after which the area of membrane carrying the bound material flows and invaginates to form a caveola, which is then pinched off to form an intracytoplasmic vesicle (see Figs. 6–9). These vesicles move to other parts of the cell and can fuse with other vesicles of similar or different character, or with another portion of the cell membrane itself. Under some circumstances, the membrane of a vesicle in the cytoplasm can be disassembled by the cell and caused to disappear, perhaps by enzymatic action, so that the contents of the vesicle come to lie in the cytoplasmic matrix (see Fig. 9).

In later studies, Chapman-Andresen, Marshall and Nachmias, Brandt and Pappas (1960, 1962) and Brandt demonstrated that these concepts pertain to the process of pinocytosis in ameba, whereas the work of Goodman and Moore, Goodman, Moore and Baker and Zucker-Franklin and Hirsch (for reviews see Hirsch 1965a, b) showed that essentially the same cell surface phenomena are obtained in phagocytosis.

Lewis' original studies of pinocytosis used the light microscope and a time-lapse cinema camera for recording surface and internal membrane movements of cells in tissue culture chambers. This type of study has been repeated many times. Films so taken, when projected so as to display the process in a compressed time scale, often show vigorous movements of the cell surface, sometimes spoken of as 'undulating membranes'. This phenomenon has been interpreted as representing a rapid formation and withdrawal of surface cytoplasmic folds or pseudopodia. Fawcett has attempted to correlate such surface movements with configurations seen in electron micrographs and has stressed that in these circumstances, folds of cell surface material appear to extend out, to bend over and to fuse with nearby areas of membrane. It can be seen from Fig. 6 that surface movements of this type form caveolae between the folds, giving rise to vesicles upon membrane fusion, recombination and pinching off. The caveola and vesicle, in this case, form in a projection or pseudopod extending from the cell surface. Fawcett also speaks of the fluid trapped in the vesicle formed in the caveolar recess. Trapping of fluid alone does not provide a mechanism for selectivity of uptake. Specific binding to surface components which become segregated in a vesicle does provide for such selectivity. The smaller the vesicle, the greater is the surface volume ratio and the greater can be the selective influence of cell surface binding groups.

It has recently been recognized that some cells have the capacity to modulate, or to modify, the chemical groupings on their surfaces in response to the appearance of certain substances in the nearby extracellular medium. This can be regarded as an adaptive mechanism permitting a cell to extend its versatility and its capacity to take up materials of value to survival of the species. Schumaker has published evidence that the capacity of the ameba cell surface to bind and to take up protein can be increased in response to the varying concentrations of protein in the surrounding medium. In the ameba, these changes in binding capacity appear not to be localized, but to be distributed widely over the surface of the cell. In some other cells, localized modulations of the binding capacity of the cell surface have been recognized. An example can be seen on the cell surface of an erythroblast in mammalian bone marrow, which is usually portrayed in electron micrographs as lacking any very striking specializations. However, Fawcett has shown that these cells, when taking up molecules of the protein, ferritin, display localized specializations of the cell surface. These areas are seen as patches perhaps 200 nm in diameter, scattered here and there over the surface of the cell and distinguished by special development (hypertrophy) of the glycocalyx and accumulation of submembranal cytoplasmic material of unknown nature, lying just under and close to the cytoplasmic surface of the cell membrane in these areas (see Fig. 7). The glycocalyx fringe in such a localized

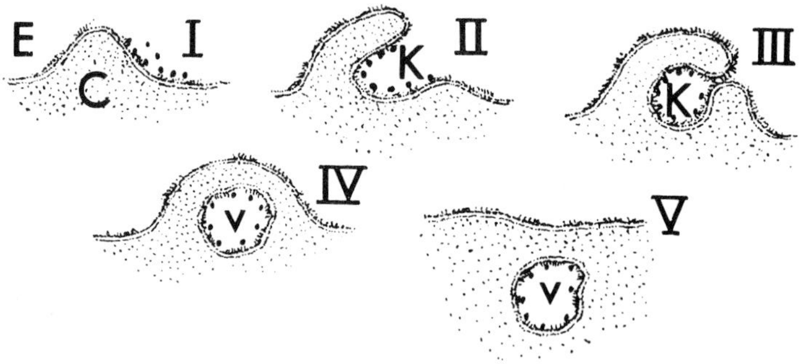

Fig. 6. A series showing cell surface configurations in 5 stages of encytosis (pinocytosis) of material in a caveola formed by a projecting cell fold such as appears to characterize the 'undulating membrane' of certain cells active in pinocytosis. The cytoplasm (C) is separated from the extracellular space (E) by a cell membrane adorned on its external surface by a delicate glycocalyx. In section I, the diagram represents several protein molecules which have been selectively bound to the external surface of the cell. The cell is envisioned as sensing the changed bonding configurations occasioned by the binding of the protein molecules and as responding to this signal by sending out a cytoplasmic fold. The bound protein molecules can be regarded as labels marking this area of cell surface. In section II, more protein molecules have been bound, the fold has grown more prominent and is bending over to form a recess or caveola (K). In section III, the cytoplasmic fold is shown as approaching a smaller apposing fold so as nearly to isolate the caveola (K) from the extracellular space. The protein molecules are represented as selectively bound to the portion of cell surface enclosed in the caveola. In IV, the two folds of cytoplasm have fused and membrane areas have recombined so as to isolate the former caveola as a vesicle (V), carrying the bound molecules and entrapped fluid and lying in a small cytoplasmic projection or pseudopod. In V, the vesicle is shown as having moved deeper into the cytoplasm, carrying the protein molecules, which mark the membrane of the vesicle as representing an area which once was on the cell surface. (Drawn after Fawcett.)

and specialized area binds ferritin and concentrates many molecules of this protein in close association with this patch of cell surface. The patch of specialized membrane then invaginates to form a caveola, which pinches off to form a vesicle enclosing a large number of protein molecules bound to the enclosed glycocalyx. The vesicle so formed, in instances of this sort, after taking its place in the cytoplasm, is surrounded on the outside by the juxtamembranal cytoplasmic material mentioned above. These accumulations, together with the exaggerated internal glycocalyx, endow the vesicles formed with a shaggy appearance which has led them to be spoken of as 'coated vesicles' (see Porter et al.; Roth and Porter).

Coated vesicles, then, represent a group in a larger class of vesicles forming in encytosis, wherein the vesicle membrane is adorned with special components derived from localized specializations of the cell surface which serve functions in selective binding and vesiculation. They reflect the capacity of some cells to modify the molecular architecture of certain parts of their surfaces in such a way as to adapt those areas for specific binding and for uptake of bound material by encytosis. This capacity makes for economy in the utilization of chemicals important in the binding and uptake processes. Anderson has described 'coated vesicles' as functioning in the uptake by encytosis of yolk protein material by oocytes, and Slautterback has noted coated vesicles in encytosis processes occurring in Hydra. However, in many cells, encytosis occurs without any localized morphological specializations of the

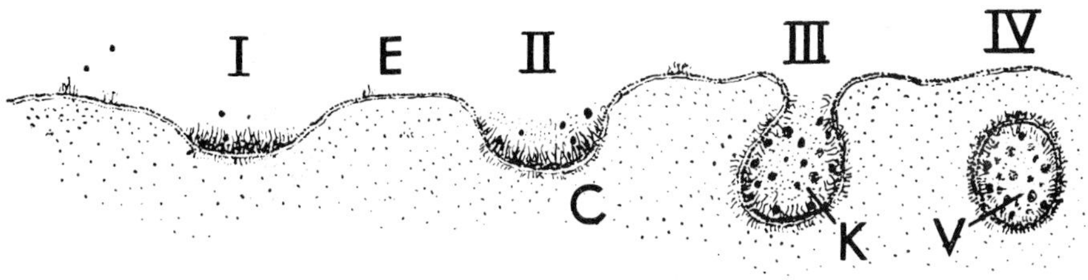

Fig. 7. Cell surface configurations in encytosis (pinocytosis) characterized by a 'coated vesicle' as seen in a mammalian bone marrow erythroblast. The stippled cytoplasm (C) of the cell is separated from the extracellular space (E) by a cell membrane which shows irregular patches of tenuous glycocalyx. Black dots in the extracellular space to the left represent ferritin molecules. At section I, the cell presents a localized and transient modification of the cell surface characterized by a special luxuriance of glycocalyx, thickened membrane and special densities in the cytoplasm immediately under the membrane. The glycocalyx is binding ferritin molecules and the cell surface is beginning to indent. In section II, one sees a further development of the glycocalyx. More ferritin has been bound to it and the invagination is deeper. In III, one sees that the process has progressed to form a well-developed caveola containing much glycocalyx material, in which many ferritin molecules are entrapped. Section IV represents a 'coated vesicle' formed by pinching off the caveola shown in III, by membrane fusion and recombination of cell surface components at the orifice of the caveola. An 'external' or cytoplasmic coating of the vesicle is represented by a radial stippling outside the vesicle membrane. However, one can think of the vesicle as having an internal coating as well, comprised of glycocalyx material carrying the enclosed and bound ferritin particles. (Drawn after Fawcett.)

membrane, other than those implicated in the binding and in the configurational maneuvers themselves.

The behavior of the cell surface in phagocytosis was first studied by Goodman and Moore and has been clarified greatly by further work of Hirsch (1965a, b) and his associates and by Marshall and Nachmias. The essential features are exemplified in Fig. 8, which is derived largely from the work of Hirsch and which represents encytosis of bacteria by a leucocyte.

It seems probable that many types of phagocytic cells can home in on bacteria or other similar prospective prey by moving up a concentration gradient of soluble, diffusible substances liberated by the bacteria. This process, known as chemotaxis, implies an interaction between components on the cell surface and the soluble substances inducing the response. Interactions of this type increase the probability of contact between phagocytic cell surface and the body producing the soluble extracellular substance.

As the cell approaches the particle to be taken in, contact is made between the glycocalyx of the cell and the surface of the particle. If the particle is a bacterium, its surface will present itself as the cell wall or glycocalyx of the bacterial cell. Bennett's (1956) hypothesis holds that if, upon contact, the chemical groupings of the surface

---

Fig. 8. Cell surface behavior in encytosis (phagocytosis) of bacteria by a leucocyte. In section I, a leucocyte is approaching two bacteria (P), probably moving up a concentration gradient of substances liberated by them. The leucocyte is represented as possessing a glycocalyx (G) on its outer surface. The cytoplasm (C) contains many lysosomes (S), which represent the 'specific granules' of the leucocyte. Each lysosome is a membrane-bound vesicle which contains hydrolytic enzymes and zymogens synthesized by the cell. In II, the cell has made contact with one of the bacteria, which has been bound to components of the cell surface. Section VIII represents hypothetical features of the contact between bacterium and cell surface. The glycocalyx (cell wall) of the bacterium is shown as engaged with and bound to the glycocalyx of the leucocyte. In III, the leucocyte is represented as having responded to the bound bacterial particle by invagination, forming a caveola (K) in which the bacterium is embedded. One of the lysosomes (S) is shown as having just fused with the caveola so as to discharge its enzymatically active contents into the caveola. In IV, the cell has made contact with and bound the second bacterial particle and has nearly completed the engulfment of the first one. Several lysosomes, or granules, are discharged into the larger caveola, the lips of which are approaching each other prior to membrane fusion and recombination. V represents the cell after completion of vesiculation of the first caveola and beginning of formation of the second. The bacterium in the vesicle is shown as degraded somewhat after enzymatic attack from the contents of many lysosomes which have emptied into the vesicle. In VI, engulfment of the second bacterial particle is also complete. The cell now contains two phagosomes (V), which are vesicles formed by encytosis containing phagocytosed material. In VII, the second phagosome is beginning to receive the contents of lysosomes, whereas the first phagosome vesicle is now mature, is receiving no more enzymes and contains the residues of the bacterium in advanced stages of digestion. The number of lysosomes (S) remaining in the cell is reduced. The leucocyte is partially degranulated. (Drawn from Hirsch 1965a, b.)

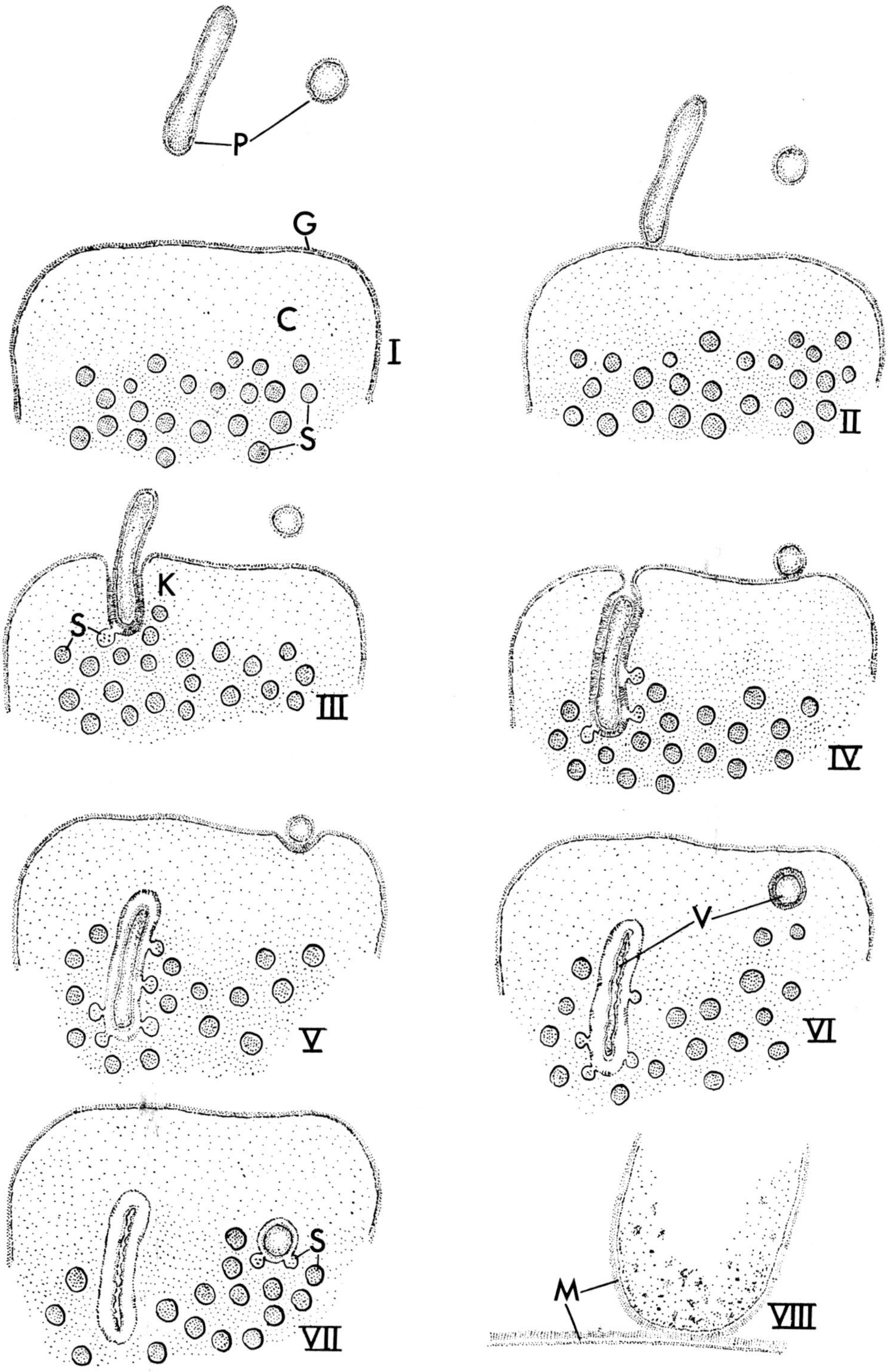

Fig. 8

molecules of cell and particle are such as to form a complementary bonding between cell and particle of sufficient strength, encytosis can proceed. If the particle is not bound to the cell surface upon contact, it is soon separated from the cell and is not taken up by it. Thus, the differing appetites of differing phagocytic cells can be explained in part, at least, in terms of variations in their respective cell surfaces.

After a particle (such as the bacterium represented in Fig. 8) has become engaged with the surface of the phagocytic cell, the changed chemical configurations at the cell surface represent information to which the cell responds by invaginating the area of membrane to which the particle is bound, forming a caveola enveloping the particle. Often more than one particle, even a large number of them, may be captured and enfolded in a single caveola. The caveola then pinches off, detaches from the cell surface and takes a position in the cytoplasm.

Many types of cells synthesize hydrolytic enzymes of various kinds and package the enzymes or their precursors in membrane-bound vesicles termed 'lysosomes' by De Duve. The so-called 'specific granules' of vertebrate eosinophilic and heterophilic (neutrophilic) leucocytes belong to this class of organelles. Cohn and Hirsch, and Archer and Hirsch have isolated the 'granules' or 'lysosomes' of eosinophils and heterophils of rabbits and other mammals and find that they are membrane-bound packets containing various proteases, nucleases, amylases, phosphatases, esterases and other hydrolases. Similar 'granules' or lysosomes are present in macrophages, amebae and many other types of phagocytic cells. These lysosomes enter into important relation with the cell surface and its derivatives during phagocytosis. In many respects, these lysosomes resemble the 'secretion granules' of pancreatic acinar cells, described earlier in this chapter (see Fig. 3).

Zucker-Franklin and Hirsch have shown that, when polymorphonuclear leucocytes are taking up bacteria or yeast cells, after a caveola of sufficient depth has formed, lysosomes move to the caveolar membrane. The membranes of lysosome and caveola then fuse and recombine in such a way as to liberate the contents of the lysosome into the caveola, where the enzymes so liberated have access to the bacteria or other particles in the pocket (see Fig. 8). Hirsch's (1962) elegant motion pictures show invagination proceeding to vesiculation as lysosome after lysosome fuses with the membrane enclosing the material undergoing encytosis. Fusion of lysosomes with enveloping membrane also occurs after the caveola has pinched off and has formed a vesicle. Such a vesicle, containing particulate material taken in by encytosis, is often termed a 'phagosome'. If the cell is heavily engaged in encytosis and takes in a sufficient number of caveolae and vesicles, the entire stock of lysosomes in the cell may be expended through the process of fusion with caveolar or vesicular membranes. Such a cell is said to be completely 'degranulated', and the process of expending lysosomes in phagocytosis has been called 'degranulation' (see Hirsch and Cohn). The degranulation of leucocytes, then, is now recognized as a process in which membrane material derived from lysosomes is combined with the cell surface membrane of caveolae, or with the membranes of phagosomic vesicles, which are, on their part, derived from the cell surface. In this process, enzymes are placed in contact with the contents of the caveolae or vesicle whilst the surrounding membranes confine the enzymes and protect the cytoplasmic matrix of the cell.

E. *Uptake of viruses.* Some further properties of the cell surface are manifested in the encytosis of certain viruses by animal cells. The essential features have been observed and diagrammed by Dales and are recapitulated in Fig. 9. These uptake mechanisms, however, are by no means confined to the encytosis of viruses, but have been noted in the uptake of ferritin and other tracers by many types of cells. It must also be recognized that all viruses do not interact with cells as outlined here. For example, the bacterial T-4 viruses attach themselves to the cell surface of bacteria and introduce their DNA into the cell without entering the cell otherwise. But in the examples cited by Dales, the virions are bound to the surface of the cells and taken in by encytosis, often several virus particles entering in a single caveola. Characteristically, several vesicles containing viruses then fuse in the cytoplasm, so that phagosomes or vesicles are formed which contain material taken in by two or more caveolae.

A similar capacity to assemble and concentrate in one vesicle material taken up by many caveolae is widespread in many types of cells. For example, Hampton showed that rat hepatocytes and Kuppfer cells take up thorium dioxide by encytosis in many caveolae and vesicles and then concentrate the colloidal material in a relatively small number of phagosomes formed by fusion of many vesicles containing the colloidal material.

The contents of such accumulation vesicles may, of course, be subjected to the action of any enzymes which may be present or introduced into the vesicle lumen. In the example of the adenovirus discussed by Dales, the virus preserves its morphological aspect in the vesicles. However, Silverstein and Dales have shown that when reovirus L-strain is taken up by animal cells, the virus particles are partially degraded in the vesicles, but the nucleic acid of that virus remains intact.

As a further stage in the process under discussion, the membrane of a vesicle containing material taken up by encytosis may, under some conditions, be disassembled entirely and disappear so that the contents of the original vesicle come to lie in the cytoplasmic matrix. In the case of the adenovirus 7, Dales has shown the virions in the matrix of HeLa cells after dissolution of the membrane in which the viruses had previously been enfolded. In the cases of the reovirus, which is destroyed in the phagosome except for its nucleic acid, the nucleic acid makes its presence felt genetically in the cell, thus demonstrating that it has taken a position in the nucleoplasm, which is in continuity with the cytoplasmic matrix. As another example, Bessis and Breton-Gorius (1957, 1959) have shown that ferritin taken into a cell by encytosis appears in the cytoplasmic matrix after dissolution of the membrane in which the protein molecules were formerly engulfed.

The sequence of events reviewed above is summarized and diagrammed in Fig. 9. It exemplifies some interesting and important properties of the cell surface. When encytosis is followed by dissolution of the membrane of the vesicle containing the engulfed material, the contents of the vesicle, which once lay outside the cell, are now found in the cytoplasmic matrix after the disappearance of the vesicle membrane. By this process, material, whatever its particulate dimensions, if capable of engulfment by encytosis, can be transferred from extracellular space on one side of the cell membrane to the cytoplasmic matrix on the opposite side of the membrane, without, in a sense, ever going through the membrane and without the formation or existence of any pore or discontinuity of the cell surface for the admission of the material. At no moment in the process is the integrity of the cell membrane compromised or its effectiveness as an ionic barrier impaired. Since material in accumulations of arbitrary size can enter cells by this process without going through a pore in the cell membrane, it follows that, in general, one cannot safely use the dimensions of a particle, molecule or ion entering a cell as a measure of sizes of hypothetical pores thought to or assumed to exist or to form in the cell membrane.

F. *Cell fusion.* The fusion of separate cells into one is an event which can be regarded as a special example of encytosis. Examples of cell fusion which are well documented include the joining of mononucleate myoblasts to form multinucleate

---

Fig. 9. Cell surface maneuvers taking place when encytosis is characterized by fusion of several encytosis vesicles and by dissolution of membrane of encytosis vesicle. This process is commonly encountered when viruses or certain proteins are taken up by cells. Section I represents a cell which has already engulfed one particle (P), which is enclosed in a vesicle in the cytoplasm. Two other particles are shown in an encytosis caveola in the process of engulfment and three more particles are shown in extracellular space (E) near the cell. In II, the encytosis of two particles has advanced so that the caveola (K) is about to pinch off and become a vesicle. The cell is beginning to engage the three particles which remain outside. Section III shows the formation of the second vesicle as complete and represents the first and second vesicles, containing one and two particles, respectively, as fusing to form a single accumulation vesicle with three particles. Meanwhile, the encytosis of the other three particles has progressed to caveola formation. IV shows the cell after the vesiculation of the caveola in III is complete. The vesicle containing the last three particles taken up is shown as fusing with the other vesicle containing three particles. V shows a single combined accumulation encytosis vesicle containing all six particles, situated in the cytoplasm (C) of the cell. In some cases not represented here, the cell adds enzymes to the contents of such a vesicle by fusion with lysosomes. Some viruses may thus be digested except for their nucleic acids. VI shows the membrane of the vesicle undergoing dissolution so that the former lumen of the vesicle is merging with the cytoplasm. VII shows the situation after complete dissolution of the encytosis vesicle membrane. The particles now lie in the cytoplasmic matrix of the cell. In cases where virus particles have been destroyed enzymatically in vesicles except for the nucleic acid, the viral nucleic acid can gain access to the cytoplasmic matrix and hence to the cell genome and the synthetic machinery of the cell by this process (see Silverstein and Dales). Alternatively, virus particles are sometimes disassembled in the cytoplasmic matrix as in VII and the viral nucleic acids are then made accessible to cell components. Comparing section I with section VIII, one sees that the particles have moved from extracellular space (E), on side of the cell membrane, to cytoplasmic matrix (C) on the other side of the cell membrane, without going through any pore in the membrane, and, in a sense, without having gone through the cell membrane at any time. (Drawn after Dales.)

muscle fibers (see Okazaki and Holtzer; Bischoff and Holtzer), and the fusion of cytotrophoblastic cells to form the syncytial trophoblast in some mammalian placentas (see Midgley et al.). Colwin and Colwin (1961c, 1963a, b) have reported that penetration of *Hydroides* and *Saccoglossus* egg by sperm involves a fusion of cell membrane of ovum to that of the sperm, so that the cytoplasm of the two cells becomes confluent. In cell fusion, the apposition, fusion and recombination of membrane involves surface areas from two separate and distinct cells, but the behavior of the

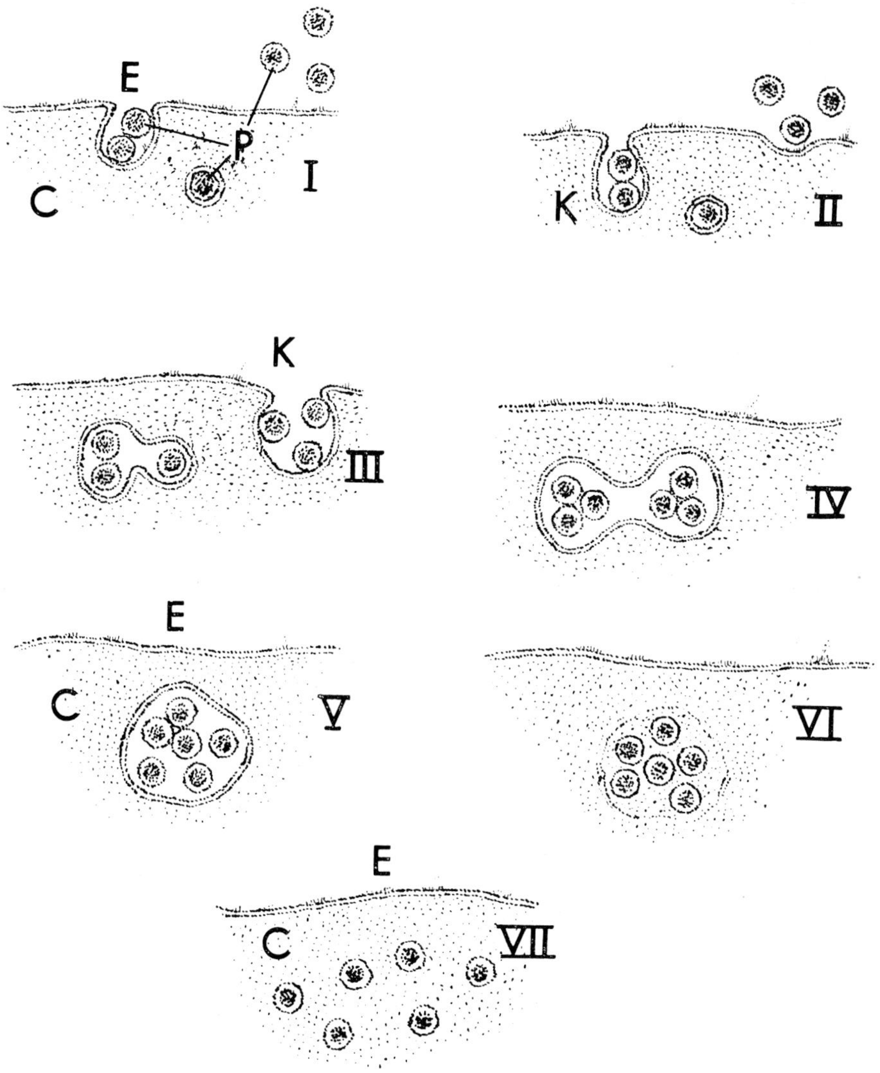

Fig. 9

membranes is not different in principle from that which is seen when two areas of membrane of the same cell fuse and recombine in phagocytosis.

In an earlier passage on eccytosis, it was pointed out that some viruses are enveloped in membrane derived from the cell surface as they are liberated from cells. When such viruses are to be taken up later by susceptible cells, it is necessary only that the membrane surrounding the virus particle and that of the cell surface fuse and recombine, whereupon the virus will be found in the cytoplasmic matrix of the susceptible cell, which will have acquired a small area of membrane from the virus, which in turn, appropriated it from the cell from which it was liberated. This provides a mechanism whereby viruses can transport cell surface material from one cell to another. The liberation of the virus represents a form of eccytosis, but uptake by this mechanism is a manifestation of encytosis.

(c) *Transport in bulk*

Encytosis and eccytosis provide mechanisms whereby material in large aggregates, embracing a few or many thousands or millions of molecules or ions, can traverse the cell surface from one side of the cell membrane to the other without going through any pore. The processes can fulfill all the requirements for active transport as set forth by Rosenberg or by Lefevre. The processes are specific and selective; they involve the utilization of energy and they do not depend primarily on diffusion or on simple charge relationships. By eccytosis and encytosis, chemical material can be accumulated in a cell or discharged from it against a concentration gradient or a chemical potential. In order to distinguish transport of material by encytosis or eccytosis from other forms of active transport, Palade (1956) has proposed that the former be spoken of as transport 'in bulk'. Karnovsky and Sbarra report that 1 to 2×10^{-15} moles of high energy phosphate are required for the engulfment of a polystyrene sphere 1.171 μm in diameter, by a polymorphonuclear leucocyte of a guinea pig. This is equivalent to the transmembranal transport of about 10^{-21} g of polystyrene per ATP molecule hydrolyzed to ADP. This mass is close to that of about 15 potassium ions, or about 26 sodium ions, or about 10 coupled pairs of sodium and potassium ions. According to Skou, about 3 Na^+ ions and less than 3 (perhaps 2) K^+ ions are transported per ATP molecule hydrolyzed in active transport of rhese ions. Thus, on the basis of mass moved per ATP hydrolyzed, uptake of polystyrene particles in bulk by encytosis appears to be about three times as efficient as coupled active transport of sodium and potassium. This speaks for the metabolic efficiency of encytosis and for the advantages of translocating materials in large bulk packages.

Acknowledgment

The author wishes to acknowledge with thanks a grant from the Sprague Foundation, which made possible the preparation of this and the previous chapter on the cell surface.

References

ANDERSON, E.: Oocyte differentiation and vitellogenesis in the roach *Periplaneta americana*. J. Cell Biol. 20 (1964) 131.

ANÉ, C.: Étude au microscope électronique de la morphogenèse d'un *Myxovirus parainfluenzae 3.* J. Microscopie 6 (1967) 31.

ARCHER, G.T. and J.G.HIRSCH: Isolation of granules from eosinophil leucocytes and study of their enzyme content. J. Exptl. Med. 118 (1963) 277.

BARGMANN, W. and A.KNOOP: Über die Morphologie der Milchsekretion. Licht- und electronenmikroskopische Studien an der Milchdrüse der Ratte. Z. Zellforsch. mikrosk. Anat. 49 (1959) 344.

BENNETT, H.S.: The concepts of membrane flow and membrane vesiculation as mechanisms for active transport and ion pumping. J. Biophys. Biochem. Cytol. Suppl. 2 (1956) 99.

BENNETT, H.S.: Moving membranes as related to cell permeability and active transport. In: S.Seno and E.V.Cowdry, eds.: Intracellular membraneous structure. Proc. 1st Intern. Symp. Cellular Chem. Okayama, Japan, Japan Society for Cell Biology, The Chugoku Press, Ltd. (1965) p. 529.

BERKALOFF, A.: Étude au microscope électronique de la morphogenèse de la particule du virus Sendai. J. Microscopie 2 (1963) 633.

BERNHARD, W.: The detection and study of tumor viruses with the electron microscope. Cancer Res. 20 (1960) 712.

BESSIS, M.C. and J.BRETON-GORIUS: Iron particles in normal erythroblasts and normal and pathological erythrocytes. J. Biophys. Biochem. Cytol. 3 (1957) 503.

BESSIS, M.C. and J.BRETON-GORIUS: Ferritin and ferruginous micelles in normal erythroblasts and hypochromic hypersideremic anemias. Blood 14 (1959) 423.

BISCHOFF, R. and H.HOLTZER: The effect of mitotic inhibitors on myogenesis *in vitro*. J. Cell Biol. 36 (1968) 111.

BRANDT, P.W.: A consideration of the extraneous coats of the plasma membrane. Circulation 26 (1962) 1075.

BRANDT, P.W. and G.D.PAPPAS: An electron microscopic study of pinocytosis in ameba I. The surface attachment phase. J. Biophys. Biochem. Cytol. 8 (1960) 675.

BRANDT, P.W. and G.D.PAPPAS: An electron microscopic study of pinocytosis in ameba II. The cytoplasmic uptake phase. J. Cell Biol. 15 (1962) 55.

BRUNS, R.R. and G.E.PALADE: Studies on blood capillaries I. General organization of blood capillaries in muscle. J. Cell Biol. 37 (1968) 244.

CHAPMAN-ANDRESEN, C.: Studies on pinocytosis in amoebae. Compt. Rend. Trav. Lab. Carlsberg 33 (1962) 73.

COHN, Z.A. and J.G.HIRSCH: The isolation and properties of the specific cytoplasmic granules of rabbit polymorphonuclear leucocytes. J. Exptl. Med. 112 (1960) 983.

COLWIN, A.L. and L.H.COLWIN: Fine structure of the spermatozoon of *Hydroides hexagonus* (Annelida), with special reference to the acrosomal region. J. Biophys. Biochem. Cytol. 10 (1961a) 211.

COLWIN, L.H. and A.L.COLWIN: Changes in the spermatozoon during fertilization in *Hydroides hexagonus* (Annelida) I. Passage of the acrosomal region through the vitelline membrane. J. Biophys. Biochem. Cytol. 10 (1961b) 231.

COLWIN, A.L. and L.H.COLWIN: Changes in the spermatozoon during fertilization in *Hydroides hexagonus* (Annelida) II. Incorporation with the egg. J. Biophys. Biochem. Cytol. 10 (1961c) 255.

COLWIN, A.L. and L.H.COLWIN: Role of the gamete membranes in fertilization in *Saccoglossus kowalevskii* (Enteropneusta) I. The acrosomal region and its changes in early stages of fertilization. J. Cell Biol. 19 (1963a) 477.

COLWIN, L.H. and A.L.COLWIN: Role of the gamete membranes in fertilization in *Saccoglossus kowalevskii* (Enteropneusta) II. Zygote formation by gamete membrane fusion. J. Cell Biol. 19 (1963b) 501.

DALES, S.: An electron microscope study of the early association between two mammalian viruses and their hosts. J. Cell Biol. 13 (1962) 303.

DE DUVE, C.: The separation and characterization of subcellular particles. Harvey Lectures Ser. 59 (1965) 49.

DE ROBERTIS, E.: Histophysiology of synapses and neurosecretion. Oxford, Pergamon Press (1964).

FAWCETT, D.W.: Surface specializations of absorbing cells. J. Histochem. Cytochem. 13 (1965) 75.

GOODMAN, J.R. and R.E.MOORE: Electron microscopic study of phagocytosis of *Staphylococcus* by human leukocytes. J. Bacteriol. 71 (1956) 547.

GOODMAN, J.R., R.E.MOORE and R.F.BAKER: Electron microscopic study of phagocytosis of *Staphylococcus* by human leucocytes II. Virulent and non-virulent *Staphylococci*. J. Bacteriol. 72 (1956) 736.

HAMPTON, J.C.: An electron microscope study of the hepatic uptake and excretion of submicroscopic particles injected into the blood stream and into the bile duct. Acta Anat. 32 (1958) 262.

HIRSCH, J.G. and Z.A.COHN: Degranulation of polymorphonuclear leucocytes following phagocytosis of microorganisms. J. Exptl. Med. 112 (1960) 1005.

HIRSCH, J.G.: Cinemicrophotographic observations on granule lysis in polymorphonuclear leucocytes during phagocytosis. J. Exptl. Med. 116 (1962) 827.

HIRSCH, J.G.: Phagocytosis. Ann. Rev. Microbiol. 19 (1965a) 339.

HIRSCH, J.G.: Neutrophil and eosinophil leucocytes. In: B.W.Zweifach, L.Grant and R.T.McClus-key, eds.: The inflammatory process. New York and London, Academic Press (1965b) 245.

HOLTER, H.: Pinocytosis. Proc. 5th Intern. Congr. Biochem. II. Oxford, Pergamon Press (1963) p. 248.

HOLTER, H.: Membrane in correlation with pinocytosis. In: S.Seno and E.V.Cowdry, eds.: Intracellular membraneous structure. Proc. 1st Intern. Symp. Cellular Chem. Okayama, Japan, Japan Society for Cell Biology, The Chugoku Press, Ltd. (1965) p. 451.

ICHIKAWA, A.: Fine structural changes in response to hormonal stimulation of the perfused canine pancreas. J. Cell Biol. 24 (1965) 369.

JAMIESON, J.D. and G.E.PALADE: Role of the Golgi complex in the intracellular transport of secretory proteins. Proc. Natl. Acad. Sci. 55 (1966) 424.

KARNOVSKY, M.L. and A.J.SBARRA: Metabolic changes accompanying the ingestion of particulate matter by cells. Am. J. Clin. Nutr. 8 (1960) 147.

KARNOVSKY, M.L.: Metabolic basis of phagocytic activity. Physiol. Rev. 42 (1962) 143.

LEFEVRE, P.G.: Active transport through animal cell membranes. In: L.V.Heilbrunn and F.Weber, eds.: Protoplasmatologia, Handbuch der Protoplasmaforschung, Bd. 8, 7a. Wien, Springer (1955) p. 1.

LEWIS, W.H.: Pinocytosis. Bull. Johns Hopkins Hosp. 49 (1931) 17.

MARSHALL, J.M. and V.T.NACHMIAS: Cell surface and pinocytosis. J. Histochem. Cytochem. 13 (1965) 92.

MAST, S.O. and W.L.DOYLE: Ingestion of fluid by amoeba. Protoplasma 20 (1934) 555.

MIDGLEY, A.R., JR., G.B.PIERCE, JR., G.A.DENEAU and J.R.G.GOSLING: Morphogenesis of syncytiotrophoblast *in vivo*: an autoradiographic demonstration. Science 141 (1963) 349.

NAKAO, K. and A.A.ANGRIST: Membrane surface specialization of blood platelet and megakaryocyte. Nature 217 (1968) 960.

ODOR, D.L.: Uptake and transfer of particulate matter from the peritoneal cavity of the rat. J. Biophys. Biochem. Cytol. Suppl. 2 (1956) 105.

OKAZAKI, K. and H.HOLTZER: Myogenesis: fusion, myosin synthesis and the mitotic cycle. Proc. Natl. Acad. Sci. 56 (1966) 1484.

PALADE, G.E.: Fine structure of blood capillaries. J. Appl. Phys. 24 (1953) 1424.

PALADE, G.E.: The endoplasmic reticulum. J. Biophys. Biochem. Cytol. Suppl. 2 (1956) 85.

PARKS, H.F. and L.D. PEACHEY: Morphological observations on cytoplasmic inclusions of phagocytosed submicroscopic particles in Kupffer cells of mice. Anat. Record 121 (1955) 348.

PARKS, H.F.: A morphological study of phagocytosis by endothelial phagocytes lining the hepatic sinusoids of the mouse. Anat. Record 125 (1956) 1.

PORTER, K.R., K. KENYON and S. BADENHAUSEN: Specializations of the unit membrane. Protoplasma 63 (1967) 262.

ROSENBERG, T.: On accumulation and active transport in biological systems I. Thermodynamic considerations. Acta Chem. Scand. 2 (1948) 14.

ROTH, T.F. and K.R. PORTER: Yolk protein uptake in the oocyte of the mosquito *Aedes aegypti L.* J. Cell Biol. 20 (1964) 313.

SCHUMAKER, V.N.: Uptake of protein from solution by *Amoeba proteus*. Exptl. Cell Res. 15 (1958) 314.

SIEKEVITZ, P. and G.E. PALADE: A cytochemical study on the pancreas of the guinea pig VI. Release of enzymes and ribonucleic acid from ribonuclear protein particles. J. Biophys. Biochem. Cytol. 7 (1960) 631.

SILVERSTEIN, S.C. and S. DALES: The penetration of reovirus RNA and initiation of its genetic function in L-strain fibroblasts. J. Cell Biol. 36 (1968) 197.

SIMPSON, C.F. and J.M. KLING: The mechanism of denucleation in circulating erythroblasts. J. Cell Biol. 35 (1967) 237.

SKOU, J.C.: Enzymatic basis for active transport of Na^+ and K^+ across cell membrane. Physiol. Rev. 45 (1965) 596.

SKUTELSKY, E. and D. DANON: An electron microscopic study of nuclear elimination from the late erythroblast. J. Cell Biol. 33 (1967) 625.

SLAUTTERBACK, D.B.: Coated vesicles in absorptive cells of *Hydra*. J. Cell Sci. 2 (1967) 563.

YAMADA, E.: The fine structure of the megakaryocyte in the mouse spleen. Acta Anat. 29 (1957) 267.

ZUCKER-FRANKLIN, D. and J.G. HIRSCH: Electron microscope studies on the degranulation of rabbit peritoneal leucocytes during phagocytosis. J. Exptl. Med. 120 (1964) 569.

CHAPTER 49

Uptake mechanism of the cell, active transport

E. SCHOFFENIELS

Department of Biochemistry, University of Liège, Belgium

Contents

1. Introduction
2. Active transport and its definitions
   (a) The classical thermodynamic approach
   (b) Biochemical aspects of the problem
3. Energy sources in active transport mechanisms
   (a) Role of ATP
   (b) Identification of a 'specific' enzyme system hydrolysing ATP
4. Mechanisms of membrane permeation
   (a) Carrier-mediated transfer
   (b) Transfer of macromolecules
5. The case of calcium ions
6. Conclusions

1. Introduction

Living organisms consist of ordered molecular structures constituting integrated and spatially organised metabolic networks. Thus, in biology, exchanges across boundaries are of the utmost importance and it is difficult to study any biological function without encountering a problem of permeability. However, different investigators may have very different theoretical and methodological approaches to such concepts as 'membrane', 'barrier' and even to cell structure.

The purpose of this chapter is to help to define the various processes by means of which substances may cross cellular membranes. Too little is known about the chemical nature and physical structure of those molecules responsible for the permeability characteristics of biological structures to allow a thorough analysis of the phenomena. Therefore the greatest caution should be exercised in order to avoid producing too narrow a definition of any particular process. On the other hand, too wide a definition might place together phenomena that may prove on further analysis to be unrelated.

The most reasonable attitude seems to decipher first the *permeability characteristics* of a living membrane, i.e. to look for what can pass through and what can not. The second step is to define the nature of the *force* responsible for the movements observed. Finally one should try to unravel the *mechanism* that explains the passage of the chemical through the membrane.

Thus instead of presenting a comprehensive survey of the literature dealing with cell permeation processes, the emphasis will be placed on the definition of operational concepts that may help to suggest new experiments aimed at the unravelling of one of the most intriguing properties of living matter.

2. Active transport and its definition

It is well known that the composition of a living cell is very different from that of its surrounding medium. In a pluricellular aquatic animal it is also known that the extracellular 'milieu intérieur' can differ in composition from the external medium. These differences have been variously interpreted and many hypotheses have been produced. On purely theoretical grounds it is evident that, by its very nature, life in all its manifestations is a reflection of a continuous exchange of matter between an organism and its surroundings. Thus the cellular membrane or at least some parts of it must be 'permeable' to various constituents of the extracellular medium. This enables us to discard any hypothesis which explains the difference in composition between a cell and its surroundings by assuming complete impermeability of the barrier limiting the cell. Isotopic studies have substantiated this conclusion by showing the generality of the principle of dynamic equilibrium at every level of cellular organization – including the atoms in molecular structures.

The one point on which everyone agrees is that the unequal distribution of ions and molecules between a cell and its surroundings is the result of complex phenomena of influx and efflux of matter. These influxes and effluxes of matter take place at various sites in the organism at the level of structures having well-defined properties and are often associated with an expenditure of metabolic energy.

However, where mechanisms of such phenomena are concerned, there are conflicting views in the literature of the last decade and these can be grouped into two main categories. The majority of research workers consider that a special structure surrounding the cell, called the 'cellular membrane', is the site of the various mechanisms which enable the cell to keep its content in the particular state observed. The opponents of this view assume that if such a thing as a membrane exists, it has no particular function, the unequal distribution of ions and molecules depends on the very special properties exhibited by macromolecules in the intracellular phase.

Physical measurements carried out on isolated cells are best interpreted if one postulates the existence of a barrier, having special properties and surrounding the cell. Electrical measurements of resistance, impedance, capacitance, potential difference, as well as surface tension and kinetic studies show that the cell interior is separated from the extracellular fluid by a barrier exhibiting a higher resistance to the movement of water, ions and molecules, than the intra- and extracellular fluids. Electrical properties of nerve indicate also that we are dealing with a structure formed by a low resistance central core surrounded by a component behaving like a poorly isolated capacitor. Arguments, stemming from recent progress in light as well as in electron microscopy, are also in favour of the existence of a clearly differentiated morphological entity at the cell surface. The problem, and it is an important one, is, however, to know if the functional barrier is related to what we see on the electron micrograph.

Despite the fact that in most studies dealing with cellular exchanges or uptake of matter by cells, the cell interior is assumed to be a homogeneous solution, it should be recognized that this is a comfortable fiction bearing no resemblance to reality. Interactions with subcellular structures as well as intracellular organelles may prove to be essential in interpreting the data. As shown below, this seems particularly true when dealing with organic ions or molecules.

The thermodynamical activity of most of the ions or molecules constituting the intracellular phase is unknown, thus leaving much doubt as to the correctness of the generally accepted assumption that the activity coefficient of many intracellular chemicals is very close to one. This last remark does not apply when dealing with exchanges between two extracellular components which are separated by a cellular layer.

(a) *The classical thermodynamic approach*

Thanks to the work of Ussing (1950) and Teorell, the concept of active transport has received a very precise meaning and this should be applied whenever possible instead of using vaguer terms such as absorption uptake or secretion. The definition rests on the thermodynamical analysis of transepithelial exchanges. Although classical thermodynamics are not of much help in elucidating the mechanism of transport, it remains, however, certain that they can give an answer as to the nature of the force responsible for the movement of matter under study.

In the actual state of our knowledge we should carefully avoid the application of the definition of active transport, given below, to any translocation of a chemical group or radical from a donor to an acceptor. More appropriately, we should consider some of the relationships established between an organism and its surroundings. For instance, how does a frog, sitting in tap water, keep its interior of different composition from the outside medium? More specifically, what is the nature of the force or forces responsible for the unequal distribution of, say, sodium and chloride ions? These problems can be discussed by considering the exchange across the skin.

In an appropriate experiment the abdominal skin of a frog is dissected and mounted as a diaphragm between two chambers. The outside of the skin, i.e. its epithelial side is bathed with a solution containing 11.5 mEq Na per liter, while the inside of the skin is bathed with ordinary frog Ringer, containing 115 mEq Na per liter. The behaviour of sodium ions may be analysed by using ^{22}Na and ^{24}Na as tracers, thus making it possible to determine influx and outflux simultaneously.

TABLE 1

The influence of 2,4-dinitrophenol (DNP) on influx (M_{in}) and outflux (M_{out}) of Na through the frog skin. Skin is bathed with ringer on the inside and ringer diluted tenfold on the outside (Schoffeniels 1955).

	1	2	3	4	5
	M_{in}	M_{out}	E(mV)	M_{in}/M_{out} Found	M_{in}/M_{out} Calc.
Control	0.34	0.093	62	3.66	0.011
DNP	0.25	1.57	−11	0.16	0.07
Control	0.445	0.145	82	3.07	0.005
DNP	0.049	0.56	−6	0.087	0.08
Control	0.228	0.008	72	28.5	0.007
DNP	0.032	0.216	−7	0.148	0.08

Table 1 shows some of the results obtained. In the controls, the electrical potential difference is rather high, the inside solution being positive with respect to the outside. The electrochemical potential for Na in the inside solution (i) is thus higher than in the outside solution (o). Nevertheless the influx of Na is always greater than the outflux, indicating a net movement of Na against the electrochemical gradient: this is a clear-cut case of active transport of an ionic species. It is thus clear that this endergonic process must be coupled to an exergonic reaction.

In the presence of 2,4-dinitrophenol (DNP), which uncouples the phosphorylation of the respiratory chain, the behaviour of Na is different, and the outflux is greater than the influx. Therefore when the metabolic integrity of the epithelium is impaired, the net flux of Na occurs along the electrochemical gradient.

Analysing the results quantitatively, we may say that the behaviour of an ion moving in the thermodynamically natural direction, is described by the following relation:

$$\ln \frac{M_{in}}{M_{out}} = \ln \frac{a_o}{a_i} - \frac{zFE}{RT} \tag{1}$$

where M_{in} is the influx, M_{out} the outflux, a_o the activity of the ion in the outside solution, a_i the activity in the inside solution, E the potential difference between the solutions i and o, z the valence of the ion, F the number of Faraday, R the gas constant, T the absolute temperature.

Applying equation (1) to the results given in Table 1, one obtains the figures given in column 5. In the controls the flux ratios found experimentally are very different from those calculated according to equation (1). In the presence of DNP, it can be seen that there is a rather good correlation between the values of the flux ratios found as compared to those calculated. The behaviour of Na is that predicted by the equation, indicating that under these conditions Na ions move according to the electrochemical gradient.

In another experiment first described by Ussing and Zerahn, identical solutions bathe the two sides of the isolated frog skin. By means of an outside electromotive force, the spontaneous potential developed by the skin is opposed, and may be set at any value. When the external battery is adjusted to just nullify the spontaneous potential difference, the skin is said to be 'short-circuited'.

In the above experiment, there is no electrochemical gradient across the preparation, therefore according to equation (1) any ion moving across the preparation in the thermodynamically natural direction will do so at equal rates in both directions.

TABLE 2

Fluxes of sodium and chloride ions measured across the isolated frog skin. Comparison with the 'short-circuit' current values. (After Koefoed-Johnsen et al.) Fluxes and current expressed in μA cm^{-2} hr^{-1}.Δ_{Na} = net sodium flux. Δ_{Cl} = net chloride flux.

Influx		Outflux				
Na	Cl	Na	Cl	Δ_{Na}	Δ_{Cl}	Current
19.3		0.9		18.4		20.2
11.8		3.3		8.5		9.5
	16.9		14.9		−2.0	45
	6.7		6.1		−0.6	57

This is obviously the case for the chloride ions as shown by the results in Table 2. However, as expected from the results shown in Table 1, there is a net flux of Na directed inwards. As first demonstrated by Ussing and Zerahn with the frog skin, the 'short-circuit' current is equal in magnitude to the net flux of Na moving inwards (Table 2). This relation also holds good with other preparations and more particularly with the toad bladder (Frazier and Leaf) or the nasal epithelium (Table 3).

TABLE 3

Comparison of net sodium flux and 'short-circuit' current through isolated pig nasal mucosa. (After Melon and Schoffeniels 1964; Schoffeniels 1967.)

No. of periods	Duration of period (min)	Mean Na influx	Mean Na outflux ($mC\ cm^{-2}\ hr^{-1}$)	Mean Na transported	Mean short-circuit current
9	60	482.01	54.04	427.97	431.22

In certain circumstances the short-circuit current may be either greater or smaller than the net flux of Na, and this suggests that other ionic species can be involved in the process under investigation. For instance, it has been shown that in frog skin under the influence of adrenaline, an extra source of electric current, amounting to up to 90 per cent of the Na current, arises.

The determination, with the aid of ^{36}Cl and ^{38}Cl, of influx and outflux of chloride ions, indicates that the nonsodium current, evoked by adrenaline stimulation of the skin, is due to active transport of chloride ions in the outward direction (Koefoed-Johnsen et al.).

With other preparations studied under normal conditions, the relation found in the isolated frog skin between net sodium flux and short-circuit current does not apply. This is observed with the isolated intestinal epithelium of the tortoise (Baillien and Schoffeniels 1961b) and with the skin of a South American species of frog, *Leptodactylus ocelatus* (Zadunaisky and Canolia).

During the last few years, it has been shown that when an unequal distribution of ions is observed between two liquid phases separated by an epithelium this is due to an active transport of one or more of the ionic species involved. Thus active transport mechanisms have been demonstrated to be operative in various tissues such as gastric mucosa, rumen, gall bladder, salivary glands, cornea and the nasal salt glands of birds and reptiles. Details may be found in recently published reviews (Andersen and Ussing 1960; Hogben; Hokin and Hokin; Schmidt-Nielsen et al.; Schoffeniels 1960, 1967; Ussing 1960).

In summary, it is evident that the behavior of sodium and chloride ions in the isolated frog skin, as described above, shows that we are dealing with two different phenomena. In the case of sodium ions the net flux which is observed results in an increase in the electrochemical potential of sodium in one of the compartments of the system. Thus, at least part of the influx of sodium ions must be coupled to an exergonic reaction. On the contrary, when dealing with chloride ions, the net flux is directed down the electrochemical gradient. Therefore it seems reasonable, as proposed by Ussing, to confine the definition of active transport to the situation found in the case of the sodium ions.

(b) *Biochemical aspects of the problem*

When dealing with the transepithelial flux of inorganic ions, it is an easy matter to define the nature of the force responsible for the observed displacement. In the case of an organic ion or molecule the problem is more complex. The molecule under study may be engaged in various metabolic sequences in addition to the undergoing transport, and thus equation (1) is deprived of all its usefulness. The study of the flux of amino acids across the cell membrane is a good case in point.

The dependence of amino-acid transport on other metabolic events has been demonstrated and also competition for transport between various amino acids has been observed. This suggests that there is a common step involved in the uptake mechanism for amino acids. Competition studies have revealed the existence of several specific sites that control the entrance into the cell of various classes of amino acids (Wiseman; Christensen and Riggs; Birt and Hird; Wilson). These studies have also shown that one generally deals with a saturation phenomenon obeying the Michaelis-Menten kinetics.

Each of the above sets of data is, however, of little value in establishing the nature of the force involved, and often one has to rely on various lines of evidence to show that the uptake is indeed active. When dealing with accumulation, in a transcellular, but extracellular compartment the nature of the forces responsible can be, at least superficially, more readily defined. Various techniques have been proposed, the most generally used being those of the everted segments of small intestine (Wilson and Wiseman) the vascularized intestinal loop *in vivo*, and the Thiry-Vella fistulas (Clarke et al.).

A technique introduced more recently (Baillien and Schoffeniels 1961a, b) meets most of the requirements necessary to ascertain unequivocally the nature of the forces responsible for the movement of an ion or molecule across the intestine epithelium. A segment of intestine is opened flat and the epithelium is gently stripped off the muscle layers. The epithelium is then inserted between two pools of fluid. Any transfer of material from one chamber to the other is made through the epithelium. The potential difference arising between the two solutions is measured while two agar bridges inserted at the end of the chambers and connected to a battery and a variable resistor make possible the passage of an electric current through the preparation, in such a way that the potential difference existing across the epithelium is abolished. At the end of an experiment the epithelium may be subjected to various biochemical analyses. The results observed are solely attributable to the activity of the epithelial cells since the muscle fibres have been stripped off.

With the isolated intestinal epithelium of the tortoise *Testudo hermanni* G. F. Gmelin, we have shown that in the case of glycine and L-alanine the influx values are of an order of magnitude higher than those of the outflux in the small intestine. In the colon the flux values in each direction are very similar and always smaller than the values found with the small intestine.

In the case of L-alanine, the influx across the small intestine is 1.3 μM cm^{-2} hr^{-1} while the outflux is 0.1 μM cm^{-2} hr^{-1}. By applying equation (1) to these results one comes to the conclusion that glycine and alanine are actively transported across the epithelium of the small intestine. On the other hand glycine moves passively across the colon.

With glutamate, in the colon as well as in the small intestine, the flux ratio is very close to 1 thus suggesting a passive behaviour for this amino acid. It may also be demonstrated that L-glutamate and L-arginine are without effect on the influx of glycine across the small intestine and the colon. On the contrary L-alanine reduces the influx of glycine across the small intestine. This result is interpreted as showing that a common step is involved in the transfer of L-alanine and glycine (Baillien and Schoffeniels 1961a).

The transepithelial electrical potential difference recorded at the level of the small intestine of many species is always very small, around 0.5 to 4 mV, the lumen being negative with respect to the serosal side (Baillien and Schoffeniels 1961b). If glucose, certain amino acids, or fatty acids are added to the physiological saline, one observes an increase in potential difference (Baillien and Schoffeniels 1962; Schoffeniels 1964, 1967).

The same result is observed with other amino acids or sugars such as glycine, L-serine or glucose. But L-glutamic acid, L-arginine and L-lysine are without effect.

The short-circuit current is also affected by these amino acids. However, in the case of L-glutamic acid, although the potential difference is never affected, the short-circuit current always goes up.

By means of microelectrodes, it is possible to determine the potential profile of the intestinal epithelium. Also by this method it is possible to locate the site(s) at which the potential profile is changed under the influence of an added amino acid or sugar. As shown in Table 4 the transepithelial potential (PD) is the algebraic sum of two

TABLE 4

Action of L-alanine and D-glucose on the electrical potential. Profile recorded in the isolated small intestine of the Greek tortoise. (After Gilles-Baillien and Schoffeniels 1965.)

L-alanine (mM/l)	PD	PD_M	PD_S	D-glucose (mM/l)	PD	PD_M	PD_S
0	3	20	23	0	2	19	21
5	13	20	33	5	8	19	27.5
20	12.5	20	33	20	7	19	25

potentials in series, the transserosal (PD_S) and the transmucosal (PD_M) potentials, opposite in sign and of different magnitude. After addition of various amounts of L-alanine or D-glucose, to the solution bathing the mucosal surface of an isolated small intestine of the Greek tortoise, it can be seen that the overall potential difference increases. This increase in potential difference is attributable solely to an increase in the transserosal potential.

In the case of L-glutamate or L-aspartate (Table 5) both transserosal and transmucosal potential increase. This explains the lack of effect observed when recording the transepithelial potential only. Dr. Gilles-Baillien and I have shown that when glutamate is added to the solution bathing the mucosal side of an isolated intestinal epithelium, L-alanine appears in the serosal fluid together with traces of unidentified amino acids. This clearly indicates that glutamate is metabolized within the cells giving rise to products that are precursors of L-alanine. Our experiments carried out *in vitro* confirm the results obtained *in vivo* on the small intestine of the dog (Neame and Wiseman).

TABLE 5

Action of L-glutamate and L-aspartate on the electrical potential profile recorded in the isolated small intestine of the tortoise (Gilles-Baillien and Schoffeniels 1968). The potentials are given in mV and the sign refers to the extracellular fluid.

L-glutamate (mM/l)	PD	PD_M	PD_S	L-aspartate	PD	PD_M	PD_S
0	2	10	12	0	0.5	10.5	11
20	2	18	20	20	1	15	16

Now, if one adds to the mucosal solution bathing a fragment of intestinal epithelium, an amino acid which is transported actively (alanine for instance), an analysis of the intracellular pool of free amino acids shows that most of the amino acids have a concentration either equal to or slightly lower than that of a control to which no alanine was added. However, the added amino acid has a higher intracellular concentration in the 'experimental' epithelium than in the 'control' but has the same concentration in the intracellular fluid as in the mucosal solution (Table 6).

When radioactive alanine is used, the results show also that amongst the different amino acids, only radioactive L-alanine appears in measurable amounts in the intracellular fluid (at least with the sensitivity of our technique). The specific activity of the intracellular L-alanine is the same in both mucosal saline and intracellular fluid (Table 7). Some radioactivity appears in the serosal solution and the results obtained show that 80% of this radioactivity belongs to L-alanine while 20% belongs to other substances (e.g. other amino acids in low concentrations or one or more substances

TABLE 6

Composition of the intracellular pool of free amino acids in the intestinal epithelium of the greek tortoise. Three hours incubation in saline containing 20 μM/ml of L-alanine. Results expressed as μM/ml of intracellular water (Schoffeniels 1967).

Amino acid	Control	20 μM/ml Ala
Tau	21.493	22.722
Asp	1.881	1.143
Thr	1.659	0.716
Ser	6.734	3.440
Glu	1.362	1.634
Pro	1.534	0.903
Gly	4.556	2.313
Ala	3.021	22.636
Cys	—	—
Val	0.890	0.427
Met	—	—
Ileu	0.516	0.331
Leu	0.669	0.748
Tyr	tr	tr
Phe	tr	tr
Lys	2.129	1.351
His	0.595	0.331
Arg	0.321	0.192

TABLE 7

Isolated intestinal epithelium of the tortoise. Specific activity of L-alanine (after Gilles-Baillien and Schoffeniels 1966). The values given have been divided by 10^4.

	Na in mucosal saline μM/ml	Mucosal saline	Intracellular fluid	Serosal saline
Exp. I	115	6.6	7.1	2.9
	11.5	6.6	6.2	3.5
Exp. II	115	3.9	4.0	2.0
Exp. III	115	4.0	4.3	2.0

which are not amino acids). Another important observation is that the specific activity of L-alanine in the serosal saline appears to be nearly half that measured in the intracellular fluid and mucosal saline (Table 7).

When the sodium concentration in the mucosal fluid was reduced tenfold, the following results were found:

(1) The intracellular concentration of L-alanine is approximately the same as that measured when ordinary saline is used on the mucosal side.

(2) In addition to radioactive L-alanine, two other radioactive substances appear in the intracellular fluid: taurine and ethionine sulfoxide. But specific activity of alanine in the intracellular fluid still has the same value as in mucosal saline (Table 7, exp. I).

(3) The amount of L-alanine crossing the serosal barrier is smaller than that found when the usual Na concentration (115 μM/ml) is present in mucosal saline. However the specific activity in the serosal saline is still nearly half that in the intracellular fluid (Table 7, exp. I).

From the above results we may conclude:

(a) L-alanine enters the cell passively at the mucosal border, as the cellular concentration is in equilibrium with that in the mucosal saline. NaCl concentration in the mucosal saline does not seem to affect this penetration.

(b) In the intracellular fluid, L-alanine is partly metabolized and the metabolic pathways followed are influenced by the mucosal NaCl concentration. Taurine and ethionine sulfoxide are among the products of the metabolic sequence(s).

(c) The active transport mechanism for alanine is localized at the serosal border as indicated by the change in permeability and the electrical characteristics of the serosal border.

(d) The serosal border is the site of L-alanine synthesis, since radioactive L-alanine appearing in the serosal saline is diluted by non-radioactive L-alanine. This mechanism must be located very near the serosal border of in the membrane itself, because the specific activity of L-alanine in the intracellular fluid is equal to that in the mucosal saline.

An interesting speculation stems from the results presented, and this is that the active transport of L-alanine could be in close connection with the synthesis of this amino acid. This view is supported by our observation that the addition of pyruvate and NH_4Cl in the mucosal saline results in an increase in the transserosal potential (as recorded with an intracellular microelectrode) identical to that obtained with L-alanine. Furthermore, L-alanine appears in the serosal saline. Experiments using doubly labelled alanine (^{14}C and ^{15}N) should allow us to evaluate the contribution of the biosynthesis of L-alanine to the transserosal transfer process. The present results demand caution in interpreting the transcellular fluxes of molecules that can be subjected to metabolic transformation. Thus the concept of active transport, as we have defined it above, could not be applied to characterize the transcellular flux of alanine if the results of further investigations were to demonstrate that the transserosal flux is solely attributable to a synthetic mechanism. On the other hand if this synthetic mechanism were responsible for only a part of the observed flux, a measurement of radioactivity alone would still lead to an erroneous estimate of the exact quantities of alanine subjected to active transport.

Finally, the results may also mean that there is more than one pool of alanine inside the cell and that each separate pool has a different turnover rate.

As shown by the results in Table 4, as soon as alanine is added, there is an increase in electrical potential across the serosal border. The question we need to ask is therefore: what is responsible for this potential change?

The results of Schultz and Zalusky on sodium flux measurements are not convincing. They interpreted their results as indicating a direct relation between potential change and Na net flux (see also Bihler et al.). We have been unable to confirm this finding in the tortoise intestine where we found an important effect of alanine on the chloride fluxes (Gilles-Baillien and Schoffeniels 1967). Our results are best interpreted by assuming that at the serosal border the passive permeability to potassium ions increases (Gilles-Baillien and Schoffeniels 1967a).

To conclude, it is most probable that the alanine appearing in the serosal fluid results partly from a biosynthesis taking place at, or very near, the serosal border of the cell. This mechanism has none of the characteristics of active transport. Thus the greatest caution has to be exercised when attempting to define the nature of the force responsible for the movement of any molecule that may enter metabolic pathways in the cell.

3. *Energy sources in active transport mechanisms*

(a) *Role of ATP*

Since we have defined active transport as a mechanism requiring an expenditure of energy, it is obvious that it must be coupled to an exergonic reaction in order to comply with the second law of thermodynamics.

The first question thus arising is: what is the nature of the free energy source utilized in the active transport? As the active transport of cations has been so far the most thoroughly investigated in this respect, let us analyse some results obtained with various cells.

When searching for the possible metabolic pathways which could provide energy for the transport mechanism, many investigators have looked either for inhibitors of transport or for substrates which could be utilized by a cell engaged in the transport process. However, these approaches do not seem to be very promising, as it may be expected that any agent which interferes with the metabolism of the cell would affect the transport mechanism.

A more direct approach which has been proposed is to consider the possible source of chemical energy available in the cell for the active transport. ATP, by analogy with its role on other systems requiring energy, is considered to be the most probable source. Experimental attempts to demonstrate a direct participation of ATP, by using 2,4-dinitrophenol (Fuhrman; Schoffeniels 1955 and Table 1; Hodgkin and Keynes 1955a, b) were not convincing, in view of the uncertainty as to the specific inhibition produced by this compound. Another indirect argument, favouring ATP as the sole donor of energy in active transport, is the persistence of active transport under anaerobic conditions, for instance in duck red cells (Tosteson and Robertson), seminal vesicle mucosa (Breuer and Whittam; Whittam and Breuer), frog skin (Leaf and Renshaw 1957a, b) and Ehrlich ascites tumour cells (Maizels et al.).

Direct evidence that ATP is involved in the active transport of cations in erythrocytes has been provided by the work of various authors. ATP was introduced into red cell ghosts by lysing the cells in diluted ATP solutions (Gardós) and the 'ghosts' were then shown to accumulate K. This early experiment was extended by Hoffman who was able to demonstrate the active transport of Na by ghosts containing ATP. An interesting finding is that ITP (inosine triphosphate) could not replace ATP.

Other findings, implicating ATP as the energy source for the active transport mechanism, were performed on the squid giant axon (Caldwell 1956, 1960; Caldwell et al. 1959, 1960). The results demonstrate that, in the absence of metabolically produced ATP, the active transport of cations is abolished and can be restored by an artificial introduction of ATP into the system.

It is true that most tissues require oxygen for their active transport mechanism. This fact has led to the so-called oxido-reduction hypothesis of active transport which was first introduced by Lund (1928a,c) to explain bioelectric potentials. The basic assumption was that a spatially organized oxidation-reduction chain transfers an electron to a site in the cell where it is finally accepted by oxygen.

This hypothesis has a quantitative limitation open to experimental verification. Four electrons are required for each molecule of oxygen utilized by the oxidation-reduction chain. Thus, in turn, four or fewer univalent ions must be transported in the reaction for every molecule of oxygen utilised.

From the results obtained with the frog skin, it appears that, on a molar basis, the net oxygen consumption amounts to about 20 per cent of the Na transported. Thus only 1 equivalent of oxygen is consumed for each 4 to 5 equivalents of Na transported. A figure of 4 equivalents of Na has been found for the toad bladder by Leaf et al.

Thus these results are inconsistent with the simple redox theory, while they are easily explained by postulating the utilization of an energy source such as ATP. They do not exclude however the possibility of a coupling between a redox system and the hydrolysis of ATP.

(b) *Identification of a 'specific' enzyme system hydrolysing ATP*

An important link in the active transport of cations must be an enzyme or an enzyme system able to hydrolyse ATP. In 1957 Skou reported results showing that in crab nerve there exists an enzyme system (located in submicroscopic particles) that hydrolyses ATP to ADP and Pi and that the activity is dependent on a combined effect of Mg, Na and K.

From analysis of the results obtained by varying the Na and K concentrations, it has been suggested that the hydrolytic activity depends on Na being present at one site and K at another site of the enzyme system (Whittam 1962a, b; Glynn 1962). In intact membranes, ATP and Na react from inside the cell.

The results of experiments using ^{32}P-labelled ATP suggest that an intermediate step in the hydrolysis of ATP is the formation of a phosphorylated compound. The formation of this compound is probably due to a transfer of an 'energy-rich bond' from ATP (Skou 1960; Post and Rosenthal; Judah et al.; Charnock and Post). The reaction requires Na, but not K, and is inhibited by Ca (Järnefelt; Ahmed and Judah 1964; Epstein and Whittam; Wins and Schoffeniels 1965).

The hydrolysis of the phosphorylated intermediate necessitates the presence of K on the outside of the cell (Whittam 1962a, b; Post et al. 1965) but Rb, Cs and NH_4^+ are good substitutes for this cation. Thus the behaviour of the enzyme system depends not only upon the concentration of substrates and cofactors but also upon the side of the cell membrane from which these are presented. This 'sidedness' is one of the main requirements expected from an active transport system.

Since the publication of the observations made by Skou, many papers have been published describing the presence, in different tissues, of an enzyme (or enzyme system) requiring Na, K and Mg ions for full activity (see Skou 1965; Schoffeniels 1967 for a survey of the pertinent literature).

In all the tissues studied, the enzyme systems have the main characteristics identified by Skou in the crab nerve. There are, however, some differences in the *p*H optima, and the affinities for Na and K.

The active transport of cations is inhibited by low concentrations of cardiac glycosides, as shown, for the first time, by Schatzmann (1953) in red cell. This observation has been extended to other cells in which an active transport of cations has been demonstrated: red cells (Glynn 1957; Kahn and Acheson; Solomon et al.; Gill and Solomon), frog skin (Koefoed-Johnsen) and nerve (Caldwell and Keynes). An interesting observation is that the compound acts only when applied from the outside of the cell, a fact that has to be related to the results showing that cardiac glycosides inhibit the activity of the 'specific' ATPase by competing with K in the hydrolysis of the phosphorylated intermediate (Post et al. 1960; Dunham and Glynn). This has been found for enzyme systems isolated from many tissues.

Bonting and Caravaggio tried to make a direct estimate of the amount of Na transported per ATP consumed by measuring, in various biological membranes, the ATPase activity that requires Na and K for full activity. They have expressed their results in terms of the unit surface of the membrane, and have related their findings to the cation flux values determined by other authors or by themselves on the same preparation (see also Bonting et al. 1963). The values found indicate that 8 to 10 Na ions are transported per 3 molecules of ATP hydrolysed, i.e. roughly 3 Na per hydrolytic cycle. This is a value that has also been proposed on the basis of oxygen consumption measurements.

In rat brain, studies of the kinetics of activation of the ATPase by Na and K have shown that one is dealing with Michaelis-Menten kinetics of the first order for K and of the second order for Na, thus indicating that 2 Na and 1 K are involved per hydrolytic cycle (Ahmed et al.; Green and Taylor; Squires).

4. *Mechanisms of membrane permeation*

As mentioned earlier in the text, the forces that may be involved to explain the displacement of matter across a membrane are the electrochemical gradient, the direct coupling of the transfer process to an exergonic reaction and a biosynthetic sequence.

Another force has sometimes been proposed as being able to promote the flux of an ion or a molecule; this is the so-called drag effect (Andersen and Ussing 1957). If an osmotic gradient is established across a membrane, there is a net flux of water down the activity gradient. Two experimental approaches have been used to estimate the magnitude of the permeability coefficient. In one case a unidirectional flux is measured using labeled water while in another case, the net flux of water arising under the influence of an osmotic gradient is measured by considering the volume change. The two methods have been applied not only to the study of transcellular fluxes but also in the case of the plasma membrane of various unicellular materials.

Whatever the case considered, the results have shown that the permeability coefficient calculated from the isotopic flux is at least an order of magnitude smaller than that estimated by measuring the change in volume. This is also found with artificial membranes (Mauro; Robbins and Mauro). The discrepancy is explained by assuming the existence of a porous membrane. This implies, among other things, that the water phase is continuous throughout the membrane and that small enough particles would cross the membrane according to the law of diffusion (as deduced from Fick's law). However, where a difference in hydrostatic (or osmotic) pressure was present across the membrane, water would flow through the pores of the membrane, dragging with it the particles in solution. This rather naive assumption has led many authors to calculate not only the radius of the pores but also their spacing.

More recently it has been suggested that if the isotopic flux of water appears to be smaller than the flux calculated from a volume change measurement, this is due to the existence of a poorly stirred layer of water on either side of the cellular membrane. A stagnant layer obviously does not disturb appreciably the results obtained when measuring an osmotic flow (Dainty) but has a profound influence on the tracer results (Hanai et al.).

In the case of a transfer down the (electro)chemical gradient, the question of the mechanism explaining the passage through the membrane is important. Are we dealing with a phenomenon related to a true diffusion process? The fact that the kinetics of the process are, in some cases, linear over a wide range of concentration, has led some authors to the conclusion that one is dealing with diffusion. One should however bear in mind that the possibility still exists that one is dealing with a system having a low affinity for the substrate or with concentrations still far from the saturation (Wilbrandt and Rosenberg).

In many instances the results obtained with animal cells or microorganisms are indicative of some sort of interaction of the permeating substance with some membrane component (see also Chappell and Haarhoff).

(a) *Carrier-mediated transfer*

The alternative to the theory of the porous membrane is that the particles crossing the membrane do so by interacting with a membrane component. Therefore, according to the chemical nature of the permeant, the interaction may vary from long range (Van der Waal's forces) down to short range (covalent bonding). If this involves a tight coupling, to the breaking of a 'high energy' bond then the process can be defined as an active transport process. In the case of a transfer down an (electro)chemical gradient, one deals with what has generally been called a carrier mediated process. Whether the carrier is mobile or not is still a matter of speculation since no experimental data have been produced to sustain any one of the many possibilities. Whatever the intimate mechanism is, the 'carrier' is not supposed to undergo any chemical alteration and the transfer across the membrane is driven solely by the concentration gradient of the substance being transported. This type of mechanism is often invoked to explain the downhill transport of various organic ions or molecules and it has been the subject of thorough investigations which have been reviewed by Wilbrandt and Rosenberg and by LeFevre (1961, 1962, 1966).

The concept of *exchange diffusion* which was created to explain part of the isotopic flux of sodium in the frog sartorius muscle (Levi and Ussing) also implies formation of a complex with a membrane component. In this biological preparation the outflux of sodium, i.e. the flux directed against the electro-chemical gradient, is much too high to be driven by the total energy that could be derived from the metabolism of the cell. However, a portion of the outflux is directly related to the concentration of the ion in the solution *towards which* the flux is directed.

In this process there is no net exchange of ions between the cell and its surroundings. The membrane component that complexes with the ion discharges that ion into one phase, and then takes up from that phase another ion of the same species. This exchange-diffusion type of mechanism has been experimentally observed for sugar transfer reactions (Park et al.; Rosenberg and Wilbrandt), amino acids (Winter and Christensen; Heinz; Heinz and Walsh) and for those of inorganic ions (Mitchell 1954).

In the case of the active transport, much work has been devoted to the study of the specific ATPase, and its possible identity with the molecular architecture responsible for the metabolically driven transfer of cations. The properties described above and more specifically those with directionality have been taken by some authors to indicate that the active sites of the ATPase are closely related, if not identical, with the specific centers of the 'carrier' molecule.

(b) *Transfer of macromolecules*

Two mechanisms are generally proposed to explain the transfer of macromolecules across the cellular membrane. The most commonly accepted view is that the molecules are accumulated in granules that come into contact with the apical membrane of the cell and attach to this surface. A small opening is formed through the apposed membranes so that the secretory substance may pass into the glandular lumen (Palade et al.). The opponents of this view assume that the secretory product diffuses across the cellular membrane (Kurosumi; Shibasaki). Results obtained in our laboratory by studying the secretion of chitinase by the gastric epithelium of various species may be interpreted as indicating that the chitinase is synthesized in the ribosomes, accumulated in zymogen granules and then released in the cytoplasm. From there it is transferred, molecule by molecule, through the cellular membrane to the glandular lumen by a mechanism that involves the energy of an oxidation-reduction system (Dandrifosse and Schoffeniels). The fact that some disaccharides such as chitobiose, lactose, trehalose, sucrose and turanose increase the rate of secretion of chitinase, is taken as indicating that the enzyme crosses the membrane as a glycoprotein. This is in keeping with the hypothesis, proposed by Eylar, that all the secreted proteins are associated with a hydrocarbon chain that gives the specificity to the transfer mechanism.

Compounds that reduce S-S groups stimulate the chitinase secretion while those that oxidize SH-groups have an inhibitory action. Cyanide, a well-known inhibitor of cytochrome a_3 promotes the secretion. Since carbon monoxide, an inhibitor of cytochrome c and a_3, is without effect on the chitinase secretion, one has to assume that an electron carrier identical to cytochrome a or having a closely related oxidation-reduction potential is involved in the transfer of chitinase across the cell membrane. The stimulating effect of cyanide could then be explained by assuming that electrons normally accepted by oxygen are now diverted to the oxidation-reduction system controlling the transfer of chitinase across the cell membrane.

5. *The case of calcium ions*

As shown above the problem of the thermodynamic activity of the chemical under study must be resolved before a definite conclusion can be drawn as to the nature of the force responsible for the fluxes under study. It is obvious that the cell interior is highly organized and that some of its specific properties are directly related to the making and the breaking of secondary bonds. When a balance sheet is drawn for the anionic and cationic contents of the cell, it is generally assumed that the inorganic ions have their full thermodynamic activity, as if they were in a dilute solution. This opinion stems from the consideration of osmotic equality between the cell interior and the extracellular space (Fredericq; Heinz; Leaf) and from the determination of the ionic mobilities in the cytoplasm (Hodgkin and Keynes 1953).

On the other hand, the use of specific glass electrodes (Hinke; Lev; MacLaughlin and Hinke) as well as the techniques of nuclear magnetic resonance and equilibrium dialysis (Cope 1965a, b, 1967; Troshin 1961, 1966) all suggest that the intracellular organic anions have a high capacity for fixation for monovalent cations. The matter is thus far from being settled and has been discussed at length many times in the case of

Na and K, both for the case of muscle as well as nerve cells (Hodgkin; Conway; Troshin 1966; Ling; Simon; Schoffeniels 1967).

In considering calcium ions the problem is even more acute, for these ions may form many different complexes. Most research workers seem to imply that, because of a dependence upon energy metabolism, the flux of calcium across any type of cellular membrane is indeed active. Recently however, evidence has been presented showing that in the intestinal epithelium the observed net flux is driven by an active transport of phosphate ions (Helbock et al.). This is an important observation when one considers the number of findings related to the behavior of calcium across any type of cell membranes.

Transport across the membranes of mitochondria has been reviewed by Lehninger et al. As for the transport across the membranes of the endoplasmic reticulum, much emphasis has been placed on the ability of these membranes to accumulate calcium in relation to a possible role in the metabolic activity of contractile tissues (Weber et al.). In both cases, however, direct evidence that one is dealing with an active transport mechanism is lacking since nothing is known about the electrochemical potential of calcium ions inside the organelle.

When dealing with red cells it is generally assumed that the main utilisation of ATP is for the active transport of monovalent cations, and this transport of cations is in turn responsible for keeping the cell volume constant (Tosteson and Hoffman). It seems, however, that this active transport mechanism is not the main consumer of ATP. As shown in our laboratory, there exist at least three different ATPases in the red cell ghost (Wins and Schoffeniels 1966a):

(a) a so-called 'specific' ATPase that requires Na and K. Its importance seems to be minor since its activity per mg of protein is rather small.

(b) A contractile system with low ATPase activity (Ohnishi). The classical methods of extraction yield rather small quantities of contractile proteins with low ATPase activity. However, Ca ions control the catalytic activity of this material and some relationship seems to exist between the activity of this system and volume changes in ghosts (Wins and Schoffeniels 1966b).

(c) The most important system, on a quantitative basis, is the one able to hydrolyse ATP in the presence of Mg ions (Wins and Schoffeniels 1966a). Its activity is low if the extraction procedure keeps the membranes intact. However it can be unmasked if the ghosts are disrupted or treated with a detergent (Wins and Schoffeniels 1967). Ca and Sr ions as well as 2,4-dinitrophenol produce a considerable increase in activity. These effects are however not additive, thus suggesting that we are dealing with a single enzymatic system. Since various types of treatment lead to the unmasking of a latent activity, this suggests that these agents are not activators of the ATPase but more probably uncouple the transfer of energy from ATP to another system.

An analogy with the situation found in the mitochondria is obvious, and this leads us to look for a system coupling the hydrolysis of ATP to an electron transfer. The Ca(or Sr)-dependent ATPase activity of the ghosts is inhibited by atebrin, sodium amytal and 2,6-dichlorophenol-indophenol. The last compound is far the best, thus suggesting the participation of flavoproteins in the system.

Consequently the questions we ask are: (a) what is the biological meaning of the stimulation by Ca ions; (b) how are the oxidation–reduction reactions coupled to the hydrolysis of ATP; (c) what kind of coupling are we dealing with?

It seems probable that the activation of an ATPase by Ca ions indicates that a transfer mechanism for Ca exists in the membranes of the ghosts. This transfer would be directed outwards. This interpretation finds an experimental support in the observations of Schatzmann (1967) who showed that the efflux of calcium from ghosts is greater if ATP is added to the system. Moreover, salyrgan inhibits this phenomenon and the effective concentration is within the range of that found to inhibit the ATPase activity. It is also worth remembering that 2,6-dichlorophenol-indophenol, an inhibitor of the ATPase activated by Ca ions, prevents the accumulation of calcium in sarcoplasmic vesicles.

The participation of flavoproteins in the transfer of calcium seems well established in the case of the membranes of the endoplasmic reticulum and very likely in the red cell ghosts. However, the nature of the enzyme system(s) involved is rather uncertain. What is known is that the membrane is able to transfer calcium ions, if ATP and Mg are present, but without further addition of any substrate which has the properties of either an electron donor or an acceptor. If it is assumed that some dehydrogenases intervene in the process, one is forced to admit that they must use substrates in catalytic amounts and that these substrates are tightly bound to the membranes. Accordingly, the oxidation-reduction system must involve a linear sequence of electron carriers endowed with an oscillating activity or else a sequence arranged in a cyclic manner.

To test these possibilities we have been looking for a possible utilisation of NADH or NADPH by red cell ghosts. We have found that they are able to oxidize the reduced nucleotides rapidly. This oxidation is followed by a partial reduction, almost to the initial level, of the NAD(P) and subsequently this is yet again oxidized. This oscillating activity is rapidly damped and the frequency is rather irregular.

So far our attempts to identify the nature of the substrate that oxidizes NAD(P) have been unsuccessful. It is also difficult, in the present state of our knowledge, to establish a firm correlation between the oscillating activity and that hydrolysis of ATP stimulated by Ca ions. However, it seems clear that to observe oscillations of amplitudes such as to permit their detection, one has to uncouple the ATPase from the dehydrogenase activity.

It is also worth noting that the oscillations in the oxidation-reduction state of NAD(P)H are paralleled by changes in the volume of the red-cell 'ghosts'. Ca ions seem to control those changes which could be due to a contractile mechanism. 2,6-dichlorophenol-indophenol inhibits the oscillations. Methylene blue is, however, less efficient. This may be related to the fact that this dye is also less efficient with regard to the ATPase activity.

6. *Conclusions*

Progress in the field of membrane permeability has long been impaired by oversimplification. In the hands of many biologists the cellular membrane has been treated as a macroscopic object thought to obey common mechanistic laws. Many models borrowed from the panoply of the physical chemist have been proposed in the hope of solving what is still challenging the ingenuity of many research workers. Thus the membrane has been compared to a sieve through which chemicals of small dimensions could diffuse freely. In the light of present results, it seems more reasonable to assume that any ion or molecule that crosses a membrane does so by interacting more or less strongly with a membrane component. This conclusion is drawn from the results of kinetic studies as well as from the consideration of the structure and the chemical nature of the cell membrane. At any rate little is known as to the type of interaction existing in the permeation process. Classical thermodynamics are obviously of little help in solving the problem, and one has to rely on other methods to elucidate the mechanisms of permeation.

Linear irreversible thermodynamics have been applied in the hope of obtaining additional insight into the factors controlling the permeability processes. Two criticisms may however be made. The first deals with the inadequacy of the theoretical approach. If, as discussed by Prigogine, organisms are open systems presenting a dissipative structure due to chemical instabilities, then all the symmetry requirements valid in the linear range of irreversible thermodynamics collapse. The second criticism concerns the difficulty of giving a physical meaning to phenomenological coefficients. In the last analysis the answer can only be given by the biochemically minded biologist.

The task of defining the force(s) responsible for the observed displacement is at least theoretically easier. As mentioned earlier in the text, the force available should always be elucidated, before applying any particular label to the phenomenon under study. Thus by analysing the fluxes of matter in the light of the second law of thermodynamics the sign of the free energy change can be decided. Any transfer directed down an (electro)chemical gradient will thus be termed passive. If the transfer is endergonic it has to be coupled to an exergonic reaction and one thus deals with an active transport – provided that the chemical remains unchanged after the transfer. Unfortunately the parameters necessary to apply equation (1) are not always at hand. This is particularly the case when dealing with fluxes between the cell interior and the surroundings for so little is known about the physicochemical state of many ions and molecules in the intracellular space that their thermodynamical activity can only be guessed.

Hasty conclusions have thus been drawn in the face of results which show that the transfer is metabolically dependent. That this is a naive attitude can be seen from the results obtained with chloride ions in the frog skin or calcium ions in the intestine. Finally, some molecules can enter metabolic pathways as well as undergoing transport. In the case of such molecules, the importance of looking for any possible transformation, occurring at the same time as transport, should be stressed. Our results obtained with the alanine fluxes in the tortoise intestine are illustrative of the type of pitfall that should be avoided.

References

AHMED, K. and J.D.JUDAH: Preparation of lipoproteins containing cation-dependent ATPase. Biochim. Biophys. Acta 93 (1964) 603.

AHMED, K., J.D.JUDAH and P.G. SCHOLEFIELD: Interaction of sodium and potassium with a cation-dependent adenosine triphosphatase system from rat brain. Biochim. Biophys. Acta 120 (1966) 351.

ANDERSEN, B. and H.H.USSING: Solvent drag on non-electrolytes during osmotic flow through isolated toad skin and its response to antidiuretic hormone. Acta Physiol. Scand. 39 (1957) 228.

ANDERSEN, B. and H.H.USSING: Active transport. In: M.Florkin and H.S.Mason, eds.: Comparative biochemistry. New York, Academic Press 2 (1960) 371.

BAILLIEN, M. and E.SCHOFFENIELS: Le transport actif d'acides aminés au niveau de l'épithélium intestinal isolé de la tortue grecque. Biochim. Biophys. Acta 53 (1961a) 521.

BAILLIEN, M. and E.SCHOFFENIELS: Origine des potentiels bioélectriques de l'épithélium intestinal de la tortue grecque. Biochim. Biophys. Acta 53 (1961b) 537.

BAILLIEN, M. and E.SCHOFFENIELS: Action des acides aminés sur la différence de potentiel électrique et sur le courant de court-circuitage au niveau de l'épithélium isolé de l'intestin grêle de la tortue grecque. Arch. Intern. Physiol. Biochim. 70 (1962) 140.

BIHLER, I., K.A.HAWKINS and R.K.CRANE: Studies on the mechanism of absorption of sugars VI. The specificity and other properties of Na^+ dependent entrance of sugars into intestinal tissue under anaerobic condition in vitro. Biochim. Biophys. Acta 59 (1962) 94.

BIRT, L.M. and F.J.R.HIRD: The uptake and metabolism of aminoacids by slices of carrot. Biochem. J. 70 (1958) 277.

BONTING, S.L. and L.L.CARAVAGGIO: Studies on sodium-potassium-activated adenosinetriphosphatase V. Correlation of enzyme activity with cation flux in six tissues. Arch. Biochem. Biophys. 101 (1963) 37.

BONTING, S.L., L.L.CARAVAGGIO and N.M.HAWKINS: Studies on sodium-potassium-activated adenosinetriphosphatase VI. Its role in cation transport in the lens of cat, calf, and rabbit. Arch. Biochem. Biophys. 101 (1963) 47.

BREUER, H. and R.WHITTAM: Ion movement in seminal vesicle mucosa. J. Physiol. (London) 135 (1957) 213.

CALDWELL, P.C.: The effects of certain metabolic inhibitors on the phosphate esters of the squid giant axon. J. Physiol. (London) 132 (1956) 35P.

CALDWELL, P.C.: The phosphorus metabolism of squid axons and its relationship to the active transport of sodium. J. Physiol. (London) 152 (1960) 545.

CALDWELL, P.C., A.L.HODGKIN and T.I.SHAW: Injection of compounds containing 'energy-rich' phosphate bonds into giant nerve fibres. J. Physiol. (London) 147 (1959) 18P.

CALDWELL, P.C., A.L.HODGKIN, R.D.KEYNES and T.I.SHAW: The effects of injecting 'energy-rich' phosphate compounds on the active transport of ions in the giant axons of *Loligo*. J. Physiol. (London) 152 (1960) 561.

CALDWELL, P.C. and R.D.KEYNES: The effect of ouabain on the efflux of sodium from a squid giant axon. J. Physiol. (London) 148 (1959) 8P.

CHAPPELL, J.B. and K.HAARHOFF: In: The biochemistry of mitochondria. Proceedings Federation European Biochemical Societies, 3rd Meeting, Warsaw, 1966.

CHARNOCK, J.S. and R.L.POST: Evidence of the mechanism of ouabain inhibition of cation activated adenosine triphosphatase. Nature 199 (1963) 910.

CHRISTENSEN, H.N. and T.R.RIGGS: Structural evidences for chelation and Schiff's base formation in amino acid transfer into cells. J. Biol. Chem. 220 (1956) 265.

CLARKE, E.W., Q.H.GIBSON, D.H.SMYTH and G.WISEMAN: Selective absorption of amino-acids from Thiry-Vella loops. J. Physiol. (London) 112 (1951) 46P.

CONWAY, E.J.: Nature and significance of concentration relations of potassium and sodium ions in skeletal muscle. Physiol. Rev. 37 (1957) 84.

COPE, F.W.: Nuclear magnetic resonance evidence for complexing of sodium ions in muscle. Proc. Natl. Acad. Sci. U.S. 54 (1965a) 225.

COPE, F.W.: A theory of ion transport across cell surfaces by a process analogous to electron transport across liquid-solid interfaces. Bull. Math. Biophys. 27 (1965b) 99.

COPE, F.W.: Nuclear magnetic resonance evidence for complexing of Na^+ in muscle, kidney and brain, and by actomyosin. The relation of cellular complexing of Na^+ to water structure and to transport kinetics. J. Gen. Physiol. 50 (1967) 1353.

DAINTY, J.: Water relations of plant cells. In: R.D.Preston, ed.: Advances in botanical research I. London, Academic Press (1963) 279.

DANDRIFOSSE, G. and E.SCHOFFENIELS: Mechanism of chitinase secretion by the gastric mucosa. Biochim. Biophys. Acta 148 (1967) 741.

DUNHAM, E.T. and I.M.GLYNN: Adenosinetriphosphatase activity and the active movements of alkali metal ions. J. Physiol. (London) 156 (1961) 274.

EPSTEIN, F.H. and R.WHITTAM: The mode of inhibition by calcium of cell membrane adenosine-triphosphatase activity. Biochem. J. 99 (1966) 232.

EYLAR, E.H.: On the biological role of glycoproteins. J. Theoret. Biol. 10 (1966) 89.

FRAZIER, H.S. and A.LEAF: Cellular mechanisms in the control of body fluids. Medicine 43 (1964) 281.

FREDERICQ, L.: Sur la concentration moleculaire du sang et des tissus chez les animaux aquatiques. Bull. Classe Sci. Acad. Roy. Belg. (1901) 428.

FUHRMAN, F.A.: Inhibition of active sodium transport in the isolated frog skin. Am. J. Physiol. 171 (1952) 266.

GARDÓS, G.: Accumulation of potassium ions in human blood cells. Acta Physiol. Acad. Sci. Hung. 6 (1954) 191.

GILL, T.J. and A.K.SOLOMON: Effect of ouabain on sodium flux in human red cells. Nature 103 (1959) 1127.

GILLES-BAILLIEN, M. and E.SCHOFFENIELS: Site of action of L-alanine and D-glucose on the potential difference across the intestine. Arch. Intern. Physiol. Biochim. 73 (1965) 355.

GILLES-BAILLIEN, M. and E.SCHOFFENIELS: Metabolic fate of L-alanine actively transported across the tortoise intestine. Life Sciences 5 (1966) 2253.

GILLES-BAILLIEN, M. and E.SCHOFFENIELS: Amino acids and bioelectric potentials in the small intestine of the greek tortoise. Life Sciences 7 (1968) 53.

GILLES-BAILLIEN, M. and E.SCHOFFENIELS: Fluxes of inorganic ions across the isolated intestinal epithelium of the greek tortoise. Arch. Intern. Physiol. Biochim. 75 (1967) 754.

GLYNN, I.M.: The action of cardiac glycosides on sodium and potassium movements in human red cells. J. Physiol. (London) 136 (1957) 148.

GLYNN, I.M.: Activation of adenosinetriphosphatase activity in a cell membrane by external potassium and internal sodium. J. Physiol. (London) 160 (1962) 18P.

GREEN, A.L. and C.B.TAYLOR: Kinetics of $(Na^+ + K^+)$-stimulated ATPase of rabbit kidney microsomes. Biochem. Biophys. Res. Commun. 14 (1964) 118.

HANAI, T., D.A.HAYDON and W.R.REDWOOD: The water permeability of artificial bimolecular leaflets: A comparison of radio tracer and osmotic methods. Ann. N.Y. Acad. Sci. 137 (1966) 731.

HEINZ, E.: The exchangeability of glycine accumulated by carcinoma cells. J. Biol. Chem. 225 (1957) 305.

HEINZ, E. and P. WALSH: Exchange diffusion, transport, and intracellular level of amino acids in Ehrlich carcinoma cells. J. Biol. Chem. 233 (1958) 1488.

HELBOCK, H.J., J.G. FORTE and P. SALTMAN: The mechanism of calcium transport by rat intestine. Biochim. Biophys. Acta 126 (1966) 81.

HINKE, J.A.M.: Glass micro-electrodes for measuring intracellular activities of sodium and potassium. Nature 184 (1959) 1257.

HODGKIN, A.L.: Ionic movements and electrical activity in giant nerves fibres. Proc. Roy. Soc. (London), Ser. B: 148 (1958) 1.

HODGKIN, A.L. and R.D. KEYNES: The mobility and diffusion coefficient of potassium in giant axons from *Sepia*. J. Physiol. (London) 119 (1953) 513.

HODGKIN, A.L. and R.D. KEYNES: Active transport of cations in giant axons from *Sepia* and *Loligo*. J. Physiol. (London) 128 (1955a) 28.

HODGKIN, A.L. and R.D. KEYNES: The potassium permeability of a giant nerve fibre. J. Physiol. (London) 128 (1955b) 61.

HOFFMAN, J.F.: The link between metabolism and the active transport of Na in human red cell ghosts. Federation Proc. 19 (1960) 127.

HOGBEN, C.A.M.: The alimentary tract. Ann. Rev. Physiol. 22 (1960) 381.

HOKIN, L.E. and M.R. HOKIN: Biological transport. Ann. Rev. Biochem. 32 (1963) 553.

JÄRNEFELT, J.: Properties and possible mechanism of the Na^+ and K^+ stimulated microsomal adenosinetriphosphatase. Biochim. Biophys. Acta 59 (1962) 643.

JUDAH, J.D., K. AHMED and A.E.M. MC LEAN: Ion transport and phosphoproteins of human red cells. Biochim. Biophys. Acta 65 (1962) 472.

KAHN, J.B. and G.H. ACHESON: Effects of cardiac glycosides and other lactones, and of certain other compounds on cation transfer in human erythrocytes. J. Pharmacol. Exptl. Therap. 115 (1955) 305.

KOEFOED-JOHNSEN, V.: The effect of g-strophanthin (ouabain) on the active transport of sodium through the isolated frog skin. Acta Physiol. Scand. 42 (1957) Suppl. 145.

KOEFOED-JOHNSEN, V., H.H. USSING and K. ZERAHN: The origin of the short-circuit current in the adrenaline stimulated frog skin. Acta Physiol. Scand. 27 (1953) 38.

KUROSUMI, K.: Electron microscopic analysis of the secretion mechanism. Intern. Rev. Cytol. 11 (1961) 1.

LEAF, A.: On the mechanism of fluid exchange of tissues in vitro. Biochem. J. 62 (1956) 241.

LEAF, A., L.B. PAGE and J. ANDERSON: Respiration and active sodium transport of isolated toad bladder. J. Biol. Chem. 234 (1959) 1625.

LEAF, A. and A. RENSHAW: Ion transport and respiration of isolated frog skin. Biochem. J. 65 (1957a) 82.

LEAF, A. and A. RENSHAW: The anaerobic active ion transport by isolated frog skin. Biochem. J. 65 (1957b) 90.

LEFEVRE, P.G.: Sugar transport in the red blood cell; structure-activity relations in substrates and antagonists. Pharmacol. Rev. 13 (1961) 39.

LEFEVRE, P.G.: Rate affinity in human red blood cell sugar transport. Am. J. Physiol. 203 (1962) 286.

LEFEVRE, P.G.: The 'dimeriser' hypothesis for sugar permeation through red cell membrane: Reinvestigation of original evidence. Biochim. Biophys. Acta 120 (1966) 395.

LEHNINGER, A.L., E. CARAFOLI and C.S. ROSSI: Energy-linked ion movements in mitochondrial systems. Advan. Enzymol. 29 (1967) 259.

LEV, A.A.: Determination of activity and activity coefficients of potassium and sodium ions in frog muscle fibers. Nature 201 (1964) 1132.

LEVI, H. and H.H. USSING: The exchange of sodium and chloride ions across the fibre membrane of the isolated frog sartorius. Acta Physiol. Scand. 16 (1949) 232.

LING, G. H.: A physical theory of the living state. New York, Blaisdell Publ. Co. (1962).

LUND, E. J.: Relation between continuous bioelectric currents and cell respiration II. J. Exptl. Zool. 51 (1928a) 265.

LUND, E. J.: Relation between continous bioelectric current and cell respiration III. Effects of concentration of oxygen on cell polarity in the frog skin. J. Exptl. Zool. 51 (1928b) 291.

LUND, E. J.: Relation between continuous bioelectric current and cell respiration V. The quantitative relation between E_P and cell oxidation as shown by the effects of cyanide and oxygen. J. Exptl. Zool. 51 (1928c) 327.

MAC LAUGHLIN, S. G. A. and J. A. M. HINKE: Sodium and water binding in single striated muscle fibers of the giant barnacle. Can. J. Physiol. Pharmacol. 44 (1966) 837.

MAIZELS, M., M. REMINGTON and R. TRUSCOE: Metabolism and sodium transfer of mouse ascites tumour cells. J. Physiol. (London) 140 (1958) 80.

MAURO, A.: Nature of solvent transfer in osmosis. Science 126 (1957) 252.

MELON, J. and E. SCHOFFENIELS: Les caractères de perméabilité de l'épithélium nasal de type épidermoïde. Atti XX Convegno Soc. Oto Rhino-laryngologica Latina, Bologna 1-5 Aprile (1964).

MITCHELL, P.: Transport of phosphate through an osmotic barrier. Symp. Soc. Exptl. Biol. 8 (1954) 254.

MITCHELL, P.: Active transport and ion accumulation. In: M. Florkin and E. H. Stotz, eds.: Comprehensive biochemistry. Amsterdam, Elsevier 22 (1967) 167.

NEAME, K. D. and G. WISEMAN: The transamination of glutamic and aspartic acids during absorption by the small intestine of the dog in vivo. J. Physiol. (London) 135 (1957) 442.

OHNISHI, T.: Extraction of actin- and myosin-like proteins from erythrocyte membrane. J. Biochem. (Tokyo) 52 (1962) 307.

PALADE, G. E., P. SIEKEVITZ and L. G. CARO: Structure, chemistry and function of the pancreatic exocrine cell. Ciba Found. Symp. Exocrine Pancreas 23 (1962) 23.

PARK, C. R., R. L. POST, C. F. KALMAN, J. H. WRIGHT, L. H. JOHNSON and H. E. MORGAN: The transport of glucose and other sugars across cell membranes and the effect of insulin. Ciba Found. Colloq. Endocrinol. 9 (1956) 240.

POST, R. L., C. R. MERRIT, C. R. KINSOLVING and C. D. ALBRIGHT: Membrane adenosine triphosphatase as a participant in the active transport of sodium and potassium in the human erythrocyte. J. Biol. Chem. 235 (1960) 1796.

POST, R. L. and A. S. ROSENTHAL: An intermediate compound in active transport. J. Gen. Physiol. 45 (1962) 614A.

POST, R. L., A. K. SEN and A. S. ROSENTHAL: A phosphorylated intermediate in adenosine triphosphate dependent sodium and potassium transport across kidney membranes. J. Biol. Chem. 240 (1965) 1437.

PRIGOGINE, I.: Structure, dissipation and life. In: Internat. Symp. Physique Théorique et Biologie, Institut de la Vie, Versailles (France) 1967.

ROBBINS, E. and A. MAURO: Experimental study of the independence of diffusion and hydrodynamic permeability coefficients in collodion membranes. J. Gen. Physiol. 43 (1960) 523.

ROSENBERG, T. and W. WILBRANDT: Uphill transport induced by counterflow. J. Gen. Physiol. 41 (1957) 289.

SCHATZMANN, H. J.: Herzglykoside als Hemmstoffe für den aktiven Kalium- und Natriumtransport durch die Erythrocytenmembran. Helv. Physiol. Pharmacol. Acta 11 (1953) 346.

SCHATZMANN, H. J.: Calcium-activated membrane ATPase of human red cells and its possible role in active Ca transport. In: H. Peeters, ed.: Protides of the biological fluids. Amsterdam, Elsevier 15 (1967) 251.

SCHMIDT-NIELSEN, K., A. BORUT, P. LEE and E. CRAWFORD: Nasal salt excretion and the possible function of the cloaca in water conservation. Science 142 (1963) 1300.

SCHOFFENIELS, E.: Action du 2,4-dinitrophénol sur le flux de Na à travers la peau de grenouille. Arch. Intern. Physiol. Biochim. 63 (1955) 361.

SCHOFFENIELS, E.: Les bases physiques et chimiques des potentiels bioélectriques chez *Electrophorus electricus* L. Arch. Intern. Physiol. Biochim. 68 (1960) 1.

SCHOFFENIELS, E.: Cellular aspects of active transport. In: M. Florkin and H.S. Mason, eds.: Comparative biochemistry. London, Academic Press 7 (1964) 137.

SCHOFFENIELS, E.: Cellular aspect of membrane permeability. Oxford, Pergamon (1967) 284 p.

SCHULTZ, S.G. and R.ZALUSKY: Interactions between active sodium transport and active amino-acid transport in isolated rabbit ileum. Nature 204 (1965) 292.

SHIBASAKI, S.: Experimental cytological and electron microscope studies on the rat gastric mucosa. Arch. Histol. (Okayama) 21 (1961) 251.

SIMON, S.E.: Ionic partition and fine structure in muscle. Nature 184 (1959) 1978.

SKOU, J.C.: The influence of some cations on an adenosine triphosphatase from peripheral nerves. Biochim. Biophys. Acta 23 (1957) 394.

SKOU, J.C.: The relationship of a (Mg^{++} + Na^+) activated K^+ stimulated enzyme or enzyme system to the active linked transport of Na^+ and K^+ across the cell membrane. In: A. Kleinzeller and A. Kotyk, eds.: Symp. CSAV: Membrane transport and metabolism. Praha, Czechoslovak Acad. Sci. (1960) 228.

SKOU, J.C.: Enzymatic basis for active transport of Na^+ and K^+ across cell membrane. Physiol. Rev. 45 (1965) 596.

SOLOMON, A.K., T.J.GILL and G.L.GOLD: The kinetics of cardiac glycoside inhibition of potassium transport in human erythrocytes. J. Gen. Physiol. 40 (1956) 327.

SQUIRES, R.F.: On the interactions of Na^+, K^+, Mg^{++}, and ATP with the Na^+ plus K^+ activated ATPase from rat brain. Biochem. Biophys. Res. Commun. 19 (1965) 27.

TEORELL, T.: Zur quantitativen Behandlung der Membranpermeabilität. Z. Elektrochem. 55 (1951) 460.

TOSTESON, D.C. and J.F.HOFFMANN: Regulation of cell volume by active cation transport in high and low potassium sheep red cells. J. Gen. Physiol. 44 (1960) 169.

TOSTESON, D.C. and J.S.ROBERTSON: Potassium transport in duck red cells. J. Cellular Comp. Physiol. 47 (1956) 147.

TROSHIN, A.S.: Sorption properties of protoplasm and their role in cell permeability. In: A. Kleinzeller and A.Kotyk, eds.: Membrane transport and metabolism. ČSAV (1961).

TROSHIN, A.S.: Problems of cell permeability. London, Pergamon Press (1966).

USSING, H.H.: The active ion transport through the isolated frog skin in the light of tracer studies. Acta Physiol. Scand. 17 (1950) 1.

USSING, H.H.: The alkali metal ions in biology. Part I. The alkali metal ions in isolated systems and tissues. In: Handbuch der experimentelle Pharmakologie. Berlin, Springer Verlag 13 (1960).

USSING, H.H. and K.ZERAHN: Active transport of sodium as the source of electric current in the short-circuited isolated frog skin. Acta Physiol. Scand. 23 (1951) 110.

WEBER, A., R.HERZ and I.REISS: Study of the kinetics of calcium transport by isolated fragmented sarcoplasmic reticulum. Biochem. Z. 345 (1966) 329.

WHITTAM, R.: Directional effects of alkali metal ions on adenosine triphosphate hydrolysis in erythrocyte ghosts. Nature 196 (1962a) 134.

WHITTAM, R.: The asymmetrical stimulation of a membrane adenosine triphosphatase in relation to active transport. Biochem. J. 84 (1962b) 110.

WHITTAM, R. and H.J.BREUER: Ion transport and metabolism in slices of guinea-pig seminal-vesicle mucosa. Biochem. J. 72 (1959) 638.

WILBRANDT, W. and T. ROSENBERG: The concept of carrier transport and its corollaries in pharmacology. Pharmacol. Rev. 13 (1961) 109.

WILSON, T.H.: Intestinal absorption. Philadelphia, Saunders Co. (1962) 263 p.

WILSON, T.H. and G.WISEMAN: The use of sacs of everted small intestine for the study of the trans-

ference of substances from the mucosal to the serosal surface. J. Physiol. (London) 123 (1954) 116.
WINS, P. and E. SCHOFFENIELS: L'activité adénosine triphosphatasique des globules rouges humains. Arch. Intern. Physiol. Biochim. 73 (1965) 160.
WINS, P. and E. SCHOFFENIELS: Studies on red-cell ghost ATPase systems: properties of a $(Mg^{2+} + Ca^{2+})$- dependent ATPase. Biochim. Biophys. Acta 120 (1966a) 341.
WINS, P. and E. SCHOFFENIELS: $(ATP + Ca^{++})$-linked contraction of red cell ghosts. Arch. Intern. Physiol. Biochim. 74 (1966b) 812.
WINS, P. and E. SCHOFFENIELS: A 'latent' dinitrophenol-stimulated ATPase in red cell ghosts. Biochim. Biophys. Acta 135 (1967) 831.
WINTER, C. G. and H. N. CHRISTENSEN: Migration of amino acid across the membrane of the human erythrocyte. J. Biol. Chem. 239 (1964) 872.
WISEMAN, G.: Absorption of amino-acids using an *in vitro* technique. J. Physiol. (London) 120 (1953) 63.
ZADUNAISKY, J. A. and O. A. CANOLIA: Active transport of sodium and chloride by the isolated skin of the South American frog *Leptodactylus ocelatus*. Nature 195 (1962) 1004.

CHAPTER 50

Cellular aspects of membrane permeability

E. SCHOFFENIELS

Department of Biochemistry, University of Liège, Belgium

Contents

1. Introduction
2. Temporo-spatial organization of the permeability characteristics
3. Hormonal effects on permeability
4. Role of inorganic ions in controlling the fate of hydrogen ions produced in the cytoplasm
   (a) Fate of the reducing equivalents originating in the cytoplasm
      Lactic dehydrogenase
      3-glycerophosphate dehydrogenase
      Glyoxylate reductase
   (b) Control of 2-ketoglutarate production
   (c) Glutamate synthesis as control of the respiration
   (d) Control of intracellular ammonia pool by inorganic ions
5. Concluding remarks

1. Introduction

The very existence of a cell is dependent on the metabolic activity of the cellular membrane. Thus, at the origin of life, and in the earliest cells the first structure that differentiated must have been endowed with those basic properties today performed by the cellular membrane. This enabled it to keep the cell volume constant. As a consequence, the cell interior differed in composition from its surroundings, and the metabolic network within must have been adapted to the specific situations created by the activity of the membrane. Thus, my basic view is that a comparative study of membrane permeability, associated with the study of the metabolic consequences of the membrane activity, should offer new material for discussing the problem of evolution and speciation.

In our previous chapter we have defined active transport as the endergonic transfer of an ion or molecule coupled to an exergonic reaction. In this context much work has been devoted to attempting to relate the behavior of an ion or molecule crossing a membrane to the metabolism of the cell. However, there is little information about the influence that activity, taking place at the cell boundary, may have on cellular metabolism. This is certainly a problem that deserves the greatest attention since it is obvious that many enzymes or even metabolic sequences must be adapted to local ionic conditions prevailing at a particular locus in the cell. Moreover such important events as the storage of information in the central nervous system must be related in one way or another, to the electrical activity of the neuronal membrane. Thus one wonders whether the exchange of ions at the cell boundary – an activity which may affect the ionic composition or concentration in certain regions of the cell – could be one of the means by which some metabolic sequences are controlled. Certainly other means are at work and the reciprocal relations that exist between various metabolic events may, on further analysis, prove to be of a more complex nature than generally assumed. Thus feedback mechanisms, allosteric regulations of enzyme activity, hormonal actions, etc. may well appear to be the crudest ways used by the cell to control its metabolism. At any rate it seems appropriate at this stage of our knowledge to discuss the available data, considering the cell as a unit both of metabolism and of structure.

In the following pages the emphasis will be placed on a possible role of the inorganic ions in the control of the activity of some key enzymes. Particular attention will be given to results obtained with euryhaline animals, since rather large variations in the ionic composition of the cell are physiologically 'normal' in these animals. Thus the repercussion of these changes or ionic composition on the activity of some metabolic sequences can be studied in biologically relevant conditions.

2. Temporo-spatial organization of the permeability characteristics

It is generally accepted that the electrical potential difference existing across the cellular membrane is the result of the metabolic activity of the cell. However, there is no agreement about the origin of this potential difference. Most workers are of the opinion that it results from the unequal distribution of inorganic ions and from the existence of specific permeability properties of the membrane. Thus, according to this view, which has been substantiated by much experimental data, one is essentially dealing with diffusion potentials, the quantitative expression of which may be found in the classical equations developed by the electrochemists. Due to the permeability characteristics of the membrane (Schoffeniels 1960a, 1961), among which are the active transport mechanisms, adequate ionic gradients are established. These give rise to diffusion potentials, the final value of which is best represented by the so-called Goldman equation (e.g. Goldman; Hodgkin and Katz).

There has been much discussion as to whether the active transport of Na is being electrogenic; if it were so it would imply a *direct* participation of this mechanism in the establishment of the measured potential. The evidence presented in favor of this view, though supporting the idea that in certain rather peculiar conditions this could indeed be the case, is not at all convincing. Most authors tend to forget that the experimental conditions, set to prove or disprove this working hypothesis, affect in a profound way the metabolism of the cell. Thus, one can hardly accept the extrapolation of results obtained, say in isotonic potassium sulfate (Bricker et al.; Klahr and Bricker) to the conditions pertaining *in vivo* (see below). Generally the electrochemical origin of the biopotentials is indicated by showing that a logarithmic relation exists between the concentration ratio for a given ion and the electrical potential difference. One thus demonstrates that the membrane is permeable to that ionic species. The comparative study of membrane permeability offers the possibility of establishing not only the distribution of the permeability characteristics in the animal kingdom but also their spatial organization within the membrane. Tables 1, 2 and 3 give the results of potential difference measurements performed upon various epithelia. It can be seen that the lumen of the intestine or the outside medium is negative with respect to the serosal fluid. Moreover, while the potential difference in certain cases may attain values up to 80 mV, in other cases, such as the small intestine, it is only a few mV.

The study of the potential profile by means of an intracellular microelectrode and of the diffusion potentials that take place at both mucosal and serosal borders of the epithelium, shows that the situation observed is due both to the spatial distribution and also to the relative permeability to the various ions. The permeability characteristics themselves are common to many cells and it is obvious that the distribution of the permeability characteristics is an important aspect of cell differentiation (Fig. 1).

TABLE 1

Potential difference across the epithelium of the digestive tract in various animal species (Schoffeniels 1961).

Species	Organ	Potential difference (mV)	Methods
Guinea-pig (*Cavia porcellus* L.)	Jejunum Ileum Colon	0.5–2 0.5–2 17–20	A
Rat (*Rattus norvegicus* Exl.)	Ileum Colon	0.5–2.5 30–40	A
Rabbit (*Oryctolagus cuniculus* L.)	Ileum Colon	1.5–2 5–10	A
Goldfish (*Carassius auratus* L.)	Small intestine	3.5	B
Carp (*Cyprinus carpio nudus* L.)	Small intestine	3.5	B
Trout (*Salmo irrideus* Gibbons)	Small intestine	0.5	B
Tortoise (*Testudo hermanni* G.F.Gmelin)	Gastric mucosa Small intestine Caecum Colon	37 2–4 10–15 20–50	BS
Turtle (*Emys orbicularis* L.)	Small intestine Colon	1.5–2.5 15–20	BS
Frog (*Rana temporaria* L.)	Gastric mucosa Rectum	30–50 10–50	BS

The potential difference is recorded on isolated preparat ions. Isolated sac (A) according to the method of Baillien and Schoffeniels (1961a, b). (B) with or without stripping of the muscle layers. (BS) with stripping of the muscle layers. Both sides of the preparation are bathed with physiological saline. The sign of the potential difference refers to the serosal fluid.

TABLE 2

Bioelectric potentials recorded in the small intestine (jejunum) and in the colon (after Gilles-Baillien and Schoffeniels 1967).

	Small intestine				Colon		
Exp.	*PD*	PD_M	PD_S	Exp.	*PD*	PD_M	PD_S
1	1	25	26	6	29	9	38
2	0.5	35	35.5	7	15	5	20
3	1.5	25	26	8	27	5	33
4	2	25	27	9	22	7	30
5	1	31	32	10	19	6	25

PD: trans-epithelial potential; PD_M: trans-mucosal potential; PD_S: trans-serosal potential. These potentials are expressed in mV, the intracellular fluid being always electrically negative with regard to the saline bathing the epithelium.

TABLE 3

Permeability coefficients and potential profiles of respiratory epithelium of various animal species (Schoffeniels 1967a).

Species	Type of epithelium	Permeability coefficients	*PD* (mV)	PD_M (mV)	PD_S (mV)
Pig	Nasal (polystratified with goblet cells)	M: $P_{Na} > P_{Cl} > P_{SO_4} > P_K$ S: $P_K > P_{Na} > P_{Cl}$	30–80	−22	+18
Rabbit	Nasal (anterior part of septum, squamous)	M: $P_{Na} \gg P_{Cl} > P_K > P_{SO_4}$ S: $P_K > P_{Na} > P_{Cl} > P_{SO_4}$			
	Nasal (posterior part of septum, ciliated; rich in glandular cells)	M: $P_{Cl} > P_{Na} > P_K$ S: $P_K > P_{Na} > P_{Cl} > P_{SO_4}$	1–6	+18	+20
	Trachea (ciliated; poor in glandular cells)	M: $P_{Cl} \gg P_{SO_4} > P_{Na} > P_K$ S: $P_K > P_{Na} > P_{Cl} = P_{SO_4}$	10–30	−7 +30	+8 +40*
Guinea-pig	Nasal	same as rabbit	1–2		
	Trachea	same as rabbit	10–20		
Man	Polyp	M: $P_{Na} > P_{Cl} > P_{SO_4} > P_K$ S: $P_K > P_{Na} > P_{Cl} > P_{SO_4}$	5–12		

* On 3 out of 10 experiments this type of profile has been obtained.
See Table 2 for abbreviations. M = mucosal; S = serosal.

It has been argued that the first negative potential jump observed with some preparations does not really indicate a potential difference across the cell membrane, but rather an extracellular potential related to the presence of a mucous layer or some other nondefined structures. To answer this criticism, the voltage variation sensed by the microelectrode has been recorded when a square pulse of current is produced through a set of stimulating electrodes. The recording obtained, after the microelectrode has indicated the first potential jump, shows the characteristically slowed onset and decay of the voltage trace, generally attributed to the membrane capacitative effect (Schoffeniels 1967a; Gilles-Baillien and Schoffeniels 1965, 1967).

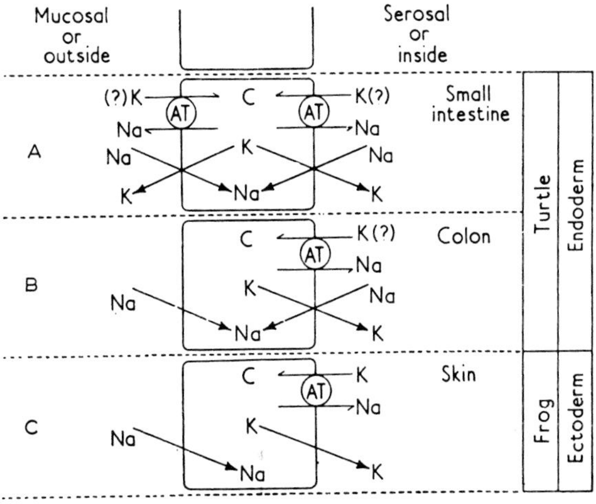

Fig. 1. Schematic representation of the spatial distribution of permeability characteristics in some epithelial cells (Schoffeniels 1961). A: turtle small intestine; B: turtle colon; C: frog skin. The oblique arrows indicate passive movement. AT is the active transport of Na coupled more or less tightly with an exchange for K in frog skin; this type of exchange has not been demonstrated in the intestine. The levels of the chemical symbols designate the concentration levels of the cations.

In conducting cells, the interior is generally negative with respect to the surrounding fluid. In certain circumstances, this potential difference, the resting potential, may alter drastically during an extremely short period of time, generally within a matter of milliseconds (action potential). Important progress in our understanding of the mechanism responsible for the action potential was made when Cole and Curtis demonstrated the breakdown of the membrane electrical resistance. Later, thanks to the work of Hodgkin, it was suggested that in resting conditions, the membrane would be essentially permeable to potassium, while during activity its permeability to sodium would increase tremendously for a very short period of time. Electrical and ionic flux measurements have so far substantiated this view.

Without going further into a detailed analysis of membrane permeability, it is apparent that cells, such as those of frog skin and respiratory or intestinal epithelium, possess the same permeability characteristics as those found in conducting cells, such as electroplaques, nerve fiber or muscle, or those present in red blood cells. But one important aspect of the epithelial cell lies in the fact that some of the permeability characteristics (e.g. high passive permeability to Na and K), although simultaneously present, may be spatially separated at a microscopic level (frog skin, tortoise colon) or may be found together in the same membrane (tortoise small intestine). This is unlike the situation found in the conducting cell where the Na-selective characteristic appears only for short periods of time (action potential).

Our results (Table 3) show that the nasal epithelium in the rabbit has a potential profile similar to that of the intestinal epithelium of the tortoise, while the profile of the trachea is in most experiments closely related to that which is found in the amphibian skin or urinary bladder, i.e. a stepwise profile. In some experiments, however, we found that the intracellular fluid was negative with respect to both the serosal or mucosal solutions. This may reflect the fact that the microelectrode has been inserted in two different types of cell. The permeability characteristics are differently distributed between the two opposing surfaces of the epithelial cells, a result in agreement with what has been found with other polar epithelia.

The permeability characteristics of the mucosal border seem to be directly related to the morphological differentiation of the cell. The rabbit trachea is a ciliated epithelium relatively poor in glandular acini or in goblet cells. It is characterized by a high chloride permeability. The epithelium isolated from the posterior part of the nasal septum is ciliated and extremely rich in glandular acini. It too is mainly permeable to chloride. The anterior part of the septum of the rabbit is a squamous epithelium but in the pig it is very often polystratified with numerous goblet cells. Both these epithelia are characterized by a high permeability to sodium ions.

Thus it seems that permeability to chloride ions is associated with the ciliated cells. A non-ciliated epithelium is characterized by a high permeability to sodium.

That the permeability characteristics are spatially separated at the cell surface is further indicated by our results obtained in collaboration with Dr. J. Melon on the composition of the human nasal mucus during an anaphylactic crisis. In patients suffering from an allergic rhinitis, an acute crisis is produced by local application of pollen extract. The mucus is collected on filter paper and its volume and composition are determined. The results of our study indicate that during the crisis the protein and the mucin concentrations of the mucus either increase or decrease according to their level in the mucus before the antigenic application. The variation of the concentration of inorganic ions as compared to control values is summarized in Table 4. Moreover, we have calculated the variation one would expect were the increase in mucus production during an anaphylactic crisis, to be the result of an ultrafiltration from blood plasma. Finally, we indicated the possible mechanisms one may evoke to explain the observed results (Table 4). It may be seen from this table that the ultrafiltration hypothesis is inadequate to explain our experimental findings, except in the case of chloride ions. One concludes that the various ionic species are crossing the cellular membranes at the level of well-differentiated and spatially separated loci.

TABLE 4

Variations in the ionic composition of human nasal mucus during an acute anaphylactic crisis induced experimentally (Schoffeniels 1967a).

Ions	Variations as % of control		Possible mechanisms
	Observed	Calculated	
Na	−13.5	+10.0	Stimulation of Na active transport inwards; inhibition of Na efflux
Cl	−20.0	−25.0	Ultrafiltration, inhibition of Cl efflux (active transport?); stimulation of Cl influx (active transport?)
K	−35.0	−61.0	Stimulation of K active transport outwards
Ca	−43.0	−23.5	Stimulation of Ca active transport inwards; inhibition of efflux

The results are expressed as per cent of the control values. The calculated variations have been obtained on the basis that the increase in secretion volume is the result of an ultrafiltration of blood plasma.

It may be concluded that the overall properties of the membrane taken as a whole are related to the temporo-spatial distribution of its permeability characteristics. Thus, as a taxonomist may define species by morphological features, we may define a living membrane by its permeability characteristics. This is why we have proposed that, at the level of membrane permeability, cellular differentiation would depend on spatial distribution and organization of the systems which are uniformly distributed at the surface of the primitive type of cell (Schoffeniels 1960a, 1961, 1964, 1967a).

It is also worth noting that both the small intestine and colon originate from the same embryonic layer, the endoderm, while the frog skin comes from the ectoderm. This means that cells originating from two different embryologic layers may evolve in the same direction (convergent differentiation).

The important question now raised is that of the chemical nature of the molecular architecture responsible for the various permeability characteristics. One may obtain information on this subject by studying the effect of various classes of compounds known to affect the permeability of living membranes. It is well known that ouabain and some ammonium derivatives affect ionic movement in a variety of cells which are either functionally different yet within the same species or which belong to species situated far apart on the evolutionary scale (bibliography in Schoffeniels 1961, 1967a). The results suggest that a common biochemical system could be responsible for all the permeability characteristics of living membranes. This would mean that we could consider the permeability characteristics as being a heterotypic expression of a common biochemical system. The concept of heterotypy is used in the sense defined by

Mason. An argument in favor of this view is offered by the observations of Tosteson and Hoffman on the permeability of sheep erythrocytes. Some sheep have red cells with high K (HK) and low Na concentrations, while other sheep have red cells with low K (LK) and high Na concentrations. Evidence obtained by Evans (cited in Goldman) suggests that the LK characteristics are inherited as a dominant gene. Tosteson and Hoffman found that the active transport of K is four times greater in HK cells than in LK cells, while active transport of Na has not been identified in LK cells. Moreover, LK cells have a greater passive permeability to K and a smaller passive permeability to Na than HK cells. Therefore it appears that a single gene might control the permeability characteristics for both active transport and passive movement of K and Na.

3. *Hormonal effects on permeability*

Hormones act on many metabolic processes including the transfer of matter across membranes. Since a relationship exists between metabolism and the permeability characteristics of the membrane, it is often difficult to know if the permeability effects observed are due to a direct action on the membrane, or whether we are witnessing the consequence of some action taking place at another level. Moreover, no agreement has so far been reached on the mechanism of action of any given hormone.

Several theories have been advanced to explain the mode of action of vasopressin and related octapeptides on the movement of water and sodium. A commercial preparation of the hormone (Pitressin) has been shown to be bound on the distal convoluted tubules and collecting ducts, but not on the proximal tubule or ascending loop of Henle. Thus this binding occurs at the known loci of water reabsorption. The antidiuretic activity of this hormone depends, among other things, on the presence of the disulphide bond. Therefore it has been suggested that a mixed disulphide is formed between the peptide and some receptor sites in the membrane. This would involve an exchange of sulphydryl groups, leading to a configurational change in the membrane, which would explain the increased permeability to water and sodium ions (Fong et al.; Holliday et al.).

A similar mechanism may explain the action of insulin on glucose uptake (Cadenas et al.). This is an interesting suggestion since the neurohypophyseal hormones exhibit some insulin-like activity, e.g. stimulation of glucose uptake by the epididymal fat pad (Pitmann et al. 1961; Mirsky and Perissuti 1962), while under certain conditions insulin can increase the net flux of sodium across the frog skin (Herrera et al.).

As further evidence that sulphydryl groups are involved in the mechanism of antidiuretic effect, we may mention the results of Molina et al. They showed that the protein-bound SH groups decrease in the cytoplasm of rat kidney tubules after injection of vasopressin. Dehydration produces the same effect. There seems to be no stoichiometric relationship between the change observed and the amount of hormone added. This is why it is suggested that the number of altered SH groups results from a 'zipper-like' action induced by vasopressin acting on some localized spot.

Orloff and Handler (1964) propose that vasopressin affects water movement through formation of cyclic 3′,5′-AMP and that the binding of the hormone is the first step in a series of events leading to the final change in permeability. Moreover, cyclic 3′,5′-AMP formation in a particulate preparation of dog kidney is stimulated by arginine-vasopressin, the natural hormone of the dog (Brown et al.). Cyclic 3′,5′-AMP increases phosphorylase activity in toad bladder, rabbit renal medulla and dog kidney (Orloff and Handler 1962; Handler and Orloff). Thus vasopressin, like epinephrine in the liver (Sutherland and Rall) and ACTH in the adrenal gland (Haynes) induces cyclic 3′,5′-AMP formation which in turn leads to stimulation of phosphorylase activity.

Results obtained with vasopressin, curare, pyridine-2-aldoxime methiodide (2-PAM) and other quaternary ammonium derivatives bring additional evidence in favor of a spatial separation of permeability characteristics. They show that it is possible to affect separately (inhibition or activation) the permeability to water and to sodium. As shown by the results of Schoffeniels and his collaborators (Schoffeniels and Tercafs; Tercafs and Schoffeniels 1961a, b, 1962; Schoffeniels et al. 1962; Köver et al.; Schoffeniels 1967a), 2-PAM is able to occupy the two sites responsible for the passive movement of Na and water, it is unable to activate these sites equally. Other compounds (e.g. atropine, curare, pilocarpine and vasopressin) are good activators of both sites. 2-PAM seems to compete with the other class of compounds for the same sites, yet is a poor activator of the site responsible for water movement. Nonetheless it is able to prevent the action of vasopressin, which is a good activator of this site. A non-ionic detergent, such as polyethylene glycol, seems to be able to activate the site responsible for the net flux of water, while it is without effect on the site responsible for the passive movement of sodium. Thus, our results obtained with 2-PAM are not easily explained on the basis that cyclic 3′,5′-AMP acts as an intracellular intermediate on the action of vasopressin. They may suggest a more complex sequence of events in which cyclic-AMP is not the compound which interacts directly with the membrane components responsible for the permeability change.

Aldosterone stimulates *in vitro* and *in vivo* the active transport of sodium across the isolated urinary bladder or the isolated ventral skin of the toad (Crabbé 1961). This effect seems to be antagonized by other steroids such as corticosterone, cortisol or progesterone (Crabbé 1964). An important characteristic of the response of the isolated urinary bladder to aldosterone is the latent period which precedes the increase in sodium transport. A pre-incubation of 6 to 12 hr in a steroid-free medium is also needed to sensitize the bladder to aldosterone.

The role of glucose or pyruvate in the stimulation of sodium transport by aldosterone has been demonstrated by showing that, in substrate-depleted bladders, hormone activity depends on an exogenous supply of these substrates. However, in substrate-enriched media, the response is characterized by a latent period of 60 to 90 min followed by a linear increase in sodium transport over a period of 4.5 to 6.5 hr (Edelman et al.). Substrates such as lactate and oxaloacetate, known to yield pyruvate in the course of their metabolism, exhibit a similar effect (Sharp and Leaf). The mechanism of action of aldosterone on the sodium transport thus appears to be very complex. Many hypotheses have been formulated but none seems to explain satisfactorily the experimental data.

Aldosterone is localized in the nucleus of the epithelial cells and its action is inhibited by actinomycin or puromycin. These observations led to the suggestion that the hormone acts by promoting DNA-dependent RNA synthesis yielding in turn an increased rate of protein synthesis, and more specifically of enzymes involved in the oxidation of pyruvate (Edelman et al.) However, recent results of Favestil show that an inhibition of DNA synthesis is without effect on aldosterone action. It has also been suggested that aldosterone acts by increasing the permeability of the outer border of the cell to sodium (Crabbé 1963).

Consequently more results are needed before drawing a definite conclusion as to a direct or secondary effect of the hormones on the permeability sites of the membrane.

4. *Role of inorganic ions in controlling the fate of hydrogen ions produced in the cytoplasm*

Little is known about the control exerted by the cell or the fate of hydrogen ions generated within the cytoplasm – yet this is a phenomenon on which many functions of the cell depend. For instance, the regulation of cell volume involves not only the existence of a cation pump, but also metabolic activity which results in the formation of nitrogen derivatives such as taurine and amino acids (for a review see Schoffeniels 1967a; Florkin and Schoffeniels 1968). Most littoral invertebrates are able to live in media of various osmolarity and thus are particularly useful for the study of the factors controlling these phenomena. In these animals the osmotic pressure of the blood is lower in a dilute medium than in a concentrated one and thus the cells themselves are subjected to an osmotic stress. If they were to behave as perfect osmometers, they would swell or shrink, with the changing extracellular osmolarity. However, when dealing with euryhaline species, the volume change is negligible. The extent to which a cell shrinks or swells may indeed be taken as a good indication of the euryhaline ability of the species (Lange). As shown by Florkin and his collaborators (see Florkin; Florkin and Schoffeniels 1965) the volume change is prevented by the control that the cell exerts on the concentration of osmotically active ions or molecules present in the intracellular fluid. Taurine and amino acids, together with inorganic ions, have been shown to be the main cellular constituents involved in the process (Florkin and Schoffeniels 1965, 1968; Schoffeniels 1967a).

On the basis of experiments performed on isolated nerves of *Eriocheir sinensis*, the Chinese crab, it has been suggested that change in the ionic composition of the intracelluar fluid is directly responsible for the observed change in the amino acid composition of the cell (Schoffeniels 1960b). As a consequence, key enzymes involved in the nitrogen metabolism or in the transfer of reducing equivalents should be differentially affected by the ions depending on the species studied.

(a) *Fate of the reducing equivalents originating in the cytoplasm*
As a result of the activity of the oxidation step leading to 1,3-diphosphoglycerate, NAD^+ is continuously reduced in the cytoplasm. Other extramitochondrial dehydrogenases may also contribute to this reduction. Despite the inability of NADH to cross the mitochondrial membrane, electrons of cytoplasmic NADH are able to reach the respiratory chain through the so-called shuttle system. Two mechanisms are generally proposed: the aceto-acetate and the dihydroxyacetone phosphate shuttles (Devlin and Bedell; Boxer and Devlin).

As a result of the functioning of the shuttles the reducing equivalents of the extramitochondrial NADH are passed into the mitochondrion while the molecules of NAD are reformed, thus permitting glycolysis to proceed.

The extramitochondrial ratio NADH/NAD is also controlled by the activity of various dehydrogenases, of which lactate and alcoholic dehydrogenases are probably the most important. The activity of these two enzymes explains why, in anaerobic conditions, glycolysis still proceeds with the production of lactate and/or ethanol. The ratio of lactate (or ethanol)/pyruvate is thus a measure of the oxidation-reduction state of the glycolytic NAD. Other synthetic systems involving the reduced dinucleotide coenzymes are undoubtedly concerned in the regulation of the oxidation-reduction state of glycolytic and respiratory coenzymes. The couples glutamate-2-ketoglutarate, hydroxypyruvate-glycerate and glyoxylate-glycollate may all play important roles in controlling the aerobic or anaerobic disposal of the reducing equivalent generated during glycolysis or in the Krebs cycle.

Lactic dehydrogenase (*E.N. 1.1.1.27*). The oxidation-reduction potentials of the couples lactate/pyruvate and NADH/NAD are such that the formation of lactate is favored. Various forms of catalytically active proteins have been identified and it has been well established that the enzyme exists in five main forms resulting from the tetrameric association of two different monomers H and M (H_4, H_3M_1, H_2M_2, H_1M_3, M_4, Kaplan). These can be separated by electrophoresis. Genetic studies have favored as well as amino acid analysis, the idea that the syntheses of the polypeptides H and M are each controlled by a different gene. H_4-LDH is maximally active at low pyruvate concentration and is inhibited by a substrate concentration of 10^{-2} M, while the M_4-LDH is maximally active at high pyruvate concentration.

The physiological significance of the various forms of LDH is not fully understood. A positive correlation may be found between the presence of the H-type in a cell and the availability of oxygen (see for instance Salthe). This points to the fact that the H form of the enzyme is associated with a predominantly aerobic metabolism. This makes sense since the H_4-LDH is inhibited at high pyruvate concentration. It is also worth noting that the LDH found in the mitochondria is of the H-type (Agostoni et al.). The proportion of the hybrids of LDH may however vary according to the conditions of the surroundings. Thus a change in oxygen tension, denervation, some pathological states, or various hormones, may all affect the structure of the LDH profoundly. It is generally assumed that this is the result of a differential effect on the synthesis of the monomers M and H. Thus estradiol favors the synthesis of the M polypeptide while a high oxygen pressure inhibits its synthesis. On the other hand oxygen enhances the synthesis of the H polypeptide (Dawson et al.). There is however little information available as to the factors that may influence the tetrameric association and the formation of hybrids.

In Crustacea there appear to be two types of LDH and the use of coenzyme analogs leads to the conclusion that, in the muscles of the species studied, the M form of the enzyme is dominant (Kaplan et al. 1960).

An interesting observation related to the problem of the control of intracellular hydrogen transport, is that the activity of the enzyme, partially purified by ammonium sulfate fractionation, is inhibited by sodium chloride. This is true for all the species we have studied so far, including mammals (Schoffeniels 1968a, b).

However, if the same experiment is performed at a concentration of pyruvate of 10^{-2} M some interesting differences are observed (Table 5). In the case of the two euryhaline species *Astacus* and *Eriocheir*, high concentrations of NaCl are inhibitory, whatever the concentration of pyruvate, while the enzyme of *Homarus*, a stenohaline species, is not inhibited by NaCl if the pyruvate concentration is high. Thus at concentrations of NaCl rather close to that which is found in the cells of marine

TABLE 5

Muscle lactic dehydrogenase of three Crustacea as a function of pyruvate and NaCl concentration (Schoffeniels 1968a).

NaCl (μM/ml)	0	50	100	200	300	400	500
			Pyruvate: 5×10^{-4} M				
Astacus fluviatilis	100	93	71	57	36	29	14
Eriocheir sinensis	100	121	121	89	44	33	22
Homarus vulgaris	100	105	100	90	80	75	65
			Pyruvate: 10^{-2} M				
Astacus fluviatilis	100	100	100	78	78	68	71
Eriocheir sinensis	100	103	100	93	77	70	57
Homarus vulgaris	100	125	125	125	125	125	125

The enzyme of *Astacus* is partially purified by ammonium sulfate precipitation between 30 and 70% saturation, while those of *Eriocheir* and *Homarus* are crude cellular extracts in distilled water.

species, there is less synthesis of lactate in the cells of the euryhaline species than in those of the stenohaline. This makes available more reducing equivalents for other purposes, e.g. glutamic acid synthesis.

3-glycerophosphate dehydrogenase (*E.N. 1.1.1.8*). The NAD-dependent glycerol-3-phosphate dehydrogenase is located in the cytoplasm whereas the cytochrome-linked enzyme is located in the mitochondria. The enzyme catalyses the reduction of phosphodihydroxyacetone into 3-phosphoglycerol and thus permits the transfer of reducing equivalents which originates in the cytoplasm to the respiratory chain in the mitochondria. Its activity is related to the ionic composition of the incubation medium and some differences exist between the enzyme extracted from euryhaline and that from stenohaline species (Table 6). At high concentration of NaCl the activity of the enzyme from stenohaline species is inhibited. However, for values of NaCl between 100 and 200 mM the activity is very much enhanced and this is particularly found when considering the euryhaline species.

Glyoxylate reductase (*E.N. 1.1.1.26*). This enzyme catalyses the reduction of glyoxylate to glycollate. It also reduces hydroxypyruvate to D-glycerate. Its metabolic importance is far from being understood but it certainly plays a role in the regulation

TABLE 6

Muscle 3-glycerophosphate dehydrogenase of some Crustacea (Schoffeniels 1968a).

NaCl μM/ml	0	100	200	300	400	500	600
Euryhaline							
Eriocheir sinensis	100	400	360	280	200	—	—
	100	300	280	240	160	120	100
Carcinus moenas	100	305	283	250	200	133	100
Portunus puber	100	212	225	206	169	131	94
Astacus fluviatilis	100	366	315	217	195	183	116
Stenohaline							
Homarus vulgaris	100	145	117	93	50	42	33
	100	155	135	105	80	—	—
Maia squinado	100	180	133	126	93	—	—
	100	158	141	125	91.5	58.5	45
Cancer pagurus							
big specimen	100	180	120	120	120	—	—
small specimen	100	126	175	126	75	—	—

The enzyme is partially purified by ammonium sulfate precipitation between 30 and 70% saturation and the concentration in dihydroxyacetone phosphate is 5×10^{-4} M. Relative activity.

of glycine concentration inside the cell. The enzyme which is extracted from muscle and nerve of Crustacea, is inhibited by inorganic ions (Table 7).

TABLE 7

Muscle glyoxylate reductase of some Crustacea (Schoffeniels 1968a).

NaCl μM/ml	0	100	200	300	400	500	600
Homarus vulgaris	390	165	95	60	40	20	25
Cancer pagurus (big specimen)	1000	160	70	40	30	25	25
Eriocheir sinensis	680	620	95	60	40	25	20
Carcinus moenas	600	185	95	45	35	25	20

The enzyme is partially purified by ammonium sulfate precipitation between 30 and 70% saturation. Initial velocity expressed in OD units per minute. The concentration in glyoxylate is 10^{-4} M.

It may thus be suggested that the inorganic composition of the intracellular fluid has a marked influence on the activity of enzymes controlling key reactions in cell metabolism. The activities of the lactic or 3-phosphoglycerol dehydrogenases from different species are differently affected by inorganic ions. This points to mechanisms which may explain euryhalinity at the molecular level.

(b) *Control of 2-ketoglutarate production*

2-ketoglutarate is a member of the tricarboxylic acid cycle and as such is located in the mitochondria. It is produced by the oxidative decarboxylation of isocitrate. The subsequent step in the cycle, i.e. the formation of succinate after decarboxylation of 2-ketoglutarate, is irreversible. The decarboxylation of 2-ketoglutarate is catalyzed by isocitrate dehydrogenase.

Two enzymes are of metabolic importance, one is located in the mitochondria (E.N. 1.1.1.41) and involves NAD as hydrogen acceptor (Ernster and Navazio; Kaplan et al. 1956). The other (E.N. 1.1.1.42) is found in the cytoplasm and is extremely concentrated in many cells. This enzyme is NADP-linked and its activity is related to the ionic composition of the medium. This is true both with a crude cellular extract and after partial purification achieved by ammonium sulfate precipitation (between 30 and 70% saturation).

The cytoplasmic enzyme is found in the muscle and nervous system of marine invertebrates. It is however more concentrated (or more soluble) in the euryhaline species than in the stenohaline species. In each type of organism the activity decreases as the salt concentration increases. This has been observed by Gilles and Schoffeniels (unpublished) in Crustacea and in Molluscs (see also Florkin and Schoffeniels 1968).

The results of experiments carried out with ^{14}C-labelled precursors, such as glucose, pyruvate, glycerol, lactate and acetate, are consistent with the interpretation that most of the 2-ketoglutarate used in glutamate synthesis finds its origin in the glycolytic activity of the cell and in the operation of the Krebs cycle (Koeppe et al.). However, Weimberg and Doudoroff have shown that *Pseudomonas saccharophila* may synthesize 2-ketoglutarate from L-arabinose without intervention of the Krebs cycle or the formation of phosphorylated intermediates. These results have also shown 2-keto-3-deoxy-arabonic acid to be an intermediary substrate (Palleroni and Doudoroff).

Datta and Katznelson have demonstrated that *Acetobacter melagenum* is able to metabolize glucose into 2-ketoglutarate by a pathway involving gluconic, 2-keto-gluconic and 2,5-diketogluconic acids as intermediaries. That arabonate may be a precursor of 2-ketoglutarate in pluricellular organisms is well demonstrated by the results of Gilles and Schoffeniels (Table 8). In the experiments reported, D-arabinose-4-^{14}C was added to the incubation medium of an isolated ventral nerve chain of lobster. The analysis of the amino acid content revealed that the radioactivity was subsequently located in taurine, aspartate and glutamate. This result is interesting since it demonstrates that 2-ketoglutarate may be produced outside the Krebs cycle. It also indicates that a metabolite of this sequence is common to both taurine and 2-ketoglutarate.

TABLE 8

Isolated ventral nerve chain of the lobster. Specific activity ($\times 10^{-3}$) of the compounds tagged after one hour incubation in the presence of arabinose-U-^{14}C in five different experiments (after Gilles and Schoffeniels, unpublished results).

Tau	19.0	18.0	36.0	13.0	20.0
Asp	3.0	2.8	2.2	3.6	0.237
Glu	9.7	9.9	2.7	44.0	8.1

(c) *Glutamate synthesis as control of the respiration*

By considering the standard oxidation-reduction potentials (E_0') of the couples glutamate/2-ketoglutarate and NADH/NAD, it is apparent that glutamic dehydrogenase favors the reductive amination of the keto acid rather than the reverse reaction. The E_0' values for the systems NADH/NAD and glutamate-2-ketoglutarate are respectively -0.32 V and -0.108 V, indicating that the presence of any concentration of ammonia, or 2-ketoglutarate, above the infinitesimal would oppose the oxidative deamination of glutamate strongly. This conclusion is of great practical consequence, for it indicates that the enzyme must play an important role in the nitrogen metabolism by controlling the *incorporation* of ammonia into organic compounds. Ammonia is the inorganic form of nitrogen commonly used in animal cells.

This key function, already noticed by Dewan and von Euler et al. many years ago, has been overlooked by many workers, especially kidney physiologists. They insisted on the importance of the enzyme in the production of ammonia (see also Hird and Marginson). However, the importance of glutamate dehydrogenase in controlling the synthesis of glutamate has now been recognized by many authors (Olson and Anfinsen; Strecker; Weil-Malherbe; Klingenberg and Pette; Tager and Slater 1963a; Schoffeniels 1964b, 1965, 1967a, b).

The enzyme found in animal tissues requires NAD as coenzyme (E.C.1.4.1.2). However, in the liver, NADP may also be used (E.C.1.4.1.4). Enzymically active, glutamate dehydrogenase consists of an association of monomers. When these are dissociated from each other, the loss of activity towards glutamate as substrate is paralleled by the appearance of catalytic properties for monocarboxylic amino acids. This situation is brought about by dilution, steroid hormones and other compounds.

Kinetic studies indicate that the catalytic activity is enhanced by ADP, some amino acids and some inorganic cations. On the contrary, the enzyme activity is inhibited by GTP, estrogenic hormones, inorganic anions, etc. (Frieden; Schoffeniels 1966a, b).

These results suggest that the enzyme activity may be directly related to the state of aggregation of the subunits according to the following scheme:

$$\text{Polymer} \overset{\text{I}}{\rightleftharpoons} \text{monomer } x \overset{\text{II}}{\rightleftharpoons} \text{monomer } y$$

Each three forms is catalytically active but the substrate specificity varies from one to another. While monomer x is primarily specific to the glutamate dehydrogenase reaction, monomer y has enhanced activity towards monocarboxylic amino acids (alanine for instance). The three forms are in equilibrium and the various agents known to affect the enzyme activity are thought to displace the equilibrium in one or the other direction. For instance ADP would favor the formation of monomer x while GTP and estrogenic hormones would shift the equilibrium towards the formation of monomer y. The form x of the monomer has a great tendency to aggregate and is antigenically different from the form y. These findings have not yet received an explanation. They point, however, to the many possible ways in which the cell could control the activity of this enzyme. Of special interest is the fact that the activity of glutamate dehydrogenase (GDH) extracted from the tissues of spiny lobster (*Palinurus vulgaris* Latr.), crayfish (*Astacus fluviatilis* L.) and lobster (*Homarus vulgaris* L.) is dependent on the ionic composition of the incubation medium (Schoffeniels and Gilles 1963; Schoffeniels 1964a, 1964b, 1965, 1966a). As far as the GDH extracted from lobster muscle is concerned, both the anion and the cation are important in determining the enzyme activity (Schoffeniels 1964b). This suggests the existence of two categories of specific sites at the surface of the enzyme. These sites may be saturated by anions and cations and, according to the species used, a variable activation of the enzyme is obtained. Thus both categories of sites would contribute to the overall enzyme activity. The kinetic studies of the reaction have shown that the anions are inhibitors of the enzyme activity by competing with 2-ketoglutarate for receptor sites on the enzyme (Schoffeniels 1966b).

There is an optimal concentration in cations above which these become inhibitory and this behaviour is also observed in the crude cellular extracts obtained from various sources (Schoffeniels 1965, 1966a). The optimal concentration is different according to the origin of the material. In mammals and freshwater species it is generally around 50 μM NaCl/ml whilst in the case of marine species it is well above that value and situated in the neighbourhood of 500 μM NaCl/ml. Since the fixation of the reduced dinucleotide on the enzyme is accompanied by an increase in the fluorescence of the coenzyme, this allows a quantitative study of the factors influencing the formation of the complex.

It has been shown that experimental conditions known to decrease the catalytic properties of the enzyme, increase the number of sites fixing the reduced coenzyme. The reverse is true when using ADP, an agent known to increase the enzyme activity.

The inorganic ions have the same effect, in that they decrease the number of binding sites for NADH (Duyckaerts and Schoffeniels). Since under the same conditions the catalytic activity of the enzyme increases, it can be concluded that the sites involved are not important in the catalysis. However, they could be related to the sites involved in the association of the monomers, or be allosteric sites controlling the transconformation of the polypeptide chain.

The results presented above point to a possible role of the inorganic components of the cell in controlling the activity of glutamate dehydrogenase and this suggestion may be of special significance when considering the adaptation to media of various salinities. Thus a euryhaline Crustacean, when introduced into brackish water or sea water, undergoes an increase in the concentration of osmotically active particles within the cell. This change in turn exerts an action on the activity of glutamate dehydrogenase. Consequently the intracellular concentration of glutamate increases, and thus contributes, via the amino transferases, to raising the intracellular osmotic pressure up to the value found in the environment.

This concept is in accordance with the fact that when *Carcinus moenas* or *Eriocheir sinensis* are transferred into diluted medium, the nitrogen excretion is increased for a certain period of time, whereas the opposite effect is observed when the crab is transferred to sea water (Needham; Florkin et al. 1964).

The activity of the lactic or the 3-phosphoglycerol dehydrogenase is affected by the inorganic ions differently, depending upon whether its origin is from a euryhaline or stenohaline animal. This suggests that this enzyme, too, may be involved in the mechanism of euryhalinity at the molecular level.

Our interpretation of the role of the glutamic dehydrogenase in controlling the synthesis of glutamate within the cell has been presented a few years ago (Schoffeniels 1964a). It finds experimental support in the results obtained by Pequin and Serfaty. These authors have shown that the infusion of glutamate in the carp, *Cyprinus carpio*, results in an effective decrease in ammonia excreted by the gills. This rules out glutamate as the source of excreted ammonia (see below).

It is obvious from the above results that the activities of many enzymes are influenced by the ionic composition of the incubation medium. We are dealing with a specific effect, as demonstrated by kinetic analysis of the results, and by the fact that some enzymes such as the L-aspartate, 2-ketoglutarate aminotransferase, or the aspartate decarboxylase are unaffected by the ions (Gilles and Schoffeniels 1966). It is also interesting to notice that in the conditions of high concentration of salts, the activity of some of the key enzymes involved in the transfer of hydrogen is modified in such a way that the cell metabolism is geared towards anaerobic conditions. This prevents some of the reducing equivalents from entering the respiratory chain and make them available for the synthesis of, for instance, glutamate. Moreover, the kinetic analysis of the effects of inorganic ions on the activity of these enzymes renders it possible to detect subtle evolutionary changes in a particular enzyme.

As is well known, the synthesis of glutamate from its corresponding keto-acid is dependent on the availability of a reducing equivalent. Therefore competition must exist between the various synthetic sequences which need NAD or NADP and consequently there should be an interaction between the respiratory chain and the synthesis of glutamate. This is indeed the case and is shown by oxygen consumption measurements in species known to synthesize amino acids at various rates according to the nature of their environment. The oxygen consumption, in most of the euryhaline species so far studied, is increased on transfer from sea water to diluted sea water (see Gilles and Schoffeniels 1965; King 1965; see also Table 9).

In the spider crabs, *Maia* and *Libinia*, which do not normally invade brackish water, respiration is significantly depressed when the animal is placed in dilute sea water (see also Schwabe). In contrast, *Carcinus* and *Callinectes*, which normally invade brackish waters, show a considerable increase in oxygen consumption. The results for *Carcinus*,

TABLE 9

Oxygen consumption of whole animals in response to diluted sea water (after King 1965).

	μl O_2/hr/g		Ratio μl O_2 in 50% sea water/ μl O_2 in 100% sea water
	In sea water	In 50% sea water	
Maia (5)	54.2 ± 4.4	28.2 ± 4.6	0.52 ± 0.04 ($P < 0.005$)
Libinia (6)	37.1 ± 3.8	26.0 ± 2.8	0.70 ± 0.03 ($P < 0.001$)
Carcinus (14)	93.6 ± 6.2	127.5 ± 9.5	1.33 ± 0.04 ($P < 0.001$)
Callinectes (6)*	97.3 ± 7.5	150.4 ± 13.8	1.53 ± 0.05 ($P < 0.001$)

* For *Callinectes*, the diluted sea water was 20%, and the ratio indicates the response at this dilution to that in full-strength water during the 'control' period. The number of animals is in parentheses. Temperature: 25 °C.

showing a 33% increase in oxygen consumption when moved from normal sea water to 50% sea water, are in agreement with those obtained by Schlieper and Schwabe. These observations are best explained if one postulates that the reduced dinucleotide coenzyme, diverted from glutamate synthesis, is oxidized via the respiratory chain in the case of a euryhaline species. In *Eriocheir*, however, the respiratory rate remains constant (Schwabe). As discussed below this can be explained if one postulates that glutamate synthesis acts as an uncoupling agent on the oxidative phosphorylation. The decrease in oxygen consumption, observed when dealing with a stenohaline species, may result from agonic reactions, since the animals did not survive more than a few hours in the experimental conditions. Other explanations could be offered and the decrease in the oxygen consumption could have more significance since a euryhaline fresh water crab such as *Paratelphusa hydrodromous* shows minimal oxygen consumption in 50% sea water and maximal values in tap water and in 100% sea water (Ramamurthi).

In our opinion glutamate dehydrogenase plays a role, as important as that generally assigned to lactic dehydrogenase or the respiratory chain, in controlling the oxidation-reduction state of the cell dinucleotide coenzymes (Schoffeniels 1968ab).

In the case of a euryhaline species the glutamate synthesis seems to control the respiratory chain by directing available reducing equivalents either towards the synthesis of glutamate or the cytochromes. This could be explained if one postulates that the glutamate dehydrogenase requires, in the mitochondria, NADP as coenzyme. The transfer of electrons from NAD to NADP would be the step under control. A stenohaline species would lack this type of control (Fig. 2).

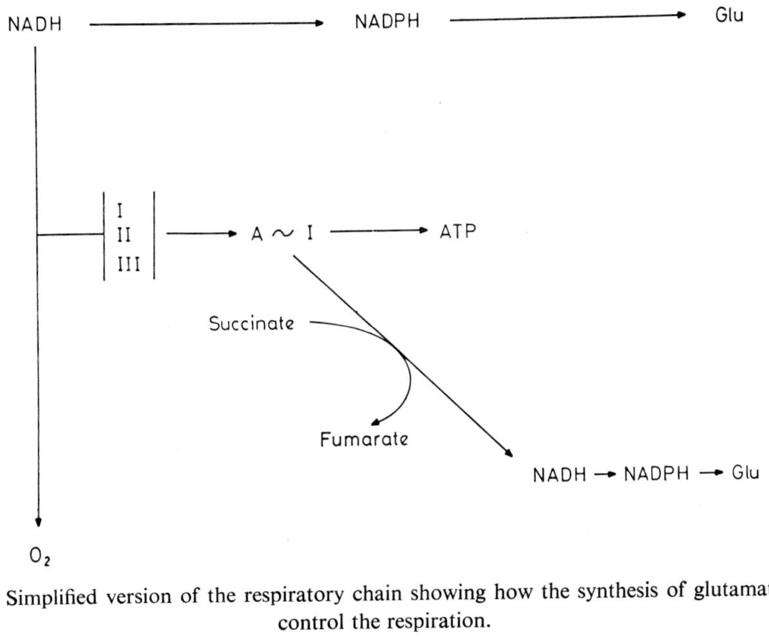

Fig. 2. Simplified version of the respiratory chain showing how the synthesis of glutamate could control the respiration.

It is worthwhile noticing that the activities of the dehydrogenases we have studied are related to the ionic composition of the incubation medium. The interesting observation is that there is an inverse relationship, as far as the salt effect is concerned, when one considers glutamate and glycerol-3-phosphate dehydrogenases on the one hand and the dehydrogenases for lactate, isocitrate and glyoxylate on the other.

In the case of a euryhaline species in a concentrated medium, the activity of the glutamate dehydrogenase is maximal, while that of the other dehydrogenases is minimal, thus suggesting that reducing equivalents produced (in the glycolytic chain for instance) are mainly used for the glutamate synthesis.

If the animal moves into a diluted medium a greater proportion of the reducing equivalents available are directed towards the respiratory chain, and this is indicated by the increase in glycerol-3-phosphate dehydrogenase activity and the decrease in glutamate dehydrogenase activity. Thus the synthesis of amino acids should decrease while the oxygen consumption and the ammonia excretion should increase. This is indeed observed in most of the euryhaline species (Florkin and Schoffeniels 1965; Schoffeniels 1967a).

This interpretation finds experimental support in the results obtained by Gilles and Schoffeniels (1965) on the isolated ventral nerve chain of the crayfish. They were able to show that the addition of NH_4Cl (10 mM) to the incubation medium of the isolated tissue increases the intracellular pool of free amino acids and produces a decrease in the oxygen consumption (from 0.876 down to 0.297 μl O_2 per hour per mg fresh weight). This is at variance with the results obtained with the lobster nerve chain where the oxygen consumption is unaffected.

In the case of *Eriocheir sinensis*, another euryhaline Crustacean, the situation is a little different, since the oxygen consumption is not affected by the transfer of the animal from fresh water to sea water or vice versa (Schwabe). But the amino acid content of the cells does follow the general pattern defined for euryhaline invertebrates. In this species the glutamate synthesis would seem to act as an uncoupling agent of the oxidative phosphorylation, by diverting the energy-rich intermediate from ATP synthesis to the benefit of the synthesis of NADH. Fig. 2 summarizes this interpretation. In this scheme a constant amount of energy-rich intermediate is produced. As shown by Tager and Slater (1963b) this can be used to reduce NAD with succinate as hydrogen donor. The distribution of its utilization between ATP or glutamate synthesis is nicely balanced, with the consequence that the oxygen consumption is not affected by the pathway that is followed. In the case of a decrease in glutamate synthesis, as happens when the animal is in fresh water, more of the energy-rich intermediate could be used for ATP synthesis, and this would in turn serve for the active transport of sodium from the dilute medium.

The relationships suggested above, if they explain satisfactorily some of the observations, are by no means considered to exclude other regulatory mechanisms. The proposed schemes are considered as tentative. More information on the intracellular localization of the enzymes involved and on the ionic composition prevailing locally is needed before a complete picture can be produced. At any rate, the comparison with the behavior of mitochondria extracted from rat liver is fruitful since, in the latter case, when the synthesis of ATP is prevented by the presence of oligomycin, glutamate synthesis increases together with an enhancement of the oxygen consumption.

(d) *Control of intracellular ammonia pool by inorganic ions*

From what we know of nitrogen metabolism, the amide glutamine and the amino acids, particulary glutamate, are the most likely candidates for control of the intracellular pool of ammonia. An interesting relationship stems from the results concerning the effect of inorganic anions on the activity of glutaminase and glutamate dehydrogenase. As is well known, glutaminase activity is enhanced by divalent anions while the converse is true as far as glutamate dehydrogenase is concerned (Schoffeniels 1966b). Thus, the ammonia pool which is mainly dependent on the activity of these two enzymes, could be controlled by the concentration of organic anions as indicated in Fig. 3. In this schematic representation, the intracellular pool of ammonia is depleted by the activity of the glutamate dehydrogenase, and by that of the glutamine synthetase. It is replenished through the deamidation catalysed by the enzyme glutaminase. In the presence of divalent anions, the intracellular concentration in ammonia tends to increase, since the production of this molecule is speeded, while its utilization is inhibited. The reverse is true when the concentration in inorganic anions is low.

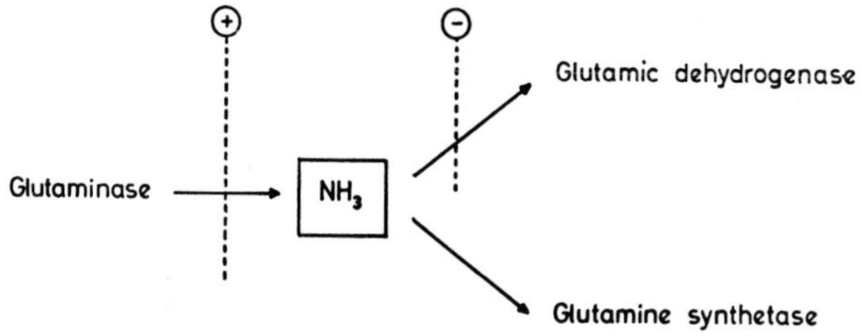

Fig. 3. Control of the intracellular pool of ammonia: effect of anions on two enzymes. +: activation, −: inhibition.

5. *Concluding remarks*

The cell membrane is certainly an organelle endowed with key functions in the general metabolism of the cell since it controls the flux of both matter and energy between the cell interior and its environment. One obvious function is to keep the cell volume constant with the unescapable consequence that the ionic composition of the cell is different from that of the surrounding medium. It is thus tempting to assume that a direct relation must exist between the activity of some metabolic sequences and the intracellular ionic concentrations. So far many results favor this view but the conclusion must be supported by further evidence. The study of metabolic pathways throughout the animal kingdom shows that important aspects of cellular differentiation arise not only from qualitative differences in the metabolic sequences present, but also from the development of specific means of control of catalytic steps common to many types of cell. This explains how the activity of a metabolic route may have various functional significances, according to the types of differentiation. The question thus raised concerns the structure of the enzymes catalyzing the *same* reaction in a large number of different cells. If, according to the type of cell considered, the enzyme is differently controlled, this would suggest that differentiation, or adaptation as the case may be, deals primarily with the development of control sites and has little effect on catalytic centers. Available data for a number of enzymes indicate that the genetic information responsible for the amino acid sequence determines the secondary and tertiary protein structure automatically, and the assumption of a folding template, carrying information differing from that contained in the amino acid code, has not yet been supported by experimental findings. If a protein has various configurations equally stable thermodynamically, the one actually found in a given tissue could result from the conditions occurring in the cytopasm. The emergence of control sites could well be related to cytoplasmic environmental influences.

Another factor that may affect the biological function of an enzyme profoundly is its intracellular location but much remains to be learnt about the factors that may control this distribution.

At present we do not have enough information to understand the relation existing between the membrane and the cell interior. The simplest interpretation is that the activity of the cellular membrane is responsible for the ionic composition of the cell interior while the ionic composition in turn influences the activity of key enzymes. Any factor that could affect the local ionic composition in a subcompartment of the cell could also be of importance. In this respect the buffering capacity of the mitochondria or of the nucleus should not be overlooked.

This working hypothesis does not exclude other regulatory mechanisms and a new dimension will be added when our knowledge of the hormonal action reaches the molecular level.

References

AGOSTONI, A., C. VERGANI and L. VILLA: Intracellular distribution of the different forms of lactic dehydrogenase. Nature 209 (1966) 1024.

BAILLIEN, M. and E. SCHOFFENIELS: Origine des potentiels bioélectriques de l'épithélium intestinal de la tortue grecque. Biochim. Biophys. Acta 53 (1961a) 537.

BAILLIEN, M. and E. SCHOFFENIELS: Le transport actif d'acides aminés au niveau de l'épithélium intestinal isolé de la tortue grecque. Biochim. Biophys. Acta 53 (1961b) 521.

BOXER, G.E. and T.M.DEVLIN: Pathways of intracellular hydrogen transport. Science 134 (1961) 1495.

BRICKER, N.S., T.BIBER and H.H.USSING: Exposure of the isolated frog skin to high potassium concentrations at the internal surface I. Bioelectric phenomena and sodium transport. J. Clin. Invest. 42 (1963) 88.

BROWN, E., D.L.CLARKE, V.ROUX and G.H.SHERMAN: The stimulation of adenosine 3′,5′-monophosphate production by antidiuretic factors. J. Biol. Chem. 238 (1963) PC852.

CADENAS, E., H.HAJI, C.R.PARK and H.RASMUSSEN: Inhibition of the insulin effect on sugar transport by N-ethylmaleimide. J. Biol. Chem. 236 (1961) PC63.

COLE, K.S. and H.J.CURTIS: Electric impedance of the squid giant axon during activity. J. Gen. Physiol. 22 (1939) 649.

CRABBÉ, J.: Stimulation of active sodium transport by the isolated toad bladder with aldosterone 'in vitro'. J. Clin. Invest. 40 (1961) 2103.

CRABBÉ, J.: Site of action of aldosterone on the bladder of the toad. Nature 200 (1963) 787.

CRABBÉ, J.: Decreased effectiveness of aldosterone on active sodium transport by the isolated toad bladder in the presence of other steroids. Acta Endocrinol. 47 (1964) 419.

CRABBÉ, J. and P.DE WEER: Action of aldosterone on the bladder and skin of the toad. Nature 202 (1964) 298.

DATTA, A.G. and H.KATZNELSON: Oxidation of 2,5-diketogluconate by a cell-free enzyme preparation from *Acetobacter melanogenum*. Nature 179 (1957) 153.

DAWSON, D.M., T.L.GOODFRIEND and N.O.KAPLAN: Lactic dehydrogenases: Functions of the two types. Science 143 (1964) 929.

DEVLIN, T.M. and B.M.BEDELL: Effect of acetoacetate on the oxidation of reduced diphosphopyridine nucleotide by intact rat liver mitochondria. J. Biol. Chem. 235 (1960) 2134.

DEWAN, J.G.: The L(+)glutamic dehydrogenase of animal tissues. Biochem. J. 32 (1938) 1378.

DUYCKAERTS, C. and E.SCHOFFENIELS: Fixation du nicotinamide-adénine-dinucléotide sur la déshydrogénase du glutamate. Arch. Intern. Physiol. Biochim. 74 (1966) 895.

EDELMAN, I.S., R.BOGOROCH and G.A.PORTER: On the mechanism of action of aldosterone on sodium transport: the role of protein synthesis. Proc. Natl. Acad. Sci. U.S. 50 (1963) 1169.

ERNSTER, L. and F.NAVAZIO: Studies on TPN-linked oxidations I. Pathways of isocitrate oxidation in rat liver mitochondria. Biochim. Biophys. Acta 26 (1957) 408.

FANESTIL, D.D.: On the mechanism of action of aldosterone on sodium transport: Effect of inhibitors of DNA synthesis. Life Sciences 7 (1968) 191.

FLORKIN, M.: Vergleichende Betrachtung des stationären Zustandes der nicht-eiweissgebundenen Aminosäuren der Tiere. 6. Colloq. Ges. Physiol. Chem. Berlin, Springer (1956) 62.

FLORKIN, M., GH.DUCHATEAU-BOSSON, CH.JEUNIAUX and E.SCHOFFENIELS: Sur le mécanisme de la régulation de la concentration intracellulaire en acides aminés libres chez *Eriocheir sinensis* au cours de l'adaptation osmotique. Arch. Intern. Physiol. Biochim. 72 (1964) 892.

FLORKIN, M. and E.SCHOFFENIELS: Euryhalinity and the concept of physiological radiation. In: K.A. Munday, ed.: Studies in comparative biochemistry. London, Pergamon Press (1965) 6.

FLORKIN, M. and E.SCHOFFENIELS: Adapted molecules: a molecular approach to ecology. New York, Academic Press (in press).

FONG, C.T.O., L.SILVER, D.R.CHRISTMAN and I.L.SCHWARTZ: On the mechanism of action of the antidiuretic hormone (Vasopressin). Proc. Natl. Acad. Scand. 46 (1960) 1273.

FRIEDEN, C.: Glutamic dehydrogenase II. The effect of various nucleotides on the association-dissociation and kinetic properties. J. Biol. Chem. 234 (1959) 815.

GILLES, R. and E.SCHOFFENIELS: Consommation d'oxygène et synthèse des acides aminés. Arch. Intern. Physiol. Biochim. 73 (1965) 144.

GILLES, R. and E.SCHOFFENIELS: Décarboxylation des acides aspartique et oxaloacetique chez le homard et l'écrevisse. Bull. Soc. Chim. Biol. 48 (1966) 397.

GILLES-BAILLIEN, M. and E. SCHOFFENIELS: Site of action of L-alanine and D-glucose on the potential difference across the intestine. Arch. Intern. Physiol. Biochim. 73 (1965) 355.

GILLES-BAILLIEN, M. and E. SCHOFFENIELS: Bioelectric potentials in the intestinal epithelium of the greek tortoise. Comp. Biochem. Physiol. 23 (1967) 95.

GOLDMAN, D. E.: Potential, impedance and rectification in membranes. J. Gen. Physiol. 27 (1943) 37.

HANDLER, J. S. and J. ORLOFF: Activation of phosphorylase in toad bladder and mammalian kidney by antidiuretic hormone. J. Am. Physiol. 205 (1963) 298.

HAYNES, C. R.: The activation of adrenal phosphorylase by the adrenocorticotropic hormone. J. Biol. Chem. 233 (1958) 1220.

HERRERA, F. C., G. WHITTEMBURY and A. PLANCHART: Effect of insulin on short-circuit current across isolated frog skin in the presence of calcium and magnesium. Biochim. Biophys. Acta 66 (1963) 170.

HIRD, F. J. R. and M. A. MARGINSON: Oxidative deamination of glutamate and transdeamination through glutamate. Arch. Biochem. Biophys. 115 (1966) 247.

HODGKIN, A. L.: The ionic-basis of electrical activity in nerve and muscle. Biol. Rev. Cambridge Phil. Soc. 26 (1951) 339.

HODGKIN, A. L. and B. KATZ: The effect of sodium ions on the electrical activity of the giant axon of the squid. J. Physiol. (London) 108 (1949) 37.

HOLLIDAY, M. A., I. L. SCHWARTZ, J. MARC-AURELE, J. HARRAH and D. ELLIOTT: Effect of *p*H and pCO_2 on response of the toad bladder to vasopressin. Federation Proc. 20 (1961) 406.

KAPLAN, N. O.: In: V. Bryson and H. J. Vogel, eds.: Evolving genes and proteins. New York, Academic Press (1965) 243.

KAPLAN, N. O., M. M. CIOTTI, M. HAMOLSKY and R. E. BIEBER: Molecular heterogeneity and evolution of enzymes. Science 131 (1960) 392.

KAPLAN, N. O., M. N. SWARTZ, M. E. FRECH and M. M. CIOTTI: Phosphorylative and nonphosphorylative pathways of electron transfer in rat-liver mitochondria. Proc. Natl. Acad. Sci. U.S. 42 (1956) 481.

KING, E.: The oxygen consumption of intact crabs and excised gills as a function of decreased salinity. Comp. Biochem. Physiol. 15 (1965) 93.

KLAHR, S. and N. S. BRICKER: On the electrogenic nature of active sodium transport across the isolated frog skin. J. Clin. Invest. 43 (1964) 922.

KLINGENBERG, M. and D. PETTE: Proportions of mitochondrial enzymes and pyridine nucleotides. Biochem. Biophys. Res. Commun. 7 (1962) 430.

KOEPPE, R. E., R. M. O'NEAL and C. H. HAHN: Pyruvate decarboxylation in thiamine-deficient (rat and chick) brain. J. Neurochem. 11 (1964) 695.

KÖVER, G., R. R. TERCAFS and E. SCHOFFENIELS: Différence de potentiel et flux net d'eau au niveau de la peau isolée de grenouille. Influence du polyéthylène-glycol '400'. Arch. Intern. Physiol. Biochim. 71 (1963) 588.

LANGE, R.: The osmotic adjustment in the echinoderm *Strongylocentrotus droebachiensis*. Comp. Biochem. Physiol. 13 (1964) 205.

MASON, H. S.: Comparative biochemistry of the phenolase complex. Advan. Enzymol. 16 (1955) 105.

MIRSKY, I. A. and G. PERISSUTI: Action of oxytocin and related peptides on epididymal adipose tissue of the rat. Endocrinology 71 (1962) 158.

MOLINA, G., A. FARAH and R. KRUSE: Effect of vasopressin and dehydration on protein-bound sulfhydryl and bisulfide groups in renal cells. J. Am. Physiol. 204 (1963) 541.

NEEDHAM, A. E.: Factors affecting nitrogen-excretion in *Carcinides maenas* (Pennant). Physiol. Comp. Oecol. 4 (1957) 209.

OLSON, J. A. and C. B. ANFINSEN: Kinetic and equilibrium studies on crystalline L-glutamic acid dehydrogenase. J. Biol. Chem. 202 (1953) 841.

ORLOFF, J. and J. S. HANDLER: The similarity of effects of vasopressin adenosine 3',5'-phosphate (cyclic AMP) and theophylline on the toad bladder. J. Clin. Invest. 41 (1962) 702.

ORLOFF, J. and J.S.HANDLER: The cellular mode of action of antidiuretic hormone. Am. J. Med. 36 (1964) 686.

PALLERONI, N.J. and M.DOUDOROFF: Characterization and properties of 2-keto-3-deoxy-D-arabonic acid. J. Biol. Chem. 223 (1956) 499.

PEQUIN, L. and A.SERFATY: Acide glutamique et excrétion azotée chez la carpe commune, *Cyprinus carpio* L. Comp. Biochem. Physiol. 18 (1966) 141.

PITMANN, J.A., B.R.BOSHELL, B.H.WILLIAMS, D.HAMMER and P.HILL: Insulin-like activity of vasopressin and oxytocin. Biochem. Biophys. Res. Commun. 6 (1961) 29.

RAMAMUSTHI, R.: Oxygen consumption of a fresh water crab, *Paratelphusa hydrodromous*, in relation to salinity stress. Comp. Biochem. Physiol. 23 (1967) 599.

SALTHE, S.N.: Comparative catalytic studies of lactic dehydrogenases in the amphibia: environmental and physiological correlations. Comp. Biochem. Physiol. 16 (1965) 393.

SCHLIEPER, C.: Über die Einwirkung niederer Salzkonzentrationen auf marine Organismen. Z. Vergleich. Physiol. 9 (1929) 478.

SCHOFFENIELS, E.: Les bases physiques et chimiques des potentiels bioélectriques chez *Electrophorus electricus* L. Arch. Intern. Physiol. Biochim. 68 (1960a) 1.

SCHOFFENIELS, E.: Origine des acides aminés intervenant dans la régulation de la pression osmotique intracellulaire de *Eriocheir sinensis* Milne Edwards. Arch. Intern. Physiol. Biochim. 68 (1960b) 696.

SCHOFFENIELS, E.: Comparative study of membrane permeability. In: T.W.Goodwin and O.Lindberg, eds.: Biological structure and function. London, Academic Press 2 (1961) 621.

SCHOFFENIELS, E.: Cellular aspect of active transport. In: M.Florkin and H.S.Mason, eds.: Comparative biochemistry. London, Academic Press 7 (1964a) 137.

SCHOFFENIELS, E.: Effect of inorganic ions on the activity of L-glutamic acid dehydrogenase. Life Sciences 3 (1964b) 845.

SCHOFFENIELS, E.: L-glutamic acid dehydrogenase activity in the gills of *Palinurus vulgaris* Latr. Arch. Intern. Physiol. Biochim. 73 (1965) 73.

SCHOFFENIELS, E.: Activité de la déshydrogénase de l'acide L-glutamique et osmorégulation. Arch. Intern. Physiol. Biochim. 74 (1966a) 333.

SCHOFFENIELS, E.: The activity of L-glutamic acid dehydrogenase. Arch. Intern. Physiol. Biochim. 74 (1966b) 665.

SCHOFFENIELS, E.: Cellular aspects of membrane permeability. New York, Pergamon Press (1967a) 284p.

SCHOFFENIELS, E.: La désamination, la désamidation et les transaminations. In: M.Javillier, M. Polonovski, M.Florkin, F.Boulanger, M.Lemoigne, J.Roche and K.Wiermser, eds.: Traité de biochimie générale. Paris, Masson et Cie 3 (1967b) 354.

SCHOFFENIELS, E.: The control of intracellular hydrogen transport by inorganic ions. Arch. Intern. Physiol. Biochim. 76 (1968a) in press.

SCHOFFENIELS, E.: Key enzyme systems in nervous tissue. In: G.H.Bourne, ed.: Structure and function of nervous system. New York, Academic Press 2 (1968b) in press.

SCHOFFENIELS, E. and R.GILLES: Effect of cations on the activity of L-glutamic acid dehydrogenase. Life Sciences 2 (1963) 834.

SCHOFFENIELS, E., R.GILLES and G.DANDRIFOSSE: Action des détergents et du calcium sur le potentiel électrique de la peau de grenouille isolée. Arch. Intern. Physiol. Biochim. 70 (1962) 335.

SCHOFFENIELS, E. and R.R.TERCAFS: Potential difference and net flux of water in the isolated amphibian skin. Biochem. Pharmacol. 11 (1962) 769.

SCHWABE, E.: Ueber die Osmoregulation verschiedener Krebse. Z. Vergleich. Physiol. 19 (1939) 183.

SHARP, G.W.G. and A.LEAF: The central role of pyruvate in the stimulation of sodium transport by aldosterone. Proc. Natl. Acad. Sci. U.S. 52 (1964) 1114.

STRECKER, H.J.: Glutamic dehydrogenase. Arch. Biochem. Biophys. 46 (1953) 128.

SUTHERLAND, E.W. and T.W.RALL: Properties of an adenine ribonucleotide produced with cellular particles, adenosinetriphosphate magnesium and adrenaline or glucagon. J. Am. Chem. Soc. 79 (1957) 3608.

TAGER, J.M. and E.C.SLATER: Synthesis of glutamate from α-oxoglutarate and ammonia in rat-liver mitochondria I. Comparison of different hydrogen donors. Biochim. Biophys. Acta 77 (1963a) 227.

TAGER, J.M. and E.C.SLATER: Synthesis of glutamate from α-oxoglutarate and ammonia in rat liver mitochondria II. Succinate as hydrogen donor. Biochim. Biophys. Acta 77 (1963b) 246.

TERCAFS, R.R. and E.SCHOFFENIELS: Action of d-tubocurarine chloride on the net flux of water across the isolated frog skin. Science 133 (1961a) 1706.

TERCAFS, R.R. and E.SCHOFFENIELS: Action du sulfate d'atropine et du chlorhydrate de pilocarpine sur le flux net d'eau au niveau de la peau isolée de *Rana temporaria* L. Arch. Intern. Physiol. Biochim. 69 (1961b) 604.

TOSTESON, D.C. and J.F.HOFFMAN: Cation transport in high and low potassium sheep red cells. J. Cellular Comp. Physiol. 52 (1958) 191.

VON EULER, H., E.ADLER, G.GUNTHER and N.B.DAS: Über den enzymatischen Abbau und Aufbau der Glutaminsäure II. In tierischen Geweben. Hoppe-Seylers Z. Physiol. Chem. 254 (1938) 61.

WEIL-MALHERBE, H.: In: D.Richter, ed.: Metabolism of the nervous system. London, Pergamon Press (1957).

WEIMBERG, R. and M.DOUDOROFF: The oxidation of L-arabinose by *Pseudomonas saccharophila*. J. Biol. Chem. 217 (1955) 607.

CHAPTER 51

Pinocytosis (endocytosis)

W. STOCKEM and K. E. WOHLFARTH-BOTTERMANN

Institute of Cytology and Micromorphology, University of Bonn

Contents

1. Introduction
2. Methods
3. Induced endocytosis
   (a) Investigation by light microscopy
      The morphology of induced endocytosis
      Factors inducing endocytosis
      Quantitative investigations
   (b) Investigation by electron microscopy
      The significance of the mucoid layer
      The formation of the endosomes
4. Permanent endocytosis
   (a) Investigation by light microscopy
      Location and kinetics of permanent endocytosis
      The relation of permanent endocytosis to amoeboid movement
      The behaviour of the cell surface
   (b) Investigation by electron microscopy
      The fine structure of the uroid
      The intracellular fate of the endosomes
5. Discussion and conclusions

1. Introduction

The original concept of the cell, as a homogeneous reaction space in a colloidal system, has been profoundly modified by electron microscopy. A principle of order, universal in its validity, underlies the intimate structure of the cell and aids in the understanding of its complex function. According to Ruska (1960, 1962) the cytoplasm is partitioned by a system of morphologically similar membranes into aqueous mixed phases (reaction spaces). The similarity of these membranes was the basis of the theory of their convertibility and kinetic properties (Wohlfarth-Bottermann 1959, 1963a, b; Komnick; Komnick and Wohlfarth-Bottermann; Schneider; Uhlig, Komnick and Wohlfarth-Bottermann). The mechanisms of membrane vesiculation and membrane flow in relation to uptake, intracellular transport, and elimination of digested or non-digestible substances represent a special case of membrane convertibility. Metschnikoff was the first to observe ingestion of food particles of light-microscopic dimensions by mesodermal cells, a process for which he coined the expression *phagocytosis* and which other workers have observed in many cell types. Terms such as *colloidopexy* (Bratianu and Llombart), *chromopexy* (Volkonsky), *athrocytosis* (Gérard and Cordier), *granulocytosis* (granulopexy, Benacerraf et al.) and *phagotrophy* (Seaman) merely express the content and size of cytoplasmic vacuoles. Yet, these terms describe processes which, from the viewpoint of cellular physiology and apart from minor morphological variations, are identical at the level of the light microscope.

In contrast to Metschnikoff's *phagocytosis*, and in order to express more accurately the vacuolar uptake of *fluid* by macrophages and sarcoma cells, Lewis (1931) applied the term *pinocytosis* to a similar mechanism visualised by phase-contrast microscopy. The higher resolving power of the electron microscope later revealed that the content of the pinocytic vacuoles, which in the light microscope has appeared homogeneous, was likewise partially granular. The pinocytotic uptake of such sub-lightmicroscopic particles has been called *rhopheocytosis* (Policard and Bessis), *micropinocytosis* (Odor), and *ultraphagocytosis* (Gosselin). The distinction between pinocytosis and phagocytosis is thus primarily a matter of microscopic resolution, in other words, a matter of identification. Yet, many expressions such as chromopexy (ingestion of pigment), athrocytosis (storage), phagotrophy (uptake of food particles in protozoa) have been introduced to designate qualitative differences. Since these expressions are often used with different meanings it is appropriate to recall that the processes they designate have a common mechanism which consists, at the morphological and metabolic-physiological level, in the uptake of substances into the cell by 'displacement of the membrane barrier from cell surface to cell interior' (Holter 1965). On the proposal of Novikoff (1961), de Duve (1963) introduced the comprehensive terms *endocytosis* (membrane vesiculation from cell surface to cell interior) and *exocytosis* (membrane vesiculation from cell interior to cell surface). Since, however, these terms do not include membrane vesiculation *inside the cell,* we consider that a third word is needed and suggest, by analogy, *intracytosis.*

The products of endocytosis are cytoplasmic vacuoles with extracellular content pinched off from the cell membrane. Straus (1958, 1959) called such vacuoles *phagosomes*, while Novikoff (1960) considered the term *pinosomes* more apt. Whether they are 'pinosomes' or 'phagosomes' they result from one and the same process, and we believe the term *endosomes*, formed on the model of 'endocytosis', to be more appropriate. Bennett attempted, with his hypothesis of membrane vesiculation and membrane flow, to explain more accurately the cellular physiology of the initial phase of endocytosis and drew attention to the functional and morphological equivalence of the many isolated findings.

Endocytosis is important chiefly because it throws light on two phenomena which are difficult to explain by the classical theory of active transport.

(1) Endocytosis enables particles, including ions, to get into the cell without having first to pass through the cell membrane. The material taken up is transported within the cell by intracytosis.

(2) Reaction-specific substances lying on the cell membrane enable certain materials to be adsorbed selectively by the cell and taken up specifically by endocytosis.

A probable additional advantage of vesicular uptake, and transport, is that the cytoplasm is separated, and thereby protected, from the substances it takes up by a membrane. Directed transport of vacuolar content to determined cell areas is easier to understand than transport of substances lying free in the cytoplasm.

The importance of endocytosis, intracytosis, and exocytosis in the metabolism of the cells of plants and animals has been demonstrated beyond dispute by a large body of research, comprehensively summarised by Holter and Holtzer; Weiling; Chapman-Andresen (1962); Wittekind; Gropp; and Willmer (1965, 1966). The most detailed studies have been carried out in amoebae (Mast and Doyle; Holter and Marshall; Brandt; Holter 1959, 1960; Chapman-Andresen 1962, 1965a; Stockem 1966; Wohlfarth-Bottermann and Stockem).

2. *Methods*

The methods that have been developed for studying endocytotic processes are aimed at elucidating the formation and intracellular fate of endosomes. Yet, by creating morphological and physiological artefacts, these same methods may distort the process of endocytosis. Our study of endocytotic processes in amoebae must therefore be preceded by a critical analysis of the main techniques employed.

The discovery of phase-contrast microscopy opened the way to observation of the cell under near-physiological conditions and to motion-picture analysis of cell motility processes. Observation of the living cell provided final proof of the existence of endocytotic processes (Lewis 1937a; Pomerat et al.). Yet, although it has many advantages, the procedure has the limitation that the fate of endosomes can be followed over short periods only. For this reason labelling of extracellular fluid with vital stains was tried, with a view to differentiating endosomes from other cytoplasmic vesicles. Most vital stains, however, such as neutral red (Lewis 1937b), toluidine blue (Rustad), and alcian blue (Chapman-Andresen 1962) have toxic effects and cause pathological reactions and morphological cell damage. Like the frequently employed fluorescent dyes (Holter and Marshall; Brandt) and fluorochromated proteins (Wolpert and O'Neill; Jeon and Bell) they often act as inducers of endocytosis. A search was therefore made for readily identifiable inert substances (melanin granules or latex spheres), or else naturally-occurring food particles (bacteria or erythrocyte ghosts). These were used in an attempt to obtain approximately physiological conditions (Gropp). Isotope techniques and autoradiography have enabled even substances not detectable in the light microscope (such as glucose and proteins) to be followed after their uptake into the cell (Chapman-Andresen and Holter; Shumaker). These results, however, were obtained chiefly in amoeboid cells in which endocytosis can be followed under the light microscope. Corresponding processes in other cell types were not demonstrated until after extensive development of electron microscopy (Odor; Karrer; Kaye and Pappas; Wessing). Here new difficulties arose, for the course of the motility processes had to be reconstructed from serial photographs taken at fixed moments in time. According to Sitte, this method will achieve results only when the following criteria are satisfied:

(1) The process must be statistically reproducible.

(2) The time interval between individual pictures must be exactly determinable and must correspond to the speed of the movement.

(3) Differentiation between individual pictures must be such that the direction of movement is clearly identifiable.

In the case of endocytosis these three conditions cannot be fulfilled without recourse to special techniques. Statistical reproducibility is difficult to achieve in practice, because endocytosis normally runs a discontinuous course and depends on the composition of the extracellular medium, which is not always quite reproducible. Moreover, endocytosis can take place so quickly, especially in its initial stage, that fixation may miss individual phases of its kinetics. Finally, endocytosis and exocytosis are morphologically identical processes. Without special techniques, therefore, and in spite of morphological differences, it is not possible to decide whether a vacuole is migrating to the cell surface (exocytosis) or from the cell surface to the cell interior (endocytosis).

These difficulties are overcome by labelling the extracellular medium with electron-dense substances which, after cell fixation, make the contents of endosomes identifiable and thus enable endocytosis and exocytosis to be differentiated. The following substances have been used successfully: mercuric sulphide (Odor); melanin granules (Felix and Dalton); ferric hydroxide and charcoal (Gieseking); ferritin (Farquhar and Palade); indian ink (Karrer); gold sol (Staubesand 1960); myofer (Schmidt 1961); various vital stains (Schmidt 1960; Hayward); thorium dioxide (Brandt and Pappas 1960, 1962); ferrlecit (Staubesand 1963); polystyrol latex (Favard and Carasso);

haemoglobin (Rudzinska et al.); copper (Wessel et al.); silicon dioxide and egg white (Stockem 1966). The use of these substances, however, is not without its difficulties. Their selection must be preceded by exhaustive trials on the test object, and be governed by the specific problem to be studied. The factors determining the choice of the method used in the investigation are: (1) the test object, (2) the labelling substance, and (3) their mutual interaction under experimental conditions. The choice will also be governed by whether the aim of the investigation is (1) to determine the endocytotic activity of the cell in its natural environment, in other words to ascertain what is the normal quantitative uptake from the extracellular medium, or (2) to find out what substances the cell is capable of incorporating by endocytosis and the effect of these substances on the course of this process.

Problem (1) is mainly physiological and calls for a labelling substance which will not affect normal endocytotic cell activity and will behave as inert material with no other action than to enable endosome content to be identified with certainty.

Problem (2) concerns the reaction of the cell to test material forced upon it experimentally. The labelling substance may greatly intensify normal endocytotic activity, resulting in increase in the quantity of material taken up. This may lead to pathological phenomena which are often followed by cell death.

Whichever of these two objectives the investigator has set himself, therefore, the choice of a suitable labelling substance is of paramount importance. This question has been investigated in detail in amoebae (Stockem 1966) and three groups of substances have been distinguished:

(1) *Coarse-particle substances* (latex, mercuric sulphide, gold sol, aerosil) which do not influence the normal endocytotic activity of amoebae in movement;

(2) *Fine-particle substances* (ferritin, myofer, ferrlecit) varying in activity;

(3) *Electron-optically amorphous solutions* (egg white, alcian blue) having vigorous inducing and intensifying action on endocytosis and producing total inhibition of cell motility.

Amoebae are excellent test objects for investigations of this kind. In this organism normal and induced endocytotic activity can be clearly differentiated in light microscopy, and they react to non-inert substances by immediate change in form and in motility pattern. Under these conditions 'aerosil', an amorphous silica preparation, may be regarded as a suitable labelling substance. In addition to all the qualities required of such a substance on technical grounds it is resistant to embedding, is readily sectioned, has no tendency to translocation and, with a particle size of 50 to 100 Å, lies within the dimensions corresponding to endocytosis and intracytosis. It can be identified with certainty in thin sections by a cytochemical method using hydrofluoric acid (Stockem 1966, 1968).

It will be readily understood that results obtained in amoebae cannot be extrapolated directly to other cell types, since the appropriate labelling substance has to be specifically ascertained each time for every test object, and with regard to each problem selected for investigation.

3. *Induced endocytosis*

(a) *Investigation by light microscopy*

The morphology of induced endocytosis. Amoebae are unicellular organisms which constantly change their shape and move by cytoplasmic streaming. Two forms can be distinguished: (1) a motile form with one or several pseudopodia (antero-posterior orientation); (2) a resting form (rounded state) the adoption of which is enforced by conditions of physiological stress (*p*H, temperature, chemical or mechanical stimulation). Change from the motile to the resting form can also be brought about by the so-called endocytosis-inducing substances, a phenomenon first described in large amoebae by Mast and Doyle, later studied by Shumaker and Brandt and thoroughly investigated by Holter and his co-workers. These findings are fully reviewed by Chapman-Andresen (1962). The present writers' phase-contrast microscopy studies on induced endocytosis (Wohlfarth-Bottermann and Stockem) were recently continued under more favourable conditions by interference phase-contrast (after Nomarski), and have shown that the process takes place as follows:

(1) The first event following replacement of the culture medium by an inducing solu-

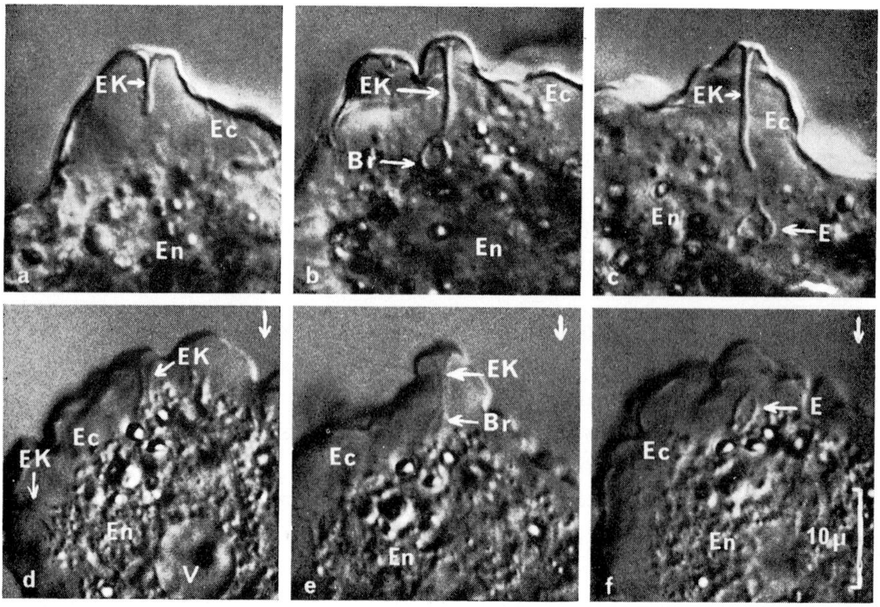

Fig. 1. Induced (a-c) and permanent (d-f) endocytosis in *Amoeba proteus.* a-c: Formation of an endocytosis channel (EK) and pinching off of an endosome (E) after 5 min incubation in 0.5% egg white. d-f: Formation of an endocytosis channel (EK) in the uroid region of a moving amoeba and pinching off of an endosome (E). Interference phase contrast after Nomarski (Zeiss). Br = dilated base of channel; Ec = ectoplasm; En = endoplasm; V = vacuole with food particles. The arrow indicates the direction of movement of the amoeba.

tion is cessation of cytoplasmic streaming. The amoeba, rounding up like a disk, changes from the motile to the resting form.

(2) Hyaline ectoplasm appears at the cell periphery and forms a border surrounding the vacuolar endoplasm; at the same time the previously smooth cell surface begins to show pronounced ruffling.

(3) The ectoplasmic envelope develops numerous pseudopodia, at first short and the membrane becomes invaginated at their tips (Fig. 1a).

(4) When the endocytosis channel, thus formed, reaches the ectoplasm-endoplasm boundary, it seems to become embedded in the surrounding cytoplasmic ground substance (groundplasm), and in consequence enlarges as the hyaline pseudopodium elongates.

(5) A large vacuole forms at the base of the endocytosis channel (Fig. 1b), becomes pinched off, and passes to the interior of the cell (Fig. 1c). The remainder of the channel splits up, as the result of clearly visible contractions, into smaller vacuoles, which are likewise carried to the cell centre.

The duration of a channel is about three minutes, and over 100 channels may be formed during one endocytosis cycle. The kinetics of the formation and disintegration of endocytosis channels may differ in directly contiguous pseudopodia belonging to the same cell. Often a channel becomes divided up as the result of elongation of the pseudopodium and thus undergoes fragmentation. The size of the membrane invaginations also varies greatly; widths range from several microns to values not measurable by the light microscope. The length may vary from 30 to 80 μ. The average width is about 2 μ and the average length 50 μ. The shape of the channel depends on the type of inducer (Chapman-Andresen 1962), the invaginations varying from tubular to bottle-shaped; the 'neck of the bottle' may be very long or very short. The diameter of the resulting endosomes ranges from several microns to some hundreds of Ångströms.

Factors inducing endocytosis. Endocytosis-inducing factors, known at present, include inorganic salts, amino acids, proteins, and certain dyes (Table 1). A decisive factor in initiating the endocytosis process is the *p*H value of the solution. The inducing power of inorganic salts is greatest in the neutral *p*H range, of amino acids in the alkaline range, and of proteins in the acid range. The action of most dyes is largely independent of *p*H. The most favourable concentration of inducing solution varies, according to the substance, between 0.1 and 0.000001 M. Optimal temperature lies between +20 and +23 °C, the minimum and maximum values being, according to the inducer, +5 and +30 °C respectively. Temperature, *p*H value, and molarity of the inducing solution are not the only factors that influence endocytosis. Zimmerman and Rustad found that a hydrostatic pressure of 3000 lb per sq. inch (210.92 kg per cm^2) causes the disappearance of endocytosis channels already formed. Metabolic inhibitors such as carbon monoxide, potassium cyanide, and 2,4-dinitrophenol can, according to Chapman-Andresen (1965b), prevent their formation.

TABLE 1

Some endocytosis inducers.

Inducing substance	*p*H Value Min.	Opt.	Max.	Concentration
Inorganic salts				
Chlorides, sulphates, and nitrates of Na, K, Mg and Li	—	7.0	—	0.1–0.15 M
Amino acids				
Aspartic acid	5.0	8.0	10.0	
Glutamic acid	5.0	8.0	10.0	
Lysine	6.0	8.0	9.0	
Arginine	6.0	8.0	9.0	
Asparagine	9.0	10.0	—	0.063 M
Triglycine	8.5	9.5	—	
Glutamine	9.0	9.5	—	
Methionine	9.5	10.0	—	
Glycine	9.0	9.5	—	
Proteins				
Bovine serum albumin	—	4.0	5.5	
Beta-lactoglobulin	—	4.0	5.0	
Bovine gamma-globulin	—	4.0	—	0.0001 M
Conalbumin	—	4.0	5.5	
Haemocyanin	—	4.0	—	0.000001 M
Insulin	—	4.0	—	
Ribonuclease	—	4.0 (7.0)	8.5	
Cytochrome C	—	4.0 (7.5)	—	0.0001 M
Lysozyme	—	4.0	—	
Clupeine	—	4.0	—	
Egg white	—	4.0–5.0	—	0.5%
Dyes				
Toluidine blue				
Methylene blue				
Methyl violet				
Thionine				
Basic fuchsine				
Janus green B	—	4–10	—	0.1–0.01%
Neutral red			—	
Acriflavine				
Brilliant cresyl blue				
Acridine orange				
Alcian blue				
Iron compounds				
Ferritin				—
Myofer	—	4–6	—	2.5%
Ferrlecit				0.6%
Buffer substances				
Phosphate buffer	—	6–8	—	0.01–0.05 M
Maleate buffer				

Whether inducers can initiate endocytosis in other cell types is not known; the work of Holter and Holtzer makes it seem at least probable. Nor is it known whether inducers must necessarily be of a chemical nature. Rinaldi found that ultraviolet radiation induced endocytosis in amoebae; the implications of this will be discussed later.

Quantitative investigations. Most of the quantitative investigations on induced endocytosis have been carried out in amoebae (Holter and Marshall; Chapman-Andresen and Holter; Chapman-Andresen and Dick; Shumaker). Only a few values (Lewis 1931; Policard and Baud) are available for cells of metazoa (Table 2). Amoebae are capable of taking up large amounts of substance during induced endocytosis. In the first phase of induction (about 20 min) the ingested volume corresponds to some

TABLE 2

Uptake of material by endocytosis.

Test object	Duration of experiment (min)	Inducing substance	Labelling substance	A	B
Chaos chaos	180	γ-globulin	Fluorescein	30–40	5
Chaos chaos	20	Bovine albumin	C^{14}-glucose	1–10	0.8
Chaos chaos	20	NaCl	Na^{22}	1–9	0.5
Chaos chaos	20	NaBr	Br^{82}	1–9	1.0
Chaos chaos	20	Coll. gold	Au^{198}	25	0.2
Chaos chaos	30	Ribonuclease	I^{131}-protein	6	—
Chaos chaos	30	Cytochrome C	I^{131}-protein	6	—
Amoeba proteus	20	Bobine albumin	I^{131}-albumin	23–200	7.5–66
Amoeba proteus	20	Bovine albumin	C^{14}-glucose	2–5	0.0001–0.00001
Amoeba proteus	20	Alcian blue	—	0.5	—
Macrophages	60	—	—	30	—
Histiocyte	60	—	—	30	—

A = Uptake expressed as percentage increase in volume calculated with reference to total volume; B = Percentage increase in total dry weight.

5 to 10% of the initial cell volume and increases of 0.5 to 1% of their dry weight have been recorded. According to Holter (1965) there is a concomitant cell membrane surface increase of up to 50% of the initial value. These results furnish a provisional answer to the question whether induced endocytosis represents primarily (a) uptake of extracellular fluid or (b) ingestion of substances adsorbed onto the cell surface from the extracellular fluid. When an inducer (bovine plasma albumin) and a non-inducer

(glucose) are offered together, with alternating labelling (cf. Table 2), they are taken up simultaneously, but the bovine albumin is taken up in quantities more than ten times greater than the glucose. Holter (1965) accordingly regards induced endocytosis as being primarily an uptake of adsorbed material; he postulates further that this selective ingestion plays an important part in the nutrition of the amoeba cell. However, a second induced endocytosis cycle cannot take place unless the amoebae are first allowed a four-hour recovery period in a normal culture medium, and the second cycle will be substantially weaker than the first. Amoebae left in an inducing solution gradually perish. Such replacement of inducing solution by normal culture medium at an appropriate time is hardly conceivable in nature. It therefore seems unlikely that endocytosis, under such special conditions, is of practical importance in cell nutrition.

(b) *Investigation by electron microscopy*

The significance of the mucoid layer. Electron microscope studies (Marshall and Nachmias; Nachmias and Marshall; Stockem 1966) have revealed the important part played by the mucoid layer in induced endocytosis. This structure consists, with some variations depending on the type of amoeba, of a homogeneous amorphous layer, 200 to 300 Å thick, lying directly upon the cell membrane, and a 1000 to 2000 Å thick filamentous zone. The mucoid layer makes up about 4% of the total dry weight of the amoeba and the biochemical analysis has shown that it is rich in an acid mucopolysaccharide of which the sugar component is mannose and which contains 4 to 5% of sulphate (Marshall and Nachmias).

Holter (1965) believes that the first step in induced endocytosis is adsorption of the inducer onto the mucoid layer. The strength of this adsorptive binding varies from one inducer to another; while salts are readily washed out, cleavage of proteins is possible only if the *p*H value rises by at least two units, and binding of certain dyes is irreversible (alcian blue, for example). Binding, according to Holter, constitutes the adsorptive stimulus (first phase) of the endocytotic process and is responsible for endocytosis channel formation. However, the present writers' own electron microscope studies on the interaction between potent inducers and the mucoid layer, have shown that endocytosis is induced only when (1) adsorption has reached a critical and at the same time quantitatively significant value (as is the case of egg white, ferritin, and thorotrast in the acid *p*H range), (2) the inducer substance destroys the mucoid layer (as does alcian blue) respectively (3) the inducer damages other cell organelles (sodium chloride) (Stockem 1966). Incomplete loading of the peripheral coat of the cell membrane with, for example, thorotrast or ferritin at neutral *p*H range will not induce endocytosis. This shows that adsorption in itself is not the sole activating factor, but that the quantity of substance adsorbed must also be important. These results lead to the further conclusion, that the initial phase of endocytosis in amoebae, is not as depicted in Bennett's hypothesis, according to which adsorbed particles induce local endocytotic invaginations. In fact, although intensive labelling of the mucoid layer with inert substances (aerosil, latex, etc.) can inhibit amoeboid movement and compel the amoebae to round up temporarily, such substances are not taken up in induced endocytosis.

In summary, we may state the following:

(1) The adsorption of the labelling substance onto the mucoid layer does not in itself suffice to induce endocytotic processes in amoeba. A more decisive factor is the quantity of substance adsorbed.

(2) Adsorptive binding certainly explains variations in concentration of these substances on the cell surface and is therefore of quantitative importance; qualitatively, however, it is less specific, since in our experience the mucoid layer adsorbs both inducers and non-inducers.

It is likewise difficult to make an inducer responsible for the induction of endocytosis by ultraviolet radiation. The production or activation of inducing substance by ultraviolet radiation, in culture medium, has been excluded by Rinaldi. Here too, damage to the mucoid layer or to other cell organelles is the more probable inducing mechanism. We believe that the factor initiating induced endocytosis is to be sought in the degree of blockage of, or damage to, the mucoid layer or other organelles. In such extreme cases the amoebae are obliged to reduce, by endocytosis, the damaged peripheral layer of their cell membrane, in order to renew it subsequently.

The formation of the endosomes. In Holter's view (Holter 1965) cell membrane invagination and endosome formation, in response to adsorptive stimulus, constitute the second phase of the endocytotic process. This aspect has also been the subject of electron microscope studies (Brandt and Pappas 1960, 1962; Chapman-Andresen and Nilson; Wohlfarth-Bottermann and Stockem). These were designed mainly to ascertain which structures generate the force necessary for invagination of the cell membrane and for fragmentation of the endocytosis channels. Present knowledge indicates that this force is furnished by an adenosine triphosphate (ATP)-sensitive contractile mechanism connected with groundplasm differentiations, the plasma-filaments (Wohlfarth-Bottermann 1964). The plasma-filaments are actively concerned with the endocytotic process in amoebae (Marshall and Nachmias; Wohlfarth-Bottermann and Stockem). Immediately after invagination of the cell membrane, the (still short) endocytosis channel, is completely surrounded by a dense groundplasmic envelope already containing discrete filaments. After the endocytotic channels have reached their maximal length, the filaments become more numereous especially in the basal channel region. Soon the filaments no longer occur singly, but arrange themselves in parallel arrays to form fibrils. They display a definite orientation, generally lying parallel to the direction in which the channels have become invaginated. There is a striking clumping of mitochondria along the endocytosis channels and at the base.

The intracellular fate of the endosomes suggests that their contents become digested. It does not differ from that of the vacuoles formed during permanent endocytosis and will therefore be discussed more fully in the next section.

4. Permanent endocytosis

(a) *Investigation by light microscopy*

Location and kinetics of permanent endocytosis. The earliest studies on endocytosis in amoebae led to the view (Chapman-Andresen 1962) that endocytotic processes in these unicellular organisms are initiated only by specific inducers and therefore run a discontinuous course. However, Wohlfarth-Bottermann's (1960) electron-microscope studies in *Hyalodiscus simplex* have shown that continuous uptake of cell membrane during locomotion is inherent in the normal behaviour of this amoeba. Wolpert and O'Neill's hypothesis that this also applies to *Amoeba proteus* has been confirmed conclusively by Wohlfarth-Bottermann and Stockem using phase contrast microscopy and electron microscopy. Interference phase contrast (after Nomarski) has enabled the kinetics of permanent endocytosis to be studied with greater precision. The formation and fragmentation of a channel in permanent endocytosis is reproduced in Fig. 1d-f. This figure shows that there are no essential differences between permanent and induced endocytosis. The stages of permanent endocytosis may be summarised as follows:

(1) Amoeboid movement is accompanied throughout by characteristic changes in the uroid (see next section) of which the first is the development of small hyaline pseudopodia.

(2) The membrane of these pseudopodia invaginates at its tip to form a broad channel leading into the cell interior (Fig. 1d).

(3) This is followed, after a brief interval, by extension and enlargement of the endocytosis channel as the result of rapid elongation of the pseudopodium (Fig. 1e).

(4) A vacuolar dilatation of the base of the channel becomes pinched off. This continues to develop actively and is carried by the cytoplasmic stream to the interior of the cell. The remainder of the channel disappears (Fig. 1f).

Endocytotic membrane invaginations often also appear in the ectoplasmic border of the uroid, between two adjacent pseudopodia. The average width of these channels is about 1 to 2 μ, and their average length 10 to 20 μ. They seldom last longer than one minute, and generally one to three channels are simultaneously formed during active amoeboid movement. It is beyond dispute that the channels appear predominantly at certain stages of the morphological transformation of the uroid region (see next section).

The principal differences between induced and permanent endocytosis are quantitative (Table 3); they concern the number, size, and duration of the channels and the part of the cell surface on which they are situated. The endosomes pinched off are similar in size. Comparison of the quantity of membrane taken up gives striking results. According to Holter (1965), amoebae in induced endocytosis take up, during a 20–30 min cycle, up to 50% of their surface membrane. If we assume the recovery period during which they cannot endocytose to be about four hours, this gives a value of 50% uptake per four and a half hours. Our own quantitative studies (not yet com-

TABLE 3

Permanent and induced endocytosis.

Endocytosis	Endocytosis channels					
	No.	Length (μ)	Width (μ)	Situation	Duration (min)	Cell membrane uptake (% with ref. to total surface)
Permanent	1–3	10–20	1–2	Uroid	1	5% per 30 min
Induced	50–100	30–80	1–2	Entire cell surface	3	50% per 30 min

pleted), on surface membrane uptake during permanent endocytosis, suggest an uptake of around 5% per 30 min, which also corresponds to some 50% per four and a half hours. Wolpert and O'Neill arrived at a similar figure. In total, membrane uptake is approximately the same during both permanent and induced endocytosis. An uptake of 50% within some four and a half hours, the maximum of which the amoebae appear to be capable, is probably a limit value determined by (a) the cell membrane surface available and (b) the time needed for synthesis of new membrane. Induced endocytosis may therefore be looked upon as a discontinuous, permanent endocytosis, speeded up some ten times and may thus be regarded as a derivative of permanent endocytosis. Permanent, in contrast to induced, endocytosis should no be considered as 'residual pinocytosis' (Holter 1965) but induced endocytosis is a markedly intensified permanent endocytosis; during it the amoebae are obliged, by inducing substances, to ingest within 30 min as much membrane as they normally take up spontaneously in four and a half hours of amoeboid movement.

The relation of permanent endocytosis to amoeboid movement. During active locomotion the uroid of amoebae undergoes typical morphological changes, the stages of which are illustrated in Fig. 2:

(1) The uroid contour is smooth, the cell surface unwrinkled, and the vacuolar endoplasm bounded externally by a narrow, continuous ectoplasmic gel tube (Fig. 2, I).

(2) Hyaline pseudopodia, of average length 10 to 50 μ, arise from the uroid (Fig. 2, II). In addition, a large pseudopodium formed of both ectoplasm and endoplasm can often be seen at one side of the caudal one third of the cell.

(3) Soon the surface of the hyaline pseudopodia begins to wrinkle and simultaneously the pseudopodia begin to retract (Fig. 2, III); the larger pseudopodium is also withdrawn.

(4) It is chiefly during this phase that the endocytosis channels are formed, as already described (Fig. 2, IV). After break up of the membrane invaginations the cell surface becomes smoothed out and the cell thus reverts to its initial state (Fig. 2, V).

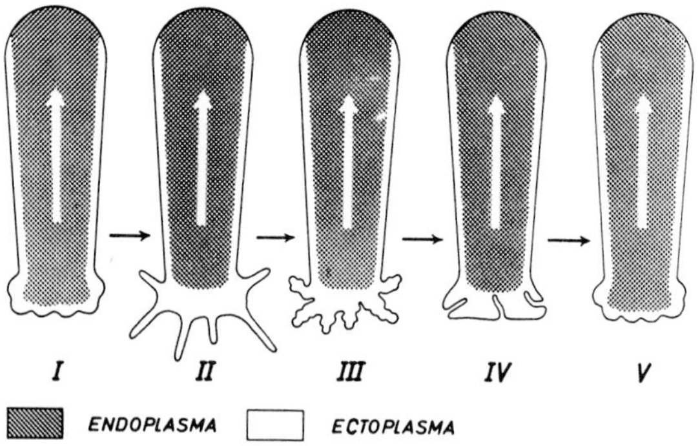

Fig. 2. Morphological change in the uroid in *Amoeba proteus* during locomotion (for explanation see text).

These morphological changes in the uroid region occur rhythmically – each cycle occupying an average of five to ten minutes – and are an important element in the ectoplasmic envelope contraction which is thought to supply the force for amoeboid movement. The rhythmical sequence of increase and decrease in volume is accompanied by regular ruffling (Fig. 3b) and unruffling (Fig. 3a) of the cell surface at the caudal pole (Czarska and Grebecki). Fig. 3a corresponds to stages I and V and Fig. 3b to stages III and IV of Fig. 2.

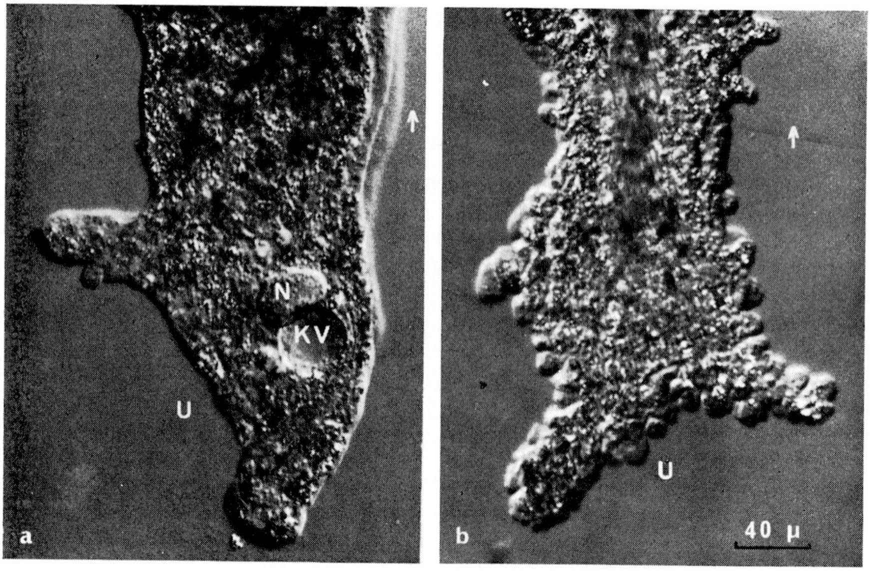

Fig. 3. (a) Uroid (U) of *Amoeba proteus* in motion. The contour is smooth and endocytotic activity weak. (b) The same uroid some minutes later. The surface membrane shows marked ruffling and there is intense endocytotic activity. Interference phase contrast after Nomarski (Zeiss). N = nucleus; KV = contractile vacuole. The arrow indicates the direction of movement of the amoeba.

The fact that endocytosis channels are formed throughout the whole of amoeboid movement with a peak during the contractile phase of the uroid (Wohlfarth-Bottermann and Stockem) suggests that permanent endocytosis is related to morphological changes in the uroid and thereby to amoeboid movement.

Feeding experiments with bacteria and with model substances of similar size (such as latex particles) have shown that permanent endocytosis plays an important part in the continuous uptake of smaller food particles (Stockem 1966).

The behaviour of the cell surface. The mucoid layer of the amoeba cell membrane must play an important role in the adsorption and concentration of material from the culture medium. According to present knowledge, however, the mucoid layer is not just an adsorptive organelle; it also performs important functions in the transport and elimination of adsorbed material. These interrelationships, in so far as they are understood at present, are illustrated in Fig. 4. Amoebae show no reaction to coarse-particle substances (see above) in concentrations of about 0.5% when these are used

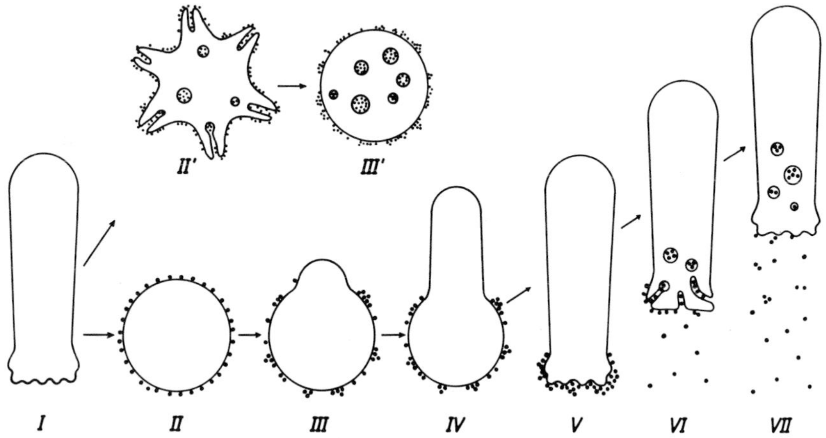

Fig. 4. Behaviour of cell suface of *Amoeba proteus* during permanent (I-VII) and induced (I, II', III') endocytosis (for description see text).

for labelling the culture medium. No change in cell shape takes place (Fig. 4, I) and the migration speed is not affected when such substances are adsorbed onto the mucoid layer and transported within a few minutes to the posterior end, where they form conglomerates visible under the light microscope (Fig. 4, V). Part of the material is taken up into the cell interior by permanent endocytosis (Fig. 4, VI) and the remainder discharged to the bottom of the culture container (Fig. 4, VII). If substantially higher concentrations of these substances are fed the amoebae rapidly round up (Fig. 4, II) and substance collects in clumps on the cell surface, leaving clear patches of surface between the clumps (Fig. 4, III); as soon as the clear areas are big enough a new large pseudopodium forms within a few minutes and amoeboid movement is resumed (Fig. 4, IV). The subsequent fate of the labelling substance corresponds to stages V to VII already described. Thus, these substances are ingested by permanent, but not by induced endocytosis.

When an inducing substance is offered the reaction is entirely different. Adsorption of the inducer is followed within a short interval by assumption of the rosette shape characteristic of induced endocytosis (Fig. 4, II′) and by vigorous uptake of inducing substance (Fig. 4, III′). The behaviour of the amoebae does not revert to normal until the inducing solution is replaced by normal culture medium. All this suggests that, in addition to its function as an adsorption organelle, the mucoid layer is also responsible for transport and discharge of particulate matter. If such matter consists of a non-inducer the mucoid layer enables the amoebae to clean their cell surface within a short time, while maintaining normal locomotor and endocytotic activity. In the most adverse circumstances they adopt the strictly time-limited resting form (Fig. 4, II to IV), but without endocytotic membrane uptake. An inducer, on the other hand, leads either to total block of the mucoid layer or to irreversible damage to this region which is so important in locomotion (see next section). The amoebae react by intense endocytosis, in an attempt to reduce the cell membrane and to replace it by a new one. If the inducer is not removed, it immediately again blocks the newly formed cell membrane, and in the end the cell's regenerative capacity becomes exhausted; under these conditions amoebae cannot survive. Such renewal of plasmalemma and mucoid layer is constantly taking place as suggested by the experimental work of Nachmias. According to present investigations the Golgi apparatus is responsible for the regeneration of new cell surface (Stockem, in press).

(b) *Investigation by electron microscopy*

The fine structure of the uroid. The difference in fine structure between the endoplasm and ectoplasm of the uroid region in large amoebae, contested by Wolpert, has recently been demonstrated by several investigators (Wohlfarth-Bottermann and Stockem; Schäfer-Danneel). Immediately under the cell membrane lies an ectoplasmic zone of varying width (Fig. 5a) containing no membranous inclusions (pure groundplasm) and next to it lies the endoplasm with its many membranous differentiations (mitochondria, Golgi apparatus, vacuoles). The constant shift in the ectoplasm : endoplasm ratio, previously noted in the light microscope, has also been visualised in the electron microscope. The related fluctuation in intensity of endocytotic activity in the uroid has also been confirmed by this study (Wohlfarth-Bottermann and Stockem). When its surface is smooth and unwrinkled (Fig. 3a), the uroid displays a membrane uptake of about 1 % in about 30 min, but when its surface is undulated and heavily wrinkled (Fig. 3b) it endocytoses up to 10 % of total cell surface during the same period. These values were ascertained using simple line grids in provisional observations on ultrathin sections. During maximal and minimal endocytosis the ectoplasm : endoplasm ratio changes in favour of the ectoplasm and the endoplasm respectively. A similar

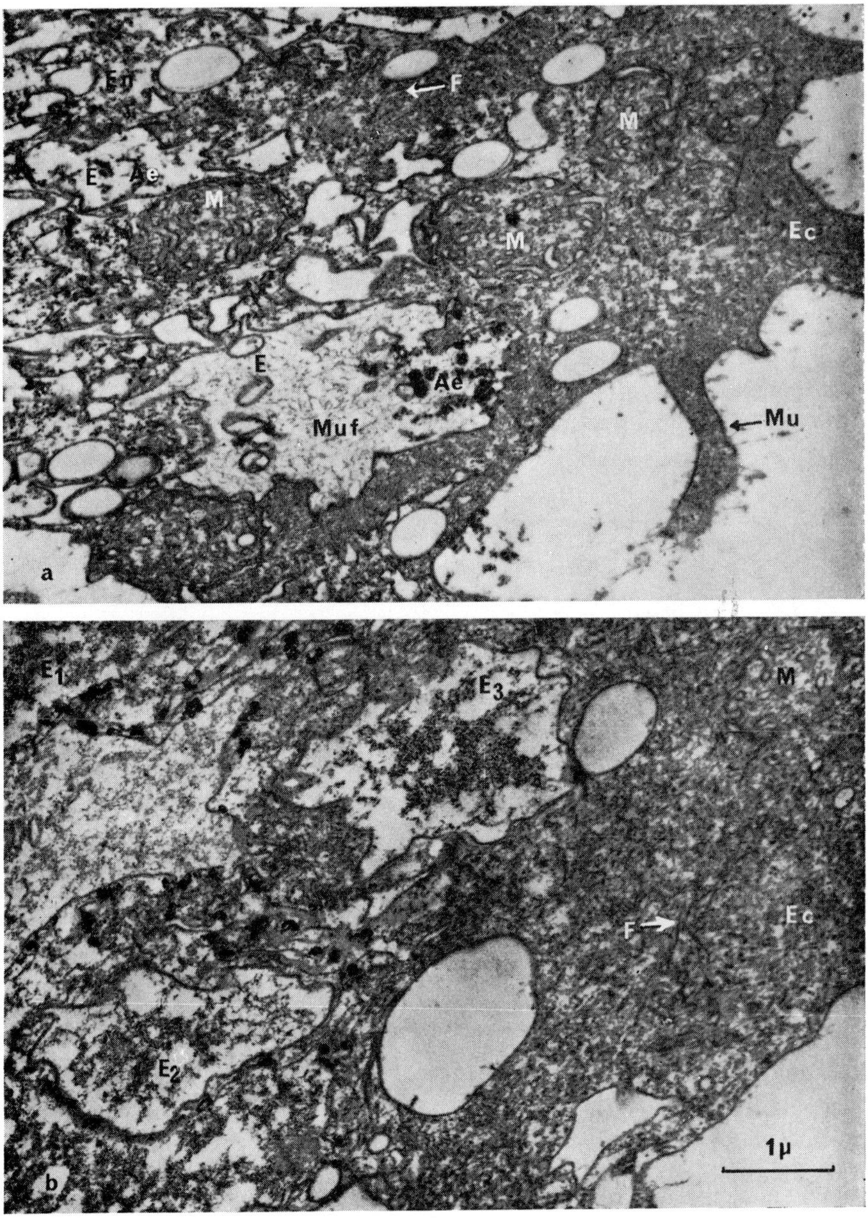

Fig. 5. (a) Section of the uroid region of *Amoeba proteus* after 15 min of permanent endocytosis in a 0.5% aerosil suspension. The endosomes (E) contain aerosil (Ae) and cast off mucoid filaments (Muf). (b) Section of an amoeba cell after 30 min of induced endocytosis in 2.5% myofer. Increase in contrast and condensation of the myofer in endosomes of different ages (E_1-E_3). Fixation in a mixture of 4% OsO_4 and 2% $K_2Cr_2O_7$; embedding in Vestopal W; Siemens ÜM 100 d; Mu = mucoid layer; Ec = ectoplasm; En = endoplasm; M = mitochondria; F = groundplasm filaments.

correlation can be detected with respect to the groundplasm filaments. They appear chiefly during the formation of the endocytosis channels (contractile phase of the uroid), and surround the channels with a dense fibrillar reticulum. Thus, invagination and pinching off, in permanent endocytosis, can be traced to the same underlying dynamic mechanism which has been described for induced endocytosis.

The intracellular fate of the endosomes. The endosomes, arising as the result of permanent and of induced endocytosis, have a similar fate (Fig. 6), as they have similar kinetics and dynamics. The first event following formation of an endocytosis channel is dilation at its base (Fig. 6, I) and pinching off of primary endosomes (Fig. 6, II). These possess an elementary membrane with adsorbed labelling material on its inner mucoid layer. Shortly after formation of the endosomes the mucoid layer begins to change. According to the labelling substance (for example, albumin), the substance

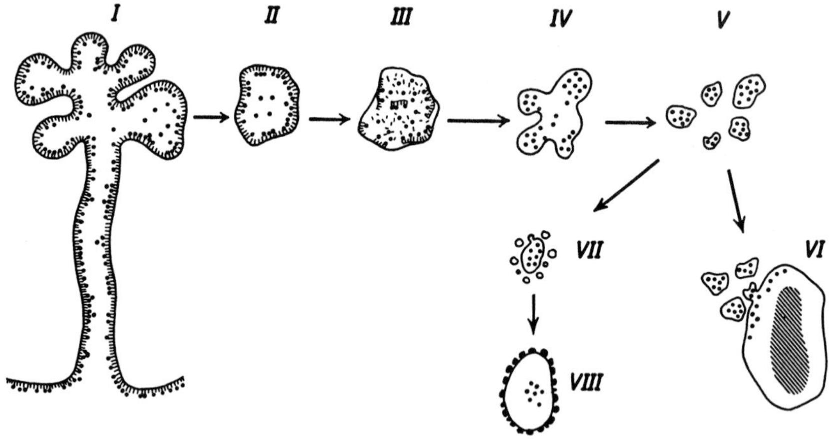

Fig. 6. Fate of the endosomes in *Amoeba proteus* after induced and permanent endocytosis (for description see text).

either becomes detached from the mucoid layer or is carried with it into the endosome interior (Fig. 5a; Fig. 6, III). The primary endosomes, hitherto relatively uniform in shape, now constrict with the production of budlike diverticula in which the labelling substance accumulates (Fig. 6, IV). At this point it is often no longer possible to identify the mucoid layer. The earliest changes in endosome content appear at this time and they vary with the type of contents. In solutions of myofer and ferrlecit, which at first appear structureless in the electron microscope, there appear numerous 'condensation nuclei' which rapidly increase in contrast and size (Fig. 5b). Soon the primary endosomes fragment by intracytosis into smaller secondary endosomes (Fig. 6, V). Their subsequent fate varies. Some coalesce – again by intracytosis – with older endosomes, which generally contain fairly large food particles, in an advanced state of digestion (paramecium) and which can therefore be called *lysosomes* (Fig. 6, VI). Others take the course represented by stages VII and VIII in Fig. 6, becoming surrounded by a dense ring of small vesicles whose contents have good contrast, which probably arise from secondary endosomes by intracytosis and which may contain digested substrate. These secretory vesicles give up their contents to the secondary endosomes by intracytotic fusion (Fig. 6, VII). This pathway has been postulated on morphological grounds only, and it has still to be proved cytochemically. In stage VII the content of the secondary endosomes clearly changes. Enzymatically hydrolysable substances undergo visible morphological digestion, while non-utilisable substances are condensed to electron-dense aggregates in the interior of the endosome. It therefore seems justifiable to compare the secondary endosomes at this point to lysosomes (de Duve 1967). The chief enzyme (acid phosphatase) has until now been demonstrated only with the light microscope (Chapman-Andresen and Lagunoff). The subsequent fate of the 'lysosomes' in amoebae has not yet been followed, with the electron microscope, further than stage VIII (Fig. 6). At this stage the outer rim acquires a border of electron-dense granules. Exocytosis of vacuoles with digested or non-digestible content has been observed in the light microscope only (Andresen and Holter), and no data on this defaecatory process are available at the present time.

We thus see that there is no significant difference between the fate of endosomes formed during induced (Brandt and Pappas 1960, 1962) or permanent endocytosis (Wohlfarth-Bottermann and Stockem). The only distinction being that the digestive process seems to take place more slowly in the former. While Brandt and Pappas (1960, 1962) do not describe stages VII and VIII (Fig. 6), they found stage VI some 24 hours after feeding the inducer. Using a non-inducer (aerosil) the present authors found stage VI after 15 min, and stages VII and VIII after about two hours, of permanent endocytosis.

5. *Discussion and conclusions*

From the study of endocytosis in amoebae and metazoan cells we can draw up a provisional diagrammatic representation of the principal methods of cellular transport of membrane and material (Fig. 7). The *uptake*, *intracellular transport*, and *excretion* of substances can be performed through two different, although probably equivalent, mechanisms, namely: (1) *vesicle transport*, also called *cytosis*; and (2) *transmembrane transport*, also called *permeation* (see also the chapter by Schoffeniels in this Handbook).

Cytosis consists of the three separate processes defined in our introductory remarks – endocytosis, intracytosis, and exocytosis. These terms appear desirable in the interest of uniformity of nomenclature and are appropriate from the viewpoint of function and morphology. The terms used (see Introduction and Fig. 7) signify no more than the uptake, transport and elimination of extracellular fluid and substances by cytosis, as observed in the light- and electron-microscopes. Differences in the morphology and kinetics of these mechanisms, are differences of degree only and are of secondary importance. We should therefore try to bring out the features which the mechanisms have in common and to characterise their established, or at least probable, physiological bases.

The most detailed studies have been made on *endocytosis* in animal and plant cells. The first phase of endocytosis (pinocytosis) starts with the adsorption of ions, mole-

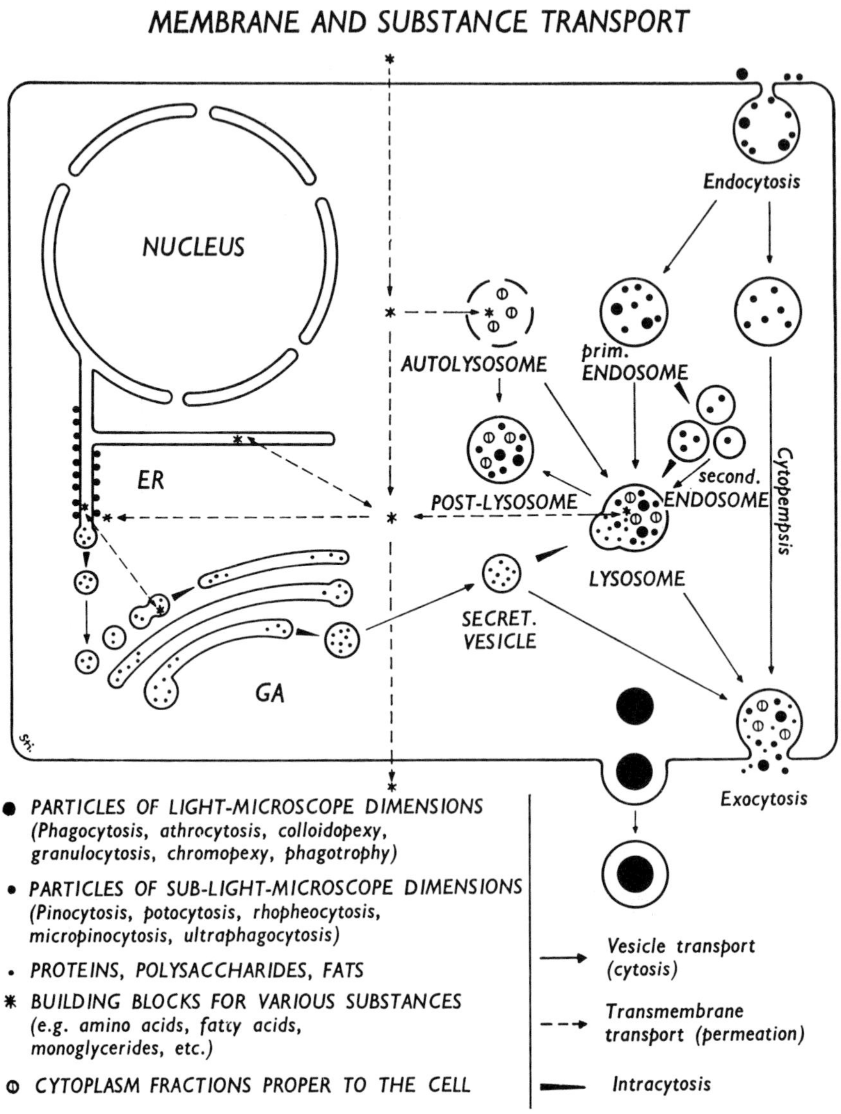

Fig. 7. Transport of membrane and material in the animal and plant cell (for description see text).

cules, or particulate substances onto a mucopolysaccharide layer (the 'mucoid layer') overlying the cell membrane. Endocytosis (phagocytosis) can also frequently be set off (in, for example, amoebae) by relatively bulky food organisms (paramecia). Improved cytochemical methods (Revel and Ito) have revealed the presence of such an extracellular mucoid layer in nearly all cell types capable of endocytosis (see the chapter by Bennett in this Handbook). The mucoid layer attains a high degree of morphological differentiation, in many amoebae, and it is in these animals that its function is most readily investigated. It has especially high affinity for the substances known as *endocytosis inducers*; these are adsorbed onto it in quantitatively significant amounts from the extracellular medium, thereby undergoing concentration prior to ingestion. This obviates premature uptake, during endocytosis, of excess fluid which the cell would have to re-excrete at the expense of energy. Non-inducing as well as inducing substances, are adsorbed in varying degrees by the mucoid layer, and are also thereby concentrated outside the cell. There is as yet no experimental proof of preferential adsorption of digestible or life-supporting substances as against non-digestible or non-utilisable material.

Substance uptake in the first phase of the endocytosis process is quantitatively important. However, it is not yet certain whether it is also of physiological importance from a qualitative point of view. Yet, there is reason to believe, that the first phase serves also in the concentration of material in metazoan cells. The definition of endocytosis has thus become modified; it is not so much the uptake from the extracellular medium by membrane vesiculation (as in the classical concept of pinocytosis), but rather the concentrated ingestion of adsorbed material. This concentrated or selective ingestion, also applies to large food particles such as paramecia, but in their case concentration on the cell surface is less significant, since food organisms of this order of magnitude, are taken up one at a time (phagocytosis). Whether adsorptive binding on the cell surface – in Holter's sense – can also be made responsible for the initiation of endocytosis is still unknown. Induced endocytosis in amoebae is simply a markedly intensified permanent endocytosis, which is going on all the time even in the absence of an inducer. It thus seems that the important factor in the induction of endocytosis is not so much the *adsorption* of material, as the *quantity* of material adsorbed, and the resultant damage to the mucoid layer. To what extent these processes differ in amoebae and other cell types is not yet known. No analogous detailed studies have been carried out in metazoan cells. Local induction of membrane invagination by surface-adsorbed particles (Bennett) does not take place in amoebae, but it cannot be excluded that it may occur in, for example, endothelial cells (Staubesand 1965). The actual inducing mechanism of endocytosis remains an open question.

The second phase of endocytosis is the pinching off of the cell membrane to form endosomes. The contents of the endosomes are either digested within the cell or transported across the cell by the shortest route and made available to adjacent cells. The latter mechanism, in which vacuoles formed endocytotically rapidly give up their contents exocytotically (Fig. 7), has been called cytopempsis (Moore and Ruska). It is a form of vesicle transport and may take place from apex to base, or *vice versa*, or in both directions at once (two-way cytopempsis (Staubesand 1965)). Cytopempsis probably serves chiefly for transport of liquid.

Normally, the contents of the primary endosomes are digested inside the cell. When, in amoebae, they consist of finely particulate material, several smaller secondary endosomes (Fig. 7) are often formed by intracytosis. The purpose of this, at least in amoebae, appears to be the qualitative separation of the vacuolar contents. When aerosil and egg white are fed together (Stockem 1966), the primary endosomes contain a mixture of both substances but the secondary endosomes only one or the other. Perhaps this is a mechanism for intracellular differentiation and separation of substances. When primary endosomes contain single large food organisms (paramecia in food vacuoles) intracytotic breakdown of the food vacuoles, into secondary endosomes, does not occur – since an undigested food organism cannot be distributed among a number of smaller vacuoles – and the digestive process (third phase) takes place in the primary endosome itself.

According to de Duve (1967) endocytosis vacuoles with undigested contents (endosomes) and those with contents in process of digestion (lysosomes) can be distinguished from each other, morphologically and biochemically, the *endosomes* containing extracellular medium only and the *lysosomes* both extracellular medium and digestive enzymes (acid phosphatase as chief enzyme). Thus, intracellular digestion begins with the transformation of primary or secondary endosomes (food vacuoles, phagosomes, pinosomes) into lysosomes. It is at this point that the morphological and histochemical changes in vacuolar content, already mentioned, take place. Food organisms are dissolved, and smaller food particles undergo condensation, and acquire increased contrast in the electron microscope. At the same time (in, for example, amoebae) the mucoid layer disappears, and acid phosphatase can now for the first time be demonstrated, cytochemically and biochemically, in the lysosomes. According to present knowledge, the digestive enzymes 'packed' into the secretory vesicles reach the lysosomes for the most part by intracytosis. The enzymes of the secretory vesicles (primary lysosomes (de Duve 1967)) arise from the ergastoplasm (ER) and, again by intracytosis, become surrounded with an intact membrane furnished by the Golgi apparatus (GA).

The digested lysosome contents are generally re-excreted from the cell by exocytosis (defaecation vacuoles). As described for amoebae (Fig. 6) and shown in the diagram (Fig. 7), secondary endosomes are not always transformed into lysosomes by the afflux of vesicles containing digestive enzymes (Gordon, Miller and Bensch); they may also coalesce by intracytosis with older lysosomes, to which they transfer their contents (Thoenes, Langer and Pfeifer).

Frequently, and for reasons as yet unexplained, the exocytotic elimination of digested lysosome contents just described, does not take place. The lysosomes then remain, as so-called *residual bodies* or *post-lysosomes*, in the cell interior, where they are stored.

In addition to the digestion of extracellular medium the cell may, in special circumstances, digest its own cytoplasm by a process in which groundplasm and cell organelles become surrounded with an non-perforated membrane. To explain the formation of this membrane a great variety of theories have been put forward (Beaulaton). The products of the process are called *autolysosomes* and their subsequent fate is similar to that of the endosomes (Fig. 7).

For the sake of completeness, the fate of substances synthesised in the cell should be mentioned briefly, since this material too is in part transported by intracytosis and by exocytosis. The best known examples of such intracellular synthesis, are the formation of new cell surface in amoebae (Stockem, in press) of the material which constitutes plant cell walls (Sievers) and the production of the zymogen granules of the exocrine pancreatic cells. In the first and second case the Golgi apparatus, in the third the endoplasmic reticulum, are the most probable formative loci. The Golgi apparatus probably serves merely as a 'packing station' – but in both cases transport is effected exclusively by intracytosis and exocytosis.

Viruses, or particles of the milk-secretion, may also be excreted by a pinching off process (see lower part of diagram, Fig. 7). Particulate elements thus become surrounded with a cell membrane of their own (plasmalemma) and are extruded together with small portions of cytoplasm into the external medium.

This brief review of the uptake, transport, digestion, synthesis, and elimination of material by cytotic mechanisms gives an idea of the importance of these processes in cell metabolism. As was mentioned at the outset, however, they cannot be considered solely responsible for it. Permeation processes (trans-membrane transport) certainly play an important part, but they lend themselves far less readily to morphological analysis, than do the kinetics of vesicle transport. For the investigation of trans-membrane transport only physiological methods are available at present. Although an attempt has been made to indicate transmembrane transport in Fig. 7, the diagram is in this respect largely hypothetical, since it shows transport pathways which have to be postulated, but have not yet been demonstrated. For instance, there is no doubt, that structural units, such as amino acids and fatty acids, pass through the cell membrane by permeation, are transported via the groundplasm, and leave the cell again by transmembrane transport. In this mechanism 'carriers' or pores in the plasmalemma play an important part. The cell is often no more than a transit station. Yet it often makes use of these structural units, synthesising them intracellularly into complex substances (fats and proteins). Synthesis of proteins begins in the ribosomes of the endoplasmic reticulum. The larger molecules are often passed on, not by transmembrane transport but (via ER, GA, secretory vesicles, and zymogen granules) by intracytosis or exocytosis. This shows that the cell is capable of effectively combining cytosis and permeation. The dynamic properties of the cytoplasm, and the convertibility of the cytoplasmic membranes, are important pre-requisites to the cell's ability to perform its basic metabolic tasks.

In the light of what has just been mentioned, endocytosis is only part of a complex series of phenomena and has to be viewed in this broad perspective if it is to be correctly explained and understood. Side by side with the continuous consumption of cell membrane by endocytosis, we have a continuous synthesis of new membrane – for the cell endeavours to keep its total surface area constant. The new membrane is provided largely through exocytosis (Stockem, in press). The formation of substances on the cell membrane is often the work of the Golgi apparatus (Revel and Ito). This alone justifies the concept of endocytosis-intracytosis-exocytosis as an interrelated whole. Amoebae, and other unicellular organisms, offer important advantages as material for further studies of this kind, since the whole series of phenomena takes place in a single cell and there is no specialisation of function as in differentiated tissues of organs.

References

ANDRESEN, N. and H. HOLTER: Cytoplasmic changes during starvation of the amoeba *Chaos chaos*. Compt. Rend. Trav. Lab. Carlsberg 25 (1945) 107.

BEAULATON, J.: Localisation d'activés lytiques dans la glande prothoracique du ver à soie du chêne (*Antheraea pernyi* Guér) au stade prénymphal II. Les vacuoles autolytiques (cytolysomes). J. Microscopie 6 (1967) 349.

BENACERRAF, B., B. N. HALPERN, C. STIFFEL, S. GRUCHAND and G. BIOZZI: Phagocytose d'une fraction du sérum chauffé et iodé par le système réticulo-endothelial et comportement consécutive de ses cellules à l'égard d'autres colloides. Ann. Inst. Pasteur 89 (1955) 601.

BENNETT, H. S.: The concepts of membrane flow and membrane vesiculation as mechanism for active transport and ion pumping. J. Biophys. Biochem. Cytol. Suppl. 2 (1956) 99.

BRANDT, PH. W.: A study for the mechanism of pinocytosis. Exptl. Cell Res. 15 (1958) 300.

BRANDT, PH. W. and G. D. PAPPAS: An electron microscopic study of pinocytosis in ameba I. The surface attachment phase. J. Biophys. Biochem. Cytol. 8 (1960) 675.

BRANDT, PH. W. and G. D. PAPPAS: An electron microscopic study of pinocytosis in ameba II. The cytoplasmic uptake phase. J. Cell Biol. 15 (1962) 55.

BRATIANU, S. and A. LLOMBART: Fonction colloido-pexique et fonction de colloido-stabilisation du système réticulo-endothelial. Compt. Rend. Soc. Biol. 101 (1929) 299.

CHAPMAN-ANDRESEN, C.: Studies on pinocytosis in amoebae. Compt. Rend. Trav. Lab. Carlsberg 33 (1962) 73.

CHAPMAN-ANDRESEN, C.: The induction of pinocytosis in amoebae. Arch. Biol. (Liège) 76 (1965a) 189.

CHAPMAN-ANDRESEN, C.: The effect of metabolic inhibitors on pinocytosis in amoebae. Progr. Protozool. Int. Congr. Ser. No. 91 (1965b) 256.

CHAPMAN-ANDRESEN, C. and D. A. T. DICK: Sodium and bromine fluxes in the amoeba *Chaos chaos*. Compt. Rend. Trav. Lab. Carlsberg 32 (1962) 445.

CHAPMAN-ANDRESEN, C. and H. HOLTER: Studies on the ingestion of ^{14}C glucose by pinocytosis in the amoeba *Chaos chaos*. Exptl. Cell Res. Suppl. 3 (1955) 52.

CHAPMAN-ANDRESEN, C. and D. LAGUNOFF: The distribution of acid phosphatase in the amoeba *Chaos chaos* L. Compt. Rend. Trav. Lab. Carlsberg 35 (1966) 419.

CHAPMAN-ANDRESEN, C. and J. R. NILSON: Electron micrographs of pinocytosis channels in *Amoeba proteus*. Exptl. Cell Res. 19 (1960) 631.

CZARSKA, L. and A. GREBECKI: Membrane folding and plasma-membrane ratio in the movement and shape transformation in *Amoeba proteus*. Acta Protozool. 4 (1966) 201.

DE DUVE, C.: Lysosomes. Ciba Foundation Symposium, 126 und 411. London, J.A.Churchill, Ltd. (1963).

DE DUVE, C.: Lysosomes and phagosomes (the vacuolar apparatus). Symp. on Biophys. and Physiol. of Biol. Transport. Vienna-New York, Springer (1967) 95.

FARQUHAR, M.G. and G.E.PALADE: Segregation of ferritin in glomerular protein absorption droplets. J. Biophys. Biochem. Cytol. 7 (1960) 297.

FAVARD, P. and N.CARASSO: Étude de la pinocytose au niveau des vacuoles digestives de ciliés péritriches. J. Microscopie 3 (1964) 671.

FELIX, M.D. and A.J.DALTON: A comparison of mesothelial cells and macrophages in mice after the intraperitoneal inoculation of melanin granules. J. Biophys. Biochem. Cytol. Suppl. 2 (1956) 109.

GÉRARD, P. and R.CORDIER: Exquisse d'une histophysiologie comparée du rein des vertébrés. Biol. Rev. Cambridge Phil. Soc. 9 (1934) 110.

GIESEKING, R.: Aufnahme und Ablagerung von Fremdstoffen in der Lunge nach elektronenoptischen Untersuchungen. Ergeb. Allgem. Pathol. Pathol. Anat. 38 (1958) 92.

GORDON, G.B., L.R.MILLER and K.G.BENSCH: Studies on the intracellular digestive process in mammalian tissue culture cells. J. Cell Biol. 25 (1965) 41.

GOSSELIN, R.E.: The uptake of radiocolloids by macrophages in vitro. J. Gen. Physiol. 39 (1956) 625.

GROPP, A.: Phagocytosis and pinocytosis. Cinemicrography in cell biology. New York and London, Academic Press (1963).

HAYWARD, A.F.: Electron microscopy of inducted pinocytosis in *Amoeba proteus*. Compt. Rend. Trav. Lab. Carlsberg 33 (1961) 535.

HOLTER, H.: Problems of pinocytosis, with special regard to amoebae. Ann. N.Y. Acad. Sci. 78 (1959) 524.

HOLTER, H.: The induction of pinocytosis. Symp. on Biol. Approaches to Cancer Chemotherapy. Louvain and London, Academic Press (1960).

HOLTER, H.: Physiologie der Pinocytose bei Amöben II. Wiss. Konf. d. Ges. Dtsch. Naturf. u. Ärzte, Schloss Reinhardsbrunn b. Friedrichroda, 1964. Funktionelle und morphologische Organisation der Zelle, Sekretion und Exkretion. Berlin-Heidelberg-New York, Springer (1965).

HOLTER, H. and M.HOLTZER: Pinocytotic uptake of fluorescein-labelled proteins by various tissue cells. Exptl. Cell Res. 18 (1959) 421.

HOLTER, H. and J.M.MARSHALL: Studies on pinocytosis in the Amoeba *Chaos chaos*. Compt. Rend. Trav. Lab. Carlsberg 29 (1954) 7.

JEON, K.W. and L.G.E.BELL: Behavior of cell membrane in relation to locomotion in *Amoeba proteus*. Exptl. Cell Res. 33 (1964) 531.

KARRER, H.E.: Electron microscopic study of the phagocytosis process in the lung. J. Biophys. Biochem. Cytol. 7 (1960) 357.

KAYE, G.J. and G.D.PAPPAS: Studies on the cornea I. The fine structure of the rabbit cornea and the uptake and transport of colloidal particles by the cornea *in vivo*. J. Cell Biol. 12 (1962) 457.

KOMNICK, H.: Elektronenmikroskopische Untersuchungen zur funktionellen Morphologie des Ionentransportes in der Salzdrüse von *Larus argentatus* III. Funktionelle Morphologie der Tubulusepithelzellen. Protoplasma 56 (1963) 605.

KOMNICK, H. and WOHLFARTH-BOTTERMANN, K.E.: Morphologie des Cytoplasmas. Fortschr. Zool. 17 (1964) 1.

LEWIS, W.H.: Pinocytose. Bull. Johns Hopkins Hosp. 49 (1931) 17.

LEWIS, W.H.: Motion picture of pinocytosis by malignant sarcoma cells. Anat. Record 67 Suppl. 3 (1937a) 64.

LEWIS, W.H.: Pinocytosis by malignant cells. Am. J. Cancer 29 (1937b) 666.

MARSHALL, J. M. and V.T.NACHMIAS: Cell surface and pinocytosis. J. Histochem. Cytochem. 13 (1965) 92.

MAST, S.O. and W.L.DOYLE: Ingestion of fluid by amoeba. Protoplasma 20 (1934) 555.

METSCHNIKOFF, E.: Untersuchungen über die mesodermalen Phagocyten einiger Wirbeltiere. Biol. Centralbl. 3 (1883) 360.

MOORE, D.H. and H.RUSKA: The fine structure of capillaries and small arteries. J. Biophys. Biochem. Cytol. 3 (1957) 457.

NACHMIAS, V.T.: A study by electron microscopy of the formation of new surface by *Chaos chaos.* Exptl. Cell Res. 43 (1966) 583.

NACHMIAS, V.T. and J.M.MARSHALL: Protein uptake by pinocytosis in Amoebae: Studies on ferritin and methylated ferritin. Symp. held in Stockholm II. New York, Academic Press (1961).

NOVIKOFF, A.B.: Biochemical and staining reactions of cytoplasmic constituents. In: D.Rudnick, ed.: Developing Cell Systems and their Control. New York, Ronald Press (1960).

NOVIKOFF, A.B.: Lysosomes and related particles. In: J.Brachet and A.E.Mirsky, eds.: The cell, Vol. II. New York and London, Academic Press (1961) 423.

ODOR, D.L.: Uptake and transfer of particulate matter from the peritoneal cavity of the rat. J. Biophys. Biochem. Cytol. Suppl. 2 (1956) 105.

POLICARD, A. and C.A.BAUD: Les structures inframicroscopiques normales et pathologiques des cellules et des tissus. Paris, Masson et Cie (1958).

POLICARD, A. and M.BESSIS: Sur un mode d'incorporation des macromolécules par la cellule, visible au microscope électronique: la rhophéocytose. Compt. Rend. 246 (1958) 3194.

POMERAT, C.M., C.G.LEFEBER and MC.D.SMITH: Quantitative cine analysis of cell organoid activity. Ann. N.Y. Acad. Sci. 58 (1954) 1311.

REVEL, J.P. and S.ITO: The surface components of cells. In: The specificity of cell surfaces. Englewood Cliffs, N. J., Prentice Hall, Inc. (1967).

RINALDI, R.A.: The induction of pinocytosis in *Amoeba proteus* by ultraviolet radiation. Exptl. Cell Res. 18 (1959) 70.

RUDZINSKA, M.A., W.TRAGER and R.S.BRAY: Pinocytotic uptake and the digestion of hemoglobin in malaria parasites. J. Protozool. 12 (4) (1965) 563.

RUSKA, H.: Der Einfluss der Elektronenmikroskopie auf die biologische Forschung. Marburger Sitzungsberichte 82 (1960) 3.

RUSKA, H.: Über funktionelle Konsequenzen der Vielphasigkeit der Zelle IV. Intern. Kongr. Neuropath. Proc. II (1962) 42.

RUSTAD, R.C.: Molecular orientation at the surface of Amoebae during pinocytosis. Nature 183 (1959) 1058.

SCHÄFER-DANNEEL, S.: Strukturelle und funktionelle Voraussetzungen für die Bewegung von *Amoeba proteus.* Z. Zellforsch. Mikroskop. Anat. 78 (1967) 441.

SCHMIDT, W.: Elektronenmikroskopische Untersuchungen über die Speicherung von Trypanblau in den Zellen des Hauptstückes der Niere. Z. Zellforsch. Mikroskop. Anat. 52 (1960) 598.

SCHMIDT, W.: Electronenmikroskopische Untersuchungen des intrazellulären Stofftransportes in der Dünndarmepithelzelle nach Markierung mit Myofer. Z. Zellforsch. Mikroskop. Anat. 54 (1961) 803.

SCHNEIDER, L.: Morphogenese und Dynamik cytoplasmatischer Membranen. Verhandl. Dtsch. Zool. Ges., Kiel (1964).

SEAMAN, G.R.: Some aspects of phagotrophy in *Tetrahymena.* J. Protozool. 8 (1961) 204.

SHUMAKER, V.N.: Uptake of protein from solution by *Amoeba proteus.* Exptl. Cell Res. 15 (1958) 314.

SIEVERS, A.: Funktion des Golgi-Apparates in pflanzlichen und tierischen Zellen II. Wiss. Konf. d. Ges. Dtsch. Naturf. u. Arzte: Funktionelle und morphologische Organisation der Zelle, Sekretion und Exkretion. Berlin-Heidelberg-New York, Springer (1965).

SITTE, H.: Beobachtung von Vorgängen im submikroskopischen: Möglichkeiten und Grenzen. Funkt. u. morph. Organ. d. Zelle. Probleme d. biol. Reduplikation, 3. wiss. Konf. d. Gesellsch. Naturforsch. u. Arzte. Wien, Semmering (1965), Berlin Springer, (1966).

STAUBESAND, J.: Experimentelle elektronenmikroskopische Untersuchungen zum Phänomen der

Membranvesikulation (Pinocytose). Klin. Wschr. 38 (1960) 1248.

STAUBESAND, J.: Histophysiologie des Herzbeutels II. Elektronenmikroskopische Untersuchungen über die Passage von Metallsolen durch mesotheliale Membranen. Z. Zellforsch. Mikroskop. Anat. 58 (1963) 915.

STAUBESAND, J.: Cytopempsis II. Wiss. Konf. d. Ges. Dtsch. Naturf. u. Ärzte: Funktionelle und morphologische Organisation der Zelle, Sekretion und Exkretion. Berlin-Heidelberg-New York, Springer (1965).

STOCKEM, W.: Pinocytose und Bewegung von Amoeben I. Die Reaktion von *Amoeba proteus* auf verschiedene Markierungssubstanzen. Z. Zellforsch. Mikroskop. Anat. 74 (1966) 372.

STOCKEM, W.: Die Eignung von Aerosil für die Untersuchung endocytotischer (pinocytotischer) Vorgänge. Mikroskopie 22 (1967) 143.

STOCKEM, W.: Pinocytose und Bewegung von Amoeben. III. Die Funktion des Golgiapparates von *Amoeba proteus* und *Chaos chaos*. Histochemie (in press).

STRAUS, W.: Colorimetric analysis with N, N-dimethyl-p-phenylenediamine of the uptake of intravenously injected horseradish peroxidase by various tissues of the rat. J. Biophys. Biochem. Cytol. 4 (1958) 541.

STRAUS, W.: Rapid cytochemical identification of phagosomes in various tissues of the rat and their differentiation from mitochondria by the peroxidase method. J. Biophys. Biochem. Cytol. 10 (1959) 292.

THOENES, W., K.H. LANGER and U. PFEIFER: Eiweissresorption, Cytoplasmaeinschmelzung und lytische Aktivitäten im Nierentubulus. Untersuchungen am Ferritin-resorbierenden Einzeltubulus der Rattenniere. Verhandl. Deutsch. Ges. Pathol. 52. Tagung. Stuttgart, Gustav Fischer Verlag (1968).

UHLIG, G., H. KOMNICK and K.E. WOHLFARTH-BOTTERMANN: Intrazelluläre Zellzotten in Nahrungsvakuolen von Ciliaten. Helgolaender Wiss. Meeresuntersuch. 12 (1965) 61.

VOLKONSKY, M.: Digestion intracellulaire et accumulation des colorants acides. Bull. Biol. Fr. Belg. 67 (1933) 135.

WEILING, F.: Über Pinocytosemechanismen im Verlaufe der Meiose bei Lycopersicum und Cucurbita unter Berücksichtigung ihrer Bedeutung sowie der Literatur über Pinocytose bei Tier und Mensch II. Kritische Besprechung und Ausdeutung der Beobachtungen. Protoplasma 55 (1962) 452.

WESSEL, W., P. GEDIGK and O. GIERSBERG: Elektronenmikroskopische und morphometrische Untersuchungen an Kaninchenlebern nach intravenöser Injektion organisch gebundenen Kupfers. Virchows Arch. Pathol. Anat. Physiol. Klin. Med. 340 (1966) 206.

WESSING, A.: Die Funktion der malpighischen Gefässe II. Wiss. Konf. d. Ges. Dtsch. Naturf. u. Ärzte, Schloss Reinhardsbrunn b. Friedrichroda 1964. Funktionelle und morphologische Organisation der Zelle, Sekretion und Exkretion. Berlin-Heidelberg-New York, Springer (1965).

WILLMER, E.N.: Cells and tissues in culture, Vol. Ia, II. London-New York, Academic Press (1965).

WILLMER, E.N.: Cells and tissues in culture, Vol. III. London-New York, Academic Press (1966).

WITTEKIND, D.: Pinocytose. Naturwissenschaften 50 (1963) 270.

WOHLFARTH-BOTTERMANN, K.E.: Die elektronenmikroskopische Untersuchung cytoplasmatischer Strukturen. Ver. Dtsch. Zool. Ges. Münster/Westf. Zool. Anz. Suppl. 23 (1959) 393.

WOHLFARTH-BOTTERMANN, K.E.: Protistenstudien X: Licht- und elektronenmikroskopische Untersuchungen an der Amöbe *Hyalodiscus simplex* n. sp. Protoplasma 52 (1960) 58.

WOHLFARTH-BOTTERMANN, K.E.: Grundelemente der Zellstruktur. Naturwissenschaften 50 (1963a) 237.

WOHLFARTH-BOTTERMANN, K.E.: Zellstrukturen und ihre Bedeutung für die amöboide Bewegung. Forsch. Ber. d. Landes Nordrhein-Westfalen, Nr. 1247. Köln, Opladen, Westdeutscher Verlag, (1963b).

WOHLFARTH-BOTTERMANN, K.E.: Cell structures and their significance for ameboid movement. Intern. Rev. Cytol. 16 (1964) 61.

WOHLFARTH-BOTTERMANN, K. E. and W. STOCKEM: Pinocytose und Bewegung von Amöben II. Permanente und induzierte Pinocytose bei *Amoeba proteus*. Z. Zellforsch. Mikroskop. Anat. 73 (1966) 444.

WOLPERT, L.: Cytoplasmic streaming and amoeboid movement. Symp. Soc. Gen. Microbiol. 15 (1965) 270.

WOLPERT, L. and C. H. O'NEILL: Dynamics of the membrane of Amoeba proteus studied with labelled specific antibody. Nature 19b (1962) 1261.

ZIMMERMAN, A. M. and R. C. RUSTAD: Effects of high pressure on pinocytosis in *Amoeba proteus*. J. Cell Biol. 25 (1965) 397.

PART XVI

Cell membranes and walls

CHAPTER 52

Molecular structure of biological membranes

J. DAVID ROBERTSON

Duke University School of Medicine, Durham, North Carolina

Contents

1. Introduction
2. The Danielli–Davson model and the unit membrane concept
3. Evidence on which the unit membrane concept is based
4. The general architectural principle
5. Viral protein coats and unit membranes

1. Introduction

In spite of the repeated reviews that have been written (Robertson 1959, 1960, 1963, 1965, 1966) stressing the origin and experimental basis of the unit membrane concept, there seems to be an inadequate appreciation of the force of the evidence on which it is based (Korn). Thus, new membrane models seem to be proposed over and over (e.g. see Sjöstrand) that are quite clearly excluded from any generality by the hard facts at hand. Occasionally, an attempt is made to apply one of these models even to the myelin sheath. However, for the most part, individuals proposing radically different models tend to shrug off the myelin sheath as a special case because they recognize that their model could not possibly fit the evidence for this particular membrane organelle. However, even they seem to be quite unimpressed by the fact that the myelin sheath is one structure in which we have a unique arrangement of membranes packed together in such a way as to make it possible to study them by several entirely different methods. A great deal of information is available about the myelin sheath and every bit of it is entirely compatible with the notion that the membrane of the myelin sheath is a fair representative of all biological membranes. To make a crude analogy, let us imagine a situation in which we have the Empire State Building to examine in detail by walking through it and determining precisely what architectural principles are used in its construction. Now suppose that we cannot examine any other building but we can see many in the distance and even look at some of them with a telescope. One would have no trouble under these circumstances in concluding that the general architectural principles that are used in the Empire State Building are like those used in practically all other buildings. To be sure there are a few buildings such as the Guggenheim Museum in New York City or circus tents in which rather different architectural principles are employed. However, this need not lessen the force of the generalization that we are able to make. This analogy, though crude, is fairly representative. We cannot say that the architectural principles used in the membranes of the myelin sheath are absolutely general; but we certainly have good reason to believe that they are broadly applicable to biological membranes of various kinds. If there are a few exceptions, so be it. However, it seems fair to point out that there are no exceptions that have been adequately validated to date. Perhaps there will be in the future, but so far we need not consider them because they do not exist. Once again, I shall, in this paper, since I have been invited and urged to do so, trace the origin of the unit membrane concept. For those readers who have read other reviews by me, there will be but little, if anything, new in what follows. However, there are certain new interpretations and thoughts about membrane structure to which I shall turn after reviewing the older material and a few bits of relevant new information.

2. The Danielli–Davson model and the unit membrane concept

It is often said that the unit membrane theory represents a confirmation of the Danielli-

Davson theory of membrane structure. There are definite similarities in the two theories, but it should be realized that each of them arose entirely independently and that in no way does either depend on the other. The Danielli–Davson theory was the culmination of a period in which there was a great surge of interest in monomolecular films following the classical work of Irving Langmuir on amphiphilic molecules. A number of biophysical facts about membranes such as surface tension, permeability properties, electrical properties and chemical composition were brought together by Danielli and Davson in a unified theory that seemed reasonable in 1935. The unit membrane theory had its origins essentially in electron microscopy, a development that came later. To be sure both theories can trace their ancestry to the work of Irving Langmuir, for without this neither theory could have reasonably been proposed.

It is appropriate to point out that, despite their similarities, there are some distinctive differences between the two theories. The original Danielli–Davson model is presented in Fig. 1. It will be seen that the membrane was pictured as consisting of a

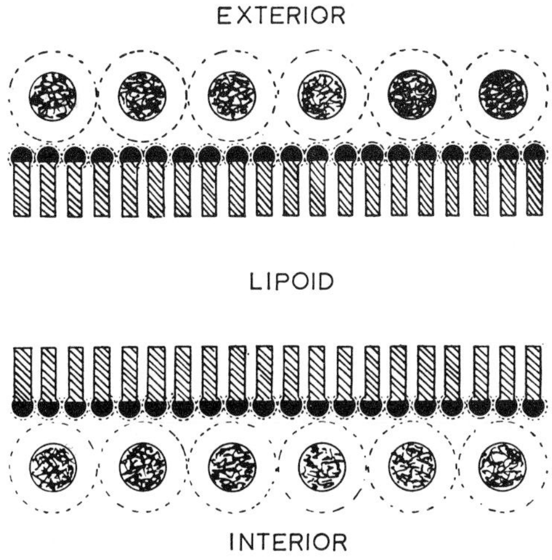

Fig. 1. The original Danielli–Davson pauci-molecular membrane model.

lipid core with the polar heads of the lipid molecules pointing outward and the non-polar carbon chains running transversely. The polar heads are covered by monolayers of protein and, in the original model, the thickness of the lipid layer was unspecified. There was a good reason for this because there simply was not enough evidence to allow a decision as to whether or not there were more than two lipid molecules in the thickness of the membrane. The only way in which this could have been done was to rely on measurements of membrane capacitance. It was known that many biological membranes had a capacitance of about 1 micro-Farad per square centimeter and this was compatible with a thickness of about one hundred Å or less and thus compatible with a single bilayer of lipid. However, it was also known that this value was not correct for several membranes, notably those of muscle fibers and marine eggs. Hence, no generalization could validly be made and it was not attempted. The unit membrane concept is represented by the diagram in Fig. 2. Here the number of lipid monolayers

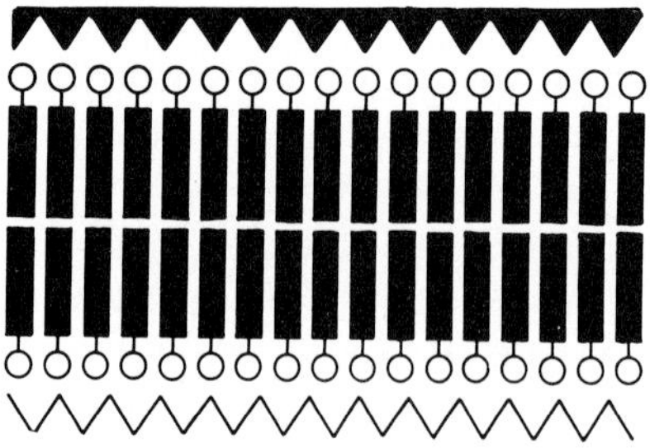

Fig. 2. Molecular diagram of the general pattern of organization of the unit membrane. The bars represent nonpolar carbon chains of lipid molecules with the circles representing their polar heads. The zig-zag lines represent monolayers of nonlipid of two different kinds. It is not intended to exclude interpenetration of the lipid carbon chains. This is not shown in the diagram, for simplicity. Indeed, some degree of interpenetration of the lipid carbon chains is very probable.

is specified. There are only two. This specification, as will be elaborated on, is based mainly on the appearances and the thicknesses of many different biological membranes as seen by electron microscopy in sectioned material. As will become clear below the densities observed are consistent with single bilayers. Further, the dimensions measured, though not constant, fall within a range consistent also with one bilayer of lipid. The variations observed are all consistent with variations in the particular lipid molecules present. The nonlipid monolayers are depicted in much the same way as in the Danielli–Davson model, but there is a new element introduced. This is the concept of chemical asymmetry. According to the unit membrane concept, there is a distinct chemical difference between the nonlipid components of the outer monolayers as compared with the one that lies next to cytoplasm. The unit membrane concept thus introduced at least two important new ideas that were not embodied in the older Danielli–Davson concept. It is also perhaps worth noting that it sets some limit on the size of the nonlipid molecules. They probably do not exceed about 25–30 Å in thickness as referred to the cross-sectional dimension of the menbrane. Thus, while both the older and the newer theories have roots in very different technical approaches, there are certain similarities as well as certain distinctive features. I shall now trace the essential evidence on which the unit membrane concept was based. I shall not review again the influence of the work of Overton; Langmuir; De Vaux; Gorter and Grendel; Cole; and Chambers, since I have done this several times in other reviews and wish to concentrate here only on the essential elements directly related to electron microscopy.

3. *Evidence on which the unit membrane concept is based*

The story begins with the work of Herbert Gasser who, toward the end of his long productive scientific career, decided to embark on an electron microscopic investigation of the 'C' fibers in peripheral nerves. These were thought to consist of syncytial Schwann cells in which were completely enclosed axons extended from the central nervous system. Gasser showed that this concept was fundamentally wrong and that instead, this kind of nerve fiber was organized as indicated in Fig. 3. This diagram

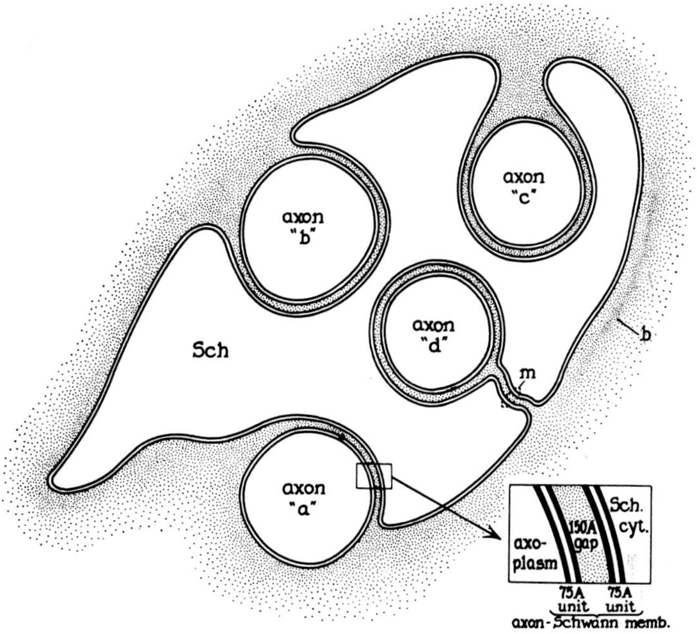

Fig. 3. Diagram of a vertebrate unmyelinated nerve fiber. See text for further explanation.

shows a cross section of a typical non-myelinated nerve fiber. Note that the axons are not enclosed in syncytial Schwann cells. Instead, the Schwann cell is an independent entity related to the axon in various ways. Some axons simply lie next to it. There are others that are pushed down into it to varying degrees. The important point is that the axon membrane never fuses with or penetrates the Schwann cell membrane. The continuity of the Schwann cell membrane is maintained throughout. Note also that there is a layer of outside substance carried down with the axon, as it is pushed down into the Schwann cell. This layer is about 100–150 Å thick and separates the axon membrane from the Schwann cell membrane in the axon-Schwann paired membrane complex. It is also extended between the apposed Schwann cell membranes carried down by the axon. The latter paired membrane complex was given the special name 'mesaxon' by Gasser. There is evidence, that I shall not go into here, that the so called gap substance between the membranes of these membrane complexes is about 90% hydrated and in certain special cases that the gap is occluded with the two membranes in intimate apposition. This kind of membrane complex was first observed and described by me in 1958 and referred to by the somewhat awkward but accurately descriptive term 'external-compound-membrane'. I adopted this term to distinguish it from similar pairs of membranes in intimate contact along their cytoplasmic surfaces that I called 'internal-compound-membranes'. Later on the term 'tight junction' was introduced for external-compound-membranes by Farquhar and Palade and this less awkward, though less precise, term is widely used at present.

Myelinated nerve fibers are organized on a plan that is basically similar to that of the non-myelinated nerve fiber as indicated in Figure 4a. During the first few days

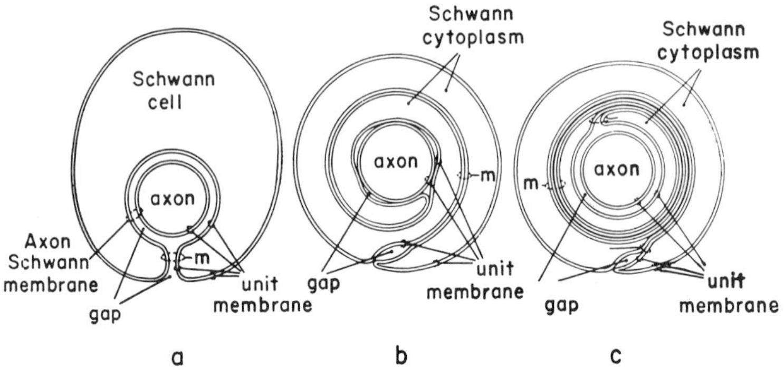

Fig. 4. Diagram summarizing the steps in the formation of nerve myelin. The mesaxon is shown at 'm'. Note that the intraperiod line originates from apposition of the two outside surfaces of the unit membranes of the mesaxon and the major dense line by apposition of the cytoplasmic surfaces of the mesaxon loops.

after birth, the mouse sciatic nerve fiber displays many stages in the formation of nerve myelin. The results from studying such nerve fibers are summarized in Fig. 4a-c. One sees some fibers in which there is simply one axon related to one Schwann cell as indicated in (a). At a little later stage of development, one sees the mesaxon elongated in a spiral along the axon, as in (b). At this stage in a permanganate fixed preparation, one characteristically sees the cleft, between the two Schwann cell membranes of the mesaxon, closed. Later on, the loops of the mesaxon come together to make an external-compound-membrane or 'tight junction'. The dense stratum made by their apposition is called the intraperiod line. Still later the cytoplasmic surfaces come

Fig. 5. At the top the characteristic appearance of myelin fixed with OsO_4 is shown. Note the regularity of the major dense line (MDL) and the irregularity of the intraperiod line (IPL) components. In the middle the characteristic appearance of myelin after $KMnO_4$ fixation is shown. Note the greater regularity of the IPL. Below is shown myelin fixed in formalin-dichromate. Note the split intraperiod line and the resulting increase in the period. This is also the characteristic appearance of myelin after fixation with glutaraldehyde followed by OsO_4. →

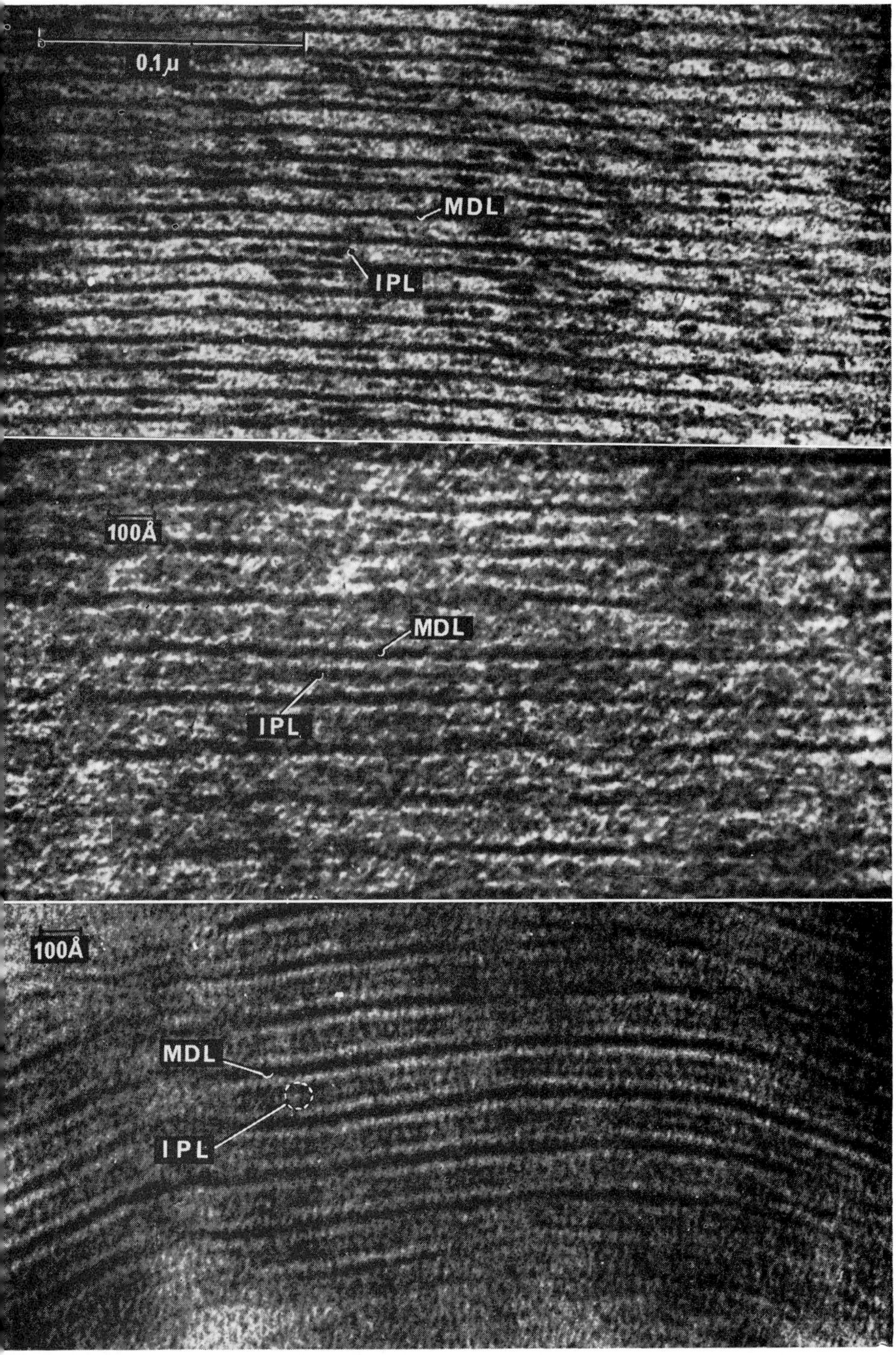
0.1μ
MDL
IPL
100Å
MDL
IPL
100Å
MDL
IPL

together as the Schwann cytoplasm between the mesaxon loops is excluded. The firm association of the cytoplasmic surfaces of the membranes along with the related pair of membranes I called an 'internal-compound-membrane'. This junction makes the so-called 'major dense line' of the compact myelin sheath. Fig. 5a-c shows portions of fully developed myelin sheaths in which the characteristic stratified structure is displayed after different fixation methods. In (a) we see the myelin sheath fixed with OsO_4. Here the major dense line is a very solid structure, whereas the intraperiod line is a tenuous structure that often is not present at all and often appears only as granules or interrupted lines. After permanganate fixation, as in (b), we see the major dense line as a solid dense structure like that in OsO_4 fixed material, but we have the intraperiod line just as well formed as the major dense line. In (c) we see the appearance of myelin after fixation with formalin followed by treatment with potassium dichromate. This particular preparation is one that I made about ten years ago and first published in 1961. It shows the intraperiod line split into two dense strata with a light zone in between that measures about 30–40 Å thick. The repeat period is increased to about 140 Å. The increase apparently is due to a separation of the membranes along the line of junction of the unit membranes normally making the intraperiod line. Much has been made recently in the literature of the fact that myelin fixed with glutaraldehyde followed by treatment with OsO_4 characteristically appears this way (Revel and Karnovsky). It may well be true that the closure of the gap between the membranes in OsO_4 or potassium permanganate fixed myelin is an artifact and that the open gap appearance is more characteristic of the living state. However, it would be premature to reach such a conclusion on present evidence. The formalin-dichromate preparations are in general very poorly fixed and when I first saw this appearance of myelin, I was inclined to regard the separation as an artifact. To be sure the repeat period in sections was relatively low and this feature provided a potential partial explanation for it. However, I believed then that the reduction in the period resulted from fixation, dehydration and embedding and represented simply a certain degree of shrinkage within the membranes themselves largely due to the removal of water. This may, however, be an incorrect interpretation since the current glutaraldehyde-osmic fixed preparations clearly are fixed in a superior manner. It may well be that in the living state, the myelin sheath is characterized by having a thin layer of outside substance between the membranes in the location of the intraperiod line. We can be sure, however, that this material is very highly hydrated since, under many conditions of fixation, it is completely obliterated. This is an important point that deserves further investigation. If, for instance, peroxidase can be shown to penetrate the sheath along this pathway in fibers that are still living and active, then we will have gone a long way toward proving that the presence of the gap is more representative of reality. At present we are also conducting X-ray diffraction studies of material fixed with glutaraldehyde-OsO_4 that may shed some light on this point. If this long thin sheet of highly hydrated material is present in the living state its influence on ion current flow radially through the myelin sheath and on saltatory conduction will have to be evaluated.

Recently, there has been considerable interest in studying membranes from which lipids have been extracted. This began when Green and his colleagues showed several years ago that mitochondria, after treatment with acetone, can be fixed with OsO_4 and shown by electron microscopy to retain their general shape. Fleischer et al. followed this with a collaborative effort and were able to demonstrate that after about 95% of the lipid had been extracted from mitochondria, the unit membrane pattern could still be demonstrated under certain conditions. More recently, Napolitano et al. have shown that beautiful preservation of the myelin structure can be obtained after extraction of 95% of the lipid. Fig. 6 is a preparation made by their technique. Note the extraordinary preservation of the general structure. Furthermore, the gap that is present in glutaraldehyde–OsO_4 fixed material between the dense strata usually seen

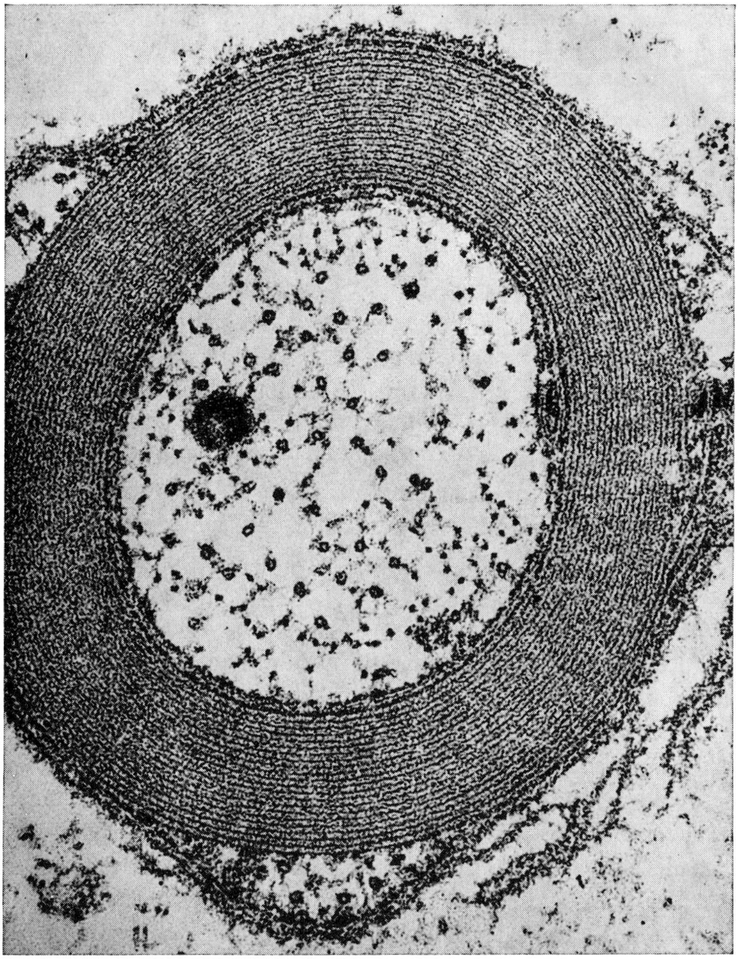

Fig. 6. Myelin structure after extraction of 95% of the lipid. See text for discussion. (Micrograph kindly supplied by Napolitano et al.) $\times$ 39,500

united to make the intraperiod line is also present here. The overall repeat period is about 160 Å. It is important to consider the preparatory procedure used in making preparations such as this. The nerve fiber is first fixed for 24-48 hr in glutaraldehyde. It is then placed in chloroform-methanol (2:1) for several hours and then into acidified chloroform-methanol. It is then put into carbon tetrachloride containing 4% OsO_4. It is taken from the carbon tetrachloride and washed in ethanol or acetone. It is then embedded and infiltrated with an epoxy embedding medium. Napolitano et al. found that if, at any stage during the chloroform-methanol extraction, the nerve is returned to aqueous media, the myelin structure is completely destroyed. Clearly what happens here is that the protein and other nonlipid components are initially fixed by the glutaraldehyde. The lipid then is slowly extracted and replaced by lipid solvents. Finally the lipid solvents are replaced by the nonpolar embedding medium. In the case of the early work of Green et al. and of Fleischer et al., the structure was not so well preserved perhaps because an aqueous fixing medium was used after lipid extraction. Many of the membranes in their preparations were indeed broken up although the emphasis was placed on the ones that were left intact. The crucial point here is that one must be very careful about the replacement of the lipid component only by solvents with a nonpolar character. If this is done, the lipid can be replaced with very little disruption of the structure. Finally, sections can be cut that display the non-lipid layers very clearly. This can be attributed to the relative efficiency of modern embedding media. Araldite, epon or other epoxy media are very tough. Furthermore, sectioning techniques today are quite good and sections are usually spread to eliminate compression artifacts by exposing them to solvent vapors after being cut.

It is interesting that about ten years ago, I performed similar extraction experiments with myelin, in which the lipid was replaced during fixation by a lipid solvent. However, in that case, the regularly spaced nonlipid lamellae that were left were seen in sections either with expanded or compressed interspaces produced by the stresses of sectioning. These preparations were embedded in methacrylate and the sections were cut with glass knives and they were not, as well as I can recall, spread after cutting by exposure to solvent vapors. Fig. 7 is such a preparation; it shows in some places the usual characteristic dense and light strata of the myelin sheath. In other places the dense strata are pushed closer together and in still others, they are separated widely with a marked increase in the spacing. This preparation was made by putting a nerve fiber into 1% PTA in ethanol and leaving it for two hours before transferring it to methacrylate for embedding. The expansion and contraction of the structure clearly depend upon compression effects resulting from the stresses of sectioning. This micrograph was first published by me in 1960. I regarded this finding at the time as very good evidence that the lipid had been removed from between the dense strata by the extraction procedure leaving the protein strata free to move about relative to one another during sectioning. This seemed to be entirely compatible with the unit membrane concept. The findings of present investigators, employing new and improved techniques that result in better preservation of such extracted membrane preparations without compression and expansion artifacts, do not in any way seem to me to suggest that this interpretation is incorrect. The embedding media and the sectioning techniques used today are simply better than they were ten years ago. It is, layers retain their relationships so exactly. Indeed, Napolitano et al. have shown that nevertheless, remarkable that it is possible to remove the lipid and have the nonlipid this procedure, if carried out on pancreatic cells, results in even better preservation of membrane structure than that normally found as indicated in one of their micrographs

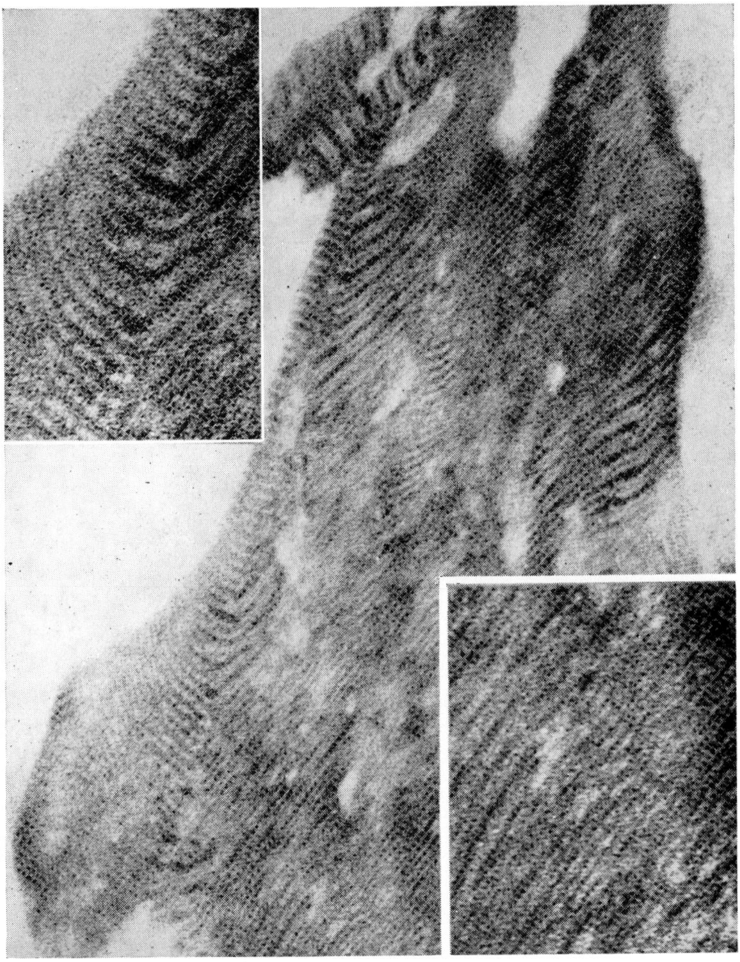

Fig. 7. Portion of a fragment of myelin placed in a solution of 1% phosphotungstic acid in absolute alcohol immediately after removal from the animal. Most of the myelin was extracted but in some regions the lamellae could be seen with heavy dense lines repeating at about 150 Å. In some regions the lines are compressed together and the difference between alternate lines is no longer seen. In such regions (inserts) the spacing is in the order of 50 Å. Methacrylate embedded. ×200,000; insets, × 330,000

(their Fig. 7). Note the unusually clear unit membrane patterns in the intracellular organelles. There is nothing in this work, however, that is incompatible with the unit membrane theory. Indeed, it seems to me to be confirmatory. The unit membrane pattern is clarified by the extraction of the lipid as indeed one might expect it to be. Before going further, I shall return to consider some of the earlier experimental evidence leading to the general theory.

It is important to consider certain studies of model systems that were done during the late 1950's in relation to the unit membrane concept. With the introduction of permanganate fixation and the demonstration of the layered structure that characterized membranes, it was important to decide what meaning could be attached to the dense and light layers observed. We saw a pair of parallel dense strata bordering a more or less uniform light central zone with the overall thickness of the whole structure amounting to somewhat under 100 Å. Rather arbitrarily, mainly because of certain electron optical uncertainties, I took a figure of 75 Å as being fairly representative though there was noted to be considerable variation in the exact thicknesses observed. It was fairly apparent from the biophysical information available about the myelin sheath that this structure most likely contained a bilayer of lipid. However, it was at first not at all apparent exactly how the lipid molecules were arranged. Any one of the three different patterns of arrangement indicated diagrammatically in Fig. 8 would have

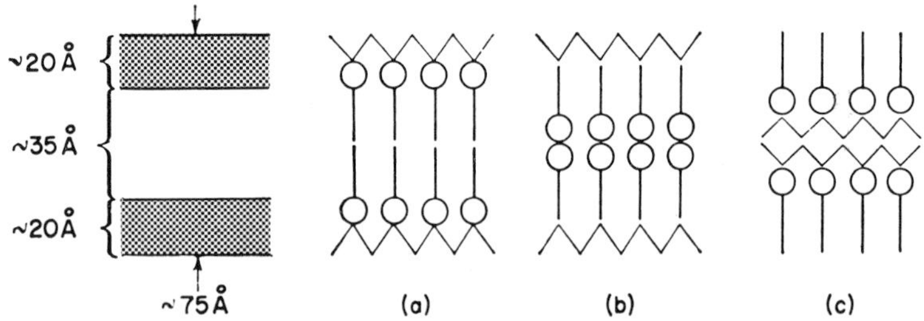

Fig. 8. Diagram of the unit membrane as seen in electron micrographs, is shown to the left, with the approximate dimensions. Three possible molecular configurations are shown in a, b and c. The zig-zag lines represent nonlipid monolayers; the circles represent lipid polar heads and the bars represent the nonpolar carbon chains of the lipid molecules.

been equally suitably in accord with the X-ray and chemical evidence available on the myelin sheath. Our problem became one of deciding precisely which one of these three patterns to choose. We went about the solution of this problem by studying the appearances of fixed and embedded preparations of crystalline proteins and of purified lipids. We already knew that pure protein components gave a fairly uniform density to the resolution at which we were working at that time ($\sim$15–20 Å). Thus, we had observed many times that both collagen fibrils and myofibrils in cross section appeared in sections of either OsO_4 or $KMnO_4$ fixed material more or less homogeneously dense. Nevertheless, we undertook to fix several different kinds of pure proteins, embed them and section them, treating them in every way as we did tissues. When we did this, we found that regardless of the fixation method used we obtained relatively homogeneous densities for pure proteins. We then studied a variety of different kinds of purified lipids representative of the types known to be found in membranes. Here we found a very different picture. Instead of homogeneous amorphous densities, we found a stratified structure consisting of dense and light strata repeating at a period of about 40 Å. Fig. 9 is a picture of purified egg cephalin treated in this way. Here we

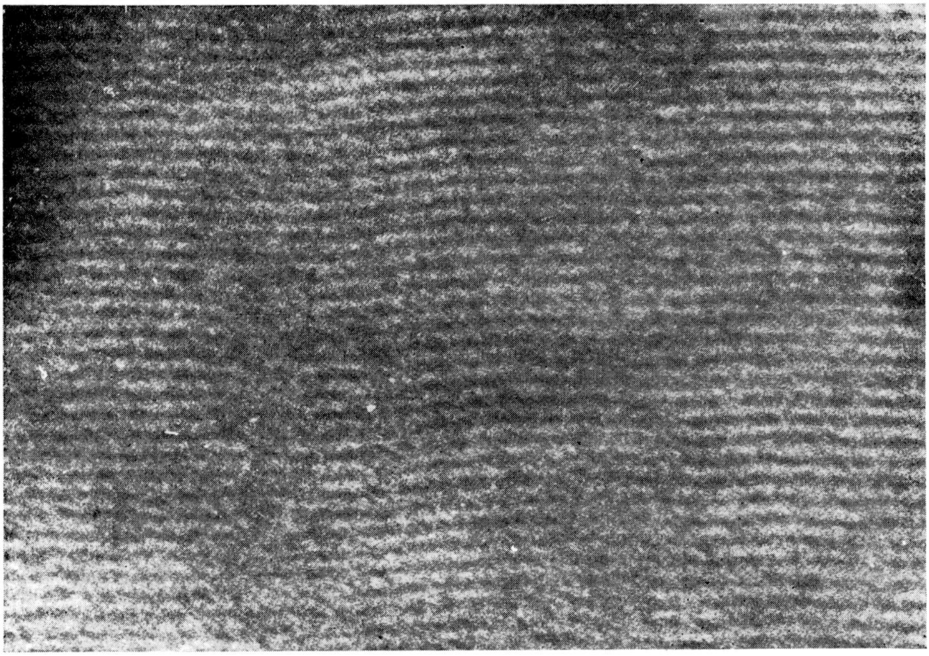

Fig. 9. Specimen of egg cephalin fixed with OsO_4, embedded in Araldite, and sectioned. × 900,000

see a regular repeating period about equal to that to be expected of layers consisting of bimolecular lipid leaflets. We knew from X-ray diffraction studies that lipids of this sort could exist in the state indicated diagrammatically in Fig. 10. This so-called smectic lamellar state is by far the most common state in which such lipids exist at room temperature at low hydration. In was quite apparent from pictures like that shown in Fig. 9 that the dense strata represented either the aligned non-polar carbon chains of the smectic bilayers or the sets of polar heads of adjacent bilayers. Our problem was to decide which of these alternatives was correct.

For a solution to this problem, we took advantage of an experiment that was reported by Schmitt et al. in 1942. They showed that dry smectic systems of lipids as in Fig. 11a could be caused to split off individual bilayers simply by hydration. We reasoned that if we could cause the bilayers to separate in this manner and could succeed in fixing them and obtain sections of them, we could decide whether the polar heads or the non-polar carbon chains were responsible for the dense strata observed. If the non-polar carbon chains were responsible for the dense strata, we should see for each bilayer a single dense stratum. If, on the other hand, the polar heads were

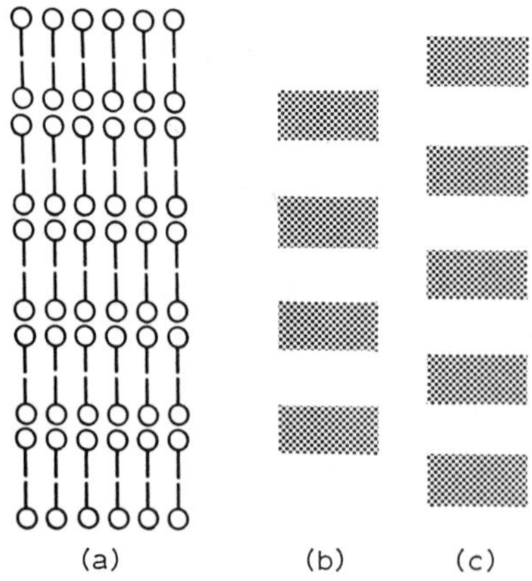

Fig. 10. Lipid molecules. (b) and (c) respectively show the possible location of the dense strata in micrographs, such as that in Fig. 9, in relation to the polar and nonpolar carbon chains (a).

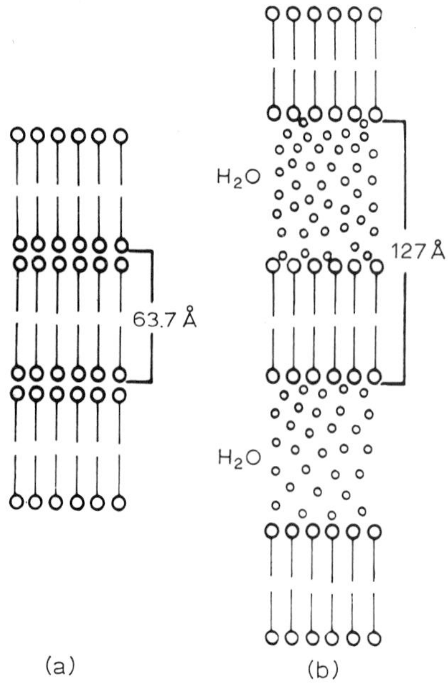

Fig. 11. Diagram taken from Schmitt et al. showing lipid molecules arranged in bilayers in the smectic state. In (a) water is excluded and the bilayers are closely approximated, in (b) water has entered along the polar heads of the molecules splitting off individual bilayers and increasing the repeat period as detected by X-ray diffraction from 63.7 Å to 127 Å.

responsible, we should see for each bilayer a pair of dense strata separated by a light central zone with the overall thickness being somewhere around 50–60 Å. We performed this experiment with the result indicated in Fig. 12. Here we see the independent bilayers split off in a partially hydrated system. We see for each bilayer a pair of parallel dense strata separated by a light central zone with approximately the appropriate dimensions. On the basis of this finding added to the studies of crystalline proteins, it seemed safe to conclude that the lipid polar heads were combined with protein to produce the dense strata seen in the unit membrane pattern. This provided us then with a firm basis on which to make some decisions about the general architectural pattern of the unit membrane, and to make a definite decision about which of the alternatives in Fig. 8 was correct. (a) was obviously the correct choice. (b) should have appeared as three dense strata and two light zones and (c) as a single broad dense band.

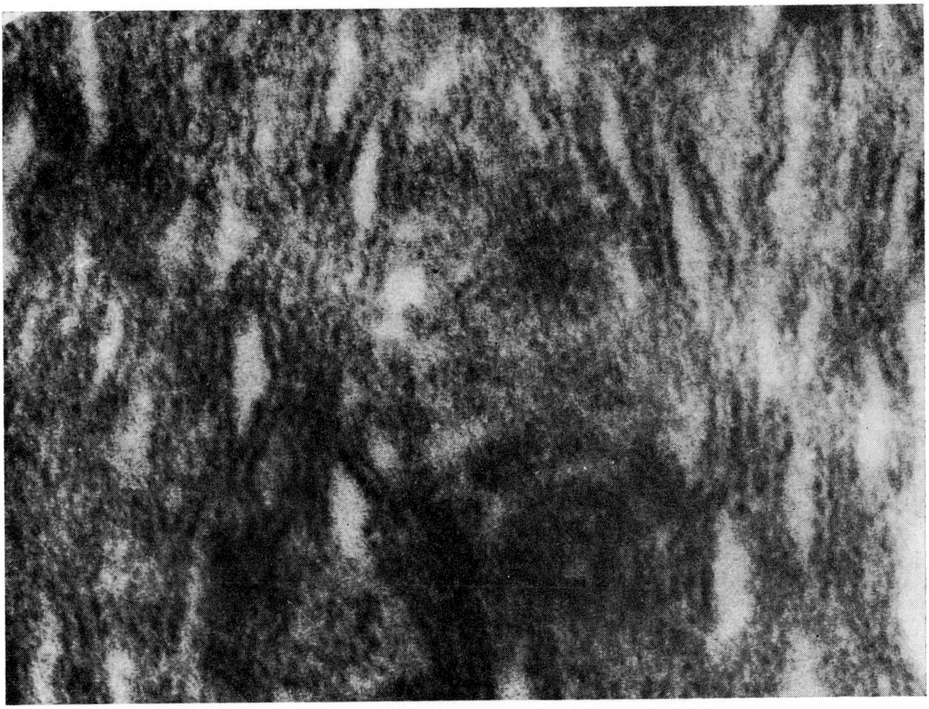

Fig. 12. Specimen of egg cephalin fixed with $KMnO_4$, embedded in Araldite and sectioned. Many individual bilayers are separated out and appear as pairs of dense strata. × 210,000

With the above information in hand, we were able to make an important interpretation of our findings on the myelin sheath that is summarized in Fig. 4. Fig. 13 is an electron micrograph showing the entry of the outer mesaxon into the compact myelin structure. Fig. 4c was drawn from such micrographs. Schmidt reported in 1935 that

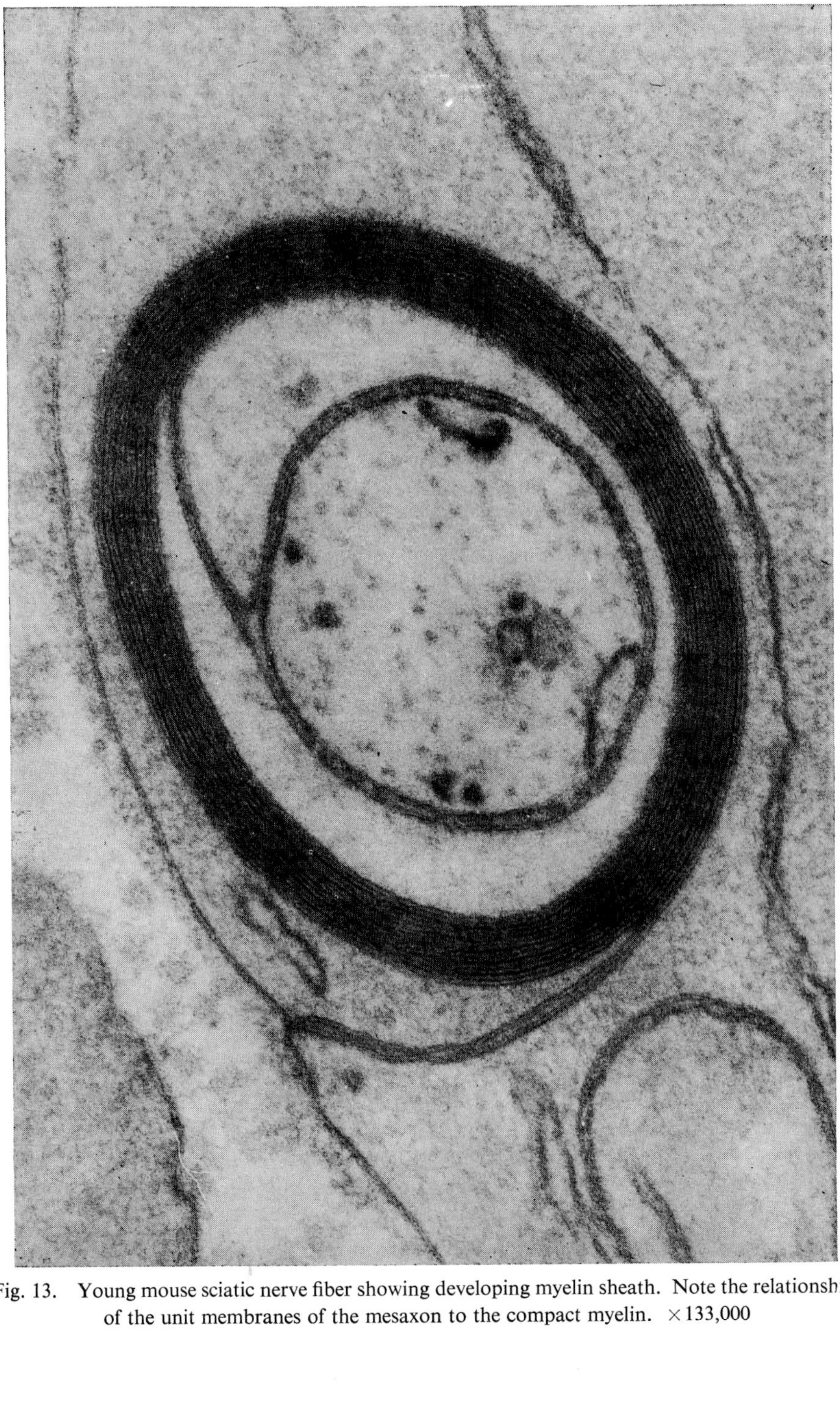

Fig. 13. Young mouse sciatic nerve fiber showing developing myelin sheath. Note the relationships of the unit membranes of the mesaxon to the compact myelin. ×133,000

the normally radially positive birefringence of the myelin sheath reversed in sign to radial negativity after extraction of lipid. This was taken to indicate that the lipid molecules were radially arranged and that after lipid extraction the weaker birefringence of tangentially arranged protein molecules became manifest. Schmidt's diagram of the structural pattern is shown in Fig. 14. In 1953, Schmitt et al. obtained

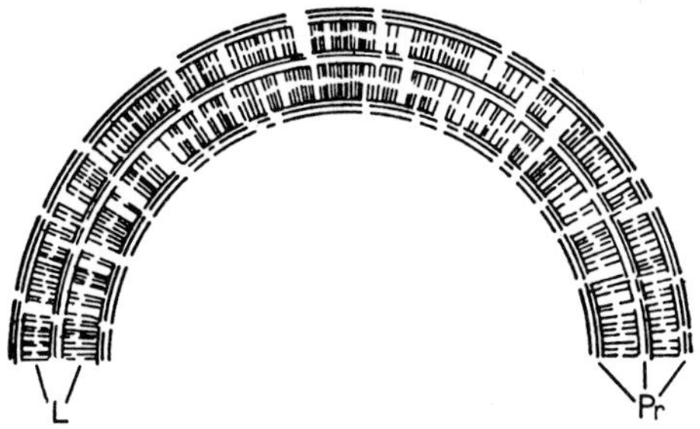

Fig. 14. Diagram from W. J. Schmidt showing his conception of the organization of lipid and protein in the myelin sheath based on polarized light studies. L: lipid; Pr: protein.

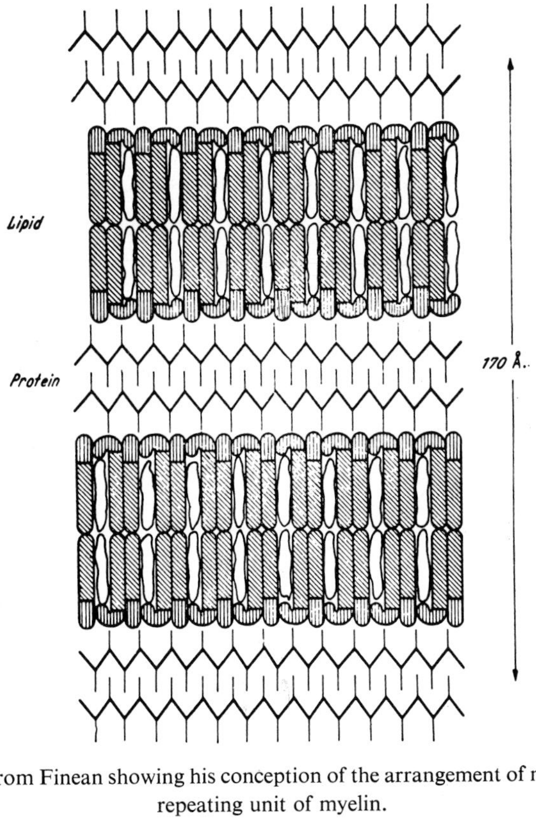

Fig. 15. Diagram from Finean showing his conception of the arrangement of molecules in the radial repeating unit of myelin.

the first small angle X-ray diffraction patterns from myelin. They found a radial repeat period of 171–186 Å depending on species. After the spiral myelin theory was presented by Dr. Geren in 1954 and its validity established by my findings in 1955, Finean proposed that the most probable molecular configuration of the radially repeating unit was that shown in Fig. 15. Assuming this diagram to be correct, I was then able to extrapolate to the unit membrane of the Schwann cell, as indicated in

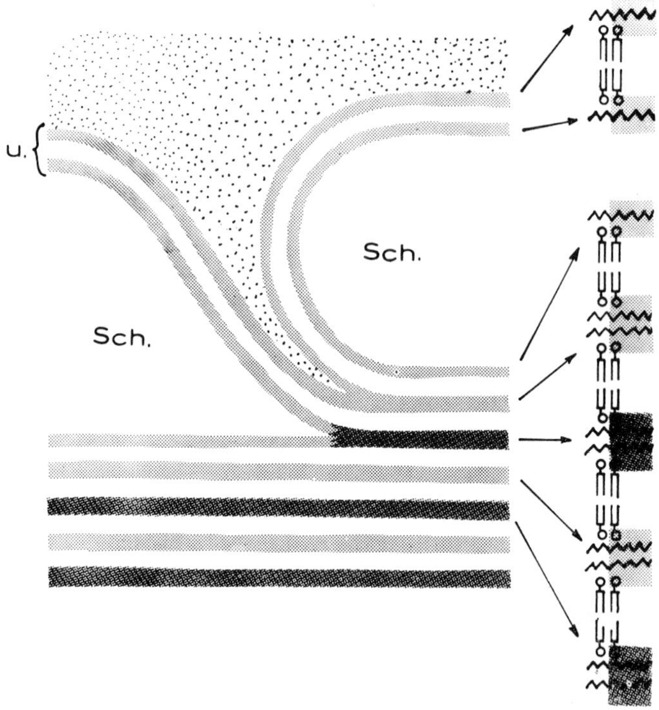

Fig. 16. Diagram of the electron microscopic appearance of myelin at its junction with the mesaxon (to the left). To the right the molecular diagram is superimposed, which is deduced partly by X-ray diffraction and partly from the studies of model systems by electron microscopy.

Fig. 16, and propose the molecular pattern for the unit membrane presented in Fig. 2. However, it was not until the model experiments described above were done that there was any firm reason to believe that Finean's diagram was correct.

It was not until 1964 that sufficient X-ray information was obtained to allow an electron density plot of the repeating unit to be made (Finean and Burge; Moody). This was consistent with the molecular pattern originally proposed. It therefore appears quite reasonable to assert that we have a firm basis for believing that the molecular pattern underlying the typical unit membrane pattern is as indicated in Fig. 2.

In 1962 Luzzati and Husson showed that pure lipid water systems need not necessarily be always in the smectic bilayer state as indicated in Fig. 10, but that in certain portions of the phase diagram the lipid may exist in various states as indicated in Fig. 17. At certain temperatures and water concentrations the lipid lamellae become

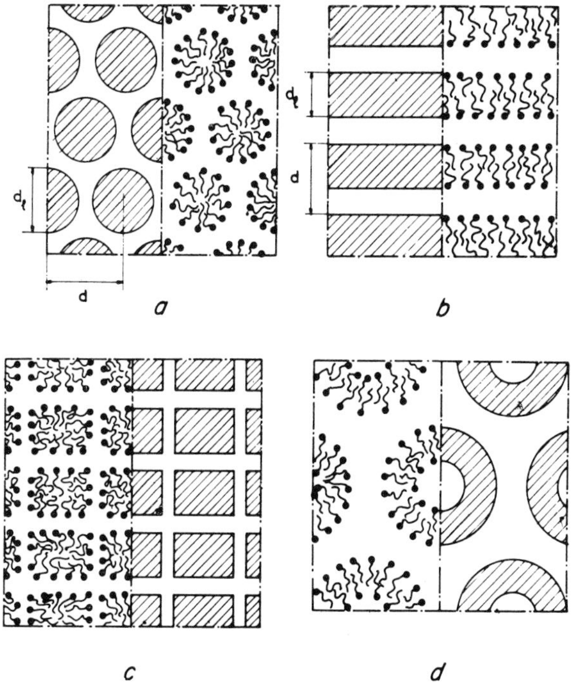

Fig. 17. Diagram showing various states in which lipids may exist in aqueous media. (From Luzzati and Husson.) See text.

converted into hexagonally arrayed regularly spaced columns with the polar heads either directed outward or inward as indicated in the diagram. Stoeckenius has shown that lipid in such a hexagonal state as indicated in Fig. 18a can be fixed with OsO_4 vapors. The polar heads of the lipid molecules are then made to show up in thin sections as dense spots in a hexagonal array as indicated in Fig. 18b. He also showed that when the lipid was caused to undergo a reversal with the polar heads pointing outward as in Fig. 17a the lipid heads could be shown up as dense strata with the overall appearance being that of a delicate honey-comb.

Fig. 19 shows portions of the phase diagram for a phospholipid-water system studied by Luzzati and Husson which consisted of an ether extract of human brain containing 52% cephalin, 35% lecithin, and 13% phospho-inositides. Phase transitions representing deviation from the usual smectic bilayer state were found in this specimen in a range that could be considered at least remotely physiological. At 37 °C and at high concentrations of lipid (low hydration) phase changes occurred as indicated in Fig. 19, by the points to the left of (b). This finding led immediately to a great deal of specula-

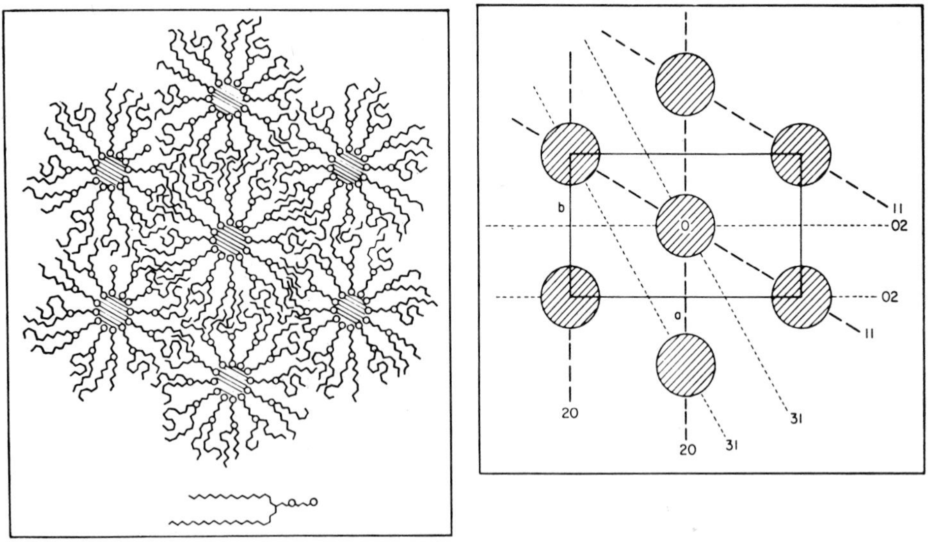

Fig. 18. Lipid in hexagonal state. (From Stoeckenius.) See text for discussion.

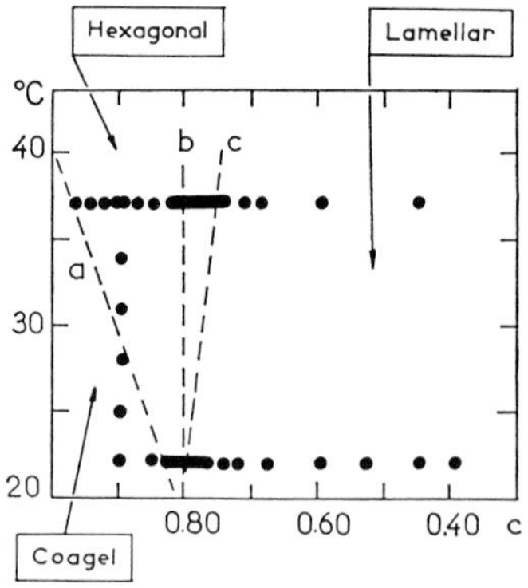

Fig. 19. Phase diagram of phospholipid-water system, and position of the experimental points. (From Luzzati and Husson.)

tion about whether or not such transitions can occur in the smectic lipid bilayers of living membranes. Obviously if they occur, the permeability properties of the membranes would be profoundly affected and the transport properties of living membranes would become understandable in entirely new terms. Seductive though this notion is, it is important to note that there is not a shred of evidence that any such transitions ever occur in living membranes. Indeed, immediately upon becoming associated with proteins, whether passively in artificial lipid-protein systems or actively in naturally occurring lipoproteins or proteolipids, lipids lose the property of undergoing such phase transitions as far as present evidence goes, since nobody has yet succeeded in producing any evidence that such phase transitions occur in such systems. This has been attempted by Husson and others with negative results. It seems apparent that the lipids are stabilized in the smectic bilayer state by association with proteins. Thus, it is highly dubious to assume that simply because some lipids in aqueous systems can undergo such phase transitions, the lipids of living biological membranes undergo any such transitions. We simply must have at least some convincing evidence that such phase transitions can occur in lipoproteins if not in membrane organelles before we take any such concept seriously in regard to the general plan of organization or function of living biological membranes.

In recent years, a great deal of interest has been aroused by consideration of another kind of artificial membrane structure. Mueller and Rudin several years ago found that it was possible to make an apparent lipid bilayer membrane at a water-to-water interface. This was done very simply by stroking a camel's hair brush containing an appropriate mixture of lipids in 2:1 chloroform-methanol over a small hole in a polyethylene container immersed completely in water. The technique for doing this is indicated in Fig. 20 taken from Thompson. As the lipid thins down interference colors are pro-

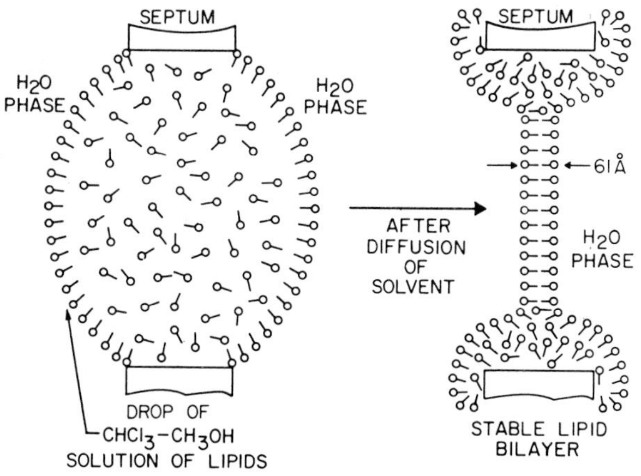

Fig. 20. Schematic drawing showing the transition of a thick lipid film to a bilayer film. (From Thompson.)

duced from light reflected from the film. Eventually the film gets so thin that no interference colors are seen and the film looks black. This is the so-called 'secondary black'. It was assumed that the secondary black regions represented true bilayers of lipid. Mueller and Rudin found that protein could be adsorbed on these artificial bilayers, and that if this were done, the electrical properties of the bilayers changed. Something vaguely resembling an action potential could be obtained by certain electrical manipulations. Thompson (1964) has studied such bilayers further and determined certain of their electrical properties as compared to those of natural membranes. Some of the relevant values are indicated in Table 1 taken from Thompson. In general the electrical properties of these artificial bilayers were found to be very similar to that of living

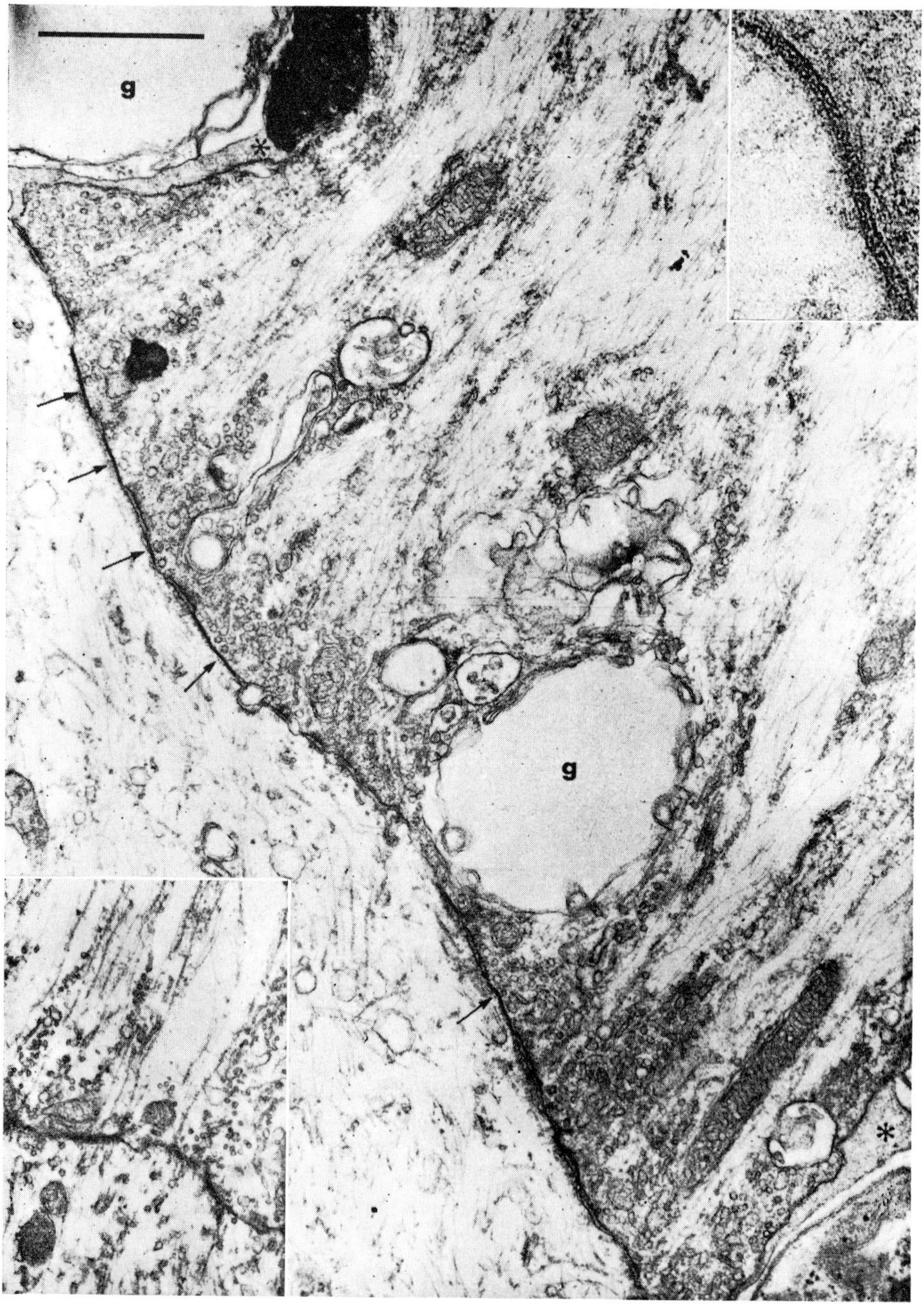

Fig. 21. High power electron micrograph of a club ending of lateral dendrite showing accumulations of vesicles near the presynaptic membrane and neurofilaments and microtubules of the terminal axons. Note the collar of extracellular matrix material surrounding the axon at the termination of the sheath. The synaptic discs are indicated by the arrows; the asterisk (*) indicates extracellular matrix material; (g) swollen glia processes; to the upper right a synaptic disc and to the lower left the termination of microtubules on the synaptic membrane complex. $\times$ 23,400. Upper inset $\times$ 152,000, lower inset $\times$ 15,200 after correction of position.

TABLE 1

Electrical properties of natural and bilayer membranes.

	Natural membranes (20–25 °C)	Bilayer membranes (36 °C)
Thickness, Å	40–45	72 ± 10
Resistance (d. c.) Ω cm^2	—	$(0.2-4.0) \times 10^6$
Resistance (1 kc) Ω cm^2	10^2–10^5	$(1.0 \pm 0.5) \times 10^6$ [1]
Capacitance (1 kc) μ f cm^{-2}	0.5–1.3	0.69 ± 0.05
Dielectric breakdown, mV	100–300	100 ± 20
H_2O permeability, micr. sec^{-1}		
isotopic	0.23–63	4.4 ± 0.5
osmotic	0.37–400	17.3–104

[1] 25 °C.

membranes except that the electrical resistance of the bilayers was found to be higher than that of living membranes. One feature of all the techniques, for making artificial membranes of this kind, is that the lipids must be mixed with a certain amount of n-decane. The late Dr. Jack Schulman pointed out on several occasions that it was highly improbable that all the n-decane was ever excluded from the bilayers. He predicted that a thin layer of n-decane molecules would always remain in the non-polar carbon chain regions of the bilayers. Eventually Thompson et al. succeeded in fixing these bilayers and obtaining electron micrographs of transverse sections of them. These showed regions of distinct widening in the light central zone of the bilayer that occurred at irregular intervals along the length of the sections. This was a very different picture from that seen in natural membranes or in artificial bilayers of the type indicated in Fig. 12. It seems very probable that the irregularities in these artificial bilayers are due to small pools of n-decane occurring in the non-polar central zones as predicted by Schulman and that a certain amount of n-decane remains distributed all along the bilayers. This provides a good explanation for smaller irregularities outside the gross deviations at the pools. The presence of this n-decane may explain at least some of the discrepancies in the electrical properties of these membranes as compared to natural membranes. Studies of such artificial bilayer membranes are now being done in a number of laboratories, and in particular Tostesan and his group are studying the effects of the macrocylic depsipeptide antibiotic 'valinomycin' on the electrical properties of the artificial membranes. When valinomycin is applied there are drastic changes in these properties. We hope this will cast considerable light on the properties of biological membranes.

4. *The general architectural principle*

The above findings on natural membranes taken together with my early model studies permitted me to specify with some confidence a general architectural principle involved in the the construction of biological membranes that seemed to be common to them all. The theory says that they are comprised of a bimolecular leaflet of lipid with the polar heads directed outward, and covered by monolayers of non-lipid. It says nothing about the particular arrangements of the lipid molecules with respect to one another nor anything about the particular lipid composition. Similarly, it says nothing about the arrangement of the non-lipid, and essentially nothing about its chemical composition, although it does say that the outside non-lipid is different from the inside non-lipid in some important way. The speculation was offered that this difference might be attributed to the fact that the outer monolayer of protein contains a high percentage of mucopolysaccharide. Essentially this principle gives no more than an overall picture of the general architectural principles involved in membrane construction.

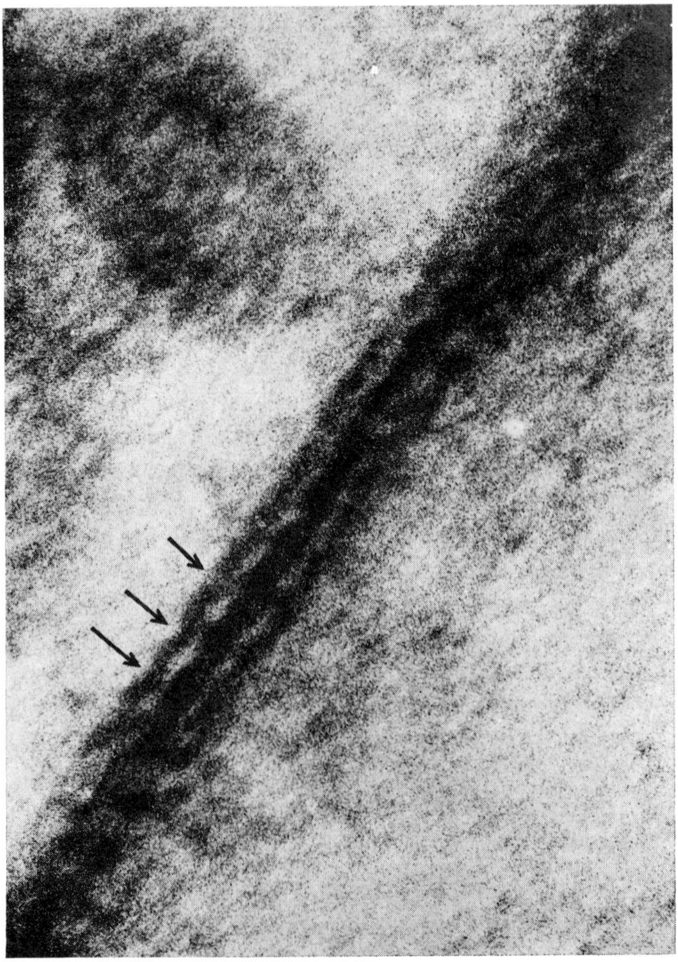

Fig. 22. High power view of synaptic discs like those indicated in Fig. 21 but in material fixed with $KMnO_4$. Arrows indicate scalloping of cytoplasmic surface. ×1,000,000

Recently we have been concerned with the possibility that there exists in unit membranes an architectural principle that goes beyond that of the earlier hypothesis. For a long time it has been speculated that there may be some kind of structural protein present in membranes, and it seems rather likely that this structural protein may have some kind of particular architectural arrangement. It may be arranged according to a limited number of architectural plans without saying anything about the particular molecules that are involved. The molecules themselves may be highly specific and may differ markedly from membrane to membrane while still being put together in a common way. Alternatively there may be for a given animal or phylum a particular species of protein molecule that has evolved to subserve this structural function very early in evolution and it may have persisted with certain essential characteristics remaining constant throughout the history of the species. This is not to say that genetic modification would not have taken place in the synthetic machinery for this particular protein, but rather that certain essential properties had to be maintained in order for survival to occur.

In 1963 we observed in our laboratory (Robertson et al.; Robertson 1963) a type of

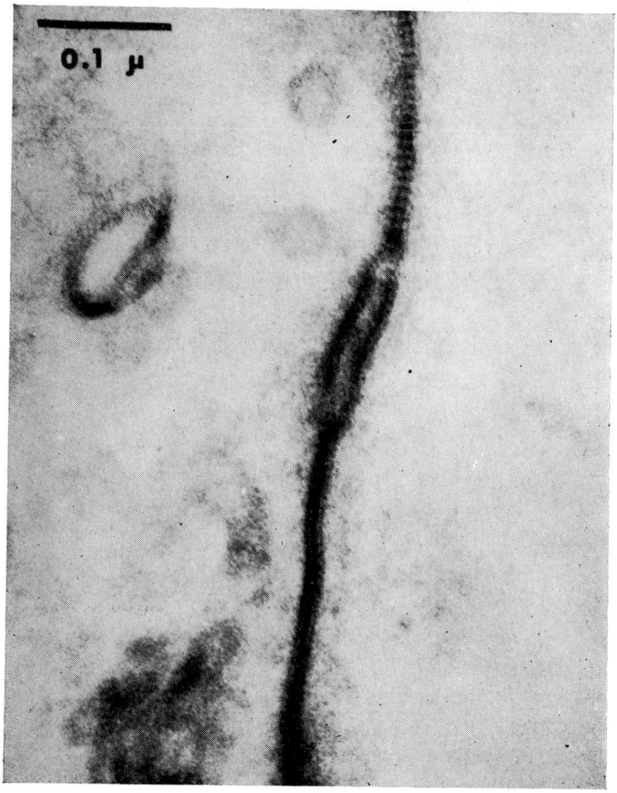

Fig. 23. Portion of two synaptic discs with intervening region with a widened cleft. Presynaptic axoplasm to the left. ×185,000

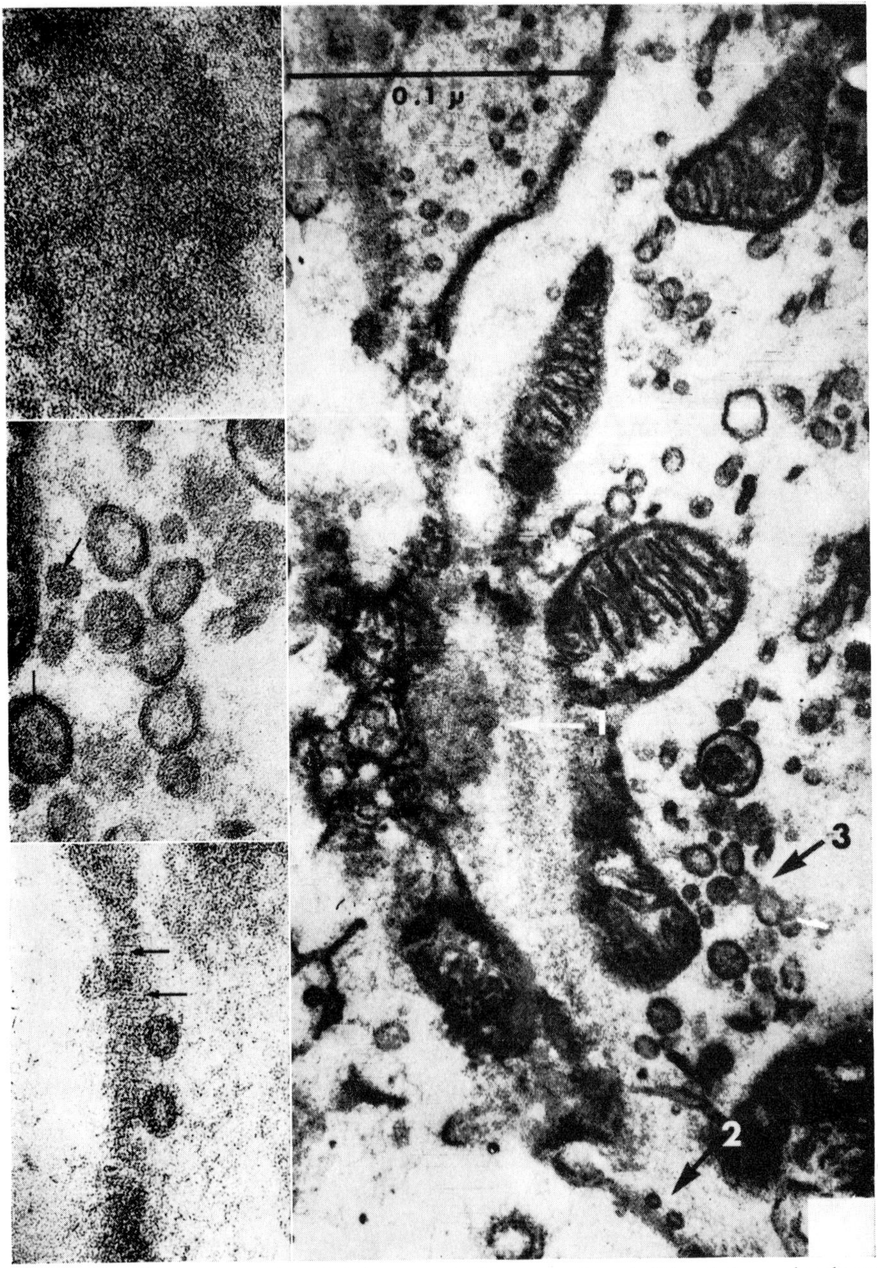

Fig. 24. Section of club ending in which the synaptic discs are sectioned obliquely to varying degrees. Some synaptic vesicles (arrow 3) are enlarged in the middle inset. They show some suggestions of subunit structure in their membranes. An obliquely sectioned disc at arrow 2 is enlarged to the lower left to show rows of dots between the dense lines that appear as the disc is tilted. A frontally sectioned disc at arrow 1 is enlarged to the upper left to show the hexagonal array of subunit facets. × 45,000. Upper inset ×130,000. Middle inset × 95,000. Lower inset ×112,000

organization in the surfaces of unit membranes making a synaptic junction in the Mauthner of cell club endings of goldfish brain, that suggested that some kind of particular architectural principle was operating in these particular membranes that might be related to a structural protein. Fig. 21 is an electron micrograph that shows a club ending at fairly high power. In some regions the pre- and postsynaptic membranes are united in disc-like structures that we called 'synaptic discs'. These are indicated by the arrows. Between the synaptic discs, the pre- and postsynaptic membranes are seen to be distinctly separated. Fig. 22 is a synaptic disc in cross section seen at very high magnification. Fig. 23 shows one synaptic disc sectioned normally with two adjacent ones sectioned obliquely. Fig. 24 shows a section of a club ending with one disc sectioned obliquely (arrow 2) and one that appears in frontal section (arrow 1). The enlargements at the bottom and top left include each of these discs respectively. I shall now try to relate the various images of the discs in cross section and oblique or frontal section.

The transversely sectioned discs show the pentalaminar structure that is characteristic of a 'tight junction' but in addition certain other features are apparent. First, there

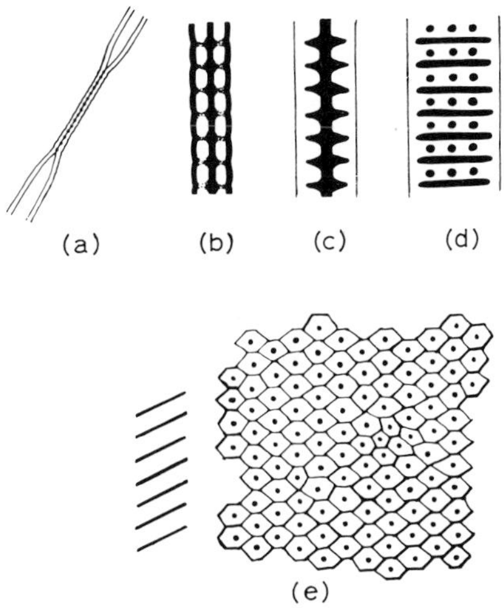

Fig. 25. Diagram of structures observed in synaptic discs in Mauthner cell club endings (a) shows the appearance of the synaptic discs at low power; (b) shows a high-power view of the central region. (c) Appearance of the synaptic disc slightly tilted. (d) Appearance of the disc at a greater degree of tilt. (e) Frontal view of the disc showing a hexagonal array of subunits repeating at a period of about 90 Å as indicated by the lines to the left. Each facet consists of a dense border and a central dense spot. The lattice is hexagonal, but there appear to be a few pentagonal facets interspersed. The facets are believed to be produced mainly by the apposed outside surfaces of the two unit membranes. This conclusion is reached mainly because of the characteristics of the image during tilt. The facet's structure is referred to as granulo-fibrillar substructure. The scalloping and vague transverse densities in (b) might indicate a micellarphase transformation in the membrane lipids, or could equally well represent some kind of optical image superimposition artifact. It is referred to as globular fine structure.

are rather regularly spaced beads along the central dense stratum which repeat at a period of about 90 Å. Opposite each of these beads there are vague transverse densities that traverse the light zones to either side. There is also a scalloping of the cytoplasmic dense strata opposite the beads. Fig. 25a, b will perhaps make these features more clear. In oblique sections the central beads are smeared out into dense strata that repeat at a period of ~ 90 Å as in Fig. 25b. With further tilt rows of dots appear between the dense strata (lower left insert in Fig. 24 and Fig. 25d). Finally in frontal sections the regular hexagonal lattice appears as in Fig. 24 (arrow 1) and Fig. 25e. Each hexagonal facet is about 90 Å in diameter and bordered by walls about 20 Å thick. There is a dot ~ 25 Å in diameter in the center of each facet. The best interpretation of the findings seems to be that the beads in the transverse sections of the disc represent the lattice lines of the hexagonal lattice seen edge on as indicated in Fig. 25d. If the lattice in Fig. 24 (upper left insert) or the diagram in Fig. 25e is turned on edge we see a set of lines that come into register at some angle. As the picture is rotated the lattice lines come into register every 60°. The lattice clearly has hexagonal symmetry. The beads seen edge on in transverse sections evidently are the lattice lines seen edge on. It seemed to me very likely that we were able to see this lattice in the synaptic disc partly because there were two membranes united with two lattices in register. Of course, the lattices are themselves not perfect, and this is a very important point. There are imperfections and occasionally it seems that there are some pentagonal facets amongst the dominant hexagonal ones. This characteristic imperfection is indicated in the diagram in Fig. 25e.

I assumed from the outset that in the synaptic disc we were seeing a manifestation of substructure in unit membranes that might not be peculiar to the synaptic disc though at first there was very little evidence for this. I have speculated that the facets themselves might be made up of aggregates of protein molecules the charred residues of which were being seen in the electron micrographs. For instance in Fig. 26a we see a portion of this lattice enlarged showing essentially what is observed in the electron micrographs and in Fig. 26b a diagrammatic representation of a conceivable living precursor of the derived structure that we actually observe. The somewhat ellipsoidal

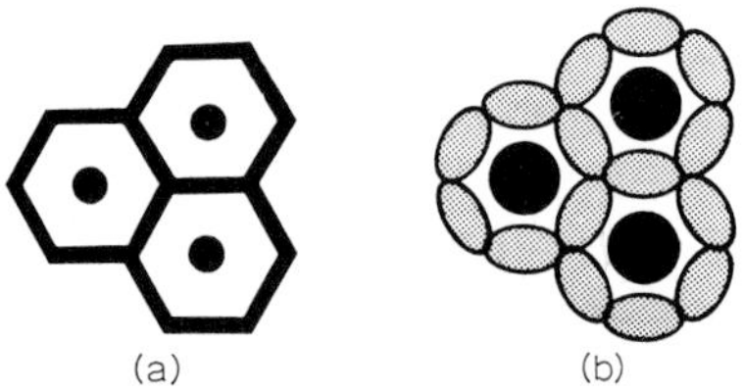

Fig. 26. (a) is a diagram of three of the hexagonally arranged facets seen in the synaptic discs. (b) is a hypothetical representation of two kinds of non-lipid molecules that might underlie this structure in the living state. The oval molecules might be structural protein and the spherical ones could be a specific protein for the particular membrane. The latter might vary from membrane to membrane or even in the same membrane. Thus it might be a mucopolysaccharide in some facets or a specific protein in others.

or cylindrical but roughly globular structures making the walls of the facets are represented as structural protein molecules. These could make up such a structure and if so might be expected to have a molecular weight of something between 15 and 20 thousand. The central globular molecule would be of similar molecular weight, although perhaps somewhat smaller. I have speculated further that the central globular molecules might represent specific molecules peculiar to the particular membrane under consideration. The structural protein molecules might be common to all the cells of the animal or the species. Such an arrangement could then subserve two functions, first, one of structural rigidity with suitable provision for deformation and, second, one of specificity for the particular function that the membrane must carry on. The first function would be served by the ellipsoidal molecules and the second by the central spherical ones. It should also be noted that there are areas of open space that could be left as a consequence of packing the molecules together. Here the polar heads of the lipid molecules deeper in the membrane might be more or less directly exposed to the outside and be available for the action of degradative enzymes such as phospholipase. There is also the possibility that the central globular molecules might be mucopolysaccharide in nature and easily pushed aside to allow lipid degradative

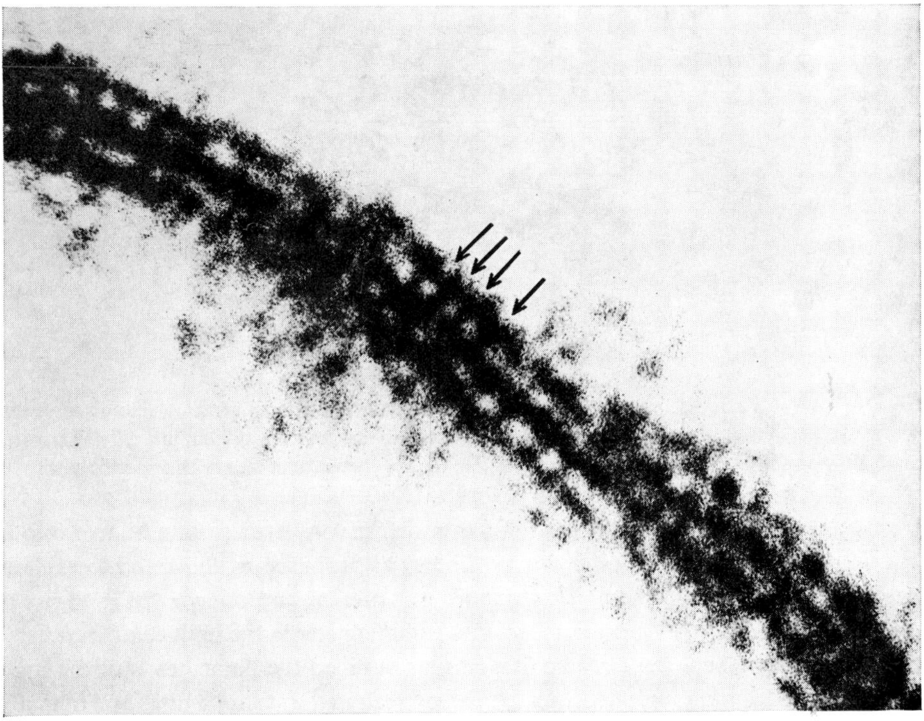

Fig. 27. Section of an octopus optic nerve fiber showing two axon membranes stuck together to make an external-compound-membrane. Note the transverse densities running across one of the unit membranes at the arrows. × 850,000

enzymes to reach the lipid polar heads without necessarily having their action either destroy the structural integrity of the membranes or reduce their protein content (see Lenard and Singer).

All of the above is based on the Mauthner cell findings, and it seemed from these studies that the highly organized structural components we had been considering probably resided in the external surfaces of the membranes. There was nothing to suggest that such structural arrangements occurred in the inner or cytoplasmic dense strata except perhaps the scalloping of the cytoplasmic surfaces in the synaptic discs. This scalloping is not widely observed but the transverse densities seen in the synaptic discs are very widely observed. For example, note the ones at the arrows in Fig. 27. Such transverse densities have given rise to the idea that there is present a so-called 'globular' fine structure in membranes in many different locations.

Sjöstrand was prominent in reporting such observations and in interpreting them in terms of the so-called 'globular fine structure'. The work of Luzzati and Husson and of Stoeckenius referred to above, provided evidence that made plausible the kind of interpretations that were made by Sjöstrand. This kind of interpretation is illustrated in the molecular diagram in Fig. 28. Here the lipid bilayer core of the unit

Fig. 28. Shows a possible molecular interpretation of observed pattern. Reasons are given in the text for believing that this arrangement of lipid molecules is not generally present in the living state in unit membranes and probably not responsible for the particular image in this specific case.

membranes of the synaptic disc are shown as being converted from a bilayer into a system of either microspheres or microcylinders as proposed by Sjöstrand to explain the transverse densities. If such a structure was present and one viewed it edge on, one might expect to see transverse densities rumming across the light central cores of the membranes where the metallic fixing agent outlined the polar heads of the lipid molecules. Such transverse densities are indeed seen in the synaptic discs and in many different membranes. Nilsson observed such structures very clearly in retinal rod outer segment membranes and Sjöstrand concluded that the so-called micellar phase transformation, represented by the conversion of the lipid bilayer core into a system of microspheres or columns of lipid, was a real phenomenon that occurred in living membranes, although these were not always fixed successfully. However, it is important to note that such phase transformations very rarely occur in lipoproteins. This alone made it seem questionable to me that such phase transformations occur in living membranes. However, the interpretation was one that could not be dismissed lightly, and for some time it was necessary to take it seriously. However, it soon occurred to me that if there were a regular hexagonal lattice in the surfaces of membranes such as I had predicted, and if it were of general occurrence one might occasionally have the membranes in exactly the right orientation, tipped precisely and correctly in the plane of the section so that one would see an image overlap artifact as indicated in the diagrams in Figs. 29–30. This artifact would exactly reproduce the images observed.

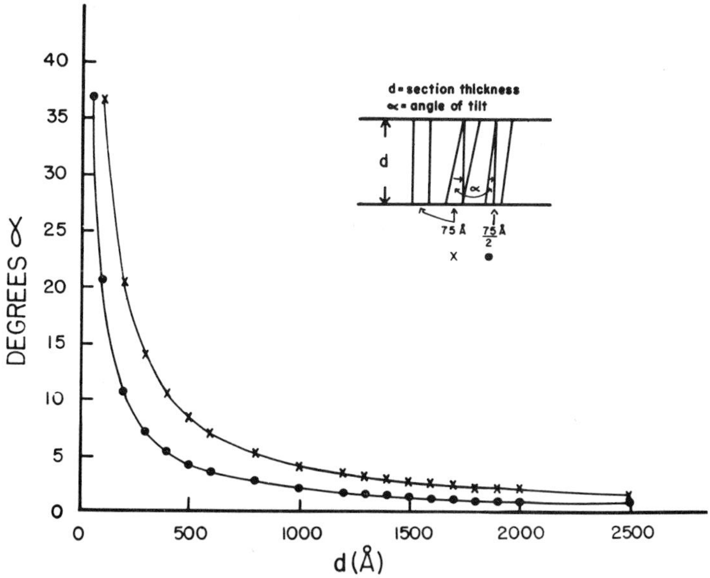

Fig. 29. Graph of angle through which a section of thickness 'd' must be tilted in order to give an overlap artifact. See text.

The theory predicts that a membrane cut transversely in a section of 500 Å or more if tilted $\sim 5°$ might show the appearance of such transverse densities. I then performed some experiments on retinal rod outer segments in which I proceeded to tilt sections of the right thickness by about 5°. I was able to demonstrate that such transverse densities could indeed be produced as indicated in Fig. 31a, b. I then began to think more seriously about the fact that the dense strata of many membranes when observed edge on as indicated in Fig. 32 are not homogeneous. They often consist rather of apparent grains that repeat at a period of about 80–90 Å. Such appearances are by no means regularly seen but they are encountered not infrequently. The appearances of these densities would seem consistent with the notion that occasionally one sees a hexagonal lattice of the type we have been discussing edge on, and that it can occur either on the inside, or the outside, or both sides of unit membranes. The fact that one does not often see this is consistent with the theory since there would only be six possible orientations out of 360° in which one would see it. Furthermore, if the patterns on the inside and outside surfaces whether the same or different were slightly out of phase with one another, then when observing membranes frontally one would normally not expect to see the pattern. I therefore began to believe that my theory about the con-

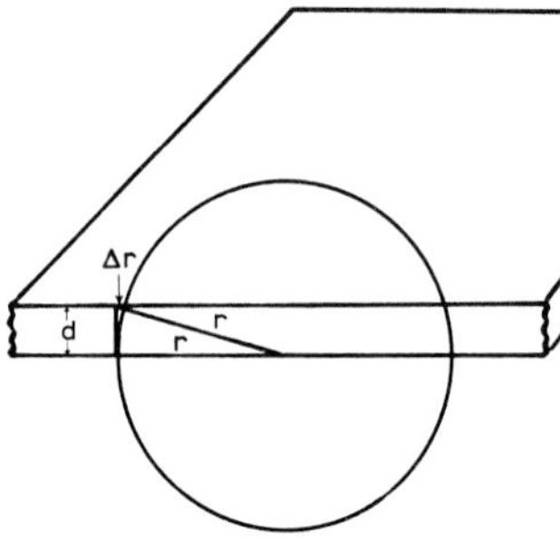

Fig. 30. Three-dimensional diagram of a section of thickness 'd' of a spherical object of radius 'r'. $\triangle$r is a measure of the degree to which the top edge of the section of a unit membrane will overlap the bottom edge. See text.

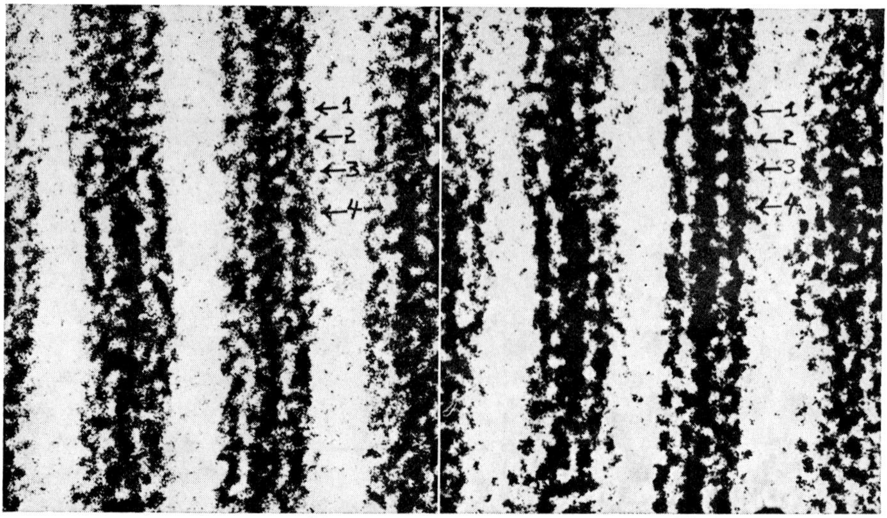

(a) (b)

Fig. 31. Two micrographs showing a few ROS lamellae in transection. Note the granular character of the images at the arrows 1–4. There are no clear-cut densities traversing the membranes. (a) The right hand micrograph (b) is of the same area after tilting the section through 5 degrees. Transverse densities now appear in the region of arrows 1–4. × 600,000

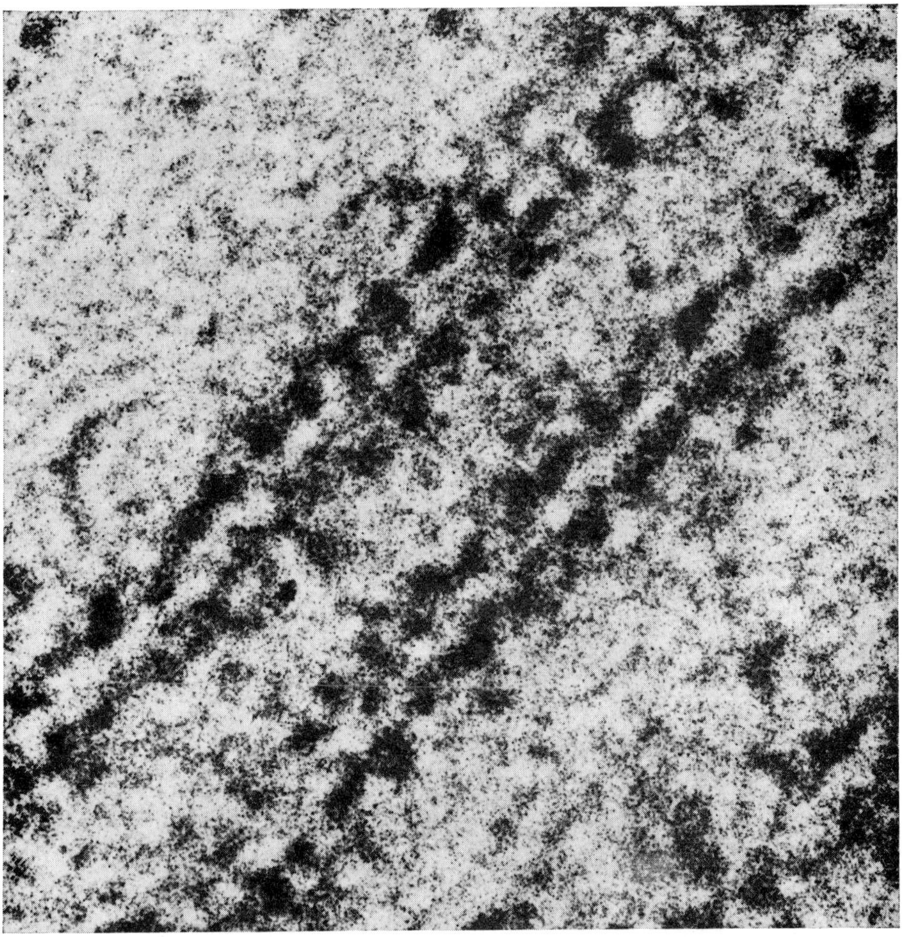

Fig. 32. Portion of transverse section of invaginated surface in epithelial cell in mouse urinary bladder fixed with $KMnO_4$, embedded in Araldite and sectioned. ~ ×1,200,000

struction of the synaptic disc membranes might have generality and that there might indeed be an architectural principle that we could define going beyond the unit membrane principle but concerning mainly the non-lipid components of the membrane.

5. *Viral protein coats and unit membranes*

I was aware of the work of Caspar and Klug on the construction of protein coats of viruses, and this new theory led me to consider further the notions concerning viral protein coats that have been built up over the last few years. I was also stimulated to consider further some of the beautiful generalities in D'Arcy Thompson's book 'On growth and form'. In the formation of protein coats for spherical viruses one is dealing with the problem of complete enclosure of space. We are also dealing with a similar problem in biological membrane systems. One of the cardinal principles of the unit membrane theory of cell structure as indicated in Fig. 33 is that living membranes always appear as continuous structures that enclose space. There is always a cytoplasmic side and always an outside substance side to any unit membrane, and these always maintain their polar relationships in the cell. These features are even maintained generally when membrane fragments are isolated from cells. Such membrane fragments by and large come out as vesicles that enclose space. Sometimes the outside surface is exposed and sometimes the inside but in general continuity is maintained. To be sure, under special conditions, Marchesi and Palade have been able to isolate sheets of membrane that do not unite to enclose space. However, this is by far the exception rather than the rule. Certainly in living cells unit membranes always enclose space.

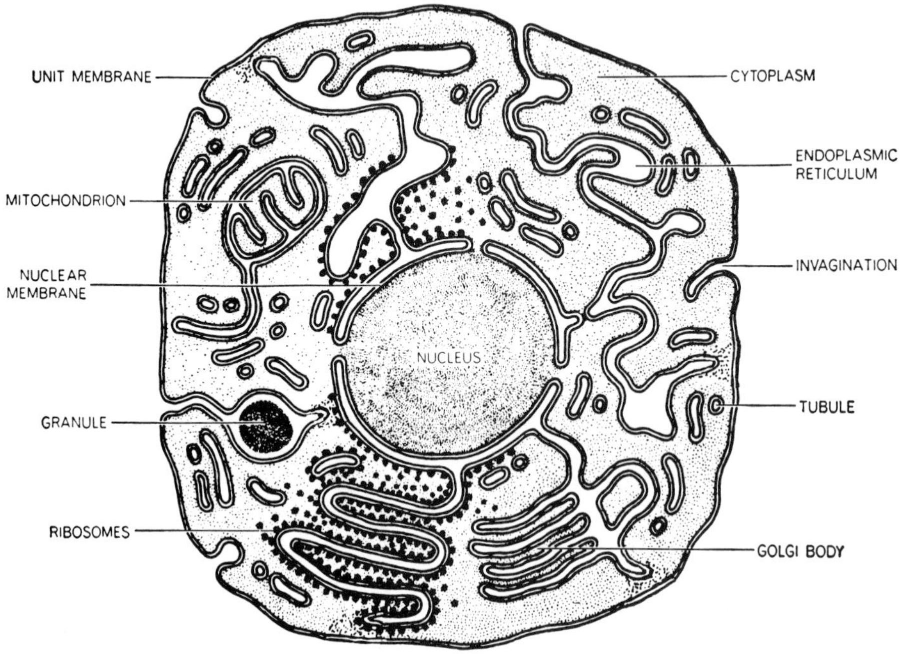

Fig. 33. Diagram of theoretical cell.

The ideas that have been developed about the enclosure of space by viral protein coats appear to me to be quite relevant to the problem of space enclosure by unit membranes. To be sure, membranes enclose relatively massive volumes as compared to viruses. One might expect then to see different structural principles employed. However, there are two striking facts about biological membranes that seem to me to suggest that perhaps similar principles are employed. First, membrane limited vesicles seem to have a minimal diameter reaching a radius of no less than about 150 Å.

Second, cells often project microvilli or so-called 'microspikes' which again do not become less than ~ 300 Å in diameter. It may well be that the lipid is primarily responsible foı this limit of ~150 Å radius, as I have suggested before (Robertson 1963). However, it may equally well be that there is something about the structural proteins that imposes such a limitation. The limiting radius of curvature is roughly comparable to that of small spherical viruses and so it seems reasonable to look for principles in membrane structural protein arrangements similar to those employed in viral protein coats. It seems appropriate therefore to consider briefly some of the principles employed in viruses.

Crick and Watson made some predictions about the way the protein coat of small spherical viruses might be constructed that have proven to be quite accurate. First, they argued that the small viruses because of space economy would have a minimal amount of their limited genetic information devoted to any one function such as the synthesis of the molecules of the protein coat. This led immediately to the idea that the protein coat might be an assembly of only one kind of small protein molecule. Clearly if this were so, this molecule must have the property of spontaneously assembling into the coat once formed. Watson and Crick went a little further and suggested that the resulting assembly would most likely have cubic symmetry. In the same year Caspar demonstrated in some X-ray diffraction studies of a small spherical virus (tomato bushy stunt) that cubic symmetry was in fact present. An essential feature of cubic symmetry is that the three coordinate directions in space are not independent. They are in fact equivalent. Thus no direction in space is preferred. Three general types of cubic symmetry exist, tetrahedral, octahedral and icosahedral. These have axes of symmetry that are respectively two-fold and three-fold (2:3) for tetrahedral, four-, three- and two-fold (4:3:2) for octahedral and five-, three- and two-fold (5:3:2) for incosahedral. Caspar found 5:3:2 symmetry in the tomato bushy stunt viruses he studied indicating icosahedral symmetry. Soon afterwards Williams and Smith produced electron micrographs of *Tipula* iridescent virus that showed clear icosahedral shape. Subsequent work has repeatedly shown icosahedral symmetry in other small spherical viruses and it appears likely that this kind of symmetry is generally present. Caspar and Klug in a beautiful analysis showed why this is so. To make their analysis clear we must briefly digress into a consideration of the forms that regular solid polyhedra can take.

D'Arcy Thompson takes up such matters in some detail. He points out that the Greeks knew that there were only a limited number of ways in which space could be enclosed with maximal cubic symmetry. It must be done with polygons which are both isogonal and isohedral, i.e. polygons that have their corners all alike and their faces all alike. There are only five regular polygons, the so-called Platonic bodies. They are: the tetrahedron, cube, octahedron, dodecahedron, and icosahedron. There is a simple theorem that was derived by Euler, a contemporary of Linnaeus, that is called Euler's law that can be used to describe the Platonic bodies. It says that in any polyhedron the faces (F) and corners (C) outnumber the edges (E) by two: $C-E+$

F = 2. The tetrahedron has four faces, the cube six, the octahedron eight, the dodecahedron twelve and the icosahedron twenty. The icosahedron has twelve corners and by Euler's law thirty edges.

There is another class of polygonal solids obtained by truncating the corners of the Platonic solids. These are thirteen in number and are called the Archimedean solids. There is one other group of thirteen known as the Catalan solids that may be formed from the Archimedean solids by replacing corners with faces. All these bodies are related to the sphere since they can be fitted into a sphere with either all the corners or all the faces intersecting its surface. The Archimedean and Catalan bodies are regular in that they either have all their corners equal or all their faces equal but only the Platonic bodies have both equal. One of the very important points that comes from examination of the properties of these various bodies is that one cannot simply put a lot of symmetrical polygons together any old way to make a closed surface. In fact, for instance, while it is possible to make a closed surface by putting squares or pentagons together it is quite impossible to do this with hexagons. If we limit ourselves to bodies with three-way corners, the following formula applies: $(6\text{-}n)\ F_n = 12$. 'n' is the number of sides of each face 'F'. This formula shows why 'n' cannot equal six. D'Arcy Thompson derived the following relation from Euler's law: $2F = (n-2)\ C + 4$. If $n = 6$, $2F = 4C + 4$. Suppose there are four faces, F, then there must be only one corner. This is clearly impossible and illustrates again why a sheet of hexagons cannot make a closed surface. However, closed surfaces can be made of mixtures of hexagons and pentagons. In this case the number of pentagons is exactly twelve. The point here is that there are only a limited number of possible ways that polygons can be combined into a closed surface. Furthermore, if only one kind of polygon is to be used it must have less than six sides.

Returning to the Platonic solids, we should note that four of the five may be constructed by folding of two simple nets, one triangular and one square. These nets when laid out in one plane have no open spaces. The dodecahedron, which is made of 12 pentagons, is exceptional in that its net when laid out in one plane does have open spaces. The folded triangular nets make a class of solids called deltahedra but only three of these belong to the Platonic bodies. Fig. 34 is a triangular net of this kind. Two asymmetric bodies have been drawn on the borders of each of the triangles. Note that there is a six-fold axis of symmetry relating each triangle. This net therefore possesses hexagonal symmetry. Thus it cannot be made to enclose space by folding without distortion. It can, however, be folded with a minimal degree of distortion to make an icosahedron. It is only necessary to make a random cut terminating in one of the six fold axes of symmetry as in Fig. 34A. The paper is then overlapped once to convert the six fold axis to a five fold axis as in Fig. 34B. This makes one corner and, if twelve such corners are made at evenly spaced positions each with the single overlap, an icosahedron results. If a double overlap to make four-fold axes is made in six such positions an octahedron results. If four triple overlaps are made to make three-fold axes a tetrahedron results. If we now consider the asymmetric figures

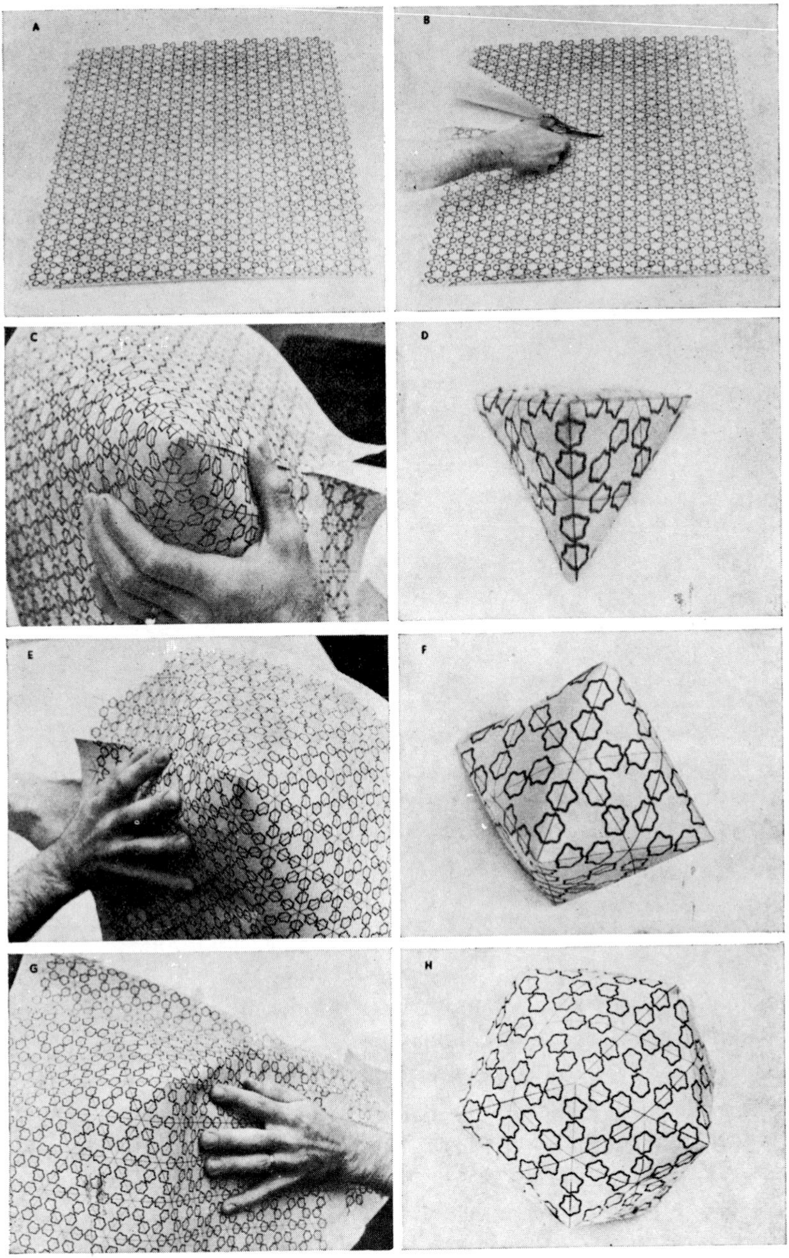

Fig. 34. A shows a triangular lattice drawn on a sheet of paper. On each side of each triangle two symmetrically disposed asymmetrical bodies have been drawn in. The apex of each triangle is a six-fold axis of symmetry. B shows a cut being made to one of the six-fold axes of symmetry of this lattice. C shows the result of overlapping the components of the lattice three times to produce a three-fold axis of symmetry. If this is done in symmetrical positions four times, one of the Platonic solids, the tetrahedron, results as shown in D. E shows the production of a corner by overlapping the figures twice. This results in a four-fold axis of symmetry and if this operation is done symmetrically six times, one of the Platonic solids, the octahedron, results as shown in F. G shows the result of overlapping the lattice once. This produces a five-fold axis of symmetry. If this operation is performed symmetrically twelve times, one of the Platonic solids, the icosahedron, results.

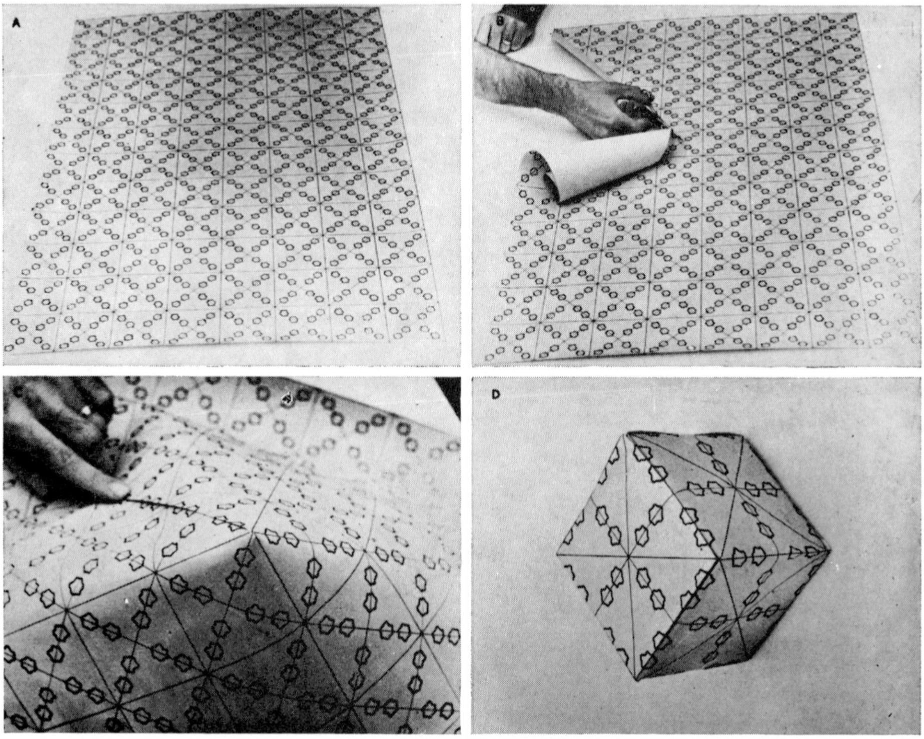

Fig. 35. A shows a lattice drawn on a sheet of paper; B, a cut is made to one of the four-fold axes of symmetry; C, the lattice is overlapped to make the corner of a solid. D shows the result of performing this operation eight times. One of the five Platonic solids, the cube, results (as in D).

drawn on the corners of the triangles to represent molecules, it will be noted that only a limited number of relationships or contacts between these units exist. These can be considered to represent chemical bonds. These bonds will be distorted by the folding and overlapping in producing the solid figures. Caspar and Klug calculated that the amount of such distortion introduced in making the icosahedron was $\sim 5°$. This is about the amount that Pauling had calculated that such bonds could be distorted. To make either the octahedron or the tetrahedron much more distortion is required and it becomes immediately apparent why the icosahedron is preferred. It should be noted that a cube can be made from a square net in a similar fashion as indicated in Fig. 35A, B. However, the distortion here is relatively great. It is a striking fact that so far all the small spherical viruses have been found to display icosahedral symmetry.

It is of considerable interest that the American architect, Buckminster Fuller, in constructing his famous domes uses the above principles. He has found that he can construct extremely rigid domes from a triangular net of steel rods having hexagonal symmetry if he introduces the right number of five-fold axes of symmetry.

Fig. 36. A dome by the architect B. Fuller. (From Caspar and Klug). See text for discussion.

A Fuller dome displaying these features taken from Caspar and Klug is shown in Fig. 36.

We have noted already that there is evidence in the synaptic disc that a hexagonal net is present in its unit membranes. Similar nets have been observed in several other biological membranes (Revel and Karnovsky). I have indicated that I believe the wide-spread occurrence of the so-called globular fine structure is explainable in terms of wide-spread occurrences of similar nets. Hexagonal nets also have been seen in bacterial cell walls (Houwink; Thiery et al.). Indeed, the only other kind of net that has ever been seen in any kind of biological membrane or bacterial cell wall is a square net (Labaw and Mosley). It seems unlikely that all this is coincidence and very likely that the principles employed in constructing biological membranes are not unrelated to those employed in constructing viral protein coats and that all are related to the elementary principles involved in constructing simple polygonal solids.

The above may seem to be rather wild speculations. Certainly, there are many speculations supported only by very weak evidence. However, speculations can be very powerful if they point the way to experiments. The ones given here clearly point the way to a number of potentially fruitful experiments that we are now performing. The near future may bring results that will elucidate new principles of unit membrane structure. These may cast light on some fundamental biological problems.

References

CASPAR, D.L.D.: Structure of bushy stunt virus. Nature 177 (1956) 475.

CASPAR, D.L.D. and A.KLUG: Physical principles on the construction of regular viruses. Symp. Quant. Biol. 27 (1962) 1.

CHAMBERS, R. and H.POLLACK: Micrurgical studies in cell physiology IV. Colorimetric determination of the nuclear and cytoplasmic *p*H in the starfish egg. J. Gen. Physiol. 10 (1927) 739.

COLE, K.S.: Surtuce forces of the arbacia egg. J. Cellular Comp. Physiol. 1 (1932) 1.

CRICK, F.H.C. and J.D.WATSON: Structure of small viruses. Nature 177 (1956) 473.

DANIELLI, J.R. and H.A.DAVSON: A contribution to the theory of permeability of thin films. J. Cell Physiol. 5 (1935) 495.

FARQUHAR, M.G. and G.E.PALADE: Functional organization of amphibian skin. Proc. Natl. Acad. Sci. U.S. 51 (1964) 569.

FINEAN, J.B. and R.E.BURGE: The determination of the Fourier transformation of the myelin layer from a study of swelling phenomena. J. Mol. Biol. 7 (1963) 672.

FLEISCHER, S., B.FLEISCHER and W.STOECKENIUS: Fine structure of lipid-depleted mitochondria. J. Cell Biol. 32 (1967) 193.

GASSER, H.S.: Olfactory nerve fibers. J. Gen. Biol. 34 (1956) 817.

GORTER, E. and R.GRENDEL: On biomolecular layers of lipoid on the chromocytes of the blood. J. Exptl. Med. 41 (1925) 439.

GREEN, D.E. and J.F.PERDUE: Correlation of mitochondrial structure and function. Ann. N.Y. Acad. Sci. 137 (1966) 667.

HOUVINK, A.L.: A macromolecular mono-layer in the cell wall of *Spirillum* Spec. Biochim. Biophys. Acta 10 (1953) 360.

KORN, E.D.: Structure of biological membranes. Science 153 (1966) 1491.

LABAW, L.W. and V.M.MOSLEY: Periodic structure in the flagella and cell walls of a bacterium. Biochim. Biophys. Acta 15 (1954) 325.

LANGMUIR, I.: The constitution and fundamental properties of solids and liquids II. Liquids. J. Am. Chem. Soc. 37 (1917) 1848.

LENARD, J. and S.J.STINGER: Structure of membranes: reaction of red blood cell membranes with phospholipase *C*. Science 159 (1968) 738.

LUZZATI, V. and R.HUSSON: The structure of the liquid-crystalline phases of lipid water systems. J. Cell Biol. 12 (1962) 207.

MARCHESI, V.T. and G.E.PALADE: The localization of Mg-Na-K-activated adenosine triphosphatase on red cell ghost membranes. J. Cell Biol. 35 (1967) 385.

MOODY, M.: X-ray diffraction pattern of nerve myelin: A method for determining the phases. Science 142 (1963) 1173.

MUELLER, P., D.O.RUDIN, H.TI TIEN and W.C.WESCOTT: Reconstitution of isolated cell membrane structure *in vitro* and its chemical transformation into an electrically excitable system. Circulation 26 (1962) 1167.

NAPOLITANO, L., F.LEBARON and J.SCALETTI: Preservation of myelin lamellar structure in the absence of lipid. A correlated chemical and morphological study. J. Cell Biol. 34 (1967) 817.

NILSSON, S.E.G.: Receptor cell outer segment development and ultrastructure of the disc membranes on the retina of the tadpole (*rana pipiens*). J. Ultrastruct. Res. 11 (1964) 581.

OVERTON, E.: Über die osmotischen Eigenschaften der lebenden Pflanzen und Tierzelle. Vjschr. Naturforsch. Ges. Zurich 40 (1895) 159.

REVEL, J.P. and KARNOVSKY: Hexagonal array of subunits in intercellular junctions of the mouse heart and liver. J. Cell Biol. 33 (1967) C7.

ROBERTSON, J.D.: The unit membrane and the Danielli–Davson model. International Symposium on Intracellular Transport, International Society for Cell Biology, Rome. New York, Academic Press

Inc. (1965) p. 1.

ROBERTSON, J.D.: Granulo-fibrillar and globular substructure in unit membranes. Ann. N.Y. Acad. Sci. 137 (1966) 421.

ROBERTSON, J.D.: Design principles of the unit membrane. In: G.E.W.Wolstenholme and M. O'Connor, eds.: Principles of bimolecular organization. Ciba Foundation. London, J. and A. Churchill Ltd. (1966) p. 357.

ROBERTSON, J.D.: Unit membranes. A review with recent new studies of experimental alterations and a new subunit structure in synaptic membranes. In: M.Locke, ed.: Cellular membranes in development. Proceedings of the XXII Symposium of the Society for the Study of Development and Growth. New York, Academic Press (1963).

ROBERTSON, J.D.: The ultrastructure of cell membranes and their derivatives. Biochem. Soc. Symp. (Cambridge, Engl.) 16 (1959) 3.

ROBERTSON, J.D.: The molecular biology of cell membranes. In: D.Nachmansohn, ed.: Molecular biology. New York, Academic Press (1960) 87.

ROBERTSON, J.D.: The molecular structure and contact relationships of cell membranes. In: B.Katz and J.A.V.Butler, eds.: Progress in biophysics. Oxford, Pergamon Press (1960) 343.

ROBERTSON, J.D.: Structural alterations in nerve fibers produced by hypotonic and hypertonic solutions. J. Biophys. Biochem. Cytol. 4 (1958) 349.

ROBERTSON, J.D.: Cell membrane and the origin of mitochondria. In: S.S.Kety and J.Bilkes, eds.: Regional neurochemistry. Proceedings of the 4th Neurochemical Symposium. Oxford, Pergamon Press (1961) 497.

ROBERTSON, J.D.: The ultrastructure of adult vertebrate peripheral myelinated fibers in relation to myelinogenesis. J. Biophys. Biochem. Cytol. 1 (1955) 271.

ROBERTSON, J.D.: The occurrence of a subunit pattern in the unit membranes of club endings in Mauthner cell synapses in goldfish brains. J. Cell Biol. 19 (1963) 201.

ROBERTSON, J.D., T.S.BODENHEIMER and D.E.STAGE: The ultrastructure of Mauthner cell synapses and nodes in goldfish brains. J. Cell Biol. 19 (1963) 159.

SCHMIDT, W.J.: Doppelbrechung und Feinbau der Markscheide der Nervenfusern. Z. Zellforsch. Mikroskop. Anat. 23 (1936) 657.

SCHMITT, F.O., R.S.BEAR and G.L.CLARK: X-ray diffraction studies on nerve. Radiology 25 (1935) 131.

SCHMITT, F.O., R.S.BEAR and K.Y.PALMER: X-ray diffraction studies on the structure of the nerve myelin sheath. J. Cellular Comp. Physiol. 18 (1941) 39.

SJÖSTRAND, F.S.: A new ultrastructural element of the membranes in mitochondria and of some cytoplasmic membranes. J. Ultrastruct. Res. 9 (1963) 340.

STOECKENIUS, W.: Some electron microscopical observations on lipid-crystalline phases in liquid-water systems. J. Cell Biol. 12 (1962) 221.

THIERY, J.P., R.BAUDOIN and D.GEROME: Etude au microscope électronique des voiles bactériens. J. Microscopie 7 (1968) 81.

THOMPSON, D'ARCY: On growth and form, 2nd ed. (1963).

THOMPSON, T.E.: The properties of biomolecular phospholipid membranes. In: M.Locke, ed.: Cellular membranes in development. New York, Academic Press (1964) 83.

THOMPSON, T.E.: Experimental bilayer membrane models. Symposium on Biophysics and Physiology of Biological Transport, Frascati. Berlin, Springer-Verlag (1965) 194.

TOSTESON, D.C., T.C.ANDRCOLI, M.TIEFFENBORG and P.COOK: The effects of macrocyclic compounds on cation transport in sheep red cells and thin and thick lipid membranes. J. Gen. Physiol. 51 (1968) 373.

UZMAN, B.G.: The formation from the Schwann cell surface of myelin in the peripheral nerves of chick embryos. Exptl. Cell Res. 7 (1954) 558.

DE VAUX, H.: cited by M.J.Kopac: The surface chemical properties of cytoplasmic proteins.

WILLIAMS, R.C. and K.M.SMITH: The polyhedral form of the *Tipula* iridescent virus. Biochim. Biophys. Acta 28 (1958) 464.

CHAPTER 53

Cell walls

D. R. KREGER

Botanical Laboratory, State University of Groningen, The Netherlands

Contents

1. Introduction
2. Molecular aspects
   (a) Polysaccharides
      Cellulose
      Other glucans
      Mannans
      Xylans
      Galactans and arabans
      Fucoidin
      Heteropolysaccharides
   (b) Polyuronides
      Pectic substances
      Alginic acid
      Heteropolymers containing uronic acids
   (c) Chitin and chitosan
   (d) Lignin
   (e) Lipids
      Waxes
      Suberin, cutin and sporopollenin
   (f) Proteins
   (g) Minerals
3. Structure
   (a) General aspects
   (b) The organization of microfibrillar constituents
      Cellulose
      Xylans
      Mannans
      Yeast glucan
      Chitin
      Polyuronides

(c) The organization of adcrusting layers
Waxes
Cuticle and cuticular layers
Cork
Sporopollenin

4. Formation and growth

(a) Formation
General aspects
Formation of microfibrils

(b) Growth
The microfibrillar aspect
Matrix and auxin

1. Introduction

The cells of plants are characteristically surrounded by a rigid envelope, the cell wall. Though some animal cells, particularly among the protozoa, develop a solid surface structure, animal cells in general do not have a solid surface. Their surface structures are discussed in the chapters by Bennett of this book. In this chapter dealing with cell walls of plants, the walls of bacteria have not been discussed because their structure is essentially different from that found elsewhere in the plant kingdom. They have been treated in the chapters on the bacterial cell by van Iterson.

Though the plant cell wall is formed outside the plasmalemma or plasma membrane it is nevertheless an important, integral part of the cell. It lends the external resistance necessary to maintain the cell in osmotic equilibrium and to withstand impact from the outside; it also gives mechanical support to the whole plant. Its molecular constitution and ultrastructural organization reflect important chemical and morphogenetic building activities of the cytoplasm, and its physical characteristics are intimately involved in the growth mechanism of cells and tissues and therefore of whole plants.

Throughout the plant kingdom the cell wall represents the most tangible, most conspicuous and most resistant product of cellular activity and it is not surprising that this was the first part of the cell to present itself to the notice of early microscopists. The first record of its appearance made by Robert Hooke in 1665 may be said to mark the beginning of cytology. Cell walls (and starch grains) were also the initial objects for study of submicroscopic cytological details; their appearance under the polarizing microscope led Nägeli in 1860 to propose the occurrence, in cell walls, of oriented, crystalline particles of cellulose which he called micelles. Similarly the discovery (von Laue in 1912) of the diffraction of X-rays in crystalline material, led quickly to the first X-ray diagrams of organic material, again in cell walls (Nishikawa and Ono in 1913). These corroborated Nägeli's postulate and, in addition, led eventually to the first data on intermolecular distances and chain periodicity in a natural high polymer. They may be regarded as the first step on a path toward a field of research later to be named 'molecular biology' by W.T. Astbury. Finally, with the advent of electron microscopy cell walls were among the first biological objects to be examined by this technique.

Because of their practical importance in the form of wood, textile fibres, and many other products, plant cell walls have formed the subject of much applied research. In a more academic field the problem of cell wall growth has long attracted the interest of physiologists and in recent years, improved methods of isolating cell walls from both higher plants, algae and fungi have given new impetus to research on their chemistry and structure.

The following pages give a rough outline of present day knowledge of the cell wall at the molecular, structural and physiological levels.

For further reading the following books and articles mentioned in the list of references, may be consulted: Aronson, Côté, Frey-Wyssling (1959), Frey-Wyssling and

Mühlethaler, Kreger (1962), Marchessault and Sarko, Mühlethaler (1967), Percival and McDowell, Preston (1952), Roelofsen (1959, 1965), Rogers and Perkins, Treiber, and Zimmermann. Original literature will be quoted here only if not mentioned in these books and articles or when a special aspect of an original paper deserves attention.

2. *Molecular aspects*

Cell walls normally contain the four groups of substances found in all living organisms, carbohydrates, lipids, proteins and minerals. Usually carbohydrates predominate in the form of polysaccharides. In addition, the walls may be encrusted with substances which do not belong to the four basic groups.

(a) *Polysaccharides*

Cellulose

Cellulose forms the most important cell wall component in all Cormophyta. However, its proportion in the walls of different kinds of cells may vary considerably. Those of cotton hairs for example consist of nearly pure cellulose, whilst in wood the proportion is normally around 40–50% and the endosperm cells of some seeds contain no more than a few percent. Certain layers of cell walls, namely the suberin layer of cork cells and the cuticle, contain no cellulose whatsoever, as is also the case with many Thallophyta.

The structural unit. The elementary composition of cellulose is $(C_6H_{10}O_5)_n$ and corresponds therefore to that of a polyanhydro-hexose. On hydrolysis it yields predominantly glucose, $C_6H_{12}O_6$. In cellulose the glucose residues are linked through glucosidic oxygen bridges between the carbon atoms 1 and 4 (Fig. 1a) to form an unbranched chain of heterocyclic six-membered rings. The stereoisomeric form of glucose underlying this chain is β-D-glucopyranose (Fig. 1b), distinguished from the α-form by the position of the OH-group on carbon atom 1 with reference to the plane of the ring. This group is in the *trans* position with respect to the OH-group on carbon 4, whereas in the α-form it is in the *cis* position (Fig. 1c). The α-form occurs in starch. The β-glucosidic linkage of the glucose residues necessitates that if the cellulose chain is to be straight each ring must be turned 180° about its C_1-C_4 axis with respect to the adjacent rings. This results in a chain with an identity period embracing two glucose residues, which is found in cellulose and appears in other linear cell wall polysaccharides consisting of *trans* linked pyranose residues; *cis* links, on the other hand, can lead to a helical chain configuration as in starch. The reason lies in the configuration of the ring which in reality is not flat (Fig. 4C).

The degree of polymerization (DP) of cellulose may vary considerably. Averages of 5000 to 10,000 and higher, corresponding to a chain-length of 2.5 to 5 μ, have been reported for carefully prepared, so-called α-celluloses. These are cell wall fractions which after adequate pretreatment remain insoluble in 24% KOH or 17.5% NaOH.

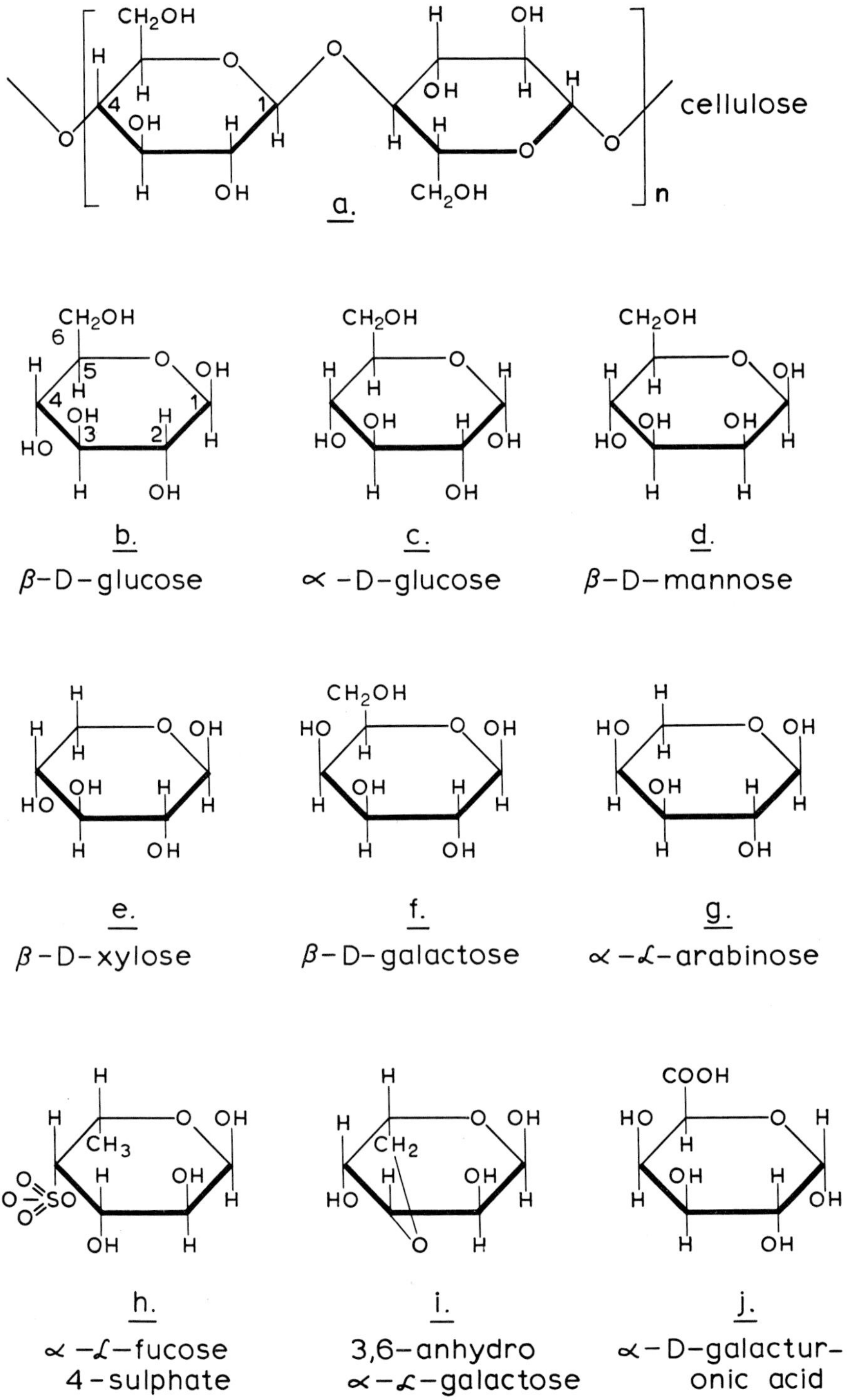
cellulose
a.
b.
β-D-glucose
c.
α-D-glucose
d.
β-D-mannose
e.
β-D-xylose
f.
β-D-galactose
g.
α-L-arabinose
h.
α-L-fucose 4-sulphate
i.
3,6-anhydro α-L-galactose
j.
α-D-galacturonic acid

Fig. 1a–j.

It may be noted that the term *α*-cellulose does not indicate a chemically defined product but refers to the residue from special extraction procedures applied to plant material. Usually the material has a high cellulose content, but it is rarely pure cellulose in the sense described above. In particular xylan and mannan are often firmly attached, and it may contain no cellulose at all when prepared from fungi or certain algae with non-cellulosic walls.

Cellulose is broken down at the glucosidic bonds by the enzyme cellulase of cellulose decomposing organisms. *In vitro* the best known solvents are alkaline solutions of cuprammonium (Schweitzer's reagent) and cupri-ethylene-diamine. Celluloses of DP below ca. 500 show solubility in alkali, the more so as the DP becomes lower.

Identification. Microchemical identification is generally based on the combined swelling and dark-blue staining reaction with chlor-zinc iodine (a solution of KI, I and $ZnCl_2$ in water) or with sulphuric acid and iodine. Several organic dyes like congo-red may also be used. However, these reactions are not quite specific for cellulose and their failure is not conclusive evidence of its absence. On the macro scale its presence is most unambiguously demonstrated by X-ray diffraction, which can commonly be used even with untreated plant material. Sometimes, however, thorough extraction of non-cellulose products is required, or the cellulose has even to be dissolved and re-precipitated. The X-ray identification is based on the property of the cellulose chains to form bundles in which they are arranged over part of their length in crystalline array with specific interchain distance.

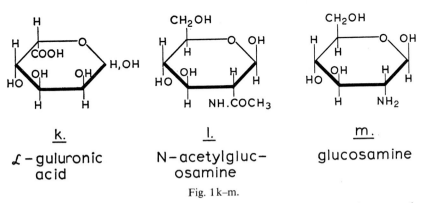

Occurrence in Thallophyta. Among the algae, cellulose is widespread. However, in only a limited number of genera is it present in the relative proportion normal in higher plants. All of these belong to the Chlorophyta and are found in particular among the Siphonocladales and Cladophorales. In these the untreated cell walls yield sharp X-ray spectra of native cellulose. In most other green algae it requires a purification step to obtain this result and even then the spectra are usually not sharp. A similar purification is also necessary in the Phaeophyta. These as well as the Rhodo-

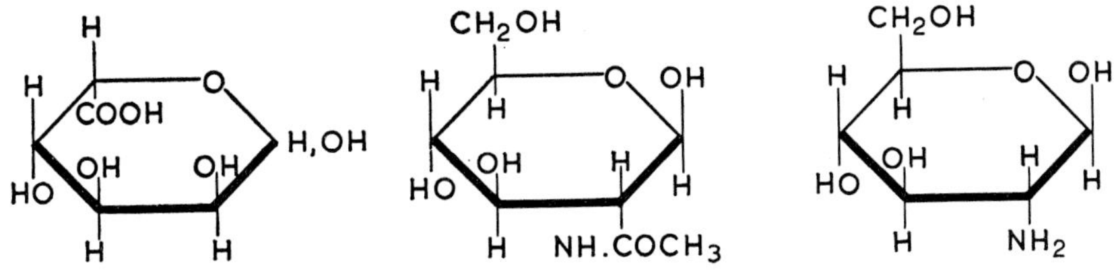

k. L-guluronic acid

l. N-acetylglucosamine

m. glucosamine

Fig. 1k–m.

Fig. 1. Structural formulae of cellulose, the monosaccharides and substituted monosaccharides composing the most important cell wall polysaccharides and their derivatives.

phyta normally contain less than 5% of cellulose on a dry-weight basis of the whole algae. Some algae (*Porphyra*, *Codium*, *Derbesia* and members of the Caulerpales and Dasycladales) have non-cellulosic walls.

Among the fungi the presence of cellulose is unusual. Its occurrence has been established in the Oomycetes, where chitin is absent, and it occurs together with chitin in *Rhizidiomyces bivellatus* (Hyphochytriales) and in *Ceratocystic ulmi* (Microascales).

Cellulose has also been found in representatives of other groups of organisms: blue-green algae, bacteria, a Myxomycete, Tunicates and certain mammalian tissues.

Other glucans

Plant cell walls may contain polymers other than cellulose which nevertheless still consist of anhydroglucose units linked by oxygen bridges. One of the most extensively studied is yeast glucan, an alkali-resistant component obtained first from baker's yeast. It constitutes about 30% of the cell wall and mainly contains chains which are β-1,3-linked, though some 20% of β-1,6-linkages have also been reported. The latter linkages have been said most recently to form a backbone chain with the 1,3-linked chains as branches (Manners and Patterson). The branches, in contrast to the 1,6-linked fraction, resist hydrolysis with dilute mineral acid and, when liberated, are alkali-soluble and yield a well defined X-ray pattern. This feature gave rise to the identification of yeast glucan in a number of yeasts other than baker's yeast and also in hyphal fungi, whilst in some species the lack of this glucan was established (Kreger 1954). The alkali resistant glucan is sometimes named R-glucan and its acid-resistant fraction hydro-glucan. This fraction has been found to be identical with the reserve carbohydrate of Euglenaceae known as paramylon.

A further type of fungal cell wall glucan was detected by its characteristic X-ray pattern and its solubility in dilute alkali in the yeast *Schizosaccharomyces*. It could also be identified similarly in a number of hyphal fungi (Kreger 1954; Wessels) and has been named S-glucan. Some alkali-soluble glucans from individual fungal species listed below have been reported whose chemical structures were studied: *Polyporus betulinus* (Duff), *Poria cocos* (Warsi and Whelan) and *Aspergillus niger* (Johnston). They were identified as 1,3-linked glucans and the one of *Aspergillus* definitely as α-1,3-linked. More recently evidence has been obtained from enzymatic, X-ray and infrared examination that the S-glucan corresponds to the α-1,3-linked type (Bacon et al. 1968).

A non-cellulosic membrane glucan from higher plants is the callose of sieve vessels which has been shown to be a β-1,3-linked glucan.

Mannans

An important constituent of many kinds of cell walls consists of mannans, i.e. polysaccharides with a monomer unit similar to that of cellulose but with the difference that the OH-group on C_2 of the pyranose ring is located on the same side of the ring as the one on C_3. The corresponding hexose is known as β-D-mannopyranose or β-D-mannose (Fig. 1d). The mannose residues may be linked by oxygen bridges in several ways which gives rise to a variety of mannan types each usually associated with a certain group of plants or kind of plant tissue.

Linear chains consisting mainly of β-1,4-linked mannose residues occur as reserve carbohydrates in the cell walls of the endosperms of palm seeds and form its main constituent. This type is known as ivory-nut mannan because the best known source is the seeds of the palm *Phytelephas macrocarpa* of which the hard endosperm is used as vegetable ivory for buttons etc. The cell walls of some genera of green algae, *Codium*, *Derbesia*, *Acetabularia* and *Batophopa* contain as the only crystalline polysaccharide this type of mannan, and in *Hydrodictyon* the walls contain 50% of these chains in an amorphous complex, the other half consisting of cellulose chains. The red alga *Porphyra* has a cuticle of ivory-nut mannan covering the whole frond (Frei and Preston 1964b). These mannan chains show a strong tendency to form microcrystalline aggregates which give a characteristic X-ray pattern.

A very different type of mannan occurs in the cell walls of most yeasts. This constitutes, in the case of the baker's yeast, about 30% of the walls and is highly branched with preponderance of α-1,2- and α-1,6-links, the latter forming a backbone chain. At least part of the yeast mannan is present as mannan protein in enzymes such as invertase and acid phosphatase located in the wall (Lampen).

Another important group of substances usually indicated as mannans, though in fact they are glucomannans, are found in the hemicelluloses of wood (i.e. the cell wall fraction which after removal of pectin and lignin is soluble in dilute alkali). In particular gymnosperm wood (so-called softwood) is rich in a compound which consists of β-1,4-linked mannose and glucose residues in the proportion 3:1, with single galactose residues and acetyl as side groups. Softwoods contain about 15% of this mannan. The wood of angyosperms (hardwood) comprises in the order of 3% of a β-1,4-linked glucomannan in which the ratio of mannose to glucose is 2:1, except for birchwood in which it is 1:1.

Xylans

Xylans are polysaccharides which are built up of anhydroresidues of the pentose xylose. The structural formula of this monosaccharide may be derived from that of glucose by replacing the CH_3OH-group on C_5 of the pyranose ring by an H atom (Fig. 1e).

Xylan forms the main portion of the non-cellulose polysaccharides in the wood of angiosperms which contains between 15% (elm) and 35% (birch) of this polysaccharide. 80–90% of the hemicellulose fraction is xylan. It consists of chains of β-1,4-linked D-xylopyranose residues with a 4-O-methyl-α-D-glucuronic acid residue linked 1,2, on every 10th residue, while 7 out of 10 xylose residues carry an acetyl group on C_3 or C_2. A high proportion of β-1,4-linked xylan also occurs in straw, cereal glumes and corn cobs. In gymnosperm wood smaller quantities of xylan (7–10%) are found which differs from that of hardwoods by a higher glucuronic acid content and the presence of arabinose residues as additional side groups.

A type of xylan which is essentially different from those already described has been found to form the cell walls of green seaweeds of the Bryopsidaceae and Caulerpales and of the wall of the red alga *Porphyra*. This consists of chains of β-1,3-linked xylose residues. In *Halicystis* walls it is linked with cellulose chains.

The β-1,4- and β-1,3-linked xylans are soluble in alkali and they are easily distinguished from each other by their X-ray pattern. The walls of the green algae mentioned above may also contain some 10% of glucose which again seems to be 1,3-linked.

Xylans have also been isolated from other red algae but association with the wall or their nature are not well established.

Galactans and arabans

Galactans and arabans are water-soluble polysaccharides which occur in the cell walls of higher plants mainly in association with pectins.

The structure of galactan corresponds to that of a cellulose in which the position of the hydroxyl group on C_4 is inverted with reference to the plane of the ring (Fig. 1f). The chains then consist of β-1,4-linked D-galactose residues. The relation with pectins is somewhat obscured by the fact that the D-galacturonic acid residues of the latter are α-1,4-linked (see Polyuronides).

Araban consists of anhydro-units of the pentose arabinose, which is usually present in the L-form. The structure of L-arabinose (Fig. 1g) may be derived from that of D-galactose by replacing the CH_3OH group by an H atom. The arabinose residues are frequently present in the furanose form, a form in which the ring-oxygen is connected with C_4 instead of C_5. The pectin of peanuts is particularly rich in araban, whereas that of the seeds of *Lupinus albus* is rich in galactan.

An important group of galactans is the gel-forming polysaccharides from red seaweeds known as agar and corrageen, which have a wide field of application in the laboratory and in the food industry. The former is extracted from *Gelidium* species and several other genera of red algae, the latter in particular from species of *Chondrus* and *Gigartina*. Agar consists in the main of about equal quantities of 1,3-linked β-D-galactose and 1,4-linked 3,6-anhydro α-L-galactose (Fig. 1i). In general the composition of carrageenan is similar but in the latter fraction the L-form is replaced by the corresponding D-form. The polysaccharide also has a considerably higher sulphate content (25%) than agar (5%). The two basic units in each of the two polysaccharides form chains in which they occur in alternating sequence.

Water-soluble sulphated polysaccharides containing both galactose and arabinose residues and a small quantity of xylose, typically in proportions of 2:2:1, are synthesized by a number of green seaweeds (*Cladophora*, *Chaetomorpha*, *Caulerpa*, *Codium*). Arabino-galactans form a constituent of gymnosperm wood, in particular of larch wood in which it comprises about 20%.

Fucoidin

Fucoidin is a water-soluble, miculaginous cell wall and intercellular component of brown seaweeds, with a high sulphate content (ca. 35%). It is composed of anhydro residues of L-fucose (6-deoxy-hexose) (Fig. 1h) the structure of which may be derived from that of L-galactose by replacing the OH group on the C_6 atom by an H atom. The mode of linkage is mainly α-1,2 and most of the sulphate groups are linked to C_4. The molecule is highly branched.

Heteropolysaccharides

Most of the polysaccharides discussed above consist of one type of monosaccharide residue either exclusively or in major part.

There are also cell wall polysaccharides containing different monoses in more nearly equal proportions. Some have already been mentioned. An important group comprises the storage products of endosperm walls in seeds. Most of these are known as amyloids since, like starch, they stain blue in solutions of iodine in potassium iodide. Amyloids contain glucose, xylose and galactose residues typically in the proportion 4:3:2 (Caesalpiniaceae, Primulaceae). In the Annonaceae the ratio is 4:1:1, and this amyloid stains brownish-violet. Structural data of the amyloids (Kooiman 1961, 1967) indicate a backbone chain of β-1,4-linked glucose residues with branches of xylose and galactose residues. Other compounds of similar occurrence which cannot be stained with iodine have been identified as galactomannans (Caesalpiniaceae, Papilionaceae) or glucomannans (Iridaceae, Liliaceae). The latter are insoluble in water but easily soluble in dilute alkali, and this fraction constitutes nearly the whole endosperm wall. The ratio of glucose to mannose is about 1:1 (Kooiman and Kreger), whereas in the galactomannans the mannose moiety is 2–3 times that of the galactose.

Some heteropolysaccharides containing uronic acid are listed in the next section.

(b) *Polyuronides*

Polyuronides are closely allied to the polysaccharides and may be derived from the latter by replacing the CH_2OH group on C_5 by a carboxyl group (–COOH). On hydrolysis they yield uronic acids such as glucuronic acid, mannuronic acid etc.

The polyuronides are represented in the plant kingdom mainly by the pectic substances and alginic acid both of which have a wide field of application in the food industry. A different polyuronide has recently been identified in the wall of a fungus (Bartnicki-Garcia and Reyes). Uronic acids also form part of many heteropolymers in particular water-soluble mucilages.

Pectic substances

The pectic substances have as their basic structure a linear chain of D-galacturonic acid (Fig. 1k) residues which are α-1,4-linked. The carboxyl groups may be esterified to varying degrees by methyl groups and partly or completely neutralized by one or more bases. This yields products of highly variable solubility and colloidal behaviour. The degree of polymerization may reach a value of 1800.

Free polygalacturonic acid is called pectic acid and the name pectinic acid indicates the partially methylated derivative. Pectic acid is insoluble in boiling water, but on esterification with methanol it becomes soluble at about 4% (w/w) methoxyl ($-OCH_3$) content. These soluble forms are called pectin. Na, K and NH_4 pectates are also soluble, but Ca^{2+} and a number of other metallics give insoluble pectates.

The insoluble pectic substances of the native cell wall are called protopectin. It is not known exactly by what conditions the insolubility is determined, but Ca^{2+} plays a prominent role. The substance is present in variable quantity in nearly all cell walls of higher plants, mostly in primary walls and intercellular spaces. In tissues rich in pectin (*Citrus* peel, 28–50%; *Petasites* collenchyma, 45%) it may be found abundant in the secondary wall. It is usually accompanied by galactan and araban.

Alginic acid

Alginic acid forms a major constituent of brown seaweeds, of which it may comprise around 13–45% with seasonal variations. It is a mixture in variable proportions, of poly-D-mannuronic acid and poly-L-guluronic acid with small amounts of poly-D-glucuronic acid. L-guluronic acid (Fig. 1b) differs from D-mannuronic acid only in that the carboxyl group is situated on the side of the ring opposite to the –OH groups on carbons 2 and 3. Both acids are 1,4-linked and the mode of linkage for the mannuronic acid has been identified as β-1,4.

The question whether the two components form part of a heteropolymer or belong to two different polymers, each made up entirely of one type of uronic acid, has not been unequivocally answered. A partial fractionation has been attained which seems to indicate the presence of two polymers, one comprising mainly mannuronic acid and the other mainly guluronic acid. They are present in the algae as the insoluble Ca alginates, the polymannuronic acid mainly in intercellular spaces and the polyguluronic acid as part of the cellulosic wall. On removal of the calcium the acids may be separately extracted. They show a more pronounced micro-crystallinity than the Ca alginate and exhibit different X-ray patterns (Frei and Preston 1962). It remains to reconcile this spatial separation and different X-ray patterns with other data suggesting that the alginate represents one molecule comprising chain fragments that over lengths of 25–30 uronic acid residues consist of either mannuronic or guluronic acid, while in other parts there is an alternating sequence of the residues (Haug et al.). In different species the ratio of the two acids may vary from about 2:1 to 1:2.

Alginic acid is extracted on a commercial scale as its soluble sodium salt, usually indicated as algin, mainly from large species as *Macrocystis pyrifera*, *Ascophyllum nodosum*, *Laminaria* and *Ecklonia* species. It is used as a stabilizer in creams, surface sizing agent of papers, thickener in textile printing pastes etc.

Heteropolymers containing uronic acids

This type of cell wall constituent may be divided into two main groups, the mucilages and the gums. The latter are usually formed under abnormal conditions and will not be discussed here.

The mucilages occur in epidermal cell walls of a number of seeds and others have been extracted from certain algae.

The seed mucilages normally consist of anhydro-units of D-galacturonic acid, D-galactose and L-arabinose, as do pectic substances, and D-xylose and L-rhamnose are also found. In several instances it has been shown that cellulose microfibrils are embedded in the mucous layers. This is the case with *Lepidium* and *Cydonia* seeds, but not with *Linum* and *Plantago*.

Some green seaweeds (*Ulva*, *Acrosiphonia*, *Enteromorpha*) produce water-soluble sulphated mucilages closely similar in constitution. The mucilage of *Ulva* has been shown to yield on hydrolysis: 32% L-rhamnose, 10% D-xylose, 8% D-glucose, and 24% D-glucuronic acid, with 19% ester sulphate linked to rhamnose.

Some brown seaweeds produce a water-insoluble sulphated glucuronoxylofucan which in *Ascophyllum nodosum* may contain up to about 50% of L-fucose residues.

(c) *Chitin and chitosan*

Chitin is a cell wall constituent found, in quantities varying from about 1% to 40% of the dry wall weight in nearly all fungi. Only in the Oomycetes and the yeast genus *Schizosaccharomyces* has its absence definitely been established.

The molecular structure may be derived schematically from that of cellulose (Fig. 1a) by replacing the OH-group at the C_2 atom by an acetamido group (–NH–CO CH_3). It is therefore composed of β-1,4-linked residues of N-acetylglucosamine (Fig. 1*l*). Chitin is insoluble in water, diluted and concentrated alkali, dilute acid and organic solvents, but is soluble in concentrated strong acids at room temperature. It is in part crystalline and yields a characteristic X-ray pattern.

Chitosan is a polyglucosamine (Fig. 1m) obtained by the deacetylation of chitin through heating in concentrated alkali. In contrast to chitin it is soluble in dilute acid, but like chitin it gives a characteristic X-ray pattern. It has so far been identified in a natural state only as a constituent of the cell walls of two species of fungi belonging to the Mucorales. Chitosansulphate forms characteristic negatively birefringent sphaerocrystals, a property used in the microchemical detection of chitin.

(d) *Lignin*

Lignin occurs as an amorphous material in all woody tissues of the Cormophyta, especially in the middle lamella. It accounts generally to about 25% of the wood and is the substance which gives the wood its characteristic properties that make it suitable as a building material. It is an aromatic high-polymer based on coniferyl alcohol (Fig. 2) in gymnosperm woods, partly replaced by sinapin alcohol in the wood of angiosperms. The structure of this compound is too complex to deal with here; reference may be made to the literature mentioned in the introduction. Lignin is easily recognized microchemically by a deep red stain with phloroglucine and hydrochloric acid, and its solubility, though not undegraded, in hot dilute alkali or bisulphite; neither test is, however, fully specific.

The heart-wood of many trees contains in addition to lignin phenolic dyestuffs, of which haematoxylin is a well known example.

(e) *Lipids*

Lipids are found particularly in epidermis outer walls, on the surfaces of plants and in the walls of cork tissue. They may be divided into two major groups, those soluble and those insoluble in normal lipid solvents. The former are mainly of a waxy nature and occur in particular on plant surfaces, the latter are high polymer, amorphous molecular networks and include cutin, suberin and perhaps sporopollenin, forming respectively the outer layers of the epidermis, the walls of cork tissue and the outer layers of walls of pollen grains.

Waxes

Most of the substances found in plants and commonly called waxes are not esters and are therefore not true waxes. They are made up of normal aliphatic long-chain compounds with corresponding physical properties, such as n. paraffins ($CH_3(CH_2)_mCH_3$), n. primary alcohols ($CH_3(CH_2)_mCH_3OH$), n. secondary alcohols ($CH_3(CH_2)_mCHOH(CH_2)_nCH_3$) and n. ketones ($CH_3(CH_2)_mCO(CH_2)_nCH$). Nevertheless esters are not uncommon, and n. aldehydes ($CH_3(CH_2)_mCHO$), diols ($HO(CH_2)_mOH$), ω-hydroxy acids ($HOOC(CH_2)_mCH_2OH$) and isomers of n. hydrocarbons, n. alcohols and fatty acids, have been detected, as well as free fatty acids, unsaturated-chain compounds and cyclic products of the pentacyclic triterpenoid type. Of the latter, ursolic acid, common in fruit skin waxes, and friedelin, a constituent of cork wax, may be mentioned (Fig. 2).

In the normal carbon chains the number of carbon atoms may vary between about 22 and 34, even-numbered chains occurring mainly in primary alcohols and fatty acids

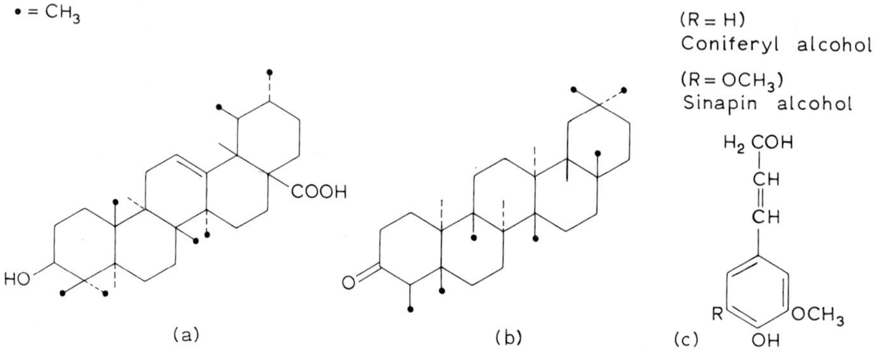

Fig. 2. Chemical structures of: (a), ursolic acid; (b), friedelin; (c), basic unit of lignin.

and odd-numbered chains in paraffins, ketones and secondary alcohols. Deviations from this odd-even rule always concern minor fractions.

The waxes are excreted as surface layers of many plants, and occur as inclusions in cutinized epidermal wall layers and suberin walls of cork tissue. Many plant waxes are of commercial value; those on the leaves of some South American palms (*Copernicia, Ceroxylon*) are of special importance in this respect.

The constitution of surface waxes of plants largely reflects natural relationships, but correspondence has also been observed between species of very divergent groups. Provisional data for a comparative phytochemistry of these waxes have been obtained from X-ray diagrams (Kreger 1948), mass spectrometry and gas chromatography (see Douglas and Eglinton). The latter methods have provided very refined data with reference to the chain length distribution in functionally homogeneous groups of wax constituents from a number of plants. Extensive data on the chemistry of plant waxes may be found in Warth and a recent review has been given by Mazliak (1968).

Suberin, cutin and sporopollenin

Suberin and cutin are polymer networks formed by esterification of dicarbonic acids and hydroxy-acids. The building units as well as their proportions in the network may differ between species.

In the suberin of the cork of commerce (*Quercus suber*) the C_{22} ω-hydroxy acid $HOCH_2(CH_2)_{20}COOH$, phellonic acid, and the C_{18} 9:10-dihydroxy dicarboxy acid $HOOC(CH_2)_7(CHOH)_2(CH_2)_7COOH$, phloionic acid, form the main products of saponification. Together they represent about 25% of the suberin, the remainder comprising related constituents and unknown products.

The cutin of the thick cutinized layers of the epidermis of *Agave americana* differs from the suberin mentioned above by the absence of C_{22} acids and the presence of C_{16} acids, all ω-hydroxy monocarbonic acids. Some of the acids, like some dicarboxy-acids of suberin, contain one or two secondary OH-groups or double linkages about half-way along the chain. Cutins are much more resistant to chemical attack than are suberins. They may be broken down by fungal enzymes (Heinen). Of none of them is the chemical structure precisely known, but a structural model in which C_{18} fatty acid chains are linked by ester and peroxide bridges has been developed on the basis of observations of cutin synthesis in leaves of *Gasteria* (Heinen and van den Brand).

Sporopollenin is a cell wall component of pollen-grains which makes up about 20–25% of the walls. It is chemically the most resistent organic product of living organisms. It remains undegraded after thousands of years burial in peat and other deposits, retaining undisturbed the shape of the grains. So far the chemical structure has not been elucidated. The elementary composition is reported to be $(C_{10}H_{16}O_3)_n$, and Brooks and Shaw have given reason to suppose that sporopollenin results from an oxydative polymerization of carotenoids and carotenoid esters.

The chemistry of the cuticle has been reviewed by Mazliak (1968) and of sporopollenin by van Gijzel.

(f) *Proteins*

Although the presence of protein in cell walls has long been a point of discussion it is now certain that the cell walls of higher plants, algae and fungi contain specific proteins. In higher plants (Lamport) and in algae (Thompson and Preston) some 5–10% of a protein has been detected in the wall. A characteristic of this protein is its content of hydroxyproline, an amino acid found in few other proteins. This protein is supposed to play a role in cell wall extension and has been provisionally called extensin. It has been suggested that polysaccharide–protein complexes isolated from yeast cell walls play a role in bud formation, agglutination reactions and enzyme (invertase) activities (Lampen). In fungi, enzyme(s) responsible for the synthesis of cell wall glucan have been localized in the wall (Wang and Bartnicki-Garcia).

(g) *Minerals*

When plant cell walls are incinerated there remains an ash which represents the minerals present in the walls. In the case of wood the ash normally contains the elements Na, K, Ca, Mg, Fe, Mn, Al, Si, S, P and C in the form of oxides or carbonates. The proportions may vary considerably but the contents of K and Ca are always fairly high. In addition, special encrustations and deposits of minerals are of frequent occurrence. These may consist of $CaCO_3$, as in wall protuberances of the cell lumen known as cystoliths (Urticales, Moraceae) in the walls of green algae, as in *Acetabularia* and in red algae (*Corallina*). Microscopic crystals of Ca oxalate, are of frequent occurrence, for example in the phloem of certain conifers, and encrustations of Ca phosphate, as in teakwood, are not uncommon. Many cell walls contain silica, for example those of the short cells in the epidermis of Gramineae, and the walls of diatoms consist entirely of this substance. Silica in cell walls is mostly amorphous and for the greater part soluble in boiling water at *p*H 8–20. In the cell walls of the fresh water alga *Chlorochytridion tuberculatum* and other algae, but also in higher plants (Sterling), has its occurrence in the form of microcrystalline quartz been observed.

3. *Structure*

(a) *General aspects*

In the preceding section the various types of molecules isolated from cell walls have been mentioned and their chemical structures described. We will now discuss the organization at the supramolecular level which arises in some groups of cell wall molecules by the tendency of molecular chains to aggregate.

Molecular aggregates may be revealed by electron microscopy and by X-ray diffraction analysis. The former method gives the size and shape of aggregates provided they are not too small. The latter technique yields proof of the presence of regions in the aggregates in which the molecules lie in the regular spatial arrangement characteristic of crystals and may provide data about this arrangement and that of the crystals. Certain structural features which might not be revealed by either of these methods, for instance a preferred orientation of molecular chains in aggregates that are not crystalline in the X-ray sense, may be detected under the polarizing microscope.

The general picture of cell wall ultrastructure under the electron microscope is one which nearly always shows long, thin threads embedded in amorphous material. These threads, usually 100–200 Å wide and about a half as thick are called microfibrils. It has been shown that the microfibrils consist mainly of polysaccharides with linear chains and that the non-mineral crystalline fraction of the wall is located in these microfibrils. Because of the belief that the collection of microfibrils act as a kind of skeleton which reinforces the wall, microfibrillar materials are often called skeletal polysaccharides and the embedding material matrix substances.

The most important skeletal materials are cellulose and chitin, but xylans and mannans are now also included in this group. All other polysaccharides as well as the polyuronides and the proteins belong to the matrix. The distinction between skeletal and matrix substances is seldom, however, as clear-cut as this; matrix substances may be closely associated with the microfibrils and may not be completely amorphous, while the crystalline component of a wall may not be organized into recognizable microfibrils.

In addition to the matrix substances already mentioned, the interfibrillar material may contain substances which are deposited at an advanced stage of development of the wall. The most important of these is lignin. Furthermore heart-wood extractives and minerals may be deposited secondarily in the interfibrillar space. These substances may be distinguished as encrusting materials.

The lipoid substances suberin, cutin and waxes do not fit into this general picture because they are deposited either on the inside (suberin) or, mainly, on the outside (cutin, waxes) of the microfibrillar wall layers. These deposits have been indicated therefore by several authors as adcrusting layers.

In the following sections we will discuss structural details of the microfibrils and of some of the non-microfibrillar materials mainly in terms of their molecular organization.

(b) *The organization of microfibrillar constituents*

Cellulose

Most plants, when treated by the standard procedures used in the isolation of α-cellulose yield a residue which under the electron microscope appears to consist entirely of long threads about 100–200 Å wide, the microfibrils mentioned above. With higher plants hydrolysis of such specimens normally produces glucose in yields ranging between 85% to almost 100%, as expected from bodies which consist largely of cellulose.

X-ray diffraction. The conclusion can be drawn from the X-ray pattern of cellulose that its molecular chains lie parallel to each other in bundles in which over at least part of their lengths, they are regularly spaced sideways in a crystal lattice (Fig. 3). These crystalline regions recall the micelles of Nägeli.

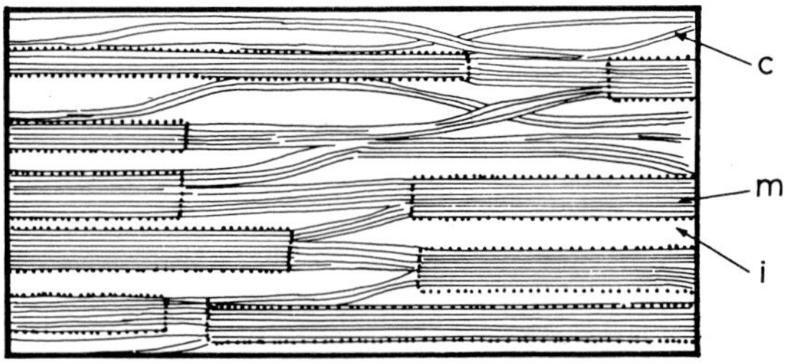

Fig. 3. Scheme of the submicroscopic structure of a cellulose fibre as proposed by Frey-Wyssling before the advent of electron microscopy. c = cellulose chains, m = crystalline cellulose (micelles), i = intermicellar space (Frey-Wyssling 1939).

The smallest repeating unit of the cellulose lattice, the unit cell, is monoclinic and of dimensions as indicated in Fig. 4A, following the Meyer and Misch proposal of 1937. In the structure as outlined here five chains traverse the unit cell, one along each vertical edge (only two are shown in Fig. 4A) and a centre chain running in the opposite direction. It should be noted that each of the chains along the edges forms part of four adjacent unit cells and that therefore in the whole structure half the chains lie in one direction and half in the other. Since each chain is, of course, represented by one repeating unit or two glucose residues, the unit cell contains four glucose residues. It is now believed that the chains are not straight, as they appear in the model of Meyer and Misch, since hydrogen bonds between the –OH on carbon 3 of one sugar ring and the ring oxygen of the next causes adjacent rings to be tilted with respect to each other (Fig. 4B; for a recent statement see Marchessault and Sarko). Fig. 4D is a diagram of the chain-packing in projection along the *b*-axis on to the basal plane. In this figure the chain direction has therefore to be thought perpendicular to the page. It should be noted that this is the structure of native cellulose or cellulose I. Cellulose that has been dissolved and reprecipitated has a different crystal structure, specified as cellulose II or regenerated cellulose.

It has been deduced from low-angle X-ray scattering and from line broadening in the high-angle X-ray pattern that in celluloses from higher plants, notably cotton and ramie cellulose, the crystalline region is in the order of 50 Å wide, and in primary walls values slightly less than 30 Å have been reported by several authors. On the other hand, the X-ray diagram of some algae (*Valonia*, members of the Cladophorales and a few related plants, all seaweeds) is exceptionally sharp and seems irreconcilable with a crystal width as small as 50 Å (Preston 1959); the most recent estimate, based on both the low-angle and the high-angle pattern, is about 140 Å (Preston, private communication).

Electron microscopy. Most plants, when treated by the standard procedures used in the isolation of α-cellulose, yield a residue which under the electron microscope appears to consist entirely of long threads, the microfibrils already mentioned. They are usually about 100–200 Å wide and about $\frac{1}{2}$–$\frac{1}{3}$ as thick, but diameters about 50 Å are not uncommon in primary walls (Fig. 5). In algae of the groups mentioned above with exceptionally sharp X-ray diagrams, they may be about 300 Å wide (Figs. 6 and 7). They are also visible in chemically untreated walls.

With higher plants, hydrolysis of α-cellulose normally produces glucose in yields ranging from 85% to almost 100%. The up to 15% non-glucose consists of sugars belonging to polysaccharides other than cellulose, and in some algae this fraction may range up to 50%. Exceptional, again, are the algae with sharp X-ray diagrams and wide and straight microfibrils; in these, sugars other than glucose have not been detected. The non-glucose polymers cannot be removed without disruption of the microfibrils. Treatment with sulphuric acid under carefully controlled conditions produces an opalescent solution of which the suspended particles are rodlets about 50 Å wide and some 20 or many more times as long. They give an X-ray diagram of cellulose I and, even when derived from microfibrils with a high content of non-glucose sugars, hydrolyse to give glucose only.

It is seen from the data mentioned above that there is a considerable difference between the width of the crystalline micelles of pure cellulose deduced for most plants and that normally observed on their microfibrils of α-cellulose. On these and other grounds a microfibril is considered to consist of a central crystalline 'core' of pure cellulose with interruptions of the crystallinity along the fibril and surrounded by a 'cortex' in which cellulose chains and chains of non-glucose polymers occur together (Preston 1959).

Other authors (see Frey-Wyssling 1959; Mühlethaler and Frey-Wyssling) have suggested that microfibrils are fasciations of 'elementary fibrils'. These are long, crystalline threads of pure cellulose about 35 Å wide, embedded in para- and non-crystalline material and are supposed to occur universally in natural celluloses. This concept has been supported in the later years by electron microscopy of specimens prepared by so-called negative staining techniques; negatively stained and dried cell wall fragments reveal microfibrils containing unstained, thin threads (Mühlethaler 1965, 1967), and ultra-thin sections of negatively stained native walls (cotton hair and ramie fibre), embedded in plastic and sectioned normal to the fibre direction, reveal unstained areas about 40 Å wide separated by stained material (Heyn). It is supposed that only in the fully crystalline part of the cellulose the stain has not been able to penetrate.

These thin threads seem to represent also what has been termed above a crystalline core, be it that the latter may be broader. In this regard it is of importance to note that the microfibrils of the exceptional algae mentioned above cannot have, because of their sharp X-ray pattern, a crystalline core of threads as thin as elementary fibrils. The 'elementary fibrils' observed on electron micrographs of the broad

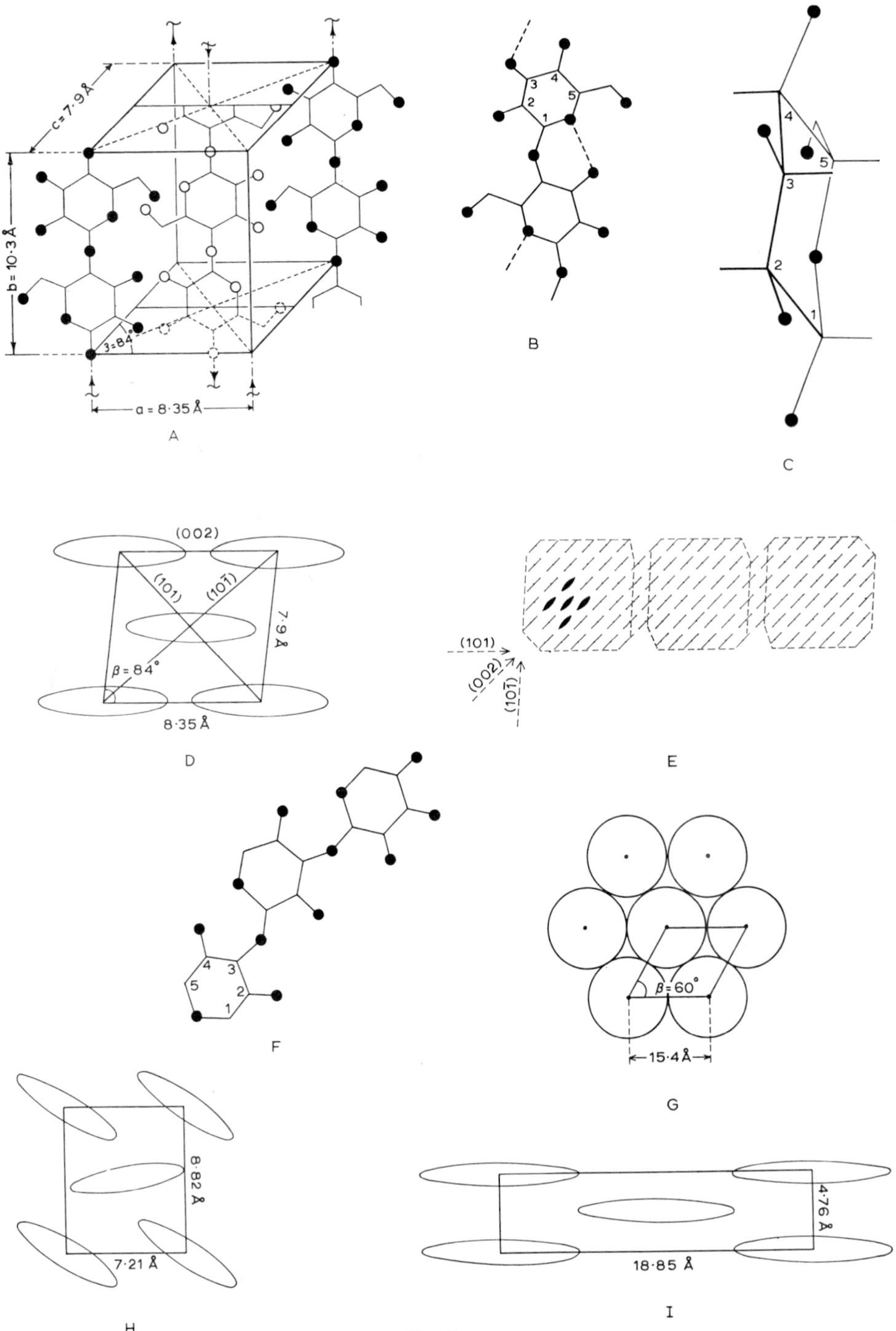
c=7·9Å
b=10·3Å
β=84°
a=8·35Å
A
B
C
(002)
(101)
(10$\bar{1}$)
7·9Å
β=84°
8·35Å
D
(101)
(002)
(10$\bar{1}$)
E
F
β=60°
15·4Å
G
8·82Å
7·21Å
H
4·76Å
18·85Å
I

Fig. 4

microfibrils of these algae after mechanical disruption (Frey-Wyssling et al.) could well represent longitudinal splitting of what was before one thread of undisturbed crystallinity in cross section. Most probably, therefore, the basic cellulose structures in native walls are long crystalline threads of cellulose I, varying in width between about 30 and 60 Å in most plants and reaching about 140 Å in some algae.

It remains to be noted that nearly all electron micrographs published so far on which microfibrils are visible have been made of chemically treated and (or) dried material in which a possible collapse of structures present in the native, wet wall could not be omitted. However, Heyn's micrographs mentioned above of embedded and sectioned material may be supposed to show the elementary fibrils or crystalline cores in the undisturbed disposition present in the native wall, and these photographs exhibit no groups of threads which form bundles of microfibrillar width. Since the same walls are known to appear microfibrillar in dried specimens, the microfibrils in such specimens can be artificial fasciations.

In almost all celluloses, both the broader faces of the microfibrils and the (101) planes of the crystallites within them tend to lie parallel to the wall surface. The plane of the glucose ring (the 002 plane) within the microfibrils must therefore lie obliquely as depicted in Fig. 4E. This fasciation of the crystallites in the plane (101) has been explained from hydrogen binding forces between the molecules which predominate in this plane. It is generally believed that the molecular chains within the microfibrils lie straight, without any appreciable folding. Although folded structures have been proposed in which the chains regularly turn back upon themselves, firm experimental evidence against such a structure has now been obtained (Muggli). Cellulose may form part of more complex polysaccharides and then may not be crystallized, as observed in *Hydrodictyon*, or be crystallized in the modification cellulose II as in *Halicystis*, both green algae.

The mutual arrangement of the cellulose microfibrils differs widely among plant cells, dependent on the type of cell involved, the developmental stage which the cell

---

Fig. 4. Survey of data on the crystal structure of skeletal cell wall polysaccharides. A: Crystal structure of cellulose according to Meyer and Misch. ● = oxygen. B: More accurate model of the cellulose chain, known as crooked chain or Hermans conformation and also adopted for crystalline ivory-nut mannan and chitin. C: Diagrammatic space-model of a glucose residue in cellulose. D: Scheme of the chain packing in cellulose in projection on the *a-c* plane. E: Mode of fasciation of elementary fibrils to form flattened microfibrils as suggested by Frey-Wyssling. F–G: Scheme of the crystal structure of the xylan of algae from data reported by Preston (1964). F: Curved chain of β-1,3-linked xylose residues. G: Hexagonal packing of xylan helices. H and I: Schemes of packing of respectively ivory-nut mannan chains (data from Preston 1968) and chitin chains in projection onto the basal plane.

has reached and the cell wall region or layer under consideration. In general, primary walls show a random array of more or less tortuous microfibrils (Fig. 5), whereas the secondary wall layers contain bundles of nearly parallel microfibrils (Fig. 6) often running in a helical direction around the cell. Often there are two opposite helical directions which alternate in successive lamallae of the secondary wall, and give rise to a feature called crossed microfibrillar orientation.

Xylans

The ultrastructural data of the β-1,4-linked xylans of hardwood and other higher plant hemicelluloses suggest that in the interfibrillar spaces they are present in a paracrystalline state with the constituent molecular chains oriented in the direction of elementary or microfibrils (Marchessault and Sarko).

The β-1,3-linked xylan in the walls of non-cellulosic algae is micro-crystalline since the walls yield X-ray patterns with well defined diffraction rings. In the electron microscope, the xylan exhibits a highly microfibrillar organization, resembling to a certain extent that of cellulose (Fig. 8). The microfibrils, which are about 100 Å wide, may lie in nearly random orientation in face view of the wall or in one of several other patterns, dependent on the wall layer and plant species concerned. A peculiar feature of some inner walls is the appearance of a more or less regular pattern of cross inter-microfibrillar connections.

On the basis of X-ray diagrams of specimens with well oriented fibrils a model for the chain configuration has been developed. In the first derivation, the molecular chains (Fig. 4F) were considered to form double-stranded helices with three xylose residues per half turn and an identity period of 6.12 Å along the axis in wet specimens (Frei and Preston 1964). The helices were oriented lengthwise in the microfibrils and packed hexagonally with a distance 15.4 Å (wet) between the helix axes (Fig. 4G).

Fig. 5. Part of a young wall of a cotton hair showing multi-net growth; more or less transverse orientation of microfibrils on the inner face (upper half of photo) changed into a more nearly axial orientation on the outer face (lower half of photo). From Roelofsen and Houwink (1953).

Fig. 6. Straight microfibrils of cellulose of uniform width in a wall of the green alga *Chaetomorpha melagonium*. From Frei and Preston (1961).

Fig. 7. Oriented files of cytoplasmic granules on the inner face of the wall of a plasmolysed cell of *Chaetomorpha*. From Frei and Preston (1961).

Fig. 8. Xylan microfibrils on the outer face of the wall of a filament of the green alga *Penicillus dumetosus*. From Frei and Preston (1964a).

Fig. 9. Net-like pattern of pits in the cuticle of a young leaf of white clover appearing after removal of wax ridges forming a similar net-pattern. From Hall (1967).

Fig. 10. Granular mannan layer in the wall of the green alga *Dasycladus vermicularis* showing grain in the direction of orientation (↑) of the mannan crystallites as determined by X-ray diffraction. From Frei and Preston (1968).

The scale in these figures corresponds to 1 μ.

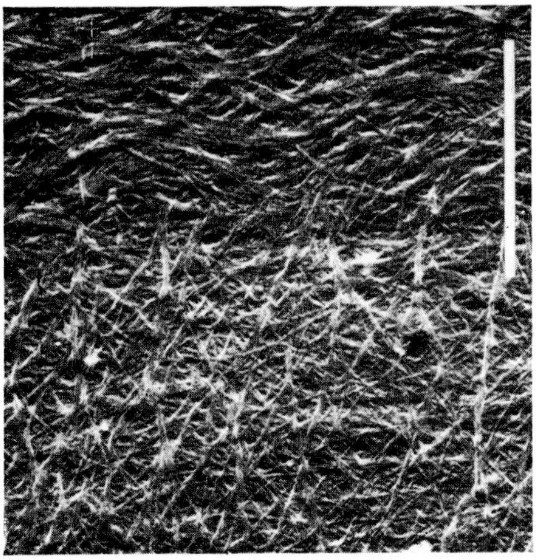
5

6

7

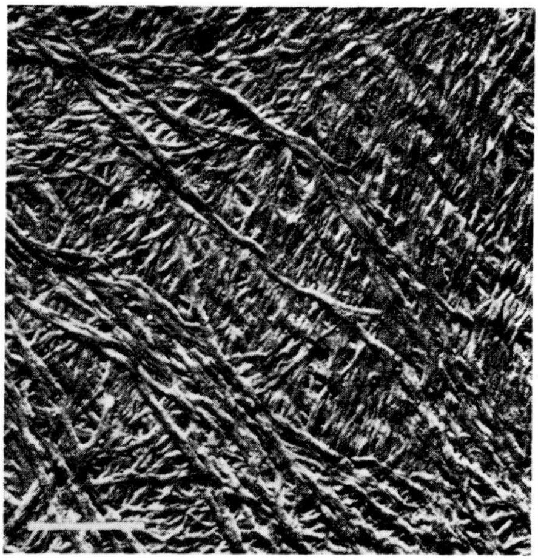
8

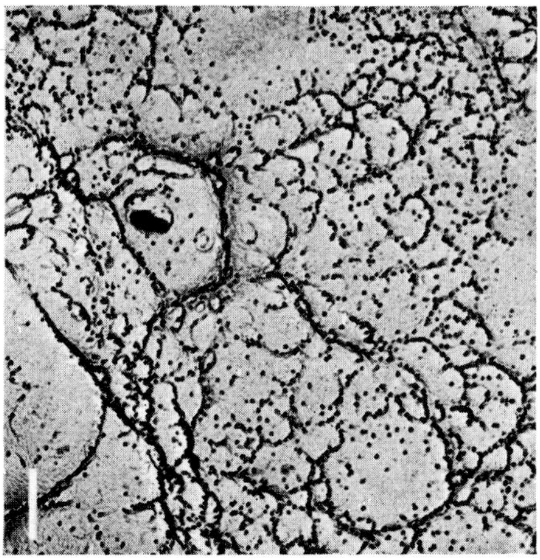
9

10

When the specimen is dry these dimensions are smaller and the crystallinity is diminished. Water clearly takes part in the structure of wet specimens. More recently, Atkins et al. have shown conclusively that the structure is based on a triple, not a double helix.

Mannans

The mannans with β-1,4-linked chains of palm seed endosperms (ivory-nut and date kernel) are said to contain a short-chain fraction with a DP ca. 15 and a fraction of DP ca. 80. The former has a granular appearance under the electron microscope and is crystalline, whereas the latter is reported to be microfibrillar but not crystalline. However, as has been noted recently (Frei and Preston 1968), the features of the latter fraction might well be explained by the presence of contaminating cellulose.

The cell walls of algae consisting of β-1,4-linked mannan do not show a structure of discrete microfibrils. Normally the most detailed structures are obtained after extraction with boiling water and these are always granular. The granular wall surfaces (Fig. 10) may show a fine striation (inner side of the wall) or corrugation (outer side) in axial or transverse direction respectively with reference to the filament axis, suggesting an opposite anistropy of the inner and outer layers (Frei and Preston 1968). Only after an exceptionally mild cleaning procedure could distinct microfibrillar networks be observed in some parts of *Codium* and *Acetabularia* walls (Mackie and Preston). These granular mannans are microcrystalline and show the X-ray pattern of ivory-nut mannan. Both polarization microscopy and X-ray fibre patterns have revealed that the crystallites are well oriented in the directions corresponding to those of the above striations.

The X-ray fibre diagrams of the oriented wall layers have enabled a preliminary unit cell to be calculated (Fig. 4H) which is orthorhombic with axes $a = 7.21$ Å, b (fibre axis) $= 10.27$ Å and $c = 8.82$ Å. The chains traverse the unit cell in opposite directions, the repeat distance 10.27 Å corresponding to two monose residues as in cellulose (Frei and Preston 1968).

The β-1,3-xylan andthe β -1,4-mannan described here may occur together in one plant as has been reported for two members of the Bangiaceae (red algae). The cell walls proper consist of xylan microfibrils while the mannan is present as a cuticle covering the whole frond and as intercellular and interfibrillar material (Frei and Preston 1964).

Yeast glucan

Yeast glucan is only faintly microfibrillar, and microfibrils are easily visible only on the innerside of the wall. The diffuse rings of the X-ray pattern reveal the presence of small crystalline regions. In most yeasts the cell is covered on the outside by an amorphous layer of mannan. Hydrolysis with dilute mineral acid removes mannan, protein and half of the glucan, leaving a highly microfibrillar and microcrystalline product, named hydroglucan. These microfibrils are considered largely to be a product of secondary aggregation. Around the bud scars of the yeast cell they form a thickened ring in which they are oriented tangentially (Houwink and Kreger).

Chitin

The ultrastructural organization of chitin in fungal cell walls resembles that of cellulose in other plants. The chitin is microcrystalline and the chains are packed to form an orthorhombic unit cell (Fig. 4I), containing 4 acetyl glucosamine residues or two chitobiose residues running in opposite direction. The position of the rings in the chain is similar to that in cellulose in that neighbouring rings are inclined to each other. The unit cell dimensions are $a = 4.76$ Å, b (fibre axis) $= 10.28$ Å and $c = 18.35$ Å. The c-axis is very long because of the protruding aminoacetyl group. The pyranose rings are about parallel to the b-c plane, and this plane has been found in the *Phycomyces* sporangiophore to be at right angles to the wall surface.

Chitin forms microfibrils which are sometimes difficult to distinguish in the electron microscope from cellulose microfibrils. In some instances, especially in extraction residues, they may appear as shorter, straight rods. Chitin granules have also been observed, both within (Houwink and Kreger) and around (Bacon et al. 1966) the bud-scar region of yeast cells. Like those of cellulose, the chitin microfibrils may show preferential orientation with reference to the long axis of the cell, and different orientations may occur in different layers of the cell wall, a feature studied extensively on *Phycomyces* sporangiophores in relation to their mode of growth.

Polyuronides

It has been shown that materials of the matrix substance, in particular polyuronides such as protopectin and Ca guluronate, are sometimes weakly crystalline. In addition, their chains may be oriented in the same direction as the cellulose microfibrils embedded in them, as has been shown for *Petasites* collenchyma (Roelofsen and Kreger) and the brown alga *Chorda filum* (Frei and Preston 1962).

(c) *The organization of adcrusting layers*

Waxes

The waxes occurring as surface coatings on leaves and stalks of numerous higher plants exhibit a great variety of microscopic and submicroscopic structures. They consist of tiny needles, rodlets, granules, scales or more complicated structures and may also appear as a continuous smooth layer. The different types of waxy coatings have been described and classified on the basis of microscopic observations by De Bary (1871). Recently, Amelunxen et al. have also given a classification which includes additional submicroscopic details.

All the wax coatings so far investigated are microcrystalline (Kreger 1948). The aliphatic hydrocarbon chains are usually packed into a rectangular lattice with axes $a = 4.97$ Å and $b = 7.45$ Å in the direction perpendicular to the chains, while the

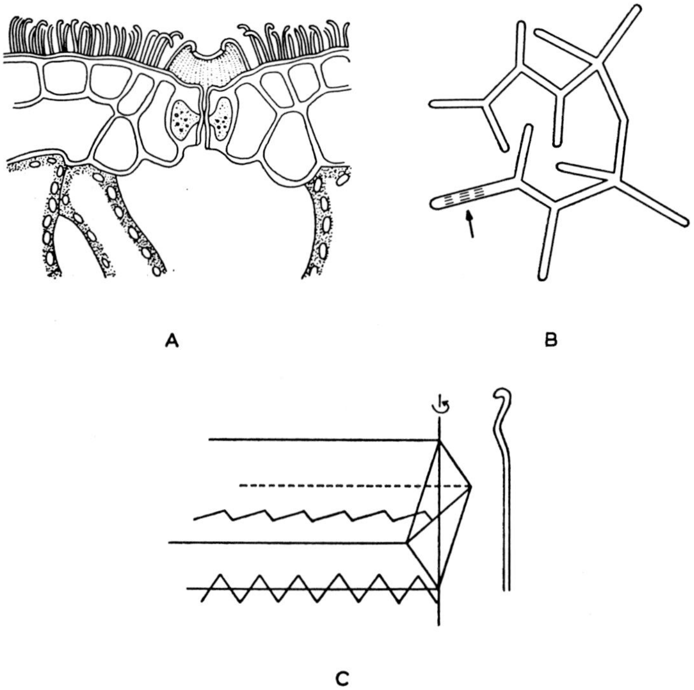

Fig. 11. Structural details of wax coatings of the rodlet type. A: Wax layer of under side of leaf of *Strelitzia ovata* with loose rodlets and cone of rodlets around stomata (De Bary 1871). B: Schematic cross section of a wax rodlet. Hydrocarbon chains indicated near arrow. C: Orientation of unit cell in a wax rodlet of sugar cane (B and C from Kreger 1948, 1958).

long *c*-axis is dependent on the chain length. In wax platelets or scales, the chains lie normal to the flat face. In rodlets they are normal to the long axis of the rodlet, and the lattice is oriented with the diagonal direction in the basal plane parallel to the long axis of the rodlet (Fig. 11C). The rodlets themselves, normally a few microns in diameter, are composed of flat ribbons adhering along their long sides (Fig. 11B) in which the chains are assumed to be oriented parallel to the ribbon face.

The rodlets may form a compact layer in which they stand perpendicular to the plant surface, but they may also be distributed as groups or singly (Fig. 11A). With particles of other shape the arrangement is usually more irregular.

The transport of wax through the underlying cuticle has been a matter of much speculation, since unambiguous evidence for the presence of pores in the cuticle has not been obtained. Recently, however, electron micrographs of replicas from cuticles have been published demonstrating the presence of 200–400 Å wide funnel shaped pits, ending in narrow pores and with a distribution correlated with sites of wax formation (Fig. 9). Whether the pores traverse the whole cuticle has not been established, but micro-channels which might serve the passage of wax are observable in the underlying wall layer of the same object (Hall 1967a, b).

Cuticle and cuticular layers

The cuticle is the thin, homogeneous layer of cutin covering the epidermis of all leaves and stems of higher plants. It generally shows a faint negative birefringence (Sitte and Rennier), which is ascribed to the presence of wax oriented normal to the wall surface, and it shows no internal structure. Inclusions of small crystals of the pentacyclic triterpenoid ursolic acid have been observed in the apple cuticle (Mazliak 1963).

Pores in the cuticle are mentioned above. Inside the cuticle many epidermis outer walls, in particular those of xerophytes, have two distinct layers (Fig. 12A), an inner one consisting mainly of cellulose and an outer layer consisting mainly of cutin. The latter is called the cuticular layer. In contrast to the cuticle the two layers are highly birefringent, with opposite signs. The optical behaviour of the cuticular layers has

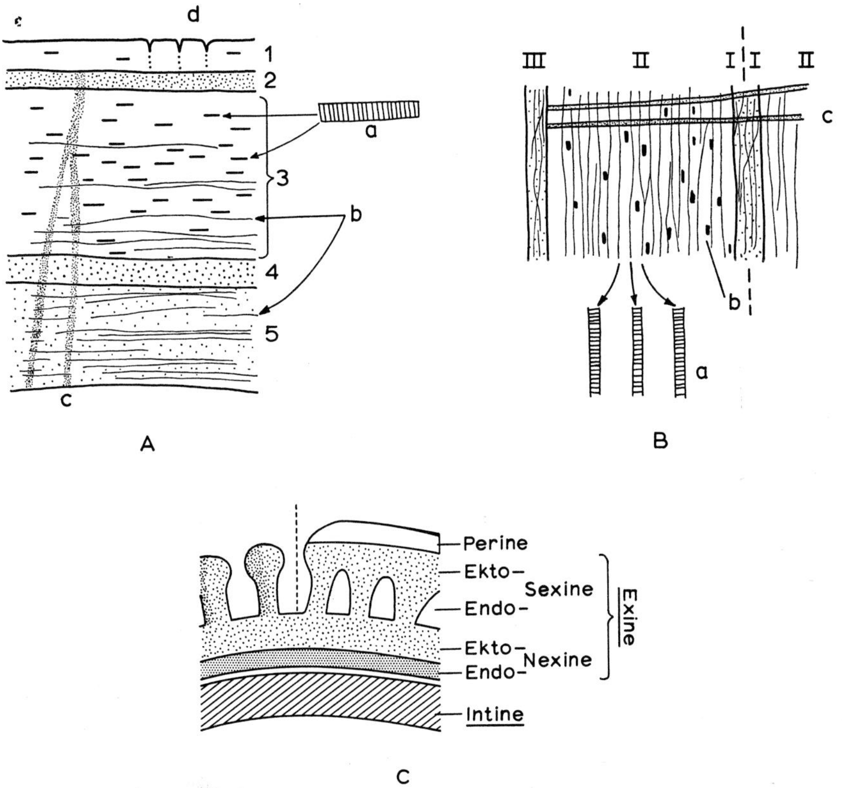

Fig. 12. Schemes of adcrusting layers. A: Cutinized epidermis outer wall. 1: cuticle; 2 and 4: pectin layers; 3: cuticular layer; 5: cellulose layer. a = wax inclusion with direction of carbon chains indicated; b = cellulose microfibrils; c = ectodesmata; d = pits in cuticle. B: Wall of a cork cell. I and III: primary and tertiary wall with cellulose and lignin; II: suberin layer with wax lamellae (a) and friedelin crystallites (b); c = former plasmodesmata. C: Scheme of a pollen wall (Sitte 1957).

led to the conclusion that they contain plate-shaped wax inclusions or wax lamellae oriented with the plane of the greatest extension tangentially in the wall, in which the wax molecules are oriented normal to the wall surface. The very few electron micrographs published so far seem to indicate a lamellar structure. This layer may also contain cellulose, the microfibrils of which are oriented, as usual, parallel to wall surface. The cellulose content generally increases through the wall from outside to inside. In many epidermal walls more or less straight, tubular regions of enhanced permeability (called ectodesmata) have been reported, running in radial direction from the inside of the wall through the cuticular layers up to the cuticle (Fig. 12A, c). They are made visible by Gilson's mercury chloride solution both for light and electron microscopy. In electron micrographs (Schnepf) they appear as a radially elongated region of disturbance of the tangentially oriented wall texture. Finally it may be mentioned that occasionally the cuticular layers are bordered on both sides by a thin pectin layer.

A comparative study of cutin in some 14 epidermises has been made by Sitte and Rennier and a recent review of data on the epidermis outer wall has been given by Franke.

Cork

In the cell walls of cork tissue three layers may generally be distinguished which, from the outside to the inside of the wall, are called primary, secondary and tertiary layers (I, II and III). Of these, I and III have been found to consist mainly of cellulose microfibrils incrusted with lignin, whereas II consists of suberin and wax while cellulose is absent (Fig. 12B). In stopper cork, from the bark of *Quercus suber*, the wax (10–20%) of whole cork) comprises both an aliphatic fraction and a pentacyclic triterpenoid fraction consisting of friedelin and cerin (2–4% of whole cork). The optical behaviour of layer II in polarized light is similar to that of the non-cellulosic part of cuticular layers. Therefore, in suberin layers as well, the wax molecules are oriented normal to the wall surface and may be supposed to form tangentially oriented platelets. In addition the electron microscope has revealed a layered structure, which in several types of cork shows lamellae about 30 Å thick alternating with layers 20–200 Å thick (Sitte 1962). The former are considered to be wax lamellae.

X-ray diagrams have demonstrated that part of the aliphatic wax fraction is crystalline and that the small cyclic fraction is well crystallized and produces the X-ray pattern of friedelin. The unit cell of friedelin is orthorhombic with axes $a = 6.42$ Å, $b = 13.75$ Å and $c = 28.3$ Å. It contains four molecules, and the b-axis is oriented radially to the cell wall. The position of the molecules in the unit cell is not known with any accuracy but the direction of their long axes may be assumed not to deviate much from that of the b-axis (Kreger 1958).

Sporopollenin

The cell walls of pollen grains consist of a cellulosic inner wall, the intine, sometimes also containing callose and an outer wall, the exine, of which the main constituent is sporopollenin. The exine, itself, may be subdivided into several layers (Fig. 12C) of which the outer layer is called sexine. The sexine exhibits structures of great variability both microscopically and submicroscopically and these structures are characteristic of plant groups and even of species. Polarization optical and electron microscopy have indicated in the non-sculptured exine layer of some species, in one instance also in the sculpturing (Horner et al.), a more or less lamellate fine structure of otherwise amorphous or finely granular sporopollenin.

4. *Formation and growth*

(a) *Formation*

General aspects

During cell division the first indication of a new wall separating the two halves of a cell is the appearance of small droplets in the equatorial plane between the daughter nuclei in late anaphase. The droplets arise as vesicles from Golgi bodies which migrate between spindle microtubuli to the equatorial plane and fuse there with larger Golgi vesicles arriving later (Whaley et al.) to form what is called the cell plate. The latter grows laterally by addition of the contents of new vesicles until it reaches the wall of the mother cell. The membranes of the emptied Golgi vesicles fuse to form the new plasmalemma lining the new separation surfaces on either side. There remain, however, narrow openings in the plate which are also lined by plasmalemma and thus form plasma connections between the daughter cells. These are called plasmodesmata and continue to exist during further wall development.

The original separation layer consists of amorphous lipoid and pectic material and represents the future middle lamella between the walls of adjoining cells. Soon after its formation a thin layer is formed on each side, which contains cellulose microfibrils identified by its birefringence. The deposition of this new layer, is followed by the deposition of new layers on the walls of the original cell and simultaneous cell extension. This extension must keep pace with the deposition of new wall material because the thickness of the wall usually does not change.

Before discussing further the process of growth of new cell walls, it should be pointed out that the formation of a new wall by centrifugal growth of a cell plate is not a universal principle. In fungi (see e.g. Moore), in a number of algae, in blue-green algae and in bacteria the process begins with an invagination of the inner side of the lateral wall which grows in a centripetal direction to form a septum, while budding (for recent details see Moor, and Marchant and Smith) as well as constriction are other forms of division.

The walls of meristematic cells in higher plants contain, on an average, 25–35% of cellulose, 34–45% of hemicellulose, 10–20% of pectin substances, 4–10% of protein and 4–7% of lipid on a dry weight basis (Roelofsen 1965, Table 1). Assuming a normal water content of about 60% in the new cell wall, the cellulose content will be in the order of 12%. The microfibrils therefore form a very loose network in a plastic mass of hydrated matrix substances.

The questions rise as to how the constituents of the wall are synthesized and in which organelles or sites of the cell synthesis is achieved. At present it is believed that matrix substances come into the wall as described above for the cell plate, that is by the deposition of the contents of Golgi vesicles, which would contain precursors and perhaps also part of the enzymes of polymerization. The plasmalemma seems to play an important role in the synthesis of cellulose.

On examining the biochemistry of these processes it appears that in cell-free systems containing synthesizing enzymes, diphosphonucleoside-linked monosaccharides and uronic acids have been found to act as precursors. By incubation of such compounds with cell-free particulate enzyme preparations from *Phaseolosus aureus* seedlings it has been possible to synthesize cellulose, pectic acid, and a glucomannan. Using an enzyme from corn cobs an arabinoxylan has also been obtained. In these experiments the nucleotides were either guanosine diphosphate (GDP) or uridine diphosphate (UDP). The former was the monosaccharide carrier in the synthesis of cellulose and glucomannan, the latter in that of the pectic acid and the arabinoxylan. In the synthesis of the bacterial cellulose of *Acetobacter xylinum* only uridine phosphates were active, and it could be shown that the cytoplasmic membrane is the structure in which the precursor of bacterial cellulose is formed (Dennis and Colvin). Another substance, so far unidentified, which seems to act as a glucose carrier in cellulose synthesis, the formation of which is induced by auxin, has been isolated from *Pisum sativum* seedlings (Winter 1967). The transformation of sugars in plants has been reviewed by Hassid.

Formation of microfibrils

The site of formation of cellulose microfibrils must lie close to the plasmalemma. The microfibrils have never been observed in the cytoplasm. They may be formed in close contact with the plasmalemma, as has been shown by electron micrographs of the innermost wall layer of cells of the alga *Chaetomorpha* which were plasmolysed before fixation. The close association with the cytoplasm surface appeared from the presence of remnants of cytoplasm in the form of granular cytoplasmic bodies on the microfibrils; these were aggregated into files in the direction of the most newly synthesized microfibrils (Fig. 7). A new microfibrillar network was formed on the surface of the plasmolysed cytoplasm. On the other hand there is evidence that microfibrils may also be formed away from the cytoplasm, as has been established in *Acetobacter xylinum*, cortical cells of pea epicotyls (Probine) and cell walls of *Chlorella* (Staehelin). The microfibril formation in *Chlorella*, as in *Chaetomorpha*, seems to be associated with granular bodies, and the latter have also been observed on the surface of the plasmalemma of other organisms (see Sassen et al.). In *Chlorella* they leave the surface of the plasmalemma and move through an amorphous matrix to the layer in which microfibrils appear.

A clear-cut answer cannot be given as yet to the question of how microfibrils arise. It could be that they arise by lateral aggregation of pre-formed cellulose chains or originate in a synthesizing enzyme particle which produces a coherent bundle of molecules, adding to the end of each molecule more and more glucose residues. The latter possibility has the advantage that it may explain the nearly uniform thickness of the microfibrils over their entire length. Also, in case of terminal synthesis, the difference in crystal structure between native and regenerated cellulose could be due to an organizing function of the enzyme particle, whereas in the case of lateral aggregation the reason of this difference would be somewhat obscure. For both possibilities of formation we are faced with the problem of how the antiparallel direction of adjacent chains in the crystal structure can be explained. Though folded chain structures have been proposed which provide a solution and are acceptable for regenerated cellulose, the occurrence of folded chains in native cellulose does not appear to be likely. Apart from this difficulty, however, there is much in favour of terminal synthesis, and in *Acetobacter* the fibrils appearing in the culture liquid, distant from the cells, have indeed been observed to grow at their tips.

As mentioned, particles have been observed at the surface of the plasmalemma and in the walls which are closely associated with microfibrils, and seem to play a role in their formation. In a culture liquid there will be sufficient freedom of movement for a particle to spin out a long microfibril, but a fixed plasmalemma particle on the inside of a cell wall can hardly be expected to produce such a thread because the end would have to be pushed away into the semi-solid matrix. This would not give rise to such long and straight microfibrils as are frequently observed. This difficulty is accounted for by a hypothesis put forward by Preston (1964) according to which, in the formation of a microfibril, files of enzyme particles would participate in such a manner that the process of terminal synthesis travels along a file of particles in which it is taken over from one particle by the next one and so on. If the plasmalemma would contain three layers of such granules in cubic close packing the model could also explain the angular relations found between successive layers of microfibrils as well as the observed phenomena of interweaving and twisting of the microfibrils. However, direct evidence for this model is not yet very extensive.

During the period of active cellulose production in secondary wall formation the cytoplasm itself shows structural details which seem to be related with this activity (see Cronshaw). Of particular importance in this respect is the appearance of so-called microtubules. These were observed first in root meristems by Ledbetter and Porter (1963) using a new fixation technique. They are about 200–270 Å wide, very long and nearly straight, with a wall about 70 Å thick, consisting of subunits. They have since been reported in an increasing number of papers on both plant and animal cytoplasmic ultrastructure. In relation to wall formation they seem to play a role in guiding the movement of Golgi vesicles during cell plate formation (see Hepler and Newcomb) and also appear during the mitotic pre-prophase, forming a temporary ring in the region where the future cell plate will reach the side wall of the mother cell (Pickett-

Heaps and Northcote). Of great interest is their appearance in close contact with the plasmalemma during secondary wall formation, when they are oriented in the direction of the microfibrils of the innermost wall layer. This could suggest that they have something to do, directly or indirectly, with microfibril formation and orientation.

(b) *Growth*

The microfibrillar aspect

The development of the cell wall usually involves two essentially different periods, one of growth in area and the other of wall thickening, which may overlap. The layer formed during the period of growth in area is usually a thin layer with a loose microfibrillar mesh and a low cellulose content. It is called the primary wall. The layers formed later as wall thickening on the inside of the primary wall are distinguished as secondary wall. They have a high cellulose content and bundles of laterally cohering parallel microfibrils, forming a variety of differentiated structures and textures. The latter will not be discussed here, and we will confine our attention to a brief treatise on the growth of the primary wall, especially in elongating cells. The anisotropy of growth of these cells offers problems not encountered in the growth of isodiametric cells.

The mechanical factors governing the process of cell elongation may be expected to be osmotic pressure, wall plasticity and wall elasticity, the last two being determined by the physical properties both of matrix and of the microfibrillar framework. In order to eliminate the role of tissue interactions the subject has been most thoroughly studied on cells growing in isolation, in particular the giant cells of algae which are easily handled. Several types of hairs and young tissue cells have also been used for this purpose.

The most important observational basis for all theories on the process of cell elongation is the distribution of the predominant microfibril directions across the cell wall. It has been shown that the orientation on the inner surface of the wall of elongating cells is nearly always transverse with respect to the longitudinal axis of the cell, whereas on the outer surface it is more nearly parallel to this axis. In between there is a gradual change from one direction of orientation to the other. This distribu-

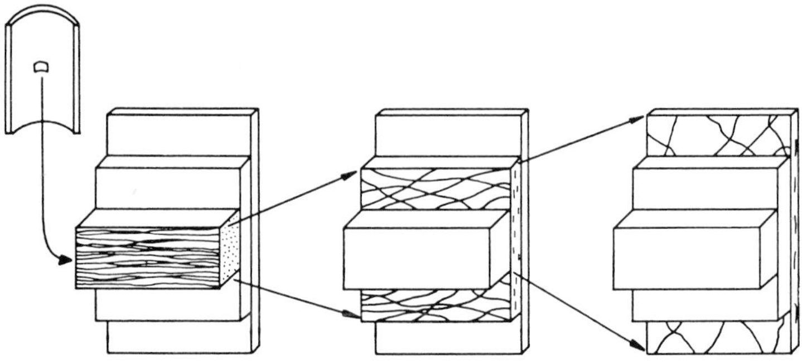

Fig. 13. Scheme of the growth of a young wall according to the principle of multi-net growth (Roelofsen 1965).

tion of orientations persists during the whole period of cell growth. The phenomenon may be explained assuming that the inner lamella of the wall in effect moves gradually towards the outside as new wall material is deposited on its inner surface. At the same time the wall undergoes a plastic deformation involving a predominantly longitudinal extension and a thinning out on account of the increase in area. In consequence, a re-orientation of the microfibrils appears from a more compact structure with a tendency to transverse orientation to a less compact structure with mainly axial orientation via intermediate structures (Figs. 5 and 13). This concept, put forward by Roelofsen and Houwink in 1953 on the basis of electron microscope studies of *Phycomyces* sporangiophores and several types of plant hairs, was termed by them 'multi-net growth'. It is now universally accepted. A theoretical mathematical treatment by Probine and Barber of the plastic and elastic properties of walls of the internodal cells of the alga *Nitella* in the growth phase has indeed shown that a mat of microfibrils with an orientation as observed in *Nitella*, embedded in a plastic matrix and under turgor pressure, would undergo longitudinal and transverse plastic extensions in the ratio observed in the growing cell.

Although it is now clear that cell growth is associated with the mechanical properties of the wall, the problem remains of the control of these properties by the living cytoplasm, and a few points concerning this aspect are mentioned below.

The stress in a cylinder wall under internal pressure is about twice as high in the transverse direction as in the longitudinal direction, and there is no reason why this would not also apply to a similarly shaped plant cell wall under turgor pressure. It has been suggested by Castle and by van Iterson in 1937 that this stress would be a directing force in the transverse orientation of the cellulose micelles in primary walls, and this orientation would then give rise to the anisotropic properties determining the mainly longitudinal growth of the wall. This wall tension theory for the orientation of micelles could later be adapted to the microfibrillar structure and was useful in considerations on multi-net growth (Roelofsen 1959). However, it has been shown (Green) that on removal of transverse stress in the wall by jacketing growing *Nitella* cells the transverse deposition of microfibrils remained. Also, colchicin could induce an isotropic deposition of microfibrils which initiated isodiametric growth. These observations seem to indicate that the oriented deposition of microfibrils must not be seen as a secondary effect of stress but as a primary causative factor of anisotropic growth, resulting from cytoplasmic organization. This, meanwhile, does not rule out the possibility that in the earliest stages of cell development, in which ordered structures are frequently not present, a particular distribution of wall expansion rates initiates orientation (Green and King).

Matrix and auxin

Another possible role of the cytoplasm in organizing wall extension might lie in the production of substances which control matrix plasticity. Changes in plasticity of the matrix must influence the ease of slip of the embedded microfibrils past each other and, therefore, may be expected to change the ratio of transverse to longitudinal extension of the wall in response to the existing distribution of stress.

With this in mind it should be pointed out that the growth-promoting substance auxin occurring in young plant tissues has been found to stimulate longitudinal growth, and much work has been and is still being done to explain this from the point of view that auxin would affect in some way the plasticity of the matrix.

According to a recent concept, the influence of auxin on wall plasticity is thought to involve a chain of metabolic events leading from auxin to the hydroxyproline-rich protein fraction found in many cell walls and called 'extensin'. The protein molecules could be cross-linked by disulfide bridges and connected with the microfibrils by galactoaraban, with which they form a complex. Auxin-induced reduction of the S–S bridges to S–H would then loosen the connection and enhance the plasticity of the system, while reoxidation by an oxydase would have the inverse effect. The various aspects of this line of thought are as yet insufficiently explored.

It can be seen from these data that the extension of young cell walls forms a rich source of problems with aspects both molecular and ultrastructural. The subject has been reviewed by Wilson and by Roelofsen (1965).

Acknowledgements

It is a pleasure to thank Professor R. D. Preston, F. R. S., Astbury Department of Biophysics, The University, Leeds, England, for making valuable suggestions, and for originals of electron micrographs. Also to Dr. D. M. Hall, Department of Scientific and Industrial Research, Lower Hutt, New Zealand, and Dr. A. L. Houwink, Department of Microbiology, Institute of Technology, Delft, The Netherlands, the author is indebted for original electron micrographs.

References

AMELUNXEN, F., K. MORGENROTH and T. PICKSAK: Untersuchungen an der Epidermis mit dem Stereoscan Electronenmicroscop. Z. Pflanzenphysiol. 57 (1967) 79.

ARONSON, J. M.: The cell wall. In: G. C. Ainsworth and A. S. Sussman, eds.: The fungi, Vol. I. New York, Academic Press (1965) p. 49.

ATKINS, E. D. T., K. D. PARKER and R. D. PRESTON: The helical structure of the β-1,3-linked xylan in some siphoneous green algae. Proc. Roy. Soc. B 173 (1969) 209.

BACON, J. S. D., E. D. DAVIDSON, D. JONES and I. F. TAYLOR: The location of chitin in the yeast cell wall. Biochem. J. 101 (1966) 36C.

BACON, J. S. D., D. JONES, V. C. FARMER and D. M. WEBLEY: The occurrence of $\alpha(1-3)$glucan in *Cryptococcus*, *Schizosaccharomyces* and *Polyporus* species, and its hydrolysis by a *Streptomyces* culture filtrate lysing cell walls of *Cryptococcus*. Biochim. Biophys. Acta 158 (1968) 313.

BARTNICKI-GARCIA, S. and E. REYES: Chemical composition of sporangiophore walls of *Mucor rouxii*. Biochim. Biophys. Acta 165 (1968) 32.

BROOKS, J. and G. SHAW: Chemical structure of the exine of pollen walls and a new function for carotenoids in nature. Nature (Lond.) 219 (1968) 532.

CÔTÉ, JR, W. A., ed.: Cellular ultrastructure of woody plants. Syracuse, N.Y. Syracuse Univ. Press (1965).

CRONSHAW, J.: Cytoplasmic fine structure and cell wall development in differentiating xylem elements. In: W. A. Côté, Jr., ed.: Cellular ultrastructure of woody plants. Syracuse, N.Y. (1965) p. 99.

DENNIS, T. D. and J. R. COLVIN: The relation between cellulose and the structure of the cell envelope in *Acetobacter xylinum*. In: W. A. Côté, Jr., ed.: Cellular ultrastructure of woody plants. Syracuse, N.Y. Syracuse Univ. Press (1965) p. 199.

DOUGLAS, A. G. and G. EGLINTON: The distribution of alkanes. In: T. Swain, ed.: Comparative phytochemistry. London, Academic Press (1966) p. 57.

DUFF, R. B.: The constitution of glucosan from the fungus *Polyporus betulinus*. J. Chem. Soc. (1952) 2592.

FRANKE, W.: Mechanisms of foliar penetration of solutions. Ann. Rev. Plant Physiol. 18 (1967) 281.

FREI, E. and R. D. PRESTON: Cell wall organization and cell growth in the filamentous green algae *Cladophora* and *Chaetomorpha*. I. The basic structure and its formation. Proc. Roy. Soc. B 154 (1961) 70.

FREI, E. and R. D. PRESTON: Configuration of alginic acid in marine Brown Algae. Nature 196 (1962) 130.

FREI, E. and R. D. PRESTON: Non-cellulosic structural polysaccharides in algal cell walls. I. Xylan in siphoneous Green Algae. Proc. Roy. Soc. B 160 (1964a) 293.

FREI, E. and R. D. PRESTON: Non-cellulosic structural polysaccharides in algal cell walls. II. Association of xylan and mannan in *Porphyra umbilicalis*. Proc. Roy. Soc. B 160 (1964b) 314.

FREI, E. and R. D. PRESTON: Non-cellulosic structural polysaccharides in algal cell walls. III. Mannan in siphoneous Green Algae. Proc. Roy. Soc. B 169 (1968) 127.

FREY-WYSSLING, A.: The submicroscopic structure of cell walls. Science Progress 134 (1939) 249.

FREY-WYSSLING, A.: Die pflanzliche Zellwand. Berlin, Springer Verlag (1959).

FREY-WYSSLING, A. and K. MÜHLETHALER: Ultrastructural plant cytology. Amsterdam, Elsevier Publ. Co. (1965).

FREY-WYSSLING, A., K. MÜHLETHALER and R. MUGGLI: Elementarfibrillen als Grundbausteine der nativen Cellulose. Holz als Roh- und Werkstoff 24 (1966) 443.

GREEN, P. B.: On mechanisms of elongation. In: M. Locke, ed.: Cytodifferentiation and macromolecular synthesis. New York, Academic Press (1963) p. 203.

GREEN, P. B. and A. KING: A mechanism for the origin of specifically oriented textures in development with special reference to *Nitella* wall texture. Austr. J. Biol. Sci. 19 (1966) 421.

HALL, D. M.: The ultrastructure of wax deposits on plant leaf surfaces. II. Cuticular pores and wax formation. J. Ultrastr. Res. 17 (1967a) 34.

HALL, D. M.: Wax microchannels in the epidermis of white clover. Science 158 (1967b) 505.

HASSID, W. Z.: Transformation of sugars in plants. Ann. Rev. Plant Physiol. 18 (1967) 253.

HAUG, A., B. LARSEN and O. SMIDSRØD: A study of the constitution of alginic acid by partial acid hydrolysis. Acta Chem. Scand. 20 (1966) 183.

HEPLER, P. K. and E. H. NEWCOMB: Fine structure of cell plate formation in the apical meristems of *Phaseolus* roots. J. Ultrastruct. Res. 19 (1967) 498.

HEINEN, W.: Über den enzymatischen Cutin-abbau. Acta Bot. Neerl. 9 (1960) 167.

HEINEN, W. and I. VAN DEN BRAND: Enzymatische Aspekte zur Biosynthese des Blatt-cutins bei *Gasteria verrucosa* Blättern nach Verletzung. Z. Naturforsch. 18 (1963) 67.

HEYN, A. N. J.: The microcrystalline structure of cellulose in cell walls of cotton, ramie and jute fibers as revealed by negative staining of sections. J. Cell Biol. 29 (1966) 181.

HORNER, H. T., N. R. LERSTEN and C. C. BOWEN: Spore development in the liverwort *Ricardia pinguis*. Amer. J. Bot. 53 (1966) 1048.

HOUWINK, A. L. and D. R. KREGER: Observations on the cell wall of yeasts. An electron microscope and X-ray diffraction study. Antonie van Leeuwenhoek 19 (1953) 1.

JOHNSTON, I. R.: The partial acid hydrolysis of a highly dextrarotatory fragment of the cell wall of *Aspergillus niger*. Isolation of the α-1,3-linked dextrin series. Biochem. J. 96 (1965) 659.

KOOIMAN, P.: The constitution of *Tamarindus* amyloid. Rec. trav. chim. Pays-Bas 80 (1961) 851.

KOOIMAN, P.: The constitution of the amyloid from the seeds of *Annona verrucata* L. Phytochem. 6 (1967) 1665.

KOOIMAN, P. and D. R. KREGER: Some observations on X-ray diffraction and monosaccharide composition in mannose containing polysaccharides from seeds. Kon. Ned. Akad. Wetensch. Proc. Ser. C 63 (1960) 613.

KREGER, D. R.: An X-ray study of waxy coatings from plants. Rec. Trav. bot. néerl. 41 (1948) 603.

KREGER, D. R.: Observations on cell walls of yeasts and some other fungi by X-ray diffraction and solubility tests. Biochim. Biophys. Acta 13 (1954) 1.

KREGER, D. R.: Wax. In: W. Ruhland, ed.: Handbuch der Pflanzenphysiologie, Vol. X. Berlin, Springer Verlag (1958a) 249.

KREGER, D. R.: X-ray diffraction of stopper cork. J. Ultrastruct. Res. 1 (1958b) 247.

KREGER, D. R.: Cell walls. In: R. Lewin, ed.: Physiology and biochemistry of algae. New York, Academic Press (1962) p. 315.

LAMPEN, J. O.: External enzymes of yeast: their nature and formation. Antonie van Leeuwenhoek 34 (1968) 1.

LAMPORT, D. T. A.: The protein component of primary cell walls. In: R. D. Preston, ed.: Advances in botanical research, 2. London, Academic Press (1965) p. 151.

MACKIE, W. and R. D. PRESTON: The occurrence of mannan microfibrils in the Green Algae *Codium fragile* and *Acetabularia crenulata*. Planta (Berl.) 79 (1968) 249.

MANNERS, D. J. and J. C. PATTERSON: A re-examination of the molecular structure of yeast glucan. Biochem. J. 98 (1966) 19C.

MARCHANT, R. and D. G. SMITH: Wall structure and bud formation in *Rhodotorula glutinis*. Arch. Mikrobiol. 58 (1967) 248.

MARCHESSAULT, R. H. and A. SARKO: X-ray structure of polysaccharides. Advances in Carbohydrate Chem. 22 (1967).

MAZLIAK, P.: La cire cuticulaire des pommes (*Pirus malus* L.). Thesis, Univ. of Paris (1963).

MAZLIAK, P.: Chemistry of plant cuticles. In: L. Reinhold and Y. Liwschitz, eds.: Progress in phytochemistry, Vol. 1. New York, Wiley-Interscience (1968) p. 49.

MOOR, H.: Endoplasmatic reticulum as the initiator of bud formation in yeast (*Saccharomyces cerevisiae*). Arch. Mikrobiol. 57 (1967) 135.

MOORE, R. T.: The ultrastructure of fungal cells. In: G. C. Ainsworth and A. S. Sussman, eds.: The fungi, Vol. 1. New York, Academic Press (1965) p. 95.

MUGGLI, R.: Über den Feinbau cellulosischer Elementarfibrillen. Cellulose Chem. and Tecnnol., Publ. Acad. Soc. Republ. Romania 2 (1968) 549.

MÜHLETHALER, K.: The fine structure of cellulose microfibrils. In: W. A. Côté, Jr., ed.: Cellular ultrastructure of woody plants. Syracuse, N.Y. Syracuse Univ. Press (1965) p. 191.

MÜHLETHALER, K.: Ultrastructure and formation of plant cell walls. Ann. Rev. Plant Physiol. 18 (1967) 1.

PERCIVAL, E. and R. H. MCDOWELL: Chemistry and enzymology of marine algal polysaccharides. London, Academic Press (1967).

PICKETT-HEAPS, J. D. and D. H. NORTHCOTE: Organization of microtubules and cytoplasmic reticulum during mitosis and cytokinesis in wheat meristems. J. Cell Sci. 1 (1966) 109.

PRESTON, R. D.: The molecular architecture of plant cell walls. London, Chapman and Hall (1952).

PRESTON, R. D.: Wall organization in plant cells. Int. Rev. Cytol. 8 (1959) 33.

PRESTON, R. D.: The structural and mechanical aspects of plant cell walls with particular reference to synthesis and growth. In: M. H. Zimmermann, ed.: The formation of wood in forest trees. New York, Academic Press (1964) p. 169.

PROBINE, M.C.: Chemical control of plant cell wall structure and cell shape. Proc. Roy. Soc. B 161 (1965) 526.

PROBINE, M.C. and N.F.BARBER: The structure and plastic properties of the cell wall of *Nitella* in relation to extension growth. Austr. J. Biol. Sci. 19 (1966) 439.

ROELOFSEN, P.A.: The plant cell-wall. Berlin, Borntraeger (1959).

ROELOFSEN, P.A.: Ultrastructure of the wall in growing cells and its relation to the direction of growth. In: R.D.Preston, ed.: Advances in botanical research, Vol. 2. London, Academic Press (1965) p. 69.

ROELOFSEN, P.A. and D.R.KREGER: The submicroscopic structure of pectin in collenchyma cell walls. J. Exp. Bot. 2 (1951) 332.

ROGERS, H.J. and H.R.PERKINS: Cell walls and membranes. London, E. and F.N.Spon Ltd. (1968).

SASSEN, M.M.A., C.C.REMSEN and W.M.HESS: Fine structure of *Penicillium megasporum* conidiospores. Protoplasma 64 (1967) 75.

SCHNEPF, E.: Untersuchungen über Darstellung und Bau der Ektodesmen und ihre Beeinflussbarkeit durch stoffliche Faktoren. Planta (Berl.) 52 (1959) 644.

SITTE, P.: Morphologie des Cutins und des Sporopollenins. In: E.Treiber, ed.: Die Chemie der Pflanzenzellwand. Berlin, Springer Verlag (1957) p. 439.

SITTE, P.: Zum Feinbau der Suberinschichten im Flaschenkork. Protoplasma 54 (1962) 555.

SITTE, P. and R.RENNIER: Untersuchungen an cuticularen Zellwandschichten. Planta (Berl.) 60 (1963) 19.

STAEHELIN, A.: Die Ultrastruktur der Zellwand des Chloroplasten von *Chlorella*. Z. f. Zellforschung 74 (1966) 325.

STERLING, C.: Crystalline silica in plants. Am. J. Bot. 54 (1967) 840.

THOMPSON, E.W. and R.D.PRESTON: Proteins in the cell walls of some Green Algae. Nature 213 (1967) 684.

TREIBER, E.: Die Chemie der Pflanzenzellwand. Berlin, Springer Verlag (1957).

VAN GIJZEL, P.: A review of the chemistry of fresh and fossil sporopollenine. Chem. Geol. (1969) in press.

WANG, M.C. and S.BARTNICKI-GARCIA: Biosynthesis of β-1,3- and β-1,6-linked glucan by *Phytophtora cinnamomi* hyphal walls. Biochem. Biophys. Res. Comm. 24 (1966) 832.

WHALEY, W.G., M.DAUWALDER and J.C.KEPHART: The Golgi apparatus and an early state in cell plate formation. J. Ultrastr. Res. 15 (1966) 169.

WARSI, S.A. and W.J.WHELAN: Structure of Pachyman, the polysaccharide component of *Poria cocos* Wolf. Chemistry Ind. (1957) 1573.

WARTH, A.H.: The chemistry and technology of waxes. New York, Reinhold Press (1960).

WESSELS, J.G.H.: Morphogenesis and biochemical processes in *Schizophyllum commune* Fr. Wentia 13 (1965) 1.

WILSON, K.: The growth of plant cell walls. Int. Rev. Cytol. 17 (1964) 1.

WINTER, H.: Effect of auxin and sugar on cell wall synthesis and growth of pea stem segments. Kon. Ned. Akad. Wetensch. Proc. Ser. C 69 (1966) 64.

WINTER, H.: The effect of IAA on sugar metabolism by growing pea stem segments. Kon. Ned. Akad. Wetensch. Proc. Ser. C 70 (1967) 294.

ZIMMERMANN, M.H., ed.: The formation of wood in forest trees. New York, Academic Press (1964).

Subject index

Bold-face numerals refer to pages where illustrations occur, italic numerals refer to pages where a subject is treated in detail.

Acanthamoeba, 1190
Acanthopachylus aculaeatus, 413, 419, 429
Acetabularia, 1027, 1062, 1063, 1070
Acetobacter melagenum, 1361
Acetobacter xylinum, 154
N-acetyl glucosamine, 155-156
N-acetyl muramic acid, 155
Acheta domesticus, 301, 303, **306**, **308**, 309, **314-317**, 319
Acheta, 305, 308, 311-313, 318
Acidic proteins in chromosomes, 504-505
  see also Chromosomes
Acid phosphatase, 446, 861
Acricotopus, 515
Acrididae, 422
Acridine orange (A.O.), 659
Acriflavin, 979
Actinomycetales, 150
Actinomycin binding, 659
Actinomycin D, 241, 548, 607, 660, 977, 988
  inhibitor of DNA synthesis, 484
  inhibitor of RNA synthesis, 512, 516
Active process (in cell uptake)
  and adrenaline, 1325
  of alanine 1327, *1328-1330*
  of amino acids, 1326
  ATPase, 1335, 1337-1338
  biochemical aspects, 1326-1331
  enzyme system hydrolysing ATP, 1332-1333
  and glutamate, 1327
  of glycine, 1327
  ion movement forces, 1326
  potential difference in epithelium, 1327
  potential profile, 1327, 1348
  short-circuited, 1324-1325
  sugars, 1327
  synthesis of amino acids, 1330
  transepithelial potential, 1327
  transmucosal potentials, 1328
  transserosal potential, 1328
  turnover rate of alanine pools, 1330
Active transport, *1321-1345*
  classical thermodynamic approach, *1322-1326*
  definition of, 1322-1323
  electrogenic Na transport, 1348
  endergonic and exergonic reactions, 1323-1324, 1331
  energy source, 1331-1334
Adaptation, and stability of doublet patterns, 78
Adenine nucleotide translocase, 926
Adenoviridae, 705
Adenovirus, 1314, 1315
Adenovirus 2, 83, 85, 100
Adenovirus 12, 693, 700, 702, 706-708
Aegilops longissima, **333**
Aerobacter aerogenes, 14
Akinetoplastic cultures, 977
Alkaline caesium chloride (CsCl), 5, 54, 60
Alkaline phosphatase, in the cell wall, 160
Allium cepa, 63, 391, 396, 403, 481, 488, 490, **1066**, **1135**
Allium fistulosa, 63
Allium porrum, **387**, 391, **400**, 401, 403, 405, 407
Amblystoma, 385
Amino acid metabolism and mitochondria, 938
Amino acid sequence of cytochrome C, 930
δ-Aminolevulinate synthetase, 936-937
Amoeba
  mucoid layer, 1382
  motile and resting form, 1378-1379
Amoeba proteus, 491, 848, 865, 1378, 1384, **1386**, 1387, **1389**, 1390
Amoeba terricola, 849
Amoeboid movement and permanent endocytosis, 1385-1387
AMP, 1355
Amphibia, 531, 541
Anaphase, 388-391
Anaplasia, 703
Annular material, 838, 845, 847-848
  structure of, 847
Annulate lamellae, *855-857*, 1120
  in cancer cells, 697
  origin of, 855
  structure of, 855
Annulus, 841
Anthoceros, 1062
Antidiuretic effect, 1354-1355
Antimongolism, 822-824
Antirrhinum, 330
Apodemus sylvaticus, 56, 58, 59, 61, 62, 64
Arbacia, 564
Arbacia puntulata, 586, 596
Arabinosylcytosine (araC), 742
Ascaris, 894
Ascaris lumbricoides, 939
Astacus, 1358
Astacus fluviatilis, 1362
ATP and active process, 1331-1332
ATP synthesis in bacteria, 183
ATPase, 564
  and active process, 1335, 1337-1338

Autolysosomes, 1395
Autophagic vacuoles, 1165
Autosomal abnormalities, 805-834
autosomal trisomy without syndromes, 815
structural abnormalities, 815-825
structural anomalies without syndromes, 825
45 XX or XY, G-, 822-824
46 XX or XY, Gq- or Gr, 822-824
46 XX or XY, Dq-, 820
46 XX or XY, 4p-, 817
46 XX or XY, 5p-, 818-819
46 XX or XY, 18p-, 820-821
46 XX or XY, 18q-, 821-822
47 XX or XY, G+, 805-810
Atresia, germ cell, 767, 769
Autosomes, 279, 290
Avian myeloblastosis virus, 109
Axoneme, 1221-1223
Azotobacter agilis, 175
Azotobacter vinelandii, 183, **185**, 209

Bacillus, 187, 206
Bacillus cereus, **128**, 175, 180, 202, 204, **209**
Bacillus lineola, 160
Bacillus maquariensis, 150
Bacillus megaterium, 128, **153**, 154, 159, **162**, 175, **177**, 204, **205**, 206
Bacillus polymyxa, 159
Bacillus subtilis, 128, **130**, 137, 141, 143, 152, **159**, 166, **178**, 181, 182, **199**, **200**, 201, **202**, **203**, **209**, 1082
Bacillus thuringensis, 209
Bacteria
ATP synthesis, 183
cell wall of, 153-160
chromosomes of, *127-145*
chromosome separation, 202
cross over in, 135
cytoplasm of, 203-204
cytoplasmic membrane, 175-178
forms, defective in cell wall materials, 160-170
internal organisation of, 197-217
L forms, 164-168
membranes of, 174-196
nucleoplasm of, 198-203
segregation of genetic material, 140-142
surface of, *148-196*
transfer of genetic information, 135-137
Balbiani rings, 505, 511, 515-516
base composition of RNA, 512
Barr bodies, 282
Basal bodies, 1223-1226
sex difference, 1226
Basal granule, 978-979
Basal laminae, 1275-1277
see also Basement membrane
Base composition, 68-69
Base sequence, 68-69
genome homology, 10
methods of measuring homology, 10
Basement membrane, 1275-1276
of capillaries, 1277
filtering action, 1277
Batrachoseps attenuatus, 542
Beggiatoa, 185
Beggiatoales, 150
Bellevalia romana, 481
Beroë ovata, **1224**
Bilateral symmetry in eggs, 642
Blaps mucronata, 424
Blaptica dubia, 413, 429
Blastomeres, development *in vitro*, 643
Blebs, 862
and mitochondria, 1000
Bodo, 977
Bombyx mori, 282
Bouquet formation, 853
Brushfield's spots, 805

Ca^{2+}
and ATPase. 1338
and cilia, 1250
and flavoproteins, 1338
flux of, 1336-1339
transport across membranes, 1337
transport in mitochondria, 924-925
as an uncoupler, 924
Calf thymus
composition of nucleohistones, 449
euchromatin and heterochromatin, 253-**254**
extraction of histones, 449
nuclear ribosomes in, 447
nucleohistones of, 230, 235-236
Callinectes, 1364
Calliphora, 880, 887
Cambarus clarkii, 413
Cancer
see Tumor and Carcinogenesis
Cancer cells
annulate lamellae, 697, 855
cell membrane of, 700-701
chromosomes in, 692-693

cilia in, 697
cytoplasm in, 693-703
ergastoplasm in, 695-696
Golgi apparatus of, 696-697
intercellular connections, 701-703
interchromatin of, 690
interchromatin granules, 690-691
lysosomes in, 699
microbodies in, 697
mitochondria in, 693-694
mitosis, 692-693
model systems of transformed cells, 706-709
nonspecific changes, 689-690
nuclear blebs, 690
nuclear membrane, 690
nucleolonema, 692
nucleolus of, 692
nucleoplasm of, 690-692
nucleus in, 690
paired cisterna, 697
pathological cytoplasmic inclusions, 697-700
pathological nuclear inclusions, 700
perichromatin granules, 690
ribosomes in, 694-696
ultrastructure of, 688-715

Capra hirca, 765, 770

Carcinogenesis, 717-731
see also Tumor
chromosome patterns in, 723-726
somatic mutation theory, 740
viral, 718

Carcinogens, chemical, 703

Carcinus moenas, 1363, 1364

Carrier transfer, 1335

Catalase, 1180, 1187-1188, 1192

Cation concentration
definition of, 22
dissociation of DNA, 31

Caulobacter, 181, 192

Caulobacter crescentus, 181

Caveolae, 1271-1272
and micropinocytosis, 1272
function of, 1271
shape of, 1271

Cavia cobaya, 286

Cavia porcellus, 58

Cell, a transit station, 1395

Cell-to-cell interaction, 672

Cell coat, 1265-1266

Cell cycle, nuclear proteins and, 660-664

Cell degeneration
endometrium, 718-719
hyperplastic, 718

Cell differentiation and nuclear proteins, *664-675*

Cell division
control of, 483-485
chromosome movements, 554-601
description of, 554-556

Cell fusion, 1314-1315

Cell hybridization, 666, 667-670
fusion of HeLa cells and erythrocytes, 667
and virus infection, 740

Cell inclusions, 212-214
crystalline inclusions, 212
microtubule structures, 212-214
storage compounds, 204-206

Cell membrane, 1263-1265
see also Membranes
in cancer cells, 700-701
configuration, 1264
encytosis, 1264
excitation of, 1264
function of, 1263-1264
morphological features, 1263
in muscles, 1265
and reactivation of the nucleus, 670
relationship to glycocalyx, 1273-1274

Cell surface
components of, *1263-1288*
configurations, *1263-1288*
enzymatic activities, 1278
folds, 1272
geometrical configurations, *1268-1273*
movements, *1295-1319*
recombinations, *1295-1319*

Cell volume, regulation of, 1356

Cell wall, 1264
in bacteria, 153-160
chemical complex of, 154-159
composition of the cell membrane, 162-164
in Enterobacteriaceae, 157
defective forms, 160-170
Gram negative, 157-159
Gram positive, 157, 162
L forms, 164-168
osmotic pressure, 160-161, 170
outermost layers, 153-154
production of, 181-182

Centrioles, 202, 567
see also Kinetosomes
atypical, 1207-1214
cartwheel structure, 1202-1203

chemical dissection of, 1215
composition of, 1214
cytochemical methods, 1215
dense lamellae in, 1213
DNA detection in, 1215-1216
fibrils in, 1203
history of, 1200
of interphase cells, 1205
kinetosome transition, 1207
life cycle, 1212-1213
in metaphase cells, 1205
and microtubules, 1205
modal pattern of replication, 1205-1207
multiple centriole production, 1209-1210
de novo formation of, 1214
and nuclear envelope, 854
occurrence in pairs, 1205-1206
reaction on fixatives, 1215
replication of, *1200-1218*
replication of atypical, 1208-1209
self-replication, 1201
short and long, 1212
striation patterns, 1204-1205
synthesis of polypeptides, 1216
synthesis of proteins, 1216
ultrastructure of, 1201-1205
wall matrix, 1203-1204
Centromere, 390-391
recognition, 64
Ceratium, 1238
Ceratium tripos, **1226**, **1235**
CF_o, 931-932
Chaos chaos, 876
Chemoreceptors, 1234
Chiasmata, *337-352*
autoradiographic demonstration, 341-342
control of, 339
DNA inhibitors, 343
DNA synthesis, 342, 532-533
environmental modification, 342-344
formation of, 340
forming at meiosis, 534
frequency, 339
gene conversion, 347-348
genetic modification, 344-345
and heat, 534
hybrid DNA hypothesis, 348-350
infrared radiation, 343
ionising radiation, 343
localisation, 340
the molecular basis of, *347-352*
native interference, 348
nutritional factors, 344
polarized conversion, 348
positive interference, 338, 339
post meiotic segregation, 348
RNA inhibitors, 343
temperature effects, 342-343, 346, 534
terminalisation, 340
time of formation, 345-347
torsion hypothesis, 347
zygotene pairing, 534-535
Chimaeras
distribution of cells, 647
double fertilization, 651-652
female progeny, 646
hermaphrodites, 645-646
human, 650-652
human hermaphrodites, 650
Chimaerism, 645
coat colour patterns, 647-650
in eyes, 648
in neural crest, 648, 649
in retinas, 648
Chironomus, 260, 501, 509, 511, 515, 516, 865, 868
Chironomus tentans, 300, **510**, 512, 514, 516
Chironomus thummi, 502, 503, 509
Chitinase, 1336
Chlamydomonas, 343, 1003, 1025-1028, 1062, 1216, 1238, 1248
Chlamydomonas reinhardi, 343, **1062**
Chloramphenicol, 1019-1020, 1093
Chlorella, 1026, 1027
Chlorobium, 185
Chlorophyceae, 1072
Chlorophylls, 1054-1057
see also Chloroplasts
Molisch's reaction, 1054
Chloroplast
absence of 5-methylcytosine, 1026-1027
asymmetric membranes, 1051
autonomy of, 950
autoradiography for nucleic acids, 1062
biogenesis of, 965-966, *1022-1046*
from blebs, 1027-1028
chlorophylls, 1054-1057
cytochemical methods for nucleic acids, 1061-1062
cytochemistry of, 1048-1076
DNA, *944-971*, 1027, *1062-1066*
DNA of plastids, 1065-1066

DNA, presence of, 1027
DNA, renaturation of, 1027
DNA, shape of, 1027
DNA, weight of, 1027
endosymbiont, 1071
enzyme treatments, 1052
episome of the cell, 1071
evolutionary origin of, 964-965
fine filaments in, 1003
genetics of, 963-964, 1023-1026, 1070-1072
grana, 1040
grana lamellae, 1048
grana lamellae, structure of, 1052
Hill reaction, 1056
information content of, 963-964
intergrana lamellae, 1048
intergrana lamellae, structure of, 1050
loss of green pigments, 1025
lamellar structures, 1048-1050
and mitochondria, 1022-1023
Molisch's reaction on chlorophylls, 1054
multi enzyme complex, 1051
nuclear control, 1023-1025
nucleic acids, 1026-1031, 1061-1072
nucleic acids, ultrastructure studies, 1062-1070
particulate structures, 1050-1052
photoreduction, 1054
photoreduction, and membranes, 1056, 1057
photosynthetic unit, 1051
photosynthetic unit, discussion on, 1053
phycobiliproteins, 1057-1061
phycobiliproteins, isolation of, 1059-1061
phycobiliproteins, localisation of, 1057-1059
pigment molecules, 1054-1061
plastid anomalies, 963
polysomal structures in, 955
quantasome-like particles, 1056
reduction of tetrazolium salts, 1054
reduction of tetrazolium salts in isolated lamellae, 1056
replication of, 957
ribosomes in, 953-957, 1028-1030, 1066-1069, 1085
ribosomes, cytoplasmic and chloroplast ribosome differences, 1069
RNA, 953-957, *944-971*, 1030-1031, 1066-1070
and sorting out, 1024
ultrastructure of, *1048-1076*
UV mutations, 963
variegation, 1024
Chloropseudomonas, 185
Chondrioids, 181
Chondrococcus columnaris, 214
Chortophaga viridifasciata, 465, 851
Chromatid, 388, 389, *479-483*, 501
Chromatin
activation, 670, 676
activation reaction, 657
active, 222, 225, 226
calcium in, 227
condensation, 633-664, 658
derepressor in active, 242
fibers, 232-235, 362, 363-365, 372
fibers, 30 Å, 237
fibers, DNA histone complex in, 365
fibers and metal binding buffers, 232-235
fibers, method for observation, 231, 235
fibers, shape of, 363, 364
fibers, substructure, 365-366
fibrils, structure of 100 Å, 235-237
hetero- and euchromatin, *see* Heterochromatin and Euchromatin
histones in active, 242
inactive chromatin, 222, 223, 225
interchromatin, 242
interchromatin area in cancer cells, 690
isolation of, 253-256
ligands in, 262-264
localization of, 375-376
localization of active, 242
magnesium in, 227
molecular complexes in active, 239-242
native, 223
perichromatin granules, 690
separation of active and inactive, 242
sex chromatin
absence of, 760
clinical significance, 762-763
DNA content, 758-759
during cell cycle, 759
during replication, 760
frequency of, 759-760
increase in, 759
late labelling, 762, 763-765
in man, 756-763
morphology of 757-759
single active X hypothesis, 763-765
size of, 757
structure of inactive, 228-239
structure in interphase, 362-366
structure in spermatids, 366-378
thickness of, 232

ultrastructure of, 361-380
Chromatin reticulum, 385, 386, 395
Chromatium okenii, 183
Chromatolysis, 1119
Chromatophores, 183
Chromocenters, 282-287
Chromomeres, 504, 509
time of DNA replication in, 509
Chromomeric regions, 504
Chromonemata, 388
Chromophil, 1119-1120
Chromosome
aberrations
and cancer, 720-721
in normal cells, 717-720
abnormalities, 717-731, 805-834
see also Autosomal abnormalities
47 XX or XY, 13+ (*see* Patau's syndrome), 813-815
47 XX or XY, 18+ (*see* Edward's syndrome), 810-813
47 XX or XY, G+ (*see* Down's syndrome), 805-810
virus induced, 733-740
virus multiplication, 744
in bacteria, *127-145*, 151
acidic proteins, 504-505
anaphase bridges, 718
arrangement of molecular components, 228-243
B chromosomes, 721
5B chromosome in wheat, 334
bineme chromosome, 481-482
biochemical activities at prophase, *541-552*
biochemical activity in interphase, 501-519
break and arginine, 744, 776
break, isolocus, 733-738, 742
break and lysosomes, 743
break, single, 733-738, 742
in cancer cells, 692-693
change, mechanism induced by virus, 740-746
chemical components, 502-505
chromatids in, 418
cores in, 413
doubleness of the lateral strands, 422
electrical surface, 329
euchromatin, fusion of, 330
fibres and chromosome movement, 573
fibrils, arranged, 431
folding, 64
fragmentation of, 733
function of, 222
heterochromatin, fusion of, 330
homologous, 329-330
human, 754-756
human, identification of, 754-756
leptotene threads, 416
metal ions in, 227
molecular components of, 222, 228
molecular organization of, 221-250
morphology of bacterial, 132-133
mosaicism, 759
movements
causes of, 573-575
during cell division, 554-601
discussion of, 594-597
energy supply, 569-572
force for, 569
multineme and unineme model, 243
multistranded, 481-482
number, optimum, 721
pairing, *326-337*
asynapsis, 331, 332, 337, 343
desynapsis, 332, 337
DNA synthesis, 525-528
environmental modification, 331
functions of, 330-331
genetic modification, 332-334
interphase pairing, 328
meiotic pairing, 328
model of, 536-538
molecular basis of, 334-337
non-homologous association, 330
primary pairing, 327-329
protein synthesis, 528-531
RNA synthesis, 531-532
secondary association, 329-330
somatic pairing, 327-328
synaptic centre, 336-337, 340
transvection effect, 331
patterns in carcinogenesis, 723-726
Philadelphia, 717, 722
polytene, 223, *501-519*
demonstration of DNA in, 502
histidine incorporation, 514
pulverization, 733, 740
replication, asynchrony in man, 294
rule of, 288-291
sex chromosome abnormalities, *753-803*
sex chromosome during meiotic prophase, 428-429
effect on stature in man, 787

females with multiple X chromosomes in man, 783-784
fine structure of, 416-427
origin of, 773-780
splitting, 479-483
stability, 720
structural continuity, 242-243
structural mapping of, 113-115
structure of, 335-336, 382-395, 502-505
structure during leptotene stage, 416-419
structure of meiotic chromosomes at division, 427-428
structure, model of, 536-538
structure in synaptene–pachytene stages, 419-427
synapsis, 419-420
synaptic ribbons, 419-420, 422
model of synaptonemal complex, 424-426
synaptonemal-like structures, 429-430
telocentric, 723
terminology of synaptonemal complex, 420-421
ultrastructure at meiosis, 413-434
unineme chromosomes, 481-482
viruses, *92-125*, *733-750*
methods to visualize, 95-97
replication of, 109-111
X chromosome
heterochromatin, 252, 278, 282-288
'hot X', 760
late labelling of, 762, 763-765
late replication of, 761
and oestrogen control, 767
origin of abnormalities in man, 785
ring, 295
46 XX males in man, 780
47 XYY males in man, 781-782
48 XXXY males in man, 781
48 XXYY males in man, 781-782
49 XXXY males in man, 781
Y chromosome
females with multiple X chromosomes in man, 783-784
females with one X chromosome, 783
organization of, 241
origin of abnormalities in man, 786
zipping process, 419
Chromulina pussilla, 876
Cilia
arm proteins, 1248
arms, 1221
ATPase, 1249
axoneme structure, 1221-1223
basal bodies, 1223-1226
beat of, 1245
bending, unilateral, 1246
biochemistry of, 1244-1258
components, 1221
compound, 1228
ctenophores, 1228
definition of, 1220
diaplectic rows, 1237
disappearing of, 1238
dynein, 1250-1251
fibril protein, central, 1252
fibril protein, outer, 1251-1252
fibrils, tubular, 1247-1248
filaments, secondary, 1222
filaments, subunit of, 1222
flexure at the base, 1247
forming of, 1238
frequency of oscillation, 1256
genetic control, 1237
history of, 1220
lateral line organ, 1270
macrocilia, 1228-1229
matrix, 1222
membrane, 1223
membranella, 1228
metachronism, 1257
movements, 1244-1247
and active processes, 1252-1258
coordinated 1257
orthoplectic rows
8 + 1 pattern, 1236
phylogenetic aspects, 1236-1237
physiology, 1244-1258
propagation, mechanism of, 1255-1256
proteins of, 1249-1250
rootlets, 1226
sensory functions, 1268-1271
sensory hairs, 1234
sensory hairs, nematode, 1236
sheat of, 1222
silverline system, 1227
size of, 1220-1221
sliding of fibrils, 1252-1255
structure at the time of the effective stroke, 1254-1255
subfiber A, 1222
timing of the bend, 1256
ultrastructure of, *1220-1242*

Cisternae
  endoplasmic reticulum of, 1103
  Golgi apparatus of, 1132
Cistrons
  rRNA, 622
    coding of, 609
    polycistrons, 609
    properties of, 622
  ribosomal, in heterochromatin, 305-315
Clostridia, 181, 206, 209
Clostridium perfringens, 30
Clostridium tetani, 160
Clupea pallasii, 463
Cnesterodon decenmaculatus, 413
Cnidocils, 1236
Coding of dipeptides, 72
C_0t, 26-28, 33, 38, 41, 43
  definition of, 23
Codonosiga botrytis, 1245
Codons, 71, 72
  terminating, 1093
Coliphage ΦX 174, 4, 6
Collemboles, **511**
Colymbetes, 309, 313
Conidia, 150
Conjugation, 151
  in bacteria, 132, 135, 136
Coptoterix gayi, **417**, 423, 424
Core–cortex interface, 615
Cortex
RNP fibers, 614-615
Crepis capillaris, 481
Cricetulus griseus, 286, 288, 762
Cri du chat syndrome, 818-819, 830
Cristae
  angular indentations, 893
  lamellar, 891
  organization of, 877, 891-895
  and starvation, 894-895
  tubular, 891
Criterion, definition of, 22
Crossing over, *337-352*
  see also Chiasmata
  autoradiographic demonstration, 341
  copy-choice model, 346, 347
  description of, 521
  environmental modifications, 342-344
  genetic modification, 344-345
  mechanism of, 521-538
  molecular base of, 347-352
  the time of formation, 345-347
Cryptobia, 977
Cryptorchidism, 781, 1237
Cyanidium caldarium, 1057
Cyanophyceae, 1057, 1062, 1071
Cycloheximide, 529, 533
Cyprinus carpio, 1363
Cysts, 150
Cytochrome C, amino acid sequence of, 930-931
Cytogenetics, developments in human, 753-754
Cytolysomes, 1165
Cytoplasm in bacteria, 203-204
  organisation of, 203-204
Cytosegresomes, 1165
Cytosis, 1391

Danielli–Davson model, 1404-1407
Dasyneura crataegi, 331
Datura, 825
Decarboxylation, control of 2-keto glutarate production, 1360-1361
Deletions, 778
  long arm, in D chromosome of man, 820
  long arm, chromosome 18 in man, 821
  presumptive, 815-825
  short arm, chromosome 4 in man, 817
  short arm, chromosome 18 in man, 820-821
Denaturation, 223
Denver classification, 754-756
Deoxyadenosine, 414, 742, 743
Deoxyribonucleoprotein, *see* DNP
Derepressor, 227, 242, 266-267
  in euchromatin and heterochromatin, 266
  nuclear SRNA as, 267
Desmosomes, *1278-1287*
  in cancer cells, 701-703
  classification of, 1279-1282
  hydraulic seal, 1285-1286
  junctional complexes, 1285-1286
  mechanical tensions, 1284
  physiological properties, 1286
  properties of, 1284
  septate, 1283, 1286
  shape of, 1279
  syncytial, 1283, 1286-1287
  terminal web in, 1285
  tonofilaments, 1283-1284
  zonal, 1279, 1284
Developmental regulation, *641-655*
Dictyosome, 1132
  enzymes of, 1137
  morphology of saccules, 1133

polysaccharides in, 1137, 1139
Didinium nasutum, **1202**
Differentiation
duration of the S-period, 477-478
in early embryos, 641-644
embryo fusion, *644-652*
'enclosure' hypothesis, 644
histone synthesis, 490-491
meiotic cells, *521-538*
permeability and, 1348
segregation of cytoplasmic material, 643
Diffusion, 1339
Digitonin, 930
Diloboderus abderus, 424
Dimethylnitrosamine, 704
2,4-Dinitrophenol, 1323, 1324, 1331
Dinoflagellates, 199-202
Diploid numbers, constant, 719
Diptera, 543
Discoglossus, 1220
Dissociation, 23
definition of, 22
Divergence
definition of, 22
of DNA, 62
DNA, 223-225
DNase, 504
of *Acheta*, 305-315
base composition of various groups of organisms, 7-9
body, 301-310
of *Acheta*, 305, 309-310
and nucleoli, 301-302
and puffs, 312
ribosomal cistrons, 308-309
RNA region of, 315-316
synaptonemal complexes, 316-318
size of, 303
ultrastructure analysis, 313-316
calf thymus, 27-**28**, 33
centrioles, 1215-1216
chemical analyses, 4, 5
chloroplast, 15-17, 40, *944-971*, *1022-1046*, *1062-1066*
genetic function, 963-964
information content, 963-964
shape of, 949
circular, 97-104, 224
'daisy chains', 224
denaturation, 23, 24, 93, 104, 223, 228
densitometer tracing of rodent DNA, **59**, **61**
double stranded, 223
doubling, autoradiographic experiments, 474
doubling, during mitosis, 473
duplexes, 10-12, 53-58
episomal, 985
euchromatin and heterochromatin, 256-262
amount of, 280
evolution of, 31, 46-50
mechanisms for increase, 5-7
extranuclear, 15-17, 40
fibrils, 503
folding in bacteria, 198
frequency spectrogram of, 41
genomes, content of, 5-7
heterologous, 55-58
histones, 663
homopolypeptides, 228-229
hybrid DNA hypothesis, 348-350
intranucleolar, 402
kinetoplast, 17, 975
kinetosomes, 1215-1216
'linkers', 227
in mitochondria, *905-906*, *944-971*, *973-1022*
autoradiographic studies, 1007
cytochemistry of, 1002-1008
'Dachs Hund' configuration, 951
denaturation of, 951-952
genetic function, 958
information content, 958-963
intercalation, 952
molecular studies, 1008-1016
multimers, circular, 953
ribosomal proteins, 962-963
shape of, 949, 985, 1010-1012
weight of, 945-949
of the mouse, *53-66*
non repetitive, 28-31, 41, 53-66
nucleolar, 606-607
nucleus, arrangement in, 374-377
physical properties, 223
plastids, 1065-1066
polyamines, 228-229
polymerase, 69-71, 94, 227, 445, 484, 524
properties, alteration, 230
proteins, enzymatic modifications, 676-677
puffs, despiralization in, 512
rate of production, 45
reassociation, 23, 24, 41, 42, 56-60
relationship of various groups, 7-9
renaturability in organelle DNA, 950
repetitious, occurrence of, 30-31

repetitive, 28-31, 41, 53-66
replication, 44-46, 64-65, 223, *277-325*, 479-483
asynchrony, 478-479
in chromocenters, 282-287
in heterochromatin, *277-325*
model for bineme choromosomes, 481-482
model, semiconservative, 479
model for unineme chromosomes, 481-482
number of replicating units, 481
in polytene chromosomes, 505-506
proteins, nuclear, 662
reorganization bands, 660
topography in polytene chromosomes, 506-509
variations in time, 287-288, 294-295
RNA synthesis, 256, 257
saltatory replication, 42-44
satellite, 9-10, *53-66*, 307, 314, 978
origin of, 62-63
secondary structure, 260-261
segregation 479-483
single strand interaction, 56-58
size in the virion, 104
strand separation, 23-24, 53, 54
strand separation model, 268-270
structural continuity, 502
subdivision of, 503
synthesis, *505-510*, 640
and chiasmata, 342, 532-533
chromosome change, virus induced, 742
chromosomes, in human meiotic, 300-301
chromosome pairing, 527-528
initiation of, 483-484, 640
late ending and late beginning, 289-291
meiosis, cytological differences, 527
meiotic prophase, 525-526
mitosis, 473-485
nuclear activation, 678
precursors, 484
regulation of, 483-485
RNA synthesis, 487-488
in S-phase, 257
in yeast, 477
template, 69, 225
tertiary structure, 261-262
tumor viruses, 9
units, length of, 503-504
viral replication, 94
viral, size and shape, 97-104
viruses, *68-87*, 705, 742, 743
DNH (DNA–histone complex), 228-232
B structure of the double helix, 231
hexagonal packing of, 231
DNP (deoxyribonucleoprotein)
changes and nuclear activation, 675-676
changes in, 671-672
changes in binding of ions, 676
complexes of, 663
cytochemical properties, *657-684*
nuclear function, *657-684*
Doublet analysis, 69-71, 73
Doublet frequencies
amino acid frequencies, 71-73
human DNA, 74-76
random expectation, 71
Doublet pattern, 73-74
host and virus, 74-76
method of comparison, 78-79
stability of, 76-78
Down's syndrome, 805-810, 830
dermatoglyphic features of, 808
and leukemia, 808
and viral infections, 810
DPN pyrophosphorylase, 227
Drosophila, 223, 225, 227, 241, 243, 252, 263, 279, 281, 340, 343, 350, 351, 413, 428, 465, 507, 511, 513, 726, 740, 765, 792, 1221, 1238
Drosophila funebris, 10-11
Drosophila hydei, 331, 505, **507**, 509, **514**, 516, 549, 842
Drosophila melanogaster, 10-11, 13, 15, 39, 40, 282, 311, 312, 331, 343, 344, 347, 501, 503, 505, 506, 509, 513, 622, 623
Drosophila neohydei, 549
Drosophila simulans, 10-11
Drosophila virilis, 506, 514
Dye binding, 659
Dynein, 1250-1251
Dysgenesis, 790
Dyskinetoplastic cultures, 977, 978
Dytiscus, 301, 309, 313

Eccytosis, 1295, *1298-1304*
cell division, 1303-1304
cell plate, 1304
liberation of the nucleus, 1303
liberation of blood platelets, 1303
liberation of viruses, 1300-1303
secretion granules, 1298
secretion by mammary gland cells, 1300
secretion by pancreatic acinar cells, 1298-1300
sperm cell, 1304

Ecdyson, 516
Echinus esculentus, 596
EDTA, 157, 161
Edwards' syndrome, 810-813, 830
  aneuploids, 813
  dermatoglyphic features, 813
Efflux, 1322
Electronmicroscope, techniques for, 415-416
Electroreceptors, 1236
Elodea, 1062
Embryo fusion, *644-652*
EMC virus, 74,79-83
Endocytosis (encytosis), 1164, 1295, *1304-1316*, *1374-1400*
  cell fusion, 1314-1316
  cell surface
    behavior of, 1387-1388
    specific binding, 1305
  coarse particle substance, 1377
  definition of, 1374
  difference between induced and permanent, 1384-1385
  duration of, 1379
  fine particle substance, 1377
  formation of endosomes, 1383
  induction, 1378-1384, 1393
  membrane flow, 1305-1306
  methods for studying, 1375-1378
  morphology of induced, 1378
  mucoid layer, binding to, 1382-1383
  mucoid layer, significance, 1382-1383
  permanent, *1384-1391*
    amoeboid movement and, 1385-1387
    localization of, 1384-1385
    kinetics of, 1384-1385
    rate of uptake, 1385
  *p*H, 1379, 1382
  phase contrast microscopy, 1375
  quantitative investigations, 1381-1382
  selectivity of, 1304
  solutions, electron-optically amorphous, 1377
  statistical reproducibility, 1376
  substance uptake, 1393
  transport in bulk, 1316
  uptake of viruses, 1313-1315
  vesiculation, 1306
  virus and enzymes, 1314-1315
  volume increase, 1381-1382
Endosomes, 1375, 1393-1394
  dilatation, 1390
  formation in endocytosis, 1383
  intracellular fate, 1390-1391
  primary, 1390
Endometrium, 718-719
Endoplasmic reticulum, 1102-1129
  absorptive activities, 1118
  accumulation of droplets, 1121-1122
  and cell injury, 1121-1123
  cisternae of, 1103
  degranulation, 1121
  dilatation, 1121
  drug detoxication, 1118-1119
  enwrapping of cytoplasmic organelles, 1122
  enzyme induction, 1122
  fluid filled system, 1103
  fragmentation, 1121
  and Golgi apparatus, 1145-1148
  median raphe, 1110
  microsomal fraction, 1111-1116
  modulations in cell function, 1121-1123
  molecular arrangement, 1123
  plasticity, 1124-1125
  pleomorphism, 1109
  rough surfaced, 1102-1117
  secretion, determination of, 1124
  secretory activities, 1118
  smooth surfaced, 1117-1119
  specializations of, 1119-1121
  tubular system, 1117
  unit membrane, 1116-1117
  vesiculation, 1121
Endospore, 150
  formation of, 206-209
Entamoeba blattae, 849
Entamoeba invadens, **1086**
Entosiphon sulcatum, **1231**
Enzymes
  classification of, 444-445
  enzymatic equipment at meiosis, 524-525
  isolation of, 444
  nuclear enzymes, 443-447
Episomes, 135, 271
  replication, 138-141
Equine rhinopneumonitis, 80-83
Ergastoplasm in cancer cells, 695-696
Eriocheir, 1358
Eriocheir sinensis, 1356, 1363, 1365, 1366
Escherichia coli, 13, 14, 26, 28, 30, 76, 98-104, 128, 129, **132**, 133, **134**, 137, 138, 141, 143, 155-156, 157, **159**, 161, 166, 175, **176**, 177, 182, 183, **190**, 198, 202-204, 206, 212, 349, 479, 903, 955, 989, 1012, 1082-1087, 1093

cell wall, 155-157, **159**, 161
membranes of, 175, **176**, 177, 182, 183
Etiology, 723
Eubacteriales, 150
Euchromatic regions, 385-386
Euchromatin, 222, 225, 252
see also Heterochromatin
as assay system, 264-268
biochemistry and biophysics: *251-276*
difference with heterochromatin, 253-255, 257-260, 262, 265, 278
fusion of chromosomes, 530
histones in, 262-264
interaction with heterochromatin, 268-271
isolation of, 253-256
polyanion–polycation complexes, 264, 268
size of the replicons, 294-300
and template activity, 262
transcription, 257
Euglena, 950, 955, 1025-1028, 1030, 1063, 1065, 1068-1070, 1072
Euglena gracilis, 945
Euoenothera, 1024, 1025
Eupagurus, 225
Euplotes, 660, 663
Euplotes eurystomus, 488, 490
Evolution of base sequence, *4-20*
Evolution of viruses, 83-85
Exosporium, 207
Exocytosis, 1374
Extinction, 658

Feulgen reaction, 658
Fibrils, peripheral, in cell envelope, 186
Fimbriae, *see* Pili
Flagella, 185-196
see also Cilia
ATPase, 1249
basal organelles, 189
base of, 187
beat of, 1244-1245
biochemistry of, 1244-1258
collar, 187
composition of, 187
contractility, 186, 189
definition of, 1220
of flatworm spermatozoa, 1230
flimmer, 1229-1230
hairy, 1223
lophotrichous, 186
molecular organisation, 1247-1252
movements of, 1244-1247
movements, active processes of, 1252-1258
9+0 pattern, 1231-1232
9+1 pattern, 1230-1231
9+7 pattern, 1232-1233
9+9 pattern, 1232-1233
peritrichous, 186
physiology of, *1244-1258*
planar undulations, 1245-1246
protozoan, 1229
Sciara type, 1233
sinusoidal shape, 186
sperm tails, 1229
ultrastructure of, *1220-1242*
undulation, 1244-1245
Flagellin, 187
5′-Fluorodeoxyuridine (FudR), 742, 743
Flimmer, 1229
Forficula, 419
Frenster model for strand separation, 268-270
Fritillaria lanceolata, 281
FSH, 767
F sex factor, 135, 139-141

G_1 period, 385, 474
G_2 period, 385, 474
constancy of duration, 476
in meiotic cells, 535-536
Galleria mellonella, 878
Gallionella ferruginea, 154
Gamma cytomembrane, 1133
Gecarcinus lateralis, 10
Gene
amplification in heterochromatin, *301-325*
major control, 332, 344
regulation during nuclear activation, 675-679
Gene activity
oocyte regulators, 550
Genes, conservative and nonconservative, 12
cytochrome C, 12
hemoglobin, 12
ribosomal R.N.A. genes, 12-15
Genes in evolution, 49, 50
size, definition of, 23
Genetic code, overall use of, 73-74
Genetic markers, outside the chromosome, 133
Genome, genetic composition in bacteria, 133-135
growth, 44, 45
loss, 45
Genophore, 151, 198, 202, 222

Glaucocystis nostochinearum, 1057, **1058-1060**, **1063**
Glucose-6-phosphatase, 446, 860, 954, 1116
Glucose-6-phosphate dehydrogenase, 486, 785, 808
Glutamate dehydrogenase, 903, 1362
  in euryhaline species, 1366
  as polymer, 1362
  quantitative study of, 1363
Glutamate synthesis, 1361-1367
  and oxygen, 1365
3-Glycerophosphate dehydrogenase, 1359
Glycocalyx, 1265-1266, 1273-1278
  attached, 1273-1274
  basal laminae, 1275-1276
  cell surface, 1273-1274
  classification of, 1266
  components of, 1265-1268
  extraneous coat, 1273
  filtering action, 1277-1278
  inorganic crystals, 1265
  intercellular matrices, 1275
  mechanical functions, 1274-1277
  mucous coats, 1276-1277
  regulatory properties, 1268
  unattached, 1274
  vertebrate red cell, 1273
Glycogen in the nucleus of cancer cells, 700
Glycolytic enzymes in nucleus, 445
Glyoxylate reductase, 1359-1360
Glyoxysomes, 1180-1195
  enzymes in, 1180
Golgi apparatus, *1131-1155*
  absence of, 1133
  acrosome production, 1139
  in cancer cells, 696-697
  cell walls, forming of, 1139, 1143
  chemical analysis, 1137-1138
  chemical composition, 1136-1138
  cisternae, 1132
  complex, 1133
  component, 1133
  cytochemical methods, 1136-1137
  dictyosomes, 1132
    see also Dictyosomes
  endoplasmic reticulum, 1145-1148
  history of, 1131-1132
  homology with mesosomes, 181-182
  origin of, 1148-1149
  physiology of, 1138-1148
  secretion, morphology of granules, 1138-1142
  secretion, forming of muco- or glycoproteins, 1145
  secretion, packing of secretory products, 1139
  sulfation of sugars, 1143
  summary of the role of, 1149
  synthesis of polysaccharides, 1142-1143
  transfer of proteins, 1143
  transition elements, 1146
  ultrastructure of, *1132-1136*
  value of the observations, 1134-1136
  vesicles of, 1133
  zymogen granules, 1139
Gram positive and negative species, 150, 157-159, 162, 177
Gregarinia melanopli, 848
Gryllidae, 429
Gryllus argentinus, 413, 418, **420**, **423**, 428-431
GTP-AMP phosphotransferase, 920-921
Gymnoplast, 162-164

H_1 virus, 79-83
Habrobracon, 228
Haemonchus contortus, **1235**
Halobacteria, 150, 160
Halobacterium halobium, 157, 160
Hare lip, 814
Harnden law, 282, 761
Helical structure, 389
Helical structure of DNA, 23, 92
Helix aspera, 465
Hemicentrotus pulcherrimus, 595
Herpes simplex, 74, 79-84, 100, 692, 705, 737
Heterochromatin, 222, 225
  as assay system, 264-268
  and autoradiographics, 281
  of autosomes in man, 294
  biochemistry and biophysics, 251
  cytological picture of, 280-281
  DNA, 256-262
  DNA replication and, *277-325*
  differences with euchromatin, 253-255, 257-260, 262, 265, 278
  fusion of chromosomes, 330
  histones in, 262-264
  history of, 252
  interaction with euchromatin, 268-271
  isolation of, 253-256
  in man, 282-287
  polytene chromosomes, 507
  regions, 385-386, 395
  replication of, 281

size of the replicons, 294-300
ribosomal cistrons in, 305-315
as a state, 280, 313
template activity, 262
transcription, 256-257
transition of, 272-273
Heterochromatinization, 290
Heteropachylloidelus robustus, 413
Heteropycnosis, negative, 280
Histoincompatibility, 720
Histones, 225-226, 262-264, 448-453, 504, 663
arginine rich, 457-461
chromatographic extraction, 452
conformation of, 226
conversion to protamines, 465
cytochemical stains, 465
definition of, 448
in DNA, 228-230
distribution in, 504
DNA body, 303
electrophoresis, 453
in eu- and heterochromatin, 262-264
fractionation of, 450-453
functions of, 466
heterogeneity, 461-463
histone-protamine transition, 666
lysine rich, 450, 453-557
metabolism, 464-466
metal ions, 228
monomers of, 459
nomenclature, 450
preparation of, 448-450
primary structure of, 464
repressor, 263-264, 268
specificity, 461-463
synthesis, 487-491
biochemical analysis, 489
cellular site, 491
and DNA synthesis, 489
HFr cell, 131, 133, 139
Higher organism, definition of, 23
Histone lack, 202
Homarus, 1358
Homarus vulgaris, 1362
Honeycomb layer, 848
Hordeum vulgare, 281
Hyalodiscus simplex, 1384
Hyalophysa, 1211
Hyalophysa chattoni, 1211
Hyalosphenia papilio, 849
Hydroides, 1315
Hydrogen ions, control of, 1356-1367
Hydroxy apatite, 28, 29, 31, 55, 60
Hyperchromicity, 34, 35
Hypernephromas, 693
Hyphae, 150

'Inactive X' hypothesis, 648-649
Influenza myxovirus, 1300-1303
Influenza virus, 104, 107
Influx, 1322
Initiation regions, 63
Initiator, 138
Ising effect, 720
Isocitrate dehydrogenase isozymes, 647
Isolabeling, 482-483
Insulin, 1354
Intracytosis, 1374
Interchromatin granules in cancer cells, 690-691
Ionic composition, influence of enzymes, 1363-1364

Jacob and Brenner initiator, 138
Jacob and Brenner model, 141-142
Jacob-Monod model, 675
Jacob and Ryter model, 182-183
Juxtamembranal cytoplasm, 1309

K_0t, *see* C_0t
K^+, transport in mitochondria, 925
Keratin fibrils, in cancer cells, 702-703
α-Keto-acid dehydrogenase complex, 903
2-Ketoglutarate, 1360-1361
Kilham rat virus, 79-83
Kinetochore, 295, 556, 558, 567, 573, 582
Kinetoplast, DNA in, 975
Kinetosome
see also Centrioles
appendages, 1204, 1211
cell surface differentiation, 1210
centriole transition, 1207
DNA in, 1215-1216
multiple kinetosome production, 1210
Klinefelter's syndrome, 773, 785

Lactate dehydrogenase, 486
Lactic dehydrogenase, 445, 1357-1359
Lactobacillus plantarum, 181
λ-Bacteriophage, 97-104, 110, 111, **114**, 133, 135
Lambda virus, 347
Lampropedia, 159
Lampbrush chromosomes, 64, 227, 239-241,

388, 395, 541
DNA synthesis during prophase of meiosis, 541-542
loop matrix protein, 543
method for observation, 232
morphological differentiation along loops, 543
significance of, 542-543
Laplatacris dispar, 413, **418**
Lathyrus odoratus, 391, 405
Lecithin and oxidation of fatty acids, 937
Lecudina, 849
Leishmania conorhini, 977
Leishmania tarentolae, 977-979
Lepisma, **1108**
Leptodactylus ocelatus, 1325
Leukemia
and Down's syndrome, 808
chronic myelogenous, 717, 722
L forms in bacteria, 164-168
nucleoplasm of, 202
proteus L form, 166, **167**
Libinia, 1364
Ligands, 262-264
counter ligands, 262-264
molecules, 252
RNA synthesis, 270-271
Lilium, 337, 343, 350, 418, 525, 536
Lilium longiflorum, 484, 490
Linkers, oligopeptide, 227
Lipid granules in bacteria, 204
Listeria monocytogenes, 160
Lithodesmium, 1231
Locomotor organelles, 185-196
Locusta migratoria, **339**
Loxa, 337
Luzatti and Nicolaieff model, 237
Lycodontis afer, 1231
Lyon hypothesis, 648, 649, 762
Lysine, 169
Lysosomes, *1160-1178*
biochemical methods, 1167-1169
biochemistry of, 1160-1178
in cancer cells, 699
and chromosome breaks, 743
DNA in, 1003
and endocytosis, 1391, 1394
enzymes, 1160-1163
free activity, 1162-1163
structure linked latency, 1161
total activity, 1162-1163
function, *1160-1178*
autophagic, 1165-1166
heterophagic, 1164-1165
inadequate, 1166
heterogeneity of, 1169-1172
history of, 1160
hyaluronidase, 1161
hydrolases, 1160
addition of, 1178
identification of acid, 1167-1168
isolation of, 1168-1169
intracellular digestion, hypothesis of, 1164
localisation, cytochemical, 1172
membrane, composition of, 1162
morphology of, 1169-1175
*p*H optimum, 1160
physical properties, 1163-1164
physiological processes, role in, 1166
primary, 1164
primary, origin of, 1165
secondary, 1164
sphingomyelinase, 1160
subcellular fractions, identification of, 1172
Lysozyme, 160-162, 181, 187
Lytechinus, 546

Macrocilia, 1228-1229
Maia, 1364
Malignancy, definition of, 688
Marsilea, 1210, 1214, 1216
Marsilea strigosa, 483
Mastigonemes, 1229
Matrix
bacteria, 128
chromosomal, 388, 404
mitochondrial, 877, 901-904, 981, 988, 1016
volume changes, 928
nucleolar, 607
RNP, discharge of, 543
Mechanoreceptors, 1234
Mecynostomum auritum, **1230**
Meiosis
achiasmatic, 534-535
biochemical activities at prophase, 541-542
biochemistry of, 521-538
DNA synthesis during prophase, 541-542
differentiation of meiotic cells, 535-538
enzymatic epuipment at, 524-525
metabolic activities, 523-524
physiological description, 522-525
RNA synthesis during prophase, 542-549
time of cytological stages, 522-523

Melanoplus, 280-282, 288
Melanoplus differentialis, 278, 282, 290
Membranes
  adielectronic, 1110
  archimedean bodies, 1438
  architectural principle, 1425-1435
  asymmetrical, 1297
  bacterial, *174-196*
  carbon chains, nonpolar, 1405-1406
  carrier transfer, 1335
  catalan bodies, 1438
  chemical pathways, 183, 203
  cytoplasmic, 175-178, 203
  Danielli–Davson model, 1404-1407
    difference with unit model, 1404-1405
  eccytosis, membrane fusion in, 1298-1300
  electrical resistance of lipid bilayers, 1425
  enclosure of space, 1436
  encytosis, flow in, 1305-1306
  encytosis, membrane fusion in, 1304
  endocytic invaginations, 1384
  exchange diffusion, 1335
  Eylar, hypothesis of, 1336
  Finean, diagram of, 1419-1420
  fusions, 1295-1298
  fusions, hypothesis for, 1296-1298
  globular fine structure, 1431-1432
  hydrogen ions, controlling of, *1356-1367*
  intracellular, 178-185
  intraperiod line, 1408-1410
  leaflet structure, bimolecular, 885-886
  limits of, 1436-1437
  lipid
    bilayer membrane, 1423-1425
    hexagonal state of, 1421-1422
    lipid–water system, 1420-1423
    molecules, 1405-1406
    without lipids, 1411-1414
  macromolecules, transfer of, 1335-1336
  mesaxon, 1407
  micellar phase transformation, 1432-1434
  mitochondrial
    composition of, 883-886
    organization of, 935-936
    transport in, 924-932
  molecular configurations, 1414-1417
  molecular structure of, *1404-1443*
  monomolecular films, 1296
  mucopolysaccharides in, 1431-1432
  myelin, formation of nerve myelin, 1408
  myelin sheath, major dense line, 1410
  nuclear
    see also Nuclear envelope
    inner nuclear membrane, 838, 839
    outer nuclear membrane, 838, 839
  permeability of, 1321, *1347-1372*
    see also Permeability
  permeation, mechanisms of, 1334
  photoreduction in chloroplasts, 1056-1057
  platonic bodies, 1437-1440
  pool, 850
  proteins
    structural proteins, 1427
    viral proteins, and Crick and Watson, 1437
  of pseudopodia, 1384
  recombinations, 1295-1298
  S, 180
  Schmidt diagram, 1419
  Schwann cells, 1407
  synaptic junction, 1429-1432
  tight junction, 1408
  transport of, 1391-1392
  unit membrane, 1116-1117, 1263
    concept of, 1404-1407
    origin of concept, *1407-1425*
    structure of, 1406
Membranella, 1228
Mercaptoethanol, 1206
Mesaxon, 1407
Mesocricetus auratus, 286, 288
Mesosomes, 178-182, 203, 214
  function of, 182-183
  in spore formation, 207
Metachronism in cilia, 1257
Metal ions, divalent, 660
Metaphase, 388-391
Metaphase figures, frequency of, 475-476
Mg^{2+}
  cilia, 1250
  mitochondria, 923
  and ribosomes, 1081, 1083, 1090
  transport in mitochondria, 924-925
Microbodies, *1180-1195*
  in cancer cells, 697
  and peroxisomes, 1182-1186
Micrococcus lysodeikticus, 99, 310
Micrococcus radiodurans, 160
Microcyst, 209-212
Microfibrils in chromosomes, 389, 396
Micromonas, 1000
Micronucleoli, 397, 407
Microtubules, 390

distribution in spindles, 582-584
and spindle fibers, 580-582
Microtus agrestis, 286
Microtus oregoni, 288, 718, 762, 765, 768
Micropinocytosis, 1374
Microvilli, 1268-1271
functions of, 1269
shape of, 1269
Mintz' clonal hypothesis, 649
Mirabilis jalapa, 1024
Mitochondria,
amino acid metabolism, 938
δ-aminolevulinate synthetase, 936-937
anastomosis in intracristal space, 899
of *Ascaris lumbricoides*, 939
autonomy of, 950
biochemistry of, 915-942
biogenesis of, 965-966, *973-1022*
in cancer cells, 693-694
and carbohydrate metabolism, 936-937
carriers
non-specific energy-linked anion carriers, 926
three anion carrier system, 926
cation pump in, 925
chemical composition, 917-919
chemic-osmotic theory, 923
chloroplasts, 1022-1023
clusters, 1000
coenzyme Q, note p. 915
compartmentation, 895-897
condensed form, 901
continuity of, 973, 999-1002
cristae, 877, 891-895
cristae and fixatives, 878-879
division of, 1000
DNA, 905-906, 944-971, 981-989, 995-996
autoradiographic studies, 1007
coding for structural components, 959
cytochemistry of, 1002-1008
'Dachs Hund' configuration, 951
denaturation of, 951-952, 981
disappearance of, 986
genetic function, 958-963
information content of, 958-963
intercalation, 952
molecular studies of, 1008-1016
multimers, circular, 953
nuclear DNA, difference with, 945
oxygen, after addition, 986-987
polymerase in yeast, 988
presence of, 944
shape of DNA, 949, 985, 1010-1012
structure of, 1004-1007
synthesis, 1012-1015
synthesis and isolated mitochondria, 987-988
T_M determinations, 944
weight of, 945-949
and drugs, 932-933
enzymatic equipment, 915
enzymes, localization of, 933-935
evolutionary origin of, 964-965
fatty acids, oxidation of, 937
fatty acids, synthesis of, 937-938
fine filaments in, 1004-1005
fine filaments, component of, 1005-1007
function of, *915-942*
genetic analysis in *Neurospora*, 993-995
genetic analysis in yeast, 979-981
and gluconeogenesis, 936
glutamate dehydrogenase, 903
glycerophosphate cycle, 936
glycine metabolism, 938
haem synthesis, 936-937
hollow cylinders, arrays of, 882
inclusions in, 904-905
intracristal space, 877, 879, 895-897
Keilin and Hartree preparation, 930
α-keto-acid dehydrogenase complex, 903
leaflet structure in membranes, 885
lipid in, 917
localization of, 933-935
and lysosomes, 1014
matrix, 877, 901-904
membranes of, 1019
components of inner membrane, 881, 886-891
composition of, 883-886
and fixatives, 878-879
inner membrane, 877, 878, 881
organization of, 935-936
outer membrane, 877, 878,
metabolic changes in, 899
methods of study, 876-877
Mitchell hypothesis, 923
morphology in cancer cells, 693-694
NADPH oxidation of, 923
NADPH reoxidation of, 923
nucleic acids, 974-975
nuclear envelope, 854
orthodox form, 901
osmotic swelling, types of, 928-929

oxidative phosphorylation, 919-924
2-oxoglutarate, 903
pediculus cristae, 895
peripheral space, 877, 895-897
phosphate potential, 921
phosphorylating systems in, 917-919
polymerases, 974-975
polysomes in, 955
proteins
soluble and insoluble, 1021
structural, 959-962, 998-999, 1020-1021
protein synthesis, 992, 1018-1022
and cytochromes, 959
pyruvate dehydrogenase, 903-904
reappearance of, 986-987
replication of, 957-958
respiratory chain, 919-924
respiratory chain fragments, 930
respiratory chain preparations, 930
respiratory control, 921-922
respiratory substrates, penetration of, 925
ribosomes in, 904-905, 953-957
RNA, *944-971*, 989-992, 996-998, 1016-1018
origin of, 991
rRNA, 991, 1017
tRNA, 989-991
synthesis, 989
of *Saccharomyces*, 939
in sperm, 1002
stalked particles, 881, 886-891
consistence of, 887-891
fixatives for, 886-887
native situation, 886-887
nature of, 888-891
synthesis of citrulline, 938
transaminases, 938
transcription, 957-958
transhydrogenase in, 923-924
translation, 957-958
translocase, adenine nucleotide, 926
translocases, 927
transport of anions, 925-926
transport of divalent cations, 924-925
transport of fatty acids, 927, 937-938
transport through membranes, *924-932*
transport of monovalent cations, 925
transport of nucleotides, 926-927
of *trypanosomes*, 975-979
ubiquinone, 915, 919
ultrastructure of, *876-913*
unusual properties, 939
variability, 974
volume, active control of, 929
volume changes, 897-899, 928-930
Mitosis in cancer cells, 692-693
Mitotic apparatus (M.A.), 556-558
biochemical analyses, 584-592
components of, 590-592
differences in components, 591-592
isolated M.A. and M.A. *in vitro*, 584-590
Mixoploids and Down's syndrome, 806-808
Mixoploidy, 759
Mn^{2+}, 4
Mnemiopsis leideyi, **1227**
Molluscum contagiosum virus, 705
Mongolism, 805-810
Morphopoiesis, 94-95
Ms 2, 26
Mucopolysaccharides in the cell wall, 159
Multicistrons, 622
Multivesicular bodies in cancer cells, 697
Murein sacculus, 154-160
Muropeptide, 154-156
Mus musculus, 53-66
Mus norvegicus albinus, 413
Mutation, 62, 76-77
temperature sensitive, 138
Mycoplasma, 160, 168-170, 175, 744
lipid content in membranes, 170
osmolarity of, 170
shape of, 170
Mycoplasma aominis, 170
Mycoplasma fermentans, **169**
Mycoplasma gallisepticum, 170
Mycoplasma hominis, 133, 137
Mycoplasma laidlawii, 168, 170
Mycoplasmatales, 150, 152, 161, 168
Myeloid bodies, 1120
Mytilus edulis, 465, **1227**
Myxobacteria, 185-186, 209
Myxobacteriales, 150
Myxococcus xanthus, 206
Myzostomum, 1231

N_1 bacteriophage, 99
NAD pyrophosphorylase, 445
NADH cytochrome C reductase, 1116
Naegleria, 1214, 1216, 1238
Neanura grassei, **511**
Neottiella rutilans, 347, 414, 424
Nephrotoma suturalis, 555, **556**, 574
Nereis, 855

Nerve myelin, formation of, 1408
Neurospora, 225, 955, 989, 991-993, 997, 1008, 1017, 1022, **1267**, 1266, 1272, 1274
mitochondria, 993-999
mitochondria, transfer of, 995
mitochondrial DNA, 995
mitochondrial RNA, 996-998
RNA polymerase, 997
Neurospora crassa, 343, 351, 881, 887, 906, 945, 993, 995, 996
Neurospora mutants, deficient in cytochromes, 994
Neurospora sitophila, 945, 994-996
Neurospora tetrasperma, 994
NH_3, control of intracellular pool, 1367
Nicotiana rustica, 1063
Nissl body, 1119-1120
Nitella, 1023
Nitrobacter agilis, 183
Nitrosocystis oceanus, 183
Nitrosomonas europea, 183
Noctiluca, 849, 862
Non-histone protein, 226-227, 263-264
Notonecta, 1220
Nuclear activation,
and DNA synthesis, 678
and protein synthesis, 679
and RNA, 677
and rRNA synthesis, 678-679
Nuclear blebs, 690
Nuclear edema, 690
Nuclear envelope, *838-871*
see also Membrane
acid phosphatase, 861
annular material, 847-848
annulate lamellae, 855-857
blebs and mitochondria, 1000
bouquet formation, 853
in cancer cells, 690
and centrioles, 854
change in properties, 662
chromatin, relationships with, 853
cytoplasmic organelles, relationships with, 854-855
different pathways in, 861-865
disruption of, 850-851
dynamic character of, 852
electrophysiological properties, 859-860
endoplasmic reticulum, 854
energy dependent process, 860
enzymatic activity, 860
enzymes, 445-446
function, 850-868
function in mitosis, 850-852
glucose-6-phosphatase, 860
interchromatin regions, 853
internal dense lamella, 838, 848-850
intranuclear channel, 853
and mitochondria, 854, 865
nucleocytoplasmic exchange, 857-868
nucleoli, 854
nucleoproteins in the nucleus, 857-858
nucleoside diphosphatase, 861
passing by pores, 858-859
peroxidase and, 863
permeability of, 857-868
*p*H and, 858
pores, 839-845
see also Nuclear pores
reformation of, 851-852
reformation of pores, 852
RNA, exchanges, 861
reverse passage in, 858
selective passage of, 857-859
structure of, 838-846
thiamine phyrophosphatase, 861
Nuclear membrane
in bacteria, 132
Nuclear pore, 839
ATPase, 861
central granules, 867
diameter of, 842-843
evolution of, 852
reformation of, 852
shape of, 843-845
Nuclear protein
accumulation of, 661
cell differentiation, 664-675
cytochemical properties, 657-684
nuclear dry mass, 660-663
nuclear function, *657-684*
protein migration, 662
synthesis of, 661
Nuclease, 97, 99
Nucleic acid, *68-87*
chloroplasts, 1061-1072
doublet pattern, 68-87
primary structure, 92
protein synthesis, 641
secondary structure, 92
starvation, 280
structure, 92-97

synthesis, regulation of, 640, 641
viral weight of, 95
viruses and host, 74-76
Nucleocytoplasmic interactions, 491
Nucleohistones, 226, 229-230
molecular structure, 230
Nucleolar DNA
synthesis of, 542
Nucleolar organizer, 402, 403, 405, 407
Nucleologenesis, 406-408
Nucleolonema in cancer cells, 692
Nucleolus, 511
in cancer cells, 692
capability of protein synthesis, 629
cleavage of 45S RNA, 626
composition of, 606-607
core, 608-613
cortex, 608, 613-617
enzymes in, 607
enzyme reactions, 397-399, 403
extrachromosomal, 623-624
fibrous component, 607-613
fine structure, 607-608
formation at telophase, 404-408
granular component, 607-608, 613-617
loops, 403
organizer, 611, 621-622
prenuclear substance, 404-406
protein to RNA ratio, 611-613
protein synthesis in, 447-448
proteins in, 606, 615
ribosome production, 621-636
rRNA synthesis, 678-679
RNA metabolism, 608
RNA species, weight of, 608
RNP fibers, 614-615
split organizer, 623
staining of, 397, 398
structure and function, *606-619*
Nucleoplasm
in bacteria, 198-203
in cancer cells, 690-692
during spore formation, 202
fibre bundles in, 198-199
L forms, 202
structure of, 198
structure, at DNA replication, 198-199
Nucleoprotamines, 229
Nucleoside diphosphate kinase, 920-921
Nucleoside triphosphatase, 227, 446
Nucleotide sequence, 38-51
bacterial, 127-132
distribution of RNA and proteins, 398-402
in evolution, 48-50
rate of production, 45
repeated sequences, 47, 48
Nucleus, 690
in bacteria, 151
differentiation, 377-378
electron opaque, 373-374, 377
enzymes, 443-447
genetic composition in bacteria, 133-135
in interphase, 382, **384**, 385
in invertebrates, 372
lamellae in, 375
proteins, 439-471
protein synthesis, 447-448
quiescent, 382-385
reactivation of hen erythrocyte, 666-667
nuclear changes, 669
ribbons and sheet-like material, 372-373
structure in, 372
in vertebrates, 371-372

Ochromonas, 1016
Oenothera, 1024
Ohno's hypothesis, 770
Osmiophilic membranous body, 981
Osmotic pressure, 160-161
and cell walls, 170, 178
Ovarian dysgenesis, 762-766
Oxidative phosphorylation, 931-932
chemi-osmotic theory, 923
general scheme, 921
Mitchell hypothesis, 923
study of, 922-923
translocases, 927
2-Oxoglutarate dehydrogenase, 903

P^{32}, in doublet analysis, 69
Pachynema, developmental patterns after, 521-522
Pair, definition of, 23
Pairing sites in meiosis, 63
Palinurus vulgaris, 1362
Panorpa nuptialis, 431
Papilloma virus, human, 79-83
Papilloma virus, Shope, 79-83
Papilloviridae, 705
Paramecium, 1003, 1211, 1215, 1216
Paramecium aurelia, 15
Paratelphusa hydrodomous, 1365

Patau's syndrome, 813-815, 830
P_1 bacteriophage, 136, 139
P_2 bacteriophage, 99
P_{22} bacteriophage, 97-104
Pectinaria, 576
Pelomyxa carolinensis, 891, 893
Penicillin sensitivity, 160
Perinuclear space, 839
Periplaneta americana, 416, **417**, **421**
Permeability
  aldosterone, 1355-1356
  cellular aspects of, *1347-1372*
  and curare, 1355
  and differentiation, 1348
  in electroplaques, 1352
  in epithelial cells, 1352
  in heterotypy, concept of, 1353-1354
  hormonal effects, 1354-1356
  and insulin, 1354
  of mucosal border, 1352
  and octapeptides, 1354
  organisation of the cell membrane, 1353
  negative potential jump, 1351
  pyridine-2-aldoxime methiodide, 1355
  spatial organisation, 1352-1353
  temporo-spatial organisation, 1348-1354
  vasopressin, 1354-1355
Permeation, 1391
  and diffusion, 1334
  drag effect, 1334
  mechanism of, 1334
Peromyscus maniculatus, 56, 58, 60, 61
Peromyscus polionotus, 56, 58, 60, 61
Peroxisomes, *1180-1195*
  catalase, 1180, 1187-1188, 1192
  enzymic reactions, 1180-1182
  glyoxylate bypass, 1190-1192
  in kidney, 1189
  and microbodies, 1182-1186
  morphology of, 1182-1186
  oxygen, influence of, 1192-1193
  peroxisomal oxidases, activity of, 1187
  physical properties, 1186-1188
  physiological role, 1191-1193
  plant cells, 1190-1191
  properties of, 1181-1191
  in protozoa, 1190
  purification, 1182
  triton WR-1339 injection, 1182
  turnover, 1188-1189
PHA (phytohemagglutinin), 666
  and acridine orange binding, 674
  histone acetylation, 673
  mechanism inducing DNP changes, 674
  RNA synthesis, 673
  stimulation, 672-675
Phagosome, 1164
Phagocytosis, *1306-1313*
  see also Pinocytosis
  and bacteria, 1310-1311
  definition of, 1306
Philadelphia chromosome, 295
Philaenus spumarius, 424, 429
Photoreceptors, 1234
Phycobiliproteins, 1057-1061
Physarum, 1007, 1015, 1016
Physarum polycephalum, 15
Φ X 174, 110, 111, 114
Pieris, 891
Pili, composition of, *185-196*
Pinocytosis, 94, *1306-1313*, *1374-1400*
  see also Endocytosis
  coated vesicles, 1309
  definition of, 1306, 1374
  hypothesis for, 1307
  and lysosomes, 1310, 1312
  and membrane flow, 1305-1306
  modulation of chemical groupings, 1307-1309
  synonyms for, 1374
  undulating membranes, 1307
Plasmalemmosomes, *see* Mesosomes
Plasmodesmata, 1287-1288
Plasmolysis and cytoplasmic membrane, 175-178
Plectonema boryanum, 30
Plethodon cinereus, 419
Pleuropneumonia-like organism, 168
Polarity in eggs, 642
Pole distal, 1133
Pole proximal, 1133
Poleward movement, 554
Polio virus, 79-83, 111
Polyanion–polycation complexes in euchromatin, 264, 268
Polycistronic loci, 405
Polygene control, 332, 344
Polymorphism of cancer cells, *688-703*
Polyoma virus, 79-83, 100, 692, 706, 738, 746
Polyribosomes, 1008
  cytoplasmic, 1083
  disaggregation of, 487
  helix of, 1082-1083
  morphology of, 1082-1085

rosettes, 1082-1083
Polysomes, 112
Polystictus versicolor, 595
Pore, *see* Nuclear pore
Pore complex, definition of, 841
Porphyridium cruentum, 1057, **1058**, **1060**
Post lysosomes, 1394
Potorus tridactylis, 481
Pox viruses, 705
PPLO (mycoplasma organism), 744
Prenucleolar bodies, 406
Primula sinensis albomaculata, 1024
Procentriole, 1206
Prokaryotic cells, 222
difference with eukaryotic cells, 214
Pronase, 235, 644,
Prophage, 94, 138
Prophase, 386
biochemical activities of chromosomes, 541-542
DNA synthesis at meiosis, 541-542
end of, 850
Protamines, 225-226, 448-453, 463-464, 663
metabolism, 464-466
protamine-histone transition, 666
Proteins
acidic proteins and RNA, 510, 511
nuclear proteins, *439-471*
acid nuclear proteins, 441-443
classification of nuclear proteins, 438-441
extraction of, 439-441
function of acid nuclear proteins, 443
nuclear ribosomal proteins, 447-448
residual nuclear proteins, 441-443
nucleolar, 606-607, 615
prophase, role in meiotic, 529
Protein synthesis, *485-492*, 542-552
and antibiotics, 1093-1094
chain elongation and ribosomes, *1089-1093*
chain initiation and ribosomes, *1089-1093*
chain termination and ribosomes, *1089-1093*
and chiasmata, 533-534
and chromosome pairing, 528-531
distinction between cytoplasmic and mitochondrial, 992, 1019
and DNA synthesis, 513-514
during meiotic prophase, 542-552
during mitosis, 485-492
histones, 487-488
inhibitors, 529
mechanism, in schematic representation, 1092
in mitochondria, 992, *1018-1022*
nuclear activation, 679
nucleic protein synthesis, 547
pattern of, 486
in polytene chromosomes, 513-515
rate of, 486-487
regulatory mechanism of, 487
time of, in polytene chromosomes, 513
Protemndon bicolor, 299
Proteus, 152, 182, 187
Proteus mirabilis, **159**, 161, **162**, 166, **189**, 198, **213**
Proteus morganii, 14
Proteus vulgaris, 157
Protoplast, 162-164
Provirus, 94
Psammechinus miliaris, 586, 596
Pseudococcus obscurus, 282
Pseudomonas, 214
Pseudomonas saccharophila, 1361
Pseudorabies, 80-83, 102
Pseudotricho nympha, 1213
Psittacosis-lymphogranuloma group, 151, 160
4 P syndrome, 817
Puffs, 311-312, 331, 396, 397, 505, 506, 510-511, 514
and chromosome abnormalities, 738
control of, 515
ecdyson sensitive, 514-515
micro, 397
structure of, 241
Pulverization, 733, 740
Purines, 92, 93
Puromycin, 1091, 1093, 1094
Pyrimidines, 92-93
Pyruvate dehydrogenase, 903-904

Raia batis, **1235**
Rana clamitans, 610, 611, **616**, 617
Rana pipiens, 893, 1003
Raphanus sativus, 385, **392**, 403
Rattus norvegicus, 58, 60
Reassociation
collision of complementary strands, 25
definition of, 22
graphical method for the presentation of the measurements, 25-27
in higher organisms, 27-30
DNA
methods of measuring, 24
rate of, 24-27

thermal chromatogram, 33
Recombination, in virus, 109
Reduction, 1357-1360
3-glycerophosphate dehydrogenase, 1359
glyoxylate reductase, 1359-1360
lactic dehydrogenase, 1357-1359
types of LDH, 1358
Reinitiation in chromosomes, 138
Related, definition of, 23
Renaturation of DNA, 23-24
see also Reassociation
Reovirus, 104, 106
Repetition, 27-34
DNA nucleotide sequences of, 22-35
DNA occurrence of, **32**
precision of, 31-34
Replication
asynchrony in man, 294
in bacteria, 137-142
in chromocenters, 282-287
control of, in bacteria, 138-139
DNA, variations in time of, 287-288, 294-295
of heterochromatin, 281-282
of human chromosomes, 293-301
and mesosomes, 182-185
model for replication control, 138
origin of in bacteria, 139
regulation in bacteria, 137
rule of chromosome, 287-290
and structures of nucleoplasm, 198-199
in virus, 109-111
Replicator, 138
Replicon, 138-139, 140, 294-300
Repressor, 263-264
Respiration, control by glutamate synthesis, 1361-1367
Respiratory chain in mitochondria, 919-924
Rhapidosomes, 212-213
Rhodnius, 863
Rhodomicrobium vannielli, 183
Rhodopseudomonas spheroides, 183
Rhodosorus marinus, 1055
Rhodospirillum, 187, 1054
Rhodospirillum molischianum, 183
Rhodospirillum rubrum, 152, 159, **183**, 185
Rhodospirillum viridis, 185
Rhopheocytosis, 1374
Rhynchosciara, 506
Rhynchosciara angelae, 738
Ribosomes
binding aminoacyl tRNA, 1089-1090
binding peptidyl tRNA, 1089-1090
biosynthesis of, 1087-1088
in cancer cells, 694-696
chain elongation, 1089-1093
chain initiation, 1089-1093
chain termination, 1089-1093
from chloroplasts, 953-957, 1066-1069, 1085
classes of, 1081-1082
'CM' particles, 1088
composition of, 1085-1088
consistence of, 1081
export to cytoplasm, 630-631
function, *1088-1100*
history of, 1080
initiation complex, 1091
Mg^{2+}, 1081, 1083, 1090
from mitochondria, 953-957
morphology of, 1082-1085
peptide formation of, 1090
polyribosomes, 1080
see also Polyribosomes
production of, *621-636*
properties of, 1080-1088
and protein structures, 1087
and protein synthesis, 1088-1089
RNA—protein ratio in mitochondria, 954-955
subribosomal particles, 398
subsequent events in the formation of, 626-632
subunits, 1082-1085
structure of, 1085-1088
synthesis of protein, 627-630
Ricinus communis, 1190
Rickettsiae, 151, 973
RNA, 225
and acidic proteins, 510
aminoacyl transfer RNA, 94, 112
in bacteria, 39
base composition in plants, animals, and bacteria, 12-15
base composition at meiosis, 547-548
in chloroplasts, 944-971, 1030-1031
in chromosomes, 396
cytoplasmic RNA and nuclear RNA, 546
distribution, in polytene chromosomes, 510
double stranded RNA, 271
genes, SRNA in, 39, 40
hybridizable, 38, 39
messenger, 38, 39, 70, 73, 112
mitochondrial, 949-971, 989-992, 996-998, 1016-1018
mouse satellite DNA, 58

nuclear, as derepressor, 267
nucleolar, 606-607, 609
and RNA synthesis, 266-267
nucleolar organizer, and 5S RNA, 623
origin of mitochondrial RNA, 991
in plastids, 1066-1070
polymerase, 227, 228, 265-267, 445, 446
in bacteria, 132
in meiotic cells, 524
pulse labelled, 38
ribosomal RNA, 71
association of the precursor with protein, 626
cleavage of the 45S component, 626-627
DNA coding for, 39-40, 621-622
genes of, 621-624
heterogeneity of, 623
hypothesis for, 628-630, 953-957
minor components, 627
mitochondrial, 991, 1017
properties of the cistron, 622
properties of the precursor, 624-626
release into the nucleoplasm, 627
ribonucleoprotein strain, 628
16–18S, 12
23–28S, 12
45S, and the precursor of, 625-626
synthesis of the precursor, 624-625
5S, 71
30S, 404
32S, 613-615
45S, 398, 403, 405, 407, 512, 609, 611
50S, 404
sedimentation patterns at meiosis, 548
synthesis, 222, 485-492,
cellular sites, 485
and chromosome pairing, 531-532
and DNA synthesis, 487, 488
during meiotic prophase, *542-552*
during mitosis, *485-492*
and ligands, 270-271
in mitochondria, 989
and nuclear activation, 677-679
and pattern of, 486-489
in polytene chromosomes, 510-513
rate of, 486-487
in yeast cultures, 486
in viruses, *68-87*, 705-706
viral replication, 94
viral, single stranded, 104, 109
viral, size and shape, 104-109
tRNA, 71, 73
difference between cytoplasmic and mitochondrial, 997-998
and mitochondria, 989-991
in *Neurospora*, 997
$tRNA_f$, 1090
RNP, 398,399, 403, 407
Robertsonian translocations, 806-807
Romalea microptera, 341-342
Rous sarcoma virus, 695-697, 701, 723, 738
R_{17} phage, 109, 111

Saccharomyces, 945
mitochondria of, 939
Saccharomyces cerevisiae, 343, 949, 979
Saccoglossus, 1315
Salmonella abortivoequina, 186
Saltatory replication, 42-45
definition of, 23
in genome growth, 45, 53
and virus, 43-44
Saprospira grandis, 212, 213
Sarcoplasmic reticulum, 1120
terminal cisternae, 1120
Satellite and rRNA, 622
Schisterocerca gregaria, 328, **329**, 342, 346, 347
Sciara, 1207, **1208**, 1209,
Sciara coprohila, 506, **508**, 509, 1233, **1235**
Sciarids, 511
Scutigera, 337
Secale, 281
Secale cereale, 279, 281, 334, 344
Segregation of genetic material in bacteria, 140-142
Selenomonas palpitans, 159
Semigymnoplast, 161
see also Spheroplast
Sendia virus, 740, 1303
Sequences
see also Nucleotide sequence
base, of the mouse, 53-54
house keeping, 63-65
nucleotide, 92
definition of, 22
repeated, definition of, 22
family of repeated, definition of, 22
repeated, length of, 34-35
Serratia marcescens, 14
Sex chromatin
see also Sex chromosomes
late replication of, 761
single X derivation of, 760-762

Sex chromosome
  abnormalities
    chromatid rearrangement, 777
    effects on psychosocial disorder in man, 787-788
    females with one X in man, 783
    nomenclature, *793-798*
    non-disjunction, 775
    origin of, 785-787
    structural rearrangement, 776
    46 XX males in man, 780
    49 XXXXY males in man, 781
    48 XXXY males in man, 781
    48 XXY males in man, 781-782
    47 XYY males in man, 781-782
  control mechanism, 791-793
  control of somatic characters, 789-790
  sex determination, *765-773*
Sex determination, *765-773*
  autosomal modification of, 770
  and cortical stimulating substance, 772-773
  and sexual infantilism, 767
  and sterility, 770-771
  the XO condition, 766
Sex factor in bacteria, 133
Shope fibroma virus, 705
Shope papilloma virus, 705
Siredon mexicanum, 1003
Skin cancers, 704
SP50 bacteriophage, 97-104
  DNA of, **96**, 101
S period, 385, 386, **387**, 474
  change of duration, during differentiation, 477-478
  constancy of duration, 476-477
  and histone synthesis, 490
Spermiogenesis, 664-666
  electronmicroscope studies of spermatogenesis *361-380*, 414
  histones and, 664-665
  histone pattern in, 226
Sperm tails, 1229
Sphaerocarpus donnellii, 347
Sphaerotilus natans, 154
Spheroplast, 161
  wall, 157
Spherules, nuclear, 396-397
Spindle, 404, 405, 556-558
  biochemical analysis, 584-592
  birefringence, 564-575
  chemical nature of, 564-565
  chromosomal spindle fibers, 556-558
  clear areas of, 579-581
  components of, 574-575
  dynamic equilibrium, 565
  fibres and microtubules, 580
  the force system, 572-573
  lesions, 569
  Mazia's 'motor mechanism', 574
  microtubules, 575-580
    and birefringence, 576-582
    difference of, 583
    distribution of, 579-584
  model of, 565-567
  model 'force insignificance', 571-572
  organisation of, 565-569
  physical nature of, 565-569
  regeneration of new fibers, 567-568
  22S protein, 590
  stability of, 565
  thickness of spindle fibers, 558
  vesicles, 580-581
Spiranthes sinensis, 281
Spirillum, 157-186
Spirillum serpens, 159
Spirochaetes, 189
Spirogyra, 973
Sporangia, 150
Spore, 206-209
  cell wall primordium of, 207
  coat, 207
  cortex of, 207
  exposporium, 207-209
  formation of, 206-209
  resistance of, 206
  transformation into the vegetative cell, 209
Stentor polymorphus, 1246
Streptobacillus moniliformis, 164
Streptomycin, 1093-1094
Structure proteins, 1020-1021
Stylocephalus longicollis, 1231
Succinyl Co A synthetase, 920-921
SV_{40} virus, 74, 79-83, 100, 693, 697, 700, 702, 705, 706, 708, 727, 738, 742
Synapsis, 419-420
  histone, 337
  meiotic pairing, 328, 330
Synaptonemal complex, 315-317, 413, 423, 424, 541
  interconnections of, 414
  model of, 424-426
  protein synthesis, 528-529

size of, 318
terminology of, 420-421
Syngamy, 541

T-antigens, 707-708
T_2 bacteriophage, 95, 97-104
T_3 bacteriophage, 97-104
T_4 bacteriophage, 26, 100, 97-104, 110, 1314
T_5 bacteriophage, 97-104
T_7 bacteriophage, 97-104, 110, 225
Tegenaria, **841**
Telomeres, 295
Telophase, 391-395
Testacella, 891
Testudo hermanni, 1327
Tetrahymena, 1012, 1016, 1017, 1018, 1212, 1214, 1215, 1223, 1249
Tetrahymena pyriformis, 15, 484, 950, 1190, 1191, 1192, 1193
Tetramitus, 1214, 1238
Thermal denaturation temperature, (T_M), 4, 53, 93
Thiospirillum jenense, 183
Thylakoid, 183, 1048
Thylaxoviridae, 705
Thymidine kinase, 484, 486, 524
Tipula, 301-304, 309, 1437
Tipula oleracea, **302**, **304**, 624
TMV, 106, 109, 111
Tomopteris helgolandica, 1237
Tonofilaments, 1281-1282
Torulopsis, 939
Tradescantia, 343, 418, 542
Tradescantia paludosa, 481
Transaminases, 938
Transcription, 223, 225
during reproductive cell cycle, 486
in lampbrush stage, 239-241
in virus, 111-113
Transduction, 94
in bacteria, 135, 139
Transfection, 94
Transformation, 136-137
viral, 738
viral and DNA synthesis, 740-743
Transition in the cell, 1395
Translation
and stability of the doublet pattern, 77-78
in virus, 111-113
Translocases, 937
and oxidative phosphorylation, 927
Transmethylation, 625
Transvection effect, 331
Transverse fission, binary, 150
Triads, 1120
Trichonympha, 1213
Trillium, 280
Trillium erectum, 523, 525, 535
Triplets, 72, 92,
mutation of, 77
Trisomic numbers, 723-724
Trisomy, 753
Trisomy G, 650, 806
Trisomy and low weight in man, 830
Triticum aestivum, 332, **333**, 334, 344
Triticum durum, 337
Triticum vulgare, **384**, **400**, 403
Triturus, 303, 364
Triturus cristatus, 543, **544**, 545
Triturus viridescens, **232**, 235, **240**, 543, **610**, 611, **614**, 615, **842**
Tropaeolum majus, **383**, 385-386, 403
Trophoblast, 641
Trophoblastic vesicle, 642
Trypanosoma brucei, 975
Trypanosoma equiperdum, 977, 978
Trypanosoma evansi, 977, 978
Trypanosoma lewisi, **976**
Trypanosoma mega, 977
T system, 1120
Tubuli in bacteria, 178-180
Tulipa gesneriana, 490
Tumor,
see also Cancer and Carcinogenesis
age, 725
antigens, 707-708
and background variation, 725
course of events, 725
murine, 720
necrobiotic phenoma, 688
primary, 722
progression, 720-722
structure of, 688
trisomic numbers, 723-724
tumor imbalance, 725
types, 722
virus, 726, *733-750*
Tumor cells
phagocytic activity, 699
and virus particles, 704-706

Ultraphagocytosis, 1374

Unique DNA, 97
  definition, 22
Uptake mechanisms, *1321-1345*
Urechis, 623
Uroid, 1388-1390
Ustilago maydis, 343, 351
UV absorption, 658-659
UV microspectrophotometry, 658

Vaccinia, 80-83
Variegation, 1024
Vibrio fetus, 189
Vibrio metschnikovii, 159-187
Vicia, 63
Vicia faba, 382, 385, 391, 403, 405, 479, 480, 482, 488, 743, 1006
Vigna, 1018
Viropexis, 94
Virus
  chromosomes, *92-125*, *733-750*
  chromosome replication, 109-111
  evolution of, 83-85
  liberation by eccytosis, 1300-1303
  multiplication and chromosome abnormalities, 744
  nucleic acid, detection in cells, 744
  oncogenic, 704-706
  origin of, *68-87*
  protein coats, 1435-1441
  RNA of, 104-109
  transcription in, 111-113
  transformation, 738
  translation, 111-113
  unit membrane, 1435-1441
Vitreocilla, 185, 202
Viviparus contectoides, **371**, **376**, 378, 1209
Volutin granules, 206

Watson-Crick model, 92-93

Xenopus, 226, 311, 391, 546, 1008, 1012
Xenopus laevis, 305, 486, 542, 611, **614**, 615, **616**, 617, 621, 623, 625, 640, 641
  hybridizable RNA, 39
  mitochondrial DNA, 40
  nuclear DNA, 40
  ribosomal genes in, 39
X and O spermatids, 430

Yeast
  crosses, 980
  cytochrome C, 981
  DNA polymerase in mitochondira, 988
  independent chromosomal alleles, 980
  neutral petites, 980
  segregational petites, 980
  suppressive petites, 980
Yersinia enterolitica, 212

Zamia, *1210*, *1214*
Zea mays, 541, **844**, 845, 1048, **1049**, 1063, 1066, **1068**
Zonula nucleum limitans, 848
Zonula pellucida, 643, 644, 1287

4
417